2013

NAUTICAL ALMANAC

2013 COMMERCIAL EDITION

Cover Design: J.Neuman

www.snowballpublishing.com

info@snowballpublishing.com

For information regarding special discounts for bulk purchases, please contact Snowball Publishing at

sales@snowballpublishing.com

ALTITUDE CORRECTION TABLES 10°–90°—SUN, STARS, PLANETS

SUN APR.–SEPT.		STARS AND PLANETS			DIP					
	Upper Limb	App. Alt.	Corrⁿ	App. Alt.	Additional Corrⁿ	Ht. of Eye	Corrⁿ	Ht. of Eye	Corrⁿ	Ht. of Eye Corrⁿ
	′	° ′	′		**2013**	m	′	ft.		m ′
	6 − 21·2	9 55	−5·3		**VENUS**	2·4	−2·8	8·0		1·0 − 1·8
	7 − 21·1	10 07	−5·2		Jan. 1–Sept. 21	2·6	−2·9	8·6		1·5 − 2·2
	8 − 21·0	10 20	−5·1		° ′	2·8	−3·0	9·2		2·0 − 2·5
	9 − 20·9	10 32	−5·1		0 +0·1	3·0	−3·1	9·8		2·5 − 2·8
	·0 − 20·8	10 46	−5·0		60	3·2	−3·2	10·5		3·0 − 3·0
	·1 − 20·7	10 59	−4·9		Sept. 22–Nov. 11	3·4	−3·3	11·2		
	·2 − 20·6	11 14	−4·8		° ′	3·6	−3·4	11·9		See table ←
	·3 − 20·5	11 29	−4·7		0 +0·2	3·8	−3·5	12·6		
	·4 − 20·4	11 44	−4·6		41 +0·1	4·0	−3·6	13·3		m ′
	·5 − 20·3	12 00	−4·5		76	4·3	−3·7	14·1		20 − 7·9
	·6 − 20·2	12 17	−4·4		Nov. 12–Dec. 5	4·5	−3·8	14·9		22 − 8·3
	·7 − 20·1	12 35	−4·3		° ′	4·7	−3·9	15·7		24 − 8·6
	·8 − 20·0	12 53	−4·2		0 +0·3	5·0	−4·0	16·5		26 − 9·0
	·9 − 19·9	13 12	−4·1		34 +0·2	5·2	−4·1	17·4		28 − 9·3
	2·0 − 19·8	13 32	−4·0		60 +0·1	5·5	−4·2	18·3		
	2·1 − 19·7	13 53	−3·9		80	5·8	−4·3	19·1		30 − 9·6
	2·2 − 19·6	14 16	−3·8		Dec. 6–Dec. 20	6·1	−4·4	20·1		32 − 10·0
	2·3 − 19·5	14 39	−3·7		° ′	6·3	−4·5	21·0		34 − 10·3
14 17 +12·6 − 19·7		14 29 +12·4 − 19·4		15 03 −3·6	29 +0·4	6·6	−4·6	22·0		36 − 10·6
14 41 +12·7 − 19·6		14 53 +12·5 − 19·3		15 29 −3·5	51 +0·3	6·9	−4·7	22·9		38 − 10·8
15 05 +12·8 − 19·5		15 18 +12·6 − 19·2		15 56 −3·4	68 +0·2	7·2	−4·8	23·9		
15 31 +12·9 − 19·4		15 45 +12·7 − 19·1		16 25 −3·3	83 +0·1	7·5	−4·9	24·9		40 − 11·1
15 59 +13·0 − 19·3		16 13 +12·8 − 19·0		16 55 −3·2	Dec. 21–Dec. 31	7·9	−5·0	26·0		42 − 11·4
16 27 +13·1 − 19·2		16 43 +12·9 − 18·9		17 27 −3·1	° ′	8·2	−5·1	27·1		44 − 11·7
16 58 +13·2 − 19·1		17 14 +13·0 − 18·8		18 01 −3·0	0 +0·5	8·5	−5·2	28·1		46 − 11·9
17 30 +13·3 − 19·0		17 47 +13·1 − 18·7		18 37 −2·9	26 +0·4	8·8	−5·3	29·2		48 − 12·2
18 05 +13·4 − 18·9		18 23 +13·2 − 18·6		19 16 −2·8	46 +0·3	9·2	−5·4	30·4		ft. ′
18 41 +13·5 − 18·8		19 00 +13·3 − 18·5		19 56 −2·7	60 +0·2	9·5	−5·5	31·5		2 − 1·4
19 20 +13·6 − 18·7		19 41 +13·4 − 18·4		20 40 −2·6	73 +0·1	9·9	−5·6	32·7		4 − 1·9
20 02 +13·7 − 18·6		20 24 +13·5 − 18·3		21 27 −2·5	84	10·3	−5·7	33·9		6 − 2·4
20 46 +13·8 − 18·5		21 10 +13·6 − 18·2		22 17 −2·4	**MARS**	10·6	−5·8	35·1		8 − 2·7
21 34 +13·9 − 18·4		21 59 +13·7 − 18·1		23 11 −2·3	Jan. 1–Dec. 31	11·0	−5·9	36·3		10 − 3·1
22 25 +14·0 − 18·3		22 52 +13·8 − 18·0		24 09 −2·2	° ′	11·4	−6·0	37·6		
23 20 +14·1 − 18·2		23 49 +13·9 − 17·9		25 12 −2·1	0 +0·1	11·8	−6·1	38·9		See table ←
24 20 +14·2 − 18·1		24 51 +14·0 − 17·8		26 20 −2·0	60	12·2	−6·2	40·1		ft. ′
25 24 +14·3 − 18·0		25 58 +14·1 − 17·7		27 34 −1·9		12·6	−6·3	41·5		70 − 8·1
26 34 +14·4 − 17·9		27 11 +14·2 − 17·6		28 54 −1·8		13·0	−6·4	42·8		75 − 8·4
27 50 +14·5 − 17·8		28 31 +14·3 − 17·5		30 22 −1·7		13·4	−6·5	44·2		80 − 8·7
29 13 +14·6 − 17·7		29 58 +14·4 − 17·4		31 58 −1·6		13·8	−6·6	45·5		85 − 8·9
30 44 +14·7 − 17·6		31 33 +14·5 − 17·3		33 43 −1·5		14·2	−6·7	46·9		90 − 9·2
32 24 +14·8 − 17·5		33 18 +14·6 − 17·2		35 38 −1·4		14·7	−6·8	48·4		95 − 9·5
34 15 +14·9 − 17·4		35 15 +14·7 − 17·1		37 45 −1·3		15·1	−6·9	49·8		
36 17 +15·0 − 17·3		37 24 +14·8 − 17·0		40 06 −1·2		15·5	−7·0	51·3		100 − 9·7
38 34 +15·1 − 17·2		39 48 +14·9 − 16·9		42 42 −1·1		16·0	−7·1	52·8		105 − 9·9
41 06 +15·2 − 17·1		42 28 +15·0 − 16·8		45 34 −1·0		16·5	−7·2	54·3		110 − 10·2
43 56 +15·3 − 17·0		45 29 +15·1 − 16·7		48 45 −0·9		16·9	−7·3	55·8		115 − 10·4
47 07 +15·4 − 16·9		48 52 +15·2 − 16·6		52 16 −0·8		17·4	−7·4	57·4		120 − 10·6
50 43 +15·5 − 16·8		52 41 +15·3 − 16·5		56 09 −0·7		17·9	−7·5	58·9		125 − 10·8
54 46 +15·6 − 16·7		56 59 +15·4 − 16·4		60 26 −0·6		18·4	−7·6	60·5		
59 21 +15·7 − 16·6		61 50 +15·5 − 16·3		65 06 −0·5		18·8	−7·7	62·1		130 − 11·1
64 28 +15·8 − 16·5		67 15 +15·6 − 16·2		70 09 −0·4		19·3	−7·8	63·8		135 − 11·3
70 10 +15·9 − 16·4		73 14 +15·7 − 16·1		75 32 −0·3		19·8	−7·9	65·4		140 − 11·5
76 24 +16·0 − 16·3		79 42 +15·8 − 16·0		81 12 −0·2		20·4	−8·0	67·1		145 − 11·7
83 05 +16·1 − 16·2		86 31 +15·9 − 15·9		87 03 −0·1		20·9	−8·1	68·8		150 − 11·9
90 00		90 00		90 00 0·0		21·4		70·5		155 − 12·1

App. Alt. = Apparent altitude = Sextant altitude corrected for index error and dip.

ALTITUDE CORRECTION TABLES 0°-10°—SUN, STARS, PLANETS A3

App. Alt.	OCT.—MAR. SUN Lower Limb	OCT.—MAR. SUN Upper Limb	APR.—SEPT. Lower Limb	APR.—SEPT. Upper Limb	STARS PLANETS	App. Alt.	OCT.—MAR. SUN Lower Limb	OCT.—MAR. SUN Upper Limb	APR.—SEPT. Lower Limb	APR.—SEPT. Upper Limb	STARS PLANETS
° ′	′	′	′	′	′	° ′	′	′	′	′	′
0 00	− 17·5	− 49·8	− 17·8	− 49·6	− 33·8	3 30	+ 3·4	− 28·9	+ 3·1	− 28·7	− 12·9
0 03	16·9	49·2	17·2	49·0	33·2	3 35	3·6	28·7	3·3	28·5	12·7
0 06	16·3	48·6	16·6	48·4	32·6	3 40	3·8	28·5	3·6	28·2	12·5
0 09	15·7	48·0	16·0	47·8	32·0	3 45	4·0	28·3	3·8	28·0	12·3
0 12	15·2	47·5	15·4	47·3	31·5	3 50	4·2	28·1	4·0	27·8	12·1
0 15	14·6	46·9	14·8	46·6	30·9	3 55	4·4	27·9	4·1	27·7	11·9
0 18	− 14·1	− 46·4	− 14·3	− 46·1	− 30·4	4 00	+ 4·6	− 27·7	+ 4·3	− 27·5	− 11·7
0 21	13·5	45·8	13·8	45·6	29·8	4 05	4·8	27·5	4·5	27·3	11·5
0 24	13·0	45·3	13·3	45·1	29·3	4 10	4·9	27·4	4·7	27·1	11·4
0 27	12·5	44·8	12·8	44·6	28·8	4 15	5·1	27·2	4·9	26·9	11·2
0 30	12·0	44·3	12·3	44·1	28·3	4 20	5·3	27·0	5·0	26·8	11·0
0 33	11·6	43·9	11·8	43·6	27·9	4 25	5·4	26·9	5·2	26·6	10·9
0 36	− 11·1	− 43·4	− 11·3	− 43·1	− 27·4	4 30	+ 5·6	− 26·7	+ 5·3	− 26·5	− 10·7
0 39	10·6	42·9	10·9	42·7	26·9	4 35	5·7	26·6	5·5	26·3	10·6
0 42	10·2	42·5	10·5	42·3	26·5	4 40	5·9	26·4	5·6	26·2	10·4
0 45	9·8	42·1	10·0	41·8	26·1	4 45	6·0	26·3	5·8	26·0	10·3
0 48	9·4	41·7	9·6	41·4	25·7	4 50	6·2	26·1	5·9	25·9	10·1
0 51	9·0	41·3	9·2	41·0	25·3	4 55	6·3	26·0	6·1	25·7	10·0
0 54	− 8·6	− 40·9	− 8·8	− 40·6	− 24·9	5 00	+ 6·4	− 25·9	+ 6·2	− 25·6	− 9·8
0 57	8·2	40·5	8·4	40·2	24·5	5 05	6·6	25·7	6·3	25·5	9·7
1 00	7·8	40·1	8·0	39·8	24·1	5 10	6·7	25·6	6·5	25·3	9·6
1 03	7·4	39·7	7·7	39·5	23·7	5 15	6·8	25·5	6·6	25·2	9·5
1 06	7·1	39·4	7·3	39·1	23·4	5 20	7·0	25·3	6·7	25·1	9·3
1 09	6·7	39·0	7·0	38·8	23·0	5 25	7·1	25·2	6·8	25·0	9·2
1 12	− 6·4	− 38·7	− 6·6	− 38·4	− 22·7	5 30	+ 7·2	− 25·1	+ 6·9	− 24·9	− 9·1
1 15	6·0	38·3	6·3	38·1	22·3	5 35	7·3	25·0	7·1	24·7	9·0
1 18	5·7	38·0	6·0	37·8	22·0	5 40	7·4	24·9	7·2	24·6	8·9
1 21	5·4	37·7	5·7	37·5	21·7	5 45	7·5	24·8	7·3	24·5	8·8
1 24	5·1	37·4	5·3	37·1	21·4	5 50	7·6	24·7	7·4	24·4	8·7
1 27	4·8	37·1	5·0	36·8	21·1	5 55	7·7	24·6	7·5	24·3	8·6
1 30	− 4·5	− 36·8	− 4·7	− 36·5	− 20·8	6 00	+ 7·8	− 24·5	+ 7·6	− 24·2	− 8·5
1 35	4·0	36·3	4·3	36·1	20·3	6 10	8·0	24·3	7·8	24·0	8·3
1 40	3·6	35·9	3·8	35·6	19·9	6 20	8·2	24·1	8·0	23·8	8·1
1 45	3·1	35·4	3·4	35·2	19·4	6 30	8·4	23·9	8·2	23·6	7·9
1 50	2·7	35·0	2·9	34·7	19·0	6 40	8·6	23·7	8·3	23·5	7·7
1 55	2·3	34·6	2·5	34·3	18·6	6 50	8·7	23·6	8·5	23·3	7·6
2 00	− 1·9	− 34·2	− 2·1	− 33·9	− 18·2	7 00	+ 8·9	− 23·4	+ 8·7	− 23·1	− 7·4
2 05	1·5	33·8	1·7	33·5	17·8	7 10	9·1	23·2	8·8	23·0	7·2
2 10	1·1	33·4	1·4	33·2	17·4	7 20	9·2	23·1	9·0	22·8	7·1
2 15	0·8	33·1	1·0	32·8	17·1	7 30	9·3	23·0	9·1	22·7	6·9
2 20	0·4	32·7	0·7	32·5	16·7	7 40	9·5	22·8	9·2	22·6	6·8
2 25	− 0·1	32·4	− 0·3	32·1	16·4	7 50	9·6	22·7	9·4	22·4	6·7
2 30	+ 0·2	− 32·1	0·0	− 31·8	− 16·1	8 00	+ 9·7	− 22·6	+ 9·5	− 22·3	− 6·6
2 35	0·5	31·8	+ 0·3	31·5	15·8	8 10	9·9	22·4	9·6	22·2	6·4
2 40	0·8	31·5	0·6	31·2	15·4	8 20	10·0	22·3	9·7	22·1	6·3
2 45	1·1	31·2	0·9	30·9	15·2	8 30	10·1	22·2	9·9	21·9	6·2
2 50	1·4	30·9	1·2	30·6	14·9	8 40	10·2	22·1	10·0	21·8	6·1
2 55	1·7	30·6	1·4	30·4	14·6	8 50	10·3	22·0	10·1	21·7	6·0
3 00	+ 2·0	− 30·3	+ 1·7	− 30·1	− 14·3	9 00	+ 10·4	− 21·9	+ 10·2	− 21·6	− 5·9
3 05	2·2	30·1	2·0	29·8	14·1	9 10	10·5	21·8	10·3	21·5	5·8
3 10	2·5	29·8	2·2	29·6	13·8	9 20	10·6	21·7	10·4	21·4	5·7
3 15	2·7	29·6	2·5	29·3	13·6	9 30	10·7	21·6	10·5	21·3	5·6
3 20	2·9	29·4	2·7	29·1	13·4	9 40	10·8	21·5	10·6	21·2	5·5
3 25	3·2	29·1	2·9	28·9	13·1	9 50	10·9	21·4	10·6	21·2	5·4
3 30	+ 3·4	− 28·9	+ 3·1	− 28·7	− 12·9	10 00	+ 11·0	− 21·3	+ 10·7	− 21·1	− 5·3

Additional corrections for temperature and pressure are given on the following page.

For bubble sextant observations ignore dip and use the star corrections for Sun, planets and stars.

A4 ALTITUDE CORRECTION TABLES—ADDITIONAL CORRECTIONS
ADDITIONAL REFRACTION CORRECTIONS FOR NON-STANDARD CONDITIONS

App. Alt.	A	B	C	D	E	F	G	H	J	K	L	M	N	P	App. Alt.
° ′	′	′	′	′	′	′	′	′	′	′	′	′	′	′	° ′
00 00	−7·3	−5·9	−4·6	−3·4	−2·2	−1·1	0·0	+1·0	+2·0	+3·0	+4·0	+4·9	+5·9	+6·9	00 00
00 30	5·5	4·5	3·5	2·6	1·7	0·8	0·0	0·8	1·6	2·3	3·1	3·8	4·5	5·3	00 30
01 00	4·4	3·5	2·8	2·0	1·3	0·7	0·0	0·6	1·2	1·8	2·4	3·0	3·6	4·2	01 00
01 30	3·5	2·9	2·2	1·7	1·1	0·5	0·0	0·5	1·0	1·5	2·0	2·5	2·9	3·4	01 30
02 00	2·9	2·4	1·9	1·4	0·9	0·4	0·0	0·4	0·8	1·3	1·7	2·0	2·4	2·8	02 00
02 30	−2·5	−2·0	−1·6	−1·2	−0·8	−0·4	0·0	+0·4	+0·7	+1·1	+1·4	+1·7	+2·1	+2·4	02 30
03 00	2·1	1·7	1·4	1·0	0·7	0·3	0·0	0·3	0·6	0·9	1·2	1·5	1·8	2·1	03 00
03 30	1·9	1·5	1·2	0·9	0·6	0·3	0·0	0·3	0·5	0·8	1·1	1·3	1·6	1·8	03 30
04 00	1·6	1·3	1·1	0·8	0·5	0·3	0·0	0·2	0·5	0·7	0·9	1·2	1·4	1·6	04 00
04 30	1·5	1·2	0·9	0·7	0·5	0·2	0·0	0·2	0·4	0·6	0·8	1·0	1·3	1·5	04 30
05 00	−1·3	−1·1	−0·9	−0·6	−0·4	−0·2	0·0	+0·2	+0·4	+0·6	+0·8	+0·9	+1·1	+1·3	05 00
06	1·1	0·9	0·7	0·5	0·3	0·2	0·0	0·2	0·3	0·5	0·6	0·8	0·9	1·1	06
07	1·0	0·8	0·6	0·5	0·3	0·1	0·0	0·1	0·3	0·4	0·5	0·7	0·8	0·9	07
08	0·8	0·7	0·5	0·4	0·3	0·1	0·0	0·1	0·2	0·4	0·5	0·6	0·7	0·8	08
09	0·7	0·6	0·5	0·4	0·2	0·1	0·0	0·1	0·2	0·3	0·4	0·5	0·6	0·7	09
10 00	−0·7	−0·5	−0·4	−0·3	−0·2	−0·1	0·0	+0·1	+0·2	+0·3	+0·4	+0·5	+0·6	+0·7	10 00
12	0·6	0·5	0·4	0·3	0·2	0·1	0·0	0·1	0·2	0·2	0·3	0·4	0·5	0·5	12
14	0·5	0·4	0·3	0·2	0·1	0·1	0·0	0·1	0·1	0·2	0·3	0·3	0·4	0·5	14
16	0·4	0·3	0·3	0·2	0·1	0·1	0·0	0·1	0·1	0·2	0·2	0·3	0·3	0·4	16
18	0·4	0·3	0·2	0·2	0·1	−0·1	0·0	+0·1	0·1	0·2	0·2	0·3	0·3	0·4	18
20 00	−0·3	−0·3	−0·2	−0·2	−0·1	0·0	0·0	0·0	+0·1	+0·1	+0·2	+0·2	+0·3	+0·3	20 00
25	0·3	0·2	0·2	0·1	0·1	0·0	0·0	0·0	0·1	0·1	0·1	0·2	0·2	0·2	25
30	0·2	0·2	0·1	0·1	0·1	0·0	0·0	0·0	+0·1	0·1	0·1	0·1	0·2	0·2	30
35	0·2	0·1	0·1	0·1	−0·1	0·0	0·0	0·0	0·0	0·1	0·1	0·1	0·1	0·2	35
40	0·1	0·1	0·1	−0·1	0·0	0·0	0·0	0·0	0·0	+0·1	0·1	0·1	0·1	0·1	40
50 00	−0·1	−0·1	−0·1	0·0	0·0	0·0	0·0	0·0	0·0	0·0	+0·1	+0·1	+0·1	+0·1	50 00

The graph is entered with arguments temperature and pressure to find a zone letter; using as arguments this zone letter and apparent altitude (sextant altitude corrected for index error and dip), a correction is taken from the table. This correction is to be applied to the sextant altitude in addition to the corrections for standard conditions (for the Sun, stars and planets from page A2-A3 and for the Moon from pages xxxiv and xxxv).

The 2013 Nautical Almanac
Commercial Edition

RELIGIOUS CALENDARS

Epiphany	Jan. 6	Low Sunday	Apr. 7
Septuagesima Sunday	Jan. 27	Rogation Sunday	May 5
Quinquagesima Sunday	Feb. 10	Ascension Day—Holy Thursday	May 9
Ash Wednesday	Feb. 13	Whit Sunday—Pentecost	May 19
Quadragesima Sunday	Feb. 17	Trinity Sunday	May 26
Palm Sunday	Mar. 24	Corpus Christi	May 30
Good Friday	Mar. 29	First Sunday in Advent	Dec. 1
Easter Day	Mar. 31	Christmas Day (Wednesday)	Dec. 25
First Day of Passover (Pesach)	Mar. 26	Day of Atonement (Yom Kippur)	Sept. 14
Feast of Weeks (Shavuot)	May 15	First day of Tabernacles (Succoth)	Sept. 19
Jewish New Year 5774 (Rosh Hashanah)	Sept. 5		
Ramadân, First day of (tabular)	July 9	Islamic New Year (1435)	Nov. 5

The Jewish and Islamic dates above are tabular dates, which begin at sunset on the previous evening and end at sunset on the date tabulated. In practice, the dates of Islamic fasts and festivals are determined by an actual sighting of the appropriate new moon.

CIVIL CALENDAR—UNITED KINGDOM

Accession of Queen Elizabeth II	Feb. 6	The Queen's Official Birthday†	June 8
St David (Wales)	Mar. 1	Birthday of Prince Philip, Duke of	
Commonwealth Day	Mar. 11	Edinburgh	June 10
St Patrick (Ireland)	Mar. 17	Remembrance Sunday	Nov. 10
Birthday of Queen Elizabeth II	Apr. 21	Birthday of the Prince of Wales	Nov. 14
St George (England)	Apr. 23	St Andrew (Scotland)	Nov. 30
Coronation Day	June 2		

PUBLIC HOLIDAYS

England and Wales—Jan. 1†, Mar. 29, Apr. 1, May 6†, May 27, Aug. 26, Dec. 25, Dec. 26

Northern Ireland—Jan. 1†, Mar. 18, Mar. 29, Apr. 1, May 6†, May 27, July 12†, Aug. 26, Dec. 25, Dec. 26

Scotland—Jan. 1, Jan. 2, Mar. 29, May 6, May 27†, Aug. 5, Dec. 25, Dec. 26†

CIVIL CALENDAR—UNITED STATES OF AMERICA

New Year's Day	Jan. 1	Labor Day	Sept. 2
Martin Luther King's Birthday	Jan. 21	Columbus Day	Oct. 14
Washington's Birthday	Feb. 18	Election Day (in certain States)	Nov. 5
Memorial Day	May 27	Veterans Day	Nov. 11
Independence Day	July 4	Thanksgiving Day	Nov. 28

†Dates subject to confirmation

PHASES OF THE MOON

New Moon			First Quarter			Full Moon			Last Quarter		
d	h	m	d	h	m	d	h	m	d	h	m
									Jan. 5	03	58
Jan. 11	19	44	Jan. 18	23	45	Jan. 27	04	38	Feb. 3	13	56
Feb. 10	07	20	Feb. 17	20	31	Feb. 25	20	26	Mar. 4	21	53
Mar. 11	19	51	Mar. 19	17	27	Mar. 27	09	27	Apr. 3	04	37
Apr. 10	09	35	Apr. 18	12	31	Apr. 25	19	57	May 2	11	14
May 10	00	28	May 18	04	35	May 25	04	25	May 31	18	58
June 8	15	56	June 16	17	24	June 23	11	32	June 30	04	54
July 8	07	14	July 16	03	18	July 22	18	16	July 29	17	43
Aug. 6	21	51	Aug. 14	10	56	Aug. 21	01	45	Aug. 28	09	35
Sept. 5	11	36	Sept. 12	17	08	Sept. 19	11	13	Sept. 27	03	55
Oct. 5	00	35	Oct. 11	23	02	Oct. 18	23	38	Oct. 26	23	40
Nov. 3	12	50	Nov. 10	05	57	Nov. 17	15	16	Nov. 25	19	28
Dec. 3	00	22	Dec. 9	15	12	Dec. 17	09	28	Dec. 25	13	48

DAYS OF THE WEEK AND DAYS OF THE YEAR

Day	JAN. Wk Yr	FEB. Wk Yr	MAR. Wk Yr	APR. Wk Yr	MAY Wk Yr	JUNE Wk Yr	JULY Wk Yr	AUG. Wk Yr	SEPT. Wk Yr	OCT. Wk Yr	NOV. Wk Yr	DEC. Wk Yr
1	Tu. 1	F. 32	F. 60	M. 91	W. 121	Sa. 152	M. 182	Th. 213	Su. 244	Tu. 274	F. 305	Su. 335
2	W. 2	Sa. 33	Sa. 61	Tu. 92	Th. 122	Su. 153	Tu. 183	F. 214	M. 245	W. 275	Sa. 306	M. 336
3	Th. 3	Su. 34	Su. 62	W. 93	F. 123	M. 154	W. 184	Sa. 215	Tu. 246	Th. 276	Su. 307	Tu. 337
4	F. 4	M. 35	M. 63	Th. 94	Sa. 124	Tu. 155	Th. 185	Su. 216	W. 247	F. 277	M. 308	W. 338
5	Sa. 5	Tu. 36	Tu. 64	F. 95	Su. 125	W. 156	F. 186	M. 217	Th. 248	Sa. 278	Tu. 309	Th. 339
6	Su. 6	W. 37	W. 65	Sa. 96	M. 126	Th. 157	Sa. 187	Tu. 218	F. 249	Su. 279	W. 310	F. 340
7	M. 7	Th. 38	Th. 66	Su. 97	Tu. 127	F. 158	Su. 188	W. 219	Sa. 250	M. 280	Th. 311	Sa. 341
8	Tu. 8	F. 39	F. 67	M. 98	W. 128	Sa. 159	M. 189	Th. 220	Su. 251	Tu. 281	F. 312	Su. 342
9	W. 9	Sa. 40	Sa. 68	Tu. 99	Th. 129	Su. 160	Tu. 190	F. 221	M. 252	W. 282	Sa. 313	M. 343
10	Th. 10	Su. 41	Su. 69	W. 100	F. 130	M. 161	W. 191	Sa. 222	Tu. 253	Th. 283	Su. 314	Tu. 344
11	F. 11	M. 42	M. 70	Th. 101	Sa. 131	Tu. 162	Th. 192	Su. 223	W. 254	F. 284	M. 315	W. 345
12	Sa. 12	Tu. 43	Tu. 71	F. 102	Su. 132	W. 163	F. 193	M. 224	Th. 255	Sa. 285	Tu. 316	Th. 346
13	Su. 13	W. 44	W. 72	Sa. 103	M. 133	Th. 164	Sa. 194	Tu. 225	F. 256	Su. 286	W. 317	F. 347
14	M. 14	Th. 45	Th. 73	Su. 104	Tu. 134	F. 165	Su. 195	W. 226	Sa. 257	M. 287	Th. 318	Sa. 348
15	Tu. 15	F. 46	F. 74	M. 105	W. 135	Sa. 166	M. 196	Th. 227	Su. 258	Tu. 288	F. 319	Su. 349
16	W. 16	Sa. 47	Sa. 75	Tu. 106	Th. 136	Su. 167	Tu. 197	F. 228	M. 259	W. 289	Sa. 320	M. 350
17	Th. 17	Su. 48	Su. 76	W. 107	F. 137	M. 168	W. 198	Sa. 229	Tu. 260	Th. 290	Su. 321	Tu. 351
18	F. 18	M. 49	M. 77	Th. 108	Sa. 138	Tu. 169	Th. 199	Su. 230	W. 261	F. 291	M. 322	W. 352
19	Sa. 19	Tu. 50	Tu. 78	F. 109	Su. 139	W. 170	F. 200	M. 231	Th. 262	Sa. 292	Tu. 323	Th. 353
20	Su. 20	W. 51	W. 79	Sa. 110	M. 140	Th. 171	Sa. 201	Tu. 232	F. 263	Su. 293	W. 324	F. 354
21	M. 21	Th. 52	Th. 80	Su. 111	Tu. 141	F. 172	Su. 202	W. 233	Sa. 264	M. 294	Th. 325	Sa. 355
22	Tu. 22	F. 53	F. 81	M. 112	W. 142	Sa. 173	M. 203	Th. 234	Su. 265	Tu. 295	F. 326	Su. 356
23	W. 23	Sa. 54	Sa. 82	Tu. 113	Th. 143	Su. 174	Tu. 204	F. 235	M. 266	W. 296	Sa. 327	M. 357
24	Th. 24	Su. 55	Su. 83	W. 114	F. 144	M. 175	W. 205	Sa. 236	Tu. 267	Th. 297	Su. 328	Tu. 358
25	F. 25	M. 56	M. 84	Th. 115	Sa. 145	Tu. 176	Th. 206	Su. 237	W. 268	F. 298	M. 329	W. 359
26	Sa. 26	Tu. 57	Tu. 85	F. 116	Su. 146	W. 177	F. 207	M. 238	Th. 269	Sa. 299	Tu. 330	Th. 360
27	Su. 27	W. 58	W. 86	Sa. 117	M. 147	Th. 178	Sa. 208	Tu. 239	F. 270	Su. 300	W. 331	F. 361
28	M. 28	Th. 59	Th. 87	Su. 118	Tu. 148	F. 179	Su. 209	W. 240	Sa. 271	M. 301	Th. 332	Sa. 362
29	Tu. 29		F. 88	M. 119	W. 149	Sa. 180	M. 210	Th. 241	Su. 272	Tu. 302	F. 333	Su. 363
30	W. 30		Sa. 89	Tu. 120	Th. 150	Su. 181	Tu. 211	F. 242	M. 273	W. 303	Sa. 334	M. 364
31	Th. 31		Su. 90		F. 151		W. 212	Sa. 243		Th. 304		Tu. 365

ECLIPSES

There are two eclipses of the Sun and one of the Moon.

1. *A partial eclipse of the Moon*, April 25 The eclipse begins at $19^h 52^m$ and ends at $20^h 23^m$. The time of maximum eclipse is $20^h 08^m$ when 0·02 of the Moon's diameter is obscured. It is visible from Africa, Europe, Asia, except the north east, Antarctica, and Australia.

2. *An annular eclipse of the Sun*, May 9-10. See map on page 6. The eclipse begins on May 9 at $21^h 25^m$ and ends at $03^h 25^m$ on May 10; the annular phase begins on May 9 at $22^h 32^m$ and ends at $02^h 18^m$ on May 10. The maximum duration of annularity is $05^m 58^s$.

3. *A total eclipse of the Sun*, November 3. See map on page 7. The eclipse begins at $10^h 05^m$ and ends at $15^h 28^m$. The total phase begins at $11^h 05^m$ and ends at $14^h 28^m$. The maximum duration of totality is $01^m 45^s$.

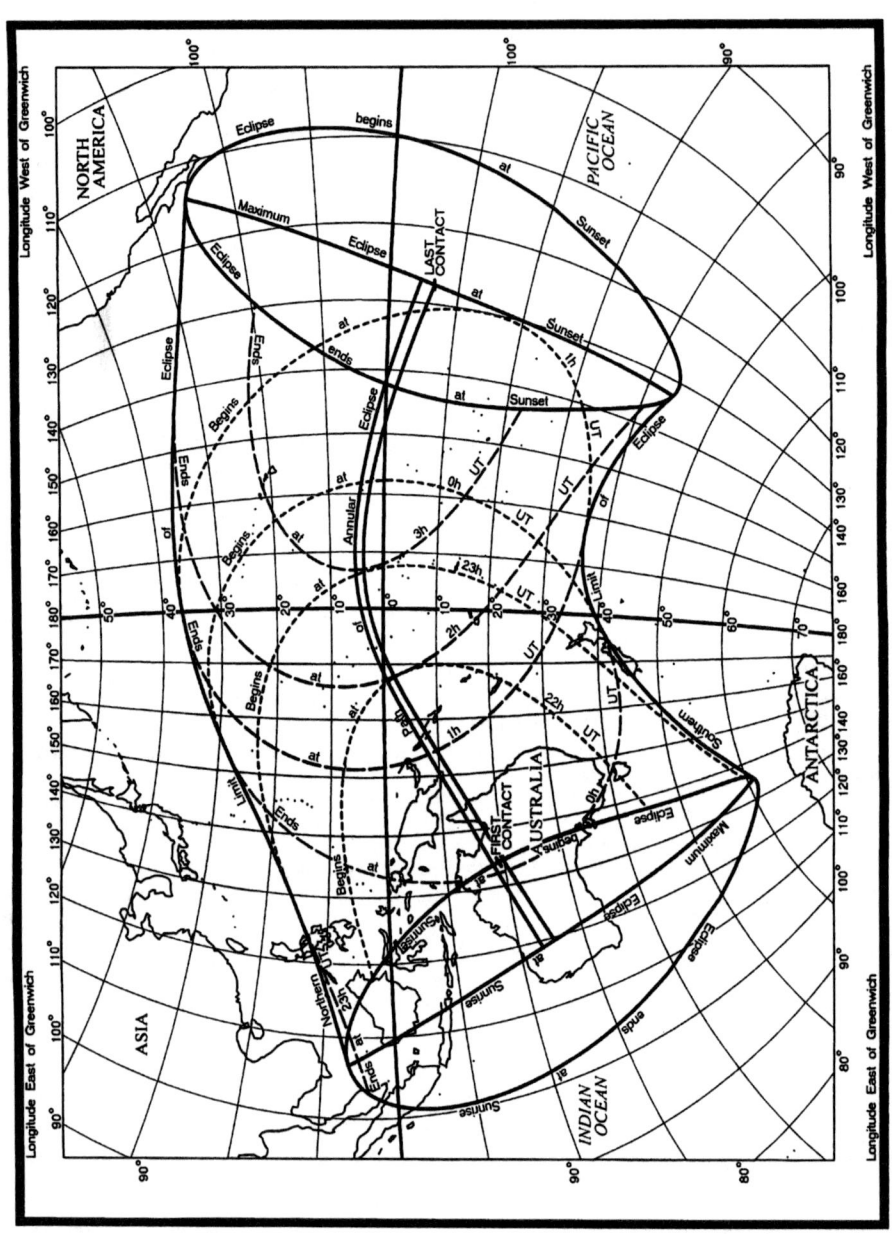

SOLAR ECLIPSE DIAGRAMS

The principal features shown on the above diagrams are: the paths of total and annular eclipses; the northern and southern limits of partial eclipse; the sunrise and sunset curves; dashed lines which show the times of beginning and end of partial eclipse at hourly intervals.

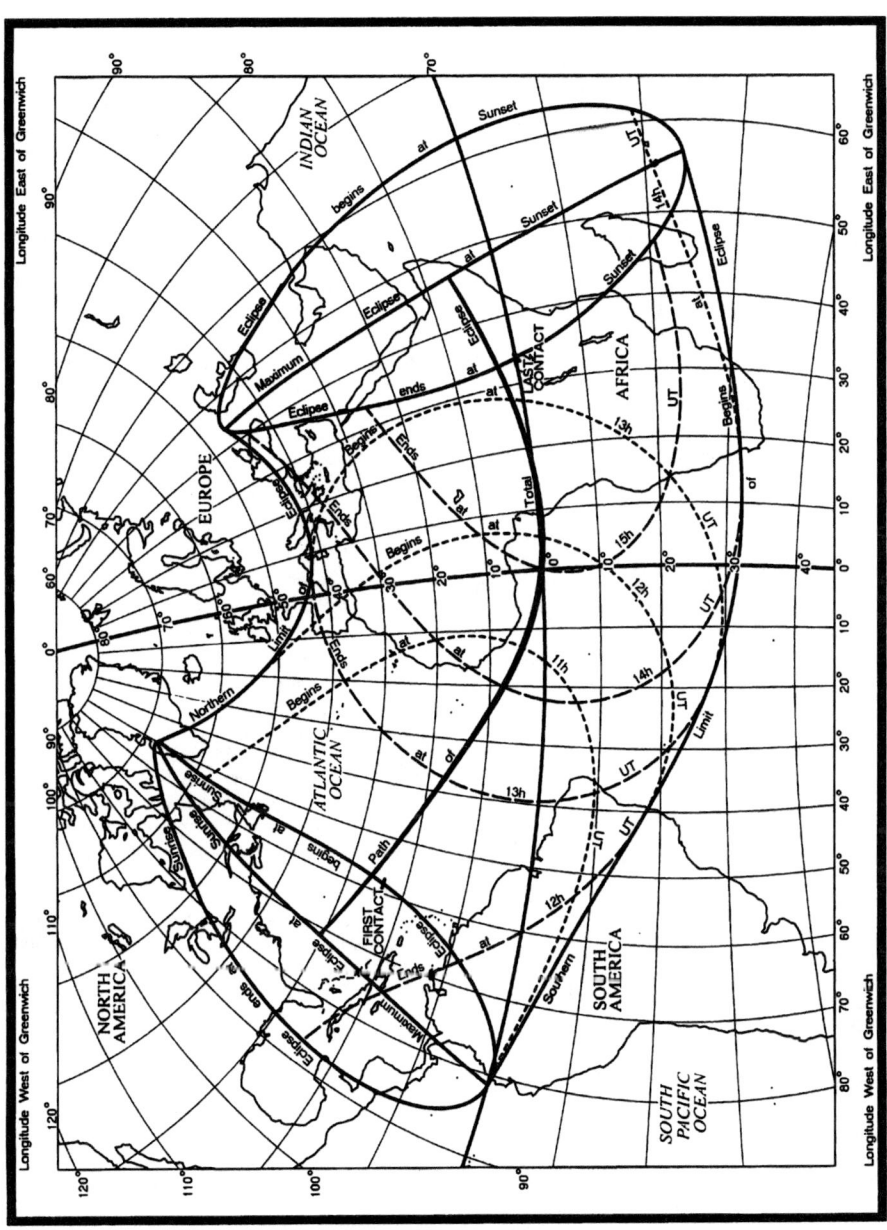

SOLAR ECLIPSE DIAGRAMS

Further details of the paths and times of central eclipse are given in
The Astronomical Almanac.

VISIBILITY OF PLANETS

VENUS is a brilliant object in the morning sky from the beginning of the year until mid-February when it becomes too close to the Sun for observation. From the end of the first week of May it reappears in the evening sky where it stays until the end of the year. Venus is in conjunction with Mercury on May 25 and June 20, with Jupiter on May 28 and with Saturn on September 20.

MARS can be seen in the evening sky in Capricornus and in Aquarius from late January until in the second week of February it becomes too close to the Sun for observation. It reappears in the morning sky during the second half of June in Taurus and moves into Gemini from mid-July (passing 6° S of *Pollux* on August 19). It remains in the morning sky for the rest of the year moving into Cancer from late August, Leo in late September (passing 1° N of *Regulus* on October 14) and Virgo from the end of November. Mars is in conjunction with Mercury on February 8 and with Jupiter on July 22.

JUPITER is in Taurus at the beginning of the year, and can be seen for more than half the night until late February after which it can only be seen in the evening sky (passing 5° N of *Aldebaran* on March 24). In the first week of June it becomes too close to the Sun for observation. It reappears in the morning sky in early July in Gemini in which constellation it remains throughout the rest of the year. Jupiter is in conjunction with Mercury on May 27, with Venus on May 28 and with Mars on July 22.

SATURN rises shortly after midnight at the beginning of the year in Libra, passes into Virgo in mid-May and once again into Libra in early September. It is at opposition on April 28 when it can be seen throughout the night, and from late July until mid-October it is visible only in the evening sky. It then becomes too close to the Sun for observation until in the second half of November it reappears, and can be seen in the morning sky for the rest of the year. Saturn is in conjunction with Venus on September 20 and with Mercury on October 10 and November 26.

MERCURY can only be seen low in the east before sunrise, or low in the west after sunset (about the time of beginning or end of civil twilight). It is visible in the mornings between the following approximate dates: January 1 (−0·6) to January 2 (−0·7), March 11 (+2·8) to May 4 (−1·3), July 19 (+2·7) to August 16 (−1·4) and November 8 (+1·5) to December 12 (−0·7) ; the planet is brighter at the end of each period. It is visible in the evenings between the following approximate dates: January 31 (−1·2) to February 26 (+2·0), May 19 (−1·5) to July 1 (+3·2) and September 4 (−0·9) to October 27 (+2·1); the planet is brighter at the beginning of each period. The figures in parentheses are the magnitudes.

PLANET DIAGRAM

General Description. The diagram on the opposite page shows, in graphical form for any date during the year, the local mean time of meridian passage of the Sun, of the five planets Mercury, Venus, Mars, Jupiter, and Saturn, and of each 30° of SHA; intermediate lines corresponding to particular stars, may be drawn in by the user if desired. It is intended to provide a general picture of the availability of planets and stars for observation.

On each side of the line marking the time of meridian passage of the Sun a band, 45^m wide, is shaded to indicate that planets and most stars crossing the meridian within 45^m of the Sun are too close to the Sun for observation.

Method of use and interpretation. For any date the diagram provides immediately the local mean times of meridian passage of the Sun, planets and stars, and thus the following information:

(a) whether a planet or star is too close to the Sun for observation;

(b) some indication of its position in the sky, especially during twilight;

(c) the proximity of other planets.

When the meridian passage of an outer planet occurs at midnight the body is in opposition to the Sun and is visible all night; a planet may then be observable during both morning and evening twilights. As the time of meridian passage decreases, the body eventually ceases to be observable in the morning, but its altitude above the eastern horizon at sunset gradually increases; this continues until the body is on the meridian during evening twilight. From then onwards the body is observable above the western horizon and its altitude at sunset gradually decreases; eventually the body becomes too close to the Sun for observation. When the body again becomes visible it is seen low in the east during morning twilight; its altitude at sunrise increases until meridian passage occurs during morning twilight. Then, as the time of meridian passage decreases to 0^h, the body is observable in the west during morning twilight with a gradually decreasing altitude, until it once again reaches opposition.

DO NOT CONFUSE

Mercury with Mars in early February and with Saturn in early October and late November; on all occasions Mercury is the brighter object.

Venus with Mercury in mid-May to early June and again in mid-June, with Jupiter in late May to early June and with Saturn in mid-September; on all occasions Venus is the brighter object.

Jupiter with Mercury in late May and with Mars in mid-July to early August; on both occasions Jupiter is the brighter object.

LOCAL MEAN TIME OF MERIDIAN PASSAGE

DIAGONALS ARE OSHA

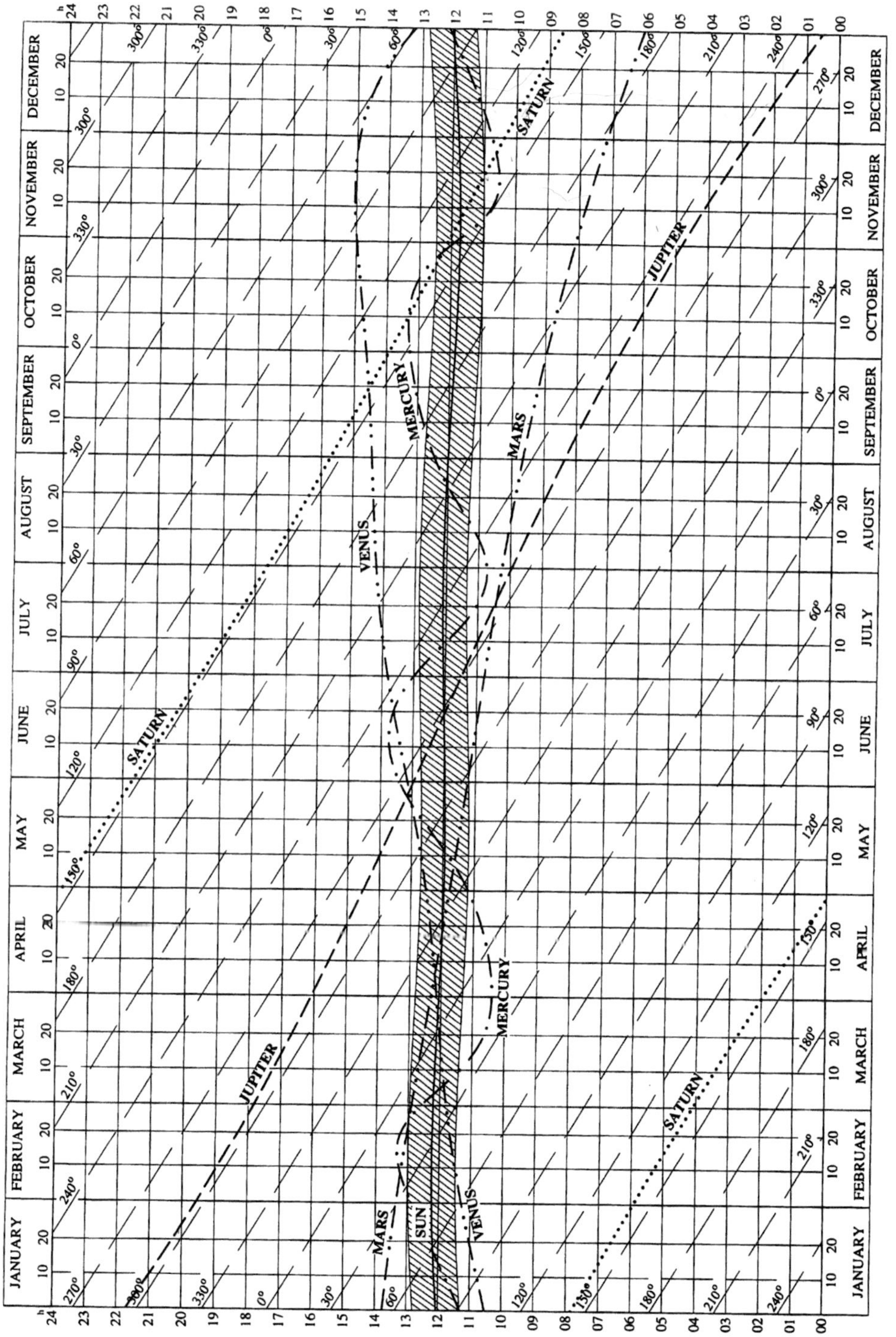

LOCAL MEAN TIME OF MERIDIAN PASSAGE

UT	ARIES GHA	VENUS −3.9 GHA	Dec	MARS +1.2 GHA	Dec	JUPITER −2.7 GHA	Dec	SATURN +0.6 GHA	Dec	STARS Name	SHA	Dec
d h	° ′	° ′	° ′	° ′	° ′	° ′	° ′	° ′	° ′		° ′	° ′
TUESDAY												
1 00	100 48.7	201 53.4	S22 20.7	153 29.8	S20 12.5	34 41.7	N20 54.3	242 54.4	S12 26.9	Acamar	315 18.3	S40 15.4
01	115 51.1	216 52.5	21.0	168 30.2	12.0	49 44.5	54.3	257 56.7	27.0	Achernar	335 26.9	S57 10.5
02	130 53.6	231 51.6	21.4	183 30.6	11.5	64 47.2	54.3	272 59.0	27.0	Acrux	173 09.5	S63 10.1
03	145 56.0	246 50.6 ..	21.7	198 31.1 ..	11.1	79 49.9 ..	54.2	288 01.2 ..	27.1	Adhara	255 12.4	S28 59.6
04	160 58.5	261 49.7	22.0	213 31.5	10.6	94 52.6	54.2	303 03.5	27.1	Aldebaran	290 49.4	N16 32.0
05	176 01.0	276 48.8	22.4	228 32.0	10.1	109 55.3	54.2	318 05.8	27.2			
06	191 03.4	291 47.9	S22 22.7	243 32.4	S20 09.6	124 58.0	N20 54.1	333 08.1	S12 27.2	Alioth	166 21.0	N55 53.0
07	206 05.9	306 47.0	23.1	258 32.8	09.1	140 00.7	54.1	348 10.3	27.3	Alkaid	152 59.3	N49 14.6
08	221 08.4	321 46.1	23.4	273 33.3	08.7	155 03.5	54.1	3 12.6	27.3	Al Na'ir	27 44.4	S46 53.9
09	236 10.8	336 45.2 ..	23.7	288 33.7 ..	08.2	170 06.2 ..	54.1	18 14.9 ..	27.4	Alnilam	275 46.3	S 1 11.8
10	251 13.3	351 44.3	24.0	303 34.1	07.7	185 08.9	54.0	33 17.2	27.5	Alphard	217 56.1	S 8 43.1
11	266 15.8	6 43.4	24.4	318 34.6	07.2	200 11.6	54.0	48 19.4	27.5			
12	281 18.2	21 42.5	S22 24.7	333 35.0	S20 06.7	215 14.3	N20 54.0	63 21.7	S12 27.6	Alphecca	126 11.5	N26 40.2
13	296 20.7	36 41.6	25.0	348 35.4	06.2	230 17.0	53.9	78 24.0	27.6	Alpheratz	357 43.8	N29 10.0
14	311 23.1	51 40.7	25.4	3 35.9	05.8	245 19.7	53.9	93 26.3	27.7	Altair	62 08.9	N 8 54.3
15	326 25.6	66 39.8 ..	25.7	18 36.3 ..	05.3	260 22.4 ..	53.9	108 28.5 ..	27.7	Ankaa	353 16.0	S42 14.3
16	341 28.1	81 38.9	26.0	33 36.8	04.8	275 25.1	53.9	123 30.8	27.8	Antares	112 26.9	S26 27.5
17	356 30.5	96 38.0	26.3	48 37.2	04.3	290 27.9	53.8	138 33.1	27.8			
18	11 33.0	111 37.1	S22 26.7	63 37.6	S20 03.8	305 30.6	N20 53.8	153 35.4	S12 27.9	Arcturus	145 56.1	N19 06.8
19	26 35.5	126 36.2	27.0	78 38.1	03.3	320 33.3	53.8	168 37.6	27.9	Atria	107 29.5	S69 02.8
20	41 37.9	141 35.3	27.3	93 38.5	02.9	335 36.0	53.7	183 39.9	28.0	Avior	234 17.5	S59 33.1
21	56 40.4	156 34.4 ..	27.6	108 38.9 ..	02.4	350 38.7 ..	53.7	198 42.2 ..	28.0	Bellatrix	278 32.0	N 6 21.5
22	71 42.9	171 33.5	27.9	123 39.4	01.9	5 41.4	53.7	213 44.5	28.1	Betelgeuse	271 01.3	N 7 24.4
23	86 45.3	186 32.6	28.2	138 39.8	01.4	20 44.1	53.7	228 46.7	28.1			
WEDNESDAY												
2 00	101 47.8	201 31.7	S22 28.6	153 40.3	S20 00.9	35 46.8	N20 53.6	243 49.0	S12 28.2	Canopus	263 55.7	S52 42.3
01	116 50.3	216 30.7	28.9	168 40.7	20 00.4	50 49.5	53.6	258 51.3	28.2	Capella	280 34.4	N46 00.6
02	131 52.7	231 29.8	29.2	183 41.1	19 59.9	65 52.2	53.6	273 53.6	28.3	Deneb	49 32.1	N45 19.9
03	146 55.2	246 28.9 ..	29.5	198 41.6 ..	59.4	80 54.9 ..	53.5	288 55.8 ..	28.3	Denebola	182 33.9	N14 29.7
04	161 57.6	261 28.0	29.8	213 42.0	59.0	95 57.6	53.5	303 58.1	28.4	Diphda	348 56.2	S17 55.0
05	177 00.1	276 27.1	30.1	228 42.5	58.5	111 00.4	53.5	319 00.4	28.4			
06	192 02.6	291 26.2	S22 30.4	243 42.9	S19 58.0	126 03.1	N20 53.5	334 02.7	S12 28.5	Dubhe	193 51.8	N61 40.4
07	207 05.0	306 25.3	30.7	258 43.3	57.5	141 05.8	53.4	349 05.0	28.6	Elnath	278 12.6	N28 37.0
08	222 07.5	321 24.4	31.0	273 43.8	57.0	156 08.5	53.4	4 07.2	28.6	Eltanin	90 46.8	N51 29.3
09	237 10.0	336 23.5 ..	31.3	288 44.2 ..	56.5	171 11.2 ..	53.4	19 09.5 ..	28.7	Enif	33 47.6	N 9 56.3
10	252 12.4	351 22.6	31.6	303 44.7	56.0	186 13.9	53.4	34 11.8	28.7	Fomalhaut	15 24.5	S29 33.2
11	267 14.9	6 21.6	31.9	318 45.1	55.5	201 16.6	53.3	49 14.1	28.8			
12	282 17.4	21 20.7	S22 32.2	333 45.5	S19 55.0	216 19.3	N20 53.3	64 16.3	S12 28.8	Gacrux	172 01.1	S57 11.0
13	297 19.8	36 19.8	32.5	348 46.0	54.5	231 22.0	53.3	79 18.6	28.9	Gienah	175 52.5	S17 36.9
14	312 22.3	51 18.9	32.8	3 46.4	54.0	246 24.7	53.2	94 20.9	28.9	Hadar	148 48.5	S60 25.9
15	327 24.8	66 18.0 ..	33.1	18 46.9 ..	53.6	261 27.4 ..	53.2	109 23.2 ..	29.0	Hamal	328 00.9	N23 31.5
16	342 27.2	81 17.1	33.4	33 47.3	53.1	276 30.1	53.2	124 25.5	29.0	Kaus Aust.	83 44.6	S34 22.5
17	357 29.7	96 16.2	33.7	48 47.7	52.6	291 32.8	53.2	139 27.7	29.1			
18	12 32.1	111 15.3	S22 34.0	63 48.2	S19 52.1	306 35.5	N20 53.1	154 30.0	S12 29.1	Kochab	137 20.7	N74 05.8
19	27 34.6	126 14.4	34.3	78 48.6	51.6	321 38.2	53.1	169 32.3	29.2	Markab	13 38.8	N15 16.7
20	42 37.1	141 13.4	34.6	93 49.1	51.1	336 40.9	53.1	184 34.6	29.2	Menkar	314 15.2	N 4 08.4
21	57 39.5	156 12.5 ..	34.9	108 49.5 ..	50.6	351 43.6 ..	53.1	199 36.8 ..	29.3	Menkent	148 08.0	S36 25.9
22	72 42.0	171 11.6	35.2	123 50.0	50.1	6 46.3	53.0	214 39.1	29.3	Miaplacidus	221 38.9	S69 46.2
23	87 44.5	186 10.7	35.5	138 50.4	49.6	21 49.0	53.0	229 41.4	29.4			
THURSDAY												
3 00	102 46.9	201 09.8	S22 35.8	153 50.8	S19 49.1	36 51.7	N20 53.0	244 43.7	S12 29.4	Mirfak	308 40.4	N49 54.6
01	117 49.4	216 08.9	36.0	168 51.3	48.6	51 54.4	52.9	259 46.0	29.5	Nunki	75 59.1	S26 16.7
02	132 51.9	231 08.0	36.3	183 51.7	48.1	66 57.1	52.9	274 48.2	29.5	Peacock	53 20.3	S56 41.5
03	147 54.3	246 07.0 ..	36.6	198 52.2 ..	47.6	81 59.8 ..	52.9	289 50.5 ..	29.6	Pollux	243 27.7	N27 59.4
04	162 56.8	261 06.1	36.9	213 52.6	47.1	97 02.5	52.9	304 52.8	29.6	Procyon	244 59.7	N 5 11.3
05	177 59.2	276 05.2	37.2	228 53.1	46.6	112 05.2	52.8	319 55.1	29.7			
06	193 01.7	291 04.3	S22 37.4	243 53.5	S19 46.1	127 07.9	N20 52.8	334 57.4	S12 29.7	Rasalhague	96 07.1	N12 33.1
07	208 04.2	306 03.4	37.7	258 53.9	45.6	142 10.6	52.8	349 59.6	29.8	Regulus	207 43.6	N11 54.0
08	223 06.6	321 02.5	38.0	273 54.4	45.1	157 13.3	52.8	5 01.9	29.8	Rigel	281 12.0	S 8 11.4
09	238 09.1	336 01.6 ..	38.3	288 54.8 ..	44.6	172 16.0 ..	52.7	20 04.2 ..	29.9	Rigil Kent.	139 52.4	S60 53.0
10	253 11.6	351 00.6	38.6	303 55.3	44.1	187 18.7	52.7	35 06.5	29.9	Sabik	102 13.2	S15 44.3
11	268 14.0	5 59.7	38.8	318 55.7	43.6	202 21.4	52.7	50 08.8	30.0			
12	283 16.5	20 58.8	S22 39.1	333 56.2	S19 43.1	217 24.1	N20 52.7	65 11.1	S12 30.0	Schedar	349 40.8	N56 36.9
13	298 19.0	35 57.9	39.4	348 56.6	42.6	232 26.8	52.6	80 13.3	30.1	Shaula	96 22.7	S37 06.6
14	313 21.4	50 57.0	39.6	3 57.1	42.1	247 29.5	52.6	95 15.6	30.1	Sirius	258 33.6	S16 44.2
15	328 23.9	65 56.0 ..	39.9	18 57.5 ..	41.6	262 32.2 ..	52.6	110 17.9 ..	30.2	Spica	158 31.6	S11 13.7
16	343 26.4	80 55.1	40.2	33 57.9	41.1	277 34.9	52.5	125 20.2	30.2	Suhail	222 52.3	S43 29.2
17	358 28.8	95 54.2	40.4	48 58.4	40.6	292 37.6	52.5	140 22.5	30.3			
18	13 31.3	110 53.3	S22 40.7	63 58.8	S19 40.1	307 40.3	N20 52.5	155 24.7	S12 30.3	Vega	80 39.6	N38 47.9
19	28 33.7	125 52.4	41.0	78 59.3	39.6	322 43.0	52.5	170 27.0	30.4	Zuben'ubi	137 05.9	S16 05.7
20	43 36.2	140 51.5	41.2	93 59.7	39.1	337 45.7	52.4	185 29.3	30.4		SHA	Mer. Pass.
21	58 38.7	155 50.5 ..	41.5	109 00.2 ..	38.6	352 48.4 ..	52.4	200 31.6 ..	30.5		° ′	h m
22	73 41.1	170 49.6	41.8	124 00.6	38.1	7 51.1	52.4	215 33.9	30.5	Venus	99 43.9	10 35
23	88 43.6	185 48.7	42.0	139 01.1	37.6	22 53.8	52.4	230 36.2	30.6	Mars	51 52.5	13 45
	h m									Jupiter	293 59.0	21 33
Mer. Pass.	17 10.0	v −0.9	d 0.3	v 0.4	d 0.5	v 2.7	d 0.0	v 2.3	d 0.1	Saturn	142 01.2	7 44

UT	SUN GHA	SUN Dec	MOON GHA	v	Dec	d	HP
d h	° '	° '	° '	'	° '	'	'
1 00	179 08.3	S23 00.1	319 18.2	13.4	N 9 42.5	10.0	55.5
01	194 08.1	22 59.9	333 50.6	13.5	9 32.5	10.0	55.5
02	209 07.8	59.7	348 23.1	13.5	9 22.5	10.1	55.6
03	224 07.5	.. 59.5	2 55.6	13.5	9 12.4	10.1	55.6
04	239 07.2	59.3	17 28.1	13.5	9 02.3	10.2	55.6
05	254 06.9	59.1	32 00.6	13.5	8 52.1	10.2	55.6
06	269 06.6	S22 58.9	46 33.1	13.5	N 8 41.9	10.2	55.6
07	284 06.3	58.7	61 05.6	13.5	8 31.7	10.3	55.7
08	299 06.0	58.5	75 38.1	13.5	8 21.4	10.4	55.7
09	314 05.7	.. 58.3	90 10.6	13.6	8 11.0	10.4	55.7
10	329 05.4	58.1	104 43.2	13.5	8 00.6	10.4	55.7
11	344 05.1	57.8	119 15.7	13.6	7 50.2	10.5	55.8
12	359 04.8	S22 57.6	133 48.3	13.5	N 7 39.7	10.5	55.8
13	14 04.5	57.4	148 20.8	13.6	7 29.2	10.5	55.8
14	29 04.2	57.2	162 53.4	13.5	7 18.7	10.6	55.8
15	44 03.9	.. 57.0	177 25.9	13.6	7 08.1	10.7	55.8
16	59 03.7	56.8	191 58.5	13.5	6 57.4	10.7	55.9
17	74 03.4	56.6	206 31.0	13.6	6 46.7	10.7	55.9
18	89 03.1	S22 56.3	221 03.6	13.5	N 6 36.0	10.7	55.9
19	104 02.8	56.1	235 36.1	13.6	6 25.3	10.8	55.9
20	119 02.5	55.9	250 08.7	13.6	6 14.5	10.8	55.9
21	134 02.2	.. 55.7	264 41.3	13.6	6 03.7	10.9	56.0
22	149 01.9	55.4	279 13.8	13.6	5 52.8	10.9	56.0
23	164 01.6	55.2	293 46.4	13.5	5 41.9	10.9	56.0
2 00	179 01.3	S22 55.0	308 18.9	13.6	N 5 31.0	10.9	56.0
01	194 01.0	54.8	322 51.5	13.5	5 20.1	11.0	56.1
02	209 00.7	54.6	337 24.0	13.6	5 09.1	11.0	56.1
03	224 00.5	.. 54.3	351 56.6	13.5	4 58.1	11.1	56.1
04	239 00.2	54.1	6 29.1	13.5	4 47.0	11.1	56.1
05	253 59.9	53.9	21 01.6	13.6	4 35.9	11.1	56.2
06	268 59.6	S22 53.6	35 34.2	13.5	N 4 24.8	11.1	56.2
07	283 59.3	53.4	50 06.7	13.5	4 13.7	11.2	56.2
08	298 59.0	53.2	64 39.2	13.5	4 02.5	11.2	56.2
09	313 58.7	.. 53.0	79 11.7	13.5	3 51.3	11.2	56.2
10	328 58.4	52.7	93 44.2	13.4	3 40.1	11.2	56.3
11	343 58.1	52.5	108 16.6	13.5	3 28.9	11.3	56.3
12	358 57.8	S22 52.3	122 49.1	13.4	N 3 17.6	11.3	56.3
13	13 57.6	52.0	137 21.5	13.5	3 06.3	11.3	56.3
14	28 57.3	51.8	151 54.0	13.4	2 55.0	11.3	56.4
15	43 57.0	.. 51.6	166 26.4	13.4	2 43.7	11.4	56.4
16	58 56.7	51.3	180 58.8	13.4	2 32.3	11.4	56.4
17	73 56.4	51.1	195 31.2	13.4	2 20.9	11.4	56.4
18	88 56.1	S22 50.8	210 03.6	13.3	N 2 09.5	11.4	56.5
19	103 55.8	50.6	224 35.9	13.4	1 58.1	11.4	56.5
20	118 55.5	50.4	239 08.3	13.3	1 46.7	11.5	56.5
21	133 55.2	.. 50.1	253 40.6	13.3	1 35.2	11.4	56.5
22	148 55.0	49.9	268 12.9	13.3	1 23.8	11.5	56.6
23	163 54.7	49.6	282 45.2	13.2	1 12.3	11.5	56.6
3 00	178 54.4	S22 49.4	297 17.4	13.3	N 1 00.8	11.5	56.6
01	193 54.1	49.2	311 49.7	13.2	0 49.3	11.6	56.7
02	208 53.8	48.9	326 21.9	13.2	0 37.7	11.5	56.7
03	223 53.5	.. 48.7	340 54.1	13.1	0 26.2	11.6	56.7
04	238 53.2	48.4	355 26.2	13.2	0 14.6	11.5	56.8
05	253 52.9	48.2	9 58.4	13.1	N 0 03.1	11.6	56.8
06	268 52.7	S22 47.9	24 30.5	13.1	S 0 08.5	11.6	56.8
07	283 52.4	47.7	39 02.6	13.0	0 20.1	11.6	56.8
08	298 52.1	47.4	53 34.6	13.1	0 31.7	11.6	56.8
09	313 51.8	.. 47.2	68 06.7	13.0	0 43.3	11.6	56.9
10	328 51.5	46.9	82 38.7	12.9	0 54.9	11.6	56.9
11	343 51.2	46.7	97 10.6	13.0	1 06.5	11.6	56.9
12	358 50.9	S22 46.4	111 42.6	12.9	S 1 18.1	11.6	56.9
13	13 50.7	46.2	126 14.5	12.8	1 29.7	11.7	57.0
14	28 50.4	45.9	140 46.3	12.9	1 41.4	11.6	57.0
15	43 50.1	.. 45.7	155 18.2	12.8	1 53.0	11.6	57.0
16	58 49.8	45.4	169 50.0	12.7	2 04.6	11.7	57.1
17	73 49.5	45.2	184 21.7	12.8	2 16.3	11.6	57.1
18	88 49.2	S22 44.9	198 53.5	12.7	S 2 27.9	11.6	57.1
19	103 49.0	44.6	213 25.2	12.6	2 39.5	11.6	57.1
20	118 48.7	44.4	227 56.8	12.6	2 51.1	11.7	57.2
21	133 48.4	.. 44.1	242 28.4	12.6	3 02.8	11.6	57.2
22	148 48.1	43.9	257 00.0	12.5	3 14.4	11.6	57.2
23	163 47.8	43.6	271 31.5	12.5	S 3 26.0	11.6	57.3
	SD 16.3	d 0.2	SD 15.2		15.3		15.5

Lat.	Twilight Naut.	Twilight Civil	Sunrise	Moonrise 1	2	3	4
°	h m	h m	h m	h m	h m	h m	h m
N 72	08 23	10 39	■	20 02	21 51	23 41	25 37
N 70	08 04	09 48	■	20 12	21 53	23 36	25 23
68	07 49	09 16	■	20 19	21 54	23 31	25 12
66	07 37	08 52	10 26	20 25	21 55	23 28	25 03
64	07 26	08 33	09 48	20 30	21 57	23 25	24 56
62	07 17	08 18	09 22	20 35	21 58	23 22	24 49
60	07 09	08 05	09 02	20 39	21 58	23 20	24 44
N 58	07 02	07 54	08 45	20 42	21 59	23 18	24 39
56	06 55	07 44	08 31	20 45	22 00	23 16	24 35
54	06 50	07 35	08 19	20 48	22 00	23 14	24 31
52	06 44	07 27	08 08	20 50	22 01	23 13	24 27
50	06 39	07 20	07 58	20 53	22 01	23 12	24 24
45	06 28	07 05	07 38	20 57	22 02	23 09	24 17
N 40	06 18	06 52	07 22	21 01	22 03	23 06	24 11
35	06 09	06 40	07 08	21 05	22 04	23 04	24 07
30	06 00	06 30	06 56	21 08	22 05	23 03	24 02
20	05 44	06 12	06 36	21 13	22 06	22 59	23 55
N 10	05 28	05 55	06 17	21 18	22 07	22 57	23 48
0	05 12	05 38	06 00	21 22	22 08	22 54	23 42
S 10	04 53	05 20	05 43	21 27	22 09	22 52	23 36
20	04 31	05 00	05 25	21 31	22 10	22 49	23 30
30	04 03	04 36	05 03	21 37	22 11	22 46	23 23
35	03 45	04 21	04 51	21 40	22 12	22 45	23 19
40	03 22	04 03	04 36	21 43	22 13	22 43	23 14
45	02 52	03 41	04 18	21 47	22 14	22 41	23 09
S 50	02 09	03 13	03 56	21 52	22 15	22 38	23 03
52	01 43	02 58	03 46	21 54	22 15	22 37	23 00
54	01 04	02 41	03 34	21 56	22 16	22 35	22 57
56	////	02 20	03 20	21 59	22 16	22 34	22 53
58	////	01 52	03 04	22 02	22 17	22 33	22 49
S 60	////	01 10	02 45	22 05	22 18	22 31	22 45

Lat.	Sunset	Twilight Civil	Twilight Naut.	Moonset 1	2	3	4
°	h m	h m	h m	h m	h m	h m	h m
N 72	■	13 30	15 46	10 42	10 29	10 16	10 03
N 70	■	14 21	16 05	10 31	10 24	10 18	10 11
68	■	14 53	16 20	10 21	10 20	10 19	10 18
66	13 43	15 17	16 32	10 14	10 17	10 20	10 23
64	14 20	15 35	16 42	10 07	10 14	10 21	10 28
62	14 47	15 50	16 52	10 02	10 12	10 22	10 32
60	15 07	16 03	17 00	09 57	10 10	10 22	10 35
N 58	15 24	16 15	17 07	09 52	10 08	10 23	10 39
56	15 38	16 24	17 13	09 48	10 06	10 23	10 41
54	15 50	16 33	17 19	09 45	10 05	10 24	10 44
52	16 01	16 41	17 24	09 42	10 03	10 24	10 46
50	16 10	16 48	17 29	09 39	10 02	10 25	10 48
45	16 30	17 04	17 41	09 32	09 59	10 26	10 53
N 40	16 46	17 17	17 51	09 27	09 57	10 26	10 57
35	17 00	17 28	18 00	09 22	09 55	10 27	11 00
30	17 12	17 38	18 08	09 18	09 53	10 27	11 03
20	17 33	17 57	18 24	09 11	09 50	10 28	11 08
N 10	17 51	18 14	18 40	09 05	09 47	10 29	11 13
0	18 08	18 30	18 56	08 59	09 44	10 30	11 17
S 10	18 25	18 48	19 15	08 53	09 41	10 31	11 21
20	18 43	19 08	19 37	08 46	09 38	10 31	11 26
30	19 05	19 32	20 05	08 39	09 35	10 32	11 31
35	19 18	19 47	20 23	08 35	09 33	10 33	11 34
40	19 32	20 05	20 46	08 30	09 31	10 33	11 37
45	19 50	20 27	21 15	08 24	09 28	10 34	11 41
S 50	20 11	20 55	21 58	08 17	09 25	10 35	11 46
52	20 22	21 10	22 24	08 14	09 24	10 35	11 48
54	20 34	21 27	23 02	08 11	09 22	10 35	11 50
56	20 47	21 47	////	08 07	09 20	10 36	11 53
58	21 03	22 15	////	08 02	09 19	10 36	11 56
S 60	21 22	22 56	////	07 57	09 16	10 37	11 59

	SUN			MOON			
Day	Eqn. of Time 00ʰ	Eqn. of Time 12ʰ	Mer. Pass.	Mer. Pass. Upper	Mer. Pass. Lower	Age	Phase
d	m s	m s	h m	h m	h m	d	%
1	03 26	03 40	12 04	02 48	15 11	19	85
2	03 54	04 08	12 04	03 33	15 56	20	77
3	04 22	04 36	12 05	04 19	16 42	21	68

TUESDAY — WEDNESDAY — THURSDAY

12   2013 JANUARY 4, 5, 6 (FRI., SAT., SUN.)

UT	ARIES GHA	VENUS −3.9 GHA	Dec	MARS +1.2 GHA	Dec	JUPITER −2.7 GHA	Dec	SATURN +0.6 GHA	Dec	STARS Name	SHA	Dec
4 00	103 46.1	200 47.8	S22 42.3	154 01.5	S19 37.1	37 56.5	N20 52.3	245 38.4	S12 30.6	Acamar	315 18.3	S40 15.4
01	118 48.5	215 46.9	42.5	169 02.0	36.6	52 59.1	52.3	260 40.7	30.7	Achernar	335 26.9	S57 10.5
02	133 51.0	230 45.9	42.8	184 02.4	36.1	68 01.8	52.3	275 43.0	30.7	Acrux	173 09.4	S63 10.1
03	148 53.5	245 45.0 ..	43.0	199 02.9 ..	35.6	83 04.5 ..	52.3	290 45.3 ..	30.8	Adhara	255 12.4	S28 59.6
04	163 55.9	260 44.1	43.3	214 03.3	35.0	98 07.2	52.2	305 47.6	30.8	Aldebaran	290 49.4	N16 32.0
05	178 58.4	275 43.2	43.5	229 03.7	34.5	113 09.9	52.2	320 49.9	30.9			
06	194 00.9	290 42.3	S22 43.8	244 04.2	S19 34.0	128 12.6	N20 52.2	335 52.1	S12 30.9	Alioth	166 21.0	N55 53.0
07	209 03.3	305 41.3	44.0	259 04.6	33.5	143 15.3	52.2	350 54.4	31.0	Alkaid	152 59.3	N49 14.6
08	224 05.8	320 40.4	44.3	274 05.1	33.0	158 18.0	52.1	5 56.7	31.0	Al Na'ir	27 44.4	S46 53.9
F 09	239 08.2	335 39.5 ..	44.5	289 05.5 ..	32.5	173 20.7 ..	52.1	20 59.0 ..	31.1	Alnilam	275 46.3	S 1 11.8
R 10	254 10.7	350 38.6	44.8	304 06.0	32.0	188 23.4	52.1	36 01.3	31.1	Alphard	217 56.1	S 8 43.1
I 11	269 13.2	5 37.6	45.0	319 06.4	31.5	203 26.1	52.1	51 03.6	31.2			
D 12	284 15.6	20 36.7	S22 45.3	334 06.9	S19 31.0	218 28.8	N20 52.0	66 05.8	S12 31.2	Alphecca	126 11.5	N26 40.2
A 13	299 18.1	35 35.8	45.5	349 07.3	30.5	233 31.4	52.0	81 08.1	31.3	Alpheratz	357 43.9	N29 10.0
Y 14	314 20.6	50 34.9	45.8	4 07.8	30.0	248 34.1	52.0	96 10.4	31.3	Altair	62 08.9	N 8 54.3
15	329 23.0	65 34.0 ..	46.0	19 08.2 ..	29.4	263 36.8 ..	51.9	111 12.7 ..	31.4	Ankaa	353 16.1	S42 14.3
16	344 25.5	80 33.0	46.2	34 08.7	28.9	278 39.5	51.9	126 15.0	31.4	Antares	112 26.9	S26 27.5
17	359 28.0	95 32.1	46.5	49 09.1	28.4	293 42.2	51.9	141 17.3	31.5			
18	14 30.4	110 31.2	S22 46.7	64 09.6	S19 27.9	308 44.9	N20 51.9	156 19.5	S12 31.5	Arcturus	145 56.1	N19 06.7
19	29 32.9	125 30.3	46.9	79 10.0	27.4	323 47.6	51.8	171 21.8	31.6	Atria	107 29.5	S69 02.8
20	44 35.3	140 29.3	47.2	94 10.5	26.9	338 50.3	51.8	186 24.1	31.6	Avior	234 17.5	S59 33.1
21	59 37.8	155 28.4 ..	47.4	109 10.9 ..	26.4	353 52.9 ..	51.8	201 26.4 ..	31.7	Bellatrix	278 32.0	N 6 21.5
22	74 40.3	170 27.5	47.6	124 11.4	25.9	8 55.6	51.8	216 28.7	31.7	Betelgeuse	271 01.3	N 7 24.4
23	89 42.7	185 26.6	47.9	139 11.8	25.4	23 58.3	51.7	231 31.0	31.8			
5 00	104 45.2	200 25.6	S22 48.1	154 12.3	S19 24.8	39 01.0	N20 51.7	246 33.3	S12 31.8	Canopus	263 55.7	S52 42.4
01	119 47.7	215 24.7	48.3	169 12.7	24.3	54 03.7	51.7	261 35.5	31.9	Capella	280 34.4	N46 00.6
02	134 50.1	230 23.8	48.6	184 13.2	23.8	69 06.4	51.7	276 37.8	31.9	Deneb	49 32.1	N45 19.9
03	149 52.6	245 22.9 ..	48.8	199 13.6 ..	23.3	84 09.1 ..	51.6	291 40.1 ..	32.0	Denebola	182 33.9	N14 29.7
04	164 55.1	260 21.9	49.0	214 14.1	22.8	99 11.7	51.6	306 42.4	32.0	Diphda	348 56.2	S17 55.0
05	179 57.5	275 21.0	49.2	229 14.5	22.3	114 14.4	51.6	321 44.7	32.1			
06	195 00.0	290 20.1	S22 49.5	244 15.0	S19 21.7	129 17.1	N20 51.6	336 47.0	S12 32.1	Dubhe	193 51.8	N61 40.4
S 07	210 02.5	305 19.2	49.7	259 15.4	21.2	144 19.8	51.6	351 49.3	32.2	Elnath	278 12.6	N28 37.0
A 08	225 04.9	320 18.2	49.9	274 15.9	20.7	159 22.5	51.5	6 51.6	32.2	Eltanin	90 46.8	N51 29.3
T 09	240 07.4	335 17.3 ..	50.1	289 16.3 ..	20.2	174 25.2 ..	51.5	21 53.8 ..	32.2	Enif	33 47.7	N 9 56.2
U 10	255 09.8	350 16.4	50.3	304 16.8	19.7	189 27.8	51.5	36 56.1	32.3	Fomalhaut	15 24.5	S29 33.2
R 11	270 12.3	5 15.4	50.5	319 17.3	19.1	204 30.5	51.5	51 58.4	32.3			
D 12	285 14.8	20 14.5	S22 50.8	334 17.7	S19 18.6	219 33.2	N20 51.4	67 00.7	S12 32.4	Gacrux	172 01.1	S57 11.0
A 13	300 17.2	35 13.6	51.0	349 18.2	18.1	234 35.9	51.4	82 03.0	32.4	Gienah	175 52.5	S17 36.9
Y 14	315 19.7	50 12.7	51.2	4 18.6	17.6	249 38.6	51.4	97 05.3	32.5	Hadar	148 48.5	S60 25.9
15	330 22.2	65 11.7 ..	51.4	19 19.1 ..	17.1	264 41.3 ..	51.4	112 07.6 ..	32.5	Hamal	328 01.0	N23 31.5
16	345 24.6	80 10.8	51.6	34 19.5	16.6	279 43.9	51.3	127 09.9	32.6	Kaus Aust.	83 44.6	S34 22.5
17	0 27.1	95 09.9	51.8	49 20.0	16.0	294 46.6	51.3	142 12.1	32.6			
18	15 29.6	110 08.9	S22 52.0	64 20.4	S19 15.5	309 49.3	N20 51.3	157 14.4	S12 32.7	Kochab	137 20.7	N74 05.8
19	30 32.0	125 08.0	52.2	79 20.9	15.0	324 52.0	51.3	172 16.7	32.7	Markab	13 38.8	N15 16.7
20	45 34.5	140 07.1	52.4	94 21.3	14.5	339 54.7	51.2	187 19.0	32.8	Menkar	314 15.2	N 4 08.4
21	60 37.0	155 06.2 ..	52.6	109 21.8 ..	13.9	354 57.3 ..	51.2	202 21.3 ..	32.8	Menkent	148 08.0	S36 25.9
22	75 39.4	170 05.2	52.8	124 22.2	13.4	10 00.0	51.2	217 23.6	32.9	Miaplacidus	221 38.9	S69 46.2
23	90 41.9	185 04.3	53.0	139 22.7	12.9	25 02.7	51.2	232 25.9	32.9			
6 00	105 44.3	200 03.4	S22 53.2	154 23.2	S19 12.4	40 05.4	N20 51.1	247 28.2	S12 33.0	Mirfak	308 40.4	N49 54.6
01	120 46.8	215 02.4	53.4	169 23.6	11.9	55 08.1	51.1	262 30.5	33.0	Nunki	75 59.1	S26 16.7
02	135 49.3	230 01.5	53.6	184 24.1	11.3	70 10.7	51.1	277 32.7	33.1	Peacock	53 20.3	S56 41.5
03	150 51.7	245 00.6 ..	53.8	199 24.5 ..	10.8	85 13.4 ..	51.1	292 35.0 ..	33.1	Pollux	243 27.7	N27 59.4
04	165 54.2	259 59.6	54.0	214 25.0	10.3	100 16.1	51.0	307 37.3	33.2	Procyon	244 59.7	N 5 11.3
05	180 56.7	274 58.7	54.2	229 25.4	09.8	115 18.8	51.0	322 39.6	33.2			
06	195 59.1	289 57.8	S22 54.4	244 25.9	S19 09.2	130 21.4	N20 51.0	337 41.9	S12 33.2	Rasalhague	96 07.1	N12 33.1
07	211 01.6	304 56.9	54.6	259 26.4	08.7	145 24.1	51.0	352 44.2	33.3	Regulus	207 43.6	N11 54.0
08	226 04.1	319 55.9	54.8	274 26.8	08.2	160 26.8	50.9	7 46.5	33.3	Rigel	281 12.0	S 8 11.4
S 09	241 06.5	334 55.0 ..	55.0	289 27.3 ..	07.7	175 29.5 ..	50.9	22 48.8 ..	33.4	Rigil Kent.	139 52.4	S60 53.0
U 10	256 09.0	349 54.1	55.2	304 27.7	07.1	190 32.1	50.9	37 51.1	33.4	Sabik	102 13.2	S15 44.3
N 11	271 11.4	4 53.1	55.4	319 28.2	06.6	205 34.8	50.9	52 53.4	33.5			
D 12	286 13.9	19 52.2	S22 55.6	334 28.6	S19 06.1	220 37.5	N20 50.9	67 55.6	S12 33.5	Schedar	349 40.8	N56 36.9
A 13	301 16.4	34 51.3	55.7	349 29.1	05.5	235 40.2	50.8	82 57.9	33.6	Shaula	96 22.7	S37 06.4
Y 14	316 18.8	49 50.3	55.9	4 29.5	05.0	250 42.8	50.8	98 00.2	33.6	Sirius	258 33.6	S16 44.2
15	331 21.3	64 49.4 ..	56.1	19 30.0 ..	04.5	265 45.5 ..	50.8	113 02.5 ..	33.7	Spica	158 31.6	S11 13.8
16	346 23.8	79 48.5	56.3	34 30.5	04.0	280 48.2	50.8	128 04.8	33.7	Suhail	222 52.2	S43 29.2
17	1 26.2	94 47.5	56.5	49 30.9	03.4	295 50.9	50.7	143 07.1	33.8			
18	16 28.7	109 46.6	S22 56.6	64 31.4	S19 02.9	310 53.5	N20 50.7	158 09.4	S12 33.8	Vega	80 39.6	N38 47.9
19	31 31.2	124 45.7	56.8	79 31.9	02.4	325 56.2	50.7	173 11.7	33.9	Zuben'ubi	137 05.9	S16 05.7
20	46 33.6	139 44.7	57.0	94 32.3	01.8	340 58.9	50.7	188 14.0	33.9		SHA	Mer.Pass.
21	61 36.1	154 43.8 ..	57.2	109 32.7 ..	01.3	356 01.5 ..	50.6	203 16.3 ..	33.9		° ′	h m
22	76 38.6	169 42.9	57.4	124 33.2	00.8	11 04.2	50.6	218 18.6	34.0	Venus	95 40.4	10 39
23	91 41.0	184 41.9	57.5	139 33.7	00.2	26 06.9	50.6	233 20.8	34.0	Mars	49 27.1	13 43
	h m									Jupiter	294 15.8	21 20
Mer.Pass. 16 58.2	v −0.9	d 0.2	v 0.5	d 0.5	v 2.7	d 0.0	v 2.3	d 0.0	Saturn	141 48.1	7 33

UT	SUN GHA	SUN Dec	MOON GHA	v	MOON Dec	d	HP
d h	° ′	° ′	° ′	′	° ′	′	′
4 00	178 47.5	S22 43.3	286 03.0	12.4	S 3 37.6	11.6	57.3
01	193 47.2	43.1	300 34.4	12.4	3 49.2	11.6	57.3
02	208 47.0	42.8	315 05.8	12.4	4 00.8	11.6	57.3
03	223 46.7	.. 42.6	329 37.2	12.3	4 12.4	11.6	57.4
04	238 46.4	42.3	344 08.5	12.3	4 24.0	11.6	57.4
05	253 46.1	42.0	358 39.8	12.2	4 35.6	11.5	57.4
06	268 45.8	S22 41.8	13 11.0	12.1	S 4 47.1	11.6	57.5
07	283 45.6	41.5	27 42.1	12.2	4 58.7	11.5	57.5
08	298 45.3	41.2	42 13.3	12.0	5 10.2	11.5	57.5
F 09	313 45.0	.. 41.0	56 44.3	12.0	5 21.7	11.5	57.6
R 10	328 44.7	40.7	71 15.3	12.0	5 33.2	11.5	57.6
I 11	343 44.4	40.4	85 46.3	11.9	5 44.7	11.5	57.6
D 12	358 44.1	S22 40.1	100 17.2	11.9	S 5 56.2	11.4	57.6
A 13	13 43.9	39.9	114 48.1	11.7	6 07.6	11.5	57.7
Y 14	28 43.6	39.6	129 18.8	11.8	6 19.1	11.4	57.7
15	43 43.3	.. 39.3	143 49.6	11.7	6 30.5	11.4	57.7
16	58 43.0	39.0	158 20.3	11.6	6 41.9	11.3	57.8
17	73 42.7	38.8	172 50.9	11.6	6 53.2	11.4	57.8
18	88 42.5	S22 38.5	187 21.5	11.5	S 7 04.6	11.3	57.8
19	103 42.2	38.2	201 52.0	11.4	7 15.9	11.3	57.9
20	118 41.9	37.9	216 22.4	11.4	7 27.2	11.2	57.9
21	133 41.6	.. 37.7	230 52.8	11.4	7 38.4	11.3	57.9
22	148 41.3	37.4	245 23.2	11.2	7 49.7	11.2	57.9
23	163 41.1	37.1	259 53.4	11.2	8 00.9	11.2	58.0
5 00	178 40.8	S22 36.8	274 23.6	11.2	S 8 12.1	11.1	58.0
01	193 40.5	36.5	288 53.8	11.0	8 23.2	11.1	58.0
02	208 40.2	36.2	303 23.8	11.0	8 34.3	11.1	58.1
03	223 39.9	.. 36.0	317 53.8	11.0	8 45.4	11.1	58.1
04	238 39.7	35.7	332 23.8	10.8	8 56.5	11.0	58.1
05	253 39.4	35.4	346 53.6	10.8	9 07.5	11.0	58.2
06	268 39.1	S22 35.1	1 23.4	10.8	S 9 18.5	10.9	58.2
S 07	283 38.8	34.8	15 53.2	10.6	9 29.4	10.9	58.2
A 08	298 38.5	34.6	30 22.8	10.6	9 40.3	10.9	58.3
T 09	313 38.3	.. 34.3	44 52.4	10.6	9 51.2	10.8	58.3
U 10	328 38.0	34.0	59 22.0	10.4	10 02.0	10.8	58.3
R 11	343 37.7	33.7	73 51.4	10.4	10 12.8	10.7	58.4
D 12	358 37.4	S22 33.4	88 20.8	10.3	S10 23.5	10.7	58.4
A 13	13 37.2	33.1	102 50.1	10.2	10 34.2	10.6	58.4
Y 14	28 36.9	32.8	117 19.3	10.2	10 44.8	10.6	58.4
15	43 36.6	.. 32.5	131 48.5	10.0	10 55.4	10.6	58.5
16	58 36.3	32.2	146 17.5	10.0	11 06.0	10.5	58.5
17	73 36.1	31.9	160 46.5	10.0	11 16.5	10.4	58.5
18	88 35.8	S22 31.7	175 15.5	9.8	S11 26.9	10.4	58.6
19	103 35.5	31.4	189 44.3	9.8	11 37.3	10.4	58.6
20	118 35.2	31.1	204 13.1	9.7	11 47.7	10.2	58.6
21	133 35.0	.. 30.8	218 41.8	9.6	11 57.9	10.3	58.7
22	148 34.7	30.5	233 10.4	9.5	12 08.2	10.1	58.7
23	163 34.4	30.2	247 38.9	9.5	12 18.3	10.1	58.7
6 00	178 34.1	S22 29.9	262 07.4	9.3	S12 28.4	10.1	58.8
01	193 33.9	29.6	276 35.7	9.3	12 38.5	10.0	58.8
02	208 33.6	29.3	291 04.0	9.2	12 48.5	9.9	58.8
03	223 33.3	.. 29.0	305 32.2	9.1	12 58.4	9.9	58.8
04	238 33.0	28.7	320 00.3	9.1	13 08.3	9.8	58.9
05	253 32.8	28.4	334 28.4	8.9	13 18.1	9.7	58.9
06	268 32.5	S22 28.1	348 56.3	8.9	S13 27.8	9.7	59.0
07	283 32.2	27.8	3 24.2	8.8	13 37.5	9.6	59.0
08	298 31.9	27.5	17 52.0	8.7	13 47.1	9.5	59.0
S 09	313 31.7	.. 27.1	32 19.7	8.6	13 56.6	9.4	59.0
U 10	328 31.4	26.8	46 47.3	8.5	14 06.0	9.4	59.1
N 11	343 31.1	26.5	61 14.8	8.5	14 15.4	9.3	59.1
D 12	358 30.8	S22 26.2	75 42.3	8.3	S14 24.7	9.2	59.1
A 13	13 30.6	25.9	90 09.6	8.3	14 33.9	9.2	59.2
Y 14	28 30.3	25.6	104 36.9	8.2	14 43.1	9.1	59.2
15	43 30.0	.. 25.3	119 04.1	8.1	14 52.2	8.9	59.2
16	58 29.8	25.0	133 31.2	8.0	15 01.1	9.0	59.2
17	73 29.5	24.7	147 58.2	7.9	15 10.1	8.8	59.3
18	88 29.2	S22 24.4	162 25.1	7.8	S15 18.9	8.7	59.3
19	103 28.9	24.0	176 51.9	7.8	15 27.6	8.7	59.3
20	118 28.7	23.7	191 18.7	7.6	15 36.3	8.5	59.4
21	133 28.4	.. 23.4	205 45.3	7.6	15 44.8	8.5	59.4
22	148 28.1	23.1	220 11.9	7.5	15 53.3	8.4	59.4
23	163 27.9	22.8	234 38.4	7.4	S16 01.7	8.3	59.5
	SD 16.3	d 0.3	SD 15.7		15.9		16.1

Lat.	Twilight Naut.	Twilight Civil	Sunrise	Moonrise 4	Moonrise 5	Moonrise 6	Moonrise 7
°	h m	h m	h m	h m	h m	h m	h m
N 72	08 19	10 29	▮	25 37	01 37	03 45	06 27
N 70	08 01	09 42	▮	25 23	01 23	03 19	05 26
68	07 47	09 12	11 27	25 12	01 12	02 59	04 51
66	07 35	08 49	10 19	25 03	01 03	02 43	04 26
64	07 25	08 31	09 44	24 56	00 56	02 30	04 07
62	07 16	08 16	09 19	24 49	00 49	02 20	03 51
60	07 08	08 04	08 59	24 44	00 44	02 10	03 38
N 58	07 01	07 53	08 43	24 39	00 39	02 02	03 27
56	06 55	07 43	08 30	24 35	00 35	01 55	03 17
54	06 49	07 35	08 18	24 31	00 31	01 49	03 09
52	06 44	07 27	08 07	24 27	00 27	01 44	03 01
50	06 28	07 05	07 38	24 24	00 24	01 39	02 54
45	06 28	07 05	07 38	24 17	00 17	01 28	02 40
N 40	06 18	06 52	07 22	24 11	00 11	01 19	02 28
35	06 09	06 41	07 09	24 07	00 07	01 11	02 17
30	06 01	06 31	06 57	24 02	00 02	01 04	02 09
20	05 45	06 12	06 36	23 55	24 53	00 53	01 53
N 10	05 29	05 56	06 19	23 48	24 43	00 43	01 40
0	05 13	05 39	06 02	23 42	24 33	00 33	01 28
S 10	04 55	05 22	05 45	23 36	24 24	00 24	01 15
20	04 33	05 02	05 27	23 30	24 14	00 14	01 02
30	04 05	04 38	05 05	23 23	24 03	00 03	00 47
35	03 47	04 24	04 53	23 19	23 57	24 39	00 39
40	03 25	04 06	04 39	23 14	23 49	24 29	00 29
45	02 56	03 45	04 21	23 09	23 41	24 18	00 18
S 50	02 14	03 16	04 00	23 03	23 31	24 04	00 04
52	01 49	03 02	03 50	23 00	23 26	23 58	24 37
54	01 13	02 45	03 38	22 57	23 21	23 51	24 28
56	////	02 25	03 25	22 53	23 15	23 43	24 19
58	////	01 59	03 09	22 49	23 09	23 34	24 07
S 60	////	01 20	02 50	22 45	23 02	23 24	23 55

Lat.	Sunset	Twilight Civil	Twilight Naut.	Moonset 4	Moonset 5	Moonset 6	Moonset 7
°	h m	h m	h m	h m	h m	h m	h m
N 72	▮	13 43	15 52	10 03	09 48	09 28	08 41
N 70	▮	14 29	16 10	10 11	10 04	09 56	09 43
68	12 44	15 00	16 25	10 18	10 17	10 17	10 19
66	13 52	15 22	16 37	10 23	10 27	10 34	10 45
64	14 27	15 40	16 47	10 28	10 36	10 48	11 05
62	14 52	15 55	16 56	10 32	10 44	10 59	11 21
60	15 12	16 08	17 03	10 35	10 51	11 09	11 35
N 58	15 28	16 18	17 10	10 39	10 58	11 18	11 46
56	15 42	16 28	17 17	10 41	11 02	11 26	11 57
54	15 54	16 37	17 22	10 44	11 06	11 33	12 06
52	16 04	16 44	17 28	10 46	11 10	11 39	12 14
50	16 13	16 51	17 32	10 48	11 14	11 44	12 21
45	16 33	17 07	17 43	10 53	11 23	11 57	12 37
N 40	16 49	17 19	17 53	10 57	11 30	12 07	12 50
35	17 03	17 31	18 02	11 00	11 36	12 15	13 00
30	17 14	17 41	18 10	11 03	11 41	12 23	13 10
20	17 33	17 59	18 26	11 08	11 50	12 36	13 27
N 10	17 52	18 15	18 41	11 13	11 59	12 48	13 41
0	18 09	18 32	18 58	11 17	12 06	12 59	13 55
S 10	18 26	18 49	19 16	11 21	12 14	13 10	14 08
20	18 44	19 09	19 38	11 26	12 22	13 21	14 23
30	19 05	19 33	20 05	11 31	12 32	13 35	14 40
35	19 18	19 47	20 23	11 34	12 37	13 42	14 49
40	19 32	20 04	20 45	11 37	12 43	13 51	15 01
45	19 49	20 26	21 14	11 41	12 50	14 02	15 14
S 50	20 11	20 54	21 56	11 46	12 59	14 14	15 30
52	20 21	21 08	22 20	11 48	13 03	14 20	15 37
54	20 32	21 25	22 55	11 50	13 08	14 27	15 46
56	20 46	21 45	////	11 53	13 12	14 34	15 55
58	21 01	22 11	////	11 56	13 18	14 42	16 06
S 60	21 20	22 49	////	11 59	13 24	14 51	16 18

	SUN Eqn. of Time 00h	SUN Eqn. of Time 12h	SUN Mer. Pass.	MOON Mer. Pass. Upper	MOON Mer. Pass. Lower	Age	Phase
d	m s	m s	h m	h m	h m	d	%
4	04 49	05 03	12 05	05 06	17 30	22	57
5	05 16	05 30	12 05	05 54	18 20	23	46
6	05 43	05 56	12 06	06 46	19 13	24	35

UT	ARIES	VENUS −3.9		MARS +1.2		JUPITER −2.7		SATURN +0.6		STARS		
	GHA	GHA	Dec	GHA	Dec	GHA	Dec	GHA	Dec	Name	SHA	Dec
d h	° ′	° ′	° ′	° ′	° ′	° ′	° ′	° ′	° ′		° ′	° ′
7 00	106 43.5	199 41.0	S22 57.7	154 34.1	S18 59.7	41 09.6	N20 50.6	248 23.1	S12 34.1	Acamar	315 18.4	S40 15.4
01	121 45.9	214 40.1	57.9	169 34.6	59.2	56 12.2	50.6	263 25.4	34.1	Achernar	335 26.9	S57 10.5
02	136 48.4	229 39.1	58.0	184 35.0	58.6	71 14.9	50.5	278 27.7	34.2	Acrux	173 09.4	S63 10.1
03	151 50.9	244 38.2 . .	58.2	199 35.5 . .	58.1	86 17.6 . .	50.5	293 30.0 . .	34.2	Adhara	255 12.4	S28 59.6
04	166 53.3	259 37.3	58.4	214 36.0	57.6	101 20.2	50.5	308 32.3	34.3	Aldebaran	290 49.4	N16 32.0
05	181 55.8	274 36.3	58.5	229 36.4	57.0	116 22.9	50.5	323 34.6	34.3			
06	196 58.3	289 35.4	S22 58.7	244 36.9	S18 56.5	131 25.6	N20 50.4	338 36.9	S12 34.4	Alioth	166 20.9	N55 53.0
07	212 00.7	304 34.5	58.9	259 37.3	56.0	146 28.2	50.4	353 39.2	34.4	Alkaid	152 59.2	N49 14.6
08	227 03.2	319 33.5	59.0	274 37.8	55.4	161 30.9	50.4	8 41.5	34.5	Al Na'ir	27 44.5	S46 53.9
M 09	242 05.7	334 32.6 . .	59.2	289 38.3 . .	54.9	176 33.6 . .	50.4	23 43.8 . .	34.5	Alnilam	275 46.3	S 1 11.8
O 10	257 08.1	349 31.6	59.3	304 38.7	54.4	191 36.2	50.4	38 46.1	34.5	Alphard	217 56.1	S 8 43.1
N 11	272 10.6	4 30.7	59.5	319 39.2	53.8	206 38.9	50.3	53 48.4	34.6			
D 12	287 13.1	19 29.8	S22 59.7	334 39.6	S18 53.3	221 41.6	N20 50.3	68 50.7	S12 34.6	Alphecca	126 11.5	N26 40.2
A 13	302 15.5	34 28.8	22 59.8	349 40.1	52.8	236 44.2	50.3	83 53.0	34.7	Alpheratz	357 43.9	N29 10.0
Y 14	317 18.0	49 27.9	23 00.0	4 40.6	52.2	251 46.9	50.3	98 55.2	34.7	Altair	62 08.8	N 8 54.3
15	332 20.4	64 27.0 . .	00.1	19 41.0 . .	51.7	266 49.6 . .	50.2	113 57.5 . .	34.8	Ankaa	353 16.1	S42 14.3
16	347 22.9	79 26.0	00.3	34 41.5	51.2	281 52.2	50.2	128 59.8	34.8	Antares	112 26.9	S26 27.5
17	2 25.4	94 25.1	00.4	49 42.0	50.6	296 54.9	50.2	144 02.1	34.9			
18	17 27.8	109 24.2	S23 00.6	64 42.4	S18 50.1	311 57.6	N20 50.2	159 04.4	S12 34.9	Arcturus	145 56.1	N19 06.7
19	32 30.3	124 23.2	00.7	79 42.9	49.5	327 00.2	50.2	174 06.7	35.0	Atria	107 29.4	S69 02.8
20	47 32.8	139 22.3	00.9	94 43.3	49.0	342 02.9	50.1	189 09.0	35.0	Avior	234 17.5	S59 33.2
21	62 35.2	154 21.3 . .	01.0	109 43.8 . .	48.5	357 05.6 . .	50.1	204 11.3 . .	35.0	Bellatrix	278 32.0	N 6 21.5
22	77 37.7	169 20.4	01.2	124 44.3	47.9	12 08.2	50.1	219 13.6	35.1	Betelgeuse	271 01.3	N 7 24.4
23	92 40.2	184 19.5	01.3	139 44.7	47.4	27 10.9	50.1	234 15.9	35.1			
8 00	107 42.6	199 18.5	S23 01.4	154 45.2	S18 46.8	42 13.6	N20 50.1	249 18.2	S12 35.2	Canopus	263 55.7	S52 42.4
01	122 45.1	214 17.6	01.6	169 45.7	46.3	57 16.2	50.0	264 20.5	35.2	Capella	280 34.4	N46 00.6
02	137 47.6	229 16.7	01.7	184 46.1	45.8	72 18.9	50.0	279 22.8	35.3	Deneb	49 32.1	N45 19.8
03	152 50.0	244 15.7 . .	01.9	199 46.6 . .	45.2	87 21.5 . .	50.0	294 25.1 . .	35.3	Denebola	182 33.8	N14 29.7
04	167 52.5	259 14.8	02.0	214 47.0	44.7	102 24.2	50.0	309 27.4	35.4	Diphda	348 56.2	S17 55.0
05	182 54.9	274 13.8	02.1	229 47.5	44.1	117 26.9	49.9	324 29.7	35.4			
06	197 57.4	289 12.9	S23 02.3	244 48.0	S18 43.6	132 29.5	N20 49.9	339 32.0	S12 35.4	Dubhe	193 51.7	N61 40.4
07	212 59.9	304 12.0	02.4	259 48.4	43.0	147 32.2	49.9	354 34.3	35.5	Elnath	278 12.6	N28 37.0
T 08	228 02.3	319 11.0	02.5	274 48.9	42.5	162 34.8	49.9	9 36.6	35.5	Eltanin	90 46.8	N51 29.3
U 09	243 04.8	334 10.1 . .	02.7	289 49.4 . .	42.0	177 37.5 . .	49.9	24 38.9 . .	35.6	Enif	33 47.7	N 9 56.2
E 10	258 07.3	349 09.1	02.8	304 49.8	41.4	192 40.2	49.8	39 41.2	35.6	Fomalhaut	15 24.5	S29 33.2
S 11	273 09.7	4 08.2	02.9	319 50.3	40.9	207 42.8	49.8	54 43.5	35.7			
D 12	288 12.2	19 07.3	S23 03.1	334 50.8	S18 40.3	222 45.5	N20 49.8	69 45.8	S12 35.7	Gacrux	172 01.1	S57 11.0
A 13	303 14.7	34 06.3	03.2	349 51.2	39.8	237 48.1	49.8	84 48.1	35.8	Gienah	175 52.5	S17 36.9
Y 14	318 17.1	49 05.4	03.3	4 51.7	39.2	252 50.8	49.8	99 50.4	35.8	Hadar	148 48.4	S60 25.9
15	333 19.6	64 04.5 . .	03.4	19 52.2 . .	38.7	267 53.5 . .	49.7	114 52.7 . .	35.8	Hamal	328 01.0	N23 31.5
16	348 22.0	79 03.5	03.6	34 52.6	38.1	282 56.1	49.7	129 54.9	35.9	Kaus Aust.	83 44.6	S34 22.5
17	3 24.5	94 02.6	03.7	49 53.1	37.6	297 58.8	49.7	144 57.2	35.9			
18	18 27.0	109 01.6	S23 03.8	64 53.6	S18 37.1	313 01.4	N20 49.7	159 59.5	S12 36.0	Kochab	137 20.6	N74 05.8
19	33 29.4	124 00.7	03.9	79 54.0	36.5	328 04.1	49.7	175 01.8	36.0	Markab	13 38.8	N15 16.7
20	48 31.9	138 59.8	04.0	94 54.5	36.0	343 06.7	49.6	190 04.1	36.1	Menkar	314 15.2	N 4 08.4
21	63 34.4	153 58.8 . .	04.1	109 55.0 . .	35.4	358 09.4 . .	49.6	205 06.4 . .	36.1	Menkent	148 08.0	S36 25.9
22	78 36.8	168 57.9	04.3	124 55.4	34.9	13 12.1	49.6	220 08.7	36.2	Miaplacidus	221 38.8	S69 46.2
23	93 39.3	183 56.9	04.4	139 55.9	34.3	28 14.7	49.6	235 11.0	36.2			
9 00	108 41.8	198 56.0	S23 04.5	154 56.4	S18 33.8	43 17.4	N20 49.6	250 13.3	S12 36.2	Mirfak	308 40.4	N49 54.6
01	123 44.2	213 55.1	04.6	169 56.8	33.2	58 20.0	49.5	265 15.6	36.3	Nunki	75 59.0	S26 16.7
02	138 46.7	228 54.1	04.7	184 57.3	32.7	73 22.7	49.5	280 17.9	36.3	Peacock	53 20.3	S56 41.5
03	153 49.2	243 53.2 . .	04.8	199 57.8 . .	32.1	88 25.3 . .	49.5	295 20.2 . .	36.4	Pollux	243 27.7	N27 59.4
04	168 51.6	258 52.2	04.9	214 58.2	31.6	103 28.0	49.5	310 22.5	36.4	Procyon	244 59.7	N 5 11.3
05	183 54.1	273 51.3	05.0	229 58.7	31.0	118 30.6	49.5	325 24.8	36.5			
06	198 56.5	288 50.3	S23 05.1	244 59.2	S18 30.5	133 33.3	N20 49.4	340 27.1	S12 36.5	Rasalhague	96 07.0	N12 33.1
W 07	213 59.0	303 49.4	05.2	259 59.6	29.9	148 35.9	49.4	355 29.4	36.6	Regulus	207 43.6	N11 54.0
E 08	229 01.5	318 48.5	05.4	275 00.1	29.4	163 38.6	49.4	10 31.7	36.6	Rigel	281 12.0	S 8 11.4
D 09	244 03.9	333 47.5 . .	05.5	290 00.6 . .	28.8	178 41.2 . .	49.4	25 34.0 . .	36.6	Rigil Kent.	139 52.3	S60 53.0
N 10	259 06.4	348 46.6	05.6	305 01.1	28.3	193 43.9	49.4	40 36.3	36.7	Sabik	102 13.2	S15 44.3
E 11	274 08.9	3 45.6	05.7	320 01.5	27.7	208 46.5	49.3	55 38.6	36.7			
S 12	289 11.3	18 44.7	S23 05.8	335 02.0	S18 27.1	223 49.2	N20 49.3	70 40.9	S12 36.8	Schedar	349 40.9	N56 36.9
D 13	304 13.8	33 43.8	05.8	350 02.5	26.6	238 51.8	49.3	85 43.2	36.8	Shaula	96 22.7	S37 06.6
A 14	319 16.3	48 42.8	05.9	5 02.9	26.0	253 54.5	49.3	100 45.5	36.9	Sirius	258 33.6	S16 44.3
Y 15	334 18.7	63 41.9 . .	06.0	20 03.4 . .	25.5	268 57.1 . .	49.3	115 47.8 . .	36.9	Spica	158 31.6	S11 13.8
16	349 21.2	78 40.9	06.1	35 03.9	24.9	283 59.8	49.2	130 50.1	36.9	Suhail	222 52.2	S43 29.2
17	4 23.7	93 40.0	06.2	50 04.3	24.4	299 02.4	49.2	145 52.4	37.0			
18	19 26.1	108 39.0	S23 06.3	65 04.8	S18 23.8	314 05.1	N20 49.2	160 54.7	S12 37.0	Vega	80 39.6	N38 47.8
19	34 28.6	123 38.1	06.4	80 05.3	23.3	329 07.7	49.2	175 57.0	37.1	Zuben'ubi	137 05.9	S16 05.7
20	49 31.0	138 37.2	06.5	95 05.8	22.7	344 10.4	49.2	190 59.3	37.1		SHA	Mer.Pass.
21	64 33.5	153 36.2 . .	06.6	110 06.2 . .	22.2	359 13.0 . .	49.1	206 01.7 . .	37.2		° ′	h m
22	79 36.0	168 35.3	06.7	125 06.7	21.6	14 15.7	49.1	221 04.0	37.2	Venus	91 35.9	10 43
23	94 38.4	183 34.3	06.8	140 07.2	21.0	29 18.3	49.1	236 06.3	37.2	Mars	47 02.6	13 41
	h m									Jupiter	294 30.9	21 07
Mer.Pass. 16 46.4		v −0.9	d 0.1	v 0.5	d 0.5	v 2.7	d 0.0	v 2.3	d 0.0	Saturn	141 35.6	7 22

UT	SUN GHA	Dec	MOON GHA	v	Dec	d	HP
d h	o '	o '	o '	'	o '	'	'
7 00	178 27.6	S22 22.5	249 04.8	7.3	S16 10.0	8.2	59.5
01	193 27.3	22.1	263 31.1	7.2	16 18.2	8.1	59.5
02	208 27.0	21.8	277 57.3	7.1	16 26.3	8.0	59.5
03	223 26.8	.. 21.5	292 23.4	7.1	16 34.3	8.0	59.6
04	238 26.5	21.2	306 49.5	6.9	16 42.3	7.8	59.6
05	253 26.2	20.9	321 15.4	6.9	16 50.1	7.7	59.6
06	268 26.0	S22 20.5	335 41.3	6.8	S16 57.8	7.6	59.7
07	283 25.7	20.2	350 07.1	6.7	17 05.4	7.5	59.7
08	298 25.4	19.9	4 32.8	6.8	17 12.9	7.4	59.7
M 09	313 25.2	.. 19.6	18 58.4	6.5	17 20.3	7.4	59.7
O 10	328 24.9	19.2	33 23.9	6.5	17 27.7	7.2	59.8
N 11	343 24.6	18.9	47 49.4	6.3	17 34.9	7.0	59.8
D 12	358 24.4	S22 18.6	62 14.7	6.3	S17 41.9	7.0	59.8
A 13	13 24.1	18.3	76 40.0	6.2	17 48.9	6.9	59.8
Y 14	28 23.8	17.9	91 05.2	6.1	17 55.8	6.8	59.9
15	43 23.6	.. 17.6	105 30.3	6.0	18 02.6	6.6	59.9
16	58 23.3	17.3	119 55.3	6.0	18 09.2	6.5	59.9
17	73 23.0	17.0	134 20.3	5.8	18 15.7	6.5	60.0
18	88 22.8	S22 16.6	148 45.1	5.8	S18 22.2	6.3	60.0
19	103 22.5	16.3	163 09.9	5.7	18 28.5	6.1	60.0
20	118 22.2	16.0	177 34.6	5.6	18 34.6	6.1	60.0
21	133 22.0	.. 15.6	191 59.2	5.6	18 40.7	6.0	60.1
22	148 21.7	15.3	206 23.8	5.4	18 46.7	5.8	60.1
23	163 21.4	15.0	220 48.2	5.4	18 52.5	5.7	60.1
8 00	178 21.2	S22 14.6	235 12.6	5.3	S18 58.2	5.5	60.1
01	193 20.9	14.3	249 36.9	5.2	19 03.7	5.5	60.2
02	208 20.6	13.9	264 01.1	5.2	19 09.2	5.3	60.2
03	223 20.4	.. 13.6	278 25.3	5.1	19 14.5	5.2	60.2
04	238 20.1	13.3	292 49.4	5.0	19 19.7	5.0	60.2
05	253 19.8	12.9	307 13.4	4.9	19 24.7	5.0	60.2
06	268 19.6	S22 12.6	321 37.3	4.9	S19 29.7	4.8	60.3
07	283 19.3	12.2	336 01.2	4.8	19 34.5	4.6	60.3
T 08	298 19.0	11.9	350 25.0	4.7	19 39.1	4.6	60.3
U 09	313 18.8	.. 11.6	4 48.7	4.7	19 43.7	4.4	60.3
E 10	328 18.5	11.2	19 12.4	4.6	19 48.1	4.2	60.4
S 11	343 18.3	10.9	33 36.0	4.5	19 52.3	4.1	60.4
D 12	358 18.0	S22 10.5	47 59.5	4.5	S19 56.4	4.0	60.4
A 13	13 17.7	10.2	62 23.0	4.4	20 00.4	3.9	60.4
Y 14	28 17.5	09.8	76 46.4	4.4	20 04.3	3.7	60.4
15	43 17.2	.. 09.5	91 09.8	4.3	20 08.0	3.5	60.5
16	58 16.9	09.1	105 33.1	4.2	20 11.5	3.5	60.5
17	73 16.7	08.8	119 56.3	4.2	20 15.0	3.2	60.5
18	88 16.4	S22 08.4	134 19.5	4.1	S20 18.2	3.2	60.5
19	103 16.2	08.1	148 42.6	4.1	20 21.4	3.0	60.5
20	118 15.9	07.7	163 05.7	4.0	20 24.4	2.8	60.5
21	133 15.6	.. 07.4	177 28.7	4.0	20 27.2	2.7	60.6
22	148 15.4	07.0	191 51.7	3.9	20 29.9	2.6	60.6
23	163 15.1	06.7	206 14.6	3.9	20 32.5	2.4	60.6
9 00	178 14.9	S22 06.3	220 37.5	3.8	S20 34.9	2.2	60.6
01	193 14.6	06.0	235 00.3	3.8	20 37.1	2.1	60.6
02	208 14.3	05.6	249 23.1	3.8	20 39.2	2.0	60.6
03	223 14.1	.. 05.3	263 45.9	3.7	20 41.2	1.8	60.7
04	238 13.8	04.9	278 08.6	3.7	20 43.0	1.6	60.7
05	253 13.6	04.6	292 31.3	3.6	20 44.6	1.5	60.7
06	268 13.3	S22 04.2	306 53.9	3.6	S20 46.1	1.4	60.7
W 07	283 13.0	03.8	321 16.5	3.6	20 47.5	1.2	60.7
E 08	298 12.8	03.5	335 39.1	3.6	20 48.7	1.0	60.7
D 09	313 12.5	.. 03.1	350 01.7	3.4	20 49.7	0.9	60.7
N 10	328 12.3	02.8	4 24.2	3.5	20 50.6	0.8	60.8
E 11	343 12.0	02.4	18 46.7	3.5	20 51.4	0.5	60.8
S 12	358 11.8	S22 02.0	33 09.2	3.4	S20 51.9	0.5	60.8
D 13	13 11.5	01.7	47 31.6	3.5	20 52.4	0.3	60.8
A 14	28 11.2	01.3	61 54.1	3.4	20 52.7	0.1	60.8
Y 15	43 11.0	.. 00.9	76 16.5	3.4	20 52.8	0.1	60.8
16	58 10.7	00.6	90 38.9	3.4	20 52.7	0.1	60.8
17	73 10.5	22 00.2	105 01.3	3.4	20 52.6	0.4	60.8
18	88 10.2	S21 59.8	119 23.7	3.3	S20 52.2	0.5	60.8
19	103 10.0	59.5	133 46.0	3.4	20 51.7	0.6	60.8
20	118 09.7	59.1	148 08.4	3.3	20 51.1	0.9	60.8
21	133 09.5	.. 58.7	162 30.7	3.4	20 50.2	0.9	60.9
22	148 09.2	58.4	176 53.1	3.3	20 49.3	1.1	60.9
23	163 08.9	58.0	191 15.4	3.4	S20 48.2	1.3	60.9
	SD 16.3	d 0.3	SD 16.3		16.5		16.6

Twilight / Sunrise / Moonrise

Lat.	Naut.	Civil	Sunrise	Moonrise 7	8	9	10
°	h m	h m	h m	h m	h m	h m	h m
N 72	08 15	10 18	■	06 27	■	■	■
N 70	07 57	09 36	■	05 26	08 07	■	■
68	07 44	09 07	11 08	04 51	06 46	08 25	09 16
66	07 32	08 46	10 12	04 26	06 08	07 34	08 31
64	07 22	08 28	09 39	04 07	05 41	07 02	08 01
62	07 14	08 14	09 16	03 51	05 20	06 38	07 38
60	07 06	08 02	08 57	03 38	05 04	06 19	07 20
N 58	07 00	07 51	08 41	03 27	04 49	06 04	07 04
56	06 54	07 42	08 28	03 17	04 37	05 50	06 51
54	06 48	07 33	08 16	03 09	04 27	05 39	06 40
52	06 43	07 26	08 06	03 01	04 18	05 29	06 30
50	06 38	07 19	07 57	02 54	04 09	05 19	06 21
45	06 27	07 04	07 38	02 40	03 52	05 00	06 02
N 40	06 18	06 52	07 22	02 28	03 37	04 44	05 47
35	06 09	06 41	07 09	02 17	03 25	04 31	05 33
30	06 01	06 31	06 57	02 09	03 14	04 20	05 22
20	05 46	06 13	06 37	01 53	02 56	04 00	05 02
N 10	05 31	05 57	06 20	01 40	02 40	03 43	04 45
0	05 15	05 41	06 03	01 28	02 26	03 27	04 29
S 10	04 57	05 24	05 46	01 15	02 11	03 11	04 14
20	04 35	05 04	05 29	01 02	01 55	02 54	03 57
30	04 08	04 41	05 09	00 47	01 38	02 34	03 37
35	03 50	04 26	04 56	00 39	01 27	02 23	03 26
40	03 29	04 09	04 41	00 29	01 16	02 10	03 13
45	03 00	03 48	04 25	00 18	01 02	01 55	02 57
S 50	02 20	03 21	04 04	00 04	00 45	01 36	02 38
52	01 56	03 07	03 54	24 37	00 37	01 27	02 29
54	01 23	02 51	03 42	24 28	00 28	01 17	02 19
56	////	02 31	03 29	24 19	00 19	01 06	02 08
58	////	02 06	03 14	24 07	00 07	00 53	01 55
S 60	////	01 30	02 56	23 55	24 38	00 38	01 40

Sunset / Twilight / Moonset

Lat.	Sunset	Civil	Naut.	Moonset 7	8	9	10
°	h m	h m	h m	h m	h m	h m	h m
N 72	■	13 56	16 00	08 41	■	■	■
N 70	■	14 38	16 17	09 43	09 05	■	■
68	13 06	15 07	16 30	10 19	10 27	10 56	12 18
66	14 02	15 29	16 42	10 45	11 06	11 48	13 03
64	14 35	15 46	16 52	11 05	11 33	12 20	13 32
62	14 58	16 00	17 00	11 21	11 54	12 44	13 55
60	15 17	16 12	17 08	11 35	12 11	13 03	14 13
N 58	15 33	16 23	17 14	11 46	12 25	13 18	14 28
56	15 46	16 32	17 20	11 57	12 38	13 32	14 41
54	15 58	16 40	17 26	12 06	12 48	13 44	14 52
52	16 08	16 48	17 31	12 14	12 58	13 54	15 02
50	16 17	16 55	17 36	12 21	13 07	14 03	15 11
45	16 36	17 10	17 46	12 37	13 25	14 23	15 29
N 40	16 52	17 22	17 56	12 50	13 40	14 38	15 44
35	17 05	17 33	18 04	13 00	13 52	14 52	15 57
30	17 17	17 43	18 12	13 10	14 03	15 03	16 08
20	17 37	18 00	18 28	13 27	14 22	15 23	16 27
N 10	17 54	18 17	18 43	13 41	14 39	15 40	16 44
0	18 10	18 33	18 59	13 55	14 54	15 57	16 59
S 10	18 27	18 50	19 17	14 08	15 10	16 13	17 15
20	18 45	19 09	19 38	14 23	15 26	16 30	17 31
30	19 06	19 33	20 05	14 40	15 45	16 49	17 50
35	19 18	19 47	20 23	14 49	15 56	17 01	18 01
40	19 32	20 04	20 44	15 01	16 09	17 14	18 13
45	19 49	20 25	21 12	15 14	16 24	17 30	18 28
S 50	20 09	20 52	21 53	15 30	16 43	17 49	18 45
52	20 19	21 06	22 16	15 37	16 51	17 58	18 54
54	20 31	21 22	22 48	15 46	17 01	18 08	19 03
56	20 43	21 41	////	15 55	17 12	18 19	19 14
58	20 58	22 06	////	16 06	17 25	18 32	19 26
S 60	21 16	22 40	////	16 18	17 39	18 48	19 40

SUN / MOON

Day	Eqn. of Time 00ʰ	12ʰ	Mer. Pass.	Mer. Pass. Upper	Lower	Age	Phase
	m s	m s	h m	h m	h m	d	%
7	06 09	06 22	12 06	07 41	20 10	25	25
8	06 35	06 47	12 07	08 40	21 11	26	15
9	07 00	07 12	12 07	09 42	22 13	27	8

UT	ARIES GHA	VENUS −3.9 GHA	Dec	MARS +1.2 GHA	Dec	JUPITER −2.7 GHA	Dec	SATURN +0.6 GHA	Dec
d h	° '	° '	° '	° '	° '	° '	° '	° '	° '
10 00	109 40.9	198 33.4	S23 06.8	155 07.6	S18 20.5	44 21.0	N20 49.1	251 08.6	S12 37.3
01	124 43.4	213 32.4	06.9	170 08.1	19.9	59 23.6	49.1	266 10.9	37.3
02	139 45.8	228 31.5	07.0	185 08.6	19.4	74 26.3	49.0	281 13.2	37.4
03	154 48.3	243 30.6 ..	07.1	200 09.1 ..	18.8	89 28.9 ..	49.0	296 15.5 ..	37.4
04	169 50.8	258 29.6	07.2	215 09.5	18.3	104 31.6	49.0	311 17.8	37.5
05	184 53.2	273 28.7	07.2	230 10.0	17.7	119 34.2	49.0	326 20.1	37.5
T 06	199 55.7	288 27.7	S23 07.3	245 10.5	S18 17.1	134 36.8	N20 49.0	341 22.4	S12 37.5
H 07	214 58.2	303 26.8	07.4	260 10.9	16.6	149 39.5	49.0	356 24.7	37.6
U 08	230 00.6	318 25.8	07.5	275 11.4	16.0	164 42.1	48.9	11 27.0	37.6
R 09	245 03.1	333 24.9 ..	07.5	290 11.9 ..	15.5	179 44.8 ..	48.9	26 29.3 ..	37.7
S 10	260 05.5	348 24.0	07.6	305 12.4	14.9	194 47.4	48.9	41 31.6	37.7
D 11	275 08.0	3 23.0	07.7	320 12.8	14.3	209 50.1	48.9	56 33.9	37.7
A 12	290 10.5	18 22.1	S23 07.7	335 13.3	S18 13.8	224 52.7	N20 48.9	71 36.2	S12 37.8
Y 13	305 12.9	33 21.1	07.8	350 13.8	13.2	239 55.3	48.8	86 38.5	37.8
14	320 15.4	48 20.2	07.9	5 14.3	12.6	254 58.0	48.8	101 40.8	37.9
15	335 17.9	63 19.2 ..	07.9	20 14.7 ..	12.1	270 00.6 ..	48.8	116 43.1 ..	37.9
16	350 20.3	78 18.3	08.0	35 15.2	11.5	285 03.3	48.8	131 45.4	38.0
17	5 22.8	93 17.4	08.1	50 15.7	11.0	300 05.9	48.8	146 47.7	38.0
18	20 25.3	108 16.4	S23 08.1	65 16.2	S18 10.4	315 08.5	N20 48.7	161 50.0	S12 38.0
19	35 27.7	123 15.5	08.2	80 16.6	09.8	330 11.2	48.7	176 52.3	38.1
20	50 30.2	138 14.5	08.2	95 17.1	09.3	345 13.8	48.7	191 54.6	38.1
21	65 32.7	153 13.6 ..	08.3	110 17.6 ..	08.7	0 16.5 ..	48.7	206 56.9 ..	38.2
22	80 35.1	168 12.6	08.4	125 18.1	08.1	15 19.1	48.7	221 59.2	38.2
23	95 37.6	183 11.7	08.4	140 18.5	07.6	30 21.7	48.7	237 01.6	38.2
11 00	110 40.0	198 10.7	S23 08.5	155 19.0	S18 07.0	45 24.4	N20 48.6	252 03.9	S12 38.3
01	125 42.5	213 09.8	08.5	170 19.5	06.4	60 27.0	48.6	267 06.2	38.3
02	140 45.0	228 08.9	08.6	185 20.0	05.9	75 29.7	48.6	282 08.5	38.4
03	155 47.4	243 07.9 ..	08.6	200 20.5 ..	05.3	90 32.3 ..	48.6	297 10.8 ..	38.4
04	170 49.9	258 07.0	08.7	215 20.9	04.8	105 34.9	48.6	312 13.1	38.5
05	185 52.4	273 06.0	08.7	230 21.4	04.2	120 37.6	48.6	327 15.4	38.5
06	200 54.8	288 05.1	S23 08.8	245 21.9	S18 03.6	135 40.2	N20 48.5	342 17.7	S12 38.5
07	215 57.3	303 04.1	08.8	260 22.4	03.0	150 42.8	48.5	357 20.0	38.6
08	230 59.8	318 03.2	08.9	275 22.8	02.5	165 45.5	48.5	12 22.3	38.6
F 09	246 02.2	333 02.2 ..	08.9	290 23.3 ..	01.9	180 48.1 ..	48.5	27 24.6 ..	38.7
R 10	261 04.7	348 01.3	08.9	305 23.8	01.3	195 50.7	48.5	42 26.9	38.7
I 11	276 07.2	3 00.3	09.0	320 24.3	00.8	210 53.4	48.5	57 29.2	38.7
D 12	291 09.6	17 59.4	S23 09.0	335 24.7	S18 00.2	225 56.0	N20 48.4	72 31.5	S12 38.8
A 13	306 12.1	32 58.5	09.1	350 25.2	17 59.6	240 58.6	48.4	87 33.9	38.8
Y 14	321 14.5	47 57.5	09.1	5 25.7	59.1	256 01.3	48.4	102 36.2	38.9
15	336 17.0	62 56.6 ..	09.1	20 26.2 ..	58.5	271 03.9 ..	48.4	117 38.5 ..	38.9
16	351 19.5	77 55.6	09.2	35 26.7	57.9	286 06.5	48.4	132 40.8	38.9
17	6 21.9	92 54.7	09.2	50 27.1	57.3	301 09.2	48.4	147 43.1	39.0
18	21 24.4	107 53.7	S23 09.2	65 27.6	S17 56.8	316 11.8	N20 48.3	162 45.4	S12 39.0
19	36 26.9	122 52.8	09.3	80 28.1	56.2	331 14.4	48.3	177 47.7	39.1
20	51 29.3	137 51.8	09.3	95 28.6	55.6	346 17.1	48.3	192 50.0	39.1
21	66 31.8	152 50.9 ..	09.3	110 29.1 ..	55.1	1 19.7 ..	48.3	207 52.3 ..	39.1
22	81 34.3	167 50.0	09.3	125 29.5	54.5	16 22.3	48.3	222 54.6	39.2
23	96 36.7	182 49.0	09.4	140 30.0	53.9	31 25.0	48.3	237 56.9	39.2
12 00	111 39.2	197 48.1	S23 09.4	155 30.5	S17 53.3	46 27.6	N20 48.2	252 59.2	S12 39.3
01	126 41.7	212 47.1	09.4	170 31.0	52.8	61 30.2	48.2	268 01.6	39.3
02	141 44.1	227 46.2	09.5	185 31.5	52.2	76 32.9	48.2	283 03.9	39.3
03	156 46.6	242 45.2 ..	09.5	200 31.9 ..	51.6	91 35.5 ..	48.2	298 06.2 ..	39.4
04	171 49.0	257 44.3	09.5	215 32.4	51.0	106 38.1	48.2	313 08.5	39.4
05	186 51.5	272 43.3	09.5	230 32.9	50.5	121 40.7	48.2	328 10.8	39.5
06	201 54.0	287 42.4	S23 09.5	245 33.4	S17 49.9	136 43.4	N20 48.1	343 13.1	S12 39.5
07	216 56.4	302 41.4	09.5	260 33.9	49.3	151 46.0	48.1	358 15.4	39.5
S 08	231 58.9	317 40.5	09.5	275 34.4	48.7	166 48.6	48.1	13 17.7	39.6
A 09	247 01.4	332 39.6 ..	09.6	290 34.8 ..	48.2	181 51.2 ..	48.1	28 20.0 ..	39.6
T 10	262 03.8	347 38.6	09.6	305 35.3	47.6	196 53.9	48.1	43 22.3	39.7
U 11	277 06.3	2 37.7	09.6	320 35.8	47.0	211 56.5	48.1	58 24.7	39.7
R 12	292 08.8	17 36.7	S23 09.6	335 36.3	S17 46.4	226 59.1	N20 48.0	73 27.0	S12 39.7
D 13	307 11.2	32 35.8	09.6	350 36.8	45.9	242 01.8	48.0	88 29.3	39.8
A 14	322 13.7	47 34.8	09.6	5 37.3	45.3	257 04.4	48.0	103 31.6	39.8
Y 15	337 16.1	62 33.9 ..	09.6	20 37.7 ..	44.7	272 07.0 ..	48.0	118 33.9 ..	39.9
16	352 18.6	77 32.9	09.6	35 38.2	44.1	287 09.6	48.0	133 36.2	39.9
17	7 21.1	92 32.0	09.6	50 38.7	43.5	302 12.2	48.0	148 38.5	39.9
18	22 23.5	107 31.0	S23 09.6	65 39.2	S17 43.0	317 14.9	N20 47.9	163 40.8	S12 40.0
19	37 26.0	122 30.1	09.6	80 39.7	42.4	332 17.5	47.9	178 43.2	40.0
20	52 28.5	137 29.2	09.6	95 40.2	41.8	347 20.1	47.9	193 45.5	40.1
21	67 30.9	152 28.2 ..	09.6	110 40.6 ..	41.2	2 22.7 ..	47.9	208 47.8 ..	40.1
22	82 33.4	167 27.3	09.6	125 41.1	40.6	17 25.4	47.9	223 50.1	40.1
23	97 35.9	182 26.3	09.6	140 41.6	40.1	32 28.0	47.9	238 52.4	40.2
Mer. Pass.	h m 16 34.6	v −0.9	d 0.0	v 0.5	d 0.6	v 2.6	d 0.0	v 2.3	d 0.0

STARS

Name	SHA	Dec
Acamar	315 18.4	S40 15.4
Achernar	335 27.0	S57 10.5
Acrux	173 09.3	S63 10.1
Adhara	255 12.3	S28 59.6
Aldebaran	290 49.4	N16 32.0
Alioth	166 20.9	N55 53.0
Alkaid	152 59.2	N49 14.6
Al Na'ir	27 44.5	S46 53.9
Alnilam	275 46.3	S 1 11.8
Alphard	217 56.1	S 8 43.1
Alphecca	126 11.5	N26 40.1
Alpheratz	357 43.9	N29 10.0
Altair	62 08.8	N 8 54.3
Ankaa	353 16.1	S42 14.3
Antares	112 26.9	S26 27.5
Arcturus	145 56.1	N19 06.7
Atria	107 29.4	S69 02.7
Avior	234 17.5	S59 33.2
Bellatrix	278 32.0	N 6 21.5
Betelgeuse	271 01.3	N 7 24.4
Canopus	263 55.7	S52 42.4
Capella	280 34.4	N46 00.6
Deneb	49 32.1	N45 19.8
Denebola	182 33.8	N14 29.7
Diphda	348 56.2	S17 55.0
Dubhe	193 51.7	N61 40.4
Elnath	278 12.6	N28 37.0
Eltanin	90 46.8	N51 29.2
Enif	33 47.7	N 9 56.2
Fomalhaut	15 24.5	S29 33.2
Gacrux	172 01.0	S57 11.0
Gienah	175 52.5	S17 36.9
Hadar	148 48.4	S60 25.9
Hamal	328 01.0	N23 31.5
Kaus Aust.	83 44.6	S34 22.5
Kochab	137 20.6	N74 05.8
Markab	13 38.8	N15 16.7
Menkar	314 15.2	N 4 08.4
Menkent	148 08.0	S36 25.9
Miaplacidus	221 38.8	S69 46.3
Mirfak	308 40.4	N49 54.6
Nunki	75 59.0	S26 16.7
Peacock	53 20.3	S56 41.5
Pollux	243 27.7	N27 59.4
Procyon	244 59.7	N 5 11.3
Rasalhague	96 07.0	N12 33.1
Regulus	207 43.6	N11 54.0
Rigel	281 12.0	S 8 11.4
Rigil Kent.	139 52.3	S60 53.0
Sabik	102 13.1	S15 44.3
Schedar	349 40.9	N56 36.9
Shaula	96 22.7	S37 06.6
Sirius	258 33.6	S16 44.3
Spica	158 31.5	S11 13.8
Suhail	222 52.2	S43 29.2
Vega	80 39.6	N38 47.8
Zuben'ubi	137 05.8	S16 05.7

	SHA	Mer. Pass.
	° '	h m
Venus	87 30.7	10 48
Mars	44 39.0	13 38
Jupiter	294 44.3	20 55
Saturn	141 23.8	7 11

SUN and MOON

UT (d h)	SUN GHA	SUN Dec	MOON GHA	v	MOON Dec	d	HP
10 00	178 08.7	S21 57.6	205 37.8	3.5	S20 46.9	1.5	60.9
01	193 08.4	57.2	220 00.1	3.4	20 45.4	1.5	60.9
02	208 08.2	56.9	234 22.5	3.4	20 43.9	1.8	60.9
03	223 07.9	.. 56.5	248 44.9	3.3	20 42.1	1.9	60.9
04	238 07.7	56.1	263 07.2	3.4	20 40.2	2.0	60.9
05	253 07.4	55.7	277 29.6	3.4	20 38.2	2.2	60.9
06	268 07.2	S21 55.4	291 52.0	3.4	S20 36.0	2.4	60.9
T 07	283 06.9	55.0	306 14.4	3.5	20 33.6	2.5	60.9
H 08	298 06.7	54.6	320 36.9	3.4	20 31.1	2.7	60.9
U 09	313 06.4	.. 54.2	334 59.3	3.5	20 28.4	2.8	60.9
R 10	328 06.2	53.9	349 21.8	3.5	20 25.6	3.0	60.9
S 11	343 05.9	53.5	3 44.3	3.5	20 22.6	3.1	60.9
D 12	358 05.7	S21 53.1	18 06.8	3.5	S20 19.5	3.3	60.9
A 13	13 05.4	52.7	32 29.3	3.6	20 16.2	3.4	60.9
Y 14	28 05.2	52.3	46 51.9	3.6	20 12.8	3.5	60.9
15	43 04.9	.. 52.0	61 14.5	3.7	20 09.3	3.8	60.9
16	58 04.7	51.6	75 37.2	3.6	20 05.5	3.8	60.9
17	73 04.4	51.2	89 59.8	3.7	20 01.7	4.0	60.9
18	88 04.2	S21 50.8	104 22.5	3.8	S19 57.7	4.2	60.9
19	103 03.9	50.4	118 45.3	3.8	19 53.5	4.3	60.9
20	118 03.7	50.0	133 08.1	3.8	19 49.2	4.5	60.9
21	133 03.4	.. 49.6	147 30.9	3.9	19 44.7	4.6	60.9
22	148 03.2	49.3	161 53.8	3.9	19 40.1	4.6	60.9
23	163 02.9	48.9	176 16.7	3.9	19 35.4	4.9	60.9
11 00	178 02.7	S21 48.5	190 39.6	4.0	S19 30.5	5.0	60.9
01	193 02.4	48.1	205 02.6	4.1	19 25.5	5.2	60.8
02	208 02.2	47.7	219 25.7	4.1	19 20.3	5.3	60.8
03	223 01.9	.. 47.3	233 48.8	4.2	19 15.0	5.4	60.8
04	238 01.7	46.9	248 12.0	4.2	19 09.6	5.6	60.8
05	253 01.4	46.5	262 35.2	4.2	19 04.0	5.7	60.8
06	268 01.2	S21 46.1	276 58.4	4.4	S18 58.3	5.9	60.8
07	283 00.9	45.7	291 21.8	4.4	18 52.4	5.9	60.8
08	298 00.7	45.3	305 45.2	4.4	18 46.5	6.2	60.8
F 09	313 00.4	.. 44.9	320 08.6	4.5	18 40.3	6.2	60.8
R 10	328 00.2	44.5	334 32.1	4.6	18 34.1	6.4	60.8
I 11	342 59.9	44.1	348 55.7	4.6	18 27.7	6.5	60.7
D 12	357 59.7	S21 43.7	3 19.3	4.7	S18 21.2	6.6	60.7
A 13	12 59.5	43.3	17 43.0	4.8	18 14.6	6.8	60.7
Y 14	27 59.2	42.9	32 06.8	4.8	18 07.8	6.9	60.7
15	42 59.0	.. 42.5	46 30.6	5.0	18 00.9	7.0	60.7
16	57 58.7	42.1	60 54.6	4.9	17 53.9	7.1	60.7
17	72 58.5	41.7	75 18.5	5.1	17 46.8	7.3	60.7
18	87 58.2	S21 41.3	89 42.6	5.1	S17 39.5	7.3	60.6
19	102 58.0	40.9	104 06.7	5.2	17 32.2	7.5	60.6
20	117 57.7	40.5	118 30.9	5.3	17 24.7	7.6	60.6
21	132 57.5	.. 40.1	132 55.2	5.3	17 17.1	7.8	60.6
22	147 57.3	39.7	147 19.5	5.4	17 09.3	7.8	60.6
23	162 57.0	39.3	161 43.9	5.5	17 01.5	7.9	60.6
12 00	177 56.8	S21 38.9	176 08.4	5.6	S16 53.6	8.1	60.5
01	192 56.5	38.5	190 33.0	5.6	16 45.5	8.2	60.5
02	207 56.3	38.1	204 57.6	5.8	16 37.3	8.3	60.5
03	222 56.1	.. 37.7	219 22.4	5.8	16 29.0	8.3	60.5
04	237 55.8	37.3	233 47.2	5.9	16 20.7	8.5	60.5
05	252 55.6	36.9	248 12.1	5.9	16 12.2	8.6	60.4
06	267 55.3	S21 36.4	262 37.0	6.1	S16 03.6	8.7	60.4
S 07	282 55.1	36.0	277 02.1	6.1	15 54.9	8.8	60.4
A 08	297 54.9	35.6	291 27.2	6.2	15 46.1	8.9	60.4
T 09	312 54.6	.. 35.2	305 52.4	6.3	15 37.2	9.0	60.4
U 10	327 54.4	34.8	320 17.7	6.4	15 28.2	9.1	60.3
R 11	342 54.1	34.4	334 43.1	6.5	15 19.1	9.2	60.3
D 12	357 53.9	S21 34.0	349 08.6	6.5	S15 09.9	9.2	60.3
A 13	12 53.7	33.5	3 34.1	6.7	15 00.7	9.4	60.3
Y 14	27 53.4	33.1	17 59.8	6.7	14 51.3	9.4	60.2
15	42 53.2	.. 32.7	32 25.5	6.8	14 41.9	9.6	60.2
16	57 52.9	32.3	46 51.3	6.9	14 32.3	9.6	60.2
17	72 52.7	31.9	61 17.2	6.9	14 22.7	9.7	60.2
18	87 52.5	S21 31.5	75 43.1	7.1	S14 13.0	9.8	60.1
19	102 52.2	31.0	90 09.2	7.2	14 03.2	9.9	60.1
20	117 52.0	30.6	104 35.4	7.2	13 53.3	9.9	60.1
21	132 51.8	.. 30.2	119 01.6	7.3	13 43.4	10.1	60.0
22	147 51.5	29.8	133 27.9	7.4	13 33.3	10.1	60.0
23	162 51.3	29.3	147 54.3	7.5	S13 23.2	10.1	60.0
	SD 16.3	d 0.4	SD 16.6		16.5		16.4

Twilight, Sunrise, Moonrise

Lat.	Naut.	Civil	Sunrise	Moonrise 10	11	12	13
N 72	08 09	10 07	■■	■■	■■	10 36	10 10
N 70	07 53	09 28	■■	■■	10 17	10 00	09 50
68	07 40	09 02	10 52	09 16	09 30	09 34	09 35
66	07 29	08 41	10 04	08 31	09 00	09 14	09 23
64	07 20	08 25	09 34	08 01	08 37	08 58	09 12
62	07 12	08 11	09 11	07 38	08 18	08 45	09 03
60	07 04	07 59	08 53	07 20	08 03	08 33	08 55
N 58	06 58	07 49	08 38	07 04	07 50	08 24	08 49
56	06 52	07 40	08 25	06 51	07 39	08 15	08 43
54	06 47	07 32	08 14	06 40	07 29	08 07	08 37
52	06 42	07 25	08 04	06 30	07 20	08 00	08 32
50	06 37	07 18	07 55	06 21	07 12	07 54	08 28
45	06 27	07 03	07 37	06 02	06 55	07 40	08 18
N 40	06 18	06 51	07 21	05 47	06 42	07 29	08 10
35	06 09	06 41	07 08	05 33	06 30	07 19	08 03
30	06 02	06 31	06 57	05 22	06 19	07 11	07 57
20	05 47	06 14	06 37	05 02	06 02	06 56	07 46
N 10	05 32	05 58	06 20	04 45	05 46	06 43	07 37
0	05 16	05 42	06 04	04 29	05 32	06 31	07 28
S 10	04 59	05 25	05 48	04 14	05 17	06 19	07 19
20	04 38	05 06	05 31	03 57	05 02	06 06	07 09
30	04 11	04 43	05 10	03 37	04 44	05 52	06 59
35	03 54	04 29	04 58	03 26	04 33	05 43	06 52
40	03 32	04 11	04 45	03 13	04 21	05 33	06 45
45	03 05	03 52	04 28	02 57	04 07	05 22	06 37
S 50	02 26	03 25	04 08	02 38	03 50	05 08	06 27
52	02 03	03 12	03 58	02 29	03 42	05 01	06 22
54	01 33	02 56	03 47	02 19	03 33	04 54	06 16
56	00 34	02 38	03 34	02 08	03 23	04 46	06 11
58	////	02 14	03 20	01 55	03 11	04 36	06 05
S 60	////	01 41	03 02	01 40	02 58	04 26	05 57

Sunset, Twilight, Moonset

Lat.	Sunset	Civil	Naut.	Moonset 10	11	12	13
N 72	■■	14 10	■■	■■		15 12	17 34
N 70	■■	14 48	16 24	■■	13 27	15 47	17 51
68	13 25	15 15	16 37	12 18	14 13	16 11	18 05
66	14 13	15 36	16 48	13 03	14 42	16 30	18 16
64	14 43	15 52	16 57	13 32	15 05	16 45	18 25
62	15 05	16 06	17 05	13 55	15 23	16 58	18 33
60	15 23	16 18	17 12	14 13	15 37	17 08	18 40
N 58	15 38	16 28	17 19	14 28	15 50	17 18	18 46
56	15 51	16 37	17 24	14 41	16 00	17 26	18 51
54	16 02	16 45	17 30	14 52	16 10	17 33	18 56
52	16 12	16 52	17 35	15 02	16 18	17 39	19 00
50	16 21	16 58	17 39	15 11	16 26	17 45	19 04
45	16 40	17 13	17 49	15 29	16 42	17 57	19 12
N 40	16 55	17 25	17 59	15 44	16 55	18 07	19 19
35	17 08	17 36	18 07	15 57	17 06	18 16	19 25
30	17 19	17 45	18 15	16 08	17 16	18 24	19 30
20	17 39	18 02	18 30	16 27	17 33	18 37	19 38
N 10	17 56	18 18	18 44	16 44	17 47	18 48	19 46
0	18 12	18 34	19 00	16 59	18 00	18 59	19 53
S 10	18 28	18 51	19 17	17 15	18 14	19 09	20 00
20	18 45	19 09	19 38	17 31	18 28	19 20	20 08
30	19 05	19 32	20 05	17 50	18 44	19 33	20 16
35	19 17	19 46	20 22	18 01	18 54	19 40	20 21
40	19 31	20 03	20 43	18 13	19 04	19 48	20 27
45	19 47	20 23	21 10	18 28	19 17	19 58	20 33
S 50	20 08	20 50	21 49	18 45	19 32	20 09	20 40
52	20 17	21 03	22 11	18 54	19 39	20 15	20 44
54	20 28	21 18	22 40	19 03	19 47	20 20	20 48
56	20 41	21 37	23 33	19 14	19 55	20 27	20 52
58	20 55	22 00	////	19 26	20 05	20 34	20 57
S 60	21 12	22 32	////	19 40	20 16	20 42	21 02

SUN and MOON

Day	SUN Eqn. of Time 00h	12h	Mer. Pass.	MOON Mer. Pass. Upper	Lower	Age	Phase
	m s	m s	h m	h m	h m	d	%
10	07 25	07 37	12 08	10 44	23 16	28	3
11	07 49	08 01	12 08	11 46	24 16	29	0
12	08 12	08 24	12 08	12 45	00 16	01	1 ●

UT	ARIES GHA	VENUS −3.9 GHA	Dec	MARS +1.2 GHA	Dec	JUPITER −2.6 GHA	Dec	SATURN +0.6 GHA	Dec	STARS Name	SHA	Dec
d h	° ′	° ′	° ′	° ′	° ′	° ′	° ′	° ′	° ′		° ′	° ′
13 00	112 38.3	197 25.4	S23 09.6	155 42.1	S17 39.5	47 30.6	N20 47.9	253 54.7	S12 40.2	Acamar	315 18.4	S40 15.4
01	127 40.8	212 24.4	09.6	170 42.6	38.9	62 33.2	47.8	268 57.0	40.2	Achernar	335 27.0	S57 10.5
02	142 43.3	227 23.5	09.6	185 43.1	38.3	77 35.8	47.8	283 59.3	40.3	Acrux	173 09.3	S63 10.1
03	157 45.7	242 22.5 ..	09.6	200 43.6 ..	37.7	92 38.5 ..	47.8	299 01.7 ..	40.3	Adhara	255 12.3	S28 59.6
04	172 48.2	257 21.6	09.6	215 44.0	37.2	107 41.1	47.8	314 04.0	40.4	Aldebaran	290 49.4	N16 32.0
05	187 50.6	272 20.6	09.6	230 44.5	36.6	122 43.7	47.8	329 06.3	40.4			
S 06	202 53.1	287 19.7	S23 09.6	245 45.0	S17 36.0	137 46.3	N20 47.8	344 08.6	S12 40.4	Alioth	166 20.9	N55 53.0
U 07	217 55.6	302 18.7	09.5	260 45.5	35.4	152 48.9	47.8	359 10.9	40.5	Alkaid	152 59.2	N49 14.6
N 08	232 58.0	317 17.8	09.5	275 46.0	34.8	167 51.6	47.7	14 13.2	40.5	Al Na'ir	27 44.5	S46 53.9
D 09	248 00.5	332 16.9 ..	09.5	290 46.5 ..	34.2	182 54.2 ..	47.7	29 15.5 ..	40.6	Alnilam	275 46.3	S 1 11.8
A 10	263 03.0	347 15.9	09.5	305 47.0	33.7	197 56.8	47.7	44 17.9	40.6	Alphard	217 56.0	S 8 43.1
Y 11	278 05.4	2 15.0	09.5	320 47.4	33.1	212 59.4	47.7	59 20.2	40.6			
12	293 07.9	17 14.0	S23 09.5	335 47.9	S17 32.5	228 02.0	N20 47.7	74 22.5	S12 40.7	Alphecca	126 11.4	N26 40.1
13	308 10.4	32 13.1	09.4	350 48.4	31.9	243 04.7	47.7	89 24.8	40.7	Alpheratz	357 43.9	N29 09.9
14	323 12.8	47 12.1	09.4	5 48.9	31.3	258 07.3	47.6	104 27.1	40.7	Altair	62 08.8	N 8 54.3
15	338 15.3	62 11.2 ..	09.4	20 49.4 ..	30.7	273 09.9 ..	47.6	119 29.4 ..	40.8	Ankaa	353 16.1	S42 14.3
16	353 17.8	77 10.2	09.4	35 49.9	30.1	288 12.5	47.6	134 31.7	40.8	Antares	112 26.8	S26 27.5
17	8 20.2	92 09.3	09.3	50 50.4	29.6	303 15.1	47.6	149 34.1	40.9			
18	23 22.7	107 08.3	S23 09.3	65 50.9	S17 29.0	318 17.7	N20 47.6	164 36.4	S12 40.9	Arcturus	145 56.0	N19 06.7
19	38 25.1	122 07.4	09.3	80 51.4	28.4	333 20.3	47.6	179 38.7	40.9	Atria	107 29.3	S69 02.7
20	53 27.6	137 06.5	09.2	95 51.8	27.8	348 23.0	47.6	194 41.0	41.0	Avior	234 17.4	S59 33.2
21	68 30.1	152 05.5 ..	09.2	110 52.3 ..	27.2	3 25.6 ..	47.6	209 43.3 ..	41.0	Bellatrix	278 32.0	N 6 21.5
22	83 32.5	167 04.6	09.2	125 52.8	26.6	18 28.2	47.5	224 45.6	41.1	Betelgeuse	271 01.3	N 7 24.4
23	98 35.0	182 03.6	09.1	140 53.3	26.0	33 30.8	47.5	239 48.0	41.1			
14 00	113 37.5	197 02.7	S23 09.1	155 53.8	S17 25.4	48 33.4	N20 47.5	254 50.3	S12 41.1	Canopus	263 55.7	S52 42.4
01	128 39.9	212 01.7	09.1	170 54.3	24.8	63 36.0	47.5	269 52.6	41.2	Capella	280 34.4	N46 00.6
02	143 42.4	227 00.8	09.0	185 54.8	24.3	78 38.6	47.5	284 54.9	41.2	Deneb	49 32.1	N45 19.8
03	158 44.9	241 59.8 ..	09.0	200 55.3 ..	23.7	93 41.2 ..	47.5	299 57.2 ..	41.2	Denebola	182 33.8	N14 29.7
04	173 47.3	256 58.9	09.0	215 55.8	23.1	108 43.9	47.4	314 59.5	41.3	Diphda	348 56.2	S17 55.0
05	188 49.8	271 58.0	08.9	230 56.3	22.5	123 46.5	47.4	330 01.9	41.3			
M 06	203 52.3	286 57.0	S23 08.9	245 56.7	S17 21.9	138 49.1	N20 47.4	345 04.2	S12 41.3	Dubhe	193 51.6	N61 40.4
O 07	218 54.7	301 56.1	08.8	260 57.2	21.3	153 51.7	47.4	0 06.5	41.4	Elnath	278 12.6	N28 37.0
N 08	233 57.2	316 55.1	08.8	275 57.7	20.7	168 54.3	47.4	15 08.8	41.4	Eltanin	90 46.8	N51 29.2
D 09	248 59.6	331 54.2 ..	08.7	290 58.2 ..	20.1	183 56.9 ..	47.4	30 11.1 ..	41.5	Enif	33 47.7	N 9 56.2
A 10	264 02.1	346 53.2	08.7	305 58.7	19.5	198 59.5	47.4	45 13.4	41.5	Fomalhaut	15 24.5	S29 33.2
Y 11	279 04.6	1 52.3	08.6	320 59.2	18.9	214 02.1	47.4	60 15.8	41.5			
12	294 07.0	16 51.3	S23 08.6	335 59.7	S17 18.3	229 04.7	N20 47.3	75 18.1	S12 41.6	Gacrux	172 01.0	S57 11.0
13	309 09.5	31 50.4	08.5	351 00.2	17.8	244 07.3	47.3	90 20.4	41.6	Gienah	175 52.4	S17 36.9
14	324 12.0	46 49.4	08.5	6 00.7	17.2	259 10.0	47.3	105 22.7	41.6	Hadar	148 48.3	S60 25.9
15	339 14.4	61 48.5 ..	08.4	21 01.2 ..	16.6	274 12.6 ..	47.3	120 25.0 ..	41.7	Hamal	328 01.0	N23 31.5
16	354 16.9	76 47.6	08.4	36 01.7	16.0	289 15.2	47.3	135 27.4	41.7	Kaus Aust.	83 44.6	S34 22.5
17	9 19.4	91 46.6	08.3	51 02.2	15.4	304 17.8	47.3	150 29.7	41.8			
18	24 21.8	106 45.7	S23 08.3	66 02.6	S17 14.8	319 20.4	N20 47.3	165 32.0	S12 41.8	Kochab	137 20.5	N74 05.8
19	39 24.3	121 44.7	08.2	81 03.1	14.2	334 23.0	47.3	180 34.3	41.8	Markab	13 38.8	N15 16.7
20	54 26.7	136 43.8	08.2	96 03.6	13.6	349 25.6	47.2	195 36.6	41.9	Menkar	314 15.2	N 4 08.4
21	69 29.2	151 42.8 ..	08.1	111 04.1 ..	13.0	4 28.2 ..	47.2	210 39.0 ..	41.9	Menkent	148 07.9	S36 25.9
22	84 31.7	166 41.9	08.0	126 04.6	12.4	19 30.8	47.2	225 41.3	41.9	Miaplacidus	221 38.8	S69 46.3
23	99 34.1	181 41.0	08.0	141 05.1	11.8	34 33.4	47.2	240 43.6	42.0			
15 00	114 36.6	196 40.0	S23 07.9	156 05.6	S17 11.2	49 36.0	N20 47.2	255 45.9	S12 42.0	Mirfak	308 40.4	N49 54.6
01	129 39.1	211 39.1	07.8	171 06.1	10.6	64 38.6	47.2	270 48.2	42.0	Nunki	75 59.0	S26 16.7
02	144 41.5	226 38.1	07.8	186 06.6	10.0	79 41.2	47.2	285 50.6	42.1	Peacock	53 20.3	S56 41.5
03	159 44.0	241 37.2 ..	07.7	201 07.1 ..	09.4	94 43.8 ..	47.2	300 52.9 ..	42.1	Pollux	243 27.7	N27 59.4
04	174 46.5	256 36.2	07.6	216 07.6	08.8	109 46.4	47.1	315 55.2	42.2	Procyon	244 59.7	N 5 11.3
05	189 48.9	271 35.3	07.6	231 08.1	08.2	124 49.0	47.1	330 57.5	42.2			
T 06	204 51.4	286 34.3	S23 07.5	246 08.6	S17 07.6	139 51.6	N20 47.1	345 59.8	S12 42.2	Rasalhague	96 07.0	N12 33.1
U 07	219 53.9	301 33.4	07.4	261 09.1	07.0	154 54.2	47.1	1 02.2	42.3	Regulus	207 43.5	N11 53.9
E 08	234 56.3	316 32.5	07.3	276 09.6	06.4	169 56.8	47.1	16 04.5	42.3	Rigel	281 12.0	S 8 11.4
S 09	249 58.8	331 31.5 ..	07.3	291 10.1 ..	05.8	184 59.4 ..	47.1	31 06.8 ..	42.3	Rigil Kent.	139 52.2	S60 53.6
D 10	265 01.2	346 30.6	07.2	306 10.6	05.2	200 02.0	47.1	46 09.1	42.4	Sabik	102 13.1	S15 44.3
A 11	280 03.7	1 29.6	07.1	321 11.1	04.6	215 04.6	47.1	61 11.5	42.4			
Y 12	295 06.2	16 28.7	S23 07.0	336 11.6	S17 04.0	230 07.2	N20 47.0	76 13.8	S12 42.4	Schedar	349 40.9	N56 36.8
13	310 08.6	31 27.7	07.0	351 12.1	03.4	245 09.8	47.0	91 16.1	42.5	Shaula	96 22.6	S37 06.6
14	325 11.1	46 26.8	06.9	6 12.6	02.8	260 12.4	47.0	106 18.4	42.5	Sirius	258 33.6	S16 44.3
15	340 13.6	61 25.8 ..	06.8	21 13.0 ..	02.2	275 15.0 ..	47.0	121 20.7 ..	42.5	Spica	158 31.5	S11 13.8
16	355 16.0	76 24.9	06.7	36 13.5	01.6	290 17.6	47.0	136 23.1	42.6	Suhail	222 52.2	S43 29.2
17	10 18.5	91 24.0	06.6	51 14.0	01.0	305 20.2	47.0	151 25.4	42.6			
18	25 21.0	106 23.0	S23 06.5	66 14.5	S17 00.4	320 22.8	N20 47.0	166 27.7	S12 42.7	Vega	80 39.6	N38 47.8
19	40 23.4	121 22.1	06.4	81 15.0	16 59.8	335 25.4	47.0	181 30.0	42.7	Zuben'ubi	137 05.8	S16 05.7
20	55 25.9	136 21.1	06.4	96 15.5	59.2	350 28.0	47.0	196 32.4	42.7		SHA	Mer. Pass.
21	70 28.3	151 20.2 ..	06.3	111 16.0 ..	58.6	5 30.6 ..	46.9	211 34.7 ..	42.8		° ′	h m
22	85 30.8	166 19.2	06.2	126 16.5	58.0	20 33.2	46.9	226 37.0	42.8	Venus	83 25.2	10 53
23	100 33.3	181 18.3	06.1	141 17.0	57.4	35 35.8	46.9	241 39.3	42.8	Mars	42 16.3	13 36
	h m									Jupiter	294 55.9	20 42
Mer. Pass.	16 22.8	v −0.9	d 0.1	v 0.5	d 0.6	v 2.6	d 0.0	v 2.3	d 0.0	Saturn	141 12.8	7 00

UT	SUN GHA	SUN Dec	MOON GHA	v	Dec	d	HP
d h	° ′	° ′	° ′	′	° ′	′	′
13 00	177 51.0	S21 28.9	162 20.8	7.6	S13 13.1	10.3	60.0
01	192 50.8	28.5	176 47.4	7.6	13 02.8	10.3	59.9
02	207 50.6	28.1	191 14.0	7.8	12 52.5	10.4	59.9
03	222 50.3	.. 27.6	205 40.8	7.8	12 42.1	10.5	59.9
04	237 50.1	27.2	220 07.6	7.9	12 31.6	10.5	59.8
05	252 49.9	26.8	234 34.5	8.1	12 21.1	10.6	59.8
06	267 49.6	S21 26.4	249 01.6	8.0	S12 10.5	10.6	59.8
07	282 49.4	25.9	263 28.6	8.2	11 59.9	10.8	59.8
08	297 49.2	25.5	277 55.8	8.3	11 49.1	10.7	59.7
S 09	312 48.9	.. 25.1	292 23.1	8.3	11 38.4	10.9	59.7
U 10	327 48.7	24.6	306 50.4	8.5	11 27.5	10.9	59.7
N 11	342 48.5	24.2	321 17.9	8.5	11 16.6	10.9	59.6
D 12	357 48.2	S21 23.8	335 45.4	8.6	S11 05.7	11.0	59.6
A 13	12 48.0	23.3	350 13.0	8.7	10 54.7	11.1	59.6
Y 14	27 47.8	22.9	4 40.7	8.7	10 43.6	11.1	59.5
15	42 47.5	.. 22.5	19 08.4	8.9	10 32.5	11.2	59.5
16	57 47.3	22.0	33 36.3	8.9	10 21.3	11.2	59.5
17	72 47.1	21.6	48 04.2	9.0	10 10.1	11.3	59.4
18	87 46.9	S21 21.2	62 32.2	9.1	S 9 58.9	11.3	59.4
19	102 46.6	20.7	77 00.3	9.2	9 47.6	11.3	59.4
20	117 46.4	20.3	91 28.5	9.2	9 36.3	11.4	59.3
21	132 46.2	.. 19.8	105 56.7	9.4	9 24.9	11.4	59.3
22	147 45.9	19.4	120 25.1	9.4	9 13.5	11.5	59.3
23	162 45.7	19.0	134 53.5	9.5	9 02.0	11.5	59.2
14 00	177 45.5	S21 18.5	149 22.0	9.6	S 8 50.5	11.5	59.2
01	192 45.2	18.1	163 50.6	9.6	8 39.0	11.6	59.1
02	207 45.0	17.6	178 19.2	9.7	8 27.4	11.6	59.1
03	222 44.8	.. 17.2	192 47.9	9.8	8 15.8	11.6	59.1
04	237 44.6	16.7	207 16.7	9.9	8 04.2	11.7	59.0
05	252 44.3	16.3	221 45.6	10.0	7 52.5	11.7	59.0
06	267 44.1	S21 15.8	236 14.6	10.0	S 7 40.8	11.7	59.0
07	282 43.9	15.4	250 43.6	10.1	7 29.1	11.7	58.9
08	297 43.7	15.0	265 12.7	10.2	7 17.4	11.8	58.9
M 09	312 43.4	.. 14.5	279 41.9	10.2	7 05.6	11.8	58.9
O 10	327 43.2	14.1	294 11.1	10.3	6 53.8	11.8	58.8
N 11	342 43.0	13.6	308 40.4	10.4	6 42.0	11.9	58.8
D 12	357 42.8	S21 13.2	323 09.8	10.5	S 6 30.1	11.8	58.7
A 13	12 42.5	12.7	337 39.3	10.5	6 18.3	11.9	58.7
Y 14	27 42.3	12.3	352 08.8	10.6	6 06.4	11.9	58.7
15	42 42.1	.. 11.8	6 38.4	10.7	5 54.5	11.9	58.6
16	57 41.9	11.4	21 08.1	10.7	5 42.6	11.9	58.6
17	72 41.6	10.9	35 37.8	10.8	5 30.7	11.9	58.6
18	87 41.4	S21 10.5	50 07.6	10.9	S 5 18.8	12.0	58.5
19	102 41.2	10.0	64 37.5	11.0	5 06.8	11.9	58.5
20	117 41.0	09.5	79 07.5	11.0	4 54.9	12.0	58.4
21	132 40.7	.. 09.1	93 37.5	11.0	4 42.9	12.0	58.4
22	147 40.5	08.6	108 07.5	11.2	4 30.9	11.9	58.4
23	162 40.3	08.2	122 37.7	11.1	4 19.0	12.0	58.3
15 00	177 40.1	S21 07.7	137 07.8	11.3	S 4 07.0	12.0	58.3
01	192 39.9	07.2	151 38.1	11.3	3 55.0	12.0	58.2
02	207 39.6	06.8	166 08.4	11.4	3 43.0	12.0	58.2
03	222 39.4	.. 06.3	180 38.8	11.4	3 31.0	12.0	58.2
04	237 39.2	05.9	195 09.2	11.5	3 19.0	12.0	58.1
05	252 39.0	05.4	209 39.7	11.5	3 07.0	12.0	58.1
06	267 38.7	S21 04.9	224 10.2	11.6	S 2 55.0	12.0	58.1
07	282 38.5	04.5	238 40.8	11.7	2 43.0	12.0	58.0
T 08	297 38.3	04.0	253 11.5	11.7	2 31.0	11.9	58.0
U 09	312 38.1	.. 03.5	267 42.2	11.8	2 19.1	12.0	57.9
E 10	327 37.9	03.1	282 13.0	11.8	2 07.1	12.0	57.9
S 11	342 37.7	02.6	296 43.8	11.9	1 55.1	12.0	57.9
D 12	357 37.4	S21 02.1	311 14.7	11.9	S 1 43.1	11.9	57.8
A 13	12 37.2	01.7	325 45.6	12.0	1 31.2	12.0	57.8
Y 14	27 37.0	01.2	340 16.6	12.0	1 19.2	11.9	57.7
15	42 36.8	.. 00.7	354 47.6	12.1	1 07.3	11.9	57.7
16	57 36.6	21 00.3	9 18.7	12.1	0 55.4	11.9	57.7
17	72 36.3	20 59.8	23 49.8	12.2	0 43.5	11.9	57.6
18	87 36.1	S20 59.3	38 21.0	12.2	S 0 31.6	11.9	57.6
19	102 35.9	58.9	52 52.2	12.2	0 19.7	11.9	57.5
20	117 35.7	58.4	67 23.4	12.4	S 0 07.8	11.8	57.5
21	132 35.5	.. 57.9	81 54.8	12.3	N 0 04.0	11.9	57.5
22	147 35.3	57.4	96 26.1	12.4	0 15.9	11.8	57.4
23	162 35.1	57.0	110 57.5	12.4	N 0 27.7	11.8	57.4
	SD 16.3	d 0.5	SD 16.2		16.0		15.8

Lat.	Twilight Naut.	Civil	Sunrise	Moonrise 13	14	15	16
°	h m	h m	h m	h m	h m	h m	h m
N 72	08 02	09 55	■■	10 10	09 53	09 39	09 27
N 70	07 47	09 20	■■	09 50	09 43	09 36	09 30
68	07 35	08 55	10 37	09 35	09 35	09 34	09 32
66	07 25	08 36	09 55	09 23	09 28	09 31	09 35
64	07 16	08 20	09 27	09 12	09 22	09 30	09 37
62	07 08	08 07	09 06	09 03	09 17	09 28	09 38
60	07 02	07 56	08 49	08 55	09 12	09 27	09 40
N 58	06 56	07 46	08 34	08 49	09 08	09 25	09 41
56	06 50	07 37	08 22	08 42	09 05	09 24	09 42
54	06 45	07 30	08 11	08 37	09 02	09 23	09 43
52	06 40	07 23	08 02	08 32	08 59	09 22	09 44
50	06 36	07 16	07 53	08 28	08 56	09 21	09 45
45	06 26	07 02	07 35	08 18	08 50	09 20	09 47
N 40	06 17	06 51	07 20	08 10	08 46	09 18	09 49
35	06 09	06 40	07 08	08 03	08 41	09 17	09 50
30	06 02	06 31	06 57	07 57	08 38	09 16	09 51
20	05 47	06 14	06 38	07 46	08 31	09 14	09 54
N 10	05 33	05 59	06 21	07 37	08 26	09 12	09 56
0	05 17	05 43	06 05	07 28	08 20	09 10	09 57
S 10	05 00	05 27	05 50	07 19	08 15	09 08	09 59
20	04 40	05 09	05 33	07 09	08 09	09 07	10 01
30	04 14	04 46	05 13	06 59	08 03	09 05	10 04
35	03 57	04 32	05 01	06 52	07 59	09 04	10 05
40	03 36	04 16	04 48	06 45	07 55	09 02	10 07
45	03 10	03 56	04 32	06 45	07 50	09 01	10 08
S 50	02 32	03 30	04 12	06 27	07 44	08 59	10 11
52	02 11	03 17	04 03	06 22	07 41	08 58	10 12
54	01 44	03 02	03 52	06 17	07 38	08 57	10 13
56	00 58	02 45	03 40	06 11	07 35	08 56	10 14
58	////	02 22	03 26	06 05	07 31	08 55	10 15
S 60	////	01 53	03 09	05 57	07 27	08 54	10 17

Lat.	Sunset	Twilight Civil	Naut.	Moonset 13	14	15	16
°	h m	h m	h m	h m	h m	h m	h m
N 72	■■	14 24	16 17	17 34	19 39	21 34	23 25
N 70	■■	14 59	16 32	17 51	19 46	21 34	23 17
68	13 42	15 24	16 44	18 05	19 52	21 34	23 11
66	14 24	15 43	16 54	18 16	19 57	21 34	23 06
64	14 51	15 59	17 03	18 25	20 02	21 34	23 02
62	15 13	16 12	17 10	18 33	20 05	21 34	22 58
60	15 30	16 23	17 17	18 40	20 09	21 34	22 55
N 58	15 44	16 33	17 23	18 46	20 11	21 34	22 53
56	15 57	16 41	17 29	18 51	20 14	21 34	22 50
54	16 07	16 49	17 34	18 56	20 16	21 34	22 48
52	16 16	16 56	17 38	19 00	20 18	21 33	22 46
50	16 25	17 02	17 43	19 04	20 20	21 33	22 44
45	16 43	17 16	17 53	19 12	20 24	21 33	22 40
N 40	16 58	17 28	18 01	19 19	20 27	21 33	22 37
35	17 11	17 38	18 09	19 25	20 30	21 33	22 34
30	17 22	17 48	18 17	19 30	20 33	21 33	22 31
20	17 41	18 04	18 31	19 38	20 37	21 33	22 27
N 10	17 57	18 20	18 46	19 46	20 41	21 33	22 23
0	18 13	18 35	19 01	19 53	20 44	21 33	22 19
S 10	18 29	18 51	19 18	20 00	20 48	21 33	22 16
20	18 46	19 10	19 38	20 08	20 52	21 33	22 12
30	19 05	19 32	20 04	20 16	20 56	21 32	22 08
35	19 16	19 46	20 21	20 21	20 58	21 32	22 05
40	19 30	20 02	20 41	20 27	21 01	21 32	22 02
45	19 46	20 22	21 08	20 33	21 04	21 32	21 59
S 50	20 05	20 47	21 45	20 40	21 07	21 32	21 55
52	20 15	21 00	22 05	20 44	21 09	21 32	21 53
54	20 25	21 15	22 32	20 48	21 11	21 32	21 51
56	20 37	21 32	23 15	20 52	21 13	21 31	21 49
58	20 51	21 54	////	20 57	21 15	21 31	21 47
S 60	21 07	22 23	////	21 02	21 17	21 31	21 44

Day	SUN Eqn. of Time 00h	12h	Mer. Pass.	MOON Mer. Pass. Upper	Lower	Age	Phase
d	m s	m s	h m	h m	h m	d	%
13	08 35	08 47	12 09	13 41	01 13	02	4
14	08 58	09 09	12 09	14 33	02 07	03	10
15	09 19	09 30	12 09	15 22	02 57	04	17

UT	ARIES GHA	VENUS −3.9 GHA	Dec	MARS +1.2 GHA	Dec	JUPITER −2.6 GHA	Dec	SATURN +0.6 GHA	Dec	STARS Name	SHA	Dec
d h	° ′	° ′	° ′	° ′	° ′	° ′	° ′	° ′	° ′		° ′	° ′
16 00	115 35.7	196 17.4	S23 06.0	156 17.5	S16 56.8	50 38.4	N20 46.9	256 41.6	S12 42.9	Acamar	315 18.4	S40 15.4
01	130 38.2	211 16.4	05.9	171 18.0	56.2	65 41.0	46.9	271 44.0	42.9	Achernar	335 27.0	S57 10.5
02	145 40.7	226 15.5	05.8	186 18.5	55.6	80 43.6	46.9	286 46.3	42.9	Acrux	173 09.3	S63 10.1
03	160 43.1	241 14.5 ..	05.7	201 19.0 ..	55.0	95 46.2 ..	46.9	301 48.6 ..	43.0	Adhara	255 12.3	S28 59.6
04	175 45.6	256 13.6	05.6	216 19.5	54.4	110 48.8	46.9	316 50.9	43.0	Aldebaran	290 49.4	N16 32.0
05	190 48.1	271 12.7	05.5	231 20.0	53.8	125 51.4	46.9	331 53.3	43.0			
06	205 50.5	286 11.7	S23 05.4	246 20.5	S16 53.2	140 54.0	N20 46.8	346 55.6	S12 43.1	Alioth	166 20.8	N55 53.0
W 07	220 53.0	301 10.8	05.3	261 21.0	52.6	155 56.6	46.8	1 57.9	43.1	Alkaid	152 59.1	N49 14.6
E 08	235 55.5	316 09.8	05.2	276 21.5	52.0	170 59.2	46.8	17 00.2	43.1	Al Na'ir	27 44.5	S46 53.9
D 09	250 57.9	331 08.9 ..	05.1	291 22.0 ..	51.3	186 01.7 ..	46.8	32 02.6 ..	43.2	Alnilam	275 46.3	S 1 11.8
N 10	266 00.4	346 07.9	05.0	306 22.5	50.7	201 04.3	46.8	47 04.9	43.2	Alphard	217 56.0	S 8 43.1
E 11	281 02.8	1 07.0	04.9	321 23.0	50.1	216 06.9	46.8	62 07.2	43.2			
S 12	296 05.3	16 06.1	S23 04.8	336 23.5	S16 49.5	231 09.5	N20 46.8	77 09.5	S12 43.3	Alphecca	126 11.4	N26 40.1
D 13	311 07.8	31 05.1	04.6	351 24.0	48.9	246 12.1	46.8	92 11.9	43.3	Alpheratz	357 43.9	N29 09.9
A 14	326 10.2	46 04.2	04.5	6 24.5	48.3	261 14.7	46.8	107 14.2	43.3	Altair	62 08.8	N 8 54.3
Y 15	341 12.7	61 03.2 ..	04.4	21 25.0 ..	47.7	276 17.3 ..	46.8	122 16.5 ..	43.4	Ankaa	353 16.1	S42 14.3
16	356 15.2	76 02.3	04.3	36 25.5	47.1	291 19.9	46.7	137 18.9	43.4	Antares	112 26.8	S26 27.5
17	11 17.6	91 01.4	04.2	51 26.0	46.5	306 22.5	46.7	152 21.2	43.5			
18	26 20.1	106 00.4	S23 04.1	66 26.5	S16 45.9	321 25.1	N20 46.7	167 23.5	S12 43.5	Arcturus	145 56.0	N19 06.7
19	41 22.6	120 59.5	04.0	81 27.0	45.3	336 27.6	46.7	182 25.8	43.5	Atria	107 29.3	S69 02.7
20	56 25.0	135 58.5	03.8	96 27.6	44.7	351 30.2	46.7	197 28.2	43.6	Avior	234 17.4	S59 33.2
21	71 27.5	150 57.6 ..	03.7	111 28.1 ..	44.0	6 32.8 ..	46.7	212 30.5 ..	43.6	Bellatrix	278 32.0	N 6 21.5
22	86 30.0	165 56.6	03.6	126 28.6	43.4	21 35.4	46.7	227 32.8	43.6	Betelgeuse	271 01.3	N 7 24.4
23	101 32.4	180 55.7	03.5	141 29.1	42.8	36 38.0	46.7	242 35.1	43.7			
17 00	116 34.9	195 54.8	S23 03.4	156 29.6	S16 42.2	51 40.6	N20 46.7	257 37.5	S12 43.7	Canopus	263 55.7	S52 42.4
01	131 37.3	210 53.8	03.2	171 30.1	41.6	66 43.2	46.7	272 39.8	43.7	Capella	280 34.4	N46 00.6
02	146 39.8	225 52.9	03.1	186 30.6	41.0	81 45.8	46.6	287 42.1	43.8	Deneb	49 32.1	N45 19.8
03	161 42.3	240 51.9 ..	03.0	201 31.1 ..	40.4	96 48.3 ..	46.6	302 44.4 ..	43.8	Denebola	182 33.8	N14 29.7
04	176 44.7	255 51.0	02.8	216 31.6	39.8	111 50.9	46.6	317 46.8	43.8	Diphda	348 56.2	S17 55.0
05	191 47.2	270 50.1	02.7	231 32.1	39.1	126 53.5	46.6	332 49.1	43.9			
06	206 49.7	285 49.1	S23 02.6	246 32.6	S16 38.5	141 56.1	N20 46.6	347 51.4	S12 43.9	Dubhe	193 51.6	N61 40.4
T 07	221 52.1	300 48.2	02.5	261 33.1	37.9	156 58.7	46.6	2 53.8	43.9	Elnath	278 12.6	N28 37.0
H 08	236 54.6	315 47.3	02.3	276 33.6	37.3	172 01.3	46.6	17 56.1	44.0	Eltanin	90 46.7	N51 29.2
U 09	251 57.1	330 46.3 ..	02.2	291 34.1 ..	36.7	187 03.8 ..	46.6	32 58.4 ..	44.0	Enif	33 47.7	N 9 56.2
R 10	266 59.5	345 45.4	02.1	306 34.6	36.1	202 06.4	46.6	48 00.8	44.0	Fomalhaut	15 24.5	S29 33.2
S 11	282 02.0	0 44.4	01.9	321 35.1	35.5	217 09.0	46.6	63 03.1	44.1			
D 12	297 04.4	15 43.5	S23 01.8	336 35.6	S16 34.8	232 11.6	N20 46.5	78 05.4	S12 44.1	Gacrux	172 01.0	S57 11.0
A 13	312 06.9	30 42.6	01.6	351 36.1	34.2	247 14.2	46.5	93 07.7	44.1	Gienah	175 52.4	S17 36.9
Y 14	327 09.4	45 41.6	01.5	6 36.6	33.6	262 16.8	46.5	108 10.1	44.2	Hadar	148 48.3	S60 25.9
15	342 11.8	60 40.7 ..	01.4	21 37.1 ..	33.0	277 19.3 ..	46.5	123 12.4 ..	44.2	Hamal	328 01.0	N23 31.5
16	357 14.3	75 39.7	01.2	36 37.6	32.4	292 21.9	46.5	138 14.7	44.2	Kaus Aust.	83 44.5	S34 22.5
17	12 16.8	90 38.8	01.1	51 38.2	31.8	307 24.5	46.5	153 17.1	44.3			
18	27 19.2	105 37.9	S23 00.9	66 38.7	S16 31.2	322 27.1	N20 46.5	168 19.4	S12 44.3	Kochab	137 20.4	N74 05.8
19	42 21.7	120 36.9	00.8	81 39.2	30.5	337 29.7	46.5	183 21.7	44.3	Markab	13 38.8	N15 16.7
20	57 24.2	135 36.0	00.6	96 39.7	29.9	352 32.2	46.5	198 24.0	44.3	Menkar	314 15.2	N 4 08.4
21	72 26.6	150 35.1 ..	00.5	111 40.2 ..	29.3	7 34.8 ..	46.5	213 26.4 ..	44.4	Menkent	148 07.9	S36 25.9
22	87 29.1	165 34.1	00.3	126 40.7	28.7	22 37.4	46.5	228 28.7	44.4	Miaplacidus	221 38.8	S69 46.3
23	102 31.6	180 33.2	00.2	141 41.2	28.1	37 40.0	46.5	243 31.0	44.4			
18 00	117 34.0	195 32.2	S23 00.0	156 41.7	S16 27.4	52 42.6	N20 46.4	258 33.4	S12 44.5	Mirfak	308 40.5	N49 54.6
01	132 36.5	210 31.3	22 59.9	171 42.2	26.8	67 45.1	46.4	273 35.7	44.5	Nunki	75 59.0	S26 16.7
02	147 38.9	225 30.4	59.7	186 42.7	26.2	82 47.7	46.4	288 38.0	44.5	Peacock	53 20.3	S56 41.5
03	162 41.4	240 29.4 ..	59.6	201 43.2 ..	25.6	97 50.3 ..	46.4	303 40.4 ..	44.6	Pollux	243 27.7	N27 59.4
04	177 43.9	255 28.5	59.4	216 43.7	25.0	112 52.9	46.4	318 42.7	44.6	Procyon	244 59.7	N 5 11.2
05	192 46.3	270 27.6	59.2	231 44.3	24.4	127 55.4	46.4	333 45.0	44.6			
06	207 48.8	285 26.6	S22 59.1	246 44.8	S16 23.7	142 58.0	N20 46.4	348 47.4	S12 44.7	Rasalhague	96 07.0	N12 33.1
07	222 51.3	300 25.7	58.9	261 45.3	23.1	158 00.6	46.4	3 49.7	44.7	Regulus	207 43.5	N11 53.9
F 08	237 53.7	315 24.7	58.7	276 45.8	22.5	173 03.2	46.4	18 52.0	44.7	Rigel	281 12.0	S 8 11.4
R 09	252 56.2	330 23.8 ..	58.6	291 46.3 ..	21.9	188 05.7 ..	46.4	33 54.4 ..	44.8	Rigil Kent.	139 52.2	S60 53.0
I 10	267 58.7	345 22.9	58.4	306 46.8	21.2	203 08.3	46.4	48 56.7	44.8	Sabik	102 13.1	S15 44.3
11	283 01.1	0 21.9	58.3	321 47.3	20.6	218 10.9	46.4	63 59.0	44.8			
D 12	298 03.6	15 21.0	S22 58.1	336 47.8	S16 20.0	233 13.5	N20 46.3	79 01.4	S12 44.9	Schedar	349 40.9	N56 36.8
A 13	313 06.1	30 20.1	57.9	351 48.3	19.4	248 16.0	46.3	94 03.7	44.9	Shaula	96 22.6	S37 06.6
Y 14	328 08.5	45 19.1	57.7	6 48.8	18.8	263 18.6	46.3	109 06.0	44.9	Sirius	258 33.6	S16 44.3
15	343 11.0	60 18.2 ..	57.6	21 49.4 ..	18.1	278 21.2 ..	46.3	124 08.4 ..	45.0	Spica	158 31.5	S11 13.8
16	358 13.4	75 17.3	57.4	36 49.9	17.5	293 23.7	46.3	139 10.7	45.0	Suhail	222 52.2	S43 29.2
17	13 15.9	90 16.3	57.2	51 50.4	16.9	308 26.3	46.3	154 13.0	45.0			
18	28 18.4	105 15.4	S22 57.0	66 50.9	S16 16.3	323 28.9	N20 46.3	169 15.4	S12 45.1	Vega	80 39.5	N38 47.8
19	43 20.8	120 14.5	56.9	81 51.4	15.6	338 31.5	46.3	184 17.7	45.1	Zuben'ubi	137 05.8	S16 05.7
20	58 23.3	135 13.5	56.7	96 51.9	15.0	353 34.0	46.3	199 20.0	45.1		SHA	Mer. Pass.
21	73 25.8	150 12.6 ..	56.5	111 52.4 ..	14.4	8 36.6 ..	46.3	214 22.4 ..	45.2		° ′	h m
22	88 28.2	165 11.7	56.3	126 52.9	13.8	23 39.2	46.3	229 24.7	45.2	Venus	79 19.9	10 57
23	103 30.7	180 10.7	56.2	141 53.4	13.1	38 41.7	46.3	244 27.0	45.2	Mars	39 54.7	13 34
	h m									Jupiter	295 05.7	20 30
Mer. Pass.	16 11.0	v −0.9	d 0.1	v 0.5	d 0.6	v 2.6	d 0.0	v 2.3	d 0.0	Saturn	141 02.6	6 48

UT	SUN GHA	SUN Dec	MOON GHA	v	MOON Dec	d	HP
d h	° ′	° ′	° ′	′	° ′	′	′
16 00	177 34.8	S20 56.5	125 28.9	12.5	N 0 39.5	11.7	57.4
01	192 34.6	56.0	140 00.4	12.5	0 51.2	11.8	57.3
02	207 34.4	55.5	154 31.9	12.6	1 03.0	11.7	57.3
03	222 34.2 ..	55.1	169 03.5	12.6	1 14.7	11.7	57.2
04	237 34.0	54.6	183 35.1	12.6	1 26.4	11.7	57.2
05	252 33.8	54.1	198 06.7	12.7	1 38.1	11.7	57.2
06	267 33.6	S20 53.6	212 38.4	12.7	N 1 49.8	11.6	57.1
W 07	282 33.3	53.1	227 10.1	12.7	2 01.4	11.6	57.1
E 08	297 33.1	52.7	241 41.8	12.8	2 13.0	11.6	57.1
D 09	312 32.9 ..	52.2	256 13.6	12.8	2 24.6	11.6	57.0
N 10	327 32.7	51.7	270 45.4	12.8	2 36.2	11.5	57.0
E 11	342 32.5	51.2	285 17.2	12.9	2 47.7	11.5	56.9
S 12	357 32.3	S20 50.7	299 49.1	12.9	N 2 59.2	11.5	56.9
D 13	12 32.1	50.2	314 21.0	13.0	3 10.7	11.4	56.9
A 14	27 31.9	49.8	328 53.0	12.9	3 22.1	11.4	56.8
Y 15	42 31.7 ..	49.3	343 24.9	13.0	3 33.5	11.4	56.8
16	57 31.4	48.8	357 56.9	13.0	3 44.9	11.3	56.8
17	72 31.2	48.3	12 28.9	13.1	3 56.2	11.3	56.7
18	87 31.0	S20 47.8	27 01.0	13.1	N 4 07.5	11.3	56.7
19	102 30.8	47.3	41 33.1	13.1	4 18.8	11.2	56.6
20	117 30.6	46.8	56 05.2	13.1	4 30.0	11.2	56.6
21	132 30.4 ..	46.3	70 37.3	13.1	4 41.2	11.2	56.6
22	147 30.2	45.9	85 09.4	13.2	4 52.4	11.1	56.5
23	162 30.0	45.4	99 41.6	13.2	5 03.5	11.1	56.5
17 00	177 29.8	S20 44.9	114 13.8	13.2	N 5 14.6	11.1	56.5
01	192 29.6	44.4	128 46.0	13.3	5 25.7	11.0	56.4
02	207 29.4	43.9	143 18.3	13.2	5 36.7	10.9	56.4
03	222 29.2 ..	43.4	157 50.5	13.3	5 47.6	11.0	56.4
04	237 29.0	42.9	172 22.8	13.3	5 58.6	10.9	56.3
05	252 28.7	42.4	186 55.1	13.3	6 09.5	10.8	56.3
06	267 28.5	S20 41.9	201 27.4	13.3	N 6 20.3	10.8	56.3
T 07	282 28.3	41.4	215 59.7	13.4	6 31.1	10.8	56.2
H 08	297 28.1	40.9	230 32.1	13.3	6 41.9	10.7	56.2
U 09	312 27.9 ..	40.4	245 04.4	13.4	6 52.6	10.6	56.2
R 10	327 27.7	39.9	259 36.8	13.4	7 03.2	10.7	56.1
S 11	342 27.5	39.4	274 09.2	13.4	7 13.9	10.6	56.1
D 12	357 27.3	S20 38.9	288 41.6	13.4	N 7 24.5	10.5	56.1
A 13	12 27.1	38.4	303 14.0	13.4	7 35.0	10.5	56.0
Y 14	27 26.9	37.9	317 46.4	13.5	7 45.5	10.4	56.0
15	42 26.7 ..	37.4	332 18.9	13.4	7 55.9	10.4	56.0
16	57 26.5	36.9	346 51.3	13.5	8 06.3	10.3	55.9
17	72 26.3	36.4	1 23.8	13.5	8 16.6	10.3	55.9
18	87 26.1	S20 35.9	15 56.3	13.4	N 8 26.9	10.3	55.9
19	102 25.9	35.4	30 28.7	13.5	8 37.2	10.2	55.8
20	117 25.7	34.9	45 01.2	13.5	8 47.4	10.1	55.8
21	132 25.5 ..	34.4	59 33.7	13.5	8 57.5	10.1	55.8
22	147 25.3	33.9	74 06.2	13.5	9 07.6	10.0	55.7
23	162 25.1	33.4	88 38.7	13.5	9 17.6	10.0	55.7
18 00	177 24.9	S20 32.9	103 11.2	13.5	N 9 27.6	9.9	55.7
01	192 24.7	32.4	117 43.7	13.5	9 37.5	9.9	55.7
02	207 24.5	31.8	132 16.2	13.5	9 47.4	9.8	55.6
03	222 24.3 ..	31.3	146 48.7	13.6	9 57.2	9.8	55.6
04	237 24.1	30.8	161 21.3	13.5	10 07.0	9.7	55.6
05	252 23.9	30.3	175 53.8	13.5	10 16.7	9.7	55.5
06	267 23.7	S20 29.8	190 26.3	13.5	N10 26.4	9.5	55.5
F 07	282 23.5	29.3	204 58.8	13.5	10 35.9	9.6	55.5
R 08	297 23.3	28.8	219 31.3	13.6	10 45.5	9.5	55.5
I 09	312 23.1 ..	28.3	234 03.9	13.5	10 55.0	9.4	55.4
D 10	327 22.9	27.7	248 36.4	13.5	11 04.4	9.4	55.4
A 11	342 22.7	27.2	263 08.9	13.5	11 13.8	9.3	55.4
Y 12	357 22.5	S20 26.7	277 41.4	13.6	N11 23.1	9.2	55.3
13	12 22.3	26.2	292 13.9	13.5	11 32.3	9.2	55.3
14	27 22.1	25.7	306 46.4	13.5	11 41.5	9.1	55.3
15	42 21.9 ..	25.2	321 18.9	13.5	11 50.6	9.1	55.3
16	57 21.8	24.6	335 51.4	13.5	11 59.7	9.0	55.2
17	72 21.6	24.1	350 23.9	13.5	12 08.7	8.9	55.2
18	87 21.4	S20 23.6	4 56.4	13.5	N12 17.6	8.9	55.2
19	102 21.2	23.1	19 28.9	13.5	12 26.5	8.8	55.2
20	117 21.0	22.6	34 01.4	13.4	12 35.3	8.8	55.1
21	132 20.8 ..	22.0	48 33.8	13.5	12 44.1	8.7	55.1
22	147 20.6	21.5	63 06.3	13.4	12 52.8	8.6	55.1
23	162 20.4	21.0	77 38.7	13.5	N13 01.4	8.5	55.1
	SD 16.3	d 0.5	SD 15.5		15.3		15.1

Lat.	Twilight Naut.	Civil	Sunrise	Moonrise 16	17	18	19
°	h m	h m	h m	h m	h m	h m	h m
N 72	07 55	09 42	■■■	09 27	09 14	09 00	08 41
N 70	07 41	09 11	11 38	09 30	09 24	09 17	09 10
68	07 30	08 48	10 23	09 32	09 32	09 31	09 31
66	07 20	08 30	09 46	09 35	09 38	09 42	09 48
64	07 12	08 15	09 20	09 37	09 44	09 52	10 02
62	07 05	08 03	09 00	09 38	09 49	10 00	10 14
60	06 59	07 52	08 44	09 40	09 53	10 07	10 24
N 58	06 53	07 43	08 30	09 41	09 57	10 14	10 33
56	06 48	07 35	08 19	09 42	10 00	10 19	10 41
54	06 43	07 27	08 08	09 43	10 03	10 24	10 48
52	06 38	07 20	07 59	09 44	10 06	10 29	10 54
50	06 34	07 14	07 51	09 45	10 08	10 33	10 59
45	06 25	07 01	07 33	09 47	10 14	10 42	11 12
N 40	06 16	06 50	07 19	09 49	10 19	10 49	11 22
35	06 09	06 40	07 07	09 50	10 23	10 56	11 31
30	06 01	06 31	06 56	09 51	10 26	11 02	11 38
20	05 47	06 14	06 38	09 54	10 33	11 12	11 52
N 10	05 33	05 59	06 22	09 55	10 38	11 20	12 03
0	05 19	05 44	06 07	09 57	10 43	11 29	12 14
S 10	05 02	05 29	05 51	09 59	10 49	11 37	12 25
20	04 42	05 11	05 35	10 01	10 54	11 46	12 37
30	04 17	04 49	05 15	10 04	11 01	11 56	12 51
35	04 00	04 35	05 04	10 05	11 05	12 02	12 59
40	03 40	04 20	04 51	10 07	11 09	12 09	13 08
45	03 15	04 00	04 36	10 08	11 14	12 17	13 18
S 50	02 39	03 35	04 17	10 11	11 20	12 27	13 31
52	02 19	03 23	04 08	10 12	11 23	12 31	13 37
54	01 54	03 09	03 57	10 13	11 26	12 36	13 44
56	01 16	02 52	03 46	10 14	11 29	12 41	13 51
58	////	02 31	03 32	10 15	11 33	12 48	14 00
S 60	////	02 04	03 17	10 17	11 37	12 55	14 09

Lat.	Sunset	Twilight Civil	Naut.	Moonset 16	17	18	19
°	h m	h m	h m	h m	h m	h m	h m
N 72	■■■	14 39	16 26	23 25	25 14	01 14	03 08
N 70	12 43	15 10	16 40	23 17	24 59	00 59	02 40
68	13 58	15 33	16 51	23 11	24 46	00 46	02 20
66	14 35	15 51	17 01	23 06	24 36	00 36	02 04
64	15 01	16 06	17 09	23 02	24 28	00 28	01 51
62	15 21	16 18	17 16	22 58	24 20	00 20	01 40
60	15 37	16 29	17 22	22 55	24 14	00 14	01 30
N 58	15 50	16 38	17 28	22 53	24 09	00 09	01 22
56	16 02	16 46	17 33	22 50	24 04	00 04	01 15
54	16 13	16 54	17 38	22 48	23 59	25 09	01 09
52	16 22	17 00	17 43	22 46	23 56	25 03	01 03
50	16 30	17 07	17 47	22 44	23 52	24 58	00 58
45	16 47	17 20	17 56	22 40	23 44	24 47	00 47
N 40	17 02	17 31	18 04	22 37	23 38	24 37	00 37
35	17 14	17 41	18 17	22 34	23 32	24 30	00 30
30	17 24	17 50	18 19	22 31	23 28	24 23	00 23
20	17 43	18 06	18 33	22 27	23 19	24 11	00 11
N 10	17 59	18 21	18 47	22 23	23 12	24 00	00 00
0	18 14	18 36	19 02	22 19	23 05	23 51	24 36
S 10	18 29	18 52	19 18	22 16	22 58	23 41	24 24
20	18 46	19 09	19 38	22 12	22 51	23 30	24 11
30	19 05	19 31	20 03	22 08	22 43	23 19	23 56
35	19 16	19 44	20 19	22 05	22 38	23 12	23 48
40	19 29	20 00	20 39	22 02	22 33	23 04	23 38
45	19 44	20 19	21 05	21 59	22 26	22 55	23 27
S 50	20 03	20 44	21 40	21 55	22 19	22 44	23 13
52	20 12	20 56	21 57	21 53	22 16	22 39	23 06
54	20 22	21 10	22 24	21 51	22 12	22 34	22 59
56	20 33	21 27	23 00	21 49	22 08	22 28	22 51
58	20 47	21 47	////	21 47	22 03	22 21	22 42
S 60	21 02	22 14	////	21 44	21 58	22 14	22 32

Day	SUN Eqn. of Time 00h	12h	Mer. Pass.	MOON Mer. Pass. Upper	Lower	Age	Phase
	m s	m s	h m	h m	h m	d	%
16	09 40	09 50	12 10	16 08	03 45	05	26
17	10 00	10 10	12 10	16 54	04 31	06	36
18	10 20	10 29	12 10	17 40	05 17	07	45

UT	ARIES	VENUS −3.9		MARS +1.2		JUPITER −2.6		SATURN +0.6		STARS		
	GHA	GHA	Dec	GHA	Dec	GHA	Dec	GHA	Dec	Name	SHA	Dec
d h	° ′	° ′	° ′	° ′	° ′	° ′	° ′	° ′	° ′		° ′	° ′
19 00	118 33.2	195 09.8	S22 56.0	156 54.0	S16 12.5	53 44.3	N20 46.3	259 29.4	S12 45.2	Acamar	315 18.4	S40 15.4
01	133 35.6	210 08.9	55.8	171 54.5	11.9	68 46.9	46.3	274 31.7	45.3	Achernar	335 27.0	S57 10.5
02	148 38.1	225 07.9	55.6	186 55.0	11.3	83 49.4	46.2	289 34.0	45.3	Acrux	173 09.2	S63 10.1
03	163 40.5	240 07.0 . .	55.4	201 55.5 . .	10.6	98 52.0 . .	46.2	304 36.4 . .	45.3	Adhara	255 12.3	S28 59.7
04	178 43.0	255 06.1	55.2	216 56.0	10.0	113 54.6	46.2	319 38.7	45.4	Aldebaran	290 49.4	N16 32.0
05	193 45.5	270 05.1	55.0	231 56.5	09.4	128 57.1	46.2	334 41.0	45.4			
06	208 47.9	285 04.2	S22 54.8	246 57.0	S16 08.8	143 59.7	N20 46.2	349 43.4	S12 45.4	Alioth	166 20.8	N55 53.0
07	223 50.4	300 03.3	54.7	261 57.6	08.1	159 02.3	46.2	4 45.7	45.5	Alkaid	152 59.1	N49 14.6
S 08	238 52.9	315 02.3	54.5	276 58.1	07.5	174 04.8	46.2	19 48.1	45.5	Al Na'ir	27 44.5	S46 53.9
A 09	253 55.3	330 01.4 . .	54.3	291 58.6 . .	06.9	189 07.4 . .	46.2	34 50.4 . .	45.5	Alnilam	275 46.3	S 1 11.8
T 10	268 57.8	345 00.5	54.1	306 59.1	06.2	204 10.0	46.2	49 52.7	45.5	Alphard	217 56.0	S 8 43.1
U 11	284 00.3	359 59.5	53.9	321 59.6	05.6	219 12.5	46.2	64 55.1	45.6			
R 12	299 02.7	14 58.6	S22 53.7	337 00.1	S16 05.0	234 15.1	N20 46.2	79 57.4	S12 45.6	Alphecca	126 11.4	N26 40.1
D 13	314 05.2	29 57.7	53.5	352 00.6	04.4	249 17.7	46.2	94 59.7	45.6	Alpheratz	357 43.9	N29 09.9
A 14	329 07.7	44 56.7	53.3	7 01.2	03.7	264 20.2	46.2	110 02.1	45.7	Altair	62 08.8	N 8 54.3
Y 15	344 10.1	59 55.8 . .	53.1	22 01.7 . .	03.1	279 22.8 . .	46.2	125 04.4 . .	45.7	Ankaa	353 16.1	S42 14.3
16	359 12.6	74 54.9	52.9	37 02.2	02.5	294 25.4	46.2	140 06.8	45.7	Antares	112 26.8	S26 27.5
17	14 15.0	89 53.9	52.7	52 02.7	01.8	309 27.9	46.2	155 09.1	45.8			
18	29 17.5	104 53.0	S22 52.5	67 03.2	S16 01.2	324 30.5	N20 46.1	170 11.4	S12 45.8	Arcturus	145 56.0	N19 06.7
19	44 20.0	119 52.1	52.3	82 03.7	16 00.6	339 33.1	46.1	185 13.8	45.8	Atria	107 29.2	S69 02.7
20	59 22.4	134 51.1	52.1	97 04.3	15 59.9	354 35.6	46.1	200 16.1	45.9	Avior	234 17.4	S59 33.2
21	74 24.9	149 50.2 . .	51.9	112 04.8 . .	59.3	9 38.2 . .	46.1	215 18.4 . .	45.9	Bellatrix	278 32.0	N 6 21.5
22	89 27.4	164 49.3	51.6	127 05.3	58.7	24 40.7	46.1	230 20.8	45.9	Betelgeuse	271 01.3	N 7 24.4
23	104 29.8	179 48.4	51.4	142 05.8	58.0	39 43.3	46.1	245 23.1	45.9			
20 00	119 32.3	194 47.4	S22 51.2	157 06.3	S15 57.4	54 45.9	N20 46.1	260 25.5	S12 46.0	Canopus	263 55.7	S52 42.4
01	134 34.8	209 46.5	51.0	172 06.8	56.8	69 48.4	46.1	275 27.8	46.0	Capella	280 34.4	N46 00.6
02	149 37.2	224 45.6	50.8	187 07.4	56.1	84 51.0	46.1	290 30.1	46.0	Deneb	49 32.1	N45 19.8
03	164 39.7	239 44.6 . .	50.6	202 07.9 . .	55.5	99 53.5 . .	46.1	305 32.5 . .	46.1	Denebola	182 33.7	N14 29.7
04	179 42.2	254 43.7	50.4	217 08.4	54.9	114 56.1	46.1	320 34.8	46.1	Diphda	348 56.3	S17 55.0
05	194 44.6	269 42.8	50.1	232 08.9	54.2	129 58.6	46.1	335 37.2	46.1			
06	209 47.1	284 41.8	S22 49.9	247 09.4	S15 53.6	145 01.2	N20 46.1	350 39.5	S12 46.1	Dubhe	193 51.6	N61 40.4
07	224 49.5	299 40.9	49.7	262 10.0	53.0	160 03.8	46.1	5 41.8	46.2	Elnath	278 12.6	N28 37.0
08	239 52.0	314 40.0	49.5	277 10.5	52.3	175 06.3	46.1	20 44.2	46.2	Eltanin	90 46.7	N51 29.2
S 09	254 54.5	329 39.1 . .	49.3	292 11.0 . .	51.7	190 08.9 . .	46.1	35 46.5 . .	46.2	Enif	33 47.7	N 9 56.2
U 10	269 56.9	344 38.1	49.0	307 11.5	51.1	205 11.4	46.1	50 48.9	46.3	Fomalhaut	15 24.5	S29 33.2
N 11	284 59.4	359 37.2	48.8	322 12.0	50.4	220 14.0	46.1	65 51.2	46.3			
D 12	300 01.9	14 36.3	S22 48.6	337 12.6	S15 49.8	235 16.5	N20 46.0	80 53.5	S12 46.3	Gacrux	172 00.9	S57 11.0
A 13	315 04.3	29 35.4	48.4	352 13.1	49.2	250 19.1	46.0	95 55.9	46.4	Gienah	175 52.4	S17 36.9
Y 14	330 06.8	44 34.4	48.1	7 13.6	48.5	265 21.7	46.0	110 58.2	46.4	Hadar	148 48.2	S60 25.9
15	345 09.3	59 33.5 . .	47.9	22 14.1 . .	47.9	280 24.2 . .	46.0	126 00.6 . .	46.4	Hamal	328 01.0	N23 31.5
16	0 11.7	74 32.6	47.7	37 14.6	47.3	295 26.8	46.0	141 02.9	46.4	Kaus Aust.	83 44.5	S34 22.5
17	15 14.2	89 31.6	47.4	52 15.2	46.6	310 29.3	46.0	156 05.2	46.5			
18	30 16.6	104 30.7	S22 47.2	67 15.7	S15 46.0	325 31.9	N20 46.0	171 07.6	S12 46.5	Kochab	137 20.4	N74 05.8
19	45 19.1	119 29.8	47.0	82 16.2	45.3	340 34.4	46.0	186 09.9	46.5	Markab	13 38.8	N15 16.7
20	60 21.6	134 28.9	46.7	97 16.7	44.7	355 37.0	46.0	201 12.3	46.6	Menkar	314 15.2	N 4 08.4
21	75 24.0	149 27.9 . .	46.5	112 17.2 . .	44.1	10 39.5 . .	46.0	216 14.6 . .	46.6	Menkent	148 07.9	S36 25.9
22	90 26.5	164 27.0	46.3	127 17.8	43.4	25 42.1	46.0	231 16.9	46.6	Miaplacidus	221 38.8	S69 46.3
23	105 29.0	179 26.1	46.0	142 18.3	42.8	40 44.6	46.0	246 19.3	46.6			
21 00	120 31.4	194 25.2	S22 45.8	157 18.8	S15 42.2	55 47.2	N20 46.0	261 21.6	S12 46.7	Mirfak	308 40.5	N49 54.6
01	135 33.9	209 24.2	45.5	172 19.3	41.5	70 49.7	46.0	276 24.0	46.7	Nunki	75 59.0	S26 16.7
02	150 36.4	224 23.3	45.3	187 19.9	40.9	85 52.3	46.0	291 26.3	46.7	Peacock	53 20.3	S56 41.5
03	165 38.8	239 22.4 . .	45.0	202 20.4 . .	40.2	100 54.8 . .	46.0	306 28.7 . .	46.8	Pollux	243 27.7	N27 59.4
04	180 41.3	254 21.5	44.8	217 20.9	39.6	115 57.4	46.0	321 31.0	46.8	Procyon	244 59.7	N 5 11.2
05	195 43.8	269 20.5	44.5	232 21.4	39.0	130 59.9	46.0	336 33.3	46.8			
06	210 46.2	284 19.6	S22 44.3	247 21.9	S15 38.3	146 02.5	N20 46.0	351 35.7	S12 46.8	Rasalhague	96 07.0	N12 33.1
07	225 48.7	299 18.7	44.0	262 22.5	37.7	161 05.0	46.0	6 38.0	46.9	Regulus	207 43.5	N11 53.9
08	240 51.1	314 17.8	43.8	277 23.0	37.0	176 07.6	46.0	21 40.4	46.9	Rigel	281 12.0	S 8 11.4
M 09	255 53.6	329 16.9 . .	43.5	292 23.5 . .	36.4	191 10.1 . .	46.0	36 42.7 . .	46.9	Rigil Kent.	139 52.1	S60 53.0
O 10	270 56.1	344 15.9	43.3	307 24.0	35.7	206 12.7	46.0	51 45.1	47.0	Sabik	102 13.1	S15 44.3
N 11	285 58.5	359 15.0	43.0	322 24.6	35.1	221 15.2	46.0	66 47.4	47.0			
D 12	301 01.0	14 14.1	S22 42.8	337 25.1	S15 34.5	236 17.8	N20 46.0	81 49.8	S12 47.0	Schedar	349 41.0	N56 36.8
A 13	316 03.5	29 13.2	42.5	352 25.6	33.8	251 20.3	45.9	96 52.1	47.0	Shaula	96 22.6	S37 06.6
Y 14	331 05.9	44 12.2	42.3	7 26.1	33.2	266 22.9	45.9	111 54.4	47.1	Sirius	258 33.6	S16 44.3
15	346 08.4	59 11.3 . .	42.0	22 26.7 . .	32.5	281 25.4 . .	45.9	126 56.8 . .	47.1	Spica	158 31.5	S11 13.8
16	1 10.9	74 10.4	41.7	37 27.2	31.9	296 28.0	45.9	141 59.1	47.1	Suhail	222 52.2	S43 29.3
17	16 13.3	89 09.5	41.5	52 27.7	31.2	311 30.5	45.9	157 01.5	47.1			
18	31 15.8	104 08.6	S22 41.2	67 28.2	S15 30.6	326 33.0	N20 45.9	172 03.8	S12 47.2	Vega	80 39.5	N38 47.8
19	46 18.3	119 07.6	41.0	82 28.8	30.0	341 35.6	45.9	187 06.2	47.2	Zuben'ubi	137 05.8	S16 05.7
20	61 20.7	134 06.7	40.7	97 29.3	29.3	356 38.1	45.9	202 08.5	47.2		SHA	Mer.Pass.
21	76 23.2	149 05.8 . .	40.4	112 29.8 . .	28.7	11 40.7 . .	45.9	217 10.9 . .	47.3		° ′	h m
22	91 25.6	164 04.9	40.2	127 30.3	28.0	26 43.2	45.9	232 13.2	47.3	Venus	75 15.1	11 02
23	106 28.1	179 03.9	39.9	142 30.9	27.4	41 45.8	45.9	247 15.6	47.3	Mars	37 34.0	13 31
	h m									Jupiter	295 13.6	20 17
Mer.Pass. 15 59.2		v −0.9	d 0.2	v 0.5	d 0.6	v 2.6	d 0.0	v 2.3	d 0.0	Saturn	140 53.2	6 37

UT	SUN GHA	SUN Dec	MOON GHA	v	MOON Dec	d	HP
d h	° ′	° ′	° ′	′	° ′	′	′
19 00	177 20.2	S20 20.5	92 11.2	13.4	N13 09.9	8.5	55.0
01	192 20.0	19.9	106 43.6	13.4	13 18.4	8.5	55.0
02	207 19.8	19.4	121 16.0	13.4	13 26.9	8.3	55.0
03	222 19.6	.. 18.9	135 48.4	13.4	13 35.2	8.3	55.0
04	237 19.4	18.4	150 20.8	13.4	13 43.5	8.2	55.0
05	252 19.3	17.8	164 53.2	13.4	13 51.7	8.2	54.9
06	267 19.1	S20 17.3	179 25.6	13.4	N13 59.9	8.1	54.9
07	282 18.9	16.8	193 58.0	13.3	14 08.0	8.0	54.9
08	297 18.7	16.3	208 30.3	13.4	14 16.0	8.0	54.9
09	312 18.5	.. 15.7	223 02.7	13.3	14 24.0	7.9	54.8
10	327 18.3	15.2	237 35.0	13.3	14 31.9	7.8	54.8
11	342 18.1	14.7	252 07.3	13.3	14 39.7	7.7	54.8
12	357 17.9	S20 14.1	266 39.6	13.3	N14 47.4	7.7	54.8
13	12 17.7	13.6	281 11.9	13.3	14 55.1	7.6	54.8
14	27 17.6	13.1	295 44.2	13.2	15 02.7	7.5	54.7
15	42 17.4	.. 12.5	310 16.4	13.3	15 10.2	7.5	54.7
16	57 17.2	12.0	324 48.7	13.2	15 17.7	7.4	54.7
17	72 17.0	11.5	339 20.9	13.2	15 25.1	7.3	54.7
18	87 16.8	S20 10.9	353 53.1	13.2	N15 32.4	7.2	54.7
19	102 16.6	10.4	8 25.3	13.2	15 39.6	7.2	54.7
20	117 16.4	09.8	22 57.5	13.1	15 46.8	7.1	54.6
21	132 16.3	.. 09.3	37 29.6	13.2	15 53.9	7.0	54.6
22	147 16.1	08.8	52 01.8	13.1	16 00.9	6.9	54.6
23	162 15.9	08.2	66 33.9	13.1	16 07.8	6.9	54.6
20 00	177 15.7	S20 07.7	81 06.0	13.1	N16 14.7	6.8	54.6
01	192 15.5	07.2	95 38.1	13.1	16 21.5	6.7	54.6
02	207 15.3	06.6	110 10.2	13.0	16 28.2	6.6	54.5
03	222 15.2	.. 06.1	124 42.2	13.1	16 34.8	6.6	54.5
04	237 15.0	05.5	139 14.3	13.0	16 41.4	6.5	54.5
05	252 14.8	05.0	153 46.3	13.0	16 47.9	6.4	54.5
06	267 14.6	S20 04.4	168 18.3	13.0	N16 54.3	6.3	54.5
07	282 14.4	03.9	182 50.3	12.9	17 00.6	6.3	54.5
08	297 14.2	03.3	197 22.2	13.0	17 06.9	6.1	54.4
09	312 14.1	.. 02.8	211 54.2	12.9	17 13.0	6.1	54.4
10	327 13.9	02.3	226 26.1	12.9	17 19.1	6.0	54.4
11	342 13.7	01.7	240 58.0	12.9	17 25.1	6.0	54.4
12	357 13.5	S20 01.2	255 29.9	12.8	N17 31.1	5.8	54.4
13	12 13.3	00.6	270 01.7	12.9	17 36.9	5.8	54.4
14	27 13.2	20 00.1	284 33.6	12.8	17 42.7	5.7	54.4
15	42 13.0	19 59.5	299 05.4	12.8	17 48.4	5.6	54.3
16	57 12.8	59.0	313 37.2	12.8	17 54.0	5.5	54.3
17	72 12.6	58.4	328 09.0	12.7	17 59.5	5.4	54.3
18	87 12.5	S19 57.9	342 40.7	12.8	N18 04.9	5.4	54.3
19	102 12.3	57.3	357 12.5	12.7	18 10.3	5.3	54.3
20	117 12.1	56.8	11 44.2	12.7	18 15.6	5.2	54.3
21	132 11.9	.. 56.2	26 15.9	12.6	18 20.8	5.1	54.3
22	147 11.7	55.6	40 47.5	12.7	18 25.9	5.0	54.3
23	162 11.6	55.1	55 19.2	12.6	18 30.9	4.9	54.3
21 00	177 11.4	S19 54.5	69 50.8	12.6	N18 35.8	4.9	54.3
01	192 11.2	54.0	84 22.4	12.6	18 40.7	4.7	54.3
02	207 11.0	53.4	98 54.0	12.6	18 45.4	4.7	54.2
03	222 10.9	.. 52.9	113 25.6	12.5	18 50.1	4.6	54.2
04	237 10.7	52.3	127 57.1	12.6	18 54.7	4.5	54.2
05	252 10.5	51.8	142 28.7	12.5	18 59.2	4.5	54.2
06	267 10.3	S19 51.2	157 00.2	12.5	N19 03.7	4.3	54.2
07	282 10.2	50.6	171 31.7	12.4	19 08.0	4.3	54.2
08	297 10.0	50.1	186 03.1	12.5	19 12.3	4.1	54.2
09	312 09.8	.. 49.5	200 34.6	12.4	19 16.4	4.1	54.2
10	327 09.7	48.9	215 06.0	12.4	19 20.5	4.0	54.2
11	342 09.5	48.4	229 37.4	12.4	19 24.5	3.9	54.2
12	357 09.3	S19 47.8	244 08.8	12.4	N19 28.4	3.8	54.2
13	12 09.1	47.3	258 40.2	12.3	19 32.2	3.7	54.2
14	27 09.0	46.7	273 11.5	12.3	19 35.9	3.7	54.2
15	42 08.8	.. 46.1	287 42.8	12.3	19 39.6	3.5	54.2
16	57 08.6	45.6	302 14.1	12.3	19 43.1	3.4	54.1
17	72 08.5	45.0	316 45.4	12.3	19 46.5	3.4	54.1
18	87 08.3	S19 44.4	331 16.7	12.2	N19 49.9	3.3	54.1
19	102 08.1	43.9	345 47.9	12.3	19 53.2	3.2	54.1
20	117 07.9	43.3	0 19.2	12.2	19 56.4	3.1	54.1
21	132 07.8	.. 42.7	14 50.4	12.2	19 59.5	3.0	54.1
22	147 07.6	42.2	29 21.6	12.1	20 02.5	2.9	54.1
23	162 07.4	41.6	43 52.7	12.3	N20 05.4	2.8	54.1
	SD 16.3	d 0.5	SD 14.9		14.8		14.9

Day labels for the UT block: SATURDAY (19), SUNDAY (20), MONDAY (21).

Twilight · Sunrise · Moonrise

Lat.	Naut.	Civil	Sunrise	19	20	21	22
°	h m	h m	h m	h m	h m	h m	h m
N 72	07 47	09 30	■■■	08 41	08 09	▭	▭
N 70	07 34	09 02	11 03	09 10	09 01	08 46	▭
68	07 24	08 40	10 09	09 31	09 34	09 40	09 57
66	07 15	08 23	09 37	09 48	09 58	10 13	10 39
64	07 08	08 10	09 13	10 02	10 17	10 37	11 08
62	07 01	07 58	08 54	10 14	10 32	10 57	11 30
60	06 55	07 48	08 39	10 24	10 45	11 12	11 48
N 58	06 49	07 39	08 26	10 33	10 56	11 26	12 03
56	06 45	07 31	08 15	10 41	11 06	11 37	12 16
54	06 40	07 24	08 05	10 48	11 15	11 47	12 27
52	06 36	07 18	07 56	10 54	11 23	11 56	12 36
50	06 32	07 12	07 48	10 59	11 30	12 04	12 45
45	06 23	06 59	07 31	11 12	11 45	12 22	13 04
N 40	06 15	06 48	07 18	11 22	11 57	12 36	13 19
35	06 08	06 39	07 06	11 31	12 08	12 48	13 32
30	06 01	06 30	06 56	11 38	12 17	12 58	13 43
20	05 47	06 14	06 38	11 52	12 33	13 17	14 02
N 10	05 34	06 00	06 22	12 03	12 47	13 32	14 19
0	05 20	05 45	06 07	12 14	13 00	13 47	14 35
S 10	05 04	05 30	05 53	12 25	13 14	14 02	14 51
20	04 44	05 13	05 37	12 37	13 28	14 18	15 08
30	04 20	04 52	05 18	12 51	13 44	14 36	15 27
35	04 04	04 39	05 07	12 59	13 54	14 47	15 38
40	03 45	04 23	04 55	13 08	14 05	14 59	15 51
45	03 20	04 05	04 40	13 18	14 18	15 14	16 07
S 50	02 46	03 41	04 21	13 31	14 33	15 32	16 26
52	02 27	03 29	04 13	13 37	14 41	15 40	16 35
54	02 04	03 16	04 03	13 44	14 49	15 50	16 45
56	01 31	03 00	03 52	13 51	14 58	16 00	16 56
58	////	02 40	03 39	14 00	15 09	16 12	17 09
S 60	////	02 15	03 24	14 09	15 21	16 27	17 25

Sunset · Twilight · Moonset

Lat.	Sunset	Civil	Naut.	19	20	21	22
°	h m	h m	h m	h m	h m	h m	h m
N 72	■■■	14 53	16 36	03 08	05 16	▭	▭
N 70	13 20	15 22	16 49	02 40	04 25	06 17	▭
68	14 14	15 43	16 59	02 20	03 53	05 23	06 45
66	14 46	16 00	17 08	02 04	03 29	04 51	06 03
64	15 10	16 13	17 16	01 51	03 11	04 27	05 34
62	15 29	16 25	17 22	01 40	02 56	04 08	05 12
60	15 44	16 35	17 28	01 30	02 44	03 53	04 55
N 58	15 57	16 44	17 33	01 22	02 33	03 39	04 40
56	16 08	16 52	17 38	01 15	02 24	03 28	04 27
54	16 18	16 59	17 43	01 09	02 15	03 18	04 16
52	16 27	17 05	17 47	01 03	02 08	03 10	04 07
50	16 35	17 11	17 51	00 58	02 01	03 02	03 58
45	16 51	17 24	18 00	00 47	01 47	02 45	03 40
N 40	17 05	17 34	18 07	00 37	01 35	02 31	03 25
35	17 17	17 44	18 15	00 30	01 25	02 20	03 12
30	17 27	17 53	18 22	00 23	01 17	02 10	03 01
20	17 45	18 08	18 35	00 11	01 02	01 52	02 42
N 10	18 01	18 22	18 48	00 00	00 49	01 37	02 26
0	18 15	18 37	19 02	24 36	00 36	01 23	02 10
S 10	18 29	18 52	19 18	24 24	00 24	01 09	01 55
20	18 45	19 09	19 37	24 11	00 11	00 54	01 38
30	19 04	19 30	20 02	23 56	24 36	00 36	01 19
35	19 15	19 43	20 18	23 48	24 26	00 26	01 08
40	19 27	19 58	20 37	23 38	24 15	00 15	00 56
45	19 42	20 17	21 01	23 27	24 01	00 01	00 41
S 50	20 00	20 40	21 35	23 13	23 45	24 23	00 23
52	20 08	20 52	21 53	23 06	23 37	24 14	00 14
54	20 18	21 05	22 15	22 59	23 29	24 05	00 05
56	20 29	21 21	22 47	22 51	23 19	23 54	24 36
58	20 41	21 40	23 53	22 42	23 08	23 41	24 23
S 60	20 56	22 04	////	22 32	22 56	23 27	24 08

SUN and MOON

Day	SUN Eqn. of Time 00h	SUN Eqn. of Time 12h	SUN Mer. Pass.	MOON Mer. Pass. Upper	MOON Mer. Pass. Lower	Age	Phase
d	m s	m s	h m	h m	h m	d	%
19	10 39	10 48	12 11	18 25	06 02	08	55
20	10 57	11 06	12 11	19 12	06 48	09	64
21	11 14	11 22	12 11	19 59	07 35	10	73

UT	ARIES GHA	VENUS −3.9 GHA	Dec	MARS +1.2 GHA	Dec	JUPITER −2.6 GHA	Dec	SATURN +0.6 GHA	Dec	STARS Name	SHA	Dec
22 00	121 30.6	194 03.0	S22 39.6	157 31.4	S15 26.7	56 48.3	N20 45.9	262 17.9	S12 47.3	Acamar	315 18.4	S40 15.4
01	136 33.0	209 02.1	39.3	172 31.9	26.1	71 50.8	45.9	277 20.2	47.4	Achernar	335 27.1	S57 10.5
02	151 35.5	224 01.2	39.1	187 32.5	25.4	86 53.4	45.9	292 22.6	47.4	Acrux	173 09.2	S63 10.1
03	166 38.0	239 00.3 ..	38.8	202 33.0 ..	24.8	101 55.9 ..	45.9	307 24.9 ..	47.4	Adhara	255 12.3	S28 59.7
04	181 40.4	253 59.4	38.5	217 33.5	24.1	116 58.5	45.9	322 27.3	47.4	Aldebaran	290 49.4	N16 32.0
05	196 42.9	268 58.4	38.3	232 34.0	23.5	132 01.0	45.9	337 29.6	47.5			
T 06	211 45.4	283 57.5	S22 38.0	247 34.6	S15 22.8	147 03.5	N20 45.9	352 32.0	S12 47.5	Alioth	166 20.8	N55 53.0
07	226 47.8	298 56.6	37.7	262 35.1	22.2	162 06.1	45.9	7 34.3	47.5	Alkaid	152 59.1	N49 14.6
U 08	241 50.3	313 55.7	37.4	277 35.6	21.6	177 08.6	45.9	22 36.7	47.6	Al Na'ir	27 44.5	S46 53.9
E 09	256 52.8	328 54.8 ..	37.1	292 36.1 ..	20.9	192 11.2 ..	45.9	37 39.0 ..	47.6	Alnilam	275 46.3	S 1 11.8
S 10	271 55.2	343 53.8	36.9	307 36.7	20.3	207 13.7	45.9	52 41.4	47.6	Alphard	217 56.0	S 8 43.1
D 11	286 57.7	358 52.9	36.6	322 37.2	19.6	222 16.2	45.9	67 43.7	47.6			
A 12	302 00.1	13 52.0	S22 36.3	337 37.7	S15 19.0	237 18.8	N20 45.9	82 46.1	S12 47.7	Alphecca	126 11.4	N26 40.1
Y 13	317 02.6	28 51.1	36.0	352 38.3	18.3	252 21.3	45.9	97 48.4	47.7	Alpheratz	357 43.9	N29 09.9
14	332 05.1	43 50.2	35.7	7 38.8	17.7	267 23.9	45.9	112 50.8	47.7	Altair	62 08.8	N 8 54.3
15	347 07.5	58 49.3 ..	35.4	22 39.3 ..	17.0	282 26.4 ..	45.9	127 53.1 ..	47.7	Ankaa	353 16.1	S42 14.3
16	2 10.0	73 48.3	35.1	37 39.9	16.4	297 28.9	45.9	142 55.5	47.8	Antares	112 26.8	S26 27.5
17	17 12.5	88 47.4	34.8	52 40.4	15.7	312 31.5	45.9	157 57.8	47.8			
18	32 14.9	103 46.5	S22 34.6	67 40.9	S15 15.1	327 34.0	N20 45.9	173 00.2	S12 47.8	Arcturus	145 56.0	N19 06.7
19	47 17.4	118 45.6	34.3	82 41.4	14.4	342 36.5	45.9	188 02.5	47.8	Atria	107 29.2	S69 02.7
20	62 19.9	133 44.7	34.0	97 42.0	13.8	357 39.1	45.9	203 04.9	47.9	Avior	234 17.4	S59 33.3
21	77 22.3	148 43.8 ..	33.7	112 42.5 ..	13.1	12 41.6 ..	45.9	218 07.2 ..	47.9	Bellatrix	278 32.0	N 6 21.5
22	92 24.8	163 42.9	33.4	127 43.0	12.5	27 44.1	45.9	233 09.6	47.9	Betelgeuse	271 01.3	N 7 24.4
23	107 27.2	178 41.9	33.1	142 43.6	11.8	42 46.7	45.9	248 11.9	48.0			
23 00	122 29.7	193 41.0	S22 32.8	157 44.1	S15 11.1	57 49.2	N20 45.9	263 14.3	S12 48.0	Canopus	263 55.7	S52 42.5
01	137 32.2	208 40.1	32.5	172 44.6	10.5	72 51.7	45.9	278 16.6	48.0	Capella	280 34.4	N46 00.6
02	152 34.6	223 39.2	32.2	187 45.2	09.8	87 54.3	45.9	293 19.0	48.0	Deneb	49 32.1	N45 19.8
03	167 37.1	238 38.3 ..	31.9	202 45.7 ..	09.2	102 56.8 ..	45.9	308 21.3 ..	48.1	Denebola	182 33.7	N14 29.7
04	182 39.6	253 37.4	31.6	217 46.2	08.5	117 59.3	45.9	323 23.7	48.1	Diphda	348 56.3	S17 55.0
05	197 42.0	268 36.5	31.3	232 46.8	07.9	133 01.9	45.9	338 26.0	48.1			
W 06	212 44.5	283 35.5	S22 31.0	247 47.3	S15 07.2	148 04.4	N20 45.9	353 28.4	S12 48.1	Dubhe	193 51.5	N61 40.5
E 07	227 47.0	298 34.6	30.7	262 47.8	06.6	163 06.9	45.9	8 30.7	48.2	Elnath	278 12.6	N28 37.0
D 08	242 49.4	313 33.7	30.4	277 48.4	05.9	178 09.5	45.9	23 33.1	48.2	Eltanin	90 46.7	N51 29.2
N 09	257 51.9	328 32.8 ..	30.0	292 48.9 ..	05.3	193 12.0 ..	45.9	38 35.4 ..	48.2	Enif	33 47.7	N 9 56.2
E 10	272 54.4	343 31.9	29.7	307 49.4	04.6	208 14.5	45.9	53 37.8	48.2	Fomalhaut	15 24.5	S29 33.2
S 11	287 56.8	358 31.0	29.4	322 50.0	04.0	223 17.1	45.9	68 40.1	48.3			
D 12	302 59.3	13 30.1	S22 29.1	337 50.5	S15 03.3	238 19.6	N20 45.9	83 42.5	S12 48.3	Gacrux	172 00.9	S57 11.0
A 13	318 01.7	28 29.2	28.8	352 51.0	02.6	253 22.1	45.9	98 44.8	48.3	Gienah	175 52.4	S17 36.9
Y 14	333 04.2	43 28.3	28.5	7 51.6	02.0	268 24.6	45.9	113 47.2	48.3	Hadar	148 48.2	S60 25.9
15	348 06.7	58 27.3 ..	28.2	22 52.1 ..	01.3	283 27.2 ..	45.9	128 49.5 ..	48.4	Hamal	328 01.0	N23 31.5
16	3 09.1	73 26.4	27.8	37 52.6	00.7	298 29.7	45.9	143 51.9	48.4	Kaus Aust.	83 44.5	S34 22.5
17	18 11.6	88 25.5	27.5	52 53.2	15 00.0	313 32.2	45.9	158 54.2	48.4			
18	33 14.1	103 24.6	S22 27.2	67 53.7	S14 59.4	328 34.7	N20 45.9	173 56.6	S12 48.4	Kochab	137 20.3	N74 05.8
19	48 16.5	118 23.7	26.9	82 54.2	58.7	343 37.3	45.9	188 58.9	48.5	Markab	13 38.8	N15 16.7
20	63 19.0	133 22.8	26.5	97 54.8	58.0	358 39.8	45.9	204 01.3	48.5	Menkar	314 15.2	N 4 08.4
21	78 21.5	148 21.9 ..	26.2	112 55.3 ..	57.4	13 42.3 ..	45.9	219 03.7 ..	48.5	Menkent	148 07.8	S36 25.9
22	93 23.9	163 21.0	25.9	127 55.8	56.7	28 44.8	45.9	234 06.0	48.5	Miaplacidus	221 38.7	S69 46.3
23	108 26.4	178 20.1	25.6	142 56.4	56.1	43 47.4	45.9	249 08.4	48.6			
24 00	123 28.9	193 19.2	S22 25.2	157 56.9	S14 55.4	58 49.9	N20 45.9	264 10.7	S12 48.6	Mirfak	308 40.5	N49 54.6
01	138 31.3	208 18.3	24.9	172 57.5	54.8	73 52.4	45.9	279 13.1	48.6	Nunki	75 59.0	S26 16.7
02	153 33.8	223 17.3	24.6	187 58.0	54.1	88 54.9	45.9	294 15.4	48.6	Peacock	53 20.3	S56 41.5
03	168 36.2	238 16.4 ..	24.3	202 58.5 ..	53.4	103 57.5 ..	45.9	309 17.8 ..	48.7	Pollux	243 27.7	N27 59.4
04	183 38.7	253 15.5	23.9	217 59.1	52.8	119 00.0	45.9	324 20.1	48.7	Procyon	244 59.7	N 5 11.2
05	198 41.2	268 14.6	23.6	232 59.6	52.1	134 02.5	45.9	339 22.5	48.7			
06	213 43.6	283 13.7	S22 23.3	248 00.1	S14 51.5	149 05.0	N20 45.9	354 24.8	S12 48.7	Rasalhague	96 07.0	N12 33.1
07	228 46.1	298 12.8	22.9	263 00.7	50.8	164 07.5	45.9	9 27.2	48.8	Regulus	207 43.5	N11 53.9
T 08	243 48.6	313 11.9	22.6	278 01.2	50.1	179 10.1	45.9	24 29.6	48.8	Rigel	281 12.0	S 8 11.4
H 09	258 51.0	328 11.0 ..	22.2	293 01.7 ..	49.5	194 12.6 ..	45.9	39 31.9 ..	48.8	Rigil Kent.	139 52.1	S60 53.0
U 10	273 53.5	343 10.1	21.9	308 02.3	48.8	209 15.1	45.9	54 34.3	48.8	Sabik	102 13.1	S15 44.3
R 11	288 56.0	358 09.2	21.6	323 02.8	48.2	224 17.6	45.9	69 36.6	48.9			
S 12	303 58.4	13 08.3	S22 21.2	338 03.4	S14 47.5	239 20.1	N20 45.9	84 39.0	S12 48.9	Schedar	349 41.0	N56 36.8
D 13	319 00.9	28 07.4	20.9	353 03.9	46.8	254 22.7	45.9	99 41.3	48.9	Shaula	96 22.6	S37 06.6
A 14	334 03.4	43 06.5	20.5	8 04.4	46.2	269 25.2	45.9	114 43.7	48.9	Sirius	258 33.6	S16 44.3
Y 15	349 05.8	58 05.6 ..	20.2	23 05.0 ..	45.5	284 27.7 ..	45.9	129 46.0 ..	48.9	Spica	158 31.4	S11 13.8
16	4 08.3	73 04.7	19.8	38 05.5	44.8	299 30.2	45.9	144 48.4	49.0	Suhail	222 52.2	S43 29.3
17	19 10.7	88 03.8	19.5	53 06.1	44.2	314 32.7	45.9	159 50.8	49.0			
18	34 13.2	103 02.9	S22 19.1	68 06.6	S14 43.5	329 35.3	N20 45.9	174 53.1	S12 49.0	Vega	80 39.5	N38 47.8
19	49 15.7	118 02.0	18.8	83 07.1	42.9	344 37.8	45.9	189 55.5	49.0	Zuben'ubi	137 05.7	S16 05.7
20	64 18.1	133 01.1	18.4	98 07.7	42.2	359 40.3	45.9	204 57.8	49.1		SHA	Mer. Pass.
21	79 20.6	148 00.2 ..	18.1	113 08.2 ..	41.5	14 42.8 ..	45.9	220 00.2 ..	49.1	Venus	71 11.3	11 06
22	94 23.1	162 59.3	17.7	128 08.8	40.9	29 45.3	45.9	235 02.5	49.1	Mars	35 14.4	13 29
23	109 25.5	177 58.4	17.4	143 09.3	40.2	44 47.8	45.9	250 04.9	49.1	Jupiter	295 19.5	20 05
Mer. Pass. 15 47.4		v −0.9	d 0.3	v 0.5	d 0.7	v 2.5	d 0.0	v 2.4	d 0.0	Saturn	140 44.5	6 26

UT	SUN GHA	SUN Dec	MOON GHA	v	MOON Dec	d	HP
d h	° ′	° ′	° ′	′	° ′	′	′
22 00	177 07.3	S19 41.0	58 23.9	12.1	N20 08.2	2.7	54.1
01	192 07.1	40.4	72 55.0	12.2	20 10.9	2.6	54.1
02	207 06.9	39.9	87 26.2	12.1	20 13.5	2.6	54.1
03	222 06.8	.. 39.3	101 57.3	12.0	20 16.1	2.4	54.1
04	237 06.6	38.7	116 28.3	12.1	20 18.5	2.4	54.1
05	252 06.4	38.1	130 59.4	12.1	20 20.9	2.2	54.1
06	267 06.3	S19 37.6	145 30.5	12.0	N20 23.1	2.2	54.1
07	282 06.1	37.0	160 01.5	12.0	20 25.3	2.1	54.1
08	297 05.9	36.4	174 32.5	12.0	20 27.4	2.0	54.1
09	312 05.8	.. 35.8	189 03.5	12.0	20 29.4	1.8	54.1
10	327 05.6	35.3	203 34.5	12.0	20 31.2	1.8	54.1
11	342 05.5	34.7	218 05.5	11.9	20 33.0	1.7	54.1
12	357 05.3	S19 34.1	232 36.4	12.0	N20 34.7	1.6	54.1
13	12 05.1	33.5	247 07.4	11.9	20 36.3	1.5	54.1
14	27 05.0	33.0	261 38.3	11.9	20 37.8	1.5	54.1
15	42 04.8	.. 32.4	276 09.2	11.9	20 39.3	1.3	54.1
16	57 04.6	31.8	290 40.1	11.9	20 40.6	1.2	54.1
17	72 04.5	31.2	305 11.0	11.9	20 41.8	1.1	54.1
18	87 04.3	S19 30.6	319 41.9	11.9	N20 42.9	1.0	54.1
19	102 04.2	30.0	334 12.8	11.8	20 43.9	1.0	54.1
20	117 04.0	29.5	348 43.6	11.8	20 44.9	0.8	54.1
21	132 03.8	28.9	3 14.4	11.9	20 45.7	0.8	54.1
22	147 03.7	28.3	17 45.3	11.8	20 46.5	0.6	54.1
23	162 03.5	27.7	32 16.1	11.8	20 47.1	0.6	54.1
23 00	177 03.3	S19 27.1	46 46.9	11.8	N20 47.7	0.4	54.1
01	192 03.2	26.5	61 17.7	11.8	20 48.1	0.4	54.1
02	207 03.0	26.0	75 48.5	11.8	20 48.5	0.2	54.1
03	222 02.9	.. 25.4	90 19.3	11.7	20 48.7	0.2	54.1
04	237 02.7	24.8	104 50.0	11.8	20 48.9	0.1	54.1
05	252 02.6	24.2	119 20.8	11.7	20 49.0	0.1	54.1
06	267 02.4	S19 23.6	133 51.5	11.8	N20 48.9	0.1	54.1
07	282 02.2	23.0	148 22.3	11.7	20 48.8	0.2	54.1
08	297 02.1	22.4	162 53.0	11.7	20 48.6	0.3	54.2
09	312 01.9	.. 21.8	177 23.7	11.8	20 48.3	0.4	54.2
10	327 01.8	21.2	191 54.5	11.7	20 47.9	0.6	54.2
11	342 01.6	20.6	206 25.2	11.7	20 47.3	0.6	54.2
12	357 01.5	S19 20.0	220 55.9	11.7	N20 46.7	0.7	54.2
13	12 01.3	19.5	235 26.6	11.7	20 46.0	0.8	54.2
14	27 01.2	18.9	249 57.3	11.7	20 45.2	0.9	54.2
15	42 01.0	.. 18.3	264 28.0	11.7	20 44.3	1.0	54.2
16	57 00.8	17.7	278 58.7	11.7	20 43.3	1.1	54.2
17	72 00.7	17.1	293 29.4	11.7	20 42.2	1.2	54.2
18	87 00.5	S19 16.5	308 00.1	11.7	N20 41.0	1.3	54.2
19	102 00.4	15.9	322 30.8	11.7	20 39.7	1.3	54.2
20	117 00.2	15.3	337 01.5	11.6	20 38.4	1.5	54.2
21	132 00.1	.. 14.7	351 32.1	11.7	20 36.9	1.6	54.2
22	146 59.9	14.1	6 02.8	11.7	20 35.3	1.7	54.2
23	161 59.8	13.5	20 33.5	11.7	20 33.6	1.8	54.3
24 00	176 59.6	S19 12.9	35 04.2	11.7	N20 31.8	1.8	54.3
01	191 59.5	12.3	49 34.9	11.6	20 30.0	2.0	54.3
02	206 59.3	11.7	64 05.5	11.7	20 28.0	2.1	54.3
03	221 59.2	.. 11.1	78 36.2	11.7	20 25.9	2.1	54.3
04	236 59.0	10.5	93 06.9	11.7	20 23.8	2.3	54.3
05	251 58.9	09.9	107 37.6	11.7	20 21.5	2.4	54.3
06	266 58.7	S19 09.3	122 08.3	11.7	N20 19.1	2.4	54.3
07	281 58.6	08.7	136 39.0	11.7	20 16.7	2.6	54.3
08	296 58.4	08.0	151 09.7	11.7	20 14.1	2.6	54.3
09	311 58.3	.. 07.4	165 40.4	11.7	20 11.5	2.7	54.3
10	326 58.1	06.8	180 11.1	11.7	20 08.8	2.9	54.4
11	341 58.0	06.2	194 41.8	11.7	20 05.9	2.9	54.4
12	356 57.8	S19 05.6	209 12.5	11.7	N20 03.0	3.0	54.4
13	11 57.7	05.0	223 43.2	11.7	20 00.0	3.2	54.4
14	26 57.5	04.4	238 13.9	11.8	19 56.8	3.2	54.4
15	41 57.4	.. 03.8	252 44.7	11.7	19 53.6	3.3	54.4
16	56 57.3	03.2	267 15.4	11.7	19 50.3	3.4	54.4
17	71 57.1	02.6	281 46.1	11.8	19 46.9	3.5	54.4
18	86 57.0	S19 02.0	296 16.9	11.7	N19 43.4	3.6	54.4
19	101 56.8	01.3	310 47.6	11.8	19 39.8	3.7	54.4
20	116 56.7	00.7	325 18.4	11.8	19 36.1	3.8	54.5
21	131 56.5	19 00.1	339 49.2	11.8	19 32.3	3.8	54.5
22	146 56.4	18 59.5	354 20.0	11.8	19 28.5	4.0	54.5
23	161 56.2	S18 58.9	8 50.8	11.8	N19 24.5	4.1	54.5
	SD 16.3	d 0.6	SD 14.7		14.8		14.8

Table of days: TUESDAY (22), WEDNESDAY (23), THURSDAY (24)

Lat.	Twilight Naut.	Twilight Civil	Sunrise	Moonrise 22	23	24	25
°	h m	h m	h m	h m	h m	h m	h m
N 72	07 39	09 17	■■■	▢	▢	▢	12 31
N 70	07 27	08 52	10 39	▢	▢	▢	12 31
68	07 17	08 32	09 56	09 57	10 36	11 46	13 14
66	07 09	08 16	09 27	10 39	11 23	12 26	13 43
64	07 02	08 04	09 05	11 08	11 53	12 53	14 05
62	06 56	07 53	08 48	11 30	12 16	13 14	14 23
60	06 51	07 43	08 33	11 48	12 34	13 31	14 37
N 58	06 46	07 35	08 21	12 03	12 49	13 45	14 50
56	06 41	07 27	08 10	12 16	13 02	13 58	15 00
54	06 37	07 21	08 01	12 27	13 14	14 08	15 10
52	06 33	07 15	07 52	12 36	13 24	14 18	15 18
50	06 29	07 09	07 45	12 45	13 33	14 26	15 25
45	06 21	06 57	07 29	13 04	13 51	14 44	15 41
N 40	06 14	06 46	07 16	13 19	14 07	14 59	15 54
35	06 07	06 37	07 04	13 32	14 20	15 11	16 06
30	06 00	06 29	06 53	13 43	14 31	15 22	16 15
20	05 47	06 14	06 37	14 02	14 51	15 41	16 32
N 10	05 35	06 00	06 22	14 19	15 07	15 57	16 46
0	05 21	05 46	06 08	14 35	15 23	16 12	17 00
S 10	05 05	05 32	05 54	14 51	15 39	16 27	17 13
20	04 47	05 15	05 39	15 08	15 56	16 43	17 28
30	04 23	04 54	05 21	15 27	16 15	17 01	17 44
35	04 08	04 42	05 10	15 38	16 27	17 12	17 54
40	03 49	04 27	04 58	15 51	16 40	17 24	18 05
45	03 25	04 09	04 44	16 07	16 55	17 39	18 18
S 50	02 53	03 46	04 26	16 26	17 14	17 57	18 33
52	02 36	03 35	04 18	16 35	17 23	18 05	18 41
54	02 14	03 22	04 09	16 45	17 33	18 14	18 49
56	01 46	03 07	03 58	16 56	17 45	18 25	18 59
58	00 57	02 49	03 46	17 09	17 58	18 37	19 08
S 60	////	02 26	03 32	17 25	18 13	18 51	19 20

Lat.	Sunset	Twilight Civil	Twilight Naut.	Moonset 22	23	24	25
°	h m	h m	h m	h m	h m	h m	h m
N 72	■■	15 08	16 47	▢	▢	▢	▢
N 70	13 45	15 33	16 58	▢	▢	▢	09 13
68	14 29	15 53	17 07	06 45	07 46	08 16	08 29
66	14 58	16 08	17 15	06 03	06 59	07 37	07 59
64	15 20	16 21	17 22	05 36	06 29	07 09	07 37
62	15 37	16 32	17 28	05 12	06 06	06 48	07 19
60	15 51	16 41	17 34	04 55	05 48	06 31	07 04
N 58	16 04	16 50	17 40	04 40	05 33	06 16	06 51
56	16 14	16 57	17 43	04 27	05 20	06 04	06 40
54	16 24	17 04	17 47	04 16	05 08	05 53	06 31
52	16 32	17 10	17 51	04 07	04 58	05 43	06 22
50	16 39	17 15	17 55	03 58	04 49	05 35	06 14
45	16 55	17 27	18 03	03 40	04 30	05 17	05 58
N 40	17 08	17 38	18 11	03 25	04 15	05 02	05 44
35	17 20	17 47	18 17	03 12	04 02	04 49	05 32
30	17 30	17 55	18 24	03 01	03 51	04 38	05 22
20	17 46	18 10	18 37	02 42	03 31	04 19	05 05
N 10	18 01	18 24	18 49	02 26	03 14	04 02	04 49
0	18 15	18 37	19 03	02 10	02 58	03 47	04 35
S 10	18 30	18 52	19 18	01 55	02 42	03 31	04 21
20	18 45	19 09	19 37	01 38	02 25	03 14	04 05
30	19 03	19 29	20 00	01 19	02 06	02 55	03 47
35	19 13	19 41	20 14	01 08	01 54	02 44	03 37
40	19 25	19 56	20 34	00 56	01 41	02 31	03 25
45	19 39	20 14	20 57	00 41	01 26	02 16	03 11
S 50	19 56	20 36	21 29	00 23	01 07	01 57	02 54
52	20 05	20 47	21 46	00 15	00 58	01 48	02 46
54	20 14	21 00	22 07	00 05	00 48	01 38	02 37
56	20 24	21 15	22 35	24 36	00 36	01 27	02 26
58	20 36	21 32	23 19	24 23	00 15	01 14	02 15
S 60	20 50	21 55	////	24 08	00 08	00 59	02 01

Day	SUN Eqn. of Time 00h	SUN Eqn. of Time 12h	SUN Mer. Pass.	MOON Mer. Pass. Upper	MOON Mer. Pass. Lower	Age	Phase
d	m s	m s	h m	h m	h m	d	%
22	11 31	11 39	12 12	20 47	08 23	11	81
23	11 46	11 54	12 12	21 35	09 11	12	88
24	12 01	12 08	12 12	22 23	09 59	13	93

UT	ARIES GHA	VENUS −3.9 GHA	VENUS Dec	MARS +1.2 GHA	MARS Dec	JUPITER −2.6 GHA	JUPITER Dec	SATURN +0.6 GHA	SATURN Dec	STARS Name	SHA	Dec
25 00	124 28.0	192 57.5	S22 17.0	158 09.8	S14 39.5	59 50.4	N20 45.9	265 07.3	S12 49.2	Acamar	315 18.5	S40 15.4
01	139 30.5	207 56.6	16.7	173 10.4	38.9	74 52.9	45.9	280 09.6	49.2	Achernar	335 27.1	S57 10.5
02	154 32.9	222 55.7	16.3	188 10.9	38.2	89 55.4	45.9	295 12.0	49.2	Acrux	173 09.1	S63 10.2
03	169 35.4	237 54.8	.. 16.0	203 11.5	.. 37.5	104 57.9	.. 45.9	310 14.3	.. 49.2	Adhara	255 12.3	S28 59.7
04	184 37.8	252 53.9	15.6	218 12.0	36.9	120 00.4	45.9	325 16.7	49.3	Aldebaran	290 49.4	N16 32.0
05	199 40.3	267 53.0	15.2	233 12.5	36.2	135 02.9	45.9	340 19.1	49.3			
06	214 42.8	282 52.1	S22 14.9	248 13.1	S14 35.5	150 05.4	N20 45.9	355 21.4	S12 49.3	Alioth	166 20.7	N55 53.0
07	229 45.2	297 51.2	14.5	263 13.6	34.9	165 08.0	45.9	10 23.8	49.3	Alkaid	152 59.0	N49 14.5
08	244 47.7	312 50.3	14.1	278 14.2	34.2	180 10.5	45.9	25 26.1	49.3	Al Na'ir	27 44.5	S46 53.9
F 09	259 50.2	327 49.4	.. 13.8	293 14.7	.. 33.5	195 13.0	.. 45.9	40 28.5	.. 49.4	Alnilam	275 46.3	S 1 11.8
R 10	274 52.6	342 48.5	13.4	308 15.3	32.9	210 15.5	45.9	55 30.9	49.4	Alphard	217 56.0	S 8 43.2
I 11	289 55.1	357 47.6	13.0	323 15.8	32.2	225 18.0	45.9	70 33.2	49.4			
D 12	304 57.6	12 46.7	S22 12.7	338 16.3	S14 31.5	240 20.5	N20 45.9	85 35.6	S12 49.4	Alphecca	126 11.3	N26 40.1
A 13	320 00.0	27 45.8	12.3	353 16.9	30.9	255 23.0	45.9	100 37.9	49.5	Alpheratz	357 43.9	N29 09.9
Y 14	335 02.5	42 44.9	11.9	8 17.4	30.2	270 25.5	45.9	115 40.3	49.5	Altair	62 08.8	N 8 54.3
15	350 05.0	57 44.0	.. 11.6	23 18.0	.. 29.5	285 28.0	.. 45.9	130 42.7	.. 49.5	Ankaa	353 16.2	S42 14.3
16	5 07.4	72 43.1	11.2	38 18.5	28.9	300 30.5	45.9	145 45.0	49.5	Antares	112 26.7	S26 27.5
17	20 09.9	87 42.2	10.8	53 19.1	28.2	315 33.1	45.9	160 47.4	49.5			
18	35 12.3	102 41.3	S22 10.4	68 19.6	S14 27.5	330 35.6	N20 45.9	175 49.7	S12 49.6	Arcturus	145 55.9	N19 06.7
19	50 14.8	117 40.4	10.0	83 20.1	26.9	345 38.1	45.9	190 52.1	49.6	Atria	107 29.1	S69 02.7
20	65 17.3	132 39.5	09.7	98 20.7	26.2	0 40.6	45.9	205 54.5	49.6	Avior	234 17.4	S59 33.3
21	80 19.7	147 38.6	.. 09.3	113 21.2	.. 25.5	15 43.1	.. 45.9	220 56.8	.. 49.6	Bellatrix	278 32.0	N 6 21.5
22	95 22.2	162 37.7	08.9	128 21.8	24.8	30 45.6	45.9	235 59.2	49.7	Betelgeuse	271 01.3	N 7 24.4
23	110 24.7	177 36.8	08.5	143 22.3	24.2	45 48.1	45.9	251 01.5	49.7			
26 00	125 27.1	192 35.9	S22 08.1	158 22.9	S14 23.5	60 50.6	N20 45.9	266 03.9	S12 49.7	Canopus	263 55.8	S52 42.5
01	140 29.6	207 35.0	07.8	173 23.4	22.8	75 53.1	45.9	281 06.3	49.7	Capella	280 34.4	N46 00.6
02	155 32.1	222 34.1	07.4	188 24.0	22.2	90 55.6	45.9	296 08.6	49.7	Deneb	49 32.1	N45 19.8
03	170 34.5	237 33.2	.. 07.0	203 24.5	.. 21.5	105 58.1	.. 45.9	311 11.0	.. 49.8	Denebola	182 33.7	N14 29.7
04	185 37.0	252 32.4	06.6	218 25.1	20.8	121 00.6	45.9	326 13.4	49.8	Diphda	348 56.3	S17 55.0
05	200 39.5	267 31.5	06.2	233 25.6	20.1	136 03.1	46.0	341 15.7	49.8			
06	215 41.9	282 30.6	S22 05.8	248 26.1	S14 19.5	151 05.6	N20 46.0	356 18.1	S12 49.8	Dubhe	193 51.5	N61 40.5
07	230 44.4	297 29.7	05.4	263 26.7	18.8	166 08.1	46.0	11 20.4	49.9	Elnath	278 12.6	N28 37.0
S 08	245 46.8	312 28.8	05.0	278 27.2	18.1	181 10.6	46.0	26 22.8	49.9	Eltanin	90 46.7	N51 29.2
A 09	260 49.3	327 27.9	.. 04.6	293 27.8	.. 17.5	196 13.2	.. 46.0	41 25.2	.. 49.9	Enif	33 47.7	N 9 56.2
T 10	275 51.8	342 27.0	04.2	308 28.3	16.8	211 15.7	46.0	56 27.5	49.9	Fomalhaut	15 24.5	S29 33.2
U 11	290 54.2	357 26.1	03.8	323 28.9	16.1	226 18.2	46.0	71 29.9	49.9			
R 12	305 56.7	12 25.2	S22 03.4	338 29.4	S14 15.4	241 20.7	N20 46.0	86 32.3	S12 50.0	Gacrux	172 00.8	S57 11.1
D 13	320 59.2	27 24.3	03.0	353 30.0	14.8	256 23.2	46.0	101 34.6	50.0	Gienah	175 52.4	S17 36.9
A 14	336 01.6	42 23.4	02.6	8 30.5	14.1	271 25.7	46.0	116 37.0	50.0	Hadar	148 48.1	S60 25.9
Y 15	351 04.1	57 22.6	.. 02.2	23 31.1	.. 13.4	286 28.2	.. 46.0	131 39.4	.. 50.0	Hamal	328 01.0	N23 31.5
16	6 06.6	72 21.7	01.8	38 31.6	12.7	301 30.7	46.0	146 41.7	50.1	Kaus Aust.	83 44.5	S34 22.5
17	21 09.0	87 20.8	01.4	53 32.2	12.1	316 33.2	46.0	161 44.1	50.1			
18	36 11.5	102 19.9	S22 01.0	68 32.7	S14 11.4	331 35.7	N20 46.0	176 46.4	S12 50.1	Kochab	137 20.2	N74 05.8
19	51 14.0	117 19.0	00.6	83 33.3	10.7	346 38.2	46.0	191 48.8	50.1	Markab	13 38.8	N15 16.6
20	66 16.4	132 18.1	22 00.2	98 33.8	10.0	1 40.7	46.0	206 51.2	50.1	Menkar	314 15.2	N 4 08.4
21	81 18.9	147 17.2	21 59.8	113 34.4	.. 09.4	16 43.2	.. 46.0	221 53.5	.. 50.2	Menkent	148 07.8	S36 25.9
22	96 21.3	162 16.3	59.4	128 34.9	08.7	31 45.7	46.0	236 55.9	50.2	Miaplacidus	221 38.7	S69 46.4
23	111 23.8	177 15.5	59.0	143 35.5	08.0	46 48.2	46.0	251 58.3	50.2			
27 00	126 26.3	192 14.6	S21 58.6	158 36.0	S14 07.3	61 50.6	N20 46.0	267 00.6	S12 50.2	Mirfak	308 40.5	N49 54.6
01	141 28.7	207 13.7	58.2	173 36.6	06.7	76 53.1	46.0	282 03.0	50.2	Nunki	75 59.0	S26 16.7
02	156 31.2	222 12.8	57.7	188 37.1	06.0	91 55.6	46.0	297 05.4	50.3	Peacock	53 20.2	S56 41.4
03	171 33.7	237 11.9	.. 57.3	203 37.7	.. 05.3	106 58.1	.. 46.0	312 07.7	.. 50.3	Pollux	243 27.7	N27 59.4
04	186 36.1	252 11.0	56.9	218 38.2	04.6	122 00.6	46.0	327 10.1	50.3	Procyon	244 59.6	N 5 11.2
05	201 38.6	267 10.2	56.5	233 38.8	03.9	137 03.1	46.1	342 12.5	50.3			
06	216 41.1	282 09.3	S21 56.1	248 39.3	S14 03.3	152 05.6	N20 46.1	357 14.8	S12 50.3	Rasalhague	96 06.9	N12 33.0
07	231 43.5	297 08.4	55.7	263 39.9	02.6	167 08.1	46.1	12 17.2	50.4	Regulus	207 43.5	N11 53.9
08	246 46.0	312 07.5	55.2	278 40.4	01.9	182 10.6	46.1	27 19.6	50.4	Rigel	281 12.0	S 8 11.4
S 09	261 48.4	327 06.6	.. 54.8	293 41.0	.. 01.2	197 13.1	.. 46.1	42 21.9	.. 50.4	Rigil Kent.	139 52.0	S60 53.0
U 10	276 50.9	342 05.7	54.4	308 41.5	14 00.5	212 15.6	46.1	57 24.3	50.4	Sabik	102 13.0	S15 44.3
N 11	291 53.4	357 04.9	54.0	323 42.1	13 59.9	227 18.1	46.1	72 26.7	50.4			
D 12	306 55.8	12 04.0	S21 53.5	338 42.6	S13 59.2	242 20.6	N20 46.1	87 29.0	S12 50.5	Schedar	349 41.0	N56 36.8
A 13	321 58.3	27 03.1	53.1	353 43.2	58.5	257 23.1	46.1	102 31.4	50.5	Shaula	96 22.5	S37 06.6
Y 14	337 00.8	42 02.2	52.7	8 43.7	57.8	272 25.6	46.1	117 33.8	50.5	Sirius	258 33.6	S16 44.3
15	352 03.2	57 01.3	.. 52.3	23 44.3	.. 57.1	287 28.1	.. 46.1	132 36.1	.. 50.5	Spica	158 31.4	S11 13.8
16	7 05.7	72 00.4	51.8	38 44.8	56.5	302 30.6	46.1	147 38.5	50.5	Suhail	222 52.1	S43 29.3
17	22 08.2	86 59.6	51.4	53 45.4	55.8	317 33.0	46.1	162 40.9	50.6			
18	37 10.6	101 58.7	S21 51.0	68 45.9	S13 55.1	332 35.5	N20 46.1	177 43.3	S12 50.6	Vega	80 39.5	N38 47.7
19	52 13.1	116 57.8	50.5	83 46.5	54.4	347 38.0	46.1	192 45.6	50.6	Zuben'ubi	137 05.7	S16 05.7
20	67 15.6	131 56.9	50.1	98 47.0	53.7	2 40.5	46.1	207 48.0	50.6		SHA	Mer. Pass.
21	82 18.0	146 56.0	.. 49.7	113 47.6	.. 53.1	17 43.0	.. 46.1	222 50.4	.. 50.6	Venus	67 08.8	11 10
22	97 20.5	161 55.2	49.2	128 48.2	52.4	32 45.5	46.1	237 52.7	50.7	Mars	32 55.7	13 26
23	112 22.9	176 54.3	48.8	143 48.7	51.7	47 48.0	46.2	252 55.1	50.7	Jupiter	295 23.5	19 53
Mer. Pass. 15 35.6		v −0.9	d 0.4	v 0.5	d 0.7	v 2.5	d 0.0	v 2.4	d 0.0	Saturn	140 36.8	6 15

UT	SUN		MOON					Lat.	Twilight		Sunrise	Moonrise			
	GHA	Dec	GHA	v	Dec	d	HP		Naut.	Civil		25	26	27	28
d h	° ′	° ′	° ′	′	° ′	′	′	°	h m	h m	h m	h m	h m	h m	h m
25 00	176 56.1	S18 58.3	23 21.6 11.8		N19 20.4	4.1	54.5	N 72	07 29	09 04	11 34	⊏⊐	13 42	15 45	17 38
01	191 56.0	57.7	37 52.4 11.8		19 16.3	4.3	54.5	N 70	07 19	08 41	10 19	12 31	14 22	16 07	17 50
02	206 55.8	57.0	52 23.2 11.8		19 12.0	4.3	54.5	68	07 10	08 23	09 42	13 14	14 48	16 24	18 00
03	221 55.7 ..	56.4	66 54.0 11.9		19 07.7	4.5	54.5	66	07 03	08 09	09 17	13 43	15 09	16 38	18 08
04	236 55.5	55.8	81 24.9 11.8		19 03.2	4.5	54.6	64	06 57	07 57	08 57	14 05	15 25	16 49	18 14
05	251 55.4	55.2	95 55.7 11.9		18 58.7	4.6	54.6	62	06 51	07 47	08 40	14 23	15 39	16 58	18 20
06	266 55.2	S18 54.6	110 26.6 11.9		N18 54.1	4.7	54.6	60	06 46	07 38	08 27	14 37	15 50	17 06	18 25
07	281 55.1	54.0	124 57.5 11.9		18 49.4	4.8	54.6	N 58	06 42	07 30	08 15	14 50	16 00	17 14	18 29
08	296 55.0	53.3	139 28.4 11.9		18 44.6	4.9	54.6	56	06 37	07 23	08 05	15 00	16 08	17 20	18 33
F 09	311 54.8 ..	52.7	153 59.3 11.9		18 39.7	5.0	54.6	54	06 33	07 17	07 56	15 10	16 16	17 25	18 37
R 10	326 54.7	52.1	168 30.2 11.9		18 34.7	5.0	54.6	52	06 30	07 11	07 49	15 18	16 23	17 30	18 40
I 11	341 54.5	51.5	183 01.1 12.0		18 29.7	5.2	54.7	50	06 19	06 54	07 26	15 25	16 29	17 35	18 43
D 12	356 54.4	S18 50.8	197 32.1 11.9		N18 24.5	5.2	54.7	45	06 19	06 54	07 26	15 41	16 42	17 45	18 49
A 13	11 54.3	50.2	212 03.0 12.0		18 19.3	5.4	54.7	N 40	06 12	06 45	07 14	15 54	16 53	17 53	18 54
Y 14	26 54.1	49.6	226 34.0 12.0		18 13.9	5.4	54.7	35	06 05	06 36	07 03	16 06	17 02	18 00	18 59
15	41 54.0 ..	49.0	241 05.0 12.0		18 08.5	5.5	54.7	30	05 59	06 28	06 53	16 15	17 10	18 06	19 02
16	56 53.9	48.3	255 36.0 12.0		18 03.0	5.6	54.7	20	05 47	06 14	06 37	16 32	17 24	18 16	19 09
17	71 53.7	47.7	270 07.0 12.1		17 57.4	5.7	54.7	N 10	05 35	06 00	06 23	16 46	17 36	18 26	19 15
18	86 53.6	S18 47.1	284 38.1 12.0		N17 51.7	5.8	54.8	0	05 22	05 47	06 09	17 00	17 48	18 34	19 21
19	101 53.4	46.5	299 09.1 12.1		17 45.9	5.8	54.8	S 10	05 07	05 33	05 55	17 13	17 59	18 43	19 26
20	116 53.3	45.8	313 40.2 12.0		17 40.1	6.0	54.8	20	04 49	05 17	05 41	17 28	18 11	18 52	19 32
21	131 53.2 ..	45.2	328 11.2 12.1		17 34.1	6.0	54.8	30	04 26	04 57	05 23	17 44	18 25	19 03	19 39
22	146 53.0	44.6	342 42.3 12.2		17 28.1	6.1	54.8	35	04 11	04 45	05 13	17 54	18 33	19 09	19 42
23	161 52.9	44.0	357 13.5 12.1		17 22.0	6.2	54.8	40	03 53	04 31	05 02	18 05	18 42	19 15	19 47
26 00	176 52.8	S18 43.3	11 44.6 12.1		N17 15.8	6.3	54.8	45	03 31	04 14	04 48	18 18	18 52	19 23	19 52
01	191 52.6	42.7	26 15.7 12.2		17 09.5	6.4	54.9	S 50	03 00	03 52	04 31	18 33	19 05	19 33	19 58
02	206 52.5	42.1	40 46.9 12.2		17 03.1	6.4	54.9	52	02 44	03 42	04 24	18 41	19 11	19 37	20 01
03	221 52.4 ..	41.4	55 18.1 12.2		16 56.7	6.6	54.9	54	02 24	03 29	04 15	18 49	19 17	19 42	20 04
04	236 52.2	40.8	69 49.3 12.2		16 50.1	6.6	54.9	56	01 59	03 15	04 05	18 58	19 25	19 47	20 07
05	251 52.1	40.2	84 20.5 12.2		16 43.5	6.7	54.9	58	01 21	02 58	03 53	19 08	19 33	19 53	20 11
06	266 52.0	S18 39.5	98 51.7 12.2		N16 36.8	6.8	54.9	S 60	////	02 37	03 40	19 20	19 42	20 00	20 15

UT	SUN		MOON					Lat.	Sunset	Twilight		Moonset			
	GHA	Dec	GHA	v	Dec	d	HP			Civil	Naut.	25	26	27	28
d h	° ′	° ′	° ′	′	° ′	′	′	°	h m	h m	h m	h m	h m	h m	h m
07	281 51.8	38.9	113 22.9 12.3		16 30.0	6.8	55.0	N 72	12 52	15 22	16 57	⊏⊐	09 42	09 17	09 01
S 08	296 51.7	38.3	127 54.2 12.3		16 23.2	7.0	55.0	N 70	14 07	15 45	17 08	09 13	09 01	08 53	08 47
A 09	311 51.6 ..	37.6	142 25.5 12.3		16 16.2	7.0	55.0	68	14 44	16 03	17 16	08 29	08 34	08 35	08 36
T 10	326 51.4	37.0	156 56.8 12.3		16 09.2	7.1	55.0	66	15 10	16 17	17 23	07 59	08 12	08 21	08 26
U 11	341 51.3	36.4	171 28.1 12.3		16 02.1	7.2	55.0	64	15 29	16 29	17 29	07 37	07 55	08 09	08 18
R 12	356 51.2	S18 35.7	185 59.4 12.4		N15 54.9	7.2	55.0	62	15 46	16 39	17 35	07 19	07 41	07 58	08 11
D 13	11 51.1	35.1	200 30.8 12.4		15 47.7	7.4	55.0	60	15 59	16 48	17 40	07 04	07 29	07 49	08 06
A 14	26 50.9	34.5	215 02.2 12.3		15 40.3	7.4	55.1	N 58	16 10	16 56	17 44	06 51	07 19	07 41	08 00
Y 15	41 50.8 ..	33.8	229 33.5 12.5		15 32.9	7.5	55.1	56	16 20	17 03	17 49	06 40	07 10	07 35	07 56
16	56 50.7	33.2	244 05.0 12.4		15 25.4	7.5	55.1	54	16 29	17 09	17 52	06 31	07 02	07 28	07 51
17	71 50.5	32.5	258 36.4 12.4		15 17.9	7.7	55.1	52	16 37	17 15	17 56	06 22	06 55	07 23	07 48
18	86 50.4	S18 31.9	273 07.8 12.5		N15 10.2	7.7	55.1	50	16 44	17 20	17 59	06 14	06 48	07 18	07 44
19	101 50.3	31.3	287 39.3 12.5		15 02.5	7.8	55.1	45	16 59	17 31	18 07	05 58	06 34	07 07	07 36
20	116 50.2	30.6	302 10.8 12.4		14 54.7	7.8	55.2	N 40	17 12	17 41	18 14	05 44	06 23	06 58	07 30
21	131 50.0 ..	30.0	316 42.2 12.6		14 46.9	8.0	55.2	35	17 23	17 50	18 20	05 32	06 13	06 50	07 25
22	146 49.9	29.3	331 13.8 12.5		14 38.9	8.0	55.2	30	17 32	17 57	18 26	05 22	06 04	06 43	07 20
23	161 49.8	28.7	345 45.3 12.5		14 30.9	8.1	55.2	20	17 48	18 12	18 38	05 05	05 49	06 31	07 11
27 00	176 49.6	S18 28.0	0 16.8 12.6		N14 22.8	8.1	55.2	N 10	18 03	18 25	18 50	04 49	05 35	06 20	07 04
01	191 49.6	27.4	14 48.4 12.6		14 14.7	8.3	55.3	0	18 16	18 38	19 03	04 35	05 23	06 10	06 57
02	206 49.4	26.8	29 20.0 12.6		14 06.4	8.2	55.3	S 10	18 30	18 52	19 18	04 21	05 10	06 00	06 49
03	221 49.3 ..	26.1	43 51.6 12.6		13 58.2	8.4	55.3	20	18 44	19 08	19 36	04 05	04 57	05 49	06 42
04	236 49.1	25.5	58 23.2 12.6		13 49.8	8.4	55.3	30	19 01	19 27	19 59	03 47	04 42	05 37	06 33
05	251 49.0	24.8	72 54.8 12.7		13 41.4	8.6	55.3	35	19 11	19 39	20 13	03 37	04 32	05 30	06 28
06	266 48.9	S18 24.2	87 26.5 12.7		N13 32.8	8.5	55.3	40	19 23	19 53	20 31	03 25	04 22	05 21	06 22
07	281 48.8	23.5	101 58.2 12.6		13 24.3	8.7	55.4	45	19 36	20 10	20 53	03 11	04 10	05 12	06 15
08	296 48.7	22.9	116 29.8 12.7		13 15.6	8.7	55.4	S 50	19 53	20 32	21 23	02 54	03 55	05 00	06 07
S 09	311 48.5 ..	22.2	131 01.5 12.8		13 06.9	8.7	55.4	52	20 01	20 42	21 39	02 46	03 48	04 55	06 03
U 10	326 48.4	21.6	145 33.3 12.7		12 58.2	8.9	55.4	54	20 09	20 54	21 58	02 37	03 41	04 49	05 59
N 11	341 48.3	20.9	160 05.0 12.7		12 49.3	8.9	55.4	56	20 19	21 08	22 23	02 26	03 32	04 42	05 54
D 12	356 48.2	S18 20.3	174 36.7 12.8		N12 40.4	8.9	55.4	58	20 30	21 25	22 59	02 15	03 22	04 34	05 49
A 13	11 48.0	19.6	189 08.5 12.8		12 31.5	9.1	55.5	S 60	20 43	21 45	////	02 01	03 11	04 26	05 44
Y 14	26 47.9	19.0	203 40.3 12.8		12 22.4	9.1	55.5								
15	41 47.8 ..	18.3	218 12.1 12.8		12 13.3	9.1	55.5		SUN			MOON			
16	56 47.7	17.7	232 43.9 12.8		12 04.2	9.2	55.5	Day	Eqn. of Time		Mer.	Mer. Pass.		Age	Phase
17	71 47.6	17.0	247 15.7 12.9		11 55.0	9.3	55.5		00ʰ	12ʰ	Pass.	Upper	Lower		
18	86 47.4	S18 16.4	261 47.6 12.8		N11 45.7	9.4	55.6	d	m s	m s	h m	h m	h m	d	%
19	101 47.3	15.7	276 19.4 12.9		11 36.3	9.3	55.6	25	12 15	12 22	12 12	23 11	10 48	14	97
20	116 47.2	15.0	290 51.3 12.9		11 27.0	9.5	55.6	26	12 29	12 35	12 13	23 59	11 35	15	99
21	131 47.1 ..	14.4	305 23.2 12.9		11 17.5	9.5	55.6	27	12 41	12 47	12 13	24 45	12 22	16	100
22	146 47.0	13.7	319 55.1 12.9		11 08.0	9.6	55.6								
23	161 46.8	13.1	334 27.0 12.9		N10 58.4	9.6	55.7								
	SD 16.3	d 0.6	SD 14.9		15.0		15.1									

UT	ARIES GHA	VENUS −3.9 GHA	Dec	MARS +1.2 GHA	Dec	JUPITER −2.5 GHA	Dec	SATURN +0.6 GHA	Dec	STARS Name	SHA	Dec
28 00	127 25.4	191 53.4	S21 48.3	158 49.3	S13 51.0	62 50.5	N20 46.2	267 57.5	S12 50.7	Acamar	315 18.5	S40 15.4
01	142 27.9	206 52.5	47.9	173 49.8	50.3	77 53.0	46.2	282 59.8	50.7	Achernar	335 27.1	S57 10.5
02	157 30.3	221 51.7	47.5	188 50.4	49.6	92 55.4	46.2	298 02.2	50.7	Acrux	173 09.1	S63 10.2
03	172 32.8	236 50.8	.. 47.0	203 50.9	.. 49.0	107 57.9	.. 46.2	313 04.6	.. 50.8	Adhara	255 12.4	S28 59.7
04	187 35.3	251 49.9	46.6	218 51.5	48.3	123 00.4	46.2	328 07.0	50.8	Aldebaran	290 49.5	N16 32.0
05	202 37.7	266 49.0	46.1	233 52.0	47.6	138 02.9	46.2	343 09.3	50.8			
06	217 40.2	281 48.2	S21 45.7	248 52.6	S13 46.9	153 05.4	N20 46.2	358 11.7	S12 50.8	Alioth	166 20.7	N55 53.0
07	232 42.7	296 47.3	45.2	263 53.1	46.2	168 07.9	46.2	13 14.1	50.8	Alkaid	152 59.0	N49 14.5
08	247 45.1	311 46.4	44.8	278 53.7	45.5	183 10.4	46.2	28 16.4	50.9	Al Na'ir	27 44.5	S46 53.9
M 09	262 47.6	326 45.5	.. 44.3	293 54.3	.. 44.9	198 12.8	.. 46.2	43 18.8	.. 50.9	Alnilam	275 46.4	S 1 11.8
O 10	277 50.1	341 44.7	43.9	308 54.8	44.2	213 15.3	46.2	58 21.2	50.9	Alphard	217 56.0	S 8 43.2
N 11	292 52.5	356 43.8	43.4	323 55.4	43.5	228 17.8	46.2	73 23.6	50.9			
D 12	307 55.0	11 42.9	S21 43.0	338 55.9	S13 42.8	243 20.3	N20 46.2	88 25.9	S12 50.9	Alphecca	126 11.3	N26 40.1
A 13	322 57.4	26 42.0	42.5	353 56.5	42.1	258 22.8	46.2	103 28.3	50.9	Alpheratz	357 43.9	N29 09.9
Y 14	337 59.9	41 41.2	42.1	8 57.0	41.4	273 25.3	46.2	118 30.7	51.0	Altair	62 08.8	N 8 54.3
15	353 02.4	56 40.3	.. 41.6	23 57.6	.. 40.8	288 27.8	.. 46.3	133 33.0	.. 51.0	Ankaa	353 16.2	S42 14.3
16	8 04.8	71 39.4	41.1	38 58.2	40.1	303 30.2	46.3	148 35.4	51.0	Antares	112 26.7	S26 27.5
17	23 07.3	86 38.5	40.7	53 58.7	39.4	318 32.7	46.3	163 37.8	51.0			
18	38 09.8	101 37.7	S21 40.2	68 59.3	S13 38.7	333 35.2	N20 46.3	178 40.2	S12 51.0	Arcturus	145 55.9	N19 06.7
19	53 12.2	116 36.8	39.8	83 59.8	38.0	348 37.7	46.3	193 42.5	51.1	Atria	107 29.1	S69 02.7
20	68 14.7	131 35.9	39.3	99 00.4	37.3	3 40.2	46.3	208 44.9	51.1	Avior	234 17.4	S59 33.3
21	83 17.2	146 35.1	.. 38.8	114 00.9	.. 36.6	18 42.6	.. 46.3	223 47.3	.. 51.1	Bellatrix	278 32.0	N 6 21.5
22	98 19.6	161 34.2	38.4	129 01.5	35.9	33 45.1	46.3	238 49.7	51.1	Betelgeuse	271 01.3	N 7 24.4
23	113 22.1	176 33.3	37.9	144 02.1	35.3	48 47.6	46.3	253 52.0	51.1			
29 00	128 24.5	191 32.5	S21 37.4	159 02.6	S13 34.6	63 50.1	N20 46.3	268 54.4	S12 51.1	Canopus	263 55.8	S52 42.5
01	143 27.0	206 31.6	37.0	174 03.2	33.9	78 52.6	46.3	283 56.8	51.2	Capella	280 34.5	N46 00.6
02	158 29.5	221 30.7	36.5	189 03.7	33.2	93 55.0	46.3	298 59.1	51.2	Deneb	49 32.1	N45 19.7
03	173 31.9	236 29.9	.. 36.0	204 04.3	.. 32.5	108 57.5	.. 46.3	314 01.5	.. 51.2	Denebola	182 33.7	N14 29.7
04	188 34.4	251 29.0	35.6	219 04.9	31.8	124 00.0	46.3	329 03.9	51.2	Diphda	348 56.3	S17 55.0
05	203 36.9	266 28.1	35.1	234 05.4	31.1	139 02.5	46.3	344 06.3	51.2			
06	218 39.3	281 27.3	S21 34.6	249 06.0	S13 30.4	154 04.9	N20 46.4	359 08.6	S12 51.3	Dubhe	193 51.5	N61 40.5
07	233 41.8	296 26.4	34.1	264 06.5	29.7	169 07.4	46.4	14 11.0	51.3	Elnath	278 12.6	N28 37.0
08	248 44.3	311 25.5	33.7	279 07.1	29.1	184 09.9	46.4	29 13.4	51.3	Eltanin	90 46.7	N51 29.1
T 09	263 46.7	326 24.7	.. 33.2	294 07.7	.. 28.4	199 12.4	.. 46.4	44 15.8	.. 51.3	Enif	33 47.7	N 9 56.2
U 10	278 49.2	341 23.8	32.7	309 08.2	27.7	214 14.9	46.4	59 18.1	51.3	Fomalhaut	15 24.5	S29 33.2
E 11	293 51.7	356 22.9	32.2	324 08.8	27.0	229 17.3	46.4	74 20.5	51.3			
S 12	308 54.1	11 22.1	S21 31.8	339 09.3	S13 26.3	244 19.8	N20 46.4	89 22.9	S12 51.4	Gacrux	172 00.8	S57 11.1
D 13	323 56.6	26 21.2	31.3	354 09.9	25.6	259 22.3	46.4	104 25.3	51.4	Gienah	175 52.3	S17 37.0
A 14	338 59.0	41 20.3	30.8	9 10.5	24.9	274 24.8	46.4	119 27.7	51.4	Hadar	148 48.1	S60 25.9
Y 15	354 01.5	56 19.5	.. 30.3	24 11.0	.. 24.2	289 27.2	.. 46.4	134 30.0	.. 51.4	Hamal	328 01.0	N23 31.5
16	9 04.0	71 18.6	29.8	39 11.6	23.5	304 29.7	46.4	149 32.4	51.4	Kaus Aust.	83 44.5	S34 22.5
17	24 06.4	86 17.7	29.3	54 12.1	22.8	319 32.2	46.5	164 34.8	51.4			
18	39 08.9	101 16.9	S21 28.8	69 12.7	S13 22.1	334 34.6	N20 46.5	179 37.2	S12 51.5	Kochab	137 20.2	N74 05.8
19	54 11.4	116 16.0	28.4	84 13.3	21.4	349 37.1	46.5	194 39.5	51.5	Markab	13 38.8	N15 16.6
20	69 13.8	131 15.2	27.9	99 13.8	20.8	4 39.6	46.5	209 41.9	51.5	Menkar	314 15.2	N 4 08.4
21	84 16.3	146 14.3	.. 27.4	114 14.4	.. 20.1	19 42.1	.. 46.5	224 44.3	.. 51.5	Menkent	148 07.8	S36 25.9
22	99 18.8	161 13.4	26.9	129 15.0	19.4	34 44.5	46.5	239 46.7	51.5	Miaplacidus	221 38.7	S69 46.4
23	114 21.2	176 12.6	26.4	144 15.5	18.7	49 47.0	46.5	254 49.0	51.5			
30 00	129 23.7	191 11.7	S21 25.9	159 16.1	S13 18.0	64 49.5	N20 46.5	269 51.4	S12 51.6	Mirfak	308 40.5	N49 54.6
01	144 26.2	206 10.9	25.4	174 16.6	17.3	79 51.9	46.5	284 53.8	51.6	Nunki	75 58.9	S26 16.7
02	159 28.6	221 10.0	24.9	189 17.2	16.6	94 54.4	46.5	299 56.2	51.6	Peacock	53 20.2	S56 41.4
03	174 31.1	236 09.1	.. 24.4	204 17.8	.. 15.9	109 56.9	.. 46.5	314 58.6	.. 51.6	Pollux	243 27.7	N27 59.4
04	189 33.5	251 08.3	23.9	219 18.3	15.2	124 59.3	46.5	330 00.9	51.6	Procyon	244 59.6	N 5 11.2
05	204 36.0	266 07.4	23.4	234 18.9	14.5	140 01.8	46.6	345 03.3	51.6			
06	219 38.5	281 06.6	S21 22.9	249 19.5	S13 13.8	155 04.3	N20 46.6	0 05.7	S12 51.7	Rasalhague	96 06.9	N12 33.0
W 07	234 40.9	296 05.7	22.4	264 20.0	13.1	170 06.8	46.6	15 08.1	51.7	Regulus	207 43.5	N11 53.9
E 08	249 43.4	311 04.8	21.9	279 20.6	12.4	185 09.2	46.6	30 10.5	51.7	Rigel	281 12.1	S 8 11.4
D 09	264 45.9	326 04.0	.. 21.4	294 21.2	.. 11.7	200 11.7	.. 46.6	45 12.8	.. 51.7	Rigil Kent.	139 52.0	S60 53.0
N 10	279 48.3	341 03.1	20.9	309 21.7	11.0	215 14.2	46.6	60 15.2	51.7	Sabik	102 13.0	S15 44.3
E 11	294 50.8	356 02.3	20.4	324 22.3	10.3	230 16.6	46.6	75 17.6	51.7			
S 12	309 53.3	11 01.4	S21 19.9	339 22.8	S13 09.6	245 19.1	N20 46.6	90 20.0	S12 51.8	Schedar	349 41.0	N56 36.8
D 13	324 55.7	26 00.6	19.4	354 23.4	08.9	260 21.6	46.6	105 22.4	51.8	Shaula	96 22.5	S37 06.6
A 14	339 58.2	40 59.7	18.9	9 24.0	08.3	275 24.0	46.6	120 24.7	51.8	Sirius	258 33.6	S16 44.3
Y 15	355 00.6	55 58.9	.. 18.4	24 24.5	.. 07.6	290 26.5	.. 46.7	135 27.1	.. 51.8	Spica	158 31.4	S11 13.8
16	10 03.1	70 58.0	17.8	39 25.1	06.9	305 28.9	46.7	150 29.5	51.8	Suhail	222 52.1	S43 29.3
17	25 05.6	85 57.1	17.3	54 25.7	06.2	320 31.4	46.7	165 31.9	51.8			
18	40 08.0	100 56.3	S21 16.8	69 26.2	S13 05.5	335 33.9	N20 46.7	180 34.3	S12 51.9	Vega	80 39.5	N38 47.7
19	55 10.5	115 55.4	16.3	84 26.8	04.8	350 36.3	46.7	195 36.6	51.9	Zuben'ubi	137 05.7	S16 05.7
20	70 13.0	130 54.6	15.8	99 27.4	04.1	5 38.8	46.7	210 39.0	51.9		SHA	Mer. Pass.
21	85 15.4	145 53.7	.. 15.3	114 27.9	.. 03.4	20 41.3	.. 46.7	225 41.4	.. 51.9		° ′	h m
22	100 17.9	160 52.9	14.7	129 28.5	02.7	35 43.8	46.7	240 43.8	51.9	Venus	63 07.9	11 14
23	115 20.4	175 52.0	14.2	144 29.1	02.0	50 46.2	46.7	255 46.2	51.9	Mars	30 38.1	13 23
h m										Jupiter	295 25.5	19 41
Mer. Pass. 15 23.8		v −0.9	d 0.5	v 0.6	d 0.7	v 2.5	d 0.0	v 2.4	d 0.0	Saturn	140 29.8	6 03

INDEX TO SELECTED STARS, 2013

Name	No	Mag	SHA	Dec
Acamar	7	3·2	315	S 40
Achernar	5	0·5	335	S 57
Acrux	30	1·3	173	S 63
Adhara	19	1·5	255	S 29
Aldebaran	10	0·9	291	N 17
Alioth	32	1·8	166	N 56
Alkaid	34	1·9	153	N 49
Al Na'ir	55	1·7	28	S 47
Alnilam	15	1·7	276	S 1
Alphard	25	2·0	218	S 9
Alphecca	41	2·2	126	N 27
Alpheratz	1	2·1	358	N 29
Altair	51	0·8	62	N 9
Ankaa	2	2·4	353	S 42
Antares	42	1·0	112	S 26
Arcturus	37	0·0	146	N 19
Atria	43	1·9	107	S 69
Avior	22	1·9	234	S 60
Bellatrix	13	1·6	279	N 6
Betelgeuse	16	Var.*	271	N 7
Canopus	17	−0·7	264	S 53
Capella	12	0·1	281	N 46
Deneb	53	1·3	50	N 45
Denebola	28	2·1	183	N 14
Diphda	4	2·0	349	S 18
Dubhe	27	1·8	194	N 62
Elnath	14	1·7	278	N 29
Eltanin	47	2·2	91	N 51
Enif	54	2·4	34	N 10
Fomalhaut	56	1·2	15	S 30
Gacrux	31	1·6	172	S 57
Gienah	29	2·6	176	S 18
Hadar	35	0·6	149	S 60
Hamal	6	2·0	328	N 24
Kaus Australis	48	1·9	84	S 34
Kochab	40	2·1	137	N 74
Markab	57	2·5	14	N 15
Menkar	8	2·5	314	N 4
Menkent	36	2·1	148	S 36
Miaplacidus	24	1·7	222	S 70
Mirfak	9	1·8	309	N 50
Nunki	50	2·0	76	S 26
Peacock	52	1·9	53	S 57
Pollux	21	1·1	243	N 28
Procyon	20	0·4	245	N 5
Rasalhague	46	2·1	96	N 13
Regulus	26	1·4	208	N 12
Rigel	11	0·1	281	S 8
Rigil Kentaurus	38	−0·3	140	S 61
Sabik	44	2·4	102	S 16
Schedar	3	2·2	350	N 57
Shaula	45	1·6	96	S 37
Sirius	18	−1·5	259	S 17
Spica	33	1·0	159	S 11
Suhail	23	2·2	223	S 43
Vega	49	0·0	81	N 39
Zubenelgenubi	39	2·8	137	S 16

No	Name	Mag	SHA	Dec
1	Alpheratz	2·1	358	N 29
2	Ankaa	2·4	353	S 42
3	Schedar	2·2	350	N 57
4	Diphda	2·0	349	S 18
5	Achernar	0·5	335	S 57
6	Hamal	2·0	328	N 24
7	Acamar	3·2	315	S 40
8	Menkar	2·5	314	N 4
9	Mirfak	1·8	309	N 50
10	Aldebaran	0·9	291	N 17
11	Rigel	0·1	281	S 8
12	Capella	0·1	281	N 46
13	Bellatrix	1·6	279	N 6
14	Elnath	1·7	278	N 29
15	Alnilam	1·7	276	S 1
16	Betelgeuse	Var.*	271	N 7
17	Canopus	−0·7	264	S 53
18	Sirius	−1·5	259	S 17
19	Adhara	1·5	255	S 29
20	Procyon	0·4	245	N 5
21	Pollux	1·1	243	N 28
22	Avior	1·9	234	S 60
23	Suhail	2·2	223	S 43
24	Miaplacidus	1·7	222	S 70
25	Alphard	2·0	218	S 9
26	Regulus	1·4	208	N 12
27	Dubhe	1·8	194	N 62
28	Denebola	2·1	183	N 14
29	Gienah	2·6	176	S 18
30	Acrux	1·3	173	S 63
31	Gacrux	1·6	172	S 57
32	Alioth	1·8	166	N 56
33	Spica	1·0	159	S 11
34	Alkaid	1·9	153	N 49
35	Hadar	0·6	149	S 60
36	Menkent	2·1	148	S 36
37	Arcturus	0·0	146	N 19
38	Rigil Kentaurus	−0·3	140	S 61
39	Zubenelgenubi	2·8	137	S 16
40	Kochab	2·1	137	N 74
41	Alphecca	2·2	126	N 27
42	Antares	1·0	112	S 26
43	Atria	1·9	107	S 69
44	Sabik	2·4	102	S 16
45	Shaula	1·6	96	S 37
46	Rasalhague	2·1	96	N 13
47	Eltanin	2·2	91	N 51
48	Kaus Australis	1·9	84	S 34
49	Vega	0·0	81	N 39
50	Nunki	2·0	76	S 26
51	Altair	0·8	62	N 9
52	Peacock	1·9	53	S 57
53	Deneb	1·3	50	N 45
54	Enif	2·4	34	N 10
55	Al Na'ir	1·7	28	S 47
56	Fomalhaut	1·2	15	S 30
57	Markab	2·5	14	N 15

*0·1 — 1·2

ALTITUDE CORRECTION TABLES 10°-90°—SUN,STARS,PLANETS

OCT.—MAR. SUN APR.—SEPT.

App. Alt.	Lower Limb	Upper Limb	App. Alt.	Lower Limb	Upper Limb
° '	'	'	° '	'	'
9 33	+10·8	−21·5	9 39	+10·6	−21·2
9 45	+10·9	−21·4	9 50	+10·7	−21·1
9 56	+11·0	−21·3	10 02	+10·8	−21·0
10 08	+11·1	−21·2	10 14	+10·9	−20·9
10 20	+11·2	−21·1	10 27	+11·0	−20·8
10 33	+11·3	−21·0	10 40	+11·1	−20·7
10 46	+11·4	−20·9	10 53	+11·2	−20·6
11 00	+11·5	−20·8	11 07	+11·3	−20·5
11 15	+11·6	−20·7	11 22	+11·4	−20·4
11 30	+11·7	−20·6	11 37	+11·5	−20·3
11 45	+11·8	−20·5	11 53	+11·6	−20·2
12 01	+11·9	−20·4	12 10	+11·7	−20·1
12 18	+12·0	−20·3	12 27	+11·8	−20·0
12 36	+12·1	−20·2	12 45	+11·9	−19·9
12 54	+12·2	−20·1	13 04	+12·0	−19·8
13 14	+12·3	−20·0	13 24	+12·1	−19·7
13 34	+12·4	−19·9	13 44	+12·2	−19·6
13 55	+12·5	−19·8	14 06	+12·3	−19·5
14 17	+12·6	−19·7	14 29	+12·4	−19·4
14 41	+12·7	−19·6	14 53	+12·5	−19·3
15 05	+12·8	−19·5	15 18	+12·6	−19·2
15 31	+12·9	−19·4	15 45	+12·7	−19·1
15 59	+13·0	−19·3	16 13	+12·8	−19·0
16 27	+13·1	−19·2	16 43	+12·9	−18·9
16 58	+13·2	−19·1	17 14	+13·0	−18·8
17 30	+13·3	−19·0	17 47	+13·1	−18·7
18 05	+13·4	−18·9	18 23	+13·2	−18·6
18 41	+13·5	−18·8	19 00	+13·3	−18·5
19 20	+13·6	−18·7	19 41	+13·4	−18·4
20 02	+13·7	−18·6	20 24	+13·5	−18·3
20 46	+13·8	−18·5	21 10	+13·6	−18·2
21 34	+13·9	−18·4	21 59	+13·7	−18·1
22 25	+14·0	−18·3	22 52	+13·8	−18·0
23 20	+14·1	−18·2	23 49	+13·9	−17·9
24 20	+14·2	−18·1	24 51	+14·0	−17·8
25 24	+14·3	−18·0	25 58	+14·1	−17·7
26 34	+14·4	−17·9	27 11	+14·2	−17·6
27 50	+14·5	−17·8	28 31	+14·3	−17·5
29 13	+14·6	−17·7	29 58	+14·4	−17·4
30 44	+14·7	−17·6	31 33	+14·5	−17·3
32 24	+14·8	−17·5	33 18	+14·6	−17·2
34 15	+14·9	−17·4	35 15	+14·7	−17·1
36 17	+15·0	−17·3	37 24	+14·8	−17·0
38 34	+15·1	−17·2	39 48	+14·9	−16·9
41 06	+15·2	−17·1	42 28	+15·0	−16·8
43 56	+15·3	−17·0	45 29	+15·1	−16·7
47 07	+15·4	−16·9	48 52	+15·2	−16·6
50 43	+15·5	−16·8	52 41	+15·3	−16·5
54 46	+15·6	−16·7	56 59	+15·4	−16·4
59 21	+15·7	−16·6	61 50	+15·5	−16·3
64 28	+15·8	−16·5	67 15	+15·6	−16·2
70 10	+15·9	−16·4	73 14	+15·7	−16·1
76 24	+16·0	−16·3	79 42	+15·8	−16·0
83 05	+16·1	−16·2	86 31	+15·9	−15·9
90 00			90 00		

STARS AND PLANETS

App Alt.	Corrⁿ
° '	'
9 55	−5·3
10 07	−5·2
10 20	−5·1
10 32	−5·0
10 46	−4·9
10 59	−4·8
11 14	−4·7
11 29	−4·6
11 44	−4·5
12 00	−4·4
12 17	−4·3
12 35	−4·2
12 53	−4·1
13 12	−4·0
13 32	−3·9
13 53	−3·8
14 16	−3·7
14 39	−3·6
15 03	−3·5
15 29	−3·4
15 56	−3·3
16 25	−3·2
16 55	−3·1
17 27	−3·0
18 01	−2·9
18 37	−2·8
19 16	−2·7
19 56	−2·6
20 40	−2·5
21 27	−2·4
22 17	−2·3
23 11	−2·2
24 09	−2·1
25 12	−2·0
26 20	−1·9
27 34	−1·8
28 54	−1·7
30 22	−1·6
31 58	−1·5
33 43	−1·4
35 38	−1·3
37 45	−1·2
40 06	−1·1
42 42	−1·0
45 34	−0·9
48 45	−0·8
52 16	−0·7
56 09	−0·6
60 26	−0·5
65 06	−0·4
70 09	−0·3
75 32	−0·2
81 12	−0·1
87 03	0·0
90 00	

App. Alt. — Additional Corrⁿ

2013

VENUS

Jan. 1–Sept. 21

°	'
60	+0·1

Sept. 22–Nov. 11

°	'
41	+0·2
76	+0·1

Nov. 12–Dec. 5

°	'
34	+0·3
60	+0·2
80	+0·1

Dec. 6–Dec. 20

°	'
29	+0·4
51	+0·3
68	+0·2
83	+0·1

Dec. 21–Dec. 31

°	'
26	+0·5
46	+0·4
60	+0·3
73	+0·2
84	+0·1

MARS

Jan. 1–Dec. 31

°	'
60	+0·1

DIP

Ht. of Eye (m)	Corrⁿ	Ht. of Eye (ft.)
2·4	−2·8	8·0
2·6	−2·9	8·6
2·8	−3·0	9·2
3·0	−3·1	9·8
3·2	−3·2	10·5
3·4	−3·3	11·2
3·6	−3·4	11·9
3·8	−3·5	12·6
4·0	−3·6	13·3
4·3	−3·7	14·1
4·5	−3·8	14·9
4·7	−3·9	15·7
5·0	−4·0	16·5
5·2	−4·1	17·4
5·5	−4·2	18·3
5·8	−4·3	19·1
6·1	−4·4	20·1
6·3	−4·5	21·0
6·6	−4·6	22·0
6·9	−4·7	22·9
7·2	−4·8	23·9
7·5	−4·9	24·9
7·9	−5·0	26·0
8·2	−5·1	27·1
8·5	−5·2	28·1
8·8	−5·3	29·2
9·2	−5·4	30·4
9·5	−5·5	31·5
9·9	−5·6	32·7
10·3	−5·7	33·9
10·6	−5·8	35·1
11·0	−5·9	36·3
11·4	−6·0	37·6
11·8	−6·1	38·9
12·2	−6·2	40·1
12·6	−6·3	41·5
13·0	−6·4	42·8
13·4	−6·5	44·2
13·8	−6·6	45·5
14·2	−6·7	46·9
14·7	−6·8	48·4
15·1	−6·9	49·8
15·5	−7·0	51·3
16·0	−7·1	52·8
16·5	−7·2	54·3
16·9	−7·3	55·8
17·4	−7·4	57·4
17·9	−7·5	58·9
18·4	−7·6	60·5
18·8	−7·7	62·1
19·3	−7·8	63·8
19·8	−7·9	65·4
20·4	−8·0	67·1
20·9	−8·1	68·8
21·4		70·5

Ht. of Eye — Corrⁿ (See table ←)

Ht. of Eye (m)	Corrⁿ
20	− 7·9
22	− 8·3
24	− 8·6
26	− 9·0
28	− 9·3
30	− 9·6
32	−10·0
34	−10·3
36	−10·6
38	−10·8
40	−11·1
42	−11·4
44	−11·7
46	−11·9
48	−12·2

Ht. of Eye (ft.)	Corrⁿ
2	− 1·4
4	− 1·9
6	− 2·4
8	− 2·7
10	− 3·1

(See table ←)

Ht. of Eye (ft.)	Corrⁿ
70	− 8·1
75	− 8·4
80	− 8·7
85	− 8·9
90	− 9·2
95	− 9·5
100	− 9·7
105	− 9·9
110	−10·2
115	−10·4
120	−10·6
125	−10·8
130	−11·1
135	−11·3
140	−11·5
145	−11·7
150	−11·9
155	−12·1

App. Alt. = Apparent altitude = Sextant altitude corrected for index error and dip.

UT	SUN GHA	SUN Dec	MOON GHA	v	MOON Dec	d	HP
d h	° ′	° ′	° ′	′	° ′	′	′
28 00	176 46.7	S18 12.4	348 58.9	13.0	N10 48.8	9.7	55.7
01	191 46.6	11.8	3 30.9	12.9	10 39.1	9.7	55.7
02	206 46.5	11.1	18 02.8	13.0	10 29.4	9.8	55.7
03	221 46.4	.. 10.4	32 34.8	13.0	10 19.6	9.9	55.7
04	236 46.3	09.8	47 06.8	12.9	10 09.7	9.9	55.7
05	251 46.1	09.1	61 38.7	13.0	9 59.8	9.9	55.8
06	266 46.0	S18 08.5	76 10.7	13.0	N 9 49.9	10.0	55.8
07	281 45.9	07.8	90 42.7	13.1	9 39.9	10.1	55.8
08	296 45.8	07.1	105 14.8	13.0	9 29.8	10.1	55.8
M 09	311 45.7	.. 06.5	119 46.8	13.0	9 19.7	10.1	55.8
O 10	326 45.6	05.8	134 18.8	13.1	9 09.6	10.2	55.9
N 11	341 45.5	05.1	148 50.9	13.0	8 59.4	10.3	55.9
D 12	356 45.3	S18 04.5	163 22.9	13.1	N 8 49.1	10.3	55.9
A 13	11 45.2	03.8	177 55.0	13.1	8 38.8	10.3	55.9
Y 14	26 45.1	03.2	192 27.1	13.0	8 28.5	10.4	55.9
15	41 45.0	.. 02.5	206 59.1	13.1	8 18.1	10.4	56.0
16	56 44.9	01.8	221 31.2	13.1	8 07.7	10.5	56.0
17	71 44.8	01.2	236 03.3	13.1	7 57.2	10.5	56.0
18	86 44.7	S18 00.5	250 35.4	13.1	N 7 46.7	10.6	56.0
19	101 44.6	17 59.8	265 07.5	13.1	7 36.1	10.6	56.0
20	116 44.4	59.2	279 39.6	13.2	7 25.5	10.6	56.1
21	131 44.3	.. 58.5	294 11.8	13.1	7 14.9	10.7	56.1
22	146 44.2	57.8	308 43.9	13.1	7 04.2	10.7	56.1
23	161 44.1	57.1	323 16.0	13.1	6 53.5	10.8	56.1
29 00	176 44.0	S17 56.5	337 48.1	13.2	N 6 42.7	10.8	56.1
01	191 43.9	55.8	352 20.3	13.1	6 31.9	10.8	56.2
02	206 43.8	55.1	6 52.4	13.1	6 21.1	10.9	56.2
03	221 43.7	.. 54.5	21 24.5	13.1	6 10.2	10.9	56.2
04	236 43.6	53.8	35 56.6	13.2	5 59.3	10.9	56.2
05	251 43.5	53.1	50 28.8	13.1	5 48.4	11.0	56.2
06	266 43.4	S17 52.4	65 00.9	13.1	N 5 37.4	11.0	56.3
07	281 43.3	51.8	79 33.0	13.2	5 26.4	11.0	56.3
T 08	296 43.1	51.1	94 05.2	13.1	5 15.4	11.1	56.3
U 09	311 43.0	.. 50.4	108 37.3	13.1	5 04.3	11.1	56.3
E 10	326 42.9	49.7	123 09.4	13.2	4 53.2	11.1	56.3
S 11	341 42.8	49.1	137 41.6	13.1	4 42.1	11.2	56.3
D 12	356 42.7	S17 48.4	152 13.7	13.1	N 4 30.9	11.2	56.4
A 13	11 42.6	47.7	166 45.8	13.1	4 19.7	11.2	56.4
Y 14	26 42.5	47.0	181 17.9	13.1	4 08.5	11.3	56.4
15	41 42.4	.. 46.3	195 50.0	13.1	3 57.3	11.3	56.4
16	56 42.3	45.7	210 22.1	13.1	3 46.0	11.3	56.5
17	71 42.2	45.0	224 54.2	13.1	3 34.7	11.3	56.5
18	86 42.1	S17 44.3	239 26.3	13.1	N 3 23.4	11.3	56.5
19	101 42.0	43.6	253 58.4	13.1	3 12.1	11.4	56.5
20	116 41.9	42.9	268 30.5	13.0	3 00.7	11.4	56.5
21	131 41.8	.. 42.2	283 02.5	13.1	2 49.3	11.4	56.6
22	146 41.7	41.6	297 34.6	13.0	2 37.9	11.4	56.6
23	161 41.6	40.9	312 06.6	13.1	2 26.5	11.4	56.6
30 00	176 41.5	S17 40.2	326 38.7	13.0	N 2 15.1	11.5	56.6
01	191 41.4	39.5	341 10.7	13.0	2 03.6	11.4	56.6
02	206 41.3	38.8	355 42.7	13.0	1 52.2	11.6	56.7
03	221 41.2	.. 38.1	10 14.7	13.0	1 40.7	11.5	56.7
04	236 41.1	37.5	24 46.7	12.9	1 29.2	11.5	56.7
05	251 41.0	36.8	39 18.6	13.0	1 17.7	11.6	56.7
06	266 40.9	S17 36.1	53 50.6	12.9	N 1 06.1	11.5	56.8
W 07	281 40.8	35.4	68 22.5	12.9	0 54.6	11.6	56.8
E 08	296 40.7	34.7	82 54.4	12.9	0 43.0	11.5	56.8
D 09	311 40.6	.. 34.0	97 26.3	12.9	0 31.5	11.6	56.8
N 10	326 40.5	33.3	111 58.2	12.9	0 19.9	11.6	56.8
E 11	341 40.4	32.6	126 30.1	12.9	N 0 08.3	11.6	56.8
S 12	356 40.3	S17 31.9	141 02.0	12.8	S 0 03.3	11.5	56.9
D 13	11 40.2	31.3	155 33.8	12.8	0 14.8	11.6	56.9
A 14	26 40.1	30.6	170 05.6	12.8	0 26.4	11.7	56.9
Y 15	41 40.0	.. 29.9	184 37.4	12.7	0 38.1	11.6	56.9
16	56 39.9	29.2	199 09.1	12.8	0 49.7	11.6	56.9
17	71 39.8	28.5	213 40.9	12.7	1 01.3	11.6	57.0
18	86 39.7	S17 27.8	228 12.6	12.7	S 1 12.9	11.6	57.0
19	101 39.6	27.1	242 44.3	12.7	1 24.5	11.6	57.0
20	116 39.5	26.4	257 16.0	12.6	1 36.1	11.6	57.0
21	131 39.5	.. 25.7	271 47.6	12.6	1 47.7	11.6	57.0
22	146 39.4	25.0	286 19.2	12.6	1 59.3	11.7	57.1
23	161 39.3	24.3	300 50.8	12.6	S 2 11.0	11.6	57.1
SD	16.3	d 0.7	SD 15.2		15.4		15.5

Twilight / Sunrise / Moonrise

Lat.	Naut.	Civil	Sunrise	28	29	30	31
°	h m	h m	h m	h m	h m	h m	h m
N 72	07 19	08 51	10 53	17 38	19 28	21 18	23 11
N 70	07 10	08 30	10 01	17 50	19 32	21 15	23 01
68	07 03	08 14	09 29	18 00	19 36	21 13	22 52
66	06 56	08 01	09 06	18 08	19 39	21 11	22 45
64	06 51	07 50	08 48	18 14	19 41	21 09	22 39
62	06 46	07 40	08 33	18 20	19 43	21 08	22 34
60	06 41	07 32	08 20	18 25	19 45	21 07	22 30
N 58	06 37	07 25	08 10	18 29	19 47	21 06	22 26
56	06 33	07 18	08 00	18 33	19 48	21 05	22 22
54	06 30	07 13	07 52	18 37	19 50	21 04	22 19
52	06 26	07 07	07 44	18 40	19 51	21 03	22 16
50	06 23	07 02	07 38	18 43	19 52	21 02	22 14
45	06 16	06 52	07 23	18 49	19 54	21 01	22 08
N 40	06 10	06 42	07 11	18 54	19 56	20 59	22 04
35	06 04	06 34	07 01	18 59	19 58	20 58	22 00
30	05 58	06 27	06 52	19 02	20 00	20 57	21 57
20	05 47	06 13	06 36	19 09	20 02	20 56	21 51
N 10	05 35	06 01	06 23	19 15	20 04	20 54	21 45
0	05 23	05 48	06 10	19 21	20 07	20 53	21 41
S 10	05 08	05 34	05 57	19 26	20 09	20 52	21 36
20	04 51	05 19	05 42	19 32	20 11	20 50	21 31
30	04 29	05 00	05 26	19 39	20 14	20 49	21 25
35	04 15	04 49	05 16	19 42	20 15	20 48	21 22
40	03 58	04 35	05 05	19 47	20 17	20 47	21 18
45	03 36	04 19	04 53	19 52	20 19	20 46	21 14
S 50	03 07	03 58	04 37	19 58	20 21	20 45	21 09
52	02 52	03 48	04 29	20 01	20 23	20 44	21 07
54	02 34	03 36	04 21	20 04	20 24	20 44	21 04
56	02 11	03 23	04 11	20 07	20 25	20 43	21 02
58	01 39	03 07	04 01	20 11	20 26	20 42	20 59
S 60	00 29	02 48	03 48	20 15	20 28	20 41	20 55

Sunset / Twilight / Moonset

Lat.	Sunset	Civil	Naut.	28	29	30	31
°	h m	h m	h m	h m	h m	h m	h m
N 72	13 34	15 37	17 08	09 01	08 47	08 35	08 23
N 70	14 26	15 57	17 17	08 47	08 41	08 35	08 29
68	14 58	16 13	17 25	08 36	08 35	08 34	08 33
66	15 21	16 26	17 31	08 26	08 30	08 34	08 37
64	15 39	16 37	17 37	08 18	08 26	08 33	08 40
62	15 54	16 47	17 42	08 11	08 23	08 33	08 43
60	16 07	16 55	17 46	08 06	08 20	08 33	08 46
N 58	16 17	17 02	17 50	08 00	08 17	08 32	08 48
56	16 27	17 09	17 54	07 56	08 14	08 32	08 50
54	16 35	17 14	17 57	07 51	08 12	08 32	08 52
52	16 43	17 20	18 01	07 48	08 10	08 32	08 54
50	16 49	17 25	18 04	07 44	08 08	08 32	08 55
45	17 04	17 35	18 11	07 36	08 04	08 31	08 58
N 40	17 16	17 44	18 17	07 30	08 01	08 31	09 01
35	17 26	17 53	18 23	07 25	07 58	08 30	09 04
30	17 35	18 00	18 29	07 20	07 55	08 30	09 06
20	17 50	18 13	18 40	07 11	07 51	08 30	09 10
N 10	18 04	18 26	18 51	07 04	07 47	08 29	09 13
0	18 17	18 38	19 04	06 57	07 43	08 29	09 16
S 10	18 30	18 52	19 18	06 49	07 39	08 28	09 19
20	18 44	19 07	19 35	06 42	07 35	08 28	09 22
30	19 00	19 26	19 57	06 33	07 30	08 27	09 26
35	19 09	19 37	20 11	06 28	07 27	08 27	09 28
40	19 20	19 50	20 27	06 22	07 24	08 26	09 30
45	19 33	20 07	20 49	06 15	07 20	08 26	09 33
S 50	19 49	20 28	21 17	06 07	07 16	08 25	09 36
52	19 56	20 37	21 32	06 03	07 14	08 25	09 38
54	20 04	20 48	21 50	05 59	07 11	08 25	09 39
56	20 13	21 01	22 12	05 54	07 09	08 25	09 41
58	20 24	21 17	22 42	05 49	07 06	08 24	09 43
S 60	20 36	21 35	23 38	05 44	07 03	08 24	09 46

SUN / MOON

Day	Eqn. of Time 00h	Eqn. of Time 12h	Mer. Pass.	Mer. Pass. Upper	Mer. Pass. Lower	Age	Phase
d	m s	m s	h m	h m	h m	d	%
28	12 53	12 58	12 13	00 45	13 09	17	98	◯
29	13 04	13 09	12 13	01 32	13 55	18	94	
30	13 14	13 19	12 13	02 18	14 41	19	89	

UT	ARIES	VENUS −3.9		MARS +1.2		JUPITER −2.5		SATURN +0.5		STARS		
d h	GHA	GHA	Dec	GHA	Dec	GHA	Dec	GHA	Dec	Name	SHA	Dec
31 00	130 22.8	190 51.2	S21 13.7	159 29.6	S13 01.3	65 48.6	N20 46.7	270 48.5	S12 51.9	Acamar	315 18.5	S40 15.4
01	145 25.3	205 50.3	13.2	174 30.2	13 00.6	80 51.1	46.8	285 50.9	52.0	Achernar	335 27.1	S57 10.5
02	160 27.8	220 49.5	12.7	189 30.8	12 59.9	95 53.6	46.8	300 53.3	52.0	Acrux	173 09.1	S63 10.2
03	175 30.2	235 48.6	.. 12.1	204 31.3	.. 59.2	110 56.0	.. 46.8	315 55.7	.. 52.0	Adhara	255 12.4	S28 59.7
04	190 32.7	250 47.8	11.6	219 31.9	58.5	125 58.5	46.8	330 58.1	52.0	Aldebaran	290 49.5	N16 32.0
05	205 35.1	265 46.9	11.1	234 32.5	57.8	141 00.9	46.8	346 00.5	52.0			
06	220 37.6	280 46.1	S21 10.6	249 33.1	S12 57.1	156 03.4	N20 46.8	1 02.8	S12 52.0	Alioth	166 20.7	N55 53.0
T 07	235 40.1	295 45.2	10.0	264 33.6	56.4	171 05.9	46.8	16 05.2	52.1	Alkaid	152 59.0	N49 14.5
H 08	250 42.5	310 44.4	09.5	279 34.2	55.7	186 08.3	46.8	31 07.6	52.1	Al Na'ir	27 44.5	S46 53.9
U 09	265 45.0	325 43.5	.. 09.0	294 34.8	.. 55.0	201 10.8	.. 46.8	46 10.0	.. 52.1	Alnilam	275 46.4	S 1 11.9
R 10	280 47.5	340 42.7	08.4	309 35.5	54.3	216 13.2	46.8	61 12.4	52.1	Alphard	217 56.0	S 8 43.2
11	295 49.9	355 41.9	07.9	324 35.9	53.6	231 15.7	46.9	76 14.8	52.1			
S 12	310 52.4	10 41.0	S21 07.4	339 36.5	S12 52.9	246 18.2	N20 46.9	91 17.1	S12 52.1	Alphecca	126 11.3	N26 40.1
D 13	325 54.9	25 40.2	06.8	354 37.0	52.2	261 20.6	46.9	106 19.5	52.1	Alpheratz	357 43.9	N29 09.9
A 14	340 57.3	40 39.3	06.3	9 37.6	51.5	276 23.1	46.9	121 21.9	52.2	Altair	62 08.8	N 8 54.2
Y 15	355 59.8	55 38.5	.. 05.8	24 38.2	.. 50.8	291 25.5	.. 46.9	136 24.3	.. 52.2	Ankaa	353 16.2	S42 14.3
16	11 02.2	70 37.6	05.2	39 38.7	50.1	306 28.0	46.9	151 26.7	52.2	Antares	112 26.7	S26 27.5
17	26 04.7	85 36.8	04.7	54 39.3	49.4	321 30.4	46.9	166 29.1	52.2			
18	41 07.2	100 35.9	S21 04.1	69 39.9	S12 48.7	336 32.9	N20 46.9	181 31.4	S12 52.2	Arcturus	145 55.9	N19 06.7
19	56 09.6	115 35.1	03.6	84 40.5	48.0	351 35.3	47.0	196 33.8	52.2	Atria	107 29.0	S69 02.7
20	71 12.1	130 34.3	03.1	99 41.0	47.2	6 37.8	47.0	211 36.2	52.2	Avior	234 17.4	S59 33.3
21	86 14.6	145 33.4	.. 02.5	114 41.6	.. 46.5	21 40.3	.. 47.0	226 38.6	.. 52.3	Bellatrix	278 32.0	N 6 21.5
22	101 17.0	160 32.6	02.0	129 42.2	45.8	36 42.7	47.0	241 41.0	52.3	Betelgeuse	271 01.3	N 7 24.4
23	116 19.5	175 31.7	01.4	144 42.7	45.1	51 45.2	47.0	256 43.4	52.3			
1 00	131 22.0	190 30.9	S21 00.9	159 43.3	S12 44.4	66 47.6	N20 47.0	271 45.8	S12 52.3	Canopus	263 55.8	S52 42.5
01	146 24.4	205 30.1	21 00.3	174 43.9	43.7	81 50.1	47.0	286 48.1	52.3	Capella	280 34.5	N46 00.6
02	161 26.9	220 29.2	20 59.8	189 44.5	43.0	96 52.5	47.0	301 50.5	52.3	Deneb	49 32.1	N45 19.7
03	176 29.4	235 28.4	.. 59.2	204 45.0	.. 42.3	111 55.0	.. 47.0	316 52.9	.. 52.3	Denebola	182 33.7	N14 29.7
04	191 31.8	250 27.5	58.7	219 45.6	41.6	126 57.4	47.1	331 55.3	52.4	Diphda	348 56.3	S17 55.0
05	206 34.3	265 26.7	58.1	234 46.2	40.9	141 59.9	47.1	346 57.7	52.4			
06	221 36.7	280 25.9	S20 57.6	249 46.7	S12 40.2	157 02.3	N20 47.1	2 00.1	S12 52.4	Dubhe	193 51.5	N61 40.5
07	236 39.2	295 25.0	57.0	264 47.3	39.5	172 04.8	47.1	17 02.5	52.4	Elnath	278 12.7	N28 37.0
08	251 41.7	310 24.2	56.5	279 47.9	38.8	187 07.2	47.1	32 04.9	52.4	Eltanin	90 46.6	N51 29.1
F 09	266 44.1	325 23.3	.. 55.9	294 48.5	.. 38.1	202 09.7	.. 47.1	47 07.2	.. 52.4	Enif	33 47.7	N 9 56.2
R 10	281 46.6	340 22.5	55.4	309 49.0	37.4	217 12.1	47.1	62 09.6	52.4	Fomalhaut	15 24.6	S29 33.2
I 11	296 49.1	355 21.7	54.8	324 49.6	36.7	232 14.6	47.1	77 12.0	52.5			
D 12	311 51.5	10 20.8	S20 54.2	339 50.2	S12 36.0	247 17.0	N20 47.2	92 14.4	S12 52.5	Gacrux	172 00.8	S57 11.1
A 13	326 54.0	25 20.0	53.7	354 50.8	35.3	262 19.5	47.2	107 16.8	52.5	Gienah	175 52.3	S17 37.0
Y 14	341 56.5	40 19.2	53.1	9 51.3	34.6	277 21.9	47.2	122 19.2	52.5	Hadar	148 48.1	S60 25.9
15	356 58.9	55 18.3	.. 52.5	24 51.9	.. 33.8	292 24.4	.. 47.2	137 21.6	.. 52.5	Hamal	328 01.1	N23 31.5
16	12 01.4	70 17.5	52.0	39 52.5	33.1	307 26.8	47.2	152 24.0	52.5	Kaus Aust.	83 44.4	S34 22.5
17	27 03.9	85 16.7	51.4	54 53.1	32.4	322 29.2	47.2	167 26.3	52.5			
18	42 06.3	100 15.8	S20 50.8	69 53.6	S12 31.7	337 31.7	N20 47.2	182 28.7	S12 52.5	Kochab	137 20.1	N74 05.8
19	57 08.8	115 15.0	50.3	84 54.2	31.0	352 34.1	47.2	197 31.1	52.6	Markab	13 38.8	N15 16.6
20	72 11.2	130 14.2	49.7	99 54.8	30.3	7 36.6	47.3	212 33.5	52.6	Menkar	314 15.3	N 4 08.4
21	87 13.7	145 13.3	.. 49.1	114 55.4	.. 29.6	22 39.0	.. 47.3	227 35.9	.. 52.6	Menkent	148 07.8	S36 25.9
22	102 16.2	160 12.5	48.6	129 55.9	28.9	37 41.5	47.3	242 38.3	52.6	Miaplacidus	221 38.7	S69 46.4
23	117 18.6	175 11.7	48.0	144 56.5	28.2	52 43.9	47.3	257 40.7	52.6			
2 00	132 21.1	190 10.8	S20 47.4	159 57.1	S12 27.5	67 46.4	N20 47.3	272 43.1	S12 52.6	Mirfak	308 40.6	N49 54.6
01	147 23.6	205 10.0	46.9	174 57.7	26.8	82 48.8	47.3	287 45.5	52.6	Nunki	75 58.9	S26 16.7
02	162 26.0	220 09.2	46.3	189 58.2	26.1	97 51.2	47.3	302 47.9	52.6	Peacock	53 20.2	S56 41.4
03	177 28.5	235 08.3	.. 45.7	204 58.8	.. 25.3	112 53.7	.. 47.3	317 50.2	.. 52.7	Pollux	243 27.7	N27 59.4
04	192 31.0	250 07.5	45.1	219 59.4	24.6	127 56.1	47.4	332 52.6	52.7	Procyon	244 59.6	N 5 11.2
05	207 33.4	265 06.7	44.5	235 00.0	23.9	142 58.6	47.4	347 55.0	52.7			
06	222 35.9	280 05.9	S20 43.9	250 00.5	S12 23.2	158 01.0	N20 47.4	2 57.4	S12 52.7	Rasalhague	96 06.9	N12 33.0
07	237 38.3	295 05.0	43.4	265 01.1	22.5	173 03.4	47.4	17 59.8	52.7	Regulus	207 43.4	N11 53.9
S 08	252 40.8	310 04.2	42.8	280 01.7	21.8	188 05.9	47.4	33 02.2	52.7	Rigel	281 12.1	S 8 11.4
A 09	267 43.3	325 03.4	.. 42.2	295 02.3	.. 21.1	203 08.3	.. 47.4	48 04.6	.. 52.7	Rigil Kent.	139 52.0	S60 53.1
T 10	282 45.7	340 02.6	41.6	310 02.9	20.4	218 10.8	47.4	63 07.0	52.7	Sabik	102 13.0	S15 44.4
U 11	297 48.2	355 01.7	41.1	325 03.4	19.7	233 13.2	47.5	78 09.4	52.8			
R 12	312 50.7	10 00.9	S20 40.5	340 04.0	S12 18.9	248 15.6	N20 47.5	93 11.8	S12 52.8	Schedar	349 41.0	N56 36.8
D 13	327 53.1	25 00.1	39.9	355 04.6	18.2	263 18.1	47.5	108 14.2	52.8	Shaula	96 22.5	S37 06.6
A 14	342 55.6	39 59.3	39.3	10 05.2	17.5	278 20.5	47.5	123 16.6	52.8	Sirius	258 33.6	S16 44.3
Y 15	357 58.1	54 58.4	.. 38.7	25 05.7	.. 16.8	293 23.0	.. 47.5	138 18.9	.. 52.8	Spica	158 31.4	S11 13.8
16	13 00.5	69 57.6	38.1	40 06.3	16.1	308 25.4	47.5	153 21.3	52.8	Suhail	222 52.1	S43 29.3
17	28 03.0	84 56.8	37.5	55 06.9	15.4	323 27.8	47.5	168 23.7	52.8			
18	43 05.5	99 56.0	S20 36.9	70 07.5	S12 14.7	338 30.3	N20 47.6	183 26.1	S12 52.8	Vega	80 39.5	N38 47.7
19	58 07.9	114 55.1	36.3	85 08.1	14.0	353 32.7	47.6	198 28.5	52.9	Zuben'ubi	137 05.7	S16 05.7
20	73 10.4	129 54.3	35.7	100 08.6	13.2	8 35.1	47.6	213 30.9	52.9		SHA	Mer.Pass.
21	88 12.8	144 53.5	.. 35.1	115 09.2	.. 12.5	23 37.6	.. 47.6	228 33.3	.. 52.9		° ′	h m
22	103 15.3	159 52.7	34.5	130 09.8	11.8	38 40.0	47.6	243 35.7	52.9	Venus	59 08.9	11 19
23	118 17.8	174 51.8	33.9	145 10.4	11.1	53 42.5	47.6	258 38.1	52.9	Mars	28 21.4	13 21
	h m									Jupiter	295 25.6	19 30
Mer.Pass. 15 12.0		v −0.8	d 0.6	v 0.6	d 0.7	v 2.4	d 0.0	v 2.4	d 0.0	Saturn	140 23.8	5 52

UT	SUN		MOON					Lat.	Twilight		Sunrise	Moonrise			
									Naut.	Civil		31	1	2	3
	GHA	Dec	GHA	v	Dec	d	HP		h m	h m	h m	h m	h m	h m	h m
d h	° ′	° ′	° ′	′	° ′	′	′	°							
31 00	176 39.2	S17 23.6	315 22.4	12.5	S 2 22.6	11.6	57.1	N 72	07 09	08 38	10 26	23 11	25 12	01 12	03 30
01	191 39.1	22.9	329 53.9	12.5	2 34.2	11.6	57.1	N 70	07 01	08 19	09 44	23 01	24 51	00 51	02 49
02	206 39.0	22.2	344 25.4	12.5	2 45.8	11.6	57.1	68	06 54	08 05	09 17	22 52	24 35	00 35	02 22
03	221 38.9	.. 21.5	358 56.9	12.4	2 57.4	11.5	57.2	66	06 49	07 53	08 56	22 45	24 22	00 22	02 01
04	236 38.8	20.8	13 28.3	12.4	3 08.9	11.6	57.2	64	06 44	07 42	08 39	22 39	24 11	00 11	01 45
05	251 38.7	20.1	27 59.7	12.4	3 20.5	11.5	57.2	62	06 40	07 34	08 25	22 34	24 02	00 02	01 31
06	266 38.6	S17 19.4	42 31.1	12.4	S 3 32.1	11.5	57.2	60	06 36	07 26	08 13	22 30	23 54	25 20	01 20
07	281 38.5	18.7	57 02.5	12.3	3 43.6	11.6	57.3	N 58	06 32	07 20	08 03	22 26	23 47	25 10	01 10
T 08	296 38.4	18.0	71 33.8	12.3	3 55.2	11.5	57.3	56	06 29	07 13	07 55	22 22	23 41	25 01	01 01
H 09	311 38.4	.. 17.3	86 05.1	12.2	4 06.7	11.5	57.3	54	06 25	07 08	07 47	22 19	23 36	24 54	00 54
U 10	326 38.3	16.6	100 36.3	12.2	4 18.2	11.5	57.3	52	06 23	07 03	07 40	22 16	23 31	24 47	00 47
R 11	341 38.2	15.9	115 07.5	12.2	4 29.7	11.5	57.3	50	06 20	06 59	07 33	22 14	23 27	24 41	00 41
S 12	356 38.1	S17 15.2	129 38.7	12.1	S 4 41.2	11.5	57.4	45	06 13	06 48	07 20	22 08	23 17	24 27	00 27
D 13	11 38.0	14.5	144 09.8	12.1	4 52.7	11.5	57.4	N 40	06 07	06 40	07 08	22 04	23 10	24 17	00 17
A 14	26 37.9	13.8	158 40.9	12.1	5 04.2	11.4	57.4	35	06 02	06 32	06 59	22 00	23 03	24 07	00 07
Y 15	41 37.8	.. 13.1	173 12.0	12.0	5 15.6	11.4	57.4	30	05 57	06 25	06 50	21 57	22 57	23 59	25 03
16	56 37.7	12.4	187 43.0	12.0	5 27.0	11.4	57.4	20	05 46	06 12	06 35	21 51	22 47	23 45	24 46
17	71 37.7	11.7	202 14.0	11.9	5 38.4	11.4	57.5	N 10	05 35	06 00	06 22	21 45	22 38	23 33	24 31
18	86 37.6	S17 11.0	216 44.9	11.9	S 5 49.8	11.4	57.5	0	05 23	05 48	06 10	21 41	22 30	23 22	24 17
19	101 37.5	10.3	231 15.8	11.8	6 01.2	11.3	57.5	S 10	05 10	05 36	05 58	21 36	22 22	23 11	24 03
20	116 37.4	09.6	245 46.6	11.9	6 12.5	11.3	57.5	20	04 53	05 21	05 44	21 31	22 13	22 59	23 49
21	131 37.3	.. 08.8	260 17.5	11.7	6 23.8	11.3	57.6	30	04 32	05 03	05 29	21 25	22 04	22 46	23 32
22	146 37.2	08.1	274 48.2	11.7	6 35.1	11.2	57.6	35	04 19	04 52	05 20	21 22	21 58	22 38	23 23
23	161 37.1	07.4	289 18.9	11.7	6 46.3	11.3	57.6	40	04 02	04 39	05 09	21 18	21 52	22 29	23 12
1 00	176 37.1	S17 06.7	303 49.6	11.6	S 6 57.6	11.2	57.6	45	03 42	04 24	04 57	21 14	21 45	22 19	22 59
01	191 37.0	06.0	318 20.2	11.6	7 08.8	11.2	57.6	S 50	03 14	04 04	04 42	21 09	21 36	22 07	22 43
02	206 36.9	05.3	332 50.8	11.6	7 20.0	11.1	57.6	52	03 00	03 54	04 35	21 07	21 32	22 01	22 36
03	221 36.8	.. 04.6	347 21.4	11.4	7 31.1	11.1	57.7	54	02 44	03 44	04 27	21 04	21 27	21 55	22 28
04	236 36.7	03.9	1 51.8	11.5	7 42.2	11.1	57.7	56	02 23	03 31	04 18	21 02	21 23	21 48	22 19
05	251 36.6	03.2	16 22.3	11.4	7 53.3	11.0	57.7	58	01 56	03 17	04 08	20 59	21 17	21 40	22 09
06	266 36.6	S17 02.4	30 52.7	11.3	S 8 04.3	11.0	57.7	S 60	01 12	02 59	03 57	20 55	21 11	21 31	21 57
07	281 36.5	01.7	45 23.0	11.3	8 15.3	11.0	57.8								
08	296 36.4	01.0	59 53.3	11.2	8 26.3	11.0	57.8	Lat.	Sunset	Twilight		Moonset			
F 09	311 36.3	17 00.3	74 23.5	11.2	8 37.3	10.9	57.8			Civil	Naut.	31	1	2	3
R 10	326 36.2	16 59.6	88 53.7	11.1	8 48.2	10.8	57.8	°	h m	h m	h m	h m	h m	h m	h m
I 11	341 36.2	58.9	103 23.8	11.1	8 59.0	10.8	57.8	N 72	14 03	15 51	17 20	08 23	08 10	07 53	07 25
D 12	356 36.1	S16 58.2	117 53.9	11.0	S 9 09.8	10.8	57.9	N 70	14 44	16 08	17 28	08 29	08 22	08 15	08 06
A 13	11 36.0	57.4	132 23.9	11.0	9 20.6	10.7	57.9	68	15 12	16 24	17 34	08 33	08 33	08 33	08 35
Y 14	26 35.9	56.7	146 53.9	10.9	9 31.3	10.7	57.9	66	15 33	16 36	17 40	08 37	08 41	08 47	08 56
15	41 35.8	.. 56.0	161 23.8	10.8	9 42.0	10.7	57.9	64	15 49	16 46	17 44	08 40	08 49	08 59	09 14
16	56 35.8	55.3	175 53.6	10.8	9 52.7	10.6	57.9	62	16 03	16 54	17 49	08 43	08 55	09 09	09 28
17	71 35.7	54.6	190 23.4	10.8	10 03.3	10.6	58.0	60	16 15	17 02	17 53	08 46	09 00	09 18	09 40
18	86 35.6	S16 53.8	204 53.2	10.7	S10 13.9	10.5	58.0	N 58	16 25	17 09	17 56	08 48	09 05	09 25	09 51
19	101 35.5	53.1	219 22.9	10.6	10 24.4	10.4	58.0	56	16 33	17 14	17 59	08 50	09 10	09 32	10 00
20	116 35.4	52.4	233 52.5	10.5	10 34.8	10.4	58.0	54	16 41	17 20	18 03	08 52	09 14	09 38	10 08
21	131 35.4	.. 51.7	248 22.0	10.5	10 45.2	10.4	58.0	52	16 48	17 25	18 06	08 54	09 17	09 44	10 15
22	146 35.3	51.0	262 51.5	10.5	10 55.6	10.3	58.1	50	16 54	17 29	18 08	08 55	09 20	09 49	10 22
23	161 35.2	50.2	277 21.0	10.4	11 05.9	10.3	58.1	45	17 08	17 39	18 14	08 58	09 27	09 59	10 36
2 00	176 35.1	S16 49.5	291 50.4	10.3	S11 16.2	10.2	58.1	N 40	17 19	17 48	18 20	09 01	09 33	10 08	10 48
01	191 35.1	48.8	306 19.7	10.2	11 26.4	10.1	58.1	35	17 29	17 55	18 26	09 04	09 38	10 16	10 58
02	206 35.0	48.1	320 48.9	10.2	11 36.5	10.1	58.2	30	17 37	18 02	18 31	09 06	09 43	10 23	11 07
03	221 34.9	.. 47.3	335 18.1	10.2	11 46.6	10.0	58.2	20	17 52	18 15	18 42	09 09	09 51	10 35	11 22
04	236 34.8	46.6	349 47.3	10.0	11 56.6	10.0	58.2	N 10	18 05	18 27	18 52	09 13	09 58	10 45	11 35
05	251 34.8	45.9	4 16.3	10.0	12 06.6	9.9	58.2	0	18 17	18 39	19 04	09 16	10 04	10 55	11 48
06	266 34.7	S16 45.2	18 45.3	10.0	S12 16.5	9.8	58.2	S 10	18 29	18 51	19 17	09 19	10 10	11 04	12 01
S 07	281 34.6	44.4	33 14.3	9.9	12 26.3	9.8	58.3	20	18 43	19 06	19 34	09 22	10 17	11 15	12 14
A 08	296 34.5	43.7	47 43.2	9.8	12 36.1	9.8	58.3	30	18 58	19 24	19 54	09 26	10 25	11 27	12 29
T 09	311 34.5	.. 43.0	62 12.0	9.7	12 45.9	9.6	58.3	35	19 07	19 35	20 08	09 28	10 30	11 34	12 38
U 10	326 34.4	42.3	76 40.7	9.7	12 55.5	9.6	58.3	40	19 17	19 47	20 24	09 30	10 35	11 41	12 49
R 11	341 34.3	41.5	91 09.4	9.6	13 05.1	9.5	58.3	45	19 29	20 03	20 44	09 33	10 41	11 51	13 01
D 12	356 34.3	S16 40.8	105 38.0	9.6	S13 14.6	9.5	58.4	S 50	19 44	20 22	21 11	09 36	10 48	12 02	13 15
A 13	11 34.2	40.0	120 06.6	9.4	13 24.1	9.4	58.4	52	19 51	20 31	21 25	09 38	10 52	12 07	13 22
Y 14	26 34.1	39.3	134 35.0	9.4	13 33.5	9.3	58.4	54	19 59	20 42	21 41	09 39	10 56	12 13	13 30
15	41 34.0	.. 38.6	149 03.4	9.4	13 42.8	9.2	58.4	56	20 08	20 54	22 01	09 41	11 00	12 19	13 38
16	56 34.0	37.9	163 31.8	9.3	13 52.0	9.2	58.4	58	20 17	21 09	22 27	09 43	11 04	12 26	13 48
17	71 33.9	37.2	178 00.1	9.2	14 01.2	9.1	58.5	S 60	20 29	21 26	23 07	09 46	11 09	12 34	13 59
18	86 33.8	S16 36.4	192 28.3	9.1	S14 10.3	9.0	58.5								
19	101 33.8	35.7	206 56.4	9.1	14 19.3	9.0	58.5			SUN			MOON		
20	116 33.7	35.0	221 24.5	9.0	14 28.3	8.9	58.5	Day	Eqn. of Time		Mer.	Mer. Pass.		Age	Phase
21	131 33.6	.. 34.2	235 52.5	8.9	14 37.2	8.7	58.5		00ʰ	12ʰ	Pass.	Upper	Lower		
22	146 33.6	33.5	250 20.4	8.9	14 45.9	8.8	58.6	d	m s	m s	h m	h m	h m	d	%
23	161 33.5	32.8	264 48.3	8.3	S14 54.7	8.6	58.6	31	13 23	13 27	12 13	03 04	15 28	20	81
								1	13 32	13 36	12 14	03 52	16 17	21	72
	SD 16.3	d 0.7	SD 15.6		15.8		15.9	2	13 39	13 43	12 14	04 42	17 08	22	62

UT	ARIES GHA	VENUS −3.9 GHA	Dec	MARS +1.2 GHA	Dec	JUPITER −2.5 GHA	Dec	SATURN +0.5 GHA	Dec	STARS Name	SHA	Dec
3 00	133 20.2	189 51.0	S20 33.4	160 11.0	S12 10.4	68 44.9	N20 47.6	273 40.5	S12 52.9	Acamar	315 18.5	S40 15.4
01	148 22.7	204 50.2	32.8	175 11.5	09.7	83 47.3	47.7	288 42.9	52.9	Achernar	335 27.2	S57 10.5
02	163 25.2	219 49.4	32.1	190 12.1	09.0	98 49.8	47.7	303 45.3	52.9	Acrux	173 09.0	S63 10.2
03	178 27.6	234 48.6	.. 31.5	205 12.7	.. 08.2	113 52.2	.. 47.7	318 47.7	.. 52.9	Adhara	255 12.4	S28 59.7
04	193 30.1	249 47.8	30.9	220 13.3	07.5	128 54.6	47.7	333 50.1	53.0	Aldebaran	290 49.5	N16 32.0
05	208 32.6	264 46.9	30.3	235 13.9	06.8	143 57.1	47.7	348 52.5	53.0			
06	223 35.0	279 46.1	S20 29.7	250 14.4	S12 06.1	158 59.5	N20 47.7	3 54.9	S12 53.0	Alioth	166 20.6	N55 53.0
07	238 37.5	294 45.3	29.1	265 15.0	05.4	174 01.9	47.7	18 57.3	53.0	Alkaid	152 59.0	N49 14.5
08	253 40.0	309 44.5	28.5	280 15.6	04.7	189 04.4	47.8	33 59.7	53.0	Al Na'ir	27 44.5	S46 53.8
S 09	268 42.4	324 43.7	.. 27.9	295 16.2	.. 04.0	204 06.8	.. 47.8	49 02.0	.. 53.0	Alnilam	275 46.4	S 1 11.9
U 10	283 44.9	339 42.8	27.3	310 16.8	03.2	219 09.2	47.8	64 04.4	53.0	Alphard	217 56.0	S 8 43.2
N 11	298 47.3	354 42.0	26.7	325 17.3	02.5	234 11.6	47.8	79 06.8	53.0			
D 12	313 49.8	9 41.2	S20 26.1	340 17.9	S12 01.8	249 14.1	N20 47.8	94 09.2	S12 53.0	Alphecca	126 11.3	N26 40.1
A 13	328 52.3	24 40.4	25.5	355 18.5	01.1	264 16.5	47.8	109 11.6	53.1	Alpheratz	357 44.0	N29 09.9
Y 14	343 54.7	39 39.6	24.9	10 19.1	12 00.4	279 18.9	47.8	124 14.0	53.1	Altair	62 08.8	N 8 54.2
15	358 57.2	54 38.8	.. 24.2	25 19.7	11 59.7	294 21.4	.. 47.9	139 16.4	.. 53.1	Ankaa	353 16.2	S42 14.3
16	13 59.7	69 38.0	23.6	40 20.3	58.9	309 23.8	47.9	154 18.8	53.1	Antares	112 26.7	S26 27.5
17	29 02.1	84 37.1	23.0	55 20.8	58.2	324 26.2	47.9	169 21.2	53.1			
18	44 04.6	99 36.3	S20 22.4	70 21.4	S11 57.5	339 28.6	N20 47.9	184 23.6	S12 53.1	Arcturus	145 55.9	N19 06.7
19	59 07.1	114 35.5	21.8	85 22.0	56.8	354 31.1	47.9	199 26.0	53.1	Atria	107 29.0	S69 02.7
20	74 09.5	129 34.7	21.2	100 22.6	56.1	9 33.5	47.9	214 28.4	53.1	Avior	234 17.4	S59 33.3
21	89 12.0	144 33.9	.. 20.5	115 23.2	.. 55.3	24 35.9	.. 48.0	229 30.8	.. 53.1	Bellatrix	278 32.0	N 6 21.5
22	104 14.4	159 33.1	19.9	130 23.8	54.6	39 38.4	48.0	244 33.2	53.1	Betelgeuse	271 01.3	N 7 24.4
23	119 16.9	174 32.3	19.3	145 24.3	53.9	54 40.8	48.0	259 35.6	53.2			
4 00	134 19.4	189 31.5	S20 18.7	160 24.9	S11 53.2	69 43.2	N20 48.0	274 38.0	S12 53.2	Canopus	263 55.8	S52 42.5
01	149 21.8	204 30.7	18.0	175 25.5	52.5	84 45.6	48.0	289 40.4	53.2	Capella	280 34.5	N46 00.6
02	164 24.3	219 29.9	17.4	190 26.1	51.8	99 48.1	48.0	304 42.8	53.2	Deneb	49 32.1	N45 19.7
03	179 26.8	234 29.0	.. 16.8	205 26.7	.. 51.0	114 50.5	.. 48.1	319 45.2	.. 53.2	Denebola	182 33.6	N14 29.7
04	194 29.2	249 28.2	16.2	220 27.3	50.3	129 52.9	48.1	334 47.6	53.2	Diphda	348 56.3	S17 55.0
05	209 31.7	264 27.4	15.5	235 27.8	49.6	144 55.3	48.1	349 50.0	53.2			
06	224 34.2	279 26.6	S20 14.9	250 28.4	S11 48.9	159 57.8	N20 48.1	4 52.4	S12 53.2	Dubhe	193 51.4	N61 40.5
07	239 36.6	294 25.8	14.3	265 29.0	48.2	175 00.2	48.1	19 54.8	53.2	Elnath	278 12.7	N28 37.0
08	254 39.1	309 25.0	13.6	280 29.6	47.4	190 02.6	48.1	34 57.2	53.2	Eltanin	90 46.6	N51 29.1
M 09	269 41.6	324 24.2	.. 13.0	295 30.2	.. 46.7	205 05.0	.. 48.2	49 59.6	.. 53.3	Enif	33 47.7	N 9 56.2
O 10	284 44.0	339 23.4	12.4	310 30.8	46.0	220 07.4	48.2	65 02.0	53.3	Fomalhaut	15 24.6	S29 33.2
N 11	299 46.5	354 22.6	11.7	325 31.4	45.3	235 09.9	48.2	80 04.4	53.3			
D 12	314 48.9	9 21.8	S20 11.1	340 31.9	S11 44.5	250 12.3	N20 48.2	95 06.8	S12 53.3	Gacrux	172 00.8	S57 11.1
A 13	329 51.4	24 21.0	10.5	355 32.5	43.8	265 14.7	48.2	110 09.2	53.3	Gienah	175 52.3	S17 37.0
Y 14	344 53.9	39 20.2	09.8	10 33.1	43.1	280 17.1	48.2	125 11.6	53.3	Hadar	148 48.0	S60 25.9
15	359 56.3	54 19.4	.. 09.2	25 33.7	.. 42.4	295 19.5	.. 48.3	140 14.0	.. 53.3	Hamal	328 01.1	N23 31.5
16	14 58.8	69 18.6	08.5	40 34.3	41.7	310 22.0	48.3	155 16.4	53.3	Kaus Aust.	83 44.4	S34 22.5
17	30 01.3	84 17.8	07.9	55 34.9	40.9	325 24.4	48.3	170 18.8	53.3			
18	45 03.7	99 17.0	S20 07.3	70 35.5	S11 40.2	340 26.8	N20 48.3	185 21.2	S12 53.3	Kochab	137 20.1	N74 05.8
19	60 06.2	114 16.2	06.6	85 36.1	39.5	355 29.2	48.3	200 23.6	53.3	Markab	13 38.8	N15 16.6
20	75 08.7	129 15.4	06.0	100 36.6	38.8	10 31.6	48.3	215 26.0	53.4	Menkar	314 15.3	N 4 08.4
21	90 11.1	144 14.6	.. 05.3	115 37.2	.. 38.0	25 34.1	.. 48.4	230 28.4	.. 53.4	Menkent	148 07.7	S36 25.9
22	105 13.6	159 13.8	04.7	130 37.8	37.3	40 36.5	48.4	245 30.8	53.4	Miaplacidus	221 38.7	S69 46.4
23	120 16.1	174 13.0	04.0	145 38.4	36.6	55 38.9	48.4	260 33.2	53.4			
5 00	135 18.5	189 12.2	S20 03.4	160 39.0	S11 35.9	70 41.3	N20 48.4	275 35.6	S12 53.4	Mirfak	308 40.6	N49 54.6
01	150 21.0	204 11.4	02.7	175 39.6	35.2	85 43.7	48.4	290 38.0	53.4	Nunki	75 58.9	S26 16.7
02	165 23.4	219 10.6	02.1	190 40.2	34.4	100 46.1	48.4	305 40.4	53.4	Peacock	53 20.2	S56 41.4
03	180 25.9	234 09.8	.. 01.4	205 40.8	.. 33.7	115 48.6	.. 48.5	320 42.8	.. 53.4	Pollux	243 27.7	N27 59.4
04	195 28.4	249 09.0	00.8	220 41.3	33.0	130 51.0	48.5	335 45.2	53.4	Procyon	244 59.7	N 5 11.2
05	210 30.8	264 08.2	20 00.1	235 41.9	32.3	145 53.4	48.5	350 47.6	53.4			
06	225 33.3	279 07.4	S19 59.5	250 42.5	S11 31.5	160 55.8	N20 48.5	5 50.0	S12 53.5	Rasalhague	96 06.9	N12 33.0
07	240 35.8	294 06.6	58.8	265 43.1	30.8	175 58.2	48.5	20 52.4	53.5	Regulus	207 43.4	N11 53.9
08	255 38.2	309 05.8	58.2	280 43.7	30.1	191 00.6	48.5	35 54.8	53.5	Rigel	281 12.1	S 8 11.5
T 09	270 40.7	324 05.0	.. 57.5	295 44.3	.. 29.4	206 03.0	.. 48.5	50 57.3	.. 53.5	Rigil Kent.	139 51.9	S60 53.1
U 10	285 43.2	339 04.2	56.8	310 44.9	28.6	221 05.5	48.6	65 59.7	53.5	Sabik	102 13.0	S15 44.4
E 11	300 45.6	354 03.4	56.2	325 45.5	27.9	236 07.9	48.6	81 02.1	53.5			
S 12	315 48.1	9 02.6	S19 55.5	340 46.1	S11 27.2	251 10.3	N20 48.6	96 04.5	S12 53.5	Schedar	349 41.1	N56 36.8
D 13	330 50.6	24 01.8	54.9	355 46.7	26.5	266 12.7	48.6	111 06.9	53.5	Shaula	96 22.5	S37 06.6
A 14	345 53.0	39 01.0	54.2	10 47.2	25.7	281 15.1	48.7	126 09.3	53.5	Sirius	258 33.6	S16 44.4
Y 15	0 55.5	54 00.3	.. 53.5	25 47.8	.. 25.0	296 17.5	.. 48.7	141 11.7	.. 53.5	Spica	158 31.4	S11 13.9
16	15 57.9	68 59.5	52.9	40 48.4	24.3	311 19.9	48.7	156 14.1	53.5	Suhail	222 52.1	S43 29.3
17	31 00.4	83 58.7	52.2	55 49.0	23.6	326 22.3	48.7	171 16.5	53.5			
18	46 02.9	98 57.9	S19 51.5	70 49.6	S11 22.8	341 24.7	N20 48.7	186 18.9	S12 53.5	Vega	80 39.5	N38 47.7
19	61 05.3	113 57.1	50.9	85 50.2	22.1	356 27.2	48.7	201 21.3	53.5	Zuben'ubi	137 05.7	S16 05.7
20	76 07.8	128 56.3	50.2	100 50.8	21.4	11 29.6	48.8	216 23.7	53.6		SHA	Mer.Pass.
21	91 10.3	143 55.5	.. 49.5	115 51.4	.. 20.6	26 32.0	.. 48.8	231 26.1	.. 53.6	Venus	55 12.1	11 23
22	106 12.7	158 54.7	48.8	130 52.0	19.9	41 34.4	48.8	246 28.5	53.6	Mars	26 05.5	13 18
23	121 15.2	173 53.9	48.2	145 52.6	19.2	56 36.8	48.8	261 30.9	53.6	Jupiter	295 23.8	19 18
Mer.Pass. 15 00.2	v −0.8 d 0.6	v 0.6	d 0.7	v 2.4	d 0.0	v 2.4	d 0.0			Saturn	140 18.6	5 41

UT	SUN GHA	SUN Dec	MOON GHA	v	MOON Dec	d	HP
d h	° '	° '	° '	'	° '	'	'
3 00	176 33.4	S16 32.0	279 16.1	8.7	S15 03.3	8.5	58.6
01	191 33.4	31.3	293 43.8	8.6	15 11.8	8.5	58.6
02	206 33.3	30.5	308 11.4	8.6	15 20.3	8.4	58.6
03	221 33.2 ..	29.8	322 39.0	8.5	15 28.7	8.3	58.7
04	236 33.2	29.1	337 06.5	8.5	15 37.0	8.2	58.7
05	251 33.1	28.3	351 34.0	8.3	15 45.2	8.1	58.7
06	266 33.0	S16 27.6	6 01.3	8.3	S15 53.3	8.0	58.7
07	281 33.0	26.9	20 28.6	8.2	16 01.3	8.0	58.7
08	296 32.9	26.1	34 55.8	8.2	16 09.3	7.8	58.8
S 09	311 32.8 ..	25.4	49 23.0	8.1	16 17.1	7.8	58.8
U 10	326 32.8	24.6	63 50.1	8.0	16 24.9	7.6	58.8
N 11	341 32.7	23.9	78 17.1	7.9	16 32.5	7.6	58.8
D 12	356 32.6	S16 23.2	92 44.0	7.9	S16 40.1	7.5	58.8
A 13	11 32.6	22.4	107 10.9	7.8	16 47.6	7.4	58.9
Y 14	26 32.5	21.7	121 37.7	7.8	16 55.0	7.2	58.9
15	41 32.5 ..	20.9	136 04.5	7.6	17 02.2	7.2	58.9
16	56 32.4	20.2	150 31.1	7.6	17 09.4	7.1	58.9
17	71 32.3	19.4	164 57.7	7.5	17 16.5	7.0	58.9
18	86 32.3	S16 18.7	179 24.2	7.5	S17 23.5	6.8	59.0
19	101 32.2	18.0	193 50.7	7.4	17 30.3	6.8	59.0
20	116 32.1	17.2	208 17.1	7.3	17 37.1	6.7	59.0
21	131 32.1 ..	16.5	222 43.4	7.3	17 43.8	6.5	59.0
22	146 32.0	15.7	237 09.7	7.1	17 50.3	6.5	59.1
23	161 32.0	15.0	251 35.8	7.2	17 56.8	6.3	59.1
4 00	176 31.9	S16 14.2	266 02.0	7.0	S18 03.1	6.2	59.1
01	191 31.8	13.5	280 28.0	7.0	18 09.3	6.2	59.1
02	206 31.8	12.7	294 54.0	6.9	18 15.5	6.0	59.1
03	221 31.7 ..	12.0	309 19.9	6.9	18 21.5	5.9	59.1
04	236 31.7	11.2	323 45.8	6.7	18 27.4	5.8	59.2
05	251 31.6	10.5	338 11.5	6.8	18 33.2	5.6	59.2
06	266 31.6	S16 09.7	352 37.3	6.6	S18 38.8	5.6	59.2
07	281 31.5	09.0	7 02.9	6.6	18 44.4	5.4	59.2
08	296 31.4	08.2	21 28.5	6.6	18 49.8	5.3	59.2
M 09	311 31.4 ..	07.5	35 54.1	6.4	18 55.1	5.2	59.2
O 10	326 31.3	06.7	50 19.5	6.4	19 00.3	5.1	59.3
N 11	341 31.3	06.0	64 44.9	6.4	19 05.4	5.0	59.3
D 12	356 31.2	S16 05.2	79 10.3	6.3	S19 10.4	4.8	59.3
A 13	11 31.2	04.5	93 35.6	6.2	19 15.2	4.7	59.3
Y 14	26 31.1	03.7	108 00.8	6.2	19 19.9	4.6	59.3
15	41 31.1 ..	03.0	122 26.0	6.1	19 24.5	4.5	59.3
16	56 31.0	02.2	136 51.1	6.0	19 29.0	4.4	59.4
17	71 31.0	01.5	151 16.1	6.0	19 33.4	4.2	59.4
18	86 30.9	S16 00.7	165 41.1	6.0	S19 37.6	4.1	59.4
19	101 30.8	16 00.0	180 06.1	5.9	19 41.7	3.9	59.4
20	116 30.8	15 59.2	194 31.0	5.8	19 45.6	3.9	59.4
21	131 30.7 ..	58.4	208 55.8	5.8	19 49.5	3.7	59.4
22	146 30.7	57.7	223 20.6	5.7	19 53.2	3.6	59.5
23	161 30.6	56.9	237 45.3	5.7	19 56.8	3.4	59.5
5 00	176 30.6	S15 56.2	252 10.0	5.7	S20 00.2	3.3	59.5
01	191 30.5	55.4	266 34.7	5.5	20 03.5	3.2	59.5
02	206 30.5	54.6	280 59.2	5.6	20 06.7	3.1	59.5
03	221 30.4 ..	53.9	295 23.8	5.5	20 09.8	2.9	59.5
04	236 30.4	53.1	309 48.3	5.4	20 12.7	2.8	59.6
05	251 30.3	52.4	324 12.7	5.5	20 15.5	2.6	59.6
06	266 30.3	S15 51.6	338 37.2	5.3	S20 18.1	2.5	59.6
07	281 30.2	50.8	353 01.5	5.4	20 20.6	2.4	59.6
T 08	296 30.2	50.1	7 25.9	5.2	20 23.0	2.2	59.6
U 09	311 30.1 ..	49.3	21 50.1	5.3	20 25.2	2.1	59.6
E 10	326 30.1	48.6	36 14.4	5.2	20 27.3	2.0	59.6
S 11	341 30.0	47.8	50 38.6	5.2	20 29.3	1.8	59.7
D 12	356 30.0	S15 47.0	65 02.8	5.1	S20 31.1	1.7	59.7
A 13	11 30.0	46.3	79 26.9	5.1	20 32.8	1.6	59.7
Y 14	26 29.9	45.5	93 51.0	5.1	20 34.4	1.4	59.7
15	41 29.9 ..	44.7	108 15.1	5.1	20 35.8	1.2	59.7
16	56 29.8	44.0	122 39.2	5.0	20 37.0	1.1	59.7
17	71 29.8	43.2	137 03.2	5.0	20 38.1	1.0	59.7
18	86 29.7	S15 42.4	151 27.2	5.0	S20 39.1	0.9	59.7
19	101 29.7	41.7	165 51.2	4.9	20 40.0	0.7	59.8
20	116 29.6	40.9	180 15.1	4.9	20 40.7	0.5	59.8
21	131 29.6 ..	40.1	194 39.0	4.9	20 41.2	0.5	59.8
22	146 29.5	39.4	209 02.9	4.9	20 41.7	0.3	59.8
23	161 29.5	38.6	223 26.8	4.9	S20 41.9	0.2	59.9
	SD 16.3	d 0.8	SD 16.0		16.2		16.3

Lat.	Twilight Naut.	Twilight Civil	Sunrise	Moonrise 3	4	5	6
°	h m	h m	h m	h m	h m	h m	h m
N 72	06 58	08 24	10 02	03 30	■■■■	■■■■	■■■■
N 70	06 51	08 08	09 28	02 49	05 01	■■■■	■■■■
68	06 46	07 55	09 04	02 22	04 12	05 55	07 06
66	06 41	07 44	08 46	02 01	03 40	05 11	06 19
64	06 37	07 35	08 30	01 45	03 17	04 41	05 48
62	06 33	07 27	08 17	01 31	02 59	04 19	05 25
60	06 30	07 20	08 06	01 20	02 44	04 01	05 06
N 58	06 27	07 14	07 57	01 10	02 31	03 46	04 51
56	06 24	07 08	07 49	01 01	02 20	03 33	04 37
54	06 21	07 03	07 41	00 54	02 10	03 22	04 26
52	06 18	06 59	07 35	00 47	02 02	03 12	04 16
50	06 16	06 54	07 29	00 41	01 54	03 04	04 07
45	06 10	06 45	07 16	00 27	01 37	02 45	03 48
N 40	06 05	06 37	07 05	00 17	01 24	02 30	03 32
35	06 00	06 30	06 56	00 07	01 13	02 17	03 19
30	05 55	06 23	06 49	25 03	01 03	02 06	03 07
20	05 45	06 12	06 34	24 46	00 46	01 47	02 48
N 10	05 35	06 00	06 22	24 31	00 31	01 30	02 31
0	05 24	05 49	06 10	24 17	00 17	01 15	02 15
S 10	05 11	05 37	05 59	24 03	00 03	01 00	01 59
20	04 55	05 23	05 46	23 49	24 43	00 43	01 42
30	04 35	05 06	05 31	23 32	24 24	00 24	01 22
35	04 22	04 55	05 23	23 23	24 14	00 14	01 11
40	04 07	04 43	05 13	23 12	24 01	00 01	00 58
45	03 47	04 28	05 01	22 59	23 46	24 43	00 43
S 50	03 22	04 10	04 47	22 43	23 29	24 24	00 24
52	03 09	04 01	04 41	22 36	23 20	24 15	00 15
54	02 53	03 51	04 33	22 28	23 11	24 05	00 05
56	02 34	03 39	04 25	22 19	23 00	23 54	25 00
58	02 10	03 26	04 16	22 09	22 48	23 41	24 48
S 60	01 36	03 09	04 05	21 57	22 34	23 26	24 33

Lat.	Sunset	Twilight Civil	Twilight Naut.	Moonset 3	4	5	6
°	h m	h m	h m	h m	h m	h m	h m
N 72	14 27	16 05	17 32	07 25	■■■■	■■■■	■■■■
N 70	15 01	16 21	17 38	08 06	07 51	■■■■	■■■■
68	15 25	16 34	17 43	08 35	08 41	08 59	09 54
66	15 44	16 45	17 48	08 56	09 13	09 44	10 41
64	15 59	16 54	17 52	09 14	09 36	10 14	11 12
62	16 12	17 02	17 56	09 28	09 55	10 36	11 35
60	16 22	17 09	17 59	09 40	10 11	10 54	11 54
N 58	16 32	17 15	18 02	09 51	10 24	11 09	12 09
56	16 40	17 20	18 05	10 00	10 36	11 22	12 22
54	16 47	17 25	18 08	10 08	10 46	11 34	12 34
52	16 54	17 30	18 10	10 15	10 54	11 43	12 44
50	17 00	17 34	18 13	10 22	11 03	11 52	12 53
45	17 12	17 43	18 18	10 36	11 20	12 11	13 12
N 40	17 23	17 51	18 23	10 48	11 34	12 27	13 27
35	17 32	17 58	18 28	10 58	11 46	12 40	13 40
30	17 40	18 05	18 33	11 07	11 56	12 51	13 51
20	17 54	18 18	18 43	11 22	12 14	13 11	14 11
N 10	18 06	18 28	18 53	11 35	12 30	13 27	14 28
0	18 17	18 39	19 04	11 48	12 44	13 43	14 43
S 10	18 29	18 51	19 17	12 01	12 59	13 59	14 59
20	18 42	19 05	19 32	12 14	13 15	14 16	15 16
30	18 56	19 22	19 52	12 29	13 33	14 35	15 35
35	19 05	19 32	20 05	12 38	13 43	14 47	15 46
40	19 14	19 44	20 22	12 49	13 55	15 00	15 59
45	19 26	19 58	20 39	13 01	14 10	15 15	16 14
S 50	19 40	20 17	21 05	13 15	14 27	15 34	16 33
52	19 46	20 26	21 17	13 22	14 35	15 43	16 41
54	19 53	20 35	21 32	13 30	14 44	15 52	16 51
56	20 01	20 47	21 51	13 38	14 55	16 04	17 02
58	20 11	21 00	22 14	13 48	15 06	16 17	17 14
S 60	20 21	21 16	22 46	13 59	15 20	16 32	17 29

	SUN			MOON			
Day	Eqn. of Time 00ʰ	Eqn. of Time 12ʰ	Mer. Pass.	Mer. Pass. Upper	Mer. Pass. Lower	Age	Phase
d	m s	m s	h m	h m	h m	d	%
3	13 46	13 49	12 14	05 35	18 02	23	51
4	13 52	13 55	12 14	06 31	19 00	24	40
5	13 58	14 00	12 14	07 29	19 59	25	29

UT	ARIES GHA	VENUS −3.9 GHA	Dec	MARS +1.2 GHA	Dec	JUPITER −2.5 GHA	Dec	SATURN +0.5 GHA	Dec	STARS Name	SHA	Dec
6 00	136 17.7	188 53.1	S19 47.5	160 53.2	S11 18.5	71 39.2	N20 48.8	276 33.3	S12 53.6	Acamar	315 18.5	S40 15.4
01	151 20.1	203 52.4	46.8	175 53.7	17.7	86 41.6	48.9	291 35.7	53.6	Achernar	335 27.2	S57 10.5
02	166 22.6	218 51.6	46.2	190 54.3	17.0	101 44.0	48.9	306 38.1	53.6	Acrux	173 09.0	S63 10.2
03	181 25.0	233 50.8 ..	45.5	205 54.9 ..	16.3	116 46.4 ..	48.9	321 40.6 ..	53.6	Adhara	255 12.4	S28 59.7
04	196 27.5	248 50.0	44.8	220 55.5	15.5	131 48.8	48.9	336 43.0	53.6	Aldebaran	290 49.5	N16 32.0
05	211 30.0	263 49.2	44.1	235 56.1	14.8	146 51.2	48.9	351 45.4	53.6			
06	226 32.4	278 48.4	S19 43.4	250 56.7	S11 14.1	161 53.6	N20 49.0	6 47.8	S12 53.6	Alioth	166 20.6	N55 53.0
W 07	241 34.9	293 47.6	42.8	265 57.3	13.4	176 56.0	49.0	21 50.2	53.6	Alkaid	152 58.9	N49 14.5
E 08	256 37.4	308 46.9	42.1	280 57.9	12.6	191 58.4	49.0	36 52.6	53.6	Al Na'ir	27 44.5	S46 53.8
D 09	271 39.8	323 46.1 ..	41.4	295 58.5 ..	11.9	207 00.9 ..	49.0	51 55.0 ..	53.7	Alnilam	275 46.4	S 1 11.9
N 10	286 42.3	338 45.3	40.7	310 59.1	11.2	222 03.3	49.0	66 57.4	53.7	Alphard	217 56.0	S 8 43.2
E 11	301 44.8	353 44.5	40.0	325 59.7	10.4	237 05.7	49.1	81 59.8	53.7			
S 12	316 47.2	8 43.7	S19 39.3	341 00.3	S11 09.7	252 08.1	N20 49.1	97 02.2	S12 53.7	Alphecca	126 11.2	N26 40.1
D 13	331 49.7	23 43.0	38.7	356 00.9	09.0	267 10.5	49.1	112 04.6	53.7	Alpheratz	357 44.0	N29 09.9
A 14	346 52.2	38 42.2	38.0	11 01.5	08.2	282 12.9	49.1	127 07.0	53.7	Altair	62 08.8	N 8 54.2
Y 15	1 54.6	53 41.4 ..	37.3	26 02.1 ..	07.5	297 15.3 ..	49.1	142 09.5 ..	53.7	Ankaa	353 16.2	S42 14.2
16	16 57.1	68 40.6	36.6	41 02.7	06.8	312 17.7	49.1	157 11.9	53.7	Antares	112 26.6	S26 27.5
17	31 59.5	83 39.8	35.9	56 03.2	06.1	327 20.1	49.2	172 14.3	53.7			
18	47 02.0	98 39.1	S19 35.2	71 03.8	S11 05.3	342 22.5	N20 49.2	187 16.7	S12 53.7	Arcturus	145 55.9	N19 06.6
19	62 04.5	113 38.3	34.5	86 04.4	04.6	357 24.9	49.2	202 19.1	53.7	Atria	107 28.9	S69 02.7
20	77 06.9	128 37.5	33.8	101 05.0	03.9	12 27.3	49.2	217 21.5	53.7	Avior	234 17.4	S59 33.4
21	92 09.4	143 36.7 ..	33.1	116 05.6 ..	03.1	27 29.7 ..	49.2	232 23.9 ..	53.7	Bellatrix	278 32.0	N 6 21.5
22	107 11.9	158 35.9	32.4	131 06.2	02.4	42 32.1	49.3	247 26.3	53.7	Betelgeuse	271 01.3	N 7 24.3
23	122 14.3	173 35.2	31.7	146 06.8	01.7	57 34.5	49.3	262 28.7	53.7			
7 00	137 16.8	188 34.4	S19 31.0	161 07.4	S11 00.9	72 36.9	N20 49.3	277 31.2	S12 53.7	Canopus	263 55.8	S52 42.5
01	152 19.3	203 33.6	30.3	176 08.0	11 00.2	87 39.3	49.3	292 33.6	53.8	Capella	280 34.5	N46 00.7
02	167 21.7	218 32.8	29.6	191 08.6	10 59.5	102 41.7	49.4	307 36.0	53.8	Deneb	49 32.1	N45 19.7
03	182 24.2	233 32.1 ..	28.9	206 09.2 ..	58.7	117 44.1 ..	49.4	322 38.4 ..	53.8	Denebola	182 33.6	N14 29.7
04	197 26.7	248 31.3	28.2	221 09.8	58.0	132 46.5	49.4	337 40.8	53.8	Diphda	348 56.3	S17 55.0
05	212 29.1	263 30.5	27.5	236 10.4	57.3	147 48.9	49.4	352 43.2	53.8			
06	227 31.6	278 29.7	S19 26.8	251 11.0	S10 56.5	162 51.3	N20 49.4	7 45.6	S12 53.8	Dubhe	193 51.4	N61 40.5
07	242 34.0	293 29.0	26.1	266 11.6	55.8	177 53.7	49.5	22 48.0	53.8	Elnath	278 12.7	N28 37.0
T 08	257 36.5	308 28.2	25.4	281 12.2	55.1	192 56.1	49.5	37 50.4	53.8	Eltanin	90 46.6	N51 29.1
H 09	272 39.0	323 27.4 ..	24.7	296 12.8 ..	54.3	207 58.4 ..	49.5	52 52.9 ..	53.8	Enif	33 47.6	N 9 56.2
U 10	287 41.4	338 26.7	24.0	311 13.4	53.6	223 00.8	49.5	67 55.3	53.8	Fomalhaut	15 24.6	S29 33.2
R 11	302 43.9	353 25.9	23.3	326 14.0	52.9	238 03.2	49.5	82 57.7	53.8			
S 12	317 46.4	8 25.1	S19 22.6	341 14.6	S10 52.1	253 05.6	N20 49.6	98 00.1	S12 53.8	Gacrux	172 00.7	S57 11.1
D 13	332 48.8	23 24.3	21.9	356 15.2	51.4	268 08.0	49.6	113 02.5	53.8	Gienah	175 52.3	S17 37.0
A 14	347 51.3	38 23.6	21.2	11 15.8	50.7	283 10.4	49.6	128 04.9	53.8	Hadar	148 48.0	S60 25.9
Y 15	2 53.8	53 22.8 ..	20.5	26 16.4 ..	49.9	298 12.8 ..	49.6	143 07.3 ..	53.8	Hamal	328 01.1	N23 31.5
16	17 56.2	68 22.0	19.8	41 17.0	49.2	313 15.2	49.6	158 09.8	53.8	Kaus Aust.	83 44.4	S34 22.5
17	32 58.7	83 21.3	19.0	56 17.6	48.5	328 17.6	49.7	173 12.2	53.8			
18	48 01.2	98 20.5	S19 18.3	71 18.2	S10 47.7	343 20.0	N20 49.7	188 14.6	S12 53.8	Kochab	137 20.0	N74 05.8
19	63 03.6	113 19.7	17.6	86 18.8	47.0	358 22.4	49.7	203 17.0	53.9	Markab	13 38.8	N15 16.6
20	78 06.1	128 19.0	16.9	101 19.4	46.3	13 24.8	49.7	218 19.4	53.9	Menkar	314 15.3	N 4 08.3
21	93 08.5	143 18.2 ..	16.2	116 20.0 ..	45.5	28 27.2 ..	49.7	233 21.8 ..	53.9	Menkent	148 07.7	S36 26.0
22	108 11.0	158 17.4	15.5	131 20.6	44.8	43 29.6	49.8	248 24.2	53.9	Miaplacidus	221 38.7	S69 46.4
23	123 13.5	173 16.7	14.7	146 21.2	44.0	58 31.9	49.8	263 26.7	53.9			
8 00	138 15.9	188 15.9	S19 14.0	161 21.8	S10 43.3	73 34.3	N20 49.8	278 29.1	S12 53.9	Mirfak	308 40.6	N49 54.6
01	153 18.4	203 15.2	13.3	176 22.4	42.6	88 36.7	49.8	293 31.5	53.9	Nunki	75 58.9	S26 16.7
02	168 20.9	218 14.4	12.6	191 23.0	41.8	103 39.1	49.9	308 33.9	53.9	Peacock	53 20.2	S56 41.4
03	183 23.3	233 13.6 ..	11.8	206 23.6 ..	41.1	118 41.5 ..	49.9	323 36.3 ..	53.9	Pollux	243 27.6	N27 59.4
04	198 25.8	248 12.9	11.1	221 24.2	40.4	133 43.9	49.9	338 38.7	53.9	Procyon	244 59.6	N 5 11.2
05	213 28.3	263 12.1	10.4	236 24.8	39.6	148 46.3	49.9	353 41.1	53.9			
06	228 30.7	278 11.3	S19 09.7	251 25.4	S10 38.9	163 48.7	N20 49.9	8 43.6	S12 53.9	Rasalhague	96 06.9	N12 33.0
07	243 33.2	293 10.6	08.9	266 26.0	38.1	178 51.1	50.0	23 46.0	53.9	Regulus	207 43.4	N11 53.9
08	258 35.7	308 09.8	08.2	281 26.6	37.4	193 53.4	50.0	38 48.4	53.9	Rigel	281 12.1	S 8 11.5
F 09	273 38.1	323 09.1 ..	07.5	296 27.2 ..	36.7	208 55.8 ..	50.0	53 50.8 ..	53.9	Rigil Kent.	139 51.9	S60 53.1
R 10	288 40.6	338 08.3	06.8	311 27.8	35.9	223 58.2	50.0	68 53.2	53.9	Sabik	102 13.0	S15 44.4
I 11	303 43.0	353 07.5	06.0	326 28.4	35.2	239 00.6	50.1	83 55.6	53.9			
D 12	318 45.5	8 06.8	S19 05.3	341 29.0	S10 34.5	254 03.0	N20 50.1	98 58.1	S12 53.9	Schedar	349 41.1	N56 36.8
A 13	333 48.0	23 06.0	04.6	356 29.6	33.7	269 05.4	50.1	114 00.5	53.9	Shaula	96 22.4	S37 06.6
Y 14	348 50.4	38 05.3	03.8	11 30.2	33.0	284 07.8	50.1	129 02.9	53.9	Sirius	258 33.6	S16 44.4
15	3 52.9	53 04.5 ..	03.1	26 30.8 ..	32.2	299 10.1 ..	50.1	144 05.3 ..	53.9	Spica	158 31.3	S11 13.9
16	18 55.4	68 03.8	02.4	41 31.4	31.5	314 12.5	50.2	159 07.7	53.9	Suhail	222 52.1	S43 29.4
17	33 57.8	83 03.0	01.6	56 32.0	30.8	329 14.9	50.2	174 10.2	54.0			
18	49 00.3	98 02.2	S19 00.9	71 32.6	S10 30.0	344 17.3	N20 50.2	189 12.6	S12 54.0	Vega	80 39.4	N38 47.7
19	64 02.8	113 01.5	19 00.1	86 33.2	29.3	359 19.7	50.2	204 15.0	54.0	Zuben'ubi	137 05.6	S16 05.7
20	79 05.2	128 00.7	18 59.4	101 33.8	28.5	14 22.1	50.3	219 17.4	54.0		SHA	Mer.Pass.
21	94 07.7	143 00.0 ..	58.7	116 34.4 ..	27.8	29 24.4 ..	50.3	234 19.8 ..	54.0		° '	h m
22	109 10.1	157 59.2	57.9	131 35.0	27.1	44 26.8	50.3	249 22.2	54.0	Venus	51 17.6	11 26
23	124 12.6	172 58.5	57.2	146 35.6	26.3	59 29.2	50.3	264 24.7	54.0	Mars	23 50.6	13 15
Mer.Pass. 14 48.4		v −0.8	d 0.7	v 0.6	d 0.7	v 2.4	d 0.0	v 2.4	d 0.0	Jupiter	295 20.1	19 06
										Saturn	140 14.4	5 29

SUN and MOON

UT	SUN GHA	SUN Dec	MOON GHA	v	Dec	d	HP
6 00	176 29.5	S15 37.8	237 50.7	4.8	S20 42.1	0.1	59.8
01	191 29.4	37.1	252 14.5	4.8	20 42.0	0.1	59.8
02	206 29.4	36.3	266 38.3	4.8	20 41.9	0.3	59.8
03	221 29.3	35.5	281 02.1	4.9	20 41.6	0.5	59.8
04	236 29.3	34.7	295 26.0	4.7	20 41.1	0.5	59.9
05	251 29.3	34.0	309 49.7	4.8	20 40.6	0.8	59.9
06	266 29.2	S15 33.2	324 13.5	4.8	S20 39.8	0.8	59.9
W 07	281 29.2	32.4	338 37.3	4.8	20 39.0	1.1	59.9
E 08	296 29.1	31.6	353 01.1	4.7	20 37.9	1.1	59.9
D 09	311 29.1	30.9	7 24.8	4.8	20 36.8	1.3	59.9
N 10	326 29.1	30.1	21 48.6	4.7	20 35.5	1.5	59.9
E 11	341 29.0	29.3	36 12.3	4.8	20 34.0	1.6	59.9
S 12	356 29.0	S15 28.5	50 36.1	4.8	S20 32.4	1.7	59.9
D 13	11 28.9	27.8	64 59.9	4.7	20 30.7	1.9	59.9
A 14	26 28.9	27.0	79 23.6	4.8	20 28.8	2.0	59.9
Y 15	41 28.9	26.2	93 47.4	4.8	20 26.8	2.2	59.9
16	56 28.8	25.4	108 11.2	4.7	20 24.6	2.3	60.0
17	71 28.8	24.7	122 34.9	4.8	20 22.3	2.4	60.0
18	86 28.7	S15 23.9	136 58.7	4.8	S20 19.9	2.6	60.0
19	101 28.7	23.1	151 22.5	4.8	20 17.3	2.8	60.0
20	116 28.7	22.3	165 46.3	4.8	20 14.5	2.8	60.0
21	131 28.6	21.6	180 10.1	4.9	20 11.7	3.1	60.0
22	146 28.6	20.8	194 34.0	4.8	20 08.6	3.1	60.0
23	161 28.6	20.0	208 57.8	4.9	20 05.5	3.3	60.0
7 00	176 28.5	S15 19.2	223 21.7	4.9	S20 02.2	3.4	60.0
01	191 28.5	18.4	237 45.6	4.9	19 58.8	3.6	60.0
02	206 28.5	17.6	252 09.5	5.0	19 55.2	3.7	60.0
03	221 28.4	16.9	266 33.5	4.9	19 51.5	3.9	60.0
04	236 28.4	16.1	280 57.4	5.0	19 47.6	4.0	60.0
05	251 28.4	15.3	295 21.4	5.0	19 43.6	4.1	60.0
06	266 28.3	S15 14.5	309 45.4	5.0	S19 39.5	4.3	60.0
T 07	281 28.3	13.7	324 09.4	5.1	19 35.2	4.4	60.0
H 08	296 28.3	12.9	338 33.5	5.1	19 30.8	4.5	60.0
U 09	311 28.2	12.2	352 57.6	5.1	19 26.3	4.7	60.0
R 10	326 28.2	11.4	7 21.7	5.2	19 21.6	4.8	60.0
S 11	341 28.2	10.6	21 45.9	5.2	19 16.8	4.9	60.0
D 12	356 28.1	S15 09.8	36 10.1	5.2	S19 11.9	5.1	60.0
A 13	11 28.1	09.0	50 34.3	5.3	19 06.8	5.2	60.0
Y 14	26 28.1	08.2	64 58.6	5.3	19 01.6	5.3	60.0
15	41 28.1	07.4	79 22.9	5.4	18 56.3	5.5	60.0
16	56 28.0	06.7	93 47.3	5.4	18 50.8	5.6	60.0
17	71 28.0	05.9	108 11.7	5.4	18 45.2	5.7	60.0
18	86 28.0	S15 05.1	122 36.1	5.5	S18 39.5	5.8	60.0
19	101 27.9	04.3	137 00.6	5.5	18 33.7	6.0	60.0
20	116 27.9	03.5	151 25.1	5.6	18 27.7	6.1	60.0
21	131 27.9	02.7	165 49.7	5.6	18 21.6	6.2	60.0
22	146 27.9	01.9	180 14.3	5.6	18 15.4	6.3	60.0
23	161 27.8	01.1	194 38.9	5.7	18 09.1	6.5	60.0
8 00	176 27.8	S15 00.3	209 03.6	5.8	S18 02.6	6.6	60.0
01	191 27.8	14 59.5	223 28.4	5.8	17 56.0	6.7	60.0
02	206 27.7	58.8	237 53.2	5.8	17 49.3	6.8	60.0
03	221 27.7	58.0	252 18.0	5.9	17 42.5	7.0	60.0
04	236 27.7	57.2	266 42.9	6.0	17 35.5	7.0	60.0
05	251 27.7	56.4	281 07.9	6.0	17 28.5	7.2	60.0
06	266 27.6	S14 55.6	295 32.9	6.1	S17 21.3	7.3	60.0
07	281 27.6	54.8	309 58.0	6.1	17 14.0	7.4	60.0
F 08	296 27.6	54.0	324 23.1	6.2	17 06.6	7.5	60.0
R 09	311 27.6	53.2	338 48.3	6.2	16 59.1	7.6	60.0
I 10	326 27.6	52.4	353 13.5	6.3	16 51.5	7.8	59.9
D 11	341 27.5	51.6	7 38.8	6.4	16 43.7	7.8	59.9
A 12	356 27.5	S14 50.8	22 04.2	6.4	S16 35.9	8.0	59.9
Y 13	11 27.5	50.0	36 29.6	6.5	16 27.9	8.0	59.9
14	26 27.5	49.2	50 55.1	6.5	16 19.9	8.2	59.9
15	41 27.4	48.4	65 20.6	6.6	16 11.7	8.3	59.9
16	56 27.4	47.6	79 46.2	6.7	16 03.4	8.3	59.9
17	71 27.4	46.8	94 11.9	6.7	15 55.1	8.5	59.9
18	86 27.4	S14 46.0	108 37.6	6.8	S15 46.6	8.6	59.9
19	101 27.4	45.2	123 03.4	6.8	15 38.0	8.6	59.9
20	116 27.3	44.4	137 29.2	6.9	15 29.4	8.8	59.8
21	131 27.3	43.6	151 55.1	7.0	15 20.6	8.8	59.8
22	146 27.3	42.8	166 21.1	7.0	15 11.8	9.0	59.8
23	161 27.3	42.0	180 47.1	7.1	S15 02.8	9.0	59.8
	SD 16.2	d 0.8	SD 16.3		16.4		16.3

Twilight / Moonrise

Lat.	Naut.	Civil	Sunrise	Moonrise 6	7	8	9
N 72	06 46	08 11	09 42	████	████	09 11	08 33
N 70	06 41	07 56	09 13	████	08 41	08 17	08 07
68	06 37	07 44	08 51	07 06	07 35	07 44	07 47
66	06 33	07 35	08 34	06 19	06 58	07 19	07 31
64	06 29	07 27	08 20	05 48	06 32	07 00	07 18
62	06 26	07 19	08 09	05 25	06 12	06 44	07 06
60	06 23	07 13	07 59	05 06	05 55	06 31	06 57
N 58	06 21	07 08	07 50	04 51	05 41	06 20	06 49
56	06 18	07 03	07 43	04 37	05 29	06 10	06 41
54	06 16	06 58	07 36	04 26	05 19	06 01	06 34
52	06 14	06 54	07 30	04 16	05 09	05 53	06 29
50	06 12	06 50	07 24	04 07	05 01	05 46	06 23
45	06 07	06 41	07 12	03 48	04 43	05 31	06 11
N 40	06 02	06 34	07 02	03 32	04 28	05 18	06 02
35	05 58	06 28	06 54	03 19	04 16	05 07	05 53
30	05 53	06 21	06 46	03 07	04 05	04 58	05 46
20	05 44	06 10	06 33	02 48	03 47	04 42	05 33
N 10	05 35	06 00	06 22	02 31	03 30	04 28	05 22
0	05 24	05 49	06 11	02 15	03 15	04 14	05 11
S 10	05 12	05 38	06 00	01 59	03 00	04 01	05 01
20	04 57	05 25	05 48	01 42	02 44	03 47	04 50
30	04 38	05 08	05 34	01 22	02 25	03 30	04 37
35	04 26	04 59	05 26	01 11	02 14	03 21	04 29
40	04 11	04 47	05 17	00 58	02 02	03 10	04 21
45	03 53	04 33	05 06	00 43	01 47	02 57	04 11
S 50	03 29	04 16	04 53	00 24	01 29	02 42	03 58
52	03 16	04 07	04 46	00 15	01 20	02 34	03 53
54	03 02	03 58	04 40	00 05	01 11	02 26	03 47
56	02 45	03 47	04 32	25 00	01 00	02 17	03 40
58	02 24	03 34	04 23	24 48	00 48	02 06	03 32
S 60	01 55	03 20	04 13	24 33	00 33	01 54	03 23

Sunset / Twilight / Moonset

Lat.	Sunset	Civil	Naut.	Moonset 6	7	8	9
N 72	14 48	16 19	17 44	████	████	12 00	14 36
N 70	15 17	16 34	17 49	████	10 26	13 25	15 01
68	15 38	16 45	17 53	09 54	11 32	13 25	15 34
66	15 55	16 55	17 57	10 41	12 07	13 49	15 34
64	16 09	17 03	18 00	11 12	12 33	14 07	15 46
62	16 21	17 10	18 03	11 35	12 53	14 22	15 56
60	16 30	17 16	18 06	11 54	13 09	14 35	16 05
N 58	16 39	17 22	18 08	12 09	13 23	14 46	16 12
56	16 47	17 27	18 11	12 22	13 34	14 55	16 19
54	16 53	17 31	18 13	12 34	13 45	15 03	16 25
52	16 59	17 35	18 15	12 44	13 54	15 11	16 30
50	17 05	17 39	18 17	12 53	14 02	15 17	16 35
45	17 17	17 47	18 22	13 12	14 19	15 32	16 46
N 40	17 26	17 55	18 27	13 27	14 33	15 43	16 54
35	17 35	18 01	18 31	13 40	14 46	15 53	17 02
30	17 42	18 07	18 36	13 51	14 56	16 02	17 08
20	17 54	18 18	18 44	14 11	15 14	16 17	17 19
N 10	18 07	18 28	18 54	14 28	15 29	16 30	17 29
0	18 18	18 39	19 04	14 43	15 44	16 42	17 38
S 10	18 29	18 50	19 17	14 59	15 58	16 54	17 46
20	18 40	19 03	19 31	15 16	16 13	17 07	17 56
30	18 54	19 19	19 49	15 35	16 31	17 21	18 07
35	19 02	19 29	20 01	15 46	16 41	17 29	18 13
40	19 11	19 40	20 16	15 59	16 52	17 39	18 20
45	19 22	19 54	20 34	16 14	17 06	17 50	18 28
S 50	19 34	20 11	20 58	16 33	17 22	18 03	18 37
52	19 41	20 19	21 10	16 41	17 30	18 09	18 42
54	19 47	20 29	21 24	16 51	17 38	18 16	18 47
56	19 55	20 39	21 40	17 02	17 48	18 24	18 52
58	20 03	20 52	22 01	17 14	17 59	18 32	18 58
S 60	20 13	21 06	22 28	17 29	18 11	18 42	19 05

SUN and MOON

Day	SUN Eqn. of Time 00h	12h	Mer. Pass.	MOON Mer. Pass. Upper	Lower	Age	Phase
	m s	m s	h m	h m	h m	d	%
6	14 02	14 04	12 14	08 29	20 59	26	19
7	14 06	14 07	12 14	09 29	21 59	27	11
8	14 09	14 10	12 14	10 28	22 57	28	5

2013 FEBRUARY 9, 10, 11 (SAT., SUN., MON.)

UT	ARIES GHA	VENUS -3.9 GHA	Dec	MARS +1.2 GHA	Dec	JUPITER -2.4 GHA	Dec	SATURN +0.5 GHA	Dec	STARS Name	SHA	Dec
d h 9 00	139 15.1	187 57.7	S18 56.4	161 36.2	S10 25.6	74 31.6	N20 50.3	279 27.1	S12 54.0	Acamar	315 18.5	S40 15.4
01	154 17.5	202 57.0	55.7	176 36.8	24.8	89 34.0	50.4	294 29.5	54.0	Achernar	335 27.2	S57 10.5
02	169 20.0	217 56.2	54.9	191 37.4	24.1	104 36.4	50.4	309 31.9	54.0	Acrux	173 09.0	S63 10.2
03	184 22.5	232 55.5	.. 54.2	206 38.0	.. 23.4	119 38.7	.. 50.4	324 34.3	.. 54.0	Adhara	255 12.4	S28 59.7
04	199 24.9	247 54.7	53.4	221 38.6	22.6	134 41.1	50.4	339 36.8	54.0	Aldebaran	290 49.5	N16 32.0
05	214 27.4	262 54.0	52.7	236 39.2	21.9	149 43.5	50.5	354 39.2	54.0			
06	229 29.9	277 53.2	S18 51.9	251 39.8	S10 21.1	164 45.9	N20 50.5	9 41.6	S12 54.0	Alioth	166 20.6	N55 53.0
07	244 32.3	292 52.5	51.2	266 40.4	20.4	179 48.3	50.5	24 44.0	54.0	Alkaid	152 58.9	N49 14.5
S 08	259 34.8	307 51.7	50.4	281 41.0	19.7	194 50.6	50.5	39 46.4	54.0	Al Na'ir	27 44.5	S46 53.8
A 09	274 37.3	322 51.0	.. 49.7	296 41.6	.. 18.9	209 53.0	.. 50.6	54 48.9	.. 54.0	Alnilam	275 46.4	S 1 11.9
T 10	289 39.7	337 50.2	48.9	311 42.3	18.2	224 55.4	50.6	69 51.3	54.0	Alphard	217 56.0	S 8 43.2
U 11	304 42.2	352 49.5	48.2	326 42.9	17.4	239 57.8	50.6	84 53.7	54.0			
R 12	319 44.6	7 48.7	S18 47.4	341 43.5	S10 16.7	255 00.1	N20 50.6	99 56.1	S12 54.0	Alphecca	126 11.2	N26 40.0
D 13	334 47.1	22 48.0	46.7	356 44.1	15.9	270 02.5	50.7	114 58.6	54.0	Alpheratz	357 44.0	N29 09.9
A 14	349 49.6	37 47.2	45.9	11 44.7	15.2	285 04.9	50.7	130 01.0	54.0	Altair	62 08.7	N 8 54.2
Y 15	4 52.0	52 46.5	.. 45.2	26 45.3	.. 14.5	300 07.3	.. 50.7	145 03.4	.. 54.0	Ankaa	353 16.2	S42 14.2
16	19 54.5	67 45.8	44.5	41 45.9	13.7	315 09.6	50.7	160 05.8	54.0	Antares	112 26.6	S26 27.5
17	34 57.0	82 45.0	43.6	56 46.5	13.0	330 12.0	50.7	175 08.2	54.0			
18	49 59.4	97 44.3	S18 42.9	71 47.1	S10 12.2	345 14.4	N20 50.8	190 10.7	S12 54.0	Arcturus	145 55.8	N19 06.6
19	65 01.9	112 43.5	42.1	86 47.7	11.5	0 16.8	50.8	205 13.1	54.0	Atria	107 28.9	S69 02.7
20	80 04.4	127 42.8	41.4	101 48.3	10.7	15 19.1	50.8	220 15.5	54.0	Avior	234 17.5	S59 33.4
21	95 06.8	142 42.0	.. 40.6	116 48.9	.. 10.0	30 21.5	.. 50.8	235 17.9	.. 54.0	Bellatrix	278 32.0	N 6 21.5
22	110 09.3	157 41.3	39.8	131 49.5	09.2	45 23.9	50.9	250 20.4	54.0	Betelgeuse	271 01.3	N 7 24.3
23	125 11.8	172 40.6	39.1	146 50.1	08.5	60 26.3	50.9	265 22.8	54.0			
10 00	140 14.2	187 39.8	S18 38.3	161 50.7	S10 07.8	75 28.6	N20 50.9	280 25.2	S12 54.0	Canopus	263 55.8	S52 42.5
01	155 16.7	202 39.1	37.5	176 51.4	07.0	90 31.0	50.9	295 27.6	54.0	Capella	280 34.5	N46 00.7
02	170 19.1	217 38.3	36.8	191 52.0	06.3	105 33.4	51.0	310 30.1	54.0	Deneb	49 32.1	N45 19.7
03	185 21.6	232 37.6	.. 36.0	206 52.6	.. 05.5	120 35.7	.. 51.0	325 32.5	.. 54.0	Denebola	182 33.6	N14 29.7
04	200 24.1	247 36.9	35.2	221 53.2	04.8	135 38.1	51.0	340 34.9	54.0	Diphda	348 56.3	S17 55.0
05	215 26.5	262 36.1	34.4	236 53.8	04.0	150 40.5	51.0	355 37.3	54.1			
06	230 29.0	277 35.4	S18 33.7	251 54.4	S10 03.3	165 42.9	N20 51.1	10 39.8	S12 54.1	Dubhe	193 51.4	N61 40.5
07	245 31.5	292 34.6	32.9	266 55.0	02.5	180 45.2	51.1	25 42.2	54.1	Elnath	278 12.7	N28 37.0
08	260 33.9	307 33.9	32.1	281 55.6	01.8	195 47.6	51.1	40 44.6	54.1	Eltanin	90 46.6	N51 29.1
S 09	275 36.4	322 33.2	.. 31.4	296 56.2	.. 01.1	210 50.0	.. 51.1	55 47.0	.. 54.1	Enif	33 47.6	N 9 56.2
U 10	290 38.9	337 32.4	30.6	311 56.8	10 00.3	225 52.3	51.2	70 49.5	54.1	Fomalhaut	15 24.6	S29 33.2
N 11	305 41.3	352 31.7	29.8	326 57.4	9 59.6	240 54.7	51.2	85 51.9	54.1			
D 12	320 43.8	7 31.0	S18 29.0	341 58.0	S 9 58.8	255 57.1	N20 51.2	100 54.3	S12 54.1	Gacrux	172 00.7	S57 11.1
A 13	335 46.2	22 30.2	28.2	356 58.7	58.1	270 59.4	51.2	115 56.7	54.1	Gienah	175 52.3	S17 37.0
Y 14	350 48.7	37 29.5	27.5	11 59.3	57.3	286 01.8	51.3	130 59.2	54.1	Hadar	148 47.9	S60 26.0
15	5 51.2	52 28.8	.. 26.7	26 59.9	.. 56.6	301 04.2	.. 51.3	146 01.6	.. 54.1	Hamal	328 01.1	N23 31.5
16	20 53.6	67 28.0	25.9	42 00.5	55.8	316 06.5	51.3	161 04.0	54.1	Kaus Aust.	83 44.4	S34 22.5
17	35 56.1	82 27.3	25.1	57 01.1	55.1	331 08.9	51.3	176 06.4	54.1			
18	50 58.6	97 26.6	S18 24.3	72 01.7	S 9 54.3	346 11.3	N20 51.4	191 08.9	S12 54.1	Kochab	137 19.9	N74 05.8
19	66 01.0	112 25.8	23.6	87 02.3	53.6	1 13.6	51.4	206 11.3	54.1	Markab	13 38.8	N15 16.6
20	81 03.5	127 25.1	22.8	102 02.9	52.8	16 16.0	51.4	221 13.7	54.1	Menkar	314 15.3	N 4 08.3
21	96 06.0	142 24.4	.. 22.0	117 03.5	.. 52.1	31 18.4	.. 51.4	236 16.1	.. 54.1	Menkent	148 07.9	S36 26.0
22	111 08.4	157 23.7	21.2	132 04.1	51.3	46 20.7	51.5	251 18.6	54.1	Miaplacidus	221 38.7	S69 46.5
23	126 10.9	172 22.9	20.4	147 04.8	50.6	61 23.1	51.5	266 21.0	54.1			
11 00	141 13.4	187 22.2	S18 19.6	162 05.4	S 9 49.9	76 25.5	N20 51.5	281 23.4	S12 54.1	Mirfak	308 40.6	N49 54.6
01	156 15.8	202 21.5	18.8	177 06.0	49.1	91 27.8	51.5	296 25.9	54.1	Nunki	75 58.9	S26 16.7
02	171 18.3	217 20.7	18.0	192 06.6	48.4	106 30.2	51.6	311 28.3	54.1	Peacock	53 20.2	S56 41.4
03	186 20.7	232 20.0	.. 17.3	207 07.2	.. 47.6	121 32.6	.. 51.6	326 30.7	.. 54.1	Pollux	243 27.6	N27 59.4
04	201 23.2	247 19.3	16.5	222 07.8	46.9	136 34.9	51.6	341 33.1	54.1	Procyon	244 59.6	N 5 11.2
05	216 25.7	262 18.6	15.7	237 08.4	46.1	151 37.3	51.6	356 35.6	54.1			
06	231 28.1	277 17.8	S18 14.9	252 09.0	S 9 45.4	166 39.6	N20 51.7	11 38.0	S12 54.1	Rasalhague	96 06.8	N12 33.0
07	246 30.6	292 17.1	14.1	267 09.7	44.6	181 42.0	51.7	26 40.4	54.1	Regulus	207 43.4	N11 53.9
08	261 33.1	307 16.4	13.3	282 10.3	43.9	196 44.4	51.7	41 42.9	54.1	Rigel	281 12.1	S 8 11.5
M 09	276 35.5	322 15.7	.. 12.5	297 10.9	.. 43.1	211 46.7	.. 51.7	56 45.3	.. 54.1	Rigil Kent.	139 51.8	S60 53.1
O 10	291 38.0	337 14.9	11.7	312 11.5	42.4	226 49.1	51.8	71 47.7	54.1	Sabik	102 12.9	S15 44.4
N 11	306 40.5	352 14.2	10.9	327 12.1	41.6	241 51.4	51.8	86 50.2	54.1			
D 12	321 42.9	7 13.5	S18 10.1	342 12.7	S 9 40.9	256 53.8	N20 51.8	101 52.6	S12 54.1	Schedar	349 41.1	N56 36.8
A 13	336 45.4	22 12.8	09.3	357 13.3	40.1	271 56.2	51.9	116 55.0	54.1	Shaula	96 22.4	S37 06.6
Y 14	351 47.9	37 12.1	08.5	12 13.9	39.4	286 58.5	51.9	131 57.4	54.1	Sirius	258 33.6	S16 44.4
15	6 50.3	52 11.3	.. 07.7	27 14.6	.. 38.6	302 00.9	.. 51.9	146 59.9	.. 54.1	Spica	158 31.3	S11 13.9
16	21 52.8	67 10.6	06.9	42 15.2	37.9	317 03.2	51.9	162 02.3	54.1	Suhail	222 52.1	S43 29.4
17	36 55.2	82 09.9	06.1	57 15.8	37.1	332 05.6	52.0	177 04.7	54.1			
18	51 57.7	97 09.2	S18 05.3	72 16.4	S 9 36.4	347 08.0	N20 52.0	192 07.2	S12 54.1	Vega	80 39.4	N38 47.7
19	67 00.2	112 08.5	04.5	87 17.0	35.6	2 10.3	52.0	207 09.6	54.1	Zuben'ubi	137 05.6	S16 05.8
20	82 02.6	127 07.7	03.7	102 17.6	34.9	17 12.7	52.0	222 12.0	54.1		SHA	Mer.Pass.
21	97 05.1	142 07.0	.. 02.9	117 18.2	.. 34.1	32 15.0	.. 52.1	237 14.5	.. 54.1		° '	h m
22	112 07.6	157 06.3	02.0	132 18.9	33.4	47 17.4	52.1	252 16.9	54.1	Venus	47 25.6	11 30
23	127 10.0	172 05.6	01.2	147 19.5	32.6	62 19.7	52.1	267 19.3	54.1	Mars	21 36.5	13 12
	h m									Jupiter	295 14.4	18 55
Mer.Pass. 14 36.7		v -0.7	d 0.8	v 0.6	d 0.7	v 2.4	d 0.0	v 2.4	d 0.0	Saturn	140 11.0	5 17

UT	SUN GHA	SUN Dec	MOON GHA	v	Dec	d	HP
SATURDAY							
9 00	176 27.3	S14 41.2	195 13.2	7.2	S14 53.8	9.2	59.8
01	191 27.2	40.4	209 39.4	7.2	14 44.6	9.2	59.8
02	206 27.2	39.6	224 05.6	7.3	14 35.4	9.3	59.8
03	221 27.2	.. 38.8	238 31.9	7.4	14 26.1	9.4	59.8
04	236 27.2	38.0	252 58.3	7.4	14 16.7	9.5	59.7
05	251 27.2	37.2	267 24.7	7.5	14 07.2	9.6	59.7
06	266 27.2	S14 36.4	281 51.2	7.6	S13 57.6	9.6	59.7
07	281 27.1	35.6	296 17.8	7.6	13 48.0	9.8	59.7
08	296 27.1	34.8	310 44.4	7.7	13 38.2	9.8	59.7
09	311 27.1	.. 34.0	325 11.1	7.8	13 28.4	9.9	59.7
10	326 27.1	33.2	339 37.9	7.8	13 18.5	10.0	59.6
11	341 27.1	32.4	354 04.7	7.9	13 08.5	10.0	59.6
12	356 27.1	S14 31.6	8 31.6	8.0	S12 58.5	10.1	59.6
13	11 27.1	30.7	22 58.6	8.0	12 48.4	10.2	59.6
14	26 27.0	29.9	37 25.6	8.1	12 38.2	10.3	59.6
15	41 27.0	.. 29.1	51 52.7	8.2	12 27.9	10.3	59.6
16	56 27.0	28.3	66 19.9	8.2	12 17.6	10.4	59.5
17	71 27.0	27.5	80 47.1	8.3	12 07.2	10.5	59.5
18	86 27.0	S14 26.7	95 14.4	8.4	S11 56.7	10.6	59.5
19	101 27.0	25.9	109 41.8	8.4	11 46.1	10.6	59.5
20	116 27.0	25.1	124 09.2	8.6	11 35.5	10.6	59.5
21	131 27.0	.. 24.3	138 36.8	8.5	11 24.9	10.7	59.4
22	146 26.9	23.5	153 04.3	8.7	11 14.2	10.8	59.4
23	161 26.9	22.7	167 32.0	8.7	11 03.4	10.9	59.4
SUNDAY							
10 00	176 26.9	S14 21.8	181 59.7	8.7	S10 52.5	10.9	59.4
01	191 26.9	21.0	196 27.4	8.9	10 41.6	10.9	59.4
02	206 26.9	20.2	210 55.3	8.9	10 30.7	11.0	59.3
03	221 26.9	.. 19.4	225 23.2	9.0	10 19.7	11.1	59.3
04	236 26.9	18.6	239 51.2	9.0	10 08.6	11.1	59.3
05	251 26.9	17.8	254 19.2	9.1	9 57.5	11.2	59.3
06	266 26.9	S14 17.0	268 47.3	9.2	S 9 46.3	11.2	59.2
07	281 26.9	16.1	283 15.5	9.2	9 35.1	11.3	59.2
08	296 26.8	15.3	297 43.7	9.3	9 23.8	11.3	59.2
09	311 26.8	.. 14.5	312 12.0	9.4	9 12.5	11.3	59.2
10	326 26.8	13.7	326 40.4	9.4	9 01.2	11.4	59.2
11	341 26.8	12.9	341 08.8	9.5	8 49.8	11.4	59.1
12	356 26.8	S14 12.1	355 37.3	9.5	S 8 38.4	11.5	59.1
13	11 26.8	11.2	10 05.8	9.6	8 26.9	11.5	59.1
14	26 26.8	10.4	24 34.4	9.7	8 15.4	11.6	59.1
15	41 26.8	.. 09.6	39 03.1	9.7	8 03.8	11.6	59.0
16	56 26.8	08.8	53 31.8	9.8	7 52.2	11.6	59.0
17	71 26.8	08.0	68 00.6	9.9	7 40.6	11.6	59.0
18	86 26.8	S14 07.2	82 29.5	9.9	S 7 29.0	11.7	59.0
19	101 26.8	06.3	96 58.4	10.0	7 17.3	11.7	58.9
20	116 26.8	05.5	111 27.4	10.0	7 05.6	11.7	58.9
21	131 26.8	.. 04.7	125 56.4	10.1	6 53.9	11.8	58.9
22	146 26.8	03.9	140 25.5	10.2	6 42.1	11.8	58.8
23	161 26.8	03.0	154 54.7	10.2	6 30.3	11.8	58.8
MONDAY							
11 00	176 26.8	S14 02.2	169 23.9	10.3	S 6 18.5	11.9	58.8
01	191 26.8	01.4	183 53.2	10.3	6 06.6	11.8	58.8
02	206 26.8	14 00.6	198 22.5	10.4	5 54.8	11.9	58.7
03	221 26.8	13 59.8	212 51.9	10.4	5 42.9	11.9	58.7
04	236 26.8	58.9	227 21.3	10.5	5 31.0	11.9	58.7
05	251 26.8	58.1	241 50.8	10.6	5 19.1	12.0	58.6
06	266 26.8	S13 57.3	256 20.4	10.6	S 5 07.1	11.9	58.6
07	281 26.8	56.5	270 50.0	10.6	4 55.2	12.0	58.6
08	296 26.8	55.6	285 19.6	10.7	4 43.2	11.9	58.6
09	311 26.8	.. 54.8	299 49.3	10.8	4 31.3	12.0	58.5
10	326 26.8	54.0	314 19.1	10.8	4 19.3	12.0	58.5
11	341 26.8	53.2	328 48.9	10.9	4 07.3	12.0	58.5
12	356 26.8	S13 52.3	343 18.8	10.9	S 3 55.3	12.1	58.4
13	11 26.8	51.5	357 48.7	11.0	3 43.2	12.0	58.4
14	26 26.8	50.7	12 18.7	11.0	3 31.2	12.0	58.4
15	41 26.8	.. 49.9	26 48.7	11.0	3 19.2	12.0	58.3
16	56 26.8	49.0	41 18.7	11.2	3 07.2	12.1	58.3
17	71 26.8	48.2	55 48.9	11.1	2 55.1	12.0	58.3
18	86 26.8	S13 47.4	70 19.0	11.2	S 2 43.1	12.0	58.3
19	101 26.8	46.5	84 49.2	11.3	2 31.1	12.1	58.2
20	116 26.8	45.7	99 19.5	11.3	2 19.0	12.0	58.2
21	131 26.8	.. 44.9	113 49.8	11.3	2 07.0	12.0	58.2
22	146 26.8	44.0	128 20.1	11.4	1 55.0	12.1	58.1
23	161 26.8	43.2	142 50.5	11.4	S 1 42.9	12.0	58.1
SD	16.2	d 0.8	SD 16.2		16.1		15.9

Twilight / Sunrise / Moonrise

Lat.	Naut.	Civil	Sunrise	Moonrise 9	10	11	12
N 72	06 35	07 57	09 23	08 33	08 14	07 59	07 47
N 70	06 31	07 44	08 57	08 07	07 59	07 53	07 47
68	06 27	07 34	08 38	07 47	07 48	07 47	07 47
66	06 24	07 25	08 23	07 31	07 38	07 43	07 47
64	06 22	07 18	08 11	07 18	07 30	07 39	07 47
62	06 19	07 12	08 00	07 06	07 23	07 35	07 47
60	06 17	07 06	07 51	06 57	07 16	07 32	07 47
N 58	06 15	07 01	07 43	06 49	07 11	07 30	07 47
56	06 13	06 57	07 36	06 41	07 06	07 27	07 47
54	06 11	06 53	07 30	06 34	07 02	07 25	07 47
52	06 09	06 49	07 24	06 29	06 58	07 23	07 47
50	06 07	06 45	07 19	06 23	06 54	07 21	07 46
45	06 03	06 38	07 08	06 11	06 46	07 18	07 46
N 40	05 59	06 31	06 59	06 02	06 40	07 14	07 46
35	05 55	06 25	06 51	05 53	06 34	07 11	07 46
30	05 51	06 19	06 44	05 46	06 29	07 09	07 46
20	05 43	06 09	06 32	05 33	06 21	07 05	07 46
N 10	05 34	05 59	06 21	05 22	06 13	07 01	07 46
0	05 25	05 49	06 11	05 11	06 06	06 57	07 46
S 10	05 13	05 39	06 00	05 01	05 58	06 54	07 46
20	04 59	05 26	05 49	04 50	05 51	06 50	07 46
30	04 41	05 11	05 36	04 37	05 42	06 45	07 47
35	04 30	05 02	05 29	04 29	05 37	06 43	07 47
40	04 16	04 51	05 20	04 21	05 31	06 40	07 47
45	03 58	04 38	05 10	04 11	05 24	06 37	07 47
S 50	03 36	04 22	04 58	03 58	05 16	06 33	07 47
52	03 24	04 14	04 52	03 53	05 12	06 31	07 47
54	03 11	04 05	04 46	03 47	05 08	06 29	07 47
56	02 56	03 55	04 39	03 40	05 04	06 27	07 47
58	02 36	03 43	04 31	03 32	04 59	06 24	07 47
S 60	02 12	03 30	04 22	03 23	04 53	06 21	07 47

Sunset / Twilight / Moonset

Lat.	Sunset	Civil	Naut.	Moonset 9	10	11	12
N 72	15 07	16 33	17 56	14 36	16 47	18 47	20 41
N 70	15 32	16 46	17 59	15 01	16 59	18 51	20 37
68	15 51	16 56	18 03	15 19	17 09	18 54	20 35
66	16 06	17 04	18 06	15 34	17 17	18 56	20 32
64	16 19	17 11	18 08	15 46	17 24	18 59	20 30
62	16 29	17 18	18 10	15 56	17 30	19 01	20 28
60	16 38	17 23	18 13	16 05	17 35	19 02	20 27
N 58	16 46	17 28	18 15	16 12	17 39	19 04	20 26
56	16 53	17 33	18 17	16 19	17 43	19 05	20 24
54	16 59	17 37	18 18	16 25	17 47	19 06	20 23
52	17 05	17 40	18 20	16 30	17 50	19 07	20 22
50	17 10	17 44	18 22	16 35	17 53	19 08	20 21
45	17 21	17 51	18 26	16 46	17 59	19 10	20 19
N 40	17 30	17 58	18 30	16 54	18 04	19 12	20 18
35	17 38	18 04	18 34	17 02	18 09	19 14	20 16
30	17 45	18 09	18 38	17 08	18 12	19 15	20 15
20	17 57	18 20	18 46	17 19	18 19	19 17	20 13
N 10	18 08	18 29	18 54	17 29	18 25	19 19	20 11
0	18 18	18 39	19 04	17 38	18 30	19 21	20 09
S 10	18 28	18 50	19 15	17 46	18 36	19 23	20 07
20	18 39	19 02	19 29	17 56	18 42	19 24	20 06
30	18 52	19 17	19 47	18 07	18 48	19 27	20 03
35	18 59	19 26	19 58	18 13	18 52	19 28	20 02
40	19 07	19 37	20 12	18 20	18 56	19 29	20 01
45	19 17	19 49	20 29	18 28	19 01	19 31	19 59
S 50	19 30	20 06	20 51	18 37	19 06	19 32	19 57
52	19 35	20 13	21 02	18 42	19 09	19 33	19 56
54	19 41	20 22	21 15	18 47	19 12	19 34	19 55
56	19 48	20 32	21 30	18 52	19 15	19 35	19 54
58	19 56	20 43	21 49	18 58	19 18	19 36	19 53
S 60	20 05	20 56	22 13	19 05	19 22	19 37	19 51

SUN / MOON

Day	Eqn. of Time 00h	12h	Mer. Pass.	Mer. Pass. Upper	Lower	Age	Phase
9	14 11	14 12	12 14	11 25	23 52	29	1
10	14 12	14 13	12 14	12 18	24 44	00	0
11	14 13	14 13	12 14	13 09	00 44	01	2

UT	ARIES	VENUS −3.9		MARS +1.2		JUPITER −2.4		SATURN +0.5		STARS		
	GHA	GHA	Dec	GHA	Dec	GHA	Dec	GHA	Dec	Name	SHA	Dec
d h	° ′	° ′	° ′	° ′	° ′	° ′	° ′	° ′	° ′		° ′	° ′
12 00	142 12.5	187 04.9	S18 00.4	162 20.1	S 9 31.9	77 22.1	N20 52.1	282 21.8	S12 54.1	Acamar	315 18.6	S40 15.4
01	157 15.0	202 04.2	17 59.6	177 20.7	31.1	92 24.4	52.2	297 24.2	54.1	Achernar	335 27.2	S57 10.5
02	172 17.4	217 03.4	58.8	192 21.3	30.4	107 26.8	52.2	312 26.6	54.1	Acrux	173 08.9	S63 10.2
03	187 19.9	232 02.7	.. 58.0	207 21.9	.. 29.6	122 29.2	.. 52.2	327 29.1	.. 54.1	Adhara	255 12.4	S28 59.7
04	202 22.3	247 02.0	57.2	222 22.5	28.8	137 31.5	52.3	342 31.5	54.1	Aldebaran	290 49.5	N16 32.0
05	217 24.8	262 01.3	56.4	237 23.2	28.1	152 33.9	52.3	357 33.9	54.1			
06	232 27.3	277 00.6	S17 55.5	252 23.8	S 9 27.3	167 36.2	N20 52.3	12 36.4	S12 54.1	Alioth	166 20.5	N55 53.0
07	247 29.7	291 59.9	54.7	267 24.4	26.6	182 38.6	52.3	27 38.8	54.1	Alkaid	152 58.9	N49 14.5
T 08	262 32.2	306 59.2	53.9	282 25.0	25.8	197 40.9	52.4	42 41.2	54.1	Al Na'ir	27 44.5	S46 53.8
U 09	277 34.7	321 58.5	.. 53.1	297 25.6	.. 25.1	212 43.3	.. 52.4	57 43.7	.. 54.1	Alnilam	275 46.4	S 1 11.9
E 10	292 37.1	336 57.7	52.3	312 26.2	24.3	227 45.6	52.4	72 46.1	54.1	Alphard	217 56.0	S 8 43.2
S 11	307 39.6	351 57.0	51.5	327 26.9	23.6	242 48.0	52.4	87 48.5	54.1			
D 12	322 42.1	6 56.3	S17 50.6	342 27.5	S 9 22.8	257 50.3	N20 52.5	102 51.0	S12 54.1	Alphecca	126 11.2	N26 40.0
A 13	337 44.5	21 55.6	49.8	357 28.1	22.1	272 52.7	52.5	117 53.4	54.1	Alpheratz	357 44.0	N29 09.9
Y 14	352 47.0	36 54.9	49.0	12 28.7	21.3	287 55.0	52.5	132 55.8	54.1	Altair	62 08.7	N 8 54.2
15	7 49.5	51 54.2	.. 48.2	27 29.3	.. 20.6	302 57.4	.. 52.6	147 58.3	.. 54.1	Ankaa	353 16.2	S42 14.2
16	22 51.9	66 53.5	47.3	42 29.9	19.8	317 59.7	52.6	163 00.7	54.1	Antares	112 26.6	S26 27.5
17	37 54.4	81 52.8	46.5	57 30.6	19.1	333 02.1	52.6	178 03.1	54.1			
18	52 56.8	96 52.1	S17 45.7	72 31.2	S 9 18.3	348 04.4	N20 52.6	193 05.6	S12 54.1	Arcturus	145 55.8	N19 06.6
19	67 59.3	111 51.4	44.9	87 31.8	17.5	3 06.8	52.7	208 08.0	54.1	Atria	107 28.8	S69 02.7
20	83 01.8	126 50.7	44.0	102 32.4	16.8	18 09.1	52.7	223 10.4	54.0	Avior	234 17.5	S59 33.4
21	98 04.2	141 50.0	.. 43.2	117 33.0	.. 16.0	33 11.5	.. 52.7	238 12.9	.. 54.0	Bellatrix	278 32.1	N 6 21.5
22	113 06.7	156 49.3	42.4	132 33.7	15.3	48 13.8	52.7	253 15.3	54.0	Betelgeuse	271 01.3	N 7 24.3
23	128 09.2	171 48.6	41.5	147 34.3	14.5	63 16.2	52.8	268 17.7	54.0			
13 00	143 11.6	186 47.9	S17 40.7	162 34.9	S 9 13.8	78 18.5	N20 52.8	283 20.2	S12 54.0	Canopus	263 55.9	S52 42.6
01	158 14.1	201 47.1	39.9	177 35.5	13.0	93 20.8	52.8	298 22.6	54.0	Capella	280 34.5	N46 00.7
02	173 16.6	216 46.4	39.1	192 36.1	12.3	108 23.2	52.9	313 25.1	54.0	Deneb	49 32.1	N45 19.7
03	188 19.0	231 45.7	.. 38.2	207 36.7	.. 11.5	123 25.5	.. 52.9	328 27.5	.. 54.0	Denebola	182 33.6	N14 29.7
04	203 21.5	246 45.0	37.4	222 37.4	10.8	138 27.9	52.9	343 29.9	54.0	Diphda	348 56.3	S17 55.0
05	218 23.9	261 44.3	36.5	237 38.0	10.0	153 30.2	52.9	358 32.4	54.0			
06	233 26.4	276 43.6	S17 35.7	252 38.6	S 9 09.2	168 32.6	N20 53.0	13 34.8	S12 54.0	Dubhe	193 51.4	N61 40.5
W 07	248 28.9	291 42.9	34.9	267 39.2	08.5	183 34.9	53.0	28 37.2	54.0	Elnath	278 12.7	N28 37.0
E 08	263 31.3	306 42.2	34.0	282 39.8	07.7	198 37.3	53.0	43 39.7	54.0	Eltanin	90 46.5	N51 29.1
D 09	278 33.8	321 41.5	.. 33.2	297 40.5	.. 07.0	213 39.6	.. 53.1	58 42.1	.. 54.0	Enif	33 47.6	N 9 56.2
N 10	293 36.3	336 40.8	32.4	312 41.1	06.2	228 41.9	53.1	73 44.6	54.0	Fomalhaut	15 24.6	S29 33.2
E 11	308 38.7	351 40.1	31.5	327 41.7	05.5	243 44.3	53.1	88 47.0	54.0			
S 12	323 41.2	6 39.5	S17 30.7	342 42.3	S 9 04.7	258 46.6	N20 53.1	103 49.4	S12 54.0	Gacrux	172 00.7	S57 11.1
D 13	338 43.7	21 38.8	29.8	357 42.9	03.9	273 49.0	53.2	118 51.9	54.0	Gienah	175 52.2	S17 37.0
A 14	353 46.1	36 38.1	29.0	12 43.6	03.2	288 51.3	53.2	133 54.3	54.0	Hadar	148 47.9	S60 26.0
Y 15	8 48.6	51 37.4	.. 28.1	27 44.2	.. 02.4	303 53.7	.. 53.2	148 56.8	.. 54.0	Hamal	328 01.1	N23 31.5
16	23 51.1	66 36.7	27.3	42 44.8	01.7	318 56.0	53.3	163 59.2	54.0	Kaus Aust.	83 44.4	S34 22.5
17	38 53.5	81 36.0	26.4	57 45.4	00.9	333 58.3	53.3	179 01.6	54.0			
18	53 56.0	96 35.3	S17 25.6	72 46.1	S 9 00.2	349 00.7	N20 53.3	194 04.1	S12 54.0	Kochab	137 19.9	N74 05.8
19	68 58.4	111 34.6	24.8	87 46.7	8 59.4	4 03.0	53.4	209 06.5	54.0	Markab	13 38.8	N15 16.6
20	84 00.9	126 33.9	23.9	102 47.3	58.6	19 05.4	53.4	224 09.0	54.0	Menkar	314 15.3	N 4 08.3
21	99 03.4	141 33.2	.. 23.1	117 47.9	.. 57.9	34 07.7	.. 53.4	239 11.4	.. 54.0	Menkent	148 07.7	S36 26.0
22	114 05.8	156 32.5	22.2	132 48.5	57.1	49 10.0	53.4	254 13.8	54.0	Miaplacidus	221 38.7	S69 46.5
23	129 08.3	171 31.8	21.4	147 49.2	56.4	64 12.4	53.5	269 16.3	54.0			
14 00	144 10.8	186 31.1	S17 20.5	162 49.8	S 8 55.6	79 14.7	N20 53.5	284 18.7	S12 54.0	Mirfak	308 40.6	N49 54.6
01	159 13.2	201 30.4	19.7	177 50.4	54.9	94 17.0	53.5	299 21.2	54.0	Nunki	75 58.9	S26 16.7
02	174 15.7	216 29.7	18.8	192 51.0	54.1	109 19.4	53.6	314 23.6	54.0	Peacock	53 20.1	S56 41.4
03	189 18.2	231 29.1	.. 17.9	207 51.7	.. 53.3	124 21.7	.. 53.6	329 26.0	.. 54.0	Pollux	243 27.7	N27 59.5
04	204 20.6	246 28.4	17.1	222 52.3	52.6	139 24.1	53.6	344 28.5	54.0	Procyon	244 59.7	N 5 11.2
05	219 23.1	261 27.7	16.2	237 52.9	51.8	154 26.4	53.6	359 30.9	54.0			
06	234 25.6	276 27.0	S17 15.4	252 53.5	S 8 51.1	169 28.7	N20 53.7	14 33.4	S12 54.0	Rasalhague	96 06.8	N12 33.0
07	249 28.0	291 26.3	14.5	267 54.1	50.3	184 31.1	53.7	29 35.8	54.0	Regulus	207 43.4	N11 53.9
T 08	264 30.5	306 25.6	13.7	282 54.8	49.5	199 33.4	53.7	44 38.3	53.9	Rigel	281 12.1	S 8 11.5
H 09	279 32.9	321 24.9	.. 12.8	297 55.4	.. 48.8	214 35.7	.. 53.8	59 40.7	.. 53.9	Rigil Kent.	139 51.8	S60 53.1
U 10	294 35.4	336 24.2	11.9	312 56.0	48.0	229 38.1	53.8	74 43.1	53.9	Sabik	102 12.9	S15 44.4
R 11	309 37.9	351 23.6	11.1	327 56.6	47.3	244 40.4	53.8	89 45.6	53.9			
S 12	324 40.3	6 22.9	S17 10.2	342 57.3	S 8 46.5	259 42.7	N20 53.9	104 48.0	S12 53.9	Schedar	349 41.1	N56 36.8
D 13	339 42.8	21 22.2	09.3	357 57.9	45.7	274 45.1	53.9	119 50.5	53.9	Shaula	96 22.4	S37 06.6
A 14	354 45.3	36 21.5	08.5	12 58.5	45.0	289 47.4	53.9	134 52.9	53.9	Sirius	258 33.6	S16 44.4
Y 15	9 47.7	51 20.8	.. 07.6	27 59.1	.. 44.2	304 49.7	.. 53.9	149 55.4	.. 53.9	Spica	158 31.3	S11 13.9
16	24 50.2	66 20.1	06.8	42 59.8	43.5	319 52.1	54.0	164 57.8	53.9	Suhail	222 52.1	S43 29.4
17	39 52.7	81 19.5	05.9	58 00.4	42.7	334 54.4	54.0	180 00.2	53.9			
18	54 55.1	96 18.8	S17 05.0	73 01.0	S 8 41.9	349 56.7	N20 54.0	195 02.7	S12 53.9	Vega	80 39.4	N38 47.7
19	69 57.6	111 18.1	04.2	88 01.6	41.2	4 59.1	54.1	210 05.1	53.9	Zuben'ubi	137 05.6	S16 05.8
20	85 00.0	126 17.4	03.3	103 02.3	40.4	20 01.4	54.1	225 07.6	53.9		SHA	Mer. Pass.
21	100 02.5	141 16.7	.. 02.4	118 02.9	.. 39.7	35 03.7	.. 54.1	240 10.0	.. 53.9		° ′	h m
22	115 05.0	156 16.1	01.5	133 03.5	38.9	50 06.1	54.2	255 12.5	53.9	Venus	43 36.2	11 33
23	130 07.4	171 15.4	00.7	148 04.1	38.1	65 08.4	54.2	270 14.9	53.9	Mars	19 23.3	13 09
	h m									Jupiter	295 06.9	18 44
Mer. Pass. 14 24.9		v −0.7	d 0.8	v 0.6	d 0.8	v 2.3	d 0.0	v 2.4	d 0.0	Saturn	140 08.6	5 06

UT	SUN		MOON					Lat.	Twilight		Sunrise	Moonrise			
									Naut.	Civil		12	13	14	15
	GHA	Dec	GHA	v	Dec	d	HP	°	h m	h m	h m	h m	h m	h m	h m
d h	° '	° '	° '	'	° '	'	'	N 72	06 22	07 43	09 04	07 47	07 35	07 22	07 07
12 00	176 26.8	S13 42.4	157 20.9	11.5	S 1 30.9	12.0	58.1	N 70	06 20	07 32	08 43	07 47	07 41	07 36	07 30
01	191 26.8	41.6	171 51.4	11.5	1 18.9	12.0	58.0	68	06 17	07 23	08 26	07 47	07 46	07 46	07 47
02	206 26.8	40.7	186 21.9	11.6	1 06.9	12.0	58.0	66	06 15	07 16	08 12	07 47	07 51	07 55	08 01
03	221 26.8	39.9	200 52.5	11.6	0 54.9	12.0	58.0	64	06 13	07 09	08 01	07 47	07 54	08 03	08 13
04	236 26.8	39.1	215 23.1	11.6	0 42.9	12.0	57.9	62	06 12	07 04	07 51	07 47	07 58	08 09	08 23
05	251 26.8	38.2	229 53.7	11.7	0 30.9	11.9	57.9	60	06 10	06 59	07 43	07 47	08 00	08 15	08 31
06	266 26.9	S13 37.4	244 24.4	11.7	S 0 19.0	12.0	57.9	N 58	06 08	06 54	07 36	07 47	08 03	08 20	08 39
07	281 26.9	36.6	258 55.1	11.8	S 0 07.0	11.9	57.8	56	06 07	06 50	07 30	07 47	08 05	08 24	08 45
08	296 26.9	35.7	273 25.9	11.7	N 0 04.9	12.0	57.8	54	06 06	06 47	07 24	07 47	08 07	08 28	08 51
T 09	311 26.9	34.9	287 56.6	11.9	0 16.9	11.9	57.8	52	06 04	06 44	07 19	07 47	08 09	08 32	08 57
U 10	326 26.9	34.1	302 27.5	11.8	0 28.8	11.8	57.7	50	06 03	06 40	07 14	07 46	08 11	08 35	09 02
E 11	341 26.9	33.2	316 58.3	11.9	0 40.6	11.9	57.7	45	05 59	06 33	07 04	07 46	08 14	08 43	09 12
S 12	356 26.9	S13 32.4	331 29.2	12.0	N 0 52.5	11.9	57.7	N 40	05 56	06 27	06 55	07 46	08 17	08 49	09 21
D 13	11 26.9	31.5	346 00.2	11.9	1 04.4	11.8	57.6	35	05 52	06 22	06 48	07 46	08 20	08 54	09 29
A 14	26 26.9	30.7	0 31.1	12.0	1 16.2	11.8	57.6	30	05 49	06 17	06 42	07 46	08 23	08 59	09 35
Y 15	41 26.9	29.9	15 02.1	12.1	1 28.0	11.8	57.6	20	05 42	06 08	06 30	07 46	08 27	09 07	09 47
16	56 26.9	29.0	29 33.2	12.0	1 39.8	11.8	57.5	N 10	05 34	05 59	06 20	07 46	08 30	09 14	09 57
17	71 27.0	28.2	44 04.2	12.1	1 51.6	11.7	57.5	0	05 25	05 50	06 11	07 46	08 34	09 21	10 07
18	86 27.0	S13 27.4	58 35.3	12.2	N 2 03.3	11.7	57.5	S 10	05 14	05 40	06 01	07 46	08 38	09 28	10 17
19	101 27.0	26.5	73 06.5	12.1	2 15.0	11.7	57.4	20	05 01	05 28	05 51	07 46	08 41	09 35	10 27
20	116 27.0	25.7	87 37.6	12.2	2 26.7	11.7	57.4	30	04 44	05 14	05 39	07 47	08 45	09 43	10 39
21	131 27.0	24.8	102 08.8	12.2	2 38.4	11.6	57.4	35	04 33	05 05	05 32	07 47	08 48	09 48	10 46
22	146 27.0	24.0	116 40.0	12.3	2 50.0	11.6	57.3	40	04 20	04 55	05 24	07 47	08 51	09 54	10 54
23	161 27.0	23.2	131 11.3	12.3	3 01.6	11.6	57.3	45	04 04	04 43	05 15	07 47	08 55	10 00	11 04
13 00	176 27.0	S13 22.3	145 42.6	12.3	N 3 13.2	11.5	57.3	S 50	03 43	04 27	05 03	07 47	08 59	10 08	11 15
01	191 27.1	21.5	160 13.9	12.3	3 24.7	11.6	57.2	52	03 32	04 20	04 58	07 47	09 01	10 12	11 20
02	206 27.1	20.6	174 45.2	12.3	3 36.3	11.4	57.2	54	03 20	04 12	04 52	07 47	09 03	10 16	11 26
03	221 27.1	19.8	189 16.5	12.4	3 47.7	11.5	57.2	56	03 06	04 03	04 46	07 47	09 05	10 20	11 33
04	236 27.1	19.0	203 47.9	12.4	3 59.2	11.4	57.1	58	02 48	03 52	04 38	07 47	09 07	10 25	11 40
05	251 27.1	18.1	218 19.3	12.4	4 10.6	11.4	57.1	S 60	02 26	03 39	04 30	07 47	09 10	10 31	11 48

UT	SUN		MOON					Lat.	Sunset	Twilight		Moonset			
										Civil	Naut.	12	13	14	15
	GHA	Dec	GHA	v	Dec	d	HP	°	h m	h m	h m	h m	h m	h m	h m
06	266 27.1	S13 17.3	232 50.7	12.5	N 4 22.0	11.3	57.1	N 72	15 26	16 47	18 08	20 41	22 33	24 25	00 25
W 07	281 27.1	16.4	247 22.2	12.5	4 33.3	11.3	57.0	N 70	15 47	16 58	18 11	20 37	22 24	24 04	00 04
E 08	296 27.2	15.6	261 53.7	12.4	4 44.6	11.3	57.0	68	16 04	17 07	18 13	20 35	22 12	23 48	25 23
D 09	311 27.2	14.7	276 25.1	12.6	4 55.9	11.2	57.0	66	16 17	17 14	18 15	20 32	22 05	23 35	25 03
N 10	326 27.2	13.9	290 56.7	12.5	5 07.1	11.2	56.9	64	16 29	17 20	18 16	20 30	21 59	23 25	24 47
E 11	341 27.2	13.0	305 28.2	12.5	5 18.3	11.2	56.9	62	16 38	17 26	18 18	20 28	21 53	23 16	24 35
S 12	356 27.2	S13 12.2	319 59.7	12.6	N 5 29.5	11.1	56.9	60	16 46	17 31	18 20	20 27	21 49	23 08	24 24
D 13	11 27.3	11.4	334 31.3	12.6	5 40.6	11.1	56.8	N 58	16 53	17 35	18 21	20 26	21 45	23 01	24 14
A 14	26 27.3	10.5	349 02.9	12.6	5 51.7	11.0	56.8	56	17 00	17 39	18 23	20 24	21 41	22 55	24 06
Y 15	41 27.3	09.7	3 34.5	12.6	6 02.7	11.0	56.8	54	17 05	17 42	18 24	20 23	21 38	22 50	23 59
16	56 27.3	08.8	18 06.1	12.7	6 13.7	10.9	56.7	52	17 10	17 46	18 25	20 22	21 35	22 45	23 52
17	71 27.3	08.0	32 37.8	12.6	6 24.6	10.9	56.7	50	17 15	17 49	18 27	20 21	21 32	22 40	23 46
18	86 27.3	S13 07.1	47 09.4	12.7	N 6 35.5	10.9	56.7	45	17 25	17 56	18 30	20 19	21 26	22 31	23 33
19	101 27.4	06.3	61 41.1	12.7	6 46.4	10.8	56.6	N 40	17 34	18 01	18 33	20 18	21 21	22 23	23 23
20	116 27.4	05.4	76 12.8	12.7	6 57.2	10.8	56.6	35	17 41	18 07	18 37	20 16	21 17	22 16	23 14
21	131 27.4	04.6	90 44.5	12.7	7 08.0	10.7	56.6	30	17 47	18 12	18 40	20 15	21 14	22 10	23 06
22	146 27.4	03.7	105 16.2	12.7	7 18.7	10.6	56.5	20	17 57	18 21	18 47	20 13	21 07	22 00	22 52
23	161 27.4	02.9	119 47.9	12.8	7 29.3	10.6	56.5	N 10	18 08	18 30	18 55	20 11	21 02	21 51	22 41
14 00	176 27.5	S13 02.0	134 19.7	12.7	N 7 39.9	10.6	56.5	0	18 18	18 39	19 03	20 09	20 56	21 43	22 30
01	191 27.5	01.2	148 51.4	12.8	7 50.5	10.5	56.5	S 10	18 27	18 49	19 14	20 07	20 51	21 35	22 19
02	206 27.5	13 00.3	163 23.2	12.8	8 01.0	10.5	56.4	20	18 37	19 00	19 27	20 06	20 46	21 27	22 07
03	221 27.5	12 59.5	177 55.0	12.7	8 11.5	10.4	56.4	30	18 49	19 14	19 44	20 03	20 39	21 16	21 53
04	236 27.6	58.6	192 26.7	12.8	8 21.9	10.4	56.4	35	18 56	19 23	19 54	20 02	20 36	21 10	21 46
05	251 27.6	57.8	206 58.5	12.8	8 32.3	10.3	56.3	40	19 04	19 33	20 07	20 01	20 32	21 03	21 37
06	266 27.6	S12 56.9	221 30.3	12.9	N 8 42.6	10.2	56.3	45	19 13	19 45	20 23	19 59	20 27	20 56	21 27
07	281 27.6	56.1	236 02.2	12.8	8 52.8	10.2	56.3	S 50	19 24	20 00	20 44	19 57	20 21	20 47	21 14
T 08	296 27.7	55.2	250 34.0	12.8	9 03.0	10.2	56.2	52	19 29	20 07	20 55	19 56	20 19	20 43	21 09
H 09	311 27.7	54.4	265 05.8	12.8	9 13.2	10.1	56.2	54	19 35	20 15	21 06	19 55	20 16	20 38	21 02
U 10	326 27.7	53.5	279 37.6	12.9	9 23.3	10.0	56.2	56	19 41	20 24	21 20	19 54	20 13	20 33	20 55
R 11	341 27.7	52.7	294 09.5	12.8	9 33.3	10.0	56.1	58	19 49	20 34	21 37	19 53	20 09	20 27	20 47
S 12	356 27.7	S12 51.8	308 41.3	12.9	N 9 43.3	9.9	56.1	S 60	19 57	20 47	21 58	19 51	20 05	20 21	20 39
D 13	11 27.8	51.0	323 13.2	12.8	9 53.2	9.9	56.1								
A 14	26 27.8	50.1	337 45.0	12.9	10 03.1	9.8	56.0			SUN			MOON		
Y 15	41 27.8	49.2	352 16.9	12.9	10 12.9	9.7	56.0	Day	Eqn. of Time		Mer.	Mer. Pass.		Age	Phase
16	56 27.9	48.4	6 48.8	12.8	10 22.6	9.7	56.0		00ʰ	12ʰ	Pass.	Upper	Lower		
17	71 27.9	47.5	21 20.6	12.9	10 32.3	9.6	56.0	d	m s	m s	h m	h m	h m	d	%
18	86 27.9	S12 46.7	35 52.5	12.9	N10 41.9	9.6	55.9	12	14 13	14 12	12 14	13 58	01 34	02	6
19	101 27.9	45.8	50 24.4	12.8	10 51.5	9.5	55.9	13	14 12	14 11	12 14	14 45	02 22	03	12
20	116 28.0	45.0	64 56.2	12.9	11 01.0	9.4	55.9	14	14 10	14 09	12 14	15 32	03 09	04	20
21	131 28.0	44.1	79 28.1	12.9	11 10.4	9.4	55.8								
22	146 28.0	43.3	94 00.0	12.9	11 19.8	9.3	55.8								
23	161 28.0	42.4	108 31.9	12.9	N11 29.1	9.3	55.8								
	SD 16.2	d 0.8	SD 15.7		15.5		15.3									

UT	ARIES GHA	VENUS −3.9 GHA	Dec	MARS +1.2 GHA	Dec	JUPITER −2.4 GHA	Dec	SATURN +0.5 GHA	Dec	Name	SHA	Dec
15 00	145 09.9	186 14.7	S16 59.8	163 04.8	S 8 37.4	80 10.7	N20 54.2	285 17.4	S12 53.9	Acamar	315 18.6	S40 15.4
01	160 12.4	201 14.0	58.9	178 05.4	36.6	95 13.0	54.3	300 19.8	53.9	Achernar	335 27.3	S57 10.5
02	175 14.8	216 13.3	58.1	193 06.0	35.9	110 15.4	54.3	315 22.2	53.9	Acrux	173 08.9	S63 10.3
03	190 17.3	231 12.7	.. 57.2	208 06.6	.. 35.1	125 17.7	.. 54.3	330 24.7	.. 53.9	Adhara	255 12.4	S28 59.8
04	205 19.8	246 12.0	56.3	223 07.3	34.3	140 20.0	54.3	345 27.1	53.9	Aldebaran	290 49.5	N16 32.0
05	220 22.2	261 11.3	55.4	238 07.9	33.6	155 22.4	54.4	0 29.6	53.9			
06	235 24.7	276 10.6	S16 54.5	253 08.5	S 8 32.8	170 24.7	N20 54.4	15 32.0	S12 53.9	Alioth	166 20.5	N55 53.0
07	250 27.2	291 10.0	53.7	268 09.1	32.0	185 27.0	54.4	30 34.5	53.8	Alkaid	152 58.8	N49 14.5
08	265 29.6	306 09.3	52.8	283 09.8	31.3	200 29.3	54.5	45 36.9	53.8	Al Na'ir	27 44.5	S46 53.8
F 09	280 32.1	321 08.6	.. 51.9	298 10.4	.. 30.5	215 31.7	.. 54.5	60 39.4	.. 53.8	Alnilam	275 46.4	S 1 11.9
R 10	295 34.5	336 07.9	51.0	313 11.0	29.8	230 34.0	54.5	75 41.8	53.8	Alphard	217 56.0	S 8 43.2
I 11	310 37.0	351 07.3	50.1	328 11.7	29.0	245 36.3	54.6	90 44.3	53.8			
D 12	325 39.5	6 06.6	S16 49.3	343 12.3	S 8 28.2	260 38.6	N20 54.6	105 46.7	S12 53.8	Alphecca	126 11.2	N26 40.0
A 13	340 41.9	21 05.9	48.4	358 12.9	27.5	275 41.0	54.6	120 49.2	53.8	Alpheratz	357 44.0	N29 09.9
Y 14	355 44.4	36 05.3	47.5	13 13.5	26.7	290 43.3	54.7	135 51.6	53.8	Altair	62 08.7	N 8 54.2
15	10 46.9	51 04.6	.. 46.6	28 14.2	.. 25.9	305 45.6	.. 54.7	150 54.0	.. 53.8	Ankaa	353 16.2	S42 14.2
16	25 49.3	66 03.9	45.7	43 14.8	25.2	320 47.9	54.7	165 56.5	53.8	Antares	112 26.6	S26 27.5
17	40 51.8	81 03.2	44.8	58 15.4	24.4	335 50.3	54.8	180 58.9	53.8			
18	55 54.3	96 02.6	S16 44.0	73 16.1	S 8 23.7	350 52.6	N20 54.8	196 01.4	S12 53.8	Arcturus	145 55.8	N19 06.6
19	70 56.7	111 01.9	43.1	88 16.7	22.9	5 54.9	54.8	211 03.8	53.8	Atria	107 28.7	S69 02.7
20	85 59.2	126 01.2	42.2	103 17.3	22.1	20 57.2	54.8	226 06.3	53.8	Avior	234 17.5	S59 33.4
21	101 01.6	141 00.6	.. 41.3	118 17.9	.. 21.4	35 59.6	.. 54.9	241 08.7	.. 53.8	Bellatrix	278 32.1	N 6 21.5
22	116 04.1	155 59.9	40.4	133 18.6	20.6	51 01.9	54.9	256 11.2	53.8	Betelgeuse	271 01.3	N 7 24.3
23	131 06.6	170 59.2	39.5	148 19.2	19.8	66 04.2	54.9	271 13.6	53.8			
16 00	146 09.0	185 58.6	S16 38.6	163 19.8	S 8 19.1	81 06.5	N20 55.0	286 16.1	S12 53.8	Canopus	263 55.9	S52 42.6
01	161 11.5	200 57.9	37.7	178 20.5	18.3	96 08.8	55.0	301 18.5	53.7	Capella	280 34.5	N46 00.7
02	176 14.0	215 57.2	36.8	193 21.1	17.5	111 11.2	55.0	316 21.0	53.7	Deneb	49 32.0	N45 19.7
03	191 16.4	230 56.6	.. 35.9	208 21.7	.. 16.8	126 13.5	.. 55.1	331 23.4	.. 53.7	Denebola	182 33.6	N14 29.7
04	206 18.9	245 55.9	35.0	223 22.3	16.0	141 15.8	55.1	346 25.9	53.7	Diphda	348 56.3	S17 55.0
05	221 21.4	260 55.2	34.1	238 23.0	15.2	156 18.1	55.1	1 28.3	53.7			
06	236 23.8	275 54.6	S16 33.2	253 23.6	S 8 14.5	171 20.4	N20 55.2	16 30.8	S12 53.7	Dubhe	193 51.3	N61 40.5
07	251 26.3	290 53.9	32.4	268 24.2	13.7	186 22.8	55.2	31 33.2	53.7	Elnath	278 12.7	N28 37.0
08	266 28.8	305 53.3	31.5	283 24.9	13.0	201 25.1	55.2	46 35.7	53.7	Eltanin	90 46.5	N51 29.1
S 09	281 31.2	320 52.6	.. 30.6	298 25.5	.. 12.2	216 27.4	.. 55.3	61 38.1	.. 53.7	Enif	33 47.6	N 9 56.2
A 10	296 33.7	335 51.9	29.7	313 26.1	11.4	231 29.7	55.3	76 40.6	53.7	Fomalhaut	15 24.6	S29 33.2
T 11	311 36.1	350 51.3	28.8	328 26.8	10.7	246 32.1	55.3	91 43.0	53.7			
U 12	326 38.6	5 50.6	S16 27.8	343 27.4	S 8 09.9	261 34.3	N20 55.4	106 45.5	S12 53.7	Gacrux	172 00.6	S57 11.2
R 13	341 41.1	20 50.0	26.9	358 28.0	09.1	276 36.7	55.4	121 47.9	53.7	Gienah	175 52.2	S17 37.0
D 14	356 43.5	35 49.3	26.0	13 28.7	08.4	291 39.0	55.4	136 50.4	53.7	Hadar	148 47.9	S60 26.0
A 15	11 46.0	50 48.6	.. 25.1	28 29.3	.. 07.6	306 41.3	.. 55.5	151 52.9	.. 53.7	Hamal	328 01.1	N23 31.5
Y 16	26 48.5	65 48.0	24.2	43 29.9	06.8	321 43.6	55.5	166 55.3	53.7	Kaus Aust.	83 44.3	S34 22.5
17	41 50.9	80 47.3	23.3	58 30.5	06.1	336 45.9	55.5	181 57.8	53.6			
18	56 53.4	95 46.7	S16 22.4	73 31.2	S 8 05.3	351 48.2	N20 55.6	197 00.2	S12 53.6	Kochab	137 19.8	N74 05.8
19	71 55.9	110 46.0	21.5	88 31.8	04.5	6 50.5	55.6	212 02.7	53.6	Markab	13 38.8	N15 16.6
20	86 58.3	125 45.4	20.6	103 32.4	03.8	21 52.9	55.6	227 05.1	53.6	Menkar	314 15.3	N 4 08.3
21	102 00.8	140 44.7	.. 19.7	118 33.1	.. 03.0	36 55.2	.. 55.7	242 07.6	.. 53.6	Menkent	148 07.6	S36 26.0
22	117 03.3	155 44.0	18.8	133 33.7	02.2	51 57.5	55.7	257 10.0	53.6	Miaplacidus	221 38.7	S69 46.5
23	132 05.7	170 43.4	17.9	148 34.3	01.5	66 59.8	55.7	272 12.5	53.6			
17 00	147 08.2	185 42.7	S16 17.0	163 35.0	S 8 00.7	82 02.1	N20 55.8	287 14.9	S12 53.6	Mirfak	308 40.6	N49 54.6
01	162 10.6	200 42.1	16.1	178 35.6	7 59.9	97 04.4	55.8	302 17.4	53.6	Nunki	75 58.8	S26 16.7
02	177 13.1	215 41.4	15.1	193 36.2	59.2	112 06.7	55.8	317 19.8	53.6	Peacock	53 20.1	S56 41.4
03	192 15.6	230 40.8	.. 14.2	208 36.9	.. 58.4	127 09.1	.. 55.9	332 22.3	.. 53.6	Pollux	243 27.7	N27 59.5
04	207 18.0	245 40.1	13.3	223 37.5	57.6	142 11.4	55.9	347 24.7	53.6	Procyon	244 59.7	N 5 11.2
05	222 20.5	260 39.5	12.4	238 38.1	56.9	157 13.7	55.9	2 27.2	53.6			
06	237 23.0	275 38.8	S16 11.5	253 38.8	S 7 56.1	172 16.0	N20 56.0	17 29.7	S12 53.5	Rasalhague	96 06.8	N12 33.0
07	252 25.4	290 38.2	10.6	268 39.4	55.3	187 18.3	56.0	32 32.1	53.5	Regulus	207 43.4	N11 53.9
08	267 27.9	305 37.5	09.6	283 40.0	54.6	202 20.6	56.0	47 34.6	53.5	Rigel	281 12.1	S 8 11.5
S 09	282 30.4	320 36.9	.. 08.7	298 40.7	.. 53.8	217 22.9	.. 56.1	62 37.0	.. 53.5	Rigil Kent.	139 51.8	S60 53.1
U 10	297 32.8	335 36.2	07.8	313 41.3	53.0	232 25.2	56.1	77 39.5	53.5	Sabik	102 12.9	S15 44.4
N 11	312 35.3	350 35.6	06.9	328 41.9	52.2	247 27.5	56.1	92 41.9	53.5			
D 12	327 37.7	5 34.9	S16 06.0	343 42.6	S 7 51.5	262 29.8	N20 56.2	107 44.4	S12 53.5	Schedar	349 41.1	N56 36.8
A 13	342 40.2	20 34.3	05.1	358 43.2	50.7	277 32.1	56.2	122 46.8	53.5	Shaula	96 22.4	S37 06.6
Y 14	357 42.7	35 33.6	04.1	13 43.8	49.9	292 34.5	56.2	137 49.3	53.5	Sirius	258 33.7	S16 44.4
15	12 45.1	50 33.0	.. 03.2	28 44.5	.. 49.2	307 36.8	.. 56.3	152 51.8	.. 53.5	Spica	158 31.3	S11 13.9
16	27 47.6	65 32.3	02.3	43 45.1	48.4	322 39.1	56.3	167 54.2	53.5	Suhail	222 52.1	S43 29.4
17	42 50.1	80 31.7	01.4	58 45.8	47.6	337 41.4	56.3	182 56.7	53.5			
18	57 52.5	95 31.1	S16 00.4	73 46.4	S 7 46.9	352 43.7	N20 56.4	197 59.1	S12 53.5	Vega	80 39.4	N38 47.7
19	72 55.0	110 30.4	15 59.5	88 47.0	46.1	7 46.0	56.4	213 01.6	53.4	Zuben'ubi	137 05.6	S16 05.8
20	87 57.5	125 29.8	58.6	103 47.7	45.3	22 48.3	56.4	228 04.0	53.4			
21	102 59.9	140 29.1	.. 57.7	118 48.3	.. 44.6	37 50.6	.. 56.5	243 06.5	.. 53.4		SHA	Mer. Pass.
22	118 02.4	155 28.5	56.7	133 48.9	43.8	52 52.9	56.5	258 09.0	53.4	Venus	39 49.5	11 37
23	133 04.9	170 27.8	55.8	148 49.6	43.0	67 55.2	56.5	273 11.4	53.4	Mars	17 10.8	13 06
										Jupiter	294 57.5	18 33
Mer. Pass. 14 13.1		v −0.7	d 0.9	v 0.6	d 0.8	v 2.3	d 0.0	v 2.5	d 0.0	Saturn	140 07.0	4 54

SUN and MOON

UT	SUN GHA	SUN Dec	MOON GHA	v	MOON Dec	d	HP
15 00	176 28.1	S12 41.5	123 03.8	12.8	N11 38.4	9.2	55.8
01	191 28.1	40.7	137 35.6	12.9	11 47.6	9.1	55.7
02	206 28.1	39.8	152 07.5	12.9	11 56.7	9.1	55.7
03	221 28.2	.. 39.0	166 39.4	12.9	12 05.8	8.9	55.7
04	236 28.2	38.1	181 11.3	12.8	12 14.7	9.0	55.6
05	251 28.2	37.2	195 43.1	12.9	12 23.7	8.8	55.6
06	266 28.3	S12 36.4	210 15.0	12.9	N12 32.5	8.8	55.6
07	281 28.3	35.5	224 46.9	12.8	12 41.3	8.7	55.5
F 08	296 28.3	34.7	239 18.7	12.9	12 50.0	8.7	55.5
R 09	311 28.4	.. 33.8	253 50.6	12.9	12 58.7	8.6	55.5
I 10	326 28.4	32.9	268 22.5	12.8	13 07.3	8.5	55.5
11	341 28.4	32.1	282 54.3	12.9	13 15.8	8.5	55.5
D 12	356 28.5	S12 31.2	297 26.2	12.8	N13 24.3	8.3	55.4
A 13	11 28.5	30.3	311 58.0	12.8	13 32.6	8.3	55.4
Y 14	26 28.5	29.5	326 29.8	12.9	13 40.9	8.3	55.4
15	41 28.6	.. 28.6	341 01.7	12.8	13 49.2	8.1	55.4
16	56 28.6	27.8	355 33.5	12.8	13 57.3	8.1	55.3
17	71 28.6	26.9	10 05.3	12.8	14 05.4	8.1	55.3
18	86 28.7	S12 26.0	24 37.1	12.8	N14 13.5	7.9	55.3
19	101 28.7	25.2	39 08.9	12.8	14 21.4	7.9	55.3
20	116 28.7	24.3	53 40.7	12.8	14 29.3	7.8	55.2
21	131 28.8	.. 23.4	68 12.5	12.8	14 37.1	7.7	55.2
22	146 28.8	22.6	82 44.3	12.8	14 44.8	7.7	55.2
23	161 28.8	21.7	97 16.1	12.7	14 52.5	7.5	55.2
16 00	176 28.9	S12 20.8	111 47.8	12.8	N15 00.0	7.5	55.1
01	191 28.9	20.0	126 19.6	12.7	15 07.5	7.5	55.1
02	206 28.9	19.1	140 51.3	12.8	15 15.0	7.3	55.1
03	221 29.0	.. 18.2	155 23.1	12.7	15 22.3	7.3	55.1
04	236 29.0	17.4	169 54.8	12.7	15 29.6	7.2	55.0
05	251 29.1	16.5	184 26.5	12.7	15 36.8	7.1	55.0
06	266 29.1	S12 15.6	198 58.2	12.7	N15 43.9	7.0	55.0
S 07	281 29.1	14.8	213 29.9	12.7	15 50.9	7.0	55.0
A 08	296 29.2	13.9	228 01.6	12.7	15 57.9	6.9	55.0
T 09	311 29.2	.. 13.0	242 33.3	12.7	16 04.8	6.8	54.9
U 10	326 29.3	12.2	257 05.0	12.6	16 11.6	6.7	54.9
R 11	341 29.3	11.3	271 36.6	12.7	16 18.3	6.7	54.9
D 12	356 29.3	S12 10.4	286 08.3	12.6	N16 25.0	6.5	54.9
A 13	11 29.4	09.5	300 39.9	12.6	16 31.5	6.5	54.9
Y 14	26 29.4	08.7	315 11.5	12.6	16 38.0	6.4	54.8
15	41 29.5	.. 07.8	329 43.1	12.6	16 44.4	6.3	54.8
16	56 29.5	06.9	344 14.7	12.6	16 50.7	6.3	54.8
17	71 29.5	06.1	358 46.3	12.6	16 57.0	6.1	54.8
18	86 29.6	S12 05.2	13 17.9	12.6	N17 03.1	6.1	54.8
19	101 29.6	04.3	27 49.5	12.5	17 09.2	6.0	54.7
20	116 29.7	03.4	42 21.0	12.6	17 15.2	5.9	54.7
21	131 29.7	.. 02.6	56 52.5	12.6	17 21.1	5.9	54.7
22	146 29.8	01.7	71 24.1	12.5	17 27.0	5.7	54.7
23	161 29.8	12 00.8	85 55.6	12.5	17 32.7	5.7	54.7
17 00	176 29.8	S11 59.9	100 27.1	12.5	N17 38.4	5.5	54.7
01	191 29.9	59.1	114 58.6	12.4	17 43.9	5.5	54.6
02	206 29.9	58.2	127 30.0	12.5	17 49.4	5.4	54.6
03	221 30.0	.. 57.3	144 01.5	12.5	17 54.8	5.4	54.6
04	236 30.0	56.4	158 33.0	12.4	18 00.2	5.2	54.6
05	251 30.1	55.6	173 04.4	12.4	18 05.4	5.2	54.6
06	266 30.1	S11 54.7	187 35.8	12.4	N18 10.6	5.0	54.6
07	281 30.2	53.8	202 07.2	12.4	18 15.6	5.0	54.6
08	296 30.2	52.9	216 38.6	12.4	18 20.6	4.9	54.5
S 09	311 30.3	.. 52.1	231 10.0	12.4	18 25.5	4.8	54.5
U 10	326 30.3	51.2	245 41.4	12.3	18 30.3	4.7	54.5
N 11	341 30.4	50.3	260 12.7	12.4	18 35.0	4.6	54.5
D 12	356 30.4	S11 49.4	274 44.1	12.3	N18 39.6	4.6	54.5
A 13	11 30.5	48.5	289 15.4	12.3	18 44.2	4.4	54.5
Y 14	26 30.5	47.7	303 46.7	12.3	18 48.6	4.4	54.5
15	41 30.6	.. 46.8	318 18.0	12.3	18 53.0	4.3	54.4
16	56 30.6	45.9	332 49.3	12.3	18 57.3	4.2	54.4
17	71 30.6	45.0	347 20.6	12.3	19 01.5	4.1	54.4
18	86 30.7	S11 44.1	1 51.9	12.2	N19 05.6	4.0	54.4
19	101 30.7	43.3	16 23.1	12.3	19 09.6	3.9	54.4
20	116 30.8	42.4	30 54.4	12.2	19 13.5	3.8	54.4
21	131 30.9	.. 41.5	45 25.6	12.2	19 17.3	3.8	54.4
22	146 30.9	40.6	59 56.8	12.2	19 21.1	3.6	54.4
23	161 31.0	39.7	74 28.0	12.2	N19 24.7	3.6	54.4
	SD 16.2	d 0.9	SD 15.1		15.0		14.8

Twilight, Sunrise and Moonrise

Lat.	Naut.	Civil	Sunrise	15	16	17	18
N 72	06 10	07 29	08 47	07 07	06 45	▭	▭
N 70	06 08	07 20	08 28	07 30	07 23	07 14	06 55
68	06 07	07 12	08 13	07 47	07 49	07 55	08 08
66	06 06	07 06	08 01	08 01	08 09	08 23	08 44
64	06 05	07 00	07 51	08 13	08 26	08 44	09 11
62	06 04	06 56	07 42	08 23	08 39	09 01	09 31
60	06 03	06 51	07 35	08 31	08 51	09 16	09 48
N 58	06 02	06 48	07 28	08 39	09 01	09 28	10 02
56	06 01	06 44	07 23	08 45	09 10	09 39	10 14
54	06 00	06 41	07 18	08 51	09 17	09 48	10 25
52	05 59	06 38	07 13	08 57	09 24	09 56	10 34
50	05 58	06 35	07 09	09 02	09 31	10 04	10 42
45	05 55	06 29	06 59	09 12	09 44	10 20	11 00
N 40	05 52	06 24	06 52	09 21	09 56	10 33	11 15
35	05 49	06 19	06 46	09 29	10 05	10 43	11 27
30	05 46	06 14	06 39	09 35	10 14	10 55	11 38
20	05 40	06 06	06 29	09 47	10 29	11 12	11 57
N 10	05 33	05 58	06 19	09 57	10 42	11 27	12 13
0	05 25	05 49	06 11	10 07	10 54	11 41	12 28
S 10	05 15	05 40	06 02	10 17	11 06	11 55	12 44
20	05 03	05 30	05 54	10 27	11 19	12 10	13 00
30	04 47	05 16	05 41	10 39	11 34	12 27	13 19
35	04 37	05 08	05 35	10 46	11 43	12 38	13 30
40	04 24	04 59	05 27	10 54	11 53	12 49	13 43
45	04 09	04 47	05 19	11 04	12 05	13 03	13 58
S 50	03 49	04 33	05 08	11 15	12 19	13 20	14 16
52	03 39	04 26	05 04	11 20	12 26	13 28	14 25
54	03 28	04 19	04 58	11 26	12 33	13 37	14 34
56	03 15	04 10	04 52	11 33	12 42	13 46	14 45
58	02 59	04 00	04 46	11 40	12 51	13 58	14 58
S 60	02 40	03 49	04 38	11 48	13 02	14 11	15 13

Sunset, Twilight and Moonset

Lat.	Sunset	Civil	Naut.	15	16	17	18
N 72	15 43	17 01	18 21	00 25	02 24	▭	▭
N 70	16 02	17 10	18 22	00 04	01 48	03 34	05 32
68	16 16	17 17	18 23	25 23	01 23	02 54	04 20
66	16 28	17 24	18 24	25 03	01 03	02 27	03 43
64	16 38	17 29	18 25	24 47	00 47	02 06	03 17
62	16 47	17 34	18 26	24 35	00 35	01 49	02 57
60	16 54	17 38	18 27	24 24	00 24	01 35	02 41
N 58	17 01	17 42	18 27	24 14	00 14	01 23	02 27
56	17 06	17 45	18 28	24 06	00 06	01 13	02 15
54	17 11	17 48	18 29	23 59	25 04	01 04	02 05
52	17 16	17 51	18 30	23 52	24 56	00 56	01 55
50	17 20	17 54	18 31	23 46	24 49	00 49	01 47
45	17 29	18 00	18 33	23 33	24 33	00 33	01 30
N 40	17 37	18 05	18 37	23 23	24 20	00 20	01 15
35	17 44	18 10	18 39	23 14	24 09	00 09	01 03
30	17 50	18 14	18 42	23 06	24 00	00 00	00 53
20	18 00	18 22	18 48	22 52	23 44	24 34	00 34
N 10	18 09	18 30	18 55	22 41	23 30	24 19	00 19
0	18 17	18 39	19 04	22 30	23 16	24 04	00 04
S 10	18 26	18 48	19 13	22 19	23 03	23 49	24 36
20	18 36	18 58	19 25	22 07	22 49	23 33	24 19
30	18 46	19 11	19 51	21 53	22 33	23 15	24 00
35	18 53	19 19	19 51	21 46	22 24	23 05	23 49
40	19 00	19 28	20 03	21 37	22 13	22 53	23 36
45	19 08	19 40	20 20	21 27	22 01	22 38	23 21
S 50	19 19	19 54	20 37	21 14	21 45	22 21	23 03
52	19 23	20 00	20 47	21 09	21 38	22 13	22 54
54	19 29	20 08	20 58	21 02	21 30	22 04	22 44
56	19 34	20 16	21 11	20 55	21 22	21 54	22 33
58	19 41	20 26	21 26	20 47	21 12	21 42	22 20
S 60	19 48	20 37	21 44	20 39	21 00	21 29	22 05

SUN and MOON notes

Day	SUN Eqn. of Time 00h	SUN Eqn. of Time 12h	SUN Mer. Pass.	MOON Mer. Pass. Upper	MOON Mer. Pass. Lower	Age	Phase
15	14 08	14 06	12 14	16 18	03 55	05	28
16	14 05	14 03	12 14	17 05	04 42	06	37
17	14 01	13 58	12 14	17 52	05 29	07	47

2013 FEBRUARY 18, 19, 20 (MON., TUES., WED.)

UT	ARIES GHA	VENUS −3.9 GHA	Dec	MARS +1.2 GHA	Dec	JUPITER −2.4 GHA	Dec	SATURN +0.5 GHA	Dec
d h	° ′	° ′	° ′	° ′	° ′	° ′	° ′	° ′	° ′
18 00	148 07.3	185 27.2	S15 54.9	163 50.2	S 7 42.3	82 57.5	N20 56.6	288 13.9	S12 53.4
01	163 09.8	200 26.6	53.9	178 50.8	41.5	97 59.8	56.6	303 16.3	53.4
02	178 12.2	215 25.9	53.0	193 51.5	40.7	113 02.1	56.6	318 18.8	53.4
03	193 14.7	230 25.3	52.1	208 52.1	39.9	128 04.4	56.7	333 21.2	53.4
04	208 17.2	245 24.6	51.1	223 52.8	39.2	143 06.7	56.7	348 23.7	53.4
05	223 19.6	260 24.0	50.2	238 53.4	38.4	158 09.0	56.7	3 26.2	53.4
06	238 22.1	275 23.4	S15 49.3	253 54.0	S 7 37.6	173 11.3	N20 56.8	18 28.6	S12 53.3
07	253 24.6	290 22.7	48.3	268 54.7	36.9	188 13.6	56.8	33 31.1	53.3
08	268 27.0	305 22.1	47.4	283 55.3	36.1	203 15.9	56.8	48 33.5	53.3
M 09	283 29.5	320 21.4	46.5	298 55.9	35.3	218 18.2	56.9	63 36.0	53.3
O 10	298 32.0	335 20.8	45.5	313 56.6	34.5	233 20.5	56.9	78 38.5	53.3
N 11	313 34.4	350 20.2	44.6	328 57.2	33.8	248 22.8	57.0	93 40.9	53.3
D 12	328 36.9	5 19.5	S15 43.6	343 57.8	S 7 33.0	263 25.1	N20 57.0	108 43.4	S12 53.3
A 13	343 39.4	20 18.9	42.7	358 58.5	32.2	278 27.4	57.0	123 45.8	53.3
Y 14	358 41.8	35 18.3	41.8	13 59.1	31.5	293 29.7	57.1	138 48.3	53.3
15	13 44.3	50 17.6	40.8	28 59.8	30.7	308 32.0	57.1	153 50.8	53.3
16	28 46.7	65 17.0	39.9	44 00.4	29.9	323 34.3	57.1	168 53.2	53.3
17	43 49.2	80 16.4	38.9	59 01.0	29.1	338 36.6	57.2	183 55.7	53.3
18	58 51.7	95 15.7	S15 38.0	74 01.7	S 7 28.4	353 38.9	N20 57.2	198 58.1	S12 53.2
19	73 54.1	110 15.1	37.1	89 02.3	27.6	8 41.2	57.2	214 00.6	53.2
20	88 56.6	125 14.5	36.1	104 03.0	26.8	23 43.5	57.3	229 03.1	53.2
21	103 59.1	140 13.8	35.2	119 03.6	26.1	38 45.8	57.3	244 05.5	53.2
22	119 01.5	155 13.2	34.2	134 04.2	25.3	53 48.1	57.3	259 08.0	53.2
23	134 04.0	170 12.6	33.3	149 04.9	24.5	68 50.4	57.4	274 10.4	53.2
19 00	149 06.5	185 12.0	S15 32.3	164 05.5	S 7 23.7	83 52.7	N20 57.4	289 12.9	S12 53.2
01	164 08.9	200 11.3	31.4	179 06.2	23.0	98 55.0	57.4	304 15.4	53.2
02	179 11.4	215 10.7	30.4	194 06.8	22.2	113 57.3	57.5	319 17.8	53.2
03	194 13.8	230 10.1	29.5	209 07.4	21.4	128 59.6	57.5	334 20.3	53.2
04	209 16.3	245 09.4	28.5	224 08.1	20.7	144 01.9	57.6	349 22.8	53.1
05	224 18.8	260 08.8	27.6	239 08.7	19.9	159 04.2	57.6	4 25.2	53.1
06	239 21.2	275 08.2	S15 26.6	254 09.4	S 7 19.1	174 06.5	N20 57.7	19 27.7	S12 53.1
07	254 23.7	290 07.6	25.7	269 10.0	18.3	189 08.8	57.7	34 30.2	53.1
T 08	269 26.2	305 06.9	24.7	284 10.6	17.6	204 11.1	57.7	49 32.6	53.1
U 09	284 28.6	320 06.3	23.8	299 11.3	16.8	219 13.4	57.7	64 35.1	53.1
E 10	299 31.1	335 05.7	22.8	314 11.9	16.0	234 15.7	57.8	79 37.5	53.1
S 11	314 33.6	350 05.1	21.8	329 12.6	15.2	249 17.9	57.8	94 40.0	53.1
D 12	329 36.0	5 04.4	S15 20.9	344 13.2	S 7 14.5	264 20.2	N20 57.9	109 42.5	S12 53.1
A 13	344 38.5	20 03.8	19.9	359 13.8	13.7	279 22.5	57.9	124 44.9	53.1
Y 14	359 41.0	35 03.2	19.0	14 14.5	12.9	294 24.8	57.9	139 47.4	53.0
15	14 43.4	50 02.6	18.0	29 15.1	12.1	309 27.1	58.0	154 49.9	53.0
16	29 45.9	65 02.0	17.0	44 15.8	11.4	324 29.4	58.0	169 52.3	53.0
17	44 48.3	80 01.3	16.1	59 16.4	10.6	339 31.7	58.0	184 54.8	53.0
18	59 50.8	95 00.7	S15 15.1	74 17.0	S 7 09.8	354 34.0	N20 58.1	199 57.3	S12 53.0
19	74 53.3	110 00.1	14.2	89 17.7	09.1	9 36.3	58.1	214 59.7	53.0
20	89 55.7	124 59.5	13.2	104 18.3	08.3	24 38.6	58.1	230 02.2	53.0
21	104 58.2	139 58.9	12.2	119 19.0	07.5	39 40.9	58.2	245 04.7	53.0
22	120 00.7	154 58.2	11.3	134 19.6	06.7	54 43.1	58.2	260 07.1	53.0
23	135 03.1	169 57.6	10.3	149 20.3	05.9	69 45.4	58.2	275 09.6	52.9
20 00	150 05.6	184 57.0	S15 09.3	164 20.9	S 7 05.2	84 47.7	N20 58.3	290 12.1	S12 52.9
01	165 08.1	199 56.4	08.4	179 21.5	04.4	99 50.0	58.3	305 14.5	52.9
02	180 10.5	214 55.8	07.4	194 22.2	03.6	114 52.3	58.4	320 17.0	52.9
03	195 13.0	229 55.2	06.4	209 22.8	02.9	129 54.6	58.4	335 19.5	52.9
04	210 15.5	244 54.5	05.5	224 23.5	02.1	144 56.9	58.4	350 21.9	52.9
05	225 17.9	259 53.9	04.5	239 24.1	01.3	159 59.2	58.5	5 24.4	52.9
06	240 20.4	274 53.3	S15 03.5	254 24.8	S 7 00.5	175 01.4	N20 58.5	20 26.9	S12 52.9
W 07	255 22.8	289 52.7	02.6	269 25.4	6 59.8	190 03.7	58.5	35 29.3	52.9
E 08	270 25.3	304 52.1	01.6	284 26.0	59.0	205 06.0	58.6	50 31.8	52.8
D 09	285 27.8	319 51.5	15 00.6	299 26.7	58.2	220 08.3	58.6	65 34.3	52.8
N 10	300 30.2	334 50.9	14 59.6	314 27.3	57.4	235 10.6	58.7	80 36.7	52.8
E 11	315 32.7	349 50.3	58.7	329 28.0	56.7	250 12.9	58.7	95 39.2	52.8
S 12	330 35.2	4 49.6	S14 57.7	344 28.6	S 6 55.9	265 15.1	N20 58.7	110 41.7	S12 52.8
D 13	345 37.6	19 49.0	56.7	359 29.3	55.1	280 17.4	58.8	125 44.1	52.8
A 14	0 40.1	34 48.4	55.7	14 29.9	54.3	295 19.7	58.8	140 46.6	52.8
Y 15	15 42.6	49 47.8	54.8	29 30.6	53.6	310 22.0	58.8	155 49.1	52.8
16	30 45.0	64 47.2	53.8	44 31.2	52.8	325 24.3	58.9	170 51.5	52.8
17	45 47.5	79 46.6	52.8	59 31.8	52.0	340 26.6	58.9	185 54.0	52.7
18	60 50.0	94 46.0	S14 51.8	74 32.5	S 6 51.2	355 28.8	N20 59.0	200 56.5	S12 52.7
19	75 52.4	109 45.4	50.9	89 33.1	50.4	10 31.1	59.0	215 59.0	52.7
20	90 54.9	124 44.8	49.9	104 33.8	49.7	25 33.4	59.0	231 01.4	52.7
21	105 57.3	139 44.2	48.9	119 34.4	48.9	40 35.7	59.1	246 03.9	52.7
22	120 59.8	154 43.6	47.9	134 35.1	48.1	55 38.0	59.1	261 06.4	52.7
23	136 02.3	169 43.0	46.9	149 35.7	47.3	70 40.2	59.1	276 08.8	52.7
Mer. Pass. 14 01.3		v −0.6	d 1.0	v 0.6	d 0.8	v 2.3	d 0.0	v 2.5	d 0.0

STARS

Name	SHA	Dec
Acamar	315 18.6	S40 15.4
Achernar	335 27.3	S57 10.5
Acrux	173 08.9	S63 10.5
Adhara	255 12.4	S28 59.8
Aldebaran	290 49.5	N16 32.0
Alioth	166 20.5	N55 53.0
Alkaid	152 58.8	N49 14.5
Al Na'ir	27 44.5	S46 53.8
Alnilam	275 46.4	S 1 11.9
Alphard	217 56.0	S 8 43.2
Alphecca	126 11.1	N26 40.0
Alpheratz	357 44.0	N29 09.9
Altair	62 08.7	N 8 54.2
Ankaa	353 16.2	S42 14.2
Antares	112 26.5	S26 27.5
Arcturus	145 55.8	N19 06.6
Atria	107 28.7	S69 02.7
Avior	234 17.5	S59 33.4
Bellatrix	278 32.1	N 6 21.5
Betelgeuse	271 01.3	N 7 24.3
Canopus	263 55.9	S52 42.6
Capella	280 34.6	N46 00.7
Deneb	49 32.0	N45 19.6
Denebola	182 33.6	N14 29.7
Diphda	348 56.3	S17 55.0
Dubhe	193 51.3	N61 40.5
Elnath	278 12.7	N28 37.0
Eltanin	90 46.5	N51 29.1
Enif	33 47.6	N 9 56.2
Fomalhaut	15 24.6	S29 33.2
Gacrux	172 00.6	S57 11.2
Gienah	175 52.2	S17 37.0
Hadar	148 47.8	S60 26.0
Hamal	328 01.1	N23 31.5
Kaus Aust.	83 44.3	S34 22.5
Kochab	137 19.7	N74 05.8
Markab	13 38.8	N15 16.6
Menkar	314 15.3	N 4 08.3
Menkent	148 07.6	S36 26.0
Miaplacidus	221 38.8	S69 46.5
Mirfak	308 40.7	N49 54.6
Nunki	75 58.8	S26 16.7
Peacock	53 20.1	S56 41.3
Pollux	243 27.7	N27 59.5
Procyon	244 59.7	N 5 11.2
Rasalhague	96 06.8	N12 33.0
Regulus	207 43.4	N11 53.9
Rigel	281 12.1	S 8 11.5
Rigil Kent.	139 51.7	S60 53.1
Sabik	102 12.9	S15 44.4
Schedar	349 41.1	N56 36.7
Shaula	96 22.3	S37 06.0
Sirius	258 33.7	S16 44.4
Spica	158 31.3	S11 13.9
Suhail	222 52.1	S43 29.4
Vega	80 39.4	N38 47.7
Zuben'ubi	137 05.5	S16 05.8

	SHA	Mer. Pass.
	° ′	h m
Venus	36 05.5	11 40
Mars	14 59.1	13 03
Jupiter	294 46.3	18 22
Saturn	140 06.5	4 42

UT	SUN GHA	SUN Dec	MOON GHA	v	MOON Dec	d	HP
18 00	176 31.0	S11 38.9	88 59.2	12.2	N19 28.3	3.5	54.4
01	191 31.1	38.0	103 30.4	12.2	19 31.8	3.4	54.3
02	206 31.1	37.1	118 01.6	12.1	19 35.2	3.2	54.3
03	221 31.2 ..	36.2	132 32.7	12.2	19 38.4	3.2	54.3
04	236 31.2	35.3	147 03.9	12.1	19 41.6	3.2	54.3
05	251 31.3	34.4	161 35.0	12.1	19 44.8	3.0	54.3
06	266 31.3	S11 33.6	176 06.1	12.2	N19 47.8	2.9	54.3
07	281 31.4	32.7	190 37.3	12.1	19 50.7	2.8	54.3
08	296 31.4	31.8	205 08.4	12.0	19 53.5	2.8	54.3
M 09	311 31.5 ..	30.9	219 39.4	12.1	19 56.3	2.6	54.3
O 10	326 31.5	30.0	234 10.5	12.1	19 58.9	2.6	54.3
N 11	341 31.6	29.1	248 41.6	12.0	20 01.5	2.4	54.3
D 12	356 31.6	S11 28.2	263 12.6	12.1	N20 03.9	2.4	54.3
A 13	11 31.7	27.4	277 43.7	12.0	20 06.3	2.3	54.3
Y 14	26 31.8	26.5	292 14.7	12.1	20 08.6	2.2	54.3
15	41 31.8 ..	25.6	306 45.8	12.0	20 10.8	2.0	54.2
16	56 31.9	24.7	321 16.8	12.0	20 12.8	2.0	54.2
17	71 31.9	23.8	335 47.8	12.0	20 14.8	1.9	54.2
18	86 32.0	S11 22.9	350 18.8	12.0	N20 16.7	1.9	54.2
19	101 32.0	22.0	4 49.8	11.9	20 18.6	1.7	54.2
20	116 32.1	21.1	19 20.7	12.0	20 20.3	1.6	54.2
21	131 32.2 ..	20.3	33 51.7	12.0	20 21.9	1.5	54.2
22	146 32.2	19.4	48 22.7	11.9	20 23.4	1.5	54.2
23	161 32.3	18.5	62 53.6	12.0	20 24.9	1.3	54.2
19 00	176 32.3	S11 17.6	77 24.6	11.9	N20 26.2	1.2	54.2
01	191 32.4	16.7	91 55.5	11.9	20 27.4	1.2	54.2
02	206 32.5	15.8	106 26.4	12.0	20 28.6	1.0	54.2
03	221 32.5 ..	14.9	120 57.4	11.9	20 29.6	1.0	54.2
04	236 32.6	14.0	135 28.3	11.9	20 30.6	0.9	54.2
05	251 32.6	13.1	149 59.2	11.9	20 31.5	0.7	54.2
06	266 32.7	S11 12.2	164 30.1	11.9	N20 32.2	0.7	54.2
07	281 32.8	11.4	179 01.0	11.9	20 32.9	0.6	54.2
T 08	296 32.8	10.5	193 31.9	11.9	20 33.5	0.5	54.2
U 09	311 32.9 ..	09.6	208 02.8	11.8	20 34.0	0.4	54.2
E 10	326 32.9	08.7	222 33.6	11.9	20 34.4	0.2	54.2
S 11	341 33.0	07.8	237 04.5	11.9	20 34.6	0.2	54.2
D 12	356 33.1	S11 06.9	251 35.4	11.9	N20 34.8	0.1	54.2
A 13	11 33.1	06.0	266 06.3	11.8	20 34.9	0.1	54.2
Y 14	26 33.2	05.1	280 37.1	11.9	20 35.0	0.1	54.2
15	41 33.3 ..	04.2	295 08.0	11.8	20 34.9	0.2	54.2
16	56 33.3	03.3	309 38.8	11.9	20 34.7	0.3	54.2
17	71 33.4	02.4	324 09.7	11.8	20 34.4	0.4	54.2
18	86 33.4	S11 01.5	338 40.5	11.9	N20 34.0	0.6	54.2
19	101 33.5	11 00.6	353 11.4	11.8	20 33.4	0.6	54.2
20	116 33.6	10 59.7	7 42.2	11.8	20 33.0	0.7	54.2
21	131 33.6 ..	58.8	22 13.0	11.9	20 32.3	0.7	54.2
22	146 33.7	57.9	36 43.9	11.8	20 31.6	0.9	54.2
23	161 33.8	57.0	51 14.7	11.8	20 30.7	0.9	54.3
20 00	176 33.8	S10 56.1	65 45.5	11.9	N20 29.8	1.1	54.3
01	191 33.9	55.3	80 16.4	11.8	20 28.7	1.1	54.3
02	206 34.0	54.4	94 47.2	11.8	20 27.6	1.2	54.3
03	221 34.0 ..	53.5	109 18.0	11.9	20 26.4	1.4	54.3
04	236 34.1	52.6	123 48.9	11.8	20 25.0	1.4	54.3
05	251 34.2	51.7	138 19.7	11.8	20 23.6	1.5	54.3
06	266 34.2	S10 50.8	152 50.5	11.9	N20 22.1	1.6	54.3
W 07	281 34.3	49.9	167 21.4	11.8	20 20.5	1.6	54.3
E 08	296 34.4	49.0	181 52.2	11.8	20 18.7	1.8	54.3
D 09	311 34.4 ..	48.1	196 23.0	11.8	20 16.9	1.9	54.3
N 10	326 34.5	47.2	210 53.8	11.9	20 15.0	2.0	54.3
E 11	341 34.6	46.3	225 24.7	11.8	20 13.0	2.1	54.3
S 12	356 34.7	S10 45.4	239 55.5	11.9	N20 10.9	2.1	54.3
D 13	11 34.7	44.5	254 26.4	11.8	20 08.8	2.3	54.3
A 14	26 34.8	43.6	268 57.2	11.9	20 06.5	2.4	54.4
Y 15	41 34.9 ..	42.7	283 28.1	11.8	20 04.1	2.5	54.4
16	56 34.9	41.8	297 58.9	11.9	20 01.6	2.5	54.4
17	71 35.0	40.9	312 29.8	11.8	19 59.1	2.7	54.4
18	86 35.1	S10 40.0	327 00.6	11.9	N19 56.4	2.7	54.4
19	101 35.1	39.1	341 31.5	11.8	19 53.7	2.9	54.4
20	116 35.2	38.2	356 02.3	11.9	19 50.8	2.9	54.4
21	131 35.3 ..	37.2	10 33.2	11.9	19 47.9	3.1	54.4
22	146 35.4	36.3	25 04.1	11.9	19 44.8	3.1	54.4
23	161 35.4	35.4	39 35.0	11.8	N19 41.7	3.2	54.4
	SD 16.2	d 0.9	SD 14.8		14.8		14.8

Lat.	Twilight Naut.	Twilight Civil	Sunrise	Moonrise 18	19	20	21
N 72	05 56	07 15	08 30	☐	☐	☐	
N 70	05 57	07 07	08 14	06 55	☐	☐	10 02
68	05 57	07 01	08 01	08 08	08 37	09 34	10 54
66	05 56	06 56	07 50	08 44	09 20	10 15	11 26
64	05 56	06 51	07 41	09 11	09 50	10 43	11 50
62	05 56	06 47	07 33	09 31	10 12	11 04	12 08
60	05 55	06 44	07 27	09 48	10 30	11 22	12 24
N 58	05 55	06 40	07 21	10 02	10 44	11 36	12 37
56	05 54	06 37	07 16	10 14	10 57	11 49	12 48
54	05 54	06 35	07 11	10 25	11 08	11 59	12 58
52	05 53	06 32	07 07	10 34	11 18	12 09	13 06
50	05 52	06 30	07 03	10 42	11 27	12 18	13 14
45	05 50	06 25	06 55	11 00	11 46	12 36	13 31
N 40	05 48	06 20	06 48	11 15	12 01	12 51	13 45
35	05 46	06 16	06 41	11 27	12 14	13 03	13 56
30	05 44	06 12	06 36	11 38	12 25	13 14	14 06
20	05 39	06 04	06 27	11 57	12 44	13 33	14 24
N 10	05 32	05 57	06 18	12 13	13 01	13 49	14 39
0	05 25	05 49	06 10	12 28	13 17	14 05	14 53
S 10	05 16	05 41	06 02	12 44	13 32	14 20	15 07
20	05 05	05 31	05 54	13 00	13 49	14 36	15 22
30	04 50	05 19	05 44	13 19	14 08	14 55	15 39
35	04 40	05 11	05 38	13 30	14 20	15 06	15 49
40	04 29	05 03	05 31	13 43	14 33	15 19	16 01
45	04 14	04 52	05 23	13 58	14 48	15 33	16 14
S 50	03 56	04 39	05 14	14 16	15 07	15 52	16 30
52	03 47	04 33	05 09	14 25	15 16	16 00	16 38
54	03 36	04 26	05 04	14 34	15 26	16 10	16 47
56	03 24	04 18	04 58	14 45	15 37	16 20	16 56
58	03 10	04 09	04 53	14 58	15 50	16 33	17 07
S 60	02 53	03 58	04 46	15 13	16 05	16 47	17 20

Lat.	Sunset	Twilight Civil	Twilight Naut.	Moonset 18	19	20	21
N 72	15 59	17 15	18 34	☐	☐	☐	☐
N 70	16 16	17 22	18 33	05 32	☐	☐	07 26
68	16 28	17 28	18 33	04 20	05 30	06 13	06 33
66	16 39	17 33	18 33	03 43	04 47	05 32	06 01
64	16 48	17 38	18 33	03 17	04 18	05 04	05 37
62	16 55	17 42	18 33	02 57	03 56	04 42	05 18
60	17 02	17 45	18 34	02 41	03 38	04 25	05 02
N 58	17 08	17 48	18 34	02 27	03 23	04 10	04 49
56	17 13	17 51	18 34	02 15	03 10	03 58	04 37
54	17 17	17 54	18 35	02 05	02 59	03 47	04 27
52	17 22	17 56	18 36	01 55	02 49	03 37	04 18
50	17 25	17 59	18 36	01 47	02 41	03 28	04 10
45	17 34	18 04	18 38	01 30	02 22	03 10	03 53
N 40	17 41	18 08	18 40	01 15	02 07	02 55	03 39
35	17 47	18 12	18 42	01 03	01 54	02 42	03 27
30	17 52	18 16	18 44	00 53	01 43	02 31	03 17
20	18 01	18 24	18 50	00 34	01 24	02 12	02 59
N 10	18 09	18 31	18 55	00 19	01 07	01 55	02 43
0	18 17	18 38	19 03	00 04	00 52	01 40	02 28
S 10	18 25	18 47	19 12	24 36	00 36	01 24	02 13
20	18 34	18 56	19 23	24 19	00 19	01 07	01 57
30	18 44	19 08	19 37	24 00	00 00	00 48	01 39
35	18 49	19 16	19 47	23 49	24 37	00 37	01 28
40	18 56	19 24	19 58	23 36	24 24	00 24	01 16
45	19 04	19 34	20 12	23 21	24 09	00 09	01 02
S 50	19 13	19 47	20 30	23 03	23 50	24 44	00 44
52	19 17	19 54	20 39	22 54	23 41	24 36	00 36
54	19 22	20 00	20 49	22 44	23 31	24 26	00 26
56	19 27	20 08	21 01	22 33	23 20	24 16	00 16
58	19 33	20 17	21 15	22 20	23 07	24 04	00 04
S 60	19 40	20 27	21 31	22 05	22 52	23 49	24 56

	SUN Eqn. of Time 00h	SUN Eqn. of Time 12h	SUN Mer. Pass.	MOON Mer. Pass. Upper	MOON Mer. Pass. Lower	Age	Phase
Day	m s	m s	h m	h m	h m	d	%
18	13 56	13 54	12 14	18 40	06 16	08	56
19	13 51	13 48	12 14	19 28	07 04	09	65
20	13 45	13 42	12 14	20 16	07 52	10	74

UT	ARIES GHA	VENUS −3.9 GHA	Dec	MARS +1.2 GHA	Dec	JUPITER −2.4 GHA	Dec	SATURN +0.5 GHA	Dec	Name	SHA	Dec
21 00	151 04.7	184 42.4	S14 45.9	164 36.4	S 6 46.6	85 42.5	N20 59.2	291 11.3	S12 52.7	Acamar	315 18.6	S40 15.4
01	166 07.2	199 41.7	.. 45.0	179 37.0	.. 45.8	100 44.8	.. 59.2	306 13.8	.. 52.6	Achernar	335 27.3	S57 10.5
02	181 09.7	214 41.1	.. 44.0	194 37.7	.. 45.0	115 47.1	.. 59.3	321 16.2	.. 52.6	Acrux	173 08.9	S63 10.3
03	196 12.1	229 40.5	.. 43.0	209 38.3	.. 44.2	130 49.4	.. 59.3	336 18.7	.. 52.6	Adhara	255 12.4	S28 59.8
04	211 14.6	244 39.9	.. 42.0	224 38.9	.. 43.5	145 51.6	.. 59.3	351 21.2	.. 52.6	Aldebaran	290 49.5	N16 32.0
05	226 17.1	259 39.3	.. 41.0	239 39.6	.. 42.7	160 53.9	.. 59.4	6 23.7	.. 52.6			
06	241 19.5	274 38.7	S14 40.0	254 40.2	S 6 41.9	175 56.2	N20 59.4	21 26.1	S12 52.6	Alioth	166 20.5	N55 53.0
07	256 22.0	289 38.1	.. 39.0	269 40.9	.. 41.1	190 58.5	.. 59.4	36 28.6	.. 52.6	Alkaid	152 58.8	N49 14.6
T 08	271 24.4	304 37.5	.. 38.1	284 41.5	.. 40.3	206 00.8	.. 59.5	51 31.1	.. 52.6	Al Na'ir	27 44.4	S46 53.8
H 09	286 26.9	319 36.9	.. 37.1	299 42.2	.. 39.6	221 03.0	.. 59.5	66 33.5	.. 52.5	Alnilam	275 46.4	S 1 11.9
U 10	301 29.4	334 36.3	.. 36.1	314 42.8	.. 38.8	236 05.3	.. 59.6	81 36.0	.. 52.5	Alphard	217 55.9	S 8 43.2
R 11	316 31.8	349 35.7	.. 35.1	329 43.5	.. 38.0	251 07.6	.. 59.6	96 38.5	.. 52.5			
S 12	331 34.3	4 35.1	S14 34.1	344 44.1	S 6 37.2	266 09.9	N20 59.6	111 41.0	S12 52.5	Alphecca	126 11.1	N26 40.0
D 13	346 36.8	19 34.5	.. 33.1	359 44.8	.. 36.5	281 12.1	.. 59.7	126 43.4	.. 52.5	Alpheratz	357 44.0	N29 09.8
A 14	1 39.2	34 33.9	.. 32.1	14 45.4	.. 35.7	296 14.4	.. 59.7	141 45.9	.. 52.5	Altair	62 08.7	N 8 54.2
Y 15	16 41.7	49 33.3	.. 31.1	29 46.1	.. 34.9	311 16.7	.. 59.8	156 48.4	.. 52.5	Ankaa	353 16.2	S42 14.2
16	31 44.2	64 32.7	.. 30.1	44 46.7	.. 34.1	326 19.0	.. 59.8	171 50.9	.. 52.4	Antares	112 26.5	S26 27.5
17	46 46.6	79 32.1	.. 29.1	59 47.4	.. 33.3	341 21.2	.. 59.8	186 53.3	.. 52.4			
18	61 49.1	94 31.5	S14 28.1	74 48.0	S 6 32.6	356 23.5	N20 59.9	201 55.8	S12 52.4	Arcturus	145 55.7	N19 06.6
19	76 51.6	109 31.0	.. 27.1	89 48.7	.. 31.8	11 25.8	.. 59.9	216 58.3	.. 52.4	Atria	107 28.6	S69 02.7
20	91 54.0	124 30.4	.. 26.1	104 49.3	.. 31.0	26 28.1	20 59.9	232 00.8	.. 52.4	Avior	234 17.5	S59 33.4
21	106 56.5	139 29.8	.. 25.1	119 50.0	.. 30.2	41 30.3	21 00.0	247 03.2	.. 52.4	Bellatrix	278 32.1	N 6 21.5
22	121 58.9	154 29.2	.. 24.1	134 50.6	.. 29.4	56 32.6	.. 00.0	262 05.7	.. 52.4	Betelgeuse	271 01.4	N 7 24.3
23	137 01.4	169 28.6	.. 23.1	149 51.3	.. 28.7	71 34.9	.. 00.1	277 08.2	.. 52.4			
22 00	152 03.9	184 28.0	S14 22.1	164 51.9	S 6 27.9	86 37.1	N21 00.1	292 10.7	S12 52.3	Canopus	263 55.9	S52 42.6
01	167 06.3	199 27.4	.. 21.1	179 52.6	.. 27.1	101 39.4	.. 00.1	307 13.1	.. 52.3	Capella	280 34.6	N46 00.7
02	182 08.8	214 26.8	.. 20.1	194 53.2	.. 26.3	116 41.7	.. 00.2	322 15.6	.. 52.3	Deneb	49 32.0	N45 19.6
03	197 11.3	229 26.2	.. 19.1	209 53.8	.. 25.6	131 44.0	.. 00.2	337 18.1	.. 52.3	Denebola	182 33.6	N14 29.7
04	212 13.7	244 25.6	.. 18.1	224 54.5	.. 24.8	146 46.2	.. 00.3	352 20.6	.. 52.3	Diphda	348 56.3	S17 55.0
05	227 16.2	259 25.0	.. 17.1	239 55.1	.. 24.0	161 48.5	.. 00.3	7 23.0	.. 52.3			
06	242 18.7	274 24.4	S14 16.1	254 55.8	S 6 23.2	176 50.8	N21 00.3	22 25.5	S12 52.3	Dubhe	193 51.3	N61 40.5
07	257 21.1	289 23.8	.. 15.1	269 56.4	.. 22.4	191 53.0	.. 00.4	37 28.0	.. 52.2	Elnath	278 12.7	N28 37.0
F 08	272 23.6	304 23.3	.. 14.1	284 57.1	.. 21.7	206 55.3	.. 00.4	52 30.5	.. 52.2	Eltanin	90 46.5	N51 29.1
R 09	287 26.1	319 22.7	.. 13.1	299 57.7	.. 20.9	221 57.6	.. 00.5	67 32.9	.. 52.2	Enif	33 47.6	N 9 56.2
I 10	302 28.5	334 22.1	.. 12.1	314 58.4	.. 20.1	236 59.8	.. 00.5	82 35.4	.. 52.2	Fomalhaut	15 24.6	S29 33.2
D 11	317 31.0	349 21.5	.. 11.1	329 59.0	.. 19.3	252 02.1	.. 00.5	97 37.9	.. 52.2			
A 12	332 33.4	4 20.9	S14 10.1	344 59.7	S 6 18.5	267 04.4	N21 00.6	112 40.4	S12 52.2	Gacrux	172 00.6	S57 11.2
Y 13	347 35.9	19 20.3	.. 09.1	0 00.3	.. 17.8	282 06.6	.. 00.6	127 42.8	.. 52.2	Gienah	175 52.2	S17 37.0
14	2 38.4	34 19.7	.. 08.1	15 01.0	.. 17.0	297 08.9	.. 00.7	142 45.3	.. 52.1	Hadar	148 47.8	S60 26.0
15	17 40.8	49 19.1	.. 07.1	30 01.7	.. 16.2	312 11.2	.. 00.7	157 47.8	.. 52.1	Hamal	328 01.1	N23 31.5
16	32 43.3	64 18.6	.. 06.1	45 02.3	.. 15.4	327 13.4	.. 00.7	172 50.3	.. 52.1	Kaus Aust.	83 44.3	S34 22.5
17	47 45.8	79 18.0	.. 05.1	60 03.0	.. 14.6	342 15.7	.. 00.8	187 52.7	.. 52.1			
18	62 48.2	94 17.4	S14 04.0	75 03.6	S 6 13.9	357 18.0	N21 00.8	202 55.2	S12 52.1	Kochab	137 19.7	N74 05.8
19	77 50.7	109 16.8	.. 03.0	90 04.3	.. 13.1	12 20.2	.. 00.9	217 57.7	.. 52.1	Markab	13 38.8	N15 16.6
20	92 53.2	124 16.2	.. 02.0	105 04.9	.. 12.3	27 22.5	.. 00.9	233 00.2	.. 52.1	Menkar	314 15.3	N 4 08.3
21	107 55.6	139 15.6	.. 01.0	120 05.6	.. 11.5	42 24.8	.. 00.9	248 02.7	.. 52.0	Menkent	148 07.6	S36 26.0
22	122 58.1	154 15.1	14 00.0	135 06.2	.. 10.7	57 27.0	.. 01.0	263 05.1	.. 52.0	Miaplacidus	221 38.8	S69 46.5
23	138 00.5	169 14.5	13 59.0	150 06.9	.. 10.0	72 29.3	.. 01.0	278 07.6	.. 52.0			
23 00	153 03.0	184 13.9	S13 58.0	165 07.5	S 6 09.2	87 31.6	N21 01.1	293 10.1	S12 52.0	Mirfak	308 40.7	N49 54.6
01	168 05.5	199 13.3	.. 56.9	180 08.2	.. 08.4	102 33.8	.. 01.1	308 12.6	.. 52.0	Nunki	75 58.8	S26 16.7
02	183 07.9	214 12.7	.. 55.9	195 08.8	.. 07.6	117 36.1	.. 01.1	323 15.1	.. 52.0	Peacock	53 20.1	S56 41.3
03	198 10.4	229 12.1	.. 54.9	210 09.5	.. 06.8	132 38.4	.. 01.2	338 17.5	.. 52.0	Pollux	243 27.7	N27 59.5
04	213 12.9	244 11.6	.. 53.9	225 10.1	.. 06.0	147 40.6	.. 01.2	353 20.0	.. 51.9	Procyon	244 59.7	N 5 11.2
05	228 15.3	259 11.0	.. 52.9	240 10.8	.. 05.3	162 42.9	.. 01.3	8 22.5	.. 51.9			
06	243 17.8	274 10.4	S13 52.0	255 11.4	S 6 04.5	177 45.1	N21 01.3	23 25.0	S12 51.9	Rasalhague	96 06.7	N12 33.0
07	258 20.3	289 09.8	.. 50.8	270 12.1	.. 03.7	192 47.4	.. 01.3	38 27.5	.. 51.9	Regulus	207 43.4	N11 53.9
S 08	273 22.7	304 09.3	.. 49.8	285 12.7	.. 02.9	207 49.7	.. 01.4	53 29.9	.. 51.9	Rigel	281 12.1	S 8 11.5
A 09	288 25.2	319 08.7	.. 48.8	300 13.4	.. 02.1	222 51.9	.. 01.4	68 32.4	.. 51.9	Rigil Kent.	139 51.7	S60 53.1
T 10	303 27.7	334 08.1	.. 47.8	315 14.0	.. 01.4	237 54.2	.. 01.5	83 34.9	.. 51.8	Sabik	102 12.8	S15 44.4
U 11	318 30.1	349 07.5	.. 46.7	330 14.7	6 00.6	252 56.5	.. 01.5	98 37.4	.. 51.8			
R 12	333 32.6	4 07.0	S13 45.7	345 15.3	S 5 59.8	267 58.7	N21 01.5	113 39.9	S12 51.8	Schedar	349 41.1	N56 36.7
D 13	348 35.0	19 06.4	.. 44.7	0 16.0	.. 59.0	283 01.0	.. 01.6	128 42.3	.. 51.8	Shaula	96 22.3	S37 06.6
A 14	3 37.5	34 05.8	.. 43.7	15 16.7	.. 58.2	298 03.2	.. 01.6	143 44.8	.. 51.8	Sirius	258 33.7	S16 44.4
Y 15	18 40.0	49 05.2	.. 42.6	30 17.3	.. 57.4	313 05.5	.. 01.7	158 47.3	.. 51.8	Spica	158 31.2	S11 13.9
16	33 42.4	64 04.7	.. 41.6	45 18.0	.. 56.7	328 07.7	.. 01.7	173 49.8	.. 51.8	Suhail	222 52.1	S43 29.4
17	48 44.9	79 04.1	.. 40.6	60 18.6	.. 55.9	343 10.0	.. 01.7	188 52.3	.. 51.7			
18	63 47.4	94 03.5	S13 39.6	75 19.3	S 5 55.1	358 12.3	N21 01.8	203 54.8	S12 51.7	Vega	80 39.3	N38 47.6
19	78 49.8	109 02.9	.. 38.5	90 19.9	.. 54.3	13 14.5	.. 01.8	218 57.2	.. 51.7	Zuben'ubi	137 05.5	S16 05.8
20	93 52.3	124 02.4	.. 37.5	105 20.6	.. 53.5	28 16.8	.. 01.9	233 59.7	.. 51.7		SHA	Mer. Pass.
21	108 54.8	139 01.8	.. 36.5	120 21.2	.. 52.8	43 19.0	.. 01.9	249 02.2	.. 51.7	Venus	32 24.1	11 43
22	123 57.2	154 01.2	.. 35.4	135 21.9	.. 52.0	58 21.3	.. 01.9	264 04.7	.. 51.7	Mars	12 48.0	13 00
23	138 59.7	169 00.6	.. 34.4	150 22.5	.. 51.2	73 23.6	.. 02.0	279 07.2	.. 51.6	Jupiter	294 33.3	18 11
Mer. Pass. 13 49.5		*v* −0.6	*d* 1.0	*v* 0.7	*d* 0.8	*v* 2.3	*d* 0.0	*v* 2.5	*d* 0.0	Saturn	140 06.8	4 31

UT	SUN GHA	SUN Dec	MOON GHA	v	MOON Dec	d	HP
d h	° '	° '	° '	'	° '	'	'
21 00	176 35.5	S10 34.5	54 05.8	11.9	N19 38.5	3.3	54.5
01	191 35.6	33.6	68 36.7	11.9	19 35.2	3.4	54.5
02	206 35.7	32.7	83 07.6	11.9	19 31.8	3.5	54.5
03	221 35.7	.. 31.8	97 38.5	11.9	19 28.3	3.6	54.5
04	236 35.8	30.9	112 09.4	11.9	19 24.7	3.7	54.5
05	251 35.9	30.0	126 40.3	12.0	19 21.0	3.8	54.5
06	266 36.0	S10 29.1	141 11.3	11.9	N19 17.2	3.9	54.5
T 07	281 36.0	28.2	155 42.2	11.9	19 13.3	3.9	54.5
H 08	296 36.1	27.3	170 13.1	12.0	19 09.4	4.1	54.6
U 09	311 36.2	.. 26.4	184 44.1	11.9	19 05.3	4.1	54.6
R 10	326 36.3	25.5	199 15.0	12.0	19 01.2	4.3	54.6
S 11	341 36.3	24.6	213 46.0	12.0	18 56.9	4.3	54.6
D 12	356 36.4	S10 23.7	228 17.0	11.9	N18 52.6	4.4	54.6
A 13	11 36.5	22.8	242 47.9	12.0	18 48.2	4.5	54.6
Y 14	26 36.6	21.9	257 18.9	12.0	18 43.7	4.6	54.6
15	41 36.6	.. 20.9	271 49.9	12.0	18 39.1	4.7	54.7
16	56 36.7	20.0	286 20.9	12.0	18 34.4	4.8	54.7
17	71 36.8	19.1	300 51.9	12.0	18 29.6	4.8	54.7
18	86 36.9	S10 18.2	315 22.9	12.1	N18 24.8	5.0	54.7
19	101 37.0	17.3	329 54.0	12.0	18 19.8	5.0	54.7
20	116 37.0	16.4	344 25.0	12.0	18 14.8	5.2	54.7
21	131 37.1	.. 15.5	358 56.0	12.1	18 09.6	5.2	54.7
22	146 37.2	14.6	13 27.1	12.1	18 04.4	5.3	54.8
23	161 37.3	13.7	27 58.2	12.0	17 59.1	5.4	54.8
22 00	176 37.3	S10 12.8	42 29.2	12.1	N17 53.7	5.5	54.8
01	191 37.4	11.9	57 00.3	12.1	17 48.2	5.6	54.8
02	206 37.5	10.9	71 31.4	12.1	17 42.6	5.6	54.8
03	221 37.6	.. 10.0	86 02.5	12.1	17 37.0	5.8	54.8
04	236 37.7	09.1	100 33.6	12.2	17 31.2	5.8	54.9
05	251 37.7	08.2	115 04.8	12.1	17 25.4	5.9	54.9
06	266 37.8	S10 07.3	129 35.9	12.2	N17 19.5	6.0	54.9
07	281 37.9	06.4	144 07.1	12.1	17 13.5	6.1	54.9
F 08	296 38.0	05.5	158 38.2	12.2	17 07.4	6.2	54.9
R 09	311 38.1	.. 04.6	173 09.4	12.2	17 01.2	6.2	55.0
I 10	326 38.2	03.6	187 40.6	12.2	16 55.0	6.4	55.0
D 11	341 38.2	02.7	202 11.8	12.2	16 48.6	6.4	55.0
A 12	356 38.3	S10 01.8	216 43.0	12.2	N16 42.2	6.5	55.0
Y 13	11 38.4	00.9	231 14.2	12.2	16 35.7	6.6	55.0
14	26 38.5	10 00.0	245 45.4	12.3	16 29.1	6.6	55.0
15	41 38.6	9 59.1	260 16.7	12.2	16 22.5	6.8	55.1
16	56 38.7	58.2	274 47.9	12.3	16 15.7	6.8	55.1
17	71 38.7	57.2	289 19.2	12.2	16 08.9	6.9	55.1
18	86 38.8	S 9 56.3	303 50.4	12.3	N16 02.0	7.0	55.1
19	101 38.9	55.4	318 21.7	12.3	15 55.0	7.1	55.1
20	116 39.0	54.5	332 53.0	12.3	15 47.9	7.1	55.2
21	131 39.1	.. 53.6	347 24.3	12.3	15 40.8	7.3	55.2
22	146 39.2	52.7	1 55.6	12.4	15 33.5	7.3	55.2
23	161 39.3	51.8	16 27.0	12.3	15 26.2	7.4	55.2
23 00	176 39.3	S 9 50.8	30 58.3	12.3	N15 18.8	7.4	55.2
01	191 39.4	49.9	45 29.6	12.4	15 11.4	7.6	55.3
02	206 39.5	49.0	60 01.0	12.4	15 03.8	7.6	55.3
03	221 39.6	.. 48.1	74 32.4	12.4	14 56.2	7.7	55.3
04	236 39.7	47.2	89 03.8	12.3	14 48.5	7.8	55.3
05	251 39.8	46.2	103 35.1	12.4	14 40.7	7.8	55.3
06	266 39.9	S 9 45.3	118 06.5	12.5	N14 32.9	7.9	55.4
07	281 40.0	44.4	132 38.0	12.4	14 25.0	8.0	55.4
S 08	296 40.0	43.5	147 09.4	12.4	14 17.0	8.1	55.4
A 09	311 40.1	.. 42.6	161 40.8	12.5	14 08.9	8.1	55.4
T 10	326 40.2	41.7	176 12.3	12.4	14 00.8	8.2	55.5
U 11	341 40.3	40.7	190 43.7	12.5	13 52.6	8.3	55.5
R 12	356 40.4	S 9 39.8	205 15.2	12.5	N13 44.3	8.4	55.5
D 13	11 40.5	38.9	219 46.7	12.4	13 35.9	8.4	55.5
A 14	26 40.6	38.0	234 18.1	12.5	13 27.5	8.5	55.5
Y 15	41 40.7	.. 37.1	248 49.6	12.5	13 19.0	8.6	55.6
16	56 40.8	36.1	263 21.1	12.5	13 10.4	8.6	55.6
17	71 40.8	35.2	277 52.6	12.6	13 01.8	8.7	55.6
18	86 40.9	S 9 34.3	292 24.2	12.5	N12 53.1	8.8	55.6
19	101 41.0	33.4	306 55.7	12.5	12 44.3	8.8	55.6
20	116 41.1	32.4	321 27.2	12.6	12 35.5	8.9	55.7
21	131 41.2	.. 31.5	335 58.8	12.5	12 26.6	9.0	55.7
22	146 41.3	30.6	350 30.3	12.6	12 17.6	9.0	55.7
23	161 41.4	29.7	5 01.9	12.5	N12 08.6	9.1	55.7
	SD 16.2	d 0.9	SD 14.9		15.0		15.1

Lat.	Twilight Naut.	Twilight Civil	Sunrise	Moonrise 21	Moonrise 22	Moonrise 23	Moonrise 24
°	h m	h m	h m	h m	h m	h m	h m
N 72	05 43	07 01	08 13	▭	11 01	13 11	15 07
N 70	05 44	06 55	07 59	10 02	11 53	13 39	15 22
68	05 46	06 50	07 48	10 54	12 24	13 59	15 35
66	05 46	06 46	07 39	11 26	12 48	14 15	15 45
64	05 47	06 42	07 31	11 50	13 06	14 28	15 53
62	05 47	06 39	07 24	12 08	13 21	14 39	16 00
60	05 47	06 36	07 18	12 24	13 33	14 48	16 06
N 58	05 48	06 33	07 13	12 37	13 44	14 56	16 12
56	05 48	06 31	07 08	12 48	13 53	15 04	16 17
54	05 47	06 28	07 04	12 58	14 02	15 10	16 21
52	05 47	06 26	07 01	13 06	14 09	15 16	16 25
50	05 47	06 24	06 57	13 14	14 16	15 21	16 28
45	05 46	06 20	06 50	13 31	14 30	15 32	16 36
N 40	05 45	06 16	06 43	13 45	14 42	15 41	16 42
35	05 43	06 12	06 38	13 56	14 52	15 49	16 48
30	05 41	06 09	06 33	14 06	15 00	15 56	16 53
20	05 37	06 02	06 25	14 24	15 15	16 08	17 01
N 10	05 31	05 56	06 17	14 39	15 28	16 18	17 08
0	05 25	05 49	06 10	14 53	15 41	16 28	17 15
S 10	05 17	05 41	06 03	15 07	15 53	16 38	17 22
20	05 06	05 32	05 55	15 22	16 06	16 48	17 29
30	04 52	05 21	05 46	15 39	16 21	17 00	17 37
35	04 43	05 14	05 41	15 49	16 29	17 07	17 42
40	04 33	05 06	05 35	16 01	16 39	17 14	17 47
45	04 19	04 57	05 27	16 14	16 50	17 23	17 53
S 50	04 02	04 45	05 19	16 30	17 04	17 34	18 01
52	03 54	04 39	05 15	16 38	17 11	17 39	18 04
54	03 44	04 32	05 11	16 47	17 18	17 44	18 08
56	03 33	04 25	05 06	16 56	17 26	17 50	18 12
58	03 20	04 17	05 00	17 07	17 35	17 57	18 16
S 60	03 05	04 07	04 54	17 20	17 45	18 05	18 21

Lat.	Sunset	Twilight Civil	Twilight Naut.	Moonset 21	Moonset 22	Moonset 23	Moonset 24
°	h m	h m	h m	h m	h m	h m	h m
N 72	16 15	17 28	18 47	▭	08 07	07 36	07 18
N 70	16 28	17 34	18 45	07 26	07 15	07 07	07 01
68	16 40	17 39	18 43	06 33	06 42	06 46	06 47
66	16 50	17 43	18 42	06 01	06 18	06 29	06 36
64	16 57	17 46	18 42	05 37	05 59	06 15	06 27
62	17 04	17 50	18 41	05 18	05 44	06 03	06 19
60	17 10	17 52	18 41	05 02	05 31	05 53	06 11
N 58	17 15	17 55	18 41	04 49	05 20	05 45	06 05
56	17 19	17 57	18 41	04 37	05 10	05 37	06 00
54	17 23	18 00	18 41	04 27	05 01	05 30	05 55
52	17 27	18 02	18 41	04 18	04 54	05 24	05 50
50	17 31	18 03	18 41	04 10	04 47	05 18	05 46
45	17 38	18 08	18 42	03 53	04 32	05 06	05 37
N 40	17 44	18 11	18 44	03 39	04 19	04 56	05 30
35	17 49	18 15	18 46	03 27	04 09	04 47	05 23
30	17 54	18 18	18 48	03 17	03 59	04 39	05 17
20	18 02	18 25	18 50	02 59	03 43	04 26	05 08
N 10	18 10	18 31	18 56	02 43	03 29	04 14	04 59
0	18 17	18 38	19 02	02 28	03 16	04 03	04 50
S 10	18 24	18 45	19 10	02 13	03 03	03 52	04 42
20	18 32	18 54	19 20	01 57	02 48	03 41	04 33
30	18 41	19 05	19 34	01 39	02 32	03 27	04 23
35	18 46	19 12	19 43	01 28	02 23	03 19	04 17
40	18 52	19 20	19 53	01 16	02 12	03 10	04 10
45	18 59	19 29	20 06	01 02	01 59	02 59	04 02
S 50	19 07	19 41	20 23	00 44	01 43	02 46	03 53
52	19 11	19 47	20 31	00 36	01 36	02 40	03 48
54	19 15	19 53	20 41	00 26	01 27	02 34	03 43
56	19 20	20 00	20 51	00 16	01 18	02 26	03 38
58	19 25	20 08	21 04	00 04	01 08	02 18	03 32
S 60	19 31	20 17	21 19	24 56	00 56	02 08	03 25

Day	SUN Eqn. of Time 00h	SUN Eqn. of Time 12h	SUN Mer. Pass.	MOON Mer. Pass. Upper	MOON Mer. Pass. Lower	Age	Phase
d	m s	m s	h m	h m	h m	d	%
21	13 38	13 35	12 14	21 04	08 40	11	82
22	13 31	13 27	12 13	21 52	09 28	12	89
23	13 23	13 19	12 13	22 39	10 16	13	94

UT	ARIES GHA	VENUS −3.9 GHA	Dec	MARS +1.2 GHA	Dec	JUPITER −2.3 GHA	Dec	SATURN +0.4 GHA	Dec	Name	SHA	Dec
d h	o ′	o ′	o ′	o ′	o ′	o ′	o ′	o ′	o ′		o ′	o ′
24 00	154 02.2	184 00.1	S13 33.4	165 23.2	S 5 50.4	88 25.8	N21 02.0	294 09.6	S12 51.6	Acamar	315 18.6	S40 15.4
01	169 04.6	198 59.5	32.3	180 23.8	49.6	103 28.1	02.1	309 12.1	51.6	Achernar	335 27.3	S57 10.4
02	184 07.1	213 58.9	31.3	195 24.5	48.8	118 30.3	02.1	324 14.6	51.6	Acrux	173 08.8	S63 10.3
03	199 09.5	228 58.4 ..	30.3	210 25.2 ..	48.1	133 32.6 ..	02.2	339 17.1 ..	51.6	Adhara	255 12.4	S28 59.8
04	214 12.0	243 57.8	29.2	225 25.8	47.3	148 34.8	02.2	354 19.6	51.6	Aldebaran	290 49.6	N16 32.0
05	229 14.5	258 57.2	28.2	240 26.5	46.5	163 37.1	02.2	9 22.1	51.5			
06	244 16.9	273 56.7	S13 27.2	255 27.1	S 5 45.7	178 39.3	N21 02.3	24 24.6	S12 51.5	Alioth	166 20.4	N55 53.0
07	259 19.4	288 56.1	26.1	270 27.8	44.9	193 41.6	02.3	39 27.0	51.5	Alkaid	152 58.8	N49 14.6
08	274 21.9	303 55.5	25.1	285 28.4	44.1	208 43.8	02.4	54 29.5	51.5	Al Na'ir	27 44.4	S46 53.8
S 09	289 24.3	318 55.0 ..	24.1	300 29.1 ..	43.4	223 46.1 ..	02.4	69 32.0 ..	51.5	Alnilam	275 46.4	S 1 11.9
U 10	304 26.8	333 54.4	23.0	315 29.7	42.6	238 48.4	02.4	84 34.5	51.5	Alphard	217 56.0	S 8 43.2
N 11	319 29.3	348 53.8	22.0	330 30.4	41.8	253 50.6	02.5	99 37.0	51.4			
D 12	334 31.7	3 53.3	S13 21.0	345 31.1	S 5 41.0	268 52.9	N21 02.5	114 39.5	S12 51.4	Alphecca	126 11.1	N26 40.0
A 13	349 34.2	18 52.7	19.9	0 31.7	40.2	283 55.1	02.6	129 41.9	51.4	Alpheratz	357 44.0	N29 09.8
Y 14	4 36.6	33 52.1	18.9	15 32.4	39.4	298 57.4	02.6	144 44.4	51.4	Altair	62 08.7	N 8 54.2
15	19 39.1	48 51.6 ..	17.8	30 33.0 ..	38.7	313 59.6 ..	02.7	159 46.9 ..	51.4	Ankaa	353 16.3	S42 14.2
16	34 41.6	63 51.0	16.8	45 33.7	37.9	329 01.9	02.7	174 49.4	51.4	Antares	112 26.5	S26 27.5
17	49 44.0	78 50.5	15.8	60 34.3	37.1	344 04.1	02.7	189 51.9	51.3			
18	64 46.5	93 49.9	S13 14.7	75 35.0	S 5 36.3	359 06.4	N21 02.8	204 54.4	S12 51.3	Arcturus	145 55.7	N19 06.6
19	79 49.0	108 49.3	13.7	90 35.7	35.5	14 08.6	02.8	219 56.9	51.3	Atria	107 28.6	S69 02.7
20	94 51.4	123 48.8	12.6	105 36.3	34.7	29 10.9	02.9	234 59.4	51.3	Avior	234 17.5	S59 33.5
21	109 53.9	138 48.2 ..	11.6	120 37.0 ..	34.0	44 13.1 ..	02.9	250 01.8 ..	51.3	Bellatrix	278 32.1	N 6 21.5
22	124 56.4	153 47.7	10.5	135 37.6	33.2	59 15.4	02.9	265 04.3	51.3	Betelgeuse	271 01.4	N 7 24.3
23	139 58.8	168 47.1	09.5	150 38.3	32.4	74 17.6	03.0	280 06.8	51.2			
25 00	155 01.3	183 46.5	S13 08.4	165 38.9	S 5 31.6	89 19.9	N21 03.0	295 09.3	S12 51.2	Canopus	263 56.0	S52 42.6
01	170 03.8	198 46.0	07.4	180 39.6	30.8	104 22.1	03.1	310 11.8	51.2	Capella	280 34.6	N46 00.7
02	185 06.2	213 45.4	06.3	195 40.3	30.0	119 24.4	03.1	325 14.3	51.2	Deneb	49 32.0	N45 19.6
03	200 08.7	228 44.9 ..	05.3	210 40.9 ..	29.2	134 26.6 ..	03.2	340 16.8 ..	51.2	Denebola	182 33.5	N14 29.7
04	215 11.1	243 44.3	04.2	225 41.6	28.5	149 28.8	03.2	355 19.3	51.1	Diphda	348 56.3	S17 55.0
05	230 13.6	258 43.8	03.2	240 42.2	27.7	164 31.1	03.2	10 21.7	51.1			
06	245 16.1	273 43.2	S13 02.1	255 42.9	S 5 26.9	179 33.3	N21 03.3	25 24.2	S12 51.1	Dubhe	193 51.3	N61 40.6
07	260 18.5	288 42.6	01.1	270 43.5	26.1	194 35.6	03.3	40 26.7	51.1	Elnath	278 12.7	N28 37.0
08	275 21.0	303 42.1	13 00.0	285 44.2	25.3	209 37.8	03.4	55 29.2	51.1	Eltanin	90 46.4	N51 29.0
M 09	290 23.5	318 41.5	12 59.0	300 44.9 ..	24.5	224 40.1 ..	03.4	70 31.7 ..	51.1	Enif	33 47.6	N 9 56.1
O 10	305 25.9	333 41.0	57.9	315 45.5	23.8	239 42.3	03.5	85 34.2	51.0	Fomalhaut	15 24.6	S29 33.2
N 11	320 28.4	348 40.4	56.9	330 46.2	23.0	254 44.6	03.5	100 36.7	51.0			
D 12	335 30.9	3 39.9	S12 55.8	345 46.8	S 5 22.2	269 46.8	N21 03.6	115 39.2	S12 51.0	Gacrux	172 00.6	S57 11.2
A 13	350 33.3	18 39.3	54.8	0 47.5	21.4	284 49.1	03.6	130 41.7	51.0	Gienah	175 52.2	S17 37.1
Y 14	5 35.8	33 38.8	53.7	15 48.2	20.6	299 51.3	03.6	145 44.1	51.0	Hadar	148 47.8	S60 26.0
15	20 38.3	48 38.2 ..	52.7	30 48.8 ..	19.8	314 53.5 ..	03.7	160 46.6 ..	51.0	Hamal	328 01.1	N23 31.5
16	35 40.7	63 37.7	51.6	45 49.5	19.0	329 55.8	03.7	175 49.1	50.9	Kaus Aust.	83 44.3	S34 22.5
17	50 43.2	78 37.1	50.6	60 50.1	18.3	344 58.0	03.8	190 51.6	50.9			
18	65 45.6	93 36.6	S12 49.5	75 50.8	S 5 17.5	0 00.3	N21 03.8	205 54.1	S12 50.9	Kochab	137 19.6	N74 05.8
19	80 48.1	108 36.0	48.4	90 51.5	16.7	15 02.5	03.8	220 56.6	50.9	Markab	13 38.8	N15 16.6
20	95 50.6	123 35.5	47.4	105 52.1	15.9	30 04.8	03.9	235 59.1	50.9	Menkar	314 15.3	N 4 08.3
21	110 53.0	138 34.9 ..	46.3	120 52.8 ..	15.1	45 07.0 ..	03.9	251 01.6 ..	50.8	Menkent	148 07.6	S36 26.0
22	125 55.5	153 34.4	45.3	135 53.4	14.3	60 09.2	04.0	266 04.1	50.8	Miaplacidus	221 38.8	S69 46.5
23	140 58.0	168 33.8	44.2	150 54.1	13.5	75 11.5	04.0	281 06.6	50.8			
26 00	156 00.4	183 33.3	S12 43.1	165 54.8	S 5 12.8	90 13.7	N21 04.1	296 09.1	S12 50.8	Mirfak	308 40.7	N49 54.6
01	171 02.9	198 32.7	42.1	180 55.4	12.0	105 16.0	04.1	311 11.5	50.8	Nunki	75 58.8	S26 16.7
02	186 05.4	213 32.2	41.0	195 56.1	11.2	120 18.2	04.1	326 14.0	50.7	Peacock	53 20.1	S56 41.3
03	201 07.8	228 31.6 ..	40.0	210 56.7 ..	10.4	135 20.4 ..	04.2	341 16.5 ..	50.7	Pollux	243 27.7	N27 59.5
04	216 10.3	243 31.1	38.9	225 57.4	09.6	150 22.7	04.2	356 19.0	50.7	Procyon	244 59.7	N 5 11.2
05	231 12.7	258 30.5	37.8	240 58.1	08.8	165 24.9	04.3	11 21.5	50.7			
06	246 15.2	273 30.0	S12 36.8	255 58.7	S 5 08.0	180 27.2	N21 04.3	26 24.0	S12 50.7	Rasalhague	96 06.7	N12 33.0
07	261 17.7	288 29.4	35.7	270 59.4	07.3	195 29.4	04.4	41 26.5	50.7	Regulus	207 43.4	N11 53.9
T 08	276 20.1	303 28.9	34.6	286 00.0	06.5	210 31.6	04.4	56 29.0	50.6	Rigel	281 12.2	S 8 11.5
U 09	291 22.6	318 28.4 ..	33.6	301 00.7 ..	05.7	225 33.9 ..	04.4	71 31.5 ..	50.6	Rigil Kent.	139 51.6	S60 53.1
E 10	306 25.1	333 27.8	32.5	316 01.4	04.9	240 36.1	04.5	86 34.0	50.6	Sabik	102 12.8	S15 44.4
S 11	321 27.5	348 27.3	31.4	331 02.0	04.1	255 38.3	04.5	101 36.5	50.6			
D 12	336 30.0	3 26.7	S12 30.4	346 02.7	S 5 03.3	270 40.6	N21 04.6	116 39.0	S12 50.6	Schedar	349 41.2	N56 36.7
A 13	351 32.5	18 26.2	29.3	1 03.4	02.5	285 42.8	04.6	131 41.5	50.5	Shaula	96 22.3	S37 06.6
Y 14	6 34.9	33 25.6	28.2	16 04.0	01.7	300 45.1	04.7	146 44.0	50.5	Sirius	258 33.7	S16 44.4
15	21 37.4	48 25.1 ..	27.2	31 04.7 ..	01.0	315 47.3 ..	04.7	161 46.4 ..	50.5	Spica	158 31.2	S11 13.9
16	36 39.9	63 24.6	26.1	46 05.3	5 00.2	330 49.5	04.8	176 48.9	50.5	Suhail	222 52.1	S43 29.5
17	51 42.3	78 24.0	25.0	61 06.0	4 59.4	345 51.8	04.8	191 51.4	50.5			
18	66 44.8	93 23.5	S12 23.9	76 06.7	S 4 58.6	0 54.0	N21 04.8	206 53.9	S12 50.4	Vega	80 39.3	N38 47.6
19	81 47.2	108 22.9	22.9	91 07.3	57.8	15 56.2	04.9	221 56.4	50.4	Zuben'ubi	137 05.5	S16 05.8
20	96 49.7	123 22.4	21.8	106 08.0	57.0	30 58.5	04.9	236 58.9	50.4		SHA	Mer. Pass.
21	111 52.2	138 21.9 ..	20.7	121 08.6 ..	56.2	46 00.7 ..	05.0	252 01.4 ..	50.4		o ′	h m
22	126 54.6	153 21.3	19.6	136 09.3	55.5	61 02.9	05.0	267 03.9	50.4	Venus	28 45.2	11 45
23	141 57.1	168 20.8	18.6	151 10.0	54.7	76 05.2	05.1	282 06.4	50.3	Mars	10 37.7	12 57
	h m									Jupiter	294 18.6	18 00
Mer. Pass. 13 37.7	v −0.6 d 1.1		v 0.7 d 0.8		v 2.2 d 0.0		v 2.5 d 0.0			Saturn	140 08.0	4 19

UT	SUN GHA	SUN Dec	MOON GHA	v	MOON Dec	d	HP
24 00	176 41.5	S 9 28.8	19 33.4	12.6	N11 59.5	9.2	55.8
01	191 41.6	27.8	34 05.0	12.6	11 50.3	9.2	55.8
02	206 41.7	26.9	48 36.6	12.6	11 41.1	9.3	55.8
03	221 41.8	.. 26.0	63 08.2	12.6	11 31.8	9.3	55.8
04	236 41.9	25.1	77 39.8	12.6	11 22.5	9.5	55.9
05	251 42.0	24.1	92 11.4	12.6	11 13.0	9.4	55.9
06	266 42.1	S 9 23.2	106 43.0	12.6	N11 03.6	9.6	55.9
07	281 42.1	22.3	121 14.6	12.6	10 54.0	9.6	55.9
08	296 42.2	21.4	135 46.2	12.7	10 44.4	9.6	56.0
S 09	311 42.3	.. 20.4	150 17.9	12.6	10 34.8	9.7	56.0
U 10	326 42.4	19.5	164 49.5	12.6	10 25.1	9.8	56.0
N 11	341 42.5	18.6	179 21.1	12.7	10 15.3	9.8	56.0
D 12	356 42.6	S 9 17.7	193 52.8	12.6	N10 05.5	9.9	56.1
A 13	11 42.7	16.7	208 24.4	12.6	9 55.6	9.9	56.1
Y 14	26 42.8	15.8	222 56.0	12.7	9 45.7	10.0	56.1
15	41 42.9	.. 14.9	237 27.7	12.6	9 35.7	10.1	56.1
16	56 43.0	14.0	251 59.3	12.7	9 25.6	10.1	56.1
17	71 43.1	13.0	266 31.0	12.7	9 15.5	10.1	56.2
18	86 43.2	S 9 12.1	281 02.7	12.6	N 9 05.4	10.2	56.2
19	101 43.3	11.2	295 34.3	12.7	8 55.2	10.3	56.2
20	116 43.4	10.3	310 06.0	12.6	8 44.9	10.3	56.2
21	131 43.5	.. 09.3	324 37.6	12.7	8 34.6	10.4	56.3
22	146 43.6	08.4	339 09.3	12.7	8 24.2	10.4	56.3
23	161 43.7	07.5	353 41.0	12.6	8 13.8	10.4	56.3
25 00	176 43.8	S 9 06.5	8 12.6	12.7	N 8 03.4	10.5	56.3
01	191 43.9	05.6	22 44.3	12.6	7 52.9	10.6	56.4
02	206 44.0	04.7	37 15.9	12.7	7 42.3	10.5	56.4
03	221 44.1	.. 03.8	51 47.6	12.6	7 31.8	10.7	56.4
04	236 44.2	02.8	66 19.2	12.7	7 21.1	10.7	56.4
05	251 44.3	01.9	80 50.9	12.6	7 10.4	10.7	56.5
06	266 44.4	S 9 01.0	95 22.5	12.7	N 6 59.7	10.7	56.5
07	281 44.5	9 00.0	109 54.2	12.6	6 49.0	10.8	56.5
08	296 44.6	8 59.1	124 25.8	12.7	6 38.2	10.9	56.5
M 09	311 44.7	.. 58.2	138 57.5	12.6	6 27.3	10.9	56.6
O 10	326 44.8	57.2	153 29.1	12.6	6 16.4	10.9	56.6
N 11	341 44.9	56.3	168 00.7	12.7	6 05.5	11.0	56.6
D 12	356 45.0	S 8 55.4	182 32.4	12.6	N 5 54.5	11.0	56.7
A 13	11 45.1	54.4	197 04.0	12.6	5 43.5	11.0	56.7
Y 14	26 45.2	53.5	211 35.6	12.6	5 32.5	11.1	56.7
15	41 45.3	.. 52.6	226 07.2	12.6	5 21.4	11.1	56.7
16	56 45.4	51.6	240 38.8	12.6	5 10.3	11.1	56.7
17	71 45.5	50.7	255 10.4	12.5	4 59.2	11.2	56.7
18	86 45.6	S 8 49.8	269 41.9	12.6	N 4 48.0	11.2	56.8
19	101 45.7	48.9	284 13.5	12.6	4 36.8	11.2	56.8
20	116 45.8	47.9	298 45.1	12.5	4 25.6	11.3	56.8
21	131 45.9	.. 47.0	313 16.6	12.5	4 14.3	11.3	56.8
22	146 46.0	46.0	327 48.2	12.5	4 03.0	11.3	56.9
23	161 46.1	45.1	342 19.7	12.5	3 51.7	11.4	56.9
26 00	176 46.2	S 8 44.2	356 51.2	12.5	N 3 40.3	11.4	56.9
01	191 46.3	43.2	11 22.7	12.5	3 28.9	11.4	56.9
02	206 46.4	42.3	25 54.2	12.5	3 17.5	11.4	57.0
03	221 46.6	.. 41.4	40 25.7	12.4	3 06.1	11.4	57.0
04	236 46.7	40.4	54 57.1	12.5	2 54.7	11.5	57.0
05	251 46.8	39.5	69 28.6	12.4	2 43.2	11.5	57.0
06	266 46.9	S 8 38.6	84 00.0	12.5	N 2 31.7	11.5	57.0
07	281 47.0	37.6	98 31.5	12.4	2 20.2	11.6	57.1
T 08	296 47.1	36.7	113 02.9	12.3	2 08.6	11.5	57.1
U 09	311 47.2	.. 35.8	127 34.2	12.4	1 57.1	11.6	57.1
E 10	326 47.3	34.8	142 05.6	12.4	1 45.5	11.6	57.1
S 11	341 47.4	33.9	156 37.0	12.3	1 33.9	11.6	57.2
D 12	356 47.5	S 8 33.0	171 08.3	12.3	N 1 22.3	11.6	57.2
A 13	11 47.6	32.0	185 39.6	12.3	1 10.7	11.7	57.2
Y 14	26 47.7	31.1	200 10.9	12.3	0 59.0	11.6	57.2
15	41 47.8	.. 30.1	214 42.2	12.2	0 47.4	11.7	57.3
16	56 47.9	29.2	229 13.4	12.3	0 35.7	11.7	57.3
17	71 48.1	28.3	243 44.7	12.2	0 24.0	11.7	57.3
18	86 48.2	S 8 27.3	258 15.9	12.2	N 0 12.3	11.7	57.3
19	101 48.3	26.4	272 47.1	12.1	N 0 00.6	11.7	57.3
20	116 48.4	25.5	287 18.2	12.2	S 0 11.1	11.7	57.4
21	131 48.5	.. 24.5	301 49.4	12.1	0 22.8	11.7	57.4
22	146 48.6	23.6	316 20.5	12.1	0 34.5	11.7	57.4
23	161 48.7	22.6	330 51.6	12.0	S 0 46.2	11.7	57.4
	SD 16.2	d 0.9	SD 15.3		15.4		15.6

Twilight / Moonrise

Lat.	Naut.	Civil	Sunrise	24	25	26	27
N 72	05 29	06 46	07 57	15 07	16 59	18 50	20 43
N 70	05 32	06 42	07 45	15 22	17 06	18 50	20 36
68	05 34	06 38	07 36	15 35	17 11	18 49	20 30
66	05 36	06 35	07 28	15 45	17 16	18 49	20 24
64	05 37	06 32	07 21	15 53	17 20	18 49	20 20
62	05 39	06 30	07 15	16 00	17 24	18 49	20 16
60	05 39	06 27	07 10	16 06	17 27	18 49	20 13
N 58	05 40	06 25	07 05	16 12	17 30	18 49	20 10
56	05 40	06 24	07 01	16 17	17 32	18 49	20 08
54	05 41	06 22	06 58	16 21	17 34	18 49	20 06
52	05 41	06 20	06 54	16 25	17 36	18 49	20 04
50	05 41	06 19	06 51	16 28	17 38	18 49	20 02
45	05 41	06 15	06 45	16 36	17 42	18 49	19 58
N 40	05 40	06 12	06 39	16 42	17 45	18 49	19 54
35	05 40	06 09	06 34	16 48	17 48	18 49	19 51
30	05 38	06 06	06 30	16 53	17 50	18 49	19 49
20	05 35	06 00	06 23	17 01	17 55	18 49	19 45
N 10	05 30	05 55	06 16	17 08	17 58	18 49	19 41
0	05 24	05 49	06 10	17 15	18 02	18 49	19 37
S 10	05 17	05 42	06 03	17 22	18 05	18 49	19 34
20	05 08	05 34	05 56	17 29	18 09	18 49	19 30
30	04 55	05 24	05 48	17 37	18 13	18 49	19 26
35	04 47	05 17	05 43	17 42	18 16	18 49	19 24
40	04 37	05 10	05 38	17 47	18 18	18 49	19 21
45	04 24	05 01	05 32	17 53	18 22	18 49	19 18
S 50	04 08	04 50	05 24	18 01	18 25	18 50	19 14
52	04 01	04 45	05 21	18 04	18 27	18 50	19 13
54	03 52	04 39	05 17	18 08	18 29	18 50	19 11
56	03 42	04 32	05 12	18 12	18 31	18 50	19 09
58	03 30	04 25	05 08	18 16	18 33	18 50	19 07
S 60	03 16	04 16	05 02	18 21	18 36	18 50	19 04

Sunset / Twilight / Moonset

Lat.	Sunset	Civil	Naut.	24	25	26	27
N 72	16 31	17 42	19 00	07 18	07 05	06 53	06 42
N 70	16 42	17 46	18 57	07 01	06 56	06 50	06 45
68	16 52	17 49	18 54	06 47	06 48	06 48	06 47
66	17 00	17 53	18 52	06 36	06 41	06 46	06 50
64	17 07	17 55	18 50	06 27	06 36	06 44	06 52
62	17 12	17 58	18 49	06 19	06 31	06 42	06 53
60	17 17	18 00	18 48	06 11	06 27	06 41	06 55
N 58	17 22	18 02	18 47	06 05	06 23	06 40	06 56
56	17 26	18 04	18 47	06 00	06 20	06 39	06 57
54	17 29	18 05	18 46	05 55	06 17	06 38	06 58
52	17 33	18 07	18 46	05 50	06 14	06 37	06 59
50	17 36	18 08	18 46	05 46	06 12	06 36	07 00
45	17 42	18 12	18 46	05 37	06 06	06 34	07 02
N 40	17 47	18 15	18 46	05 30	06 02	06 33	07 04
35	17 52	18 18	18 47	05 23	05 50	06 31	07 05
30	17 56	18 20	18 48	05 17	05 54	06 30	07 06
20	18 03	18 26	18 52	05 08	05 48	06 28	07 08
N 10	18 10	18 31	18 56	04 59	05 42	06 26	07 10
0	18 16	18 37	19 02	04 50	05 37	06 24	07 12
S 10	18 23	18 44	19 10	04 42	05 32	06 22	07 14
20	18 30	18 52	19 18	04 33	05 27	06 21	07 15
30	18 37	19 02	19 31	04 23	05 20	06 18	07 18
35	18 42	19 08	19 39	04 17	05 16	06 17	07 19
40	18 47	19 15	19 48	04 10	05 12	06 16	07 20
45	18 53	19 24	20 01	04 02	05 07	06 14	07 22
S 50	19 01	19 35	20 16	03 53	05 01	06 12	07 23
52	19 04	19 40	20 24	03 48	04 59	06 11	07 24
54	19 08	19 46	20 32	03 43	04 56	06 10	07 25
56	19 12	19 52	20 42	03 38	04 52	06 09	07 26
58	19 17	19 59	20 53	03 32	04 49	06 07	07 27
S 60	19 22	20 08	21 07	03 25	04 44	06 06	07 29

SUN / MOON

Day	Eqn. of Time 00h	Eqn. of Time 12h	Mer. Pass.	Mer. Pass. Upper	Mer. Pass. Lower	Age	Phase
24	13 14	13 10	12 13	23 26	11 03	14	98
25	13 05	13 00	12 13	24 13	11 50	15	100
26	12 55	12 50	12 13	00 13	12 37	16	99

UT (d h)	ARIES GHA	VENUS −3.9 GHA	Dec	MARS +1.2 GHA	Dec	JUPITER −2.3 GHA	Dec	SATURN +0.4 GHA	Dec	STARS Name	SHA	Dec
27 00	156 59.6	183 20.3	S12 17.5	166 10.6	S 4 53.9	91 07.4	N21 05.1	297 08.9	S12 50.3	Acamar	315 18.7	S40 15.4
01	172 02.0	198 19.7	16.4	181 11.3	53.1	106 09.6	05.2	312 11.4	50.3	Achernar	335 27.3	S57 10.4
02	187 04.5	213 19.2	15.3	196 12.0	52.3	121 11.9	05.2	327 13.9	50.3	Acrux	173 08.8	S63 10.3
03	202 07.0	228 18.6	.. 14.3	211 12.6	.. 51.5	136 14.1	.. 05.2	342 16.4	.. 50.3	Adhara	255 12.4	S28 59.8
04	217 09.4	243 18.1	13.2	226 13.3	50.7	151 16.3	05.3	357 18.9	50.2	Aldebaran	290 49.6	N16 32.0
05	232 11.9	258 17.6	12.1	241 14.0	49.9	166 18.6	05.3	12 21.4	50.2			
06	247 14.3	273 17.0	S12 11.0	256 14.6	S 4 49.2	181 20.8	N21 05.4	27 23.9	S12 50.2	Alioth	166 20.4	N55 53.0
W 07	262 16.8	288 16.5	10.0	271 15.3	48.4	196 23.0	05.4	42 26.4	50.2	Alkaid	152 58.7	N49 14.6
E 08	277 19.3	303 16.0	08.9	286 15.9	47.6	211 25.3	05.5	57 28.9	50.2	Al Na'ir	27 44.4	S46 53.7
D 09	292 21.7	318 15.4	.. 07.8	301 16.6	.. 46.8	226 27.5	.. 05.5	72 31.4	.. 50.1	Alnilam	275 46.5	S 1 11.9
N 10	307 24.2	333 14.9	06.7	316 17.3	46.0	241 29.7	05.6	87 33.9	50.1	Alphard	217 56.0	S 8 43.2
E 11	322 26.7	348 14.4	05.6	331 17.9	45.2	256 31.9	05.6	102 36.4	50.1			
S 12	337 29.1	3 13.8	S12 04.6	346 18.6	S 4 44.4	271 34.2	N21 05.6	117 38.9	S12 50.1	Alphecca	126 11.1	N26 40.0
D 13	352 31.6	18 13.3	03.5	1 19.3	43.6	286 36.4	05.7	132 41.4	50.1	Alpheratz	357 44.0	N29 09.8
A 14	7 34.1	33 12.8	02.4	16 19.9	42.8	301 38.6	05.7	147 43.9	50.0	Altair	62 08.7	N 8 54.2
Y 15	22 36.5	48 12.2	.. 01.3	31 20.6	.. 42.1	316 40.9	.. 05.8	162 46.4	.. 50.0	Ankaa	353 16.3	S42 14.2
16	37 39.0	63 11.7	12 00.2	46 21.3	41.3	331 43.1	05.8	177 48.9	50.0	Antares	112 26.5	S26 27.5
17	52 41.5	78 11.2	11 59.1	61 21.9	40.5	346 45.3	05.9	192 51.4	50.0			
18	67 43.9	93 10.7	S11 58.0	76 22.6	S 4 39.7	1 47.5	N21 05.9	207 53.9	S12 50.0	Arcturus	145 55.7	N19 06.6
19	82 46.4	108 10.1	57.0	91 23.3	38.9	16 49.8	06.0	222 56.4	49.9	Atria	107 28.5	S69 02.7
20	97 48.8	123 09.6	55.9	106 23.9	38.1	31 52.0	06.0	237 58.9	49.9	Avior	234 17.5	S59 33.5
21	112 51.3	138 09.1	.. 54.8	121 24.6	.. 37.3	46 54.2	.. 06.0	253 01.4	.. 49.9	Bellatrix	278 32.1	N 6 21.5
22	127 53.8	153 08.5	53.7	136 25.2	36.5	61 56.4	06.1	268 03.9	49.9	Betelgeuse	271 01.4	N 7 24.3
23	142 56.2	168 08.0	52.6	151 25.9	35.8	76 58.7	06.1	283 06.4	49.8			
28 00	157 58.7	183 07.5	S11 51.5	166 26.6	S 4 35.0	92 00.9	N21 06.2	298 08.9	S12 49.8	Canopus	263 56.0	S52 42.6
01	173 01.2	198 07.0	50.4	181 27.2	34.2	107 03.1	06.2	313 11.4	49.8	Capella	280 34.6	N46 00.7
02	188 03.6	213 06.4	49.3	196 27.9	33.4	122 05.4	06.3	328 13.9	49.8	Deneb	49 32.0	N45 19.6
03	203 06.1	228 05.9	.. 48.3	211 28.6	.. 32.6	137 07.6	.. 06.3	343 16.4	.. 49.8	Denebola	182 33.5	N14 29.7
04	218 08.6	243 05.4	47.2	226 29.2	31.8	152 09.8	06.4	358 18.9	49.7	Diphda	348 56.4	S17 55.0
05	233 11.0	258 04.9	46.1	241 29.9	31.0	167 12.0	06.4	13 21.4	49.7			
06	248 13.5	273 04.3	S11 45.0	256 30.6	S 4 30.2	182 14.2	N21 06.5	28 23.9	S12 49.7	Dubhe	193 51.3	N61 40.6
T 07	263 15.9	288 03.8	43.9	271 31.2	29.4	197 16.5	06.5	43 26.4	49.7	Elnath	278 12.8	N28 37.0
H 08	278 18.4	303 03.3	42.8	286 31.9	28.7	212 18.7	06.5	58 28.9	49.7	Eltanin	90 46.4	N51 29.0
U 09	293 20.9	318 02.8	.. 41.7	301 32.6	.. 27.9	227 20.9	.. 06.6	73 31.4	.. 49.6	Enif	33 47.6	N 9 56.1
R 10	308 23.3	333 02.3	40.6	316 33.2	27.1	242 23.1	06.6	88 33.9	49.6	Fomalhaut	15 24.6	S29 33.1
S 11	323 25.8	348 01.7	39.5	331 33.9	26.3	257 25.4	06.6	103 36.4	49.6			
D 12	338 28.3	3 01.2	S11 38.4	346 34.6	S 4 25.5	272 27.6	N21 06.7	118 38.9	S12 49.6	Gacrux	172 00.6	S57 11.2
A 13	353 30.7	18 00.7	37.3	1 35.2	24.7	287 29.8	06.8	133 41.4	49.5	Gienah	175 52.2	S17 37.1
Y 14	8 33.2	33 00.2	36.2	16 35.9	23.9	302 32.0	06.8	148 43.9	49.5	Hadar	148 47.7	S60 26.0
15	23 35.7	47 59.6	.. 35.1	31 36.6	.. 23.1	317 34.2	.. 06.9	163 46.4	.. 49.5	Hamal	328 01.2	N23 31.5
16	38 38.1	62 59.1	34.0	46 37.2	22.3	332 36.5	06.9	178 48.9	49.5	Kaus Aust.	83 44.2	S34 22.5
17	53 40.6	77 58.6	32.9	61 37.9	21.5	347 38.7	07.0	193 51.4	49.5			
18	68 43.1	92 58.1	S11 31.8	76 38.6	S 4 20.8	2 40.9	N21 07.0	208 53.9	S12 49.4	Kochab	137 19.5	N74 05.8
19	83 45.5	107 57.6	30.7	91 39.2	20.0	17 43.1	07.0	223 56.4	49.4	Markab	13 38.8	N15 16.6
20	98 48.0	122 57.0	29.6	106 39.9	19.2	32 45.3	07.1	238 58.9	49.4	Menkar	314 15.4	N 4 08.3
21	113 50.4	137 56.5	.. 28.5	121 40.6	.. 18.4	47 47.6	.. 07.1	254 01.4	.. 49.4	Menkent	148 07.5	S36 26.0
22	128 52.9	152 56.0	27.4	136 41.2	17.6	62 49.8	07.2	269 03.9	49.3	Miaplacidus	221 38.8	S69 46.6
23	143 55.4	167 55.5	26.3	151 41.9	16.8	77 52.0	07.2	284 06.4	49.3			
1 00	158 57.8	182 55.0	S11 25.2	166 42.6	S 4 16.0	92 54.2	N21 07.3	299 08.9	S12 49.3	Mirfak	308 40.7	N49 54.6
01	174 00.3	197 54.5	24.1	181 43.2	15.2	107 56.4	07.3	314 11.4	49.3	Nunki	75 58.7	S26 16.6
02	189 02.8	212 53.9	23.0	196 43.9	14.4	122 58.7	07.4	329 13.9	49.2	Peacock	53 20.0	S56 41.3
03	204 05.2	227 53.4	.. 21.9	211 44.6	.. 13.7	138 00.9	.. 07.4	344 16.4	.. 49.2	Pollux	243 27.7	N27 59.5
04	219 07.7	242 52.9	20.8	226 45.2	12.9	153 03.1	07.5	359 18.9	49.2	Procyon	244 59.7	N 5 11.2
05	234 10.2	257 52.4	19.7	241 45.9	12.1	168 05.3	07.5	14 21.4	49.2			
06	249 12.6	272 51.9	S11 18.6	256 46.6	S 4 11.3	183 07.5	N21 07.6	29 23.9	S12 49.2	Rasalhague	96 06.7	N12 33.0
07	264 15.1	287 51.4	17.5	271 47.3	10.5	198 09.7	07.6	44 26.4	49.1	Regulus	207 43.4	N11 53.9
F 08	279 17.6	302 50.9	16.4	286 47.9	09.7	213 12.0	07.6	59 28.9	49.1	Rigel	281 12.2	S 8 11.5
R 09	294 20.0	317 50.4	.. 15.3	301 48.6	.. 08.9	228 14.2	.. 07.7	74 31.4	.. 49.1	Rigil Kent.	139 51.6	S60 53.1
I 10	309 22.5	332 49.8	14.2	316 49.3	08.1	243 16.4	07.7	89 33.9	49.1	Sabik	102 12.8	S15 44.4
D 11	324 24.9	347 49.3	13.1	331 49.9	07.3	258 18.6	07.8	104 36.5	49.1			
A 12	339 27.4	2 48.8	S11 12.0	346 50.6	S 4 06.5	273 20.8	N21 07.8	119 39.0	S12 49.0	Schedar	349 41.2	N56 36.7
Y 13	354 29.9	17 48.3	10.9	1 51.3	05.7	288 23.0	07.9	134 41.5	49.0	Shaula	96 22.3	S37 06.6
14	9 32.3	32 47.8	09.8	16 51.9	05.0	303 25.2	07.9	149 44.0	49.0	Sirius	258 33.7	S16 44.4
15	24 34.8	47 47.3	.. 08.6	31 52.6	.. 04.2	318 27.5	.. 08.0	164 46.5	.. 49.0	Spica	158 31.2	S11 13.9
16	39 37.3	62 46.8	07.5	46 53.3	03.4	333 29.7	08.0	179 49.0	48.9	Suhail	222 52.2	S43 29.5
17	54 39.7	77 46.3	06.4	61 53.9	02.6	348 31.9	08.1	194 51.5	48.9			
18	69 42.2	92 45.8	S11 05.3	76 54.6	S 4 01.8	3 34.1	N21 08.1	209 54.0	S12 48.9	Vega	80 39.3	N38 47.6
19	84 44.7	107 45.2	04.2	91 55.3	01.0	18 36.3	08.2	224 56.5	48.9	Zuben'ubi	137 05.5	S16 05.8
20	99 47.1	122 44.7	03.1	106 56.0	4 00.2	33 38.5	08.2	239 59.0	48.8		SHA	Mer. Pass.
21	114 49.6	137 44.2	.. 02.0	121 56.6	3 59.4	48 40.7	.. 08.3	255 01.5	.. 48.8			h m
22	129 52.0	152 43.7	11 00.9	136 57.3	58.6	63 42.9	08.3	270 04.0	48.8	Venus	25 08.8	11 48
23	144 54.5	167 43.2	S10 59.7	151 58.0	57.8	78 45.1	08.3	285 06.5	48.8	Mars	8 27.9	12 54
	h m									Jupiter	294 02.2	17 49
Mer. Pass. 13 25.9	v −0.5　d 1.1			v 0.7　d 0.8		v 2.2　d 0.0		v 2.5　d 0.0		Saturn	140 10.2	4 07

UT	SUN GHA	SUN Dec	MOON GHA	v	MOON Dec	d	HP
d h	° ′	° ′	° ′	′	° ′	′	′
27 00	176 48.8	S 8 21.7	345 22.6	12.1	S 0 57.9	11.8	57.5
01	191 48.9	20.8	359 53.7	12.0	1 09.7	11.7	57.5
02	206 49.0	19.8	14 24.7	12.0	1 21.4	11.7	57.5
03	221 49.2	.. 18.9	28 55.7	11.9	1 33.1	11.8	57.5
04	236 49.3	17.9	43 26.6	12.0	1 44.9	11.7	57.5
05	251 49.4	17.0	57 57.6	11.9	1 56.6	11.7	57.5
W 06	266 49.5	S 8 16.1	72 28.5	11.8	S 2 08.3	11.8	57.6
E 07	281 49.6	15.1	86 59.3	11.9	2 20.1	11.7	57.6
D 08	296 49.7	14.2	101 30.2	11.8	2 31.8	11.7	57.6
N 09	311 49.8	.. 13.2	116 01.0	11.8	2 43.5	11.7	57.6
E 10	326 49.9	12.3	130 31.8	11.7	2 55.2	11.7	57.7
S 11	341 50.1	11.3	145 02.5	11.7	3 06.9	11.7	57.7
D 12	356 50.2	S 8 10.4	159 33.2	11.7	S 3 18.6	11.7	57.7
A 13	11 50.3	09.5	174 03.9	11.7	3 30.3	11.7	57.7
Y 14	26 50.4	08.5	188 34.6	11.6	3 42.0	11.6	57.7
15	41 50.5	.. 07.6	203 05.2	11.5	3 53.6	11.7	57.8
16	56 50.6	06.6	217 35.7	11.6	4 05.3	11.6	57.8
17	71 50.7	05.7	232 06.3	11.5	4 16.9	11.6	57.8
18	86 50.9	S 8 04.7	246 36.8	11.5	S 4 28.5	11.6	57.8
19	101 51.0	03.8	261 07.3	11.4	4 40.1	11.6	57.8
20	116 51.1	02.9	275 37.7	11.4	4 51.7	11.6	57.9
21	131 51.2	.. 01.9	290 08.1	11.3	5 03.3	11.5	57.9
22	146 51.3	01.0	304 38.4	11.4	5 14.8	11.6	57.9
23	161 51.4	8 00.0	319 08.8	11.2	5 26.4	11.5	57.9
28 00	176 51.5	S 7 59.1	333 39.0	11.3	S 5 37.9	11.4	57.9
01	191 51.7	58.1	348 09.3	11.2	5 49.3	11.5	58.0
02	206 51.8	57.2	2 39.5	11.1	6 00.8	11.4	58.0
03	221 51.9	.. 56.3	17 09.6	11.1	6 12.2	11.4	58.0
04	236 52.0	55.3	31 39.7	11.1	6 23.6	11.4	58.0
05	251 52.1	54.4	46 09.8	11.0	6 35.0	11.4	58.0
T 06	266 52.2	S 7 53.4	60 39.8	11.0	S 6 46.4	11.3	58.0
H 07	281 52.4	52.5	75 09.8	10.9	6 57.7	11.3	58.1
U 08	296 52.5	51.5	89 39.8	10.9	7 09.0	11.2	58.1
R 09	311 52.6	.. 50.6	104 09.7	10.8	7 20.2	11.2	58.1
S 10	326 52.7	49.6	118 39.5	10.8	7 31.4	11.2	58.1
D 11	341 52.8	48.7	133 09.3	10.8	7 42.6	11.2	58.1
A 12	356 53.0	S 7 47.7	147 39.1	10.7	S 7 53.8	11.1	58.1
Y 13	11 53.1	46.8	162 08.8	10.7	8 04.9	11.1	58.2
14	26 53.2	45.8	176 38.5	10.6	8 16.0	11.0	58.2
15	41 53.3	.. 44.9	191 08.1	10.5	8 27.0	11.0	58.2
16	56 53.4	43.9	205 37.6	10.6	8 38.0	11.0	58.2
17	71 53.6	43.0	220 07.2	10.4	8 49.0	10.9	58.2
18	86 53.7	S 7 42.1	234 36.6	10.5	S 8 59.9	10.8	58.3
19	101 53.8	41.1	249 06.1	10.3	9 10.7	10.9	58.3
20	116 53.9	40.2	263 35.4	10.4	9 21.6	10.7	58.3
21	131 54.0	.. 39.2	278 04.8	10.3	9 32.3	10.8	58.3
22	146 54.2	38.3	292 34.0	10.3	9 43.1	10.6	58.3
23	161 54.3	37.3	307 03.3	10.1	9 53.7	10.7	58.3
1 00	176 54.4	S 7 36.4	321 32.4	10.1	S 10 04.4	10.5	58.4
01	191 54.5	35.4	336 01.5	10.1	10 14.9	10.6	58.4
02	206 54.6	34.5	350 30.6	10.0	10 25.5	10.4	58.4
03	221 54.8	.. 33.5	4 59.6	10.0	10 35.9	10.5	58.4
04	236 54.9	32.6	19 28.6	9.9	10 46.4	10.3	58.4
05	251 55.0	31.6	33 57.5	9.9	10 56.7	10.3	58.4
F 06	266 55.1	S 7 30.7	48 26.4	9.8	S 11 07.0	10.3	58.5
R 07	281 55.3	29.7	62 55.2	9.7	11 17.3	10.2	58.5
I 08	296 55.4	28.8	77 23.9	9.7	11 27.5	10.1	58.5
D 09	311 55.5	.. 27.8	91 52.6	9.6	11 37.6	10.1	58.5
A 10	326 55.6	26.9	106 21.2	9.6	11 47.7	10.0	58.5
Y 11	341 55.7	25.9	120 49.8	9.5	11 57.7	9.9	58.5
12	356 55.9	S 7 25.0	135 18.3	9.5	S 12 07.6	9.9	58.5
13	11 56.0	24.0	149 46.8	9.4	12 17.5	9.8	58.5
14	26 56.1	23.0	164 15.2	9.4	12 27.3	9.7	58.6
15	41 56.2	.. 22.1	178 43.6	9.3	12 37.0	9.7	58.6
16	56 56.4	21.1	193 11.9	9.2	12 46.7	9.6	58.6
17	71 56.5	20.2	207 40.1	9.2	12 56.3	9.5	58.6
18	86 56.6	S 7 19.2	222 08.3	9.1	S 13 05.8	9.5	58.6
19	101 56.9	18.3	236 36.4	9.1	13 15.3	9.4	58.6
20	116 56.9	17.3	251 04.5	9.0	13 24.7	9.3	58.6
21	131 57.0	.. 16.4	265 32.5	9.0	13 34.0	9.2	58.6
22	146 57.1	15.4	280 00.5	8.9	13 43.2	9.2	58.7
23	161 57.2	14.5	294 28.4	8.8	S 13 52.4	9.0	58.7
SD	16.2	d 0.9	SD 15.7		15.8		15.9

Twilight / Sunrise / Moonrise

Lat.	Naut.	Civil	Sunrise	27	28	1	2
°	h m	h m	h m	h m	h m	h m	h m
N 72	05 14	06 32	07 41	20 43	22 42	24 53	00 53
N 70	05 19	06 29	07 31	20 36	22 26	24 22	00 22
68	05 22	06 27	07 23	20 30	22 13	23 59	25 47
66	05 25	06 24	07 16	20 24	22 02	23 41	25 20
64	05 28	06 22	07 10	20 20	21 53	23 27	25 00
62	05 30	06 21	07 05	20 16	21 45	23 15	24 44
60	05 31	06 19	07 01	20 13	21 39	23 05	24 30
N 58	05 32	06 18	06 57	20 10	21 33	22 56	24 18
56	05 33	06 16	06 54	20 08	21 28	22 49	24 08
54	05 34	06 15	06 51	20 06	21 23	22 42	23 59
52	05 35	06 14	06 48	20 04	21 19	22 36	23 51
50	05 35	06 13	06 45	20 02	21 16	22 30	23 44
45	05 36	06 10	06 40	19 58	21 08	22 18	23 29
N 40	05 36	06 08	06 35	19 54	21 01	22 08	23 16
35	05 36	06 05	06 31	19 51	20 55	22 00	23 05
30	05 35	06 03	06 27	19 49	20 50	21 53	22 56
20	05 33	05 58	06 20	19 45	20 42	21 40	22 40
N 10	05 29	05 54	06 15	19 41	20 34	21 29	22 26
0	05 24	05 48	06 09	19 37	20 27	21 19	22 13
S 10	05 18	05 42	06 04	19 34	20 20	21 09	22 01
20	05 09	05 35	05 57	19 30	20 13	20 58	21 47
30	04 57	05 26	05 50	19 26	20 05	20 46	21 32
35	04 50	05 20	05 46	19 24	20 00	20 39	21 23
40	04 41	05 14	05 41	19 21	19 54	20 31	21 12
45	04 29	05 06	05 36	19 18	19 48	20 22	21 00
S 50	04 15	04 56	05 29	19 14	19 41	20 11	20 46
52	04 07	04 51	05 26	19 13	19 37	20 06	20 39
54	03 59	04 45	05 23	19 11	19 34	20 00	20 32
56	03 50	04 40	05 19	19 09	19 30	19 54	20 24
58	03 40	04 33	05 15	19 07	19 25	19 47	20 14
S 60	03 27	04 25	05 10	19 04	19 20	19 39	20 04

Sunset / Twilight / Moonset

Lat.	Sunset	Civil	Naut.	27	28	1	2
°	h m	h m	h m	h m	h m	h m	h m
N 72	16 46	17 55	19 14	06 42	06 29	06 15	05 54
N 70	16 55	17 58	19 09	06 45	06 39	06 33	06 25
68	17 04	18 00	19 05	06 47	06 47	06 48	06 50
66	17 10	18 02	19 02	06 50	06 54	07 00	07 09
64	17 16	18 04	18 59	06 52	07 00	07 10	07 24
62	17 21	18 06	18 57	06 53	07 05	07 19	07 37
60	17 25	18 07	18 55	06 55	07 09	07 27	07 48
N 58	17 29	18 08	18 54	06 56	07 13	07 33	07 57
56	17 32	18 10	18 53	06 57	07 17	07 39	08 06
54	17 35	18 11	18 52	06 58	07 20	07 44	08 13
52	17 38	18 12	18 51	06 59	07 23	07 49	08 20
50	17 41	18 13	18 51	07 00	07 25	07 53	08 26
45	17 46	18 16	18 50	07 02	07 31	08 03	08 39
N 40	17 51	18 18	18 49	07 04	07 36	08 11	08 49
35	17 55	18 20	18 50	07 05	07 40	08 18	08 59
30	17 58	18 22	18 50	07 06	07 44	08 24	09 07
20	18 05	18 27	18 56	07 08	07 50	08 34	09 21
N 10	18 10	18 32	18 56	07 10	07 56	08 43	09 33
0	18 16	18 37	19 01	07 12	08 01	08 52	09 45
S 10	18 21	18 43	19 07	07 14	08 06	09 00	09 56
20	18 27	18 50	19 16	07 15	08 12	09 09	10 09
30	18 34	18 58	19 27	07 18	08 18	09 20	10 23
35	18 38	19 04	19 34	07 19	08 22	09 26	10 31
40	18 43	19 11	19 43	07 20	08 26	09 33	10 41
45	18 48	19 18	19 55	07 22	08 31	09 41	10 52
S 50	18 55	19 28	20 09	07 23	08 37	09 51	11 05
52	18 58	19 33	20 16	07 24	08 39	09 55	11 11
54	19 01	19 38	20 24	07 25	08 42	10 00	11 18
56	19 05	19 44	20 33	07 26	08 46	10 06	11 26
58	19 09	19 50	20 43	07 27	08 49	10 12	11 35
S 60	19 13	19 58	20 55	07 29	08 53	10 19	11 45

	SUN			MOON			
Day	Eqn. of Time 00h	12h	Mer. Pass.	Mer. Pass. Upper	Lower	Age	Phase
d	m s	m s	h m	h m	h m	d	%
27	12 45	12 40	12 13	01 00	13 25	17	97
28	12 34	12 28	12 12	01 49	14 14	18	92
1	12 23	12 17	12 12	02 39	15 05	19	85

2013 MARCH 2, 3, 4 (SAT., SUN., MON.)

UT	ARIES GHA	VENUS −3.9 GHA	VENUS Dec	MARS +1.2 GHA	MARS Dec	JUPITER −2.3 GHA	JUPITER Dec	SATURN +0.4 GHA	SATURN Dec	STARS Name	SHA	Dec
d h	° ′	° ′	° ′	° ′	° ′	° ′	° ′	° ′	° ′		° ′	° ′
2 00	159 57.0	182 42.7	S10 58.6	166 58.6	S 3 57.1	93 47.4	N21 08.4	300 09.0	S12 48.7	Acamar	315 18.7	S40 15.4
01	174 59.4	197 42.2	.. 57.5	181 59.3	56.3	108 49.6	08.4	315 11.6	48.7	Achernar	335 27.4	S57 10.4
02	190 01.9	212 41.7	56.4	197 00.0	55.5	123 51.8	08.5	330 14.1	48.7	Acrux	173 08.8	S63 10.3
03	205 04.4	227 41.2	.. 55.3	212 00.6	.. 54.7	138 54.0	.. 08.5	345 16.6	.. 48.7	Adhara	255 12.5	S28 59.8
04	220 06.8	242 40.7	54.2	227 01.3	53.9	153 56.2	08.6	0 19.1	48.7	Aldebaran	290 49.6	N16 32.0
05	235 09.3	257 40.2	53.1	242 02.0	53.1	168 58.4	08.6	15 21.6	48.6			
06	250 11.8	272 39.7	S10 51.9	257 02.7	S 3 52.3	184 00.6	N21 08.7	30 24.1	S12 48.6	Alioth	166 20.4	N55 53.0
07	265 14.2	287 39.2	50.8	272 03.3	51.5	199 02.8	08.7	45 26.6	48.6	Alkaid	152 58.7	N49 14.6
S 08	280 16.7	302 38.7	49.7	287 04.0	50.7	214 05.0	08.8	60 29.1	48.6	Al Na'ir	27 44.4	S46 53.7
A 09	295 19.2	317 38.2	.. 48.6	302 04.7	.. 49.9	229 07.2	.. 08.8	75 31.6	.. 48.5	Alnilam	275 46.5	S 1 11.9
T 10	310 21.6	332 37.7	47.5	317 05.3	49.1	244 09.4	08.9	90 34.1	48.5	Alphard	217 56.0	S 8 43.2
U 11	325 24.1	347 37.2	46.3	332 06.0	48.4	259 11.7	08.9	105 36.6	48.5			
R 12	340 26.5	2 36.7	S10 45.2	347 06.7	S 3 47.6	274 13.9	N21 09.0	120 39.2	S12 48.5	Alphecca	126 11.1	N26 40.0
D 13	355 29.0	17 36.2	44.1	2 07.3	46.8	289 16.1	09.0	135 41.7	48.4	Alpheratz	357 44.0	N29 09.8
A 14	10 31.5	32 35.7	43.0	17 08.0	46.0	304 18.3	09.1	150 44.2	48.4	Altair	62 08.6	N 8 54.2
Y 15	25 33.9	47 35.2	.. 41.9	32 08.7	.. 45.2	319 20.5	.. 09.1	165 46.7	.. 48.4	Ankaa	353 16.3	S42 14.2
16	40 36.4	62 34.7	40.7	47 09.4	44.4	334 22.7	09.2	180 49.2	48.4	Antares	112 26.4	S26 27.5
17	55 38.9	77 34.2	39.6	62 10.0	43.6	349 24.9	09.2	195 51.7	48.3			
18	70 41.3	92 33.7	S10 38.5	77 10.7	S 3 42.8	4 27.1	N21 09.2	210 54.2	S12 48.3	Arcturus	145 55.7	N19 06.6
19	85 43.8	107 33.2	37.4	92 11.4	42.0	19 29.3	09.3	225 56.7	48.3	Atria	107 28.5	S69 02.7
20	100 46.3	122 32.7	36.2	107 12.1	41.2	34 31.5	09.3	240 59.2	48.3	Avior	234 17.6	S59 33.5
21	115 48.7	137 32.2	.. 35.1	122 12.7	.. 40.4	49 33.7	.. 09.4	256 01.8	.. 48.2	Bellatrix	278 32.1	N 6 21.5
22	130 51.2	152 31.7	34.0	137 13.4	39.6	64 35.9	09.4	271 04.3	48.2	Betelgeuse	271 01.4	N 7 24.3
23	145 53.6	167 31.2	32.9	152 14.1	38.9	79 38.1	09.5	286 06.8	48.2			
3 00	160 56.1	182 30.7	S10 31.7	167 14.7	S 3 38.1	94 40.3	N21 09.5	301 09.3	S12 48.2	Canopus	263 56.0	S52 42.6
01	175 58.6	197 30.2	30.6	182 15.4	37.3	109 42.5	09.6	316 11.8	48.1	Capella	280 34.6	N46 00.7
02	191 01.0	212 29.7	29.5	197 16.1	36.5	124 44.7	09.6	331 14.3	48.1	Deneb	49 32.0	N45 19.6
03	206 03.5	227 29.2	.. 28.4	212 16.8	.. 35.7	139 46.9	.. 09.7	346 16.8	.. 48.1	Denebola	182 33.5	N14 29.7
04	221 06.0	242 28.7	27.2	227 17.4	34.9	154 49.1	09.7	1 19.3	48.1	Diphda	348 56.4	S17 55.0
05	236 08.4	257 28.2	26.1	242 18.1	34.1	169 51.3	09.8	16 21.9	48.0			
06	251 10.9	272 27.7	S10 25.0	257 18.8	S 3 33.3	184 53.5	N21 09.8	31 24.4	S12 48.0	Dubhe	193 51.3	N61 40.6
07	266 13.4	287 27.2	23.8	272 19.4	32.5	199 55.7	09.9	46 26.9	48.0	Elnath	278 12.8	N28 37.0
S 08	281 15.8	302 26.7	22.7	287 20.1	31.7	214 57.9	09.9	61 29.4	48.0	Eltanin	90 46.4	N51 29.0
U 09	296 18.3	317 26.2	.. 21.6	302 20.8	.. 30.9	230 00.1	.. 10.0	76 31.9	.. 47.9	Enif	33 47.6	N 9 56.1
N 10	311 20.8	332 25.7	20.4	317 21.5	30.1	245 02.3	10.0	91 34.4	47.9	Fomalhaut	15 24.5	S29 33.1
11	326 23.2	347 25.2	19.3	332 22.1	29.3	260 04.5	10.1	106 36.9	47.9			
D 12	341 25.7	2 24.7	S10 18.2	347 22.8	S 3 28.6	275 06.7	N21 10.1	121 39.5	S12 47.9	Gacrux	172 00.5	S57 11.2
A 13	356 28.1	17 24.2	17.1	2 23.5	27.8	290 08.9	10.2	136 42.0	47.8	Gienah	175 52.2	S17 37.1
Y 14	11 30.6	32 23.8	15.9	17 24.2	27.0	305 11.1	10.2	151 44.5	47.8	Hadar	148 47.7	S60 26.0
15	26 33.1	47 23.3	.. 14.8	32 24.8	.. 26.2	320 13.3	.. 10.3	166 47.0	.. 47.8	Hamal	328 01.2	N23 31.5
16	41 35.5	62 22.8	13.7	47 25.5	25.4	335 15.5	10.3	181 49.5	47.8	Kaus Aust.	83 44.2	S34 22.5
17	56 38.0	77 22.3	12.5	62 26.2	24.6	350 17.7	10.4	196 52.0	47.7			
18	71 40.5	92 21.8	S10 11.4	77 26.9	S 3 23.8	5 19.9	N21 10.4	211 54.5	S12 47.7	Kochab	137 19.5	N74 05.8
19	86 42.9	107 21.3	10.2	92 27.5	23.0	20 22.1	10.5	226 57.1	47.7	Markab	13 38.8	N15 16.6
20	101 45.4	122 20.8	09.1	107 28.2	22.2	35 24.3	10.5	241 59.6	47.7	Menkar	314 15.4	N 4 08.3
21	116 47.9	137 20.3	.. 08.0	122 28.9	.. 21.4	50 26.5	.. 10.6	257 02.1	.. 47.6	Menkent	148 07.5	S36 26.0
22	131 50.3	152 19.8	06.8	137 29.6	20.6	65 28.7	10.6	272 04.6	47.6	Miaplacidus	221 38.8	S69 46.6
23	146 52.8	167 19.3	05.7	152 30.2	19.8	80 30.9	10.6	287 07.1	47.6			
4 00	161 55.3	182 18.9	S10 04.6	167 30.9	S 3 19.0	95 33.1	N21 10.7	302 09.6	S12 47.6	Mirfak	308 40.8	N49 54.6
01	176 57.7	197 18.4	03.4	182 31.6	18.3	110 35.3	10.7	317 12.2	47.5	Nunki	75 58.7	S26 16.6
02	192 00.2	212 17.9	02.3	197 32.2	17.5	125 37.5	10.8	332 14.7	47.5	Peacock	53 20.0	S56 41.3
03	207 02.6	227 17.4	.. 01.1	212 32.9	.. 16.7	140 39.7	.. 10.8	347 17.2	.. 47.5	Pollux	243 27.7	N27 57.9
04	222 05.1	242 16.9	10 00.0	227 33.6	15.9	155 41.9	10.9	2 19.7	47.5	Procyon	244 59.7	N 5 11.2
05	237 07.6	257 16.4	9 58.9	242 34.3	15.1	170 44.1	10.9	17 22.2	47.4			
06	252 10.0	272 15.9	S 9 57.7	257 34.9	S 3 14.3	185 46.3	N21 11.0	32 24.7	S12 47.4	Rasalhague	96 06.7	N12 33.0
07	267 12.5	287 15.5	56.6	272 35.6	13.5	200 48.5	11.0	47 27.3	47.4	Regulus	207 43.4	N11 53.9
08	282 15.0	302 15.0	55.4	287 36.3	12.7	215 50.7	11.1	62 29.8	47.3	Rigel	281 12.2	S 8 11.5
M 09	297 17.4	317 14.5	.. 54.3	302 37.0	.. 11.9	230 52.9	.. 11.1	77 32.3	.. 47.3	Rigil Kent.	139 51.6	S60 53.1
O 10	312 19.9	332 14.0	53.2	317 37.6	11.1	245 55.1	11.2	92 34.8	47.3	Sabik	102 12.8	S15 44.4
N 11	327 22.4	347 13.5	52.0	332 38.3	10.3	260 57.2	11.2	107 37.3	47.3			
D 12	342 24.8	2 13.0	S 9 50.9	347 39.0	S 3 09.5	275 59.4	N21 11.3	122 39.8	S12 47.2	Schedar	349 41.2	N56 36.7
A 13	357 27.3	17 12.6	49.7	2 39.7	08.7	291 01.6	11.3	137 42.4	47.2	Shaula	96 22.2	S37 06.6
Y 14	12 29.8	32 12.1	48.6	17 40.3	08.0	306 03.8	11.4	152 44.9	47.2	Sirius	258 33.7	S16 44.4
15	27 32.2	47 11.6	.. 47.4	32 41.0	.. 07.2	321 06.0	.. 11.4	167 47.4	.. 47.2	Spica	158 31.2	S11 13.9
16	42 34.7	62 11.1	46.3	47 41.7	06.4	336 08.2	11.5	182 49.9	47.1	Suhail	222 52.2	S43 29.5
17	57 37.1	77 10.6	45.1	62 42.4	05.6	351 10.4	11.5	197 52.4	47.1			
18	72 39.6	92 10.1	S 9 44.0	77 43.1	S 3 04.8	6 12.6	N21 11.6	212 55.0	S12 47.1	Vega	80 39.3	N38 47.6
19	87 42.1	107 09.7	42.9	92 43.7	04.0	21 14.8	11.6	227 57.5	47.1	Zuben'ubi	137 05.5	S16 05.8
20	102 44.5	122 09.2	41.7	107 44.4	03.2	36 17.0	11.7	243 00.0	47.0		SHA	Mer. Pass.
21	117 47.0	137 08.7	.. 40.6	122 45.1	.. 02.4	51 19.2	.. 11.7	258 02.5	47.0		° ′	h m
22	132 49.5	152 08.2	39.4	137 45.8	01.6	66 21.3	11.8	273 05.0	47.0	Venus	21 34.6	11 50
23	147 51.9	167 07.7	38.3	152 46.4	00.8	81 23.5	11.8	288 07.6	46.9	Mars	6 18.6	12 50
	h m									Jupiter	293 44.2	17 39
Mer. Pass. 13 14.1		v −0.5	d 1.1	v 0.7	d 0.8	v 2.2	d 0.0	v 2.5	d 0.0	Saturn	140 13.2	3 55

UT	SUN GHA	SUN Dec	MOON GHA	v	MOON Dec	d	HP
d h	° '	° '	° '	'	° '	'	'
2 00	176 57.4	S 7 13.5	308 56.2	8.8	S14 01.4	9.0	58.7
01	191 57.5	12.6	323 24.0	8.6	14 10.4	8.9	58.7
02	206 57.6	11.6	337 51.8	8.6	14 19.3	8.9	58.7
03	221 57.8	.. 10.7	352 19.4	8.7	14 28.2	8.7	58.7
04	236 57.9	09.7	6 47.1	8.5	14 36.9	8.7	58.7
05	251 58.0	08.7	21 14.6	8.5	14 45.6	8.6	58.7
06	266 58.1	S 7 07.8	35 42.1	8.5	S14 54.2	8.5	58.8
07	281 58.3	06.8	50 09.6	8.3	15 02.7	8.4	58.8
S 08	296 58.4	05.9	64 36.9	8.4	15 11.1	8.3	58.8
A 09	311 58.5	.. 04.9	79 04.3	8.2	15 19.4	8.3	58.8
T 10	326 58.6	04.0	93 31.5	8.3	15 27.7	8.1	58.8
U 11	341 58.8	03.0	107 58.8	8.1	15 35.8	8.1	58.8
R 12	356 58.9	S 7 02.1	122 25.9	8.1	S15 43.9	7.9	58.8
D 13	11 59.0	01.1	136 53.0	8.1	15 51.8	7.9	58.8
A 14	26 59.2	7 00.1	151 20.1	8.0	15 59.7	7.8	58.8
Y 15	41 59.3	6 59.2	165 47.1	7.9	16 07.5	7.6	58.8
16	56 59.4	58.2	180 14.0	7.9	16 15.1	7.6	58.9
17	71 59.6	57.3	194 40.9	7.8	16 22.7	7.5	58.9
18	86 59.7	S 6 56.3	209 07.7	7.7	S16 30.2	7.4	58.9
19	101 59.8	55.4	223 34.4	7.7	16 37.6	7.2	58.9
20	116 59.9	54.4	238 01.1	7.7	16 44.8	7.2	58.9
21	132 00.1	.. 53.4	252 27.8	7.6	16 52.0	7.1	58.9
22	147 00.2	52.5	266 54.4	7.5	16 59.1	7.0	58.9
23	162 00.3	51.5	281 20.9	7.5	17 06.1	6.9	58.9
3 00	177 00.5	S 6 50.6	295 47.4	7.5	S17 13.0	6.7	58.9
01	192 00.6	49.6	310 13.9	7.4	17 19.7	6.7	58.9
02	207 00.7	48.7	324 40.3	7.3	17 26.4	6.5	59.0
03	222 00.9	.. 47.7	339 06.6	7.3	17 32.9	6.5	59.0
04	237 01.0	46.7	353 32.9	7.2	17 39.4	6.3	59.0
05	252 01.1	45.8	7 59.1	7.2	17 45.7	6.2	59.0
06	267 01.3	S 6 44.8	22 25.3	7.1	S17 51.9	6.2	59.0
07	282 01.4	43.9	36 51.4	7.1	17 58.1	6.0	59.0
08	297 01.5	42.9	51 17.5	7.0	18 04.1	5.8	59.0
S 09	312 01.7	.. 41.9	65 43.5	7.0	18 09.9	5.8	59.0
U 10	327 01.8	41.0	80 09.5	6.9	18 15.7	5.7	59.0
N 11	342 01.9	40.0	94 35.4	6.9	18 21.4	5.5	59.0
D 12	357 02.1	S 6 39.1	109 01.3	6.9	S18 26.9	5.5	59.0
A 13	12 02.2	38.1	123 27.2	6.7	18 32.4	5.3	59.0
Y 14	27 02.3	37.1	137 52.9	6.8	18 37.7	5.2	59.1
15	42 02.5	.. 36.2	152 18.7	6.7	18 42.9	5.1	59.1
16	57 02.6	35.2	166 44.4	6.6	18 48.0	4.9	59.1
17	72 02.7	34.3	181 10.0	6.7	18 52.9	4.9	59.1
18	87 02.9	S 6 33.3	195 35.7	6.5	S18 57.8	4.7	59.1
19	102 03.0	32.3	210 01.2	6.6	19 02.5	4.6	59.1
20	117 03.1	31.4	224 26.8	6.5	19 07.1	4.5	59.1
21	132 03.3	.. 30.4	238 52.3	6.4	19 11.6	4.3	59.1
22	147 03.4	29.5	253 17.7	6.4	19 15.9	4.2	59.1
23	162 03.5	28.5	267 43.1	6.4	19 20.1	4.2	59.1
4 00	177 03.7	S 6 27.5	282 08.5	6.3	S19 24.3	3.9	59.1
01	192 03.8	26.6	296 33.8	6.3	19 28.2	3.9	59.1
02	207 03.9	25.6	310 59.1	6.3	19 32.1	3.7	59.1
03	222 04.1	.. 24.6	325 24.4	6.2	19 35.8	3.5	59.1
04	237 04.2	23.7	339 49.6	6.2	19 39.4	3.5	59.1
05	252 04.4	22.7	354 14.8	6.2	19 42.9	3.3	59.1
06	267 04.5	S 6 21.8	8 40.0	6.1	S19 46.2	3.3	59.2
07	282 04.6	20.8	23 05.1	6.1	19 49.5	3.0	59.2
08	297 04.8	19.8	37 30.2	6.1	19 52.5	3.0	59.2
M 09	312 04.9	.. 18.9	51 55.3	6.0	19 55.5	2.8	59.2
O 10	327 05.0	17.9	66 20.3	6.0	19 58.3	2.7	59.2
N 11	342 05.2	16.9	80 45.3	6.0	20 01.0	2.6	59.2
D 12	357 05.3	S 6 16.0	95 10.3	6.0	S20 03.6	2.4	59.2
A 13	12 05.5	15.0	109 35.3	5.9	20 06.0	2.3	59.2
Y 14	27 05.6	14.0	124 00.2	5.9	20 08.3	2.2	59.2
15	42 05.7	.. 13.1	138 25.1	5.9	20 10.5	2.1	59.2
16	57 05.9	12.1	152 50.0	5.9	20 12.6	1.9	59.2
17	72 06.0	11.2	167 14.9	5.8	20 14.5	1.7	59.2
18	87 06.1	S 6 10.2	181 39.7	5.9	S20 16.2	1.7	59.2
19	102 06.3	09.2	196 04.6	5.8	20 17.9	1.5	59.2
20	117 06.4	08.3	210 29.4	5.8	20 19.4	1.4	59.2
21	132 06.6	.. 07.3	224 54.2	5.8	20 20.8	1.2	59.2
22	147 06.7	06.3	239 19.0	5.7	20 22.0	1.1	59.2
23	162 06.8	05.4	253 43.7	5.8	S20 23.1	1.0	59.2
	SD 16.2	d 1.0	SD 16.0		16.1		16.1

Lat.	Twilight Naut.	Twilight Civil	Sunrise	Moonrise 2	Moonrise 3	Moonrise 4	Moonrise 5
°	h m	h m	h m	h m	h m	h m	h m
N 72	04 59	06 17	07 25	■■	03 49	■■	■■
N 70	05 05	06 16	07 17	00 22	02 26	04 55	■■
68	05 10	06 15	07 11	25 47	01 47	03 31	04 53
66	05 14	06 13	07 05	25 20	01 20	02 53	04 07
64	05 18	06 12	07 00	25 00	01 00	02 26	03 38
62	05 20	06 12	06 56	24 44	00 44	02 06	03 15
60	05 23	06 11	06 52	24 30	00 30	01 49	02 57
N 58	05 24	06 10	06 49	24 18	00 18	01 35	02 42
56	05 26	06 09	06 46	24 08	00 08	01 23	02 29
54	05 27	06 08	06 44	23 59	25 12	01 12	02 17
52	05 28	06 07	06 41	23 51	25 03	01 03	02 08
50	05 29	06 07	06 39	23 44	24 54	00 54	01 59
45	05 31	06 05	06 34	23 29	24 36	00 36	01 40
N 40	05 32	06 03	06 30	23 16	24 22	00 22	01 24
35	05 32	06 01	06 27	23 05	24 10	00 10	01 11
30	05 31	06 00	06 24	22 56	23 59	25 00	01 00
20	05 31	05 56	06 18	22 40	23 41	24 41	00 41
N 10	05 28	05 52	06 13	22 26	23 25	24 24	00 24
0	05 24	05 48	06 09	22 13	23 10	24 08	00 08
S 10	05 18	05 43	06 04	22 01	22 55	23 53	24 52
20	05 10	05 36	05 58	21 47	22 40	23 36	24 35
30	05 00	05 28	05 52	21 32	22 22	23 17	24 16
35	04 53	05 23	05 49	21 23	22 11	23 06	24 05
40	04 44	05 17	05 45	21 12	21 59	22 53	23 53
45	04 34	05 10	05 40	21 00	21 45	22 38	23 38
S 50	04 21	05 01	05 34	20 46	21 28	22 20	23 20
52	04 14	04 57	05 32	20 39	21 20	22 11	23 11
54	04 07	04 52	05 29	20 32	21 12	22 01	23 02
56	03 58	04 47	05 25	20 24	21 02	21 50	22 51
58	03 49	04 40	05 22	20 14	20 50	21 38	22 38
S 60	03 37	04 34	05 18	20 04	20 37	21 23	22 24

Lat.	Sunset	Twilight Civil	Twilight Naut.	Moonset 2	Moonset 3	Moonset 4	Moonset 5
°	h m	h m	h m	h m	h m	h m	h m
N 72	17 00	18 09	19 28	05 54	04 53	■■	■■
N 70	17 09	18 10	19 21	06 26	06 17	05 47	■■
68	17 15	18 11	19 16	06 50	06 56	07 11	07 52
66	17 20	18 12	19 11	07 09	07 24	07 50	08 37
64	17 25	18 13	19 08	07 24	07 45	08 17	09 07
62	17 29	18 14	19 05	07 37	08 02	08 38	09 30
60	17 33	18 14	19 03	07 48	08 16	08 55	09 48
N 58	17 36	18 15	19 01	07 57	08 28	09 09	10 03
56	17 39	18 16	18 59	08 06	08 39	09 22	10 16
54	17 41	18 17	18 58	08 13	08 48	09 32	10 27
52	17 43	18 17	18 56	08 20	08 57	09 42	10 37
50	17 46	18 18	18 55	08 26	09 04	09 51	10 46
45	17 50	18 20	18 54	08 39	09 20	10 09	11 05
N 40	17 54	18 21	18 53	08 49	09 33	10 24	11 20
35	17 57	18 23	18 52	08 59	09 45	10 36	11 33
30	18 00	18 24	18 52	09 07	09 55	10 47	11 45
20	18 05	18 26	18 54	09 21	10 12	11 06	12 04
N 10	18 11	18 32	18 56	09 33	10 26	11 22	12 21
0	18 15	18 36	19 00	09 45	10 40	11 38	12 36
S 10	18 20	18 41	19 06	09 56	10 54	11 53	12 52
20	18 25	18 47	19 13	10 09	11 09	12 10	13 09
30	18 31	18 55	19 23	10 23	11 26	12 28	13 28
35	18 34	19 00	19 30	10 31	11 36	12 39	13 39
40	18 38	19 06	19 38	10 41	11 48	12 52	13 52
45	18 43	19 13	19 49	10 52	12 01	13 07	14 07
S 50	18 49	19 22	20 02	11 05	12 17	13 25	14 25
52	18 51	19 26	20 08	11 11	12 23	13 34	14 34
54	18 54	19 30	20 15	11 18	12 34	13 43	14 44
56	18 57	19 35	20 24	11 26	12 43	13 54	14 55
58	19 01	19 42	20 33	11 35	12 54	14 07	15 07
S 60	19 04	19 48	20 44	11 45	13 07	14 21	15 22

Day	SUN Eqn. of Time 00ʰ	SUN Eqn. of Time 12ʰ	SUN Mer. Pass.	MOON Mer. Pass. Upper	MOON Mer. Pass. Lower	Age	Phase
d	m s	m s	h m	h m	h m	d	%
2	12 11	12 05	12 12	03 32	15 59	20	76
3	11 58	11 52	12 12	04 27	16 55	21	66
4	11 46	11 39	12 12	05 24	17 53	22	55

UT	ARIES GHA	VENUS −3.9 GHA	VENUS Dec	MARS +1.2 GHA	MARS Dec	JUPITER −2.3 GHA	JUPITER Dec	SATURN +0.4 GHA	SATURN Dec	STARS Name	SHA	Dec
d h	° ′	° ′	° ′	° ′	° ′	° ′	° ′	° ′	° ′		° ′	° ′
5 00	162 54.4	182 07.3	S 9 37.1	167 47.1	S 3 00.0	96 25.7	N21 11.9	303 10.1	S12 46.9	Acamar	315 18.7	S40 15.4
01	177 56.9	197 06.8	36.0	182 47.8	2 59.2	111 27.9	11.9	318 12.6	46.9	Achernar	335 27.4	S57 10.4
02	192 59.3	212 06.3	34.8	197 48.5	58.4	126 30.1	12.0	333 15.1	46.9	Acrux	173 08.8	S63 10.4
03	208 01.8	227 05.8	.. 33.7	212 49.1	.. 57.6	141 32.3	.. 12.0	348 17.6	.. 46.8	Adhara	255 12.5	S28 59.8
04	223 04.2	242 05.4	32.5	227 49.8	56.8	156 34.5	12.1	3 20.2	46.8	Aldebaran	290 49.6	N16 32.0
05	238 06.7	257 04.9	31.4	242 50.5	56.1	171 36.7	12.1	18 22.7	46.8			
06	253 09.2	272 04.4	S 9 30.2	257 51.2	S 2 55.3	186 38.8	N21 12.2	33 25.2	S12 46.8	Alioth	166 20.4	N55 53.0
07	268 11.6	287 03.9	29.1	272 51.8	54.5	201 41.0	12.2	48 27.7	46.7	Alkaid	152 58.7	N49 14.6
08	283 14.1	302 03.5	27.9	287 52.5	53.7	216 43.2	12.3	63 30.2	46.7	Al Na'ir	27 44.4	S46 53.7
09	298 16.6	317 03.0	.. 26.8	302 53.2	.. 52.9	231 45.4	.. 12.3	78 32.8	.. 46.7	Alnilam	275 46.5	S 1 11.9
10	313 19.0	332 02.5	25.6	317 53.9	52.1	246 47.6	12.4	93 35.3	46.6	Alphard	217 56.0	S 8 43.3
11	328 21.5	347 02.0	24.5	332 54.6	51.3	261 49.8	12.4	108 37.8	46.6			
12	343 24.0	2 01.6	S 9 23.3	347 55.2	S 2 50.5	276 52.0	N21 12.5	123 40.3	S12 46.6	Alphecca	126 11.0	N26 40.0
13	358 26.4	17 01.1	22.1	2 55.9	49.7	291 54.2	12.5	138 42.9	46.6	Alpheratz	357 44.0	N29 09.8
14	13 28.9	32 00.6	21.0	17 56.6	48.9	306 56.3	12.6	153 45.4	46.5	Altair	62 08.6	N 8 54.2
15	28 31.4	47 00.1	.. 19.8	32 57.3	.. 48.1	321 58.5	.. 12.6	168 47.9	.. 46.5	Ankaa	353 16.3	S42 14.2
16	43 33.8	61 59.7	18.7	47 57.9	47.3	337 00.7	12.7	183 50.4	46.5	Antares	112 26.4	S26 27.5
17	58 36.3	76 59.2	17.5	62 58.6	46.5	352 02.9	12.7	198 52.9	46.4			
18	73 38.7	91 58.7	S 9 16.4	77 59.3	S 2 45.7	7 05.1	N21 12.8	213 55.5	S12 46.4	Arcturus	145 55.7	N19 06.6
19	88 41.2	106 58.2	15.2	93 00.0	44.9	22 07.3	12.8	228 58.0	46.4	Atria	107 28.4	S69 02.7
20	103 43.7	121 57.8	14.0	108 00.7	44.2	37 09.4	12.9	244 00.5	46.4	Avior	234 17.6	S59 33.5
21	118 46.1	136 57.3	.. 12.9	123 01.3	.. 43.4	52 11.6	.. 12.9	259 03.0	.. 46.3	Bellatrix	278 32.1	N 6 21.5
22	133 48.6	151 56.8	11.7	138 02.0	42.6	67 13.8	13.0	274 05.6	46.3	Betelgeuse	271 01.4	N 7 24.3
23	148 51.1	166 56.4	10.6	153 02.7	41.8	82 16.0	13.0	289 08.1	46.3			
6 00	163 53.5	181 55.9	S 9 09.4	168 03.4	S 2 41.0	97 18.2	N21 13.1	304 10.6	S12 46.3	Canopus	263 56.0	S52 42.6
01	178 56.0	196 55.4	08.3	183 04.0	40.2	112 20.3	13.1	319 13.1	46.2	Capella	280 34.7	N46 00.7
02	193 58.5	211 54.9	07.1	198 04.7	39.4	127 22.5	13.2	334 15.7	46.2	Deneb	49 31.9	N45 19.6
03	209 00.9	226 54.5	.. 05.9	213 05.4	.. 38.6	142 24.7	.. 13.2	349 18.2	.. 46.2	Denebola	182 33.5	N14 29.7
04	224 03.4	241 54.0	04.8	228 06.1	37.8	157 26.9	13.3	4 20.7	46.1	Diphda	348 56.4	S17 55.0
05	239 05.9	256 53.5	03.6	243 06.8	37.0	172 29.1	13.3	19 23.2	46.1			
06	254 08.3	271 53.1	S 9 02.4	258 07.4	S 2 36.2	187 31.2	N21 13.4	34 25.8	S12 46.1	Dubhe	193 51.3	N61 40.6
07	269 10.8	286 52.6	01.3	273 08.1	35.4	202 33.4	13.4	49 28.3	46.1	Elnath	278 12.8	N28 37.0
08	284 13.2	301 52.1	9 00.1	288 08.8	34.6	217 35.6	13.5	64 30.8	46.0	Eltanin	90 46.3	N51 29.0
09	299 15.7	316 51.7	8 59.0	303 09.5	.. 33.8	232 37.8	.. 13.5	79 33.3	.. 46.0	Enif	33 47.6	N 9 56.1
10	314 18.2	331 51.2	57.8	318 10.2	33.0	247 40.0	13.6	94 35.9	46.0	Fomalhaut	15 24.5	S29 33.1
11	329 20.6	346 50.7	56.6	333 10.8	32.2	262 42.1	13.6	109 38.4	45.9			
12	344 23.1	1 50.3	S 8 55.5	348 11.5	S 2 31.5	277 44.3	N21 13.7	124 40.9	S12 45.9	Gacrux	172 00.5	S57 11.3
13	359 25.6	16 49.8	54.3	3 12.2	30.7	292 46.5	13.7	139 43.4	45.9	Gienah	175 52.2	S17 37.1
14	14 28.0	31 49.3	53.1	18 12.9	29.9	307 48.7	13.8	154 46.0	45.8	Hadar	148 47.7	S60 26.1
15	29 30.5	46 48.9	.. 52.0	33 13.5	.. 29.1	322 50.9	.. 13.8	169 48.5	.. 45.8	Hamal	328 01.2	N23 31.5
16	44 33.0	61 48.4	50.8	48 14.2	28.3	337 53.0	13.9	184 51.0	45.8	Kaus Aust.	83 44.2	S34 22.5
17	59 35.4	76 47.9	49.6	63 14.9	27.5	352 55.2	13.9	199 53.5	45.8			
18	74 37.9	91 47.5	S 8 48.5	78 15.6	S 2 26.7	7 57.4	N21 14.0	214 56.1	S12 45.7	Kochab	137 19.4	N74 05.8
19	89 40.4	106 47.0	47.3	93 16.3	25.9	22 59.6	14.0	229 58.6	45.7	Markab	13 38.8	N15 16.6
20	104 42.8	121 46.6	46.1	108 16.9	25.1	38 01.7	14.1	245 01.1	45.7	Menkar	314 15.4	N 4 08.3
21	119 45.3	136 46.1	.. 45.0	123 17.6	.. 24.3	53 03.9	.. 14.1	260 03.7	.. 45.6	Menkent	148 07.5	S36 26.1
22	134 47.7	151 45.6	43.8	138 18.3	23.5	68 06.1	14.2	275 06.2	45.6	Miaplacidus	221 38.8	S69 46.6
23	149 50.2	166 45.2	42.6	153 19.0	22.7	83 08.3	14.2	290 08.7	45.6			
7 00	164 52.7	181 44.7	S 8 41.5	168 19.7	S 2 21.9	98 10.4	N21 14.3	305 11.2	S12 45.6	Mirfak	308 40.8	N49 54.6
01	179 55.1	196 44.2	40.3	183 20.3	21.1	113 12.6	14.4	320 13.8	45.5	Nunki	75 58.7	S26 16.6
02	194 57.6	211 43.8	39.1	198 21.0	20.3	128 14.8	14.4	335 16.3	45.5	Peacock	53 20.0	S56 41.3
03	210 00.1	226 43.3	.. 38.0	213 21.7	.. 19.5	143 17.0	.. 14.5	350 18.8	.. 45.5	Pollux	243 27.7	N27 59.5
04	225 02.5	241 42.9	36.8	228 22.4	18.8	158 19.1	14.5	5 21.4	45.4	Procyon	244 59.7	N 5 11.2
05	240 05.0	256 42.4	35.6	243 23.1	18.0	173 21.3	14.6	20 23.9	45.4			
06	255 07.5	271 41.9	S 8 34.4	258 23.7	S 2 17.2	188 23.5	N21 14.6	35 26.4	S12 45.3	Rasalhague	96 06.7	N12 33.0
07	270 09.9	286 41.5	33.3	273 24.4	16.4	203 25.7	14.7	50 28.9	45.3	Regulus	207 43.4	N11 53.9
08	285 12.4	301 41.0	32.1	288 25.1	15.6	218 27.8	14.7	65 31.5	45.3	Rigel	281 12.2	S 8 11.5
09	300 14.8	316 40.6	.. 30.9	303 25.8	.. 14.8	233 30.0	.. 14.8	80 34.0	.. 45.3	Rigil Kent.	139 51.5	S60 53.2
10	315 17.3	331 40.1	29.8	318 26.5	14.0	248 32.2	14.8	95 36.5	45.3	Sabik	102 12.7	S15 44.4
11	330 19.8	346 39.6	28.6	333 27.2	13.2	263 34.3	14.9	110 39.1	45.2			
12	345 22.2	1 39.2	S 8 27.4	348 27.8	S 2 12.4	278 36.5	N21 14.9	125 41.6	S12 45.2	Schedar	349 41.2	N56 36.7
13	0 24.7	16 38.7	26.2	3 28.5	11.6	293 38.7	15.0	140 44.1	45.2	Shaula	96 22.2	S37 06.6
14	15 27.2	31 38.3	25.1	18 29.2	10.8	308 40.9	15.0	155 46.7	45.1	Sirius	258 33.7	S16 44.4
15	30 29.6	46 37.8	.. 23.9	33 29.9	.. 10.0	323 43.0	.. 15.1	170 49.2	.. 45.1	Spica	158 31.2	S11 13.9
16	45 32.1	61 37.4	22.7	48 30.6	09.2	338 45.2	15.1	185 51.7	45.1	Suhail	222 52.2	S43 29.5
17	60 34.6	76 36.9	21.5	63 31.2	08.4	353 47.4	15.2	200 54.2	45.0			
18	75 37.0	91 36.4	S 8 20.4	78 31.9	S 2 07.6	8 49.5	N21 15.2	215 56.8	S12 45.0	Vega	80 39.2	N38 47.6
19	90 39.5	106 36.0	19.2	93 32.6	06.8	23 51.7	15.3	230 59.3	45.0	Zuben'ubi	137 05.4	S16 05.8
20	105 42.0	121 35.5	18.0	108 33.3	06.0	38 53.9	15.3	246 01.8	45.0		SHA	Mer. Pass.
21	120 44.4	136 35.1	.. 16.8	123 34.0	.. 05.3	53 56.0	.. 15.4	261 04.4	.. 44.9		° ′	h m
22	135 46.9	151 34.6	15.6	138 34.6	04.5	68 58.2	15.4	276 06.9	44.9	Venus	18 02.4	11 53
23	150 49.3	166 34.2	14.5	153 35.3	03.7	84 00.4	15.5	291 09.4	44.9	Mars	4 09.8	12 47
	h m									Jupiter	293 24.6	17 28
Mer. Pass. 13 02.3		v −0.5	d 1.2	v 0.7	d 0.8	v 2.2	d 0.1	v 2.5	d 0.0	Saturn	140 17.1	3 43

Left margin days: TUESDAY, WEDNESDAY, THURSDAY

UT	SUN GHA	SUN Dec	MOON GHA	v	MOON Dec	d	HP
d h	° ′	° ′	° ′	′	° ′	′	′
5 00	177 07.0	S 6 04.4	268 08.5	5.7	S20 24.1	0.8	59.2
01	192 07.1	03.4	282 33.2	5.8	20 24.9	0.7	59.2
02	207 07.3	02.5	296 58.0	5.7	20 25.6	0.6	59.2
03	222 07.4	.. 01.5	311 22.7	5.7	20 26.2	0.4	59.2
04	237 07.6	6 00.5	325 47.4	5.7	20 26.6	0.3	59.2
05	252 07.7	5 59.6	340 12.1	5.7	20 26.9	0.1	59.2
06	267 07.8	S 5 58.6	354 36.8	5.7	S20 27.0	0.1	59.2
07	282 08.0	57.6	9 01.5	5.8	20 27.1	0.2	59.3
08	297 08.1	56.7	23 26.3	5.6	20 26.9	0.2	59.3
T 09	312 08.3	.. 55.7	37 50.9	5.7	20 26.7	0.4	59.3
U 10	327 08.4	54.7	52 15.6	5.7	20 26.3	0.5	59.3
E 11	342 08.5	53.8	66 40.3	5.7	20 25.8	0.7	59.3
S 12	357 08.7	S 5 52.8	81 05.0	5.7	S20 25.1	0.8	59.3
D 13	12 08.8	51.8	95 29.7	5.8	20 24.3	0.9	59.3
A 14	27 09.0	50.9	109 54.5	5.7	20 23.4	1.1	59.3
Y 15	42 09.1	.. 49.9	124 19.2	5.7	20 22.3	1.2	59.3
16	57 09.3	48.9	138 43.9	5.7	20 21.1	1.3	59.3
17	72 09.4	48.0	153 08.6	5.8	20 19.8	1.5	59.3
18	87 09.5	S 5 47.0	167 33.4	5.7	S20 18.3	1.6	59.3
19	102 09.7	46.0	181 58.1	5.8	20 16.7	1.7	59.3
20	117 09.8	45.1	196 22.9	5.7	20 15.0	1.9	59.3
21	132 10.0	.. 44.1	210 47.6	5.8	20 13.1	2.0	59.3
22	147 10.1	43.1	225 12.4	5.8	20 11.1	2.1	59.3
23	162 10.3	42.1	239 37.2	5.8	20 09.0	2.3	59.3
6 00	177 10.4	S 5 41.2	254 02.0	5.9	S20 06.7	2.4	59.3
01	192 10.6	40.2	268 26.9	5.8	20 04.3	2.6	59.3
02	207 10.7	39.2	282 51.7	5.9	20 01.7	2.6	59.3
03	222 10.8	.. 38.3	297 16.6	5.9	19 59.1	2.8	59.3
04	237 11.0	37.3	311 41.5	5.9	19 56.3	3.0	59.3
05	252 11.1	36.3	326 06.4	6.0	19 53.3	3.0	59.3
06	267 11.3	S 5 35.4	340 31.4	5.9	S19 50.3	3.2	59.3
W 07	282 11.4	34.4	354 56.3	6.0	19 47.1	3.4	59.3
E 08	297 11.6	33.4	9 21.3	6.0	19 43.7	3.4	59.3
D 09	312 11.7	.. 32.5	23 46.3	6.1	19 40.3	3.6	59.3
N 10	327 11.9	31.5	38 11.4	6.1	19 36.7	3.7	59.3
E 11	342 12.0	30.5	52 36.5	6.1	19 33.0	3.9	59.3
S 12	357 12.2	S 5 29.5	67 01.6	6.1	S19 29.1	3.9	59.3
D 13	12 12.3	28.6	81 26.7	6.2	19 25.2	4.1	59.3
A 14	27 12.4	27.6	95 51.9	6.1	19 21.1	4.2	59.3
Y 15	42 12.6	.. 26.6	110 17.0	6.3	19 16.9	4.4	59.3
16	57 12.7	25.7	124 42.3	6.2	19 12.5	4.5	59.2
17	72 12.9	24.7	139 07.5	6.3	19 08.0	4.6	59.2
18	87 13.0	S 5 23.7	153 32.8	6.4	S19 03.4	4.7	59.2
19	102 13.2	22.7	167 58.2	6.4	18 58.7	4.8	59.2
20	117 13.3	21.8	182 23.6	6.4	18 53.9	5.0	59.2
21	132 13.5	.. 20.8	196 49.0	6.4	18 48.9	5.1	59.2
22	147 13.6	19.8	211 14.4	6.5	18 43.8	5.2	59.2
23	162 13.8	18.9	225 39.9	6.5	18 38.6	5.3	59.2
7 00	177 13.9	S 5 17.9	240 05.4	6.6	S18 33.3	5.5	59.2
01	192 14.1	16.9	254 31.0	6.6	18 27.8	5.5	59.2
02	207 14.2	15.9	268 56.6	6.7	18 22.3	5.7	59.2
03	222 14.4	.. 15.0	283 22.3	6.7	18 16.6	5.8	59.2
04	237 14.5	14.0	297 48.0	6.7	18 10.8	5.9	59.2
05	252 14.7	13.0	312 13.7	6.8	18 04.9	6.1	59.2
06	267 14.8	S 5 12.0	326 39.5	6.8	S17 58.8	6.1	59.2
T 07	282 15.0	11.1	341 05.3	6.9	17 52.7	6.3	59.2
H 08	297 15.1	10.1	355 31.2	6.9	17 46.4	6.3	59.2
U 09	312 15.3	.. 09.1	9 57.1	7.0	17 40.1	6.5	59.2
R 10	327 15.4	08.2	24 23.1	7.0	17 33.6	6.6	59.2
S 11	342 15.6	07.2	38 49.1	7.1	17 27.0	6.7	59.2
D 12	357 15.7	S 5 06.2	53 15.2	7.1	S17 20.3	6.8	59.2
A 13	12 15.9	05.2	67 41.3	7.2	17 13.5	6.9	59.2
Y 14	27 16.0	04.3	82 07.5	7.2	17 06.6	7.0	59.2
15	42 16.2	.. 03.3	96 33.7	7.3	16 59.6	7.2	59.1
16	57 16.3	02.3	111 00.0	7.3	16 52.4	7.2	59.1
17	72 16.5	01.3	125 26.3	7.4	16 45.2	7.3	59.1
18	87 16.6	S 5 00.4	139 52.7	7.4	S16 37.9	7.5	59.1
19	102 16.8	4 59.4	154 19.1	7.5	16 30.4	7.5	59.1
20	117 16.9	58.4	168 45.6	7.6	16 22.9	7.6	59.1
21	132 17.1	.. 57.4	183 12.2	7.5	16 15.3	7.8	59.1
22	147 17.2	56.5	197 38.7	7.7	16 07.5	7.8	59.1
23	162 17.4	55.5	212 05.4	7.7	S15 59.7	7.9	59.1
	SD 16.1	d 1.0	SD 16.1		16.1		16.1

Lat.	Twilight Naut.	Twilight Civil	Sunrise	Moonrise 5	6	7	8
°	h m	h m	h m	h m	h m	h m	h m
N 72	04 43	06 02	07 10	■■■■	■■■■	07 57	06 53
N 70	04 52	06 02	07 03	■■■■	07 01	06 30	06 20
68	04 58	06 03	06 56	04 53	05 34	05 50	05 56
66	05 03	06 02	06 53	04 07	04 56	05 22	05 37
64	05 07	06 02	06 50	03 38	04 28	05 01	05 22
62	05 11	06 02	06 46	03 15	04 07	04 44	05 09
60	05 14	06 02	06 43	02 57	03 50	04 30	04 58
N 58	05 16	06 02	06 41	02 42	03 36	04 17	04 49
56	05 18	06 01	06 39	02 29	03 24	04 07	04 41
54	05 20	06 01	06 36	02 17	03 13	03 57	04 33
52	05 22	06 01	06 35	02 08	03 03	03 49	04 26
50	05 23	06 01	06 33	01 59	02 55	03 41	04 20
45	05 23	06 00	06 29	01 40	02 36	03 25	04 07
N 40	05 27	05 59	06 26	01 24	02 21	03 12	03 57
35	05 28	05 58	06 23	01 11	02 09	03 01	03 47
30	05 29	05 56	06 20	01 00	01 58	02 51	03 39
20	05 28	05 54	06 16	00 41	01 39	02 34	03 25
N 10	05 26	05 51	06 12	00 24	01 23	02 19	03 13
0	05 23	05 47	06 08	00 08	01 07	02 05	03 01
S 10	05 18	05 43	06 04	24 52	00 52	01 51	02 50
20	05 11	05 37	06 00	24 35	00 35	01 36	02 37
30	05 02	05 30	05 54	24 16	00 16	01 19	02 23
35	04 56	05 26	05 51	24 05	00 05	01 09	02 15
40	04 48	05 21	05 48	23 53	24 58	00 58	02 05
45	04 39	05 14	05 44	23 38	24 44	00 44	01 54
S 50	04 26	05 06	05 39	23 20	24 28	00 28	01 41
52	04 20	05 02	05 37	23 11	24 20	00 20	01 34
54	04 14	04 58	05 34	23 02	24 11	00 11	01 27
56	04 06	04 53	05 32	22 51	24 02	00 02	01 20
58	03 57	04 48	05 29	22 38	23 51	25 11	01 11
S 60	03 47	04 42	05 25	22 24	23 38	25 01	01 01

Lat.	Sunset	Twilight Civil	Twilight Naut.	Moonset 5	6	7	8
°	h m	h m	h m	h m	h m	h m	h m
N 72	17 15	18 22	19 42	■■■■	■■■■	08 52	11 53
N 70	17 21	18 22	19 34	■■■■	07 47	10 19	12 24
68	17 26	18 22	19 27	07 52	09 13	10 58	12 47
66	17 30	18 22	19 21	08 37	09 51	11 24	13 05
64	17 34	18 22	19 17	09 07	10 18	11 45	13 19
62	17 37	18 22	19 13	09 30	10 39	12 02	13 31
60	17 40	18 22	19 10	09 48	10 56	12 15	13 41
N 58	17 43	18 22	19 07	10 03	11 10	12 27	13 50
56	17 45	18 22	19 05	10 16	11 22	12 37	13 57
54	17 47	18 22	19 03	10 27	11 33	12 46	14 04
52	17 49	18 23	19 02	10 37	11 42	12 54	14 10
50	17 51	18 23	19 00	10 46	11 51	13 02	14 16
45	17 54	18 24	18 58	11 05	12 08	13 17	14 28
N 40	17 57	18 24	18 56	11 20	12 23	13 29	14 38
35	18 00	18 25	18 55	11 33	12 35	13 40	14 46
30	18 03	18 26	18 54	11 45	12 46	13 49	14 53
20	18 07	18 29	18 54	12 04	13 04	14 05	15 06
N 10	18 11	18 32	18 56	12 21	13 20	14 19	15 17
0	18 14	18 35	18 59	12 36	13 35	14 32	15 27
S 10	18 18	18 39	19 04	12 52	13 50	14 45	15 37
20	18 23	18 45	19 11	13 09	14 05	14 59	15 48
30	18 27	18 52	19 20	13 28	14 23	15 14	16 00
35	18 30	18 56	19 26	13 39	14 34	15 23	16 07
40	18 34	19 01	19 33	13 52	14 46	15 33	16 15
45	18 38	19 07	19 43	14 07	15 00	15 45	16 24
S 50	18 42	19 15	19 55	14 25	15 17	16 00	16 35
52	18 44	19 19	20 00	14 34	15 25	16 06	16 41
54	18 47	19 23	20 07	14 44	15 34	16 14	16 46
56	18 49	19 28	20 14	14 55	15 44	16 22	16 52
58	18 52	19 33	20 23	15 07	15 55	16 31	16 59
S 60	18 55	19 39	20 33	15 22	16 08	16 42	17 07

Day	SUN Eqn. of Time 00h	12h	Mer. Pass.	MOON Mer. Pass. Upper	Lower	Age	Phase
d	m s	m s	h m	h m	h m	d	%
5	11 32	11 26	12 11	06 22	18 52	23	43
6	11 19	11 12	12 11	07 21	19 50	24	32
7	11 05	10 57	12 11	08 19	20 47	25	22

UT	ARIES GHA	VENUS −3.9 GHA	Dec	MARS +1.2 GHA	Dec	JUPITER −2.2 GHA	Dec	SATURN +0.4 GHA	Dec	STARS Name	SHA	Dec
8 00	165 51.8	181 33.7	S 8 13.3	168 36.0	S 2 02.9	99 02.5	N21 15.5	306 12.0	S12 44.8	Acamar	315 18.7	S40 15.4
01	180 54.3	196 33.3	12.1	183 36.7	02.1	114 04.7	15.6	321 14.5	44.8	Achernar	335 27.4	S57 10.4
02	195 56.7	211 32.8	10.9	198 37.4	01.3	129 06.9	15.6	336 17.0	44.8	Acrux	173 08.8	S63 10.4
03	210 59.2	226 32.4 ..	09.8	213 38.1	2 00.5	144 09.0 ..	15.7	351 19.6 ..	44.7	Adhara	255 12.5	S28 59.8
04	226 01.7	241 31.9	08.6	228 38.7	1 59.7	159 11.2	15.7	6 22.1	44.7	Aldebaran	290 49.6	N16 32.0
05	241 04.1	256 31.4	07.4	243 39.4	58.9	174 13.4	15.8	21 24.6	44.7			
06	256 06.6	271 31.0	S 8 06.2	258 40.1	S 1 58.1	189 15.5	N21 15.9	36 27.2	S12 44.6	Alioth	166 20.3	N55 53.0
07	271 09.1	286 30.5	05.0	273 40.8	57.3	204 17.7	15.9	51 29.7	44.6	Alkaid	152 58.7	N49 14.6
F 08	286 11.5	301 30.1	03.8	288 41.5	56.5	219 19.9	16.0	66 32.2	44.6	Al Na'ir	27 44.4	S46 53.7
R 09	301 14.0	316 29.6 ..	02.7	303 42.1 ..	55.7	234 22.0 ..	16.0	81 34.8 ..	44.6	Alnilam	275 46.5	S 1 11.9
I 10	316 16.5	331 29.2	01.5	318 42.8	54.9	249 24.2	16.1	96 37.3	44.5	Alphard	217 56.0	S 8 43.3
D 11	331 18.9	346 28.7	8 00.3	333 43.5	54.1	264 26.4	16.1	111 39.8	44.5			
A 12	346 21.4	1 28.3	S 7 59.1	348 44.2	S 1 53.3	279 28.5	N21 16.2	126 42.4	S12 44.5	Alphecca	126 11.0	N26 40.0
Y 13	1 23.8	16 27.8	57.9	3 44.9	52.5	294 30.7	16.2	141 44.9	44.4	Alpheratz	357 44.0	N29 09.8
14	16 26.3	31 27.4	56.8	18 45.6	51.7	309 32.9	16.3	156 47.4	44.4	Altair	62 08.6	N 8 54.2
15	31 28.8	46 26.9 ..	55.6	33 46.2 ..	51.0	324 35.0 ..	16.3	171 50.0 ..	44.4	Ankaa	353 16.3	S42 14.1
16	46 31.2	61 26.5	54.4	48 46.9	50.2	339 37.2	16.4	186 52.5	44.3	Antares	112 26.4	S26 27.5
17	61 33.7	76 26.0	53.2	63 47.6	49.4	354 39.3	16.4	201 55.0	44.3			
18	76 36.2	91 25.6	S 7 52.0	78 48.3	S 1 48.6	9 41.5	N21 16.5	216 57.6	S12 44.3	Arcturus	145 55.6	N19 06.6
19	91 38.6	106 25.1	50.8	93 49.0	47.8	24 43.7	16.5	232 00.1	44.2	Atria	107 28.3	S69 02.7
20	106 41.1	121 24.7	49.6	108 49.7	47.0	39 45.8	16.6	247 02.7	44.2	Avior	234 17.6	S59 33.5
21	121 43.6	136 24.3 ..	48.5	123 50.3 ..	46.2	54 48.0 ..	16.6	262 05.2 ..	44.2	Bellatrix	278 32.2	N 6 21.5
22	136 46.0	151 23.8	47.3	138 51.0	45.4	69 50.2	16.7	277 07.7	44.1	Betelgeuse	271 01.4	N 7 24.3
23	151 48.5	166 23.4	46.1	153 51.7	44.6	84 52.3	16.7	292 10.3	44.1			
9 00	166 50.9	181 22.9	S 7 44.9	168 52.4	S 1 43.8	99 54.5	N21 16.8	307 12.8	S12 44.1	Canopus	263 56.1	S52 42.6
01	181 53.4	196 22.5	43.7	183 53.1	43.0	114 56.6	16.9	322 15.3	44.1	Capella	280 34.7	N46 00.7
02	196 55.9	211 22.0	42.5	198 53.8	42.2	129 58.8	16.9	337 17.9	44.0	Deneb	49 31.9	N45 19.6
03	211 58.3	226 21.6 ..	41.3	213 54.4 ..	41.4	145 01.0 ..	17.0	352 20.4 ..	44.0	Denebola	182 33.5	N14 29.7
04	227 00.8	241 21.1	40.1	228 55.1	40.6	160 03.1	17.0	7 22.9	44.0	Diphda	348 56.4	S17 55.0
05	242 03.3	256 20.7	39.0	243 55.8	39.8	175 05.3	17.1	22 25.5	43.9			
06	257 05.7	271 20.2	S 7 37.8	258 56.5	S 1 39.0	190 07.4	N21 17.1	37 28.0	S12 43.9	Dubhe	193 51.3	N61 40.6
07	272 08.2	286 19.8	36.6	273 57.2	38.2	205 09.6	17.2	52 30.6	43.9	Elnath	278 12.8	N28 37.0
S 08	287 10.7	301 19.4	35.4	288 57.9	37.5	220 11.7	17.2	67 33.1	43.8	Eltanin	90 46.3	N51 29.0
A 09	302 13.1	316 18.9 ..	34.2	303 58.5 ..	36.7	235 13.9 ..	17.3	82 35.6 ..	43.8	Enif	33 47.6	N 9 56.1
T 10	317 15.6	331 18.5	33.0	318 59.2	35.9	250 16.1	17.3	97 38.2	43.8	Fomalhaut	15 24.5	S29 33.1
U 11	332 18.1	346 18.0	31.8	333 59.9	35.1	265 18.2	17.4	112 40.7	43.7			
R 12	347 20.5	1 17.6	S 7 30.6	349 00.6	S 1 34.3	280 20.4	N21 17.4	127 43.2	S12 43.7	Gacrux	172 00.5	S57 11.3
D 13	2 23.0	16 17.1	29.4	4 01.3	33.5	295 22.5	17.5	142 45.8	43.7	Gienah	175 52.1	S17 37.1
A 14	17 25.4	31 16.7	28.2	19 02.0	32.7	310 24.7	17.5	157 48.3	43.6	Hadar	148 47.6	S60 26.1
Y 15	32 27.9	46 16.3 ..	27.0	34 02.7 ..	31.9	325 26.9 ..	17.6	172 50.9 ..	43.6	Hamal	328 01.2	N23 31.5
16	47 30.4	61 15.8	25.8	49 03.3	31.1	340 29.0	17.6	187 53.4	43.6	Kaus Aust.	83 44.1	S34 22.5
17	62 32.8	76 15.4	24.7	64 04.0	30.3	355 31.2	17.7	202 55.9	43.5			
18	77 35.3	91 14.9	S 7 23.5	79 04.7	S 1 29.5	10 33.3	N21 17.8	217 58.5	S12 43.5	Kochab	137 19.4	N74 05.8
19	92 37.8	106 14.5	22.3	94 05.4	28.7	25 35.5	17.8	233 01.0	43.5	Markab	13 38.8	N15 16.6
20	107 40.2	121 14.0	21.1	109 06.1	27.9	40 37.6	17.9	248 03.6	43.4	Menkar	314 15.4	N 4 08.3
21	122 42.7	136 13.6 ..	19.9	124 06.8 ..	27.1	55 39.8 ..	17.9	263 06.1 ..	43.4	Menkent	148 07.5	S36 26.1
22	137 45.2	151 13.2	18.7	139 07.4	26.3	70 41.9	18.0	278 08.6	43.4	Miaplacidus	221 38.9	S69 46.6
23	152 47.6	166 12.7	17.5	154 08.1	25.5	85 44.1	18.0	293 11.2	43.3			
10 00	167 50.1	181 12.3	S 7 16.3	169 08.8	S 1 24.7	100 46.2	N21 18.1	308 13.7	S12 43.3	Mirfak	308 40.8	N49 54.5
01	182 52.6	196 11.9	15.1	184 09.5	23.9	115 48.4	18.1	323 16.3	43.3	Nunki	75 58.7	S26 16.6
02	197 55.0	211 11.4	13.9	199 10.2	23.2	130 50.6	18.2	338 18.8	43.2	Peacock	53 19.9	S56 41.3
03	212 57.5	226 11.0 ..	12.7	214 10.9 ..	22.4	145 52.7 ..	18.2	353 21.3 ..	43.2	Pollux	243 27.7	N27 59.5
04	227 59.9	241 10.5	11.5	229 11.6	21.6	160 54.9	18.3	8 23.9	43.2	Procyon	244 59.7	N 5 11.2
05	243 02.4	256 10.1	10.3	244 12.2	20.8	175 57.0	18.3	23 26.4	43.1			
06	258 04.9	271 09.7	S 7 09.1	259 12.9	S 1 20.0	190 59.2	N21 18.4	38 29.0	S12 43.1	Rasalhague	96 06.6	N12 33.0
07	273 07.3	286 09.2	07.9	274 13.6	19.2	206 01.3	18.4	53 31.5	43.1	Regulus	207 43.4	N11 53.9
S 08	288 09.8	301 08.8	06.7	289 14.3	18.4	221 03.5	18.5	68 34.0	43.0	Rigel	281 12.2	S 8 11.5
U 09	303 12.3	316 08.4 ..	05.5	304 15.0 ..	17.6	236 05.6 ..	18.6	83 36.6 ..	43.0	Rigil Kent.	139 51.5	S60 53.2
N 10	318 14.7	331 07.9	04.3	319 15.7	16.8	251 07.8	18.6	98 39.1	43.0	Sabik	102 12.7	S15 44.4
D 11	333 17.2	346 07.5	03.1	334 16.4	16.0	266 09.9	18.7	113 41.7	42.9			
A 12	348 19.7	1 07.0	S 7 01.9	349 17.0	S 1 15.2	281 12.1	N21 18.7	128 44.2	S12 42.9	Schedar	349 41.2	N56 36.7
Y 13	3 22.1	16 06.6	7 00.7	4 17.7	14.4	296 14.2	18.8	143 46.7	42.9	Shaula	96 22.2	S37 06.6
14	18 24.6	31 06.2	6 59.5	19 18.4	13.6	311 16.4	18.8	158 49.3	42.8	Sirius	258 33.7	S16 44.4
15	33 27.0	46 05.7 ..	58.3	34 19.1 ..	12.8	326 18.5 ..	18.9	173 51.8 ..	42.8	Spica	158 31.2	S11 13.9
16	48 29.5	61 05.3	57.1	49 19.8	12.0	341 20.7	18.9	188 54.4	42.8	Suhail	222 52.2	S43 29.5
17	63 32.0	76 04.9	55.9	64 20.5	11.2	356 22.8	19.0	203 56.9	42.7			
18	78 34.4	91 04.4	S 6 54.7	79 21.2	S 1 10.5	11 25.0	N21 19.0	218 59.5	S12 42.7	Vega	80 39.2	N38 47.6
19	93 36.9	106 04.0	53.5	94 21.8	09.7	26 27.1	19.1	234 02.0	42.7	Zuben'ubi	137 05.4	S16 05.8
20	108 39.4	121 03.6	52.3	109 22.5	08.9	41 29.3	19.1	249 04.5	42.6		SHA	Mer.Pass.
21	123 41.8	136 03.1 ..	51.1	124 23.2 ..	08.1	56 31.4 ..	19.2	264 07.1 ..	42.6	Venus	14 32.0	11 55
22	138 44.3	151 02.7	49.9	139 23.9	07.3	71 33.6	19.3	279 09.6	42.6	Mars	2 01.4	12 44
23	153 46.8	166 02.3	48.7	154 24.6	06.5	86 35.7	19.3	294 12.2	42.5	Jupiter	293 03.5	17 18
Mer.Pass. 12 50.5		v −0.4	d 1.2	v 0.7	d 0.8	v 2.2	d 0.1	v 2.5	d 0.0	Saturn	140 21.8	3 31

UT	SUN GHA	SUN Dec	MOON GHA	v	MOON Dec	d	HP
8 FRIDAY	° ′	° ′	° ′	′	° ′	′	′
00	177 17.5	S 4 54.5	226 32.1	7.7	S15 51.8	8.1	59.1
01	192 17.7	53.5	240 58.8	7.8	15 43.7	8.1	59.1
02	207 17.8	52.6	255 25.6	7.9	15 35.6	8.2	59.1
03	222 18.0	.. 51.6	269 52.5	7.9	15 27.4	8.3	59.1
04	237 18.1	50.6	284 19.4	8.0	15 19.1	8.4	59.0
05	252 18.3	49.6	298 46.4	8.0	15 10.7	8.5	59.0
06	267 18.5	S 4 48.7	313 13.4	8.1	S15 02.2	8.6	59.0
07	282 18.6	47.7	327 40.5	8.1	14 53.6	8.7	59.0
08	297 18.8	46.7	342 07.6	8.2	14 44.9	8.7	59.0
09	312 18.9	.. 45.7	356 34.8	8.2	14 36.2	8.9	59.0
10	327 19.1	44.8	11 02.0	8.3	14 27.3	8.9	59.0
11	342 19.2	43.8	25 29.3	8.4	14 18.4	9.0	59.0
12	357 19.4	S 4 42.8	39 56.7	8.4	S14 09.4	9.2	59.0
13	12 19.5	41.8	54 24.1	8.5	14 00.3	9.1	59.0
14	27 19.7	40.9	68 51.6	8.5	13 51.2	9.3	58.9
15	42 19.8	39.9	83 19.1	8.6	13 41.9	9.3	58.9
16	57 20.0	38.9	97 46.7	8.7	13 32.6	9.4	58.9
17	72 20.1	37.9	112 14.4	8.6	13 23.2	9.5	58.9
18	87 20.3	S 4 36.9	126 42.0	8.8	S13 13.7	9.6	58.9
19	102 20.5	36.0	141 09.8	8.8	13 04.1	9.6	58.9
20	117 20.6	35.0	155 37.6	8.9	12 54.5	9.7	58.9
21	132 20.8	.. 34.0	170 05.5	8.9	12 44.8	9.8	58.9
22	147 20.9	33.0	184 33.4	9.0	12 35.0	9.8	58.9
23	162 21.1	32.1	199 01.4	9.0	12 25.2	9.9	58.9
9 SATURDAY							
00	177 21.2	S 4 31.1	213 29.4	9.1	S12 15.3	10.0	58.8
01	192 21.4	30.1	227 57.5	9.2	12 05.3	10.1	58.8
02	207 21.5	29.1	242 25.7	9.2	11 55.2	10.1	58.8
03	222 21.7	.. 28.1	256 53.9	9.2	11 45.1	10.1	58.8
04	237 21.9	27.2	271 22.1	9.3	11 35.0	10.3	58.8
05	252 22.0	26.2	285 50.4	9.4	11 24.7	10.3	58.8
06	267 22.2	S 4 25.2	300 18.8	9.4	S11 14.4	10.3	58.7
07	282 22.3	24.2	314 47.2	9.5	11 04.1	10.4	58.7
08	297 22.5	23.3	329 15.7	9.5	10 53.7	10.5	58.7
09	312 22.6	.. 22.3	343 44.2	9.6	10 43.2	10.6	58.7
10	327 22.8	21.3	358 12.8	9.6	10 32.6	10.5	58.7
11	342 23.0	20.3	12 41.4	9.7	10 22.1	10.7	58.7
12	357 23.1	S 4 19.3	27 10.1	9.8	S10 11.4	10.7	58.7
13	12 23.3	18.4	41 38.9	9.8	10 00.7	10.7	58.6
14	27 23.4	17.4	56 07.7	9.8	9 50.0	10.8	58.6
15	42 23.6	.. 16.4	70 36.5	9.9	9 39.2	10.8	58.6
16	57 23.7	15.4	85 05.4	10.0	9 28.4	10.9	58.6
17	72 23.9	14.4	99 34.4	10.0	9 17.5	11.0	58.6
18	87 24.1	S 4 13.5	114 03.4	10.0	S 9 06.5	11.0	58.5
19	102 24.2	12.5	128 32.4	10.1	8 55.5	11.0	58.5
20	117 24.4	11.5	143 01.5	10.2	8 44.5	11.0	58.5
21	132 24.5	.. 10.5	157 30.7	10.2	8 33.5	11.0	58.5
22	147 24.7	09.5	171 59.9	10.2	8 22.3	11.1	58.5
23	162 24.9	08.6	186 29.1	10.3	8 11.2	11.2	58.5
10 SUNDAY							
00	177 25.0	S 4 07.6	200 58.4	10.4	S 8 00.0	11.2	58.5
01	192 25.2	06.6	215 27.8	10.4	7 48.8	11.3	58.4
02	207 25.3	05.6	229 57.2	10.4	7 37.5	11.3	58.4
03	222 25.5	.. 04.6	244 26.6	10.5	7 26.2	11.3	58.4
04	237 25.7	03.7	258 56.1	10.5	7 14.9	11.4	58.4
05	252 25.8	02.7	273 25.6	10.6	7 03.5	11.4	58.4
06	267 26.0	S 4 01.7	287 55.2	10.6	S 6 52.1	11.4	58.4
07	282 26.1	4 00.7	302 24.8	10.7	6 40.7	11.4	58.3
08	297 26.3	3 59.7	316 54.5	10.7	6 29.3	11.5	58.3
09	312 26.5	.. 58.8	331 24.2	10.8	6 17.8	11.5	58.3
10	327 26.6	57.8	345 54.0	10.8	6 06.3	11.6	58.3
11	342 26.8	56.8	0 23.8	10.9	5 54.7	11.5	58.3
12	357 26.9	S 3 55.8	14 53.7	10.9	S 5 43.2	11.6	58.2
13	12 27.1	54.8	29 23.6	10.9	5 31.6	11.6	58.2
14	27 27.3	53.9	43 53.5	11.0	5 20.0	11.6	58.2
15	42 27.4	.. 52.9	58 23.5	11.0	5 08.4	11.7	58.2
16	57 27.6	51.9	72 53.5	11.0	4 56.7	11.6	58.2
17	72 27.8	50.9	87 23.5	11.1	4 45.1	11.7	58.1
18	87 27.9	S 3 49.9	101 53.6	11.2	S 4 33.4	11.7	58.1
19	102 28.1	49.0	116 23.8	11.2	4 21.7	11.7	58.1
20	117 28.2	48.0	130 54.0	11.2	4 10.0	11.7	58.1
21	132 28.4	.. 47.0	145 24.2	11.2	3 58.3	11.7	58.1
22	147 28.6	46.0	159 54.4	11.3	3 46.6	11.8	58.0
23	162 28.7	45.0	174 24.7	11.3	S 3 34.8	11.7	58.0
	SD 16.1	d 1.0	SD 16.1		16.0		15.9

Lat.	Twilight Naut.	Twilight Civil	Sunrise	Moonrise 8	9	10	11
	h m	h m	h m	h m	h m	h m	h m
N 72	04 27	05 47	06 54	06 53	06 32	06 17	06 05
N 70	04 37	05 49	06 49	06 20	06 13	06 07	06 02
68	04 45	05 50	06 45	05 56	05 58	05 59	05 59
66	04 51	05 51	06 42	05 37	05 46	05 53	05 57
64	04 57	05 52	06 39	05 22	05 36	05 47	05 55
62	05 01	05 53	06 37	05 09	05 28	05 42	05 54
60	05 05	05 53	06 35	04 58	05 20	05 37	05 52
N 58	05 08	05 54	06 33	04 49	05 13	05 34	05 51
56	05 11	05 54	06 31	04 41	05 08	05 30	05 50
54	05 13	05 54	06 29	04 33	05 02	05 27	05 49
52	05 15	05 54	06 28	04 26	04 57	05 24	05 48
50	05 17	05 54	06 26	04 20	04 53	05 22	05 47
45	05 20	05 54	06 23	04 07	04 44	05 16	05 45
N 40	05 23	05 54	06 21	03 57	04 36	05 11	05 44
35	05 24	05 54	06 19	03 47	04 29	05 07	05 43
30	05 25	05 53	06 17	03 39	04 23	05 03	05 41
20	05 26	05 51	06 13	03 25	04 13	04 57	05 39
N 10	05 25	05 49	06 10	03 13	04 04	04 52	05 38
0	05 22	05 46	06 07	03 01	03 55	04 47	05 36
S 10	05 18	05 43	06 04	02 50	03 46	04 41	05 34
20	05 13	05 38	06 01	02 37	03 37	04 36	05 32
30	05 04	05 32	05 56	02 23	03 27	04 29	05 30
35	04 59	05 29	05 54	02 15	03 21	04 26	05 29
40	04 52	05 24	05 51	02 05	03 14	04 21	05 28
45	04 44	05 18	05 48	01 54	03 06	04 17	05 27
S 50	04 32	05 11	05 44	01 41	02 56	04 11	05 25
52	04 27	05 08	05 42	01 34	02 51	04 08	05 24
54	04 21	05 04	05 40	01 27	02 46	04 05	05 23
56	04 14	05 00	05 38	01 20	02 41	04 02	05 22
58	04 06	04 55	05 36	01 11	02 34	03 58	05 21
S 60	03 57	04 50	05 33	01 01	02 27	03 54	05 20

Lat.	Sunset	Twilight Civil	Twilight Naut.	Moonset 8	9	10	11
	h m	h m	h m	h m	h m	h m	h m
N 72	17 29	18 36	19 57	11 53	14 05	16 05	18 00
N 70	17 33	18 34	19 47	12 24	14 21	16 13	18 00
68	17 37	18 33	19 38	12 47	14 34	16 19	18 00
66	17 40	18 32	19 32	13 05	14 45	16 24	18 00
64	17 43	18 31	19 26	13 19	14 54	16 28	18 00
62	17 46	18 30	19 22	13 31	15 02	16 32	18 00
60	17 48	18 29	19 18	13 41	15 08	16 35	18 00
N 58	17 50	18 29	19 14	13 50	15 14	16 38	17 59
56	17 51	18 28	19 12	13 57	15 19	16 40	17 59
54	17 53	18 28	19 09	14 04	15 24	16 42	17 59
52	17 54	18 28	19 05	14 10	15 28	16 44	17 59
50	17 55	18 28	19 05	14 16	15 31	16 46	17 59
45	17 58	18 27	19 02	14 28	15 39	16 50	17 59
N 40	18 00	18 28	18 59	14 38	15 46	16 53	17 59
35	18 03	18 28	18 57	14 46	15 52	16 56	17 59
30	18 04	18 28	18 56	14 53	15 57	16 59	17 59
20	18 08	18 30	18 55	15 06	16 05	17 03	17 59
N 10	18 11	18 32	18 56	15 17	16 13	17 07	17 59
0	18 14	18 34	18 59	15 27	16 20	17 10	17 59
S 10	18 17	18 38	19 02	15 37	16 27	17 14	17 59
20	18 20	18 42	19 08	15 48	16 34	17 17	17 59
30	18 24	18 48	19 16	16 00	16 42	17 21	17 59
35	18 26	18 52	19 22	16 07	16 47	17 24	17 58
40	18 29	18 56	19 28	16 15	16 52	17 26	17 58
45	18 32	19 02	19 37	16 24	16 59	17 29	17 58
S 50	18 36	19 08	19 48	16 35	17 06	17 33	17 58
52	18 38	19 12	19 54	16 41	17 09	17 35	17 58
54	18 39	19 15	19 59	16 46	17 13	17 36	17 58
56	18 41	19 19	20 05	16 52	17 17	17 38	17 58
58	18 44	19 24	20 13	16 59	17 22	17 40	17 57
S 60	18 46	19 29	20 22	17 07	17 27	17 43	17 57

Day	SUN Eqn. of Time 00h	SUN Eqn. of Time 12h	SUN Mer. Pass.	MOON Mer. Pass. Upper	MOON Mer. Pass. Lower	Age	Phase
	m s	m s	h m	h m	h m	d	%
8	10 50	10 43	12 11	09 14	21 41	26	14
9	10 35	10 28	12 10	10 07	22 33	27	7
10	10 20	10 13	12 10	10 58	23 23	28	2

UT	ARIES GHA	VENUS −3.9 GHA	Dec	MARS +1.2 GHA	Dec	JUPITER −2.2 GHA	Dec	SATURN +0.4 GHA	Dec	STARS Name	SHA	Dec
11 00	168 49.2	181 01.8	S 6 47.5	169 25.3	S 1 05.7	101 37.9	N21 19.4	309 14.7	S12 42.5	Acamar	315 18.7	S40 15.4
01	183 51.7	196 01.4	46.3	184 26.0	04.9	116 40.0	19.4	324 17.3	42.5	Achernar	335 27.4	S57 10.4
02	198 54.2	211 01.0	45.1	199 26.7	04.1	131 42.1	19.5	339 19.8	42.4	Acrux	173 08.8	S63 10.4
03	213 56.6	226 00.5	.. 43.9	214 27.3	.. 03.3	146 44.3	.. 19.5	354 22.4	.. 42.4	Adhara	255 12.5	S28 59.8
04	228 59.1	241 00.1	42.7	229 28.0	02.5	161 46.4	19.6	9 24.9	42.4	Aldebaran	290 49.6	N16 32.0
05	244 01.5	255 59.7	41.5	244 28.7	01.7	176 48.6	19.6	24 27.4	42.3			
06	259 04.0	270 59.2	S 6 40.3	259 29.4	S 1 00.9	191 50.7	N21 19.7	39 30.0	S12 42.3	Alioth	166 20.3	N55 53.1
07	274 06.5	285 58.8	39.1	274 30.1	1 00.1	206 52.9	19.7	54 32.5	42.3	Alkaid	152 58.6	N49 14.6
08	289 08.9	300 58.4	37.9	289 30.8	0 59.3	221 55.0	19.8	69 35.1	42.2	Al Na'ir	27 44.4	S46 53.7
M 09	304 11.4	315 58.0	.. 36.7	304 31.5	.. 58.5	236 57.2	.. 19.9	84 37.6	.. 42.2	Alnilam	275 46.5	S 1 11.9
O 10	319 13.9	330 57.5	35.5	319 32.1	57.8	251 59.3	19.9	99 40.2	42.2	Alphard	217 56.0	S 8 43.3
N 11	334 16.3	345 57.1	34.2	334 32.8	57.0	267 01.5	20.0	114 42.7	42.1			
D 12	349 18.8	0 56.7	S 6 33.0	349 33.5	S 0 56.2	282 03.6	N21 20.0	129 45.3	S12 42.1	Alphecca	126 11.0	N26 40.0
A 13	4 21.3	15 56.2	31.8	4 34.2	55.4	297 05.7	20.1	144 47.8	42.1	Alpheratz	357 44.0	N29 09.8
Y 14	19 23.7	30 55.8	30.6	19 34.9	54.6	312 07.9	20.1	159 50.4	42.0	Altair	62 08.6	N 8 54.2
15	34 26.2	45 55.4	.. 29.4	34 35.6	.. 53.8	327 10.0	.. 20.2	174 52.9	.. 42.0	Ankaa	353 16.3	S42 14.1
16	49 28.6	60 55.0	28.2	49 36.3	53.0	342 12.2	20.2	189 55.4	42.0	Antares	112 26.4	S26 27.6
17	64 31.1	75 54.5	27.0	64 37.0	52.2	357 14.3	20.3	204 58.0	41.9			
18	79 33.6	90 54.1	S 6 25.8	79 37.6	S 0 51.4	12 16.5	N21 20.3	220 00.5	S12 41.9	Arcturus	145 55.6	N19 06.6
19	94 36.0	105 53.7	24.6	94 38.3	50.6	27 18.6	20.4	235 03.1	41.8	Atria	107 28.3	S69 02.7
20	109 38.5	120 53.2	23.4	109 39.0	49.8	42 20.7	20.5	250 05.6	41.8	Avior	234 17.6	S59 33.5
21	124 41.0	135 52.8	.. 22.2	124 39.7	.. 49.0	57 22.9	.. 20.5	265 08.2	.. 41.8	Bellatrix	278 32.2	N 6 21.5
22	139 43.4	150 52.4	20.9	139 40.4	48.2	72 25.0	20.6	280 10.7	41.7	Betelgeuse	271 01.4	N 7 24.3
23	154 45.9	165 52.0	19.7	154 41.1	47.4	87 27.2	20.6	295 13.3	41.7			
12 00	169 48.4	180 51.5	S 6 18.5	169 41.8	S 0 46.6	102 29.3	N21 20.7	310 15.8	S12 41.7	Canopus	263 56.1	S52 42.6
01	184 50.8	195 51.1	17.3	184 42.5	45.8	117 31.4	20.7	325 18.4	41.6	Capella	280 34.7	N46 00.7
02	199 53.3	210 50.7	16.1	199 43.2	45.1	132 33.6	20.8	340 20.9	41.6	Deneb	49 31.9	N45 19.6
03	214 55.8	225 50.3	.. 14.9	214 43.8	.. 44.3	147 35.7	.. 20.8	355 23.5	.. 41.6	Denebola	182 33.5	N14 29.7
04	229 58.2	240 49.8	13.7	229 44.5	43.5	162 37.9	20.9	10 26.0	41.5	Diphda	348 56.4	S17 55.0
05	245 00.7	255 49.4	12.5	244 45.2	42.7	177 40.0	20.9	25 28.6	41.5			
06	260 03.1	270 49.0	S 6 11.2	259 45.9	S 0 41.9	192 42.1	N21 21.0	40 31.1	S12 41.5	Dubhe	193 51.3	N61 40.6
07	275 05.6	285 48.6	10.0	274 46.6	41.1	207 44.3	21.1	55 33.7	41.4	Elnath	278 12.8	N28 37.0
08	290 08.1	300 48.1	08.8	289 47.3	40.3	222 46.4	21.1	70 36.2	41.4	Eltanin	90 46.3	N51 29.4
T 09	305 10.5	315 47.7	.. 07.6	304 48.0	.. 39.5	237 48.5	.. 21.2	85 38.8	.. 41.4	Enif	33 47.6	N 9 56.1
U 10	320 13.0	330 47.3	06.4	319 48.7	38.7	252 50.7	21.2	100 41.3	41.3	Fomalhaut	15 24.5	S29 33.1
E 11	335 15.5	345 46.9	05.2	334 49.3	37.9	267 52.8	21.3	115 43.9	41.3			
S 12	350 17.9	0 46.5	S 6 04.0	349 50.0	S 0 37.1	282 55.0	N21 21.3	130 46.4	S12 41.2	Gacrux	172 00.5	S57 11.3
D 13	5 20.4	15 46.0	02.8	4 50.7	36.3	297 57.1	21.4	145 49.0	41.2	Gienah	175 52.1	S17 37.1
A 14	20 22.9	30 45.6	01.5	19 51.4	35.5	312 59.2	21.4	160 51.5	41.2	Hadar	148 47.6	S60 26.1
Y 15	35 25.3	45 45.2	6 00.3	34 52.1	.. 34.7	328 01.4	.. 21.5	175 54.1	.. 41.1	Hamal	328 01.2	N23 31.4
16	50 27.8	60 44.8	5 59.1	49 52.8	33.9	343 03.5	21.5	190 56.6	41.1	Kaus Aust.	83 44.1	S34 22.5
17	65 30.2	75 44.3	57.9	64 53.5	33.2	358 05.6	21.6	205 59.2	41.1			
18	80 32.7	90 43.9	S 5 56.7	79 54.2	S 0 32.4	13 07.8	N21 21.7	221 01.7	S12 41.0	Kochab	137 19.3	N74 05.8
19	95 35.2	105 43.5	55.5	94 54.9	31.6	28 09.9	21.7	236 04.3	41.0	Markab	13 38.8	N15 16.6
20	110 37.6	120 43.1	54.2	109 55.5	30.8	43 12.0	21.8	251 06.8	41.0	Menkar	314 15.4	N 4 08.3
21	125 40.1	135 42.7	.. 53.0	124 56.2	.. 30.0	58 14.2	.. 21.8	266 09.4	.. 40.9	Menkent	148 07.5	S36 26.1
22	140 42.6	150 42.2	51.8	139 56.9	29.2	73 16.3	21.9	281 11.9	40.9	Miaplacidus	221 38.9	S69 46.6
23	155 45.0	165 41.8	50.6	154 57.6	28.4	88 18.4	21.9	296 14.5	40.9			
13 00	170 47.5	180 41.4	S 5 49.4	169 58.3	S 0 27.6	103 20.6	N21 22.0	311 17.0	S12 40.8	Mirfak	308 40.8	N49 54.5
01	185 50.0	195 41.0	48.2	184 59.0	26.8	118 22.7	22.0	326 19.6	40.8	Nunki	75 58.7	S26 16.6
02	200 52.4	210 40.6	46.9	199 59.7	26.0	133 24.9	22.1	341 22.1	40.7	Peacock	53 19.9	S56 41.3
03	215 54.9	225 40.1	.. 45.7	215 00.4	.. 25.2	148 27.0	.. 22.2	356 24.7	.. 40.7	Pollux	243 27.7	N27 59.5
04	230 57.4	240 39.7	44.5	230 01.1	24.4	163 29.1	22.2	11 27.2	40.7	Procyon	244 59.7	N 5 11.2
05	245 59.8	255 39.3	43.3	245 01.8	23.6	178 31.2	22.3	26 29.8	40.6			
06	261 02.3	270 38.9	S 5 42.1	260 02.4	S 0 22.8	193 33.4	N21 22.3	41 32.3	S12 40.6	Rasalhague	96 06.6	N12 33.0
W 07	276 04.7	285 38.5	40.8	275 03.1	22.0	208 35.5	22.4	56 34.9	40.6	Regulus	207 43.4	N11 53.9
E 08	291 07.2	300 38.1	39.6	290 03.8	21.3	223 37.6	22.4	71 37.4	40.5	Rigel	281 12.2	S 8 11.5
D 09	306 09.7	315 37.6	.. 38.4	305 04.5	.. 20.5	238 39.8	.. 22.5	86 40.0	.. 40.5	Rigil Kent.	139 51.5	S60 53.2
N 10	321 12.1	330 37.2	37.2	320 05.2	19.7	253 41.9	22.5	101 42.5	40.5	Sabik	102 12.7	S15 44.4
E 11	336 14.6	345 36.8	36.0	335 05.9	18.9	268 44.0	22.6	116 45.1	40.4			
S 12	351 17.1	0 36.4	S 5 34.7	350 06.6	S 0 18.1	283 46.2	N21 22.7	131 47.6	S12 40.4	Schedar	349 41.2	N56 36.7
D 13	6 19.5	15 36.0	33.5	5 07.3	17.3	298 48.3	22.7	146 50.2	40.3	Shaula	96 22.2	S37 06.6
A 14	21 22.0	30 35.6	32.3	20 08.0	16.5	313 50.4	22.8	161 52.7	40.3	Sirius	258 33.7	S16 44.4
Y 15	36 24.5	45 35.1	.. 31.1	35 08.7	.. 15.7	328 52.6	.. 22.8	176 55.3	.. 40.3	Spica	158 31.1	S11 13.9
16	51 26.9	60 34.7	29.9	50 09.3	14.9	343 54.7	22.9	191 57.9	40.2	Suhail	222 52.2	S43 29.5
17	66 29.4	75 34.3	28.6	65 10.0	14.1	358 56.8	22.9	207 00.4	40.2			
18	81 31.9	90 33.9	S 5 27.4	80 10.7	S 0 13.3	13 58.9	N21 23.0	222 03.0	S12 40.2	Vega	80 39.2	N38 47.6
19	96 34.3	105 33.5	26.2	95 11.4	12.5	29 01.1	23.0	237 05.5	40.1	Zuben'ubi	137 05.4	S16 05.8
20	111 36.8	120 33.1	25.0	110 12.1	11.7	44 03.2	23.1	252 08.1	40.1		SHA	Mer. Pass.
21	126 39.2	135 32.6	.. 23.7	125 12.8	.. 10.9	59 05.3	.. 23.2	267 10.6	.. 40.0	Venus	11 03.2	11 57
22	141 41.7	150 32.2	22.5	140 13.5	10.2	74 07.5	23.2	282 13.2	40.0	Mars	359 53.4	12 41
23	156 44.2	165 31.8	21.3	155 14.2	09.4	89 09.6	23.3	297 15.7	40.0	Jupiter	292 40.9	17 08
Mer. Pass. 12 38.7		v −0.4 d 1.2		v 0.7 d 0.8		v 2.1 d 0.1		v 2.5 d 0.0		Saturn	140 27.5	3 18

UT	SUN GHA	SUN Dec	MOON GHA	v	MOON Dec	d	HP
d h	° ′	° ′	° ′	′	° ′	′	′
11 00	177 28.9	S 3 44.0	188 55.0	11.4	S 3 23.1	11.8	58.0
01	192 29.1	43.1	203 25.4	11.4	3 11.3	11.8	58.0
02	207 29.2	42.1	217 55.8	11.4	2 59.5	11.7	57.9
03	222 29.4 ..	41.1	232 26.2	11.5	2 47.8	11.8	57.9
04	237 29.5	40.1	246 56.7	11.5	2 36.0	11.8	57.9
05	252 29.7	39.1	261 27.2	11.5	2 24.2	11.8	57.9
06	267 29.9	S 3 38.1	275 57.7	11.6	S 2 12.4	11.8	57.9
M 07	282 30.0	37.2	290 28.3	11.6	2 00.6	11.8	57.8
O 08	297 30.2	36.2	304 58.9	11.6	1 48.8	11.8	57.8
N 09	312 30.4 ..	35.2	319 29.5	11.7	1 37.0	11.8	57.8
D 10	327 30.5	34.2	334 00.2	11.7	1 25.2	11.8	57.8
A 11	342 30.7	33.2	348 30.9	11.7	1 13.4	11.7	57.7
Y 12	357 30.9	S 3 32.3	3 01.6	11.8	S 1 01.7	11.8	57.7
13	12 31.0	31.3	17 32.4	11.7	0 49.9	11.8	57.7
14	27 31.2	30.3	32 03.1	11.8	0 38.1	11.8	57.7
15	42 31.3 ..	29.3	46 34.0	11.8	0 26.3	11.7	57.6
16	57 31.5	28.3	61 04.8	11.9	0 14.6	11.8	57.6
17	72 31.7	27.3	75 35.7	11.8	S 0 02.8	11.7	57.6
18	87 31.8	S 3 26.4	90 06.5	12.0	N 0 08.9	11.7	57.6
19	102 32.0	25.4	104 37.5	11.9	0 20.6	11.8	57.5
20	117 32.2	24.4	119 08.4	12.0	0 32.4	11.7	57.5
21	132 32.3 ..	23.4	133 39.4	12.0	0 44.1	11.6	57.5
22	147 32.5	22.4	148 10.4	12.0	0 55.7	11.7	57.5
23	162 32.7	21.4	162 41.4	12.0	1 07.4	11.7	57.4
12 00	177 32.8	S 3 20.5	177 12.4	12.1	N 1 19.1	11.6	57.4
01	192 33.0	19.5	191 43.5	12.0	1 30.7	11.6	57.4
02	207 33.2	18.5	206 14.5	12.1	1 42.3	11.7	57.4
03	222 33.3 ..	17.5	220 45.6	12.2	1 54.0	11.5	57.3
04	237 33.5	16.5	235 16.8	12.1	2 05.5	11.6	57.3
05	252 33.7	15.5	249 47.9	12.2	2 17.1	11.5	57.3
06	267 33.8	S 3 14.6	264 19.1	12.2	N 2 28.6	11.6	57.3
T 07	282 34.0	13.6	278 50.3	12.2	2 40.2	11.5	57.2
U 08	297 34.2	12.6	293 21.5	12.2	2 51.7	11.4	57.2
E 09	312 34.3 ..	11.6	307 52.7	12.2	3 03.1	11.5	57.2
S 10	327 34.5	10.6	322 23.9	12.3	3 14.6	11.4	57.2
D 11	342 34.7	09.6	336 55.2	12.2	3 26.0	11.4	57.1
A 12	357 34.8	S 3 08.6	351 26.4	12.3	N 3 37.4	11.3	57.1
Y 13	12 35.0	07.7	5 57.7	12.3	3 48.7	11.4	57.1
14	27 35.2	06.7	20 29.0	12.3	4 00.1	11.3	57.1
15	42 35.3 ..	05.7	35 00.3	12.3	4 11.4	11.2	57.0
16	57 35.5	04.7	49 31.6	12.4	4 22.6	11.3	57.0
17	72 35.7	03.7	64 03.0	12.3	4 33.9	11.2	57.0
18	87 35.8	S 3 02.7	78 34.3	12.4	N 4 45.1	11.1	57.0
19	102 36.0	01.8	93 05.7	12.4	4 56.2	11.2	56.9
20	117 36.2	3 00.8	107 37.1	12.4	5 07.4	11.1	56.9
21	132 36.3 ..	2 59.8	122 08.5	12.4	5 18.5	11.0	56.9
22	147 36.5	58.8	136 39.9	12.4	5 29.5	11.0	56.9
23	162 36.7	57.8	151 11.3	12.4	5 40.5	11.0	56.8
13 00	177 36.9	S 2 56.8	165 42.7	12.5	N 5 51.5	11.0	56.8
01	192 37.0	55.8	180 14.2	12.4	6 02.5	10.9	56.8
02	207 37.2	54.9	194 45.6	12.5	6 13.4	10.8	56.7
03	222 37.4 ..	53.9	209 17.1	12.4	6 24.2	10.8	56.7
04	237 37.5	52.9	223 48.5	12.5	6 35.0	10.8	56.7
05	252 37.7	51.9	238 20.0	12.5	6 45.8	10.8	56.7
06	267 37.9	S 2 50.9	252 51.5	12.4	N 6 56.6	10.6	56.6
W 07	282 38.0	49.9	267 22.9	12.5	7 07.2	10.7	56.6
E 08	297 38.2	48.9	281 54.4	12.5	7 17.9	10.6	56.6
D 09	312 38.4 ..	48.0	296 25.9	12.5	7 28.5	10.6	56.6
N 10	327 38.6	47.0	310 57.4	12.5	7 39.0	10.5	56.5
E 11	342 38.7	46.0	325 28.9	12.5	7 49.5	10.5	56.5
S 12	357 38.9	S 2 45.0	340 00.4	12.5	N 8 00.0	10.4	56.5
D 13	12 39.1	44.0	354 31.9	12.6	8 10.4	10.4	56.5
A 14	27 39.2	43.0	9 03.5	12.5	8 20.8	10.3	56.4
Y 15	42 39.4 ..	42.0	23 35.0	12.5	8 31.1	10.2	56.4
16	57 39.6	41.1	38 06.5	12.5	8 41.3	10.2	56.4
17	72 39.7	40.1	52 38.0	12.6	8 51.5	10.2	56.4
18	87 39.9	S 2 39.1	67 09.6	12.5	N 9 01.7	10.1	56.3
19	102 40.1	38.1	81 41.1	12.5	9 11.8	10.0	56.3
20	117 40.3	37.1	96 12.6	12.5	9 21.8	10.0	56.3
21	132 40.4 ..	36.1	110 44.1	12.6	9 31.8	9.9	56.2
22	147 40.6	35.1	125 15.7	12.5	9 41.7	9.9	56.2
23	162 40.8	34.2	139 47.2	12.5	N 9 51.6	9.8	56.2
	SD 16.1	d 1.0	SD 15.7		15.6		15.4

Lat.	Twilight Naut.	Civil	Sunrise	Moonrise 11	12	13	14
°	h m	h m	h m	h m	h m	h m	h m
N 72	04 10	05 32	06 39	06 05	05 54	05 42	05 30
N 70	04 22	05 35	06 36	06 02	05 57	05 52	05 47
68	04 32	05 38	06 33	05 59	05 59	06 00	06 01
66	04 39	05 40	06 31	05 57	06 02	06 06	06 12
64	04 46	05 42	06 29	05 55	06 04	06 12	06 22
62	04 51	05 43	06 27	05 54	06 05	06 17	06 30
60	04 55	05 44	06 26	05 52	06 07	06 21	06 37
N 58	04 59	05 45	06 24	05 51	06 08	06 25	06 43
56	05 03	05 46	06 23	05 50	06 09	06 28	06 49
54	05 06	05 47	06 22	05 49	06 10	06 31	06 54
52	05 08	05 47	06 21	05 48	06 11	06 34	06 58
50	05 10	05 48	06 20	05 47	06 12	06 37	07 03
45	05 15	05 49	06 18	05 45	06 14	06 42	07 11
N 40	05 18	05 49	06 16	05 44	06 15	06 47	07 19
35	05 20	05 50	06 15	05 43	06 17	06 51	07 26
30	05 22	05 50	06 13	05 41	06 18	06 54	07 31
20	05 23	05 49	06 11	05 39	06 20	07 01	07 41
N 10	05 23	05 48	06 09	05 38	06 22	07 06	07 50
0	05 22	05 46	06 06	05 36	06 24	07 11	07 58
S 10	05 19	05 43	06 04	05 34	06 26	07 17	08 07
20	05 14	05 39	06 01	05 32	06 28	07 22	08 16
30	05 06	05 34	05 58	05 30	06 30	07 29	08 26
35	05 01	05 31	05 57	05 29	06 32	07 32	08 32
40	04 55	05 27	05 54	05 28	06 33	07 37	08 39
45	04 47	05 22	05 51	05 27	06 35	07 42	08 47
S 50	04 37	05 16	05 49	05 25	06 37	07 48	08 56
52	04 33	05 14	05 48	05 24	06 38	07 50	09 01
54	04 27	05 10	05 46	05 23	06 39	07 54	09 06
56	04 21	05 07	05 44	05 22	06 40	07 57	09 11
58	04 14	05 03	05 43	05 21	06 42	08 01	09 17
S 60	04 06	04 58	05 40	05 20	06 43	08 05	09 24

Lat.	Sunset	Twilight Civil	Naut.	Moonset 11	12	13	14
°	h m	h m	h m	h m	h m	h m	h m
N 72	17 43	18 50	20 13	18 00	19 51	21 43	23 38
N 70	17 46	18 47	20 00	18 00	19 44	21 27	23 11
68	17 48	18 44	19 50	18 00	19 38	21 15	22 50
66	17 50	18 41	19 42	18 00	19 33	21 05	22 34
64	17 52	18 40	19 36	18 00	19 29	20 56	22 21
62	17 54	18 38	19 30	18 00	19 25	20 49	22 10
60	17 55	18 37	19 25	18 00	19 22	20 43	22 01
N 58	17 56	18 35	19 21	17 59	19 19	20 37	21 53
56	17 57	18 35	19 18	17 59	19 17	20 32	21 45
54	17 59	18 34	19 15	17 59	19 15	20 28	21 39
52	17 59	18 33	19 12	17 59	19 13	20 24	21 33
50	18 00	18 32	19 10	17 59	19 11	20 21	21 28
45	18 02	18 31	19 06	17 59	19 07	20 13	21 17
N 40	18 04	18 31	19 02	17 59	19 04	20 07	21 08
35	18 05	18 30	19 00	17 59	19 01	20 01	21 00
30	18 06	18 30	18 58	17 59	18 58	19 56	20 53
20	18 09	18 31	18 56	17 59	18 54	19 48	20 41
N 10	18 11	18 32	18 56	17 59	18 50	19 41	20 31
0	18 13	18 34	18 58	17 59	18 47	19 34	20 21
S 10	18 15	18 36	19 01	17 59	18 43	19 27	20 11
20	18 18	18 40	19 05	17 59	18 39	19 20	20 01
30	18 20	18 44	19 12	17 58	18 35	19 12	19 49
35	18 22	18 48	19 17	17 58	18 33	19 07	19 42
40	18 24	18 51	19 23	17 58	18 30	19 01	19 35
45	18 27	18 56	19 31	17 58	18 26	18 55	19 26
S 50	18 29	19 02	19 41	17 58	18 23	18 48	19 15
52	18 31	19 05	19 45	17 58	18 21	18 45	19 10
54	18 32	19 08	19 51	17 58	18 19	18 41	19 04
56	18 33	19 11	19 57	17 58	18 17	18 37	18 58
58	18 35	19 15	20 04	17 58	18 14	18 32	18 52
S 60	18 37	19 20	20 12	17 57	18 12	18 27	18 44

	SUN Eqn. of Time 00h	12h	Mer. Pass.	MOON Mer. Pass. Upper	Lower	Age	Phase
Day	m s	m s	h m	h m	h m	d	%
11	10 05	09 57	12 10	11 47	24 12	29	0
12	09 49	09 41	12 10	12 35	00 12	01	1
13	09 33	09 25	12 09	13 23	00 59	02	3

UT	ARIES GHA	VENUS −3.9 GHA	Dec	MARS +1.2 GHA	Dec	JUPITER −2.2 GHA	Dec	SATURN +0.3 GHA	Dec	STARS Name	SHA	Dec
14 00	171 46.6	180 31.4	S 5 20.1	170 14.9	S 0 08.6	104 11.7	N21 23.3	312 18.3	S12 39.9	Acamar	315 18.7	S40 15.4
01	186 49.1	195 31.0	18.8	185 15.6	07.8	119 13.8	23.4	327 20.8	39.9	Achernar	335 27.4	S57 10.4
02	201 51.6	210 30.6	17.6	200 16.3	07.0	134 16.0	23.4	342 23.4	39.9	Acrux	173 08.7	S63 10.4
03	216 54.0	225 30.2	.. 16.4	215 16.9	.. 06.2	149 18.1	.. 23.5	357 26.0	.. 39.8	Adhara	255 12.5	S28 59.8
04	231 56.5	240 29.8	15.2	230 17.6	05.4	164 20.2	23.6	12 28.5	39.8	Aldebaran	290 49.6	N16 32.0
05	246 59.0	255 29.3	14.0	245 18.3	04.6	179 22.3	23.6	27 31.1	39.7			
06	262 01.4	270 28.9	S 5 12.7	260 19.0	S 0 03.8	194 24.5	N21 23.7	42 33.6	S12 39.7	Alioth	166 20.3	N55 53.1
07	277 03.9	285 28.5	11.5	275 19.7	03.0	209 26.6	23.7	57 36.2	39.7	Alkaid	152 58.6	N49 14.6
T 08	292 06.3	300 28.1	10.3	290 20.4	02.2	224 28.7	23.8	72 38.7	39.6	Al Na'ir	27 44.4	S46 53.7
H 09	307 08.8	315 27.7	.. 09.0	305 21.1	.. 01.4	239 30.8	.. 23.8	87 41.3	.. 39.6	Alnilam	275 46.5	S 1 11.9
U 10	322 11.3	330 27.3	07.8	320 21.8	S 00.6	254 33.0	23.9	102 43.9	39.6	Alphard	217 56.0	S 8 43.3
R 11	337 13.7	345 26.9	06.6	335 22.5	N 00.1	269 35.1	23.9	117 46.4	39.5			
S 12	352 16.2	0 26.5	S 5 05.4	350 23.2	N 0 00.9	284 37.2	N21 24.0	132 49.0	S12 39.5	Alphecca	126 11.0	N26 40.0
D 13	7 18.7	15 26.0	04.1	5 23.9	01.7	299 39.3	24.1	147 51.5	39.4	Alpheratz	357 44.0	N29 09.8
A 14	22 21.1	30 25.6	02.9	20 24.5	02.5	314 41.5	24.1	162 54.1	39.4	Altair	62 08.6	N 8 54.2
Y 15	37 23.6	45 25.2	.. 01.7	35 25.2	.. 03.3	329 43.6	.. 24.2	177 56.6	.. 39.4	Ankaa	353 16.3	S42 14.1
16	52 26.1	60 24.8	5 00.5	50 25.9	04.1	344 45.7	24.2	192 59.2	39.3	Antares	112 26.3	S26 27.6
17	67 28.5	75 24.4	4 59.2	65 26.6	04.9	359 47.8	24.3	208 01.8	39.3			
18	82 31.0	90 24.0	S 4 58.0	80 27.3	N 0 05.7	14 50.0	N21 24.3	223 04.3	S12 39.3	Arcturus	145 55.6	N19 06.6
19	97 33.5	105 23.6	56.8	95 28.0	06.5	29 52.1	24.4	238 06.9	39.2	Atria	107 28.2	S69 02.7
20	112 35.9	120 23.2	55.5	110 28.7	07.3	44 54.2	24.4	253 09.4	39.2	Avior	234 17.7	S59 33.5
21	127 38.4	135 22.8	.. 54.3	125 29.4	.. 08.1	59 56.3	.. 24.5	268 12.0	.. 39.1	Bellatrix	278 32.2	N 6 21.5
22	142 40.8	150 22.4	53.1	140 30.1	08.9	74 58.4	24.6	283 14.5	39.1	Betelgeuse	271 01.4	N 7 24.3
23	157 43.3	165 21.9	51.9	155 30.8	09.6	90 00.6	24.6	298 17.1	39.1			
15 00	172 45.8	180 21.5	S 4 50.6	170 31.5	N 0 10.4	105 02.7	N21 24.7	313 19.7	S12 39.0	Canopus	263 56.1	S52 42.6
01	187 48.2	195 21.1	49.4	185 32.2	11.2	120 04.8	24.7	328 22.2	39.0	Capella	280 34.7	N46 00.7
02	202 50.7	210 20.7	48.2	200 32.8	12.0	135 06.9	24.8	343 24.8	39.0	Deneb	49 31.9	N45 19.6
03	217 53.2	225 20.3	.. 46.9	215 33.5	.. 12.8	150 09.0	.. 24.8	358 27.3	.. 38.9	Denebola	182 33.5	N14 29.7
04	232 55.6	240 19.9	45.7	230 34.2	13.6	165 11.2	24.9	13 29.9	38.9	Diphda	348 56.4	S17 54.9
05	247 58.1	255 19.5	44.5	245 34.9	14.4	180 13.3	25.0	28 32.5	38.8			
06	263 00.6	270 19.1	S 4 43.2	260 35.6	N 0 15.2	195 15.4	N21 25.0	43 35.0	S12 38.8	Dubhe	193 51.3	N61 40.6
07	278 03.0	285 18.7	42.0	275 36.3	16.0	210 17.5	25.1	58 37.6	38.8	Elnath	278 12.8	N28 37.0
08	293 05.5	300 18.3	40.8	290 37.0	16.8	225 19.6	25.1	73 40.1	38.7	Eltanin	90 46.3	N51 29.0
F 09	308 07.9	315 17.9	.. 39.6	305 37.7	.. 17.6	240 21.8	.. 25.2	88 42.7	.. 38.7	Enif	33 47.6	N 9 56.1
R 10	323 10.4	330 17.5	38.3	320 38.4	18.4	255 23.9	25.2	103 45.3	38.6	Fomalhaut	15 24.5	S29 33.1
I 11	338 12.9	345 17.1	37.1	335 39.1	19.1	270 26.0	25.3	118 47.8	38.6			
D 12	353 15.3	0 16.7	S 4 35.9	350 39.8	N 0 19.9	285 28.1	N21 25.4	133 50.4	S12 38.6	Gacrux	172 00.5	S57 11.3
A 13	8 17.8	15 16.2	34.6	5 40.5	20.7	300 30.2	25.4	148 52.9	38.5	Gienah	175 52.1	S17 37.1
Y 14	23 20.3	30 15.8	33.4	20 41.2	21.5	315 32.3	25.5	163 55.5	38.5	Hadar	148 47.6	S60 26.1
15	38 22.7	45 15.4	.. 32.2	35 41.9	.. 22.3	330 34.5	.. 25.5	178 58.1	.. 38.4	Hamal	328 01.2	N23 31.4
16	53 25.2	60 15.0	30.9	50 42.5	23.1	345 36.6	25.6	194 00.6	38.4	Kaus Aust.	83 44.1	S34 22.5
17	68 27.7	75 14.6	29.7	65 43.2	23.9	0 38.7	25.6	209 03.2	38.4			
18	83 30.1	90 14.2	S 4 28.5	80 43.9	N 0 24.7	15 40.8	N21 25.7	224 05.7	S12 38.3	Kochab	137 19.3	N74 05.8
19	98 32.6	105 13.8	27.2	95 44.6	25.5	30 42.9	25.8	239 08.3	38.3	Markab	13 38.8	N15 16.6
20	113 35.1	120 13.4	26.0	110 45.3	26.3	45 45.0	25.8	254 10.9	38.3	Menkar	314 15.4	N 4 08.3
21	128 37.5	135 13.0	.. 24.8	125 46.0	.. 27.1	60 47.2	.. 25.9	269 13.4	.. 38.2	Menkent	148 07.4	S36 26.1
22	143 40.0	150 12.6	23.5	140 46.7	27.8	75 49.3	25.9	284 16.0	38.2	Miaplacidus	221 38.9	S69 46.6
23	158 42.4	165 12.2	22.3	155 47.4	28.6	90 51.5	26.0	299 18.6	38.1			
16 00	173 44.9	180 11.8	S 4 21.1	170 48.1	N 0 29.4	105 53.5	N21 26.0	314 21.1	S12 38.1	Mirfak	308 40.8	N49 54.5
01	188 47.4	195 11.4	19.8	185 48.8	30.2	120 55.6	26.1	329 23.7	38.1	Nunki	75 58.6	S26 16.6
02	203 49.8	210 11.0	18.6	200 49.5	31.0	135 57.7	26.2	344 26.2	38.0	Peacock	53 19.9	S56 41.3
03	218 52.3	225 10.6	.. 17.3	215 50.2	.. 31.8	150 59.8	.. 26.2	359 28.8	.. 38.0	Pollux	243 27.7	N27 59.5
04	233 54.8	240 10.2	16.1	230 50.9	32.6	166 02.0	26.3	14 31.4	37.9	Procyon	244 59.7	N 5 11.2
05	248 57.2	255 09.8	14.9	245 51.6	33.4	181 04.1	26.3	29 33.9	37.9			
06	263 59.7	270 09.4	S 4 13.6	260 52.3	N 0 34.2	196 06.2	N21 26.4	44 36.5	S12 37.9	Rasalhague	96 06.6	N12 33.0
07	279 02.2	285 09.0	12.4	275 52.9	35.0	211 08.3	26.4	59 39.1	37.8	Regulus	207 43.4	N11 53.9
S 08	294 04.6	300 08.6	11.2	290 53.6	35.8	226 10.4	26.5	74 41.6	37.8	Rigel	281 12.2	S 8 11.5
A 09	309 07.1	315 08.2	.. 09.9	305 54.3	.. 36.6	241 12.5	.. 26.6	89 44.2	.. 37.7	Rigil Kent.	139 51.4	S60 53.2
T 10	324 09.6	330 07.8	08.7	320 55.0	37.3	256 14.6	26.6	104 46.7	37.7	Sabik	102 12.7	S15 44.4
U 11	339 12.0	345 07.4	07.5	335 55.7	38.1	271 16.7	26.7	119 49.3	37.7			
R 12	354 14.5	0 07.0	S 4 06.2	350 56.4	N 0 38.9	286 18.9	N21 26.7	134 51.9	S12 37.6	Schedar	349 41.2	N56 36.6
D 13	9 16.9	15 06.6	05.0	5 57.1	39.7	301 21.0	26.8	149 54.4	37.6	Shaula	96 22.1	S37 06.6
A 14	24 19.4	30 06.2	03.7	20 57.8	40.5	316 23.1	26.8	164 57.0	37.5	Sirius	258 33.8	S16 44.4
Y 15	39 21.9	45 05.8	.. 02.5	35 58.5	.. 41.3	331 25.2	.. 26.9	179 59.6	.. 37.5	Spica	158 31.1	S11 13.9
16	54 24.3	60 05.4	01.3	50 59.2	42.1	346 27.3	27.0	195 02.1	37.5	Suhail	222 52.2	S43 29.5
17	69 26.8	75 05.0	4 00.0	65 59.9	42.9	1 29.4	27.0	210 04.7	37.4			
18	84 29.3	90 04.6	S 3 58.8	81 00.6	N 0 43.7	16 31.5	N21 27.1	225 07.3	S12 37.4	Vega	80 39.2	N38 47.6
19	99 31.7	105 04.2	57.6	96 01.3	44.4	31 33.6	27.1	240 09.8	37.3	Zuben'ubi	137 05.4	S16 05.8
20	114 34.2	120 03.8	56.3	111 02.0	45.2	46 35.7	27.2	255 12.4	37.3		SHA	Mer. Pass.
21	129 36.7	135 03.4	.. 55.1	126 02.7	.. 46.0	61 37.8	.. 27.2	270 15.0	.. 37.3		° '	h m
22	144 39.1	150 03.0	53.8	141 03.4	46.8	76 40.0	27.3	285 17.5	37.2	Venus	7 35.8	11 59
23	159 41.6	165 02.6	52.6	156 04.0	47.6	91 42.1	27.4	300 20.1	37.2	Mars	357 45.7	12 37
	h m									Jupiter	292 16.9	16 57
Mer. Pass.	12 26.9	v −0.4	d 1.2	v 0.7	d 0.8	v 2.1	d 0.1	v 2.6	d 0.0	Saturn	140 33.9	3 06

UT	SUN GHA	SUN Dec	MOON GHA	v	MOON Dec	d	HP
d h	° '	° '	° '	'	° '	'	'
14 00	177 40.9	S 2 33.2	154 18.7	12.6	N10 01.4	9.8	56.2
01	192 41.1	32.2	168 50.3	12.5	10 11.2	9.7	56.1
02	207 41.3	31.2	183 21.8	12.5	10 20.9	9.6	56.1
03	222 41.5	.. 30.2	197 53.3	12.6	10 30.5	9.6	56.1
04	237 41.6	29.2	212 24.9	12.5	10 40.1	9.5	56.1
05	252 41.8	28.2	226 56.4	12.5	10 49.6	9.5	56.0
06	267 42.0	S 2 27.2	241 27.9	12.5	N10 59.1	9.4	56.0
T 07	282 42.1	26.3	255 59.4	12.6	11 08.5	9.3	56.0
H 08	297 42.3	25.3	270 31.0	12.5	11 17.8	9.3	56.0
U 09	312 42.5	.. 24.3	285 02.5	12.5	11 27.1	9.2	55.9
R 10	327 42.7	23.3	299 34.0	12.5	11 36.3	9.2	55.9
S 11	342 42.8	22.3	314 05.5	12.5	11 45.5	9.1	55.9
D 12	357 43.0	S 2 21.3	328 37.0	12.5	N11 54.5	9.1	55.9
A 13	12 43.2	20.3	343 08.5	12.5	12 03.6	8.9	55.8
Y 14	27 43.4	19.4	357 40.0	12.5	12 12.5	8.9	55.8
15	42 43.5	.. 18.4	12 11.5	12.5	12 21.4	8.8	55.8
16	57 43.7	17.4	26 43.0	12.5	12 30.2	8.8	55.8
17	72 43.9	16.4	41 14.5	12.4	12 39.0	8.6	55.7
18	87 44.1	S 2 15.4	55 45.9	12.5	N12 47.6	8.6	55.7
19	102 44.2	14.4	70 17.4	12.5	12 56.2	8.6	55.7
20	117 44.4	13.4	84 48.9	12.4	13 04.8	8.5	55.7
21	132 44.6	.. 12.4	99 20.3	12.5	13 13.3	8.4	55.6
22	147 44.8	11.5	113 51.8	12.4	13 21.7	8.3	55.6
23	162 44.9	10.5	128 23.2	12.5	13 30.0	8.2	55.6
15 00	177 45.1	S 2 09.5	142 54.7	12.4	N13 38.2	8.2	55.6
01	192 45.3	08.5	157 26.1	12.4	13 46.4	8.1	55.5
02	207 45.4	07.5	171 57.5	12.4	13 54.5	8.1	55.5
03	222 45.6	.. 06.5	186 28.9	12.4	14 02.6	7.9	55.5
04	237 45.8	05.5	201 00.3	12.4	14 10.5	7.9	55.5
05	252 46.0	04.5	215 31.7	12.4	14 18.4	7.9	55.4
06	267 46.1	S 2 03.6	230 03.1	12.4	N14 26.3	7.7	55.4
07	282 46.3	02.6	244 34.5	12.4	14 34.0	7.7	55.4
F 08	297 46.5	01.6	259 05.9	12.4	14 41.7	7.6	55.4
R 09	312 46.7	2 00.6	273 37.3	12.3	14 49.3	7.5	55.3
I 10	327 46.8	1 59.6	288 08.6	12.4	14 56.8	7.4	55.3
D 11	342 47.0	58.6	302 40.0	12.3	15 04.2	7.4	55.3
A 12	357 47.2	S 1 57.6	317 11.3	12.4	N15 11.6	7.2	55.3
Y 13	12 47.4	56.6	331 42.7	12.3	15 18.8	7.2	55.3
14	27 47.6	55.7	346 14.0	12.3	15 26.0	7.2	55.2
15	42 47.7	.. 54.7	0 45.3	12.3	15 33.2	7.0	55.2
16	57 47.9	53.7	15 16.6	12.3	15 40.2	7.0	55.2
17	72 48.1	52.7	29 47.9	12.3	15 47.2	6.9	55.2
18	87 48.3	S 1 51.7	44 19.2	12.3	N15 54.1	6.8	55.2
19	102 48.4	50.7	58 50.5	12.3	16 00.9	6.7	55.1
20	117 48.6	49.7	73 21.8	12.3	16 07.6	6.6	55.1
21	132 48.8	.. 48.7	87 53.1	12.2	16 14.2	6.6	55.1
22	147 49.0	47.8	102 24.3	12.3	16 20.8	6.5	55.1
23	162 49.1	46.8	116 55.6	12.2	16 27.3	6.4	55.1
16 00	177 49.3	S 1 45.8	131 26.8	12.2	N16 33.7	6.3	55.0
01	192 49.5	44.8	145 58.0	12.2	16 40.0	6.2	55.0
02	207 49.7	43.8	160 29.3	12.2	16 46.2	6.1	55.0
03	222 49.8	.. 42.8	175 00.5	12.2	16 52.3	6.1	55.0
04	237 50.0	41.8	189 31.7	12.2	16 58.4	6.0	55.0
05	252 50.2	40.8	204 02.9	12.2	17 04.4	5.9	54.9
06	267 50.4	S 1 39.9	218 34.1	12.1	N17 10.3	5.8	54.9
S 07	282 50.6	38.9	233 05.2	12.2	17 16.1	5.7	54.9
A 08	297 50.7	37.9	247 36.4	12.2	17 21.8	5.6	54.9
T 09	312 50.9	.. 36.9	262 07.6	12.1	17 27.4	5.6	54.9
U 10	327 51.1	35.9	276 38.7	12.1	17 33.0	5.4	54.8
R 11	342 51.3	34.9	291 09.8	12.2	17 38.4	5.4	54.8
D 12	357 51.4	S 1 33.9	305 41.0	12.1	N17 43.8	5.3	54.8
A 13	12 51.6	32.9	320 12.1	12.1	17 49.1	5.2	54.8
Y 14	27 51.8	31.9	334 43.2	12.1	17 54.3	5.1	54.8
15	42 52.0	.. 31.0	349 14.3	12.1	17 59.4	5.1	54.8
16	57 52.2	30.0	3 45.4	12.1	18 04.5	4.9	54.7
17	72 52.3	29.0	18 16.5	12.1	18 09.4	4.9	54.7
18	87 52.5	S 1 28.0	32 47.6	12.1	N18 14.3	4.7	54.7
19	102 52.7	27.0	47 18.7	12.0	18 19.0	4.7	54.7
20	117 52.9	26.0	61 49.7	12.1	18 23.7	4.6	54.7
21	132 53.1	.. 25.0	76 20.8	12.0	18 28.3	4.5	54.7
22	147 53.2	24.0	90 51.8	12.1	18 32.8	4.4	54.7
23	162 53.4	23.1	105 22.9	12.0	N18 37.2	4.3	54.6
	SD 16.1	d 1.0	SD 15.2		15.1		14.9

Lat.	Naut.	Civil	Sunrise	Moonrise 14	15	16	17
°	h m	h m	h m	h m	h m	h m	h m
N 72	03 53	05 16	06 23	05 30	05 13	04 45	▭
N 70	04 07	05 21	06 22	05 47	05 42	05 36	05 28
68	04 18	05 25	06 20	06 01	06 03	06 08	06 18
66	04 27	05 28	06 19	06 12	06 20	06 32	06 50
64	04 35	05 31	06 18	06 22	06 34	06 50	07 14
62	04 41	05 33	06 17	06 30	06 46	07 06	07 33
60	04 46	05 35	06 16	06 37	06 56	07 19	07 48
N 58	04 51	05 37	06 16	06 43	07 04	07 30	08 01
56	04 55	05 38	06 15	06 49	07 12	07 40	08 13
54	04 58	05 39	06 15	06 54	07 19	07 48	08 23
52	05 01	05 40	06 14	06 58	07 25	07 56	08 31
50	05 04	05 41	06 14	07 03	07 31	08 03	08 39
45	05 09	05 43	06 12	07 11	07 43	08 18	08 56
N 40	05 13	05 45	06 11	07 19	07 53	08 30	09 10
35	05 16	05 45	06 11	07 26	08 02	08 41	09 22
30	05 18	05 46	06 10	07 31	08 10	08 50	09 33
20	05 21	05 46	06 08	07 41	08 23	09 06	09 51
N 10	05 22	05 46	06 07	07 50	08 34	09 20	10 06
0	05 21	05 45	06 06	07 58	08 45	09 33	10 21
S 10	05 19	05 43	06 04	08 07	08 57	09 46	10 36
20	05 15	05 40	06 02	08 16	09 08	10 00	10 51
30	05 08	05 36	06 00	08 26	09 22	10 17	11 09
35	05 04	05 34	05 59	08 32	09 30	10 26	11 20
40	04 59	05 31	05 58	08 39	09 39	10 37	11 32
45	04 52	05 27	05 56	08 47	09 50	10 50	11 46
S 50	04 43	05 21	05 54	08 56	10 02	11 05	12 04
52	04 39	05 19	05 53	09 01	10 08	11 13	12 12
54	04 34	05 16	05 52	09 06	10 15	11 21	12 21
56	04 28	05 13	05 51	09 11	10 23	11 30	12 32
58	04 22	05 10	05 49	09 17	10 31	11 40	12 44
S 60	04 14	05 06	05 48	09 24	10 41	11 52	12 58

Lat.	Sunset	Civil	Naut.	Moonset 14	15	16	17
°	h m	h m	h m	h m	h m	h m	h m
N 72	17 57	19 04	20 29	23 38	25 45	01 45	▭
N 70	17 58	18 59	20 14	23 11	24 55	00 55	02 42
68	17 59	18 56	20 03	22 50	24 24	00 24	01 52
66	18 00	18 51	19 53	22 34	24 00	00 00	01 21
64	18 01	18 48	19 45	22 21	23 42	24 58	00 58
62	18 02	18 46	19 39	22 10	23 28	24 39	00 39
60	18 03	18 44	19 33	22 01	23 15	24 24	00 24
N 58	18 03	18 42	19 29	21 53	23 04	24 11	00 11
56	18 04	18 41	19 24	21 45	22 55	24 00	00 00
54	18 04	18 39	19 21	21 39	22 47	23 50	24 48
52	18 05	18 38	19 18	21 33	22 40	23 42	24 38
50	18 05	18 37	19 15	21 28	22 33	23 34	24 30
45	18 06	18 35	19 10	21 17	22 19	23 17	24 12
N 40	18 07	18 34	19 05	21 08	22 07	23 04	23 57
35	18 08	18 33	19 02	21 00	21 57	22 52	23 45
30	18 08	18 32	19 00	20 53	21 48	22 42	23 34
20	18 10	18 32	18 57	20 41	21 34	22 25	23 15
N 10	18 11	18 32	18 56	20 31	21 20	22 10	22 59
0	18 12	18 33	18 57	20 21	21 08	21 56	22 44
S 10	18 13	18 34	18 59	20 11	20 56	21 42	22 29
20	18 15	18 37	19 03	20 01	20 43	21 27	22 13
30	18 17	18 41	19 09	19 49	20 28	21 10	21 54
35	18 18	18 43	19 13	19 42	20 20	21 00	21 43
40	18 19	18 46	19 18	19 35	20 10	20 49	21 31
45	18 21	18 50	19 25	19 26	19 59	20 35	21 16
S 50	18 23	18 55	19 34	19 15	19 45	20 19	20 58
52	18 24	18 58	19 38	19 10	19 38	20 11	20 50
54	18 25	19 00	19 43	19 04	19 31	20 03	20 41
56	18 26	19 03	19 48	18 58	19 24	19 54	20 30
58	18 27	19 06	19 54	18 52	19 15	19 43	20 18
S 60	18 28	19 10	20 01	18 44	19 04	19 30	20 04

Day	SUN Eqn. of Time 00h	12h	Mer. Pass.	MOON Mer. Pass. Upper	Lower	Age	Phase
d	m s	m s	h m	h m	h m	d	%
14	09 17	09 08	12 09	14 10	01 46	03	8
15	09 00	08 52	12 09	14 57	02 33	04	14
16	08 43	08 35	12 09	15 44	03 21	05	21

UT	ARIES GHA	VENUS −3.9 GHA	Dec	MARS +1.2 GHA	Dec	JUPITER −2.2 GHA	Dec	SATURN +0.3 GHA	Dec	STARS Name	SHA	Dec
d h	° ′	° ′	° ′	° ′	° ′	° ′	° ′	° ′	° ′		° ′	° ′
17 00	174 44.0	180 02.2	S 3 51.4	171 04.7	N 0 48.4	106 44.2	N21 27.4	315 22.7	S12 37.1	Acamar	315 18.7	S40 15.4
01	189 46.5	195 01.8	50.1	186 05.4	49.2	121 46.3	27.5	330 25.2	37.1	Achernar	335 27.4	S57 10.4
02	204 49.0	210 01.4	48.9	201 06.1	50.0	136 48.4	27.5	345 27.8	37.1	Acrux	173 08.7	S63 10.4
03	219 51.4	225 01.0 ..	47.6	216 06.8 ..	50.8	151 50.5 ..	27.6	0 30.4 ..	37.0	Adhara	255 12.5	S28 59.8
04	234 53.9	240 00.6	46.4	231 07.5	51.6	166 52.6	27.6	15 32.9	37.0	Aldebaran	290 49.7	N16 32.0
05	249 56.4	255 00.2	45.2	246 08.2	52.3	181 54.7	27.7	30 35.5	36.9			
06	264 58.8	269 59.8	S 3 43.9	261 08.9	N 0 53.1	196 56.8	N21 27.8	45 38.1	S12 36.9	Alioth	166 20.3	N55 53.1
07	280 01.3	284 59.4	42.7	276 09.6	53.9	211 58.9	27.8	60 40.6	36.9	Alkaid	152 58.6	N49 14.6
08	295 03.8	299 59.0	41.4	291 10.3	54.7	227 01.0	27.9	75 43.2	36.8	Al Na'ir	27 44.4	S46 53.7
S 09	310 06.2	314 58.6 ..	40.2	306 11.0 ..	55.5	242 03.1 ..	27.9	90 45.8 ..	36.8	Alnilam	275 46.5	S 1 11.9
U 10	325 08.7	329 58.2	39.0	321 11.7	56.3	257 05.2	28.0	105 48.3	36.7	Alphard	217 56.0	S 8 43.3
N 11	340 11.2	344 57.8	37.7	336 12.4	57.1	272 07.3	28.0	120 50.9	36.7			
D 12	355 13.6	359 57.4	S 3 36.5	351 13.1	N 0 57.9	287 09.5	N21 28.1	135 53.5	S12 36.7	Alphecca	126 11.0	N26 40.0
A 13	10 16.1	14 57.0	35.2	6 13.8	58.7	302 11.6	28.2	150 56.0	36.6	Alpheratz	357 44.0	N29 09.8
Y 14	25 18.5	29 56.6	34.0	21 14.5	0 59.5	317 13.7	28.2	165 58.6	36.6	Altair	62 08.5	N 8 54.2
15	40 21.0	44 56.2 ..	32.7	36 15.2	1 00.2	332 15.8 ..	28.3	181 01.2 ..	36.5	Ankaa	353 16.3	S42 14.1
16	55 23.5	59 55.8	31.5	51 15.9	01.0	347 17.9	28.3	196 03.7	36.5	Antares	112 26.3	S26 27.6
17	70 25.9	74 55.4	30.3	66 16.6	01.8	2 20.0	28.4	211 06.3	36.5			
18	85 28.4	89 55.0	S 3 29.0	81 17.2	N 1 02.6	17 22.1	N21 28.5	226 08.9	S12 36.4	Arcturus	145 55.6	N19 06.6
19	100 30.9	104 54.6	27.8	96 17.9	03.4	32 24.2	28.5	241 11.4	36.4	Atria	107 28.2	S69 02.7
20	115 33.3	119 54.2	26.5	111 18.6	04.2	47 26.3	28.6	256 14.0	36.3	Avior	234 17.7	S59 33.5
21	130 35.8	134 53.8 ..	25.3	126 19.3 ..	05.0	62 28.4 ..	28.6	271 16.6 ..	36.3	Bellatrix	278 32.2	N 6 21.5
22	145 38.3	149 53.4	24.0	141 20.0	05.8	77 30.5	28.7	286 19.1	36.2	Betelgeuse	271 01.5	N 7 24.3
23	160 40.7	164 53.0	22.8	156 20.7	06.6	92 32.6	28.7	301 21.7	36.2			
18 00	175 43.2	179 52.7	S 3 21.6	171 21.4	N 1 07.3	107 34.7	N21 28.8	316 24.3	S12 36.2	Canopus	263 56.1	S52 42.6
01	190 45.7	194 52.3	20.3	186 22.1	08.1	122 36.8	28.9	331 26.9	36.1	Capella	280 34.7	N46 00.7
02	205 48.1	209 51.9	19.1	201 22.8	08.9	137 38.9	28.9	346 29.4	36.1	Deneb	49 31.9	N45 19.6
03	220 50.6	224 51.5 ..	17.8	216 23.5 ..	09.7	152 41.0 ..	29.0	1 32.0 ..	36.0	Denebola	182 33.5	N14 29.7
04	235 53.0	239 51.1	16.6	231 24.2	10.5	167 43.1	29.0	16 34.6	36.0	Diphda	348 56.4	S17 54.9
05	250 55.5	254 50.7	15.3	246 24.9	11.3	182 45.2	29.1	31 37.1	36.0			
06	265 58.0	269 50.3	S 3 14.1	261 25.6	N 1 12.1	197 47.3	N21 29.1	46 39.7	S12 35.9	Dubhe	193 51.3	N61 40.7
07	281 00.4	284 49.9	12.8	276 26.3	12.9	212 49.4	29.2	61 42.3	35.9	Elnath	278 12.9	N28 37.0
08	296 02.9	299 49.5	11.6	291 27.0	13.7	227 51.5	29.3	76 44.8	35.8	Eltanin	90 46.2	N51 29.0
M 09	311 05.4	314 49.1 ..	10.4	306 27.7 ..	14.4	242 53.6 ..	29.3	91 47.4 ..	35.8	Enif	33 47.5	N 9 56.1
O 10	326 07.8	329 48.7	09.1	321 28.4	15.2	257 55.7	29.4	106 50.0	35.7	Fomalhaut	15 24.5	S29 33.1
N 11	341 10.3	344 48.3	07.9	336 29.1	16.0	272 57.8	29.4	121 52.6	35.7			
D 12	356 12.8	359 47.9	S 3 06.6	351 29.8	N 1 16.8	287 59.9	N21 29.5	136 55.1	S12 35.7	Gacrux	172 00.5	S57 11.3
A 13	11 15.2	14 47.5	05.4	6 30.5	17.6	303 02.0	29.6	151 57.7	35.6	Gienah	175 52.1	S17 37.1
Y 14	26 17.7	29 47.1	04.1	21 31.2	18.4	318 04.1	29.6	167 00.3	35.6	Hadar	148 47.5	S60 26.1
15	41 20.1	44 46.8 ..	02.9	36 31.9 ..	19.2	333 06.2 ..	29.7	182 02.8 ..	35.5	Hamal	328 01.2	N23 31.4
16	56 22.6	59 46.4	01.6	51 32.6	20.0	348 08.3	29.7	197 05.4	35.5	Kaus Aust.	83 44.1	S34 22.5
17	71 25.1	74 46.0	3 00.4	66 33.2	20.7	3 10.4	29.8	212 08.0	35.5			
18	86 27.5	89 45.6	S 2 59.1	81 33.9	N 1 21.5	18 12.5	N21 29.8	227 10.6	S12 35.4	Kochab	137 19.2	N74 05.8
19	101 30.0	104 45.2	57.9	96 34.6	22.3	33 14.6	29.9	242 13.1	35.4	Markab	13 38.8	N15 16.6
20	116 32.5	119 44.8	56.6	111 35.3	23.1	48 16.7	30.0	257 15.7	35.3	Menkar	314 15.4	N 4 08.3
21	131 34.9	134 44.4 ..	55.4	126 36.0 ..	23.9	63 18.8 ..	30.0	272 18.3 ..	35.3	Menkent	148 07.4	S36 26.1
22	146 37.4	149 44.0	54.2	141 36.7	24.7	78 20.9	30.1	287 20.8	35.2	Miaplacidus	221 39.0	S69 46.7
23	161 39.9	164 43.6	52.9	156 37.4	25.5	93 23.0	30.1	302 23.4	35.2			
19 00	176 42.3	179 43.2	S 2 51.7	171 38.1	N 1 26.3	108 25.1	N21 30.2	317 26.0	S12 35.2	Mirfak	308 40.8	N49 54.5
01	191 44.8	194 42.8	50.4	186 38.8	27.0	123 27.2	30.3	332 28.6	35.1	Nunki	75 58.6	S26 16.6
02	206 47.3	209 42.4	49.2	201 39.5	27.8	138 29.3	30.3	347 31.1	35.1	Peacock	53 19.9	S56 41.2
03	221 49.7	224 42.1 ..	47.9	216 40.2 ..	28.6	153 31.4 ..	30.4	2 33.7 ..	35.0	Pollux	243 27.8	N27 59.5
04	236 52.2	239 41.7	46.7	231 40.9	29.4	168 33.4	30.4	17 36.3	35.0	Procyon	244 59.8	N 5 11.2
05	251 54.6	254 41.3	45.4	246 41.6	30.2	183 35.5	30.5	32 38.9	34.9			
06	266 57.1	269 40.9	S 2 44.2	261 42.3	N 1 31.0	198 37.6	N21 30.5	47 41.4	S12 34.9	Rasalhague	96 06.6	N12 33.0
07	281 59.6	284 40.5	42.9	276 43.0	31.8	213 39.7	30.6	62 44.0	34.9	Regulus	207 43.4	N11 53.9
T 08	297 02.0	299 40.1	41.7	291 43.7	32.6	228 41.8	30.7	77 46.6	34.8	Rigel	281 12.3	S 8 11.5
U 09	312 04.5	314 39.7 ..	40.4	306 44.4 ..	33.3	243 43.9 ..	30.7	92 49.2 ..	34.8	Rigil Kent.	139 51.4	S60 53.2
E 10	327 07.0	329 39.3	39.2	321 45.1	34.1	258 46.0	30.8	107 51.7	34.7	Sabik	102 12.7	S15 44.4
S 11	342 09.4	344 38.9	37.9	336 45.8	34.9	273 48.1	30.8	122 54.3	34.7			
D 12	357 11.9	359 38.6	S 2 36.7	351 46.5	N 1 35.7	288 50.2	N21 30.9	137 56.9	S12 34.7	Schedar	349 41.2	N56 36.6
A 13	12 14.4	14 38.2	35.4	6 47.2	36.5	303 52.3	31.0	152 59.5	34.6	Shaula	96 22.1	S37 06.6
Y 14	27 16.8	29 37.8	34.2	21 47.9	37.3	318 54.4	31.0	168 02.0	34.6	Sirius	258 33.8	S16 44.4
15	42 19.3	44 37.4 ..	32.9	36 48.6 ..	38.1	333 56.5 ..	31.1	183 04.6 ..	34.5	Spica	158 31.1	S11 14.0
16	57 21.8	59 37.0	31.7	51 49.3	38.8	348 58.6	31.1	198 07.2	34.5	Suhail	222 52.2	S43 29.5
17	72 24.2	74 36.6	30.4	66 50.0	39.6	4 00.7	31.2	213 09.8	34.4			
18	87 26.7	89 36.2	S 2 29.2	81 50.7	N 1 40.4	19 02.8	N21 31.3	228 12.3	S12 34.4	Vega	80 39.1	N38 47.6
19	102 29.1	104 35.8	27.9	96 51.4	41.2	34 04.8	31.3	243 14.9	34.4	Zuben'ubi	137 05.4	S16 05.8
20	117 31.6	119 35.4	26.7	111 52.1	42.0	49 06.9	31.4	258 17.5	34.3		SHA	Mer.Pass.
21	132 34.1	134 35.1 ..	25.4	126 52.8 ..	42.8	64 09.0 ..	31.4	273 20.1 ..	34.3		° ′	h m
22	147 36.5	149 34.7	24.2	141 53.5	43.6	79 11.1	31.5	288 22.6	34.2	Venus	4 09.5	12 01
23	162 39.0	164 34.3	22.9	156 54.1	44.4	94 13.2	31.5	303 25.2	34.2	Mars	355 38.2	12 34
	h m									Jupiter	291 51.5	16 47
Mer.Pass. 12 15.1		v −0.4	d 1.2	v 0.7	d 0.8	v 2.1	d 0.1	v 2.6	d 0.0	Saturn	140 41.1	2 54

UT	SUN GHA	SUN Dec	MOON GHA	v	Dec	d	HP
d h	° ′	° ′	° ′	′	° ′	′	′
17 00	177 53.6	S 1 22.1	119 53.9	12.0	N18 41.5	4.2	54.6
01	192 53.8	21.1	134 24.9	12.0	18 45.7	4.2	54.6
02	207 53.9	20.1	148 55.9	12.1	18 49.9	4.0	54.6
03	222 54.1	19.1	163 27.0	12.1	18 53.9	4.0	54.6
04	237 54.3	18.1	177 58.0	12.0	18 57.9	3.8	54.6
05	252 54.5	17.1	192 29.0	12.0	19 01.7	3.8	54.6
06	267 54.7	S 1 16.1	207 00.0	11.9	N19 05.5	3.7	54.5
07	282 54.8	15.1	221 30.9	12.0	19 09.2	3.6	54.5
08	297 55.0	14.2	236 01.9	12.0	19 12.8	3.5	54.5
S 09	312 55.2	13.2	250 32.9	12.0	19 16.3	3.4	54.5
U 10	327 55.4	12.2	265 03.9	11.9	19 19.7	3.3	54.5
N 11	342 55.6	11.2	279 34.8	12.0	19 23.0	3.2	54.5
D 12	357 55.7	S 1 10.2	294 05.8	11.9	N19 26.2	3.1	54.5
A 13	12 55.9	09.2	308 36.7	12.0	19 29.3	3.1	54.5
Y 14	27 56.1	08.2	323 07.7	11.9	19 32.4	2.9	54.4
15	42 56.3	07.2	337 38.6	11.9	19 35.3	2.9	54.4
16	57 56.5	06.2	352 09.5	12.0	19 38.2	2.7	54.4
17	72 56.6	05.3	6 40.5	11.9	19 40.9	2.7	54.4
18	87 56.8	S 1 04.3	21 11.4	11.9	N19 43.6	2.6	54.4
19	102 57.0	03.3	35 42.3	11.9	19 46.2	2.4	54.4
20	117 57.2	02.3	50 13.2	12.0	19 48.6	2.4	54.4
21	132 57.4	01.3	64 44.2	11.9	19 51.0	2.3	54.4
22	147 57.6	1 00.3	79 15.1	11.9	19 53.3	2.2	54.4
23	162 57.7	0 59.3	93 46.0	11.9	19 55.5	2.1	54.4
18 00	177 57.9	S 0 58.3	108 16.9	11.9	N19 57.6	2.0	54.4
01	192 58.1	57.4	122 47.8	11.9	19 59.6	2.0	54.3
02	207 58.3	56.4	137 18.7	11.9	20 01.6	1.8	54.3
03	222 58.5	55.4	151 49.6	11.9	20 03.4	1.7	54.3
04	237 58.6	54.4	166 20.5	11.9	20 05.1	1.6	54.3
05	252 58.8	53.4	180 51.4	11.9	20 06.7	1.6	54.3
06	267 59.0	S 0 52.4	195 22.3	11.9	N20 08.3	1.4	54.3
07	282 59.2	51.4	209 53.2	11.9	20 09.7	1.4	54.3
08	297 59.4	50.4	224 24.1	11.9	20 11.1	1.2	54.3
M 09	312 59.5	49.4	238 54.9	11.9	20 12.3	1.2	54.3
N 10	327 59.7	48.5	253 25.8	11.9	20 13.5	1.1	54.3
N 11	342 59.9	47.5	267 56.7	11.9	20 14.6	1.0	54.3
D 12	358 00.1	S 0 46.5	282 27.6	11.9	N20 15.6	0.8	54.3
A 13	13 00.3	45.5	296 58.5	11.9	20 16.4	0.8	54.3
Y 14	28 00.5	44.5	311 29.4	11.9	20 17.2	0.7	54.3
15	43 00.6	43.5	326 00.3	11.9	20 17.9	0.6	54.3
16	58 00.8	42.5	340 31.2	11.9	20 18.5	0.5	54.3
17	73 01.0	41.5	355 02.1	11.9	20 19.0	0.4	54.3
18	88 01.2	S 0 40.5	9 33.0	11.9	N20 19.4	0.3	54.3
19	103 01.4	39.6	24 03.9	11.9	20 19.7	0.3	54.3
20	118 01.6	38.6	38 34.8	11.9	20 20.0	0.1	54.2
21	133 01.7	37.6	53 05.7	11.9	20 20.1	0.0	54.2
22	148 01.9	36.6	67 36.6	11.9	20 20.1	0.1	54.2
23	163 02.1	35.6	82 07.5	11.9	20 20.0	0.1	54.2
19 00	178 02.3	S 0 34.6	96 38.4	11.9	N20 19.9	0.3	54.2
01	193 02.5	33.6	111 09.3	11.9	20 19.6	0.3	54.2
02	208 02.7	32.6	125 40.2	12.0	20 19.3	0.5	54.2
03	223 02.8	31.7	140 11.2	11.9	20 18.8	0.5	54.2
04	238 03.0	30.7	154 42.1	11.9	20 18.3	0.6	54.2
05	253 03.2	29.7	169 13.0	11.9	20 17.7	0.7	54.2
06	268 03.4	S 0 28.7	183 43.9	12.0	N20 17.0	0.9	54.2
07	283 03.6	27.7	198 14.9	11.9	20 16.1	0.9	54.2
T 08	298 03.8	26.7	212 45.8	11.9	20 15.2	1.0	54.2
U 09	313 03.9	25.7	227 16.8	11.9	20 14.2	1.1	54.2
E 10	328 04.1	24.7	241 47.7	12.0	20 13.1	1.2	54.2
S 11	343 04.3	23.7	256 18.7	11.9	20 11.9	1.3	54.2
D 12	358 04.5	S 0 22.8	270 49.6	12.0	N20 10.6	1.3	54.3
A 13	13 04.7	21.8	285 20.6	12.0	20 09.3	1.5	54.3
Y 14	28 04.9	20.8	299 51.6	12.0	20 07.8	1.6	54.3
15	43 05.0	19.8	314 22.6	12.0	20 06.2	1.6	54.3
16	58 05.2	18.8	328 53.6	12.0	20 04.6	1.8	54.3
17	73 05.4	17.8	343 24.6	12.0	20 02.8	1.8	54.3
18	88 05.6	S 0 16.8	357 55.6	12.0	N20 01.0	2.0	54.3
19	103 05.8	15.8	12 26.6	12.0	19 59.0	2.0	54.3
20	118 06.0	14.9	26 57.6	12.0	19 57.0	2.1	54.3
21	133 06.1	13.9	41 28.6	12.1	19 54.9	2.3	54.3
22	148 06.3	12.9	55 59.7	12.0	19 52.6	2.3	54.3
23	163 06.5	11.9	70 30.7	12.1	N19 50.3	2.4	54.3
	SD 16.1 d 1.0		SD 14.8		14.8		14.8

Twilight — Moonrise

Lat.	Naut.	Civil	Sunrise	17	18	19	20
°	h m	h m	h m	h m	h m	h m	h m
N 72	03 34	05 01	06 08	▢	▢	▢	▢
N 70	03 51	05 07	06 08	05 28	▢	▢	07 35
68	04 04	05 12	06 08	06 18	06 41	07 26	08 36
66	04 14	05 17	06 08	06 50	07 20	08 07	09 11
64	04 23	05 20	06 08	07 14	07 48	08 35	09 36
62	04 30	05 23	06 08	07 33	08 09	08 56	09 55
60	04 37	05 26	06 07	07 48	08 26	09 14	10 11
N 58	04 42	05 28	06 07	08 01	08 40	09 28	10 25
56	04 46	05 30	06 07	08 13	08 53	09 41	10 36
54	04 50	05 32	06 07	08 23	09 03	09 51	10 46
52	04 54	05 34	06 07	08 31	09 13	10 01	10 55
50	04 57	05 35	06 07	08 39	09 22	10 10	11 03
45	05 03	05 38	06 07	08 56	09 40	10 28	11 21
N 40	05 08	05 40	06 07	09 10	09 55	10 43	11 35
35	05 12	05 41	06 06	09 22	10 07	10 55	11 47
30	05 15	05 42	06 06	09 33	10 18	11 06	11 57
20	05 18	05 44	06 06	09 51	10 37	11 25	12 15
N 10	05 20	05 44	06 05	10 06	10 53	11 42	12 30
0	05 20	05 44	06 05	10 21	11 09	11 57	12 45
S 10	05 19	05 43	06 04	10 36	11 24	12 12	12 59
20	05 16	05 41	06 03	10 51	11 41	12 29	13 15
30	05 10	05 38	06 02	11 09	12 00	12 48	13 33
35	05 07	05 36	06 02	11 20	12 11	12 59	13 43
40	05 02	05 34	06 01	11 32	12 24	13 11	13 55
45	04 56	05 31	06 00	11 46	12 39	13 26	14 09
S 50	04 48	05 26	05 59	12 04	12 57	13 44	14 26
52	04 44	05 24	05 58	12 12	13 06	13 53	14 34
54	04 40	05 22	05 58	12 22	13 16	14 03	14 43
56	04 35	05 20	05 57	12 32	13 27	14 13	14 52
58	04 29	05 17	05 56	12 44	13 39	14 26	15 04
S 60	04 23	05 14	05 55	12 58	13 54	14 40	15 17

Sunset — Twilight — Moonset

Lat.	Sunset	Civil	Naut.	17	18	19	20
°	h m	h m	h m	h m	h m	h m	h m
N 72	18 10	19 18	20 47	▢	▢	▢	▢
N 70	18 10	19 12	20 29	02 42	▢	▢	05 35
68	18 10	19 06	20 15	01 52	03 09	04 04	04 34
66	18 10	19 01	20 04	01 21	02 30	03 23	03 59
64	18 10	18 58	19 55	00 58	02 03	02 55	03 34
62	18 10	18 54	19 48	00 39	01 42	02 34	03 14
60	18 10	18 52	19 41	00 24	01 25	02 16	02 58
N 58	18 10	18 49	19 36	00 11	01 11	02 02	02 44
56	18 10	18 47	19 31	00 00	00 59	01 49	02 32
54	18 10	18 45	19 27	24 48	00 48	01 38	02 22
52	18 10	18 44	19 23	24 38	00 38	01 29	02 13
50	18 10	18 42	19 20	24 30	00 30	01 20	02 04
45	18 10	18 39	19 14	24 12	00 12	01 02	01 47
N 40	18 10	18 37	19 09	23 57	24 47	00 47	01 32
35	18 10	18 35	19 05	23 45	24 34	00 34	01 20
30	18 10	18 34	19 02	23 34	24 23	00 23	01 10
20	18 10	18 32	18 58	23 15	24 04	00 04	00 53
N 10	18 11	18 32	18 56	22 59	23 48	24 35	00 35
0	18 11	18 32	18 56	22 44	23 32	24 20	00 20
S 10	18 12	18 33	18 57	22 29	23 17	24 05	00 05
20	18 12	18 34	19 00	22 13	23 00	23 49	24 39
30	18 13	18 37	19 05	21 54	22 41	23 30	24 22
35	18 14	18 39	19 09	21 43	22 30	23 20	24 12
40	18 15	18 42	19 13	21 31	22 17	23 07	24 01
45	18 15	18 45	19 19	21 16	22 02	22 52	23 47
S 50	18 16	18 49	19 27	20 58	21 44	22 34	23 31
52	18 17	18 51	19 30	20 50	21 35	22 26	23 23
54	18 17	18 53	19 35	20 41	21 25	22 16	23 14
56	18 18	18 55	19 39	20 30	21 14	22 06	23 05
58	18 19	18 58	19 45	20 18	21 01	21 53	22 54
S 60	18 19	19 01	19 51	20 04	20 46	21 39	22 41

SUN — MOON

Day	Eqn. of Time 00ʰ	Eqn. of Time 12ʰ	Mer. Pass.	Mer. Pass. Upper	Mer. Pass. Lower	Age	Phase
d	m s	m s	h m	h m	h m	d	%
17	08 26	08 17	12 08	16 32	04 08	06	30
18	08 09	08 00	12 08	17 21	04 56	07	39
19	07 51	07 42	12 08	18 09	05 45	08	48

UT	ARIES GHA	VENUS −4.0 GHA	Dec	MARS +1.2 GHA	Dec	JUPITER −2.2 GHA	Dec	SATURN +0.3 GHA	Dec
20 00	177 41.5	179 33.9	S 2 21.7	171 54.8	N 1 45.1	109 15.3	N21 31.6	318 27.8	S12 34.1
01	192 43.9	194 33.5	20.4	186 55.5	45.9	124 17.4	31.7	333 30.4	34.1
02	207 46.4	209 33.1	19.2	201 56.2	46.7	139 19.5	31.7	348 32.9	34.0
03	222 48.9	224 32.7	.. 17.9	216 56.9	.. 47.5	154 21.6	.. 31.8	3 35.5	.. 34.0
04	237 51.3	239 32.3	16.7	231 57.6	48.3	169 23.7	31.8	18 38.1	34.0
05	252 53.8	254 32.0	15.4	246 58.3	49.1	184 25.7	31.9	33 40.7	33.9
06	267 56.2	269 31.6	S 2 14.2	261 59.0	N 1 49.9	199 27.8	N21 32.0	48 43.2	S12 33.9
W 07	282 58.7	284 31.2	12.9	276 59.7	50.6	214 29.9	32.0	63 45.8	33.8
E 08	298 01.2	299 30.8	11.7	292 00.4	51.4	229 32.0	32.1	78 48.4	33.8
D 09	313 03.6	314 30.4	.. 10.4	307 01.1	.. 52.2	244 34.1	.. 32.1	93 51.0	.. 33.7
N 10	328 06.1	329 30.0	09.2	322 01.8	53.0	259 36.2	32.2	108 53.6	33.7
E 11	343 08.6	344 29.6	07.9	337 02.5	53.8	274 38.3	32.3	123 56.1	33.7
S 12	358 11.0	359 29.2	S 2 06.7	352 03.2	N 1 54.6	289 40.4	N21 32.3	138 58.7	S12 33.6
D 13	13 13.5	14 28.9	05.4	7 03.9	55.4	304 42.4	32.4	154 01.3	33.6
A 14	28 16.0	29 28.5	04.2	22 04.6	56.1	319 44.5	32.4	169 03.9	33.5
Y 15	43 18.4	44 28.1	.. 02.9	37 05.3	.. 56.9	334 46.6	.. 32.5	184 06.4	.. 33.5
16	58 20.9	59 27.7	01.7	52 06.0	57.7	349 48.7	32.6	199 09.0	33.4
17	73 23.4	74 27.3	2 00.4	67 06.7	58.5	4 50.8	32.6	214 11.6	33.4
18	88 25.8	89 26.9	S 1 59.2	82 07.4	N 1 59.3	19 52.9	N21 32.7	229 14.2	S12 33.4
19	103 28.3	104 26.5	57.9	97 08.1	2 00.1	34 55.0	32.7	244 16.8	33.3
20	118 30.7	119 26.2	56.6	112 08.8	00.8	49 57.0	32.8	259 19.3	33.3
21	133 33.2	134 25.8	.. 55.4	127 09.5	.. 01.6	64 59.1	.. 32.8	274 21.9	.. 33.2
22	148 35.7	149 25.4	54.1	142 10.2	02.4	80 01.2	32.9	289 24.5	33.2
23	163 38.1	164 25.0	52.9	157 10.9	03.2	95 03.3	33.0	304 27.1	33.1
21 00	178 40.6	179 24.6	S 1 51.6	172 11.6	N 2 04.0	110 05.4	N21 33.0	319 29.7	S12 33.1
01	193 43.1	194 24.2	50.4	187 12.3	04.8	125 07.5	33.1	334 32.2	33.0
02	208 45.5	209 23.9	49.1	202 13.0	05.6	140 09.5	33.1	349 34.8	33.0
03	223 48.0	224 23.5	.. 47.9	217 13.7	.. 06.3	155 11.6	.. 33.2	4 37.4	.. 33.0
04	238 50.5	239 23.1	46.6	232 14.4	07.1	170 13.7	33.3	19 40.0	32.9
05	253 52.9	254 22.7	45.4	247 15.1	07.9	185 15.8	33.3	34 42.6	32.9
06	268 55.4	269 22.3	S 1 44.1	262 15.8	N 2 08.7	200 17.9	N21 33.4	49 45.1	S12 32.8
T 07	283 57.9	284 21.9	42.9	277 16.5	09.5	215 20.0	33.4	64 47.7	32.8
H 08	299 00.3	299 21.6	41.6	292 17.2	10.3	230 22.0	33.5	79 50.3	32.7
U 09	314 02.8	314 21.2	.. 40.3	307 17.9	.. 11.0	245 24.1	.. 33.6	94 52.9	.. 32.7
R 10	329 05.2	329 20.8	39.1	322 18.6	11.8	260 26.2	33.6	109 55.5	32.6
S 11	344 07.7	344 20.4	37.8	337 19.3	12.6	275 28.3	33.7	124 58.0	32.6
D 12	359 10.2	359 20.0	S 1 36.6	352 20.0	N 2 13.4	290 30.4	N21 33.7	140 00.6	S12 32.6
A 13	14 12.6	14 19.6	35.3	7 20.7	14.2	305 32.5	33.8	155 03.2	32.5
Y 14	29 15.1	29 19.3	34.1	22 21.4	15.0	320 34.5	33.9	170 05.8	32.5
15	44 17.6	44 18.9	.. 32.8	37 22.1	.. 15.7	335 36.6	.. 33.9	185 08.4	.. 32.4
16	59 20.0	59 18.5	31.6	52 22.8	16.5	350 38.7	34.0	200 10.9	32.4
17	74 22.5	74 18.1	30.3	67 23.5	17.3	5 40.8	34.0	215 13.5	32.3
18	89 25.0	89 17.7	S 1 29.1	82 24.2	N 2 18.1	20 42.9	N21 34.1	230 16.1	S12 32.3
19	104 27.4	104 17.3	27.8	97 24.9	18.9	35 44.9	34.2	245 18.7	32.2
20	119 29.9	119 17.0	26.5	112 25.6	19.7	50 47.0	34.2	260 21.3	32.2
21	134 32.3	134 16.6	.. 25.3	127 26.3	.. 20.4	65 49.1	.. 34.3	275 23.9	.. 32.2
22	149 34.8	149 16.2	24.0	142 27.0	21.2	80 51.2	34.3	290 26.4	32.1
23	164 37.3	164 15.8	22.8	157 27.7	22.0	95 53.2	34.4	305 29.0	32.1
22 00	179 39.7	179 15.4	S 1 21.5	172 28.4	N 2 22.8	110 55.3	N21 34.5	320 31.6	S12 32.0
01	194 42.2	194 15.0	20.3	187 29.0	23.6	125 57.4	34.5	335 34.2	32.0
02	209 44.7	209 14.7	19.0	202 29.7	24.4	140 59.5	34.6	350 36.8	31.9
03	224 47.1	224 14.3	.. 17.8	217 30.4	.. 25.1	156 01.6	.. 34.6	5 39.3	.. 31.9
04	239 49.6	239 13.9	16.5	232 31.1	25.9	171 03.6	34.7	20 41.9	31.8
05	254 52.1	254 13.5	15.2	247 31.8	26.7	186 05.7	34.8	35 44.5	31.8
06	269 54.5	269 13.1	S 1 14.0	262 32.5	N 2 27.5	201 07.8	N21 34.8	50 47.1	S12 31.8
07	284 57.0	284 12.8	12.7	277 33.2	28.3	216 09.9	34.9	65 49.7	31.7
08	299 59.5	299 12.4	11.5	292 33.9	29.1	231 11.9	34.9	80 52.3	31.7
F 09	315 01.9	314 12.0	.. 10.2	307 34.6	.. 29.8	246 14.0	.. 35.0	95 54.8	.. 31.6
R 10	330 04.4	329 11.6	09.0	322 35.3	30.6	261 16.1	35.0	110 57.4	31.6
I 11	345 06.8	344 11.2	07.7	337 36.0	31.4	276 18.2	35.1	126 00.0	31.5
D 12	0 09.3	359 10.8	S 1 06.5	352 36.7	N 2 32.2	291 20.2	N21 35.2	141 02.6	S12 31.5
A 13	15 11.8	14 10.5	05.2	7 37.4	33.0	306 22.3	35.2	156 05.2	31.4
Y 14	30 14.2	29 10.1	03.9	22 38.1	33.7	321 24.4	35.3	171 07.8	31.4
15	45 16.7	44 09.7	.. 02.7	37 38.8	.. 34.5	336 26.5	.. 35.4	186 10.4	.. 31.3
16	60 19.2	59 09.3	01.4	52 39.5	35.3	351 28.5	35.4	201 13.0	31.3
17	75 21.6	74 08.9	1 00.2	67 40.2	36.1	6 30.6	35.5	216 15.5	31.3
18	90 24.1	89 08.6	S 0 58.9	82 40.9	N 2 36.9	21 32.7	N21 35.5	231 18.1	S12 31.2
19	105 26.6	104 08.2	57.7	97 41.6	37.7	36 34.8	35.6	246 20.7	31.2
20	120 29.0	119 07.8	56.4	112 42.3	38.4	51 36.8	35.6	261 23.3	31.1
21	135 31.5	134 07.4	.. 55.1	127 43.0	.. 39.2	66 38.9	.. 35.7	276 25.9	.. 31.1
22	150 34.0	149 07.0	53.9	142 43.7	40.0	81 41.0	35.8	291 28.5	31.0
23	165 36.4	164 06.7	52.6	157 44.4	40.8	96 43.1	35.8	306 31.0	31.0
	h m								
Mer. Pass. 12 03.3	v −0.4 d 1.3	v 0.7 d 0.8		v 2.1 d 0.1		v 2.6 d 0.0			

STARS

Name	SHA	Dec
Acamar	315 18.8	S40 15.4
Achernar	335 27.4	S57 10.3
Acrux	173 08.7	S63 10.4
Adhara	255 12.6	S28 59.8
Aldebaran	290 49.7	N16 32.0
Alioth	166 20.3	N55 53.1
Alkaid	152 58.6	N49 14.6
Al Na'ir	27 44.3	S46 53.7
Alnilam	275 46.6	S 1 11.9
Alphard	217 56.0	S 8 43.3
Alphecca	126 10.9	N26 40.0
Alpheratz	357 44.0	N29 09.8
Altair	62 08.5	N 8 54.2
Ankaa	353 16.3	S42 14.1
Antares	112 26.3	S26 27.6
Arcturus	145 55.6	N19 06.6
Atria	107 28.1	S69 02.7
Avior	234 17.7	S59 33.6
Bellatrix	278 32.2	N 6 21.5
Betelgeuse	271 01.5	N 7 24.3
Canopus	263 56.2	S52 42.6
Capella	280 34.8	N46 00.7
Deneb	49 31.8	N45 19.5
Denebola	182 33.5	N14 29.7
Diphda	348 56.4	S17 54.9
Dubhe	193 51.3	N61 40.7
Elnath	278 12.9	N28 37.0
Eltanin	90 46.2	N51 29.0
Enif	33 47.5	N 9 56.1
Fomalhaut	15 24.5	S29 33.1
Gacrux	172 00.5	S57 11.3
Gienah	175 52.1	S17 37.1
Hadar	148 47.5	S60 26.1
Hamal	328 01.2	N23 31.4
Kaus Aust.	83 44.0	S34 22.5
Kochab	137 19.2	N74 05.8
Markab	13 38.8	N15 16.6
Menkar	314 15.4	N 4 08.3
Menkent	148 07.4	S36 26.1
Miaplacidus	221 39.0	S69 46.7
Mirfak	308 40.9	N49 54.5
Nunki	75 58.6	S26 16.6
Peacock	53 19.8	S56 41.2
Pollux	243 27.8	N27 59.5
Procyon	244 59.8	N 5 11.2
Rasalhague	96 06.6	N12 33.0
Regulus	207 43.4	N11 53.9
Rigel	281 12.3	S 8 11.5
Rigil Kent.	139 51.4	S60 53.2
Sabik	102 12.6	S15 44.4
Schedar	349 41.2	N56 36.6
Shaula	96 22.1	S37 06.6
Sirius	258 33.8	S16 44.4
Spica	158 31.1	S11 14.0
Suhail	222 52.2	S43 29.6
Vega	80 39.1	N38 47.6
Zuben'ubi	137 05.3	S16 05.8

	SHA	Mer. Pass.
	o ′	h m
Venus	0 44.0	12 03
Mars	353 31.0	12 31
Jupiter	291 24.8	16 37
Saturn	140 49.0	2 42

UT	SUN GHA	SUN Dec	MOON GHA	v	MOON Dec	d	HP
d h	° '	° '	° '	'	° '	'	'
20 00	178 06.7	S 0 10.9	85 01.8	12.0	N19 47.9	2.5	54.3
01	193 06.9	09.9	99 32.8	12.1	19 45.4	2.6	54.3
02	208 07.1	08.9	114 03.9	12.1	19 42.8	2.6	54.3
03	223 07.3	.. 07.9	128 35.0	12.1	19 40.2	2.8	54.3
04	238 07.4	06.9	143 06.1	12.1	19 37.4	2.9	54.3
05	253 07.6	06.0	157 37.2	12.1	19 34.5	2.9	54.3
06	268 07.8	S 0 05.0	172 08.3	12.1	N19 31.6	3.1	54.3
W 07	283 08.0	04.0	186 39.4	12.1	19 28.5	3.1	54.4
E 08	298 08.2	03.0	201 10.5	12.2	19 25.4	3.2	54.4
D 09	313 08.4	.. 02.0	215 41.7	12.1	19 22.2	3.3	54.4
N 10	328 08.5	S 01.0	230 12.8	12.1	19 18.9	3.4	54.4
E 11	343 08.7	00.0	244 43.9	12.0	19 15.5	3.5	54.4
S 12	358 08.9	N 0 01.0	259 15.1	12.2	N19 12.0	3.6	54.4
D 13	13 09.1	01.9	273 46.3	12.2	19 08.4	3.7	54.4
A 14	28 09.3	02.9	288 17.5	12.2	19 04.7	3.8	54.4
Y 15	43 09.5	.. 03.9	302 48.7	12.2	19 00.9	3.8	54.4
16	58 09.7	04.9	317 19.9	12.2	18 57.1	4.0	54.4
17	73 09.8	05.9	331 51.1	12.2	18 53.1	4.0	54.4
18	88 10.0	N 0 06.9	346 22.3	12.3	N18 49.1	4.1	54.5
19	103 10.2	07.9	0 53.6	12.2	18 45.0	4.2	54.5
20	118 10.4	08.9	15 24.8	12.3	18 40.8	4.3	54.5
21	133 10.6	.. 09.8	29 56.1	12.2	18 36.5	4.4	54.5
22	148 10.8	10.8	44 27.3	12.3	18 32.1	4.5	54.5
23	163 11.0	11.8	58 58.6	12.3	18 27.6	4.5	54.5
21 00	178 11.1	N 0 12.8	73 29.9	12.3	N18 23.1	4.7	54.5
01	193 11.3	13.8	88 01.2	12.3	18 18.4	4.7	54.5
02	208 11.5	14.8	102 32.5	12.4	18 13.7	4.8	54.6
03	223 11.7	.. 15.8	117 03.9	12.3	18 08.9	4.9	54.6
04	238 11.9	16.8	131 35.2	12.3	18 04.0	5.0	54.6
05	253 12.1	17.7	146 06.5	12.4	17 59.0	5.1	54.6
06	268 12.3	N 0 18.7	160 37.9	12.4	N17 53.9	5.1	54.6
T 07	283 12.5	19.7	175 09.3	12.3	17 48.8	5.3	54.6
H 08	298 12.6	20.7	189 40.6	12.4	17 43.5	5.3	54.7
U 09	313 12.8	.. 21.7	204 12.0	12.4	17 38.2	5.4	54.7
R 10	328 13.0	22.7	218 43.4	12.5	17 32.8	5.5	54.7
S 11	343 13.2	23.7	233 14.9	12.4	17 27.3	5.6	54.7
D 12	358 13.4	N 0 24.7	247 46.3	12.4	N17 21.7	5.7	54.7
A 13	13 13.6	25.6	262 17.7	12.5	17 16.0	5.7	54.7
Y 14	28 13.8	26.6	276 49.2	12.4	17 10.3	5.9	54.8
15	43 13.9	.. 27.6	291 20.6	12.5	17 04.4	5.9	54.8
16	58 14.1	28.6	305 52.1	12.5	16 58.5	6.0	54.8
17	73 14.3	29.6	320 23.6	12.5	16 52.5	6.0	54.8
18	88 14.5	N 0 30.6	334 55.1	12.5	N16 46.5	6.2	54.8
19	103 14.7	31.6	349 26.6	12.5	16 40.3	6.2	54.9
20	118 14.9	32.5	3 58.1	12.5	16 34.1	6.4	54.9
21	133 15.1	.. 33.5	18 29.6	12.5	16 27.7	6.4	54.9
22	148 15.3	34.5	33 01.1	12.6	16 21.3	6.4	54.9
23	163 15.4	35.5	47 32.7	12.5	16 14.9	6.6	54.9
22 00	178 15.6	N 0 36.5	62 04.2	12.6	N16 08.3	6.6	54.9
01	193 15.8	37.5	76 35.8	12.6	16 01.7	6.8	55.0
02	208 16.0	38.5	91 07.4	12.5	15 54.9	6.8	55.0
03	223 16.2	.. 39.5	105 38.9	12.6	15 48.1	6.8	55.0
04	238 16.4	40.4	120 10.5	12.6	15 41.3	7.0	55.0
05	253 16.6	41.4	134 42.1	12.6	15 34.3	7.0	55.0
06	268 16.8	N 0 42.4	149 13.7	12.7	N15 27.3	7.1	55.1
07	283 16.9	43.4	163 45.4	12.6	15 20.2	7.2	55.1
F 08	298 17.1	44.4	178 17.0	12.6	15 13.0	7.3	55.1
R 09	313 17.3	.. 45.4	192 48.6	12.7	15 05.7	7.3	55.1
I 10	328 17.5	46.4	207 20.3	12.6	14 58.4	7.4	55.2
D 11	343 17.7	47.3	221 51.9	12.7	14 51.0	7.5	55.2
A 12	358 17.9	N 0 48.3	236 23.6	12.6	N14 43.5	7.6	55.2
Y 13	13 18.1	49.3	250 55.2	12.7	14 35.9	7.6	55.2
14	28 18.3	50.3	265 26.9	12.7	14 28.3	7.7	55.2
15	43 18.4	.. 51.3	279 58.6	12.7	14 20.6	7.8	55.3
16	58 18.6	52.3	294 30.3	12.7	14 12.8	7.9	55.3
17	73 18.8	53.3	309 02.0	12.7	14 04.9	7.9	55.3
18	88 19.0	N 0 54.2	323 33.7	12.7	N13 57.0	8.0	55.3
19	103 19.2	55.2	338 05.4	12.7	13 49.0	8.0	55.3
20	118 19.4	56.2	352 37.1	12.7	13 41.0	8.2	55.4
21	133 19.6	.. 57.2	7 08.8	12.8	13 32.8	8.2	55.4
22	148 19.8	58.2	21 40.6	12.7	13 24.6	8.3	55.4
23	163 20.0	59.2	36 12.3	12.7	N13 16.3	8.3	55.5
	SD 16.1	d 1.0	SD 14.8		14.9		15.0

Lat.	Twilight Naut.	Civil	Sunrise	Moonrise 20	21	22	23
°	h m	h m	h m	h m	h m	h m	h m
N 72	03 14	04 44	05 53	▭	08 11	10 34	12 31
N 70	03 34	04 53	05 54	07 35	09 24	11 08	12 50
68	03 49	04 59	05 55	08 36	10 01	11 32	13 06
66	04 01	05 05	05 56	09 11	10 27	11 50	13 18
64	04 11	05 09	05 57	09 36	10 47	12 05	13 28
62	04 20	05 13	05 58	09 55	11 03	12 18	13 37
60	04 27	05 17	05 58	10 11	11 17	12 28	13 44
N 58	04 33	05 20	05 59	10 25	11 28	12 38	13 51
56	04 38	05 22	05 59	10 36	11 38	12 46	13 57
54	04 43	05 25	06 00	10 46	11 47	12 53	14 02
52	04 47	05 27	06 00	10 55	11 55	12 59	14 06
50	04 50	05 28	06 01	11 03	12 02	13 05	14 11
45	04 58	05 32	06 01	11 21	12 17	13 17	14 20
N 40	05 03	05 35	06 02	11 35	12 30	13 27	14 27
35	05 08	05 37	06 02	11 47	12 40	13 36	14 34
30	05 11	05 39	06 03	11 57	12 50	13 44	14 39
20	05 16	05 41	06 03	12 15	13 05	13 57	14 49
N 10	05 18	05 43	06 04	12 30	13 19	14 08	14 58
0	05 19	05 43	06 04	12 45	13 32	14 19	15 06
S 10	05 19	05 43	06 04	12 59	13 45	14 30	15 14
20	05 17	05 42	06 04	13 15	13 59	14 41	15 23
30	05 12	05 40	06 04	13 33	14 15	14 54	15 32
35	05 09	05 39	06 04	13 43	14 24	15 02	15 38
40	05 05	05 37	06 04	13 55	14 34	15 10	15 44
45	05 00	05 34	06 04	14 09	14 46	15 20	15 51
S 50	04 53	05 31	06 03	14 26	15 01	15 32	16 00
52	04 50	05 30	06 03	14 34	15 08	15 38	16 04
54	04 46	05 28	06 03	14 42	15 16	15 44	16 09
56	04 42	05 26	06 03	14 52	15 24	15 51	16 14
58	04 37	05 24	06 03	15 04	15 34	15 59	16 19
S 60	04 31	05 21	06 03	15 17	15 45	16 07	16 25

Lat.	Sunset	Twilight Civil	Naut.	Moonset 20	21	22	23
°	h m	h m	h m	h m	h m	h m	h m
N 72	18 24	19 33	21 06	▭	06 39	05 54	05 35
N 70	18 22	19 24	20 45	05 35	05 25	05 19	05 14
68	18 21	19 17	20 28	04 34	04 48	04 54	04 57
66	18 20	19 12	20 16	03 59	04 21	04 35	04 44
64	18 19	19 07	20 05	03 34	04 00	04 19	04 32
62	18 18	19 03	19 57	03 14	03 44	04 06	04 23
60	18 17	18 59	19 49	02 58	03 30	03 55	04 15
N 58	18 17	18 56	19 43	02 44	03 18	03 45	04 07
56	18 16	18 53	19 38	02 32	03 07	03 36	04 01
54	18 16	18 51	19 33	02 22	02 58	03 29	03 55
52	18 15	18 49	19 25	02 13	02 50	03 22	03 50
50	18 15	18 47	19 25	02 04	02 43	03 16	03 45
45	18 14	18 43	19 18	01 47	02 27	03 03	03 35
N 40	18 13	18 40	19 12	01 32	02 14	02 52	03 26
35	18 13	18 38	19 07	01 20	02 03	02 42	03 19
30	18 12	18 36	19 04	01 10	01 53	02 34	03 12
20	18 11	18 33	18 59	00 51	01 36	02 19	03 03
N 10	18 11	18 32	18 56	00 35	01 21	02 07	02 51
0	18 10	18 31	18 55	00 20	01 08	01 55	02 42
S 10	18 10	18 31	18 55	00 05	00 54	01 43	02 32
20	18 10	18 32	18 57	24 39	00 39	01 30	02 22
30	18 10	18 34	19 01	24 22	00 22	01 16	02 10
35	18 10	18 35	19 04	24 12	00 12	01 07	02 04
40	18 10	18 37	19 08	24 01	00 01	00 57	01 56
45	18 10	18 39	19 13	23 47	24 46	00 46	01 47
S 50	18 10	18 42	19 20	23 31	24 32	00 32	01 36
52	18 10	18 43	19 23	23 23	24 25	00 25	01 31
54	18 10	18 45	19 27	23 14	24 18	00 18	01 25
56	18 10	18 47	19 31	23 05	24 10	00 10	01 19
58	18 10	18 49	19 36	22 54	24 01	00 01	01 12
S 60	18 10	18 52	19 41	22 41	23 50	25 04	01 04

Day	SUN Eqn. of Time 00h	12h	Mer. Pass.	MOON Mer. Pass. Upper	Lower	Age	Phase
d	m s	m s	h m	h m	h m	d	%
20	07 34	07 25	12 07	18 56	06 32	09	57
21	07 16	07 07	12 07	19 44	07 20	10	67
22	06 58	06 49	12 07	20 30	08 07	11	75

UT	ARIES	VENUS −4.0		MARS +1.2		JUPITER −2.2		SATURN +0.3		STARS		
	GHA	GHA	Dec	GHA	Dec	GHA	Dec	GHA	Dec	Name	SHA	Dec
d h	° ′	° ′	° ′	° ′	° ′	° ′	° ′	° ′	° ′		° ′	° ′
23 00	180 38.9	179 06.3	S 0 51.4	172 45.1	N 2 41.6	111 45.1	N21 35.9	321 33.6	S12 30.9	Acamar	315 18.8	S40 15.4
01	195 41.3	194 05.9	50.1	187 45.8	42.3	126 47.2	35.9	336 36.2	30.9	Achernar	335 27.4	S57 10.3
02	210 43.8	209 05.5	48.9	202 46.5	43.1	141 49.3	36.0	351 38.8	30.8	Acrux	173 08.7	S63 10.5
03	225 46.3	224 05.1	.. 47.6	217 47.2	.. 43.9	156 51.3	.. 36.1	6 41.4	.. 30.8	Adhara	255 12.6	S28 59.8
04	240 48.7	239 04.8	46.3	232 47.9	44.7	171 53.4	36.1	21 44.0	30.7	Aldebaran	290 49.7	N16 32.0
05	255 51.2	254 04.4	45.1	247 48.6	45.5	186 55.5	36.2	36 46.6	30.7			
06	270 53.7	269 04.0	S 0 43.8	262 49.3	N 2 46.2	201 57.6	N21 36.3	51 49.1	S12 30.7	Alioth	166 20.3	N55 53.1
07	285 56.1	284 03.6	42.6	277 50.0	47.0	216 59.6	36.3	66 51.7	30.6	Alkaid	152 58.6	N49 14.6
S 08	300 58.6	299 03.2	41.3	292 50.7	47.8	232 01.7	36.4	81 54.3	30.6	Al Na'ir	27 44.3	S46 53.6
A 09	316 01.1	314 02.9	.. 40.1	307 51.4	.. 48.6	247 03.8	.. 36.4	96 56.9	.. 30.5	Alnilam	275 46.6	S 1 11.9
T 10	331 03.5	329 02.5	38.8	322 52.1	49.4	262 05.8	36.5	111 59.5	30.5	Alphard	217 56.0	S 8 43.3
U 11	346 06.0	344 02.1	37.5	337 52.8	50.1	277 07.9	36.6	127 02.1	30.4			
R 12	1 08.4	359 01.7	S 0 36.3	352 53.5	N 2 50.9	292 10.0	N21 36.6	142 04.7	S12 30.4	Alphecca	126 10.9	N26 40.0
D 13	16 10.9	14 01.3	35.0	7 54.2	51.7	307 12.1	36.7	157 07.3	30.3	Alpheratz	357 44.0	N29 09.8
A 14	31 13.4	29 01.0	33.8	22 54.9	52.5	322 14.1	36.7	172 09.8	30.3	Altair	62 08.5	N 8 54.2
Y 15	46 15.8	44 00.6	.. 32.5	37 55.6	.. 53.3	337 16.2	.. 36.8	187 12.4	.. 30.2	Ankaa	353 16.3	S42 14.1
16	61 18.3	59 00.2	31.2	52 56.3	54.1	352 18.3	36.9	202 15.0	30.2	Antares	112 26.3	S26 27.6
17	76 20.8	73 59.8	30.0	67 57.0	54.8	7 20.3	36.9	217 17.6	30.1			
18	91 23.2	88 59.4	S 0 28.7	82 57.7	N 2 55.6	22 22.4	N21 37.0	232 20.2	S12 30.1	Arcturus	145 55.6	N19 06.6
19	106 25.7	103 59.1	27.5	97 58.4	56.4	37 24.5	37.0	247 22.8	30.1	Atria	107 28.1	S69 02.7
20	121 28.2	118 58.7	26.2	112 59.1	57.2	52 26.5	37.1	262 25.4	30.0	Avior	234 17.7	S59 33.6
21	136 30.6	133 58.3	.. 25.0	127 59.8	.. 57.9	67 28.6	.. 37.2	277 28.0	.. 30.0	Bellatrix	278 32.2	N 6 21.5
22	151 33.1	148 57.9	23.7	143 00.5	58.7	82 30.7	37.2	292 30.5	29.9	Betelgeuse	271 01.5	N 7 24.3
23	166 35.6	163 57.6	22.4	158 01.2	2 59.5	97 32.7	37.3	307 33.1	29.9			
24 00	181 38.0	178 57.2	S 0 21.2	173 01.9	N 3 00.3	112 34.8	N21 37.3	322 35.7	S12 29.8	Canopus	263 56.2	S52 42.6
01	196 40.5	193 56.8	19.9	188 02.6	01.1	127 36.9	37.4	337 38.3	29.8	Capella	280 34.8	N46 00.7
02	211 42.9	208 56.4	18.7	203 03.3	01.8	142 38.9	37.5	352 40.9	29.7	Deneb	49 31.8	N45 19.5
03	226 45.4	223 56.0	.. 17.4	218 04.0	.. 02.6	157 41.0	.. 37.5	7 43.5	.. 29.7	Denebola	182 33.5	N14 29.7
04	241 47.9	238 55.7	16.1	233 04.7	03.4	172 43.1	37.6	22 46.1	29.6	Diphda	348 56.4	S17 54.9
05	256 50.3	253 55.3	14.9	248 05.4	04.2	187 45.1	37.6	37 48.7	29.6			
06	271 52.8	268 54.9	S 0 13.6	263 06.1	N 3 05.0	202 47.2	N21 37.7	52 51.3	S12 29.5	Dubhe	193 51.3	N61 40.7
07	286 55.3	283 54.5	12.4	278 06.8	05.7	217 49.3	37.8	67 53.9	29.5	Elnath	278 12.9	N28 37.0
S 08	301 57.7	298 54.1	11.1	293 07.5	06.5	232 51.3	37.8	82 56.4	29.4	Eltanin	90 46.2	N51 29.0
U 09	317 00.2	313 53.8	.. 09.9	308 08.2	.. 07.3	247 53.4	.. 37.9	97 59.0	.. 29.4	Enif	33 47.5	N 9 56.1
N 10	332 02.7	328 53.4	08.6	323 08.9	08.1	262 55.5	37.9	113 01.6	29.4	Fomalhaut	15 24.5	S29 33.1
D 11	347 05.1	343 53.0	07.3	338 09.6	08.9	277 57.5	38.0	128 04.2	29.3			
A 12	2 07.6	358 52.6	S 0 06.1	353 10.3	N 3 09.6	292 59.6	N21 38.1	143 06.8	S12 29.3	Gacrux	172 00.5	S57 11.4
Y 13	17 10.1	13 52.3	04.8	8 11.0	10.4	308 01.7	38.1	158 09.4	29.2	Gienah	175 52.1	S17 37.1
14	32 12.5	28 51.9	03.6	23 11.7	11.2	323 03.7	38.2	173 12.0	29.2	Hadar	148 47.5	S60 26.1
15	47 15.0	43 51.5	.. 02.3	38 12.4	.. 12.0	338 05.8	.. 38.2	188 14.6	.. 29.1	Hamal	328 01.2	N23 31.4
16	62 17.4	58 51.1	S 01.0	53 13.1	12.7	353 07.8	38.3	203 17.2	29.1	Kaus Aust.	83 44.0	S34 22.5
17	77 19.9	73 50.7	N 00.2	68 13.8	13.5	8 09.9	38.4	218 19.8	29.0			
18	92 22.4	88 50.4	N 0 01.5	83 14.5	N 3 14.3	23 12.0	N21 38.4	233 22.3	S12 29.0	Kochab	137 19.2	N74 05.9
19	107 24.8	103 50.0	02.7	98 15.2	15.1	38 14.0	38.5	248 24.9	28.9	Markab	13 38.8	N15 16.5
20	122 27.3	118 49.6	04.0	113 15.9	15.9	53 16.1	38.5	263 27.5	28.9	Menkar	314 15.4	N 4 08.3
21	137 29.8	133 49.2	.. 05.2	128 16.6	.. 16.6	68 18.2	.. 38.6	278 30.1	.. 28.8	Menkent	148 07.4	S36 26.1
22	152 32.2	148 48.9	06.5	143 17.3	17.4	83 20.2	38.7	293 32.7	28.8	Miaplacidus	221 39.0	S69 46.7
23	167 34.7	163 48.5	07.8	158 18.0	18.2	98 22.3	38.7	308 35.3	28.7			
25 00	182 37.2	178 48.1	N 0 09.0	173 18.7	N 3 19.0	113 24.3	N21 38.8	323 37.9	S12 28.7	Mirfak	308 40.9	N49 54.5
01	197 39.6	193 47.7	10.3	188 19.4	19.7	128 26.4	38.8	338 40.5	28.6	Nunki	75 58.6	S26 16.6
02	212 42.1	208 47.3	11.5	203 20.1	20.5	143 28.5	38.9	353 43.1	28.6	Peacock	53 19.8	S56 41.2
03	227 44.5	223 47.0	.. 12.8	218 20.8	.. 21.3	158 30.5	.. 39.0	8 45.7	.. 28.5	Pollux	243 27.8	N27 59.5
04	242 47.0	238 46.6	14.1	233 21.5	22.1	173 32.6	39.0	23 48.3	28.5	Procyon	244 59.8	N 5 11.2
05	257 49.5	253 46.2	15.3	248 22.2	22.8	188 34.6	39.1	38 50.9	28.5			
06	272 51.9	268 45.8	N 0 16.6	263 22.9	N 3 23.6	203 36.7	N21 39.1	53 53.5	S12 28.4	Rasalhague	96 06.5	N12 33.0
07	287 54.4	283 45.5	17.8	278 23.6	24.4	218 38.8	39.2	68 56.0	28.4	Regulus	207 43.4	N11 53.9
08	302 56.9	298 45.1	19.1	293 24.3	25.2	233 40.8	39.3	83 58.6	28.3	Rigel	281 12.3	S 8 11.5
M 09	317 59.3	313 44.7	.. 20.4	308 25.0	.. 26.0	248 42.9	.. 39.3	99 01.2	.. 28.3	Rigil Kent.	139 51.4	S60 53.2
O 10	333 01.8	328 44.3	21.6	323 25.7	26.7	263 44.9	39.4	114 03.8	28.2	Sabik	102 12.6	S15 44.4
N 11	348 04.3	343 43.9	22.9	338 26.4	27.5	278 47.0	39.5	129 06.4	28.2			
D 12	3 06.7	358 43.6	N 0 24.1	353 27.1	N 3 28.3	293 49.1	N21 39.5	144 09.0	S12 28.1	Schedar	349 41.2	N56 36.6
A 13	18 09.2	13 43.2	25.4	8 27.8	29.1	308 51.1	39.6	159 11.6	28.1	Shaula	96 22.0	S37 06.6
Y 14	33 11.7	28 42.8	26.7	23 28.5	29.8	323 53.2	39.6	174 14.2	28.0	Sirius	258 33.8	S16 44.4
15	48 14.1	43 42.4	.. 27.9	38 29.2	.. 30.6	338 55.2	.. 39.7	189 16.8	.. 28.0	Spica	158 31.1	S11 14.0
16	63 16.6	58 42.1	29.2	53 29.9	31.4	353 57.3	39.8	204 19.4	27.9	Suhail	222 52.2	S43 29.6
17	78 19.0	73 41.7	30.4	68 30.6	32.2	8 59.4	39.8	219 22.0	27.9			
18	93 21.5	88 41.3	N 0 31.7	83 31.3	N 3 32.9	24 01.4	N21 39.9	234 24.6	S12 27.8	Vega	80 39.1	N38 47.6
19	108 24.0	103 40.9	33.0	98 32.0	33.7	39 03.5	39.9	249 27.2	27.8	Zuben'ubi	137 05.3	S16 05.8
20	123 26.4	118 40.6	34.2	113 32.7	34.5	54 05.5	40.0	264 29.8	27.7		SHA	Mer. Pass.
21	138 28.9	133 40.2	.. 35.5	128 33.4	.. 35.3	69 07.6	.. 40.1	279 32.4	.. 27.7	Venus	357 19.2	12 04
22	153 31.4	148 39.8	36.7	143 34.1	36.0	84 09.6	40.1	294 35.0	27.6	Mars	351 23.9	12 27
23	168 33.8	163 39.4	38.0	158 34.8	36.8	99 11.7	40.2	309 37.5	27.6	Jupiter	290 56.8	16 27
Mer. Pass.	h m 11 51.5	v −0.4	d 1.3	v 0.7	d 0.8	v 2.1	d 0.1	v 2.6	d 0.0	Saturn	140 57.7	2 29

UT	SUN GHA	SUN Dec	MOON GHA	v	Dec	d	HP
d h	° ′	° ′	° ′	′	° ′	′	′
23 00	178 20.1	N 1 00.2	50 44.0	12.8	N13 08.0	8.4	55.5
01	193 20.3	01.1	65 15.8	12.7	12 59.6	8.5	55.5
02	208 20.5	02.1	79 47.5	12.8	12 51.1	8.6	55.5
03	223 20.7	.. 03.1	94 19.3	12.7	12 42.5	8.6	55.6
04	238 20.9	04.1	108 51.0	12.8	12 33.9	8.7	55.6
05	253 21.1	05.1	123 22.8	12.7	12 25.2	8.8	55.6
S 06	268 21.3	N 1 06.1	137 54.5	12.8	N12 16.4	8.8	55.6
A 07	283 21.5	07.1	152 26.3	12.7	12 07.6	8.9	55.7
T 08	298 21.7	08.0	166 58.0	12.8	11 58.7	8.9	55.7
U 09	313 21.8	.. 09.0	181 29.8	12.8	11 49.8	9.0	55.7
R 10	328 22.0	10.0	196 01.6	12.7	11 40.8	9.1	55.8
D 11	343 22.2	11.0	210 33.3	12.8	11 31.7	9.2	55.8
A 12	358 22.4	N 1 12.0	225 05.1	12.8	N11 22.5	9.2	55.8
Y 13	13 22.6	13.0	239 36.9	12.7	11 13.3	9.2	55.8
14	28 22.8	13.9	254 08.6	12.8	11 04.1	9.4	55.9
15	43 23.0	.. 14.9	268 40.4	12.8	10 54.7	9.3	55.9
16	58 23.2	15.9	283 12.2	12.7	10 45.4	9.5	55.9
17	73 23.3	16.9	297 43.9	12.8	10 35.9	9.5	55.9
18	88 23.5	N 1 17.9	312 15.7	12.8	N10 26.4	9.6	56.0
19	103 23.7	18.9	326 47.5	12.7	10 16.8	9.6	56.0
20	118 23.9	19.9	341 19.2	12.8	10 07.2	9.7	56.0
21	133 24.1	.. 20.8	355 51.0	12.7	9 57.5	9.7	56.1
22	148 24.3	21.8	10 22.7	12.8	9 47.8	9.8	56.1
23	163 24.5	22.8	24 54.5	12.7	9 38.0	9.9	56.1
24 00	178 24.7	N 1 23.8	39 26.2	12.8	N 9 28.1	9.9	56.1
01	193 24.9	24.8	53 58.0	12.7	9 18.2	9.9	56.2
02	208 25.1	25.8	68 29.7	12.7	9 08.3	10.1	56.2
03	223 25.2	.. 26.7	83 01.4	12.8	8 58.2	10.0	56.2
04	238 25.4	27.7	97 33.2	12.7	8 48.2	10.2	56.3
05	253 25.6	28.7	112 04.9	12.7	8 38.0	10.1	56.3
S 06	268 25.8	N 1 29.7	126 36.6	12.7	N 8 27.9	10.3	56.3
U 07	283 26.0	30.7	141 08.3	12.7	8 17.6	10.2	56.3
N 08	298 26.2	31.7	155 40.0	12.7	8 07.4	10.4	56.4
D 09	313 26.4	.. 32.6	170 11.7	12.6	7 57.0	10.3	56.4
A 10	328 26.6	33.6	184 43.3	12.7	7 46.7	10.5	56.4
Y 11	343 26.8	34.6	199 15.0	12.7	7 36.2	10.4	56.5
12	358 26.9	N 1 35.6	213 46.7	12.6	N 7 25.8	10.6	56.5
13	13 27.1	36.6	228 18.3	12.6	7 15.2	10.5	56.5
14	28 27.3	37.6	242 49.9	12.7	7 04.7	10.6	56.6
15	43 27.5	.. 38.5	257 21.6	12.6	6 54.1	10.7	56.6
16	58 27.7	39.5	271 53.2	12.6	6 43.4	10.7	56.6
17	73 27.9	40.5	286 24.8	12.6	6 32.7	10.7	56.6
18	88 28.1	N 1 41.5	300 56.4	12.5	N 6 22.0	10.8	56.7
19	103 28.3	42.5	315 27.9	12.6	6 11.2	10.9	56.7
20	118 28.5	43.5	329 59.5	12.5	6 00.3	10.8	56.7
21	133 28.7	.. 44.4	344 31.0	12.5	5 49.5	10.9	56.8
22	148 28.8	45.4	359 02.5	12.6	5 38.6	11.0	56.8
23	163 29.0	46.4	13 34.1	12.4	5 27.6	11.0	56.8
25 00	178 29.2	N 1 47.4	28 05.5	12.5	N 5 16.6	11.0	56.9
01	193 29.4	48.4	42 37.0	12.5	5 05.6	11.1	56.9
02	208 29.6	49.3	57 08.5	12.4	4 54.5	11.1	56.9
03	223 29.8	.. 50.3	71 39.9	12.4	4 43.4	11.1	57.0
04	238 30.0	51.3	86 11.3	12.4	4 32.3	11.2	57.0
05	253 30.2	52.3	100 42.7	12.4	4 21.1	11.2	57.0
M 06	268 30.4	N 1 53.3	115 14.1	12.4	N 4 09.9	11.2	57.0
O 07	283 30.5	54.3	129 45.5	12.3	3 58.7	11.3	57.1
N 08	298 30.7	55.2	144 16.8	12.3	3 47.4	11.3	57.1
D 09	313 30.9	.. 56.2	158 48.1	12.3	3 36.1	11.3	57.1
A 10	328 31.1	57.2	173 19.4	12.3	3 24.8	11.4	57.2
Y 11	343 31.3	58.2	187 50.7	12.3	3 13.4	11.3	57.2
12	358 31.5	N 1 59.2	202 22.0	12.2	N 3 02.1	11.5	57.2
13	13 31.7	2 00.2	216 53.2	12.2	2 50.6	11.4	57.3
14	28 31.9	01.1	231 24.4	12.2	2 39.2	11.5	57.3
15	43 32.1	.. 02.1	245 55.6	12.1	2 27.7	11.5	57.3
16	58 32.3	03.1	260 26.7	12.1	2 16.2	11.5	57.4
17	73 32.4	04.1	274 57.8	12.1	2 04.7	11.5	57.4
18	88 32.6	N 2 05.1	289 28.9	12.1	N 1 53.2	11.6	57.4
19	103 32.8	06.0	304 00.0	12.0	1 41.6	11.6	57.4
20	118 33.0	07.0	318 31.0	12.0	1 30.0	11.6	57.5
21	133 33.2	.. 08.0	333 02.0	12.0	1 18.4	11.6	57.5
22	148 33.4	09.0	347 33.0	12.0	1 06.8	11.6	57.5
23	163 33.6	10.0	2 04.0	11.9	N 0 55.2	11.7	57.6
	SD 16.1	d 1.0	SD 15.2		15.4		15.6

Lat.	Twilight Naut.	Twilight Civil	Sunrise	Moonrise 23	24	25	26
°	h m	h m	h m	h m	h m	h m	h m
N 72	02 52	04 28	05 37	12 31	14 22	16 13	18 06
N 70	03 16	04 38	05 40	12 50	14 33	16 16	18 02
68	03 34	04 46	05 43	13 06	14 41	16 18	17 58
66	03 48	04 53	05 45	13 18	14 48	16 20	17 55
64	03 59	04 59	05 46	13 28	14 54	16 22	17 53
62	04 09	05 03	05 48	13 37	14 59	16 24	17 51
60	04 17	05 07	05 49	13 44	15 03	16 25	17 49
N 58	04 24	05 11	05 50	13 51	15 07	16 26	17 47
56	04 29	05 14	05 51	13 57	15 11	16 27	17 46
54	04 35	05 17	05 52	14 02	15 14	16 28	17 45
52	04 39	05 19	05 53	14 06	15 16	16 29	17 43
50	04 43	05 22	05 54	14 11	15 19	16 30	17 42
45	04 52	05 26	05 56	14 20	15 25	16 31	17 40
N 40	04 58	05 30	05 57	14 27	15 29	16 33	17 38
35	05 03	05 33	05 58	14 34	15 33	16 34	17 36
30	05 07	05 35	05 59	14 39	15 36	16 35	17 35
20	05 13	05 39	06 01	14 49	15 43	16 37	17 33
N 10	05 16	05 41	06 02	14 58	15 48	16 38	17 30
0	05 18	05 42	06 03	15 06	15 53	16 40	17 28
S 10	05 19	05 43	06 04	15 14	15 58	16 42	17 27
20	05 17	05 43	06 05	15 23	16 03	16 43	17 24
30	05 14	05 42	06 06	15 32	16 09	16 45	17 22
35	05 12	05 41	06 06	15 38	16 12	16 46	17 21
40	05 08	05 40	06 07	15 44	16 16	16 48	17 19
45	05 04	05 38	06 08	15 51	16 21	16 49	17 18
S 50	04 58	05 36	06 08	16 00	16 28	16 51	17 16
52	04 55	05 35	06 09	16 04	16 28	16 52	17 15
54	04 52	05 34	06 09	16 09	16 31	16 52	17 14
56	04 48	05 32	06 10	16 14	16 34	16 53	17 11
58	04 44	05 30	06 10	16 19	16 37	16 54	17 11
S 60	04 39	05 28	06 10	16 25	16 41	16 56	17 10

Lat.	Sunset	Twilight Civil	Twilight Naut.	Moonset 23	24	25	26
°	h m	h m	h m	h m	h m	h m	h m
N 72	18 38	19 48	21 26	05 35	05 21	05 10	04 59
N 70	18 35	19 37	21 01	05 14	05 09	05 04	04 59
68	18 32	19 29	20 42	04 57	04 59	04 59	04 59
66	18 30	19 22	20 28	04 44	04 50	04 55	05 00
64	18 28	19 16	20 16	04 32	04 43	04 52	05 00
62	18 26	19 11	20 06	04 23	04 37	04 49	05 00
60	18 25	19 07	19 58	04 15	04 31	04 46	05 01
N 58	18 23	19 03	19 51	04 07	04 27	04 44	05 01
56	18 22	19 00	19 45	04 01	04 22	04 42	05 01
54	18 21	18 57	19 39	03 55	04 18	04 40	05 01
52	18 20	18 54	19 35	03 50	04 15	04 38	05 01
50	18 19	18 52	19 31	03 45	04 12	04 37	05 01
45	18 18	18 47	19 22	03 35	04 05	04 33	05 02
N 40	18 16	18 43	19 15	03 26	03 59	04 31	05 02
35	18 15	18 40	19 09	03 19	03 54	04 28	05 02
30	18 14	18 38	19 06	03 12	03 49	04 26	05 02
20	18 12	18 34	19 00	03 01	03 42	04 22	05 03
N 10	18 11	18 32	18 57	02 51	03 35	04 18	05 03
0	18 09	18 30	18 54	02 42	03 28	04 15	05 03
S 10	18 08	18 29	18 54	02 32	03 22	04 12	05 03
20	18 07	18 29	18 55	02 22	03 15	04 08	05 03
30	18 06	18 30	18 58	02 10	03 07	04 04	05 04
35	18 05	18 31	19 00	02 04	03 02	04 02	05 04
40	18 05	18 33	19 04	01 56	02 57	03 59	05 04
45	18 04	18 33	19 07	01 47	02 50	03 56	05 04
S 50	18 03	18 35	19 13	01 36	02 43	03 52	05 04
52	18 03	18 36	19 16	01 31	02 40	03 51	05 04
54	18 02	18 38	19 19	01 25	02 36	03 49	05 04
56	18 02	18 39	19 23	01 19	02 32	03 47	05 04
58	18 02	18 41	19 27	01 12	02 27	03 45	05 04
S 60	18 01	18 42	19 32	01 04	02 21	03 42	05 04

Day	SUN Eqn. of Time 00h	SUN Eqn. of Time 12h	SUN Mer. Pass.	MOON Mer. Pass. Upper	MOON Mer. Pass. Lower	Age	Phase
d	m s	m s	h m	h m	h m	d	%
23	06 40	06 31	12 07	21 17	08 54	12	83
24	06 22	06 13	12 06	22 04	09 40	13	90
25	06 04	05 54	12 06	22 51	10 28	14	96

UT	ARIES GHA	VENUS −4.0 GHA	Dec	MARS +1.2 GHA	Dec	JUPITER −2.1 GHA	Dec	SATURN +0.3 GHA	Dec	Star Name	SHA	Dec
26 00	183 36.3	178 39.0	N 0 39.2	173 35.5	N 3 37.6	114 13.7	N21 40.2	324 40.1	S12 27.5	Acamar	315 18.8	S40 15.4
01	198 38.8	193 38.7	40.5	188 36.2	38.4	129 15.8	40.3	339 42.7	27.5	Achernar	335 27.5	S57 10.3
02	213 41.2	208 38.3	41.8	203 36.9	39.1	144 17.9	40.4	354 45.3	27.4	Acrux	173 08.7	S63 10.5
03	228 43.7	223 37.9	.. 43.0	218 37.6	.. 39.9	159 19.9	.. 40.4	9 47.9	.. 27.4	Adhara	255 12.6	S28 59.8
04	243 46.1	238 37.5	44.3	233 38.3	40.7	174 22.0	40.5	24 50.5	27.3	Aldebaran	290 49.7	N16 32.0
05	258 48.6	253 37.2	45.5	248 39.0	41.5	189 24.0	40.5	39 53.1	27.3			
06	273 51.1	268 36.8	N 0 46.8	263 39.7	N 3 42.2	204 26.1	N21 40.6	54 55.7	S12 27.2	Alioth	166 20.3	N55 53.1
07	288 53.5	283 36.4	48.1	278 40.4	43.0	219 28.1	40.7	69 58.3	27.2	Alkaid	152 58.6	N49 14.6
08	303 56.0	298 36.0	49.3	293 41.1	43.8	234 30.2	40.7	85 00.9	27.2	Al Na'ir	27 44.3	S46 53.6
09	318 58.5	313 35.7	.. 50.6	308 41.8	.. 44.6	249 32.2	.. 40.8	100 03.5	.. 27.1	Alnilam	275 46.6	S 1 11.9
10	334 00.9	328 35.3	51.8	323 42.5	45.3	264 34.3	40.9	115 06.1	27.1	Alphard	217 56.0	S 8 43.3
11	349 03.4	343 34.9	53.1	338 43.2	46.1	279 36.3	40.9	130 08.7	27.0			
12	4 05.9	358 34.5	N 0 54.4	353 43.9	N 3 46.9	294 38.4	N21 41.0	145 11.3	S12 27.0	Alphecca	126 10.9	N26 40.0
13	19 08.3	13 34.2	55.6	8 44.6	47.7	309 40.5	41.0	160 13.9	26.9	Alpheratz	357 44.0	N29 09.8
14	34 10.8	28 33.8	56.9	23 45.3	48.4	324 42.5	41.1	175 16.5	26.9	Altair	62 08.5	N 8 54.2
15	49 13.3	43 33.4	.. 58.1	38 46.0	.. 49.2	339 44.6	.. 41.2	190 19.1	.. 26.8	Ankaa	353 16.3	S42 14.1
16	64 15.7	58 33.0	0 59.4	53 46.7	50.0	354 46.6	41.2	205 21.7	26.8	Antares	112 26.3	S26 27.6
17	79 18.2	73 32.6	1 00.7	68 47.4	50.8	9 48.7	41.3	220 24.3	26.7			
18	94 20.6	88 32.3	N 1 01.9	83 48.1	N 3 51.5	24 50.7	N21 41.3	235 26.9	S12 26.7	Arcturus	145 55.6	N19 06.6
19	109 23.1	103 31.9	03.2	98 48.9	52.3	39 52.8	41.4	250 29.5	26.6	Atria	107 28.0	S69 02.7
20	124 25.6	118 31.5	04.4	113 49.6	53.1	54 54.8	41.5	265 32.1	26.6	Avior	234 17.8	S59 33.6
21	139 28.0	133 31.1	.. 05.7	128 50.3	.. 53.8	69 56.9	.. 41.5	280 34.7	.. 26.5	Bellatrix	278 32.2	N 6 21.5
22	154 30.5	148 30.8	06.9	143 51.0	54.6	84 58.9	41.6	295 37.3	26.5	Betelgeuse	271 01.5	N 7 24.3
23	169 33.0	163 30.4	08.2	158 51.7	55.4	100 01.0	41.6	310 39.9	26.4			
27 00	184 35.4	178 30.0	N 1 09.5	173 52.4	N 3 56.2	115 03.0	N21 41.7	325 42.5	S12 26.4	Canopus	263 56.2	S52 42.6
01	199 37.9	193 29.6	10.7	188 53.1	56.9	130 05.1	41.8	340 45.1	26.3	Capella	280 34.8	N46 00.7
02	214 40.4	208 29.3	12.0	203 53.8	57.7	145 07.1	41.8	355 47.7	26.3	Deneb	49 31.8	N45 19.5
03	229 42.8	223 28.9	.. 13.2	218 54.5	.. 58.5	160 09.2	.. 41.9	10 50.3	.. 26.2	Denebola	182 33.5	N14 29.7
04	244 45.3	238 28.5	14.5	233 55.2	3 59.3	175 11.2	41.9	25 52.9	26.2	Diphda	348 56.4	S17 54.9
05	259 47.7	253 28.1	15.8	248 55.9	4 00.0	190 13.3	42.0	40 55.5	26.1			
06	274 50.2	268 27.7	N 1 17.0	263 56.6	N 4 00.8	205 15.3	N21 42.1	55 58.1	S12 26.1	Dubhe	193 51.3	N61 40.7
07	289 52.7	283 27.4	18.3	278 57.3	01.6	220 17.4	42.1	71 00.7	26.0	Elnath	278 12.9	N28 37.0
08	304 55.1	298 27.0	19.5	293 58.0	02.3	235 19.4	42.2	86 03.2	26.0	Eltanin	90 46.1	N51 29.0
09	319 57.6	313 26.6	.. 20.8	308 58.7	.. 03.1	250 21.5	.. 42.3	101 05.8	.. 25.9	Enif	33 47.5	N 9 56.1
10	335 00.1	328 26.2	22.1	323 59.4	03.9	265 23.5	42.3	116 08.4	25.9	Fomalhaut	15 24.5	S29 33.1
11	350 02.5	343 25.9	23.3	339 00.1	04.7	280 25.6	42.4	131 11.0	25.8			
12	5 05.0	358 25.5	N 1 24.6	354 00.8	N 4 05.4	295 27.6	N21 42.4	146 13.6	S12 25.8	Gacrux	172 00.5	S57 11.4
13	20 07.5	13 25.1	25.8	9 01.5	06.2	310 29.7	42.5	161 16.2	25.7	Gienah	175 52.1	S17 37.1
14	35 09.9	28 24.7	27.1	24 02.2	07.0	325 31.7	42.6	176 18.8	25.7	Hadar	148 47.5	S60 26.2
15	50 12.4	43 24.4	.. 28.3	39 02.9	.. 07.7	340 33.8	.. 42.6	191 21.4	.. 25.6	Hamal	328 01.2	N23 31.4
16	65 14.9	58 24.0	29.6	54 03.6	08.5	355 35.8	42.7	206 24.0	25.6	Kaus Aust.	83 44.0	S34 22.5
17	80 17.3	73 23.6	30.9	69 04.3	09.3	10 37.8	42.7	221 26.6	25.5			
18	95 19.8	88 23.2	N 1 32.1	84 05.0	N 4 10.1	25 39.9	N21 42.8	236 29.2	S12 25.5	Kochab	137 19.1	N74 05.9
19	110 22.2	103 22.9	33.4	99 05.7	10.8	40 41.9	42.9	251 31.8	25.4	Markab	13 38.8	N15 16.5
20	125 24.7	118 22.5	34.6	114 06.4	11.6	55 44.0	42.9	266 34.4	25.4	Menkar	314 15.4	N 4 08.3
21	140 27.2	133 22.1	.. 35.9	129 07.1	.. 12.4	70 46.0	.. 43.0	281 37.0	.. 25.3	Menkent	148 07.4	S36 26.1
22	155 29.6	148 21.7	37.2	144 07.8	13.1	85 48.1	43.0	296 39.6	25.3	Miaplacidus	221 39.1	S69 46.7
23	170 32.1	163 21.3	38.4	159 08.5	13.9	100 50.1	43.1	311 42.2	25.2			
28 00	185 34.6	178 21.0	N 1 39.7	174 09.2	N 4 14.7	115 52.2	N21 43.2	326 44.8	S12 25.2	Mirfak	308 40.9	N49 54.5
01	200 37.0	193 20.6	40.9	189 09.9	15.5	130 54.2	43.2	341 47.4	25.1	Nunki	75 58.5	S26 16.6
02	215 39.5	208 20.2	42.2	204 10.6	16.2	145 56.3	43.3	356 50.0	25.1	Peacock	53 19.8	S56 41.2
03	230 42.0	223 19.8	.. 43.4	219 11.3	.. 17.0	160 58.3	.. 43.4	11 52.7	.. 25.0	Pollux	243 27.8	N27 59.5
04	245 44.4	238 19.5	44.7	234 12.0	17.8	176 00.3	43.4	26 55.3	25.0	Procyon	244 59.8	N 5 11.2
05	260 46.9	253 19.1	46.0	249 12.7	18.5	191 02.4	43.5	41 57.9	24.9			
06	275 49.3	268 18.7	N 1 47.2	264 13.4	N 4 19.3	206 04.4	N21 43.5	57 00.5	S12 24.9	Rasalhague	96 06.5	N12 33.0
07	290 51.8	283 18.3	48.5	279 14.1	20.1	221 06.5	43.6	72 03.1	24.8	Regulus	207 43.4	N11 53.9
08	305 54.3	298 18.0	49.7	294 14.8	20.8	236 08.5	43.7	87 05.7	24.8	Rigel	281 12.3	S 8 11.5
09	320 56.7	313 17.6	.. 51.0	309 15.5	.. 21.6	251 10.6	.. 43.7	102 08.3	.. 24.7	Rigil Kent.	139 51.3	S60 53.2
10	335 59.2	328 17.2	52.3	324 16.2	22.4	266 12.6	43.8	117 10.9	24.7	Sabik	102 12.6	S15 44.4
11	351 01.7	343 16.8	53.5	339 16.9	23.2	281 14.7	43.8	132 13.5	24.6			
12	6 04.1	358 16.4	N 1 54.8	354 17.6	N 4 23.9	296 16.7	N21 43.9	147 16.1	S12 24.6	Schedar	349 41.2	N56 36.6
13	21 06.6	13 16.1	56.0	9 18.3	24.7	311 18.7	44.0	162 18.7	24.5	Shaula	96 22.0	S37 06.6
14	36 09.1	28 15.7	57.3	24 19.0	25.5	326 20.8	44.0	177 21.3	24.5	Sirius	258 33.8	S16 44.4
15	51 11.5	43 15.3	.. 58.5	39 19.7	.. 26.2	341 22.8	.. 44.1	192 23.9	.. 24.4	Spica	158 31.1	S11 14.0
16	66 14.0	58 14.9	1 59.8	54 20.4	27.0	356 24.9	44.2	207 26.5	24.4	Suhail	222 52.3	S43 29.6
17	81 16.5	73 14.6	2 01.1	69 21.1	27.8	11 26.9	44.2	222 29.1	24.3			
18	96 18.9	88 14.2	N 2 02.3	84 21.8	N 4 28.5	26 28.9	N21 44.3	237 31.7	S12 24.3	Vega	80 39.1	N38 47.6
19	111 21.4	103 13.8	03.6	99 22.5	29.3	41 31.0	44.3	252 34.3	24.2	Zuben'ubi	137 05.3	S16 05.8
20	126 23.8	118 13.4	04.8	114 23.2	30.1	56 33.0	44.4	267 36.9	24.2		SHA	Mer.Pass.
21	141 26.3	133 13.0	.. 06.1	129 23.9	.. 30.8	71 35.1	.. 44.5	282 39.5	.. 24.1	Venus	353 54.6	12 06
22	156 28.8	148 12.7	07.3	144 24.6	31.6	86 37.1	44.5	297 42.1	24.1	Mars	349 16.9	12 24
23	171 31.2	163 12.3	08.6	159 25.3	32.4	101 39.1	44.6	312 44.7	24.0	Jupiter	290 27.6	16 18
Mer. Pass. 11 39.7		v −0.4	d 1.3	v 0.7	d 0.8	v 2.0	d 0.1	v 2.6	d 0.0	Saturn	141 07.0	2 17

UT	SUN		MOON					Lat.	Twilight		Sunrise	Moonrise			
									Naut.	Civil		26	27	28	29
	GHA	Dec	GHA	v	Dec	d	HP	°	h m	h m	h m	h m	h m	h m	h m
d h	° ′	° ′	° ′	′	° ′	′	′	N 72	02 27	04 10	05 22	18 06	20 04	22 12	24 39
26 00	178 33.8	N 2 10.9	16 34.9	11.9	N 0 43.5	11.6	57.6	N 70	02 56	04 23	05 26	18 02	19 52	21 47	23 50
01	193 34.0	11.9	31 05.8	11.8	0 31.9	11.7	57.6	68	03 17	04 33	05 30	17 58	19 42	21 29	23 19
02	208 34.2	12.9	45 36.6	11.9	0 20.2	11.7	57.6	66	03 34	04 41	05 33	17 55	19 33	21 14	22 56
03	223 34.3 ..	13.9	60 07.5	11.8	N 0 08.5	11.7	57.7	64	03 47	04 47	05 36	17 53	19 26	21 02	22 38
04	238 34.5	14.9	74 38.3	11.7	S 0 03.2	11.8	57.7	62	03 57	04 53	05 38	17 51	19 20	20 52	22 24
05	253 34.7	15.8	89 09.0	11.7	0 15.0	11.7	57.7	60	04 06	04 58	05 40	17 49	19 15	20 44	22 11
06	268 34.9	N 2 16.8	103 39.7	11.7	S 0 26.7	11.7	57.8	N 58	04 14	05 02	05 42	17 47	19 11	20 36	22 01
07	283 35.1	17.8	118 10.4	11.7	0 38.4	11.8	57.8	56	04 21	05 06	05 44	17 46	19 07	20 29	21 52
08	298 35.3	18.8	132 41.1	11.6	0 50.2	11.8	57.8	54	04 27	05 09	05 45	17 45	19 03	20 23	21 43
T 09	313 35.5 ..	19.8	147 11.7	11.6	1 02.0	11.7	57.8	52	04 32	05 12	05 46	17 43	19 00	20 18	21 36
U 10	328 35.7	20.7	161 42.3	11.5	1 13.7	11.8	57.9	50	04 36	05 15	05 47	17 42	18 57	20 13	21 30
E 11	343 35.9	21.7	176 12.8	11.5	1 25.5	11.8	57.9	45	04 46	05 21	05 50	17 40	18 51	20 03	21 16
S 12	358 36.1	N 2 22.7	190 43.3	11.5	S 1 37.3	11.8	57.9	N 40	04 53	05 25	05 52	17 38	18 45	19 54	21 04
D 13	13 36.2	23.7	205 13.8	11.4	1 49.1	11.7	58.0	35	04 59	05 28	05 54	17 36	18 41	19 47	20 54
A 14	28 36.4	24.7	219 44.2	11.4	2 00.8	11.8	58.0	30	05 03	05 31	05 55	17 35	18 37	19 41	20 46
Y 15	43 36.6 ..	25.6	234 14.6	11.3	2 12.6	11.8	58.0	20	05 10	05 36	05 58	17 33	18 30	19 30	20 31
16	58 36.8	26.6	248 44.9	11.3	2 24.4	11.8	58.0	N 10	05 15	05 39	06 00	17 30	18 24	19 20	20 18
17	73 37.0	27.6	263 15.2	11.3	2 36.2	11.8	58.1	0	05 17	05 41	06 02	17 28	18 19	19 11	20 06
18	88 37.2	N 2 28.6	277 45.5	11.2	S 2 48.0	11.8	58.1	S 10	05 18	05 43	06 04	17 27	18 13	19 02	19 55
19	103 37.4	29.6	292 15.7	11.2	2 59.8	11.7	58.1	20	05 18	05 44	06 06	17 24	18 07	18 53	19 42
20	118 37.6	30.5	306 45.9	11.1	3 11.5	11.8	58.2	30	05 16	05 44	06 08	17 22	18 01	18 42	19 28
21	133 37.8 ..	31.5	321 16.0	11.1	3 23.3	11.8	58.2	35	05 14	05 44	06 09	17 21	17 57	18 36	19 20
22	148 38.0	32.5	335 46.1	11.0	3 35.1	11.7	58.2	40	05 12	05 43	06 10	17 19	17 53	18 29	19 10
23	163 38.1	33.5	350 16.1	11.0	3 46.8	11.7	58.2	45	05 08	05 42	06 11	17 18	17 48	18 21	18 59
27 00	178 38.3	N 2 34.5	4 46.1	11.0	S 3 58.5	11.8	58.3	S 50	05 03	05 41	06 13	17 16	17 42	18 12	18 46
01	193 38.5	35.4	19 16.1	10.9	4 10.3	11.7	58.3	52	05 01	05 40	06 14	17 15	17 40	18 07	18 40
02	208 38.7	36.4	33 46.0	10.9	4 22.0	11.7	58.3	54	04 58	05 39	06 14	17 14	17 37	18 03	18 33
03	223 38.9 ..	37.4	48 15.9	10.8	4 33.7	11.7	58.3	56	04 55	05 38	06 15	17 13	17 33	17 57	18 26
04	238 39.1	38.4	62 45.7	10.7	4 45.4	11.7	58.4	58	04 51	05 37	06 16	17 11	17 30	17 51	18 17
05	253 39.3	39.3	77 15.4	10.7	4 57.1	11.6	58.4	S 60	04 47	05 36	06 17	17 10	17 26	17 45	18 08
06	268 39.5	N 2 40.3	91 45.1	10.7	S 5 08.7	11.7	58.4								
W 07	283 39.7	41.3	106 14.8	10.6	5 20.4	11.6	58.4	Lat.	Sunset	Twilight		Moonset			
E 08	298 39.9	42.3	120 44.4	10.6	5 32.0	11.6	58.5			Civil	Naut.	26	27	28	29
D 09	313 40.0 ..	43.3	135 14.0	10.5	5 43.6	11.6	58.5	°	h m	h m	h m	h m	h m	h m	h m
N 10	328 40.2	44.2	149 43.5	10.5	5 55.2	11.5	58.5	N 72	18 52	20 04	21 50	04 59	04 47	04 34	04 18
E 11	343 40.4	45.2	164 13.0	10.4	6 06.7	11.6	58.5	N 70	18 47	19 51	21 19	04 59	04 54	04 49	04 43
S 12	358 40.6	N 2 46.2	178 42.4	10.5	S 6 18.3	11.5	58.6	68	18 43	19 41	20 57	04 59	05 00	05 01	05 03
D 13	13 40.8	47.2	193 11.8	10.3	6 29.8	11.4	58.6	66	18 39	19 32	20 40	05 00	05 05	05 11	05 19
A 14	28 41.0	48.1	207 41.1	10.2	6 41.2	11.5	58.6	64	18 37	19 25	20 27	05 00	05 09	05 19	05 32
Y 15	43 41.2 ..	49.1	222 10.3	10.2	6 52.7	11.4	58.6	62	18 34	19 19	20 16	05 00	05 12	05 26	05 43
16	58 41.4	50.1	236 39.5	10.2	7 04.1	11.4	58.7	60	18 32	19 14	20 06	05 01	05 15	05 32	05 53
17	73 41.6	51.1	251 08.7	10.1	7 15.5	11.4	58.7								
18	88 41.8	N 2 52.0	265 37.8	10.0	S 7 26.9	11.3	58.7	N 58	18 30	19 10	19 58	05 01	05 18	05 38	06 01
19	103 41.9	53.0	280 06.8	10.0	7 38.2	11.3	58.7	56	18 28	19 06	19 51	05 01	05 21	05 43	06 08
20	118 42.1	54.0	294 35.8	9.9	7 49.5	11.3	58.8	54	18 27	19 03	19 46	05 01	05 23	05 47	06 15
21	133 42.3 ..	55.0	309 04.7	9.9	8 00.8	11.2	58.8	52	18 25	18 59	19 40	05 01	05 25	05 51	06 21
22	148 42.5	56.0	323 33.6	9.8	8 12.0	11.2	58.8	50	18 24	18 57	19 36	05 01	05 27	05 55	06 26
23	163 42.7	56.9	338 02.4	9.8	8 23.2	11.1	58.8	45	18 21	18 51	19 26	05 02	05 31	06 02	06 38
28 00	178 42.9	N 2 57.9	352 31.2	9.7	S 8 34.3	11.1	58.8	N 40	18 19	18 46	19 18	05 02	05 34	06 09	06 47
01	193 43.1	58.9	6 59.9	9.7	8 45.4	11.1	58.9	35	18 17	18 43	19 13	05 02	05 37	06 15	06 56
02	208 43.3	2 59.9	21 28.6	9.5	8 56.5	11.0	58.9	30	18 16	18 40	19 08	05 02	05 40	06 20	07 03
03	223 43.5	3 00.8	35 57.1	9.6	9 07.5	10.9	58.9	20	18 13	18 35	19 01	05 03	05 44	06 28	07 16
04	238 43.7	01.8	50 25.7	9.5	9 18.4	11.0	58.9	N 10	18 11	18 32	18 56	05 03	05 48	06 36	07 27
05	253 43.8	02.8	64 54.2	9.4	9 29.4	10.8	59.0	0	18 09	18 29	18 53	05 03	05 52	06 43	07 37
06	268 44.0	N 3 03.8	79 22.6	9.3	S 9 40.2	10.9	59.0	S 10	18 07	18 28	18 52	05 03	05 56	06 51	07 48
07	283 44.2	04.7	93 50.9	9.3	9 51.1	10.7	59.0	20	18 05	18 27	18 52	05 03	06 00	06 58	07 59
T 08	298 44.4	05.7	108 19.2	9.3	10 01.8	10.8	59.0	30	18 02	18 26	18 54	05 04	06 04	07 07	08 12
H 09	313 44.6 ..	06.7	122 47.5	9.1	10 12.6	10.6	59.0	35	18 01	18 26	18 56	05 04	06 07	07 12	08 19
U 10	328 44.8	07.6	137 15.6	9.2	10 23.2	10.6	59.1	40	18 00	18 27	18 59	05 04	06 10	07 18	08 27
R 11	343 45.0	08.6	151 43.8	9.0	10 33.8	10.6	59.1	45	17 58	18 28	19 02	05 04	06 13	07 25	08 37
S 12	358 45.2	N 3 09.6	166 11.8	9.0	S10 44.4	10.5	59.1	S 50	17 57	18 29	19 06	05 04	06 18	07 33	08 49
D 13	13 45.4	10.6	180 39.8	9.0	10 54.9	10.4	59.1	52	17 56	18 29	19 09	05 04	06 20	07 37	08 55
A 14	28 45.6	11.6	195 07.8	8.8	11 05.3	10.4	59.1	54	17 55	18 30	19 11	05 04	06 22	07 41	09 01
Y 15	43 45.7 ..	12.5	209 35.6	8.9	11 15.7	10.3	59.1	56	17 54	18 31	19 14	05 04	06 24	07 46	09 08
16	58 45.9	13.5	224 03.5	8.7	11 26.0	10.3	59.2	58	17 53	18 32	19 18	05 04	06 27	07 51	09 16
17	73 46.1	14.5	238 31.2	8.7	11 36.3	10.2	59.2	S 60	17 52	18 33	19 22	05 04	06 29	07 57	09 25
18	88 46.3	N 3 15.5	252 58.9	8.7	S11 46.5	10.1	59.2								
19	103 46.5	16.4	267 26.6	8.5	11 56.6	10.1	59.2			SUN			MOON		
20	118 46.7	17.4	281 54.1	8.5	12 06.7	10.0	59.2	Day	Eqn. of Time		Mer.	Mer. Pass.		Age	Phase
21	133 46.9 ..	18.4	296 21.6	8.5	12 16.7	9.9	59.2		00ʰ	12ʰ	Pass.	Upper	Lower		
22	148 47.1	19.4	310 49.1	8.4	12 26.6	9.9	59.3	d	m s	m s	h m	h m	h m	d	%
23	163 47.3	20.3	325 16.5	8.3	S12 36.5	9.8	59.3	26	05 45	05 36	12 06	23 40	11 16	15	99
								27	05 27	05 18	12 05	24 31	12 05	16	100
	SD 16.1	d 1.0	SD 15.8		16.0		16.1	28	05 09	05 00	12 05	00 31	12 57	17	98

UT	ARIES GHA	VENUS −4.0 GHA	Dec	MARS +1.2 GHA	Dec	JUPITER −2.1 GHA	Dec	SATURN +0.3 GHA	Dec	STARS Name	SHA	Dec
d h	° ′	° ′	° ′	° ′	° ′	° ′	° ′	° ′	° ′		° ′	° ′
29 00	186 33.7	178 11.9	N 2 09.9	174 26.0	N 4 33.1	116 41.2	N21 44.6	327 47.3	S12 24.0	Acamar	315 18.8	S40 15.4
01	201 36.2	193 11.5	11.1	189 26.7	33.9	131 43.2	44.7	342 49.9	23.9	Achernar	335 27.5	S57 10.3
02	216 38.6	208 11.2	12.4	204 27.4	34.7	146 45.3	44.8	357 52.5	23.9	Acrux	173 08.7	S63 10.5
03	231 41.1	223 10.8	. . 13.6	219 28.1	. . 35.5	161 47.3	. . 44.8	12 55.1	. . 23.8	Adhara	255 12.6	S28 59.8
04	246 43.6	238 10.4	14.9	234 28.8	36.2	176 49.3	44.9	27 57.7	23.8	Aldebaran	290 49.7	N16 32.0
05	261 46.0	253 10.0	16.1	249 29.5	37.0	191 51.4	44.9	43 00.3	23.7			
06	276 48.5	268 09.6	N 2 17.4	264 30.2	N 4 37.8	206 53.4	N21 45.0	58 02.9	S12 23.7	Alioth	166 20.3	N55 53.1
07	291 51.0	283 09.3	18.6	279 30.9	38.5	221 55.5	45.1	73 05.5	23.6	Alkaid	152 58.6	N49 14.7
08	306 53.4	298 08.9	19.9	294 31.6	39.3	236 57.5	45.1	88 08.1	23.6	Al Na'ir	27 44.3	S46 53.6
09	321 55.9	313 08.5	. . 21.2	309 32.3	. . 40.1	251 59.5	. . 45.2	103 10.7	. . 23.5	Alnilam	275 46.6	S 1 11.9
10	336 58.3	328 08.1	22.4	324 33.0	40.8	267 01.6	45.3	118 13.3	23.5	Alphard	217 56.0	S 8 43.3
11	352 00.8	343 07.8	23.7	339 33.7	41.6	282 03.6	45.3	133 15.9	23.4			
12	7 03.3	358 07.4	N 2 24.9	354 34.4	N 4 42.4	297 05.7	N21 45.4	148 18.6	S12 23.4	Alphecca	126 10.9	N26 40.1
13	22 05.7	13 07.0	26.2	9 35.1	43.1	312 07.7	45.4	163 21.2	23.3	Alpheratz	357 44.0	N29 09.8
14	37 08.2	28 06.6	27.4	24 35.8	43.9	327 09.7	45.5	178 23.8	23.3	Altair	62 08.5	N 8 54.2
15	52 10.7	43 06.2	. . 28.7	39 36.5	. . 44.7	342 11.8	. . 45.6	193 26.4	. . 23.2	Ankaa	353 16.3	S42 14.1
16	67 13.1	58 05.9	30.0	54 37.2	45.4	357 13.8	45.6	208 29.0	23.2	Antares	112 26.2	S26 27.6
17	82 15.6	73 05.5	31.2	69 37.9	46.2	12 15.8	45.7	223 31.6	23.1			
18	97 18.1	88 05.1	N 2 32.5	84 38.6	N 4 47.0	27 17.9	N21 45.7	238 34.2	S12 23.1	Arcturus	145 55.6	N19 06.6
19	112 20.5	103 04.7	33.7	99 39.3	47.7	42 19.9	45.8	253 36.8	23.0	Atria	107 28.0	S69 02.7
20	127 23.0	118 04.4	35.0	114 40.0	48.5	57 21.9	45.9	268 39.4	23.0	Avior	234 17.8	S59 33.6
21	142 25.4	133 04.0	. . 36.2	129 40.7	. . 49.3	72 24.0	. . 45.9	283 42.0	. . 22.9	Bellatrix	278 32.3	N 6 21.5
22	157 27.9	148 03.6	37.5	144 41.4	50.0	87 26.0	46.0	298 44.6	22.9	Betelgeuse	271 01.5	N 7 24.3
23	172 30.4	163 03.2	38.7	159 42.1	50.8	102 28.1	46.1	313 47.2	22.8			
30 00	187 32.8	178 02.8	N 2 40.0	174 42.8	N 4 51.6	117 30.1	N21 46.1	328 49.8	S12 22.8	Canopus	263 56.2	S52 42.6
01	202 35.3	193 02.5	41.3	189 43.5	52.3	132 32.1	46.2	343 52.4	22.7	Capella	280 34.8	N46 00.7
02	217 37.8	208 02.1	42.5	204 44.2	53.1	147 34.2	46.2	358 55.0	22.6	Deneb	49 13.8	N45 19.5
03	232 40.2	223 01.7	. . 43.8	219 44.9	. . 53.8	162 36.2	. . 46.3	13 57.6	. . 22.6	Denebola	182 33.5	N14 29.7
04	247 42.7	238 01.3	45.0	234 45.6	54.6	177 38.2	46.4	29 00.2	22.5	Diphda	348 56.4	S17 54.9
05	262 45.2	253 00.9	46.3	249 46.3	55.4	192 40.3	46.4	44 02.9	22.5			
06	277 47.6	268 00.6	N 2 47.5	264 47.0	N 4 56.1	207 42.3	N21 46.5	59 05.5	S12 22.4	Dubhe	193 51.3	N61 40.7
07	292 50.1	283 00.2	48.8	279 47.7	56.9	222 44.3	46.5	74 08.1	22.4	Elnath	278 12.9	N28 37.0
08	307 52.6	297 59.8	50.0	294 48.4	57.7	237 46.4	46.6	89 10.7	22.3	Eltanin	90 46.1	N51 29.0
09	322 55.0	312 59.4	. . 51.3	309 49.1	. . 58.4	252 48.4	. . 46.7	104 13.3	. . 22.3	Enif	33 47.5	N 9 56.1
10	337 57.5	327 59.1	52.5	324 49.8	4 59.2	267 50.4	46.7	119 15.9	22.2	Fomalhaut	15 24.5	S29 33.1
11	352 59.9	342 58.7	53.8	339 50.5	5 00.0	282 52.5	46.8	134 18.5	22.2			
12	8 02.4	357 58.3	N 2 55.1	354 51.2	N 5 00.7	297 54.5	N21 46.9	149 21.1	S12 22.1	Gacrux	172 00.4	S57 11.4
13	23 04.9	12 57.9	56.3	9 51.9	01.5	312 56.5	46.9	164 23.7	22.1	Gienah	175 52.1	S17 37.1
14	38 07.3	27 57.5	57.6	24 52.7	02.3	327 58.6	47.0	179 26.3	22.0	Hadar	148 47.5	S60 26.2
15	53 09.8	42 57.2	2 58.8	39 53.4	. . 03.0	343 00.6	. . 47.0	194 28.9	. . 22.0	Hamal	328 01.2	N23 31.4
16	68 12.3	57 56.8	3 00.1	54 54.1	03.8	358 02.6	47.1	209 31.5	21.9	Kaus Aust.	83 44.0	S34 22.5
17	83 14.7	72 56.4	01.3	69 54.8	04.5	13 04.6	47.2	224 34.1	21.9			
18	98 17.2	87 56.0	N 3 02.6	84 55.5	N 5 05.3	28 06.7	N21 47.2	239 36.8	S12 21.8	Kochab	137 19.1	N74 05.9
19	113 19.7	102 55.6	03.8	99 56.2	06.1	43 08.7	47.3	254 39.4	21.8	Markab	13 38.8	N15 16.5
20	128 22.1	117 55.3	05.1	114 56.9	06.8	58 10.7	47.3	269 42.0	21.7	Menkar	314 15.5	N 4 08.3
21	143 24.6	132 54.9	. . 06.3	129 57.6	. . 07.6	73 12.8	. . 47.4	284 44.6	. . 21.7	Menkent	148 07.4	S36 26.1
22	158 27.1	147 54.5	07.6	144 58.3	08.4	88 14.8	47.5	299 47.2	21.6	Miaplacidus	221 39.1	S69 46.7
23	173 29.5	162 54.1	08.8	159 59.0	09.1	103 16.8	47.5	314 49.8	21.6			
31 00	188 32.0	177 53.7	N 3 10.1	174 59.7	N 5 09.9	118 18.9	N21 47.6	329 52.4	S12 21.5	Mirfak	308 40.9	N49 54.5
01	203 34.4	192 53.4	11.3	190 00.4	10.7	133 20.9	47.7	344 55.0	21.5	Nunki	75 58.5	S26 16.6
02	218 36.9	207 53.0	12.6	205 01.1	11.4	148 22.9	47.7	359 57.6	21.4	Peacock	53 19.7	S56 41.2
03	233 39.4	222 52.6	. . 13.9	220 01.8	. . 12.2	163 24.9	. . 47.8	15 00.2	. . 21.4	Pollux	243 27.8	N27 59.5
04	248 41.8	237 52.2	15.1	235 02.5	12.9	178 27.0	47.8	30 02.8	21.3	Procyon	244 59.8	N 5 11.2
05	263 44.3	252 51.8	16.4	250 03.2	13.7	193 29.0	47.9	45 05.4	21.2			
06	278 46.8	267 51.4	N 3 17.6	265 03.9	N 5 14.5	208 31.0	N21 48.0	60 08.1	S12 21.2	Rasalhague	96 06.5	N12 33.0
07	293 49.2	282 51.1	18.9	280 04.6	15.2	223 33.1	48.0	75 10.7	21.1	Regulus	207 43.4	N11 53.9
08	308 51.7	297 50.7	20.1	295 05.3	16.0	238 35.1	48.1	90 13.3	21.1	Rigel	281 12.3	S 8 11.5
09	323 54.2	312 50.3	. . 21.4	310 06.0	. . 16.8	253 37.1	. . 48.1	105 15.9	. . 21.0	Rigil Kent.	139 51.3	S60 53.3
10	338 56.6	327 49.9	22.6	325 06.7	17.5	268 39.1	48.2	120 18.5	21.0	Sabik	102 12.6	S15 44.4
11	353 59.1	342 49.5	23.9	340 07.4	18.3	283 41.2	48.3	135 21.1	20.9			
12	9 01.5	357 49.2	N 3 25.1	355 08.1	N 5 19.0	298 43.2	N21 48.3	150 23.7	S12 20.9	Schedar	349 41.2	N56 36.6
13	24 04.0	12 48.8	26.4	10 08.8	19.8	313 45.2	48.4	165 26.3	20.8	Shaula	96 22.0	S37 06.6
14	39 06.5	27 48.4	27.6	25 09.5	20.6	328 47.3	48.5	180 28.9	20.8	Sirius	258 33.8	S16 44.4
15	54 08.9	42 48.0	. . 28.9	40 10.2	. . 21.3	343 49.3	. . 48.5	195 31.6	. . 20.7	Spica	158 31.1	S11 14.0
16	69 11.4	57 47.6	30.1	55 10.9	22.1	358 51.3	48.6	210 34.2	20.7	Suhail	222 52.3	S43 29.6
17	84 13.9	72 47.3	31.4	70 11.6	22.8	13 53.3	48.6	225 36.8	20.6			
18	99 16.3	87 46.9	N 3 32.6	85 12.3	N 5 23.6	28 55.4	N21 48.7	240 39.4	S12 20.6	Vega	80 39.0	N38 47.6
19	114 18.8	102 46.5	33.9	100 13.0	24.4	43 57.4	48.8	255 42.0	20.5	Zuben'ubi	137 05.3	S16 05.8
20	129 21.3	117 46.1	35.1	115 13.7	25.1	58 59.4	48.8	270 44.6	20.5		SHA	Mer.Pass.
21	144 23.7	132 45.7	. . 36.4	130 14.4	. . 25.9	74 01.4	. . 48.9	285 47.2	. . 20.4		° ′	h m
22	159 26.2	147 45.3	37.6	145 15.1	26.6	89 03.5	49.0	300 49.8	20.4	Venus	350 30.0	12 08
23	174 28.7	162 45.0	38.9	160 15.8	27.4	104 05.5	49.0	315 52.4	20.3	Mars	347 10.0	12 21
	h m									Jupiter	289 57.2	16 08
Mer.Pass.	11 27.9	v −0.4 d 1.3		v 0.7 d 0.8		v 2.0 d 0.1		v 2.6 d 0.1		Saturn	141 17.0	2 04

SUN and MOON

UT	SUN GHA	SUN Dec	MOON GHA	v	MOON Dec	d	HP
29 00	178 47.4	N 3 21.3	339 43.8	8.3	S12 46.3	9.7	59.3
01	193 47.6	22.3	354 11.1	8.2	12 56.0	9.6	59.3
02	208 47.8	23.3	8 38.3	8.1	13 05.6	9.6	59.3
03	223 48.0	.. 24.2	23 05.4	8.1	13 15.2	9.4	59.3
04	238 48.2	25.2	37 32.5	8.0	13 24.6	9.4	59.3
05	253 48.4	26.2	51 59.5	8.0	13 34.0	9.4	59.4
06	268 48.6	N 3 27.1	66 26.5	7.9	S13 43.4	9.2	59.4
07	283 48.8	28.1	80 53.4	7.8	13 52.6	9.2	59.4
08	298 49.0	29.1	95 20.2	7.8	14 01.8	9.0	59.4
F 09	313 49.2	.. 30.1	109 47.0	7.7	14 10.8	9.0	59.4
R 10	328 49.3	31.0	124 13.7	7.7	14 19.8	8.9	59.4
I 11	343 49.5	32.0	138 40.4	7.6	14 28.7	8.8	59.4
D 12	358 49.7	N 3 33.0	153 07.0	7.5	S14 37.5	8.8	59.4
A 13	13 49.9	34.0	167 33.5	7.5	14 46.3	8.6	59.5
Y 14	28 50.1	34.9	182 00.0	7.5	14 54.9	8.5	59.5
15	43 50.3	.. 35.9	196 26.5	7.3	15 03.4	8.5	59.5
16	58 50.5	36.9	210 52.8	7.3	15 11.9	8.4	59.5
17	73 50.7	37.8	225 19.1	7.3	15 20.3	8.2	59.5
18	88 50.9	N 3 38.8	239 45.4	7.2	S15 28.5	8.2	59.5
19	103 51.0	39.8	254 11.6	7.1	15 36.7	8.1	59.5
20	118 51.2	40.8	268 37.7	7.1	15 44.8	7.9	59.5
21	133 51.4	.. 41.7	283 03.8	7.0	15 52.7	7.9	59.5
22	148 51.6	42.7	297 29.8	7.0	16 00.6	7.8	59.5
23	163 51.8	43.7	311 55.8	6.9	16 08.4	7.6	59.6
30 00	178 52.0	N 3 44.6	326 21.7	6.8	S16 16.0	7.6	59.6
01	193 52.2	45.6	340 47.5	6.8	16 23.6	7.5	59.6
02	208 52.4	46.6	355 13.3	6.8	16 31.1	7.3	59.6
03	223 52.5	.. 47.6	9 39.1	6.7	16 38.4	7.3	59.6
04	238 52.7	48.5	24 04.8	6.6	16 45.7	7.1	59.6
05	253 52.9	49.5	38 30.4	6.6	16 52.8	7.0	59.6
06	268 53.1	N 3 50.5	52 56.0	6.6	S16 59.8	6.9	59.6
07	283 53.3	51.4	67 21.6	6.5	17 06.7	6.8	59.6
S 08	298 53.5	52.4	81 47.1	6.4	17 13.5	6.7	59.6
A 09	313 53.7	.. 53.4	96 12.5	6.4	17 20.2	6.6	59.6
T 10	328 53.9	54.4	110 37.9	6.4	17 26.8	6.5	59.6
U 11	343 54.1	55.3	125 03.3	6.3	17 33.3	6.4	59.6
R 12	358 54.2	N 3 56.3	139 28.6	6.2	S17 39.7	6.1	59.6
D 13	13 54.4	57.3	153 53.8	6.2	17 45.9	6.1	59.6
A 14	28 54.6	58.2	168 19.0	6.2	17 52.0	6.0	59.6
Y 15	43 54.8	3 59.2	182 44.2	6.1	17 58.0	5.9	59.6
16	58 55.0	4 00.2	197 09.3	6.1	18 03.9	5.8	59.6
17	73 55.2	01.1	211 34.4	6.0	18 09.7	5.6	59.7
18	88 55.4	N 4 02.1	225 59.4	6.0	S18 15.3	5.5	59.7
19	103 55.6	03.1	240 24.4	6.0	18 20.8	5.4	59.7
20	118 55.7	04.0	254 49.4	5.9	18 26.2	5.3	59.7
21	133 55.9	.. 05.0	269 14.3	5.9	18 31.5	5.2	59.7
22	148 56.1	06.0	283 39.2	5.8	18 36.7	5.0	59.7
23	163 56.3	06.9	298 04.0	5.8	18 41.7	4.9	59.7
31 00	178 56.5	N 4 07.9	312 28.8	5.8	S18 46.6	4.8	59.7
01	193 56.7	08.9	326 53.6	5.8	18 51.4	4.6	59.7
02	208 56.9	09.9	341 18.4	5.7	18 56.0	4.5	59.7
03	223 57.1	.. 10.8	355 43.1	5.6	19 00.5	4.4	59.7
04	238 57.3	11.8	10 07.7	5.7	19 04.9	4.3	59.7
05	253 57.4	12.8	24 32.4	5.6	19 09.2	4.1	59.7
06	268 57.6	N 4 13.7	38 57.0	5.6	S19 13.3	4.0	59.7
07	283 57.8	14.7	53 21.6	5.6	19 17.3	3.9	59.7
08	298 58.0	15.7	67 46.2	5.5	19 21.2	3.8	59.7
S 09	313 58.2	.. 16.6	82 10.7	5.5	19 25.0	3.6	59.7
U 10	328 58.4	17.6	96 35.2	5.5	19 28.6	3.4	59.7
N 11	343 58.6	18.6	110 59.7	5.5	19 32.0	3.4	59.7
D 12	358 58.7	N 4 19.5	125 24.2	5.4	S19 35.4	3.2	59.7
A 13	13 58.9	20.5	139 48.6	5.4	19 38.6	3.1	59.7
Y 14	28 59.1	21.5	154 13.0	5.4	19 41.7	2.9	59.7
15	43 59.3	.. 22.4	168 37.4	5.4	19 44.6	2.8	59.7
16	58 59.5	23.4	183 01.8	5.4	19 47.4	2.7	59.6
17	73 59.7	24.4	197 26.2	5.4	19 50.1	2.6	59.6
18	88 59.9	N 4 25.3	211 50.6	5.3	S19 52.7	2.4	59.6
19	104 00.1	26.3	226 14.9	5.4	19 55.1	2.2	59.6
20	119 00.2	27.2	240 39.3	5.3	19 57.3	2.2	59.6
21	134 00.4	.. 28.2	255 03.6	5.3	19 59.5	2.0	59.6
22	149 00.6	29.2	269 27.9	5.3	20 01.5	1.8	59.6
23	164 00.8	30.1	283 52.2	5.3	S20 03.3	1.7	59.6
	SD 16.0	d 1.0	SD 16.2		16.2		16.3

Twilight, Sunrise and Moonrise

Lat.	Naut.	Civil	Sunrise	Moonrise 29	30	31	1
N 72	01 59	03 53	05 06	24 39	00 39	▬	▬
N 70	02 35	04 07	05 12	23 50	26 03	02 03	▬
68	03 00	04 19	05 17	23 19	25 07	01 07	02 39
66	03 19	04 28	05 22	22 56	24 34	00 34	01 56
64	03 34	04 36	05 25	22 38	24 09	00 09	01 27
62	03 46	04 43	05 28	22 24	23 50	25 06	01 06
60	03 56	04 49	05 31	22 11	23 35	24 48	00 48
N 58	04 05	04 54	05 33	22 01	23 21	24 33	00 33
56	04 12	04 58	05 36	21 52	23 10	24 21	00 21
54	04 18	05 02	05 38	21 43	23 00	24 09	00 09
52	04 24	05 05	05 39	21 36	22 51	24 00	00 00
50	04 29	05 08	05 41	21 30	22 43	23 51	24 50
45	04 39	05 15	05 44	21 16	22 26	23 33	24 32
N 40	04 48	05 20	05 47	21 04	22 12	23 18	24 17
35	04 54	05 24	05 50	20 54	22 01	23 05	24 04
30	05 00	05 28	05 52	20 46	21 51	22 54	23 53
20	05 07	05 33	05 55	20 31	21 33	22 35	23 34
N 10	05 13	05 37	05 58	20 18	21 18	22 18	23 18
0	05 16	05 40	06 01	20 06	21 04	22 03	23 02
S 10	05 18	05 43	06 04	19 55	20 50	21 48	22 47
20	05 19	05 44	06 07	19 42	20 35	21 31	22 30
30	05 18	05 46	06 09	19 28	20 18	21 13	22 12
35	05 17	05 46	06 11	19 20	20 08	21 02	22 01
40	05 15	05 46	06 13	19 10	19 57	20 49	21 48
45	05 12	05 46	06 15	18 59	19 43	20 34	21 33
S 50	05 08	05 45	06 18	18 46	19 27	20 17	21 15
52	05 06	05 45	06 19	18 40	19 20	20 08	21 06
54	05 04	05 45	06 20	18 33	19 11	19 59	20 57
56	05 01	05 44	06 21	18 26	19 02	19 48	20 46
58	04 58	05 44	06 23	18 17	18 51	19 36	20 33
S 60	04 54	05 43	06 25	18 08	18 39	19 22	20 19

Sunset, Twilight and Moonset

Lat.	Sunset	Civil	Naut.	Moonset 29	30	31	1
N 72	19 06	20 20	22 19	04 18	03 47	▬	▬
N 70	18 59	20 05	21 39	04 43	04 37	04 25	▬
68	18 54	19 53	21 13	05 03	05 09	05 21	05 54
66	18 49	19 43	20 53	05 19	05 32	05 55	06 37
64	18 45	19 35	20 38	05 32	05 51	06 20	07 05
62	18 42	19 28	20 26	05 43	06 06	06 39	07 27
60	18 39	19 22	20 15	05 53	06 19	06 56	07 45
N 58	18 37	19 17	20 06	06 01	06 30	07 09	08 00
56	18 34	19 12	19 59	06 08	06 40	07 21	08 13
54	18 32	19 08	19 52	06 15	06 49	07 31	08 24
52	18 31	19 05	19 46	06 21	06 56	07 40	08 33
50	18 29	19 02	19 41	06 26	07 03	07 48	08 42
45	18 25	18 55	19 30	06 38	07 18	08 06	09 01
N 40	18 22	18 50	19 22	06 47	07 31	08 20	09 16
35	18 20	18 45	19 15	06 56	07 41	08 32	09 29
30	18 18	18 42	19 10	07 03	07 51	08 43	09 40
20	18 14	18 36	19 02	07 16	08 06	09 01	09 59
N 10	18 11	18 32	18 56	07 27	08 20	09 17	10 16
0	18 08	18 28	18 52	07 37	08 33	09 32	10 31
S 10	18 05	18 26	18 50	07 48	08 47	09 47	10 47
20	18 02	18 24	18 50	07 59	09 01	10 03	11 03
30	17 59	18 23	18 50	08 12	09 17	10 21	11 22
35	17 57	18 22	18 52	08 19	09 26	10 32	11 33
40	17 55	18 22	18 54	08 27	09 37	10 46	11 46
45	17 53	18 22	18 56	08 37	09 49	10 58	12 01
S 50	17 50	18 22	19 00	08 49	10 05	11 16	12 19
52	17 49	18 23	19 02	08 55	10 12	11 24	12 28
54	17 48	18 23	19 04	09 01	10 20	11 33	12 38
56	17 46	18 23	19 06	09 08	10 29	11 44	12 49
58	17 45	18 24	19 09	09 16	10 39	11 56	13 01
S 60	17 43	18 24	19 13	09 25	10 51	12 09	13 16

SUN and MOON

Day	SUN Eqn. of Time 00h	12h	Mer. Pass.	MOON Mer. Pass. Upper	Lower	Age	Phase
29	04 51	04 42	12 05	01 24	13 52	18	94
30	04 32	04 23	12 04	02 20	14 49	19	88
31	04 14	04 05	12 04	03 18	15 47	20	79

UT	ARIES GHA	VENUS −4.0 GHA	Dec	MARS +1.2 GHA	Dec	JUPITER −2.1 GHA	Dec	SATURN +0.2 GHA	Dec	STARS Name	SHA	Dec
1 00	189 31.1	177 44.6	N 3 40.1	175 16.5	N 5 28.2	119 07.5	N21 49.1	330 55.0	S12 20.3	Acamar	315 18.8	S40 15.3
01	204 33.6	192 44.2	41.4	190 17.2	28.9	134 09.5	49.1	345 57.7	20.2	Achernar	335 27.5	S57 10.3
02	219 36.0	207 43.8	42.6	205 17.9	29.7	149 11.6	49.2	1 00.3	20.1	Acrux	173 08.7	S63 10.5
03	234 38.5	222 43.4 ..	43.9	220 18.6 ..	30.4	164 13.6 ..	49.3	16 02.9 ..	20.1	Adhara	255 12.6	S28 59.8
04	249 41.0	237 43.0	45.1	235 19.3	31.2	179 15.6	49.3	31 05.5	20.0	Aldebaran	290 49.7	N16 32.0
05	264 43.4	252 42.7	46.4	250 20.0	32.0	194 17.6	49.4	46 08.1	20.0			
06	279 45.9	267 42.3	N 3 47.6	265 20.7	N 5 32.7	209 19.7	N21 49.4	61 10.7	S12 19.9	Alioth	166 20.3	N55 53.1
M 07	294 48.4	282 41.9	48.9	280 21.4	33.5	224 21.7	49.5	76 13.3	19.9	Alkaid	152 58.6	N49 14.7
O 08	309 50.8	297 41.5	50.1	295 22.1	34.2	239 23.7	49.6	91 15.9	19.8	Al Na'ir	27 44.3	S46 53.6
N 09	324 53.3	312 41.1 ..	51.4	310 22.8 ..	35.0	254 25.7 ..	49.6	106 18.6 ..	19.8	Alnilam	275 46.6	S 1 11.9
D 10	339 55.8	327 40.7	52.6	325 23.5	35.8	269 27.7	49.7	121 21.2	19.7	Alphard	217 56.0	S 8 43.3
A 11	354 58.2	342 40.4	53.9	340 24.2	36.5	284 29.8	49.8	136 23.8	19.7			
Y 12	10 00.7	357 40.0	N 3 55.1	355 24.9	N 5 37.3	299 31.8	N21 49.8	151 26.4	S12 19.6	Alphecca	126 10.9	N26 40.1
13	25 03.2	12 39.6	56.4	10 25.6	38.0	314 33.8	49.9	166 29.0	19.6	Alpheratz	357 44.0	N29 09.7
14	40 05.6	27 39.2	57.6	25 26.3	38.8	329 35.8	49.9	181 31.6	19.5	Altair	62 08.4	N 8 54.2
15	55 08.1	42 38.8	3 58.9	40 27.0 ..	39.6	344 37.9 ..	50.0	196 34.2 ..	19.5	Ankaa	353 16.3	S42 14.0
16	70 10.5	57 38.4	4 00.1	55 27.7	40.3	359 39.9	50.1	211 36.8	19.4	Antares	112 26.2	S26 27.6
17	85 13.0	72 38.1	01.4	70 28.4	41.1	14 41.9	50.1	226 39.5	19.4			
18	100 15.5	87 37.7	N 4 02.6	85 29.1	N 5 41.8	29 43.9	N21 50.2	241 42.1	S12 19.3	Arcturus	145 55.5	N19 06.7
19	115 17.9	102 37.3	03.9	100 29.8	42.6	44 45.9	50.2	256 44.7	19.2	Atria	107 27.9	S69 02.7
20	130 20.4	117 36.9	05.1	115 30.5	43.3	59 48.0	50.3	271 47.3	19.2	Avior	234 17.8	S59 33.6
21	145 22.9	132 36.5 ..	06.4	130 31.2 ..	44.1	74 50.0 ..	50.4	286 49.9 ..	19.1	Bellatrix	278 32.3	N 6 21.5
22	160 25.3	147 36.1	07.6	145 31.9	44.9	89 52.0	50.4	301 52.5	19.1	Betelgeuse	271 01.5	N 7 24.3
23	175 27.8	162 35.8	08.8	160 32.6	45.6	104 54.0	50.5	316 55.1	19.0			
2 00	190 30.3	177 35.4	N 4 10.1	175 33.3	N 5 46.4	119 56.0	N21 50.6	331 57.8	S12 19.0	Canopus	263 56.3	S52 42.6
01	205 32.7	192 35.0	11.3	190 34.0	47.1	134 58.1	50.6	347 00.4	18.9	Capella	280 34.8	N46 00.6
02	220 35.2	207 34.6	12.6	205 34.7	47.9	150 00.1	50.7	2 03.0	18.9	Deneb	49 31.8	N45 19.5
03	235 37.7	222 34.2 ..	13.8	220 35.4 ..	48.6	165 02.1 ..	50.7	17 05.6 ..	18.8	Denebola	182 33.5	N14 29.7
04	250 40.1	237 33.8	15.1	235 36.1	49.4	180 04.1	50.8	32 08.2	18.8	Diphda	348 56.4	S17 54.9
05	265 42.6	252 33.4	16.3	250 36.8	50.2	195 06.1	50.9	47 10.8	18.7			
06	280 45.0	267 33.1	N 4 17.6	265 37.5	N 5 50.9	210 08.2	N21 50.9	62 13.4	S12 18.7	Dubhe	193 51.3	N61 40.7
T 07	295 47.5	282 32.7	18.8	280 38.2	51.7	225 10.2	51.0	77 16.1	18.6	Elnath	278 12.9	N28 37.0
U 08	310 50.0	297 32.3	20.1	295 38.9	52.4	240 12.2	51.1	92 18.7	18.6	Eltanin	90 46.1	N51 29.0
E 09	325 52.4	312 31.9 ..	21.3	310 39.6 ..	53.2	255 14.2 ..	51.1	107 21.3 ..	18.5	Enif	33 47.5	N 9 56.1
S 10	340 54.9	327 31.5	22.6	325 40.3	53.9	270 16.2	51.2	122 23.9	18.4	Fomalhaut	15 24.5	S29 33.0
D 11	355 57.4	342 31.1	23.8	340 41.0	54.7	285 18.3	51.2	137 26.5	18.4			
A 12	10 59.8	357 30.7	N 4 25.0	355 41.7	N 5 55.4	300 20.3	N21 51.3	152 29.1	S12 18.3	Gacrux	172 00.4	S57 11.4
Y 13	26 02.3	12 30.4	26.3	10 42.4	56.2	315 22.3	51.4	167 31.7	18.3	Gienah	175 52.1	S17 37.1
14	41 04.8	27 30.0	27.5	25 43.1	57.0	330 24.3	51.4	182 34.4	18.2	Hadar	148 47.4	S60 26.2
15	56 07.2	42 29.6 ..	28.8	40 43.8 ..	57.7	345 26.3 ..	51.5	197 37.0 ..	18.2	Hamal	328 01.2	N23 31.4
16	71 09.7	57 29.2	30.0	55 44.5	58.5	0 28.3	51.5	212 39.6	18.1	Kaus Aust.	83 43.9	S34 22.5
17	86 12.1	72 28.8	31.3	70 45.2	5 59.2	15 30.3	51.6	227 42.2	18.1			
18	101 14.6	87 28.4	N 4 32.5	85 45.9	N 6 00.0	30 32.4	N21 51.7	242 44.8	S12 18.0	Kochab	137 19.1	N74 05.9
19	116 17.1	102 28.0	33.8	100 46.6	00.7	45 34.4	51.7	257 47.4	18.0	Markab	13 38.7	N15 16.5
20	131 19.5	117 27.6	35.0	115 47.3	01.5	60 36.4	51.8	272 50.1	17.9	Menkar	314 15.5	N 4 08.3
21	146 22.0	132 27.3 ..	36.2	130 48.0 ..	02.2	75 38.4 ..	51.9	287 52.7 ..	17.9	Menkent	148 07.3	S36 26.1
22	161 24.5	147 26.9	37.5	145 48.7	03.0	90 40.4	51.9	302 55.3	17.8	Miaplacidus	221 39.1	S69 46.7
23	176 26.9	162 26.5	38.7	160 49.4	03.8	105 42.4	52.0	317 57.9	17.7			
3 00	191 29.4	177 26.1	N 4 40.0	175 50.1	N 6 04.5	120 44.4	N21 52.0	333 00.5	S12 17.7	Mirfak	308 40.9	N49 54.5
01	206 31.9	192 25.7	41.2	190 50.8	05.3	135 46.5	52.1	348 03.1	17.6	Nunki	75 58.5	S26 16.6
02	221 34.3	207 25.3	42.5	205 51.5	06.0	150 48.5	52.2	3 05.8	17.6	Peacock	53 19.7	S56 41.2
03	236 36.8	222 24.9 ..	43.7	220 52.2 ..	06.8	165 50.5 ..	52.2	18 08.4 ..	17.5	Pollux	243 27.8	N27 59.5
04	251 39.3	237 24.5	44.9	235 52.9	07.5	180 52.5	52.3	33 11.0	17.5	Procyon	244 59.8	N 5 11.2
05	266 41.7	252 24.2	46.2	250 53.6	08.3	195 54.5	52.4	48 13.6	17.4			
06	281 44.2	267 23.8	N 4 47.4	265 54.3	N 6 09.0	210 56.5	N21 52.4	63 16.2	S12 17.4	Rasalhague	96 06.5	N12 33.0
W 07	296 46.6	282 23.4	48.7	280 55.0	09.8	225 58.5	52.5	78 18.8	17.3	Regulus	207 43.4	N11 53.9
E 08	311 49.1	297 23.0	49.9	295 55.7	10.5	241 00.6	52.5	93 21.5	17.3	Rigel	281 12.3	S 8 11.5
D 09	326 51.6	312 22.6 ..	51.2	310 56.4 ..	11.3	256 02.6 ..	52.6	108 24.1 ..	17.2	Rigil Kent.	139 51.3	S60 53.3
N 10	341 54.0	327 22.2	52.4	325 57.1	12.0	271 04.6	52.7	123 26.7	17.2	Sabik	102 12.5	S15 44.4
E 11	356 56.5	342 21.8	53.6	340 57.8	12.8	286 06.6	52.7	138 29.3	17.1			
S 12	11 59.0	357 21.4	N 4 54.9	355 58.5	N 6 13.5	301 08.6	N21 52.8	153 31.9	S12 17.0	Schedar	349 41.2	N56 36.6
D 13	27 01.4	12 21.0	56.1	10 59.2	14.3	316 10.6	52.8	168 34.5	17.0	Shaula	96 22.0	S37 06.6
A 14	42 03.9	27 20.6	57.4	25 59.9	15.1	331 12.6	52.9	183 37.2	16.9	Sirius	258 33.9	S16 44.4
Y 15	57 06.4	42 20.3 ..	58.6	41 00.6 ..	15.8	346 14.6 ..	53.0	198 39.8 ..	16.9	Spica	158 31.1	S11 14.0
16	72 08.8	57 19.9	4 59.8	56 01.3	16.6	1 16.7	53.0	213 42.4	16.8	Suhail	222 52.3	S43 29.6
17	87 11.3	72 19.5	5 01.1	71 02.0	17.3	16 18.7	53.1	228 45.0	16.8			
18	102 13.8	87 19.1	N 5 02.3	86 02.7	N 6 18.1	31 20.7	N21 53.2	243 47.6	S12 16.7	Vega	80 39.0	N38 47.6
19	117 16.2	102 18.7	03.6	101 03.4	18.8	46 22.7	53.2	258 50.3	16.7	Zuben'ubi	137 05.3	S16 05.9
20	132 18.7	117 18.3	04.8	116 04.1	19.6	61 24.7	53.3	273 52.9	16.6		SHA	Mer.Pass.
21	147 21.1	132 17.9 ..	06.0	131 04.8 ..	20.3	76 26.7 ..	53.3	288 55.5 ..	16.6		° ′	h m
22	162 23.6	147 17.5	07.3	146 05.5	21.1	91 28.7	53.4	303 58.1	16.5	Venus	347 05.1	12 10
23	177 26.1	162 17.1	08.5	161 06.2	21.8	106 30.7	53.5	319 00.7	16.4	Mars	345 03.0	12 17
	h m									Jupiter	289 25.8	15 58
Mer.Pass. 11 16.1	v −0.4 d 1.2	v 0.7	d 0.8	v 2.0	d 0.1	v 2.6	d 0.1			Saturn	141 27.5	1 52

SUN / MOON

UT	SUN GHA	Dec	MOON GHA	v	Dec	d	HP
d h	° '	° '	° '	'	° '	'	'
1 00	179 01.0	N 4 31.1	298 16.5	5.3	S20 05.0	1.6	59.6
01	194 01.2	32.1	312 40.8	5.3	20 06.6	1.5	59.6
02	209 01.4	33.0	327 05.1	5.3	20 08.1	1.3	59.6
03	224 01.6	34.0	341 29.4	5.3	20 09.4	1.1	59.6
04	239 01.7	35.0	355 53.7	5.3	20 10.5	1.1	59.6
05	254 01.9	35.9	10 18.0	5.3	20 11.6	0.9	59.6
06	269 02.1	N 4 36.9	24 42.3	5.3	S20 12.5	0.7	59.6
07	284 02.3	37.9	39 06.6	5.3	20 13.2	0.7	59.6
08	299 02.5	38.8	53 30.9	5.3	20 13.9	0.4	59.6
M 09	314 02.7	39.8	67 55.2	5.4	20 14.3	0.4	59.6
O 10	329 02.9	40.8	82 19.6	5.3	20 14.7	0.2	59.6
N 11	344 03.0	41.7	96 43.9	5.3	20 14.9	0.1	59.6
D 12	359 03.2	N 4 42.7	111 08.2	5.4	S20 15.0	0.1	59.5
A 13	14 03.4	43.6	125 32.6	5.3	20 14.9	0.2	59.5
Y 14	29 03.6	44.6	139 56.9	5.4	20 14.7	0.3	59.5
15	44 03.8	45.6	154 21.3	5.4	20 14.4	0.5	59.5
16	59 04.0	46.5	168 45.7	5.4	20 13.9	0.6	59.5
17	74 04.2	47.5	183 10.1	5.4	20 13.3	0.8	59.5
18	89 04.3	N 4 48.5	197 34.5	5.5	S20 12.5	0.9	59.5
19	104 04.5	49.4	211 59.0	5.4	20 11.6	1.0	59.5
20	119 04.7	50.4	226 23.5	5.4	20 10.6	1.1	59.5
21	134 04.9	51.3	240 47.9	5.5	20 09.5	1.3	59.5
22	149 05.1	52.3	255 12.4	5.6	20 08.2	1.5	59.5
23	164 05.3	53.3	269 37.0	5.5	20 06.7	1.5	59.5
2 00	179 05.5	N 4 54.2	284 01.5	5.6	S20 05.2	1.7	59.4
01	194 05.6	55.2	298 26.1	5.6	20 03.5	1.9	59.4
02	209 05.8	56.1	312 50.7	5.7	20 01.6	1.9	59.4
03	224 06.0	57.1	327 15.4	5.7	19 59.7	2.1	59.4
04	239 06.2	58.1	341 40.1	5.7	19 57.6	2.2	59.4
05	254 06.4	4 59.0	356 04.8	5.7	19 55.4	2.4	59.4
06	269 06.6	N 5 00.0	10 29.5	5.8	S19 53.0	2.5	59.4
07	284 06.7	01.0	24 54.3	5.8	19 50.5	2.6	59.4
08	299 06.9	01.9	39 19.1	5.8	19 47.9	2.8	59.4
T 09	314 07.1	02.9	53 43.9	5.9	19 45.1	2.9	59.4
U 10	329 07.3	03.8	68 08.8	5.9	19 42.2	3.0	59.3
E 11	344 07.5	04.8	82 33.7	6.0	19 39.2	3.1	59.3
S 12	359 07.7	N 5 05.8	96 58.7	5.9	S19 36.1	3.3	59.3
D 13	14 07.9	06.7	111 23.6	6.1	19 32.8	3.4	59.3
A 14	29 08.0	07.7	125 48.7	6.1	19 29.4	3.5	59.3
Y 15	44 08.2	08.6	140 13.8	6.1	19 25.9	3.7	59.3
16	59 08.4	09.6	154 38.9	6.1	19 22.2	3.7	59.3
17	74 08.6	10.5	169 04.0	6.3	19 18.5	3.9	59.3
18	89 08.8	N 5 11.5	183 29.3	6.2	S19 14.6	4.1	59.2
19	104 09.0	12.5	197 54.5	6.3	19 10.5	4.1	59.2
20	119 09.1	13.4	212 19.8	6.4	19 06.4	4.3	59.2
21	134 09.3	14.4	226 45.2	6.4	19 02.1	4.4	59.2
22	149 09.5	15.3	241 10.6	6.4	18 57.7	4.5	59.2
23	164 09.7	16.3	255 36.0	6.5	18 53.2	4.6	59.2
3 00	179 09.9	N 5 17.0	270 01.5	6.5	S18 40.6	4.0	59.2
01	194 10.1	18.2	284 27.0	6.6	18 43.8	4.8	59.2
02	209 10.2	19.2	298 52.6	6.7	18 39.0	5.0	59.1
03	224 10.4	20.1	313 18.3	6.7	18 34.0	5.1	59.1
04	239 10.6	21.1	327 44.0	6.7	18 28.9	5.2	59.1
05	254 10.8	22.0	342 09.7	6.9	18 23.7	5.4	59.1
06	269 11.0	N 5 23.0	356 35.6	6.8	S18 18.3	5.4	59.1
W 07	284 11.2	24.0	11 01.4	6.9	18 12.9	5.5	59.1
E 08	299 11.3	24.9	25 27.3	7.0	18 07.3	5.6	59.1
D 09	314 11.5	25.9	39 53.3	7.0	18 01.7	5.8	59.0
N 10	329 11.7	26.8	54 19.3	7.1	17 55.9	5.9	59.0
E 11	344 11.9	27.8	68 45.4	7.2	17 50.0	6.0	59.0
S 12	359 12.1	N 5 28.7	83 11.6	7.2	S17 44.0	6.1	59.0
D 13	14 12.3	29.7	97 37.8	7.2	17 37.9	6.3	59.0
A 14	29 12.4	30.6	112 04.0	7.4	17 31.6	6.3	59.0
Y 15	44 12.6	31.6	126 30.4	7.3	17 25.3	6.4	59.0
16	59 12.8	32.6	140 56.7	7.5	17 18.9	6.5	59.0
17	74 13.0	33.5	155 23.2	7.5	17 12.4	6.7	58.9
18	89 13.2	N 5 34.5	169 49.7	7.5	S17 05.7	6.7	58.9
19	104 13.3	35.4	184 16.2	7.6	16 59.0	6.9	58.9
20	119 13.5	36.4	198 42.8	7.7	16 52.1	6.9	58.9
21	134 13.7	37.3	213 09.5	7.8	16 45.2	7.0	58.9
22	149 13.9	38.3	227 36.3	7.8	16 38.2	7.2	58.9
23	164 14.1	39.2	242 03.1	7.8	S16 31.0	7.2	58.9
	SD 16.0	d 1.0	SD 16.2		16.2		16.1

Twilight / Sunrise / Moonrise

Lat.	Twilight Naut.	Twilight Civil	Sunrise	Moonrise 1	2	3	4
°	h m	h m	h m	h m	h m	h m	h m
N 72	01 23	03 34	04 50	■■■■	■■■■	■■■■	05 10
N 70	02 12	03 51	04 58	■■■■	■■■■	04 40	04 31
68	02 42	04 05	05 05	02 39	03 33	03 55	04 04
66	03 03	04 16	05 10	01 56	02 53	03 25	03 44
64	03 20	04 25	05 15	01 27	02 25	03 03	03 27
62	03 34	04 32	05 19	01 06	02 04	02 45	03 13
60	03 45	04 39	05 22	00 48	01 46	02 30	03 01
N 58	03 55	04 45	05 25	00 33	01 32	02 17	02 51
56	04 03	04 50	05 28	00 21	01 19	02 06	02 42
54	04 10	04 54	05 30	00 09	01 09	01 56	02 34
52	04 17	04 58	05 32	00 00	00 59	01 48	02 27
50	04 22	05 02	05 34	24 50	00 50	01 40	02 21
45	04 34	05 09	05 39	24 32	00 32	01 23	02 07
N 40	04 43	05 15	05 42	24 17	00 17	01 09	01 55
35	04 50	05 20	05 45	24 04	00 04	00 58	01 46
30	04 56	05 24	05 48	23 53	24 48	00 48	01 37
20	05 05	05 31	05 53	23 34	24 30	00 30	01 22
N 10	05 11	05 36	05 57	23 18	24 15	00 15	01 09
0	05 15	05 39	06 00	23 02	24 01	00 01	00 57
S 10	05 18	05 43	06 04	22 47	23 46	24 44	00 44
20	05 20	05 45	06 07	22 30	23 31	24 31	00 31
30	05 20	05 47	06 11	22 12	23 13	24 16	00 16
35	05 19	05 48	06 14	22 01	23 03	24 08	00 08
40	05 18	05 49	06 16	21 48	22 51	23 58	25 05
45	05 16	05 50	06 19	21 33	22 38	23 46	24 56
S 50	05 13	05 50	06 22	21 15	22 21	23 32	24 45
52	05 11	05 50	06 24	21 06	22 13	23 25	24 40
54	05 09	05 50	06 26	20 57	22 04	23 17	24 34
56	05 07	05 50	06 27	20 46	21 54	23 09	24 28
58	05 05	05 50	06 29	20 33	21 42	23 00	24 21
S 60	05 02	05 50	06 32	20 19	21 29	22 49	24 13

Sunset / Twilight / Moonset

Lat.	Sunset	Twilight Civil	Twilight Naut.	Moonset 1	2	3	4
°	h m	h m	h m	h m	h m	h m	h m
N 72	19 20	20 37	22 58	■■■■	■■■■	■■■■	09 24
N 70	19 12	20 19	22 02	■■■■	■■■■	07 58	10 02
68	19 05	20 05	21 30	05 54	07 04	08 42	10 28
66	18 59	19 54	21 07	06 37	07 43	09 11	10 48
64	18 54	19 44	20 50	07 05	08 11	09 33	11 04
62	18 50	19 37	20 36	07 27	08 32	09 51	11 17
60	18 47	19 30	20 24	07 45	08 49	10 05	11 28
N 58	18 43	19 24	20 14	08 00	09 03	10 17	11 37
56	18 40	19 19	20 06	08 13	09 16	10 28	11 46
54	18 38	19 14	19 58	08 24	09 27	10 38	11 53
52	18 36	19 10	19 52	08 33	09 36	10 46	12 00
50	18 34	19 07	19 46	08 42	09 45	10 53	12 06
45	18 29	18 59	19 34	09 01	10 03	11 09	12 19
N 40	18 25	18 53	19 25	09 16	10 17	11 22	12 29
35	18 22	18 48	19 18	09 29	10 30	11 34	12 38
30	18 19	18 43	19 12	09 40	10 41	11 43	12 46
20	18 15	18 37	19 03	09 59	10 59	12 00	13 00
N 10	18 11	18 32	18 56	10 16	11 15	12 14	13 12
0	18 07	18 28	18 52	10 31	11 30	12 28	13 23
S 10	18 03	18 24	18 49	10 47	11 45	12 41	13 33
20	17 59	18 21	18 47	11 03	12 01	12 55	13 45
30	17 55	18 19	18 47	11 22	12 19	13 11	13 58
35	17 53	18 18	18 47	11 33	12 30	13 21	14 06
40	17 50	18 17	18 49	11 46	12 42	13 31	14 14
45	17 47	18 17	18 51	12 01	12 57	13 44	14 24
S 50	17 44	18 16	18 53	12 19	13 14	13 59	14 36
52	17 43	18 16	18 55	12 28	13 22	14 06	14 42
54	17 40	18 16	18 57	12 38	13 31	14 14	14 48
56	17 39	18 16	18 59	12 49	13 41	14 23	14 55
58	17 36	18 15	19 01	13 01	13 53	14 33	15 03
S 60	17 34	18 15	19 04	13 16	14 07	14 44	15 11

SUN / MOON

Day	SUN Eqn. of Time 00ʰ	SUN Eqn. of Time 12ʰ	SUN Mer. Pass.	MOON Mer. Pass. Upper	MOON Mer. Pass. Lower	Age	Phase
d	m s	m s	h m	h m	h m	d	%
1	03 56	03 47	12 04	04 17	16 47	21	69
2	03 39	03 30	12 03	05 16	17 45	22	58
3	03 21	03 12	12 03	06 14	18 42	23	47

UT	ARIES GHA	VENUS −4.0 GHA	Dec	MARS +1.2 GHA	Dec	JUPITER −2.1 GHA	Dec	SATURN +0.2 GHA	Dec	STARS Name	SHA	Dec
4 00	192 28.5	177 16.7	N 5 09.8	176 06.9	N 6 22.6	121 32.7	N21 53.5	334 03.3	S12 16.4	Acamar	315 18.8	S40 15.3
01	207 31.0	192 16.4	11.0	191 07.6	23.3	136 34.8	53.6	349 06.0	16.3	Achernar	335 27.5	S57 10.3
02	222 33.5	207 16.0	12.2	206 08.3	24.1	151 36.8	53.7	4 08.6	16.3	Acrux	173 08.7	S63 10.5
03	237 35.9	222 15.6	.. 13.5	221 09.0	.. 24.8	166 38.8	.. 53.7	19 11.2	.. 16.2	Adhara	255 12.6	S28 59.8
04	252 38.4	237 15.2	14.7	236 09.7	25.6	181 40.8	53.8	34 13.8	16.2	Aldebaran	290 49.7	N16 32.0
05	267 40.9	252 14.8	15.9	251 10.4	26.3	196 42.8	53.8	49 16.4	16.1			
06	282 43.3	267 14.4	N 5 17.2	266 11.1	N 6 27.1	211 44.8	N21 53.9	64 19.1	S12 16.1	Alioth	166 20.3	N55 53.2
07	297 45.8	282 14.0	18.4	281 11.8	27.8	226 46.8	54.0	79 21.7	16.0	Alkaid	152 58.5	N49 14.7
T 08	312 48.3	297 13.6	19.7	296 12.5	28.6	241 48.8	54.0	94 24.3	16.0	Al Na'ir	27 44.2	S46 53.6
H 09	327 50.7	312 13.2	.. 20.9	311 13.2	.. 29.3	256 50.8	.. 54.1	109 26.9	.. 15.9	Alnilam	275 46.6	S 1 11.9
U 10	342 53.2	327 12.8	22.1	326 13.9	30.1	271 52.8	54.1	124 29.5	15.8	Alphard	217 56.0	S 8 43.3
R 11	357 55.6	342 12.4	23.4	341 14.6	30.8	286 54.8	54.2	139 32.2	15.8			
S 12	12 58.1	357 12.0	N 5 24.6	356 15.3	N 6 31.6	301 56.8	N21 54.3	154 34.8	S12 15.7	Alphecca	126 10.8	N26 40.1
D 13	28 00.6	12 11.6	25.8	11 16.0	32.3	316 58.9	54.3	169 37.4	15.7	Alpheratz	357 44.0	N29 09.7
A 14	43 03.0	27 11.2	27.1	26 16.7	33.1	332 00.9	54.4	184 40.0	15.6	Altair	62 08.4	N 8 54.2
Y 15	58 05.5	42 10.9	.. 28.3	41 17.4	.. 33.8	347 02.9	.. 54.5	199 42.6	.. 15.6	Ankaa	353 16.3	S42 14.0
16	73 08.0	57 10.5	29.6	56 18.1	34.6	2 04.9	54.5	214 45.3	15.5	Antares	112 26.2	S26 27.6
17	88 10.4	72 10.1	30.8	71 18.8	35.3	17 06.9	54.6	229 47.9	15.5			
18	103 12.9	87 09.7	N 5 32.0	86 19.5	N 6 36.1	32 08.9	N21 54.6	244 50.5	S12 15.4	Arcturus	145 55.5	N19 06.7
19	118 15.4	102 09.3	33.3	101 20.2	36.8	47 10.9	54.7	259 53.1	15.4	Atria	107 27.8	S69 02.8
20	133 17.8	117 08.9	34.5	116 20.9	37.6	62 12.9	54.8	274 55.7	15.3	Avior	234 17.8	S59 33.6
21	148 20.3	132 08.5	.. 35.7	131 21.6	.. 38.3	77 14.9	.. 54.8	289 58.4	.. 15.2	Bellatrix	278 32.3	N 6 21.5
22	163 22.7	147 08.1	37.0	146 22.3	39.1	92 16.9	54.9	305 01.0	15.2	Betelgeuse	271 01.5	N 7 24.3
23	178 25.2	162 07.7	38.2	161 23.0	39.8	107 18.9	55.0	320 03.6	15.1			
5 00	193 27.7	177 07.3	N 5 39.4	176 23.7	N 6 40.6	122 20.9	N21 55.0	335 06.2	S12 15.1	Canopus	263 56.3	S52 42.6
01	208 30.1	192 06.9	40.7	191 24.4	41.3	137 22.9	55.1	350 08.8	15.0	Capella	280 34.8	N46 00.6
02	223 32.6	207 06.5	41.9	206 25.1	42.0	152 24.9	55.1	5 11.5	15.0	Deneb	49 31.7	N45 19.5
03	238 35.1	222 06.1	.. 43.1	221 25.8	.. 42.8	167 26.9	.. 55.2	20 14.1	.. 14.9	Denebola	182 33.5	N14 29.7
04	253 37.5	237 05.7	44.4	236 26.5	43.5	182 28.9	55.3	35 16.7	14.9	Diphda	348 56.4	S17 54.9
05	268 40.0	252 05.3	45.6	251 27.2	44.3	197 30.9	55.3	50 19.3	14.8			
06	283 42.5	267 04.9	N 5 46.8	266 27.9	N 6 45.0	212 33.0	N21 55.4	65 22.0	S12 14.7	Dubhe	193 51.3	N61 40.7
07	298 44.9	282 04.5	48.1	281 28.6	45.8	227 35.0	55.4	80 24.6	14.7	Elnath	278 12.9	N28 37.0
08	313 47.4	297 04.1	49.3	296 29.3	46.5	242 37.0	55.5	95 27.2	14.6	Eltanin	90 46.0	N51 29.0
F 09	328 49.9	312 03.7	.. 50.5	311 30.0	.. 47.3	257 39.0	.. 55.6	110 29.8	.. 14.6	Enif	33 47.4	N 9 56.1
R 10	343 52.3	327 03.3	51.8	326 30.7	48.0	272 41.0	55.6	125 32.4	14.5	Fomalhaut	15 24.4	S29 33.0
I 11	358 54.8	342 02.9	53.0	341 31.4	48.8	287 43.0	55.7	140 35.1	14.5			
D 12	13 57.2	357 02.6	N 5 54.2	356 32.1	N 6 49.5	302 45.0	N21 55.8	155 37.7	S12 14.4	Gacrux	172 00.4	S57 11.4
A 13	28 59.7	12 02.2	55.5	11 32.8	50.3	317 47.0	55.8	170 40.3	14.4	Gienah	175 52.1	S17 37.2
Y 14	44 02.2	27 01.8	56.7	26 33.5	51.0	332 49.0	55.9	185 42.9	14.3	Hadar	148 47.4	S60 26.2
15	59 04.6	42 01.4	.. 57.9	41 34.2	.. 51.8	347 51.0	.. 55.9	200 45.6	.. 14.2	Hamal	328 01.2	N23 31.4
16	74 07.1	57 01.0	5 59.1	56 34.9	52.5	2 53.0	56.0	215 48.2	14.2	Kaus Aust.	83 43.9	S34 22.5
17	89 09.6	72 00.6	6 00.4	71 35.6	53.2	17 55.0	56.1	230 50.8	14.1			
18	104 12.0	87 00.2	N 6 01.6	86 36.3	N 6 54.0	32 57.0	N21 56.1	245 53.4	S12 14.1	Kochab	137 19.0	N74 05.9
19	119 14.5	101 59.8	02.8	101 37.0	54.7	47 59.0	56.2	260 56.0	14.0	Markab	13 38.7	N15 16.5
20	134 17.0	116 59.4	04.1	116 37.7	55.5	63 01.0	56.3	275 58.7	14.0	Menkar	314 15.5	N 4 08.3
21	149 19.4	131 59.0	.. 05.3	131 38.4	.. 56.2	78 03.0	.. 56.3	291 01.3	.. 13.9	Menkent	148 07.3	S36 26.2
22	164 21.9	146 58.6	06.5	146 39.1	57.0	93 05.0	56.4	306 03.9	13.9	Miaplacidus	221 39.2	S69 46.7
23	179 24.3	161 58.2	07.8	161 39.7	57.7	108 07.0	56.4	321 06.5	13.8			
6 00	194 26.8	176 57.8	N 6 09.0	176 40.4	N 6 58.5	123 09.0	N21 56.5	336 09.2	S12 13.7	Mirfak	308 40.9	N49 54.5
01	209 29.3	191 57.4	10.2	191 41.1	59.2	138 11.0	56.6	351 11.8	13.7	Nunki	75 58.5	S26 16.6
02	224 31.7	206 57.0	11.4	206 41.8	6 59.9	153 13.0	56.6	6 14.4	13.6	Peacock	53 19.7	S56 41.2
03	239 34.2	221 56.6	.. 12.7	221 42.5	7 00.7	168 15.0	.. 56.7	21 17.0	.. 13.6	Pollux	243 27.8	N27 59.5
04	254 36.7	236 56.2	13.9	236 43.2	01.4	183 17.0	56.7	36 19.7	13.5	Procyon	244 59.8	N 5 11.2
05	269 39.1	251 55.8	15.1	251 43.9	02.2	198 19.0	56.8	51 22.3	13.5			
06	284 41.6	266 55.4	N 6 16.3	266 44.6	N 7 02.9	213 21.0	N21 56.9	66 24.9	S12 13.4	Rasalhague	96 06.4	N12 33.0
07	299 44.1	281 55.0	17.6	281 45.3	03.7	228 23.0	56.9	81 27.5	13.4	Regulus	207 43.4	N11 53.9
S 08	314 46.5	296 54.6	18.8	296 46.0	04.4	243 25.0	57.0	96 30.1	13.3	Rigel	281 12.3	S 8 11.5
A 09	329 49.0	311 54.2	.. 20.0	311 46.7	.. 05.1	258 27.0	.. 57.1	111 32.8	.. 13.2	Rigil Kent.	139 51.3	S60 53.3
T 10	344 51.5	326 53.8	21.3	326 47.4	05.9	273 29.0	57.1	126 35.4	13.2	Sabik	102 12.5	S15 44.4
U 11	359 53.9	341 53.4	22.5	341 48.1	06.6	288 31.0	57.2	141 38.0	13.1			
R 12	14 56.4	356 53.0	N 6 23.7	356 48.8	N 7 07.4	303 33.0	N21 57.2	156 40.6	S12 13.1	Schedar	349 41.2	N56 36.6
D 13	29 58.8	11 52.6	24.9	11 49.5	08.1	318 35.0	57.3	171 43.3	13.0	Shaula	96 21.9	S37 06.6
A 14	45 01.3	26 52.2	26.2	26 50.2	08.9	333 37.0	57.4	186 45.9	13.0	Sirius	258 33.9	S16 44.4
Y 15	60 03.8	41 51.8	.. 27.4	41 50.9	.. 09.6	348 39.0	.. 57.4	201 48.5	.. 12.9	Spica	158 31.1	S11 14.0
16	75 06.2	56 51.4	28.6	56 51.6	10.3	3 41.0	57.5	216 51.1	12.9	Suhail	222 52.3	S43 29.6
17	90 08.7	71 51.0	29.8	71 52.3	11.1	18 43.0	57.6	231 53.8	12.8			
18	105 11.2	86 50.6	N 6 31.1	86 53.0	N 7 11.8	33 45.0	N21 57.6	246 56.4	S12 12.7	Vega	80 39.0	N38 47.6
19	120 13.6	101 50.1	32.3	101 53.7	12.6	48 47.0	57.7	261 59.0	12.7	Zuben'ubi	137 05.3	S16 05.9
20	135 16.1	116 49.7	33.5	116 54.4	13.3	63 49.0	57.7	277 01.6	12.6			
21	150 18.6	131 49.3	.. 34.7	131 55.1	.. 14.1	78 51.0	.. 57.8	292 04.3	.. 12.6		SHA	Mer. Pass.
22	165 21.0	146 48.9	36.0	146 55.8	14.8	93 53.0	57.9	307 06.9	12.5	Venus	343 39.6	12 12
23	180 23.5	161 48.5	37.2	161 56.5	15.5	108 54.9	57.9	322 09.5	12.5	Mars	342 56.0	12 14
										Jupiter	288 53.2	15 48
Mer. Pass. 11 04.3		v −0.4	d 1.2	v 0.7	d 0.7	v 2.0	d 0.1	v 2.6	d 0.1	Saturn	141 38.6	1 39

UT	SUN GHA	SUN Dec	MOON GHA	MOON ʋ	MOON Dec	MOON d	MOON HP	Lat.	Twilight Naut.	Twilight Civil	Sunrise	Moonrise 4	Moonrise 5	Moonrise 6	Moonrise 7
d h	° '	° '	° '	'	° '	'	'	°	h m	h m	h m	h m	h m	h m	h m
4 00	179 14.3	N 5 40.2	256 29.9	7.9	S16 23.8	7.4	58.8	N 72	////	03 15	04 34	05 10	04 47	04 32	04 21
01	194 14.4	41.1	270 56.8	8.0	16 16.4	7.4	58.8	N 70	01 44	03 35	04 44	04 31	04 25	04 20	04 15
02	209 14.6	42.1	285 23.8	8.1	16 09.0	7.5	58.8	68	02 22	03 50	04 52	04 04	04 08	04 10	04 11
03	224 14.8 ..	43.1	299 50.9	8.1	16 01.5	7.6	58.8	66	02 47	04 03	04 58	03 44	03 55	04 02	04 07
04	239 15.0	44.0	314 18.0	8.2	15 53.9	7.7	58.8	64	03 06	04 13	05 04	03 27	03 43	03 55	04 04
05	254 15.2	45.0	328 45.2	8.2	15 46.2	7.8	58.8	62	03 22	04 22	05 09	03 13	03 33	03 49	04 01
06	269 15.3	N 5 45.9	343 12.4	8.3	S15 38.4	7.9	58.7	60	03 34	04 29	05 13	03 01	03 25	03 43	03 59
07	284 15.5	46.9	357 39.7	8.4	15 30.5	8.0	58.7	N 58	03 45	04 36	05 17	02 51	03 17	03 38	03 57
T 08	299 15.7	47.8	12 07.1	8.4	15 22.5	8.0	58.7	56	03 54	04 41	05 20	02 42	03 11	03 34	03 55
H 09	314 15.9 ..	48.8	26 34.5	8.5	15 14.5	8.2	58.7	54	04 02	04 46	05 23	02 34	03 05	03 30	03 53
U 10	329 16.1	49.7	41 02.0	8.5	15 06.3	8.2	58.7	52	04 09	04 51	05 26	02 27	03 00	03 27	03 51
R 11	344 16.2	50.7	55 29.5	8.6	14 58.1	8.3	58.7	50	04 15	04 55	05 28	02 21	02 55	03 24	03 50
S 12	359 16.4	N 5 51.6	69 57.1	8.7	S14 49.8	8.4	58.7	N 40	04 38	05 16	05 38	01 55	02 35	03 11	03 44
D 13	14 16.6	52.6	84 24.8	8.7	14 41.4	8.5	58.6	35	04 46	05 16	05 41	01 46	02 28	03 06	03 42
A 14	29 16.8	53.5	98 52.5	8.8	14 32.9	8.6	58.6	30	04 52	05 20	05 45	01 37	02 21	03 02	03 40
Y 15	44 17.0 ..	54.5	113 20.3	8.9	14 24.3	8.6	58.6	20	05 02	05 28	05 50	01 22	02 10	02 54	03 36
16	59 17.2	55.4	127 48.2	8.9	14 15.7	8.8	58.6	N 10	05 09	05 34	05 55	01 09	02 00	02 48	03 33
17	74 17.3	56.4	142 16.1	9.0	14 06.9	8.8	58.6	0	05 14	05 39	05 59	00 57	01 50	02 41	03 30
18	89 17.5	N 5 57.3	156 44.1	9.0	S13 58.1	8.8	58.6	S 10	05 18	05 43	06 04	00 44	01 41	02 35	03 27
19	104 17.7	58.3	171 12.1	9.1	13 49.3	9.0	58.5	20	05 20	05 46	06 08	00 31	01 31	02 28	03 24
20	119 17.9	5 59.2	185 40.2	9.2	13 40.3	9.0	58.5	30	05 21	05 49	06 13	00 16	01 19	02 20	03 21
21	134 18.1	6 00.2	200 08.4	9.2	13 31.3	9.1	58.5	35	05 21	05 51	06 16	00 08	01 12	02 16	03 19
22	149 18.2	01.1	214 36.6	9.3	13 22.2	9.2	58.5	40	05 21	05 52	06 19	25 05	01 05	02 11	03 16
23	164 18.4	02.1	229 04.9	9.4	13 13.0	9.2	58.5	45	05 19	05 53	06 23	24 56	00 56	02 05	03 14
5 00	179 18.6	N 6 03.0	243 33.3	9.4	S13 03.8	9.3	58.5	S 50	05 17	05 55	06 27	24 45	00 45	01 58	03 10
01	194 18.8	04.0	258 01.7	9.4	12 54.5	9.4	58.4	52	05 16	05 55	06 29	24 40	00 40	01 55	03 09
02	209 19.0	04.9	272 30.1	9.6	12 45.1	9.4	58.4	54	05 15	05 56	06 31	24 34	00 34	01 51	03 07
03	224 19.1 ..	05.9	286 58.7	9.6	12 35.7	9.6	58.4	56	05 13	05 56	06 33	24 28	00 28	01 47	03 06
04	239 19.3	06.8	301 27.3	9.6	12 26.1	9.5	58.4	58	05 11	05 57	06 36	24 21	00 21	01 43	03 04
05	254 19.5	07.8	315 55.9	9.7	12 16.6	9.7	58.4	S 60	05 09	05 57	06 39	24 13	00 13	01 38	03 01

UT	SUN GHA	SUN Dec	MOON GHA	MOON ʋ	MOON Dec	MOON d	MOON HP	Lat.	Sunset	Twilight Civil	Twilight Naut.	Moonset 4	Moonset 5	Moonset 6	Moonset 7
d h	° '	° '	° '	'	° '	'	'	°	h m	h m	h m	h m	h m	h m	h m
06	269 19.7	N 6 08.7	330 24.6	9.8	S12 06.9	9.7	58.4	N 72	19 34	20 55	////	09 24	11 38	13 37	15 30
07	284 19.8	09.7	344 53.4	9.8	11 57.2	9.7	58.3	N 70	19 24	20 34	22 30	10 02	11 58	13 47	15 33
08	299 20.0	10.6	359 22.2	9.9	11 47.5	9.9	58.3	68	19 16	20 18	21 49	10 28	12 13	13 56	15 35
F 09	314 20.2 ..	11.6	13 51.1	9.9	11 37.6	9.8	58.3	66	19 09	20 05	21 22	10 48	12 26	14 02	15 37
R 10	329 20.4	12.5	28 20.0	10.0	11 27.8	10.0	58.3	64	19 03	19 54	21 02	11 04	12 36	14 08	15 38
I 11	344 20.6	13.5	42 49.0	10.1	11 17.8	10.0	58.3	62	18 58	19 45	20 46	11 17	12 45	14 13	15 39
D 12	359 20.7	N 6 14.4	57 18.1	10.1	S11 07.8	10.1	58.2	60	18 54	19 38	20 33	11 28	12 53	14 17	15 41
A 13	14 20.9	15.4	71 47.2	10.1	10 57.8	10.1	58.2	N 58	18 50	19 31	20 23	11 37	12 59	14 21	15 42
Y 14	29 21.1	16.3	86 16.3	10.3	10 47.7	10.2	58.2	56	18 47	19 25	20 13	11 46	13 05	14 24	15 42
15	44 21.3 ..	17.3	100 45.6	10.2	10 37.5	10.2	58.2	54	18 44	19 20	20 05	11 53	13 11	14 27	15 43
16	59 21.5	18.2	115 14.8	10.4	10 27.3	10.3	58.2	52	18 41	19 16	19 58	12 00	13 15	14 30	15 44
17	74 21.6	19.1	129 44.2	10.3	10 17.0	10.3	58.2	50	18 38	19 11	19 52	12 06	13 20	14 33	15 45
18	89 21.8	N 6 20.1	144 13.5	10.5	S10 06.7	10.4	58.1	45	18 33	19 03	19 39	12 19	13 29	14 38	15 46
19	104 22.0	21.0	158 43.0	10.5	9 56.3	10.4	58.1	N 40	18 28	18 56	19 29	12 29	13 36	14 42	15 47
20	119 22.2	22.0	173 12.5	10.5	9 45.9	10.5	58.1	35	18 25	18 50	19 20	12 38	13 43	14 46	15 48
21	134 22.3 ..	22.9	187 42.0	10.6	9 35.4	10.5	58.1	30	18 21	18 45	19 14	12 46	13 49	14 49	15 49
22	149 22.5	23.9	202 11.6	10.6	9 24.9	10.5	58.1	20	18 15	18 38	19 04	13 00	13 58	14 55	15 51
23	164 22.7	24.8	216 41.2	10.7	9 14.4	10.6	58.1	N 10	18 10	18 32	18 56	13 12	14 07	15 00	15 52
6 00	179 22.9	N 6 25.8	231 10.9	10.8	S 9 03.8	10.6	58.0	0	18 06	18 27	18 51	13 23	14 15	15 05	15 53
01	194 23.1	26.7	245 40.7	10.8	8 53.2	10.7	58.0	S 10	18 01	18 23	18 47	13 33	14 23	15 09	15 54
02	209 23.2	27.7	260 10.5	10.8	8 42.5	10.7	58.0	20	17 57	18 19	18 45	13 45	14 31	15 14	15 55
03	224 23.4 ..	28.6	274 40.3	10.9	8 31.8	10.8	58.0	30	17 52	18 16	18 43	13 58	14 41	15 20	15 57
04	239 23.6	29.5	289 10.2	11.0	8 21.0	10.8	57.9	35	17 49	18 14	18 43	14 06	14 46	15 23	15 58
05	254 23.8	30.5	303 40.2	10.9	8 10.2	10.8	57.9	40	17 46	18 13	18 44	14 14	14 52	15 26	15 58
06	269 23.9	N 6 31.4	318 10.1	11.1	S 7 59.4	10.9	57.9	45	17 42	18 11	18 45	14 24	14 59	15 31	15 59
S 07	284 24.1	32.4	332 40.2	11.1	7 48.5	10.9	57.9	S 50	17 37	18 10	18 47	14 36	15 08	15 35	16 01
A 08	299 24.3	33.3	347 10.3	11.1	7 37.6	11.0	57.9	52	17 35	18 09	18 48	14 42	15 12	15 38	16 01
T 09	314 24.5 ..	34.3	1 40.4	11.2	7 26.6	10.9	57.9	54	17 33	18 09	18 49	14 48	15 16	15 40	16 02
U 10	329 24.6	35.2	16 10.6	11.2	7 15.7	11.0	57.8	56	17 31	18 08	18 51	14 55	15 21	15 43	16 02
R 11	344 24.8	36.2	30 40.8	11.2	7 04.7	11.1	57.8	58	17 28	18 07	18 53	15 03	15 26	15 46	16 03
D 12	359 25.0	N 6 37.1	45 11.0	11.3	S 6 53.6	11.0	57.8	S 60	17 25	18 07	18 55	15 11	15 32	15 49	16 04
A 13	14 25.2	38.0	59 41.3	11.4	6 42.6	11.1	57.8								
Y 14	29 25.4	39.0	74 11.7	11.4	6 31.5	11.1	57.8								
15	44 25.5 ..	39.9	88 42.1	11.4	6 20.4	11.2	57.8								
16	59 25.7	40.9	103 12.5	11.5	6 09.2	11.2	57.7								
17	74 25.9	41.8	117 43.0	11.5	5 58.0	11.1	57.7								
18	89 26.1	N 6 42.7	132 13.5	11.5	S 5 46.9	11.3	57.7								
19	104 26.2	43.7	146 44.0	11.6	5 35.6	11.2	57.7								
20	119 26.4	44.6	161 14.6	11.7	5 24.4	11.3	57.7								
21	134 26.6 ..	45.6	175 45.3	11.6	5 13.1	11.2	57.6								
22	149 26.8	46.5	190 15.9	11.7	5 01.9	11.3	57.6								
23	164 26.9	47.5	204 46.6	11.8	S 4 50.6	11.4	57.6								

	SUN				MOON			
Day	Eqn. of Time 00ʰ	Eqn. of Time 12ʰ	Mer. Pass.	Mer. Pass. Upper	Mer. Pass. Lower	Age	Phase	
d	m s	m s	h m	h m	h m	d	%	
4	03 03	02 55	12 03	07 10	19 36	24	36	
5	02 46	02 37	12 03	08 03	20 28	25	25	
6	02 29	02 20	12 02	08 53	21 18	26	16	

SUN SD	SUN d	MOON SD (4)	MOON SD (5)	MOON SD (6)
16.0	0.9	16.0	15.9	15.8

UT	ARIES	VENUS −3.9		MARS +1.2		JUPITER −2.1		SATURN +0.2		STARS		
d h	GHA	GHA	Dec	GHA	Dec	GHA	Dec	GHA	Dec	Name	SHA	Dec
7 00	195 26.0	176 48.1	N 6 38.4	176 57.2	N 7 16.3	123 56.9	N21 58.0	337 12.1	S12 12.4	Acamar	315 18.8	S40 15.3
01	210 28.4	191 47.7	39.6	191 57.9	17.0	138 58.9	58.0	352 14.8	12.3	Achernar	335 27.5	S57 10.2
02	225 30.9	206 47.3	40.8	206 58.6	17.8	154 00.9	58.1	7 17.4	12.3	Acrux	173 08.7	S63 10.5
03	240 33.3	221 46.9 ..	42.1	221 59.3 ..	18.5	169 02.9 ..	58.2	22 20.0 ..	12.2	Adhara	255 12.7	S28 59.8
04	255 35.8	236 46.5	43.3	237 00.0	19.2	184 04.9	58.2	37 22.6	12.2	Aldebaran	290 49.7	N16 32.0
05	270 38.3	251 46.1	44.5	252 00.7	20.0	199 06.9	58.3	52 25.3	12.1			
06	285 40.7	266 45.7	N 6 45.7	267 01.4	N 7 20.7	214 08.9	N21 58.4	67 27.9	S12 12.1	Alioth	166 20.3	N55 53.2
07	300 43.2	281 45.3	47.0	282 02.1	21.5	229 10.9	58.4	82 30.5	12.0	Alkaid	152 58.5	N49 14.7
08	315 45.7	296 44.9	48.2	297 02.8	22.2	244 12.9	58.5	97 33.2	12.0	Al Na'ir	27 44.2	S46 53.6
S 09	330 48.1	311 44.5 ..	49.4	312 03.5 ..	22.9	259 14.9 ..	58.5	112 35.8 ..	11.9	Alnilam	275 46.6	S 1 11.9
U 10	345 50.6	326 44.1	50.6	327 04.2	23.7	274 16.9	58.6	127 38.4	11.8	Alphard	217 56.0	S 8 43.3
N 11	0 53.1	341 43.7	51.8	342 04.9	24.4	289 18.9	58.7	142 41.0	11.8			
D 12	15 55.5	356 43.3	N 6 53.1	357 05.6	N 7 25.2	304 20.9	N21 58.7	157 43.7	S12 11.7	Alphecca	126 10.8	N26 40.1
A 13	30 58.0	11 42.9	54.3	12 06.3	25.9	319 22.9	58.8	172 46.3	11.7	Alpheratz	357 44.0	N29 09.7
Y 14	46 00.4	26 42.5	55.5	27 07.0	26.6	334 24.9	58.8	187 48.9	11.6	Altair	62 08.4	N 8 54.2
15	61 02.9	41 42.0 ..	56.7	42 07.7 ..	27.4	349 26.9 ..	58.9	202 51.5 ..	11.6	Ankaa	353 16.3	S42 14.0
16	76 05.4	56 41.6	57.9	57 08.4	28.1	4 28.9	59.0	217 54.2	11.5	Antares	112 26.2	S26 27.6
17	91 07.8	71 41.2	6 59.1	72 09.1	28.8	19 30.8	59.0	232 56.8	11.4			
18	106 10.3	86 40.8	N 7 00.4	87 09.8	N 7 29.6	34 32.8	N21 59.1	247 59.4	S12 11.4	Arcturus	145 55.5	N19 06.7
19	121 12.8	101 40.4	01.6	102 10.5	30.3	49 34.8	59.2	263 02.0	11.3	Atria	107 27.8	S69 02.8
20	136 15.2	116 40.0	02.8	117 11.2	31.1	64 36.8	59.2	278 04.7	11.3	Avior	234 17.9	S59 33.6
21	151 17.7	131 39.6 ..	04.0	132 11.8 ..	31.8	79 38.8 ..	59.3	293 07.3 ..	11.2	Bellatrix	278 32.3	N 6 21.5
22	166 20.2	146 39.2	05.2	147 12.5	32.5	94 40.8	59.3	308 09.9	11.2	Betelgeuse	271 01.6	N 7 24.3
23	181 22.6	161 38.8	06.5	162 13.2	33.3	109 42.8	59.4	323 12.6	11.1			
8 00	196 25.1	176 38.4	N 7 07.7	177 13.9	N 7 34.0	124 44.8	N21 59.5	338 15.2	S12 11.0	Canopus	263 56.3	S52 42.6
01	211 27.6	191 38.0	08.9	192 14.6	34.7	139 46.8	59.5	353 17.8	11.0	Capella	280 34.9	N46 00.6
02	226 30.0	206 37.6	10.1	207 15.3	35.5	154 48.8	59.6	8 20.4	10.9	Deneb	49 31.7	N45 19.5
03	241 32.5	221 37.1 ..	11.3	222 16.0 ..	36.2	169 50.8 ..	59.7	23 23.1 ..	10.9	Denebola	182 33.5	N14 29.7
04	256 34.9	236 36.7	12.5	237 16.7	37.0	184 52.8	59.7	38 25.7	10.8	Diphda	348 56.3	S17 54.9
05	271 37.4	251 36.3	13.7	252 17.4	37.7	199 54.7	59.8	53 28.3	10.8			
06	286 39.9	266 35.9	N 7 15.0	267 18.1	N 7 38.4	214 56.7	N21 59.9	68 30.9	S12 10.7	Dubhe	193 51.3	N61 40.7
07	301 42.3	281 35.5	16.2	282 18.8	39.2	229 58.7	21 59.9	83 33.6	10.7	Elnath	278 12.9	N28 37.0
08	316 44.8	296 35.1	17.4	297 19.5	39.9	245 00.7	22 00.0	98 36.2	10.6	Eltanin	90 46.0	N51 29.0
M 09	331 47.3	311 34.7 ..	18.6	312 20.2 ..	40.6	260 02.7 ..	00.0	113 38.8 ..	10.5	Enif	33 47.4	N 9 56.1
O 10	346 49.7	326 34.3	19.8	327 20.9	41.4	275 04.7	00.1	128 41.5	10.5	Fomalhaut	15 24.4	S29 33.0
N 11	1 52.2	341 33.9	21.0	342 21.6	42.1	290 06.7	00.1	143 44.1	10.4			
D 12	16 54.7	356 33.4	N 7 22.2	357 22.3	N 7 42.8	305 08.7	N22 00.2	158 46.7	S12 10.4	Gacrux	172 00.4	S57 11.4
A 13	31 57.1	11 33.0	23.5	12 23.0	43.6	320 10.7	00.3	173 49.3	10.3	Gienah	175 52.1	S17 37.2
Y 14	46 59.6	26 32.6	24.7	27 23.7	44.3	335 12.6	00.3	188 52.0	10.3	Hadar	148 47.4	S60 26.2
15	62 02.0	41 32.2 ..	25.9	42 24.4 ..	45.1	350 14.6 ..	00.4	203 54.6 ..	10.2	Hamal	328 01.2	N23 31.4
16	77 04.5	56 31.8	27.1	57 25.1	45.8	5 16.6	00.5	218 57.2	10.1	Kaus Aust.	83 43.9	S34 22.5
17	92 07.0	71 31.4	28.3	72 25.8	46.5	20 18.6	00.5	233 59.9	10.1			
18	107 09.4	86 31.0	N 7 29.5	87 26.5	N 7 47.3	35 20.6	N22 00.6	249 02.5	S12 10.0	Kochab	137 19.0	N74 05.9
19	122 11.9	101 30.6	30.7	102 27.2	48.0	50 22.6	00.6	264 05.1	10.0	Markab	13 38.7	N15 16.5
20	137 14.4	116 30.1	31.9	117 27.9	48.7	65 24.6	00.7	279 07.7	09.9	Menkar	314 15.5	N 4 08.3
21	152 16.8	131 29.7 ..	33.2	132 28.6 ..	49.5	80 26.6 ..	00.8	294 10.4 ..	09.9	Menkent	148 07.3	S36 26.2
22	167 19.3	146 29.3	34.4	147 29.3	50.2	95 28.6	00.8	309 13.0	09.8	Miaplacidus	221 39.2	S69 46.7
23	182 21.8	161 28.9	35.6	162 30.0	50.9	110 30.5	00.9	324 15.6	09.7			
9 00	197 24.2	176 28.5	N 7 36.8	177 30.7	N 7 51.7	125 32.5	N22 00.9	339 18.3	S12 09.7	Mirfak	308 40.9	N49 54.5
01	212 26.7	191 28.1	38.0	192 31.4	52.4	140 34.5	01.0	354 20.9	09.6	Nunki	75 58.4	S26 16.6
02	227 29.2	206 27.7	39.2	207 32.1	53.1	155 36.5	01.1	9 23.5	09.6	Peacock	53 19.6	S56 41.2
03	242 31.6	221 27.2 ..	40.4	222 32.7 ..	53.9	170 38.5 ..	01.1	24 26.1 ..	09.5	Pollux	243 27.9	N27 59.5
04	257 34.1	236 26.8	41.6	237 33.4	54.6	185 40.5	01.2	39 28.8	09.5	Procyon	244 59.8	N 5 11.2
05	272 36.5	251 26.4	42.8	252 34.1	55.3	200 42.5	01.3	54 31.4	09.4			
06	287 39.0	266 26.0	N 7 44.0	267 34.8	N 7 56.1	215 44.4	N22 01.3	69 34.0	S12 09.3	Rasalhague	96 06.4	N12 33.0
07	302 41.5	281 25.6	45.2	282 35.5	56.8	230 46.4	01.4	84 36.7	09.3	Regulus	207 43.4	N11 53.9
08	317 43.9	296 25.2	46.4	297 36.2	57.5	245 48.4	01.4	99 39.3	09.2	Rigel	281 12.3	S 8 11.5
T 09	332 46.4	311 24.8 ..	47.7	312 36.9 ..	58.3	260 50.4 ..	01.5	114 41.9 ..	09.2	Rigil Kent.	139 51.2	S60 53.3
U 10	347 48.9	326 24.3	48.9	327 37.6	59.0	275 52.4	01.6	129 44.6	09.1	Sabik	102 12.5	S15 44.4
E 11	2 51.3	341 23.9	50.1	342 38.3	7 59.7	290 54.4	01.6	144 47.2	09.1			
S 12	17 53.8	356 23.5	N 7 51.3	357 39.0	N 8 00.5	305 56.4	N22 01.7	159 49.8	S12 09.0	Schedar	349 41.2	N56 36.5
D 13	32 56.3	11 23.1	52.5	12 39.7	01.2	320 58.3	01.7	174 52.4	08.9	Shaula	96 21.9	S37 06.6
A 14	47 58.7	26 22.7	53.7	27 40.4	01.9	336 00.3	01.8	189 55.1	08.9	Sirius	258 33.9	S16 44.4
Y 15	63 01.2	41 22.2 ..	54.9	42 41.1 ..	02.6	351 02.3 ..	01.9	204 57.7 ..	08.8	Spica	158 31.1	S11 14.0
16	78 03.6	56 21.8	56.1	57 41.8	03.4	6 04.3	01.9	220 00.3	08.8	Suhail	222 52.3	S43 29.6
17	93 06.1	71 21.4	57.3	72 42.5	04.1	21 06.3	02.0	235 03.0	08.7			
18	108 08.6	86 21.0	N 7 58.5	87 43.2	N 8 04.8	36 08.3	N22 02.1	250 05.6	S12 08.6	Vega	80 39.0	N38 47.6
19	123 11.0	101 20.6	7 59.7	102 43.9	05.6	51 10.2	02.1	265 08.2	08.6	Zuben'ubi	137 05.3	S16 05.9
20	138 13.5	116 20.2	8 00.9	117 44.6	06.3	66 12.2	02.2	280 10.9	08.5		SHA	Mer.Pass.
21	153 16.0	131 19.7 ..	02.1	132 45.3 ..	07.0	81 14.2 ..	02.2	295 13.5 ..	08.5	Venus	340 13.3	12 14
22	168 18.4	146 19.3	03.3	147 46.0	07.8	96 16.2	02.3	310 16.1	08.4	Mars	340 48.9	12 11
23	183 20.9	161 18.9	04.5	162 46.7	08.5	111 18.2	02.4	325 18.8	08.4	Jupiter	288 19.7	15 39
Mer. Pass. 10 52.5		v −0.4	d 1.2	v 0.7	d 0.7	v 2.0	d 0.1	v 2.6	d 0.1	Saturn	141 50.1	1 27

UT	SUN GHA	SUN Dec	MOON GHA	MOON v	MOON Dec	MOON d	MOON HP
d h	° '	° '	° '	'	° '	'	'
7 00	179 27.1	N 6 48.4	219 17.4 11.7	S 4 39.2	11.3	57.6
01	194 27.3	49.3	233 48.1 11.9	4 27.9 11.3	57.6
02	209 27.5	50.3	248 19.0 11.8	4 16.6 11.4	57.5
03	224 27.6 ..	51.2	262 49.8 11.9	4 05.2 11.4	57.5
04	239 27.8	52.2	277 20.7 11.9	3 53.8 11.4	57.5
05	254 28.0	53.1	291 51.6 11.9	3 42.4 11.4	57.5
06	269 28.2	N 6 54.0	306 22.5 12.0	S 3 31.0 11.4	57.4
07	284 28.3	55.0	320 53.5 12.0	3 19.6 11.4	57.4
08	299 28.5	55.9	335 24.5 12.1	3 08.2 11.4	57.4
S 09	314 28.7 ..	56.9	349 55.6 12.0	2 56.8 11.5	57.4
U 10	329 28.9	57.8	4 26.6 12.1	2 45.3 11.4	57.4
N 11	344 29.0	58.7	18 57.7 12.1	2 33.9 11.5	57.4
D 12	359 29.2	N 6 59.7	33 28.8 12.2	S 2 22.4 11.4	57.3
A 13	14 29.4	7 00.6	48 00.0 12.2	2 11.0 11.5	57.3
Y 14	29 29.5	01.5	62 31.2 12.2	1 59.5 11.5	57.3
15	44 29.7 ..	02.5	77 02.4 12.2	1 48.0 11.4	57.3
16	59 29.9	03.4	91 33.6 12.3	1 36.6 11.5	57.3
17	74 30.1	04.4	106 04.9 12.3	1 25.1 11.4	57.2
18	89 30.2	N 7 05.3	120 36.2 12.3	S 1 13.7 11.5	57.2
19	104 30.4	06.2	135 07.5 12.3	1 02.2 11.5	57.2
20	119 30.6	07.2	149 38.8 12.4	0 50.7 11.4	57.2
21	134 30.8 ..	08.1	164 10.2 12.3	0 39.3 11.5	57.2
22	149 30.9	09.0	178 41.5 12.4	0 27.8 11.4	57.1
23	164 31.1	10.0	193 12.9 12.4	0 16.4 11.5	57.1
8 00	179 31.3	N 7 10.9	207 44.3 12.5	S 0 04.9 11.4	57.1
01	194 31.5	11.8	222 15.8 12.4	N 0 06.5 11.4	57.1
02	209 31.6	12.8	236 47.2 12.5	0 17.9 11.4	57.1
03	224 31.8 ..	13.7	251 18.7 12.5	0 29.3 11.4	57.0
04	239 32.0	14.6	265 50.2 12.5	0 40.7 11.4	57.0
05	254 32.1	15.6	280 21.7 12.6	0 52.1 11.4	57.0
06	269 32.3	N 7 16.5	294 53.3 12.5	N 1 03.5 11.4	57.0
07	284 32.5	17.5	309 24.8 12.6	1 14.9 11.4	57.0
08	299 32.7	18.4	323 56.4 12.5	1 26.3 11.3	56.9
M 09	314 32.8 ..	19.3	338 27.9 12.6	1 37.6 11.3	56.9
O 10	329 33.0	20.3	352 59.5 12.6	1 48.9 11.3	56.9
N 11	344 33.2	21.2	7 31.1 12.6	2 00.2 11.3	56.9
D 12	359 33.3	N 7 22.1	22 02.7 12.7	N 2 11.5 11.3	56.9
A 13	14 33.5	23.1	36 34.4 12.6	2 22.8 11.3	56.8
Y 14	29 33.7	24.0	51 06.0 12.7	2 34.1 11.2	56.8
15	44 33.9 ..	24.9	65 37.7 12.6	2 45.3 11.2	56.8
16	59 34.0	25.8	80 09.3 12.7	2 56.5 11.2	56.8
17	74 34.2	26.8	94 41.0 12.7	3 07.7 11.2	56.8
18	89 34.4	N 7 27.7	109 12.7 12.7	N 3 18.9 11.1	56.7
19	104 34.5	28.6	123 44.4 12.7	3 30.0 11.1	56.7
20	119 34.7	29.6	138 16.1 12.7	3 41.1 11.1	56.7
21	134 34.9 ..	30.5	152 47.8 12.7	3 52.2 11.1	56.7
22	149 35.1	31.4	167 19.5 12.8	4 03.3 11.0	56.7
23	164 35.2	32.4	181 51.3 12.7	4 14.3 11.1	56.6
9 00	179 35.4	N 7 33.3	196 23.0 12.7	N 4 25.4 10.9	56.6
01	194 35.6	34.2	210 54.7 12.8	4 36.3 11.0	56.6
02	209 35.7	35.2	225 26.5 12.7	4 47.3 10.9	56.6
03	224 35.9 ..	36.1	239 58.2 12.8	4 58.2 10.9	56.5
04	239 36.1	37.0	254 30.0 12.8	5 09.1 10.9	56.5
05	254 36.2	37.9	269 01.8 12.7	5 20.0 10.8	56.5
06	269 36.4	N 7 38.9	283 33.5 12.8	N 5 30.8 10.8	56.5
07	284 36.6	39.8	298 05.3 12.8	5 41.6 10.8	56.5
08	299 36.7	40.7	312 37.1 12.7	5 52.4 10.7	56.4
T 09	314 36.9 ..	41.7	327 08.8 12.8	6 03.1 10.7	56.4
U 10	329 37.1	42.6	341 40.6 12.8	6 13.8 10.6	56.4
E 11	344 37.3	43.5	356 12.4 12.7	6 24.4 10.6	56.4
S 12	359 37.4	N 7 44.4	10 44.1 12.8	N 6 35.0 10.6	56.4
D 13	14 37.6	45.4	25 15.9 12.8	6 45.6 10.5	56.3
A 14	29 37.8	46.3	39 47.7 12.8	6 56.1 10.5	56.3
Y 15	44 37.9 ..	47.2	54 19.5 12.7	7 06.6 10.5	56.3
16	59 38.1	48.2	68 51.2 12.8	7 17.1 10.4	56.3
17	74 38.3	49.1	83 23.0 12.8	7 27.5 10.3	56.3
18	89 38.4	N 7 50.0	97 54.8 12.7	N 7 37.8 10.4	56.2
19	104 38.6	50.9	112 26.5 12.8	7 48.2 10.2	56.2
20	119 38.8	51.9	126 58.3 12.7	7 58.4 10.3	56.2
21	134 38.9 ..	52.8	141 30.0 12.8	8 08.7 10.2	56.2
22	149 39.1	53.7	156 01.8 12.7	8 18.9 10.1	56.2
23	164 39.3	54.6	170 33.5 12.8	N 8 29.0 10.1	56.1
	SD 16.0	d 0.9	SD 15.6	15.5	15.4

Lat.	Twilight Naut.	Twilight Civil	Sunrise	Moonrise 7	Moonrise 8	Moonrise 9	Moonrise 10
°	h m	h m	h m	h m	h m	h m	h m
N 72	////	02 54	04 18	04 21	04 10	03 59	03 48
N 70	01 07	03 18	04 29	04 15	04 11	04 06	04 02
68	01 59	03 36	04 39	04 11	04 11	04 12	04 13
66	02 29	03 50	04 47	04 07	04 12	04 17	04 22
64	02 52	04 02	04 53	04 04	04 12	04 21	04 30
62	03 09	04 11	04 59	04 01	04 13	04 24	04 37
60	03 23	04 20	05 04	03 59	04 13	04 27	04 43
N 58	03 35	04 27	05 08	03 57	04 13	04 30	04 48
56	03 45	04 33	05 12	03 55	04 14	04 33	04 52
54	03 53	04 39	05 16	03 53	04 14	04 35	04 57
52	04 01	04 44	05 19	03 51	04 14	04 37	05 00
50	04 08	04 48	05 22	03 50	04 14	04 39	05 04
45	04 22	04 58	05 28	03 47	04 15	04 43	05 11
N 40	04 32	05 05	05 33	03 44	04 15	04 46	05 18
35	04 41	05 12	05 37	03 42	04 16	04 49	05 23
30	04 48	05 17	05 41	03 40	04 16	04 52	05 28
20	04 59	05 25	05 48	03 36	04 17	04 57	05 37
N 10	05 07	05 32	05 53	03 33	04 17	05 01	05 44
0	05 13	05 38	05 58	03 30	04 18	05 04	05 51
S 10	05 18	05 42	06 04	03 27	04 18	05 08	05 58
20	05 21	05 47	06 09	03 24	04 19	05 13	06 06
30	05 23	05 51	06 15	03 21	04 20	05 17	06 15
35	05 23	05 53	06 18	03 19	04 20	05 20	06 20
40	05 23	05 55	06 22	03 16	04 20	05 23	06 25
45	05 23	05 57	06 26	03 14	04 21	05 27	06 32
S 50	05 22	05 59	06 32	03 10	04 22	05 32	06 40
52	05 21	06 00	06 34	03 09	04 22	05 34	06 44
54	05 20	06 01	06 37	03 07	04 22	05 36	06 48
56	05 19	06 02	06 39	03 06	04 23	05 38	06 53
58	05 18	06 03	06 43	03 04	04 23	05 41	06 58
S 60	05 16	06 04	06 46	03 01	04 24	05 44	07 04

Lat.	Sunset	Twilight Civil	Twilight Naut.	Moonset 7	Moonset 8	Moonset 9	Moonset 10
°	h m	h m	h m	h m	h m	h m	h m
N 72	19 49	21 15	////	15 30	17 20	19 09	21 01
N 70	19 37	20 50	23 12	15 33	17 15	18 57	20 39
68	19 27	20 31	22 12	15 35	17 12	18 47	20 22
66	19 19	20 16	21 39	15 37	17 09	18 40	20 09
64	19 12	20 04	21 16	15 38	17 06	18 33	19 58
62	19 06	19 54	20 43	15 39	17 04	18 27	19 49
60	19 01	19 46	20 43	15 41	17 02	18 22	19 41
N 58	18 57	19 38	20 31	15 42	17 00	18 18	19 34
56	18 53	19 32	20 21	15 42	16 59	18 14	19 27
54	18 49	19 26	20 12	15 43	16 58	18 11	19 22
52	18 46	19 21	20 04	15 44	16 56	18 07	19 17
50	18 43	19 16	19 57	15 45	16 55	18 05	19 13
45	18 37	19 07	19 43	15 46	16 53	17 58	19 03
N 40	18 31	18 59	19 32	15 47	16 51	17 53	18 55
35	18 27	18 53	19 23	15 48	16 49	17 49	18 48
30	18 23	18 47	19 15	15 49	16 47	17 45	18 42
20	18 16	18 39	19 05	15 51	16 45	17 38	18 31
N 10	18 10	18 32	18 56	15 52	16 42	17 32	18 22
0	18 05	18 26	18 50	15 53	16 40	17 27	18 14
S 10	18 00	18 21	18 45	15 54	16 38	17 21	18 05
20	17 54	18 17	18 42	15 55	16 36	17 15	17 56
30	17 48	18 12	18 40	15 57	16 33	17 09	17 46
35	17 45	18 10	18 39	15 58	16 31	17 05	17 40
40	17 41	18 08	18 39	15 58	16 29	17 01	17 33
45	17 36	18 06	18 40	15 59	16 27	16 56	17 25
S 50	17 31	18 04	18 41	16 01	16 25	16 50	17 16
52	17 29	18 03	18 41	16 01	16 24	16 47	17 11
54	17 26	18 02	18 42	16 02	16 23	16 44	17 07
56	17 23	18 00	18 43	16 02	16 21	16 41	17 02
58	17 20	17 59	18 45	16 03	16 20	16 37	16 56
S 60	17 16	17 58	18 46	16 04	16 18	16 33	16 49

	SUN			MOON			
Day	Eqn. of Time 00ʰ	Eqn. of Time 12ʰ	Mer. Pass.	Mer. Pass. Upper	Mer. Pass. Lower	Age	Phase
d	m s	m s	h m	h m	h m	d	%
7	02 12	02 04	12 02	09 42	22 05	27	9
8	01 55	01 47	12 02	10 29	22 52	28	4
9	01 39	01 31	12 02	11 16	23 39	29	1

UT	ARIES GHA	VENUS −3.9 GHA	Dec	MARS +1.2 GHA	Dec	JUPITER −2.1 GHA	Dec	SATURN +0.2 GHA	Dec	Name	SHA	Dec
10 00	198 23.4	176 18.5	N 8 05.7	177 47.4	N 8 09.2	126 20.2	N22 02.4	340 21.4	S12 08.3	Acamar	315 18.8	S40 15.3
01	213 25.8	191 18.1	06.9	192 48.1	09.9	141 22.1	02.5	355 24.0	08.2	Achernar	335 27.5	S57 10.2
02	228 28.3	206 17.6	08.1	207 48.7	10.7	156 24.1	02.5	10 26.7	08.2	Acrux	173 08.7	S63 10.6
03	243 30.8	221 17.2 ..	09.3	222 49.4 ..	11.4	171 26.1 ..	02.6	25 29.3 ..	08.1	Adhara	255 12.7	S28 59.8
04	258 33.2	236 16.8	10.5	237 50.1	12.1	186 28.1	02.7	40 31.9	08.1	Aldebaran	290 49.8	N16 32.0
05	273 35.7	251 16.4	11.7	252 50.8	12.9	201 30.1	02.7	55 34.5	08.0			
W 06	288 38.1	266 16.0	N 8 12.9	267 51.5	N 8 13.6	216 32.0	N22 02.8	70 37.2	S12 08.0	Alioth	166 20.3	N55 53.2
E 07	303 40.6	281 15.5	14.1	282 52.2	14.3	231 34.0	02.9	85 39.8	07.9	Alkaid	152 58.5	N49 14.7
D 08	318 43.1	296 15.1	15.3	297 52.9	15.0	246 36.0	02.9	100 42.4	07.8	Al Na'ir	27 44.2	S46 53.6
N 09	333 45.5	311 14.7 ..	16.5	312 53.6 ..	15.8	261 38.0 ..	03.0	115 45.1 ..	07.8	Alnilam	275 46.6	S 1 11.9
E 10	348 48.0	326 14.3	17.7	327 54.3	16.5	276 40.0	03.0	130 47.7	07.7	Alphard	217 56.1	S 8 43.3
S 11	3 50.5	341 13.8	18.9	342 55.0	17.2	291 42.0	03.1	145 50.3	07.7			
D 12	18 52.9	356 13.4	N 8 20.1	357 55.7	N 8 18.0	306 43.9	N22 03.2	160 53.0	S12 07.6	Alphecca	126 10.8	N26 40.1
A 13	33 55.4	11 13.0	21.3	12 56.4	18.7	321 45.9	03.2	175 55.6	07.6	Alpheratz	357 44.0	N29 09.7
Y 14	48 57.9	26 12.6	22.5	27 57.1	19.4	336 47.9	03.3	190 58.2	07.5	Altair	62 08.4	N 8 54.2
15	64 00.3	41 12.1 ..	23.7	42 57.8 ..	20.1	351 49.9 ..	03.3	206 00.9 ..	07.4	Ankaa	353 16.2	S42 14.0
16	79 02.8	56 11.7	24.9	57 58.5	20.9	6 51.9	03.4	221 03.5	07.4	Antares	112 26.2	S26 27.6
17	94 05.3	71 11.3	26.1	72 59.2	21.6	21 53.8	03.4	236 06.1	07.3			
18	109 07.7	86 10.9	N 8 27.3	87 59.9	N 8 22.3	36 55.8	N22 03.5	251 08.8	S12 07.3	Arcturus	145 55.5	N19 06.7
19	124 10.2	101 10.4	28.5	103 00.6	23.1	51 57.8	03.6	266 11.4	07.2	Atria	107 27.8	S69 02.8
20	139 12.6	116 10.0	29.7	118 01.3	23.8	66 59.8	03.6	281 14.0	07.1	Avior	234 17.9	S59 33.6
21	154 15.1	131 09.6 ..	30.9	133 02.0 ..	24.5	82 01.7 ..	03.7	296 16.7 ..	07.1	Bellatrix	278 32.3	N 6 21.5
22	169 17.6	146 09.2	32.1	148 02.6	25.2	97 03.7	03.8	311 19.3	07.0	Betelgeuse	271 01.6	N 7 24.3
23	184 20.0	161 08.7	33.3	163 03.3	26.0	112 05.7	03.8	326 21.9	07.0			
11 00	199 22.5	176 08.3	N 8 34.5	178 04.0	N 8 26.7	127 07.7	N22 03.9	341 24.6	S12 06.9	Canopus	263 56.4	S52 42.6
01	214 25.0	191 07.9	35.7	193 04.7	27.4	142 09.7	04.0	356 27.2	06.9	Capella	280 34.9	N46 00.6
02	229 27.4	206 07.5	36.9	208 05.4	28.1	157 11.6	04.0	11 29.8	06.8	Deneb	49 31.7	N45 19.5
03	244 29.9	221 07.0 ..	38.1	223 06.1 ..	28.9	172 13.6 ..	04.1	26 32.5 ..	06.7	Denebola	182 33.5	N14 29.7
04	259 32.4	236 06.6	39.3	238 06.8	29.6	187 15.6	04.1	41 35.1	06.7	Diphda	348 56.3	S17 54.9
05	274 34.8	251 06.2	40.4	253 07.5	30.3	202 17.6	04.2	56 37.7	06.6			
T 06	289 37.3	266 05.8	N 8 41.6	268 08.2	N 8 31.0	217 19.5	N22 04.3	71 40.4	S12 06.6	Dubhe	193 51.4	N61 40.8
H 07	304 39.7	281 05.3	42.8	283 08.9	31.8	232 21.5	04.3	86 43.0	06.5	Elnath	278 13.0	N28 37.0
U 08	319 42.2	296 04.9	44.0	298 09.6	32.5	247 23.5	04.4	101 45.6	06.5	Eltanin	90 46.0	N51 29.1
R 09	334 44.7	311 04.5 ..	45.2	313 10.3 ..	33.2	262 25.5 ..	04.4	116 48.3 ..	06.4	Enif	33 47.4	N 9 56.1
S 10	349 47.1	326 04.0	46.4	328 11.0	33.9	277 27.5	04.5	131 50.9	06.3	Fomalhaut	15 24.4	S29 33.0
D 11	4 49.6	341 03.6	47.6	343 11.7	34.7	292 29.4	04.6	146 53.5	06.3			
A 12	19 52.1	356 03.2	N 8 48.8	358 12.4	N 8 35.4	307 31.4	N22 04.6	161 56.2	S12 06.2	Gacrux	172 00.4	S57 11.4
Y 13	34 54.5	11 02.8	50.0	13 13.1	36.1	322 33.4	04.7	176 58.8	06.2	Gienah	175 52.1	S17 37.2
14	49 57.0	26 02.3	51.2	28 13.8	36.8	337 35.4	04.8	192 01.4	06.1	Hadar	148 47.4	S60 26.2
15	64 59.5	41 01.9 ..	52.4	43 14.5 ..	37.5	352 37.3 ..	04.8	207 04.1 ..	06.0	Hamal	328 01.2	N23 31.4
16	80 01.9	56 01.5	53.5	58 15.1	38.3	7 39.3	04.9	222 06.7	06.0	Kaus Aust.	83 43.9	S34 22.5
17	95 04.4	71 01.0	54.7	73 15.8	39.0	22 41.3	04.9	237 09.3	05.9			
18	110 06.9	86 00.6	N 8 55.9	88 16.5	N 8 39.7	37 43.3	N22 05.0	252 12.0	S12 05.9	Kochab	137 19.0	N74 05.9
19	125 09.3	101 00.2	57.1	103 17.2	40.4	52 45.2	05.1	267 14.6	05.8	Markab	13 38.7	N15 16.5
20	140 11.8	115 59.7	58.3	118 17.9	41.2	67 47.2	05.1	282 17.2	05.8	Menkar	314 15.5	N 4 08.3
21	155 14.2	130 59.3	8 59.5	133 18.6 ..	41.9	82 49.2 ..	05.2	297 19.9 ..	05.7	Menkent	148 07.3	S36 26.2
22	170 16.7	145 58.9	9 00.7	148 19.3	42.6	97 51.2	05.2	312 22.5	05.6	Miaplacidus	221 39.3	S69 46.8
23	185 19.2	160 58.4	01.9	163 20.0	43.3	112 53.1	05.3	327 25.1	05.6			
12 00	200 21.6	175 58.0	N 9 03.0	178 20.7	N 8 44.0	127 55.1	N22 05.4	342 27.8	S12 05.5	Mirfak	308 40.9	N49 54.5
01	215 24.1	190 57.6	04.2	193 21.4	44.8	142 57.1	05.4	357 30.4	05.5	Nunki	75 58.4	S26 16.6
02	230 26.6	205 57.1	05.4	208 22.1	45.5	157 59.1	05.5	12 33.0	05.4	Peacock	53 19.6	S56 41.2
03	245 29.0	220 56.7 ..	06.6	223 22.8 ..	46.2	173 01.0 ..	05.5	27 35.7 ..	05.3	Pollux	243 27.9	N27 59.5
04	260 31.5	235 56.3	07.8	238 23.5	46.9	188 03.0	05.6	42 38.3	05.3	Procyon	244 59.9	N 5 11.2
05	275 34.0	250 55.8	09.0	253 24.2	47.7	203 05.0	05.7	57 40.9	05.2			
F 06	290 36.4	265 55.4	N 9 10.2	268 24.9	N 8 48.4	218 06.9	N22 05.7	72 43.6	S12 05.2	Rasalhague	96 06.4	N12 33.0
R 07	305 38.9	280 55.0	11.3	283 25.6	49.1	233 08.9	05.8	87 46.2	05.1	Regulus	207 43.5	N11 53.9
I 08	320 41.3	295 54.5	12.5	298 26.2	49.8	248 10.9	05.8	102 48.8	05.1	Rigel	281 12.4	S 8 11.5
D 09	335 43.8	310 54.1 ..	13.7	313 26.9 ..	50.5	263 12.9 ..	05.9	117 51.5 ..	05.0	Rigil Kent.	139 51.2	S60 53.3
A 10	350 46.3	325 53.7	14.9	328 27.6	51.3	278 14.8	06.0	132 54.1	04.9	Sabik	102 12.5	S15 44.4
Y 11	5 48.7	340 53.2	16.1	343 28.3	52.0	293 16.8	06.0	147 56.8	04.9			
12	20 51.2	355 52.8	N 9 17.3	358 29.0	N 8 52.7	308 18.8	N22 06.1	162 59.4	S12 04.8	Schedar	349 41.2	N56 36.5
13	35 53.7	10 52.4	18.4	13 29.7	53.4	323 20.8	06.2	178 02.0	04.8	Shaula	96 21.9	S37 06.6
14	50 56.1	25 51.9	19.6	28 30.4	54.1	338 22.7	06.2	193 04.7	04.7	Sirius	258 33.9	S16 44.4
15	65 58.6	40 51.5 ..	20.8	43 31.1 ..	54.9	353 24.7 ..	06.3	208 07.3 ..	04.6	Spica	158 31.1	S11 14.0
16	81 01.1	55 51.0	22.0	58 31.8	55.6	8 26.7	06.3	223 09.9	04.6	Suhail	222 52.3	S43 29.6
17	96 03.5	70 50.6	23.2	73 32.5	56.3	23 28.6	06.4	238 12.6	04.5			
18	111 06.0	85 50.2	N 9 24.3	88 33.2	N 8 57.0	38 30.6	N22 06.5	253 15.2	S12 04.5	Vega	80 38.9	N38 47.6
19	126 08.5	100 49.7	25.5	103 33.9	57.7	53 32.6	06.5	268 17.8	04.4	Zuben'ubi	137 05.2	S16 05.9
20	141 10.9	115 49.3	26.7	118 34.6	58.4	68 34.5	06.6	283 20.5	04.4		SHA	Mer. Pass.
21	156 13.4	130 48.9 ..	27.9	133 35.3 ..	59.2	83 36.5 ..	06.6	298 23.1 ..	04.3	Venus	336 45.8	12 16
22	171 15.8	145 48.4	29.0	148 35.9	8 59.9	98 38.5	06.7	313 25.7	04.2	Mars	338 41.5	12 07
23	186 18.3	160 48.0	30.2	163 36.6	N 9 00.6	113 40.5	06.8	328 28.4	04.2	Jupiter	287 45.2	15 29
Mer. Pass. 10 40.7		v −0.4	d 1.2	v 0.7	d 0.7	v 2.0	d 0.1	v 2.6	d 0.1	Saturn	142 02.1	1 14

UT	SUN GHA	SUN Dec	MOON GHA	v	Dec	d	HP
10 00	179 39.4	N 7 55.6	185 05.3	12.7	N 8 39.1	10.0	56.1
01	194 39.6	56.5	199 37.0	12.8	8 49.1	10.0	56.1
02	209 39.8	57.4	214 08.8	12.7	8 59.1	10.0	56.1
03	224 39.9	.. 58.3	228 40.5	12.7	9 09.1	9.9	56.0
04	239 40.1	7 59.3	243 12.2	12.7	9 19.0	9.8	56.0
05	254 40.3	8 00.2	257 43.9	12.7	9 28.8	9.8	56.0
W 06	269 40.4	N 8 01.1	272 15.6	12.7	N 9 38.6	9.7	56.0
E 07	284 40.6	02.0	286 47.3	12.7	9 48.3	9.7	56.0
D 08	299 40.8	02.9	301 19.0	12.7	9 58.0	9.6	55.9
N 09	314 40.9	.. 03.9	315 50.7	12.7	10 07.6	9.6	55.9
E 10	329 41.1	04.8	330 22.4	12.7	10 17.2	9.5	55.9
S 11	344 41.3	05.7	344 54.1	12.6	10 26.7	9.5	55.9
D 12	359 41.4	N 8 06.6	359 25.7	12.7	N10 36.2	9.4	55.9
A 13	14 41.6	07.6	13 57.4	12.6	10 45.6	9.3	55.8
Y 14	29 41.8	08.5	28 29.0	12.7	10 54.9	9.3	55.8
15	44 41.9	.. 09.4	43 00.7	12.6	11 04.2	9.2	55.8
16	59 42.1	10.3	57 32.3	12.6	11 13.4	9.2	55.8
17	74 42.3	11.2	72 03.9	12.6	11 22.6	9.1	55.8
18	89 42.4	N 8 12.2	86 35.5	12.6	N11 31.7	9.1	55.7
19	104 42.6	13.1	101 07.1	12.6	11 40.8	9.0	55.7
20	119 42.8	14.0	115 38.7	12.6	11 49.8	8.9	55.7
21	134 42.9	.. 14.9	130 10.3	12.5	11 58.7	8.8	55.7
22	149 43.1	15.8	144 41.8	12.6	12 07.5	8.8	55.7
23	164 43.3	16.8	159 13.4	12.5	12 16.3	8.8	55.6
11 00	179 43.4	N 8 17.7	173 44.9	12.6	N12 25.1	8.6	55.6
01	194 43.6	18.6	188 16.5	12.5	12 33.7	8.6	55.6
02	209 43.7	19.5	202 48.0	12.5	12 42.3	8.6	55.6
03	224 43.9	.. 20.4	217 19.5	12.5	12 50.9	8.4	55.5
04	239 44.1	21.4	231 51.0	12.5	12 59.3	8.4	55.5
05	254 44.2	22.3	246 22.5	12.4	13 07.7	8.4	55.5
T 06	269 44.4	N 8 23.2	260 53.9	12.5	N13 16.1	8.2	55.5
H 07	284 44.6	24.1	275 25.4	12.4	13 24.3	8.2	55.5
U 08	299 44.7	25.0	289 56.8	12.5	13 32.5	8.1	55.5
R 09	314 44.9	.. 26.0	304 28.3	12.4	13 40.6	8.1	55.4
S 10	329 45.1	26.9	318 59.7	12.4	13 48.7	8.0	55.4
D 11	344 45.2	27.8	333 31.1	12.4	13 56.7	7.9	55.4
A 12	359 45.4	N 8 28.7	348 02.5	12.4	N14 04.6	7.8	55.4
Y 13	14 45.5	29.6	2 33.9	12.3	14 12.4	7.8	55.4
14	29 45.7	30.5	17 05.2	12.4	14 20.2	7.7	55.3
15	44 45.9	.. 31.4	31 36.6	12.3	14 27.9	7.6	55.3
16	59 46.0	32.4	46 07.9	12.4	14 35.5	7.5	55.3
17	74 46.2	33.3	60 39.3	12.3	14 43.0	7.5	55.3
18	89 46.4	N 8 34.2	75 10.6	12.3	N14 50.5	7.4	55.3
19	104 46.5	35.1	89 41.9	12.3	14 57.9	7.3	55.2
20	119 46.7	36.0	104 13.2	12.3	15 05.2	7.2	55.2
21	134 46.8	.. 36.9	118 44.5	12.2	15 12.4	7.2	55.2
22	149 47.0	37.8	133 15.7	12.3	15 19.6	7.1	55.2
23	164 47.2	38.8	147 47.0	12.2	15 26.7	7.0	55.2
12 00	179 47.3	N 8 39.7	162 18.2	12.2	N15 33.7	6.9	55.2
01	194 47.5	40.6	176 49.4	12.2	15 40.6	6.9	55.1
02	209 47.6	41.5	191 20.6	12.2	15 47.5	6.7	55.1
03	224 47.8	.. 42.4	205 51.8	12.2	15 54.2	6.7	55.1
04	239 48.0	43.3	220 23.0	12.2	16 00.9	6.6	55.1
05	254 48.1	44.2	234 54.2	12.2	16 07.5	6.6	55.1
F 06	269 48.3	N 8 45.2	249 25.4	12.1	N16 14.1	6.4	55.0
R 07	284 48.4	46.1	263 56.5	12.1	16 20.5	6.4	55.0
I 08	299 48.6	47.0	278 27.6	12.2	16 26.9	6.3	55.0
D 09	314 48.8	.. 47.9	292 58.8	12.1	16 33.2	6.2	55.0
A 10	329 48.9	48.8	307 29.9	12.1	16 39.4	6.1	55.0
Y 11	344 49.1	49.7	322 01.0	12.1	16 45.5	6.0	55.0
12	359 49.2	N 8 50.6	336 32.1	12.0	N16 51.5	6.0	54.9
13	14 49.4	51.5	351 03.1	12.1	16 57.5	5.8	54.9
14	29 49.6	52.4	5 34.2	12.1	17 03.3	5.8	54.9
15	44 49.7	.. 53.3	20 05.3	12.0	17 09.1	5.7	54.9
16	59 49.9	54.3	34 36.3	12.0	17 14.8	5.6	54.9
17	74 50.0	55.2	49 07.3	12.0	17 20.4	5.6	54.9
18	89 50.2	N 8 56.1	63 38.3	12.0	N17 26.0	5.4	54.8
19	104 50.4	57.0	78 09.3	12.0	17 31.4	5.4	54.8
20	119 50.5	57.9	92 40.3	12.0	17 36.8	5.2	54.8
21	134 50.7	.. 58.8	107 11.3	12.0	17 42.0	5.2	54.8
22	149 50.8	8 59.7	121 42.3	12.0	17 47.2	5.1	54.8
23	164 51.0	N 9 00.6	136 13.3	11.9	N17 52.3	5.0	54.8
	SD 16.0	d 0.9	SD 15.2		15.1		15.0

Twilight / Sunrise / Moonrise

Lat.	Naut.	Civil	Sunrise	10	11	12	13
N 72	////	02 31	04 01	03 48	03 34	03 14	▭
N 70	////	03 00	04 15	04 02	03 57	03 52	03 47
68	01 32	03 20	04 26	04 13	04 15	04 19	04 28
66	02 10	03 37	04 35	04 22	04 29	04 40	04 56
64	02 36	03 50	04 43	04 30	04 41	04 56	05 17
62	02 56	04 01	04 49	04 37	04 51	05 10	05 34
60	03 11	04 11	04 55	04 43	05 00	05 21	05 48
N 58	03 24	04 18	05 00	04 48	05 08	05 32	06 01
56	03 35	04 25	05 04	04 52	05 15	05 40	06 11
54	03 45	04 31	05 08	04 57	05 21	05 48	06 21
52	03 53	04 37	05 12	05 00	05 26	05 55	06 29
50	04 01	04 42	05 15	05 04	05 31	06 02	06 37
45	04 16	04 52	05 22	05 11	05 42	06 16	06 53
N 40	04 27	05 00	05 28	05 18	05 51	06 27	07 06
35	04 37	05 07	05 33	05 23	05 59	06 37	07 17
30	04 45	05 13	05 38	05 28	06 06	06 45	07 27
20	04 57	05 23	05 45	05 37	06 18	07 00	07 44
N 10	05 06	05 30	05 52	05 44	06 28	07 13	07 59
0	05 13	05 37	05 58	05 51	06 38	07 25	08 13
S 10	05 18	05 42	06 04	05 58	06 48	07 38	08 27
20	05 22	05 48	06 10	06 06	06 59	07 51	08 43
30	05 25	05 53	06 17	06 15	07 11	08 06	09 00
35	05 26	05 55	06 21	06 20	07 18	08 15	09 10
40	05 26	05 58	06 25	06 25	07 26	08 25	09 22
45	05 27	06 01	06 30	06 32	07 36	08 37	09 35
S 50	05 26	06 04	06 36	06 40	07 47	08 51	09 52
52	05 26	06 05	06 39	06 44	07 52	08 58	10 00
54	05 25	06 06	06 42	06 48	07 58	09 06	10 09
56	05 25	06 08	06 45	06 53	08 05	09 14	10 19
58	05 24	06 09	06 49	06 58	08 12	09 24	10 30
S 60	05 23	06 11	06 53	07 04	08 21	09 35	10 43

Sunset / Twilight / Moonset

Lat.	Sunset	Civil	Naut.	10	11	12	13
N 72	20 04	21 37	////	21 01	22 59	▭	▭
N 70	19 50	21 07	////	20 39	22 22	24 07	00 07
68	19 39	20 45	22 39	20 22	21 56	23 27	24 49
66	19 29	20 28	21 57	20 09	21 36	22 59	24 14
64	19 21	20 15	21 30	19 58	21 20	22 38	23 48
62	19 14	20 03	21 09	19 49	21 07	22 22	23 28
60	19 09	19 54	20 53	19 41	20 56	22 08	23 12
N 58	19 03	19 46	20 40	19 34	20 47	21 56	22 58
56	18 59	19 39	20 28	19 27	20 38	21 45	22 47
54	18 55	19 32	20 19	19 22	20 31	21 36	22 36
52	18 51	19 27	20 10	19 17	20 24	21 28	22 27
50	18 48	19 22	20 03	19 12	20 18	21 21	22 19
45	18 40	19 11	19 48	19 03	20 05	21 05	22 02
N 40	18 34	18 55	19 36	18 55	19 55	20 53	21 48
35	18 29	18 55	19 26	18 48	19 46	20 42	21 36
30	18 25	18 49	19 18	18 42	19 38	20 32	21 25
20	18 17	18 39	19 06	18 31	19 24	20 15	21 07
N 10	18 10	18 32	18 56	18 22	19 12	20 02	20 51
0	18 04	18 25	18 49	18 14	19 01	19 49	20 37
S 10	17 58	18 19	18 44	18 05	18 50	19 35	20 22
20	17 52	18 14	18 40	17 56	18 38	19 21	20 06
30	17 45	18 09	18 37	17 46	18 24	19 05	19 48
35	17 41	18 06	18 36	17 40	18 16	18 55	19 38
40	17 36	18 04	18 35	17 33	18 08	18 45	19 26
45	17 31	18 01	18 35	17 25	17 57	18 32	19 12
S 50	17 25	17 57	18 35	17 16	17 45	18 17	18 55
52	17 22	17 56	18 35	17 11	17 39	18 10	18 47
54	17 19	17 55	18 35	17 07	17 32	18 02	18 38
56	17 16	17 53	18 36	17 02	17 25	17 53	18 28
58	17 12	17 51	18 37	16 56	17 17	17 44	18 16
S 60	17 07	17 50	18 38	16 49	17 08	17 32	18 03

SUN / MOON

Day	Eqn. of Time 00h	Eqn. of Time 12h	Mer. Pass.	Mer. Pass. Upper	Mer. Pass. Lower	Age	Phase
	m s	m s	h m	h m	h m	d	%
10	01 23	01 15	12 01	12 02	24 26	00	0
11	01 07	00 59	12 01	12 49	00 26	01	1
12	00 51	00 43	12 01	13 37	01 13	02	4

UT	ARIES	VENUS −3.9		MARS +1.2		JUPITER −2.0		SATURN +0.2		STARS		
	GHA	GHA	Dec	GHA	Dec	GHA	Dec	GHA	Dec	Name	SHA	Dec
d h	° ′	° ′	° ′	° ′	° ′	° ′	° ′	° ′	° ′		° ′	° ′
13 00	201 20.8	175 47.5	N 9 31.4	178 37.3	N 9 01.3	128 42.4	N22 06.8	343 31.0	S12 04.1	Acamar	315 18.8	S40 15.3
01	216 23.2	190 47.1	32.6	193 38.0	02.0	143 44.4	06.9	358 33.7	04.1	Achernar	335 27.5	S57 10.2
02	231 25.7	205 46.7	33.8	208 38.7	02.8	158 46.4	06.9	13 36.3	04.0	Acrux	173 08.7	S63 10.6
03	246 28.2	220 46.2	.. 34.9	223 39.4	.. 03.5	173 48.3	.. 07.0	28 38.9	.. 03.9	Adhara	255 12.7	S28 59.8
04	261 30.6	235 45.8	36.1	238 40.1	04.2	188 50.3	07.1	43 41.6	03.9	Aldebaran	290 49.8	N16 32.0
05	276 33.1	250 45.3	37.3	253 40.8	04.9	203 52.3	07.1	58 44.2	03.8			
S 06	291 35.6	265 44.9	N 9 38.5	268 41.5	N 9 05.6	218 54.2	N22 07.2	73 46.8	S12 03.8	Alioth	166 20.3	N55 53.2
A 07	306 38.0	280 44.5	39.6	283 42.2	06.3	233 56.2	07.3	88 49.5	03.7	Alkaid	152 58.5	N49 14.7
T 08	321 40.5	295 44.0	40.8	298 42.9	07.0	248 58.2	07.3	103 52.1	03.6	Al Na'ir	27 44.2	S46 53.6
U 09	336 43.0	310 43.6	.. 42.0	313 43.6	.. 07.8	264 00.1	.. 07.4	118 54.7	.. 03.6	Alnilam	275 46.7	S 1 11.9
R 10	351 45.4	325 43.1	43.2	328 44.3	08.5	279 02.1	07.4	133 57.4	03.5	Alphard	217 56.1	S 8 43.3
D 11	6 47.9	340 42.7	44.3	343 44.9	09.2	294 04.1	07.5	149 00.0	03.5			
A 12	21 50.3	355 42.2	N 9 45.5	358 45.6	N 9 09.9	309 06.1	N22 07.6	164 02.7	S12 03.4	Alphecca	126 10.8	N26 40.1
Y 13	36 52.8	10 41.8	46.7	13 46.3	10.6	324 08.0	07.6	179 05.3	03.4	Alpheratz	357 43.9	N29 09.7
14	51 55.3	25 41.4	47.8	28 47.0	11.3	339 10.0	07.7	194 07.9	03.3	Altair	62 08.4	N 8 54.2
15	66 57.7	40 40.9	.. 49.0	43 47.7	.. 12.1	354 12.0	.. 07.7	209 10.6	.. 03.2	Ankaa	353 16.2	S42 14.0
16	82 00.2	55 40.5	50.2	58 48.4	12.8	9 13.9	07.8	224 13.2	03.2	Antares	112 26.1	S26 27.6
17	97 02.7	70 40.0	51.4	73 49.1	13.5	24 15.9	07.9	239 15.8	03.1			
18	112 05.1	85 39.6	N 9 52.5	88 49.8	N 9 14.2	39 17.9	N22 07.9	254 18.5	S12 03.1	Arcturus	145 55.5	N19 06.7
19	127 07.6	100 39.1	53.7	103 50.5	14.9	54 19.8	08.0	269 21.1	03.0	Atria	107 27.7	S69 02.8
20	142 10.1	115 38.7	54.9	118 51.2	15.6	69 21.8	08.0	284 23.8	02.9	Avior	234 17.9	S59 33.6
21	157 12.5	130 38.2	.. 56.0	133 51.9	.. 16.3	84 23.8	.. 08.1	299 26.4	.. 02.9	Bellatrix	278 32.3	N 6 21.5
22	172 15.0	145 37.8	57.2	148 52.6	17.1	99 25.7	08.2	314 29.0	02.8	Betelgeuse	271 01.6	N 7 24.3
23	187 17.4	160 37.4	58.4	163 53.3	17.8	114 27.7	08.2	329 31.7	02.8			
14 00	202 19.9	175 36.9	N 9 59.5	178 53.9	N 9 18.5	129 29.7	N22 08.3	344 34.3	S12 02.7	Canopus	263 56.4	S52 42.6
01	217 22.4	190 36.5	10 00.7	193 54.6	19.2	144 31.6	08.3	359 36.9	02.6	Capella	280 34.9	N46 00.6
02	232 24.8	205 36.0	01.9	208 55.3	19.9	159 33.6	08.4	14 39.6	02.6	Deneb	49 31.7	N45 19.5
03	247 27.3	220 35.6	.. 03.0	223 56.0	.. 20.6	174 35.5	.. 08.5	29 42.2	.. 02.5	Denebola	182 33.5	N14 29.7
04	262 29.8	235 35.1	04.2	238 56.7	21.3	189 37.5	08.5	44 44.9	02.5	Diphda	348 56.3	S17 54.9
05	277 32.2	250 34.7	05.4	253 57.4	22.0	204 39.5	08.6	59 47.5	02.4			
S 06	292 34.7	265 34.2	N10 06.5	268 58.1	N 9 22.8	219 41.4	N22 08.6	74 50.1	S12 02.4	Dubhe	193 51.4	N61 40.8
U 07	307 37.2	280 33.8	07.7	283 58.8	23.5	234 43.4	08.7	89 52.8	02.3	Elnath	278 13.0	N28 37.0
N 08	322 39.6	295 33.3	08.9	298 59.5	24.2	249 45.4	08.8	104 55.4	02.2	Eltanin	90 46.0	N51 29.1
D 09	337 42.1	310 32.9	.. 10.0	314 00.2	.. 24.9	264 47.3	.. 08.8	119 58.0	.. 02.2	Enif	33 47.4	N 9 56.1
A 10	352 44.6	325 32.4	11.2	329 00.9	25.6	279 49.3	08.9	135 00.7	02.1	Fomalhaut	15 24.4	S29 33.0
Y 11	7 47.0	340 32.0	12.4	344 01.5	26.3	294 51.3	09.0	150 03.3	02.1			
12	22 49.5	355 31.5	N10 13.5	359 02.2	N 9 27.0	309 53.2	N22 09.0	165 06.0	S12 02.0	Gacrux	172 00.4	S57 11.5
13	37 51.9	10 31.1	14.7	14 02.9	27.7	324 55.2	09.1	180 08.6	01.9	Gienah	175 52.1	S17 37.2
14	52 54.4	25 30.6	15.8	29 03.6	28.4	339 57.2	09.1	195 11.2	01.9	Hadar	148 47.4	S60 26.2
15	67 56.9	40 30.2	.. 17.0	44 04.3	.. 29.2	354 59.1	.. 09.2	210 13.9	.. 01.8	Hamal	328 01.2	N23 31.4
16	82 59.3	55 29.7	18.2	59 05.0	29.9	10 01.1	09.3	225 16.5	01.8	Kaus Aust.	83 43.8	S34 22.5
17	98 01.8	70 29.3	19.3	74 05.7	30.6	25 03.0	09.3	240 19.1	01.7			
18	113 04.3	85 28.8	N10 20.5	89 06.4	N 9 31.3	40 05.0	N22 09.4	255 21.8	S12 01.6	Kochab	137 19.0	N74 06.0
19	128 06.7	100 28.4	21.6	104 07.1	32.0	55 07.0	09.4	270 24.4	01.6	Markab	13 38.7	N15 16.5
20	143 09.2	115 27.9	22.8	119 07.8	32.7	70 08.9	09.5	285 27.1	01.5	Menkar	314 15.5	N 4 08.3
21	158 11.7	130 27.5	.. 24.0	134 08.5	.. 33.4	85 10.9	.. 09.6	300 29.7	.. 01.5	Menkent	148 07.3	S36 26.2
22	173 14.1	145 27.0	25.1	149 09.2	34.1	100 12.9	09.6	315 32.3	01.4	Miaplacidus	221 39.3	S69 46.8
23	188 16.6	160 26.5	26.3	164 09.8	34.8	115 14.8	09.7	330 35.0	01.3			
15 00	203 19.1	175 26.1	N10 27.4	179 10.5	N 9 35.5	130 16.8	N22 09.7	345 37.6	S12 01.3	Mirfak	308 40.9	N49 54.4
01	218 21.5	190 25.6	28.6	194 11.2	36.3	145 18.7	09.8	0 40.3	01.2	Nunki	75 58.4	S26 16.6
02	233 24.0	205 25.2	29.8	209 11.9	37.0	160 20.7	09.9	15 42.9	01.2	Peacock	53 19.6	S56 41.2
03	248 26.4	220 24.7	.. 30.9	224 12.6	.. 37.7	175 22.7	.. 09.9	30 45.5	.. 01.1	Pollux	243 27.9	N27 59.5
04	263 28.9	235 24.3	32.1	239 13.3	38.4	190 24.6	10.0	45 48.2	01.1	Procyon	244 59.9	N 5 11.2
05	278 31.4	250 23.8	33.2	254 14.0	39.1	205 26.6	10.0	60 50.8	01.0			
M 06	293 33.8	265 23.4	N10 34.4	269 14.7	N 9 39.8	220 28.5	N22 10.1	75 53.5	S12 00.9	Rasalhague	96 06.4	N12 33.0
O 07	308 36.3	280 22.9	35.5	284 15.4	40.5	235 30.5	10.2	90 56.1	00.9	Regulus	207 43.5	N11 53.9
N 08	323 38.8	295 22.4	36.7	299 16.1	41.2	250 32.5	10.2	105 58.7	00.8	Rigel	281 12.4	S 8 11.5
D 09	338 41.2	310 22.0	.. 37.8	314 16.7	.. 41.9	265 34.4	.. 10.3	121 01.4	.. 00.8	Rigil Kent.	139 51.2	S60 53.3
A 10	353 43.7	325 21.5	39.0	329 17.4	42.6	280 36.4	10.3	136 04.0	00.7	Sabik	102 12.5	S15 44.4
Y 11	8 46.2	340 21.1	40.1	344 18.1	43.3	295 38.3	10.4	151 06.6	00.6			
12	23 48.6	355 20.6	N10 41.3	359 18.8	N 9 44.0	310 40.3	N22 10.5	166 09.3	S12 00.6	Schedar	349 41.2	N56 36.5
13	38 51.1	10 20.2	42.5	14 19.5	44.7	325 42.3	10.5	181 11.9	00.5	Shaula	96 21.9	S37 06.6
14	53 53.6	25 19.7	43.6	29 20.2	45.4	340 44.2	10.6	196 14.6	00.5	Sirius	258 33.9	S16 44.4
15	68 56.0	40 19.2	.. 44.8	44 20.9	.. 46.2	355 46.2	.. 10.6	211 17.2	.. 00.4	Spica	158 31.1	S11 14.0
16	83 58.5	55 18.8	45.9	59 21.6	46.9	10 48.1	10.7	226 19.8	00.3	Suhail	222 52.4	S43 29.6
17	99 00.9	70 18.3	47.1	74 22.3	47.6	25 50.1	10.8	241 22.5	00.3			
18	114 03.4	85 17.9	N10 48.2	89 23.0	N 9 48.3	40 52.1	N22 10.8	256 25.1	S12 00.2	Vega	80 38.9	N38 47.6
19	129 05.9	100 17.4	49.4	104 23.6	49.0	55 54.0	10.9	271 27.8	00.2	Zuben'ubi	137 05.2	S16 05.9
20	144 08.3	115 16.9	50.5	119 24.3	49.7	70 56.0	10.9	286 30.4	00.1		SHA	Mer. Pass.
21	159 10.8	130 16.5	.. 51.7	134 25.0	.. 50.4	85 57.9	.. 11.0	301 33.0	.. 00.0		° ′	h m
22	174 13.3	145 16.0	52.8	149 25.7	51.1	100 59.9	11.1	316 35.7	12 00.0	Venus	333 17.0	12 18
23	189 15.7	160 15.6	54.0	164 26.4	51.8	116 01.9	11.1	331 38.3	S11 59.9	Mars	336 34.0	12 04
	h m									Jupiter	287 09.7	15 20
Mer. Pass. 10 29.0	v −0.5 d 1.2		v 0.7 d 0.7		v 2.0 d 0.1		v 2.6 d 0.1			Saturn	142 14.4	1 02

UT	SUN GHA	Dec	MOON GHA	v	Dec	d	HP
13 00	179 51.2	N 9 01.5	150 44.2	12.0	N17 57.3	4.9	54.7
01	194 51.3	02.4	165 15.2	11.9	18 02.2	4.9	54.7
02	209 51.5	03.3	179 46.1	11.9	18 07.1	4.7	54.7
03	224 51.6	.. 04.2	194 17.0	11.9	18 11.8	4.6	54.7
04	239 51.8	05.1	208 47.9	12.0	18 16.4	4.6	54.7
05	254 51.9	06.1	223 18.9	11.9	18 21.0	4.5	54.7
06	269 52.1	N 9 07.0	237 49.8	11.8	N18 25.5	4.4	54.7
07	284 52.3	07.9	252 20.6	11.9	18 29.9	4.3	54.6
S 08	299 52.4	08.8	266 51.5	11.9	18 34.2	4.2	54.6
A 09	314 52.6	.. 09.7	281 22.4	11.9	18 38.4	4.1	54.6
T 10	329 52.7	10.6	295 53.3	11.8	18 42.5	4.0	54.6
U 11	344 52.9	11.5	310 24.1	11.9	18 46.5	3.9	54.6
R 12	359 53.0	N 9 12.4	324 55.0	11.9	N18 50.4	3.9	54.6
D 13	14 53.2	13.3	339 25.9	11.8	18 54.3	3.7	54.6
A 14	29 53.4	14.2	353 56.7	11.8	18 58.0	3.7	54.5
Y 15	44 53.5	.. 15.1	8 27.5	11.9	19 01.7	3.5	54.5
16	59 53.7	16.0	22 58.4	11.8	19 05.2	3.5	54.5
17	74 53.8	16.9	37 29.2	11.8	19 08.7	3.4	54.5
18	89 54.0	N 9 17.8	52 00.0	11.8	N19 12.1	3.3	54.5
19	104 54.1	18.7	66 30.8	11.8	19 15.4	3.2	54.5
20	119 54.3	19.6	81 01.6	11.9	19 18.6	3.1	54.5
21	134 54.4	.. 20.5	95 32.5	11.8	19 21.7	3.0	54.5
22	149 54.6	21.4	110 03.3	11.8	19 24.7	2.9	54.5
23	164 54.8	22.3	124 34.1	11.8	19 27.6	2.8	54.4
14 00	179 54.9	N 9 23.2	139 04.9	11.8	N19 30.4	2.8	54.4
01	194 55.1	24.1	153 35.7	11.8	19 33.2	2.6	54.4
02	209 55.2	25.0	168 06.5	11.8	19 35.8	2.5	54.4
03	224 55.4	.. 25.9	182 37.3	11.7	19 38.3	2.5	54.4
04	239 55.5	26.8	197 08.0	11.8	19 40.8	2.3	54.4
05	254 55.7	27.7	211 38.8	11.8	19 43.1	2.3	54.4
06	269 55.8	N 9 28.6	226 09.6	11.8	N19 45.4	2.2	54.4
07	284 56.0	29.5	240 40.4	11.8	19 47.6	2.0	54.4
08	299 56.1	30.4	255 11.2	11.8	19 49.6	2.0	54.3
S 09	314 56.3	.. 31.3	269 42.0	11.8	19 51.6	1.9	54.3
U 10	329 56.4	32.2	284 12.8	11.8	19 53.5	1.8	54.3
N 11	344 56.6	33.1	298 43.6	11.8	19 55.3	1.7	54.3
D 12	359 56.8	N 9 34.0	313 14.4	11.8	N19 57.0	1.6	54.3
A 13	14 56.9	34.9	327 45.2	11.8	19 58.6	1.5	54.3
Y 14	29 57.1	35.8	342 16.0	11.8	20 00.1	1.4	54.3
15	44 57.2	.. 36.7	356 46.8	11.8	20 01.5	1.3	54.3
16	59 57.4	37.6	11 17.6	11.8	20 02.8	1.3	54.3
17	74 57.5	38.5	25 48.4	11.8	20 04.1	1.1	54.3
18	89 57.7	N 9 39.4	40 19.2	11.8	N20 05.2	1.0	54.3
19	104 57.8	40.3	54 50.0	11.8	20 06.2	1.0	54.3
20	119 58.0	41.2	69 20.8	11.8	20 07.2	0.8	54.3
21	134 58.1	.. 42.1	83 51.6	11.8	20 08.0	0.8	54.2
22	149 58.3	43.0	98 22.4	11.8	20 08.8	0.6	54.2
23	164 58.4	43.9	112 53.3	11.8	20 09.4	0.6	54.2
15 00	179 58.6	N 9 44.8	127 24.1	11.9	N20 10.0	0.5	54.2
01	194 58.7	45.6	141 55.0	11.8	20 10.5	0.3	54.2
02	209 58.9	46.5	156 25.8	11.9	20 10.8	0.3	54.2
03	224 59.0	.. 47.4	170 56.7	11.8	20 11.1	0.2	54.2
04	239 59.2	48.3	185 27.5	11.9	20 11.3	0.1	54.2
05	254 59.3	49.2	199 58.4	11.9	20 11.4	0.0	54.2
06	269 59.5	N 9 50.1	214 29.3	11.9	N20 11.4	0.1	54.2
07	284 59.6	51.0	229 00.2	11.8	20 11.3	0.2	54.2
08	299 59.8	51.9	243 31.0	11.9	20 11.1	0.3	54.2
M 09	314 59.9	.. 52.8	258 01.9	12.0	20 10.8	0.4	54.2
O 10	330 00.1	53.7	272 32.9	11.9	20 10.4	0.4	54.2
N 11	345 00.2	54.6	287 03.8	11.9	20 10.0	0.6	54.2
D 12	0 00.4	N 9 55.5	301 34.7	11.9	N20 09.4	0.6	54.2
A 13	15 00.5	56.4	316 05.6	12.0	20 08.8	0.8	54.2
Y 14	30 00.7	57.2	330 36.6	12.0	20 08.0	0.8	54.2
15	45 00.8	.. 58.1	345 07.6	11.9	20 07.2	1.0	54.2
16	60 01.0	59.0	359 38.5	12.0	20 06.2	1.0	54.2
17	75 01.1	9 59.9	14 09.5	12.0	20 05.2	1.1	54.2
18	90 01.3	N10 00.8	28 40.5	12.0	N20 04.1	1.3	54.2
19	105 01.4	01.7	43 11.5	12.0	20 02.8	1.3	54.2
20	120 01.6	02.6	57 42.5	12.0	20 01.5	1.4	54.2
21	135 01.7	.. 03.5	72 13.5	12.1	20 00.1	1.5	54.2
22	150 01.9	04.4	86 44.6	12.0	19 58.6	1.6	54.2
23	165 02.0	05.2	101 15.6	12.1	N19 57.0	1.6	54.2
	SD 16.0	d 0.9	SD 14.9		14.8		14.8

Lat.	Twilight Naut.	Civil	Sunrise	Moonrise 13	14	15	16
	h m	h m	h m	h m	h m	h m	h m
N 72	////	02 06	03 44	▭	▭	▭	▭
N 70	////	02 40	04 00	03 47	03 40	▭	05 11
68	00 54	03 04	04 13	04 28	04 45	05 21	06 22
66	01 49	03 23	04 23	04 56	05 21	06 01	06 58
64	02 20	03 38	04 32	05 17	05 47	06 29	07 24
62	02 42	03 50	04 40	05 34	06 07	06 50	07 44
60	03 00	04 00	04 46	05 48	06 23	07 07	08 01
N 58	03 14	04 09	04 52	06 01	06 37	07 21	08 14
56	03 26	04 17	04 57	06 11	06 49	07 34	08 26
54	03 36	04 24	05 01	06 21	06 59	07 45	08 37
52	03 45	04 30	05 05	06 29	07 09	07 54	08 46
50	03 53	04 35	05 09	06 37	07 17	08 03	08 54
45	04 10	04 46	05 17	06 53	07 35	08 21	09 12
N 40	04 22	04 56	05 24	07 06	07 49	08 36	09 26
35	04 32	05 03	05 29	07 17	08 01	08 48	09 38
30	04 41	05 10	05 34	07 27	08 12	08 59	09 49
20	04 53	05 20	05 43	07 44	08 30	09 18	10 07
N 10	05 04	05 29	05 50	07 59	08 47	09 35	10 23
0	05 12	05 36	05 57	08 13	09 02	09 50	10 38
S 10	05 18	05 42	06 04	08 27	09 17	10 05	10 53
20	05 23	05 48	06 11	08 43	09 33	10 22	11 08
30	05 26	05 54	06 18	09 00	09 52	10 41	11 27
35	05 28	05 57	06 23	09 10	10 02	10 52	11 37
40	05 29	06 01	06 28	09 22	10 15	11 04	11 49
45	05 30	06 04	06 34	09 35	10 30	11 19	12 03
S 50	05 31	06 08	06 41	09 52	10 48	11 37	12 21
52	05 31	06 10	06 44	10 00	10 56	11 46	12 29
54	05 31	06 12	06 48	10 09	11 06	11 56	12 38
56	05 30	06 14	06 51	10 19	11 17	12 07	12 48
58	05 30	06 16	06 56	10 30	11 29	12 19	13 00
S 60	05 30	06 18	07 01	10 43	11 43	12 34	13 14

Lat.	Sunset	Twilight Civil	Naut.	Moonset 13	14	15	16
	h m	h m	h m	h m	h m	h m	h m
N 72	20 20	22 02	////	▭	▭	▭	▭
N 70	20 03	21 25	////	00 07	01 54	▭	03 44
68	19 50	21 00	23 24	24 49	00 49	01 53	02 33
66	19 39	20 41	22 19	24 14	00 14	01 14	01 56
64	19 30	20 25	21 45	23 48	24 46	00 46	01 30
62	19 23	20 13	21 22	23 28	24 25	00 25	01 09
60	19 16	20 02	21 04	23 12	24 08	00 08	00 53
N 58	19 10	19 53	20 49	22 58	23 53	24 39	00 39
56	19 05	19 45	20 36	22 47	23 41	24 27	00 27
54	19 00	19 38	20 26	22 36	23 30	24 16	00 16
52	18 56	19 32	20 17	22 27	23 21	24 07	00 07
50	18 52	19 27	20 09	22 19	23 12	23 59	24 23
45	18 44	19 15	19 52	22 02	22 54	23 41	24 23
N 40	18 37	19 06	19 39	21 48	22 39	23 26	24 09
35	18 32	18 58	19 29	21 36	22 26	23 14	23 57
30	18 27	18 51	19 20	21 25	22 15	23 03	23 47
20	18 18	18 40	19 07	21 07	21 57	22 45	23 30
N 10	18 10	18 32	18 57	20 51	21 40	22 28	23 15
0	18 04	18 25	18 49	20 37	21 25	22 13	23 01
S 10	17 57	18 18	18 43	20 22	21 10	21 58	22 46
20	17 50	18 12	18 38	20 06	20 53	21 42	22 31
30	17 42	18 06	18 34	19 48	20 34	21 23	22 13
35	17 37	18 03	18 32	19 38	20 23	21 12	22 03
40	17 32	17 59	18 31	19 26	20 11	20 59	21 51
45	17 26	17 56	18 30	19 12	19 56	20 45	21 37
S 50	17 19	17 52	18 29	18 55	19 38	20 26	21 20
52	17 16	17 50	18 29	18 47	19 29	20 18	21 12
54	17 12	17 48	18 29	18 38	19 19	20 08	21 03
56	17 08	17 46	18 29	18 28	19 09	19 57	20 53
58	17 04	17 44	18 29	18 16	18 56	19 45	20 42
S 60	16 59	17 41	18 29	18 03	18 42	19 31	20 29

Day	SUN Eqn. of Time 00h	12h	Mer. Pass.	MOON Mer. Pass. Upper	Lower	Age	Phase
d	m s	m s	h m	h m	h m	d %	
13	00 36	00 28	12 00	14 25	02 01	03 9	
14	00 21	00 13	12 00	15 13	02 49	04 15	
15	00 06	00 01	12 00	16 01	03 37	05 23	

UT	ARIES GHA	VENUS −3.9 GHA	Dec	MARS +1.2 GHA	Dec	JUPITER −2.0 GHA	Dec	SATURN +0.2 GHA	Dec	STARS Name	SHA	Dec
d h	° ′	° ′	° ′	° ′	° ′	° ′	° ′	° ′	° ′		° ′	° ′
16 00	204 18.2	175 15.1	N10 55.1	179 27.1	N 9 52.5	131 03.8	N22 11.2	346 41.0	S11 59.9	Acamar	315 18.8	S40 15.3
01	219 20.7	190 14.6	56.2	194 27.8	53.2	146 05.8	11.2	1 43.6	59.8	Achernar	335 27.5	S57 10.2
02	234 23.1	205 14.2	57.4	209 28.5	53.9	161 07.7	11.3	16 46.2	59.7	Acrux	173 08.7	S63 10.6
03	249 25.6	220 13.7 ..	58.5	224 29.2 ..	54.6	176 09.7 ..	11.4	31 48.9 ..	59.7	Adhara	255 12.7	S28 59.8
04	264 28.0	235 13.2	10 59.7	239 29.9	55.3	191 11.6	11.4	46 51.5	59.6	Aldebaran	290 49.8	N16 32.0
05	279 30.5	250 12.8	11 00.8	254 30.5	56.0	206 13.6	11.5	61 54.2	59.6			
06	294 33.0	265 12.3	N11 02.0	269 31.2	N 9 56.7	221 15.6	N22 11.5	76 56.8	S11 59.5	Alioth	166 20.3	N55 53.2
07	309 35.4	280 11.8	03.1	284 31.9	57.4	236 17.5	11.6	91 59.4	59.5	Alkaid	152 58.5	N49 14.7
T 08	324 37.9	295 11.4	04.3	299 32.6	58.1	251 19.5	11.7	107 02.1	59.4	Al Na'ir	27 44.1	S46 53.5
U 09	339 40.4	310 10.9 ..	05.4	314 33.3 ..	58.8	266 21.4 ..	11.7	122 04.7 ..	59.3	Alnilam	275 46.7	S 1 11.9
E 10	354 42.8	325 10.5	06.5	329 34.0	9 59.5	281 23.4	11.8	137 07.4	59.3	Alphard	217 56.1	S 8 43.3
S 11	9 45.3	340 10.0	07.7	344 34.7	10 00.2	296 25.3	11.8	152 10.0	59.2			
D 12	24 47.8	355 09.5	N11 08.8	359 35.4	N10 00.9	311 27.3	N22 11.9	167 12.7	S11 59.2	Alphecca	126 10.8	N26 40.1
A 13	39 50.2	10 09.1	10.0	14 36.1	01.6	326 29.2	12.0	182 15.3	59.1	Alpheratz	357 43.9	N29 09.7
Y 14	54 52.7	25 08.6	11.1	29 36.7	02.3	341 31.2	12.0	197 17.9	59.0	Altair	62 08.3	N 8 54.2
15	69 55.2	40 08.1 ..	12.3	44 37.4 ..	03.0	356 33.2 ..	12.1	212 20.6 ..	59.0	Ankaa	353 16.2	S42 14.0
16	84 57.6	55 07.7	13.4	59 38.1	03.7	11 35.1	12.1	227 23.2	58.9	Antares	112 26.1	S26 27.6
17	100 00.1	70 07.2	14.5	74 38.8	04.4	26 37.1	12.2	242 25.9	58.9			
18	115 02.5	85 06.7	N11 15.7	89 39.5	N10 05.1	41 39.0	N22 12.3	257 28.5	S11 58.8	Arcturus	145 55.5	N19 06.7
19	130 05.0	100 06.2	16.8	104 40.2	05.8	56 41.0	12.3	272 31.1	58.7	Atria	107 27.6	S69 02.8
20	145 07.5	115 05.8	18.0	119 40.9	06.5	71 42.9	12.4	287 33.8	58.7	Avior	234 18.0	S59 33.6
21	160 09.9	130 05.3 ..	19.1	134 41.6 ..	07.2	86 44.9 ..	12.4	302 36.4 ..	58.6	Bellatrix	278 32.3	N 6 21.5
22	175 12.4	145 04.8	20.2	149 42.3	07.9	101 46.8	12.5	317 39.1	58.6	Betelgeuse	271 01.6	N 7 24.3
23	190 14.9	160 04.4	21.4	164 42.9	08.6	116 48.8	12.6	332 41.7	58.5			
17 00	205 17.3	175 03.9	N11 22.5	179 43.6	N10 09.3	131 50.8	N22 12.6	347 44.3	S11 58.4	Canopus	263 56.4	S52 42.6
01	220 19.8	190 03.4	23.6	194 44.3	10.0	146 52.7	12.7	2 47.0	58.4	Capella	280 34.9	N46 00.6
02	235 22.3	205 03.0	24.8	209 45.0	10.7	161 54.7	12.7	17 49.6	58.3	Deneb	49 31.6	N45 19.5
03	250 24.7	220 02.5 ..	25.9	224 45.7 ..	11.4	176 56.6 ..	12.8	32 52.3 ..	58.3	Denebola	182 33.5	N14 29.7
04	265 27.2	235 02.0	27.0	239 46.4	12.1	191 58.6	12.9	47 54.9	58.2	Diphda	348 56.3	S17 54.9
05	280 29.7	250 01.5	28.2	254 47.1	12.8	207 00.5	12.9	62 57.6	58.1			
06	295 32.1	265 01.1	N11 29.3	269 47.8	N10 13.5	222 02.5	N22 13.0	78 00.2	S11 58.1	Dubhe	193 51.4	N61 40.8
W 07	310 34.6	280 00.6	30.4	284 48.4	14.2	237 04.4	13.0	93 02.8	58.0	Elnath	278 13.0	N28 37.0
E 08	325 37.0	295 00.1	31.6	299 49.1	14.9	252 06.4	13.1	108 05.5	58.0	Eltanin	90 45.9	N51 29.1
D 09	340 39.5	309 59.7 ..	32.7	314 49.8 ..	15.6	267 08.3 ..	13.2	123 08.1 ..	57.9	Enif	33 47.4	N 9 56.1
N 10	355 42.0	324 59.2	33.8	329 50.5	16.3	282 10.3	13.2	138 10.8	57.8	Fomalhaut	15 24.4	S29 33.0
E 11	10 44.4	339 58.7	35.0	344 51.2	17.0	297 12.2	13.3	153 13.4	57.8			
S 12	25 46.9	354 58.2	N11 36.1	359 51.9	N10 17.7	312 14.2	N22 13.3	168 16.0	S11 57.7	Gacrux	172 00.4	S57 11.5
D 13	40 49.4	9 57.8	37.2	14 52.6	18.4	327 16.1	13.4	183 18.7	57.7	Gienah	175 52.1	S17 37.2
A 14	55 51.8	24 57.3	38.4	29 53.3	19.1	342 18.1	13.5	198 21.3	57.6	Hadar	148 47.4	S60 26.3
Y 15	70 54.3	39 56.8 ..	39.5	44 53.9 ..	19.8	357 20.0 ..	13.5	213 24.0 ..	57.5	Hamal	328 01.2	N23 31.4
16	85 56.8	54 56.3	40.6	59 54.6	20.5	12 22.0	13.6	228 26.6	57.5	Kaus Aust.	83 43.8	S34 22.5
17	100 59.2	69 55.9	41.7	74 55.3	21.2	27 23.9	13.6	243 29.3	57.4			
18	116 01.7	84 55.4	N11 42.9	89 56.0	N10 21.9	42 25.9	N22 13.7	258 31.9	S11 57.4	Kochab	137 18.9	N74 06.0
19	131 04.1	99 54.9	44.0	104 56.7	22.6	57 27.8	13.8	273 34.5	57.3	Markab	13 38.7	N15 16.5
20	146 06.6	114 54.4	45.1	119 57.4	23.3	72 29.8	13.8	288 37.2	57.2	Menkar	314 15.5	N 4 08.3
21	161 09.1	129 53.9 ..	46.3	134 58.1 ..	24.0	87 31.7 ..	13.9	303 39.8 ..	57.2	Menkent	148 07.3	S36 26.2
22	176 11.5	144 53.5	47.4	149 58.8	24.7	102 33.7	13.9	318 42.5	57.1	Miaplacidus	221 39.3	S69 46.8
23	191 14.0	159 53.0	48.5	164 59.5	25.4	117 35.6	14.0	333 45.1	57.1			
18 00	206 16.5	174 52.5	N11 49.6	180 00.1	N10 26.1	132 37.6	N22 14.1	348 47.8	S11 57.0	Mirfak	308 40.9	N49 54.4
01	221 18.9	189 52.0	50.8	195 00.8	26.8	147 39.6	14.1	3 50.4	56.9	Nunki	75 58.4	S26 16.6
02	236 21.4	204 51.6	51.9	210 01.5	27.5	162 41.5	14.2	18 53.0	56.9	Peacock	53 19.5	S56 41.2
03	251 23.9	219 51.1 ..	53.0	225 02.2 ..	28.2	177 43.4 ..	14.2	33 55.7 ..	56.8	Pollux	243 27.9	N27 59.5
04	266 26.3	234 50.6	54.1	240 02.9	28.9	192 45.4	14.3	48 58.3	56.8	Procyon	244 59.9	N 5 11.2
05	281 28.8	249 50.1	55.2	255 03.6	29.5	207 47.3	14.4	64 01.0	56.7			
06	296 31.3	264 49.6	N11 56.4	270 04.3	N10 30.2	222 49.3	N22 14.4	79 03.6	S11 56.6	Rasalhague	96 06.4	N12 33.0
07	311 33.7	279 49.1	57.5	285 04.9	30.9	237 51.2	14.5	94 06.2	56.6	Regulus	207 43.5	N11 53.9
T 08	326 36.2	294 48.7	58.6	300 05.6	31.6	252 53.2	14.5	109 08.9	56.5	Rigel	281 12.4	S 8 11.5
H 09	341 38.6	309 48.2	11 59.7	315 06.3 ..	32.3	267 55.1 ..	14.6	124 11.5 ..	56.5	Rigil Kent.	139 51.2	S60 53.3
U 10	356 41.1	324 47.7	12 00.9	330 07.0	33.0	282 57.1	14.7	139 14.2	56.4	Sabik	102 12.4	S15 44.4
R 11	11 43.6	339 47.2	02.0	345 07.7	33.7	297 59.0	14.7	154 16.8	56.3			
S 12	26 46.0	354 46.7	N12 03.1	0 08.4	N10 34.4	313 01.0	N22 14.8	169 19.5	S11 56.3	Schedar	349 41.2	N56 36.5
D 13	41 48.5	9 46.3	04.2	15 09.1	35.1	328 02.9	14.8	184 22.1	56.2	Shaula	96 21.8	S37 06.6
A 14	56 51.0	24 45.8	05.3	30 09.8	35.8	343 04.9	14.9	199 24.7	56.2	Sirius	258 33.9	S16 44.4
Y 15	71 53.4	39 45.3 ..	06.4	45 10.4 ..	36.5	358 06.8 ..	14.9	214 27.4 ..	56.1	Spica	158 31.0	S11 14.0
16	86 55.9	54 44.8	07.6	60 11.1	37.2	13 08.8	15.0	229 30.0	56.0	Suhail	222 52.4	S43 29.6
17	101 58.4	69 44.3	08.7	75 11.8	37.9	28 10.7	15.1	244 32.7	56.0			
18	117 00.8	84 43.8	N12 09.8	90 12.5	N10 38.5	43 12.7	N22 15.1	259 35.3	S11 55.9	Vega	80 38.9	N38 47.6
19	132 03.3	99 43.3	10.9	105 13.2	39.2	58 14.6	15.2	274 38.0	55.9	Zuben'ubi	137 05.2	S16 05.9
20	147 05.8	114 42.9	12.0	120 13.9	39.9	73 16.6	15.2	289 40.6	55.8		SHA	Mer.Pass.
21	162 08.2	129 42.4 ..	13.1	135 14.6 ..	40.6	88 18.5 ..	15.3	304 43.3 ..	55.7		° ′	h m
22	177 10.7	144 41.9	14.3	150 15.3	41.3	103 20.5	15.4	319 45.9	55.7	Venus	329 46.6	12 20
23	192 13.1	159 41.4	15.4	165 15.9	42.0	118 22.4	15.4	334 48.5	55.6	Mars	334 26.3	12 01
	h m									Jupiter	286 33.4	15 11
Mer. Pass. 10 17.2		v −0.5	d 1.1	v 0.7	d 0.7	v 2.0	d 0.1	v 2.6	d 0.1	Saturn	142 27.0	0 49

UT	SUN GHA	SUN Dec	MOON GHA	v	Dec	d	HP
d h	° ′	° ′	° ′	′	° ′	′	′
16 00	180 02.2	N10 06.1	115 46.7	12.1	N19 55.4	1.8	54.2
01	195 02.3	07.0	130 17.8	12.1	19 53.6	1.9	54.2
02	210 02.5	07.9	144 48.9	12.1	19 51.7	1.9	54.2
03	225 02.6	.. 08.8	159 20.0	12.1	19 49.8	2.1	54.2
04	240 02.8	09.7	173 51.1	12.1	19 47.7	2.1	54.2
05	255 02.9	10.6	188 22.2	12.2	19 45.6	2.2	54.2
06	270 03.1	N10 11.4	202 53.4	12.2	N19 43.4	2.4	54.2
07	285 03.2	12.3	217 24.6	12.1	19 41.0	2.4	54.2
T 08	300 03.3	13.2	231 55.7	12.2	19 38.6	2.5	54.2
U 09	315 03.5	.. 14.1	246 26.9	12.2	19 36.1	2.5	54.2
E 10	330 03.6	15.0	260 58.1	12.3	19 33.6	2.7	54.2
S 11	345 03.8	15.9	275 29.4	12.2	19 30.9	2.8	54.2
D 12	0 03.9	N10 16.8	290 00.6	12.3	N19 28.1	2.9	54.2
A 13	15 04.1	17.6	304 31.9	12.2	19 25.2	2.9	54.2
Y 14	30 04.2	18.5	319 03.1	12.3	19 22.3	3.0	54.2
15	45 04.4	.. 19.4	333 34.4	12.3	19 19.3	3.2	54.2
16	60 04.5	20.3	348 05.7	12.3	19 16.1	3.2	54.2
17	75 04.7	21.2	2 37.0	12.4	19 12.9	3.3	54.2
18	90 04.8	N10 22.0	17 08.4	12.3	N19 09.6	3.4	54.2
19	105 04.9	22.9	31 39.7	12.4	19 06.2	3.4	54.2
20	120 05.1	23.8	46 11.1	12.4	19 02.8	3.6	54.2
21	135 05.2	.. 24.7	60 42.5	12.4	18 59.2	3.7	54.2
22	150 05.4	25.6	75 13.9	12.4	18 55.5	3.7	54.2
23	165 05.5	26.5	89 45.3	12.4	18 51.8	3.8	54.2
17 00	180 05.7	N10 27.3	104 16.7	12.5	N18 48.0	3.9	54.3
01	195 05.8	28.2	118 48.2	12.5	18 44.1	4.0	54.3
02	210 06.0	29.1	133 19.7	12.4	18 40.1	4.1	54.3
03	225 06.1	.. 30.0	147 51.1	12.5	18 36.0	4.2	54.3
04	240 06.2	30.9	162 22.6	12.6	18 31.8	4.2	54.3
05	255 06.4	31.7	176 54.2	12.5	18 27.6	4.4	54.3
06	270 06.5	N10 32.6	191 25.7	12.6	N18 23.2	4.4	54.3
W 07	285 06.7	33.5	205 57.3	12.5	18 18.8	4.5	54.3
E 08	300 06.8	34.4	220 28.8	12.6	18 14.3	4.6	54.3
D 09	315 07.0	.. 35.2	235 00.4	12.6	18 09.7	4.7	54.3
N 10	330 07.1	36.1	249 32.0	12.6	18 05.0	4.7	54.3
E 11	345 07.2	37.0	264 03.6	12.7	18 00.3	4.8	54.3
S 12	0 07.4	N10 37.9	278 35.3	12.6	N17 55.5	5.0	54.4
D 13	15 07.5	38.7	293 06.9	12.7	17 50.5	5.0	54.4
A 14	30 07.7	39.6	307 38.6	12.7	17 45.5	5.1	54.4
Y 15	45 07.8	.. 40.5	322 10.3	12.7	17 40.4	5.1	54.4
16	60 08.0	41.4	336 42.0	12.7	17 35.3	5.3	54.4
17	75 08.1	42.2	351 13.7	12.8	17 30.0	5.3	54.4
18	90 08.2	N10 43.1	5 45.5	12.7	N17 24.7	5.4	54.4
19	105 08.4	44.0	20 17.2	12.8	17 19.3	5.5	54.4
20	120 08.5	44.9	34 49.0	12.8	17 13.8	5.6	54.5
21	135 08.7	.. 45.7	49 20.8	12.8	17 08.2	5.6	54.5
22	150 08.8	46.6	63 52.6	12.8	17 02.6	5.8	54.5
23	165 08.9	47.5	78 24.4	12.9	16 56.8	5.8	54.5
18 00	180 09.1	N10 48.4	92 56.3	12.8	N16 51.0	5.9	54.5
01	195 09.2	49.2	107 28.1	12.9	16 45.1	5.9	54.5
02	210 09.4	50.1	122 00.0	12.9	16 39.2	6.1	54.5
03	225 09.5	.. 51.0	136 31.9	12.9	16 33.1	6.1	54.6
04	240 09.6	51.9	151 03.8	12.9	16 27.0	6.2	54.6
05	255 09.8	52.7	165 35.7	13.0	16 20.8	6.3	54.6
06	270 09.9	N10 53.6	180 07.7	12.9	N16 14.5	6.3	54.6
07	285 10.1	54.5	194 39.6	13.0	16 08.2	6.5	54.6
T 08	300 10.2	55.3	209 11.6	13.0	16 01.7	6.5	54.6
H 09	315 10.3	.. 56.2	223 43.6	12.9	15 55.2	6.6	54.7
U 10	330 10.5	57.1	238 15.5	13.1	15 48.6	6.6	54.7
R 11	345 10.6	57.9	252 47.6	13.0	15 42.0	6.7	54.7
S 12	0 10.7	N10 58.8	267 19.6	13.0	N15 35.3	6.8	54.7
D 13	15 10.9	10 59.7	281 51.6	13.1	15 28.5	6.9	54.7
A 14	30 11.0	11 00.6	296 23.7	13.0	15 21.6	7.0	54.7
Y 15	45 11.2	.. 01.4	310 55.7	13.1	15 14.6	7.0	54.8
16	60 11.3	02.3	325 27.8	13.1	15 07.6	7.1	54.8
17	75 11.4	03.2	339 59.9	13.1	15 00.5	7.2	54.8
18	90 11.6	N11 04.0	354 32.0	13.1	N14 53.3	7.2	54.8
19	105 11.7	04.9	9 04.1	13.1	14 46.1	7.3	54.8
20	120 11.8	05.8	23 36.2	13.1	14 38.8	7.4	54.9
21	135 12.0	.. 06.6	38 08.3	13.2	14 31.4	7.5	54.9
22	150 12.1	07.5	52 40.5	13.1	14 23.9	7.5	54.9
23	165 12.3	08.4	67 12.6	13.2	N14 16.4	7.6	54.9
	SD 16.0	d 0.9	SD 14.8		14.8		14.9

Lat.	Twilight Naut.	Civil	Sunrise	Moonrise 16	17	18	19
°	h m	h m	h m	h m	h m	h m	h m
N 72	////	01 36	03 27	▭	▭	07 57	09 55
N 70	////	02 19	03 45	05 11	06 57	08 39	10 20
68	////	02 48	04 00	06 22	07 40	09 07	10 38
66	01 23	03 09	04 12	06 58	08 09	09 29	10 53
64	02 02	03 26	04 22	07 24	08 31	09 45	11 05
62	02 28	03 39	04 30	07 44	08 48	09 59	11 15
60	02 47	03 50	04 37	08 01	09 03	10 11	11 24
N 58	03 03	04 00	04 44	08 14	09 15	10 21	11 31
56	03 17	04 09	04 49	08 26	09 25	10 30	11 38
54	03 28	04 18	04 54	08 37	09 35	10 38	11 44
52	03 38	04 23	04 59	08 46	09 43	10 45	11 49
50	03 46	04 29	05 03	08 54	09 51	10 51	11 54
45	04 04	04 41	05 12	09 12	10 06	11 04	12 05
N 40	04 17	04 51	05 19	09 26	10 19	11 15	12 13
35	04 28	04 59	05 25	09 38	10 31	11 25	12 21
30	04 37	05 06	05 31	09 49	10 40	11 33	12 27
20	04 52	05 18	05 40	10 07	10 57	11 47	12 38
N 10	05 02	05 27	05 49	10 23	11 11	12 00	12 48
0	05 11	05 35	05 56	10 38	11 25	12 11	12 57
S 10	05 18	05 42	06 04	10 53	11 38	12 23	13 07
20	05 23	05 49	06 11	11 08	11 53	12 35	13 16
30	05 28	05 56	06 20	11 27	12 09	12 50	13 27
35	05 30	06 00	06 25	11 37	12 19	12 58	13 34
40	05 32	06 04	06 31	11 49	12 30	13 07	13 41
45	05 34	06 08	06 38	12 03	12 43	13 18	13 50
S 50	05 35	06 13	06 45	12 21	12 58	13 31	14 00
52	05 35	06 15	06 49	12 29	13 06	13 37	14 04
54	05 36	06 17	06 53	12 38	13 14	13 44	14 09
56	05 36	06 19	06 57	12 48	13 23	13 51	14 15
58	05 36	06 22	07 02	13 00	13 33	14 00	14 21
S 60	05 36	06 25	07 08	13 14	13 45	14 09	14 29

Lat.	Sunset	Twilight Civil	Naut.	Moonset 16	17	18	19
°	h m	h m	h m	h m	h m	h m	h m
N 72	20 36	22 34	////	▭	▭	04 14	03 52
N 70	20 17	21 45	////	03 44	03 36	03 31	03 26
68	20 02	21 15	////	02 33	02 52	03 02	03 06
66	19 50	20 53	22 45	01 56	02 23	02 40	02 51
64	19 39	20 36	22 03	01 30	02 01	02 22	02 38
62	19 31	20 22	21 35	01 09	01 43	02 08	02 27
60	19 23	20 11	21 15	00 53	01 28	01 56	02 17
N 58	19 17	20 01	20 58	00 39	01 16	01 45	02 09
56	19 11	19 52	20 45	00 27	01 05	01 36	02 02
54	19 06	19 44	20 33	00 16	00 55	01 28	01 55
52	19 01	19 38	20 23	00 07	00 47	01 21	01 50
50	18 57	19 32	20 14	24 39	00 39	01 14	01 44
45	18 48	19 19	19 57	24 23	00 23	01 00	01 33
N 40	18 41	19 09	19 43	24 09	00 09	00 48	01 23
35	18 34	19 00	19 32	23 57	24 38	00 38	01 15
30	18 29	18 53	19 22	23 47	24 29	00 29	01 08
20	18 19	18 41	19 08	23 30	24 14	00 14	00 55
N 10	18 11	18 32	18 57	23 15	24 00	00 00	00 44
0	18 03	18 24	18 48	23 01	23 47	24 34	00 34
S 10	17 55	18 17	18 41	22 46	23 35	24 23	00 23
20	17 47	18 11	18 36	22 31	23 21	24 12	00 12
30	17 38	18 03	18 30	22 13	23 06	23 59	24 54
35	17 33	17 59	18 28	22 03	22 56	23 52	24 48
40	17 27	17 55	18 26	21 51	22 46	23 43	24 42
45	17 21	17 51	18 25	21 37	22 34	23 33	24 34
S 50	17 13	17 46	18 23	21 20	22 19	23 21	24 25
52	17 09	17 44	18 23	21 12	22 12	23 15	24 21
54	17 05	17 41	18 22	21 03	22 04	23 09	24 17
56	17 01	17 39	18 22	20 53	21 55	23 02	24 12
58	16 56	17 36	18 21	20 42	21 45	22 54	24 06
S 60	16 50	17 33	18 21	20 29	21 34	22 45	23 59

Day	SUN Eqn. of Time 00h	12h	Mer. Pass.	MOON Mer. Pass. Upper	Lower	Age	Phase
	m s	m s	h m	h m	h m	d	%
16	00 08	00 15	12 00	16 49	04 25	06	31
17	00 22	00 29	12 00	17 36	05 13	07	40
18	00 36	00 43	11 59	18 23	05 59	08	50

UT	ARIES GHA	VENUS −3.9 GHA	Dec	MARS +1.2 GHA	Dec	JUPITER −2.0 GHA	Dec	SATURN +0.2 GHA	Dec
19 00	207 15.6	174 40.9	N12 16.5	180 16.6	N10 42.7	133 24.4	N22 15.5	349 51.2	S11 55.6
01	222 18.1	189 40.4	17.6	195 17.3	43.4	148 26.3	15.5	4 53.8	55.5
02	237 20.5	204 39.9	18.7	210 18.0	44.1	163 28.3	15.6	19 56.5	55.4
03	252 23.0	219 39.4 ..	19.8	225 18.7 ..	44.8	178 30.2 ..	15.7	34 59.1 ..	55.4
04	267 25.5	234 39.0	20.9	240 19.4	45.5	193 32.1	15.7	50 01.8	55.3
05	282 27.9	249 38.5	22.0	255 20.1	46.1	208 34.1	15.8	65 04.4	55.3
06	297 30.4	264 38.0	N12 23.1	270 20.7	N10 46.8	223 36.0	N22 15.8	80 07.0	S11 55.2
F 07	312 32.9	279 37.5	24.3	285 21.4	47.5	238 38.0	15.9	95 09.7	55.1
R 08	327 35.3	294 37.0	25.4	300 22.1	48.2	253 39.9	16.0	110 12.3	55.1
I 09	342 37.8	309 36.5 ..	26.5	315 22.8 ..	48.9	268 41.9 ..	16.0	125 15.0 ..	55.0
D 10	357 40.2	324 36.0	27.6	330 23.5	49.6	283 43.8	16.1	140 17.6	55.0
A 11	12 42.7	339 35.5	28.7	345 24.2	50.3	298 45.8	16.1	155 20.3	54.9
Y 12	27 45.2	354 35.0	N12 29.8	0 24.9	N10 51.0	313 47.7	N22 16.2	170 22.9	S11 54.8
13	42 47.6	9 34.5	30.9	15 25.5	51.7	328 49.7	16.3	185 25.5	54.8
14	57 50.1	24 34.0	32.0	30 26.2	52.3	343 51.6	16.3	200 28.2	54.7
15	72 52.6	39 33.6 ..	33.1	45 26.9 ..	53.0	358 53.5 ..	16.4	215 30.8 ..	54.7
16	87 55.0	54 33.1	34.2	60 27.6	53.7	13 55.5	16.4	230 33.5	54.6
17	102 57.5	69 32.6	35.3	75 28.3	54.4	28 57.4	16.5	245 36.1	54.6
18	118 00.0	84 32.1	N12 36.4	90 29.0	N10 55.1	43 59.4	N22 16.5	260 38.8	S11 54.5
19	133 02.4	99 31.6	37.5	105 29.6	55.8	59 01.3	16.6	275 41.4	54.4
20	148 04.9	114 31.1	38.6	120 30.3	56.5	74 03.3	16.7	290 44.1	54.4
21	163 07.4	129 30.6 ..	39.7	135 31.0 ..	57.1	89 05.2 ..	16.7	305 46.7 ..	54.3
22	178 09.8	144 30.1	40.8	150 31.7	57.8	104 07.1	16.8	320 49.3	54.2
23	193 12.3	159 29.6	41.9	165 32.4	58.5	119 09.1	16.8	335 52.0	54.2
20 00	208 14.7	174 29.1	N12 43.0	180 33.1	N10 59.2	134 11.0	N22 16.9	350 54.6	S11 54.1
01	223 17.2	189 28.6	44.1	195 33.8	10 59.9	149 13.0	17.0	5 57.3	54.1
02	238 19.7	204 28.1	45.2	210 34.4	11 00.6	164 14.9	17.0	20 59.9	54.0
03	253 22.1	219 27.6 ..	46.3	225 35.1 ..	01.3	179 16.9 ..	17.1	36 02.6 ..	53.9
04	268 24.6	234 27.1	47.4	240 35.8	01.9	194 18.8	17.1	51 05.2	53.9
05	283 27.1	249 26.6	48.5	255 36.5	02.6	209 20.7	17.2	66 07.9	53.8
06	298 29.5	264 26.1	N12 49.6	270 37.2	N11 03.3	224 22.7	N22 17.3	81 10.5	S11 53.8
S 07	313 32.0	279 25.6	50.7	285 37.9	04.0	239 24.6	17.3	96 13.1	53.7
A 08	328 34.5	294 25.1	51.8	300 38.5	04.7	254 26.6	17.4	111 15.8	53.6
T 09	343 36.9	309 24.6 ..	53.0	315 39.2 ..	05.4	269 28.5 ..	17.4	126 18.4 ..	53.6
U 10	358 39.4	324 24.1	54.0	330 39.9	06.0	284 30.5	17.5	141 21.1	53.5
R 11	13 41.9	339 23.6	55.1	345 40.6	06.7	299 32.4	17.5	156 23.7	53.5
D 12	28 44.3	354 23.1	N12 56.2	0 41.3	N11 07.4	314 34.3	N22 17.6	171 26.4	S11 53.4
A 13	43 46.8	9 22.6	57.3	15 42.0	08.1	329 36.3	17.7	186 29.0	53.3
Y 14	58 49.2	24 22.1	58.4	30 42.7	08.8	344 38.2	17.7	201 31.7	53.3
15	73 51.7	39 21.6	12 59.5	45 43.3 ..	09.5	359 40.2 ..	17.8	216 34.3 ..	53.2
16	88 54.2	54 21.1	13 00.6	60 44.0	10.1	14 42.1	17.8	231 36.9	53.2
17	103 56.6	69 20.6	01.7	75 44.7	10.8	29 44.0	17.9	246 39.6	53.1
18	118 59.1	84 20.1	N13 02.7	90 45.4	N11 11.5	44 46.0	N22 18.0	261 42.2	S11 53.0
19	134 01.6	99 19.6	03.8	105 46.1	12.2	59 47.9	18.0	276 44.9	53.0
20	149 04.0	114 19.1	04.9	120 46.8	12.9	74 49.9	18.1	291 47.5	52.9
21	164 06.5	129 18.6 ..	06.0	135 47.4 ..	13.5	89 51.8 ..	18.1	306 50.2 ..	52.9
22	179 09.0	144 18.1	07.1	150 48.1	14.2	104 53.7	18.2	321 52.8	52.8
23	194 11.4	159 17.6	08.2	165 48.8	14.9	119 55.7	18.3	336 55.5	52.7
21 00	209 13.9	174 17.1	N13 09.3	180 49.5	N11 15.6	134 57.6	N22 18.3	351 58.1	S11 52.7
01	224 16.3	189 16.6	10.4	195 50.2	16.3	149 59.6	18.4	7 00.7	52.6
02	239 18.8	204 16.0	11.5	210 50.9	16.9	165 01.5	18.4	22 03.4	52.6
03	254 21.3	219 15.5 ..	12.5	225 51.5 ..	17.6	180 03.4 ..	18.5	37 06.0 ..	52.5
04	269 23.7	234 15.0	13.6	240 52.2	18.3	195 05.4	18.5	52 08.7	52.4
05	284 26.2	249 14.5	14.7	255 52.9	19.0	210 07.3	18.6	67 11.3	52.4
06	299 28.7	264 14.0	N13 15.8	270 53.6	N11 19.7	225 09.3	N22 18.7	82 14.0	S11 52.3
S 07	314 31.1	279 13.5	16.9	285 54.3	20.3	240 11.2	18.7	97 16.6	52.3
U 08	329 33.6	294 13.0	18.0	300 55.0	21.0	255 13.1	18.8	112 19.3	52.2
N 09	344 36.1	309 12.5 ..	19.0	315 55.6 ..	21.7	270 15.1 ..	18.8	127 21.9 ..	52.1
D 10	359 38.5	324 12.0	20.1	330 56.3	22.4	285 17.0	18.9	142 24.6	52.1
A 11	14 41.0	339 11.5	21.2	345 57.0	23.1	300 18.9	19.0	157 27.2	52.0
Y 12	29 43.5	354 11.0	N13 22.3	0 57.7	N11 23.7	315 20.9	N22 19.0	172 29.8	S11 52.0
13	44 45.9	9 10.4	23.4	15 58.4	24.4	330 22.8	19.1	187 32.5	51.9
14	59 48.4	24 09.9	24.5	30 59.1	25.1	345 24.8	19.1	202 35.1	51.8
15	74 50.8	39 09.4 ..	25.5	45 59.7 ..	25.8	0 26.7 ..	19.2	217 37.8 ..	51.8
16	89 53.3	54 08.9	26.6	61 00.4	26.4	15 28.6	19.2	232 40.4	51.7
17	104 55.8	69 08.4	27.7	76 01.1	27.1	30 30.6	19.3	247 43.1	51.7
18	119 58.2	84 07.9	N13 28.8	91 01.8	N11 27.8	45 32.5	N22 19.4	262 45.7	S11 51.6
19	135 00.7	99 07.4	29.8	106 02.5	28.5	60 34.4	19.4	277 48.4	51.5
20	150 03.2	114 06.9	31.0	121 03.1	29.1	75 36.3	19.5	292 51.0	51.5
21	165 05.6	129 06.3 ..	32.0	136 03.8 ..	29.8	90 38.3 ..	19.5	307 53.7 ..	51.4
22	180 08.1	144 05.8	33.1	151 04.5	30.5	105 40.2	19.6	322 56.3	51.4
23	195 10.6	159 05.3	34.1	166 05.2	31.2	120 42.2	19.6	337 58.9	51.3
Mer. Pass.	10 05.4	v −0.5	d 1.1	v 0.7	d 0.7	v 1.9	d 0.1	v 2.6	d 0.1

STARS

Name	SHA	Dec
Acamar	315 18.8	S40 15.3
Achernar	335 27.5	S57 10.2
Acrux	173 08.7	S63 10.6
Adhara	255 12.7	S28 59.8
Aldebaran	290 49.8	N16 32.0
Alioth	166 20.3	N55 53.2
Alkaid	152 58.5	N49 14.7
Al Na'ir	27 44.1	S46 53.5
Alnilam	275 46.7	S 1 11.9
Alphard	217 56.1	S 8 43.3
Alphecca	126 10.8	N26 40.1
Alpheratz	357 43.9	N29 09.7
Altair	62 08.3	N 8 54.2
Ankaa	353 16.2	S42 14.0
Antares	112 26.1	S26 27.6
Arcturus	145 55.5	N19 06.7
Atria	107 27.6	S69 02.8
Avior	234 18.0	S59 33.6
Bellatrix	278 32.3	N 6 21.5
Betelgeuse	271 01.6	N 7 24.3
Canopus	263 56.4	S52 42.6
Capella	280 34.9	N46 00.6
Deneb	49 31.6	N45 19.5
Denebola	182 33.5	N14 29.7
Diphda	348 56.3	S17 54.8
Dubhe	193 51.4	N61 40.8
Elnath	278 13.0	N28 37.0
Eltanin	90 45.9	N51 29.1
Enif	33 47.4	N 9 56.1
Fomalhaut	15 24.4	S29 33.0
Gacrux	172 00.4	S57 11.5
Gienah	175 52.1	S17 37.2
Hadar	148 47.4	S60 26.3
Hamal	328 01.2	N23 31.4
Kaus Aust.	83 43.8	S34 22.5
Kochab	137 18.9	N74 06.0
Markab	13 38.7	N15 16.5
Menkar	314 15.5	N 4 08.3
Menkent	148 07.3	S36 26.2
Miaplacidus	221 39.4	S69 46.8
Mirfak	308 41.0	N49 54.4
Nunki	75 58.3	S26 16.6
Peacock	53 19.5	S56 41.2
Pollux	243 27.9	N27 59.5
Procyon	244 59.9	N 5 11.2
Rasalhague	96 06.3	N12 33.0
Regulus	207 43.5	N11 53.9
Rigel	281 12.4	S 8 11.5
Rigil Kent.	139 51.2	S60 53.4
Sabik	102 12.4	S15 44.4
Schedar	349 41.1	N56 36.5
Shaula	96 21.8	S37 06.6
Sirius	258 33.9	S16 44.4
Spica	158 31.0	S11 14.0
Suhail	222 52.4	S43 29.6
Vega	80 38.9	N38 47.6
Zuben'ubi	137 05.2	S16 05.9

	SHA	Mer. Pass.
Venus	326 14.3	12 22
Mars	332 18.3	11 57
Jupiter	285 56.3	15 01
Saturn	142 39.9	0 36

UT	SUN GHA	Dec	MOON GHA	v	Dec	d	HP
d h	° ′	° ′	° ′	′	° ′	′	′
19 00	180 12.4	N11 09.2	81 44.8	13.2	N14 08.8	7.6	54.9
01	195 12.5	10.1	96 17.0	13.2	14 01.2	7.8	55.0
02	210 12.7	10.9	110 49.2	13.1	13 53.4	7.8	55.0
03	225 12.8	.. 11.8	125 21.3	13.2	13 45.6	7.8	55.0
04	240 12.9	12.7	139 53.5	13.3	13 37.8	8.0	55.0
05	255 13.1	13.5	154 25.8	13.2	13 29.8	8.0	55.1
06	270 13.2	N11 14.4	168 58.0	13.2	N13 21.8	8.1	55.1
07	285 13.3	15.3	183 30.2	13.2	13 13.7	8.1	55.1
08	300 13.5	16.1	198 02.4	13.3	13 05.6	8.2	55.1
F 09	315 13.6	.. 17.0	212 34.7	13.2	12 57.4	8.3	55.1
R 10	330 13.7	17.9	227 06.9	13.3	12 49.1	8.3	55.2
I 11	345 13.9	18.7	241 39.2	13.2	12 40.8	8.4	55.2
D 12	0 14.0	N11 19.6	256 11.4	13.3	N12 32.4	8.4	55.2
A 13	15 14.1	20.4	270 43.7	13.3	12 24.0	8.6	55.2
Y 14	30 14.3	21.3	285 16.0	13.2	12 15.4	8.6	55.3
15	45 14.4	.. 22.2	299 48.2	13.3	12 06.8	8.6	55.3
16	60 14.5	23.0	314 20.5	13.3	11 58.2	8.7	55.3
17	75 14.7	23.9	328 52.8	13.3	11 49.5	8.8	55.3
18	90 14.8	N11 24.7	343 25.1	13.2	N11 40.7	8.8	55.4
19	105 14.9	25.6	357 57.3	13.3	11 31.9	8.9	55.4
20	120 15.1	26.5	12 29.6	13.3	11 23.0	9.0	55.4
21	135 15.2	.. 27.3	27 01.9	13.3	11 14.0	9.0	55.4
22	150 15.3	28.2	41 34.2	13.3	11 05.0	9.1	55.5
23	165 15.5	29.0	56 06.5	13.3	10 55.9	9.1	55.5
20 00	180 15.6	N11 29.9	70 38.8	13.3	N10 46.8	9.2	55.5
01	195 15.7	30.7	85 11.1	13.2	10 37.6	9.2	55.6
02	210 15.9	31.6	99 43.3	13.3	10 28.4	9.3	55.6
03	225 16.0	.. 32.5	114 15.6	13.3	10 19.1	9.4	55.6
04	240 16.1	33.3	128 47.9	13.3	10 09.7	9.4	55.6
05	255 16.3	34.2	143 20.2	13.2	10 00.3	9.5	55.7
06	270 16.4	N11 35.0	157 52.4	13.3	N9 50.8	9.5	55.7
S 07	285 16.5	35.9	172 24.7	13.3	9 41.3	9.6	55.7
A 08	300 16.7	36.7	186 57.0	13.2	9 31.7	9.7	55.8
T 09	315 16.8	.. 37.6	201 29.2	13.3	9 22.0	9.6	55.8
U 10	330 16.9	38.4	216 01.5	13.2	9 12.4	9.8	55.8
R 11	345 17.0	39.3	230 33.7	13.3	9 02.6	9.8	55.8
D 12	0 17.2	N11 40.1	245 06.0	13.2	N8 52.8	9.8	55.9
A 13	15 17.3	41.0	259 38.2	13.2	8 43.0	9.9	55.9
Y 14	30 17.4	41.9	274 10.4	13.3	8 33.1	10.0	55.9
15	45 17.6	.. 42.7	288 42.7	13.2	8 23.1	10.0	56.0
16	60 17.7	43.6	303 14.9	13.2	8 13.1	10.0	56.0
17	75 17.8	44.4	317 47.1	13.1	8 03.1	10.1	56.0
18	90 18.0	N11 45.3	332 19.2	13.2	N7 53.0	10.2	56.1
19	105 18.1	46.1	346 51.4	13.2	7 42.8	10.2	56.1
20	120 18.2	47.0	1 23.6	13.1	7 32.6	10.2	56.1
21	135 18.3	.. 47.8	15 55.7	13.2	7 22.4	10.3	56.2
22	150 18.5	48.7	30 27.9	13.1	7 12.1	10.3	56.2
23	165 18.6	49.5	45 00.0	13.1	7 01.8	10.4	56.2
21 00	180 18.7	N11 50.4	59 32.1	13.1	N6 51.4	10.4	56.3
01	195 18.8	51.2	74 04.2	13.1	6 41.0	10.5	56.3
02	210 19.0	52.1	88 36.3	13.0	6 30.5	10.5	56.3
03	225 19.1	.. 52.9	103 08.3	13.1	6 20.0	10.6	56.4
04	240 19.2	53.8	117 40.4	13.0	6 09.4	10.6	56.4
05	255 19.4	54.6	132 12.4	13.0	5 58.8	10.6	56.4
06	270 19.5	N11 55.5	146 44.4	13.0	N5 48.2	10.7	56.5
07	285 19.6	56.3	161 16.4	12.9	5 37.5	10.7	56.5
08	300 19.7	57.1	175 48.3	13.0	5 26.8	10.8	56.5
S 09	315 19.9	.. 58.0	190 20.3	12.9	5 16.0	10.8	56.6
U 10	330 20.0	58.8	204 52.2	12.9	5 05.3	10.9	56.6
N 11	345 20.1	11 59.7	219 24.1	12.9	4 54.4	10.8	56.6
D 12	0 20.2	N12 00.5	233 56.0	12.9	N4 43.6	11.0	56.7
A 13	15 20.4	01.4	248 27.8	12.9	4 32.6	10.9	56.7
Y 14	30 20.5	02.2	262 59.7	12.8	4 21.7	11.0	56.7
15	45 20.6	.. 03.1	277 31.5	12.8	4 10.7	11.0	56.8
16	60 20.7	03.9	292 03.3	12.7	3 59.7	11.0	56.8
17	75 20.9	04.8	306 35.0	12.7	3 48.7	11.1	56.8
18	90 21.0	N12 05.6	321 06.7	12.7	N3 37.6	11.1	56.9
19	105 21.1	06.4	335 38.4	12.7	3 26.5	11.1	56.9
20	120 21.2	07.3	350 10.1	12.7	3 15.4	11.2	56.9
21	135 21.4	.. 08.1	4 41.8	12.6	3 04.2	11.2	57.0
22	150 21.5	09.0	19 13.4	12.5	2 53.0	11.2	57.0
23	165 21.6	09.8	33 44.9	12.6	N2 41.8	11.3	57.0
	SD 15.9	d 0.9	SD 15.0		15.2		15.4

Twilight / Moonrise

Lat.	Naut.	Civil	Sunrise	19	20	21	22
°	h m	h m	h m	h m	h m	h m	h m
N 72	////	00 53	03 09	09 55	11 45	13 33	15 23
N 70	////	01 56	03 30	10 20	11 59	13 40	15 23
68	////	02 30	03 47	10 38	12 11	13 45	15 22
66	00 46	02 54	04 00	10 53	12 20	13 49	15 21
64	01 41	03 13	04 11	11 05	12 27	13 53	15 21
62	02 12	03 28	04 21	11 15	12 34	13 56	15 21
60	02 35	03 41	04 29	11 24	12 40	13 59	15 20
N 58	02 52	03 51	04 36	11 31	12 45	14 01	15 20
56	03 07	04 01	04 42	11 38	12 49	14 03	15 20
54	03 19	04 09	04 47	11 44	12 53	14 05	15 19
52	03 30	04 16	04 52	11 49	12 57	14 07	15 19
50	03 39	04 22	04 57	11 54	13 00	14 08	15 19
45	03 58	04 36	05 07	12 05	13 07	14 12	15 19
N 40	04 12	04 46	05 15	12 13	13 13	14 15	15 18
35	04 24	04 55	05 22	12 21	13 18	14 17	15 18
30	04 34	05 03	05 28	12 27	13 23	14 19	15 18
20	04 49	05 16	05 38	12 38	13 30	14 23	15 17
N 10	05 01	05 26	05 47	12 48	13 37	14 26	15 17
0	05 10	05 34	05 56	12 57	13 43	14 29	15 17
S 10	05 18	05 42	06 04	13 07	13 50	14 33	15 16
20	05 24	05 50	06 12	13 16	13 56	14 36	15 16
30	05 30	05 58	06 22	13 27	14 04	14 40	15 16
35	05 32	06 02	06 28	13 34	14 08	14 42	15 16
40	05 35	06 06	06 34	13 41	14 13	14 44	15 15
45	05 37	06 11	06 41	13 50	14 19	14 47	15 15
S 50	05 39	06 17	06 50	14 00	14 26	14 50	15 15
52	05 40	06 19	06 54	14 04	14 29	14 52	15 15
54	05 41	06 22	06 59	14 09	14 32	14 54	15 15
56	05 42	06 25	07 03	14 15	14 36	14 56	15 15
58	05 42	06 28	07 09	14 21	14 40	14 58	15 15
S 60	05 43	06 32	07 15	14 29	14 45	15 00	15 14

Sunset / Twilight / Moonset

Lat.	Sunset	Civil	Naut.	19	20	21	22
°	h m	h m	h m	h m	h m	h m	h m
N 72	20 54	23 27	////	03 52	03 37	03 26	03 15
N 70	20 31	22 09	////	03 26	03 21	03 17	03 12
68	20 14	21 32	////	03 06	03 09	03 11	03 10
66	20 00	21 07	23 31	02 51	02 58	03 04	03 09
64	19 49	20 48	22 23	02 38	02 49	02 59	03 07
62	19 39	20 32	21 50	02 27	02 42	02 55	03 06
60	19 31	20 19	21 26	02 17	02 35	02 51	03 05
N 58	19 24	20 08	21 08	02 09	02 29	02 47	03 04
56	19 17	19 59	20 53	02 02	02 24	02 44	03 03
54	19 12	19 51	20 41	01 55	02 20	02 42	03 02
52	19 06	19 43	20 30	01 50	02 15	02 39	03 02
50	19 02	19 37	20 20	01 44	02 12	02 37	03 01
45	18 52	19 23	20 01	01 33	02 03	02 32	03 00
N 40	18 44	19 12	19 46	01 23	01 56	02 28	02 58
35	18 37	19 03	19 34	01 15	01 50	02 24	02 57
30	18 30	18 55	19 25	01 08	01 45	02 21	02 56
20	18 20	18 42	19 09	00 55	01 35	02 15	02 55
N 10	18 11	18 32	18 57	00 44	01 27	02 10	02 53
0	18 02	18 23	18 48	00 34	01 19	02 05	02 52
S 10	17 54	18 15	18 40	00 23	01 12	02 01	02 50
20	17 45	18 07	18 33	00 12	01 03	01 55	02 49
30	17 35	18 00	18 28	24 54	00 54	01 50	02 47
35	17 30	17 55	18 25	24 48	00 48	01 46	02 46
40	17 23	17 51	18 22	24 42	00 42	01 42	02 45
45	17 16	17 46	18 20	24 34	00 34	01 38	02 43
S 50	17 07	17 40	18 17	24 25	00 25	01 32	02 42
52	17 03	17 38	18 17	24 21	00 21	01 30	02 41
54	16 58	17 35	18 16	24 17	00 17	01 27	02 40
56	16 53	17 32	18 15	24 12	00 12	01 24	02 39
58	16 48	17 29	18 14	24 06	00 06	01 21	02 38
S 60	16 42	17 25	18 14	23 59	25 17	01 17	02 37

SUN / MOON

Day	Eqn. of Time 00ʰ	12ʰ	Mer. Pass.	Mer. Pass. Upper	Lower	Age	Phase
d	m s	m s	h m	h m	h m	d %	
19	00 49	00 56	11 59	19 08	06 46	09 60	
20	01 02	01 08	11 59	19 54	07 31	10 69	◑
21	01 15	01 21	11 59	20 41	08 17	11 78	

UT	ARIES GHA	VENUS −3.9 GHA	Dec	MARS +1.2 GHA	Dec	JUPITER −2.0 GHA	Dec	SATURN +0.1 GHA	Dec	Name	SHA	Dec
22 00	210 13.0	174 04.8	N13 35.2	181 05.9	N11 31.9	135 44.1	N22 19.7	353 01.6	S11 51.2	Acamar	315 18.9	S40 15.2
01	225 15.5	189 04.3	36.3	196 06.6	32.5	150 46.1	19.8	8 04.2	51.2	Achernar	335 27.5	S57 10.2
02	240 17.9	204 03.8	37.4	211 07.2	33.2	165 48.0	19.8	23 06.9	51.1	Acrux	173 08.7	S63 10.6
03	255 20.4	219 03.2 ..	38.4	226 07.9 ..	33.9	180 49.9 ..	19.9	38 09.5 ..	51.1	Adhara	255 12.7	S28 59.8
04	270 22.9	234 02.7	39.5	241 08.6	34.6	195 51.9	19.9	53 12.2	51.0	Aldebaran	290 49.8	N16 32.0
05	285 25.3	249 02.2	40.6	256 09.3	35.2	210 53.8	20.0	68 14.8	50.9			
06	300 27.8	264 01.7	N13 41.6	271 10.0	N11 35.9	225 55.7	N22 20.1	83 17.5	S11 50.9	Alioth	166 20.3	N55 53.2
07	315 30.3	279 01.2	42.7	286 10.6	36.6	240 57.7	20.1	98 20.1	50.8	Alkaid	152 58.5	N49 14.8
M 08	330 32.7	294 00.7	43.8	301 11.3	37.2	255 59.6	20.2	113 22.8	50.8	Al Na'ir	27 44.1	S46 53.5
O 09	345 35.2	309 00.1 ..	44.8	316 12.0 ..	37.9	271 01.5 ..	20.2	128 25.4 ..	50.7	Alnilam	275 46.7	S 1 11.9
N 10	0 37.7	323 59.6	45.9	331 12.7	38.6	286 03.5	20.3	143 28.1	50.6	Alphard	217 56.1	S 8 43.3
D 11	15 40.1	338 59.1	47.0	346 13.4	39.3	301 05.4	20.3	158 30.7	50.6			
A 12	30 42.6	353 58.6	N13 48.0	1 14.1	N11 39.9	316 07.3	N22 20.4	173 33.3	S11 50.5	Alphecca	126 10.8	N26 40.1
Y 13	45 45.1	8 58.1	49.1	16 14.7	40.6	331 09.3	20.5	188 36.0	50.5	Alpheratz	357 43.9	N29 09.7
14	60 47.5	23 57.5	50.2	31 15.4	41.3	346 11.2	20.5	203 38.6	50.4	Altair	62 08.3	N 8 54.2
15	75 50.0	38 57.0 ..	51.2	46 16.1 ..	42.0	1 13.1 ..	20.6	218 41.3 ..	50.3	Ankaa	353 16.2	S42 13.9
16	90 52.4	53 56.5	52.3	61 16.8	42.6	16 15.1	20.6	233 43.9	50.3	Antares	112 26.1	S26 27.6
17	105 54.9	68 56.0	53.4	76 17.5	43.3	31 17.0	20.7	248 46.6	50.2			
18	120 57.4	83 55.4	N13 54.4	91 18.1	N11 44.0	46 18.9	N22 20.7	263 49.2	S11 50.2	Arcturus	145 55.5	N19 06.7
19	135 59.8	98 54.9	55.5	106 18.8	44.6	61 20.9	20.8	278 51.9	50.1	Atria	107 27.6	S69 02.8
20	151 02.3	113 54.4	56.6	121 19.5	45.3	76 22.8	20.9	293 54.5	50.0	Avior	234 18.0	S59 33.6
21	166 04.8	128 53.9 ..	57.6	136 20.2 ..	46.0	91 24.7 ..	20.9	308 57.2 ..	50.0	Bellatrix	278 32.3	N 6 21.5
22	181 07.2	143 53.4	58.7	151 20.9	46.7	106 26.7	21.0	323 59.8	49.9	Betelgeuse	271 01.6	N 7 24.3
23	196 09.7	158 52.8	13 59.7	166 21.5	47.3	121 28.6	21.0	339 02.4	49.9			
23 00	211 12.2	173 52.3	N14 00.8	181 22.2	N11 48.0	136 30.5	N22 21.1	354 05.1	S11 49.8	Canopus	263 56.5	S52 42.6
01	226 14.6	188 51.8	01.9	196 22.9	48.7	151 32.5	21.2	9 07.7	49.7	Capella	280 34.9	N46 00.6
02	241 17.1	203 51.2	03.0	211 23.6	49.3	166 34.4	21.2	24 10.4	49.7	Deneb	49 31.6	N45 19.5
03	256 19.6	218 50.7 ..	04.0	226 24.3 ..	50.0	181 36.3 ..	21.3	39 13.0 ..	49.6	Denebola	182 33.5	N14 29.7
04	271 22.0	233 50.2	05.0	241 24.9	50.7	196 38.3	21.3	54 15.7	49.6	Diphda	348 56.3	S17 54.8
05	286 24.5	248 49.7	06.1	256 25.6	51.3	211 40.2	21.4	69 18.3	49.5			
06	301 26.9	263 49.1	N14 07.2	271 26.3	N11 52.0	226 42.1	N22 21.4	84 21.0	S11 49.4	Dubhe	193 51.4	N61 40.8
07	316 29.4	278 48.6	08.2	286 27.0	52.7	241 44.1	21.5	99 23.6	49.4	Elnath	278 13.0	N28 37.0
T 08	331 31.9	293 48.1	09.3	301 27.7	53.3	256 46.0	21.6	114 26.3	49.3	Eltanin	90 45.9	N51 29.1
U 09	346 34.3	308 47.6 ..	10.3	316 28.3 ..	54.0	271 47.9 ..	21.6	129 28.9 ..	49.3	Enif	33 47.3	N 9 56.1
E 10	1 36.8	323 47.0	11.4	331 29.0	54.7	286 49.9	21.7	144 31.6	49.2	Fomalhaut	15 24.3	S29 33.0
S 11	16 39.3	338 46.5	12.4	346 29.7	55.3	301 51.8	21.7	159 34.2	49.1			
D 12	31 41.7	353 46.0	N14 13.5	1 30.4	N11 56.0	316 53.7	N22 21.8	174 36.9	S11 49.1	Gacrux	172 00.5	S57 11.5
A 13	46 44.2	8 45.4	14.5	16 31.1	56.7	331 55.7	21.8	189 39.5	49.0	Gienah	175 52.1	S17 37.2
Y 14	61 46.7	23 44.9	15.6	31 31.7	57.3	346 57.6	21.9	204 42.1	49.0	Hadar	148 47.3	S60 26.3
15	76 49.1	38 44.4 ..	16.6	46 32.4 ..	58.0	1 59.5 ..	22.0	219 44.8 ..	48.9	Hamal	328 01.2	N23 31.4
16	91 51.6	53 43.8	17.7	61 33.1	58.7	17 01.4	22.0	234 47.4	48.8	Kaus Aust.	83 43.8	S34 22.5
17	106 54.0	68 43.3	18.7	76 33.8	11 59.3	32 03.4	22.1	249 50.1	48.8			
18	121 56.5	83 42.8	N14 19.8	91 34.5	N12 00.0	47 05.3	N22 22.1	264 52.7	S11 48.7	Kochab	137 18.9	N74 06.0
19	136 59.0	98 42.2	20.8	106 35.1	00.7	62 07.2	22.2	279 55.4	48.6	Markab	13 38.6	N15 16.6
20	152 01.4	113 41.7	21.9	121 35.8	01.3	77 09.2	22.3	294 58.0	48.6	Menkar	314 15.5	N 4 08.3
21	167 03.9	128 41.2 ..	22.9	136 36.5 ..	02.0	92 11.1 ..	22.3	310 00.7 ..	48.5	Menkent	148 07.3	S36 26.2
22	182 06.4	143 40.6	24.0	151 37.2	02.7	107 13.0	22.4	325 03.3	48.5	Miaplacidus	221 39.4	S69 46.8
23	197 08.8	158 40.1	25.0	166 37.9	03.3	122 15.0	22.4	340 06.0	48.4			
24 00	212 11.3	173 39.6	N14 26.1	181 38.5	N12 04.0	137 16.9	N22 22.5	355 08.6	S11 48.3	Mirfak	308 41.0	N49 54.4
01	227 13.8	188 39.0	27.1	196 39.2	04.7	152 18.8	22.5	10 11.3	48.3	Nunki	75 58.3	S26 16.6
02	242 16.2	203 38.5	28.1	211 39.9	05.3	167 20.7	22.6	25 13.9	48.2	Peacock	53 19.4	S56 41.1
03	257 18.7	218 38.0 ..	29.2	226 40.6 ..	06.0	182 22.7 ..	22.6	40 16.6 ..	48.2	Pollux	243 27.9	N27 59.5
04	272 21.2	233 37.4	30.2	241 41.2	06.7	197 24.6	22.7	55 19.2	48.1	Procyon	244 59.9	N 5 11.2
05	287 23.6	248 36.9	31.3	256 41.9	07.3	212 26.5	22.8	70 21.8	48.0			
06	302 26.1	263 36.3	N14 32.3	271 42.6	N12 08.0	227 28.5	N22 22.8	85 24.5	S11 48.0	Rasalhague	96 06.3	N12 33.0
W 07	317 28.5	278 35.8	33.4	286 43.3	08.6	242 30.4	22.9	100 27.1	47.9	Regulus	207 43.5	N11 53.9
E 08	332 31.0	293 35.3	34.4	301 44.0	09.3	257 32.3	22.9	115 29.8	47.9	Rigel	281 12.4	S 8 11.5
D 09	347 33.5	308 34.7 ..	35.4	316 44.6 ..	10.0	272 34.2 ..	23.0	130 32.4 ..	47.8	Rigil Kent.	139 51.2	S60 53.4
N 10	2 35.9	323 34.2	36.5	331 45.3	10.6	287 36.2	23.0	145 35.1	47.7	Sabik	102 12.4	S15 44.4
E 11	17 38.4	338 33.6	37.5	346 46.0	11.3	302 38.1	23.1	160 37.7	47.7			
S 12	32 40.9	353 33.1	N14 38.5	1 46.7	N12 12.0	317 40.0	N22 23.2	175 40.4	S11 47.6	Schedar	349 41.1	N56 36.5
D 13	47 43.3	8 32.6	39.6	16 47.4	12.6	332 42.0	23.2	190 43.0	47.6	Shaula	96 21.8	S37 06.6
A 14	62 45.8	23 32.0	40.6	31 48.0	13.3	347 43.9	23.3	205 45.7	47.5	Sirius	258 34.0	S16 44.4
Y 15	77 48.3	38 31.5 ..	41.7	46 48.7 ..	13.9	2 45.8 ..	23.3	220 48.3 ..	47.4	Spica	158 31.0	S11 14.0
16	92 50.7	53 30.9	42.7	61 49.4	14.6	17 47.7	23.4	235 51.0	47.4	Suhail	222 52.4	S43 29.6
17	107 53.2	68 30.4	43.7	76 50.1	15.3	32 49.7	23.4	250 53.6	47.3			
18	122 55.6	83 29.8	N14 44.8	91 50.7	N12 15.9	47 51.6	N22 23.5	265 56.3	S11 47.3	Vega	80 38.8	N38 47.6
19	137 58.1	98 29.3	45.8	106 51.4	16.6	62 53.5	23.6	280 59.0	47.2	Zuben'ubi	137 05.2	S16 05.9
20	153 00.6	113 28.8	46.8	121 52.1	17.2	77 55.4	23.6	296 01.6	47.1		SHA	Mer.Pass.
21	168 03.0	128 28.2 ..	47.9	136 52.8 ..	17.9	92 57.4 ..	23.7	311 04.2 ..	47.1	Venus	322 40.1	12 25
22	183 05.5	143 27.7	48.9	151 53.5	18.5	107 59.3	23.7	326 06.8	47.0	Mars	330 10.1	11 54
23	198 08.0	158 27.1	49.9	166 54.1	19.2	123 01.2	23.8	341 09.5	47.0	Jupiter	285 18.4	14 52
Mer.Pass. 9 53.6		v −0.5	d 1.1	v 0.7	d 0.7	v 1.9	d 0.1	v 2.6	d 0.1	Saturn	142 52.9	0 24

UT	SUN GHA	SUN Dec	MOON GHA	v	MOON Dec	d	HP
d h	° ′	° ′	° ′	′	° ′	′	′
22 00	180 21.7	N12 10.6	48 16.5	12.5	N 2 30.5	11.3	57.1
01	195 21.9	11.5	62 48.0	12.5	2 19.2	11.3	57.1
02	210 22.0	12.3	77 19.5	12.4	2 07.9	11.3	57.2
03	225 22.1	.. 13.2	91 50.9	12.5	1 56.6	11.4	57.2
04	240 22.2	14.0	106 22.4	12.3	1 45.2	11.4	57.2
05	255 22.3	14.8	120 53.7	12.4	1 33.8	11.4	57.3
06	270 22.5	N12 15.7	135 25.1	12.3	N 1 22.4	11.4	57.3
07	285 22.6	16.5	149 56.4	12.3	1 11.0	11.4	57.3
M 08	300 22.7	17.4	164 27.7	12.2	0 59.6	11.5	57.4
O 09	315 22.8	.. 18.2	178 58.9	12.2	0 48.1	11.5	57.4
N 10	330 23.0	19.0	193 30.1	12.1	0 36.6	11.5	57.4
11	345 23.1	19.9	208 01.2	12.1	0 25.1	11.5	57.5
D 12	0 23.2	N12 20.7	222 32.3	12.1	N 0 13.6	11.6	57.5
A 13	15 23.3	21.5	237 03.4	12.0	N 0 02.0	11.5	57.6
Y 14	30 23.4	22.4	251 34.4	12.0	S 0 09.5	11.6	57.6
15	45 23.6	.. 23.2	266 05.4	12.0	0 21.1	11.6	57.6
16	60 23.7	24.1	280 36.4	11.9	0 32.7	11.6	57.7
17	75 23.8	24.9	295 07.3	11.8	0 44.3	11.6	57.7
18	90 23.9	N12 25.7	309 38.1	11.8	S 0 55.9	11.6	57.7
19	105 24.0	26.6	324 08.9	11.8	1 07.5	11.6	57.8
20	120 24.2	27.4	338 39.7	11.7	1 19.1	11.7	57.8
21	135 24.3	.. 28.2	353 10.4	11.7	1 30.8	11.6	57.8
22	150 24.4	29.1	7 41.1	11.6	1 42.4	11.7	57.9
23	165 24.5	29.9	22 11.7	11.5	1 54.1	11.6	57.9
23 00	180 24.6	N12 30.7	36 42.2	11.6	S 2 05.7	11.7	58.0
01	195 24.7	31.6	51 12.8	11.4	2 17.4	11.7	58.0
02	210 24.9	32.4	65 43.2	11.4	2 29.1	11.6	58.0
03	225 25.0	.. 33.2	80 13.6	11.4	2 40.7	11.7	58.1
04	240 25.1	34.1	94 44.0	11.3	2 52.4	11.7	58.1
05	255 25.2	34.9	109 14.3	11.3	3 04.1	11.6	58.1
06	270 25.3	N12 35.7	123 44.6	11.2	S 3 15.7	11.7	58.2
07	285 25.5	36.5	138 14.8	11.1	3 27.4	11.7	58.2
T 08	300 25.6	37.4	152 44.9	11.1	3 39.1	11.6	58.2
U 09	315 25.7	.. 38.2	167 15.0	11.0	3 50.7	11.7	58.3
E 10	330 25.8	39.0	181 45.0	11.0	4 02.4	11.6	58.3
S 11	345 25.9	39.9	196 15.0	10.9	4 14.0	11.7	58.3
D 12	0 26.0	N12 40.7	210 44.9	10.9	S 4 25.7	11.6	58.4
A 13	15 26.2	41.5	225 14.8	10.8	4 37.3	11.6	58.4
Y 14	30 26.3	42.3	239 44.6	10.7	4 48.9	11.6	58.5
15	45 26.4	.. 43.2	254 14.3	10.7	5 00.5	11.6	58.5
16	60 26.5	44.0	268 44.0	10.6	5 12.1	11.6	58.5
17	75 26.6	44.8	283 13.6	10.6	5 23.7	11.6	58.6
18	90 26.7	N12 45.7	297 43.2	10.5	S 5 35.3	11.5	58.6
19	105 26.8	46.5	312 12.7	10.4	5 46.8	11.5	58.6
20	120 27.0	47.3	326 42.1	10.4	5 58.3	11.6	58.7
21	135 27.1	.. 48.1	341 11.5	10.3	6 09.9	11.5	58.7
22	150 27.2	49.0	355 40.8	10.2	6 21.4	11.4	58.7
23	165 27.3	49.8	10 10.0	10.2	6 32.8	11.5	58.8
24 00	180 27.4	N12 50.6	24 39.2	10.1	S 6 44.3	11.4	58.8
01	195 27.5	51.4	39 08.3	10.0	6 55.7	11.4	58.8
02	210 27.6	52.2	53 37.3	10.0	7 07.1	11.4	58.9
03	225 27.8	.. 53.1	68 06.3	9.9	7 18.5	11.3	58.9
04	240 27.9	53.9	82 35.2	9.8	7 29.8	11.3	58.9
05	255 28.0	54.7	97 04.0	9.8	7 41.1	11.3	59.0
06	270 28.1	N12 55.5	111 32.8	9.7	S 7 52.4	11.3	59.0
W 07	285 28.2	56.4	126 01.5	9.6	8 03.7	11.2	59.0
E 08	300 28.3	57.2	140 30.1	9.6	8 14.9	11.2	59.1
D 09	315 28.4	.. 58.0	154 58.7	9.5	8 26.1	11.1	59.1
N 10	330 28.5	58.8	169 27.2	9.4	8 37.2	11.1	59.1
E 11	345 28.7	12 59.6	183 55.6	9.3	8 48.3	11.1	59.2
S 12	0 28.8	N13 00.5	198 23.9	9.3	S 8 59.4	11.0	59.2
D 13	15 28.9	01.3	212 52.2	9.2	9 10.4	11.0	59.2
A 14	30 29.0	02.1	227 20.4	9.1	9 21.4	11.0	59.2
Y 15	45 29.1	.. 02.9	241 48.5	9.1	9 32.4	10.9	59.3
16	60 29.2	03.7	256 16.6	8.9	9 43.3	10.8	59.3
17	75 29.3	04.5	270 44.5	8.9	9 54.1	10.9	59.3
18	90 29.4	N13 05.4	285 12.4	8.9	S10 05.0	10.7	59.4
19	105 29.5	06.2	299 40.3	8.7	10 15.7	10.7	59.4
20	120 29.7	07.0	314 08.0	8.7	10 26.4	10.7	59.4
21	135 29.8	.. 07.8	328 35.7	8.6	10 37.1	10.6	59.5
22	150 29.9	08.6	343 03.3	8.5	10 47.7	10.5	59.5
23	165 30.0	09.4	357 30.8	8.5	S10 58.2	10.5	59.5
	SD 15.9	d 0.8	SD 15.7		15.9		16.1

Lat.	Twilight Naut.	Twilight Civil	Sunrise	Moonrise 22	Moonrise 23	Moonrise 24	Moonrise 25
°	h m	h m	h m	h m	h m	h m	h m
N 72	////	////	02 50	15 23	17 18	19 21	21 38
N 70	////	01 28	03 14	15 23	17 10	19 03	21 04
68	////	02 11	03 33	15 22	17 03	18 49	20 40
66	////	02 39	03 48	15 21	16 57	18 37	20 21
64	01 17	03 00	04 01	15 21	16 53	18 28	20 06
62	01 56	03 17	04 11	15 21	16 49	18 20	19 53
60	02 21	03 31	04 20	15 20	16 45	18 13	19 43
N 58	02 41	03 42	04 28	15 20	16 42	18 07	19 34
56	02 57	03 52	04 35	15 20	16 39	18 02	19 25
54	03 10	04 01	04 41	15 19	16 37	17 57	19 18
52	03 22	04 09	04 46	15 19	16 35	17 52	19 12
50	03 32	04 16	04 51	15 19	16 32	17 49	19 06
45	03 52	04 30	05 02	15 19	16 28	17 40	18 54
N 40	04 07	04 42	05 11	15 18	16 24	17 33	18 44
35	04 20	04 52	05 18	15 18	16 21	17 27	18 35
30	04 30	05 00	05 25	15 18	16 19	17 22	18 27
20	04 47	05 13	05 36	15 17	16 14	17 13	18 14
N 10	04 59	05 24	05 46	15 17	16 10	17 05	18 03
0	05 09	05 34	05 55	15 17	16 06	16 58	17 52
S 10	05 18	05 42	06 04	15 16	16 02	16 50	17 42
20	05 25	05 51	06 13	15 16	15 58	16 43	17 31
30	05 31	06 00	06 24	15 16	15 54	16 34	17 18
35	05 35	06 04	06 30	15 15	15 51	16 29	17 11
40	05 38	06 09	06 37	15 15	15 48	16 23	17 03
45	05 40	06 15	06 45	15 15	15 45	16 17	16 53
S 50	05 43	06 21	06 55	15 15	15 41	16 09	16 42
52	05 45	06 24	06 59	15 15	15 39	16 05	16 36
54	05 46	06 27	07 04	15 15	15 37	16 01	16 30
56	05 47	06 30	07 09	15 15	15 35	15 57	16 24
58	05 48	06 34	07 15	15 15	15 32	15 52	16 17
S 60	05 49	06 38	07 22	15 14	15 30	15 47	16 08

Lat.	Sunset	Twilight Civil	Twilight Naut.	Moonset 22	Moonset 23	Moonset 24	Moonset 25
°	h m	h m	h m	h m	h m	h m	h m
N 72	21 12	////	////	03 15	03 04	02 53	02 38
N 70	20 46	22 38	////	03 12	03 08	03 03	02 58
68	20 26	21 51	////	03 10	03 11	03 12	03 14
66	20 11	21 21	////	03 09	03 14	03 19	03 27
64	19 58	20 59	22 48	03 07	03 16	03 25	03 37
62	19 47	20 42	22 06	03 06	03 18	03 31	03 46
60	19 38	20 28	21 39	03 05	03 20	03 35	03 54
N 58	19 30	20 16	21 18	03 04	03 21	03 40	04 01
56	19 23	20 06	21 02	03 03	03 22	03 43	04 07
54	19 17	19 57	20 48	03 02	03 24	03 47	04 13
52	19 11	19 49	20 36	03 02	03 25	03 50	04 18
50	19 06	19 42	20 26	03 01	03 26	03 52	04 22
45	18 56	19 27	20 06	03 00	03 28	03 59	04 32
N 40	18 47	19 15	19 50	02 58	03 30	04 04	04 41
35	18 39	19 06	19 37	02 57	03 32	04 08	04 48
30	18 32	18 57	19 27	02 56	03 33	04 12	04 54
20	18 21	18 44	19 10	02 55	03 36	04 19	05 05
N 10	18 11	18 32	18 58	02 53	03 38	04 25	05 14
0	18 02	18 23	18 47	02 52	03 40	04 30	05 23
S 10	17 53	18 14	18 39	02 50	03 42	04 36	05 32
20	17 43	18 05	18 31	02 49	03 44	04 42	05 42
30	17 32	17 57	18 25	02 47	03 47	04 48	05 53
35	17 26	17 52	18 22	02 46	03 48	04 52	05 59
40	17 19	17 47	18 18	02 45	03 50	04 57	06 06
45	17 11	17 41	18 15	02 43	03 51	05 02	06 15
S 50	17 01	17 35	18 12	02 42	03 54	05 08	06 25
52	16 57	17 32	18 11	02 41	03 55	05 11	06 30
54	16 52	17 29	18 10	02 40	03 56	05 14	06 35
56	16 46	17 25	18 09	02 39	03 57	05 18	06 41
58	16 40	17 21	18 07	02 38	03 58	05 22	06 47
S 60	16 33	17 17	18 06	02 37	04 00	05 26	06 55

Day	SUN Eqn. of Time 00h	SUN Eqn. of Time 12h	SUN Mer. Pass.	MOON Mer. Pass. Upper	MOON Mer. Pass. Lower	Age	Phase
d	m s	m s	h m	h m	h m	d	%
22	01 27	01 33	11 58	21 28	09 04	12	86
23	01 38	01 44	11 58	22 18	09 53	13	93
24	01 49	01 55	11 58	23 10	10 44	14	98

UT	ARIES GHA	VENUS −3.9 GHA	Dec	MARS +1.2 GHA	Dec	JUPITER −2.0 GHA	Dec	SATURN +0.1 GHA	Dec	STARS Name	SHA	Dec
25 00	213 10.4	173 26.6	N14 51.0	181 54.8	N12 19.9	138 03.1	N22 23.8	356 12.1	S11 46.9	Acamar	315 18.9	S40 15.2
01	228 12.9	188 26.0	52.0	196 55.5	20.5	153 05.1	23.9	11 14.8	46.8	Achernar	335 27.5	S57 10.1
02	243 15.4	203 25.5	53.0	211 56.2	21.2	168 07.0	24.0	26 17.4	46.8	Acrux	173 08.7	S63 10.6
03	258 17.8	218 24.9	.. 54.0	226 56.8	.. 21.9	183 08.9	.. 24.0	41 20.1	.. 46.7	Adhara	255 12.8	S28 59.8
04	273 20.3	233 24.4	55.1	241 57.5	22.5	198 10.8	24.1	56 22.7	46.7	Aldebaran	290 49.8	N16 32.0
05	288 22.8	248 23.8	56.1	256 58.2	23.2	213 12.8	24.1	71 25.4	46.6			
06	303 25.2	263 23.3	N14 57.1	271 58.9	N12 23.8	228 14.7	N22 24.2	86 28.0	S11 46.5	Alioth	166 20.3	N55 53.3
T 07	318 27.7	278 22.7	58.1	286 59.6	24.5	243 16.6	24.2	101 30.7	46.5	Alkaid	152 58.5	N49 14.8
H 08	333 30.1	293 22.2	14 59.2	302 00.2	25.2	258 18.5	24.3	116 33.3	46.4	Al Na'ir	27 44.1	S46 53.5
U 09	348 32.6	308 21.6	15 00.2	317 00.9	.. 25.8	273 20.5	.. 24.3	131 36.0	.. 46.4	Alnilam	275 46.7	S 1 11.9
R 10	3 35.1	323 21.1	01.2	332 01.6	26.5	288 22.4	24.4	146 38.6	46.3	Alphard	217 56.1	S 8 43.3
S 11	18 37.5	338 20.5	02.2	347 02.3	27.1	303 24.3	24.5	161 41.3	46.2			
D 12	33 40.0	353 20.0	N15 03.3	2 02.9	N12 27.8	318 26.2	N22 24.5	176 43.9	S11 46.2	Alphecca	126 10.8	N26 40.1
A 13	48 42.5	8 19.4	04.3	17 03.6	28.4	333 28.2	24.6	191 46.6	46.1	Alpheratz	357 43.9	N29 09.7
Y 14	63 44.9	23 18.9	05.3	32 04.3	29.1	348 30.1	24.6	206 49.2	46.1	Altair	62 08.3	N 8 54.2
15	78 47.4	38 18.3	.. 06.3	47 05.0	.. 29.7	3 32.0	.. 24.7	221 51.9	.. 46.0	Ankaa	353 16.2	S42 13.9
16	93 49.9	53 17.8	07.3	62 05.6	30.4	18 33.9	24.7	236 54.5	45.9	Antares	112 26.1	S26 27.6
17	108 52.3	68 17.2	08.4	77 06.3	31.1	33 35.9	24.8	251 57.1	45.9			
18	123 54.8	83 16.7	N15 09.4	92 07.0	N12 31.7	48 37.8	N22 24.9	266 59.8	S11 45.8	Arcturus	145 55.5	N19 06.7
19	138 57.3	98 16.1	10.4	107 07.7	32.4	63 39.7	24.9	282 02.4	45.8	Atria	107 27.5	S69 02.8
20	153 59.7	113 15.6	11.4	122 08.3	33.0	78 41.6	25.0	297 05.1	45.7	Avior	234 18.1	S59 33.6
21	169 02.2	128 15.0	.. 12.4	137 09.0	.. 33.7	93 43.6	.. 25.0	312 07.7	.. 45.6	Bellatrix	278 32.4	N 6 21.5
22	184 04.6	143 14.4	13.4	152 09.7	34.3	108 45.5	25.1	327 10.4	45.6	Betelgeuse	271 01.6	N 7 24.3
23	199 07.1	158 13.9	14.5	167 10.4	35.0	123 47.4	25.1	342 13.0	45.5			
26 00	214 09.6	173 13.3	N15 15.5	182 11.0	N12 35.6	138 49.3	N22 25.2	357 15.7	S11 45.5	Canopus	263 56.5	S52 42.6
01	229 12.0	188 12.8	16.5	197 11.7	36.3	153 51.3	25.2	12 18.3	45.4	Capella	280 34.9	N46 00.6
02	244 14.5	203 12.2	17.5	212 12.4	36.9	168 53.2	25.3	27 21.0	45.3	Deneb	49 31.5	N45 19.5
03	259 17.0	218 11.7	.. 18.5	227 13.1	.. 37.6	183 55.1	.. 25.4	42 23.6	.. 45.3	Denebola	182 33.5	N14 29.7
04	274 19.4	233 11.1	19.5	242 13.8	38.3	198 57.0	25.4	57 26.3	45.2	Diphda	348 56.3	S17 54.8
05	289 21.9	248 10.5	20.5	257 14.4	38.9	213 58.9	25.5	72 28.9	45.2			
06	304 24.4	263 10.0	N15 21.5	272 15.1	N12 39.6	229 00.9	N22 25.5	87 31.6	S11 45.1	Dubhe	193 51.5	N61 40.8
07	319 26.8	278 09.4	22.6	287 15.8	40.2	244 02.8	25.6	102 34.2	45.0	Elnath	278 13.0	N28 37.0
F 08	334 29.3	293 08.9	23.6	302 16.5	40.9	259 04.7	25.6	117 36.9	45.0	Eltanin	90 45.9	N51 29.1
R 09	349 31.7	308 08.3	.. 24.6	317 17.1	.. 41.5	274 06.6	.. 25.7	132 39.5	.. 44.9	Enif	33 47.3	N 9 56.2
I 10	4 34.2	323 07.7	25.6	332 17.8	42.2	289 08.6	25.8	147 42.2	44.9	Fomalhaut	15 24.3	S29 33.0
D 11	19 36.7	338 07.2	26.6	347 18.5	42.8	304 10.5	25.8	162 44.8	44.8			
A 12	34 39.1	353 06.6	N15 27.6	2 19.2	N12 43.5	319 12.4	N22 25.9	177 47.4	S11 44.7	Gacrux	172 00.5	S57 11.5
Y 13	49 41.6	8 06.1	28.6	17 19.8	44.1	334 14.3	25.9	192 50.1	44.7	Gienah	175 52.1	S17 37.2
14	64 44.1	23 05.5	29.6	32 20.5	44.8	349 16.2	26.0	207 52.7	44.6	Hadar	148 47.3	S60 26.3
15	79 46.5	38 04.9	.. 30.6	47 21.2	.. 45.4	4 18.2	.. 26.0	222 55.4	.. 44.6	Hamal	328 01.2	N23 31.4
16	94 49.0	53 04.4	31.6	62 21.9	46.1	19 20.1	26.1	237 58.0	44.5	Kaus Aust.	83 43.7	S34 22.5
17	109 51.5	68 03.8	32.6	77 22.5	46.7	34 22.0	26.1	253 00.7	44.4			
18	124 53.9	83 03.2	N15 33.6	92 23.2	N12 47.4	49 23.9	N22 26.2	268 03.3	S11 44.3	Kochab	137 18.9	N74 06.0
19	139 56.4	98 02.7	34.6	107 23.9	48.0	64 25.8	26.3	283 06.0	44.3	Markab	13 38.6	N15 16.6
20	154 58.9	113 02.1	35.6	122 24.5	48.7	79 27.8	26.3	298 08.6	44.3	Menkar	314 15.5	N 4 08.3
21	170 01.3	128 01.5	.. 36.6	137 25.2	.. 49.3	94 29.7	.. 26.4	313 11.3	.. 44.2	Menkent	148 07.3	S36 26.2
22	185 03.8	143 01.0	37.6	152 25.9	50.0	109 31.6	26.4	328 13.9	44.1	Miaplacidus	221 39.5	S69 46.8
23	200 06.2	158 00.4	38.6	167 26.6	50.6	124 33.5	26.5	343 16.6	44.1			
27 00	215 08.7	172 59.8	N15 39.6	182 27.2	N12 51.3	139 35.4	N22 26.5	358 19.2	S11 44.0	Mirfak	308 41.0	N49 54.4
01	230 11.2	187 59.3	40.6	197 27.9	51.9	154 37.4	26.6	13 21.9	44.0	Nunki	75 58.3	S26 16.6
02	245 13.6	202 58.7	41.6	212 28.6	52.6	169 39.3	26.6	28 24.5	43.9	Peacock	53 19.4	S56 41.1
03	260 16.1	217 58.1	.. 42.6	227 29.3	.. 53.2	184 41.2	.. 26.7	43 27.2	.. 43.8	Pollux	243 27.9	N27 59.5
04	275 18.6	232 57.6	43.6	242 29.9	53.9	199 43.1	26.8	58 29.8	43.8	Procyon	244 59.9	N 5 11.2
05	290 21.0	247 57.0	44.6	257 30.6	54.5	214 45.0	26.8	73 32.5	43.7			
06	305 23.5	262 56.4	N15 45.6	272 31.3	N12 55.1	229 47.0	N22 26.9	88 35.1	S11 43.7	Rasalhague	96 06.3	N12 33.0
07	320 26.0	277 55.9	46.6	287 32.0	55.8	244 48.9	26.9	103 37.8	43.6	Regulus	207 43.5	N11 53.9
S 08	335 28.4	292 55.3	47.6	302 32.6	56.4	259 50.8	27.0	118 40.4	43.5	Rigel	281 12.4	S 8 11.5
A 09	350 30.9	307 54.7	.. 48.6	317 33.3	.. 57.1	274 52.7	.. 27.0	133 43.0	.. 43.5	Rigil Kent.	139 51.2	S60 53.4
T 10	5 33.4	322 54.1	49.6	332 34.0	57.7	289 54.6	27.1	148 45.7	43.4	Sabik	102 12.4	S15 44.4
U 11	20 35.8	337 53.6	50.6	347 34.7	58.4	304 56.5	27.1	163 48.3	43.4			
R 12	35 38.3	352 53.0	N15 51.5	2 35.3	N12 59.0	319 58.5	N22 27.2	178 51.0	S11 43.3	Schedar	349 41.1	N56 36.5
D 13	50 40.7	7 52.4	52.5	17 36.0	59.7	335 00.4	27.3	193 53.6	43.2	Shaula	96 21.8	S37 06.6
A 14	65 43.2	22 51.8	53.5	32 36.7	13 00.3	350 02.3	27.3	208 56.3	43.2	Sirius	258 34.0	S16 44.4
Y 15	80 45.7	37 51.3	.. 54.5	47 37.3	.. 01.0	5 04.2	.. 27.4	223 58.9	.. 43.1	Spica	158 31.0	S11 14.0
16	95 48.1	52 50.7	55.5	62 38.0	01.6	20 06.1	27.4	239 01.6	43.1	Suhail	222 52.4	S43 29.6
17	110 50.6	67 50.1	56.5	77 38.7	02.2	35 08.1	27.5	254 04.2	43.0			
18	125 53.1	82 49.5	N15 57.5	92 39.4	N13 02.9	50 10.0	N22 27.5	269 06.9	S11 42.9	Vega	80 38.8	N38 47.7
19	140 55.5	97 49.0	58.5	107 40.0	03.5	65 11.9	27.6	284 09.5	42.9	Zuben'ubi	137 05.2	S16 05.9
20	155 58.0	112 48.4	15 59.4	122 40.7	04.2	80 13.8	27.6	299 12.2	42.8		SHA	Mer.Pass.
21	171 00.5	127 47.8	16 00.4	137 41.4	.. 04.8	95 15.7	.. 27.7	314 14.8	.. 42.8	Venus	319 03.8	12 28
22	186 02.9	142 47.2	01.4	152 42.1	05.5	110 17.6	27.8	329 17.5	42.7	Mars	328 01.5	11 51
23	201 05.4	157 46.7	02.4	167 42.7	06.1	125 19.6	27.8	344 20.1	42.6	Jupiter	284 39.8	14 43
Mer.Pass.	9 41.8	v −0.6	d 1.0	v 0.7	d 0.7	v 1.9	d 0.1	v 2.6	d 0.1	Saturn	143 06.1	0 11

UT	SUN GHA	SUN Dec	MOON GHA	v	MOON Dec	d	HP
d h	° ′	° ′	° ′	′	° ′	′	′
25 00	180 30.1	N13 10.3	11 58.3	8.4	S11 08.7	10.5	59.5
01	195 30.2	11.1	26 25.7	8.3	11 19.2	10.3	59.6
02	210 30.3	11.9	40 53.0	8.2	11 29.5	10.3	59.6
03	225 30.4	.. 12.7	55 20.2	8.2	11 39.8	10.3	59.6
04	240 30.5	13.5	69 47.4	8.0	11 50.1	10.2	59.6
05	255 30.6	14.3	84 14.4	8.0	12 00.3	10.1	59.7
06	270 30.7	N13 15.1	98 41.4	8.0	S12 10.4	10.1	59.7
07	285 30.8	16.0	113 08.4	7.8	12 20.5	10.0	59.7
T 08	300 31.0	16.8	127 35.2	7.8	12 30.5	9.9	59.7
H 09	315 31.1	.. 17.6	142 02.0	7.7	12 40.4	9.8	59.8
U 10	330 31.2	18.4	156 28.7	7.6	12 50.2	9.8	59.8
R 11	345 31.3	19.2	170 55.3	7.5	13 00.0	9.7	59.8
S 12	0 31.4	N13 20.0	185 21.8	7.5	S13 09.7	9.6	59.8
D 13	15 31.5	20.8	199 48.3	7.4	13 19.3	9.6	59.9
A 14	30 31.6	21.6	214 14.7	7.3	13 28.9	9.4	59.9
Y 15	45 31.7	.. 22.4	228 41.0	7.2	13 38.3	9.4	59.9
16	60 31.8	23.3	243 07.2	7.2	13 47.7	9.3	59.9
17	75 31.9	24.1	257 34.4	7.1	13 57.0	9.3	60.0
18	90 32.0	N13 24.9	271 59.5	7.0	S14 06.3	9.1	60.0
19	105 32.1	25.7	286 25.5	6.9	14 15.4	9.0	60.0
20	120 32.2	26.5	300 51.4	6.9	14 24.4	9.0	60.0
21	135 32.3	.. 27.3	315 17.3	6.8	14 33.4	8.9	60.0
22	150 32.4	28.1	329 43.1	6.7	14 42.3	8.8	60.1
23	165 32.5	28.9	344 08.8	6.6	14 51.1	8.7	60.1
26 00	180 32.6	N13 29.7	358 34.4	6.6	S14 59.8	8.6	60.1
01	195 32.7	30.5	13 00.0	6.5	15 08.4	8.5	60.1
02	210 32.9	31.3	27 25.5	6.4	15 16.9	8.4	60.1
03	225 33.0	.. 32.1	41 50.9	6.4	15 25.3	8.3	60.2
04	240 33.1	32.9	56 16.3	6.3	15 33.6	8.2	60.2
05	255 33.2	33.7	70 41.6	6.2	15 41.8	8.1	60.2
06	270 33.3	N13 34.5	85 06.8	6.1	S15 49.9	8.0	60.2
07	285 33.4	35.3	99 31.9	6.1	15 57.9	7.9	60.2
F 08	300 33.5	36.1	113 57.0	6.0	16 05.8	7.8	60.2
R 09	315 33.6	.. 36.9	128 22.0	5.9	16 13.6	7.7	60.3
I 10	330 33.7	37.7	142 46.9	5.9	16 21.3	7.6	60.3
11	345 33.8	38.5	157 11.8	5.8	16 28.9	7.5	60.3
D 12	0 33.9	N13 39.3	171 36.6	5.7	S16 36.4	7.4	60.3
A 13	15 34.0	40.1	186 01.3	5.7	16 43.8	7.2	60.3
Y 14	30 34.1	40.9	200 26.0	5.6	16 51.0	7.2	60.3
15	45 34.2	.. 41.7	214 50.6	5.6	16 58.2	7.0	60.3
16	60 34.3	42.5	229 15.2	5.5	17 05.2	6.9	60.4
17	75 34.4	43.3	243 39.7	5.4	17 12.1	6.8	60.4
18	90 34.5	N13 44.1	258 04.1	5.3	S17 18.9	6.7	60.4
19	105 34.6	44.9	272 28.4	5.3	17 25.6	6.6	60.4
20	120 34.7	45.7	286 52.7	5.3	17 32.2	6.4	60.4
21	135 34.8	.. 46.5	301 17.0	5.2	17 38.6	6.3	60.4
22	150 34.9	47.3	315 41.2	5.1	17 44.9	6.2	60.4
23	165 35.0	48.1	330 05.3	5.1	17 51.1	6.1	60.4
27 00	180 35.1	N13 48.9	344 29.4	5.0	S17 57.2	6.0	60.4
01	195 35.2	49.7	358 53.4	5.0	18 03.2	5.8	60.4
02	210 35.3	50.5	13 17.4	4.9	18 09.0	5.7	60.5
03	225 35.4	.. 51.3	27 41.3	4.9	18 14.7	5.6	60.5
04	240 35.5	52.1	42 05.2	4.8	18 20.3	5.4	60.5
05	255 35.6	52.9	56 29.0	4.8	18 25.7	5.3	60.5
06	270 35.7	N13 53.7	70 52.8	4.7	S18 31.0	5.2	60.5
07	285 35.8	54.5	85 16.5	4.7	18 36.2	5.1	60.5
S 08	300 35.9	55.3	99 40.2	4.7	18 41.3	4.9	60.5
A 09	315 36.0	.. 56.1	114 03.9	4.6	18 46.2	4.8	60.5
T 10	330 36.1	56.9	128 27.5	4.5	18 51.0	4.6	60.5
U 11	345 36.1	57.7	142 51.0	4.6	18 55.6	4.6	60.5
R 12	0 36.2	N13 58.5	157 14.6	4.4	S19 00.2	4.3	60.5
D 13	15 36.3	13 59.3	171 38.0	4.4	19 04.5	4.3	60.5
A 14	30 36.4	14 00.0	186 01.5	4.4	19 08.8	4.1	60.5
Y 15	45 36.5	.. 00.8	200 24.9	4.4	19 12.9	4.0	60.5
16	60 36.6	01.6	214 48.3	4.4	19 16.9	3.9	60.5
17	75 36.7	02.4	229 11.7	4.3	19 20.7	3.7	60.5
18	90 36.8	N14 03.2	243 35.0	4.3	S19 24.4	3.6	60.5
19	105 36.9	04.0	257 58.3	4.2	19 28.0	3.4	60.5
20	120 37.0	04.8	272 21.5	4.3	19 31.4	3.2	60.5
21	135 37.1	.. 05.6	286 44.8	4.2	19 34.6	3.2	60.5
22	150 37.2	06.4	301 08.0	4.2	19 37.8	3.0	60.5
23	165 37.3	07.1	315 31.2	4.2	S19 40.8	2.8	60.5
	SD 15.9	d 0.8	SD 16.3		16.4		16.5

Lat.	Twilight Naut.	Civil	Sunrise	Moonrise 25	26	27	28
°	h m	h m	h m	h m	h m	h m	h m
N 72	////	////	02 29	21 38	■	■	■
N 70	////	00 50	02 58	21 04	23 14	25 54	01 54
68	////	01 50	03 20	20 40	22 32	24 16	00 16
66	////	02 23	03 37	20 21	22 04	23 37	24 46
64	00 44	02 47	03 50	20 06	21 42	23 09	24 18
62	01 37	03 06	04 02	19 53	21 25	22 48	23 56
60	02 07	03 21	04 11	19 43	21 11	22 31	23 38
N 58	02 30	03 34	04 20	19 34	20 59	22 17	23 23
56	02 47	03 44	04 27	19 25	20 48	22 05	23 11
54	03 02	03 54	04 34	19 18	20 39	21 54	23 00
52	03 14	04 02	04 40	19 12	20 31	21 45	22 50
50	03 25	04 10	04 45	19 06	20 23	21 36	22 41
45	03 46	04 25	04 57	18 54	20 08	21 18	22 23
N 40	04 03	04 38	05 06	18 44	19 55	21 04	22 08
35	04 16	04 48	05 15	18 35	19 44	20 51	21 55
30	04 27	04 57	05 22	18 27	19 34	20 40	21 44
20	04 44	05 11	05 34	18 14	19 18	20 22	21 24
N 10	04 58	05 24	05 45	18 03	19 04	20 06	21 08
0	05 08	05 33	05 54	17 52	18 50	19 51	20 52
S 10	05 18	05 43	06 04	17 42	18 37	19 36	20 37
20	05 26	05 52	06 14	17 31	18 23	19 20	20 20
30	05 33	06 01	06 26	17 18	18 07	19 02	20 01
35	05 37	06 06	06 33	17 11	17 58	18 51	19 50
40	05 40	06 12	06 40	17 03	17 48	18 39	19 38
45	05 44	06 18	06 49	16 53	17 35	18 25	19 23
S 50	05 47	06 25	06 59	16 42	17 21	18 08	19 05
52	05 49	06 29	07 04	16 36	17 14	18 00	18 56
54	05 51	06 32	07 09	16 30	17 06	17 51	18 46
56	05 52	06 36	07 15	16 24	16 57	17 41	18 36
58	05 54	06 40	07 22	16 17	16 48	17 29	18 23
S 60	05 56	06 45	07 29	16 08	16 37	17 16	18 09

Lat.	Sunset	Twilight Civil	Naut.	Moonset 25	26	27	28
°	h m	h m	h m	h m	h m	h m	h m
N 72	21 32	////	////	02 38	02 17	■	■
N 70	21 01	23 25	////	02 58	02 52	02 45	02 13
68	20 39	22 12	////	03 14	03 18	03 28	03 51
66	20 22	21 36	////	03 27	03 38	03 57	04 31
64	20 07	21 11	23 29	03 37	03 54	04 19	04 58
62	19 56	20 52	22 24	03 46	04 07	04 36	05 19
60	19 46	20 37	21 52	03 54	04 18	04 51	05 37
N 58	19 37	20 24	21 29	04 01	04 28	05 04	05 51
56	19 29	20 13	21 11	04 07	04 37	05 15	06 03
54	19 23	20 03	20 56	04 13	04 45	05 24	06 14
52	19 17	19 55	20 43	04 18	04 52	05 33	06 24
50	19 11	19 47	20 32	04 22	04 58	05 41	06 33
45	18 59	19 31	20 11	04 32	05 11	05 57	06 51
N 40	18 50	19 19	19 54	04 41	05 22	06 11	07 06
35	18 41	19 08	19 40	04 48	05 32	06 22	07 18
30	18 34	18 59	19 29	04 54	05 40	06 32	07 29
20	18 22	18 45	19 12	05 05	05 55	06 50	07 48
N 10	18 11	18 33	18 58	05 14	06 08	07 05	08 05
0	18 01	18 22	18 47	05 23	06 20	07 19	08 20
S 10	17 51	18 13	18 38	05 32	06 32	07 33	08 36
20	17 41	18 04	18 30	05 42	06 44	07 48	08 52
30	17 29	17 54	18 22	05 53	06 59	08 06	09 11
35	17 23	17 49	18 18	05 59	07 08	08 16	09 22
40	17 15	17 43	18 15	06 06	07 17	08 28	09 34
45	17 06	17 37	18 11	06 15	07 29	08 41	09 49
S 50	16 56	17 29	18 07	06 25	07 43	08 58	10 07
52	16 51	17 26	18 06	06 30	07 49	09 06	10 16
54	16 45	17 22	18 04	06 35	07 56	09 15	10 25
56	16 39	17 19	18 02	06 41	08 04	09 25	10 36
58	16 33	17 15	18 01	06 47	08 14	09 36	10 49
S 60	16 25	17 10	17 59	06 55	08 24	09 49	11 03

	SUN			MOON			
Day	Eqn. of Time 00h	12h	Mer. Pass.	Mer. Pass. Upper	Lower	Age	Phase
d	m s	m s	h m	h m	h m	d	%
25	02 00	02 05	11 58	24 06	11 38	15	100
26	02 10	02 15	11 58	00 06	12 35	16	99
27	02 20	02 25	11 58	01 05	13 35	17	96

UT	ARIES	VENUS −3.9		MARS +1.2		JUPITER −2.0		SATURN +0.1		STARS		
	GHA	GHA	Dec	GHA	Dec	GHA	Dec	GHA	Dec	Name	SHA	Dec
d h	° ′	° ′	° ′	° ′	° ′	° ′	° ′	° ′	° ′		° ′	° ′
28 00	216 07.9	172 46.1	N16 03.4	182 43.4	N13 06.7	140 21.5	N22 27.9	359 22.8	S11 42.6	Acamar	315 18.9	S40 15.2
01	231 10.3	187 45.5	04.4	197 44.1	07.4	155 23.4	27.9	14 25.4	42.5	Achernar	335 27.5	S57 10.1
02	246 12.8	202 44.9	05.3	212 44.7	08.0	170 25.3	28.0	29 28.1	42.5	Acrux	173 08.7	S63 10.7
03	261 15.2	217 44.3 ..	06.3	227 45.4 ..	08.7	185 27.2 ..	28.0	44 30.7 ..	42.4	Adhara	255 12.8	S28 59.8
04	276 17.7	232 43.8	07.3	242 46.1	09.3	200 29.1	28.1	59 33.4	42.3	Aldebaran	290 49.8	N16 32.0
05	291 20.2	247 43.2	08.3	257 46.8	10.0	215 31.1	28.1	74 36.0	42.3			
06	306 22.6	262 42.6	N16 09.2	272 47.4	N13 10.6	230 33.0	N22 28.2	89 38.7	S11 42.2	Alioth	166 20.3	N55 53.3
07	321 25.1	277 42.0	10.2	287 48.1	11.2	245 34.9	28.3	104 41.3	42.2	Alkaid	152 58.5	N49 14.8
08	336 27.6	292 41.4	11.2	302 48.8	11.9	260 36.8	28.3	119 43.9	42.1	Al Na'ir	27 44.0	S46 53.5
S 09	351 30.0	307 40.8 ..	12.2	317 49.5 ..	12.5	275 38.7 ..	28.4	134 46.6 ..	42.0	Alnilam	275 46.7	S 1 11.9
U 10	6 32.5	322 40.3	13.2	332 50.1	13.2	290 40.6	28.4	149 49.2	42.0	Alphard	217 56.1	S 8 43.3
N 11	21 35.0	337 39.7	14.1	347 50.8	13.8	305 42.5	28.5	164 51.9	41.9			
D 12	36 37.4	352 39.1	N16 15.1	2 51.5	N13 14.4	320 44.5	N22 28.5	179 54.5	S11 41.9	Alphecca	126 10.7	N26 40.1
A 13	51 39.9	7 38.5	16.1	17 52.1	15.1	335 46.4	28.6	194 57.2	41.8	Alpheratz	357 43.9	N29 09.7
Y 14	66 42.3	22 37.9	17.0	32 52.8	15.7	350 48.3	28.6	209 59.8	41.7	Altair	62 08.2	N 8 54.2
15	81 44.8	37 37.3 ..	18.0	47 53.5 ..	16.4	5 50.2 ..	28.7	225 02.5 ..	41.7	Ankaa	353 16.2	S42 13.9
16	96 47.3	52 36.8	19.0	62 54.2	17.0	20 52.1	28.7	240 05.1	41.6	Antares	112 26.0	S26 27.6
17	111 49.7	67 36.2	20.0	77 54.8	17.6	35 54.0	28.8	255 07.8	41.6			
18	126 52.2	82 35.6	N16 20.9	92 55.5	N13 18.3	50 56.0	N22 28.9	270 10.4	S11 41.5	Arcturus	145 55.5	N19 06.7
19	141 54.7	97 35.0	21.9	107 56.2	18.9	65 57.9	28.9	285 13.1	41.4	Atria	107 27.5	S69 02.8
20	156 57.1	112 34.4	22.9	122 56.8	19.5	80 59.8	29.0	300 15.7	41.4	Avior	234 18.1	S59 33.6
21	171 59.6	127 33.8 ..	23.8	137 57.5 ..	20.2	96 01.7 ..	29.0	315 18.4 ..	41.3	Bellatrix	278 32.4	N 6 21.5
22	187 02.1	142 33.2	24.8	152 58.2	20.8	111 03.6	29.1	330 21.0	41.3	Betelgeuse	271 01.6	N 7 24.3
23	202 04.5	157 32.6	25.8	167 58.8	21.5	126 05.5	29.1	345 23.7	41.2			
29 00	217 07.0	172 32.0	N16 26.7	182 59.5	N13 22.1	141 07.4	N22 29.2	0 26.3	S11 41.1	Canopus	263 56.5	S52 42.6
01	232 09.5	187 31.5	27.7	198 00.2	22.7	156 09.3	29.2	15 29.0	41.1	Capella	280 34.9	N46 00.6
02	247 11.9	202 30.9	28.6	213 00.9	23.4	171 11.3	29.3	30 31.6	41.0	Deneb	49 31.5	N45 19.5
03	262 14.4	217 30.3 ..	29.6	228 01.5 ..	24.0	186 13.2 ..	29.3	45 34.3 ..	41.0	Denebola	182 33.5	N14 29.7
04	277 16.8	232 29.7	30.6	243 02.2	24.6	201 15.1	29.4	60 36.9	40.9	Diphda	348 56.3	S17 54.8
05	292 19.3	247 29.1	31.5	258 02.9	25.3	216 17.0	29.5	75 39.6	40.8			
06	307 21.8	262 28.5	N16 32.5	273 03.5	N13 25.9	231 18.9	N22 29.5	90 42.2	S11 40.8	Dubhe	193 51.5	N61 40.8
07	322 24.2	277 27.9	33.5	288 04.2	26.5	246 20.8	29.6	105 44.9	40.7	Elnath	278 13.0	N28 37.0
08	337 26.7	292 27.3	34.4	303 04.9	27.2	261 22.7	29.6	120 47.5	40.7	Eltanin	90 45.8	N51 29.1
M 09	352 29.2	307 26.7 ..	35.4	318 05.5 ..	27.8	276 24.7 ..	29.7	135 50.1 ..	40.6	Enif	33 47.3	N 9 56.2
O 10	7 31.6	322 26.1	36.3	333 06.2	28.4	291 26.6	29.7	150 52.8	40.5	Fomalhaut	15 24.3	S29 32.9
N 11	22 34.1	337 25.5	37.3	348 06.9	29.1	306 28.5	29.8	165 55.4	40.5			
D 12	37 36.6	352 24.9	N16 38.2	3 07.6	N13 29.7	321 30.4	N22 29.8	180 58.1	S11 40.4	Gacrux	172 00.5	S57 11.5
A 13	52 39.0	7 24.3	39.2	18 08.2	30.4	336 32.3	29.9	196 00.7	40.4	Gienah	175 52.1	S17 37.2
Y 14	67 41.5	22 23.7	40.1	33 08.9	31.0	351 34.2	29.9	211 03.4	40.3	Hadar	148 47.3	S60 26.3
15	82 44.0	37 23.1 ..	41.1	48 09.6 ..	31.6	6 36.1 ..	30.0	226 06.0 ..	40.2	Hamal	328 01.2	N23 31.4
16	97 46.4	52 22.5	42.1	63 10.2	32.2	21 38.0	30.1	241 08.7	40.2	Kaus Aust.	83 43.7	S34 22.5
17	112 48.9	67 21.9	43.0	78 10.9	32.9	36 39.9	30.1	256 11.3	40.1			
18	127 51.3	82 21.3	N16 44.0	93 11.6	N13 33.5	51 41.9	N22 30.2	271 14.0	S11 40.1	Kochab	137 18.9	N74 06.0
19	142 53.8	97 20.7	44.9	108 12.2	34.1	66 43.8	30.2	286 16.6	40.0	Markab	13 38.6	N15 16.6
20	157 56.3	112 20.2	45.9	123 12.9	34.8	81 45.7	30.3	301 19.3	40.0	Menkar	314 15.5	N 4 08.4
21	172 58.7	127 19.6 ..	46.8	138 13.6 ..	35.4	96 47.6 ..	30.3	316 21.9 ..	39.9	Menkent	148 07.3	S36 26.2
22	188 01.2	142 19.0	47.8	153 14.3	36.0	111 49.5	30.4	331 24.6	39.8	Miaplacidus	221 39.5	S69 46.9
23	203 03.7	157 18.3	48.7	168 14.9	36.7	126 51.4	30.4	346 27.2	39.8			
30 00	218 06.1	172 17.7	N16 49.6	183 15.6	N13 37.3	141 53.3	N22 30.5	1 29.9	S11 39.7	Mirfak	308 41.0	N49 54.4
01	233 08.6	187 17.1	50.6	198 16.3	37.9	156 55.2	30.5	16 32.5	39.7	Nunki	75 58.3	S26 16.6
02	248 11.1	202 16.5	51.5	213 16.9	38.6	171 57.1	30.6	31 35.2	39.6	Peacock	53 19.4	S56 41.1
03	263 13.5	217 15.9 ..	52.5	228 17.6 ..	39.2	186 59.1 ..	30.7	46 37.8 ..	39.5	Pollux	243 28.0	N27 59.5
04	278 16.0	232 15.3	53.4	243 18.3	39.8	202 01.0	30.7	61 40.5	39.5	Procyon	244 59.9	N 5 11.2
05	293 18.5	247 14.7	54.4	258 18.9	40.5	217 02.9	30.8	76 43.1	39.4			
06	308 20.9	262 14.1	N16 55.3	273 19.6	N13 41.1	232 04.8	N22 30.8	91 45.8	S11 39.4	Rasalhague	96 06.3	N12 33.0
07	323 23.4	277 13.5	56.3	288 20.3	41.7	247 06.7	30.9	106 48.4	39.3	Regulus	207 43.5	N11 53.9
08	338 25.8	292 12.9	57.2	303 20.9	42.3	262 08.6	30.9	121 51.0	39.2	Rigel	281 12.4	S 8 11.4
T 09	353 28.3	307 12.3 ..	58.1	318 21.6 ..	43.0	277 10.5 ..	31.0	136 53.7 ..	39.2	Rigil Kent.	139 51.1	S60 53.4
U 10	8 30.8	322 11.7	16 59.1	333 22.3	43.6	292 12.4	31.0	151 56.3	39.1	Sabik	102 12.4	S15 44.4
E 11	23 33.2	337 11.1	17 00.0	348 22.9	44.2	307 14.3	31.1	166 59.0	39.1			
S 12	38 35.7	352 10.5	N17 01.0	3 23.6	N13 44.9	322 16.2	N22 31.1	182 01.6	S11 39.0	Schedar	349 41.1	N56 36.5
D 13	53 38.2	7 09.9	01.9	18 24.3	45.5	337 18.2	31.2	197 04.3	38.9	Shaula	96 21.7	S37 06.6
A 14	68 40.6	22 09.3	02.8	33 24.9	46.1	352 20.1	31.2	212 06.9	38.9	Sirius	258 34.0	S16 44.4
Y 15	83 43.1	37 08.7 ..	03.8	48 25.6 ..	46.7	7 22.0 ..	31.3	227 09.6 ..	38.8	Spica	158 31.0	S11 14.0
16	98 45.6	52 08.1	04.7	63 26.3	47.4	22 23.9	31.4	242 12.2	38.8	Suhail	222 52.4	S43 29.6
17	113 48.0	67 07.5	05.6	78 26.9	48.0	37 25.8	31.4	257 14.9	38.7			
18	128 50.5	82 06.8	N17 06.6	93 27.6	N13 48.6	52 27.7	N22 31.5	272 17.5	S11 38.6	Vega	80 38.8	N38 47.7
19	143 53.0	97 06.2	07.5	108 28.3	49.2	67 29.6	31.5	287 20.2	38.6	Zuben'ubi	137 05.2	S16 05.9
20	158 55.4	112 05.6	08.4	123 28.9	49.9	82 31.5	31.6	302 22.8	38.5		SHA	Mer.Pass.
21	173 57.9	127 05.0 ..	09.4	138 29.6 ..	50.5	97 33.4 ..	31.6	317 25.5 ..	38.5		° ′	h m
22	189 00.3	142 04.4	10.3	153 30.3	51.1	112 35.3	31.7	332 28.1	38.4	Venus	315 25.1	12 30
23	204 02.8	157 03.8	11.2	168 30.9	51.7	127 37.2	31.7	347 30.8	38.3	Mars	325 52.5	11 48
	h m									Jupiter	284 00.4	14 34
Mer.Pass. 9 30.0		v −0.6	d 1.0	v 0.7	d 0.6	v 1.9	d 0.1	v 2.6	d 0.1	Saturn	143 19.3	23 54

UT	SUN GHA	SUN Dec	MOON GHA	v	Dec	d	HP	Lat.	Twilight Naut.	Twilight Civil	Sunrise	Moonrise 28	Moonrise 29	Moonrise 30	Moonrise 1
d h	° ′	° ′	° ′	′	° ′	′	′	°	h m	h m	h m	h m	h m	h m	h m
								N 72	////	////	02 08	■■	■■	■■	03 32
28 00	180 37.4	N14 07.9	329 54.4	4.2	S19 43.6	2.7	60.5	N 70	////	////	02 42	01 54	■■	02 54	02 44
01	195 37.5	08.7	344 17.6	4.1	19 46.3	2.6	60.5	68	////	01 26	03 06	00 16	01 28	02 01	02 13
02	210 37.6	09.5	358 40.7	4.1	19 48.9	2.4	60.5	66	////	02 07	03 25	24 46	00 46	01 28	01 50
03	225 37.7 ..	10.3	13 03.8	4.2	19 51.3	2.3	60.5	64	////	02 34	03 40	24 18	00 18	01 03	01 32
04	240 37.7	11.1	27 27.0	4.1	19 53.6	2.1	60.5	62	01 16	02 55	03 52	23 56	24 44	00 44	01 17
05	255 37.8	11.9	41 50.1	4.1	19 55.7	2.0	60.5	60	01 53	03 11	04 03	23 38	24 28	00 28	01 04
06	270 37.9	N14 12.6	56 13.2	4.0	S19 57.7	1.8	60.5	N 58	02 18	03 25	04 12	23 23	24 15	00 15	00 53
07	285 38.0	13.4	70 36.2	4.1	19 59.5	1.7	60.5	56	02 37	03 37	04 20	23 11	24 03	00 03	00 44
08	300 38.0	14.2	84 59.3	4.1	20 01.2	1.5	60.5	54	02 53	03 47	04 28	23 00	23 53	24 35	00 35
S 09	315 38.2 ..	15.0	99 22.4	4.1	20 02.7	1.5	60.5	52	03 06	03 56	04 34	22 50	23 44	24 27	00 27
U 10	330 38.3	15.8	113 45.5	4.1	20 04.2	1.2	60.5	50	03 18	04 04	04 40	22 41	23 36	24 21	00 21
N 11	345 38.4	16.6	128 08.6	4.0	20 05.4	1.1	60.5	45	03 41	04 20	04 52	22 23	23 19	24 06	00 06
D 12	0 38.5	N14 17.3	142 31.6	4.1	S20 06.5	1.0	60.5	N 40	03 58	04 33	05 03	22 08	23 04	23 54	24 36
A 13	15 38.6	18.1	156 54.7	4.1	20 07.5	0.8	60.5	35	04 12	04 44	05 11	21 55	22 52	23 43	24 28
Y 14	30 38.7	18.9	171 17.8	4.1	20 08.3	0.7	60.5	30	04 24	04 54	05 19	21 44	22 42	23 34	24 21
15	45 38.8 ..	19.7	185 40.9	4.1	20 09.0	0.5	60.5	20	04 42	05 09	05 32	21 24	22 24	23 18	24 08
16	60 38.8	20.5	200 04.0	4.1	20 09.5	0.4	60.4	N 10	04 56	05 22	05 43	21 08	22 08	23 04	23 57
17	75 38.9	21.2	214 27.1	4.1	20 09.9	0.2	60.4	0	05 08	05 33	05 54	20 52	21 53	22 52	23 47
18	90 39.0	N14 22.0	228 50.2	4.2	S20 10.1	0.1	60.4	S 10	05 18	05 43	06 04	20 37	21 38	22 39	23 36
19	105 39.1	22.8	243 13.4	4.1	20 10.2	0.1	60.4	20	05 26	05 53	06 15	20 20	21 23	22 25	23 25
20	120 39.2	23.6	257 36.5	4.2	20 10.1	0.2	60.4	30	05 35	06 03	06 28	20 01	21 04	22 09	23 13
21	135 39.3 ..	24.4	271 59.7	4.2	20 09.9	0.3	60.4	35	05 39	06 09	06 35	19 50	20 54	22 00	23 05
22	150 39.4	25.1	286 22.9	4.2	20 09.6	0.5	60.4	40	05 43	06 15	06 43	19 38	20 42	21 49	22 57
23	165 39.5	25.9	300 46.1	4.2	20 09.1	0.7	60.4	45	05 47	06 22	06 52	19 23	20 28	21 37	22 47
29 00	180 39.6	N14 26.7	315 09.3	4.2	S20 08.4	0.7	60.4	S 50	05 51	06 30	07 04	19 05	20 10	21 21	22 35
01	195 39.6	27.5	329 32.5	4.3	20 07.7	1.0	60.3	52	05 53	06 33	07 09	18 56	20 02	21 14	22 30
02	210 39.7	28.2	343 55.8	4.3	20 06.7	1.0	60.3	54	05 55	06 37	07 15	18 46	19 53	21 06	22 24
03	225 39.8 ..	29.0	358 19.1	4.3	20 05.7	1.3	60.3	56	05 57	06 41	07 21	18 36	19 42	20 58	22 17
04	240 39.9	29.8	12 42.4	4.4	20 04.4	1.3	60.3	58	05 59	06 46	07 28	18 23	19 31	20 48	22 09
05	255 40.0	30.6	27 05.8	4.4	20 03.1	1.5	60.3	S 60	06 02	06 51	07 36	18 09	19 17	20 36	22 00

UT	SUN GHA	SUN Dec	MOON GHA	v	Dec	d	HP	Lat.	Sunset	Twilight Civil	Twilight Naut.	Moonset 28	Moonset 29	Moonset 30	Moonset 1
06	270 40.1	N14 31.4	41 29.2	4.4	S20 01.6	1.7	60.3	°	h m	h m	h m	h m	h m	h m	h m
07	285 40.2	32.1	55 52.6	4.5	19 59.9	1.7	60.3	N 72	21 53	////	////	■■	■■	■■	06 52
08	300 40.2	32.9	70 16.1	4.5	19 58.2	2.0	60.3	N 70	21 17	////	////	02 13	■■	05 28	07 38
M 09	315 40.3 ..	33.7	84 39.6	4.5	19 56.2	2.0	60.2	68	20 52	22 37	////	03 51	04 48	06 21	08 08
O 10	330 40.4	34.4	99 03.1	4.6	19 54.2	2.2	60.2	66	20 32	21 53	////	04 31	05 30	06 54	08 31
N 11	345 40.5	35.2	113 26.7	4.6	19 52.0	2.4	60.2	64	20 17	21 24	////	04 58	05 58	07 18	08 48
D 12	0 40.6	N14 36.0	127 50.3	4.6	S19 49.6	2.5	60.2	62	20 04	21 03	22 46	05 19	06 20	07 37	09 03
A 13	15 40.7	36.8	142 13.9	4.7	19 47.1	2.6	60.2	60	19 53	20 46	22 06	05 37	06 37	07 52	09 15
Y 14	30 40.8	37.5	156 37.6	4.8	19 44.5	2.7	60.2	N 58	19 44	20 32	21 40	05 52	06 52	08 05	09 25
15	45 40.8 ..	38.3	171 01.4	4.7	19 41.8	2.9	60.2	56	19 36	20 21	21 20	06 03	07 05	08 16	09 34
16	60 40.9	39.1	185 25.1	4.9	19 38.9	3.1	60.1	54	19 28	20 09	21 04	06 14	07 16	08 26	09 42
17	75 41.0	39.8	199 49.0	4.9	19 35.8	3.1	60.1	52	19 22	20 00	20 50	06 24	07 25	08 35	09 50
18	90 41.1	N14 40.6	214 12.9	4.9	S19 32.7	3.3	60.1	50	19 16	19 52	20 39	06 33	07 34	08 43	09 56
19	105 41.2	41.4	228 36.8	5.0	19 29.4	3.5	60.1	45	19 03	19 35	20 15	06 51	07 52	09 00	10 10
20	120 41.3	42.2	243 00.8	5.0	19 25.9	3.5	60.1	N 40	18 53	19 22	19 57	07 06	08 07	09 13	10 21
21	135 41.3 ..	42.9	257 24.8	5.1	19 22.4	3.7	60.1	35	18 44	19 11	19 43	07 18	08 20	09 25	10 31
22	150 41.4	43.7	271 48.9	5.2	19 18.7	3.9	60.0	30	18 36	19 01	19 31	07 29	08 31	09 35	10 39
23	165 41.5	44.5	286 13.1	5.2	19 14.8	3.9	60.0	20	18 23	18 46	19 13	07 48	08 50	09 52	10 54
30 00	180 41.6	N14 45.2	300 37.3	5.2	S19 10.9	4.1	60.0	N 10	18 11	18 33	18 59	08 05	09 06	10 07	11 07
01	195 41.7	46.0	315 01.5	5.4	19 06.8	4.2	60.0	0	18 01	18 22	18 47	08 20	09 22	10 21	11 18
02	210 41.8	46.8	329 25.9	5.3	19 02.6	4.4	60.0	S 10	17 50	18 12	18 37	08 36	09 37	10 35	11 30
03	225 41.8 ..	47.5	343 50.2	5.5	18 58.2	4.4	59.9	20	17 39	18 02	18 28	08 52	09 53	10 50	11 42
04	240 41.9	48.3	358 14.7	5.5	18 53.8	4.6	59.9	30	17 27	17 51	18 20	09 11	10 12	11 07	11 56
05	255 42.0	49.1	12 39.2	5.5	18 49.2	4.8	59.9	35	17 19	17 45	18 15	09 22	10 23	11 17	12 05
06	270 42.1	N14 49.8	27 03.7	5.7	S18 44.4	4.8	59.9	40	17 11	17 39	18 11	09 34	10 35	11 28	12 14
07	285 42.2	50.6	41 28.4	5.7	18 39.6	5.0	59.9	45	17 02	17 32	18 07	09 49	10 50	11 41	12 25
08	300 42.2	51.3	55 53.1	5.7	18 34.6	5.0	59.8	S 50	16 50	17 24	18 02	10 07	11 07	11 57	12 38
T 09	315 42.3 ..	52.1	70 17.8	5.9	18 29.6	5.3	59.8	52	16 45	17 21	18 00	10 16	11 16	12 04	12 44
U 10	330 42.4	52.9	84 42.7	5.8	18 24.3	5.3	59.8	54	16 39	17 17	17 58	10 25	11 25	12 13	12 50
E 11	345 42.5	53.6	99 07.5	6.0	18 19.0	5.4	59.8	56	16 33	17 12	17 56	10 36	11 36	12 22	12 58
S 12	0 42.6	N14 54.4	113 32.5	6.0	S18 13.6	5.6	59.8	58	16 25	17 08	17 54	10 49	11 48	12 33	13 06
D 13	15 42.6	55.2	127 57.5	6.1	18 08.0	5.7	59.7	S 60	16 17	17 02	17 52	11 03	12 02	12 44	13 15
A 14	30 42.7	55.9	142 22.6	6.2	18 02.3	5.8	59.7								
Y 15	45 42.8 ..	56.7	156 47.8	6.2	17 56.5	5.9	59.7								
16	60 42.9	57.4	171 13.0	6.3	17 50.6	6.0	59.7								
17	75 42.9	58.2	185 38.3	6.4	17 44.6	6.1	59.6			SUN			MOON		
18	90 43.0	N14 59.0	200 03.7	6.5	S17 38.5	6.3	59.6								
19	105 43.1	14 59.7	214 29.2	6.5	17 32.2	6.3	59.6	Day	Eqn. of Time 00h	Eqn. of Time 12h	Mer. Pass.	Mer. Pass. Upper	Mer. Pass. Lower	Age	Phase
20	120 43.2	15 00.5	228 54.7	6.6	17 25.9	6.5	59.6								
21	135 43.3 ..	01.2	243 20.3	6.7	17 19.4	6.5	59.6	d	m s	m s	h m	h m	h m	d	%
22	150 43.3	02.0	257 46.0	6.7	17 12.9	6.7	59.5	28	02 29	02 34	11 57	02 06	14 36	18	90
23	165 43.4	02.8	272 11.7	6.9	S17 06.2	6.8	59.5	29	02 38	02 42	11 57	03 07	15 37	19	82
	SD 15.9	d 0.8	SD 16.5		16.4		16.3	30	02 46	02 50	11 57	04 07	16 37	20	72

UT	ARIES	VENUS −3.9		MARS +1.3		JUPITER −2.0		SATURN +0.1		STARS		
	GHA	GHA	Dec	GHA	Dec	GHA	Dec	GHA	Dec	Name	SHA	Dec
d h	° ′	° ′	° ′	° ′	° ′	° ′	° ′	° ′	° ′		° ′	° ′
1 00	219 05.3	172 03.2	N17 12.1	183 31.6	N13 52.4	142 39.1	N22 31.8	2 33.4	S11 38.3	Acamar	315 18.8	S40 15.2
01	234 07.7	187 02.6	13.1	198 32.3	53.0	157 41.1	31.8	17 36.1	38.2	Achernar	335 27.4	S57 10.1
02	249 10.2	202 01.9	14.0	213 32.9	53.6	172 43.0	31.9	32 38.7	38.2	Acrux	173 08.7	S63 10.7
03	264 12.7	217 01.3 . .	14.9	228 33.6 . .	54.2	187 44.9 . .	31.9	47 41.4 . .	38.1	Adhara	255 12.8	S28 59.8
04	279 15.1	232 00.7	15.9	243 34.3	54.9	202 46.8	32.0	62 44.0	38.1	Aldebaran	290 49.8	N16 32.0
05	294 17.6	247 00.1	16.8	258 34.9	55.5	217 48.7	32.1	77 46.7	38.0			
06	309 20.1	261 59.5	N17 17.7	273 35.6	N13 56.1	232 50.6	N22 32.1	92 49.3	S11 37.9	Alioth	166 20.3	N55 53.3
W 07	324 22.5	276 58.9	18.6	288 36.3	56.7	247 52.5	32.2	107 51.9	37.9	Alkaid	152 58.5	N49 14.8
E 08	339 25.0	291 58.3	19.6	303 36.9	57.4	262 54.4	32.2	122 54.6	37.8	Al Na'ir	27 44.0	S46 53.5
D 09	354 27.4	306 57.6 . .	20.5	318 37.6 . .	58.0	277 56.3 . .	32.3	137 57.2 . .	37.8	Alnilam	275 46.7	S 1 11.9
N 10	9 29.9	321 57.0	21.4	333 38.3	58.6	292 58.2	32.3	152 59.9	37.7	Alphard	217 56.1	S 8 43.3
E 11	24 32.4	336 56.4	27.8	348 38.9	59.2	308 00.1	32.4	168 02.5	37.6			
S 12	39 34.8	351 55.8	N17 23.2	3 39.6	N13 59.9	323 02.0	N22 32.4	183 05.2	S11 37.6	Alphecca	126 10.7	N26 40.1
D 13	54 37.3	6 55.2	24.2	18 40.3	14 00.5	338 03.9	32.5	198 07.8	37.5	Alpheratz	357 43.8	N29 09.7
A 14	69 39.8	21 54.5	25.1	33 40.9	01.1	353 05.8	32.5	213 10.5	37.5	Altair	62 08.2	N 8 54.2
Y 15	84 42.2	36 53.9 . .	26.0	48 41.6 . .	01.7	8 07.7 . .	32.6	228 13.1 . .	37.4	Ankaa	353 16.2	S42 13.9
16	99 44.7	51 53.3	26.9	63 42.3	02.3	23 09.7	32.6	243 15.8	37.3	Antares	112 26.0	S26 27.6
17	114 47.2	66 52.7	27.8	78 42.9	03.0	38 11.6	32.7	258 18.4	37.3			
18	129 49.6	81 52.1	N17 28.7	93 43.6	N14 03.6	53 13.5	N22 32.7	273 21.1	S11 37.2	Arcturus	145 55.5	N19 06.7
19	144 52.1	96 51.4	29.6	108 44.3	04.2	68 15.4	32.8	288 23.7	37.2	Atria	107 27.4	S69 02.8
20	159 54.6	111 50.8	30.6	123 44.9	04.8	83 17.3	32.9	303 26.4	37.1	Avior	234 18.1	S59 33.6
21	174 57.0	126 50.2 . .	31.5	138 45.6 . .	05.4	98 19.2 . .	32.9	318 29.0 . .	37.0	Bellatrix	278 32.4	N 6 21.5
22	189 59.5	141 49.6	32.4	153 46.3	06.1	113 21.1	33.0	333 31.7	37.0	Betelgeuse	271 01.6	N 7 24.3
23	205 01.9	156 48.9	33.3	168 46.9	06.7	128 23.0	33.0	348 34.3	36.9			
2 00	220 04.4	171 48.3	N17 34.2	183 47.6	N14 07.3	143 24.9	N22 33.1	3 37.0	S11 36.9	Canopus	263 56.5	S52 42.6
01	235 06.9	186 47.7	35.1	198 48.3	07.9	158 26.8	33.1	18 39.6	36.8	Capella	280 35.0	N46 00.6
02	250 09.3	201 47.1	36.0	213 48.9	08.5	173 28.7	33.2	33 42.3	36.8	Deneb	49 31.5	N45 19.5
03	265 11.8	216 46.4 . .	36.9	228 49.6 . .	09.2	188 30.6 . .	33.2	48 44.9 . .	36.7	Denebola	182 33.5	N14 29.7
04	280 14.3	231 45.8	37.8	243 50.3	09.8	203 32.5	33.3	63 47.5	36.6	Diphda	348 56.3	S17 54.8
05	295 16.7	246 45.2	38.7	258 50.9	10.4	218 34.4	33.3	78 50.2	36.6			
06	310 19.2	261 44.6	N17 39.6	273 51.6	N14 11.0	233 36.3	N22 33.4	93 52.8	S11 36.5	Dubhe	193 51.5	N61 40.8
07	325 21.7	276 43.9	40.6	288 52.2	11.6	248 38.2	33.4	108 55.5	36.5	Elnath	278 13.0	N28 37.0
T 08	340 24.1	291 43.3	41.5	303 52.9	12.2	263 40.1	33.5	123 58.1	36.4	Eltanin	90 45.8	N51 29.1
H 09	355 26.6	306 42.7 . .	42.4	318 53.6 . .	12.9	278 42.0 . .	33.5	139 00.8 . .	36.3	Enif	33 47.3	N 9 56.2
U 10	10 29.1	321 42.0	43.3	333 54.2	13.5	293 43.9	33.6	154 03.4	36.3	Fomalhaut	15 24.3	S29 32.9
R 11	25 31.5	336 41.4	44.2	348 54.9	14.1	308 45.8	33.6	169 06.1	36.2			
S 12	40 34.0	351 40.8	N17 45.1	3 55.6	N14 14.7	323 47.7	N22 33.7	184 08.7	S11 36.2	Gacrux	172 00.5	S57 11.5
D 13	55 36.4	6 40.2	46.0	18 56.2	15.3	338 49.6	33.7	199 11.4	36.1	Gienah	175 52.1	S17 37.2
A 14	70 38.9	21 39.5	46.9	33 56.9	15.9	353 51.5	33.8	214 14.0	36.0	Hadar	148 47.3	S60 26.3
Y 15	85 41.4	36 38.9 . .	47.8	48 57.6 . .	16.5	8 53.5 . .	33.9	229 16.7 . .	36.0	Hamal	328 01.2	N23 31.4
16	100 43.8	51 38.3	48.7	63 58.2	17.2	23 55.4	33.9	244 19.3	35.9	Kaus Aust.	83 43.7	S34 22.5
17	115 46.3	66 37.6	49.6	78 58.9	17.8	38 57.3	34.0	259 22.0	35.9			
18	130 48.8	81 37.0	N17 50.5	93 59.5	N14 18.4	53 59.2	N22 34.0	274 24.6	S11 35.8	Kochab	137 18.9	N74 06.0
19	145 51.2	96 36.4	51.3	109 00.2	19.0	69 01.1	34.1	289 27.3	35.7	Markab	13 38.6	N15 16.6
20	160 53.7	111 35.7	52.2	124 00.9	19.6	84 03.0	34.1	304 29.9	35.7	Menkar	314 15.5	N 4 08.4
21	175 56.2	126 35.1 . .	53.1	139 01.5 . .	20.2	99 04.9 . .	34.2	319 32.6 . .	35.6	Menkent	148 07.3	S36 26.2
22	190 58.6	141 34.5	54.0	154 02.2	20.8	114 06.8	34.2	334 35.2	35.6	Miaplacidus	221 39.6	S69 46.8
23	206 01.1	156 33.8	54.9	169 02.9	21.5	129 08.7	34.3	349 37.8	35.5			
3 00	221 03.5	171 33.2	N17 55.8	184 03.5	N14 22.1	144 10.6	N22 34.3	4 40.5	S11 35.5	Mirfak	308 40.9	N49 54.4
01	236 06.0	186 32.5	56.7	199 04.2	22.7	159 12.5	34.4	19 43.1	35.4	Nunki	75 58.2	S26 16.6
02	251 08.5	201 31.9	57.6	214 04.9	23.3	174 14.4	34.4	34 45.8	35.3	Peacock	53 19.3	S56 41.1
03	266 10.9	216 31.3 . .	58.5	229 05.5 . .	23.9	189 16.3 . .	34.5	49 48.4 . .	35.3	Pollux	243 28.0	N27 59.5
04	281 13.4	231 30.6	17 59.4	244 06.2	24.5	204 18.2	34.5	64 51.1	35.2	Procyon	244 59.9	N 5 11.2
05	296 15.9	246 30.0	18 00.3	259 06.8	25.1	219 20.1	34.6	79 53.7	35.2			
06	311 18.3	261 29.4	N18 01.1	274 07.5	N14 25.7	234 22.0	N22 34.6	94 56.4	S11 35.1	Rasalhague	96 06.3	N12 33.0
07	326 20.8	276 28.7	02.0	289 08.2	26.4	249 23.9	34.7	109 59.0	35.0	Regulus	207 43.5	N11 53.9
08	341 23.3	291 28.1	02.9	304 08.8	27.0	264 25.8	34.7	125 01.7	35.0	Rigel	281 12.4	S 8 11.4
F 09	356 25.7	306 27.4 . .	03.8	319 09.5 . .	27.6	279 27.7 . .	34.8	140 04.3 . .	34.9	Rigil Kent.	139 51.1	S60 53.4
R 10	11 28.2	321 26.8	04.7	334 10.2	28.2	294 29.6	34.8	155 07.0	34.9	Sabik	102 12.4	S15 44.4
I 11	26 30.7	336 26.2	05.6	349 10.8	28.8	309 31.5	34.9	170 09.6	34.8			
D 12	41 33.1	351 25.5	N18 06.4	4 11.5	N14 29.4	324 33.4	N22 35.0	185 12.3	S11 34.8	Schedar	349 41.1	N56 36.5
A 13	56 35.6	6 24.9	07.3	19 12.1	30.0	339 35.3	35.0	200 14.9	34.7	Shaula	96 21.7	S37 06.6
Y 14	71 38.0	21 24.2	08.2	34 12.8	30.6	354 37.2	35.1	215 17.6	34.6	Sirius	258 34.0	S16 44.4
15	86 40.5	36 23.6 . .	09.1	49 13.5 . .	31.2	9 39.1 . .	35.1	230 20.2 . .	34.6	Spica	158 31.0	S11 14.0
16	101 43.0	51 22.9	10.0	64 14.1	31.8	24 41.0	35.2	245 22.8	34.5	Suhail	222 52.5	S43 29.6
17	116 45.4	66 22.3	10.8	79 14.8	32.5	39 42.9	35.2	260 25.5	34.5			
18	131 47.9	81 21.7	N18 11.7	94 15.4	N14 33.1	54 44.8	N22 35.3	275 28.1	S11 34.4	Vega	80 38.8	N38 47.7
19	146 50.4	96 21.0	12.6	109 16.1	33.7	69 46.7	35.3	290 30.8	34.3	Zuben'ubi	137 05.2	S16 05.9
20	161 52.8	111 20.4	13.5	124 16.8	34.3	84 48.6	35.4	305 33.4	34.3		SHA	Mer.Pass.
21	176 55.3	126 19.7 . .	14.3	139 17.4 . .	34.9	99 50.5 . .	35.4	320 36.1 . .	34.2		° ′	h m
22	191 57.8	141 19.1	15.2	154 18.1	35.5	114 52.4	35.5	335 38.7	34.2	Venus	311 43.9	12 33
23	207 00.2	156 18.4	16.1	169 18.8	36.1	129 54.3	35.5	350 41.4	34.1	Mars	323 43.2	11 44
	h m									Jupiter	283 20.5	14 25
Mer. Pass. 9 18.2		v −0.6	d 0.9	v 0.7	d 0.6	v 1.9	d 0.1	v 2.6	d 0.1	Saturn	143 32.5	23 41

UT	SUN GHA	SUN Dec	MOON GHA	v	MOON Dec	d	HP
d h	° ′	° ′	° ′	′	° ′	′	′
1 00	180 43.5	N15 03.5	286 37.6	6.9	S16 59.4	6.9	59.5
01	195 43.6	04.3	301 03.5	6.9	16 52.5	6.9	59.5
02	210 43.6	05.0	315 29.4	7.1	16 45.6	7.1	59.4
03	225 43.7 ..	05.8	329 55.5	7.1	16 38.5	7.2	59.4
04	240 43.8	06.5	344 21.6	7.2	16 31.3	7.3	59.4
05	255 43.9	07.3	358 47.8	7.3	16 24.0	7.3	59.4
W 06	270 43.9	N15 08.0	13 14.1	7.3	S16 16.7	7.5	59.3
E 07	285 44.0	08.8	27 40.4	7.5	16 09.2	7.6	59.3
D 08	300 44.1	09.6	42 06.9	7.5	16 01.6	7.6	59.3
N 09	315 44.2 ..	10.3	56 33.4	7.6	15 54.0	7.8	59.3
E 10	330 44.2	11.1	71 00.0	7.6	15 46.2	7.8	59.2
S 11	345 44.3	11.8	85 26.6	7.8	15 38.4	8.0	59.2
D 12	0 44.4	N15 12.6	99 53.4	7.8	S15 30.4	8.0	59.2
A 13	15 44.5	13.3	114 20.2	7.9	15 22.4	8.1	59.2
Y 14	30 44.5	14.1	128 47.1	8.0	15 14.3	8.2	59.1
15	45 44.6 ..	14.8	143 14.1	8.0	15 06.1	8.3	59.1
16	60 44.7	15.6	157 41.1	8.2	14 57.8	8.3	59.1
17	75 44.8	16.3	172 08.3	8.2	14 49.5	8.5	59.1
18	90 44.8	N15 17.1	186 35.5	8.2	S14 41.0	8.5	59.0
19	105 44.9	17.8	201 02.7	8.4	14 32.5	8.6	59.0
20	120 45.0	18.6	215 30.1	8.4	14 23.9	8.7	59.0
21	135 45.0 ..	19.3	229 57.5	8.6	14 15.2	8.8	59.0
22	150 45.1	20.1	244 25.1	8.5	14 06.4	8.8	58.9
23	165 45.2	20.8	258 52.6	8.7	13 57.6	8.9	58.9
2 00	180 45.3	N15 21.5	273 20.3	8.7	S13 48.7	9.0	58.9
01	195 45.3	22.3	287 48.0	8.9	13 39.7	9.0	58.9
02	210 45.4	23.0	302 15.9	8.9	13 30.7	9.2	58.8
03	225 45.5 ..	23.8	316 43.8	8.9	13 21.5	9.2	58.8
04	240 45.5	24.5	331 11.7	9.1	13 12.3	9.2	58.8
05	255 45.6	25.3	345 39.8	9.1	13 03.1	9.4	58.8
T 06	270 45.7	N15 26.0	0 07.9	9.2	S12 53.7	9.4	58.7
H 07	285 45.7	26.8	14 36.1	9.2	12 44.3	9.4	58.7
U 08	300 45.8	27.5	29 04.3	9.4	12 34.9	9.5	58.7
R 09	315 45.9 ..	28.2	43 32.7	9.4	12 25.4	9.6	58.6
S 10	330 45.9	29.0	58 01.1	9.5	12 15.8	9.7	58.6
D 11	345 46.0	29.7	72 29.6	9.5	12 06.1	9.7	58.6
A 12	0 46.1	N15 30.5	86 58.1	9.7	S11 56.4	9.8	58.5
Y 13	15 46.1	31.2	101 26.8	9.7	11 46.6	9.8	58.5
14	30 46.2	32.0	115 55.5	9.7	11 36.8	9.9	58.5
15	45 46.3 ..	32.7	130 24.2	9.9	11 26.9	9.9	58.5
16	60 46.3	33.4	144 53.1	9.9	11 17.0	10.0	58.5
17	75 46.4	34.2	159 22.0	9.9	11 07.0	10.0	58.4
18	90 46.5	N15 34.9	173 50.9	10.1	S10 57.0	10.1	58.4
19	105 46.5	35.7	188 20.0	10.1	10 46.9	10.2	58.4
20	120 46.6	36.4	202 49.1	10.2	10 36.7	10.2	58.4
21	135 46.7 ..	37.1	217 18.3	10.2	10 26.5	10.2	58.3
22	150 46.7	37.9	231 47.5	10.3	10 16.3	10.3	58.3
23	165 46.8	38.6	246 16.8	10.4	10 06.0	10.4	58.3
3 00	180 46.9	N15 39.3	260 46.2	10.4	S 9 55.6	10.3	58.2
01	195 46.9	40.1	275 15.6	10.6	9 45.3	10.5	58.2
02	210 47.0	40.8	289 45.2	10.5	9 34.8	10.4	58.2
03	225 47.1 ..	41.5	304 14.7	10.7	9 24.4	10.5	58.2
04	240 47.1	42.3	318 44.4	10.6	9 13.9	10.6	58.1
05	255 47.2	43.0	333 14.0	10.8	9 03.3	10.6	58.1
F 06	270 47.3	N15 43.7	347 43.8	10.8	S 8 52.7	10.6	58.1
R 07	285 47.3	44.5	2 13.6	10.9	8 42.1	10.7	58.1
I 08	300 47.4	45.2	16 43.5	10.9	8 31.4	10.6	58.0
D 09	315 47.4 ..	45.9	31 13.4	11.0	8 20.8	10.8	58.0
A 10	330 47.5	46.7	45 43.4	11.1	8 10.0	10.7	58.0
Y 11	345 47.6	47.4	60 13.5	11.1	7 59.3	10.8	58.0
12	0 47.6	N15 48.1	74 43.6	11.1	S 7 48.5	10.9	57.9
13	15 47.7	48.9	89 13.7	11.3	7 37.6	10.8	57.9
14	30 47.8	49.6	103 44.0	11.2	7 26.8	10.9	57.9
15	45 47.8 ..	50.3	118 14.2	11.4	7 15.9	10.9	57.8
16	60 47.9	51.0	132 44.6	11.3	7 05.0	11.0	57.8
17	75 47.9	51.8	147 14.9	11.5	6 54.0	11.0	57.8
18	90 48.0	N15 52.5	161 45.4	11.5	S 6 43.0	11.0	57.8
19	105 48.1	53.2	176 15.9	11.5	6 32.0	11.0	57.7
20	120 48.1	54.0	190 46.4	11.6	6 21.0	11.0	57.7
21	135 48.2 ..	54.7	205 17.0	11.6	6 10.0	11.1	57.7
22	150 48.2	55.4	219 47.6	11.7	5 58.9	11.1	57.7
23	165 48.3	56.1	234 18.3	11.8	S 5 47.8	11.1	57.6
	SD 15.9	d 0.7	SD 16.1		16.0		15.8

Moonrise

Lat.	Twilight Naut.	Twilight Civil	Sunrise	1	2	3	4
°	h m	h m	h m	h m	h m	h m	h m
N 72	////	////	01 43	03 32	03 04	02 48	02 36
N 70	////	////	02 24	02 44	02 38	02 33	02 28
68	////	00 53	02 52	02 13	02 19	02 21	02 23
66	////	01 48	03 13	01 50	02 03	02 12	02 18
64	////	02 20	03 30	01 32	01 50	02 03	02 13
62	00 47	02 43	03 43	01 17	01 40	01 56	02 10
60	01 36	03 01	03 55	01 04	01 30	01 50	02 06
N 58	02 05	03 16	04 05	00 53	01 22	01 45	02 03
56	02 27	03 29	04 14	00 44	01 15	01 40	02 01
54	02 44	03 40	04 21	00 35	01 08	01 35	01 59
52	02 58	03 49	04 28	00 27	01 02	01 31	01 56
50	03 11	03 58	04 35	00 21	00 57	01 28	01 54
45	03 35	04 15	04 48	00 06	00 46	01 20	01 50
N 40	03 54	04 29	04 59	24 36	00 36	01 13	01 47
35	04 08	04 41	05 08	24 28	00 28	01 07	01 44
30	04 21	04 51	05 16	24 21	00 21	01 02	01 41
20	04 40	05 07	05 30	24 08	00 08	00 54	01 36
N 10	04 55	05 20	05 42	23 57	24 46	00 46	01 32
0	05 07	05 32	05 54	23 47	24 39	00 39	01 28
S 10	05 18	05 43	06 05	23 36	24 32	00 32	01 24
20	05 27	05 54	06 16	23 25	24 24	00 24	01 20
30	05 36	06 05	06 30	23 13	24 15	00 15	01 15
35	05 41	06 11	06 37	23 05	24 10	00 10	01 13
40	05 46	06 18	06 46	22 57	24 04	00 04	01 09
45	05 50	06 25	06 56	22 47	23 57	25 06	01 06
S 50	05 55	06 34	07 08	22 35	23 49	25 02	01 02
52	05 58	06 38	07 14	22 30	23 45	25 00	01 00
54	06 00	06 42	07 20	22 24	23 41	24 57	00 57
56	06 02	06 47	07 27	22 17	23 37	24 55	00 55
58	06 05	06 52	07 35	22 09	23 31	24 52	00 52
S 60	06 08	06 58	07 44	22 00	23 26	24 49	00 49

Moonset

Lat.	Sunset	Twilight Civil	Twilight Naut.	1	2	3	4
°	h m	h m	h m	h m	h m	h m	h m
N 72	22 19	////	////	06 52	09 14	11 16	13 09
N 70	21 34	////	////	07 38	09 37	11 29	13 14
68	21 05	23 15	////	08 08	09 56	11 39	13 18
66	20 44	22 11	////	08 31	10 10	11 47	13 21
64	20 26	21 38	////	08 48	10 22	11 54	13 24
62	20 12	21 14	23 19	09 03	10 32	12 00	13 26
60	20 01	20 55	22 23	09 15	10 40	12 05	13 28
N 58	19 50	20 40	21 52	09 25	10 48	12 10	13 30
56	19 42	20 27	21 30	09 34	10 54	12 14	13 32
54	19 34	20 16	21 12	09 42	11 00	12 18	13 33
52	19 27	20 06	20 57	09 50	11 06	12 21	13 34
50	19 20	19 57	20 45	09 56	11 10	12 24	13 35
45	19 07	19 39	20 20	10 10	11 21	12 30	13 38
N 40	18 56	19 26	20 01	10 21	11 29	12 35	13 40
35	18 46	19 13	19 46	10 31	11 36	12 40	13 42
30	18 38	19 03	19 34	10 39	11 43	12 44	13 44
20	18 24	18 47	19 14	10 54	11 54	12 51	13 46
N 10	18 12	18 34	18 59	11 07	12 03	12 57	13 49
0	18 00	18 22	18 47	11 18	12 12	13 03	13 51
S 10	17 49	18 11	18 36	11 30	12 21	13 08	13 53
20	17 37	18 00	18 26	11 42	12 30	13 14	13 55
30	17 24	17 49	18 17	11 56	12 41	13 21	13 58
35	17 16	17 43	18 13	12 05	12 47	13 25	14 00
40	17 07	17 36	18 08	12 14	12 54	13 29	14 01
45	16 57	17 28	18 03	12 25	13 02	13 34	14 03
S 50	16 45	17 19	17 58	12 38	13 11	13 40	14 05
52	16 39	17 15	17 55	12 44	13 15	13 42	14 06
54	16 33	17 11	17 53	12 50	13 20	13 45	14 08
56	16 26	17 06	17 51	12 58	13 26	13 49	14 09
58	16 18	17 01	17 48	13 06	13 32	13 52	14 10
S 60	16 09	16 55	17 45	13 15	13 38	13 56	14 12

	SUN			MOON			
Day	Eqn. of Time 00h	Eqn. of Time 12h	Mer. Pass.	Mer. Pass. Upper	Mer. Pass. Lower	Age	Phase
d	m s	m s	h m	h m	h m	d	%
1	02 54	02 57	11 57	05 05	17 33	21	61
2	03 01	03 04	11 57	05 59	18 25	22	50
3	03 07	03 10	11 57	06 51	19 15	23	39

UT	ARIES	VENUS −3.9		MARS +1.3		JUPITER −2.0		SATURN +0.2	
d h	GHA	GHA	Dec	GHA	Dec	GHA	Dec	GHA	Dec
4 00	222 02.7	171 17.8	N18 16.9	184 19.4	N14 36.7	144 56.2	N22 35.6	5 44.0	S11 34.0
01	237 05.2	186 17.1	17.8	199 20.1	37.3	159 58.1	35.6	20 46.7	34.0
02	252 07.6	201 16.5	18.7	214 20.7	37.9	175 00.0	35.7	35 49.3	33.9
03	267 10.1	216 15.8	19.6	229 21.4	38.5	190 01.9	35.7	50 52.0	33.9
04	282 12.5	231 15.2	20.4	244 22.1	39.1	205 03.8	35.8	65 54.6	33.9
05	297 15.0	246 14.5	21.3	259 22.7	39.7	220 05.7	35.8	80 57.3	33.8
06	312 17.5	261 13.9	N18 22.2	274 23.4	N14 40.3	235 07.6	N22 35.9	95 59.9	S11 33.7
07	327 19.9	276 13.2	23.0	289 24.0	40.9	250 09.5	35.9	111 02.5	33.6
S 08	342 22.4	291 12.6	23.9	304 24.7	41.5	265 11.4	36.0	126 05.2	33.6
A 09	357 24.9	306 11.9	24.7	319 25.4	42.2	280 13.3	36.0	141 07.8	33.5
T 10	12 27.3	321 11.3	25.6	334 26.0	42.8	295 15.2	36.1	156 10.5	33.5
U 11	27 29.8	336 10.6	26.5	349 26.7	43.4	310 17.1	36.1	171 13.1	33.4
R 12	42 32.3	351 10.0	N18 27.3	4 27.3	N14 44.0	325 19.0	N22 36.2	186 15.8	S11 33.3
D 13	57 34.7	6 09.3	28.2	19 28.0	44.6	340 20.9	36.2	201 18.4	33.3
A 14	72 37.2	21 08.6	29.1	34 28.7	45.2	355 22.8	36.3	216 21.1	33.2
Y 15	87 39.6	36 08.0	29.9	49 29.3	45.8	10 24.7	36.3	231 23.7	33.2
16	102 42.1	51 07.3	30.8	64 30.0	46.4	25 26.6	36.4	246 26.4	33.1
17	117 44.6	66 06.7	31.6	79 30.6	47.0	40 28.5	36.5	261 29.0	33.1
18	132 47.0	81 06.0	N18 32.5	94 31.3	N14 47.6	55 30.4	N22 36.5	276 31.7	S11 33.0
19	147 49.5	96 05.4	33.3	109 32.0	48.2	70 32.3	36.6	291 34.3	32.9
20	162 52.0	111 04.7	34.2	124 32.6	48.8	85 34.2	36.6	306 37.0	32.9
21	177 54.4	126 04.1	35.0	139 33.3	49.4	100 36.1	36.7	321 39.6	32.8
22	192 56.9	141 03.4	35.9	154 33.9	50.0	115 37.9	36.7	336 42.2	32.8
23	207 59.4	156 02.7	36.8	169 34.6	50.6	130 39.8	36.8	351 44.9	32.7
5 00	223 01.8	171 02.1	N18 37.6	184 35.3	N14 51.2	145 41.7	N22 36.8	6 47.5	S11 32.7
01	238 04.3	186 01.4	38.5	199 35.9	51.8	160 43.6	36.9	21 50.2	32.6
02	253 06.8	201 00.8	39.3	214 36.6	52.4	175 45.5	36.9	36 52.8	32.5
03	268 09.2	216 00.1	40.2	229 37.2	53.0	190 47.4	37.0	51 55.5	32.5
04	283 11.7	230 59.4	41.0	244 37.9	53.6	205 49.3	37.0	66 58.1	32.4
05	298 14.1	245 58.8	42.3	259 38.5	54.2	220 51.2	37.1	82 00.8	32.4
06	313 16.6	260 58.1	N18 42.7	274 39.2	N14 54.8	235 53.1	N22 37.1	97 03.4	S11 32.3
07	328 19.1	275 57.4	43.5	289 39.9	55.4	250 55.0	37.2	112 06.1	32.2
S 08	343 21.5	290 56.8	44.4	304 40.5	56.0	265 56.9	37.2	127 08.7	32.2
U 09	358 24.0	305 56.1	45.2	319 41.2	56.6	280 58.8	37.3	142 11.4	32.1
N 10	13 26.5	320 55.4	46.1	334 41.8	57.2	296 00.7	37.3	157 14.0	32.1
D 11	28 28.9	335 54.8	46.9	349 42.5	57.8	311 02.6	37.4	172 16.6	32.0
A 12	43 31.4	350 54.1	N18 47.7	4 43.2	N14 58.4	326 04.5	N22 37.4	187 19.3	S11 32.0
Y 13	58 33.9	5 53.5	48.6	19 43.8	59.0	341 06.4	37.5	202 21.9	31.9
14	73 36.3	20 52.8	49.4	34 44.5	14 59.6	356 08.3	37.5	217 24.6	31.8
15	88 38.8	35 52.1	50.3	49 45.1	15 00.2	11 10.2	37.6	232 27.2	31.8
16	103 41.2	50 51.5	51.1	64 45.8	00.8	26 12.1	37.6	247 29.9	31.7
17	118 43.7	65 50.8	51.9	79 46.4	01.3	41 14.0	37.7	262 32.5	31.7
18	133 46.2	80 50.1	N18 52.8	94 47.1	N15 01.9	56 15.9	N22 37.7	277 35.2	S11 31.6
19	148 48.6	95 49.4	53.6	109 47.8	02.5	71 17.8	37.8	292 37.8	31.5
20	163 51.1	110 48.8	54.4	124 48.4	03.1	86 19.7	37.8	307 40.5	31.5
21	178 53.6	125 48.1	55.3	139 49.1	03.7	101 21.5	37.9	322 43.1	31.4
22	193 56.0	140 47.4	56.1	154 49.7	04.3	116 23.4	37.9	337 45.7	31.4
23	208 58.5	155 46.8	56.9	169 50.4	04.9	131 25.3	38.0	352 48.4	31.3
6 00	224 01.0	170 46.1	N18 57.8	184 51.0	N15 05.5	146 27.2	N22 38.0	7 51.0	S11 31.3
01	239 03.4	185 45.4	58.6	199 51.7	06.1	161 29.1	38.1	22 53.7	31.2
02	254 05.9	200 44.8	18 59.4	214 52.4	06.7	176 31.0	38.1	37 56.3	31.1
03	269 08.4	215 44.1	19 00.3	229 53.0	07.3	191 32.9	38.2	52 59.0	31.1
04	284 10.8	230 43.4	01.1	244 53.7	07.9	206 34.8	38.2	68 01.6	31.0
05	299 13.3	245 42.7	01.9	259 54.3	08.5	221 36.7	38.3	83 04.3	31.0
06	314 15.7	260 42.1	N19 02.7	274 55.0	N15 09.1	236 38.6	N22 38.3	98 06.9	S11 30.9
07	329 18.2	275 41.4	03.6	289 55.6	09.7	251 40.5	38.4	113 09.6	30.9
08	344 20.7	290 40.7	04.4	304 56.3	10.2	266 42.4	38.4	128 12.2	30.8
M 09	359 23.1	305 40.0	05.2	319 57.0	10.8	281 44.3	38.5	143 14.8	30.7
O 10	14 25.6	320 39.4	06.0	334 57.6	11.4	296 46.2	38.5	158 17.5	30.7
N 11	29 28.1	335 38.7	06.8	349 58.3	12.0	311 48.1	38.6	173 20.1	30.6
D 12	44 30.5	350 38.0	N19 07.7	4 58.9	N15 12.6	326 49.9	N22 38.6	188 22.8	S11 30.6
A 13	59 33.0	5 37.3	08.5	19 59.6	13.2	341 51.8	38.7	203 25.4	30.5
Y 14	74 35.5	20 36.6	09.3	35 00.2	13.8	356 53.7	38.7	218 28.1	30.5
15	89 37.9	35 36.0	10.1	50 00.9	14.4	11 55.6	38.8	233 30.7	30.4
16	104 40.4	50 35.3	10.9	65 01.5	15.0	26 57.5	38.8	248 33.4	30.3
17	119 42.9	65 34.6	11.8	80 02.2	15.6	41 59.4	38.9	263 36.0	30.3
18	134 45.3	80 33.9	N19 12.6	95 02.9	N15 16.2	57 01.3	N22 38.9	278 38.7	S11 30.2
19	149 47.8	95 33.2	13.4	110 03.5	16.7	72 03.2	39.0	293 41.3	30.2
20	164 50.2	110 32.6	14.2	125 04.2	17.3	87 05.1	39.0	308 43.9	30.1
21	179 52.7	125 31.9	15.0	140 04.8	17.9	102 07.0	39.1	323 46.6	30.1
22	194 55.2	140 31.2	15.8	155 05.5	18.5	117 08.9	39.1	338 49.2	30.0
23	209 57.6	155 30.5	16.6	170 06.1	19.1	132 10.8	39.2	353 51.9	29.9
Mer.Pass.	h m 9 06.4	v −0.7	d 0.8	v 0.7	d 0.6	v 1.9	d 0.1	v 2.6	d 0.1

STARS

Name	SHA	Dec
Acamar	315 18.8	S40 15.2
Achernar	335 27.4	S57 10.1
Acrux	173 08.8	S63 10.7
Adhara	255 12.8	S28 59.8
Aldebaran	290 49.8	N16 32.0
Alioth	166 20.3	N55 53.3
Alkaid	152 58.5	N49 14.8
Al Na'ir	27 44.0	S46 53.5
Alnilam	275 46.7	S 1 11.9
Alphard	217 56.1	S 8 43.3
Alphecca	126 10.7	N26 40.2
Alpheratz	357 43.8	N29 09.7
Altair	62 08.2	N 8 54.2
Ankaa	353 16.1	S42 13.9
Antares	112 26.0	S26 27.6
Arcturus	145 55.5	N19 06.7
Atria	107 27.4	S69 02.8
Avior	234 18.1	S59 33.6
Bellatrix	278 32.4	N 6 21.5
Betelgeuse	271 01.6	N 7 24.3
Canopus	263 56.5	S52 42.6
Capella	280 35.0	N46 00.6
Deneb	49 31.5	N45 19.5
Denebola	182 33.5	N14 29.7
Diphda	348 56.3	S17 54.8
Dubhe	193 51.5	N61 40.8
Elnath	278 13.0	N28 37.0
Eltanin	90 45.8	N51 29.1
Enif	33 47.2	N 9 56.2
Fomalhaut	15 24.3	S29 32.9
Gacrux	172 00.5	S57 11.6
Gienah	175 52.1	S17 37.2
Hadar	148 47.3	S60 26.3
Hamal	328 01.2	N23 31.4
Kaus Aust.	83 43.7	S34 22.5
Kochab	137 18.9	N74 06.1
Markab	13 38.6	N15 16.6
Menkar	314 15.5	N 4 08.4
Menkent	148 07.3	S36 26.2
Miaplacidus	221 39.6	S69 46.8
Mirfak	308 40.9	N49 54.4
Nunki	75 58.2	S26 16.6
Peacock	53 19.3	S56 41.1
Pollux	243 28.0	N27 59.5
Procyon	245 00.0	N 5 11.2
Rasalhague	96 06.3	N12 33.0
Regulus	207 43.5	N11 53.9
Rigel	281 12.4	S 8 11.4
Rigil Kent.	139 51.1	S60 53.4
Sabik	102 12.3	S15 44.4
Schedar	349 41.0	N56 36.5
Shaula	96 21.7	S37 06.6
Sirius	258 34.0	S16 44.4
Spica	158 31.0	S11 14.0
Suhail	222 52.5	S43 29.6
Vega	80 38.8	N38 47.7
Zuben'ubi	137 05.2	S16 05.9

	SHA	Mer.Pass.
	° ′	h m
Venus	308 00.2	12 36
Mars	321 33.4	11 41
Jupiter	282 39.9	14 15
Saturn	143 45.7	23 29

UT	SUN GHA	Dec	MOON GHA	v	Dec	d	HP
4							
00	180 48.4	N15 56.9	248 49.1	11.7	S 5 36.7	11.1	57.6
01	195 48.4	57.6	263 19.8	11.9	5 25.6	11.1	57.6
02	210 48.5	58.3	277 50.7	11.8	5 14.5	11.2	57.6
03	225 48.5	.. 59.0	292 21.5	12.0	5 03.3	11.2	57.5
04	240 48.6	15 59.8	306 52.5	11.9	4 52.1	11.2	57.5
05	255 48.6	16 00.5	321 23.4	12.0	4 40.9	11.2	57.5
06	270 48.7	N16 01.2	335 54.4	12.1	S 4 29.7	11.2	57.5
07	285 48.8	01.9	350 25.5	12.1	4 18.5	11.2	57.4
08	300 48.8	02.6	4 56.6	12.1	4 07.3	11.3	57.4
09	315 48.9	.. 03.4	19 27.7	12.2	3 56.0	11.2	57.4
10	330 48.9	04.1	33 58.9	12.2	3 44.8	11.3	57.4
11	345 49.0	04.8	48 30.1	12.2	3 33.5	11.2	57.3
12	0 49.0	N16 05.5	63 01.3	12.3	S 3 22.3	11.3	57.3
13	15 49.1	06.2	77 32.6	12.3	3 11.0	11.3	57.3
14	30 49.1	07.0	92 03.9	12.4	2 59.7	11.3	57.3
15	45 49.2	.. 07.7	106 35.3	12.4	2 48.4	11.3	57.2
16	60 49.3	08.4	121 06.7	12.4	2 37.1	11.3	57.2
17	75 49.3	09.1	135 38.1	12.5	2 25.8	11.3	57.2
18	90 49.4	N16 09.8	150 09.6	12.5	S 2 14.5	11.3	57.2
19	105 49.4	10.6	164 41.1	12.5	2 03.2	11.3	57.1
20	120 49.5	11.3	179 12.6	12.6	1 51.9	11.3	57.1
21	135 49.5	.. 12.0	193 44.2	12.6	1 40.6	11.3	57.1
22	150 49.6	12.7	208 15.8	12.6	1 29.3	11.3	57.1
23	165 49.6	13.4	222 47.4	12.6	1 18.0	11.3	57.0
5							
00	180 49.7	N16 14.1	237 19.0	12.7	S 1 06.7	11.2	57.0
01	195 49.7	14.8	251 50.7	12.7	0 55.5	11.3	57.0
02	210 49.8	15.6	266 22.4	12.7	0 44.2	11.3	57.0
03	225 49.8	.. 16.3	280 54.1	12.8	0 32.9	11.3	56.9
04	240 49.9	17.0	295 25.9	12.8	0 21.6	11.3	56.9
05	255 49.9	17.7	309 57.7	12.8	S 0 10.3	11.2	56.9
06	270 50.0	N16 18.4	324 29.5	12.8	N 0 00.9	11.3	56.9
07	285 50.1	19.1	339 01.3	12.9	0 12.2	11.2	56.8
08	300 50.1	19.8	353 33.2	12.9	0 23.4	11.3	56.8
09	315 50.2	.. 20.5	8 05.1	12.9	0 34.7	11.2	56.8
10	330 50.2	21.2	22 37.0	12.9	0 45.9	11.2	56.8
11	345 50.3	21.9	37 08.9	12.9	0 57.1	11.2	56.7
12	0 50.3	N16 22.7	51 40.8	13.0	N 1 08.3	11.2	56.7
13	15 50.4	23.4	66 12.8	12.9	1 19.5	11.1	56.7
14	30 50.4	24.1	80 44.7	13.0	1 30.6	11.2	56.7
15	45 50.5	.. 24.8	95 16.7	13.0	1 41.8	11.1	56.6
16	60 50.5	25.5	109 48.7	13.1	1 52.9	11.1	56.6
17	75 50.5	26.2	124 20.8	13.0	2 04.0	11.1	56.6
18	90 50.6	N16 26.9	138 52.8	13.1	N 2 15.1	11.1	56.6
19	105 50.6	27.6	153 24.9	13.0	2 26.2	11.1	56.5
20	120 50.7	28.3	167 56.9	13.1	2 37.3	11.0	56.5
21	135 50.7	.. 29.0	182 29.0	13.1	2 48.3	11.0	56.5
22	150 50.8	29.7	197 01.1	13.1	2 59.3	11.0	56.5
23	165 50.8	30.4	211 33.2	13.1	3 10.3	11.0	56.5
6							
00	180 50.9	N16 31.1	226 05.3	13.2	N 3 21.3	11.0	56.4
01	195 50.9	31.8	240 37.5	13.1	3 32.3	10.9	56.4
02	210 51.0	32.5	255 09.6	13.1	3 43.2	10.9	56.4
03	225 51.0	.. 33.2	269 41.7	13.2	3 54.1	10.9	56.4
04	240 51.1	33.9	284 13.9	13.2	4 05.0	10.8	56.3
05	255 51.1	34.6	298 46.1	13.1	4 15.8	10.9	56.3
06	270 51.2	N16 35.3	313 18.2	13.2	N 4 26.7	10.7	56.3
07	285 51.2	36.0	327 50.4	13.2	4 37.4	10.8	56.3
08	300 51.2	36.7	342 22.6	13.2	4 48.2	10.8	56.3
09	315 51.3	.. 37.4	356 54.8	13.2	4 59.0	10.7	56.2
10	330 51.3	38.1	11 27.0	13.2	5 09.7	10.6	56.2
11	345 51.4	38.8	25 59.2	13.2	5 20.3	10.7	56.2
12	0 51.4	N16 39.5	40 31.4	13.2	N 5 31.0	10.6	56.2
13	15 51.5	40.2	55 03.6	13.2	5 41.6	10.6	56.2
14	30 51.5	40.9	69 35.8	13.2	5 52.2	10.5	56.1
15	45 51.6	.. 41.6	84 08.0	13.2	6 02.7	10.5	56.1
16	60 51.6	42.3	98 40.2	13.2	6 13.2	10.5	56.1
17	75 51.6	43.0	113 12.4	13.2	6 23.7	10.4	56.1
18	90 51.7	N16 43.7	127 44.6	13.2	N 6 34.1	10.4	56.0
19	105 51.7	44.4	142 16.8	13.2	6 44.5	10.4	56.0
20	120 51.8	45.1	156 49.0	13.2	6 54.9	10.3	56.0
21	135 51.8	.. 45.8	171 21.2	13.2	7 05.2	10.3	56.0
22	150 51.8	46.5	185 53.4	13.2	7 15.5	10.2	56.0
23	165 51.9	47.1	200 25.6	13.2	N 7 25.7	10.2	55.9
SD	15.9	d 0.7	SD 15.6		15.5		15.3

Moonrise

Lat.	Twilight Naut.	Civil	Sunrise	4	5	6	7
N 72	////	////	01 12	02 36	02 25	02 15	02 04
N 70	////	////	02 06	02 28	02 24	02 20	02 15
68	////	////	02 38	02 23	02 23	02 24	02 24
66	////	01 28	03 01	02 18	02 22	02 27	02 32
64	////	02 05	03 20	02 13	02 22	02 30	02 39
62	////	02 31	03 34	02 10	02 21	02 33	02 44
60	01 18	02 51	03 47	02 06	02 21	02 35	02 49
N 58	01 52	03 08	03 58	02 03	02 20	02 37	02 54
56	02 16	03 21	04 07	02 01	02 20	02 39	02 58
54	02 35	03 33	04 15	01 59	02 20	02 40	03 01
52	02 51	03 43	04 23	01 56	02 19	02 42	03 05
50	03 04	03 52	04 29	01 54	02 19	02 43	03 07
45	03 30	04 11	04 44	01 50	02 18	02 46	03 14
N 40	03 49	04 26	04 55	01 47	02 18	02 48	03 19
35	04 05	04 38	05 05	01 44	02 18	02 51	03 24
30	04 18	04 48	05 14	01 41	02 17	02 53	03 28
20	04 38	05 05	05 29	01 36	02 17	02 56	03 35
N 10	04 54	05 19	05 41	01 32	02 16	02 59	03 42
0	05 07	05 32	05 53	01 28	02 15	03 02	03 48
S 10	05 18	05 43	06 05	01 24	02 15	03 05	03 54
20	05 28	05 55	06 17	01 20	02 14	03 08	04 00
30	05 38	06 07	06 32	01 15	02 14	03 11	04 08
35	05 43	06 13	06 40	01 13	02 14	03 13	04 12
40	05 48	06 20	06 49	01 09	02 13	03 16	04 17
45	05 53	06 29	07 00	01 06	02 13	03 18	04 23
S 50	05 59	06 38	07 13	01 02	02 12	03 22	04 29
52	06 02	06 42	07 19	01 00	02 12	03 23	04 33
54	06 04	06 47	07 25	00 57	02 12	03 25	04 36
56	06 07	06 52	07 33	00 55	02 12	03 27	04 40
58	06 10	06 58	07 41	00 52	02 11	03 29	04 44
S 60	06 14	07 04	07 51	00 49	02 11	03 31	04 49

Moonset

Lat.	Sunset	Twilight Civil	Naut.	4	5	6	7
N 72	22 52	////	////	13 09	14 58	16 45	18 34
N 70	21 53	////	////	13 14	14 56	16 36	18 16
68	21 19	////	////	13 18	14 54	16 28	18 02
66	20 55	22 33	////	13 21	14 53	16 22	17 51
64	20 36	21 52	////	13 24	14 51	16 17	17 41
62	20 21	21 25	////	13 26	14 50	16 12	17 33
60	20 08	21 04	22 42	13 28	14 49	16 08	17 26
N 58	19 57	20 48	22 05	13 30	14 48	16 05	17 20
56	19 48	20 34	21 40	13 32	14 47	16 02	17 15
54	19 39	20 22	21 20	13 33	14 47	15 59	17 10
52	19 31	20 12	21 04	13 34	14 46	15 56	17 05
50	19 25	20 02	20 51	13 35	14 46	15 54	17 01
45	19 11	19 44	20 25	13 38	14 44	15 49	16 53
N 40	18 59	19 29	20 05	13 40	14 43	15 45	16 46
35	18 49	19 16	19 49	13 42	14 42	15 42	16 40
30	18 40	19 06	19 36	13 44	14 42	15 38	16 35
20	18 25	18 48	19 16	13 46	14 40	15 33	16 25
N 10	18 12	18 34	19 00	13 49	14 39	15 28	16 17
0	18 00	18 22	18 47	13 51	14 38	15 24	16 10
S 10	17 48	18 10	18 35	13 53	14 37	15 19	16 02
20	17 36	17 59	18 25	13 55	14 35	15 15	15 54
30	17 21	17 46	18 15	13 58	14 34	15 09	15 45
35	17 13	17 40	18 10	14 00	14 33	15 06	15 40
40	17 03	17 32	18 05	14 01	14 32	15 03	15 34
45	16 53	17 24	17 59	14 03	14 31	14 58	15 27
S 50	16 40	17 15	17 53	14 05	14 30	14 54	15 19
52	16 34	17 11	17 51	14 06	14 29	14 51	15 15
54	16 27	17 06	17 48	14 08	14 28	14 49	15 11
56	16 20	17 01	17 45	14 09	14 28	14 46	15 06
58	16 11	16 55	17 43	14 10	14 27	14 43	15 01
S 60	16 02	16 48	17 39	14 12	14 26	14 40	14 55

	SUN Eqn. of Time 00h	12h	Mer. Pass.	MOON Mer. Pass. Upper	Lower	Age	Phase
Day	m s	m s	h m	h m	h m	d	%
4	03 13	03 16	11 57	07 40	20 03	24	29
5	03 19	03 21	11 57	08 27	20 50	25	20
6	03 23	03 26	11 57	09 13	21 36	26	12

UT	ARIES	VENUS −3.9		MARS +1.3		JUPITER −2.0		SATURN +0.2		STARS		
	GHA	GHA	Dec	GHA	Dec	GHA	Dec	GHA	Dec	Name	SHA	Dec
d h	° ′	° ′	° ′	° ′	° ′	° ′	° ′	° ′	° ′		° ′	° ′
7 00	225 00.1	170 29.8	N19 17.4	185 06.8	N15 19.7	147 12.7	N22 39.2	8 54.5	S11 29.9	Acamar	315 18.8	S40 15.2
01	240 02.6	185 29.2	18.2	200 07.4	20.3	162 14.5	39.3	23 57.2	29.8	Achernar	335 27.4	S57 10.1
02	255 05.0	200 28.5	19.0	215 08.1	20.9	177 16.4	39.3	38 59.8	29.8	Acrux	173 08.8	S63 10.7
03	270 07.5	215 27.8 ..	19.9	230 08.8 ..	21.4	192 18.3 ..	39.4	54 02.5 ..	29.7	Adhara	255 12.8	S28 59.8
04	285 10.0	230 27.1	20.7	245 09.4	22.0	207 20.2	39.4	69 05.1	29.7	Aldebaran	290 49.8	N16 32.0
05	300 12.4	245 26.4	21.5	260 10.1	22.6	222 22.1	39.5	84 07.7	29.6			
06	315 14.9	260 25.7	N19 22.3	275 10.7	N15 23.2	237 24.0	N22 39.5	99 10.4	S11 29.5	Alioth	166 20.3	N55 53.3
07	330 17.3	275 25.0	23.1	290 11.4	23.8	252 25.9	39.6	114 13.0	29.5	Alkaid	152 58.5	N49 14.8
08	345 19.8	290 24.4	23.9	305 12.0	24.4	267 27.8	39.6	129 15.7	29.4	Al Na'ir	27 44.0	S46 53.5
09	0 22.3	305 23.7 ..	24.7	320 12.7 ..	25.0	282 29.7 ..	39.7	144 18.3 ..	29.4	Alnilam	275 46.7	S 1 11.9
10	15 24.7	320 23.0	25.5	335 13.3	25.5	297 31.6	39.7	159 21.0	29.3	Alphard	217 56.2	S 8 43.3
11	30 27.2	335 22.3	26.3	350 14.0	26.1	312 33.5	39.8	174 23.6	29.3			
12	45 29.7	350 21.6	N19 27.1	5 14.6	N15 26.7	327 35.3	N22 39.8	189 26.3	S11 29.2	Alphecca	126 10.7	N26 40.2
13	60 32.1	5 20.9	27.9	20 15.3	27.3	342 37.2	39.9	204 28.9	29.1	Alpheratz	357 43.8	N29 09.7
14	75 34.6	20 20.2	28.7	35 16.0	27.9	357 39.1	39.9	219 31.6	29.1	Altair	62 08.2	N 8 54.3
15	90 37.1	35 19.5 ..	29.5	50 16.6 ..	28.5	12 41.0 ..	40.0	234 34.2 ..	29.0	Ankaa	353 16.1	S42 13.9
16	105 39.5	50 18.8	30.3	65 17.3	29.0	27 42.9	40.0	249 36.8	29.0	Antares	112 26.0	S26 27.6
17	120 42.0	65 18.1	31.1	80 17.9	29.6	42 44.8	40.1	264 39.5	28.9			
18	135 44.5	80 17.5	N19 31.8	95 18.6	N15 30.2	57 46.7	N22 40.1	279 42.1	S11 28.9	Arcturus	145 55.5	N19 06.7
19	150 46.9	95 16.8	32.6	110 19.2	30.8	72 48.6	40.2	294 44.8	28.8	Atria	107 27.4	S69 02.9
20	165 49.4	110 16.1	33.4	125 19.9	31.4	87 50.5	40.2	309 47.4	28.7	Avior	234 18.2	S59 33.6
21	180 51.8	125 15.4 ..	34.2	140 20.5 ..	32.0	102 52.4 ..	40.3	324 50.1 ..	28.7	Bellatrix	278 32.4	N 6 21.5
22	195 54.3	140 14.7	35.0	155 21.2	32.5	117 54.2	40.3	339 52.7	28.6	Betelgeuse	271 01.6	N 7 24.3
23	210 56.8	155 14.0	35.8	170 21.8	33.1	132 56.1	40.4	354 55.3	28.6			
8 00	225 59.2	170 13.3	N19 36.6	185 22.5	N15 33.7	147 58.0	N22 40.4	9 58.0	S11 28.5	Canopus	263 56.6	S52 42.6
01	241 01.7	185 12.6	37.4	200 23.1	34.3	162 59.9	40.5	25 00.6	28.5	Capella	280 35.0	N46 00.6
02	256 04.2	200 11.9	38.2	215 23.8	34.9	178 01.8	40.5	40 03.3	28.4	Deneb	49 31.4	N45 19.5
03	271 06.6	215 11.2 ..	38.9	230 24.4 ..	35.4	193 03.7 ..	40.6	55 05.9 ..	28.3	Denebola	182 33.6	N14 29.7
04	286 09.1	230 10.5	39.7	245 25.1	36.0	208 05.6	40.6	70 08.6	28.3	Diphda	348 56.2	S17 54.8
05	301 11.6	245 09.8	40.5	260 25.7	36.6	223 07.5	40.7	85 11.2	28.2			
06	316 14.0	260 09.1	N19 41.3	275 26.4	N15 37.2	238 09.4	N22 40.7	100 13.9	S11 28.2	Dubhe	193 51.6	N61 40.8
07	331 16.5	275 08.4	42.1	290 27.1	37.8	253 11.2	40.8	115 16.5	28.1	Elnath	278 13.0	N28 37.0
08	346 18.9	290 07.7	42.9	305 27.7	38.3	268 13.1	40.8	130 19.1	28.1	Eltanin	90 45.8	N51 29.2
09	1 21.4	305 07.0 ..	43.6	320 28.4 ..	38.9	283 15.0 ..	40.9	145 21.8 ..	28.0	Enif	33 47.2	N 9 56.2
10	16 23.9	320 06.3	44.4	335 29.0	39.5	298 16.9	40.9	160 24.4	27.9	Fomalhaut	15 24.2	S29 32.9
11	31 26.3	335 05.6	45.2	350 29.7	40.1	313 18.8	41.0	175 27.1	27.9			
12	46 28.8	350 04.9	N19 46.0	5 30.3	N15 40.6	328 20.7	N22 41.0	190 29.7	S11 27.8	Gacrux	172 00.5	S57 11.6
13	61 31.3	5 04.2	46.7	20 31.0	41.2	343 22.6	41.0	205 32.4	27.8	Gienah	175 52.1	S17 37.2
14	76 33.7	20 03.5	47.5	35 31.6	41.8	358 24.5	41.1	220 35.0	27.7	Hadar	148 47.3	S60 26.4
15	91 36.2	35 02.8 ..	48.3	50 32.3 ..	42.4	13 26.3 ..	41.1	235 37.7 ..	27.7	Hamal	328 01.2	N23 31.4
16	106 38.7	50 02.1	49.1	65 32.9	42.9	28 28.2	41.2	250 40.3	27.6	Kaus Aust.	83 43.6	S34 22.5
17	121 41.1	65 01.4	49.8	80 33.6	43.5	43 30.1	41.2	265 42.9	27.5			
18	136 43.6	80 00.7	N19 50.6	95 34.2	N15 44.1	58 32.0	N22 41.3	280 45.6	S11 27.5	Kochab	137 18.9	N74 06.1
19	151 46.1	95 00.0	51.4	110 34.9	44.7	73 33.9	41.3	295 48.2	27.4	Markab	13 38.6	N15 16.6
20	166 48.5	109 59.3	52.1	125 35.5	45.3	88 35.8	41.4	310 50.9	27.4	Menkar	314 15.5	N 4 08.4
21	181 51.0	124 58.6 ..	52.9	140 36.2 ..	45.8	103 37.7 ..	41.4	325 53.5 ..	27.3	Menkent	148 07.5	S36 26.2
22	196 53.4	139 57.9	53.7	155 36.8	46.4	118 39.6	41.5	340 56.2	27.3	Miaplacidus	221 39.7	S69 46.8
23	211 55.9	154 57.2	54.4	170 37.5	47.0	133 41.4	41.5	355 58.8	27.2			
9 00	226 58.4	169 56.5	N19 55.2	185 38.1	N15 47.6	148 43.3	N22 41.6	11 01.4	S11 27.2	Mirfak	308 40.9	N49 54.4
01	242 00.8	184 55.8	56.0	200 38.8	48.1	163 45.2	41.6	26 04.1	27.1	Nunki	75 58.2	S26 16.6
02	257 03.3	199 55.1	56.7	215 39.4	48.7	178 47.1	41.7	41 06.7	27.0	Peacock	53 19.3	S56 41.1
03	272 05.8	214 54.4 ..	57.5	230 40.1 ..	49.3	193 49.0 ..	41.7	56 09.4 ..	27.0	Pollux	243 28.0	N27 59.5
04	287 08.2	229 53.6	58.3	245 40.7	49.8	208 50.9	41.8	71 12.0	26.9	Procyon	245 00.0	N 5 11.2
05	302 10.7	244 52.9	59.0	260 41.4	50.4	223 52.8	41.8	86 14.7	26.9			
06	317 13.2	259 52.2	N19 59.8	275 42.0	N15 51.0	238 54.6	N22 41.9	101 17.3	S11 26.8	Rasalhague	96 06.2	N12 33.0
07	332 15.6	274 51.5	20 00.5	290 42.7	51.6	253 56.5	41.9	116 19.9	26.8	Regulus	207 43.5	N11 54.0
08	347 18.1	289 50.8	01.3	305 43.3	52.1	268 58.4	42.0	131 22.6	26.7	Rigel	281 12.4	S 8 11.4
09	2 20.6	304 50.1 ..	02.1	320 44.0 ..	52.7	284 00.3 ..	42.0	146 25.2 ..	26.6	Rigil Kent.	139 51.1	S60 53.4
10	17 23.0	319 49.4	02.8	335 44.6	53.3	299 02.2	42.1	161 27.9	26.6	Sabik	102 12.3	S15 44.4
11	32 25.5	334 48.7	03.6	350 45.3	53.8	314 04.1	42.1	176 30.5	26.5			
12	47 27.9	349 48.0	N20 04.3	5 45.9	N15 54.4	329 06.0	N22 42.2	191 33.2	S11 26.5	Schedar	349 41.0	N56 36.5
13	62 30.4	4 47.2	05.1	20 46.6	55.0	344 07.8	42.2	206 35.8	26.4	Shaula	96 21.7	S37 06.6
14	77 32.9	19 46.5	05.8	35 47.2	55.6	359 09.7	42.3	221 38.4	26.4	Sirius	258 34.0	S16 44.4
15	92 35.3	34 45.8 ..	06.6	50 47.9 ..	56.1	14 11.6 ..	42.3	236 41.1 ..	26.3	Spica	158 31.0	S11 14.0
16	107 37.8	49 45.1	07.3	65 48.5	56.7	29 13.5	42.4	251 43.7	26.3	Suhail	222 52.5	S43 29.6
17	122 40.3	64 44.4	08.1	80 49.2	57.3	44 15.4	42.4	266 46.4	26.2			
18	137 42.7	79 43.7	N20 08.8	95 49.8	N15 57.8	59 17.3	N22 42.4	281 49.0	S11 26.1	Vega	80 38.7	N38 47.7
19	152 45.2	94 43.0	09.6	110 50.5	58.4	74 19.2	42.5	296 51.7	26.1	Zuben'ubi	137 05.2	S16 05.9
20	167 47.7	109 42.3	10.3	125 51.1	59.0	89 21.0	42.5	311 54.3	26.0		SHA	Mer. Pass.
21	182 50.1	124 41.5 ..	11.1	140 51.8	15 59.5	104 22.9 ..	42.6	326 56.9 ..	26.0		° ′	h m
22	197 52.6	139 40.8	11.8	155 52.4	16 00.1	119 24.8	42.6	341 59.6	25.9	Venus	304 14.1	12 40
23	212 55.0	154 40.1	12.6	170 53.1	N16 00.7	134 26.7	42.7	357 02.2	25.9	Mars	319 23.2	11 38
	h m									Jupiter	281 58.8	14 06
Mer. Pass. 8 54.6		v −0.7	d 0.8	v 0.7	d 0.6	v 1.9	d 0.0	v 2.6	d 0.1	Saturn	143 58.8	23 16

UT	SUN GHA	SUN Dec	MOON GHA	v	MOON Dec	d	HP
d h	° ′	° ′	° ′	′	° ′	′	′
7 00	180 51.9	N16 47.8	214 57.8	13.2	N 7 35.9	10.2	55.9
01	195 52.0	48.5	229 30.0	13.2	7 46.1	10.1	55.9
02	210 52.0	49.2	244 02.2	13.2	7 56.2	10.1	55.9
03	225 52.0	.. 49.9	258 34.4	13.1	8 06.3	10.0	55.9
04	240 52.1	50.6	273 06.5	13.2	8 16.3	10.0	55.9
05	255 52.1	51.3	287 38.7	13.2	8 26.3	9.9	55.8
06	270 52.2	N16 52.0	302 10.9	13.1	N 8 36.2	9.9	55.8
07	285 52.2	52.7	316 43.0	13.2	8 46.1	9.9	55.8
T 08	300 52.2	53.3	331 15.2	13.1	8 56.0	9.8	55.8
U 09	315 52.3	.. 54.0	345 47.3	13.1	9 05.8	9.7	55.7
E 10	330 52.3	54.7	0 19.4	13.2	9 15.5	9.7	55.7
S 11	345 52.4	55.4	14 51.6	13.1	9 25.2	9.7	55.7
D 12	0 52.4	N16 56.1	29 23.7	13.1	N 9 34.9	9.6	55.7
A 13	15 52.4	56.8	43 55.8	13.1	9 44.5	9.5	55.7
Y 14	30 52.5	57.5	58 27.9	13.1	9 54.0	9.5	55.6
15	45 52.5	.. 58.1	73 00.0	13.0	10 03.5	9.5	55.6
16	60 52.5	58.8	87 32.0	13.1	10 13.0	9.4	55.6
17	75 52.6	16 59.5	102 04.1	13.1	10 22.4	9.3	55.6
18	90 52.6	N17 00.2	116 36.2	13.0	N10 31.7	9.3	55.6
19	105 52.7	00.9	131 08.2	13.0	10 41.0	9.2	55.5
20	120 52.7	01.6	145 40.2	13.0	10 50.2	9.2	55.5
21	135 52.7	.. 02.2	160 12.2	13.0	10 59.4	9.1	55.5
22	150 52.8	02.9	174 44.2	13.0	11 08.5	9.1	55.5
23	165 52.8	03.6	189 16.2	13.0	11 17.6	9.0	55.5
8 00	180 52.8	N17 04.3	203 48.2	13.0	N11 26.6	9.0	55.5
01	195 52.9	05.0	218 20.2	12.9	11 35.6	8.8	55.4
02	210 52.9	05.6	232 52.1	12.9	11 44.4	8.9	55.4
03	225 52.9	.. 06.3	247 24.0	13.0	11 53.3	8.8	55.4
04	240 53.0	07.0	261 56.0	12.9	12 02.1	8.7	55.4
05	255 53.0	07.7	276 27.9	12.9	12 10.8	8.6	55.4
06	270 53.0	N17 08.3	290 59.8	12.8	N12 19.4	8.6	55.3
W 07	285 53.1	09.0	305 31.6	12.9	12 28.0	8.5	55.3
E 08	300 53.1	09.7	320 03.5	12.8	12 36.5	8.5	55.3
D 09	315 53.1	.. 10.4	334 35.3	12.8	12 45.0	8.4	55.3
N 10	330 53.2	11.0	349 07.1	12.9	12 53.4	8.3	55.3
E 11	345 53.2	11.7	3 39.0	12.7	13 01.7	8.3	55.3
S 12	0 53.2	N17 12.4	18 10.7	12.8	N13 10.0	8.2	55.2
D 13	15 53.3	13.1	32 42.5	12.8	13 18.2	8.1	55.2
A 14	30 53.3	13.7	47 14.3	12.7	13 26.3	8.1	55.2
Y 15	45 53.3	.. 14.4	61 46.0	12.8	13 34.4	8.0	55.2
16	60 53.4	15.1	76 17.8	12.7	13 42.4	8.0	55.2
17	75 53.4	15.7	90 49.5	12.6	13 50.4	7.8	55.2
18	90 53.4	N17 16.4	105 21.1	12.7	N13 58.2	7.8	55.1
19	105 53.4	17.1	119 52.8	12.7	14 06.0	7.8	55.1
20	120 53.5	17.8	134 24.5	12.6	14 13.8	7.6	55.1
21	135 53.5	.. 18.4	148 56.1	12.6	14 21.4	7.6	55.1
22	150 53.5	19.1	163 27.7	12.6	14 29.0	7.5	55.1
23	165 53.6	19.8	177 59.3	12.6	14 36.5	7.5	55.1
9 00	180 53.6	N17 20.4	192 30.9	12.6	N14 44.0	7.3	55.0
01	195 53.6	21.1	207 02.5	12.5	14 51.3	7.3	55.0
02	210 53.6	21.8	221 34.0	12.6	14 58.6	7.3	55.0
03	225 53.7	.. 22.4	236 05.6	12.5	15 05.9	7.1	55.0
04	240 53.7	23.1	250 37.1	12.5	15 13.0	7.1	55.0
05	255 53.7	23.8	265 08.6	12.5	15 20.1	7.0	55.0
06	270 53.8	N17 24.4	279 40.1	12.4	N15 27.1	6.9	54.9
07	285 53.8	25.1	294 11.5	12.5	15 34.0	6.9	54.9
T 08	300 53.8	25.8	308 43.0	12.4	15 40.9	6.8	54.9
H 09	315 53.8	.. 26.4	323 14.4	12.4	15 47.7	6.7	54.9
U 10	330 53.9	27.1	337 45.8	12.4	15 54.4	6.6	54.9
R 11	345 53.9	27.7	352 17.2	12.3	16 01.0	6.5	54.9
S 12	0 53.9	N17 28.4	6 48.5	12.4	N16 07.5	6.5	54.9
D 13	15 53.9	29.1	21 19.9	12.4	16 14.0	6.4	54.8
A 14	30 54.0	29.7	35 51.2	12.4	16 20.4	6.3	54.8
Y 15	45 54.0	.. 30.4	50 22.6	12.3	16 26.7	6.2	54.8
16	60 54.0	31.0	64 53.9	12.2	16 32.9	6.2	54.8
17	75 54.0	31.7	79 25.1	12.3	16 39.1	6.0	54.8
18	90 54.1	N17 32.4	93 56.4	12.3	N16 45.1	6.0	54.8
19	105 54.1	33.0	108 27.7	12.2	16 51.1	5.9	54.7
20	120 54.1	33.7	122 58.9	12.2	16 57.0	5.8	54.7
21	135 54.1	.. 34.3	137 30.1	12.2	17 02.8	5.8	54.7
22	150 54.2	35.0	152 01.3	12.2	17 08.6	5.6	54.7
23	165 54.2	35.6	166 32.5	12.2	N17 14.2	5.6	54.7
	SD 15.9	d 0.7	SD 15.2		15.1		14.9

Lat.	Twilight Naut.	Twilight Civil	Sunrise	Moonrise 7	8	9	10
°	h m	h m	h m	h m	h m	h m	h m
N 72	////	////	00 20	02 04	01 51	01 35	01 03
N 70	////	////	01 45	02 15	02 11	02 06	02 02
68	////	////	02 23	02 24	02 26	02 29	02 36
66	////	01 02	02 49	02 32	02 39	02 48	03 01
64	////	01 50	03 10	02 39	02 49	03 02	03 21
62	////	02 20	03 26	02 44	02 58	03 15	03 37
60	00 55	02 42	03 39	02 49	03 06	03 26	03 50
N 58	01 39	02 59	03 51	02 54	03 13	03 35	04 02
56	02 06	03 14	04 01	02 58	03 19	03 43	04 12
54	02 26	03 26	04 10	03 01	03 24	03 50	04 21
52	02 43	03 37	04 17	03 05	03 29	03 57	04 28
50	02 57	03 47	04 24	03 07	03 34	04 03	04 36
45	03 25	04 06	04 39	03 14	03 43	04 15	04 51
N 40	03 45	04 22	04 52	03 19	03 51	04 26	05 04
35	04 01	04 35	05 02	03 24	03 58	04 35	05 14
30	04 15	04 46	05 11	03 28	04 05	04 43	05 24
20	04 36	05 04	05 27	03 35	04 15	04 57	05 40
N 10	04 53	05 18	05 40	03 42	04 25	05 09	05 55
0	05 06	05 31	05 53	03 48	04 34	05 20	06 08
S 10	05 18	05 43	06 05	03 54	04 43	05 32	06 21
20	05 29	05 56	06 19	04 00	04 52	05 44	06 36
30	05 40	06 08	06 33	04 08	05 03	05 58	06 53
35	05 45	06 15	06 42	04 12	05 10	06 07	07 02
40	05 51	06 23	06 52	04 17	05 17	06 16	07 13
45	05 57	06 32	07 04	04 23	05 26	06 27	07 26
S 50	06 03	06 42	07 17	04 29	05 36	06 41	07 42
52	06 06	06 47	07 23	04 33	05 41	06 47	07 50
54	06 09	06 53	07 31	04 36	05 46	06 54	07 58
56	06 12	06 57	07 38	04 40	05 52	07 02	08 08
58	06 16	07 03	07 47	04 44	05 59	07 11	08 18
S 60	06 19	07 10	07 58	04 49	06 06	07 21	08 31

Lat.	Sunset	Twilight Civil	Twilight Naut.	Moonset 7	8	9	10
°	h m	h m	h m	h m	h m	h m	h m
N 72	☐	☐	☐	18 34	20 27	22 38	☐
N 70	22 14	////	////	18 16	19 57	21 40	23 25
68	21 34	////	////	18 02	19 35	21 06	22 32
66	21 06	23 00	////	17 51	19 18	20 42	21 59
64	20 46	22 07	////	17 41	19 04	20 23	21 36
62	20 29	21 37	////	17 33	18 52	20 07	21 17
60	20 15	21 14	23 06	17 26	18 42	19 54	21 01
N 58	20 04	20 56	22 20	17 20	18 33	19 43	20 48
56	19 53	20 41	21 50	17 15	18 26	19 34	20 37
54	19 45	20 28	21 29	17 10	18 19	19 25	20 27
52	19 37	20 17	21 12	17 05	18 13	19 17	20 18
50	19 29	20 08	20 57	17 01	18 07	19 11	20 10
45	19 14	19 48	20 30	16 53	17 55	18 56	19 54
N 40	19 02	19 32	20 09	16 46	17 46	18 44	19 40
35	18 51	19 19	19 52	16 40	17 37	18 34	19 28
30	18 42	19 08	19 39	16 35	17 30	18 25	19 18
20	18 26	18 50	19 19	16 25	17 17	18 09	19 01
N 10	18 13	18 35	19 01	16 17	17 06	17 56	18 45
0	18 00	18 22	18 47	16 10	16 56	17 43	18 31
S 10	17 47	18 09	18 35	16 02	16 46	17 31	18 17
20	17 34	17 57	18 24	15 54	16 35	17 17	18 02
30	17 19	17 44	18 13	15 45	16 23	17 02	17 44
35	17 11	17 37	18 07	15 40	16 15	16 53	17 34
40	17 01	17 29	18 02	15 34	16 07	16 43	17 23
45	16 49	17 21	17 56	15 27	15 58	16 31	17 09
S 50	16 35	17 10	17 49	15 19	15 46	16 17	16 53
52	16 29	17 06	17 46	15 15	15 41	16 11	16 45
54	16 22	17 01	17 43	15 11	15 35	16 03	16 36
56	16 14	16 55	17 40	15 06	15 29	15 55	16 27
58	16 05	16 49	17 37	15 01	15 21	15 46	16 16
S 60	15 54	16 42	17 33	14 55	15 13	15 35	16 03

Day	SUN Eqn. of Time 00h	12h	Mer. Pass.	MOON Mer. Pass. Upper	Lower	Age	Phase
d	m s	m s	h m	h m	h m	d	%
7	03 28	03 30	11 57	09 59	22 22	27	6
8	03 31	03 33	11 56	10 45	23 08	28	2
9	03 34	03 36	11 56	11 32	23 56	29	0

UT	ARIES GHA	VENUS −3.9 GHA	Dec	MARS +1.3 GHA	Dec	JUPITER −2.0 GHA	Dec	SATURN +0.2 GHA	Dec
10 00	227 57.5	169 39.4	N20 13.3	185 53.7	N16 01.2	149 28.6	N22 42.7	12 04.9	S11 25.8
01	243 00.0	184 38.7	14.0	200 54.4	01.8	164 30.5	42.8	27 07.5	25.7
02	258 02.4	199 37.9	14.8	215 55.0	02.4	179 32.3	42.8	42 10.1	25.7
03	273 04.9	214 37.2	.. 15.5	230 55.7	.. 02.9	194 34.2	.. 42.9	57 12.8	.. 25.6
04	288 07.4	229 36.5	16.3	245 56.3	03.5	209 36.1	42.9	72 15.4	25.6
05	303 09.8	244 35.8	17.0	260 57.0	04.1	224 38.0	43.0	87 18.1	25.5
06	318 12.3	259 35.1	N20 17.7	275 57.6	N16 04.6	239 39.9	N22 43.0	102 20.7	S11 25.5
07	333 14.8	274 34.3	18.5	290 58.3	05.2	254 41.8	43.1	117 23.4	25.4
08	348 17.2	289 33.6	19.2	305 58.9	05.8	269 43.6	43.1	132 26.0	25.4
F 09	3 19.7	304 32.9	.. 19.9	320 59.6	.. 06.3	284 45.5	.. 43.2	147 28.6	.. 25.3
R 10	18 22.2	319 32.2	20.7	336 00.2	06.9	299 47.4	43.2	162 31.3	25.2
I 11	33 24.6	334 31.5	21.4	351 00.9	07.5	314 49.3	43.3	177 33.9	25.2
D 12	48 27.1	349 30.7	N20 22.1	6 01.5	N16 08.0	329 51.2	N22 43.3	192 36.6	S11 25.1
A 13	63 29.5	4 30.0	22.9	21 02.2	08.6	344 53.1	43.4	207 39.2	25.1
Y 14	78 32.0	19 29.3	23.6	36 02.8	09.2	359 54.9	43.4	222 41.9	25.0
15	93 34.5	34 28.6	.. 24.3	51 03.5	.. 09.7	14 56.8	.. 43.4	237 44.5	.. 25.0
16	108 36.9	49 27.8	25.1	66 04.1	10.3	29 58.7	43.5	252 47.1	24.9
17	123 39.4	64 27.1	25.8	81 04.8	10.8	45 00.6	43.5	267 49.8	24.9
18	138 41.9	79 26.4	N20 26.5	96 05.4	N16 11.4	60 02.5	N22 43.6	282 52.4	S11 24.8
19	153 44.3	94 25.7	27.2	111 06.1	12.0	75 04.4	43.6	297 55.1	24.7
20	168 46.8	109 24.9	28.0	126 06.7	12.5	90 06.2	43.7	312 57.7	24.7
21	183 49.3	124 24.2	.. 28.7	141 07.3	.. 13.1	105 08.1	.. 43.7	328 00.3	.. 24.6
22	198 51.7	139 23.5	29.4	156 08.0	13.7	120 10.0	43.8	343 03.0	24.6
23	213 54.2	154 22.7	30.3	171 08.6	14.2	135 11.9	43.8	358 05.6	24.5
11 00	228 56.7	169 22.0	N20 30.8	186 09.3	N16 14.8	150 13.8	N22 43.9	13 08.3	S11 24.5
01	243 59.1	184 21.3	31.6	201 09.9	15.3	165 15.7	43.9	28 10.9	24.4
02	259 01.6	199 20.6	32.3	216 10.6	15.9	180 17.5	44.0	43 13.5	24.4
03	274 04.0	214 19.8	.. 33.0	231 11.2	.. 16.5	195 19.4	.. 44.0	58 16.2	.. 24.3
04	289 06.5	229 19.1	33.7	246 11.9	17.0	210 21.3	44.1	73 18.8	24.2
05	304 09.0	244 18.3	34.4	261 12.5	17.6	225 23.2	44.1	88 21.5	24.2
06	319 11.4	259 17.6	N20 35.1	276 13.2	N16 18.1	240 25.1	N22 44.1	103 24.1	S11 24.1
07	334 13.9	274 16.9	35.9	291 13.8	18.7	255 26.9	44.2	118 26.8	24.1
S 08	349 16.4	289 16.2	36.6	306 14.5	19.3	270 28.8	44.2	133 29.4	24.0
A 09	4 18.8	304 15.4	.. 37.3	321 15.1	.. 19.8	285 30.7	.. 44.3	148 32.0	.. 24.0
T 10	19 21.3	319 14.7	38.0	336 15.8	20.4	300 32.6	44.3	163 34.7	23.9
U 11	34 23.8	334 14.0	38.7	351 16.4	20.9	315 34.5	44.4	178 37.3	23.9
R 12	49 26.2	349 13.2	N20 39.4	6 17.0	N16 21.5	330 36.3	N22 44.4	193 40.0	S11 23.8
D 13	64 28.7	4 12.5	40.1	21 17.7	22.0	345 38.2	44.5	208 42.6	23.8
A 14	79 31.2	19 11.8	40.8	36 18.3	22.6	0 40.1	44.5	223 45.2	23.7
Y 15	94 33.6	34 11.0	.. 41.5	51 19.0	.. 23.2	15 42.0	.. 44.6	238 47.9	.. 23.6
16	109 36.1	49 10.3	42.2	66 19.6	23.7	30 43.9	44.6	253 50.5	23.6
17	124 38.5	64 09.6	42.9	81 20.3	24.3	45 45.8	44.7	268 53.2	23.5
18	139 41.0	79 08.8	N20 43.6	96 20.9	N16 24.8	60 47.6	N22 44.7	283 55.8	S11 23.5
19	154 43.5	94 08.1	44.3	111 21.6	25.4	75 49.5	44.8	298 58.4	23.4
20	169 45.9	109 07.3	45.0	126 22.2	25.9	90 51.4	44.8	314 01.1	23.4
21	184 48.4	124 06.6	.. 45.7	141 22.9	.. 26.5	105 53.3	.. 44.8	329 03.7	.. 23.3
22	199 50.9	139 05.9	46.4	156 23.5	27.0	120 55.2	44.9	344 06.4	23.3
23	214 53.3	154 05.1	47.1	171 24.2	27.6	135 57.0	44.9	359 09.0	23.2
12 00	229 55.8	169 04.4	N20 47.8	186 24.8	N16 28.1	150 58.9	N22 45.0	14 11.6	S11 23.1
01	244 58.3	184 03.6	48.5	201 25.4	28.7	166 00.8	45.0	29 14.3	23.1
02	260 00.7	199 02.9	49.2	216 26.1	29.3	181 02.7	45.1	44 16.9	23.0
03	275 03.2	214 02.2	.. 49.9	231 26.7	.. 29.8	196 04.6	.. 45.1	59 19.6	.. 23.0
04	290 05.6	229 01.4	50.6	246 27.4	30.4	211 06.4	45.2	74 22.2	22.9
05	305 08.1	244 00.7	51.3	261 28.0	30.9	226 08.3	45.2	89 24.8	22.9
06	320 10.6	258 59.9	N20 52.0	276 28.7	N16 31.5	241 10.2	N22 45.3	104 27.5	S11 22.8
07	335 13.0	273 59.2	52.7	291 29.3	32.0	256 12.1	45.3	119 30.1	22.8
08	350 15.5	288 58.4	53.4	306 30.0	32.6	271 13.9	45.4	134 32.8	22.7
S 09	5 18.0	303 57.7	.. 54.0	321 30.6	.. 33.1	286 15.8	.. 45.4	149 35.4	.. 22.7
U 10	20 20.4	318 57.0	54.7	336 31.3	33.7	301 17.7	45.4	164 38.0	22.6
N 11	35 22.9	333 56.2	55.4	351 31.9	34.2	316 19.6	45.5	179 40.7	22.5
D 12	50 25.4	348 55.5	N20 56.1	6 32.5	N16 34.8	331 21.5	N22 45.5	194 43.3	S11 22.5
A 13	65 27.8	3 54.7	56.8	21 33.2	35.3	346 23.3	45.6	209 45.9	22.4
Y 14	80 30.3	18 54.0	57.5	36 33.8	35.9	1 25.2	45.6	224 48.6	22.4
15	95 32.8	33 53.2	.. 58.1	51 34.5	.. 36.4	16 27.1	.. 45.7	239 51.2	.. 22.3
16	110 35.2	48 52.5	58.8	66 35.1	37.0	31 29.0	45.7	254 53.9	22.3
17	125 37.7	63 51.7	20 59.5	81 35.8	37.5	46 30.9	45.8	269 56.5	22.2
18	140 40.1	78 51.0	N21 00.2	96 36.4	N16 38.1	61 32.7	N22 45.8	284 59.1	S11 22.2
19	155 42.6	93 50.2	00.9	111 37.0	38.6	76 34.6	45.9	300 01.8	22.1
20	170 45.1	108 49.5	01.5	126 37.7	39.2	91 36.5	45.9	315 04.4	22.1
21	185 47.5	123 48.7	.. 02.2	141 38.3	.. 39.7	106 38.4	.. 45.9	330 07.1	.. 22.0
22	200 50.0	138 48.0	02.9	156 39.0	40.3	121 40.2	46.0	345 09.7	22.0
23	215 52.5	153 47.2	03.6	171 39.6	40.8	136 42.1	46.0	0 12.3	21.9
Mer. Pass.	h m 8 42.8	v −0.7	d 0.7	v 0.6	d 0.6	v 1.9	d 0.0	v 2.6	d 0.1

STARS

Name	SHA	Dec
Acamar	315 18.8	S40 15.2
Achernar	335 27.4	S57 10.0
Acrux	173 08.8	S63 10.7
Adhara	255 12.8	S28 59.8
Aldebaran	290 49.8	N16 32.0
Alioth	166 20.4	N55 53.3
Alkaid	152 58.5	N49 14.8
Al Na'ir	27 43.9	S46 53.5
Alnilam	275 46.7	S 1 11.8
Alphard	217 56.2	S 8 43.3
Alphecca	126 10.7	N26 40.2
Alpheratz	357 43.8	N29 09.7
Altair	62 08.2	N 8 54.3
Ankaa	353 16.1	S42 13.8
Antares	112 26.0	S26 27.6
Arcturus	145 55.5	N19 06.8
Atria	107 27.3	S69 02.9
Avior	234 18.2	S59 33.6
Bellatrix	278 32.4	N 6 21.5
Betelgeuse	271 01.6	N 7 24.3
Canopus	263 56.6	S52 42.5
Capella	280 35.0	N46 00.6
Deneb	49 31.4	N45 19.6
Denebola	182 33.6	N14 29.7
Diphda	348 56.2	S17 54.8
Dubhe	193 51.6	N61 40.8
Elnath	278 13.0	N28 37.0
Eltanin	90 45.7	N51 29.2
Enif	33 47.2	N 9 56.2
Fomalhaut	15 24.2	S29 32.9
Gacrux	172 00.5	S57 11.6
Gienah	175 52.1	S17 37.2
Hadar	148 47.3	S60 26.4
Hamal	328 01.2	N23 31.4
Kaus Aust.	83 43.6	S34 22.5
Kochab	137 18.9	N74 06.1
Markab	13 38.5	N15 16.6
Menkar	314 15.5	N 4 08.4
Menkent	148 07.3	S36 26.3
Miaplacidus	221 39.7	S69 46.8
Mirfak	308 40.9	N49 54.4
Nunki	75 58.2	S26 16.6
Peacock	53 19.2	S56 41.1
Pollux	243 28.0	N27 59.5
Procyon	245 00.0	N 5 11.2
Rasalhague	96 06.2	N12 33.1
Regulus	207 43.6	N11 54.0
Rigel	281 12.4	S 8 11.4
Rigil Kent.	139 51.1	S60 53.4
Sabik	102 12.3	S15 44.4
Schedar	349 41.0	N56 36.4
Shaula	96 21.7	S37 06.4
Sirius	258 34.0	S16 44.4
Spica	158 31.0	S11 14.0
Suhail	222 52.5	S43 29.6
Vega	80 38.7	N38 47.7
Zuben'ubi	137 05.2	S16 05.9

	SHA	Mer. Pass.
	° ′	h m
Venus	300 25.4	12 43
Mars	317 12.6	11 35
Jupiter	281 17.1	13 57
Saturn	144 11.6	23 03

UT	SUN GHA	SUN Dec	MOON GHA	MOON v	MOON Dec	MOON d	MOON HP	Lat.	Twilight Naut.	Twilight Civil	Sunrise	Moonrise 10	Moonrise 11	Moonrise 12	Moonrise 13
	° '	° '	° '	'	° '	'	'	°	h m	h m	h m	h m	h m	h m	h m
d h								N 72	▭	▭	▭	01 03	▭	▭	▭
10 00	180 54.2	N17 36.3						N 70	////	////	01 22	02 02	01 56	01 40	02 41
01	195 54.2	37.0	An annular eclipse of					68	////	////	02 08	02 36	02 50	03 18	04 09
02	210 54.2	37.6	the Sun occurs on this					66	////	00 21	02 38	03 01	03 23	03 57	04 48
03	225 54.3 ..	38.3	date. See page 5.					64	////	01 33	03 00	03 21	03 47	04 24	05 15
04	240 54.3	38.9						62	////	02 07	03 17	03 37	04 06	04 45	05 35
05	255 54.3	39.6						60	00 19	02 32	03 32	03 50	04 22	05 02	05 52
06	270 54.3	N17 40.2	268 10.3 12.1	12.1	N17 51.4	5.0	54.6	N 58	01 24	02 51	03 44	04 02	04 35	05 16	06 06
07	285 54.4	40.9	282 41.4 12.1	12.1	17 56.4	4.9	54.6	56	01 55	03 06	03 55	04 12	04 47	05 29	06 18
08	300 54.4	41.5	297 12.5 12.0	12.0	18 01.3	4.8	54.6	54	02 18	03 20	04 04	04 21	04 57	05 39	06 29
F 09	315 54.4 ..	42.2	311 43.5 12.0	12.0	18 06.1	4.7	54.6	52	02 36	03 31	04 12	04 28	05 06	05 49	06 39
R 10	330 54.4	42.8	326 14.5 12.0	12.0	18 10.8	4.7	54.5	50	02 51	03 41	04 20	04 36	05 14	05 57	06 47
I 11	345 54.4	43.5	340 45.5 12.0	12.0	18 15.5	4.5	54.5	45	03 20	04 02	04 36	04 51	05 31	06 16	07 05
D 12	0 54.5	N17 44.1	355 16.5 12.0	12.0	N18 20.0	4.5	54.5	N 40	03 41	04 18	04 49	05 04	05 45	06 30	07 19
A 13	15 54.5	44.8	9 47.5 12.0	12.0	18 24.5	4.3	54.5	35	03 58	04 32	05 00	05 14	05 57	06 43	07 32
Y 14	30 54.5	45.4	24 18.5 11.9	11.9	18 28.8	4.3	54.5	30	04 12	04 43	05 09	05 24	06 07	06 54	07 43
15	45 54.5 ..	46.1	38 49.4 12.0	12.0	18 33.1	4.2	54.5	20	04 34	05 02	05 26	05 40	06 26	07 13	08 01
16	60 54.5	46.7	53 20.4 11.9	11.9	18 37.3	4.1	54.5	N 10	04 52	05 18	05 40	05 55	06 41	07 29	08 17
17	75 54.5	47.4	67 51.3 11.9	11.9	18 41.4	4.0	54.5	0	05 06	05 31	05 53	06 08	06 56	07 44	08 32
18	90 54.6	N17 48.0	82 22.2 11.9	11.9	N18 45.4	3.9	54.5	S 10	05 18	05 44	06 06	06 21	07 11	08 00	08 47
19	105 54.6	48.6	96 53.1 11.9	11.9	18 49.3	3.8	54.4	20	05 30	05 57	06 20	06 36	07 27	08 16	09 04
20	120 54.6	49.3	111 24.0 11.9	11.9	18 53.1	3.8	54.4	30	05 41	06 10	06 35	06 53	07 45	08 35	09 22
21	135 54.6 ..	49.9	125 54.9 11.9	11.9	18 56.9	3.6	54.4	35	05 47	06 18	06 44	07 02	07 56	08 46	09 33
22	150 54.6	50.6	140 25.8 11.9	11.9	19 00.5	3.6	54.4	40	05 53	06 26	06 55	07 13	08 08	08 59	09 45
23	165 54.7	51.2	154 56.7 11.9	11.9	19 04.1	3.4	54.4	45	06 00	06 35	07 07	07 26	08 22	09 14	10 00
11 00	180 54.7	N17 51.9	169 27.6 11.8	11.8	N19 07.5	3.4	54.4	S 50	06 07	06 46	07 21	07 42	08 40	09 32	10 18
01	195 54.7	52.5	183 58.4 11.9	11.9	19 10.9	3.3	54.4	52	06 10	06 51	07 28	07 50	08 48	09 41	10 26
02	210 54.7	53.2	198 29.3 11.8	11.8	19 14.2	3.2	54.4	54	06 13	06 56	07 36	07 58	08 58	09 50	10 35
03	225 54.7 ..	53.8	213 00.1 11.9	11.9	19 17.4	3.1	54.4	56	06 17	07 02	07 44	08 08	09 08	10 01	10 46
04	240 54.7	54.4	227 31.0 11.8	11.8	19 20.5	3.0	54.3	58	06 21	07 09	07 54	08 18	09 20	10 14	10 58
05	255 54.8	55.1	242 01.8 11.8	11.8	19 23.5	2.9	54.3	S 60	06 25	07 16	08 05	08 31	09 34	10 28	11 12

UT	SUN GHA	SUN Dec	MOON GHA	MOON v	MOON Dec	MOON d	MOON HP	Lat.	Sunset	Twilight Civil	Twilight Naut.	Moonset 10	Moonset 11	Moonset 12	Moonset 13
06	270 54.8	N17 55.7	256 32.6 11.8	11.8	N19 26.4	2.8	54.3								
07	285 54.8	56.4	271 03.4 11.8	11.8	19 29.2	2.7	54.3	Lat.	Sunset	Civil	Naut.	10	11	12	13
S 08	300 54.8	57.0	285 34.2 11.8	11.8	19 31.9	2.7	54.3								
A 09	315 54.8 ..	57.6	300 05.0 11.8	11.8	19 34.6	2.5	54.3	°	h m	h m	h m	h m	h m	h m	h m
T 10	330 54.8	58.3	314 35.8 11.8	11.8	19 37.1	2.5	54.3	N 72	▭	▭	▭	▭	▭	▭	▭
U 11	345 54.8	58.9	329 06.6 11.8	11.8	19 39.6	2.3	54.3	N 70	22 39	////	////	23 25	25 22	01 22	02 01
R 12	0 54.9	N17 59.5	343 37.4 11.8	11.8	N19 41.9	2.3	54.3	68	21 49	////	////	22 32	23 44	24 33	00 33
D 13	15 54.9	18 00.2	358 08.2 11.8	11.8	19 44.2	2.2	54.3	66	21 18	////	////	21 59	23 05	23 54	24 26
A 14	30 54.9	00.8	12 39.0 11.8	11.8	19 46.4	2.0	54.2	64	20 55	22 25	////	21 36	22 38	23 27	24 03
Y 15	45 54.9 ..	01.4	27 09.8 11.8	11.8	19 48.4	2.0	54.2	62	20 38	21 49	////	21 17	22 17	23 06	23 44
16	60 54.9	02.1	41 40.6 11.8	11.8	19 50.4	1.9	54.2	60	20 23	21 24	////	21 01	22 00	22 49	23 28
17	75 54.9	02.7	56 11.4 11.7	11.7	19 52.3	1.8	54.2								
18	90 54.9	N18 03.3	70 42.1 11.8	11.8	N19 54.1	1.7	54.2	N 58	20 10	21 04	22 34	20 48	21 46	22 35	23 15
19	105 54.9	04.0	85 12.9 11.8	11.8	19 55.8	1.6	54.2	56	19 59	20 48	22 01	20 37	21 34	22 23	23 04
20	120 55.0	04.6	99 43.7 11.8	11.8	19 57.4	1.5	54.2	54	19 50	20 34	21 37	20 27	21 23	22 12	22 54
21	135 55.0 ..	05.2	114 14.5 11.8	11.8	19 58.9	1.4	54.2	52	19 41	20 23	21 19	20 18	21 14	22 03	22 45
22	150 55.0	05.9	128 45.3 11.7	11.7	20 00.3	1.3	54.2	50	19 34	20 13	21 04	20 10	21 05	21 54	22 37
23	165 55.0	06.5	143 16.0 11.8	11.8	20 01.6	1.3	54.2	45	19 18	19 52	20 34	19 54	20 47	21 36	22 20
12 00	180 55.0	N18 07.1	157 46.8 11.8	11.8	N20 02.9	1.1	54.2	N 40	19 05	19 35	20 12	19 40	20 33	21 21	22 06
01	195 55.0	07.8	172 17.6 11.8	11.8	20 04.0	1.0	54.2	35	18 54	19 21	19 55	19 28	20 20	21 09	21 54
02	210 55.0	08.4	186 48.4 11.8	11.8	20 05.0	1.0	54.2	30	18 44	19 10	19 41	19 18	20 09	20 58	21 44
03	225 55.0 ..	09.0	201 19.2 11.8	11.8	20 06.0	0.8	54.2	20	18 27	18 51	19 19	19 01	19 51	20 39	21 26
04	240 55.0	09.7	215 50.0 11.8	11.8	20 06.8	0.8	54.1	N 10	18 13	18 35	19 01	18 45	19 35	20 23	21 10
05	255 55.1	10.3	230 20.8 11.8	11.8	20 07.6	0.7	54.1	0	18 00	18 22	18 47	18 31	19 19	20 08	20 55
06	270 55.1	N18 10.9	244 51.6 11.8	11.8	N20 08.3	0.5	54.1	S 10	17 47	18 09	18 34	18 17	19 04	19 52	20 41
07	285 55.1	11.5	259 22.4 11.8	11.8	20 08.8	0.5	54.1	20	17 33	17 56	18 23	18 02	18 48	19 36	20 25
08	300 55.1	12.2	273 53.2 11.8	11.8	20 09.3	0.4	54.1	30	17 17	17 42	18 11	17 44	18 29	19 17	20 07
S 09	315 55.1 ..	12.8	288 24.0 11.9	11.9	20 09.7	0.3	54.1	35	17 08	17 35	18 05	17 34	18 19	19 06	19 56
U 10	330 55.1	13.4	302 54.9 11.8	11.8	20 10.0	0.2	54.1	40	16 58	17 26	17 59	17 23	18 06	18 53	19 44
N 11	345 55.1	14.0	317 25.7 11.9	11.9	20 10.2	0.1	54.1	45	16 46	17 17	17 53	17 09	17 51	18 38	19 30
D 12	0 55.1	N18 14.7	331 56.6 11.8	11.8	N20 10.3	0.0	54.1	S 50	16 31	17 06	17 45	16 53	17 34	18 20	19 12
A 13	15 55.1	15.3	346 27.4 11.9	11.9	20 10.3	0.1	54.1	52	16 24	17 01	17 42	16 45	17 25	18 12	19 04
Y 14	30 55.1	15.9	0 58.3 11.9	11.9	20 10.2	0.2	54.1	54	16 16	16 56	17 39	16 36	17 16	18 02	18 55
15	45 55.1 ..	16.5	15 29.1 11.9	11.9	20 10.0	0.3	54.1	56	16 08	16 50	17 35	16 27	17 05	17 51	18 44
16	60 55.1	17.1	30 00.0 11.9	11.9	20 09.7	0.4	54.1	58	15 58	16 43	17 31	16 16	16 53	17 38	18 32
17	75 55.1	17.8	44 30.9 11.9	11.9	20 09.3	0.4	54.1	S 60	15 47	16 36	17 27	16 03	16 39	17 24	18 19
18	90 55.2	N18 18.4	59 01.8 11.9	11.9	N20 08.9	0.6	54.1								
19	105 55.2	19.0	73 32.7 11.9	11.9	20 08.3	0.7	54.1								
20	120 55.2	19.6	88 03.6 11.9	11.9	20 07.6	0.7	54.1								
21	135 55.2 ..	20.2	102 34.5 12.0	12.0	20 06.9	0.8	54.1								
22	150 55.2	20.9	117 05.5 11.9	11.9	20 06.1	1.0	54.1								
23	165 55.2	21.5	131 36.4 12.0	12.0	N20 05.1	1.0	54.1								

	SUN			MOON			
Day	Eqn. of Time 00h	Eqn. of Time 12h	Mer. Pass.	Mer. Pass. Upper	Mer. Pass. Lower	Age	Phase
d	m s	m s	h m	h m	h m	d	%
10	03 37	03 38	11 56	12 20	24 44	00	0
11	03 39	03 39	11 56	13 08	00 44	01	2
12	03 40	03 40	11 56	13 56	01 32	02	6

SD 15.9	d 0.6	SD 14.9	14.8	14.7

UT	ARIES	VENUS −3.9		MARS +1.3		JUPITER −1.9		SATURN +0.2		STARS		
	GHA	GHA	Dec	GHA	Dec	GHA	Dec	GHA	Dec	Name	SHA	Dec
d h	° ′	° ′	° ′	° ′	° ′	° ′	° ′	° ′	° ′		° ′	° ′
13 00	230 54.9	168 46.5	N21 04.2	186 40.3	N16 41.3	151 44.0	N22 46.1	15 15.0	S11 21.8	Acamar	315 18.8	S40 15.1
01	245 57.4	183 45.7	04.9	201 40.9	41.9	166 45.9	46.1	30 17.6	21.8	Achernar	335 27.4	S57 10.0
02	260 59.9	198 45.0	05.6	216 41.5	42.4	181 47.8	46.2	45 20.3	21.7	Acrux	173 08.8	S63 10.7
03	276 02.3	213 44.2 ..	06.2	231 42.2 ..	43.0	196 49.6 ..	46.2	60 22.9 ..	21.7	Adhara	255 12.8	S28 59.8
04	291 04.8	228 43.5	06.9	246 42.8	43.5	211 51.5	46.3	75 25.5	21.6	Aldebaran	290 49.8	N16 32.0
05	306 07.3	243 42.7	07.6	261 43.5	44.1	226 53.4	46.3	90 28.2	21.6			
06	321 09.7	258 42.0	N21 08.2	276 44.1	N16 44.6	241 55.3	N22 46.4	105 30.8	S11 21.5	Alioth	166 20.4	N55 53.3
07	336 12.2	273 41.2	08.9	291 44.8	45.2	256 57.1	46.4	120 33.4	21.5	Alkaid	152 58.5	N49 14.9
08	351 14.6	288 40.5	09.6	306 45.4	45.7	271 59.0	46.4	135 36.1	21.4	Al Na'ir	27 43.9	S46 53.4
M 09	6 17.1	303 39.7 ..	10.2	321 46.0 ..	46.3	287 00.9 ..	46.5	150 38.7 ..	21.4	Alnilam	275 46.7	S 1 11.8
O 10	21 19.6	318 39.0	10.9	336 46.7	46.8	302 02.8	46.5	165 41.4	21.3	Alphard	217 56.2	S 8 43.3
N 11	36 22.0	333 38.2	11.6	351 47.3	47.3	317 04.7	46.6	180 44.0	21.2			
D 12	51 24.5	348 37.4	N21 12.2	6 48.0	N16 47.9	332 06.5	N22 46.6	195 46.6	S11 21.2	Alphecca	126 10.7	N26 40.2
A 13	66 27.0	3 36.7	12.9	21 48.6	48.4	347 08.4	46.7	210 49.3	21.1	Alpheratz	357 43.8	N29 09.7
Y 14	81 29.4	18 35.9	13.5	36 49.3	49.0	2 10.3	46.7	225 51.9	21.1	Altair	62 08.1	N 8 54.3
15	96 31.9	33 35.2 ..	14.2	51 49.9 ..	49.5	17 12.2 ..	46.8	240 54.6 ..	21.0	Ankaa	353 16.1	S42 13.8
16	111 34.4	48 34.4	14.9	66 50.5	50.1	32 14.0	46.8	255 57.2	21.0	Antares	112 26.0	S26 27.6
17	126 36.8	63 33.7	15.5	81 51.2	50.6	47 15.9	46.9	270 59.8	20.9			
18	141 39.3	78 32.9	N21 16.2	96 51.8	N16 51.1	62 17.8	N22 46.9	286 02.5	S11 20.9	Arcturus	145 55.5	N19 06.8
19	156 41.8	93 32.1	16.8	111 52.5	51.7	77 19.7	46.9	301 05.1	20.8	Atria	107 27.3	S69 02.9
20	171 44.2	108 31.4	17.5	126 53.1	52.2	92 21.5	47.0	316 07.7	20.8	Avior	234 18.2	S59 33.6
21	186 46.7	123 30.6 ..	18.1	141 53.7 ..	52.8	107 23.4 ..	47.0	331 10.4 ..	20.7	Bellatrix	278 32.4	N 6 21.5
22	201 49.1	138 29.9	18.8	156 54.4	53.3	122 25.3	47.1	346 13.0	20.7	Betelgeuse	271 01.7	N 7 24.3
23	216 51.6	153 29.1	19.4	171 55.0	53.8	137 27.2	47.1	1 15.6	20.6			
14 00	231 54.1	168 28.3	N21 20.1	186 55.7	N16 54.4	152 29.0	N22 47.2	16 18.3	S11 20.6	Canopus	263 56.6	S52 42.5
01	246 56.5	183 27.6	20.7	201 56.3	54.9	167 30.9	47.2	31 20.9	20.5	Capella	280 35.0	N46 00.6
02	261 59.0	198 26.8	21.4	216 57.0	55.5	182 32.8	47.3	46 23.6	20.4	Deneb	49 31.4	N45 19.6
03	277 01.5	213 26.0 ..	22.0	231 57.6 ..	56.0	197 34.7 ..	47.3	61 26.2 ..	20.4	Denebola	182 33.6	N14 29.7
04	292 03.9	228 25.3	22.7	246 58.2	56.5	212 36.5	47.3	76 28.8	20.3	Diphda	348 56.2	S17 54.8
05	307 06.4	243 24.5	23.3	261 58.9	57.1	227 38.4	47.4	91 31.5	20.3			
06	322 08.9	258 23.8	N21 23.9	276 59.5	N16 57.6	242 40.3	N22 47.4	106 34.1	S11 20.2	Dubhe	193 51.6	N61 40.9
07	337 11.3	273 23.0	24.6	292 00.2	58.1	257 42.2	47.5	121 36.7	20.2	Elnath	278 13.0	N28 37.0
T 08	352 13.8	288 22.2	25.2	307 00.8	58.7	272 44.0	47.5	136 39.4	20.1	Eltanin	90 45.7	N51 29.2
U 09	7 16.2	303 21.5 ..	25.9	322 01.4 ..	59.2	287 45.9 ..	47.6	151 42.0 ..	20.1	Enif	33 47.2	N 9 56.2
E 10	22 18.7	318 20.7	26.5	337 02.1	16 59.8	302 47.8	47.6	166 44.7	20.0	Fomalhaut	15 24.2	S29 32.9
S 11	37 21.2	333 19.9	27.1	352 02.7	17 00.3	317 49.7	47.7	181 47.3	20.0			
D 12	52 23.6	348 19.2	N21 27.8	7 03.4	N17 00.8	332 51.5	N22 47.7	196 49.9	S11 19.9	Gacrux	172 00.5	S57 11.6
A 13	67 26.1	3 18.4	28.4	22 04.0	01.4	347 53.4	47.7	211 52.6	19.9	Gienah	175 52.1	S17 37.2
Y 14	82 28.6	18 17.6	29.0	37 04.6	01.9	2 55.3	47.8	226 55.2	19.8	Hadar	148 47.3	S60 26.4
15	97 31.0	33 16.9 ..	29.7	52 05.3 ..	02.4	17 57.2 ..	47.8	241 57.8 ..	19.8	Hamal	328 01.1	N23 31.4
16	112 33.5	48 16.1	30.3	67 05.9	03.0	32 59.0	47.9	257 00.5	19.7	Kaus Aust.	83 43.6	S34 22.5
17	127 36.0	63 15.3	30.9	82 06.6	03.5	48 00.9	47.9	272 03.1	19.6			
18	142 38.4	78 14.6	N21 31.6	97 07.2	N17 04.0	63 02.8	N22 48.0	287 05.7	S11 19.6	Kochab	137 18.9	N74 06.1
19	157 40.9	93 13.8	32.2	112 07.8	04.6	78 04.7	48.0	302 08.4	19.5	Markab	13 38.5	N15 16.6
20	172 43.4	108 13.0	32.8	127 08.5	05.1	93 06.5	48.0	317 11.0	19.5	Menkar	314 15.4	N 4 08.4
21	187 45.8	123 12.2 ..	33.4	142 09.1 ..	05.6	108 08.4 ..	48.1	332 13.7 ..	19.4	Menkent	148 07.2	S36 26.3
22	202 48.3	138 11.5	34.1	157 09.8	06.2	123 10.3	48.1	347 16.3	19.4	Miaplacidus	221 39.7	S69 46.8
23	217 50.7	153 10.7	34.7	172 10.4	06.7	138 12.2	48.2	2 18.9	19.3			
15 00	232 53.2	168 09.9	N21 35.3	187 11.0	N17 07.2	153 14.0	N22 48.2	17 21.6	S11 19.3	Mirfak	308 40.9	N49 54.4
01	247 55.7	183 09.2	35.9	202 11.7	07.8	168 15.9	48.3	32 24.2	19.2	Nunki	75 58.2	S26 16.6
02	262 58.1	198 08.4	36.6	217 12.3	08.3	183 17.8	48.3	47 26.8	19.2	Peacock	53 19.2	S56 41.1
03	278 00.6	213 07.6 ..	37.2	232 13.0 ..	08.8	198 19.7 ..	48.4	62 29.5 ..	19.1	Pollux	243 28.0	N27 59.5
04	293 03.1	228 06.8	37.8	247 13.6	09.4	213 21.5	48.4	77 32.1	19.1	Procyon	245 00.0	N 5 11.2
05	308 05.5	243 06.1	38.4	262 14.2	09.9	228 23.4	48.4	92 34.7	19.0			
06	323 08.0	258 05.3	N21 39.0	277 14.9	N17 10.4	243 25.3	N22 48.5	107 37.4	S11 19.0	Rasalhague	96 06.2	N12 33.1
W 07	338 10.5	273 04.5	39.6	292 15.5	11.0	258 27.1	48.5	122 40.0	18.9	Regulus	207 43.6	N11 54.0
E 08	353 12.9	288 03.7	40.3	307 16.2	11.5	273 29.0	48.6	137 42.6	18.9	Rigel	281 12.4	S 8 11.4
D 09	8 15.4	303 03.0 ..	40.9	322 16.8 ..	12.0	288 30.9 ..	48.6	152 45.3 ..	18.8	Rigil Kent.	139 51.1	S60 53.5
N 10	23 17.9	318 02.2	41.5	337 17.4	12.6	303 32.8	48.7	167 47.9	18.7	Sabik	102 12.3	S15 44.4
E 11	38 20.3	333 01.4	42.1	352 18.1	13.1	318 34.6	48.7	182 50.6	18.7			
S 12	53 22.8	348 00.6	N21 42.7	7 18.7	N17 13.6	333 36.5	N22 48.7	197 53.2	S11 18.6	Schedar	349 41.0	N56 36.4
D 13	68 25.2	2 59.9	43.3	22 19.4	14.1	348 38.4	48.8	212 55.8	18.6	Shaula	96 21.6	S37 06.6
A 14	83 27.7	17 59.1	43.9	37 20.0	14.7	3 40.3	48.8	227 58.5	18.5	Sirius	258 34.0	S16 44.4
Y 15	98 30.2	32 58.3 ..	44.5	52 20.6 ..	15.2	18 42.1 ..	48.9	243 01.1 ..	18.5	Spica	158 31.0	S11 14.0
16	113 32.6	47 57.5	45.1	67 21.3	15.7	33 44.0	48.9	258 03.7	18.4	Suhail	222 52.5	S43 29.6
17	128 35.1	62 56.7	45.8	82 21.9	16.2	48 45.9	49.0	273 06.4	18.4			
18	143 37.6	77 56.0	N21 46.4	97 22.5	N17 16.8	63 47.7	N22 49.0	288 09.0	S11 18.3	Vega	80 38.7	N38 47.7
19	158 40.0	92 55.2	47.0	112 23.2	17.3	78 49.6	49.1	303 11.6	18.3	Zuben'ubi	137 05.1	S16 05.9
20	173 42.5	107 54.4	47.6	127 23.8	17.8	93 51.5	49.1	318 14.3	18.2			SHA
21	188 45.0	122 53.6 ..	48.2	142 24.4 ..	18.3	108 53.4 ..	49.1	333 16.9 ..	18.2			Mer. Pass.
22	203 47.4	137 52.8	48.8	157 25.1	18.9	123 55.2	49.2	348 19.5	18.1	Venus	296 34.3	12 47
23	218 49.9	152 52.1	49.4	172 25.7	19.4	138 57.1	49.2	3 22.2	18.1	Mars	315 01.6	11 32
	h m									Jupiter	280 35.0	13 48
Mer. Pass. 8 31.0		v −0.8	d 0.6	v 0.6	d 0.5	v 1.9	d 0.0	v 2.6	d 0.1	Saturn	144 24.2	22 51

UT	SUN GHA	SUN Dec	MOON GHA	v	MOON Dec	d	HP
d h	° '	° '	° '	'	° '	'	'
13 00	180 55.2	N18 22.1	146 07.4	12.0	N20 04.1	1.1	54.1
01	195 55.2	22.7	160 38.4	12.0	20 03.0	1.2	54.0
02	210 55.2	23.3	175 09.4	12.0	20 01.8	1.3	54.0
03	225 55.2	.. 24.0	189 40.4	12.0	20 00.5	1.4	54.0
04	240 55.2	24.6	204 11.4	12.0	19 59.1	1.5	54.0
05	255 55.2	25.2	218 42.4	12.1	19 57.6	1.6	54.0
06	270 55.2	N18 25.8	233 13.5	12.0	N19 56.0	1.7	54.0
07	285 55.2	26.4	247 44.5	12.1	19 54.3	1.7	54.0
08	300 55.2	27.0	262 15.6	12.1	19 52.6	1.9	54.0
M 09	315 55.2	.. 27.6	276 46.7	12.1	19 50.7	1.9	54.0
O 10	330 55.2	28.2	291 17.8	12.1	19 48.8	2.1	54.0
N 11	345 55.2	28.9	305 48.9	12.2	19 46.7	2.1	54.0
D 12	0 55.2	N18 29.5	320 20.1	12.1	N19 44.6	2.2	54.0
A 13	15 55.2	30.1	334 51.2	12.2	19 42.4	2.3	54.0
Y 14	30 55.2	30.7	349 22.4	12.2	19 40.1	2.4	54.0
15	45 55.2	.. 31.3	3 53.6	12.2	19 37.7	2.5	54.0
16	60 55.2	31.9	18 24.8	12.3	19 35.2	2.6	54.0
17	75 55.2	32.5	32 56.1	12.2	19 32.6	2.7	54.0
18	90 55.2	N18 33.1	47 27.3	12.3	N19 29.9	2.7	54.0
19	105 55.2	33.7	61 58.6	12.3	19 27.2	2.9	54.0
20	120 55.2	34.3	76 29.9	12.3	19 24.3	2.9	54.0
21	135 55.2	.. 34.9	91 01.2	12.3	19 21.4	3.0	54.0
22	150 55.2	35.5	105 32.5	12.4	19 18.4	3.1	54.0
23	165 55.2	36.2	120 03.9	12.4	19 15.3	3.2	54.0
14 00	180 55.2	N18 36.8	134 35.3	12.3	N19 12.1	3.3	54.0
01	195 55.2	37.4	149 06.6	12.5	19 08.8	3.4	54.0
02	210 55.2	38.0	163 38.1	12.4	19 05.4	3.4	54.0
03	225 55.2	.. 38.6	178 09.5	12.4	19 02.0	3.6	54.1
04	240 55.2	39.2	192 40.9	12.5	18 58.4	3.6	54.1
05	255 55.2	39.8	207 12.4	12.5	18 54.8	3.7	54.1
06	270 55.2	N18 40.4	221 43.9	12.5	N18 51.1	3.8	54.1
07	285 55.2	41.0	236 15.4	12.6	18 47.3	3.9	54.1
08	300 55.2	41.6	250 47.0	12.5	18 43.4	4.0	54.1
T 09	315 55.2	.. 42.2	265 18.5	12.6	18 39.4	4.0	54.1
U 10	330 55.2	42.8	279 50.1	12.6	18 35.4	4.2	54.1
E 11	345 55.2	43.4	294 21.7	12.6	18 31.2	4.2	54.1
S 12	0 55.2	N18 44.0	308 53.3	12.7	N18 27.0	4.3	54.1
D 13	15 55.2	44.6	323 25.0	12.7	18 22.7	4.4	54.1
A 14	30 55.2	45.2	337 56.7	12.7	18 18.3	4.5	54.1
Y 15	45 55.2	.. 45.8	352 28.4	12.7	18 13.8	4.5	54.1
16	60 55.2	46.4	7 00.1	12.7	18 09.3	4.6	54.1
17	75 55.2	46.9	21 31.8	12.8	18 04.7	4.8	54.1
18	90 55.2	N18 47.5	36 03.6	12.8	N17 59.9	4.8	54.1
19	105 55.2	48.1	50 35.4	12.8	17 55.1	4.8	54.1
20	120 55.2	48.7	65 07.2	12.8	17 50.3	5.0	54.1
21	135 55.2	.. 49.3	79 39.0	12.9	17 45.3	5.0	54.1
22	150 55.2	49.9	94 10.9	12.8	17 40.3	5.2	54.2
23	165 55.1	50.5	108 42.7	12.9	17 35.1	5.2	54.2
15 00	180 55.1	N18 51.1	123 14.6	12.9	N17 29.9	5.2	54.2
01	195 55.1	51.7	137 46.5	13.0	17 24.7	5.4	54.2
02	210 55.1	52.3	152 18.5	13.0	17 19.3	5.4	54.2
03	225 55.1	.. 52.9	166 50.5	12.9	17 13.9	5.5	54.2
04	240 55.1	53.5	181 22.4	13.1	17 08.4	5.6	54.2
05	255 55.1	54.0	195 54.5	13.0	17 02.8	5.7	54.2
06	270 55.1	N18 54.6	210 26.5	13.0	N16 57.1	5.8	54.2
W 07	285 55.1	55.2	224 58.5	13.1	16 51.3	5.8	54.2
E 08	300 55.1	55.8	239 30.6	13.1	16 45.5	5.9	54.2
D 09	315 55.1	.. 56.4	254 02.7	13.1	16 39.6	5.9	54.3
N 10	330 55.1	57.0	268 34.8	13.2	16 33.7	6.1	54.3
E 11	345 55.1	57.6	283 07.0	13.2	16 27.6	6.1	54.3
S 12	0 55.0	N18 58.1	297 39.2	13.1	N16 21.5	6.2	54.3
D 13	15 55.0	58.7	312 11.3	13.3	16 15.3	6.3	54.3
A 14	30 55.0	59.3	326 43.6	13.2	16 09.0	6.3	54.3
Y 15	45 55.0	18 59.9	341 15.8	13.2	16 02.7	6.4	54.3
16	60 55.0	19 00.5	355 48.0	13.3	15 56.3	6.5	54.3
17	75 55.0	01.1	10 20.3	13.3	15 49.8	6.6	54.3
18	90 55.0	N19 01.6	24 52.6	13.3	N15 43.2	6.6	54.4
19	105 55.0	02.2	39 24.9	13.4	15 36.6	6.7	54.4
20	120 55.0	02.8	53 57.3	13.3	15 29.9	6.8	54.4
21	135 54.9	.. 03.4	68 29.6	13.4	15 23.1	6.8	54.4
22	150 54.9	04.0	83 02.0	13.4	15 16.3	6.9	54.4
23	165 54.9	04.5	97 34.4	13.4	N15 09.4	7.0	54.4
	SD 15.8	d 0.6	SD 14.7		14.7		14.8

Twilight / Sunrise / Moonrise

Lat.	Naut.	Civil	Sunrise	Moonrise 13	14	15	16
°	h m	h m	h m	h m	h m	h m	h m
N 72	☐	☐	☐	☐	☐	05 19	07 24
N 70	////	////	00 52	02 41	04 31	06 14	07 53
68	////	////	01 52	04 09	05 22	06 47	08 15
66	////	////	02 26	04 48	05 54	07 10	08 32
64	////	01 14	02 50	05 15	06 17	07 29	08 46
62	////	01 55	03 09	05 35	06 36	07 44	08 58
60	////	02 22	03 24	05 52	06 51	07 57	09 07
N 58	01 07	02 43	03 38	06 06	07 04	08 08	09 16
56	01 44	02 59	03 49	06 18	07 15	08 17	09 23
54	02 09	03 14	03 59	06 29	07 25	08 26	09 30
52	02 28	03 26	04 08	06 39	07 34	08 33	09 36
50	02 44	03 36	04 15	06 47	07 42	08 40	09 42
45	03 15	03 58	04 32	07 05	07 58	08 55	09 53
N 40	03 37	04 15	04 46	07 19	08 12	09 06	10 03
35	03 55	04 29	04 57	07 32	08 23	09 17	10 11
30	04 10	04 41	05 07	07 43	08 33	09 25	10 18
20	04 33	05 01	05 24	08 01	08 51	09 41	10 31
N 10	04 51	05 17	05 39	08 17	09 06	09 54	10 42
0	05 06	05 31	05 53	08 32	09 20	10 06	10 52
S 10	05 19	05 44	06 06	08 47	09 34	10 19	11 02
20	05 31	05 58	06 21	09 04	09 49	10 32	11 13
30	05 43	06 12	06 37	09 22	10 06	10 47	11 25
35	05 49	06 20	06 47	09 33	10 16	10 56	11 32
40	05 56	06 28	06 57	09 45	10 27	11 06	11 40
45	06 03	06 38	07 10	10 00	10 41	11 17	11 50
S 50	06 10	06 50	07 25	10 18	10 57	11 31	12 01
52	06 14	06 55	07 33	10 26	11 05	11 38	12 06
54	06 17	07 01	07 41	10 35	11 13	11 45	12 12
56	06 21	07 07	07 50	10 46	11 23	11 53	12 18
58	06 25	07 14	08 00	10 58	11 34	12 02	12 25
S 60	06 30	07 22	08 11	11 12	11 46	12 13	12 34

Sunset / Twilight / Moonset

Lat.	Sunset	Civil	Naut.	Moonset 13	14	15	16
°	h m	h m	h m	h m	h m	h m	h m
N 72	☐	☐	☐	☐	☐	02 40	02 11
N 70	23 14	////	////	02 01	01 50	01 45	01 40
68	22 05	////	////	00 33	00 59	01 11	01 17
66	21 30	////	////	24 26	00 26	00 47	00 59
64	21 05	22 45	////	24 03	00 03	00 27	00 45
62	20 46	22 01	////	23 44	24 12	00 12	00 32
60	20 30	21 33	////	23 28	23 58	24 22	00 22
N 58	20 17	21 12	22 52	23 15	23 47	24 13	00 13
56	20 05	20 55	22 12	23 04	23 37	24 05	00 05
54	19 55	20 41	21 46	22 54	23 29	23 58	24 23
52	19 46	20 28	21 26	22 45	23 21	23 51	24 18
50	19 38	20 18	21 10	22 37	23 14	23 45	24 13
45	19 21	19 55	20 39	22 20	22 58	23 33	24 04
N 40	19 08	19 38	20 16	22 06	22 46	23 22	23 56
35	18 56	19 24	19 58	21 54	22 35	23 13	23 49
30	18 46	19 12	19 43	21 44	22 26	23 05	23 42
20	18 29	18 52	19 19	21 26	22 10	22 52	23 32
N 10	18 14	18 36	19 02	21 10	21 56	22 40	23 22
0	18 00	18 22	18 47	20 55	21 42	22 28	23 14
S 10	17 46	18 08	18 34	20 41	21 29	22 17	23 05
20	17 32	17 55	18 22	20 25	21 15	22 05	22 55
30	17 15	17 41	18 09	20 07	20 58	21 51	22 44
35	17 06	17 33	18 03	19 56	20 49	21 43	22 38
40	16 55	17 24	17 57	19 44	20 38	21 33	22 31
45	16 42	17 14	17 50	19 30	20 25	21 22	22 22
S 50	16 27	17 02	17 42	19 12	20 09	21 09	22 12
52	16 19	16 57	17 38	19 04	20 02	21 03	22 07
54	16 11	16 51	17 35	18 55	19 53	20 56	22 02
56	16 03	16 45	17 31	18 44	19 44	20 48	21 56
58	15 52	16 38	17 26	18 32	19 34	20 40	21 49
S 60	15 41	16 30	17 22	18 19	19 21	20 30	21 42

SUN / MOON

Day	SUN Eqn. of Time 00ʰ	12ʰ	Mer. Pass.	MOON Mer. Pass. Upper	Lower	Age	Phase
d	m s	m s	h m	h m	h m	d	%
13	03 41	03 41	11 56	14 44	02 20	03	11
14	03 41	03 41	11 56	15 31	03 08	04	17
15	03 41	03 40	11 56	16 17	03 54	05	25

UT	ARIES GHA	VENUS −3.9 GHA	Dec	MARS +1.3 GHA	Dec	JUPITER −1.9 GHA	Dec	SATURN +0.2 GHA	Dec	STARS Name	SHA	Dec
16 00	233 52.4	167 51.3	N21 50.0	187 26.4	N17 19.9	153 59.0	N22 49.3	18 24.8	S11 18.0	Acamar	315 18.8	S40 15.1
01	248 54.8	182 50.5	50.6	202 27.0	20.4	169 00.8	49.3	33 27.4	18.0	Achernar	335 27.4	S57 10.0
02	263 57.3	197 49.7	51.2	217 27.6	21.0	184 02.7	49.4	48 30.1	17.9	Acrux	173 08.8	S63 10.7
03	278 59.7	212 48.9 ..	51.7	232 28.3 ..	21.5	199 04.6 ..	49.4	63 32.7 ..	17.9	Adhara	255 12.8	S28 59.8
04	294 02.2	227 48.1	52.3	247 28.9	22.0	214 06.5	49.4	78 35.3	17.8	Aldebaran	290 49.8	N16 32.0
05	309 04.7	242 47.4	52.9	262 29.5	22.5	229 08.3	49.5	93 38.0	17.8			
06	324 07.1	257 46.6	N21 53.5	277 30.2	N17 23.1	244 10.2	N22 49.5	108 40.6	S11 17.7	Alioth	166 20.4	N55 53.3
07	339 09.6	272 45.8	54.1	292 30.8	23.6	259 12.1	49.6	123 43.2	17.7	Alkaid	152 58.5	N49 14.9
T 08	354 12.1	287 45.0	54.7	307 31.5	24.1	274 13.9	49.6	138 45.9	17.6	Al Na'ir	27 43.9	S46 53.4
H 09	9 14.5	302 44.2 ..	55.3	322 32.1 ..	24.6	289 15.8 ..	49.7	153 48.5 ..	17.5	Alnilam	275 46.7	S 1 11.8
U 10	24 17.0	317 43.4	55.9	337 32.7	25.2	304 17.7	49.7	168 51.1	17.5	Alphard	217 56.2	S 8 43.3
R 11	39 19.5	332 42.6	56.5	352 33.4	25.7	319 19.6	49.7	183 53.8	17.4			
S 12	54 21.9	347 41.9	N21 57.1	7 34.0	N17 26.2	334 21.4	N22 49.8	198 56.4	S11 17.4	Alphecca	126 10.7	N26 40.2
D 13	69 24.4	2 41.1	57.6	22 34.6	26.7	349 23.3	49.8	213 59.0	17.3	Alpheratz	357 43.7	N29 09.7
A 14	84 26.8	17 40.3	58.2	37 35.3	27.2	4 25.2	49.9	229 01.7	17.3	Altair	62 08.1	N 8 54.3
Y 15	99 29.3	32 39.5 ..	58.8	52 35.9 ..	27.8	19 27.0 ..	49.9	244 04.3 ..	17.2	Ankaa	353 16.1	S42 13.8
16	114 31.8	47 38.7	21 59.4	67 36.6	28.3	34 28.9	50.0	259 06.9	17.2	Antares	112 26.0	S26 27.6
17	129 34.2	62 37.9	22 00.0	82 37.2	28.8	49 30.8	50.0	274 09.6	17.1			
18	144 36.7	77 37.1	N22 00.5	97 37.8	N17 29.3	64 32.7	N22 50.0	289 12.2	S11 17.1	Arcturus	145 55.5	N19 06.8
19	159 39.2	92 36.3	01.1	112 38.5	29.8	79 34.5	50.1	304 14.8	17.0	Atria	107 27.3	S69 02.9
20	174 41.6	107 35.6	01.7	127 39.1	30.4	94 36.4	50.1	319 17.5	17.0	Avior	234 18.3	S59 33.6
21	189 44.1	122 34.8 ..	02.3	142 39.7 ..	30.9	109 38.3 ..	50.2	334 20.1 ..	16.9	Bellatrix	278 32.4	N 6 21.5
22	204 46.6	137 34.0	02.8	157 40.4	31.4	124 40.1	50.2	349 22.7	16.9	Betelgeuse	271 01.7	N 7 24.4
23	219 49.0	152 33.2	03.4	172 41.0	31.9	139 42.0	50.3	4 25.4	16.8			
17 00	234 51.5	167 32.4	N22 04.0	187 41.6	N17 32.4	154 43.9	N22 50.3	19 28.0	S11 16.8	Canopus	263 56.6	S52 42.5
01	249 54.0	182 31.6	04.6	202 42.3	33.0	169 45.7	50.3	34 30.6	16.7	Capella	280 35.0	N46 00.6
02	264 56.4	197 30.8	05.1	217 42.9	33.5	184 47.6	50.4	49 33.3	16.7	Deneb	49 31.3	N45 19.6
03	279 58.9	212 30.0 ..	05.7	232 43.5 ..	34.0	199 49.5 ..	50.4	64 35.9 ..	16.6	Denebola	182 33.6	N14 29.8
04	295 01.3	227 29.2	06.3	247 44.2	34.5	214 51.3	50.5	79 38.5	16.6	Diphda	348 56.2	S17 54.7
05	310 03.8	242 28.4	06.8	262 44.8	35.0	229 53.2	50.5	94 41.2	16.5			
06	325 06.3	257 27.6	N22 07.4	277 45.5	N17 35.5	244 55.1	N22 50.6	109 43.8	S11 16.5	Dubhe	193 51.6	N61 40.9
07	340 08.7	272 26.8	08.0	292 46.1	36.1	259 57.0	50.6	124 46.4	16.4	Elnath	278 13.0	N28 37.0
08	355 11.2	287 26.0	08.5	307 46.7	36.6	274 58.8	50.6	139 49.1	16.4	Eltanin	90 45.7	N51 29.2
F 09	10 13.7	302 25.2 ..	09.1	322 47.4 ..	37.1	290 00.7 ..	50.7	154 51.7 ..	16.3	Enif	33 47.2	N 9 56.2
R 10	25 16.1	317 24.4	09.7	337 48.0	37.6	305 02.6	50.7	169 54.3	16.3	Fomalhaut	15 24.2	S29 32.9
I 11	40 18.6	332 23.7	10.2	352 48.6	38.1	320 04.4	50.8	184 56.9	16.2			
D 12	55 21.1	347 22.9	N22 10.8	7 49.3	N17 38.6	335 06.3	N22 50.8	199 59.6	S11 16.2	Gacrux	172 00.5	S57 11.6
A 13	70 23.5	2 22.1	11.3	22 49.9	39.1	350 08.2	50.8	215 02.2	16.1	Gienah	175 52.1	S17 37.2
Y 14	85 26.0	17 21.3	11.9	37 50.5	39.7	5 10.0	50.9	230 04.9	16.1	Hadar	148 47.3	S60 26.4
15	100 28.5	32 20.5 ..	12.5	52 51.2 ..	40.2	20 11.9 ..	50.9	245 07.5 ..	16.0	Hamal	328 01.1	N23 31.4
16	115 30.9	47 19.7	13.0	67 51.8	40.7	35 13.8	51.0	260 10.1	16.0	Kaus Aust.	83 43.6	S34 22.5
17	130 33.4	62 18.9	13.6	82 52.4	41.2	50 15.6	51.0	275 12.7	15.9			
18	145 35.8	77 18.1	N22 14.1	97 53.1	N17 41.7	65 17.5	N22 51.0	290 15.4	S11 15.9	Kochab	137 18.9	N74 06.1
19	160 38.3	92 17.3	14.7	112 53.7	42.2	80 19.4	51.1	305 18.0	15.8	Markab	13 38.5	N15 16.6
20	175 40.8	107 16.5	15.2	127 54.3	42.7	95 21.3	51.1	320 20.6	15.7	Menkar	314 15.4	N 4 08.4
21	190 43.2	122 15.7 ..	15.8	142 55.0 ..	43.2	110 23.1 ..	51.2	335 23.3 ..	15.7	Menkent	148 07.2	S36 26.3
22	205 45.7	137 14.9	16.3	157 55.6	43.8	125 25.0	51.2	350 25.9	15.6	Miaplacidus	221 39.8	S69 46.8
23	220 48.2	152 14.1	16.9	172 56.2	44.3	140 26.9	51.3	5 28.5	15.6			
18 00	235 50.6	167 13.3	N22 17.4	187 56.9	N17 44.8	155 28.7	N22 51.3	20 31.2	S11 15.5	Mirfak	308 40.9	N49 54.3
01	250 53.1	182 12.5	18.0	202 57.5	45.3	170 30.6	51.3	35 33.8	15.5	Nunki	75 58.1	S26 16.6
02	265 55.6	197 11.7	18.5	217 58.1	45.8	185 32.5	51.4	50 36.4	15.4	Peacock	53 19.5	S56 41.1
03	280 58.0	212 11.0 ..	19.0	232 58.8 ..	46.3	200 34.3 ..	51.4	65 39.1 ..	15.4	Pollux	243 28.0	N27 59.5
04	296 00.5	227 10.1	19.6	247 59.4	46.8	215 36.2	51.5	80 41.7	15.3	Procyon	245 00.0	N 5 11.2
05	311 02.9	242 09.3	20.1	263 00.0	47.3	230 38.1	51.5	95 44.3	15.3			
06	326 05.4	257 08.5	N22 20.7	278 00.7	N17 47.8	245 39.9	N22 51.5	110 46.9	S11 15.2	Rasalhague	96 06.2	N12 33.1
07	341 07.9	272 07.7	21.2	293 01.3	48.3	260 41.8	51.6	125 49.6	15.2	Regulus	207 43.6	N11 54.0
S 08	356 10.3	287 06.8	21.7	308 01.9	48.8	275 43.7	51.6	140 52.2	15.1	Rigel	281 12.4	S 8 11.4
A 09	11 12.8	302 06.0 ..	22.3	323 02.6 ..	49.4	290 45.5 ..	51.7	155 54.8 ..	15.1	Rigil Kent.	139 51.1	S60 53.5
T 10	26 15.3	317 05.2	22.8	338 03.2	49.9	305 47.4	51.7	170 57.5	15.0	Sabik	102 12.3	S15 44.4
U 11	41 17.7	332 04.4	23.3	353 03.8	50.4	320 49.3	51.8	186 00.1	15.0			
R 12	56 20.2	347 03.6	N22 23.9	8 04.5	N17 50.9	335 51.1	N22 51.8	201 02.7	S11 14.9	Schedar	349 40.9	N56 36.4
D 13	71 22.7	2 02.8	24.4	23 05.1	51.4	350 53.0	51.8	216 05.4	14.9	Shaula	96 21.6	S37 06.6
A 14	86 25.1	17 02.0	24.9	38 05.7	51.9	5 54.9	51.9	231 08.0	14.8	Sirius	258 34.0	S16 44.4
Y 15	101 27.6	32 01.2 ..	25.5	53 06.4 ..	52.4	20 56.7 ..	51.9	246 10.6 ..	14.8	Spica	158 31.0	S11 14.0
16	116 30.1	47 00.4	26.0	68 07.0	52.9	35 58.6	52.0	261 13.2	14.7	Suhail	222 52.6	S43 29.6
17	131 32.5	61 59.6	26.5	83 07.6	53.4	51 00.5	52.0	276 15.9	14.7			
18	146 35.0	76 58.8	N22 27.1	98 08.3	N17 53.9	66 02.3	N22 52.0	291 18.5	S11 14.6	Vega	80 38.7	N38 47.7
19	161 37.4	91 58.0	27.6	113 08.9	54.4	81 04.2	52.1	306 21.1	14.6	Zuben'ubi	137 05.1	S16 05.9
20	176 39.9	106 57.2	28.1	128 09.5	54.9	96 06.1	52.1	321 23.8	14.5		SHA	Mer.Pass.
21	191 42.4	121 56.4 ..	28.6	143 10.2 ..	55.4	111 07.9 ..	52.2	336 26.4 ..	14.5	Venus	292 40.9	12 51
22	206 44.8	136 55.5	29.2	158 10.8	55.9	126 09.8	52.2	351 29.0	14.4	Mars	312 50.1	11 29
23	221 47.3	151 54.7	29.7	173 11.4	56.4	141 11.7	52.2	6 31.7	14.4	Jupiter	279 52.4	13 39
Mer.Pass. 8 19.2		v −0.8	d 0.6	v 0.6	d 0.5	v 1.9	d 0.0	v 2.6	d 0.1	Saturn	144 36.5	22 38

UT	SUN		MOON					Lat.	Twilight		Sunrise	Moonrise			
									Naut.	Civil		16	17	18	19
	GHA	Dec	GHA	v	Dec	d	HP								
d h	° ′	° ′	° ′	′	° ′	′	′	°	h m	h m	h m	h m	h m	h m	h m
16 00	180 54.9	N19 05.1	112 06.8	13.4	N15 02.4	7.1	54.4	N 72	▭	▭	▭	07 24	09 14	10 59	12 45
01	195 54.9	05.7	126 39.2	13.5	14 55.3	7.1	54.5	N 70	▭	▭	▭	07 53	09 31	11 09	12 48
02	210 54.9	06.3	141 11.7	13.4	14 48.2	7.2	54.5	68	////	////	01 35	08 15	09 45	11 17	12 50
03	225 54.9 ..	06.9	155 44.1	13.5	14 41.0	7.2	54.5	66	////	00 51	02 14	08 32	09 57	11 23	12 51
04	240 54.9	07.4	170 16.6	13.5	14 33.8	7.4	54.5	64	////	01 42	02 40	08 46	10 06	11 28	12 53
05	255 54.8	08.0	184 49.1	13.5	14 26.4	7.4	54.5	62	////	02 12	03 01	08 58	10 14	11 33	12 54
06	270 54.8	N19 08.6	199 21.6	13.6	N14 19.0	7.4	54.5	60	////	02 12	03 18	09 07	10 21	11 37	12 55
07	285 54.8	09.1	213 54.2	13.5	14 11.6	7.5	54.5	N 58	00 46	02 35	03 31	09 16	10 27	11 40	12 56
T 08	300 54.8	09.7	228 26.7	13.6	14 04.1	7.6	54.5	56	01 32	02 53	03 43	09 23	10 32	11 43	12 57
H 09	315 54.8 ..	10.3	242 59.3	13.6	13 56.5	7.7	54.6	54	02 00	03 08	03 54	09 30	10 37	11 46	12 57
U 10	330 54.8	10.9	257 31.9	13.6	13 48.8	7.7	54.6	52	02 21	03 20	04 03	09 36	10 41	11 49	12 58
R 11	345 54.8	11.4	272 04.5	13.6	13 41.1	7.8	54.6	50	02 38	03 32	04 11	09 42	10 45	11 51	12 59
S 12	0 54.7	N19 12.0	286 37.1	13.6	N13 33.3	7.8	54.6	45	03 10	03 54	04 29	09 53	10 54	11 56	13 00
D 13	15 54.7	12.6	301 09.7	13.7	13 25.5	7.9	54.6	N 40	03 34	04 12	04 43	10 03	11 01	12 00	13 01
A 14	30 54.7	13.2	315 42.4	13.7	13 17.6	8.0	54.7	35	03 52	04 27	04 55	10 11	11 07	12 04	13 02
Y 15	45 54.7 ..	13.7	330 15.1	13.6	13 09.6	8.0	54.7	30	04 08	04 39	05 05	10 18	11 12	12 07	13 03
16	60 54.7	14.3	344 47.7	13.7	13 01.6	8.1	54.7	20	04 31	04 59	05 23	10 31	11 21	12 12	13 05
17	75 54.7	14.9	359 20.4	13.7	12 53.5	8.2	54.7	N 10	04 50	05 16	05 39	10 42	11 29	12 17	13 06
18	90 54.6	N19 15.4	13 53.1	13.8	N12 45.3	8.2	54.7	0	05 05	05 31	05 53	10 52	11 37	12 22	13 07
19	105 54.6	16.0	28 25.8	13.8	12 37.1	8.3	54.8	S 10	05 19	05 45	06 07	11 02	11 44	12 26	13 08
20	120 54.6	16.6	42 58.6	13.7	12 28.8	8.3	54.8	20	05 32	05 59	06 22	11 13	11 52	12 31	13 10
21	135 54.6 ..	17.1	57 31.3	13.7	12 20.5	8.4	54.8	30	05 45	06 14	06 39	11 25	12 01	12 36	13 11
22	150 54.6	17.7	72 04.0	13.8	12 12.1	8.5	54.8	35	05 51	06 22	06 49	11 32	12 07	12 40	13 12
23	165 54.6	18.3	86 36.8	13.8	12 03.6	8.5	54.8	40	05 58	06 31	07 00	11 40	12 12	12 43	13 13
17 00	180 54.5	N19 18.8	101 09.6	13.8	N11 55.1	8.6	54.9	45	06 06	06 41	07 13	11 50	12 19	12 47	13 14
01	195 54.5	19.4	115 42.3	13.8	11 46.5	8.6	54.9	S 50	06 14	06 54	07 30	12 01	12 27	12 52	13 16
02	210 54.5	19.9	130 15.1	13.8	11 37.9	8.7	54.9	52	06 18	06 59	07 37	12 06	12 31	12 54	13 17
03	225 54.5 ..	20.5	144 47.9	13.8	11 29.2	8.7	54.9	54	06 21	07 05	07 45	12 12	12 35	12 57	13 17
04	240 54.5	21.1	159 20.7	13.8	11 20.5	8.8	55.0	56	06 26	07 12	07 55	12 18	12 40	12 59	13 18
05	255 54.4	21.6	173 53.5	13.9	11 11.7	8.9	55.0	58	06 30	07 19	08 06	12 25	12 45	13 02	13 19
06	270 54.4	N19 22.2	188 26.4	13.8	N11 02.8	8.9	55.0	S 60	06 35	07 28	08 18	12 34	12 51	13 06	13 20

UT	SUN		MOON					Lat.	Sunset	Twilight		Moonset			
										Civil	Naut.	16	17	18	19
d h	° ′	° ′	° ′	′	° ′	′	′	°	h m	h m	h m	h m	h m	h m	h m
07	285 54.4	22.8	202 59.2	13.8	10 53.9	9.0	55.0	N 72	▭	▭	▭	02 11	01 55	01 42	01 32
08	300 54.4	23.3	217 32.0	13.8	10 44.9	9.0	55.0	N 70	▭	▭	▭	01 40	01 35	01 31	01 27
F 09	315 54.4 ..	23.9	232 04.8	13.9	10 35.9	9.1	55.1	68	22 23	////	////	01 17	01 20	01 22	01 22
R 10	330 54.4	24.4	246 37.7	13.8	10 26.8	9.1	55.1	66	21 42	////	////	00 59	01 08	01 14	01 19
I 11	345 54.3	25.0	261 10.5	13.9	10 17.7	9.2	55.1	64	21 15	23 11	////	00 45	00 57	01 07	01 16
D 12	0 54.3	N19 25.5	275 43.4	13.8	N10 08.5	9.2	55.1	62	20 54	22 15	////	00 32	00 48	01 02	01 13
A 13	15 54.3	26.1	290 16.2	13.9	9 59.3	9.3	55.2	60	20 37	21 43	////	00 22	00 41	00 57	01 11
Y 14	30 54.3	26.7	304 49.1	13.8	9 50.0	9.3	55.2	N 58	20 23	21 20	23 15	00 13	00 34	00 52	01 09
15	45 54.2 ..	27.2	319 21.9	13.9	9 40.7	9.4	55.2	56	20 11	21 02	22 24	00 05	00 28	00 48	01 07
16	60 54.2	27.8	333 54.8	13.8	9 31.3	9.4	55.2	54	20 00	20 47	21 55	24 23	00 23	00 45	01 05
17	75 54.2	28.3	348 27.6	13.9	9 21.9	9.5	55.3	52	19 51	20 34	21 34	24 18	00 18	00 42	01 04
18	90 54.2	N19 28.9	3 00.5	13.8	N 9 12.4	9.6	55.3	50	19 42	20 23	21 16	24 13	00 13	00 39	01 02
19	105 54.2	29.4	17 33.3	13.9	9 02.8	9.5	55.3	45	19 25	19 59	20 43	24 04	00 04	00 32	00 59
20	120 54.1	30.0	32 06.2	13.8	8 53.3	9.7	55.3	N 40	19 10	19 41	20 20	23 56	24 27	00 27	00 57
21	135 54.1 ..	30.5	46 39.0	13.9	8 43.6	9.7	55.4	35	18 58	19 27	20 01	23 49	24 22	00 22	00 55
22	150 54.1	31.1	61 11.9	13.8	8 33.9	9.7	55.4	30	18 48	19 14	19 46	23 42	24 18	00 18	00 53
23	165 54.1	31.6	75 44.7	13.9	8 24.2	9.7	55.4	20	18 30	18 54	19 22	23 32	24 11	00 11	00 49
18 00	180 54.0	N19 32.2	90 17.6	13.8	N 8 14.5	9.9	55.4	N 10	18 14	18 37	19 03	23 22	24 04	00 04	00 46
01	195 54.0	32.7	104 50.4	13.8	8 04.6	9.8	55.5	0	18 00	18 22	18 47	23 14	23 58	24 43	00 43
02	210 54.0	33.3	119 23.2	13.9	7 54.8	9.9	55.5	S 10	17 46	18 08	18 34	23 05	23 52	24 40	00 40
03	225 54.0 ..	33.8	133 56.1	13.8	7 44.9	10.0	55.5	20	17 31	17 54	18 21	22 55	23 46	24 37	00 37
04	240 53.9	34.4	148 28.9	13.8	7 34.9	10.0	55.6	30	17 13	17 39	18 08	22 44	23 38	24 34	00 34
05	255 53.9	34.9	163 01.7	13.8	7 24.9	10.0	55.6	35	17 03	17 31	18 01	22 38	23 34	24 32	00 32
06	270 53.9	N19 35.5	177 34.5	13.8	N 7 14.9	10.1	55.6	40	16 52	17 22	17 54	22 31	23 29	24 29	00 29
S 07	285 53.9	36.0	192 07.3	13.7	7 04.8	10.1	55.6	45	16 39	17 11	17 47	22 22	23 23	24 26	00 26
A 08	300 53.8	36.6	206 40.0	13.8	6 54.7	10.2	55.7	S 50	16 23	16 59	17 38	22 12	23 17	24 23	00 23
T 09	315 53.8 ..	37.1	221 12.8	13.8	6 44.5	10.2	55.7	52	16 15	16 53	17 35	22 07	23 13	24 22	00 22
U 10	330 53.8	37.7	235 45.6	13.7	6 34.3	10.2	55.7	54	16 07	16 47	17 31	22 02	23 10	24 20	00 20
R 11	345 53.8	38.2	250 18.3	13.8	6 24.1	10.3	55.8	56	15 57	16 40	17 27	21 56	23 06	24 18	00 18
D 12	0 53.7	N19 38.7	264 51.1	13.7	N 6 13.8	10.4	55.8	58	15 47	16 33	17 22	21 49	23 02	24 16	00 16
A 13	15 53.7	39.3	279 23.8	13.7	6 03.4	10.3	55.8	S 60	15 34	16 24	17 17	21 42	22 57	24 14	00 14
Y 14	30 53.7	39.8	293 56.5	13.7	5 53.1	10.4	55.9								
15	45 53.7 ..	40.4	308 29.2	13.7	5 42.7	10.5	55.9								
16	60 53.6	40.9	323 01.9	13.6	5 32.2	10.4	55.9								
17	75 53.6	41.5	337 34.5	13.7	5 21.8	10.5	56.0								
18	90 53.6	N19 42.0	352 07.2	13.6	N 5 11.3	10.6	56.0				SUN			MOON	
19	105 53.5	42.5	6 39.8	13.6	5 00.7	10.6	56.0	Day	Eqn. of Time		Mer.	Mer. Pass.		Age	Phase
20	120 53.5	43.1	21 12.4	13.6	4 50.1	10.6	56.1		00ʰ	12ʰ	Pass.	Upper	Lower		
21	135 53.5 ..	43.6	35 45.0	13.5	4 39.5	10.6	56.1	d	m s	m s	h m	h m	h m	d	%
22	150 53.5	44.2	50 17.5	13.6	4 28.9	10.7	56.1	16	03 40	03 39	11 56	17 03	04 40	06	34
23	165 53.4	44.7	64 50.1	13.5	N 4 18.2	10.7	56.1	17	03 38	03 37	11 56	17 48	05 25	07	43
	SD 15.8	d 0.6	SD 14.9		15.0		15.2	18	03 36	03 35	11 56	18 33	06 10	08	53

UT	ARIES GHA	VENUS −3.9 GHA	Dec	MARS +1.3 GHA	Dec	JUPITER −1.9 GHA	Dec	SATURN +0.3 GHA	Dec	STARS Name	SHA	Dec
d h	° ′	° ′	° ′	° ′	° ′	° ′	° ′	° ′	° ′		° ′	° ′
19 00	236 49.8	166 53.9 N22 30.2		188 12.1 N17 56.9		156 13.5 N22 52.3		21 34.3 S11 14.3		Acamar	315 18.8	S40 15.1
01	251 52.2	181 53.1	30.7	203 12.7	57.4	171 15.4	52.3	36 36.9	14.3	Achernar	335 27.4	S57 10.0
02	266 54.7	196 52.3	31.2	218 13.3	57.9	186 17.3	52.4	51 39.5	14.2	Acrux	173 08.8	S63 10.7
03	281 57.2	211 51.5 . .	31.8	233 14.0 . .	58.4	201 19.1 . .	52.4	66 42.2 . .	14.2	Adhara	255 12.8	S28 59.8
04	296 59.6	226 50.7	32.3	248 14.6	58.9	216 21.0	52.4	81 44.8	14.1	Aldebaran	290 49.8	N16 32.0
05	312 02.1	241 49.9	32.8	263 15.2	59.4	231 22.9	52.5	96 47.4	14.1			
06	327 04.6	256 49.1 N22 33.3		278 15.8 N17 59.9		246 24.7 N22 52.5		111 50.1 S11 14.0		Alioth	166 20.4	N55 53.4
07	342 07.0	271 48.2	33.8	293 16.5	18 00.4	261 26.6	52.6	126 52.7	14.0	Alkaid	152 58.6	N49 14.9
08	357 09.5	286 47.4	34.3	308 17.1	00.9	276 28.5	52.6	141 55.3	13.9	Al Na'ir	27 43.8	S46 53.4
S 09	12 11.9	301 46.6 . .	34.8	323 17.7 . .	01.4	291 30.3 . .	52.6	156 57.9 . .	13.9	Alnilam	275 46.7	S 1 11.8
U 10	27 14.4	316 45.8	35.3	338 18.4	01.9	306 32.2	52.7	172 00.6	13.8	Alphard	217 56.2	S 8 43.3
N 11	42 16.9	331 45.0	35.8	353 19.0	02.4	321 34.1	52.7	187 03.2	13.8			
D 12	57 19.3	346 44.2 N22 36.4		8 19.6 N18 02.9		336 35.9 N22 52.8		202 05.8 S11 13.7		Alphecca	126 10.7	N26 40.2
A 13	72 21.8	1 43.4	36.9	23 20.3	03.4	351 37.8	52.8	217 08.5	13.7	Alpheratz	357 43.7	N29 09.7
Y 14	87 24.3	16 42.5	37.4	38 20.9	03.9	6 39.7	52.8	232 11.1	13.6	Altair	62 08.1	N 8 54.3
15	102 26.7	31 41.7 . .	37.9	53 21.5 . .	04.4	21 41.5 . .	52.9	247 13.7 . .	13.6	Ankaa	353 16.0	S42 13.8
16	117 29.2	46 40.9	38.4	68 22.2	04.9	36 43.4	52.9	262 16.3	13.5	Antares	112 25.9	S26 27.6
17	132 31.7	61 40.1	38.9	83 22.8	05.4	51 45.3	53.0	277 19.0	13.5			
18	147 34.1	76 39.3 N22 39.4		98 23.4 N18 05.9		66 47.1 N22 53.0		292 21.6 S11 13.4		Arcturus	145 55.5	N19 06.8
19	162 36.6	91 38.5	39.9	113 24.0	06.4	81 49.0	53.0	307 24.2	13.4	Atria	107 27.3	S69 02.9
20	177 39.0	106 37.6	40.4	128 24.7	06.9	96 50.8	53.1	322 26.8	13.3	Avior	234 18.3	S59 33.6
21	192 41.5	121 36.8 . .	40.9	143 25.3 . .	07.4	111 52.7 . .	53.1	337 29.5 . .	13.3	Bellatrix	278 32.4	N 6 21.5
22	207 44.0	136 36.0	41.4	158 25.9	07.9	126 54.6	53.2	352 32.1	13.2	Betelgeuse	271 01.7	N 7 24.4
23	222 46.4	151 35.2	41.9	173 26.6	08.4	141 56.4	53.2	7 34.7	13.2			
20 00	237 48.9	166 34.4 N22 42.3		188 27.2 N18 08.9		156 58.3 N22 53.2		22 37.4 S11 13.1		Canopus	263 56.6	S52 42.5
01	252 51.4	181 33.6	42.8	203 27.8	09.4	172 00.2	53.3	37 40.0	13.1	Capella	280 35.0	N46 00.5
02	267 53.8	196 32.7	43.3	218 28.5	09.9	187 02.0	53.3	52 42.6	13.1	Deneb	49 31.3	N45 19.6
03	282 56.3	211 31.9 . .	43.8	233 29.1 . .	10.4	202 03.9 . .	53.4	67 45.2 . .	13.0	Denebola	182 33.6	N14 29.8
04	297 58.8	226 31.1	44.3	248 29.7	10.9	217 05.8	53.4	82 47.9	13.0	Diphda	348 56.2	S17 54.7
05	313 01.2	241 30.3	44.8	263 30.4	11.4	232 07.6	53.4	97 50.5	12.9			
06	328 03.7	256 29.5 N22 45.3		278 31.0 N18 11.9		247 09.5 N22 53.5		112 53.1 S11 12.9		Dubhe	193 51.7	N61 40.9
07	343 06.2	271 28.6	45.8	293 31.6	12.4	262 11.4	53.5	127 55.7	12.8	Elnath	278 13.0	N28 37.0
08	358 08.6	286 27.8	46.3	308 32.2	12.9	277 13.2	53.6	142 58.4	12.8	Eltanin	90 45.7	N51 29.2
M 09	13 11.1	301 27.0 . .	46.7	323 32.9 . .	13.4	292 15.1 . .	53.6	158 01.0 . .	12.7	Enif	33 47.1	N 9 56.2
O 10	28 13.5	316 26.2	47.2	338 33.5	13.8	307 17.0	53.6	173 03.6	12.7	Fomalhaut	15 24.1	S29 32.9
N 11	43 16.0	331 25.3	47.7	353 34.1	14.3	322 18.8	53.7	188 06.2	12.6			
D 12	58 18.5	346 24.5 N22 48.2		8 34.8 N18 14.8		337 20.7 N22 53.7		203 08.9 S11 12.6		Gacrux	172 00.5	S57 11.6
A 13	73 20.9	1 23.7	48.7	23 35.4	15.3	352 22.5	53.8	218 11.5	12.5	Gienah	175 52.2	S17 37.2
Y 14	88 23.4	16 22.9	49.1	38 36.0	15.8	7 24.4	53.8	233 14.1	12.5	Hadar	148 47.3	S60 26.4
15	103 25.9	31 22.0 . .	49.6	53 36.6 . .	16.3	22 26.3 . .	53.8	248 16.8 . .	12.4	Hamal	328 01.1	N23 31.4
16	118 28.3	46 21.2	50.1	68 37.3	16.8	37 28.1	53.9	263 19.4	12.4	Kaus Aust.	83 43.6	S34 22.5
17	133 30.8	61 20.4	50.6	83 37.9	17.3	52 30.0	53.9	278 22.0	12.3			
18	148 33.3	76 19.6 N22 51.0		98 38.5 N18 17.8		67 31.9 N22 54.0		293 24.6 S11 12.3		Kochab	137 19.0	N74 06.1
19	163 35.7	91 18.7	51.5	113 39.2	18.3	82 33.7	54.0	308 27.3	12.2	Markab	13 38.5	N15 16.6
20	178 38.2	106 17.9	52.0	128 39.8	18.8	97 35.6	54.0	323 29.9	12.2	Menkar	314 15.4	N 4 08.4
21	193 40.6	121 17.1 . .	52.5	143 40.4 . .	19.2	112 37.4 . .	54.1	338 32.5 . .	12.1	Menkent	148 07.3	S36 26.3
22	208 43.1	136 16.3	52.9	158 41.0	19.7	127 39.3	54.1	353 35.1	12.1	Miaplacidus	221 39.8	S69 46.8
23	223 45.6	151 15.4	53.4	173 41.7	20.2	142 41.2	54.1	8 37.8	12.0			
21 00	238 48.0	166 14.6 N22 53.9		188 42.3 N18 20.7		157 43.0 N22 54.2		23 40.4 S11 12.0		Mirfak	308 40.9	N49 54.3
01	253 50.5	181 13.8	54.3	203 42.9	21.2	172 44.9	54.2	38 43.0	11.9	Nunki	75 58.1	S26 16.6
02	268 53.0	196 13.0	54.8	218 43.6	21.7	187 46.8	54.3	53 45.6	11.9	Peacock	53 19.1	S56 41.1
03	283 55.4	211 12.1 . .	55.2	233 44.2 . .	22.2	202 48.6 . .	54.3	68 48.3 . .	11.8	Pollux	243 28.0	N27 59.5
04	298 57.9	226 11.3	55.7	248 44.8	22.7	217 50.5	54.3	83 50.9	11.8	Procyon	245 00.0	N 5 11.2
05	314 00.4	241 10.5	56.2	263 45.4	23.1	232 52.4	54.4	98 53.5	11.7			
06	329 02.8	256 09.6 N22 56.6		278 46.1 N18 23.6		247 54.2 N22 54.4		113 56.1 S11 11.7		Rasalhague	96 06.2	N12 33.1
07	344 05.3	271 08.8	57.1	293 46.7	24.1	262 56.1	54.5	128 58.8	11.6	Regulus	207 43.6	N11 54.0
08	359 07.8	286 08.0	57.5	308 47.3	24.6	277 57.9	54.5	144 01.4	11.6	Rigel	281 12.4	S 8 11.4
T 09	14 10.2	301 07.2 . .	58.0	323 48.0 . .	25.1	292 59.8 . .	54.5	159 04.0 . .	11.5	Rigil Kent.	139 51.1	S60 53.5
U 10	29 12.7	316 06.3	58.5	338 48.6	25.6	308 01.7	54.6	174 06.6	11.5	Sabik	102 12.3	S15 44.4
E 11	44 15.1	331 05.5	58.9	353 49.2	26.1	323 03.5	54.6	189 09.3	11.4			
S 12	59 17.6	346 04.7 N22 59.4		8 49.8 N18 26.5		338 05.4 N22 54.7		204 11.9 S11 11.4		Schedar	349 40.9	N56 36.4
D 13	74 20.1	1 03.8	22 59.8	23 50.5	27.0	353 07.3	54.7	219 14.5	11.4	Shaula	96 21.6	S37 06.6
A 14	89 22.5	16 03.0	23 00.3	38 51.1	27.5	8 09.1	54.7	234 17.1	11.3	Sirius	258 34.0	S16 44.4
Y 15	104 25.0	31 02.2 . .	00.7	53 51.7 . .	28.0	23 11.0 . .	54.8	249 19.7 . .	11.3	Spica	158 31.0	S11 14.0
16	119 27.5	46 01.3	01.2	68 52.3	28.5	38 12.8	54.8	264 22.4	11.2	Suhail	222 52.6	S43 29.6
17	134 29.9	61 00.5	01.6	83 53.0	29.0	53 14.7	54.8	279 25.0	11.2			
18	149 32.4	75 59.7 N23 02.1		98 53.6 N18 29.4		68 16.6 N22 54.9		294 27.6 S11 11.1		Vega	80 38.7	N38 47.7
19	164 34.9	90 58.8	02.5	113 54.2	29.9	83 18.4	54.9	309 30.2	11.1	Zuben'ubi	137 05.1	S16 05.9
20	179 37.3	105 58.0	02.9	128 54.8	30.4	98 20.3	55.0	324 32.9	11.0		SHA	Mer.Pass.
21	194 39.8	120 57.2 . .	03.4	143 55.5 . .	30.9	113 22.1 . .	55.0	339 35.5 . .	11.0		° ′	h m
22	209 42.3	135 56.3	03.8	158 56.1	31.4	128 24.0	55.0	354 38.1	10.9	Venus	288 45.5	12 54
23	224 44.7	150 55.5	04.3	173 56.7	31.8	143 25.9	55.1	9 40.7	10.9	Mars	310 38.3	11 26
	h m									Jupiter	279 09.4	13 30
Mer.Pass.	8 07.4	v −0.8	d 0.5	v 0.6	d 0.5	v 1.9	d 0.0	v 2.6	d 0.0	Saturn	144 48.5	22 26

UT	SUN GHA	SUN Dec	MOON GHA	v	Dec	d	HP
d h	° ′	° ′	° ′	′	° ′	′	′
19 00	180 53.4	N19 45.2	79 22.6	13.5	N 4 07.5	10.8	56.2
01	195 53.4	45.8	93 55.1	13.5	3 56.7	10.8	56.2
02	210 53.3	46.3	108 27.6	13.4	3 45.9	10.8	56.2
03	225 53.3	.. 46.8	123 00.0	13.5	3 35.1	10.8	56.3
04	240 53.3	47.4	137 32.5	13.4	3 24.3	10.9	56.3
05	255 53.3	47.9	152 04.9	13.3	3 13.4	10.9	56.3
06	270 53.2	N19 48.4	166 37.2	13.4	N 3 02.5	10.9	56.4
07	285 53.2	49.0	181 09.6	13.3	2 51.6	11.0	56.4
S 08	300 53.2	49.5	195 41.9	13.3	2 40.6	10.9	56.5
U 09	315 53.1	.. 50.0	210 14.2	13.2	2 29.7	11.0	56.5
N 10	330 53.1	50.6	224 46.4	13.3	2 18.7	11.1	56.5
D 11	345 53.1	51.1	239 18.7	13.2	2 07.6	11.0	56.6
A 12	0 53.0	N19 51.6	253 50.9	13.1	N 1 56.6	11.1	56.6
Y 13	15 53.0	52.1	268 23.0	13.1	1 45.5	11.1	56.6
14	30 53.0	52.7	282 55.1	13.1	1 34.4	11.1	56.7
15	45 52.9	.. 53.2	297 27.2	13.1	1 23.3	11.2	56.7
16	60 52.9	53.7	311 59.3	13.0	1 12.1	11.1	56.7
17	75 52.9	54.3	326 31.3	13.0	1 01.0	11.2	56.8
18	90 52.8	N19 54.8	341 03.3	12.9	N 0 49.8	11.2	56.8
19	105 52.8	55.3	355 35.2	13.0	0 38.6	11.2	56.9
20	120 52.8	55.8	10 07.2	12.8	0 27.4	11.3	56.9
21	135 52.7	.. 56.4	24 39.0	12.8	0 16.1	11.2	56.9
22	150 52.7	56.9	39 10.8	12.8	N 0 04.9	11.3	57.0
23	165 52.7	57.4	53 42.6	12.8	S 0 06.4	11.3	57.0
20 00	180 52.6	N19 57.9	68 14.4	12.7	S 0 17.7	11.3	57.0
01	195 52.6	58.4	82 46.1	12.6	0 29.0	11.3	57.1
02	210 52.6	59.0	97 17.7	12.6	0 40.3	11.3	57.1
03	225 52.5	19 59.5	111 49.3	12.6	0 51.6	11.3	57.2
04	240 52.5	20 00.0	126 20.9	12.5	1 02.9	11.4	57.2
05	255 52.5	00.5	140 52.4	12.5	1 14.3	11.3	57.2
06	270 52.4	N20 01.0	155 23.9	12.4	S 1 25.6	11.4	57.3
07	285 52.4	01.6	169 55.3	12.4	1 37.0	11.4	57.3
M 08	300 52.4	02.1	184 26.7	12.3	1 48.4	11.4	57.3
O 09	315 52.3	.. 02.6	198 58.0	12.3	1 59.8	11.3	57.4
N 10	330 52.3	03.1	213 29.3	12.2	2 11.1	11.4	57.4
N 11	345 52.2	03.6	228 00.5	12.2	2 22.5	11.4	57.5
D 12	0 52.2	N20 04.1	242 31.7	12.1	S 2 33.9	11.4	57.5
A 13	15 52.2	04.7	257 02.8	12.0	2 45.3	11.4	57.5
Y 14	30 52.1	05.2	271 33.8	12.0	2 56.7	11.4	57.6
15	45 52.1	.. 05.7	286 04.8	12.0	3 08.1	11.4	57.6
16	60 52.1	06.2	300 35.8	11.9	3 19.5	11.4	57.7
17	75 52.0	06.7	315 06.7	11.8	3 30.9	11.4	57.7
18	90 52.0	N20 07.2	329 37.5	11.8	S 3 42.3	11.4	57.7
19	105 51.9	07.7	344 08.3	11.7	3 53.7	11.4	57.8
20	120 51.9	08.2	358 39.0	11.6	4 05.1	11.4	57.8
21	135 51.9	.. 08.8	13 09.6	11.6	4 16.5	11.4	57.9
22	150 51.8	09.3	27 40.2	11.5	4 27.9	11.4	57.9
23	165 51.8	09.8	42 10.7	11.5	4 39.3	11.4	57.9
21 00	180 51.7	N20 10.3	56 41.2	11.4	S 4 50.7	11.3	58.0
01	195 51.7	10.8	71 11.6	11.3	5 02.0	11.4	58.0
02	210 51.7	11.3	85 41.9	11.3	5 13.4	11.3	58.1
03	225 51.6	.. 11.8	100 12.2	11.2	5 24.7	11.4	58.1
04	240 51.6	12.3	114 42.4	11.1	5 36.1	11.3	58.1
05	255 51.5	12.8	129 12.5	11.1	5 47.4	11.3	58.2
06	270 51.5	N20 13.3	143 42.6	11.0	S 5 58.7	11.3	58.2
07	285 51.5	13.8	158 12.6	10.9	6 10.0	11.3	58.3
T 08	300 51.4	14.3	172 42.5	10.9	6 21.3	11.2	58.3
U 09	315 51.4	.. 14.8	187 12.4	10.8	6 32.5	11.2	58.3
E 10	330 51.3	15.3	201 42.2	10.7	6 43.7	11.3	58.4
S 11	345 51.3	15.8	216 11.9	10.6	6 55.0	11.2	58.4
D 12	0 51.2	N20 16.3	230 41.5	10.6	S 7 06.2	11.1	58.4
A 13	15 51.2	16.8	245 11.1	10.5	7 17.3	11.3	58.5
Y 14	30 51.2	17.3	259 40.6	10.4	7 28.5	11.1	58.5
15	45 51.1	.. 17.8	274 10.0	10.3	7 39.6	11.1	58.6
16	60 51.1	18.3	288 39.3	10.3	7 50.7	11.1	58.6
17	75 51.0	18.8	303 08.6	10.2	8 01.8	11.0	58.6
18	90 51.0	N20 19.3	317 37.8	10.1	S 8 12.8	11.0	58.7
19	105 50.9	19.8	332 06.9	10.0	8 23.8	11.0	58.7
20	120 50.9	20.3	346 35.9	10.0	8 34.8	10.9	58.8
21	135 50.8	.. 20.8	1 04.9	9.8	8 45.7	11.0	58.8
22	150 50.8	21.3	15 33.7	9.8	8 56.7	10.8	58.8
23	165 50.8	21.8	30 02.5	9.7	S 9 07.5	10.9	58.9
	SD 15.8	d 0.5	SD 15.4		15.7		15.9

Twilight / Sunrise / Moonrise

Lat.	Twilight Naut.	Twilight Civil	Sunrise	Moonrise 19	20	21	22
°	h m	h m	h m	h m	h m	h m	h m
N 72	▭	▭	▭	12 45	14 34	16 30	18 37
N 70	▭	▭	▭	12 48	14 30	16 17	18 13
68	////	////	01 16	12 50	14 26	16 07	17 54
66	////	////	02 02	12 51	14 23	15 59	17 40
64	////	00 09	02 31	12 53	14 20	15 52	17 27
62	////	01 28	02 53	12 54	14 18	15 46	17 17
60	////	02 03	03 11	12 55	14 16	15 41	17 09
N 58	00 07	02 27	03 26	12 56	14 14	15 36	17 01
56	01 20	02 46	03 38	12 57	14 13	15 32	16 54
54	01 51	03 02	03 49	12 57	14 11	15 28	16 48
52	02 14	03 15	03 59	12 58	14 10	15 25	16 43
50	02 32	03 27	04 08	12 59	14 09	15 22	16 38
45	03 06	03 51	04 26	13 00	14 07	15 16	16 28
N 40	03 31	04 09	04 40	13 01	14 05	15 10	16 19
35	03 50	04 25	04 53	13 02	14 03	15 06	16 12
30	04 05	04 37	05 04	13 03	14 01	15 02	16 05
20	04 30	04 58	05 22	13 05	13 59	14 55	15 54
N 10	04 49	05 16	05 38	13 06	13 56	14 49	15 45
0	05 05	05 31	05 53	13 07	13 54	14 43	15 36
S 10	05 20	05 45	06 08	13 08	13 52	14 38	15 27
20	05 33	06 00	06 23	13 10	13 50	14 32	15 17
30	05 46	06 15	06 41	13 11	13 47	14 25	15 07
35	05 53	06 24	06 51	13 12	13 46	14 21	15 01
40	06 00	06 33	07 03	13 13	13 44	14 17	14 54
45	06 08	06 44	07 17	13 14	13 42	14 12	14 46
S 50	06 17	06 57	07 33	13 16	13 40	14 06	14 36
52	06 21	07 03	07 41	13 17	13 39	14 04	14 32
54	06 25	07 09	07 50	13 17	13 38	14 01	14 27
56	06 30	07 16	08 00	13 18	13 37	13 57	14 21
58	06 35	07 24	08 11	13 19	13 36	13 54	14 15
S 60	06 40	07 33	08 24	13 20	13 34	13 50	14 09

Sunset / Twilight / Moonset

Lat.	Sunset	Twilight Civil	Twilight Naut.	Moonset 19	20	21	22
°	h m	h m	h m	h m	h m	h m	h m
N 72	▭	▭	▭	01 32	01 21	01 10	00 58
N 70	▭	▭	▭	01 27	01 22	01 17	01 13
68	22 44	////	////	01 22	01 23	01 23	01 25
66	21 55	////	////	01 19	01 23	01 28	01 34
64	21 24	////	////	01 16	01 24	01 33	01 43
62	21 02	22 29	////	01 13	01 24	01 36	01 50
60	20 44	21 53	////	01 11	01 25	01 39	01 56
N 58	20 29	21 28	////	01 09	01 25	01 42	02 02
56	20 16	21 09	22 37	01 07	01 25	01 45	02 07
54	20 05	20 52	22 04	01 05	01 26	01 47	02 11
52	19 55	20 39	21 41	01 04	01 26	01 49	02 15
50	19 46	20 27	21 22	01 02	01 26	01 51	02 19
45	19 28	20 03	20 48	00 59	01 27	01 55	02 27
N 40	19 13	19 44	20 23	00 57	01 27	01 59	02 33
35	19 01	19 29	20 04	00 55	01 28	02 02	02 39
30	18 50	19 16	19 48	00 53	01 28	02 05	02 44
20	18 31	18 55	19 23	00 49	01 28	02 09	02 53
N 10	18 15	18 37	19 04	00 46	01 29	02 13	03 01
0	18 00	18 22	18 48	00 43	01 29	02 17	03 08
S 10	17 45	18 08	18 33	00 40	01 30	02 21	03 15
20	17 30	17 53	18 20	00 37	01 30	02 25	03 23
30	17 12	17 38	18 07	00 34	01 31	02 30	03 32
35	17 02	17 29	18 00	00 32	01 31	02 33	03 37
40	16 51	17 19	17 52	00 29	01 31	02 36	03 43
45	16 36	17 08	17 44	00 26	01 32	02 39	03 50
S 50	16 19	16 55	17 35	00 23	01 32	02 43	03 58
52	16 11	16 50	17 31	00 22	01 32	02 45	04 02
54	16 02	16 43	17 27	00 20	01 32	02 48	04 06
56	15 53	16 36	17 23	00 18	01 33	02 50	04 11
58	15 41	16 28	17 18	00 16	01 33	02 53	04 16
S 60	15 28	16 19	17 12	00 14	01 33	02 56	04 22

Day	SUN Eqn. of Time 00h	12h	Mer. Pass.	MOON Mer. Pass. Upper	Lower	Age	Phase
d	m s	m s	h m	h m	h m	d	%
19	03 34	03 32	11 56	19 18	06 55	09	63
20	03 31	03 29	11 57	20 06	07 42	10	73
21	03 27	03 25	11 57	20 56	08 30	11	82

UT	ARIES GHA	VENUS −3.9 GHA	Dec	MARS +1.4 GHA	Dec	JUPITER −1.9 GHA	Dec	SATURN +0.3 GHA	Dec	STARS Name	SHA	Dec
d h	° ′	° ′	° ′	° ′	° ′	° ′	° ′	° ′	° ′		° ′	° ′
22 00	239 47.2	165 54.7	N23 04.7	188 57.4	N18 32.3	158 27.7	N22 55.1	24 43.4	S11 10.8	Acamar	315 18.8	S40 15.1
01	254 49.6	180 53.8	05.1	203 58.0	32.8	173 29.6	55.1	39 46.0	10.8	Achernar	335 27.3	S57 10.0
02	269 52.1	195 53.0	05.6	218 58.6	33.3	188 31.5	55.2	54 48.6	10.7	Acrux	173 08.9	S63 10.7
03	284 54.6	210 52.2 ..	06.0	233 59.2 ..	33.8	203 33.3 ..	55.2	69 51.2 ..	10.7	Adhara	255 12.9	S28 59.7
04	299 57.0	225 51.3	06.5	248 59.9	34.2	218 35.2	55.3	84 53.9	10.6	Aldebaran	290 49.8	N16 32.0
05	314 59.5	240 50.5	06.9	264 00.5	34.7	233 37.0	55.3	99 56.5	10.6			
06	330 02.0	255 49.6	N23 07.3	279 01.1	N18 35.2	248 38.9	N22 55.3	114 59.1	S11 10.5	Alioth	166 20.4	N55 53.4
W 07	345 04.4	270 48.8	07.7	294 01.7	35.7	263 40.8	55.4	130 01.7	10.5	Alkaid	152 58.6	N49 14.9
E 08	0 06.9	285 48.0	08.2	309 02.4	36.2	278 42.6	55.4	145 04.3	10.4	Al Na'ir	27 43.8	S46 53.4
D 09	15 09.4	300 47.1 ..	08.6	324 03.0 ..	36.6	293 44.5 ..	55.5	160 07.0 ..	10.4	Alnilam	275 46.7	S 1 11.8
N 10	30 11.8	315 46.3	09.0	339 03.6	37.1	308 46.3	55.5	175 09.6	10.4	Alphard	217 56.2	S 8 43.3
E 11	45 14.3	330 45.5	09.5	354 04.2	37.6	323 48.2	55.5	190 12.2	10.3			
S 12	60 16.7	345 44.6	N23 09.9	9 04.9	N18 38.1	338 50.1	N22 55.6	205 14.8	S11 10.3	Alphecca	126 10.7	N26 40.2
D 13	75 19.2	0 43.8	10.3	24 05.5	38.5	353 51.9	55.6	220 17.5	10.2	Alpheratz	357 43.7	N29 09.7
A 14	90 21.7	15 42.9	10.7	39 06.1	39.0	8 53.8	55.6	235 20.1	10.2	Altair	62 08.1	N 8 54.3
Y 15	105 24.1	30 42.1 ..	11.2	54 06.7 ..	39.5	23 55.6 ..	55.7	250 22.7 ..	10.1	Ankaa	353 16.0	S42 13.8
16	120 26.6	45 41.3	11.6	69 07.4	40.0	38 57.5	55.7	265 25.3	10.1	Antares	112 25.9	S26 27.6
17	135 29.1	60 40.4	12.0	84 08.0	40.4	53 59.4	55.8	280 27.9	10.0			
18	150 31.5	75 39.6	N23 12.4	99 08.6	N18 40.9	69 01.2	N22 55.8	295 30.6	S11 10.0	Arcturus	145 55.5	N19 06.8
19	165 34.0	90 38.7	12.8	114 09.2	41.4	84 03.1	55.8	310 33.2	09.9	Atria	107 27.2	S69 02.9
20	180 36.5	105 37.9	13.2	129 09.9	41.9	99 04.9	55.9	325 35.8	09.9	Avior	234 18.3	S59 33.6
21	195 38.9	120 37.1 ..	13.7	144 10.5 ..	42.3	114 06.8 ..	55.9	340 38.4 ..	09.8	Bellatrix	278 32.4	N 6 21.5
22	210 41.4	135 36.2	14.1	159 11.1	42.8	129 08.7	55.9	355 41.0	09.8	Betelgeuse	271 01.7	N 7 24.4
23	225 43.9	150 35.4	14.5	174 11.7	43.3	144 10.5	56.0	10 43.7	09.7			
23 00	240 46.3	165 34.5	N23 14.9	189 12.4	N18 43.7	159 12.4	N22 56.0	25 46.3	S11 09.7	Canopus	263 56.6	S52 42.5
01	255 48.8	180 33.7	15.3	204 13.0	44.2	174 14.2	56.0	40 48.9	09.7	Capella	280 35.0	N46 00.5
02	270 51.2	195 32.8	15.7	219 13.6	44.7	189 16.1	56.1	55 51.5	09.6	Deneb	49 31.3	N45 19.6
03	285 53.7	210 32.0 ..	16.1	234 14.2 ..	45.2	204 18.0 ..	56.1	70 54.2 ..	09.6	Denebola	182 33.6	N14 29.8
04	300 56.2	225 31.2	16.5	249 14.9	45.6	219 19.8	56.2	85 56.8	09.5	Diphda	348 56.2	S17 54.7
05	315 58.6	240 30.3	16.9	264 15.5	46.1	234 21.7	56.2	100 59.4	09.5			
06	331 01.1	255 29.5	N23 17.3	279 16.1	N18 46.6	249 23.5	N22 56.2	116 02.0	S11 09.4	Dubhe	193 51.7	N61 40.9
07	346 03.6	270 28.6	17.7	294 16.7	47.0	264 25.4	56.3	131 04.6	09.4	Elnath	278 13.0	N28 36.9
T 08	1 06.0	285 27.8	18.1	309 17.4	47.5	279 27.3	56.3	146 07.3	09.3	Eltanin	90 45.7	N51 29.2
H 09	16 08.5	300 26.9 ..	18.5	324 18.0 ..	48.0	294 29.1 ..	56.3	161 09.9 ..	09.3	Enif	33 47.1	N 9 56.2
U 10	31 11.0	315 26.1	18.9	339 18.6	48.5	309 31.0	56.4	176 12.5	09.2	Fomalhaut	15 24.1	S29 32.9
R 11	46 13.4	330 25.2	19.3	354 19.2	48.9	324 32.8	56.4	191 15.1	09.2			
S 12	61 15.9	345 24.4	N23 19.7	9 19.9	N18 49.4	339 34.7	N22 56.5	206 17.7	S11 09.1	Gacrux	172 00.6	S57 11.6
D 13	76 18.4	0 23.6	20.1	24 20.5	49.9	354 36.6	56.5	221 20.4	09.1	Gienah	175 52.2	S17 37.2
A 14	91 20.8	15 22.7	20.5	39 21.1	50.3	9 38.4	56.5	236 23.0	09.0	Hadar	148 47.3	S60 26.4
Y 15	106 23.3	30 21.9 ..	20.9	54 21.7 ..	50.8	24 40.3 ..	56.6	251 25.6 ..	09.0	Hamal	328 01.1	N23 31.4
16	121 25.7	45 21.0	21.3	69 22.3	51.3	39 42.1	56.6	266 28.2	09.0	Kaus Aust.	83 43.5	S34 22.5
17	136 28.2	60 20.2	21.7	84 23.0	51.7	54 44.0	56.6	281 30.8	08.9			
18	151 30.7	75 19.3	N23 22.1	99 23.6	N18 52.2	69 45.9	N22 56.7	296 33.5	S11 08.9	Kochab	137 19.0	N74 06.2
19	166 33.1	90 18.5	22.5	114 24.2	52.7	84 47.7	56.7	311 36.1	08.8	Markab	13 38.4	N15 16.6
20	181 35.6	105 17.6	22.9	129 24.8	53.1	99 49.6	56.7	326 38.7	08.8	Menkar	314 15.4	N 4 08.4
21	196 38.1	120 16.8 ..	23.3	144 25.5 ..	53.6	114 51.4 ..	56.8	341 41.3 ..	08.7	Menkent	148 07.3	S36 26.3
22	211 40.5	135 15.9	23.7	159 26.1	54.1	129 53.3	56.8	356 43.9	08.7	Miaplacidus	221 39.9	S69 46.8
23	226 43.0	150 15.1	24.0	174 26.7	54.5	144 55.2	56.9	11 46.5	08.6			
24 00	241 45.5	165 14.2	N23 24.4	189 27.3	N18 55.0	159 57.0	N22 56.9	26 49.2	S11 08.6	Mirfak	308 40.9	N49 54.3
01	256 47.9	180 13.4	24.8	204 28.0	55.5	174 58.9	56.9	41 51.8	08.5	Nunki	75 58.1	S26 16.6
02	271 50.4	195 12.5	25.2	219 28.6	55.9	190 00.7	57.0	56 54.4	08.5	Peacock	53 19.1	S56 41.1
03	286 52.8	210 11.7 ..	25.6	234 29.2 ..	56.4	205 02.6 ..	57.0	71 57.0 ..	08.5	Pollux	243 28.0	N27 59.5
04	301 55.3	225 10.8	25.9	249 29.8	56.8	220 04.4	57.0	86 59.6	08.4	Procyon	245 00.0	N 5 11.2
05	316 57.8	240 10.0	26.3	264 30.4	57.3	235 06.3	57.1	102 02.3	08.4			
06	332 00.2	255 09.1	N23 26.7	279 31.1	N18 57.8	250 08.2	N22 57.1	117 04.9	S11 08.3	Rasalhague	96 06.2	N12 33.1
07	347 02.7	270 08.3	27.1	294 31.7	58.2	265 10.0	57.2	132 07.5	08.3	Regulus	207 43.6	N11 54.0
08	2 05.2	285 07.4	27.4	309 32.3	58.7	280 11.9	57.2	147 10.1	08.2	Rigel	281 12.4	S 8 11.4
F 09	17 07.6	300 06.6 ..	27.8	324 32.9 ..	59.2	295 13.7 ..	57.2	162 12.7 ..	08.2	Rigil Kent.	139 51.1	S60 53.5
R 10	32 10.1	315 05.7	28.2	339 33.6	59.6	310 15.6	57.3	177 15.4	08.1	Sabik	102 12.3	S15 44.4
I 11	47 12.6	330 04.9	28.6	354 34.2	19 00.1	325 17.5	57.3	192 18.0	08.1			
D 12	62 15.0	345 04.0	N23 28.9	9 34.8	N19 00.5	340 19.3	N22 57.3	207 20.6	S11 08.0	Schedar	349 40.9	N56 36.4
A 13	77 17.5	0 03.2	29.3	24 35.4	01.0	355 21.2	57.4	222 23.2	08.0	Shaula	96 21.6	S37 06.6
Y 14	92 20.0	15 02.3	29.7	39 36.0	01.5	10 23.0	57.4	237 25.8	08.0	Sirius	258 34.0	S16 44.4
15	107 22.4	30 01.4 ..	30.0	54 36.7 ..	01.9	25 24.9 ..	57.4	252 28.4 ..	07.9	Spica	158 31.0	S11 14.0
16	122 24.9	45 00.6	30.4	69 37.3	02.4	40 26.7	57.5	267 31.1	07.9	Suhail	222 52.6	S43 29.6
17	137 27.3	59 59.7	30.8	84 37.9	02.8	55 28.6	57.5	282 33.7	07.8			
18	152 29.8	74 58.9	N23 31.1	99 38.5	N19 03.3	70 30.5	N22 57.5	297 36.3	S11 07.8	Vega	80 38.6	N38 47.8
19	167 32.3	89 58.0	31.5	114 39.2	03.8	85 32.3	57.6	312 38.9	07.7	Zuben'ubi	137 05.1	S16 05.9
20	182 34.7	104 57.2	31.8	129 39.8	04.2	100 34.2	57.6	327 41.5	07.7		SHA	Mer.Pass.
21	197 37.2	119 56.3 ..	32.2	144 40.4 ..	04.7	115 36.0 ..	57.6	342 44.1 ..	07.6		° ′	h m
22	212 39.7	134 55.5	32.6	159 41.0	05.1	130 37.9	57.7	357 46.8	07.6	Venus	284 48.2	12 58
23	227 42.1	149 54.6	32.9	174 41.6	05.6	145 39.7	57.7	12 49.4	07.5	Mars	308 26.0	11 23
	h m									Jupiter	278 26.1	13 22
Mer. Pass. 7 55.6		v −0.8	d 0.4	v 0.6	d 0.5	v 1.9	d 0.0	v 2.6	d 0.0	Saturn	145 00.0	22 13

UT	SUN GHA	SUN Dec	MOON GHA	v	Dec	d	HP
22 00	180 50.7	N20 22.3	44 31.2	9.7	S 9 18.4	10.8	58.9
01	195 50.7	22.8	58 59.9	9.5	9 29.2	10.7	59.0
02	210 50.6	23.3	73 28.4	9.5	9 39.9	10.8	59.0
03	225 50.6 ..	23.8	87 56.9	9.4	9 50.7	10.6	59.0
04	240 50.5	24.3	102 25.3	9.3	10 01.3	10.7	59.1
05	255 50.5	24.8	116 53.6	9.2	10 12.0	10.6	59.1
06	270 50.4	N20 25.2	131 21.8	9.1	S10 22.6	10.5	59.2
W 07	285 50.4	25.7	145 49.9	9.0	10 33.1	10.5	59.2
E 08	300 50.3	26.2	160 17.9	9.0	10 43.6	10.5	59.2
D 09	315 50.3 ..	26.7	174 45.9	8.9	10 54.1	10.4	59.2
N 10	330 50.2	27.2	189 13.8	8.7	11 04.5	10.3	59.3
E 11	345 50.2	27.7	203 41.5	8.7	11 14.8	10.3	59.3
S 12	0 50.2	N20 28.2	218 09.2	8.6	S11 25.1	10.3	59.4
D 13	15 50.1	28.7	232 36.8	8.6	11 35.4	10.1	59.4
A 14	30 50.1	29.1	247 04.4	8.4	11 45.5	10.2	59.4
Y 15	45 50.0 ..	29.6	261 31.8	8.3	11 55.7	10.0	59.5
16	60 50.0	30.1	275 59.1	8.3	12 05.7	10.0	59.5
17	75 49.9	30.6	290 26.4	8.1	12 15.7	10.0	59.6
18	90 49.9	N20 31.1	304 53.5	8.1	S12 25.7	9.9	59.6
19	105 49.8	31.6	319 20.6	8.0	12 35.6	9.8	59.6
20	120 49.8	32.0	333 47.6	7.9	12 45.4	9.7	59.7
21	135 49.7 ..	32.5	348 14.5	7.8	12 55.1	9.7	59.7
22	150 49.7	33.0	2 41.3	7.7	13 04.8	9.6	59.7
23	165 49.6	33.5	17 08.0	7.6	13 14.4	9.5	59.8
23 00	180 49.6	N20 34.0	31 34.6	7.6	S13 23.9	9.5	59.8
01	195 49.5	34.4	46 01.2	7.4	13 33.4	9.4	59.8
02	210 49.5	34.9	60 27.6	7.4	13 42.8	9.3	59.9
03	225 49.4 ..	35.4	74 54.0	7.2	13 52.1	9.2	59.9
04	240 49.4	35.9	89 20.2	7.2	14 01.3	9.2	59.9
05	255 49.3	36.3	103 46.4	7.1	14 10.5	9.1	60.0
06	270 49.2	N20 36.8	118 12.5	7.0	S14 19.6	9.0	60.0
T 07	285 49.2	37.3	132 38.5	6.9	14 28.6	8.9	60.0
H 08	300 49.1	37.8	147 04.4	6.8	14 37.5	8.8	60.1
U 09	315 49.1 ..	38.2	161 30.2	6.7	14 46.3	8.8	60.1
R 10	330 49.0	38.7	175 55.9	6.7	14 55.1	8.6	60.1
S 11	345 49.0	39.2	190 21.6	6.5	15 03.7	8.6	60.2
D 12	0 48.9	N20 39.7	204 47.1	6.5	S15 12.3	8.4	60.2
A 13	15 48.9	40.1	219 12.6	6.3	15 20.7	8.4	60.2
Y 14	30 48.8	40.6	233 37.9	6.3	15 29.1	8.3	60.2
15	45 48.8 ..	41.1	248 03.2	6.2	15 37.4	8.2	60.3
16	60 48.7	41.5	262 28.4	6.1	15 45.6	8.1	60.3
17	75 48.7	42.0	276 53.5	6.0	15 53.7	7.9	60.3
18	90 48.6	N20 42.5	291 18.5	6.0	S16 01.6	7.9	60.4
19	105 48.6	42.9	305 43.5	5.8	16 09.5	7.8	60.4
20	120 48.5	43.4	320 08.3	5.8	16 17.3	7.7	60.4
21	135 48.4 ..	43.9	334 33.1	5.7	16 25.0	7.6	60.4
22	150 48.4	44.3	348 57.8	5.6	16 32.6	7.4	60.5
23	165 48.3	44.8	3 22.4	5.5	16 40.0	7.4	60.5
24 00	180 48.3	N20 45.3	17 46.9	5.4	S16 47.4	7.3	60.5
01	195 48.2	45.7	32 11.3	5.3	16 54.7	7.1	60.5
02	210 48.2	46.2	46 35.6	5.3	17 01.8	7.0	60.6
03	225 48.1 ..	46.7	60 59.9	5.2	17 08.8	6.9	60.6
04	240 48.1	47.1	75 24.1	5.1	17 15.7	6.8	60.6
05	255 48.0	47.6	89 48.2	5.0	17 22.5	6.7	60.6
06	270 47.9	N20 48.0	104 12.2	5.0	S17 29.2	6.6	60.7
07	285 47.9	48.5	118 36.2	4.9	17 35.8	6.4	60.7
08	300 47.8	49.0	133 00.1	4.8	17 42.2	6.4	60.7
F 09	315 47.8 ..	49.4	147 23.9	4.7	17 48.6	6.2	60.7
R 10	330 47.7	49.9	161 47.6	4.7	17 54.8	6.0	60.8
I 11	345 47.6	50.3	176 11.3	4.6	18 00.8	6.0	60.8
D 12	0 47.6	N20 50.8	190 34.9	4.5	S18 06.8	5.8	60.8
A 13	15 47.5	51.2	204 58.4	4.4	18 12.6	5.7	60.8
Y 14	30 47.5	51.7	219 21.8	4.4	18 18.3	5.6	60.8
15	45 47.4 ..	52.2	233 45.2	4.3	18 23.9	5.4	60.9
16	60 47.4	52.6	248 08.5	4.3	18 29.3	5.4	60.9
17	75 47.3	53.1	262 31.8	4.1	18 34.7	5.1	60.9
18	90 47.2	N20 53.5	276 54.9	4.2	S18 39.8	5.1	60.9
19	105 47.2	54.0	291 18.1	4.0	18 44.9	4.9	60.9
20	120 47.1	54.4	305 41.1	4.0	18 49.8	4.8	60.9
21	135 47.1 ..	54.9	320 04.1	4.0	18 54.6	4.6	61.0
22	150 47.0	55.3	334 27.1	3.9	18 59.2	4.5	61.0
23	165 46.9	55.8	348 50.0	3.8	S19 03.7	4.4	61.0
	SD 15.8	d 0.5	SD 16.2		16.4		16.6

Twilight / Moonrise

Lat.	Naut.	Civil	Sunrise	22	23	24	25
N 72	□	□	□	18 37	21 08	■	■
N 70	□	□	□	18 13	20 18	22 36	■
68	////	////	00 53	17 54	19 46	21 38	23 11
66	////	////	01 49	17 40	19 23	21 04	22 28
64	////	////	02 22	17 27	19 05	20 39	22 00
62	////	01 14	02 46	17 17	18 50	20 20	21 38
60	////	01 53	03 05	17 09	18 38	20 04	21 20
N 58	////	02 20	03 20	17 01	18 27	19 51	21 05
56	01 07	02 40	03 34	16 54	18 18	19 39	20 53
54	01 43	02 57	03 45	16 48	18 10	19 29	20 41
52	02 08	03 11	03 55	16 43	18 02	19 20	20 32
50	02 27	03 23	04 04	16 38	17 56	19 12	20 23
45	03 02	03 48	04 23	16 28	17 42	18 55	20 04
N 40	03 28	04 07	04 38	16 19	17 30	18 41	19 49
35	03 48	04 23	04 51	16 12	17 20	18 29	19 37
30	04 04	04 36	05 02	16 05	17 12	18 19	19 25
20	04 29	04 57	05 21	15 54	16 57	18 01	19 06
N 10	04 49	05 15	05 38	15 45	16 44	17 46	18 50
0	05 05	05 31	05 53	15 36	16 32	17 32	18 34
S 10	05 20	05 46	06 08	15 27	16 20	17 18	18 19
20	05 34	06 02	06 24	15 17	16 08	17 03	18 03
30	05 48	06 17	06 43	15 07	15 53	16 45	17 44
35	05 55	06 26	06 53	15 01	15 45	16 35	17 33
40	06 03	06 36	07 05	14 54	15 35	16 24	17 20
45	06 11	06 47	07 20	14 46	15 25	16 11	17 06
S 50	06 20	07 00	07 37	14 36	15 11	15 55	16 48
52	06 24	07 07	07 45	14 32	15 05	15 47	16 39
54	06 29	07 13	07 55	14 27	14 58	15 39	16 30
56	06 34	07 21	08 05	14 21	14 51	15 29	16 19
58	06 39	07 29	08 17	14 15	14 43	15 18	16 07
S 60	06 45	07 38	08 30	14 09	14 33	15 06	15 53

Sunset / Twilight / Moonset

Lat.	Sunset	Civil	Naut.	22	23	24	25
N 72	□	□	□	00 58	00 41	00 09	■
N 70	□	□	□	01 13	01 07	01 01	00 49
68	23 10	////	////	01 25	01 27	01 33	01 48
66	22 08	////	////	01 34	01 43	01 57	02 23
64	21 34	22 44	////	01 43	01 56	02 16	02 48
62	21 09	22 44	////	01 50	02 07	02 32	03 08
60	20 50	22 03	////	01 56	02 17	02 45	03 24
N 58	20 34	21 36	////	02 02	02 25	02 56	03 37
56	20 21	21 15	22 51	02 07	02 33	03 06	03 49
54	20 09	20 58	22 13	02 11	02 39	03 15	04 00
52	19 59	20 44	21 48	02 15	02 45	03 22	04 09
50	19 50	20 34	21 28	02 19	02 51	03 29	04 17
45	19 31	20 07	20 52	02 27	03 02	03 44	04 35
N 40	19 16	19 47	20 26	02 33	03 12	03 57	04 49
35	19 03	19 31	20 06	02 39	03 20	04 07	05 01
30	18 51	19 18	19 50	02 44	03 28	04 17	05 12
20	18 32	18 56	19 25	02 53	03 40	04 33	05 30
N 10	18 16	18 38	19 05	03 01	03 52	04 47	05 46
0	18 00	18 22	18 48	03 08	04 02	05 00	06 01
S 10	17 45	18 07	18 33	03 15	04 13	05 13	06 16
20	17 29	17 52	18 19	03 23	04 24	05 27	06 32
30	17 11	17 36	18 06	03 32	04 37	05 44	06 51
35	17 00	17 27	17 58	03 37	04 44	05 53	07 01
40	16 48	17 17	17 51	03 43	04 53	06 04	07 14
45	16 33	17 06	17 42	03 50	05 03	06 16	07 28
S 50	16 16	16 53	17 33	03 58	05 15	06 32	07 46
52	16 08	16 46	17 29	04 02	05 20	06 39	07 54
54	15 58	16 40	17 24	04 06	05 27	06 47	08 03
56	15 48	16 32	17 19	04 11	05 33	06 56	08 14
58	15 36	16 24	17 14	04 16	05 41	07 06	08 26
S 60	15 23	16 15	17 08	04 22	05 50	07 16	08 40

SUN / MOON

Day	Eqn. of Time 00h	Eqn. of Time 12h	Mer. Pass.	Mer. Pass. Upper	Mer. Pass. Lower	Age	Phase
	m s	m s	h m	h m	h m	d	%
22	03 23	03 21	11 57	21 49	09 22	12	90
23	03 18	03 16	11 57	22 46	10 17	13	96
24	03 13	03 10	11 57	23 47	11 16	14	99

UT	ARIES	VENUS −3.9		MARS +1.4		JUPITER −1.9		SATURN +0.3		STARS		
	GHA	GHA	Dec	GHA	Dec	GHA	Dec	GHA	Dec	Name	SHA	Dec
25 00	242 44.6	164 53.8	N23 33.3	189 42.3	N19 06.0	160 41.6	N22 57.8	27 52.0	S11 07.5	Acamar	315 18.8	S40 15.1
01	257 47.1	179 52.9	33.6	204 42.9	06.5	175 43.5	57.8	42 54.6	07.5	Achernar	335 27.3	S57 10.0
02	272 49.5	194 52.0	34.0	219 43.5	07.0	190 45.3	57.8	57 57.2	07.4	Acrux	173 08.9	S63 10.7
03	287 52.0	209 51.2 ..	34.3	234 44.1 ..	07.4	205 47.2 ..	57.9	72 59.8 ..	07.4	Adhara	255 12.9	S28 59.7
04	302 54.5	224 50.3	34.7	249 44.7	07.9	220 49.0	57.9	88 02.5	07.3	Aldebaran	290 49.8	N16 32.0
05	317 56.9	239 49.5	35.0	264 45.4	08.3	235 50.9	57.9	103 05.1	07.3			
06	332 59.4	254 48.6	N23 35.4	279 46.0	N19 08.8	250 52.7	N22 58.0	118 07.7	S11 07.2	Alioth	166 20.4	N55 53.4
S 07	348 01.8	269 47.8	35.7	294 46.6	09.2	265 54.6	58.0	133 10.3	07.2	Alkaid	152 58.6	N49 14.9
A 08	3 04.3	284 46.9	36.1	309 47.2	09.7	280 56.5	58.0	148 12.9	07.1	Al Na'ir	27 43.8	S46 53.4
T 09	18 06.8	299 46.0 ..	36.4	324 47.8 ..	10.1	295 58.3 ..	58.1	163 15.5 ..	07.1	Alnilam	275 46.7	S 1 11.8
U 10	33 09.2	314 45.2	36.8	339 48.5	10.6	311 00.2	58.1	178 18.2	07.1	Alphard	217 56.2	S 8 43.3
R 11	48 11.7	329 44.3	37.1	354 49.1	11.1	326 02.0	58.1	193 20.8	07.0			
D 12	63 14.2	344 43.5	N23 37.4	9 49.7	N19 11.5	341 03.9	N22 58.2	208 23.4	S11 07.0	Alphecca	126 10.7	N26 40.2
A 13	78 16.6	359 42.6	37.8	24 50.3	12.0	356 05.7	58.2	223 26.0	06.9	Alpheratz	357 43.7	N29 09.7
Y 14	93 19.1	14 41.7	38.1	39 50.9	12.4	11 07.6	58.2	238 28.6	06.9	Altair	62 08.1	N 8 54.3
15	108 21.6	29 40.9 ..	38.5	54 51.6 ..	12.9	26 09.4 ..	58.3	253 31.2 ..	06.8	Ankaa	353 16.0	S42 13.8
16	123 24.0	44 40.0	38.8	69 52.2	13.3	41 11.3	58.3	268 33.8	06.8	Antares	112 25.9	S26 27.6
17	138 26.5	59 39.2	39.1	84 52.8	13.8	56 13.2	58.3	283 36.5	06.7			
18	153 29.0	74 38.3	N23 39.5	99 53.4	N19 14.2	71 15.0	N22 58.4	298 39.1	S11 06.7	Arcturus	145 55.5	N19 06.8
19	168 31.4	89 37.4	39.8	114 54.0	14.7	86 16.9	58.4	313 41.7	06.7	Atria	107 27.2	S69 02.9
20	183 33.9	104 36.6	40.1	129 54.7	15.1	101 18.7	58.5	328 44.3	06.6	Avior	234 18.3	S59 33.6
21	198 36.3	119 35.7 ..	40.5	144 55.3 ..	15.6	116 20.6 ..	58.5	343 46.9 ..	06.6	Bellatrix	278 32.4	N 6 21.5
22	213 38.8	134 34.9	40.8	159 55.9	16.0	131 22.4	58.5	358 49.5	06.5	Betelgeuse	271 01.7	N 7 24.4
23	228 41.3	149 34.0	41.1	174 56.5	16.5	146 24.3	58.6	13 52.2	06.5			
26 00	243 43.7	164 33.1	N23 41.4	189 57.1	N19 16.9	161 26.2	N22 58.6	28 54.8	S11 06.4	Canopus	263 56.6	S52 42.5
01	258 46.2	179 32.3	41.8	204 57.8	17.4	176 28.0	58.6	43 57.4	06.4	Capella	280 35.0	N46 00.5
02	273 48.7	194 31.4	42.1	219 58.4	17.8	191 29.9	58.7	59 00.0	06.4	Deneb	49 31.3	N45 19.6
03	288 51.1	209 30.5 ..	42.4	234 59.0 ..	18.3	206 31.7 ..	58.7	74 02.6 ..	06.3	Denebola	182 33.6	N14 29.8
04	303 53.6	224 29.7	42.7	249 59.6	18.7	221 33.6	58.7	89 05.2	06.3	Diphda	348 56.1	S17 54.7
05	318 56.1	239 28.8	43.1	265 00.2	19.2	236 35.4	58.8	104 07.8	06.2			
06	333 58.5	254 28.0	N23 43.4	280 00.9	N19 19.6	251 37.3	N22 58.8	119 10.4	S11 06.2	Dubhe	193 51.7	N61 40.9
07	349 01.0	269 27.1	43.7	295 01.5	20.0	266 39.1	58.8	134 13.1	06.1	Elnath	278 13.0	N28 36.9
08	4 03.5	284 26.2	44.0	310 02.1	20.5	281 41.0	58.9	149 15.7	06.1	Eltanin	90 45.7	N51 29.2
S 09	19 05.9	299 25.4 ..	44.3	325 02.7 ..	20.9	296 42.9 ..	58.9	164 18.3 ..	06.0	Enif	33 47.1	N 9 56.2
U 10	34 08.4	314 24.5	44.6	340 03.3	21.4	311 44.7	58.9	179 20.9	06.0	Fomalhaut	15 24.1	S29 32.8
N 11	49 10.8	329 23.6	45.0	355 03.9	21.8	326 46.6	59.0	194 23.5	06.0			
D 12	64 13.3	344 22.8	N23 45.3	10 04.6	N19 22.3	341 48.4	N22 59.0	209 26.1	S11 05.9	Gacrux	172 00.6	S57 11.6
A 13	79 15.8	359 21.9	45.6	25 05.2	22.7	356 50.3	59.0	224 28.7	05.9	Gienah	175 52.2	S17 37.2
Y 14	94 18.2	14 21.0	45.9	40 05.8	23.2	11 52.1	59.1	239 31.4	05.8	Hadar	148 47.3	S60 26.4
15	109 20.7	29 20.2 ..	46.2	55 06.4 ..	23.6	26 54.0 ..	59.1	254 34.0 ..	05.8	Hamal	328 01.1	N23 31.4
16	124 23.2	44 19.3	46.5	70 07.0	24.1	41 55.8	59.1	269 36.6	05.7	Kaus Aust.	83 43.5	S34 22.5
17	139 25.6	59 18.4	46.8	85 07.7	24.5	56 57.7	59.2	284 39.2	05.7			
18	154 28.1	74 17.6	N23 47.1	100 08.3	N19 24.9	71 59.5	N22 59.2	299 41.8	S11 05.7	Kochab	137 19.0	N74 06.2
19	169 30.6	89 16.7	47.4	115 08.9	25.4	87 01.4	59.2	314 44.4	05.6	Markab	13 38.4	N15 16.6
20	184 33.0	104 15.8	47.7	130 09.5	25.8	102 03.3	59.3	329 47.0	05.6	Menkar	314 15.4	N 4 08.4
21	199 35.5	119 15.0 ..	48.0	145 10.1 ..	26.3	117 05.1 ..	59.3	344 49.6 ..	05.5	Menkent	148 07.3	S36 26.3
22	214 37.9	134 14.1	48.3	160 10.7	26.7	132 07.0	59.3	359 52.3	05.5	Miaplacidus	221 39.9	S69 46.8
23	229 40.4	149 13.2	48.6	175 11.4	27.2	147 08.8	59.4	14 54.9	05.4			
27 00	244 42.9	164 12.4	N23 48.9	190 12.0	N19 27.6	162 10.7	N22 59.4	29 57.5	S11 05.4	Mirfak	308 40.9	N49 54.3
01	259 45.3	179 11.5	49.2	205 12.6	28.0	177 12.5	59.4	45 00.1	05.4	Nunki	75 58.1	S26 16.6
02	274 47.8	194 10.6	49.5	220 13.2	28.5	192 14.4	59.5	60 02.7	05.3	Peacock	53 19.0	S56 41.1
03	289 50.3	209 09.8 ..	49.8	235 13.8 ..	28.9	207 16.2 ..	59.5	75 05.3 ..	05.3	Pollux	243 28.0	N27 59.5
04	304 52.7	224 08.9	50.1	250 14.4	29.4	222 18.1	59.5	90 07.9	05.2	Procyon	245 00.0	N 5 11.2
05	319 55.2	239 08.0	50.4	265 15.1	29.8	237 19.9	59.6	105 10.5	05.2			
06	334 57.7	254 07.2	N23 50.7	280 15.7	N19 30.2	252 21.8	N22 59.6	120 13.1	S11 05.1	Rasalhague	96 06.2	N12 33.1
07	350 00.1	269 06.3	51.0	295 16.3	30.7	267 23.7	59.6	135 15.8	05.1	Regulus	207 43.6	N11 54.0
08	5 02.6	284 05.4	51.3	310 16.9	31.1	282 25.5	59.7	150 18.4	05.1	Rigel	281 12.4	S 8 11.4
M 09	20 05.1	299 04.6 ..	51.6	325 17.5 ..	31.5	297 27.4 ..	59.7	165 21.0 ..	05.0	Rigil Kent.	139 51.1	S60 53.5
O 10	35 07.5	314 03.7	51.8	340 18.1	32.0	312 29.2	59.7	180 23.6	05.0	Sabik	102 12.2	S15 44.4
N 11	50 10.0	329 02.8	52.1	355 18.8	32.4	327 31.1	59.8	195 26.2	04.9			
D 12	65 12.4	344 01.9	N23 52.4	10 19.4	N19 32.9	342 32.9	N22 59.8	210 28.8	S11 04.9	Schedar	349 40.8	N56 36.4
A 13	80 14.9	359 01.1	52.7	25 20.0	33.3	357 34.8	59.8	225 31.4	04.8	Shaula	96 21.6	S37 06.6
Y 14	95 17.4	14 00.2	53.0	40 20.6	33.7	12 36.6	59.9	240 34.0	04.8	Sirius	258 34.0	S16 44.4
15	110 19.8	28 59.3 ..	53.3	55 21.2 ..	34.2	27 38.5 ..	59.9	255 36.6 ..	04.8	Spica	158 31.0	S11 14.0
16	125 22.3	43 58.5	53.5	70 21.8	34.6	42 40.3	22 59.9	270 39.3	04.7	Suhail	222 52.6	S43 29.6
17	140 24.8	58 57.6	53.8	85 22.5	35.0	57 42.2	23 00.0	285 41.9	04.7			
18	155 27.2	73 56.7	N23 54.1	100 23.1	N19 35.5	72 44.0	N23 00.0	300 44.5	S11 04.6	Vega	80 38.6	N38 47.8
19	170 29.7	88 55.9	54.4	115 23.7	35.9	87 45.9	00.0	315 47.1	04.6	Zuben'ubi	137 05.1	S16 05.9
20	185 32.2	103 55.0	54.6	130 24.3	36.3	102 47.8	00.1	330 49.7	04.5		SHA	Mer. Pass.
21	200 34.6	118 54.1 ..	54.9	145 24.9 ..	36.8	117 49.6 ..	00.1	345 52.3 ..	04.5	Venus	280 49.4	13 03
22	215 37.1	133 53.2	55.2	160 25.5	37.2	132 51.5	00.1	0 54.9	04.5	Mars	306 13.4	11 20
23	230 39.6	148 52.4	55.4	175 26.2	37.6	147 53.3	00.2	15 57.5	04.4	Jupiter	277 42.4	13 13
Mer. Pass.	7 43.8	v −0.9	d 0.3	v 0.6	d 0.4	v 1.9	d 0.0	v 2.6	d 0.0	Saturn	145 11.0	22 01

SUN and MOON

UT	SUN GHA	SUN Dec	MOON GHA	v	MOON Dec	d	HP
d h	° ′	° ′	° ′	′	° ′	′	′
25 00	180 46.9	N20 56.2	3 12.8	3.8	S19 08.1	4.2	61.0
01	195 46.8	56.7	17 35.6	3.7	19 12.3	4.1	61.0
02	210 46.7	57.1	31 58.3	3.7	19 16.4	3.9	61.0
03	225 46.7	.. 57.6	46 21.0	3.6	19 20.3	3.8	61.0
04	240 46.6	58.0	60 43.6	3.6	19 24.1	3.7	61.1
05	255 46.6	58.5	75 06.2	3.6	19 27.8	3.5	61.1
06	270 46.5	N20 58.9	89 28.8	3.5	S19 31.3	3.4	61.1
07	285 46.4	59.3	103 51.3	3.4	19 34.7	3.2	61.1
S 08	300 46.4	20 59.8	118 13.7	3.4	19 37.9	3.1	61.1
A 09	315 46.3	21 00.2	132 36.1	3.4	19 41.0	2.9	61.1
T 10	330 46.2	00.7	146 58.5	3.4	19 43.9	2.8	61.1
U 11	345 46.2	01.1	161 20.9	3.3	19 46.7	2.6	61.1
R 12	0 46.1	N21 01.6	175 43.2	3.3	S19 49.3	2.5	61.1
D 13	15 46.1	02.0	190 05.5	3.2	19 51.8	2.3	61.1
A 14	30 46.0	02.4	204 27.7	3.3	19 54.1	2.2	61.1
Y 15	45 45.9	.. 02.9	218 50.0	3.2	19 56.3	2.1	61.2
16	60 45.9	03.3	233 12.2	3.1	19 58.4	1.8	61.2
17	75 45.8	03.8	247 34.3	3.2	20 00.2	1.8	61.2
18	90 45.7	N21 04.2	261 56.5	3.1	S20 02.0	1.6	61.2
19	105 45.7	04.6	276 18.6	3.2	20 03.6	1.4	61.2
20	120 45.6	05.1	290 40.8	3.1	20 05.0	1.3	61.2
21	135 45.5	.. 05.5	305 02.9	3.1	20 06.3	1.1	61.2
22	150 45.5	05.9	319 25.0	3.1	20 07.4	1.0	61.2
23	165 45.4	06.4	333 47.1	3.0	20 08.4	0.8	61.2
26 00	180 45.3	N21 06.8	348 09.1	3.1	S20 09.2	0.6	61.2
01	195 45.3	07.2	2 31.2	3.1	20 09.8	0.5	61.2
02	210 45.2	07.7	16 53.3	3.0	20 10.3	0.4	61.2
03	225 45.1	.. 08.1	31 15.3	3.1	20 10.7	0.2	61.2
04	240 45.1	08.5	45 37.4	3.1	20 10.9	0.1	61.2
05	255 45.0	09.0	59 59.5	3.0	20 11.0	0.1	61.2
06	270 44.9	N21 09.4	74 21.5	3.1	S20 10.9	0.3	61.2
07	285 44.9	09.8	88 43.6	3.1	20 10.6	0.4	61.2
S 08	300 44.8	10.3	103 05.7	3.1	20 10.2	0.6	61.2
U 09	315 44.7	.. 10.7	117 27.8	3.1	20 09.6	0.7	61.2
N 10	330 44.7	11.1	131 49.9	3.1	20 08.9	0.9	61.2
11	345 44.6	11.5	146 12.0	3.1	20 08.0	1.0	61.2
D 12	0 44.5	N21 12.0	160 34.1	3.2	S20 07.0	1.2	61.2
A 13	15 44.5	12.4	174 56.3	3.2	20 05.8	1.3	61.2
Y 14	30 44.4	12.8	189 18.5	3.2	20 04.5	1.5	61.2
15	45 44.3	.. 13.2	203 40.7	3.2	20 03.0	1.6	61.1
16	60 44.3	13.7	218 02.9	3.2	20 01.4	1.8	61.1
17	75 44.2	14.1	232 25.1	3.3	19 59.6	1.9	61.1
18	90 44.1	N21 14.5	246 47.4	3.3	S19 57.7	2.1	61.1
19	105 44.0	14.9	261 09.7	3.4	19 55.6	2.2	61.1
20	120 44.0	15.4	275 32.1	3.3	19 53.4	2.4	61.1
21	135 43.9	.. 15.8	289 54.4	3.5	19 51.0	2.5	61.1
22	150 43.8	16.2	304 16.9	3.4	19 48.5	2.7	61.1
23	165 43.8	16.6	318 39.3	3.5	19 45.8	2.8	61.1
27 00	180 43.7	N21 17.0	333 01.8	3.5	S19 43.0	3.0	61.1
01	195 43.6	17.5	347 24.3	3.6	19 40.0	3.1	61.0
02	210 43.5	17.9	1 46.9	3.6	19 36.9	3.3	61.0
03	225 43.5	.. 18.3	16 09.5	3.7	19 33.6	3.4	61.0
04	240 43.4	18.7	30 32.2	3.7	19 30.2	3.5	61.0
05	255 43.3	19.1	44 54.9	3.8	19 26.7	3.7	61.0
06	270 43.3	N21 19.5	59 17.7	3.8	S19 23.0	3.8	61.0
07	285 43.2	20.0	73 40.5	3.8	19 19.2	4.0	61.0
08	300 43.1	20.4	88 03.3	4.0	19 15.2	4.1	60.9
M 09	315 43.0	.. 20.8	102 26.3	4.0	19 11.1	4.2	60.9
O 10	330 43.0	21.2	116 49.3	4.0	19 06.9	4.4	60.9
N 11	345 42.9	21.6	131 12.3	4.1	19 02.5	4.5	60.9
D 12	0 42.8	N21 22.0	145 35.4	4.2	S18 58.0	4.7	60.9
A 13	15 42.7	22.4	159 58.6	4.2	18 53.3	4.8	60.9
Y 14	30 42.7	22.8	174 21.8	4.3	18 48.5	4.9	60.8
15	45 42.6	.. 23.2	188 45.1	4.3	18 43.6	5.1	60.8
16	60 42.5	23.7	203 08.4	4.4	18 38.5	5.1	60.8
17	75 42.4	24.1	217 31.8	4.4	18 33.4	5.4	60.8
18	90 42.4	N21 24.5	231 55.3	4.6	S18 28.0	5.4	60.8
19	105 42.3	24.9	246 18.9	4.6	18 22.6	5.6	60.7
20	120 42.2	25.3	260 42.5	4.7	18 17.0	5.7	60.7
21	135 42.1	.. 25.7	275 06.2	4.8	18 11.3	5.8	60.7
22	150 42.1	26.1	289 30.0	4.8	18 05.5	5.9	60.7
23	165 42.0	26.5	303 53.8	4.9	S17 59.6	6.1	60.7
	SD 15.8	d 0.4	SD 16.7		16.7		16.6

Twilight, Sunrise and Moonrise

Lat.	Naut.	Civil	Sunrise	Moonrise 25	26	27	28
°	h m	h m	h m	h m	h m	h m	h m
N 72	□	□	□	■	■	■	02 19
N 70	□	□	□	■	01 19	01 01	
68	////	////	00 13	23 11	24 02	00 02	00 22
66	////	////	01 37	22 28	23 24	23 55	24 12
64	////	////	02 13	22 00	22 58	23 34	23 57
62	////	00 58	02 39	21 38	22 37	23 17	23 45
60	////	01 44	02 59	21 20	22 20	23 03	23 34
N 58	////	02 13	03 15	21 05	22 06	22 51	23 25
56	00 52	02 34	03 29	20 53	21 53	22 40	23 16
54	01 34	02 52	03 41	20 41	21 43	22 31	23 09
52	02 01	03 07	03 52	20 32	21 33	22 23	23 02
50	02 22	03 19	04 01	20 23	21 24	22 15	22 56
45	02 59	03 45	04 20	20 04	21 06	21 59	22 44
N 40	03 25	04 05	04 36	19 49	20 52	21 46	22 33
35	03 45	04 21	04 50	19 37	20 39	21 35	22 24
30	04 02	04 34	05 01	19 25	20 28	21 25	22 16
20	04 28	04 57	05 21	19 06	20 09	21 08	22 02
N 10	04 48	05 15	05 38	18 50	19 53	20 53	21 50
0	05 05	05 31	05 53	18 34	19 38	20 39	21 38
S 10	05 21	05 47	06 09	18 19	19 22	20 26	21 27
20	05 35	06 02	06 26	18 03	19 06	20 11	21 14
30	05 49	06 19	06 44	17 44	18 47	19 54	21 00
35	05 57	06 28	06 55	17 33	18 36	19 44	20 52
40	06 05	06 38	07 08	17 20	18 24	19 32	20 43
45	06 13	06 50	07 23	17 06	18 09	19 19	20 32
S 50	06 23	07 04	07 41	16 48	17 51	19 03	20 19
52	06 28	07 10	07 49	16 39	17 43	18 55	20 13
54	06 32	07 17	07 59	16 30	17 33	18 47	20 06
56	06 37	07 25	08 09	16 19	17 22	18 37	19 58
58	06 43	07 33	08 22	16 07	17 10	18 26	19 49
S 60	06 49	07 43	08 36	15 53	16 56	18 13	19 40

Sunset, Twilight and Moonset

Lat.	Sunset	Civil	Naut.	Moonset 25	26	27	28
°	h m	h m	h m	h m	h m	h m	h m
N 72	□	□	□	■	■	■	03 41
N 70	□	□	□	00 49	■	02 31	04 58
68	22 21	////	////	01 48	02 27	03 48	05 36
66	21 43	////	////	02 23	03 10	04 26	06 02
64	21 17	23 02	////	02 48	03 38	04 52	06 22
62	20 56	22 13	////	03 08	04 00	05 13	06 39
60	20 40	21 43	////	03 24	04 18	05 29	06 52
N 58	20 26	21 21	23 07	03 37	04 33	05 43	07 04
56	20 14	21 03	22 22	03 49	04 46	05 55	07 14
54	20 03	20 49	21 55	04 00	04 57	06 06	07 23
52	19 54	20 36	21 34	04 09	05 07	06 15	07 31
50	19 34	20 10	20 56	04 17	05 15	06 24	07 38
45	19 18	19 50	20 30	04 35	05 34	06 41	07 53
N 40	19 18	19 50	20 30	04 49	05 49	06 56	08 06
35	19 05	19 34	20 09	05 01	06 02	07 08	08 16
30	18 53	19 20	19 52	05 12	06 13	07 19	08 26
20	18 33	18 58	19 26	05 30	06 32	07 37	08 41
N 10	18 16	18 39	19 06	05 46	06 49	07 53	08 55
0	18 01	18 23	18 49	06 01	07 05	08 07	09 08
S 10	17 45	18 07	18 33	06 16	07 20	08 22	09 21
20	17 28	17 52	18 19	06 32	07 37	08 38	09 34
30	17 08	17 35	18 05	06 51	07 56	08 56	09 50
35	16 58	17 26	17 57	07 01	08 07	09 06	09 58
40	16 46	17 16	17 49	07 14	08 19	09 18	10 09
45	16 31	17 04	17 40	07 28	08 34	09 32	10 20
S 50	16 13	16 50	17 30	07 46	08 52	09 49	10 35
52	16 04	16 44	17 26	07 54	09 01	09 57	10 41
54	15 55	16 37	17 21	08 03	09 11	10 05	10 49
56	15 44	16 29	17 16	08 14	09 21	10 15	10 57
58	15 32	16 20	17 11	08 26	09 34	10 27	11 06
S 60	15 17	16 05	17 05	08 40	09 48	10 40	11 16

SUN and MOON

Day	SUN Eqn. of Time 00h	SUN Eqn. of Time 12h	SUN Mer. Pass.	MOON Mer. Pass. Upper	MOON Mer. Pass. Lower	Age	Phase
d	m s	m s	h m	h m	h m	d %	
25	03 08	03 05	11 57	12 18	24 49	15 100	
26	03 02	02 58	11 57	00 49	13 21	16 97	○
27	02 55	02 51	11 57	01 53	14 24	17 92	

UT	ARIES	VENUS −3.8		MARS +1.4		JUPITER −1.9		SATURN +0.3		STARS		
	GHA	GHA	Dec	GHA	Dec	GHA	Dec	GHA	Dec	Name	SHA	Dec
d h	° ′	° ′	° ′	° ′	° ′	° ′	° ′	° ′	° ′		° ′	° ′
28 00	245 42.0	163 51.5	N23 55.7	190 26.8	N19 38.1	162 55.2	N23 00.2	31 00.1	S11 04.4	Acamar	315 18.8	S40 15.1
01	260 44.5	178 50.6	56.0	205 27.4	38.5	177 57.0	00.2	46 02.7	04.3	Achernar	335 27.3	S57 09.9
02	275 46.9	193 49.7	56.3	220 28.0	38.9	192 58.9	00.3	61 05.4	04.3	Acrux	173 08.9	S63 10.8
03	290 49.4	208 48.9 ..	56.5	235 28.6 ..	39.4	208 00.7 ..	00.3	76 08.0 ..	04.3	Adhara	255 12.9	S28 59.7
04	305 51.9	223 48.0	56.8	250 29.2	39.8	223 02.6	00.3	91 10.6	04.2	Aldebaran	290 49.8	N16 32.0
05	320 54.3	238 47.1	57.0	265 29.8	40.2	238 04.4	00.4	106 13.2	04.2			
06	335 56.8	253 46.3	N23 57.3	280 30.5	N19 40.7	253 06.3	N23 00.4	121 15.8	S11 04.1	Alioth	166 20.4	N55 53.4
07	350 59.3	268 45.4	57.6	295 31.1	41.1	268 08.1	00.4	136 18.4	04.1	Alkaid	152 58.6	N49 14.9
T 08	6 01.7	283 44.5	57.8	310 31.7	41.5	283 10.0	00.5	151 21.0	04.0	Al Na'ir	27 43.7	S46 53.4
U 09	21 04.2	298 43.6 ..	58.1	325 32.3 ..	42.0	298 11.8 ..	00.5	166 23.6 ..	04.0	Alnilam	275 46.7	S 1 11.8
E 10	36 06.7	313 42.8	58.3	340 32.9	42.4	313 13.7	00.5	181 26.2	04.0	Alphard	217 56.2	S 8 43.3
S 11	51 09.1	328 41.9	58.6	355 33.5	42.8	328 15.5	00.6	196 28.8	03.9			
D 12	66 11.6	343 41.0	N23 58.9	10 34.2	N19 43.2	343 17.4	N23 00.6	211 31.4	S11 03.9	Alphecca	126 10.7	N26 40.3
A 13	81 14.1	358 40.1	59.1	25 34.8	43.7	358 19.3	00.6	226 34.1	03.8	Alpheratz	357 43.6	N29 09.7
Y 14	96 16.5	13 39.3	59.4	40 35.4	44.1	13 21.1	00.7	241 36.7	03.8	Altair	62 08.0	N 8 54.3
15	111 19.0	28 38.4 ..	59.6	55 36.0 ..	44.5	28 23.0 ..	00.7	256 39.3 ..	03.8	Ankaa	353 16.0	S42 13.8
16	126 21.4	43 37.5	23 59.9	70 36.6	45.0	43 24.8	00.7	271 41.9	03.7	Antares	112 25.9	S26 27.6
17	141 23.9	58 36.6	24 00.1	85 37.2	45.4	58 26.7	00.7	286 44.5	03.7			
18	156 26.4	73 35.8	N24 00.4	100 37.8	N19 45.8	73 28.5	N23 00.8	301 47.1	S11 03.6	Arcturus	145 55.5	N19 06.8
19	171 28.8	88 34.9	00.6	115 38.5	46.2	88 30.4	00.8	316 49.7	03.6	Atria	107 27.2	S69 02.9
20	186 31.3	103 34.0	00.8	130 39.1	46.7	103 32.2	00.8	331 52.3	03.6	Avior	234 18.4	S59 33.6
21	201 33.8	118 33.1 ..	01.1	145 39.7 ..	47.1	118 34.1 ..	00.9	346 54.9 ..	03.5	Bellatrix	278 32.4	N 6 21.5
22	216 36.2	133 32.2	01.3	160 40.3	47.5	133 35.9	00.9	1 57.5	03.5	Betelgeuse	271 01.7	N 7 24.4
23	231 38.7	148 31.4	01.6	175 40.9	47.9	148 37.8	00.9	17 00.1	03.4			
29 00	246 41.2	163 30.5	N24 01.8	190 41.5	N19 48.4	163 39.6	N23 01.0	32 02.7	S11 03.4	Canopus	263 56.7	S52 42.5
01	261 43.6	178 29.6	02.1	205 42.1	48.8	178 41.5	01.0	47 05.3	03.3	Capella	280 35.0	N46 00.5
02	276 46.1	193 28.7	02.3	220 42.8	49.2	193 43.3	01.0	62 07.9	03.3	Deneb	49 31.2	N45 19.6
03	291 48.6	208 27.9 ..	02.5	235 43.4 ..	49.6	208 45.2 ..	01.1	77 10.6 ..	03.3	Denebola	182 33.6	N14 29.8
04	306 51.0	223 27.0	02.8	250 44.0	50.1	223 47.0	01.1	92 13.2	03.2	Diphda	348 56.1	S17 54.7
05	321 53.5	238 26.1	03.0	265 44.6	50.5	238 48.9	01.1	107 15.8	03.2			
06	336 55.9	253 25.2	N24 03.2	280 45.2	N19 50.9	253 50.7	N23 01.2	122 18.4	S11 03.1	Dubhe	193 51.7	N61 40.9
07	351 58.4	268 24.3	03.5	295 45.8	51.3	268 52.6	01.2	137 21.0	03.1	Elnath	278 13.0	N28 36.9
W 08	7 00.9	283 23.5	03.7	310 46.4	51.8	283 54.4	01.2	152 23.6	03.1	Eltanin	90 45.6	N51 29.3
E 09	22 03.3	298 22.6 ..	03.9	325 47.0 ..	52.2	298 56.3 ..	01.3	167 26.2 ..	03.0	Enif	33 47.1	N 9 56.2
D 10	37 05.8	313 21.7	04.1	340 47.7	52.6	313 58.1	01.3	182 28.8	03.0	Fomalhaut	15 24.1	S29 32.8
N 11	52 08.3	328 20.8	04.4	355 48.3	53.0	329 00.0	01.3	197 31.4	02.9			
E 12	67 10.7	343 20.0	N24 04.6	10 48.9	N19 53.4	344 01.9	N23 01.3	212 34.0	S11 02.9	Gacrux	172 00.6	S57 11.6
S 13	82 13.2	358 19.1	04.8	25 49.5	53.9	359 03.7	01.4	227 36.6	02.9	Gienah	175 52.2	S17 37.2
D 14	97 15.7	13 18.2	05.0	40 50.1	54.3	14 05.6	01.4	242 39.2	02.8	Hadar	148 47.3	S60 26.4
A 15	112 18.1	28 17.3 ..	05.3	55 50.7 ..	54.7	29 07.4 ..	01.4	257 41.8 ..	02.8	Hamal	328 01.1	N23 31.4
Y 16	127 20.6	43 16.4	05.5	70 51.3	55.1	44 09.3	01.5	272 44.4	02.7	Kaus Aust.	83 43.5	S34 22.5
17	142 23.0	58 15.6	05.7	85 51.9	55.5	59 11.1	01.5	287 47.0	02.7			
18	157 25.5	73 14.7	N24 05.9	100 52.6	N19 56.0	74 13.0	N23 01.5	302 49.6	S11 02.7	Kochab	137 19.0	N74 06.2
19	172 28.0	88 13.8	06.1	115 53.2	56.4	89 14.8	01.6	317 52.2	02.6	Markab	13 38.4	N15 16.6
20	187 30.4	103 12.9	06.4	130 53.8	56.8	104 16.7	01.6	332 54.9	02.6	Menkar	314 15.4	N 4 08.4
21	202 32.9	118 12.0 ..	06.6	145 54.4 ..	57.2	119 18.5 ..	01.6	347 57.5 ..	02.5	Menkent	148 07.2	S36 26.3
22	217 35.4	133 11.2	06.8	160 55.0	57.6	134 20.4	01.6	3 00.1	02.5	Miaplacidus	221 39.9	S69 46.8
23	232 37.8	148 10.3	07.0	175 55.6	58.1	149 22.2	01.7	18 02.7	02.5			
30 00	247 40.3	163 09.4	N24 07.2	190 56.2	N19 58.5	164 24.1	N23 01.7	33 05.3	S11 02.4	Mirfak	308 40.9	N49 54.3
01	262 42.8	178 08.5	07.4	205 56.8	58.9	179 25.9	01.8	48 07.9	02.4	Nunki	75 58.0	S26 16.6
02	277 45.2	193 07.6	07.6	220 57.5	59.3	194 27.8	01.8	63 10.5	02.3	Peacock	53 19.0	S56 41.1
03	292 47.7	208 06.8 ..	07.8	235 58.1	19 59.7	209 29.6 ..	01.8	78 13.1 ..	02.3	Pollux	243 28.0	N27 59.5
04	307 50.2	223 05.9	08.0	250 58.7	20 00.1	224 31.5	01.8	93 15.7	02.3	Procyon	245 00.0	N 5 11.2
05	322 52.6	238 05.0	08.2	265 59.3	00.5	239 33.3	01.9	108 18.3	02.2			
06	337 55.1	253 04.1	N24 08.4	280 59.9	N20 01.0	254 35.2	N23 01.9	123 20.9	S11 02.2	Rasalhague	96 06.1	N12 33.1
07	352 57.5	268 03.2	08.6	296 00.5	01.4	269 37.0	01.9	138 23.5	02.1	Regulus	207 43.6	N11 54.0
T 08	8 00.0	283 02.3	08.8	311 01.1	01.8	284 38.9	02.0	153 26.1	02.1	Rigel	281 12.4	S 8 11.4
H 09	23 02.5	298 01.5 ..	09.0	326 01.7 ..	02.2	299 40.7 ..	02.0	168 28.7 ..	02.1	Rigil Kent.	139 51.1	S60 53.5
U 10	38 04.9	313 00.6	09.2	341 02.4	02.6	314 42.6	02.0	183 31.3	02.0	Sabik	102 12.2	S15 44.4
R 11	53 07.4	327 59.7	09.4	356 03.0	03.0	329 44.4	02.1	198 33.9	02.0			
S 12	68 09.9	342 58.8	N24 09.6	11 03.6	N20 03.4	344 46.3	N23 02.1	213 36.5	S11 01.9	Schedar	349 40.8	N56 36.4
D 13	83 12.3	357 57.9	09.8	26 04.2	03.9	359 48.1	02.1	228 39.1	01.9	Shaula	96 21.5	S37 06.6
A 14	98 14.8	12 57.0	10.0	41 04.8	04.3	14 50.0	02.1	243 41.7	01.9	Sirius	258 34.0	S16 44.3
Y 15	113 17.3	27 56.2 ..	10.2	56 05.4 ..	04.7	29 51.8 ..	02.2	258 44.3 ..	01.8	Spica	158 31.0	S11 14.0
16	128 19.7	42 55.3	10.4	71 06.0	05.1	44 53.7	02.2	273 46.9	01.8	Suhail	222 52.6	S43 29.6
17	143 22.2	57 54.4	10.6	86 06.6	05.5	59 55.5	02.2	288 49.5	01.7			
18	158 24.7	72 53.5	N24 10.8	101 07.2	N20 05.9	74 57.4	N23 02.3	303 52.1	S11 01.7	Vega	80 38.6	N38 47.8
19	173 27.1	87 52.6	11.0	116 07.9	06.3	89 59.2	02.3	318 54.7	01.7	Zuben'ubi	137 05.1	S16 05.9
20	188 29.6	102 51.7	11.2	131 08.5	06.7	105 01.1	02.3	333 57.3	01.6		SHA	Mer. Pass.
21	203 32.0	117 50.9	11.3	146 09.1 ..	07.1	120 02.9 ..	02.4	348 59.9 ..	01.6		° ′	h m
22	218 34.5	132 50.0	11.5	161 09.7	07.6	135 04.8	02.4	4 02.5	01.5	Venus	276 49.3	13 07
23	233 37.0	147 49.1	11.7	176 10.3	08.0	150 06.6	02.4	19 05.1	01.5	Mars	304 00.4	11 17
	h m									Jupiter	276 58.5	13 04
Mer. Pass. 7 32.0		v −0.9	d 0.2	v 0.6	d 0.4	v 1.9	d 0.0	v 2.6	d 0.0	Saturn	145 21.6	21 48

UT	SUN		MOON					Lat.	Twilight		Sunrise	Moonrise			
									Naut.	Civil		28	29	30	31
	GHA	Dec	GHA	v	Dec	d	HP	°	h m	h m	h m	h m	h m	h m	h m
d h	° ′	° ′	° ′	′	° ′	′	′	N 72	▭	▭	▭	02 19	01 25	01 06	00 53
28 00	180 41.9	N21 26.9	318 17.7	5.0	S17 53.5	6.2	60.6	N 70	▭	▭	▭	01 01	00 54	00 48	00 43
01	195 41.8	27.3	332 41.7	5.1	17 47.3	6.3	60.6	68	▭	▭	▭	00 22	00 30	00 34	00 35
02	210 41.8	27.7	347 05.8	5.1	17 41.0	6.4	60.6	66	////	////	01 25	24 12	00 12	00 22	00 29
03	225 41.7	.. 28.1	1 29.9	5.3	17 34.6	6.6	60.6	64	////	////	02 05	23 57	24 12	00 12	00 23
04	240 41.6	28.5	15 54.2	5.3	17 28.0	6.6	60.5	62	////	00 38	02 33	23 45	24 04	00 04	00 18
05	255 41.5	28.9	30 18.5	5.4	17 21.4	6.8	60.5	60	////	01 35	02 54	23 34	23 56	24 14	00 14
06	270 41.5	N21 29.3	44 42.9	5.4	S17 14.6	6.9	60.5	N 58	////	02 06	03 11	23 25	23 50	24 10	00 10
07	285 41.4	29.7	59 07.3	5.6	17 07.7	7.0	60.5	56	00 34	02 29	03 25	23 16	23 44	24 07	00 07
T 08	300 41.3	30.1	73 31.9	5.6	17 00.7	7.1	60.4	54	01 26	02 47	03 38	23 09	23 39	24 04	00 04
U 09	315 41.2	.. 30.5	87 56.5	5.7	16 53.6	7.2	60.4	52	01 55	03 03	03 49	23 02	23 34	24 01	00 01
E 10	330 41.1	30.9	102 21.2	5.8	16 46.4	7.3	60.4	50	02 17	03 16	03 58	22 56	23 30	23 59	24 24
S 11	345 41.1	31.3	116 46.0	5.9	16 39.1	7.5	60.4	45	02 56	03 42	04 18	22 44	23 21	23 53	24 23
D 12	0 41.0	N21 31.7	131 10.9	5.9	S16 31.6	7.5	60.3	N 40	03 23	04 03	04 35	22 33	23 13	23 49	24 21
A 13	15 40.9	32.1	145 35.8	6.1	16 24.1	7.6	60.3	35	03 44	04 19	04 48	22 24	23 07	23 45	24 20
Y 14	30 40.8	32.5	160 00.9	6.1	16 16.5	7.8	60.3	30	04 01	04 33	05 00	22 16	23 01	23 41	24 19
15	45 40.8	.. 32.9	174 26.0	6.2	16 08.7	7.8	60.3	20	04 27	04 56	05 20	22 02	22 51	23 35	24 17
16	60 40.7	33.3	188 51.2	6.3	16 00.9	7.9	60.2	N 10	04 48	05 15	05 38	21 50	22 42	23 30	24 15
17	75 40.6	33.7	203 16.5	6.4	15 53.0	8.1	60.2	0	05 06	05 32	05 54	21 38	22 33	23 25	24 14
18	90 40.5	N21 34.1	217 41.9	6.5	S15 44.9	8.1	60.2	S 10	05 21	05 47	06 10	21 27	22 25	23 20	24 12
19	105 40.4	34.4	232 07.4	6.6	15 36.8	8.2	60.1	20	05 36	06 03	06 27	21 14	22 16	23 14	24 10
20	120 40.4	34.8	246 33.0	6.6	15 28.6	8.4	60.1	30	05 51	06 20	06 46	21 00	22 06	23 08	24 08
21	135 40.3	.. 35.2	260 58.6	6.7	15 20.2	8.4	60.1	35	05 58	06 30	06 57	20 52	22 00	23 05	24 07
22	150 40.2	35.6	275 24.3	6.9	15 11.8	8.5	60.1	40	06 07	06 40	07 10	20 43	21 53	23 01	24 06
23	165 40.1	36.0	289 50.2	6.9	15 03.3	8.6	60.0	45	06 16	06 52	07 25	20 32	21 45	22 56	24 05
29 00	180 40.0	N21 36.4	304 16.1	7.0	S14 54.7	8.6	60.0	S 50	06 26	07 07	07 44	20 19	21 35	22 50	24 03
01	195 39.9	36.8	318 42.1	7.1	14 46.1	8.8	60.0	52	06 31	07 13	07 53	20 13	21 31	22 48	24 02
02	210 39.9	37.2	333 08.2	7.2	14 37.3	8.8	59.9	54	06 36	07 21	08 03	20 06	21 26	22 45	24 01
03	225 39.8	.. 37.6	347 34.4	7.2	14 28.5	9.0	59.9	56	06 41	07 29	08 14	19 58	21 21	22 42	24 00
04	240 39.7	37.9	2 00.6	7.4	14 19.5	9.0	59.9	58	06 47	07 38	08 27	19 49	21 15	22 38	23 59
05	255 39.6	38.3	16 27.0	7.4	14 10.5	9.1	59.8	S 60	06 53	07 48	08 42	19 40	21 08	22 34	23 58
06	270 39.5	N21 38.7	30 53.4	7.5	S14 01.4	9.1	59.8	Lat.	Sunset	Twilight		Moonset			
W 07	285 39.5	39.1	45 19.9	7.7	13 52.3	9.3	59.8			Civil	Naut.	28	29	30	31
E 08	300 39.4	39.5	59 46.6	7.7	13 43.0	9.3	59.7								
D 09	315 39.3	.. 39.9	74 13.3	7.7	13 33.7	9.4	59.7	°	h m	h m	h m	h m	h m	h m	h m
N 10	330 39.2	40.2	88 40.0	7.9	13 24.3	9.5	59.7	N 72	▭	▭	▭	03 41	06 35	08 47	10 46
E 11	345 39.1	40.6	103 06.9	8.0	13 14.8	9.5	59.7	N 70	▭	▭	▭	04 58	07 06	09 03	10 53
S 12	0 39.0	N21 41.0	117 33.9	8.0	S13 05.3	9.6	59.6	68	▭	▭	▭	05 36	07 28	09 16	10 59
D 13	15 39.0	41.4	132 00.9	8.2	12 55.7	9.7	59.6	66	22 34	////	////	06 02	07 45	09 26	11 04
A 14	30 38.9	41.8	146 28.1	8.2	12 46.0	9.7	59.5	64	21 52	////	////	06 22	07 59	09 35	11 08
Y 15	45 38.8	.. 42.1	160 55.3	8.3	12 36.3	9.8	59.5	62	21 24	23 25	////	06 39	08 11	09 42	11 11
16	60 38.7	42.5	175 22.6	8.4	12 26.5	9.9	59.5	60	21 02	22 23	////	06 52	08 21	09 49	11 14
17	75 38.6	42.9	189 50.0	8.5	12 16.6	9.9	59.5								
18	90 38.5	N21 43.3	204 17.5	8.6	S12 06.7	10.0	59.4	N 58	20 45	21 51	////	07 04	08 29	09 54	11 17
19	105 38.5	43.6	218 45.1	8.6	11 56.7	10.1	59.4	56	20 30	21 27	23 28	07 14	08 37	09 59	11 19
20	120 38.4	44.0	233 12.7	8.7	11 46.6	10.1	59.4	54	20 18	21 08	22 31	07 23	08 44	10 04	11 21
21	135 38.3	.. 44.4	247 40.4	8.9	11 36.5	10.2	59.3	52	20 07	20 53	22 01	07 31	08 50	10 08	11 23
22	150 38.2	44.8	262 08.3	8.8	11 26.3	10.2	59.3	50	19 57	20 40	21 39	07 38	08 55	10 11	11 25
23	165 38.1	45.1	276 36.1	9.0	11 16.1	10.3	59.3	45	19 37	20 13	21 00	07 53	09 07	10 19	11 29
30 00	180 38.0	N21 45.5	291 04.1	9.1	S11 05.8	10.3	59.2	N 40	19 21	19 53	20 33	08 06	09 16	10 25	11 32
01	195 37.9	45.9	305 32.2	9.1	10 55.5	10.4	59.2	35	19 07	19 36	20 12	08 16	09 25	10 31	11 35
02	210 37.9	46.3	320 00.3	9.3	10 45.1	10.4	59.2	30	18 55	19 22	19 54	08 26	09 32	10 36	11 37
03	225 37.8	.. 46.6	334 28.6	9.3	10 34.7	10.5	59.1	20	18 35	18 59	19 28	08 41	09 44	10 44	11 41
04	240 37.7	47.0	348 56.9	9.4	10 24.2	10.5	59.1	N 10	18 18	18 40	19 07	08 55	09 55	10 51	11 45
05	255 37.6	47.4	3 25.3	9.4	10 13.7	10.6	59.0	0	18 01	18 23	18 49	09 08	10 05	10 58	11 48
06	270 37.5	N21 47.7	17 53.7	9.6	S10 03.1	10.6	59.0	S 10	17 45	18 08	18 34	09 21	10 15	11 05	11 52
T 07	285 37.4	48.1	32 22.3	9.6	9 52.5	10.7	59.0	20	17 28	17 52	18 19	09 34	10 25	11 12	11 55
H 08	300 37.3	48.5	46 50.9	9.7	9 41.8	10.7	58.9	30	17 08	17 34	18 04	09 50	10 37	11 20	11 59
U 09	315 37.2	.. 48.8	61 19.6	9.8	9 31.1	10.7	58.9	35	16 57	17 25	17 56	09 58	10 44	11 25	12 01
R 10	330 37.2	49.2	75 48.4	9.8	9 20.4	10.8	58.9	40	16 44	17 14	17 48	10 09	10 52	11 30	12 04
S 11	345 37.1	49.6	90 17.2	9.9	9 09.6	10.9	58.8	45	16 29	17 02	17 39	10 20	11 01	11 36	12 07
D 12	0 37.0	N21 49.9	104 46.1	10.0	S 8 58.7	10.8	58.8	S 50	16 10	16 48	17 28	10 35	11 12	11 43	12 10
A 13	15 36.9	50.3	119 15.1	10.1	8 47.9	10.9	58.8	52	16 02	16 41	17 24	10 41	11 17	11 46	12 12
Y 14	30 36.8	50.7	133 44.2	10.2	8 37.0	11.0	58.7	54	15 52	16 34	17 19	10 49	11 22	11 50	12 13
15	45 36.7	.. 51.0	148 13.4	10.2	8 26.1	11.0	58.7	56	15 41	16 26	17 14	10 57	11 29	11 54	12 15
16	60 36.6	51.4	162 42.6	10.3	8 15.1	11.0	58.7	58	15 28	16 17	17 08	11 06	11 35	11 58	12 17
17	75 36.5	51.7	177 11.9	10.3	8 04.1	11.0	58.6	S 60	15 13	16 07	17 01	11 16	11 43	12 03	12 20
18	90 36.4	N21 52.1	191 41.2	10.5	S 7 53.1	11.1	58.6		SUN			MOON			
19	105 36.4	52.5	206 10.7	10.5	7 42.0	11.1	58.6	Day	Eqn. of Time		Mer.	Mer. Pass.		Age	Phase
20	120 36.3	52.8	220 40.2	10.5	7 30.9	11.1	58.5		00ʰ	12ʰ	Pass.	Upper	Lower		
21	135 36.2	.. 53.2	235 09.7	10.7	7 19.8	11.1	58.5	d	m s	m s	h m	h m	h m	d %	
22	150 36.1	53.5	249 39.4	10.7	7 08.7	11.2	58.5	28	02 48	02 44	11 57	02 54	15 23	18 84	
23	165 36.0	53.9	264 09.1	10.8	S 6 57.5	11.2	58.4	29	02 40	02 36	11 57	03 52	16 19	19 75	
	SD 15.8	d 0.4	SD 16.4		16.2		16.0	30	02 32	02 28	11 58	04 46	17 12	20 64	

UT (d h)	ARIES GHA	VENUS −3.8 GHA	Dec	MARS +1.4 GHA	Dec	JUPITER −1.9 GHA	Dec	SATURN +0.3 GHA	Dec	Star Name	SHA	Dec
31 00	248 39.4	162 48.2	N24 11.9	191 10.9	N20 08.4	165 08.5	N23 02.4	34 07.7	S11 01.5	Acamar	315 18.8	S40 15.0
01	263 41.9	177 47.3	12.1	206 11.5	08.8	180 10.3	02.5	49 10.3	01.4	Achernar	335 27.3	S57 09.9
02	278 44.4	192 46.4	12.3	221 12.1	09.2	195 12.2	02.5	64 12.9	01.4	Acrux	173 08.9	S63 10.8
03	293 46.8	207 45.6 ..	12.4	236 12.7 ..	09.6	210 14.0 ..	02.5	79 15.6 ..	01.4	Adhara	255 12.9	S28 59.7
04	308 49.3	222 44.7	12.6	251 13.3	10.0	225 15.9	02.6	94 18.2	01.3	Aldebaran	290 49.8	N16 32.0
05	323 51.8	237 43.8	12.8	266 14.0	10.4	240 17.7	02.6	109 20.8	01.3			
06	338 54.2	252 42.9	N24 13.0	281 14.6	N20 10.8	255 19.6	N23 02.6	124 23.4	S11 01.2	Alioth	166 20.5	N55 53.4
07	353 56.7	267 42.0	13.1	296 15.2	11.2	270 21.4	02.7	139 26.0	01.2	Alkaid	152 58.6	N49 14.9
08	8 59.2	282 41.1	13.3	311 15.8	11.6	285 23.3	02.7	154 28.6	01.2	Al Na'ir	27 43.7	S46 53.4
F 09	24 01.6	297 40.2 ..	13.5	326 16.4 ..	12.0	300 25.1 ..	02.7	169 31.2 ..	01.1	Alnilam	275 46.7	S 1 11.8
R 10	39 04.1	312 39.4	13.6	341 17.0	12.4	315 27.0	02.7	184 33.8	01.1	Alphard	217 56.2	S 8 43.3
I 11	54 06.5	327 38.5	13.8	356 17.6	12.8	330 28.8	02.8	199 36.4	01.0			
D 12	69 09.0	342 37.6	N24 13.2	11 18.2	N20 13.2	345 30.7	N23 02.8	214 39.0	S11 01.0	Alphecca	126 10.7	N26 40.3
A 13	84 11.5	357 36.7	14.1	26 18.8	13.7	0 32.5	02.8	229 41.6	01.0	Alpheratz	357 43.6	N29 09.7
Y 14	99 13.9	12 35.8	14.3	41 19.4	14.1	15 34.4	02.9	244 44.2	00.9	Altair	62 08.0	N 8 54.3
15	114 16.4	27 34.9 ..	14.5	56 20.1 ..	14.5	30 36.2 ..	02.9	259 46.8 ..	00.9	Ankaa	353 15.9	S42 13.8
16	129 18.9	42 34.0	14.6	71 20.7	14.9	45 38.1	02.9	274 49.4	00.9	Antares	112 25.9	S26 27.6
17	144 21.3	57 33.2	14.8	86 21.3	15.3	60 39.9	03.0	289 52.0	00.8			
18	159 23.8	72 32.3	N24 14.9	101 21.9	N20 15.7	75 41.8	N23 03.0	304 54.6	S11 00.8	Arcturus	145 55.5	N19 06.8
19	174 26.3	87 31.4	15.1	116 22.5	16.1	90 43.6	03.0	319 57.2	00.7	Atria	107 27.2	S69 03.0
20	189 28.7	102 30.5	15.3	131 23.1	16.5	105 45.5	03.0	334 59.8	00.7	Avior	234 18.4	S59 33.6
21	204 31.2	117 29.6 ..	15.4	146 23.7 ..	16.9	120 47.3 ..	03.1	350 02.4 ..	00.7	Bellatrix	278 32.4	N 6 21.5
22	219 33.6	132 28.7	15.6	161 24.3	17.3	135 49.2	03.1	5 05.0	00.6	Betelgeuse	271 01.7	N 7 24.4
23	234 36.1	147 27.8	15.7	176 24.9	17.7	150 51.0	03.1	20 07.6	00.6			
1 00	249 38.6	162 26.9	N24 15.9	191 25.5	N20 18.1	165 52.9	N23 03.2	35 10.2	S11 00.5	Canopus	263 56.7	S52 42.5
01	264 41.0	177 26.1	16.0	206 26.1	18.5	180 54.7	03.2	50 12.8	00.5	Capella	280 35.0	N46 00.5
02	279 43.5	192 25.2	16.2	221 26.8	18.9	195 56.5	03.2	65 15.4	00.5	Deneb	49 31.2	N45 19.6
03	294 46.0	207 24.3 ..	16.3	236 27.4 ..	19.3	210 58.4 ..	03.2	80 18.0 ..	00.4	Denebola	182 33.6	N14 29.8
04	309 48.4	222 23.4	16.5	251 28.0	19.7	226 00.2	03.3	95 20.6	00.4	Diphda	348 56.1	S17 54.7
05	324 50.9	237 22.5	16.6	266 28.6	20.1	241 02.1	03.3	110 23.2	00.4			
06	339 53.4	252 21.6	N24 16.8	281 29.2	N20 20.5	256 03.9	N23 03.3	125 25.7	S11 00.3	Dubhe	193 51.8	N61 40.9
07	354 55.8	267 20.7	16.9	296 29.8	20.9	271 05.8	03.4	140 28.3	00.3	Elnath	278 13.0	N28 36.9
S 08	9 58.3	282 19.8	17.0	311 30.4	21.3	286 07.6	03.4	155 30.9	00.2	Eltanin	90 45.6	N51 29.3
A 09	25 00.8	297 19.0 ..	17.2	326 31.0 ..	21.7	301 09.5 ..	03.4	170 33.5 ..	00.2	Enif	33 47.0	N 9 56.3
T 10	40 03.2	312 18.1	17.3	341 31.6	22.1	316 11.3	03.4	185 36.1	00.2	Fomalhaut	15 24.0	S29 32.8
U 11	55 05.7	327 17.2	17.5	356 32.2	22.5	331 13.2	03.5	200 38.7	00.1			
R 12	70 08.1	342 16.3	N24 17.6	11 32.8	N20 22.9	346 15.0	N23 03.5	215 41.3	S11 00.1	Gacrux	172 00.6	S57 11.6
D 13	85 10.6	357 15.4	17.7	26 33.4	23.3	1 16.9	03.5	230 43.9	00.1	Gienah	175 52.2	S17 37.2
A 14	100 13.1	12 14.5	17.9	41 34.0	23.6	16 18.7	03.6	245 46.5	00.0	Hadar	148 47.3	S60 26.4
Y 15	115 15.5	27 13.6 ..	18.0	56 34.7 ..	24.0	31 20.6 ..	03.6	260 49.1	11 00.0	Hamal	328 01.0	N23 31.4
16	130 18.0	42 12.7	18.1	71 35.3	24.4	46 22.4	03.6	275 51.7	10 59.9	Kaus Aust.	83 43.5	S34 22.5
17	145 20.5	57 11.9	18.3	86 35.9	24.8	61 24.3	03.6	290 54.3	59.9			
18	160 22.9	72 11.0	N24 18.4	101 36.5	N20 25.2	76 26.1	N23 03.7	305 56.9	S10 59.9	Kochab	137 19.1	N74 06.2
19	175 25.4	87 10.1	18.5	116 37.1	25.6	91 28.0	03.7	320 59.5	59.8	Markab	13 38.4	N15 16.6
20	190 27.9	102 09.2	18.6	131 37.7	26.0	106 29.8	03.7	336 02.1	59.8	Menkar	314 15.4	N 4 08.4
21	205 30.3	117 08.3 ..	18.8	146 38.3 ..	26.4	121 31.7 ..	03.8	351 04.7 ..	59.8	Menkent	148 07.3	S36 26.3
22	220 32.8	132 07.4	18.9	161 38.9	26.8	136 33.5	03.8	6 07.3	59.7	Miaplacidus	221 40.0	S69 46.8
23	235 35.2	147 06.5	19.0	176 39.5	27.2	151 35.4	03.8	21 09.9	59.7			
2 00	250 37.7	162 05.6	N24 19.1	191 40.1	N20 27.6	166 37.2	N23 03.8	36 12.5	S10 59.7	Mirfak	308 40.8	N49 54.3
01	265 40.2	177 04.7	19.3	206 40.7	28.0	181 39.1	03.9	51 15.1	59.6	Nunki	75 58.0	S26 16.6
02	280 42.6	192 03.9	19.3	221 41.3	28.4	196 40.9	03.9	66 17.7	59.6	Peacock	53 19.0	S56 41.1
03	295 45.1	207 03.0 ..	19.5	236 41.9 ..	28.8	211 42.8 ..	03.9	81 20.3 ..	59.5	Pollux	243 28.1	N27 59.5
04	310 47.6	222 02.1	19.6	251 42.6	29.1	226 44.6	03.9	96 22.9	59.5	Procyon	245 00.0	N 5 11.2
05	325 50.0	237 01.2	19.7	266 43.2	29.5	241 46.4	04.0	111 25.5	59.5			
06	340 52.5	252 00.3	N24 19.8	281 43.8	N20 29.9	256 48.3	N23 04.0	126 28.1	S10 59.4	Rasalhague	96 06.1	N12 33.1
07	355 55.0	266 59.4	20.0	296 44.4	30.3	271 50.1	04.0	141 30.7	59.4	Regulus	207 43.6	N11 54.0
08	10 57.4	281 58.5	20.1	311 45.0	30.7	286 52.0	04.0	156 33.3	59.4	Rigel	281 12.4	S 8 11.4
S 09	25 59.9	296 57.6 ..	20.2	326 45.6 ..	31.1	301 53.8 ..	04.1	171 35.9 ..	59.3	Rigil Kent.	139 51.1	S60 53.5
U 10	41 02.4	311 56.7	20.3	341 46.2	31.5	316 55.7	04.1	186 38.5	59.3	Sabik	102 12.2	S15 44.4
N 11	56 04.8	326 55.8	20.4	356 46.8	31.9	331 57.5	04.1	201 41.1	59.3			
D 12	71 07.3	341 55.0	N24 20.5	11 47.4	N20 32.3	346 59.4	N23 04.2	216 43.6	S10 59.2	Schedar	349 40.8	N56 36.4
A 13	86 09.7	356 54.1	20.6	26 48.0	32.6	2 01.2	04.2	231 46.2	59.2	Shaula	96 21.5	S37 06.6
Y 14	101 12.2	11 53.2	20.8	41 48.6	33.0	17 03.1	04.2	246 48.8	59.1	Sirius	258 34.0	S16 44.3
15	116 14.7	26 52.3 ..	20.8	56 49.2 ..	33.4	32 04.9 ..	04.2	261 51.4 ..	59.1	Spica	158 31.1	S11 14.0
16	131 17.1	41 51.4	20.9	71 49.8	33.8	47 06.8	04.3	276 54.0	59.1	Suhail	222 52.6	S43 29.6
17	146 19.6	56 50.5	21.0	86 50.4	34.2	62 08.6	04.3	291 56.6	59.0			
18	161 22.1	71 49.6	N24 21.1	101 51.0	N20 34.6	77 10.5	N23 04.3	306 59.2	S10 59.0	Vega	80 38.6	N38 47.8
19	176 24.5	86 48.7	21.2	116 51.6	35.0	92 12.3	04.4	322 01.8	59.0	Zuben'ubi	137 05.1	S16 05.9
20	191 27.0	101 47.8	21.3	131 52.3	35.4	107 14.2	04.4	337 04.4	58.9		SHA	Mer. Pass.
21	206 29.5	116 46.9 ..	21.4	146 52.9 ..	35.7	122 16.0 ..	04.4	352 07.0 ..	58.9	Venus	272 48.4	13 11
22	221 31.9	131 46.1	21.5	161 53.5	36.1	137 17.8	04.4	7 09.6	58.9	Mars	301 47.0	11 14
23	236 34.4	146 45.2	21.6	176 54.1	36.5	152 19.7	04.5	22 12.2	58.8	Jupiter	276 14.3	12 55
Mer. Pass. 7 20.2		v −0.9	d 0.1	v 0.6	d 0.4	v 1.8	d 0.0	v 2.6	d 0.0	Saturn	145 31.6	21 36

UT	SUN GHA	SUN Dec	MOON GHA	v	MOON Dec	d	HP
d h	o '	o '	o '	'	o '	'	'
31 00	180 35.9	N21 54.2	278 38.9	10.8	S 6 46.3	11.2	58.4
01	195 35.8	54.6	293 08.7	10.9	6 35.1	11.2	58.3
02	210 35.7	55.0	307 38.6	11.0	6 23.9	11.3	58.3
03	225 35.6	.. 55.3	322 08.6	11.0	6 12.6	11.3	58.3
04	240 35.5	55.7	336 38.6	11.1	6 01.4	11.3	58.2
05	255 35.5	56.0	351 08.7	11.1	5 50.1	11.3	58.2
06	270 35.4	N21 56.4	5 38.8	11.2	S 5 38.8	11.3	58.2
07	285 35.3	56.7	20 09.0	11.3	5 27.5	11.4	58.1
F 08	300 35.2	57.1	34 39.3	11.3	5 16.1	11.3	58.1
R 09	315 35.1	.. 57.4	49 09.6	11.4	5 04.8	11.4	58.1
I 10	330 35.0	57.8	63 40.0	11.5	4 53.4	11.4	58.0
11	345 34.9	58.1	78 10.5	11.5	4 42.0	11.3	58.0
D 12	0 34.8	N21 58.5	92 41.0	11.5	S 4 30.7	11.4	58.0
A 13	15 34.7	58.8	107 11.5	11.6	4 19.3	11.4	57.9
Y 14	30 34.6	59.2	121 42.1	11.7	4 07.9	11.5	57.9
15	45 34.5	.. 59.5	136 12.8	11.7	3 56.4	11.4	57.9
16	60 34.4	21 59.9	150 43.5	11.8	3 45.0	11.4	57.8
17	75 34.3	22 00.2	165 14.3	11.8	3 33.6	11.4	57.8
18	90 34.2	N22 00.6	179 45.1	11.8	S 3 22.2	11.4	57.8
19	105 34.2	00.9	194 15.9	12.0	3 10.8	11.5	57.7
20	120 34.1	01.2	208 46.9	11.9	2 59.3	11.4	57.7
21	135 34.0	.. 01.6	223 17.8	12.0	2 47.9	11.5	57.7
22	150 33.9	01.9	237 48.8	12.1	2 36.4	11.4	57.6
23	165 33.8	02.3	252 19.9	12.1	2 25.0	11.4	57.6
1 00	180 33.7	N22 02.6	266 51.0	12.1	S 2 13.6	11.4	57.6
01	195 33.6	02.9	281 22.1	12.2	2 02.2	11.5	57.5
02	210 33.5	03.3	295 53.3	12.3	1 50.7	11.4	57.5
03	225 33.4	.. 03.6	310 24.6	12.2	1 39.3	11.4	57.5
04	240 33.3	04.0	324 55.8	12.4	1 27.9	11.4	57.4
05	255 33.2	04.3	339 27.2	12.3	1 16.5	11.4	57.4
06	270 33.1	N22 04.6	353 58.5	12.4	S 1 05.1	11.4	57.4
07	285 33.0	05.0	8 29.9	12.4	0 53.7	11.4	57.3
S 08	300 32.9	05.3	23 01.3	12.5	0 42.3	11.4	57.3
A 09	315 32.8	.. 05.6	37 32.8	12.5	0 30.9	11.4	57.3
T 10	330 32.7	06.0	52 04.3	12.6	0 19.5	11.3	57.2
U 11	345 32.6	06.3	66 35.9	12.5	S 0 08.2	11.4	57.2
R 12	0 32.5	N22 06.6	81 07.4	12.6	N 0 03.2	11.3	57.2
D 13	15 32.4	07.0	95 39.0	12.7	0 14.5	11.3	57.1
A 14	30 32.3	07.3	110 10.7	12.7	0 25.8	11.4	57.1
Y 15	45 32.2	.. 07.6	124 42.4	12.7	0 37.2	11.2	57.1
16	60 32.1	08.0	139 14.1	12.7	0 48.4	11.3	57.0
17	75 32.0	08.3	153 45.8	12.8	0 59.7	11.3	57.0
18	90 31.9	N22 08.6	168 17.6	12.8	N 1 11.0	11.2	57.0
19	105 31.8	08.9	182 49.4	12.8	1 22.2	11.2	56.9
20	120 31.7	09.3	197 21.2	12.9	1 33.4	11.2	56.9
21	135 31.6	.. 09.6	211 53.1	12.8	1 44.6	11.2	56.9
22	150 31.6	09.9	226 24.9	12.9	1 55.8	11.2	56.9
23	165 31.5	10.3	240 56.8	13.0	2 07.0	11.1	56.8
2 00	180 31.4	N22 10.6	255 28.8	12.9	N 2 18.1	11.2	56.8
01	195 31.3	10.9	270 00.7	13.0	2 29.3	11.0	56.8
02	210 31.2	11.2	284 32.7	13.0	2 40.3	11.1	56.7
03	225 31.1	.. 11.5	299 04.7	13.0	2 51.4	11.1	56.7
04	240 31.0	11.9	313 36.7	13.1	3 02.5	11.0	56.7
05	255 30.9	12.2	328 08.8	13.0	3 13.5	11.0	56.6
06	270 30.8	N22 12.5	342 40.8	13.1	N 3 24.5	11.0	56.6
07	285 30.7	12.8	357 12.9	13.1	3 35.5	10.9	56.6
08	300 30.6	13.1	11 45.0	13.1	3 46.4	10.9	56.5
S 09	315 30.5	.. 13.5	26 17.1	13.1	3 57.3	10.9	56.5
U 10	330 30.4	13.8	40 49.2	13.2	4 08.2	10.8	56.5
N 11	345 30.3	14.1	55 21.4	13.1	4 19.0	10.9	56.5
D 12	0 30.1	N22 14.4	69 53.5	13.2	N 4 29.9	10.8	56.4
A 13	15 30.0	14.7	84 25.7	13.2	4 40.7	10.7	56.4
Y 14	30 29.9	15.0	98 57.9	13.2	4 51.4	10.7	56.4
15	45 29.8	.. 15.4	113 30.1	13.2	5 02.1	10.7	56.3
16	60 29.7	15.7	128 02.3	13.2	5 12.8	10.7	56.3
17	75 29.6	16.0	142 34.6	13.2	5 23.5	10.6	56.3
18	90 29.5	N22 16.3	157 06.8	13.2	N 5 34.1	10.6	56.3
19	105 29.4	16.6	171 39.0	13.3	5 44.7	10.6	56.2
20	120 29.3	16.9	186 11.3	13.3	5 55.3	10.5	56.2
21	135 29.2	.. 17.2	200 43.6	13.2	6 05.8	10.5	56.2
22	150 29.1	17.5	215 15.8	13.3	6 16.3	10.4	56.1
23	165 29.0	17.9	229 48.1	13.3	N 6 26.7	10.4	56.1
	SD 15.8	d 0.3	SD 15.8		15.6		15.4

Twilight / Sunrise / Moonrise

Lat.	Naut.	Civil	Sunrise	31	1	2	3
o	h m	h m	h m	h m	h m	h m	h m
N 72	□	□	□	00 53	00 41	00 31	00 20
N 70	□	□	□	00 43	00 39	00 34	00 30
68	□	□	□	00 35	00 36	00 37	00 37
66	////	////	01 12	00 29	00 34	00 39	00 44
64	////	////	01 58	00 23	00 32	00 41	00 49
62	////	////	02 27	00 18	00 31	00 42	00 54
60	////	01 26	02 49	00 14	00 29	00 44	00 58
N 58	////	02 00	03 07	00 10	00 28	00 45	01 01
56	////	02 24	03 22	00 07	00 27	00 46	01 05
54	01 18	02 44	03 35	00 04	00 26	00 47	01 08
52	01 50	02 59	03 46	00 01	00 25	00 48	01 10
50	02 13	03 13	03 56	24 24	00 24	00 49	01 13
45	02 53	03 40	04 17	24 23	00 23	00 50	01 18
N 40	03 21	04 01	04 33	24 21	00 21	00 52	01 23
35	03 42	04 18	04 47	24 20	00 20	00 53	01 27
30	04 00	04 32	04 59	24 19	00 19	00 55	01 30
20	04 27	04 56	05 20	24 17	00 17	00 57	01 36
N 10	04 48	05 15	05 38	24 15	00 15	00 59	01 41
0	05 06	05 32	05 54	24 14	00 14	01 00	01 46
S 10	05 22	05 48	06 11	24 12	00 12	01 02	01 51
20	05 37	06 04	06 28	24 10	00 10	01 04	01 57
30	05 52	06 22	06 48	24 08	00 08	01 07	02 03
35	06 00	06 31	06 59	24 07	00 07	01 08	02 07
40	06 09	06 42	07 12	24 06	00 06	01 09	02 11
45	06 18	06 55	07 28	24 05	00 05	01 11	02 16
S 50	06 29	07 10	07 47	24 03	00 03	01 13	02 21
52	06 33	07 16	07 56	24 02	00 02	01 14	02 24
54	06 38	07 24	08 06	24 01	00 01	01 15	02 27
56	06 44	07 32	08 18	24 00	00 00	01 16	02 30
58	06 50	07 41	08 31	23 59	25 18	01 18	02 34
S 60	06 57	07 52	08 47	23 58	25 19	01 19	02 38

Sunset / Twilight / Moonset

Lat.	Sunset	Civil	Naut.	31	1	2	3
o	h m	h m	h m	h m	h m	h m	h m
N 72	□	□	□	10 46	12 37	14 25	16 12
N 70	□	□	□	10 53	12 37	14 18	15 57
68	□	□	□	10 59	12 37	14 12	15 46
66	22 48	////	////	11 04	12 37	14 07	15 36
64	22 00	////	////	11 08	12 37	14 03	15 28
62	21 30	////	////	11 11	12 37	14 00	15 21
60	21 08	22 33	////	11 14	12 37	13 57	15 15
N 58	20 50	21 57	////	11 17	12 37	13 54	15 10
56	20 35	21 33	////	11 19	12 37	13 52	15 05
54	20 22	21 13	22 40	11 21	12 37	13 50	15 01
52	20 10	20 57	22 07	11 23	12 37	13 48	14 57
50	20 00	20 43	21 44	11 25	12 37	13 46	14 54
45	19 40	20 16	21 04	11 29	12 37	13 42	14 46
N 40	19 23	19 55	20 35	11 32	12 37	13 39	14 40
35	19 09	19 38	20 14	11 35	12 37	13 36	14 35
30	18 57	19 24	19 56	11 37	12 36	13 34	14 30
20	18 36	19 00	19 29	11 41	12 36	13 30	14 22
N 10	18 18	18 41	19 08	11 45	12 36	13 26	14 15
0	18 01	18 24	18 50	11 48	12 36	13 23	14 08
S 10	17 45	18 08	18 34	11 52	12 36	13 19	14 02
20	17 28	17 51	18 19	11 55	12 36	13 15	13 55
30	17 08	17 34	18 03	11 59	12 36	13 11	13 47
35	16 56	17 24	17 55	12 01	12 36	13 09	13 42
40	16 43	17 13	17 47	12 04	12 35	13 06	13 37
45	16 27	17 01	17 37	12 07	12 35	13 03	13 31
S 50	16 08	16 46	17 27	12 10	12 35	12 59	13 24
52	15 59	16 39	17 22	12 12	12 35	12 57	13 20
54	15 49	16 32	17 17	12 13	12 35	12 56	13 17
56	15 37	16 23	17 11	12 15	12 35	12 53	13 13
58	15 24	16 13	17 05	12 17	12 35	12 50	13 08
S 60	15 09	16 03	16 59	12 20	12 34	12 49	13 03

	SUN		MOON			
Day	Eqn. of Time 00h	Eqn. of Time 12h	Mer. Pass.	Mer. Pass. Upper	Mer. Pass. Lower	Age Phase
d	m s	m s	h m	h m	h m	d %
31	02 24	02 19	11 58	05 37	18 01	21 53
1	02 15	02 10	11 58	06 25	18 48	22 43
2	02 06	02 01	11 58	07 11	19 34	23 32

UT	ARIES GHA	VENUS −3.8 GHA	Dec	MARS +1.4 GHA	Dec	JUPITER −1.9 GHA	Dec	SATURN +0.4 GHA	Dec	STARS Name	SHA	Dec
d h	° '	° '	° '	° '	° '	° '	° '	° '	° '		° '	° '
3 00	251 36.9	161 44.3	N24 21.7	191 54.7	N20 36.9	167 21.5	N23 04.5	37 14.8	S10 58.8	Acamar	315 18.8	S40 15.0
01	266 39.3	176 43.4	21.8	206 55.3	37.3	182 23.4	04.5	52 17.4	58.7	Achernar	335 27.2	S57 09.9
02	281 41.8	191 42.5	21.9	221 55.9	37.7	197 25.2	04.5	67 20.0	58.7	Acrux	173 08.9	S63 10.8
03	296 44.2	206 41.6	.. 22.0	236 56.5	.. 38.0	212 27.1	.. 04.6	82 22.6	.. 58.7	Adhara	255 12.9	S28 59.7
04	311 46.7	221 40.7	22.0	251 57.1	38.4	227 28.9	04.6	97 25.2	58.6	Aldebaran	290 49.7	N16 32.0
05	326 49.2	236 39.8	22.1	266 57.7	38.8	242 30.8	04.6	112 27.7	58.6			
M 06	341 51.6	251 38.9	N24 22.2	281 58.3	N20 39.2	257 32.6	N23 04.7	127 30.3	S10 58.6	Alioth	166 20.5	N55 53.4
O 07	356 54.1	266 38.0	22.3	296 58.9	39.6	272 34.5	04.7	142 32.9	58.5	Alkaid	152 58.6	N49 14.9
N 08	11 56.6	281 37.1	22.4	311 59.5	39.9	287 36.3	04.7	157 35.5	58.5	Al Na'ir	27 43.7	S46 53.4
D 09	26 59.0	296 36.3	.. 22.5	327 00.1	.. 40.3	302 38.2	.. 04.7	172 38.1	.. 58.5	Alnilam	275 46.7	S 1 11.8
A 10	42 01.5	311 35.4	22.5	342 00.7	40.7	317 40.0	04.8	187 40.7	58.4	Alphard	217 56.2	S 8 43.3
Y 11	57 04.0	326 34.5	22.6	357 01.3	41.1	332 41.9	04.8	202 43.3	58.4			
12	72 06.4	341 33.6	N24 22.7	12 01.9	N20 41.5	347 43.7	N23 04.8	217 45.9	S10 58.4	Alphecca	126 10.7	N26 40.3
13	87 08.9	356 32.7	22.8	27 02.5	41.8	2 45.5	04.8	232 48.5	58.3	Alpheratz	357 43.6	N29 09.8
14	102 11.3	11 31.8	22.8	42 03.2	42.2	17 47.4	04.9	247 51.1	58.3	Altair	62 08.0	N 8 54.3
15	117 13.8	26 30.9	.. 22.9	57 03.8	.. 42.6	32 49.2	.. 04.9	262 53.7	.. 58.3	Ankaa	353 15.9	S42 13.7
16	132 16.3	41 30.0	23.0	72 04.4	43.0	47 51.1	04.9	277 56.3	58.2	Antares	112 25.9	S26 27.6
17	147 18.7	56 29.1	23.1	87 05.0	43.4	62 52.9	04.9	292 58.9	58.2			
18	162 21.2	71 28.2	N24 23.1	102 05.6	N20 43.7	77 54.8	N23 05.0	308 01.4	S10 58.1	Arcturus	145 55.5	N19 06.8
19	177 23.7	86 27.3	23.2	117 06.2	44.1	92 56.6	05.0	323 04.0	58.1	Atria	107 27.1	S69 03.0
20	192 26.1	101 26.5	23.3	132 06.8	44.5	107 58.5	05.0	338 06.6	58.1	Avior	234 18.4	S59 33.6
21	207 28.6	116 25.6	.. 23.3	147 07.4	.. 44.9	123 00.3	.. 05.0	353 09.2	.. 58.0	Bellatrix	278 32.4	N 6 21.5
22	222 31.1	131 24.7	23.4	162 08.0	45.2	138 02.2	05.1	8 11.8	58.0	Betelgeuse	271 01.7	N 7 24.4
23	237 33.5	146 23.8	23.5	177 08.6	45.6	153 04.0	05.1	23 14.4	58.0			
4 00	252 36.0	161 22.9	N24 23.5	192 09.2	N20 46.0	168 05.9	N23 05.1	38 17.0	S10 57.9	Canopus	263 56.7	S52 42.4
01	267 38.5	176 22.0	23.6	207 09.8	46.4	183 07.7	05.2	53 19.6	57.9	Capella	280 35.0	N46 00.5
02	282 40.9	191 21.1	23.6	222 10.4	46.7	198 09.5	05.2	68 22.2	57.9	Deneb	49 31.2	N45 19.6
03	297 43.4	206 20.2	.. 23.7	237 11.0	.. 47.1	213 11.4	.. 05.2	83 24.8	.. 57.8	Denebola	182 33.6	N14 29.8
04	312 45.8	221 19.3	23.8	252 11.6	47.5	228 13.2	05.2	98 27.4	57.8	Diphda	348 56.1	S17 54.7
05	327 48.3	236 18.4	23.8	267 12.2	47.9	243 15.1	05.3	113 29.9	57.8			
T 06	342 50.8	251 17.5	N24 23.9	282 12.8	N20 48.2	258 16.9	N23 05.3	128 32.5	S10 57.7	Dubhe	193 51.8	N61 40.9
U 07	357 53.2	266 16.6	23.9	297 13.4	48.6	273 18.8	05.3	143 35.1	57.7	Elnath	278 13.0	N28 36.9
E 08	12 55.7	281 15.8	24.0	312 14.0	49.0	288 20.6	05.3	158 37.7	57.7	Eltanin	90 45.6	N51 29.3
S 09	27 58.2	296 14.9	.. 24.0	327 14.6	.. 49.4	303 22.5	.. 05.4	173 40.3	.. 57.6	Enif	33 47.0	N 9 56.3
D 10	43 00.6	311 14.0	24.1	342 15.2	49.7	318 24.3	05.4	188 42.9	57.6	Fomalhaut	15 24.0	S29 32.8
A 11	58 03.1	326 13.1	24.1	357 15.8	50.1	333 26.2	05.4	203 45.5	57.6			
Y 12	73 05.6	341 12.2	N24 24.2	12 16.4	N20 50.5	348 28.0	N23 05.5	218 48.1	S10 57.5	Gacrux	172 00.6	S57 11.6
13	88 08.0	356 11.3	24.2	27 17.0	50.8	3 29.8	05.5	233 50.7	57.5	Gienah	175 52.2	S17 37.2
14	103 10.5	11 10.4	24.3	42 17.6	51.2	18 31.7	05.5	248 53.2	57.5	Hadar	148 47.4	S60 26.5
15	118 13.0	26 09.5	.. 24.3	57 18.3	.. 51.6	33 33.5	.. 05.5	263 55.8	.. 57.4	Hamal	328 01.0	N23 31.4
16	133 15.4	41 08.6	24.3	72 18.9	52.0	48 35.4	05.5	278 58.4	57.4	Kaus Aust.	83 43.5	S34 22.5
17	148 17.9	56 07.7	24.4	87 19.5	52.3	63 37.2	05.6	294 01.0	57.4			
18	163 20.3	71 06.8	N24 24.4	102 20.1	N20 52.7	78 39.1	N23 05.6	309 03.6	S10 57.3	Kochab	137 19.1	N74 06.2
19	178 22.8	86 05.9	24.5	117 20.7	53.1	93 40.9	05.6	324 06.2	57.3	Markab	13 38.3	N15 16.6
20	193 25.3	101 05.1	24.5	132 21.3	53.4	108 42.8	05.6	339 08.8	57.3	Menkar	314 15.4	N 4 08.4
21	208 27.7	116 04.2	.. 24.5	147 21.9	.. 53.8	123 44.6	.. 05.7	354 11.4	.. 57.2	Menkent	148 07.3	S36 26.3
22	223 30.2	131 03.3	24.6	162 22.5	54.2	138 46.5	05.7	9 14.0	57.2	Miaplacidus	221 40.0	S69 46.8
23	238 32.7	146 02.4	24.6	177 23.1	54.5	153 48.3	05.7	24 16.5	57.2			
5 00	253 35.1	161 01.5	N24 24.6	192 23.7	N20 54.9	168 50.1	N23 05.7	39 19.1	S10 57.1	Mirfak	308 40.8	N49 54.3
01	268 37.6	176 00.6	24.7	207 24.3	55.3	183 52.0	05.8	54 21.7	57.1	Nunki	75 58.0	S26 16.6
02	283 40.1	190 59.7	24.7	222 24.9	55.6	198 53.8	05.8	69 24.3	57.1	Peacock	53 18.9	S56 41.1
03	298 42.5	205 58.8	.. 24.7	237 25.5	.. 56.0	213 55.7	.. 05.8	84 26.9	.. 57.0	Pollux	243 28.1	N27 59.5
04	313 45.0	220 57.9	24.7	252 26.1	56.4	228 57.5	05.8	99 29.5	57.0	Procyon	245 00.0	N 5 11.2
05	328 47.4	235 57.0	24.8	267 26.7	56.7	243 59.4	05.9	114 32.1	57.0			
W 06	343 49.9	250 56.1	N24 24.8	282 27.3	N20 57.1	259 01.2	N23 05.9	129 34.7	S10 56.9	Rasalhague	96 06.1	N12 33.1
E 07	358 52.4	265 55.2	24.8	297 27.9	57.5	274 03.1	05.9	144 37.2	56.9	Regulus	207 43.6	N11 54.0
D 08	13 54.8	280 54.4	24.8	312 28.5	57.8	289 04.9	05.9	159 39.8	56.9	Rigel	281 12.4	S 8 11.4
N 09	28 57.3	295 53.5	.. 24.9	327 29.1	.. 58.2	304 06.7	.. 06.0	174 42.4	.. 56.8	Rigil Kent.	139 51.1	S60 53.5
E 10	43 59.8	310 52.6	24.9	342 29.7	58.5	319 08.6	06.0	189 45.0	56.8	Sabik	102 12.2	S15 44.4
S 11	59 02.2	325 51.7	24.9	357 30.3	58.9	334 10.4	06.0	204 47.6	56.8			
D 12	74 04.7	340 50.8	N24 24.9	12 30.9	N20 59.3	349 12.3	N23 06.0	219 50.2	S10 56.7	Schedar	349 40.7	N56 36.4
A 13	89 07.2	355 49.9	24.9	27 31.5	20 59.6	4 14.1	06.1	234 52.8	56.7	Shaula	96 21.5	S37 06.6
Y 14	104 09.6	10 49.0	25.0	42 32.1	21 00.0	19 16.0	06.1	249 55.3	56.7	Sirius	258 34.1	S16 44.3
15	119 12.1	25 48.1	.. 25.0	57 32.7	.. 00.4	34 17.8	.. 06.1	264 57.9	.. 56.6	Spica	158 31.1	S11 14.0
16	134 14.6	40 47.2	25.0	72 33.3	00.7	49 19.7	06.1	280 00.5	56.6	Suhail	222 52.6	S43 29.6
17	149 17.0	55 46.3	25.0	87 33.9	01.1	64 21.5	06.2	295 03.1	56.6			
18	164 19.5	70 45.4	N24 25.0	102 34.5	N21 01.4	79 23.3	N23 06.2	310 05.7	S10 56.5	Vega	80 38.6	N38 47.8
19	179 21.9	85 44.5	25.0	117 35.1	01.8	94 25.2	06.2	325 08.3	56.5	Zuben'ubi	137 05.1	S16 05.9
20	194 24.4	100 43.7	25.0	132 35.7	02.2	109 27.0	06.3	340 10.9	56.5		SHA	Mer. Pass.
21	209 26.9	115 42.8	.. 25.0	147 36.3	.. 02.5	124 28.9	.. 06.3	355 13.4	.. 56.4	Venus	268 46.9	13 15
22	224 29.3	130 41.9	25.0	162 36.9	02.9	139 30.7	06.3	10 16.0	56.4	Mars	299 33.2	11 11
23	239 31.8	145 41.0	25.0	177 37.5	03.2	154 32.6	06.3	25 18.6	56.4	Jupiter	275 29.9	12 46
Mer. Pass. 7 08.4		v −0.9	d 0.0	v 0.6	d 0.4	v 1.8	d 0.0	v 2.6	d 0.0	Saturn	145 41.0	21 23

UT	SUN GHA	SUN Dec	MOON GHA	v	MOON Dec	d	HP
d h	° ′	° ′	° ′	′	° ′	′	′
3 00	180 28.9	N22 18.2	244 20.4	13.3	N 6 37.1	10.4	56.1
01	195 28.8	18.5	258 52.7	13.3	6 47.5	10.3	56.1
02	210 28.7	18.8	273 25.0	13.3	6 57.8	10.3	56.0
03	225 28.6	.. 19.1	287 57.3	13.3	7 08.1	10.2	56.0
04	240 28.5	19.4	302 29.6	13.3	7 18.3	10.2	56.0
05	255 28.4	19.7	317 01.9	13.3	7 28.5	10.2	56.0
M 06	270 28.3	N22 20.0	331 34.2	13.3	N 7 38.7	10.1	55.9
07	285 28.2	20.3	346 06.5	13.3	7 48.8	10.0	55.9
O 08	300 28.1	20.6	0 38.8	13.3	7 58.8	10.1	55.9
N 09	315 28.0	.. 20.9	15 11.1	13.3	8 08.9	9.9	55.9
10	330 27.9	21.2	29 43.4	13.4	8 18.8	10.0	55.8
D 11	345 27.8	21.5	44 15.8	13.3	8 28.8	9.9	55.8
A 12	0 27.7	N22 21.8	58 48.1	13.3	N 8 38.7	9.8	55.8
Y 13	15 27.6	22.1	73 20.4	13.3	8 48.5	9.8	55.8
14	30 27.5	22.4	87 52.7	13.3	8 58.3	9.7	55.7
15	45 27.4	.. 22.7	102 25.0	13.3	9 08.0	9.7	55.7
16	60 27.2	23.0	116 57.3	13.3	9 17.7	9.7	55.7
17	75 27.1	23.3	131 29.6	13.3	9 27.4	9.6	55.7
18	90 27.0	N22 23.6	146 01.9	13.3	N 9 37.0	9.5	55.6
19	105 26.9	23.9	160 34.2	13.2	9 46.5	9.5	55.6
20	120 26.8	24.2	175 06.4	13.3	9 56.0	9.4	55.6
21	135 26.7	.. 24.5	189 38.7	13.3	10 05.4	9.4	55.6
22	150 26.6	24.8	204 11.0	13.2	10 14.8	9.4	55.5
23	165 26.5	25.1	218 43.2	13.3	10 24.2	9.2	55.5
4 00	180 26.4	N22 25.4	233 15.5	13.2	N10 33.4	9.3	55.5
01	195 26.3	25.7	247 47.7	13.3	10 42.7	9.1	55.5
02	210 26.2	25.9	262 20.0	13.2	10 51.8	9.1	55.4
03	225 26.1	.. 26.2	276 52.2	13.2	11 00.9	9.1	55.4
04	240 26.0	26.5	291 24.4	13.2	11 10.0	9.0	55.4
05	255 25.9	26.8	305 56.6	13.2	11 19.0	8.9	55.4
T 06	270 25.8	N22 27.1	320 28.8	13.2	N11 27.9	8.9	55.4
U 07	285 25.7	27.4	335 01.0	13.2	11 36.8	8.9	55.4
E 08	300 25.5	27.7	349 33.2	13.1	11 45.7	8.7	55.3
S 09	315 25.4	.. 28.0	4 05.3	13.2	11 54.4	8.7	55.3
D 10	330 25.3	28.2	18 37.5	13.1	12 03.1	8.7	55.3
A 11	345 25.2	28.5	33 09.6	13.2	12 11.8	8.6	55.3
Y 12	0 25.1	N22 28.8	47 41.8	13.1	N12 20.4	8.5	55.2
13	15 25.0	29.1	62 13.9	13.1	12 28.9	8.4	55.2
14	30 24.9	29.4	76 46.0	13.1	12 37.3	8.4	55.2
15	45 24.8	.. 29.7	91 18.1	13.0	12 45.7	8.4	55.2
16	60 24.7	29.9	105 50.1	13.1	12 54.1	8.3	55.2
17	75 24.6	30.2	120 22.2	13.0	13 02.4	8.2	55.1
18	90 24.4	N22 30.5	134 54.2	13.1	N13 10.6	8.1	55.1
19	105 24.3	30.8	149 26.3	13.0	13 18.7	8.1	55.1
20	120 24.2	31.1	163 58.3	13.0	13 26.8	8.0	55.1
21	135 24.1	.. 31.3	178 30.3	13.0	13 34.8	8.0	55.1
22	150 24.0	31.6	193 02.3	12.9	13 42.8	7.8	55.1
23	165 23.9	31.9	207 34.2	13.0	13 50.6	7.9	55.0
5 00	180 23.8	N22 32.2	222 06.2	12.9	N13 58.5	7.7	55.0
01	195 23.7	32.4	236 38.1	12.9	14 06.2	7.7	55.0
02	210 23.6	32.7	251 10.0	12.9	14 13.9	7.6	55.0
03	225 23.4	.. 33.0	265 41.9	12.9	14 21.5	7.5	55.0
04	240 23.3	33.3	280 13.8	12.9	14 29.0	7.5	54.9
05	255 23.2	33.5	294 45.7	12.8	14 36.5	7.4	54.9
W 06	270 23.1	N22 33.8	309 17.5	12.8	N14 43.9	7.3	54.9
E 07	285 23.0	34.1	323 49.3	12.9	14 51.2	7.3	54.9
D 08	300 22.9	34.3	338 21.2	12.7	14 58.5	7.2	54.9
N 09	315 22.8	.. 34.6	352 52.9	12.8	15 05.7	7.1	54.9
E 10	330 22.7	34.9	7 24.7	12.8	15 12.8	7.0	54.8
S 11	345 22.6	35.1	21 56.5	12.7	15 19.8	7.0	54.8
D 12	0 22.4	N22 35.4	36 28.2	12.7	N15 26.8	6.9	54.8
A 13	15 22.3	35.7	50 59.9	12.8	15 33.7	6.8	54.8
Y 14	30 22.2	35.9	65 31.7	12.6	15 40.5	6.7	54.8
15	45 22.1	.. 36.2	80 03.3	12.7	15 47.2	6.7	54.8
16	60 22.0	36.5	94 35.0	12.7	15 53.9	6.6	54.7
17	75 21.9	36.7	109 06.7	12.6	16 00.5	6.5	54.7
18	90 21.8	N22 37.0	123 38.3	12.6	N16 07.0	6.4	54.7
19	105 21.6	37.3	138 09.9	12.6	16 13.4	6.4	54.7
20	120 21.5	37.5	152 41.5	12.5	16 19.8	6.3	54.7
21	135 21.4	.. 37.8	167 13.1	12.5	16 26.1	6.2	54.7
22	150 21.3	38.1	181 44.6	12.6	16 32.3	6.1	54.6
23	165 21.2	38.3	196 16.2	12.5	N16 38.4	6.0	54.6
	SD 15.8	d 0.3	SD 15.2		15.1		14.9

Lat.	Twilight Naut.	Twilight Civil	Sunrise	Moonrise 3	4	5	6
°	h m	h m	h m	h m	h m	h m	h m
N 72	□	□	□	00 20	{00 23 / 00 54}	23 30	□
N 70	□	□	□	00 30	00 25	00 21	00 16
68	□	□	□	00 37	00 38	00 41	00 46
66	////	////	00 58	00 44	00 49	00 57	01 09
64	////	////	01 51	00 49	00 59	01 11	01 27
62	////	////	02 22	00 54	01 07	01 22	01 42
60	////	01 17	02 45	00 58	01 13	01 32	01 54
N 58	////	01 55	03 04	01 01	01 19	01 40	02 05
56	////	02 20	03 19	01 05	01 25	01 48	02 14
54	01 10	02 40	03 32	01 08	01 30	01 54	02 23
52	01 45	02 57	03 44	01 10	01 34	02 00	02 30
50	02 09	03 11	03 54	01 13	01 38	02 06	02 37
45	02 50	03 38	04 15	01 18	01 47	02 18	02 52
N 40	03 19	04 00	04 32	01 23	01 54	02 27	03 04
35	03 41	04 17	04 46	01 27	02 00	02 36	03 14
30	03 59	04 32	04 59	01 30	02 06	02 43	03 23
20	04 27	04 55	05 20	01 36	02 16	02 56	03 38
N 10	04 48	05 15	05 38	01 41	02 24	03 07	03 52
0	05 06	05 32	05 55	01 46	02 32	03 18	04 05
S 10	05 22	05 49	06 11	01 51	02 40	03 29	04 18
20	05 38	06 05	06 29	01 57	02 49	03 40	04 32
30	05 53	06 23	06 49	02 03	02 59	03 54	04 48
35	06 02	06 33	07 01	02 07	03 05	04 01	04 57
40	06 10	06 44	07 14	02 11	03 11	04 10	05 07
45	06 20	06 57	07 30	02 16	03 19	04 20	05 20
S 50	06 31	07 12	07 50	02 21	03 28	04 33	05 35
52	06 36	07 19	07 59	02 24	03 32	04 39	05 42
54	06 41	07 27	08 10	02 27	03 37	04 45	05 50
56	06 47	07 35	08 21	02 30	03 42	04 52	05 59
58	06 53	07 45	08 35	02 34	03 48	05 00	06 09
S 60	07 00	07 56	08 51	02 38	03 55	05 10	06 21

Lat.	Sunset	Twilight Civil	Twilight Naut.	Moonset 3	4	5	6
°	h m	h m	h m	h m	h m	h m	h m
N 72	□	□	□	16 12	18 03	20 04	□
N 70	□	□	□	15 57	17 37	19 19	21 03
68	□	□	□	15 46	17 18	18 49	20 17
66	23 03	////	////	15 36	17 03	18 27	19 47
64	22 08	////	////	15 28	16 50	18 10	19 25
62	21 36	////	////	15 21	16 40	17 56	19 07
60	21 13	22 42	////	15 15	16 31	17 44	18 53
N 58	20 54	22 04	////	15 10	16 23	17 34	18 40
56	20 38	21 38	////	15 05	16 16	17 25	18 29
54	20 25	21 17	22 49	15 01	16 10	17 17	18 20
52	20 14	21 01	22 13	14 57	16 04	17 09	18 11
50	20 03	20 47	21 49	14 54	15 59	17 03	18 04
45	19 42	20 19	21 07	14 46	15 49	16 49	17 47
N 40	19 25	19 57	20 38	14 40	15 40	16 30	17 34
35	19 10	19 40	20 16	14 35	15 32	16 28	17 23
30	18 58	19 25	19 58	14 30	15 25	16 20	17 13
20	18 37	19 01	19 30	14 22	15 14	16 05	16 56
N 10	18 18	18 42	19 09	14 15	15 04	15 53	16 42
0	18 02	18 24	18 50	14 08	14 54	15 41	16 28
S 10	17 45	18 08	18 34	14 02	14 45	15 29	16 14
20	17 28	17 51	18 19	13 55	14 35	15 16	15 59
30	17 07	17 33	18 03	13 47	14 23	15 02	15 43
35	16 55	17 23	17 55	13 42	14 17	14 53	15 33
40	16 41	17 12	17 46	13 37	14 09	14 44	15 22
45	16 26	16 59	17 36	13 31	14 01	14 33	15 09
S 50	16 06	16 44	17 25	13 24	13 50	14 19	14 53
52	15 57	16 37	17 20	13 20	13 45	14 13	14 46
54	15 47	16 30	17 15	13 17	13 40	14 06	14 37
56	15 35	16 21	17 09	13 13	13 34	13 59	14 28
58	15 23	16 12	17 03	13 08	13 28	13 51	14 18
S 60	15 05	16 01	16 56	13 03	13 20	13 40	14 06

	SUN Eqn. of Time 00h	SUN Eqn. of Time 12h	SUN Mer. Pass.	MOON Mer. Pass. Upper	MOON Mer. Pass. Lower	Age	Phase
Day							
d	m s	m s	h m	h m	h m	d	%
3	01 56	01 51	11 58	07 57	20 20	24	23
4	01 46	01 41	11 58	08 43	21 06	25	15
5	01 35	01 30	11 59	09 29	21 53	26	9

2013 JUNE 6, 7, 8 (THURS., FRI., SAT.)

UT	ARIES GHA	VENUS −3.8 GHA	Dec	MARS +1.4 GHA	Dec	JUPITER −1.9 GHA	Dec	SATURN +0.4 GHA	Dec	STARS Name	SHA	Dec
d h	° ′	° ′	° ′	° ′	° ′	° ′	° ′	° ′	° ′		° ′	° ′
6 00	254 34.3	160 40.1	N24 25.0	192 38.1	N21 03.6	169 34.4	N23 06.3	40 21.2	S10 56.3	Acamar	315 18.7	S40 15.0
01	269 36.7	175 39.2	25.0	207 38.7	04.0	184 36.3	06.3	55 23.8	56.3	Achernar	335 27.2	S57 09.9
02	284 39.2	190 38.3	25.0	222 39.3	04.3	199 38.1	06.4	70 26.4	56.3	Acrux	173 09.0	S63 10.8
03	299 41.7	205 37.4 . .	25.0	237 39.9 . .	04.7	214 39.9 . .	06.4	85 28.9 . .	56.2	Adhara	255 12.9	S28 59.7
04	314 44.1	220 36.5	25.0	252 40.5	05.0	229 41.8	06.4	100 31.5	56.2	Aldebaran	290 49.7	N16 32.0
05	329 46.6	235 35.6	25.0	267 41.1	05.4	244 43.6	06.4	115 34.1	56.2			
06	344 49.1	250 34.7	N24 25.0	282 41.7	N21 05.7	259 45.5	N23 06.5	130 36.7	S10 56.1	Alioth	166 20.5	N55 53.4
07	359 51.5	265 33.9	25.0	297 42.3	06.1	274 47.3	06.5	145 39.3	56.1	Alkaid	152 58.6	N49 15.0
T 08	14 54.0	280 33.0	25.0	312 42.9	06.5	289 49.2	06.5	160 41.9	56.1	Al Na'ir	27 43.7	S46 53.4
H 09	29 56.4	295 32.1 . .	25.0	327 43.5 . .	06.8	304 51.0 . .	06.5	175 44.5 . .	56.0	Alnilam	275 46.7	S 1 11.8
U 10	44 58.9	310 31.2	25.0	342 44.1	07.2	319 52.9	06.6	190 47.0	56.0	Alphard	217 56.2	S 8 43.3
R 11	60 01.4	325 30.3	25.0	357 44.7	07.5	334 54.7	06.6	205 49.6	56.0			
S 12	75 03.8	340 29.4	N24 25.0	12 45.3	N21 07.9	349 56.5	N23 06.6	220 52.2	S10 56.0	Alphecca	126 10.7	N26 40.3
D 13	90 06.3	355 28.5	24.9	27 45.9	08.2	4 58.4	06.6	235 54.8	55.9	Alpheratz	357 43.6	N29 08.8
A 14	105 08.8	10 27.6	24.9	42 46.5	08.6	20 00.2	06.7	250 57.4	55.9	Altair	62 08.0	N 8 54.4
Y 15	120 11.2	25 26.7 . .	24.9	57 47.1 . .	08.9	35 02.1 . .	06.7	266 00.0 . .	55.9	Ankaa	353 15.9	S42 13.7
16	135 13.7	40 25.8	24.9	72 47.7	09.3	50 03.9	06.7	281 02.5	55.8	Antares	112 25.9	S26 27.6
17	150 16.2	55 24.9	24.9	87 48.3	09.6	65 05.8	06.7	296 05.1	55.8			
18	165 18.6	70 24.1	N24 24.9	102 48.9	N21 10.0	80 07.6	N23 06.8	311 07.7	S10 55.8	Arcturus	145 55.5	N19 06.8
19	180 21.1	85 23.2	24.8	117 49.5	10.3	95 09.5	06.8	326 10.3	55.7	Atria	107 27.1	S69 03.0
20	195 23.5	100 22.3	24.8	132 50.1	10.7	110 11.3	06.8	341 12.9	55.7	Avior	234 18.4	S59 33.6
21	210 26.0	115 21.4 . .	24.8	147 50.7 . .	11.0	125 13.1 . .	06.8	356 15.4 . .	55.7	Bellatrix	278 32.4	N 6 21.5
22	225 28.5	130 20.5	24.8	162 51.3	11.4	140 15.0	06.8	11 18.0	55.6	Betelgeuse	271 01.6	N 7 24.4
23	240 30.9	145 19.6	24.7	177 51.9	11.7	155 16.8	06.9	26 20.6	55.6			
7 00	255 33.4	160 18.7	N24 24.7	192 52.5	N21 12.1	170 18.7	N23 06.9	41 23.2	S10 55.6	Canopus	263 56.7	S52 42.4
01	270 35.9	175 17.8	24.7	207 53.1	12.4	185 20.5	06.9	56 25.8	55.5	Capella	280 34.9	N46 00.5
02	285 38.3	190 16.9	24.6	222 53.7	12.8	200 22.4	06.9	71 28.4	55.5	Deneb	49 31.2	N45 19.7
03	300 40.8	205 16.0 . .	24.6	237 54.3 . .	13.1	215 24.2 . .	07.0	86 30.9 . .	55.5	Denebola	182 33.6	N14 29.8
04	315 43.3	220 15.2	24.6	252 54.9	13.5	230 26.0	07.0	101 33.5	55.5	Diphda	348 56.1	S17 54.7
05	330 45.7	235 14.3	24.5	267 55.5	13.8	245 27.9	07.0	116 36.1	55.4			
06	345 48.2	250 13.4	N24 24.5	282 56.1	N21 14.2	260 29.7	N23 07.0	131 38.7	S10 55.4	Dubhe	193 51.8	N61 40.9
07	0 50.7	265 12.5	24.5	297 56.7	14.5	275 31.6	07.1	146 41.3	55.4	Elnath	278 13.0	N28 36.9
08	15 53.1	280 11.6	24.4	312 57.3	14.9	290 33.4	07.1	161 43.8	55.3	Eltanin	90 45.6	N51 29.3
F 09	30 55.6	295 10.7 . .	24.4	327 57.9 . .	15.2	305 35.3 . .	07.1	176 46.4 . .	55.3	Enif	33 47.0	N 9 56.3
R 10	45 58.0	310 09.8	24.4	342 58.5	15.6	320 37.1	07.1	191 49.0	55.3	Fomalhaut	15 24.0	S29 32.8
I 11	61 00.5	325 08.9	24.3	357 59.1	15.9	335 38.9	07.1	206 51.6	55.2			
D 12	76 03.0	340 08.0	N24 24.3	12 59.7	N21 16.3	350 40.8	N23 07.2	221 54.2	S10 55.2	Gacrux	172 00.6	S57 11.6
A 13	91 05.4	355 07.2	24.2	28 00.3	16.6	5 42.6	07.2	236 56.7	55.2	Gienah	175 52.2	S17 37.2
Y 14	106 07.9	10 06.3	24.2	43 00.9	17.0	20 44.5	07.2	251 59.3	55.1	Hadar	148 47.4	S60 26.5
15	121 10.4	25 05.4 . .	24.1	58 01.5 . .	17.3	35 46.3 . .	07.2	267 01.9 . .	55.1	Hamal	328 01.0	N23 31.4
16	136 12.8	40 04.5	24.1	73 02.1	17.6	50 48.2	07.3	282 04.5	55.1	Kaus Aust.	83 43.4	S34 22.5
17	151 15.3	55 03.6	24.0	88 02.7	18.0	65 50.0	07.3	297 07.1	55.1			
18	166 17.8	70 02.7	N24 24.0	103 03.3	N21 18.3	80 51.8	N23 07.3	312 09.6	S10 55.0	Kochab	137 19.1	N74 06.2
19	181 20.2	85 01.8	23.9	118 03.9	18.7	95 53.7	07.3	327 12.2	55.0	Markab	13 38.3	N15 16.6
20	196 22.7	100 00.9	23.9	133 04.5	19.0	110 55.5	07.4	342 14.8	55.0	Menkar	314 15.3	N 4 08.4
21	211 25.2	115 00.0 . .	23.8	148 05.1 . .	19.4	125 57.4 . .	07.4	357 17.4 . .	54.9	Menkent	148 07.3	S36 26.3
22	226 27.6	129 59.2	23.8	163 05.7	19.7	140 59.2	07.4	12 20.0	54.9	Miaplacidus	221 40.1	S69 46.8
23	241 30.1	144 58.3	23.7	178 06.3	20.0	156 01.1	07.4	27 22.5	54.9			
8 00	256 32.5	159 57.4	N24 23.7	193 06.9	N21 20.4	171 02.9	N23 07.4	42 25.1	S10 54.8	Mirfak	308 40.8	N49 54.3
01	271 35.0	174 56.5	23.6	208 07.5	20.7	186 04.7	07.5	57 27.7	54.8	Nunki	75 58.0	S26 16.6
02	286 37.5	189 55.6	23.5	223 08.1	21.1	201 06.6	07.5	72 30.3	54.8	Peacock	53 18.9	S56 41.1
03	301 39.9	204 54.7 . .	23.5	238 08.7 . .	21.4	216 08.4 . .	07.5	87 32.8 . .	54.8	Pollux	243 28.1	N27 59.5
04	316 42.4	219 53.8	23.4	253 09.3	21.7	231 10.3	07.5	102 35.4	54.7	Procyon	245 00.0	N 5 11.2
05	331 44.9	234 52.9	23.4	268 09.9	22.1	246 12.1	07.5	117 38.0	54.7			
06	346 47.3	249 52.0	N24 23.3	283 10.5	N21 22.4	261 14.0	N23 07.6	132 40.6	S10 54.7	Rasalhague	96 06.1	N12 33.1
07	1 49.8	264 51.2	23.2	298 11.1	22.8	276 15.8	07.6	147 43.2	54.6	Regulus	207 43.6	N11 54.0
S 08	16 52.3	279 50.3	23.2	313 11.7	23.1	291 17.6	07.6	162 45.7	54.6	Rigel	281 12.4	S 8 11.4
A 09	31 54.7	294 49.4 . .	23.1	328 12.3 . .	23.4	306 19.5 . .	07.6	177 48.3 . .	54.6	Rigil Kent.	139 51.1	S60 53.5
T 10	46 57.2	309 48.5	23.0	343 12.9	23.8	321 21.3	07.6	192 50.9	54.6	Sabik	102 12.2	S15 44.4
U 11	61 59.7	324 47.6	22.9	358 13.5	24.1	336 23.2	07.7	207 53.5	54.5			
R 12	77 02.1	339 46.7	N24 22.9	13 14.1	N21 24.5	351 25.0	N23 07.7	222 56.0	S10 54.5	Schedar	349 40.7	N56 36.4
D 13	92 04.6	354 45.8	22.8	28 14.7	24.8	6 26.9	07.7	237 58.6	54.5	Shaula	96 21.5	S37 06.6
A 14	107 07.0	9 44.9	22.7	43 15.3	25.1	21 28.7	07.7	253 01.2	54.4	Sirius	258 34.1	S16 44.3
Y 15	122 09.5	24 44.1 . .	22.6	58 15.9 . .	25.5	36 30.5 . .	07.8	268 03.8 . .	54.4	Spica	158 31.1	S11 14.0
16	137 12.0	39 43.2	22.6	73 16.5	25.8	51 32.4	07.8	283 06.3	54.4	Suhail	222 52.7	S43 29.6
17	152 14.4	54 42.3	22.5	88 17.1	26.1	66 34.2	07.8	298 08.9	54.3			
18	167 16.9	69 41.4	N24 22.4	103 17.7	N21 26.5	81 36.1	N23 07.8	313 11.5	S10 54.3	Vega	80 38.6	N38 47.8
19	182 19.4	84 40.5	22.3	118 18.3	26.8	96 37.9	07.8	328 14.1	54.3	Zuben'ubi	137 05.1	S16 05.9
20	197 21.8	99 39.6	22.2	133 18.9	27.1	111 39.8	07.9	343 16.7	54.3		SHA	Mer.Pass.
21	212 24.3	114 38.7 . .	22.2	148 19.5 . .	27.5	126 41.6 . .	07.9	358 19.2 . .	54.2		° ′	h m
22	227 26.8	129 37.9	22.1	163 20.1	27.8	141 43.4	07.9	13 21.8	54.2	Venus	264 45.3	13 20
23	242 29.2	144 37.0	22.0	178 20.7	28.1	156 45.3	07.9	28 24.4	54.2	Mars	297 19.1	11 08
	h m									Jupiter	274 45.3	12 37
Mer. Pass. 6 56.6		v −0.9	d 0.0	v 0.6	d 0.3	v 1.8	d 0.0	v 2.6	d 0.0	Saturn	145 49.8	21 11

SUN / MOON

UT	SUN GHA	SUN Dec	MOON GHA	v	MOON Dec	d	HP
THURSDAY							
6 00	180 21.1	N22 38.6	210 47.7	12.5	N16 44.4	6.0	54.6
01	195 21.0	38.8	225 19.2	12.5	16 50.4	5.9	54.6
02	210 20.8	39.1	239 50.7	12.4	16 56.3	5.8	54.6
03	225 20.7 ..	39.3	254 22.1	12.5	17 02.1	5.7	54.6
04	240 20.6	39.6	268 53.6	12.4	17 07.8	5.7	54.6
05	255 20.5	39.9	283 25.0	12.4	17 13.5	5.5	54.6
06	270 20.4	N22 40.1	297 56.4	12.4	N17 19.0	5.5	54.5
07	285 20.3	40.4	312 27.8	12.4	17 24.5	5.4	54.5
08	300 20.2	40.6	326 59.2	12.3	17 29.9	5.3	54.5
09	315 20.0 ..	40.9	341 30.5	12.4	17 35.2	5.3	54.5
10	330 19.9	41.1	356 01.9	12.3	17 40.5	5.1	54.5
11	345 19.8	41.4	10 33.2	12.3	17 45.6	5.1	54.5
12	0 19.7	N22 41.6	25 04.5	12.3	N17 50.7	5.0	54.5
13	15 19.6	41.9	39 35.8	12.3	17 55.7	4.9	54.4
14	30 19.5	42.1	54 07.1	12.2	18 00.6	4.8	54.4
15	45 19.3 ..	42.4	68 38.3	12.3	18 05.4	4.7	54.4
16	60 19.2	42.6	83 09.6	12.2	18 10.1	4.7	54.4
17	75 19.1	42.9	97 40.8	12.2	18 14.8	4.5	54.4
18	90 19.0	N22 43.1	112 12.0	12.2	N18 19.3	4.5	54.4
19	105 18.9	43.4	126 43.2	12.1	18 23.8	4.4	54.4
20	120 18.8	43.6	141 14.3	12.2	18 28.2	4.3	54.4
21	135 18.6 ..	43.9	155 45.5	12.2	18 32.5	4.2	54.4
22	150 18.5	44.1	170 16.7	12.1	18 36.7	4.1	54.3
23	165 18.4	44.3	184 47.8	12.1	18 40.8	4.0	54.3
FRIDAY							
7 00	180 18.3	N22 44.6	199 18.9	12.1	N18 44.8	4.0	54.3
01	195 18.2	44.8	213 50.0	12.1	18 48.8	3.8	54.3
02	210 18.1	45.1	228 21.1	12.1	18 52.6	3.8	54.3
03	225 17.9 ..	45.3	242 52.2	12.0	18 56.4	3.7	54.3
04	240 17.8	45.5	257 23.2	12.1	19 00.1	3.6	54.3
05	255 17.7	45.8	271 54.3	12.0	19 03.7	3.5	54.3
06	270 17.6	N22 46.0	286 25.3	12.1	N19 07.2	3.4	54.3
07	285 17.5	46.3	300 56.4	12.0	19 10.6	3.3	54.2
08	300 17.4	46.5	315 27.4	12.0	19 13.9	3.2	54.2
09	315 17.2 ..	46.7	329 58.4	12.0	19 17.1	3.2	54.2
10	330 17.1	47.0	344 29.4	11.9	19 20.3	3.0	54.2
11	345 17.0	47.2	359 00.3	12.0	19 23.3	3.0	54.2
12	0 16.9	N22 47.4	13 31.3	12.0	N19 26.3	2.8	54.2
13	15 16.8	47.7	28 02.3	11.9	19 29.1	2.8	54.2
14	30 16.6	47.9	42 33.2	12.0	19 31.9	2.7	54.2
15	45 16.5 ..	48.1	57 04.2	11.9	19 34.6	2.6	54.2
16	60 16.4	48.4	71 35.1	11.9	19 37.2	2.5	54.2
17	75 16.3	48.6	86 06.0	12.0	19 39.7	2.4	54.2
18	90 16.2	N22 48.8	100 37.0	11.9	N19 42.1	2.3	54.2
19	105 16.0	49.1	115 07.9	11.9	19 44.4	2.2	54.1
20	120 15.9	49.3	129 38.8	11.9	19 46.6	2.2	54.1
21	135 15.8 ..	49.5	144 09.7	11.9	19 48.8	2.0	54.1
22	150 15.7	49.7	158 40.6	11.9	19 50.8	1.9	54.1
23	165 15.6	50.0	173 11.5	11.9	19 52.7	1.9	54.1
SATURDAY							
8 00	180 15.4	N22 50.2	187 42.4	11.8	N19 54.6	1.8	54.1
01	195 15.3	50.4	202 13.2	11.9	19 56.4	1.6	54.1
02	210 15.2	50.6	216 44.1	11.9	19 58.0	1.5	54.1
03	225 15.1 ..	50.9	231 15.0	11.9	19 59.6	1.5	54.1
04	240 15.0	51.1	245 45.9	11.8	20 01.1	1.4	54.1
05	255 14.8	51.3	260 16.7	11.9	20 02.5	1.3	54.1
06	270 14.7	N22 51.5	274 47.6	11.9	N20 03.8	1.2	54.1
07	285 14.6	51.8	289 18.5	11.8	20 05.0	1.1	54.1
08	300 14.5	52.0	303 49.3	11.9	20 06.1	1.0	54.1
09	315 14.4 ..	52.2	318 20.2	11.8	20 07.1	0.9	54.0
10	330 14.2	52.4	332 51.0	11.9	20 08.0	0.8	54.0
11	345 14.1	52.6	347 21.9	11.9	20 08.8	0.7	54.0
12	0 14.0	N22 52.9	1 52.8	11.8	N20 09.5	0.7	54.0
13	15 13.9	53.1	16 23.6	11.9	20 10.2	0.5	54.0
14	30 13.7	53.3	30 54.5	11.9	20 10.7	0.5	54.0
15	45 13.6 ..	53.5	45 25.4	11.8	20 11.2	0.3	54.0
16	60 13.5	53.7	59 56.2	11.9	20 11.5	0.3	54.0
17	75 13.4	53.9	74 27.1	11.9	20 11.8	0.1	54.0
18	90 13.3	N22 54.1	88 58.0	11.9	N20 11.9	0.1	54.0
19	105 13.1	54.4	103 28.9	11.9	20 12.0	0.0	54.0
20	120 13.0	54.6	117 59.8	11.9	20 12.0	0.1	54.0
21	135 12.9 ..	54.8	132 30.7	11.9	20 11.9	0.2	54.0
22	150 12.8	55.0	147 01.6	11.9	20 11.7	0.3	54.0
23	165 12.6	55.2	161 32.5	11.9	N20 11.4	0.4	54.0
	SD 15.8	d 0.2	SD 14.8		14.8		14.7

Twilight / Sunrise / Moonrise

Lat.	Twilight Naut.	Twilight Civil	Sunrise	Moonrise 6	7	8	9
N 72	□	□	□	□	□	□	□
N 70	□	□	□	00 16	00 10	00 01	□
68	□	□	□	00 46	00 57	01 18	02 01
66	////	////	00 44	01 09	01 27	01 56	02 40
64	////	////	01 44	01 27	01 50	02 22	03 08
62	////	////	02 18	01 42	02 08	02 43	03 29
60	////	01 09	02 42	01 54	02 23	03 00	03 46
N 58	////	01 50	03 01	02 05	02 36	03 14	04 01
56	////	02 17	03 17	02 14	02 47	03 26	04 13
54	01 03	02 37	03 30	02 23	02 56	03 37	04 24
52	01 41	02 54	03 42	02 30	03 05	03 46	04 33
50	02 06	03 09	03 52	02 37	03 13	03 55	04 42
45	02 48	03 37	04 14	02 52	03 30	04 12	05 00
N 40	03 18	03 59	04 31	03 04	03 43	04 27	05 15
35	03 40	04 16	04 46	03 14	03 55	04 40	05 27
30	03 58	04 31	04 58	03 23	04 05	04 50	05 38
20	04 26	04 56	05 20	03 38	04 23	05 09	05 57
N 10	04 48	05 15	05 38	03 52	04 38	05 25	06 13
0	05 07	05 33	05 55	04 05	04 53	05 41	06 29
S 10	05 23	05 49	06 12	04 18	05 07	05 56	06 44
20	05 39	06 06	06 30	04 32	05 22	06 12	07 00
30	05 55	06 24	06 51	04 48	05 40	06 31	07 19
35	06 03	06 35	07 03	04 57	05 51	06 42	07 30
40	06 12	06 46	07 16	05 07	06 03	06 55	07 43
45	06 22	06 59	07 33	05 20	06 17	07 09	07 57
S 50	06 33	07 14	07 52	05 35	06 34	07 28	08 16
52	06 38	07 22	08 02	05 42	06 42	07 36	08 24
54	06 44	07 29	08 13	05 50	06 51	07 46	08 34
56	06 49	07 38	08 25	05 59	07 01	07 57	08 45
58	06 56	07 48	08 39	06 09	07 13	08 09	08 57
S 60	07 03	07 59	08 55	06 21	07 26	08 24	09 11

Sunset / Twilight / Moonset

Lat.	Sunset	Twilight Civil	Twilight Naut.	Moonset 6	7	8	9
N 72	□	□	□	21 03	22 52	□	□
N 70	□	□	□	20 17	21 35	22 33	23 06
68	□	□	□	19 47	20 58	21 53	22 31
66	23 19	////	////	19 25	20 31	21 25	22 05
64	22 15	////	////	19 07	20 11	21 04	21 46
62	21 41	////	////	18 53	19 54	20 47	21 29
60	21 17	22 51	////	18 40	19 40	20 32	21 16
N 58	20 58	22 09	////	18 29	19 28	20 20	21 04
56	20 42	21 42	////	18 20	19 18	20 09	20 53
54	20 28	21 21	22 57	18 11	19 08	20 00	20 44
52	20 16	21 04	22 18	18 04	19 00	19 51	20 36
50	20 06	20 50	21 53	17 58	18 52	19 43	20 27
45	19 44	20 21	21 10	17 47	18 42	19 33	20 18
N 40	19 27	19 59	20 40	17 34	18 28	19 18	20 04
35	19 12	19 42	20 18	17 23	18 16	19 05	19 52
30	18 59	19 27	20 00	17 13	18 05	18 55	19 41
20	18 38	19 02	19 32	16 56	17 47	18 36	19 23
N 10	18 20	18 43	19 10	16 42	17 31	18 19	19 07
0	18 03	18 25	18 51	16 28	17 16	18 04	18 52
S 10	17 46	18 08	18 35	16 14	17 01	17 48	18 37
20	17 28	17 51	18 19	15 59	16 45	17 32	18 21
30	17 07	17 33	18 03	15 43	16 27	17 13	18 02
35	16 55	17 23	17 55	15 33	16 16	17 02	17 51
40	16 41	17 12	17 46	15 22	16 04	16 49	17 39
45	16 25	16 59	17 36	15 09	15 49	16 34	17 24
S 50	16 05	16 43	17 24	14 53	15 32	16 16	17 06
52	15 56	16 36	17 19	14 46	15 23	16 07	16 58
54	15 45	16 28	17 14	14 37	15 14	15 58	16 48
56	15 33	16 19	17 08	14 28	15 04	15 47	16 38
58	15 19	16 10	17 02	14 18	14 52	15 34	16 25
S 60	15 02	15 59	16 55	14 06	14 38	15 20	16 11

SUN / MOON

Day	SUN Eqn. of Time 00ʰ	12ʰ	Mer. Pass.	MOON Mer. Pass. Upper	Lower	Age	Phase
	m s	m s	h m	h m	h m	d	%
6	01 25	01 19	11 59	10 16	22 40	27	4
7	01 13	01 08	11 59	11 04	23 28	28	1
8	01 02	00 56	11 59	11 52	24 16	29	0

UT	ARIES	VENUS −3.8		MARS +1.4		JUPITER −1.9		SATURN +0.4		STARS		
	GHA	GHA	Dec	GHA	Dec	GHA	Dec	GHA	Dec	Name	SHA	Dec
d h	° ′	° ′	° ′	° ′	° ′	° ′	° ′	° ′	° ′		° ′	° ′
9 00	257 31.7	159 36.1	N24 21.9	193 21.3	N21 28.5	171 47.1	N23 07.9	43 27.0	S10 54.1	Acamar	315 18.7	S40 15.0
01	272 34.2	174 35.2	21.8	208 21.9	28.8	186 49.0	08.0	58 29.5	54.1	Achernar	335 27.2	S57 09.9
02	287 36.6	189 34.3	21.7	223 22.5	29.1	201 50.8	08.0	73 32.1	54.1	Acrux	173 09.0	S63 10.8
03	302 39.1	204 33.4 ..	21.6	238 23.1 ..	29.5	216 52.7 ..	08.0	88 34.7 ..	54.1	Adhara	255 12.9	S28 59.7
04	317 41.5	219 32.5	21.5	253 23.7	29.8	231 54.5	08.0	103 37.3	54.0	Aldebaran	290 49.7	N16 32.0
05	332 44.0	234 31.7	21.4	268 24.3	30.1	246 56.3	08.1	118 39.8	54.0			
06	347 46.5	249 30.8	N24 21.3	283 24.9	N21 30.5	261 58.2	N23 08.1	133 42.4	S10 54.0	Alioth	166 20.5	N55 53.4
07	2 48.9	264 29.9	21.2	298 25.5	30.8	277 00.0	08.1	148 45.0	53.9	Alkaid	152 58.6	N49 15.0
08	17 51.4	279 29.0	21.2	313 26.1	31.1	292 01.9	08.1	163 47.6	53.9	Al Na'ir	27 43.6	S46 53.4
S 09	32 53.9	294 28.1 ..	21.1	328 26.7 ..	31.5	307 03.7 ..	08.1	178 50.1 ..	53.9	Alnilam	275 46.7	S 1 11.8
U 10	47 56.3	309 27.2	21.0	343 27.3	31.8	322 05.6	08.2	193 52.7	53.9	Alphard	217 56.3	S 8 43.3
N 11	62 58.8	324 26.3	20.9	358 27.9	32.1	337 07.4	08.2	208 55.3	53.8			
D 12	78 01.3	339 25.5	N24 20.7	13 28.5	N21 32.4	352 09.2	N23 08.2	223 57.8	S10 53.8	Alphecca	126 10.7	N26 40.3
A 13	93 03.7	354 24.6	20.6	28 29.1	32.8	7 11.1	08.2	239 00.4	53.8	Alpheratz	357 43.6	N29 09.8
Y 14	108 06.2	9 23.7	20.5	43 29.7	33.1	22 12.9	08.2	254 03.0	53.7	Altair	62 08.0	N 8 54.4
15	123 08.6	24 22.8 ..	20.4	58 30.3 ..	33.4	37 14.8 ..	08.3	269 05.6 ..	53.7	Ankaa	353 15.9	S42 13.7
16	138 11.1	39 21.9	20.3	73 30.9	33.7	52 16.6	08.3	284 08.1	53.7	Antares	112 25.9	S26 27.6
17	153 13.6	54 21.0	20.2	88 31.5	34.1	67 18.4	08.3	299 10.7	53.7			
18	168 16.0	69 20.2	N24 20.1	103 32.1	N21 34.4	82 20.3	N23 08.3	314 13.3	S10 53.6	Arcturus	145 55.5	N19 06.8
19	183 18.5	84 19.3	20.0	118 32.7	34.7	97 22.1	08.3	329 15.9	53.6	Atria	107 27.1	S69 03.0
20	198 21.0	99 18.4	19.9	133 33.3	35.1	112 24.0	08.4	344 18.4	53.6	Avior	234 18.4	S59 33.5
21	213 23.4	114 17.5 ..	19.8	148 33.9 ..	35.4	127 25.8 ..	08.4	359 21.0 ..	53.6	Bellatrix	278 32.4	N 6 21.5
22	228 25.9	129 16.6	19.7	163 34.4	35.7	142 27.7	08.4	14 23.6	53.5	Betelgeuse	271 01.6	N 7 24.4
23	243 28.4	144 15.7	19.5	178 35.0	36.4	157 29.5	08.4	29 26.1	53.5			
10 00	258 30.8	159 14.9	N24 19.4	193 35.6	N21 36.4	172 31.3	N23 08.4	44 28.7	S10 53.5	Canopus	263 56.7	S52 42.4
01	273 33.3	174 14.0	19.3	208 36.2	36.7	187 33.2	08.5	59 31.3	53.4	Capella	280 34.9	N46 00.5
02	288 35.8	189 13.1	19.2	223 36.8	37.0	202 35.0	08.5	74 33.9	53.4	Deneb	49 31.1	N45 19.7
03	303 38.2	204 12.2 ..	19.1	238 37.4 ..	37.3	217 36.9 ..	08.5	89 36.4 ..	53.4	Denebola	182 33.6	N14 29.8
04	318 40.7	219 11.3	18.9	253 38.0	37.6	232 38.7	08.5	104 39.0	53.4	Diphda	348 56.0	S17 54.7
05	333 43.1	234 10.5	18.8	268 38.6	38.0	247 40.5	08.5	119 41.6	53.3			
06	348 45.6	249 09.6	N24 18.7	283 39.2	N21 38.3	262 42.4	N23 08.6	134 44.2	S10 53.3	Dubhe	193 51.8	N61 40.9
07	3 48.1	264 08.7	18.6	298 39.8	38.6	277 44.2	08.6	149 46.7	53.3	Elnath	278 13.0	N28 36.9
08	18 50.5	279 07.8	18.4	313 40.4	38.9	292 46.1	08.6	164 49.3	53.3	Eltanin	90 45.6	N51 29.3
M 09	33 53.0	294 06.9 ..	18.3	328 41.0 ..	39.3	307 47.9 ..	08.6	179 51.9 ..	53.2	Enif	33 47.0	N 9 56.3
O 10	48 55.5	309 06.0	18.2	343 41.6	39.6	322 49.8	08.7	194 54.4	53.2	Fomalhaut	15 24.0	S29 32.8
N 11	63 57.9	324 05.2	18.0	358 42.2	39.9	337 51.6	08.7	209 57.0	53.2			
D 12	79 00.4	339 04.3	N24 17.9	13 42.8	N21 40.2	352 53.4	N23 08.7	224 59.6	S10 53.1	Gacrux	172 00.6	S57 11.6
A 13	94 02.9	354 03.4	17.8	28 43.4	40.5	7 55.3	08.7	240 02.1	53.1	Gienah	175 52.2	S17 37.2
Y 14	109 05.3	9 02.5	17.6	43 44.0	40.9	22 57.1	08.7	255 04.7	53.1	Hadar	148 47.4	S60 26.5
15	124 07.8	24 01.6 ..	17.5	58 44.6 ..	41.2	37 59.0 ..	08.7	270 07.3 ..	53.1	Hamal	328 01.0	N23 31.4
16	139 10.3	39 00.8	17.4	73 45.2	41.5	53 00.8	08.8	285 09.9	53.0	Kaus Aust.	83 43.4	S34 22.5
17	154 12.7	53 59.9	17.2	88 45.8	41.8	68 02.6	08.8	300 12.4	53.0			
18	169 15.2	68 59.0	N24 17.1	103 46.4	N21 42.1	83 04.5	N23 08.8	315 15.0	S10 53.0	Kochab	137 19.2	N74 06.2
19	184 17.6	83 58.1	17.0	118 47.0	42.4	98 06.3	08.8	330 17.6	53.0	Markab	13 38.3	N15 16.7
20	199 20.1	98 57.2	16.8	133 47.6	42.8	113 08.2	08.8	345 20.1	52.9	Menkar	314 15.3	N 4 08.4
21	214 22.6	113 56.4 ..	16.7	148 48.2 ..	43.1	128 10.0 ..	08.9	0 22.7 ..	52.9	Menkent	148 07.3	S36 26.3
22	229 25.0	128 55.5	16.5	163 48.8	43.4	143 11.9	08.9	15 25.3	52.9	Miaplacidus	221 40.1	S69 46.8
23	244 27.5	143 54.6	16.4	178 49.4	43.7	158 13.7	08.9	30 27.8	52.9			
11 00	259 30.0	158 53.7	N24 16.2	193 50.0	N21 44.0	173 15.5	N23 08.9	45 30.4	S10 52.8	Mirfak	308 40.8	N49 54.3
01	274 32.4	173 52.8	16.1	208 50.6	44.3	188 17.4	08.9	60 33.0	52.8	Nunki	75 58.0	S26 16.6
02	289 34.9	188 52.0	15.9	223 51.1	44.7	203 19.2	08.9	75 35.5	52.8	Peacock	53 18.9	S56 41.1
03	304 37.4	203 51.1 ..	15.8	238 51.7 ..	45.0	218 21.1 ..	09.0	90 38.1 ..	52.8	Pollux	243 28.1	N27 59.5
04	319 39.8	218 50.2	15.6	253 52.3	45.3	233 22.9	09.0	105 40.7	52.7	Procyon	245 00.0	N 5 11.2
05	334 42.3	233 49.3	15.5	268 52.9	45.6	248 24.7	09.0	120 43.3	52.7			
06	349 44.8	248 48.5	N24 15.3	283 53.5	N21 45.9	263 26.6	N23 09.0	135 45.8	S10 52.7	Rasalhague	96 06.1	N12 33.1
07	4 47.2	263 47.6	15.2	298 54.1	46.2	278 28.4	09.0	150 48.4	52.6	Regulus	207 43.6	N11 54.0
T 08	19 49.7	278 46.7	15.0	313 54.7	46.5	293 30.3	09.1	165 51.0	52.6	Rigel	281 12.4	S 8 11.3
U 09	34 52.1	293 45.8 ..	14.8	328 55.3 ..	46.8	308 32.1 ..	09.1	180 53.5 ..	52.6	Rigil Kent.	139 51.1	S60 53.6
E 10	49 54.6	308 44.9	14.7	343 55.9	47.2	323 34.0	09.1	195 56.1	52.6	Sabik	102 12.2	S15 44.4
S 11	64 57.1	323 44.1	14.5	358 56.5	47.5	338 35.8	09.1	210 58.7	52.5			
D 12	79 59.5	338 43.2	N24 14.4	13 57.1	N21 47.8	353 37.6	N23 09.1	226 01.2	S10 52.5	Schedar	349 40.7	N56 36.4
A 13	95 02.0	353 42.3	14.2	28 57.7	48.1	8 39.5	09.2	241 03.8	52.5	Shaula	96 21.5	S37 06.6
Y 14	110 04.5	8 41.4	14.0	43 58.3	48.4	23 41.3	09.2	256 06.4	52.5	Sirius	258 34.1	S16 44.3
15	125 06.9	23 40.6 ..	13.9	58 58.9 ..	48.7	38 43.2 ..	09.2	271 08.9 ..	52.4	Spica	158 31.1	S11 14.0
16	140 09.4	38 39.7	13.7	73 59.5	49.0	53 45.0	09.2	286 11.5	52.4	Suhail	222 52.7	S43 29.6
17	155 11.9	53 38.8	13.5	89 00.1	49.3	68 46.8	09.2	301 14.1	52.4			
18	170 14.3	68 37.9	N24 13.4	104 00.7	N21 49.6	83 48.7	N23 09.2	316 16.6	S10 52.4	Vega	80 38.5	N38 47.9
19	185 16.8	83 37.1	13.2	119 01.3	49.9	98 50.5	09.3	331 19.2	52.3	Zuben'ubi	137 05.1	S16 05.9
20	200 19.2	98 36.2	13.0	134 01.9	50.3	113 52.4	09.3	346 21.8	52.3		SHA	Mer. Pass.
21	215 21.7	113 35.3 ..	12.8	149 02.5 ..	50.6	128 54.2 ..	09.3	1 24.3 ..	52.3		° ′	h m
22	230 24.2	128 34.4	12.7	164 03.1	50.9	143 56.0	09.3	16 26.9	52.3	Venus	260 44.0	13 24
23	245 26.6	143 33.6	12.5	179 03.7	51.2	158 57.9	09.3	31 29.5	52.2	Mars	295 04.8	11 05
	h m									Jupiter	274 00.5	12 28
Mer. Pass. 6 44.8		v −0.9	d 0.1	v 0.6	d 0.3	v 1.8	d 0.0	v 2.6	d 0.0	Saturn	145 57.9	20 58

SUN and MOON — GHA and Declination

UT	SUN GHA	SUN Dec	MOON GHA	v	Dec	d	HP
d h	° '	° '	° '	'	° '	'	'
9 00	180 12.5	N22 55.4	176 03.4	11.9	N20 11.0	0.5	54.0
01	195 12.4	55.6	190 34.3	11.9	20 10.5	0.6	54.0
02	210 12.3	55.8	205 05.2	12.0	20 09.9	0.7	54.0
03	225 12.2 ..	56.0	219 36.2	11.9	20 09.2	0.7	54.0
04	240 12.0	56.2	234 07.1	12.0	20 08.5	0.9	54.0
05	255 11.9	56.4	248 38.1	11.9	20 07.6	1.0	54.0
06	270 11.8	N22 56.6	263 09.0	12.0	N20 06.6	1.0	54.0
07	285 11.7	56.9	277 40.0	12.0	20 05.6	1.2	54.0
S 08	300 11.5	57.1	292 11.0	12.0	20 04.4	1.2	54.0
U 09	315 11.4 ..	57.3	306 42.0	12.0	20 03.2	1.3	54.0
N 10	330 11.3	57.5	321 13.0	12.0	20 01.9	1.4	54.0
D 11	345 11.2	57.7	335 44.0	12.1	20 00.5	1.5	54.0
A 12	0 11.0	N22 57.9	350 15.1	12.0	N19 59.0	1.6	54.0
Y 13	15 10.9	58.1	4 46.1	12.1	19 57.4	1.7	53.9
14	30 10.8	58.3	19 17.2	12.0	19 55.7	1.8	53.9
15	45 10.7 ..	58.5	33 48.2	12.1	19 53.9	1.9	53.9
16	60 10.5	58.7	48 19.3	12.1	19 52.0	2.0	53.9
17	75 10.4	58.9	62 50.4	12.1	19 50.0	2.0	53.9
18	90 10.3	N22 59.1	77 21.5	12.2	N19 48.0	2.2	53.9
19	105 10.2	59.2	91 52.7	12.1	19 45.8	2.2	53.9
20	120 10.0	59.4	106 23.8	12.2	19 43.6	2.3	53.9
21	135 09.9 ..	59.6	120 55.0	12.2	19 41.3	2.5	53.9
22	150 09.8	22 59.8	135 26.2	12.2	19 38.8	2.5	53.9
23	165 09.7	23 00.0	149 57.4	12.2	19 36.3	2.6	53.9
10 00	180 09.5	N23 00.2	164 28.6	12.2	N19 33.7	2.7	53.9
01	195 09.4	00.4	178 59.8	12.3	19 31.0	2.7	53.9
02	210 09.3	00.6	193 31.1	12.3	19 28.3	2.9	53.9
03	225 09.2 ..	00.8	208 02.4	12.2	19 25.4	3.0	53.9
04	240 09.0	01.0	222 33.6	12.4	19 22.4	3.0	53.9
05	255 08.9	01.2	237 05.0	12.3	19 19.4	3.1	53.9
06	270 08.8	N23 01.4	251 36.3	12.3	N19 16.3	3.2	53.9
07	285 08.7	01.5	266 07.6	12.4	19 13.1	3.3	54.0
M 08	300 08.5	01.7	280 39.0	12.4	19 09.8	3.4	54.0
O 09	315 08.4 ..	01.9	295 10.4	12.4	19 06.4	3.5	54.0
N 10	330 08.3	02.1	309 41.8	12.4	19 02.9	3.6	54.0
D 11	345 08.2	02.3	324 13.2	12.5	18 59.3	3.6	54.0
A 12	0 08.0	N23 02.5	338 44.7	12.5	N18 55.7	3.8	54.0
Y 13	15 07.9	02.7	353 16.2	12.5	18 51.9	3.8	54.0
14	30 07.8	02.8	7 47.7	12.5	18 48.1	3.9	54.0
15	45 07.6 ..	03.0	22 19.2	12.5	18 44.2	4.0	54.0
16	60 07.5	03.2	36 50.7	12.6	18 40.2	4.1	54.0
17	75 07.4	03.4	51 22.3	12.6	18 36.1	4.1	54.0
18	90 07.3	N23 03.6	65 53.9	12.6	N18 32.0	4.3	54.0
19	105 07.1	03.7	80 25.5	12.6	18 27.7	4.3	54.0
20	120 07.0	03.9	94 57.1	12.7	18 23.4	4.4	54.0
21	135 06.9 ..	04.1	109 28.8	12.7	18 19.0	4.5	54.0
22	150 06.8	04.3	124 00.5	12.7	18 14.5	4.6	54.0
23	165 06.6	04.4	138 32.2	12.7	18 09.9	4.6	54.0
11 00	180 06.5	N23 04.6	153 03.9	12.8	N18 05.3	4.8	54.0
01	195 06.4	04.8	167 35.7	12.7	18 00.5	4.8	54.0
02	210 06.2	05.0	182 07.4	12.9	17 55.7	4.9	54.0
03	225 06.1 ..	05.1	196 39.3	12.8	17 50.8	5.0	54.0
04	240 06.0	05.3	211 11.1	12.8	17 45.8	5.0	54.0
05	255 05.9	05.5	225 42.9	12.9	17 40.8	5.1	54.0
06	270 05.7	N23 05.7	240 14.8	12.9	N17 35.7	5.3	54.0
07	285 05.6	05.8	254 46.7	12.9	17 30.4	5.3	54.0
T 08	300 05.5	06.0	269 18.6	13.0	17 25.1	5.3	54.0
U 09	315 05.3 ..	06.2	283 50.6	13.0	17 19.8	5.5	54.0
E 10	330 05.2	06.3	298 22.6	13.0	17 14.3	5.5	54.1
S 11	345 05.1	06.5	312 54.6	13.0	17 08.8	5.6	54.1
D 12	0 05.0	N23 06.7	327 26.6	13.1	N17 03.2	5.7	54.1
A 13	15 04.8	06.8	341 58.7	13.0	16 57.5	5.7	54.1
Y 14	30 04.7	07.0	356 30.7	13.1	16 51.8	5.9	54.1
15	45 04.6 ..	07.2	11 02.8	13.2	16 45.9	5.9	54.1
16	60 04.4	07.3	25 35.0	13.1	16 40.0	6.0	54.1
17	75 04.3	07.5	40 07.1	13.2	16 34.0	6.0	54.1
18	90 04.2	N23 07.7	54 39.3	13.2	N16 28.0	6.1	54.1
19	105 04.1	07.8	69 11.5	13.2	16 21.9	6.2	54.1
20	120 03.9	08.0	83 43.7	13.3	16 15.7	6.3	54.1
21	135 03.8 ..	08.1	98 16.0	13.3	16 09.4	6.4	54.1
22	150 03.7	08.3	112 48.3	13.3	16 03.0	6.4	54.1
23	165 03.5	08.5	127 20.6	13.3	N15 56.6	6.5	54.2
	SD 15.8	d 0.2	SD 14.7		14.7		14.7

Twilight, Sunrise and Moonrise

Lat.	Twilight Naut.	Civil	Sunrise	Moonrise 9	10	11	12
°	h m	h m	h m	h m	h m	h m	h m
N 72	□	□	□	□	□	02 27	04 55
N 70	□	□	□	□	02 06	03 50	05 31
68	□	□	□	02 01	03 07	04 29	05 56
66	////	////	00 28	02 40	03 42	04 55	06 16
64	////	////	01 39	03 08	04 07	05 16	06 31
62	////	////	02 14	03 29	04 26	05 32	06 44
60	////	01 02	02 39	03 46	04 42	05 46	06 55
N 58	////	01 46	02 59	04 01	04 56	05 58	07 04
56	////	02 14	03 15	04 13	05 07	06 08	07 13
54	00 57	02 35	03 29	04 24	05 18	06 17	07 20
52	01 37	02 52	03 41	04 33	05 27	06 25	07 27
50	02 03	03 07	03 51	04 42	05 35	06 32	07 33
45	02 47	03 36	04 13	05 00	05 52	06 47	07 45
N 40	03 17	03 58	04 31	05 15	06 06	07 00	07 56
35	03 39	04 16	04 46	05 27	06 18	07 11	08 05
30	03 58	04 31	04 58	05 38	06 28	07 20	08 13
20	04 26	04 55	05 20	05 57	06 46	07 36	08 26
N 10	04 49	05 16	05 39	06 13	07 02	07 50	08 38
0	05 07	05 33	05 56	06 29	07 16	08 03	08 49
S 10	05 24	05 50	06 13	06 44	07 31	08 16	09 00
20	05 40	06 07	06 31	07 00	07 46	08 30	09 12
30	05 55	06 26	06 52	07 19	08 04	08 46	09 25
35	06 04	06 36	07 04	07 30	08 15	08 55	09 33
40	06 14	06 48	07 18	07 43	08 26	09 06	09 42
45	06 24	07 01	07 34	07 57	08 40	09 18	09 52
S 50	06 35	07 16	07 55	08 16	08 57	09 33	10 04
52	06 40	07 24	08 04	08 24	09 05	09 40	10 10
54	06 46	07 32	08 15	08 34	09 14	09 48	10 16
56	06 52	07 41	08 27	08 45	09 24	09 57	10 23
58	06 58	07 51	08 42	08 57	09 36	10 07	10 31
S 60	07 05	08 02	08 59	09 11	09 49	10 18	10 40

Sunset, Twilight and Moonset

Lat.	Sunset	Twilight Civil	Naut.	Moonset 9	10	11	12
°	h m	h m	h m	h m	h m	h m	h m
N 72	□	□	□	□	□	01 24	00 33
N 70	□	□	□	23 06	00 07	(00 01)(23 56)	23 51
68	□	□	□	23 06	23 22	23 29	23 33
66	23 38	////	////	22 31	22 54	23 09	23 19
64	22 21	////	////	22 05	22 33	22 53	23 07
62	21 46	////	////	21 46	22 16	22 39	22 57
60	21 21	22 59	////	21 29	22 02	22 28	22 48
N 58	21 01	22 14	////	21 16	21 50	22 19	22 40
56	20 45	21 46	////	21 04	21 40	22 09	22 34
54	20 31	21 24	23 04	20 53	21 30	22 01	22 28
52	20 19	21 07	22 23	20 44	21 22	21 54	22 22
50	20 08	20 52	21 56	20 36	21 15	21 48	22 17
45	19 46	20 23	21 12	20 18	20 59	21 35	22 06
N 40	19 28	20 01	20 42	20 04	20 46	21 23	21 57
35	19 14	19 43	20 20	19 52	20 35	21 14	21 50
30	19 01	19 28	20 01	19 41	20 25	21 05	21 43
20	18 39	19 04	19 33	19 23	20 08	20 50	21 31
N 10	18 20	18 43	19 10	19 07	19 53	20 38	21 21
0	18 03	18 26	18 52	18 52	19 39	20 25	21 11
S 10	17 46	18 09	18 35	18 37	19 25	20 13	21 01
20	17 28	17 52	18 21	18 21	19 10	20 00	20 50
30	17 07	17 33	18 03	18 02	18 53	19 45	20 38
35	16 55	17 23	17 54	17 51	18 43	19 37	20 31
40	16 41	17 11	17 45	17 39	18 32	19 27	20 23
45	16 24	16 58	17 35	17 24	18 18	19 15	20 14
S 50	16 04	16 42	17 24	17 06	18 02	19 01	20 02
52	15 54	16 33	17 19	16 58	17 54	18 54	19 57
54	15 44	16 27	17 13	16 48	17 45	18 47	19 51
56	15 31	16 18	17 07	16 38	17 35	18 38	19 45
58	15 17	16 08	17 00	16 25	17 24	18 29	19 37
S 60	15 00	15 57	16 53	16 11	17 11	18 18	19 29

SUN and MOON — daily data

Day	Eqn. of Time 00h	12h	Mer. Pass.	Mer. Pass. Upper	Lower	Age	Phase
d	m s	m s	h m	h m	h m	d	%
9	00 50	00 44	11 59	12 40	00 16	01	1
10	00 38	00 32	11 59	13 28	01 04	02	3
11	00 26	00 20	12 00	14 14	01 51	03	7

● (new moon phase)

2013 JUNE 12, 13, 14 (WED., THURS., FRI.)

UT	ARIES GHA	VENUS −3.8 GHA	Dec	MARS +1.5 GHA	Dec	JUPITER −1.9 GHA	Dec	SATURN +0.4 GHA	Dec	STARS Name	SHA	Dec
12 00	260 29.1	158 32.7	N24 12.3	194 04.3	N21 51.5	173 59.7	N23 09.4	46 32.0	S10 52.2	Acamar	315 18.7	S40 15.0
01	275 31.6	173 31.8	12.1	209 04.8	51.8	189 01.6	09.4	61 34.6	52.2	Achernar	335 27.2	S57 09.9
02	290 34.0	188 30.9	12.0	224 05.4	52.1	204 03.4	09.4	76 37.1	52.2	Acrux	173 09.0	S63 10.8
03	305 36.5	203 30.1 ..	11.8	239 06.0 ..	52.4	219 05.2 ..	09.4	91 39.7 ..	52.1	Adhara	255 12.9	S28 59.7
04	320 39.0	218 29.2	11.6	254 06.6	52.7	234 07.1	09.4	106 42.3	52.1	Aldebaran	290 49.7	N16 32.0
05	335 41.4	233 28.3	11.4	269 07.2	53.0	249 08.9	09.4	121 44.8	52.1			
W 06	350 43.9	248 27.4	N24 11.2	284 07.8	N21 53.3	264 10.8	N23 09.5	136 47.4	S10 52.1	Alioth	166 20.5	N55 53.4
E 07	5 46.4	263 26.6	11.0	299 08.4	53.6	279 12.6	09.5	151 50.0	52.0	Alkaid	152 58.6	N49 15.0
D 08	20 48.8	278 25.7	10.9	314 09.0	53.9	294 14.5	09.5	166 52.5	52.0	Al Na'ir	27 43.6	S46 53.4
N 09	35 51.3	293 24.8 ..	10.7	329 09.6 ..	54.2	309 16.3 ..	09.5	181 55.1 ..	52.0	Alnilam	275 46.7	S 1 11.8
E 10	50 53.7	308 24.0	10.5	344 10.2	54.5	324 18.1	09.5	196 57.7	52.0	Alphard	217 56.3	S 8 43.2
S 11	65 56.2	323 23.1	10.3	359 10.8	54.8	339 20.0	09.6	212 00.2	51.9			
D 12	80 58.7	338 22.2	N24 10.1	14 11.4	N21 55.1	354 21.8	N23 09.6	227 02.8	S10 51.9	Alphecca	126 10.7	N26 40.3
A 13	96 01.1	353 21.3	09.9	29 12.0	55.4	9 23.7	09.6	242 05.4	51.9	Alpheratz	357 43.5	N29 09.8
Y 14	111 03.6	8 20.5	09.7	44 12.6	55.7	24 25.5	09.6	257 07.9	51.9	Altair	62 07.9	N 8 54.4
15	126 06.1	23 19.6 ..	09.5	59 13.2 ..	56.0	39 27.3 ..	09.6	272 10.5 ..	51.8	Ankaa	353 15.8	S42 13.7
16	141 08.5	38 18.7	09.3	74 13.8	56.3	54 29.2	09.6	287 13.0	51.8	Antares	112 25.9	S26 27.6
17	156 11.0	53 17.9	09.1	89 14.4	56.6	69 31.0	09.7	302 15.6	51.8			
18	171 13.5	68 17.0	N24 08.9	104 15.0	N21 56.9	84 32.9	N23 09.7	317 18.2	S10 51.8	Arcturus	145 55.5	N19 06.8
19	186 15.9	83 16.1	08.7	119 15.6	57.2	99 34.7	09.7	332 20.7	51.8	Atria	107 27.1	S69 03.0
20	201 18.4	98 15.2	08.5	134 16.1	57.5	114 36.5	09.7	347 23.3	51.7	Avior	234 18.5	S59 33.5
21	216 20.9	113 14.4 ..	08.3	149 16.7 ..	57.8	129 38.4 ..	09.7	2 25.9 ..	51.7	Bellatrix	278 32.3	N 6 21.5
22	231 23.3	128 13.5	08.1	164 17.3	58.1	144 40.2	09.7	17 28.4	51.7	Betelgeuse	271 01.6	N 7 24.4
23	246 25.8	143 12.6	07.9	179 17.9	58.4	159 42.1	09.8	32 31.0	51.7			
13 00	261 28.2	158 11.8	N24 07.7	194 18.5	N21 58.7	174 43.9	N23 09.8	47 33.5	S10 51.6	Canopus	263 56.7	S52 42.4
01	276 30.7	173 10.9	07.5	209 19.1	59.0	189 45.7	09.8	62 36.1	51.6	Capella	280 34.9	N46 00.5
02	291 33.2	188 10.0	07.3	224 19.7	59.3	204 47.6	09.8	77 38.7	51.6	Deneb	49 31.1	N45 19.7
03	306 35.6	203 09.2 ..	07.1	239 20.3 ..	59.6	219 49.4 ..	09.8	92 41.2 ..	51.6	Denebola	182 33.6	N14 29.8
04	321 38.1	218 08.3	06.9	254 20.9	21 59.9	234 51.3	09.8	107 43.8	51.5	Diphda	348 56.0	S17 54.6
05	336 40.6	233 07.4	06.7	269 21.5	22 00.2	249 53.1	09.9	122 46.4	51.5			
T 06	351 43.0	248 06.5	N24 06.4	284 22.1	N22 00.5	264 55.0	N23 09.9	137 48.9	S10 51.5	Dubhe	193 51.9	N61 40.9
H 07	6 45.5	263 05.7	06.2	299 22.7	00.8	279 56.8	09.9	152 51.5	51.5	Elnath	278 13.0	N28 36.9
U 08	21 48.0	278 04.8	06.0	314 23.3	01.1	294 58.6	09.9	167 54.0	51.4	Eltanin	90 45.6	N51 29.3
R 09	36 50.4	293 03.9 ..	05.8	329 23.9 ..	01.4	310 00.5 ..	09.9	182 56.6 ..	51.4	Enif	33 47.0	N 9 56.3
S 10	51 52.9	308 03.1	05.6	344 24.5	01.7	325 02.3	09.9	197 59.2	51.4	Fomalhaut	15 23.9	S29 32.8
D 11	66 55.4	323 02.2	05.4	359 25.1	02.0	340 04.2	10.0	213 01.7	51.4			
A 12	81 57.8	338 01.3	N24 05.1	14 25.7	N22 02.3	355 06.0	N23 10.0	228 04.3	S10 51.4	Gacrux	172 00.7	S57 11.6
Y 13	97 00.3	353 00.5	04.9	29 26.3	02.6	10 07.8	10.0	243 06.8	51.3	Gienah	175 52.2	S17 37.2
14	112 02.7	7 59.6	04.7	44 26.8	02.9	25 09.7	10.0	258 09.4	51.3	Hadar	148 47.4	S60 26.5
15	127 05.2	22 58.7 ..	04.5	59 27.4 ..	03.2	40 11.5 ..	10.0	273 12.0 ..	51.3	Hamal	328 01.0	N23 31.4
16	142 07.7	37 57.9	04.2	74 28.0	03.5	55 13.4	10.0	288 14.5	51.3	Kaus Aust.	83 43.4	S34 22.5
17	157 10.1	52 57.0	04.0	89 28.6	03.7	70 15.2	10.0	303 17.1	51.2			
18	172 12.6	67 56.2	N24 03.8	104 29.2	N22 04.0	85 17.0	N23 10.1	318 19.6	S10 51.2	Kochab	137 19.2	N74 06.3
19	187 15.1	82 55.3	03.5	119 29.8	04.3	100 18.9	10.1	333 22.2	51.2	Markab	13 38.3	N15 16.7
20	202 17.5	97 54.4	03.3	134 30.4	04.6	115 20.7	10.1	348 24.8	51.2	Menkar	314 15.3	N 4 08.4
21	217 20.0	112 53.6 ..	03.1	149 31.0 ..	04.9	130 22.6 ..	10.1	3 27.3 ..	51.1	Menkent	148 07.3	S36 26.3
22	232 22.5	127 52.7	02.8	164 31.6	05.2	145 24.4	10.1	18 29.9	51.1	Miaplacidus	221 40.1	S69 46.8
23	247 24.9	142 51.8	02.6	179 32.2	05.5	160 26.2	10.2	33 32.4	51.1			
14 00	262 27.4	157 51.0	N24 02.4	194 32.8	N22 05.8	175 28.1	N23 10.2	48 35.0	S10 51.1	Mirfak	308 40.8	N49 54.3
01	277 29.8	172 50.1	02.1	209 33.4	06.1	190 29.9	10.2	63 37.6	51.1	Nunki	75 58.0	S26 16.6
02	292 32.3	187 49.2	01.9	224 34.0	06.4	205 31.8	10.2	78 40.1	51.0	Peacock	53 18.8	S56 41.1
03	307 34.8	202 48.4 ..	01.7	239 34.6 ..	06.6	220 33.6 ..	10.2	93 42.7 ..	51.0	Pollux	243 28.1	N27 59.5
04	322 37.2	217 47.5	01.4	254 35.2	06.9	235 35.4	10.2	108 45.2	51.0	Procyon	245 00.0	N 5 11.2
05	337 39.7	232 46.7	01.2	269 35.8	07.2	250 37.3	10.3	123 47.8	51.0			
F 06	352 42.2	247 45.8	N24 00.9	284 36.3	N22 07.5	265 39.1	N23 10.3	138 50.3	S10 50.9	Rasalhague	96 06.1	N12 33.2
R 07	7 44.6	262 44.9	00.7	299 36.9	07.8	280 41.0	10.3	153 52.9	50.9	Regulus	207 43.6	N11 54.0
I 08	22 47.1	277 44.1	00.4	314 37.5	08.1	295 42.8	10.3	168 55.5	50.9	Rigel	281 12.4	S 8 11.3
D 09	37 49.6	292 43.2 ..	00.2	329 38.1 ..	08.4	310 44.6 ..	10.3	183 58.0 ..	50.9	Rigil Kent.	139 51.2	S60 53.6
A 10	52 52.0	307 42.3	24 00.0	344 38.7	08.7	325 46.5	10.3	199 00.6	50.9	Sabik	102 12.5	S15 44.4
Y 11	67 54.5	322 41.5	23 59.7	359 39.3	08.9	340 48.3	10.4	214 03.1	50.8			
12	82 57.0	337 40.6	N23 59.5	14 39.9	N22 09.2	355 50.2	N23 10.4	229 05.7	S10 50.8	Schedar	349 40.6	N56 36.4
13	97 59.4	352 39.8	59.2	29 40.5	09.5	10 52.0	10.4	244 08.2	50.8	Shaula	96 21.5	S37 06.6
14	113 01.9	7 38.9	58.9	44 41.1	09.8	25 53.8	10.4	259 10.8	50.8	Sirius	258 34.0	S16 44.3
15	128 04.3	22 38.0 ..	58.7	59 41.7 ..	10.1	40 55.7 ..	10.4	274 13.4 ..	50.7	Spica	158 31.1	S11 14.0
16	143 06.8	37 37.2	58.4	74 42.3	10.4	55 57.5	10.4	289 15.9	50.7	Suhail	222 52.7	S43 29.6
17	158 09.3	52 36.3	58.2	89 42.9	10.6	70 59.4	10.4	304 18.5	50.7			
18	173 11.7	67 35.5	N23 57.9	104 43.5	N22 10.9	86 01.2	N23 10.5	319 21.0	S10 50.7	Vega	80 38.5	N38 47.9
19	188 14.2	82 34.6	57.7	119 44.1	11.2	101 03.0	10.5	334 23.6	50.7	Zuben'ubi	137 05.1	S16 05.9
20	203 16.7	97 33.7	57.4	134 44.7	11.5	116 04.9	10.5	349 26.1	50.6		SHA	Mer. Pass.
21	218 19.1	112 32.9 ..	57.1	149 45.2 ..	11.8	131 06.7 ..	10.5	4 28.7 ..	50.6	Venus	256 43.5	13 28
22	233 21.6	127 32.0	56.9	164 45.8	12.1	146 08.6	10.5	19 31.2	50.6	Mars	292 50.3	11 02
23	248 24.1	142 31.2	56.6	179 46.4	12.3	161 10.4	10.5	34 33.8	50.6	Jupiter	273 15.7	12 20
Mer. Pass. 6 33.0		v −0.9	d 0.2	v 0.6	d 0.3	v 1.8	d 0.0	v 2.6	d 0.0	Saturn	146 05.3	20 46

UT	SUN GHA	SUN Dec	MOON GHA	MOON v	MOON Dec	MOON d	MOON HP
d h	° '	° '	° '	'	° '	'	'
12 00	180 03.4	N23 08.6	141 52.9 13.4		N15 50.1	6.5	54.2
01	195 03.3	08.8	156 25.3 13.3		15 43.6	6.7	54.2
02	210 03.2	08.9	170 57.6 13.4		15 36.9	6.7	54.2
03	225 03.0 ..	09.1	185 30.0 13.5		15 30.2	6.7	54.2
04	240 02.9	09.2	200 02.5 13.4		15 23.5	6.9	54.2
05	255 02.8	09.4	214 34.9 13.5		15 16.6	6.9	54.2
06	270 02.6	N23 09.6	229 07.4 13.5		N15 09.7	7.0	54.2
W 07	285 02.5	09.7	243 39.9 13.5		15 02.7	7.0	54.2
E 08	300 02.4	09.9	258 12.4 13.6		14 55.7	7.1	54.2
D 09	315 02.2 ..	10.0	272 45.0 13.6		14 48.6	7.2	54.3
N 10	330 02.1	10.2	287 17.5 13.6		14 41.4	7.2	54.3
E 11	345 02.0	10.3	301 50.1 13.6		14 34.2	7.3	54.3
S 12	0 01.9	N23 10.5	316 22.7 13.7		N14 26.9	7.4	54.3
D 13	15 01.7	10.6	330 55.4 13.6		14 19.5	7.4	54.3
A 14	30 01.6	10.8	345 28.0 13.7		14 12.1	7.5	54.3
Y 15	45 01.5 ..	10.9	0 00.7 13.7		14 04.6	7.6	54.3
16	60 01.3	11.1	14 33.4 13.7		13 57.0	7.6	54.3
17	75 01.2	11.2	29 06.1 13.8		13 49.4	7.7	54.4
18	90 01.1	N23 11.3	43 38.9 13.7		N13 41.7	7.8	54.4
19	105 00.9	11.5	58 11.6 13.8		13 33.9	7.8	54.4
20	120 00.8	11.6	72 44.4 13.8		13 26.1	7.8	54.4
21	135 00.7 ..	11.8	87 17.2 13.9		13 18.3	8.0	54.4
22	150 00.5	11.9	101 50.1 13.8		13 10.3	8.0	54.4
23	165 00.4	12.1	116 22.9 13.9		13 02.3	8.0	54.4
13 00	180 00.3	N23 12.2	130 55.8 13.8		N12 54.3	8.1	54.4
01	195 00.2	12.3	145 28.6 13.9		12 46.2	8.2	54.5
02	210 00.0	12.5	160 01.5 13.9		12 38.0	8.2	54.5
03	224 59.9 ..	12.6	174 34.5 13.9		12 29.8	8.3	54.5
04	239 59.8	12.8	189 07.4 13.9		12 21.5	8.4	54.5
05	254 59.6	12.9	203 40.3 14.0		12 13.1	8.4	54.5
06	269 59.5	N23 13.0	218 13.3 14.0		N12 04.7	8.4	54.5
T 07	284 59.4	13.2	232 46.3 14.0		11 56.3	8.5	54.6
H 08	299 59.2	13.3	247 19.3 14.0		11 47.8	8.6	54.6
U 09	314 59.1 ..	13.4	261 52.3 14.1		11 39.2	8.6	54.6
R 10	329 59.0	13.6	276 25.4 14.0		11 30.6	8.7	54.6
S 11	344 58.8	13.7	290 58.4 14.1		11 21.9	8.7	54.6
D 12	359 58.7	N23 13.8	305 31.5 14.0		N11 13.2	8.8	54.6
A 13	14 58.6	14.0	320 04.5 14.1		11 04.4	8.8	54.7
Y 14	29 58.4	14.1	334 37.6 14.1		10 55.6	8.9	54.7
15	44 58.3 ..	14.2	349 10.7 14.1		10 46.7	8.9	54.7
16	59 58.2	14.4	3 43.8 14.2		10 37.8	9.0	54.7
17	74 58.0	14.5	18 17.0 14.1		10 28.8	9.0	54.7
18	89 57.9	N23 14.6	32 50.1 14.2		N10 19.8	9.1	54.7
19	104 57.8	14.8	47 23.3 14.1		10 10.7	9.1	54.8
20	119 57.6	14.9	61 56.4 14.2		10 01.6	9.2	54.8
21	134 57.5 ..	15.0	76 29.6 14.1		9 52.4	9.2	54.8
22	149 57.4	15.1	91 02.7 14.2		9 43.2	9.3	54.8
23	164 57.2	15.3	105 35.9 14.2		9 33.9	9.3	54.8
14 00	179 57.1	N23 15.4	120 09.1 14.2		N 9 24.6	9.4	54.9
01	194 57.0	15.5	134 42.3 14.2		9 15.2	9.4	54.9
02	209 56.8	15.6	149 15.5 14.2		9 05.8	9.5	54.9
03	224 56.7 ..	15.8	163 48.7 14.3		8 56.3	9.5	54.9
04	239 56.6	15.9	178 22.0 14.2		8 46.8	9.5	54.9
05	254 56.5	16.0	192 55.2 14.2		8 37.3	9.6	55.0
06	269 56.3	N23 16.1	207 28.4 14.2		N 8 27.7	9.6	55.0
07	284 56.2	16.2	222 01.6 14.3		8 18.1	9.7	55.0
08	299 56.1	16.3	236 34.9 14.2		8 08.4	9.7	55.0
F 09	314 55.9 ..	16.5	251 08.1 14.2		7 58.7	9.8	55.0
R 10	329 55.8	16.6	265 41.3 14.3		7 48.9	9.8	55.1
I 11	344 55.7	16.8	280 14.6 14.2		7 39.1	9.8	55.1
D 12	359 55.5	N23 16.8	294 47.8 14.3		N 7 29.3	9.9	55.1
A 13	14 55.4	16.9	309 21.1 14.2		7 19.4	9.9	55.1
Y 14	29 55.3	17.1	323 54.3 14.2		7 09.5	10.0	55.2
15	44 55.1 ..	17.2	338 27.5 14.3		6 59.5	10.0	55.2
16	59 55.0	17.3	353 00.8 14.2		6 49.5	10.0	55.2
17	74 54.9	17.4	7 34.0 14.2		6 39.5	10.1	55.2
18	89 54.7	N23 17.5	22 07.2 14.2		N 6 29.4	10.1	55.3
19	104 54.6	17.6	36 40.4 14.3		6 19.3	10.1	55.3
20	119 54.5	17.7	51 13.7 14.2		6 09.2	10.2	55.3
21	134 54.3 ..	17.8	65 46.9 14.2		5 59.0	10.2	55.3
22	149 54.2	17.9	80 20.1 14.2		5 48.8	10.2	55.4
23	164 54.1	18.1	94 53.3 14.2		N 5 38.6	10.3	55.4
	SD 15.8 d 0.1		SD 14.8	14.9			15.0

Lat.	Twilight Naut.	Twilight Civil	Sunrise	Moonrise 12	Moonrise 13	Moonrise 14	Moonrise 15
°	h m	h m	h m	h m	h m	h m	h m
N 72	▭	▭	▭	04 55	06 47	08 33	10 16
N 70	▭	▭	▭	05 31	07 09	08 45	10 22
68	▭	▭	▭	05 56	07 25	08 55	10 26
66	▭	▭	▭	06 16	07 39	09 03	10 29
64	////	////	01 35	06 31	07 50	09 10	10 32
62	////	////	02 11	06 44	07 59	09 16	10 35
60	////	00 56	02 37	06 55	08 07	09 21	10 37
N 58	////	01 43	02 57	07 04	08 14	09 26	10 39
56	////	02 12	03 14	07 13	08 20	09 30	10 41
54	00 51	02 34	03 28	07 20	08 26	09 33	10 42
52	01 34	02 51	03 40	07 27	08 31	09 36	10 44
50	02 01	03 06	03 50	07 33	08 35	09 39	10 45
45	02 46	03 35	04 13	07 45	08 45	09 46	10 48
N 40	03 16	03 58	04 31	07 56	08 53	09 51	10 50
35	03 39	04 16	04 45	08 05	09 00	09 56	10 52
30	03 58	04 31	04 58	08 13	09 06	10 00	10 54
20	04 26	04 56	05 20	08 26	09 16	10 06	10 57
N 10	04 49	05 16	05 39	08 38	09 25	10 13	11 00
0	05 08	05 34	05 56	08 49	09 34	10 18	11 02
S 10	05 25	05 51	06 14	09 00	09 42	10 24	11 05
20	05 41	06 08	06 32	09 12	09 52	10 30	11 08
30	05 57	06 27	06 53	09 25	10 02	10 37	11 11
35	06 06	06 37	07 05	09 33	10 08	10 41	11 13
40	06 15	06 49	07 19	09 42	10 14	10 45	11 15
45	06 25	07 02	07 36	09 52	10 22	10 50	11 17
S 50	06 37	07 18	07 57	10 04	10 32	10 56	11 20
52	06 42	07 26	08 06	10 10	10 36	10 59	11 21
54	06 47	07 34	08 17	10 16	10 41	11 02	11 23
56	06 54	07 43	08 30	10 23	10 46	11 06	11 24
58	07 00	07 53	08 44	10 31	10 52	11 10	11 26
S 60	07 08	08 04	09 02	10 40	10 58	11 14	11 28

Lat.	Sunset	Twilight Civil	Twilight Naut.	Moonset 12	Moonset 13	Moonset 14	Moonset 15
°	h m	h m	h m	h m	h m	h m	h m
N 72	▭	▭	▭	00 33	00 14	(00 01 / 23 44)	23 39
N 70	▭	▭	▭	23 51	23 46	23 42	23 38
68	▭	▭	▭	23 33	23 35	23 36	23 36
66	▭	▭	▭	23 19	23 26	23 31	23 35
64	22 26	////	////	23 07	23 18	23 26	23 34
62	21 49	////	////	22 57	23 11	23 23	23 33
60	21 24	23 06	////	22 48	23 05	23 19	23 33
N 58	21 04	22 18	////	22 40	22 59	23 16	23 32
56	20 47	21 49	////	22 34	22 55	23 14	23 32
54	20 33	21 27	23 10	22 28	22 50	23 11	23 31
52	20 21	21 09	22 26	22 22	22 47	23 09	23 31
50	20 10	20 54	21 59	22 17	22 43	23 07	23 30
45	19 48	20 25	21 14	22 06	22 35	23 03	23 29
N 40	19 30	20 03	20 44	21 57	22 29	22 59	23 28
35	19 15	19 44	20 21	21 50	22 23	22 56	23 28
30	19 02	19 29	20 03	21 43	22 18	22 53	23 27
20	18 40	19 05	19 34	21 31	22 10	22 48	23 26
N 10	18 21	18 44	19 11	21 21	22 02	22 44	23 25
0	18 04	18 26	18 52	21 11	21 55	22 39	23 24
S 10	17 46	18 09	18 36	21 01	21 48	22 35	23 23
20	17 28	17 52	18 20	20 50	21 40	22 31	23 22
30	17 07	17 33	18 03	20 38	21 32	22 26	23 21
35	16 55	17 23	17 55	20 31	21 27	22 23	23 20
40	16 41	17 11	17 45	20 23	21 21	22 19	23 19
45	16 24	16 58	17 35	20 14	21 14	22 15	23 18
S 50	16 04	16 42	17 23	20 02	21 06	22 11	23 17
52	15 54	16 35	17 18	19 57	21 02	22 08	23 16
54	15 43	16 26	17 13	19 51	20 58	22 06	23 16
56	15 30	16 17	17 06	19 45	20 53	22 03	23 15
58	15 16	16 07	17 00	19 37	20 48	22 00	23 14
S 60	14 59	15 56	16 52	19 29	20 42	21 57	23 14

	SUN	SUN	SUN	MOON	MOON	MOON	MOON
Day	Eqn. of Time 00h	Eqn. of Time 12h	Mer. Pass.	Mer. Pass. Upper	Mer. Pass. Lower	Age	Phase
d	m s	m s	h m	h m	h m	d	%
12	00 14	00 08	12 00	15 00	02 37	04	13
13	00 01	00 05	12 00	15 45	03 22	05	20
14	00 11	00 18	12 00	16 29	04 07	06	28

2013 JUNE 15, 16, 17 (SAT., SUN., MON.)

UT	ARIES	VENUS −3.8		MARS +1.5		JUPITER −1.9		SATURN +0.4		STARS		
	GHA	GHA	Dec	GHA	Dec	GHA	Dec	GHA	Dec	Name	SHA	Dec
d h	° ′	° ′	° ′	° ′	° ′	° ′	° ′	° ′	° ′		° ′	° ′
15 00	263 26.5	157 30.3 N23 56.4		194 47.0 N22 12.6		176 12.2 N23 10.6		49 36.4 S10 50.6		Acamar	315 18.7	S40 15.0
01	278 29.0	172 29.5	56.1	209 47.6	12.9	191 14.1	10.6	64 38.9	50.5	Achernar	335 27.1	S57 09.9
02	293 31.5	187 28.6	55.8	224 48.2	13.2	206 15.9	10.6	79 41.5	50.5	Acrux	173 09.0	S63 10.8
03	308 33.9	202 27.7 ..	55.6	239 48.8 ..	13.5	221 17.8 ..	10.6	94 44.0 ..	50.5	Adhara	255 12.9	S28 59.7
04	323 36.4	217 26.9	55.3	254 49.4	13.7	236 19.6	10.6	109 46.6	50.5	Aldebaran	290 49.7	N16 32.0
05	338 38.8	232 26.0	55.0	269 50.0	14.0	251 21.4	10.6	124 49.1	50.5			
06	353 41.3	247 25.2 N23 54.7		284 50.6 N22 14.3		266 23.3 N23 10.6		139 51.7 S10 50.4		Alioth	166 20.6	N55 53.4
07	8 43.8	262 24.3	54.5	299 51.2	14.6	281 25.1	10.7	154 54.2	50.4	Alkaid	152 58.7	N49 15.0
S 08	23 46.2	277 23.5	54.2	314 51.8	14.8	296 27.0	10.7	169 56.8	50.4	Al Na'ir	27 43.6	S46 53.4
A 09	38 48.7	292 22.6 ..	53.9	329 52.4 ..	15.1	311 28.8 ..	10.7	184 59.3 ..	50.4	Alnilam	275 46.7	S 1 11.8
T 10	53 51.2	307 21.8	53.6	344 53.0	15.4	326 30.6	10.7	200 01.9	50.4	Alphard	217 56.3	S 8 43.2
U 11	68 53.6	322 20.9	53.4	359 53.6	15.7	341 32.5	10.7	215 04.5	50.3			
R 12	83 56.1	337 20.0 N23 53.1		14 54.1 N22 15.9		356 34.3 N23 10.7		230 07.0 S10 50.3		Alphecca	126 10.7	N26 40.3
D 13	98 58.6	352 19.2	52.8	29 54.7	16.2	11 36.2	10.7	245 09.6	50.3	Alpheratz	357 43.5	N29 09.8
A 14	114 01.0	7 18.3	52.5	44 55.3	16.5	26 38.0	10.8	260 12.1	50.3	Altair	62 07.9	N 8 54.4
Y 15	129 03.5	22 17.5 ..	52.2	59 55.9 ..	16.8	41 39.8 ..	10.8	275 14.7 ..	50.2	Ankaa	353 15.8	S42 13.7
16	144 05.9	37 16.6	51.9	74 56.5	17.0	56 41.7	10.8	290 17.2	50.2	Antares	112 25.9	S26 27.6
17	159 08.4	52 15.8	51.7	89 57.1	17.3	71 43.5	10.8	305 19.8	50.2			
18	174 10.9	67 14.9 N23 51.4		104 57.7 N22 17.6		86 45.4 N23 10.8		320 22.3 S10 50.2		Arcturus	145 55.5	N19 06.8
19	189 13.3	82 14.1	51.1	119 58.3	17.9	101 47.2	10.8	335 24.9	50.2	Atria	107 27.1	S69 03.0
20	204 15.8	97 13.2	50.8	134 58.9	18.1	116 49.0	10.8	350 27.4	50.1	Avior	234 18.5	S59 33.5
21	219 18.3	112 12.4 ..	50.5	149 59.5 ..	18.4	131 50.9 ..	10.9	5 30.0 ..	50.1	Bellatrix	278 32.3	N 6 21.5
22	234 20.7	127 11.5	50.2	165 00.1	18.7	146 52.7	10.9	20 32.5	50.1	Betelgeuse	271 01.6	N 7 24.4
23	249 23.2	142 10.7	49.9	180 00.7	19.0	161 54.6	10.9	35 35.1	50.1			
16 00	264 25.7	157 09.8 N23 49.6		195 01.3 N22 19.2		176 56.4 N23 10.9		50 37.6 S10 50.1		Canopus	263 56.7	S52 42.4
01	279 28.1	172 09.0	49.3	210 01.8	19.5	191 58.2	10.9	65 40.2	50.0	Capella	280 34.9	N46 00.5
02	294 30.6	187 08.1	49.0	225 02.4	19.8	207 00.1	10.9	80 42.7	50.0	Deneb	49 31.1	N45 19.7
03	309 33.1	202 07.3 ..	48.7	240 03.0 ..	20.0	222 01.9 ..	10.9	95 45.3 ..	50.0	Denebola	182 33.7	N14 29.8
04	324 35.5	217 06.4	48.4	255 03.6	20.3	237 03.8	11.0	110 47.8	50.0	Diphda	348 56.0	S17 54.6
05	339 38.0	232 05.6	48.1	270 04.2	20.6	252 05.6	11.0	125 50.4	50.0			
06	354 40.4	247 04.7 N23 47.8		285 04.8 N22 20.9		267 07.4 N23 11.0		140 52.9 S10 50.0		Dubhe	193 51.9	N61 40.9
07	9 42.9	262 03.9	47.5	300 05.4	21.1	282 09.3	11.0	155 55.5	49.9	Elnath	278 13.0	N28 36.9
08	24 45.4	277 03.0	47.2	315 06.0	21.4	297 11.1	11.0	170 58.0	49.9	Eltanin	90 45.6	N51 29.4
S 09	39 47.8	292 02.2 ..	46.9	330 06.6 ..	21.7	312 13.0 ..	11.0	186 00.6 ..	49.9	Enif	33 46.9	N 9 56.3
U 10	54 50.3	307 01.3	46.6	345 07.2	21.9	327 14.8	11.0	201 03.1	49.9	Fomalhaut	15 23.9	S29 32.8
N 11	69 52.8	322 00.5	46.3	0 07.8	22.2	342 16.6	11.1	216 05.7	49.9			
D 12	84 55.2	336 59.6 N23 46.0		15 08.4 N22 22.5		357 18.5 N23 11.1		231 08.2 S10 49.8		Gacrux	172 00.7	S57 11.6
A 13	99 57.7	351 58.8	45.7	30 09.0	22.7	12 20.3	11.1	246 10.8	49.8	Gienah	175 52.2	S17 37.2
Y 14	115 00.2	6 57.9	45.4	45 09.6	23.0	27 22.2	11.1	261 13.3	49.8	Hadar	148 47.4	S60 26.5
15	130 02.6	21 57.1 ..	45.1	60 10.1 ..	23.3	42 24.0 ..	11.1	276 15.9 ..	49.8	Hamal	328 00.9	N23 31.4
16	145 05.1	36 56.3	44.8	75 10.7	23.5	57 25.8	11.1	291 18.4	49.8	Kaus Aust.	83 43.4	S34 22.5
17	160 07.6	51 55.4	44.4	90 11.3	23.8	72 27.7	11.1	306 21.0	49.7			
18	175 10.0	66 54.6 N23 44.1		105 11.9 N22 24.1		87 29.5 N23 11.1		321 23.5 S10 49.7		Kochab	137 19.2	N74 06.3
19	190 12.5	81 53.7	43.8	120 12.5	24.3	102 31.4	11.2	336 26.1	49.7	Markab	13 38.3	N15 16.7
20	205 14.9	96 52.9	43.5	135 13.1	24.6	117 33.2	11.2	351 28.6	49.7	Menkar	314 15.3	N 4 08.5
21	220 17.4	111 52.0 ..	43.2	150 13.7 ..	24.8	132 35.0 ..	11.2	6 31.2 ..	49.7	Menkent	148 07.3	S36 26.3
22	235 19.9	126 51.2	42.9	165 14.3	25.1	147 36.9	11.2	21 33.7	49.6	Miaplacidus	221 40.2	S69 46.8
23	250 22.3	141 50.3	42.5	180 14.9	25.4	162 38.7	11.2	36 36.3	49.6			
17 00	265 24.8	156 49.5 N23 42.2		195 15.5 N22 25.6		177 40.6 N23 11.2		51 38.8 S10 49.6		Mirfak	308 40.7	N49 54.3
01	280 27.3	171 48.7	41.9	210 16.1	25.9	192 42.4	11.2	66 41.4	49.6	Nunki	75 58.0	S26 16.6
02	295 29.7	186 47.8	41.6	225 16.7	26.2	207 44.2	11.3	81 43.9	49.6	Peacock	53 18.8	S56 41.1
03	310 32.2	201 47.0 ..	41.2	240 17.3 ..	26.4	222 46.1 ..	11.3	96 46.5 ..	49.6	Pollux	243 28.1	N27 59.5
04	325 34.7	216 46.1	40.9	255 17.8	26.7	237 47.9	11.3	111 49.0	49.5	Procyon	245 00.0	N 5 11.2
05	340 37.1	231 45.3	40.6	270 18.4	26.9	252 49.8	11.3	126 51.6	49.5			
06	355 39.6	246 44.5 N23 40.2		285 19.0 N22 27.2		267 51.6 N23 11.3		141 54.1 S10 49.5		Rasalhague	96 06.1	N12 33.2
07	10 42.0	261 43.6	39.9	300 19.6	27.5	282 53.4	11.3	156 56.7	49.5	Regulus	207 43.7	N11 54.0
08	25 44.5	276 42.8	39.6	315 20.2	27.7	297 55.3	11.3	171 59.2	49.5	Rigel	281 12.4	S 8 11.3
M 09	40 47.0	291 41.9 ..	39.2	330 20.8 ..	28.0	312 57.1 ..	11.3	187 01.8 ..	49.4	Rigil Kent.	139 51.2	S60 53.6
O 10	55 49.4	306 41.1	38.9	345 21.4	28.2	327 59.0	11.4	202 04.3	49.4	Sabik	102 12.2	S15 44.4
N 11	70 51.9	321 40.3	38.6	0 22.0	28.5	343 00.8	11.4	217 06.9	49.4			
D 12	85 54.4	336 39.4 N23 38.2		15 22.6 N22 28.8		358 02.6 N23 11.4		232 09.4 S10 49.4		Schedar	349 40.6	N56 36.4
A 13	100 56.8	351 38.6	37.9	30 23.2	29.0	13 04.5	11.4	247 12.0	49.4	Shaula	96 21.5	S37 06.7
Y 14	115 59.3	6 37.7	37.6	45 23.8	29.3	28 06.3	11.4	262 14.5	49.4	Sirius	258 34.0	S16 44.3
15	131 01.8	21 36.9 ..	37.2	60 24.4 ..	29.5	43 08.2 ..	11.4	277 17.0 ..	49.3	Spica	158 31.1	S11 14.0
16	146 04.2	36 36.1	36.9	75 24.9	29.8	58 10.0	11.4	292 19.6	49.3	Suhail	222 52.7	S43 29.6
17	161 06.7	51 35.2	36.5	90 25.5	30.0	73 11.8	11.4	307 22.1	49.3			
18	176 09.2	66 34.4 N23 36.2		105 26.1 N22 30.3		88 13.7 N23 11.5		322 24.7 S10 49.3		Vega	80 38.5	N38 47.9
19	191 11.6	81 33.5	35.8	120 26.7	30.6	103 15.5	11.5	337 27.2	49.3	Zuben'ubi	137 05.1	S16 05.9
20	206 14.1	96 32.7	35.5	135 27.3	30.8	118 17.4	11.5	352 29.8	49.3		SHA	Mer. Pass.
21	221 16.5	111 31.9 ..	35.2	150 27.9 ..	31.1	133 19.2 ..	11.5	7 32.3 ..	49.2		° ′	h m
22	236 19.0	126 31.0	34.8	165 28.5	31.3	148 21.0	11.5	22 34.9	49.2	Venus	252 44.2	13 32
23	251 21.5	141 30.2	34.5	180 29.1	31.6	163 22.9	11.5	37 37.4	49.2	Mars	290 35.6	10 59
	h m									Jupiter	272 30.7	12 11
Mer. Pass. 6 21.2		v −0.8 d 0.3		v 0.6 d 0.3		v 1.8 d 0.0		v 2.5 d 0.0		Saturn	146 12.0	20 34

UT	SUN GHA	SUN Dec	MOON GHA	v	Dec	d	HP
15 00	179 53.9	N23 18.2	109 26.5	14.1	N 5 28.3	10.3	55.4
01	194 53.8	18.3	123 59.6	14.2	5 18.0	10.3	55.4
02	209 53.7	18.4	138 32.8	14.2	5 07.7	10.4	55.5
03	224 53.5	.. 18.5	153 06.0	14.1	4 57.3	10.4	55.5
04	239 53.4	18.6	167 39.1	14.2	4 46.9	10.4	55.5
05	254 53.3	18.7	182 12.3	14.1	4 36.5	10.5	55.5
06	269 53.1	N23 18.8	196 45.4	14.1	N 4 26.0	10.5	55.6
07	284 53.0	18.9	211 18.5	14.1	4 15.5	10.5	55.6
S 08	299 52.9	19.0	225 51.6	14.1	4 05.0	10.6	55.6
A 09	314 52.7	.. 19.1	240 24.7	14.0	3 54.4	10.5	55.6
T 10	329 52.6	19.2	254 57.7	14.1	3 43.9	10.6	55.7
U 11	344 52.4	19.3	269 30.8	14.0	3 33.3	10.6	55.7
R 12	359 52.3	N23 19.4	284 03.8	14.0	N 3 22.7	10.7	55.7
D 13	14 52.2	19.5	298 36.8	14.0	3 12.0	10.7	55.8
A 14	29 52.0	19.6	313 09.8	14.0	3 01.3	10.7	55.8
Y 15	44 51.9	.. 19.7	327 42.8	14.0	2 50.6	10.7	55.8
16	59 51.8	19.8	342 15.8	13.9	2 39.9	10.7	55.8
17	74 51.6	19.9	356 48.7	13.9	2 29.2	10.8	55.9
18	89 51.5	N23 20.0	11 21.6	13.9	N 2 18.4	10.8	55.9
19	104 51.4	20.1	25 54.5	13.9	2 07.6	10.8	55.9
20	119 51.2	20.2	40 27.4	13.8	1 56.8	10.8	56.0
21	134 51.1	.. 20.2	55 00.2	13.8	1 46.0	10.9	56.0
22	149 51.0	20.3	69 33.0	13.8	1 35.1	10.8	56.0
23	164 50.8	20.4	84 05.8	13.8	1 24.3	10.9	56.1
16 00	179 50.7	N23 20.5	98 38.6	13.7	N 1 13.4	10.9	56.1
01	194 50.6	20.6	113 11.3	13.7	1 02.5	10.9	56.1
02	209 50.4	20.7	127 44.0	13.7	0 51.6	11.0	56.1
03	224 50.2	.. 20.8	142 16.7	13.6	0 40.6	10.9	56.2
04	239 50.2	20.9	156 49.3	13.6	0 29.7	11.0	56.2
05	254 50.0	21.0	171 21.9	13.6	0 18.7	11.0	56.2
06	269 49.9	N23 21.0	185 54.5	13.6	N 0 07.7	10.9	56.3
07	284 49.8	21.1	200 27.1	13.5	S 0 03.2	11.0	56.3
08	299 49.6	21.2	214 59.6	13.4	0 14.2	11.1	56.3
S 09	314 49.5	.. 21.3	229 32.0	13.5	0 25.3	11.0	56.4
U 10	329 49.4	21.4	244 04.5	13.4	0 36.3	11.0	56.4
N 11	344 49.2	21.5	258 36.9	13.3	0 47.3	11.1	56.4
D 12	359 49.1	N23 21.5	273 09.2	13.4	S 0 58.4	11.0	56.5
A 13	14 48.9	21.6	287 41.6	13.3	1 09.4	11.1	56.5
Y 14	29 48.8	21.7	302 13.9	13.2	1 20.5	11.0	56.5
15	44 48.7	.. 21.8	316 46.1	13.2	1 31.5	11.1	56.6
16	59 48.5	21.9	331 18.3	13.2	1 42.6	11.1	56.6
17	74 48.4	21.9	345 50.5	13.1	1 53.7	11.1	56.6
18	89 48.3	N23 22.0	0 22.6	13.1	S 2 04.8	11.1	56.7
19	104 48.1	22.1	14 54.7	13.0	2 15.9	11.0	56.7
20	119 48.0	22.2	29 26.7	13.0	2 27.0	11.0	56.7
21	134 47.9	.. 22.2	43 58.7	12.9	2 38.0	11.1	56.8
22	149 47.7	22.3	58 30.6	12.9	2 49.1	11.0	56.8
23	164 47.6	22.4	73 02.5	12.8	3 00.2	11.1	56.9
17 00	179 47.5	N23 22.5	87 34.3	12.8	S 3 11.2	11.1	56.9
01	194 47.3	22.5	102 06.1	12.7	3 22.4	11.0	56.9
02	209 47.2	22.6	116 37.8	12.7	3 33.5	11.1	57.0
03	224 47.1	.. 22.7	131 09.5	12.7	3 44.6	11.0	57.0
04	239 46.9	22.7	145 41.2	12.5	3 55.7	11.1	57.0
05	254 46.8	22.8	160 12.7	12.6	4 06.8	11.0	57.1
06	269 46.7	N23 22.9	174 44.3	12.4	S 4 17.8	11.1	57.1
07	284 46.5	23.0	189 15.7	12.5	4 28.9	11.1	57.1
08	299 46.4	23.0	203 47.2	12.3	4 40.0	11.0	57.2
M 09	314 46.2	.. 23.1	218 18.5	12.3	4 51.0	11.1	57.2
O 10	329 46.1	23.2	232 49.8	12.2	5 02.1	11.0	57.3
N 11	344 46.0	23.2	247 21.0	12.2	5 13.1	11.0	57.3
D 12	359 45.8	N23 23.3	261 52.2	12.1	S 5 24.1	11.0	57.3
A 13	14 45.7	23.3	276 23.3	12.1	5 35.1	11.0	57.4
Y 14	29 45.6	23.4	290 54.4	12.0	5 46.1	11.0	57.4
15	44 45.4	.. 23.5	305 25.4	11.9	5 57.1	11.0	57.4
16	59 45.3	23.5	319 56.3	11.9	6 08.1	10.9	57.5
17	74 45.2	23.6	334 27.2	11.8	6 19.0	11.0	57.5
18	89 45.0	N23 23.7	348 58.0	11.7	S 6 30.0	10.9	57.6
19	104 44.9	23.7	3 28.7	11.7	6 40.9	10.9	57.6
20	119 44.8	23.8	17 59.4	11.6	6 51.8	10.9	57.6
21	134 44.6	.. 23.8	32 30.0	11.5	7 02.7	10.8	57.7
22	149 44.5	23.9	47 00.5	11.5	7 13.5	10.9	57.7
23	164 44.4	23.9	61 31.0	11.4	S 7 24.4	10.8	57.8
	SD 15.8	d 0.1	SD 15.2		15.4		15.6

Twilight / Moonrise

Lat.	Naut.	Civil	Sunrise	Moonrise 15	16	17	18
N 72	▢	▢	▢	10 16	12 01	13 50	15 47
N 70	▢	▢	▢	10 22	11 59	13 41	15 29
68	▢	▢	▢	10 26	11 58	13 34	15 15
66	▢	▢	▢	10 29	11 57	13 28	15 04
64	////	////	01 32	10 32	11 56	13 23	14 54
62	////	////	02 10	10 35	11 55	13 19	14 46
60	////	00 52	02 36	10 37	11 55	13 15	14 39
N 58	////	01 41	02 56	10 39	11 54	13 12	14 33
56	////	02 11	03 13	10 41	11 54	13 09	14 28
54	00 47	02 33	03 27	10 42	11 53	13 07	14 23
52	01 33	02 51	03 39	10 44	11 53	13 04	14 18
50	02 00	03 06	03 50	10 45	11 52	13 02	14 14
45	02 46	03 35	04 13	10 48	11 52	12 58	14 06
N 40	03 16	03 58	04 31	10 50	11 51	12 54	13 59
35	03 39	04 16	04 46	10 52	11 50	12 50	13 53
30	03 58	04 31	04 59	10 54	11 50	12 48	13 48
20	04 27	04 56	05 21	10 57	11 49	12 43	13 39
N 10	04 49	05 16	05 40	11 00	11 48	12 38	13 31
0	05 08	05 35	05 57	11 02	11 47	12 34	13 23
S 10	05 25	05 52	06 14	11 05	11 47	12 30	13 16
20	05 41	06 09	06 33	11 08	11 46	12 26	13 08
30	05 58	06 28	06 54	11 11	11 45	12 21	13 00
35	06 07	06 38	07 07	11 13	11 45	12 18	12 55
40	06 16	06 50	07 21	11 15	11 44	12 15	12 49
45	06 26	07 04	07 37	11 17	11 44	12 12	12 42
S 50	06 38	07 20	07 58	11 20	11 43	12 08	12 34
52	06 43	07 27	08 08	11 21	11 43	12 06	12 31
54	06 49	07 35	08 19	11 23	11 43	12 04	12 27
56	06 55	07 44	08 32	11 24	11 42	12 01	12 23
58	07 02	07 54	08 46	11 26	11 42	11 59	12 18
S 60	07 09	08 06	09 04	11 28	11 41	11 56	12 12

Sunset / Twilight / Moonset

Lat.	Sunset	Civil	Naut.	Moonset 15	16	17	18
N 72	▢	▢	▢	23 39	23 29	23 18	23 04
N 70	▢	▢	▢	23 38	23 33	23 28	23 23
68	▢	▢	▢	23 36	23 37	23 39	23 39
66	▢	▢	▢	23 35	23 40	23 45	23 52
64	22 30	////	////	23 34	23 42	23 51	24 02
62	21 52	////	////	23 33	23 44	23 57	24 11
60	21 26	23 11	////	23 33	23 46	24 01	00 01
N 58	21 06	22 21	////	23 32	23 48	24 06	00 06
56	20 49	21 51	////	23 32	23 50	24 10	00 10
54	20 35	21 29	23 15	23 31	23 51	24 13	00 13
52	20 22	21 11	22 29	23 31	23 52	24 16	00 16
50	20 11	20 56	22 01	23 30	23 54	24 19	00 19
45	19 49	20 26	21 16	23 29	23 56	24 25	00 25
N 40	19 31	20 04	20 45	23 28	23 59	24 30	00 30
35	19 16	19 46	20 22	23 28	24 02	00 02	00 35
30	19 03	19 30	20 04	23 27	24 05	00 05	00 39
20	18 41	19 05	19 35	23 26	24 08	00 08	00 46
N 10	18 22	18 45	19 12	23 25	24 10	00 10	00 52
0	18 04	18 27	18 53	23 24	24 12	00 12	00 57
S 10	17 47	18 10	18 36	23 23	24 14	00 14	01 03
20	17 28	17 51	18 18	23 22	24 16	00 16	01 09
30	17 07	17 34	18 04	23 21	24 19	00 19	01 15
35	16 55	17 23	17 55	23 20	24 21	00 21	01 20
40	16 41	17 12	17 51	23 19	24 23	00 23	01 25
45	16 24	16 58	17 35	23 18	24 25	00 25	01 30
S 50	16 03	16 42	17 23	23 17	24 27	00 27	01 36
52	15 53	16 34	17 18	23 16	24 28	00 28	01 39
54	15 42	16 26	17 12	23 16	24 29	00 29	01 42
56	15 30	16 17	17 06	23 15	24 31	00 31	01 46
58	15 15	16 07	17 00	23 14	24 33	00 33	01 50
S 60	14 58	15 55	16 52	23 14	24 33	00 33	01 54

	SUN			MOON			
Day	Eqn. of Time 00ʰ	12ʰ	Mer. Pass.	Mer. Pass. Upper	Lower	Age	Phase
d	m s	m s	h m	h m	h m	d	%
15	00 24	00 30	12 01	17 13	04 51	07	38
16	00 37	00 43	12 01	17 58	05 36	08	48
17	00 50	00 56	12 01	18 46	06 22	09	58

UT	ARIES GHA	VENUS −3.8 GHA	Dec	MARS +1.5 GHA	Dec	JUPITER −1.9 GHA	Dec	SATURN +0.5 GHA	Dec	STARS Name	SHA	Dec
18 00	266 23.9	156 29.4	N23 34.1	195 29.7	N22 31.8	178 24.7	N23 11.5	52 39.9	S10 49.2	Acamar	315 18.7	S40 15.0
01	281 26.4	171 28.5	33.7	210 30.3	32.1	193 26.6	11.5	67 42.5	49.2	Achernar	335 27.1	S57 09.8
02	296 28.9	186 27.7	33.4	225 30.9	32.3	208 28.4	11.5	82 45.0	49.1	Acrux	173 09.1	S63 10.8
03	311 31.3	201 26.9 ..	33.0	240 31.5 ..	32.6	223 30.2 ..	11.6	97 47.6 ..	49.1	Adhara	255 12.9	S28 59.7
04	326 33.8	216 26.0	32.7	255 32.1	32.8	238 32.1	11.6	112 50.1	49.1	Aldebaran	290 49.7	N16 32.0
05	341 36.3	231 25.2	32.3	270 32.6	33.1	253 33.9	11.6	127 52.7	49.1			
06	356 38.7	246 24.4	N23 32.0	285 33.2	N22 33.3	268 35.8	N23 11.6	142 55.2	S10 49.1	Alioth	166 20.6	N55 53.4
T 07	11 41.2	261 23.5	31.6	300 33.8	33.6	283 37.6	11.6	157 57.8	49.1	Alkaid	152 58.7	N49 15.0
U 08	26 43.6	276 22.7	31.2	315 34.4	33.8	298 39.4	11.6	173 00.3	49.0	Al Na'ir	27 43.5	S46 53.4
E 09	41 46.1	291 21.9 ..	30.9	330 35.0 ..	34.1	313 41.3 ..	11.6	188 02.8 ..	49.0	Alnilam	275 46.7	S 1 11.8
S 10	56 48.6	306 21.0	30.5	345 35.6	34.3	328 43.1	11.6	203 05.4	49.0	Alphard	217 56.3	S 8 43.2
D 11	71 51.0	321 20.2	30.2	0 36.2	34.6	343 45.0	11.7	218 07.9	49.0			
A 12	86 53.5	336 19.4	N23 29.8	15 36.8	N22 34.8	358 46.8	N23 11.7	233 10.5	S10 49.0	Alphecca	126 10.7	N26 40.3
Y 13	101 56.0	351 18.5	29.4	30 37.4	35.1	13 48.6	11.7	248 13.0	49.0	Alpheratz	357 43.5	N29 09.8
14	116 58.4	6 17.7	29.1	45 38.0	35.3	28 50.5	11.7	263 15.6	48.9	Altair	62 07.9	N 8 54.4
15	132 00.9	21 16.9 ..	28.7	60 38.6 ..	35.6	43 52.3 ..	11.7	278 18.1 ..	48.9	Ankaa	353 15.8	S42 13.7
16	147 03.4	36 16.1	28.3	75 39.2	35.8	58 54.2	11.7	293 20.6	48.9	Antares	112 25.9	S26 27.6
17	162 05.8	51 15.2	27.9	90 39.7	36.1	73 56.0	11.7	308 23.2	48.9			
18	177 08.3	66 14.4	N23 27.6	105 40.3	N22 36.3	88 57.8	N23 11.7	323 25.7	S10 48.9	Arcturus	145 55.5	N19 06.9
19	192 10.8	81 13.6	27.2	120 40.9	36.6	103 59.7	11.7	338 28.3	48.9	Atria	107 27.1	S69 03.0
20	207 13.2	96 12.7	26.8	135 41.5	36.8	119 01.5	11.8	353 30.8	48.8	Avior	234 18.5	S59 33.5
21	222 15.7	111 11.9 ..	26.4	150 42.1 ..	37.1	134 03.4 ..	11.8	8 33.4 ..	48.8	Bellatrix	278 32.3	N 6 21.5
22	237 18.1	126 11.1	26.1	165 42.7	37.3	149 05.2	11.8	23 35.9	48.8	Betelgeuse	271 01.6	N 7 24.4
23	252 20.6	141 10.3	25.7	180 43.3	37.6	164 07.0	11.8	38 38.4	48.8			
19 00	267 23.1	156 09.4	N23 25.3	195 43.9	N22 37.8	179 08.9	N23 11.8	53 41.0	S10 48.8	Canopus	263 56.7	S52 42.4
01	282 25.5	171 08.6	24.9	210 44.5	38.1	194 10.7	11.8	68 43.5	48.8	Capella	280 34.9	N46 00.5
02	297 28.0	186 07.8	24.5	225 45.1	38.3	209 12.6	11.8	83 46.1	48.8	Deneb	49 31.1	N45 19.7
03	312 30.5	201 07.0 ..	24.2	240 45.7 ..	38.5	224 14.4 ..	11.8	98 48.6 ..	48.7	Denebola	182 33.7	N14 29.8
04	327 32.9	216 06.1	23.8	255 46.3	38.8	239 16.2	11.8	113 51.1	48.7	Diphda	348 56.0	S17 54.6
05	342 35.4	231 05.3	23.4	270 46.8	39.0	254 18.1	11.8	128 53.7	48.7			
06	357 37.9	246 04.5	N23 23.0	285 47.4	N22 39.3	269 19.9	N23 11.9	143 56.2	S10 48.7	Dubhe	193 51.9	N61 40.9
W 07	12 40.3	261 03.7	22.6	300 48.0	39.5	284 21.8	11.9	158 58.8	48.7	Elnath	278 13.0	N28 36.9
E 08	27 42.8	276 02.8	22.2	315 48.6	39.8	299 23.6	11.9	174 01.3	48.7	Eltanin	90 45.6	N51 29.4
D 09	42 45.3	291 02.0 ..	21.8	330 49.2 ..	40.0	314 25.4 ..	11.9	189 03.8 ..	48.6	Enif	33 46.9	N 9 56.3
N 10	57 47.7	306 01.2	21.5	345 49.8	40.2	329 27.3	11.9	204 06.4	48.6	Fomalhaut	15 23.9	S29 32.8
E 11	72 50.2	321 00.4	21.1	0 50.4	40.5	344 29.1	11.9	219 08.9	48.6			
S 12	87 52.6	335 59.5	N23 20.7	15 51.0	N22 40.7	359 31.0	N23 11.9	234 11.5	S10 48.6	Gacrux	172 00.7	S57 11.6
D 13	102 55.1	350 58.7	20.3	30 51.6	41.0	14 32.8	11.9	249 14.0	48.6	Gienah	175 52.2	S17 37.2
A 14	117 57.6	5 57.9	19.9	45 52.2	41.2	29 34.6	11.9	264 16.5	48.6	Hadar	148 47.4	S60 26.5
Y 15	133 00.0	20 57.1 ..	19.5	60 52.8 ..	41.4	44 36.5 ..	11.9	279 19.1 ..	48.6	Hamal	328 00.9	N23 31.4
16	148 02.5	35 56.3	19.1	75 53.3	41.7	59 38.3	11.9	294 21.6	48.5	Kaus Aust.	83 43.4	S34 22.5
17	163 05.0	50 55.4	18.7	90 53.9	41.9	74 40.2	12.0	309 24.1	48.5			
18	178 07.4	65 54.6	N23 18.3	105 54.5	N22 42.2	89 42.0	N23 12.0	324 26.7	S10 48.5	Kochab	137 19.3	N74 06.3
19	193 09.9	80 53.8	17.9	120 55.1	42.4	104 43.9	12.0	339 29.2	48.5	Markab	13 38.2	N15 16.7
20	208 12.4	95 53.0	17.5	135 55.7	42.6	119 45.7	12.0	354 31.8	48.5	Menkar	314 15.3	N 4 08.5
21	223 14.8	110 52.2 ..	17.1	150 56.3 ..	42.9	134 47.5 ..	12.0	9 34.3 ..	48.5	Menkent	148 07.3	S36 26.3
22	238 17.3	125 51.4	16.7	165 56.9	43.1	149 49.4	12.0	24 36.8	48.4	Miaplacidus	221 40.2	S69 46.7
23	253 19.8	140 50.5	16.3	180 57.5	43.3	164 51.2	12.0	39 39.4	48.4			
20 00	268 22.2	155 49.7	N23 15.8	195 58.1	N22 43.6	179 53.1	N23 12.0	54 41.9	S10 48.4	Mirfak	308 40.7	N49 54.3
01	283 24.7	170 48.9	15.4	210 58.7	43.8	194 54.9	12.1	69 44.5	48.4	Nunki	75 57.9	S26 16.6
02	298 27.1	185 48.1	15.0	225 59.3	44.0	209 56.7	12.1	84 47.0	48.4	Peacock	53 18.8	S56 41.1
03	313 29.6	200 47.3 ..	14.6	240 59.9 ..	44.3	224 58.6 ..	12.1	99 49.5 ..	48.4	Pollux	243 28.1	N27 59.5
04	328 32.1	215 46.5	14.2	256 00.4	44.5	240 00.4	12.1	114 52.1	48.4	Procyon	245 00.0	N 5 11.2
05	343 34.5	230 45.6	13.8	271 01.0	44.7	255 02.3	12.1	129 54.6	48.3			
06	358 37.0	245 44.8	N23 13.4	286 01.6	N22 45.0	270 04.1	N23 12.1	144 57.1	S10 48.3	Rasalhague	96 06.1	N12 33.2
T 07	13 39.5	260 44.0	13.0	301 02.2	45.2	285 05.9	12.1	159 59.7	48.3	Regulus	207 43.7	N11 54.0
H 08	28 41.9	275 43.2	12.5	316 02.8	45.4	300 07.8	12.1	175 02.2	48.3	Rigel	281 12.4	S 8 11.3
U 09	43 44.4	290 42.4 ..	12.1	331 03.4 ..	45.7	315 09.6 ..	12.1	190 04.7 ..	48.3	Rigil Kent.	139 51.2	S60 53.6
R 10	58 46.9	305 41.6	11.7	346 04.0	45.9	330 11.5	12.1	205 07.3	48.3	Sabik	102 12.2	S15 44.4
S 11	73 49.3	320 40.8	11.3	1 04.6	46.1	345 13.3	12.2	220 09.8	48.3			
D 12	88 51.8	335 39.9	N23 10.9	16 05.2	N22 46.4	0 15.1	N23 12.2	235 12.4	S10 48.2	Schedar	349 40.6	N56 36.4
A 13	103 54.2	350 39.1	10.4	31 05.8	46.6	15 17.0	12.2	250 14.9	48.2	Shaula	96 21.5	S37 06.7
Y 14	118 56.7	5 38.3	10.0	46 06.4	46.8	30 18.8	12.2	265 17.4	48.2	Sirius	258 34.0	S16 44.3
15	133 59.2	20 37.5 ..	09.6	61 06.9 ..	47.1	45 20.7 ..	12.2	280 20.0 ..	48.2	Spica	158 31.1	S11 14.0
16	149 01.6	35 36.7	09.2	76 07.5	47.3	60 22.5	12.2	295 22.5	48.2	Suhail	222 52.7	S43 29.6
17	164 04.1	50 35.9	08.7	91 08.1	47.5	75 24.3	12.2	310 25.0	48.2			
18	179 06.6	65 35.1	N23 08.3	106 08.7	N22 47.8	90 26.2	N23 12.2	325 27.6	S10 48.2	Vega	80 38.5	N38 47.9
19	194 09.0	80 34.3	07.9	121 09.3	48.0	105 28.0	12.2	340 30.1	48.2	Zuben'ubi	137 05.1	S16 05.9
20	209 11.5	95 33.5	07.4	136 09.9	48.2	120 29.9	12.2	355 32.6	48.1		SHA	Mer.Pass.
21	224 14.0	110 32.6 ..	07.0	151 10.5 ..	48.4	135 31.7 ..	12.3	10 35.2 ..	48.1		° ′	h m
22	239 16.4	125 31.8	06.6	166 11.1	48.7	150 33.5	12.3	25 37.7	48.1	Venus	248 46.4	13 36
23	254 18.9	140 31.0	06.1	181 11.7	48.9	165 35.4	12.3	40 40.2	48.1	Mars	288 20.8	10 57
	h m									Jupiter	271 45.8	12 02
Mer.Pass.	6 09.5	v −0.8	d 0.4	v 0.6	d 0.2	v 1.8	d 0.0	v 2.5	d 0.0	Saturn	146 17.9	20 22

UT	SUN		MOON					Lat.	Twilight		Sunrise	Moonrise			
									Naut.	Civil		18	19	20	21
	GHA	Dec	GHA	v	Dec	d	HP								
d h	o '	o '	o '	'	o '	'	'	N 72	h m	h m	h m	15 47	17 59	▬	▬
18 00	179 44.2	N23 24.0	76 01.4	11.3	S 7 35.2	10.8	57.8	N 70	▭	▭	▭	15 29	17 26	19 33	22 10
01	194 44.1	24.1	90 31.7	11.3	7 46.0	10.7	57.8	68	▭	▭	▭	15 15	17 02	18 52	20 37
02	209 43.9	24.1	105 02.0	11.1	7 56.7	10.8	57.9	66	▭	▭	▭	15 04	16 43	18 24	19 58
03	224 43.8	.. 24.2	119 32.1	11.1	8 07.5	10.7	57.9	64	////	////	01 31	14 54	16 28	18 03	19 31
04	239 43.7	24.2	134 02.2	11.1	8 18.2	10.6	57.9	62	////	////	02 09	14 46	16 16	17 46	19 10
05	254 43.5	24.3	148 32.3	10.9	8 28.8	10.7	58.0	60	////	00 49	02 36	14 39	16 05	17 32	18 53
06	269 43.4	N23 24.3	163 02.2	10.9	S 8 39.5	10.6	58.0	N 58	////	01 40	02 56	14 33	15 56	17 20	18 39
07	284 43.3	24.4	177 32.1	10.8	8 50.1	10.6	58.1	56	////	02 10	03 13	14 28	15 48	17 10	18 27
08	299 43.1	24.4	192 01.9	10.7	9 00.7	10.6	58.1	54	00 45	02 33	03 27	14 23	15 41	17 00	18 16
T 09	314 43.0	.. 24.5	206 31.6	10.7	9 11.3	10.5	58.1	52	01 32	02 51	03 39	14 18	15 35	16 52	18 07
U 10	329 42.9	24.5	221 01.3	10.5	9 21.8	10.5	58.2	50	02 00	03 06	03 50	14 14	15 29	16 45	17 58
E 11	344 42.7	24.6	235 30.8	10.5	9 32.3	10.4	58.2	45	02 46	03 35	04 13	14 06	15 17	16 29	17 40
S 12	359 42.6	N23 24.6	250 00.3	10.4	S 9 42.7	10.4	58.3	N 40	03 16	03 58	04 31	13 59	15 07	16 17	17 26
D 13	14 42.5	24.7	264 29.7	10.3	9 53.1	10.4	58.3	35	03 40	04 16	04 46	13 53	14 58	16 06	17 13
A 14	29 42.3	24.7	278 59.0	10.3	10 03.5	10.3	58.3	30	03 58	04 32	04 59	13 48	14 51	15 56	17 03
Y 15	44 42.2	.. 24.7	293 28.3	10.1	10 13.8	10.3	58.4	20	04 27	04 57	05 21	13 39	14 38	15 40	16 44
16	59 42.0	24.8	307 57.4	10.1	10 24.1	10.3	58.4	N 10	04 50	05 17	05 40	13 31	14 27	15 26	16 28
17	74 41.9	24.8	322 26.5	10.0	10 34.4	10.2	58.5	0	05 09	05 35	05 58	13 23	14 16	15 13	16 13
18	89 41.8	N23 24.9	336 55.5	9.9	S10 44.6	10.1	58.5	S 10	05 26	05 52	06 15	13 16	14 06	15 00	15 58
19	104 41.6	24.9	351 24.4	9.8	10 54.7	10.1	58.5	20	05 42	06 10	06 34	13 08	13 55	14 46	15 43
20	119 41.5	25.0	5 53.2	9.7	11 04.8	10.1	58.6	30	05 59	06 29	06 55	13 00	13 42	14 30	15 24
21	134 41.4	.. 25.0	20 21.9	9.7	11 14.9	10.0	58.6	35	06 07	06 39	07 07	12 55	13 35	14 21	15 14
22	149 41.2	25.0	34 50.6	9.6	11 24.9	10.0	58.7	40	06 17	06 51	07 22	12 49	13 27	14 10	15 02
23	164 41.1	25.1	49 19.2	9.4	11 34.9	9.9	58.7	45	06 27	07 04	07 38	12 42	13 17	13 58	14 48
19 00	179 41.0	N23 25.1	63 47.6	9.4	S11 44.8	9.8	58.7	S 50	06 39	07 21	07 59	12 34	13 06	13 44	14 31
01	194 40.8	25.2	78 16.0	9.3	11 54.6	9.8	58.8	52	06 44	07 28	08 09	12 31	13 00	13 37	14 22
02	209 40.7	25.2	92 44.3	9.2	12 04.4	9.8	58.8	54	06 50	07 36	08 20	12 27	12 55	13 29	14 13
03	224 40.6	.. 25.2	107 12.5	9.1	12 14.2	9.7	58.9	56	06 56	07 45	08 33	12 23	12 48	13 21	14 03
04	239 40.4	25.3	121 40.6	9.0	12 23.9	9.6	58.9	58	07 03	07 56	08 48	12 18	12 41	13 11	13 52
05	254 40.3	25.3	136 08.6	9.0	12 33.5	9.6	58.9	S 60	07 10	08 07	09 05	12 12	12 33	13 00	13 39

UT	SUN		MOON					Lat.	Sunset	Twilight		Moonset			
										Civil	Naut.	18	19	20	21
06	269 40.1	N23 25.3	150 36.6	8.8	S12 43.1	9.5	59.0								
W 07	284 40.0	25.4	165 04.4	8.8	12 52.6	9.4	59.0	o	h m	h m	h m	h m	h m	h m	h m
E 08	299 39.9	25.4	179 32.2	8.6	13 02.0	9.4	59.0	N 72	▭	▭	▭	23 04	22 43	▬	▬
D 09	314 39.7	.. 25.4	193 59.8	8.6	13 11.4	9.3	59.1	N 70	▭	▭	▭	23 23	23 18	23 10	22 42
N 10	329 39.6	25.5	208 27.4	8.5	13 20.7	9.3	59.1	68	▭	▭	▭	23 39	23 43	23 52	24 14
E 11	344 39.5	25.5	222 54.9	8.3	13 30.0	9.1	59.2	66	▭	▭	▭	23 52	24 02	00 02	00 20
S 12	359 39.3	N23 25.5	237 22.2	8.3	S13 39.1	9.2	59.2	64	22 32	////	////	24 02	00 02	00 18	00 42
D 13	14 39.2	25.6	251 49.5	8.2	13 48.3	9.0	59.2	62	21 54	////	////	24 11	00 11	00 31	01 00
A 14	29 39.1	25.6	266 16.7	8.1	13 57.3	9.0	59.3	60	21 27	23 14	////	00 01	00 19	00 42	01 14
Y 15	44 38.9	.. 25.6	280 43.8	8.0	14 06.3	8.9	59.3	N 58	21 07	22 23	////	00 06	00 26	00 52	01 27
16	59 38.8	25.6	295 10.8	7.9	14 15.2	8.8	59.4	56	20 50	21 53	////	00 10	00 32	01 01	01 38
17	74 38.7	25.7	309 37.7	7.9	14 24.0	8.7	59.4	54	20 36	21 30	23 18	00 13	00 38	01 08	01 47
18	89 38.5	N23 25.7	324 04.6	7.7	S14 32.7	8.7	59.4	52	20 23	21 12	22 31	00 16	00 43	01 15	01 56
19	104 38.4	25.7	338 31.3	7.6	14 41.4	8.6	59.5	50	20 12	20 57	22 03	00 19	00 47	01 21	02 03
20	119 38.2	25.7	352 57.9	7.5	14 50.0	8.5	59.5	45	19 50	20 27	21 17	00 25	00 57	01 35	02 20
21	134 38.1	.. 25.8	7 24.4	7.5	14 58.5	8.4	59.5	N 40	19 32	20 05	20 46	00 30	01 05	01 46	02 33
22	149 38.0	25.8	21 50.9	7.3	15 06.9	8.3	59.6	35	19 17	19 46	20 23	00 35	01 13	01 55	02 45
23	164 37.8	25.8	36 17.2	7.3	15 15.2	8.3	59.6	30	19 04	19 31	20 05	00 39	01 19	02 04	02 55
20 00	179 37.7	N23 25.8	50 43.5	7.1	S15 23.5	8.2	59.7	20	18 42	19 06	19 35	00 46	01 30	02 18	03 12
01	194 37.6	25.8	65 09.6	7.1	15 31.7	8.0	59.7	N 10	18 23	18 46	19 13	00 52	01 39	02 31	03 27
02	209 37.4	25.9	79 35.7	6.9	15 39.7	8.0	59.7	0	18 05	18 28	18 54	00 57	01 48	02 43	03 41
03	224 37.3	.. 25.9	94 01.6	6.9	15 47.7	7.9	59.8	S 10	17 48	18 10	18 37	01 03	01 57	02 54	03 55
04	239 37.2	25.9	108 27.5	6.8	15 55.6	7.8	59.8	20	17 29	17 53	18 21	01 09	02 07	03 07	04 10
05	254 37.0	25.9	122 53.3	6.7	16 03.4	7.7	59.8	30	17 08	17 34	18 04	01 16	02 17	03 22	04 28
06	269 36.9	N23 25.9	137 19.0	6.5	S16 11.1	7.6	59.9	35	16 55	17 24	17 55	01 20	02 24	03 30	04 38
T 07	284 36.8	26.0	151 44.5	6.5	16 18.7	7.5	59.9	40	16 41	17 12	17 46	01 25	02 31	03 40	04 49
H 08	299 36.6	26.0	166 10.0	6.4	16 26.2	7.5	59.9	45	16 24	16 58	17 36	01 30	02 39	03 51	05 03
U 09	314 36.5	.. 26.0	180 35.4	6.4	16 33.7	7.3	60.0	S 50	16 04	16 42	17 24	01 36	02 50	04 05	05 20
R 10	329 36.3	26.0	195 00.8	6.2	16 41.0	7.2	60.0	52	15 54	16 35	17 18	01 39	02 54	04 11	05 27
S 11	344 36.2	26.0	209 26.0	6.1	16 48.2	7.1	60.0	54	15 43	16 26	17 13	01 42	02 59	04 18	05 36
D 12	359 36.1	N23 26.0	223 51.1	6.0	S16 55.3	7.0	60.1	56	15 30	16 17	17 07	01 46	03 05	04 26	05 46
A 13	14 35.9	26.0	238 16.1	6.0	17 02.3	6.9	60.1	58	15 15	16 07	17 00	01 50	03 12	04 35	05 57
Y 14	29 35.8	26.1	252 41.1	5.8	17 09.2	6.8	60.1	S 60	14 58	15 55	16 52	01 54	03 19	04 46	06 10
15	44 35.7	.. 26.1	267 05.9	5.8	17 16.0	6.7	60.2								
16	59 35.5	26.1	281 30.7	5.7	17 22.7	6.5	60.2		SUN			MOON			
17	74 35.4	26.1	295 55.4	5.5	17 29.2	6.5	60.2								
18	89 35.3	N23 26.1	310 19.9	5.5	S17 35.7	6.4	60.3	Day	Eqn. of Time		Mer.	Mer. Pass.		Age	Phase
19	104 35.1	26.1	324 44.4	5.4	17 42.1	6.2	60.3		00h	12h	Pass.	Upper	Lower		
20	119 35.0	26.1	339 08.8	5.4	17 48.3	6.1	60.3	d	m s	m s	h m	h m	h m	d	%
21	134 34.9	.. 26.1	353 33.2	5.2	17 54.4	6.0	60.4	18	01 03	01 09	12 01	19 36	07 10	10	69
22	149 34.7	26.1	7 57.4	5.2	18 00.4	5.9	60.4	19	01 16	01 22	12 01	20 29	08 02	11	79
23	164 34.6	26.1	22 21.6	5.0	S18 06.3	5.8	60.4	20	01 29	01 35	12 02	21 27	08 58	12	87
	SD 15.8	d 0.0	SD 15.9		16.1		16.4									

UT	ARIES GHA	VENUS −3.8 GHA	Dec	MARS +1.5 GHA	Dec	JUPITER −1.9 GHA	Dec	SATURN +0.5 GHA	Dec	STARS Name	SHA	Dec
21 00	269 21.4	155 30.2	N23 05.7	196 12.3	N22 49.1	180 37.2	N23 12.3	55 42.8	S10 48.1	Acamar	315 18.7	S40 14.9
01	284 23.8	170 29.4	05.3	211 12.9	49.4	195 39.1	12.3	70 45.3	48.1	Achernar	335 27.1	S57 09.8
02	299 26.3	185 28.6	04.8	226 13.5	49.6	210 40.9	12.3	85 47.8	48.1	Acrux	173 09.1	S63 10.8
03	314 28.7	200 27.8	.. 04.4	241 14.0	.. 49.8	225 42.7	.. 12.3	100 50.4	.. 48.0	Adhara	255 12.9	S28 59.6
04	329 31.2	215 27.0	04.0	256 14.6	50.0	240 44.6	12.3	115 52.9	48.0	Aldebaran	290 49.7	N16 32.0
05	344 33.7	230 26.2	03.5	271 15.2	50.3	255 46.4	12.3	130 55.4	48.0			
06	359 36.1	245 25.4	N23 03.1	286 15.8	N22 50.5	270 48.3	N23 12.3	145 58.0	S10 48.0	Alioth	166 20.6	N55 53.4
07	14 38.6	260 24.6	02.6	301 16.4	50.7	285 50.1	12.3	161 00.5	48.0	Alkaid	152 58.7	N49 15.0
08	29 41.1	275 23.8	02.2	316 17.0	50.9	300 51.9	12.4	176 03.0	48.0	Al Na'ir	27 43.5	S46 53.4
F 09	44 43.5	290 23.0	.. 01.7	331 17.6	.. 51.2	315 53.8	.. 12.4	191 05.6	.. 48.0	Alnilam	275 46.7	S 1 11.8
R 10	59 46.0	305 22.2	01.3	346 18.2	51.4	330 55.6	12.4	206 08.1	48.0	Alphard	217 56.3	S 8 43.2
I 11	74 48.5	320 21.4	00.8	1 18.8	51.6	345 57.5	12.4	221 10.6	47.9			
D 12	89 50.9	335 20.6	N23 00.4	16 19.4	N22 51.8	0 59.3	N23 12.4	236 13.2	S10 47.9	Alphecca	126 10.7	N26 40.3
A 13	104 53.4	350 19.8	22 59.9	31 20.0	52.0	16 01.1	12.4	251 15.7	47.9	Alpheratz	357 43.4	N29 09.8
Y 14	119 55.9	5 19.0	59.5	46 20.5	52.3	31 03.0	12.4	266 18.2	47.9	Altair	62 07.9	N 8 54.4
15	134 58.3	20 18.2	.. 59.0	61 21.1	.. 52.5	46 04.8	.. 12.4	281 20.8	.. 47.9	Ankaa	353 15.8	S42 13.7
16	150 00.8	35 17.4	58.6	76 21.7	52.7	61 06.7	12.4	296 23.3	47.9	Antares	112 25.9	S26 27.6
17	165 03.2	50 16.5	58.1	91 22.3	52.9	76 08.5	12.4	311 25.8	47.9			
18	180 05.7	65 15.7	N22 57.7	106 22.9	N22 53.2	91 10.3	N23 12.4	326 28.3	S10 47.9	Arcturus	145 55.5	N19 06.9
19	195 08.2	80 14.9	57.2	121 23.5	53.4	106 12.2	12.4	341 30.9	47.8	Atria	107 27.1	S69 03.0
20	210 10.6	95 14.1	56.8	136 24.1	53.6	121 14.0	12.5	356 33.4	47.8	Avior	234 18.5	S59 33.5
21	225 13.1	110 13.4	.. 56.3	151 24.7	.. 53.8	136 15.9	.. 12.5	11 35.9	.. 47.8	Bellatrix	278 32.3	N 6 21.5
22	240 15.6	125 12.6	55.8	166 25.3	54.0	151 17.7	12.5	26 38.5	47.8	Betelgeuse	271 01.6	N 7 24.4
23	255 18.0	140 11.8	55.3	181 25.9	54.2	166 19.5	12.5	41 41.0	47.8			
22 00	270 20.5	155 11.0	N22 54.9	196 26.5	N22 54.5	181 21.4	N23 12.5	56 43.5	S10 47.8	Canopus	263 56.7	S52 42.4
01	285 23.0	170 10.2	54.4	211 27.0	54.7	196 23.2	12.5	71 46.1	47.8	Capella	280 34.9	N46 00.5
02	300 25.4	185 09.4	54.0	226 27.6	54.9	211 25.1	12.5	86 48.6	47.8	Deneb	49 31.1	N45 19.7
03	315 27.9	200 08.6	.. 53.5	241 28.2	.. 55.1	226 26.9	.. 12.5	101 51.1	.. 47.8	Denebola	182 33.7	N14 29.8
04	330 30.4	215 07.8	53.0	256 28.8	55.3	241 28.7	12.5	116 53.7	47.7	Diphda	348 55.9	S17 54.6
05	345 32.8	230 07.0	52.6	271 29.4	55.5	256 30.6	12.5	131 56.2	47.7			
06	0 35.3	245 06.2	N22 52.1	286 30.0	N22 55.8	271 32.4	N23 12.5	146 58.7	S10 47.7	Dubhe	193 51.9	N61 40.9
07	15 37.7	260 05.4	51.6	301 30.6	56.0	286 34.3	12.5	162 01.2	47.7	Elnath	278 13.0	N28 36.9
S 08	30 40.2	275 04.6	51.2	316 31.2	56.2	301 36.1	12.5	177 03.8	47.7	Eltanin	90 45.6	N51 29.4
A 09	45 42.7	290 03.8	.. 50.7	331 31.8	.. 56.4	316 37.9	.. 12.6	192 06.3	.. 47.7	Enif	33 46.9	N 9 56.3
T 10	60 45.1	305 03.0	50.2	346 32.4	56.6	331 39.8	12.6	207 08.8	47.7	Fomalhaut	15 23.9	S29 32.8
U 11	75 47.6	320 02.2	49.7	1 33.0	56.8	346 41.6	12.6	222 11.4	47.7			
R 12	90 50.1	335 01.4	N22 49.3	16 33.6	N22 57.1	1 43.5	N23 12.6	237 13.9	S10 47.6	Gacrux	172 00.7	S57 11.7
D 13	105 52.5	350 00.6	48.8	31 34.1	57.3	16 45.3	12.6	252 16.4	47.6	Gienah	175 52.2	S17 37.2
A 14	120 55.0	4 59.8	48.3	46 34.7	57.5	31 47.1	12.6	267 18.9	47.6	Hadar	148 47.4	S60 26.5
Y 15	135 57.5	19 59.0	.. 47.8	61 35.3	.. 57.7	46 49.0	.. 12.6	282 21.5	.. 47.6	Hamal	328 00.9	N23 31.4
16	150 59.9	34 58.2	47.3	76 35.9	57.9	61 50.8	12.6	297 24.0	47.6	Kaus Aust.	83 43.4	S34 22.5
17	166 02.4	49 57.5	46.9	91 36.5	58.1	76 52.7	12.6	312 26.5	47.6			
18	181 04.9	64 56.7	N22 46.4	106 37.1	N22 58.3	91 54.5	N23 12.6	327 29.0	S10 47.6	Kochab	137 19.3	N74 06.3
19	196 07.3	79 55.9	45.9	121 37.7	58.5	106 56.3	12.6	342 31.6	47.6	Markab	13 38.2	N15 16.7
20	211 09.8	94 55.1	45.4	136 38.3	58.7	121 58.2	12.6	357 34.1	47.6	Menkar	314 15.3	N 4 08.5
21	226 12.2	109 54.3	.. 44.9	151 38.9	.. 59.0	137 00.0	.. 12.6	12 36.6	.. 47.6	Menkent	148 07.3	S36 26.3
22	241 14.7	124 53.5	44.4	166 39.5	59.2	152 01.9	12.6	27 39.2	47.5	Miaplacidus	221 40.2	S69 46.7
23	256 17.2	139 52.7	43.9	181 40.1	59.4	167 03.7	12.7	42 41.7	47.5			
23 00	271 19.6	154 51.9	N22 43.5	196 40.6	N22 59.6	182 05.6	N23 12.7	57 44.2	S10 47.5	Mirfak	308 40.7	N49 54.3
01	286 22.1	169 51.2	43.0	211 41.2	22 59.8	197 07.4	12.7	72 46.7	47.5	Nunki	75 57.9	S26 16.6
02	301 24.6	184 50.4	42.5	226 41.8	23 00.0	212 09.2	12.7	87 49.3	47.5	Peacock	53 18.7	S56 41.1
03	316 27.0	199 49.6	.. 42.0	241 42.4	.. 00.2	227 11.1	.. 12.7	102 51.8	.. 47.5	Pollux	243 28.1	N27 59.5
04	331 29.5	214 48.8	41.5	256 43.0	00.4	242 12.9	12.7	117 54.3	47.5	Procyon	245 00.0	N 5 11.2
05	346 32.0	229 48.0	41.0	271 43.6	00.6	257 14.8	12.7	132 56.8	47.5			
06	1 34.4	244 47.2	N22 40.5	286 44.2	N23 00.8	272 16.6	N23 12.7	147 59.4	S10 47.4	Rasalhague	96 06.1	N12 33.2
07	16 36.9	259 46.4	40.0	301 44.8	01.0	287 18.4	12.7	163 01.9	47.4	Regulus	207 43.7	N11 54.0
08	31 39.4	274 45.7	39.5	316 45.4	01.2	302 20.3	12.7	178 04.4	47.4	Rigel	281 12.4	S 8 11.3
S 09	46 41.8	289 44.9	.. 39.0	331 46.0	.. 01.5	317 22.1	.. 12.7	193 06.9	.. 47.4	Rigil Kent.	139 51.2	S60 53.6
U 10	61 44.3	304 44.1	38.5	346 46.5	01.7	332 24.0	12.7	208 09.5	47.4	Sabik	102 12.2	S15 44.3
N 11	76 46.7	319 43.3	38.0	1 47.1	01.9	347 25.8	12.7	223 12.0	47.4			
D 12	91 49.2	334 42.5	N22 37.5	16 47.7	N23 02.1	2 27.6	N23 12.7	238 14.5	S10 47.4	Schedar	349 40.5	N56 36.4
A 13	106 51.7	349 41.7	37.0	31 48.3	02.3	17 29.5	12.8	253 17.0	47.4	Shaula	96 21.5	S37 06.7
Y 14	121 54.1	4 41.0	36.5	46 48.9	02.5	32 31.3	12.8	268 19.6	47.4	Sirius	258 34.0	S16 44.3
15	136 56.6	19 40.2	.. 36.0	61 49.5	.. 02.7	47 33.2	.. 12.8	283 22.1	.. 47.4	Spica	158 31.1	S11 14.0
16	151 59.1	34 39.4	35.5	76 50.1	02.9	62 35.0	12.8	298 24.6	47.4	Suhail	222 52.7	S43 29.6
17	167 01.5	49 38.6	35.0	91 50.7	03.1	77 36.8	12.8	313 27.1	47.4			
18	182 04.0	64 37.8	N22 34.4	106 51.3	N23 03.3	92 38.7	N23 12.8	328 29.7	S10 47.3	Vega	80 38.5	N38 47.9
19	197 06.5	79 37.1	33.9	121 51.9	03.5	107 40.5	12.8	343 32.2	47.3	Zuben'ubi	137 05.1	S16 05.9
20	212 08.9	94 36.3	33.4	136 52.5	03.7	122 42.4	12.8	358 34.7	47.3		SHA	Mer. Pass.
21	227 11.4	109 35.5	.. 32.9	151 53.1	.. 03.9	137 44.2	.. 12.8	13 37.2	.. 47.3	Venus	244 50.5	13 40
22	242 13.8	124 34.7	32.4	166 53.6	04.1	152 46.0	12.8	28 39.8	47.3	Mars	286 06.0	10 54
23	257 16.3	139 34.0	31.9	181 54.2	04.3	167 47.9	12.8	43 42.3	47.3	Jupiter	271 00.9	11 53
Mer. Pass. 5 57.7		*v* −0.8	*d* 0.5	*v* 0.6	*d* 0.2	*v* 1.8	*d* 0.0	*v* 2.5	*d* 0.0	Saturn	146 23.0	20 10

UT	SUN GHA	SUN Dec	MOON GHA	v	MOON Dec	d	HP
d h	° ′	° ′	° ′	′	° ′	′	′
21 00	179 34.5	N23 26.1	36 45.6	5.0	S18 12.1	5.6	60.5
01	194 34.3	26.1	51 09.6	4.9	18 17.7	5.5	60.5
02	209 34.2	26.1	65 33.5	4.9	18 23.2	5.4	60.5
03	224 34.0	.. 26.1	79 57.4	4.7	18 28.6	5.3	60.6
04	239 33.9	26.1	94 21.1	4.7	18 33.9	5.1	60.6
05	254 33.8	26.1	108 44.8	4.6	18 39.0	5.0	60.6
06	269 33.6	N23 26.1	123 08.4	4.5	S18 44.0	4.9	60.6
07	284 33.5	26.1	137 31.9	4.4	18 48.9	4.8	60.7
F 08	299 33.4	26.1	151 55.3	4.4	18 53.7	4.6	60.7
R 09	314 33.2	.. 26.1	166 18.7	4.3	18 58.3	4.5	60.7
I 10	329 33.1	26.1	180 42.0	4.2	19 02.8	4.4	60.7
11	344 33.0	26.1	195 05.2	4.2	19 07.2	4.2	60.8
D 12	359 32.8	N23 26.1	209 28.4	4.1	S19 11.4	4.1	60.8
A 13	14 32.7	26.1	223 51.5	4.0	19 15.5	3.9	60.8
Y 14	29 32.6	26.1	238 14.5	3.9	19 19.4	3.8	60.8
15	44 32.4	.. 26.1	252 37.4	3.9	19 23.2	3.7	60.9
16	59 32.3	26.1	267 00.3	3.9	19 26.9	3.6	60.9
17	74 32.2	26.1	281 23.2	3.7	19 30.5	3.3	60.9
18	89 32.0	N23 26.1	295 45.9	3.7	S19 33.8	3.3	60.9
19	104 31.9	26.1	310 08.6	3.7	19 37.1	3.1	61.0
20	119 31.8	26.1	324 31.3	3.6	19 40.2	3.0	61.0
21	134 31.6	.. 26.0	338 53.9	3.5	19 43.2	2.8	61.0
22	149 31.5	26.0	353 16.4	3.5	19 46.0	2.7	61.0
23	164 31.3	26.0	7 38.9	3.5	19 48.7	2.5	61.0
22 00	179 31.2	N23 26.0	22 01.4	3.4	S19 51.2	2.4	61.1
01	194 31.1	26.0	36 23.8	3.3	19 53.6	2.2	61.1
02	209 30.9	26.0	50 46.1	3.3	19 55.8	2.1	61.1
03	224 30.8	.. 26.0	65 08.4	3.3	19 57.9	1.9	61.1
04	239 30.7	25.9	79 30.7	3.2	19 59.8	1.8	61.1
05	254 30.5	25.9	93 52.9	3.2	20 01.6	1.7	61.2
06	269 30.4	N23 25.9	108 15.1	3.1	S20 03.3	1.5	61.2
07	284 30.3	25.9	122 37.2	3.1	20 04.8	1.3	61.2
S 08	299 30.1	25.9	136 59.3	3.1	20 06.1	1.2	61.2
A 09	314 30.0	.. 25.9	151 21.4	3.1	20 07.3	1.0	61.2
T 10	329 29.9	25.8	165 43.5	3.0	20 08.3	0.9	61.2
U 11	344 29.7	25.8	180 05.5	3.0	20 09.2	0.7	61.3
R 12	359 29.6	N23 25.8	194 27.5	2.9	S20 09.9	0.6	61.3
D 13	14 29.5	25.8	208 49.4	3.0	20 10.5	0.4	61.3
A 14	29 29.3	25.7	223 11.4	2.9	20 10.9	0.2	61.3
Y 15	44 29.2	.. 25.7	237 33.3	2.9	20 11.1	0.2	61.3
16	59 29.1	25.7	251 55.2	2.9	20 11.3	0.1	61.3
17	74 28.9	25.7	266 17.1	2.9	20 11.2	0.2	61.3
18	89 28.8	N23 25.6	280 39.0	2.8	S20 11.0	0.4	61.3
19	104 28.7	25.6	295 00.8	2.9	20 10.6	0.5	61.3
20	119 28.5	25.6	309 22.7	2.8	20 10.1	0.6	61.4
21	134 28.4	.. 25.6	323 44.5	2.9	20 09.5	0.9	61.4
22	149 28.3	25.5	338 06.4	2.8	20 08.6	0.9	61.4
23	164 28.1	25.5	352 28.2	2.9	20 07.7	1.2	61.4
23 00	179 28.0	N23 25.5	6 50.1	2.8	S20 06.5	1.3	61.4
01	194 27.9	25.4	21 11.9	2.8	20 05.2	1.4	61.4
02	209 27.7	25.4	35 33.7	2.9	20 03.8	1.6	61.4
03	224 27.6	.. 25.4	49 55.6	2.8	20 02.2	1.7	61.4
04	239 27.5	25.3	64 17.4	2.9	20 00.5	2.0	61.4
05	254 27.3	25.3	78 39.3	2.9	19 58.5	2.0	61.4
06	269 27.2	N23 25.3	93 01.2	2.9	S19 56.5	2.2	61.4
07	284 27.1	25.2	107 23.1	2.9	19 54.3	2.4	61.4
08	299 26.9	25.2	121 45.0	2.9	19 51.9	2.5	61.4
S 09	314 26.8	.. 25.2	136 06.9	3.0	19 49.4	2.7	61.4
U 10	329 26.7	25.1	150 28.9	2.9	19 46.7	2.8	61.4
N 11	344 26.5	25.1	164 50.8	3.0	19 43.9	3.0	61.4
D 12	359 26.4	N23 25.1	179 12.8	3.0	S19 40.9	3.1	61.4
A 13	14 26.3	25.0	193 34.8	3.1	19 37.8	3.3	61.4
Y 14	29 26.1	25.0	207 56.9	3.1	19 34.5	3.4	61.4
15	44 26.0	.. 24.9	222 19.0	3.1	19 31.1	3.6	61.4
16	59 25.9	24.9	236 41.1	3.1	19 27.5	3.7	61.4
17	74 25.7	24.8	251 03.2	3.2	19 23.8	3.9	61.4
18	89 25.6	N23 24.8	265 25.4	3.2	S19 19.9	4.0	61.4
19	104 25.5	24.8	279 47.6	3.3	19 15.9	4.1	61.4
20	119 25.3	24.7	294 09.9	3.3	19 11.8	4.3	61.4
21	134 25.2	.. 24.7	308 32.2	3.3	19 07.5	4.5	61.4
22	149 25.1	24.6	322 54.5	3.4	19 03.0	4.6	61.4
23	164 24.9	24.6	337 16.9	3.4	S18 58.4	4.7	61.4
	SD 15.8	d 0.0	SD 16.6		16.7		16.7

Lat.	Twilight Naut.	Twilight Civil	Sunrise	Moonrise 21	22	23	24
°	h m	h m	h m	h m	h m	h m	h m
N 72	▭	▭	▭	▬	▬		23 56
N 70	▭	▭	▭	22 10	▬	23 21	23 11
68	▭	▭	▭	20 37	21 53	22 28	22 41
66	▭	▭	▭	19 58	21 11	21 55	22 18
64	////	////	01 31	19 31	20 42	21 30	22 00
62	////	////	02 10	19 10	20 20	21 11	21 45
60		00 49	02 36	18 53	20 03	20 55	21 33
N 58	////	01 41	02 57	18 39	19 48	20 42	21 22
56	////	02 11	03 13	18 27	19 35	20 30	21 13
54	00 45	02 33	03 28	18 16	19 24	20 20	21 04
52	01 33	02 51	03 40	18 07	19 14	20 11	20 57
50	02 01	03 06	03 51	17 58	19 05	20 03	20 50
45	02 46	03 36	04 13	17 40	18 47	19 45	20 35
N 40	03 17	03 59	04 32	17 26	18 32	19 31	20 23
35	03 40	04 17	04 47	17 13	18 19	19 19	20 13
30	03 59	04 32	05 00	17 03	18 08	19 09	20 04
20	04 28	04 57	05 22	16 44	17 48	18 50	19 48
N 10	04 51	05 18	05 41	16 28	17 32	18 35	19 35
0	05 10	05 36	05 58	16 13	17 16	18 20	19 22
S 10	05 27	05 53	06 16	15 58	17 01	18 05	19 09
20	05 43	06 10	06 34	15 43	16 44	17 49	18 55
30	05 59	06 29	06 56	15 24	16 25	17 31	18 40
35	06 08	06 40	07 08	15 14	16 14	17 21	18 30
40	06 18	06 52	07 22	15 02	16 02	17 08	18 20
45	06 28	07 05	07 39	14 48	15 47	16 54	18 08
S 50	06 40	07 21	08 00	14 31	15 28	16 37	17 53
52	06 45	07 29	08 10	14 22	15 20	16 28	17 46
54	06 51	07 37	08 21	14 13	15 10	16 19	17 38
56	06 57	07 46	08 34	14 03	14 59	16 09	17 29
58	07 04	07 56	08 48	13 52	14 47	15 57	17 19
S 60	07 11	08 08	09 06	13 39	14 32	15 43	17 08

Lat.	Sunset	Twilight Civil	Twilight Naut.	Moonset 21	22	23	24
°	h m	h m	h m	h m	h m	h m	h m
N 72	▭	▭	▭	▬	▬		
N 70	▭	▭	▭	22 42	▬		01 57
68	▭	▭	▭	24 14	00 14	01 12	02 50
66	▭	▭	▭	00 20	00 54	01 54	03 22
64	22 32	////	////	00 42	01 21	02 22	03 46
62	21 54	////	////	01 00	01 42	02 44	04 05
60	21 28	23 14	////	01 14	01 59	03 02	04 20
N 58	21 07	22 23	////	01 27	02 14	03 16	04 34
56	20 51	21 53	////	01 38	02 29	03 29	04 45
54	20 36	21 31	23 18	01 47	02 37	03 40	04 55
52	20 24	21 13	22 31	01 56	02 47	03 50	05 04
50	20 08	20 58	22 03	02 03	02 55	03 59	05 11
45	19 51	20 28	21 18	02 20	03 14	04 17	05 28
N 40	19 32	20 05	20 47	02 33	03 29	04 32	05 42
35	19 17	19 47	20 24	02 45	03 41	04 45	05 53
30	19 04	19 32	20 05	02 55	03 52	04 56	06 03
20	18 42	19 07	19 36	03 12	04 11	05 15	06 21
N 10	18 23	18 46	19 13	03 27	04 28	05 31	06 36
0	18 06	18 28	18 54	03 41	04 43	05 47	06 50
S 10	17 48	18 11	18 37	03 55	04 58	06 02	07 04
20	17 30	17 54	18 21	04 10	05 15	06 18	07 18
30	17 08	17 35	18 05	04 28	05 34	06 37	07 35
35	16 56	17 24	17 56	04 38	05 45	06 48	07 45
40	16 42	17 12	17 47	04 49	05 57	07 00	07 56
45	16 25	16 59	17 36	05 03	06 12	07 15	08 09
S 50	16 04	16 43	17 24	05 20	06 30	07 33	08 25
52	15 54	16 35	17 19	05 27	06 39	07 41	08 32
54	15 43	16 27	17 13	05 36	06 48	07 50	08 41
56	15 31	16 18	17 07	05 46	06 59	08 01	08 50
58	15 17	16 08	17 00	05 57	07 12	08 13	09 00
S 60	14 58	15 56	16 53	06 10	07 26	08 27	09 12

	SUN			MOON			
Day	Eqn. of Time 00h	12h	Mer. Pass.	Mer. Pass. Upper	Lower	Age	Phase
d	m s	m s	h m	h m	h m	d	%
21	01 42	01 48	12 02	22 28	09 57	13	94
22	01 55	02 01	12 02	23 31	11 00	14	98
23	02 08	02 14	12 02	24 35	12 03	15	100

UT	ARIES GHA	VENUS GHA	VENUS Dec	MARS GHA	MARS Dec	JUPITER GHA	JUPITER Dec	SATURN GHA	SATURN Dec	STARS Name	SHA	Dec
24 00	272 18.8	154 33.2	N22 31.4	196 54.8	N23 04.5	182 49.7	N23 12.8	58 44.8	S10 47.3	Acamar	315 18.6	S40 14.9
01	287 21.2	169 32.4	30.8	211 55.4	04.7	197 51.6	12.8	73 47.3	47.3	Achernar	335 27.0	S57 09.8
02	302 23.7	184 31.6	30.3	226 56.0	04.9	212 53.4	12.8	88 49.8	47.3	Acrux	173 09.1	S63 10.8
03	317 26.2	199 30.8 ..	29.8	241 56.6 ..	05.1	227 55.2 ..	12.8	103 52.4 ..	47.3	Adhara	255 12.9	S28 59.6
04	332 28.6	214 30.1	29.3	256 57.2	05.3	242 57.1	12.8	118 54.9	47.2	Aldebaran	290 49.7	N16 32.0
05	347 31.1	229 29.3	28.8	271 57.8	05.5	257 58.9	12.8	133 57.4	47.2			
06	2 33.6	244 28.5	N22 28.2	286 58.4	N23 05.7	273 00.8	N23 12.9	148 59.9	S10 47.2	Alioth	166 20.6	N55 53.4
07	17 36.0	259 27.8	27.7	301 59.0	05.9	288 02.6	12.9	164 02.5	47.2	Alkaid	152 58.7	N49 15.0
08	32 38.5	274 27.0	27.2	316 59.6	06.1	303 04.5	12.9	179 05.0	47.2	Al Na'ir	27 43.5	S46 53.4
M 09	47 41.0	289 26.2 ..	26.7	332 00.2 ..	06.3	318 06.3 ..	12.9	194 07.5 ..	47.2	Alnilam	275 46.7	S 1 11.8
O 10	62 43.4	304 25.4	26.1	347 00.7	06.5	333 08.1	12.9	209 10.0	47.2	Alphard	217 56.3	S 8 43.2
N 11	77 45.9	319 24.7	25.6	2 01.3	06.6	348 10.0	12.9	224 12.5	47.2			
D 12	92 48.3	334 23.9	N22 25.1	17 01.9	N23 06.9	3 11.8	N23 12.9	239 15.1	S10 47.2	Alphecca	126 10.7	N26 40.4
A 13	107 50.8	349 23.1	24.5	32 02.5	07.1	18 13.7	12.9	254 17.6	47.2	Alpheratz	357 43.4	N29 09.8
Y 14	122 53.3	4 22.4	24.0	47 03.1	07.3	33 15.5	12.9	269 20.1	47.2	Altair	62 07.9	N 8 54.4
15	137 55.7	19 21.6 ..	23.5	62 03.7 ..	07.5	48 17.3 ..	12.9	284 22.6 ..	47.2	Ankaa	353 15.7	S42 13.7
16	152 58.2	34 20.8	22.9	77 04.3	07.6	63 19.2	12.9	299 25.1	47.1	Antares	112 25.9	S26 27.6
17	168 00.7	49 20.0	22.4	92 04.9	07.8	78 21.0	12.9	314 27.7	47.1			
18	183 03.1	64 19.3	N22 21.9	107 05.5	N23 08.0	93 22.9	N23 12.9	329 30.2	S10 47.1	Arcturus	145 55.5	N19 06.9
19	198 05.6	79 18.5	21.3	122 06.1	08.2	108 24.7	12.9	344 32.7	47.1	Atria	107 27.1	S69 03.1
20	213 08.1	94 17.7	20.8	137 06.7	08.4	123 26.5	12.9	359 35.2	47.1	Avior	234 18.5	S59 33.5
21	228 10.5	109 17.0 ..	20.2	152 07.2 ..	08.6	138 28.4 ..	12.9	14 37.7 ..	47.1	Bellatrix	278 32.3	N 6 21.5
22	243 13.0	124 16.2	19.7	167 07.8	08.8	153 30.2	12.9	29 40.3	47.1	Betelgeuse	271 01.6	N 7 24.4
23	258 15.5	139 15.4	19.2	182 08.4	09.0	168 32.1	12.9	44 42.8	47.1			
25 00	273 17.9	154 14.7	N22 18.6	197 09.0	N23 09.2	183 33.9	N23 13.0	59 45.3	S10 47.1	Canopus	263 56.7	S52 42.3
01	288 20.4	169 13.9	18.1	212 09.6	09.4	198 35.7	13.0	74 47.8	47.1	Capella	280 34.9	N46 00.5
02	303 22.8	184 13.1	17.5	227 10.2	09.6	213 37.6	13.0	89 50.3	47.1	Deneb	49 31.0	N45 19.7
03	318 25.3	199 12.4 ..	17.0	242 10.8 ..	09.8	228 39.4 ..	13.0	104 52.9 ..	47.1	Denebola	182 33.7	N14 29.8
04	333 27.8	214 11.6	16.4	257 11.4	09.9	243 41.3	13.0	119 55.4	47.1	Diphda	348 55.9	S17 54.6
05	348 30.2	229 10.9	15.9	272 12.0	10.1	258 43.1	13.0	134 57.9	47.0			
06	3 32.7	244 10.1	N22 15.3	287 12.6	N23 10.3	273 45.0	N23 13.0	150 00.4	S10 47.0	Dubhe	193 52.0	N61 40.9
07	18 35.2	259 09.3	14.8	302 13.2	10.5	288 46.8	13.0	165 02.9	47.0	Elnath	278 12.9	N28 36.9
08	33 37.6	274 08.6	14.2	317 13.7	10.7	303 48.6	13.0	180 05.4	47.0	Eltanin	90 45.6	N51 29.4
T 09	48 40.1	289 07.8 ..	13.7	332 14.3 ..	10.9	318 50.5 ..	13.0	195 08.0 ..	47.0	Enif	33 46.9	N 9 56.3
U 10	63 42.6	304 07.0	13.1	347 14.9	11.1	333 52.3	13.0	210 10.5	47.0	Fomalhaut	15 23.8	S29 32.8
E 11	78 45.0	319 06.3	12.6	2 15.5	11.3	348 54.2	13.0	225 13.0	47.0			
S 12	93 47.5	334 05.5	N22 12.0	17 16.1	N23 11.5	3 56.0	N23 13.0	240 15.5	S10 47.0	Gacrux	172 00.7	S57 11.7
D 13	108 50.0	349 04.8	11.4	32 16.7	11.6	18 57.8	13.0	255 18.0	47.0	Gienah	175 52.2	S17 37.2
A 14	123 52.4	4 04.0	10.9	47 17.3	11.8	33 59.7	13.0	270 20.5	47.0	Hadar	148 47.4	S60 26.5
Y 15	138 54.9	19 03.3 ..	10.3	62 17.9 ..	12.0	49 01.5 ..	13.0	285 23.1 ..	47.0	Hamal	328 00.9	N23 31.4
16	153 57.3	34 02.5	09.8	77 18.5	12.2	64 03.4	13.0	300 25.6	47.0	Kaus Aust.	83 43.4	S34 22.5
17	168 59.8	49 01.7	09.2	92 19.1	12.4	79 05.2	13.0	315 28.1	47.0			
18	184 02.3	64 01.0	N22 08.6	107 19.7	N23 12.6	94 07.0	N23 13.0	330 30.6	S10 47.0	Kochab	137 19.4	N74 06.3
19	199 04.7	79 00.2	08.1	122 20.3	12.8	109 08.9	13.0	345 33.1	46.9	Markab	13 38.2	N15 16.7
20	214 07.2	93 59.5	07.5	137 20.8	12.9	124 10.7	13.0	0 35.6	46.9	Menkar	314 15.2	N 4 08.5
21	229 09.7	108 58.7 ..	06.9	152 21.4 ..	13.1	139 12.6 ..	13.0	15 38.2 ..	46.9	Menkent	148 07.3	S36 26.3
22	244 12.1	123 58.0	06.4	167 22.0	13.3	154 14.4	13.1	30 40.7	46.9	Miaplacidus	221 40.3	S69 46.7
23	259 14.6	138 57.2	05.8	182 22.6	13.5	169 16.3	13.1	45 43.2	46.9			
26 00	274 17.1	153 56.4	N22 05.2	197 23.2	N23 13.7	184 18.1	N23 13.1	60 45.7	S10 46.9	Mirfak	308 40.6	N49 54.3
01	289 19.5	168 55.7	04.7	212 23.8	13.9	199 19.9	13.1	75 48.2	46.9	Nunki	75 57.9	S26 16.6
02	304 22.0	183 54.9	04.1	227 24.4	14.0	214 21.8	13.1	90 50.7	46.9	Peacock	53 18.7	S56 41.1
03	319 24.5	198 54.2 ..	03.5	242 25.0 ..	14.2	229 23.6 ..	13.1	105 53.3 ..	46.9	Pollux	243 28.1	N27 59.5
04	334 26.9	213 53.4	03.0	257 25.6	14.4	244 25.5	13.1	120 55.8	46.9	Procyon	245 00.0	N 5 11.2
05	349 29.4	228 52.7	02.4	272 26.2	14.6	259 27.3	13.1	135 58.3	46.9			
06	4 31.8	243 51.9	N22 01.8	287 26.8	N23 14.8	274 29.1	N23 13.1	151 00.8	S10 46.9	Rasalhague	96 06.1	N12 33.2
W 07	19 34.3	258 51.2	01.2	302 27.4	14.9	289 31.0	13.1	166 03.3	46.9	Regulus	207 43.7	N11 54.0
E 08	34 36.8	273 50.4	00.6	317 27.9	15.1	304 32.8	13.1	181 05.8	46.9	Rigel	281 12.4	S 8 11.3
D 09	49 39.2	288 49.7	22 00.1	332 28.5 ..	15.3	319 34.7 ..	13.1	196 08.3 ..	46.9	Rigil Kent.	139 51.2	S60 53.6
N 10	64 41.7	303 48.9	21 59.5	347 29.1	15.5	334 36.5	13.1	211 10.9	46.9	Sabik	102 12.2	S15 44.3
E 11	79 44.2	318 48.2	58.9	2 29.7	15.6	349 38.4	13.1	226 13.4	46.8			
S 12	94 46.6	333 47.4	N21 58.3	17 30.3	N23 15.8	4 40.2	N23 13.1	241 15.9	S10 46.8	Schedar	349 40.5	N56 36.5
D 13	109 49.1	348 46.7	57.7	32 30.9	16.0	19 42.0	13.1	256 18.4	46.8	Shaula	96 21.4	S37 06.7
A 14	124 51.6	3 45.9	57.2	47 31.5	16.2	34 43.9	13.1	271 20.9	46.8	Sirius	258 34.0	S16 44.3
Y 15	139 54.0	18 45.2 ..	56.6	62 32.1 ..	16.4	49 45.7 ..	13.1	286 23.4 ..	46.8	Spica	158 31.1	S11 14.0
16	154 56.5	33 44.5	56.0	77 32.7	16.5	64 47.6	13.1	301 25.9	46.8	Suhail	222 52.7	S43 29.5
17	169 58.9	48 43.7	55.4	92 33.3	16.7	79 49.4	13.1	316 28.4	46.8			
18	185 01.4	63 43.0	N21 54.8	107 33.9	N23 16.9	94 51.2	N23 13.1	331 31.0	S10 46.8	Vega	80 38.5	N38 47.9
19	200 03.9	78 42.2	54.2	122 34.4	17.1	109 53.1	13.1	346 33.5	46.8	Zuben'ubi	137 05.1	S16 05.9
20	215 06.3	93 41.5	53.6	137 35.0	17.2	124 54.9	13.1	1 36.0	46.8		SHA	Mer. Pass.
21	230 08.8	108 40.7 ..	53.0	152 35.6 ..	17.4	139 56.8 ..	13.1	16 38.5 ..	46.8		° '	h m
22	245 11.3	123 40.0	52.4	167 36.2	17.6	154 58.6	13.1	31 41.0	46.8	Venus	240 56.8	13 44
23	260 13.7	138 39.2	51.8	182 36.8	17.8	170 00.5	13.1	46 43.5	46.8	Mars	283 51.1	10 51
	h m									Jupiter	270 16.0	11 44
Mer. Pass. 5 45.9		v −0.8	d 0.6	v 0.6	d 0.2	v 1.8	d 0.0	v 2.5	d 0.0	Saturn	146 27.4	19 58

SUN and MOON

Day	UT (d h)	SUN GHA	SUN Dec	MOON GHA	v	Dec	d	HP
	24 00	179 24.8	N23 24.5	351 39.3	3.5	S18 53.7	4.9	61.4
	01	194 24.7	24.5	6 01.8	3.5	18 48.8	5.0	61.4
	02	209 24.5	24.4	20 24.3	3.6	18 43.8	5.2	61.4
	03	224 24.4	.. 24.3	34 46.9	3.7	18 38.6	5.3	61.3
	04	239 24.3	24.3	49 09.6	3.7	18 33.3	5.4	61.3
	05	254 24.1	24.3	63 32.3	3.7	18 27.9	5.5	61.3
	06	269 24.0	N23 24.2	77 55.0	3.8	S18 22.4	5.7	61.3
	07	284 23.9	24.2	92 17.8	3.9	18 16.7	5.9	61.3
M	08	299 23.7	24.1	106 40.7	3.9	18 10.8	5.9	61.3
O	09	314 23.6	.. 24.1	121 03.6	4.0	18 04.9	6.1	61.3
N	10	329 23.5	24.0	135 26.6	4.1	17 58.8	6.3	61.3
D	11	344 23.3	24.0	149 49.7	4.1	17 52.5	6.3	61.3
A	12	359 23.2	N23 23.9	164 12.8	4.2	S17 46.2	6.5	61.2
Y	13	14 23.1	23.8	178 36.0	4.2	17 39.7	6.6	61.2
	14	29 22.9	23.8	192 59.2	4.4	17 33.1	6.7	61.2
	15	44 22.8	.. 23.7	207 22.6	4.4	17 26.4	6.9	61.2
	16	59 22.7	23.7	221 46.0	4.4	17 19.5	7.0	61.2
	17	74 22.5	23.6	236 09.4	4.6	17 12.5	7.1	61.2
	18	89 22.4	N23 23.6	250 33.0	4.6	S17 05.4	7.2	61.1
	19	104 22.3	23.5	264 56.6	4.7	16 58.2	7.3	61.1
	20	119 22.1	23.4	279 20.3	4.7	16 50.9	7.5	61.1
	21	134 22.0	.. 23.4	293 44.0	4.9	16 43.4	7.5	61.1
	22	149 21.9	23.3	308 07.9	4.9	16 35.9	7.7	61.1
	23	164 21.7	23.2	322 31.8	5.0	16 28.2	7.8	61.1
	25 00	179 21.6	N23 23.2	336 55.8	5.1	S16 20.4	7.9	61.0
	01	194 21.5	23.1	351 19.9	5.1	16 12.5	8.0	61.0
	02	209 21.3	23.0	5 44.0	5.2	16 04.5	8.1	61.0
	03	224 21.2	.. 23.0	20 08.2	5.4	15 56.4	8.2	61.0
	04	239 21.1	22.9	34 32.6	5.4	15 48.2	8.3	60.9
	05	254 20.9	22.8	48 57.0	5.4	15 39.9	8.5	60.9
	06	269 20.8	N23 22.8	63 21.4	5.6	S15 31.4	8.5	60.9
	07	284 20.7	22.7	77 46.0	5.6	15 22.9	8.6	60.9
T	08	299 20.5	22.6	92 10.6	5.8	15 14.3	8.7	60.9
U	09	314 20.4	.. 22.6	106 35.4	5.8	15 05.6	8.9	60.8
E	10	329 20.3	22.5	121 00.2	5.9	14 56.7	8.9	60.8
S	11	344 20.2	22.4	135 25.1	6.0	14 47.8	9.0	60.8
D	12	359 20.0	N23 22.3	149 50.1	6.0	S14 38.8	9.1	60.8
A	13	14 19.9	22.3	164 15.1	6.2	14 29.7	9.2	60.7
Y	14	29 19.8	22.2	178 40.3	6.2	14 20.5	9.2	60.7
	15	44 19.6	.. 22.1	193 05.5	6.4	14 11.3	9.4	60.7
	16	59 19.5	22.0	207 30.9	6.4	14 01.9	9.4	60.6
	17	74 19.4	22.0	221 56.3	6.5	13 52.5	9.6	60.6
	18	89 19.2	N23 21.9	236 21.8	6.6	S13 42.9	9.6	60.6
	19	104 19.1	21.8	250 47.4	6.6	13 33.3	9.7	60.6
	20	119 19.0	21.7	265 13.0	6.8	13 23.6	9.7	60.5
	21	134 18.8	.. 21.7	279 38.8	6.9	13 13.9	9.9	60.5
	22	149 18.7	21.6	294 04.7	6.9	13 04.0	9.9	60.5
	23	164 18.6	21.5	308 30.6	7.0	12 54.1	10.0	60.4
	26 00	179 18.4	N23 21.4	322 56.6	7.1	S12 44.1	10.1	60.4
	01	194 18.3	21.3	337 22.7	7.2	12 34.0	10.1	60.4
	02	209 18.2	21.2	351 48.9	7.3	12 23.9	10.2	60.4
	03	224 18.1	.. 21.2	6 15.2	7.4	12 13.7	10.3	60.3
	04	239 17.9	21.1	20 41.6	7.4	12 03.4	10.3	60.3
	05	254 17.8	21.0	35 08.0	7.6	11 53.1	10.4	60.3
	06	269 17.7	N23 20.9	49 34.6	7.6	S11 42.7	10.5	60.2
W	07	284 17.5	20.8	64 01.2	7.7	11 32.2	10.6	60.2
E	08	299 17.4	20.7	78 27.9	7.8	11 21.7	10.6	60.2
D	09	314 17.3	.. 20.6	92 54.7	7.9	11 11.1	10.6	60.1
N	10	329 17.1	20.6	107 21.6	8.0	11 00.5	10.7	60.1
E	11	344 17.0	20.5	121 48.6	8.1	10 49.8	10.8	60.1
S	12	359 16.9	N23 20.4	136 15.7	8.1	S10 39.0	10.8	60.0
D	13	14 16.8	20.3	150 42.8	8.2	10 28.2	10.8	60.0
A	14	29 16.6	20.2	165 10.0	8.3	10 17.4	10.9	60.0
Y	15	44 16.5	.. 20.1	179 37.3	8.4	10 06.5	11.0	59.9
	16	59 16.4	20.0	194 04.7	8.5	9 55.5	11.0	59.9
	17	74 16.2	19.9	208 32.2	8.6	9 44.5	11.0	59.8
	18	89 16.1	N23 19.8	222 59.8	8.6	S 9 33.5	11.1	59.8
	19	104 16.0	19.7	237 27.4	8.7	9 22.4	11.1	59.8
	20	119 15.8	19.6	251 55.1	8.8	9 11.3	11.2	59.7
	21	134 15.7	.. 19.5	266 22.9	8.9	9 00.1	11.2	59.7
	22	149 15.6	19.4	280 50.8	9.0	8 48.9	11.2	59.7
	23	164 15.5	19.3	295 18.8	9.0	S 8 37.7	11.3	59.6
	SD	15.8	d 0.1	SD 16.7		16.6		16.4

Twilight, Sunrise, Moonrise

Lat.	Naut.	Civil	Sunrise	Moonrise 24	25	26	27
N 72	□	□	□	23 56	23 28	23 12	23 00
N 70	□	□	□	23 11	23 05	22 59	22 55
68	□	□	□	22 41	22 46	22 49	22 50
66	□	□	□	22 18	22 32	22 40	22 46
64	////	////	01 33	21 45	22 09	22 33	22 43
62	////	////	02 11	21 45	22 09	22 26	22 40
60	////	00 52	02 37	21 33	22 00	22 21	22 37
N 58	////	01 42	02 58	21 21	21 52	22 16	22 35
56	////	02 12	03 15	21 13	21 45	22 11	22 33
54	00 48	02 34	03 29	21 04	21 39	22 07	22 31
52	01 34	02 52	03 41	20 57	21 33	22 04	22 30
50	02 02	03 07	03 52	20 50	21 28	22 00	22 28
45	02 47	03 37	04 14	20 35	21 17	21 53	22 25
N 40	03 18	04 00	04 32	20 23	21 08	21 47	22 22
35	03 41	04 18	04 47	20 13	21 00	21 42	22 19
30	04 00	04 33	05 00	20 04	20 53	21 37	22 17
20	04 29	04 58	05 22	19 48	20 45	21 29	22 14
N 10	04 51	05 18	05 41	19 35	20 31	21 22	22 10
0	05 10	05 36	05 59	19 22	20 21	21 16	22 07
S 10	05 27	05 54	06 16	19 09	20 11	21 09	22 04
20	05 43	06 11	06 35	18 55	20 00	21 02	22 01
30	06 00	06 30	06 56	18 40	19 48	20 54	21 57
35	06 09	06 40	07 08	18 30	19 41	20 49	21 55
40	06 18	06 52	07 23	18 20	19 33	20 44	21 53
45	06 28	07 06	07 39	18 08	19 23	20 38	21 50
S 50	06 40	07 22	08 00	17 53	19 12	20 30	21 47
52	06 45	07 29	08 10	17 46	19 06	20 27	21 45
54	06 51	07 37	08 21	17 38	19 01	20 23	21 43
56	06 57	07 46	08 34	17 29	18 54	20 19	21 42
58	07 04	07 57	08 48	17 19	18 47	20 14	21 40
S 60	07 11	08 08	09 06	17 08	18 38	20 09	21 37

Sunset, Twilight, Moonset

Lat.	Sunset	Civil	Naut.	Moonset 24	25	26	27
N 72	□	□	□	■■■■	03 32	06 00	08 09
N 70	□	□	□	01 57	04 16	06 22	08 19
68	□	□	□	02 50	04 45	06 39	08 28
66	□	□	□	03 22	05 06	06 52	08 35
64	22 31	////	////	03 46	05 23	07 04	08 41
62	21 54	////	////	04 05	05 37	07 13	08 46
60	21 28	23 12	////	04 20	05 49	07 21	08 51
N 58	21 07	22 23	////	04 34	05 59	07 28	08 55
56	20 51	21 53	////	04 45	06 08	07 34	08 58
54	20 36	21 31	23 17	04 55	06 16	07 40	09 01
52	20 24	21 13	22 31	05 04	06 23	07 45	09 04
50	20 13	20 58	22 03	05 13	06 30	07 50	09 07
45	19 51	20 28	21 18	05 28	06 43	07 59	09 12
N 40	19 33	20 06	20 47	05 42	06 54	08 07	09 17
35	19 18	19 48	20 24	05 53	07 04	08 14	09 21
30	19 05	19 32	20 06	06 03	07 12	08 20	09 25
20	18 43	19 07	19 37	06 21	07 26	08 30	09 31
N 10	18 24	18 47	19 14	06 38	07 39	08 39	09 36
0	18 06	18 29	18 55	06 50	07 50	08 47	09 41
S 10	17 49	18 12	18 38	07 04	08 02	08 56	09 45
20	17 30	17 54	18 22	07 18	08 14	09 04	09 51
30	17 09	17 36	18 05	07 35	08 28	09 14	09 56
35	16 57	17 25	17 57	07 45	08 36	09 20	10 00
40	16 43	17 13	17 47	07 56	08 45	09 26	10 03
45	16 26	17 00	17 37	08 09	08 55	09 34	10 07
S 50	16 05	16 44	17 25	08 25	09 08	09 43	10 13
52	15 55	16 36	17 20	08 32	09 14	09 47	10 15
54	15 44	16 28	17 14	08 41	09 20	09 51	10 17
56	15 32	16 19	17 08	08 50	09 27	09 56	10 20
58	15 17	16 09	17 01	09 00	09 35	10 02	10 23
S 60	15 00	15 57	16 54	09 12	09 44	10 08	10 27

SUN and MOON

Day	SUN Eqn. of Time 00h	12h	Mer. Pass.	MOON Mer. Pass. Upper	Lower	Age	Phase
	m s	m s	h m	h m	h m	d	%
24	02 21	02 27	12 02	00 35	13 06	16	98
25	02 33	02 40	12 03	01 36	14 06	17	94
26	02 46	02 52	12 03	02 34	15 02	18	87

UT	ARIES GHA	VENUS −3.8 GHA	Dec	MARS +1.5 GHA	Dec	JUPITER −1.9 GHA	Dec	SATURN +0.5 GHA	Dec
27 00	275 16.2	153 38.5	N21 51.2	197 37.4	N23 17.9	185 02.3	N23 13.1	61 46.0	S10 46.8
01	290 18.7	168 37.8	50.6	212 38.0	18.1	200 04.1	13.1	76 48.5	46.8
02	305 21.1	183 37.0	50.1	227 38.6	18.3	215 06.0	13.1	91 51.0	46.8
03	320 23.6	198 36.3 ..	49.5	242 39.2 ..	18.4	230 07.8 ..	13.1	106 53.6 ..	46.8
04	335 26.1	213 35.5	48.9	257 39.8	18.6	245 09.7	13.2	121 56.1	46.8
05	350 28.5	228 34.8	48.3	272 40.4	18.8	260 11.5	13.2	136 58.6	46.8
06	5 31.0	243 34.1	N21 47.7	287 41.0	N23 19.0	275 13.3	N23 13.2	152 01.1	S10 46.7
07	20 33.4	258 33.3	47.0	302 41.5	19.1	290 15.2	13.2	167 03.6	46.7
T 08	35 35.9	273 32.6	46.4	317 42.1	19.3	305 17.0	13.2	182 06.1	46.7
H 09	50 38.4	288 31.8 ..	45.8	332 42.7 ..	19.5	320 18.9 ..	13.2	197 08.6 ..	46.7
U 10	65 40.8	303 31.1	45.2	347 43.3	19.6	335 20.7	13.2	212 11.1	46.7
R 11	80 43.3	318 30.4	44.6	2 43.9	19.8	350 22.6	13.2	227 13.6	46.7
S 12	95 45.8	333 29.6	N21 44.0	17 44.5	N23 20.0	5 24.4	N23 13.2	242 16.2	S10 46.7
D 13	110 48.2	348 28.9	43.4	32 45.1	20.1	20 26.2	13.2	257 18.7	46.7
A 14	125 50.7	3 28.2	42.8	47 45.7	20.3	35 28.1	13.2	272 21.2	46.7
Y 15	140 53.2	18 27.4 ..	42.2	62 46.3 ..	20.5	50 29.9 ..	13.2	287 23.7 ..	46.7
16	155 55.6	33 26.7	41.6	77 46.9	20.6	65 31.8	13.2	302 26.2	46.7
17	170 58.1	48 26.0	41.0	92 47.5	20.8	80 33.6	13.2	317 28.7	46.7
18	186 00.6	63 25.2	N21 40.3	107 48.1	N23 21.0	95 35.4	N23 13.2	332 31.2	S10 46.7
19	201 03.0	78 24.5	39.7	122 48.7	21.1	110 37.3	13.2	347 33.7	46.7
20	216 05.5	93 23.8	39.1	137 49.2	21.3	125 39.1	13.2	2 36.2	46.7
21	231 07.9	108 23.0 ..	38.5	152 49.8 ..	21.5	140 41.0 ..	13.2	17 38.7 ..	46.7
22	246 10.4	123 22.3	37.9	167 50.4	21.6	155 42.8	13.2	32 41.2	46.7
23	261 12.9	138 21.6	37.3	182 51.0	21.8	170 44.7	13.2	47 43.7	46.7
28 00	276 15.3	153 20.8	N21 36.6	197 51.6	N23 22.0	185 46.5	N23 13.2	62 46.3	S10 46.7
01	291 17.8	168 20.1	36.0	212 52.2	22.1	200 48.3	13.2	77 48.8	46.7
02	306 20.3	183 19.4	35.4	227 52.8	22.3	215 50.2	13.2	92 51.3	46.7
03	321 22.7	198 18.6 ..	34.8	242 53.4 ..	22.5	230 52.0 ..	13.2	107 53.8 ..	46.7
04	336 25.2	213 17.9	34.1	257 54.0	22.6	245 53.9	13.2	122 56.3	46.7
05	351 27.7	228 17.2	33.5	272 54.6	22.8	260 55.7	13.2	137 58.8	46.7
06	6 30.1	243 16.5	N21 32.9	287 55.2	N23 23.0	275 57.6	N23 13.2	153 01.3	S10 46.7
07	21 32.6	258 15.7	32.3	302 55.8	23.1	290 59.4	13.2	168 03.8	46.6
F 08	36 35.0	273 15.0	31.6	317 56.3	23.3	306 01.2	13.2	183 06.3	46.6
R 09	51 37.5	288 14.3 ..	31.0	332 56.9 ..	23.4	321 03.1 ..	13.2	198 08.8 ..	46.6
I 10	66 40.0	303 13.6	30.4	347 57.5	23.6	336 04.9	13.2	213 11.3	46.6
11	81 42.4	318 12.8	29.7	2 58.1	23.8	351 06.8	13.2	228 13.8	46.6
D 12	96 44.9	333 12.1	N21 29.1	17 58.7	N23 23.9	6 08.6	N23 13.2	243 16.3	S10 46.6
A 13	111 47.4	348 11.4	28.5	32 59.3	24.1	21 10.5	13.2	258 18.8	46.6
Y 14	126 49.8	3 10.7	27.8	47 59.9	24.2	36 12.3	13.2	273 21.3	46.6
15	141 52.3	18 09.9 ..	27.2	63 00.5 ..	24.4	51 14.1 ..	13.2	288 23.9 ..	46.6
16	156 54.8	33 09.2	26.6	78 01.1	24.5	66 16.0	13.2	303 26.4	46.6
17	171 57.2	48 08.5	25.9	93 01.7	24.7	81 17.8	13.2	318 28.9	46.6
18	186 59.7	63 07.8	N21 25.3	108 02.3	N23 24.9	96 19.7	N23 13.2	333 31.4	S10 46.6
19	202 02.2	78 07.1	24.6	123 02.9	25.0	111 21.5	13.2	348 33.9	46.6
20	217 04.6	93 06.3	24.0	138 03.5	25.2	126 23.4	13.2	3 36.4	46.6
21	232 07.1	108 05.6 ..	23.4	153 04.0 ..	25.3	141 25.2 ..	13.2	18 38.9 ..	46.6
22	247 09.5	123 04.9	22.7	168 04.6	25.5	156 27.0	13.2	33 41.4	46.6
23	262 12.0	138 04.2	22.1	183 05.2	25.6	171 28.9	13.2	48 43.9	46.6
29 00	277 14.5	153 03.5	N21 21.4	198 05.8	N23 25.8	186 30.7	N23 13.2	63 46.4	S10 46.6
01	292 16.9	168 02.7	20.8	213 06.4	26.0	201 32.6	13.2	78 48.9	46.6
02	307 19.4	183 02.0	20.1	228 07.0	26.1	216 34.4	13.2	93 51.4	46.6
03	322 21.9	198 01.3 ..	19.5	243 07.6 ..	26.3	231 36.3 ..	13.2	108 53.9 ..	46.6
04	337 24.3	213 00.6	18.8	258 08.2	26.4	246 38.1	13.2	123 56.4	46.6
05	352 26.8	227 59.9	18.2	273 08.8	26.6	261 39.9	13.2	138 58.9	46.6
06	7 29.3	242 59.2	N21 17.5	288 09.4	N23 26.7	276 41.8	N23 13.2	154 01.4	S10 46.6
07	22 31.7	257 58.5	16.9	303 10.0	26.9	291 43.6	13.2	169 03.9	46.6
S 08	37 34.2	272 57.7	16.2	318 10.6	27.0	306 45.5	13.2	184 06.4	46.6
A 09	52 36.7	287 57.0 ..	15.6	333 11.2 ..	27.2	321 47.3 ..	13.2	199 08.9 ..	46.6
T 10	67 39.1	302 56.3	14.9	348 11.8	27.3	336 49.2	13.2	214 11.4	46.6
U 11	82 41.6	317 55.6	14.2	3 12.3	27.5	351 51.0	13.2	229 13.9	46.6
R 12	97 44.0	332 54.9	N21 13.6	18 12.9	N23 27.6	6 52.8	N23 13.2	244 16.4	S10 46.6
D 13	112 46.5	347 54.2	12.9	33 13.5	27.8	21 54.7	13.2	259 18.9	46.6
A 14	127 49.0	2 53.5	12.3	48 14.1	27.9	36 56.5	13.2	274 21.4	46.6
Y 15	142 51.4	17 52.8 ..	11.6	63 14.7 ..	28.1	51 58.4 ..	13.2	289 23.9 ..	46.6
16	157 53.9	32 52.1	10.9	78 15.3	28.2	67 00.2	13.2	304 26.4	46.6
17	172 56.4	47 51.3	10.3	93 15.9	28.4	82 02.1	13.2	319 28.9	46.6
18	187 58.8	62 50.6	N21 09.6	108 16.5	N23 28.5	97 03.9	N23 13.2	334 31.4	S10 46.6
19	203 01.3	77 49.9	09.0	123 17.1	28.7	112 05.7	13.2	349 33.9	46.6
20	218 03.8	92 49.2	08.3	138 17.7	28.8	127 07.6	13.2	4 36.4	46.6
21	233 06.2	107 48.5 ..	07.6	153 18.3 ..	29.0	142 09.4 ..	13.2	19 38.9 ..	46.6
22	248 08.7	122 47.8	07.0	168 18.9	29.1	157 11.3	13.2	34 41.4	46.6
23	263 11.1	137 47.1	06.3	183 19.5	29.3	172 13.1	13.2	49 43.9	46.6
Mer.Pass. 5 34.1	v −0.7 d 0.6	v 0.6 d 0.2		v 1.8 d 0.0		v 2.5 d 0.0			

STARS

Name	SHA	Dec
Acamar	315 18.6	S40 14.9
Achernar	335 27.0	S57 09.8
Acrux	173 09.1	S63 10.8
Adhara	255 12.9	S28 59.6
Aldebaran	290 49.6	N16 32.0
Alioth	166 20.6	N55 53.4
Alkaid	152 58.7	N49 15.0
Al Na'ir	27 43.4	S46 53.4
Alnilam	275 46.7	S 1 11.7
Alphard	217 56.3	S 8 43.2
Alphecca	126 10.7	N26 40.4
Alpheratz	357 43.4	N29 09.8
Altair	62 07.9	N 8 54.4
Ankaa	353 15.7	S42 13.7
Antares	112 25.9	S26 27.6
Arcturus	145 55.5	N19 06.9
Atria	107 27.1	S69 03.1
Avior	234 18.5	S59 33.5
Bellatrix	278 32.3	N 6 21.6
Betelgeuse	271 01.6	N 7 24.4
Canopus	263 56.7	S52 42.3
Capella	280 34.8	N46 00.5
Deneb	49 31.0	N45 19.8
Denebola	182 33.7	N14 29.8
Diphda	348 55.9	S17 54.6
Dubhe	193 52.0	N61 40.9
Elnath	278 12.9	N28 36.9
Eltanin	90 45.6	N51 29.4
Enif	33 46.9	N 9 56.3
Fomalhaut	15 23.8	S29 32.7
Gacrux	172 00.8	S57 11.7
Gienah	175 52.3	S17 37.2
Hadar	148 47.5	S60 26.5
Hamal	328 00.8	N23 31.4
Kaus Aust.	83 43.3	S34 22.5
Kochab	137 19.4	N74 06.3
Markab	13 38.2	N15 16.7
Menkar	314 15.2	N 4 08.5
Menkent	148 07.3	S36 26.3
Miaplacidus	221 40.3	S69 46.7
Mirfak	308 40.6	N49 54.3
Nunki	75 57.9	S26 16.6
Peacock	53 18.7	S56 41.1
Pollux	243 28.1	N27 59.5
Procyon	245 00.0	N 5 11.3
Rasalhague	96 06.1	N12 33.2
Regulus	207 43.7	N11 54.0
Rigel	281 12.3	S 8 11.3
Rigil Kent.	139 51.2	S60 53.6
Sabik	102 12.2	S15 44.3
Schedar	349 40.4	N56 36.5
Shaula	96 21.4	S37 06.7
Sirius	258 34.0	S16 44.3
Spica	158 31.1	S11 14.0
Suhail	222 52.7	S43 29.5
Vega	80 38.5	N38 47.9
Zuben'ubi	137 05.2	S16 05.9

	SHA	Mer.Pass.
Venus	237 05.5	13 47
Mars	281 36.3	10 48
Jupiter	269 31.2	11 35
Saturn	146 30.9	19 46

UT	SUN GHA	SUN Dec	MOON GHA	v	MOON Dec	d	HP
d h	° ′	° ′	° ′	′	° ′	′	′
27 00	179 15.3	N23 19.2	309 46.8	9.1	S 8 26.4	11.4	59.6
01	194 15.2	19.1	324 14.9	9.2	8 15.0	11.3	59.5
02	209 15.1	19.0	338 43.1	9.3	8 03.7	11.4	59.5
03	224 14.9	.. 18.9	353 11.4	9.4	7 52.3	11.4	59.5
04	239 14.8	18.8	7 39.8	9.4	7 40.9	11.4	59.4
05	254 14.7	18.7	22 08.2	9.5	7 29.5	11.5	59.4
06	269 14.6	N23 18.6	36 36.7	9.6	S 7 18.0	11.5	59.4
07	284 14.4	18.5	51 05.3	9.6	7 06.5	11.5	59.3
T 08	299 14.3	18.4	65 33.9	9.8	6 55.0	11.6	59.3
H 09	314 14.2	.. 18.3	80 02.7	9.8	6 43.4	11.6	59.3
U 10	329 14.0	18.2	94 31.5	9.8	6 31.8	11.5	59.2
R 11	344 13.9	18.1	109 00.3	10.0	6 20.3	11.7	59.2
S 12	359 13.8	N23 18.0	123 29.3	10.0	S 6 08.6	11.6	59.1
D 13	14 13.7	17.9	137 58.3	10.1	5 57.0	11.6	59.1
A 14	29 13.5	17.8	152 27.4	10.1	5 45.4	11.7	59.1
Y 15	44 13.4	.. 17.7	166 56.5	10.2	5 33.7	11.7	59.0
16	59 13.3	17.6	181 25.7	10.3	5 22.0	11.7	59.0
17	74 13.1	17.4	195 55.0	10.4	5 10.3	11.7	58.9
18	89 13.0	N23 17.3	210 24.4	10.4	S 4 58.6	11.7	58.9
19	104 12.9	17.2	224 53.8	10.5	4 46.9	11.7	58.9
20	119 12.8	17.1	239 23.3	10.5	4 35.2	11.7	58.8
21	134 12.6	.. 17.0	253 52.8	10.6	4 23.5	11.8	58.8
22	149 12.5	16.9	268 22.4	10.7	4 11.7	11.7	58.7
23	164 12.4	16.8	282 52.1	10.7	4 00.0	11.8	58.7
28 00	179 12.2	N23 16.6	297 21.8	10.8	S 3 48.2	11.7	58.7
01	194 12.1	16.5	311 51.6	10.9	3 36.5	11.8	58.6
02	209 12.0	16.4	326 21.5	10.9	3 24.7	11.7	58.6
03	224 11.9	.. 16.3	340 51.4	11.0	3 13.0	11.8	58.6
04	239 11.7	16.2	355 21.4	11.0	3 01.2	11.8	58.5
05	254 11.6	16.1	9 51.4	11.1	2 49.4	11.7	58.5
06	269 11.5	N23 15.9	24 21.5	11.1	S 2 37.7	11.8	58.4
07	284 11.4	15.8	38 51.6	11.2	2 25.9	11.7	58.4
F 08	299 11.2	15.7	53 21.8	11.3	2 14.2	11.8	58.4
R 09	314 11.1	.. 15.6	67 52.1	11.3	2 02.4	11.7	58.3
I 10	329 11.0	15.4	82 22.4	11.3	1 50.7	11.7	58.3
11	344 10.8	15.3	96 52.7	11.4	1 39.0	11.8	58.2
D 12	359 10.7	N23 15.2	111 23.1	11.5	S 1 27.2	11.7	58.2
A 13	14 10.6	15.1	125 53.6	11.5	1 15.5	11.7	58.2
Y 14	29 10.5	14.9	140 24.1	11.5	1 03.8	11.7	58.1
15	44 10.3	.. 14.8	154 54.6	11.6	0 52.1	11.7	58.1
16	59 10.2	14.7	169 25.2	11.7	0 40.4	11.6	58.0
17	74 10.1	14.6	183 55.9	11.7	0 28.8	11.7	58.0
18	89 10.0	N23 14.4	198 26.6	11.7	S 0 17.1	11.6	58.0
19	104 09.8	14.3	212 57.3	11.8	S 0 05.5	11.7	57.9
20	119 09.7	14.2	227 28.1	11.8	N 0 06.2	11.6	57.9
21	134 09.6	.. 14.0	241 58.9	11.9	0 17.8	11.6	57.8
22	149 09.5	13.9	256 29.8	11.9	0 29.4	11.5	57.8
23	164 09.3	13.8	271 00.7	12.0	0 40.9	11.6	57.8
29 00	179 09.2	N23 13.6	285 31.7	12.0	N 0 52.5	11.5	57.7
01	194 09.1	13.5	300 02.7	12.0	1 04.0	11.5	57.7
02	209 09.0	13.4	314 33.7	12.1	1 15.5	11.5	57.7
03	224 08.8	.. 13.2	329 04.8	12.1	1 27.0	11.5	57.6
04	239 08.7	13.1	343 35.9	12.1	1 38.5	11.4	57.6
05	254 08.6	13.0	358 07.0	12.2	1 49.9	11.5	57.6
06	269 08.5	N23 12.8	12 38.2	12.2	N 2 01.4	11.4	57.5
07	284 08.3	12.7	27 09.4	12.3	2 12.8	11.3	57.5
S 08	299 08.2	12.6	41 40.7	12.3	2 24.1	11.4	57.4
A 09	314 08.1	.. 12.4	56 12.0	12.3	2 35.5	11.3	57.4
T 10	329 08.0	12.3	70 43.3	12.3	2 46.8	11.3	57.3
U 11	344 07.8	12.1	85 14.6	12.4	2 58.1	11.2	57.3
R 12	359 07.7	N23 12.0	99 46.0	12.4	N 3 09.3	11.2	57.3
D 13	14 07.6	11.9	114 17.4	12.5	3 20.5	11.2	57.2
A 14	29 07.5	11.7	128 48.9	12.4	3 31.7	11.2	57.2
Y 15	44 07.3	.. 11.6	143 20.3	12.5	3 42.9	11.1	57.2
16	59 07.2	11.4	157 51.8	12.5	3 54.0	11.1	57.1
17	74 07.1	11.3	172 23.3	12.6	4 05.1	11.1	57.1
18	89 07.0	N23 11.1	186 54.9	12.6	N 4 16.2	11.0	57.0
19	104 06.8	11.0	201 26.5	12.6	4 27.2	11.0	57.0
20	119 06.7	10.8	215 58.1	12.6	4 38.2	10.9	57.0
21	134 06.6	.. 10.7	230 29.7	12.6	4 49.1	10.9	56.9
22	149 06.5	10.5	245 01.3	12.7	5 00.0	10.9	56.9
23	164 06.3	10.4	259 33.0	12.7	N 5 10.9	10.9	56.9
SD	15.8 d 0.1		SD 16.1		15.9		15.6

Twilight — Sunrise — Moonrise

Lat.	Naut.	Civil	Sunrise	Moonrise 27	28	29	30
°	h m	h m	h m	h m	h m	h m	h m
N 72	▭	▭	▭	23 00	22 49	22 39	22 28
N 70	▭	▭	▭	22 55	22 50	22 46	22 41
68	▭	▭	▭	22 50	22 51	22 51	22 52
66	▭	▭	▭	22 46	22 51	22 56	23 02
64	////	////	01 37	22 43	22 52	23 00	23 09
62	////	////	02 14	22 40	22 52	23 04	23 16
60	////	00 57	02 39	22 37	22 52	23 07	23 22
N 58	////	01 45	03 00	22 35	22 53	23 09	23 27
56	////	02 14	03 16	22 33	22 53	23 12	23 32
54	00 52	02 36	03 30	22 31	22 53	23 14	23 36
52	01 37	02 54	03 42	22 30	22 53	23 16	23 40
50	02 04	03 09	03 53	22 28	22 53	23 18	23 43
45	02 49	03 38	04 16	22 25	22 54	23 22	23 51
N 40	03 19	04 01	04 34	22 22	22 54	23 26	23 57
35	03 42	04 19	04 48	22 19	22 55	23 28	24 02
30	04 01	04 34	05 01	22 17	22 55	23 31	24 07
20	04 30	04 59	05 23	22 14	22 55	23 36	24 16
N 10	04 52	05 19	05 42	22 10	22 56	23 40	24 23
0	05 11	05 37	06 00	22 07	22 56	23 44	24 30
S 10	05 28	05 54	06 17	22 04	22 57	23 48	24 37
20	05 44	06 11	06 35	22 01	22 57	23 52	24 45
30	06 00	06 30	06 56	21 57	22 58	23 57	24 53
35	06 09	06 41	07 09	21 55	22 58	23 59	24 58
40	06 18	06 52	07 23	21 53	22 59	24 03	00 03
45	06 28	07 06	07 39	21 50	22 59	24 06	00 06
S 50	06 40	07 22	08 00	21 47	23 00	24 11	00 11
52	06 45	07 29	08 10	21 45	23 00	24 13	00 13
54	06 51	07 37	08 21	21 43	23 01	24 15	00 15
56	06 57	07 46	08 33	21 42	23 01	24 17	00 17
58	07 04	07 56	08 48	21 40	23 01	24 20	00 20
S 60	07 11	08 08	09 05	21 37	23 02	24 23	00 23

Sunset — Twilight — Moonset

Lat.	Sunset	Civil	Naut.	Moonset 27	28	29	30
°	h m	h m	h m	h m	h m	h m	h m
N 72	▭	▭	▭	08 09	10 06	11 58	13 47
N 70	▭	▭	▭	08 19	10 09	11 54	13 36
68	▭	▭	▭	08 28	10 11	11 50	13 26
66	▭	▭	▭	08 35	10 13	11 47	13 18
64	22 29	////	////	08 41	10 15	11 45	13 12
62	21 52	////	////	08 46	10 16	11 43	13 06
60	21 27	23 08	////	08 51	10 18	11 41	13 01
N 58	21 07	22 21	////	08 55	10 19	11 39	12 57
56	20 50	21 52	////	08 58	10 20	11 38	12 53
54	20 36	21 30	23 13	09 01	10 20	11 36	12 49
52	20 24	21 12	22 29	09 04	10 21	11 35	12 46
50	20 14	20 57	22 02	09 07	10 22	11 34	12 43
45	19 51	20 28	21 17	09 12	10 23	11 32	12 37
N 40	19 33	20 06	20 47	09 17	10 25	11 30	12 32
35	19 18	19 48	20 24	09 21	10 26	11 28	12 28
30	19 05	19 32	20 06	09 25	10 27	11 26	12 24
20	18 43	19 08	19 37	09 31	10 28	11 24	12 17
N 10	18 24	18 47	19 14	09 36	10 30	11 21	12 11
0	18 06	18 29	18 56	09 41	10 31	11 19	12 06
S 10	17 50	18 12	18 39	09 45	10 32	11 17	12 00
20	17 31	17 55	18 23	09 51	10 34	11 15	11 55
30	17 10	17 36	18 06	09 56	10 35	11 12	11 48
35	16 58	17 26	17 58	10 00	10 36	11 10	11 44
40	16 44	17 14	17 48	10 03	10 37	11 09	11 40
45	16 28	17 01	17 38	10 07	10 38	11 07	11 35
S 50	16 07	16 45	17 27	10 13	10 39	11 04	11 29
52	15 57	16 38	17 21	10 15	10 40	11 03	11 26
54	15 46	16 30	17 16	10 17	10 40	11 02	11 23
56	15 33	16 21	17 10	10 20	10 41	11 00	11 20
58	15 19	16 10	17 03	10 23	10 42	10 59	11 16
S 60	15 02	15 59	16 56	10 27	10 43	10 57	11 12

SUN / MOON

Day	Eqn. of Time 00h	12h	Mer. Pass.	Mer. Pass. Upper	Lower	Age	Phase
d	m s	m s	h m	h m	h m	d	%
27	02 58	03 05	12 03	03 28	15 54	19	78
28	03 11	03 17	12 03	04 19	16 44	20	68
29	03 23	03 29	12 03	05 08	17 31	21	58

UT	ARIES GHA	VENUS −3.8 GHA	Dec	MARS +1.5 GHA	Dec	JUPITER −1.9 GHA	Dec	SATURN +0.5 GHA	Dec	STARS Name	SHA	Dec
30 00	278 13.6	152 46.4	N21 05.6	198 20.1	N23 29.4	187 15.0	N23 13.2	64 46.4	S10 46.6	Acamar	315 18.6	S40 14.9
01	293 16.1	167 45.7	04.9	213 20.6	29.6	202 16.8	13.2	79 48.9	46.6	Achernar	335 27.0	S57 09.8
02	308 18.5	182 45.0	04.3	228 21.2	29.7	217 18.6	13.2	94 51.4	46.6	Acrux	173 09.2	S63 10.8
03	323 21.0	197 44.3	.. 03.6	243 21.8	.. 29.9	232 20.5	.. 13.2	109 53.9	.. 46.6	Adhara	255 12.9	S28 59.6
04	338 23.5	212 43.6	02.9	258 22.4	30.0	247 22.3	13.2	124 56.4	46.6	Aldebaran	290 49.6	N16 32.0
05	353 25.9	227 42.9	02.2	273 23.0	30.1	262 24.2	13.2	139 58.9	46.6			
06	8 28.4	242 42.2	N21 01.6	288 23.6	N23 30.3	277 26.0	N23 13.2	155 01.4	S10 46.6	Alioth	166 20.7	N55 53.4
07	23 30.9	257 41.5	00.9	303 24.2	30.4	292 27.9	13.2	170 03.9	46.6	Alkaid	152 58.7	N49 15.0
08	38 33.3	272 40.8	21 00.2	318 24.8	30.6	307 29.7	13.2	185 06.4	46.6	Al Na'ir	27 43.4	S46 53.4
S 09	53 35.8	287 40.1	20 59.5	333 25.4	.. 30.7	322 31.5	.. 13.2	200 08.9	.. 46.6	Alnilam	275 46.6	S 1 11.7
U 10	68 38.3	302 39.4	58.9	348 26.0	30.9	337 33.4	13.2	215 11.4	46.6	Alphard	217 56.3	S 8 43.2
N 11	83 40.7	317 38.7	58.2	3 26.6	31.0	352 35.2	13.2	230 13.9	46.6			
D 12	98 43.2	332 38.0	N20 57.5	18 27.2	N23 31.1	7 37.1	N23 13.2	245 16.4	S10 46.6	Alphecca	126 10.7	N26 40.4
A 13	113 45.6	347 37.3	56.8	33 27.8	31.3	22 38.9	13.2	260 18.9	46.6	Alpheratz	357 43.4	N29 08.8
Y 14	128 48.1	2 36.6	56.1	48 28.4	31.4	37 40.8	13.2	275 21.4	46.6	Altair	62 07.9	N 8 54.4
15	143 50.6	17 35.9	.. 55.4	63 28.9	.. 31.6	52 42.6	.. 13.2	290 23.9	.. 46.6	Ankaa	353 15.7	S42 13.7
16	158 53.0	32 35.2	54.7	78 29.5	31.7	67 44.4	13.2	305 26.4	46.6	Antares	112 25.9	S26 27.6
17	173 55.5	47 34.5	54.1	93 30.1	31.8	82 46.3	13.2	320 28.9	46.6			
18	188 58.0	62 33.8	N20 53.4	108 30.7	N23 32.0	97 48.1	N23 13.2	335 31.4	S10 46.6	Arcturus	145 55.6	N19 06.9
19	204 00.4	77 33.1	52.7	123 31.3	32.1	112 50.0	13.2	350 33.9	46.6	Atria	107 27.1	S69 03.1
20	219 02.9	92 32.4	52.0	138 31.9	32.3	127 51.8	13.2	5 36.4	46.6	Avior	234 18.5	S59 33.5
21	234 05.4	107 31.7	.. 51.3	153 32.5	.. 32.4	142 53.7	.. 13.2	20 38.9	.. 46.6	Bellatrix	278 32.3	N 6 21.6
22	249 07.8	122 31.0	50.6	168 33.1	32.5	157 55.5	13.2	35 41.4	46.6	Betelgeuse	271 01.6	N 7 24.4
23	264 10.3	137 30.3	49.9	183 33.7	32.7	172 57.4	13.2	50 43.9	46.6			
1 00	279 12.7	152 29.6	N20 49.2	198 34.3	N23 32.8	187 59.2	N23 13.2	65 46.4	S10 46.6	Canopus	263 56.7	S52 42.3
01	294 15.2	167 28.9	48.5	213 34.9	32.9	203 01.0	13.2	80 48.9	46.6	Capella	280 34.8	N46 00.5
02	309 17.7	182 28.2	47.8	228 35.5	33.1	218 02.9	13.2	95 51.4	46.6	Deneb	49 31.0	N45 19.8
03	324 20.1	197 27.6	.. 47.1	243 36.1	.. 33.2	233 04.7	.. 13.2	110 53.9	.. 46.6	Denebola	182 33.7	N14 29.8
04	339 22.6	212 26.9	46.4	258 36.7	33.4	248 06.6	13.2	125 56.4	46.6	Diphda	348 55.9	S17 54.6
05	354 25.1	227 26.2	45.7	273 37.3	33.5	263 08.4	13.2	140 58.9	46.6			
06	9 27.5	242 25.5	N20 45.0	288 37.9	N23 33.6	278 10.3	N23 13.2	156 01.4	S10 46.6	Dubhe	193 52.0	N61 40.9
07	24 30.0	257 24.8	44.3	303 38.4	33.8	293 12.1	13.2	171 03.9	46.6	Elnath	278 12.9	N28 36.9
08	39 32.5	272 24.1	43.6	318 39.0	33.9	308 14.0	13.2	186 06.4	46.6	Eltanin	90 45.6	N51 29.4
M 09	54 34.9	287 23.4	.. 42.9	333 39.6	.. 34.0	323 15.8	.. 13.2	201 08.9	.. 46.6	Enif	33 46.8	N 9 56.4
O 10	69 37.4	302 22.7	42.2	348 40.2	34.2	338 17.6	13.2	216 11.3	46.6	Fomalhaut	15 23.8	S29 32.7
N 11	84 39.9	317 22.0	41.5	3 40.8	34.3	353 19.5	13.2	231 13.8	46.6			
D 12	99 42.3	332 21.4	N20 40.8	18 41.4	N23 34.4	8 21.3	N23 13.2	246 16.3	S10 46.6	Gacrux	172 00.8	S57 11.7
A 13	114 44.8	347 20.7	40.1	33 42.0	34.6	23 23.2	13.2	261 18.8	46.6	Gienah	175 52.3	S17 37.2
Y 14	129 47.2	2 20.0	39.4	48 42.6	34.7	38 25.0	13.2	276 21.3	46.6	Hadar	148 47.5	S60 26.5
15	144 49.7	17 19.3	.. 38.7	63 43.2	.. 34.8	53 26.9	.. 13.2	291 23.8	.. 46.6	Hamal	328 00.8	N23 31.4
16	159 52.2	32 18.6	38.0	78 43.8	35.0	68 28.7	13.2	306 26.3	46.6	Kaus Aust.	83 43.3	S34 22.5
17	174 54.6	47 17.9	37.3	93 44.4	35.1	83 30.5	13.2	321 28.8	46.6			
18	189 57.1	62 17.3	N20 36.5	108 45.0	N23 35.2	98 32.4	N23 13.2	336 31.3	S10 46.6	Kochab	137 19.5	N74 06.3
19	204 59.6	77 16.6	35.8	123 45.6	35.3	113 34.2	13.2	351 33.8	46.6	Markab	13 38.1	N15 16.7
20	220 02.0	92 15.9	35.1	138 46.2	35.5	128 36.1	13.2	6 36.3	46.6	Menkar	314 15.2	N 4 08.5
21	235 04.5	107 15.2	.. 34.4	153 46.8	.. 35.6	143 37.9	.. 13.2	21 38.8	.. 46.6	Menkent	148 07.3	S36 26.3
22	250 07.0	122 14.5	33.7	168 47.4	35.7	158 39.8	13.2	36 41.3	46.6	Miaplacidus	221 40.3	S69 46.7
23	265 09.4	137 13.9	33.0	183 48.0	35.9	173 41.6	13.2	51 43.8	46.6			
2 00	280 11.9	152 13.2	N20 32.2	198 48.5	N23 36.0	188 43.5	N23 13.2	66 46.3	S10 46.6	Mirfak	308 40.6	N49 54.3
01	295 14.4	167 12.5	31.5	213 49.1	36.1	203 45.3	13.2	81 48.7	46.6	Nunki	75 57.9	S26 16.6
02	310 16.8	182 11.8	30.8	228 49.7	36.2	218 47.1	13.2	96 51.2	46.6	Peacock	53 18.7	S56 41.2
03	325 19.3	197 11.1	.. 30.1	243 50.3	.. 36.4	233 49.0	.. 13.2	111 53.7	.. 46.6	Pollux	243 28.1	N27 59.5
04	340 21.7	212 10.5	29.4	258 50.9	36.5	248 50.8	13.2	126 56.2	46.6	Procyon	245 00.0	N 5 11.3
05	355 24.2	227 09.8	28.6	273 51.5	36.6	263 52.7	13.2	141 58.7	46.6			
06	10 26.7	242 09.1	N20 27.9	288 52.1	N23 36.8	278 54.5	N23 13.2	157 01.2	S10 46.6	Rasalhague	96 06.1	N12 33.2
07	25 29.1	257 08.4	27.2	303 52.7	36.9	293 56.4	13.2	172 03.7	46.6	Regulus	207 43.7	N11 54.0
T 08	40 31.6	272 07.8	26.5	318 53.3	37.0	308 58.2	13.2	187 06.2	46.6	Rigel	281 12.3	S 8 11.3
U 09	55 34.1	287 07.1	.. 25.7	333 53.9	.. 37.1	324 00.1	.. 13.2	202 08.7	.. 46.6	Rigil Kent.	139 51.2	S60 53.6
E 10	70 36.5	302 06.4	25.0	348 54.5	37.3	339 01.9	13.2	217 11.2	46.6	Sabik	102 12.2	S15 44.3
S 11	85 39.0	317 05.7	24.3	3 55.1	37.4	354 03.8	13.2	232 13.7	46.6			
D 12	100 41.5	332 05.1	N20 23.5	18 55.7	N23 37.5	9 05.6	N23 13.2	247 16.2	S10 46.6	Schedar	349 40.4	N56 36.5
A 13	115 43.9	347 04.4	22.8	33 56.3	37.6	24 07.4	13.2	262 18.6	46.6	Shaula	96 21.4	S37 06.7
Y 14	130 46.4	2 03.7	22.1	48 56.9	37.8	39 09.3	13.2	277 21.1	46.6	Sirius	258 34.0	S16 44.2
15	145 48.9	17 03.0	.. 21.4	63 57.5	.. 37.9	54 11.1	.. 13.2	292 23.6	.. 46.6	Spica	158 31.1	S11 14.0
16	160 51.3	32 02.4	20.6	78 58.1	38.0	69 13.0	13.2	307 26.1	46.6	Suhail	222 52.7	S43 29.5
17	175 53.8	47 01.7	19.9	93 58.7	38.1	84 14.8	13.2	322 28.6	46.6			
18	190 56.2	62 01.0	N20 19.2	108 59.2	N23 38.2	99 16.7	N23 13.1	337 31.1	S10 46.6	Vega	80 38.5	N38 48.0
19	205 58.7	77 00.4	18.4	123 59.8	38.4	114 18.5	13.1	352 33.6	46.6	Zuben'ubi	137 05.2	S16 05.9
20	221 01.2	91 59.7	17.7	139 00.4	38.5	129 20.4	13.1	7 36.1	46.6			
21	236 03.6	106 59.0	.. 17.0	154 01.0	.. 38.6	144 22.2	.. 13.1	22 38.6	.. 46.6			
22	251 06.1	121 58.4	16.2	169 01.6	38.7	159 24.0	13.1	37 41.0	46.6			
23	266 08.6	136 57.7	15.5	184 02.2	38.8	174 25.9	13.1	52 43.5	46.6			
	h m										SHA	Mer. Pass.
Mer. Pass.	5 22.3	v −0.7	d 0.7	v 0.6	d 0.1	v 1.8	d 0.0	v 2.5	d 0.0	Venus	233 16.9	13 51
										Mars	279 21.5	10 45
										Jupiter	268 46.5	11 27
										Saturn	146 33.6	19 34

UT	SUN GHA	Dec	MOON GHA	v	Dec	d	HP
30 00	179 06.2	N23 10.2	274 04.7	12.7	N 5 21.8	10.8	56.8
01	194 06.1	10.1	288 36.4	12.7	5 32.6	10.7	56.8
02	209 06.0	09.9	303 08.1	12.7	5 43.3	10.7	56.8
03	224 05.8	.. 09.8	317 39.8	12.8	5 54.0	10.7	56.7
04	239 05.7	09.6	332 11.6	12.8	6 04.7	10.6	56.7
05	254 05.6	09.5	346 43.4	12.8	6 15.3	10.6	56.7
06	269 05.5	N23 09.3	1 15.2	12.8	N 6 25.9	10.6	56.6
07	284 05.4	09.2	15 47.0	12.8	6 36.5	10.5	56.6
S 08	299 05.2	09.0	30 18.8	12.9	6 47.0	10.5	56.6
U 09	314 05.1	.. 08.9	44 50.7	12.8	6 57.5	10.4	56.5
N 10	329 05.0	08.7	59 22.5	12.9	7 07.9	10.3	56.5
D 11	344 04.9	08.5	73 54.4	12.9	7 18.2	10.4	56.5
A 12	359 04.7	N23 08.4	88 26.3	12.9	N 7 28.6	10.2	56.4
Y 13	14 04.6	08.2	102 58.2	12.9	7 38.8	10.3	56.4
14	29 04.5	08.1	117 30.1	12.9	7 49.1	10.1	56.4
15	44 04.4	.. 07.9	132 02.0	12.9	7 59.2	10.2	56.3
16	59 04.2	07.7	146 33.9	12.9	8 09.4	10.1	56.3
17	74 04.1	07.6	161 05.8	13.0	8 19.5	10.0	56.3
18	89 04.0	N23 07.4	175 37.8	12.9	N 8 29.5	10.0	56.2
19	104 03.9	07.3	190 09.7	13.0	8 39.5	9.9	56.2
20	119 03.8	07.1	204 41.7	13.0	8 49.4	9.9	56.2
21	134 03.6	.. 06.9	219 13.7	12.9	8 59.3	9.8	56.1
22	149 03.5	06.8	233 45.6	13.0	9 09.1	9.8	56.1
23	164 03.4	06.6	248 17.6	13.0	9 18.9	9.7	56.1
1 00	179 03.3	N23 06.4	262 49.6	13.0	N 9 28.6	9.7	56.0
01	194 03.2	06.3	277 21.6	13.0	9 38.3	9.6	56.0
02	209 03.0	06.1	291 53.6	12.9	9 47.9	9.5	55.9
03	224 02.9	.. 05.9	306 25.5	13.0	9 57.4	9.5	55.9
04	239 02.8	05.8	320 57.5	13.0	10 06.9	9.5	55.9
05	254 02.7	05.6	335 29.5	13.0	10 16.4	9.4	55.9
06	269 02.5	N23 05.4	350 01.5	13.0	N10 25.8	9.3	55.9
07	284 02.4	05.2	4 33.5	13.0	10 35.1	9.2	55.8
M 08	299 02.3	05.1	19 05.5	13.0	10 44.3	9.3	55.8
O 09	314 02.2	.. 04.9	33 37.5	13.0	10 53.6	9.1	55.8
N 10	329 02.1	04.7	48 09.5	13.0	11 02.7	9.1	55.7
D 11	344 01.9	04.5	62 41.5	13.0	11 11.8	9.0	55.7
A 12	359 01.8	N23 04.4	77 13.5	13.0	N11 20.8	9.0	55.7
Y 13	14 01.7	04.2	91 45.5	13.0	11 29.8	8.9	55.7
14	29 01.6	04.0	106 17.5	12.9	11 38.7	8.9	55.6
15	44 01.5	.. 03.8	120 49.4	13.0	11 47.6	8.7	55.6
16	59 01.3	03.7	135 21.4	13.0	11 56.3	8.8	55.6
17	74 01.2	03.5	149 53.4	12.9	12 05.1	8.6	55.5
18	89 01.1	N23 03.3	164 25.3	13.0	N12 13.7	8.6	55.5
19	104 01.0	03.1	178 57.3	13.0	12 22.3	8.6	55.5
20	119 00.9	02.9	193 29.3	12.9	12 30.9	8.4	55.5
21	134 00.8	.. 02.8	208 01.2	13.0	12 39.3	8.4	55.4
22	149 00.6	02.6	222 33.2	12.9	12 47.7	8.4	55.4
23	164 00.5	02.4	237 05.1	12.9	12 56.1	8.2	55.4
2 00	179 00.4	N23 02.2	251 37.0	12.9	N13 04.3	8.2	55.3
01	194 00.3	02.0	266 08.9	13.0	13 12.5	8.2	55.3
02	209 00.2	01.8	280 40.9	12.9	13 20.7	8.0	55.3
03	224 00.0	.. 01.7	295 12.8	12.9	13 28.7	8.0	55.3
04	238 59.9	01.5	309 44.7	12.8	13 36.7	8.0	55.3
05	253 59.8	01.3	324 16.5	12.9	13 44.7	7.8	55.2
06	268 59.7	N23 01.1	338 48.4	12.9	N13 52.5	7.8	55.2
07	283 59.6	00.9	353 20.3	12.9	14 00.3	7.7	55.2
T 08	298 59.5	00.7	7 52.2	12.8	14 08.0	7.7	55.2
U 09	313 59.3	.. 00.5	22 24.0	12.8	14 15.7	7.6	55.1
E 10	328 59.2	00.3	36 55.8	12.9	14 23.3	7.5	55.1
S 11	343 59.1	00.1	51 27.7	12.8	14 30.8	7.4	55.1
D 12	358 59.0	N23 00.0	65 59.5	12.8	N14 38.2	7.4	55.1
A 13	13 58.9	22 59.8	80 31.3	12.8	14 45.6	7.3	55.1
Y 14	28 58.7	59.6	95 03.1	12.7	14 52.9	7.2	55.0
15	43 58.6	.. 59.4	109 34.8	12.8	15 00.1	7.2	55.0
16	58 58.5	59.2	124 06.6	12.8	15 07.3	7.0	55.0
17	73 58.4	59.0	138 38.4	12.7	15 14.3	7.0	55.0
18	88 58.3	N22 58.8	153 10.1	12.7	N15 21.3	7.0	54.9
19	103 58.2	58.6	167 41.8	12.7	15 28.3	6.8	54.9
20	118 58.0	58.4	182 13.5	12.8	15 35.1	6.8	54.9
21	133 57.9	.. 58.2	196 45.3	12.6	15 41.9	6.7	54.9
22	148 57.8	58.0	211 16.9	12.7	15 48.6	6.6	54.9
23	163 57.7	57.8	225 48.6	12.7	N15 55.2	6.5	54.8
	SD 15.8	d 0.2	SD 15.4		15.2		15.0

Lat.	Twilight Naut.	Civil	Sunrise	Moonrise 30	1	2	3
N 72	▭	▭	▭	22 28	22 14	21 55	21 01
N 70	▭	▭	▭	22 41	22 37	22 32	22 28
68	▭	▭	▭	22 52	22 54	22 59	23 07
66	////	////	00 21	23 02	23 09	23 19	23 34
64	////	////	01 41	23 09	23 21	23 35	23 55
62	////	////	02 17	23 16	23 31	23 49	24 12
60	////	01 04	02 42	23 22	23 39	24 00	00 00
N 58	////	01 49	03 02	23 27	23 47	24 10	00 10
56	////	02 17	03 18	23 32	23 54	24 19	00 19
54	00 58	02 39	03 32	23 36	24 00	00 00	00 27
52	01 40	02 56	03 44	23 40	24 05	00 05	00 34
50	02 07	03 11	03 55	23 43	24 10	00 10	00 40
45	02 51	03 40	04 17	23 51	24 21	00 21	00 54
N 40	03 21	04 02	04 35	23 57	24 30	00 30	01 05
35	03 44	04 20	04 50	24 02	00 02	00 38	01 15
30	04 02	04 35	05 02	24 07	00 07	00 44	01 23
20	04 31	05 00	05 24	24 16	00 16	00 56	01 38
N 10	04 53	05 20	05 43	24 23	00 23	01 07	01 51
0	05 12	05 38	06 00	24 30	00 30	01 16	02 03
S 10	05 28	05 55	06 17	24 37	00 37	01 26	02 15
20	05 44	06 12	06 36	24 45	00 45	01 37	02 28
30	06 00	06 30	06 57	24 53	00 53	01 49	02 43
35	06 09	06 41	07 09	24 58	00 58	01 56	02 52
40	06 18	06 52	07 23	00 03	01 04	02 04	03 02
45	06 28	07 05	07 39	00 06	01 11	02 13	03 14
S 50	06 40	07 21	07 59	00 11	01 19	02 25	03 28
52	06 45	07 28	08 09	00 13	01 23	02 30	03 35
54	06 50	07 36	08 20	00 15	01 27	02 36	03 42
56	06 57	07 45	08 32	00 17	01 31	02 42	03 50
58	07 03	07 55	08 47	00 20	01 36	02 50	04 00
S 60	07 10	08 07	09 04	00 23	01 42	02 58	04 11

Lat.	Sunset	Twilight Civil	Naut.	Moonset 30	1	2	3
N 72	▭	▭	▭	13 47	15 37	17 34	20 06
N 70	▭	▭	▭	13 36	15 16	16 57	18 40
68	▭	▭	▭	13 26	15 00	16 32	18 01
66	23 39	////	////	13 18	14 47	16 12	17 34
64	22 25	////	////	13 12	14 36	15 57	17 14
62	21 50	////	////	13 06	14 26	15 44	16 57
60	21 25	23 02	////	13 01	14 18	15 33	16 43
N 58	21 05	22 18	////	12 57	14 12	15 23	16 31
56	20 49	21 50	////	12 53	14 05	15 15	16 21
54	20 35	21 29	23 07	12 49	14 00	15 08	16 12
52	20 23	21 11	22 27	12 46	13 55	15 01	16 04
50	20 12	20 56	22 01	12 43	13 51	14 55	15 57
45	19 50	20 27	21 17	12 37	13 41	14 43	15 42
N 40	19 33	20 05	20 47	12 32	13 33	14 32	15 29
35	19 18	19 47	20 24	12 28	13 26	14 23	15 18
30	19 05	19 32	20 06	12 24	13 20	14 15	15 09
20	18 43	19 08	19 37	12 17	13 10	14 02	14 53
N 10	18 25	18 48	19 15	12 11	13 01	13 50	14 39
0	18 08	18 30	18 56	12 06	12 52	13 39	14 26
S 10	17 50	18 13	18 39	12 00	12 44	13 28	14 12
20	17 32	17 56	18 24	11 55	12 35	13 16	13 58
30	17 11	17 38	18 07	11 48	12 25	13 02	13 42
35	16 59	17 27	17 59	11 44	12 19	12 55	13 33
40	16 45	17 16	17 40	11 40	12 12	12 46	13 23
45	16 29	17 02	17 40	11 35	12 04	12 36	13 10
S 50	16 08	16 47	17 28	11 29	11 55	12 23	12 55
52	15 59	16 39	17 23	11 26	11 51	12 18	12 48
54	15 48	16 31	17 17	11 23	11 46	12 11	12 40
56	15 36	16 23	17 11	11 20	11 41	12 04	12 32
58	15 21	16 13	17 05	11 15	11 36	11 56	12 22
S 60	15 04	16 01	16 58	11 12	11 28	11 47	12 11

Day	SUN Eqn. of Time 00h	12h	Mer. Pass.	MOON Mer. Pass. Upper	Lower	Age	Phase
	m s	m s	h m	h m	h m	d	%
30	03 35	03 41	12 04	05 55	18 18	22	47
1	03 47	03 52	12 04	06 41	19 04	23	37
2	03 58	04 04	12 04	07 28	19 51	24	28

2013 JULY 3, 4, 5 (WED., THURS., FRI.)

UT	ARIES GHA	VENUS −3.8 GHA	Dec	MARS +1.5 GHA	Dec	JUPITER −1.9 GHA	Dec	SATURN +0.5 GHA	Dec	STARS Name	SHA	Dec
d h	° ′	° ′	° ′	° ′	° ′	° ′	° ′	° ′	° ′		° ′	° ′
3 00	281 11.0	151 57.0	N20 14.7	199 02.8	N23 39.0	189 27.7	N23 13.1	67 46.0	S10 46.6	Acamar	315 18.6	S40 14.9
01	296 13.5	166 56.4	14.0	214 03.4	39.1	204 29.6	13.1	82 48.5	46.6	Achernar	335 26.9	S57 09.8
02	311 16.0	181 55.7	13.2	229 04.0	39.2	219 31.4	13.1	97 51.0	46.7	Acrux	173 09.2	S63 10.8
03	326 18.4	196 55.0 ..	12.5	244 04.6 ..	39.3	234 33.3 ..	13.1	112 53.5 ..	46.7	Adhara	255 12.9	S28 59.6
04	341 20.9	211 54.4	11.7	259 05.2	39.4	249 35.1	13.1	127 56.0	46.7	Aldebaran	290 49.6	N16 32.0
05	356 23.3	226 53.7	11.0	274 05.8	39.6	264 37.0	13.1	142 58.5	46.7			
06	11 25.8	241 53.0	N20 10.2	289 06.4	N23 39.7	279 38.8	N23 13.1	158 01.0	S10 46.7	Alioth	166 20.7	N55 53.4
W 07	26 28.3	256 52.4	09.5	304 07.0	39.8	294 40.7	13.1	173 03.4	46.7	Alkaid	152 58.8	N49 15.0
E 08	41 30.7	271 51.7	08.7	319 07.6	39.9	309 42.5	13.1	188 05.9	46.7	Al Na'ir	27 43.4	S46 53.4
D 09	56 33.2	286 51.1 ..	08.0	334 08.2 ..	40.0	324 44.3 ..	13.1	203 08.4 ..	46.7	Alnilam	275 46.6	S 1 11.7
N 10	71 35.7	301 50.4	07.2	349 08.8	40.1	339 46.2	13.1	218 10.9	46.7	Alphard	217 56.3	S 8 43.2
E 11	86 38.1	316 49.7	06.5	4 09.4	40.2	354 48.0	13.1	233 13.4	46.7			
S 12	101 40.6	331 49.1	N20 05.7	19 10.0	N23 40.4	9 49.9	N23 13.1	248 15.9	S10 46.7	Alphecca	126 10.7	N26 40.4
D 13	116 43.1	346 48.4	05.0	34 10.6	40.5	24 51.7	13.1	263 18.4	46.7	Alpheratz	357 43.3	N29 09.8
A 14	131 45.5	1 47.8	04.2	49 11.2	40.6	39 53.6	13.1	278 20.8	46.7	Altair	62 07.9	N 8 54.5
Y 15	146 48.0	16 47.1 ..	03.5	64 11.8 ..	40.7	54 55.4 ..	13.1	293 23.3 ..	46.7	Ankaa	353 15.6	S42 13.6
16	161 50.5	31 46.4	02.7	79 12.3	40.8	69 57.3	13.1	308 25.8	46.7	Antares	112 25.9	S26 27.6
17	176 52.9	46 45.8	02.0	94 12.9	40.9	84 59.1	13.1	323 28.3	46.7			
18	191 55.4	61 45.1	N20 01.2	109 13.5	N23 41.0	100 01.0	N23 13.1	338 30.8	S10 46.7	Arcturus	145 55.6	N19 06.9
19	206 57.8	76 44.5	20 00.4	124 14.1	41.2	115 02.8	13.1	353 33.3	46.7	Atria	107 27.1	S69 03.1
20	222 00.3	91 43.8	19 59.7	139 14.7	41.3	130 04.6	13.1	8 35.8	46.7	Avior	234 18.6	S59 33.4
21	237 02.8	106 43.2 ..	58.9	154 15.3 ..	41.4	145 06.5 ..	13.1	23 38.2 ..	46.7	Bellatrix	278 32.3	N 6 21.6
22	252 05.2	121 42.5	58.2	169 15.9	41.5	160 08.3	13.1	38 40.7	46.7	Betelgeuse	271 01.6	N 7 24.4
23	267 07.7	136 41.9	57.4	184 16.5	41.6	175 10.2	13.0	53 43.2	46.7			
4 00	282 10.2	151 41.2	N19 56.6	199 17.1	N23 41.7	190 12.0	N23 13.0	68 45.7	S10 46.7	Canopus	263 56.7	S52 42.3
01	297 12.6	166 40.6	55.9	214 17.7	41.8	205 13.9	13.0	83 48.2	46.7	Capella	280 34.8	N46 00.4
02	312 15.1	181 39.9	55.1	229 18.3	41.9	220 15.7	13.0	98 50.7	46.7	Deneb	49 31.0	N45 19.8
03	327 17.6	196 39.2 ..	54.3	244 18.9 ..	42.0	235 17.6 ..	13.0	113 53.2 ..	46.8	Denebola	182 33.7	N14 29.8
04	342 20.0	211 38.6	53.6	259 19.5	42.1	250 19.4	13.0	128 55.6	46.8	Diphda	348 55.8	S17 54.6
05	357 22.5	226 37.9	52.8	274 20.1	42.3	265 21.3	13.0	143 58.1	46.8			
06	12 25.0	241 37.3	N19 52.0	289 20.7	N23 42.4	280 23.1	N23 13.0	159 00.6	S10 46.8	Dubhe	193 52.0	N61 40.8
T 07	27 27.4	256 36.6	51.2	304 21.3	42.5	295 25.0	13.0	174 03.1	46.8	Elnath	278 12.9	N28 36.9
H 08	42 29.9	271 36.0	50.5	319 21.9	42.6	310 26.8	13.0	189 05.6	46.8	Eltanin	90 45.6	N51 29.5
U 09	57 32.3	286 35.4 ..	49.7	334 22.5 ..	42.7	325 28.6 ..	13.0	204 08.1 ..	46.8	Enif	33 46.8	N 9 56.4
R 10	72 34.8	301 34.7	48.9	349 23.1	42.8	340 30.5	13.0	219 10.5	46.8	Fomalhaut	15 23.8	S29 32.7
S 11	87 37.3	316 34.1	48.1	4 23.7	42.9	355 32.3	13.0	234 13.0	46.8			
D 12	102 39.7	331 33.4	N19 47.4	19 24.3	N23 43.0	10 34.2	N23 13.0	249 15.5	S10 46.8	Gacrux	172 00.8	S57 11.7
A 13	117 42.2	346 32.8	46.6	34 24.9	43.1	25 36.0	13.0	264 18.0	46.8	Gienah	175 52.3	S17 37.2
Y 14	132 44.7	1 32.1	45.8	49 25.5	43.2	40 37.9	13.0	279 20.5	46.8	Hadar	148 47.5	S60 26.5
15	147 47.1	16 31.5 ..	45.0	64 26.1 ..	43.3	55 39.7 ..	13.0	294 22.9 ..	46.8	Hamal	328 00.8	N23 31.5
16	162 49.6	31 30.8	44.3	79 26.7	43.4	70 41.6	13.0	309 25.4	46.8	Kaus Aust.	83 43.3	S34 22.5
17	177 52.1	46 30.2	43.5	94 27.3	43.5	85 43.4	13.0	324 27.9	46.8			
18	192 54.5	61 29.5	N19 42.7	109 27.9	N23 43.6	100 45.3	N23 13.0	339 30.4	S10 46.8	Kochab	137 19.5	N74 06.3
19	207 57.0	76 28.9	41.9	124 28.5	43.7	115 47.1	13.0	354 32.9	46.8	Markab	13 38.1	N15 16.7
20	222 59.4	91 28.3	41.1	139 29.0	43.8	130 49.0	13.0	9 35.4	46.8	Menkar	314 15.2	N 4 08.5
21	238 01.9	106 27.6 ..	40.3	154 29.6 ..	43.9	145 50.8 ..	13.0	24 37.8 ..	46.8	Menkent	148 07.3	S36 26.3
22	253 04.4	121 27.0	39.6	169 30.2	44.0	160 52.7	12.9	39 40.3	46.9	Miaplacidus	221 26.5	S69 46.7
23	268 06.8	136 26.3	38.8	184 30.8	44.1	175 54.5	12.9	54 42.8	46.9			
5 00	283 09.3	151 25.7	N19 38.0	199 31.4	N23 44.2	190 56.3	N23 12.9	69 45.3	S10 46.9	Mirfak	308 40.6	N49 54.3
01	298 11.8	166 25.1	37.2	214 32.0	44.3	205 58.2	12.9	84 47.8	46.9	Nunki	75 57.9	S26 16.6
02	313 14.2	181 24.4	36.4	229 32.6	44.4	221 00.0	12.9	99 50.2	46.9	Peacock	53 18.6	S56 41.2
03	328 16.7	196 23.8 ..	35.6	244 33.2 ..	44.5	236 01.9 ..	12.9	114 52.7 ..	46.9	Pollux	243 28.1	N27 59.5
04	343 19.2	211 23.1	34.8	259 33.8	44.6	251 03.7	12.9	129 55.2	46.9	Procyon	245 00.0	N 5 11.3
05	358 21.6	226 22.5	34.0	274 34.4	44.7	266 05.6	12.9	144 57.7	46.9			
06	13 24.1	241 21.9	N19 33.2	289 35.0	N23 44.8	281 07.4	N23 12.9	160 00.2	S10 46.9	Rasalhague	96 06.1	N12 33.2
07	28 26.6	256 21.2	32.5	304 35.6	44.9	296 09.3	12.9	175 02.6	46.9	Regulus	207 43.7	N11 54.0
08	43 29.0	271 20.6	31.7	319 36.2	45.0	311 11.1	12.9	190 05.1	46.9	Rigel	281 03.2	S 8 11.3
F 09	58 31.5	286 20.0 ..	30.9	334 36.8 ..	45.1	326 13.0 ..	12.9	205 07.6 ..	46.9	Rigil Kent.	139 51.3	S60 53.6
R 10	73 33.9	301 19.3	30.1	349 37.4	45.2	341 14.8	12.9	220 10.1	46.9	Sabik	102 12.2	S15 44.3
I 11	88 36.4	316 18.7	29.3	4 38.0	45.3	356 16.7	12.9	235 12.6	46.9			
D 12	103 38.9	331 18.1	N19 28.5	19 38.6	N23 45.4	11 18.5	N23 12.9	250 15.0	S10 46.9	Schedar	349 40.4	N56 36.5
A 13	118 41.3	346 17.4	27.7	34 39.2	45.5	26 20.4	12.9	265 17.5	47.0	Shaula	96 21.4	S37 06.7
Y 14	133 43.8	1 16.8	26.9	49 39.8	45.6	41 22.2	12.9	280 20.0	47.0	Sirius	258 34.0	S16 44.2
15	148 46.3	16 16.2 ..	26.1	64 40.4 ..	45.7	56 24.1 ..	12.9	295 22.5 ..	47.0	Spica	158 31.1	S11 14.0
16	163 48.7	31 15.5	25.3	79 41.0	45.8	71 25.9	12.9	310 25.0	47.0	Suhail	222 52.8	S43 29.5
17	178 51.2	46 14.9	24.5	94 41.6	45.9	86 27.7	12.8	325 27.4	47.0			
18	193 53.7	61 14.3	N19 23.7	109 42.2	N23 46.0	101 29.6	N23 12.8	340 29.9	S10 47.0	Vega	80 38.5	N38 48.0
19	208 56.1	76 13.7	22.9	124 42.8	46.1	116 31.4	12.8	355 32.4	47.0	Zuben'ubi	137 05.2	S16 05.9
20	223 58.6	91 13.0	22.1	139 43.4	46.2	131 33.3	12.8	10 34.9	47.0		SHA	Mer.Pass.
21	239 01.1	106 12.4 ..	21.2	154 44.0 ..	46.3	146 35.1 ..	12.8	25 37.3 ..	47.0	Venus	229 31.0	13 54
22	254 03.5	121 11.8	20.4	169 44.6	46.4	161 37.0	12.8	40 39.8	47.0	Mars	277 06.9	10 42
23	269 06.0	136 11.1	19.6	184 45.2	46.5	176 38.8	12.8	55 42.3	47.0	Jupiter	268 01.9	11 18
Mer. Pass. 5 10.5		v −0.6 d 0.8		v 0.6 d 0.1		v 1.8 d 0.0		v 2.5 d 0.0		Saturn	146 35.5	19 22

UT	SUN GHA	SUN Dec	MOON GHA	v	MOON Dec	d	HP
d h	° '	° '	° '	'	° '	'	'
3 00	178 57.6	N22 57.6	240 20.3	12.6	N16 01.7	6.5	54.8
01	193 57.5	57.4	254 51.9	12.7	16 08.2	6.4	54.8
02	208 57.4	57.2	269 23.6	12.6	16 14.6	6.3	54.8
03	223 57.2	.. 57.0	283 55.2	12.6	16 20.9	6.2	54.8
04	238 57.1	56.8	298 26.8	12.6	16 27.1	6.2	54.8
05	253 57.0	56.6	312 58.4	12.5	16 33.3	6.1	54.7
06	268 56.9	N22 56.4	327 29.9	12.6	N16 39.4	6.0	54.7
W 07	283 56.8	56.2	342 01.5	12.6	16 45.4	5.9	54.7
E 08	298 56.7	56.0	356 33.1	12.5	16 51.3	5.8	54.7
D 09	313 56.5	.. 55.8	11 04.6	12.5	16 57.1	5.8	54.7
N 10	328 56.4	55.5	25 36.1	12.5	17 02.9	5.6	54.6
E 11	343 56.3	55.3	40 07.6	12.5	17 08.5	5.6	54.6
S 12	358 56.2	N22 55.1	54 39.1	12.5	N17 14.1	5.5	54.6
D 13	13 56.1	54.9	69 10.6	12.4	17 19.6	5.5	54.6
A 14	28 56.0	54.7	83 42.0	12.5	17 25.1	5.3	54.6
Y 15	43 55.9	.. 54.5	98 13.5	12.4	17 30.4	5.3	54.6
16	58 55.7	54.3	112 44.9	12.4	17 35.7	5.1	54.5
17	73 55.6	54.1	127 16.3	12.4	17 40.8	5.1	54.5
18	88 55.5	N22 53.9	141 47.7	12.4	N17 45.9	5.1	54.5
19	103 55.4	53.6	156 19.1	12.4	17 51.0	4.9	54.5
20	118 55.3	53.4	170 50.5	12.4	17 55.9	4.8	54.5
21	133 55.2	.. 53.2	185 21.9	12.3	18 00.7	4.8	54.5
22	148 55.1	53.0	199 53.2	12.3	18 05.5	4.7	54.5
23	163 55.0	52.8	214 24.5	12.4	18 10.2	4.6	54.4
4 00	178 54.8	N22 52.6	228 55.9	12.3	N18 14.8	4.5	54.4
01	193 54.7	52.4	243 27.2	12.3	18 19.3	4.4	54.4
02	208 54.6	52.1	257 58.5	12.2	18 23.7	4.3	54.4
03	223 54.5	.. 51.9	272 29.7	12.3	18 28.0	4.2	54.4
04	238 54.4	51.7	287 01.0	12.3	18 32.2	4.2	54.4
05	253 54.3	51.5	301 32.3	12.2	18 36.4	4.1	54.4
06	268 54.2	N22 51.3	316 03.5	12.2	N18 40.5	4.0	54.3
T 07	283 54.1	51.0	330 34.7	12.2	18 44.5	3.9	54.3
H 08	298 53.9	50.8	345 05.9	12.2	18 48.4	3.8	54.3
U 09	313 53.8	.. 50.6	359 37.1	12.2	18 52.2	3.7	54.3
R 10	328 53.7	50.4	14 08.3	12.2	18 55.9	3.6	54.3
S 11	343 53.6	50.1	28 39.5	12.2	18 59.5	3.6	54.3
D 12	358 53.5	N22 49.9	43 10.7	12.1	N19 03.1	3.4	54.3
A 13	13 53.4	49.7	57 41.8	12.2	19 06.5	3.4	54.3
Y 14	28 53.3	49.5	72 13.0	12.1	19 09.9	3.2	54.3
15	43 53.2	.. 49.2	86 44.1	12.1	19 13.1	3.2	54.2
16	58 53.1	49.0	101 15.2	12.1	19 16.3	3.1	54.2
17	73 52.9	48.8	115 46.3	12.1	19 19.4	3.0	54.2
18	88 52.8	N22 48.6	130 17.4	12.1	N19 22.4	3.0	54.2
19	103 52.7	48.3	144 48.5	12.1	19 25.4	2.8	54.2
20	118 52.6	48.1	159 19.6	12.1	19 28.2	2.7	54.2
21	133 52.5	.. 47.9	173 50.7	12.0	19 30.9	2.7	54.2
22	148 52.4	47.6	188 21.7	12.1	19 33.6	2.5	54.2
23	163 52.3	47.4	202 52.8	12.0	19 36.1	2.5	54.2
5 00	178 52.2	N22 47.2	217 23.8	12.1	N19 38.6	2.3	54.2
01	193 52.1	46.9	231 54.9	12.0	19 40.9	2.3	54.1
02	208 52.0	46.7	246 25.9	12.0	19 43.2	2.2	54.1
03	223 51.8	.. 46.4	260 56.9	12.1	19 45.4	2.1	54.1
04	238 51.7	46.2	275 28.0	12.0	19 47.5	2.0	54.1
05	253 51.6	46.0	289 59.0	12.0	19 49.5	1.9	54.1
06	268 51.5	N22 45.7	304 30.0	12.0	N19 51.4	1.8	54.1
F 07	283 51.4	45.5	319 01.0	12.0	19 53.2	1.8	54.1
R 08	298 51.3	45.3	333 32.0	11.9	19 55.0	1.6	54.1
I 09	313 51.2	.. 45.0	348 02.9	12.0	19 56.6	1.6	54.1
D 10	328 51.1	44.8	2 33.9	12.0	19 58.2	1.4	54.1
A 11	343 51.0	44.5	17 04.9	12.0	19 59.6	1.4	54.1
Y 12	358 50.9	N22 44.3	31 35.9	12.0	N20 01.0	1.2	54.1
13	13 50.8	44.0	46 06.9	11.9	20 02.2	1.2	54.1
14	28 50.7	43.8	60 37.8	12.0	20 03.4	1.1	54.0
15	43 50.5	.. 43.6	75 08.8	12.0	20 04.5	1.0	54.0
16	58 50.4	43.3	89 39.8	11.9	20 05.5	0.9	54.0
17	73 50.3	43.1	104 10.7	12.0	20 06.4	0.8	54.0
18	88 50.2	N22 42.8	118 41.7	11.9	N20 07.2	0.7	54.0
19	103 50.1	42.6	133 12.6	12.0	20 07.9	0.6	54.0
20	118 50.0	42.3	147 43.6	12.0	20 08.5	0.5	54.0
21	133 49.9	.. 42.1	162 14.6	11.9	20 09.0	0.4	54.0
22	148 49.8	41.8	176 45.5	12.0	20 09.4	0.4	54.0
23	163 49.7	41.6	191 16.5	11.9	N20 09.8	0.2	54.0
	SD 15.8	d 0.2	SD 14.9		14.8		14.7

Lat.	Twilight Naut.	Twilight Civil	Sunrise	Moonrise 3	4	5	6
°	h m	h m	h m	h m	h m	h m	h m
N 72	□	□	□	21 01	□	□	□
N 70	□	□	□	22 28	22 22	□	23 42
68	□	□	□	23 07	23 24	23 58	24 56
66	////	////	00 42	23 34	23 59	24 37	00 37
64	////	////	01 47	23 55	24 24	00 24	01 05
62	////	////	02 21	24 12	00 12	00 44	01 26
60	////	01 11	02 46	00 00	00 26	01 00	01 43
N 58	////	01 53	03 05	00 10	00 39	01 14	01 57
56	////	02 21	03 21	00 19	00 49	01 26	02 10
54	01 06	02 42	03 35	00 27	00 58	01 36	02 21
52	01 44	02 59	03 47	00 34	01 07	01 45	02 30
50	02 10	03 13	03 57	00 40	01 14	01 54	02 39
45	02 51	03 43	04 19	00 54	01 30	02 11	02 57
N 40	03 23	04 04	04 36	01 05	01 43	02 26	03 12
35	03 45	04 22	04 51	01 15	01 55	02 38	03 24
30	04 03	04 36	05 04	01 23	02 04	02 48	03 35
20	04 32	05 01	05 25	01 38	02 21	03 07	03 54
N 10	04 54	05 21	05 44	01 51	02 36	03 23	04 10
0	05 12	05 38	06 01	02 03	02 50	03 38	04 26
S 10	05 29	05 55	06 18	02 15	03 04	03 53	04 41
20	05 44	06 12	06 36	02 28	03 19	04 09	04 58
30	06 00	06 30	06 56	02 43	03 36	04 27	05 16
35	06 09	06 40	07 08	02 52	03 46	04 38	05 27
40	06 18	06 52	07 22	03 02	03 58	04 51	05 40
45	06 28	07 05	07 38	03 14	04 11	05 05	05 55
S 50	06 39	07 20	07 59	03 28	04 28	05 23	06 13
52	06 44	07 28	08 08	03 35	04 36	05 32	06 22
54	06 50	07 35	08 19	03 42	04 44	05 41	06 32
56	06 56	07 44	08 31	03 50	04 54	05 52	06 42
58	07 02	07 54	08 45	04 00	05 05	06 04	06 55
S 60	07 09	08 05	09 01	04 11	05 18	06 19	07 10

Lat.	Sunset	Twilight Civil	Twilight Naut.	Moonset 3	4	5	6
°	h m	h m	h m	h m	h m	h m	h m
N 72	□	□	□	20 06	□	□	□
N 70	□	□	□	18 40	□	□	22 24
68	□	□	□	18 01	19 23	20 29	21 10
66	23 21	////	////	17 34	18 48	19 49	20 33
64	22 20	////	////	17 14	18 23	19 22	20 03
62	21 46	////	////	16 57	18 03	19 00	19 46
60	21 22	22 55	////	16 43	17 47	18 43	19 29
N 58	21 03	22 14	////	16 31	17 34	18 29	19 15
56	20 47	21 47	////	16 21	17 22	18 17	19 03
54	20 34	21 26	23 01	16 12	17 12	18 06	18 53
52	20 22	21 09	22 23	16 04	17 03	17 56	18 43
50	20 11	20 55	21 58	15 57	16 55	17 48	18 35
45	19 50	20 26	21 15	15 42	16 38	17 30	18 17
N 40	19 32	20 05	20 46	15 29	16 24	17 15	18 02
35	19 18	19 47	20 23	15 18	16 12	17 02	17 50
30	19 05	19 32	20 05	15 09	16 01	16 51	17 39
20	18 44	19 08	19 37	14 53	15 43	16 33	17 20
N 10	18 25	18 48	19 15	14 39	15 28	16 16	17 04
0	18 08	18 31	18 57	14 26	15 13	16 01	16 49
S 10	17 51	18 14	18 40	14 12	14 59	15 46	16 34
20	17 33	17 57	18 24	13 58	14 43	15 29	16 17
30	17 13	17 39	18 09	13 42	14 25	15 11	15 59
35	17 01	17 29	18 00	13 33	14 15	15 00	15 48
40	16 47	17 17	17 51	13 23	14 03	14 47	15 35
45	16 31	17 04	17 41	13 10	13 49	14 32	15 20
S 50	16 11	16 49	17 30	12 55	13 32	14 14	15 02
52	16 01	16 41	17 25	12 48	13 24	14 06	14 54
54	15 50	16 34	17 19	12 40	13 15	13 56	14 44
56	15 38	16 25	17 14	12 32	13 05	13 45	14 33
58	15 24	16 15	17 07	12 22	12 53	13 33	14 21
S 60	15 08	16 04	17 00	12 11	12 40	13 18	14 06

Day	SUN Eqn. of Time 00h	SUN Eqn. of Time 12h	SUN Mer. Pass.	MOON Mer. Pass. Upper	MOON Mer. Pass. Lower	Age	Phase
	m s	m s	h m	h m	h m	d	%
3	04 09	04 15	12 04	08 14	20 38	25	20
4	04 20	04 26	12 04	09 02	21 25	26	13
5	04 31	04 36	12 05	09 49	22 13	27	7

UT	ARIES	VENUS −3.9		MARS +1.5		JUPITER −1.9		SATURN +0.6		STARS		
	GHA	GHA	Dec	GHA	Dec	GHA	Dec	GHA	Dec	Name	SHA	Dec
d h	° ′	° ′	° ′	° ′	° ′	° ′	° ′	° ′	° ′		° ′	° ′
6 00	284 08.4	151 10.5	N19 18.8	199 45.8	N23 46.6	191 40.7	N23 12.8	70 44.8	S10 47.0	Acamar	315 18.5	S40 14.9
01	299 10.9	166 09.9	18.0	214 46.4	46.7	206 42.5	12.8	85 47.2	47.0	Achernar	335 26.9	S57 09.8
02	314 13.4	181 09.3	17.2	229 47.0	46.8	221 44.4	12.8	100 49.7	47.0	Acrux	173 09.2	S63 10.8
03	329 15.8	196 08.6 . .	16.4	244 47.6 . .	46.8	236 46.2 . .	12.8	115 52.2 . .	47.1	Adhara	255 12.9	S28 59.6
04	344 18.3	211 08.0	15.6	259 48.2	46.9	251 48.1	12.8	130 54.7	47.1	Aldebaran	290 49.6	N16 32.0
05	359 20.8	226 07.4	14.8	274 48.8	47.0	266 49.9	12.8	145 57.2	47.1			
06	14 23.2	241 06.8	N19 14.0	289 49.4	N23 47.1	281 51.8	N23 12.8	160 59.6	S10 47.1	Alioth	166 20.7	N55 53.4
07	29 25.7	256 06.2	13.1	304 50.0	47.2	296 53.6	12.8	176 02.1	47.1	Alkaid	152 58.8	N49 15.0
S 08	44 28.2	271 05.5	12.3	319 50.6	47.3	311 55.5	12.8	191 04.6	47.1	Al Na'ir	27 43.4	S46 53.4
A 09	59 30.6	286 04.9 . .	11.5	334 51.2 . .	47.4	326 57.3 . .	12.8	206 07.1 . .	47.1	Alnilam	275 46.6	S 1 11.7
T 10	74 33.1	301 04.3	10.7	349 51.8	47.5	341 59.2	12.7	221 09.5	47.1	Alphard	217 56.3	S 8 43.2
U 11	89 35.6	316 03.7	09.9	4 52.4	47.6	357 01.0	12.7	236 12.0	47.1			
R 12	104 38.0	331 03.1	N19 09.0	19 53.0	N23 47.6	12 02.9	N23 12.7	251 14.5	S10 47.1	Alphecca	126 10.7	N26 40.4
D 13	119 40.5	346 02.4	08.2	34 53.6	47.7	27 04.7	12.7	266 17.0	47.1	Alpheratz	357 43.3	N29 09.9
A 14	134 42.9	1 01.8	07.4	49 54.2	47.8	42 06.6	12.7	281 19.4	47.1	Altair	62 07.8	N 8 54.5
Y 15	149 45.4	16 01.2 . .	06.6	64 54.8 . .	47.9	57 08.4 . .	12.7	296 21.9 . .	47.1	Ankaa	353 15.6	S42 13.6
16	164 47.9	31 00.6	05.8	79 55.4	48.0	72 10.2	12.7	311 24.4	47.2	Antares	112 25.9	S26 27.6
17	179 50.3	46 00.0	04.9	94 56.0	48.1	87 12.1	12.7	326 26.8	47.2			
18	194 52.8	60 59.4	N19 04.1	109 56.6	N23 48.2	102 13.9	N23 12.7	341 29.3	S10 47.2	Arcturus	145 55.6	N19 06.9
19	209 55.3	75 58.7	03.3	124 57.2	48.3	117 15.8	12.7	356 31.8	47.2	Atria	107 27.1	S69 03.1
20	224 57.7	90 58.1	02.5	139 57.8	48.3	132 17.6	12.7	11 34.3	47.2	Avior	234 18.6	S59 33.4
21	240 00.2	105 57.5 . .	01.6	154 58.4 . .	48.4	147 19.5 . .	12.7	26 36.7 . .	47.2	Bellatrix	278 32.3	N 6 21.6
22	255 02.7	120 56.9	00.8	169 59.0	48.5	162 21.3	12.7	41 39.2	47.2	Betelgeuse	271 01.6	N 7 24.4
23	270 05.1	135 56.3	19 00.0	184 59.6	48.6	177 23.2	12.7	56 41.7	47.2			
7 00	285 07.6	150 55.7	N18 59.1	200 00.2	N23 48.7	192 25.0	N23 12.7	71 44.2	S10 47.2	Canopus	263 56.7	S52 42.3
01	300 10.1	165 55.1	58.3	215 00.8	48.8	207 26.9	12.6	86 46.6	47.2	Capella	280 34.8	N46 00.4
02	315 12.5	180 54.4	57.5	230 01.4	48.8	222 28.7	12.6	101 49.1	47.2	Deneb	49 31.0	N45 19.8
03	330 15.0	195 53.8 . .	56.6	245 02.0 . .	48.9	237 30.6 . .	12.6	116 51.6 . .	47.3	Denebola	182 33.7	N14 29.8
04	345 17.4	210 53.2	55.8	260 02.6	49.0	252 32.4	12.6	131 54.1	47.3	Diphda	348 55.8	S17 54.6
05	0 19.9	225 52.6	55.0	275 03.2	49.1	267 34.3	12.6	146 56.5	47.3			
06	15 22.4	240 52.0	N18 54.1	290 03.8	N23 49.2	282 36.1	N23 12.6	161 59.0	S10 47.3	Dubhe	193 52.1	N61 40.8
07	30 24.8	255 51.4	53.3	305 04.4	49.2	297 38.0	12.6	177 01.5	47.3	Elnath	278 12.9	N28 36.9
08	45 27.3	270 50.8	52.5	320 05.0	49.3	312 39.8	12.6	192 03.9	47.3	Eltanin	90 45.6	N51 29.5
S 09	60 29.8	285 50.2 . .	51.6	335 05.6 . .	49.4	327 41.7 . .	12.6	207 06.4 . .	47.3	Enif	33 46.8	N 9 56.4
U 10	75 32.2	300 49.6	50.8	350 06.2	49.5	342 43.5	12.6	222 08.9	47.3	Fomalhaut	15 23.7	S29 32.7
N 11	90 34.7	315 49.0	49.9	5 06.8	49.6	357 45.4	12.6	237 11.4	47.3			
D 12	105 37.2	330 48.4	N18 49.1	20 07.4	N23 49.7	12 47.2	N23 12.6	252 13.8	S10 47.3	Gacrux	172 00.8	S57 11.7
A 13	120 39.6	345 47.8	48.3	35 08.0	49.7	27 49.1	12.6	267 16.3	47.3	Gienah	175 52.3	S17 37.2
Y 14	135 42.1	0 47.2	47.4	50 08.6	49.8	42 50.9	12.6	282 18.8	47.4	Hadar	148 47.5	S60 26.5
15	150 44.5	15 46.6 . .	46.6	65 09.2 . .	49.9	57 52.8 . .	12.5	297 21.2 . .	47.4	Hamal	328 00.8	N23 31.5
16	165 47.0	30 46.0	45.7	80 09.8	50.0	72 54.6	12.5	312 23.7	47.4	Kaus Aust.	83 43.3	S34 22.5
17	180 49.5	45 45.3	44.9	95 10.4	50.0	87 56.5	12.5	327 26.2	47.4			
18	195 51.9	60 44.7	N18 44.0	110 11.0	N23 50.1	102 58.3	N23 12.5	342 28.6	S10 47.4	Kochab	137 19.6	N74 06.3
19	210 54.4	75 44.1	43.2	125 11.6	50.2	118 00.2	12.5	357 31.1	47.4	Markab	13 38.1	N15 16.8
20	225 56.9	90 43.5	42.3	140 12.2	50.3	133 02.0	12.5	12 33.6	47.4	Menkar	314 15.2	N 4 08.5
21	240 59.3	105 42.9 . .	41.5	155 12.8 . .	50.3	148 03.9 . .	12.5	27 36.1 . .	47.4	Menkent	148 07.3	S36 26.3
22	256 01.8	120 42.3	40.6	170 13.4	50.4	163 05.7	12.5	42 38.5	47.4	Miaplacidus	221 40.4	S69 46.7
23	271 04.3	135 41.7	39.8	185 14.0	50.5	178 07.6	12.5	57 41.0	47.4			
8 00	286 06.7	150 41.1	N18 38.9	200 14.6	N23 50.6	193 09.4	N23 12.5	72 43.5	S10 47.5	Mirfak	308 40.5	N49 54.3
01	301 09.2	165 40.5	38.1	215 15.2	50.6	208 11.3	12.5	87 45.9	47.5	Nunki	75 57.9	S26 16.6
02	316 11.7	180 40.0	37.2	230 15.8	50.7	223 13.1	12.5	102 48.4	47.5	Peacock	53 18.6	S56 41.2
03	331 14.1	195 39.4 . .	36.4	245 16.4 . .	50.8	238 15.0 . .	12.5	117 50.9 . .	47.5	Pollux	243 28.0	N27 59.5
04	346 16.6	210 38.8	35.5	260 17.0	50.9	253 16.8	12.4	132 53.3	47.5	Procyon	245 00.0	N 5 11.3
05	1 19.0	225 38.2	34.7	275 17.6	50.9	268 18.7	12.4	147 55.8	47.5			
06	16 21.5	240 37.6	N18 33.8	290 18.2	N23 51.0	283 20.5	N23 12.4	162 58.3	S10 47.5	Rasalhague	96 06.1	N12 33.2
07	31 24.0	255 37.0	33.0	305 18.8	51.1	298 22.4	12.4	178 00.7	47.5	Regulus	207 43.7	N11 54.0
08	46 26.4	270 36.4	32.1	320 19.4	51.2	313 24.2	12.4	193 03.2	47.5	Rigel	281 12.3	S 8 11.3
M 09	61 28.9	285 35.8 . .	31.2	335 20.0 . .	51.2	328 26.1 . .	12.4	208 05.7 . .	47.5	Rigil Kent.	139 51.3	S60 53.6
O 10	76 31.4	300 35.2	30.4	350 20.6	51.3	343 27.9	12.4	223 08.1	47.6	Sabik	102 12.2	S15 44.3
N 11	91 33.8	315 34.6	29.5	5 21.2	51.4	358 29.8	12.4	238 10.6	47.6			
D 12	106 36.3	330 34.0	N18 28.7	20 21.8	N23 51.4	13 31.6	N23 12.4	253 13.1	S10 47.6	Schedar	349 40.3	N56 36.5
A 13	121 38.8	345 33.4	27.8	35 22.4	51.5	28 33.5	12.4	268 15.5	47.6	Shaula	96 21.4	S37 06.7
Y 14	136 41.2	0 32.8	26.9	50 23.0	51.6	43 35.3	12.4	283 18.0	47.6	Sirius	258 34.0	S16 44.2
15	151 43.7	15 32.2 . .	26.1	65 23.6 . .	51.6	58 37.2 . .	12.4	298 20.5 . .	47.6	Spica	158 31.1	S11 14.0
16	166 46.2	30 31.6	25.2	80 24.2	51.7	73 39.0	12.3	313 22.9	47.6	Suhail	222 52.8	S43 29.5
17	181 48.6	45 31.1	24.3	95 24.8	51.8	88 40.9	12.3	328 25.4	47.6			
18	196 51.1	60 30.5	N18 23.5	110 25.4	N23 51.9	103 42.7	N23 12.3	343 27.9	S10 47.6	Vega	80 38.5	N38 48.0
19	211 53.5	75 29.9	22.6	125 26.0	51.9	118 44.6	12.3	358 30.3	47.7	Zuben'ubi	137 05.2	S16 05.9
20	226 56.0	90 29.3	21.7	140 26.6	52.0	133 46.4	12.3	13 32.8	47.7		SHA	Mer. Pass.
21	241 58.5	105 28.7 . .	20.9	155 27.2 . .	52.1	148 48.3 . .	12.3	28 35.3 . .	47.7		° ′	h m
22	257 00.9	120 28.1	20.0	170 27.8	52.1	163 50.1	12.3	43 37.7	47.7	Venus	225 48.1	13 57
23	272 03.4	135 27.5	19.1	185 28.4	52.2	178 52.0	12.3	58 40.2	47.7	Mars	274 52.6	10 40
	h m									Jupiter	267 17.5	11 09
Mer. Pass.	4 58.7	v −0.6	d 0.8	v 0.6	d 0.1	v 1.8	d 0.0	v 2.5	d 0.0	Saturn	146 36.6	19 10

UT	SUN GHA	Dec	MOON GHA	v	Dec	d	HP
d h	° ′	° ′	° ′	′	° ′	′	′
6 00	178 49.6	N22 41.3	205 47.4	12.0	N20 10.0	0.2	54.0
01	193 49.5	41.1	220 18.4	12.0	20 10.2	0.0	54.0
02	208 49.4	40.8	234 49.4	11.9	20 10.2	0.0	54.0
03	223 49.3	.. 40.6	249 20.3	12.0	20 10.2	0.1	54.0
04	238 49.2	40.3	263 51.3	12.0	20 10.1	0.2	54.0
05	253 49.1	40.1	278 22.3	11.9	20 09.9	0.4	54.0
06	268 49.0	N22 39.8	292 53.2	12.0	N20 09.5	0.4	54.0
07	283 48.8	39.6	307 24.2	12.0	20 09.1	0.5	54.0
S 08	298 48.7	39.3	321 55.2	12.0	20 08.6	0.6	54.0
A 09	313 48.6	.. 39.1	336 26.2	12.0	20 08.0	0.7	54.0
T 10	328 48.5	38.8	350 57.2	12.0	20 07.3	0.7	54.0
U 11	343 48.4	38.5	5 28.2	12.0	20 06.6	0.9	54.0
R 12	358 48.3	N22 38.3	19 59.2	12.0	N20 05.7	1.0	54.0
D 13	13 48.2	38.0	34 30.2	12.1	20 04.7	1.0	54.0
A 14	28 48.1	37.8	49 01.3	12.0	20 03.7	1.2	54.0
Y 15	43 48.0	.. 37.5	63 32.3	12.0	20 02.5	1.2	54.0
16	58 47.9	37.2	78 03.3	12.1	20 01.3	1.3	53.9
17	73 47.8	37.0	92 34.4	12.0	20 00.0	1.5	53.9
18	88 47.7	N22 36.7	107 05.4	12.1	N19 58.5	1.5	53.9
19	103 47.6	36.5	121 36.5	12.1	19 57.0	1.6	53.9
20	118 47.5	36.2	136 07.6	12.1	19 55.4	1.7	53.9
21	133 47.4	.. 35.9	150 38.7	12.1	19 53.7	1.8	53.9
22	148 47.3	35.7	165 09.8	12.1	19 51.9	1.9	53.9
23	163 47.2	35.4	179 40.9	12.1	19 50.0	1.9	53.9
7 00	178 47.1	N22 35.1	194 12.0	12.1	N19 48.1	2.1	53.9
01	193 47.0	34.9	208 43.1	12.2	19 46.0	2.1	53.9
02	208 46.9	34.6	223 14.3	12.1	19 43.9	2.3	53.9
03	223 46.8	.. 34.3	237 45.4	12.2	19 41.6	2.3	53.9
04	238 46.7	34.1	252 16.6	12.2	19 39.3	2.4	53.9
05	253 46.6	33.8	266 47.8	12.2	19 36.8	2.5	53.9
06	268 46.5	N22 33.5	281 19.0	12.2	N19 34.3	2.6	53.9
07	283 46.4	33.2	295 50.2	12.2	19 31.7	2.7	53.9
08	298 46.3	33.0	310 21.4	12.3	19 29.0	2.7	53.9
S 09	313 46.2	.. 32.7	324 52.7	12.2	19 26.3	2.9	53.9
U 10	328 46.1	32.4	339 23.9	12.3	19 23.4	3.0	53.9
N 11	343 46.0	32.1	353 55.2	12.3	19 20.4	3.0	54.0
D 12	358 45.9	N22 31.9	8 26.5	12.3	N19 17.4	3.2	54.0
A 13	13 45.8	31.6	22 57.8	12.3	19 14.2	3.2	54.0
Y 14	28 45.7	31.3	37 29.1	12.4	19 11.0	3.3	54.0
15	43 45.6	.. 31.0	52 00.5	12.3	19 07.7	3.4	54.0
16	58 45.5	30.8	66 31.8	12.4	19 04.3	3.5	54.0
17	73 45.4	30.5	81 03.2	12.4	19 00.8	3.5	54.0
18	88 45.3	N22 30.2	95 34.6	12.4	N18 57.3	3.7	54.0
19	103 45.2	29.9	110 06.0	12.5	18 53.6	3.7	54.0
20	118 45.1	29.7	124 37.5	12.4	18 49.9	3.9	54.0
21	133 45.0	.. 29.4	139 08.9	12.5	18 46.0	3.9	54.0
22	148 44.9	29.1	153 40.4	12.5	18 42.1	4.0	54.0
23	163 44.8	28.8	168 11.9	12.5	18 38.1	4.1	54.0
8 00	178 44.7	N22 28.5	182 43.4	12.5	N18 34.0	4.1	54.0
01	193 44.6	28.2	197 14.9	12.6	18 29.9	4.3	54.0
02	208 44.5	28.0	211 46.5	12.6	18 25.6	4.3	54.0
03	223 44.4	.. 27.7	226 18.1	12.6	18 21.3	4.4	54.0
04	238 44.3	27.4	240 49.7	12.6	18 16.9	4.5	54.0
05	253 44.2	27.1	255 21.3	12.6	18 12.4	4.6	54.0
06	268 44.1	N22 26.8	269 52.9	12.7	N18 07.8	4.7	54.0
07	283 44.0	26.5	284 24.6	12.7	18 03.1	4.7	54.0
08	298 43.9	26.2	298 56.3	12.7	17 58.4	4.9	54.0
M 09	313 43.8	.. 26.0	313 28.0	12.7	17 53.5	4.9	54.0
O 10	328 43.7	25.7	327 59.7	12.7	17 48.6	5.0	54.0
N 11	343 43.6	25.4	342 31.4	12.8	17 43.6	5.0	54.0
D 12	358 43.5	N22 25.1	357 03.2	12.8	N17 38.6	5.2	54.0
A 13	13 43.4	24.8	11 35.0	12.8	17 33.4	5.2	54.0
Y 14	28 43.3	24.5	26 06.8	12.9	17 28.2	5.3	54.1
15	43 43.2	.. 24.2	40 38.7	12.8	17 22.9	5.4	54.1
16	58 43.1	23.9	55 10.5	12.9	17 17.5	5.5	54.1
17	73 43.0	23.6	69 42.4	12.9	17 12.0	5.5	54.1
18	88 42.9	N22 23.3	84 14.3	13.0	N17 06.5	5.6	54.1
19	103 42.9	23.0	98 46.3	12.9	17 00.9	5.7	54.1
20	118 42.8	22.7	113 18.2	13.0	16 55.2	5.8	54.1
21	133 42.7	.. 22.4	127 50.2	13.0	16 49.4	5.9	54.1
22	148 42.6	22.1	142 22.2	13.0	16 43.5	5.9	54.1
23	163 42.5	21.8	156 54.2	13.1	N16 37.6	6.0	54.1
	SD 15.8	d 0.3	SD 14.7		14.7		14.7

Lat.	Twilight Naut.	Civil	Sunrise	Moonrise 6	7	8	9
°	h m	h m	h m	h m	h m	h m	h m
N 72	....	....	....	□	□	□	02 26
N 70	....	....	....	23 42	25 28	01 28	03 10
68	....	....	....	24 56	00 56	02 13	03 39
66	////	////	00 58	00 37	01 33	02 43	04 01
64	////	////	01 54	01 05	01 59	03 05	04 18
62	////	////	02 26	01 26	02 19	03 22	04 33
60	////	01 20	02 50	01 43	02 36	03 37	04 45
N 58	////	01 59	03 09	01 57	02 50	03 49	04 55
56	////	02 25	03 24	02 10	03 02	04 00	05 04
54	01 14	02 45	03 38	02 21	03 12	04 10	05 12
52	01 49	03 02	03 49	02 30	03 21	04 18	05 19
50	02 14	03 16	04 00	02 39	03 30	04 26	05 25
45	02 56	03 44	04 21	02 57	03 47	04 42	05 39
N 40	03 25	04 06	04 38	03 12	04 02	04 55	05 50
35	03 47	04 23	04 53	03 24	04 14	05 06	06 00
30	04 05	04 38	05 05	03 35	04 25	05 16	06 08
20	04 33	05 02	05 26	03 54	04 43	05 33	06 23
N 10	04 55	05 22	05 44	04 10	04 59	05 47	06 35
0	05 13	05 39	06 01	04 26	05 14	06 01	06 47
S 10	05 29	05 55	06 18	04 41	05 29	06 15	06 59
20	05 45	06 12	06 36	04 58	05 44	06 29	07 12
30	06 00	06 30	06 56	05 16	06 03	06 46	07 26
35	06 09	06 40	07 08	05 27	06 13	06 55	07 34
40	06 17	06 51	07 21	05 40	06 25	07 07	07 44
45	06 27	07 04	07 37	05 55	06 40	07 19	07 55
S 50	06 38	07 19	07 57	06 13	06 57	07 35	08 08
52	06 43	07 26	08 06	06 22	07 05	07 43	08 14
54	06 48	07 34	08 17	06 32	07 15	07 51	08 21
56	06 54	07 43	08 29	06 42	07 25	08 00	08 29
58	07 00	07 52	08 43	06 55	07 37	08 10	08 37
S 60	07 07	08 03	08 59	07 10	07 50	08 22	08 47

Lat.	Sunset	Twilight Civil	Naut.	Moonset 6	7	8	9
°	h m	h m	h m	h m	h m	h m	h m
N 72	□	□	□	□	□	22 57	22 34
N 70	□	□	□	22 24	22 16	22 11	22 07
68	□	□	□	22 10	22 31	21 41	21 46
66	23 07	////	////	20 33	21 01	21 19	21 30
64	22 14	////	////	20 06	20 38	21 01	21 17
62	21 42	////	////	19 46	20 20	20 46	21 05
60	21 19	22 47	////	19 29	20 06	20 34	20 56
N 58	21 00	22 10	////	19 15	19 53	20 23	20 47
56	20 45	21 44	////	19 03	19 42	20 14	20 40
54	20 32	21 24	22 54	18 53	19 32	20 05	20 33
52	20 20	21 07	22 19	18 43	19 23	19 58	20 27
50	20 10	20 53	21 55	18 35	19 16	19 51	20 21
45	19 48	20 25	21 13	18 17	18 59	19 37	20 10
N 40	19 31	20 04	20 45	18 02	18 45	19 26	20 00
35	19 17	19 46	20 23	17 50	18 34	19 14	19 52
30	19 05	19 32	20 05	17 39	18 24	19 05	19 44
20	18 44	19 08	19 37	17 20	18 06	18 50	19 31
N 10	18 25	18 48	19 15	17 04	17 51	18 36	19 20
0	18 09	18 31	18 57	16 49	17 37	18 23	19 09
S 10	17 52	18 15	18 41	16 34	17 22	18 11	18 59
20	17 34	17 58	18 25	16 17	17 07	17 57	18 47
30	17 14	17 40	18 10	15 59	16 49	17 41	18 34
35	17 02	17 30	18 01	15 48	16 39	17 32	18 26
40	16 49	17 19	17 43	15 35	16 27	17 21	18 17
45	16 33	17 06	17 43	15 20	16 13	17 09	18 07
S 50	16 13	16 51	17 32	15 02	15 56	16 54	17 55
52	16 04	16 44	17 27	14 54	15 48	16 47	17 49
54	15 53	16 36	17 22	14 44	15 39	16 39	17 43
56	15 41	16 28	17 16	14 33	15 29	16 30	17 35
58	15 28	16 18	17 10	14 21	15 17	16 20	17 27
S 60	15 12	16 07	17 03	14 06	15 03	16 08	17 18

	SUN		MOON			
Day	Eqn. of Time 00h	12h	Mer. Pass.	Mer. Pass. Upper	Lower	Age	Phase
d	m s	m s	h m	h m	h m	d	%
6	04 41	04 46	12 05	23 01	10 37	28	3
7	04 51	04 56	12 05	11 25	23 49	29	1
8	05 01	05 06	12 05	12 12	24 35	00	0

UT	ARIES GHA	VENUS −3.9 GHA	Dec	MARS +1.6 GHA	Dec	JUPITER −1.9 GHA	Dec	SATURN +0.6 GHA	Dec	STARS Name	SHA	Dec
9 00	287 05.9	150 27.0	N18 18.3	200 29.0	N23 52.3	193 53.8	N23 12.3	73 42.7	S10 47.7	Acamar	315 18.5	S40 14.9
01	302 08.3	165 26.4	.. 17.4	215 29.6	.. 52.3	208 55.7	.. 12.3	88 45.1	.. 47.7	Achernar	335 26.9	S57 09.8
02	317 10.8	180 25.8	.. 16.5	230 30.2	.. 52.4	223 57.5	.. 12.3	103 47.6	.. 47.7	Acrux	173 09.2	S63 10.8
03	332 13.3	195 25.2	.. 15.6	245 30.8	.. 52.4	238 59.4	.. 12.2	118 50.1	.. 47.8	Adhara	255 12.8	S28 59.6
04	347 15.7	210 24.6	.. 14.8	260 31.4	.. 52.5	254 01.2	.. 12.2	133 52.5	.. 47.8	Aldebaran	290 49.6	N16 32.0
05	2 18.2	225 24.0	.. 13.9	275 32.0	.. 52.6	269 03.1	.. 12.2	148 55.0	.. 47.8			
06	17 20.7	240 23.5	N18 13.0	290 32.6	N23 52.6	284 04.9	N23 12.2	163 57.5	S10 47.8	Alioth	166 20.7	N55 53.4
07	32 23.1	255 22.9	.. 12.1	305 33.2	.. 52.7	299 06.8	.. 12.2	178 59.9	.. 47.8	Alkaid	152 58.8	N49 15.0
T 08	47 25.6	270 22.3	.. 11.2	320 33.8	.. 52.8	314 08.6	.. 12.2	194 02.4	.. 47.8	Al Na'ir	27 43.3	S46 53.4
U 09	62 28.0	285 21.7	.. 10.4	335 34.4	.. 52.8	329 10.5	.. 12.2	209 04.8	.. 47.8	Alnilam	275 46.6	S 1 11.7
E 10	77 30.5	300 21.1	.. 09.5	350 35.0	.. 52.9	344 12.3	.. 12.2	224 07.3	.. 47.8	Alphard	217 56.3	S 8 43.2
S 11	92 33.0	315 20.6	.. 08.6	5 35.6	.. 52.9	359 14.2	.. 12.2	239 09.8	.. 47.8			
D 12	107 35.4	330 20.0	N18 07.7	20 36.3	N23 53.0	14 16.0	N23 12.2	254 12.2	S10 47.9	Alphecca	126 10.7	N26 40.4
A 13	122 37.9	345 19.4	.. 06.8	35 36.9	.. 53.1	29 17.9	.. 12.2	269 14.7	.. 47.9	Alpheratz	357 43.3	N29 09.9
Y 14	137 40.4	0 18.8	.. 06.0	50 37.5	.. 53.1	44 19.7	.. 12.1	284 17.2	.. 47.9	Altair	62 07.8	N 8 54.5
15	152 42.8	15 18.3	.. 05.1	65 38.1	.. 53.2	59 21.6	.. 12.1	299 19.6	.. 47.9	Ankaa	353 15.6	S42 13.6
16	167 45.3	30 17.7	.. 04.2	80 38.7	.. 53.3	74 23.4	.. 12.1	314 22.1	.. 47.9	Antares	112 25.9	S26 27.6
17	182 47.8	45 17.1	.. 03.3	95 39.3	.. 53.3	89 25.3	.. 12.1	329 24.5	.. 47.9			
18	197 50.2	60 16.5	N18 02.4	110 39.9	N23 53.4	104 27.1	N23 12.1	344 27.0	S10 47.9	Arcturus	145 55.6	N19 06.9
19	212 52.7	75 16.0	.. 01.5	125 40.5	.. 53.4	119 29.0	.. 12.1	359 29.5	.. 47.9	Atria	107 27.1	S69 03.1
20	227 55.1	90 15.4	18 00.6	140 41.1	.. 53.5	134 30.9	.. 12.1	14 31.9	.. 48.0	Avior	234 18.6	S59 33.4
21	242 57.6	105 14.8	17 59.7	155 41.7	.. 53.5	149 32.7	.. 12.1	29 34.4	.. 48.0	Bellatrix	278 32.2	N 6 21.6
22	258 00.1	120 14.2	.. 58.9	170 42.3	.. 53.6	164 34.6	.. 12.1	44 36.9	.. 48.0	Betelgeuse	271 01.5	N 7 24.4
23	273 02.5	135 13.7	.. 58.0	185 42.9	.. 53.7	179 36.4	.. 12.1	59 39.3	.. 48.0			
10 00	288 05.0	150 13.1	N17 57.1	200 43.5	N23 53.7	194 38.3	N23 12.1	74 41.8	S10 48.0	Canopus	263 56.7	S52 42.3
01	303 07.5	165 12.5	.. 56.2	215 44.1	.. 53.8	209 40.1	.. 12.0	89 44.2	.. 48.0	Capella	280 34.8	N46 00.4
02	318 09.9	180 12.0	.. 55.3	230 44.7	.. 53.8	224 42.0	.. 12.0	104 46.7	.. 48.0	Deneb	49 31.0	N45 19.8
03	333 12.4	195 11.4	.. 54.4	245 45.3	.. 53.9	239 43.8	.. 12.0	119 49.2	.. 48.1	Denebola	182 33.7	N14 29.8
04	348 14.9	210 10.8	.. 53.5	260 45.9	.. 53.9	254 45.7	.. 12.0	134 51.6	.. 48.1	Diphda	348 55.8	S17 54.6
05	3 17.3	225 10.2	.. 52.6	275 46.5	.. 54.0	269 47.5	.. 12.0	149 54.1	.. 48.1			
06	18 19.8	240 09.7	N17 51.7	290 47.1	N23 54.1	284 49.4	N23 12.0	164 56.5	S10 48.1	Dubhe	193 52.1	N61 40.8
W 07	33 22.3	255 09.1	.. 50.8	305 47.7	.. 54.1	299 51.2	.. 12.0	179 59.0	.. 48.1	Elnath	278 12.9	N28 36.9
E 08	48 24.7	270 08.5	.. 49.9	320 48.3	.. 54.2	314 53.1	.. 12.0	195 01.5	.. 48.1	Eltanin	90 45.6	N51 29.5
D 09	63 27.2	285 08.0	.. 49.0	335 48.9	.. 54.2	329 54.9	.. 12.0	210 03.9	.. 48.1	Enif	33 46.8	N 9 56.4
N 10	78 29.6	300 07.4	.. 48.1	350 49.5	.. 54.3	344 56.8	.. 12.0	225 06.4	.. 48.1	Fomalhaut	15 23.7	S29 32.7
E 11	93 32.1	315 06.8	.. 47.2	5 50.2	.. 54.3	359 58.6	.. 11.9	240 08.8	.. 48.2			
S 12	108 34.6	330 06.3	N17 46.3	20 50.8	N23 54.4	15 00.5	N23 11.9	255 11.3	S10 48.2	Gacrux	172 00.8	S57 11.6
D 13	123 37.0	345 05.7	.. 45.4	35 51.4	.. 54.4	30 02.3	.. 11.9	270 13.8	.. 48.2	Gienah	175 52.3	S17 37.2
A 14	138 39.5	0 05.2	.. 44.5	50 52.0	.. 54.5	45 04.2	.. 11.9	285 16.2	.. 48.2	Hadar	148 47.5	S60 26.5
Y 15	153 42.0	15 04.6	.. 43.6	65 52.6	.. 54.5	60 06.0	.. 11.9	300 18.7	.. 48.2	Hamal	328 00.8	N23 31.5
16	168 44.4	30 04.0	.. 42.7	80 53.2	.. 54.6	75 07.9	.. 11.9	315 21.1	.. 48.2	Kaus Aust.	83 43.3	S34 22.5
17	183 46.9	45 03.5	.. 41.8	95 53.8	.. 54.6	90 09.7	.. 11.9	330 23.6	.. 48.2			
18	198 49.4	60 02.9	N17 40.9	110 54.4	N23 54.7	105 11.6	N23 11.9	345 26.0	S10 48.3	Kochab	137 19.6	N74 06.3
19	213 51.8	75 02.4	.. 40.0	125 55.0	.. 54.7	120 13.5	.. 11.9	0 28.5	.. 48.3	Markab	13 38.1	N15 16.8
20	228 54.3	90 01.8	.. 39.1	140 55.6	.. 54.8	135 15.3	.. 11.8	15 31.0	.. 48.3	Menkar	314 15.1	N 4 08.5
21	243 56.8	105 01.2	.. 38.2	155 56.2	.. 54.8	150 17.2	.. 11.8	30 33.4	.. 48.3	Menkent	148 07.3	S36 26.3
22	258 59.2	120 00.7	.. 37.2	170 56.8	.. 54.9	165 19.0	.. 11.8	45 35.9	.. 48.3	Miaplacidus	221 40.4	S69 46.7
23	274 01.7	135 00.1	.. 36.3	185 57.4	.. 54.9	180 20.9	.. 11.8	60 38.3	.. 48.3			
11 00	289 04.1	149 59.6	N17 35.4	200 58.0	N23 55.0	195 22.7	N23 11.8	75 40.8	S10 48.3	Mirfak	308 40.5	N49 54.3
01	304 06.6	164 59.0	.. 34.5	215 58.6	.. 55.0	210 24.6	.. 11.8	90 43.2	.. 48.4	Nunki	75 57.9	S26 16.6
02	319 09.1	179 58.4	.. 33.6	230 59.2	.. 55.1	225 26.4	.. 11.8	105 45.7	.. 48.4	Peacock	53 18.6	S56 41.2
03	334 11.5	194 57.9	.. 32.7	245 59.8	.. 55.1	240 28.3	.. 11.8	120 48.2	.. 48.4	Pollux	243 28.0	N27 59.5
04	349 14.0	209 57.3	.. 31.8	261 00.4	.. 55.2	255 30.1	.. 11.8	135 50.6	.. 48.4	Procyon	245 00.0	N 5 11.3
05	4 16.5	224 56.8	.. 30.9	276 01.1	.. 55.2	270 32.0	.. 11.8	150 53.1	.. 48.4			
06	19 18.9	239 56.2	N17 29.9	291 01.7	N23 55.3	285 33.8	N23 11.7	165 55.5	S10 48.4	Rasalhague	96 06.1	N12 33.2
07	34 21.4	254 55.7	.. 29.0	306 02.3	.. 55.3	300 35.7	.. 11.7	180 58.0	.. 48.4	Regulus	207 43.7	N11 54.0
T 08	49 23.9	269 55.1	.. 28.1	321 02.9	.. 55.3	315 37.5	.. 11.7	196 00.4	.. 48.5	Rigel	281 12.3	S 8 11.3
H 09	64 26.3	284 54.6	.. 27.2	336 03.5	.. 55.4	330 39.4	.. 11.7	211 02.9	.. 48.5	Rigil Kent.	139 51.3	S60 53.6
U 10	79 28.8	299 54.0	.. 26.3	351 04.1	.. 55.4	345 41.3	.. 11.7	226 05.3	.. 48.5	Sabik	102 12.1	S15 44.3
R 11	94 31.3	314 53.5	.. 25.3	6 04.7	.. 55.5	0 43.1	.. 11.7	241 07.8	.. 48.5			
S 12	109 33.7	329 52.9	N17 24.4	21 05.3	N23 55.5	15 45.0	N23 11.7	256 10.3	S10 48.5	Schedar	349 40.3	N56 36.5
D 13	124 36.2	344 52.4	.. 23.5	36 05.9	.. 55.6	30 46.8	.. 11.7	271 12.7	.. 48.5	Shaula	96 21.4	S37 06.7
A 14	139 38.6	359 51.8	.. 22.6	51 06.5	.. 55.6	45 48.7	.. 11.7	286 15.2	.. 48.5	Sirius	258 34.0	S16 44.2
Y 15	154 41.1	14 51.3	.. 21.7	66 07.1	.. 55.7	60 50.5	.. 11.6	301 17.6	.. 48.6	Spica	158 31.1	S11 14.0
16	169 43.6	29 50.7	.. 20.7	81 07.7	.. 55.7	75 52.4	.. 11.6	316 20.1	.. 48.6	Suhail	222 52.8	S43 29.5
17	184 46.0	44 50.2	.. 19.8	96 08.3	.. 55.7	90 54.2	.. 11.6	331 22.5	.. 48.6			
18	199 48.5	59 49.6	N17 18.9	111 08.9	N23 55.8	105 56.1	N23 11.6	346 25.0	S10 48.6	Vega	80 38.5	N38 48.0
19	214 51.0	74 49.1	.. 18.0	126 09.6	.. 55.8	120 57.9	.. 11.6	1 27.4	.. 48.6	Zuben'ubi	137 05.2	S16 05.9
20	229 53.4	89 48.5	.. 17.0	141 10.2	.. 55.9	135 59.8	.. 11.6	16 29.9	.. 48.6		SHA	Mer.Pass.
21	244 55.9	104 48.0	.. 16.1	156 10.8	.. 55.9	151 01.6	.. 11.6	31 32.3	.. 48.7		° '	h m
22	259 58.4	119 47.4	.. 15.2	171 11.4	.. 55.9	166 03.5	.. 11.6	46 34.8	.. 48.7	Venus	222 08.1	14 00
23	275 00.8	134 46.9	.. 14.2	186 12.0	.. 56.0	181 05.4	.. 11.6	61 37.3	.. 48.7	Mars	272 38.5	10 37
	h m									Jupiter	266 33.3	11 00
Mer. Pass.	4 46.9	v −0.6	d 0.9	v 0.6	d 0.1	v 1.9	d 0.0	v 2.5	d 0.0	Saturn	146 36.8	18 58

UT	SUN GHA	SUN Dec	MOON GHA	MOON v	MOON Dec	MOON d	MOON HP
d h	° '	° '	° '	'	° '	'	'
9 00	178 42.4	N22 21.5	171 26.3 13.1	N16 31.6	6.0	54.1
01	193 42.3	21.2	185 58.4 13.1	16 25.6	6.2	54.1
02	208 42.2	20.9	200 30.5 13.1	16 19.4	6.2	54.1
03	223 42.1 ..	20.6	215 02.6 13.1	16 13.2	6.3	54.1
04	238 42.0	20.3	229 34.7 13.1	16 06.9	6.4	54.2
05	253 41.9	20.0	244 06.9 13.2	16 00.5	6.4	54.2
06	268 41.8	N22 19.7	258 39.1 13.2	N15 54.1	6.5	54.2
07	283 41.7	19.4	273 11.3 13.3	15 47.6	6.6	54.2
08	298 41.6	19.1	287 43.6 13.3	15 41.0	6.7	54.2
09	313 41.5 ..	18.8	302 15.9 13.3	15 34.3	6.7	54.2
10	328 41.4	18.5	316 48.2 13.3	15 27.6	6.8	54.2
11	343 41.4	18.2	331 20.5 13.3	15 20.8	6.8	54.2
12	358 41.3	N22 17.9	345 52.8 13.4	N15 14.0	7.0	54.2
13	13 41.2	17.6	0 25.2 13.4	15 07.0	7.0	54.2
14	28 41.1	17.3	14 57.6 13.4	15 00.0	7.0	54.2
15	43 41.0 ..	17.0	29 30.0 13.4	14 53.0	7.1	54.2
16	58 40.9	16.7	44 02.4 13.5	14 45.9	7.2	54.3
17	73 40.8	16.4	58 34.9 13.5	14 38.7	7.3	54.3
18	88 40.7	N22 16.0	73 07.4 13.5	N14 31.4	7.3	54.3
19	103 40.6	15.7	87 39.9 13.5	14 24.1	7.4	54.3
20	118 40.5	15.4	102 12.4 13.6	14 16.7	7.5	54.3
21	133 40.4 ..	15.1	116 44.9 13.6	14 09.2	7.5	54.3
22	148 40.4	14.8	131 17.5 13.6	14 01.7	7.6	54.3
23	163 40.3	14.5	145 50.1 13.6	13 54.1	7.6	54.3
10 00	178 40.2	N22 14.2	160 22.7 13.7	N13 46.5	7.8	54.3
01	193 40.1	13.8	174 55.4 13.6	13 38.7	7.7	54.4
02	208 40.0	13.5	189 28.0 13.7	13 31.0	7.9	54.4
03	223 39.9 ..	13.2	204 00.7 13.7	13 23.1	7.9	54.4
04	238 39.8	12.9	218 33.4 13.8	13 15.2	7.9	54.4
05	253 39.7	12.6	233 06.2 13.7	13 07.3	8.0	54.4
06	268 39.6	N22 12.3	247 38.9 13.8	N12 59.3	8.1	54.4
07	283 39.6	11.9	262 11.7 13.8	12 51.2	8.1	54.4
08	298 39.5	11.6	276 44.5 13.8	12 43.1	8.2	54.4
09	313 39.4 ..	11.3	291 17.3 13.8	12 34.9	8.3	54.4
10	328 39.3	11.0	305 50.1 13.9	12 26.6	8.3	54.5
11	343 39.2	10.7	320 23.0 13.8	12 18.3	8.3	54.5
12	358 39.1	N22 10.3	334 55.8 13.9	N12 10.0	8.4	54.5
13	13 39.0	10.0	349 28.7 13.9	12 01.6	8.5	54.5
14	28 38.9	09.7	4 01.6 13.9	11 53.1	8.5	54.5
15	43 38.9 ..	09.4	18 34.5 14.0	11 44.6	8.6	54.5
16	58 38.8	09.0	33 07.5 13.9	11 36.0	8.6	54.5
17	73 38.7	08.7	47 40.4 14.0	11 27.4	8.7	54.6
18	88 38.6	N22 08.4	62 13.4 14.0	N11 18.7	8.8	54.6
19	103 38.5	08.1	76 46.4 14.0	11 09.9	8.7	54.6
20	118 38.4	07.7	91 19.4 14.0	11 01.2	8.9	54.6
21	133 38.3 ..	07.4	105 52.4 14.1	10 52.3	8.9	54.6
22	148 38.3	07.1	120 25.5 14.0	10 43.4	8.9	54.6
23	163 38.2	06.7	134 58.5 14.1	10 34.5	9.0	54.6
11 00	178 38.1	N22 06.4	149 31.6 14.1	N10 25.5	9.0	54.6
01	193 38.0	06.1	164 04.7 14.1	10 16.5	9.1	54.7
02	208 37.9	05.7	178 37.8 14.1	10 07.4	9.1	54.7
03	223 37.8 ..	05.4	193 10.9 14.1	9 58.3	9.2	54.7
04	238 37.7	05.1	207 44.0 14.2	9 49.1	9.2	54.7
05	253 37.7	04.7	222 17.2 14.1	9 39.9	9.3	54.7
06	268 37.6	N22 04.4	236 50.3 14.2	N 9 30.6	9.3	54.7
07	283 37.5	04.1	251 23.5 14.2	9 21.3	9.4	54.8
08	298 37.4	03.7	265 56.7 14.2	9 11.9	9.4	54.8
09	313 37.3 ..	03.4	280 29.9 14.1	9 02.5	9.4	54.8
10	328 37.2	03.1	295 03.0 14.3	8 53.1	9.5	54.8
11	343 37.2	02.7	309 36.3 14.2	8 43.6	9.6	54.8
12	358 37.1	N22 02.4	324 09.5 14.2	N 8 34.0	9.5	54.8
13	13 37.0	02.0	338 42.7 14.2	8 24.5	9.6	54.9
14	28 36.9	01.7	353 15.9 14.3	8 14.9	9.7	54.9
15	43 36.8 ..	01.4	7 49.2 14.2	8 05.2	9.7	54.9
16	58 36.8	01.0	22 22.4 14.3	7 55.5	9.7	54.9
17	73 36.7	00.7	36 55.7 14.2	7 45.8	9.8	54.9
18	88 36.6	N22 00.3	51 28.9 14.3	N 7 36.0	9.8	54.9
19	103 36.5	22 00.0	66 02.2 14.3	7 26.2	9.6	54.9
20	118 36.4	21 59.7	80 35.5 14.2	7 16.4	9.9	55.0
21	133 36.3 ..	59.3	95 08.7 14.3	7 06.5	9.9	55.0
22	148 36.3	59.0	109 42.0 14.3	6 56.6	10.0	55.0
23	163 36.2	58.6	124 15.3 14.3	N 6 46.6	10.0	55.0
	SD 15.8	d 0.3	SD 14.8		14.8		14.9

Side labels: TUESDAY, WEDNESDAY, THURSDAY

Lat.	Twilight Naut.	Twilight Civil	Sunrise	Moonrise 9	Moonrise 10	Moonrise 11	Moonrise 12
°	h m	h m	h m	h m	h m	h m	h m
N 72	▭	▭	▭	02 26	04 23	06 11	07 54
N 70	▭	▭	▭	03 10	04 49	06 26	08 02
68	▭	▭	▭	03 39	05 08	06 38	08 08
66	////	////	01 13	04 01	05 24	06 48	08 13
64	////	////	02 02	04 18	05 36	06 56	08 17
62	////	////	02 32	04 33	05 47	07 03	08 21
60	////	01 29	02 55	04 45	05 56	07 09	08 24
N 58	////	02 05	03 13	04 55	06 04	07 15	08 27
56	////	02 30	03 28	05 04	06 11	07 20	08 30
54	01 22	02 49	03 41	05 12	06 17	07 24	08 32
52	01 55	03 06	03 52	05 19	06 22	07 28	08 34
50	02 18	03 19	04 02	05 25	06 27	07 31	08 36
45	02 59	03 47	04 23	05 39	06 36	07 39	08 40
N 40	03 27	04 08	04 40	05 50	06 47	07 45	08 44
35	03 49	04 25	04 54	06 00	06 55	07 50	08 46
30	04 07	04 39	05 07	06 08	07 01	07 55	08 49
20	04 34	05 03	05 27	06 23	07 13	08 03	08 54
N 10	04 56	05 22	05 45	06 35	07 23	08 10	08 58
0	05 13	05 39	06 02	06 47	07 33	08 17	09 01
S 10	05 29	05 56	06 18	06 59	07 42	08 24	09 05
20	05 45	06 12	06 36	07 12	07 52	08 31	09 09
30	06 00	06 30	06 56	07 26	08 04	08 39	09 13
35	06 08	06 39	07 07	07 34	08 10	08 44	09 16
40	06 17	06 50	07 20	07 44	08 18	08 49	09 19
45	06 26	07 03	07 36	07 55	08 26	08 55	09 22
S 50	06 37	07 18	07 55	08 08	08 37	09 02	09 26
52	06 42	07 25	08 04	08 14	08 42	09 06	09 28
54	06 47	07 32	08 15	08 21	08 47	09 09	09 30
56	06 52	07 40	08 26	08 29	08 53	09 13	09 32
58	06 58	07 50	08 40	08 37	08 59	09 18	09 35
S 60	07 05	08 00	08 55	08 47	09 07	09 23	09 37

Lat.	Sunset	Twilight Civil	Twilight Naut.	Moonset 9	Moonset 10	Moonset 11	Moonset 12
°	h m	h m	h m	h m	h m	h m	h m
N 72	▭	▭	▭	22 34	22 19	22 08	21 58
N 70	▭	▭	▭	22 07	22 02	21 58	21 54
68	▭	▭	▭	21 46	21 49	21 50	21 51
66	22 54	////	////	21 30	21 38	21 44	21 48
64	22 07	////	////	21 17	21 29	21 38	21 46
62	21 37	////	////	21 05	21 21	21 33	21 44
60	21 15	22 39	////	20 56	21 14	21 29	21 43
N 58	20 57	22 04	////	20 47	21 07	21 25	21 41
56	20 42	21 40	////	20 40	21 02	21 22	21 40
54	20 29	21 20	22 46	20 33	20 57	21 19	21 39
52	20 18	21 04	22 14	20 27	20 53	21 16	21 37
50	20 08	20 51	21 51	20 22	20 49	21 13	21 36
45	19 47	20 23	21 11	20 10	20 40	21 08	21 34
N 40	19 30	20 02	20 43	20 00	20 33	21 03	21 32
35	19 16	19 45	20 21	19 52	20 26	20 59	21 31
30	19 04	19 31	20 04	19 44	20 21	20 55	21 29
20	18 43	19 08	19 36	19 31	20 11	20 49	21 27
N 10	18 26	18 48	19 15	19 20	20 02	20 44	21 25
0	18 09	18 31	18 57	19 09	19 54	20 38	21 22
S 10	17 53	18 15	18 41	18 59	19 46	20 33	21 20
20	17 35	17 59	18 26	18 47	19 37	20 27	21 18
30	17 15	17 41	18 11	18 34	19 27	20 21	21 15
35	17 04	17 32	18 03	18 26	19 21	20 17	21 14
40	16 51	17 21	17 54	18 17	19 15	20 13	21 12
45	16 35	17 08	17 45	18 07	19 07	20 08	21 10
S 50	16 16	16 53	17 34	17 55	18 58	20 02	21 08
52	16 07	16 46	17 29	17 49	18 53	19 59	21 06
54	15 56	16 39	17 24	17 43	18 49	19 56	21 05
56	15 45	16 31	17 19	17 35	18 43	19 53	21 04
58	15 32	16 21	17 13	17 27	18 37	19 49	21 02
S 60	15 16	16 11	17 06	17 18	18 31	19 45	21 01

Day	SUN Eqn. of Time 00h	SUN Eqn. of Time 12h	SUN Mer. Pass.	MOON Mer. Pass. Upper	MOON Mer. Pass. Lower	Age	Phase
d	m s	m s	h m	h m	h m	d	%
9	05 10	05 15	12 05	12 58	00 35	01	1
10	05 19	05 23	12 05	13 43	01 21	02	5
11	05 27	05 32	12 06	14 28	02 06	03	9

UT	ARIES	VENUS −3.9		MARS +1.6		JUPITER −1.9		SATURN +0.6		STARS		
	GHA	GHA	Dec	GHA	Dec	GHA	Dec	GHA	Dec	Name	SHA	Dec
d h	° ′	° ′	° ′	° ′	° ′	° ′	° ′	° ′	° ′		° ′	° ′
12 00	290 03.3	149 46.4	N17 13.3	201 12.6	N23 56.0	196 07.2	N23 11.5	76 39.7	S10 48.7	Acamar	315 18.5	S40 14.8
01	305 05.7	164 45.8	12.4	216 13.2	56.1	211 09.1	11.5	91 42.2	48.7	Achernar	335 26.8	S57 09.8
02	320 08.2	179 45.3	11.4	231 13.8	56.1	226 10.9	11.5	106 44.6	48.7	Acrux	173 09.3	S63 10.8
03	335 10.7	194 44.7 ..	10.5	246 14.4 ..	56.1	241 12.8 ..	11.5	121 47.1 ..	48.8	Adhara	255 12.8	S28 59.6
04	350 13.1	209 44.2	09.6	261 15.0	56.2	256 14.6	11.5	136 49.5	48.8	Aldebaran	290 49.6	N16 32.0
05	5 15.6	224 43.7	08.6	276 15.6	56.2	271 16.5	11.5	151 52.0	48.8			
06	20 18.1	239 43.1	N17 07.7	291 16.2	N23 56.2	286 18.3	N23 11.5	166 54.4	S10 48.8	Alioth	166 20.8	N55 53.4
07	35 20.5	254 42.6	06.8	306 16.8	56.3	301 20.2	11.5	181 56.9	48.8	Alkaid	152 58.8	N49 15.0
08	50 23.0	269 42.0	05.8	321 17.5	56.3	316 22.0	11.4	196 59.3	48.8	Al Na'ir	27 43.3	S46 53.4
F 09	65 25.5	284 41.5 ..	04.9	336 18.1 ..	56.4	331 23.9 ..	11.4	212 01.8 ..	48.8	Alnilam	275 46.6	S 1 11.7
R 10	80 27.9	299 41.0	04.0	351 18.7	56.4	346 25.8	11.4	227 04.2	48.9	Alphard	217 56.3	S 8 43.2
I 11	95 30.4	314 40.4	03.0	6 19.3	56.4	1 27.6	11.4	242 06.7	48.9			
D 12	110 32.9	329 39.9	N17 02.1	21 19.9	N23 56.5	16 29.5	N23 11.4	257 09.1	S10 48.9	Alphecca	126 10.7	N26 40.4
A 13	125 35.3	344 39.4	01.1	36 20.5	56.5	31 31.3	11.4	272 11.6	48.9	Alpheratz	357 43.3	N29 09.9
Y 14	140 37.8	359 38.8	17 00.2	51 21.1	56.5	46 33.2	11.4	287 14.0	48.9	Altair	62 07.8	N 8 54.5
15	155 40.2	14 38.3	16 59.3	66 21.7 ..	56.6	61 35.0 ..	11.4	302 16.5 ..	48.9	Ankaa	353 15.6	S42 13.6
16	170 42.7	29 37.7	58.3	81 22.3	56.6	76 36.9	11.3	317 18.9	49.0	Antares	112 25.9	S26 27.6
17	185 45.2	44 37.2	57.4	96 22.9	56.6	91 38.7	11.3	332 21.4	49.0			
18	200 47.6	59 36.7	N16 56.4	111 23.5	N23 56.7	106 40.6	N23 11.3	347 23.8	S10 49.0	Arcturus	145 55.6	N19 06.9
19	215 50.1	74 36.1	55.5	126 24.2	56.7	121 42.5	11.3	2 26.3	49.0	Atria	107 27.1	S69 03.1
20	230 52.6	89 35.6	54.5	141 24.8	56.7	136 44.3	11.3	17 28.7	49.0	Avior	234 18.6	S59 33.4
21	245 55.0	104 35.1 ..	53.6	156 25.4 ..	56.8	151 46.2 ..	11.3	32 31.2 ..	49.0	Bellatrix	278 32.2	N 6 21.6
22	260 57.5	119 34.6	52.6	171 26.0	56.8	166 48.0	11.3	47 33.6	49.1	Betelgeuse	271 01.5	N 7 24.4
23	276 00.0	134 34.0	51.7	186 26.6	56.8	181 49.9	11.3	62 36.1	49.1			
13 00	291 02.4	149 33.5	N16 50.7	201 27.2	N23 56.8	196 51.7	N23 11.2	77 38.5	S10 49.1	Canopus	263 56.6	S52 42.2
01	306 04.9	164 33.0	49.8	216 27.8	56.9	211 53.6	11.2	92 41.0	49.1	Capella	280 34.7	N46 00.4
02	321 07.3	179 32.4	48.8	231 28.4	56.9	226 55.4	11.2	107 43.4	49.1	Deneb	49 30.9	N45 19.8
03	336 09.8	194 31.9 ..	47.9	246 29.0 ..	56.9	241 57.3 ..	11.2	122 45.9 ..	49.1	Denebola	182 33.7	N14 29.8
04	351 12.3	209 31.4	46.9	261 29.6	57.0	256 59.2	11.2	137 48.3	49.2	Diphda	348 55.8	S17 54.5
05	6 14.7	224 30.9	46.0	276 30.3	57.0	272 01.0	11.2	152 50.8	49.2			
06	21 17.2	239 30.3	N16 45.0	291 30.9	N23 57.0	287 02.9	N23 11.2	167 53.2	S10 49.2	Dubhe	193 52.1	N61 40.8
07	36 19.7	254 29.8	44.1	306 31.5	57.1	302 04.7	11.2	182 55.7	49.2	Elnath	278 12.9	N28 36.9
S 08	51 22.1	269 29.3	43.1	321 32.1	57.1	317 06.6	11.1	197 58.1	49.2	Eltanin	90 45.6	N51 29.5
A 09	66 24.6	284 28.8 ..	42.2	336 32.7 ..	57.1	332 08.4 ..	11.1	213 00.6 ..	49.3	Enif	33 46.8	N 9 56.4
T 10	81 27.1	299 28.2	41.2	351 33.3	57.1	347 10.3	11.1	228 03.0	49.3	Fomalhaut	15 23.7	S29 32.7
U 11	96 29.5	314 27.7	40.3	6 33.9	57.2	2 12.2	11.1	243 05.5	49.3			
R 12	111 32.0	329 27.2	N16 39.3	21 34.5	N23 57.2	17 14.0	N23 11.1	258 07.9	S10 49.3	Gacrux	172 00.9	S57 11.6
D 13	126 34.5	344 26.7	38.3	36 35.1	57.2	32 15.9	11.1	273 10.4	49.3	Gienah	175 52.3	S17 37.1
A 14	141 36.9	359 26.1	37.4	51 35.7	57.2	47 17.7	11.1	288 12.8	49.3	Hadar	148 47.6	S60 26.5
Y 15	156 39.4	14 25.6 ..	36.4	66 36.4 ..	57.3	62 19.6 ..	11.1	303 15.2 ..	49.4	Hamal	328 00.7	N23 31.5
16	171 41.8	29 25.1	35.5	81 37.0	57.3	77 21.4	11.0	318 17.7	49.4	Kaus Aust.	83 43.3	S34 22.5
17	186 44.3	44 24.6	34.5	96 37.6	57.3	92 23.3	11.0	333 20.1	49.4			
18	201 46.8	59 24.1	N16 33.5	111 38.2	N23 57.3	107 25.1	N23 11.0	348 22.6	S10 49.4	Kochab	137 19.7	N74 06.3
19	216 49.2	74 23.5	32.6	126 38.8	57.4	122 27.0	11.0	3 25.0	49.4	Markab	13 38.1	N15 16.8
20	231 51.7	89 23.0	31.6	141 39.4	57.4	137 28.9	11.0	18 27.5	49.5	Menkar	314 15.1	N 4 08.5
21	246 54.2	104 22.5 ..	30.6	156 40.0 ..	57.4	152 30.7 ..	11.0	33 29.9 ..	49.5	Menkent	148 07.4	S36 26.3
22	261 56.6	119 22.0	29.7	171 40.6	57.4	167 32.6	11.0	48 32.4	49.5	Miaplacidus	221 40.4	S69 46.5
23	276 59.1	134 21.5	28.7	186 41.3	57.4	182 34.4	11.0	63 34.8	49.5			
14 00	292 01.6	149 21.0	N16 27.7	201 41.9	N23 57.5	197 36.3	N23 10.9	78 37.3	S10 49.5	Mirfak	308 40.5	N49 54.3
01	307 04.0	164 20.4	26.8	216 42.5	57.5	212 38.1	10.9	93 39.7	49.5	Nunki	75 57.9	S26 16.6
02	322 06.5	179 19.9	25.8	231 43.1	57.5	227 40.0	10.9	108 42.2	49.6	Peacock	53 18.6	S56 41.2
03	337 09.0	194 19.4 ..	24.8	246 43.7 ..	57.5	242 41.9 ..	10.9	123 44.6 ..	49.6	Pollux	243 28.0	N27 59.5
04	352 11.4	209 18.9	23.9	261 44.3	57.6	257 43.7	10.9	138 47.0	49.6	Procyon	245 00.0	N 5 11.3
05	7 13.9	224 18.4	22.9	276 44.9	57.6	272 45.6	10.9	153 49.5	49.6			
06	22 16.3	239 17.9	N16 21.9	291 45.5	N23 57.6	287 47.4	N23 10.9	168 51.9	S10 49.6	Rasalhague	96 06.1	N12 33.3
07	37 18.8	254 17.4	20.9	306 46.2	57.6	302 49.3	10.8	183 54.4	49.7	Regulus	207 43.7	N11 54.0
08	52 21.3	269 16.8	20.0	321 46.8	57.6	317 51.1	10.8	198 56.8	49.7	Rigel	281 12.3	S 8 11.2
S 09	67 23.7	284 16.3 ..	19.0	336 47.4 ..	57.6	332 53.0 ..	10.8	213 59.3 ..	49.7	Rigil Kent.	139 51.3	S60 53.6
U 10	82 26.2	299 15.8	18.0	351 48.0	57.7	347 54.9	10.8	229 01.7	49.7	Sabik	102 12.2	S15 44.3
N 11	97 28.7	314 15.3	17.1	6 48.6	57.7	2 56.7	10.8	244 04.1	49.7			
D 12	112 31.1	329 14.8	N16 16.1	21 49.2	N23 57.7	17 58.6	N23 10.8	259 06.6	S10 49.8	Schedar	349 40.3	N56 36.5
A 13	127 33.6	344 14.3	15.1	36 49.8	57.7	33 00.4	10.8	274 09.0	49.8	Shaula	96 21.4	S37 06.7
Y 14	142 36.1	359 13.8	14.1	51 50.4	57.7	48 02.3	10.7	289 11.5	49.8	Sirius	258 34.0	S16 44.2
15	157 38.5	14 13.3 ..	13.1	66 51.1 ..	57.8	63 04.2 ..	10.7	304 13.9 ..	49.8	Spica	158 31.2	S11 13.9
16	172 41.0	29 12.8	12.2	81 51.7	57.8	78 06.0	10.7	319 16.4	49.8	Suhail	222 52.8	S43 29.5
17	187 43.4	44 12.3	11.2	96 52.3	57.8	93 07.9	10.7	334 18.8	49.8			
18	202 45.9	59 11.8	N16 10.2	111 52.9	N23 57.8	108 09.7	N23 10.7	349 21.2	S10 49.9	Vega	80 38.5	N38 48.0
19	217 48.4	74 11.3	09.2	126 53.5	57.8	123 11.6	10.7	4 23.7	49.9	Zuben'ubi	137 05.2	S16 05.9
20	232 50.8	89 10.8	08.2	141 54.1	57.8	138 13.4	10.7	19 26.1	49.9		SHA	Mer. Pass.
21	247 53.3	104 10.3 ..	07.3	156 54.7 ..	57.8	153 15.3 ..	10.6	34 28.6 ..	49.9		° ′	h m
22	262 55.8	119 09.7	06.3	171 55.3	57.9	168 17.2	10.6	49 31.0	49.9	Venus	218 31.1	14 02
23	277 58.2	134 09.2	05.3	186 56.0	57.9	183 19.0	10.6	64 33.5	50.0	Mars	270 24.8	10 34
	h m									Jupiter	265 49.3	10 51
Mer. Pass. 4 35.1		v −0.5	d 1.0	v 0.6	d 0.0	v 1.9	d 0.0	v 2.4	d 0.0	Saturn	146 36.1	18 46

UT	SUN		MOON					Lat.	Twilight		Sunrise	Moonrise			
									Naut.	Civil		12	13	14	15
	GHA	Dec	GHA	v	Dec	d	HP		h m	h m	h m	h m	h m	h m	h m
d h	° '	° '	° '	'	° '	'	'	°							
12 00	178 36.1	N21 58.3	138 48.6	14.3	N 6 36.6	10.0	55.1	N 72	▭	▭	▭	07 54	09 37	11 22	13 12
01	193 36.0	57.9	153 21.9	14.3	6 26.6	10.1	55.1	N 70	▭	▭	▭	08 02	09 38	11 16	12 59
02	208 35.9	57.6	167 55.2	14.3	6 16.5	10.0	55.1	68	▭	▭	▭	08 08	09 39	11 11	12 48
03	223 35.9	57.2	182 28.5	14.2	6 06.5	10.2	55.1	66	///	///	01 27	08 13	09 39	11 07	12 39
04	238 35.8	56.9	197 01.7	14.3	5 56.3	10.1	55.1	64	///	///	02 10	08 17	09 40	11 04	12 31
05	253 35.7	56.5	211 35.0	14.3	5 46.2	10.2	55.1	62	///	00 35	02 38	08 21	09 40	11 01	12 25
06	268 35.6	N21 56.2	226 08.3	14.3	N 5 36.0	10.2	55.2	60	///	01 39	03 00	08 24	09 41	10 59	12 19
07	283 35.6	55.8	240 41.6	14.3	5 25.8	10.3	55.2	N 58	////	02 12	03 17	08 27	09 41	10 57	12 14
08	298 35.5	55.5	255 14.9	14.3	5 15.5	10.2	55.2	56	00 30	02 35	03 32	08 30	09 41	10 55	12 10
F 09	313 35.4	55.1	269 48.2	14.2	5 05.3	10.3	55.2	54	01 31	02 54	03 45	08 32	09 42	10 53	12 06
R 10	328 35.3	54.8	284 21.4	14.3	4 55.0	10.4	55.2	52	02 01	03 10	03 56	08 34	09 42	10 51	12 03
I 11	343 35.2	54.4	298 54.7	14.3	4 44.6	10.3	55.3	50	02 23	03 23	04 05	08 36	09 42	10 50	11 59
D 12	358 35.2	N21 54.1	313 28.0	14.3	N 4 34.3	10.4	55.3	45	03 03	03 50	04 26	08 40	09 43	10 47	11 52
A 13	13 35.1	53.7	328 01.3	14.2	4 23.9	10.4	55.3	N 40	03 30	04 10	04 42	08 44	09 43	10 44	11 47
Y 14	28 35.0	53.4	342 34.5	14.3	4 13.5	10.4	55.3	35	03 51	04 27	04 56	08 46	09 44	10 42	11 42
15	43 34.9	53.0	357 07.8	14.2	4 03.1	10.5	55.4	30	04 08	04 41	05 08	08 49	09 44	10 40	11 38
16	58 34.9	52.6	11 41.0	14.2	3 52.6	10.5	55.4	20	04 35	05 04	05 28	08 54	09 44	10 36	11 30
17	73 34.8	52.3	26 14.2	14.3	3 42.1	10.5	55.4	N 10	04 56	05 23	05 46	08 58	'09 45	10 33	11 24
18	88 34.7	N21 51.9	40 47.5	14.2	N 3 31.6	10.5	55.4	0	05 14	05 40	06 02	09 01	09 46	10 31	11 18
19	103 34.6	51.6	55 20.7	14.2	3 21.1	10.5	55.4	S 10	05 30	05 56	06 18	09 05	09 46	10 28	11 12
20	118 34.5	51.2	69 53.9	14.2	3 10.6	10.6	55.5	20	05 44	06 12	06 35	09 09	09 47	10 25	11 05
21	133 34.5	50.8	84 27.1	14.2	3 00.0	10.6	55.5	30	05 59	06 29	06 55	09 13	09 47	10 22	10 58
22	148 34.4	50.5	99 00.3	14.1	2 49.4	10.6	55.5	35	06 07	06 39	07 06	09 16	09 48	10 20	10 54
23	163 34.3	50.1	113 33.4	14.2	2 38.8	10.6	55.5	40	06 16	06 49	07 19	09 19	09 48	10 18	10 50
								45	06 25	07 01	07 34	09 22	09 49	10 16	10 44
13 00	178 34.2	N21 49.8	128 06.6	14.1	N 2 28.2	10.7	55.6	S 50	06 35	07 16	07 53	09 26	09 49	10 13	10 38
01	193 34.2	49.4	142 39.7	14.1	2 17.5	10.6	55.6	52	06 40	07 23	08 02	09 28	09 50	10 11	10 35
02	208 34.1	49.0	157 12.8	14.1	2 06.9	10.7	55.6	54	06 45	07 30	08 12	09 30	09 50	10 10	10 32
03	223 34.0	48.7	171 45.9	14.1	1 56.2	10.7	55.6	56	06 50	07 38	08 23	09 32	09 50	10 09	10 28
04	238 33.9	48.3	186 19.0	14.1	1 45.5	10.7	55.6	58	06 56	07 47	08 36	09 35	09 51	10 07	10 24
05	253 33.9	47.9	200 52.1	14.1	1 34.8	10.8	55.7	S 60	07 02	07 57	08 51	09 37	09 51	10 05	10 20
06	268 33.8	N21 47.6	215 25.2	14.0	N 1 24.0	10.7	55.7								
S 07	283 33.7	47.2	229 58.2	14.0	1 13.3	10.8	55.7	Lat.	Sunset	Twilight		Moonset			
A 08	298 33.7	46.8	244 31.2	14.0	1 02.5	10.7	55.7			Civil	Naut.	12	13	14	15
T 09	313 33.6	46.5	259 04.2	14.0	0 51.8	10.8	55.8	°	h m	h m	h m	h m	h m	h m	h m
U 10	328 33.5	46.1	273 37.2	14.0	0 41.0	10.8	55.8	N 72	▭	▭	▭	21 58	21 48	21 37	21 25
R 11	343 33.4	45.7	288 10.2	13.9	0 30.2	10.8	55.8	N 70	▭	▭	▭	21 54	21 50	21 45	21 41
D 12	358 33.4	N21 45.4	302 43.1	13.9	N 0 19.4	10.8	55.8	68	▭	▭	▭	21 51	21 51	21 52	21 53
A 13	13 33.3	45.0	317 16.0	13.9	N 0 08.6	10.8	55.9	66	22 41	///	///	21 48	21 53	21 58	22 04
Y 14	28 33.2	44.6	331 48.9	13.9	S 0 02.2	10.9	55.9	64	21 59	///	///	21 46	21 54	22 02	22 12
15	43 33.1	44.3	346 21.8	13.8	0 13.1	10.8	55.9	62	21 31	23 29	///	21 44	21 55	22 07	22 20
16	58 33.0	43.9	0 54.6	13.8	0 23.9	10.9	55.9	60	21 10	22 30	///	21 43	21 56	22 10	22 26
17	73 33.0	43.5	15 27.4	13.8	0 34.8	10.8	56.0	N 58	20 53	21 58	////	21 41	21 57	22 13	22 32
18	88 32.9	N21 43.1	30 00.2	13.8	S 0 45.6	10.9	56.0	56	20 39	21 35	23 33	21 40	21 58	22 16	22 37
19	103 32.9	42.8	44 33.0	13.7	0 56.5	10.8	56.0	54	20 26	21 16	22 38	21 39	21 58	22 19	22 42
20	118 32.8	42.4	59 05.7	13.7	1 07.3	10.9	56.0	52	20 15	21 01	22 09	21 37	21 59	22 21	22 46
21	133 32.7	42.0	73 38.4	13.6	1 18.2	10.9	56.1	50	20 05	20 48	21 47	21 36	21 59	22 23	22 50
22	148 32.6	41.6	88 11.0	13.7	1 29.1	10.9	56.1	45	19 45	20 21	21 08	21 34	22 01	22 28	22 58
23	163 32.6	41.3	102 43.7	13.6	1 40.0	10.8	56.1								
14 00	178 32.5	N21 40.9	117 16.3	13.5	S 1 50.8	10.9	56.2	N 40	19 29	20 01	20 41	21 32	22 02	22 32	23 05
01	193 32.4	40.5	131 48.8	13.6	2 01.7	10.9	56.2	35	19 15	19 44	20 20	21 31	22 03	22 36	23 11
02	208 32.4	40.1	146 21.4	13.5	2 12.6	10.9	56.2	30	19 03	19 30	20 03	21 29	22 03	22 39	23 16
03	223 32.3	39.7	160 53.9	13.4	2 23.5	10.9	56.2	20	18 43	19 07	19 36	21 27	22 05	22 44	23 25
04	238 32.2	39.4	175 26.3	13.4	2 34.4	10.8	56.3	N 10	18 26	18 48	19 15	21 25	22 06	22 49	23 33
05	253 32.2	39.0	189 58.8	13.4	2 45.2	10.9	56.3	0	18 09	18 32	18 56	21 22	22 07	22 53	23 41
06	268 32.1	N21 38.6	204 31.2	13.3	S 2 56.1	10.9	56.3	S 10	17 53	18 16	18 42	21 20	22 08	22 57	23 49
07	283 32.0	38.2	219 03.5	13.3	3 07.0	10.8	56.3	20	17 36	18 00	18 27	21 18	22 09	23 02	23 57
08	298 32.0	37.8	233 35.8	13.3	3 17.8	10.9	56.4	30	17 17	17 43	18 12	21 16	22 11	23 07	24 06
S 09	313 31.9	37.4	248 08.1	13.2	3 28.7	10.9	56.4	35	17 06	17 33	18 04	21 14	22 11	23 10	24 11
U 10	328 31.8	37.1	262 40.3	13.2	3 39.6	10.8	56.4	40	16 53	17 23	17 56	21 12	22 12	23 14	24 17
N 11	343 31.8	36.7	277 12.5	13.2	3 50.4	10.8	56.5	45	16 37	17 10	17 47	21 10	22 13	23 18	24 25
D 12	358 31.7	N21 36.3	291 44.7	13.1	S 4 01.2	10.9	56.5	S 50	16 19	16 56	17 37	21 08	22 14	23 23	24 33
A 13	13 31.6	35.9	306 16.8	13.0	4 12.1	10.8	56.5	52	16 10	16 49	17 32	21 06	22 15	23 25	24 37
Y 14	28 31.6	35.5	320 48.8	13.0	4 22.9	10.8	56.5	54	16 00	16 42	17 27	21 05	22 15	23 28	24 41
15	43 31.5	35.1	335 20.8	13.0	4 33.7	10.8	56.6	56	15 49	16 34	17 22	21 04	22 16	23 30	24 46
16	58 31.4	34.7	349 52.8	12.9	4 44.5	10.8	56.6	58	15 36	16 25	17 16	21 02	22 17	23 33	24 52
17	73 31.4	34.4	4 24.7	12.9	4 55.3	10.8	56.6	S 60	15 21	16 15	17 10	21 01	22 18	23 36	24 58
18	88 31.3	N21 34.0	18 56.6	12.8	S 5 06.1	10.8	56.7		SUN			MOON			
19	103 31.2	33.6	33 28.4	12.8	5 16.9	10.7	56.7		Eqn. of Time		Mer.	Mer. Pass.		Age	Phase
20	118 31.2	33.2	48 00.2	12.7	5 27.6	10.7	56.7	Day	00h	12h	Pass.	Upper	Lower		
21	133 31.1	32.8	62 31.9	12.7	5 38.3	10.8	56.8	d	m s	m s	h m	h m	h m	d %	
22	148 31.0	32.4	77 03.6	12.7	5 49.1	10.7	56.8	12	05 35	05 39	12 06	15 12	02 50	04 16	
23	163 31.0	32.0	91 35.3	12.5	S 5 59.8	10.7	56.8	13	05 43	05 46	12 06	15 56	03 34	05 24	
	SD 15.8	d 0.4	SD 15.1		15.2		15.4	14	05 50	05 53	12 06	16 42	04 19	06 33	◗

UT	ARIES GHA	VENUS −3.9 GHA	Dec	MARS +1.6 GHA	Dec	JUPITER −1.9 GHA	Dec	SATURN +0.6 GHA	Dec	STARS Name	SHA	Dec
d h	° ′	° ′	° ′	° ′	° ′	° ′	° ′	° ′	° ′		° ′	° ′
15 00	293 00.7	149 08.7	N16 04.3	201 56.6	N23 57.9	198 20.9	N23 10.6	79 35.9	S10 50.0	Acamar	315 18.5	S40 14.8
01	308 03.2	164 08.2	03.3	216 57.2	57.9	213 22.7	10.6	94 38.3	50.0	Achernar	335 26.8	S57 09.8
02	323 05.6	179 07.7	02.3	231 57.8	57.9	228 24.6	10.6	109 40.8	50.0	Acrux	173 09.3	S63 10.8
03	338 08.1	194 07.2 ..	01.4	246 58.4 ..	57.9	243 26.5 ..	10.6	124 43.2 ..	50.0	Adhara	255 12.8	S28 59.5
04	353 10.6	209 06.7	16 00.4	261 59.0	57.9	258 28.3	10.5	139 45.7	50.1	Aldebaran	290 49.5	N16 32.0
05	8 13.0	224 06.2	15 59.4	276 59.6	57.9	273 30.2	10.5	154 48.1	50.1			
06	23 15.5	239 05.7	N15 58.4	292 00.3	N23 58.0	288 32.0	N23 10.5	169 50.5	S10 50.1	Alioth	166 20.8	N55 53.4
07	38 17.9	254 05.2	57.4	307 00.9	58.0	303 33.9	10.5	184 53.0	50.1	Alkaid	152 58.8	N49 15.0
08	53 20.4	269 04.7	56.4	322 01.5	58.0	318 35.8	10.5	199 55.4	50.1	Al Na'ir	27 43.3	S46 53.4
M 09	68 22.9	284 04.2 ..	55.4	337 02.1 ..	58.0	333 37.6 ..	10.5	214 57.9 ..	50.2	Alnilam	275 46.6	S 1 11.7
O 10	83 25.3	299 03.7	54.4	352 02.7	58.0	348 39.5	10.5	230 00.3	50.2	Alphard	217 56.3	S 8 43.2
N 11	98 27.8	314 03.3	53.4	7 03.3	58.0	3 41.3	10.4	245 02.7	50.2			
D 12	113 30.3	329 02.8	N15 52.4	22 04.0	N23 58.0	18 43.2	N23 10.4	260 05.2	S10 50.2	Alphecca	126 10.8	N26 40.4
A 13	128 32.7	344 02.3	51.4	37 04.6	58.0	33 45.0	10.4	275 07.6	50.2	Alpheratz	357 43.3	N29 09.9
Y 14	143 35.2	359 01.8	50.4	52 05.2	58.0	48 46.9	10.4	290 10.1	50.3	Altair	62 07.8	N 8 54.5
15	158 37.7	14 01.3 ..	49.5	67 05.8 ..	58.0	63 48.8 ..	10.4	305 12.5 ..	50.3	Ankaa	353 15.5	S42 13.6
16	173 40.1	29 00.8	48.5	82 06.4	58.0	78 50.6	10.4	320 14.9	50.3	Antares	112 25.9	S26 27.6
17	188 42.6	44 00.3	47.5	97 07.0	58.0	93 52.5	10.4	335 17.4	50.3			
18	203 45.1	58 59.8	N15 46.5	112 07.6	N23 58.1	108 54.3	N23 10.3	350 19.8	S10 50.4	Arcturus	145 55.6	N19 06.9
19	218 47.5	73 59.3	45.5	127 08.3	58.1	123 56.2	10.3	5 22.2	50.4	Atria	107 27.2	S69 03.1
20	233 50.0	88 58.8	44.5	142 08.9	58.1	138 58.1	10.3	20 24.7	50.4	Avior	234 18.6	S59 33.4
21	248 52.4	103 58.3 ..	43.5	157 09.5 ..	58.1	153 59.9 ..	10.3	35 27.1 ..	50.4	Bellatrix	278 32.2	N 6 21.6
22	263 54.9	118 57.8	42.5	172 10.1	58.1	169 01.8	10.3	50 29.6	50.4	Betelgeuse	271 01.5	N 7 24.4
23	278 57.4	133 57.3	41.5	187 10.7	58.1	184 03.6	10.3	65 32.0	50.5			
16 00	293 59.8	148 56.9	N15 40.5	202 11.3	N23 58.1	199 05.5	N23 10.2	80 34.4	S10 50.5	Canopus	263 56.6	S52 42.2
01	309 02.3	163 56.4	39.5	217 12.0	58.1	214 07.4	10.2	95 36.9	50.5	Capella	280 34.7	N46 00.4
02	324 04.8	178 55.9	38.5	232 12.6	58.1	229 09.2	10.2	110 39.3	50.5	Deneb	49 30.9	N45 19.9
03	339 07.2	193 55.4 ..	37.5	247 13.2 ..	58.1	244 11.1 ..	10.2	125 41.7 ..	50.5	Denebola	182 33.7	N14 29.8
04	354 09.7	208 54.9	36.5	262 13.8	58.1	259 12.9	10.2	140 44.2	50.6	Diphda	348 55.8	S17 54.5
05	9 12.2	223 54.4	35.4	277 14.4	58.1	274 14.8	10.2	155 46.6	50.6			
06	24 14.6	238 53.9	N15 34.4	292 15.0	N23 58.1	289 16.7	N23 10.2	170 49.1	S10 50.6	Dubhe	193 52.1	N61 40.8
07	39 17.1	253 53.4	33.4	307 15.7	58.1	304 18.5	10.1	185 51.5	50.6	Elnath	278 12.8	N28 36.9
T 08	54 19.5	268 53.0	32.4	322 16.3	58.1	319 20.4	10.1	200 53.9	50.6	Eltanin	90 45.6	N51 29.5
U 09	69 22.0	283 52.5 ..	31.4	337 16.9 ..	58.1	334 22.2 ..	10.1	215 56.4 ..	50.7	Enif	33 46.8	N 9 56.4
E 10	84 24.5	298 52.0	30.4	352 17.5	58.1	349 24.1	10.1	230 58.8	50.7	Fomalhaut	15 23.7	S29 32.7
S 11	99 26.9	313 51.5	29.4	7 18.1	58.1	4 26.0	10.1	246 01.2	50.7			
D 12	114 29.4	328 51.0	N15 28.4	22 18.7	N23 58.1	19 27.8	N23 10.1	261 03.7	S10 50.7	Gacrux	172 00.9	S57 11.6
A 13	129 31.9	343 50.6	27.4	37 19.4	58.1	34 29.7	10.0	276 06.1	50.8	Gienah	175 52.3	S17 37.1
Y 14	144 34.3	358 50.1	26.4	52 20.0	58.1	49 31.6	10.0	291 08.5	50.8	Hadar	148 47.6	S60 26.5
15	159 36.8	13 49.6 ..	25.4	67 20.6 ..	58.1	64 33.4 ..	10.0	306 11.0 ..	50.8	Hamal	328 00.7	N23 31.5
16	174 39.3	28 49.1	24.3	82 21.2	58.1	79 35.3	10.0	321 13.4	50.8	Kaus Aust.	83 43.3	S34 22.5
17	189 41.7	43 48.6	23.3	97 21.8	58.1	94 37.1	10.0	336 15.8	50.8			
18	204 44.2	58 48.2	N15 22.3	112 22.5	N23 58.1	109 39.0	N23 10.0	351 18.3	S10 50.9	Kochab	137 .19.7	N74 06.3
19	219 46.7	73 47.7	21.3	127 23.1	58.1	124 40.9	10.0	6 20.7	50.9	Markab	13 38.0	N15 16.8
20	234 49.1	88 47.2	20.3	142 23.7	58.1	139 42.7	09.9	21 23.1	50.9	Menkar	314 15.1	N 4 08.5
21	249 51.6	103 46.7 ..	19.3	157 24.3 ..	58.1	154 44.6 ..	09.9	36 25.6 ..	50.9	Menkent	148 07.4	S36 26.3
22	264 54.0	118 46.2	18.3	172 24.9	58.1	169 46.4	09.9	51 28.0	51.0	Miaplacidus	221 40.4	S69 46.6
23	279 56.5	133 45.8	17.2	187 25.5	58.1	184 48.3	09.9	66 30.4	51.0			
17 00	294 59.0	148 45.3	N15 16.2	202 26.2	N23 58.1	199 50.2	N23 09.9	81 32.9	S10 51.0	Mirfak	308 40.4	N49 54.3
01	310 01.4	163 44.8	15.2	217 26.8	58.1	214 52.0	09.9	96 35.3	51.0	Nunki	75 57.9	S26 16.6
02	325 03.9	178 44.3	14.2	232 27.4	58.1	229 53.9	09.8	111 37.7	51.0	Peacock	53 18.6	S56 41.2
03	340 06.4	193 43.9 ..	13.2	247 28.0 ..	58.1	244 55.8 ..	09.8	126 40.2 ..	51.1	Pollux	243 28.0	N27 59.5
04	355 08.8	208 43.4	12.1	262 28.6	58.1	259 57.6	09.8	141 42.6	51.1	Procyon	245 00.0	N 5 11.3
05	10 11.3	223 42.9	11.1	277 29.3	58.1	274 59.5	09.8	156 45.0	51.1			
06	25 13.8	238 42.5	N15 10.1	292 29.9	N23 58.0	290 01.3	N23 09.8	171 47.5	S10 51.1	Rasalhague	96 06.1	N12 33.3
W 07	40 16.2	253 42.0	09.1	307 30.5	58.0	305 03.2	09.8	186 49.9	51.2	Regulus	207 43.7	N11 54.0
E 08	55 18.7	268 41.5	08.0	322 31.1	58.0	320 05.1	09.7	201 52.3	51.2	Rigel	281 12.3	S 8 11.2
D 09	70 21.2	283 41.0 ..	07.0	337 31.7 ..	58.0	335 06.9 ..	09.7	216 54.8 ..	51.2	Rigil Kent.	139 51.4	S60 53.6
N 10	85 23.6	298 40.6	06.0	352 32.4	58.0	350 08.8	09.7	231 57.2	51.2	Sabik	102 12.2	S15 44.3
E 11	100 26.1	313 40.1	05.0	7 33.0	58.0	5 10.6	09.7	246 59.6	51.3			
S 12	115 28.5	328 39.6	N15 03.9	22 33.6	N23 58.0	20 12.5	N23 09.7	262 02.1	S10 51.3	Schedar	349 40.2	N56 36.5
D 13	130 31.0	343 39.2	02.9	37 34.2	58.0	35 14.4	09.7	277 04.5	51.3	Shaula	96 21.4	S37 06.7
A 14	145 33.5	358 38.7	01.9	52 34.8	58.0	50 16.2	09.6	292 06.9	51.3	Sirius	258 34.0	S16 44.2
Y 15	160 35.9	13 38.2	15 00.9	67 35.5 ..	58.0	65 18.1 ..	09.6	307 09.4 ..	51.3	Spica	158 31.2	S11 13.9
16	175 38.4	28 37.8	14 59.8	82 36.1	58.0	80 20.0	09.6	322 11.8	51.4	Suhail	222 52.8	S43 29.5
17	190 40.9	43 37.3	58.8	97 36.7	57.9	95 21.8	09.6	337 14.2	51.4			
18	205 43.3	58 36.8	N14 57.8	112 37.3	N23 57.9	110 23.7	N23 09.6	352 16.7	S10 51.4	Vega	80 38.5	N38 48.0
19	220 45.8	73 36.4	56.7	127 37.9	57.9	125 25.6	09.6	7 19.1	51.4	Zuben'ubi	137 05.2	S16 05.9
20	235 48.3	88 35.9	55.7	142 38.6	57.9	140 27.4	09.5	22 21.5	51.5		SHA	Mer.Pass.
21	250 50.7	103 35.4 ..	54.7	157 39.2 ..	57.9	155 29.3 ..	09.5	37 23.9 ..	51.5		° ′	h m
22	265 53.2	118 35.0	53.6	172 39.8	57.9	170 31.1	09.5	52 26.4	51.5	Venus	214 57.0	14 05
23	280 55.6	133 34.5	52.6	187 40.4	57.9	185 33.0	09.5	67 28.8	51.5	Mars	268 11.5	10 31
	h m									Jupiter	265 05.7	10 42
Mer.Pass. 4 23.3		v −0.5 d 1.0		v 0.6 d 0.0		v 1.9 d 0.0		v 2.4 d 0.0		Saturn	146 34.6	18 35

UT	SUN		MOON				Lat.	Twilight		Sunrise	Moonrise			
								Naut.	Civil		15	16	17	18
	GHA	Dec	GHA	v	Dec	d	HP							
d h	° ′	° ′	° ′	′	° ′	′	′	°	h m	h m	h m	h m	h m	h m	h m
15 00	178 30.9	N21 31.6	106 06.8	12.5	S 6 10.5	10.6	56.8	N 72	▭	▭	▭	13 12	15 12	17 34	■
01	193 30.8	31.2	120 38.3	12.5	6 21.1	10.7	56.9	N 70	▭	▭	▭	12 59	14 47	16 44	18 53
02	208 30.8	30.8	135 09.8	12.4	6 31.8	10.6	56.9	68	▭	▭	▭	12 48	14 28	16 13	17 59
03	223 30.7 ..	30.4	149 41.2	12.4	6 42.4	10.6	56.9	66	////	////	01 40	12 39	14 13	15 51	17 26
04	238 30.6	30.0	164 12.6	12.3	6 53.0	10.6	57.0	64	////	////	02 19	12 31	14 01	15 33	17 02
05	253 30.6	29.6	178 43.9	12.2	7 03.6	10.6	57.0	62	////	00 58	02 45	12 25	13 51	15 18	16 43
06	268 30.5	N21 29.3	193 15.1	12.2	S 7 14.2	10.5	57.0	60	////	01 49	03 06	12 19	13 42	15 06	16 27
07	283 30.5	28.9	207 46.3	12.1	7 24.7	10.5	57.1	N 58	////	02 19	03 22	12 14	13 34	14 55	16 13
08	298 30.4	28.5	222 17.4	12.1	7 35.2	10.5	57.1	56	00 53	02 41	03 36	12 10	13 27	14 46	16 03
M 09	313 30.3 ..	28.1	236 48.5	12.0	7 45.7	10.4	57.1	54	01 40	02 59	03 49	12 06	13 21	14 38	15 53
O 10	328 30.3	27.7	251 19.5	11.9	7 56.1	10.5	57.2	52	02 07	03 14	03 59	12 03	13 16	14 30	15 44
N 11	343 30.2	27.3	265 50.4	11.9	8 06.6	10.4	57.2	50	02 28	03 27	04 09	11 59	13 11	14 24	15 36
D 12	358 30.1	N21 26.9	280 21.3	11.8	S 8 17.0	10.4	57.2	45	03 06	03 53	04 29	11 52	13 00	14 10	15 19
A 13	13 30.1	26.5	294 52.1	11.8	8 27.4	10.3	57.3	N 40	03 33	04 13	04 45	11 47	12 52	13 58	15 05
Y 14	28 30.0	26.1	309 22.9	11.7	8 37.7	10.3	57.3	35	03 54	04 29	04 58	11 42	12 44	13 48	14 54
15	43 30.0 ..	25.7	323 53.6	11.6	8 48.0	10.3	57.3	30	04 10	04 43	05 10	11 38	12 38	13 40	14 44
16	58 29.9	25.3	338 24.2	11.6	8 58.3	10.2	57.4	20	04 37	05 05	05 30	11 30	12 26	13 25	14 26
17	73 29.8	24.8	352 54.8	11.5	9 08.5	10.2	57.4	N 10	04 57	05 24	05 47	11 24	12 16	13 12	14 11
18	88 29.8	N21 24.4	7 25.3	11.4	S 9 18.7	10.2	57.4	0	05 14	05 40	06 02	11 18	12 07	13 00	13 57
19	103 29.7	24.0	21 55.7	11.3	9 28.9	10.1	57.5	S 10	05 30	05 56	06 18	11 12	11 58	12 49	13 43
20	118 29.7	23.6	36 26.0	11.3	9 39.0	10.1	57.5	20	05 44	06 11	06 35	11 05	11 49	12 36	13 28
21	133 29.6 ..	23.2	50 56.3	11.2	9 49.1	10.1	57.5	30	05 59	06 28	06 54	10 58	11 38	12 22	13 11
22	148 29.5	22.8	65 26.5	11.2	9 59.2	10.0	57.6	35	06 06	06 37	07 05	10 54	11 31	12 13	13 01
23	163 29.5	22.4	79 56.7	11.0	10 09.2	10.0	57.6	40	06 14	06 48	07 18	10 50	11 24	12 04	12 50
16 00	178 29.4	N21 22.0	94 26.7	11.0	S10 19.2	9.9	57.6	45	06 23	07 00	07 32	10 44	11 16	11 53	12 37
01	193 29.4	21.6	108 56.7	11.0	10 29.1	9.9	57.7	S 50	06 33	07 14	07 51	10 38	11 06	11 40	12 21
02	208 29.3	21.2	123 26.7	10.8	10 39.0	9.9	57.7	52	06 38	07 20	07 59	10 35	11 02	11 34	12 13
03	223 29.2 ..	20.8	137 56.5	10.8	10 48.9	9.8	57.7	54	06 42	07 27	08 09	10 32	10 57	11 27	12 05
04	238 29.2	20.4	152 26.3	10.7	10 58.7	9.7	57.8	56	06 47	07 35	08 20	10 28	10 51	11 19	11 56
05	253 29.1	20.0	166 56.0	10.6	11 08.4	9.7	57.8	58	06 53	07 44	08 32	10 24	10 45	11 11	11 45
06	268 29.1	N21 19.5	181 25.6	10.6	S11 18.1	9.7	57.8	S 60	06 59	07 53	08 47	10 20	10 38	11 01	11 33
07	283 29.0	19.1	195 55.2	10.5	11 27.8	9.6	57.9								
T 08	298 29.0	18.7	210 24.7	10.4	11 37.4	9.5	57.9	Lat.	Sunset	Twilight		Moonset			
U 09	313 28.9 ..	18.3	224 54.1	10.3	11 46.9	9.5	57.9			Civil	Naut.	15	16	17	18
E 10	328 28.8	17.9	239 23.4	10.2	11 56.4	9.5	57.9								
S 11	343 28.8	17.5	253 52.6	10.2	12 05.9	9.4	58.0	°	h m	h m	h m	h m	h m	h m	h m
D 12	358 28.7	N21 17.1	268 21.8	10.1	S12 15.3	9.3	58.0	N 72	▭	▭	▭	21 25	21 09	20 40	■
A 13	13 28.7	16.6	282 50.9	10.0	12 24.6	9.3	58.1	N 70	▭	▭	▭	21 41	21 36	21 30	21 22
Y 14	28 28.6	16.2	297 19.9	9.9	12 33.9	9.2	58.1	68	▭	▭	▭	21 53	21 56	22 02	22 17
15	43 28.6 ..	15.8	311 48.8	9.9	12 43.1	9.2	58.1	66	22 28	////	////	22 04	22 12	22 26	22 50
16	58 28.5	15.4	326 17.7	9.7	12 52.3	9.1	58.2	64	21 51	////	////	22 12	22 26	22 45	23 14
17	73 28.5	15.0	340 46.4	9.7	13 01.4	9.0	58.2	62	21 25	23 08	////	22 20	22 37	23 00	23 34
18	88 28.4	N21 14.6	355 15.1	9.6	S13 10.4	9.0	58.2	60	21 05	22 21	////	22 26	22 46	23 13	23 50
19	103 28.3	14.1	9 43.7	9.5	13 19.4	8.9	58.3	N 58	20 49	21 52	////	22 32	22 55	23 24	24 03
20	118 28.3	13.7	24 12.2	9.4	13 28.3	8.9	58.3	56	20 35	21 30	23 14	22 37	23 02	23 34	24 15
21	133 28.2 ..	13.3	38 40.6	9.4	13 37.2	8.8	58.4	54	20 23	21 12	22 30	22 42	23 09	23 42	24 25
22	148 28.2	12.9	53 09.0	9.3	13 46.0	8.7	58.4	52	20 12	20 57	22 03	22 46	23 15	23 50	24 34
23	163 28.1	12.4	67 37.3	9.1	13 54.7	8.6	58.4	50	20 03	20 44	21 42	22 50	23 20	23 57	24 42
17 00	178 28.1	N21 12.0	82 06.4	9.1	S14 03.3	8.6	58.5	45	19 43	20 19	21 05	22 58	23 32	24 12	00 12
01	193 28.0	11.6	96 33.5	9.0	14 11.9	8.5	58.5	N 40	19 27	19 59	20 39	23 05	23 43	24 34	00 34
02	208 28.0	11.2	111 01.5	8.9	14 20.4	8.5	58.5	35	19 14	19 43	20 18	23 11	23 50	24 45	00 45
03	223 27.9 ..	10.7	125 29.4	8.9	14 28.9	8.3	58.6	30	19 02	19 29	20 01	23 16	23 58	24 44	00 44
04	238 27.9	10.3	139 57.3	8.7	14 37.2	8.3	58.6	20	18 42	19 07	19 35	23 25	24 10	00 10	01 00
05	253 27.8	09.9	154 25.0	8.7	14 45.5	8.2	58.6	N 10	18 25	18 48	19 15	23 33	24 22	00 22	01 24
06	268 27.8	N21 09.5	168 52.7	8.6	S14 53.7	8.1	58.7	0	18 10	18 32	18 58	23 41	24 32	00 32	01 27
W 07	283 27.7	09.0	183 20.3	8.4	15 01.8	8.1	58.7	S 10	17 54	18 17	18 42	23 49	24 43	00 43	01 40
E 08	298 27.7	08.6	197 47.7	8.4	15 09.9	8.0	58.7	20	17 37	18 01	18 28	23 57	24 54	00 54	01 54
D 09	313 27.6 ..	08.2	212 15.1	8.4	15 17.9	7.9	58.8	30	17 18	17 44	18 14	24 06	00 06	01 07	02 10
N 10	328 27.6	07.8	226 42.5	8.2	15 25.8	7.8	58.8	35	17 07	17 35	18 06	24 11	00 11	01 14	02 19
E 11	343 27.5	07.3	241 09.7	8.1	15 33.6	7.7	58.8	40	16 55	17 25	17 58	24 17	00 17	01 23	02 30
S 12	358 27.5	N21 06.9	255 36.8	8.1	S15 41.3	7.6	58.9	45	16 40	17 13	17 49	24 25	00 25	01 33	02 43
D 13	13 27.4	06.5	270 03.9	7.9	15 48.9	7.6	58.9	S 50	16 22	16 59	17 39	24 33	00 33	01 45	02 58
A 14	28 27.4	06.0	284 30.8	7.9	15 56.5	7.4	58.9	52	16 13	16 53	17 35	24 37	00 37	01 51	03 05
Y 15	43 27.3 ..	05.6	298 57.7	7.8	16 03.9	7.4	59.0	54	16 04	16 46	17 30	24 41	00 41	01 57	03 13
16	58 27.3	05.2	313 24.5	7.7	16 11.3	7.3	59.0	56	15 53	16 38	17 25	24 46	00 46	02 04	03 22
17	73 27.2	04.7	327 51.2	7.6	16 18.6	7.2	59.0	58	15 41	16 29	17 20	24 52	00 52	02 12	03 32
18	88 27.2	N21 04.3	342 17.8	7.5	S16 25.8	7.1	59.1	S 60	15 26	16 19	17 14	24 58	00 58	02 21	03 44
19	103 27.1	03.9	356 44.3	7.5	16 32.9	7.0	59.1								
20	118 27.1	03.4	11 10.8	7.3	16 39.9	6.9	59.2		SUN			MOON			
21	133 27.0 ..	03.0	25 37.1	7.3	16 46.8	6.8	59.2	Day	Eqn. of Time		Mer.	Mer. Pass.		Age	Phase
22	148 27.0	02.6	40 03.4	7.2	16 53.6	6.7	59.2		00ʰ	12ʰ	Pass.	Upper	Lower		
23	163 26.9	02.1	54 29.6	7.1	S17 00.3	6.7	59.3	d	m s	m s	h m	h m	h m	d %	
								15	05 56	05 59	12 06	17 29	05 05	07 43	
	SD 15.8	d 0.4	SD 15.6		15.8		16.0	16	06 02	06 05	12 06	18 20	05 54	08 54	◑
								17	06 08	06 10	12 06	19 14	06 46	09 65	

UT	ARIES GHA	VENUS −3.9 GHA	Dec	MARS +1.6 GHA	Dec	JUPITER −1.9 GHA	Dec	SATURN +0.6 GHA	Dec	STARS Name	SHA	Dec
18 00	295 58.1	148 34.0	N14 51.6	202 41.0	N23 57.9	200 34.9	N23 09.5	82 31.2	S10 51.6	Acamar	315 18.4	S40 14.8
01	311 00.6	163 33.6	50.5	217 41.7	57.9	215 36.7	09.5	97 33.7	51.6	Achernar	335 26.8	S57 09.8
02	326 03.0	178 33.1	49.5	232 42.3	57.8	230 38.6	09.4	112 36.1	51.6	Acrux	173 09.3	S63 10.8
03	341 05.5	193 32.7 ..	48.5	247 42.9 ..	57.8	245 40.5 ..	09.4	127 38.5 ..	51.6	Adhara	255 12.8	S28 59.5
04	356 08.0	208 32.2	47.4	262 43.5	57.8	260 42.3	09.4	142 40.9	51.7	Aldebaran	290 49.5	N16 32.0
05	11 10.4	223 31.7	46.4	277 44.2	57.8	275 44.2	09.4	157 43.4	51.7			
06	26 12.9	238 31.3	N14 45.4	292 44.8	N23 57.8	290 46.0	N23 09.4	172 45.8	S10 51.7	Alioth	166 20.8	N55 53.4
07	41 15.4	253 30.8	44.3	307 45.4	57.8	305 47.9	09.4	187 48.2	51.7	Alkaid	152 58.9	N49 15.0
T 08	56 17.8	268 30.4	43.3	322 46.0	57.7	320 49.8	09.3	202 50.7	51.8	Al Na'ir	27 43.3	S46 53.4
H 09	71 20.3	283 29.9 ..	42.2	337 46.6 ..	57.7	335 51.6 ..	09.3	217 53.1 ..	51.8	Alnilam	275 46.6	S 1 11.7
U 10	86 22.8	298 29.5	41.2	352 47.3	57.7	350 53.5	09.3	232 55.5	51.8	Alphard	217 56.3	S 8 43.2
R 11	101 25.2	313 29.0	40.2	7 47.9	57.7	5 55.4	09.3	247 57.9	51.8			
S 12	116 27.7	328 28.5	N14 39.1	22 48.5	N23 57.7	20 57.2	N23 09.3	263 00.4	S10 51.9	Alphecca	126 10.8	N26 40.4
D 13	131 30.1	343 28.1	38.1	37 49.1	57.7	35 59.1	09.2	278 02.8	51.9	Alpheratz	357 43.2	N29 09.9
A 14	146 32.6	358 27.6	37.0	52 49.7	57.6	51 01.0	09.2	293 05.2	51.9	Altair	62 07.8	N 8 54.5
Y 15	161 35.1	13 27.2 ..	36.0	67 50.4 ..	57.6	66 02.8 ..	09.2	308 07.7 ..	51.9	Ankaa	353 15.5	S42 13.6
16	176 37.5	28 26.7	34.9	82 51.0	57.6	81 04.7	09.2	323 10.1	51.9	Antares	112 25.9	S26 27.6
17	191 40.0	43 26.3	33.9	97 51.6	57.6	96 06.6	09.2	338 12.5	51.9			
18	206 42.5	58 25.8	N14 32.9	112 52.2	N23 57.6	111 08.4	N23 09.2	353 14.9	S10 52.0	Arcturus	145 55.6	N19 06.9
19	221 44.9	73 25.4	31.8	127 52.9	57.5	126 10.3	09.1	8 17.4	52.0	Atria	107 27.2	S69 03.1
20	236 47.4	88 24.9	30.8	142 53.5	57.5	141 12.1	09.1	23 19.8	52.0	Avior	234 18.5	S59 33.4
21	251 49.9	103 24.5 ..	29.7	157 54.1 ..	57.5	156 14.0 ..	09.1	38 22.2 ..	52.1	Bellatrix	278 32.2	N 6 21.6
22	266 52.3	118 24.0	28.7	172 54.7	57.5	171 15.9	09.1	53 24.6	52.1	Betelgeuse	271 01.5	N 7 24.4
23	281 54.8	133 23.6	27.6	187 55.4	57.5	186 17.7	09.1	68 27.1	52.1			
19 00	296 57.3	148 23.1	N14 26.6	202 56.0	N23 57.4	201 19.6	N23 09.1	83 29.5	S10 52.1	Canopus	263 56.6	S52 42.2
01	311 59.7	163 22.7	25.5	217 56.6	57.4	216 21.5	09.0	98 31.9	52.1	Capella	280 34.7	N46 00.4
02	327 02.2	178 22.2	24.5	232 57.2	57.4	231 23.3	09.0	113 34.3	52.2	Deneb	49 30.9	N45 19.9
03	342 04.6	193 21.8 ..	23.4	247 57.9 ..	57.4	246 25.2 ..	09.0	128 36.8 ..	52.2	Denebola	182 33.7	N14 29.8
04	357 07.1	208 21.3	22.4	262 58.5	57.4	261 27.1	09.0	143 39.2	52.2	Diphda	348 55.7	S17 54.5
05	12 09.6	223 20.9	21.3	277 59.1	57.3	276 28.9	09.0	158 41.6	52.3			
06	27 12.0	238 20.4	N14 20.2	292 59.7	N23 57.3	291 30.8	N23 08.9	173 44.0	S10 52.3	Dubhe	193 52.1	N61 40.8
07	42 14.5	253 20.0	19.2	308 00.3	57.3	306 32.7	08.9	188 46.5	52.3	Elnath	278 12.8	N28 36.9
F 08	57 17.0	268 19.5	18.1	323 01.0	57.3	321 34.5	08.9	203 48.9	52.4	Eltanin	90 45.6	N51 29.5
R 09	72 19.4	283 19.1 ..	17.1	338 01.6 ..	57.2	336 36.4 ..	08.9	218 51.3 ..	52.4	Enif	33 46.7	N 9 56.4
I 10	87 21.9	298 18.7	16.0	353 02.2	57.2	351 38.3	08.9	233 53.7	52.4	Fomalhaut	15 23.7	S29 32.7
D 11	102 24.4	313 18.2	15.0	8 02.8	57.2	6 40.1	08.9	248 56.2	52.4			
A 12	117 26.8	328 17.8	N14 13.9	23 03.5	N23 57.2	21 42.0	N23 08.8	263 58.6	S10 52.5	Gacrux	172 00.9	S57 11.6
Y 13	132 29.3	343 17.3	12.9	38 04.1	57.1	36 43.9	08.8	279 01.0	52.5	Gienah	175 52.3	S17 37.1
14	147 31.8	358 16.9	11.8	53 04.7	57.1	51 45.7	08.8	294 03.4	52.5	Hadar	148 47.6	S60 26.5
15	162 34.2	13 16.4 ..	10.7	68 05.3 ..	57.1	66 47.6 ..	08.8	309 05.9 ..	52.5	Hamal	328 00.7	N23 31.5
16	177 36.7	28 16.0	09.7	83 06.0	57.0	81 49.5	08.8	324 08.3	52.6	Kaus Aust.	83 43.3	S34 22.5
17	192 39.1	43 15.6	08.6	98 06.6	57.0	96 51.3	08.7	339 10.7	52.6			
18	207 41.6	58 15.1	N14 07.6	113 07.2	N23 57.0	111 53.2	N23 08.7	354 13.1	S10 52.6	Kochab	137 19.8	N74 06.3
19	222 44.1	73 14.7	06.5	128 07.9	57.0	126 55.1	08.7	9 15.5	52.6	Markab	13 38.0	N15 16.8
20	237 46.5	88 14.2	05.4	143 08.5	56.9	141 56.9	08.7	24 18.0	52.7	Menkar	314 15.1	N 4 08.5
21	252 49.0	103 13.8 ..	04.4	158 09.1 ..	56.9	156 58.8 ..	08.7	39 20.4 ..	52.7	Menkent	148 07.4	S36 26.3
22	267 51.5	118 13.4	03.3	173 09.7	56.9	172 00.7	08.7	54 22.8	52.7	Miaplacidus	221 40.4	S69 46.6
23	282 53.9	133 12.9	02.2	188 10.4	56.8	187 02.5	08.6	69 25.2	52.7			
20 00	297 56.4	148 12.5	N14 01.2	203 11.0	N23 56.8	202 04.4	N23 08.6	84 27.7	S10 52.8	Mirfak	308 40.4	N49 54.3
01	312 58.9	163 12.1	14 00.1	218 11.6	56.8	217 06.3	08.6	99 30.1	52.8	Nunki	75 57.8	S26 16.6
02	328 01.3	178 11.6	13 59.1	233 12.2	56.8	232 08.1	08.6	114 32.5	52.8	Peacock	53 18.6	S56 41.2
03	343 03.8	193 11.2 ..	58.0	248 12.9 ..	56.7	247 10.0 ..	08.6	129 34.9 ..	52.9	Pollux	243 28.0	N27 59.5
04	358 06.3	208 10.8	56.9	263 13.5	56.7	262 11.9	08.5	144 37.3	52.9	Procyon	245 00.0	N 5 11.3
05	13 08.7	223 10.3	55.9	278 14.1	56.7	277 13.7	08.5	159 39.8	52.9			
06	28 11.2	238 09.9	N13 54.8	293 14.7	N23 56.6	292 15.6	N23 08.5	174 42.2	S10 52.9	Rasalhague	96 06.1	N12 33.3
07	43 13.6	253 09.5	53.7	308 15.4	56.6	307 17.5	08.5	189 44.6	53.0	Regulus	207 43.7	N11 54.0
S 08	58 16.1	268 09.0	52.6	323 16.0	56.6	322 19.3	08.5	204 47.0	53.0	Rigel	281 12.2	S 8 11.2
A 09	73 18.6	283 08.6 ..	51.6	338 16.6 ..	56.5	337 21.2 ..	08.4	219 49.4 ..	53.0	Rigil Kent.	139 51.4	S60 53.6
T 10	88 21.0	298 08.2	50.5	353 17.2	56.5	352 23.1	08.4	234 51.9	53.0	Sabik	102 12.2	S15 44.3
U 11	103 23.5	313 07.7	49.4	8 17.9	56.5	7 24.9	08.4	249 54.3	53.1			
R 12	118 26.0	328 07.3	N13 48.4	23 18.5	N23 56.4	22 26.8	N23 08.4	264 56.7	S10 53.1	Schedar	349 40.2	N56 36.5
D 13	133 28.4	343 06.9	47.3	38 19.1	56.4	37 28.7	08.4	279 59.1	53.1	Shaula	96 21.4	S37 06.7
A 14	148 30.9	358 06.4	46.2	53 19.8	56.4	52 30.5	08.3	295 01.5	53.1	Sirius	258 34.0	S16 44.2
Y 15	163 33.4	13 06.0 ..	45.1	68 20.4 ..	56.3	67 32.4 ..	08.3	310 04.0 ..	53.2	Spica	158 31.2	S11 13.9
16	178 35.8	28 05.6	44.1	83 21.0	56.3	82 34.3	08.3	325 06.4	53.2	Suhail	222 52.8	S43 29.4
17	193 38.3	43 05.2	43.0	98 21.6	56.3	97 36.1	08.3	340 08.8	53.2			
18	208 40.7	58 04.7	N13 41.9	113 22.3	N23 56.2	112 38.0	N23 08.3	355 11.2	S10 53.3	Vega	80 38.5	N38 48.1
19	223 43.2	73 04.3	40.8	128 22.9	56.2	127 39.9	08.3	10 13.6	53.3	Zuben'ubi	137 05.2	S16 05.9
20	238 45.7	88 03.9	39.8	143 23.5	56.1	142 41.7	08.2	25 16.1	53.3		SHA	Mer. Pass.
21	253 48.1	103 03.5 ..	38.7	158 24.2 ..	56.1	157 43.6 ..	08.2	40 18.5 ..	53.3	Venus	211 25.9	14 07
22	268 50.6	118 03.0	37.6	173 24.8	56.1	172 45.5	08.2	55 20.9	53.4	Mars	265 58.7	10 28
23	283 53.1	133 02.6	36.5	188 25.4	56.0	187 47.3	08.2	70 23.3	53.4	Jupiter	264 22.4	10 33
Mer. Pass. 4 11.5		v −0.4	d 1.1	v 0.6	d 0.0	v 1.9	d 0.0	v 2.4	d 0.0	Saturn	146 32.2	18 23

UT	SUN GHA	SUN Dec	MOON GHA	v	Dec	d	HP
d h	° '	° '	° '	'	° '	'	'
18 00	178 26.9	N21 01.7	68 55.7	7.0	S17 07.0	6.5	59.3
01	193 26.8	01.2	83 21.7	6.9	17 13.5	6.4	59.3
02	208 26.8	00.8	97 47.6	6.8	17 19.9	6.3	59.4
03	223 26.7	21 00.4	112 13.4	6.8	17 26.2	6.2	59.4
04	238 26.7	20 59.9	126 39.2	6.6	17 32.4	6.1	59.4
05	253 26.6	59.5	141 04.8	6.6	17 38.5	6.0	59.5
06	268 26.6	N20 59.0	155 30.4	6.5	S17 44.5	5.9	59.5
07	283 26.5	58.6	169 55.9	6.4	17 50.4	5.8	59.5
T 08	298 26.5	58.2	184 21.3	6.3	17 56.2	5.6	59.6
H 09	313 26.4 ..	57.7	198 46.6	6.3	18 01.8	5.6	59.6
U 10	328 26.4	57.3	213 11.9	6.1	18 07.4	5.4	59.6
R 11	343 26.4	56.8	227 37.0	6.1	18 12.8	5.4	59.7
S 12	358 26.3	N20 56.4	242 02.1	6.0	S18 18.2	5.2	59.7
D 13	13 26.3	55.9	256 27.1	5.9	18 23.4	5.1	59.7
A 14	28 26.2	55.5	270 52.0	5.9	18 28.5	5.0	59.7
Y 15	43 26.2 ..	55.0	285 16.9	5.8	18 33.5	4.8	59.8
16	58 26.1	54.6	299 41.7	5.6	18 38.3	4.8	59.8
17	73 26.1	54.1	314 06.3	5.6	18 43.1	4.6	59.8
18	88 26.0	N20 53.7	328 30.9	5.6	S18 47.7	4.5	59.9
19	103 26.0	53.2	342 55.5	5.4	18 52.2	4.4	59.9
20	118 26.0	52.8	357 19.9	5.4	18 56.6	4.2	59.9
21	133 25.9 ..	52.3	11 44.3	5.3	19 00.8	4.1	60.0
22	148 25.9	51.9	26 08.6	5.3	19 04.9	4.0	60.0
23	163 25.9	51.4	40 32.9	5.2	19 08.9	3.9	60.0
19 00	178 25.8	N20 51.0	54 57.1	5.1	S19 12.8	3.7	60.1
01	193 25.8	50.5	69 21.2	5.0	19 16.5	3.7	60.1
02	208 25.7	50.1	83 45.2	5.0	19 20.2	3.4	60.1
03	223 25.7 ..	49.6	98 09.2	4.9	19 23.6	3.4	60.1
04	238 25.6	49.2	112 33.1	4.8	19 27.0	3.2	60.2
05	253 25.6	48.7	126 56.9	4.8	19 30.2	3.1	60.2
06	268 25.5	N20 48.3	141 20.7	4.7	S19 33.3	2.9	60.2
07	283 25.5	47.8	155 44.4	4.6	19 36.2	2.9	60.3
08	298 25.5	47.3	170 08.0	4.6	19 39.1	2.6	60.3
F 09	313 25.4 ..	46.9	184 31.6	4.5	19 41.7	2.6	60.3
R 10	328 25.4	46.4	198 55.1	4.5	19 44.3	2.4	60.3
I 11	343 25.4	46.0	213 18.6	4.4	19 46.7	2.2	60.4
D 12	358 25.3	N20 45.5	227 42.0	4.4	S19 48.9	2.2	60.4
A 13	13 25.3	45.0	242 05.4	4.3	19 51.1	2.0	60.4
Y 14	28 25.2	44.6	256 28.7	4.2	19 53.1	1.8	60.4
15	43 25.2 ..	44.1	270 51.9	4.2	19 54.9	1.7	60.5
16	58 25.2	43.7	285 15.1	4.2	19 56.6	1.6	60.5
17	73 25.1	43.2	299 38.3	4.1	19 58.2	1.4	60.5
18	88 25.1	N20 42.7	314 01.4	4.1	S19 59.6	1.3	60.5
19	103 25.0	42.3	328 24.5	4.0	20 00.9	1.1	60.6
20	118 25.0	41.8	342 47.5	4.0	20 02.0	1.0	60.6
21	133 25.0 ..	41.3	357 10.5	3.9	20 03.0	0.8	60.6
22	148 24.9	40.9	11 33.4	3.9	20 03.8	0.7	60.6
23	163 24.9	40.4	25 56.3	3.9	20 04.5	0.6	60.7
20 00	178 24.9	N20 39.9	40 19.2	3.8	S20 05.1	0.4	60.7
01	193 24.8	39.5	54 42.0	3.8	20 05.5	0.2	60.7
02	208 24.8	39.0	69 04.8	3.8	20 05.7	0.1	60.7
03	223 24.8 ..	38.5	83 27.6	3.7	20 05.8	0.0	60.7
04	238 24.7	38.1	97 50.3	3.8	20 05.8	0.2	60.8
05	253 24.7	37.6	112 13.1	3.6	20 05.6	0.3	60.8
06	268 24.7	N20 37.1	126 35.7	3.7	S20 05.3	0.5	60.8
07	283 24.6	36.7	140 58.4	3.6	20 04.8	0.6	60.8
S 08	298 24.6	36.2	155 21.0	3.6	20 04.2	0.8	60.8
A 09	313 24.6 ..	35.7	169 43.6	3.6	20 03.4	1.0	60.9
T 10	328 24.5	35.2	184 06.2	3.6	20 02.5	1.1	60.9
U 11	343 24.5	34.8	198 28.8	3.6	20 01.4	1.2	60.9
R 12	358 24.5	N20 34.3	212 51.4	3.5	S20 00.2	1.4	60.9
D 13	13 24.4	33.8	227 13.9	3.6	19 58.8	1.6	60.9
A 14	28 24.4	33.3	241 36.5	3.5	19 57.2	1.6	60.9
Y 15	43 24.4 ..	32.9	255 59.0	3.5	19 55.6	1.9	61.0
16	58 24.3	32.4	270 21.5	3.5	19 53.7	1.9	61.0
17	73 24.3	31.9	284 44.1	3.5	19 51.8	2.1	61.0
18	88 24.3	N20 31.4	299 06.6	3.5	S19 49.7	2.3	61.0
19	103 24.2	31.0	313 29.1	3.5	19 47.4	2.4	61.0
20	118 24.2	30.5	327 51.6	3.5	19 45.0	2.6	61.0
21	133 24.2 ..	30.0	342 14.1	3.5	19 42.4	2.7	61.0
22	148 24.1	29.5	356 36.6	3.5	19 39.7	2.9	61.0
23	163 24.1	29.0	10 59.2	3.5	S19 36.8	3.0	61.1
SD 15.8	d 0.5		SD 16.3		16.5		16.6

Lat.	Twilight Naut.	Civil	Sunrise	Moonrise 18	19	20	21
°	h m	h m	h m	h m	h m	h m	h m
N 72	////	////	////	■■■■	■■■■	■■■■	22 55
N 70	////	////	////	18 53	■■■■	21 43	21 27
68	////	////	00 47	17 59	19 30	20 24	20 47
66	////	////	01 53	17 26	18 48	19 46	20 20
64	////	////	02 28	17 02	18 20	19 19	19 58
62	////	01 16	02 52	16 43	17 59	18 58	19 41
60	////	01 58	03 12	16 27	17 41	18 41	19 27
N 58	////	02 26	03 28	16 14	17 26	18 27	19 14
56	01 09	02 47	03 41	16 03	17 14	18 15	19 04
54	01 48	03 04	03 53	15 53	17 03	18 04	18 54
52	02 14	03 18	04 03	15 44	16 53	17 55	18 46
50	02 34	03 31	04 12	15 36	16 45	17 46	18 38
45	03 10	03 56	04 31	15 19	16 26	17 28	18 22
N 40	03 36	04 15	04 47	15 05	16 11	17 13	18 09
35	03 56	04 31	05 00	14 54	15 59	17 01	17 58
30	04 12	04 45	05 11	14 44	15 48	16 50	17 48
20	04 38	05 07	05 31	14 26	15 29	16 31	17 31
N 10	04 58	05 25	05 47	14 11	15 12	16 15	17 16
0	05 15	05 41	06 03	13 57	14 57	15 59	17 02
S 10	05 30	05 56	06 18	13 43	14 42	15 44	16 48
20	05 44	06 11	06 34	13 28	14 26	15 28	16 33
30	05 58	06 27	06 53	13 11	14 07	15 09	16 16
35	06 05	06 36	07 03	13 01	13 56	14 58	16 06
40	06 13	06 46	07 16	12 50	13 44	14 46	15 54
45	06 21	06 58	07 30	12 37	13 29	14 31	15 41
S 50	06 31	07 11	07 48	12 21	13 11	14 13	15 24
52	06 35	07 17	07 56	12 13	13 03	14 04	15 16
54	06 40	07 24	08 05	12 05	12 54	13 55	15 08
56	06 44	07 31	08 16	11 56	12 43	13 44	14 58
58	06 50	07 40	08 28	11 45	12 31	13 32	14 47
S 60	06 56	07 49	08 41	11 33	12 17	13 18	14 34

Lat.	Sunset	Twilight Civil	Naut.	Moonset 18	19	20	21
°	h m	h m	h m	h m	h m	h m	h m
N 72	////	////	////	21 22	■■■■	22 50	23 49
N 70	////	////	////	21 22	22 50	22 50	25 17
68	23 15	////	////	22 17	22 52	24 09	00 09
66	22 16	////	////	22 50	23 34	24 46	00 46
64	21 43	////	////	23 14	24 02	00 02	01 13
62	21 18	22 52	////	23 34	24 24	00 24	01 34
60	20 59	22 12	////	23 50	24 41	00 41	01 50
N 58	20 44	21 45	////	24 03	00 03	00 56	02 04
56	20 30	21 24	22 59	24 15	00 15	01 09	02 16
54	20 19	21 07	22 22	24 25	00 25	01 20	02 27
52	20 09	20 53	21 57	24 34	00 34	01 29	02 36
50	20 00	20 41	21 37	24 42	00 42	01 38	02 45
45	19 41	20 16	21 01	00 12	01 00	01 57	03 03
N 40	19 25	19 57	20 36	00 24	01 14	02 12	03 17
35	19 12	19 41	20 16	00 35	01 26	02 24	03 29
30	19 01	19 28	20 00	00 44	01 37	02 36	03 40
20	18 43	19 06	19 34	01 00	01 50	02 55	03 58
N 10	18 25	18 48	19 14	01 14	02 11	03 11	04 14
0	18 10	18 32	18 58	01 27	02 25	03 27	04 29
S 10	17 55	18 17	18 43	01 40	02 40	03 42	04 44
20	17 39	18 02	18 29	01 54	02 56	03 58	04 59
30	17 20	17 46	18 15	02 10	03 14	04 17	05 17
35	17 09	17 37	18 08	02 19	03 25	04 28	05 28
40	16 57	17 27	18 00	02 30	03 37	04 41	05 40
45	16 43	17 15	17 52	02 43	03 51	04 56	05 54
S 50	16 25	17 02	17 42	02 58	04 09	05 14	06 11
52	16 17	16 56	17 38	03 05	04 17	05 22	06 19
54	16 08	16 49	17 34	03 13	04 26	05 32	06 28
56	15 57	16 42	17 29	03 22	04 35	05 43	06 38
58	15 46	16 33	17 23	03 32	04 48	05 55	06 49
S 60	15 32	16 24	17 18	03 44	05 02	06 09	07 02

Day	SUN Eqn. of Time 00h	12h	Mer. Pass.	MOON Mer. Pass. Upper	Lower	Age	Phase
	m s	m s	h m	h m	h m	d	%
18	06 12	06 15	12 06	20 11	07 42	10	75
19	06 17	06 19	12 06	21 12	08 41	11	85
20	06 20	06 22	12 06	22 14	09 43	12	92

2013 JULY 21, 22, 23 (SUN., MON., TUES.)

UT	ARIES GHA	VENUS −3.9 GHA	Dec	MARS +1.6 GHA	Dec	JUPITER −1.9 GHA	Dec	SATURN +0.6 GHA	Dec	STARS Name	SHA	Dec
21 00	298 55.5	148 02.2	N13 35.4	203 26.0	N23 56.0	202 49.2	N23 08.2	85 25.7	S10 53.4	Acamar	315 18.4	S40 14.8
01	313 58.0	163 01.8	.. 34.4	218 26.7	.. 55.9	217 51.1	.. 08.1	100 28.1	.. 53.5	Achernar	335 26.7	S57 09.8
02	329 00.5	178 01.3	.. 33.3	233 27.3	.. 55.9	232 52.9	.. 08.1	115 30.6	.. 53.5	Acrux	173 09.3	S63 10.8
03	344 02.9	193 00.9	.. 32.2	248 27.9	.. 55.9	247 54.8	.. 08.1	130 33.0	.. 53.5	Adhara	255 12.8	S28 59.5
04	359 05.4	208 00.5	.. 31.1	263 28.6	.. 55.8	262 56.7	.. 08.1	145 35.4	.. 53.5	Aldebaran	290 49.5	N16 32.0
05	14 07.9	223 00.1	.. 30.0	278 29.2	.. 55.8	277 58.6	.. 08.1	160 37.8	.. 53.6			
06	29 10.3	237 59.7	N13 29.0	293 29.8	N23 55.7	293 00.4	N23 08.0	175 40.2	S10 53.6	Alioth	166 20.8	N55 53.4
07	44 12.8	252 59.2	.. 27.9	308 30.4	.. 55.7	308 02.3	.. 08.0	190 42.6	.. 53.6	Alkaid	152 58.9	N49 15.0
08	59 15.2	267 58.8	.. 26.8	323 31.1	.. 55.7	323 04.2	.. 08.0	205 45.1	.. 53.7	Al Na'ir	27 43.2	S46 53.4
S 09	74 17.7	282 58.4	.. 25.7	338 31.7	.. 55.6	338 06.0	.. 08.0	220 47.5	.. 53.7	Alnilam	275 46.5	S 1 11.7
U 10	89 20.2	297 58.0	.. 24.6	353 32.3	.. 55.6	353 07.9	.. 08.0	235 49.9	.. 53.7	Alphard	217 56.3	S 8 43.2
N 11	104 22.6	312 57.6	.. 23.5	8 33.0	.. 55.5	8 09.8	.. 07.9	250 52.3	.. 53.7			
D 12	119 25.1	327 57.1	N13 22.5	23 33.6	N23 55.5	23 11.6	N23 07.9	265 54.7	S10 53.8	Alphecca	126 10.8	N26 40.4
A 13	134 27.6	342 56.7	.. 21.4	38 34.2	.. 55.5	38 13.5	.. 07.9	280 57.1	.. 53.8	Alpheratz	357 43.2	N29 09.9
Y 14	149 30.0	357 56.3	.. 20.3	53 34.9	.. 55.4	53 15.4	.. 07.9	295 59.6	.. 53.8	Altair	62 07.8	N 8 54.5
15	164 32.5	12 55.9	.. 19.2	68 35.5	.. 55.4	68 17.2	.. 07.9	311 02.0	.. 53.9	Ankaa	353 15.5	S42 13.6
16	179 35.0	27 55.5	.. 18.1	83 36.1	.. 55.3	83 19.1	.. 07.8	326 04.4	.. 53.9	Antares	112 25.9	S26 27.6
17	194 37.4	42 55.1	.. 17.0	98 36.8	.. 55.3	98 21.0	.. 07.8	341 06.8	.. 53.9			
18	209 39.9	57 54.7	N13 15.9	113 37.4	N23 55.2	113 22.9	N23 07.8	356 09.2	S10 53.9	Arcturus	145 55.6	N19 06.9
19	224 42.4	72 54.2	.. 14.8	128 38.0	.. 55.2	128 24.7	.. 07.8	11 11.6	.. 54.0	Atria	107 27.2	S69 03.2
20	239 44.8	87 53.8	.. 13.7	143 38.6	.. 55.1	143 26.6	.. 07.8	26 14.0	.. 54.0	Avior	234 18.6	S59 33.4
21	254 47.3	102 53.4	.. 12.6	158 39.3	.. 55.1	158 28.5	.. 07.7	41 16.5	.. 54.0	Bellatrix	278 32.2	N 6 21.6
22	269 49.7	117 53.0	.. 11.6	173 39.9	.. 55.0	173 30.3	.. 07.7	56 18.9	.. 54.1	Betelgeuse	271 01.5	N 7 24.4
23	284 52.2	132 52.6	.. 10.5	188 40.5	.. 55.0	188 32.2	.. 07.7	71 21.3	.. 54.1			
22 00	299 54.7	147 52.2	N13 09.4	203 41.2	N23 55.0	203 34.1	N23 07.7	86 23.7	S10 54.1	Canopus	263 56.6	S52 42.2
01	314 57.1	162 51.8	.. 08.3	218 41.8	.. 54.9	218 35.9	.. 07.7	101 26.1	.. 54.1	Capella	280 34.7	N46 00.4
02	329 59.6	177 51.4	.. 07.2	233 42.4	.. 54.9	233 37.8	.. 07.6	116 28.5	.. 54.2	Deneb	49 30.9	N45 19.9
03	345 02.1	192 50.9	.. 06.1	248 43.1	.. 54.8	248 39.7	.. 07.6	131 30.9	.. 54.2	Denebola	182 33.7	N14 29.8
04	0 04.5	207 50.5	.. 05.0	263 43.7	.. 54.8	263 41.6	.. 07.6	146 33.4	.. 54.2	Diphda	348 55.7	S17 54.5
05	15 07.0	222 50.1	.. 03.9	278 44.3	.. 54.7	278 43.4	.. 07.6	161 35.8	.. 54.3			
06	30 09.5	237 49.7	N13 02.8	293 45.0	N23 54.7	293 45.3	N23 07.6	176 38.2	S10 54.3	Dubhe	193 52.1	N61 40.8
07	45 11.9	252 49.3	.. 01.7	308 45.6	.. 54.6	308 47.2	.. 07.5	191 40.6	.. 54.3	Elnath	278 12.8	N28 36.9
08	60 14.4	267 48.9	13 00.6	323 46.2	.. 54.6	323 49.0	.. 07.5	206 43.0	.. 54.3	Eltanin	90 45.6	N51 29.5
M 09	75 16.9	282 48.5	12 59.5	338 46.9	.. 54.5	338 50.9	.. 07.5	221 45.4	.. 54.4	Enif	33 46.7	N 9 56.4
O 10	90 19.3	297 48.1	.. 58.4	353 47.5	.. 54.5	353 52.8	.. 07.5	236 47.8	.. 54.4	Fomalhaut	15 23.6	S29 32.7
N 11	105 21.8	312 47.7	.. 57.3	8 48.1	.. 54.4	8 54.7	.. 07.5	251 50.2	.. 54.4			
D 12	120 24.2	327 47.3	N12 56.2	23 48.8	N23 54.4	23 56.5	N23 07.4	266 52.7	S10 54.5	Gacrux	172 00.9	S57 11.6
A 13	135 26.7	342 46.9	.. 55.1	38 49.4	.. 54.3	38 58.4	.. 07.4	281 55.1	.. 54.5	Gienah	175 52.3	S17 37.1
Y 14	150 29.2	357 46.5	.. 54.0	53 50.0	.. 54.3	54 00.3	.. 07.4	296 57.5	.. 54.5	Hadar	148 47.6	S60 26.5
15	165 31.6	12 46.1	.. 52.9	68 50.7	.. 54.2	69 02.1	.. 07.4	311 59.9	.. 54.6	Hamal	328 00.6	N23 31.5
16	180 34.1	27 45.7	.. 51.8	83 51.3	.. 54.2	84 04.0	.. 07.3	327 02.3	.. 54.6	Kaus Aust.	83 43.3	S34 22.5
17	195 36.6	42 45.3	.. 50.7	98 51.9	.. 54.1	99 05.9	.. 07.3	342 04.7	.. 54.6			
18	210 39.0	57 44.9	N12 49.6	113 52.6	N23 54.0	114 07.7	N23 07.3	357 07.1	S10 54.6	Kochab	137 19.8	N74 06.3
19	225 41.5	72 44.5	.. 48.5	128 53.2	.. 54.0	129 09.6	.. 07.3	12 09.5	.. 54.7	Markab	13 38.0	N15 16.8
20	240 44.0	87 44.1	.. 47.4	143 53.8	.. 53.9	144 11.5	.. 07.2	27 12.0	.. 54.7	Menkar	314 15.0	N 4 08.6
21	255 46.4	102 43.7	.. 46.3	158 54.5	.. 53.9	159 13.4	.. 07.2	42 14.4	.. 54.7	Menkent	148 07.4	S36 26.3
22	270 48.9	117 43.3	.. 45.2	173 55.1	.. 53.8	174 15.2	.. 07.2	57 16.8	.. 54.8	Miaplacidus	221 40.5	S69 46.6
23	285 51.4	132 42.9	.. 44.1	188 55.7	.. 53.8	189 17.1	.. 07.2	72 19.2	.. 54.8			
23 00	300 53.8	147 42.5	N12 43.0	203 56.4	N23 53.7	204 19.0	N23 07.2	87 21.6	S10 54.8	Mirfak	308 40.4	N49 54.3
01	315 56.3	162 42.1	.. 41.9	218 57.0	.. 53.7	219 20.9	.. 07.2	102 24.0	.. 54.9	Nunki	75 57.8	S26 16.6
02	330 58.7	177 41.7	.. 40.7	233 57.6	.. 53.6	234 22.7	.. 07.1	117 26.4	.. 54.9	Peacock	53 18.5	S56 41.2
03	346 01.2	192 41.3	.. 39.6	248 58.3	.. 53.6	249 24.6	.. 07.1	132 28.8	.. 54.9	Pollux	243 28.0	N27 59.5
04	1 03.7	207 40.9	.. 38.5	263 58.9	.. 53.5	264 26.5	.. 07.1	147 31.2	.. 55.0	Procyon	245 00.0	N 5 11.3
05	16 06.1	222 40.5	.. 37.4	278 59.5	.. 53.4	279 28.3	.. 07.1	162 33.6	.. 55.0			
06	31 08.6	237 40.1	N12 36.3	294 00.2	N23 53.4	294 30.2	N23 07.0	177 36.1	S10 55.0	Rasalhague	96 06.1	N12 33.3
07	46 11.1	252 39.7	.. 35.2	309 00.8	.. 53.3	309 32.1	.. 07.0	192 38.5	.. 55.0	Regulus	207 43.7	N11 54.0
T 08	61 13.5	267 39.3	.. 34.1	324 01.4	.. 53.3	324 34.0	.. 07.0	207 40.9	.. 55.1	Rigel	281 12.2	S 8 11.2
U 09	76 16.0	282 38.9	.. 33.0	339 02.1	.. 53.2	339 35.8	.. 07.0	222 43.3	.. 55.1	Rigil Kent.	139 51.4	S60 53.6
E 10	91 18.5	297 38.5	.. 31.9	354 02.7	.. 53.1	354 37.7	.. 07.0	237 45.7	.. 55.1	Sabik	102 12.2	S15 44.3
S 11	106 20.9	312 38.1	.. 30.8	9 03.3	.. 53.1	9 39.6	.. 06.9	252 48.1	.. 55.2			
D 12	121 23.4	327 37.7	N12 29.6	24 04.0	N23 53.0	24 41.5	N23 06.9	267 50.5	S10 55.2	Schedar	349 40.1	N56 36.5
A 13	136 25.8	342 37.3	.. 28.5	39 04.6	.. 53.0	39 43.3	.. 06.9	282 52.9	.. 55.3	Shaula	96 21.4	S37 06.7
Y 14	151 28.3	357 36.9	.. 27.4	54 05.3	.. 52.9	54 45.2	.. 06.9	297 55.3	.. 55.3	Sirius	258 34.0	S16 44.2
15	166 30.8	12 36.5	.. 26.3	69 05.9	.. 52.8	69 47.1	.. 06.9	312 57.7	.. 55.3	Spica	158 31.2	S11 13.9
16	181 33.2	27 36.1	.. 25.2	84 06.5	.. 52.8	84 48.9	.. 06.8	328 00.1	.. 55.3	Suhail	222 52.8	S43 29.4
17	196 35.7	42 35.8	.. 24.1	99 07.2	.. 52.7	99 50.8	.. 06.8	343 02.5	.. 55.4			
18	211 38.2	57 35.4	N12 22.9	114 07.8	N23 52.7	114 52.7	N23 06.8	358 04.9	S10 55.4	Vega	80 38.5	N38 48.1
19	226 40.6	72 35.0	.. 21.8	129 08.4	.. 52.6	129 54.6	.. 06.8	13 07.4	.. 55.4	Zuben'ubi	137 05.2	S16 05.9
20	241 43.1	87 34.6	.. 20.7	144 09.1	.. 52.5	144 56.4	.. 06.7	28 09.8	.. 55.4		SHA	Mer.Pass.
21	256 45.6	102 34.2	.. 19.6	159 09.7	.. 52.5	159 58.3	.. 06.7	43 12.2	.. 55.5		° '	h m
22	271 48.0	117 33.8	.. 18.5	174 10.3	.. 52.4	175 00.2	.. 06.7	58 14.6	.. 55.5	Venus	207 57.5	14 09
23	286 50.5	132 33.4	.. 17.4	189 11.0	.. 52.3	190 02.1	.. 06.7	73 17.0	.. 55.5	Mars	263 46.5	10 25
Mer. Pass. 3 59.7		v −0.4 d 1.1		v 0.6 d 0.1		v 1.9 d 0.0		v 2.4 d 0.0		Jupiter	263 39.4	10 24
										Saturn	146 29.0	18 11

UT	SUN GHA	SUN Dec	MOON GHA	v	MOON Dec	d	HP
d h	o '	o '	o '	'	o '	'	'
21 00	178 24.1	N20 28.6	25 21.7	3.5	S19 33.8	3.2	61.1
01	193 24.1	28.1	39 44.2	3.6	19 30.6	3.3	61.1
02	208 24.0	27.6	54 06.8	3.6	19 27.3	3.4	61.1
03	223 24.0	.. 27.1	68 29.4	3.5	19 23.9	3.6	61.1
04	238 24.0	26.6	82 51.9	3.6	19 20.3	3.8	61.1
05	253 23.9	26.1	97 14.5	3.7	19 16.5	3.9	61.1
06	268 23.9	N20 25.6	111 37.2	3.6	S19 12.6	4.0	61.1
07	283 23.9	25.2	125 59.8	3.6	19 08.6	4.2	61.1
08	298 23.9	24.7	140 22.4	3.7	19 04.4	4.3	61.1
S 09	313 23.8	.. 24.2	154 45.1	3.7	19 00.1	4.5	61.1
U 10	328 23.8	23.7	169 07.8	3.8	18 55.6	4.6	61.2
N 11	343 23.8	23.2	183 30.6	3.7	18 51.0	4.7	61.2
D 12	358 23.7	N20 22.7	197 53.3	3.8	S18 46.3	4.9	61.2
A 13	13 23.7	22.2	212 16.1	3.8	18 41.4	5.0	61.2
Y 14	28 23.7	21.7	226 38.9	3.9	18 36.4	5.2	61.2
15	43 23.7	.. 21.3	241 01.8	3.9	18 31.2	5.3	61.2
16	58 23.6	20.8	255 24.7	3.9	18 25.9	5.4	61.2
17	73 23.6	20.3	269 47.6	4.0	18 20.5	5.6	61.2
18	88 23.6	N20 19.8	284 10.6	4.0	S18 14.9	5.7	61.2
19	103 23.6	19.3	298 33.6	4.0	18 09.2	5.8	61.2
20	118 23.5	18.8	312 56.6	4.1	18 03.4	6.0	61.2
21	133 23.5	.. 18.3	327 19.7	4.2	17 57.4	6.1	61.2
22	148 23.5	17.8	341 42.9	4.2	17 51.3	6.3	61.2
23	163 23.5	17.3	356 06.1	4.2	17 45.0	6.3	61.2
22 00	178 23.4	N20 16.8	10 29.3	4.3	S17 38.7	6.5	61.2
01	193 23.4	16.3	24 52.6	4.3	17 32.2	6.6	61.2
02	208 23.4	15.8	39 15.9	4.4	17 25.6	6.8	61.2
03	223 23.4	.. 15.3	53 39.3	4.4	17 18.8	6.9	61.2
04	238 23.3	14.8	68 02.7	4.5	17 11.9	7.0	61.2
05	253 23.3	14.3	82 26.2	4.5	17 04.9	7.1	61.2
06	268 23.3	N20 13.8	96 49.7	4.6	S16 57.8	7.2	61.2
07	283 23.3	13.3	111 13.3	4.6	16 50.6	7.4	61.2
08	298 23.3	12.8	125 36.9	4.8	16 43.2	7.5	61.1
M 09	313 23.2	.. 12.3	140 00.7	4.7	16 35.7	7.6	61.1
O 10	328 23.2	11.8	154 24.4	4.8	16 28.1	7.7	61.1
N 11	343 23.2	11.3	168 48.2	4.9	16 20.4	7.8	61.1
D 12	358 23.2	N20 10.8	183 12.1	5.0	S16 12.6	7.9	61.1
A 13	13 23.2	10.3	197 36.1	5.0	16 04.7	8.1	61.1
Y 14	28 23.1	09.8	212 00.1	5.1	15 56.6	8.2	61.1
15	43 23.1	.. 09.3	226 24.2	5.1	15 48.4	8.2	61.1
16	58 23.1	08.8	240 48.3	5.2	15 40.2	8.4	61.1
17	73 23.1	08.3	255 12.5	5.3	15 31.8	8.5	61.1
18	88 23.1	N20 07.8	269 36.8	5.3	S15 23.3	8.6	61.1
19	103 23.0	07.3	284 01.1	5.4	15 14.7	8.7	61.0
20	118 23.0	06.8	298 25.5	5.5	15 06.0	8.8	61.0
21	133 23.0	.. 06.3	312 50.0	5.5	14 57.2	8.9	61.0
22	148 23.0	05.8	327 14.5	5.6	14 48.3	9.0	61.0
23	163 23.0	05.3	341 39.1	5.7	14 39.3	9.1	61.0
23 00	178 22.9	N20 04.7	356 03.8	5.8	S14 30.2	9.2	61.0
01	193 22.9	04.2	10 28.6	5.8	14 21.0	9.2	61.0
02	208 22.9	03.7	24 53.4	5.9	14 11.8	9.4	60.9
03	223 22.9	.. 03.2	39 18.3	6.0	14 02.4	9.5	60.9
04	238 22.9	02.7	53 43.3	6.0	13 52.9	9.5	60.9
05	253 22.9	02.2	68 08.3	6.1	13 43.4	9.7	60.9
06	268 22.8	N20 01.7	82 33.4	6.2	S13 33.7	9.7	60.9
07	283 22.8	01.2	96 58.6	6.2	13 24.0	9.8	60.9
08	298 22.8	00.6	111 23.8	6.4	13 14.2	9.9	60.8
T 09	313 22.8	20 00.1	125 49.2	6.4	13 04.3	10.0	60.8
U 10	328 22.8	19 59.6	140 14.6	6.5	12 54.3	10.0	60.8
E 11	343 22.8	59.1	154 40.1	6.5	12 44.3	10.2	60.8
S 12	358 22.7	N19 58.6	169 05.6	6.7	S12 34.1	10.2	60.8
D 13	13 22.7	58.1	183 31.3	6.7	12 23.9	10.3	60.7
A 14	28 22.7	57.5	197 57.0	6.7	12 13.6	10.3	60.7
Y 15	43 22.7	.. 57.0	212 22.7	6.9	12 03.3	10.4	60.7
16	58 22.7	56.5	226 48.6	6.9	11 52.9	10.5	60.7
17	73 22.7	56.0	241 14.5	7.0	11 42.4	10.6	60.6
18	88 22.7	N19 55.5	255 40.5	7.1	S11 31.8	10.6	60.6
19	103 22.7	54.9	270 06.6	7.2	11 21.2	10.7	60.6
20	118 22.6	54.4	284 32.8	7.2	11 10.5	10.8	60.6
21	133 22.6	.. 53.9	298 59.0	7.3	10 59.7	10.8	60.6
22	148 22.6	53.4	313 25.3	7.4	10 48.9	10.9	60.5
23	163 22.6	52.9	327 51.7	7.4	S10 38.0	11.0	60.5
	SD 15.8	d 0.5	SD 16.7		16.7		16.6

Twilight / Moonrise

Lat.	Naut.	Civil	Sunrise	21	22	23	24
o	h m	h m	h m	h m	h m	h m	h m
N 72	▭	▭	▭	22 55	21 53	21 33	21 20
N 70	▭	▭	▭	21 27	21 21	21 15	21 11
68	////	////	01 15	20 47	20 57	21 01	21 03
66	////	////	02 06	20 20	20 38	20 49	20 57
64	////	////	02 37	19 58	20 23	20 39	20 52
62	////	01 32	03 00	19 41	20 10	20 31	20 47
60	////	02 08	03 18	19 27	19 59	20 24	20 43
N 58	////	02 34	03 33	19 14	19 50	20 17	20 39
56	01 24	02 53	03 46	19 04	19 42	20 11	20 36
54	01 57	03 10	03 57	18 54	19 34	20 06	20 33
52	02 21	03 23	04 07	18 46	19 28	20 02	20 30
50	02 40	03 35	04 16	18 38	19 22	19 57	20 28
45	03 14	03 59	04 34	18 22	19 08	19 48	20 23
N 40	03 39	04 18	04 49	18 09	18 58	19 40	20 18
35	03 59	04 34	05 02	17 58	18 48	19 34	20 14
30	04 17	04 47	05 13	17 48	18 40	19 28	20 11
20	04 40	05 08	05 32	17 31	18 26	19 18	20 05
N 10	04 59	05 25	05 48	17 16	18 14	19 09	20 00
0	05 15	05 41	06 03	17 02	18 02	19 00	19 55
S 10	05 30	05 55	06 18	16 48	17 51	18 52	19 50
20	05 43	06 10	06 33	16 33	17 38	18 43	19 45
30	05 56	06 26	06 51	16 16	17 24	18 32	19 39
35	06 04	06 34	07 02	16 06	17 16	18 27	19 35
40	06 11	06 44	07 14	15 54	17 06	18 20	19 32
45	06 19	06 55	07 28	15 41	16 55	18 12	19 27
S 50	06 28	07 08	07 44	15 24	16 42	18 02	19 22
52	06 32	07 14	07 52	15 16	16 36	17 58	19 19
54	06 36	07 20	08 01	15 08	16 29	17 53	19 16
56	06 41	07 28	08 11	14 58	16 21	17 47	19 13
58	06 46	07 36	08 23	14 47	16 12	17 41	19 10
S 60	06 51	07 45	08 36	14 34	16 02	17 34	19 06

Twilight / Moonset

Lat.	Sunset	Civil	Naut.	21	22	23	24
o	h m	h m	h m	h m	h m	h m	h m
N 72	▭	▭	▭	23 49	26 58	02 58	05 16
N 70	25 17	01 17	03 29	23 17	00 17	03 29	05 32
68	22 51	////	////	00 09	01 56	03 51	05 45
66	22 04	////	////	00 46	02 23	04 09	05 55
64	21 34	////	////	01 13	02 43	04 23	06 04
62	21 11	22 37	////	01 34	03 00	04 35	06 11
60	20 53	22 02	////	01 50	03 14	04 45	06 18
N 58	20 38	21 37	////	02 04	03 26	04 54	06 23
56	20 26	21 18	22 45	02 16	03 36	05 01	06 28
54	20 15	21 02	22 13	02 27	03 45	05 08	06 32
52	20 05	20 48	21 50	02 36	03 53	05 14	06 36
50	19 56	20 37	21 32	02 45	04 00	05 20	06 40
45	19 38	20 13	20 58	03 03	04 15	05 31	06 48
N 40	19 23	19 54	20 33	03 17	04 28	05 41	06 54
35	19 10	19 39	20 14	03 29	04 39	05 50	07 00
30	19 00	19 26	19 58	03 40	04 48	05 57	07 04
20	18 41	19 05	19 33	03 58	05 04	06 09	07 13
N 10	18 25	18 47	19 14	04 14	05 18	06 20	07 20
0	18 10	18 32	18 58	04 29	05 31	06 30	07 27
S 10	17 55	18 18	18 43	04 44	05 44	06 40	07 33
20	17 40	18 03	18 30	04 59	05 57	06 51	07 40
30	17 22	17 47	18 17	05 17	06 13	07 03	07 48
35	17 11	17 39	18 10	05 28	06 22	07 10	07 53
40	17 00	17 29	18 02	05 40	06 32	07 18	07 58
45	16 46	17 18	17 54	05 54	06 44	07 27	08 04
S 50	16 29	17 05	17 45	06 11	06 58	07 38	08 11
52	16 21	16 59	17 41	06 19	07 05	07 43	08 14
54	16 12	16 53	17 37	06 28	07 13	07 48	08 18
56	16 02	16 46	17 33	06 38	07 21	07 55	08 22
58	15 51	16 38	17 28	06 49	07 30	08 01	08 26
S 60	15 38	16 29	17 22	07 02	07 41	08 09	08 31

SUN / MOON

Day	Eqn. of Time 00h	Eqn. of Time 12h	Mer. Pass.	Mer. Pass. Upper	Mer. Pass. Lower	Age	Phase
d	m s	m s	h m	h m	h m	d	%
21	06 24	06 25	12 06	23 16	10 45	13	97
22	06 26	06 27	12 06	24 16	11 47	14	100
23	06 28	06 29	12 06	00 16	12 45	15	99

UT	ARIES GHA	VENUS −3.9 GHA	Dec	MARS +1.6 GHA	Dec	JUPITER −1.9 GHA	Dec	SATURN +0.6 GHA	Dec	STARS Name	SHA	Dec
24 00	301 53.0	147 33.0	N12 16.2	204 11.6	N23 52.3	205 03.9	N23 06.7	88 19.4	S10 55.6	Acamar	315 18.4	S40 14.8
01	316 55.4	162 32.6	15.1	219 12.3	52.2	220 05.8	06.6	103 21.8	55.6	Achernar	335 26.7	S57 09.7
02	331 57.9	177 32.3	14.0	234 12.9	52.2	235 07.7	06.6	118 24.2	55.6	Acrux	173 09.4	S63 10.8
03	347 00.3	192 31.9 ..	12.9	249 13.5 ..	52.1	250 09.6 ..	06.6	133 26.6 ..	55.7	Adhara	255 12.8	S28 59.5
04	2 02.8	207 31.5	11.8	264 14.2	52.0	265 11.4	06.5	148 29.0	55.7	Aldebaran	290 49.5	N16 32.1
05	17 05.3	222 31.1	10.6	279 14.8	52.0	280 13.3	06.5	163 31.4	55.7			
W 06	32 07.7	237 30.7	N12 09.5	294 15.4	N23 51.9	295 15.2	N23 06.5	178 33.8	S10 55.8	Alioth	166 20.8	N55 53.4
E 07	47 10.2	252 30.3	08.4	309 16.1	51.8	310 17.1	06.5	193 36.2	55.8	Alkaid	152 58.9	N49 15.0
D 08	62 12.7	267 29.9	07.3	324 16.7	51.8	325 18.9	06.5	208 38.6	55.8	Al Na'ir	27 43.2	S46 53.4
N 09	77 15.1	282 29.6 ..	06.1	339 17.4 ..	51.7	340 20.8 ..	06.5	223 41.0 ..	55.9	Alnilam	275 46.5	S 1 11.7
E 10	92 17.6	297 29.2	05.0	354 18.0	51.6	355 22.7	06.4	238 43.4	55.9	Alphard	217 56.3	S 8 43.2
S 11	107 20.1	312 28.8	03.9	9 18.6	51.6	10 24.6	06.4	253 45.8	55.9			
D 12	122 22.5	327 28.4	N12 02.8	24 19.3	N23 51.5	25 26.4	N23 06.4	268 48.3	S10 56.0	Alphecca	126 10.8	N26 40.4
A 13	137 25.0	342 28.0	01.6	39 19.9	51.4	40 28.3	06.4	283 50.7	56.0	Alpheratz	357 43.2	N29 09.9
Y 14	152 27.5	357 27.7	12 00.5	54 20.6	51.3	55 30.2	06.3	298 53.1	56.0	Altair	62 07.8	N 8 54.5
15	167 29.9	12 27.3	11 59.4	69 21.2 ..	51.3	70 32.1 ..	06.3	313 55.5 ..	56.1	Ankaa	353 15.4	S42 13.6
16	182 32.4	27 26.9	58.2	84 21.8	51.2	85 33.9	06.3	328 57.9	56.1	Antares	112 25.9	S26 27.6
17	197 34.8	42 26.5	57.1	99 22.5	51.1	100 35.8	06.3	344 00.3	56.1			
18	212 37.3	57 26.1	N11 56.0	114 23.1	N23 51.1	115 37.7	N23 06.3	359 02.7	S10 56.2	Arcturus	145 55.6	N19 06.9
19	227 39.8	72 25.8	54.9	129 23.8	51.0	130 39.6	06.2	14 05.1	56.2	Atria	107 27.2	S69 03.2
20	242 42.2	87 25.4	53.7	144 24.4	50.9	145 41.4	06.2	29 07.5	56.2	Avior	234 18.6	S59 33.3
21	257 44.7	102 25.0 ..	52.6	159 25.0 ..	50.9	160 43.3 ..	06.2	44 09.9 ..	56.3	Bellatrix	278 32.2	N 6 21.6
22	272 47.2	117 24.6	51.5	174 25.7	50.8	175 45.2	06.2	59 12.3	56.3	Betelgeuse	271 01.5	N 7 24.4
23	287 49.6	132 24.3	50.3	189 26.3	50.7	190 47.1	06.1	74 14.7	56.3			
25 00	302 52.1	147 23.9	N11 49.2	204 27.0	N23 50.6	205 48.9	N23 06.1	89 17.1	S10 56.4	Canopus	263 56.6	S52 42.2
01	317 54.6	162 23.5	48.1	219 27.6	50.6	220 50.8	06.1	104 19.5	56.4	Capella	280 34.6	N46 00.4
02	332 57.0	177 23.1	46.9	234 28.2	50.5	235 52.7	06.1	119 21.9	56.4	Deneb	49 30.9	N45 19.9
03	347 59.5	192 22.8 ..	45.8	249 28.9 ..	50.4	250 54.6 ..	06.1	134 24.3 ..	56.5	Denebola	182 33.8	N14 29.8
04	3 01.9	207 22.4	44.7	264 29.5	50.4	265 56.4	06.0	149 26.7	56.5	Diphda	348 55.7	S17 54.5
05	18 04.4	222 22.0	43.5	279 30.2	50.3	280 58.3	06.0	164 29.1	56.5			
T 06	33 06.9	237 21.6	N11 42.4	294 30.8	N23 50.2	296 00.2	N23 06.0	179 31.5	S10 56.6	Dubhe	193 52.1	N61 40.8
H 07	48 09.3	252 21.3	41.3	309 31.4	50.1	311 02.1	06.0	194 33.9	56.6	Elnath	278 12.8	N28 36.9
U 08	63 11.8	267 20.9	40.1	324 32.1	50.0	326 03.9	05.9	209 36.3	56.6	Eltanin	90 45.6	N51 29.6
R 09	78 14.3	282 20.5 ..	39.0	339 32.7 ..	50.0	341 05.8 ..	05.9	224 38.7 ..	56.7	Enif	33 46.7	N 9 56.4
S 10	93 16.7	297 20.2	37.9	354 33.4	49.9	356 07.7	05.9	239 41.1	56.7	Fomalhaut	15 23.6	S29 32.7
11	108 19.2	312 19.8	36.7	9 34.0	49.8	11 09.5	05.9	254 43.5	56.7			
D 12	123 21.7	327 19.4	N11 35.6	24 34.6	N23 49.7	26 11.5	N23 05.8	269 45.9	S10 56.8	Gacrux	172 00.9	S57 11.6
A 13	138 24.1	342 19.0	34.4	39 35.3	49.7	41 13.3	05.8	284 48.3	56.8	Gienah	175 52.3	S17 37.1
Y 14	153 26.6	357 18.7	33.3	54 35.9	49.6	56 15.2	05.8	299 50.7	56.8	Hadar	148 47.7	S60 26.5
15	168 29.1	12 18.3 ..	32.2	69 36.6 ..	49.5	71 17.1 ..	05.8	314 53.1 ..	56.9	Hamal	328 00.6	N23 31.5
16	183 31.5	27 17.9	31.0	84 37.2	49.4	86 19.0	05.8	329 55.5	56.9	Kaus Aust.	83 43.3	S34 22.5
17	198 34.0	42 17.6	29.9	99 37.9	49.4	101 20.8	05.8	344 57.9	56.9			
18	213 36.4	57 17.2	N11 28.7	114 38.5	N23 49.3	116 22.7	N23 05.7	0 00.3	S10 57.0	Kochab	137 19.9	N74 06.3
19	228 38.9	72 16.8	27.6	129 39.1	49.2	131 24.6	05.7	15 02.7	57.0	Markab	13 38.0	N15 16.8
20	243 41.4	87 16.5	26.4	144 39.8	49.1	146 26.5	05.7	30 05.1	57.0	Menkar	314 15.0	N 4 08.6
21	258 43.8	102 16.1 ..	25.3	159 40.4 ..	49.0	161 28.3 ..	05.6	45 07.5 ..	57.1	Menkent	148 07.4	S36 26.3
22	273 46.3	117 15.7	24.2	174 41.1	49.0	176 30.2	05.6	60 09.9	57.1	Miaplacidus	221 40.5	S69 46.6
23	288 48.8	132 15.4	23.0	189 41.7	48.9	191 32.1	05.6	75 12.3	57.1			
26 00	303 51.2	147 15.0	N11 21.9	204 42.4	N23 48.8	206 34.0	N23 05.6	90 14.7	S10 57.2	Mirfak	308 40.3	N49 54.3
01	318 53.7	162 14.6	20.7	219 43.0	48.7	221 35.9	05.5	105 17.1	57.2	Nunki	75 57.8	S26 16.6
02	333 56.2	177 14.3	19.6	234 43.6	48.6	236 37.7	05.5	120 19.5	57.2	Peacock	53 18.5	S56 41.2
03	348 58.6	192 13.9 ..	18.4	249 44.3 ..	48.6	251 39.6 ..	05.5	135 21.9 ..	57.3	Pollux	243 28.0	N27 59.5
04	4 01.1	207 13.6	17.3	264 44.9	48.5	266 41.5	05.5	150 24.3	57.3	Procyon	245 00.0	N 5 11.3
05	19 03.6	222 13.2	16.1	279 45.6	48.4	281 43.4	05.4	165 26.7	57.3			
F 06	34 06.0	237 12.8	N11 15.0	294 46.2	N23 48.3	296 45.3	N23 05.4	180 29.1	S10 57.4	Rasalhague	96 06.1	N12 33.3
R 07	49 08.5	252 12.5	13.8	309 46.9	48.2	311 47.1	05.4	195 31.5	57.4	Regulus	207 43.7	N11 54.0
I 08	64 10.9	267 12.1	12.7	324 47.5	48.1	326 49.0	05.4	210 33.9	57.4	Rigel	281 12.2	S 8 11.2
D 09	79 13.4	282 11.7 ..	11.6	339 48.1 ..	48.1	341 50.9 ..	05.3	225 36.3 ..	57.5	Rigil Kent.	139 51.4	S60 53.6
A 10	94 15.9	297 11.4	10.4	354 48.8	48.0	356 52.8	05.3	240 38.7	57.5	Sabik	102 12.2	S15 44.3
Y 11	109 18.3	312 11.0	09.3	9 49.4	47.9	11 54.6	05.3	255 41.1	57.5			
12	124 20.8	327 10.7	N11 08.1	24 50.1	N23 47.8	26 56.5	N23 05.3	270 43.5	S10 57.6	Schedar	349 40.1	N56 36.5
13	139 23.3	342 10.3	07.0	39 50.7	47.7	41 58.4	05.3	285 45.9	57.6	Shaula	96 21.4	S37 06.7
14	154 25.7	357 10.0	05.8	54 51.4	47.6	57 00.3	05.2	300 48.3	57.6	Sirius	258 33.9	S16 44.2
15	169 28.2	12 09.6 ..	04.6	69 52.0 ..	47.6	72 02.2 ..	05.2	315 50.7 ..	57.7	Spica	158 31.2	S11 13.9
16	184 30.7	27 09.2	03.5	84 52.7	47.5	87 04.0	05.2	330 53.1	57.7	Suhail	222 52.8	S43 29.4
17	199 33.1	42 08.9	02.3	99 53.3	47.4	102 05.9	05.2	345 55.5	57.8			
18	214 35.6	57 08.5	N11 01.2	114 53.9	N23 47.3	117 07.8	N23 05.1	0 57.9	S10 57.8	Vega	80 38.5	N38 48.1
19	229 38.0	72 08.2	11 00.0	129 54.6	47.2	132 09.7	05.1	16 00.2	57.8	Zuben'ubi	137 05.2	S16 05.8
20	244 40.5	87 07.8	10 58.9	144 55.2	47.1	147 11.6	05.1	31 02.6	57.9		SHA	Mer.Pass.
21	259 43.0	102 07.5 ..	57.7	159 55.9 ..	47.0	162 13.4 ..	05.1	46 05.0 ..	57.9		° '	h m
22	274 45.4	117 07.1	56.6	174 56.5	46.9	177 15.3	05.0	61 07.4	57.9	Venus	204 31.8	14 11
23	289 47.9	132 06.8	55.4	189 57.2	46.9	192 17.2	05.0	76 09.8	58.0	Mars	261 34.9	10 22
	h m									Jupiter	262 56.8	10 15
Mer.Pass.	3 47.9	v −0.4	d 1.1	v 0.6	d 0.1	v 1.9	d 0.0	v 2.4	d 0.0	Saturn	146 25.0	18 00

UT	SUN GHA	SUN Dec	MOON GHA	v	MOON Dec	d	HP
24 WED							
00	178 22.6	N19 52.3	342 18.1	7.6	S10 27.0	11.0	60.5
01	193 22.6	51.8	356 44.7	7.6	10 16.0	11.0	60.4
02	208 22.6	51.3	11 11.3	7.7	10 05.0	11.1	60.4
03	223 22.6	.. 50.8	25 38.0	7.7	9 53.9	11.2	60.4
04	238 22.5	50.2	40 04.7	7.9	9 42.7	11.2	60.4
05	253 22.5	49.7	54 31.6	7.9	9 31.5	11.2	60.3
06	268 22.5	N19 49.2	68 58.5	7.9	S 9 20.3	11.4	60.3
07	283 22.5	48.7	83 25.4	8.1	9 08.9	11.3	60.3
08	298 22.5	48.1	97 52.5	8.1	8 57.6	11.4	60.3
09	313 22.5	.. 47.6	112 19.6	8.2	8 46.2	11.4	60.2
10	328 22.5	47.1	126 46.8	8.3	8 34.8	11.5	60.2
11	343 22.5	46.5	141 14.1	8.3	8 23.3	11.5	60.2
12	358 22.5	N19 46.0	155 41.4	8.4	S 8 11.8	11.6	60.1
13	13 22.5	45.5	170 08.8	8.5	8 00.2	11.6	60.1
14	28 22.5	44.9	184 36.3	8.6	7 48.6	11.6	60.1
15	43 22.4	.. 44.4	199 03.9	8.6	7 37.0	11.7	60.0
16	58 22.4	43.9	213 31.5	8.7	7 25.3	11.7	60.0
17	73 22.4	43.3	227 59.2	8.7	7 13.6	11.7	60.0
18	88 22.4	N19 42.8	242 26.9	8.9	S 7 01.9	11.7	59.9
19	103 22.4	42.3	256 54.8	8.9	6 50.2	11.8	59.9
20	118 22.4	41.7	271 22.7	8.9	6 38.4	11.8	59.9
21	133 22.4	.. 41.2	285 50.6	9.1	6 26.6	11.8	59.9
22	148 22.4	40.7	300 18.7	9.1	6 14.8	11.9	59.8
23	163 22.4	40.1	314 46.8	9.1	6 02.9	11.9	59.8
25 THU							
00	178 22.4	N19 39.6	329 14.9	9.3	S 5 51.0	11.9	59.7
01	193 22.4	39.1	343 43.2	9.3	5 39.1	11.9	59.7
02	208 22.4	38.5	358 11.5	9.3	5 27.2	11.9	59.7
03	223 22.4	.. 38.0	12 39.8	9.5	5 15.3	11.9	59.6
04	238 22.4	37.4	27 08.3	9.5	5 03.4	12.0	59.6
05	253 22.4	36.9	41 36.8	9.5	4 51.4	12.0	59.6
06	268 22.4	N19 36.4	56 05.3	9.6	S 4 39.4	11.9	59.5
07	283 22.4	35.8	70 33.9	9.7	4 27.5	12.0	59.5
08	298 22.3	35.3	85 02.6	9.7	4 15.5	12.0	59.5
09	313 22.3	.. 34.7	99 31.3	9.8	4 03.5	12.0	59.4
10	328 22.3	34.2	114 00.1	9.9	3 51.5	12.1	59.4
11	343 22.3	33.6	128 29.0	9.9	3 39.4	12.0	59.3
12	358 22.3	N19 33.1	142 57.9	10.0	S 3 27.4	12.0	59.3
13	13 22.3	32.6	157 26.9	10.0	3 15.4	12.0	59.3
14	28 22.3	32.0	171 55.9	10.1	3 03.4	12.0	59.2
15	43 22.3	.. 31.5	186 25.0	10.2	2 51.4	12.1	59.2
16	58 22.3	30.9	200 54.2	10.2	2 39.3	12.0	59.2
17	73 22.3	30.4	215 23.4	10.2	2 27.3	12.0	59.1
18	88 22.3	N19 29.8	229 52.6	10.3	S 2 15.3	12.0	59.1
19	103 22.3	29.3	244 21.9	10.4	2 03.3	12.0	59.0
20	118 22.3	28.7	258 51.3	10.4	1 51.3	12.0	59.0
21	133 22.3	.. 28.2	273 20.7	10.5	1 39.3	12.0	59.0
22	148 22.3	27.6	287 50.2	10.5	1 27.3	12.0	58.9
23	163 22.3	27.1	302 19.7	10.6	1 15.3	12.0	58.9
26 FRI							
00	178 22.3	N19 26.5	316 49.5	10.6	S 1 03.0	12.0	58.9
01	193 22.3	26.0	331 18.9	10.7	0 51.3	11.9	58.8
02	208 22.3	25.4	345 48.6	10.7	0 39.4	12.0	58.8
03	223 22.3	.. 24.9	0 18.3	10.7	0 27.4	11.9	58.7
04	238 22.3	24.3	14 48.0	10.9	0 15.5	11.9	58.7
05	253 22.3	23.8	29 17.9	10.8	S 0 03.6	11.9	58.7
06	268 22.3	N19 23.2	43 47.7	10.9	N 0 08.3	11.9	58.6
07	283 22.3	22.7	58 17.6	11.0	0 20.2	11.8	58.6
08	298 22.3	22.1	72 47.6	11.0	0 32.0	11.9	58.5
09	313 22.3	.. 21.5	87 17.6	11.0	0 43.9	11.8	58.5
10	328 22.3	21.0	101 47.6	11.1	0 55.7	11.8	58.5
11	343 22.3	20.4	116 17.7	11.1	1 07.5	11.7	58.4
12	358 22.3	N19 19.9	130 47.8	11.2	N 1 19.2	11.8	58.4
13	13 22.4	19.3	145 18.0	11.2	1 31.0	11.7	58.3
14	28 22.4	18.8	159 48.2	11.2	1 42.7	11.7	58.3
15	43 22.4	.. 18.2	174 18.4	11.3	1 54.4	11.7	58.3
16	58 22.4	17.6	188 48.7	11.3	2 06.1	11.6	58.2
17	73 22.4	17.1	203 19.0	11.4	2 17.7	11.6	58.2
18	88 22.4	N19 16.5	217 49.4	11.3	N 2 29.3	11.6	58.1
19	103 22.4	16.0	232 19.7	11.5	2 40.9	11.6	58.1
20	118 22.4	15.4	246 50.2	11.4	2 52.5	11.5	58.1
21	133 22.4	.. 14.8	261 20.6	11.5	3 04.0	11.5	58.0
22	148 22.4	14.3	275 51.1	11.6	3 15.5	11.4	58.0
23	163 22.4	13.7	290 21.7	11.5	N 3 26.9	11.4	57.9
	SD 15.8	d 0.5	SD 16.4		16.2		15.9

Twilight / Sunrise / Moonrise

Lat.	Naut.	Civil	Sunrise	Moonrise 24	25	26	27
N 72	▭	▭	▭	21 26	21 09	20 58	20 48
N 70	▭	▭	▭	21 11	21 07	21 02	20 58
68	////	////	01 36	21 03	21 05	21 06	21 07
66	////	////	02 18	20 57	21 03	21 08	21 14
64	////	00 46	02 46	20 52	21 02	21 11	21 20
62	////	01 46	03 08	20 47	21 00	21 13	21 25
60	////	02 18	03 25	20 43	20 59	21 15	21 30
N 58	00 42	02 41	03 39	20 39	20 58	21 16	21 34
56	01 36	03 00	03 51	20 36	20 57	21 18	21 38
54	02 06	03 15	04 02	20 33	20 57	21 19	21 41
52	02 28	03 28	04 11	20 30	20 56	21 20	21 44
50	02 46	03 40	04 20	20 28	20 55	21 21	21 47
45	03 19	04 03	04 38	20 23	20 54	21 24	21 53
N 40	03 43	04 21	04 52	20 18	20 53	21 26	21 58
35	04 01	04 36	05 04	20 14	20 52	21 27	22 02
30	04 17	04 48	05 15	20 11	20 51	21 29	22 06
20	04 41	05 09	05 33	20 05	20 49	21 32	22 13
N 10	05 00	05 26	05 49	20 00	20 48	21 34	22 19
0	05 16	05 41	06 03	19 55	20 47	21 36	22 25
S 10	05 29	05 55	06 17	19 50	20 46	21 39	22 30
20	05 42	06 09	06 33	19 45	20 44	21 41	22 36
30	05 55	06 24	06 50	19 39	20 43	21 44	22 43
35	06 02	06 33	07 00	19 35	20 42	21 46	22 47
40	06 09	06 42	07 11	19 32	20 41	21 48	22 52
45	06 17	06 52	07 25	19 27	20 40	21 50	22 57
S 50	06 25	07 05	07 41	19 22	20 39	21 53	23 04
52	06 29	07 10	07 48	19 19	20 38	21 54	23 07
54	06 33	07 17	07 57	19 16	20 37	21 55	23 10
56	06 37	07 23	08 06	19 13	20 37	21 57	23 14
58	06 42	07 31	08 17	19 10	20 36	21 58	23 18
S 60	06 47	07 39	08 30	19 06	20 35	22 00	23 22

Sunset / Twilight / Moonset

Lat.	Sunset	Civil	Naut.	Moonset 24	25	26	27
N 72	▭	▭	▭	05 16	07 22	09 19	11 13
N 70	▭	▭	▭	05 32	07 28	09 18	11 04
68	22 32	////	////	05 45	07 34	09 18	10 57
66	21 52	////	////	05 55	07 38	09 17	10 52
64	21 24	23 17	////	06 04	07 42	09 17	10 47
62	21 03	22 23	////	06 11	07 45	09 16	10 43
60	20 47	21 52	////	06 18	07 48	09 16	10 40
N 58	20 33	21 30	23 22	06 23	07 51	09 15	10 36
56	20 20	21 12	22 33	06 28	07 53	09 15	10 34
54	20 10	20 56	22 04	06 32	07 55	09 15	10 31
52	20 01	20 43	21 43	06 36	07 57	09 14	10 29
50	19 52	20 32	21 26	06 40	07 58	09 14	10 27
45	19 35	20 09	20 53	06 46	08 02	09 14	10 22
N 40	19 20	19 51	20 30	06 54	08 05	09 13	10 19
35	19 08	19 37	20 11	07 00	08 07	09 13	10 16
30	18 58	19 24	19 56	07 04	08 10	09 12	10 13
20	18 40	19 04	19 32	07 13	08 13	09 12	10 08
N 10	18 24	18 45	19 11	07 20	08 17	09 11	10 04
0	18 10	18 32	18 57	07 27	08 20	09 11	09 59
S 10	17 56	18 18	18 44	07 33	08 23	09 10	09 55
20	17 41	18 04	18 31	07 40	08 26	09 09	09 51
30	17 23	17 49	18 18	07 48	08 30	09 09	09 46
35	17 14	17 41	18 11	07 53	08 32	09 08	09 44
40	17 02	17 21	17 57	07 58	08 34	09 08	09 40
45	16 49	17 21	17 57	08 04	08 37	09 07	09 37
S 50	16 33	17 09	17 48	08 11	08 40	09 07	09 32
52	16 25	17 03	17 45	08 14	08 41	09 06	09 30
54	16 17	16 57	17 41	08 18	08 43	09 06	09 28
56	16 07	16 50	17 36	08 22	08 45	09 06	09 26
58	15 56	16 43	17 32	08 26	08 47	09 05	09 23
S 60	15 44	16 34	17 27	08 31	08 49	09 05	09 20

SUN / MOON

Day	SUN Eqn. of Time 00h	12h	Mer. Pass.	MOON Mer. Pass. Upper	Lower	Age	Phase
d	m s	m s	h m	h m	h m	d %	
24	06 30	06 30	12 07	01 14	13 41	16 95	
25	06 30	06 31	12 07	02 07	14 33	17 89	◑
26	06 31	06 31	12 07	02 59	15 24	18 82	

UT	ARIES GHA	VENUS −3.9 GHA	Dec	MARS +1.6 GHA	Dec	JUPITER −1.9 GHA	Dec	SATURN +0.6 GHA	Dec	Name	SHA	Dec
27 00	304 50.4	147 06.4	N10 54.3	204 57.8	N23 46.8	207 19.1	N23 05.0	91 12.2	S10 58.0	Acamar	315 18.4	S40 14.8
01	319 52.8	162 06.0	53.1	219 58.5	46.7	222 21.0	05.0	106 14.6	58.0	Achernar	335 26.7	S57 09.7
02	334 55.3	177 05.7	51.9	234 59.1	46.6	237 22.8	04.9	121 17.0	58.1	Acrux	173 09.4	S63 10.8
03	349 57.8	192 05.3	.. 50.8	249 59.8	.. 46.5	252 24.7	.. 04.9	136 19.4	.. 58.1	Adhara	255 12.8	S28 59.5
04	5 00.2	207 05.0	49.6	265 00.4	46.4	267 26.6	04.9	151 21.8	58.1	Aldebaran	290 49.5	N16 32.1
05	20 02.7	222 04.6	48.5	280 01.1	46.3	282 28.5	04.9	166 24.2	58.2			
06	35 05.2	237 04.3	N10 47.3	295 01.7	N23 46.2	297 30.4	N23 04.8	181 26.6	S10 58.2	Alioth	166 20.9	N55 53.4
07	50 07.6	252 03.9	46.2	310 02.3	46.1	312 32.2	04.8	196 29.0	58.3	Alkaid	152 58.9	N49 15.0
S 08	65 10.1	267 03.6	45.0	325 03.0	46.0	327 34.1	04.8	211 31.4	58.3	Al Na'ir	27 43.2	S46 53.4
A 09	80 12.5	282 03.2	.. 43.8	340 03.6	.. 46.0	342 36.0	.. 04.8	226 33.8	.. 58.3	Alnilam	275 46.5	S 1 11.7
T 10	95 15.0	297 02.9	42.7	355 04.3	45.9	357 37.9	04.7	241 36.2	58.4	Alphard	217 56.3	S 8 43.2
U 11	110 17.5	312 02.5	41.5	10 04.9	45.8	12 39.8	04.7	256 38.6	58.4			
R 12	125 19.9	327 02.2	N10 40.4	25 05.6	N23 45.7	27 41.6	N23 04.7	271 40.9	S10 58.4	Alphecca	126 10.8	N26 40.4
D 13	140 22.4	342 01.8	39.2	40 06.2	45.6	42 43.5	04.7	286 43.3	58.5	Alpheratz	357 43.2	N29 09.9
A 14	155 24.9	357 01.5	38.0	55 06.9	45.5	57 45.4	04.6	301 45.7	58.5	Altair	62 07.8	N 8 54.5
Y 15	170 27.3	12 01.1	.. 36.9	70 07.5	.. 45.4	72 47.3	.. 04.6	316 48.1	.. 58.5	Ankaa	353 15.4	S42 13.6
16	185 29.8	27 00.8	35.7	85 08.2	45.3	87 49.2	04.6	331 50.5	58.6	Antares	112 25.9	S26 27.6
17	200 32.3	42 00.5	34.5	100 08.8	45.2	102 51.1	04.6	346 52.9	58.6			
18	215 34.7	57 00.1	N10 33.4	115 09.5	N23 45.1	117 52.9	N23 04.5	1 55.3	S10 58.7	Arcturus	145 55.6	N19 06.9
19	230 37.2	71 59.8	32.2	130 10.1	45.0	132 54.8	04.5	16 57.7	58.7	Atria	107 27.2	S69 03.2
20	245 39.6	86 59.4	31.0	145 10.8	44.9	147 56.7	04.5	32 00.1	58.7	Avior	234 18.6	S59 33.3
21	260 42.1	101 59.1	.. 29.9	160 11.4	.. 44.8	162 58.6	.. 04.5	47 02.5	.. 58.8	Bellatrix	278 32.1	N 6 21.6
22	275 44.6	116 58.7	28.7	175 12.1	44.7	178 00.5	04.4	62 04.9	58.8	Betelgeuse	271 01.5	N 7 24.5
23	290 47.0	131 58.4	27.5	190 12.7	44.6	193 02.3	04.4	77 07.3	58.8			
28 00	305 49.5	146 58.0	N10 26.4	205 13.4	N23 44.5	208 04.2	N23 04.4	92 09.7	S10 58.9	Canopus	263 56.6	S52 42.2
01	320 52.0	161 57.7	25.2	220 14.0	44.4	223 06.1	04.4	107 12.0	58.9	Capella	280 34.6	N46 00.4
02	335 54.4	176 57.4	24.0	235 14.7	44.3	238 08.0	04.3	122 14.4	58.9	Deneb	49 30.9	N45 19.9
03	350 56.9	191 57.0	.. 22.9	250 15.3	.. 44.2	253 09.9	.. 04.3	137 16.8	.. 59.0	Denebola	182 33.8	N14 29.8
04	5 59.4	206 56.7	21.7	265 16.0	44.1	268 11.8	04.3	152 19.2	59.0	Diphda	348 55.7	S17 54.5
05	21 01.8	221 56.3	20.5	280 16.6	44.0	283 13.6	04.3	167 21.6	59.0			
06	36 04.3	236 56.0	N10 19.4	295 17.3	N23 43.9	298 15.5	N23 04.2	182 24.0	S10 59.1	Dubhe	193 52.2	N61 40.8
07	51 06.8	251 55.7	18.2	310 17.9	43.8	313 17.4	04.2	197 26.4	59.1	Elnath	278 12.8	N28 36.9
08	66 09.2	266 55.3	17.0	325 18.6	43.7	328 19.3	04.2	212 28.8	59.2	Eltanin	90 45.7	N51 29.6
S 09	81 11.7	281 55.0	.. 15.9	340 19.2	.. 43.6	343 21.2	.. 04.2	227 31.2	.. 59.2	Enif	33 46.7	N 9 56.5
U 10	96 14.1	296 54.6	14.7	355 19.9	43.5	358 23.1	04.1	242 33.6	59.2	Fomalhaut	15 23.6	S29 32.7
N 11	111 16.6	311 54.3	13.5	10 20.5	43.4	13 24.9	04.1	257 35.9	59.3			
D 12	126 19.1	326 54.0	N10 12.3	25 21.2	N23 43.3	28 26.8	N23 04.1	272 38.3	S10 59.3	Gacrux	172 01.0	S57 11.6
A 13	141 21.5	341 53.6	11.2	40 21.8	43.2	43 28.7	04.1	287 40.7	59.4	Gienah	175 52.3	S17 37.1
Y 14	156 24.0	356 53.3	10.0	55 22.5	43.1	58 30.6	04.0	302 43.1	59.4	Hadar	148 47.7	S60 26.5
15	171 26.5	11 53.0	.. 08.8	70 23.1	.. 43.0	73 32.5	.. 04.0	317 45.5	.. 59.4	Hamal	328 00.6	N23 31.5
16	186 28.9	26 52.6	07.6	85 23.8	42.9	88 34.4	04.0	332 47.9	59.5	Kaus Aust.	83 43.3	S34 22.5
17	201 31.4	41 52.3	06.5	100 24.4	42.8	103 36.2	04.0	347 50.3	59.5			
18	216 33.9	56 51.9	N10 05.3	115 25.1	N23 42.7	118 38.1	N23 03.9	2 52.7	S10 59.6	Kochab	137 19.9	N74 06.3
19	231 36.3	71 51.6	04.1	130 25.7	42.6	133 40.0	03.9	17 55.1	59.6	Markab	13 38.0	N15 16.8
20	246 38.8	86 51.3	02.9	145 26.4	42.5	148 41.9	03.9	32 57.4	59.6	Menkar	314 15.0	N 4 08.6
21	261 41.3	101 50.9	.. 01.8	160 27.0	.. 42.4	163 43.8	.. 03.9	47 59.8	.. 59.7	Menkent	148 07.4	S36 26.3
22	276 43.7	116 50.6	10 00.6	175 27.7	42.3	178 45.7	03.8	63 02.2	59.7	Miaplacidus	221 40.5	S69 46.6
23	291 46.2	131 50.3	9 59.4	190 28.3	42.2	193 47.5	03.8	78 04.6	59.7			
29 00	306 48.6	146 49.9	N 9 58.2	205 29.0	N23 42.1	208 49.4	N23 03.8	93 07.0	S10 59.8	Mirfak	308 40.3	N49 54.3
01	321 51.1	161 49.6	57.1	220 29.6	42.0	223 51.3	03.7	108 09.4	59.8	Nunki	75 57.8	S26 16.6
02	336 53.6	176 49.3	55.9	235 30.3	41.9	238 53.2	03.7	123 11.8	59.8	Peacock	53 18.5	S56 41.2
03	351 56.0	191 49.0	.. 54.7	250 31.0	.. 41.8	253 55.1	.. 03.7	138 14.2	.. 59.9	Pollux	243 28.0	N27 59.5
04	6 58.5	206 48.6	53.5	265 31.6	41.7	268 57.0	03.7	153 16.5	10 59.9	Procyon	244 59.9	N 5 11.3
05	22 01.0	221 48.3	52.3	280 32.3	41.6	283 58.8	03.6	168 18.9	11 00.0			
06	37 03.4	236 48.0	N 9 51.2	295 32.9	N23 41.5	299 00.7	N23 03.6	183 21.3	S11 00.0	Rasalhague	96 06.1	N12 33.3
07	52 05.9	251 47.6	50.0	310 33.6	41.4	314 02.6	03.6	198 23.7	00.0	Regulus	207 43.7	N11 54.0
08	67 08.4	266 47.3	48.8	325 34.2	41.2	329 04.5	03.6	213 26.1	00.1	Rigel	281 12.2	S 8 11.2
M 09	82 10.8	281 47.0	.. 47.6	340 34.9	.. 41.1	344 06.4	.. 03.5	228 28.5	.. 00.1	Rigil Kent.	139 51.5	S60 53.6
O 10	97 13.3	296 46.6	46.4	355 35.5	41.0	359 08.3	03.5	243 30.9	00.2	Sabik	102 12.2	S15 44.3
N 11	112 15.7	311 46.3	45.2	10 36.2	40.9	14 10.2	03.5	258 33.2	00.2			
D 12	127 18.2	326 46.0	N 9 44.1	25 36.8	N23 40.8	29 12.0	N23 03.5	273 35.6	S11 00.2	Schedar	349 40.1	N56 36.5
A 13	142 20.7	341 45.7	42.9	40 37.5	40.7	44 13.9	03.4	288 38.0	00.3	Shaula	96 21.4	S37 06.7
Y 14	157 23.1	356 45.3	41.7	55 38.1	40.6	59 15.8	03.4	303 40.4	00.3	Sirius	258 33.9	S16 44.2
15	172 25.6	11 45.0	.. 40.5	70 38.8	.. 40.5	74 17.7	.. 03.4	318 42.8	.. 00.3	Spica	158 31.2	S11 13.9
16	187 28.1	26 44.7	39.3	85 39.5	40.4	89 19.6	03.4	333 45.2	00.4	Suhail	222 52.8	S43 29.4
17	202 30.5	41 44.4	38.1	100 40.1	40.3	104 21.5	03.3	348 47.6	00.4			
18	217 33.0	56 44.0	N 9 37.0	115 40.8	N23 40.2	119 23.4	N23 03.3	3 49.9	S11 00.5	Vega	80 38.5	N38 48.1
19	232 35.5	71 43.7	35.8	130 41.4	40.0	134 25.2	03.3	18 52.3	00.5	Zuben'ubi	137 05.2	S16 05.8
20	247 37.9	86 43.4	34.6	145 42.1	39.9	149 27.1	03.2	33 54.7	00.5		SHA	Mer.Pass.
21	262 40.4	101 43.1	.. 33.4	160 42.7	.. 39.8	164 29.0	.. 03.2	48 57.1	.. 00.6	Venus	201 08.5	14 12
22	277 42.9	116 42.7	32.2	175 43.4	39.7	179 30.9	03.2	63 59.5	00.6	Mars	259 23.9	10 19
23	292 45.3	131 42.4	31.0	190 44.0	39.6	194 32.8	03.2	79 01.9	00.7	Jupiter	262 14.7	10 06
Mer.Pass. 3 36.1	v −0.3 d 1.2	v 0.7	d 0.1	v 1.9	d 0.0	v 2.4	d 0.0			Saturn	146 20.1	17 49

UT	SUN GHA	SUN Dec	MOON GHA	v	Dec	d	HP
d h	° ,	° ,	° ,	,	° ,	,	,
27 00	178 22.4	N19 13.1	304 52.2	11.6	N 3 38.3	11.4	57.9
01	193 22.4	12.6	319 22.8	11.7	3 49.7	11.4	57.9
02	208 22.4	12.0	333 53.5	11.6	4 01.1	11.3	57.8
03	223 22.4	.. 11.4	348 24.1	11.7	4 12.4	11.3	57.8
04	238 22.4	10.9	2 54.8	11.7	4 23.7	11.2	57.7
05	253 22.4	10.3	17 25.5	11.8	4 34.9	11.2	57.7
06	268 22.5	N19 09.7	31 56.3	11.7	N 4 46.1	11.1	57.7
07	283 22.5	09.2	46 27.0	11.8	4 57.2	11.1	57.6
08	298 22.5	08.6	60 57.8	11.9	5 08.3	11.1	57.6
09	313 22.5	08.0	75 28.7	11.8	5 19.4	11.0	57.6
10	328 22.5	07.5	89 59.5	11.9	5 30.4	11.0	57.5
11	343 22.5	06.9	104 30.4	11.9	5 41.4	11.0	57.5
12	358 22.5	N19 06.3	119 01.3	11.9	N 5 52.4	10.9	57.4
13	13 22.5	05.7	133 32.2	12.0	6 03.3	10.8	57.4
14	28 22.5	05.2	148 03.2	12.0	6 14.1	10.8	57.4
15	43 22.5	.. 04.6	162 34.2	12.0	6 24.9	10.8	57.3
16	58 22.5	04.0	177 05.2	12.0	6 35.7	10.7	57.3
17	73 22.6	03.5	191 36.2	12.0	6 46.4	10.6	57.2
18	88 22.6	N19 02.9	206 07.2	12.1	N 6 57.0	10.6	57.2
19	103 22.6	02.3	220 38.3	12.1	7 07.6	10.6	57.2
20	118 22.6	01.7	235 09.4	12.1	7 18.2	10.5	57.1
21	133 22.6	.. 01.2	249 40.5	12.1	7 28.7	10.5	57.1
22	148 22.6	00.6	264 11.6	12.1	7 39.2	10.4	57.0
23	163 22.6	19 00.0	278 42.7	12.1	7 49.6	10.3	57.0
28 00	178 22.6	N18 59.4	293 13.8	12.2	N 7 59.9	10.3	57.0
01	193 22.7	58.8	307 45.0	12.2	8 10.2	10.3	56.9
02	208 22.7	58.3	322 16.2	12.2	8 20.5	10.2	56.9
03	223 22.7	.. 57.7	336 47.4	12.2	8 30.7	10.1	56.9
04	238 22.7	57.1	351 18.6	12.2	8 40.8	10.1	56.8
05	253 22.7	56.5	5 49.8	12.3	8 50.9	10.0	56.8
06	268 22.7	N18 55.9	20 21.1	12.2	N 9 00.9	10.0	56.8
07	283 22.7	55.4	34 52.3	12.3	9 10.9	9.9	56.7
08	298 22.8	54.8	49 23.6	12.2	9 20.8	9.8	56.7
09	313 22.8	.. 54.2	63 54.8	12.3	9 30.6	9.8	56.6
10	328 22.8	53.6	78 26.1	12.3	9 40.4	9.7	56.6
11	343 22.8	53.0	92 57.4	12.3	9 50.1	9.7	56.6
12	358 22.8	N18 52.5	107 28.7	12.3	N 9 59.8	9.6	56.5
13	13 22.8	51.9	122 00.0	12.3	10 09.4	9.5	56.5
14	28 22.8	51.3	136 31.4	12.3	10 18.9	9.5	56.5
15	43 22.9	.. 50.7	151 02.7	12.3	10 28.4	9.4	56.4
16	58 22.9	50.1	165 34.0	12.3	10 37.8	9.4	56.4
17	73 22.9	49.5	180 05.4	12.3	10 47.2	9.3	56.4
18	88 22.9	N18 48.9	194 36.7	12.4	N10 56.5	9.2	56.3
19	103 22.9	48.3	209 08.1	12.3	11 05.7	9.2	56.3
20	118 22.9	47.8	223 39.4	12.4	11 14.9	9.1	56.3
21	133 23.0	.. 47.2	238 10.8	12.4	11 24.0	9.0	56.2
22	148 23.0	46.6	252 42.2	12.4	11 33.0	9.0	56.2
23	163 23.0	46.0	267 13.6	12.3	11 42.0	8.9	56.2
29 00	178 23.0	N18 45.4	281 44.9	12.4	N11 50.9	8.8	56.1
01	193 23.0	44.8	296 16.3	12.4	11 59.7	8.8	56.1
02	208 23.1	44.2	310 47.7	12.4	12 08.5	8.7	56.1
03	223 23.1	.. 43.6	325 19.1	12.4	12 17.2	8.6	56.0
04	238 23.1	43.0	339 50.5	12.4	12 25.8	8.6	56.0
05	253 23.1	42.4	354 21.9	12.4	12 34.4	8.5	56.0
06	268 23.1	N18 41.8	8 53.3	12.4	N12 42.9	8.4	55.9
07	283 23.2	41.3	23 24.7	12.4	12 51.3	8.4	55.9
08	298 23.2	40.7	37 56.1	12.4	12 59.7	8.3	55.9
09	313 23.2	.. 40.1	52 27.5	12.4	13 08.0	8.2	55.8
10	328 23.2	39.5	66 58.9	12.4	13 16.2	8.1	55.8
11	343 23.2	38.9	81 30.3	12.4	13 24.3	8.1	55.8
12	358 23.3	N18 38.3	96 01.7	12.4	N13 32.4	8.0	55.7
13	13 23.3	37.7	110 33.1	12.4	13 40.4	7.9	55.7
14	28 23.3	37.1	125 04.5	12.4	13 48.3	7.8	55.7
15	43 23.3	.. 36.5	139 35.9	12.4	13 56.1	7.8	55.7
16	58 23.4	35.9	154 07.3	12.4	14 03.9	7.7	55.6
17	73 23.4	35.3	168 38.7	12.4	14 11.6	7.6	55.6
18	88 23.4	N18 34.7	183 10.1	12.3	N14 19.2	7.6	55.6
19	103 23.4	34.1	197 41.4	12.4	14 26.8	7.5	55.5
20	118 23.4	33.5	212 12.8	12.4	14 34.2	7.4	55.5
21	133 23.5	.. 32.9	226 44.2	12.4	14 41.6	7.4	55.5
22	148 23.5	32.3	241 15.6	12.3	14 49.0	7.2	55.5
23	163 23.5	31.7	255 46.9	12.4	N14 56.2	7.2	55.4
	SD 15.8	d 0.6	SD 15.6		15.4		15.2

Days marked in left margin: S A T U R D A Y (27), S U N D A Y (28), M O N D A Y (29).

Lat.	Twilight Naut.	Twilight Civil	Sunrise	Moonrise 27	28	29	30
°	h m	h m	h m	h m	h m	h m	h m
N 72	▭	▭	▭	20 48	20 36	20 21	19 54
N 70	////	////	00 39	20 58	20 54	20 51	20 47
68	////	////	01 54	21 07	21 09	21 13	21 20
66	////	////	02 30	21 14	21 21	21 30	21 44
64	////	01 14	02 56	21 20	21 31	21 45	22 03
62	////	01 59	03 15	21 25	21 40	21 57	22 18
60	////	02 28	03 32	21 30	21 47	22 07	22 31
N 58	01 07	02 49	03 45	21 34	21 54	22 16	22 43
56	01 48	03 07	03 57	21 38	22 00	22 24	22 52
54	02 15	03 21	04 07	21 41	22 05	22 31	23 01
52	02 35	03 33	04 16	21 44	22 09	22 37	23 09
50	02 52	03 44	04 24	21 47	22 14	22 43	23 16
45	03 23	04 07	04 41	21 53	22 23	22 56	23 31
N 40	03 46	04 24	04 55	21 58	22 31	23 06	23 43
35	04 06	04 38	05 07	22 02	22 38	23 15	23 54
30	04 19	04 50	05 17	22 06	22 44	23 23	24 03
20	04 42	05 10	05 34	22 13	22 54	23 36	24 19
N 10	05 01	05 27	05 49	22 19	23 03	23 48	24 33
0	05 16	05 41	06 03	22 25	23 12	23 59	24 47
S 10	05 29	05 55	06 17	22 30	23 21	24 10	00 10
20	05 41	06 08	06 31	22 36	23 30	24 23	00 23
30	05 54	06 23	06 48	22 43	23 41	24 36	00 36
35	06 00	06 31	06 58	22 47	23 47	24 44	00 44
40	06 07	06 39	07 09	22 52	23 54	24 54	00 54
45	06 14	06 49	07 21	22 57	24 02	00 02	01 04
S 50	06 22	07 01	07 37	23 04	24 12	00 12	01 18
52	06 25	07 07	07 44	23 07	24 17	00 17	01 24
54	06 29	07 12	07 52	23 10	24 22	00 22	01 31
56	06 33	07 19	08 01	23 14	24 28	00 28	01 38
58	06 37	07 26	08 12	23 18	24 34	00 34	01 47
S 60	06 42	07 34	08 23	23 22	24 41	00 41	01 56

Lat.	Sunset	Twilight Civil	Twilight Naut.	Moonset 27	28	29	30
°	h m	h m	h m	h m	h m	h m	h m
N 72	▭	▭	▭	11 13	13 04	14 58	17 04
N 70	23 19	////	////	11 04	12 47	14 30	16 12
68	22 14	////	////	10 57	12 34	14 09	15 40
66	21 40	////	////	10 52	12 23	13 52	15 16
64	21 15	22 53	////	10 47	12 14	13 38	14 58
62	20 56	22 10	////	10 43	12 07	13 27	14 43
60	20 40	21 43	////	10 40	12 00	13 17	14 30
N 58	20 26	21 22	23 00	10 36	11 54	13 09	14 19
56	20 15	21 05	22 21	10 34	11 49	13 02	14 10
54	20 05	20 50	21 56	10 31	11 45	12 55	14 02
52	19 56	20 38	21 36	10 29	11 41	12 49	13 54
50	19 48	20 28	21 20	10 27	11 37	12 44	13 48
45	19 31	20 06	20 49	10 22	11 29	12 32	13 33
N 40	19 18	19 48	20 26	10 19	11 22	12 23	13 21
35	19 06	19 34	20 08	10 16	11 16	12 15	13 11
30	18 56	19 22	19 53	10 13	11 11	12 08	13 03
20	18 39	19 02	19 30	10 08	11 02	11 55	12 47
N 10	18 24	18 46	19 12	10 04	10 54	11 43	12 34
0	18 10	18 32	18 57	09 59	10 47	11 35	12 22
S 10	17 56	18 18	18 44	09 55	10 40	11 25	12 10
20	17 42	18 05	18 32	09 51	10 32	11 14	11 57
30	17 25	17 51	18 20	09 46	10 24	11 02	11 42
35	17 16	17 43	18 13	09 44	10 19	10 55	11 33
40	17 05	17 34	18 07	09 40	10 13	10 47	11 22
45	16 52	17 24	18 00	09 37	10 06	10 38	11 12
S 50	16 37	17 12	17 52	09 32	09 59	10 27	10 58
52	16 30	17 07	17 48	09 30	09 55	10 21	10 51
54	16 21	17 01	17 45	09 28	09 51	10 16	10 44
56	16 12	16 55	17 41	09 26	09 47	10 10	10 36
58	16 02	16 48	17 36	09 23	09 42	10 02	10 27
S 60	15 50	16 40	17 32	09 20	09 36	09 55	10 17

Day	SUN Eqn. of Time 00h	12h	SUN Mer. Pass.	MOON Mer. Pass. Upper	Lower	Age	Phase
d	m s	m s	h m	h m	h m	d %	
27	06 30	06 30	12 06	03 48	16 12	19 72	
28	06 29	06 29	12 06	04 36	17 00	20 63	
29	06 28	06 27	12 06	05 23	17 47	21 53	

UT	ARIES	VENUS −3.9		MARS +1.6		JUPITER −1.9		SATURN +0.6		STARS		
	GHA	GHA	Dec	GHA	Dec	GHA	Dec	GHA	Dec	Name	SHA	Dec
d h	° ′	° ′	° ′	° ′	° ′	° ′	° ′	° ′	° ′		° ′	° ′
30 00	307 47.8	146 42.1 N 9 29.8		205 44.7 N23 39.5		209 34.7 N23 03.1		94 04.2 S11 00.7		Acamar	315 18.3	S40 14.8
01	322 50.2	161 41.8	28.6	220 45.4	39.4	224 36.6	03.1	109 06.6	00.7	Achernar	335 26.6	S57 09.7
02	337 52.7	176 41.4	27.5	235 46.0	39.3	239 38.4	03.1	124 09.0	00.8	Acrux	173 09.4	S63 10.7
03	352 55.2	191 41.1 . .	26.3	250 46.7 . .	39.1	254 40.3 . .	03.1	139 11.4 . .	00.8	Adhara	255 12.8	S28 59.5
04	7 57.6	206 40.8	25.1	265 47.3	39.0	269 42.2	03.0	154 13.8	00.9	Aldebaran	290 49.4	N16 32.1
05	23 00.1	221 40.5	23.9	280 48.0	38.9	284 44.1	03.0	169 16.2	00.9			
06	38 02.6	236 40.2 N 9 22.7		295 48.6 N23 38.8		299 46.0 N23 03.0		184 18.5 S11 00.9		Alioth	166 20.9	N55 53.4
07	53 05.0	251 39.8	21.5	310 49.3	38.7	314 47.9	03.0	199 20.9	01.0	Alkaid	152 58.9	N49 15.0
T 08	68 07.5	266 39.5	20.3	325 49.9	38.6	329 49.8	02.9	214 23.3	01.0	Al Na'ir	27 43.2	S46 53.4
U 09	83 10.0	281 39.2 . .	19.1	340 50.6 . .	38.4	344 51.7 . .	02.9	229 25.7 . .	01.1	Alnilam	275 46.5	S 1 11.7
E 10	98 12.4	296 38.9	17.9	355 51.3	38.3	359 53.5	02.9	244 28.1	01.1	Alphard	217 56.3	S 8 43.2
S 11	113 14.9	311 38.6	16.7	10 51.9	38.2	14 55.4	02.8	259 30.4	01.1			
D 12	128 17.4	326 38.2 N 9 15.5		25 52.6 N23 38.1		29 57.3 N23 02.8		274 32.8 S11 01.2		Alphecca	126 10.8	N26 40.4
A 13	143 19.8	341 37.9	14.4	40 53.2	38.0	44 59.2	02.8	289 35.2	01.2	Alpheratz	357 43.1	N29 09.9
Y 14	158 22.3	356 37.6	13.2	55 53.9	37.9	60 01.1	02.8	304 37.6	01.3	Altair	62 07.8	N 8 54.5
15	173 24.7	11 37.3 . .	12.0	70 54.5 . .	37.7	75 03.0 . .	02.7	319 40.0 . .	01.3	Ankaa	353 15.4	S42 13.6
16	188 27.2	26 37.0	10.8	85 55.2	37.6	90 04.9	02.7	334 42.4	01.3	Antares	112 25.9	S26 27.6
17	203 29.7	41 36.7	09.6	100 55.9	37.5	105 06.8	02.7	349 44.7	01.4			
18	218 32.1	56 36.3 N 9 08.4		115 56.5 N23 37.4		120 08.6 N23 02.7		4 47.1 S11 01.4		Arcturus	145 55.7	N19 06.9
19	233 34.6	71 36.0	07.2	130 57.2	37.3	135 10.5	02.6	19 49.5	01.5	Atria	107 27.3	S69 03.2
20	248 37.1	86 35.7	06.0	145 57.8	37.1	150 12.4	02.6	34 51.9	01.5	Avior	234 18.6	S59 33.3
21	263 39.5	101 35.4 . .	04.8	160 58.5 . .	37.0	165 14.3 . .	02.6	49 54.3 . .	01.5	Bellatrix	278 32.1	N 6 21.6
22	278 42.0	116 35.1	03.6	175 59.2	36.9	180 16.2	02.5	64 56.6	01.6	Betelgeuse	271 01.4	N 7 24.5
23	293 44.5	131 34.8	02.4	190 59.8	36.8	195 18.1	02.5	79 59.0	01.6			
31 00	308 46.9	146 34.5 N 9 01.2		206 00.5 N23 36.7		210 20.0 N23 02.5		95 01.4 S11 01.7		Canopus	263 56.6	S52 42.2
01	323 49.4	161 34.1 9 00.0		221 01.1	36.5	225 21.9	02.5	110 03.8	01.7	Capella	280 34.6	N46 00.4
02	338 51.8	176 33.8 8 58.8		236 01.8	36.4	240 23.8	02.4	125 06.2	01.7	Deneb	49 30.9	N45 19.9
03	353 54.3	191 33.5 . . 57.6		251 02.5 . .	36.3	255 25.6 . .	02.4	140 08.5 . .	01.8	Denebola	182 33.8	N14 29.8
04	8 56.8	206 33.2	56.4	266 03.1	36.2	270 27.5	02.4	155 10.9	01.8	Diphda	348 55.6	S17 54.5
05	23 59.2	221 32.9	55.2	281 03.8	36.0	285 29.4	02.4	170 13.3	01.9			
06	39 01.7	236 32.6 N 8 54.0		296 04.4 N23 35.9		300 31.3 N23 02.3		185 15.7 S11 01.9		Dubhe	193 52.2	N61 40.8
07	54 04.2	251 32.3	52.8	311 05.1	35.8	315 33.2	02.3	200 18.1	01.9	Elnath	278 12.7	N28 36.9
W 08	69 06.6	266 32.0	51.6	326 05.8	35.7	330 35.1	02.3	215 20.4	02.0	Eltanin	90 45.7	N51 29.6
E 09	84 09.1	281 31.7 . .	50.4	341 06.4 . .	35.6	345 37.0 . .	02.2	230 22.8 . .	02.0	Enif	33 46.7	N 9 56.5
D 10	99 11.6	296 31.4	49.2	356 07.1	35.4	0 38.9	02.2	245 25.2	02.1	Fomalhaut	15 23.6	S29 32.7
N 11	114 14.0	311 31.0	48.0	11 07.7	35.3	15 40.8	02.2	260 27.6	02.1			
E 12	129 16.5	326 30.7 N 8 46.8		26 08.4 N23 35.2		30 42.7 N23 02.2		275 29.9 S11 02.2		Gacrux	172 01.0	S57 11.6
S 13	144 19.0	341 30.4	45.6	41 09.1	35.1	45 44.5	02.1	290 32.3	02.2	Gienah	175 52.4	S17 37.1
D 14	159 21.4	356 30.1	44.4	56 09.7	34.9	60 46.4	02.1	305 34.7	02.2	Hadar	148 47.7	S60 26.5
A 15	174 23.9	11 29.8 . .	43.2	71 10.4 . .	34.8	75 48.3 . .	02.1	320 37.1 . .	02.3	Hamal	328 00.6	N23 31.5
Y 16	189 26.3	26 29.5	42.0	86 11.0	34.7	90 50.2	02.0	335 39.5	02.3	Kaus Aust.	83 43.3	S34 22.5
17	204 28.8	41 29.2	40.8	101 11.7	34.5	105 52.1	02.0	350 41.8	02.4			
18	219 31.3	56 28.9 N 8 39.6		116 12.4 N23 34.4		120 54.0 N23 02.0		5 44.2 S11 02.4		Kochab	137 20.0	N74 06.3
19	234 33.7	71 28.6	38.4	131 13.0	34.3	135 55.9	02.0	20 46.6	02.4	Markab	13 37.9	N15 16.8
20	249 36.2	86 28.3	37.2	146 13.7	34.2	150 57.8	01.9	35 49.0	02.5	Menkar	314 15.0	N 4 08.6
21	264 38.7	101 28.0 . .	36.0	161 14.4 . .	34.0	165 59.7 . .	01.9	50 51.3 . .	02.5	Menkent	148 07.4	S36 26.3
22	279 41.1	116 27.7	34.8	176 15.0	33.9	181 01.6	01.9	65 53.7	02.6	Miaplacidus	221 40.5	S69 46.6
23	294 43.6	131 27.4	33.6	191 15.7	33.8	196 03.5	01.9	80 56.1	02.6			
1 00	309 46.1	146 27.1 N 8 32.3		206 16.3 N23 33.7		211 05.3 N23 01.8		95 58.5 S11 02.6		Mirfak	308 40.3	N49 54.3
01	324 48.5	161 26.8	31.1	221 17.0	33.5	226 07.2	01.8	111 00.8	02.7	Nunki	75 57.8	S26 16.6
02	339 51.0	176 26.5	29.9	236 17.7	33.4	241 09.1	01.8	126 03.2	02.7	Peacock	53 18.5	S56 41.2
03	354 53.5	191 26.2 . .	28.7	251 18.3 . .	33.3	256 11.0 . .	01.7	141 05.6 . .	02.8	Pollux	243 28.0	N27 59.4
04	9 55.9	206 25.9	27.5	266 19.0	33.1	271 12.9	01.7	156 08.0	02.8	Procyon	244 59.9	N 5 11.3
05	24 58.4	221 25.5	26.3	281 19.7	33.0	286 14.8	01.7	171 10.3	02.9			
06	40 00.8	236 25.2 N 8 25.1		296 20.3 N23 32.9		301 16.7 N23 01.7		186 12.7 S11 02.9		Rasalhague	96 06.1	N12 33.3
07	55 03.3	251 24.9	23.9	311 21.0	32.7	316 18.6	01.6	201 15.1	02.9	Regulus	207 43.7	N11 54.0
T 08	70 05.8	266 24.6	22.7	326 21.6	32.6	331 20.5	01.6	216 17.5	03.0	Rigel	281 12.2	S 8 11.2
H 09	85 08.2	281 24.3 . .	21.5	341 22.3 . .	32.5	346 22.4 . .	01.6	231 19.8 . .	03.0	Rigil Kent.	139 51.5	S60 53.6
U 10	100 10.7	296 24.0	20.3	356 23.0	32.3	1 24.3	01.5	246 22.2	03.1	Sabik	102 12.2	S15 44.3
R 11	115 13.2	311 23.7	19.0	11 23.6	32.2	16 26.2	01.5	261 24.6	03.1			
S 12	130 15.6	326 23.4 N 8 17.8		26 24.3 N23 32.1		31 28.0 N23 01.5		276 27.0 S11 03.2		Schedar	349 40.1	N56 36.6
D 13	145 18.1	341 23.1	16.6	41 25.0	31.9	46 29.9	01.5	291 29.3	03.2	Shaula	96 21.5	S37 06.7
A 14	160 20.6	356 22.8	15.4	56 25.6	31.8	61 31.8	01.4	306 31.7	03.2	Sirius	258 33.9	S16 44.1
Y 15	175 23.0	11 22.5 . .	14.2	71 26.3 . .	31.7	76 33.7 . .	01.4	321 34.1 . .	03.3	Spica	158 31.2	S11 13.9
16	190 25.5	26 22.3	13.0	86 27.0	31.5	91 35.6	01.4	336 36.5	03.3	Suhail	222 52.8	S43 29.4
17	205 28.0	41 22.0	11.8	101 27.6	31.4	106 37.5	01.3	351 38.8	03.4			
18	220 30.4	56 21.7 N 8 10.6		116 28.3 N23 31.3		121 39.4 N23 01.3		6 41.2 S11 03.4		Vega	80 38.5	N38 48.1
19	235 32.9	71 21.4	09.3	131 29.0	31.1	136 41.3	01.3	21 43.6	03.5	Zuben'ubi	137 05.2	S16 05.8
20	250 35.3	86 21.1	08.1	146 29.6	31.0	151 43.2	01.3	36 46.0	03.5		SHA	Mer.Pass.
21	265 37.8	101 20.8 . .	06.9	161 30.3 . .	30.9	166 45.1 . .	01.2	51 48.3 . .	03.5		° ′	h m
22	280 40.3	116 20.5	05.7	176 31.0	30.7	181 47.0	01.2	66 50.7	03.6	Venus	197 47.5	14 14
23	295 42.7	131 20.2	04.5	191 31.6	30.6	196 48.9	01.2	81 53.1	03.6	Mars	257 13.6	10 16
	h m									Jupiter	261 33.1	9 57
Mer. Pass. 3 24.3		v −0.3	d 1.2	v 0.7	d 0.1	v 1.9	d 0.0	v 2.4	d 0.0	Saturn	146 14.5	17 37

SUN / MOON

UT	SUN GHA	SUN Dec	MOON GHA	v	MOON Dec	d	HP
30 00	178 23.5	N18 31.1	270 18.3	12.4	N15 03.4	7.1	55.4
01	193 23.6	30.5	284 49.7	12.3	15 10.5	7.0	55.4
02	208 23.6	29.9	299 21.0	12.4	15 17.5	6.9	55.4
03	223 23.6	.. 29.3	313 52.4	12.3	15 24.4	6.9	55.3
04	238 23.6	28.6	328 23.7	12.4	15 31.3	6.7	55.3
05	253 23.7	28.0	342 55.1	12.3	15 38.0	6.7	55.3
06	268 23.7	N18 27.4	357 26.4	12.3	N15 44.7	6.7	55.2
07	283 23.7	26.8	11 57.7	12.3	15 51.4	6.5	55.2
T 08	298 23.7	26.2	26 29.0	12.4	15 57.9	6.4	55.2
U 09	313 23.8	.. 25.6	41 00.4	12.3	16 04.3	6.4	55.2
E 10	328 23.8	25.0	55 31.7	12.3	16 10.7	6.3	55.1
S 11	343 23.8	24.4	70 03.0	12.3	16 17.0	6.2	55.1
D 12	358 23.9	N18 23.8	84 34.3	12.3	N16 23.2	6.2	55.1
A 13	13 23.9	23.2	99 05.6	12.3	16 29.4	6.0	55.1
Y 14	28 23.9	22.6	113 36.9	12.2	16 35.4	6.0	55.1
15	43 23.9	.. 22.0	128 08.1	12.3	16 41.4	5.9	55.0
16	58 24.0	21.3	142 39.4	12.3	16 47.3	5.8	55.0
17	73 24.0	20.7	157 10.7	12.2	16 53.1	5.7	55.0
18	88 24.0	N18 20.1	171 41.9	12.3	N16 58.8	5.6	55.0
19	103 24.1	19.5	186 13.2	12.2	17 04.4	5.6	54.9
20	118 24.1	18.9	200 44.4	12.3	17 10.0	5.4	54.9
21	133 24.1	.. 18.3	215 15.7	12.2	17 15.4	5.4	54.9
22	148 24.2	17.7	229 46.9	12.2	17 20.8	5.3	54.9
23	163 24.2	17.0	244 18.1	12.2	17 26.1	5.2	54.9
31 00	178 24.2	N18 16.4	258 49.3	12.2	N17 31.3	5.2	54.8
01	193 24.2	15.8	273 20.5	12.2	17 36.5	5.0	54.8
02	208 24.3	15.2	287 51.7	12.2	17 41.5	5.0	54.8
03	223 24.3	.. 14.6	302 22.9	12.2	17 46.5	4.8	54.8
04	238 24.3	14.0	316 54.1	12.2	17 51.3	4.8	54.8
05	253 24.4	13.3	331 25.3	12.1	17 56.1	4.7	54.7
06	268 24.4	N18 12.7	345 56.4	12.2	N18 00.8	4.6	54.7
W 07	283 24.4	12.1	0 27.6	12.2	18 05.4	4.6	54.7
E 08	298 24.5	11.5	14 58.8	12.1	18 10.0	4.4	54.7
D 09	313 24.5	.. 10.9	29 29.9	12.2	18 14.4	4.4	54.7
N 10	328 24.5	10.2	44 01.1	12.1	18 18.8	4.2	54.6
E 11	343 24.6	09.6	58 32.2	12.1	18 23.0	4.2	54.6
S 12	358 24.6	N18 09.0	73 03.3	12.1	N18 27.2	4.1	54.6
D 13	13 24.6	08.4	87 34.4	12.1	18 31.3	4.0	54.6
A 14	28 24.7	07.8	102 05.5	12.2	18 35.3	3.9	54.6
Y 15	43 24.7	.. 07.1	116 36.7	12.1	18 39.2	3.8	54.6
16	58 24.7	06.5	131 07.8	12.1	18 43.0	3.7	54.5
17	73 24.8	05.9	145 38.8	12.1	18 46.7	3.7	54.5
18	88 24.8	N18 05.3	160 09.9	12.1	N18 50.4	3.5	54.5
19	103 24.8	04.6	174 41.0	12.1	18 53.9	3.5	54.5
20	118 24.9	04.0	189 12.1	12.1	18 57.4	3.4	54.5
21	133 24.9	.. 03.4	203 43.2	12.0	19 00.8	3.3	54.5
22	148 25.0	02.7	218 14.2	12.1	19 04.1	3.2	54.4
23	163 25.0	02.1	232 45.3	12.0	19 07.3	3.1	54.4
1 00	178 25.0	N18 01.5	247 16.3	12.1	N19 10.4	3.0	54.4
01	193 25.1	00.9	261 47.4	12.0	19 13.4	2.9	54.4
02	208 25.1	18 00.2	276 18.4	12.1	19 16.3	2.9	54.4
03	223 25.1	17 59.6	290 49.5	12.0	19 19.2	2.7	54.4
04	238 25.2	59.0	305 20.5	12.0	19 21.9	2.6	54.4
05	253 25.2	58.3	319 51.5	12.0	19 24.5	2.6	54.3
06	268 25.3	N17 57.7	334 22.5	12.1	N19 27.1	2.5	54.3
07	283 25.3	57.1	348 53.6	12.0	19 29.6	2.4	54.3
T 08	298 25.3	56.4	3 24.6	12.0	19 32.0	2.3	54.3
H 09	313 25.4	.. 55.8	17 55.6	12.0	19 34.3	2.1	54.3
U 10	328 25.4	55.2	32 26.6	12.0	19 36.4	2.2	54.3
R 11	343 25.5	54.5	46 57.6	12.0	19 38.6	2.0	54.3
S 12	358 25.5	N17 53.9	61 28.6	12.0	N19 40.6	1.9	54.3
D 13	13 25.5	53.3	75 59.6	12.0	19 42.5	1.8	54.3
A 14	28 25.6	52.6	90 30.6	12.0	19 44.3	1.8	54.2
Y 15	43 25.6	.. 52.0	105 01.6	12.0	19 46.1	1.6	54.2
16	58 25.7	51.4	119 32.6	12.0	19 47.7	1.6	54.2
17	73 25.7	50.7	134 03.6	12.0	19 49.3	1.6	54.2
18	88 25.7	N17 50.1	148 34.6	12.0	N19 50.7	1.4	54.2
19	103 25.8	49.5	163 05.6	11.9	19 52.1	1.3	54.2
20	118 25.8	48.8	177 36.5	12.0	19 53.4	1.2	54.2
21	133 25.9	.. 48.2	192 07.5	12.0	19 54.6	1.1	54.2
22	148 25.9	47.5	206 38.5	12.0	19 55.7	1.0	54.2
23	163 26.0	46.9	221 09.5	12.0	N19 56.7	0.9	54.2
	SD 15.8	d 0.6	SD 15.0		14.9		14.8

Twilight / Sunrise / Moonrise

Lat.	Naut.	Civil	Sunrise	30	31	1	2
N 72	////	////	□	19 54	□	□	□
N 70	////	////	01 18	20 47	20 44	20 44	21 31
68	////	////	02 10	21 20	21 33	22 01	22 49
66	////	////	02 42	21 44	22 05	22 38	23 27
64	////	01 34	03 05	22 03	22 28	23 05	23 54
62	////	02 11	03 23	22 18	22 47	23 25	24 14
60	////	02 37	03 39	22 31	23 02	23 42	24 31
N 58	01 25	02 57	03 51	22 43	23 15	23 56	24 45
56	02 00	03 13	04 02	22 52	23 27	24 08	00 08
54	02 24	03 27	04 12	23 01	23 37	24 19	00 19
52	02 42	03 39	04 20	23 09	23 46	24 28	00 28
50	02 58	03 49	04 28	23 16	23 53	24 37	00 37
45	03 27	04 10	04 44	23 31	24 10	00 10	00 54
N 40	03 50	04 27	04 57	23 43	24 24	00 24	01 09
35	04 07	04 41	05 09	23 54	24 36	00 36	01 21
30	04 21	04 52	05 18	24 03	00 03	00 46	01 32
20	04 44	05 12	05 35	24 19	00 19	01 04	01 51
N 10	05 01	05 27	05 49	24 33	00 33	01 20	02 07
0	05 16	05 41	06 03	24 47	00 47	01 34	02 22
S 10	05 29	05 54	06 16	00 10	01 00	01 49	02 37
20	05 40	06 07	06 30	00 23	01 14	02 05	02 54
30	05 52	06 21	06 46	00 36	01 30	02 23	03 12
35	05 58	06 28	06 55	00 44	01 40	02 33	03 23
40	06 04	06 37	07 06	00 54	01 51	02 45	03 36
45	06 11	06 46	07 18	01 04	02 04	02 59	03 51
S 50	06 18	06 57	07 33	01 18	02 19	03 17	04 09
52	06 21	07 02	07 40	01 24	02 27	03 25	04 17
54	06 25	07 08	07 47	01 31	02 35	03 34	04 27
56	06 28	07 14	07 56	01 38	02 44	03 44	04 38
58	06 32	07 21	08 06	01 47	02 55	03 56	04 50
S 60	06 37	07 28	08 17	01 56	03 07	04 10	05 05

Sunset / Twilight / Moonset

Lat.	Sunset	Civil	Naut.	30	31	1	2
N 72	□	////	////	17 04	□	□	□
N 70	22 46	////	////	16 12	17 54	19 34	20 27
68	21 58	////	////	15 40	17 05	18 17	19 08
66	21 28	////	////	15 16	16 34	17 40	18 30
64	21 05	22 33	////	14 58	16 11	17 14	18 04
62	20 47	21 58	////	14 43	15 52	16 53	17 43
60	20 33	21 33	////	14 30	15 37	16 36	17 26
N 58	20 20	21 14	22 42	14 19	15 24	16 22	17 12
56	20 09	20 58	22 12	14 10	15 13	16 10	17 00
54	20 00	20 44	21 47	14 02	15 04	16 00	16 49
52	19 51	20 33	21 29	13 54	14 55	15 51	16 40
50	19 44	20 22	21 13	13 48	14 47	15 42	16 31
45	19 28	20 02	20 44	13 33	14 31	15 24	16 13
N 40	19 15	19 45	20 22	13 21	14 17	15 10	15 59
35	19 04	19 31	20 05	13 11	14 06	14 58	15 46
30	18 54	19 20	19 51	13 03	13 56	14 47	15 36
20	18 37	19 01	19 29	12 47	13 39	14 29	15 17
N 10	18 23	18 45	19 11	12 34	13 24	14 12	15 01
0	18 10	18 32	18 57	12 22	13 10	13 57	14 45
S 10	17 57	18 19	18 44	12 10	12 56	13 42	14 30
20	17 43	18 06	18 33	11 57	12 41	13 26	14 14
30	17 27	17 52	18 21	11 42	12 24	13 08	13 55
35	17 18	17 45	18 15	11 33	12 14	12 57	13 44
40	17 07	17 36	18 09	11 23	12 02	12 45	13 32
45	16 55	17 26	18 02	11 12	11 49	12 31	13 17
S 50	16 41	17 16	17 55	10 58	11 33	12 13	12 59
52	16 34	17 11	17 52	10 51	11 25	12 05	12 50
54	16 26	17 05	17 49	10 44	11 17	11 55	12 41
56	16 17	16 59	17 45	10 36	11 07	11 45	12 30
58	16 08	16 53	17 41	10 27	10 56	11 33	12 18
S 60	15 57	16 45	17 37	10 17	10 44	11 19	12 03

SUN / MOON

Day	Eqn. of Time 00h	Eqn. of Time 12h	Mer. Pass.	Mer. Pass. Upper	Mer. Pass. Lower	Age d	Phase %
30	06 26	06 25	12 06	06 11	18 34	22	43
31	06 23	06 22	12 06	06 58	19 22	23	33
1	06 20	06 18	12 06	07 46	20 10	24	25

UT	ARIES GHA	VENUS −3.9 GHA	Dec	MARS +1.6 GHA	Dec	JUPITER −1.9 GHA	Dec	SATURN +0.7 GHA	Dec	STARS Name	SHA	Dec
2 00	310 45.2	146 19.9	N 8 03.3	206 32.3	N23 30.5	211 50.8	N23 01.1	96 55.4	S11 03.7	Acamar	315 18.3	S40 14.8
01	325 47.7	161 19.6	02.1	221 33.0	30.3	226 52.7	01.1	111 57.8	03.7	Achernar	335 26.6	S57 09.7
02	340 50.1	176 19.3	8 00.8	236 33.6	30.2	241 54.6	01.1	127 00.2	03.8	Acrux	173 09.4	S63 10.7
03	355 52.6	191 19.0	7 59.6	251 34.3 ..	30.0	256 56.4 ..	01.1	142 02.6 ..	03.8	Adhara	255 12.8	S28 59.5
04	10 55.1	206 18.7	58.4	266 35.0	29.9	271 58.3	01.0	157 04.9	03.8	Aldebaran	290 49.4	N16 32.1
05	25 57.5	221 18.4	57.2	281 35.6	29.8	287 00.2	01.0	172 07.3	03.9			
06	41 00.0	236 18.1	N 7 56.0	296 36.3	N23 29.6	302 02.1	N23 01.0	187 09.7	S11 03.9	Alioth	166 20.9	N55 53.4
07	56 02.4	251 17.8	54.8	311 37.0	29.5	317 04.0	00.9	202 12.0	04.0	Alkaid	152 58.9	N49 15.0
08	71 04.9	266 17.5	53.5	326 37.6	29.3	332 05.9	00.9	217 14.4	04.0	Al Na'ir	27 43.2	S46 53.4
F 09	86 07.4	281 17.2 ..	52.3	341 38.3 ..	29.2	347 07.8 ..	00.9	232 16.8 ..	04.1	Alnilam	275 46.5	S 1 11.7
R 10	101 09.8	296 17.0	51.1	356 39.0	29.1	2 09.7	00.9	247 19.2	04.1	Alphard	217 56.3	S 8 43.1
I 11	116 12.3	311 16.7	49.9	11 39.6	28.9	17 11.6	00.8	262 21.5	04.1			
D 12	131 14.8	326 16.4	N 7 48.7	26 40.3	N23 28.8	32 13.5	N23 00.8	277 23.9	S11 04.2	Alphecca	126 10.8	N26 40.4
A 13	146 17.2	341 16.1	47.4	41 41.0	28.6	47 15.4	00.8	292 26.3	04.2	Alpheratz	357 43.1	N29 10.0
Y 14	161 19.7	356 15.8	46.2	56 41.6	28.5	62 17.3	00.7	307 28.6	04.3	Altair	62 07.8	N 8 54.5
15	176 22.2	11 15.5 ..	45.0	71 42.3 ..	28.4	77 19.2 ..	00.7	322 31.0 ..	04.3	Ankaa	353 15.4	S42 13.6
16	191 24.6	26 15.2	43.8	86 43.0	28.2	92 21.1	00.7	337 33.4	04.4	Antares	112 25.9	S26 27.6
17	206 27.1	41 14.9	42.6	101 43.6	28.1	107 23.0	00.6	352 35.8	04.4			
18	221 29.6	56 14.6	N 7 41.3	116 44.3	N23 27.9	122 24.9	N23 00.6	7 38.1	S11 04.5	Arcturus	145 55.7	N19 06.9
19	236 32.0	71 14.3	40.1	131 45.0	27.8	137 26.8	00.6	22 40.5	04.5	Atria	107 27.3	S69 03.2
20	251 34.5	86 14.1	38.9	146 45.6	27.6	152 28.7	00.6	37 42.9	04.5	Avior	234 18.6	S59 33.3
21	266 36.9	101 13.8 ..	37.7	161 46.3 ..	27.5	167 30.6 ..	00.5	52 45.2 ..	04.6	Bellatrix	278 32.1	N 6 21.6
22	281 39.4	116 13.5	36.4	176 47.0	27.4	182 32.4	00.5	67 47.6	04.6	Betelgeuse	271 01.4	N 7 24.5
23	296 41.9	131 13.2	35.2	191 47.7	27.2	197 34.3	00.5	82 50.0	04.7			
3 00	311 44.3	146 12.9	N 7 34.0	206 48.3	N23 27.1	212 36.2	N23 00.4	97 52.3	S11 04.7	Canopus	263 56.5	S52 42.1
01	326 46.8	161 12.6	32.8	221 49.0	26.9	227 38.1	00.4	112 54.7	04.8	Capella	280 34.6	N46 00.4
02	341 49.3	176 12.3	31.6	236 49.7	26.8	242 40.0	00.4	127 57.1	04.8	Deneb	49 30.9	N45 20.0
03	356 51.7	191 12.1 ..	30.3	251 50.3 ..	26.6	257 41.9 ..	00.4	142 59.4 ..	04.8	Denebola	182 33.8	N14 29.8
04	11 54.2	206 11.8	29.1	266 51.0	26.5	272 43.8	00.3	158 01.8	04.9	Diphda	348 55.6	S17 54.5
05	26 56.7	221 11.5	27.9	281 51.7	26.3	287 45.7	00.3	173 04.2	04.9			
06	41 59.1	236 11.2	N 7 26.6	296 52.4	N23 26.2	302 47.6	N23 00.2	188 06.5	S11 05.0	Dubhe	193 52.2	N61 40.8
07	57 01.6	251 10.9	25.4	311 53.0	26.0	317 49.5	00.2	203 08.9	05.0	Elnath	278 12.7	N28 36.9
S 08	72 04.1	266 10.6	24.2	326 53.7	25.9	332 51.4	00.2	218 11.3	05.1	Eltanin	90 45.7	N51 29.6
A 09	87 06.5	281 10.3 ..	23.0	341 54.4 ..	25.7	347 53.3 ..	00.2	233 13.6 ..	05.1	Enif	33 46.7	N 9 56.5
T 10	102 09.0	296 10.1	21.7	356 55.0 +	25.6	2 55.2	00.1	248 16.0	05.2	Fomalhaut	15 23.6	S29 32.7
U 11	117 11.4	311 09.8	20.5	11 55.7	25.4	17 57.1	00.1	263 18.4	05.2			
R 12	132 13.9	326 09.5	N 7 19.3	26 56.4	N23 25.3	32 59.0	N23 00.1	278 20.7	S11 05.3	Gacrux	172 01.0	S57 11.6
D 13	147 16.4	341 09.2	18.1	41 57.1	25.1	48 00.9	00.1	293 23.1	05.3	Gienah	175 52.4	S17 37.1
A 14	162 18.8	356 08.9	16.8	56 57.7	25.0	63 02.8	00.0	308 25.5	05.3	Hadar	148 47.7	S60 26.5
Y 15	177 21.3	11 08.7 ..	15.6	71 58.4 ..	24.8	78 04.7 ..	00.0	323 27.8 ..	05.4	Hamal	328 00.6	N23 31.5
16	192 23.8	26 08.4	14.4	86 59.1	24.7	93 06.6	23 00.0	338 30.2	05.4	Kaus Aust.	83 43.3	S34 22.5
17	207 26.2	41 08.1	13.1	101 59.7	24.5	108 08.5	22 59.9	353 32.6	05.5			
18	222 28.7	56 07.8	N 7 11.9	117 00.4	N23 24.4	123 10.4	N22 59.9	8 34.9	S11 05.5	Kochab	137 20.1	N74 06.3
19	237 31.2	71 07.5	10.7	132 01.1	24.2	138 12.3	59.9	23 37.3	05.6	Markab	13 37.9	N15 16.9
20	252 33.6	86 07.3	09.5	147 01.8	24.1	153 14.2	59.8	38 39.7	05.6	Menkar	314 15.0	N 4 08.6
21	267 36.1	101 07.0 ..	08.2	162 02.4 ..	23.9	168 16.1 ..	59.8	53 42.0 ..	05.7	Menkent	148 07.4	S36 26.3
22	282 38.6	116 06.7	07.0	177 03.1	23.8	183 18.0	59.8	68 44.4	05.7	Miaplacidus	221 40.5	S69 46.6
23	297 41.0	131 06.4	05.8	192 03.8	23.6	198 19.9	59.8	83 46.8	05.7			
4 00	312 43.5	146 06.1	N 7 04.5	207 04.5	N23 23.5	213 21.8	N22 59.7	98 49.1	S11 05.8	Mirfak	308 40.2	N49 54.3
01	327 45.9	161 05.9	03.3	222 05.1	23.3	228 23.7	59.7	113 51.5	05.8	Nunki	75 57.8	S26 16.6
02	342 48.4	176 05.6	02.1	237 05.8	23.2	243 25.6	59.7	128 53.9	05.9	Peacock	53 18.5	S56 41.2
03	357 50.9	191 05.3	7 00.8	252 06.5 ..	23.0	258 27.5 ..	59.6	143 56.2 ..	05.9	Pollux	243 28.0	N27 59.4
04	12 53.3	206 05.0	6 59.6	267 07.2	22.9	273 29.4	59.6	158 58.6	06.0	Procyon	244 59.9	N 5 11.3
05	27 55.8	221 04.8	58.4	282 07.8	22.7	288 31.3	59.6	174 01.0	06.0			
06	42 58.3	236 04.5	N 6 57.1	297 08.5	N23 22.6	303 33.2	N22 59.5	189 03.3	S11 06.1	Rasalhague	96 06.1	N12 33.3
07	58 00.7	251 04.2	55.9	312 09.2	22.4	318 35.1	59.5	204 05.7	06.1	Regulus	207 43.7	N11 54.0
08	73 03.2	266 03.9	54.7	327 09.8	22.3	333 37.0	59.5	219 08.0	06.2	Rigel	281 12.2	S 8 11.2
S 09	88 05.7	281 03.6 ..	53.4	342 10.5 ..	22.1	348 38.9 ..	59.5	234 10.4 ..	06.2	Rigil Kent.	139 51.5	S60 53.6
U 10	103 08.1	296 03.4	52.2	357 11.2	21.9	3 40.8	59.4	249 12.8	06.3	Sabik	102 12.2	S15 44.3
N 11	118 10.6	311 03.1	51.0	12 11.9	21.8	18 42.7	59.4	264 15.1	06.3			
D 12	133 13.0	326 02.8	N 6 49.7	27 12.6	N23 21.6	33 44.6	N22 59.4	279 17.5	S11 06.3	Schedar	349 40.0	N56 36.6
A 13	148 15.5	341 02.5	48.5	42 13.2	21.5	48 46.5	59.3	294 19.9	06.4	Shaula	96 21.5	S37 06.7
Y 14	163 18.0	356 02.2	47.3	57 13.9	21.3	63 48.4	59.3	309 22.2	06.4	Sirius	258 33.9	S16 44.1
15	178 20.4	11 02.0 ..	46.0	72 14.6 ..	21.2	78 50.3 ..	59.3	324 24.6 ..	06.5	Spica	158 31.2	S11 13.9
16	193 22.9	26 01.7	44.8	87 15.3	21.0	93 52.2	59.2	339 27.0	06.5	Suhail	222 52.8	S43 29.4
17	208 25.4	41 01.5	43.6	102 15.9	20.8	108 54.1	59.2	354 29.3	06.6			
18	223 27.8	56 01.2	N 6 42.3	117 16.6	N23 20.7	123 56.0	N22 59.2	9 31.7	S11 06.6	Vega	80 38.5	N38 48.1
19	238 30.3	71 00.9	41.1	132 17.3	20.5	138 57.9	59.1	24 34.0	06.7	Zuben'ubi	137 05.3	S16 05.8
20	253 32.8	86 00.6	39.8	147 18.0	20.4	153 59.8	59.1	39 36.4	06.7			
21	268 35.2	101 00.4 ..	38.6	162 18.6 ..	20.2	169 01.7 ..	59.1	54 38.8 ..	06.8			
22	283 37.7	116 00.1	37.4	177 19.3	20.0	184 03.6	59.1	69 41.1	06.8			
23	298 40.2	130 59.8	36.1	192 20.0	19.9	199 05.5	59.0	84 43.5	06.9			

	h m										SHA	Mer.Pass.
Mer.Pass.	3 12.5	v −0.3	d 1.2	v 0.7	d 0.1	v 1.9	d 0.0	v 2.4	d 0.0	Venus	194 28.6	14 15
										Mars	255 04.0	10 12
										Jupiter	260 51.9	9 48
										Saturn	146 08.0	17 26

UT	SUN GHA	SUN Dec	MOON GHA	v	MOON Dec	d	HP
d h	° ′	° ′	° ′	′	° ′	′	′
2 00	178 26.0	N17 46.3	235 40.5	12.0	N19 57.6	0.8	54.2
01	193 26.0	45.6	250 11.5	12.0	19 58.4	0.7	54.1
02	208 26.1	45.0	264 42.5	12.0	19 59.1	0.6	54.1
03	223 26.1	.. 44.3	279 13.5	12.0	19 59.7	0.6	54.1
04	238 26.2	43.7	293 44.5	11.9	20 00.3	0.4	54.1
05	253 26.2	43.0	308 15.4	12.0	20 00.7	0.4	54.1
06	268 26.3	N17 42.4	322 46.4	12.0	N20 01.1	0.2	54.1
07	283 26.3	41.8	337 17.4	12.0	20 01.3	0.2	54.1
08	298 26.4	41.1	351 48.4	12.1	20 01.5	0.1	54.1
F 09	313 26.4	.. 40.5	6 19.5	12.0	20 01.6	0.0	54.1
R 10	328 26.4	39.8	20 50.5	12.0	20 01.6	0.0	54.1
I 11	343 26.5	39.2	35 21.5	12.0	20 01.5	0.2	54.1
D 12	358 26.5	N17 38.5	49 52.5	12.0	N20 01.3	0.3	54.1
A 13	13 26.6	37.9	64 23.5	12.0	20 01.0	0.4	54.1
Y 14	28 26.6	37.2	78 54.5	12.1	20 00.6	0.5	54.1
15	43 26.7	.. 36.6	93 25.6	12.0	20 00.1	0.6	54.1
16	58 26.7	35.9	107 56.6	12.1	19 59.6	0.7	54.1
17	73 26.8	35.3	122 27.7	12.0	19 58.9	0.8	54.1
18	88 26.8	N17 34.6	136 58.7	12.1	N19 58.1	0.8	54.1
19	103 26.9	34.0	151 29.8	12.0	19 57.3	0.9	54.1
20	118 26.9	33.3	166 00.8	12.1	19 56.4	1.1	54.0
21	133 27.0	.. 32.7	180 31.9	12.1	19 55.3	1.1	54.0
22	148 27.0	32.0	195 03.0	12.0	19 54.2	1.2	54.0
23	163 27.1	31.4	209 34.0	12.1	19 53.0	1.3	54.0
3 00	178 27.1	N17 30.7	224 05.1	12.1	N19 51.7	1.4	54.0
01	193 27.2	30.1	238 36.2	12.2	19 50.3	1.5	54.0
02	208 27.2	29.4	253 07.4	12.1	19 48.8	1.5	54.0
03	223 27.3	.. 28.8	267 38.5	12.1	19 47.3	1.7	54.0
04	238 27.3	28.1	282 09.6	12.1	19 45.6	1.8	54.0
05	253 27.4	27.5	296 40.7	12.2	19 43.8	1.8	54.0
06	268 27.4	N17 26.8	311 11.9	12.1	N19 42.0	1.9	54.0
S 07	283 27.5	26.2	325 43.0	12.2	19 40.1	2.1	54.0
A 08	298 27.5	25.5	340 14.2	12.2	19 38.0	2.1	54.0
T 09	313 27.6	.. 24.8	354 45.4	12.2	19 35.9	2.2	54.0
U 10	328 27.6	24.2	9 16.6	12.2	19 33.7	2.3	54.0
R 11	343 27.7	23.5	23 47.8	12.2	19 31.4	2.4	54.0
D 12	358 27.7	N17 22.9	38 19.0	12.2	N19 29.0	2.4	54.0
A 13	13 27.8	22.2	52 50.2	12.3	19 26.6	2.6	54.0
Y 14	28 27.8	21.5	67 21.5	12.2	19 24.0	2.6	54.0
15	43 27.9	.. 20.9	81 52.7	12.3	19 21.4	2.7	54.0
16	58 27.9	20.2	96 24.0	12.3	19 18.6	2.8	54.0
17	73 28.0	19.6	110 55.3	12.3	19 15.8	2.9	54.0
18	88 28.0	N17 18.9	125 26.6	12.3	N19 12.9	3.0	54.0
19	103 28.1	18.2	139 57.9	12.3	19 09.9	3.1	54.0
20	118 28.2	17.6	154 29.2	12.3	19 06.8	3.2	54.0
21	133 28.2	.. 16.9	169 00.5	12.4	19 03.6	3.3	54.0
22	148 28.3	16.3	183 31.9	12.3	19 00.3	3.3	54.0
23	163 28.3	15.6	198 03.3	12.3	18 57.0	3.5	54.1
4 00	178 28.4	N17 14.9	212 34.6	12.4	N18 53.5	3.5	54.1
01	193 28.4	14.3	227 06.0	12.4	18 50.0	3.6	54.1
02	208 28.5	13.6	241 37.4	12.5	18 46.4	3.7	54.1
03	223 28.5	.. 12.9	256 08.9	12.4	18 42.7	3.8	54.1
04	238 28.6	12.3	270 40.3	12.5	18 38.9	3.9	54.1
05	253 28.7	11.6	285 11.8	12.5	18 35.0	3.9	54.1
06	268 28.7	N17 10.9	299 43.3	12.5	N18 31.1	4.0	54.1
07	283 28.8	10.3	314 14.8	12.5	18 27.1	4.2	54.1
08	298 28.8	09.6	328 46.3	12.5	18 22.9	4.2	54.1
S 09	313 28.9	.. 08.9	343 17.8	12.5	18 18.7	4.3	54.1
U 10	328 28.9	08.3	357 49.3	12.6	18 14.4	4.3	54.1
N 11	343 29.0	07.6	12 20.9	12.6	18 10.1	4.5	54.1
D 12	358 29.1	N17 06.9	26 52.5	12.6	N18 05.6	4.5	54.1
A 13	13 29.1	06.2	41 24.1	12.6	18 01.1	4.7	54.1
Y 14	28 29.2	05.6	55 55.7	12.6	17 56.4	4.7	54.1
15	43 29.2	.. 04.9	70 27.3	12.7	17 51.7	4.7	54.1
16	58 29.3	04.2	84 59.0	12.7	17 47.0	4.9	54.1
17	73 29.4	03.6	99 30.7	12.7	17 42.1	5.0	54.1
18	88 29.4	N17 02.9	114 02.4	12.7	N17 37.1	5.0	54.1
19	103 29.5	02.2	128 34.1	12.7	17 32.1	5.1	54.1
20	118 29.5	01.5	143 05.8	12.8	17 27.0	5.2	54.1
21	133 29.6	.. 00.9	157 37.6	12.7	17 21.8	5.2	54.2
22	148 29.7	17 00.2	172 09.3	12.8	17 16.6	5.4	54.2
23	163 29.7	N16 59.5	186 41.1	12.8	N17 11.2	5.4	54.2
	SD 15.8	d 0.7	SD 14.7		14.7		14.7

Lat.	Twilight Naut.	Twilight Civil	Sunrise	Moonrise 2	3	4	5
°	h m	h m	h m	h m	h m	h m	h m
N 72						23 53	25 59
N 70	////	////	01 44	21 31	23 09	24 50	00 50
68	////	////	02 26	22 49	24 00	00 00	01 23
66	////	00 55	02 54	23 27	24 32	00 32	01 47
64	////	01 52	03 15	23 54	24 55	00 55	02 06
62	////	02 23	03 32	24 14	00 14	01 14	02 21
60	00 49	02 47	03 46	24 31	00 31	01 29	02 34
N 58	01 41	03 05	03 58	24 45	00 45	01 42	02 45
56	02 10	03 20	04 08	00 08	00 57	01 53	02 55
54	02 32	03 33	04 17	00 19	01 07	02 03	03 03
52	02 49	03 44	04 25	00 28	01 17	02 11	03 11
50	03 04	03 54	04 32	00 37	01 25	02 19	03 18
45	03 32	04 14	04 48	00 54	01 43	02 36	03 32
N 40	03 53	04 30	05 00	01 09	01 58	02 50	03 44
35	04 10	04 43	05 11	01 21	02 10	03 01	03 54
30	04 23	04 54	05 20	01 32	02 21	03 11	04 03
20	04 45	05 13	05 36	01 51	02 39	03 28	04 19
N 10	05 02	05 28	05 50	02 07	02 55	03 44	04 32
0	05 16	05 41	06 03	02 22	03 10	03 58	04 44
S 10	05 28	05 53	06 15	02 37	03 25	04 12	04 57
20	05 39	06 06	06 29	02 54	03 41	04 27	05 10
30	05 50	06 19	06 44	03 12	04 00	04 44	05 25
35	05 56	06 26	06 53	03 23	04 10	04 54	05 34
40	06 01	06 34	07 03	03 36	04 23	05 05	05 44
45	06 08	06 43	07 14	03 51	04 37	05 19	05 56
S 50	06 14	06 53	07 28	04 09	04 55	05 35	06 10
52	06 17	06 58	07 35	04 17	05 03	05 43	06 17
54	06 20	07 03	07 42	04 27	05 13	05 51	06 24
56	06 23	07 09	07 50	04 38	05 23	06 01	06 32
58	06 27	07 15	07 59	04 50	05 35	06 12	06 41
S 60	06 31	07 22	08 10	05 05	05 49	06 24	06 52

Lat.	Sunset	Twilight Civil	Twilight Naut.	Moonset 2	3	4	5
°	h m	h m	h m	h m	h m	h m	h m
N 72						21 21	20 52
N 70	22 22	////	////	20 27	20 27	20 24	20 21
68	21 43	////	////	19 08	19 36	19 50	19 58
66	21 16	23 07	////	18 30	19 04	19 26	19 39
64	20 50	22 16	////	18 04	18 40	19 06	19 25
62	20 39	21 46	////	17 43	18 21	18 50	19 12
60	20 25	21 23	23 13	17 26	18 06	18 37	19 02
N 58	20 13	21 05	22 27	17 12	17 53	18 26	18 52
56	20 03	20 50	21 59	17 00	17 41	18 16	18 44
54	19 54	20 38	21 38	16 49	17 31	18 07	18 37
52	19 46	20 27	21 21	16 40	17 23	17 59	18 30
50	19 39	20 17	21 07	16 31	17 15	17 52	18 24
45	19 24	19 57	20 39	16 13	16 57	17 37	18 12
N 40	19 11	19 41	20 18	15 59	16 44	17 24	18 01
35	19 01	19 28	20 02	15 46	16 32	17 14	17 52
30	18 52	19 17	19 48	15 36	16 21	17 04	17 44
20	18 36	18 59	19 27	15 17	16 03	16 48	17 30
N 10	18 22	18 44	19 10	15 01	15 48	16 34	17 18
0	18 10	18 31	18 56	14 45	15 33	16 20	17 07
S 10	17 57	18 19	18 44	14 30	15 18	16 07	16 55
20	17 44	18 07	18 33	14 14	15 03	15 53	16 43
30	17 29	17 54	18 23	13 55	14 45	15 36	16 29
35	17 20	17 47	18 17	13 44	14 34	15 26	16 21
40	17 10	17 39	18 11	13 32	14 22	15 16	16 11
45	16 59	17 30	18 05	13 17	14 08	15 03	16 00
S 50	16 45	17 20	17 59	12 59	13 50	14 47	15 47
52	16 38	17 15	17 56	12 50	13 42	14 39	15 41
54	16 31	17 10	17 53	12 41	13 33	14 31	15 34
56	16 23	17 04	17 49	12 30	13 22	14 22	15 26
58	16 14	16 58	17 46	12 18	13 11	14 11	15 17
S 60	16 03	16 51	17 42	12 03	12 57	13 59	15 07

Day	SUN Eqn. of Time 00h	12h	SUN Mer. Pass.	MOON Mer. Pass. Upper	Lower	Age	Phase
d	m s	m s	h m	h m	h m	d	%
2	06 16	06 14	12 06	08 34	20 58	25	17
3	06 12	06 09	12 06	09 22	21 45	26	11
4	06 07	06 04	12 06	10 09	22 32	27	5

UT	ARIES GHA	VENUS −3.9 GHA	Dec	MARS +1.6 GHA	Dec	JUPITER −1.9 GHA	Dec	SATURN +0.7 GHA	Dec	STARS Name	SHA	Dec
5 00	313 42.6	145 59.6	N 6 34.9	207 20.7	N23 19.7	214 07.4	N22 59.0	99 45.8	S11 06.9	Acamar	315 18.3	S40 14.8
01	328 45.1	160 59.3	33.7	222 21.3	19.6	229 09.3	59.0	114 48.2	06.9	Achernar	335 26.6	S57 09.7
02	343 47.5	175 59.0	32.4	237 22.0	19.4	244 11.2	58.9	129 50.6	07.0	Acrux	173 09.5	S63 10.7
03	358 50.0	190 58.7	.. 31.2	252 22.7	.. 19.2	259 13.1	.. 58.9	144 52.9	.. 07.0	Adhara	255 12.8	S28 59.5
04	13 52.5	205 58.5	29.9	267 23.4	19.1	274 15.0	58.9	159 55.3	07.1	Aldebaran	290 49.4	N16 32.1
05	28 54.9	220 58.2	28.7	282 24.1	18.9	289 16.9	58.8	174 57.7	07.1			
06	43 57.4	235 57.9	N 6 27.5	297 24.7	N23 18.8	304 18.8	N22 58.8	190 00.0	S11 07.2	Alioth	166 20.9	N55 53.4
07	58 59.9	250 57.7	26.2	312 25.4	18.6	319 20.7	58.8	205 02.4	07.2	Alkaid	152 59.0	N49 15.0
08	74 02.3	265 57.4	25.0	327 26.1	18.4	334 22.6	58.7	220 04.7	07.3	Al Na'ir	27 43.2	S46 53.4
M 09	89 04.8	280 57.1	.. 23.7	342 26.8	.. 18.3	349 24.5	.. 58.7	235 07.1	.. 07.3	Alnilam	275 46.5	S 1 11.7
O 10	104 07.3	295 56.9	22.5	357 27.5	18.1	4 26.4	58.7	250 09.5	07.4	Alphard	217 56.3	S 8 43.1
N 11	119 09.7	310 56.6	21.2	12 28.1	17.9	19 28.3	58.7	265 11.8	07.4			
D 12	134 12.2	325 56.3	N 6 20.0	27 28.8	N23 17.8	34 30.2	N22 58.6	280 14.2	S11 07.5	Alphecca	126 10.8	N26 40.4
A 13	149 14.7	340 56.1	18.8	42 29.5	17.6	49 32.1	58.6	295 16.5	07.5	Alpheratz	357 43.1	N29 10.0
Y 14	164 17.1	355 55.8	17.5	57 30.2	17.4	64 34.0	58.5	310 18.9	07.6	Altair	62 07.8	N 8 54.6
15	179 19.6	10 55.5	.. 16.3	72 30.9	.. 17.3	79 35.9	.. 58.5	325 21.2	.. 07.6	Ankaa	353 15.4	S42 13.6
16	194 22.0	25 55.3	15.0	87 31.5	17.1	94 37.8	58.5	340 23.6	07.7	Antares	112 25.9	S26 27.6
17	209 24.5	40 55.0	13.8	102 32.2	17.0	109 39.7	58.5	355 26.0	07.7			
18	224 27.0	55 54.7	N 6 12.5	117 32.9	N23 16.8	124 41.6	N22 58.4	10 28.3	S11 07.7	Arcturus	145 55.7	N19 06.9
19	239 29.4	70 54.5	11.3	132 33.6	16.6	139 43.5	58.4	25 30.7	07.8	Atria	107 27.3	S69 03.2
20	254 31.9	85 54.2	10.1	147 34.3	16.5	154 45.4	58.4	40 33.0	07.8	Avior	234 18.6	S59 33.3
21	269 34.4	100 54.0	.. 08.8	162 34.9	.. 16.3	169 47.3	.. 58.3	55 35.4	.. 07.9	Bellatrix	278 32.1	N 6 21.6
22	284 36.8	115 53.7	07.6	177 35.6	16.1	184 49.2	58.3	70 37.8	07.9	Betelgeuse	271 01.4	N 7 24.5
23	299 39.3	130 53.4	06.3	192 36.3	15.9	199 51.1	58.3	85 40.1	08.0			
6 00	314 41.8	145 53.2	N 6 05.1	207 37.0	N23 15.8	214 53.1	N22 58.2	100 42.5	S11 08.0	Canopus	263 56.5	S52 42.1
01	329 44.2	160 52.9	03.8	222 37.7	15.6	229 55.0	58.2	115 44.8	08.1	Capella	280 34.5	N46 00.4
02	344 46.7	175 52.6	02.6	237 38.3	15.4	244 56.9	58.2	130 47.2	08.1	Deneb	49 30.9	N45 20.0
03	359 49.2	190 52.4	.. 01.3	252 39.0	.. 15.3	259 58.8	.. 58.1	145 49.5	.. 08.2	Denebola	182 33.8	N14 29.8
04	14 51.6	205 52.1	6 00.1	267 39.7	15.1	275 00.7	58.1	160 51.9	08.2	Diphda	348 55.6	S17 54.5
05	29 54.1	220 51.9	5 58.9	282 40.4	14.9	290 02.6	58.1	175 54.3	08.3			
06	44 56.5	235 51.6	N 5 57.6	297 41.1	N23 14.8	305 04.5	N22 58.1	190 56.6	S11 08.3	Dubhe	193 52.2	N61 40.7
07	59 59.0	250 51.3	56.4	312 41.8	14.6	320 06.4	58.0	205 59.0	08.4	Elnath	278 12.7	N28 36.9
T 08	75 01.5	265 51.1	55.1	327 42.4	14.4	335 08.3	58.0	221 01.3	08.4	Eltanin	90 45.7	N51 29.6
U 09	90 03.9	280 50.8	.. 53.9	342 43.1	.. 14.3	350 10.2	.. 58.0	236 03.7	.. 08.5	Enif	33 46.7	N 9 56.5
E 10	105 06.4	295 50.5	52.6	357 43.8	14.1	5 12.1	57.9	251 06.0	08.5	Fomalhaut	15 23.5	S29 32.7
S 11	120 08.9	310 50.3	51.4	12 44.5	13.9	20 14.0	57.9	266 08.4	08.6			
D 12	135 11.3	325 50.0	N 5 50.1	27 45.2	N23 13.7	35 15.9	N22 57.9	281 10.8	S11 08.6	Gacrux	172 01.0	S57 11.6
A 13	150 13.8	340 49.8	48.9	42 45.9	13.6	50 17.8	57.8	296 13.1	08.7	Gienah	175 52.4	S17 37.1
Y 14	165 16.3	355 49.5	47.6	57 46.5	13.4	65 19.7	57.8	311 15.5	08.7	Hadar	148 47.8	S60 26.5
15	180 18.7	10 49.3	.. 46.4	72 47.2	.. 13.2	80 21.6	.. 57.8	326 17.8	.. 08.8	Hamal	328 00.5	N23 31.5
16	195 21.2	25 49.0	45.1	87 47.9	13.0	95 23.5	57.7	341 20.2	08.8	Kaus Aust.	83 43.3	S34 22.5
17	210 23.6	40 48.7	43.9	102 48.6	12.9	110 25.4	57.7	356 22.5	08.9			
18	225 26.1	55 48.5	N 5 42.6	117 49.3	N23 12.7	125 27.3	N22 57.7	11 24.9	S11 08.9	Kochab	137 20.1	N74 06.3
19	240 28.6	70 48.2	41.4	132 50.0	12.5	140 29.3	57.6	26 27.2	08.9	Markab	13 37.9	N15 16.9
20	255 31.0	85 48.0	40.1	147 50.6	12.4	155 31.2	57.6	41 29.6	09.0	Menkar	314 14.9	N 4 08.6
21	270 33.5	100 47.7	.. 38.9	162 51.3	.. 12.2	170 33.1	.. 57.6	56 31.9	.. 09.0	Menkent	148 07.5	S36 26.3
22	285 36.0	115 47.5	37.6	177 52.0	12.0	185 35.0	57.5	71 34.3	09.1	Miaplacidus	221 40.5	S69 46.5
23	300 38.4	130 47.2	36.4	192 52.7	11.8	200 36.9	57.5	86 36.7	09.1			
7 00	315 40.9	145 46.9	N 5 35.1	207 53.4	N23 11.7	215 38.8	N22 57.5	101 39.0	S11 09.2	Mirfak	308 40.2	N49 54.3
01	330 43.4	160 46.7	33.9	222 54.1	11.5	230 40.7	57.5	116 41.4	09.2	Nunki	75 57.8	S26 16.6
02	345 45.8	175 46.4	32.6	237 54.8	11.3	245 42.6	57.4	131 43.7	09.3	Peacock	53 18.5	S56 41.3
03	0 48.3	190 46.2	.. 31.4	252 55.4	.. 11.1	260 44.5	.. 57.4	146 46.1	.. 09.3	Pollux	243 27.9	N27 59.4
04	15 50.8	205 45.9	30.1	267 56.1	11.0	275 46.4	57.4	161 48.4	09.4	Procyon	244 59.9	N 5 11.3
05	30 53.2	220 45.7	28.9	282 56.8	10.8	290 48.3	57.3	176 50.8	09.4			
06	45 55.7	235 45.4	N 5 27.6	297 57.5	N23 10.6	305 50.2	N22 57.3	191 53.1	S11 09.5	Rasalhague	96 06.1	N12 33.3
W 07	60 58.1	250 45.2	26.3	312 58.2	10.4	320 52.1	57.3	206 55.5	09.5	Regulus	207 43.7	N11 54.0
E 08	76 00.6	265 44.9	25.1	327 58.9	10.2	335 54.0	57.2	221 57.8	09.6	Rigel	281 12.1	S 8 11.2
D 09	91 03.1	280 44.7	.. 23.8	342 59.6	.. 10.1	350 56.0	.. 57.2	237 00.2	.. 09.6	Rigil Kent.	139 51.5	S60 53.6
N 10	106 05.5	295 44.4	22.6	358 00.3	09.9	5 57.9	57.2	252 02.5	09.7	Sabik	102 12.2	S15 44.3
E 11	121 08.0	310 44.1	21.3	13 00.9	09.7	20 59.8	57.1	267 04.9	09.7			
S 12	136 10.5	325 43.9	N 5 20.1	28 01.6	N23 09.5	36 01.7	N22 57.1	282 07.2	S11 09.8	Schedar	349 40.0	N56 36.6
D 13	151 12.9	340 43.6	18.8	43 02.3	09.3	51 03.6	57.1	297 09.6	09.8	Shaula	96 21.5	S37 06.7
A 14	166 15.4	355 43.4	17.6	58 03.0	09.2	66 05.5	57.0	312 12.0	09.9	Sirius	258 33.9	S16 44.1
Y 15	181 17.9	10 43.1	.. 16.3	73 03.7	.. 09.0	81 07.4	.. 57.0	327 14.3	.. 09.9	Spica	158 31.2	S11 13.9
16	196 20.3	25 42.9	15.1	88 04.4	08.8	96 09.3	57.0	342 16.7	10.0	Suhail	222 52.8	S43 29.4
17	211 22.8	40 42.6	13.8	103 05.1	08.6	111 11.2	56.9	357 19.0	10.0			
18	226 25.2	55 42.4	N 5 12.5	118 05.8	N23 08.4	126 13.1	N22 56.9	12 21.4	S11 10.1	Vega	80 38.5	N38 48.1
19	241 27.7	70 42.1	11.3	133 06.4	08.3	141 15.0	56.9	27 23.7	10.1	Zuben'ubi	137 05.3	S16 05.8
20	256 30.2	85 41.9	10.0	148 07.1	08.1	156 16.9	56.8	42 26.1	10.2		SHA	Mer. Pass.
21	271 32.6	100 41.6	.. 08.8	163 07.8	.. 07.9	171 18.9	.. 56.8	57 28.4	.. 10.2		° '	h m
22	286 35.1	115 41.4	07.5	178 08.5	07.7	186 20.8	56.8	72 30.8	10.3	Venus	191 11.4	14 17
23	301 37.6	130 41.1	06.3	193 09.2	07.5	201 22.7	56.7	87 33.1	10.3	Mars	252 55.2	10 09
										Jupiter	260 11.3	9 39
Mer. Pass. 3 00.7		v −0.3	d 1.2	v 0.7	d 0.2	v 1.9	d 0.0	v 2.4	d 0.0	Saturn	146 00.7	17 14

SUN / MOON

UT	SUN GHA	SUN Dec	MOON GHA	v	MOON Dec	d	HP
5 00	178 29.8	N16 58.8	201 12.9	12.9	N17 05.8	5.5	54.2
01	193 29.9	58.2	215 44.8	12.8	17 00.3	5.6	54.2
02	208 29.9	57.5	230 16.6	12.9	16 54.7	5.7	54.2
03	223 30.0	56.8	244 48.5	12.9	16 49.0	5.7	54.2
04	238 30.0	56.1	259 20.4	12.9	16 43.3	5.8	54.2
05	253 30.1	55.5	273 52.3	12.9	16 37.5	5.9	54.2
06	268 30.2	N16 54.8	288 24.2	13.0	N16 31.6	6.0	54.2
07	283 30.2	54.1	302 56.2	12.9	16 25.6	6.0	54.2
M 08	298 30.3	53.4	317 28.1	13.0	16 19.6	6.1	54.2
O 09	313 30.4	52.7	332 00.1	13.0	16 13.5	6.2	54.3
N 10	328 30.4	52.1	346 32.1	13.1	16 07.3	6.3	54.3
D 11	343 30.5	51.4	1 04.2	13.0	16 01.0	6.3	54.3
A 12	358 30.5	N16 50.7	15 36.2	13.1	N15 54.7	6.4	54.3
Y 13	13 30.6	50.0	30 08.3	13.1	15 48.3	6.5	54.3
14	28 30.7	49.3	44 40.4	13.1	15 41.8	6.5	54.3
15	43 30.7	48.6	59 12.5	13.1	15 35.3	6.7	54.3
16	58 30.8	48.0	73 44.6	13.2	15 28.6	6.6	54.3
17	73 30.9	47.3	88 16.8	13.2	15 22.0	6.8	54.3
18	88 30.9	N16 46.6	102 49.0	13.1	N15 15.2	6.8	54.3
19	103 31.0	45.9	117 21.1	13.3	15 08.4	7.0	54.4
20	118 31.1	45.2	131 53.4	13.2	15 01.4	6.9	54.4
21	133 31.1	44.5	146 25.6	13.2	14 54.5	7.1	54.4
22	148 31.2	43.8	160 57.8	13.3	14 47.4	7.1	54.4
23	163 31.3	43.2	175 30.1	13.3	14 40.3	7.2	54.4
6 00	178 31.3	N16 42.5	190 02.4	13.3	N14 33.1	7.2	54.4
01	193 31.4	41.8	204 34.7	13.3	14 25.9	7.3	54.4
02	208 31.5	41.1	219 07.1	13.3	14 18.6	7.4	54.4
03	223 31.6	40.4	233 39.4	13.4	14 11.2	7.4	54.4
04	238 31.6	39.7	248 11.8	13.4	14 03.8	7.5	54.4
05	253 31.7	39.0	262 44.2	13.4	13 56.3	7.6	54.5
06	268 31.8	N16 38.3	277 16.6	13.4	N13 48.7	7.6	54.5
07	283 31.8	37.7	291 49.0	13.4	13 41.1	7.7	54.5
T 08	298 31.9	37.0	306 21.4	13.5	13 33.4	7.8	54.5
U 09	313 32.0	36.3	320 53.9	13.5	13 25.6	7.8	54.5
E 10	328 32.0	35.6	335 26.4	13.5	13 17.8	7.9	54.5
S 11	343 32.1	34.9	349 58.9	13.5	13 09.9	8.0	54.5
D 12	358 32.2	N16 34.2	4 31.4	13.5	N13 01.9	8.0	54.5
A 13	13 32.3	33.5	19 03.9	13.6	12 53.9	8.0	54.6
Y 14	28 32.3	32.8	33 36.5	13.6	12 45.9	8.2	54.6
15	43 32.4	32.1	48 09.1	13.6	12 37.7	8.2	54.6
16	58 32.5	31.4	62 41.7	13.6	12 29.5	8.2	54.6
17	73 32.5	30.7	77 14.3	13.6	12 21.3	8.3	54.6
18	88 32.6	N16 30.0	91 46.9	13.6	N12 13.0	8.4	54.6
19	103 32.7	29.3	106 19.5	13.7	12 04.6	8.4	54.6
20	118 32.8	28.6	120 52.2	13.7	11 56.2	8.5	54.7
21	133 32.8	27.9	135 24.9	13.6	11 47.7	8.5	54.7
22	148 32.9	27.2	149 57.5	13.7	11 39.2	8.6	54.7
23	163 33.0	26.5	164 30.2	13.8	11 30.6	8.6	54.7
7 00	178 33.1	N16 25.8	179 03.0	13.7	N11 22.0	8.7	54.7
01	193 33.2	25.1	193 35.7	13.7	11 13.3	8.7	54.7
02	208 33.2	24.4	208 08.4	13.8	11 04.6	8.8	54.7
03	223 33.3	23.7	222 41.2	13.8	10 55.8	8.9	54.7
04	238 33.4	23.0	237 14.0	13.8	10 46.9	8.9	54.8
05	253 33.4	22.3	251 46.8	13.8	10 38.0	8.9	54.8
06	268 33.5	N16 21.6	266 19.6	13.8	N10 29.1	9.0	54.8
W 07	283 33.6	20.9	280 52.4	13.8	10 20.1	9.1	54.8
E 08	298 33.7	20.2	295 25.2	13.9	10 11.0	9.1	54.8
D 09	313 33.7	19.5	309 58.1	13.8	10 01.9	9.1	54.8
N 10	328 33.8	18.8	324 30.9	13.9	9 52.8	9.2	54.9
E 11	343 33.9	18.1	339 03.8	13.8	9 43.6	9.3	54.9
S 12	358 34.0	N16 17.4	353 36.6	13.9	N9 34.3	9.3	54.9
D 13	13 34.0	16.7	8 09.5	13.9	9 25.0	9.3	54.9
A 14	28 34.1	16.0	22 42.4	13.9	9 15.7	9.4	54.9
Y 15	43 34.2	15.3	37 15.3	14.0	9 06.3	9.4	54.9
16	58 34.3	14.6	51 48.3	13.9	8 56.9	9.5	54.9
17	73 34.4	13.9	66 21.2	13.9	8 47.4	9.5	54.9
18	88 34.4	N16 13.2	80 54.1	14.0	N8 37.9	9.5	55.0
19	103 34.5	12.5	95 27.1	13.9	8 28.4	9.6	55.0
20	118 34.6	11.8	110 00.0	14.0	8 18.8	9.6	55.0
21	133 34.7	11.1	124 33.0	13.9	8 09.1	9.6	55.0
22	148 34.8	10.4	139 05.9	14.0	7 59.5	9.8	55.0
23	163 34.8	09.7	153 38.9	14.0	N7 49.7	9.7	55.1
SD	15.8	d 0.7	SD 14.8		14.9		15.0

Moonrise / Twilight

Lat.	Twilight Naut.	Twilight Civil	Sunrise	Moonrise 5	6	7	8
N 72	////	////	01 00	25 59	01 59	03 48	05 33
N 70	////	////	02 05	00 50	02 29	04 07	05 43
68	////	////	02 40	01 23	02 51	04 21	05 51
66	////	01 24	03 05	01 47	03 09	04 33	05 58
64	////	02 07	03 24	02 06	03 23	04 42	06 04
62	////	02 35	03 40	02 21	03 34	04 51	06 08
60	01 16	02 56	03 53	02 34	03 44	04 58	06 13
N 58	01 55	03 13	04 04	02 45	03 53	05 04	06 16
56	02 21	03 27	04 14	02 55	04 01	05 09	06 20
54	02 40	03 39	04 22	03 03	04 08	05 14	06 23
52	02 56	03 50	04 30	03 11	04 14	05 19	06 25
50	03 10	03 59	04 37	03 18	04 19	05 23	06 28
45	03 37	04 18	04 51	03 32	04 31	05 31	06 33
N 40	03 57	04 33	05 03	03 44	04 41	05 39	06 37
35	04 13	04 46	05 13	03 54	04 49	05 45	06 41
30	04 26	04 56	05 22	04 03	04 56	05 50	06 45
20	04 46	05 14	05 37	04 19	05 09	06 00	06 50
N 10	05 02	05 28	05 50	04 32	05 20	06 08	06 55
0	05 16	05 41	06 02	04 44	05 30	06 16	07 00
S 10	05 27	05 53	06 14	04 57	05 41	06 23	07 05
20	05 38	06 04	06 27	05 10	05 52	06 31	07 10
30	05 48	06 17	06 42	05 25	06 04	06 41	07 16
35	05 53	06 23	06 50	05 34	06 11	06 46	07 19
40	05 58	06 31	06 59	05 44	06 19	06 52	07 23
45	06 04	06 39	07 10	05 56	06 29	06 59	07 27
S 50	06 10	06 49	07 23	06 10	06 40	07 07	07 32
52	06 13	06 53	07 30	06 17	06 46	07 11	07 35
54	06 16	06 58	07 36	06 24	06 52	07 16	07 37
56	06 18	07 03	07 44	06 32	06 58	07 20	07 40
58	06 22	07 09	07 53	06 41	07 05	07 25	07 43
S 60	06 25	07 15	08 02	06 52	07 14	07 31	07 47

Moonset / Twilight

Lat.	Sunset	Twilight Civil	Twilight Naut.	Moonset 5	6	7	8
N 72	22 59	////	////	20 52	20 37	20 25	20 15
N 70	22 01	////	////	20 21	20 17	20 13	20 10
68	21 28	////	////	19 58	20 02	20 04	20 05
66	21 04	22 40	////	19 39	19 49	19 56	20 01
64	20 45	22 00	////	19 25	19 38	19 49	19 58
62	20 30	21 34	////	19 12	19 29	19 43	19 55
60	20 17	21 13	22 49	19 02	19 21	19 38	19 52
N 58	20 06	20 57	22 13	18 52	19 14	19 33	19 50
56	19 57	20 43	21 48	18 44	19 08	19 29	19 48
54	19 48	20 31	21 29	18 37	19 03	19 25	19 46
52	19 41	20 21	21 13	18 30	18 58	19 22	19 44
50	19 34	20 12	21 00	18 24	18 53	19 19	19 43
45	19 20	19 53	20 34	18 12	18 43	19 12	19 39
N 40	19 08	19 38	20 11	18 01	18 35	19 07	19 37
35	18 58	19 25	19 58	17 52	18 28	19 02	19 34
30	18 49	19 15	19 45	17 44	18 22	18 57	19 32
20	18 34	18 58	19 25	17 30	18 11	18 50	19 28
N 10	18 21	18 43	19 09	17 18	18 01	18 43	19 25
0	18 09	18 31	18 56	17 07	17 52	18 37	19 22
S 10	17 57	18 19	18 45	16 55	17 43	18 31	19 18
20	17 45	18 08	18 34	16 43	17 33	18 24	19 15
30	17 32	17 55	18 24	16 29	17 22	18 16	19 11
35	17 22	17 49	18 19	16 21	17 16	18 12	19 09
40	17 13	17 41	18 14	16 11	17 08	18 07	19 06
45	17 02	17 33	18 08	16 00	17 00	18 01	19 03
S 50	16 49	17 24	18 02	15 47	16 49	17 54	18 59
52	16 43	17 19	18 00	15 41	16 45	17 50	18 58
54	16 36	17 14	17 57	15 34	16 39	17 47	18 56
56	16 28	17 09	17 54	15 26	16 33	17 43	18 54
58	16 20	17 03	17 51	15 17	16 27	17 38	18 51
S 60	16 10	16 57	17 48	15 07	16 20	17 33	18 49

SUN / MOON

Day	Eqn. of Time 00h	Eqn. of Time 12h	Mer. Pass.	Mer. Pass. Upper	Mer. Pass. Lower	Age	Phase
	m s	m s	h m	h m	h m	d	%
5	06 01	05 58	12 06	10 56	23 19	28	2
6	05 55	05 51	12 06	11 41	24 04	29	0
7	05 48	05 44	12 06	12 26	00 04	01	1

UT	ARIES GHA	VENUS −3.9 GHA	Dec	MARS +1.6 GHA	Dec	JUPITER −2.0 GHA	Dec	SATURN +0.7 GHA	Dec	STARS Name	SHA	Dec
8 00	316 40.0	145 40.9	N 5 05.0	208 09.9	N23 07.3	216 24.6	N22 56.7	102 35.5	S11 10.4	Acamar	315 18.3	S40 14.8
01	331 42.5	160 40.6	03.7	223 10.6	07.2	231 26.5	56.7	117 37.8	10.4	Achernar	335 26.5	S57 09.7
02	346 45.0	175 40.4	02.5	238 11.3	07.0	246 28.4	56.6	132 40.2	10.5	Acrux	173 09.5	S63 10.7
03	1 47.4	190 40.1	.. 01.2	253 12.0	.. 06.8	261 30.3	.. 56.6	147 42.5	.. 10.5	Adhara	255 12.7	S28 59.4
04	16 49.9	205 39.9	5 00.0	268 12.6	06.6	276 32.2	56.6	162 44.9	10.6	Aldebaran	290 49.4	N16 32.1
05	31 52.4	220 39.6	4 58.7	283 13.3	06.4	291 34.1	56.5	177 47.2	10.6			
06	46 54.8	235 39.4	N 4 57.5	298 14.0	N23 06.2	306 36.0	N22 56.5	192 49.6	S11 10.7	Alioth	166 20.9	N55 53.4
T 07	61 57.3	250 39.2	56.2	313 14.7	06.1	321 38.0	56.5	207 51.9	10.7	Alkaid	152 59.0	N49 15.0
H 08	76 59.7	265 38.9	54.9	328 15.4	05.9	336 39.9	56.4	222 54.3	10.8	Al Na'ir	27 43.1	S46 53.4
U 09	92 02.2	280 38.7	.. 53.7	343 16.1	.. 05.7	351 41.8	.. 56.4	237 56.6	.. 10.8	Alnilam	275 46.4	S 1 11.7
R 10	107 04.7	295 38.4	52.4	358 16.8	05.5	6 43.7	56.4	252 59.0	10.9	Alphard	217 56.3	S 8 43.1
S 11	122 07.1	310 38.2	51.2	13 17.5	05.3	21 45.6	56.3	268 01.3	10.9			
D 12	137 09.6	325 37.9	N 4 49.9	28 18.2	N23 05.1	36 47.5	N22 56.3	283 03.7	S11 11.0	Alphecca	126 10.9	N26 40.4
A 13	152 12.1	340 37.7	48.6	43 18.9	04.9	51 49.4	56.3	298 06.0	11.0	Alpheratz	357 43.1	N29 10.0
Y 14	167 14.5	355 37.4	47.4	58 19.6	04.8	66 51.3	56.2	313 08.4	11.1	Altair	62 07.8	N 8 54.6
15	182 17.0	10 37.2	.. 46.1	73 20.3	.. 04.6	81 53.2	.. 56.2	328 10.7	.. 11.1	Ankaa	353 15.3	S42 13.6
16	197 19.5	25 36.9	44.9	88 20.9	04.4	96 55.2	56.2	343 13.0	11.2	Antares	112 25.9	S26 27.6
17	212 21.9	40 36.7	43.6	103 21.6	04.2	111 57.1	56.1	358 15.4	11.2			
18	227 24.4	55 36.4	N 4 42.3	118 22.3	N23 04.0	126 59.0	N22 56.1	13 17.7	S11 11.3	Arcturus	145 55.7	N19 06.9
19	242 26.9	70 36.2	41.1	133 23.0	03.8	142 00.9	56.1	28 20.1	11.3	Atria	107 27.3	S69 03.2
20	257 29.3	85 36.0	39.8	148 23.7	03.6	157 02.8	56.0	43 22.4	11.4	Avior	234 18.6	S59 33.3
21	272 31.8	100 35.7	.. 38.6	163 24.4	.. 03.4	172 04.7	.. 56.0	58 24.8	.. 11.4	Bellatrix	278 32.1	N 6 21.6
22	287 34.2	115 35.5	37.3	178 25.1	03.2	187 06.6	56.0	73 27.1	11.5	Betelgeuse	271 01.4	N 7 24.5
23	302 36.7	130 35.2	36.0	193 25.8	03.0	202 08.5	55.9	88 29.5	11.5			
9 00	317 39.2	145 35.0	N 4 34.8	208 26.5	N23 02.9	217 10.5	N22 55.9	103 31.8	S11 11.6	Canopus	263 56.5	S52 42.1
01	332 41.6	160 34.7	33.5	223 27.2	02.7	232 12.4	55.9	118 34.2	11.6	Capella	280 34.5	N46 00.4
02	347 44.1	175 34.5	32.2	238 27.9	02.5	247 14.3	55.8	133 36.5	11.7	Deneb	49 30.9	N45 20.0
03	2 46.6	190 34.3	.. 31.0	253 28.6	.. 02.3	262 16.2	.. 55.8	148 38.9	.. 11.8	Denebola	182 33.8	N14 29.8
04	17 49.0	205 34.0	29.7	268 29.3	02.1	277 18.1	55.8	163 41.2	11.8	Diphda	348 55.6	S17 54.5
05	32 51.5	220 33.8	28.4	283 30.0	01.9	292 20.0	55.7	178 43.6	11.9			
06	47 54.0	235 33.5	N 4 27.2	298 30.7	N23 01.7	307 21.9	N22 55.7	193 45.9	S11 11.9	Dubhe	193 52.2	N61 40.7
07	62 56.4	250 33.3	25.9	313 31.4	01.5	322 23.8	55.6	208 48.3	12.0	Elnath	278 12.7	N28 36.9
F 08	77 58.9	265 33.1	24.7	328 32.0	01.3	337 25.8	55.6	223 50.6	12.0	Eltanin	90 45.7	N51 29.6
R 09	93 01.3	280 32.8	.. 23.4	343 32.7	.. 01.1	352 27.7	.. 55.6	238 52.9	.. 12.1	Enif	33 46.7	N 9 56.5
I 10	108 03.8	295 32.6	22.1	358 33.4	00.9	7 29.6	55.6	253 55.3	12.1	Fomalhaut	15 23.5	S29 32.7
D 11	123 06.3	310 32.3	20.9	13 34.1	00.7	22 31.5	55.5	268 57.6	12.2			
A 12	138 08.7	325 32.1	N 4 19.6	28 34.8	N23 00.5	37 33.4	N22 55.5	284 00.0	S11 12.2	Gacrux	172 01.0	S57 11.6
Y 13	153 11.2	340 31.9	18.3	43 35.5	00.4	52 35.3	55.5	299 02.3	12.3	Gienah	175 52.4	S17 37.1
14	168 13.7	355 31.6	17.1	58 36.2	00.2	67 37.2	55.4	314 04.7	12.3	Hadar	148 47.8	S60 26.5
15	183 16.1	10 31.4	.. 15.8	73 36.9	23 00.0	82 39.2	.. 55.4	329 07.0	.. 12.4	Hamal	328 00.5	N23 31.5
16	198 18.6	25 31.1	14.5	88 37.6	22 59.8	97 41.1	55.3	344 09.4	12.4	Kaus Aust.	83 43.3	S34 22.5
17	213 21.1	40 30.9	13.3	103 38.3	59.6	112 43.0	55.3	359 11.7	12.5			
18	228 23.5	55 30.7	N 4 12.0	118 39.0	N22 59.4	127 44.9	N22 55.3	14 14.0	S11 12.5	Kochab	137 20.2	N74 06.3
19	243 26.0	70 30.4	10.7	133 39.7	59.2	142 46.8	55.3	29 16.4	12.6	Markab	13 37.9	N15 16.9
20	258 28.5	85 30.2	09.5	148 40.4	59.0	157 48.7	55.2	44 18.7	12.6	Menkar	314 14.9	N 4 08.6
21	273 30.9	100 30.0	.. 08.2	163 41.1	.. 58.8	172 50.7	.. 55.2	59 21.1	.. 12.7	Menkent	148 07.5	S36 26.3
22	288 33.4	115 29.7	06.9	178 41.8	58.6	187 52.6	55.2	74 23.4	12.7	Miaplacidus	221 40.5	S69 46.5
23	303 35.8	130 29.5	05.7	193 42.5	58.4	202 54.5	55.1	89 25.8	12.8			
10 00	318 38.3	145 29.2	N 4 04.4	208 43.2	N22 58.2	217 56.4	N22 55.1	104 28.1	S11 12.8	Mirfak	308 40.2	N49 54.3
01	333 40.8	160 29.0	03.1	223 43.9	58.0	232 58.3	55.1	119 30.5	12.9	Nunki	75 57.8	S26 16.6
02	348 43.2	175 28.8	01.9	238 44.6	57.8	248 00.2	55.0	134 32.8	12.9	Peacock	53 18.5	S56 41.3
03	3 45.7	190 28.5	4 00.6	253 45.3	.. 57.6	263 02.1	.. 55.0	149 35.1	.. 13.0	Pollux	243 27.9	N27 59.4
04	18 48.2	205 28.3	3 59.3	268 46.0	57.4	278 04.1	55.0	164 37.5	13.0	Procyon	244 59.9	N 5 11.3
05	33 50.6	220 28.1	58.1	283 46.7	57.2	293 06.0	54.9	179 39.8	13.1			
06	48 53.1	235 27.8	N 3 56.8	298 47.4	N22 57.0	308 07.9	N22 54.9	194 42.2	S11 13.2	Rasalhague	96 06.1	N12 33.3
07	63 55.6	250 27.6	55.5	313 48.1	56.8	323 09.8	54.9	209 44.5	13.2	Regulus	207 43.7	N11 54.0
S 08	78 58.0	265 27.4	54.3	328 48.8	56.6	338 11.7	54.8	224 46.8	13.3	Rigel	281 12.1	S 8 11.2
A 09	94 00.5	280 27.1	.. 53.0	343 49.5	.. 56.4	353 13.6	.. 54.8	239 49.2	.. 13.3	Rigil Kent.	139 51.6	S60 53.6
T 10	109 02.9	295 26.9	51.7	358 50.2	56.2	8 15.6	54.8	254 51.5	13.4	Sabik	102 12.2	S15 44.3
U 11	124 05.4	310 26.7	50.5	13 50.9	56.0	23 17.5	54.7	269 53.9	13.4			
R 12	139 07.9	325 26.4	N 3 49.2	28 51.6	N22 55.8	38 19.4	N22 54.7	284 56.2	S11 13.5	Schedar	349 40.0	N56 36.6
D 13	154 10.3	340 26.2	47.9	43 52.3	55.6	53 21.3	54.7	299 58.6	13.5	Shaula	96 21.5	S37 06.7
A 14	169 12.8	355 26.0	46.6	58 53.0	55.4	68 23.2	54.6	315 00.9	13.6	Sirius	258 33.9	S16 44.1
Y 15	184 15.3	10 25.7	.. 45.4	73 53.7	.. 55.2	83 25.1	.. 54.6	330 03.2	.. 13.6	Spica	158 31.2	S11 13.9
16	199 17.7	25 25.5	44.1	88 54.4	55.0	98 27.1	54.6	345 05.6	13.7	Suhail	222 52.8	S43 29.4
17	214 20.2	40 25.3	42.8	103 55.1	54.8	113 29.0	54.5	0 07.9	13.7			
18	229 22.7	55 25.0	N 3 41.6	118 55.8	N22 54.5	128 30.9	N22 54.5	15 10.3	S11 13.8	Vega	80 38.5	N38 48.1
19	244 25.1	70 24.8	40.3	133 56.5	54.4	143 32.8	54.5	30 12.6	13.8	Zuben'ubi	137 05.3	S16 05.8
20	259 27.6	85 24.6	39.0	148 57.2	54.4	158 34.7	54.4	45 14.9	13.9		SHA	Mer. Pass.
21	274 30.1	100 24.3	.. 37.7	163 57.9	.. 54.0	173 36.7	.. 54.4	60 17.3	.. 13.9	Venus	187 55.8	14 18
22	289 32.5	115 24.1	36.5	178 58.6	53.8	188 38.6	54.4	75 19.6	14.0	Mars	250 47.3	10 06
23	304 35.0	130 23.9	35.2	193 59.3	53.6	203 40.5	54.3	90 22.0	14.1	Jupiter	259 31.3	9 30
Mer. Pass.	2 48.9	v −0.2	d 1.3	v 0.7	d 0.2	v 1.9	d 0.0	v 2.3	d 0.1	Saturn	145 52.7	17 03

UT	SUN GHA	SUN Dec	MOON GHA	v	MOON Dec	d	HP
8 00	178 34.9	N16 08.9	168 11.9	14.0	N 7 40.0	9.8	55.1
01	193 35.0	08.2	182 44.9	13.9	7 30.2	9.8	55.1
02	208 35.1	07.5	197 17.8	14.0	7 20.4	9.9	55.1
03	223 35.2	.. 06.8	211 50.8	14.0	7 10.5	9.9	55.1
04	238 35.2	06.1	226 23.8	14.0	7 00.6	10.0	55.1
05	253 35.3	05.4	240 56.8	14.0	6 50.6	9.9	55.2
06	268 35.4	N16 04.7	255 29.3	14.1	N 6 40.7	10.0	55.2
07	283 35.5	04.0	270 02.9	14.0	6 30.7	10.1	55.2
T 08	298 35.6	03.3	284 35.9	14.0	6 20.6	10.1	55.2
H 09	313 35.6	.. 02.5	299 08.9	14.0	6 10.5	10.1	55.2
U 10	328 35.7	01.8	313 41.9	14.0	6 00.4	10.1	55.2
R 11	343 35.8	01.1	328 14.9	14.0	5 50.3	10.2	55.3
S 12	358 35.9	N16 00.4	342 47.9	14.0	N 5 40.1	10.2	55.3
D 13	13 36.0	15 59.7	357 20.9	14.0	5 29.9	10.2	55.3
A 14	28 36.1	59.0	11 53.9	14.1	5 19.7	10.3	55.3
Y 15	43 36.1	.. 58.3	26 27.0	14.0	5 09.4	10.3	55.3
16	58 36.2	57.5	41 00.0	14.0	4 59.1	10.3	55.4
17	73 36.3	56.8	55 33.0	14.0	4 48.8	10.4	55.4
18	88 36.4	N15 56.1	70 06.0	14.0	N 4 38.4	10.3	55.4
19	103 36.5	55.4	84 39.0	14.0	4 28.1	10.4	55.4
20	118 36.6	54.7	99 12.0	14.0	4 17.7	10.4	55.4
21	133 36.7	.. 54.0	113 45.0	14.0	4 07.3	10.5	55.4
22	148 36.7	53.2	128 18.0	13.9	3 56.8	10.5	55.5
23	163 36.8	52.5	142 50.9	14.0	3 46.3	10.5	55.5
9 00	178 36.9	N15 51.8	157 23.9	14.0	N 3 35.8	10.5	55.5
01	193 37.0	51.1	171 56.9	13.9	3 25.3	10.5	55.5
02	208 37.1	50.4	186 29.8	14.0	3 14.8	10.6	55.5
03	223 37.2	.. 49.6	201 02.8	13.9	3 04.2	10.6	55.6
04	238 37.3	48.9	215 35.7	14.0	2 53.7	10.6	55.6
05	253 37.4	48.2	230 08.7	13.9	2 43.1	10.6	55.6
06	268 37.4	N15 47.5	244 41.6	13.9	N 2 32.5	10.7	55.6
07	283 37.5	46.7	259 14.5	13.9	2 21.8	10.6	55.6
F 08	298 37.6	46.0	273 47.4	13.9	2 11.2	10.7	55.7
R 09	313 37.7	.. 45.3	288 20.3	13.9	2 00.5	10.7	55.7
I 10	328 37.8	44.6	302 53.2	13.8	1 49.8	10.7	55.7
D 11	343 37.9	43.8	317 26.0	13.9	1 39.1	10.7	55.7
A 12	358 38.0	N15 43.1	331 58.9	13.8	N 1 28.4	10.7	55.7
Y 13	13 38.1	42.4	346 31.7	13.8	1 17.7	10.7	55.8
14	28 38.2	41.7	1 04.5	13.8	1 07.0	10.8	55.8
15	43 38.2	.. 40.9	15 37.3	13.8	0 56.2	10.7	55.8
16	58 38.3	40.2	30 10.1	13.8	0 45.5	10.8	55.8
17	73 38.4	39.5	44 42.9	13.8	0 34.7	10.8	55.8
18	88 38.5	N15 38.8	59 15.7	13.7	N 0 23.9	10.8	55.9
19	103 38.6	38.0	73 48.4	13.7	0 13.1	10.7	55.9
20	118 38.7	37.3	88 21.1	13.7	N 0 02.4	10.8	55.9
21	133 38.8	.. 36.6	102 53.8	13.7	S 0 08.4	10.8	55.9
22	148 38.9	35.8	117 26.5	13.6	0 19.2	10.8	55.9
23	163 39.0	35.1	131 59.1	13.7	0 30.1	10.8	56.0
10 00	178 39.1	N15 34.4	146 51.8	13.6	S 0 40.9	10.8	56.0
01	193 39.2	33.7	161 04.4	13.6	0 51.7	10.8	56.0
02	208 39.3	32.9	175 37.0	13.6	1 02.5	10.8	56.0
03	223 39.3	.. 32.2	190 09.5	13.6	1 13.3	10.9	56.0
04	238 39.4	31.5	204 42.1	13.5	1 24.2	10.8	56.1
05	253 39.5	30.7	219 14.6	13.5	1 35.0	10.8	56.1
06	268 39.6	N15 30.0	233 47.1	13.4	S 1 45.8	10.8	56.1
07	283 39.7	29.3	248 19.5	13.5	1 56.6	10.9	56.1
S 08	298 39.8	28.5	262 52.0	13.4	2 07.5	10.8	56.1
A 09	313 39.9	.. 27.8	277 24.4	13.3	2 18.3	10.8	56.2
T 10	328 40.0	27.1	291 56.7	13.4	2 29.1	10.8	56.2
U 11	343 40.1	26.3	306 29.1	13.3	2 39.9	10.8	56.2
R 12	358 40.2	N15 25.6	321 01.4	13.3	S 2 50.7	10.8	56.2
D 13	13 40.3	24.9	335 33.7	13.3	3 01.5	10.8	56.3
A 14	28 40.4	24.1	350 06.0	13.2	3 12.3	10.8	56.3
Y 15	43 40.5	.. 23.4	4 38.2	13.2	3 23.1	10.8	56.3
16	58 40.6	22.6	19 10.4	13.1	3 33.9	10.8	56.3
17	73 40.7	21.9	33 42.5	13.2	3 44.7	10.7	56.3
18	88 40.8	N15 21.2	48 14.7	13.0	S 3 55.4	10.8	56.4
19	103 40.9	20.4	62 46.7	13.1	4 06.2	10.7	56.4
20	118 41.0	19.7	77 18.8	13.0	4 16.9	10.7	56.4
21	133 41.1	.. 19.0	91 50.8	13.0	4 27.6	10.7	56.4
22	148 41.2	18.2	106 22.8	12.9	4 38.3	10.7	56.5
23	163 41.3	17.5	120 54.7	12.9	S 4 49.0	10.7	56.5
	SD 15.8	d 0.7	SD 15.1		15.2		15.3

Twilight / Sunrise / Moonrise

Lat.	Naut.	Civil	Sunrise	Moonrise 8	9	10	11
N 72	////	////	01 36	05 33	07 16	09 00	10 48
N 70	////	////	02 24	05 43	07 19	08 57	10 37
68	////	00 32	02 54	05 51	07 22	08 54	10 28
66	////	01 47	03 16	05 58	07 24	08 52	10 21
64	////	02 21	03 34	06 04	07 26	08 50	10 15
62	00 29	02 46	03 48	06 08	07 28	08 48	10 10
60	01 36	03 05	04 00	06 13	07 29	08 47	10 06
N 58	02 07	03 21	04 10	06 16	07 30	08 45	10 02
56	02 30	03 34	04 19	06 20	07 31	08 44	09 58
54	02 48	03 45	04 27	06 23	07 32	08 43	09 55
52	03 03	03 55	04 34	06 25	07 33	08 42	09 52
50	03 16	04 04	04 41	06 28	07 34	08 41	09 50
45	03 41	04 22	04 55	06 33	07 36	08 39	09 44
N 40	04 00	04 36	05 06	06 37	07 37	08 38	09 40
35	04 15	04 48	05 15	06 41	07 38	08 36	09 36
30	04 28	04 58	05 24	06 45	07 40	08 35	09 32
20	04 48	05 15	05 38	06 50	07 41	08 33	09 26
N 10	05 03	05 29	05 51	06 55	07 43	08 32	09 21
0	05 16	05 41	06 02	07 00	07 45	08 30	09 16
S 10	05 26	05 52	06 13	07 05	07 46	08 28	09 11
20	05 36	06 03	06 25	07 10	07 48	08 27	09 06
30	05 46	06 14	06 39	07 16	07 50	08 25	09 00
35	05 50	06 20	06 47	07 19	07 51	08 24	08 57
40	05 55	06 27	06 56	07 23	07 53	08 22	08 53
45	06 00	06 35	07 06	07 27	07 54	08 21	08 49
S 50	06 06	06 44	07 18	07 32	07 56	08 19	08 44
52	06 08	06 48	07 24	07 35	07 57	08 19	08 42
54	06 10	06 53	07 31	07 37	07 58	08 18	08 39
56	06 13	06 57	07 38	07 40	07 59	08 17	08 36
58	06 16	07 03	07 46	07 43	08 00	08 16	08 33
S 60	06 19	07 09	07 55	07 47	08 01	08 15	08 30

Sunset / Twilight / Moonset

Lat.	Sunset	Civil	Naut.	Moonset 8	9	10	11
N 72	22 26	////	////	20 15	20 06	19 56	19 45
N 70	21 42	////	////	20 10	20 06	20 02	19 58
68	21 14	23 19	////	20 05	20 06	20 07	20 08
66	20 52	22 19	////	20 01	20 06	20 11	20 17
64	20 35	21 46	////	19 58	20 06	20 14	20 24
62	20 21	21 22	23 25	19 55	20 06	20 18	20 30
60	20 09	21 03	22 30	19 52	20 06	20 20	20 36
N 58	19 59	20 48	22 00	19 50	20 06	20 23	20 41
56	19 50	20 35	21 38	19 48	20 06	20 25	20 45
54	19 42	20 24	21 20	19 46	20 06	20 27	20 49
52	19 35	20 15	21 06	19 44	20 06	20 28	20 52
50	19 29	20 06	20 53	19 43	20 06	20 30	20 56
45	19 16	19 48	20 29	19 39	20 06	20 34	21 03
N 40	19 04	19 34	20 10	19 37	20 06	20 36	21 08
35	18 55	19 22	19 55	19 34	20 06	20 39	21 13
30	18 47	19 12	19 42	19 32	20 06	20 41	21 18
20	18 33	18 56	19 23	19 28	20 06	20 45	21 26
N 10	18 20	18 42	19 08	19 25	20 06	20 49	21 33
0	18 09	18 30	18 55	19 22	20 06	20 52	21 39
S 10	17 58	18 19	18 45	19 18	20 06	20 55	21 45
20	17 46	18 09	18 35	19 15	20 06	20 59	21 52
30	17 32	17 57	18 26	19 11	20 06	21 02	22 00
35	17 24	17 51	18 21	19 09	20 06	21 05	22 05
40	17 16	17 44	18 16	19 06	20 06	21 07	22 10
45	17 05	17 36	18 11	19 03	20 06	21 10	22 16
S 50	16 53	17 27	18 06	18 59	20 06	21 14	22 23
52	16 47	17 23	18 04	18 58	20 06	21 15	22 26
54	16 41	17 19	18 01	18 56	20 06	21 17	22 30
56	16 34	17 14	17 59	18 54	20 06	21 19	22 34
58	16 27	17 09	17 56	18 51	20 06	21 21	22 39
S 60	16 17	17 03	17 53	18 49	20 06	21 24	22 44

SUN / MOON

Day	Eqn. of Time 00h	12h	Mer. Pass.	Mer. Pass. Upper	Lower	Age	Phase
d	m s	m s	h m	h m	h m	d	%
8	05 41	05 37	12 06	13 11	00 49	02	3
9	05 33	05 28	12 05	13 56	01 33	03	7
10	05 24	05 19	12 05	14 41	02 18	04	13

2013 AUGUST 11, 12, 13 (SUN., MON., TUES.)

UT	ARIES GHA	VENUS −3.9 GHA	Dec	MARS +1.6 GHA	Dec	JUPITER −2.0 GHA	Dec	SATURN +0.7 GHA	Dec
11 00	319 37.4	145 23.6	N 3 33.9	209 00.0	N22 53.4	218 42.4	N22 54.3	105 24.3	S11 14.1
01	334 39.9	160 23.4	32.7	224 00.7	53.1	233 44.3	54.3	120 26.6	14.2
02	349 42.4	175 23.2	31.4	239 01.4	52.9	248 46.3	54.2	135 29.0	14.2
03	4 44.8	190 22.9	30.1	254 02.1	52.7	263 48.2	54.2	150 31.3	14.3
04	19 47.3	205 22.7	28.8	269 02.8	52.5	278 50.1	54.2	165 33.7	14.3
05	34 49.8	220 22.5	27.6	284 03.5	52.3	293 52.0	54.1	180 36.0	14.4
06	49 52.2	235 22.3	N 3 26.3	299 04.2	N22 52.1	308 53.9	N22 54.1	195 38.3	S11 14.4
07	64 54.7	250 22.0	25.0	314 04.9	51.9	323 55.8	54.1	210 40.7	14.5
08	79 57.2	265 21.8	23.7	329 05.6	51.7	338 57.8	54.0	225 43.0	14.5
S 09	94 59.6	280 21.6	22.5	344 06.3	51.5	353 59.7	54.0	240 45.4	14.6
U 10	110 02.1	295 21.3	21.2	359 07.0	51.3	9 01.6	53.9	255 47.7	14.6
N 11	125 04.6	310 21.1	19.9	14 07.7	51.1	24 03.5	53.9	270 50.0	14.7
D 12	140 07.0	325 20.9	N 3 18.7	29 08.4	N22 50.9	39 05.4	N22 53.8	285 52.4	S11 14.8
A 13	155 09.5	340 20.7	17.4	44 09.1	50.7	54 07.4	53.8	300 54.7	14.8
Y 14	170 11.9	355 20.4	16.1	59 09.9	50.5	69 09.3	53.8	315 57.0	14.9
15	185 14.4	10 20.2	14.8	74 10.6	50.2	84 11.2	53.8	330 59.4	14.9
16	200 16.9	25 20.0	13.6	89 11.3	50.0	99 13.1	53.7	346 01.7	15.0
17	215 19.3	40 19.7	12.3	104 12.0	49.8	114 15.1	53.7	1 04.1	15.0
18	230 21.8	55 19.5	N 3 11.0	119 12.7	N22 49.6	129 17.0	N22 53.6	16 06.4	S11 15.1
19	245 24.3	70 19.3	09.7	134 13.4	49.4	144 18.9	53.6	31 08.7	15.1
20	260 26.7	85 19.1	08.5	149 14.1	49.2	159 20.8	53.6	46 11.1	15.2
21	275 29.2	100 18.8	07.2	164 14.8	49.0	174 22.7	53.5	61 13.4	15.2
22	290 31.7	115 18.6	05.9	179 15.5	48.8	189 24.7	53.5	76 15.7	15.3
23	305 34.1	130 18.4	04.6	194 16.2	48.6	204 26.6	53.5	91 18.1	15.3
12 00	320 36.6	145 18.2	N 3 03.4	209 16.9	N22 48.3	219 28.5	N22 53.5	106 20.4	S11 15.4
01	335 39.0	160 17.9	02.1	224 17.6	48.1	234 30.4	53.4	121 22.7	15.5
02	350 41.5	175 17.7	3 00.8	239 18.3	47.9	249 32.3	53.4	136 25.1	15.5
03	5 44.0	190 17.5	2 59.5	254 19.0	47.7	264 34.3	53.4	151 27.4	15.6
04	20 46.4	205 17.3	58.3	269 19.7	47.5	279 36.2	53.3	166 29.8	15.6
05	35 48.9	220 17.0	57.0	284 20.4	47.3	294 38.1	53.3	181 32.1	15.7
06	50 51.4	235 16.8	N 2 55.7	299 21.2	N22 47.1	309 40.0	N22 53.3	196 34.4	S11 15.7
07	65 53.8	250 16.6	54.4	314 21.9	46.8	324 42.0	53.2	211 36.8	15.8
08	80 56.3	265 16.4	53.1	329 22.6	46.6	339 43.9	53.2	226 39.1	15.8
M 09	95 58.8	280 16.1	51.9	344 23.3	46.4	354 45.8	53.1	241 41.4	15.9
O 10	111 01.2	295 15.9	50.6	359 24.0	46.2	9 47.7	53.1	256 43.8	15.9
N 11	126 03.7	310 15.7	49.3	14 24.7	46.0	24 49.6	53.1	271 46.1	16.0
D 12	141 06.2	325 15.5	N 2 48.0	29 25.4	N22 45.8	39 51.6	N22 53.0	286 48.4	S11 16.1
A 13	156 08.6	340 15.2	46.8	44 26.1	45.6	54 53.5	53.0	301 50.8	16.1
Y 14	171 11.1	355 15.0	45.5	59 26.8	45.3	69 55.4	53.0	316 53.1	16.2
15	186 13.5	10 14.8	44.2	74 27.5	45.1	84 57.3	52.9	331 55.4	16.2
16	201 16.0	25 14.6	42.9	89 28.2	44.9	99 59.3	52.9	346 57.8	16.3
17	216 18.5	40 14.4	41.7	104 28.9	44.7	115 01.2	52.9	2 00.1	16.3
18	231 20.9	55 14.1	N 2 40.4	119 29.7	N22 44.5	130 03.1	N22 52.8	17 02.4	S11 16.4
19	246 23.4	70 13.9	39.1	134 30.4	44.2	145 05.0	52.8	32 04.8	16.4
20	261 25.9	85 13.7	37.8	149 31.1	44.0	160 07.0	52.8	47 07.1	16.5
21	276 28.3	100 13.5	36.5	164 31.8	43.8	175 08.9	52.7	62 09.4	16.5
22	291 30.8	115 13.3	35.3	179 32.5	43.6	190 10.8	52.7	77 11.8	16.6
23	306 33.3	130 13.0	34.0	194 33.2	43.4	205 12.7	52.7	92 14.1	16.7
13 00	321 35.7	145 12.8	N 2 32.7	209 33.9	N22 43.2	220 14.7	N22 52.6	107 16.4	S11 16.7
01	336 38.2	160 12.6	31.4	224 34.6	42.9	235 16.6	52.6	122 18.8	16.8
02	351 40.6	175 12.4	30.1	239 35.3	42.7	250 18.5	52.5	137 21.1	16.8
03	6 43.1	190 12.2	28.9	254 36.1	42.5	265 20.4	52.5	152 23.4	16.9
04	21 45.6	205 11.9	27.6	269 36.8	42.3	280 22.4	52.5	167 25.8	16.9
05	36 48.0	220 11.7	26.3	284 37.5	42.1	295 24.3	52.4	182 28.1	17.0
06	51 50.5	235 11.5	N 2 25.0	299 38.2	N22 41.8	310 26.2	N22 52.4	197 30.4	S11 17.1
07	66 53.0	250 11.3	23.7	314 38.9	41.6	325 28.1	52.4	212 32.8	17.1
08	81 55.4	265 11.1	22.5	329 39.6	41.4	340 30.1	52.3	227 35.1	17.2
T 09	96 57.9	280 10.8	21.2	344 40.3	41.2	355 32.0	52.3	242 37.4	17.2
U 10	112 00.4	295 10.6	19.9	359 41.0	40.9	10 33.9	52.3	257 39.8	17.3
E 11	127 02.8	310 10.4	18.6	14 41.8	40.7	25 35.8	52.2	272 42.1	17.3
S 12	142 05.3	325 10.2	N 2 17.3	29 42.5	N22 40.5	40 37.8	N22 52.2	287 44.4	S11 17.4
D 13	157 07.8	340 10.0	16.1	44 43.2	40.3	55 39.7	52.2	302 46.8	17.4
A 14	172 10.2	355 09.7	14.8	59 43.9	40.0	70 41.6	52.1	317 49.1	17.5
Y 15	187 12.7	10 09.5	13.5	74 44.6	39.8	85 43.6	52.1	332 51.4	17.6
16	202 15.1	25 09.3	12.2	89 45.3	39.6	100 45.5	52.0	347 53.7	17.6
17	217 17.6	40 09.1	10.9	104 46.0	39.4	115 47.4	52.0	2 56.1	17.7
18	232 20.1	55 08.9	N 2 09.7	119 46.8	N22 39.1	130 49.3	N22 52.0	17 58.4	S11 17.7
19	247 22.5	70 08.7	08.4	134 47.5	38.9	145 51.3	51.9	33 00.7	17.8
20	262 25.0	85 08.4	07.1	149 48.2	38.7	160 53.2	51.9	48 03.1	17.8
21	277 27.5	100 08.2	05.8	164 48.9	38.5	175 55.1	51.9	63 05.4	17.9
22	292 29.9	115 08.0	04.5	179 49.6	38.2	190 57.0	51.8	78 07.7	18.0
23	307 32.4	130 07.8	03.3	194 50.3	38.0	205 59.0	51.8	93 10.1	18.0
Mer.Pass.	h m 2 37.1	v −0.2	d 1.3	v 0.7	d 0.2	v 1.9	d 0.0	v 2.3	d 0.1

STARS

Name	SHA	Dec
Acamar	315 18.2	S40 14.8
Achernar	335 26.5	S57 09.7
Acrux	173 09.5	S63 10.7
Adhara	255 12.7	S28 59.4
Aldebaran	290 49.3	N16 32.1
Alioth	166 21.0	N55 53.4
Alkaid	152 59.0	N49 15.0
Al Na'ir	27 43.1	S46 53.4
Alnilam	275 46.4	S 1 11.6
Alphard	217 56.3	S 8 43.1
Alphecca	126 10.9	N26 40.4
Alpheratz	357 43.1	N29 10.0
Altair	62 07.8	N 8 54.6
Ankaa	353 15.3	S42 13.6
Antares	112 26.0	S26 27.6
Arcturus	145 55.7	N19 06.9
Atria	107 27.4	S69 03.2
Avior	234 18.5	S59 33.2
Bellatrix	278 32.0	N 6 21.6
Betelgeuse	271 01.4	N 7 24.5
Canopus	263 56.5	S52 42.1
Capella	280 34.5	N46 00.4
Deneb	49 30.9	N45 20.0
Denebola	182 33.8	N14 29.8
Diphda	348 55.6	S17 54.5
Dubhe	193 52.2	N61 40.7
Elnath	278 12.7	N28 36.9
Eltanin	90 45.7	N51 29.6
Enif	33 46.7	N 9 56.5
Fomalhaut	15 23.5	S29 32.7
Gacrux	172 01.1	S57 11.6
Gienah	175 52.4	S17 37.1
Hadar	148 47.8	S60 26.5
Hamal	328 00.5	N23 31.6
Kaus Aust.	83 43.3	S34 22.5
Kochab	137 20.2	N74 06.3
Markab	13 37.9	N15 16.9
Menkar	314 14.9	N 4 08.6
Menkent	148 07.5	S36 26.3
Miaplacidus	221 40.5	S69 46.5
Mirfak	308 40.2	N49 54.3
Nunki	75 57.9	S26 16.6
Peacock	53 18.5	S56 41.3
Pollux	243 27.9	N27 59.4
Procyon	244 59.9	N 5 11.3
Rasalhague	96 06.1	N12 33.3
Regulus	207 43.7	N11 54.0
Rigel	281 12.1	S 8 11.2
Rigil Kent.	139 51.6	S60 53.6
Sabik	102 12.2	S15 44.3
Schedar	349 39.9	N56 36.6
Shaula	96 21.5	S37 06.7
Sirius	258 33.9	S16 44.1
Spica	158 31.2	S11 13.9
Suhail	222 52.8	S43 29.3
Vega	80 38.5	N38 48.2
Zuben'ubi	137 05.3	S16 05.8

	SHA	Mer.Pass.
		h m
Venus	184 41.6	14 19
Mars	248 40.3	10 02
Jupiter	258 51.9	9 21
Saturn	145 43.8	16 52

SUN and MOON

UT	SUN GHA	SUN Dec	MOON GHA	MOON v	MOON Dec	MOON d	MOON HP
d h	° '	° '	° '	'	° '	'	'
11 00	178 41.4	N15 16.7	135 26.6 12.9	S 4 59.7	10.7	56.5
01	193 41.5	16.0	149 58.5 12.8	5 10.4	10.6	56.5
02	208 41.6	15.2	164 30.3 12.8	5 21.0	10.7	56.5
03	223 41.7 ..	14.5	179 02.1 12.8	5 31.7	10.6	56.6
04	238 41.8	13.8	193 33.9 12.7	5 42.3	10.6	56.6
05	253 41.9	13.0	208 05.6 12.6	5 52.9	10.5	56.6
06	268 42.0	N15 12.3	222 37.2 12.6	S 6 03.4	10.6	56.6
07	283 42.1	11.5	237 08.8 12.6	6 14.0	10.5	56.7
08	298 42.2	10.8	251 40.4 12.5	6 24.5	10.5	56.7
S 09	313 42.3 ..	10.0	266 11.9 12.5	6 35.0	10.5	56.7
U 10	328 42.4	09.3	280 43.4 12.5	6 45.5	10.5	56.7
N 11	343 42.5	08.6	295 14.9 12.3	6 56.0	10.4	56.8
D 12	358 42.6	N15 07.8	309 46.2 12.4	S 7 06.4	10.4	56.8
A 13	13 42.7	07.1	324 17.6 12.3	7 16.8	10.4	56.8
Y 14	28 42.9	06.3	338 48.9 12.2	7 27.2	10.3	56.8
15	43 42.9 ..	05.6	353 20.1 12.2	7 37.5	10.4	56.9
16	58 43.0	04.8	7 51.3 12.2	7 47.9	10.2	56.9
17	73 43.1	04.1	22 22.5 12.1	7 58.1	10.3	56.9
18	88 43.2	N15 03.3	36 53.6 12.0	S 8 08.4	10.2	56.9
19	103 43.3	02.6	51 24.6 12.0	8 18.6	10.2	57.0
20	118 43.4	01.8	65 55.6 11.9	8 28.8	10.2	57.0
21	133 43.5 ..	01.1	80 26.5 11.9	8 39.0	10.1	57.0
22	148 43.6	15 00.3	94 57.4 11.8	8 49.1	10.1	57.0
23	163 43.7	14 59.6	109 28.2 11.8	8 59.2	10.0	57.0
12 00	178 43.8	N14 59.8	123 59.0 11.7	S 9 09.2	10.0	57.1
01	193 43.9	58.1	138 29.7 11.7	9 19.2	10.0	57.1
02	208 44.0	57.3	153 00.4 11.6	9 29.2	9.9	57.1
03	223 44.1 ..	56.6	167 31.0 11.6	9 39.1	9.9	57.1
04	238 44.2	55.8	182 01.6 11.4	9 49.0	9.9	57.2
05	253 44.3	55.1	196 32.0 11.5	9 58.9	9.8	57.2
06	268 44.4	N14 54.3	211 02.5 11.4	S10 08.7	9.7	57.2
07	283 44.5	53.6	225 32.9 11.3	10 18.4	9.7	57.2
08	298 44.7	52.8	240 03.2 11.2	10 28.1	9.7	57.3
M 09	313 44.8 ..	52.1	254 33.4 11.2	10 37.8	9.6	57.3
O 10	328 44.9	51.3	269 03.6 11.2	10 47.4	9.6	57.3
N 11	343 45.0	50.5	283 33.8 11.0	10 57.0	9.5	57.4
D 12	358 45.1	N14 49.8	298 03.8 11.0	S11 06.5	9.5	57.4
A 13	13 45.2	49.0	312 33.8 11.0	11 16.0	9.4	57.4
Y 14	28 45.3	48.3	327 03.8 10.9	11 25.4	9.4	57.4
15	43 45.4 ..	47.5	341 33.7 10.8	11 34.8	9.3	57.5
16	58 45.5	46.8	356 03.5 10.7	11 44.1	9.3	57.5
17	73 45.6	46.0	10 33.2 10.7	11 53.4	9.2	57.5
18	88 45.7	N14 45.2	25 02.9 10.7	S12 02.6	9.2	57.5
19	103 45.8	44.5	39 32.6 10.5	12 11.8	9.1	57.6
20	118 45.9	43.7	54 02.1 10.5	12 20.9	9.0	57.6
21	133 46.1 ..	43.0	68 31.6 10.4	12 29.9	9.0	57.6
22	148 46.2	42.2	83 01.0 10.4	12 38.9	8.9	57.6
23	163 46.3	41.5	97 30.4 10.3	12 47.8	8.8	57.7
13 00	170 46.4	N14 40.7	111 59.7 10.2	S12 56.6	8.8	57.7
01	193 46.5	39.9	126 28.9 10.2	13 05.4	8.8	57.7
02	208 46.6	39.2	140 58.1 10.1	13 14.2	8.6	57.7
03	223 46.7 ..	38.4	155 27.2 10.0	13 22.8	8.6	57.8
04	238 46.8	37.6	169 56.2 9.9	13 31.4	8.6	57.8
05	253 46.9	36.9	184 25.1 9.9	13 40.0	8.4	57.8
06	268 47.1	N14 36.1	198 54.0 9.8	S13 48.4	8.4	57.8
07	283 47.2	35.4	213 22.8 9.8	13 56.8	8.4	57.9
T 08	298 47.3	34.6	227 51.6 9.6	14 05.2	8.2	57.9
U 09	313 47.4 ..	33.8	242 20.2 9.6	14 13.4	8.2	57.9
E 10	328 47.5	33.1	256 48.8 9.6	14 21.6	8.1	57.9
S 11	343 47.6	32.3	271 17.4 9.4	14 29.7	8.0	58.0
D 12	358 47.7	N14 31.5	285 45.8 9.4	S14 37.7	8.0	58.0
A 13	13 47.9	30.8	300 14.2 9.3	14 45.7	7.9	58.0
Y 14	28 48.0	30.0	314 42.5 9.2	14 53.6	7.8	58.1
15	43 48.1 ..	29.2	329 10.7 9.2	15 01.4	7.7	58.1
16	58 48.2	28.5	343 38.9 9.1	15 09.1	7.7	58.1
17	73 48.3	27.7	358 07.0 9.0	15 16.8	7.5	58.1
18	88 48.4	N14 26.9	12 35.0 9.0	S15 24.3	7.5	58.2
19	103 48.5	26.2	27 03.0 8.9	15 31.8	7.4	58.2
20	118 48.7	25.4	41 30.9 8.8	15 39.2	7.3	58.2
21	133 48.8 ..	24.6	55 58.7 8.7	15 46.5	7.3	58.2
22	148 48.9	23.9	70 26.4 8.7	15 53.8	7.1	58.3
23	163 49.0	23.1	84 54.1 8.5	S16 00.9	7.1	58.3
	SD 15.8	d 0.8	SD 15.5	15.6			15.8

Twilight, Sunrise and Moonrise

Lat.	Twilight Naut.	Twilight Civil	Sunrise	Moonrise 11	Moonrise 12	Moonrise 13	Moonrise 14
°	h m	h m	h m	h m	h m	h m	h m
N 72	////	////	02 03	10 48	12 42	14 48	■
N 70	////	////	02 41	10 37	12 22	14 12	16 10
68	////	01 18	03 07	10 28	12 06	13 47	15 29
66	////	02 05	03 27	10 21	11 53	13 28	15 01
64	////	02 35	03 43	10 15	11 43	13 12	14 40
62	01 09	02 57	03 56	10 10	11 34	12 59	14 23
60	01 52	03 14	04 07	10 06	11 27	12 48	14 09
N 58	02 19	03 29	04 17	10 02	11 20	12 39	13 57
56	02 40	03 41	04 25	09 58	11 14	12 31	13 46
54	02 56	03 51	04 33	09 55	11 09	12 23	13 37
52	03 10	04 01	04 39	09 52	11 04	12 17	13 29
50	03 22	04 09	04 45	09 50	11 00	12 11	13 22
45	03 46	04 26	04 58	09 44	10 51	11 58	13 06
N 40	04 04	04 39	05 09	09 40	10 43	11 48	12 53
35	04 18	04 51	05 18	09 36	10 37	11 39	12 42
30	04 30	05 00	05 26	09 32	10 31	11 31	12 33
20	04 49	05 16	05 39	09 26	10 21	11 18	12 16
N 10	05 03	05 29	05 51	09 21	10 12	11 06	12 02
0	05 15	05 40	06 02	09 16	10 04	10 55	11 49
S 10	05 26	05 51	06 12	09 11	09 56	10 44	11 36
20	05 35	06 01	06 24	09 06	09 48	10 33	11 22
30	05 43	06 12	06 36	09 00	09 39	10 20	11 06
35	05 48	06 19	06 44	08 57	09 33	10 12	10 57
40	05 52	06 24	06 52	08 53	09 27	10 04	10 46
45	05 56	06 31	07 02	08 49	09 20	09 54	10 34
S 50	06 01	06 39	07 13	08 44	09 11	09 42	10 19
52	06 03	06 43	07 19	08 42	09 07	09 37	10 12
54	06 05	06 47	07 25	08 39	09 03	09 31	10 05
56	06 07	06 51	07 31	08 36	08 58	09 24	09 56
58	06 10	06 56	07 39	08 33	08 53	09 16	09 46
S 60	06 12	07 02	07 47	08 30	08 47	09 08	09 35

Sunset, Twilight and Moonset

Lat.	Sunset	Twilight Civil	Twilight Naut.	Moonset 11	Moonset 12	Moonset 13	Moonset 14
°	h m	h m	h m	h m	h m	h m	h m
N 72	22 01	////	////	19 45	19 32	19 13	■
N 70	21 25	////	////	19 58	19 54	19 50	19 46
68	21 00	22 43	////	20 08	20 11	20 16	20 27
66	20 40	22 00	////	20 17	20 25	20 36	20 56
64	20 25	21 32	////	20 24	20 36	20 53	21 18
62	20 12	21 11	22 53	20 30	20 46	21 06	21 35
60	20 01	20 54	22 14	20 36	20 54	21 18	21 50
N 58	19 52	20 39	21 48	20 41	21 02	21 28	22 02
56	19 43	20 28	21 28	20 45	21 08	21 37	22 13
54	19 36	20 17	21 12	20 49	21 14	21 45	22 22
52	19 30	20 08	20 58	20 52	21 19	21 52	22 31
50	19 24	20 00	20 46	20 56	21 24	21 58	22 38
45	19 11	19 43	20 23	21 03	21 35	22 12	22 55
N 40	19 01	19 30	20 05	21 08	21 43	22 23	23 08
35	18 52	19 19	19 51	21 13	21 51	22 32	23 20
30	18 44	19 09	19 39	21 18	21 57	22 41	23 30
20	18 31	18 54	19 21	21 26	22 09	22 56	23 47
N 10	18 19	18 41	19 06	21 33	22 19	23 10	24 02
0	18 08	18 30	18 55	21 39	22 28	23 21	24 16
S 10	17 58	18 19	18 45	21 45	22 38	23 33	24 30
20	17 47	18 09	18 36	21 52	22 48	23 46	24 45
30	17 34	17 59	18 27	22 00	22 59	24 00	00 00
35	17 27	17 53	18 23	22 05	23 06	24 09	00 09
40	17 18	17 47	18 19	22 10	23 14	24 19	00 19
45	17 09	17 40	18 14	22 16	23 23	24 30	00 30
S 50	16 57	17 31	18 10	22 23	23 33	24 44	00 44
52	16 52	17 28	18 08	22 26	23 38	24 51	00 51
54	16 46	17 24	18 06	22 30	23 44	24 58	00 58
56	16 40	17 19	18 04	22 34	23 50	25 06	01 06
58	16 32	17 15	18 01	22 39	23 57	25 15	01 15
S 60	16 24	17 09	17 59	22 44	24 05	00 05	01 26

SUN and MOON

Day	SUN Eqn. of Time 00ʰ	SUN Eqn. of Time 12ʰ	SUN Mer. Pass.	MOON Mer. Pass. Upper	MOON Mer. Pass. Lower	Age	Phase
d	m s	m s	h m	h m	h m	d	%
11	05 15	05 10	12 05	15 28	03 04	05	20
12	05 05	05 00	12 05	16 16	03 52	06	29
13	04 55	04 49	12 05	17 08	04 42	07	40

UT	ARIES	VENUS −3.9		MARS +1.6		JUPITER −2.0		SATURN +0.7		STARS		
	GHA	GHA	Dec	GHA	Dec	GHA	Dec	GHA	Dec	Name	SHA	Dec
d h	° ′	° ′	° ′	° ′	° ′	° ′	° ′	° ′	° ′		° ′	° ′
14 00	322 34.9	145 07.6	N 2 02.0	209 51.0	N22 37.8	221 00.9	N22 51.8	108 12.4	S11 18.1	Acamar	315 18.2	S40 14.8
01	337 37.3	160 07.4	2 00.7	224 51.8	37.6	236 02.8	51.7	123 14.7	18.1	Achernar	335 26.5	S57 09.7
02	352 39.8	175 07.1	1 59.4	239 52.5	37.3	251 04.8	51.7	138 17.0	18.2	Acrux	173 09.5	S63 10.7
03	7 42.3	190 06.9	.. 58.1	254 53.2	.. 37.1	266 06.7	.. 51.7	153 19.4	.. 18.2	Adhara	255 12.7	S28 59.4
04	22 44.7	205 06.7	56.8	269 53.9	36.9	281 08.6	51.6	168 21.7	18.3	Aldebaran	290 49.3	N16 32.1
05	37 47.2	220 06.5	55.6	284 54.6	36.7	296 10.5	51.6	183 24.0	18.4			
06	52 49.6	235 06.3	N 1 54.3	299 55.3	N22 36.4	311 12.5	N22 51.5	198 26.4	S11 18.4	Alioth	166 21.0	N55 53.4
W 07	67 52.1	250 06.1	53.0	314 56.1	36.2	326 14.4	51.5	213 28.7	18.5	Alkaid	152 59.0	N49 15.0
E 08	82 54.6	265 05.9	51.7	329 56.8	36.0	341 16.3	51.5	228 31.0	18.5	Al Na'ir	27 43.1	S46 53.4
D 09	97 57.0	280 05.6	.. 50.4	344 57.5	.. 35.7	356 18.3	.. 51.4	243 33.3	.. 18.6	Alnilam	275 46.4	S 1 11.6
N 10	112 59.5	295 05.4	49.1	359 58.2	35.5	11 20.2	51.4	258 35.7	18.6	Alphard	217 56.3	S 8 43.1
E 11	128 02.0	310 05.2	47.9	14 58.9	35.3	26 22.1	51.4	273 38.0	18.7			
S 12	143 04.4	325 05.0	N 1 46.6	29 59.6	N22 35.1	41 24.1	N22 51.3	288 40.3	S11 18.8	Alphecca	126 10.9	N26 40.5
D 13	158 06.9	340 04.8	45.3	45 00.4	34.8	56 26.0	51.3	303 42.7	18.8	Alpheratz	357 43.0	N29 10.0
A 14	173 09.4	355 04.6	44.0	60 01.1	34.6	71 27.9	51.3	318 45.0	18.9	Altair	62 07.8	N 8 54.6
Y 15	188 11.8	10 04.4	.. 42.7	75 01.8	.. 34.4	86 29.8	.. 51.2	333 47.3	.. 18.9	Ankaa	353 15.3	S42 13.6
16	203 14.3	25 04.1	41.4	90 02.5	34.1	101 31.8	51.2	348 49.6	19.0	Antares	112 26.0	S26 27.6
17	218 16.7	40 03.9	40.2	105 03.2	33.9	116 33.7	51.1	3 52.0	19.0			
18	233 19.2	55 03.7	N 1 38.9	120 04.0	N22 33.7	131 35.6	N22 51.1	18 54.3	S11 19.1	Arcturus	145 55.7	N19 06.9
19	248 21.7	70 03.5	37.6	135 04.7	33.4	146 37.6	51.0	33 56.6	19.2	Atria	107 27.4	S69 03.2
20	263 24.1	85 03.3	36.3	150 05.4	33.2	161 39.5	51.0	48 58.9	19.2	Avior	234 18.5	S59 33.2
21	278 26.6	100 03.1	.. 35.0	165 06.1	.. 33.0	176 41.4	.. 51.0	64 01.3	.. 19.3	Bellatrix	278 32.0	N 6 21.6
22	293 29.1	115 02.9	33.7	180 06.8	32.7	191 43.4	51.0	79 03.6	19.3	Betelgeuse	271 01.3	N 7 24.5
23	308 31.5	130 02.7	32.5	195 07.6	32.5	206 45.3	50.9	94 05.9	19.4			
15 00	323 34.0	145 02.4	N 1 31.2	210 08.3	N22 32.3	221 47.2	N22 50.9	109 08.2	S11 19.4	Canopus	263 56.5	S52 42.1
01	338 36.5	160 02.2	29.9	225 09.0	32.0	236 49.2	50.9	124 10.6	19.5	Capella	280 34.5	N46 00.4
02	353 38.9	175 02.0	28.6	240 09.7	31.8	251 51.1	50.8	139 12.9	19.6	Deneb	49 30.9	N45 20.0
03	8 41.4	190 01.8	.. 27.3	255 10.4	.. 31.6	266 53.0	.. 50.8	154 15.2	.. 19.6	Denebola	182 33.8	N14 29.8
04	23 43.9	205 01.6	26.0	270 11.2	31.3	281 55.0	50.7	169 17.6	19.7	Diphda	348 55.5	S17 54.5
05	38 46.3	220 01.4	24.8	285 11.9	31.1	296 56.9	50.7	184 19.9	19.7			
06	53 48.8	235 01.2	N 1 23.5	300 12.6	N22 30.9	311 58.8	N22 50.7	199 22.2	S11 19.8	Dubhe	193 52.2	N61 40.7
T 07	68 51.2	250 01.0	22.2	315 13.3	30.6	327 00.8	50.6	214 24.5	19.8	Elnath	278 12.6	N28 36.9
H 08	83 53.7	265 00.8	20.9	330 14.0	30.4	342 02.7	50.6	229 26.9	19.9	Eltanin	90 45.8	N51 29.6
U 09	98 56.2	280 00.5	.. 19.6	345 14.8	.. 30.2	357 04.6	.. 50.6	244 29.2	.. 20.0	Enif	33 46.7	N 9 56.5
R 10	113 58.6	295 00.3	18.3	0 15.5	29.9	12 06.5	50.5	259 31.5	20.0	Fomalhaut	15 23.5	S29 32.7
S 11	129 01.1	310 00.1	17.0	15 16.2	29.7	27 08.5	50.5	274 33.8	20.1			
D 12	144 03.6	324 59.9	N 1 15.8	30 16.9	N22 29.4	42 10.4	N22 50.4	289 36.1	S11 20.1	Gacrux	172 01.1	S57 11.6
A 13	159 06.0	339 59.7	14.5	45 17.7	29.2	57 12.3	50.4	304 38.5	20.2	Gienah	175 52.4	S17 37.1
Y 14	174 08.5	354 59.5	13.2	60 18.4	29.0	72 14.3	50.4	319 40.8	20.3	Hadar	148 47.8	S60 26.5
15	189 11.0	9 59.3	.. 11.9	75 19.1	.. 28.7	87 16.2	.. 50.3	334 43.1	.. 20.3	Hamal	328 00.5	N23 31.6
16	204 13.4	24 59.1	10.6	90 19.8	28.5	102 18.1	50.3	349 45.4	20.4	Kaus Aust.	83 43.3	S34 22.5
17	219 15.9	39 58.9	09.3	105 20.5	28.3	117 20.1	50.3	4 47.8	20.4			
18	234 18.4	54 58.7	N 1 08.0	120 21.3	N22 28.0	132 22.0	N22 50.2	19 50.1	S11 20.5	Kochab	137 20.3	N74 06.3
19	249 20.8	69 58.5	06.8	135 22.0	27.8	147 24.0	50.2	34 52.4	20.5	Markab	13 37.9	N15 16.9
20	264 23.3	84 58.2	05.5	150 22.7	27.5	162 25.9	50.2	49 54.7	20.6	Menkar	314 14.9	N 4 08.6
21	279 25.7	99 58.0	.. 04.2	165 23.4	.. 27.3	177 27.8	.. 50.1	64 57.1	.. 20.7	Menkent	148 07.5	S36 26.3
22	294 28.2	114 57.8	02.9	180 24.2	27.1	192 29.8	50.1	79 59.4	20.7	Miaplacidus	221 40.5	S69 46.5
23	309 30.7	129 57.6	01.6	195 24.9	26.8	207 31.7	50.1	95 01.7	20.8			
16 00	324 33.1	144 57.4	N 1 00.3	210 25.6	N22 26.6	222 33.6	N22 50.0	110 04.0	S11 20.8	Mirfak	308 40.1	N49 54.3
01	339 35.6	159 57.2	0 59.0	225 26.3	26.3	237 35.6	50.0	125 06.4	20.9	Nunki	75 57.9	S26 16.6
02	354 38.1	174 57.0	57.8	240 27.1	26.1	252 37.5	49.9	140 08.7	21.0	Peacock	53 18.5	S56 41.3
03	9 40.5	189 56.8	.. 56.5	255 27.8	.. 25.8	267 39.4	.. 49.9	155 11.0	.. 21.0	Pollux	243 27.9	N27 59.4
04	24 43.0	204 56.6	55.2	270 28.5	25.6	282 41.4	49.9	170 13.3	21.1	Procyon	244 59.9	N 5 11.3
05	39 45.5	219 56.4	53.9	285 29.2	25.4	297 43.3	49.8	185 15.6	21.1			
06	54 47.9	234 56.2	N 0 52.6	300 30.0	N22 25.1	312 45.2	N22 49.8	200 18.0	S11 21.2	Rasalhague	96 06.1	N12 33.3
07	69 50.4	249 56.0	51.3	315 30.7	24.9	327 47.2	49.8	215 20.3	21.3	Regulus	207 43.7	N11 54.0
08	84 52.9	264 55.8	50.0	330 31.4	24.6	342 49.1	49.7	230 22.6	21.3	Rigel	281 12.1	S 8 11.2
F 09	99 55.3	279 55.5	.. 48.7	345 32.1	.. 24.4	357 51.0	.. 49.7	245 24.9	.. 21.4	Rigil Kent.	139 51.6	S60 53.6
R 10	114 57.8	294 55.3	47.5	0 32.9	24.2	12 53.0	49.6	260 27.2	21.4	Sabik	102 12.2	S15 44.3
I 11	130 00.2	309 55.1	46.2	15 33.6	23.9	27 54.9	49.6	275 29.6	21.5			
D 12	145 02.7	324 54.9	N 0 44.9	30 34.3	N22 23.7	42 56.9	N22 49.6	290 31.9	S11 21.6	Schedar	349 39.9	N56 36.6
A 13	160 05.2	339 54.7	43.6	45 35.1	23.4	57 58.8	49.5	305 34.2	21.6	Shaula	96 21.5	S37 06.7
Y 14	175 07.6	354 54.5	42.3	60 35.8	23.2	73 00.7	49.5	320 36.5	21.7	Sirius	258 33.8	S16 44.1
15	190 10.1	9 54.3	.. 41.0	75 36.5	.. 22.9	88 02.7	.. 49.5	335 38.9	.. 21.7	Spica	158 31.3	S11 13.9
16	205 12.6	24 54.1	39.7	90 37.2	22.7	103 04.6	49.4	350 41.2	21.8	Suhail	222 52.8	S43 29.3
17	220 15.0	39 53.9	38.4	105 38.0	22.4	118 06.5	49.4	5 43.5	21.8			
18	235 17.5	54 53.7	N 0 37.2	120 38.7	N22 22.2	133 08.5	N22 49.3	20 45.8	S11 21.9	Vega	80 38.5	N38 48.2
19	250 20.0	69 53.5	35.9	135 39.4	21.9	148 10.4	49.3	35 48.1	22.0	Zuben'ubi	137 05.3	S16 05.8
20	265 22.4	84 53.3	34.6	150 40.1	21.7	163 12.4	49.3	50 50.5	22.0		SHA	Mer. Pass.
21	280 24.9	99 53.1	.. 33.3	165 40.9	.. 21.5	178 14.3	.. 49.2	65 52.8	.. 22.1		° ′	h m
22	295 27.4	114 52.9	32.0	180 41.6	21.2	193 16.2	49.2	80 55.1	22.1	Venus	181 28.4	14 20
23	310 29.8	129 52.7	30.7	195 42.3	21.0	208 18.2	49.2	95 57.4	22.2	Mars	246 34.3	9 59
	h m									Jupiter	258 13.2	9 12
Mer. Pass.	2 25.3	v −0.2	d 1.3	v 0.7	d 0.2	v 1.9	d 0.0	v 2.3	d 0.1	Saturn	145 34.2	16 41

UT	SUN GHA	SUN Dec	MOON GHA	v	MOON Dec	d	HP
d h	° ´	° ´	° ´	´	° ´	´	´
14 00	178 49.1	N14 22.3	99 21.6	8.6	S16 08.0	6.9	58.3
01	193 49.2	21.6	113 49.2	8.4	16 14.9	6.9	58.4
02	208 49.4	20.8	128 16.6	8.4	16 21.8	6.8	58.4
03	223 49.5 ..	20.0	142 44.0	8.3	16 28.6	6.7	58.4
04	238 49.6	19.2	157 11.3	8.2	16 35.3	6.6	58.4
05	253 49.7	18.5	171 38.5	8.1	16 41.9	6.5	58.5
06	268 49.8	N14 17.7	186 05.6	8.1	S16 48.4	6.5	58.5
W 07	283 49.9	16.9	200 32.7	8.0	16 54.9	6.3	58.5
E 08	298 50.1	16.2	214 59.7	8.0	17 01.2	6.2	58.5
D 09	313 50.2 ..	15.4	229 26.7	7.8	17 07.4	6.1	58.6
N 10	328 50.3	14.6	243 53.5	7.8	17 13.5	6.1	58.6
E 11	343 50.4	13.8	258 20.3	7.7	17 19.6	5.9	58.6
S 12	358 50.5	N14 13.1	272 47.0	7.7	S17 25.5	5.8	58.6
D 13	13 50.7	12.3	287 13.7	7.6	17 31.3	5.7	58.7
A 14	28 50.8	11.5	301 40.3	7.5	17 37.0	5.7	58.7
Y 15	43 50.9 ..	10.7	316 06.8	7.4	17 42.7	5.5	58.7
16	58 51.0	10.0	330 33.2	7.4	17 48.2	5.4	58.8
17	73 51.1	09.2	344 59.6	7.3	17 53.6	5.3	58.8
18	88 51.3	N14 08.4	359 25.9	7.2	S17 58.9	5.2	58.8
19	103 51.4	07.6	13 52.1	7.2	18 04.1	5.1	58.8
20	118 51.5	06.8	28 18.3	7.1	18 09.2	5.0	58.9
21	133 51.6 ..	06.1	42 44.4	7.0	18 14.2	4.8	58.9
22	148 51.7	05.3	57 10.4	7.0	18 19.0	4.8	58.9
23	163 51.9	04.5	71 36.4	6.9	18 23.8	4.7	58.9
15 00	178 52.0	N14 03.7	86 02.3	6.8	S18 28.5	4.5	59.0
01	193 52.1	02.9	100 28.1	6.8	18 33.0	4.4	59.0
02	208 52.2	02.2	114 53.9	6.7	18 37.4	4.3	59.0
03	223 52.4 ..	01.4	129 19.6	6.6	18 41.7	4.2	59.0
04	238 52.5	14 00.6	143 45.2	6.6	18 45.9	4.1	59.1
05	253 52.6	13 59.8	158 10.8	6.5	18 50.0	4.0	59.1
06	268 52.7	N13 59.0	172 36.3	6.4	S18 54.0	3.8	59.1
T 07	283 52.8	58.3	187 01.7	6.4	18 57.8	3.7	59.1
H 08	298 53.0	57.5	201 27.1	6.4	19 01.5	3.6	59.2
U 09	313 53.1 ..	56.7	215 52.5	6.2	19 05.1	3.5	59.2
R 10	328 53.2	55.9	230 17.7	6.2	19 08.6	3.4	59.2
S 11	343 53.3	55.1	244 42.9	6.2	19 12.0	3.2	59.2
D 12	358 53.5	N13 54.3	259 08.1	6.1	S19 15.2	3.1	59.3
A 13	13 53.6	53.6	273 33.2	6.0	19 18.3	3.0	59.3
Y 14	28 53.7	52.8	287 58.2	6.0	19 21.3	2.9	59.3
15	43 53.8 ..	52.0	302 23.2	6.0	19 24.2	2.7	59.3
16	58 54.0	51.2	316 48.2	5.9	19 26.9	2.6	59.4
17	73 54.1	50.4	331 13.1	5.8	19 29.5	2.5	59.4
18	88 54.2	N13 49.6	345 37.9	5.8	S19 32.0	2.3	59.4
19	103 54.4	48.8	0 02.7	5.7	19 34.3	2.3	59.4
20	118 54.5	48.1	14 27.4	5.7	19 36.6	2.1	59.5
21	133 54.6 ..	47.3	28 52.1	5.6	19 38.7	1.9	59.5
22	148 54.7	46.5	43 16.7	5.6	19 40.6	1.9	59.5
23	163 54.9	45.7	57 41.3	5.5	19 42.5	1.7	59.5
16 00	178 55.0	N13 44.9	72 05.8	5.5	S19 44.2	1.6	59.6
01	193 55.2	44.1	86 30.3	5.5	19 45.8	1.5	59.6
02	208 55.3	43.3	100 54.8	5.4	19 47.2	1.3	59.6
03	223 55.4 ..	42.5	115 19.2	5.4	19 48.5	1.2	59.6
04	238 55.5	41.8	129 43.6	5.3	19 49.7	1.0	59.7
05	253 55.6	41.0	144 07.9	5.3	19 50.7	0.9	59.7
06	268 55.8	N13 40.2	158 32.2	5.3	S19 51.6	0.8	59.7
F 07	283 55.9	39.4	172 56.5	5.2	19 52.4	0.5	59.7
R 08	298 56.0	38.6	187 20.7	5.2	19 53.1	0.5	59.7
I 09	313 56.2 ..	37.8	201 44.9	5.1	19 53.6	0.3	59.8
D 10	328 56.3	37.0	216 09.0	5.2	19 53.9	0.3	59.8
A 11	343 56.4	36.2	230 33.2	5.0	19 54.2	0.0	59.8
Y 12	358 56.5	N13 35.4	244 57.2	5.1	S19 54.2	0.0	59.8
13	13 56.7	34.6	259 21.3	5.0	19 54.2	0.2	59.8
14	28 56.8	33.8	273 45.3	5.1	19 54.0	0.3	59.9
15	43 56.9 ..	33.0	288 09.4	4.9	19 53.7	0.4	59.9
16	58 57.1	32.2	302 33.3	5.0	19 53.3	0.6	59.9
17	73 57.2	31.4	316 57.3	4.9	19 52.7	0.8	59.9
18	88 57.3	N13 30.7	331 21.2	5.0	S19 51.9	0.8	59.9
19	103 57.5	29.9	345 45.2	4.8	19 51.1	1.0	60.0
20	118 57.6	29.1	0 09.0	4.9	19 50.1	1.2	60.0
21	133 57.7 ..	28.3	14 32.9	4.9	19 48.9	1.3	60.0
22	148 57.9	27.5	28 56.8	4.8	19 47.6	1.4	60.0
23	163 58.0	26.7	43 20.6	4.9	S19 46.2	1.6	60.0
	SD 15.8	d 0.8	SD 16.0		16.1		16.3

Lat.	Twilight Naut.	Twilight Civil	Sunrise	Moonrise 14	Moonrise 15	Moonrise 16	Moonrise 17
°	h m	h m	h m	h m	h m	h m	h m
N 72	////	////	02 25	■■■	■■■	■■■	■■■
N 70	////	////	02 57	16 10	18 17	19 54	19 38
68	////	01 44	03 20	15 29	17 04	18 13	18 48
66	////	02 22	03 38	15 01	16 27	17 33	18 16
64	////	02 47	03 52	14 40	16 00	17 06	17 53
62	01 33	03 07	04 04	14 23	15 40	16 45	17 34
60	02 07	03 23	04 14	14 09	15 24	16 28	17 18
N 58	02 30	03 36	04 23	13 57	15 10	16 13	17 05
56	02 49	03 48	04 31	13 46	14 58	16 01	16 54
54	03 04	03 57	04 38	13 37	14 47	15 50	16 44
52	03 17	04 06	04 44	13 29	14 38	15 41	16 35
50	03 28	04 14	04 50	13 22	14 29	15 32	16 27
45	03 50	04 30	05 02	13 06	14 12	15 14	16 10
N 40	04 07	04 43	05 12	12 53	13 57	14 59	15 56
35	04 21	04 53	05 20	12 42	13 45	14 46	15 44
30	04 32	05 02	05 27	12 33	13 35	14 35	15 33
20	04 50	05 17	05 41	12 16	13 16	14 17	15 16
N 10	05 04	05 29	05 51	12 02	13 01	14 00	15 00
0	05 15	05 40	06 01	11 49	12 46	13 45	14 45
S 10	05 24	05 49	06 11	11 36	12 31	13 30	14 31
20	05 33	05 59	06 22	11 22	12 16	13 14	14 15
30	05 41	06 09	06 34	11 06	11 58	12 55	13 57
35	05 44	06 14	06 40	10 57	11 47	12 44	13 47
40	05 48	06 20	06 48	10 46	11 35	12 32	13 35
45	05 52	06 27	06 57	10 34	11 21	12 17	13 21
S 50	05 56	06 34	07 08	10 19	11 04	11 59	13 04
52	05 58	06 38	07 13	10 12	10 56	11 51	12 56
54	06 00	06 41	07 18	10 05	10 47	11 41	12 47
56	06 01	06 45	07 24	09 56	10 37	11 31	12 36
58	06 03	06 49	07 31	09 46	10 26	11 18	12 25
S 60	06 05	06 54	07 39	09 35	10 13	11 04	12 11

Lat.	Sunset	Twilight Civil	Twilight Naut.	Moonset 14	Moonset 15	Moonset 16	Moonset 17
°	h m	h m	h m	h m	h m	h m	h m
N 72	21 38	////	////	■■■	■■■	■■■	■■■
N 70	21 08	23 28	////	19 46	19 39	20 06	22 29
68	20 46	22 18	////	20 27	20 52	21 48	23 19
66	20 29	21 43	////	20 56	21 30	22 27	23 50
64	20 14	21 18	23 32	21 18	21 56	22 54	24 13
62	20 03	20 59	22 30	21 35	22 16	23 15	24 32
60	19 53	20 44	21 58	21 50	22 33	23 32	24 47
N 58	19 44	20 31	21 36	22 02	22 47	23 47	25 00
56	19 36	20 20	21 18	22 13	23 00	23 59	25 11
54	19 30	20 10	21 03	22 22	23 10	24 10	00 10
52	19 24	20 02	20 50	22 31	23 20	24 19	00 19
50	19 18	19 54	20 39	22 38	23 28	24 28	00 28
45	19 06	19 38	20 17	22 55	23 46	24 46	00 46
N 40	18 57	19 26	20 01	23 08	24 01	00 01	01 01
35	18 48	19 15	19 47	23 20	24 13	00 13	01 13
30	18 41	19 06	19 36	23 30	24 24	00 24	01 24
20	18 29	18 51	19 18	23 47	24 43	00 43	01 42
N 10	18 18	18 40	19 05	24 02	00 02	00 59	01 59
0	18 08	18 29	18 54	24 16	00 16	01 14	02 14
S 10	17 58	18 20	18 44	24 30	00 30	01 29	02 29
20	17 47	18 10	18 36	24 45	00 45	01 45	02 45
30	17 36	18 00	18 29	00 00	01 02	02 04	03 03
35	17 29	17 55	18 25	00 09	01 12	02 14	03 14
40	17 21	17 49	18 21	00 19	01 24	02 27	03 28
45	17 12	17 43	18 17	00 30	01 37	02 41	03 40
S 50	17 02	17 35	18 14	00 44	01 54	02 59	03 58
52	16 57	17 32	18 12	00 51	02 02	03 08	04 06
54	16 51	17 29	18 10	00 58	02 10	03 17	04 15
56	16 45	17 25	18 09	01 06	02 20	03 28	04 26
58	16 38	17 20	18 07	01 15	02 31	03 40	04 38
S 60	16 31	17 16	18 05	01 26	02 44	03 54	04 51

Day	SUN Eqn. of Time 00h	SUN Eqn. of Time 12h	SUN Mer. Pass.	MOON Mer. Pass. Upper	MOON Mer. Pass. Lower	Age	Phase
d	m s	m s	h m	h m	h m	d %	
14	04 44	04 38	12 05	18 02	05 35	08 51	
15	04 32	04 26	12 04	19 00	06 31	09 62	
16	04 20	04 14	12 04	19 59	07 29	10 73	

UT (d h)	ARIES GHA	VENUS −4.0 GHA	Dec	MARS +1.6 GHA	Dec	JUPITER −2.0 GHA	Dec	SATURN +0.7 GHA	Dec
17 00	325 32.3	144 52.5	N 0 29.4	210 43.1	N22 20.7	223 20.1	N22 49.1	110 59.7	S11 22.3
01	340 34.7	159 52.3	28.1	225 43.8	20.5	238 22.0	49.1	126 02.1	22.3
02	355 37.2	174 52.1	26.9	240 44.5	20.2	253 24.0	49.1	141 04.4	22.4
03	10 39.7	189 51.9	.. 25.6	255 45.3	.. 20.0	268 25.9	.. 49.0	156 06.7	.. 22.4
04	25 42.1	204 51.7	24.3	270 46.0	19.7	283 27.9	49.0	171 09.0	22.5
05	40 44.6	219 51.4	23.0	285 46.7	19.5	298 29.8	48.9	186 11.3	22.6
06	55 47.1	234 51.2	N 0 21.7	300 47.4	N22 19.2	313 31.7	N22 48.9	201 13.6	S11 22.6
07	70 49.5	249 51.0	20.4	315 48.2	19.0	328 33.7	48.9	216 16.0	22.7
S 08	85 52.0	264 50.8	19.1	330 48.9	18.7	343 35.6	48.8	231 18.3	22.7
A 09	100 54.5	279 50.6	.. 17.8	345 49.6	.. 18.5	358 37.6	.. 48.8	246 20.6	.. 22.8
T 10	115 56.9	294 50.4	16.6	0 50.4	18.2	13 39.5	48.8	261 22.9	22.9
U 11	130 59.4	309 50.2	15.3	15 51.1	18.0	28 41.4	48.7	276 25.2	22.9
R 12	146 01.8	324 50.0	N 0 14.0	30 51.8	N22 17.7	43 43.4	N22 48.7	291 27.6	S11 23.0
D 13	161 04.3	339 49.8	12.7	45 52.6	17.5	58 45.3	48.6	306 29.9	23.0
A 14	176 06.8	354 49.6	11.4	60 53.3	17.2	73 47.3	48.6	321 32.2	23.1
Y 15	191 09.2	9 49.4	.. 10.1	75 54.0	.. 17.0	88 49.2	.. 48.5	336 34.5	.. 23.2
16	206 11.7	24 49.2	08.8	90 54.8	16.7	103 51.1	48.5	351 36.8	23.2
17	221 14.2	39 49.0	07.5	105 55.5	16.5	118 53.1	48.5	6 39.1	23.3
18	236 16.6	54 48.8	N 0 06.2	120 56.2	N22 16.2	133 55.0	N22 48.4	21 41.5	S11 23.3
19	251 19.1	69 48.6	05.0	135 57.0	16.0	148 57.0	48.4	36 43.8	23.4
20	266 21.6	84 48.4	03.7	150 57.7	15.7	163 58.9	48.4	51 46.1	23.5
21	281 24.0	99 48.2	.. 02.4	165 58.4	.. 15.5	179 00.8	.. 48.3	66 48.4	.. 23.5
22	296 26.5	114 48.0	N 01.1	180 59.2	15.2	194 02.8	48.3	81 50.7	23.6
23	311 29.0	129 47.8	S 00.2	195 59.9	14.9	209 04.7	48.3	96 53.0	23.6
18 00	326 31.4	144 47.6	S 0 01.5	211 00.6	N22 14.7	224 06.7	N22 48.2	111 55.4	S11 23.7
01	341 33.9	159 47.4	02.8	226 01.4	14.4	239 08.6	48.2	126 57.7	23.8
02	356 36.3	174 47.2	04.1	241 02.1	14.2	254 10.6	48.2	142 00.0	23.8
03	11 38.8	189 47.0	.. 05.4	256 02.8	.. 13.9	269 12.5	.. 48.1	157 02.3	.. 23.9
04	26 41.3	204 46.8	06.6	271 03.6	13.7	284 14.4	48.1	172 04.6	23.9
05	41 43.7	219 46.6	07.9	286 04.3	13.4	299 16.4	48.0	187 06.9	24.0
06	56 46.2	234 46.4	S 0 09.2	301 05.0	N22 13.2	314 18.3	N22 48.0	202 09.2	S11 24.1
07	71 48.7	249 46.2	10.5	316 05.8	12.9	329 20.3	48.0	217 11.6	24.1
08	86 51.1	264 46.0	11.8	331 06.5	12.6	344 22.2	47.9	232 13.9	24.2
S 09	101 53.6	279 45.8	.. 13.1	346 07.2	.. 12.4	359 24.2	.. 47.9	247 16.2	.. 24.3
U 10	116 56.1	294 45.6	14.4	1 08.0	12.1	14 26.1	47.8	262 18.5	24.3
N 11	131 58.5	309 45.4	15.7	16 08.7	11.9	29 28.0	47.8	277 20.8	24.4
D 12	147 01.0	324 45.2	S 0 17.0	31 09.4	N22 11.6	44 30.0	N22 47.8	292 23.1	S11 24.4
A 13	162 03.5	339 45.0	18.2	46 10.2	11.4	59 31.9	47.7	307 25.5	24.5
Y 14	177 05.9	354 44.8	19.5	61 10.9	11.1	74 33.9	47.7	322 27.8	24.6
15	192 08.4	9 44.6	.. 20.8	76 11.7	.. 10.8	89 35.8	.. 47.7	337 30.1	.. 24.6
16	207 10.8	24 44.4	22.1	91 12.4	10.6	104 37.8	47.6	352 32.4	24.7
17	222 13.3	39 44.2	23.4	106 13.1	10.3	119 39.7	47.6	7 34.7	24.7
18	237 15.8	54 44.0	S 0 24.7	121 13.9	N22 10.1	134 41.6	N22 47.5	22 37.0	S11 24.8
19	252 18.2	69 43.8	26.0	136 14.6	09.8	149 43.6	47.5	37 39.3	24.9
20	267 20.7	84 43.6	27.3	151 15.3	09.5	164 45.5	47.5	52 41.6	24.9
21	282 23.2	99 43.4	.. 28.6	166 16.1	.. 09.3	179 47.5	.. 47.4	67 44.0	.. 25.0
22	297 25.6	114 43.2	29.8	181 16.8	09.0	194 49.4	47.4	82 46.3	25.1
23	312 28.1	129 43.0	31.1	196 17.6	08.8	209 51.4	47.4	97 48.6	25.1
19 00	327 30.6	144 42.8	S 0 32.4	211 18.3	N22 08.5	224 53.3	N22 47.3	112 50.9	S11 25.2
01	342 33.0	159 42.6	33.7	226 19.0	08.2	239 55.3	47.3	127 53.2	25.2
02	357 35.5	174 42.4	35.0	241 19.8	07.9	254 57.2	47.2	142 55.5	25.3
03	12 38.0	189 42.2	.. 36.3	256 20.5	.. 07.7	269 59.2	.. 47.2	157 57.8	.. 25.4
04	27 40.4	204 42.0	37.6	271 21.2	07.5	285 01.1	47.2	173 00.1	25.4
05	42 42.9	219 41.8	38.9	286 22.0	07.2	300 03.0	47.1	188 02.5	25.5
06	57 45.3	234 41.6	S 0 40.2	301 22.7	N22 06.9	315 05.0	N22 47.1	203 04.8	S11 25.5
07	72 47.8	249 41.4	41.5	316 23.5	06.7	330 06.9	47.0	218 07.1	25.6
08	87 50.3	264 41.2	42.7	331 24.2	06.4	345 08.9	47.0	233 09.4	25.7
M 09	102 52.7	279 41.0	.. 44.0	346 24.9	.. 06.1	0 10.8	.. 47.0	248 11.7	.. 25.7
O 10	117 55.2	294 40.8	45.3	1 25.7	05.9	15 12.8	46.9	263 14.0	25.8
N 11	132 57.7	309 40.6	46.6	16 26.4	05.6	30 14.7	46.9	278 16.3	25.9
D 12	148 00.1	324 40.4	S 0 47.9	31 27.2	N22 05.4	45 16.7	N22 46.9	293 18.6	S11 25.9
A 13	163 02.6	339 40.2	49.2	46 27.9	05.1	60 18.6	46.8	308 21.0	26.0
Y 14	178 05.1	354 40.0	50.5	61 28.7	04.8	75 20.6	46.8	323 23.3	26.0
15	193 07.5	9 39.8	.. 51.8	76 29.4	.. 04.6	90 22.5	.. 46.7	338 25.6	.. 26.1
16	208 10.0	24 39.6	53.1	91 30.1	04.3	105 24.5	46.7	353 27.9	26.2
17	223 12.4	39 39.4	54.3	106 30.9	04.0	120 26.4	46.7	8 30.2	26.2
18	238 14.9	54 39.3	S 0 55.6	121 31.6	N22 03.8	135 28.4	N22 46.6	23 32.5	S11 26.3
19	253 17.4	69 39.1	56.9	136 32.4	03.5	150 30.3	46.6	38 34.8	26.4
20	268 19.8	84 38.9	58.2	151 33.1	03.2	165 32.3	46.5	53 37.1	26.4
21	283 22.3	99 38.7	0 59.5	166 33.8	.. 03.0	180 34.2	.. 46.5	68 39.4	.. 26.5
22	298 24.8	114 38.5	1 00.8	181 34.6	02.7	195 36.2	46.5	83 41.7	26.5
23	313 27.2	129 38.3	S 1 02.1	196 35.3	02.4	210 38.1	46.4	98 44.1	26.6
Mer. Pass.	h m 2 13.5	v −0.2	d 1.3	v 0.7	d 0.3	v 1.9	d 0.0	v 2.3	d 0.1

STARS

Name	SHA	Dec
Acamar	315 18.2	S40 14.8
Achernar	335 26.4	S57 09.7
Acrux	173 09.5	S63 10.7
Adhara	255 12.7	S28 59.4
Aldebaran	290 49.3	N16 32.1
Alioth	166 21.0	N55 53.4
Alkaid	152 59.0	N49 15.0
Al Na'ir	27 43.1	S46 53.4
Alnilam	275 46.4	S 1 11.6
Alphard	217 56.3	S 8 43.1
Alphecca	126 10.9	N26 40.5
Alpheratz	357 43.0	N29 10.0
Altair	62 07.8	N 8 54.6
Ankaa	353 15.3	S42 13.6
Antares	112 26.0	S26 27.6
Arcturus	145 55.7	N19 06.9
Atria	107 27.4	S69 03.2
Avior	234 18.5	S59 33.2
Bellatrix	278 32.0	N 6 21.6
Betelgeuse	271 01.3	N 7 24.5
Canopus	263 56.4	S52 42.1
Capella	280 34.4	N46 00.4
Deneb	49 30.9	N45 20.0
Denebola	182 33.8	N14 29.8
Diphda	348 55.5	S17 54.5
Dubhe	193 52.2	N61 40.7
Elnath	278 12.6	N28 36.9
Eltanin	90 45.8	N51 29.6
Enif	33 46.6	N 9 56.5
Fomalhaut	15 23.5	S29 32.7
Gacrux	172 01.1	S57 11.6
Gienah	175 52.4	S17 37.1
Hadar	148 47.9	S60 26.5
Hamal	328 00.4	N23 31.6
Kaus Aust.	83 43.4	S34 22.5
Kochab	137 20.3	N74 06.3
Markab	13 37.9	N15 16.9
Menkar	314 14.8	N 4 08.6
Menkent	148 07.5	S36 26.3
Miaplacidus	221 40.5	S69 46.5
Mirfak	308 40.1	N49 54.3
Nunki	75 57.9	S26 16.6
Peacock	53 18.5	S56 41.3
Pollux	243 27.9	N27 59.4
Procyon	244 59.9	N 5 11.3
Rasalhague	96 06.2	N12 33.3
Regulus	207 43.7	N11 54.0
Rigel	281 12.1	S 8 11.2
Rigil Kent.	139 51.6	S60 53.6
Sabik	102 12.2	S15 44.3
Schedar	349 39.9	N56 36.6
Shaula	96 21.5	S37 06.7
Sirius	258 33.8	S16 44.1
Spica	158 31.3	S11 13.9
Suhail	222 52.7	S43 29.3
Vega	80 38.6	N38 48.2
Zuben'ubi	137 05.3	S16 05.8

	SHA	Mer. Pass.
	° '	h m
Venus	178 16.2	14 21
Mars	244 29.2	9 55
Jupiter	257 35.3	9 02
Saturn	145 23.9	16 30

UT	SUN GHA	SUN Dec	MOON GHA	MOON v	MOON Dec	MOON d	MOON HP	Lat.	Twilight Naut.	Twilight Civil	Sunrise	Moonrise 17	Moonrise 18	Moonrise 19	Moonrise 20
d h	° ′	° ′	° ′	′	° ′	′	′	°	h m	h m	h m	h m	h m	h m	h m
17 00	178 58.1	N13 25.9	57 44.5	4.8	S19 44.6	1.7	60.1	N 72	////	////	02 45	▬	20 19	19 53	19 39
01	193 58.3	25.1	72 08.3	4.8	19 42.9	1.8	60.1	N 70	////	01 15	03 12	19 38	19 29	19 29	19 26
02	208 58.4	24.3	86 32.1	4.8	19 41.1	2.0	60.1	68	////	02 06	03 32	18 48	19 04	19 11	19 15
03	223 58.5 ..	23.5	100 55.9	4.8	19 39.1	2.1	60.1	66	////	02 37	03 48	18 16	18 41	18 56	19 06
04	238 58.7	22.7	115 19.7	4.8	19 37.0	2.3	60.1	64	01 06	02 59	04 01	17 53	18 23	18 44	18 58
05	253 58.8	21.9	129 43.5	4.8	19 34.7	2.4	60.1	62	01 51	03 17	04 12	17 34	18 08	18 33	18 52
06	268 58.9	N13 21.1	144 07.3	4.7	S19 32.3	2.5	60.2	60	02 20	03 32	04 22	17 18	17 56	18 24	18 46
07	283 59.1	20.3	158 31.0	4.8	19 29.8	2.7	60.2	N 58	02 41	03 44	04 30	17 05	17 45	18 16	18 41
S 08	298 59.2	19.5	172 54.8	4.8	19 27.1	2.8	60.2	56	02 58	03 54	04 37	16 54	17 36	18 09	18 36
A 09	313 59.3 ..	18.7	187 18.6	4.8	19 24.3	2.9	60.2	54	03 12	04 03	04 43	16 44	17 27	18 03	18 32
T 10	328 59.5	17.9	201 42.4	4.7	19 21.4	3.1	60.2	52	03 24	04 11	04 49	16 35	17 20	17 57	18 28
U 11	343 59.6	17.1	216 06.1	4.8	19 18.3	3.2	60.2	50	03 34	04 19	04 54	16 27	17 13	17 52	18 25
R 12	358 59.8	N13 16.3	230 29.9	4.8	S19 15.1	3.4	60.2	45	03 55	04 34	05 05	16 10	16 59	17 41	18 18
D 13	13 59.9	15.5	244 53.7	4.8	19 11.7	3.5	60.3	N 40	04 11	04 46	05 14	15 56	16 46	17 31	18 12
A 14	29 00.0	14.7	259 17.5	4.8	19 08.2	3.6	60.3	35	04 24	04 56	05 22	15 44	16 36	17 24	18 06
Y 15	44 00.2 ..	13.9	273 41.3	4.8	19 04.6	3.8	60.3	30	04 34	05 04	05 29	15 33	16 27	17 16	18 02
16	59 00.3	13.1	288 05.1	4.8	19 00.8	3.9	60.3	20	04 51	05 18	05 41	15 16	16 12	17 04	17 53
17	74 00.4	12.3	302 28.9	4.9	18 56.9	4.0	60.3	N 10	05 04	05 29	05 51	15 00	15 58	16 54	17 46
18	89 00.6	N13 11.5	316 52.8	4.8	S18 52.9	4.2	60.3	0	05 15	05 39	06 00	14 45	15 45	16 44	17 40
19	104 00.7	10.7	331 16.6	4.8	18 48.7	4.3	60.3	S 10	05 23	05 48	06 10	14 31	15 32	16 34	17 33
20	119 00.9	09.8	345 40.4	4.9	18 44.4	4.5	60.4	20	05 31	05 57	06 21	14 15	15 19	16 23	17 26
21	134 01.0 ..	09.0	0 04.3	4.9	18 39.9	4.5	60.4	30	05 38	06 06	06 31	13 57	15 03	16 10	17 17
22	149 01.1	08.2	14 28.2	4.9	18 35.4	4.7	60.4	35	05 41	06 11	06 37	13 47	14 54	16 03	17 13
23	164 01.3	07.4	28 52.1	4.9	18 30.7	4.9	60.4	40	05 45	06 16	06 44	13 35	14 44	15 55	17 07
18 00	179 01.4	N13 06.6	43 16.0	5.0	S18 25.8	5.0	60.4	45	05 48	06 22	06 52	13 21	14 31	15 46	17 01
01	194 01.5	05.8	57 40.0	5.0	18 20.8	5.1	60.4	S 50	05 51	06 29	07 02	13 04	14 16	15 34	16 53
02	209 01.7	05.0	72 04.0	5.0	18 15.7	5.2	60.4	52	05 52	06 32	07 07	12 57	14 10	15 29	16 50
03	224 01.8 ..	04.2	86 28.0	5.0	18 10.5	5.3	60.4	54	05 54	06 35	07 12	12 47	14 02	15 23	16 46
04	239 02.0	03.4	100 52.0	5.0	18 05.2	5.5	60.4	56	05 55	06 39	07 18	12 36	13 53	15 16	16 42
05	254 02.1	02.6	115 16.0	5.1	17 59.7	5.7	60.4	58	05 56	06 43	07 25	12 25	13 43	15 09	16 37
06	269 02.2	N13 01.8	129 40.1	5.1	S17 54.0	5.7	60.5	S 60	05 58	06 47	07 31	12 11	13 32	15 00	16 32

UT	SUN GHA	SUN Dec	MOON GHA	MOON v	MOON Dec	MOON d	MOON HP	Lat.	Sunset	Twilight Civil	Twilight Naut.	Moonset 17	Moonset 18	Moonset 19	Moonset 20
07	284 02.4	01.0	144 04.2	5.1	17 48.3	5.9	60.5	°	h m	h m	h m	h m	h m	h m	h m
08	299 02.5	13 00.2	158 28.3	5.2	17 42.4	6.0	60.5	N 72	21 18	////	////	▬	23 55	26 21	02 21
S 09	314 02.7	12 59.4	172 52.5	5.2	17 36.4	6.1	60.5	N 70	20 52	22 42	////	22 29	24 38	00 38	02 43
U 10	329 02.8	58.5	187 16.7	5.2	17 30.3	6.2	60.5	68	20 32	21 56	////	23 19	25 07	01 07	03 00
N 11	344 03.0	57.7	201 40.9	5.2	17 24.1	6.4	60.5	66	20 17	21 27	////	23 50	25 29	01 29	03 14
D 12	359 03.1	N12 56.9	216 05.1	5.3	S17 17.7	6.5	60.5	64	20 04	21 05	22 53	24 13	00 13	01 46	03 25
A 13	14 03.2	56.1	230 29.4	5.4	17 11.2	6.6	60.5	62	19 53	20 48	22 11	24 32	00 32	02 00	03 35
Y 14	29 03.4	55.3	244 53.8	5.3	17 04.6	6.7	60.5	60	19 44	20 34	21 44	24 47	00 47	02 12	03 43
15	44 03.5 ..	54.5	259 18.1	5.4	16 57.9	6.9	60.5	N 58	19 36	20 22	21 24	25 00	01 00	02 22	03 50
16	59 03.7	53.7	273 42.5	5.5	16 51.0	6.9	60.5	56	19 29	20 12	21 08	25 11	01 11	02 31	03 56
17	74 03.8	52.9	288 07.0	5.5	16 44.1	7.1	60.5	54	19 23	20 03	20 54	00 10	01 20	02 39	04 02
18	89 03.9	N12 52.1	302 31.5	5.5	S16 37.0	7.2	60.5	52	19 17	19 55	20 42	00 19	01 29	02 46	04 07
19	104 04.1	51.2	316 56.0	5.5	16 29.8	7.3	60.5	50	19 12	19 48	20 32	00 28	01 37	02 53	04 11
20	119 04.2	50.4	331 20.5	5.6	16 22.5	7.4	60.5	45	19 01	19 33	20 13	00 46	01 55	03 06	04 21
21	134 04.4 ..	49.6	345 45.1	5.7	16 15.1	7.6	60.5	N 40	18 52	19 21	19 56	01 01	02 07	03 17	04 29
22	149 04.5	48.8	0 09.8	5.7	16 07.5	7.6	60.5	35	18 45	19 11	19 43	01 13	02 18	03 27	04 36
23	164 04.7	48.0	14 34.5	5.7	15 59.9	7.8	60.5	30	18 38	19 03	19 33	01 24	02 28	03 35	04 42
19 00	179 04.8	N12 47.2	28 59.2	5.8	S15 52.1	7.8	60.5	20	18 26	18 49	19 16	01 42	02 45	03 49	04 53
01	194 05.0	46.4	43 24.0	5.8	15 44.3	8.0	60.5	N 10	18 16	18 38	19 03	01 59	03 00	04 02	05 02
02	209 05.1	45.5	57 48.8	5.9	15 36.3	8.1	60.5	0	18 07	18 28	18 53	02 14	03 14	04 13	05 10
03	224 05.2 ..	44.7	72 13.7	5.9	15 28.2	8.2	60.5	S 10	17 58	18 19	18 44	02 29	03 28	04 25	05 19
04	239 05.4	43.9	86 38.6	6.0	15 20.0	8.3	60.5	20	17 48	18 11	18 37	02 45	03 42	04 37	05 28
05	254 05.5	43.1	101 03.6	6.1	15 11.7	8.4	60.5	30	17 37	18 02	18 30	03 03	03 59	04 51	05 38
06	269 05.7	N12 42.3	115 28.6	6.1	S15 03.3	8.5	60.5	35	17 31	17 57	18 27	03 14	04 09	04 59	05 44
07	284 05.8	41.5	129 53.7	6.1	14 54.8	8.6	60.5	40	17 24	17 52	18 24	03 26	04 20	05 08	05 50
08	299 06.0	40.6	144 18.8	6.2	14 46.2	8.6	60.5	45	17 16	17 46	18 21	03 40	04 33	05 18	05 58
M 09	314 06.1 ..	39.8	158 44.0	6.2	14 37.6	8.8	60.5	S 50	17 06	17 40	18 17	03 58	04 48	05 31	06 07
O 10	329 06.3	39.0	173 09.2	6.3	14 28.8	8.9	60.5	52	17 01	17 37	18 16	04 06	04 56	05 37	06 11
N 11	344 06.4	38.2	187 34.5	6.3	14 19.9	9.0	60.5	54	16 56	17 33	18 15	04 15	05 04	05 43	06 16
D 12	359 06.6	N12 37.4	201 59.8	6.4	S14 10.9	9.1	60.5	56	16 51	17 30	18 14	04 26	05 13	05 51	06 21
A 13	14 06.7	36.6	216 25.2	6.5	14 01.8	9.2	60.5	58	16 45	17 26	18 12	04 38	05 23	05 59	06 26
Y 14	29 06.9	35.7	230 50.7	6.5	13 52.6	9.2	60.5	S 60	16 38	17 22	18 11	04 51	05 35	06 08	06 33
15	44 07.0 ..	34.9	245 16.2	6.5	13 43.4	9.4	60.5								
16	59 07.1	34.1	259 41.7	6.6	13 34.0	9.4	60.5								
17	74 07.3	33.3	274 07.3	6.7	13 24.6	9.5	60.5								
18	89 07.4	N12 32.5	288 33.0	6.7	S13 15.1	9.6	60.5								
19	104 07.6	31.6	302 58.7	6.7	13 05.4	9.7	60.5								
20	119 07.7	30.8	317 24.4	6.9	12 55.7	9.7	60.5								
21	134 07.9 ..	30.0	331 50.3	6.8	12 46.0	9.9	60.4								
22	149 08.0	29.2	346 16.1	7.0	12 36.1	9.9	60.4								
23	164 08.2	28.3	0 42.1	7.0	S12 26.2	10.1	60.4								

	SUN SD	SUN d	MOON SD		MOON SD
	15.8	0.8	16.4	16.5	16.5

	SUN Eqn. of Time 00h	SUN Eqn. of Time 12h	SUN Mer. Pass.	MOON Mer. Pass. Upper	MOON Mer. Pass. Lower	MOON Age	MOON Phase
Day	m s	m s	h m	h m	h m	d	%
17	04 08	04 01	12 04	21 00	08 30	11	82
18	03 55	03 48	12 04	21 59	09 30	12	91
19	03 41	03 34	12 04	22 57	10 28	13	96

UT	ARIES GHA	VENUS −4.0 GHA	Dec	MARS +1.6 GHA	Dec	JUPITER −2.0 GHA	Dec	SATURN +0.7 GHA	Dec	STARS Name	SHA	Dec
20 00	328 29.7	144 38.1	S 1 03.4	211 36.1	N22 02.2	225 40.1	N22 46.4	113 46.4	S11 26.7	Acamar	315 18.2	S40 14.8
01	343 32.2	159 37.9	04.7	226 36.8	01.9	240 42.0	46.4	128 48.7	26.7	Achernar	335 26.4	S57 09.8
02	358 34.6	174 37.7	06.0	241 37.6	01.6	255 43.9	46.3	143 51.0	26.8	Acrux	173 09.6	S63 10.7
03	13 37.1	189 37.5	.. 07.2	256 38.3	.. 01.4	270 45.9	.. 46.3	158 53.3	.. 26.9	Adhara	255 12.7	S28 59.4
04	28 39.6	204 37.3	08.5	271 39.0	01.1	285 47.8	46.2	173 55.6	26.9	Aldebaran	290 49.3	N16 32.1
05	43 42.0	219 37.1	09.8	286 39.8	00.8	300 49.8	46.2	188 57.9	27.0			
06	58 44.5	234 36.9	S 1 11.1	301 40.5	N22 00.5	315 51.7	N22 46.2	204 00.2	S11 27.0	Alioth	166 21.0	N55 53.4
07	73 46.9	249 36.7	12.4	316 41.3	00.3	330 53.7	46.1	219 02.5	27.1	Alkaid	152 59.1	N49 15.0
08	88 49.4	264 36.5	13.7	331 42.0	22 00.0	345 55.6	46.1	234 04.8	27.2	Al Na'ir	27 43.1	S46 53.4
T 09	103 51.9	279 36.3	.. 15.0	346 42.8	21 59.7	0 57.6	.. 46.1	249 07.1	.. 27.2	Alnilam	275 46.4	S 1 11.6
U 10	118 54.3	294 36.1	16.3	1 43.5	59.5	15 59.5	46.0	264 09.5	27.2	Alphard	217 56.3	S 8 43.1
E 11	133 56.8	309 35.9	17.6	16 44.3	59.2	31 01.5	46.0	279 11.8	27.4			
S 12	148 59.3	324 35.7	S 1 18.8	31 45.0	N21 58.9	46 03.4	N22 45.9	294 14.1	S11 27.4	Alphecca	126 10.9	N26 40.5
D 13	164 01.7	339 35.5	20.1	46 45.8	58.7	61 05.4	45.9	309 16.4	27.5	Alpheratz	357 43.0	N29 10.0
A 14	179 04.2	354 35.3	21.4	61 46.5	58.4	76 07.4	45.9	324 18.7	27.6	Altair	62 07.8	N 8 54.6
Y 15	194 06.7	9 35.1	.. 22.7	76 47.2	.. 58.1	91 09.3	.. 45.8	339 21.0	.. 27.6	Ankaa	353 15.2	S42 13.6
16	209 09.1	24 34.9	24.0	91 48.0	57.8	106 11.3	45.8	354 23.3	27.7	Antares	112 26.0	S26 27.6
17	224 11.6	39 34.7	25.3	106 48.7	57.6	121 13.2	45.7	9 25.6	27.7			
18	239 14.1	54 34.6	S 1 26.6	121 49.5	N21 57.3	136 15.2	N22 45.7	24 27.9	S11 27.8	Arcturus	145 55.7	N19 06.9
19	254 16.5	69 34.4	27.9	136 50.2	57.0	151 17.1	45.7	39 30.2	27.9	Atria	107 27.5	S69 03.2
20	269 19.0	84 34.2	29.2	151 51.0	56.8	166 19.1	45.6	54 32.5	27.9	Avior	234 18.5	S59 33.2
21	284 21.4	99 34.0	.. 30.5	166 51.7	.. 56.5	181 21.0	.. 45.6	69 34.8	.. 28.0	Bellatrix	278 32.0	N 6 21.6
22	299 23.9	114 33.8	31.7	181 52.5	56.2	196 23.0	45.5	84 37.1	28.1	Betelgeuse	271 01.3	N 7 24.5
23	314 26.4	129 33.6	33.0	196 53.2	55.9	211 24.9	45.5	99 39.4	28.1			
21 00	329 28.8	144 33.4	S 1 34.3	211 54.0	N21 55.7	226 26.9	N22 45.5	114 41.8	S11 28.2	Canopus	263 56.4	S52 42.1
01	344 31.3	159 33.2	35.6	226 54.7	55.4	241 28.8	45.4	129 44.1	28.2	Capella	280 34.4	N46 00.4
02	359 33.8	174 33.0	36.9	241 55.5	55.1	256 30.8	45.4	144 46.4	28.3	Deneb	49 30.9	N45 20.1
03	14 36.2	189 32.8	.. 38.2	256 56.2	.. 54.8	271 32.7	.. 45.4	159 48.7	.. 28.4	Denebola	182 33.8	N14 29.8
04	29 38.7	204 32.6	39.5	271 57.0	54.6	286 34.7	45.3	174 51.0	28.4	Diphda	348 55.5	S17 54.5
05	44 41.2	219 32.4	40.8	286 57.7	54.3	301 36.6	45.3	189 53.3	28.5			
06	59 43.6	234 32.2	S 1 42.1	301 58.5	N21 54.0	316 38.6	N22 45.2	204 55.6	S11 28.6	Dubhe	193 52.2	N61 40.7
W 07	74 46.1	249 32.0	43.3	316 59.2	53.7	331 40.5	45.2	219 57.9	28.6	Elnath	278 12.6	N28 36.9
E 08	89 48.5	264 31.8	44.6	332 00.0	53.5	346 42.5	45.2	235 00.2	28.7	Eltanin	90 45.8	N51 29.7
D 09	104 51.0	279 31.6	.. 45.9	347 00.7	.. 53.2	1 44.5	.. 45.1	250 02.5	.. 28.8	Enif	33 46.6	N 9 56.5
N 10	119 53.5	294 31.4	47.2	2 01.5	52.9	16 46.4	45.1	265 04.8	28.8	Fomalhaut	15 23.5	S29 32.7
E 11	134 55.9	309 31.3	48.5	17 02.2	52.6	31 48.4	45.0	280 07.1	28.9			
S 12	149 58.4	324 31.1	S 1 49.8	32 03.0	N21 52.3	46 50.3	N22 45.0	295 09.4	S11 29.0	Gacrux	172 01.1	S57 11.5
D 13	165 00.9	339 30.9	51.1	47 03.7	52.1	61 52.3	45.0	310 11.7	29.0	Gienah	175 52.4	S17 37.1
A 14	180 03.3	354 30.7	52.4	62 04.5	51.8	76 54.2	44.9	325 14.0	29.1	Hadar	148 47.9	S60 26.5
Y 15	195 05.8	9 30.5	.. 53.7	77 05.2	.. 51.5	91 56.2	.. 44.9	340 16.3	.. 29.1	Hamal	328 00.4	N23 31.6
16	210 08.3	24 30.3	54.9	92 06.0	51.2	106 58.1	44.8	355 18.6	29.2	Kaus Aust.	83 43.4	S34 22.5
17	225 10.7	39 30.1	56.2	107 06.7	51.0	122 00.1	44.8	10 20.9	29.3			
18	240 13.2	54 29.9	S 1 57.5	122 07.5	N21 50.7	137 02.0	N22 44.8	25 23.2	S11 29.3	Kochab	137 20.4	N74 06.3
19	255 15.7	69 29.7	1 58.8	137 08.2	50.4	152 04.0	44.7	40 25.5	29.4	Markab	13 37.9	N15 16.9
20	270 18.1	84 29.5	2 00.1	152 09.0	50.1	167 06.0	44.7	55 27.9	29.5	Menkar	314 14.8	N 4 08.6
21	285 20.6	99 29.3	.. 01.4	167 09.7	.. 49.8	182 07.9	.. 44.7	70 30.2	.. 29.5	Menkent	148 07.5	S36 26.3
22	300 23.0	114 29.1	02.7	182 10.5	49.6	197 09.9	44.6	85 32.5	29.6	Miaplacidus	221 40.5	S69 46.5
23	315 25.5	129 28.9	04.0	197 11.2	49.3	212 11.8	44.6	100 34.8	29.7			
22 00	330 28.0	144 28.7	S 2 05.2	212 12.0	N21 49.0	227 13.8	N22 44.5	115 37.1	S11 29.7	Mirfak	308 40.0	N49 54.3
01	345 30.4	159 28.5	06.5	227 12.7	48.7	242 15.7	44.5	130 39.4	29.8	Nunki	75 57.9	S26 16.6
02	0 32.9	174 28.4	07.8	242 13.5	48.4	257 17.7	44.5	145 41.7	29.9	Peacock	53 18.5	S56 41.3
03	15 35.4	189 28.2	.. 09.1	257 14.2	.. 48.2	272 19.6	.. 44.4	160 44.0	.. 29.9	Pollux	243 27.9	N27 59.4
04	30 37.8	204 28.0	10.4	272 15.0	47.9	287 21.6	44.4	175 46.3	30.0	Procyon	244 59.8	N 5 11.3
05	45 40.3	219 27.8	11.7	287 15.7	47.7	302 23.6	44.3	190 48.6	30.0			
06	60 42.8	234 27.6	S 2 13.0	302 16.5	N21 47.3	317 25.5	N22 44.3	205 50.9	S11 30.1	Rasalhague	96 06.2	N12 33.3
07	75 45.2	249 27.4	14.3	317 17.2	47.0	332 27.5	44.3	220 53.2	30.2	Regulus	207 43.7	N11 54.0
T 08	90 47.7	264 27.2	15.6	332 18.0	46.7	347 29.4	44.2	235 55.5	30.2	Rigel	281 12.0	S 8 11.1
H 09	105 50.1	279 27.0	.. 16.8	347 18.8	.. 46.5	2 31.4	.. 44.2	250 57.8	.. 30.3	Rigil Kent.	139 51.7	S60 53.6
U 10	120 52.6	294 26.8	18.1	2 19.5	46.2	17 33.4	44.1	266 00.1	30.4	Sabik	102 12.2	S15 44.3
R 11	135 55.1	309 26.6	19.4	17 20.3	45.9	32 35.3	44.1	281 02.4	30.4			
S 12	150 57.5	324 26.4	S 2 20.7	32 21.0	N21 45.6	47 37.3	N22 44.1	296 04.7	S11 30.5	Schedar	349 39.9	N56 36.7
D 13	166 00.0	339 26.2	22.0	47 21.8	45.3	62 39.2	44.0	311 07.0	30.6	Shaula	96 21.5	S37 06.7
A 14	181 02.5	354 26.0	23.3	62 22.5	45.0	77 41.2	44.0	326 09.3	30.6	Sirius	258 33.8	S16 44.1
Y 15	196 04.9	9 25.9	.. 24.6	77 23.3	.. 44.8	92 43.1	.. 43.9	341 11.6	.. 30.7	Spica	158 31.3	S11 13.9
16	211 07.4	24 25.7	25.9	92 24.0	44.5	107 45.1	43.9	356 13.9	30.8	Suhail	222 52.7	S43 29.3
17	226 09.9	39 25.5	27.1	107 24.8	44.2	122 47.1	43.9	11 16.2	30.8			
18	241 12.3	54 25.3	S 2 28.4	122 25.5	N21 43.9	137 49.0	N22 43.8	26 18.5	S11 30.9	Vega	80 38.6	N38 48.2
19	256 14.8	69 25.1	29.7	137 26.3	43.6	152 51.0	43.8	41 20.8	31.0	Zuben'ubi	137 05.3	S16 05.8
20	271 17.3	84 24.9	31.0	152 27.1	43.3	167 52.9	43.7	56 23.1	31.0		SHA	Mer.Pass.
21	286 19.7	99 24.7	.. 32.3	167 27.8	.. 43.0	182 54.9	.. 43.7	71 25.4	.. 31.1		° ′	h m
22	301 22.2	114 24.5	33.6	182 28.6	42.8	197 56.9	43.7	86 27.7	31.2	Venus	175 04.6	14 22
23	316 24.6	129 24.3	34.9	197 29.3	42.5	212 58.8	43.6	101 30.0	31.2	Mars	242 25.1	9 52
Mer.Pass.	h m 2 01.7	v −0.2	d 1.3	v 0.8	d 0.3	v 2.0	d 0.0	v 2.3	d 0.1	Jupiter	256 58.0	8 53
										Saturn	145 12.9	16 19

SUN / MOON

UT	SUN GHA	SUN Dec	MOON GHA	v	MOON Dec	d	HP
20 00	179 08.3	N12 27.5	15 08.1	7.0	S12 16.1	10.0	60.4
01	194 08.5	26.7	29 34.1	7.1	12 06.1	10.2	60.4
02	209 08.6	25.9	44 00.2	7.2	11 55.9	10.3	60.4
03	224 08.8	.. 25.0	58 26.4	7.2	11 45.6	10.3	60.4
04	239 08.9	24.2	72 52.6	7.3	11 35.3	10.4	60.4
05	254 09.1	23.4	87 18.9	7.3	11 24.9	10.4	60.4
06	269 09.2	N12 22.6	101 45.2	7.4	S11 14.5	10.5	60.3
07	284 09.4	21.8	116 11.6	7.5	11 04.0	10.6	60.3
T 08	299 09.5	20.9	130 38.1	7.5	10 53.4	10.7	60.3
U 09	314 09.7	.. 20.1	145 04.6	7.6	10 42.7	10.7	60.3
E 10	329 09.8	19.3	159 31.2	7.6	10 32.0	10.8	60.3
S 11	344 10.0	18.4	173 57.8	7.7	10 21.2	10.8	60.3
D 12	359 10.1	N12 17.6	188 24.5	7.7	S10 10.4	10.9	60.3
A 13	14 10.3	16.8	202 51.2	7.8	9 59.5	11.0	60.3
Y 14	29 10.5	16.0	217 18.0	7.9	9 48.5	11.0	60.2
15	44 10.6	.. 15.1	231 44.9	7.9	9 37.5	11.1	60.2
16	59 10.8	14.3	246 11.8	8.0	9 26.4	11.1	60.2
17	74 10.9	13.5	260 38.8	8.0	9 15.3	11.2	60.2
18	89 11.1	N12 12.7	275 05.8	8.1	S 9 04.1	11.2	60.2
19	104 11.2	11.8	289 32.9	8.1	8 52.9	11.3	60.2
20	119 11.4	11.0	304 00.0	8.2	8 41.6	11.3	60.1
21	134 11.5	.. 10.2	318 27.2	8.3	8 30.3	11.4	60.1
22	149 11.7	09.3	332 54.5	8.3	8 18.9	11.4	60.1
23	164 11.8	08.5	347 21.8	8.4	8 07.5	11.4	60.1
21 00	179 12.0	N12 07.7	1 49.2	8.4	S 7 56.1	11.5	60.1
01	194 12.1	06.8	16 16.6	8.5	7 44.6	11.5	60.0
02	209 12.3	06.0	30 44.1	8.5	7 33.1	11.6	60.0
03	224 12.5	.. 05.2	45 11.6	8.6	7 21.5	11.6	60.0
04	239 12.6	04.3	59 39.2	8.6	7 09.9	11.7	60.0
05	254 12.8	03.5	74 06.8	8.7	6 58.2	11.6	59.9
06	269 12.9	N12 02.7	88 34.5	8.8	S 6 46.6	11.7	59.9
W 07	284 13.1	01.8	103 02.3	8.8	6 34.9	11.8	59.9
E 08	299 13.2	01.0	117 30.1	8.8	6 23.1	11.7	59.9
D 09	314 13.4	12 00.2	131 57.9	9.0	6 11.4	11.8	59.9
N 10	329 13.5	11 59.3	146 25.9	8.9	5 59.6	11.8	59.8
E 11	344 13.7	58.5	160 53.8	9.0	5 47.8	11.9	59.8
S 12	359 13.9	N11 57.7	175 21.8	9.1	S 5 35.9	11.9	59.8
D 13	14 14.0	56.8	189 49.9	9.1	5 24.0	11.8	59.8
A 14	29 14.2	56.0	204 18.0	9.2	5 12.2	12.0	59.7
Y 15	44 14.3	.. 55.2	218 46.2	9.2	5 00.2	11.9	59.7
16	59 14.5	54.3	233 14.4	9.3	4 48.3	11.9	59.7
17	74 14.6	53.5	247 42.7	9.3	4 36.4	12.0	59.7
18	89 14.8	N11 52.7	262 11.0	9.4	S 4 24.4	12.0	59.6
19	104 15.0	51.8	276 39.4	9.4	4 12.4	11.9	59.6
20	119 15.1	51.0	291 07.8	9.5	4 00.5	12.0	59.6
21	134 15.3	.. 50.1	305 36.3	9.5	3 48.5	12.1	59.6
22	149 15.4	49.3	320 04.8	9.6	3 36.4	12.0	59.5
23	164 15.6	48.5	334 33.4	9.6	3 24.4	12.0	59.5
22 00	179 15.8	N11 47.6	349 02.0	9.6	S 3 12.4	12.0	59.5
01	194 15.9	46.8	3 30.6	9.7	3 00.4	12.1	59.4
02	209 16.1	45.9	17 59.3	9.8	2 48.3	12.0	59.4
03	224 16.2	.. 45.1	32 28.1	9.8	2 36.3	12.1	59.4
04	239 16.4	44.3	46 56.9	9.8	2 24.2	12.0	59.4
05	254 16.6	43.4	61 25.7	9.9	2 12.2	12.1	59.3
06	269 16.7	N11 42.6	75 54.6	9.9	S 2 00.1	12.0	59.3
07	284 16.9	41.7	90 23.5	10.0	1 48.1	12.0	59.3
T 08	299 17.0	40.9	104 52.5	10.0	1 36.1	12.1	59.2
H 09	314 17.2	.. 40.1	119 21.5	10.1	1 24.0	12.0	59.2
U 10	329 17.4	39.2	133 50.6	10.1	1 12.0	12.0	59.2
R 11	344 17.5	38.4	148 19.7	10.1	1 00.0	12.1	59.1
S 12	359 17.7	N11 37.5	162 48.8	10.2	S 0 47.9	12.0	59.1
D 13	14 17.8	36.7	177 18.0	10.2	0 35.9	12.0	59.1
A 14	29 18.0	35.8	191 47.2	10.2	0 23.9	11.9	59.0
Y 15	44 18.2	.. 35.0	206 16.4	10.3	S 0 12.0	12.0	59.0
16	59 18.3	34.2	220 45.7	10.4	0 00.0	12.0	59.0
17	74 18.5	33.3	235 15.1	10.3	N 0 12.0	11.9	58.9
18	89 18.6	N11 32.5	249 44.4	10.4	N 0 23.9	11.9	58.9
19	104 18.8	31.6	264 13.8	10.5	0 35.8	12.0	58.9
20	119 19.0	30.8	278 43.3	10.4	0 47.8	11.8	58.8
21	134 19.1	.. 29.9	293 12.7	10.6	0 59.6	11.9	58.8
22	149 19.3	29.1	307 42.3	10.5	1 11.5	11.9	58.8
23	164 19.5	28.2	322 11.8	10.6	N 1 23.4	11.8	58.7
	SD 15.8	d 0.8	SD 16.4		16.3		16.1

Twilight / Sunrise / Moonrise

Lat.	Twilight Naut.	Civil	Sunrise	Moonrise 20	21	22	23
N 72	////	////	03 03	19 39	19 28	19 18	19 08
N 70	////	01 46	03 27	19 26	19 22	19 18	19 15
68	////	02 25	03 44	19 15	19 17	19 19	19 20
66	////	02 51	03 59	19 06	19 13	19 19	19 25
64	01 33	03 11	04 10	18 58	19 10	19 20	19 30
62	02 08	03 27	04 20	18 52	19 07	19 20	19 33
60	02 32	03 40	04 29	18 46	19 04	19 20	19 36
N 58	02 51	03 51	04 36	18 41	19 02	19 21	19 39
56	03 06	04 01	04 43	18 36	19 00	19 21	19 42
54	03 19	04 09	04 49	18 32	18 58	19 21	19 44
52	03 30	04 17	04 54	18 28	18 56	19 21	19 46
50	03 40	04 24	04 59	18 25	18 54	19 22	19 48
45	03 59	04 38	05 09	18 18	18 51	19 22	19 52
N 40	04 14	04 49	05 17	18 12	18 48	19 22	19 56
35	04 27	04 58	05 25	18 06	18 46	19 23	19 59
30	04 37	05 06	05 31	18 02	18 43	19 23	20 01
20	04 52	05 19	05 42	17 53	18 40	19 24	20 06
N 10	05 04	05 30	05 51	17 46	18 36	19 24	20 10
0	05 14	05 39	06 00	17 40	18 33	19 25	20 14
S 10	05 23	05 47	06 08	17 33	18 30	19 25	20 18
20	05 29	05 55	06 17	17 26	18 27	19 26	20 23
30	05 35	06 03	06 27	17 17	18 23	19 26	20 28
35	05 38	06 07	06 33	17 13	18 21	19 27	20 31
40	05 41	06 12	06 40	17 07	18 18	19 27	20 34
45	05 43	06 17	06 47	17 01	18 15	19 28	20 38
S 50	05 45	06 23	06 57	16 53	18 12	19 28	20 42
52	05 47	06 26	07 01	16 50	18 10	19 29	20 44
54	05 48	06 29	07 05	16 46	18 08	19 29	20 47
56	05 49	06 32	07 10	16 42	18 06	19 29	20 49
58	05 49	06 35	07 16	16 37	18 04	19 30	20 52
S 60	05 50	06 39	07 22	16 32	18 02	19 30	20 55

Sunset / Twilight / Moonset

Lat.	Sunset	Twilight Civil	Naut.	Moonset 20	21	22	23
N 72	20 58	23 28	////	02 21	04 31	06 32	08 29
N 70	20 36	22 13	////	02 43	04 42	06 35	08 24
68	20 19	21 37	////	03 00	04 51	06 37	08 21
66	20 05	21 12	23 33	03 14	04 58	06 39	08 17
64	19 54	20 52	22 27	03 25	05 04	06 41	08 15
62	19 44	20 37	21 54	03 35	05 10	06 43	08 13
60	19 36	20 24	21 31	03 43	05 14	06 44	08 11
N 58	19 28	20 13	21 13	03 50	05 18	06 45	08 09
56	19 22	20 04	20 58	03 56	05 22	06 46	08 08
54	19 16	19 55	20 45	04 02	05 25	06 47	08 06
52	19 11	19 48	20 34	04 07	05 28	06 48	08 05
50	19 06	19 41	20 25	04 11	05 31	06 48	08 04
45	18 56	19 28	20 06	04 21	05 36	06 50	08 01
N 40	18 48	19 17	19 51	04 29	05 41	06 51	07 59
35	18 41	19 07	19 39	04 36	05 45	06 52	07 57
30	18 35	19 00	19 29	04 42	05 49	06 53	07 56
20	18 24	18 47	19 13	04 53	05 55	06 55	07 53
N 10	18 15	18 36	19 02	05 02	06 00	06 56	07 51
0	18 06	18 28	18 52	05 10	06 05	06 58	07 48
S 10	17 58	18 19	18 44	05 19	06 10	06 59	07 46
20	17 49	18 12	18 37	05 28	06 15	07 00	07 44
30	17 39	18 03	18 31	05 38	06 21	07 02	07 41
35	17 33	17 59	18 29	05 44	06 25	07 03	07 39
40	17 27	17 55	18 26	05 50	06 28	07 04	07 38
45	17 19	17 49	18 24	05 58	06 33	07 05	07 35
S 50	17 10	17 44	18 21	06 07	06 38	07 06	07 33
52	17 06	17 41	18 20	06 11	06 40	07 07	07 32
54	17 02	17 38	18 20	06 16	06 43	07 07	07 31
56	16 57	17 35	18 19	06 21	06 46	07 08	07 29
58	16 51	17 32	18 18	06 26	06 49	07 09	07 28
S 60	16 45	17 28	18 17	06 33	06 53	07 10	07 26

SUN / MOON

Day	SUN Eqn. of Time 00h	12h	Mer. Pass.	MOON Mer. Pass. Upper	Lower	Age	Phase
d	m s	m s	h m	h m	h m	d %	
20	03 27	03 20	12 03	23 52	11 25	14 99	
21	03 12	03 05	12 03	24 45	12 19	15 100	◯
22	02 57	02 50	12 03	00 45	13 11	16 97	

UT	ARIES GHA	VENUS −4.0 GHA	Dec	MARS +1.6 GHA	Dec	JUPITER −2.0 GHA	Dec	SATURN +0.7 GHA	Dec
23 00	331 27.1	144 24.1	S 2 36.2	212 30.1	N21 42.2	228 00.8	N22 43.6	116 32.3	S11 31.3
01	346 29.6	159 23.9	37.4	227 30.8	41.9	243 02.7	43.5	131 34.6	31.3
02	1 32.0	174 23.7	38.7	242 31.6	41.6	258 04.7	43.5	146 36.9	31.4
03	16 34.5	189 23.6	.. 40.0	257 32.4	.. 41.3	273 06.7	.. 43.5	161 39.2	.. 31.5
04	31 37.0	204 23.4	41.3	272 33.1	41.0	288 08.6	43.4	176 41.5	31.5
05	46 39.4	219 23.2	42.6	287 33.9	40.7	303 10.6	43.4	191 43.8	31.6
06	61 41.9	234 23.0	S 2 43.9	302 34.6	N21 40.5	318 12.5	N22 43.4	206 46.1	S11 31.7
07	76 44.4	249 22.8	45.2	317 35.4	40.2	333 14.5	43.3	221 48.4	31.7
08	91 46.8	264 22.6	46.5	332 36.2	39.9	348 16.5	43.3	236 50.7	31.8
F 09	106 49.3	279 22.4	.. 47.7	347 36.9	.. 39.6	3 18.4	.. 43.2	251 53.0	.. 31.9
R 10	121 51.8	294 22.2	49.0	2 37.7	39.3	18 20.4	43.2	266 55.3	31.9
I 11	136 54.2	309 22.0	50.3	17 38.4	39.0	33 22.3	43.2	281 57.6	32.0
D 12	151 56.7	324 21.8	S 2 51.6	32 39.2	N21 38.7	48 24.3	N22 43.1	296 59.9	S11 32.1
A 13	166 59.1	339 21.6	52.9	47 39.9	38.4	63 26.3	43.1	312 02.2	32.1
Y 14	182 01.6	354 21.4	54.2	62 40.7	38.1	78 28.2	43.0	327 04.5	32.2
15	197 04.1	9 21.3	.. 55.5	77 41.5	.. 37.8	93 30.2	.. 43.0	342 06.8	.. 32.3
16	212 06.5	24 21.1	56.7	92 42.2	37.6	108 32.2	43.0	357 09.1	32.3
17	227 09.0	39 20.9	58.0	107 43.0	37.3	123 34.1	42.9	12 11.4	32.4
18	242 11.5	54 20.7	S 2 59.3	122 43.8	N21 37.0	138 36.1	N22 42.9	27 13.7	S11 32.5
19	257 13.9	69 20.5	3 00.6	137 44.5	36.7	153 38.0	42.8	42 16.0	32.5
20	272 16.4	84 20.3	01.9	152 45.3	36.4	168 40.0	42.8	57 18.3	32.6
21	287 18.9	99 20.1	.. 03.2	167 46.0	.. 36.1	183 42.0	.. 42.8	72 20.6	.. 32.7
22	302 21.3	114 19.9	04.5	182 46.8	35.8	198 43.9	42.7	87 22.9	32.7
23	317 23.8	129 19.7	05.7	197 47.6	35.5	213 45.9	42.7	102 25.2	32.8
24 00	332 26.2	144 19.5	S 3 07.0	212 48.3	N21 35.2	228 47.9	N22 42.6	117 27.5	S11 32.9
01	347 28.7	159 19.3	08.3	227 49.1	34.9	243 49.8	42.6	132 29.8	32.9
02	2 31.2	174 19.2	09.6	242 49.8	34.6	258 51.8	42.6	147 32.1	33.0
03	17 33.6	189 19.0	.. 10.9	257 50.6	.. 34.3	273 53.8	.. 42.5	162 34.4	.. 33.1
04	32 36.1	204 18.8	12.2	272 51.4	34.0	288 55.7	42.5	177 36.7	33.1
05	47 38.6	219 18.6	13.5	287 52.1	33.7	303 57.7	42.4	192 38.9	33.2
06	62 41.0	234 18.4	S 3 14.7	302 52.9	N21 33.4	318 59.7	N22 42.4	207 41.2	S11 33.3
07	77 43.5	249 18.2	16.0	317 53.7	33.2	334 01.6	42.4	222 43.5	33.3
S 08	92 46.0	264 18.0	17.3	332 54.4	32.9	349 03.6	42.3	237 45.8	33.4
A 09	107 48.4	279 17.8	.. 18.6	347 55.2	.. 32.6	4 05.5	.. 42.3	252 48.1	.. 33.5
T 10	122 50.9	294 17.6	19.9	2 55.9	32.3	19 07.5	42.2	267 50.4	33.5
U 11	137 53.4	309 17.4	21.2	17 56.7	32.0	34 09.5	42.2	282 52.7	33.6
R 12	152 55.8	324 17.2	S 3 22.4	32 57.5	N21 31.7	49 11.4	N22 42.2	297 55.0	S11 33.7
D 13	167 58.3	339 17.0	23.7	47 58.2	31.4	64 13.4	42.1	312 57.3	33.7
A 14	183 00.7	354 16.9	25.0	62 59.0	31.1	79 15.4	42.1	327 59.6	33.8
Y 15	198 03.2	9 16.7	.. 26.3	77 59.8	.. 30.8	94 17.3	.. 42.0	343 01.9	.. 33.9
16	213 05.7	24 16.5	27.6	93 00.5	30.5	109 19.3	42.0	358 04.2	33.9
17	228 08.1	39 16.3	28.9	108 01.3	30.2	124 21.3	42.0	13 06.5	34.0
18	243 10.6	54 16.1	S 3 30.2	123 02.1	N21 29.9	139 23.2	N22 41.9	28 08.8	S11 34.1
19	258 13.1	69 15.9	31.4	138 02.8	29.6	154 25.2	41.9	43 11.1	34.1
20	273 15.5	84 15.7	32.7	153 03.6	29.3	169 27.2	41.8	58 13.4	34.2
21	288 18.0	99 15.5	.. 34.0	168 04.4	.. 29.0	184 29.1	.. 41.8	73 15.7	.. 34.3
22	303 20.5	114 15.3	35.3	183 05.1	28.7	199 31.1	41.8	88 18.0	34.3
23	318 22.9	129 15.1	36.6	198 05.9	28.4	214 33.1	41.7	103 20.3	34.4
25 00	333 25.4	144 14.9	S 3 37.9	213 06.7	N21 28.1	229 35.0	N22 41.7	118 22.6	S11 34.5
01	348 27.8	159 14.7	39.1	228 07.4	27.8	244 37.0	41.6	133 24.8	34.5
02	3 30.3	174 14.6	40.4	243 08.2	27.5	259 39.0	41.6	148 27.1	34.6
03	18 32.8	189 14.4	.. 41.7	258 09.0	.. 27.2	274 41.0	.. 41.6	163 29.4	.. 34.7
04	33 35.2	204 14.2	43.0	273 09.7	26.9	289 42.9	41.5	178 31.7	34.7
05	48 37.7	219 14.0	44.3	288 10.5	26.6	304 44.9	41.5	193 34.0	34.8
06	63 40.2	234 13.8	S 3 45.6	303 11.3	N21 26.3	319 46.9	N22 41.4	208 36.3	S11 34.9
07	78 42.6	249 13.6	46.8	318 12.0	26.0	334 48.8	41.4	223 38.6	34.9
08	93 45.1	264 13.4	48.1	333 12.8	25.7	349 50.8	41.4	238 40.9	35.0
S 09	108 47.6	279 13.2	.. 49.4	348 13.6	.. 25.4	4 52.8	.. 41.3	253 43.2	.. 35.1
U 10	123 50.0	294 13.0	50.7	3 14.3	25.1	19 54.7	41.3	268 45.5	35.1
N 11	138 52.5	309 12.8	52.0	18 15.1	24.8	34 56.7	41.2	283 47.8	35.2
D 12	153 55.0	324 12.7	S 3 53.2	33 15.9	N21 24.5	49 58.7	N22 41.2	298 50.1	S11 35.3
A 13	168 57.4	339 12.5	54.5	48 16.6	24.2	65 00.6	41.2	313 52.4	35.3
Y 14	183 59.9	354 12.3	55.8	63 17.4	23.9	80 02.6	41.1	328 54.7	35.4
15	199 02.3	9 12.1	.. 57.1	78 18.2	.. 23.6	95 04.6	.. 41.1	343 56.9	.. 35.5
16	214 04.8	24 11.9	58.4	93 19.0	23.3	110 06.6	41.0	358 59.2	35.5
17	229 07.3	39 11.7	3 59.7	108 19.7	23.0	125 08.5	41.0	14 01.5	35.6
18	244 09.7	54 11.5	S 4 00.9	123 20.5	N21 22.7	140 10.5	N22 41.0	29 03.8	S11 35.7
19	259 12.2	69 11.3	02.2	138 21.3	22.4	155 12.5	40.9	44 06.1	35.8
20	274 14.7	84 11.1	03.5	153 22.0	22.0	170 14.4	40.9	59 08.4	35.8
21	289 17.1	99 10.9	.. 04.8	168 22.8	.. 21.7	185 16.4	.. 40.8	74 10.7	.. 35.9
22	304 19.6	114 10.7	06.1	183 23.6	21.4	200 18.4	40.8	89 13.0	36.0
23	319 22.1	129 10.6	07.3	198 24.3	21.1	215 20.4	40.7	104 15.3	36.0
Mer.Pass. 1 49.9	v −0.2	d 1.3	v 0.8	d 0.3	v 2.0	d 0.0	v 2.3	d 0.1

STARS

Name	SHA	Dec
Acamar	315 18.1	S40 14.8
Achernar	335 26.4	S57 09.8
Acrux	173 09.6	S63 10.7
Adhara	255 12.7	S28 59.4
Aldebaran	290 49.2	N16 32.1
Alioth	166 21.0	N55 53.3
Alkaid	152 59.1	N49 15.0
Al Na'ir	27 43.1	S46 53.4
Alnilam	275 46.3	S 1 11.6
Alphard	217 56.3	S 8 43.1
Alphecca	126 10.9	N26 40.5
Alpheratz	357 43.0	N29 10.0
Altair	62 07.8	N 8 54.6
Ankaa	353 15.2	S42 13.6
Antares	112 26.0	S26 27.6
Arcturus	145 55.7	N19 06.9
Atria	107 27.5	S69 03.2
Avior	234 18.5	S59 33.2
Bellatrix	278 32.0	N 6 21.7
Betelgeuse	271 01.3	N 7 24.5
Canopus	263 56.4	S52 42.1
Capella	280 34.4	N46 00.4
Deneb	49 30.9	N45 20.1
Denebola	182 33.8	N14 29.8
Diphda	348 55.5	S17 54.5
Dubhe	193 52.2	N61 40.7
Elnath	278 12.6	N28 36.9
Eltanin	90 45.8	N51 29.7
Enif	33 46.6	N 9 56.5
Fomalhaut	15 23.5	S29 32.7
Gacrux	172 01.1	S57 11.5
Gienah	175 52.4	S17 37.1
Hadar	148 47.9	S60 26.5
Hamal	328 00.4	N23 31.6
Kaus Aust.	83 43.4	S34 22.5
Kochab	137 20.5	N74 06.3
Markab	13 37.8	N15 16.9
Menkar	314 14.8	N 4 08.6
Menkent	148 07.5	S36 26.3
Miaplacidus	221 40.5	S69 46.4
Mirfak	308 40.0	N49 54.3
Nunki	75 57.9	S26 16.6
Peacock	53 18.5	S56 41.3
Pollux	243 27.9	N27 59.4
Procyon	244 59.8	N 5 11.3
Rasalhague	96 06.2	N12 33.3
Regulus	207 43.7	N11 54.0
Rigel	281 12.0	S 8 11.1
Rigil Kent.	139 51.7	S60 53.6
Sabik	102 12.3	S15 44.3
Schedar	349 39.8	N56 36.7
Shaula	96 21.5	S37 06.7
Sirius	258 33.8	S16 44.1
Spica	158 31.3	S11 13.9
Suhail	222 52.7	S43 29.3
Vega	80 38.6	N38 48.2
Zuben'ubi	137 05.3	S16 05.8

	SHA	Mer.Pass.
Venus	171 53.3	14 23
Mars	240 22.1	9 48
Jupiter	256 21.6	8 44
Saturn	145 01.2	16 08

UT	SUN		MOON					Lat.	Twilight		Sunrise	Moonrise			
									Naut.	Civil		23	24	25	26
	GHA	Dec	GHA	v	Dec	d	HP	°	h m	h m	h m	h m	h m	h m	h m
d h	° '	° '	° '	'	° '	'	'	N 72	////	01 16	03 20	19 08	18 57	18 45	18 27
23 00	179 19.6	N11 27.4	336 41.4	10.6	N 1 35.2	11.8	58.7	N 70	////	02 10	03 40	19 15	19 11	19 08	19 06
01	194 19.8	26.5	351 11.0	10.6	1 47.0	11.8	58.7	68	////	02 41	03 56	19 20	19 23	19 26	19 33
02	209 20.0	25.7	5 40.6	10.7	1 58.8	11.7	58.6	66	01 06	03 04	04 09	19 25	19 32	19 41	19 54
03	224 20.1 . .	24.9	20 10.3	10.7	2 10.5	11.8	58.6	64	01 53	03 22	04 19	19 30	19 40	19 53	20 10
04	239 20.3	24.0	34 40.0	10.8	2 22.3	11.7	58.6	62	02 22	03 36	04 28	19 33	19 47	20 04	20 24
05	254 20.4	23.2	49 09.8	10.7	2 34.0	11.6	58.5	60	02 44	03 48	04 36	19 36	19 53	20 13	20 36
06	269 20.6	N11 22.3	63 39.5	10.8	N 2 45.6	11.7	58.5	N 58	03 00	03 59	04 43	19 39	19 59	20 20	20 46
07	284 20.8	21.5	78 09.3	10.9	2 57.3	11.6	58.5	56	03 14	04 08	04 49	19 42	20 03	20 27	20 55
08	299 20.9	20.6	92 39.2	10.8	3 08.9	11.6	58.4	54	03 26	04 15	04 54	19 44	20 08	20 34	21 03
F 09	314 21.1 . .	19.8	107 09.0	10.9	3 20.5	11.5	58.4	52	03 37	04 22	04 59	19 46	20 12	20 39	21 10
R 10	329 21.3	18.9	121 38.9	10.9	3 32.0	11.5	58.4	50	03 45	04 28	05 03	19 48	20 15	20 44	21 16
I 11	344 21.4	18.1	136 08.8	11.0	3 43.5	11.5	58.3	45	04 04	04 41	05 12	19 52	20 23	20 55	21 30
D 12	359 21.6	N11 17.2	150 38.8	10.9	N 3 55.0	11.4	58.3	N 40	04 18	04 52	05 20	19 56	20 29	21 04	21 42
A 13	14 21.8	16.4	165 08.7	11.0	4 06.4	11.4	58.2	35	04 29	05 01	05 27	19 59	20 35	21 12	21 51
Y 14	29 21.9	15.5	179 38.7	11.1	4 17.8	11.4	58.2	30	04 39	05 08	05 33	20 01	20 40	21 19	22 00
15	44 22.1 . .	14.7	194 08.8	11.0	4 29.2	11.3	58.2	20	04 53	05 20	05 42	20 06	20 49	21 31	22 15
16	59 22.3	13.8	208 38.8	11.1	4 40.5	11.3	58.2	N 10	05 05	05 30	05 51	20 10	20 56	21 42	22 28
17	74 22.4	13.0	223 08.9	11.1	4 51.8	11.3	58.1	0	05 13	05 38	05 59	20 14	21 03	21 52	22 40
18	89 22.6	N11 12.1	237 39.0	11.1	N 5 03.1	11.2	58.1	S 10	05 21	05 45	06 07	20 18	21 11	22 02	22 53
19	104 22.8	11.3	252 09.1	11.1	5 14.3	11.1	58.0	20	05 27	05 53	06 15	20 23	21 18	22 13	23 06
20	119 22.9	10.4	266 39.2	11.2	5 25.4	11.1	58.0	30	05 32	06 00	06 24	20 28	21 27	22 25	23 21
21	134 23.1 . .	09.5	281 09.4	11.2	5 36.5	11.1	58.0	35	05 34	06 04	06 30	20 31	21 32	22 32	23 30
22	149 23.3	08.7	295 39.6	11.2	5 47.6	11.0	57.9	40	05 36	06 08	06 35	20 34	21 38	22 41	23 40
23	164 23.4	07.8	310 09.8	11.2	5 58.6	11.0	57.9	45	05 38	06 13	06 42	20 38	21 45	22 50	23 52
24 00	179 23.6	N11 07.0	324 40.0	11.3	N 6 09.6	11.0	57.9	S 50	05 40	06 18	06 51	20 42	21 54	23 02	24 06
01	194 23.8	06.1	339 10.3	11.2	6 20.6	10.8	57.8	52	05 41	06 20	06 54	20 44	21 57	23 07	24 13
02	209 23.9	05.3	353 40.5	11.3	6 31.4	10.9	57.8	54	05 41	06 22	06 59	20 47	22 02	23 13	24 21
03	224 24.1 . .	04.4	8 10.8	11.3	6 42.3	10.8	57.8	56	05 42	06 25	07 03	20 49	22 06	23 20	24 29
04	239 24.3	03.6	22 41.1	11.4	6 53.1	10.7	57.7	58	05 42	06 28	07 08	20 52	22 12	23 27	24 39
05	254 24.5	02.7	37 11.5	11.3	7 03.8	10.7	57.7	S 60	05 43	06 31	07 14	20 55	22 18	23 36	24 50
06	269 24.6	N11 01.9	51 41.8	11.4	N 7 14.5	10.6	57.7	Lat.	Sunset	Twilight		Moonset			
07	284 24.8	01.0	66 12.2	11.3	7 25.1	10.6	57.6			Civil	Naut.	23	24	25	26
S 08	299 25.0	11 00.1	80 42.5	11.4	7 35.7	10.5	57.6								
A 09	314 25.1	10 59.3	95 12.9	11.4	7 46.2	10.5	57.5	°	h m	h m	h m	h m	h m	h m	h m
T 10	329 25.3	58.4	109 43.3	11.5	7 56.7	10.4	57.5	N 72	20 40	22 37	////	08 29	10 23	12 17	14 16
U 11	344 25.5	57.6	124 13.8	11.4	8 07.1	10.4	57.5	N 70	20 21	21 49	////	08 24	10 10	11 55	13 38
R 12	359 25.6	N10 56.7	138 44.2	11.5	N 8 17.5	10.3	57.4	68	20 06	21 19	////	08 21	10 00	11 38	13 12
D 13	14 25.8	55.9	153 14.7	11.4	8 27.8	10.3	57.4	66	19 53	20 57	22 48	08 17	09 52	11 24	12 52
A 14	29 26.0	55.0	167 45.1	11.5	8 38.1	10.1	57.4	64	19 43	20 40	22 06	08 15	09 46	11 13	12 36
Y 15	44 26.2 . .	54.1	182 15.6	11.5	8 48.2	10.2	57.3	62	19 34	20 26	21 39	08 13	09 40	11 03	12 23
16	59 26.3	53.3	196 46.1	11.5	8 58.4	10.1	57.3	60	19 27	20 14	21 18	08 11	09 35	10 55	12 11
17	74 26.5	52.4	211 16.6	11.5	9 08.5	10.0	57.3								
18	89 26.7	N10 51.6	225 47.1	11.6	N 9 18.5	9.9	57.2	N 58	19 20	20 04	21 02	08 09	09 30	10 48	12 02
19	104 26.8	50.7	240 17.7	11.5	9 28.4	9.9	57.2	56	19 15	19 55	20 48	08 07	09 26	10 42	11 53
20	119 27.0	49.8	254 48.2	11.6	9 38.2	9.8	57.1	54	19 11	19 48	20 36	08 06	09 23	10 36	11 46
21	134 27.2 . .	49.0	269 18.8	11.5	9 48.1	9.8	57.1	52	19 05	19 41	20 26	08 05	09 19	10 31	11 39
22	149 27.4	48.1	283 49.3	11.6	9 57.9	9.7	57.1	50	19 00	19 35	20 18	08 04	09 17	10 26	11 33
23	164 27.5	47.3	298 19.9	11.6	10 07.6	9.6	57.0	45	18 51	19 22	20 02	08 01	09 10	10 17	11 22
25 00	179 27.7	N10 46.4	312 50.5	11.6	N10 17.2	9.6	57.0	N 40	18 44	19 12	19 46	07 59	09 05	10 08	11 09
01	194 27.9	45.5	327 21.1	11.6	10 26.8	9.5	57.0	35	18 37	19 03	19 35	07 57	09 00	10 01	11 00
02	209 28.0	44.7	341 51.7	11.6	10 36.3	9.5	56.9	30	18 32	18 56	19 25	07 56	08 56	09 55	10 52
03	224 28.2 . .	43.8	356 22.3	11.7	10 45.8	9.3	56.9	20	18 22	18 44	19 11	07 53	08 50	09 45	10 38
04	239 28.4	42.9	10 53.0	11.6	10 55.1	9.3	56.9	N 10	18 13	18 35	19 00	07 51	08 44	09 35	10 26
05	254 28.6	42.1	25 23.6	11.6	11 04.4	9.3	56.9	0	18 05	18 27	18 51	07 48	08 38	09 27	10 15
06	269 28.7	N10 41.2	39 54.2	11.7	N11 13.7	9.1	56.8	S 10	17 58	18 19	18 44	07 46	08 32	09 18	10 04
07	284 28.9	40.4	54 24.9	11.6	11 22.8	9.1	56.8	20	17 50	18 12	18 38	07 44	08 26	09 09	09 52
08	299 29.1	39.5	68 55.5	11.7	11 31.9	9.1	56.7	30	17 41	18 05	18 33	07 41	08 19	08 58	09 38
S 09	314 29.3 . .	38.6	83 26.2	11.7	11 41.0	8.9	56.7	35	17 36	18 01	18 31	07 39	08 15	08 52	09 30
U 10	329 29.4	37.8	97 56.9	11.6	11 49.9	8.9	56.7	40	17 30	17 57	18 29	07 38	08 11	08 45	09 21
N 11	344 29.6	36.9	112 27.5	11.7	11 58.8	8.8	56.6	45	17 23	17 53	18 27	07 35	08 06	08 37	09 11
D 12	359 29.8	N10 36.0	126 58.2	11.7	N12 07.6	8.8	56.5	S 50	17 15	17 48	18 25	07 33	08 00	08 28	08 58
A 13	14 30.0	35.2	141 28.9	11.7	12 16.4	8.7	56.5	52	17 11	17 46	18 25	07 32	07 57	08 23	08 52
Y 14	29 30.1	34.3	155 59.6	11.7	12 25.1	8.6	56.5	54	17 07	17 43	18 24	07 31	07 54	08 18	08 46
15	44 30.3 . .	33.4	170 30.3	11.7	12 33.7	8.5	56.5	56	17 02	17 41	18 24	07 29	07 50	08 13	08 39
16	59 30.5	32.6	185 01.0	11.7	12 42.2	8.5	56.4	58	16 57	17 38	18 23	07 28	07 47	08 07	08 31
17	74 30.7	31.7	199 31.7	11.7	12 50.7	8.3	56.4	S 60	16 52	17 35	18 23	07 26	07 42	08 00	08 21
18	89 30.8	N10 30.8	214 02.4	11.7	N12 59.0	8.3	56.4		SUN			MOON			
19	104 31.0	30.0	228 33.1	11.8	13 07.3	8.3	56.3	Day	Eqn. of Time		Mer.	Mer. Pass.		Age	Phase
20	119 31.2	29.1	243 03.9	11.7	13 15.6	8.1	56.3		00h	12h	Pass.	Upper	Lower		
21	134 31.4 . .	28.2	257 34.6	11.7	13 23.7	8.1	56.3	d	m s	m s	h m	h m	h m	d %	
22	149 31.5	27.4	272 05.3	11.7	13 31.8	8.0	56.2	23	02 42	02 34	12 03	01 36	14 01	17 92	
23	164 31.7	26.5	286 36.0	11.8	N13 39.8	7.9	56.2	24	02 26	02 18	12 02	02 26	14 51	18 86	
	SD 15.8	d 0.9	SD 15.9		15.6		15.4	25	02 10	02 01	12 02	03 15	15 39	19 77	

UT	ARIES	VENUS −4.0		MARS +1.6		JUPITER −2.0		SATURN +0.7		STARS		
	GHA	GHA	Dec	GHA	Dec	GHA	Dec	GHA	Dec	Name	SHA	Dec
d h	° ′	° ′	° ′	° ′	° ′	° ′	° ′	° ′	° ′		° ′	° ′
26 00	334 24.5	144 10.4	S 4 08.6	213 25.1	N21 20.8	230 22.3	N22 40.7	119 17.6	S11 36.1	Acamar	315 18.1	S40 14.8
01	349 27.0	159 10.2	09.9	228 25.9	20.5	245 24.3	40.7	134 19.9	36.2	Achernar	335 26.3	S57 09.8
02	4 29.5	174 10.0	11.2	243 26.7	20.2	260 26.3	40.6	149 22.1	36.2	Acrux	173 09.6	S63 10.7
03	19 31.9	189 09.8 ..	12.5	258 27.4 ..	19.9	275 28.2 ..	40.6	164 24.4 ..	36.3	Adhara	255 12.6	S28 59.4
04	34 34.4	204 09.6	13.8	273 28.2	19.6	290 30.2	40.5	179 26.7	36.4	Aldebaran	290 49.2	N16 32.1
05	49 36.8	219 09.4	15.0	288 29.0	19.3	305 32.2	40.5	194 29.0	36.4			
06	64 39.3	234 09.2	S 4 16.3	303 29.8	N21 19.0	320 34.2	N22 40.5	209 31.3	S11 36.5	Alioth	166 21.0	N55 53.3
07	79 41.8	249 09.0	17.6	318 30.5	18.7	335 36.1	40.4	224 33.6	36.6	Alkaid	152 59.1	N49 15.0
08	94 44.2	264 08.8	18.9	333 31.3	18.4	350 38.1	40.4	239 35.9	36.6	Al Na'ir	27 43.1	S46 53.5
M 09	109 46.7	279 08.6 ..	20.2	348 32.1 ..	18.1	5 40.1 ..	40.3	254 38.2 ..	36.7	Alnilam	275 46.3	S 1 11.6
O 10	124 49.2	294 08.5	21.4	3 32.8	17.8	20 42.1	40.3	269 40.5	36.8	Alphard	217 56.2	S 8 43.1
N 11	139 51.6	309 08.3	22.7	18 33.6	17.4	35 44.0	40.3	284 42.8	36.8			
D 12	154 54.1	324 08.1	S 4 24.0	33 34.4	N21 17.1	50 46.0	N22 40.2	299 45.0	S11 36.9	Alphecca	126 10.9	N26 40.5
A 13	169 56.6	339 07.9	25.3	48 35.2	16.8	65 48.0	40.2	314 47.3	37.0	Alpheratz	357 43.0	N29 10.1
Y 14	184 59.0	354 07.7	26.5	63 35.9	16.5	80 49.9	40.1	329 49.6	37.1	Altair	62 07.8	N 8 54.6
15	200 01.5	9 07.5 ..	27.8	78 36.7 ..	16.2	95 51.9 ..	40.1	344 51.9 ..	37.1	Ankaa	353 15.2	S42 13.6
16	215 03.9	24 07.3	29.1	93 37.5	15.9	110 53.9	40.1	359 54.2	37.2	Antares	112 26.0	S26 27.6
17	230 06.4	39 07.1	30.4	108 38.3	15.6	125 55.9	40.0	14 56.5	37.3			
18	245 08.9	54 06.9	S 4 31.7	123 39.0	N21 15.3	140 57.8	N22 40.0	29 58.8	S11 37.3	Arcturus	145 55.8	N19 06.9
19	260 11.3	69 06.7	32.9	138 39.8	15.0	155 59.8	39.9	45 01.1	37.4	Atria	107 27.6	S69 03.2
20	275 13.8	84 06.5	34.2	153 40.6	14.7	171 01.8	39.9	60 03.4	37.5	Avior	234 18.5	S59 33.2
21	290 16.3	99 06.3 ..	35.5	168 41.4 ..	14.3	186 03.8 ..	39.9	75 05.6 ..	37.5	Bellatrix	278 31.9	N 6 21.7
22	305 18.7	114 06.2	36.8	183 42.1	14.0	201 05.7	39.8	90 07.9	37.6	Betelgeuse	271 01.3	N 7 24.5
23	320 21.2	129 06.0	38.1	198 42.9	13.7	216 07.7	39.8	105 10.2	37.7			
27 00	335 23.7	144 05.8	S 4 39.3	213 43.7	N21 13.4	231 09.7	N22 39.7	120 12.5	S11 37.7	Canopus	263 56.4	S52 42.0
01	350 26.1	159 05.6	40.6	228 44.5	13.1	246 11.7	39.7	135 14.8	37.8	Capella	280 34.3	N46 00.4
02	5 28.6	174 05.4	41.9	243 45.2	12.8	261 13.7	39.7	150 17.1	37.9	Deneb	49 30.9	N45 20.1
03	20 31.1	189 05.2 ..	43.2	258 46.0 ..	12.5	276 15.6 ..	39.6	165 19.4 ..	37.9	Denebola	182 33.8	N14 29.8
04	35 33.5	204 05.0	44.4	273 46.8	12.2	291 17.6	39.6	180 21.7	38.0	Diphda	348 55.5	S17 54.5
05	50 36.0	219 04.8	45.7	288 47.6	11.8	306 19.6	39.5	195 23.9	38.1			
06	65 38.4	234 04.6	S 4 47.0	303 48.4	N21 11.5	321 21.6	N22 39.5	210 26.2	S11 38.2	Dubhe	193 52.2	N61 40.6
07	80 40.9	249 04.4	48.3	318 49.1	11.2	336 23.5	39.5	225 28.5	38.2	Elnath	278 12.5	N28 36.9
T 08	95 43.4	264 04.2	49.6	333 49.9	10.9	351 25.5	39.4	240 30.8	38.3	Eltanin	90 45.8	N51 29.7
U 09	110 45.8	279 04.0 ..	50.8	348 50.7 ..	10.6	6 27.5 ..	39.4	255 33.1 ..	38.4	Enif	33 46.6	N 9 56.5
E 10	125 48.3	294 03.8	52.1	3 51.5	10.3	21 29.5	39.3	270 35.4	38.4	Fomalhaut	15 23.5	S29 32.7
S 11	140 50.8	309 03.7	53.4	18 52.2	10.0	36 31.4	39.3	285 37.7	38.5			
D 12	155 53.2	324 03.5	S 4 54.7	33 53.0	N21 09.6	51 33.4	N22 39.2	300 39.9	S11 38.6	Gacrux	172 01.1	S57 11.5
A 13	170 55.7	339 03.3	55.9	48 53.8	09.3	66 35.4	39.2	315 42.2	38.6	Gienah	175 52.4	S17 37.1
Y 14	185 58.2	354 03.1	57.2	63 54.6	09.0	81 37.4	39.1	330 44.5	38.7	Hadar	148 47.9	S60 26.5
15	201 00.6	9 02.9 ..	58.5	78 55.4 ..	08.7	96 39.4 ..	39.1	345 46.8 ..	38.8	Hamal	328 00.4	N23 31.6
16	216 03.1	24 02.7	4 59.8	93 56.1	08.4	111 41.3	39.1	0 49.1	38.8	Kaus Aust.	83 43.4	S34 22.5
17	231 05.6	39 02.5	5 01.0	108 56.9	08.1	126 43.3	39.0	15 51.4	38.9			
18	246 08.0	54 02.3	S 5 02.3	123 57.7	N21 07.7	141 45.3	N22 39.0	30 53.7	S11 39.0	Kochab	137 20.5	N74 06.3
19	261 10.5	69 02.1	03.6	138 58.5	07.4	156 47.3	39.0	45 55.9	39.1	Markab	13 37.8	N15 16.9
20	276 12.9	84 01.9	04.9	153 59.3	07.1	171 49.3	38.9	60 58.2	39.1	Menkar	314 14.8	N 4 08.6
21	291 15.4	99 01.7 ..	06.1	169 00.0 ..	06.8	186 51.2 ..	38.9	76 00.5 ..	39.2	Menkent	148 07.6	S36 26.3
22	306 17.9	114 01.5	07.4	184 00.8	06.5	201 53.2	38.8	91 02.8	39.3	Miaplacidus	221 40.4	S69 46.4
23	321 20.3	129 01.3	08.7	199 01.6	06.2	216 55.2	38.8	106 05.1	39.3			
28 00	336 22.8	144 01.2	S 5 10.0	214 02.4	N21 05.8	231 57.2	N22 38.8	121 07.4	S11 39.4	Mirfak	308 40.0	N49 54.3
01	351 25.3	159 01.0	11.2	229 03.2	05.5	246 59.1	38.7	136 09.7	39.5	Nunki	75 57.9	S26 16.6
02	6 27.7	174 00.8	12.5	244 03.9	05.2	262 01.1	38.7	151 11.9	39.5	Peacock	53 18.5	S56 41.3
03	21 30.2	189 00.6 ..	13.8	259 04.7 ..	04.9	277 03.1 ..	38.6	166 14.2 ..	39.6	Pollux	243 27.8	N27 59.4
04	36 32.7	204 00.4	15.1	274 05.5	04.6	292 05.1	38.6	181 16.5	39.7	Procyon	244 59.8	N 5 11.3
05	51 35.1	219 00.2	16.3	289 06.3	04.3	307 07.1	38.6	196 18.8	39.8			
06	66 37.6	234 00.0	S 5 17.6	304 07.1	N21 03.9	322 09.1	N22 38.5	211 21.1	S11 39.8	Rasalhague	96 06.2	N12 33.3
W 07	81 40.0	248 59.8	18.9	319 07.9	03.6	337 11.0	38.5	226 23.4	39.9	Regulus	207 43.7	N11 54.0
E 08	96 42.5	263 59.6	20.1	334 08.6	03.3	352 13.0	38.4	241 25.6	40.0	Rigel	281 12.0	S 8 11.1
D 09	111 45.0	278 59.4 ..	21.4	349 09.4 ..	03.0	7 15.0 ..	38.4	256 27.9 ..	40.0	Rigil Kent.	139 51.7	S60 53.6
N 10	126 47.4	293 59.2	22.7	4 10.2	02.7	22 17.0	38.3	271 30.2	40.1	Sabik	102 12.3	S15 44.3
E 11	141 49.9	308 59.0	24.0	19 11.0	02.3	37 19.0	38.3	286 32.5	40.2			
S 12	156 52.4	323 58.8	S 5 25.2	34 11.8	N21 02.0	52 20.9	N22 38.3	301 34.8	S11 40.2	Schedar	349 39.8	N56 36.7
D 13	171 54.8	338 58.6	26.5	49 12.6	01.7	67 22.9	38.2	316 37.1	40.3	Shaula	96 21.6	S37 06.7
A 14	186 57.3	353 58.5	27.8	64 13.3	01.4	82 24.9	38.2	331 39.3	40.4	Sirius	258 33.6	S16 44.1
Y 15	201 59.8	8 58.3 ..	29.1	79 14.1 ..	01.0	97 26.9 ..	38.1	346 41.6 ..	40.5	Spica	158 31.3	S11 13.9
16	217 02.2	23 58.1	30.3	94 14.9	00.7	112 28.9	38.1	1 43.9	40.5	Suhail	222 52.7	S43 29.3
17	232 04.7	38 57.9	31.6	109 15.7	00.4	127 30.9	38.1	16 46.2	40.6			
18	247 07.2	53 57.7	S 5 32.9	124 16.5	N21 00.1	142 32.8	N22 38.0	31 48.5	S11 40.7	Vega	80 38.6	N38 48.2
19	262 09.6	68 57.5	34.1	139 17.3	20 59.8	157 34.8	38.0	46 50.8	40.7	Zuben'ubi	137 05.3	S16 05.8
20	277 12.1	83 57.3	35.4	154 18.0	59.4	172 36.8	37.9	61 53.0	40.8		SHA	Mer.Pass.
21	292 14.5	98 57.1 ..	36.7	169 18.8 ..	59.1	187 38.8 ..	37.9	76 55.3 ..	40.9	Venus	168 42.1	14 24
22	307 17.0	113 56.9	38.0	184 19.6	58.8	202 40.8	37.9	91 57.6	41.0	Mars	238 20.0	9 45
23	322 19.5	128 56.7	39.2	199 20.4	58.5	217 42.8	37.8	106 59.9	41.0	Jupiter	255 46.0	8 34
Mer. Pass. 1 38.2		v −0.2	d 1.3	v 0.8	d 0.3	v 2.0	d 0.0	v 2.3	d 0.1	Saturn	144 48.8	15 57

UT	SUN GHA	SUN Dec	MOON GHA	v	Dec	d	HP
26 00	179 31.9	N10 25.6	301 06.8	11.7	N13 47.7	7.9	56.2
01	194 32.1	24.8	315 37.5	11.7	13 55.6	7.8	56.2
02	209 32.2	23.9	330 08.2	11.8	14 03.4	7.6	56.1
03	224 32.4	.. 23.0	344 39.0	11.7	14 11.0	7.7	56.1
04	239 32.6	22.2	359 09.7	11.8	14 18.7	7.5	56.1
05	254 32.8	21.3	13 40.5	11.7	14 26.2	7.4	56.0
06	269 32.9	N10 20.4	28 11.2	11.7	N14 33.6	7.4	56.0
07	284 33.1	19.5	42 41.9	11.8	14 41.0	7.3	56.0
M 08	299 33.3	18.7	57 12.7	11.7	14 48.3	7.2	55.9
O 09	314 33.5	.. 17.8	71 43.4	11.8	14 55.5	7.1	55.9
N 10	329 33.7	16.9	86 14.2	11.7	15 02.6	7.1	55.9
D 11	344 33.8	16.1	100 44.9	11.8	15 09.7	7.0	55.8
A 12	359 34.0	N10 15.2	115 15.7	11.8	N15 16.7	6.8	55.8
Y 13	14 34.2	14.3	129 46.5	11.7	15 23.5	6.9	55.8
14	29 34.4	13.4	144 17.2	11.8	15 30.4	6.7	55.8
15	44 34.5	.. 12.6	158 48.0	11.7	15 37.1	6.6	55.7
16	59 34.7	11.7	173 18.7	11.8	15 43.7	6.6	55.7
17	74 34.9	10.8	187 49.5	11.7	15 50.3	6.4	55.7
18	89 35.1	N10 10.0	202 20.2	11.8	N15 56.7	6.4	55.6
19	104 35.3	09.1	216 51.0	11.7	16 03.1	6.3	55.6
20	119 35.4	08.2	231 21.7	11.8	16 09.4	6.2	55.6
21	134 35.6	.. 07.3	245 52.5	11.7	16 15.6	6.2	55.6
22	149 35.8	06.5	260 23.2	11.8	16 21.8	6.0	55.5
23	164 36.0	05.6	274 54.0	11.8	16 27.8	6.0	55.5
27 00	179 36.2	N10 04.7	289 24.8	11.7	N16 33.8	5.8	55.5
01	194 36.3	03.8	303 55.5	11.8	16 39.6	5.8	55.4
02	209 36.5	03.0	318 26.3	11.7	16 45.4	5.7	55.4
03	224 36.7	.. 02.1	332 57.0	11.8	16 51.1	5.6	55.4
04	239 36.9	01.2	347 27.8	11.7	16 56.7	5.5	55.4
05	254 37.1	10 00.3	1 58.5	11.8	17 02.2	5.5	55.3
06	269 37.2	N 9 59.4	16 29.3	11.7	N17 07.7	5.3	55.3
07	284 37.4	58.6	31 00.0	11.8	17 13.0	5.3	55.3
T 08	299 37.6	57.7	45 30.8	11.7	17 18.3	5.2	55.3
U 09	314 37.8	.. 56.8	60 01.5	11.8	17 23.5	5.1	55.2
E 10	329 38.0	55.9	74 32.3	11.7	17 28.6	5.0	55.2
S 11	344 38.2	55.1	89 03.0	11.8	17 33.6	4.9	55.2
D 12	359 38.3	N 9 54.2	103 33.8	11.8	N17 38.5	4.8	55.2
A 13	14 38.5	53.3	118 04.6	11.7	17 43.3	4.7	55.1
Y 14	29 38.7	52.4	132 35.3	11.8	17 48.0	4.7	55.1
15	44 38.9	.. 51.5	147 06.1	11.7	17 52.7	4.5	55.1
16	59 39.1	50.7	161 36.8	11.8	17 57.2	4.5	55.1
17	74 39.3	49.8	176 07.6	11.7	18 01.7	4.3	55.0
18	89 39.4	N 9 48.9	190 38.3	11.8	N18 06.0	4.3	55.0
19	104 39.6	48.0	205 09.1	11.7	18 10.3	4.2	55.0
20	119 39.8	47.1	219 39.8	11.8	18 14.5	4.1	55.0
21	134 40.0	.. 46.3	234 10.6	11.7	18 18.6	4.0	55.0
22	149 40.2	45.4	248 41.3	11.8	18 22.6	3.9	54.9
23	164 40.4	44.5	263 12.1	11.7	18 26.5	3.9	54.9
28 00	179 40.5	N 9 43.6	277 42.8	11.8	N18 30.4	3.7	54.9
01	194 40.7	42.7	292 13.6	11.8	18 34.1	3.7	54.9
02	209 40.9	41.8	306 44.4	11.7	18 37.8	3.5	54.9
03	224 41.1	.. 41.0	321 15.1	11.8	18 41.3	3.5	54.8
04	239 41.3	40.1	335 45.9	11.8	18 44.8	3.4	54.8
05	254 41.5	39.2	350 16.7	11.7	18 48.2	3.2	54.8
06	269 41.6	N 9 38.3	4 47.4	11.8	N18 51.4	3.2	54.8
W 07	284 41.8	37.4	19 18.2	11.8	18 54.6	3.1	54.8
E 08	299 42.0	36.5	33 49.0	11.7	18 57.7	3.0	54.7
D 09	314 42.2	.. 35.7	48 19.7	11.8	19 00.7	3.0	54.7
N 10	329 42.4	34.8	62 50.5	11.8	19 03.7	2.8	54.7
E 11	344 42.6	33.9	77 21.3	11.7	19 06.5	2.7	54.7
S 12	359 42.8	N 9 33.0	91 52.0	11.8	N19 09.2	2.6	54.7
D 13	14 42.9	32.1	106 22.8	11.8	19 11.8	2.6	54.7
A 14	29 43.1	31.2	120 53.6	11.8	19 14.4	2.4	54.6
Y 15	44 43.3	.. 30.4	135 24.4	11.8	19 16.8	2.4	54.6
16	59 43.5	29.5	149 55.2	11.8	19 19.2	2.3	54.6
17	74 43.7	28.6	164 26.0	11.8	19 21.5	2.1	54.6
18	89 43.9	N 9 27.7	178 56.8	11.8	N19 23.6	2.1	54.6
19	104 44.1	26.8	193 27.6	11.8	19 25.7	2.0	54.6
20	119 44.2	25.9	207 58.4	11.8	19 27.7	1.9	54.5
21	134 44.4	.. 25.0	222 29.2	11.8	19 29.6	1.8	54.5
22	149 44.6	24.1	237 00.0	11.8	19 31.4	1.7	54.5
23	164 44.8	23.3	251 30.8	11.9	N19 33.1	1.7	54.5
	SD 15.9	d 0.9	SD 15.2		15.0		14.9

Lat.	Naut.	Civil	Sunrise	Moonrise 26	27	28	29
N 72	////	01 51	03 36	18 27	17 31	▢	▢
N 70	////	02 30	03 54	19 06	19 05	19 08	19 35
68	////	02 57	04 08	19 33	19 44	20 06	20 47
66	01 35	03 17	04 19	19 54	20 12	20 41	21 23
64	02 11	03 33	04 28	20 10	20 33	21 05	21 49
62	02 36	03 46	04 36	20 24	20 50	21 25	22 10
60	02 54	03 57	04 43	20 36	21 05	21 41	22 26
N 58	03 10	04 06	04 49	20 46	21 17	21 54	22 40
56	03 22	04 14	04 55	20 55	21 27	22 06	22 52
54	03 33	04 21	04 59	21 03	21 37	22 16	23 03
52	03 43	04 28	05 04	21 10	21 45	22 26	23 12
50	03 51	04 33	05 08	21 16	21 52	22 34	23 20
45	04 08	04 45	05 16	21 30	22 08	22 51	23 38
N 40	04 21	04 55	05 23	21 42	22 22	23 05	23 53
35	04 32	05 03	05 29	21 51	22 33	23 17	24 05
30	04 41	05 10	05 34	22 00	22 43	23 28	24 16
20	04 54	05 21	05 43	22 15	23 00	23 46	24 34
N 10	05 05	05 30	05 51	22 28	23 15	24 02	00 02
0	05 13	05 37	05 58	22 40	23 29	24 17	00 17
S 10	05 19	05 44	06 05	22 53	23 43	24 32	00 32
20	05 25	05 50	06 13	23 06	23 57	24 48	00 48
30	05 29	05 57	06 21	23 21	24 15	00 15	01 06
35	05 31	06 00	06 26	23 30	24 25	00 25	01 17
40	05 33	06 04	06 31	23 40	24 36	00 36	01 29
45	05 33	06 07	06 37	23 52	24 50	00 50	01 43
S 50	05 34	06 12	06 45	24 06	00 06	01 06	02 01
52	05 35	06 14	06 48	24 13	00 13	01 14	02 09
54	05 35	06 16	06 52	24 21	00 21	01 23	02 19
56	05 35	06 18	06 56	24 29	00 29	01 33	02 29
58	05 35	06 20	07 00	24 39	00 39	01 44	02 41
S 60	05 35	06 23	07 05	24 50	00 50	01 57	02 55

Lat.	Sunset	Civil	Naut.	Moonset 26	27	28	29
N 72	20 23	22 04	////	14 16	16 53	▭	▭
N 70	20 06	21 27	////	13 38	15 20	16 57	18 10
68	19 53	21 02	23 25	13 12	14 41	15 59	16 59
66	19 42	20 43	22 20	12 52	14 13	15 25	16 22
64	19 33	20 27	21 47	12 36	13 53	15 00	15 56
62	19 25	20 15	21 24	12 23	13 36	14 41	15 36
60	19 18	20 04	21 06	12 11	13 21	14 25	15 19
N 58	19 12	19 55	20 51	12 02	13 10	14 12	15 05
56	19 07	19 47	20 38	11 53	13 00	14 00	14 53
54	19 02	19 41	20 28	11 46	12 51	13 50	14 42
52	18 58	19 34	20 18	11 39	12 43	13 41	14 33
50	18 54	19 28	20 10	11 33	12 36	13 33	14 25
45	18 46	19 17	19 54	11 20	12 20	13 16	14 07
N 40	18 39	19 07	19 41	11 09	12 07	13 02	13 53
35	18 33	18 59	19 30	11 00	11 57	12 50	13 40
30	18 28	18 53	19 22	10 52	11 47	12 40	13 30
20	18 19	18 42	19 08	10 38	11 31	12 22	13 11
N 10	18 12	18 33	18 58	10 26	11 17	12 06	12 55
0	18 05	18 26	18 50	10 15	11 03	11 52	12 40
S 10	17 58	18 19	18 44	10 04	10 50	11 37	12 25
20	17 51	18 13	18 39	09 52	10 36	11 22	12 09
30	17 44	18 07	18 34	09 38	10 20	11 04	11 50
35	17 38	18 03	18 33	09 30	10 11	10 54	11 40
40	17 32	18 00	18 31	09 21	10 00	10 42	11 27
45	17 26	17 56	18 30	09 11	09 47	10 28	11 13
S 50	17 19	17 52	18 29	08 58	09 32	10 11	10 55
52	17 16	17 50	18 29	08 52	09 25	10 03	10 47
54	17 12	17 48	18 29	08 46	09 17	09 54	10 37
56	17 08	17 46	18 29	08 39	09 09	09 44	10 27
58	17 04	17 44	18 29	08 31	08 59	09 33	10 14
S 60	16 59	17 41	18 30	08 21	08 47	09 20	10 00

Day	Eqn. of Time 00h	12h	Mer. Pass.	Mer. Pass. Upper	Lower	Age	Phase
26	01 53	01 44	12 02	04 03	16 28	20	68
27	01 36	01 27	12 01	04 52	17 16	21	59
28	01 18	01 09	12 01	05 40	18 04	22	49

UT	ARIES GHA	VENUS −4.0 GHA	Dec	MARS +1.6 GHA	Dec	JUPITER −2.0 GHA	Dec	SATURN +0.7 GHA	Dec
d h	° ′	° ′	° ′	° ′	° ′	° ′	° ′	° ′	° ′
29 00	337 21.9	143 56.5	S 5 40.5	214 21.2	N20 58.1	232 44.7	N22 37.8	122 02.2	S11 41.1
01	352 24.4	158 56.3	41.8	229 22.0	57.8	247 46.7	37.7	137 04.4	41.2
02	7 26.9	173 56.1	43.0	244 22.8	57.5	262 48.7	37.7	152 06.7	41.2
03	22 29.3	188 55.9 ..	44.3	259 23.5 ..	57.2	277 50.7 ..	37.7	167 09.0 ..	41.3
04	37 31.8	203 55.7	45.6	274 24.3	56.8	292 52.7	37.6	182 11.3	41.4
05	52 34.3	218 55.5	46.8	289 25.1	56.5	307 54.7	37.6	197 13.6	41.4
06	67 36.7	233 55.3	S 5 48.1	304 25.9	N20 56.2	322 56.6	N22 37.5	212 15.9	S11 41.5
07	82 39.2	248 55.2	49.4	319 26.7	55.9	337 58.6	37.5	227 18.1	41.6
T 08	97 41.7	263 55.0	50.7	334 27.5	55.5	353 00.6	37.4	242 20.4	41.7
H 09	112 44.1	278 54.8 ..	51.9	349 28.3 ..	55.2	8 02.6 ..	37.4	257 22.7 ..	41.7
U 10	127 46.6	293 54.6	53.2	4 29.1	54.9	23 04.6	37.4	272 25.0	41.8
R 11	142 49.0	308 54.4	54.5	19 29.8	54.6	38 06.6	37.3	287 27.3	41.9
S 12	157 51.5	323 54.2	S 5 55.7	34 30.6	N20 54.2	53 08.6	N22 37.3	302 29.5	S11 41.9
D 13	172 54.0	338 54.0	57.0	49 31.4	53.9	68 10.5	37.2	317 31.8	42.0
A 14	187 56.4	353 53.8	58.3	64 32.2	53.6	83 12.5	37.2	332 34.1	42.1
Y 15	202 58.9	8 53.6	5 59.5	79 33.0 ..	53.3	98 14.5 ..	37.2	347 36.4 ..	42.2
16	218 01.4	23 53.4	6 00.8	94 33.8	52.9	113 16.5	37.1	2 38.7	42.2
17	233 03.8	38 53.2	02.1	109 34.6	52.6	128 18.5	37.1	17 40.9	42.3
18	248 06.3	53 53.0	S 6 03.3	124 35.4	N20 52.3	143 20.5	N22 37.0	32 43.2	S11 42.4
19	263 08.8	68 52.8	04.6	139 36.2	51.9	158 22.5	37.0	47 45.5	42.4
20	278 11.2	83 52.6	05.9	154 36.9	51.6	173 24.5	37.0	62 47.8	42.5
21	293 13.7	98 52.4 ..	07.1	169 37.7 ..	51.3	188 26.4 ..	36.9	77 50.1 ..	42.6
22	308 16.1	113 52.2	08.4	184 38.5	51.0	203 28.4	36.9	92 52.3	42.7
23	323 18.6	128 52.0	09.7	199 39.3	50.6	218 30.4	36.8	107 54.6	42.7
30 00	338 21.1	143 51.8	S 6 10.9	214 40.1	N20 50.3	233 32.4	N22 36.8	122 56.9	S11 42.8
01	353 23.5	158 51.6	12.2	229 40.9	50.0	248 34.4	36.7	137 59.2	42.9
02	8 26.0	173 51.4	13.5	244 41.7	49.6	263 36.4	36.7	153 01.4	42.9
03	23 28.5	188 51.2 ..	14.7	259 42.5 ..	49.3	278 38.4 ..	36.7	168 03.7 ..	43.0
04	38 30.9	203 51.0	16.0	274 43.3	49.0	293 40.4	36.6	183 06.0	43.1
05	53 33.4	218 50.9	17.3	289 44.1	48.6	308 42.4	36.6	198 08.3	43.2
06	68 35.9	233 50.7	S 6 18.5	304 44.9	N20 48.3	323 44.3	N22 36.5	213 10.6	S11 43.2
07	83 38.3	248 50.5	19.8	319 45.7	48.0	338 46.3	36.5	228 12.8	43.3
F 08	98 40.8	263 50.3	21.1	334 46.4	47.6	353 48.3	36.5	243 15.1	43.4
R 09	113 43.3	278 50.1 ..	22.3	349 47.2 ..	47.3	8 50.3 ..	36.4	258 17.4 ..	43.4
I 10	128 45.7	293 49.9	23.6	4 48.0	47.0	23 52.3	36.4	273 19.7	43.5
D 11	143 48.2	308 49.7	24.9	19 48.8	46.7	38 54.3	36.4	288 21.9	43.6
A 12	158 50.6	323 49.5	S 6 26.1	34 49.6	N20 46.3	53 56.3	N22 36.3	303 24.2	S11 43.7
Y 13	173 53.1	338 49.3	27.4	49 50.4	46.0	68 58.3	36.3	318 26.5	43.7
14	188 55.6	353 49.1	28.6	64 51.2	45.7	84 00.3	36.2	333 28.8	43.8
15	203 58.0	8 48.9 ..	29.9	79 52.0 ..	45.3	99 02.3 ..	36.2	348 31.1 ..	43.9
16	219 00.5	23 48.7	31.2	94 52.8	45.0	114 04.2	36.1	3 33.3	44.0
17	234 03.0	38 48.5	32.4	109 53.6	44.7	129 06.2	36.1	18 35.6	44.0
18	249 05.4	53 48.3	S 6 33.7	124 54.4	N20 44.3	144 08.2	N22 36.0	33 37.9	S11 44.1
19	264 07.9	68 48.1	35.0	139 55.2	44.0	159 10.2	36.0	48 40.2	44.2
20	279 10.4	83 47.9	36.2	154 56.0	43.7	174 12.2	36.0	63 42.4	44.2
21	294 12.8	98 47.7 ..	37.5	169 56.8 ..	43.3	189 14.2 ..	35.9	78 44.7 ..	44.3
22	309 15.3	113 47.5	38.7	184 57.6	43.0	204 16.2	35.9	93 47.0	44.4
23	324 17.8	128 47.3	40.0	199 58.4	42.6	219 18.2	35.8	108 49.3	44.5
31 00	339 20.2	143 47.1	S 6 41.3	214 59.1	N20 42.3	234 20.2	N22 35.8	123 51.5	S11 44.5
01	354 22.7	158 46.9	42.5	229 59.9	42.0	249 22.2	35.8	138 53.8	44.6
02	9 25.1	173 46.7	43.8	245 00.7	41.6	264 24.2	35.7	153 56.1	44.7
03	24 27.6	188 46.5 ..	45.0	260 01.5 ..	41.3	279 26.2 ..	35.7	168 58.4 ..	44.7
04	39 30.1	203 46.3	46.3	275 02.3	41.0	294 28.2	35.6	184 00.6	44.8
05	54 32.5	218 46.1	47.6	290 03.1	40.6	309 30.2	35.6	199 02.9	44.9
06	69 35.0	233 45.9	S 6 48.8	305 03.9	N20 40.3	324 32.1	N22 35.5	214 05.2	S11 45.0
07	84 37.5	248 45.7	50.1	320 04.7	40.0	339 34.1	35.5	229 07.5	45.0
S 08	99 39.9	263 45.5	51.3	335 05.5	39.6	354 36.1	35.5	244 09.7	45.1
A 09	114 42.4	278 45.3 ..	52.6	350 06.3 ..	39.3	9 38.1 ..	35.4	259 12.0 ..	45.2
T 10	129 44.9	293 45.1	53.9	5 07.1	38.9	24 40.1	35.4	274 14.3	45.3
U 11	144 47.3	308 44.9	55.1	20 07.9	38.6	39 42.1	35.3	289 16.6	45.3
R 12	159 49.8	323 44.7	S 6 56.4	35 08.7	N20 38.3	54 44.1	N22 35.3	304 18.8	S11 45.4
D 13	174 52.2	338 44.5	57.6	50 09.5	37.9	69 46.1	35.3	319 21.1	45.5
A 14	189 54.7	353 44.3	6 58.9	65 10.3	37.6	84 48.1	35.2	334 23.4	45.5
Y 15	204 57.2	8 44.1	7 00.2	80 11.1 ..	37.2	99 50.1 ..	35.2	349 25.7 ..	45.6
16	219 59.6	23 43.9	01.4	95 11.9	36.9	114 52.1	35.1	4 27.9	45.7
17	235 02.1	38 43.7	02.7	110 12.7	36.6	129 54.1	35.1	19 30.2	45.8
18	250 04.6	53 43.5	S 7 03.9	125 13.5	N20 36.2	144 56.1	N22 35.1	34 32.5	S11 45.8
19	265 07.0	68 43.3	05.2	140 14.3	35.9	159 58.1	35.0	49 34.8	45.9
20	280 09.5	83 43.1	06.4	155 15.1	35.6	175 00.1	35.0	64 37.0	46.0
21	295 12.0	98 42.9 ..	07.7	170 15.9 ..	35.2	190 02.1 ..	34.9	79 39.3 ..	46.1
22	310 14.4	113 42.7	09.0	185 16.7	34.9	205 04.1	34.9	94 41.6	46.1
23	325 16.9	128 42.5	10.2	200 17.5	34.5	220 06.1	34.8	109 43.9	46.2
Mer. Pass.	h m 1 26.4	v −0.2	d 1.3	v 0.8	d 0.3	v 2.0	d 0.0	v 2.3	d 0.1

STARS

Name	SHA	Dec
Acamar	315 18.1	S40 14.8
Achernar	335 26.3	S57 09.8
Acrux	173 09.6	S63 10.6
Adhara	255 12.6	S28 59.4
Aldebaran	290 49.2	N16 32.1
Alioth	166 21.0	N55 53.3
Alkaid	152 59.1	N49 15.0
Al Na'ir	27 43.1	S46 53.5
Alnilam	275 46.3	S 1 11.6
Alphard	217 56.2	S 8 43.1
Alphecca	126 11.0	N26 40.5
Alpheratz	357 43.0	N29 10.1
Altair	62 07.8	N 8 54.6
Ankaa	353 15.2	S42 13.6
Antares	112 26.0	S26 27.6
Arcturus	145 55.8	N19 06.9
Atria	107 27.6	S69 03.2
Avior	234 18.5	S59 33.2
Bellatrix	278 31.9	N 6 21.7
Betelgeuse	271 01.2	N 7 24.5
Canopus	263 56.3	S52 42.0
Capella	280 34.3	N46 00.4
Deneb	49 30.9	N45 20.1
Denebola	182 33.8	N14 29.8
Diphda	348 55.5	S17 54.5
Dubhe	193 52.2	N61 40.6
Elnath	278 12.5	N28 36.9
Eltanin	90 45.9	N51 29.7
Enif	33 46.6	N 9 56.6
Fomalhaut	15 23.5	S29 32.7
Gacrux	172 01.1	S57 11.5
Gienah	175 52.4	S17 37.1
Hadar	148 48.0	S60 26.5
Hamal	328 00.4	N23 31.6
Kaus Aust.	83 43.4	S34 22.5
Kochab	137 20.6	N74 06.3
Markab	13 37.8	N15 17.0
Menkar	314 14.8	N 4 08.6
Menkent	148 07.6	S36 26.3
Miaplacidus	221 40.4	S69 46.4
Mirfak	308 40.0	N49 54.3
Nunki	75 57.9	S26 16.6
Peacock	53 18.5	S56 41.3
Pollux	243 27.8	N27 59.4
Procyon	244 59.8	N 5 11.3
Rasalhague	96 06.2	N12 33.3
Regulus	207 43.7	N11 54.0
Rigel	281 12.0	S 8 11.1
Rigil Kent.	139 51.7	S60 53.6
Sabik	102 12.3	S15 44.3
Schedar	349 39.8	N56 36.7
Shaula	96 21.6	S37 06.7
Sirius	258 33.8	S16 44.1
Spica	158 31.3	S11 13.9
Suhail	222 52.7	S43 29.3
Vega	80 38.6	N38 48.2
Zuben'ubi	137 05.4	S16 05.8

	SHA	Mer. Pass.
		h m
Venus	165 30.8	14 25
Mars	236 19.0	9 41
Jupiter	255 11.3	8 25
Saturn	144 35.8	15 46

SUN and MOON

UT	SUN GHA	Dec	MOON GHA	v	Dec	d	HP
29 00	179 45.0	N 9 22.4	266 01.7	11.8	N19 34.8	1.5	54.5
01	194 45.2	21.5	280 32.5	11.8	19 36.3	1.4	54.5
02	209 45.4	20.6	295 03.3	11.9	19 37.7	1.4	54.5
03	224 45.6	.. 19.7	309 34.2	11.8	19 39.1	1.2	54.4
04	239 45.7	18.8	324 05.0	11.8	19 40.3	1.2	54.4
05	254 45.9	17.9	338 35.8	11.9	19 41.5	1.0	54.4
06	269 46.1	N 9 17.0	353 06.7	11.9	N19 42.5	1.0	54.4
07	284 46.3	16.1	7 37.6	11.8	19 43.5	0.9	54.4
T 08	299 46.5	15.3	22 08.4	11.9	19 44.4	0.8	54.4
H 09	314 46.7	.. 14.4	36 39.3	11.9	19 45.2	0.7	54.4
U 10	329 46.9	13.5	51 10.2	11.9	19 45.9	0.6	54.4
R 11	344 47.1	12.6	65 41.1	11.9	19 46.5	0.5	54.3
S 12	359 47.3	N 9 11.7	80 12.0	11.9	N19 47.0	0.4	54.3
D 13	14 47.4	10.8	94 42.9	11.9	19 47.4	0.3	54.3
A 14	29 47.6	09.9	109 13.8	11.9	19 47.7	0.3	54.3
Y 15	44 47.8	.. 09.0	123 44.7	12.0	19 48.0	0.1	54.3
16	59 48.0	08.1	138 15.7	11.9	19 48.1	0.1	54.3
17	74 48.2	07.2	152 46.6	11.9	19 48.2	0.1	54.3
18	89 48.4	N 9 06.3	167 17.5	12.0	N19 48.1	0.1	54.3
19	104 48.6	05.4	181 48.5	12.0	19 48.0	0.2	54.3
20	119 48.8	04.5	196 19.5	11.9	19 47.8	0.4	54.3
21	134 49.0	.. 03.7	210 50.4	12.0	19 47.4	0.4	54.3
22	149 49.2	02.8	225 21.4	12.0	19 47.0	0.5	54.2
23	164 49.3	01.9	239 52.4	12.0	19 46.5	0.6	54.2
30 00	179 49.5	N 9 01.0	254 23.4	12.0	N19 46.0	0.7	54.2
01	194 49.7	9 00.1	268 54.4	12.1	19 45.2	0.7	54.2
02	209 49.9	8 59.2	283 25.5	12.0	19 44.5	0.9	54.2
03	224 50.1	.. 58.3	297 56.5	12.1	19 43.6	1.0	54.2
04	239 50.3	57.4	312 27.6	12.0	19 42.6	1.0	54.2
05	254 50.5	56.5	326 58.6	12.1	19 41.6	1.1	54.2
06	269 50.7	N 8 55.6	341 29.7	12.1	N19 40.5	1.3	54.2
07	284 50.9	54.7	356 00.8	12.1	19 39.2	1.3	54.2
F 08	299 51.1	53.8	10 31.9	12.1	19 37.9	1.4	54.2
R 09	314 51.3	.. 52.9	25 03.0	12.1	19 36.5	1.5	54.2
I 10	329 51.4	52.0	39 34.1	12.1	19 35.0	1.6	54.2
11	344 51.6	51.1	54 05.2	12.2	19 33.4	1.7	54.2
D 12	359 51.8	N 8 50.2	68 36.4	12.1	N19 31.7	1.8	54.2
A 13	14 52.0	49.3	83 07.5	12.2	19 29.9	1.8	54.2
Y 14	29 52.2	48.4	97 38.7	12.2	19 28.1	2.0	54.2
15	44 52.4	.. 47.5	112 09.9	12.2	19 26.1	2.0	54.2
16	59 52.6	46.6	126 41.1	12.2	19 24.1	2.1	54.2
17	74 52.8	45.7	141 12.3	12.2	19 22.0	2.2	54.2
18	89 53.0	N 8 44.8	155 43.5	12.3	N19 19.8	2.3	54.2
19	104 53.2	43.9	170 14.8	12.2	19 17.5	2.4	54.2
20	119 53.4	43.0	184 46.0	12.3	19 15.1	2.5	54.2
21	134 53.6	.. 42.1	199 17.3	12.3	19 12.6	2.6	54.2
22	149 53.8	41.2	213 48.6	12.3	19 10.0	2.6	54.2
23	164 54.0	40.3	228 19.9	12.3	19 07.4	2.8	54.2
31 00	179 54.2	N 8 39.4	242 51.2	12.3	N19 04.6	2.8	54.2
01	194 54.3	38.5	257 22.5	12.3	19 01.8	2.9	54.2
02	209 54.5	37.6	271 53.8	12.4	18 58.9	3.0	54.2
03	224 54.7	.. 36.7	286 25.2	12.4	18 55.9	3.1	54.2
04	239 54.9	35.8	300 56.6	12.4	18 52.8	3.2	54.2
05	254 55.1	34.9	315 28.0	12.4	18 49.6	3.3	54.2
06	269 55.3	N 8 34.0	329 59.4	12.4	N18 46.3	3.3	54.2
07	284 55.5	33.1	344 30.8	12.4	18 43.0	3.4	54.2
S 08	299 55.7	32.2	359 02.2	12.5	18 39.6	3.6	54.2
A 09	314 55.9	.. 31.3	13 33.7	12.4	18 36.0	3.6	54.2
T 10	329 56.1	30.4	28 05.1	12.5	18 32.4	3.7	54.2
U 11	344 56.3	29.5	42 36.6	12.5	18 28.7	3.7	54.2
R 12	359 56.5	N 8 28.6	57 08.1	12.6	N18 25.0	3.9	54.2
D 13	14 56.7	27.7	71 39.7	12.5	18 21.1	3.9	54.2
A 14	29 56.9	26.8	86 11.2	12.5	18 17.2	4.1	54.2
Y 15	44 57.1	.. 25.9	100 42.7	12.6	18 13.1	4.1	54.2
16	59 57.3	25.0	115 14.3	12.6	18 09.0	4.2	54.2
17	74 57.5	24.1	129 45.9	12.6	18 04.8	4.2	54.2
18	89 57.7	N 8 23.2	144 17.5	12.6	N18 00.6	4.4	54.2
19	104 57.9	22.3	158 49.1	12.7	17 56.2	4.4	54.2
20	119 58.1	21.4	173 20.8	12.6	17 51.8	4.5	54.2
21	134 58.3	.. 20.5	187 52.4	12.7	17 47.3	4.6	54.2
22	149 58.5	19.6	202 24.1	12.7	17 42.7	4.7	54.2
23	164 58.6	18.7	216 55.8	12.7	N17 38.0	4.8	54.2
	SD 15.9	d 0.9	SD 14.8		14.8		14.8

Twilight / Sunrise / Moonrise

Lat.	Twilight Naut.	Twilight Civil	Sunrise	Moonrise 29	30	31	1
N 72	////	02 17	03 52	▭	▭	21 14	23 31
N 70	////	02 49	04 07	19 35	20 53	22 29	24 07
68	01 11	03 11	04 19	20 47	21 49	23 07	24 32
66	01 58	03 29	04 29	21 23	22 22	23 33	24 52
64	02 27	03 43	04 37	21 49	22 46	23 53	25 08
62	02 48	03 55	04 44	22 10	23 05	24 10	00 10
60	03 05	04 05	04 50	22 26	23 21	24 23	00 23
N 58	03 19	04 13	04 56	22 40	23 34	24 35	00 35
56	03 30	04 21	05 00	22 52	23 45	24 45	00 45
54	03 40	04 27	05 05	23 03	23 55	24 54	00 54
52	03 49	04 33	05 09	23 12	24 04	00 04	01 02
50	03 57	04 38	05 12	23 20	24 12	00 12	01 09
45	04 12	04 49	05 20	23 38	24 29	00 29	01 24
N 40	04 25	04 58	05 26	23 53	24 43	00 43	01 37
35	04 34	05 05	05 31	24 05	00 05	00 55	01 47
30	04 43	05 11	05 36	24 16	00 16	01 05	01 57
20	04 55	05 22	05 44	24 34	00 34	01 23	02 13
N 10	05 05	05 30	05 51	00 02	00 50	01 38	02 27
0	05 12	05 36	05 57	00 17	01 05	01 53	02 40
S 10	05 18	05 42	06 04	00 32	01 20	02 07	02 53
20	05 22	05 48	06 10	00 48	01 36	02 22	03 06
30	05 26	05 53	06 18	01 06	01 54	02 40	03 22
35	05 27	05 56	06 22	01 17	02 05	02 50	03 32
40	05 28	05 59	06 26	01 29	02 17	03 02	03 42
45	05 28	06 02	06 32	01 43	02 32	03 16	03 54
S 50	05 28	06 06	06 38	02 01	02 50	03 32	04 09
52	05 28	06 07	06 41	02 09	02 58	03 40	04 16
54	05 28	06 09	06 45	02 19	03 08	03 49	04 24
56	05 28	06 11	06 48	02 29	03 18	03 59	04 33
58	05 27	06 12	06 52	02 41	03 30	04 10	04 42
S 60	05 26	06 14	06 57	02 55	03 44	04 23	04 53

Sunset / Twilight / Moonset

Lat.	Sunset	Twilight Civil	Twilight Naut.	Moonset 29	30	31	1
N 72	20 06	21 38	////	▭	▭	19 50	19 09
N 70	19 51	21 08	////	18 10	18 31	18 34	18 32
68	19 40	20 46	22 40	16 59	17 36	17 55	18 06
66	19 30	20 29	21 58	16 22	17 02	17 29	17 46
64	19 22	20 15	21 30	15 56	16 38	17 08	17 29
62	19 15	20 04	21 10	15 36	16 19	16 51	17 16
60	19 09	19 54	20 54	15 19	16 03	16 37	17 04
N 58	19 04	19 46	20 40	15 05	15 49	16 25	16 54
56	19 00	19 39	20 29	14 53	15 38	16 15	16 46
54	18 55	19 33	20 19	14 42	15 28	16 06	16 38
52	18 51	19 27	20 11	14 33	15 19	15 58	16 31
50	18 48	19 22	20 03	14 25	15 10	15 50	16 25
45	18 41	19 11	19 48	14 07	14 53	15 34	16 11
N 40	18 35	19 02	19 36	13 53	14 39	15 21	16 00
35	18 29	18 55	19 26	13 40	14 27	15 10	15 50
30	18 25	18 49	19 18	13 30	14 17	15 01	15 42
20	18 17	18 39	19 05	13 11	13 59	14 44	15 27
N 10	18 10	18 31	18 56	12 54	13 43	14 29	15 14
0	18 04	18 25	18 49	12 40	13 28	14 15	15 02
S 10	17 58	18 19	18 43	12 25	13 13	14 02	14 50
20	17 52	18 13	18 39	12 09	12 57	13 47	14 37
30	17 44	18 08	18 36	11 50	12 39	13 30	14 22
35	17 40	18 05	18 35	11 40	12 29	13 20	14 13
40	17 35	18 03	18 34	11 27	12 16	13 08	14 03
45	17 30	17 59	18 34	11 13	12 02	12 55	13 52
S 50	17 23	17 56	18 34	10 55	11 44	12 39	13 37
52	17 21	17 55	18 34	10 47	11 36	12 31	13 31
54	17 17	17 53	18 34	10 37	11 27	12 22	13 23
56	17 14	17 52	18 35	10 27	11 16	12 13	13 13
58	17 10	17 50	18 35	10 14	11 04	12 06	13 06
S 60	17 06	17 48	18 36	10 00	10 50	11 49	12 55

SUN / MOON

	SUN			MOON			
Day	Eqn. of Time 00h	12h	Mer. Pass.	Mer. Pass. Upper	Lower	Age	Phase
d	m s	m s	h m	h m	h m	d %	
29	01 00	00 51	12 01	06 28	18 53	23 40	
30	00 42	00 33	12 01	07 16	19 40	24 31	
31	00 24	00 14	12 00	08 04	20 27	25 22	

2013 SEPTEMBER 1, 2, 3 (SUN., MON., TUES.)

UT	ARIES GHA	VENUS −4.0 GHA	Dec	MARS +1.6 GHA	Dec	JUPITER −2.0 GHA	Dec	SATURN +0.7 GHA	Dec	STARS Name	SHA	Dec
1 00	340 19.4	143 42.3	S 7 11.5	215 18.3	N20 34.2	235 08.1	N22 34.8	124 46.1	S11 46.3	Acamar	315 18.1	S40 14.8
01	355 21.8	158 42.1	12.7	230 19.1	33.8	250 10.1	34.8	139 48.4	46.3	Achernar	335 26.3	S57 09.8
02	10 24.3	173 41.9	14.0	245 19.9	33.5	265 12.1	34.7	154 50.7	46.4	Acrux	173 09.6	S63 10.6
03	25 26.7	188 41.7	.. 15.2	260 20.7	.. 33.2	280 14.1	.. 34.7	169 52.9	.. 46.5	Adhara	255 12.6	S28 59.4
04	40 29.2	203 41.5	16.5	275 21.5	32.8	295 16.1	34.6	184 55.2	46.6	Aldebaran	290 49.2	N16 32.1
05	55 31.7	218 41.3	17.7	290 22.3	32.5	310 18.1	34.6	199 57.5	46.6			
06	70 34.1	233 41.1	S 7 19.0	305 23.1	N20 32.1	325 20.1	N22 34.6	214 59.8	S11 46.7	Alioth	166 21.1	N55 53.3
07	85 36.6	248 40.9	20.3	320 23.9	31.8	340 22.1	34.5	230 02.0	46.8	Alkaid	152 59.1	N49 15.0
08	100 39.1	263 40.7	21.5	335 24.7	31.5	355 24.1	34.5	245 04.3	46.9	Al Na'ir	27 43.1	S46 53.5
S 09	115 41.5	278 40.5	.. 22.8	350 25.5	.. 31.1	10 26.0	.. 34.4	260 06.6	.. 46.9	Alnilam	275 46.3	S 1 11.6
U 10	130 44.0	293 40.3	24.0	5 26.3	30.8	25 28.0	34.4	275 08.8	47.0	Alphard	217 56.2	S 8 43.1
N 11	145 46.5	308 40.1	25.3	20 27.1	30.4	40 30.0	34.3	290 11.1	47.1			
D 12	160 48.9	323 39.9	S 7 26.5	35 27.9	N20 30.1	55 32.0	N22 34.3	305 13.4	S11 47.2	Alphecca	126 11.0	N26 40.5
A 13	175 51.4	338 39.7	27.8	50 28.7	29.7	70 34.0	34.3	320 15.7	47.2	Alpheratz	357 43.0	N29 10.1
Y 14	190 53.9	353 39.5	29.0	65 29.5	29.4	85 36.0	34.2	335 17.9	47.3	Altair	62 07.8	N 8 54.6
15	205 56.3	8 39.3	.. 30.3	80 30.3	.. 29.0	100 38.0	.. 34.2	350 20.2	.. 47.4	Ankaa	353 15.2	S42 13.6
16	220 58.8	23 39.1	31.5	95 31.1	28.7	115 40.0	34.1	5 22.5	47.5	Antares	112 26.0	S26 27.6
17	236 01.2	38 38.9	32.8	110 32.0	28.4	130 42.0	34.1	20 24.7	47.5			
18	251 03.7	53 38.7	S 7 34.0	125 32.8	N20 28.0	145 44.0	N22 34.1	35 27.0	S11 47.6	Arcturus	145 55.8	N19 06.9
19	266 06.2	68 38.5	35.3	140 33.6	27.7	160 46.0	34.0	50 29.3	47.7	Atria	107 27.6	S69 03.2
20	281 08.6	83 38.3	36.5	155 34.4	27.3	175 48.0	34.0	65 31.6	47.7	Avior	234 18.4	S59 33.1
21	296 11.1	98 38.1	.. 37.8	170 35.2	.. 27.0	190 50.1	.. 33.9	80 33.8	.. 47.8	Bellatrix	278 31.9	N 6 21.7
22	311 13.6	113 37.9	39.0	185 36.0	26.6	205 52.1	33.9	95 36.1	47.9	Betelgeuse	271 01.2	N 7 24.5
23	326 16.0	128 37.7	40.3	200 36.8	26.3	220 54.1	33.8	110 38.4	48.0			
2 00	341 18.5	143 37.5	S 7 41.5	215 37.6	N20 25.9	235 56.1	N22 33.8	125 40.6	S11 48.0	Canopus	263 56.3	S52 42.0
01	356 21.0	158 37.3	42.8	230 38.4	25.6	250 58.1	33.8	140 42.9	48.1	Capella	280 34.3	N46 00.4
02	11 23.4	173 37.1	44.0	245 39.2	25.2	266 00.1	33.7	155 45.2	48.2	Deneb	49 30.9	N45 20.1
03	26 25.9	188 36.9	.. 45.3	260 40.0	.. 24.9	281 02.1	.. 33.7	170 47.5	.. 48.3	Denebola	182 33.8	N14 29.8
04	41 28.4	203 36.7	46.5	275 40.8	24.5	296 04.1	33.6	185 49.7	48.3	Diphda	348 55.4	S17 54.5
05	56 30.8	218 36.5	47.8	290 41.6	24.2	311 06.1	33.6	200 52.0	48.4			
06	71 33.3	233 36.3	S 7 49.0	305 42.4	N20 23.8	326 08.1	N22 33.5	215 54.3	S11 48.5	Dubhe	193 52.2	N61 40.6
07	86 35.7	248 36.1	50.3	320 43.2	23.5	341 10.1	33.5	230 56.5	48.6	Elnath	278 12.5	N28 36.9
08	101 38.2	263 35.8	51.5	335 44.0	23.2	356 12.1	33.5	245 58.8	48.6	Eltanin	90 45.9	N51 29.7
M 09	116 40.7	278 35.6	.. 52.8	350 44.8	.. 22.8	11 14.1	.. 33.4	261 01.1	.. 48.7	Enif	33 46.6	N 9 56.6
O 10	131 43.1	293 35.4	54.0	5 45.7	22.5	26 16.1	33.4	276 03.3	48.8	Fomalhaut	15 23.5	S29 32.7
N 11	146 45.6	308 35.2	55.3	20 46.5	22.2	41 18.1	33.4	291 05.6	48.9			
D 12	161 48.1	323 35.0	S 7 56.5	35 47.3	N20 21.8	56 20.1	N22 33.3	306 07.9	S11 48.9	Gacrux	172 01.2	S57 11.5
A 13	176 50.5	338 34.8	57.8	50 48.1	21.4	71 22.1	33.3	321 10.1	49.0	Gienah	175 52.4	S17 37.1
Y 14	191 53.0	353 34.6	7 59.0	65 48.9	21.1	86 24.1	33.2	336 12.4	49.1	Hadar	148 48.0	S60 26.5
15	206 55.5	8 34.4	8 00.3	80 49.7	.. 20.7	101 26.1	.. 33.1	351 14.7	.. 49.2	Hamal	328 00.3	N23 31.6
16	221 57.9	23 34.2	01.5	95 50.5	20.4	116 28.1	33.1	6 16.9	49.2	Kaus Aust.	83 43.4	S34 22.6
17	237 00.4	38 34.0	02.8	110 51.3	20.0	131 30.1	33.1	21 19.2	49.3			
18	252 02.8	53 33.8	S 8 04.0	125 52.1	N20 19.7	146 32.1	N22 33.1	36 21.5	S11 49.4	Kochab	137 20.6	N74 06.3
19	267 05.3	68 33.6	05.3	140 52.9	19.3	161 34.1	33.0	51 23.8	49.5	Markab	13 37.8	N15 17.0
20	282 07.8	83 33.4	06.5	155 53.7	19.0	176 36.1	33.0	66 26.0	49.5	Menkar	314 14.7	N 4 08.6
21	297 10.2	98 33.2	.. 07.7	170 54.6	.. 18.6	191 38.1	.. 32.9	81 28.3	.. 49.6	Menkent	148 07.6	S36 26.3
22	312 12.7	113 33.0	09.0	185 55.4	18.2	206 40.1	32.9	96 30.6	49.7	Miaplacidus	221 40.4	S69 46.4
23	327 15.2	128 32.8	10.2	200 56.2	17.9	221 42.1	32.9	111 32.8	49.8			
3 00	342 17.6	143 32.6	S 8 11.5	215 57.0	N20 17.5	236 44.2	N22 32.8	126 35.1	S11 49.8	Mirfak	308 39.9	N49 54.3
01	357 20.1	158 32.4	12.7	230 57.8	17.2	251 46.2	32.8	141 37.4	49.9	Nunki	75 57.9	S26 16.6
02	12 22.6	173 32.1	14.0	245 58.6	16.8	266 48.2	32.7	156 39.6	50.0	Peacock	53 18.5	S56 41.3
03	27 25.0	188 31.9	.. 15.2	260 59.4	.. 16.5	281 50.2	.. 32.7	171 41.9	.. 50.0	Pollux	243 27.8	N27 59.4
04	42 27.5	203 31.7	16.5	276 00.2	16.1	296 52.2	32.6	186 44.2	50.1	Procyon	244 59.8	N 5 11.3
05	57 30.0	218 31.5	17.7	291 01.0	15.8	311 54.2	32.6	201 46.4	50.2			
06	72 32.4	233 31.3	S 8 18.9	306 01.9	N20 15.4	326 56.2	N22 32.5	216 48.7	S11 50.3	Rasalhague	96 06.2	N12 33.4
07	87 34.9	248 31.1	20.2	321 02.7	15.1	341 58.2	32.5	231 51.0	50.3	Regulus	207 43.7	N11 54.0
08	102 37.3	263 30.9	21.4	336 03.5	14.7	357 00.2	32.5	246 53.2	50.4	Rigel	281 11.9	S 8 11.1
T 09	117 39.8	278 30.7	.. 22.7	351 04.3	.. 14.4	12 02.2	.. 32.4	261 55.5	.. 50.5	Rigil Kent.	139 51.8	S60 53.6
U 10	132 42.3	293 30.5	23.9	6 05.1	14.0	27 04.2	32.4	276 57.8	50.6	Sabik	102 12.3	S15 44.3
E 11	147 44.7	308 30.3	25.1	21 05.9	13.7	42 06.2	32.4	292 00.0	50.6			
S 12	162 47.2	323 30.1	S 8 26.4	36 06.7	N20 13.3	57 08.2	N22 32.3	307 02.3	S11 50.7	Schedar	349 39.8	N56 36.7
D 13	177 49.7	338 29.9	27.6	51 07.5	12.9	72 10.3	32.3	322 04.6	50.8	Shaula	96 21.6	S37 06.7
A 14	192 52.1	353 29.7	28.9	66 08.4	12.6	87 12.3	32.2	337 06.8	50.9	Sirius	258 33.7	S16 44.1
Y 15	207 54.6	8 29.4	.. 30.1	81 09.2	.. 12.2	102 14.3	.. 32.2	352 09.1	.. 50.9	Spica	158 31.3	S11 13.9
16	222 57.1	23 29.2	31.3	96 10.0	11.9	117 16.3	32.1	7 11.3	51.0	Suhail	222 52.7	S43 29.3
17	237 59.5	38 29.0	32.6	111 10.8	11.5	132 18.3	32.1	22 13.6	51.1			
18	253 02.0	53 28.8	S 8 33.8	126 11.6	N20 11.2	147 20.3	N22 32.1	37 15.9	S11 51.2	Vega	80 38.6	N38 48.2
19	268 04.4	68 28.6	35.1	141 12.4	10.8	162 22.3	32.0	52 18.1	51.2	Zuben'ubi	137 05.4	S16 05.8
20	283 06.9	83 28.4	36.3	156 13.2	10.5	177 24.3	32.0	67 20.4	51.3		SHA	Mer. Pass.
21	298 09.4	98 28.2	.. 37.5	171 14.1	.. 10.1	192 26.3	.. 31.9	82 22.7	.. 51.4	Venus	162 19.0	14 26
22	313 11.8	113 28.0	38.8	186 14.9	09.7	207 28.3	31.9	97 24.9	51.5	Mars	234 19.1	9 37
23	328 14.3	128 27.8	40.0	201 15.7	09.4	222 30.3	31.9	112 27.2	51.6	Jupiter	254 37.6	8 15
Mer. Pass. 1 14.6		v −0.2	d 1.2	v 0.8	d 0.3	v 2.0	d 0.0	v 2.3	d 0.1	Saturn	144 22.1	15 35

UT	SUN GHA	Dec	MOON GHA	v	Dec	d	HP
d h	° ′	° ′	° ′	′	° ′	′	′
1 00	179 58.8	N 8 17.7	231 27.5 12.7	N17 33.2	4.8	54.2	
01	194 59.0	16.8	245 59.2 12.8	17 28.4	4.9	54.2	
02	209 59.2	15.9	260 31.0 12.7	17 23.5	5.0	54.2	
03	224 59.4	15.0	275 02.7 12.8	17 18.5	5.1	54.3	
04	239 59.6	14.1	289 34.5 12.8	17 13.4	5.2	54.3	
05	254 59.8	13.2	304 06.3 12.8	17 08.2	5.2	54.3	
06	270 00.0	N 8 12.3	318 38.1 12.9	N17 03.0	5.3	54.3	
07	285 00.2	11.4	333 10.0 12.8	16 57.7	5.4	54.3	
08	300 00.4	10.5	347 41.8 12.9	16 52.3	5.5	54.3	
S 09	315 00.6	09.6	2 13.7 12.9	16 46.8	5.6	54.3	
U 10	330 00.8	08.7	16 45.6 12.9	16 41.2	5.6	54.3	
N 11	345 01.0	07.8	31 17.5 13.0	16 35.6	5.7	54.3	
D 12	0 01.2	N 8 06.9	45 49.4 12.9	N16 29.9	5.8	54.3	
A 13	15 01.4	05.9	60 21.3 13.0	16 24.1	5.8	54.3	
Y 14	30 01.6	05.0	74 53.3 12.9	16 18.3	5.9	54.3	
15	45 01.8	04.1	89 25.2 13.0	16 12.4	6.0	54.4	
16	60 02.0	03.2	103 57.2 13.0	16 06.4	6.1	54.4	
17	75 02.2	02.3	118 29.2 13.1	16 00.3	6.2	54.4	
18	90 02.4	N 8 01.4	133 01.3 13.0	N15 54.1	6.2	54.4	
19	105 02.6	8 00.5	147 33.3 13.1	15 47.9	6.3	54.4	
20	120 02.8	7 59.6	162 05.4 13.0	15 41.6	6.4	54.4	
21	135 03.0	58.7	176 37.4 13.1	15 35.2	6.4	54.4	
22	150 03.2	57.8	191 09.5 13.1	15 28.8	6.5	54.4	
23	165 03.4	56.8	205 41.6 13.2	15 22.3	6.6	54.4	
2 00	180 03.6	N 7 55.9	220 13.8 13.1	N15 15.7	6.7	54.4	
01	195 03.8	55.0	234 45.9 13.2	15 09.0	6.7	54.5	
02	210 04.0	54.1	249 18.1 13.1	15 02.3	6.8	54.5	
03	225 04.2	53.2	263 50.2 13.2	14 55.5	6.9	54.5	
04	240 04.4	52.3	278 22.4 13.2	14 48.6	6.9	54.5	
05	255 04.6	51.4	292 54.6 13.2	14 41.7	7.0	54.5	
06	270 04.8	N 7 50.5	307 26.8 13.3	N14 34.7	7.1	54.5	
07	285 05.0	49.5	321 59.1 13.2	14 27.6	7.1	54.5	
M 08	300 05.2	48.6	336 31.3 13.3	14 20.5	7.2	54.5	
O 09	315 05.4	47.7	351 03.6 13.3	14 13.3	7.3	54.6	
N 10	330 05.6	46.8	5 35.9 13.3	14 06.0	7.4	54.6	
D 11	345 05.8	45.9	20 08.2 13.3	13 58.6	7.4	54.6	
A 12	0 06.0	N 7 45.0	34 40.5 13.3	N13 51.2	7.5	54.6	
Y 13	15 06.2	44.1	49 12.8 13.4	13 43.7	7.5	54.6	
14	30 06.4	43.1	63 45.2 13.3	13 36.2	7.6	54.6	
15	45 06.6	42.2	78 17.5 13.4	13 28.6	7.7	54.6	
16	60 06.8	41.3	92 49.9 13.4	13 20.9	7.7	54.7	
17	75 07.0	40.4	107 22.3 13.4	13 13.2	7.8	54.7	
18	90 07.2	N 7 39.5	121 54.7 13.4	N13 05.4	7.8	54.7	
19	105 07.4	38.6	136 27.1 13.4	12 57.6	8.0	54.7	
20	120 07.6	37.7	150 59.5 13.5	12 49.6	7.9	54.7	
21	135 07.8	36.7	165 32.0 13.4	12 41.7	8.1	54.7	
22	150 08.0	35.8	180 04.4 13.5	12 33.6	8.1	54.7	
23	165 08.2	34.9	194 36.9 13.5	12 25.5	8.1	54.8	
3 00	180 08.4	N 7 34.0	209 09.4 13.4	N12 17.4	8.3	54.8	
01	195 08.6	33.1	223 41.8 13.5	12 09.1	8.2	54.8	
02	210 08.9	32.2	238 14.3 13.6	12 00.9	8.4	54.8	
03	225 09.1	31.2	252 46.9 13.5	11 52.5	8.4	54.8	
04	240 09.3	30.3	267 19.4 13.5	11 44.1	8.4	54.8	
05	255 09.5	29.4	281 51.9 13.5	11 35.7	8.5	54.9	
06	270 09.7	N 7 28.5	296 24.4 13.6	N11 27.2	8.6	54.9	
07	285 09.9	27.6	310 57.0 13.6	11 18.6	8.6	54.9	
T 08	300 10.1	26.6	325 29.6 13.5	11 10.0	8.7	54.9	
U 09	315 10.3	25.7	340 02.1 13.6	11 01.3	8.7	54.9	
E 10	330 10.5	24.8	354 34.7 13.6	10 52.6	8.8	54.9	
S 11	345 10.7	23.9	9 07.3 13.6	10 43.8	8.8	55.0	
D 12	0 10.9	N 7 23.0	23 39.9 13.6	N10 35.0	8.9	55.0	
A 13	15 11.1	22.1	38 12.5 13.6	10 26.1	9.0	55.0	
Y 14	30 11.3	21.1	52 45.1 13.6	10 17.1	9.0	55.0	
15	45 11.5	20.2	67 17.7 13.7	10 08.1	9.0	55.0	
16	60 11.7	19.3	81 50.4 13.6	9 59.1	9.1	55.0	
17	75 11.9	18.4	96 23.0 13.7	9 50.0	9.1	55.1	
18	90 12.1	N 7 17.5	110 55.7 13.6	N 9 40.9	9.2	55.1	
19	105 12.3	16.5	125 28.3 13.7	9 31.7	9.3	55.1	
20	120 12.5	15.6	140 01.0 13.6	9 22.4	9.3	55.1	
21	135 12.7	14.7	154 33.6 13.7	9 13.1	9.3	55.1	
22	150 12.9	13.8	169 06.3 13.6	9 03.8	9.4	55.1	
23	165 13.1	12.8	183 38.9 13.7	N 8 54.4	9.4	55.2	
	SD 15.9	d 0.9	SD 14.8		14.9		15.0

Lat.	Twilight Naut.	Civil	Sunrise	Moonrise 1	2	3	4
°	h m	h m	h m	h m	h m	h m	h m
N 72	////	02 39	04 07	23 31	25 22	01 22	03 08
N 70	00 19	03 06	04 20	24 07	00 07	01 44	03 21
68	01 41	03 25	04 30	24 32	00 32	02 01	03 31
66	02 16	03 41	04 39	24 52	00 52	02 15	03 40
64	02 41	03 53	04 46	25 08	01 08	02 26	03 47
62	03 00	04 04	04 52	00 23	01 20	02 35	03 53
60	03 15	04 13	04 57	00 23	01 31	02 44	03 58
N 58	03 27	04 20	05 02	00 35	01 41	02 51	04 03
56	03 38	04 27	05 06	00 45	01 49	02 57	04 07
54	03 47	04 33	05 10	00 54	01 57	03 02	04 10
52	03 55	04 38	05 13	01 02	02 03	03 07	04 14
50	04 02	04 43	05 17	01 09	02 09	03 12	04 17
45	04 17	04 53	05 23	01 24	02 22	03 22	04 23
N 40	04 28	05 01	05 29	01 37	02 32	03 30	04 29
35	04 37	05 08	05 33	01 47	02 41	03 37	04 33
30	04 45	05 13	05 38	01 57	02 49	03 43	04 37
20	04 56	05 22	05 45	02 13	03 03	03 54	04 45
N 10	05 05	05 29	05 51	02 27	03 15	04 03	04 51
0	05 11	05 35	05 56	02 40	03 26	04 11	04 57
S 10	05 16	05 41	06 02	02 53	03 37	04 20	05 02
20	05 20	05 45	06 08	03 06	03 49	04 29	05 09
30	05 22	05 50	06 14	03 22	04 02	04 40	05 16
35	05 23	05 52	06 18	03 32	04 10	04 46	05 20
40	05 23	05 55	06 22	03 42	04 19	04 53	05 24
45	05 23	05 57	06 27	03 54	04 29	05 00	05 30
S 50	05 22	06 00	06 32	04 09	04 41	05 10	05 36
52	05 22	06 01	06 35	04 16	04 47	05 14	05 39
54	05 21	06 02	06 38	04 24	04 54	05 19	05 42
56	05 20	06 04	06 41	04 33	05 01	05 24	05 46
58	05 19	06 05	06 44	04 42	05 09	05 30	05 49
S 60	05 18	06 06	06 48	04 53	05 18	05 37	05 54

Lat.	Sunset	Twilight Civil	Naut.	Moonset 1	2	3	4
°	h m	h m	h m	h m	h m	h m	h m
N 72	19 49	21 15	////	19 09	18 53	18 41	18 31
N 70	19 37	20 50	23 12	18 32	18 30	18 27	18 24
68	19 27	20 31	22 11	18 06	18 12	18 15	18 17
66	19 18	20 16	21 38	17 46	17 57	18 05	18 12
64	19 11	20 04	21 15	17 29	17 45	17 57	18 07
62	19 05	19 53	20 57	17 16	17 35	17 50	18 03
60	19 00	19 45	20 42	17 04	17 26	17 44	18 00
N 58	18 56	19 37	20 30	16 54	17 18	17 39	17 57
56	18 52	19 31	20 19	16 46	17 11	17 34	17 54
54	18 48	19 25	20 11	16 38	17 05	17 29	17 51
52	18 45	19 20	20 03	16 31	17 00	17 25	17 49
50	18 42	19 15	19 56	16 25	16 55	17 22	17 47
45	18 35	19 05	19 42	16 11	16 44	17 14	17 42
N 40	18 30	18 57	19 30	16 00	16 35	17 08	17 39
35	18 25	18 51	19 21	15 50	16 27	17 02	17 35
30	18 21	18 45	19 14	15 42	16 20	16 57	17 32
20	18 14	18 37	19 03	15 27	16 08	16 48	17 27
N 10	18 08	18 30	18 54	15 14	15 58	16 41	17 23
0	18 03	18 24	18 48	15 02	15 48	16 33	17 18
S 10	17 58	18 19	18 43	14 50	15 38	16 26	17 14
20	17 52	18 14	18 40	14 37	15 27	16 18	17 09
30	17 46	18 10	18 37	14 22	15 15	16 09	17 04
35	17 42	18 07	18 37	14 13	15 08	16 04	17 01
40	17 38	18 05	18 37	14 03	15 00	15 58	16 57
45	17 33	18 03	18 37	13 52	14 50	15 51	16 53
S 50	17 28	18 00	18 38	13 37	14 39	15 43	16 48
52	17 25	17 59	18 38	13 31	14 34	15 39	16 46
54	17 23	17 58	18 39	13 23	14 28	15 35	16 44
56	17 20	17 57	18 40	13 15	14 21	15 30	16 41
58	17 16	17 56	18 41	13 06	14 14	15 25	16 38
S 60	17 12	17 54	18 43	12 55	14 05	15 19	16 34

	SUN			MOON			
Day	Eqn. of Time 00h	12h	Mer. Pass.	Mer. Pass. Upper	Lower	Age	Phase
d	m s	m s	h m	h m	h m	d	%
1	00 05	00 04	12 00	08 51	21 14	26	15	
2	00 14	00 24	12 00	09 37	22 00	27	9	
3	00 33	00 43	11 59	10 22	22 45	28	4	

UT	ARIES GHA	VENUS −4.1 GHA	Dec	MARS +1.6 GHA	Dec	JUPITER −2.1 GHA	Dec	SATURN +0.7 GHA	Dec
d 4 00	343 16.8	143 27.6	S 8 41.3	216 16.5	N20 09.0	237 32.4	N22 31.8	127 29.5	S11 51.6
01	358 19.2	158 27.4	42.5	231 17.3	08.7	252 34.4	31.8	142 31.7	51.7
02	13 21.7	173 27.1	43.7	246 18.1	08.3	267 36.4	31.7	157 34.0	51.8
03	28 24.2	188 26.9	.. 45.0	261 19.0	.. 08.0	282 38.4	.. 31.7	172 36.3	.. 51.9
04	43 26.6	203 26.7	46.2	276 19.8	07.6	297 40.4	31.6	187 38.5	51.9
05	58 29.1	218 26.5	47.4	291 20.6	07.2	312 42.4	31.6	202 40.8	52.0
W 06	73 31.6	233 26.3	S 8 48.7	306 21.4	N20 06.9	327 44.4	N22 31.6	217 43.1	S11 52.1
E 07	88 34.0	248 26.1	49.9	321 22.2	06.5	342 46.4	31.5	232 45.3	52.2
D 08	103 36.5	263 25.9	51.1	336 23.0	06.2	357 48.5	31.5	247 47.6	52.2
N 09	118 38.9	278 25.7	.. 52.4	351 23.9	.. 05.8	12 50.5	.. 31.4	262 49.8	.. 52.3
E 10	133 41.4	293 25.5	53.6	6 24.7	05.4	27 52.5	31.4	277 52.1	52.4
S 11	148 43.9	308 25.2	54.8	21 25.5	05.1	42 54.5	31.4	292 54.4	52.5
D 12	163 46.3	323 25.0	S 8 56.1	36 26.3	N20 04.7	57 56.5	N22 31.3	307 56.6	S11 52.5
A 13	178 48.8	338 24.8	57.3	51 27.1	04.4	72 58.5	31.3	322 58.9	52.6
Y 14	193 51.3	353 24.6	58.5	66 28.0	04.0	88 00.5	31.2	338 01.2	52.7
15	208 53.7	8 24.4	8 59.8	81 28.8	.. 03.6	103 02.5	.. 31.2	353 03.4	.. 52.8
16	223 56.2	23 24.2	9 01.0	96 29.6	03.3	118 04.6	31.1	8 05.7	52.8
17	238 58.7	38 24.0	02.2	111 30.4	02.9	133 06.6	31.1	23 07.9	52.9
18	254 01.1	53 23.8	S 9 03.5	126 31.2	N20 02.6	148 08.6	N22 31.1	38 10.2	S11 53.0
19	269 03.6	68 23.5	04.7	141 32.0	02.2	163 10.6	31.0	53 12.5	53.1
20	284 06.1	83 23.3	05.9	156 32.9	01.8	178 12.6	31.0	68 14.7	53.1
21	299 08.5	98 23.1	.. 07.2	171 33.7	.. 01.5	193 14.6	.. 30.9	83 17.0	.. 53.2
22	314 11.0	113 22.9	08.4	186 34.5	01.1	208 16.7	30.9	98 19.3	53.3
23	329 13.4	128 22.7	09.6	201 35.3	00.7	223 18.7	30.9	113 21.5	53.4
5 00	344 15.9	143 22.5	S 9 10.9	216 36.2	N20 00.4	238 20.7	N22 30.8	128 23.8	S11 53.4
01	359 18.4	158 22.3	12.1	231 37.0	20 00.0	253 22.7	30.8	143 26.0	53.5
02	14 20.8	173 22.1	13.3	246 37.8	19 59.7	268 24.7	30.7	158 28.3	53.6
03	29 23.3	188 21.8	.. 14.6	261 38.6	.. 59.3	283 26.7	.. 30.7	173 30.6	.. 53.7
04	44 25.8	203 21.6	15.8	276 39.4	58.9	298 28.7	30.6	188 32.8	53.8
05	59 28.2	218 21.4	17.0	291 40.3	58.6	313 30.8	30.6	203 35.1	53.8
T 06	74 30.7	233 21.2	S 9 18.2	306 41.1	N19 58.2	328 32.8	N22 30.6	218 37.3	S11 53.9
H 07	89 33.2	248 21.0	19.5	321 41.9	57.8	343 34.8	30.5	233 39.6	54.0
U 08	104 35.6	263 20.8	20.7	336 42.7	57.5	358 36.8	30.5	248 41.9	54.1
R 09	119 38.1	278 20.5	.. 21.9	351 43.5	.. 57.1	13 38.8	.. 30.4	263 44.1	.. 54.1
S 10	134 40.5	293 20.3	23.1	6 44.4	56.7	28 40.9	30.4	278 46.4	54.2
D 11	149 43.0	308 20.1	24.4	21 45.2	56.4	43 42.9	30.4	293 48.7	54.3
A 12	164 45.5	323 19.9	S 9 25.6	36 46.0	N19 56.0	58 44.9	N22 30.3	308 50.9	S11 54.4
Y 13	179 47.9	338 19.7	26.8	51 46.8	55.6	73 46.9	30.3	323 53.2	54.4
14	194 50.4	353 19.5	28.1	66 47.7	55.3	88 48.9	30.2	338 55.4	54.5
15	209 52.9	8 19.3	.. 29.3	81 48.5	.. 54.9	103 50.9	.. 30.2	353 57.7	.. 54.6
16	224 55.3	23 19.0	30.5	96 49.3	54.5	118 53.0	30.1	9 00.0	54.7
17	239 57.8	38 18.8	31.7	111 50.1	54.2	133 55.0	30.1	24 02.2	54.7
18	255 00.3	53 18.6	S 9 33.0	126 51.0	N19 53.8	148 57.0	N22 30.1	39 04.5	S11 54.8
19	270 02.7	68 18.4	34.2	141 51.8	53.4	163 59.0	30.0	54 06.7	54.9
20	285 05.2	83 18.2	35.4	156 52.6	53.1	179 01.0	30.0	69 09.0	55.0
21	300 07.7	98 18.0	.. 36.6	171 53.4	.. 52.7	194 03.1	.. 29.9	84 11.2	.. 55.1
22	315 10.1	113 17.7	37.8	186 54.3	52.3	209 05.1	29.9	99 13.5	55.1
23	330 12.6	128 17.5	39.1	201 55.1	52.0	224 07.1	29.9	114 15.8	55.2
6 00	345 15.0	143 17.3	S 9 40.3	216 55.9	N19 51.6	239 09.1	N22 29.8	129 18.0	S11 55.3
01	0 17.5	158 17.1	41.5	231 56.7	51.2	254 11.1	29.8	144 20.3	55.4
02	15 20.0	173 16.9	42.7	246 57.6	50.9	269 13.2	29.7	159 22.5	55.4
03	30 22.4	188 16.6	.. 44.0	261 58.4	.. 50.5	284 15.2	.. 29.7	174 24.8	.. 55.5
04	45 24.9	203 16.4	45.2	276 59.2	50.1	299 17.2	29.6	189 27.1	55.6
05	60 27.4	218 16.2	46.4	292 00.1	49.8	314 19.2	29.6	204 29.3	55.7
F 06	75 29.8	233 16.0	S 9 47.6	307 00.9	N19 49.4	329 21.2	N22 29.6	219 31.6	S11 55.7
R 07	90 32.3	248 15.8	48.8	322 01.7	49.0	344 23.3	29.5	234 33.8	55.8
I 08	105 34.8	263 15.6	50.1	337 02.5	48.7	359 25.3	29.5	249 36.1	55.9
D 09	120 37.2	278 15.3	.. 51.3	352 03.4	.. 48.3	14 27.3	.. 29.4	264 38.4	.. 56.0
A 10	135 39.7	293 15.1	52.5	7 04.2	47.9	29 29.3	29.4	279 40.6	56.1
Y 11	150 42.1	308 14.9	53.7	22 05.0	47.5	44 31.4	29.4	294 42.9	56.1
12	165 44.6	323 14.7	S 9 54.9	37 05.8	N19 47.2	59 33.4	N22 29.3	309 45.1	S11 56.2
13	180 47.1	338 14.5	56.2	52 06.7	46.8	74 35.4	29.3	324 47.4	56.3
14	195 49.5	353 14.2	57.4	67 07.5	46.4	89 37.4	29.2	339 49.6	56.4
15	210 52.0	8 14.0	.. 58.6	82 08.3	.. 46.1	104 39.5	.. 29.2	354 51.9	.. 56.4
16	225 54.5	23 13.8	9 59.8	97 09.2	45.7	119 41.5	29.1	9 54.2	56.5
17	240 56.9	38 13.6	10 01.0	112 10.0	45.3	134 43.5	29.1	24 56.4	56.6
18	255 59.4	53 13.4	S10 02.2	127 10.8	N19 44.9	149 45.5	N22 29.1	39 58.7	S11 56.7
19	271 01.9	68 13.1	03.5	142 11.7	44.6	164 47.5	29.0	55 00.9	56.7
20	286 04.3	83 12.9	04.7	157 12.5	44.2	179 49.6	29.0	70 03.2	56.8
21	301 06.8	98 12.7	.. 05.9	172 13.3	.. 43.8	194 51.6	.. 28.9	85 05.4	.. 56.9
22	316 09.3	113 12.5	07.1	187 14.1	43.5	209 53.6	28.9	100 07.7	57.0
23	331 11.7	128 12.2	08.3	202 15.0	43.1	224 55.6	28.9	115 10.0	57.1
Mer.Pass.	h m 1 02.8	v −0.2	d 1.2	v 0.8	d 0.4	v 2.0	d 0.0	v 2.3	d 0.1

STARS

Name	SHA	Dec
Acamar	315 18.0	S40 14.8
Achernar	335 26.3	S57 09.8
Acrux	173 09.6	S63 10.6
Adhara	255 12.6	S28 59.4
Aldebaran	290 49.2	N16 32.1
Alioth	166 21.1	N55 53.3
Alkaid	152 59.1	N49 14.9
Al Na'ir	27 43.1	S46 53.5
Alnilam	275 46.3	S 1 11.6
Alphard	217 56.2	S 8 43.1
Alphecca	126 11.0	N26 40.4
Alpheratz	357 43.0	N29 10.1
Altair	62 07.8	N 8 54.6
Ankaa	353 15.2	S42 13.7
Antares	112 26.1	S26 27.6
Arcturus	145 55.8	N19 06.9
Atria	107 27.7	S69 03.2
Avior	234 18.4	S59 33.1
Bellatrix	278 31.9	N 6 21.7
Betelgeuse	271 01.2	N 7 24.5
Canopus	263 56.3	S52 42.0
Capella	280 34.2	N46 00.4
Deneb	49 31.0	N45 20.1
Denebola	182 33.8	N14 29.8
Diphda	348 55.4	S17 54.5
Dubhe	193 52.2	N61 40.6
Elnath	278 12.5	N28 36.9
Eltanin	90 45.9	N51 29.7
Enif	33 46.6	N 9 56.6
Fomalhaut	15 23.4	S29 32.7
Gacrux	172 01.2	S57 11.5
Gienah	175 52.4	S17 37.1
Hadar	148 48.0	S60 26.5
Hamal	328 00.3	N23 31.6
Kaus Aust.	83 43.4	S34 22.6
Kochab	137 20.7	N74 06.3
Markab	13 37.8	N15 17.0
Menkar	314 14.7	N 4 08.6
Menkent	148 07.6	S36 26.2
Miaplacidus	221 40.4	S69 46.4
Mirfak	308 39.9	N49 54.4
Nunki	75 57.9	S26 16.6
Peacock	53 18.5	S56 41.4
Pollux	243 27.8	N27 59.4
Procyon	244 59.8	N 5 11.3
Rasalhague	96 06.2	N12 33.4
Regulus	207 43.7	N11 54.0
Rigel	281 11.9	S 8 11.1
Rigil Kent.	139 51.8	S60 53.6
Sabik	102 12.3	S15 44.3
Schedar	349 39.8	N56 36.7
Shaula	96 21.6	S37 06.7
Sirius	258 33.7	S16 44.1
Spica	158 31.3	S11 13.9
Suhail	222 52.7	S43 29.2
Vega	80 38.7	N38 48.2
Zuben'ubi	137 05.4	S16 05.8

	SHA	Mer.Pass.
		h m
Venus	159 06.6	14 27
Mars	232 20.2	9 33
Jupiter	254 04.8	8 06
Saturn	144 07.9	15 24

SUN and MOON

UT	SUN GHA	SUN Dec	MOON GHA	MOON v	MOON Dec	MOON d	MOON HP
d h	° ′	° ′	° ′	′	° ′	′	′
4 00	180 13.3	N 7 11.9	198 11.6	13.7	N 8 45.0	9.5	55.2
01	195 13.5	11.0	212 44.3	13.7	8 35.5	9.5	55.2
02	210 13.8	10.1	227 17.0	13.7	8 26.0	9.6	55.2
03	225 14.0	.. 09.2	241 49.7	13.6	8 16.4	9.6	55.2
04	240 14.2	08.2	256 22.3	13.7	8 06.8	9.6	55.3
05	255 14.4	07.3	270 55.0	13.7	7 57.2	9.7	55.3
06	270 14.6	N 7 06.4	285 27.7	13.7	N 7 47.5	9.7	55.3
W 07	285 14.8	05.5	300 00.4	13.7	7 37.8	9.8	55.3
E 08	300 15.0	04.5	314 33.1	13.7	7 28.0	9.8	55.3
D 09	315 15.2	.. 03.6	329 05.8	13.7	7 18.2	9.9	55.4
N 10	330 15.4	02.7	343 38.5	13.7	7 08.3	9.9	55.4
E 11	345 15.6	01.8	358 11.2	13.6	6 58.4	9.9	55.4
S 12	0 15.8	N 7 00.8	12 43.8	13.7	N 6 48.5	9.9	55.4
D 13	15 16.0	6 59.9	27 16.5	13.7	6 38.6	10.0	55.4
A 14	30 16.2	59.0	41 49.2	13.7	6 28.6	10.1	55.5
Y 15	45 16.4	.. 58.1	56 21.9	13.7	6 18.5	10.1	55.5
16	60 16.6	57.1	70 54.6	13.6	6 08.4	10.1	55.5
17	75 16.8	56.2	85 27.2	13.7	5 58.3	10.1	55.5
18	90 17.1	N 6 55.3	99 59.9	13.7	N 5 48.2	10.2	55.5
19	105 17.3	54.4	114 32.6	13.6	5 38.0	10.2	55.6
20	120 17.5	53.4	129 05.2	13.7	5 27.8	10.2	55.6
21	135 17.7	.. 52.5	143 37.9	13.7	5 17.6	10.3	55.6
22	150 17.9	51.6	158 10.6	13.6	5 07.3	10.3	55.6
23	165 18.1	50.7	172 43.2	13.6	4 57.0	10.3	55.6
5 00	180 18.3	N 6 49.7	187 15.8	13.7	N 4 46.7	10.4	55.7
01	195 18.5	48.8	201 48.5	13.6	4 36.3	10.4	55.7
02	210 18.7	47.9	216 21.1	13.6	4 25.9	10.4	55.7
03	225 18.9	.. 47.0	230 53.7	13.6	4 15.5	10.4	55.7
04	240 19.1	46.0	245 26.3	13.6	4 05.1	10.5	55.7
05	255 19.3	45.1	259 58.9	13.6	3 54.6	10.5	55.8
06	270 19.6	N 6 44.2	274 31.5	13.6	N 3 44.1	10.5	55.8
07	285 19.8	43.2	289 04.1	13.5	3 33.6	10.5	55.8
T 08	300 20.0	42.3	303 36.6	13.6	3 23.1	10.6	55.8
H 09	315 20.2	.. 41.4	318 09.2	13.5	3 12.5	10.6	55.8
U 10	330 20.4	40.5	332 41.7	13.5	3 01.9	10.6	55.9
R 11	345 20.6	39.5	347 14.2	13.5	2 51.3	10.6	55.9
S 12	0 20.8	N 6 38.6	1 46.7	13.5	N 2 40.7	10.7	55.9
D 13	15 21.0	37.7	16 19.2	13.5	2 30.0	10.7	55.9
A 14	30 21.2	36.7	30 51.7	13.5	2 19.4	10.7	55.9
Y 15	45 21.4	.. 35.8	45 24.2	13.4	2 08.7	10.7	56.0
16	60 21.6	34.9	59 56.6	13.5	1 58.0	10.7	56.0
17	75 21.8	34.0	74 29.1	13.4	1 47.3	10.8	56.0
18	90 22.1	N 6 33.0	89 01.5	13.4	N 1 36.5	10.7	56.0
19	105 22.3	32.1	103 33.9	13.4	1 25.8	10.8	56.0
20	120 22.5	31.2	118 06.3	13.4	1 15.0	10.8	56.1
21	135 22.7	.. 30.2	132 38.7	13.3	1 04.2	10.8	56.1
22	150 22.9	29.3	147 11.0	13.3	0 53.4	10.8	56.1
23	165 23.1	28.4	161 43.3	13.3	0 42.6	10.8	56.1
6 00	180 23.3	N 6 27.4	176 15.6	13.3	N 0 31.8	10.8	56.2
01	195 23.5	26.5	190 47.9	13.3	0 21.0	10.8	56.2
02	210 23.7	25.6	205 20.2	13.2	N 0 10.2	10.9	56.2
03	225 23.9	.. 24.7	219 52.4	13.3	S 0 00.7	10.8	56.2
04	240 24.2	23.7	234 24.7	13.2	0 11.5	10.9	56.2
05	255 24.4	22.8	248 56.9	13.1	0 22.4	10.8	56.3
06	270 24.6	N 6 21.9	263 29.0	13.2	S 0 33.2	10.9	56.3
07	285 24.8	20.9	278 01.2	13.1	0 44.1	10.9	56.3
08	300 25.0	20.0	292 33.3	13.1	0 55.0	10.9	56.3
F 09	315 25.2	.. 19.1	307 05.4	13.1	1 05.8	10.9	56.3
R 10	330 25.4	18.1	321 37.5	13.1	1 16.7	10.9	56.4
I 11	345 25.6	17.2	336 09.6	13.0	1 27.6	10.9	56.4
D 12	0 25.8	N 6 16.3	350 41.6	13.0	S 1 38.5	10.8	56.4
A 13	15 26.1	15.3	5 13.6	12.9	1 49.3	10.9	56.4
Y 14	30 26.3	14.4	19 45.5	13.0	2 00.2	10.9	56.5
15	45 26.5	.. 13.5	34 17.5	12.9	2 11.1	10.9	56.5
16	60 26.7	12.5	48 49.4	12.9	2 22.0	10.8	56.5
17	75 26.9	11.6	63 21.3	12.8	2 32.8	10.9	56.5
18	90 27.1	N 6 10.7	77 53.1	12.8	S 2 43.7	10.8	56.5
19	105 27.3	09.7	92 24.9	12.8	2 54.5	10.9	56.6
20	120 27.5	08.8	106 56.7	12.8	3 05.4	10.8	56.6
21	135 27.7	.. 07.9	121 28.5	12.7	3 16.2	10.9	56.6
22	150 28.0	06.9	136 00.2	12.7	3 27.1	10.8	56.6
23	165 28.2	06.0	150 31.9	12.6	S 3 37.9	10.8	56.6
	SD 15.9	d 0.9	SD 15.1		15.2		15.4

Twilight, Sunrise and Moonrise

Lat.	Twilight Naut.	Twilight Civil	Sunrise	Moonrise 4	Moonrise 5	Moonrise 6	Moonrise 7
°	h m	h m	h m	h m	h m	h m	h m
N 72	////	02 59	04 21	03 08	04 52	06 37	08 24
N 70	01 18	03 21	04 32	03 21	04 58	06 36	08 16
68	02 04	03 38	04 41	03 31	05 02	06 35	08 09
66	02 33	03 52	04 48	03 40	05 06	06 34	08 04
64	02 54	04 03	04 55	03 47	05 09	06 34	07 59
62	03 11	04 12	05 00	03 53	05 12	06 33	07 56
60	03 24	04 21	05 05	03 58	05 15	06 33	07 52
N 58	03 35	04 27	05 09	04 03	05 17	06 32	07 49
56	03 45	04 33	05 12	04 07	05 18	06 32	07 46
54	03 54	04 39	05 15	04 10	05 20	06 31	07 44
52	04 01	04 43	05 18	04 14	05 22	06 31	07 42
50	04 07	04 48	05 21	04 17	05 23	06 31	07 40
45	04 21	04 57	05 27	04 23	05 26	06 30	07 36
N 40	04 31	05 04	05 32	04 29	05 29	06 30	07 32
35	04 40	05 10	05 36	04 33	05 31	06 29	07 29
30	04 46	05 15	05 39	04 37	05 33	06 29	07 26
20	04 57	05 23	05 45	04 45	05 36	06 28	07 22
N 10	05 05	05 29	05 51	04 51	05 39	06 28	07 18
0	05 10	05 35	05 55	04 57	05 42	06 27	07 14
S 10	05 14	05 39	06 00	05 02	05 45	06 27	07 10
20	05 17	05 43	06 05	05 09	05 47	06 26	07 06
30	05 19	05 46	06 10	05 16	05 51	06 26	07 02
35	05 19	05 48	06 14	05 20	05 53	06 26	06 59
40	05 19	05 50	06 17	05 24	05 55	06 25	06 57
45	05 18	05 52	06 21	05 30	05 57	06 25	06 53
S 50	05 16	05 53	06 26	05 36	06 00	06 25	06 49
52	05 15	05 54	06 28	05 39	06 02	06 24	06 48
54	05 14	05 55	06 30	05 42	06 03	06 24	06 46
56	05 13	05 56	06 33	05 46	06 05	06 24	06 43
58	05 11	05 57	06 36	05 49	06 07	06 24	06 41
S 60	05 09	05 57	06 39	05 54	06 09	06 23	06 38

Sunset, Twilight and Moonset

Lat.	Sunset	Twilight Civil	Twilight Naut.	Moonset 4	Moonset 5	Moonset 6	Moonset 7
°	h m	h m	h m	h m	h m	h m	h m
N 72	19 33	20 53	////	18 31	18 22	18 13	18 04
N 70	19 22	20 32	22 28	18 24	18 20	18 17	18 14
68	19 14	20 16	21 47	18 17	18 19	18 20	18 22
66	19 07	20 03	21 20	18 12	18 17	18 23	18 29
64	19 01	19 52	21 00	18 07	18 16	18 25	18 35
62	18 56	19 43	20 44	18 03	18 15	18 27	18 40
60	18 51	19 35	20 31	18 00	18 14	18 29	18 45
N 58	18 47	19 28	20 20	17 57	18 14	18 30	18 48
56	18 44	19 22	20 10	17 54	18 13	18 32	18 52
54	18 41	19 17	20 02	17 51	18 12	18 33	18 55
52	18 38	19 13	19 49	17 49	18 12	18 34	18 58
50	18 35	19 08	19 49	17 47	18 11	18 35	19 01
45	18 30	19 00	19 35	17 42	18 10	18 38	19 07
N 40	18 25	18 53	19 25	17 39	18 09	18 40	19 11
35	18 21	18 47	19 17	17 35	18 08	18 41	19 16
30	18 18	18 42	19 10	17 32	18 07	18 43	19 19
20	18 12	18 34	19 00	17 27	18 06	18 45	19 26
N 10	18 07	18 28	18 52	17 23	18 05	18 47	19 32
0	18 02	18 23	18 47	17 18	18 04	18 50	19 37
S 10	17 57	18 18	18 43	17 14	18 02	18 52	19 42
20	17 53	18 13	18 43	17 09	18 01	18 54	19 48
30	17 47	18 11	18 39	17 04	18 00	18 56	19 54
35	17 44	18 10	18 39	17 01	17 59	18 58	19 58
40	17 41	18 08	18 40	16 57	17 58	19 00	20 02
45	17 37	18 06	18 40	16 53	17 57	19 01	20 07
S 50	17 32	18 05	18 42	16 48	17 55	19 04	20 13
52	17 30	18 04	18 43	16 46	17 55	19 05	20 16
54	17 28	18 03	18 44	16 44	17 54	19 06	20 19
56	17 25	18 03	18 46	16 41	17 53	19 07	20 22
58	17 23	18 02	18 47	16 38	17 52	19 09	20 26
S 60	17 19	18 01	18 49	16 34	17 51	19 10	20 30

SUN and MOON

Day	SUN Eqn. of Time 00h	SUN Eqn. of Time 12h	SUN Mer. Pass.	MOON Mer. Pass. Upper	MOON Mer. Pass. Lower	Age	Phase
d	m s	m s	h m	h m	h m	d	%
4	00 53	01 03	11 59	11 07	23 30	29	1
5	01 13	01 23	11 59	11 53	24 15	00	0
6	01 33	01 43	11 58	12 38	00 15	01	1

UT	ARIES	VENUS −4.1		MARS +1.6		JUPITER −2.1		SATURN +0.7		STARS		
	GHA	GHA	Dec	GHA	Dec	GHA	Dec	GHA	Dec	Name	SHA	Dec
d h	° ′	° ′	° ′	° ′	° ′	° ′	° ′	° ′	° ′		° ′	° ′
7 00	346 14.2	143 12.0	S10 09.5	217 15.8	N19 42.7	239 57.7	N22 28.8	130 12.2	S11 57.1	Acamar	315 18.0	S40 14.8
01	1 16.6	158 11.8	10.8	232 16.6	42.3	254 59.7	28.8	145 14.5	57.2	Achernar	335 26.2	S57 09.8
02	16 19.1	173 11.6	12.0	247 17.5	42.0	270 01.7	28.7	160 16.7	57.3	Acrux	173 09.7	S63 10.6
03	31 21.6	188 11.4 . .	13.2	262 18.3 . .	41.6	285 03.8 . .	28.7	175 19.0 . .	57.4	Adhara	255 12.6	S28 59.4
04	46 24.0	203 11.1	14.4	277 19.1	41.2	300 05.8	28.6	190 21.2	57.4	Aldebaran	290 49.1	N16 32.1
05	61 26.5	218 10.9	15.6	292 20.0	40.8	315 07.8	28.6	205 23.5	57.5			
06	76 29.0	233 10.7	S10 16.8	307 20.8	N19 40.5	330 09.8	N22 28.6	220 25.7	S11 57.6	Alioth	166 21.1	N55 53.3
07	91 31.4	248 10.5	18.0	322 21.6	40.1	345 11.9	28.5	235 28.0	57.7	Alkaid	152 59.2	N49 14.9
S 08	106 33.9	263 10.2	19.2	337 22.5	39.7	0 13.9	28.5	250 30.3	57.8	Al Na'ir	27 43.1	S46 53.5
A 09	121 36.4	278 10.0 . .	20.5	352 23.3 . .	39.3	15 15.9 . .	28.4	265 32.5 . .	57.8	Alnilam	275 46.2	S 1 11.6
T 10	136 38.8	293 09.8	21.7	7 24.1	39.0	30 17.9	28.4	280 34.8	57.9	Alphard	217 56.2	S 8 43.1
U 11	151 41.3	308 09.6	22.9	22 25.0	38.6	45 20.0	28.4	295 37.0	58.0			
R 12	166 43.7	323 09.3	S10 24.1	37 25.8	N19 38.2	60 22.0	N22 28.3	310 39.3	S11 58.1	Alphecca	126 11.0	N26 40.4
D 13	181 46.2	338 09.1	25.3	52 26.6	37.8	75 24.0	28.3	325 41.5	58.1	Alpheratz	357 42.9	N29 10.1
A 14	196 48.7	353 08.9	26.5	67 27.5	37.5	90 26.1	28.2	340 43.8	58.2	Altair	62 07.9	N 8 54.6
Y 15	211 51.1	8 08.7 . .	27.7	82 28.3 . .	37.1	105 28.1 . .	28.2	355 46.0 . .	58.3	Ankaa	353 15.2	S42 13.7
16	226 53.6	23 08.4	28.9	97 29.1	36.7	120 30.1	28.1	10 48.3	58.4	Antares	112 26.1	S26 27.6
17	241 56.1	38 08.2	30.1	112 30.0	36.3	135 32.1	28.1	25 50.5	58.5			
18	256 58.5	53 08.0	S10 31.3	127 30.8	N19 36.0	150 34.2	N22 28.1	40 52.8	S11 58.5	Arcturus	145 55.8	N19 06.9
19	272 01.0	68 07.8	32.5	142 31.6	35.6	165 36.2	28.0	55 55.1	58.6	Atria	107 27.7	S69 03.2
20	287 03.5	83 07.5	33.8	157 32.5	35.2	180 38.2	28.0	70 57.3	58.7	Avior	234 18.4	S59 33.1
21	302 05.9	98 07.3 . .	35.0	172 33.3 . .	34.8	195 40.3 . .	27.9	85 59.6 . .	58.8	Bellatrix	278 31.9	N 6 21.7
22	317 08.4	113 07.1	36.2	187 34.1	34.4	210 42.3	27.9	101 01.8	58.8	Betelgeuse	271 01.2	N 7 24.5
23	332 10.9	128 06.9	37.4	202 35.0	34.1	225 44.3	27.9	116 04.1	58.9			
8 00	347 13.3	143 06.6	S10 38.6	217 35.8	N19 33.7	240 46.3	N22 27.8	131 06.3	S11 59.0	Canopus	263 56.2	S52 42.0
01	2 15.8	158 06.4	39.8	232 36.7	33.3	255 48.4	27.8	146 08.6	59.1	Capella	280 34.2	N46 00.4
02	17 18.2	173 06.2	41.0	247 37.5	32.9	270 50.4	27.7	161 10.8	59.2	Deneb	49 31.0	N45 20.1
03	32 20.7	188 06.0 . .	42.2	262 38.3 . .	32.5	285 52.4 . .	27.7	176 13.1 . .	59.2	Denebola	182 33.8	N14 29.8
04	47 23.2	203 05.7	43.4	277 39.2	32.2	300 54.5	27.6	191 15.3	59.3	Diphda	348 55.4	S17 54.5
05	62 25.6	218 05.5	44.6	292 40.0	31.8	315 56.5	27.6	206 17.6	59.4			
06	77 28.1	233 05.3	S10 45.8	307 40.8	N19 31.4	330 58.5	N22 27.6	221 19.8	S11 59.5	Dubhe	193 52.2	N61 40.6
07	92 30.6	248 05.0	47.0	322 41.7	31.0	346 00.6	27.5	236 22.1	59.6	Elnath	278 12.4	N28 36.9
08	107 33.0	263 04.8	48.2	337 42.5	30.7	1 02.6	27.5	251 24.4	59.6	Eltanin	90 45.9	N51 29.7
S 09	122 35.5	278 04.6 . .	49.4	352 43.4 . .	30.3	16 04.6 . .	27.4	266 26.6 . .	59.7	Enif	33 46.6	N 9 56.6
U 10	137 38.0	293 04.4	50.6	7 44.2	29.9	31 06.7	27.4	281 28.9	59.8	Fomalhaut	15 23.4	S29 32.8
N 11	152 40.4	308 04.1	51.8	22 45.0	29.5	46 08.7	27.4	296 31.1	59.9			
D 12	167 42.9	323 03.9	S10 53.0	37 45.9	N19 29.1	61 10.7	N22 27.3	311 33.4	S11 59.9	Gacrux	172 01.2	S57 11.5
A 13	182 45.3	338 03.7	54.2	52 46.7	28.7	76 12.8	27.3	326 35.6	12 00.0	Gienah	175 52.4	S17 37.0
Y 14	197 47.8	353 03.4	55.4	67 47.6	28.4	91 14.8	27.2	341 37.9	00.1	Hadar	148 48.0	S60 26.4
15	212 50.3	8 03.2 . .	56.6	82 48.4 . .	28.0	106 16.8 . .	27.2	356 40.1 . .	00.2	Hamal	328 00.3	N23 31.6
16	227 52.7	23 03.0	57.8	97 49.2	27.6	121 18.9	27.1	11 42.4	00.3	Kaus Aust.	83 43.4	S34 22.6
17	242 55.2	38 02.7	10 59.0	112 50.1	27.2	136 20.9	27.1	26 44.6	00.3			
18	257 57.7	53 02.5	S11 00.2	127 50.9	N19 26.8	151 22.9	N22 27.1	41 46.9	S12 00.4	Kochab	137 20.7	N74 06.3
19	273 00.1	68 02.3	01.4	142 51.8	26.5	166 25.0	27.0	56 49.1	00.5	Markab	13 37.8	N15 17.0
20	288 02.6	83 02.1	02.6	157 52.6	26.1	181 27.0	27.0	71 51.4	00.6	Menkar	314 14.7	N 4 08.6
21	303 05.1	98 01.8 . .	03.8	172 53.4 . .	25.7	196 29.0 . .	26.9	86 53.6 . .	00.7	Menkent	148 07.6	S36 26.2
22	318 07.5	113 01.6	05.0	187 54.3	25.3	211 31.1	26.9	101 55.9	00.7	Miaplacidus	221 40.4	S69 46.4
23	333 10.0	128 01.4	06.2	202 55.1	24.9	226 33.1	26.9	116 58.1	00.8			
9 00	348 12.5	143 01.1	S11 07.4	217 56.0	N19 24.5	241 35.1	N22 26.8	132 00.4	S12 00.9	Mirfak	308 39.9	N49 54.4
01	3 14.9	158 00.9	08.6	232 56.8	24.2	256 37.2	26.8	147 02.6	01.0	Nunki	75 57.9	S26 16.6
02	18 17.4	173 00.7	09.8	247 57.6	23.8	271 39.2	26.7	162 04.9	01.0	Peacock	53 18.6	S56 41.4
03	33 19.8	188 00.4 . .	11.0	262 58.5 . .	23.4	286 41.2 . .	26.7	177 07.1 . .	01.1	Pollux	243 27.8	N27 59.4
04	48 22.3	203 00.2	12.2	277 59.3	23.0	301 43.3	26.6	192 09.4	01.2	Procyon	244 59.8	N 5 11.3
05	63 24.8	218 00.0	13.4	293 00.2	22.6	316 45.3	26.6	207 11.6	01.3			
06	78 27.2	232 59.7	S11 14.6	308 01.0	N19 22.2	331 47.4	N22 26.6	222 13.9	S12 01.4	Rasalhague	96 06.2	N12 33.4
07	93 29.7	247 59.5	15.8	323 01.9	21.9	346 49.4	26.5	237 16.1	01.4	Regulus	207 43.7	N11 54.0
08	108 32.2	262 59.3	17.0	338 02.7	21.5	1 51.4	26.5	252 18.4	01.5	Rigel	281 11.9	S 8 11.1
M 09	123 34.6	277 59.0 . .	18.2	353 03.5 . .	21.1	16 53.5 . .	26.4	267 20.6 . .	01.6	Rigil Kent.	139 51.8	S60 53.6
O 10	138 37.1	292 58.8	19.4	8 04.4	20.7	31 55.5	26.4	282 22.9	01.7	Sabik	102 12.3	S15 44.3
N 11	153 39.6	307 58.6	20.6	23 05.2	20.3	46 57.5	26.4	297 25.1	01.8			
D 12	168 42.0	322 58.3	S11 21.7	38 06.1	N19 19.9	61 59.6	N22 26.3	312 27.4	S12 01.8	Schedar	349 39.7	N56 36.8
A 13	183 44.5	337 58.1	22.9	53 06.9	19.5	77 01.6	26.3	327 29.6	01.9	Shaula	96 21.6	S37 06.7
Y 14	198 47.0	352 57.9	24.1	68 07.8	19.2	92 03.7	26.2	342 31.9	02.0	Sirius	258 33.7	S16 44.1
15	213 49.4	7 57.6 . .	25.3	83 08.6 . .	18.8	107 05.7 . .	26.2	357 34.1 . .	02.1	Spica	158 31.3	S11 13.9
16	228 51.9	22 57.4	26.5	98 09.5	18.4	122 07.7	26.1	12 36.4	02.2	Suhail	222 52.7	S43 29.2
17	243 54.3	37 57.2	27.7	113 10.3	18.0	137 09.8	26.1	27 38.6	02.2			
18	258 56.8	52 56.9	S11 28.9	128 11.1	N19 17.6	152 11.8	N22 26.1	42 40.9	S12 02.3	Vega	80 38.7	N38 48.2
19	273 59.3	67 56.7	30.1	143 12.0	17.2	167 13.9	26.0	57 43.1	02.4	Zuben'ubi	137 05.4	S16 05.8
20	289 01.7	82 56.5	31.3	158 12.8	16.8	182 15.9	26.0	72 45.4	02.5		SHA	Mer.Pass.
21	304 04.2	97 56.2 . .	32.5	173 13.7 . .	16.4	197 17.9 . .	25.9	87 47.6 . .	02.6		° ′	h m
22	319 06.7	112 56.0	33.7	188 14.5	16.1	212 20.0	25.9	102 49.9	02.6	Venus	155 53.3	14 28
23	334 09.1	127 55.7	34.8	203 15.4	15.7	227 22.0	25.9	117 52.1	02.7	Mars	230 22.5	9 29
	h m									Jupiter	253 33.0	7 56
Mer.Pass. 0 51.0		v −0.2	d 1.2	v 0.8	d 0.4	v 2.0	d 0.0	v 2.3	d 0.1	Saturn	143 53.0	15 13

UT	SUN GHA	SUN Dec	MOON GHA	v	MOON Dec	d	HP
d h	° ′	° ′	° ′	′	° ′	′	′
7 00	180 28.4	N 6 05.0	165 03.5	12.7	S 3 48.7	10.8	56.7
01	195 28.6	04.1	179 35.2	12.5	3 59.5	10.8	56.7
02	210 28.8	03.2	194 06.7	12.6	4 10.3	10.8	56.7
03	225 29.0	.. 02.2	208 38.3	12.5	4 21.1	10.7	56.7
04	240 29.2	01.3	223 09.8	12.5	4 31.8	10.8	56.7
05	255 29.4	6 00.4	237 41.3	12.4	4 42.6	10.7	56.8
06	270 29.7	N 5 59.4	252 12.7	12.4	S 4 53.3	10.7	56.8
07	285 29.9	58.5	266 44.1	12.4	5 04.0	10.7	56.8
S 08	300 30.1	57.6	281 15.5	12.3	5 14.7	10.7	56.8
A 09	315 30.3	.. 56.6	295 46.8	12.3	5 25.4	10.7	56.9
T 10	330 30.5	55.7	310 18.1	12.2	5 36.1	10.6	56.9
U 11	345 30.7	54.7	324 49.3	12.2	5 46.7	10.6	56.9
R 12	0 30.9	N 5 53.8	339 20.5	12.2	S 5 57.3	10.6	56.9
D 13	15 31.2	52.9	353 51.7	12.1	6 07.9	10.6	56.9
A 14	30 31.4	51.9	8 22.8	12.1	6 18.5	10.6	57.0
Y 15	45 31.6	.. 51.0	22 53.9	12.0	6 29.1	10.5	57.0
16	60 31.8	50.1	37 24.9	12.0	6 39.6	10.5	57.0
17	75 32.0	49.1	51 55.9	11.9	6 50.1	10.5	57.0
18	90 32.2	N 5 48.2	66 26.8	11.9	S 7 00.5	10.5	57.0
19	105 32.4	47.2	80 57.7	11.9	7 11.0	10.4	57.1
20	120 32.6	46.3	95 28.6	11.8	7 21.4	10.4	57.1
21	135 32.9	.. 45.4	109 59.4	11.8	7 31.8	10.3	57.1
22	150 33.1	44.4	124 30.2	11.7	7 42.1	10.3	57.1
23	165 33.3	43.5	139 00.9	11.6	7 52.4	10.3	57.1
8 00	180 33.5	N 5 42.5	153 31.5	11.7	S 8 02.7	10.3	57.2
01	195 33.7	41.6	168 02.2	11.5	8 13.0	10.2	57.2
02	210 33.9	40.7	182 32.7	11.6	8 23.2	10.2	57.2
03	225 34.1	.. 39.7	197 03.3	11.4	8 33.4	10.1	57.2
04	240 34.4	38.8	211 33.7	11.5	8 43.5	10.1	57.2
05	255 34.6	37.8	226 04.2	11.3	8 53.6	10.1	57.3
06	270 34.8	N 5 36.9	240 34.5	11.4	S 9 03.7	10.0	57.3
07	285 35.0	36.0	255 04.9	11.2	9 13.7	10.0	57.3
S 08	300 35.2	35.0	269 35.1	11.3	9 23.7	9.9	57.3
U 09	315 35.4	34.1	284 05.4	11.1	9 33.6	9.9	57.3
N 10	330 35.6	33.1	298 35.5	11.2	9 43.5	9.8	57.4
11	345 35.9	32.2	313 05.7	11.0	9 53.3	9.9	57.4
D 12	0 36.1	N 5 31.3	327 35.7	11.0	S10 03.2	9.7	57.4
A 13	15 36.3	30.3	342 05.7	11.0	10 12.9	9.7	57.4
Y 14	30 36.5	29.4	356 35.7	10.9	10 22.6	9.7	57.4
15	45 36.7	.. 28.4	11 05.6	10.9	10 32.3	9.6	57.5
16	60 36.9	27.5	25 35.5	10.7	10 41.9	9.5	57.5
17	75 37.2	26.6	40 05.2	10.8	10 51.4	9.5	57.5
18	90 37.4	N 5 25.6	54 35.0	10.7	S11 00.9	9.5	57.5
19	105 37.6	24.7	69 04.7	10.6	11 10.4	9.4	57.5
20	120 37.8	23.7	83 34.3	10.6	11 19.8	9.3	57.6
21	135 38.0	.. 22.8	98 03.9	10.5	11 29.1	9.3	57.6
22	150 38.2	21.8	112 33.4	10.5	11 38.4	9.3	57.6
23	165 38.4	20.9	127 02.9	10.4	11 47.7	9.1	57.6
9 00	180 38.7	N 5 20.0	141 32.3	10.3	S11 56.8	9.2	57.6
01	195 38.9	19.0	156 01.6	10.3	12 06.0	9.0	57.7
02	210 39.1	18.1	170 30.9	10.2	12 15.0	9.0	57.7
03	225 39.3	.. 17.1	185 00.1	10.2	12 24.0	8.9	57.7
04	240 39.5	16.2	199 29.3	10.1	12 32.9	8.9	57.7
05	255 39.7	15.2	213 58.4	10.1	12 41.8	8.8	57.7
06	270 40.0	N 5 14.3	228 27.5	10.0	S12 50.6	8.7	57.8
07	285 40.2	13.3	242 56.5	9.9	12 59.3	8.7	57.8
M 08	300 40.4	12.4	257 25.4	9.9	13 08.0	8.6	57.8
O 09	315 40.6	.. 11.5	271 54.3	9.8	13 16.6	8.5	57.8
N 10	330 40.8	10.5	286 23.1	9.8	13 25.1	8.5	57.8
11	345 41.0	09.6	300 51.9	9.7	13 33.6	8.4	57.9
D 12	0 41.3	N 5 08.6	315 20.6	9.7	S13 42.0	8.3	57.9
A 13	15 41.5	07.7	329 49.3	9.5	13 50.3	8.3	57.9
Y 14	30 41.7	06.7	344 17.8	9.6	13 58.6	8.1	57.9
15	45 41.9	.. 05.8	358 46.4	9.4	14 06.7	8.1	57.9
16	60 42.1	04.8	13 14.8	9.4	14 14.8	8.1	58.0
17	75 42.3	03.9	27 43.2	9.4	14 22.9	7.9	58.0
18	90 42.6	N 5 02.9	42 11.6	9.3	S14 30.8	7.9	58.0
19	105 42.8	02.0	56 39.9	9.2	14 38.7	7.8	58.0
20	120 43.0	01.1	71 08.1	9.2	14 46.5	7.7	58.0
21	135 43.2	5 00.1	85 36.3	9.1	14 54.2	7.6	58.0
22	150 43.4	4 59.2	100 04.4	9.0	15 01.8	7.5	58.1
23	165 43.7	N 4 58.2	114 32.4	9.0	S15 09.3	7.5	58.1
	SD 15.9	d 0.9	SD 15.5		15.6		15.8

Moonrise

Lat.	Twilight Naut.	Twilight Civil	Sunrise	7	8	9	10
°	h m	h m	h m	h m	h m	h m	h m
N 72	00 40	03 17	04 35	08 24	10 16	12 17	14 40
N 70	01 49	03 36	04 45	08 16	10 00	11 48	13 42
68	02 24	03 51	04 52	08 09	09 47	11 27	13 08
66	02 48	04 03	04 58	08 04	09 36	11 10	12 43
64	03 06	04 13	05 03	07 59	09 27	10 56	12 24
62	03 21	04 21	05 08	07 56	09 20	10 45	12 09
60	03 33	04 28	05 12	07 52	09 13	10 35	11 56
N 58	03 44	04 34	05 15	07 49	09 08	10 27	11 45
56	03 52	04 40	05 18	07 46	09 03	10 19	11 35
54	04 00	04 44	05 21	07 44	08 58	10 13	11 27
52	04 07	04 49	05 23	07 42	08 54	10 07	11 19
50	04 13	04 52	05 25	07 40	08 50	10 02	11 12
45	04 25	05 00	05 30	07 36	08 42	09 50	10 58
N 40	04 34	05 07	05 34	07 32	08 36	09 41	10 46
35	04 42	05 12	05 38	07 29	08 30	09 32	10 35
30	04 48	05 17	05 41	07 26	08 25	09 25	10 27
20	04 58	05 24	05 46	07 22	08 17	09 13	10 11
N 10	05 05	05 29	05 50	07 18	08 09	09 03	09 58
0	05 09	05 34	05 54	07 14	08 02	08 53	09 46
S 10	05 13	05 37	05 58	07 10	07 55	08 43	09 33
20	05 15	05 40	06 02	07 06	07 48	08 32	09 20
30	05 15	05 43	06 07	07 02	07 40	08 21	09 05
35	05 15	05 44	06 09	06 59	07 35	08 14	08 57
40	05 14	05 45	06 12	06 57	07 30	08 06	08 47
45	05 12	05 46	06 15	06 53	07 24	07 57	08 35
S 50	05 10	05 47	06 19	06 49	07 16	07 46	08 22
52	05 08	05 47	06 21	06 48	07 13	07 41	08 15
54	05 07	05 48	06 23	06 46	07 09	07 36	08 08
56	05 05	05 48	06 25	06 43	07 05	07 30	08 00
58	05 03	05 48	06 27	06 41	07 00	07 23	07 51
S 60	05 00	05 49	06 30	06 38	06 55	07 15	07 41

Moonset

Lat.	Sunset	Twilight Civil	Twilight Naut.	7	8	9	10
°	h m	h m	h m	h m	h m	h m	h m
N 72	19 17	20 34	22 56	18 04	17 52	17 37	17 06
N 70	19 08	20 19	21 59	18 14	18 10	18 08	18 05
68	19 01	20 01	21 26	18 22	18 25	18 30	18 40
66	18 55	19 50	21 03	18 29	18 37	18 48	19 05
64	18 50	19 40	20 46	18 35	18 47	19 02	19 25
62	18 46	19 32	20 31	18 40	18 55	19 14	19 41
60	18 42	19 25	20 20	18 45	19 03	19 25	19 54
N 58	18 39	19 19	20 10	18 48	19 09	19 34	20 06
56	18 36	19 14	20 01	18 52	19 15	19 42	20 16
54	18 33	19 09	19 54	18 55	19 20	19 49	20 24
52	18 31	19 05	19 47	18 58	19 25	19 55	20 32
50	18 29	19 02	19 41	19 01	19 29	20 01	20 40
45	18 24	18 54	19 29	19 07	19 38	20 14	20 55
N 40	18 20	18 48	19 20	19 11	19 46	20 24	21 08
35	18 17	18 42	19 12	19 16	19 53	20 33	21 18
30	18 14	18 38	19 06	19 19	19 58	20 41	21 28
20	18 09	18 31	18 57	19 26	20 09	20 55	21 44
N 10	18 05	18 26	18 50	19 32	20 18	21 06	21 58
0	18 01	18 22	18 46	19 37	20 26	21 18	22 12
S 10	17 57	18 18	18 43	19 42	20 34	21 29	22 25
20	17 53	18 15	18 40	19 48	20 44	21 41	22 39
30	17 49	18 13	18 40	19 54	20 54	21 54	22 56
35	17 46	18 12	18 41	19 58	21 00	22 02	23 05
40	17 44	18 11	18 42	20 02	21 07	22 13	23 16
45	17 40	18 10	18 44	20 07	21 15	22 22	23 29
S 50	17 37	18 09	18 46	20 13	21 24	22 35	23 45
52	17 35	18 09	18 48	20 16	21 28	22 41	23 52
54	17 33	18 09	18 49	20 19	21 33	22 48	24 00
56	17 31	18 08	18 51	20 22	21 39	22 55	24 09
58	17 29	18 08	18 53	20 26	21 45	23 04	24 24
S 60	17 26	18 08	18 56	20 30	21 52	23 13	24 32

	SUN Eqn. of Time 00h	SUN Eqn. of Time 12h	SUN Mer. Pass.	MOON Mer. Pass. Upper	MOON Mer. Pass. Lower	Age	Phase
Day	m s	m s	h m	h m	h m	d	%
7	01 53	02 03	11 58	13 25	01 02	02	4
8	02 14	02 24	11 58	14 14	01 49	03	10
9	02 34	02 45	11 57	15 05	02 39	04	17

UT	ARIES GHA	VENUS −4.1 GHA	Dec	MARS +1.6 GHA	Dec	JUPITER −2.1 GHA	Dec	SATURN +0.7 GHA	Dec	STARS Name	SHA	Dec
10 00	349 11.6	142 55.5	S11 36.0	218 16.2	N19 15.3	242 24.1	N22 25.8	132 54.4	S12 02.8	Acamar	315 18.0	S40 14.8
01	4 14.1	157 55.3	37.2	233 17.1	14.9	257 26.1	25.8	147 56.6	02.9	Achernar	335 26.2	S57 09.8
02	19 16.5	172 55.0	38.4	248 17.9	14.5	272 28.1	25.7	162 58.9	02.9	Acrux	173 09.7	S63 10.6
03	34 19.0	187 54.8	.. 39.6	263 18.8	.. 14.1	287 30.2	.. 25.7	178 01.1	.. 03.0	Adhara	255 12.5	S28 59.4
04	49 21.4	202 54.6	40.8	278 19.6	13.7	302 32.2	25.6	193 03.4	03.1	Aldebaran	290 49.1	N16 32.1
05	64 23.9	217 54.3	42.0	293 20.5	13.3	317 34.3	25.6	208 05.6	03.2			
06	79 26.4	232 54.1	S11 43.1	308 21.3	N19 13.0	332 36.3	N22 25.6	223 07.9	S12 03.3	Alioth	166 21.1	N55 53.3
07	94 28.8	247 53.8	44.3	323 22.2	12.6	347 38.3	25.5	238 10.1	03.3	Alkaid	152 59.2	N49 14.9
T 08	109 31.3	262 53.6	45.5	338 23.0	12.2	2 40.4	25.5	253 12.4	03.4	Al Na'ir	27 43.1	S46 53.5
U 09	124 33.8	277 53.4	.. 46.7	353 23.9	.. 11.8	17 42.4	.. 25.4	268 14.6	.. 03.5	Alnilam	275 46.2	S 1 11.6
E 10	139 36.2	292 53.1	47.9	8 24.7	11.4	32 44.5	25.4	283 16.9	03.6	Alphard	217 56.2	S 8 43.1
S 11	154 38.7	307 52.9	49.1	23 25.5	11.0	47 46.5	25.4	298 19.1	03.7			
D 12	169 41.2	322 52.7	S11 50.2	38 26.4	N19 10.6	62 48.6	N22 25.3	313 21.4	S12 03.7	Alphecca	126 11.0	N26 40.4
A 13	184 43.6	337 52.4	51.4	53 27.2	10.2	77 50.6	25.3	328 23.6	03.8	Alpheratz	357 42.9	N29 10.1
Y 14	199 46.1	352 52.2	52.6	68 28.1	09.8	92 52.6	25.2	343 25.8	03.9	Altair	62 07.9	N 8 54.6
15	214 48.6	7 51.9	.. 53.8	83 28.9	.. 09.4	107 54.7	.. 25.2	358 28.1	.. 04.0	Ankaa	353 15.1	S42 13.7
16	229 51.0	22 51.7	55.0	98 29.8	09.0	122 56.7	25.2	13 30.3	04.1	Antares	112 26.1	S26 27.6
17	244 53.5	37 51.5	56.1	113 30.6	08.7	137 58.8	25.1	28 32.6	04.1			
18	259 55.9	52 51.2	S11 57.3	128 31.5	N19 08.3	153 00.8	N22 25.1	43 34.8	S12 04.2	Arcturus	145 55.8	N19 06.9
19	274 58.4	67 51.0	58.5	143 32.4	07.9	168 02.9	25.0	58 37.1	04.3	Atria	107 27.8	S69 03.2
20	290 00.9	82 50.7	11 59.7	158 33.2	07.5	183 04.9	25.0	73 39.3	04.4	Avior	234 18.4	S59 33.1
21	305 03.3	97 50.5	12 00.9	173 34.1	.. 07.1	198 07.0	.. 24.9	88 41.6	.. 04.5	Bellatrix	278 31.8	N 6 21.7
22	320 05.8	112 50.3	02.0	188 34.9	06.7	213 09.0	24.9	103 43.8	04.5	Betelgeuse	271 01.2	N 7 24.5
23	335 08.3	127 50.0	03.2	203 35.8	06.3	228 11.0	24.9	118 46.1	04.6			
11 00	350 10.7	142 49.8	S12 04.4	218 36.6	N19 05.9	243 13.1	N22 24.8	133 48.3	S12 04.7	Canopus	263 56.2	S52 42.0
01	5 13.2	157 49.5	05.6	233 37.5	05.5	258 15.1	24.8	148 50.6	04.8	Capella	280 34.2	N46 00.4
02	20 15.7	172 49.3	06.8	248 38.3	05.1	273 17.2	24.7	163 52.8	04.9	Deneb	49 31.0	N45 20.2
03	35 18.1	187 49.0	.. 07.9	263 39.2	.. 04.7	288 19.2	.. 24.7	178 55.0	.. 04.9	Denebola	182 33.8	N14 29.8
04	50 20.6	202 48.8	09.1	278 40.0	04.3	303 21.3	24.7	193 57.3	05.0	Diphda	348 55.4	S17 54.5
05	65 23.1	217 48.6	10.3	293 40.9	03.9	318 23.3	24.6	208 59.5	05.1			
06	80 25.5	232 48.3	S12 11.5	308 41.7	N19 03.5	333 25.4	N22 24.6	224 01.8	S12 05.2	Dubhe	193 52.2	N61 40.6
W 07	95 28.0	247 48.1	12.6	323 42.6	03.2	348 27.4	24.5	239 04.0	05.3	Elnath	278 12.4	N28 36.9
E 08	110 30.4	262 47.8	13.8	338 43.4	02.8	3 29.5	24.5	254 06.3	05.3	Eltanin	90 46.0	N51 29.7
D 09	125 32.9	277 47.6	.. 15.0	353 44.3	.. 02.4	18 31.5	.. 24.4	269 08.5	.. 05.4	Enif	33 46.6	N 9 56.6
N 10	140 35.4	292 47.3	16.2	8 45.1	02.0	33 33.6	24.4	284 10.8	05.5	Fomalhaut	15 23.4	S29 32.8
E 11	155 37.8	307 47.1	17.3	23 46.0	01.6	48 35.6	24.4	299 13.0	05.6			
S 12	170 40.3	322 46.8	S12 18.5	38 46.8	N19 01.2	63 37.7	N22 24.3	314 15.3	S12 05.7	Gacrux	172 01.2	S57 11.5
D 13	185 42.8	337 46.6	19.7	53 47.7	00.8	78 39.7	24.3	329 17.5	05.8	Gienah	175 52.4	S17 37.0
A 14	200 45.2	352 46.4	20.8	68 48.6	00.4	93 41.8	24.2	344 19.7	05.8	Hadar	148 48.0	S60 26.4
Y 15	215 47.7	7 46.1	.. 22.0	83 49.4	19 00.0	108 43.8	.. 24.2	359 22.0	.. 05.9	Hamal	328 00.3	N23 31.6
16	230 50.2	22 45.9	23.2	98 50.3	18 59.6	123 45.9	24.2	14 24.2	06.0	Kaus Aust.	83 43.5	S34 22.6
17	245 52.6	37 45.6	24.4	113 51.1	59.2	138 47.9	24.1	29 26.5	06.1			
18	260 55.1	52 45.4	S12 25.5	128 52.0	N18 58.8	153 50.0	N22 24.1	44 28.7	S12 06.2	Kochab	137 20.8	N74 06.3
19	275 57.5	67 45.1	26.7	143 52.8	58.4	168 52.0	24.0	59 31.0	06.2	Markab	13 37.8	N15 17.0
20	291 00.0	82 44.9	27.9	158 53.7	58.0	183 54.1	24.0	74 33.2	06.3	Menkar	314 14.7	N 4 08.7
21	306 02.5	97 44.6	.. 29.0	173 54.5	.. 57.6	198 56.1	.. 24.0	89 35.5	.. 06.4	Menkent	148 07.6	S36 26.2
22	321 04.9	112 44.4	30.2	188 55.4	57.2	213 58.2	23.9	104 37.7	06.5	Miaplacidus	221 40.3	S69 46.4
23	336 07.4	127 44.1	31.4	203 56.3	56.8	229 00.2	23.9	119 39.9	06.6			
12 00	351 09.9	142 43.9	S12 32.5	218 57.1	N18 56.4	244 02.3	N22 23.8	134 42.2	S12 06.6	Mirfak	308 39.8	N49 54.4
01	6 12.3	157 43.6	33.7	233 58.0	56.0	259 04.3	23.8	149 44.4	06.7	Nunki	75 57.9	S26 16.6
02	21 14.8	172 43.4	34.9	248 58.8	55.6	274 06.4	23.7	164 46.7	06.8	Peacock	53 18.6	S56 41.4
03	36 17.3	187 43.1	.. 36.1	263 59.7	.. 55.2	289 08.4	.. 23.7	179 48.9	.. 06.9	Pollux	243 27.7	N27 59.4
04	51 19.7	202 42.9	37.2	279 00.6	54.8	304 10.5	23.7	194 51.2	07.0	Procyon	244 59.7	N 5 11.3
05	66 22.2	217 42.7	38.4	294 01.4	54.4	319 12.5	23.6	209 53.4	07.0			
06	81 24.7	232 42.4	S12 39.5	309 02.3	N18 54.0	334 14.6	N22 23.6	224 55.6	S12 07.1	Rasalhague	96 06.3	N12 33.4
07	96 27.1	247 42.2	40.7	324 03.1	53.6	349 16.6	23.5	239 57.9	07.2	Regulus	207 43.6	N11 54.0
T 08	111 29.6	262 41.9	41.9	339 04.0	53.2	4 18.7	23.5	255 00.1	07.3	Rigel	281 11.9	S 8 11.1
H 09	126 32.0	277 41.7	.. 43.0	354 04.8	.. 52.8	19 20.7	.. 23.5	270 02.4	.. 07.4	Rigil Kent.	139 51.8	S60 53.6
U 10	141 34.5	292 41.4	44.2	9 05.7	52.4	34 22.8	23.4	285 04.6	07.4	Sabik	102 12.3	S15 44.3
R 11	156 37.0	307 41.2	45.3	24 06.6	52.0	49 24.8	23.4	300 06.9	07.5			
S 12	171 39.4	322 40.9	S12 46.5	39 07.4	N18 51.6	64 26.9	N22 23.3	315 09.1	S12 07.6	Schedar	349 39.7	N56 36.8
D 13	186 41.9	337 40.7	47.7	54 08.3	51.2	79 28.9	23.3	330 11.3	07.7	Shaula	96 21.6	S37 06.7
A 14	201 44.4	352 40.4	48.8	69 09.1	50.8	94 31.0	23.3	345 13.6	07.8	Sirius	258 33.7	S16 44.1
Y 15	216 46.8	7 40.2	.. 50.0	84 10.0	.. 50.4	109 33.1	.. 23.2	0 15.8	.. 07.9	Spica	158 31.3	S11 13.9
16	231 49.3	22 39.9	51.1	99 10.9	50.0	124 35.1	23.2	15 18.1	07.9	Suhail	222 52.7	S43 29.2
17	246 51.8	37 39.6	52.3	114 11.7	49.6	139 37.2	23.1	30 20.3	08.0			
18	261 54.2	52 39.4	S12 53.5	129 12.6	N18 49.2	154 39.2	N22 23.1	45 22.5	S12 08.1	Vega	80 38.7	N38 48.2
19	276 56.7	67 39.1	54.6	144 13.4	48.8	169 41.3	23.1	60 24.8	08.2	Zuben'ubi	137 05.4	S16 05.8
20	291 59.2	82 38.9	55.8	159 14.3	48.4	184 43.3	23.0	75 27.0	08.3		SHA	Mer. Pass.
21	307 01.6	97 38.6	.. 56.9	174 15.2	.. 48.0	199 45.4	.. 23.0	90 29.3	.. 08.3	Venus	152 39.0	14 29
22	322 04.1	112 38.4	58.1	189 16.0	47.6	214 47.4	22.9	105 31.5	08.4	Mars	228 25.9	9 25
23	337 06.5	127 38.1	59.3	204 16.9	47.2	229 49.5	22.9	120 33.8	08.5	Jupiter	253 02.4	7 46
Mer. Pass.	0 39.2	v −0.2	d 1.2	v 0.9	d 0.4	v 2.0	d 0.0	v 2.2	d 0.1	Saturn	143 37.6	15 03

UT	SUN GHA	Dec	MOON GHA	v	Dec	d	HP
d h	° ′	° ′	° ′	′	° ′	′	′
10 00	180 43.9	N 4 57.3	129 00.4	8.9	S15 16.8	7.4	58.1
01	195 44.1	56.3	143 28.3	8.9	15 24.2	7.3	58.1
02	210 44.3	55.4	157 56.2	8.8	15 31.5	7.2	58.1
03	225 44.5 ..	54.4	172 24.0	8.7	15 38.7	7.1	58.2
04	240 44.7	53.5	186 51.7	8.7	15 45.8	7.0	58.2
05	255 45.0	52.5	201 19.4	8.6	15 52.8	7.0	58.2
06	270 45.2	N 4 51.6	215 47.0	8.6	S15 59.8	6.8	58.2
07	285 45.4	50.6	230 14.6	8.5	16 06.6	6.8	58.2
T 08	300 45.6	49.7	244 42.1	8.5	16 13.4	6.7	58.2
U 09	315 45.8 ..	48.7	259 09.6	8.4	16 20.1	6.5	58.3
E 10	330 46.0	47.8	273 37.0	8.3	16 26.6	6.5	58.3
S 11	345 46.3	46.8	288 04.3	8.3	16 33.1	6.4	58.3
D 12	0 46.5	N 4 45.9	302 31.6	8.2	S16 39.5	6.3	58.3
A 13	15 46.7	44.9	316 58.8	8.1	16 45.8	6.2	58.3
Y 14	30 46.9	44.0	331 25.9	8.1	16 52.0	6.1	58.4
15	45 47.1 ..	43.0	345 53.0	8.1	16 58.1	6.0	58.4
16	60 47.4	42.1	0 20.1	8.0	17 04.1	5.9	58.4
17	75 47.6	41.2	14 47.1	7.9	17 10.0	5.8	58.4
18	90 47.8	N 4 40.2	29 14.0	7.9	S17 15.8	5.7	58.4
19	105 48.0	39.3	43 40.9	7.8	17 21.5	5.6	58.4
20	120 48.2	38.3	58 07.7	7.7	17 27.1	5.5	58.5
21	135 48.5 ..	37.4	72 34.4	7.8	17 32.6	5.4	58.5
22	150 48.7	36.4	87 01.2	7.6	17 38.0	5.3	58.5
23	165 48.9	35.5	101 27.8	7.6	17 43.3	5.1	58.5
11 00	180 49.1	N 4 34.5	115 54.4	7.6	S17 48.4	5.1	58.5
01	195 49.3	33.6	130 21.0	7.5	17 53.5	5.0	58.5
02	210 49.6	32.6	144 47.5	7.4	17 58.5	4.8	58.6
03	225 49.8 ..	31.7	159 13.9	7.4	18 03.3	4.8	58.6
04	240 50.0	30.7	173 40.3	7.3	18 08.1	4.6	58.6
05	255 50.2	29.7	188 06.6	7.3	18 12.7	4.5	58.6
06	270 50.4	N 4 28.8	202 32.9	7.3	S18 17.2	4.4	58.6
W 07	285 50.6	27.8	216 59.2	7.2	18 21.6	4.4	58.6
E 08	300 50.9	26.9	231 25.4	7.1	18 26.0	4.1	58.7
D 09	315 51.1 ..	25.9	245 51.5	7.1	18 30.1	4.1	58.7
N 10	330 51.3	25.0	260 17.6	7.0	18 34.2	4.0	58.7
E 11	345 51.5	24.0	274 43.6	7.0	18 38.2	3.8	58.7
S 12	0 51.7	N 4 23.1	289 09.6	7.0	S18 42.0	3.8	58.7
D 13	15 52.0	22.1	303 35.6	6.9	18 45.8	3.6	58.7
A 14	30 52.2	21.2	318 01.5	6.9	18 49.4	3.5	58.8
Y 15	45 52.4 ..	20.2	332 27.4	6.8	18 52.9	3.3	58.8
16	60 52.6	19.3	346 53.2	6.8	18 56.2	3.3	58.8
17	75 52.8	18.3	1 19.0	6.7	18 59.5	3.2	58.8
18	90 53.1	N 4 17.4	15 44.7	6.7	S19 02.7	3.0	58.8
19	105 53.3	16.4	30 10.4	6.7	19 05.7	2.9	58.8
20	120 53.5	15.5	44 36.1	6.6	19 08.6	2.8	58.8
21	135 53.7 ..	14.5	59 01.7	6.6	19 11.4	2.6	58.9
22	150 53.9	13.6	73 27.3	6.5	19 14.0	2.6	58.9
23	165 54.2	12.6	87 52.8	6.5	19 16.6	2.4	58.9
12 00	180 54.4	N 4 11.7	102 18.3	6.5	S19 19.0	2.3	58.9
01	195 54.6	10.7	116 43.8	6.4	19 21.3	2.1	58.9
02	210 54.8	09.8	131 09.2	6.4	19 23.4	2.1	58.9
03	225 55.0 ..	08.8	145 34.6	6.4	19 25.5	1.9	58.9
04	240 55.3	07.8	160 00.0	6.3	19 27.4	1.8	59.0
05	255 55.5	06.9	174 25.3	6.3	19 29.2	1.7	59.0
06	270 55.7	N 4 05.9	188 50.6	6.3	S19 30.9	1.5	59.0
T 07	285 55.9	05.0	203 15.9	6.3	19 32.4	1.4	59.0
H 08	300 56.2	04.0	217 41.2	6.2	19 33.8	1.3	59.0
U 09	315 56.4 ..	03.1	232 06.4	6.2	19 35.1	1.2	59.0
R 10	330 56.6	02.1	246 31.6	6.2	19 36.3	1.0	59.1
S 11	345 56.8	01.2	260 56.8	6.1	19 37.3	0.9	59.1
D 12	0 57.0	N 4 00.2	275 21.9	6.1	S19 38.2	0.8	59.1
A 13	15 57.3	3 59.3	289 47.0	6.1	19 39.0	0.7	59.1
Y 14	30 57.5	58.3	304 12.1	6.1	19 39.7	0.5	59.1
15	45 57.7 ..	57.3	318 37.2	6.0	19 40.2	0.4	59.1
16	60 57.9	56.4	333 02.2	6.1	19 40.6	0.2	59.1
17	75 58.1	55.4	347 27.3	6.0	19 40.8	0.2	59.1
18	90 58.4	N 3 54.5	1 52.3	6.0	S19 41.0	0.0	59.2
19	105 58.6	53.5	16 17.3	6.0	19 41.0	0.1	59.2
20	120 58.8	52.6	30 42.3	5.9	19 40.9	0.3	59.2
21	135 59.0 ..	51.6	45 07.2	6.0	19 40.6	0.4	59.2
22	150 59.3	50.7	59 32.2	5.9	19 40.2	0.5	59.2
23	165 59.5	49.7	73 57.1	6.0	S19 39.7	0.6	59.2
	SD 15.9	d 1.0	SD 15.9		16.0		16.1

Lat.	Twilight Naut.	Civil	Sunrise	Moonrise 10	11	12	13
°	h m	h m	h m	h m	h m	h m	h m
N 72	01 29	03 34	04 49	14 40	■■	■■	■■
N 70	02 13	03 50	04 57	13 42	15 38	17 20	17 43
68	02 41	04 03	05 03	13 08	14 44	16 01	16 46
66	03 02	04 14	05 08	12 43	14 11	15 23	16 12
64	03 18	04 22	05 12	12 24	13 47	14 56	15 48
62	03 31	04 29	05 15	12 09	13 28	14 35	15 28
60	03 42	04 36	05 19	11 56	13 12	14 18	15 12
N 58	03 51	04 41	05 21	11 45	12 59	14 04	14 59
56	03 59	04 46	05 24	11 35	12 47	13 52	14 47
54	04 06	04 50	05 26	11 27	12 37	13 42	14 37
52	04 12	04 54	05 28	11 19	12 28	13 32	14 28
50	04 18	04 57	05 30	11 12	12 20	13 24	14 20
45	04 29	05 04	05 34	10 58	12 04	13 06	14 02
N 40	04 38	05 10	05 37	10 46	11 50	12 51	13 48
35	04 44	05 14	05 40	10 35	11 38	12 39	13 36
30	04 50	05 18	05 42	10 27	11 28	12 28	13 25
20	04 59	05 24	05 47	10 11	11 10	12 09	13 07
N 10	05 04	05 29	05 50	09 58	10 55	11 53	12 51
0	05 09	05 33	05 53	09 46	10 41	11 38	12 37
S 10	05 11	05 35	05 56	09 33	10 27	11 23	12 22
20	05 12	05 38	06 00	09 20	10 12	11 07	12 06
30	05 12	05 39	06 03	09 05	09 55	10 49	11 48
35	05 11	05 40	06 05	08 57	09 45	10 38	11 38
40	05 09	05 40	06 07	08 47	09 33	10 26	11 26
45	05 07	05 41	06 10	08 35	09 20	10 12	11 11
S 50	05 03	05 41	06 13	08 22	09 04	09 54	10 54
52	05 02	05 41	06 14	08 15	08 56	09 46	10 46
54	05 00	05 40	06 16	08 08	08 48	09 37	10 37
56	04 57	05 40	06 17	08 00	08 38	09 27	10 26
58	04 55	05 40	06 19	07 51	08 27	09 15	10 15
S 60	04 51	05 40	06 21	07 41	08 15	09 01	10 01

Lat.	Sunset	Twilight Civil	Naut.	Moonset 10	11	12	13
°	h m	h m	h m	h m	h m	h m	h m
N 72	19 01	20 15	22 14	17 06	■■	■■	■■
N 70	18 54	19 59	21 34	18 05	18 05	18 24	20 04
68	18 48	19 47	21 07	18 40	19 00	19 44	21 00
66	18 44	19 37	20 48	19 05	19 34	20 22	21 33
64	18 39	19 29	20 32	19 25	19 58	20 48	21 58
62	18 36	19 22	20 19	19 41	20 17	21 09	22 17
60	18 33	19 16	20 09	19 54	20 33	21 26	22 33
N 58	18 30	19 10	20 00	20 06	20 47	21 40	22 46
56	18 28	19 06	19 52	20 16	20 58	21 52	22 58
54	18 26	19 02	19 45	20 24	21 08	22 03	23 08
52	18 24	18 58	19 39	20 32	21 18	22 12	23 17
50	18 22	18 55	19 34	20 40	21 26	22 21	23 25
45	18 18	18 48	19 23	20 55	21 43	22 39	23 42
N 40	18 15	18 43	19 15	21 08	21 57	22 53	23 55
35	18 13	18 38	19 08	21 18	22 09	23 06	24 07
30	18 10	18 34	19 02	21 28	22 20	23 16	24 17
20	18 06	18 28	18 54	21 44	22 38	23 35	24 35
N 10	18 03	18 24	18 48	21 58	22 53	23 51	24 50
0	18 00	18 21	18 45	22 12	23 08	24 06	00 06
S 10	17 57	18 18	18 42	22 25	23 23	24 21	00 21
20	17 54	18 16	18 41	22 39	23 39	24 37	00 37
30	17 50	18 14	18 42	22 56	23 57	24 55	00 55
35	17 49	18 14	18 43	23 05	24 07	00 07	01 06
40	17 46	18 13	18 45	23 16	24 19	00 19	01 18
45	17 44	18 13	18 47	23 29	24 33	00 33	01 33
S 50	17 41	18 13	18 51	23 45	24 51	00 51	01 50
52	17 40	18 14	18 53	23 52	24 59	00 59	01 59
54	17 38	18 14	18 55	24 00	00 00	01 08	02 08
56	17 37	18 14	18 57	24 09	00 09	01 18	02 18
58	17 35	18 14	19 00	24 20	00 20	01 30	02 30
S 60	17 33	18 15	19 03	24 32	00 32	01 43	02 44

Day	SUN Eqn. of Time 00h	12h	Mer. Pass.	MOON Mer. Pass. Upper	Lower	Age	Phase
d	m s	m s	h m	h m	h m	d %	
10	02 55	03 06	11 57	15 59	03 32	05 26	
11	03 16	03 27	11 57	16 55	04 26	06 37	
12	03 37	03 48	11 56	17 52	05 23	07 48	

UT	ARIES GHA	VENUS −4.1 GHA	VENUS Dec	MARS +1.6 GHA	MARS Dec	JUPITER −2.1 GHA	JUPITER Dec	SATURN +0.7 GHA	SATURN Dec	STARS Name	SHA	Dec
d h	° ′	° ′	° ′	° ′	° ′	° ′	° ′	° ′	° ′		° ′	° ′
13 00	352 09.0	142 37.9	S13 00.4	219 17.8	N18 46.8	244 51.6	N22 22.8	135 36.0	S12 08.6	Acamar	315 18.0	S40 14.8
01	7 11.5	157 37.6	01.6	234 18.6	46.8	259 53.6	22.8	150 38.2	08.7	Achernar	335 26.2	S57 09.8
02	22 13.9	172 37.4	02.7	249 19.5	46.0	274 55.7	22.8	165 40.5	08.7	Acrux	173 09.7	S63 10.6
03	37 16.4	187 37.1 ..	03.9	264 20.3 ..	45.6	289 57.7 ..	22.7	180 42.7 ..	08.8	Adhara	255 12.5	S28 59.4
04	52 18.9	202 36.9	05.0	279 21.2	45.2	304 59.8	22.7	195 45.0	08.9	Aldebaran	290 49.1	N16 32.1
05	67 21.3	217 36.6	06.2	294 22.1	44.8	320 01.8	22.6	210 47.2	09.0			
06	82 23.8	232 36.4	S13 07.3	309 22.9	N18 44.4	335 03.9	N22 22.6	225 49.4	S12 09.1	Alioth	166 21.1	N55 53.3
07	97 26.3	247 36.1	08.5	324 23.8	44.0	350 06.0	22.6	240 51.7	09.2	Alkaid	152 59.2	N49 14.9
08	112 28.7	262 35.8	09.6	339 24.7	43.6	5 08.0	22.5	255 53.9	09.2	Al Na'ir	27 43.1	S46 53.5
F 09	127 31.2	277 35.6 ..	10.8	354 25.5 ..	43.2	20 10.1 ..	22.5	270 56.2 ..	09.3	Alnilam	275 46.2	S 1 11.6
R 10	142 33.7	292 35.3	11.9	9 26.4	42.8	35 12.1	22.4	285 58.4	09.4	Alphard	217 56.2	S 8 43.1
I 11	157 36.1	307 35.1	13.1	24 27.3	42.4	50 14.2	22.4	301 00.6	09.5			
D 12	172 38.6	322 34.8	S13 14.2	39 28.1	N18 42.0	65 16.2	N22 22.4	316 02.9	S12 09.6	Alphecca	126 11.0	N26 40.4
A 13	187 41.0	337 34.6	15.4	54 29.0	41.6	80 18.3	22.3	331 05.1	09.6	Alpheratz	357 42.9	N29 10.1
Y 14	202 43.5	352 34.3	16.5	69 29.9	41.2	95 20.4	22.3	346 07.4	09.7	Altair	62 07.9	N 8 54.6
15	217 46.0	7 34.1 ..	17.7	84 30.7 ..	40.8	110 22.4 ..	22.2	1 09.6 ..	09.8	Ankaa	353 15.1	S42 13.7
16	232 48.4	22 33.8	18.8	99 31.6	40.4	125 24.5	22.2	16 11.8	09.9	Antares	112 26.1	S26 27.6
17	247 50.9	37 33.5	20.0	114 32.5	40.0	140 26.5	22.1	31 14.1	10.0			
18	262 53.4	52 33.3	S13 21.1	129 33.3	N18 39.6	155 28.6	N22 22.1	46 16.3	S12 10.1	Arcturus	145 55.8	N19 06.9
19	277 55.8	67 33.0	22.3	144 34.2	39.1	170 30.7	22.1	61 18.6	10.1	Atria	107 27.8	S69 03.2
20	292 58.3	82 32.8	23.4	159 35.1	38.7	185 32.7	22.0	76 20.8	10.2	Avior	234 18.3	S59 33.1
21	308 00.8	97 32.5 ..	24.6	174 35.9 ..	38.3	200 34.8 ..	22.0	91 23.0 ..	10.3	Bellatrix	278 31.8	N 6 21.7
22	323 03.2	112 32.3	25.7	189 36.8	37.9	215 36.8	21.9	106 25.3	10.4	Betelgeuse	271 01.1	N 7 24.5
23	338 05.7	127 32.0	26.9	204 37.7	37.5	230 38.9	21.9	121 27.5	10.5			
14 00	353 08.1	142 31.7	S13 28.0	219 38.5	N18 37.1	245 41.0	N22 21.9	136 29.8	S12 10.5	Canopus	263 56.2	S52 42.0
01	8 10.6	157 31.5	29.2	234 39.4	36.7	260 43.0	21.8	151 32.0	10.6	Capella	280 34.1	N46 00.4
02	23 13.1	172 31.2	30.3	249 40.3	36.3	275 45.1	21.8	166 34.2	10.7	Deneb	49 31.0	N45 20.2
03	38 15.5	187 31.0 ..	31.4	264 41.1 ..	35.9	290 47.2 ..	21.7	181 36.5 ..	10.8	Denebola	182 33.8	N14 29.8
04	53 18.0	202 30.7	32.6	279 42.0	35.5	305 49.2	21.7	196 38.7	10.9	Diphda	348 55.4	S17 54.5
05	68 20.5	217 30.4	33.7	294 42.9	35.1	320 51.3	21.7	211 40.9	11.0			
06	83 22.9	232 30.2	S13 34.9	309 43.7	N18 34.7	335 53.3	N22 21.6	226 43.2	S12 11.0	Dubhe	193 52.2	N61 40.5
07	98 25.4	247 29.9	36.0	324 44.6	34.3	350 55.4	21.6	241 45.4	11.1	Elnath	278 12.4	N28 36.9
S 08	113 27.9	262 29.7	37.2	339 45.5	33.9	5 57.5	21.5	256 47.7	11.2	Eltanin	90 46.0	N51 29.7
A 09	128 30.3	277 29.4 ..	38.3	354 46.3 ..	33.4	20 59.5 ..	21.5	271 49.9 ..	11.3	Enif	33 46.6	N 9 56.6
T 10	143 32.8	292 29.1	39.4	9 47.2	33.0	36 01.6	21.5	286 52.1	11.4	Fomalhaut	15 23.4	S29 32.8
U 11	158 35.3	307 28.9	40.6	24 48.1	32.6	51 03.7	21.4	301 54.4	11.4			
R 12	173 37.7	322 28.6	S13 41.7	39 48.9	N18 32.2	66 05.7	N22 21.4	316 56.6	S12 11.5	Gacrux	172 01.2	S57 11.4
D 13	188 40.2	337 28.3	42.9	54 49.8	31.8	81 07.8	21.3	331 58.8	11.6	Gienah	175 52.4	S17 37.0
A 14	203 42.6	352 28.1	44.0	69 50.7	31.4	96 09.9	21.3	347 01.1	11.7	Hadar	148 48.0	S60 26.4
Y 15	218 45.1	7 27.8 ..	45.1	84 51.6 ..	31.0	111 11.9 ..	21.3	2 03.3 ..	11.8	Hamal	328 00.3	N23 31.6
16	233 47.6	22 27.6	46.3	99 52.4	30.6	126 14.0	21.2	17 05.6	11.9	Kaus Aust.	83 43.5	S34 22.6
17	248 50.0	37 27.3	47.4	114 53.3	30.2	141 16.1	21.2	32 07.8	11.9			
18	263 52.5	52 27.0	S13 48.5	129 54.2	N18 29.8	156 18.1	N22 21.1	47 10.0	S12 12.0	Kochab	137 20.8	N74 06.3
19	278 55.0	67 26.8	49.7	144 55.0	29.3	171 20.2	21.1	62 12.3	12.1	Markab	13 37.8	N15 17.0
20	293 57.4	82 26.5	50.8	159 55.9	28.9	186 22.3	21.0	77 14.5	12.2	Menkar	314 14.7	N 4 08.7
21	308 59.9	97 26.2 ..	51.9	174 56.8 ..	28.5	201 24.3 ..	21.0	92 16.7 ..	12.3	Menkent	148 07.6	S36 26.2
22	324 02.4	112 26.0	53.1	189 57.7	28.1	216 26.4	21.0	107 19.0	12.4	Miaplacidus	221 46.3	S69 46.3
23	339 04.8	127 25.7	54.2	204 58.5	27.7	231 28.5	20.9	122 21.2	12.4			
15 00	354 07.3	142 25.4	S13 55.3	219 59.4	N18 27.3	246 30.5	N22 20.9	137 23.5	S12 12.5	Mirfak	308 39.8	N49 54.4
01	9 09.8	157 25.2	56.5	235 00.3	26.9	261 32.6	20.8	152 25.7	12.6	Nunki	75 58.0	S26 16.6
02	24 12.2	172 24.9	57.6	250 01.2	26.5	276 34.7	20.8	167 27.9	12.7	Peacock	53 18.6	S56 41.4
03	39 14.7	187 24.6 ..	58.7	265 02.0 ..	26.1	291 36.7 ..	20.8	182 30.2 ..	12.8	Pollux	243 27.7	N27 59.4
04	54 17.1	202 24.4	13 59.9	280 02.9	25.6	306 38.8	20.7	197 32.4	12.8	Procyon	244 59.7	N 5 11.3
05	69 19.6	217 24.1	14 01.0	295 03.8	25.2	321 40.9	20.7	212 34.6	12.9			
06	84 22.1	232 23.8	S14 02.1	310 04.6	N18 24.8	336 42.9	N22 20.6	227 36.9	S12 13.0	Rasalhague	96 06.3	N12 33.4
07	99 24.5	247 23.6	03.3	325 05.5	24.4	351 45.0	20.6	242 39.1	13.1	Regulus	207 43.6	N11 54.0
08	114 27.0	262 23.3	04.4	340 06.4	24.0	6 47.1	20.6	257 41.3	13.2	Rigel	281 11.9	S 8 11.1
S 09	129 29.5	277 23.0 ..	05.5	355 07.3 ..	23.6	21 49.1 ..	20.5	272 43.6 ..	13.3	Rigil Kent.	139 51.9	S60 53.6
U 10	144 31.9	292 22.8	06.6	10 08.1	23.2	36 51.2	20.5	287 45.8	13.3	Sabik	102 12.3	S15 44.3
N 11	159 34.4	307 22.5	07.8	25 09.0	22.8	51 53.3	20.4	302 48.0	13.4			
D 12	174 36.9	322 22.2	S14 08.9	40 09.9	N18 22.3	66 55.4	N22 20.4	317 50.3	S12 13.5	Schedar	349 39.7	N56 36.8
A 13	189 39.3	337 22.0	10.0	55 10.8	21.9	81 57.4	20.4	332 52.5	13.6	Shaula	96 21.6	S37 06.7
Y 14	204 41.8	352 21.7	11.2	70 11.6	21.5	96 59.5	20.3	347 54.7	13.7	Sirius	258 33.7	S16 44.1
15	219 44.3	7 21.4 ..	12.3	85 12.5 ..	21.1	112 01.6 ..	20.3	2 57.0 ..	13.8	Spica	158 31.3	S11 13.9
16	234 46.7	22 21.2	13.4	100 13.4	20.7	127 03.6	20.2	17 59.2	13.8	Suhail	222 52.6	S43 29.2
17	249 49.2	37 20.9	14.5	115 14.3	20.3	142 05.7	20.2	33 01.5	13.9			
18	264 51.6	52 20.6	S14 15.6	130 15.2	N18 19.9	157 07.8	N22 20.2	48 03.7	S12 14.0	Vega	80 38.7	N38 48.2
19	279 54.1	67 20.4	16.8	145 16.0	19.4	172 09.8	20.1	63 05.9	14.1	Zuben'ubi	137 05.4	S16 05.8
20	294 56.6	82 20.1	17.9	160 16.9	19.0	187 11.9	20.1	78 08.2	14.2		SHA	Mer. Pass.
21	309 59.0	97 19.8 ..	19.0	175 17.8 ..	18.6	202 14.0 ..	20.0	93 10.4 ..	14.3		° ′	h m
22	325 01.5	112 19.5	20.1	190 18.7	18.2	217 16.1	20.0	108 12.6	14.3	Venus	149 23.6	14 30
23	340 04.0	127 19.3	21.3	205 19.5	17.8	232 18.1	20.0	123 14.9	14.4	Mars	226 30.4	9 21
	h m									Jupiter	252 32.8	7 36
Mer. Pass. 0 27.4		v −0.3	d 1.1	v 0.9	d 0.4	v 2.1	d 0.0	v 2.2	d 0.1	Saturn	143 21.6	14 52

UT	SUN GHA	Dec	MOON GHA	v	Dec	d	HP
d h	° ′	° ′	° ′	′	° ′	′	′
13 00	180 59.7	N 3 48.7	88 22.1	5.9	S19 39.1	0.8	59.2
01	195 59.9	47.8	102 47.0	5.9	19 38.3	0.9	59.2
02	211 00.1	46.8	117 11.9	5.9	19 37.4	1.0	59.3
03	226 00.4	.. 45.9	131 36.8	5.9	19 36.4	1.2	59.3
04	241 00.6	44.9	146 01.7	5.9	19 35.2	1.3	59.3
05	256 00.8	44.0	160 26.6	5.8	19 33.9	1.4	59.3
06	271 01.0	N 3 43.0	174 51.4	5.9	S19 32.5	1.6	59.3
07	286 01.2	42.0	189 16.3	5.9	19 30.9	1.6	59.3
F 08	301 01.5	41.1	203 41.2	5.9	19 29.3	1.8	59.3
R 09	316 01.7	.. 40.1	218 06.1	5.8	19 27.5	2.0	59.3
I 10	331 01.9	39.2	232 30.9	5.9	19 25.5	2.1	59.4
D 11	346 02.1	38.2	246 55.8	5.9	19 23.4	2.2	59.4
A 12	1 02.4	N 3 37.3	261 20.7	5.9	S19 21.2	2.3	59.4
Y 13	16 02.6	36.3	275 45.6	5.9	19 18.9	2.4	59.4
14	31 02.8	35.3	290 10.5	5.9	19 16.5	2.6	59.4
15	46 03.0	.. 34.4	304 35.3	5.9	19 13.9	2.8	59.4
16	61 03.2	33.4	319 00.2	5.9	19 11.1	2.8	59.4
17	76 03.5	32.5	333 25.1	5.9	19 08.3	3.0	59.4
18	91 03.7	N 3 31.5	347 50.0	6.0	S19 05.3	3.1	59.4
19	106 03.9	30.6	2 15.0	5.9	19 02.2	3.2	59.4
20	121 04.1	29.6	16 39.9	5.9	18 59.0	3.4	59.5
21	136 04.4	.. 28.6	31 04.8	6.0	18 55.6	3.4	59.5
22	151 04.6	27.7	45 29.8	5.9	18 52.2	3.7	59.5
23	166 04.8	26.7	59 54.7	6.0	18 48.5	3.7	59.5
14 00	181 05.0	N 3 25.8	74 19.7	6.0	S18 44.8	3.8	59.5
01	196 05.2	24.8	88 44.7	6.0	18 41.0	4.0	59.5
02	211 05.5	23.8	103 09.7	6.1	18 37.0	4.1	59.5
03	226 05.7	.. 22.9	117 34.8	6.0	18 32.9	4.3	59.5
04	241 05.9	21.9	131 59.8	6.1	18 28.6	4.3	59.5
05	256 06.1	21.0	146 24.9	6.1	18 24.3	4.5	59.5
06	271 06.4	N 3 20.0	160 50.0	6.1	S18 19.8	4.6	59.5
07	286 06.6	19.0	175 15.1	6.1	18 15.2	4.7	59.6
S 08	301 06.8	18.1	189 40.2	6.2	18 10.5	4.9	59.6
A 09	316 07.0	.. 17.1	204 05.4	6.1	18 05.6	5.0	59.6
T 10	331 07.3	16.2	218 30.5	6.2	18 00.6	5.0	59.6
U 11	346 07.5	15.2	232 55.7	6.3	17 55.6	5.3	59.6
R 12	1 07.7	N 3 14.2	247 21.0	6.2	S17 50.3	5.3	59.6
D 13	16 07.9	13.3	261 46.2	6.3	17 45.0	5.4	59.6
A 14	31 08.1	12.3	276 11.5	6.3	17 39.6	5.6	59.6
Y 15	46 08.4	.. 11.4	290 36.8	6.3	17 34.0	5.7	59.6
16	61 08.6	10.4	305 02.1	6.4	17 28.3	5.8	59.6
17	76 08.8	09.4	319 27.5	6.4	17 22.5	5.9	59.6
18	91 09.0	N 3 08.5	333 52.9	6.4	S17 16.6	6.0	59.6
19	106 09.3	07.5	348 18.3	6.5	17 10.6	6.1	59.6
20	121 09.5	06.6	2 43.8	6.5	17 04.5	6.3	59.6
21	136 09.7	.. 05.6	17 09.3	6.5	16 58.2	6.3	59.6
22	151 09.9	04.6	31 34.8	6.6	16 51.9	6.5	59.6
23	166 10.1	03.7	46 00.4	6.6	16 45.4	6.6	59.6
15 00	181 10.4	N 3 02.7	60 26.0	6.6	S16 38.8	6.7	59.7
01	196 10.6	01.8	74 51.6	6.7	16 32.1	6.8	59.7
02	211 10.8	3 00.8	89 17.3	6.7	16 25.3	6.9	59.7
03	226 11.0	2 59.8	103 43.0	6.7	16 18.4	7.0	59.7
04	241 11.3	58.9	118 08.7	6.8	16 11.4	7.2	59.7
05	256 11.5	57.9	132 34.5	6.8	16 04.2	7.2	59.7
06	271 11.7	N 2 56.9	147 00.3	6.9	S15 57.0	7.3	59.7
07	286 11.9	56.0	161 26.2	6.9	15 49.7	7.5	59.7
08	301 12.2	55.0	175 52.1	6.9	15 42.2	7.5	59.7
S 09	316 12.4	.. 54.1	190 18.0	7.0	15 34.7	7.6	59.7
U 10	331 12.6	53.1	204 44.0	7.0	15 27.1	7.8	59.7
N 11	346 12.8	52.1	219 10.0	7.0	15 19.3	7.8	59.7
D 12	1 13.1	N 2 51.2	233 36.0	7.1	S15 11.5	7.9	59.7
A 13	16 13.3	50.2	248 02.1	7.2	15 03.6	8.1	59.7
Y 14	31 13.5	49.3	262 28.3	7.2	14 55.5	8.1	59.7
15	46 13.7	.. 48.3	276 54.5	7.2	14 47.4	8.2	59.7
16	61 13.9	47.3	291 20.7	7.2	14 39.2	8.4	59.7
17	76 14.2	46.4	305 46.9	7.4	14 30.8	8.4	59.7
18	91 14.4	N 2 45.4	320 13.3	7.3	S14 22.4	8.5	59.7
19	106 14.6	44.4	334 39.6	7.4	14 13.9	8.6	59.7
20	121 14.8	43.5	349 06.0	7.4	14 05.3	8.6	59.7
21	136 15.1	.. 42.5	3 32.4	7.5	13 56.7	8.8	59.7
22	151 15.3	41.5	17 58.9	7.5	13 47.9	8.9	59.7
23	166 15.5	40.6	32 25.4	7.6	S13 39.0	8.9	59.7
SD	15.9	d 1.0	SD 16.2		16.2		16.3

Lat.	Twilight Naut.	Civil	Sunrise	Moonrise 13	14	15	16
°	h m	h m	h m	h m	h m	h m	h m
N 72	02 00	03 50	05 03	▬	18 43	18 11	17 55
N 70	02 34	04 04	05 09	17 43	17 43	17 41	17 38
68	02 57	04 15	05 13	16 46	17 08	17 19	17 24
66	03 15	04 24	05 17	16 12	16 43	17 01	17 13
64	03 29	04 31	05 20	15 48	16 23	16 47	17 03
62	03 41	04 38	05 23	15 28	16 07	16 35	16 55
60	03 51	04 44	05 26	15 12	15 53	16 24	16 48
N 58	03 59	04 48	05 28	14 59	15 42	16 15	16 42
56	04 06	04 52	05 30	14 47	15 32	16 07	16 36
54	04 12	04 56	05 31	14 37	15 23	16 00	16 31
52	04 18	04 59	05 33	14 28	15 15	15 54	16 27
50	04 23	05 02	05 34	14 20	15 08	15 48	16 23
45	04 33	05 08	05 37	14 02	14 52	15 36	16 14
N 40	04 41	05 13	05 40	13 48	14 39	15 25	16 06
35	04 47	05 17	05 42	13 36	14 29	15 16	16 00
30	04 52	05 20	05 44	13 25	14 19	15 08	15 54
20	04 59	05 25	05 47	13 07	14 03	14 55	15 44
N 10	05 04	05 29	05 50	12 51	13 48	14 43	15 35
0	05 08	05 32	05 52	12 37	13 35	14 32	15 27
S 10	05 09	05 34	05 55	12 22	13 21	14 21	15 19
20	05 09	05 35	05 57	12 06	13 07	14 09	15 10
30	05 08	05 36	05 59	11 48	12 51	13 55	15 00
35	05 06	05 36	06 01	11 38	12 41	13 47	14 55
40	05 03	05 35	06 02	11 26	12 30	13 38	14 48
45	05 01	05 35	06 04	11 11	12 17	13 28	14 40
S 50	04 57	05 34	06 06	10 54	12 02	13 15	14 31
52	04 55	05 34	06 07	10 46	11 54	13 09	14 27
54	04 52	05 33	06 08	10 37	11 46	13 02	14 22
56	04 49	05 32	06 09	10 26	11 37	12 55	14 17
58	04 46	05 32	06 11	10 15	11 26	12 46	14 11
S 60	04 42	05 31	06 12	10 01	11 14	12 37	14 04

Lat.	Sunset	Twilight Civil	Naut.	Moonset 13	14	15	16
°	h m	h m	h m	h m	h m	h m	h m
N 72	18 45	19 57	21 44	▬	21 06	23 37	25 47
N 70	18 40	19 44	21 12	20 04	22 05	24 05	00 05
68	18 36	19 33	20 50	21 00	22 39	24 26	00 26
66	18 32	19 25	20 33	21 33	23 04	24 43	00 43
64	18 29	19 17	20 19	21 58	23 23	24 56	00 56
62	18 26	19 11	20 08	22 17	23 38	25 08	01 08
60	18 24	19 06	19 58	22 33	23 52	25 17	01 17
N 58	18 22	19 02	19 50	22 46	24 03	00 03	01 26
56	18 20	18 58	19 43	22 58	24 12	00 12	01 33
54	18 18	18 54	19 37	23 08	24 21	00 21	01 39
52	18 17	18 51	19 32	23 17	24 29	00 29	01 45
50	18 16	18 48	19 27	23 25	24 35	00 35	01 51
45	18 13	18 42	19 17	23 42	24 50	00 50	02 02
N 40	18 10	18 37	19 09	23 55	25 02	01 02	02 11
35	18 08	18 34	19 03	24 07	00 07	01 12	02 19
30	18 07	18 30	18 59	24 17	00 17	01 21	02 26
20	18 04	18 26	18 51	24 35	00 35	01 37	02 38
N 10	18 01	18 22	18 46	24 50	00 50	01 50	02 49
0	17 59	18 19	18 43	00 06	01 05	02 02	02 59
S 10	17 57	18 18	18 42	00 21	01 19	02 15	03 08
20	17 54	18 16	18 42	00 37	01 34	02 28	03 18
30	17 52	18 16	18 44	00 55	01 51	02 43	03 30
35	17 51	18 16	18 45	01 06	02 01	02 51	03 37
40	17 49	18 16	18 48	01 18	02 13	03 01	03 44
45	17 48	18 17	18 51	01 33	02 26	03 13	03 53
S 50	17 46	18 18	18 55	01 50	02 42	03 26	04 04
52	17 45	18 18	18 58	01 59	02 50	03 33	04 09
54	17 44	18 19	19 00	02 08	02 58	03 40	04 14
56	17 43	18 20	19 03	02 18	03 08	03 48	04 20
58	17 42	18 21	19 07	02 30	03 19	03 57	04 27
S 60	17 40	18 22	19 11	02 44	03 31	04 07	04 34

Day	SUN Eqn. of Time 00ʰ	12ʰ	Mer. Pass.	MOON Mer. Pass. Upper	Lower	Age	Phase
d	m s	m s	h m	h m	h m	d	%
13	03 58	04 09	11 56	18 51	06 21	08	59
14	04 20	04 30	11 55	19 49	07 20	09	70
15	04 41	04 52	11 55	20 45	08 17	10	80

UT	ARIES GHA	VENUS −4.1 GHA	Dec	MARS +1.6 GHA	Dec	JUPITER −2.1 GHA	Dec	SATURN +0.7 GHA	Dec
16 00	355 06.4	142 19.0	S14 22.4	220 20.4	N18 17.4	247 20.2	N22 19.9	138 17.1	S12 14.5
01	10 08.9	157 18.7	23.5	235 21.3	17.0	262 22.3	19.9	153 19.3	14.6
02	25 11.4	172 18.5	24.6	250 22.2	16.5	277 24.4	19.8	168 21.6	14.7
03	40 13.8	187 18.2 ..	25.7	265 23.0 ..	16.1	292 26.4 ..	19.8	183 23.8 ..	14.8
04	55 16.3	202 17.9	26.9	280 23.9	15.7	307 28.5	19.8	198 26.0	14.8
05	70 18.7	217 17.6	28.0	295 24.8	15.3	322 30.6	19.7	213 28.3	14.9
06	85 21.2	232 17.4	S14 29.1	310 25.7	N18 14.9	337 32.7	N22 19.7	228 30.5	S12 15.0
07	100 23.7	247 17.1	30.2	325 26.6	14.5	352 34.7	19.6	243 32.7	15.1
08	115 26.1	262 16.8	31.3	340 27.4	14.0	7 36.8	19.6	258 35.0	15.2
M 09	130 28.6	277 16.6 ..	32.4	355 28.3 ..	13.6	22 38.9 ..	19.6	273 37.2 ..	15.3
O 10	145 31.1	292 16.3	33.6	10 29.2	13.2	37 41.0	19.5	288 39.4	15.3
N 11	160 33.5	307 16.0	34.7	25 30.1	12.8	52 43.0	19.5	303 41.7	15.4
D 12	175 36.0	322 15.7	S14 35.8	40 31.0	N18 12.4	67 45.1	N22 19.4	318 43.9	S12 15.5
A 13	190 38.5	337 15.5	36.9	55 31.8	12.0	82 47.2	19.4	333 46.1	15.6
Y 14	205 40.9	352 15.2	38.0	70 32.7	11.5	97 49.3	19.4	348 48.4	15.7
15	220 43.4	7 14.9 ..	39.1	85 33.6 ..	11.1	112 51.3 ..	19.3	3 50.6 ..	15.8
16	235 45.9	22 14.6	40.2	100 34.5	10.7	127 53.4	19.3	18 52.8	15.8
17	250 48.3	37 14.4	41.3	115 35.4	10.3	142 55.5	19.2	33 55.1	15.9
18	265 50.8	52 14.1	S14 42.5	130 36.3	N18 09.9	157 57.6	N22 19.2	48 57.3	S12 16.0
19	280 53.2	67 13.8	43.6	145 37.1	09.4	172 59.6	19.2	63 59.5	16.1
20	295 55.7	82 13.5	44.7	160 38.0	09.0	188 01.7	19.1	79 01.8	16.2
21	310 58.2	97 13.3 ..	45.8	175 38.9 ..	08.6	203 03.8 ..	19.1	94 04.0 ..	16.3
22	326 00.6	112 13.0	46.9	190 39.8	08.2	218 05.9	19.0	109 06.2	16.3
23	341 03.1	127 12.7	48.0	205 40.7	07.8	233 07.9	19.0	124 08.5	16.4
17 00	356 05.6	142 12.4	S14 49.1	220 41.5	N18 07.3	248 10.0	N22 19.0	139 10.7	S12 16.5
01	11 08.0	157 12.1	50.2	235 42.4	06.9	263 12.1	18.9	154 12.9	16.6
02	26 10.5	172 11.9	51.3	250 43.3	06.5	278 14.2	18.9	169 15.1	16.7
03	41 13.0	187 11.6 ..	52.4	265 44.2 ..	06.1	293 16.3 ..	18.8	184 17.4 ..	16.8
04	56 15.4	202 11.3	53.5	280 45.1	05.7	308 18.3	18.8	199 19.6	16.8
05	71 17.9	217 11.0	54.6	295 46.0	05.2	323 20.4	18.8	214 21.8	16.9
06	86 20.3	232 10.7	S14 55.8	310 46.8	N18 04.8	338 22.5	N22 18.7	229 24.1	S12 17.0
07	101 22.8	247 10.5	56.9	325 47.7	04.4	353 24.6	18.7	244 26.3	17.1
T 08	116 25.3	262 10.2	58.0	340 48.6	04.0	8 26.7	18.6	259 28.5	17.2
U 09	131 27.7	277 09.9	14 59.1	355 49.5 ..	03.6	23 28.7 ..	18.6	274 30.8 ..	17.3
E 10	146 30.2	292 09.6	15 00.2	10 50.4	03.1	38 30.8	18.6	289 33.0	17.3
S 11	161 32.7	307 09.3	01.3	25 51.3	02.7	53 32.9	18.5	304 35.2	17.4
D 12	176 35.1	322 09.1	S15 02.4	40 52.2	N18 02.3	68 35.0	N22 18.5	319 37.5	S12 17.5
A 13	191 37.6	337 08.8	03.5	55 53.0	01.9	83 37.1	18.4	334 39.7	17.6
Y 14	206 40.1	352 08.5	04.6	70 53.9	01.4	98 39.2	18.4	349 41.9	17.7
15	221 42.5	7 08.2 ..	05.7	85 54.8 ..	01.0	113 41.2 ..	18.4	4 44.1 ..	17.7
16	236 45.0	22 07.9	06.8	100 55.7	00.6	128 43.3	18.3	19 46.4	17.8
17	251 47.5	37 07.7	07.9	115 56.6	18 00.2	143 45.4	18.3	34 48.6	17.9
18	266 49.9	52 07.4	S15 09.0	130 57.5	N17 59.8	158 47.5	N22 18.2	49 50.8	S12 18.0
19	281 52.4	67 07.1	10.1	145 58.4	59.3	173 49.6	18.2	64 53.1	18.1
20	296 54.8	82 06.8	11.2	160 59.3	58.9	188 51.6	18.2	79 55.3	18.2
21	311 57.3	97 06.5 ..	12.3	176 00.1 ..	58.5	203 53.7 ..	18.1	94 57.5 ..	18.3
22	326 59.8	112 06.2	13.3	191 01.0	58.1	218 55.8	18.1	109 59.8	18.3
23	342 02.2	127 06.0	14.4	206 01.9	57.6	233 57.9	18.0	125 02.0	18.4
18 00	357 04.7	142 05.7	S15 15.5	221 02.8	N17 57.2	249 00.0	N22 18.0	140 04.2	S12 18.5
01	12 07.2	157 05.4	16.6	236 03.7	56.8	264 02.1	18.0	155 06.4	18.6
02	27 09.6	172 05.1	17.7	251 04.6	56.4	279 04.2	17.9	170 08.7	18.7
03	42 12.1	187 04.8 ..	18.8	266 05.5 ..	55.9	294 06.2 ..	17.9	185 10.9 ..	18.8
04	57 14.6	202 04.5	19.9	281 06.4	55.5	309 08.3	17.8	200 13.1	18.9
05	72 17.0	217 04.2	21.0	296 07.2	55.1	324 10.4	17.8	215 15.4	18.9
06	87 19.5	232 04.0	S15 22.1	311 08.1	N17 54.7	339 12.5	N22 17.8	230 17.6	S12 19.0
W 07	102 22.0	247 03.7	23.2	326 09.0	54.2	354 14.6	17.7	245 19.8	19.1
E 08	117 24.4	262 03.4	24.3	341 09.9	53.8	9 16.7	17.7	260 22.1	19.2
D 09	132 26.9	277 03.1 ..	25.4	356 10.8 ..	53.4	24 18.8 ..	17.6	275 24.3 ..	19.3
N 10	147 29.3	292 02.8	26.5	11 11.7	53.0	39 20.8	17.6	290 26.5	19.4
E 11	162 31.8	307 02.5	27.5	26 12.6	52.5	54 22.9	17.6	305 28.7	19.4
S 12	177 34.3	322 02.2	S15 28.6	41 13.5	N17 52.1	69 25.0	N22 17.5	320 31.0	S12 19.5
D 13	192 36.7	337 02.0	29.7	56 14.4	51.7	84 27.1	17.5	335 33.2	19.6
A 14	207 39.2	352 01.7	30.8	71 15.3	51.3	99 29.2	17.4	350 35.4	19.7
Y 15	222 41.7	7 01.4 ..	31.9	86 16.1 ..	50.8	114 31.3 ..	17.4	5 37.6 ..	19.8
16	237 44.1	22 01.1	33.0	101 17.0	50.4	129 33.4	17.4	20 39.9	19.9
17	252 46.6	37 00.8	34.1	116 17.9	50.0	144 35.4	17.3	35 42.1	19.9
18	267 49.1	52 00.5	S15 35.1	131 18.8	N17 49.6	159 37.5	N22 17.3	50 44.3	S12 20.0
19	282 51.5	67 00.2	36.2	146 19.7	49.1	174 39.6	17.2	65 46.6	20.1
20	297 54.0	81 59.9	37.3	161 20.6	48.7	189 41.7	17.2	80 48.8	20.2
21	312 56.4	96 59.6 ..	38.4	176 21.5 ..	48.3	204 43.8 ..	17.2	95 51.0 ..	20.3
22	327 58.9	111 59.4	39.5	191 22.4	47.8	219 45.9	17.1	110 53.2	20.4
23	343 01.4	126 59.1	40.6	206 23.3	47.4	234 48.0	17.1	125 55.5	20.5
Mer.Pass. 0 15.6		v −0.3 d 1.1		v 0.9 d 0.4		v 2.1 d 0.0		v 2.2 d 0.1	

STARS

Name	SHA	Dec
Acamar	315 18.0	S40 14.8
Achernar	335 26.2	S57 09.8
Acrux	173 09.7	S63 10.6
Adhara	255 12.5	S28 59.4
Aldebaran	290 49.1	N16 32.1
Alioth	166 21.1	N55 53.2
Alkaid	152 59.2	N49 14.9
Al Na'ir	27 43.1	S46 53.5
Alnilam	275 46.2	S 1 11.6
Alphard	217 56.2	S 8 43.1
Alphecca	126 11.0	N26 40.4
Alpheratz	357 42.9	N29 10.1
Altair	62 07.9	N 8 54.6
Ankaa	353 15.1	S42 13.7
Antares	112 26.1	S26 27.6
Arcturus	145 55.8	N19 06.9
Atria	107 27.8	S69 03.2
Avior	234 18.3	S59 33.1
Bellatrix	278 31.8	N 6 21.7
Betelgeuse	271 01.1	N 7 24.5
Canopus	263 56.2	S52 42.0
Capella	280 34.1	N46 00.4
Deneb	49 31.0	N45 20.2
Denebola	182 33.8	N14 29.8
Diphda	348 55.4	S17 54.5
Dubhe	193 52.2	N61 40.5
Elnath	278 12.4	N28 36.9
Eltanin	90 46.0	N51 29.7
Enif	33 46.6	N 9 56.6
Fomalhaut	15 23.4	S29 32.8
Gacrux	172 01.2	S57 11.4
Gienah	175 52.4	S17 37.0
Hadar	148 48.1	S60 26.4
Hamal	328 00.3	N23 31.7
Kaus Aust.	83 43.5	S34 22.6
Kochab	137 20.9	N74 06.2
Markab	13 37.8	N15 17.0
Menkar	314 14.6	N 4 08.7
Menkent	148 07.6	S36 26.2
Miaplacidus	221 40.3	S69 46.3
Mirfak	308 39.8	N49 54.4
Nunki	75 58.0	S26 16.6
Peacock	53 18.6	S56 41.4
Pollux	243 27.7	N27 59.4
Procyon	244 59.7	N 5 11.3
Rasalhague	96 06.3	N12 33.4
Regulus	207 43.6	N11 54.0
Rigel	281 11.8	S 8 11.1
Rigil Kent.	139 51.9	S60 53.5
Sabik	102 12.4	S15 44.3
Schedar	349 39.7	N56 36.8
Shaula	96 21.7	S37 06.7
Sirius	258 33.6	S16 44.1
Spica	158 31.3	S11 13.9
Suhail	222 52.6	S43 29.2
Vega	80 38.7	N38 48.2
Zuben'ubi	137 05.4	S16 05.8

	SHA	Mer.Pass.
Venus	146 06.9	14 31
Mars	224 36.0	9 17
Jupiter	252 04.5	7 26
Saturn	143 05.1	14 41

UT	SUN GHA	SUN Dec	MOON GHA	v	MOON Dec	d	HP
d h	o ′	o ′	o ′	′	o ′	′	′
16 00	181 15.7	N 2 39.6	46 52.0	7.6	S13 30.1	9.0	59.7
01	196 16.0	38.7	61 18.6	7.7	13 21.1	9.2	59.7
02	211 16.2	37.7	75 45.3	7.7	13 11.9	9.1	59.7
03	226 16.4	.. 36.7	90 12.0	7.8	13 02.8	9.3	59.7
04	241 16.6	35.8	104 38.8	7.8	12 53.5	9.4	59.7
05	256 16.9	34.8	119 05.6	7.8	12 44.1	9.4	59.7
06	271 17.1	N 2 33.8	133 32.4	7.9	S12 34.7	9.5	59.7
07	286 17.3	32.9	147 59.3	7.9	12 25.2	9.6	59.7
08	301 17.5	31.9	162 26.2	8.0	12 15.6	9.7	59.7
M 09	316 17.7	.. 30.9	176 53.2	8.0	12 05.9	9.7	59.7
O 10	331 18.0	30.0	191 20.2	8.1	11 56.2	9.8	59.6
N 11	346 18.2	29.0	205 47.3	8.1	11 46.4	9.9	59.6
D 12	1 18.4	N 2 28.1	220 14.4	8.2	S11 36.5	10.0	59.6
A 13	16 18.6	27.1	234 41.6	8.2	11 26.5	10.0	59.6
Y 14	31 18.9	26.1	249 08.8	8.2	11 16.5	10.1	59.6
15	46 19.1	.. 25.2	263 36.0	8.3	11 06.4	10.1	59.6
16	61 19.3	24.2	278 03.3	8.4	10 56.3	10.2	59.6
17	76 19.5	23.2	292 30.7	8.4	10 46.1	10.3	59.6
18	91 19.8	N 2 22.3	306 58.1	8.4	S10 35.8	10.4	59.6
19	106 20.0	21.3	321 25.5	8.5	10 25.4	10.4	59.6
20	121 20.2	20.3	335 53.0	8.5	10 15.0	10.5	59.6
21	136 20.4	.. 19.4	350 20.5	8.6	10 04.5	10.5	59.6
22	151 20.7	18.4	4 48.1	8.6	9 54.0	10.6	59.6
23	166 20.9	17.4	19 15.7	8.7	9 43.4	10.6	59.6
17 00	181 21.1	N 2 16.5	33 43.4	8.7	S 9 32.8	10.7	59.5
01	196 21.3	15.5	48 11.1	8.7	9 22.1	10.7	59.5
02	211 21.6	14.5	62 38.8	8.8	9 11.4	10.8	59.5
03	226 21.8	.. 13.6	77 06.6	8.9	9 00.6	10.9	59.5
04	241 22.0	12.6	91 34.5	8.8	8 49.7	10.9	59.5
05	256 22.2	11.6	106 02.3	9.0	8 38.8	10.9	59.5
06	271 22.5	N 2 10.7	120 30.3	8.9	S 8 27.9	11.0	59.5
07	286 22.7	09.7	134 58.2	9.0	8 16.9	11.1	59.5
T 08	301 22.9	08.7	149 26.2	9.1	8 05.8	11.1	59.5
U 09	316 23.1	.. 07.8	163 54.3	9.1	7 54.7	11.1	59.5
E 10	331 23.3	06.8	178 22.4	9.1	7 43.6	11.2	59.4
S 11	346 23.6	05.8	192 50.5	9.2	7 32.4	11.2	59.4
D 12	1 23.8	N 2 04.9	207 18.7	9.2	S 7 21.2	11.2	59.4
A 13	16 24.0	03.9	221 46.9	9.3	7 10.0	11.3	59.4
Y 14	31 24.2	02.9	236 15.2	9.3	6 58.7	11.4	59.4
15	46 24.5	.. 02.0	250 43.5	9.3	6 47.3	11.3	59.4
16	61 24.7	01.0	265 11.8	9.4	6 36.0	11.4	59.4
17	76 24.9	2 00.0	279 40.2	9.4	6 24.6	11.4	59.4
18	91 25.1	N 1 59.1	294 08.6	9.4	S 6 13.2	11.5	59.3
19	106 25.4	58.1	308 37.0	9.5	6 01.7	11.5	59.3
20	121 25.6	57.1	323 05.5	9.6	5 50.2	11.5	59.3
21	136 25.8	.. 56.2	337 34.1	9.5	5 38.7	11.5	59.3
22	151 26.0	55.2	352 02.6	9.7	5 27.2	11.6	59.3
23	166 26.3	54.2	6 31.3	9.6	5 15.6	11.6	59.3
18 00	181 26.5	N 1 53.3	20 59.9	9.7	S 5 04.0	11.6	59.2
01	196 26.7	52.3	35 28.6	9.7	4 52.4	11.6	59.2
02	211 26.9	51.3	49 57.3	9.8	4 40.8	11.7	59.2
03	226 27.2	.. 50.4	64 26.1	9.7	4 29.1	11.7	59.2
04	241 27.4	49.4	78 54.8	9.9	4 17.4	11.7	59.2
05	256 27.6	48.4	93 23.7	9.8	4 05.7	11.7	59.2
06	271 27.8	N 1 47.5	107 52.5	9.9	S 3 54.0	11.7	59.1
W 07	286 28.0	46.5	122 21.4	10.0	3 42.3	11.8	59.1
E 08	301 28.3	45.5	136 50.4	9.9	3 30.5	11.7	59.1
D 09	316 28.5	.. 44.6	151 19.3	10.0	3 18.8	11.8	59.1
N 10	331 28.7	43.6	165 48.3	10.0	3 07.0	11.8	59.1
E 11	346 28.9	42.6	180 17.3	10.1	2 55.2	11.8	59.1
S 12	1 29.2	N 1 41.7	194 46.4	10.1	S 2 43.4	11.7	59.0
D 13	16 29.4	40.7	209 15.5	10.1	2 31.7	11.8	59.0
A 14	31 29.6	39.7	223 44.6	10.2	2 19.9	11.9	59.0
Y 15	46 29.8	.. 38.8	238 13.8	10.1	2 08.0	11.8	59.0
16	61 30.1	37.8	252 42.9	10.3	1 56.2	11.8	59.0
17	76 30.3	36.8	267 12.2	10.2	1 44.4	11.8	58.9
18	91 30.5	N 1 35.9	281 41.4	10.3	S 1 32.6	11.8	58.9
19	106 30.7	34.9	296 10.7	10.3	1 20.8	11.8	58.9
20	121 31.0	33.9	310 40.0	10.3	1 09.0	11.8	58.9
21	136 31.2	.. 33.0	325 09.3	10.3	0 57.2	11.8	58.9
22	151 31.4	32.0	339 38.6	10.4	0 45.4	11.8	58.8
23	166 31.6	31.0	354 08.0	10.4	S 0 33.6	11.8	58.8
	SD 15.9	d 1.0	SD 16.2		16.2		16.1

Lat.	Twilight Naut.	Twilight Civil	Sunrise	Moonrise 16	17	18	19
o	h m	h m	h m	h m	h m	h m	h m
N 72	02 25	04 06	05 17	17 55	17 44	17 34	17 25
N 70	02 52	04 17	05 21	17 38	17 35	17 32	17 29
68	03 12	04 27	05 24	17 24	17 28	17 30	17 32
66	03 27	04 34	05 27	17 13	17 21	17 28	17 35
64	03 40	04 41	05 29	17 03	17 16	17 27	17 37
62	03 50	04 46	05 31	16 55	17 12	17 26	17 39
60	03 59	04 51	05 33	16 48	17 08	17 25	17 41
N 58	04 06	04 55	05 34	16 42	17 04	17 24	17 43
56	04 13	04 58	05 36	16 36	17 01	17 23	17 44
54	04 18	05 01	05 37	16 31	16 58	17 22	17 45
52	04 23	05 04	05 38	16 27	16 55	17 21	17 47
50	04 28	05 06	05 39	16 23	16 53	17 21	17 48
45	04 37	05 12	05 41	16 14	16 48	17 19	17 50
N 40	04 44	05 16	05 43	16 06	16 43	17 18	17 52
35	04 49	05 19	05 44	16 00	16 40	17 17	17 54
30	04 54	05 22	05 46	15 54	16 36	17 16	17 55
20	05 00	05 26	05 48	15 44	16 30	17 15	17 58
N 10	05 04	05 29	05 50	15 35	16 25	17 13	18 00
0	05 06	05 31	05 51	15 27	16 21	17 12	18 03
S 10	05 07	05 32	05 53	15 19	16 16	17 11	18 05
20	05 07	05 32	05 54	15 10	16 11	17 10	18 07
30	05 04	05 32	05 56	15 00	16 05	17 08	18 10
35	05 02	05 31	05 57	14 55	16 01	17 07	18 12
40	04 59	05 31	05 57	14 48	15 58	17 06	18 14
45	04 55	05 29	05 59	14 40	15 53	17 05	18 16
S 50	04 50	05 28	06 00	14 31	15 48	17 04	18 19
52	04 47	05 27	06 00	14 27	15 45	17 03	18 20
54	04 44	05 26	06 01	14 22	15 43	17 03	18 21
56	04 41	05 25	06 01	14 17	15 40	17 02	18 23
58	04 37	05 23	06 02	14 11	15 36	17 01	18 24
S 60	04 33	05 22	06 03	14 04	15 33	17 00	18 26

Lat.	Sunset	Twilight Civil	Twilight Naut.	Moonset 16	17	18	19
o	h m	h m	h m	h m	h m	h m	h m
N 72	18 30	19 40	21 18	25 47	01 47	03 48	05 45
N 70	18 26	19 29	20 52	00 05	02 02	03 55	05 44
68	18 23	19 20	20 33	00 26	02 14	04 00	05 43
66	18 20	19 12	20 18	00 43	02 24	04 04	05 43
64	18 18	19 06	20 06	00 56	02 32	04 08	05 42
62	18 16	19 01	19 56	01 08	02 40	04 11	05 42
60	18 15	18 57	19 48	01 17	02 46	04 14	05 41
N 58	18 13	18 53	19 41	01 26	02 51	04 17	05 41
56	18 12	18 49	19 34	01 33	02 56	04 19	05 40
54	18 11	18 46	19 29	01 39	03 00	04 21	05 40
52	18 10	18 44	19 24	01 45	03 04	04 22	05 40
50	18 09	18 41	19 20	01 51	03 07	04 24	05 40
45	18 07	18 36	19 11	02 02	03 15	04 28	05 39
N 40	18 05	18 32	19 04	02 11	03 21	04 31	05 39
35	18 04	18 29	18 59	02 19	03 26	04 33	05 38
30	18 03	18 27	18 55	02 26	03 31	04 35	05 38
20	18 01	18 23	18 48	02 38	03 39	04 39	05 37
N 10	17 59	18 20	18 45	02 49	03 46	04 42	05 37
0	17 58	18 18	18 42	02 59	03 53	04 45	05 36
S 10	17 56	18 17	18 42	03 08	03 59	04 48	05 36
20	17 55	18 17	18 43	03 18	04 06	04 51	05 35
30	17 54	18 17	18 45	03 30	04 14	04 55	05 34
35	17 53	18 18	18 47	03 37	04 18	04 57	05 34
40	17 51	18 18	18 51	03 43	04 23	04 59	05 33
45	17 51	18 20	18 55	03 53	04 29	05 02	05 33
S 50	17 50	18 22	19 00	04 04	04 36	05 05	05 32
52	17 50	18 23	19 03	04 09	04 39	05 07	05 32
54	17 49	18 24	19 06	04 14	04 43	05 08	05 32
56	17 49	18 26	19 09	04 20	04 47	05 10	05 31
58	17 48	18 27	19 13	04 27	04 51	05 12	05 31
S 60	17 47	18 29	19 18	04 34	04 56	05 14	05 31

Day	SUN Eqn. of Time 00h	12h	Mer. Pass.	MOON Mer. Pass. Upper	Lower	Age	Phase
d	m s	m s	h m	h m	h m	d	%
16	05 02	05 13	11 55	21 40	09 13	11	89
17	05 24	05 35	11 54	22 33	10 07	12	95
18	05 45	05 56	11 54	23 24	10 59	13	99

UT	ARIES GHA	VENUS −4.2 GHA	Dec	MARS +1.6 GHA	Dec	JUPITER −2.1 GHA	Dec	SATURN +0.7 GHA	Dec	Name	SHA	Dec
19 00	358 03.8	141 58.8	S15 41.6	221 24.2	N17 47.0	249 50.1	N22 17.0	140 57.7	S12 20.5	Acamar	315 17.9	S40 14.8
01	13 06.3	156 58.5	42.7	236 25.1	46.6	264 52.2	17.0	155 59.9	20.6	Achernar	335 26.2	S57 09.8
02	28 08.8	171 58.2	43.8	251 26.0	46.1	279 54.3	17.0	171 02.2	20.7	Acrux	173 09.7	S63 10.5
03	43 11.2	186 57.9 · ·	44.9	266 26.9 · ·	45.7	294 56.3 · ·	16.9	186 04.4 · ·	20.8	Adhara	255 12.5	S28 59.3
04	58 13.7	201 57.6	46.0	281 27.8	45.3	309 58.4	16.9	201 06.6	20.9	Aldebaran	290 49.0	N16 32.1
05	73 16.2	216 57.3	47.0	296 28.6	44.8	325 00.5	16.8	216 08.8	21.0			
06	88 18.6	231 57.0	S15 48.1	311 29.5	N17 44.4	340 02.6	N22 16.8	231 11.1	S12 21.0	Alioth	166 21.1	N55 53.2
07	103 21.1	246 56.7	49.2	326 30.4	44.0	355 04.7	16.8	246 13.3	21.1	Alkaid	152 59.2	N49 14.9
T 08	118 23.6	261 56.4	50.3	341 31.3	43.6	10 06.8	16.7	261 15.5	21.2	Al Na'ir	27 43.1	S46 53.5
H 09	133 26.0	276 56.1 · ·	51.3	356 32.2 · ·	43.1	25 08.9 · ·	16.7	276 17.7 · ·	21.3	Alnilam	275 46.2	S 1 11.6
U 10	148 28.5	291 55.8	52.4	11 33.1	42.7	40 11.0	16.6	291 20.0	21.4	Alphard	217 56.2	S 8 43.1
R 11	163 30.9	306 55.6	53.5	26 34.0	42.3	55 13.1	16.6	306 22.2	21.5			
S 12	178 33.4	321 55.3	S15 54.6	41 34.9	N17 41.8	70 15.2	N22 16.6	321 24.4	S12 21.6	Alphecca	126 11.1	N26 40.4
D 13	193 35.9	336 55.0	55.6	56 35.8	41.4	85 17.3	16.5	336 26.6	21.6	Alpheratz	357 42.9	N29 10.1
A 14	208 38.3	351 54.7	56.7	71 36.7	41.0	100 19.4	16.5	351 28.9	21.7	Altair	62 07.9	N 8 54.6
Y 15	223 40.8	6 54.4 · ·	57.8	86 37.6 · ·	40.5	115 21.5 · ·	16.5	6 31.1 · ·	21.8	Ankaa	353 15.1	S42 13.7
16	238 43.3	21 54.1	58.9	101 38.5	40.1	130 23.5	16.4	21 33.3	21.9	Antares	112 26.1	S26 27.6
17	253 45.7	36 53.8	15 59.9	116 39.4	39.7	145 25.6	16.4	36 35.5	22.0			
18	268 48.2	51 53.5	S16 01.0	131 40.3	N17 39.2	160 27.7	N22 16.3	51 37.8	S12 22.1	Arcturus	145 55.8	N19 06.9
19	283 50.7	66 53.2	02.1	146 41.2	38.8	175 29.8	16.3	66 40.0	22.1	Atria	107 27.9	S69 03.2
20	298 53.1	81 52.9	03.1	161 42.1	38.4	190 31.9	16.3	81 42.2	22.2	Avior	234 18.3	S59 33.1
21	313 55.6	96 52.6 · ·	04.2	176 43.0 · ·	38.0	205 34.0 · ·	16.2	96 44.5 · ·	22.3	Bellatrix	278 31.8	N 6 21.7
22	328 58.0	111 52.3	05.3	191 43.9	37.5	220 36.1	16.2	111 46.7	22.4	Betelgeuse	271 01.1	N 7 24.5
23	344 00.5	126 52.0	06.3	206 44.8	37.1	235 38.2	16.1	126 48.9	22.5			
20 00	359 03.0	141 51.7	S16 07.4	221 45.7	N17 36.7	250 40.3	N22 16.1	141 51.1	S12 22.6	Canopus	263 56.1	S52 42.0
01	14 05.4	156 51.4	08.5	236 46.6	36.2	265 42.4	16.1	156 53.4	22.7	Capella	280 34.1	N46 00.4
02	29 07.9	171 51.1	09.5	251 47.5	35.8	280 44.5	16.0	171 55.6	22.7	Deneb	49 31.0	N45 20.2
03	44 10.4	186 50.8 · ·	10.6	266 48.4 · ·	35.4	295 46.6 · ·	16.0	186 57.8 · ·	22.8	Denebola	182 33.8	N14 29.8
04	59 12.8	201 50.5	11.7	281 49.3	34.9	310 48.7	15.9	202 00.0	22.9	Diphda	348 55.4	S17 54.5
05	74 15.3	216 50.2	12.7	296 50.2	34.5	325 50.8	15.9	217 02.3	23.0			
06	89 17.8	231 49.9	S16 13.8	311 51.1	N17 34.1	340 52.9	N22 15.9	232 04.5	S12 23.0	Dubhe	193 52.2	N61 40.5
07	104 20.2	246 49.6	14.9	326 52.0	33.6	355 55.0	15.8	247 06.7	23.1	Elnath	278 12.3	N28 36.9
08	119 22.7	261 49.3	15.9	341 52.9	33.2	10 57.1	15.8	262 08.9	23.2	Eltanin	90 46.0	N51 29.7
F 09	134 25.2	276 49.0 · ·	17.0	356 53.8 · ·	32.8	25 59.2 · ·	15.7	277 11.1 · ·	23.3	Enif	33 46.7	N 9 56.6
R 10	149 27.6	291 48.7	18.0	11 54.7	32.3	41 01.3	15.7	292 13.4	23.4	Fomalhaut	15 23.4	S29 32.8
I 11	164 30.1	306 48.4	19.1	26 55.6	31.9	56 03.4	15.7	307 15.6	23.5			
D 12	179 32.5	321 48.1	S16 20.2	41 56.5	N17 31.5	71 05.5	N22 15.6	322 17.8	S12 23.6	Gacrux	172 01.2	S57 11.4
A 13	194 35.0	336 47.8	21.2	56 57.4	31.0	86 07.6	15.6	337 20.0	23.7	Gienah	175 52.4	S17 37.0
Y 14	209 37.5	351 47.5	22.3	71 58.3	30.6	101 09.7	15.6	352 22.3	23.8	Hadar	148 48.1	S60 26.4
15	224 39.9	6 47.2 · ·	23.3	86 59.2 · ·	30.2	116 11.8 · ·	15.5	7 24.5 · ·	23.8	Hamal	328 00.2	N23 31.7
16	239 42.4	21 46.9	24.4	102 00.1	29.7	131 13.9	15.5	22 26.7	23.9	Kaus Aust.	83 43.5	S34 22.6
17	254 44.9	36 46.6	25.4	117 01.0	29.3	146 16.0	15.4	37 28.9	24.0			
18	269 47.3	51 46.3	S16 26.5	132 01.9	N17 28.8	161 18.1	N22 15.4	52 31.2	S12 24.1	Kochab	137 20.9	N74 06.2
19	284 49.8	66 46.0	27.6	147 02.8	28.4	176 20.2	15.4	67 33.4	24.2	Markab	13 37.8	N15 17.0
20	299 52.3	81 45.7	28.6	162 03.7	28.0	191 22.3	15.3	82 35.6	24.3	Menkar	314 14.6	N 4 08.7
21	314 54.7	96 45.4 · ·	29.7	177 04.6 · ·	27.5	206 24.4 · ·	15.3	97 37.8 · ·	24.4	Menkent	148 07.6	S36 26.2
22	329 57.2	111 45.1	30.7	192 05.5	27.1	221 26.5	15.2	112 40.1	24.4	Miaplacidus	221 40.3	S69 46.3
23	344 59.6	126 44.8	31.8	207 06.4	26.7	236 28.6	15.2	127 42.3	24.5			
21 00	0 02.1	141 44.5	S16 32.8	222 07.3	N17 26.2	251 30.7	N22 15.2	142 44.5	S12 24.6	Mirfak	308 39.8	N49 54.4
01	15 04.6	156 44.2	33.9	237 08.2	25.8	266 32.8	15.1	157 46.7	24.7	Nunki	75 58.0	S26 16.6
02	30 07.0	171 43.9	34.9	252 09.1	25.4	281 34.9	15.1	172 48.9	24.8	Peacock	53 18.6	S56 41.4
03	45 09.5	186 43.6 · ·	36.0	267 10.0 · ·	24.9	296 37.0 · ·	15.1	187 51.2 · ·	24.9	Pollux	243 27.7	N27 59.4
04	60 12.0	201 43.3	37.0	282 10.9	24.5	311 39.1	15.0	202 53.4	25.0	Procyon	244 59.7	N 5 11.3
05	75 14.4	216 42.9	38.1	297 11.8	24.0	326 41.2	15.0	217 55.6	25.0			
06	90 16.9	231 42.6	S16 39.1	312 12.7	N17 23.6	341 43.3	N22 14.9	232 57.8	S12 25.1	Rasalhague	96 06.3	N12 33.4
07	105 19.4	246 42.3	40.2	327 13.6	23.2	356 45.4	14.9	248 00.1	25.2	Regulus	207 43.6	N11 54.0
S 08	120 21.8	261 42.0	41.2	342 14.5	22.7	11 47.5	14.9	263 02.3	25.3	Rigel	281 11.8	S 8 11.1
A 09	135 24.3	276 41.7 · ·	42.3	357 15.4 · ·	22.3	26 49.6 · ·	14.8	278 04.5 · ·	25.4	Rigil Kent.	139 51.9	S60 53.5
T 10	150 26.8	291 41.4	43.3	12 16.3	21.9	41 51.7	14.8	293 06.7	25.5	Sabik	102 12.4	S15 44.3
U 11	165 29.2	306 41.1	44.4	27 17.2	21.4	56 53.8	14.7	308 09.0	25.6			
R 12	180 31.7	321 40.8	S16 45.4	42 18.1	N17 21.0	71 55.9	N22 14.7	323 11.2	S12 25.6	Schedar	349 39.7	N56 36.8
D 13	195 34.1	336 40.5	46.4	57 19.1	20.5	86 58.0	14.7	338 13.4	25.7	Shaula	96 21.7	S37 06.7
A 14	210 36.6	351 40.2	47.5	72 20.0	20.1	102 00.1	14.6	353 15.6	25.8	Sirius	258 33.6	S16 44.1
Y 15	225 39.1	6 39.9 · ·	48.5	87 20.9 · ·	19.7	117 02.2 · ·	14.6	8 17.8 · ·	25.9	Spica	158 31.3	S11 13.9
16	240 41.5	21 39.6	49.6	102 21.8	19.2	132 04.3	14.5	23 20.1	26.0	Suhail	222 52.6	S43 29.2
17	255 44.0	36 39.3	50.6	117 22.7	18.8	147 06.4	14.5	38 22.3	26.1			
18	270 46.5	51 38.9	S16 51.7	132 23.6	N17 18.4	162 08.5	N22 14.5	53 24.5	S12 26.2	Vega	80 38.7	N38 48.2
19	285 48.9	66 38.6	52.7	147 24.5	17.9	177 10.7	14.4	68 26.7	26.2	Zuben'ubi	137 05.4	S16 05.8
20	300 51.4	81 38.3	53.7	162 25.4	17.5	192 12.8	14.4	83 28.9	26.3		SHA	Mer.Pass.
21	315 53.9	96 38.0 · ·	54.8	177 26.3 · ·	17.0	207 14.9 · ·	14.4	98 31.2 · ·	26.4		° ′	h m
22	330 56.3	111 37.7	55.8	192 27.2	16.6	222 17.0	14.3	113 33.4	26.5	Venus	142 48.7	14 33
23	345 58.8	126 37.4	56.8	207 28.1	16.2	237 19.1	14.3	128 35.6	26.6	Mars	222 42.7	9 12
	h m									Jupiter	251 37.3	7 16
Mer.Pass.	0 03.8	v −0.3	d 1.1	v 0.9	d 0.4	v 2.1	d 0.0	v 2.2	d 0.1	Saturn	142 48.2	14 30

UT	SUN		MOON				Lat.	Twilight		Sunrise	Moonrise			
								Naut.	Civil		19	20	21	22
	GHA	Dec	GHA	v	Dec	d	HP							
d h	° ′	° ′	° ′	′	° ′	′	′	°	h m	h m	h m	h m	h m	h m	h m
19 00	181 31.9	N 1 30.0	8 37.4	10.5	S 0 21.8	11.8	58.8	N 72	02 46	04 21	05 30	17 25	17 16	17 05	16 52
01	196 32.1	29.1	23 06.9	10.4	S 0 10.0	11.8	58.8	N 70	03 09	04 30	05 32	17 29	17 26	17 24	17 22
02	211 32.3	28.1	37 36.3	10.5	N 0 01.8	11.8	58.7	68	03 26	04 38	05 34	17 32	17 35	17 38	17 44
03	226 32.5	.. 27.1	52 05.8	10.5	0 13.6	11.7	58.7	66	03 39	04 44	05 36	17 35	17 42	17 50	18 02
04	241 32.7	26.2	66 35.3	10.5	0 25.3	11.8	58.7	64	03 50	04 49	05 37	17 37	17 48	18 00	18 16
05	256 33.0	25.2	81 04.8	10.6	0 37.1	11.7	58.7	62	03 59	04 54	05 39	17 39	17 53	18 09	18 28
06	271 33.2	N 1 24.2	95 34.4	10.6	N 0 48.8	11.8	58.7	60	04 07	04 58	05 40	17 41	17 58	18 17	18 38
07	286 33.4	23.3	110 04.0	10.6	1 00.6	11.7	58.6	N 58	04 14	05 01	05 41	17 43	18 02	18 23	18 47
T 08	301 33.6	22.3	124 33.6	10.6	1 12.3	11.7	58.6	56	04 19	05 04	05 41	17 44	18 06	18 29	18 55
H 09	316 33.9	.. 21.3	139 03.2	10.6	1 24.0	11.6	58.6	54	04 24	05 07	05 42	17 45	18 09	18 34	19 02
U 10	331 34.1	20.4	153 32.8	10.7	1 35.6	11.7	58.6	52	04 29	05 09	05 43	17 47	18 12	18 39	19 09
R 11	346 34.3	19.4	168 02.5	10.7	1 47.3	11.6	58.5	50	04 33	05 11	05 43	17 48	18 15	18 43	19 15
S 12	1 34.5	N 1 18.4	182 32.2	10.7	N 1 58.9	11.6	58.5	45	04 41	05 15	05 45	17 50	18 21	18 53	19 27
D 13	16 34.8	17.4	197 01.9	10.7	2 10.5	11.6	58.5	N 40	04 47	05 19	05 46	17 52	18 26	19 01	19 37
A 14	31 35.0	16.5	211 31.6	10.8	2 22.1	11.6	58.5	35	04 52	05 21	05 47	17 54	18 30	19 07	19 46
Y 15	46 35.2	.. 15.5	226 01.4	10.7	2 33.7	11.5	58.4	30	04 55	05 23	05 47	17 55	18 34	19 13	19 54
16	61 35.4	14.5	240 31.1	10.8	2 45.2	11.6	58.4	20	05 01	05 26	05 48	17 58	18 41	19 24	20 08
17	76 35.7	13.6	255 00.9	10.8	2 56.8	11.5	58.4	N 10	05 04	05 28	05 49	18 00	18 47	19 33	20 20
18	91 35.9	N 1 12.6	269 30.7	10.8	N 3 08.3	11.4	58.4	0	05 05	05 29	05 50	18 03	18 52	19 42	20 31
19	106 36.1	11.6	284 00.5	10.9	3 19.7	11.5	58.3	S 10	05 04	05 30	05 51	18 05	18 58	19 50	20 42
20	121 36.3	10.7	298 30.4	10.8	3 31.2	11.4	58.3	20	05 04	05 29	05 51	18 07	19 04	20 00	20 54
21	136 36.5	.. 09.7	313 00.2	10.9	3 42.6	11.3	58.3	30	05 00	05 28	05 52	18 10	19 11	20 10	21 08
22	151 36.8	08.7	327 30.1	10.9	3 53.9	11.4	58.2	35	04 58	05 27	05 52	18 12	19 15	20 17	21 16
23	166 37.0	07.7	342 00.0	10.9	4 05.3	11.3	58.2	40	04 54	05 26	05 53	18 14	19 20	20 24	21 25
20 00	181 37.2	N 1 06.8	356 29.9	10.9	N 4 16.6	11.3	58.2	45	04 49	05 24	05 53	18 16	19 25	20 32	21 36
01	196 37.4	05.8	10 59.8	10.9	4 27.9	11.2	58.2	S 50	04 43	05 21	05 53	18 19	19 32	20 42	21 49
02	211 37.7	04.8	25 29.7	11.0	4 39.1	11.2	58.1	52	04 40	05 20	05 53	18 20	19 35	20 47	21 55
03	226 37.9	.. 03.9	39 59.7	10.9	4 50.3	11.2	58.1	54	04 37	05 18	05 53	18 21	19 38	20 52	22 02
04	241 38.1	02.9	54 29.6	11.0	5 01.5	11.1	58.1	56	04 33	05 17	05 54	18 23	19 42	20 58	22 10
05	256 38.3	01.9	68 59.6	11.0	5 12.6	11.1	58.1	58	04 28	05 15	05 54	18 24	19 46	21 04	22 18
06	271 38.6	N 1 01.0	83 29.6	11.0	N 5 23.7	11.1	58.0	S 60	04 23	05 12	05 54	18 26	19 50	21 11	22 28

Lat.	Sunset	Twilight		Moonset			
		Civil	Naut.	19	20	21	22
°	h m	h m	h m	h m	h m	h m	h m
N 72	18 14	19 23	20 56	05 45	07 39	09 33	11 29
N 70	18 12	19 14	20 34	05 44	07 31	09 16	11 01
68	18 10	19 06	20 18	05 43	07 24	09 03	10 39
66	18 09	19 00	20 05	05 43	07 18	08 52	10 23
64	18 08	18 55	19 54	05 42	07 14	08 43	10 09
62	18 07	18 51	19 45	05 42	07 10	08 35	09 58
60	18 06	18 47	19 38	05 41	07 06	08 29	09 48
N 58	18 05	18 44	19 31	05 41	07 03	08 23	09 40
56	18 04	18 41	19 26	05 40	07 00	08 18	09 32
54	18 03	18 39	19 21	05 40	06 58	08 13	09 26
52	18 03	18 37	19 17	05 40	06 56	08 09	09 20
50	18 02	18 35	19 13	05 40	06 54	08 05	09 14
45	18 01	18 31	19 05	05 39	06 49	07 57	09 03
N 40	18 00	18 27	18 59	05 39	06 45	07 51	08 53
35	18 00	18 25	18 54	05 38	06 42	07 45	08 45
30	17 59	18 23	18 51	05 38	06 39	07 40	08 38
20	17 58	18 20	18 46	05 37	06 35	07 31	08 26
N 10	17 57	18 18	18 43	05 37	06 30	07 23	08 15
0	17 57	18 17	18 41	05 36	06 26	07 16	08 05
S 10	17 56	18 17	18 41	05 36	06 22	07 09	07 55
20	17 56	18 18	18 43	05 35	06 18	07 01	07 44
30	17 55	18 19	18 47	05 34	06 13	06 52	07 32
35	17 55	18 20	18 50	05 34	06 10	06 47	07 25
40	17 55	18 22	18 53	05 34	06 07	06 42	07 17
45	17 55	18 24	18 58	05 33	06 04	06 35	07 08
S 50	17 55	18 27	19 05	05 32	05 59	06 27	06 57
52	17 54	18 28	19 08	05 32	05 57	06 23	06 52
54	17 54	18 30	19 11	05 32	05 55	06 19	06 46
56	17 54	18 31	19 15	05 31	05 53	06 15	06 40
58	17 54	18 33	19 20	05 31	05 50	06 10	06 33
S 60	17 54	18 36	19 25	05 31	05 47	06 05	06 25

UT	SUN		MOON				
	GHA	Dec	GHA	v	Dec	d	HP
07	286 38.8	1 00.0	97 59.6	11.0	5 34.8	11.0	58.0
08	301 39.0	0 59.0	112 29.6	11.0	5 45.8	10.9	58.0
F 09	316 39.2	.. 58.0	126 59.6	11.0	5 56.7	11.0	57.9
R 10	331 39.4	57.1	141 29.6	11.1	6 07.7	10.8	57.9
I 11	346 39.7	56.1	155 59.7	11.0	6 18.5	10.9	57.9
D 12	1 39.9	N 0 55.1	170 29.7	11.1	N 6 29.4	10.8	57.9
A 13	16 40.1	54.2	184 59.8	11.0	6 40.2	10.7	57.8
Y 14	31 40.3	53.2	199 29.8	11.1	6 50.9	10.7	57.8
15	46 40.6	.. 52.2	213 59.9	11.1	7 01.6	10.7	57.8
16	61 40.8	51.3	228 30.0	11.1	7 12.3	10.6	57.7
17	76 41.0	50.3	243 00.1	11.1	7 22.9	10.5	57.7
18	91 41.2	N 0 49.3	257 30.2	11.1	N 7 33.4	10.5	57.6
19	106 41.4	48.3	272 00.3	11.1	7 43.9	10.5	57.6
20	121 41.7	47.4	286 30.4	11.2	7 54.4	10.3	57.6
21	136 41.9	.. 46.4	301 00.6	11.1	8 04.7	10.4	57.6
22	151 42.1	45.4	315 30.7	11.2	8 15.1	10.3	57.6
23	166 42.3	44.5	330 00.9	11.1	8 25.4	10.2	57.5
21 00	181 42.6	N 0 43.5	344 31.0	11.2	N 8 35.6	10.2	57.5
01	196 42.8	42.5	359 01.2	11.1	8 45.8	10.1	57.5
02	211 43.0	41.5	13 31.3	11.2	8 55.9	10.0	57.4
03	226 43.2	.. 40.6	28 01.5	11.2	9 05.9	10.0	57.4
04	241 43.4	39.6	42 31.7	11.1	9 15.9	10.0	57.4
05	256 43.7	38.6	57 01.8	11.2	9 25.9	9.9	57.3
06	271 43.9	N 0 37.7	71 32.0	11.2	N 9 35.8	9.8	57.3
07	286 44.1	36.7	86 02.2	11.2	9 45.6	9.7	57.3
S 08	301 44.3	35.7	100 32.4	11.2	9 55.3	9.7	57.3
A 09	316 44.6	.. 34.7	115 02.6	11.2	10 05.0	9.7	57.2
T 10	331 44.8	33.8	129 32.8	11.2	10 14.7	9.5	57.2
U 11	346 45.0	32.8	144 03.0	11.2	10 24.2	9.5	57.2
R 12	1 45.2	N 0 31.8	158 33.2	11.2	N 10 33.7	9.5	57.1
D 13	16 45.4	30.9	173 03.4	11.3	10 43.2	9.3	57.1
A 14	31 45.7	29.9	187 33.6	11.2	10 52.5	9.3	57.1
Y 15	46 45.9	.. 28.9	202 03.8	11.3	11 01.8	9.3	57.0
16	61 46.1	27.9	216 34.1	11.2	11 11.1	9.1	57.0
17	76 46.3	27.0	231 04.3	11.2	11 20.2	9.1	57.0
18	91 46.6	N 0 26.0	245 34.5	11.2	N 11 29.3	9.1	57.0
19	106 46.8	25.0	260 04.7	11.2	11 38.4	8.9	56.9
20	121 47.0	24.0	274 34.9	11.3	11 47.3	8.9	56.9
21	136 47.2	.. 23.1	289 05.2	11.2	11 56.2	8.8	56.9
22	151 47.4	22.1	303 35.4	11.2	12 05.0	8.8	56.8
23	166 47.7	21.1	318 05.6	11.3	N 12 13.8	8.7	56.8
	SD 16.0	d 1.0	SD 15.9		15.8		15.6

	SUN			MOON			
Day	Eqn. of Time		Mer.	Mer. Pass.		Age	Phase
	00ʰ	12ʰ	Pass.	Upper	Lower		
d	m s	m s	h m	h m	h m	d %	
19	06 07	06 18	11 54	24 14	11 50	14 100	
20	06 28	06 39	11 53	00 14	12 39	15 99	◯
21	06 50	07 00	11 53	01 04	13 29	16 95	

UT	ARIES GHA	VENUS −4.2 GHA	VENUS Dec	MARS +1.6 GHA	MARS Dec	JUPITER −2.1 GHA	JUPITER Dec	SATURN +0.7 GHA	SATURN Dec
22 00	1 01.2	141 37.1	S16 57.9	222 29.0	N17 15.7	252 21.2	N22 14.2	143 37.8	S12 26.7
01	16 03.7	156 36.8	16 58.9	237 29.9	15.3	267 23.3	14.2	158 40.1	26.8
02	31 06.2	171 36.5	17 00.0	252 30.8	14.8	282 25.4	14.2	173 42.3	26.8
03	46 08.6	186 36.1	.. 01.0	267 31.8	.. 14.4	297 27.5	.. 14.1	188 44.5	.. 26.9
04	61 11.1	201 35.8	02.0	282 32.7	14.0	312 29.6	14.1	203 46.7	27.0
05	76 13.6	216 35.5	03.1	297 33.6	13.5	327 31.7	14.0	218 48.9	27.1
S 06	91 16.0	231 35.2	S17 04.1	312 34.5	N17 13.1	342 33.8	N22 14.0	233 51.2	S12 27.2
U 07	106 18.5	246 34.9	05.1	327 35.4	12.6	357 35.9	14.0	248 53.4	27.3
N 08	121 21.0	261 34.6	06.2	342 36.3	12.2	12 38.1	13.9	263 55.6	27.4
D 09	136 23.4	276 34.3	.. 07.2	357 37.2	.. 11.7	27 40.2	.. 13.9	278 57.8	.. 27.4
A 10	151 25.9	291 33.9	08.2	12 38.1	11.3	42 42.3	13.9	294 00.0	27.5
Y 11	166 28.4	306 33.6	09.2	27 39.0	10.9	57 44.4	13.8	309 02.3	27.6
12	181 30.8	321 33.3	S17 10.3	42 39.9	N17 10.4	72 46.5	N22 13.8	324 04.5	S12 27.7
13	196 33.3	336 33.0	11.3	57 40.9	10.0	87 48.6	13.7	339 06.7	27.8
14	211 35.7	351 32.7	12.3	72 41.8	09.5	102 50.7	13.7	354 08.9	27.9
15	226 38.2	6 32.4	.. 13.4	87 42.7	.. 09.1	117 52.8	.. 13.7	9 11.1	.. 28.0
16	241 40.7	21 32.0	14.4	102 43.6	08.7	132 54.9	13.6	24 13.4	28.0
17	256 43.1	36 31.7	15.4	117 44.5	08.2	147 57.1	13.6	39 15.6	28.1
18	271 45.6	51 31.4	S17 16.4	132 45.4	N17 07.8	162 59.2	N22 13.5	54 17.8	S12 28.2
19	286 48.1	66 31.1	17.5	147 46.3	07.3	178 01.3	13.5	69 20.0	28.3
20	301 50.5	81 30.8	18.5	162 47.2	06.9	193 03.4	13.5	84 22.2	28.4
21	316 53.0	96 30.5	.. 19.5	177 48.1	.. 06.4	208 05.5	.. 13.4	99 24.4	.. 28.5
22	331 55.5	111 30.1	20.5	192 49.1	06.0	223 07.6	13.4	114 26.7	28.6
23	346 57.9	126 29.8	21.6	207 50.0	05.5	238 09.7	13.4	129 28.9	28.7
23 00	2 00.4	141 29.5	S17 22.6	222 50.9	N17 05.1	253 11.8	N22 13.3	144 31.1	S12 28.7
01	17 02.9	156 29.2	23.6	237 51.8	04.7	268 14.0	13.3	159 33.3	28.8
02	32 05.3	171 28.9	24.6	252 52.7	04.2	283 16.1	13.2	174 35.5	28.9
03	47 07.8	186 28.5	.. 25.6	267 53.6	.. 03.8	298 18.2	.. 13.2	189 37.8	.. 29.0
04	62 10.2	201 28.2	26.7	282 54.5	03.3	313 20.3	13.2	204 40.0	29.1
05	77 12.7	216 27.9	27.7	297 55.5	02.9	328 22.4	13.1	219 42.2	29.2
M 06	92 15.2	231 27.6	S17 28.7	312 56.4	N17 02.5	343 24.5	N22 13.1	234 44.4	S12 29.3
O 07	107 17.6	246 27.3	29.7	327 57.3	02.0	358 26.6	13.1	249 46.6	29.3
N 08	122 20.1	261 26.9	30.7	342 58.2	01.5	13 28.8	13.0	264 48.9	29.4
D 09	137 22.6	276 26.6	.. 31.7	357 59.1	.. 01.1	28 30.9	.. 13.0	279 51.1	.. 29.5
A 10	152 25.0	291 26.3	32.8	13 00.0	00.7	43 33.0	12.9	294 53.3	29.6
Y 11	167 27.5	306 26.0	33.8	28 00.9	17 00.2	58 35.1	12.9	309 55.5	29.7
12	182 30.0	321 25.7	S17 34.8	43 01.9	N16 59.8	73 37.2	N22 12.9	324 57.7	S12 29.8
13	197 32.4	336 25.3	35.8	58 02.8	59.3	88 39.3	12.8	339 59.9	29.9
14	212 34.9	351 25.0	36.8	73 03.7	58.9	103 41.5	12.8	355 02.2	29.9
15	227 37.3	6 24.7	.. 37.8	88 04.6	.. 58.4	118 43.6	.. 12.8	10 04.4	.. 30.0
16	242 39.8	21 24.4	38.8	103 05.5	58.0	133 45.7	12.7	25 06.6	30.1
17	257 42.3	36 24.0	39.8	118 06.4	57.5	148 47.8	12.7	40 08.8	30.2
18	272 44.7	51 23.7	S17 40.9	133 07.4	N16 57.1	163 49.9	N22 12.6	55 11.0	S12 30.3
19	287 47.2	66 23.4	41.9	148 08.3	56.6	178 52.0	12.6	70 13.2	30.4
20	302 49.7	81 23.1	42.9	163 09.2	56.2	193 54.2	12.6	85 15.5	30.5
21	317 52.1	96 22.7	.. 43.9	178 10.1	.. 55.7	208 56.3	.. 12.5	100 17.7	.. 30.6
22	332 54.6	111 22.4	44.9	193 11.0	55.3	223 58.4	12.5	115 19.9	30.6
23	347 57.1	126 22.1	45.9	208 11.9	54.8	239 00.5	12.5	130 22.1	30.7
24 00	2 59.5	141 21.8	S17 46.9	223 12.9	N16 54.4	254 02.6	N22 12.4	145 24.3	S12 30.8
01	18 02.0	156 21.4	47.9	238 13.8	54.0	269 04.8	12.4	160 26.6	30.9
02	33 04.5	171 21.1	48.9	253 14.7	53.5	284 06.9	12.3	175 28.8	31.0
03	48 06.9	186 20.8	.. 49.9	268 15.6	.. 53.1	299 09.0	.. 12.3	190 31.0	.. 31.1
04	63 09.4	201 20.5	50.9	283 16.5	52.6	314 11.1	12.3	205 33.2	31.2
05	78 11.8	216 20.1	51.9	298 17.5	52.2	329 13.2	12.2	220 35.4	31.2
T 06	93 14.3	231 19.8	S17 52.9	313 18.4	N16 51.7	344 15.4	N22 12.2	235 37.6	S12 31.3
U 07	108 16.8	246 19.5	53.9	328 19.3	51.3	359 17.5	12.2	250 39.8	31.4
E 08	123 19.2	261 19.1	54.9	343 20.2	50.8	14 19.6	12.1	265 42.1	31.5
S 09	138 21.7	276 18.8	.. 55.9	358 21.1	.. 50.4	29 21.7	.. 12.1	280 44.3	.. 31.6
D 10	153 24.2	291 18.5	56.9	13 22.0	49.9	44 23.9	12.0	295 46.5	31.7
A 11	168 26.6	306 18.2	57.9	28 23.0	49.5	59 26.0	12.0	310 48.7	31.8
Y 12	183 29.1	321 17.8	S17 58.9	43 23.9	N16 49.0	74 28.1	N22 12.0	325 50.9	S12 31.9
13	198 31.6	336 17.5	17 59.9	58 24.8	48.6	89 30.2	11.9	340 53.1	31.9
14	213 34.0	351 17.2	18 00.9	73 25.7	48.1	104 32.3	11.9	355 55.4	32.0
15	228 36.5	6 16.8	.. 01.9	88 26.7	.. 47.7	119 34.5	.. 11.9	10 57.6	.. 32.1
16	243 39.0	21 16.5	02.9	103 27.6	47.2	134 36.6	11.8	26 59.8	32.2
17	258 41.4	36 16.2	03.9	118 28.5	46.8	149 38.7	11.8	41 02.0	32.3
18	273 43.9	51 15.8	S18 04.9	133 29.4	N16 46.3	164 40.8	N22 11.7	56 04.2	S12 32.4
19	288 46.3	66 15.5	05.9	148 30.3	45.9	179 43.0	11.7	71 06.4	32.5
20	303 48.8	81 15.2	06.9	163 31.3	45.4	194 45.1	11.7	86 08.7	32.5
21	318 51.3	96 14.8	.. 07.9	178 32.2	.. 45.0	209 47.2	.. 11.6	101 10.9	.. 32.6
22	333 53.7	111 14.5	08.8	193 33.1	44.5	224 49.3	11.6	116 13.1	32.7
23	348 56.2	126 14.2	09.8	208 34.0	44.1	239 51.5	11.6	131 15.3	32.8
Mer. Pass.	23 48.1	v −0.3	d 1.0	v 0.9	d 0.4	v 2.1	d 0.0	v 2.2	d 0.1

STARS

Name	SHA	Dec
Acamar	315 17.9	S40 14.8
Achernar	335 26.2	S57 09.8
Acrux	173 09.7	S63 10.5
Adhara	255 12.5	S28 59.3
Aldebaran	290 49.0	N16 32.1
Alioth	166 21.1	N55 53.2
Alkaid	152 59.2	N49 14.9
Al Na'ir	27 43.1	S46 53.5
Alnilam	275 46.1	S 1 11.6
Alphard	217 56.1	S 8 43.1
Alphecca	126 11.1	N26 40.4
Alpheratz	357 42.9	N29 10.2
Altair	62 07.9	N 8 54.6
Ankaa	353 15.1	S42 13.7
Antares	112 26.2	S26 27.6
Arcturus	145 55.8	N19 06.9
Atria	107 27.9	S69 03.2
Avior	234 18.3	S59 33.1
Bellatrix	278 31.7	N 6 21.7
Betelgeuse	271 01.1	N 7 24.5
Canopus	263 56.1	S52 42.0
Capella	280 34.1	N46 00.4
Deneb	49 31.0	N45 20.2
Denebola	182 33.8	N14 29.8
Diphda	348 55.4	S17 54.5
Dubhe	193 52.2	N61 40.5
Elnath	278 12.3	N28 36.9
Eltanin	90 46.1	N51 29.7
Enif	33 46.7	N 9 56.6
Fomalhaut	15 23.4	S29 32.8
Gacrux	172 01.2	S57 11.4
Gienah	175 52.4	S17 37.0
Hadar	148 48.1	S60 26.4
Hamal	328 00.2	N23 31.7
Kaus Aust.	83 43.5	S34 22.6
Kochab	137 21.0	N74 06.2
Markab	13 37.8	N15 17.0
Menkar	314 14.6	N 4 08.7
Menkent	148 07.7	S36 26.2
Miaplacidus	221 40.2	S69 46.3
Mirfak	308 39.7	N49 54.4
Nunki	75 58.0	S26 16.6
Peacock	53 18.6	S56 41.4
Pollux	243 27.7	N27 59.4
Procyon	244 59.7	N 5 11.3
Rasalhague	96 06.3	N12 33.4
Regulus	207 43.6	N11 54.0
Rigel	281 11.8	S 8 11.1
Rigil Kent.	139 51.9	S60 53.5
Sabik	102 12.4	S15 44.3
Schedar	349 39.7	N56 36.8
Shaula	96 21.7	S37 06.7
Sirius	258 33.6	S16 44.1
Spica	158 31.3	S11 13.9
Suhail	222 52.6	S43 29.2
Vega	80 38.8	N38 48.2
Zuben'ubi	137 05.4	S16 05.8

	SHA	Mer. Pass.
Venus	139 29.1	14 34
Mars	220 50.5	9 08
Jupiter	251 11.5	7 06
Saturn	142 30.7	14 20

UT	SUN		MOON					Lat.	Twilight		Sunrise	Moonrise			
									Naut.	Civil		22	23	24	25
	GHA	Dec	GHA	v	Dec	d	HP								
d h	° ′	° ′	° ′	′	° ′	′	′	°	h m	h m	h m	h m	h m	h m	h m
22 00	181 47.9	N 0 20.2	332 35.9	11.2	N12 22.5	8.5	56.8	N 72	03 05	04 35	05 43	16 52	16 29	▭	▭
01	196 48.1	19.2	347 06.1	11.2	12 31.0	8.6	56.7	N 70	03 24	04 43	05 44	17 22	17 22	17 25	17 42
02	211 48.3	18.2	1 36.3	11.3	12 39.6	8.4	56.7	68	03 39	04 49	05 45	17 44	17 54	18 12	18 45
03	226 48.5	.. 17.2	16 06.6	11.2	12 48.0	8.4	56.7	66	03 51	04 54	05 45	18 02	18 18	18 43	19 20
04	241 48.8	16.3	30 36.8	11.2	12 56.4	8.3	56.6	64	04 00	04 58	05 46	18 16	18 37	19 06	19 45
05	256 49.0	15.3	45 07.0	11.3	13 04.7	8.2	56.6	62	04 08	05 02	05 46	18 28	18 52	19 24	20 05
06	271 49.2	N 0 14.3	59 37.3	11.2	N13 12.9	8.2	56.6	60	04 15	05 05	05 47	18 38	19 05	19 39	20 21
07	286 49.4	13.4	74 07.5	11.3	13 21.1	8.0	56.6	N 58	04 21	05 08	05 47	18 47	19 16	19 52	20 35
08	301 49.6	12.4	88 37.8	11.2	13 29.1	8.0	56.5	56	04 26	05 10	05 47	18 55	19 26	20 03	20 47
S 09	316 49.9	.. 11.4	103 08.0	11.2	13 37.1	7.9	56.5	54	04 30	05 12	05 48	19 02	19 35	20 13	20 57
U 10	331 50.1	10.4	117 38.2	11.3	13 45.0	7.9	56.5	52	04 34	05 14	05 48	19 09	19 43	20 21	21 06
N 11	346 50.3	09.5	132 08.5	11.2	13 52.9	7.7	56.4	50	04 38	05 16	05 48	19 15	19 50	20 29	21 14
D 12	1 50.5	N 0 08.5	146 38.7	11.3	N14 00.6	7.7	56.4	45	04 45	05 19	05 48	19 27	20 05	20 46	21 32
A 13	16 50.8	07.5	161 09.0	11.2	14 08.3	7.6	56.4	N 40	04 50	05 21	05 49	19 37	20 17	21 00	21 46
Y 14	31 51.0	06.5	175 39.2	11.3	14 15.9	7.5	56.4	35	04 54	05 23	05 49	19 46	20 28	21 11	21 58
15	46 51.2	.. 05.6	190 09.5	11.2	14 23.4	7.4	56.3	30	04 57	05 25	05 49	19 54	20 37	21 22	22 09
16	61 51.4	04.6	204 39.7	11.2	14 30.8	7.4	56.3	20	05 01	05 27	05 49	20 08	20 53	21 39	22 27
17	76 51.6	03.6	219 09.9	11.3	14 38.2	7.2	56.3	N 10	05 04	05 28	05 49	20 20	21 07	21 55	22 43
18	91 51.9	N 0 02.7	233 40.2	11.2	N14 45.4	7.2	56.2	0	05 04	05 28	05 49	20 31	21 20	22 09	22 58
19	106 52.1	01.7	248 10.4	11.3	14 52.6	7.1	56.2	S 10	05 04	05 28	05 49	20 42	21 33	22 23	23 13
20	121 52.3	N 00.7	262 40.7	11.2	14 59.7	7.1	56.2	20	05 01	05 27	05 49	20 54	21 47	22 39	23 28
21	136 52.5	S 00.3	277 10.9	11.3	15 06.8	6.9	56.1	30	04 57	05 24	05 48	21 08	22 04	22 57	23 47
22	151 52.7	01.2	291 41.2	11.2	15 13.7	6.8	56.1	35	04 53	05 23	05 48	21 16	22 13	23 07	23 57
23	166 53.0	02.2	306 11.4	11.3	15 20.5	6.8	56.1	40	04 49	05 21	05 48	21 25	22 24	23 19	24 10
23 00	181 53.2	S 0 03.2	320 41.7	11.2	N15 27.3	6.7	56.1	45	04 43	05 18	05 47	21 36	22 37	23 33	24 24
01	196 53.4	04.2	335 11.9	11.2	15 34.0	6.6	56.0	S 50	04 36	05 14	05 46	21 49	22 52	23 50	24 42
02	211 53.6	05.1	349 42.1	11.3	15 40.6	6.5	56.0	52	04 33	05 13	05 46	21 55	23 00	23 58	24 50
03	226 53.8	.. 06.1	4 12.4	11.2	15 47.1	6.4	56.0	54	04 29	05 11	05 46	22 02	23 08	24 07	00 07
04	241 54.1	07.1	18 42.6	11.3	15 53.5	6.3	55.9	56	04 24	05 08	05 45	22 10	23 17	24 17	00 17
05	256 54.3	08.0	33 12.9	11.2	15 59.8	6.3	55.9	58	04 19	05 06	05 45	22 18	23 27	24 29	00 29
06	271 54.5	S 0 09.0	47 43.1	11.3	N16 06.1	6.2	55.9	S 60	04 13	05 03	05 45	22 28	23 39	24 42	00 42
07	286 54.7	10.0	62 13.4	11.2	16 12.3	6.0	55.9								

UT	SUN		MOON					Lat.	Sunset	Twilight		Moonset			
										Civil	Naut.	22	23	24	25
d h								°	h m	h m	h m	h m	h m	h m	h m
08	301 54.9	11.0	76 43.6	11.3	16 18.3	6.0	55.8	N 72	17 59	19 07	20 35	11 29	13 35	▭	▭
M 09	316 55.2	.. 11.9	91 13.9	11.2	16 24.3	5.9	55.8	N 70	17 58	18 59	20 17	11 01	12 44	14 22	15 47
O 10	331 55.4	12.9	105 44.1	11.3	16 30.2	5.8	55.8	68	17 58	18 53	20 03	10 39	12 12	13 36	14 44
N 11	346 55.6	13.9	120 14.4	11.3	16 36.0	5.7	55.8	66	17 57	18 48	19 51	10 23	11 48	13 05	14 09
D 12	1 55.8	S 0 14.9	134 44.7	11.2	N16 41.7	5.7	55.7	64	17 57	18 44	19 42	10 09	11 30	12 43	13 44
A 13	16 56.0	15.8	149 14.9	11.3	16 47.4	5.5	55.7	62	17 57	18 41	19 34	09 58	11 15	12 25	13 24
Y 14	31 56.2	16.8	163 45.2	11.2	16 52.9	5.5	55.7	60	17 56	18 38	19 28	09 48	11 02	12 10	13 08
15	46 56.5	.. 17.8	178 15.4	11.3	16 58.4	5.3	55.6	N 58	17 56	18 35	19 21	09 40	10 52	11 57	12 55
16	61 56.7	18.8	192 45.7	11.2	17 03.7	5.3	55.6	56	17 56	18 33	19 17	09 32	10 42	11 46	12 43
17	76 56.9	19.7	207 16.0	11.2	17 09.0	5.2	55.6	54	17 56	18 31	19 13	09 26	10 34	11 37	12 33
18	91 57.1	S 0 20.7	221 46.2	11.3	N17 14.2	5.1	55.6	52	17 56	18 29	19 09	09 20	10 27	11 28	12 24
19	106 57.3	21.7	236 16.5	11.3	17 19.3	5.0	55.5	50	17 56	18 28	19 06	09 14	10 20	11 20	12 15
20	121 57.6	22.6	250 46.8	11.3	17 24.3	4.9	55.5	45	17 56	18 25	18 59	09 03	10 06	11 04	11 58
21	136 57.8	.. 23.6	265 17.1	11.3	17 29.2	4.8	55.5	N 40	17 55	18 22	18 54	08 53	09 54	10 51	11 44
22	151 58.0	24.6	279 47.4	11.2	17 34.0	4.7	55.5	35	17 55	18 20	18 50	08 45	09 44	10 39	11 32
23	166 58.2	25.6	294 17.6	11.3	17 38.7	4.6	55.4	30	17 55	18 19	18 47	08 38	09 35	10 29	11 21
24 00	181 58.4	S 0 26.6	308 47.9	11.3	N17 43.3	4.6	55.4	20	17 55	18 17	18 43	08 26	09 20	10 12	11 03
01	196 58.7	27.5	323 18.2	11.3	17 47.9	4.4	55.4	N 10	17 55	18 16	18 41	08 15	09 07	09 58	10 47
02	211 58.9	28.5	337 48.5	11.3	17 52.3	4.4	55.4	0	17 56	18 16	18 40	08 05	08 54	09 44	10 33
03	226 59.1	.. 29.5	352 18.8	11.3	17 56.7	4.3	55.3	S 10	17 56	18 17	18 41	07 55	08 42	09 30	10 18
04	241 59.3	30.4	6 49.1	11.3	18 01.0	4.1	55.3	20	17 56	18 19	18 44	07 44	08 29	09 15	10 02
05	256 59.5	31.4	21 19.4	11.3	18 05.1	4.1	55.3	30	17 57	18 21	18 49	07 32	08 14	08 58	09 44
06	271 59.7	S 0 32.4	35 49.7	11.4	N18 09.2	4.0	55.3	35	17 57	18 23	18 52	07 25	08 05	08 48	09 33
07	287 00.0	33.3	50 20.1	11.3	18 13.2	3.9	55.3	40	17 57	18 25	18 57	07 17	07 56	08 37	09 21
T 08	302 00.2	34.3	64 50.4	11.3	18 17.1	3.8	55.2	45	17 58	18 28	19 02	07 08	07 44	08 23	09 07
U 09	317 00.4	.. 35.3	79 20.7	11.4	18 20.9	3.7	55.2	S 50	17 59	18 31	19 10	06 57	07 30	08 07	08 50
E 10	332 00.6	36.3	93 51.1	11.3	18 24.6	3.6	55.2	52	17 59	18 33	19 13	06 52	07 23	08 00	08 41
S 11	347 00.8	37.2	108 21.4	11.3	18 28.2	3.5	55.2	54	18 00	18 35	19 17	06 46	07 16	07 51	08 32
D 12	2 01.1	S 0 38.2	122 51.7	11.4	N18 31.7	3.5	55.1	56	18 00	18 37	19 22	06 40	07 08	07 42	08 22
A 13	17 01.3	39.2	137 22.1	11.3	18 35.2	3.3	55.1	58	18 01	18 40	19 27	06 33	06 59	07 31	08 11
Y 14	32 01.5	40.2	151 52.4	11.4	18 38.5	3.2	55.1	S 60	18 01	18 43	19 33	06 25	06 49	07 19	07 57
15	47 01.7	.. 41.1	166 22.8	11.4	18 41.7	3.2	55.1								
16	62 01.9	42.1	180 53.2	11.4	18 44.9	3.0	55.1								
17	77 02.1	43.1	195 23.6	11.4	18 47.9	3.0	55.0								
18	92 02.4	S 0 44.1	209 54.0	11.4	N18 50.9	2.9	55.0								
19	107 02.6	45.0	224 24.4	11.4	18 53.8	2.7	55.0			SUN			MOON		
20	122 02.8	46.0	238 54.8	11.4	18 56.5	2.7	55.0	Day	Eqn. of Time		Mer.	Mer. Pass.		Age	Phase
21	137 03.0	.. 47.0	253 25.2	11.4	18 59.2	2.6	54.9		00ʰ	12ʰ	Pass.	Upper	Lower		
22	152 03.2	48.0	267 55.6	11.4	19 01.8	2.5	54.9	d	m s	m s	h m	h m	h m	d	%
23	167 03.4	48.9	282 26.0	11.5	N19 04.3	2.4	54.9	22	07 11	07 22	11 53	01 53	14 18	17	90
	SD 16.0	d 1.0	SD 15.4		15.2		15.0	23	07 32	07 43	11 52	02 43	15 07	18	83
								24	07 53	08 04	11 52	03 32	15 56	19	75

UT	ARIES GHA	VENUS −4.2 GHA	Dec	MARS +1.6 GHA	Dec	JUPITER −2.2 GHA	Dec	SATURN +0.7 GHA	Dec	STARS Name	SHA	Dec
25 00	3 58.7	141 13.8	S18 10.8	223 35.0	N16 43.6	254 53.6	N22 11.5	146 17.5	S12 32.9	Acamar	315 17.9	S40 14.8
01	19 01.1	156 13.5	11.8	238 35.9	43.2	269 55.7	11.5	161 19.7	33.0	Achernar	335 26.1	S57 09.9
02	34 03.6	171 13.2	12.8	253 36.8	42.7	284 57.8	11.5	176 21.9	33.1	Acrux	173 09.7	S63 10.5
03	49 06.1	186 12.8 ..	13.8	268 37.7 ..	42.3	300 00.0 ..	11.4	191 24.2 ..	33.2	Adhara	255 12.4	S28 59.3
04	64 08.5	201 12.5	14.8	283 38.6	41.8	315 02.1	11.4	206 26.4	33.3	Aldebaran	290 49.0	N16 32.1
05	79 11.0	216 12.2	15.8	298 39.6	41.4	330 04.2	11.3	221 28.6	33.3			
06	94 13.4	231 11.8	S18 16.7	313 40.5	N16 40.9	345 06.4	N22 11.3	236 30.8	S12 33.4	Alioth	166 21.1	N55 53.2
W 07	109 15.9	246 11.5	17.7	328 41.4	40.4	0 08.5	11.3	251 33.0	33.5	Alkaid	152 59.2	N49 14.9
E 08	124 18.4	261 11.2	18.7	343 42.3	40.0	15 10.6	11.2	266 35.2	33.6	Al Na'ir	27 43.1	S46 53.6
D 09	139 20.8	276 10.8 ..	19.7	358 43.3 ..	39.5	30 12.7 ..	11.2	281 37.4 ..	33.7	Alnilam	275 46.1	S 1 11.6
N 10	154 23.3	291 10.5	20.7	13 44.2	39.1	45 14.9	11.2	296 39.7	33.8	Alphard	217 56.1	S 8 43.1
E 11	169 25.8	306 10.2	21.7	28 45.1	38.6	60 17.0	11.1	311 41.9	33.9			
S 12	184 28.2	321 09.8	S18 22.6	43 46.0	N16 38.2	75 19.1	N22 11.1	326 44.1	S12 33.9	Alphecca	126 11.1	N26 40.4
D 13	199 30.7	336 09.5	23.6	58 47.0	37.7	90 21.3	11.0	341 46.3	34.0	Alpheratz	357 42.9	N29 10.2
A 14	214 33.2	351 09.1	24.6	73 47.9	37.3	105 23.4	11.0	356 48.5	34.1	Altair	62 07.9	N 8 54.6
Y 15	229 35.6	6 08.8 ..	25.6	88 48.8 ..	36.8	120 25.5 ..	11.0	11 50.7 ..	34.2	Ankaa	353 15.1	S42 13.7
16	244 38.1	21 08.5	26.6	103 49.7	36.4	135 27.6	10.9	26 52.9	34.3	Antares	112 26.2	S26 27.6
17	259 40.6	36 08.1	27.5	118 50.7	35.9	150 29.8	10.9	41 55.2	34.4			
18	274 43.0	51 07.8	S18 28.5	133 51.6	N16 35.5	165 31.9	N22 10.9	56 57.4	S12 34.5	Arcturus	145 55.8	N19 06.9
19	289 45.5	66 07.4	29.5	148 52.5	35.0	180 34.0	10.8	71 59.6	34.6	Atria	107 27.9	S69 03.2
20	304 47.9	81 07.1	30.5	163 53.5	34.6	195 36.2	10.8	87 01.8	34.6	Avior	234 18.2	S59 33.1
21	319 50.4	96 06.8 ..	31.4	178 54.4 ..	34.1	210 38.3 ..	10.8	102 04.0 ..	34.7	Bellatrix	278 31.7	N 6 21.7
22	334 52.9	111 06.4	32.4	193 55.3	33.6	225 40.4	10.7	117 06.2	34.8	Betelgeuse	271 01.1	N 7 24.5
23	349 55.3	126 06.1	33.4	208 56.2	33.2	240 42.6	10.7	132 08.4	34.9			
26 00	4 57.8	141 05.7	S18 34.4	223 57.2	N16 32.7	255 44.7	N22 10.6	147 10.6	S12 35.0	Canopus	263 56.1	S52 42.0
01	20 00.3	156 05.4	35.3	238 58.1	32.3	270 46.8	10.6	162 12.9	35.1	Capella	280 34.0	N46 00.4
02	35 02.7	171 05.1	36.3	253 59.0	31.8	285 49.0	10.6	177 15.1	35.2	Deneb	49 31.0	N45 20.2
03	50 05.2	186 04.7 ..	37.3	269 00.0 ..	31.4	300 51.1 ..	10.5	192 17.3 ..	35.3	Denebola	182 33.8	N14 29.8
04	65 07.7	201 04.4	38.2	284 00.9	30.9	315 53.2	10.5	207 19.5	35.3	Diphda	348 55.4	S17 54.5
05	80 10.1	216 04.0	39.2	299 01.8	30.5	330 55.4	10.5	222 21.7	35.4			
06	95 12.6	231 03.7	S18 40.2	314 02.7	N16 30.0	345 57.5	N22 10.4	237 23.9	S12 35.5	Dubhe	193 52.2	N61 40.5
T 07	110 15.1	246 03.4	41.1	329 03.7	29.5	0 59.6	10.4	252 26.1	35.6	Elnath	278 12.3	N28 36.9
H 08	125 17.5	261 03.0	42.1	344 04.6	29.1	16 01.8	10.4	267 28.3	35.7	Eltanin	90 46.1	N51 29.7
U 09	140 20.0	276 02.7 ..	43.1	359 05.5 ..	28.6	31 03.9 ..	10.3	282 30.6 ..	35.8	Enif	33 46.7	N 9 56.6
R 10	155 22.4	291 02.3	44.0	14 06.5	28.2	46 06.0	10.3	297 32.8	35.9	Fomalhaut	15 23.4	S29 32.8
11	170 24.9	306 02.0	45.0	29 07.4	27.7	61 08.2	10.2	312 35.0	36.0			
S 12	185 27.4	321 01.6	S18 46.0	44 08.3	N16 27.3	76 10.3	N22 10.2	327 37.2	S12 36.1	Gacrux	172 01.2	S57 11.4
D 13	200 29.8	336 01.3	46.9	59 09.2	26.8	91 12.4	10.2	342 39.4	36.1	Gienah	175 52.4	S17 37.0
A 14	215 32.3	351 00.9	47.9	74 10.2	26.4	106 14.6	10.1	357 41.6	36.2	Hadar	148 48.1	S60 26.4
Y 15	230 34.8	6 00.6 ..	48.9	89 11.1 ..	25.9	121 16.7 ..	10.1	12 43.8 ..	36.3	Hamal	328 00.2	N23 31.7
16	245 37.2	21 00.3	49.8	104 12.0	25.4	136 18.8	10.1	27 46.0	36.4	Kaus Aust.	83 43.5	S34 22.6
17	260 39.7	35 59.9	50.8	119 13.0	25.0	151 21.0	10.0	42 48.3	36.5			
18	275 42.2	50 59.6	S18 51.7	134 13.9	N16 24.5	166 23.1	N22 10.0	57 50.5	S12 36.6	Kochab	137 21.0	N74 06.2
19	290 44.6	65 59.2	52.7	149 14.8	24.1	181 25.3	10.0	72 52.7	36.7	Markab	13 37.8	N15 17.0
20	305 47.1	80 58.9	53.7	164 15.8	23.6	196 27.4	09.9	87 54.9	36.8	Menkar	314 14.6	N 4 08.7
21	320 49.5	95 58.5 ..	54.6	179 16.7 ..	23.2	211 29.5 ..	09.9	102 57.1 ..	36.8	Menkent	148 07.7	S36 26.2
22	335 52.0	110 58.2	55.6	194 17.6	22.7	226 31.7	09.8	117 59.3	36.9	Miaplacidus	221 40.2	S69 46.3
23	350 54.5	125 57.8	56.5	209 18.6	22.2	241 33.8	09.8	133 01.5	37.0			
27 00	5 56.9	140 57.5	S18 57.5	224 19.5	N16 21.8	256 35.9	N22 09.8	148 03.7	S12 37.1	Mirfak	308 39.7	N49 54.4
01	20 59.4	155 57.1	58.4	239 20.4	21.3	271 38.1	09.7	163 05.9	37.2	Nunki	75 58.0	S26 16.6
02	36 01.9	170 56.8	18 59.4	254 21.4	20.9	286 40.2	09.7	178 08.1	37.3	Peacock	53 18.7	S56 41.4
03	51 04.3	185 56.4	19 00.3	269 22.3 ..	20.4	301 42.4 ..	09.7	193 10.4 ..	37.4	Pollux	243 27.6	N27 59.4
04	66 06.8	200 56.1	01.3	284 23.2	19.9	316 44.5	09.6	208 12.6	37.5	Procyon	244 59.6	N 5 11.3
05	81 09.3	215 55.7	02.2	299 24.2	19.5	331 46.6	09.6	223 14.8	37.5			
06	96 11.7	230 55.4	S19 03.2	314 25.1	N16 19.0	346 48.8	N22 09.6	238 17.0	S12 37.6	Rasalhague	96 06.3	N12 33.4
07	111 14.2	245 55.0	04.1	329 26.0	18.6	1 50.9	09.5	253 19.2	37.7	Regulus	207 43.6	N11 54.0
F 08	126 16.7	260 54.7	05.1	344 27.0	18.1	16 53.1	09.5	268 21.4	37.8	Rigel	281 11.8	S 8 11.1
R 09	141 19.1	275 54.3 ..	06.0	359 27.9 ..	17.6	31 55.2 ..	09.5	283 23.6 ..	37.9	Rigil Kent.	139 51.9	S60 53.5
I 10	156 21.6	290 54.0	07.0	14 28.8	17.2	46 57.3	09.4	298 25.8	38.0	Sabik	102 12.4	S15 44.3
11	171 24.0	305 53.6	07.9	29 29.8	16.7	61 59.5	09.4	313 28.0	38.1			
D 12	186 26.5	320 53.3	S19 08.9	44 30.7	N16 16.3	77 01.6	N22 09.3	328 30.3	S12 38.2	Schedar	349 39.7	N56 36.8
A 13	201 29.0	335 52.9	09.8	59 31.6	15.8	92 03.8	09.3	343 32.5	38.2	Shaula	96 21.7	S37 06.7
Y 14	216 31.4	350 52.6	10.8	74 32.6	15.3	107 05.9	09.3	358 34.7	38.3	Sirius	258 33.6	S16 44.1
15	231 33.9	5 52.2 ..	11.7	89 33.5 ..	14.9	122 08.1 ..	09.2	13 36.9 ..	38.3	Spica	158 31.3	S11 13.9
16	246 36.4	20 51.9	12.7	104 34.5	14.4	137 10.2	09.2	28 39.1	38.5	Suhail	222 52.6	S43 29.2
17	261 38.8	35 51.5	13.6	119 35.4	14.0	152 12.3	09.2	43 41.3	38.6			
18	276 41.3	50 51.2	S19 14.5	134 36.3	N16 13.5	167 14.5	N22 09.1	58 43.5	S12 38.7	Vega	80 38.8	N38 48.3
19	291 43.8	65 50.8	15.5	149 37.3	13.0	182 16.6	09.1	73 45.7	38.8	Zuben'ubi	137 05.4	S16 05.8
20	306 46.2	80 50.5	16.4	164 38.2	12.6	197 18.8	09.1	88 47.9	38.9		SHA	Mer.Pass.
21	321 48.7	95 50.1 ..	17.4	179 39.1 ..	12.1	212 20.9 ..	09.0	103 50.1 ..	39.0		° '	h m
22	336 51.2	110 49.7	18.3	194 40.1	11.7	227 23.1	09.0	118 52.3	39.0	Venus	136 07.9	14 36
23	351 53.6	125 49.4	19.2	209 41.0	11.2	242 25.2	09.0	133 54.6	39.1	Mars	218 59.4	9 04
	h m									Jupiter	250 46.9	6 56
Mer.Pass.	23 36.3	v −0.3	d 1.0	v 0.9	d 0.5	v 2.1	d 0.0	v 2.2	d 0.1	Saturn	142 12.8	14 09

UT	SUN GHA	SUN Dec	MOON GHA	v	MOON Dec	d	HP
25 00	182 03.7	S 0 49.9	296 56.5	11.4	N19 06.7	2.3	54.9
01	197 03.9	50.9	311 26.9	11.5	19 09.0	2.2	54.9
02	212 04.1	51.8	325 57.4	11.4	19 11.2	2.1	54.9
03	227 04.3	.. 52.8	340 27.8	11.5	19 13.3	2.0	54.8
04	242 04.5	53.8	354 58.3	11.5	19 15.3	1.9	54.8
05	257 04.7	54.8	9 28.8	11.5	19 17.2	1.8	54.8
06	272 05.0	S 0 55.7	23 59.3	11.5	N19 19.0	1.8	54.8
W 07	287 05.2	56.7	38 29.8	11.5	19 20.8	1.6	54.8
E 08	302 05.4	57.7	53 00.3	11.6	19 22.4	1.6	54.7
D 09	317 05.6	.. 58.7	67 30.9	11.5	19 24.0	1.4	54.7
N 10	332 05.8	0 59.6	82 01.4	11.5	19 25.4	1.4	54.7
N 11	347 06.0	1 00.6	96 31.9	11.6	19 26.8	1.2	54.7
E 12	2 06.3	S 1 01.6	111 02.5	11.6	N19 28.0	1.2	54.7
S 13	17 06.5	02.6	125 33.1	11.6	19 29.2	1.1	54.7
D 14	32 06.7	03.5	140 03.7	11.6	19 30.3	1.0	54.6
A 15	47 06.9	.. 04.5	154 34.3	11.6	19 31.3	0.9	54.6
Y 16	62 07.1	05.5	169 04.9	11.6	19 32.2	0.8	54.6
17	77 07.3	06.4	183 35.5	11.7	19 33.0	0.7	54.6
18	92 07.5	S 1 07.4	198 06.2	11.6	N19 33.7	0.6	54.6
19	107 07.8	08.4	212 36.8	11.7	19 34.3	0.5	54.6
20	122 08.0	09.4	227 07.5	11.7	19 34.8	0.4	54.6
21	137 08.2	.. 10.3	241 38.2	11.7	19 35.2	0.3	54.5
22	152 08.4	11.3	256 08.9	11.7	19 35.5	0.3	54.5
23	167 08.6	12.3	270 39.6	11.8	19 35.8	0.1	54.5
26 00	182 08.8	S 1 13.3	285 10.4	11.7	N19 35.9	0.1	54.5
01	197 09.0	14.2	299 41.1	11.8	19 36.0	0.1	54.5
02	212 09.3	15.2	314 11.9	11.7	19 35.9	0.1	54.5
03	227 09.5	.. 16.2	328 42.6	11.8	19 35.8	0.2	54.5
04	242 09.7	17.2	343 13.4	11.8	19 35.6	0.3	54.5
05	257 09.9	18.1	357 44.2	11.9	19 35.3	0.3	54.4
06	272 10.1	S 1 19.1	12 15.1	11.8	N19 34.8	0.5	54.4
T 07	287 10.3	20.1	26 45.9	11.9	19 34.3	0.5	54.4
H 08	302 10.5	21.1	41 16.8	11.9	19 33.8	0.7	54.4
U 09	317 10.8	.. 22.0	55 47.7	11.9	19 33.1	0.8	54.4
R 10	332 11.0	23.0	70 18.6	11.9	19 32.3	0.9	54.4
11	347 11.2	24.0	84 49.5	11.9	19 31.4	0.9	54.4
S 12	2 11.4	S 1 24.9	99 20.4	11.9	N19 30.5	1.1	54.4
D 13	17 11.6	25.9	113 51.3	12.0	19 29.4	1.1	54.4
A 14	32 11.8	26.9	128 22.3	12.0	19 28.3	1.2	54.4
Y 15	47 12.0	.. 27.9	142 53.3	12.0	19 27.1	1.4	54.3
16	62 12.3	28.8	157 24.3	12.0	19 25.7	1.4	54.3
17	77 12.5	29.8	171 55.3	12.1	19 24.3	1.5	54.3
18	92 12.7	S 1 30.8	186 26.4	12.0	N19 22.8	1.6	54.3
19	107 12.9	31.8	200 57.4	12.1	19 21.2	1.6	54.3
20	122 13.1	32.7	215 28.5	12.1	19 19.6	1.8	54.3
21	137 13.3	.. 33.7	229 59.6	12.1	19 17.8	1.9	54.3
22	152 13.5	34.7	244 30.7	12.1	19 15.9	1.9	54.3
23	167 13.7	35.7	259 01.8	12.2	19 14.0	2.0	54.3
27 00	182 14.0	S 1 36.6	273 33.0	12.2	N19 12.0	2.1	54.3
01	197 14.2	37.6	288 04.2	12.2	19 09.9	2.3	54.3
02	212 14.4	38.6	302 35.4	12.2	19 07.6	2.2	54.3
03	227 14.6	.. 39.5	317 06.6	12.2	19 05.4	2.4	54.3
04	242 14.8	40.5	331 37.8	12.3	19 03.0	2.5	54.3
05	257 15.0	41.5	346 09.1	12.2	19 00.5	2.6	54.3
06	272 15.2	S 1 42.5	0 40.3	12.3	N18 57.9	2.6	54.3
F 07	287 15.4	43.4	15 11.6	12.4	18 55.3	2.7	54.3
R 08	302 15.7	44.4	29 43.0	12.3	18 52.6	2.8	54.3
I 09	317 15.9	.. 45.4	44 14.3	12.4	18 49.8	2.9	54.2
D 10	332 16.1	46.4	58 45.7	12.3	18 46.9	3.0	54.2
11	347 16.3	47.3	73 17.0	12.4	18 43.9	3.1	54.2
A 12	2 16.5	S 1 48.3	87 48.4	12.5	N18 40.8	3.2	54.2
Y 13	17 16.7	49.3	102 19.9	12.4	18 37.6	3.2	54.2
14	32 16.9	50.2	116 51.3	12.5	18 34.4	3.3	54.2
15	47 17.1	.. 51.2	131 22.8	12.4	18 31.1	3.4	54.2
16	62 17.3	52.2	145 54.2	12.5	18 27.7	3.5	54.2
17	77 17.6	53.2	160 25.7	12.6	18 24.2	3.6	54.2
18	92 17.8	S 1 54.1	174 57.3	12.5	N18 20.6	3.7	54.2
19	107 18.0	55.1	189 28.8	12.6	18 16.9	3.7	54.2
20	122 18.2	56.1	204 00.4	12.6	18 13.2	3.8	54.2
21	137 18.4	.. 57.1	218 32.0	12.6	18 09.4	3.9	54.2
22	152 18.6	58.0	233 03.6	12.6	18 05.5	4.0	54.2
23	167 18.8	59.0	247 35.2	12.7	N18 01.5	4.1	54.2
	SD 16.0	d 1.0	SD 14.9		14.8		14.8

Twilight / Sunrise / Moonrise

Lat.	Naut.	Civil	Sunrise	Moonrise 25	26	27	28
N 72	03 23	04 49	05 57	▭	▭	▭	20 59
N 70	03 39	04 55	05 56	17 42	18 40	20 08	21 43
68	03 51	05 00	05 55	18 45	19 38	20 50	22 12
66	04 02	05 04	05 55	19 20	20 12	21 18	22 34
64	04 10	05 07	05 55	19 45	20 37	21 40	22 51
62	04 17	05 10	05 54	20 05	20 56	21 57	23 05
60	04 23	05 12	05 54	20 21	21 12	22 11	23 17
N 58	04 28	05 14	05 53	20 35	21 26	22 23	23 27
56	04 32	05 16	05 53	20 47	21 37	22 34	23 36
54	04 36	05 18	05 53	20 57	21 47	22 43	23 44
52	04 39	05 19	05 53	21 06	21 56	22 52	23 51
50	04 42	05 20	05 52	21 14	22 04	22 59	23 57
45	04 48	05 23	05 52	21 32	22 21	23 16	24 11
N 40	04 53	05 24	05 51	21 46	22 35	23 28	24 22
35	04 56	05 26	05 51	21 58	22 47	23 39	24 32
30	04 59	05 27	05 51	22 09	22 58	23 48	24 40
20	05 02	05 28	05 50	22 27	23 16	24 05	00 05
N 10	05 04	05 28	05 49	22 43	23 31	24 19	00 19
0	05 03	05 27	05 48	22 58	23 46	24 33	00 33
S 10	05 02	05 26	05 47	23 13	24 00	00 00	00 46
20	04 58	05 24	05 46	23 28	24 16	00 16	01 01
30	04 53	05 21	05 44	23 47	24 34	00 34	01 17
35	04 49	05 18	05 44	23 57	24 44	00 44	01 27
40	04 44	05 16	05 43	24 10	00 10	00 56	01 38
45	04 37	05 12	05 41	24 24	00 24	01 10	01 51
S 50	04 29	05 08	05 40	24 42	00 42	01 27	02 06
52	04 25	05 05	05 39	24 50	00 50	01 35	02 13
54	04 21	05 03	05 38	00 07	00 59	01 44	02 22
56	04 16	05 00	05 38	00 17	01 10	01 54	02 31
58	04 10	04 57	05 37	00 29	01 22	02 06	02 41
S 60	04 03	04 54	05 36	00 42	01 36	02 19	02 53

Sunset / Twilight / Moonset

Lat.	Sunset	Civil	Naut.	Moonset 25	26	27	28
N 72	17 43	18 51	20 16	▭	▭	▭	17 26
N 70	17 44	18 45	20 00	15 47	16 29	16 40	16 41
68	17 45	18 40	19 48	14 44	15 31	15 57	16 12
66	17 46	18 37	19 38	14 09	14 57	15 29	15 50
64	17 46	18 34	19 30	13 44	14 32	15 07	15 32
62	17 47	18 31	19 24	13 24	14 12	14 49	15 17
60	17 47	18 29	19 18	13 08	13 56	14 35	15 05
N 58	17 48	18 27	19 13	12 55	13 43	14 22	14 54
56	17 48	18 25	19 09	12 43	13 31	14 12	14 45
54	17 49	18 24	19 05	12 33	13 21	14 02	14 37
52	17 49	18 22	19 02	12 24	13 12	13 54	14 29
50	17 49	18 21	18 59	12 15	13 04	13 46	14 22
45	17 50	18 19	18 53	11 58	12 46	13 30	14 08
N 40	17 51	18 17	18 49	11 44	12 32	13 16	13 56
35	17 51	18 16	18 46	11 32	12 20	13 05	13 46
30	17 52	18 15	18 43	11 21	12 10	12 55	13 37
20	17 53	18 14	18 40	11 03	11 52	12 38	13 22
N 10	17 53	18 14	18 39	10 47	11 36	12 23	13 08
0	17 54	18 15	18 39	10 33	11 21	12 09	12 55
S 10	17 56	18 17	18 41	10 18	11 06	11 55	12 43
20	17 57	18 19	18 45	10 02	10 50	11 39	12 29
30	17 59	18 22	18 50	09 44	10 32	11 22	12 13
35	17 59	18 25	18 54	09 33	10 21	11 12	12 04
40	18 01	18 28	19 00	09 21	10 09	11 00	11 54
45	18 02	18 31	19 06	09 07	09 55	10 47	11 41
S 50	18 04	18 36	19 14	08 50	09 37	10 30	11 26
52	18 04	18 38	19 19	08 41	09 29	10 22	11 19
54	18 05	18 41	19 23	08 32	09 20	10 13	11 12
56	18 06	18 44	19 28	08 22	09 09	10 03	11 03
58	18 07	18 47	19 34	08 10	08 57	09 52	10 53
S 60	18 08	18 50	19 41	07 57	08 43	09 39	10 42

SUN / MOON

Day	Eqn. of Time 00h	12h	Mer. Pass.	Mer. Pass. Upper	Lower	Age	Phase
	m s	m s	h m	h m	h m	d	%
25	08 14	08 25	11 52	04 21	16 45	20	66
26	08 35	08 45	11 51	05 09	17 33	21	56
27	08 55	09 06	11 51	05 57	18 21	22	47

UT	ARIES	VENUS −4.2		MARS +1.6		JUPITER −2.2		SATURN +0.7		STARS		
d h	GHA	GHA	Dec	GHA	Dec	GHA	Dec	GHA	Dec	Name	SHA	Dec
28 00	6 56.1	140 49.0	S19 20.2	224 41.9	N16 10.7	257 27.4	N22 08.9	148 56.8	S12 39.2	Acamar	315 17.9	S40 14.8
01	21 58.5	155 48.7	21.1	239 42.9	10.3	272 29.5	08.9	163 59.0	39.3	Achernar	335 26.1	S57 09.9
02	37 01.0	170 48.3	22.1	254 43.8	09.8	287 31.6	08.8	179 01.2	39.4	Acrux	173 09.7	S63 10.5
03	52 03.5	185 48.0 ..	23.0	269 44.8 ..	09.3	302 33.8 ..	08.8	194 03.4 ..	39.5	Adhara	255 12.4	S28 59.3
04	67 05.9	200 47.6	23.9	284 45.7	08.9	317 35.9	08.8	209 05.6	39.6	Aldebaran	290 49.0	N16 32.1
05	82 08.4	215 47.3	24.9	299 46.6	08.4	332 38.1	08.7	224 07.8	39.7			
06	97 10.9	230 46.9	S19 25.8	314 47.6	N16 08.0	347 40.2	N22 08.7	239 10.0	S12 39.7	Alioth	166 21.1	N55 53.2
07	112 13.3	245 46.5	26.7	329 48.5	07.5	2 42.4	08.7	254 12.2	39.8	Alkaid	152 59.2	N49 14.9
08	127 15.8	260 46.2	27.7	344 49.5	07.0	17 44.5	08.6	269 14.4	39.9	Al Na'ir	27 43.1	S46 53.6
09	142 18.3	275 45.8 ..	28.6	359 50.4 ..	06.6	32 46.7 ..	08.6	284 16.6 ..	40.0	Alnilam	275 46.1	S 1 11.6
10	157 20.7	290 45.5	29.5	14 51.3	06.1	47 48.8	08.6	299 18.9	40.1	Alphard	217 56.1	S 8 43.1
11	172 23.2	305 45.1	30.4	29 52.3	05.6	62 51.0	08.5	314 21.1	40.2			
12	187 25.7	320 44.7	S19 31.4	44 53.2	N16 05.2	77 53.1	N22 08.5	329 23.3	S12 40.3	Alphecca	126 11.1	N26 40.4
13	202 28.1	335 44.4	32.3	59 54.2	04.7	92 55.3	08.5	344 25.5	40.4	Alpheratz	357 42.9	N29 10.2
14	217 30.6	350 44.0	33.2	74 55.1	04.3	107 57.4	08.4	359 27.7	40.5	Altair	62 07.9	N 8 54.6
15	232 33.0	5 43.7 ..	34.2	89 56.0 ..	03.8	122 59.6 ..	08.4	14 29.9 ..	40.5	Ankaa	353 15.1	S42 13.7
16	247 35.5	20 43.3	35.1	104 57.0	03.3	138 01.7	08.4	29 32.1	40.6	Antares	112 26.2	S26 27.6
17	262 38.0	35 42.9	36.0	119 57.9	02.9	153 03.9	08.3	44 34.3	40.7			
18	277 40.4	50 42.6	S19 36.9	134 58.9	N16 02.4	168 06.0	N22 08.3	59 36.5	S12 40.8	Arcturus	145 55.9	N19 06.9
19	292 42.9	65 42.2	37.9	149 59.8	01.9	183 08.2	08.2	74 38.7	40.9	Atria	107 28.0	S69 03.2
20	307 45.4	80 41.9	38.8	165 00.7	01.5	198 10.3	08.2	89 40.9	41.0	Avior	234 18.2	S59 33.1
21	322 47.8	95 41.5 ..	39.7	180 01.7 ..	01.0	213 12.5 ..	08.2	104 43.1 ..	41.1	Bellatrix	278 31.7	N 6 21.7
22	337 50.3	110 41.1	40.6	195 02.6	00.5	228 14.6	08.1	119 45.3	41.2	Betelgeuse	271 01.0	N 7 24.5
23	352 52.8	125 40.8	41.5	210 03.6	16 00.1	243 16.8	08.1	134 47.6	41.3			
29 00	7 55.2	140 40.4	S19 42.5	225 04.5	N15 59.6	258 18.9	N22 08.1	149 49.8	S12 41.3	Canopus	263 56.0	S52 42.0
01	22 57.7	155 40.1	43.4	240 05.5	59.2	273 21.1	08.0	164 52.0	41.4	Capella	280 34.0	N46 00.4
02	38 00.1	170 39.7	44.3	255 06.4	58.7	288 23.2	08.0	179 54.2	41.5	Deneb	49 31.1	N45 20.2
03	53 02.6	185 39.3 ..	45.2	270 07.3 ..	58.2	303 25.4 ..	08.0	194 56.4 ..	41.6	Denebola	182 33.8	N14 29.8
04	68 05.1	200 39.0	46.1	285 08.3	57.8	318 27.5	07.9	209 58.6	41.7	Diphda	348 55.4	S17 54.5
05	83 07.5	215 38.6	47.0	300 09.2	57.3	333 29.7	07.9	225 00.8	41.8			
06	98 10.0	230 38.2	S19 48.0	315 10.2	N15 56.9	348 31.8	N22 07.9	240 03.0	S12 41.9	Dubhe	193 52.1	N61 40.5
07	113 12.5	245 37.9	48.9	330 11.1	56.4	3 34.0	07.8	255 05.2	42.0	Elnath	278 12.3	N28 36.9
08	128 14.9	260 37.5	49.8	345 12.1	55.9	18 36.1	07.8	270 07.4	42.0	Eltanin	90 46.1	N51 29.7
09	143 17.4	275 37.1 ..	50.7	0 13.0 ..	55.4	33 38.3 ..	07.8	285 09.6 ..	42.1	Enif	33 46.7	N 9 56.6
10	158 19.9	290 36.8	51.6	15 14.0	55.0	48 40.5	07.7	300 11.8	42.2	Fomalhaut	15 23.4	S29 32.8
11	173 22.3	305 36.4	52.5	30 14.9	54.5	63 42.6	07.7	315 14.0	42.3			
12	188 24.8	320 36.0	S19 53.4	45 15.8	N15 54.0	78 44.8	N22 07.7	330 16.2	S12 42.4	Gacrux	172 01.2	S57 11.4
13	203 27.3	335 35.7	54.3	60 16.8	53.6	93 46.9	07.6	345 18.4	42.5	Gienah	175 52.4	S17 37.0
14	218 29.7	350 35.3	55.2	75 17.7	53.1	108 49.1	07.6	0 20.7	42.6	Hadar	148 48.1	S60 26.4
15	233 32.2	5 34.9 ..	56.2	90 18.7 ..	52.6	123 51.2 ..	07.6	15 22.9 ..	42.7	Hamal	328 00.2	N23 31.7
16	248 34.6	20 34.6	57.1	105 19.6	52.2	138 53.4	07.5	30 25.1	42.8	Kaus Aust.	83 43.5	S34 22.6
17	263 37.1	35 34.2	58.0	120 20.6	51.7	153 55.5	07.5	45 27.3	42.8			
18	278 39.6	50 33.8	S19 58.9	135 21.5	N15 51.2	168 57.7	N22 07.5	60 29.5	S12 42.9	Kochab	137 21.1	N74 06.2
19	293 42.0	65 33.5	19 59.8	150 22.5	50.8	183 59.8	07.4	75 31.7	43.0	Markab	13 37.8	N15 17.0
20	308 44.5	80 33.1	20 00.7	165 23.4	50.3	199 02.0	07.4	90 33.9	43.1	Menkar	314 14.6	N 4 08.7
21	323 47.0	95 32.7 ..	01.6	180 24.4 ..	49.8	214 04.2 ..	07.4	105 36.1 ..	43.2	Menkent	148 07.7	S36 26.2
22	338 49.4	110 32.4	02.5	195 25.3	49.4	229 06.3	07.3	120 38.3	43.3	Miaplacidus	221 40.1	S69 46.3
23	353 51.9	125 32.0	03.4	210 26.3	48.9	244 08.5	07.3	135 40.5	43.4			
30 00	8 54.4	140 31.6	S20 04.3	225 27.2	N15 48.4	259 10.6	N22 07.2	150 42.7	S12 43.5	Mirfak	308 39.7	N49 54.4
01	23 56.8	155 31.3	05.2	240 28.1	48.0	274 12.8	07.2	165 44.9	43.6	Nunki	75 58.0	S26 16.6
02	38 59.3	170 30.9	06.1	255 29.1	47.5	289 15.0	07.2	180 47.1	43.6	Peacock	53 18.7	S56 41.4
03	54 01.8	185 30.5 ..	07.0	270 30.0 ..	47.0	304 17.1 ..	07.1	195 49.3 ..	43.7	Pollux	243 27.6	N27 59.4
04	69 04.2	200 30.1	07.9	285 31.0	46.5	319 19.3	07.1	210 51.5	43.8	Procyon	244 59.6	N 5 11.3
05	84 06.7	215 29.8	08.8	300 31.9	46.1	334 21.4	07.1	225 53.7	43.9			
06	99 09.1	230 29.4	S20 09.7	315 32.9	N15 45.6	349 23.6	N22 07.0	240 55.9	S12 44.0	Rasalhague	96 06.3	N12 33.4
07	114 11.6	245 29.0	10.6	330 33.8	45.1	4 25.8	07.0	255 58.1	44.1	Regulus	207 43.6	N11 54.0
08	129 14.1	260 28.7	11.5	345 34.8	44.7	19 27.9	07.0	271 00.4	44.2	Rigel	281 11.8	S 8 11.1
09	144 16.5	275 28.3 ..	12.4	0 35.7 ..	44.2	34 30.1 ..	06.9	286 02.6 ..	44.3	Rigil Kent.	139 51.9	S60 53.5
10	159 19.0	290 27.9	13.2	15 36.7	43.7	49 32.2	06.9	301 04.8	44.4	Sabik	102 12.4	S15 44.3
11	174 21.5	305 27.5	14.1	30 37.6	43.3	64 34.4	06.9	316 07.0	44.4			
12	189 23.9	320 27.2	S20 15.0	45 38.6	N15 42.8	79 36.6	N22 06.8	331 09.2	S12 44.5	Schedar	349 39.7	N56 36.9
13	204 26.4	335 26.8	15.9	60 39.5	42.3	94 38.7	06.8	346 11.4	44.6	Shaula	96 21.7	S37 06.7
14	219 28.9	350 26.4	16.8	75 40.5	41.9	109 40.9	06.8	1 13.6	44.7	Sirius	258 33.6	S16 44.1
15	234 31.3	5 26.0 ..	17.7	90 41.4 ..	41.4	124 43.0 ..	06.7	16 15.8 ..	44.8	Spica	158 31.3	S11 13.9
16	249 33.8	20 25.7	18.6	105 42.4	40.9	139 45.2	06.7	31 18.0	44.9	Suhail	222 52.5	S43 29.2
17	264 36.2	35 25.3	19.5	120 43.3	40.4	154 47.4	06.7	46 20.2	45.0			
18	279 38.7	50 24.9	S20 20.4	135 44.3	N15 40.0	169 49.5	N22 06.6	61 22.4	S12 45.1	Vega	80 38.8	N38 48.3
19	294 41.2	65 24.5	21.2	150 45.2	39.5	184 51.7	06.6	76 24.6	45.2	Zuben'ubi	137 05.4	S16 05.8
20	309 43.6	80 24.2	22.1	165 46.2	39.0	199 53.9	06.6	91 26.8	45.3		SHA	Mer.Pass.
21	324 46.1	95 23.8 ..	23.0	180 47.1 ..	38.6	214 56.0 ..	06.5	106 29.0 ..	45.3	Venus	132 45.2	14 38
22	339 48.6	110 23.4	23.9	195 48.1	38.1	229 58.2	06.5	121 31.2	45.4	Mars	217 09.3	8 59
23	354 51.0	125 23.0	24.8	210 49.1	37.6	245 00.4	06.5	136 33.4	45.5	Jupiter	250 23.7	6 46
Mer.Pass. 23 24.5		v −0.4 d 0.9		v 0.9 d 0.5		v 2.2 d 0.0		v 2.2 d 0.1		Saturn	141 54.5	13 59

Day markers (left margin): 28 — SATURDAY; 29 — SUNDAY; 30 — MONDAY

UT	SUN GHA	SUN Dec	MOON GHA	v	MOON Dec	d	HP
d h	° ′	° ′	° ′	′	° ′	′	′
28 00	182 19.0	S 2 00.0	262 06.9	12.6	N17 57.4	4.2	54.2
01	197 19.2	01.0	276 38.5	12.7	17 53.2	4.2	54.2
02	212 19.4	01.9	291 10.2	12.7	17 49.0	4.3	54.2
03	227 19.7	.. 02.9	305 41.9	12.8	17 44.7	4.4	54.2
04	242 19.9	03.9	320 13.7	12.7	17 40.3	4.5	54.2
05	257 20.1	04.8	334 45.4	12.8	17 35.8	4.5	54.3
06	272 20.3	S 2 05.8	349 17.2	12.8	N17 31.3	4.7	54.3
S 07	287 20.5	06.8	3 49.0	12.8	17 26.6	4.7	54.3
A 08	302 20.7	07.8	18 20.8	12.9	17 21.9	4.8	54.3
T 09	317 20.9	.. 08.7	32 52.7	12.8	17 17.1	4.8	54.3
U 10	332 21.1	09.7	47 24.5	12.7	17 12.3	5.0	54.3
R 11	347 21.3	10.7	61 56.4	12.9	17 07.3	5.0	54.3
D 12	2 21.5	S 2 11.6	76 28.3	12.9	N17 02.3	5.1	54.3
A 13	17 21.8	12.6	91 00.2	13.0	16 57.2	5.2	54.3
Y 14	32 22.0	13.6	105 32.2	12.9	16 52.0	5.2	54.3
15	47 22.2	.. 14.6	120 04.1	13.0	16 46.8	5.4	54.3
16	62 22.4	15.5	134 36.1	13.0	16 41.4	5.4	54.3
17	77 22.6	16.5	149 08.1	13.0	16 36.0	5.4	54.3
18	92 22.8	S 2 17.5	163 40.1	13.1	N16 30.6	5.6	54.3
19	107 23.0	18.5	178 12.2	13.0	16 25.0	5.6	54.3
20	122 23.2	19.4	192 44.2	13.1	16 19.4	5.7	54.3
21	137 23.4	.. 20.4	207 16.3	13.1	16 13.7	5.8	54.3
22	152 23.6	21.4	221 48.4	13.1	16 07.9	5.9	54.3
23	167 23.8	22.3	236 20.5	13.2	16 02.0	5.9	54.3
29 00	182 24.0	S 2 23.3	250 52.7	13.1	N15 56.1	6.0	54.4
01	197 24.2	24.3	265 24.8	13.2	15 50.1	6.1	54.4
02	212 24.5	25.3	279 57.0	13.2	15 44.0	6.1	54.4
03	227 24.7	.. 26.2	294 29.2	13.2	15 37.9	6.2	54.4
04	242 24.9	27.2	309 01.4	13.2	15 31.7	6.3	54.4
05	257 25.1	28.2	323 33.6	13.3	15 25.4	6.4	54.4
06	272 25.3	S 2 29.1	338 05.9	13.2	N15 19.0	6.4	54.4
S 07	287 25.5	30.1	352 38.1	13.3	15 12.6	6.5	54.4
U 08	302 25.7	31.1	7 10.4	13.3	15 06.1	6.6	54.4
N 09	317 25.9	.. 32.1	21 42.7	13.3	14 59.5	6.6	54.5
D 10	332 26.1	33.0	36 15.0	13.3	14 52.9	6.7	54.5
A 11	347 26.3	34.0	50 47.3	13.4	14 46.2	6.8	54.5
Y 12	2 26.5	S 2 35.0	65 19.7	13.4	N14 39.4	6.8	54.5
13	17 26.7	35.9	79 52.1	13.3	14 32.6	6.9	54.5
14	32 26.9	36.9	94 24.4	13.4	14 25.7	7.0	54.5
15	47 27.1	.. 37.9	108 56.8	13.4	14 18.7	7.1	54.5
16	62 27.3	38.9	123 29.2	13.4	14 11.6	7.1	54.5
17	77 27.5	39.8	138 01.6	13.5	14 04.5	7.1	54.6
18	92 27.8	S 2 40.8	152 34.1	13.4	N13 57.4	7.3	54.6
19	107 28.0	41.8	167 06.5	13.5	13 50.1	7.3	54.6
20	122 28.2	42.7	181 39.0	13.5	13 42.8	7.4	54.6
21	137 28.4	.. 43.7	196 11.5	13.5	13 35.4	7.4	54.6
22	152 28.6	44.7	210 44.0	13.5	13 28.0	7.5	54.6
23	167 28.8	45.7	225 16.5	13.5	13 20.5	7.5	54.6
30 00	182 29.0	S 2 46.6	239 49.0	13.5	N13 13.0	7.7	54.7
01	197 29.2	47.6	254 21.5	13.5	13 05.3	7.7	54.7
02	212 29.4	48.6	268 54.0	13.6	12 57.6	7.7	54.7
03	227 29.6	.. 49.5	283 26.6	13.6	12 49.9	7.8	54.7
04	242 29.8	50.5	297 59.2	13.5	12 42.1	7.9	54.7
05	257 30.0	51.5	312 31.7	13.6	12 34.2	7.9	54.7
06	272 30.2	S 2 52.5	327 04.3	13.6	N12 26.3	8.0	54.7
M 07	287 30.4	53.4	341 36.9	13.6	12 18.3	8.0	54.8
O 08	302 30.6	54.4	356 09.5	13.6	12 10.3	8.2	54.8
N 09	317 30.8	.. 55.4	10 42.1	13.7	12 02.1	8.1	54.8
10	332 31.0	56.3	25 14.8	13.6	11 54.0	8.2	54.8
11	347 31.2	57.3	39 47.4	13.6	11 45.8	8.3	54.8
D 12	2 31.4	S 2 58.3	54 20.0	13.7	N11 37.5	8.4	54.9
A 13	17 31.6	2 59.3	68 52.7	13.6	11 29.1	8.4	54.9
Y 14	32 31.8	3 00.2	83 25.3	13.7	11 20.7	8.4	54.9
15	47 32.0	.. 01.2	97 58.0	13.6	11 12.3	8.5	54.9
16	62 32.2	02.2	112 30.6	13.7	11 03.8	8.6	54.9
17	77 32.4	03.1	127 03.3	13.7	10 55.2	8.6	54.9
18	92 32.6	S 3 04.1	141 36.0	13.7	N10 46.6	8.7	55.0
19	107 32.8	05.1	156 08.7	13.7	10 37.9	8.7	55.0
20	122 33.0	06.0	170 41.4	13.7	10 29.2	8.8	55.0
21	137 33.3	.. 07.0	185 14.1	13.7	10 20.4	8.8	55.0
22	152 33.5	08.0	199 46.8	13.7	10 11.6	8.9	55.0
23	167 33.7	09.0	214 19.5	13.7	N10 02.7	8.9	55.1
	SD 16.0	d 1.0	SD 14.8		14.8		14.9

Twilight / Sunrise / Moonrise

Lat.	Naut.	Civil	Sunrise	Moonrise 28	29	30	1
°	h m	h m	h m	h m	h m	h m	h m
N 72	03 39	05 03	06 10	20 59	22 53	24 39	00 39
N 70	03 53	05 07	06 08	21 43	23 19	24 55	00 55
68	04 04	05 11	06 06	22 12	23 39	25 07	01 07
66	04 12	05 13	06 04	22 34	23 54	25 18	01 18
64	04 19	05 16	06 03	22 51	24 07	00 07	01 26
62	04 25	05 18	06 02	23 05	24 18	00 18	01 34
60	04 30	05 19	06 01	23 17	24 27	00 27	01 40
N 58	04 35	05 21	06 00	23 27	24 35	00 35	01 45
56	04 38	05 22	05 59	23 36	24 42	00 42	01 50
54	04 42	05 23	05 58	23 44	24 48	00 48	01 55
52	04 45	05 24	05 58	23 51	24 54	00 54	01 59
50	04 47	05 25	05 57	23 57	24 59	00 59	02 02
45	04 52	05 26	05 56	24 11	00 11	01 10	02 10
N 40	04 56	05 27	05 54	24 22	00 22	01 19	02 17
35	04 59	05 28	05 53	24 32	00 32	01 27	02 22
30	05 01	05 28	05 52	24 40	00 40	01 33	02 27
20	05 03	05 28	05 50	00 05	00 55	01 45	02 36
N 10	05 03	05 28	05 49	00 19	01 08	01 55	02 43
0	05 02	05 26	05 47	00 33	01 19	02 05	02 50
S 10	05 00	05 24	05 45	00 46	01 31	02 15	02 57
20	04 55	05 21	05 43	01 01	01 44	02 25	03 04
30	04 49	05 14	05 41	01 17	01 58	02 36	03 13
35	04 44	05 14	05 39	01 27	02 06	02 43	03 18
40	04 39	05 11	05 38	01 38	02 16	02 51	03 23
45	04 31	05 07	05 36	01 51	02 27	02 59	03 29
S 50	04 22	05 01	05 33	02 06	02 40	03 10	03 37
52	04 18	04 58	05 32	02 13	02 46	03 15	03 41
54	04 13	04 55	05 31	02 22	02 53	03 20	03 44
56	04 07	04 52	05 30	02 31	03 01	03 26	03 49
58	04 00	04 49	05 28	02 41	03 09	03 33	03 53
S 60	03 53	04 44	05 26	02 53	03 19	03 41	03 58

Sunset / Twilight / Moonset

Lat.	Sunset	Civil	Naut.	Moonset 28	29	30	1
°	h m	h m	h m	h m	h m	h m	h m
N 72	17 28	18 35	19 58	17 26	17 08	16 56	16 46
N 70	17 31	18 31	19 45	16 41	16 41	16 36	16 36
68	17 33	18 28	19 34	16 12	16 20	16 25	16 28
66	17 34	18 25	19 26	15 50	16 03	16 13	16 21
64	17 36	18 23	19 19	15 32	15 50	16 04	16 15
62	17 37	18 21	19 13	15 17	15 38	15 55	16 09
60	17 38	18 20	19 08	15 05	15 29	15 48	16 05
N 58	17 39	18 18	19 04	14 54	15 20	15 42	16 01
56	17 40	18 17	19 01	14 45	15 13	15 36	15 57
54	17 41	18 16	18 57	14 37	15 06	15 31	15 54
52	17 42	18 15	18 55	14 29	15 00	15 27	15 51
50	17 43	18 15	18 52	14 22	14 54	15 23	15 48
45	17 44	18 13	18 47	14 08	14 42	15 14	15 43
N 40	17 46	18 12	18 44	13 56	14 32	15 06	15 38
35	17 47	18 12	18 41	13 46	14 24	15 00	15 33
30	17 48	18 12	18 39	13 37	14 17	14 54	15 30
20	17 50	18 12	18 37	13 22	14 04	14 44	15 23
N 10	17 52	18 13	18 37	13 08	13 52	14 35	15 17
0	17 53	18 14	18 38	12 55	13 41	14 27	15 12
S 10	17 55	18 16	18 41	12 43	13 31	14 18	15 06
20	17 58	18 20	18 45	12 29	13 19	14 09	15 00
30	18 00	18 24	18 52	12 13	13 06	13 59	14 53
35	18 02	18 27	18 57	12 04	12 58	13 53	14 50
40	18 04	18 31	19 03	11 54	12 49	13 46	14 45
45	18 06	18 35	19 10	11 41	12 39	13 39	14 40
S 50	18 08	18 41	19 19	11 26	12 26	13 29	14 34
52	18 09	18 43	19 24	11 19	12 21	13 25	14 31
54	18 11	18 46	19 29	11 12	12 14	13 20	14 27
56	18 12	18 50	19 35	11 03	12 07	13 14	14 24
58	18 14	18 53	19 42	10 53	11 59	13 08	14 20
S 60	18 15	18 58	19 50	10 42	11 50	13 01	14 16

	SUN			MOON			
Day	Eqn. of Time 00ʰ	12ʰ	Mer. Pass.	Mer. Pass. Upper	Lower	Age	Phase
d	m s	m s	h m	h m	h m	d	%
28	09 16	09 26	11 51	06 44	19 07	23	38
29	09 36	09 46	11 50	07 30	19 53	24	29
30	09 56	10 05	11 50	08 16	20 38	25	20

UT	ARIES GHA	VENUS −4.2 GHA	Dec	MARS +1.6 GHA	Dec	JUPITER −2.2 GHA	Dec	SATURN +0.6 GHA	Dec	STARS Name	SHA	Dec
d h	° ′	° ′	° ′	° ′	° ′	° ′	° ′	° ′	° ′		° ′	° ′
1 00	9 53.5	140 22.7	S20 25.7	225 50.0	N15 37.1	260 02.5	N22 06.4	151 35.6	S12 45.6	Acamar	315 17.9	S40 14.8
01	24 56.0	155 22.3	26.5	240 51.0	36.7	275 04.7	06.4	166 37.8	45.7	Achernar	335 26.1	S57 09.9
02	39 58.4	170 21.9	27.4	255 51.9	36.2	290 06.9	06.4	181 40.0	45.8	Acrux	173 09.7	S63 10.5
03	55 00.9	185 21.5	.. 28.3	270 52.9	.. 35.7	305 09.0	.. 06.3	196 42.2	.. 45.9	Adhara	255 12.4	S28 59.3
04	70 03.4	200 21.2	29.2	285 53.8	35.3	320 11.2	06.3	211 44.4	46.0	Aldebaran	290 49.0	N16 32.1
05	85 05.8	215 20.8	30.1	300 54.8	34.8	335 13.4	06.3	226 46.6	46.1			
06	100 08.3	230 20.4	S20 30.9	315 55.7	N15 34.3	350 15.5	N22 06.2	241 48.8	S12 46.1	Alioth	166 21.1	N55 53.2
07	115 10.7	245 20.0	31.8	330 56.7	33.8	5 17.7	06.2	256 51.0	46.2	Alkaid	152 59.2	N49 14.8
T 08	130 13.2	260 19.6	32.7	345 57.6	33.4	20 19.9	06.2	271 53.2	46.3	Al Na'ir	27 43.1	S46 53.6
U 09	145 15.7	275 19.3	.. 33.6	0 58.6	.. 32.9	35 22.0	.. 06.1	286 55.4	.. 46.4	Alnilam	275 46.1	S 1 11.6
E 10	160 18.1	290 18.9	34.4	15 59.5	32.4	50 24.2	06.1	301 57.7	46.5	Alphard	217 56.1	S 8 43.1
S 11	175 20.6	305 18.5	35.3	31 00.5	32.0	65 26.4	06.1	316 59.9	46.6			
D 12	190 23.1	320 18.1	S20 36.2	46 01.5	N15 31.5	80 28.5	N22 06.0	332 02.1	S12 46.7	Alphecca	126 11.1	N26 40.4
A 13	205 25.5	335 17.7	37.1	61 02.4	31.0	95 30.7	06.0	347 04.3	46.8	Alpheratz	357 42.9	N29 10.2
Y 14	220 28.0	350 17.4	37.9	76 03.4	30.5	110 32.9	06.0	2 06.5	46.9	Altair	62 07.9	N 8 54.6
15	235 30.5	5 17.0	.. 38.8	91 04.3	.. 30.1	125 35.0	.. 05.9	17 08.7	.. 46.9	Ankaa	353 15.1	S42 13.7
16	250 32.9	20 16.6	39.7	106 05.3	29.6	140 37.2	05.9	32 10.9	47.0	Antares	112 26.2	S26 27.6
17	265 35.4	35 16.2	40.5	121 06.2	29.1	155 39.4	05.9	47 13.1	47.1			
18	280 37.8	50 15.8	S20 41.4	136 07.2	N15 28.6	170 41.5	N22 05.8	62 15.3	S12 47.2	Arcturus	145 55.9	N19 06.8
19	295 40.3	65 15.5	42.3	151 08.1	28.2	185 43.7	05.8	77 17.5	47.3	Atria	107 28.0	S69 03.2
20	310 42.8	80 15.1	43.1	166 09.1	27.7	200 45.9	05.8	92 19.7	47.4	Avior	234 18.2	S59 33.1
21	325 45.2	95 14.7	.. 44.0	181 10.1	.. 27.2	215 48.1	.. 05.7	107 21.9	.. 47.5	Bellatrix	278 31.7	N 6 21.7
22	340 47.7	110 14.3	44.9	196 11.0	26.8	230 50.2	05.7	122 24.1	47.6	Betelgeuse	271 01.0	N 7 24.5
23	355 50.2	125 13.9	45.7	211 12.0	26.3	245 52.4	05.7	137 26.3	47.7			
2 00	10 52.6	140 13.5	S20 46.6	226 12.9	N15 25.8	260 54.6	N22 05.6	152 28.5	S12 47.8	Canopus	263 56.0	S52 42.0
01	25 55.1	155 13.2	47.4	241 13.9	25.3	275 56.7	05.6	167 30.7	47.8	Capella	280 34.0	N46 00.4
02	40 57.6	170 12.8	48.3	256 14.8	24.9	290 58.9	05.6	182 32.9	47.9	Deneb	49 31.1	N45 20.2
03	56 00.0	185 12.4	.. 49.2	271 15.8	.. 24.4	306 01.1	.. 05.5	197 35.1	.. 48.0	Denebola	182 33.8	N14 29.7
04	71 02.5	200 12.0	50.0	286 16.8	23.9	321 03.3	05.5	212 37.3	48.1	Diphda	348 55.4	S17 54.5
05	86 05.0	215 11.6	50.9	301 17.7	23.4	336 05.4	05.5	227 39.5	48.2			
06	101 07.4	230 11.2	S20 51.7	316 18.7	N15 23.0	351 07.6	N22 05.4	242 41.7	S12 48.3	Dubhe	193 52.1	N61 40.4
W 07	116 09.9	245 10.9	52.6	331 19.6	22.5	6 09.8	05.4	257 43.9	48.4	Elnath	278 12.2	N28 36.9
E 08	131 12.3	260 10.5	53.5	346 20.6	22.0	21 12.0	05.4	272 46.1	48.5	Eltanin	90 46.1	N51 29.7
D 09	146 14.8	275 10.1	.. 54.3	1 21.6	.. 21.5	36 14.1	.. 05.3	287 48.3	.. 48.6	Enif	33 46.7	N 9 56.6
N 10	161 17.3	290 09.7	55.2	16 22.5	21.1	51 16.3	05.3	302 50.5	48.6	Fomalhaut	15 23.4	S29 32.8
11	176 19.7	305 09.3	56.0	31 23.5	20.6	66 18.5	05.3	317 52.7	48.7			
E 12	191 22.2	320 08.9	S20 56.9	46 24.4	N15 20.1	81 20.7	N22 05.2	332 54.9	S12 48.8	Gacrux	172 01.2	S57 11.4
S 13	206 24.7	335 08.5	57.7	61 25.4	19.6	96 22.8	05.2	347 57.1	48.9	Gienah	175 52.4	S17 37.0
D 14	221 27.1	350 08.1	58.6	76 26.4	19.2	111 25.0	05.2	2 59.3	49.0	Hadar	148 48.1	S60 26.4
A 15	236 29.6	5 07.8	20 59.4	91 27.3	.. 18.7	126 27.2	.. 05.1	18 01.5	.. 49.1	Hamal	328 00.2	N23 31.7
Y 16	251 32.1	20 07.4	21 00.3	106 28.3	18.2	141 29.4	05.1	33 03.7	49.2	Kaus Aust.	83 43.6	S34 22.6
17	266 34.5	35 07.0	01.1	121 29.2	17.7	156 31.5	05.1	48 05.9	49.3			
18	281 37.0	50 06.6	S21 02.0	136 30.2	N15 17.2	171 33.7	N22 05.0	63 08.1	S12 49.4	Kochab	137 21.1	N74 06.2
19	296 39.4	65 06.2	02.8	151 31.2	16.8	186 35.9	05.0	78 10.3	49.5	Markab	13 37.8	N15 17.0
20	311 41.9	80 05.8	03.7	166 32.1	16.3	201 38.1	05.0	93 12.5	49.5	Menkar	314 14.6	N 4 08.7
21	326 44.4	95 05.4	.. 04.5	181 33.1	.. 15.8	216 40.2	.. 04.9	108 14.7	.. 49.6	Menkent	148 07.7	S36 26.2
22	341 46.8	110 05.0	05.3	196 34.0	15.3	231 42.4	04.9	123 16.9	49.7	Miaplacidus	221 40.1	S69 46.3
23	356 49.3	125 04.6	06.2	211 35.0	14.9	246 44.6	04.9	138 19.1	49.8			
3 00	11 51.8	140 04.3	S21 07.0	226 36.0	N15 14.4	261 46.8	N22 04.9	153 21.3	S12 49.9	Mirfak	308 39.6	N49 54.4
01	26 54.2	155 03.9	07.9	241 36.9	13.9	276 49.0	04.8	168 23.5	50.0	Nunki	75 58.0	S26 16.6
02	41 56.7	170 03.5	08.7	256 37.9	13.4	291 51.1	04.8	183 25.7	50.1	Peacock	53 18.7	S56 41.4
03	56 59.2	185 03.1	.. 09.6	271 38.9	.. 13.0	306 53.3	.. 04.7	198 27.9	.. 50.2	Pollux	243 27.6	N27 59.4
04	72 01.6	200 02.7	10.4	286 39.8	12.5	321 55.5	04.7	213 30.1	50.3	Procyon	244 59.6	N 5 11.3
05	87 04.1	215 02.3	11.2	301 40.8	12.0	336 57.7	04.7	228 32.3	50.4			
06	102 06.6	230 01.9	S21 12.1	316 41.8	N15 11.5	351 59.9	N22 04.7	243 34.5	S12 50.5	Rasalhague	96 06.4	N12 33.4
07	117 09.0	245 01.5	12.9	331 42.7	11.0	7 02.0	04.6	258 36.7	50.5	Regulus	207 43.6	N11 53.9
T 08	132 11.5	260 01.1	13.7	346 43.7	10.6	22 04.2	04.6	273 38.9	50.6	Rigel	281 11.7	S 8 11.1
H 09	147 13.9	275 00.7	.. 14.6	1 44.6	.. 10.1	37 06.4	.. 04.6	288 41.1	.. 50.7	Rigil Kent.	139 52.0	S60 53.5
U 10	162 16.4	290 00.3	15.4	16 45.6	09.6	52 08.6	04.5	303 43.3	50.8	Sabik	102 12.4	S15 44.3
R 11	177 18.9	305 00.0	16.2	31 46.6	09.1	67 10.8	04.5	318 45.5	50.9			
S 12	192 21.3	319 59.6	S21 17.1	46 47.5	N15 08.7	82 12.9	N22 04.5	333 47.7	S12 51.0	Schedar	349 39.6	N56 36.9
D 13	207 23.8	334 59.2	17.9	61 48.5	08.2	97 15.1	04.4	348 49.9	51.1	Shaula	96 21.7	S37 06.7
A 14	222 26.3	349 58.8	18.7	76 49.5	07.7	112 17.3	04.4	3 52.1	51.2	Sirius	258 33.5	S16 44.1
Y 15	237 28.7	4 58.4	.. 19.6	91 50.4	.. 07.2	127 19.5	.. 04.4	18 54.3	.. 51.2	Spica	158 31.3	S11 13.9
16	252 31.2	19 58.0	20.4	106 51.4	06.7	142 21.7	04.3	33 56.5	51.3	Suhail	222 52.5	S43 29.2
17	267 33.7	34 57.6	21.2	121 52.4	06.3	157 23.9	04.3	48 58.7	51.4			
18	282 36.1	49 57.2	S21 22.1	136 53.3	N15 05.8	172 26.0	N22 04.3	64 00.9	S12 51.5	Vega	80 38.8	N38 48.2
19	297 38.6	64 56.8	22.9	151 54.3	05.3	187 28.2	04.3	79 03.1	51.6	Zuben'ubi	137 05.5	S16 05.8
20	312 41.1	79 56.4	23.7	166 55.3	04.8	202 30.4	04.2	94 05.3	51.7		SHA	Mer.Pass.
21	327 43.5	94 56.0	.. 24.5	181 56.2	.. 04.3	217 32.6	.. 04.2	109 07.5	.. 51.8		° ′	h m
22	342 46.0	109 55.6	25.4	196 57.2	03.9	232 34.8	04.2	124 09.7	51.9	Venus	129 20.9	14 39
23	357 48.4	124 55.2	26.2	211 58.2	03.4	247 37.0	04.1	139 11.9	52.0	Mars	215 20.3	8 55
	h m									Jupiter	250 01.9	6 35
Mer.Pass. 23 12.7	v −0.4 d 0.9			v 1.0 d 0.5		v 2.2 d 0.0		v 2.2 d 0.1		Saturn	141 35.9	13 48

UT	SUN GHA	SUN Dec	MOON GHA	v	Dec	d	HP
	° ′	° ′	° ′	′	° ′	′	′
d h							
1 00	182 33.9	S 3 09.9	228 52.2	13.7	N 9 53.8	9.0	55.1
01	197 34.1	10.9	243 24.9	13.7	9 44.8	9.0	55.1
02	212 34.3	11.9	257 57.6	13.7	9 35.8	9.1	55.1
03	227 34.5	.. 12.8	272 30.3	13.7	9 26.7	9.1	55.1
04	242 34.7	13.8	287 03.0	13.7	9 17.6	9.2	55.2
05	257 34.9	14.8	301 35.7	13.7	9 08.4	9.3	55.2
06	272 35.1	S 3 15.7	316 08.4	13.7	N 8 59.1	9.2	55.2
07	287 35.3	16.7	330 41.1	13.7	8 49.9	9.4	55.2
08	302 35.5	17.7	345 13.8	13.7	8 40.5	9.3	55.2
09	317 35.7	.. 18.6	359 46.5	13.8	8 31.2	9.4	55.3
10	332 35.9	19.6	14 19.3	13.7	8 21.8	9.5	55.3
11	347 36.1	20.6	28 52.0	13.7	8 12.3	9.5	55.3
12	2 36.3	S 3 21.6	43 24.7	13.7	N 8 02.8	9.6	55.3
13	17 36.5	22.5	57 57.4	13.7	7 53.2	9.6	55.4
14	32 36.7	23.5	72 30.1	13.6	7 43.6	9.6	55.4
15	47 36.9	.. 24.5	87 02.7	13.7	7 34.0	9.7	55.4
16	62 37.1	25.4	101 35.4	13.7	7 24.3	9.7	55.4
17	77 37.3	26.4	116 08.1	13.7	7 14.6	9.8	55.5
18	92 37.5	S 3 27.4	130 40.8	13.6	N 7 04.8	9.8	55.5
19	107 37.7	28.3	145 13.4	13.7	6 55.0	9.8	55.5
20	122 37.9	29.3	159 46.1	13.7	6 45.2	9.9	55.5
21	137 38.1	.. 30.3	174 18.8	13.6	6 35.3	9.9	55.5
22	152 38.3	31.2	188 51.4	13.6	6 25.4	10.0	55.6
23	167 38.5	32.2	203 24.0	13.7	6 15.4	9.9	55.6
2 00	182 38.7	S 3 33.2	217 56.7	13.6	N 6 05.5	10.1	55.6
01	197 38.9	34.1	232 29.3	13.6	5 55.4	10.0	55.6
02	212 39.1	35.1	247 01.9	13.6	5 45.4	10.2	55.7
03	227 39.3	.. 36.1	261 34.5	13.6	5 35.2	10.1	55.7
04	242 39.4	37.0	276 07.1	13.5	5 25.1	10.2	55.7
05	257 39.6	38.0	290 39.6	13.6	5 14.9	10.2	55.7
06	272 39.8	S 3 39.0	305 12.2	13.5	N 5 04.7	10.2	55.8
07	287 40.0	40.0	319 44.7	13.6	4 54.5	10.3	55.8
08	302 40.2	40.9	334 17.3	13.5	4 44.2	10.3	55.8
09	317 40.4	.. 41.9	348 49.8	13.5	4 33.9	10.3	55.8
10	332 40.6	42.9	3 22.3	13.5	4 23.6	10.4	55.9
11	347 40.8	43.8	17 54.8	13.5	4 13.2	10.4	55.9
12	2 41.0	S 3 44.8	32 27.3	13.4	N 4 02.8	10.4	55.9
13	17 41.2	45.8	46 59.7	13.4	3 52.4	10.4	55.9
14	32 41.4	46.7	61 32.1	13.5	3 42.0	10.5	56.0
15	47 41.6	.. 47.7	76 04.6	13.4	3 31.5	10.5	56.0
16	62 41.8	48.7	90 37.0	13.3	3 21.0	10.6	56.0
17	77 42.0	49.6	105 09.3	13.4	3 10.5	10.6	56.0
18	92 42.2	S 3 50.6	119 41.7	13.4	N 2 59.9	10.5	56.1
19	107 42.4	51.6	134 14.1	13.3	2 49.4	10.6	56.1
20	122 42.6	52.5	148 46.4	13.3	2 38.8	10.7	56.1
21	137 42.8	.. 53.5	163 18.7	13.2	2 28.1	10.6	56.1
22	152 43.0	54.5	177 50.9	13.3	2 17.5	10.7	56.2
23	167 43.2	55.4	192 23.2	13.2	2 06.8	10.6	56.2
3 00	182 43.4	S 3 56.4	206 55.4	13.2	N 1 56.2	10.8	56.2
01	197 43.6	57.4	221 27.6	13.2	1 45.4	10.7	56.3
02	212 43.8	58.3	235 59.8	13.2	1 34.7	10.7	56.3
03	227 44.0	3 59.3	250 32.0	13.1	1 24.0	10.8	56.3
04	242 44.2	4 00.3	265 04.1	13.1	1 13.2	10.7	56.3
05	257 44.4	01.2	279 36.2	13.1	1 02.5	10.8	56.4
06	272 44.5	S 4 02.2	294 08.3	13.1	N 0 51.7	10.8	56.4
07	287 44.7	03.2	308 40.4	13.0	0 40.9	10.8	56.4
08	302 44.9	04.1	323 12.4	13.0	0 30.1	10.9	56.4
09	317 45.1	.. 05.1	337 44.4	13.0	0 19.2	10.8	56.5
10	332 45.3	06.1	352 16.4	12.9	N 0 08.4	10.9	56.5
11	347 45.5	07.0	6 48.3	12.9	S 0 02.5	10.8	56.5
12	2 45.7	S 4 08.0	21 20.2	12.9	S 0 13.3	10.9	56.5
13	17 45.9	08.9	35 52.1	12.8	0 24.2	10.9	56.6
14	32 46.1	09.9	50 23.9	12.8	0 35.1	10.9	56.6
15	47 46.3	.. 10.9	64 55.7	12.8	0 46.0	10.9	56.6
16	62 46.5	11.8	79 27.5	12.8	0 56.9	10.9	56.6
17	77 46.7	12.8	93 59.3	12.7	1 07.8	10.9	56.7
18	92 46.9	S 4 13.8	108 31.0	12.6	S 1 18.7	10.9	56.7
19	107 47.1	14.7	123 02.6	12.7	1 29.6	10.9	56.7
20	122 47.2	15.7	137 34.3	12.6	1 40.5	10.9	56.8
21	137 47.4	.. 16.7	152 05.9	12.6	1 51.4	10.9	56.8
22	152 47.6	17.6	166 37.5	12.5	2 02.3	10.9	56.8
23	167 47.8	18.6	181 09.0	12.5	S 2 13.2	11.0	56.8
	SD 16.0	d 1.0	SD 15.1		15.2		15.4

Day rows: TUESDAY (1 00–23), WEDNESDAY (2 00–23), THURSDAY (3 00–23)

Lat.	Twilight Naut.	Twilight Civil	Sunrise	Moonrise 1	2	3	4
°	h m	h m	h m	h m	h m	h m	h m
N 72	03 55	05 16	06 24	00 39	02 23	04 07	05 53
N 70	04 06	05 19	06 20	00 55	02 31	04 08	05 48
68	04 15	05 21	06 17	01 07	02 38	04 09	05 44
66	04 23	05 23	06 14	01 18	02 43	04 11	05 40
64	04 29	05 24	06 12	01 26	02 48	04 11	05 37
62	04 34	05 26	06 10	01 34	02 52	04 12	05 35
60	04 38	05 27	06 08	01 40	02 55	04 13	05 33
N 58	04 42	05 27	06 06	01 45	02 58	04 13	05 31
56	04 45	05 28	06 05	01 50	03 01	04 14	05 29
54	04 47	05 29	06 04	01 55	03 04	04 14	05 27
52	04 50	05 29	06 03	01 59	03 06	04 15	05 26
50	04 52	05 29	06 02	02 02	03 08	04 15	05 25
45	04 56	05 30	05 59	02 10	03 12	04 16	05 22
N 40	04 59	05 30	05 57	02 17	03 16	04 17	05 19
35	05 01	05 30	05 56	02 22	03 19	04 18	05 17
30	05 02	05 30	05 54	02 27	03 22	04 18	05 16
20	05 04	05 29	05 51	02 36	03 27	04 19	05 13
N 10	05 03	05 28	05 49	02 43	03 31	04 20	05 10
0	05 01	05 25	05 46	02 50	03 35	04 21	05 08
S 10	04 58	05 22	05 43	02 57	03 39	04 22	05 05
20	04 53	05 18	05 40	03 04	03 43	04 23	05 03
30	04 45	05 13	05 37	03 13	03 48	04 24	05 00
35	04 40	05 10	05 35	03 18	03 51	04 24	04 58
40	04 33	05 06	05 33	03 23	03 54	04 25	04 56
45	04 25	05 00	05 30	03 29	03 58	04 26	04 54
S 50	04 15	04 54	05 27	03 37	04 02	04 27	04 52
52	04 10	04 51	05 25	03 41	04 04	04 27	04 50
54	04 05	04 48	05 24	03 44	04 06	04 28	04 49
56	03 58	04 44	05 22	03 49	04 09	04 28	04 48
58	03 51	04 40	05 20	03 53	04 11	04 29	04 46
S 60	03 42	04 35	05 17	03 58	04 14	04 29	04 45

Lat.	Sunset	Twilight Civil	Twilight Naut.	Moonset 1	2	3	4
°	h m	h m	h m	h m	h m	h m	h m
N 72	17 13	18 20	19 40	16 46	16 37	16 29	16 20
N 70	17 17	18 17	19 29	16 36	16 33	16 30	16 27
68	17 20	18 15	19 21	16 28	16 30	16 32	16 34
66	17 23	18 14	19 14	16 21	16 27	16 33	16 39
64	17 25	18 12	19 08	16 15	16 24	16 34	16 43
62	17 27	18 11	19 03	16 09	16 22	16 34	16 47
60	17 29	18 11	18 59	16 05	16 20	16 35	16 51
N 58	17 31	18 10	18 55	16 01	16 18	16 36	16 54
56	17 32	18 09	18 52	15 57	16 17	16 36	16 56
54	17 34	18 09	18 50	15 54	16 15	16 37	16 59
52	17 35	18 08	18 48	15 51	16 14	16 37	17 01
50	17 36	18 08	18 46	15 48	16 13	16 38	17 03
45	17 39	18 08	18 42	15 43	16 11	16 38	17 07
N 40	17 41	18 08	18 39	15 38	16 08	16 39	17 11
35	17 43	18 08	18 37	15 33	16 07	16 40	17 14
30	17 44	18 08	18 36	15 30	16 05	16 40	17 17
20	17 47	18 09	18 35	15 23	16 02	16 41	17 22
N 10	17 50	18 11	18 35	15 17	15 59	16 42	17 26
0	17 53	18 13	18 37	15 12	15 57	16 43	17 31
S 10	17 55	18 16	18 41	15 06	15 55	16 44	17 35
20	17 58	18 20	18 46	15 00	15 52	16 45	17 39
30	18 02	18 26	18 54	14 53	15 49	16 46	17 44
35	18 04	18 30	18 59	14 50	15 47	16 46	17 47
40	18 06	18 34	19 06	14 45	15 45	16 47	17 50
45	18 09	18 39	19 14	14 40	15 43	16 47	17 54
S 50	18 13	18 46	19 25	14 34	15 40	16 48	17 58
52	18 14	18 49	19 30	14 31	15 39	16 49	18 00
54	18 16	18 52	19 36	14 27	15 37	16 49	18 03
56	18 18	18 56	19 42	14 24	15 36	16 49	18 05
58	18 20	19 00	19 50	14 20	15 34	16 50	18 08
S 60	18 23	19 05	19 58	14 16	15 32	16 50	18 11

	SUN		MOON			
Day	Eqn. of Time 00ʰ	12ʰ	Mer. Pass.	Mer. Pass. Upper	Lower	Age Phase
d	m s	m s	h m	h m	h m	d %
1	10 15	10 25	11 50	09 01	21 23	26 13
2	10 34	10 44	11 49	09 46	22 09	27 7
3	10 53	11 02	11 49	10 32	22 55	28 3

2013 OCTOBER 4, 5, 6 (FRI., SAT., SUN.)

UT	ARIES	VENUS −4.3		MARS +1.6		JUPITER −2.2		SATURN +0.6		STARS		
	GHA	GHA	Dec	GHA	Dec	GHA	Dec	GHA	Dec	Name	SHA	Dec
d h	° ′	° ′	° ′	° ′	° ′	° ′	° ′	° ′	° ′		° ′	° ′
4 00	12 50.9	139 54.8	S21 27.0	226 59.1	N15 02.9	262 39.2	N22 04.1	154 14.1	S12 52.1	Acamar	315 17.8	S40 14.8
01	27 53.4	154 54.4	27.8	242 00.1	02.4	277 41.3	04.1	169 16.3	52.1	Achernar	335 26.1	S57 09.9
02	42 55.8	169 54.0	28.6	257 01.1	01.9	292 43.5	04.0	184 18.5	52.2	Acrux	173 09.7	S63 10.5
03	57 58.3	184 53.6	. . 29.5	272 02.0	. . 01.5	307 45.7	. . 04.0	199 20.7	. . 52.3	Adhara	255 12.4	S28 59.3
04	73 00.8	199 53.2	30.3	287 03.0	01.0	322 47.9	04.0	214 22.9	52.4	Aldebaran	290 48.9	N16 32.1
05	88 03.2	214 52.8	31.1	302 04.0	00.5	337 50.1	03.9	229 25.1	52.5			
06	103 05.7	229 52.4	S21 31.9	317 04.9	N15 00.0	352 52.3	N22 03.9	244 27.3	S12 52.6	Alioth	166 21.1	N55 53.2
07	118 08.2	244 52.0	32.7	332 05.9	14 59.5	7 54.5	03.9	259 29.5	52.7	Alkaid	152 59.2	N49 14.8
08	133 10.6	259 51.6	33.5	347 06.9	59.1	22 56.7	03.8	274 31.7	52.8	Al Na'ir	27 43.2	S46 53.6
F 09	148 13.1	274 51.2	. . 34.4	2 07.9	. . 58.6	37 58.8	. . 03.8	289 33.9	. . 52.9	Alnilam	275 46.1	S 1 11.6
R 10	163 15.5	289 50.8	35.2	17 08.8	58.1	53 01.0	03.8	304 36.1	53.0	Alphard	217 56.1	S 8 43.1
I 11	178 18.0	304 50.4	36.0	32 09.8	57.6	68 03.2	03.8	319 38.3	53.0			
D 12	193 20.5	319 50.0	S21 36.8	47 10.8	N14 57.1	83 05.4	N22 03.7	334 40.5	S12 53.1	Alphecca	126 11.1	N26 40.4
A 13	208 22.9	334 49.6	37.6	62 11.7	56.7	98 07.6	03.7	349 42.7	53.2	Alpheratz	357 42.9	N29 10.2
Y 14	223 25.4	349 49.2	38.4	77 12.7	56.2	113 09.8	03.7	4 44.9	53.3	Altair	62 08.0	N 8 54.6
15	238 27.9	4 48.8	. . 39.2	92 13.7	. . 55.7	128 12.0	. . 03.6	19 47.1	. . 53.4	Ankaa	353 15.1	S42 13.8
16	253 30.3	19 48.4	40.0	107 14.6	55.2	143 14.2	03.6	34 49.3	53.5	Antares	112 26.2	S26 27.6
17	268 32.8	34 48.0	40.8	122 15.6	54.7	158 16.4	03.6	49 51.5	53.6			
18	283 35.3	49 47.6	S21 41.7	137 16.6	N14 54.2	173 18.6	N22 03.5	64 53.7	S12 53.7	Arcturus	145 55.9	N19 06.8
19	298 37.7	64 47.2	42.5	152 17.6	53.8	188 20.7	03.5	79 55.9	53.8	Atria	107 28.1	S69 03.2
20	313 40.2	79 46.8	43.3	167 18.5	53.3	203 22.9	03.5	94 58.1	53.9	Avior	234 18.1	S59 33.1
21	328 42.7	94 46.4	. . 44.1	182 19.5	. . 52.8	218 25.1	. . 03.4	110 00.2	. . 53.9	Bellatrix	278 31.7	N 6 21.7
22	343 45.1	109 46.0	44.9	197 20.5	52.3	233 27.3	03.4	125 02.4	54.0	Betelgeuse	271 01.0	N 7 24.5
23	358 47.6	124 45.6	45.7	212 21.4	51.8	248 29.5	03.4	140 04.6	54.1			
5 00	13 50.0	139 45.2	S21 46.5	227 22.4	N14 51.4	263 31.7	N22 03.3	155 06.8	S12 54.2	Canopus	263 56.0	S52 42.0
01	28 52.5	154 44.8	47.3	242 23.4	50.9	278 33.9	03.3	170 09.0	54.3	Capella	280 33.9	N46 00.4
02	43 55.0	169 44.4	48.1	257 24.4	50.4	293 36.1	03.3	185 11.2	54.4	Deneb	49 31.1	N45 20.2
03	58 57.4	184 44.0	. . 48.9	272 25.3	. . 49.9	308 38.3	. . 03.3	200 13.4	. . 54.5	Denebola	182 33.8	N14 29.7
04	73 59.9	199 43.6	49.7	287 26.3	49.4	323 40.5	03.2	215 15.6	54.6	Diphda	348 55.4	S17 54.5
05	89 02.4	214 43.2	50.5	302 27.3	48.9	338 42.7	03.2	230 17.8	54.7			
06	104 04.8	229 42.8	S21 51.3	317 28.3	N14 48.5	353 44.9	N22 03.2	245 20.0	S12 54.8	Dubhe	193 52.1	N61 40.4
07	119 07.3	244 42.4	52.1	332 29.2	48.0	8 47.1	03.1	260 22.2	54.9	Elnath	278 12.2	N28 36.9
S 08	134 09.8	259 42.0	52.9	347 30.2	47.5	23 49.3	03.1	275 24.4	54.9	Eltanin	90 46.2	N51 29.7
A 09	149 12.2	274 41.6	. . 53.6	2 31.2	. . 47.0	38 51.5	. . 03.1	290 26.6	. . 55.0	Enif	33 46.7	N 9 56.6
T 10	164 14.7	289 41.2	54.4	17 32.2	46.5	53 53.6	03.0	305 28.8	55.1	Fomalhaut	15 23.5	S29 32.8
U 11	179 17.1	304 40.8	55.2	32 33.1	46.0	68 55.8	03.0	320 31.0	55.2			
R 12	194 19.6	319 40.4	S21 56.0	47 34.1	N14 45.6	83 58.0	N22 03.0	335 33.2	S12 55.3	Gacrux	172 01.2	S57 11.4
D 13	209 22.1	334 40.0	56.8	62 35.1	45.1	99 00.2	03.0	350 35.4	55.4	Gienah	175 52.4	S17 37.0
A 14	224 24.5	349 39.6	57.6	77 36.1	44.6	114 02.4	02.9	5 37.6	55.5	Hadar	148 48.1	S60 26.3
Y 15	239 27.0	4 39.2	. . 58.4	92 37.0	. . 44.1	129 04.6	. . 02.9	20 39.8	. . 55.6	Hamal	328 00.2	N23 31.7
16	254 29.5	19 38.8	21 59.2	107 38.0	43.6	144 06.8	02.9	35 42.0	55.7	Kaus Aust.	83 43.6	S34 22.6
17	269 31.9	34 38.3	22 00.0	122 39.0	43.1	159 09.0	02.8	50 44.2	55.8			
18	284 34.4	49 37.9	S22 00.8	137 40.0	N14 42.6	174 11.2	N22 02.8	65 46.4	S12 55.8	Kochab	137 21.1	N74 06.2
19	299 36.9	64 37.5	01.5	152 40.9	42.2	189 13.4	02.8	80 48.6	55.9	Markab	13 37.8	N15 17.0
20	314 39.3	79 37.1	02.3	167 41.9	41.7	204 15.6	02.7	95 50.8	56.0	Menkar	314 14.6	N 4 08.7
21	329 41.8	94 36.7	. . 03.1	182 42.9	. . 41.2	219 17.8	. . 02.7	110 53.0	. . 56.1	Menkent	148 07.7	S36 26.2
22	344 44.3	109 36.3	03.9	197 43.9	40.7	234 20.0	02.7	125 55.2	56.2	Miaplacidus	221 40.1	S69 46.3
23	359 46.7	124 35.9	04.7	212 44.8	40.2	249 22.2	02.7	140 57.4	56.3			
6 00	14 49.2	139 35.5	S22 05.5	227 45.8	N14 39.7	264 24.4	N22 02.6	155 59.5	S12 56.4	Mirfak	308 39.6	N49 54.4
01	29 51.6	154 35.1	06.2	242 46.8	39.3	279 26.6	02.6	171 01.7	56.5	Nunki	75 58.1	S26 16.6
02	44 54.1	169 34.7	07.0	257 47.8	38.8	294 28.8	02.6	186 03.9	56.6	Peacock	53 18.7	S56 41.4
03	59 56.6	184 34.3	. . 07.8	272 48.7	. . 38.3	309 31.0	. . 02.5	201 06.1	. . 56.7	Pollux	243 27.6	N27 59.4
04	74 59.0	199 33.9	08.6	287 49.7	37.8	324 33.2	02.5	216 08.3	56.7	Procyon	244 59.6	N 5 11.3
05	90 01.5	214 33.5	09.3	302 50.7	37.3	339 35.4	02.5	231 10.5	56.8			
06	105 04.0	229 33.0	S22 10.1	317 51.7	N14 36.8	354 37.6	N22 02.4	246 12.7	S12 56.9	Rasalhague	96 06.4	N12 33.4
07	120 06.4	244 32.6	10.9	332 52.7	36.3	9 39.8	02.4	261 14.9	57.0	Regulus	207 43.5	N11 53.9
08	135 08.9	259 32.2	11.7	347 53.6	35.9	24 42.0	02.4	276 17.1	57.1	Rigel	281 11.7	S 8 11.1
S 09	150 11.4	274 31.8	. . 12.4	2 54.6	. . 35.4	39 44.2	. . 02.4	291 19.3	. . 57.2	Rigil Kent.	139 52.0	S60 53.5
U 10	165 13.8	289 31.4	13.2	17 55.6	34.9	54 46.4	02.3	306 21.5	57.3	Sabik	102 12.4	S15 44.3
N 11	180 16.3	304 31.0	14.0	32 56.6	34.4	69 48.6	02.3	321 23.7	57.4			
D 12	195 18.7	319 30.6	S22 14.7	47 57.6	N14 33.9	84 50.8	N22 02.3	336 25.9	S12 57.5	Schedar	349 39.6	N56 36.9
A 13	210 21.2	334 30.2	15.5	62 58.5	33.4	99 53.0	02.2	351 28.1	57.6	Shaula	96 21.8	S37 06.7
Y 14	225 23.7	349 29.8	16.3	77 59.5	32.9	114 55.3	02.2	6 30.3	57.7	Sirius	258 33.5	S16 44.1
15	240 26.1	4 29.3	. . 17.1	93 00.5	. . 32.4	129 57.5	. . 02.2	21 32.5	. . 57.7	Spica	158 31.3	S11 13.9
16	255 28.6	19 28.9	17.8	108 01.5	32.0	144 59.7	02.1	36 34.7	57.8	Suhail	222 52.5	S43 29.2
17	270 31.1	34 28.5	18.6	123 02.5	31.5	160 01.9	02.1	51 36.9	57.9			
18	285 33.5	49 28.1	S22 19.3	138 03.4	N14 31.0	175 04.1	N22 02.1	66 39.1	S12 58.0	Vega	80 38.8	N38 48.2
19	300 36.0	64 27.7	20.1	153 04.4	30.5	190 06.3	02.1	81 41.2	58.1	Zuben'ubi	137 05.5	S16 05.8
20	315 38.5	79 27.3	20.9	168 05.4	30.0	205 08.5	02.0	96 43.4	58.2		SHA	Mer.Pass.
21	330 40.9	94 26.9	. . 21.6	183 06.4	. . 29.5	220 10.7	. . 02.0	111 45.6	. . 58.3		° ′	h m
22	345 43.4	109 26.5	22.4	198 07.4	29.0	235 12.9	02.0	126 47.8	58.4	Venus	125 55.2	14 41
23	0 45.9	124 26.0	23.2	213 08.4	28.5	250 15.1	01.9	141 50.0	58.5	Mars	213 32.4	8 50
	h m									Jupiter	249 41.7	6 25
Mer.Pass. 23 00.9		v −0.4	d 0.8	v 1.0	d 0.5	v 2.2	d 0.0	v 2.2	d 0.1	Saturn	141 16.8	13 38

UT	SUN GHA	SUN Dec	MOON GHA	MOON v	MOON Dec	MOON d	MOON HP	Lat.	Twilight Naut.	Twilight Civil	Sunrise	Moonrise 4	Moonrise 5	Moonrise 6	Moonrise 7
	° '	° '	° '	'	° '	'	'	°	h m	h m	h m	h m	h m	h m	h m
d h								N 72	04 10	05 30	06 37	05 53	07 45	09 44	11 57
4 00	182 48.0	S 4 19.6	195 40.5	12.4	S 2 24.2	10.9	56.9	N 70	04 19	05 31	06 32	05 48	07 32	09 20	11 14
01	197 48.2	20.5	210 11.9	12.5	2 35.1	10.9	56.9	68	04 27	05 32	06 27	05 44	07 21	09 02	10 45
02	212 48.4	21.5	224 43.4	12.3	2 46.0	10.9	56.9	66	04 33	05 33	06 24	05 40	07 13	08 48	10 24
03	227 48.6	.. 22.5	239 14.7	12.4	2 56.9	10.9	56.9	64	04 38	05 33	06 20	05 37	07 06	08 36	10 07
04	242 48.8	23.4	253 46.1	12.3	3 07.8	10.9	57.0	62	04 42	05 33	06 18	05 35	07 00	08 26	09 53
05	257 49.0	24.4	268 17.4	12.2	3 18.7	10.9	57.0	60	04 45	05 34	06 15	05 33	06 54	08 18	09 41
06	272 49.2	S 4 25.3	282 48.6	12.2	S 3 29.6	10.9	57.0	N 58	04 48	05 34	06 13	05 31	06 50	08 10	09 31
07	287 49.3	26.3	297 19.8	12.2	3 40.5	10.9	57.0	56	04 51	05 34	06 11	05 29	06 46	08 04	09 22
08	302 49.5	27.3	311 51.0	12.1	3 51.4	10.8	57.1	54	04 53	05 34	06 09	05 27	06 42	07 58	09 14
F 09	317 49.7	.. 28.2	326 22.1	12.1	4 02.2	10.9	57.1	52	04 55	05 34	06 08	05 26	06 39	07 53	09 07
R 10	332 49.9	29.2	340 53.2	12.1	4 13.1	10.9	57.1	50	04 56	05 34	06 06	05 25	06 36	07 48	09 01
I 11	347 50.1	30.2	355 24.3	12.0	4 24.0	10.8	57.1	45	05 00	05 34	06 00	05 22	06 29	07 38	08 47
D 12	2 50.3	S 4 31.1	9 55.3	11.9	S 4 34.8	10.8	57.2	N 40	05 02	05 33	06 00	05 19	06 24	07 30	08 36
A 13	17 50.5	32.1	24 26.2	11.9	4 45.6	10.8	57.2	35	05 03	05 33	05 58	05 17	06 19	07 22	08 27
Y 14	32 50.7	33.1	38 57.1	11.9	4 56.4	10.8	57.2	30	05 04	05 32	05 56	05 16	06 15	07 16	08 18
15	47 50.9	.. 34.0	53 28.0	11.8	5 07.2	10.8	57.3	20	05 04	05 30	05 52	05 13	06 08	07 05	08 04
16	62 51.1	35.0	67 58.8	11.8	5 18.0	10.8	57.3	N 10	05 03	05 27	05 48	05 10	06 02	06 56	07 52
17	77 51.2	35.9	82 29.6	11.7	5 28.8	10.7	57.3	0	05 00	05 24	05 45	05 08	05 56	06 47	07 40
18	92 51.4	S 4 36.9	97 00.3	11.7	S 5 39.5	10.7	57.3	S 10	04 56	05 21	05 42	05 05	05 50	06 38	07 29
19	107 51.6	37.9	111 31.0	11.6	5 50.2	10.7	57.4	20	04 50	05 16	05 38	05 03	05 44	06 29	07 16
20	122 51.8	38.8	126 01.6	11.6	6 00.9	10.7	57.4	30	04 41	05 09	05 33	05 00	05 38	06 18	07 03
21	137 52.0	.. 39.8	140 32.2	11.5	6 11.6	10.7	57.4	35	04 35	05 05	05 31	04 58	05 34	06 12	06 55
22	152 52.2	40.8	155 02.7	11.5	6 22.3	10.6	57.4	40	04 28	05 01	05 28	04 56	05 29	06 05	06 45
23	167 52.4	41.7	169 33.2	11.4	6 32.9	10.6	57.5	45	04 19	04 55	05 24	04 54	05 24	05 57	06 35
5 00	182 52.6	S 4 42.7	184 03.6	11.4	S 6 43.5	10.6	57.5	S 50	04 08	04 47	05 20	04 52	05 18	05 48	06 22
01	197 52.7	43.6	198 34.0	11.3	6 54.1	10.6	57.5	52	04 03	04 44	05 18	04 50	05 15	05 43	06 16
02	212 52.9	44.6	213 04.3	11.3	7 04.7	10.5	57.6	54	03 56	04 40	05 16	04 49	05 12	05 39	06 10
03	227 53.1	.. 45.6	227 34.6	11.2	7 15.2	10.5	57.6	56	03 49	04 36	05 14	04 48	05 09	05 33	06 02
04	242 53.3	46.5	242 04.8	11.1	7 25.7	10.5	57.6	58	03 41	04 31	05 11	04 46	05 05	05 27	05 54
05	257 53.5	47.5	256 34.9	11.2	7 36.2	10.4	57.6	S 60	03 32	04 25	05 08	04 45	05 01	05 21	05 45

UT	SUN GHA	SUN Dec	MOON GHA	MOON v	MOON Dec	MOON d	MOON HP	Lat.	Sunset	Twilight Civil	Twilight Naut.	Moonset 4	Moonset 5	Moonset 6	Moonset 7
06	272 53.7	S 4 48.5	271 05.1	11.0	S 7 46.6	10.4	57.6								
07	287 53.9	49.4	285 35.1	11.0	7 57.0	10.4	57.6	Lat.	Sunset	Civil	Naut.	4	5	6	7
S 08	302 54.1	50.4	300 05.1	11.0	8 07.4	10.3	57.7								
A 09	317 54.2	.. 51.3	314 35.1	10.9	8 17.7	10.3	57.7	°	h m	h m	h m	h m	h m	h m	h m
T 10	332 54.4	52.3	329 05.0	10.8	8 28.0	10.3	57.7	N 72	16 57	18 04	19 24	16 20	16 10	15 57	15 37
U 11	347 54.6	53.3	343 34.8	10.8	8 38.3	10.2	57.7	N 70	17 03	18 04	19 15	16 27	16 25	16 22	16 21
R 12	2 54.8	S 4 54.2	358 04.6	10.7	S 8 48.5	10.2	57.8	68	17 08	18 03	19 08	16 34	16 37	16 41	16 50
D 13	17 55.0	55.2	12 34.3	10.7	8 58.7	10.1	57.8	66	17 11	18 02	19 02	16 39	16 46	16 57	17 12
A 14	32 55.2	56.1	27 04.0	10.6	9 08.8	10.1	57.8	64	17 15	18 02	18 57	16 43	16 55	17 10	17 30
Y 15	47 55.4	.. 57.1	41 33.6	10.5	9 18.9	10.1	57.8	62	17 18	18 02	18 53	16 47	17 02	17 20	17 45
16	62 55.5	58.1	56 03.1	10.5	9 29.0	10.0	57.9	60	17 20	18 02	18 50	16 51	17 08	17 30	17 57
17	77 55.7	4 59.0	70 32.6	10.5	9 39.0	10.0	57.9	N 58	17 23	18 02	18 47	16 54	17 14	17 38	18 08
18	92 55.9	S 5 00.0	85 02.1	10.4	S 9 49.0	9.9	57.9	56	17 25	18 02	18 45	16 56	17 19	17 45	18 17
19	107 56.1	00.9	99 31.5	10.3	9 58.9	9.9	57.9	54	17 26	18 02	18 42	16 59	17 23	17 51	18 25
20	122 56.3	01.9	114 00.8	10.3	10 08.8	9.8	57.9	52	17 28	18 02	18 41	17 01	17 27	17 57	18 33
21	137 56.5	.. 02.9	128 30.1	10.2	10 18.6	9.8	58.0	50	17 30	18 02	18 39	17 03	17 31	18 02	18 40
22	152 56.6	03.8	142 59.3	10.1	10 28.4	9.6	58.0	45	17 33	18 02	18 36	17 07	17 39	18 14	18 54
23	167 56.8	04.8	157 28.4	10.1	10 38.2	9.6	58.0								
6 00	182 57.0	S 5 05.7	171 57.5	10.0	S 10 47.0	9.7	58.0	N 40	17 36	18 03	18 34	17 11	17 45	18 23	19 06
01	197 57.2	06.7	186 26.5	10.0	10 57.5	9.5	58.1	35	17 38	18 04	18 33	17 14	17 51	18 31	19 16
02	212 57.4	07.7	200 55.5	9.9	11 07.0	9.6	58.1	30	17 41	18 04	18 32	17 17	17 56	18 38	19 25
03	227 57.6	.. 08.6	215 24.4	9.9	11 16.6	9.4	58.1	20	17 45	18 07	18 32	17 22	18 05	18 51	19 40
04	242 57.7	09.6	229 53.3	9.7	11 26.0	9.4	58.1	N 10	17 48	18 09	18 34	17 26	18 13	19 02	19 54
05	257 57.9	10.5	244 22.0	9.8	11 35.4	9.4	58.1	0	17 52	18 12	18 36	17 31	18 20	19 12	20 06
06	272 58.1	S 5 11.5	258 50.8	9.6	S 11 44.8	9.3	58.2	S 10	17 55	18 16	18 41	17 35	18 27	19 22	20 19
07	287 58.3	12.5	273 19.4	9.6	11 54.1	9.2	58.2	20	17 59	18 21	18 47	17 39	18 35	19 33	20 33
08	302 58.5	13.4	287 48.0	9.6	12 03.3	9.1	58.2	30	18 04	18 28	18 56	17 44	18 44	19 46	20 48
S 09	317 58.7	.. 14.4	302 16.6	9.5	12 12.4	9.1	58.2	35	18 06	18 32	19 02	17 47	18 49	19 53	20 57
U 10	332 58.8	15.3	316 45.1	9.4	12 21.5	9.1	58.2	40	18 10	18 37	19 09	17 50	18 55	20 01	21 07
N 11	347 59.0	16.3	331 13.5	9.3	12 30.6	8.9	58.3	45	18 13	18 43	19 18	17 54	19 02	20 11	21 20
D 12	2 59.2	S 5 17.2	345 41.8	9.3	S 12 39.5	8.9	58.3	S 50	18 17	18 50	19 30	17 58	19 10	20 23	21 34
A 13	17 59.4	18.2	0 10.1	9.3	12 48.4	8.9	58.3	52	18 19	18 54	19 36	18 00	19 14	20 28	21 41
Y 14	32 59.6	19.2	14 38.4	9.2	12 57.3	8.7	58.3	54	18 22	18 58	19 42	18 03	19 18	20 34	21 49
15	47 59.8	.. 20.1	29 06.6	9.1	13 06.0	8.7	58.3	56	18 24	19 02	19 49	18 05	19 23	20 41	21 57
16	62 59.9	21.1	43 34.7	9.0	13 14.7	8.6	58.4	58	18 27	19 07	19 58	18 08	19 28	20 48	22 07
17	78 00.1	22.0	58 02.7	9.0	13 23.3	8.5	58.4	S 60	18 30	19 13	20 07	18 11	19 34	20 57	22 18
18	93 00.3	S 5 23.0	72 30.7	9.0	S 13 31.9	8.5	58.4								
19	108 00.5	24.0	86 58.7	8.8	13 40.4	8.4	58.4			SUN			MOON		
20	123 00.7	24.9	101 26.5	8.8	13 48.8	8.3	58.4	Day	Eqn. of Time 00h	Eqn. of Time 12h	Mer. Pass.	Mer. Pass. Upper	Mer. Pass. Lower	Age	Phase
21	138 00.8	.. 25.9	115 54.3	8.8	13 57.1	8.2	58.5								
22	153 01.0	26.8	130 22.1	8.7	14 05.3	8.2	58.5	d	m s	m s	h m	h m	h m	d %	
23	168 01.2	27.8	144 49.8	8.6	S 14 13.5	8.1	58.5	4	11 12	11 21	11 49	11 19	23 43	29 0	●
								5	11 30	11 39	11 48	12 08	24 33	00 0	
	SD 16.0	d 1.0	SD 15.6		15.7		15.9	6	11 48	11 56	11 48	12 59	00 33	01 3	

UT	ARIES GHA	VENUS −4.3 GHA	Dec	MARS +1.6 GHA	Dec	JUPITER −2.2 GHA	Dec	SATURN +0.6 GHA	Dec	STARS Name	SHA	Dec
7 00	15 48.3	139 25.6	S22 23.9	228 09.3	N14 28.1	265 17.3	N22 01.9	156 52.2	S12 58.6	Acamar	315 17.8	S40 14.8
01	30 50.8	154 25.2	24.7	243 10.3	27.6	280 19.5	01.9	171 54.4	58.6	Achernar	335 26.1	S57 09.9
02	45 53.2	169 24.8	25.4	258 11.3	27.1	295 21.7	01.9	186 56.6	58.7	Acrux	173 09.6	S63 10.5
03	60 55.7	184 24.4	.. 26.2	273 12.3	.. 26.6	310 23.9	.. 01.8	201 58.8	.. 58.8	Adhara	255 12.3	S28 59.4
04	75 58.2	199 24.0	26.9	288 13.3	26.1	325 26.1	01.8	217 01.0	58.9	Aldebaran	290 48.9	N16 32.1
05	91 00.6	214 23.6	27.7	303 14.2	25.6	340 28.3	01.8	232 03.2	59.0			
06	106 03.1	229 23.1	S22 28.5	318 15.2	N14 25.1	355 30.6	N22 01.7	247 05.4	S12 59.1	Alioth	166 21.1	N55 53.1
07	121 05.6	244 22.7	29.2	333 16.2	24.6	10 32.8	01.7	262 07.6	59.2	Alkaid	152 59.2	N49 14.8
08	136 08.0	259 22.3	30.0	348 17.2	24.2	25 35.0	01.7	277 09.8	59.3	Al Na'ir	27 43.2	S46 53.6
M 09	151 10.5	274 21.9	.. 30.7	3 18.2	.. 23.7	40 37.2	.. 01.7	292 12.0	.. 59.4	Alnilam	275 46.0	S 1 11.6
O 10	166 13.0	289 21.5	31.5	18 19.2	23.2	55 39.4	01.6	307 14.2	59.5	Alphard	217 56.1	S 8 43.1
N 11	181 15.4	304 21.1	32.2	33 20.2	22.7	70 41.6	01.6	322 16.3	59.6			
D 12	196 17.9	319 20.6	S22 33.0	48 21.1	N14 22.2	85 43.8	N22 01.6	337 18.5	S12 59.6	Alphecca	126 11.1	N26 40.4
A 13	211 20.4	334 20.2	33.7	63 22.1	21.7	100 46.0	01.5	352 20.7	59.7	Alpheratz	357 42.9	N29 10.2
Y 14	226 22.8	349 19.8	34.5	78 23.1	21.2	115 48.2	01.5	7 22.9	59.8	Altair	62 08.0	N 8 54.6
15	241 25.3	4 19.4	.. 35.2	93 24.1	.. 20.7	130 50.5	.. 01.5	22 25.1	12 59.9	Ankaa	353 15.1	S42 13.8
16	256 27.7	19 19.0	35.9	108 25.1	20.2	145 52.7	01.4	37 27.3	13 00.0	Antares	112 26.2	S26 27.6
17	271 30.2	34 18.6	36.7	123 26.1	19.8	160 54.9	01.4	52 29.5	00.1			
18	286 32.7	49 18.1	S22 37.4	138 27.1	N14 19.3	175 57.1	N22 01.4	67 31.7	S13 00.2	Arcturus	145 55.9	N19 06.8
19	301 35.1	64 17.7	38.2	153 28.0	18.8	190 59.3	01.4	82 33.9	00.3	Atria	107 28.1	S69 03.2
20	316 37.6	79 17.3	38.9	168 29.0	18.3	206 01.5	01.3	97 36.1	00.4	Avior	234 18.1	S59 33.0
21	331 40.1	94 16.9	.. 39.7	183 30.0	.. 17.8	221 03.7	.. 01.3	112 38.3	.. 00.5	Bellatrix	278 31.6	N 6 21.7
22	346 42.5	109 16.5	40.4	198 31.0	17.3	236 05.9	01.3	127 40.5	00.6	Betelgeuse	271 01.0	N 7 24.5
23	1 45.0	124 16.1	41.1	213 32.0	16.8	251 08.2	01.3	142 42.7	00.6			
8 00	16 47.5	139 15.6	S22 41.9	228 33.0	N14 16.3	266 10.4	N22 01.2	157 44.9	S13 00.7	Canopus	263 55.9	S52 42.0
01	31 49.9	154 15.2	42.6	243 34.0	15.8	281 12.6	01.2	172 47.0	00.8	Capella	280 33.9	N46 00.4
02	46 52.4	169 14.8	43.3	258 34.9	15.3	296 14.8	01.2	187 49.2	00.9	Deneb	49 31.1	N45 20.2
03	61 54.8	184 14.4	.. 44.1	273 35.9	.. 14.9	311 17.0	.. 01.1	202 51.4	.. 01.0	Denebola	182 33.8	N14 29.7
04	76 57.3	199 14.0	44.8	288 36.9	14.4	326 19.2	01.1	217 53.6	01.1	Diphda	348 55.4	S17 54.5
05	91 59.8	214 13.5	45.5	303 37.9	14.0	341 21.4	01.1	232 55.8	01.2			
06	107 02.2	229 13.1	S22 46.3	318 38.9	N14 13.4	356 23.7	N22 01.1	247 58.0	S13 01.3	Dubhe	193 52.1	N61 40.4
07	122 04.7	244 12.7	47.0	333 39.9	12.9	11 25.9	01.0	263 00.2	01.4	Elnath	278 12.2	N28 36.9
T 08	137 07.2	259 12.3	47.7	348 40.9	12.4	26 28.1	01.0	278 02.4	01.5	Eltanin	90 46.2	N51 29.3
U 09	152 09.6	274 11.9	.. 48.5	3 41.9	.. 11.9	41 30.3	.. 01.0	293 04.6	.. 01.6	Enif	33 46.7	N 9 56.6
E 10	167 12.1	289 11.4	49.2	18 42.9	11.4	56 32.5	00.9	308 06.8	01.6	Fomalhaut	15 23.5	S29 32.8
S 11	182 14.6	304 11.0	49.9	33 43.8	10.9	71 34.8	00.9	323 09.0	01.7			
D 12	197 17.0	319 10.6	S22 50.6	48 44.8	N14 10.4	86 37.0	N22 00.9	338 11.2	S13 01.8	Gacrux	172 01.2	S57 11.3
A 13	212 19.5	334 10.2	51.4	63 45.8	09.9	101 39.2	00.9	353 13.4	01.9	Gienah	175 52.4	S17 37.0
Y 14	227 22.0	349 09.8	52.1	78 46.8	09.5	116 41.4	00.8	8 15.5	02.0	Hadar	148 48.1	S60 26.3
15	242 24.4	4 09.3	.. 52.8	93 47.8	.. 09.0	131 43.6	.. 00.8	23 17.7	.. 02.1	Hamal	328 00.2	N23 31.7
16	257 26.9	19 08.9	53.5	108 48.8	08.5	146 45.8	00.8	38 19.9	02.2	Kaus Aust.	83 43.6	S34 22.6
17	272 29.3	34 08.5	54.3	123 49.8	08.0	161 48.1	00.7	53 22.1	02.3			
18	287 31.8	49 08.1	S22 55.0	138 50.8	N14 07.5	176 50.3	N22 00.7	68 24.3	S13 02.4	Kochab	137 21.2	N74 06.1
19	302 34.3	64 07.6	55.7	153 51.8	07.0	191 52.5	00.7	83 26.5	02.5	Markab	13 37.8	N15 17.0
20	317 36.7	79 07.2	56.4	168 52.8	06.5	206 54.7	00.7	98 28.7	02.6	Menkar	314 14.5	N 4 08.7
21	332 39.2	94 06.8	.. 57.1	183 53.8	.. 06.0	221 56.9	.. 00.6	113 30.9	.. 02.6	Menkent	148 07.7	S36 26.2
22	347 41.7	109 06.4	57.9	198 54.7	05.5	236 59.2	00.6	128 33.1	02.7	Miaplacidus	221 40.0	S69 46.3
23	2 44.1	124 06.0	58.6	213 55.7	05.0	252 01.4	00.6	143 35.3	02.8			
9 00	17 46.6	139 05.5	S22 59.3	228 56.7	N14 04.5	267 03.6	N22 00.6	158 37.5	S13 02.9	Mirfak	308 39.6	N49 54.4
01	32 49.1	154 05.1	23 00.0	243 57.7	04.0	282 05.8	00.5	173 39.6	03.0	Nunki	75 58.1	S26 16.6
02	47 51.5	169 04.7	00.7	258 58.7	03.5	297 08.1	00.5	188 41.8	03.1	Peacock	53 18.8	S56 41.4
03	62 54.0	184 04.3	.. 01.4	273 59.7	.. 03.1	312 10.3	.. 00.5	203 44.0	.. 03.2	Pollux	243 27.5	N27 59.4
04	77 56.5	199 03.8	02.1	289 00.7	02.6	327 12.5	00.4	218 46.2	03.3	Procyon	244 59.6	N 5 11.3
05	92 58.9	214 03.4	02.9	304 01.7	02.1	342 14.7	00.4	233 48.4	03.4			
06	108 01.4	229 03.0	S23 03.6	319 02.7	N14 01.6	357 16.9	N22 00.4	248 50.6	S13 03.5	Rasalhague	96 06.4	N12 33.4
W 07	123 03.8	244 02.6	04.3	334 03.7	01.1	12 19.2	00.4	263 52.8	03.6	Regulus	207 43.5	N11 53.9
E 08	138 06.3	259 02.1	05.0	349 04.7	00.6	27 21.4	00.3	278 55.0	03.6	Rigel	281 11.7	S 8 11.1
D 09	153 08.8	274 01.7	.. 05.7	4 05.7	14 00.1	42 23.6	.. 00.3	293 57.2	.. 03.7	Rigil Kent.	139 52.6	S60 53.5
N 10	168 11.2	289 01.3	06.4	19 06.7	13 59.6	57 25.8	00.3	308 59.4	03.8	Sabik	102 12.5	S15 44.3
E 11	183 13.7	304 00.9	07.1	34 07.7	59.1	72 28.1	00.3	324 01.6	03.9			
S 12	198 16.2	319 00.4	S23 07.8	49 08.6	N13 58.6	87 30.3	N22 00.2	339 03.7	S13 04.0	Schedar	349 39.6	N56 36.9
D 13	213 18.6	334 00.0	08.5	64 09.6	58.1	102 32.5	00.2	354 05.9	04.1	Shaula	96 21.8	S37 06.7
A 14	228 21.1	348 59.6	09.2	79 10.6	57.6	117 34.7	00.2	9 08.1	04.2	Sirius	258 33.5	S16 44.1
Y 15	243 23.6	3 59.2	.. 09.9	94 11.6	.. 57.1	132 37.0	.. 00.1	24 10.3	.. 04.3	Spica	158 31.3	S11 13.9
16	258 26.0	18 58.7	10.6	109 12.6	56.6	147 39.2	00.1	39 12.5	04.4	Suhail	222 52.5	S43 29.2
17	273 28.5	33 58.3	11.3	124 13.6	56.1	162 41.4	00.1	54 14.7	04.5			
18	288 30.9	48 57.9	S23 12.0	139 14.6	N13 55.6	177 43.7	N22 00.1	69 16.9	S13 04.6	Vega	80 38.9	N38 48.2
19	303 33.4	63 57.5	12.7	154 15.6	55.2	192 45.9	00.0	84 19.1	04.6	Zuben'ubi	137 05.5	S16 05.8
20	318 35.9	78 57.0	13.4	169 16.6	54.7	207 48.1	00.0	99 21.3	04.7			
21	333 38.3	93 56.6	.. 14.1	184 17.6	.. 54.2	222 50.3	.. 00.0	114 23.5	.. 04.8			
22	348 40.8	108 56.2	14.8	199 18.6	53.7	237 52.6	22 00.0	129 25.6	04.9			
23	3 43.3	123 55.8	15.5	214 19.6	53.2	252 54.8	N21 59.9	144 27.8	05.0			

											SHA	Mer. Pass.
											° '	h m
										Venus	122 28.2	14 43
										Mars	211 45.5	8 45
										Jupiter	249 22.9	6 14
Mer. Pass. 22 49.1	v −0.4 d 0.7			v 1.0 d 0.5		v 2.2 d 0.0		v 2.2 d 0.1		Saturn	140 57.4	13 27

SUN and MOON

UT (d h)	SUN GHA	SUN Dec	MOON GHA	v	MOON Dec	d	HP
7 00	183 01.4	S 5 28.7	159 17.4	8.6	S14 21.6	8.0	58.5
01	198 01.6	29.7	173 45.0	8.5	14 29.6	7.9	58.5
02	213 01.7	30.7	188 12.5	8.4	14 37.5	7.9	58.5
03	228 01.9	.. 31.6	202 39.9	8.4	14 45.4	7.7	58.6
04	243 02.1	32.6	217 07.3	8.3	14 53.1	7.7	58.6
05	258 02.3	33.5	231 34.6	8.3	15 00.8	7.6	58.6
06	273 02.4	S 5 34.5	246 01.9	8.2	S15 08.4	7.5	58.6
07	288 02.6	35.4	260 29.1	8.2	15 15.9	7.4	58.6
08	303 02.8	36.4	274 56.3	8.1	15 23.3	7.3	58.6
M 09	318 03.0	.. 37.3	289 23.4	8.0	15 30.6	7.2	58.7
O 10	333 03.2	38.3	303 50.4	8.0	15 37.8	7.2	58.7
N 11	348 03.3	39.3	318 17.4	7.9	15 45.0	7.0	58.7
D 12	3 03.5	S 5 40.2	332 44.3	7.8	S15 52.0	7.0	58.7
A 13	18 03.7	41.2	347 11.1	7.8	15 59.0	6.8	58.7
Y 14	33 03.9	42.1	1 37.9	7.8	16 05.8	6.8	58.7
15	48 04.0	.. 43.1	16 04.7	7.7	16 12.6	6.6	58.7
16	63 04.2	44.0	30 31.4	7.6	16 19.2	6.6	58.8
17	78 04.4	45.0	44 58.0	7.6	16 25.8	6.5	58.8
18	93 04.6	S 5 45.9	59 24.6	7.5	S16 32.3	6.3	58.8
19	108 04.8	46.9	73 51.1	7.5	16 38.6	6.3	58.8
20	123 04.9	47.9	88 17.6	7.4	16 44.9	6.2	58.8
21	138 05.1	.. 48.8	102 44.0	7.4	16 51.1	6.0	58.8
22	153 05.3	49.8	117 10.4	7.3	16 57.1	6.0	58.8
23	168 05.5	50.7	131 36.7	7.3	17 03.1	5.8	58.9
8 00	183 05.6	S 5 51.7	146 03.0	7.2	S17 08.9	5.8	58.9
01	198 05.8	52.6	160 29.2	7.2	17 14.7	5.6	58.9
02	213 06.0	53.6	174 55.4	7.1	17 20.3	5.5	58.9
03	228 06.2	.. 54.5	189 21.5	7.0	17 25.8	5.5	58.9
04	243 06.3	55.5	203 47.5	7.1	17 31.3	5.3	58.9
05	258 06.5	56.4	218 13.6	6.9	17 36.6	5.2	58.9
06	273 06.7	S 5 57.4	232 39.5	7.0	S17 41.8	5.1	58.9
07	288 06.9	58.3	247 05.5	6.8	17 46.9	5.0	59.0
T 08	303 07.0	5 59.3	261 31.3	6.9	17 51.9	4.8	59.0
U 09	318 07.2	6 00.2	275 57.2	6.8	17 56.7	4.8	59.0
E 10	333 07.4	01.2	290 23.0	6.7	18 01.5	4.6	59.0
S 11	348 07.6	02.1	304 48.7	6.7	18 06.1	4.5	59.0
D 12	3 07.7	S 6 03.1	319 14.4	6.7	S18 10.6	4.5	59.0
A 13	18 07.9	04.1	333 40.1	6.6	18 15.1	4.3	59.0
Y 14	33 08.1	05.0	348 05.7	6.6	18 19.4	4.1	59.0
15	48 08.2	.. 06.0	2 31.3	6.5	18 23.5	4.1	59.0
16	63 08.4	06.9	16 56.8	6.5	18 27.6	3.9	59.0
17	78 08.6	07.9	31 22.3	6.5	18 31.5	3.9	59.1
18	93 08.8	S 6 08.8	45 47.8	6.5	S18 35.4	3.7	59.1
19	108 08.9	09.8	60 13.3	6.4	18 39.1	3.5	59.1
20	123 09.1	10.7	74 38.7	6.3	18 42.6	3.5	59.1
21	138 09.3	.. 11.7	89 04.0	6.4	18 46.1	3.3	59.1
22	153 09.4	12.6	103 29.4	6.3	18 49.4	3.3	59.1
23	168 09.6	13.6	117 54.7	6.2	18 52.7	3.1	59.1
9 00	183 09.8	S 6 14.5	132 19.9	6.3	S18 55.8	2.9	59.1
01	198 10.0	15.5	146 45.2	6.2	18 58.7	2.9	59.1
02	213 10.1	16.4	161 10.4	6.2	19 01.6	2.7	59.1
03	228 10.3	.. 17.4	175 35.6	6.1	19 04.3	2.6	59.1
04	243 10.5	18.3	190 00.7	6.2	19 06.9	2.5	59.1
05	258 10.6	19.3	204 25.9	6.1	19 09.4	2.3	59.2
06	273 10.8	S 6 20.2	218 51.0	6.0	S19 11.7	2.3	59.2
W 07	288 11.0	21.2	233 16.0	6.1	19 14.0	2.1	59.2
E 08	303 11.2	22.1	247 41.1	6.0	19 16.1	1.9	59.2
D 09	318 11.3	.. 23.1	262 06.1	6.1	19 18.0	1.9	59.2
N 10	333 11.5	24.0	276 31.2	6.0	19 19.9	1.7	59.2
E 11	348 11.7	25.0	290 56.2	6.0	19 21.6	1.6	59.2
S 12	3 11.8	S 6 25.9	305 21.2	5.9	S19 23.2	1.4	59.2
D 13	18 12.0	26.9	319 46.1	6.0	19 24.6	1.4	59.2
A 14	33 12.2	27.8	334 11.1	5.9	19 26.0	1.2	59.2
Y 15	48 12.3	.. 28.8	348 36.0	5.9	19 27.2	1.1	59.2
16	63 12.5	29.7	3 00.9	6.0	19 28.3	0.9	59.2
17	78 12.7	30.7	17 25.9	5.9	19 29.2	0.8	59.2
18	93 12.8	S 6 31.6	31 50.8	5.9	S19 30.0	0.7	59.2
19	108 13.0	32.5	46 15.7	5.8	19 30.7	0.6	59.2
20	123 13.2	33.5	60 40.5	5.9	19 31.3	0.4	59.2
21	138 13.3	.. 34.4	75 05.4	5.9	19 31.7	0.3	59.2
22	153 13.5	35.4	89 30.3	5.9	19 32.0	0.2	59.2
23	168 13.7	36.3	103 55.2	5.8	S19 32.2	0.0	59.2
	SD 16.0	d 1.0	SD 16.0		16.1		16.1

Twilight and Moonrise

Lat.	Naut.	Civil	Sunrise	Moonrise 7	8	9	10
N 72	04 24	05 43	06 51	11 57	▬	▬	▬
N 70	04 32	05 43	06 44	11 14	13 10	14 58	15 46
68	04 38	05 42	06 38	10 45	12 25	13 50	14 45
66	04 42	05 42	06 33	10 24	11 55	13 13	14 10
64	04 46	05 42	06 29	10 07	11 33	12 48	13 45
62	04 50	05 41	06 26	09 53	11 15	12 27	13 25
60	04 53	05 41	06 22	09 41	11 00	12 11	13 09
N 58	04 55	05 40	06 20	09 31	10 48	11 57	12 55
56	04 57	05 40	06 17	09 22	10 37	11 45	12 43
54	04 59	05 39	06 15	09 14	10 27	11 35	12 33
52	05 00	05 39	06 13	09 07	10 19	11 25	12 24
50	05 01	05 39	06 11	09 01	10 11	11 17	12 16
45	05 03	05 37	06 07	08 47	09 55	10 59	11 58
N 40	05 05	05 36	06 03	08 36	09 42	10 45	11 44
35	05 06	05 35	06 00	08 27	09 31	10 33	11 32
30	05 06	05 34	05 57	08 18	09 21	10 22	11 21
20	05 05	05 31	05 53	08 04	09 04	10 04	11 03
N 10	05 03	05 27	05 48	07 52	08 50	09 48	10 47
0	04 59	05 23	05 44	07 40	08 36	09 34	10 32
S 10	04 54	05 19	05 40	07 29	08 22	09 19	10 17
20	04 47	05 13	05 35	07 16	08 08	09 03	10 01
30	04 37	05 06	05 30	07 03	07 51	08 45	09 43
35	04 31	05 01	05 27	06 55	07 42	08 35	09 33
40	04 23	04 56	05 23	06 45	07 31	08 23	09 21
45	04 13	04 49	05 19	06 35	07 18	08 09	09 06
S 50	04 01	04 41	05 14	06 22	07 03	07 52	08 49
52	03 55	04 37	05 11	06 16	06 56	07 44	08 41
54	03 48	04 32	05 09	06 10	06 48	07 35	08 32
56	03 40	04 28	05 06	06 02	06 39	07 25	08 21
58	03 31	04 22	05 03	05 54	06 29	07 13	08 09
S 60	03 21	04 16	04 59	05 45	06 17	07 00	07 56

Sunset, Twilight and Moonset

Lat.	Sunset	Civil	Naut.	Moonset 7	8	9	10
N 72	16 42	17 49	19 08	15 37	▬	▬	▬
N 70	16 49	17 50	19 01	16 21	16 22	16 35	17 50
68	16 55	17 51	18 55	16 50	17 07	17 44	18 50
66	17 00	17 51	18 50	17 12	17 38	18 20	19 25
64	17 04	17 52	18 47	17 30	18 00	18 46	19 50
62	17 08	17 52	18 44	17 45	18 19	19 06	20 10
60	17 11	17 53	18 41	17 57	18 34	19 23	20 26
N 58	17 14	17 53	18 39	18 08	18 47	19 37	20 39
56	17 17	17 54	18 37	18 17	18 58	19 49	20 51
54	17 19	17 54	18 35	18 25	19 07	19 59	21 01
52	17 21	17 55	18 34	18 33	19 16	20 08	21 10
50	17 23	17 55	18 33	18 40	19 24	20 17	21 18
45	17 27	17 57	18 31	18 54	19 41	20 35	21 35
N 40	17 31	17 58	18 29	19 06	19 54	20 49	21 50
35	17 34	18 00	18 29	19 16	20 06	21 01	22 02
30	17 37	18 01	18 29	19 25	20 16	21 12	22 12
20	17 42	18 04	18 30	19 40	20 34	21 30	22 30
N 10	17 46	18 08	18 32	19 54	20 49	21 46	22 45
0	17 51	18 12	18 36	20 06	21 03	22 01	23 00
S 10	17 55	18 16	18 41	20 19	21 18	22 16	23 14
20	18 00	18 22	18 48	20 33	21 33	22 32	23 30
30	18 06	18 30	18 58	20 48	21 50	22 50	23 47
35	18 09	18 34	19 05	20 57	22 00	23 01	23 57
40	18 13	18 40	19 13	21 07	22 12	23 13	24 09
45	18 17	18 47	19 23	21 20	22 26	23 28	24 23
S 50	18 22	18 55	19 35	21 34	22 43	23 45	24 39
52	18 25	18 59	19 42	21 41	22 51	23 53	24 47
54	18 27	19 04	19 49	21 49	22 59	24 02	00 02
56	18 30	19 09	19 57	22 07	23 09	24 13	00 13
58	18 34	19 15	20 06	22 07	23 21	24 25	00 25
S 60	18 37	19 21	20 17	22 18	23 34	24 38	00 38

SUN and MOON

Day	Eqn. of Time 00h	12h	Mer. Pass.	Mer. Pass. Upper	Lower	Age	Phase
d	m s	m s	h m	h m	h m	d	%
7	12 05	12 14	11 48	13 53	01 26	02	7
8	12 22	12 31	11 47	14 50	02 21	03	14
9	12 39	12 47	11 47	15 47	03 18	04	23

UT	ARIES	VENUS −4.3		MARS +1.6		JUPITER −2.2		SATURN +0.6		STARS		
	GHA	GHA	Dec	GHA	Dec	GHA	Dec	GHA	Dec	Name	SHA	Dec
d h	° ′	° ′	° ′	° ′	° ′	° ′	° ′	° ′	° ′		° ′	° ′
10 00	18 45.7	138 55.3	S23 16.2	229 20.6	N13 52.7	267 57.0	N21 59.9	159 30.0	S13 05.1	Acamar	315 17.8	S40 14.9
01	33 48.2	153 54.9	16.9	244 21.6	52.2	282 59.3	59.9	174 32.2	05.2	Achernar	335 26.1	S57 09.9
02	48 50.7	168 54.5	17.6	259 22.6	51.7	298 01.5	59.8	189 34.4	05.3	Acrux	173 09.6	S63 10.5
03	63 53.1	183 54.0	.. 18.3	274 23.6	.. 51.2	313 03.7	.. 59.8	204 36.6	.. 05.4	Adhara	255 12.3	S28 59.4
04	78 55.6	198 53.6	18.9	289 24.6	50.7	328 05.9	59.8	219 38.8	05.5	Aldebaran	290 48.9	N16 32.1
05	93 58.1	213 53.2	19.6	304 25.6	50.2	343 08.2	59.8	234 41.0	05.6			
06	109 00.5	228 52.8	S23 20.3	319 26.6	N13 49.7	358 10.4	N21 59.7	249 43.2	S13 05.6	Alioth	166 21.1	N55 53.1
07	124 03.0	243 52.3	21.0	334 27.6	49.2	13 12.6	59.7	264 45.3	05.7	Alkaid	152 59.2	N49 14.8
T 08	139 05.4	258 51.9	21.7	349 28.6	48.7	28 14.9	59.7	279 47.5	05.8	Al Na'ir	27 43.2	S46 53.6
H 09	154 07.9	273 51.5	.. 22.4	4 29.6	.. 48.2	43 17.1	.. 59.7	294 49.7	.. 05.9	Alnilam	275 46.0	S 1 11.6
U 10	169 10.4	288 51.0	23.1	19 30.6	47.7	58 19.3	59.6	309 51.9	06.0	Alphard	217 56.0	S 8 43.1
R 11	184 12.8	303 50.6	23.7	34 31.6	47.2	73 21.6	59.6	324 54.1	06.1			
S 12	199 15.3	318 50.2	S23 24.4	49 32.6	N13 46.7	88 23.8	N21 59.6	339 56.3	S13 06.2	Alphecca	126 11.1	N26 40.4
D 13	214 17.8	333 49.8	25.1	64 33.6	46.2	103 26.0	59.6	354 58.5	06.3	Alpheratz	357 42.9	N29 10.2
A 14	229 20.2	348 49.3	25.8	79 34.6	45.7	118 28.3	59.5	10 00.7	06.4	Altair	62 08.0	N 8 54.6
Y 15	244 22.7	3 48.9	.. 26.5	94 35.6	.. 45.2	133 30.5	.. 59.5	25 02.9	.. 06.5	Ankaa	353 15.1	S42 13.8
16	259 25.2	18 48.5	27.1	109 36.6	44.7	148 32.7	59.5	40 05.1	06.6	Antares	112 26.2	S26 27.6
17	274 27.6	33 48.0	27.8	124 37.6	44.3	163 35.0	59.5	55 07.2	06.7			
18	289 30.1	48 47.6	S23 28.5	139 38.6	N13 43.8	178 37.2	N21 59.4	70 09.4	S13 06.7	Arcturus	145 55.9	N19 06.8
19	304 32.6	63 47.2	29.2	154 39.6	43.3	193 39.4	59.4	85 11.6	06.8	Atria	107 28.1	S69 03.2
20	319 35.0	78 46.8	29.8	169 40.6	42.8	208 41.7	59.4	100 13.8	06.9	Avior	234 18.1	S59 33.0
21	334 37.5	93 46.3	.. 30.5	184 41.6	.. 42.3	223 43.9	.. 59.4	115 16.0	.. 07.0	Bellatrix	278 31.6	N 6 21.7
22	349 39.9	108 45.9	31.2	199 42.6	41.8	238 46.1	59.3	130 18.2	07.1	Betelgeuse	271 00.9	N 7 24.5
23	4 42.4	123 45.5	31.9	214 43.6	41.3	253 48.4	59.3	145 20.4	07.2			
11 00	19 44.9	138 45.0	S23 32.5	229 44.6	N13 40.8	268 50.6	N21 59.3	160 22.6	S13 07.3	Canopus	263 55.9	S52 42.0
01	34 47.3	153 44.6	33.2	244 45.6	40.3	283 52.9	59.2	175 24.7	07.4	Capella	280 33.9	N46 00.4
02	49 49.8	168 44.2	33.9	259 46.6	39.8	298 55.1	59.2	190 26.9	07.5	Deneb	49 31.1	N45 20.2
03	64 52.3	183 43.7	.. 34.5	274 47.6	.. 39.3	313 57.3	.. 59.2	205 29.1	.. 07.6	Denebola	182 33.8	N14 29.7
04	79 54.7	198 43.3	35.2	289 48.6	38.8	328 59.6	59.2	220 31.3	07.7	Diphda	348 55.4	S17 54.5
05	94 57.2	213 42.9	35.9	304 49.6	38.3	344 01.8	59.1	235 33.5	07.7			
06	109 59.7	228 42.4	S23 36.5	319 50.6	N13 37.8	359 04.0	N21 59.1	250 35.7	S13 07.8	Dubhe	193 52.1	N61 40.4
07	125 02.1	243 42.0	37.2	334 51.6	37.3	14 06.3	59.1	265 37.9	07.9	Elnath	278 12.2	N28 36.9
08	140 04.6	258 41.6	37.8	349 52.6	36.8	29 08.5	59.1	280 40.1	08.0	Eltanin	90 46.2	N51 29.7
F 09	155 07.1	273 41.1	.. 38.5	4 53.6	.. 36.3	44 10.8	.. 59.0	295 42.3	.. 08.1	Enif	33 46.7	N 9 56.6
R 10	170 09.5	288 40.7	39.2	19 54.6	35.8	59 13.0	59.0	310 44.4	08.2	Fomalhaut	15 23.5	S29 32.8
I 11	185 12.0	303 40.3	39.8	34 55.6	35.3	74 15.2	59.0	325 46.6	08.3			
D 12	200 14.4	318 39.9	S23 40.5	49 56.6	N13 34.8	89 17.5	N21 59.0	340 48.8	S13 08.4	Gacrux	172 01.2	S57 11.3
A 13	215 16.9	333 39.4	41.1	64 57.6	34.3	104 19.7	58.9	355 51.0	08.5	Gienah	175 52.4	S17 37.0
Y 14	230 19.4	348 39.0	41.8	79 58.6	33.8	119 22.0	58.9	10 53.2	08.6	Hadar	148 48.1	S60 26.3
15	245 21.8	3 38.6	.. 42.5	94 59.6	.. 33.3	134 24.2	.. 58.9	25 55.4	.. 08.7	Hamal	328 00.2	N23 31.7
16	260 24.3	18 38.1	43.1	110 00.7	32.8	149 26.5	58.9	40 57.6	08.8	Kaus Aust.	83 43.6	S34 22.6
17	275 26.8	33 37.7	43.8	125 01.7	32.3	164 28.7	58.8	55 59.8	08.8			
18	290 29.2	48 37.3	S23 44.4	140 02.7	N13 31.8	179 30.9	N21 58.8	71 01.9	S13 08.9	Kochab	137 21.2	N74 06.1
19	305 31.7	63 36.8	45.1	155 03.7	31.3	194 33.2	58.8	86 04.1	09.0	Markab	13 37.8	N15 17.0
20	320 34.2	78 36.4	45.7	170 04.7	30.8	209 35.4	58.8	101 06.3	09.1	Menkar	314 14.5	N 4 08.7
21	335 36.6	93 36.0	.. 46.4	185 05.7	.. 30.3	224 37.7	.. 58.7	116 08.5	.. 09.2	Menkent	148 07.3	S36 26.2
22	350 39.1	108 35.5	47.0	200 06.7	29.8	239 39.9	58.7	131 10.7	09.3	Miaplacidus	221 40.0	S69 46.3
23	5 41.5	123 35.1	47.7	215 07.7	29.3	254 42.2	58.7	146 12.9	09.4			
12 00	20 44.0	138 34.7	S23 48.3	230 08.7	N13 28.8	269 44.4	N21 58.7	161 15.1	S13 09.5	Mirfak	308 39.6	N49 54.5
01	35 46.5	153 34.2	49.0	245 09.7	28.3	284 46.6	58.6	176 17.3	09.6	Nunki	75 58.1	S26 16.6
02	50 48.9	168 33.8	49.6	260 10.7	27.8	299 48.9	58.6	191 19.4	09.7	Peacock	53 18.8	S56 41.4
03	65 51.4	183 33.4	.. 50.3	275 11.7	.. 27.3	314 51.1	.. 58.6	206 21.6	.. 09.8	Pollux	243 27.5	N27 59.3
04	80 53.9	198 32.9	50.9	290 12.7	26.8	329 53.4	58.6	221 23.8	09.8	Procyon	244 59.5	N 5 11.3
05	95 56.3	213 32.5	51.5	305 13.7	26.3	344 55.6	58.5	236 26.0	09.9			
06	110 58.8	228 32.1	S23 52.2	320 14.7	N13 25.8	359 57.9	N21 58.5	251 28.2	S13 10.0	Rasalhague	96 06.4	N12 33.3
07	126 01.3	243 31.6	52.8	335 15.8	25.3	15 00.1	58.5	266 30.4	10.1	Regulus	207 43.5	N11 53.9
S 08	141 03.7	258 31.2	53.5	350 16.8	24.8	30 02.4	58.5	281 32.6	10.2	Rigel	281 11.7	S 8 11.1
A 09	156 06.2	273 30.8	.. 54.1	5 17.8	.. 24.3	45 04.6	.. 58.4	296 34.7	.. 10.3	Rigil Kent.	139 52.0	S60 53.4
T 10	171 08.7	288 30.3	54.7	20 18.8	23.8	60 06.9	58.4	311 36.9	10.4	Sabik	102 12.5	S15 44.3
U 11	186 11.1	303 29.9	55.4	35 19.8	23.3	75 09.1	58.4	326 39.1	10.5			
R 12	201 13.6	318 29.4	S23 56.0	50 20.8	N13 22.8	90 11.4	N21 58.4	341 41.3	S13 10.6	Schedar	349 39.6	N56 36.9
D 13	216 16.0	333 29.0	56.6	65 21.8	22.3	105 13.6	58.3	356 43.5	10.7	Shaula	96 21.8	S37 06.7
A 14	231 18.5	348 28.6	57.3	80 22.8	21.8	120 15.8	58.3	11 45.7	10.8	Sirius	258 33.5	S16 44.1
Y 15	246 21.0	3 28.1	.. 57.9	95 23.8	.. 21.3	135 18.1	.. 58.3	26 47.9	.. 10.9	Spica	158 31.3	S11 13.9
16	261 23.4	18 27.7	58.5	110 24.8	20.8	150 20.3	58.3	41 50.0	10.9	Suhail	222 52.5	S43 29.2
17	276 25.9	33 27.3	59.2	125 25.8	20.3	165 22.6	58.2	56 52.2	11.0			
18	291 28.4	48 26.8	S23 59.8	140 26.9	N13 19.8	180 24.8	N21 58.2	71 54.4	S13 11.1	Vega	80 38.9	N38 48.2
19	306 30.8	63 26.4	24 00.4	155 27.9	19.3	195 27.1	58.2	86 56.6	11.2	Zuben'ubi	137 05.5	S16 05.8
20	321 33.3	78 26.0	01.1	170 28.9	18.8	210 29.3	58.2	101 58.8	11.3		SHA	Mer. Pass.
21	336 35.8	93 25.5	.. 01.7	185 29.9	.. 18.3	225 31.6	.. 58.2	117 01.0	.. 11.4		° ′	h m
22	351 38.2	108 25.1	02.3	200 30.9	17.8	240 33.9	58.1	132 03.2	11.5	Venus	119 00.2	14 45
23	6 40.7	123 24.7	02.9	215 31.9	17.3	255 36.1	58.1	147 05.4	11.6	Mars	209 59.7	8 40
	h m									Jupiter	249 05.7	6 04
Mer. Pass. 22 37.3		v −0.4	d 0.7	v 1.0	d 0.5	v 2.2	d 0.0	v 2.2	d 0.1	Saturn	140 37.7	13 17

UT	SUN GHA	SUN Dec	MOON GHA	v	MOON Dec	d	HP
10 **00**	183 13.8	S 6 37.3	118 20.0	5.9	S19 32.2	0.1	59.3
01	198 14.0	38.2	132 44.9	5.9	19 32.1	0.2	59.3
02	213 14.2	39.2	147 09.8	5.8	19 31.9	0.3	59.3
03	228 14.3	.. 40.1	161 34.6	5.9	19 31.6	0.5	59.3
04	243 14.5	41.1	175 59.5	5.9	19 31.1	0.6	59.3
05	258 14.7	42.0	190 24.4	5.8	19 30.5	0.7	59.3
06	273 14.8	S 6 43.0	204 49.2	5.9	S19 29.8	0.9	59.3
07	288 15.0	43.9	219 14.1	5.9	19 28.9	1.0	59.3
T 08	303 15.2	44.9	233 39.0	5.9	19 27.9	1.1	59.3
H 09	318 15.3	.. 45.8	248 03.9	5.9	19 26.8	1.3	59.3
U 10	333 15.5	46.7	262 28.8	5.9	19 25.5	1.4	59.3
R 11	348 15.7	47.7	276 53.7	5.9	19 24.1	1.5	59.3
S 12	3 15.8	S 6 48.6	291 18.6	5.9	S19 22.6	1.6	59.3
D 13	18 16.0	49.6	305 43.5	6.0	19 21.0	1.8	59.3
A 14	33 16.1	50.5	320 08.5	5.9	19 19.2	1.9	59.3
Y 15	48 16.3	.. 51.5	334 33.4	6.0	19 17.3	2.0	59.3
16	63 16.5	52.4	348 58.4	6.0	19 15.3	2.1	59.3
17	78 16.6	53.4	3 23.4	6.0	19 13.2	2.3	59.3
18	93 16.8	S 6 54.3	17 48.4	6.0	S19 10.9	2.4	59.3
19	108 17.0	55.2	32 13.4	6.0	19 08.5	2.5	59.3
20	123 17.1	56.2	46 38.4	6.1	19 06.0	2.7	59.3
21	138 17.3	.. 57.1	61 03.5	6.1	19 03.3	2.8	59.3
22	153 17.5	58.1	75 28.6	6.1	19 00.5	2.9	59.3
23	168 17.6	6 59.0	89 53.7	6.1	18 57.6	3.0	59.3
11 00	183 17.8	S 7 00.0	104 18.8	6.2	S18 54.6	3.2	59.3
01	198 17.9	00.9	118 44.0	6.1	18 51.4	3.2	59.3
02	213 18.1	01.8	133 09.1	6.2	18 48.2	3.4	59.3
03	228 18.3	.. 02.8	147 34.3	6.3	18 44.8	3.6	59.3
04	243 18.4	03.7	161 59.6	6.2	18 41.2	3.6	59.3
05	258 18.6	04.7	176 24.8	6.3	18 37.6	3.8	59.3
06	273 18.7	S 7 05.6	190 50.1	6.3	S18 33.8	3.9	59.3
07	288 18.9	06.6	205 15.4	6.4	18 29.9	4.0	59.3
F 08	303 19.1	07.5	219 40.8	6.4	18 25.9	4.1	59.3
R 09	318 19.2	.. 08.4	234 06.2	6.4	18 21.8	4.3	59.3
I 10	333 19.4	09.4	248 31.6	6.4	18 17.5	4.3	59.3
11	348 19.5	10.3	262 57.0	6.5	18 13.2	4.5	59.3
D 12	3 19.7	S 7 11.3	277 22.5	6.5	S18 08.7	4.6	59.3
A 13	18 19.9	12.2	291 48.0	6.6	18 04.1	4.7	59.3
Y 14	33 20.0	13.1	306 13.6	6.6	17 59.4	4.9	59.3
15	48 20.2	.. 14.1	320 39.2	6.6	17 54.5	4.9	59.3
16	63 20.3	15.0	335 04.8	6.6	17 49.6	5.1	59.3
17	78 20.5	16.0	349 30.4	6.7	17 44.5	5.2	59.3
18	93 20.7	S 7 16.9	3 56.1	6.8	S17 39.3	5.2	59.3
19	108 20.8	17.8	18 21.9	6.8	17 34.1	5.5	59.3
20	123 21.0	18.8	32 47.7	6.8	17 28.6	5.5	59.3
21	138 21.1	.. 19.7	47 13.5	6.8	17 23.1	5.6	59.3
22	153 21.3	20.7	61 39.3	6.9	17 17.5	5.7	59.3
23	168 21.4	21.6	76 05.2	7.0	17 11.8	5.9	59.3
12 00	183 21.6	S 7 22.5	90 31.2	7.0	S17 05.9	5.9	59.3
01	198 21.8	23.5	104 57.2	7.0	17 00.0	6.1	59.2
02	213 21.9	24.4	119 23.2	7.1	16 53.9	6.2	59.2
03	228 22.1	.. 25.4	133 49.3	7.1	16 47.7	6.2	59.2
04	243 22.2	26.3	148 15.4	7.2	16 41.5	6.4	59.2
05	258 22.4	27.2	162 41.6	7.2	16 35.1	6.5	59.2
06	273 22.5	S 7 28.2	177 07.8	7.2	S16 28.6	6.6	59.2
S 07	288 22.7	29.1	191 34.0	7.3	16 22.0	6.7	59.2
A 08	303 22.8	30.0	206 00.3	7.4	16 15.3	6.7	59.2
T 09	318 23.0	.. 31.0	220 26.7	7.4	16 08.6	6.9	59.2
U 10	333 23.2	31.9	234 53.1	7.4	16 01.7	7.0	59.2
R 11	348 23.3	32.9	249 19.5	7.5	15 54.7	7.1	59.2
D 12	3 23.5	S 7 33.8	263 46.0	7.5	S15 47.6	7.2	59.2
A 13	18 23.6	34.7	278 12.5	7.6	15 40.4	7.3	59.2
Y 14	33 23.8	35.7	292 39.1	7.6	15 33.1	7.3	59.2
15	48 23.9	.. 36.6	307 05.7	7.7	15 25.8	7.5	59.2
16	63 24.1	37.5	321 32.4	7.7	15 18.3	7.6	59.2
17	78 24.2	38.5	335 59.1	7.8	15 10.7	7.6	59.2
18	93 24.4	S 7 39.4	350 25.9	7.8	S15 03.1	7.8	59.2
19	108 24.5	40.3	4 52.7	7.9	14 55.3	7.8	59.2
20	123 24.7	41.3	19 19.6	7.9	14 47.5	7.9	59.2
21	138 24.8	.. 42.2	33 46.5	8.0	14 39.6	8.0	59.1
22	153 25.0	43.1	48 13.5	8.0	14 31.6	8.1	59.1
23	168 25.1	44.1	62 40.5	8.1	S14 23.5	8.2	59.1
	SD 16.0	d 0.9	SD 16.2		16.2		16.1

Lat.	Twilight Naut.	Twilight Civil	Sunrise	Moonrise 10	11	12	13
N 72	04 38	05 56	07 05	■	17 15	16 27	16 10
N 70	04 44	05 55	06 57	15 46	15 52	15 52	15 50
68	04 48	05 53	06 49	14 45	15 13	15 26	15 34
66	04 52	05 51	06 43	14 10	14 46	15 07	15 20
64	04 55	05 50	06 38	13 45	14 25	14 51	15 09
62	04 58	05 49	06 34	13 25	14 08	14 38	15 00
60	05 00	05 48	06 30	13 09	13 53	14 27	14 52
N 58	05 01	05 47	06 26	12 55	13 41	14 17	14 45
56	05 03	05 46	06 23	12 43	13 31	14 08	14 39
54	05 04	05 45	06 20	12 33	13 21	14 01	14 33
52	05 05	05 44	06 18	12 24	13 13	13 54	14 28
50	05 06	05 43	06 16	12 16	13 06	13 48	14 23
45	05 07	05 41	06 11	11 58	12 50	13 34	14 13
N 40	05 08	05 39	06 06	11 44	12 36	13 23	14 05
35	05 08	05 37	06 03	11 32	12 25	13 14	13 57
30	05 08	05 35	05 59	11 21	12 15	13 05	13 51
20	05 06	05 31	05 54	11 03	11 59	12 51	13 40
N 10	05 03	05 27	05 48	10 47	11 44	12 38	13 30
0	04 58	05 23	05 43	10 32	11 30	12 27	13 21
S 10	04 52	05 17	05 38	10 17	11 16	12 15	13 12
20	04 45	05 11	05 33	10 01	11 01	12 02	13 02
30	04 34	05 02	05 26	09 43	10 44	11 48	12 51
35	04 27	04 57	05 23	09 33	10 35	11 39	12 45
40	04 18	04 51	05 18	09 21	10 23	11 30	12 37
45	04 07	04 43	05 13	09 06	10 10	11 18	12 29
S 50	03 54	04 34	05 07	08 49	09 54	11 05	12 18
52	03 47	04 30	05 05	08 41	09 46	10 58	12 13
54	03 40	04 25	05 02	08 32	09 38	10 51	12 08
56	03 31	04 19	04 58	08 21	09 28	10 43	12 02
58	03 21	04 13	04 54	08 09	09 18	10 34	11 55
S 60	03 10	04 06	04 50	07 56	09 05	10 24	11 48

Lat.	Sunset	Twilight Civil	Twilight Naut.	Moonset 10	11	12	13
N 72	16 26	17 35	18 53	■	18 22	21 08	23 17
N 70	16 35	17 37	18 47	17 50	19 44	21 42	23 36
68	16 42	17 39	18 43	18 50	20 23	22 06	23 50
66	16 49	17 40	18 39	19 25	20 49	22 24	24 02
64	16 54	17 42	18 36	19 50	21 10	22 39	24 12
62	16 58	17 43	18 34	20 10	21 27	22 52	24 21
60	17 02	17 44	18 32	20 26	21 40	23 02	24 28
N 58	17 06	17 45	18 31	20 39	21 52	23 12	24 34
56	17 09	17 46	18 29	20 51	22 02	23 20	24 40
54	17 12	17 47	18 28	21 01	22 11	23 27	24 45
52	17 15	17 48	18 27	21 10	22 19	23 33	24 49
50	17 17	17 49	18 27	21 18	22 26	23 39	24 53
45	17 22	17 52	18 25	21 35	22 42	23 51	25 02
N 40	17 26	17 54	18 25	21 50	22 54	24 01	00 01
35	17 30	17 56	18 25	22 02	23 05	24 10	00 10
30	17 34	17 58	18 25	22 12	23 14	24 18	00 18
20	17 40	18 02	18 27	22 30	23 30	24 31	00 31
N 10	17 45	18 06	18 31	22 45	23 44	24 42	00 42
0	17 50	18 11	18 35	23 00	23 57	24 53	00 53
S 10	17 55	18 16	18 41	23 14	24 10	00 10	01 03
20	18 01	18 23	18 49	23 30	24 24	00 24	01 15
30	18 07	18 32	19 00	23 47	24 39	00 39	01 27
35	18 11	18 37	19 07	23 57	24 48	00 48	01 35
40	18 16	18 43	19 16	24 09	00 09	00 56	01 43
45	18 21	18 51	19 27	24 23	00 23	01 11	01 52
S 50	18 27	19 00	19 41	24 39	00 39	01 25	02 04
52	18 30	19 05	19 48	24 47	00 47	01 32	02 09
54	18 33	19 10	19 56	00 02	00 56	01 40	02 15
56	18 36	19 16	20 04	00 13	01 06	01 48	02 22
58	18 40	19 22	20 14	00 25	01 17	01 57	02 29
S 60	18 45	19 29	20 26	00 38	01 29	02 08	02 37

Day	SUN Eqn. of Time 00h	SUN Eqn. of Time 12h	SUN Mer. Pass.	MOON Mer. Pass. Upper	MOON Mer. Pass. Lower	Age	Phase
10	12 55	13 03	11 47	16 46	04 17	05	34
11	13 11	13 18	11 47	17 44	05 15	06	45
12	13 26	13 34	11 46	18 40	06 12	07	56

UT	ARIES GHA	VENUS −4.4 GHA	Dec	MARS +1.6 GHA	Dec	JUPITER −2.3 GHA	Dec	SATURN +0.6 GHA	Dec	STARS Name	SHA	Dec
13 00	21 43.2	138 24.2	S24 03.6	230 32.9	N13 16.8	270 38.4	N21 58.1	162 07.5	S13 11.7	Acamar	315 17.8	S40 14.9
01	36 45.6	153 23.8	04.2	245 33.9	16.3	285 40.6	58.1	177 09.7	11.8	Achernar	335 26.1	S57 09.9
02	51 48.1	168 23.3	04.8	260 35.0	15.8	300 42.9	58.0	192 11.9	11.9	Acrux	173 09.6	S63 10.4
03	66 50.5	183 22.9	.. 05.4	275 36.0	.. 15.3	315 45.1	.. 58.0	207 14.1	.. 11.9	Adhara	255 12.3	S28 59.4
04	81 53.0	198 22.5	06.0	290 37.0	14.8	330 47.4	58.0	222 16.3	12.0	Aldebaran	290 48.9	N16 32.1
05	96 55.5	213 22.0	06.7	305 38.0	14.3	345 49.6	58.0	237 18.5	12.1			
06	111 57.9	228 21.6	S24 07.3	320 39.0	N13 13.8	0 51.9	N21 57.9	252 20.7	S13 12.2	Alioth	166 21.1	N55 53.1
07	127 00.4	243 21.2	07.9	335 40.0	13.3	15 54.1	57.9	267 22.8	12.3	Alkaid	152 59.2	N49 14.8
08	142 02.9	258 20.7	08.5	350 41.0	12.8	30 56.4	57.9	282 25.0	12.4	Al Na'ir	27 43.2	S46 53.6
S 09	157 05.3	273 20.3	.. 09.1	5 42.0	.. 12.3	45 58.6	.. 57.9	297 27.2	.. 12.5	Alnilam	275 46.0	S 1 11.6
U 10	172 07.8	288 19.9	09.7	20 43.1	11.8	61 00.9	57.8	312 29.4	12.6	Alphard	217 56.0	S 8 43.1
N 11	187 10.3	303 19.4	10.3	35 44.1	11.3	76 03.1	57.8	327 31.6	12.7			
D 12	202 12.7	318 19.0	S24 11.0	50 45.1	N13 10.8	91 05.4	N21 57.8	342 33.8	S13 12.8	Alphecca	126 11.1	N26 40.4
A 13	217 15.2	333 18.5	11.6	65 46.1	10.3	106 07.7	57.8	357 35.9	12.9	Alpheratz	357 42.9	N29 10.2
Y 14	232 17.7	348 18.1	12.2	80 47.1	09.8	121 09.9	57.8	12 38.1	13.0	Altair	62 08.0	N 8 54.6
15	247 20.1	3 17.7	.. 12.8	95 48.1	.. 09.3	136 12.2	.. 57.7	27 40.3	.. 13.0	Ankaa	353 15.1	S42 13.8
16	262 22.6	18 17.2	13.4	110 49.1	08.8	151 14.4	57.7	42 42.5	13.1	Antares	112 26.2	S26 27.6
17	277 25.0	33 16.8	14.0	125 50.2	08.3	166 16.7	57.7	57 44.7	13.2			
18	292 27.5	48 16.4	S24 14.6	140 51.2	N13 07.8	181 18.9	N21 57.7	72 46.9	S13 13.3	Arcturus	145 55.9	N19 06.8
19	307 30.0	63 15.9	15.2	155 52.2	07.3	196 21.2	57.6	87 49.1	13.4	Atria	107 28.1	S69 03.2
20	322 32.4	78 15.5	15.8	170 53.2	06.8	211 23.5	57.6	102 51.2	13.5	Avior	234 18.0	S59 33.0
21	337 34.9	93 15.0	.. 16.4	185 54.2	.. 06.3	226 25.7	.. 57.6	117 53.4	.. 13.6	Bellatrix	278 31.6	N 6 21.7
22	352 37.4	108 14.6	17.0	200 55.2	05.8	241 28.0	57.6	132 55.6	13.7	Betelgeuse	271 00.9	N 7 24.5
23	7 39.8	123 14.2	17.6	215 56.3	05.3	256 30.2	57.5	147 57.8	13.8			
14 00	22 42.3	138 13.7	S24 18.2	230 57.3	N13 04.8	271 32.5	N21 57.5	163 00.0	S13 13.9	Canopus	263 55.9	S52 42.0
01	37 44.8	153 13.3	18.8	245 58.3	04.3	286 34.8	57.5	178 02.2	14.0	Capella	280 33.8	N46 00.4
02	52 47.2	168 12.9	19.4	260 59.3	03.7	301 37.0	57.5	193 04.4	14.1	Deneb	49 31.2	N45 20.2
03	67 49.7	183 12.4	.. 20.0	276 00.3	.. 03.2	316 39.3	.. 57.5	208 06.5	.. 14.1	Denebola	182 33.7	N14 29.7
04	82 52.1	198 12.0	20.6	291 01.3	02.7	331 41.5	57.4	223 08.7	14.2	Diphda	348 55.3	S17 54.5
05	97 54.6	213 11.5	21.2	306 02.4	02.2	346 43.8	57.4	238 10.9	14.3			
06	112 57.1	228 11.1	S24 21.8	321 03.4	N13 01.7	1 46.1	N21 57.4	253 13.1	S13 14.4	Dubhe	193 52.0	N61 40.4
07	127 59.5	243 10.7	22.4	336 04.4	01.2	16 48.3	57.4	268 15.3	14.5	Elnath	278 12.1	N28 37.0
08	143 02.0	258 10.2	23.0	351 05.4	00.7	31 50.6	57.3	283 17.5	14.6	Eltanin	90 46.2	N51 29.7
M 09	158 04.5	273 09.8	.. 23.6	6 06.4	13 00.2	46 52.8	.. 57.3	298 19.6	.. 14.7	Enif	33 46.7	N 9 56.6
O 10	173 06.9	288 09.4	24.2	21 07.4	12 59.7	61 55.1	57.3	313 21.8	14.8	Fomalhaut	15 23.5	S29 32.8
N 11	188 09.4	303 08.9	24.8	36 08.5	59.2	76 57.4	57.3	328 24.0	14.9			
D 12	203 11.9	318 08.5	S24 25.4	51 09.5	N12 58.7	91 59.6	N21 57.2	343 26.2	S13 15.0	Gacrux	172 01.1	S57 11.3
A 13	218 14.3	333 08.0	25.9	66 10.5	58.2	107 01.9	57.2	358 28.4	15.1	Gienah	175 52.4	S17 37.0
Y 14	233 16.8	348 07.6	26.5	81 11.5	57.7	122 04.2	57.2	13 30.6	15.2	Hadar	148 48.1	S60 26.3
15	248 19.3	3 07.2	.. 27.1	96 12.5	.. 57.2	137 06.4	.. 57.2	28 32.7	.. 15.2	Hamal	328 00.1	N23 31.7
16	263 21.7	18 06.7	27.7	111 13.6	56.7	152 08.7	57.2	43 34.9	15.3	Kaus Aust.	83 43.6	S34 22.6
17	278 24.2	33 06.3	28.3	126 14.6	56.2	167 11.0	57.1	58 37.1	15.4			
18	293 26.6	48 05.9	S24 28.8	141 15.6	N12 55.7	182 13.2	N21 57.1	73 39.3	S13 15.5	Kochab	137 21.2	N74 06.1
19	308 29.1	63 05.4	29.4	156 16.6	55.2	197 15.5	57.1	88 41.5	15.6	Markab	13 37.8	N15 17.0
20	323 31.6	78 05.0	30.0	171 17.6	54.7	212 17.8	57.1	103 43.7	15.7	Menkar	314 14.5	N 4 08.7
21	338 34.0	93 04.5	.. 30.6	186 18.7	.. 54.2	227 20.0	.. 57.0	118 45.9	.. 15.8	Menkent	148 07.7	S36 26.2
22	353 36.5	108 04.1	31.2	201 19.7	53.7	242 22.3	57.0	133 48.0	15.9	Miaplacidus	221 39.9	S69 46.3
23	8 39.0	123 03.7	31.7	216 20.7	53.2	257 24.6	57.0	148 50.2	16.0			
15 00	23 41.4	138 03.2	S24 32.3	231 21.7	N12 52.7	272 26.8	N21 57.0	163 52.4	S13 16.1	Mirfak	308 39.6	N49 54.5
01	38 43.9	153 02.8	32.9	246 22.7	52.1	287 29.1	57.0	178 54.6	16.2	Nunki	75 58.1	S26 16.6
02	53 46.4	168 02.3	33.5	261 23.8	51.6	302 31.4	56.9	193 56.8	16.3	Peacock	53 18.8	S56 41.4
03	68 48.8	183 01.9	.. 34.0	276 24.8	.. 51.1	317 33.6	.. 56.9	208 59.0	.. 16.3	Pollux	243 27.5	N27 59.3
04	83 51.3	198 01.5	34.6	291 25.8	50.6	332 35.9	56.9	224 01.5	16.4	Procyon	244 59.5	N 5 11.3
05	98 53.7	213 01.0	35.2	306 26.8	50.1	347 38.2	56.9	239 03.3	16.5			
06	113 56.2	228 00.6	S24 35.7	321 27.9	N12 49.6	2 40.4	N21 56.8	254 05.5	S13 16.6	Rasalhague	96 06.4	N12 33.3
07	128 58.7	243 00.1	36.3	336 28.9	49.1	17 42.7	56.8	269 07.7	16.7	Regulus	207 43.5	N11 53.9
08	144 01.1	257 59.7	36.9	351 29.9	48.6	32 45.0	56.8	284 09.9	16.8	Rigel	281 11.7	S 8 11.1
T 09	159 03.6	272 59.3	.. 37.5	6 30.9	.. 48.1	47 47.2	.. 56.8	299 12.1	.. 16.9	Rigil Kent.	139 52.0	S60 53.4
U 10	174 06.1	287 58.8	38.0	21 31.9	47.6	62 49.5	56.8	314 14.2	17.0	Sabik	102 12.5	S15 44.3
E 11	189 08.5	302 58.4	38.6	36 33.0	47.1	77 51.8	56.7	329 16.4	17.1			
S 12	204 11.0	317 58.0	S24 39.1	51 34.0	N12 46.6	92 54.1	N21 56.7	344 18.6	S13 17.2	Schedar	349 39.6	N56 36.9
D 13	219 13.5	332 57.5	39.7	66 35.0	46.1	107 56.3	56.7	359 20.8	17.3	Shaula	96 21.8	S37 06.7
A 14	234 15.9	347 57.1	40.3	81 36.0	45.6	122 58.6	56.7	14 23.0	17.4	Sirius	258 33.4	S16 44.1
Y 15	249 18.4	2 56.6	.. 40.8	96 37.1	.. 45.1	138 00.9	.. 56.7	29 25.1	.. 17.4	Spica	158 31.3	S11 13.9
16	264 20.9	17 56.2	41.4	111 38.1	44.6	153 03.1	56.6	44 27.3	17.5	Suhail	222 52.4	S43 29.2
17	279 23.3	32 55.8	42.0	126 39.1	44.1	168 05.4	56.6	59 29.5	17.6			
18	294 25.8	47 55.3	S24 42.5	141 40.1	N12 43.5	183 07.7	N21 56.6	74 31.7	S13 17.7	Vega	80 38.9	N38 48.2
19	309 28.2	62 54.9	43.1	156 41.2	43.0	198 10.0	56.6	89 33.9	17.8	Zuben'ubi	137 05.5	S16 05.8
20	324 30.7	77 54.4	43.6	171 42.2	42.5	213 12.2	56.5	104 36.1	17.9		SHA	Mer.Pass.
21	339 33.2	92 54.0	.. 44.2	186 43.2	.. 42.0	228 14.5	.. 56.5	119 38.2	.. 18.0	Venus	115 21.4	14 48
22	354 35.6	107 53.6	44.7	201 44.2	41.5	243 16.8	56.5	134 40.4	18.1	Mars	208 15.0	8 36
23	9 38.1	122 53.1	45.3	216 45.3	41.0	258 19.1	56.5	149 42.6	18.2	Jupiter	248 50.2	5 53
Mer.Pass. 22 25.5		v −0.4 d 0.6		v 1.0 d 0.5		v 2.3 d 0.0		v 2.2 d 0.1		Saturn	140 17.7	13 06

UT	SUN GHA	SUN Dec	MOON GHA	v	MOON Dec	d	HP
d h	° ′	° ′	° ′	′	° ′	′	′
13 00	183 25.3	S 7 45.0	77 07.6	8.1	S14 15.3	8.3	59.1
01	198 25.4	46.0	91 34.7	8.2	14 07.0	8.4	59.1
02	213 25.6	46.9	106 01.9	8.2	13 58.6	8.4	59.1
03	228 25.8	.. 47.8	120 29.1	8.3	13 50.2	8.5	59.1
04	243 25.9	48.8	134 56.4	8.3	13 41.7	8.6	59.1
05	258 26.1	49.7	149 23.7	8.4	13 33.1	8.7	59.1
06	273 26.2	S 7 50.6	163 51.1	8.4	S13 24.4	8.8	59.1
07	288 26.4	51.6	178 18.5	8.5	13 15.6	8.8	59.1
08	303 26.5	52.5	192 46.0	8.5	13 06.8	8.9	59.1
S 09	318 26.7	.. 53.4	207 13.5	8.6	12 57.9	9.0	59.1
U 10	333 26.8	54.4	221 41.1	8.6	12 48.9	9.1	59.1
N 11	348 27.0	55.3	236 08.7	8.6	12 39.8	9.1	59.1
D 12	3 27.1	S 7 56.2	250 36.3	8.7	S12 30.7	9.2	59.0
A 13	18 27.2	57.1	265 04.0	8.8	12 21.5	9.3	59.0
Y 14	33 27.4	58.1	279 31.8	8.8	12 12.2	9.4	59.0
15	48 27.5	.. 59.0	293 59.6	8.9	12 02.8	9.4	59.0
16	63 27.7	7 59.9	308 27.5	8.9	11 53.4	9.5	59.0
17	78 27.8	8 00.9	322 55.4	9.0	11 43.9	9.6	59.0
18	93 28.0	S 8 01.8	337 23.4	9.0	S11 34.3	9.6	59.0
19	108 28.1	02.7	351 51.4	9.0	11 24.7	9.7	59.0
20	123 28.3	03.7	6 19.4	9.1	11 15.0	9.7	59.0
21	138 28.4	.. 04.6	20 47.5	9.2	11 05.3	9.8	59.0
22	153 28.6	05.5	35 15.7	9.1	10 55.5	9.9	59.0
23	168 28.7	06.5	49 43.8	9.3	10 45.6	9.9	59.0
14 00	183 28.9	S 8 07.4	64 12.1	9.3	S10 35.7	10.0	58.9
01	198 29.0	08.3	78 40.4	9.3	10 25.7	10.1	58.9
02	213 29.2	09.2	93 08.7	9.4	10 15.6	10.1	58.9
03	228 29.3	.. 10.2	107 37.1	9.4	10 05.5	10.1	58.9
04	243 29.5	11.1	122 05.5	9.5	9 55.4	10.3	58.9
05	258 29.6	12.0	136 34.0	9.5	9 45.1	10.2	58.9
06	273 29.7	S 8 13.0	151 02.5	9.5	S 9 34.9	10.4	58.9
07	288 29.9	13.9	165 31.0	9.6	9 24.5	10.3	58.9
08	303 30.0	14.8	179 59.6	9.7	9 14.2	10.5	58.9
M 09	318 30.2	.. 15.7	194 28.3	9.7	9 03.7	10.4	58.8
O 10	333 30.3	16.7	208 57.0	9.7	8 53.3	10.5	58.8
N 11	348 30.5	17.6	223 25.7	9.8	8 42.8	10.6	58.8
D 12	3 30.6	S 8 18.5	237 54.5	9.8	S 8 32.2	10.6	58.8
A 13	18 30.8	19.5	252 23.3	9.8	8 21.6	10.7	58.8
Y 14	33 30.9	20.4	266 52.1	9.9	8 10.9	10.7	58.8
15	48 31.0	.. 21.3	281 21.0	10.0	8 00.2	10.7	58.8
16	63 31.2	22.2	295 50.0	9.9	7 49.5	10.8	58.8
17	78 31.3	23.2	310 18.9	10.0	7 38.7	10.8	58.8
18	93 31.5	S 8 24.1	324 47.9	10.1	S 7 27.9	10.8	58.7
19	108 31.6	25.0	339 17.0	10.1	7 17.1	10.9	58.7
20	123 31.8	25.9	353 46.1	10.1	7 06.2	11.0	58.7
21	138 31.9	.. 26.9	8 15.2	10.2	6 55.2	10.9	58.7
22	153 32.0	27.8	22 44.4	10.2	6 44.3	11.0	58.7
23	168 32.2	28.7	37 13.6	10.2	6 33.3	11.1	58.7
15 00	183 32.3	S 8 29.6	51 42.8	10.3	S 6 22.2	11.0	58.7
01	198 32.5	30.6	66 12.1	10.3	6 11.2	11.1	58.7
02	213 32.6	31.5	80 41.4	10.3	6 00.1	11.1	58.6
03	228 32.7	.. 32.4	95 10.7	10.4	5 49.0	11.2	58.6
04	243 32.9	33.3	109 40.1	10.4	5 37.8	11.1	58.6
05	258 33.0	34.3	124 09.5	10.5	5 26.7	11.2	58.6
06	273 33.2	S 8 35.2	138 39.0	10.5	S 5 15.5	11.3	58.6
07	288 33.3	36.1	153 08.5	10.5	5 04.2	11.2	58.6
08	303 33.4	37.0	167 38.0	10.5	4 53.0	11.3	58.6
T 09	318 33.6	.. 38.0	182 07.5	10.6	4 41.7	11.3	58.5
U 10	333 33.7	38.9	196 37.1	10.6	4 30.4	11.3	58.5
E 11	348 33.8	39.8	211 06.7	10.6	4 19.1	11.3	58.5
S 12	3 34.0	S 8 40.7	225 36.3	10.7	S 4 07.8	11.4	58.5
D 13	18 34.1	41.6	240 06.0	10.7	3 56.4	11.3	58.5
A 14	33 34.3	42.6	254 35.7	10.7	3 45.1	11.4	58.5
Y 15	48 34.4	.. 43.5	269 05.4	10.7	3 33.7	11.4	58.5
16	63 34.5	44.4	283 35.1	10.8	3 22.3	11.4	58.4
17	78 34.7	45.3	298 04.9	10.8	3 10.9	11.4	58.4
18	93 34.8	S 8 46.3	312 34.7	10.9	S 2 59.5	11.5	58.4
19	108 34.9	47.2	327 04.6	10.8	2 48.0	11.4	58.4
20	123 35.1	48.1	341 34.4	10.9	2 36.6	11.4	58.4
21	138 35.2	.. 49.0	356 04.3	10.9	2 25.2	11.5	58.4
22	153 35.4	49.9	10 34.2	10.9	2 13.7	11.5	58.4
23	168 35.5	50.9	25 04.1	11.0	S 2 02.2	11.4	58.3
	SD 16.1	d 0.9	SD 16.1		16.0		15.9

Lat.	Twilight Naut.	Twilight Civil	Sunrise	Moonrise 13	14	15	16
°	h m	h m	h m	h m	h m	h m	h m
N 72	04 51	06 10	07 20	16 10	15 59	15 49	15 41
N 70	04 56	06 06	07 09	15 50	15 47	15 45	15 42
68	04 59	06 03	07 00	15 34	15 38	15 41	15 43
66	05 02	06 01	06 53	15 20	15 30	15 37	15 44
64	05 04	05 59	06 47	15 09	15 23	15 35	15 45
62	05 05	05 57	06 42	15 00	15 17	15 32	15 46
60	05 07	05 55	06 37	14 52	15 12	15 30	15 46
N 58	05 08	05 53	06 33	14 45	15 08	15 28	15 47
56	05 09	05 52	06 29	14 39	15 04	15 26	15 47
54	05 09	05 50	06 26	14 33	15 00	15 25	15 48
52	05 10	05 49	06 23	14 28	14 57	15 23	15 48
50	05 10	05 48	06 20	14 23	14 54	15 22	15 48
45	05 11	05 45	06 14	14 13	14 48	15 19	15 49
N 40	05 11	05 42	06 09	14 05	14 42	15 17	15 50
35	05 10	05 40	06 05	13 57	14 37	15 15	15 51
30	05 09	05 37	06 01	13 51	14 33	15 13	15 51
20	05 07	05 32	05 54	13 40	14 26	15 10	15 52
N 10	05 03	05 27	05 48	13 30	14 20	15 07	15 53
0	04 58	05 22	05 43	13 21	14 14	15 04	15 54
S 10	04 51	05 16	05 37	13 12	14 08	15 02	15 55
20	04 42	05 08	05 30	13 02	14 01	14 59	15 56
30	04 30	04 59	05 23	12 51	13 54	14 56	15 57
35	04 22	04 53	05 19	12 45	13 50	14 54	15 58
40	04 13	04 46	05 14	12 37	13 45	14 52	15 58
45	04 03	04 38	05 08	12 29	13 39	14 50	15 59
S 50	03 47	04 28	05 01	12 18	13 33	14 47	16 00
52	03 39	04 23	04 58	12 13	13 30	14 46	16 01
54	03 31	04 17	04 54	12 08	13 26	14 44	16 01
56	03 22	04 11	04 51	12 02	13 22	14 43	16 02
58	03 11	04 04	04 46	11 55	13 18	14 41	16 03
S 60	02 58	03 56	04 41	11 48	13 13	14 39	16 03

Lat.	Sunset	Twilight Civil	Twilight Naut.	Moonset 13	14	15	16
°	h m	h m	h m	h m	h m	h m	h m
N 72	16 10	17 20	18 38	23 17	25 16	01 16	03 11
N 70	16 21	17 24	18 34	23 36	25 26	01 26	03 13
68	16 30	17 27	18 31	23 50	25 34	01 34	03 15
66	16 37	17 29	18 28	24 02	00 02	01 40	03 16
64	16 44	17 32	18 27	24 12	00 12	01 45	03 17
62	16 49	17 34	18 25	24 21	00 21	01 50	03 18
60	16 54	17 36	18 24	24 28	00 28	01 54	03 19
N 58	16 58	17 37	18 23	24 34	00 34	01 57	03 20
56	17 02	17 39	18 22	24 40	00 40	02 00	03 20
54	17 05	17 41	18 21	24 45	00 45	02 03	03 21
52	17 08	17 42	18 21	24 49	00 49	02 06	03 21
50	17 11	17 43	18 21	24 53	00 53	02 08	03 22
45	17 17	17 46	18 20	25 02	01 02	02 13	03 23
N 40	17 22	17 48	18 20	00 01	01 09	02 17	03 24
35	17 26	17 52	18 21	00 10	01 16	02 21	03 25
30	17 30	17 54	18 22	00 18	01 21	02 24	03 25
20	17 37	17 59	18 25	00 31	01 31	02 29	03 26
N 10	17 43	18 05	18 29	00 42	01 39	02 34	03 27
0	17 49	18 10	18 34	00 53	01 46	02 38	03 28
S 10	17 55	18 17	18 41	01 03	01 54	02 42	03 29
20	18 02	18 24	18 50	01 15	02 02	02 47	03 30
30	18 09	18 34	19 03	01 27	02 11	02 52	03 31
35	18 14	18 40	19 10	01 35	02 16	02 55	03 31
40	18 19	18 47	19 20	01 43	02 22	02 58	03 32
45	18 25	18 55	19 32	01 52	02 29	03 02	03 33
S 50	18 32	19 06	19 47	02 04	02 37	03 06	03 34
52	18 35	19 11	19 54	02 09	02 41	03 08	03 34
54	18 39	19 16	20 03	02 15	02 45	03 11	03 34
56	18 43	19 22	20 12	02 22	02 49	03 13	03 35
58	18 47	19 29	20 23	02 29	02 54	03 16	03 35
S 60	18 52	19 37	20 36	02 37	03 00	03 19	03 36

	SUN Eqn. of Time 00h	12h	Mer. Pass.	MOON Mer. Pass. Upper	Lower	Age	Phase
Day	m s	m s	h m	h m	h m	d	%
13	13 41	13 48	11 46	19 34	07 07	08	67
14	13 55	14 02	11 46	20 26	08 00	09	77
15	14 09	14 16	11 46	21 16	08 51	10	86

UT	ARIES GHA	VENUS −4.4 GHA	Dec	MARS +1.6 GHA	Dec	JUPITER −2.3 GHA	Dec	SATURN +0.6 GHA	Dec	STARS Name	SHA	Dec
16 00	24 40.6	137 52.7	S24 45.8	231 46.3	N12 40.5	273 21.3	N21 56.5	164 44.8	S13 18.3	Acamar	315 17.8	S40 14.9
01	39 43.0	152 52.2	46.4	246 47.3	40.0	288 23.6	56.4	179 47.0	18.4	Achernar	335 26.1	S57 10.0
02	54 45.5	167 51.8	46.9	261 48.3	39.5	303 25.9	56.4	194 49.2	18.4	Acrux	173 09.6	S63 10.4
03	69 48.0	182 51.4 ..	47.5	276 49.4 ..	39.0	318 28.2 ..	56.4	209 51.5 ..	18.5	Adhara	255 12.3	S28 59.4
04	84 50.4	197 50.9	48.0	291 50.4	38.5	333 30.4	56.4	224 53.5	18.6	Aldebaran	290 48.9	N16 32.1
05	99 52.9	212 50.5	48.6	306 51.4	38.0	348 32.7	56.4	239 55.7	18.7			
W 06	114 55.4	227 50.0	S24 49.1	321 52.4	N12 37.5	3 35.0	N21 56.3	254 57.9	S13 18.8	Alioth	166 21.1	N55 53.1
E 07	129 57.8	242 49.6	49.7	336 53.5	37.0	18 37.3	56.3	270 00.1	18.9	Alkaid	152 59.2	N49 14.8
D 08	145 00.3	257 49.2	50.2	351 54.5	36.4	33 39.5	56.3	285 02.2	19.0	Al Na'ir	27 43.2	S46 53.6
N 09	160 02.7	272 48.7 ..	50.8	6 55.5 ..	35.9	48 41.8 ..	56.3	300 04.4 ..	19.1	Alnilam	275 46.0	S 1 11.6
E 10	175 05.2	287 48.3	51.3	21 56.6	35.4	63 44.1	56.3	315 06.6	19.2	Alphard	217 56.0	S 8 43.1
S 11	190 07.7	302 47.9	51.8	36 57.6	34.9	78 46.4	56.2	330 08.8	19.3			
D 12	205 10.1	317 47.4	S24 52.4	51 58.6	N12 34.4	93 48.7	N21 56.2	345 11.0	S13 19.4	Alphecca	126 11.1	N26 40.4
A 13	220 12.6	332 47.0	52.9	66 59.6	33.9	108 50.9	56.2	0 13.2	19.5	Alpheratz	357 42.9	N29 10.2
Y 14	235 15.1	347 46.5	53.4	82 00.7	33.4	123 53.2	56.2	15 15.3	19.5	Altair	62 08.0	N 8 54.6
15	250 17.5	2 46.1 ..	54.0	97 01.7 ..	32.9	138 55.5 ..	56.2	30 17.5 ..	19.6	Ankaa	353 15.1	S42 13.8
16	265 20.0	17 45.7	54.5	112 02.7	32.4	153 57.8	56.1	45 19.7	19.7	Antares	112 26.2	S26 27.6
17	280 22.5	32 45.2	55.1	127 03.8	31.9	169 00.1	56.1	60 21.9	19.8			
18	295 24.9	47 44.8	S24 55.6	142 04.8	N12 31.4	184 02.3	N21 56.1	75 24.1	S13 19.9	Arcturus	145 55.9	N19 06.8
19	310 27.4	62 44.3	56.1	157 05.8	30.9	199 04.6	56.1	90 26.2	20.0	Atria	107 28.2	S69 03.1
20	325 29.8	77 43.9	56.6	172 06.8	30.4	214 06.9	56.0	105 28.4	20.1	Avior	234 18.0	S59 33.0
21	340 32.3	92 43.5 ..	57.2	187 07.9 ..	29.8	229 09.2 ..	56.0	120 30.6 ..	20.2	Bellatrix	278 31.6	N 6 21.7
22	355 34.8	107 43.0	57.7	202 08.9	29.3	244 11.5	56.0	135 32.8	20.3	Betelgeuse	271 00.9	N 7 24.5
23	10 37.2	122 42.6	58.2	217 09.9	28.8	259 13.8	56.0	150 35.0	20.4			
17 00	25 39.7	137 42.1	S24 58.8	232 11.0	N12 28.3	274 16.0	N21 56.0	165 37.2	S13 20.5	Canopus	263 55.9	S52 42.0
01	40 42.2	152 41.7	59.3	247 12.0	27.8	289 18.3	56.0	180 39.3	20.6	Capella	280 33.8	N46 00.4
02	55 44.6	167 41.3	24 59.8	262 13.0	27.3	304 20.6	55.9	195 41.5	20.6	Deneb	49 31.2	N45 20.2
03	70 47.1	182 40.8	25 00.3	277 14.1 ..	26.8	319 22.9 ..	55.9	210 43.7 ..	20.7	Denebola	182 33.7	N14 29.7
04	85 49.6	197 40.4	00.9	292 15.1	26.3	334 25.2	55.9	225 45.9	20.8	Diphda	348 55.4	S17 54.5
05	100 52.0	212 39.9	01.4	307 16.1	25.8	349 27.5	55.9	240 48.1	20.9			
T 06	115 54.5	227 39.5	S25 01.9	322 17.2	N12 25.3	4 29.7	N21 55.9	255 50.2	S13 21.0	Dubhe	193 52.0	N61 40.4
H 07	130 57.0	242 39.1	02.4	337 18.2	24.8	19 32.0	55.8	270 52.4	21.1	Elnath	278 12.1	N28 37.0
U 08	145 59.4	257 38.6	02.9	352 19.2	24.2	34 34.3	55.8	285 54.6	21.2	Eltanin	90 46.3	N51 29.7
R 09	161 01.9	272 38.2 ..	03.5	7 20.3 ..	23.7	49 36.6 ..	55.8	300 56.8 ..	21.3	Enif	33 46.7	N 9 56.6
S 10	176 04.3	287 37.8	04.0	22 21.3	23.2	64 38.9	55.8	315 59.0	21.4	Fomalhaut	15 23.5	S29 32.8
D 11	191 06.8	302 37.3	04.5	37 22.3	22.7	79 41.2	55.8	331 01.1	21.5			
A 12	206 09.3	317 36.9	S25 05.0	52 23.4	N12 22.2	94 43.5	N21 55.7	346 03.3	S13 21.6	Gacrux	172 01.1	S57 11.3
Y 13	221 11.7	332 36.4	05.5	67 24.4	21.7	109 45.7	55.7	1 05.5	21.7	Gienah	175 52.4	S17 37.0
14	236 14.2	347 36.0	06.0	82 25.4	21.2	124 48.0	55.7	16 07.7	21.7	Hadar	148 48.1	S60 26.3
15	251 16.7	2 35.6 ..	06.5	97 26.5 ..	20.7	139 50.3 ..	55.7	31 09.9 ..	21.8	Hamal	328 00.1	N23 31.7
16	266 19.1	17 35.1	07.1	112 27.5	20.2	154 52.6	55.7	46 12.1	21.9	Kaus Aust.	83 43.6	S34 22.6
17	281 21.6	32 34.7	07.6	127 28.5	19.7	169 54.9	55.6	61 14.2	22.0			
18	296 24.1	47 34.2	S25 08.1	142 29.6	N12 19.1	184 57.2	N21 55.6	76 16.4	S13 22.1	Kochab	137 21.2	N74 06.1
19	311 26.5	62 33.8	08.6	157 30.6	18.6	199 59.5	55.6	91 18.6	22.2	Markab	13 37.8	N15 17.0
20	326 29.0	77 33.4	09.1	172 31.6	18.1	215 01.8	55.6	106 20.8	22.3	Menkar	314 14.5	N 4 08.7
21	341 31.4	92 32.9 ..	09.6	187 32.7 ..	17.6	230 04.1 ..	55.6	121 23.0 ..	22.4	Menkent	148 07.7	S36 26.1
22	356 33.9	107 32.5	10.1	202 33.7	17.1	245 06.3	55.5	136 25.1	22.5	Miaplacidus	221 39.9	S69 46.2
23	11 36.4	122 32.1	10.6	217 34.7	16.6	260 08.6	55.5	151 27.3	22.6			
18 00	26 38.8	137 31.6	S25 11.1	232 35.8	N12 16.1	275 10.9	N21 55.5	166 29.5	S13 22.7	Mirfak	308 39.5	N49 54.5
01	41 41.3	152 31.2	11.6	247 36.8	15.6	290 13.2	55.5	181 31.7	22.8	Nunki	75 58.1	S26 16.6
02	56 43.8	167 30.7	12.1	262 37.8	15.1	305 15.5	55.5	196 33.9	22.8	Peacock	53 18.8	S56 41.4
03	71 46.2	182 30.3 ..	12.6	277 38.9 ..	14.6	320 17.8 ..	55.4	211 36.0 ..	22.9	Pollux	243 27.5	N27 59.3
04	86 48.7	197 29.9	13.1	292 39.9	14.0	335 20.1	55.4	226 38.2	23.0	Procyon	244 59.5	N 5 11.3
05	101 51.2	212 29.4	13.6	307 40.9	13.5	350 22.4	55.4	241 40.4	23.1			
F 06	116 53.6	227 29.0	S25 14.1	322 42.0	N12 13.0	5 24.7	N21 55.4	256 42.6	S13 23.2	Rasalhague	96 06.4	N12 33.3
R 07	131 56.1	242 28.6	14.6	337 43.0	12.5	20 27.0	55.4	271 44.8	23.3	Regulus	207 43.5	N11 53.9
I 08	146 58.6	257 28.1	15.1	352 44.0	12.0	35 29.3	55.4	286 46.9	23.4	Rigel	281 11.6	S 8 11.1
D 09	162 01.0	272 27.7 ..	15.6	7 45.1 ..	11.5	50 31.6 ..	55.3	301 49.1 ..	23.5	Rigil Kent.	139 52.0	S60 53.4
A 10	177 03.5	287 27.2	16.1	22 46.1	11.0	65 33.9	55.3	316 51.3	23.6	Sabik	102 12.5	S15 44.3
Y 11	192 05.9	302 26.8	16.6	37 47.2	10.5	80 36.1	55.3	331 53.5	23.7			
12	207 08.4	317 26.4	S25 17.0	52 48.2	N12 10.0	95 38.4	N21 55.3	346 55.7	S13 23.8	Schedar	349 40.9	N56 37.0
13	222 10.9	332 25.9	17.5	67 49.2	09.4	110 40.7	55.3	1 57.8	23.9	Shaula	96 21.8	S37 06.7
14	237 13.3	347 25.5	18.0	82 50.3	08.9	125 43.0	55.2	17 00.0	23.9	Sirius	258 33.4	S16 44.1
15	252 15.8	2 25.1 ..	18.5	97 51.3 ..	08.4	140 45.3 ..	55.2	32 02.2 ..	24.0	Spica	158 31.3	S11 13.9
16	267 18.3	17 24.6	19.0	112 52.4	07.9	155 47.6	55.2	47 04.4	24.1	Suhail	222 52.4	S43 29.2
17	282 20.7	32 24.2	19.5	127 53.4	07.4	170 49.9	55.2	62 06.6	24.2			
18	297 23.2	47 23.7	S25 20.0	142 54.4	N12 06.9	185 52.2	N21 55.2	77 08.7	S13 24.3	Vega	80 38.9	N38 48.2
19	312 25.7	62 23.3	20.4	157 55.5	06.4	200 54.5	55.2	92 10.9	24.4	Zuben'ubi	137 05.5	S16 05.8
20	327 28.1	77 22.9	20.9	172 56.5	05.9	215 56.8	55.1	107 13.1	24.5		SHA	Mer.Pass.
21	342 30.6	92 22.4 ..	21.4	187 57.5 ..	05.4	230 59.1 ..	55.1	122 15.3 ..	24.6	Venus	112 02.4	14 50
22	357 33.0	107 22.0	21.9	202 58.6	04.8	246 01.4	55.1	137 17.5	24.7	Mars	206 31.3	8 31
23	12 35.5	122 21.6	22.4	217 59.6	04.3	261 03.7	55.1	152 19.6	24.8	Jupiter	248 36.3	5 42
Mer.Pass. 22 13.7	v −0.4 d 0.5	v 1.0 d 0.5		v 2.3 d 0.0		v 2.2 d 0.1				Saturn	139 57.5	12 56

UT	SUN GHA	Dec	MOON GHA	v	Dec	d	HP
d h	o ′	o ′	o ′	′	o ′	′	′
16 00	183 35.6	S 8 51.8	39 34.1	10.9	S 1 50.8	11.5	58.3
01	198 35.8	52.7	54 04.0	11.0	1 39.3	11.5	58.3
02	213 35.9	53.6	68 34.0	11.0	1 27.8	11.4	58.3
03	228 36.0	.. 54.5	83 04.0	11.1	1 16.4	11.5	58.3
04	243 36.2	55.5	97 34.1	11.0	1 04.9	11.5	58.3
05	258 36.3	56.4	112 04.1	11.1	0 53.4	11.5	58.2
06	273 36.4	S 8 57.3	126 34.2	11.1	S 0 41.9	11.4	58.2
W 07	288 36.6	58.2	141 04.3	11.1	0 30.5	11.5	58.2
E 08	303 36.7	8 59.1	155 34.4	11.1	0 19.0	11.5	58.2
D 09	318 36.8	9 00.0	170 04.5	11.2	S 0 07.5	11.4	58.2
N 10	333 37.0	01.0	184 34.7	11.2	N 0 03.9	11.5	58.1
E 11	348 37.1	01.9	199 04.9	11.1	0 15.4	11.4	58.1
S 12	3 37.2	S 9 02.8	213 35.0	11.2	N 0 26.8	11.5	58.1
D 13	18 37.4	03.7	228 05.2	11.3	0 38.3	11.4	58.1
A 14	33 37.5	04.6	242 35.5	11.2	0 49.7	11.4	58.1
Y 15	48 37.6	.. 05.5	257 05.7	11.2	1 01.1	11.4	58.1
16	63 37.8	06.5	271 35.9	11.3	1 12.5	11.4	58.0
17	78 37.9	07.4	286 06.2	11.3	1 23.9	11.4	58.0
18	93 38.0	S 9 08.3	300 36.5	11.2	N 1 35.3	11.4	58.0
19	108 38.1	09.2	315 06.7	11.3	1 46.7	11.3	58.0
20	123 38.3	10.1	329 37.0	11.3	1 58.0	11.3	58.0
21	138 38.4	.. 11.0	344 07.3	11.4	2 09.3	11.4	57.9
22	153 38.5	12.0	358 37.7	11.3	2 20.7	11.3	57.9
23	168 38.7	12.9	13 08.0	11.3	2 32.0	11.3	57.9
17 00	183 38.8	S 9 13.8	27 38.3	11.4	S 2 43.2	11.3	57.9
01	198 38.9	14.7	42 08.7	11.3	2 54.5	11.2	57.9
02	213 39.0	15.6	56 39.0	11.4	3 05.7	11.2	57.9
03	228 39.2	.. 16.5	71 09.4	11.4	3 16.9	11.2	57.8
04	243 39.3	17.4	85 39.8	11.3	3 28.1	11.2	57.8
05	258 39.4	18.4	100 10.1	11.4	3 39.3	11.1	57.8
06	273 39.6	S 9 19.3	114 40.5	11.4	N 3 50.4	11.1	57.8
T 07	288 39.7	20.2	129 10.9	11.4	4 01.5	11.1	57.8
H 08	303 39.8	21.1	143 41.3	11.4	4 12.6	11.0	57.7
U 09	318 39.9	.. 22.0	158 11.7	11.4	4 23.6	11.0	57.7
R 10	333 40.1	22.9	172 42.1	11.5	4 34.6	11.0	57.7
S 11	348 40.2	23.8	187 12.6	11.4	4 45.6	11.0	57.7
D 12	3 40.3	S 9 24.7	201 43.0	11.4	N 4 56.6	10.9	57.6
A 13	18 40.4	25.6	216 13.4	11.4	5 07.5	10.9	57.6
Y 14	33 40.6	26.6	230 43.8	11.5	5 18.4	10.8	57.6
15	48 40.7	.. 27.5	245 14.3	11.4	5 29.2	10.8	57.6
16	63 40.8	28.4	259 44.7	11.4	5 40.0	10.8	57.6
17	78 40.9	29.3	274 15.1	11.5	5 50.8	10.7	57.5
18	93 41.1	S 9 30.2	288 45.6	11.4	N 6 01.5	10.7	57.5
19	108 41.2	31.1	303 16.0	11.5	6 12.2	10.7	57.5
20	123 41.3	32.0	317 46.5	11.4	6 22.9	10.6	57.5
21	138 41.4	.. 32.9	332 16.9	11.4	6 33.5	10.6	57.5
22	153 41.6	33.8	346 47.3	11.5	6 44.1	10.5	57.4
23	168 41.7	34.7	1 17.8	11.4	6 54.6	10.5	57.4
18 00	183 41.8	S 9 35.7	15 48.2	11.5	N 7 05.1	10.5	57.4
01	198 41.9	36.6	30 18.7	11.4	7 15.6	10.4	57.4
02	213 42.1	37.5	44 49.1	11.4	7 26.0	10.3	57.3
03	228 42.2	.. 38.4	59 19.5	11.5	7 36.3	10.4	57.3
04	243 42.3	39.3	73 50.0	11.4	7 46.7	10.2	57.3
05	258 42.4	40.2	88 20.4	11.4	7 56.9	10.2	57.3
06	273 42.5	S 9 41.1	102 50.8	11.5	N 8 07.1	10.2	57.2
07	288 42.7	42.0	117 21.3	11.4	8 17.3	10.1	57.2
F 08	303 42.8	42.9	131 51.7	11.4	8 27.4	10.1	57.2
R 09	318 42.9	.. 43.8	146 22.1	11.4	8 37.5	10.0	57.2
I 10	333 43.0	44.7	160 52.5	11.4	8 47.5	9.9	57.2
D 11	348 43.1	45.6	175 22.9	11.5	8 57.4	9.9	57.1
A 12	3 43.3	S 9 46.5	189 53.4	11.4	N 9 07.3	9.9	57.1
Y 13	18 43.4	47.4	204 23.8	11.4	9 17.2	9.8	57.1
14	33 43.5	48.4	218 54.2	11.4	9 27.0	9.7	57.1
15	48 43.6	.. 49.3	233 24.6	11.4	9 36.7	9.7	57.1
16	63 43.7	50.2	247 55.0	11.3	9 46.4	9.6	57.0
17	78 43.9	51.1	262 25.3	11.4	9 56.0	9.6	57.0
18	93 44.0	S 9 52.0	276 55.7	11.4	N10 05.6	9.5	57.0
19	108 44.1	52.9	291 26.1	11.4	10 15.1	9.4	57.0
20	123 44.2	53.8	305 56.5	11.3	10 24.5	9.4	56.9
21	138 44.3	.. 54.7	320 26.8	11.4	10 33.9	9.3	56.9
22	153 44.5	55.6	334 57.2	11.3	10 43.2	9.3	56.9
23	168 44.6	56.5	349 27.5	11.4	N10 52.5	9.2	56.9
	SD 16.1	d 0.9	SD 15.8		15.7		15.6

Lat.	Twilight Naut.	Civil	Sunrise	Moonrise 16	17	18	19
o	h m	h m	h m	h m	h m	h m	h m
N 72	05 04	06 23	07 35	15 41	15 32	15 22	15 11
N 70	05 07	06 18	07 22	15 42	15 39	15 37	15 35
68	05 09	06 14	07 12	15 43	15 46	15 49	15 54
66	05 11	06 10	07 03	15 44	15 51	15 59	16 09
64	05 12	06 07	06 56	15 45	15 55	16 07	16 21
62	05 13	06 04	06 50	15 46	15 59	16 14	16 32
60	05 14	06 02	06 44	15 46	16 03	16 20	16 41
N 58	05 14	06 00	06 40	15 47	16 06	16 26	16 49
56	05 15	05 58	06 36	15 47	16 08	16 31	16 56
54	05 15	05 56	06 32	15 48	16 11	16 35	17 02
52	05 15	05 54	06 28	15 48	16 13	16 39	17 07
50	05 15	05 52	06 25	15 48	16 15	16 43	17 13
45	05 15	05 49	06 18	15 49	16 19	16 50	17 24
N 40	05 14	05 45	06 13	15 50	16 23	16 57	17 33
35	05 13	05 42	06 08	15 51	16 26	17 03	17 41
30	05 11	05 39	06 03	15 51	16 29	17 08	17 48
20	05 07	05 33	05 55	15 52	16 34	17 17	18 00
N 10	05 03	05 27	05 49	15 53	16 39	17 25	18 11
0	04 57	05 21	05 42	15 54	16 43	17 32	18 21
S 10	04 49	05 14	05 35	15 55	16 47	17 39	18 31
20	04 39	05 06	05 28	15 56	16 52	17 47	18 42
30	04 26	04 55	05 20	15 57	16 57	17 56	18 55
35	04 18	04 49	05 15	15 58	17 00	18 02	19 02
40	04 08	04 41	05 09	15 58	17 04	18 08	19 10
45	03 55	04 31	05 03	15 59	17 08	18 15	19 20
S 50	03 39	04 21	04 55	16 00	17 12	18 23	19 32
52	03 32	04 16	04 51	16 01	17 15	18 27	19 37
54	03 23	04 10	04 47	16 01	17 17	18 31	19 43
56	03 12	04 03	04 43	16 02	17 20	18 36	19 50
58	03 01	03 55	04 38	16 03	17 23	18 42	19 58
S 60	02 46	03 47	04 32	16 03	17 26	18 48	20 06

Lat.	Sunset	Twilight Civil	Naut.	Moonset 16	17	18	19
o	h m	h m	h m	h m	h m	h m	h m
N 72	15 54	17 06	18 24	03 11	05 03	06 55	08 49
N 70	16 07	17 11	18 21	03 13	04 58	06 42	08 26
68	16 17	17 15	18 19	03 15	04 54	06 32	08 09
66	16 26	17 19	18 18	03 16	04 50	06 23	07 55
64	16 33	17 22	18 17	03 18	04 47	06 16	07 43
62	16 40	17 25	18 16	03 18	04 45	06 10	07 34
60	16 45	17 27	18 15	03 19	04 43	06 05	07 25
N 58	16 50	17 30	18 15	03 20	04 41	06 00	07 18
56	16 54	17 32	18 15	03 20	04 39	05 56	07 12
54	16 58	17 34	18 15	03 21	04 37	05 53	07 06
52	17 01	17 36	18 15	03 21	04 36	05 49	07 01
50	17 05	17 37	18 15	03 22	04 35	05 46	06 56
45	17 12	17 41	18 15	03 23	04 32	05 40	06 46
N 40	17 17	17 45	18 16	03 24	04 30	05 34	06 38
35	17 23	17 48	18 17	03 25	04 28	05 30	06 31
30	17 27	17 51	18 19	03 25	04 26	05 26	06 24
20	17 35	17 57	18 23	03 26	04 23	05 18	06 14
N 10	17 42	18 03	18 28	03 27	04 20	05 12	06 04
0	17 49	18 10	18 34	03 28	04 17	05 06	05 55
S 10	17 55	18 17	18 42	03 29	04 15	05 00	05 47
20	18 03	18 25	18 52	03 30	04 12	04 54	05 37
30	18 11	18 36	19 05	03 31	04 09	04 47	05 27
35	18 16	18 42	19 13	03 31	04 07	04 43	05 21
40	18 22	18 50	19 24	03 32	04 05	04 39	05 13
45	18 29	18 59	19 36	03 33	04 03	04 33	05 05
S 50	18 37	19 11	19 53	03 34	04 00	04 27	04 56
52	18 40	19 16	20 01	03 34	03 59	04 24	04 51
54	18 45	19 22	20 10	03 34	03 57	04 21	04 46
56	18 49	19 29	20 20	03 35	03 56	04 17	04 41
58	18 54	19 37	20 33	03 35	03 54	04 13	04 35
S 60	19 00	19 46	20 47	03 36	03 52	04 09	04 28

	SUN			MOON			
Day	Eqn. of Time 00h	12h	Mer. Pass.	Mer. Pass. Upper	Lower	Age	Phase
d	m s	m s	h m	h m	h m	d	%
16	14 22	14 29	11 46	22 06	09 41	11	93
17	14 35	14 41	11 45	22 55	10 30	12	97
18	14 47	14 53	11 45	23 44	11 19	13	100

2013 OCTOBER 19, 20, 21 (SAT., SUN., MON.)

UT	ARIES GHA	VENUS −4.4 GHA	Dec	MARS +1.5 GHA	Dec	JUPITER −2.3 GHA	Dec	SATURN +0.6 GHA	Dec	STARS Name	SHA	Dec
19 00	27 38.0	137 21.1	S25 22.8	233 00.7	N12 03.8	276 06.0	N21 55.1	167 21.8	S13 24.9	Acamar	315 17.8	S40 14.9
01	42 40.4	152 20.7	23.3	248 01.7	03.3	291 08.3	55.0	182 24.0	25.0	Achernar	335 26.1	S57 10.0
02	57 42.9	167 20.3	23.8	263 02.7	02.8	306 10.6	55.0	197 26.2	25.0	Acrux	173 09.6	S63 10.4
03	72 45.4	182 19.8 ..	24.3	278 03.8 ..	02.3	321 12.9 ..	55.0	212 28.3 ..	25.1	Adhara	255 12.2	S28 59.4
04	87 47.8	197 19.4	24.7	293 04.8	01.8	336 15.2	55.0	227 30.5	25.2	Aldebaran	290 48.9	N16 32.1
05	102 50.3	212 18.9	25.2	308 05.9	01.3	351 17.5	55.0	242 32.7	25.3			
06	117 52.8	227 18.5	S25 25.7	323 06.9	N12 00.7	6 19.8	N21 55.0	257 34.9	S13 25.4	Alioth	166 21.1	N55 53.1
07	132 55.2	242 18.1	26.2	338 07.9	12 00.2	21 22.1	54.9	272 37.1	25.5	Alkaid	152 59.3	N49 14.7
S 08	147 57.7	257 17.6	26.6	353 09.0	11 59.7	36 24.4	54.9	287 39.2	25.6	Al Na'ir	27 43.2	S46 53.6
A 09	163 00.2	272 17.2 ..	27.1	8 10.0 ..	59.2	51 26.7 ..	54.9	302 41.4 ..	25.7	Alnilam	275 46.0	S 1 11.6
T 10	178 02.6	287 16.8	27.6	23 11.1	58.7	66 29.0	54.9	317 43.6	25.8	Alphard	217 56.0	S 8 43.1
U 11	193 05.1	302 16.3	28.0	38 12.1	58.2	81 31.3	54.9	332 45.8	25.9			
R 12	208 07.5	317 15.9	S25 28.5	53 13.2	N11 57.7	96 33.6	N21 54.8	347 48.0	S13 26.0	Alphecca	126 11.2	N26 40.4
D 13	223 10.0	332 15.5	29.0	68 14.2	57.2	111 35.9	54.8	2 50.1	26.1	Alpheratz	357 42.9	N29 10.2
A 14	238 12.5	347 15.0	29.4	83 15.2	56.6	126 38.2	54.8	17 52.3	26.1	Altair	62 08.0	N 8 54.6
Y 15	253 14.9	2 14.6 ..	29.9	98 16.3 ..	56.1	141 40.5 ..	54.8	32 54.5 ..	26.2	Ankaa	353 15.1	S42 13.8
16	268 17.4	17 14.2	30.3	113 17.3	55.6	156 42.8	54.8	47 56.7	26.3	Antares	112 26.2	S26 27.6
17	283 19.9	32 13.7	30.8	128 18.4	55.1	171 45.1	54.8	62 58.9	26.4			
18	298 22.3	47 13.3	S25 31.3	143 19.4	N11 54.6	186 47.4	N21 54.7	78 01.0	S13 26.5	Arcturus	145 55.9	N19 06.8
19	313 24.8	62 12.9	31.7	158 20.5	54.1	201 49.7	54.7	93 03.2	26.6	Atria	107 28.2	S69 03.1
20	328 27.3	77 12.4	32.2	173 21.5	53.6	216 52.1	54.7	108 05.4	26.7	Avior	234 17.9	S59 33.0
21	343 29.7	92 12.0 ..	32.6	188 22.5 ..	53.0	231 54.4 ..	54.7	123 07.6 ..	26.8	Bellatrix	278 31.6	N 6 21.7
22	358 32.2	107 11.5	33.1	203 23.6	52.5	246 56.7	54.7	138 09.7	26.9	Betelgeuse	271 00.9	N 7 24.5
23	13 34.7	122 11.1	33.5	218 24.6	52.0	261 59.0	54.7	153 11.9	27.0			
20 00	28 37.1	137 10.7	S25 34.0	233 25.7	N11 51.5	277 01.3	N21 54.6	168 14.1	S13 27.1	Canopus	263 55.8	S52 42.0
01	43 39.6	152 10.2	34.4	248 26.7	51.0	292 03.6	54.6	183 16.3	27.2	Capella	280 33.8	N46 00.4
02	58 42.0	167 09.8	34.9	263 27.8	50.5	307 05.9	54.6	198 18.5	27.2	Deneb	49 31.2	N45 20.2
03	73 44.5	182 09.4 ..	35.3	278 28.8 ..	50.0	322 08.2 ..	54.6	213 20.6 ..	27.3	Denebola	182 33.7	N14 29.7
04	88 47.0	197 08.9	35.8	293 29.9	49.5	337 10.5	54.6	228 22.8	27.4	Diphda	348 55.4	S17 54.5
05	103 49.4	212 08.5	36.2	308 30.9	48.9	352 12.8	54.6	243 25.0	27.5			
06	118 51.9	227 08.1	S25 36.7	323 31.9	N11 48.4	7 15.1	N21 54.5	258 27.2	S13 27.6	Dubhe	193 52.0	N61 40.4
07	133 54.4	242 07.6	37.1	338 33.0	47.9	22 17.4	54.5	273 29.4	27.7	Elnath	278 12.1	N28 37.0
S 08	148 56.8	257 07.2	37.6	353 34.0	47.4	37 19.7	54.5	288 31.5	27.8	Eltanin	90 46.3	N51 29.7
U 09	163 59.3	272 06.8 ..	38.0	8 35.1 ..	46.9	52 22.1 ..	54.5	303 33.7 ..	27.9	Enif	33 46.7	N 9 56.6
N 10	179 01.8	287 06.3	38.5	23 36.1	46.4	67 24.4	54.5	318 35.9	28.0	Fomalhaut	15 23.5	S29 32.8
D 11	194 04.2	302 05.9	38.9	38 37.2	45.9	82 26.7	54.5	333 38.1	28.1			
A 12	209 06.7	317 05.5	S25 39.3	53 38.2	N11 45.3	97 29.0	N21 54.4	348 40.2	S13 28.2	Gacrux	172 01.1	S57 11.3
Y 13	224 09.1	332 05.0	39.8	68 39.3	44.8	112 31.3	54.4	3 42.4	28.3	Gienah	175 52.4	S17 37.0
14	239 11.6	347 04.6	40.2	83 40.3	44.3	127 33.6	54.4	18 44.6	28.3	Hadar	148 48.1	S60 26.3
15	254 14.1	2 04.2 ..	40.6	98 41.4 ..	43.8	142 35.9 ..	54.4	33 46.8 ..	28.4	Hamal	328 00.1	N23 31.7
16	269 16.5	17 03.8	41.1	113 42.4	43.3	157 38.2	54.4	48 49.0	28.5	Kaus Aust.	83 43.7	S34 22.6
17	284 19.0	32 03.3	41.5	128 43.5	42.8	172 40.5	54.4	63 51.1	28.6			
18	299 21.5	47 02.9	S25 41.9	143 44.5	N11 42.3	187 42.9	N21 54.3	78 53.3	S13 28.7	Kochab	137 21.3	N74 06.1
19	314 23.9	62 02.5	42.4	158 45.6	41.7	202 45.2	54.3	93 55.5	28.8	Markab	13 37.8	N15 17.0
20	329 26.4	77 02.0	42.8	173 46.6	41.2	217 47.5	54.3	108 57.7	28.9	Menkar	314 14.5	N 4 08.7
21	344 28.9	92 01.6 ..	43.2	188 47.7 ..	40.7	232 49.8 ..	54.3	123 59.8 ..	29.0	Menkent	148 07.7	S36 26.1
22	359 31.3	107 01.2	43.7	203 48.7	40.2	247 52.1	54.3	139 02.0	29.1	Miaplacidus	221 39.8	S69 46.2
23	14 33.8	122 00.7	44.1	218 49.7	39.7	262 54.4	54.3	154 04.2	29.2			
21 00	29 36.3	137 00.3	S25 44.5	233 50.8	N11 39.2	277 56.7	N21 54.3	169 06.4	S13 29.3	Mirfak	308 39.5	N49 54.5
01	44 38.7	151 59.9	45.0	248 51.8	38.7	292 59.1	54.2	184 08.6	29.3	Nunki	75 58.1	S26 16.6
02	59 41.2	166 59.4	45.4	263 52.9	38.1	308 01.4	54.2	199 10.7	29.4	Peacock	53 18.9	S56 41.5
03	74 43.6	181 59.0 ..	45.8	278 53.9 ..	37.6	323 03.7 ..	54.2	214 12.9 ..	29.5	Pollux	243 27.4	N27 59.3
04	89 46.1	196 58.6	46.2	293 55.0	37.1	338 06.0	54.2	229 15.1	29.6	Procyon	244 59.5	N 5 11.3
05	104 48.6	211 58.1	46.6	308 56.0	36.6	353 08.3	54.2	244 17.3	29.7			
06	119 51.0	226 57.7	S25 47.1	323 57.1	N11 36.1	8 10.6	N21 54.1	259 19.4	S13 29.8	Rasalhague	96 06.4	N12 33.3
07	134 53.5	241 57.3	47.5	338 58.1	35.6	23 13.0	54.1	274 21.6	29.9	Regulus	207 43.5	N11 53.9
08	149 56.0	256 56.9	47.9	353 59.2	35.0	38 15.3	54.1	289 23.8	30.0	Rigel	281 11.6	S 8 11.1
M 09	164 58.4	271 56.4 ..	48.3	9 00.2 ..	34.5	53 17.6 ..	54.1	304 26.0 ..	30.1	Rigil Kent.	139 52.0	S60 53.4
O 10	180 00.9	286 56.0	48.7	24 01.3	34.0	68 19.9	54.1	319 28.1	30.2	Sabik	102 12.5	S15 44.3
N 11	195 03.4	301 55.6	49.2	39 02.3	33.5	83 22.2	54.1	334 30.3	30.3			
D 12	210 05.8	316 55.1	S25 49.6	54 03.4	N11 33.0	98 24.5	N21 54.0	349 32.5	S13 30.4	Schedar	349 39.6	N56 37.0
A 13	225 08.3	331 54.7	50.0	69 04.4	32.5	113 26.9	54.0	4 34.7	30.5	Shaula	96 21.8	S37 06.7
Y 14	240 10.8	346 54.3	50.4	84 05.5	31.9	128 29.2	54.0	19 36.9	30.5	Sirius	258 33.4	S16 44.1
15	255 13.2	1 53.9 ..	50.8	99 06.6 ..	31.4	143 31.5 ..	54.0	34 39.0 ..	30.6	Spica	158 31.3	S11 13.9
16	270 15.7	16 53.4	51.2	114 07.6	30.9	158 33.8	54.0	49 41.2	30.7	Suhail	222 52.4	S43 29.2
17	285 18.1	31 53.0	51.6	129 08.7	30.4	173 36.1	54.0	64 43.4	30.8			
18	300 20.6	46 52.6	S25 52.0	144 09.7	N11 29.9	188 38.5	N21 54.0	79 45.6	S13 30.9	Vega	80 38.9	N38 48.2
19	315 23.1	61 52.1	52.4	159 10.8	29.4	203 40.8	54.0	94 47.7	31.0	Zuben'ubi	137 05.5	S16 05.8
20	330 25.5	76 51.7	52.8	174 11.8	28.9	218 43.1	53.9	109 49.9	31.1		SHA	Mer. Pass.
21	345 28.0	91 51.3 ..	53.2	189 12.9 ..	28.3	233 45.4 ..	53.9	124 52.1 ..	31.2		° ′	h m
22	0 30.5	106 50.9	53.7	204 13.9	27.8	248 47.8	53.9	139 54.3	31.3	Venus	108 33.6	14 52
23	15 32.9	121 50.4	54.1	219 15.0	27.3	263 50.1	53.9	154 56.4	31.4	Mars	204 48.6	8 26
	h m									Jupiter	248 24.2	5 31
Mer. Pass. 22 01.9	v −0.4	d 0.4	v 1.0	d 0.5	v 2.3	d 0.0	v 2.2	d 0.1	Saturn	139 37.0	12 45

Upper table — SUN, MOON, Twilight, Sunrise, Moonrise

UT	SUN GHA	SUN Dec	MOON GHA	v	MOON Dec	d	HP	Lat.	Twilight Naut.	Twilight Civil	Sunrise	Moonrise 19	Moonrise 20	Moonrise 21	Moonrise 22
d h	° ′	° ′	° ′	′	° ′	′	′	°	h m	h m	h m	h m	h m	h m	h m
19 00	183 44.7	S 9 57.4	3 57.9	11.3	N11 01.7	9.1	56.8	N 72	05 17	06 36	07 50	15 11	14 55	14 07	⟥
01	198 44.8	58.3	18 28.2	11.4	11 10.8	9.1	56.8	N 70	05 19	06 30	07 35	15 35	15 35	15 37	15 48
02	213 44.9	9 59.2	32 58.6	11.3	11 19.9	9.0	56.8	68	05 19	06 24	07 23	15 54	16 02	16 16	16 43
03	228 45.0	10 00.1	47 28.9	11.3	11 28.9	8.9	56.8	66	05 20	06 20	07 13	16 09	16 23	16 44	17 16
04	243 45.1	01.0	61 59.2	11.3	11 37.8	8.9	56.8	64	05 21	06 16	07 05	16 21	16 40	17 05	17 40
05	258 45.3	01.9	76 29.5	11.3	11 46.7	8.8	56.7	62	05 21	06 12	06 58	16 32	16 54	17 22	17 59
06	273 45.4	S10 02.8	90 59.8	11.3	N11 55.5	8.7	56.7	60	05 21	06 09	06 52	16 41	17 05	17 36	18 15
07	288 45.5	03.7	105 30.1	11.3	12 04.2	8.7	56.7	N 58	05 21	06 06	06 47	16 49	17 16	17 48	18 28
S 08	303 45.6	04.6	120 00.4	11.3	12 12.9	8.6	56.7	56	05 20	06 04	06 42	16 56	17 25	17 59	18 40
A 09	318 45.7 ..	05.5	134 30.7	11.3	12 21.5	8.5	56.6	54	05 20	06 01	06 37	17 02	17 32	18 08	18 50
T 10	333 45.8	06.4	149 01.0	11.2	12 30.0	8.4	56.6	52	05 20	05 59	06 34	17 07	17 40	18 17	18 59
U 11	348 45.9	07.3	163 31.2	11.3	12 38.4	8.4	56.6	50	05 19	05 57	06 30	17 13	17 46	18 24	19 07
R 12	3 46.1	S10 08.2	178 01.5	11.2	N12 46.8	8.3	56.6	45	05 18	05 52	06 22	17 24	18 00	18 40	19 24
D 13	18 46.2	09.1	192 31.7	11.3	12 55.1	8.2	56.5	N 40	05 17	05 48	06 16	17 33	18 11	18 53	19 38
A 14	33 46.3	10.0	207 02.0	11.2	13 03.3	8.2	56.5	35	05 15	05 45	06 10	17 41	18 21	19 04	19 50
Y 15	48 46.4 ..	10.9	221 32.2	11.3	13 11.5	8.1	56.5	30	05 13	05 41	06 05	17 48	18 30	19 14	20 01
16	63 46.5	11.8	236 02.5	11.2	13 19.6	8.0	56.5	20	05 08	05 34	05 57	18 00	18 45	19 31	20 19
17	78 46.6	12.7	250 32.7	11.2	13 27.6	7.9	56.4	N 10	05 03	05 27	05 49	18 11	18 58	19 46	20 35
18	93 46.7	S10 13.6	265 02.9	11.2	N13 35.5	7.9	56.4	0	04 56	05 20	05 41	18 21	19 10	20 00	20 49
19	108 46.8	14.5	279 33.1	11.2	13 43.4	7.8	56.4	S 10	04 48	05 13	05 34	18 31	19 23	20 14	21 04
20	123 47.0	15.4	294 03.3	11.2	13 51.2	7.7	56.4	20	04 37	05 03	05 26	18 42	19 36	20 29	21 20
21	138 47.1 ..	16.3	308 33.5	11.2	13 58.9	7.6	56.3	30	04 23	04 52	05 17	18 55	19 51	20 46	21 38
22	153 47.2	17.2	323 03.7	11.2	14 06.5	7.5	56.3	35	04 14	04 45	05 11	19 02	20 00	20 56	21 48
23	168 47.3	18.1	337 33.9	11.1	14 14.0	7.5	56.3	40	04 03	04 37	05 05	19 10	20 10	21 07	22 01
20 00	183 47.4	S10 19.0	352 04.0	11.2	N14 21.5	7.4	56.3	45	03 50	04 27	04 58	19 20	20 22	21 21	22 15
01	198 47.5	19.9	6 34.2	11.2	14 28.9	7.3	56.2	S 50	03 32	04 15	04 49	19 32	20 37	21 38	22 32
02	213 47.6	20.8	21 04.4	11.2	14 36.2	7.2	56.2	52	03 24	04 09	04 45	19 37	20 44	21 45	22 41
03	228 47.7 ..	21.7	35 34.5	11.2	14 43.4	7.2	56.2	54	03 14	04 02	04 40	19 43	20 51	21 54	22 50
04	243 47.8	22.6	50 04.7	11.1	14 50.6	7.1	56.2	56	03 03	03 55	04 35	19 50	21 00	22 04	23 00
05	258 47.9	23.5	64 34.8	11.1	14 57.7	6.9	56.2	58	02 50	03 47	04 30	19 58	21 09	22 15	23 12
06	273 48.1	S10 24.4	79 04.9	11.2	N15 04.6	6.9	56.1	S 60	02 34	03 37	04 24	20 06	21 20	22 28	23 26

UT	SUN GHA	SUN Dec	MOON GHA	v	MOON Dec	d	HP	Lat.	Sunset	Twilight Civil	Twilight Naut.	Moonset 19	Moonset 20	Moonset 21	Moonset 22
07	288 48.2	25.3	93 35.1	11.1	15 11.5	6.8	56.1	°	h m	h m	h m	h m	h m	h m	h m
08	303 48.3	26.1	108 05.2	11.1	15 18.3	6.8	56.1	N 72	15 38	16 52	18 10	08 49	10 48	13 19	⟥
S 09	318 48.4 ..	27.0	122 35.3	11.1	15 25.1	6.6	56.0	N 70	15 53	16 58	18 10	08 26	10 09	11 50	13 22
U 10	333 48.5	27.9	137 05.4	11.1	15 31.7	6.6	56.0	68	16 05	17 04	18 09	08 09	09 43	11 11	12 28
N 11	348 48.6	28.8	151 35.5	11.1	15 38.3	6.5	56.0	66	16 15	17 08	18 08	07 55	09 23	10 44	11 55
D 12	3 48.7	S10 29.7	166 05.6	11.1	N15 44.8	6.4	56.0	64	16 23	17 12	18 08	07 43	09 06	10 23	11 30
A 13	18 48.8	30.6	180 35.7	11.1	15 51.2	6.3	56.0	62	16 30	17 16	18 07	07 34	08 53	10 07	11 11
Y 14	33 48.9	31.5	195 05.8	11.1	15 57.5	6.2	55.9	60	16 36	17 19	18 08	07 25	08 42	09 53	10 56
15	48 49.0 ..	32.4	209 35.9	11.0	16 03.7	6.1	55.9	N 58	16 42	17 22	18 08	07 18	08 32	09 41	10 43
16	63 49.1	33.3	224 05.9	11.1	16 09.8	6.1	55.9	56	16 47	17 25	18 08	07 12	08 24	09 31	10 31
17	78 49.2	34.2	238 36.0	11.1	16 15.9	5.9	55.9	54	16 51	17 27	18 08	07 06	08 16	09 22	10 21
18	93 49.3	S10 35.1	253 06.1	11.1	N16 21.8	5.9	55.8	52	16 55	17 30	18 09	07 01	08 09	09 14	10 12
19	108 49.4	36.0	267 36.2	11.0	16 27.7	5.8	55.8	50	16 59	17 32	18 09	06 56	08 03	09 06	10 04
20	123 49.5	36.9	282 06.2	11.1	16 33.5	5.7	55.8	45	17 07	17 36	18 10	06 46	07 50	08 51	09 47
21	138 49.6 ..	37.8	296 36.3	11.0	16 39.2	5.6	55.8	N 40	17 13	17 41	18 12	06 38	07 39	08 38	09 33
22	153 49.7	38.6	311 06.3	11.1	16 44.8	5.5	55.7	35	17 19	17 44	18 14	06 31	07 30	08 27	09 22
23	168 49.8	39.5	325 36.4	11.0	16 50.3	5.4	55.7	30	17 24	17 48	18 16	06 24	07 22	08 18	09 11
21 00	183 50.0	S10 40.4	340 06.4	11.0	N16 55.7	5.4	55.7	20	17 33	17 55	18 21	06 14	07 08	08 02	08 54
01	198 50.1	41.3	354 36.5	11.0	17 01.1	5.2	55.7	N 10	17 41	18 02	18 27	06 04	06 56	07 47	08 38
02	213 50.2	42.2	9 06.5	11.1	17 06.3	5.2	55.6	0	17 48	18 09	18 34	05 55	06 45	07 34	08 24
03	228 50.3 ..	43.1	23 36.6	11.0	17 11.5	5.0	55.6	S 10	17 56	18 17	18 42	05 47	06 33	07 21	08 09
04	243 50.4	44.0	38 06.6	11.1	17 16.5	5.0	55.6	20	18 04	18 26	18 53	05 37	06 21	07 07	07 54
05	258 50.5	44.9	52 36.7	11.0	17 21.5	4.9	55.6	30	18 13	18 38	19 07	05 27	06 08	06 51	07 36
06	273 50.6	S10 45.8	67 06.7	11.1	N17 26.4	4.8	55.5	35	18 19	18 45	19 15	05 20	06 00	06 41	07 26
07	288 50.7	46.6	81 36.8	11.0	17 31.2	4.7	55.5	40	18 25	18 54	19 27	05 13	05 51	06 31	07 14
08	303 50.8	47.5	96 06.8	11.1	17 35.9	4.6	55.5	45	18 33	19 04	19 41	05 05	05 40	06 18	07 00
M 09	318 50.9 ..	48.4	110 36.9	11.0	17 40.5	4.5	55.5	S 50	18 42	19 16	19 59	04 56	05 27	06 03	06 43
O 10	333 51.0	49.3	125 06.9	11.0	17 45.0	4.4	55.5	52	18 46	19 22	20 07	04 51	05 21	05 56	06 36
N 11	348 51.1	50.2	139 36.9	11.1	17 49.4	4.4	55.4	54	18 50	19 29	20 17	04 46	05 15	05 48	06 27
D 12	3 51.2	S10 51.1	154 07.0	11.0	N17 53.8	4.2	55.4	56	18 55	19 36	20 29	04 41	05 08	05 39	06 17
A 13	18 51.3	52.0	168 37.0	11.1	17 58.0	4.1	55.4	58	19 01	19 45	20 42	04 35	04 59	05 29	06 05
Y 14	33 51.4	52.9	183 07.1	11.0	18 02.1	4.1	55.4	S 60	19 08	19 55	20 58	04 28	04 50	05 18	05 52
15	48 51.5 ..	53.7	197 37.1	11.0	18 06.2	4.0	55.4								
16	63 51.6	54.6	212 07.2	11.1	18 10.2	3.8	55.3								
17	78 51.7	55.5	226 37.3	11.0	18 14.0	3.8	55.3								
18	93 51.8	S10 56.4	241 07.3	11.1	N18 17.8	3.7	55.3		SUN			MOON			
19	108 51.9	57.3	255 37.4	11.1	18 21.5	3.5	55.3	Day	Eqn. of Time 00ʰ	Eqn. of Time 12ʰ	Mer. Pass.	Mer. Pass. Upper	Mer. Pass. Lower	Age	Phase
20	123 52.0	58.2	270 07.5	11.0	18 25.0	3.5	55.3	d	m s	m s	h m	h m	h m	d %	
21	138 52.0 ..	59.1	284 37.5	11.1	18 28.5	3.4	55.2	19	14 59	15 04	11 45	24 33	12 08	14 100	
22	153 52.1	10 59.9	299 07.6	11.0	18 31.9	3.3	55.2	20	15 09	15 15	11 45	00 33	12 58	15 98	◯
23	168 52.2	S11 00.8	313 37.7	11.1	N18 35.2	3.2	55.2	21	15 20	15 24	11 45	01 22	13 47	16 94	
	SD 16.1	d 0.9	SD 15.4		15.3		15.1									

UT	ARIES GHA	VENUS −4.4 GHA	VENUS Dec	MARS +1.5 GHA	MARS Dec	JUPITER −2.3 GHA	JUPITER Dec	SATURN +0.6 GHA	SATURN Dec	STARS Name	SHA	Dec
d h	° ′	° ′	° ′	° ′	° ′	° ′	° ′	° ′	° ′		° ′	° ′
22 00	30 35.4	136 50.0	S25 54.5	234 16.0	N11 26.8	278 52.4	N21 53.9	169 58.6	S13 31.5	Acamar	315 17.8	S40 14.9
01	45 37.9	151 49.6	54.9	249 17.1	26.3	293 54.7	53.9	185 00.8	31.6	Achernar	335 26.1	S57 10.0
02	60 40.3	166 49.2	55.3	264 18.1	25.8	308 57.1	53.9	200 03.0	31.6	Acrux	173 09.6	S63 10.4
03	75 42.8	181 48.7	. . 55.7	279 19.2	. . 25.2	323 59.4	. . 53.8	215 05.2	. . 31.7	Adhara	255 12.2	S28 59.4
04	90 45.2	196 48.3	56.1	294 20.2	24.7	339 01.7	53.8	230 07.3	31.8	Aldebaran	290 48.8	N16 32.1
05	105 47.7	211 47.9	56.4	309 21.3	24.2	354 04.0	53.8	245 09.5	31.9			
06	120 50.2	226 47.5	S25 56.8	324 22.4	N11 23.7	9 06.3	N21 53.8	260 11.7	S13 32.0	Alioth	166 21.1	N55 53.0
07	135 52.6	241 47.0	57.2	339 23.4	23.2	24 08.7	53.8	275 13.9	32.1	Alkaid	152 59.2	N49 14.7
08	150 55.1	256 46.6	57.6	354 24.5	22.7	39 11.0	53.8	290 16.0	32.2	Al Na'ir	27 43.2	S46 53.6
T 09	165 57.6	271 46.2	. . 58.0	9 25.5	. . 22.1	54 13.3	. . 53.8	305 18.2	. . 32.3	Alnilam	275 45.9	S 1 11.6
U 10	181 00.0	286 45.7	58.4	24 26.6	21.6	69 15.7	53.7	320 20.4	32.4	Alphard	217 56.0	S 8 43.1
E 11	196 02.5	301 45.3	58.8	39 27.6	21.1	84 18.0	53.7	335 22.6	32.5			
S 12	211 05.0	316 44.9	S25 59.2	54 28.7	N11 20.6	99 20.3	N21 53.7	350 24.7	S13 32.6	Alphecca	126 11.2	N26 40.3
D 13	226 07.4	331 44.5	25 59.6	69 29.7	20.1	114 22.6	53.7	5 26.9	32.7	Alpheratz	357 42.9	N29 10.2
A 14	241 09.9	346 44.1	26 00.0	84 30.8	19.6	129 25.0	53.7	20 29.1	32.7	Altair	62 08.0	N 8 54.6
Y 15	256 12.4	1 43.6	. . 00.4	99 31.9	. . 19.0	144 27.3	. . 53.7	35 31.3	. . 32.8	Ankaa	353 15.1	S42 13.8
16	271 14.8	16 43.2	00.7	114 32.9	18.5	159 29.6	53.7	50 33.4	32.9	Antares	112 26.3	S26 27.6
17	286 17.3	31 42.8	01.1	129 34.0	18.0	174 31.9	53.6	65 35.6	33.0			
18	301 19.7	46 42.4	S26 01.5	144 35.0	N11 17.5	189 34.3	N21 53.6	80 37.8	S13 33.1	Arcturus	145 55.9	N19 06.8
19	316 22.2	61 41.9	01.9	159 36.1	17.0	204 36.6	53.6	95 40.0	33.2	Atria	107 28.2	S69 03.1
20	331 24.7	76 41.5	02.3	174 37.1	16.4	219 38.9	53.6	110 42.1	33.3	Avior	234 17.9	S59 33.0
21	346 27.1	91 41.1	. . 02.6	189 38.2	. . 15.9	234 41.3	. . 53.6	125 44.3	. . 33.4	Bellatrix	278 31.5	N 6 21.7
22	1 29.6	106 40.7	03.0	204 39.2	15.4	249 43.6	53.6	140 46.5	33.5	Betelgeuse	271 00.9	N 7 24.5
23	16 32.1	121 40.2	03.4	219 40.3	14.9	264 45.9	53.6	155 48.7	33.6			
23 00	31 34.5	136 39.8	S26 03.8	234 41.4	N11 14.4	279 48.3	N21 53.5	170 50.8	S13 33.7	Canopus	263 55.8	S52 42.0
01	46 37.0	151 39.4	04.1	249 42.4	13.9	294 50.6	53.5	185 53.0	33.8	Capella	280 33.8	N46 00.4
02	61 39.5	166 39.0	04.5	264 43.5	13.3	309 52.9	53.5	200 55.2	33.8	Deneb	49 31.2	N45 20.3
03	76 41.9	181 38.6	. . 04.9	279 44.5	. . 12.8	324 55.3	. . 53.5	215 57.4	. . 33.9	Denebola	182 33.7	N14 29.7
04	91 44.4	196 38.1	05.3	294 45.6	12.3	339 57.6	53.5	230 59.6	34.0	Diphda	348 55.4	S17 54.5
05	106 46.9	211 37.7	05.6	309 46.7	11.8	354 59.9	53.5	246 01.7	34.1			
06	121 49.3	226 37.3	S26 06.0	324 47.7	N11 11.3	10 02.3	N21 53.5	261 03.9	S13 34.2	Dubhe	193 52.0	N61 40.3
W 07	136 51.8	241 36.9	06.4	339 48.8	10.8	25 04.6	53.5	276 06.1	34.3	Elnath	278 12.1	N28 37.0
E 08	151 54.2	256 36.5	06.7	354 49.8	10.2	40 06.9	53.4	291 08.3	34.4	Eltanin	90 46.3	N51 29.7
D 09	166 56.7	271 36.0	. . 07.1	9 50.9	. . 09.7	55 09.3	. . 53.4	306 10.4	. . 34.5	Enif	33 46.8	N 9 56.6
N 10	181 59.2	286 35.6	07.5	24 52.0	09.2	70 11.6	53.4	321 12.6	34.6	Fomalhaut	15 23.5	S29 32.9
N 11	197 01.6	301 35.2	07.8	39 53.0	08.7	85 13.9	53.4	336 14.8	34.7			
E 12	212 04.1	316 34.8	S26 08.2	54 54.1	N11 08.2	100 16.3	N21 53.4	351 17.0	S13 34.8	Gacrux	172 01.1	S57 11.3
S 13	227 06.6	331 34.4	08.6	69 55.1	07.6	115 18.6	53.4	6 19.1	34.8	Gienah	175 52.3	S17 37.0
D 14	242 09.0	346 33.9	08.9	84 56.2	07.1	130 20.9	53.4	21 21.3	34.9	Hadar	148 48.1	S60 26.3
A 15	257 11.5	1 33.5	. . 09.3	99 57.3	. . 06.6	145 23.3	. . 53.3	36 23.5	. . 35.0	Hamal	328 00.1	N23 31.7
Y 16	272 14.0	16 33.1	09.6	114 58.3	06.1	160 25.6	53.3	51 25.7	35.1	Kaus Aust.	83 43.7	S34 22.6
17	287 16.4	31 32.7	10.0	129 59.4	05.6	175 27.9	53.3	66 27.8	35.2			
18	302 18.9	46 32.3	S26 10.4	145 00.4	N11 05.1	190 30.3	N21 53.3	81 30.0	S13 35.3	Kochab	137 21.3	N74 06.1
19	317 21.3	61 31.8	10.7	160 01.5	04.5	205 32.6	53.3	96 32.2	35.4	Markab	13 37.9	N15 17.1
20	332 23.8	76 31.4	11.1	175 02.6	04.0	220 35.0	53.3	111 34.4	35.5	Menkar	314 14.5	N 4 08.7
21	347 26.3	91 31.0	. . 11.4	190 03.6	. . 03.5	235 37.3	. . 53.3	126 36.5	. . 35.6	Menkent	148 07.7	S36 26.1
22	2 28.7	106 30.6	11.8	205 04.7	03.0	250 39.6	53.3	141 38.7	35.7	Miaplacidus	221 39.8	S69 46.2
23	17 31.2	121 30.2	12.1	220 05.7	02.5	265 42.0	53.2	156 40.9	35.8			
24 00	32 33.7	136 29.8	S26 12.5	235 06.8	N11 01.9	280 44.3	N21 53.2	171 43.1	S13 35.9	Mirfak	308 39.5	N49 54.5
01	47 36.1	151 29.3	12.8	250 07.9	01.4	295 46.7	53.2	186 45.2	35.9	Nunki	75 58.1	S26 16.6
02	62 38.6	166 28.9	13.2	265 08.9	00.9	310 49.0	53.2	201 47.4	36.0	Peacock	53 18.9	S56 41.5
03	77 41.1	181 28.5	. . 13.5	280 10.0	11 00.4	325 51.3	. . 53.2	216 49.6	. . 36.1	Pollux	243 27.4	N27 59.3
04	92 43.5	196 28.1	13.9	295 11.1	10 59.9	340 53.7	53.2	231 51.8	36.2	Procyon	244 59.4	N 5 11.3
05	107 46.0	211 27.7	14.2	310 12.1	59.3	355 56.0	53.2	246 53.9	36.3			
06	122 48.5	226 27.3	S26 14.6	325 13.2	N10 58.8	10 58.4	N21 53.2	261 56.1	S13 36.4	Rasalhague	96 06.4	N12 33.3
07	137 50.9	241 26.8	14.9	340 14.3	58.3	26 00.7	53.1	276 58.3	36.5	Regulus	207 43.4	N11 53.9
T 08	152 53.4	256 26.4	15.2	355 15.3	57.8	41 03.0	53.1	292 00.5	36.6	Rigel	281 11.6	S 8 11.2
H 09	167 55.8	271 26.0	. . 15.6	10 16.4	. . 57.3	56 05.4	. . 53.1	307 02.6	. . 36.7	Rigil Kent.	139 52.0	S60 53.4
U 10	182 58.3	286 25.6	15.9	25 17.4	56.7	71 07.7	53.1	322 04.8	36.8	Sabik	102 12.5	S15 44.3
R 11	198 00.8	301 25.2	16.3	40 18.5	56.2	86 10.1	53.1	337 07.0	36.9			
S 12	213 03.2	316 24.8	S26 16.6	55 19.6	N10 55.7	101 12.4	N21 53.1	352 09.2	S13 37.0	Schedar	349 39.6	N56 37.0
D 13	228 05.7	331 24.4	16.9	70 20.6	55.2	116 14.8	53.1	7 11.3	37.0	Shaula	96 21.8	S37 06.7
A 14	243 08.2	346 24.0	17.3	85 21.7	54.7	131 17.1	53.1	22 13.5	37.1	Sirius	258 33.4	S16 44.1
Y 15	258 10.6	1 23.5	. . 17.6	100 22.8	. . 54.2	146 19.5	. . 53.1	37 15.7	. . 37.2	Spica	158 31.3	S11 13.9
16	273 13.1	16 23.1	17.9	115 23.8	53.6	161 21.8	53.0	52 17.9	37.3	Suhail	222 52.3	S43 29.2
17	288 15.6	31 22.7	18.3	130 24.9	53.1	176 24.1	53.0	67 20.0	37.4			
18	303 18.0	46 22.3	S26 18.6	145 26.0	N10 52.6	191 26.5	N21 53.0	82 22.2	S13 37.5	Vega	80 39.0	N38 48.2
19	318 20.5	61 21.9	18.9	160 27.0	52.1	206 28.8	53.0	97 24.4	37.6	Zuben'ubi	137 05.5	S16 05.8
20	333 23.0	76 21.5	19.3	175 28.1	51.6	221 31.2	53.0	112 26.6	37.7		SHA	Mer.Pass.
21	348 25.4	91 21.1	. . 19.6	190 29.2	. . 51.0	236 33.5	. . 53.0	127 28.7	. . 37.8		° ′	h m
22	3 27.9	106 20.7	19.9	205 30.2	50.5	251 35.9	53.0	142 30.9	37.9	Venus	105 05.3	14 54
23	18 30.3	121 20.2	20.2	220 31.3	50.0	266 38.2	53.0	157 33.1	38.0	Mars	203 06.8	8 21
	h m									Jupiter	248 13.7	5 20
Mer.Pass. 21 50.1		v −0.4	d 0.4	v 1.1	d 0.5	v 2.3	d 0.0	v 2.2	d 0.1	Saturn	139 16.3	12 35

UT	SUN GHA	SUN Dec	MOON GHA	v	MOON Dec	d	HP
d h	o ′	o ′	o ′	′	o ′	′	′
22 00	183 52.3	S11 01.7	328 07.8	11.1	N18 38.4	3.1	55.2
01	198 52.4	02.6	342 37.9	11.1	18 41.5	3.0	55.2
02	213 52.5	03.5	357 08.0	11.1	18 44.5	2.9	55.1
03	228 52.6	.. 04.4	11 38.1	11.2	18 47.4	2.8	55.1
04	243 52.7	05.2	26 08.3	11.1	18 50.2	2.8	55.1
05	258 52.8	06.1	40 38.4	11.1	18 53.0	2.6	55.1
06	273 52.9	S11 07.0	55 08.5	11.2	N18 55.6	2.5	55.1
07	288 53.0	07.9	69 38.7	11.1	18 58.1	2.5	55.0
T 08	303 53.1	08.8	84 08.8	11.2	19 00.6	2.3	55.0
U 09	318 53.2	.. 09.6	98 39.0	11.2	19 02.9	2.3	55.0
E 10	333 53.3	10.5	113 09.2	11.2	19 05.2	2.1	55.0
S 11	348 53.4	11.4	127 39.4	11.2	19 07.3	2.1	55.0
D 12	3 53.5	S11 12.3	142 09.6	11.2	N19 09.4	1.9	54.9
A 13	18 53.6	13.2	156 39.8	11.2	19 11.3	1.9	54.9
Y 14	33 53.7	14.0	171 10.0	11.2	19 13.2	1.8	54.9
15	48 53.7	.. 14.9	185 40.2	11.3	19 15.0	1.6	54.9
16	63 53.8	15.8	200 10.5	11.2	19 16.6	1.6	54.9
17	78 53.9	16.7	214 40.7	11.3	19 18.2	1.5	54.9
18	93 54.0	S11 17.6	229 11.0	11.3	N19 19.7	1.4	54.8
19	108 54.1	18.4	243 41.3	11.3	19 21.1	1.3	54.8
20	123 54.2	19.3	258 11.6	11.3	19 22.4	1.2	54.8
21	138 54.3	.. 20.2	272 41.9	11.3	19 23.6	1.1	54.8
22	153 54.4	21.1	287 12.2	11.4	19 24.7	1.0	54.8
23	168 54.5	22.0	301 42.6	11.3	19 25.7	0.9	54.7
23 00	183 54.6	S11 22.8	316 12.9	11.4	N19 26.6	0.8	54.7
01	198 54.6	23.7	330 43.3	11.4	19 27.4	0.8	54.7
02	213 54.7	24.6	345 13.7	11.4	19 28.2	0.6	54.7
03	228 54.8	.. 25.5	359 44.1	11.4	19 28.8	0.5	54.7
04	243 54.9	26.3	14 14.5	11.5	19 29.3	0.5	54.7
05	258 55.0	27.2	28 45.0	11.4	19 29.8	0.3	54.7
06	273 55.1	S11 28.1	43 15.4	11.5	N19 30.1	0.3	54.6
W 07	288 55.2	29.0	57 45.9	11.5	19 30.4	0.1	54.6
E 08	303 55.3	29.8	72 16.4	11.5	19 30.5	0.1	54.6
D 09	318 55.3	.. 30.7	86 46.9	11.6	19 30.6	0.0	54.6
N 10	333 55.4	31.6	101 17.5	11.5	19 30.6	0.1	54.6
E 11	348 55.5	32.5	115 48.0	11.6	19 30.5	0.3	54.6
S 12	3 55.6	S11 33.3	130 18.6	11.6	N19 30.2	0.4	54.5
D 13	18 55.7	34.2	144 49.2	11.6	19 29.9	0.4	54.5
A 14	33 55.8	35.1	159 19.8	11.6	19 29.5	0.4	54.5
Y 15	48 55.8	.. 35.9	173 50.4	11.7	19 29.1	0.6	54.5
16	63 55.9	36.8	188 21.1	11.7	19 28.5	0.7	54.5
17	78 56.0	37.7	202 51.8	11.7	19 27.8	0.8	54.5
18	93 56.1	S11 38.6	217 22.5	11.7	N19 27.0	0.8	54.5
19	108 56.2	39.4	231 53.2	11.8	19 26.2	1.0	54.5
20	123 56.3	40.3	246 24.0	11.7	19 25.2	1.0	54.5
21	138 56.3	.. 41.2	260 54.7	11.8	19 24.2	1.2	54.4
22	153 56.4	42.0	275 25.5	11.8	19 23.0	1.2	54.4
23	168 56.5	42.9	289 56.3	11.9	19 21.8	1.3	54.4
24 00	183 56.6	S11 43.8	304 27.2	11.8	N19 20.5	1.4	54.4
01	198 56.7	44.6	318 58.0	11.9	19 19.1	1.5	54.4
02	213 56.8	45.5	333 28.9	11.9	19 17.6	1.6	54.4
03	228 56.8	.. 46.4	347 59.8	12.0	19 16.0	1.7	54.4
04	243 56.9	47.3	2 30.8	11.9	19 14.3	1.7	54.4
05	258 57.0	48.1	17 01.7	12.0	19 12.6	1.9	54.4
06	273 57.1	S11 49.0	31 32.7	12.0	N19 10.7	1.9	54.4
07	288 57.2	49.9	46 03.7	12.0	19 08.8	2.0	54.3
T 08	303 57.2	50.7	60 34.7	12.1	19 06.8	2.2	54.3
H 09	318 57.3	.. 51.6	75 05.8	12.1	19 04.6	2.2	54.3
U 10	333 57.4	52.5	89 36.9	12.1	19 02.4	2.2	54.3
R 11	348 57.5	53.3	104 08.0	12.1	19 00.2	2.4	54.3
S 12	3 57.5	S11 54.2	118 39.1	12.2	N18 57.8	2.5	54.3
D 13	18 57.6	55.1	133 10.3	12.2	18 55.3	2.5	54.3
A 14	33 57.7	55.9	147 41.5	12.2	18 52.8	2.7	54.3
Y 15	48 57.8	.. 56.8	162 12.7	12.3	18 50.1	2.7	54.3
16	63 57.9	57.6	176 44.0	12.2	18 47.4	2.8	54.3
17	78 57.9	58.5	191 15.2	12.3	18 44.6	2.9	54.3
18	93 58.0	S11 59.4	205 46.5	12.3	N18 41.7	3.0	54.3
19	108 58.1	12 00.2	220 17.8	12.4	18 38.7	3.1	54.3
20	123 58.2	01.1	234 49.2	12.4	18 35.6	3.1	54.3
21	138 58.2	.. 02.0	249 20.6	12.4	18 32.5	3.2	54.2
22	153 58.3	02.8	263 52.0	12.4	18 29.3	3.4	54.2
23	168 58.4	03.7	278 23.4	12.5	N18 25.9	3.4	54.2
	SD 16.1	d 0.9	SD 15.0		14.9		14.8

Twilight / Sunrise / Moonrise

Lat.	Twilight Naut.	Twilight Civil	Sunrise	Moonrise 22	23	24	25
o	h m	h m	h m	h m	h m	h m	h m
N 72	05 30	06 49	08 06	▢	▢	▢	18 22
N 70	05 30	06 41	07 48	15 48	16 27	17 46	19 18
68	05 30	06 35	07 35	16 43	17 28	18 33	19 51
66	05 29	06 29	07 24	17 16	18 02	19 03	20 15
64	05 29	06 24	07 14	17 40	18 27	19 26	20 34
62	05 28	06 20	07 06	17 59	18 47	19 44	20 49
60	05 28	06 16	06 59	18 15	19 03	19 59	21 02
N 58	05 27	06 13	06 53	18 28	19 16	20 12	21 13
56	05 26	06 10	06 48	18 40	19 28	20 23	21 23
54	05 26	06 07	06 43	18 50	19 38	20 32	21 31
52	05 25	06 04	06 39	18 59	19 47	20 41	21 39
50	05 24	06 02	06 35	19 07	19 56	20 49	21 46
45	05 22	05 56	06 26	19 24	20 13	21 05	22 00
N 40	05 20	05 51	06 19	19 38	20 27	21 18	22 12
35	05 17	05 47	06 13	19 50	20 39	21 30	22 22
30	05 15	05 43	06 07	20 01	20 50	21 40	22 31
20	05 09	05 35	05 58	20 19	21 08	21 57	22 46
N 10	05 03	05 28	05 49	20 35	21 23	22 12	23 00
0	04 55	05 20	05 41	20 49	21 38	22 26	23 12
S 10	04 46	05 11	05 33	21 04	21 53	22 40	23 25
20	04 35	05 01	05 24	21 20	22 08	22 55	23 38
30	04 19	04 49	05 13	21 38	22 26	23 12	23 53
35	04 10	04 41	05 08	21 48	22 37	23 22	24 02
40	03 58	04 32	05 01	22 01	22 49	23 33	24 12
45	03 44	04 22	04 53	22 15	23 03	23 46	24 24
S 50	03 25	04 08	04 43	22 32	23 21	24 02	00 02
52	03 16	04 02	04 39	22 41	23 29	24 10	00 10
54	03 05	03 55	04 34	22 50	23 38	24 18	00 18
56	02 53	03 47	04 28	23 00	23 48	24 28	00 28
58	02 39	03 38	04 22	23 12	24 00	00 00	00 39
S 60	02 22	03 27	04 15	23 26	24 13	00 13	00 51

Sunset / Twilight / Moonset

Lat.	Sunset	Twilight Civil	Twilight Naut.	Moonset 22	23	24	25
o	h m	h m	h m	h m	h m	h m	h m
N 72	15 21	16 37	17 56	▢	▢	▢	15 48
N 70	15 39	16 46	17 57	13 22	14 25	14 46	14 51
68	15 52	16 52	17 57	12 28	13 24	13 59	14 18
66	16 04	16 58	17 58	11 55	12 50	13 28	13 53
64	16 13	17 03	17 58	11 30	12 24	13 05	13 34
62	16 21	17 07	17 59	11 11	12 05	12 46	13 18
60	16 28	17 11	18 00	10 56	11 49	12 31	13 05
N 58	16 34	17 15	18 01	10 43	11 35	12 18	12 53
56	16 40	17 18	18 01	10 31	11 23	12 07	12 43
54	16 44	17 21	18 02	10 21	11 13	11 57	12 35
52	16 49	17 24	18 03	10 12	11 04	11 49	12 27
50	16 53	17 26	18 04	10 04	10 56	11 41	12 20
45	17 02	17 32	18 06	09 47	10 38	11 24	12 05
N 40	17 09	17 37	18 08	09 33	10 24	11 10	11 52
35	17 15	17 41	18 11	09 22	10 12	10 59	11 41
30	17 21	17 45	18 13	09 11	10 02	10 49	11 32
20	17 31	17 53	18 19	08 54	09 43	10 31	11 16
N 10	17 39	18 01	18 26	08 38	09 28	10 16	11 02
0	17 48	18 09	18 33	08 24	09 13	10 01	10 48
S 10	17 56	18 18	18 43	08 09	08 58	09 47	10 35
20	18 05	18 28	18 54	07 54	08 42	09 31	10 21
30	18 16	18 40	19 10	07 36	08 24	09 14	10 04
35	18 22	18 48	19 19	07 26	08 13	09 03	09 55
40	18 29	18 57	19 31	07 14	08 01	08 51	09 44
45	18 37	19 08	19 46	07 00	07 47	08 37	09 31
S 50	18 47	19 22	20 05	06 43	07 29	08 20	09 15
52	18 51	19 28	20 14	06 36	07 21	08 12	09 08
54	18 56	19 35	20 25	06 27	07 12	08 03	09 00
56	19 02	19 43	20 38	06 17	07 01	07 53	08 51
58	19 08	19 53	20 52	06 05	06 50	07 41	08 40
S 60	19 15	20 04	21 10	05 52	06 36	07 28	08 28

SUN / MOON

Day	SUN Eqn. of Time 00h	12h	Mer. Pass.	MOON Mer. Pass. Upper	Lower	Age	Phase
d	m s	m s	h m	h m	h m	d	%
22	15 29	15 34	11 44	02 12	14 37	17	88
23	15 38	15 42	11 44	03 01	15 25	18	81
24	15 46	15 50	11 44	03 50	16 14	19	73

UT	ARIES GHA	VENUS −4.5 GHA	Dec	MARS +1.5 GHA	Dec	JUPITER −2.3 GHA	Dec	SATURN +0.6 GHA	Dec	STARS Name	SHA	Dec
25 00	33 32.8	136 19.8	S26 20.6	235 32.4	N10 49.5	281 40.6	N21 52.9	172 35.2	S13 38.1	Acamar	315 17.8	S40 14.9
01	48 35.3	151 19.4	20.9	250 33.4	49.0	296 42.9	52.9	187 37.4	38.1	Achernar	335 26.1	S57 10.0
02	63 37.7	166 19.0	21.2	265 34.5	48.4	311 45.3	52.9	202 39.6	38.2	Acrux	173 09.5	S63 10.4
03	78 40.2	181 18.6 . .	21.5	280 35.6 . .	47.9	326 47.6 . .	52.9	217 41.8 . .	38.3	Adhara	255 12.2	S28 59.4
04	93 42.7	196 18.2	21.9	295 36.6	47.4	341 50.0	52.9	232 43.9	38.4	Aldebaran	290 48.8	N16 32.1
05	108 45.1	211 17.8	22.2	310 37.7	46.9	356 52.3	52.9	247 46.1	38.5			
06	123 47.6	226 17.4	S26 22.5	325 38.8	N10 46.4	11 54.7	N21 52.9	262 48.3	S13 38.6	Alioth	166 21.1	N55 53.0
07	138 50.1	241 17.0	22.8	340 39.8	45.8	26 57.0	52.9	277 50.5	38.7	Alkaid	152 59.2	N49 14.7
08	153 52.5	256 16.6	23.1	355 40.9	45.3	41 59.4	52.9	292 52.6	38.8	Al Na'ir	27 43.3	S46 53.6
F 09	168 55.0	271 16.2 . .	23.4	10 42.0 . .	44.8	57 01.7 . .	52.8	307 54.8 . .	38.9	Alnilam	275 45.9	S 1 11.6
R 10	183 57.5	286 15.8	23.8	25 43.0	44.3	72 04.1	52.8	322 57.0	39.0	Alphard	217 55.9	S 8 43.1
I 11	198 59.9	301 15.3	24.1	40 44.1	43.8	87 06.4	52.8	337 59.2	39.1			
D 12	214 02.4	316 14.9	S26 24.4	55 45.2	N10 43.2	102 08.8	N21 52.8	353 01.3	S13 39.1	Alphecca	126 11.2	N26 40.3
A 13	229 04.8	331 14.5	24.7	70 46.3	42.7	117 11.1	52.8	8 03.5	39.2	Alpheratz	357 42.9	N29 10.2
Y 14	244 07.3	346 14.1	25.0	85 47.3	42.2	132 13.5	52.8	23 05.7	39.3	Altair	62 08.0	N 8 54.6
15	259 09.8	1 13.7 . .	25.3	100 48.4 . .	41.7	147 15.8 . .	52.8	38 07.9 . .	39.4	Ankaa	353 15.1	S42 13.8
16	274 12.2	16 13.3	25.6	115 49.5	41.1	162 18.2	52.8	53 10.0	39.5	Antares	112 26.3	S26 27.6
17	289 14.7	31 12.9	25.9	130 50.5	40.6	177 20.5	52.8	68 12.2	39.6			
18	304 17.2	46 12.5	S26 26.2	145 51.6	N10 40.1	192 22.9	N21 52.8	83 14.4	S13 39.7	Arcturus	145 55.9	N19 06.8
19	319 19.6	61 12.1	26.5	160 52.7	39.6	207 25.3	52.7	98 16.6	39.8	Atria	107 28.2	S69 03.1
20	334 22.1	76 11.7	26.8	175 53.7	39.1	222 27.6	52.7	113 18.7	39.9	Avior	234 17.9	S59 33.1
21	349 24.6	91 11.3 . .	27.1	190 54.8 . .	38.5	237 30.0 . .	52.7	128 20.9 . .	40.0	Bellatrix	278 31.5	N 6 21.7
22	4 27.0	106 10.9	27.4	205 55.9	38.0	252 32.3	52.7	143 23.1	40.1	Betelgeuse	271 00.8	N 7 24.5
23	19 29.5	121 10.5	27.7	220 57.0	37.5	267 34.7	52.7	158 25.2	40.2			
26 00	34 31.9	136 10.1	S26 28.0	235 58.0	N10 37.0	282 37.0	N21 52.7	173 27.4	S13 40.2	Canopus	263 55.8	S52 42.1
01	49 34.4	151 09.7	28.3	250 59.1	36.5	297 39.4	52.7	188 29.6	40.3	Capella	280 33.7	N46 00.5
02	64 36.9	166 09.3	28.6	266 00.2	35.9	312 41.7	52.7	203 31.8	40.4	Deneb	49 31.2	N45 20.3
03	79 39.3	181 08.9 . .	28.9	281 01.2 . .	35.4	327 44.1 . .	52.7	218 33.9 . .	40.5	Denebola	182 33.7	N14 29.7
04	94 41.8	196 08.5	29.2	296 02.3	34.9	342 46.5	52.7	233 36.1	40.6	Diphda	348 55.4	S17 54.6
05	109 44.3	211 08.1	29.5	311 03.4	34.4	357 48.8	52.6	248 38.3	40.7			
06	124 46.7	226 07.7	S26 29.8	326 04.5	N10 33.9	12 51.2	N21 52.6	263 40.5	S13 40.8	Dubhe	193 51.9	N61 40.3
07	139 49.2	241 07.3	30.1	341 05.5	33.3	27 53.5	52.6	278 42.6	40.9	Elnath	278 12.1	N28 37.0
S 08	154 51.7	256 06.9	30.4	356 06.6	32.8	42 55.9	52.6	293 44.8	41.0	Eltanin	90 46.3	N51 29.7
A 09	169 54.1	271 06.5 . .	30.7	11 07.7 . .	32.3	57 58.3 . .	52.6	308 47.0 . .	41.1	Enif	33 46.8	N 9 56.6
T 10	184 56.6	286 06.1	31.0	26 08.8	31.8	73 00.6	52.6	323 49.2	41.2	Fomalhaut	15 23.5	S29 32.9
U 11	199 59.1	301 05.7	31.2	41 09.8	31.2	88 03.0	52.6	338 51.3	41.2			
R 12	215 01.5	316 05.3	S26 31.5	56 10.9	N10 30.7	103 05.3	N21 52.6	353 53.5	S13 41.3	Gacrux	172 01.1	S57 11.3
D 13	230 04.0	331 04.9	31.8	71 12.0	30.2	118 07.7	52.6	8 55.7	41.4	Gienah	175 52.3	S17 37.0
A 14	245 06.4	346 04.6	32.1	86 13.0	29.7	133 10.1	52.6	23 57.8	41.5	Hadar	148 48.1	S60 26.3
Y 15	260 08.9	1 04.1 . .	32.4	101 14.1 . .	29.2	148 12.4 . .	52.5	39 00.0 . .	41.6	Hamal	328 00.1	N23 31.7
16	275 11.4	16 03.7	32.7	116 15.2	28.6	163 14.8	52.5	54 02.2	41.7	Kaus Aust.	83 43.7	S34 22.6
17	290 13.8	31 03.3	32.9	131 16.3	28.1	178 17.1	52.5	69 04.4	41.8			
18	305 16.3	46 02.9	S26 33.2	146 17.3	N10 27.6	193 19.5	N21 52.5	84 06.5	S13 41.9	Kochab	137 21.3	N74 06.0
19	320 18.8	61 02.5	33.5	161 18.4	27.1	208 21.9	52.5	99 08.7	42.0	Markab	13 37.9	N15 17.1
20	335 21.2	76 02.1	33.8	176 19.5	26.6	223 24.2	52.5	114 10.9	42.1	Menkar	314 14.5	N 4 08.7
21	350 23.7	91 01.7 . .	34.1	191 20.6 . .	26.0	238 26.6 . .	52.5	129 13.1 . .	42.2	Menkent	148 07.7	S36 26.1
22	5 26.2	106 01.3	34.3	206 21.6	25.5	253 29.0	52.5	144 15.2	42.3	Miaplacidus	221 39.7	S69 46.2
23	20 28.6	121 00.9	34.6	221 22.7	25.0	268 31.3	52.5	159 17.4	42.3			
27 00	35 31.1	136 00.5	S26 34.9	236 23.8	N10 24.5	283 33.7	N21 52.5	174 19.6	S13 42.4	Mirfak	308 39.5	N49 54.5
01	50 33.6	151 00.1	35.2	251 24.9	23.9	298 36.1	52.5	189 21.8	42.5	Nunki	75 58.2	S26 16.6
02	65 36.0	165 59.7	35.4	266 25.9	23.4	313 38.4	52.4	204 23.9	42.6	Peacock	53 18.9	S56 41.5
03	80 38.5	180 59.4 . .	35.7	281 27.0 . .	22.9	328 40.8 . .	52.4	219 26.1 . .	42.7	Pollux	243 27.4	N27 59.3
04	95 40.9	195 59.0	36.0	296 28.1	22.4	343 43.2	52.4	234 28.3	42.8	Procyon	244 59.4	N 5 11.3
05	110 43.4	210 58.6	36.2	311 29.2	21.9	358 45.5	52.4	249 30.4	42.9			
06	125 45.9	225 58.2	S26 36.5	326 30.3	N10 21.3	13 47.9	N21 52.4	264 32.6	S13 43.0	Rasalhague	96 06.5	N12 33.3
07	140 48.3	240 57.8	36.8	341 31.3	20.8	28 50.3	52.4	279 34.8	43.1	Regulus	207 43.4	N11 53.9
08	155 50.8	255 57.4	37.0	356 32.4	20.3	43 52.6	52.4	294 37.0	43.2	Rigel	281 11.6	S 8 11.2
S 09	170 53.3	270 57.0 . .	37.3	11 33.5 . .	19.8	58 55.0 . .	52.4	309 39.1 . .	43.3	Rigil Kent.	139 52.0	S60 53.4
U 10	185 55.7	285 56.6	37.6	26 34.6	19.2	73 57.4	52.4	324 41.3	43.3	Sabik	102 12.5	S15 44.3
N 11	200 58.2	300 56.2	37.8	41 35.6	18.7	88 59.7	52.4	339 43.5	43.4			
D 12	216 00.7	315 55.8	S26 38.1	56 36.7	N10 18.2	104 02.1	N21 52.4	354 45.7	S13 43.5	Schedar	349 39.6	N56 37.0
A 13	231 03.1	330 55.4	38.3	71 37.8	17.7	119 04.5	52.4	9 47.8	43.6	Shaula	96 21.9	S37 06.7
Y 14	246 05.6	345 55.1	38.6	86 38.9	17.2	134 06.8	52.3	24 50.0	43.7	Sirius	258 33.4	S16 44.1
15	261 08.0	0 54.7 . .	38.8	101 40.0 . .	16.6	149 09.2 . .	52.3	39 52.2 . .	43.8	Spica	158 31.3	S11 13.9
16	276 10.5	15 54.3	39.1	116 41.0	16.1	164 11.6	52.3	54 54.3	43.9	Suhail	222 52.3	S43 29.2
17	291 13.0	30 53.9	39.4	131 42.1	15.6	179 14.0	52.3	69 56.5	44.0			
18	306 15.4	45 53.5	S26 39.6	146 43.2	N10 15.1	194 16.3	N21 52.3	84 58.7	S13 44.1	Vega	80 39.0	N38 48.2
19	321 17.9	60 53.1	39.9	161 44.3	14.5	209 18.7	52.3	100 00.9	44.2	Zuben'ubi	137 05.5	S16 05.8
20	336 20.4	75 52.7	40.1	176 45.4	14.0	224 21.1	52.3	115 03.0	44.3		SHA	Mer.Pass.
21	351 22.8	90 52.3 . .	40.4	191 46.4 . .	13.5	239 23.4 . .	52.3	130 05.2 . .	44.3		° ′	h m
22	6 25.3	105 52.0	40.6	206 47.5	13.0	254 25.8	52.3	145 07.4	44.4	Venus	101 38.1	14 56
23	21 27.8	120 51.6	40.9	221 48.6	12.5	269 28.2	52.3	160 09.5	44.5	Mars	201 26.1	8 16
	h m									Jupiter	248 05.1	5 09
Mer.Pass.	21 38.3	v −0.4	d 0.3	v 1.1	d 0.5	v 2.4	d 0.0	v 2.2	d 0.1	Saturn	138 55.5	12 24

SUN / MOON

UT	SUN GHA	SUN Dec	MOON GHA	v	MOON Dec	d	HP
d h	° ′	° ′	° ′	′	° ′	′	′
25 00	183 58.5	S12 04.5	292 54.9	12.5	N18 22.5	3.4	54.2
01	198 58.5	05.4	307 26.4	12.5	18 19.1	3.6	54.2
02	213 58.6	06.3	321 57.9	12.5	18 15.5	3.6	54.2
03	228 58.7	.. 07.1	336 29.4	12.6	18 11.9	3.8	54.2
04	243 58.7	08.0	351 01.0	12.6	18 08.1	3.8	54.2
05	258 58.8	08.9	5 32.6	12.6	18 04.3	3.9	54.2
06	273 58.9	S12 09.7	20 04.2	12.6	N18 00.4	4.0	54.2
07	288 59.0	10.6	34 35.8	12.7	17 56.4	4.0	54.2
F 08	303 59.0	11.4	49 07.5	12.7	17 52.4	4.1	54.2
R 09	318 59.1	.. 12.3	63 39.2	12.8	17 48.3	4.2	54.2
I 10	333 59.2	13.2	78 11.0	12.7	17 44.1	4.3	54.2
D 11	348 59.2	14.0	92 42.7	12.8	17 39.8	4.4	54.2
A 12	3 59.3	S12 14.9	107 14.5	12.8	N17 35.4	4.5	54.2
Y 13	18 59.4	15.7	121 46.3	12.9	17 30.9	4.5	54.2
14	33 59.5	16.6	136 18.2	12.8	17 26.4	4.6	54.2
15	48 59.5	.. 17.4	150 50.0	12.9	17 21.8	4.7	54.2
16	63 59.6	18.3	165 21.9	13.0	17 17.1	4.7	54.2
17	78 59.7	19.2	179 53.9	12.9	17 12.4	4.9	54.2
18	93 59.7	S12 20.0	194 25.8	13.0	N17 07.5	4.9	54.2
19	108 59.8	20.9	208 57.8	13.0	17 02.6	5.0	54.2
20	123 59.9	21.7	223 29.8	13.0	16 57.6	5.0	54.2
21	138 59.9	.. 22.6	238 01.8	13.1	16 52.6	5.2	54.2
22	154 00.0	23.4	252 33.9	13.0	16 47.4	5.2	54.2
23	169 00.1	24.3	267 05.9	13.2	16 42.2	5.3	54.2
26 00	184 00.1	S12 25.1	281 38.1	13.1	N16 36.9	5.3	54.2
01	199 00.2	26.0	296 10.2	13.1	16 31.6	5.5	54.2
02	214 00.3	26.8	310 42.3	13.2	16 26.1	5.5	54.2
03	229 00.3	.. 27.7	325 14.5	13.2	16 20.6	5.5	54.2
04	244 00.4	28.6	339 46.7	13.3	16 15.1	5.7	54.2
05	259 00.5	29.4	354 19.0	13.2	16 09.4	5.7	54.2
06	274 00.5	S12 30.3	8 51.2	13.3	N16 03.7	5.8	54.2
07	289 00.6	31.1	23 23.5	13.3	15 57.9	5.9	54.2
S 08	304 00.6	32.0	37 55.8	13.4	15 52.0	5.9	54.2
A 09	319 00.7	.. 32.8	52 28.2	13.3	15 46.1	6.0	54.3
T 10	334 00.8	33.7	67 00.5	13.4	15 40.1	6.1	54.3
U 11	349 00.8	34.5	81 32.9	13.4	15 34.0	6.1	54.3
R 12	4 00.9	S12 35.4	96 05.3	13.4	N15 27.9	6.2	54.3
D 13	19 01.0	36.2	110 37.7	13.5	15 21.7	6.3	54.3
A 14	34 01.0	37.1	125 10.2	13.5	15 15.4	6.4	54.3
Y 15	49 01.1	.. 37.9	139 42.7	13.5	15 09.0	6.4	54.3
16	64 01.1	38.8	154 15.2	13.5	15 02.6	6.5	54.3
17	79 01.2	39.6	168 47.7	13.5	14 56.1	6.5	54.3
18	94 01.3	S12 40.5	183 20.2	13.6	N14 49.6	6.7	54.3
19	109 01.3	41.3	197 52.8	13.6	14 42.9	6.6	54.3
20	124 01.4	42.1	212 25.4	13.6	14 36.3	6.8	54.3
21	139 01.4	.. 43.0	226 58.0	13.6	14 29.5	6.8	54.3
22	154 01.5	43.8	241 30.6	13.6	14 22.7	6.9	54.4
23	169 01.6	44.7	256 03.2	13.7	14 15.8	6.9	54.4
27 00	184 01.6	S12 45.5	270 35.9	13.7	N14 08.9	7.0	54.4
01	199 01.7	46.4	285 08.6	13.7	14 01.9	7.1	54.4
02	214 01.7	47.2	299 41.3	13.7	13 54.8	7.1	54.4
03	229 01.8	.. 48.1	314 14.0	13.7	13 47.7	7.2	54.4
04	244 01.9	48.9	328 46.7	13.8	13 40.5	7.3	54.4
05	259 01.9	49.8	343 19.5	13.7	13 33.2	7.3	54.4
06	274 02.0	S12 50.6	357 52.2	13.8	N13 25.9	7.4	54.4
07	289 02.0	51.4	12 25.0	13.8	13 18.5	7.4	54.5
S 08	304 02.1	52.3	26 57.8	13.9	13 11.1	7.5	54.5
U 09	319 02.1	.. 53.1	41 30.7	13.8	13 03.6	7.6	54.5
N 10	334 02.2	54.0	56 03.5	13.9	12 56.0	7.6	54.5
D 11	349 02.2	54.8	70 36.4	13.8	12 48.4	7.7	54.5
A 12	4 02.3	S12 55.7	85 09.2	13.9	N12 40.7	7.7	54.5
Y 13	19 02.4	56.5	99 42.1	13.9	12 33.0	7.8	54.5
14	34 02.4	57.3	114 15.0	13.9	12 25.2	7.9	54.5
15	49 02.5	.. 58.2	128 47.9	13.9	12 17.3	7.9	54.6
16	64 02.5	59.0	143 20.8	14.0	12 09.4	8.0	54.6
17	79 02.6	12 59.9	157 53.8	13.9	12 01.4	8.0	54.6
18	94 02.6	S13 00.7	172 26.7	14.0	N11 53.4	8.1	54.6
19	109 02.7	01.5	186 59.7	13.9	11 45.3	8.1	54.6
20	124 02.7	02.4	201 32.6	14.0	11 37.2	8.2	54.6
21	139 02.8	.. 03.2	216 05.6	14.0	11 29.0	8.3	54.7
22	154 02.8	04.1	230 38.6	14.0	11 20.7	8.3	54.7
23	169 02.9	04.9	245 11.6	14.0	N11 12.4	8.3	54.7
	SD 16.1	d 0.8	SD 14.8		14.8		14.9

Twilight, Sunrise, Moonrise

Lat.	Naut.	Civil	Sunrise	Moonrise 25	26	27	28
°	h m	h m	h m	h m	h m	h m	h m
N 72	05 42	07 03	08 22	18 22	20 21	22 07	23 50
N 70	05 41	06 53	08 02	19 18	20 52	22 27	24 01
68	05 39	06 45	07 47	19 51	21 15	22 42	24 10
66	05 38	06 38	07 34	20 15	21 33	22 54	24 18
64	05 37	06 33	07 24	20 34	21 48	23 05	24 24
62	05 36	06 28	07 15	20 49	22 00	23 13	24 29
60	05 34	06 23	07 07	21 02	22 10	23 21	24 34
N 58	05 33	06 19	07 00	21 13	22 19	23 27	24 38
56	05 32	06 16	06 54	21 23	22 26	23 33	24 42
54	05 31	06 12	06 49	21 31	22 33	23 38	24 45
52	05 30	06 09	06 44	21 39	22 40	23 43	24 48
50	05 29	06 06	06 40	21 46	22 45	23 47	24 51
45	05 26	06 00	06 30	22 00	22 57	23 56	24 57
N 40	05 23	05 55	06 22	22 12	23 07	24 04	00 04
35	05 20	05 50	06 15	22 22	23 16	24 10	00 10
30	05 17	05 45	06 09	22 31	23 23	24 16	00 16
20	05 10	05 36	05 59	22 46	23 36	24 26	00 26
N 10	05 03	05 28	05 49	23 00	23 47	24 35	00 35
0	04 55	05 19	05 41	23 12	23 58	24 43	00 43
S 10	04 45	05 10	05 32	23 25	24 08	00 08	00 51
20	04 32	04 59	05 22	23 38	24 20	00 20	00 59
30	04 16	04 46	05 11	23 53	24 32	00 32	01 09
35	04 06	04 38	05 04	24 02	00 02	00 40	01 15
40	03 53	04 28	04 57	24 12	00 12	00 48	01 21
45	03 38	04 16	04 48	24 24	00 24	00 58	01 28
S 50	03 18	04 02	04 37	00 02	00 38	01 10	01 37
52	03 08	03 55	04 32	00 10	00 45	01 15	01 41
54	02 57	03 48	04 27	00 18	00 52	01 21	01 46
56	02 44	03 39	04 21	00 28	01 00	01 28	01 51
58	02 28	03 29	04 14	00 39	01 10	01 35	01 56
S 60	02 08	03 17	04 06	00 51	01 20	01 43	02 03

Sunset, Twilight, Moonset

Lat.	Sunset	Civil	Naut.	Moonset 25	26	27	28
°	h m	h m	h m	h m	h m	h m	h m
N 72	15 04	16 23	17 43	15 48	15 24	15 11	15 01
N 70	15 24	16 33	17 45	14 51	14 52	14 50	14 48
68	15 40	16 41	17 47	14 18	14 34	14 34	14 38
66	15 53	16 48	17 48	13 53	14 09	14 21	14 29
64	16 03	16 54	17 50	13 34	13 54	14 09	14 21
62	16 12	16 59	17 51	13 18	13 42	14 00	14 15
60	16 20	17 04	17 52	13 05	13 31	13 52	14 09
N 58	16 27	17 08	17 54	12 53	13 21	13 45	14 04
56	16 34	17 12	17 55	12 43	13 13	13 38	14 00
54	16 38	17 15	17 56	12 35	13 06	13 32	13 56
52	16 43	17 18	17 57	12 27	12 59	13 27	13 52
50	16 47	17 21	17 58	12 20	12 53	13 23	13 49
45	16 57	17 27	18 01	12 05	12 40	13 12	13 42
N 40	17 05	17 33	18 04	11 52	12 30	13 04	13 36
35	17 12	17 38	18 07	11 41	12 20	12 56	13 31
30	17 18	17 43	18 11	11 32	12 12	12 50	13 26
20	17 29	17 51	18 17	11 16	11 58	12 39	13 18
N 10	17 38	18 00	18 25	11 02	11 46	12 29	13 11
0	17 47	18 09	18 33	10 48	11 34	12 20	13 04
S 10	17 56	18 18	18 43	10 35	11 23	12 10	12 57
20	18 06	18 29	18 56	10 21	11 11	12 00	12 50
30	18 18	18 43	19 12	10 04	10 56	11 49	12 42
35	18 24	18 51	19 23	09 55	10 48	11 42	12 37
40	18 32	19 01	19 35	09 44	10 38	11 34	12 32
45	18 41	19 12	19 51	09 31	10 27	11 25	12 25
S 50	18 52	19 27	20 11	09 15	10 14	11 15	12 18
52	18 57	19 34	20 22	09 08	10 07	11 10	12 14
54	19 02	19 42	20 33	09 00	10 00	11 04	12 10
56	19 08	19 51	20 47	08 51	09 53	10 58	12 06
58	19 15	20 01	21 03	08 40	09 44	10 51	12 01
S 60	19 23	20 13	21 23	08 28	09 34	10 43	11 55

SUN and MOON

Day	SUN Eqn. of Time 00h	12h	Mer. Pass.	MOON Mer. Pass. Upper	Lower	Age	Phase
d	m s	m s	h m	h m	h m	d %	
25	15 54	15 57	11 44	04 37	17 00	20 64	
26	16 00	16 03	11 44	05 23	17 46	21 55	
27	16 06	16 09	11 44	06 09	18 31	22 45	◗

UT	ARIES GHA	VENUS −4.5 GHA	Dec	MARS +1.5 GHA	Dec	JUPITER −2.4 GHA	Dec	SATURN +0.6 GHA	Dec	STARS Name	SHA	Dec
d h	° ′	° ′	° ′	° ′	° ′	° ′	° ′	° ′	° ′		° ′	° ′
28 00	36 30.2	135 51.2	S26 41.1	236 49.7	N10 11.9	284 30.6	N21 52.3	175 11.7	S13 44.6	Acamar	315 17.8	S40 14.9
01	51 32.7	150 50.8	41.4	251 50.8	11.4	299 32.9	52.3	190 13.9	44.7	Achernar	335 26.1	S57 10.0
02	66 35.2	165 50.4	41.6	266 51.8	10.9	314 35.3	52.3	205 16.1	44.8	Acrux	173 09.5	S63 10.4
03	81 37.6	180 50.0 ..	41.8	281 52.9 ..	10.4	329 37.7 ..	52.2	220 18.2 ..	44.9	Adhara	255 12.2	S28 59.4
04	96 40.1	195 49.7	42.1	296 54.0	09.8	344 40.1	52.2	235 20.4	45.0	Aldebaran	290 48.8	N16 32.1
05	111 42.5	210 49.3	42.3	311 55.1	09.3	359 42.4	52.2	250 22.6	45.1			
06	126 45.0	225 48.9	S26 42.6	326 56.2	N10 08.8	14 44.8	N21 52.2	265 24.8	S13 45.2	Alioth	166 21.1	N55 53.0
07	141 47.5	240 48.5	42.8	341 57.2	08.3	29 47.2	52.2	280 26.9	45.3	Alkaid	152 59.2	N49 14.7
08	156 49.9	255 48.1	43.0	356 58.3	07.8	44 49.6	52.2	295 29.1	45.3	Al Na'ir	27 43.3	S46 53.6
M 09	171 52.4	270 47.7 ..	43.3	11 59.4 ..	07.2	59 51.9 ..	52.2	310 31.3 ..	45.4	Alnilam	275 45.9	S 1 11.6
O 10	186 54.9	285 47.4	43.5	27 00.5	06.7	74 54.3	52.2	325 33.4	45.5	Alphard	217 55.9	S 8 43.1
N 11	201 57.3	300 47.0	43.8	42 01.6	06.2	89 56.7	52.2	340 35.6	45.6			
D 12	216 59.8	315 46.6	S26 44.0	57 02.7	N10 05.7	104 59.1	N21 52.2	355 37.8	S13 45.7	Alphecca	126 11.2	N26 40.3
A 13	232 02.3	330 46.2	44.2	72 03.7	05.1	120 01.4	52.2	10 40.0	45.8	Alpheratz	357 42.9	N29 10.3
Y 14	247 04.7	345 45.8	44.5	87 04.8	04.6	135 03.8	52.2	25 42.1	45.9	Altair	62 08.1	N 8 54.6
15	262 07.2	0 45.5 ..	44.7	102 05.9 ..	04.1	150 06.2 ..	52.2	40 44.3 ..	46.0	Ankaa	353 15.1	S42 13.8
16	277 09.7	15 45.1	44.9	117 07.0	03.6	165 08.6	52.2	55 46.5	46.1	Antares	112 26.3	S26 27.6
17	292 12.1	30 44.7	45.1	132 08.1	03.0	180 11.0	52.1	70 48.6	46.2			
18	307 14.6	45 44.3	S26 45.4	147 09.2	N10 02.5	195 13.3	N21 52.1	85 50.8	S13 46.3	Arcturus	145 55.9	N19 06.8
19	322 17.0	60 44.0	45.6	162 10.2	02.0	210 15.7	52.1	100 53.0	46.3	Atria	107 28.3	S69 03.1
20	337 19.5	75 43.6	45.8	177 11.3	01.5	225 18.1	52.1	115 55.2	46.4	Avior	234 17.8	S59 33.1
21	352 22.0	90 43.2 ..	46.0	192 12.4 ..	00.9	240 20.5 ..	52.1	130 57.3 ..	46.5	Bellatrix	278 31.5	N 6 21.6
22	7 24.4	105 42.8	46.3	207 13.5	10 00.4	255 22.9	52.1	145 59.5	46.6	Betelgeuse	271 00.8	N 7 24.5
23	22 26.9	120 42.5	46.5	222 14.6	9 59.9	270 25.2	52.1	161 01.7	46.7			
29 00	37 29.4	135 42.1	S26 46.7	237 15.7	N 9 59.4	285 27.6	N21 52.1	176 03.8	S13 46.8	Canopus	263 55.7	S52 42.1
01	52 31.8	150 41.7	46.9	252 16.7	58.9	300 30.0	52.1	191 06.0	46.9	Capella	280 33.7	N46 00.5
02	67 34.3	165 41.3	47.2	267 17.8	58.3	315 32.4	52.1	206 08.2	47.0	Deneb	49 31.3	N45 20.3
03	82 36.8	180 41.0 ..	47.4	282 18.9 ..	57.8	330 34.8 ..	52.1	221 10.4 ..	47.1	Denebola	182 33.7	N14 29.7
04	97 39.2	195 40.6	47.6	297 20.0	57.3	345 37.2	52.1	236 12.5	47.2	Diphda	348 55.4	S17 54.6
05	112 41.7	210 40.2	47.8	312 21.1	56.8	0 39.5	52.1	251 14.7	47.3			
06	127 44.1	225 39.8	S26 48.0	327 22.2	N 9 56.2	15 41.9	N21 52.1	266 16.9	S13 47.3	Dubhe	193 51.9	N61 40.3
07	142 46.6	240 39.5	48.2	342 23.3	55.7	30 44.3	52.1	281 19.0	47.4	Elnath	278 12.0	N28 37.0
T 08	157 49.1	255 39.1	48.4	357 24.3	55.2	45 46.7	52.0	296 21.2	47.5	Eltanin	90 46.4	N51 29.6
U 09	172 51.5	270 38.7 ..	48.7	12 25.4 ..	54.7	60 49.1 ..	52.0	311 23.4 ..	47.6	Enif	33 46.8	N 9 56.6
E 10	187 54.0	285 38.4	48.9	27 26.5	54.1	75 51.5	52.0	326 25.6	47.7	Fomalhaut	15 23.5	S29 32.9
S 11	202 56.5	300 38.0	49.1	42 27.6	53.6	90 53.9	52.0	341 27.7	47.8			
D 12	217 58.9	315 37.6	S26 49.3	57 28.7	N 9 53.1	105 56.2	N21 52.0	356 29.9	S13 47.9	Gacrux	172 01.1	S57 11.3
A 13	233 01.4	330 37.3	49.5	72 29.8	52.6	120 58.6	52.0	11 32.1	48.0	Gienah	175 52.3	S17 37.0
Y 14	248 03.9	345 36.9	49.7	87 30.9	52.0	136 01.0	52.0	26 34.2	48.1	Hadar	148 48.1	S60 26.2
15	263 06.3	0 36.5 ..	49.9	102 32.0 ..	51.5	151 03.4 ..	52.0	41 36.4 ..	48.2	Hamal	328 00.1	N23 31.7
16	278 08.8	15 36.2	50.1	117 33.0	51.0	166 05.8	52.0	56 38.6	48.3	Kaus Aust.	83 43.7	S34 22.6
17	293 11.3	30 35.8	50.3	132 34.1	50.5	181 08.2	52.0	71 40.8	48.3			
18	308 13.7	45 35.4	S26 50.5	147 35.2	N 9 50.0	196 10.6	N21 52.0	86 42.9	S13 48.4	Kochab	137 21.3	N74 06.0
19	323 16.2	60 35.1	50.7	162 36.3	49.4	211 13.0	52.0	101 45.1	48.5	Markab	13 37.9	N15 17.1
20	338 18.6	75 34.7	50.9	177 37.4	48.9	226 15.3	52.0	116 47.3	48.6	Menkar	314 14.5	N 4 08.7
21	353 21.1	90 34.3 ..	51.1	192 38.5 ..	48.4	241 17.7 ..	52.0	131 49.4 ..	48.7	Menkent	148 07.7	S36 26.1
22	8 23.6	105 34.0	51.3	207 39.6	47.9	256 20.1	52.0	146 51.6	48.8	Miaplacidus	221 39.7	S69 46.2
23	23 26.0	120 33.6	51.5	222 40.7	47.3	271 22.5	52.0	161 53.8	48.9			
30 00	38 28.5	135 33.2	S26 51.7	237 41.7	N 9 46.8	286 24.9	N21 52.0	176 56.0	S13 49.0	Mirfak	308 39.5	N49 54.5
01	53 31.0	150 32.9	51.9	252 42.8	46.3	301 27.3	52.0	191 58.1	49.1	Nunki	75 58.2	S26 16.6
02	68 33.4	165 32.5	52.1	267 43.9	45.8	316 29.7	51.9	207 00.3	49.2	Peacock	53 18.9	S56 41.5
03	83 35.9	180 32.2 ..	52.3	282 45.0 ..	45.2	331 32.1 ..	51.9	222 02.5 ..	49.3	Pollux	243 27.4	N27 59.3
04	98 38.4	195 31.8	52.5	297 46.1	44.7	346 34.5	51.9	237 04.6	49.3	Procyon	244 59.4	N 5 11.3
05	113 40.8	210 31.4	52.7	312 47.2	44.2	1 36.9	51.9	252 06.8	49.4			
06	128 43.3	225 31.1	S26 52.9	327 48.3	N 9 43.7	16 39.3	N21 51.9	267 09.0	S13 49.5	Rasalhague	96 06.5	N12 33.3
W 07	143 45.7	240 30.7	53.0	342 49.4	43.1	31 41.7	51.9	282 11.2	49.6	Regulus	207 43.4	N11 53.9
E 08	158 48.2	255 30.4	53.2	357 50.5	42.6	46 44.0	51.9	297 13.3	49.7	Rigel	281 11.6	S 8 11.2
D 09	173 50.7	270 30.0 ..	53.4	12 51.6 ..	42.1	61 46.4 ..	51.9	312 15.5 ..	49.8	Rigil Kent.	139 52.0	S60 53.4
N 10	188 53.1	285 29.6	53.6	27 52.7	41.6	76 48.8	51.9	327 17.7	49.9	Sabik	102 12.5	S15 44.3
E 11	203 55.6	300 29.3	53.8	42 53.7	41.0	91 51.2	51.9	342 19.8	50.0			
S 12	218 58.1	315 28.9	S26 54.0	57 54.8	N 9 40.5	106 53.6	N21 51.9	357 22.0	S13 50.1	Schedar	349 39.6	N56 37.0
D 13	234 00.5	330 28.6	54.1	72 55.9	40.0	121 56.0	51.9	12 24.2	50.2	Shaula	96 21.9	S37 06.7
A 14	249 03.0	345 28.2	54.3	87 57.0	39.5	136 58.4	51.9	27 26.4	50.3	Sirius	258 33.3	S16 44.1
Y 15	264 05.5	0 27.9 ..	54.5	102 58.1 ..	38.9	152 00.8 ..	51.9	42 28.5 ..	50.3	Spica	158 31.3	S11 13.9
16	279 07.9	15 27.5	54.7	117 59.2	38.4	167 03.2	51.9	57 30.7	50.4	Suhail	222 52.3	S43 29.2
17	294 10.4	30 27.2	54.9	133 00.3	37.9	182 05.6	51.9	72 32.9	50.5			
18	309 12.9	45 26.8	S26 55.0	148 01.4	N 9 37.4	197 08.0	N21 51.9	87 35.0	S13 50.6	Vega	80 39.0	N38 48.2
19	324 15.3	60 26.4	55.2	163 02.5	36.8	212 10.4	51.9	102 37.2	50.7	Zuben'ubi	137 05.5	S16 05.8
20	339 17.8	75 26.1	55.4	178 03.6	36.3	227 12.8	51.9	117 39.4	50.8		SHA	Mer.Pass.
21	354 20.2	90 25.7 ..	55.6	193 04.7 ..	35.8	242 15.2 ..	51.9	132 41.6 ..	50.9		° ′	h m
22	9 22.7	105 25.4	55.7	208 05.8	35.3	257 17.6	51.9	147 43.7	51.0	Venus	98 12.7	14 58
23	24 25.2	120 25.0	55.9	223 06.9	34.7	272 20.0	51.9	162 45.9	51.1	Mars	199 46.3	8 10
	h m									Jupiter	247 58.3	4 57
Mer. Pass. 21 26.5	v −0.4 d 0.2			v 1.1 d 0.5		v 2.4 d 0.0		v 2.2 d 0.1		Saturn	138 34.5	12 14

UT	SUN GHA	Dec	MOON GHA	v	Dec	d	HP
d h	° ′	° ′	° ′	′	° ′	′	′
28 00	184 02.9	S13 05.7	259 44.6	14.0	N11 04.1	8.4	54.7
01	199 03.0	06.6	274 17.6	14.1	10 55.7	8.5	54.7
02	214 03.0	07.4	288 50.7	14.0	10 47.2	8.5	54.7
03	229 03.1	.. 08.2	303 23.7	14.0	10 38.7	8.6	54.8
04	244 03.1	09.1	317 56.7	14.1	10 30.1	8.6	54.8
05	259 03.2	09.9	332 29.8	14.0	10 21.5	8.6	54.8
06	274 03.2	S13 10.8	347 02.8	14.1	N10 12.9	8.7	54.8
07	289 03.3	11.6	1 35.9	14.0	10 04.2	8.8	54.8
M 08	304 03.3	12.4	16 08.9	14.1	9 55.4	8.8	54.8
O 09	319 03.4	.. 13.3	30 42.0	14.1	9 46.6	8.9	54.9
N 10	334 03.4	14.1	45 15.1	14.1	9 37.7	8.9	54.9
D 11	349 03.5	14.9	59 48.2	14.0	9 28.8	9.0	54.9
A 12	4 03.5	S13 15.8	74 21.2	14.1	N 9 19.8	9.0	54.9
Y 13	19 03.5	16.6	88 54.3	14.1	9 10.8	9.0	55.0
14	34 03.6	17.4	103 27.4	14.1	9 01.8	9.1	55.0
15	49 03.6	.. 18.3	118 00.5	14.0	8 52.7	9.2	55.0
16	64 03.7	19.1	132 33.5	14.1	8 43.5	9.2	55.0
17	79 03.7	19.9	147 06.6	14.1	8 34.3	9.2	55.0
18	94 03.8	S13 20.8	161 39.7	14.1	N 8 25.1	9.3	55.1
19	109 03.8	21.6	176 12.8	14.0	8 15.8	9.3	55.1
20	124 03.9	22.4	190 45.8	14.1	8 06.5	9.4	55.1
21	139 03.9	.. 23.2	205 18.9	14.1	7 57.1	9.4	55.1
22	154 03.9	24.1	219 52.0	14.0	7 47.7	9.4	55.1
23	169 04.0	24.9	234 25.0	14.1	7 38.3	9.5	55.2
29 00	184 04.0	S13 25.7	248 58.1	14.0	N 7 28.8	9.6	55.2
01	199 04.1	26.6	263 31.1	14.1	7 19.2	9.5	55.2
02	214 04.1	27.4	278 04.2	14.0	7 09.7	9.7	55.2
03	229 04.2	.. 28.2	292 37.2	14.0	7 00.0	9.6	55.3
04	244 04.2	29.0	307 10.2	14.0	6 50.4	9.7	55.3
05	259 04.2	29.9	321 43.2	14.0	6 40.7	9.8	55.3
06	274 04.3	S13 30.7	336 16.2	14.0	N 6 30.9	9.7	55.3
07	289 04.3	31.5	350 49.2	14.0	6 21.2	9.8	55.4
T 08	304 04.4	32.4	5 22.2	14.0	6 11.4	9.9	55.4
U 09	319 04.4	.. 33.2	19 55.2	14.0	6 01.5	9.9	55.4
E 10	334 04.4	34.0	34 28.2	13.9	5 51.6	9.9	55.4
S 11	349 04.5	34.8	49 01.1	14.0	5 41.7	9.9	55.5
D 12	4 04.5	S13 35.7	63 34.1	13.9	N 5 31.8	10.0	55.5
A 13	19 04.5	36.5	78 07.0	13.9	5 21.8	10.0	55.5
Y 14	34 04.6	37.3	92 39.9	13.9	5 11.8	10.1	55.6
15	49 04.6	.. 38.1	107 12.8	13.9	5 01.7	10.1	55.6
16	64 04.7	39.0	121 45.7	13.9	4 51.6	10.1	55.6
17	79 04.7	39.8	136 18.6	13.8	4 41.5	10.2	55.6
18	94 04.7	S13 40.6	150 51.4	13.8	N 4 31.3	10.2	55.7
19	109 04.8	41.4	165 24.2	13.9	4 21.1	10.2	55.7
20	124 04.8	42.2	179 57.1	13.7	4 10.9	10.2	55.7
21	139 04.8	.. 43.1	194 29.8	13.8	4 00.7	10.3	55.7
22	154 04.9	43.9	209 02.6	13.8	3 50.4	10.3	55.8
23	169 04.9	44.7	223 35.4	13.7	3 40.1	10.3	55.8
30 00	184 04.9	S13 45.5	238 08.1	13.7	N 3 29.8	10.4	55.8
01	199 05.0	46.3	252 40.0	13.7	3 19.4	10.4	55.9
02	214 05.0	47.2	267 13.5	13.7	3 09.0	10.4	55.9
03	229 05.0	.. 48.0	281 46.2	13.6	2 58.6	10.4	55.9
04	244 05.1	48.8	296 18.8	13.6	2 48.2	10.5	55.9
05	259 05.1	49.6	310 51.4	13.6	2 37.7	10.4	56.0
06	274 05.1	S13 50.4	325 24.0	13.5	N 2 27.3	10.5	56.0
W 07	289 05.2	51.3	339 56.5	13.6	2 16.8	10.6	56.0
E 08	304 05.2	52.1	354 29.1	13.5	2 06.2	10.5	56.1
D 09	319 05.2	.. 52.9	9 01.6	13.5	1 55.7	10.6	56.1
N 10	334 05.3	53.7	23 34.1	13.4	1 45.1	10.6	56.1
E 11	349 05.3	54.5	38 06.5	13.4	1 34.5	10.6	56.2
S 12	4 05.3	S13 55.3	52 38.9	13.4	N 1 23.9	10.6	56.2
D 13	19 05.4	56.1	67 11.3	13.4	1 13.3	10.7	56.2
A 14	34 05.4	57.0	81 43.7	13.3	1 02.6	10.6	56.3
Y 15	49 05.4	.. 57.8	96 16.0	13.3	0 52.0	10.7	56.3
16	64 05.4	58.6	110 48.3	13.2	0 41.3	10.7	56.3
17	79 05.5	13 59.4	125 20.5	13.2	0 30.6	10.7	56.3
18	94 05.5	S14 00.2	139 52.7	13.2	N 0 19.9	10.8	56.4
19	109 05.5	01.0	154 24.9	13.2	N 0 09.1	10.7	56.4
20	124 05.6	01.8	168 57.1	13.1	S 0 01.6	10.8	56.4
21	139 05.6	.. 02.7	183 29.2	13.0	0 12.4	10.7	56.5
22	154 05.6	03.5	198 01.2	13.1	0 23.1	10.8	56.5
23	169 05.6	04.3	212 33.3	13.0	S 0 33.9	10.8	56.5
	SD 16.1	d 0.8	SD 15.0		15.1		15.3

Lat.	Twilight Naut.	Civil	Sunrise	Moonrise 28	29	30	31
°	h m	h m	h m	h m	h m	h m	h m
N 72	05 55	07 16	08 39	23 50	25 32	01 32	03 16
N 70	05 52	07 05	08 16	24 01	00 01	01 36	03 14
68	05 49	06 56	07 59	24 10	00 10	01 40	03 12
66	05 47	06 48	07 45	24 18	00 18	01 43	03 11
64	05 45	06 41	07 33	24 24	00 24	01 45	03 09
62	05 43	06 35	07 23	24 29	00 29	01 48	03 08
60	05 41	06 30	07 15	24 34	00 34	01 50	03 08
N 58	05 39	06 26	07 07	24 38	00 38	01 51	03 07
56	05 38	06 22	07 01	24 42	00 42	01 53	03 06
54	05 36	06 18	06 55	24 45	00 45	01 54	03 05
52	05 35	06 14	06 50	24 48	00 48	01 55	03 05
50	05 33	06 11	06 45	24 51	00 51	01 57	03 04
45	05 29	06 04	06 34	24 57	00 57	01 59	03 03
N 40	05 26	05 58	06 26	00 04	01 02	02 01	03 02
35	05 22	05 52	06 18	00 10	01 06	02 03	03 02
30	05 19	05 47	06 12	00 16	01 10	02 04	03 01
20	05 11	05 38	06 00	00 26	01 16	02 07	03 00
N 10	05 03	05 28	05 50	00 35	01 22	02 10	02 59
0	04 54	05 19	05 40	00 43	01 27	02 12	02 58
S 10	04 44	05 09	05 31	00 51	01 32	02 14	02 57
20	04 30	04 57	05 20	00 59	01 38	02 17	02 56
30	04 13	04 43	05 08	01 09	01 44	02 19	02 55
35	04 02	04 34	05 01	01 15	01 48	02 21	02 54
40	03 49	04 24	04 53	01 21	01 52	02 23	02 53
45	03 32	04 11	04 43	01 28	01 57	02 25	02 53
S 50	03 11	03 56	04 32	01 37	02 03	02 27	02 52
52	03 00	03 49	04 26	01 41	02 06	02 28	02 51
54	02 48	03 40	04 20	01 46	02 08	02 30	02 51
56	02 34	03 31	04 14	01 51	02 12	02 31	02 50
58	02 16	03 20	04 06	01 56	02 15	02 33	02 50
S 60	01 54	03 08	03 58	02 03	02 19	02 34	02 49

Lat.	Sunset	Twilight Civil	Naut.	Moonset 28	29	30	31
°	h m	h m	h m	h m	h m	h m	h m
N 72	14 47	16 10	17 31	15 01	14 53	14 44	14 36
N 70	15 10	16 21	17 34	14 48	14 46	14 43	14 40
68	15 27	16 30	17 37	14 38	14 40	14 42	14 44
66	15 41	16 38	17 39	14 29	14 36	14 42	14 48
64	15 53	16 45	17 41	14 21	14 32	14 41	14 50
62	16 03	16 51	17 43	14 15	14 28	14 40	14 53
60	16 12	16 56	17 45	14 09	14 25	14 40	14 55
N 58	16 19	17 01	17 47	14 04	14 22	14 39	14 57
56	16 26	17 05	17 49	14 00	14 20	14 39	14 59
54	16 32	17 09	17 50	13 56	14 18	14 39	15 00
52	16 37	17 12	17 52	13 52	14 16	14 38	15 01
50	16 42	17 16	17 54	13 49	14 14	14 38	15 03
45	16 52	17 23	17 57	13 42	14 10	14 37	15 06
N 40	17 01	17 29	18 01	13 36	14 06	14 37	15 08
35	17 09	17 35	18 05	13 31	14 03	14 36	15 10
30	17 15	17 40	18 08	13 26	14 01	14 36	15 12
20	17 27	17 50	18 16	13 18	13 56	14 35	15 15
N 10	17 37	17 59	18 24	13 11	13 52	14 34	15 18
0	17 47	18 08	18 33	13 04	13 49	14 34	15 20
S 10	17 57	18 19	18 44	12 57	13 45	14 33	15 23
20	18 08	18 31	18 57	12 50	13 41	14 32	15 25
30	18 20	18 45	19 15	12 42	13 36	14 31	15 29
35	18 27	18 54	19 26	12 37	13 33	14 31	15 30
40	18 35	19 04	19 39	12 32	13 30	14 30	15 32
45	18 45	19 17	19 56	12 25	13 26	14 30	15 35
S 50	18 57	19 33	20 18	12 18	13 22	14 29	15 37
52	19 02	19 40	20 29	12 14	13 20	14 28	15 39
54	19 08	19 49	20 41	12 10	13 18	14 28	15 40
56	19 15	19 58	20 56	12 06	13 15	14 27	15 42
58	19 23	20 09	21 14	12 01	13 13	14 27	15 43
S 60	19 31	20 22	21 37	11 55	13 10	14 26	15 45

Day	SUN Eqn. of Time 00h	12h	Mer. Pass.	MOON Mer. Pass. Upper	Lower	Age	Phase
d	m s	m s	h m	h m	h m	d %	
28	16 12	16 14	11 44	06 53	19 16	23 36	
29	16 16	16 18	11 44	07 38	20 00	24 27	
30	16 20	16 21	11 44	08 23	20 46	25 18	

UT	ARIES GHA	VENUS −4.5 GHA	Dec	MARS +1.5 GHA	Dec	JUPITER −2.4 GHA	Dec	SATURN +0.5 GHA	Dec	STARS Name	SHA	Dec
31 00	39 27.6	135 24.7	S26 56.1	238 08.0	N 9 34.2	287 22.4	N21 51.8	177 48.1	S13 51.2	Acamar	315 17.8	S40 14.9
01	54 30.1	150 24.3	56.2	253 09.0	33.7	302 24.8	51.8	192 50.2	51.2	Achernar	335 26.1	S57 10.0
02	69 32.6	165 24.0	56.4	268 10.1	33.2	317 27.2	51.8	207 52.4	51.3	Acrux	173 09.5	S63 10.4
03	84 35.0	180 23.6 ..	56.6	283 11.2 ..	32.6	332 29.6 ..	51.8	222 54.6 ..	51.4	Adhara	255 12.2	S28 59.4
04	99 37.5	195 23.3	56.7	298 12.3	32.1	347 32.0	51.8	237 56.7	51.5	Aldebaran	290 48.8	N16 32.1
05	114 40.0	210 22.9	56.9	313 13.4	31.6	2 34.4	51.8	252 58.9	51.6			
T 06	129 42.4	225 22.6	S26 57.1	328 14.5	N 9 31.1	17 36.8	N21 51.8	268 01.1	S13 51.7	Alioth	166 21.1	N55 53.0
H 07	144 44.9	240 22.3	57.2	343 15.6	30.5	32 39.2	51.8	283 03.3	51.8	Alkaid	152 59.2	N49 14.7
U 08	159 47.4	255 21.9	57.4	358 16.7	30.0	47 41.6	51.8	298 05.4	51.9	Al Na'ir	27 43.3	S46 53.7
R 09	174 49.8	270 21.6 ..	57.6	13 17.8 ..	29.5	62 44.0 ..	51.8	313 07.6 ..	52.0	Alnilam	275 45.9	S 1 11.6
S 10	189 52.3	285 21.2	57.7	28 18.9	29.0	77 46.4	51.8	328 09.8	52.1	Alphard	217 55.9	S 8 43.1
D 11	204 54.7	300 20.9	57.9	43 20.0	28.4	92 48.8	51.8	343 11.9	52.2			
A 12	219 57.2	315 20.5	S26 58.0	58 21.1	N 9 27.9	107 51.2	N21 51.8	358 14.1	S13 52.2	Alphecca	126 11.2	N26 40.3
Y 13	234 59.7	330 20.2	58.2	73 22.2	27.4	122 53.6	51.8	13 16.3	52.3	Alpheratz	357 42.9	N29 10.3
14	250 02.1	345 19.8	58.3	88 23.3	26.9	137 56.0	51.8	28 18.5	52.4	Altair	62 08.1	N 8 54.6
15	265 04.6	0 19.5 ..	58.5	103 24.4 ..	26.3	152 58.4 ..	51.8	43 20.6 ..	52.5	Ankaa	353 15.1	S42 13.9
16	280 07.1	15 19.2	58.6	118 25.5	25.8	168 00.8	51.8	58 22.8	52.6	Antares	112 26.3	S26 27.6
17	295 09.5	30 18.8	58.8	133 26.6	25.3	183 03.2	51.8	73 25.0	52.7			
18	310 12.0	45 18.5	S26 58.9	148 27.7	N 9 24.8	198 05.6	N21 51.8	88 27.1	S13 52.8	Arcturus	145 55.9	N19 06.8
19	325 14.5	60 18.1	59.1	163 28.8	24.2	213 08.1	51.8	103 29.3	52.9	Atria	107 28.3	S69 03.1
20	340 16.9	75 17.8	59.2	178 29.9	23.7	228 10.5	51.8	118 31.5	53.0	Avior	234 17.8	S59 33.1
21	355 19.4	90 17.5 ..	59.4	193 31.0 ..	23.2	243 12.9 ..	51.8	133 33.6 ..	53.1	Bellatrix	278 31.5	N 6 21.6
22	10 21.8	105 17.1	59.5	208 32.1	22.7	258 15.3	51.8	148 35.8	53.1	Betelgeuse	271 00.8	N 7 24.5
23	25 24.3	120 16.8	59.7	223 33.2	22.1	273 17.7	51.8	163 38.0	53.2			
1 00	40 26.8	135 16.4	S26 59.8	238 34.3	N 9 21.6	288 20.1	N21 51.8	178 40.2	S13 53.3	Canopus	263 55.7	S52 42.1
01	55 29.2	150 16.1	27 00.0	253 35.4	21.1	303 22.5	51.8	193 42.3	53.4	Capella	280 33.7	N46 00.5
02	70 31.7	165 15.8	00.1	268 36.5	20.6	318 24.9	51.8	208 44.5	53.5	Deneb	49 31.3	N45 20.3
03	85 34.2	180 15.4 ..	00.2	283 37.6 ..	20.0	333 27.3 ..	51.8	223 46.7 ..	53.6	Denebola	182 33.7	N14 29.7
04	100 36.6	195 15.1	00.4	298 38.7	19.5	348 29.7	51.8	238 48.8	53.7	Diphda	348 55.4	S17 54.6
05	115 39.1	210 14.8	00.5	313 39.8	19.0	3 32.1	51.8	253 51.0	53.8			
F 06	130 41.6	225 14.4	S27 00.7	328 40.9	N 9 18.5	18 34.5	N21 51.8	268 53.2	S13 53.9	Dubhe	193 51.9	N61 40.3
R 07	145 44.0	240 14.1	00.8	343 42.0	17.9	33 37.0	51.8	283 55.3	54.0	Elnath	278 12.0	N28 37.0
I 08	160 46.5	255 13.8	00.9	358 43.1	17.4	48 39.4	51.7	298 57.5	54.0	Eltanin	90 46.4	N51 29.6
D 09	175 49.0	270 13.4 ..	01.1	13 44.2 ..	16.9	63 41.8 ..	51.7	313 59.7 ..	54.1	Enif	33 46.8	N 9 56.6
A 10	190 51.4	285 13.1	01.2	28 45.3	16.4	78 44.2	51.7	329 01.9	54.2	Fomalhaut	15 23.5	S29 32.9
Y 11	205 53.9	300 12.8	01.3	43 46.4	15.8	93 46.6	51.7	344 04.0	54.3			
12	220 56.3	315 12.5	S27 01.5	58 47.5	N 9 15.3	108 49.0	N21 51.7	359 06.2	S13 54.4	Gacrux	172 01.0	S57 11.3
13	235 58.8	330 12.1	01.6	73 48.6	14.8	123 51.4	51.7	14 08.4	54.5	Gienah	175 52.3	S17 37.0
14	251 01.3	345 11.8	01.7	88 49.7	14.3	138 53.8	51.7	29 10.5	54.6	Hadar	148 48.1	S60 26.2
15	266 03.7	0 11.5 ..	01.9	103 50.8 ..	13.7	153 56.3 ..	51.7	44 12.7 ..	54.7	Hamal	328 00.1	N23 31.7
16	281 06.2	15 11.1	02.0	118 51.9	13.2	168 58.7	51.7	59 14.9	54.8	Kaus Aust.	83 43.7	S34 22.5
17	296 08.7	30 10.8	02.1	133 53.0	12.7	184 01.1	51.7	74 17.0	54.9			
18	311 11.1	45 10.5	S27 02.2	148 54.1	N 9 12.2	199 03.5	N21 51.7	89 19.2	S13 55.0	Kochab	137 21.3	N74 06.0
19	326 13.6	60 10.2	02.4	163 55.2	11.6	214 05.9	51.7	104 21.4	55.0	Markab	13 37.9	N15 17.1
20	341 16.1	75 09.8	02.5	178 56.3	11.1	229 08.3	51.7	119 23.6	55.1	Menkar	314 14.5	N 4 08.7
21	356 18.5	90 09.5 ..	02.6	193 57.4 ..	10.6	244 10.7 ..	51.7	134 25.7 ..	55.2	Menkent	148 07.6	S36 26.1
22	11 21.0	105 09.2	02.7	208 58.5	10.1	259 13.2	51.7	149 27.9	55.3	Miaplacidus	221 39.6	S69 46.2
23	26 23.4	120 08.9	02.8	223 59.6	09.5	274 15.6	51.7	164 30.1	55.4			
2 00	41 25.9	135 08.6	S27 03.0	239 00.7	N 9 09.0	289 18.0	N21 51.7	179 32.2	S13 55.5	Mirfak	308 39.5	N49 54.5
01	56 28.4	150 08.2	03.1	254 01.8	08.5	304 20.4	51.7	194 34.4	55.6	Nunki	75 58.2	S26 16.6
02	71 30.8	165 07.9	03.2	269 02.9	08.0	319 22.8	51.7	209 36.6	55.7	Peacock	53 19.0	S56 41.5
03	86 33.3	180 07.6 ..	03.3	284 04.0 ..	07.4	334 25.3 ..	51.7	224 38.7 ..	55.8	Pollux	243 27.3	N27 59.3
04	101 35.8	195 07.3	03.4	299 05.1	06.9	349 27.7	51.7	239 40.9	55.9	Procyon	244 59.4	N 5 11.3
05	116 38.2	210 07.0	03.5	314 06.2	06.4	4 30.1	51.7	254 43.1	55.9			
S 06	131 40.7	225 06.6	S27 03.6	329 07.3	N 9 05.9	19 32.5	N21 51.7	269 45.3	S13 56.0	Rasalhague	96 06.5	N12 33.3
A 07	146 43.2	240 06.3	03.8	344 08.4	05.3	34 34.9	51.7	284 47.4	56.1	Regulus	207 43.4	N11 53.9
T 08	161 45.6	255 06.0	03.9	359 09.5	04.8	49 37.3	51.7	299 49.6	56.2	Rigel	281 11.6	S 8 11.2
U 09	176 48.1	270 05.7 ..	04.0	14 10.6 ..	04.3	64 39.8 ..	51.7	314 51.8 ..	56.3	Rigil Kent.	139 52.0	S60 53.4
R 10	191 50.6	285 05.4	04.1	29 11.7	03.8	79 42.2	51.7	329 53.9	56.4	Sabik	102 12.5	S15 44.3
D 11	206 53.0	300 05.1	04.2	44 12.8	03.2	94 44.6	51.7	344 56.1	56.5			
A 12	221 55.5	315 04.7	S27 04.3	59 13.9	N 9 02.7	109 47.0	N21 51.7	359 58.3	S13 56.6	Schedar	349 39.7	N56 37.0
Y 13	236 57.9	330 04.4	04.4	74 15.0	02.2	124 49.5	51.7	15 00.4	56.7	Shaula	96 21.9	S37 06.7
14	252 00.4	345 04.1	04.5	89 16.1	01.7	139 51.9	51.7	30 02.6	56.8	Sirius	258 33.3	S16 44.1
15	267 02.9	0 03.8 ..	04.6	104 17.2 ..	01.1	154 54.3 ..	51.7	45 04.8 ..	56.8	Spica	158 31.3	S11 13.9
16	282 05.3	15 03.5	04.7	119 18.4	00.6	169 56.7	51.7	60 07.0	56.9	Suhail	222 52.3	S43 29.2
17	297 07.8	30 03.2	04.8	134 19.5	9 00.1	184 59.1	51.7	75 09.1	57.0			
18	312 10.3	45 02.9	S27 04.9	149 20.6	N 8 59.5	200 01.6	N21 51.7	90 11.3	S13 57.1	Vega	80 39.0	N38 48.2
19	327 12.7	60 02.6	05.0	164 21.7	59.0	215 04.0	51.7	105 13.5	57.2	Zuben'ubi	137 05.5	S16 05.8
20	342 15.2	75 02.3	05.1	179 22.8	58.5	230 06.4	51.7	120 15.6	57.3		SHA	Mer.Pass.
21	357 17.7	90 02.0 ..	05.2	194 23.9 ..	58.0	245 08.8 ..	51.7	135 17.8 ..	57.4	Venus	94 49.7	14 59
22	12 20.1	105 01.6	05.3	209 25.0	57.4	260 11.3	51.7	150 20.0	57.5	Mars	198 07.5	8 05
23	27 22.6	120 01.3	05.4	224 26.1	56.9	275 13.7	51.7	165 22.1	57.6	Jupiter	247 53.3	4 46
Mer.Pass. 21 14.7		v −0.3	d 0.1	v 1.1	d 0.5	v 2.4	d 0.0	v 2.2	d 0.1	Saturn	138 13.4	12 04

UT	SUN GHA	SUN Dec	MOON GHA	v	MOON Dec	d	HP
d h	° ′	° ′	° ′	′	° ′	′	′
31 00	184 05.7	S14 05.1	227 05.3	12.9	S 0 44.7	10.8	56.6
01	199 05.7	05.9	241 37.2	12.9	0 55.5	10.8	56.6
02	214 05.7	06.7	256 09.1	12.9	1 06.3	10.8	56.6
03	229 05.7	.. 07.5	270 41.0	12.8	1 17.1	10.8	56.7
04	244 05.8	08.3	285 12.8	12.8	1 27.9	10.9	56.7
05	259 05.8	09.1	299 44.6	12.8	1 38.8	10.8	56.7
06	274 05.8	S14 09.9	314 16.4	12.7	S 1 49.6	10.8	56.8
07	289 05.8	10.8	328 48.1	12.6	2 00.4	10.9	56.8
T 08	304 05.8	11.6	343 19.7	12.6	2 11.3	10.8	56.8
H 09	319 05.9	.. 12.4	357 51.3	12.6	2 22.1	10.9	56.9
U 10	334 05.9	13.2	12 22.9	12.5	2 33.0	10.8	56.9
R 11	349 05.9	14.0	26 54.4	12.5	2 43.8	10.9	56.9
S 12	4 05.9	S14 14.8	41 25.9	12.4	S 2 54.7	10.8	57.0
D 13	19 06.0	15.6	55 57.3	12.4	3 05.5	10.9	57.0
A 14	34 06.0	16.4	70 28.7	12.3	3 16.4	10.8	57.0
Y 15	49 06.0	.. 17.2	85 00.0	12.3	3 27.2	10.9	57.1
16	64 06.0	18.0	99 31.2	12.3	3 38.1	10.8	57.1
17	79 06.0	18.8	114 02.5	12.1	3 48.9	10.8	57.1
18	94 06.1	S14 19.6	128 33.6	12.1	S 3 59.7	10.9	57.2
19	109 06.1	20.4	143 04.7	12.1	4 10.6	10.8	57.2
20	124 06.1	21.2	157 35.8	12.0	4 21.4	10.8	57.2
21	139 06.1	.. 22.0	172 06.8	12.0	4 32.2	10.8	57.3
22	154 06.1	22.8	186 37.8	11.9	4 43.0	10.7	57.3
23	169 06.2	23.6	201 08.7	11.8	4 53.8	10.7	57.3
1 00	184 06.2	S14 24.4	215 39.5	11.8	S 5 04.5	10.8	57.4
01	199 06.2	25.2	230 10.3	11.7	5 15.3	10.8	57.4
02	214 06.2	26.0	244 41.0	11.7	5 26.1	10.7	57.4
03	229 06.2	.. 26.8	259 11.7	11.6	5 36.8	10.7	57.5
04	244 06.2	27.6	273 42.3	11.5	5 47.5	10.7	57.5
05	259 06.3	28.4	288 12.8	11.5	5 58.2	10.7	57.5
06	274 06.3	S14 29.2	302 43.3	11.4	S 6 08.9	10.7	57.6
07	289 06.3	30.0	317 13.7	11.4	6 19.6	10.6	57.6
08	304 06.3	30.8	331 44.1	11.3	6 30.2	10.7	57.6
F 09	319 06.3	.. 31.6	346 14.4	11.3	6 40.9	10.6	57.7
R 10	334 06.3	32.4	0 44.7	11.1	6 51.5	10.6	57.7
I 11	349 06.3	33.2	15 14.8	11.2	7 02.1	10.5	57.7
D 12	4 06.3	S14 34.0	29 45.0	11.0	S 7 12.6	10.6	57.8
A 13	19 06.4	34.8	44 15.0	11.0	7 23.2	10.5	57.8
Y 14	34 06.4	35.6	58 45.0	10.9	7 33.7	10.4	57.8
15	49 06.4	.. 36.4	73 14.9	10.9	7 44.1	10.5	57.9
16	64 06.4	37.2	87 44.8	10.8	7 54.6	10.4	57.9
17	79 06.4	38.0	102 14.6	10.7	8 05.0	10.4	57.9
18	94 06.4	S14 38.8	116 44.3	10.7	S 8 15.4	10.4	58.0
19	109 06.4	39.6	131 14.0	10.6	8 25.8	10.3	58.0
20	124 06.4	40.4	145 43.6	10.5	8 36.1	10.3	58.0
21	139 06.5	.. 41.2	160 13.1	10.4	8 46.4	10.2	58.1
22	154 06.5	42.0	174 42.5	10.4	8 56.6	10.3	58.1
23	169 06.5	42.8	189 11.9	10.3	9 06.9	10.1	58.1
2 00	184 06.5	S14 43.6	203 41.2	10.3	S 9 17.0	10.2	58.1
01	199 06.5	44.3	218 10.5	10.2	9 27.2	10.1	58.2
02	214 06.5	45.1	232 39.7	10.1	9 37.3	10.0	58.2
03	229 06.5	.. 45.9	247 08.8	10.0	9 47.3	10.0	58.2
04	244 06.5	46.7	261 37.8	10.0	9 57.3	10.0	58.3
05	259 06.5	47.5	276 06.8	9.9	10 07.3	9.9	58.3
06	274 06.5	S14 48.3	290 35.7	9.8	S10 17.2	9.9	58.3
07	289 06.5	49.1	305 04.5	9.7	10 27.1	9.8	58.4
S 08	304 06.5	49.9	319 33.2	9.7	10 36.9	9.8	58.4
A 09	319 06.5	.. 50.7	334 01.9	9.6	10 46.7	9.8	58.4
T 10	334 06.5	51.4	348 30.5	9.5	10 56.5	9.6	58.5
U 11	349 06.6	52.2	2 59.0	9.5	11 06.1	9.7	58.5
R 12	4 06.6	S14 53.0	17 27.5	9.4	S11 15.8	9.5	58.5
D 13	19 06.6	53.8	31 55.9	9.3	11 25.3	9.5	58.5
A 14	34 06.6	54.6	46 24.2	9.2	11 34.8	9.5	58.6
Y 15	49 06.6	.. 55.4	60 52.4	9.2	11 44.3	9.4	58.6
16	64 06.6	56.2	75 20.6	9.1	11 53.7	9.3	58.6
17	79 06.6	56.9	89 48.7	9.0	12 03.0	9.3	58.7
18	94 06.6	S14 57.7	104 16.7	8.9	S12 12.3	9.2	58.7
19	109 06.6	58.5	118 44.6	8.9	12 21.5	9.2	58.7
20	124 06.6	14 59.3	133 12.5	8.8	12 30.7	9.1	58.7
21	139 06.6	15 00.1	147 40.3	8.7	12 39.8	9.0	58.8
22	154 06.6	00.9	162 08.0	8.6	12 48.8	8.9	58.8
23	169 06.6	01.6	176 35.6	8.6	S12 57.7	8.9	58.8
	SD 16.1	d 0.8	SD 15.5		15.7		15.9

Twilight — Sunrise — Moonrise

Lat.	Naut.	Civil	Sunrise	31	1	2	3
°	h m	h m	h m	h m	h m	h m	h m
N 72	06 07	07 30	08 58	03 16	05 04	07 00	09 08
N 70	06 02	07 17	08 31	03 14	04 55	06 42	08 35
68	05 59	07 06	08 11	03 12	04 48	06 28	08 12
66	05 56	06 57	07 56	03 11	04 42	06 16	07 54
64	05 53	06 50	07 43	03 09	04 37	06 07	07 39
62	05 50	06 43	07 32	03 08	04 32	05 59	07 27
60	05 48	06 37	07 22	03 08	04 28	05 52	07 17
N 58	05 45	06 32	07 14	03 07	04 25	05 46	07 08
56	05 43	06 27	07 07	03 06	04 22	05 40	07 00
54	05 41	06 23	07 01	03 05	04 19	05 35	06 53
52	05 39	06 19	06 55	03 05	04 17	05 31	06 47
50	05 38	06 16	06 50	03 04	04 14	05 27	06 41
45	05 33	06 08	06 38	03 03	04 10	05 18	06 29
N 40	05 29	06 01	06 29	03 02	04 06	05 11	06 19
35	05 25	05 55	06 21	03 02	04 02	05 05	06 10
30	05 21	05 49	06 14	03 01	03 59	05 00	06 03
20	05 13	05 39	06 01	03 00	03 54	04 51	05 50
N 10	05 04	05 29	05 51	02 59	03 49	04 43	05 39
0	04 54	05 19	05 40	02 58	03 45	04 35	05 28
S 10	04 42	05 08	05 30	02 57	03 41	04 28	05 18
20	04 28	04 55	05 18	02 56	03 37	04 20	05 07
30	04 10	04 40	05 05	02 55	03 32	04 11	04 55
35	03 58	04 31	04 58	02 54	03 29	04 06	04 47
40	03 44	04 20	04 49	02 53	03 26	04 00	04 39
45	03 27	04 07	04 39	02 53	03 22	03 54	04 30
S 50	03 04	03 50	04 26	02 52	03 17	03 46	04 18
52	02 53	03 42	04 21	02 51	03 15	03 42	04 13
54	02 39	03 33	04 14	02 51	03 13	03 38	04 07
56	02 24	03 23	04 07	02 50	03 11	03 34	04 01
58	02 04	03 11	03 59	02 50	03 08	03 29	03 54
S 60	01 39	02 58	03 50	02 49	03 05	03 23	03 46

Sunset — Twilight — Moonset

Lat.	Sunset	Civil	Naut.	31	1	2	3
°	h m	h m	h m	h m	h m	h m	h m
N 72	14 28	15 56	17 19	14 36	14 26	14 15	14 00
N 70	14 55	16 09	17 23	14 40	14 38	14 35	14 33
68	15 15	16 20	17 27	14 44	14 47	14 51	14 58
66	15 30	16 29	17 30	14 48	14 55	15 04	15 17
64	15 43	16 36	17 33	14 50	15 01	15 14	15 32
62	15 54	16 43	17 36	14 53	15 07	15 23	15 45
60	16 04	16 49	17 38	14 55	15 12	15 31	15 56
N 58	16 12	16 54	17 41	14 57	15 16	15 38	16 06
56	16 19	16 59	17 43	14 59	15 20	15 44	16 14
54	16 26	17 03	17 45	15 00	15 23	15 50	16 22
52	16 31	17 07	17 47	15 01	15 27	15 55	16 29
50	16 37	17 11	17 49	15 03	15 29	16 00	16 35
45	16 48	17 19	17 53	15 06	15 36	16 09	16 48
N 40	16 58	17 26	17 58	15 08	15 41	16 18	16 59
35	17 06	17 32	18 02	15 10	15 46	16 25	17 09
30	17 13	17 38	18 06	15 12	15 50	16 31	17 16
20	17 25	17 48	18 14	15 15	15 57	16 42	17 31
N 10	17 37	17 58	18 23	15 18	16 03	16 51	17 43
0	17 47	18 08	18 33	15 20	16 09	17 00	17 55
S 10	17 58	18 19	18 45	15 23	16 15	17 09	18 06
20	18 09	18 32	18 59	15 25	16 21	17 19	18 19
30	18 22	18 48	19 18	15 29	16 28	17 30	18 33
35	18 30	18 57	19 29	15 30	16 32	17 36	18 42
40	18 39	19 08	19 44	15 32	16 37	17 43	18 51
45	18 49	19 22	20 01	15 35	16 42	17 52	19 02
S 50	19 02	19 38	20 25	15 37	16 49	18 02	19 16
52	19 08	19 46	20 36	15 39	16 52	18 06	19 22
54	19 14	19 55	20 50	15 40	16 55	18 12	19 29
56	19 22	20 06	21 06	15 42	16 59	18 17	19 37
58	19 30	20 18	21 26	15 43	17 03	18 24	19 46
S 60	19 39	20 32	21 52	15 45	17 07	18 31	19 56

SUN and MOON

Day	Eqn. of Time 00h	Eqn. of Time 12h	Mer. Pass.	Mer. Pass. Upper	Mer. Pass. Lower	Age	Phase
d	m s	m s	h m	h m	h m	d	%
31	16 23	16 24	11 44	09 09	21 33	26	11
1	16 25	16 25	11 44	09 57	22 22	27	5
2	16 26	16 26	11 44	10 48	23 14	28	1 ●

2013 NOVEMBER 3, 4, 5 (SUN., MON., TUES.)

UT	ARIES GHA	VENUS −4.6 GHA	Dec	MARS +1.5 GHA	Dec	JUPITER −2.4 GHA	Dec	SATURN +0.5 GHA	Dec	Name	SHA	Dec
d h	° ′	° ′	° ′	° ′	° ′	° ′	° ′	° ′	° ′		° ′	° ′
3 00	42 25.1	135 01.0	S27 05.5	239 27.2	N 8 56.4	290 16.1	N21 51.7	180 24.3	S13 57.7	Acamar	315 17.7	S40 15.0
01	57 27.5	150 00.7	05.6	254 28.3	55.9	305 18.5	51.7	195 26.5	57.7	Achernar	335 26.1	S57 10.0
02	72 30.0	165 00.4	05.7	269 29.4	55.3	320 21.0	51.7	210 28.6	57.8	Acrux	173 09.5	S63 10.4
03	87 32.4	180 00.1 ..	05.8	284 30.5 ..	54.8	335 23.4 ..	51.7	225 30.8 ..	57.9	Adhara	255 12.1	S28 59.4
04	102 34.9	194 59.8	05.8	299 31.6	54.3	350 25.8	51.7	240 33.0	58.0	Aldebaran	290 48.8	N16 32.1
05	117 37.4	209 59.5	05.9	314 32.7	53.8	5 28.3	51.7	255 35.2	58.1			
06	132 39.8	224 59.2	S27 06.0	329 33.9	N 8 53.2	20 30.7	N21 51.7	270 37.3	S13 58.2	Alioth	166 21.0	N55 53.0
07	147 42.3	239 58.9	06.1	344 35.0	52.7	35 33.1	51.7	285 39.5	58.3	Alkaid	152 59.2	N49 14.7
08	162 44.8	254 58.6	06.2	359 36.1	52.2	50 35.5	51.7	300 41.7	58.4	Al Na'ir	27 43.3	S46 53.7
09	177 47.2	269 58.3 ..	06.3	14 37.2 ..	51.7	65 38.0 ..	51.7	315 43.8 ..	58.5	Alnilam	275 45.9	S 1 11.7
10	192 49.7	284 58.0	06.4	29 38.3	51.1	80 40.4	51.7	330 46.0	58.6	Alphard	217 55.9	S 8 43.1
11	207 52.2	299 57.7	06.4	44 39.4	50.6	95 42.8	51.7	345 48.2	58.6			
12	222 54.6	314 57.4	S27 06.5	59 40.5	N 8 50.1	110 45.3	N21 51.7	0 50.3	S13 58.7	Alphecca	126 11.2	N26 40.3
13	237 57.1	329 57.1	06.6	74 41.6	49.6	125 47.7	51.7	15 52.5	58.8	Alpheratz	357 42.9	N29 10.3
14	252 59.5	344 56.8	06.7	89 42.7	49.0	140 50.1	51.7	30 54.7	58.9	Altair	62 08.1	N 8 54.6
15	268 02.0	359 56.5 ..	06.8	104 43.8 ..	48.5	155 52.5 ..	51.7	45 56.8 ..	59.0	Ankaa	353 15.1	S42 13.9
16	283 04.5	14 56.2	06.8	119 45.0	48.0	170 55.0	51.7	60 59.0	59.1	Antares	112 26.3	S26 27.6
17	298 06.9	29 55.9	06.9	134 46.1	47.5	185 57.4	51.7	76 01.2	59.2			
18	313 09.4	44 55.7	S27 07.0	149 47.2	N 8 46.9	200 59.8	N21 51.7	91 03.4	S13 59.3	Arcturus	145 55.9	N19 06.7
19	328 11.9	59 55.4	07.1	164 48.3	46.4	216 02.3	51.7	106 05.5	59.4	Atria	107 28.3	S69 03.1
20	343 14.3	74 55.1	07.1	179 49.4	45.9	231 04.7	51.7	121 07.7	59.4	Avior	234 17.8	S59 33.1
21	358 16.8	89 54.8 ..	07.2	194 50.5 ..	45.3	246 07.1 ..	51.7	136 09.9 ..	59.5	Bellatrix	278 31.5	N 6 21.6
22	13 19.3	104 54.5	07.3	209 51.6	44.8	261 09.6	51.7	151 12.0	59.6	Betelgeuse	271 00.8	N 7 24.5
23	28 21.7	119 54.2	07.3	224 52.7	44.3	276 12.0	51.7	166 14.2	59.7			
4 00	43 24.2	134 53.9	S27 07.4	239 53.8	N 8 43.8	291 14.4	N21 51.7	181 16.4	S13 59.8	Canopus	263 55.7	S52 42.1
01	58 26.7	149 53.6	07.5	254 55.0	43.2	306 16.9	51.7	196 18.5	13 59.9	Capella	280 33.7	N46 00.5
02	73 29.1	164 53.3	07.5	269 56.1	42.7	321 19.3	51.7	211 20.7	14 00.0	Deneb	49 31.3	N45 20.3
03	88 31.6	179 53.0 ..	07.6	284 57.2 ..	42.2	336 21.8 ..	51.7	226 22.9 ..	00.1	Denebola	182 33.6	N14 29.6
04	103 34.0	194 52.8	07.7	299 58.3	41.7	351 24.2	51.7	241 25.0	00.2	Diphda	348 55.4	S17 54.6
05	118 36.5	209 52.5	07.7	314 59.4	41.1	6 26.6	51.7	256 27.2	00.3			
06	133 39.0	224 52.2	S27 07.8	330 00.5	N 8 40.6	21 29.1	N21 51.7	271 29.4	S14 00.3	Dubhe	193 51.8	N61 40.3
07	148 41.4	239 51.9	07.8	345 01.6	40.1	36 31.5	51.7	286 31.6	00.4	Elnath	278 12.0	N28 37.0
08	163 43.9	254 51.6	07.9	0 02.7	39.6	51 33.9	51.7	301 33.7	00.5	Eltanin	90 46.4	N51 29.6
09	178 46.4	269 51.3 ..	08.0	15 03.9 ..	39.0	66 36.4 ..	51.7	316 35.9 ..	00.6	Enif	33 46.8	N 9 56.6
10	193 48.8	284 51.1	08.0	30 05.0	38.5	81 38.8	51.7	331 38.1	00.7	Fomalhaut	15 23.5	S29 32.9
11	208 51.3	299 50.8	08.1	45 06.1	38.0	96 41.3	51.7	346 40.2	00.8			
12	223 53.8	314 50.5	S27 08.1	60 07.2	N 8 37.5	111 43.7	N21 51.7	1 42.4	S14 00.9	Gacrux	172 01.0	S57 11.3
13	238 56.2	329 50.2	08.2	75 08.3	36.9	126 46.1	51.7	16 44.6	01.0	Gienah	175 52.3	S17 37.0
14	253 58.7	344 50.0	08.2	90 09.4	36.4	141 48.6	51.7	31 46.7	01.1	Hadar	148 48.1	S60 26.2
15	269 01.2	359 49.7 ..	08.3	105 10.5 ..	35.9	156 51.0 ..	51.7	46 48.9 ..	01.2	Hamal	328 00.1	N23 31.7
16	284 03.6	14 49.4	08.3	120 11.7	35.3	171 53.4	51.7	61 51.1	01.2	Kaus Aust.	83 43.7	S34 22.5
17	299 06.1	29 49.1	08.4	135 12.8	34.8	186 55.9	51.7	76 53.2	01.3			
18	314 08.5	44 48.8	S27 08.4	150 13.9	N 8 34.3	201 58.3	N21 51.7	91 55.4	S14 01.4	Kochab	137 21.3	N74 06.0
19	329 11.0	59 48.6	08.5	165 15.0	33.8	217 00.8	51.7	106 57.6	01.5	Markab	13 37.9	N15 17.1
20	344 13.5	74 48.3	08.5	180 16.1	33.2	232 03.2	51.7	121 59.8	01.6	Menkar	314 14.5	N 4 08.7
21	359 15.9	89 48.0 ..	08.6	195 17.2 ..	32.7	247 05.7 ..	51.7	137 01.9 ..	01.7	Menkent	148 07.6	S36 26.1
22	14 18.4	104 47.8	08.6	210 18.4	32.2	262 08.1	51.7	152 04.1	01.8	Miaplacidus	221 39.6	S69 46.2
23	29 20.9	119 47.5	08.7	225 19.5	31.7	277 10.5	51.7	167 06.3	01.9			
5 00	44 23.3	134 47.2	S27 08.7	240 20.6	N 8 31.1	292 13.0	N21 51.7	182 08.4	S14 02.0	Mirfak	308 39.4	N49 54.5
01	59 25.8	149 47.0	08.7	255 21.7	30.6	307 15.4	51.7	197 10.6	02.0	Nunki	75 58.2	S26 16.6
02	74 28.3	164 46.7	08.8	270 22.8	30.1	322 17.9	51.7	212 12.8	02.1	Peacock	53 19.0	S56 41.5
03	89 30.7	179 46.4 ..	08.8	285 23.9 ..	29.6	337 20.3 ..	51.8	227 14.9 ..	02.2	Pollux	243 27.3	N27 59.3
04	104 33.2	194 46.1	08.9	300 25.1	29.0	352 22.8	51.8	242 17.1	02.3	Procyon	244 59.4	N 5 11.2
05	119 35.6	209 45.9	08.9	315 26.2	28.5	7 25.2	51.8	257 19.3	02.4			
06	134 38.1	224 45.6	S27 08.9	330 27.3	N 8 28.0	22 27.7	N21 51.8	272 21.4	S14 02.5	Rasalhague	96 06.5	N12 33.3
07	149 40.6	239 45.4	09.0	345 28.4	27.5	37 30.1	51.8	287 23.6	02.6	Regulus	207 43.4	N11 53.9
08	164 43.0	254 45.1	09.0	0 29.5	26.9	52 32.5	51.8	302 25.8	02.7	Rigel	281 11.5	S 8 11.2
09	179 45.5	269 44.8 ..	09.1	15 30.7 ..	26.4	67 35.0 ..	51.8	317 28.0 ..	02.8	Rigil Kent.	139 52.0	S60 53.4
10	194 48.0	284 44.6	09.1	30 31.8	25.9	82 37.4	51.8	332 30.1	02.8	Sabik	102 12.5	S15 44.3
11	209 50.4	299 44.3	09.1	45 32.9	25.3	97 39.9	51.8	347 32.3	02.9			
12	224 52.9	314 44.0	S27 09.1	60 34.0	N 8 24.8	112 42.3	N21 51.8	2 34.5	S14 03.0	Schedar	349 39.7	N56 37.0
13	239 55.4	329 43.8	09.2	75 35.1	24.3	127 44.8	51.8	17 36.6	03.1	Shaula	96 21.9	S37 06.7
14	254 57.8	344 43.5	09.2	90 36.2	23.8	142 47.2	51.8	32 38.8	03.2	Sirius	258 33.3	S16 44.1
15	270 00.3	359 43.3 ..	09.2	105 37.4 ..	23.2	157 49.7 ..	51.8	47 41.0 ..	03.3	Spica	158 31.3	S11 13.9
16	285 02.8	14 43.0	09.3	120 38.5	22.7	172 52.1	51.8	62 43.1	03.4	Suhail	222 52.2	S43 29.2
17	300 05.2	29 42.8	09.3	135 39.6	22.2	187 54.6	51.8	77 45.3	03.5			
18	315 07.7	44 42.5	S27 09.3	150 40.7	N 8 21.7	202 57.0	N21 51.8	92 47.5	S14 03.6	Vega	80 39.0	N38 48.2
19	330 10.1	59 42.3	09.3	165 41.8	21.1	217 59.5	51.8	107 49.6	03.7	Zuben'ubi	137 05.5	S16 05.8
20	345 12.6	74 42.0	09.4	180 43.0	20.6	233 01.9	51.8	122 51.8	03.7		SHA	Mer. Pass.
21	0 15.1	89 41.7 ..	09.4	195 44.1 ..	20.1	248 04.4 ..	51.8	137 54.0 ..	03.8		° ′	h m
22	15 17.5	104 41.5	09.4	210 45.2	19.6	263 06.8	51.8	152 56.1	03.9	Venus	91 29.7	15 01
23	30 20.0	119 41.2	09.4	225 46.3	19.0	278 09.3	51.8	167 58.3	04.0	Mars	196 29.7	8 00
	h m									Jupiter	247 50.3	4 34
Mer. Pass. 21 02.9		v −0.3	d 0.1	v 1.1	d 0.5	v 2.4	d 0.0	v 2.2	d 0.1	Saturn	137 52.2	11 53

UT	SUN GHA	SUN Dec	MOON GHA	v	MOON Dec	d	HP
d h	° ′	° ′	° ′	′	° ′	′	′
3 00	184 06.6	S15 02.4	191 03.2	8.5	S13 06.6	8.8	58.9
01	199 06.6	03.2	205 30.7	8.4	13 15.4	8.8	58.9
02	214 06.6	04.0	219 58.1	8.3	13 24.2	8.7	58.9
03	229 06.6	.. 04.8	234 25.4	8.3	13 32.9	8.6	58.9
04	244 06.6	05.5	248 52.7	8.2	13 41.5	8.5	59.0
05	259 06.6	06.3	263 19.9	8.1	13 50.0	8.4	59.0
06	274 06.6	S15 07.1	277 47.0	8.0	S13 58.4	8.4	59.0
07	289 06.6	07.9	292 14.0	8.0	14 06.8	8.3	59.0
08	304 06.6	08.7	306 41.0	7.9	14 15.1	8.2	59.1
S 09	319 06.6	.. 09.4	321 07.9	7.8	14 23.3	8.1	59.1
U 10	334 06.6	10.2	335 34.7	7.8	14 31.4	8.0	59.1
N 11	349 06.6	11.0	350 01.5	7.6	S14 39.4	8.0	59.1
D 12	4 06.6	S15 11.8					
A 13	19 06.6	12.6					
Y 14	34 06.6	13.3	A total eclipse of				
15	49 06.5	.. 14.1	the Sun occurs on this				
16	64 06.5	14.9	date. See page 5.				
17	79 06.5	15.7					
18	94 06.5	S15 16.4	91 06.7	7.2	S15 33.3	7.3	59.3
19	109 06.5	17.2	105 32.9	7.1	15 40.6	7.3	59.3
20	124 06.5	18.0	119 59.0	7.0	15 47.9	7.1	59.3
21	139 06.5	.. 18.7	134 25.0	7.0	15 55.0	7.1	59.4
22	154 06.5	19.5	148 51.0	6.9	16 02.1	6.9	59.4
23	169 06.5	20.3	163 16.9	6.8	16 09.0	6.8	59.4
4 00	184 06.5	S15 21.1	177 42.7	6.8	S16 15.8	6.8	59.4
01	199 06.5	21.8	192 08.5	6.7	16 22.6	6.6	59.5
02	214 06.5	22.6	206 34.2	6.6	16 29.2	6.6	59.5
03	229 06.5	.. 23.4	220 59.8	6.6	16 35.8	6.4	59.5
04	244 06.5	24.1	235 25.4	6.5	16 42.2	6.3	59.5
05	259 06.4	24.9	249 50.9	6.4	16 48.5	6.3	59.5
06	274 06.4	S15 25.7	264 16.3	6.4	S16 54.8	6.1	59.5
07	289 06.4	26.4	278 41.7	6.3	17 00.9	6.0	59.6
08	304 06.4	27.2	293 07.0	6.3	17 06.9	5.9	59.6
M 09	319 06.4	.. 28.0	307 32.3	6.2	17 12.8	5.8	59.6
O 10	334 06.4	28.7	321 57.5	6.1	17 18.6	5.7	59.6
N 11	349 06.4	29.5	336 22.6	6.1	17 24.3	5.5	59.6
D 12	4 06.4	S15 30.3	350 47.7	6.0	S17 29.8	5.5	59.6
A 13	19 06.4	31.0	5 12.7	6.0	17 35.3	5.3	59.7
Y 14	34 06.3	31.8	19 37.7	5.9	17 40.6	5.2	59.7
15	49 06.3	.. 32.6	34 02.6	5.9	17 45.8	5.1	59.7
16	64 06.3	33.3	48 27.5	5.8	17 50.9	5.0	59.7
17	79 06.3	34.1	62 52.3	5.7	17 55.9	4.9	59.7
18	94 06.3	S15 34.9	77 17.0	5.7	S18 00.8	4.7	59.7
19	109 06.3	35.6	91 41.7	5.7	18 05.5	4.7	59.8
20	124 06.3	36.4	106 06.4	5.6	18 10.2	4.5	59.8
21	139 06.2	.. 37.2	120 31.0	5.6	18 14.7	4.3	59.8
22	154 06.2	37.9	134 55.6	5.4	18 19.0	4.3	59.8
23	169 06.2	38.7	149 20.1	5.4	18 23.3	4.1	59.8
5 00	184 06.2	S15 39.4	163 44.5	5.5	S18 27.4	4.1	59.8
01	199 06.2	40.2	178 09.0	5.4	18 31.5	3.8	59.8
02	214 06.2	41.0	192 33.4	5.3	18 35.3	3.8	59.8
03	229 06.1	.. 41.7	206 57.7	5.3	18 39.1	3.6	59.9
04	244 06.1	42.5	221 22.0	5.3	18 42.7	3.5	59.9
05	259 06.1	43.2	235 46.3	5.2	18 46.2	3.4	59.9
06	274 06.1	S15 44.0	250 10.5	5.2	S18 49.6	3.2	59.9
07	289 06.1	44.8	264 34.7	5.2	18 52.8	3.2	59.9
08	304 06.0	45.5	278 58.9	5.1	18 56.0	3.0	59.9
T 09	319 06.0	.. 46.3	293 23.0	5.1	18 59.0	2.8	59.9
U 10	334 06.0	47.0	307 47.1	5.0	19 01.8	2.7	59.9
E 11	349 06.0	47.8	322 11.1	5.1	19 04.5	2.6	59.9
S 12	4 06.0	S15 48.5	336 35.2	5.0	S19 07.1	2.5	59.9
D 13	19 05.9	49.3	350 59.2	5.0	19 09.6	2.3	59.9
A 14	34 05.9	50.0	5 23.2	4.9	19 11.9	2.2	60.0
Y 15	49 05.9	.. 50.8	19 47.1	5.0	19 14.1	2.1	60.0
16	64 05.9	51.5	34 11.1	4.9	19 16.2	1.9	60.0
17	79 05.8	52.3	48 35.0	4.9	19 18.1	1.8	60.0
18	94 05.8	S15 53.1	62 58.9	4.9	S19 19.9	1.6	60.0
19	109 05.8	53.8	77 22.8	4.8	19 21.5	1.5	60.0
20	124 05.8	54.6	91 46.6	4.9	19 23.0	1.4	60.0
21	139 05.8	.. 55.3	106 10.5	4.8	19 24.4	1.3	60.0
22	154 05.7	56.1	120 34.3	4.8	19 25.7	1.1	60.0
23	169 05.7	56.8	134 58.1	4.8	S19 26.8	1.0	60.0
	SD 16.2	d 0.8	SD 16.1		16.3		16.3

Lat.	Twilight Naut.	Twilight Civil	Sunrise	Moonrise 3	4	5	6
°	h m	h m	h m	h m	h m	h m	h m
N 72	06 18	07 43	09 17	09 08	11 49	■■■	■■■
N 70	06 13	07 29	08 46	08 35	10 34	12 32	13 49
68	06 08	07 16	08 24	08 12	09 57	11 32	12 41
66	06 04	07 06	08 06	07 54	09 30	10 58	12 05
64	06 01	06 58	07 52	07 39	09 10	10 33	11 39
62	05 57	06 51	07 40	07 27	08 54	10 13	11 19
60	05 54	06 44	07 30	07 17	08 40	09 57	11 02
N 58	05 51	06 38	07 21	07 08	08 29	09 44	10 48
56	05 49	06 33	07 14	07 00	08 18	09 32	10 36
54	05 47	06 29	07 07	06 53	08 10	09 22	10 26
52	05 44	06 24	07 00	06 47	08 02	09 13	10 16
50	05 42	06 20	06 55	06 41	07 54	09 05	10 08
45	05 37	06 12	06 43	06 29	07 39	08 47	09 50
N 40	05 32	06 04	06 33	06 19	07 27	08 33	09 36
35	05 27	05 58	06 24	06 10	07 16	08 21	09 24
30	05 23	05 51	06 16	06 03	07 07	08 11	09 13
20	05 14	05 40	06 03	05 50	06 51	07 53	08 54
N 10	05 04	05 29	05 51	05 39	06 37	07 38	08 38
0	04 54	05 19	05 40	05 28	06 25	07 23	08 23
S 10	04 41	05 07	05 29	05 18	06 12	07 09	08 09
20	04 27	04 54	05 17	05 07	05 58	06 54	07 53
30	04 07	04 37	05 03	04 55	05 43	06 36	07 34
35	03 55	04 28	04 55	04 47	05 34	06 26	07 24
40	03 40	04 16	04 45	04 39	05 23	06 14	07 12
45	03 22	04 02	04 34	04 30	05 12	06 01	06 57
S 50	02 57	03 44	04 21	04 18	04 57	05 44	06 40
52	02 45	03 36	04 15	04 13	04 50	05 36	06 32
54	02 31	03 26	04 08	04 07	04 43	05 28	06 22
56	02 14	03 16	04 00	04 01	04 35	05 18	06 12
58	01 52	03 03	03 52	03 54	04 26	05 07	06 00
S 60	01 23	02 48	03 42	03 46	04 15	04 54	05 47

Lat.	Sunset	Twilight Civil	Twilight Naut.	Moonset 3	4	5	6
°	h m	h m	h m	h m	h m	h m	h m
N 72	14 09	15 42	17 07	14 00	13 18	■■■	■■■
N 70	14 39	15 57	17 13	14 33	14 33	14 39	15 29
68	15 02	16 09	17 17	14 58	15 11	15 39	16 36
66	15 20	16 20	17 22	15 17	15 38	16 14	17 12
64	15 34	16 28	17 25	15 32	15 59	16 39	17 38
62	15 46	16 36	17 29	15 46	16 16	16 59	17 58
60	15 56	16 42	17 32	15 56	16 30	17 15	18 15
N 58	16 05	16 48	17 35	16 06	16 42	17 29	18 29
56	16 13	16 53	17 37	16 14	16 52	17 41	18 41
54	16 20	16 58	17 40	16 22	17 02	17 51	18 51
52	16 26	17 02	17 42	16 29	17 10	18 00	19 00
50	16 32	17 06	17 44	16 35	17 17	18 08	19 09
45	16 44	17 15	17 50	16 48	17 33	18 26	19 26
N 40	16 54	17 22	17 55	16 59	17 46	18 40	19 41
35	17 03	17 29	17 59	17 08	17 57	18 52	19 53
30	17 11	17 35	18 04	17 16	18 07	19 03	20 03
20	17 24	17 47	18 13	17 31	18 24	19 21	20 22
N 10	17 36	17 58	18 23	17 43	18 39	19 37	20 37
0	17 47	18 09	18 33	17 55	18 52	19 52	20 52
S 10	17 58	18 20	18 46	18 06	19 06	20 07	21 07
20	18 11	18 34	19 01	18 19	19 21	20 22	21 23
30	18 25	18 50	19 21	18 33	19 38	20 41	21 41
35	18 33	19 00	19 33	18 42	19 47	20 51	21 51
40	18 42	19 12	19 48	18 52	19 59	21 03	22 03
45	18 54	19 26	20 07	19 02	20 12	21 18	22 17
S 50	19 07	19 44	20 32	19 16	20 28	21 35	22 34
52	19 13	19 53	20 44	19 22	20 35	21 43	22 42
54	19 20	20 02	20 59	19 28	20 44	21 52	22 51
56	19 28	20 13	21 16	19 37	20 53	22 02	23 01
58	19 37	20 26	21 39	19 46	21 04	22 14	23 12
S 60	19 47	20 42	22 09	19 56	21 16	22 26	23 26

Day	SUN Eqn. of Time 00h	SUN Eqn. of Time 12h	SUN Mer. Pass.	MOON Mer. Pass. Upper	MOON Mer. Pass. Lower	Age	Phase
d	m s	m s	h m	h m	h m	d	%
3	16 26	16 26	11 44	11 44	24 10	29	0	●
4	16 26	16 25	11 44	12 38	00 10	01	1
5	16 25	16 24	11 44	13 38	01 08	02	5

UT	ARIES GHA	VENUS −4.6 GHA	Dec	MARS +1.4 GHA	Dec	JUPITER −2.4 GHA	Dec	SATURN +0.5 GHA	Dec
d h 6 00	45 22.5	134 41.0	S27 09.4	240 47.5	N 8 18.5	293 11.7	N21 51.8	183 00.5	S14 04.1
01	60 24.9	149 40.7	09.4	255 48.6	18.0	308 14.2	51.8	198 02.7	04.2
02	75 27.4	164 40.5	09.5	270 49.7	17.5	323 16.6	51.8	213 04.8	04.3
03	90 29.9	179 40.2 ..	09.5	285 50.8 ..	16.9	338 19.1 ..	51.8	228 07.0 ..	04.4
04	105 32.3	194 40.0	09.5	300 51.9	16.4	353 21.6	51.8	243 09.2	04.5
05	120 34.8	209 39.8	09.5	315 53.1	15.9	8 24.0	51.8	258 11.3	04.5
W 06	135 37.3	224 39.5	S27 09.5	330 54.2	N 8 15.3	23 26.5	N21 51.8	273 13.5	S14 04.6
E 07	150 39.7	239 39.3	09.5	345 55.3	14.8	38 28.9	51.8	288 15.7	04.7
D 08	165 42.2	254 39.0	09.5	0 56.4	14.3	53 31.4	51.8	303 17.8	04.8
N 09	180 44.6	269 38.8 ..	09.5	15 57.6 ..	13.8	68 33.8 ..	51.9	318 20.0 ..	04.9
E 10	195 47.1	284 38.5	09.6	30 58.7	13.2	83 36.3	51.9	333 22.2	05.0
S 11	210 49.6	299 38.3	09.6	45 59.8	12.7	98 38.7	51.9	348 24.3	05.1
D 12	225 52.0	314 38.1	S27 09.6	61 00.9	N 8 12.2	113 41.2	N21 51.9	3 26.5	S14 05.2
A 13	240 54.5	329 37.8	09.6	76 02.0	11.7	128 43.7	51.9	18 28.7	05.3
Y 14	255 57.0	344 37.6	09.6	91 03.2	11.1	143 46.1	51.9	33 30.8	05.3
15	270 59.4	359 37.4 ..	09.6	106 04.3 ..	10.6	158 48.6 ..	51.9	48 33.0 ..	05.4
16	286 01.9	14 37.1	09.6	121 05.4	10.1	173 51.0	51.9	63 35.2	05.5
17	301 04.4	29 36.9	09.6	136 06.5	09.6	188 53.5	51.9	78 37.4	05.6
18	316 06.8	44 36.6	S27 09.6	151 07.7	N 8 09.0	203 55.9	N21 51.9	93 39.5	S14 05.7
19	331 09.3	59 36.4	09.6	166 08.8	08.5	218 58.4	51.9	108 41.7	05.8
20	346 11.8	74 36.2	09.6	181 09.9	08.0	234 00.9	51.9	123 43.9	05.9
21	1 14.2	89 36.0 ..	09.6	196 11.0 ..	07.4	249 03.3 ..	51.9	138 46.0 ..	06.0
22	16 16.7	104 35.7	09.6	211 12.2	06.9	264 05.8	51.9	153 48.2	06.1
23	31 19.1	119 35.5	09.6	226 13.3	06.4	279 08.3	51.9	168 50.4	06.1
7 00	46 21.6	134 35.3	S27 09.6	241 14.4	N 8 05.9	294 10.7	N21 51.9	183 52.5	S14 06.2
01	61 24.1	149 35.0	09.5	256 15.5	05.3	309 13.2	51.9	198 54.7	06.3
02	76 26.5	164 34.8	09.5	271 16.7	04.8	324 15.6	51.9	213 56.9	06.4
03	91 29.0	179 34.6 ..	09.5	286 17.8 ..	04.3	339 18.1 ..	51.9	228 59.0 ..	06.5
04	106 31.5	194 34.4	09.5	301 18.9	03.8	354 20.6	51.9	244 01.2	06.6
05	121 33.9	209 34.1	09.5	316 20.1	03.2	9 23.0	51.9	259 03.4	06.7
T 06	136 36.4	224 33.9	S27 09.5	331 21.2	N 8 02.7	24 25.5	N21 52.0	274 05.5	S14 06.8
H 07	151 38.9	239 33.7	09.5	346 22.3	02.2	39 28.0	52.0	289 07.7	06.9
U 08	166 41.3	254 33.5	09.5	1 23.4	01.7	54 30.4	52.0	304 09.9	06.9
R 09	181 43.8	269 33.2 ..	09.4	16 24.6 ..	01.1	69 32.9 ..	52.0	319 12.1 ..	07.0
S 10	196 46.3	284 33.0	09.4	31 25.7	00.6	84 35.3	52.0	334 14.2	07.1
D 11	211 48.7	299 32.8	09.4	46 26.8	8 00.1	99 37.8	52.0	349 16.4	07.2
A 12	226 51.2	314 32.6	S27 09.4	61 27.9	N 7 59.6	114 40.3	N21 52.0	4 18.6	S14 07.3
Y 13	241 53.6	329 32.4	09.4	76 29.1	59.0	129 42.7	52.0	19 20.7	07.4
14	256 56.1	344 32.2	09.4	91 30.2	58.5	144 45.2	52.0	34 22.9	07.5
15	271 58.6	359 31.9 ..	09.3	106 31.3 ..	58.0	159 47.7 ..	52.0	49 25.1 ..	07.6
16	287 01.0	14 31.7	09.3	121 32.5	57.4	174 50.1	52.0	64 27.2	07.7
17	302 03.5	29 31.5	09.3	136 33.6	56.9	189 52.6	52.0	79 29.4	07.7
18	317 06.0	44 31.3	S27 09.3	151 34.7	N 7 56.4	204 55.1	N21 52.0	94 31.6	S14 07.8
19	332 08.4	59 31.1	09.2	166 35.8	55.9	219 57.5	52.0	109 33.7	07.9
20	347 10.9	74 30.9	09.2	181 37.0	55.3	235 00.0	52.0	124 35.9	08.0
21	2 13.4	89 30.7 ..	09.2	196 38.1 ..	54.8	250 02.5 ..	52.0	139 38.1 ..	08.1
22	17 15.8	104 30.5	09.1	211 39.2	54.3	265 05.0	52.0	154 40.2	08.2
23	32 18.3	119 30.3	09.1	226 40.4	53.8	280 07.4	52.0	169 42.4	08.3
8 00	47 20.7	134 30.1	S27 09.1	241 41.5	N 7 53.2	295 09.9	N21 52.1	184 44.6	S14 08.4
01	62 23.2	149 29.9	09.1	256 42.6	52.7	310 12.4	52.1	199 46.8	08.5
02	77 25.7	164 29.7	09.0	271 43.8	52.2	325 14.8	52.1	214 48.9	08.5
03	92 28.1	179 29.5 ..	09.0	286 44.9 ..	51.7	340 17.3 ..	52.1	229 51.1 ..	08.6
04	107 30.6	194 29.3	09.0	301 46.0	51.1	355 19.8	52.1	244 53.3	08.7
05	122 33.1	209 29.1	08.9	316 47.2	50.6	10 22.2	52.1	259 55.4	08.8
F 06	137 35.5	224 28.9	S27 08.9	331 48.3	N 7 50.1	25 24.7	N21 52.1	274 57.6	S14 08.9
R 07	152 38.0	239 28.7	08.8	346 49.4	49.6	40 27.2	52.1	289 59.8	09.0
I 08	167 40.5	254 28.5	08.8	1 50.6	49.0	55 29.7	52.1	305 01.9	09.1
D 09	182 42.9	269 28.3 ..	08.8	16 51.7 ..	48.5	70 32.1 ..	52.1	320 04.1 ..	09.2
A 10	197 45.4	284 28.1	08.7	31 52.8	48.0	85 34.6	52.1	335 06.3	09.3
Y 11	212 47.9	299 27.9	08.7	46 53.9	47.4	100 37.1	52.1	350 08.4	09.3
12	227 50.3	314 27.7	S27 08.6	61 55.1	N 7 46.9	115 39.6	N21 52.1	5 10.6	S14 09.4
13	242 52.8	329 27.5	08.6	76 56.2	46.4	130 42.0	52.1	20 12.8	09.5
14	257 55.2	344 27.3	08.6	91 57.3	45.9	145 44.5	52.1	35 14.9	09.6
15	272 57.7	359 27.1 ..	08.5	106 58.5 ..	45.3	160 47.0 ..	52.2	50 17.1 ..	09.7
16	288 00.2	14 26.9	08.5	121 59.6	44.8	175 49.5	52.2	65 19.3	09.8
17	303 02.6	29 26.7	08.4	137 00.7	44.3	190 51.9	52.2	80 21.5	09.9
18	318 05.1	44 26.5	S27 08.4	152 01.9	N 7 43.8	205 54.4	N21 52.2	95 23.6	S14 10.0
19	333 07.6	59 26.3	08.3	167 03.0	43.2	220 56.9	52.2	110 25.8	10.0
20	348 10.0	74 26.2	08.3	182 04.2	42.7	235 59.4	52.2	125 28.0	10.1
21	3 12.5	89 26.0 ..	08.2	197 05.3 ..	42.2	251 01.9 ..	52.2	140 30.1 ..	10.2
22	18 15.0	104 25.8	08.2	212 06.4	41.7	266 04.3	52.2	155 32.3	10.3
23	33 17.4	119 25.6	08.1	227 07.6	41.1	281 06.8	52.2	170 34.5	10.4
Mer. Pass. 20 51.1	*v* −0.2 *d* 0.0			*v* 1.1 *d* 0.5		*v* 2.5 *d* 0.0		*v* 2.2 *d* 0.1	

STARS

Name	SHA	Dec
Acamar	315 17.7	S40 15.0
Achernar	335 26.1	S57 10.1
Acrux	173 09.4	S63 10.4
Adhara	255 12.1	S28 59.4
Aldebaran	290 48.8	N16 32.1
Alioth	166 21.0	N55 53.0
Alkaid	152 59.2	N49 14.6
Al Na'ir	27 43.3	S46 53.7
Alnilam	275 45.8	S 1 11.7
Alphard	217 55.9	S 8 43.1
Alphecca	126 11.2	N26 40.3
Alpheratz	357 42.9	N29 10.3
Altair	62 08.1	N 8 54.6
Ankaa	353 15.1	S42 13.9
Antares	112 26.3	S26 27.6
Arcturus	145 55.8	N19 06.7
Atria	107 28.3	S69 03.1
Avior	234 17.7	S59 33.1
Bellatrix	278 31.4	N 6 21.6
Betelgeuse	271 00.8	N 7 24.5
Canopus	263 55.7	S52 42.1
Capella	280 33.6	N46 00.5
Deneb	49 31.3	N45 20.3
Denebola	182 33.6	N14 29.6
Diphda	348 55.4	S17 54.6
Dubhe	193 51.8	N61 40.3
Elnath	278 12.0	N28 37.0
Eltanin	90 46.4	N51 29.6
Enif	33 46.8	N 9 56.6
Fomalhaut	15 23.6	S29 32.9
Gacrux	172 01.0	S57 11.2
Gienah	175 52.3	S17 37.0
Hadar	148 48.1	S60 26.2
Hamal	328 00.3	N23 31.8
Kaus Aust.	83 43.7	S34 22.5
Kochab	137 21.4	N74 06.0
Markab	13 37.9	N15 17.1
Menkar	314 14.4	N 4 08.6
Menkent	148 07.6	S36 26.1
Miaplacidus	221 39.5	S69 46.2
Mirfak	308 39.4	N49 54.6
Nunki	75 58.2	S26 16.6
Peacock	53 19.0	S56 41.5
Pollux	243 27.3	N27 59.3
Procyon	244 59.3	N 5 11.2
Rasalhague	96 06.5	N12 33.3
Regulus	207 43.3	N11 53.9
Rigel	281 11.5	S 8 11.2
Rigil Kent.	139 52.0	S60 53.3
Sabik	102 12.5	S15 44.3
Schedar	349 39.7	N56 37.0
Shaula	96 21.9	S37 06.7
Sirius	258 33.3	S16 44.1
Spica	158 31.3	S11 13.9
Suhail	222 52.2	S43 29.2
Vega	80 39.0	N38 48.2
Zuben'ubi	137 05.4	S16 05.8

	SHA	Mer. Pass.
	° ′	h m
Venus	88 13.7	15 02
Mars	194 52.8	7 54
Jupiter	247 49.1	4 23
Saturn	137 30.9	11 43

UT	SUN GHA	SUN Dec	MOON GHA	v	Dec	d	HP
d h	° '	° '	° '	'	° '	'	'
6 00	184 05.7	S15 57.6	149 21.9	4.8	S19 27.8	0.8	60.0
01	199 05.7	58.3	163 45.7	4.8	19 28.6	0.7	60.0
02	214 05.6	59.1	178 09.5	4.8	19 29.3	0.6	60.0
03	229 05.6	15 59.8	192 33.3	4.8	19 29.9	0.4	60.0
04	244 05.6	16 00.6	206 57.1	4.8	19 30.3	0.3	60.0
05	259 05.5	01.3	221 20.9	4.8	19 30.6	0.2	60.0
06	274 05.5	S16 02.0	235 44.7	4.8	S19 30.8	0.0	60.0
W 07	289 05.5	02.8	250 08.5	4.7	19 30.8	0.1	60.0
E 08	304 05.5	03.5	264 32.2	4.8	19 30.7	0.3	60.0
D 09	319 05.4 ..	04.3	278 56.0	4.8	19 30.4	0.4	60.0
N 10	334 05.4	05.0	293 19.8	4.8	19 30.0	0.5	60.0
E 11	349 05.4	05.8	307 43.6	4.8	19 29.5	0.7	60.0
S 12	4 05.3	S16 06.5	322 07.4	4.9	S19 28.8	0.8	60.0
D 13	19 05.3	07.3	336 31.3	4.8	19 28.0	0.9	60.0
A 14	34 05.3	08.0	350 55.1	4.8	19 27.1	1.1	60.0
Y 15	49 05.3 ..	08.7	5 18.9	4.9	19 26.0	1.2	60.0
16	64 05.2	09.5	19 42.8	4.9	19 24.8	1.4	60.0
17	79 05.2	10.2	34 06.7	4.9	19 23.4	1.4	60.0
18	94 05.2	S16 11.0	48 30.6	4.9	S19 22.0	1.7	60.0
19	109 05.1	11.7	62 54.5	4.9	19 20.3	1.7	60.0
20	124 05.1	12.5	77 18.4	4.9	19 18.6	1.9	60.0
21	139 05.1 ..	13.2	91 42.3	5.0	19 16.7	2.0	60.0
22	154 05.0	13.9	106 06.3	5.0	19 14.7	2.2	60.0
23	169 05.0	14.7	120 30.3	5.0	19 12.5	2.3	60.0
7 00	184 05.0	S16 15.4	134 54.3	5.1	S19 10.2	2.4	60.0
01	199 04.9	16.2	149 18.4	5.1	19 07.8	2.5	60.0
02	214 04.9	16.9	163 42.5	5.1	19 05.3	2.7	60.0
03	229 04.9 ..	17.6	178 06.6	5.1	19 02.6	2.8	60.0
04	244 04.8	18.4	192 30.7	5.2	18 59.8	3.0	60.0
05	259 04.8	19.1	206 54.9	5.2	18 56.8	3.0	60.0
06	274 04.8	S16 19.8	221 19.1	5.2	S18 53.8	3.2	59.9
07	289 04.7	20.6	235 43.3	5.3	18 50.6	3.4	59.9
T 08	304 04.7	21.3	250 07.6	5.3	18 47.2	3.4	59.9
H 09	319 04.6 ..	22.0	264 31.9	5.4	18 43.8	3.6	59.9
U 10	334 04.6	22.8	278 56.3	5.4	18 40.2	3.7	59.9
R 11	349 04.6	23.5	293 20.7	5.4	18 36.5	3.9	59.9
S 12	4 04.5	S16 24.2	307 45.1	5.5	S18 32.6	3.9	59.9
D 13	19 04.5	25.0	322 09.6	5.5	18 28.7	4.1	59.9
A 14	34 04.5	25.7	336 34.1	5.6	18 24.6	4.3	59.9
Y 15	49 04.4 ..	26.4	350 58.7	5.6	18 20.3	4.3	59.9
16	64 04.4	27.2	5 23.3	5.7	18 16.0	4.5	59.9
17	79 04.3	27.9	19 48.0	5.7	18 11.5	4.5	59.9
18	94 04.3	S16 28.6	34 12.7	5.7	S18 07.0	4.7	59.8
19	109 04.3	29.4	48 37.4	5.8	18 02.3	4.9	59.8
20	124 04.2	30.1	63 02.2	5.9	17 57.4	4.9	59.8
21	139 04.2 ..	30.8	77 27.1	5.9	17 52.5	5.1	59.8
22	154 04.1	31.5	91 52.0	5.9	17 47.4	5.1	59.8
23	169 04.1	32.3	106 16.9	6.0	17 42.3	5.3	59.8
8 00	184 04.0	S16 33.0	120 41.9	6.1	S17 37.0	5.4	59.8
01	199 04.0	33.7	135 07.0	6.1	17 31.6	5.5	59.8
02	214 04.0	34.4	149 32.1	6.2	17 26.1	5.7	59.8
03	229 03.9 ..	35.2	163 57.3	6.2	17 20.4	5.7	59.8
04	244 03.9	35.9	178 22.5	6.3	17 14.7	5.9	59.7
05	259 03.8	36.6	192 47.8	6.3	17 08.8	5.9	59.7
06	274 03.8	S16 37.3	207 13.1	6.4	S17 02.9	6.1	59.7
07	289 03.7	38.1	221 38.5	6.5	16 56.8	6.2	59.7
08	304 03.7	38.8	236 04.0	6.5	16 50.6	6.3	59.7
F 09	319 03.6 ..	39.5	250 29.5	6.6	16 44.3	6.4	59.7
R 10	334 03.6	40.2	264 55.1	6.6	16 37.9	6.5	59.7
I 11	349 03.6	41.0	279 20.7	6.7	16 31.4	6.6	59.6
D 12	4 03.5	S16 41.7	293 46.4	6.8	S16 24.8	6.7	59.6
A 13	19 03.5	42.4	308 12.2	6.8	16 18.1	6.8	59.6
Y 14	34 03.4	43.1	322 38.0	6.9	16 11.3	6.9	59.6
15	49 03.4 ..	43.8	337 03.9	6.9	16 04.4	7.1	59.6
16	64 03.3	44.6	351 29.8	7.0	15 57.3	7.1	59.6
17	79 03.3	45.3	5 55.8	7.1	15 50.2	7.2	59.6
18	94 03.2	S16 46.0	20 21.9	7.1	S15 43.0	7.3	59.5
19	109 03.2	46.7	34 48.0	7.2	15 35.7	7.4	59.5
20	124 03.1	47.4	49 14.2	7.3	15 28.3	7.5	59.5
21	139 03.1 ..	48.2	63 40.5	7.3	15 20.8	7.6	59.5
22	154 03.0	48.9	78 06.8	7.4	15 13.2	7.6	59.5
23	169 03.0	49.6	92 33.2	7.4	S15 05.6	7.8	59.5
	SD 16.2	d 0.7	SD 16.4		16.3		16.2

Lat.	Twilight Naut.	Twilight Civil	Sunrise	Moonrise 6	Moonrise 7	Moonrise 8	Moonrise 9
°	h m	h m	h m	h m	h m	h m	h m
N 72	06 30	07 57	09 39	■■	■■	14 47	14 27
N 70	06 23	07 40	09 02	13 49	14 03	14 04	14 03
68	06 17	07 27	08 37	12 41	13 18	13 36	13 44
66	06 13	07 16	08 18	12 05	12 48	13 14	13 29
64	06 08	07 06	08 02	11 39	12 26	12 56	13 17
62	06 04	06 58	07 49	11 19	12 08	12 42	13 07
60	06 01	06 51	07 38	11 02	11 53	12 30	12 58
N 58	05 57	06 45	07 28	10 48	11 40	12 19	12 50
56	05 54	06 39	07 20	10 36	11 29	12 10	12 43
54	05 52	06 34	07 12	10 26	11 19	12 02	12 36
52	05 49	06 29	07 06	10 16	11 10	11 55	12 31
50	05 46	06 25	07 00	10 08	11 02	11 48	12 26
45	05 41	06 16	06 47	09 50	10 46	11 34	12 15
N 40	05 35	06 07	06 36	09 36	10 32	11 22	12 05
35	05 30	06 00	06 27	09 24	10 21	11 12	11 57
30	05 25	05 54	06 19	09 13	10 10	11 03	11 50
20	05 15	05 42	06 04	08 54	09 53	10 48	11 38
N 10	05 05	05 30	05 52	08 38	09 38	10 34	11 28
0	04 54	05 19	05 40	08 23	09 23	10 22	11 18
S 10	04 41	05 06	05 28	08 09	09 09	10 09	11 08
20	04 25	04 52	05 15	07 53	08 54	09 56	10 57
30	04 05	04 35	05 01	07 34	08 37	09 41	10 45
35	03 52	04 25	04 52	07 24	08 26	09 32	10 38
40	03 36	04 12	04 42	07 12	08 15	09 21	10 30
45	03 17	03 58	04 30	06 57	08 01	09 09	10 20
S 50	02 51	03 39	04 16	06 40	07 44	08 55	10 09
52	02 38	03 30	04 10	06 32	07 36	08 48	10 03
54	02 22	03 20	04 02	06 22	07 28	08 40	09 57
56	02 03	03 08	03 54	06 12	07 18	08 32	09 51
58	01 39	02 54	03 45	06 00	07 07	08 22	09 44
S 60	01 04	02 38	03 34	05 47	06 54	08 11	09 35

Lat.	Sunset	Twilight Civil	Twilight Naut.	Moonset 6	Moonset 7	Moonset 8	Moonset 9
°	h m	h m	h m	h m	h m	h m	h m
N 72	13 47	15 29	16 56	■■	■■	18 38	20 53
N 70	14 24	15 46	17 03	15 29	17 19	19 19	21 15
68	14 49	15 59	17 09	16 36	18 04	19 47	21 32
66	15 09	16 11	17 14	17 12	18 33	20 08	21 46
64	15 25	16 20	17 18	17 38	18 56	20 24	21 57
62	15 38	16 28	17 22	17 58	19 13	20 38	22 07
60	15 49	16 35	17 26	18 15	19 28	20 50	22 15
N 58	15 58	16 42	17 29	18 29	19 40	21 00	22 22
56	16 07	16 47	17 32	18 41	19 51	21 08	22 29
54	16 14	16 53	17 35	18 51	20 01	21 16	22 34
52	16 21	16 57	17 38	19 00	20 09	21 23	22 39
50	16 27	17 02	17 40	19 09	20 17	21 29	22 44
45	16 40	17 11	17 46	19 26	20 33	21 43	22 54
N 40	16 51	17 19	17 52	19 41	20 46	21 54	23 02
35	17 00	17 27	17 57	19 53	20 57	22 03	23 09
30	17 08	17 33	18 02	20 03	21 07	22 11	23 15
20	17 23	17 46	18 12	20 22	21 23	22 25	23 25
N 10	17 35	17 57	18 22	20 37	21 38	22 37	23 35
0	17 47	18 09	18 34	20 52	21 52	22 49	23 43
S 10	17 59	18 21	18 47	21 07	22 05	23 00	23 52
20	18 12	18 35	19 03	21 23	22 19	23 12	24 01
30	18 27	18 53	19 23	21 41	22 36	23 26	24 11
35	18 36	19 03	19 36	21 51	22 45	23 34	24 17
40	18 46	19 16	19 52	22 03	22 56	23 42	24 23
45	18 58	19 31	20 12	22 17	23 09	23 53	24 31
S 50	19 12	19 50	20 38	22 34	23 24	24 05	00 05
52	19 19	19 59	20 52	22 42	23 31	24 11	00 11
54	19 26	20 09	21 08	22 51	23 39	24 18	00 18
56	19 35	20 21	21 27	23 01	23 48	24 25	00 25
58	19 44	20 35	21 52	23 12	23 58	24 33	00 33
S 60	19 55	20 52	22 29	23 26	24 09	00 09	00 42

Day	SUN Eqn. of Time 00h	SUN Eqn. of Time 12h	SUN Mer. Pass.	MOON Mer. Pass. Upper	MOON Mer. Pass. Lower	Age	Phase
d	m s	m s	h m	h m	h m	d %	
6	16 23	16 21	11 44	14 38	02 08	03 12	
7	16 20	16 18	11 44	15 38	03 08	04 20	
8	16 16	16 14	11 44	16 35	04 07	05 31	

UT	ARIES GHA	VENUS −4.6 GHA	Dec	MARS +1.4 GHA	Dec	JUPITER −2.5 GHA	Dec	SATURN +0.5 GHA	Dec	STARS Name	SHA	Dec
d h	° ′	° ′	° ′	° ′	° ′	° ′	° ′	° ′	° ′		° ′	° ′
9 00	48 19.9	134 25.4	S27 08.0	242 08.7	N 7 40.6	296 09.3	N21 52.2	185 36.6	S14 10.5	Acamar	315 17.7	S40 15.0
01	63 22.4	149 25.2	08.0	257 09.8	40.1	311 11.8	52.2	200 38.8	10.6	Achernar	335 26.1	S57 10.1
02	78 24.8	164 25.1	07.9	272 11.0	39.6	326 14.2	52.2	215 41.0	10.7	Acrux	173 09.4	S63 10.4
03	93 27.3	179 24.9 ..	07.9	287 12.1 ..	39.0	341 16.7 ..	52.2	230 43.1 ..	10.8	Adhara	255 12.1	S28 59.4
04	108 29.7	194 24.7	07.8	302 13.2	38.5	356 19.2	52.2	245 45.3	10.8	Aldebaran	290 48.7	N16 32.1
05	123 32.2	209 24.5	07.8	317 14.4	38.0	11 21.7	52.2	260 47.5	10.9			
06	138 34.7	224 24.4	S27 07.7	332 15.5	N 7 37.5	26 24.2	N21 52.3	275 49.6	S14 11.0	Alioth	166 21.0	N55 52.9
07	153 37.1	239 24.2	07.6	347 16.6	36.9	41 26.7	52.3	290 51.8	11.1	Alkaid	152 59.2	N49 14.6
S 08	168 39.6	254 24.0	07.6	2 17.8	36.4	56 29.1	52.3	305 54.0	11.2	Al Na'ir	27 43.3	S46 53.7
A 09	183 42.1	269 23.8 ..	07.5	17 18.9 ..	35.9	71 31.6 ..	52.3	320 56.1 ..	11.3	Alnilam	275 45.8	S 1 11.7
T 10	198 44.5	284 23.7	07.4	32 20.1	35.3	86 34.1	52.3	335 58.3	11.4	Alphard	217 55.8	S 8 43.1
U 11	213 47.0	299 23.5	07.4	47 21.2	34.8	101 36.6	52.3	351 00.5	11.5			
R 12	228 49.5	314 23.3	S27 07.3	62 22.3	N 7 34.3	116 39.1	N21 52.3	6 02.7	S14 11.5	Alphecca	126 11.2	N26 40.3
D 13	243 51.9	329 23.2	07.2	77 23.5	33.8	131 41.6	52.3	21 04.8	11.6	Alpheratz	357 42.9	N29 10.3
A 14	258 54.4	344 23.0	07.2	92 24.6	33.2	146 44.0	52.3	36 07.0	11.7	Altair	62 08.1	N 8 54.6
Y 15	273 56.9	359 22.8 ..	07.1	107 25.7 ..	32.7	161 46.5 ..	52.3	51 09.2 ..	11.8	Ankaa	353 15.2	S42 13.9
16	288 59.3	14 22.7	07.0	122 26.9	32.2	176 49.0	52.3	66 11.3	11.9	Antares	112 26.3	S26 27.6
17	304 01.8	29 22.5	07.0	137 28.0	31.7	191 51.5	52.4	81 13.5	12.0			
18	319 04.2	44 22.3	S27 06.9	152 29.2	N 7 31.1	206 54.0	N21 52.4	96 15.7	S14 12.1	Arcturus	145 55.8	N19 06.7
19	334 06.7	59 22.2	06.8	167 30.3	30.6	221 56.5	52.4	111 17.8	12.2	Atria	107 28.3	S69 03.1
20	349 09.2	74 22.0	06.7	182 31.4	30.1	236 58.9	52.4	126 20.0	12.3	Avior	234 17.7	S59 33.1
21	4 11.6	89 21.9 ..	06.7	197 32.6 ..	29.6	252 01.4 ..	52.4	141 22.2 ..	12.3	Bellatrix	278 31.4	N 6 21.6
22	19 14.1	104 21.7	06.6	212 33.7	29.0	267 03.9	52.4	156 24.3	12.4	Betelgeuse	271 00.7	N 7 24.5
23	34 16.6	119 21.6	06.5	227 34.8	28.5	282 06.4	52.4	171 26.5	12.5			
10 00	49 19.0	134 21.4	S27 06.4	242 36.0	N 7 28.0	297 08.9	N21 52.4	186 28.7	S14 12.6	Canopus	263 55.6	S52 42.1
01	64 21.5	149 21.2	06.3	257 37.1	27.5	312 11.4	52.4	201 30.8	12.7	Capella	280 33.6	N46 00.5
02	79 24.0	164 21.1	06.3	272 38.3	26.9	327 13.9	52.4	216 33.0	12.8	Deneb	49 31.3	N45 20.3
03	94 26.4	179 20.9 ..	06.2	287 39.4 ..	26.4	342 16.4 ..	52.4	231 35.2 ..	12.9	Denebola	182 33.6	N14 29.6
04	109 28.9	194 20.8	06.1	302 40.5	25.9	357 18.9	52.5	246 37.4	13.0	Diphda	348 55.4	S17 54.6
05	124 31.3	209 20.6	06.0	317 41.7	25.4	12 21.3	52.5	261 39.5	13.0			
06	139 33.8	224 20.5	S27 05.9	332 42.8	N 7 24.8	27 23.8	N21 52.5	276 41.7	S14 13.1	Dubhe	193 51.8	N61 40.2
07	154 36.3	239 20.3	05.8	347 44.0	24.3	42 26.3	52.5	291 43.9	13.2	Elnath	278 11.9	N28 37.0
08	169 38.7	254 20.2	05.8	2 45.1	23.8	57 28.8	52.5	306 46.0	13.3	Eltanin	90 46.4	N51 29.6
S 09	184 41.2	269 20.0 ..	05.7	17 46.3 ..	23.3	72 31.3 ..	52.5	321 48.2 ..	13.4	Enif	33 46.8	N 9 56.6
U 10	199 43.7	284 19.9	05.6	32 47.4	22.7	87 33.8	52.5	336 50.4	13.5	Fomalhaut	15 23.6	S29 32.9
N 11	214 46.1	299 19.8	05.5	47 48.5	22.2	102 36.3	52.5	351 52.5	13.6			
D 12	229 48.6	314 19.6	S27 05.4	62 49.7	N 7 21.7	117 38.8	N21 52.5	6 54.7	S14 13.7	Gacrux	172 01.0	S57 11.2
A 13	244 51.1	329 19.5	05.3	77 50.8	21.1	132 41.3	52.5	21 56.9	13.7	Gienah	175 52.2	S17 37.0
Y 14	259 53.5	344 19.3	05.2	92 52.0	20.6	147 43.8	52.5	36 59.0	13.8	Hadar	148 48.1	S60 26.2
15	274 56.0	359 19.2 ..	05.1	107 53.1 ..	20.1	162 46.3 ..	52.6	52 01.2 ..	13.9	Hamal	328 00.1	N23 31.8
16	289 58.5	14 19.1	05.0	122 54.2	19.6	177 48.8	52.6	67 03.4	14.0	Kaus Aust.	83 43.7	S34 22.5
17	305 00.9	29 18.9	04.9	137 55.4	19.0	192 51.2	52.6	82 05.5	14.1			
18	320 03.4	44 18.8	S27 04.8	152 56.5	N 7 18.5	207 53.7	N21 52.6	97 07.7	S14 14.2	Kochab	137 21.4	N74 05.9
19	335 05.8	59 18.7	04.7	167 57.7	18.0	222 56.2	52.6	112 09.9	14.3	Markab	13 37.9	N15 17.1
20	350 08.3	74 18.5	04.6	182 58.8	17.5	237 58.7	52.6	127 12.1	14.4	Menkar	314 14.4	N 4 08.6
21	5 10.8	89 18.4 ..	04.5	198 00.0 ..	16.9	253 01.2 ..	52.6	142 14.2 ..	14.4	Menkent	148 07.6	S36 26.1
22	20 13.2	104 18.3	04.4	213 01.1	16.4	268 03.7	52.6	157 16.4	14.5	Miaplacidus	221 39.5	S69 46.2
23	35 15.7	119 18.1	04.3	228 02.3	15.9	283 06.2	52.6	172 18.6	14.6			
11 00	50 18.2	134 18.0	S27 04.2	243 03.4	N 7 15.4	298 08.7	N21 52.6	187 20.7	S14 14.7	Mirfak	308 39.4	N49 54.6
01	65 20.6	149 17.9	04.1	258 04.5	14.8	313 11.2	52.7	202 22.9	14.8	Nunki	75 58.2	S26 16.6
02	80 23.1	164 17.7	04.0	273 05.7	14.3	328 13.7	52.7	217 25.1	14.9	Peacock	53 19.0	S56 41.5
03	95 25.6	179 17.6 ..	03.9	288 06.8 ..	13.8	343 16.2 ..	52.7	232 27.2 ..	15.0	Pollux	243 27.3	N27 59.3
04	110 28.0	194 17.5	03.8	303 08.0	13.3	358 18.7	52.7	247 29.4	15.1	Procyon	244 59.3	N 5 11.2
05	125 30.5	209 17.4	03.7	318 09.1	12.7	13 21.2	52.7	262 31.6	15.1			
06	140 33.0	224 17.3	S27 03.6	333 10.3	N 7 12.2	28 23.7	N21 52.7	277 33.7	S14 15.2	Rasalhague	96 06.5	N12 33.3
07	155 35.4	239 17.1	03.5	348 11.4	11.7	43 26.2	52.7	292 35.9	15.3	Regulus	207 43.3	N11 53.8
08	170 37.9	254 17.0	03.4	3 12.6	11.2	58 28.7	52.7	307 38.1	15.4	Rigel	281 11.5	S 8 11.2
M 09	185 40.3	269 16.9 ..	03.3	18 13.7 ..	10.6	73 31.2 ..	52.7	322 40.2 ..	15.5	Rigil Kent.	139 51.9	S60 53.3
O 10	200 42.8	284 16.8	03.2	33 14.8	10.1	88 33.7	52.7	337 42.4	15.6	Sabik	102 12.5	S15 44.3
N 11	215 45.3	299 16.7	03.1	48 16.0	09.6	103 36.2	52.7	352 44.6	15.7			
D 12	230 47.7	314 16.5	S27 02.9	63 17.1	N 7 09.1	118 38.7	N21 52.8	7 46.8	S14 15.8	Schedar	349 39.7	N56 37.1
A 13	245 50.2	329 16.4	02.8	78 18.3	08.5	133 41.2	52.8	22 48.9	15.8	Shaula	96 21.9	S37 06.7
Y 14	260 52.7	344 16.3	02.7	93 19.4	08.0	148 43.7	52.8	37 51.1	15.9	Sirius	258 33.3	S16 44.1
15	275 55.1	359 16.2 ..	02.6	108 20.6 ..	07.5	163 46.2 ..	52.8	52 53.3 ..	16.0	Spica	158 31.3	S11 13.9
16	290 57.6	14 16.1	02.5	123 21.7	07.0	178 48.7	52.8	67 55.4	16.1	Suhail	222 52.2	S43 29.2
17	306 00.1	29 16.0	02.4	138 22.9	06.4	193 51.2	52.8	82 57.6	16.2			
18	321 02.5	44 15.9	S27 02.2	153 24.0	N 7 05.9	208 53.7	N21 52.8	97 59.8	S14 16.3	Vega	80 39.1	N38 48.2
19	336 05.0	59 15.8	02.1	168 25.2	05.4	223 56.2	52.8	113 01.9	16.4	Zuben'ubi	137 05.5	S16 05.8
20	351 07.4	74 15.7	02.0	183 26.3	04.9	238 58.7	52.9	128 04.1	16.5		SHA	Mer. Pass.
21	6 09.9	89 15.6 ..	01.9	198 27.5 ..	04.3	254 01.2 ..	52.9	143 06.3 ..	16.5		° ′	h m
22	21 12.4	104 15.5	01.8	213 28.6	03.8	269 03.7	52.9	158 08.4	16.6	Venus	85 02.4	15 03
23	36 14.8	119 15.4	01.6	228 29.8	03.3	284 06.2	52.9	173 10.6	16.7	Mars	193 17.0	7 49
	h m									Jupiter	247 49.9	4 11
Mer. Pass. 20 39.3	v −0.1 d 0.1	v 1.1 d 0.5		v 2.5 d 0.0		v 2.2 d 0.1				Saturn	137 09.7	11 32

UT	SUN GHA	Dec	MOON GHA	v	Dec	d	HP
d h	° ′	° ′	° ′	′	° ′	′	′
9 00	184 02.9	S16 50.3	106 59.6	7.5	S14 57.8	7.9	59.5
01	199 02.9	51.0	121 26.1	7.6	14 49.9	7.9	59.4
02	214 02.8	51.7	135 52.7	7.6	14 42.0	8.1	59.4
03	229 02.8	.. 52.4	150 19.3	7.8	14 33.9	8.1	59.4
04	244 02.7	53.2	164 46.1	7.7	14 25.8	8.2	59.4
05	259 02.7	53.9	179 12.8	7.9	14 17.6	8.3	59.4
06	274 02.6	S16 54.6	193 39.7	7.9	S14 09.3	8.3	59.4
S 07	289 02.6	55.3	208 06.6	7.9	14 01.0	8.5	59.3
A 08	304 02.5	56.0	222 33.5	8.1	13 52.5	8.5	59.3
T 09	319 02.4	.. 56.7	237 00.6	8.1	13 44.0	8.6	59.3
U 10	334 02.4	57.4	251 27.7	8.1	13 35.4	8.7	59.3
R 11	349 02.3	58.1	265 54.8	8.2	13 26.7	8.8	59.3
D 12	4 02.3	S16 58.8	280 22.0	8.3	S13 17.9	8.8	59.3
A 13	19 02.2	16 59.6	294 49.3	8.4	13 09.1	8.9	59.2
Y 14	34 02.2	17 00.3	309 16.7	8.4	13 00.2	9.0	59.2
15	49 02.1	.. 01.0	323 44.1	8.5	12 51.2	9.1	59.2
16	64 02.1	01.7	338 11.6	8.5	12 42.1	9.1	59.2
17	79 02.0	02.4	352 39.1	8.6	12 33.0	9.2	59.2
18	94 01.9	S17 03.1	7 06.7	8.7	S12 23.8	9.3	59.1
19	109 01.9	03.8	21 34.4	8.8	12 14.5	9.3	59.1
20	124 01.8	04.5	36 02.2	8.7	12 05.2	9.4	59.1
21	139 01.8	.. 05.2	50 29.9	8.9	11 55.8	9.5	59.1
22	154 01.7	05.9	64 57.8	8.9	11 46.3	9.5	59.1
23	169 01.6	06.6	79 25.7	9.0	11 36.8	9.6	59.1
10 00	184 01.6	S17 07.3	93 53.7	9.1	S11 27.2	9.6	59.0
01	199 01.5	08.0	108 21.8	9.1	11 17.6	9.8	59.0
02	214 01.5	08.7	122 49.9	9.1	11 07.8	9.7	59.0
03	229 01.4	.. 09.4	137 18.0	9.3	10 58.1	9.8	59.0
04	244 01.3	10.1	151 46.3	9.2	10 48.3	9.9	59.0
05	259 01.3	10.8	166 14.5	9.4	10 38.4	10.0	58.9
06	274 01.2	S17 11.5	180 42.9	9.4	S10 28.4	10.0	58.9
S 07	289 01.2	12.2	195 11.3	9.5	10 18.4	10.0	58.9
U 08	304 01.1	12.9	209 39.8	9.5	10 08.4	10.1	58.9
N 09	319 01.0	.. 13.6	224 08.3	9.6	9 58.3	10.1	58.9
D 10	334 01.0	14.3	238 36.9	9.6	9 48.2	10.2	58.8
A 11	349 00.9	15.0	253 05.5	9.7	9 38.0	10.3	58.8
Y 12	4 00.8	S17 15.7	267 34.2	9.7	S 9 27.7	10.3	58.8
13	19 00.8	16.4	282 02.9	9.8	9 17.4	10.3	58.8
14	34 00.7	17.1	296 31.7	9.9	9 07.1	10.4	58.8
15	49 00.7	.. 17.8	311 00.6	9.9	8 56.7	10.4	58.7
16	64 00.6	18.5	325 29.5	10.0	8 46.3	10.5	58.7
17	79 00.5	19.2	339 58.5	10.0	8 35.8	10.5	58.7
18	94 00.5	S17 19.9	354 27.5	10.1	S 8 25.3	10.5	58.7
19	109 00.4	20.6	8 56.6	10.1	8 14.8	10.6	58.7
20	124 00.3	21.3	23 25.7	10.2	8 04.2	10.6	58.6
21	139 00.3	.. 22.0	37 54.9	10.2	7 53.6	10.7	58.6
22	154 00.2	22.7	52 24.1	10.3	7 42.9	10.7	58.6
23	169 00.1	23.3	66 53.4	10.3	7 32.2	10.7	58.6
11 00	184 00.1	S17 24.0	81 22.7	10.4	S 7 21.5	10.8	58.6
01	199 00.0	24.7	95 52.1	10.4	7 10.7	10.8	58.5
02	213 59.9	25.4	110 21.5	10.5	6 59.9	10.8	58.5
03	228 59.8	.. 26.1	124 51.0	10.5	6 49.1	10.9	58.5
04	243 59.8	26.8	139 20.5	10.5	6 38.2	10.9	58.5
05	258 59.7	27.5	153 50.0	10.6	6 27.3	10.9	58.5
06	273 59.6	S17 28.2	168 19.6	10.7	S 6 16.4	10.9	58.4
M 07	288 59.6	28.9	182 49.3	10.7	6 05.5	11.0	58.4
O 08	303 59.5	29.5	197 19.0	10.7	5 54.5	11.0	58.4
N 09	318 59.4	.. 30.2	211 48.7	10.8	5 43.5	11.0	58.4
D 10	333 59.4	30.9	226 18.5	10.8	5 32.5	11.0	58.4
A 11	348 59.3	31.6	240 48.3	10.9	5 21.5	11.1	58.3
Y 12	3 59.2	S17 32.3	255 18.2	10.9	S 5 10.4	11.1	58.3
13	18 59.1	33.0	269 48.1	11.0	4 59.3	11.1	58.3
14	33 59.1	33.7	284 18.1	11.0	4 48.2	11.1	58.3
15	48 59.0	.. 34.3	298 48.1	11.0	4 37.1	11.1	58.3
16	63 58.9	35.0	313 18.1	11.0	4 26.0	11.2	58.2
17	78 58.8	35.7	327 48.1	11.1	4 14.8	11.2	58.2
18	93 58.8	S17 36.4	342 18.2	11.2	S 4 03.7	11.2	58.2
19	108 58.7	37.1	356 48.4	11.2	3 52.5	11.2	58.2
20	123 58.6	37.7	11 18.6	11.2	3 41.3	11.2	58.2
21	138 58.5	.. 38.4	25 48.8	11.2	3 30.1	11.2	58.1
22	153 58.5	39.1	40 19.0	11.3	3 18.9	11.3	58.1
23	168 58.4	39.8	54 49.3	11.3	S 3 07.6	11.2	58.1
	SD 16.2	d 0.7	SD 16.1		16.0		15.9

Lat.	Twilight Naut.	Twilight Civil	Sunrise	Moonrise 9	10	11	12
°	h m	h m	h m	h m	h m	h m	h m
N 72	06 41	08 11	10 04	14 27	14 14	14 05	13 56
N 70	06 33	07 52	09 19	14 03	14 00	13 58	13 55
68	06 27	07 37	08 50	13 44	13 49	13 52	13 55
66	06 21	07 25	08 29	13 29	13 40	13 48	13 54
64	06 16	07 15	08 12	13 17	13 32	13 44	13 54
62	06 11	07 06	07 57	13 07	13 25	13 40	13 54
60	06 07	06 58	07 46	12 58	13 19	13 37	13 53
N 58	06 03	06 51	07 35	12 50	13 14	13 34	13 53
56	06 00	06 45	07 26	12 43	13 09	13 32	13 53
54	05 57	06 39	07 18	12 36	13 05	13 30	13 53
52	05 54	06 34	07 11	12 31	13 01	13 28	13 53
50	05 51	06 30	07 05	12 26	12 58	13 26	13 52
45	05 44	06 20	06 51	12 15	12 50	13 22	13 52
N 40	05 38	06 11	06 39	12 05	12 44	13 19	13 52
35	05 33	06 03	06 30	11 57	12 38	13 16	13 52
30	05 27	05 56	06 21	11 50	12 33	13 13	13 51
20	05 17	05 43	06 06	11 38	12 25	13 09	13 51
N 10	05 06	05 31	05 53	11 28	12 18	13 05	13 51
0	04 54	05 19	05 40	11 18	12 11	13 01	13 50
S 10	04 40	05 06	05 28	11 08	12 04	12 58	13 50
20	04 23	04 51	05 14	10 57	11 56	12 54	13 50
30	04 02	04 33	04 59	10 45	11 48	12 49	13 50
35	03 49	04 22	04 50	10 38	11 43	12 47	13 50
40	03 32	04 09	04 39	10 30	11 37	12 44	13 49
45	03 12	03 53	04 27	10 20	11 31	12 41	13 49
S 50	02 44	03 34	04 12	10 09	11 23	12 37	13 49
52	02 30	03 24	04 05	10 03	11 19	12 35	13 49
54	02 13	03 13	03 57	09 57	11 15	12 33	13 49
56	01 53	03 01	03 48	09 51	11 11	12 31	13 49
58	01 25	02 46	03 38	09 44	11 06	12 28	13 49
S 60	00 41	02 28	03 26	09 35	11 01	12 25	13 48

Lat.	Sunset	Twilight Civil	Twilight Naut.	Moonset 9	10	11	12
°	h m	h m	h m	h m	h m	h m	h m
N 72	13 23	15 15	16 45	20 53	22 54	24 48	00 48
N 70	14 07	15 34	16 53	21 15	23 06	24 52	00 52
68	14 36	15 49	17 00	21 32	23 15	24 56	00 56
66	14 58	16 02	17 06	21 46	23 23	24 58	00 58
64	15 15	16 12	17 11	21 57	23 30	25 01	01 01
62	15 30	16 21	17 16	22 07	23 36	25 03	01 03
60	15 42	16 29	17 20	22 15	23 41	25 05	01 05
N 58	15 52	16 36	17 24	22 22	23 45	25 06	01 06
56	16 01	16 42	17 27	22 29	23 49	25 08	01 08
54	16 09	16 48	17 30	22 34	23 52	25 09	01 09
52	16 16	16 53	17 34	22 39	23 55	25 10	01 10
50	16 23	16 58	17 36	22 44	23 58	25 11	01 11
45	16 36	17 08	17 43	22 54	24 04	00 04	01 13
N 40	16 48	17 17	17 49	23 02	24 09	00 09	01 15
35	16 58	17 25	17 55	23 09	24 14	00 14	01 17
30	17 07	17 32	18 00	23 15	24 17	00 17	01 18
20	17 22	17 45	18 11	23 25	24 24	00 24	01 21
N 10	17 35	17 57	18 22	23 35	24 30	00 30	01 23
0	17 47	18 09	18 34	23 43	24 35	00 35	01 25
S 10	18 00	18 22	18 48	23 52	24 40	00 40	01 27
20	18 14	18 37	19 05	24 01	00 01	00 46	01 29
30	18 30	18 55	19 26	24 11	00 11	00 52	01 31
35	18 39	19 07	19 40	24 17	00 17	00 56	01 32
40	18 49	19 20	19 57	24 23	00 23	01 00	01 34
45	19 02	19 35	20 17	24 31	00 31	01 05	01 36
S 50	19 17	19 55	20 45	00 05	00 40	01 10	01 38
52	19 24	20 05	21 00	00 11	00 44	01 13	01 39
54	19 32	20 16	21 17	00 18	00 49	01 16	01 40
56	19 41	20 29	21 38	00 25	00 54	01 19	01 41
58	19 52	20 44	22 07	00 33	01 00	01 22	01 42
S 60	20 03	21 02	22 56	00 42	01 06	01 26	01 43

Day	SUN Eqn. of Time 00h	SUN Eqn. of Time 12h	Mer. Pass.	MOON Mer. Pass. Upper	MOON Mer. Pass. Lower	Age	Phase
d	m s	m s	h m	h m	h m	d	%
9	16 12	16 09	11 44	17 30	05 03	06	42
10	16 06	16 04	11 44	18 23	05 57	07	53
11	16 00	15 57	11 44	19 13	06 48	08	64

UT	ARIES GHA	VENUS −4.7 GHA	Dec	MARS +1.4 GHA	Dec	JUPITER −2.5 GHA	Dec	SATURN +0.5 GHA	Dec	STARS Name	SHA	Dec
12 00	51 17.3	134 15.3	S27 01.5	243 30.9	N 7 02.8	299 08.8	N21 52.9	188 12.8	S14 16.8	Acamar	315 17.7	S40 15.0
01	66 19.8	149 15.2	01.4	258 32.1	02.2	314 11.3	52.9	203 14.9	16.9	Achernar	335 26.1	S57 10.1
02	81 22.2	164 15.1	01.3	273 33.2	01.7	329 13.8	52.9	218 17.1	17.0	Acrux	173 09.4	S63 10.3
03	96 24.7	179 15.0	.. 01.1	288 34.4	.. 01.2	344 16.3	.. 52.9	233 19.3	.. 17.1	Adhara	255 12.1	S28 59.4
04	111 27.2	194 14.9	01.0	303 35.5	00.7	359 18.8	52.9	248 21.5	17.2	Aldebaran	290 48.7	N16 32.1
05	126 29.6	209 14.8	00.9	318 36.7	7 00.1	14 21.3	53.0	263 23.6	17.2			
06	141 32.1	224 14.7	S27 00.7	333 37.8	N 6 59.6	29 23.8	N21 53.0	278 25.8	S14 17.3	Alioth	166 21.0	N55 52.9
07	156 34.6	239 14.6	00.6	348 39.0	59.1	44 26.3	53.0	293 28.0	17.4	Alkaid	152 59.2	N49 14.6
T 08	171 37.0	254 14.5	00.5	3 40.1	58.6	59 28.8	53.0	308 30.1	17.5	Al Na'ir	27 43.4	S46 53.7
U 09	186 39.5	269 14.4	.. 00.3	18 41.3	.. 58.0	74 31.3	.. 53.0	323 32.3	.. 17.6	Alnilam	275 45.8	S 1 11.7
E 10	201 41.9	284 14.3	00.2	33 42.4	57.5	89 33.8	53.0	338 34.5	17.7	Alphard	217 55.8	S 8 43.1
S 11	216 44.4	299 14.3	27 00.1	48 43.6	57.0	104 36.3	53.0	353 36.6	17.8			
D 12	231 46.9	314 14.2	S26 59.9	63 44.7	N 6 56.5	119 38.9	N21 53.0	8 38.8	S14 17.9	Alphecca	126 11.2	N26 40.3
A 13	246 49.3	329 14.1	59.8	78 45.9	55.9	134 41.4	53.0	23 41.0	17.9	Alpheratz	357 42.9	N29 10.3
Y 14	261 51.8	344 14.0	59.7	93 47.0	55.4	149 43.9	53.1	38 43.1	18.0	Altair	62 08.1	N 8 54.6
15	276 54.3	359 13.9	.. 59.5	108 48.2	.. 54.9	164 46.4	.. 53.1	53 45.3	.. 18.1	Ankaa	353 15.2	S42 13.9
16	291 56.7	14 13.8	59.4	123 49.3	54.4	179 48.9	53.1	68 47.5	18.2	Antares	112 26.3	S26 27.6
17	306 59.2	29 13.8	59.2	138 50.5	53.8	194 51.4	53.1	83 49.6	18.3			
18	322 01.7	44 13.7	S26 59.1	153 51.6	N 6 53.3	209 53.9	N21 53.1	98 51.8	S14 18.4	Arcturus	145 55.8	N19 06.7
19	337 04.1	59 13.6	58.9	168 52.8	52.8	224 56.4	53.1	113 54.0	18.5	Atria	107 28.3	S69 03.0
20	352 06.6	74 13.5	58.8	183 53.9	52.3	239 58.9	53.1	128 56.2	18.5	Avior	234 17.6	S59 33.1
21	7 09.0	89 13.5	.. 58.7	198 55.1	.. 51.7	255 01.5	.. 53.1	143 58.3	.. 18.6	Bellatrix	278 31.4	N 6 21.6
22	22 11.5	104 13.4	58.5	213 56.2	51.2	270 04.0	53.2	159 00.5	18.7	Betelgeuse	271 00.7	N 7 24.5
23	37 14.0	119 13.3	58.4	228 57.4	50.7	285 06.5	53.2	174 02.7	18.8			
13 00	52 16.4	134 13.2	S26 58.2	243 58.5	N 6 50.2	300 09.0	N21 53.2	189 04.8	S14 18.9	Canopus	263 55.6	S52 42.1
01	67 18.9	149 13.2	58.1	258 59.7	49.6	315 11.5	53.2	204 07.0	19.0	Capella	280 33.6	N46 00.5
02	82 21.4	164 13.1	57.9	274 00.8	49.1	330 14.0	53.2	219 09.2	19.1	Deneb	49 31.4	N45 20.2
03	97 23.8	179 13.0	.. 57.8	289 02.0	.. 48.6	345 16.5	.. 53.2	234 11.3	.. 19.2	Denebola	182 33.6	N14 29.6
04	112 26.3	194 13.0	57.6	304 03.2	48.1	0 19.1	53.2	249 13.5	19.2	Diphda	348 55.4	S17 54.6
05	127 28.8	209 12.9	57.5	319 04.3	47.5	15 21.6	53.2	264 15.7	19.3			
06	142 31.2	224 12.9	S26 57.3	334 05.5	N 6 47.0	30 24.1	N21 53.3	279 17.8	S14 19.4	Dubhe	193 51.7	N61 40.2
W 07	157 33.7	239 12.8	57.2	349 06.6	46.5	45 26.6	53.3	294 20.0	19.5	Elnath	278 11.9	N28 37.0
E 08	172 36.2	254 12.7	57.0	4 07.8	46.0	60 29.1	53.3	309 22.2	19.6	Eltanin	90 46.5	N51 29.6
D 09	187 38.6	269 12.7	.. 56.8	19 08.9	.. 45.4	75 31.6	.. 53.3	324 24.4	.. 19.7	Enif	33 46.8	N 9 56.6
N 10	202 41.1	284 12.6	56.7	34 10.1	44.9	90 34.2	53.3	339 26.5	19.8	Fomalhaut	15 23.6	S29 32.9
E 11	217 43.5	299 12.6	56.5	49 11.2	44.4	105 36.7	53.3	354 28.7	19.9			
S 12	232 46.0	314 12.5	S26 56.4	64 12.4	N 6 43.9	120 39.2	N21 53.3	9 30.9	S14 19.9	Gacrux	172 00.9	S57 11.2
D 13	247 48.5	329 12.5	56.2	79 13.6	43.3	135 41.7	53.4	24 33.0	20.0	Gienah	175 52.2	S17 37.0
A 14	262 50.9	344 12.4	56.1	94 14.7	42.8	150 44.2	53.4	39 35.2	20.1	Hadar	148 48.0	S60 26.2
Y 15	277 53.4	359 12.4	.. 55.9	109 15.9	.. 42.3	165 46.8	.. 53.4	54 37.4	.. 20.2	Hamal	328 00.1	N23 31.8
16	292 55.9	14 12.3	55.7	124 17.0	41.8	180 49.3	53.4	69 39.5	20.3	Kaus Aust.	83 43.8	S34 22.5
17	307 58.3	29 12.3	55.6	139 18.2	41.2	195 51.8	53.4	84 41.7	20.4			
18	323 00.8	44 12.2	S26 55.4	154 19.3	N 6 40.7	210 54.3	N21 53.4	99 43.9	S14 20.4	Kochab	137 21.3	N74 05.9
19	338 03.3	59 12.2	55.2	169 20.5	40.2	225 56.8	53.4	114 46.0	20.5	Markab	13 37.9	N15 17.1
20	353 05.7	74 12.1	55.1	184 21.6	39.7	240 59.4	53.4	129 48.2	20.6	Menkar	314 14.4	N 4 08.6
21	8 08.2	89 12.1	.. 54.9	199 22.8	.. 39.1	256 01.9	.. 53.5	144 50.4	.. 20.7	Menkent	148 07.6	S36 26.1
22	23 10.7	104 12.0	54.7	214 24.0	38.6	271 04.4	53.5	159 52.6	20.8	Miaplacidus	221 39.4	S69 46.3
23	38 13.1	119 12.0	54.6	229 25.1	38.1	286 06.9	53.5	174 54.7	20.9			
14 00	53 15.6	134 12.0	S26 54.4	244 26.3	N 6 37.6	301 09.5	N21 53.5	189 56.9	S14 21.0	Mirfak	308 39.4	N49 54.6
01	68 18.0	149 11.9	54.2	259 27.4	37.0	316 12.0	53.5	204 59.1	21.1	Nunki	75 58.2	S26 16.6
02	83 20.5	164 11.9	54.1	274 28.6	36.5	331 14.5	53.5	220 01.2	21.1	Peacock	53 19.0	S56 41.5
03	98 23.0	179 11.9	.. 53.9	289 29.7	.. 36.0	346 17.0	.. 53.5	235 03.4	.. 21.2	Pollux	243 27.2	N27 59.3
04	113 25.4	194 11.8	53.7	304 30.9	35.5	1 19.6	53.6	250 05.6	21.3	Procyon	244 59.3	N 5 11.2
05	128 27.9	209 11.8	53.5	319 32.1	34.9	16 22.1	53.6	265 07.7	21.4			
06	143 30.4	224 11.8	S26 53.4	334 33.2	N 6 34.4	31 24.6	N21 53.6	280 09.9	S14 21.5	Rasalhague	96 06.5	N12 33.3
07	158 32.8	239 11.7	53.2	349 34.4	33.9	46 27.1	53.6	295 12.1	21.6	Regulus	207 43.3	N11 53.8
T 08	173 35.3	254 11.7	53.0	4 35.5	33.4	61 29.7	53.6	310 14.2	21.7	Rigel	281 11.5	S 8 11.2
H 09	188 37.8	269 11.7	.. 52.8	19 36.7	.. 32.8	76 32.2	.. 53.6	325 16.4	.. 21.8	Rigil Kent.	139 51.9	S60 53.3
U 10	203 40.2	284 11.7	52.6	34 37.9	32.3	91 34.7	53.6	340 18.6	21.8	Sabik	102 12.5	S15 44.3
R 11	218 42.7	299 11.6	52.5	49 39.0	31.8	106 37.2	53.7	355 20.7	21.9			
S 12	233 45.1	314 11.6	S26 52.3	64 40.2	N 6 31.3	121 39.8	N21 53.7	10 22.9	S14 22.0	Schedar	349 39.7	N56 37.1
D 13	248 47.6	329 11.6	52.1	79 41.3	30.8	136 42.3	53.7	25 25.1	22.1	Shaula	96 21.9	S37 06.7
A 14	263 50.1	344 11.6	51.9	94 42.5	30.2	151 44.8	53.7	40 27.3	22.2	Sirius	258 33.2	S16 44.1
Y 15	278 52.5	359 11.5	.. 51.7	109 43.7	.. 29.7	166 47.4	.. 53.7	55 29.4	.. 22.3	Spica	158 31.2	S11 13.9
16	293 55.0	14 11.5	51.6	124 44.8	29.2	181 49.9	53.7	70 31.6	22.4	Suhail	222 52.2	S43 29.2
17	308 57.5	29 11.5	51.4	139 46.0	28.7	196 52.4	53.7	85 33.8	22.4			
18	323 59.9	44 11.5	S26 51.2	154 47.1	N 6 28.1	211 54.9	N21 53.8	100 35.9	S14 22.5	Vega	80 39.1	N38 48.2
19	339 02.4	59 11.5	51.0	169 48.3	27.6	226 57.5	53.8	115 38.1	22.6	Zuben'ubi	137 05.4	S16 05.8
20	354 04.9	74 11.5	50.8	184 49.5	27.1	242 00.0	53.8	130 40.3	22.7		SHA	Mer. Pass.
21	9 07.3	89 11.5	.. 50.6	199 50.6	.. 26.6	257 02.5	.. 53.8	145 42.4	.. 22.8		° ′	h m
22	24 09.8	104 11.5	50.4	214 51.8	26.0	272 05.1	53.8	160 44.6	22.9	Venus	81 56.8	15 03
23	39 12.3	119 11.5	50.2	229 53.0	25.5	287 07.6	53.8	175 46.8	23.0	Mars	191 42.1	7 44
	h m									Jupiter	247 52.6	3 59
Mer. Pass. 20 27.5		v −0.1 d 0.2		v 1.2 d 0.5		v 2.5 d 0.0		v 2.2 d 0.1		Saturn	136 48.4	11 22

UT	SUN GHA	SUN Dec	MOON GHA	MOON v	MOON Dec	MOON d	MOON HP	Lat.	Twilight Naut.	Twilight Civil	Sunrise	Moonrise 12	Moonrise 13	Moonrise 14	Moonrise 15
d h	° '	° '	° '	'	° '	'	'	°	h m	h m	h m	h m	h m	h m	h m
12 00	183 58.3	S17 40.5	69 19.6	11.3	S 2 56.4	11.2	58.1	N 72	06 53	08 25	10 35	13 56	13 47	13 38	13 28
01	198 58.2	41.1	83 49.9	11.4	2 45.2	11.3	58.0	N 70	06 43	08 04	09 37	13 55	13 53	13 50	13 48
02	213 58.2	41.8	98 20.3	11.4	2 33.9	11.2	58.0	68	06 35	07 48	09 04	13 55	13 57	14 00	14 04
03	228 58.1 ..	42.5	112 50.7	11.5	2 22.7	11.3	58.0	66	06 29	07 34	08 40	13 54	14 01	14 08	14 17
04	243 58.0	43.2	127 21.2	11.4	2 11.4	11.3	58.0	64	06 23	07 23	08 21	13 54	14 04	14 15	14 28
05	258 57.9	43.8	141 51.6	11.5	2 00.1	11.2	58.0	62	06 18	07 13	08 06	13 54	14 07	14 21	14 37
06	273 57.8	S17 44.5	156 22.1	11.5	S 1 48.9	11.3	57.9	60	06 13	07 05	07 53	13 53	14 09	14 26	14 45
07	288 57.8	45.2	170 52.6	11.6	1 37.6	11.3	57.9	N 58	06 09	06 57	07 42	13 53	14 11	14 30	14 52
T 08	303 57.7	45.9	185 23.2	11.5	1 26.3	11.2	57.9	56	06 05	06 51	07 33	13 53	14 13	14 35	14 58
U 09	318 57.6 ..	46.5	199 53.7	11.6	1 15.1	11.3	57.9	54	06 02	06 45	07 24	13 53	14 15	14 38	15 03
E 10	333 57.5	47.2	214 24.3	11.7	1 03.8	11.3	57.9	52	05 58	06 39	07 17	13 53	14 17	14 42	15 08
S 11	348 57.4	47.9	228 55.0	11.6	0 52.5	11.2	57.8	50	05 55	06 34	07 10	13 52	14 18	14 45	15 13
D 12	3 57.4	S17 48.6	243 25.6	11.7	S 0 41.3	11.3	57.8	45	05 48	06 23	06 55	13 52	14 21	14 51	15 23
A 13	18 57.3	49.2	257 56.3	11.7	0 30.0	11.3	57.8	N 40	05 41	06 14	06 43	13 52	14 24	14 57	15 31
Y 14	33 57.2	49.9	272 27.0	11.7	0 18.7	11.2	57.8	35	05 35	06 06	06 33	13 52	14 26	15 02	15 38
15	48 57.1 ..	50.6	286 57.7	11.7	S 0 07.5	11.3	57.8	30	05 29	05 58	06 23	13 51	14 29	15 06	15 45
16	63 57.0	51.2	301 28.4	11.8	N 0 03.8	11.2	57.7	20	05 18	05 45	06 08	13 51	14 32	15 13	15 56
17	78 56.9	51.9	315 59.2	11.8	0 15.0	11.2	57.7	N 10	05 06	05 32	05 54	13 51	14 35	15 20	16 05
18	93 56.9	S17 52.6	330 30.0	11.8	N 0 26.2	11.2	57.7	0	04 54	05 19	05 41	13 50	14 39	15 26	16 14
19	108 56.8	53.2	345 00.8	11.8	0 37.4	11.3	57.7	S 10	04 39	05 05	05 28	13 50	14 42	15 33	16 24
20	123 56.7	53.9	359 31.6	11.8	0 48.7	11.1	57.6	20	04 22	04 50	05 13	13 50	14 45	15 39	16 33
21	138 56.6 ..	54.6	14 02.4	11.8	0 59.8	11.2	57.6	30	04 00	04 31	04 57	13 50	14 49	15 47	16 45
22	153 56.5	55.2	28 33.2	11.9	1 11.0	11.2	57.6	35	03 46	04 19	04 47	13 50	14 51	15 52	16 51
23	168 56.4	55.9	43 04.1	11.9	1 22.2	11.2	57.6	40	03 29	04 06	04 36	13 49	14 54	15 57	16 59
13 00	183 56.4	S17 56.6	57 35.0	11.9	N 1 33.4	11.1	57.6	45	03 07	03 50	04 23	13 49	14 57	16 03	17 07
01	198 56.3	57.2	72 05.9	11.9	1 44.5	11.1	57.5	S 50	02 38	03 29	04 07	13 49	15 00	16 10	17 18
02	213 56.2	57.9	86 36.8	11.9	1 55.6	11.1	57.5	52	02 23	03 19	04 00	13 49	15 02	16 13	17 23
03	228 56.1 ..	58.6	101 07.7	12.0	2 06.7	11.1	57.5	54	02 05	03 07	03 51	13 49	15 04	16 17	17 28
04	243 56.0	59.2	115 38.7	11.9	2 17.8	11.1	57.5	56	01 42	02 54	03 42	13 49	15 06	16 21	17 34
05	258 55.9	17 59.9	130 09.6	12.0	2 28.9	11.1	57.5	58	01 10	02 38	03 31	13 49	15 08	16 25	17 41
06	273 55.8	S18 00.6	144 40.6	11.9	N 2 40.0	11.0	57.4	S 60	////	02 19	03 19	13 48	15 10	16 31	17 49
W 07	288 55.7	01.2	159 11.5	12.0	2 51.0	11.0	57.4								
E 08	303 55.7	01.9	173 42.5	12.0	3 02.0	11.0	57.4	Lat.	Sunset	Twilight Civil	Twilight Naut.	Moonset 12	Moonset 13	Moonset 14	Moonset 15
D 09	318 55.6 ..	02.5	188 13.5	12.0	3 13.0	11.0	57.4								
N 10	333 55.5	03.2	202 44.5	12.0	3 24.0	10.9	57.4	°	h m	h m	h m	h m	h m	h m	h m
E 11	348 55.4	03.9	217 15.5	12.1	3 34.9	10.9	57.3	N 72	12 53	15 02	16 35	00 48	02 38	04 28	06 18
S 12	3 55.3	S18 04.5	231 46.6	12.0	N 3 45.8	10.9	57.3	N 70	13 50	15 23	16 44	00 52	02 36	04 18	05 59
D 13	18 55.2	05.2	246 17.6	12.0	3 56.7	10.9	57.3	68	14 24	15 40	16 52	00 56	02 33	04 10	05 45
A 14	33 55.1	05.8	260 48.6	12.1	4 07.6	10.8	57.3	66	14 48	15 54	16 59	00 58	02 31	04 03	05 33
Y 15	48 55.0 ..	06.5	275 19.7	12.0	4 18.4	10.8	57.2	64	15 06	16 05	17 05	01 01	02 30	03 57	05 23
16	63 54.9	07.1	289 50.7	12.0	4 29.2	10.8	57.2	62	15 22	16 15	17 10	01 03	02 29	03 53	05 15
17	78 54.8	07.8	304 21.7	12.1	4 40.0	10.7	57.2	60	15 35	16 23	17 15	01 05	02 27	03 48	05 08
18	93 54.8	S18 08.5	318 52.8	12.1	N 4 50.7	10.8	57.2	N 58	15 46	16 31	17 19	01 06	02 26	03 45	05 02
19	108 54.7	09.1	333 23.9	12.0	5 01.5	10.6	57.2	56	15 55	16 37	17 23	01 08	02 25	03 41	04 56
20	123 54.6	09.8	347 54.9	12.1	5 12.1	10.7	57.1	54	16 04	16 43	17 26	01 09	02 24	03 39	04 51
21	138 54.5 ..	10.4	2 26.0	12.0	5 22.8	10.6	57.1	52	16 12	16 49	17 30	01 10	02 24	03 36	04 47
22	153 54.4	11.1	16 57.0	12.1	5 33.4	10.6	57.1	50	16 18	16 54	17 33	01 11	02 23	03 33	04 43
23	168 54.3	11.7	31 28.1	12.1	5 44.0	10.5	57.1	45	16 33	17 05	17 40	01 13	02 21	03 28	04 34
14 00	183 54.2	S18 12.4	45 59.2	12.0	N 5 54.5	10.6	57.1	N 40	16 45	17 14	17 47	01 15	02 20	03 24	04 27
01	198 54.1	13.0	60 30.2	12.1	6 05.1	10.4	57.0	35	16 56	17 23	17 53	01 17	02 19	03 20	04 20
02	213 54.0	13.7	75 01.3	12.1	6 15.5	10.5	57.0	30	17 05	17 30	17 59	01 18	02 18	03 17	04 15
03	228 53.9 ..	14.3	89 32.4	12.0	6 26.0	10.4	57.0	20	17 21	17 44	18 10	01 21	02 16	03 11	04 05
04	243 53.8	15.0	104 03.4	12.1	6 36.4	10.3	57.0	N 10	17 35	17 57	18 22	01 23	02 15	03 06	03 57
05	258 53.7	15.6	118 34.5	12.1	6 46.7	10.4	57.0	0	17 48	18 10	18 35	01 25	02 13	03 01	03 49
06	273 53.6	S18 16.3	133 05.6	12.0	N 6 57.1	10.2	56.9	S 10	18 01	18 23	18 49	01 27	02 12	02 57	03 42
T 07	288 53.5	16.9	147 36.6	12.1	7 07.3	10.3	56.9	20	18 16	18 39	19 07	01 29	02 10	02 52	03 33
H 08	303 53.4	17.6	162 07.7	12.0	7 17.6	10.2	56.9	30	18 32	18 58	19 29	01 31	02 09	02 46	03 24
U 09	318 53.3 ..	18.2	176 38.7	12.1	7 27.8	10.1	56.9	35	18 42	19 10	19 44	01 32	02 08	02 43	03 19
R 10	333 53.2	18.9	191 09.8	12.0	7 37.9	10.1	56.9	40	18 53	19 24	20 23	01 34	02 07	02 39	03 12
S 11	348 53.1	19.5	205 40.8	12.1	7 48.0	10.1	56.8	45	19 06	19 40	20 23	01 36	02 05	02 35	03 05
D 12	3 53.0	S18 20.2	220 11.9	12.0	N 7 58.1	10.0	56.8	S 50	19 22	20 01	20 52	01 38	02 04	02 30	02 57
A 13	18 52.9	20.8	234 42.9	12.0	8 08.1	10.0	56.8	52	19 30	20 11	21 08	01 39	02 03	02 27	02 53
Y 14	33 52.8	21.4	249 13.9	12.0	8 18.1	9.9	56.8	54	19 38	20 23	21 26	01 40	02 02	02 25	02 49
15	48 52.7 ..	22.1	263 44.9	12.0	8 28.0	9.9	56.8	56	19 48	20 37	21 50	01 41	02 01	02 22	02 44
16	63 52.6	22.7	278 15.9	12.1	8 37.9	9.8	56.7	58	19 59	20 54	22 24	01 42	02 00	02 19	02 39
17	78 52.5	23.4	292 47.0	12.0	8 47.7	9.8	56.7	S 60	20 12	21 13	////	01 43	01 59	02 15	02 33
18	93 52.4	S18 24.0	307 18.0	11.9	N 8 57.5	9.7	56.7								
19	108 52.3	24.7	321 48.9	12.0	9 07.2	9.7	56.7		SUN			MOON			
20	123 52.2	25.3	336 19.9	12.0	9 16.9	9.6	56.7	Day	Eqn. of Time 00ʰ	Eqn. of Time 12ʰ	Mer. Pass.	Mer. Pass. Upper	Mer. Pass. Lower	Age	Phase
21	138 52.1 ..	25.9	350 50.9	12.0	9 26.5	9.6	56.6								
22	153 52.0	26.6	5 21.9	11.9	9 36.1	9.5	56.6	d	m s	m s	h m	h m	h m	d	%
23	168 51.9	27.2	19 52.8	12.0	N 9 45.6	9.4	56.6	12	15 53	15 50	11 44	20 02	07 38	09	74
								13	15 46	15 41	11 44	20 50	08 26	10	83
	SD 16.2	d 0.7	SD 15.8		15.6		15.5	14	15 37	15 32	11 44	21 38	09 14	11	90

UT	ARIES GHA	VENUS −4.7 GHA	Dec	MARS +1.4 GHA	Dec	JUPITER −2.5 GHA	Dec	SATURN +0.5 GHA	Dec	STARS Name	SHA	Dec
15 00	54 14.7	134 11.5	S26 50.0	244 54.1	N 6 25.0	302 10.1	N21 53.8	190 49.0	S14 23.0	Acamar	315 17.7	S40 15.0
01	69 17.2	149 11.5	49.9	259 55.3	24.5	317 12.7	53.9	205 51.1	23.1	Achernar	335 26.1	S57 10.1
02	84 19.6	164 11.5	49.7	274 56.4	23.9	332 15.2	53.9	220 53.3	23.2	Acrux	173 09.3	S63 10.3
03	99 22.1	179 11.5 ..	49.5	289 57.6 ..	23.4	347 17.7 ..	53.9	235 55.5 ..	23.3	Adhara	255 12.0	S28 59.5
04	114 24.6	194 11.5	49.3	304 58.8	22.9	2 20.3	53.9	250 57.6	23.4	Aldebaran	290 48.7	N16 32.1
05	129 27.0	209 11.5	49.1	319 59.9	22.4	17 22.8	53.9	265 59.8	23.5			
06	144 29.5	224 11.5	S26 48.9	335 01.1	N 6 21.8	32 25.3	N21 53.9	281 02.0	S14 23.6	Alioth	166 21.0	N55 52.9
07	159 32.0	239 11.5	48.7	350 02.3	21.3	47 27.9	54.0	296 04.1	23.6	Alkaid	152 59.2	N49 14.6
08	174 34.4	254 11.5	48.5	5 03.4	20.8	62 30.4	54.0	311 06.3	23.7	Al Na'ir	27 43.4	S46 53.7
F 09	189 36.9	269 11.5 ..	48.3	20 04.6 ..	20.3	77 32.9 ..	54.0	326 08.5 ..	23.8	Alnilam	275 45.8	S 1 11.7
R 10	204 39.4	284 11.5	48.1	35 05.7	19.8	92 35.5	54.0	341 10.6	23.9	Alphard	217 55.8	S 8 43.2
I 11	219 41.8	299 11.5	47.9	50 06.9	19.2	107 38.0	54.0	356 12.8	24.0			
D 12	234 44.3	314 11.5	S26 47.7	65 08.1	N 6 18.7	122 40.5	N21 54.0	11 15.0	S14 24.1	Alphecca	126 11.2	N26 40.2
A 13	249 46.8	329 11.5	47.5	80 09.2	18.2	137 43.1	54.0	26 17.2	24.2	Alpheratz	357 43.0	N29 10.3
Y 14	264 49.2	344 11.5	47.3	95 10.4	17.7	152 45.6	54.1	41 19.3	24.3	Altair	62 08.1	N 8 54.6
15	279 51.7	359 11.6 ..	47.1	110 11.6 ..	17.1	167 48.2 ..	54.1	56 21.5 ..	24.3	Ankaa	353 15.2	S42 13.9
16	294 54.1	14 11.6	46.9	125 12.7	16.6	182 50.7	54.1	71 23.7	24.4	Antares	112 26.3	S26 27.6
17	309 56.6	29 11.6	46.6	140 13.9	16.1	197 53.2	54.1	86 25.8	24.5			
18	324 59.1	44 11.6	S26 46.4	155 15.1	N 6 15.6	212 55.8	N21 54.1	101 28.0	S14 24.6	Arcturus	145 55.8	N19 06.7
19	340 01.5	59 11.6	46.2	170 16.2	15.0	227 58.3	54.1	116 30.2	24.7	Atria	107 28.3	S69 03.0
20	355 04.0	74 11.7	46.0	185 17.4	14.5	243 00.9	54.2	131 32.3	24.8	Avior	234 17.6	S59 33.1
21	10 06.5	89 11.7 ..	45.8	200 18.6 ..	14.0	258 03.4 ..	54.2	146 34.5 ..	24.9	Bellatrix	278 31.4	N 6 21.6
22	25 08.9	104 11.7	45.6	215 19.7	13.5	273 05.9	54.2	161 36.7	24.9	Betelgeuse	271 00.7	N 7 24.4
23	40 11.4	119 11.7	45.4	230 20.9	13.0	288 08.5	54.2	176 38.9	25.0			
16 00	55 13.9	134 11.8	S26 45.2	245 22.1	N 6 12.4	303 11.0	N21 54.2	191 41.0	S14 25.1	Canopus	263 55.6	S52 42.1
01	70 16.3	149 11.8	45.0	260 23.2	11.9	318 13.6	54.2	206 43.2	25.2	Capella	280 33.6	N46 00.5
02	85 18.8	164 11.8	44.7	275 24.4	11.4	333 16.1	54.3	221 45.4	25.3	Deneb	49 31.4	N45 20.2
03	100 21.2	179 11.9 ..	44.5	290 25.6 ..	10.9	348 18.6 ..	54.3	236 47.5 ..	25.4	Denebola	182 33.6	N14 29.6
04	115 23.7	194 11.9	44.3	305 26.7	10.3	3 21.2	54.3	251 49.7	25.4	Diphda	348 55.4	S17 54.6
05	130 26.2	209 11.9	44.1	320 27.9	09.8	18 23.7	54.3	266 51.9	25.5			
06	145 28.6	224 12.0	S26 43.9	335 29.1	N 6 09.3	33 26.3	N21 54.3	281 54.0	S14 25.6	Dubhe	193 51.7	N61 40.2
07	160 31.1	239 12.0	43.7	350 30.2	08.8	48 28.8	54.3	296 56.2	25.7	Elnath	278 11.9	N28 37.0
08	175 33.6	254 12.1	43.4	5 31.4	08.2	63 31.4	54.4	311 58.4	25.8	Eltanin	90 46.5	N51 29.6
S 09	190 36.0	269 12.1 ..	43.2	20 32.6 ..	07.7	78 33.9 ..	54.4	327 00.5 ..	25.9	Enif	33 46.8	N 9 56.6
A 10	205 38.5	284 12.2	43.0	35 33.7	07.2	93 36.4	54.4	342 02.7	26.0	Fomalhaut	15 23.6	S29 32.9
T 11	220 41.0	299 12.2	42.8	50 34.9	06.7	108 39.0	54.4	357 04.9	26.0			
U 12	235 43.4	314 12.3	S26 42.5	65 36.1	N 6 06.2	123 41.5	N21 54.4	12 07.1	S14 26.1	Gacrux	172 00.9	S57 11.2
R 13	250 45.9	329 12.3	42.3	80 37.3	05.6	138 44.1	54.4	27 09.2	26.2	Gienah	175 52.2	S17 37.0
D 14	265 48.4	344 12.4	42.1	95 38.4	05.1	153 46.6	54.5	42 11.4	26.3	Hadar	148 48.0	S60 26.2
A 15	280 50.8	359 12.4 ..	41.9	110 39.6 ..	04.6	168 49.2 ..	54.5	57 13.6 ..	26.4	Hamal	328 00.1	N23 31.8
Y 16	295 53.3	14 12.5	41.6	125 40.8	04.1	183 51.7	54.5	72 15.7	26.5	Kaus Aust.	83 43.8	S34 22.5
17	310 55.7	29 12.5	41.4	140 41.9	03.5	198 54.3	54.5	87 17.9	26.6			
18	325 58.2	44 12.6	S26 41.2	155 43.1	N 6 03.0	213 56.8	N21 54.5	102 20.1	S14 26.6	Kochab	137 21.3	N74 05.9
19	341 00.7	59 12.6	41.0	170 44.3	02.5	228 59.4	54.5	117 22.2	26.7	Markab	13 37.9	N15 17.1
20	356 03.1	74 12.7	40.7	185 45.4	02.0	244 01.9	54.6	132 24.4	26.8	Menkar	314 14.4	N 4 08.6
21	11 05.6	89 12.7 ..	40.5	200 46.6 ..	01.5	259 04.5 ..	54.6	147 26.6 ..	26.9	Menkent	148 07.6	S36 26.1
22	26 08.1	104 12.8	40.3	215 47.8	00.9	274 07.0	54.6	162 28.8	27.0	Miaplacidus	221 39.4	S69 46.3
23	41 10.5	119 12.9	40.0	230 49.0	6 00.4	289 09.6	54.6	177 30.9	27.1			
17 00	56 13.0	134 12.9	S26 39.8	245 50.1	N 5 59.9	304 12.1	N21 54.6	192 33.1	S14 27.2	Mirfak	308 39.4	N49 54.6
01	71 15.5	149 13.0	39.6	260 51.3	59.4	319 14.7	54.6	207 35.3	27.2	Nunki	75 58.2	S26 16.6
02	86 17.9	164 13.1	39.3	275 52.5	58.8	334 17.2	54.7	222 37.4	27.3	Peacock	53 19.1	S56 41.4
03	101 20.4	179 13.1 ..	39.1	290 53.6 ..	58.3	349 19.8 ..	54.7	237 39.6 ..	27.4	Pollux	243 27.2	N27 59.3
04	116 22.9	194 13.2	38.9	305 54.8	57.8	4 22.3	54.7	252 41.8	27.5	Procyon	244 59.3	N 5 11.2
05	131 25.3	209 13.3	38.6	320 56.0	57.3	19 24.9	54.7	267 43.9	27.6			
06	146 27.8	224 13.4	S26 38.4	335 57.2	N 5 56.8	34 27.4	N21 54.7	282 46.1	S14 27.7	Rasalhague	96 06.5	N12 33.3
07	161 30.2	239 13.4	38.1	350 58.3	56.2	49 30.0	54.8	297 48.3	27.8	Regulus	207 43.3	N11 53.8
08	176 32.7	254 13.5	37.9	5 59.5	55.7	64 32.5	54.8	312 50.5	27.8	Rigel	281 11.5	S 8 11.2
S 09	191 35.2	269 13.6 ..	37.7	21 00.7 ..	55.2	79 35.1 ..	54.8	327 52.6 ..	27.9	Rigil Kent.	139 51.9	S60 53.3
U 10	206 37.6	284 13.7	37.4	36 01.8	54.7	94 37.6	54.8	342 54.8	28.0	Sabik	102 12.5	S15 44.3
N 11	221 40.1	299 13.8	37.2	51 03.0	54.1	109 40.2	54.8	357 57.0	28.1			
D 12	236 42.6	314 13.9	S26 36.9	66 04.2	N 5 53.6	124 42.7	N21 54.8	12 59.1	S14 28.2	Schedar	349 39.7	N56 37.1
A 13	251 45.0	329 13.9	36.7	81 05.4	53.1	139 45.3	54.9	28 01.3	28.3	Shaula	96 21.9	S37 06.7
Y 14	266 47.5	344 14.0	36.4	96 06.5	52.6	154 47.8	54.9	43 03.5	28.3	Sirius	258 33.2	S16 44.2
15	281 50.0	359 14.1 ..	36.2	111 07.7 ..	52.1	169 50.4 ..	54.9	58 05.6 ..	28.4	Spica	158 31.2	S11 13.9
16	296 52.4	14 14.2	35.9	126 08.9	51.5	184 52.9	54.9	73 07.8	28.5	Suhail	222 52.1	S43 29.2
17	311 54.9	29 14.3	35.7	141 10.1	51.0	199 55.5	54.9	88 10.0	28.6			
18	326 57.3	44 14.4	S26 35.4	156 11.2	N 5 50.5	214 58.1	N21 55.0	103 12.2	S14 28.7	Vega	80 39.1	N38 48.2
19	341 59.8	59 14.5	35.2	171 12.4	50.0	230 00.6	55.0	118 14.3	28.8	Zuben'ubi	137 05.4	S16 05.8
20	357 02.3	74 14.6	34.9	186 13.6	49.4	245 03.2	55.0	133 16.5	28.9			
21	12 04.7	89 14.7 ..	34.7	201 14.8 ..	48.9	260 05.7 ..	55.0	148 18.7 ..	28.9		SHA	Mer. Pass.
22	27 07.2	104 14.8	34.4	216 15.9	48.4	275 08.3	55.0	163 20.8	29.0	Venus	78 57.9	15 03
23	42 09.7	119 14.9	34.2	231 17.1	47.9	290 10.8	55.0	178 23.0	29.1	Mars	190 08.2	7 38
Mer. Pass. 20 15.7		v 0.0	d 0.2	v 1.2	d 0.5	v 2.5	d 0.0	v 2.2	d 0.1	Jupiter	247 57.2	3 47
										Saturn	136 27.2	11 12

UT	SUN GHA	SUN Dec	MOON GHA	v	MOON Dec	d	HP
d h	° ′	° ′	° ′	′	° ′	′	′
15 00	183 51.8	S18 27.9	34 23.8	11.9	N 9 55.0	9.4	56.6
01	198 51.7	28.5	48 54.7	11.9	10 04.4	9.4	56.5
02	213 51.6	29.1	63 25.6	12.0	10 13.8	9.3	56.5
03	228 51.5	.. 29.8	77 56.6	11.9	10 23.1	9.2	56.5
04	243 51.4	30.4	92 27.5	11.9	10 32.3	9.2	56.5
05	258 51.3	31.0	106 58.4	11.9	10 41.5	9.1	56.5
06	273 51.2	S18 31.7	121 29.3	11.8	N10 50.6	9.1	56.4
07	288 51.1	32.3	136 00.1	11.9	10 59.7	9.0	56.4
F 08	303 51.0	33.0	150 31.0	11.8	11 08.7	8.9	56.4
R 09	318 50.9	.. 33.6	165 01.8	11.9	11 17.6	8.9	56.4
I 10	333 50.8	34.2	179 32.7	11.8	11 26.5	8.8	56.4
11	348 50.7	34.8	194 03.5	11.8	11 35.3	8.8	56.3
D 12	3 50.6	S18 35.5	208 34.3	11.8	N11 44.1	8.7	56.3
A 13	18 50.5	36.1	223 05.1	11.8	11 52.8	8.6	56.3
Y 14	33 50.4	36.7	237 35.9	11.8	12 01.4	8.5	56.3
15	48 50.2	.. 37.4	252 06.7	11.7	12 09.9	8.5	56.3
16	63 50.1	38.0	266 37.4	11.8	12 18.4	8.5	56.2
17	78 50.0	38.6	281 08.2	11.7	12 26.9	8.3	56.2
18	93 49.9	S18 39.3	295 38.9	11.8	N12 35.2	8.3	56.2
19	108 49.8	39.9	310 09.7	11.7	12 43.5	8.2	56.2
20	123 49.7	40.5	324 40.4	11.7	12 51.7	8.2	56.1
21	138 49.6	.. 41.1	339 11.1	11.6	12 59.9	8.1	56.1
22	153 49.5	41.8	353 41.7	11.7	13 08.0	8.0	56.1
23	168 49.4	42.4	8 12.4	11.7	13 16.0	8.0	56.1
16 00	183 49.3	S18 43.0	22 43.1	11.6	N13 24.0	7.8	56.1
01	198 49.1	43.6	37 13.7	11.6	13 31.8	7.8	56.1
02	213 49.0	44.3	51 44.3	11.6	13 39.6	7.8	56.0
03	228 48.9	.. 44.9	66 14.9	11.6	13 47.4	7.6	56.0
04	243 48.8	45.5	80 45.5	11.6	13 55.0	7.6	56.0
05	258 48.7	46.1	95 16.1	11.6	14 02.6	7.5	56.0
06	273 48.6	S18 46.8	109 46.7	11.5	N14 10.1	7.4	56.0
S 07	288 48.5	47.4	124 17.2	11.6	14 17.5	7.4	55.9
A 08	303 48.3	48.0	138 47.8	11.5	14 24.9	7.3	55.9
T 09	318 48.2	.. 48.6	153 18.3	11.5	14 32.2	7.2	55.9
U 10	333 48.1	49.2	167 48.8	11.5	14 39.4	7.1	55.9
R 11	348 48.0	49.9	182 19.3	11.5	14 46.5	7.1	55.9
D 12	3 47.9	S18 50.5	196 49.8	11.5	N14 53.6	6.9	55.8
A 13	18 47.8	51.1	211 20.3	11.4	15 00.5	6.9	55.8
Y 14	33 47.7	51.7	225 50.7	11.4	15 07.4	6.8	55.8
15	48 47.5	.. 52.3	240 21.2	11.4	15 14.2	6.8	55.8
16	63 47.4	52.9	254 51.6	11.4	15 21.0	6.6	55.8
17	78 47.3	53.6	269 22.0	11.4	15 27.6	6.6	55.8
18	93 47.2	S18 54.2	283 52.4	11.4	N15 34.2	6.5	55.7
19	108 47.1	54.8	298 22.8	11.4	15 40.7	6.4	55.7
20	123 46.9	55.4	312 53.2	11.4	15 47.1	6.3	55.7
21	138 46.8	.. 56.0	327 23.6	11.4	15 53.4	6.2	55.7
22	153 46.7	56.6	341 54.0	11.3	15 59.6	6.2	55.7
23	168 46.6	57.2	356 24.3	11.3	16 05.8	6.1	55.6
17 00	183 46.5	S18 57.8	10 54.6	11.4	N16 11.9	6.0	55.6
01	198 46.3	58.5	25 25.0	11.3	16 17.9	5.9	55.6
02	213 46.2	59.1	39 55.3	11.3	16 23.8	5.8	55.6
03	228 46.1	18 59.7	54 25.6	11.3	16 29.6	5.7	55.6
04	243 46.0	19 00.3	68 55.9	11.2	16 35.3	5.7	55.5
05	258 45.9	00.9	83 26.1	11.3	16 41.0	5.5	55.5
06	273 45.7	S19 01.5	97 56.4	11.3	N16 46.5	5.5	55.5
07	288 45.6	02.1	112 26.7	11.2	16 52.0	5.4	55.5
08	303 45.5	02.7	126 56.9	11.3	16 57.4	5.3	55.5
S 09	318 45.4	.. 03.3	141 27.2	11.2	17 02.7	5.2	55.4
U 10	333 45.2	03.9	155 57.4	11.2	17 07.9	5.1	55.4
N 11	348 45.1	04.5	170 27.6	11.2	17 13.0	5.1	55.4
D 12	3 45.0	S19 05.1	184 57.8	11.2	N17 18.1	4.9	55.4
A 13	18 44.9	05.7	199 28.0	11.2	17 23.0	4.9	55.4
Y 14	33 44.7	06.3	213 58.2	11.2	17 27.9	4.7	55.3
15	48 44.6	.. 06.9	228 28.4	11.2	17 32.6	4.7	55.3
16	63 44.5	07.5	242 58.6	11.2	17 37.3	4.6	55.3
17	78 44.4	08.1	257 28.8	11.2	17 41.9	4.5	55.3
18	93 44.2	S19 08.7	271 59.0	11.1	N17 46.4	4.4	55.3
19	108 44.1	09.3	286 29.1	11.2	17 50.8	4.3	55.3
20	123 44.0	09.9	300 59.3	11.2	17 55.1	4.2	55.2
21	138 43.9	.. 10.5	315 29.5	11.1	17 59.3	4.2	55.2
22	153 43.7	11.1	329 59.6	11.2	18 03.5	4.0	55.2
23	168 43.6	11.7	344 29.8	11.1	N18 07.5	3.9	55.2
	SD 16.2	d 0.6	SD 15.3		15.2		15.1

Twilight / Sunrise / Moonrise

Lat.	Naut.	Civil	Sunrise	Moonrise 15	16	17	18
°	h m	h m	h m	h m	h m	h m	h m
N 72	07 03	08 40	■■■	13 28	13 15	12 50	▭
N 70	06 53	08 16	09 57	13 48	13 47	13 47	13 53
68	06 44	07 58	09 18	14 04	14 10	14 22	14 42
66	06 37	07 43	08 51	14 17	14 29	14 46	15 13
64	06 30	07 31	08 31	14 28	14 44	15 06	15 37
62	06 24	07 20	08 14	14 37	14 56	15 22	15 55
60	06 19	07 11	08 01	14 45	15 07	15 35	16 10
N 58	06 15	07 03	07 49	14 52	15 16	15 47	16 23
56	06 11	06 56	07 39	14 58	15 25	15 57	16 35
54	06 06	06 50	07 30	15 03	15 32	16 05	16 45
52	06 02	06 44	07 22	15 08	15 39	16 13	16 53
50	05 59	06 39	07 15	15 13	15 45	16 20	17 01
45	05 52	06 27	06 59	15 23	15 57	16 36	17 18
N 40	05 44	06 17	06 46	15 31	16 08	16 48	17 32
35	05 38	06 08	06 35	15 38	16 17	16 59	17 44
30	05 32	06 01	06 26	15 45	16 25	17 08	17 54
20	05 19	05 46	06 09	15 56	16 39	17 25	18 12
N 10	05 07	05 33	05 55	16 05	16 52	17 39	18 27
0	04 54	05 19	05 41	16 14	17 03	17 52	18 42
S 10	04 39	05 05	05 27	16 24	17 15	18 06	18 56
20	04 21	04 49	05 13	16 33	17 27	18 20	19 12
30	03 58	04 29	04 55	16 45	17 41	18 37	19 30
35	03 43	04 17	04 45	16 51	17 50	18 46	19 40
40	03 25	04 03	04 34	16 59	17 59	18 57	19 52
45	03 03	03 46	04 20	17 07	18 10	19 10	20 06
S 50	02 32	03 24	04 03	17 18	18 24	19 26	20 23
52	02 16	03 13	03 55	17 23	18 30	19 34	20 31
54	01 56	03 01	03 46	17 28	18 37	19 42	20 41
56	01 31	02 47	03 36	17 34	18 45	19 51	20 51
58	00 52	02 30	03 25	17 41	18 54	20 02	21 02
S 60	////	02 09	03 12	17 49	19 04	20 14	21 16

Sunset / Twilight / Moonset

Lat.	Sunset	Civil	Naut.	Moonset 15	16	17	18
°	h m	h m	h m	h m	h m	h m	h m
N 72	■■■	14 49	16 25	06 18	08 12	10 20	▭
N 70	13 32	15 13	16 36	05 59	07 41	09 23	11 00
68	14 11	15 31	16 44	05 45	07 19	08 49	10 11
66	14 37	15 46	16 52	05 33	07 01	08 25	09 40
64	14 58	15 58	16 59	05 23	06 47	08 06	09 17
62	15 15	16 09	17 04	05 15	06 35	07 51	08 59
60	15 28	16 18	17 10	05 08	06 25	07 38	08 44
N 58	15 40	16 26	17 14	05 02	06 16	07 27	08 31
56	15 50	16 33	17 19	04 56	06 08	07 17	08 20
54	15 59	16 40	17 23	04 51	06 01	07 08	08 10
52	16 07	16 45	17 26	04 47	05 55	07 01	08 02
50	16 15	16 50	17 30	04 43	05 50	06 54	07 54
45	16 30	17 02	17 38	04 34	05 38	06 39	07 37
N 40	16 43	17 12	17 45	04 27	05 28	06 27	07 24
35	16 54	17 21	17 51	04 20	05 19	06 17	07 12
30	17 04	17 29	17 58	04 15	05 12	06 08	07 02
20	17 20	17 43	18 10	04 05	04 59	05 53	06 45
N 10	17 35	17 57	18 22	03 57	04 48	05 39	06 30
0	17 48	18 10	18 36	03 49	04 38	05 27	06 16
S 10	18 02	18 25	18 51	03 42	04 27	05 14	06 02
20	18 17	18 41	19 09	03 33	04 16	05 01	05 47
30	18 34	19 01	19 32	03 24	04 04	04 45	05 30
35	18 45	19 13	19 47	03 19	03 56	04 37	05 20
40	18 57	19 27	20 05	03 12	03 48	04 26	05 08
45	19 12	19 45	20 28	03 05	03 38	04 15	04 55
S 50	19 27	20 07	20 59	02 57	03 27	04 00	04 39
52	19 35	20 18	21 16	02 53	03 21	03 54	04 31
54	19 44	20 30	21 36	02 49	03 15	03 46	04 22
56	19 54	20 45	22 03	02 44	03 09	03 38	04 13
58	20 06	21 02	22 44	02 39	03 02	03 29	04 02
S 60	20 19	21 23	////	02 33	02 53	03 18	03 50

SUN / MOON

Day	Eqn. of Time 00h	12h	Mer. Pass.	Mer. Pass. Upper	Lower	Age	Phase
d	m s	m s	h m	h m	h m	d	%
15	15 28	15 22	11 45	22 26	10 02	12	95
16	15 17	15 12	11 45	23 15	10 50	13	99
17	15 06	15 00	11 45	24 04	11 39	14	100

UT (d h)	ARIES GHA	VENUS −4.7 GHA	Dec	MARS +1.3 GHA	Dec	JUPITER −2.5 GHA	Dec	SATURN +0.5 GHA	Dec	Star	SHA	Dec
18 00	57 12.1	134 15.0	S26 33.9	246 18.3	N 5 47.4	305 13.4	N21 55.1	193 25.2	S14 29.2	Acamar	315 17.7	S40 15.0
01	72 14.6	149 15.1	33.7	261 19.5	46.8	320 16.0	55.1	208 27.4	29.3	Achernar	335 26.1	S57 10.1
02	87 17.1	164 15.2	33.4	276 20.6	46.3	335 18.5	55.1	223 29.5	29.4	Acrux	173 09.3	S63 10.3
03	102 19.5	179 15.3	.. 33.2	291 21.8	.. 45.8	350 21.1	.. 55.1	238 31.7	.. 29.5	Adhara	255 12.0	S28 59.5
04	117 22.0	194 15.4	32.9	306 23.0	45.3	5 23.6	55.1	253 33.9	29.5	Aldebaran	290 48.7	N16 32.1
05	132 24.5	209 15.5	32.6	321 24.2	44.8	20 26.2	55.2	268 36.0	29.6			
06	147 26.9	224 15.6	S26 32.4	336 25.3	N 5 44.2	35 28.8	N21 55.2	283 38.2	S14 29.7	Alioth	166 20.9	N55 52.9
07	162 29.4	239 15.8	32.1	351 26.5	43.7	50 31.3	55.2	298 40.4	29.8	Alkaid	152 59.2	N49 14.6
08	177 31.8	254 15.9	31.9	6 27.7	43.2	65 33.9	55.2	313 42.5	29.9	Al Na'ir	27 43.4	S46 53.7
M 09	192 34.3	269 16.0	.. 31.6	21 28.9	.. 42.7	80 36.4	.. 55.2	328 44.7	.. 30.0	Alnilam	275 45.8	S 1 11.7
O 10	207 36.8	284 16.1	31.3	36 30.1	42.1	95 39.0	55.3	343 46.9	30.0	Alphard	217 55.8	S 8 43.2
N 11	222 39.2	299 16.2	31.1	51 31.2	41.6	110 41.6	55.3	358 49.1	30.1			
D 12	237 41.7	314 16.4	S26 30.8	66 32.4	N 5 41.1	125 44.1	N21 55.3	13 51.2	S14 30.2	Alphecca	126 11.2	N26 40.2
A 13	252 44.2	329 16.5	30.5	81 33.6	40.6	140 46.7	55.3	28 53.4	30.3	Alpheratz	357 43.0	N29 10.3
Y 14	267 46.6	344 16.6	30.3	96 34.8	40.1	155 49.3	55.3	43 55.6	30.4	Altair	62 08.1	N 8 54.6
15	282 49.1	359 16.7	.. 30.0	111 35.9	.. 39.5	170 51.8	.. 55.4	58 57.7	.. 30.5	Ankaa	353 15.2	S42 13.9
16	297 51.6	14 16.9	29.7	126 37.1	39.0	185 54.4	55.4	73 59.9	30.6	Antares	112 26.3	S26 27.6
17	312 54.0	29 17.0	29.5	141 38.3	38.5	200 57.0	55.4	89 02.1	30.6			
18	327 56.5	44 17.1	S26 29.2	156 39.5	N 5 38.0	215 59.5	N21 55.4	104 04.3	S14 30.7	Arcturus	145 55.8	N19 06.7
19	342 59.0	59 17.3	28.9	171 40.7	37.5	231 02.1	55.4	119 06.4	30.8	Atria	107 28.3	S69 03.0
20	358 01.4	74 17.4	28.7	186 41.8	36.9	246 04.7	55.5	134 08.6	30.9	Avior	234 17.6	S59 33.1
21	13 03.9	89 17.5	.. 28.4	201 43.0	.. 36.4	261 07.2	.. 55.5	149 10.8	.. 31.0	Bellatrix	278 31.4	N 6 21.6
22	28 06.3	104 17.7	28.1	216 44.2	35.9	276 09.8	55.5	164 12.9	31.1	Betelgeuse	271 00.7	N 7 24.4
23	43 08.8	119 17.8	27.8	231 45.4	35.4	291 12.4	55.5	179 15.1	31.1			
19 00	58 11.3	134 18.0	S26 27.6	246 46.6	N 5 34.9	306 14.9	N21 55.5	194 17.3	S14 31.2	Canopus	263 55.6	S52 42.2
01	73 13.7	149 18.1	27.3	261 47.7	34.3	321 17.5	55.6	209 19.4	31.3	Capella	280 33.6	N46 00.5
02	88 16.2	164 18.3	27.0	276 48.9	33.8	336 20.1	55.6	224 21.6	31.4	Deneb	49 31.4	N45 20.2
03	103 18.7	179 18.4	.. 26.7	291 50.1	.. 33.3	351 22.6	.. 55.6	239 23.8	.. 31.5	Denebola	182 33.5	N14 29.6
04	118 21.1	194 18.6	26.5	306 51.3	32.8	6 25.2	55.6	254 26.0	31.6	Diphda	348 55.4	S17 54.6
05	133 23.6	209 18.7	26.2	321 52.5	32.2	21 27.8	55.6	269 28.1	31.7			
06	148 26.1	224 18.9	S26 25.9	336 53.6	N 5 31.7	36 30.3	N21 55.7	284 30.3	S14 31.7	Dubhe	193 51.7	N61 40.2
07	163 28.5	239 19.0	25.6	351 54.8	31.2	51 32.9	55.7	299 32.5	31.8	Elnath	278 11.9	N28 37.0
T 08	178 31.0	254 19.2	25.3	6 56.0	30.7	66 35.5	55.7	314 34.6	31.9	Eltanin	90 46.5	N51 29.6
U 09	193 33.5	269 19.3	.. 25.1	21 57.2	.. 30.2	81 38.0	.. 55.7	329 36.8	.. 32.0	Enif	33 46.9	N 9 56.6
E 10	208 35.9	284 19.5	24.8	36 58.4	29.6	96 40.6	55.7	344 39.0	32.1	Fomalhaut	15 23.6	S29 32.9
S 11	223 38.4	299 19.7	24.5	51 59.6	29.1	111 43.2	55.8	359 41.2	32.2			
D 12	238 40.8	314 19.8	S26 24.2	67 00.7	N 5 28.6	126 45.8	N21 55.8	14 43.3	S14 32.2	Gacrux	172 00.9	S57 11.2
A 13	253 43.3	329 20.0	23.9	82 01.9	28.1	141 48.3	55.8	29 45.5	32.3	Gienah	175 52.2	S17 37.0
Y 14	268 45.8	344 20.1	23.6	97 03.1	27.6	156 50.9	55.8	44 47.7	32.4	Hadar	148 48.0	S60 26.2
15	283 48.2	359 20.3	.. 23.4	112 04.3	.. 27.0	171 53.5	.. 55.8	59 49.8	.. 32.5	Hamal	328 00.1	N23 31.8
16	298 50.7	14 20.5	23.1	127 05.5	26.5	186 56.0	55.9	74 52.0	32.6	Kaus Aust.	83 43.8	S34 22.5
17	313 53.2	29 20.7	22.8	142 06.6	26.0	201 58.6	55.9	89 54.2	32.7			
18	328 55.6	44 20.8	S26 22.5	157 07.8	N 5 25.5	217 01.2	N21 55.9	104 56.4	S14 32.7	Kochab	137 21.3	N74 05.9
19	343 58.1	59 21.0	22.2	172 09.0	25.0	232 03.8	55.9	119 58.5	32.8	Markab	13 37.9	N15 17.1
20	359 00.6	74 21.2	21.9	187 10.2	24.4	247 06.3	55.9	135 00.7	32.9	Menkar	314 14.4	N 4 08.6
21	14 03.0	89 21.4	.. 21.6	202 11.4	.. 23.9	262 08.9	.. 56.0	150 02.9	.. 33.0	Menkent	148 07.6	S36 26.1
22	29 05.5	104 21.5	21.3	217 12.6	23.4	277 11.5	56.0	165 05.0	33.1	Miaplacidus	221 39.3	S69 46.3
23	44 07.9	119 21.7	21.0	232 13.8	22.9	292 14.1	56.0	180 07.2	33.2			
20 00	59 10.4	134 21.9	S26 20.7	247 14.9	N 5 22.4	307 16.6	N21 56.0	195 09.4	S14 33.2	Mirfak	308 39.4	N49 54.6
01	74 12.9	149 22.1	20.5	262 16.1	21.8	322 19.2	56.0	210 11.6	33.3	Nunki	75 58.2	S26 16.6
02	89 15.3	164 22.3	20.2	277 17.3	21.3	337 21.8	56.1	225 13.7	33.4	Peacock	53 19.1	S56 41.4
03	104 17.8	179 22.5	.. 19.9	292 18.5	.. 20.8	352 24.4	.. 56.1	240 15.9	.. 33.5	Pollux	243 27.2	N27 59.3
04	119 20.3	194 22.7	19.6	307 19.7	20.3	7 26.9	56.1	255 18.1	33.6	Procyon	244 59.2	N 5 11.2
05	134 22.7	209 22.9	19.3	322 20.9	19.8	22 29.5	56.1	270 20.2	33.7			
06	149 25.2	224 23.0	S26 19.0	337 22.0	N 5 19.2	37 32.1	N21 56.2	285 22.4	S14 33.8	Rasalhague	96 06.5	N12 33.3
W 07	164 27.7	239 23.2	18.7	352 23.2	18.7	52 34.7	56.2	300 24.6	33.8	Regulus	207 43.2	N11 53.8
E 08	179 30.1	254 23.4	18.4	7 24.4	18.2	67 37.3	56.2	315 26.8	33.9	Rigel	281 11.5	S 8 11.2
D 09	194 32.6	269 23.6	.. 18.1	22 25.6	.. 17.7	82 39.8	.. 56.2	330 28.9	.. 34.0	Rigil Kent.	139 51.9	S60 53.3
N 10	209 35.1	284 23.8	17.8	37 26.8	17.2	97 42.4	56.2	345 31.1	34.1	Sabik	102 12.5	S15 44.3
E 11	224 37.5	299 24.0	17.5	52 28.0	16.7	112 45.0	56.3	0 33.3	34.2			
S 12	239 40.0	314 24.2	S26 17.2	67 29.2	N 5 16.1	127 47.6	N21 56.3	15 35.4	S14 34.3	Schedar	349 39.7	N56 37.1
D 13	254 42.4	329 24.5	16.9	82 30.4	15.6	142 50.2	56.3	30 37.6	34.3	Shaula	96 21.9	S37 06.7
A 14	269 44.9	344 24.7	16.6	97 31.5	15.1	157 52.7	56.3	45 39.8	34.4	Sirius	258 33.2	S16 44.2
Y 15	284 47.4	359 24.9	.. 16.3	112 32.7	.. 14.6	172 55.3	.. 56.4	60 42.0	.. 34.5	Spica	158 31.2	S11 13.9
16	299 49.8	14 25.1	15.9	127 33.9	14.1	187 57.9	56.4	75 44.1	34.6	Suhail	222 52.1	S43 29.2
17	314 52.3	29 25.3	15.6	142 35.1	13.5	203 00.5	56.4	90 46.3	34.7			
18	329 54.8	44 25.5	S26 15.3	157 36.3	N 5 13.0	218 03.1	N21 56.4	105 48.5	S14 34.8	Vega	80 39.1	N38 48.2
19	344 57.2	59 25.7	15.0	172 37.5	12.5	233 05.6	56.4	120 50.6	34.8	Zuben'ubi	137 05.4	S16 05.8
20	359 59.7	74 26.0	14.7	187 38.7	12.0	248 08.2	56.5	135 52.8	34.9		SHA	Mer.Pass.
21	15 02.2	89 26.2	.. 14.4	202 39.9	.. 11.5	263 10.8	.. 56.5	150 55.0	.. 35.0	Venus	76 06.7	15 03
22	30 04.6	104 26.4	14.1	217 41.0	10.9	278 13.4	56.5	165 57.2	35.1	Mars	188 35.3	7 32
23	45 07.1	119 26.6	13.8	232 42.2	10.4	293 16.0	56.5	180 59.3	35.2	Jupiter	248 03.6	3 34
Mer. Pass. 20 04.0		v 0.2	d 0.3	v 1.2	d 0.5	v 2.6	d 0.0	v 2.2	d 0.1	Saturn	136 06.0	11 01

SUN and MOON

UT	SUN GHA	SUN Dec	MOON GHA	v	MOON Dec	d	HP
18 00	183 43.5	S19 12.3	358 59.9	11.1	N18 11.4	3.9	55.2
01	198 43.3	12.9	13 30.0	11.2	18 15.3	3.8	55.2
02	213 43.2	13.5	28 00.2	11.1	18 19.1	3.6	55.1
03	228 43.1	.. 14.1	42 30.3	11.2	18 22.7	3.6	55.1
04	243 43.0	14.7	57 00.5	11.1	18 26.3	3.5	55.1
05	258 42.8	15.3	71 30.6	11.1	18 29.8	3.4	55.1
06	273 42.7	S19 15.9	86 00.7	11.2	N18 33.2	3.3	55.1
M 07	288 42.6	16.5	100 30.9	11.1	18 36.5	3.2	55.1
O 08	303 42.4	17.1	115 01.0	11.1	18 39.7	3.1	55.0
N 09	318 42.3	.. 17.7	129 31.1	11.2	18 42.8	3.0	55.0
D 10	333 42.2	18.3	144 01.3	11.1	18 45.8	2.9	55.0
A 11	348 42.0	18.9	158 31.4	11.1	18 48.7	2.8	55.0
Y 12	3 41.9	S19 19.5	173 01.5	11.2	N18 51.5	2.8	55.0
13	18 41.8	20.0	187 31.7	11.1	18 54.3	2.6	55.0
14	33 41.6	20.6	202 01.8	11.2	18 56.9	2.5	54.9
15	48 41.5	.. 21.2	216 32.0	11.1	18 59.4	2.5	54.9
16	63 41.4	21.8	231 02.1	11.2	19 01.9	2.3	54.9
17	78 41.2	22.4	245 32.3	11.1	19 04.2	2.3	54.9
18	93 41.1	S19 23.0	260 02.4	11.2	N19 06.5	2.1	54.9
19	108 41.0	23.6	274 32.6	11.2	19 08.6	2.1	54.9
20	123 40.8	24.1	289 02.8	11.1	19 10.7	2.0	54.8
21	138 40.7	.. 24.7	303 32.9	11.2	19 12.7	1.8	54.8
22	153 40.5	25.3	318 03.1	11.2	19 14.5	1.8	54.8
23	168 40.4	25.9	332 33.3	11.2	19 16.3	1.7	54.8
19 00	183 40.3	S19 26.5	347 03.5	11.2	N19 18.0	1.6	54.8
01	198 40.1	27.1	1 33.7	11.3	19 19.6	1.5	54.8
02	213 40.0	27.6	16 04.0	11.2	19 21.1	1.4	54.8
03	228 39.9	.. 28.2	30 34.2	11.2	19 22.5	1.3	54.7
04	243 39.7	28.8	45 04.4	11.3	19 23.8	1.2	54.7
05	258 39.6	29.4	59 34.7	11.2	19 25.0	1.1	54.7
06	273 39.4	S19 30.0	74 04.9	11.3	N19 26.1	1.0	54.7
T 07	288 39.3	30.5	88 35.2	11.3	19 27.1	1.0	54.7
U 08	303 39.2	31.1	103 05.5	11.3	19 28.1	0.8	54.7
E 09	318 39.0	.. 31.7	117 35.8	11.3	19 28.9	0.7	54.7
S 10	333 38.9	32.3	132 06.1	11.3	19 29.6	0.7	54.6
D 11	348 38.7	32.8	146 36.4	11.4	19 30.3	0.5	54.6
A 12	3 38.6	S19 33.4	161 06.8	11.3	N19 30.8	0.4	54.6
Y 13	18 38.5	34.0	175 37.1	11.4	19 31.2	0.4	54.6
14	33 38.3	34.6	190 07.5	11.4	19 31.6	0.3	54.6
15	48 38.2	.. 35.1	204 37.9	11.4	19 31.9	0.1	54.6
16	63 38.0	35.7	219 08.3	11.4	19 32.0	0.1	54.6
17	78 37.9	36.3	233 38.7	11.4	19 32.1	0.0	54.5
18	93 37.7	S19 36.9	248 09.1	11.5	N19 32.1	0.1	54.5
19	108 37.6	37.4	262 39.6	11.5	19 32.0	0.3	54.5
20	123 37.4	38.0	277 10.1	11.4	19 31.7	0.3	54.5
21	138 37.3	.. 38.6	291 40.5	11.6	19 31.4	0.4	54.5
22	153 37.2	39.1	306 11.1	11.5	19 31.0	0.4	54.5
23	168 37.0	39.7	320 41.6	11.5	19 30.6	0.6	54.5
20 00	183 36.9	S19 40.3	335 12.1	11.6	N19 30.0	0.7	54.5
01	198 36.7	40.8	349 42.7	11.6	19 29.3	0.8	54.4
02	213 36.6	41.4	4 13.3	11.6	19 28.5	0.8	54.4
03	228 36.4	.. 42.0	18 43.9	11.6	19 27.7	1.0	54.4
04	243 36.3	42.5	33 14.5	11.7	19 26.7	1.0	54.4
05	258 36.1	43.1	47 45.2	11.7	19 25.7	1.2	54.4
06	273 36.0	S19 43.7	62 15.9	11.7	N19 24.5	1.2	54.4
W 07	288 35.8	44.2	76 46.6	11.7	19 23.3	1.3	54.4
E 08	303 35.7	44.8	91 17.3	11.7	19 22.0	1.4	54.4
D 09	318 35.5	.. 45.4	105 48.0	11.8	19 20.6	1.5	54.4
N 10	333 35.4	45.9	120 18.8	11.8	19 19.1	1.6	54.3
E 11	348 35.2	46.5	134 49.6	11.8	19 17.5	1.7	54.3
S 12	3 35.1	S19 47.0	149 20.4	11.9	N19 15.8	1.8	54.3
D 13	18 34.9	47.6	163 51.3	11.9	19 14.0	1.8	54.3
A 14	33 34.8	48.2	178 22.2	11.9	19 12.2	2.0	54.3
Y 15	48 34.6	.. 48.7	192 53.1	11.9	19 10.2	2.0	54.3
16	63 34.5	49.3	207 24.0	11.9	19 08.2	2.1	54.3
17	78 34.3	49.8	221 54.9	12.0	19 06.1	2.2	54.3
18	93 34.2	S19 50.4	236 25.9	12.0	N19 03.9	2.3	54.3
19	108 34.0	50.9	250 56.9	12.0	19 01.6	2.4	54.3
20	123 33.9	51.5	265 27.9	12.1	18 59.2	2.5	54.2
21	138 33.7	.. 52.1	279 59.0	12.1	18 56.7	2.6	54.2
22	153 33.6	52.6	294 30.1	12.1	18 54.1	2.6	54.2
23	168 33.4	53.2	309 01.2	12.2	N18 51.5	2.8	54.2
	SD 16.2	d 0.6	SD 15.0		14.9		14.8

Twilight, Sunrise, Moonrise

Lat.	Naut.	Civil	Sunrise	Moonrise 18	19	20	21
N 72	07 14	08 54	■	□	□	□	15 27
N 70	07 02	08 28	10 19	13 53	14 17	15 22	16 52
68	06 52	08 08	09 33	14 42	15 19	16 16	17 31
66	06 44	07 52	09 03	15 13	15 54	16 49	17 57
64	06 37	07 38	08 41	15 37	16 19	17 13	18 18
62	06 31	07 27	08 23	15 55	16 38	17 32	18 35
60	06 25	07 18	08 08	16 10	16 55	17 48	18 48
N 58	06 20	07 09	07 56	16 23	17 08	18 01	19 00
56	06 15	07 02	07 45	16 35	17 20	18 12	19 10
54	06 11	06 55	07 35	16 45	17 30	18 22	19 19
52	06 07	06 49	07 27	16 53	17 39	18 31	19 27
50	06 03	06 43	07 19	17 01	17 48	18 39	19 35
45	05 55	06 31	07 03	17 18	18 05	18 56	19 50
N 40	05 47	06 20	06 50	17 32	18 19	19 10	20 03
35	05 40	06 10	06 38	17 44	18 31	19 22	20 13
30	05 34	06 03	06 28	17 54	18 42	19 32	20 23
20	05 21	05 48	06 11	18 12	19 00	19 49	20 39
N 10	05 08	05 34	05 56	18 27	19 16	20 05	20 53
0	04 54	05 20	05 42	18 42	19 31	20 19	21 06
S 10	04 39	05 05	05 27	18 56	19 46	20 33	21 20
20	04 20	04 48	05 12	19 12	20 01	20 49	21 34
30	03 56	04 28	04 54	19 30	20 20	21 06	21 50
35	03 41	04 15	04 44	19 40	20 30	21 17	21 59
40	03 22	04 01	04 31	19 52	20 43	21 28	22 10
45	02 58	03 43	04 17	20 06	20 57	21 42	22 22
S 50	02 26	03 20	04 00	20 23	21 14	21 59	22 37
52	02 09	03 08	03 51	20 31	21 23	22 07	22 44
54	01 47	02 55	03 42	20 41	21 32	22 16	22 52
56	01 19	02 40	03 31	20 51	21 42	22 26	23 01
58	00 30	02 22	03 19	21 02	21 54	22 37	23 11
S 60	////	01 59	03 05	21 16	22 08	22 50	23 22

Sunset, Twilight, Moonset

Lat.	Sunset	Civil	Naut.	Moonset 18	19	20	21
N 72	■	14 36	16 16	□	□	□	14 29
N 70	13 11	15 02	16 28	11 00	12 19	12 54	13 04
68	13 57	15 22	16 37	10 11	11 17	12 00	12 24
66	14 27	15 36	16 46	09 40	10 42	11 27	11 57
64	14 50	15 52	16 53	09 17	10 17	11 03	11 36
62	15 07	16 03	16 59	08 59	09 57	10 44	11 19
60	15 22	16 12	17 05	08 44	09 41	10 28	11 05
N 58	15 35	16 21	17 10	08 31	09 28	10 15	10 53
56	15 45	16 29	17 15	08 20	09 16	10 03	10 42
54	15 55	16 36	17 20	08 10	09 06	09 53	10 33
52	16 03	16 41	17 23	08 02	08 56	09 44	10 25
50	16 11	16 47	17 27	07 54	08 48	09 36	10 18
45	16 27	16 59	17 35	07 37	08 31	09 19	10 02
N 40	16 41	17 10	17 43	07 24	08 17	09 05	09 48
35	16 52	17 19	17 50	07 12	08 05	08 53	09 37
30	17 02	17 28	17 57	07 02	07 54	08 43	09 28
20	17 19	17 43	18 10	06 45	07 36	08 25	09 11
N 10	17 35	17 57	18 23	06 30	07 20	08 09	08 56
0	17 49	18 11	18 36	06 16	07 05	07 54	08 42
S 10	18 03	18 26	18 52	06 02	06 51	07 40	08 28
20	18 19	18 43	19 11	05 47	06 35	07 24	08 13
30	18 37	19 04	19 34	05 30	06 17	07 06	07 56
35	18 48	19 16	19 51	05 20	06 06	06 55	07 46
40	19 00	19 31	20 09	05 08	05 54	06 43	07 35
45	19 14	19 49	20 33	04 55	05 40	06 29	07 21
S 50	19 32	20 12	21 07	04 39	05 22	06 11	07 05
52	19 41	20 24	21 24	04 31	05 14	06 03	06 57
54	19 50	20 37	21 46	04 22	05 05	05 54	06 49
56	20 01	20 52	22 16	04 13	04 55	05 44	06 39
58	20 13	21 11	23 11	04 02	04 43	05 32	06 28
S 60	20 27	21 34	////	03 50	04 29	05 18	06 15

SUN and MOON

	SUN Eqn. of Time 00h	12h	Mer. Pass.	MOON Mer. Pass. Upper	Lower	Age	Phase
Day	m s	m s	h m	h m	h m	d	%
18	14 54	14 48	11 45	00 04	12 29	15	99
19	14 41	14 35	11 45	00 54	13 18	16	97
20	14 28	14 21	11 46	01 43	14 07	17	92

UT	ARIES GHA	VENUS −4.8 GHA	Dec	MARS +1.3 GHA	Dec	JUPITER −2.5 GHA	Dec	SATURN +0.6 GHA	Dec	STARS Name	SHA	Dec
d h	° ′	° ′	° ′	° ′	° ′	° ′	° ′	° ′	° ′		° ′	° ′
21 00	60 09.6	134 26.8	S26 13.5	247 43.4	N 5 09.9	308 18.6	N21 56.5	196 01.5	S14 35.3	Acamar	315 17.7	S40 15.0
01	75 12.0	149 27.1	13.2	262 44.6	09.4	323 21.2	56.6	211 03.7	35.3	Achernar	335 26.1	S57 10.1
02	90 14.5	164 27.3	12.8	277 45.8	08.9	338 23.7	56.6	226 05.8	35.4	Acrux	173 09.2	S63 10.3
03	105 16.9	179 27.5	.. 12.5	292 47.0	.. 08.3	353 26.3	.. 56.6	241 08.0	.. 35.5	Adhara	255 12.0	S28 59.5
04	120 19.4	194 27.8	12.2	307 48.2	07.8	8 28.9	56.6	256 10.2	35.6	Aldebaran	290 48.7	N16 32.1
05	135 21.9	209 28.0	11.9	322 49.4	07.3	23 31.5	56.7	271 12.4	35.7			
06	150 24.3	224 28.2	S26 11.6	337 50.6	N 5 06.8	38 34.1	N21 56.7	286 14.5	S14 35.8	Alioth	166 20.9	N55 52.9
07	165 26.8	239 28.5	11.3	352 51.8	06.3	53 36.7	56.7	301 16.7	35.8	Alkaid	152 59.1	N49 14.6
T 08	180 29.3	254 28.7	10.9	7 52.9	05.8	68 39.3	56.7	316 18.9	35.9	Al Na'ir	27 43.4	S46 53.7
H 09	195 31.7	269 29.0	.. 10.6	22 54.1	.. 05.2	83 41.8	.. 56.8	331 21.0	.. 36.0	Alnilam	275 45.8	S 1 11.7
U 10	210 34.2	284 29.2	10.3	37 55.3	04.7	98 44.4	56.8	346 23.2	36.1	Alphard	217 55.7	S 8 43.2
R 11	225 36.7	299 29.5	10.0	52 56.5	04.2	113 47.0	56.8	1 25.4	36.2			
S 12	240 39.1	314 29.7	S26 09.7	67 57.7	N 5 03.7	128 49.6	N21 56.8	16 27.6	S14 36.3	Alphecca	126 11.1	N26 40.2
D 13	255 41.6	329 30.0	09.3	82 58.9	03.2	143 52.2	56.8	31 29.7	36.3	Alpheratz	357 43.0	N29 10.3
A 14	270 44.1	344 30.2	09.0	98 00.1	02.6	158 54.8	56.9	46 31.9	36.4	Altair	62 08.1	N 8 54.6
Y 15	285 46.5	359 30.5	.. 08.7	113 01.3	.. 02.1	173 57.4	.. 56.9	61 34.1	.. 36.5	Ankaa	353 15.2	S42 13.9
16	300 49.0	14 30.7	08.4	128 02.5	01.6	189 00.0	56.9	76 36.3	36.6	Antares	112 26.3	S26 27.6
17	315 51.4	29 31.0	08.0	143 03.7	01.1	204 02.6	56.9	91 38.4	36.7			
18	330 53.9	44 31.2	S26 07.7	158 04.9	N 5 00.6	219 05.2	N21 57.0	106 40.6	S14 36.8	Arcturus	145 55.8	N19 06.7
19	345 56.4	59 31.5	07.4	173 06.1	5 00.0	234 07.7	57.0	121 42.8	36.8	Atria	107 28.3	S69 03.0
20	0 58.8	74 31.8	07.1	188 07.2	4 59.5	249 10.3	57.0	136 44.9	36.9	Avior	234 17.5	S59 33.1
21	16 01.3	89 32.0	.. 06.7	203 08.4	.. 59.0	264 12.9	.. 57.0	151 47.1	.. 37.0	Bellatrix	278 31.4	N 6 21.6
22	31 03.8	104 32.3	06.4	218 09.6	58.5	279 15.5	57.1	166 49.3	37.1	Betelgeuse	271 00.7	N 7 24.4
23	46 06.2	119 32.6	06.1	233 10.8	58.0	294 18.1	57.1	181 51.5	37.2			
22 00	61 08.7	134 32.8	S26 05.7	248 12.0	N 4 57.5	309 20.7	N21 57.1	196 53.6	S14 37.3	Canopus	263 55.5	S52 42.2
01	76 11.2	149 33.1	05.4	263 13.2	57.0	324 23.3	57.1	211 55.8	37.3	Capella	280 33.5	N46 00.5
02	91 13.6	164 33.4	05.1	278 14.4	56.4	339 25.9	57.2	226 58.0	37.4	Deneb	49 31.4	N45 20.2
03	106 16.1	179 33.6	.. 04.7	293 15.6	.. 55.9	354 28.5	.. 57.2	242 00.1	.. 37.5	Denebola	182 33.5	N14 29.6
04	121 18.5	194 33.9	04.4	308 16.8	55.4	9 31.1	57.2	257 02.3	37.6	Diphda	348 55.4	S17 54.6
05	136 21.0	209 34.2	04.1	323 18.0	54.9	24 33.7	57.2	272 04.5	37.7			
06	151 23.5	224 34.5	S26 03.7	338 19.2	N 4 54.4	39 36.3	N21 57.2	287 06.7	S14 37.8	Dubhe	193 51.6	N61 40.2
07	166 25.9	239 34.8	03.4	353 20.4	53.9	54 38.9	57.3	302 08.8	37.8	Elnath	278 11.9	N28 37.0
08	181 28.4	254 35.1	03.1	8 21.6	53.3	69 41.5	57.3	317 11.0	37.9	Eltanin	90 46.5	N51 29.6
F 09	196 30.9	269 35.3	.. 02.7	23 22.8	.. 52.8	84 44.1	.. 57.3	332 13.2	.. 38.0	Enif	33 46.9	N 9 56.6
R 10	211 33.3	284 35.6	02.4	38 24.0	52.3	99 46.7	57.3	347 15.4	38.1	Fomalhaut	15 23.6	S29 32.9
I 11	226 35.8	299 35.9	02.1	53 25.2	51.8	114 49.3	57.4	2 17.5	38.2			
D 12	241 38.3	314 36.2	S26 01.7	68 26.4	N 4 51.3	129 51.8	N21 57.4	17 19.7	S14 38.2	Gacrux	172 00.8	S57 11.2
A 13	256 40.7	329 36.5	01.4	83 27.6	50.7	144 54.4	57.4	32 21.9	38.3	Gienah	175 52.2	S17 37.0
Y 14	271 43.2	344 36.8	01.0	98 28.8	50.2	159 57.0	57.4	47 24.0	38.4	Hadar	148 48.0	S60 26.2
15	286 45.7	359 37.1	.. 00.7	113 29.9	.. 49.7	174 59.6	.. 57.5	62 26.2	.. 38.5	Hamal	328 00.1	N23 31.8
16	301 48.1	14 37.4	00.3	128 31.1	49.2	190 02.2	57.5	77 28.4	38.6	Kaus Aust.	83 43.8	S34 22.5
17	316 50.6	29 37.7	26 00.0	143 32.3	48.7	205 04.8	57.5	92 30.6	38.7			
18	331 53.0	44 38.0	S25 59.7	158 33.5	N 4 48.2	220 07.4	N21 57.5	107 32.7	S14 38.7	Kochab	137 21.3	N74 05.9
19	346 55.5	59 38.3	59.3	173 34.7	47.6	235 10.0	57.6	122 34.9	38.8	Markab	13 37.9	N15 17.1
20	1 58.0	74 38.6	59.0	188 35.9	47.1	250 12.6	57.6	137 37.1	38.9	Menkar	314 14.4	N 4 08.6
21	17 00.4	89 38.9	.. 58.6	203 37.1	.. 46.6	265 15.2	.. 57.6	152 39.3	.. 39.0	Menkent	148 07.5	S36 26.1
22	32 02.9	104 39.3	58.3	218 38.3	46.1	280 17.8	57.6	167 41.4	39.1	Miaplacidus	221 39.3	S69 46.3
23	47 05.4	119 39.6	57.9	233 39.5	45.6	295 20.4	57.7	182 43.6	39.2			
23 00	62 07.8	134 39.9	S25 57.6	248 40.7	N 4 45.1	310 23.0	N21 57.7	197 45.8	S14 39.2	Mirfak	308 39.4	N49 54.6
01	77 10.3	149 40.2	57.2	263 41.9	44.5	325 25.6	57.7	212 47.9	39.3	Nunki	75 58.2	S26 16.6
02	92 12.8	164 40.5	56.9	278 43.1	44.0	340 28.3	57.7	227 50.1	39.4	Peacock	53 19.1	S56 41.4
03	107 15.2	179 40.8	.. 56.5	293 44.3	.. 43.5	355 30.9	.. 57.8	242 52.3	.. 39.5	Pollux	243 27.2	N27 59.3
04	122 17.7	194 41.2	56.2	308 45.5	43.0	10 33.5	57.8	257 54.5	39.6	Procyon	244 59.2	N 5 11.2
05	137 20.2	209 41.5	55.8	323 46.7	42.5	25 36.1	57.8	272 56.6	39.7			
06	152 22.6	224 41.8	S25 55.5	338 47.9	N 4 42.0	40 38.7	N21 57.8	287 58.8	S14 39.7	Rasalhague	96 06.5	N12 33.3
07	167 25.1	239 42.2	55.1	353 49.1	41.5	55 41.3	57.9	303 01.0	39.8	Regulus	207 43.2	N11 53.8
S 08	182 27.5	254 42.5	54.8	8 50.3	40.9	70 43.9	57.9	318 03.2	39.9	Rigel	281 11.4	S 8 11.2
A 09	197 30.0	269 42.8	.. 54.4	23 51.5	.. 40.4	85 46.5	.. 57.9	333 05.3	.. 40.0	Rigil Kent.	139 51.9	S60 53.3
T 10	212 32.5	284 43.2	54.1	38 52.7	39.9	100 49.1	57.9	348 07.5	40.1	Sabik	102 12.5	S15 44.3
U 11	227 34.9	299 43.5	53.7	53 53.9	39.4	115 51.7	58.0	3 09.7	40.1			
R 12	242 37.4	314 43.8	S25 53.4	68 55.1	N 4 38.9	130 54.3	N21 58.0	18 11.9	S14 40.2	Schedar	349 39.7	N56 37.1
D 13	257 39.9	329 44.2	53.0	83 56.3	38.4	145 56.9	58.0	33 14.0	40.3	Shaula	96 21.9	S37 06.7
A 14	272 42.3	344 44.5	52.6	98 57.5	37.8	160 59.5	58.0	48 16.2	40.4	Sirius	258 33.2	S16 44.2
Y 15	287 44.8	359 44.9	.. 52.3	113 58.7	.. 37.3	176 02.1	.. 58.1	63 18.4	.. 40.5	Spica	158 31.2	S11 13.9
16	302 47.3	14 45.2	51.9	128 59.9	36.8	191 04.7	58.1	78 20.5	40.6	Suhail	222 52.1	S43 29.2
17	317 49.7	29 45.6	51.6	144 01.1	36.3	206 07.3	58.1	93 22.7	40.6			
18	332 52.2	44 45.9	S25 51.2	159 02.3	N 4 35.8	221 09.9	N21 58.1	108 24.9	S14 40.7	Vega	80 39.1	N38 48.2
19	347 54.7	59 46.3	50.8	174 03.5	35.3	236 12.5	58.2	123 27.1	40.8	Zuben'ubi	137 05.4	S16 05.8
20	2 57.1	74 46.6	50.5	189 04.7	34.7	251 15.2	58.2	138 29.2	40.9		SHA	Mer. Pass.
21	17 59.6	89 47.0	.. 50.1	204 05.9	.. 34.2	266 17.8	.. 58.2	153 31.4	.. 41.0		° ′	h m
22	33 02.0	104 47.3	49.8	219 07.1	33.7	281 20.4	58.2	168 33.6	41.1	Venus	73 24.1	15 02
23	48 04.5	119 47.7	49.4	234 08.3	33.2	296 23.0	58.3	183 35.8	41.1	Mars	187 03.3	7 27
	h m									Jupiter	248 12.0	3 22
Mer. Pass. 19 52.2		v 0.3	d 0.3	v 1.2	d 0.5	v 2.6	d 0.0	v 2.2	d 0.1	Saturn	135 44.9	10 51

SUN and MOON

UT	SUN GHA	SUN Dec	MOON GHA	v	MOON Dec	d	HP
21 00	183 33.3	S19 53.7	323 32.4	12.1	N18 48.7	2.8	54.2
01	198 33.1	54.3	338 03.5	12.2	18 45.9	2.9	54.2
02	213 32.9	54.8	352 34.7	12.3	18 43.0	3.0	54.2
03	228 32.8	.. 55.4	7 06.0	12.2	18 40.0	3.1	54.2
04	243 32.6	55.9	21 37.2	12.3	18 36.9	3.1	54.2
05	258 32.5	56.5	36 08.5	12.3	18 33.8	3.3	54.2
06	273 32.3	S19 57.0	50 39.8	12.4	N18 30.5	3.3	54.2
07	288 32.2	57.6	65 11.2	12.4	18 27.2	3.4	54.2
T 08	303 32.0	58.1	79 42.6	12.4	18 23.8	3.5	54.2
H 09	318 31.8	.. 58.7	94 14.0	12.4	18 20.3	3.6	54.2
U 10	333 31.7	59.2	108 45.4	12.5	18 16.7	3.6	54.2
R 11	348 31.5	19 59.8	123 16.9	12.5	18 13.1	3.8	54.1
S 12	3 31.4	S20 00.3	137 48.4	12.6	N18 09.3	3.8	54.1
D 13	18 31.2	00.8	152 20.0	12.5	18 05.5	3.9	54.1
A 14	33 31.1	01.4	166 51.5	12.6	18 01.6	4.0	54.1
Y 15	48 30.9	.. 01.9	181 23.1	12.7	17 57.6	4.1	54.1
16	63 30.7	02.5	195 54.8	12.6	17 53.5	4.1	54.1
17	78 30.6	03.0	210 26.4	12.7	17 49.4	4.2	54.1
18	93 30.4	S20 03.6	224 58.1	12.7	N17 45.2	4.3	54.1
19	108 30.2	04.1	239 29.8	12.8	17 40.9	4.4	54.1
20	123 30.1	04.6	254 01.6	12.8	17 36.5	4.5	54.1
21	138 29.9	.. 05.2	268 33.4	12.8	17 32.0	4.5	54.1
22	153 29.8	05.7	283 05.2	12.9	17 27.5	4.6	54.1
23	168 29.6	06.3	297 37.1	12.8	17 22.9	4.7	54.1
22 00	183 29.4	S20 06.8	312 08.9	13.0	N17 18.2	4.8	54.1
01	198 29.3	07.3	326 40.9	12.9	17 13.4	4.8	54.1
02	213 29.1	07.9	341 12.8	13.0	17 08.6	4.9	54.1
03	228 28.9	.. 08.4	355 44.8	13.0	17 03.7	5.0	54.1
04	243 28.8	08.9	10 16.8	13.0	16 58.7	5.1	54.1
05	258 28.6	09.5	24 48.8	13.1	16 53.6	5.1	54.1
06	273 28.5	S20 10.0	39 20.9	13.1	N16 48.5	5.2	54.1
07	288 28.3	10.5	53 53.0	13.1	16 43.3	5.3	54.1
08	303 28.1	11.1	68 25.1	13.2	16 38.0	5.4	54.1
F 09	318 28.0	.. 11.6	82 57.3	13.2	16 32.6	5.4	54.1
R 10	333 27.8	12.1	97 29.5	13.2	16 27.2	5.5	54.1
I 11	348 27.6	12.7	112 01.7	13.3	16 21.7	5.6	54.1
D 12	3 27.5	S20 13.2	126 34.0	13.3	N16 16.1	5.6	54.1
A 13	18 27.3	13.7	141 06.3	13.3	16 10.5	5.7	54.1
Y 14	33 27.1	14.3	155 38.6	13.4	16 04.8	5.8	54.1
15	48 26.9	.. 14.8	170 11.0	13.4	15 59.0	5.9	54.1
16	63 26.8	15.3	184 43.4	13.4	15 53.1	5.9	54.1
17	78 26.6	15.8	199 15.8	13.4	15 47.2	6.0	54.1
18	93 26.4	S20 16.4	213 48.2	13.5	N15 41.2	6.1	54.1
19	108 26.3	16.9	228 20.7	13.5	15 35.1	6.1	54.1
20	123 26.1	17.4	242 53.2	13.5	15 29.0	6.2	54.1
21	138 25.9	.. 17.9	257 25.7	13.6	15 22.8	6.2	54.1
22	153 25.8	18.5	271 58.3	13.6	15 16.6	6.4	54.1
23	168 25.6	19.0	286 30.9	13.6	15 10.2	6.4	54.1
23 00	183 25.4	S20 19.5	301 03.5	13.6	N15 03.8	6.4	54.1
01	198 25.2	20.0	315 36.1	13.7	14 57.4	6.5	54.1
02	213 25.1	20.5	330 08.8	13.7	14 50.9	6.6	54.1
03	228 24.9	.. 21.1	344 41.5	13.7	14 44.3	6.7	54.1
04	243 24.7	21.6	359 14.2	13.8	14 37.6	6.7	54.1
05	258 24.6	22.1	13 47.0	13.8	14 30.9	6.8	54.1
06	273 24.4	S20 22.6	28 19.8	13.8	N14 24.1	6.8	54.1
07	288 24.2	23.1	42 52.6	13.8	14 17.3	6.9	54.1
S 08	303 24.0	23.7	57 25.4	13.9	14 10.4	7.0	54.1
A 09	318 23.9	.. 24.2	71 58.3	13.9	14 03.4	7.0	54.2
T 10	333 23.7	24.7	86 31.2	13.9	13 56.4	7.1	54.2
U 11	348 23.5	25.2	101 04.1	13.9	13 49.3	7.1	54.2
R 12	3 23.3	S20 25.7	115 37.0	14.0	N13 42.2	7.2	54.2
D 13	18 23.2	26.2	130 10.0	14.0	13 35.0	7.3	54.2
A 14	33 23.0	26.7	144 43.0	14.0	13 27.7	7.3	54.2
Y 15	48 22.8	.. 27.3	159 16.0	14.0	13 20.4	7.4	54.2
16	63 22.6	27.8	173 49.0	14.1	13 13.0	7.4	54.2
17	78 22.5	28.3	188 22.1	14.1	13 05.6	7.5	54.2
18	93 22.3	S20 28.8	202 55.2	14.1	N12 58.1	7.6	54.2
19	108 22.1	29.3	217 28.3	14.1	12 50.5	7.6	54.2
20	123 21.9	29.8	232 01.4	14.1	12 42.9	7.7	54.2
21	138 21.7	.. 30.3	246 34.5	14.2	12 35.3	7.8	54.2
22	153 21.6	30.8	261 07.7	14.2	12 27.5	7.7	54.3
23	168 21.4	31.3	275 40.9	14.2	N12 19.8	7.9	54.3
	SD 16.2	d 0.5	SD 14.8		14.7		14.8

Twilight, Sunrise, Moonrise

Lat.	Naut.	Civil	Sunrise	Moonrise 21	22	23	24
N 72	07 24	09 08	■	15 27	17 47	19 36	21 18
N 70	07 11	08 39	10 46	16 52	18 26	20 00	21 33
68	07 00	08 17	09 48	17 31	18 53	20 18	21 45
66	06 51	08 00	09 14	17 57	19 13	20 33	21 54
64	06 44	07 46	08 50	18 18	19 30	20 45	22 02
62	06 37	07 34	08 31	18 35	19 43	20 55	22 09
60	06 31	07 24	08 15	18 48	19 54	21 04	22 15
N 58	06 25	07 15	08 02	19 00	20 04	21 11	22 20
56	06 20	07 07	07 51	19 10	20 13	21 18	22 25
54	06 16	07 00	07 41	19 19	20 20	21 24	22 29
52	06 11	06 53	07 32	19 27	20 27	21 29	22 33
50	06 07	06 47	07 24	19 35	20 33	21 34	22 36
45	05 58	06 35	07 07	19 50	20 46	21 44	22 43
N 40	05 50	06 24	06 53	20 03	20 57	21 53	22 50
35	05 43	06 14	06 41	20 13	21 07	22 00	22 55
30	05 36	06 05	06 31	20 23	21 15	22 07	22 59
20	05 23	05 50	06 13	20 39	21 29	22 18	23 07
N 10	05 09	05 35	05 57	20 53	21 41	22 28	23 14
0	04 55	05 21	05 43	21 06	21 52	22 37	23 21
S 10	04 39	05 05	05 28	21 20	22 04	22 46	23 27
20	04 19	04 48	05 12	21 34	22 16	22 56	23 34
30	03 55	04 26	04 53	21 50	22 30	23 07	23 42
35	03 39	04 12	04 42	21 59	22 38	23 13	23 47
40	03 19	03 58	04 29	22 10	22 47	23 20	23 52
45	02 55	03 40	04 15	22 22	22 57	23 29	23 58
S 50	02 20	03 16	03 56	22 37	23 10	23 39	24 05
52	02 02	03 04	03 47	22 44	23 16	23 44	24 08
54	01 39	02 50	03 38	22 52	23 23	23 49	24 12
56	01 06	02 34	03 27	23 01	23 30	23 54	24 16
58	////	02 15	03 14	23 11	23 38	24 01	00 01
S 60	////	01 50	02 59	23 22	23 48	24 08	00 08

Sunset, Twilight, Moonset

Lat.	Sunset	Civil	Naut.	Moonset 21	22	23	24
N 72	■	14 23	16 07	14 29	13 45	13 29	13 19
N 70	12 45	14 52	16 20	13 04	13 05	13 04	13 02
68	13 44	15 14	16 31	12 24	12 38	12 45	12 49
66	14 17	15 31	16 40	11 57	12 17	12 29	12 39
64	14 42	15 46	16 48	11 36	12 00	12 17	12 30
62	15 01	15 58	16 55	11 19	11 46	12 06	12 22
60	15 16	16 08	17 01	11 05	11 34	11 57	12 15
N 58	15 30	16 17	17 06	10 53	11 24	11 48	12 09
56	15 41	16 25	17 11	10 42	11 15	11 41	12 04
54	15 51	16 32	17 16	10 33	11 07	11 35	11 59
52	16 00	16 38	17 20	10 25	11 00	11 29	11 55
50	16 08	16 44	17 24	10 18	10 53	11 24	11 51
45	16 25	16 57	17 33	10 02	10 39	11 12	11 43
N 40	16 39	17 08	17 42	09 40	10 28	11 03	11 35
35	16 51	17 18	17 49	09 37	10 18	10 55	11 29
30	17 01	17 27	17 56	09 28	10 09	10 48	11 24
20	17 19	17 43	18 10	09 11	09 54	10 35	11 14
N 10	17 35	17 57	18 23	08 56	09 41	10 24	11 06
0	17 50	18 12	18 37	08 42	09 29	10 14	10 58
S 10	18 05	18 27	18 54	08 28	09 16	10 04	10 50
20	18 21	18 43	19 13	08 13	09 03	09 53	10 42
30	18 40	19 06	19 38	07 56	08 48	09 40	10 32
35	18 51	19 19	19 54	07 46	08 39	09 32	10 27
40	19 03	19 35	20 14	07 35	08 29	09 24	10 20
45	19 18	19 54	20 39	07 21	08 17	09 14	10 13
S 50	19 37	20 18	21 13	07 05	08 02	09 02	10 04
52	19 46	20 30	21 32	06 57	07 56	08 57	09 59
54	19 56	20 44	21 56	06 49	07 48	08 50	09 55
56	20 07	21 00	22 30	06 39	07 40	08 44	09 50
58	20 20	21 20	////	06 28	07 30	08 37	09 44
S 60	20 35	21 45	////	06 15	07 19	08 27	09 37

SUN and MOON

Day	Eqn. of Time 00h	12h	Mer. Pass.	Mer. Pass. Upper	Lower	Age	Phase
21	14 13	14 06	11 46	02 31	14 54	18	87
22	13 58	13 50	11 46	03 18	15 41	19	80
23	13 42	13 34	11 46	04 03	16 25	20	71

UT	ARIES GHA	VENUS −4.8 GHA	Dec	MARS +1.3 GHA	Dec	JUPITER −2.5 GHA	Dec	SATURN +0.6 GHA	Dec	STARS Name	SHA	Dec
d h	° ′	° ′	° ′	° ′	° ′	° ′	° ′	° ′	° ′		° ′	° ′
24 00	63 07.0	134 48.1	S25 49.0	249 09.5	N 4 32.7	311 25.6	N21 58.3	198 37.9	S14 41.2	Acamar	315 17.7	S40 15.1
01	78 09.4	149 48.4	48.7	264 10.7	32.2	326 28.2	58.3	213 40.1	41.3	Achernar	335 26.2	S57 10.1
02	93 11.9	164 48.8	48.3	279 11.9	31.7	341 30.8	58.3	228 42.3	41.4	Acrux	173 09.2	S63 10.3
03	108 14.4	179 49.2 ..	47.9	294 13.2 ..	31.1	356 33.4 ..	58.4	243 44.5 ..	41.5	Adhara	255 12.0	S28 59.5
04	123 16.8	194 49.5	47.6	309 14.4	30.6	11 36.0	58.4	258 46.6	41.5	Aldebaran	290 48.7	N16 32.1
05	138 19.3	209 49.9	47.2	324 15.6	30.1	26 38.6	58.4	273 48.8	41.6			
06	153 21.8	224 50.3	S25 46.8	339 16.8	N 4 29.6	41 41.3	N21 58.4	288 51.0	S14 41.7	Alioth	166 20.9	N55 52.9
07	168 24.2	239 50.7	46.5	354 18.0	29.1	56 43.9	58.5	303 53.1	41.8	Alkaid	152 59.1	N49 14.5
08	183 26.7	254 51.1	46.1	9 19.2	28.6	71 46.5	58.5	318 55.3	41.9	Al Na'ir	27 43.4	S46 53.7
S 09	198 29.1	269 51.4 ..	45.7	24 20.4 ..	28.1	86 49.1 ..	58.5	333 57.5 ..	42.0	Alnilam	275 45.7	S 1 11.7
U 10	213 31.6	284 51.8	45.3	39 21.6	27.5	101 51.7	58.6	348 59.7	42.0	Alphard	217 55.7	S 8 43.2
N 11	228 34.1	299 52.2	45.0	54 22.8	27.0	116 54.3	58.6	4 01.8	42.1			
D 12	243 36.5	314 52.6	S25 44.6	69 24.0	N 4 26.5	131 56.9	N21 58.6	19 04.0	S14 42.2	Alphecca	126 11.1	N26 40.2
A 13	258 39.0	329 53.0	44.2	84 25.2	26.0	146 59.6	58.6	34 06.2	42.3	Alpheratz	357 43.0	N29 10.3
Y 14	273 41.5	344 53.4	43.8	99 26.4	25.5	162 02.2	58.7	49 08.4	42.3	Altair	62 08.2	N 8 54.6
15	288 43.9	359 53.8 ..	43.5	114 27.6 ..	25.0	177 04.8 ..	58.7	64 10.5 ..	42.4	Ankaa	353 15.2	S42 13.9
16	303 46.4	14 54.2	43.1	129 28.8	24.5	192 07.4	58.7	79 12.7	42.5	Antares	112 26.3	S26 27.6
17	318 48.9	29 54.6	42.7	144 30.0	23.9	207 10.0	58.7	94 14.9	42.6			
18	333 51.3	44 55.0	S25 42.3	159 31.2	N 4 23.4	222 12.6	N21 58.8	109 17.1	S14 42.7	Arcturus	145 55.8	N19 06.7
19	348 53.8	59 55.4	42.0	174 32.4	22.9	237 15.3	58.8	124 19.2	42.8	Atria	107 28.3	S69 03.0
20	3 56.3	74 55.8	41.6	189 33.6	22.4	252 17.9	58.8	139 21.4	42.8	Avior	234 17.5	S59 33.1
21	18 58.7	89 56.2 ..	41.2	204 34.8 ..	21.9	267 20.5 ..	58.8	154 23.6 ..	42.9	Bellatrix	278 31.4	N 6 21.6
22	34 01.2	104 56.6	40.8	219 36.1	21.4	282 23.1	58.9	169 25.8	43.0	Betelgeuse	271 00.7	N 7 24.4
23	49 03.6	119 57.0	40.4	234 37.3	20.9	297 25.7	58.9	184 27.9	43.1			
25 00	64 06.1	134 57.4	S25 40.1	249 38.5	N 4 20.3	312 28.3	N21 58.9	199 30.1	S14 43.2	Canopus	263 55.5	S52 42.2
01	79 08.6	149 57.8	39.7	264 39.7	19.8	327 31.0	59.0	214 32.3	43.3	Capella	280 33.5	N46 00.5
02	94 11.0	164 58.2	39.3	279 40.9	19.3	342 33.6	59.0	229 34.5	43.3	Deneb	49 31.4	N45 20.2
03	109 13.5	179 58.7 ..	38.9	294 42.1 ..	18.8	357 36.2 ..	59.0	244 36.6 ..	43.5	Denebola	182 33.5	N14 29.6
04	124 16.0	194 59.1	38.5	309 43.3	18.3	12 38.8	59.0	259 38.8	43.5	Diphda	348 55.4	S17 54.6
05	139 18.4	209 59.5	38.1	324 44.5	17.8	27 41.4	59.1	274 41.0	43.6			
06	154 20.9	224 59.9	S25 37.8	339 45.7	N 4 17.3	42 44.1	N21 59.1	289 43.2	S14 43.7	Dubhe	193 51.6	N61 40.2
07	169 23.4	240 00.4	37.4	354 46.9	16.8	57 46.7	59.1	304 45.3	43.7	Elnath	278 11.9	N28 37.0
08	184 25.8	255 00.8	37.0	9 48.1	16.2	72 49.3	59.1	319 47.5	43.8	Eltanin	90 46.5	N51 29.5
M 09	199 28.3	270 01.2 ..	36.6	24 49.3 ..	15.7	87 51.9 ..	59.2	334 49.7 ..	43.9	Enif	33 46.9	N 9 56.6
O 10	214 30.8	285 01.7	36.2	39 50.6	15.2	102 54.5	59.2	349 51.9	44.0	Fomalhaut	15 23.6	S29 32.9
N 11	229 33.2	300 02.1	35.8	54 51.8	14.7	117 57.2	59.2	4 54.0	44.1			
D 12	244 35.7	315 02.5	S25 35.4	69 53.0	N 4 14.2	132 59.8	N21 59.3	19 56.2	S14 44.2	Gacrux	172 00.8	S57 11.2
A 13	259 38.1	330 03.0	35.0	84 54.2	13.7	148 02.4	59.3	34 58.4	44.2	Gienah	175 52.1	S17 37.0
Y 14	274 40.6	345 03.4	34.6	99 55.4	13.2	163 05.0	59.3	50 00.6	44.3	Hadar	148 47.9	S60 26.2
15	289 43.1	0 03.9 ..	34.3	114 56.6 ..	12.6	178 07.7 ..	59.3	65 02.7 ..	44.4	Hamal	328 00.1	N23 31.8
16	304 45.5	15 04.3	33.9	129 57.8	12.1	193 10.3	59.4	80 04.9	44.5	Kaus Aust.	83 43.8	S34 22.5
17	319 48.0	30 04.8	33.5	144 59.0	11.6	208 12.9	59.4	95 07.1	44.6			
18	334 50.5	45 05.2	S25 33.1	160 00.2	N 4 11.1	223 15.5	N21 59.4	110 09.3	S14 44.6	Kochab	137 21.3	N74 05.8
19	349 52.9	60 05.7	32.7	175 01.5	10.6	238 18.2	59.5	125 11.4	44.7	Markab	13 38.0	N15 17.1
20	4 55.4	75 06.1	32.3	190 02.7	10.1	253 20.8	59.5	140 13.6	44.8	Menkar	314 14.4	N 4 08.6
21	19 57.9	90 06.6 ..	31.9	205 03.9 ..	09.6	268 23.4 ..	59.5	155 15.8 ..	44.9	Menkent	148 07.5	S36 26.1
22	35 00.3	105 07.0	31.5	220 05.1	09.1	283 26.0	59.5	170 18.0	45.0	Miaplacidus	221 39.2	S69 46.3
23	50 02.8	120 07.5	31.1	235 06.3	08.5	298 28.7	59.6	185 20.1	45.0			
26 00	65 05.2	135 08.0	S25 30.7	250 07.5	N 4 08.0	313 31.3	N21 59.6	200 22.3	S14 45.1	Mirfak	308 39.4	N49 54.6
01	80 07.7	150 08.4	30.3	265 08.7	07.5	328 33.9	59.6	215 24.5	45.2	Nunki	75 58.2	S26 16.6
02	95 10.2	165 08.9	29.9	280 09.9	07.0	343 36.5	59.6	230 26.7	45.3	Peacock	53 19.1	S56 41.4
03	110 12.6	180 09.4 ..	29.5	295 11.1 ..	06.5	358 39.2 ..	59.7	245 28.8 ..	45.4	Pollux	243 27.1	N27 59.3
04	125 15.1	195 09.8	29.1	310 12.4	06.0	13 41.8	59.7	260 31.0	45.4	Procyon	244 59.2	N 5 11.2
05	140 17.6	210 10.3	28.7	325 13.6	05.5	28 44.4	59.7	275 33.2	45.5			
06	155 20.0	225 10.8	S25 28.3	340 14.8	N 4 05.0	43 47.1	N21 59.8	290 35.4	S14 45.6	Rasalhague	96 06.5	N12 33.3
07	170 22.5	240 11.3	27.9	355 16.0	04.5	58 49.7	59.8	305 37.5	45.7	Regulus	207 43.2	N11 53.8
08	185 25.0	255 11.8	27.5	10 17.2	03.9	73 52.3	59.8	320 39.7	45.8	Rigel	281 11.4	S 8 11.2
T 09	200 27.4	270 12.2 ..	27.1	25 18.4 ..	03.4	88 55.0 ..	59.8	335 41.9 ..	45.9	Rigil Kent.	139 51.9	S60 53.3
U 10	215 29.9	285 12.7	26.7	40 19.6	02.9	103 57.6	59.9	350 44.1	45.9	Sabik	102 12.5	S15 44.3
E 11	230 32.4	300 13.2	26.3	55 20.9	02.4	119 00.2	59.9	5 46.2	46.0			
S 12	245 34.8	315 13.7	S25 25.9	70 22.1	N 4 01.9	134 02.8	N21 59.9	20 48.4	S14 46.1	Schedar	349 39.7	N56 37.1
D 13	260 37.3	330 14.2	25.5	85 23.3	01.4	149 05.5	22 00.0	35 50.6	46.2	Shaula	96 21.9	S37 06.7
A 14	275 39.7	345 14.7	25.1	100 24.5	00.9	164 08.1	00.0	50 52.8	46.3	Sirius	258 33.2	S16 44.2
Y 15	290 42.2	0 15.2 ..	24.7	115 25.7	4 00.4	179 10.7 ..	00.0	65 54.9 ..	46.3	Spica	158 31.2	S11 13.9
16	305 44.7	15 15.7	24.3	130 26.9	3 59.8	194 13.4	00.1	80 57.1	46.4	Suhail	222 52.0	S43 29.2
17	320 47.1	30 16.2	23.9	145 28.1	59.3	209 16.0	00.1	95 59.3	46.5			
18	335 49.6	45 16.7	S25 23.4	160 29.4	N 3 58.8	224 18.6	N22 00.1	111 01.5	S14 46.6	Vega	80 39.1	N38 48.1
19	350 52.1	60 17.2	23.0	175 30.6	58.3	239 21.3	00.1	126 03.6	46.7	Zuben'ubi	137 05.4	S16 05.8
20	5 54.5	75 17.7	22.6	190 31.8	57.8	254 23.9	00.2	141 05.8	46.7		SHA	Mer. Pass.
21	20 57.0	90 18.2 ..	22.2	205 33.0 ..	57.3	269 26.5 ..	00.2	156 08.0 ..	46.8		° ′	h m
22	35 59.5	105 18.7	21.8	220 34.2	56.8	284 29.2	00.2	171 10.2	46.9	Venus	70 51.3	15 00
23	51 01.9	120 19.2	21.4	235 35.4	56.3	299 31.8	00.3	186 12.3	47.0	Mars	185 32.4	7 21
Mer. Pass.	h m 19 40.4	v 0.4	d 0.4	v 1.2	d 0.5	v 2.6	d 0.0	v 2.2	d 0.1	Jupiter	248 22.2	3 10
										Saturn	135 24.0	10 40

UT	SUN GHA	SUN Dec	MOON GHA	v	Dec	d	HP
d h	o '	o '	o '	'	o '	'	'
24 00	183 21.2	S20 31.8	290 14.1	14.2	N12 11.9	7.8	54.3
01	198 21.0	32.3	304 47.3	14.2	12 04.1	8.0	54.3
02	213 20.8	32.9	319 20.5	14.3	11 56.1	8.0	54.3
03	228 20.7	.. 33.4	333 53.8	14.3	11 48.1	8.0	54.3
04	243 20.5	33.9	348 27.1	14.3	11 40.1	8.1	54.3
05	258 20.3	34.4	3 00.4	14.3	11 32.0	8.2	54.3
06	273 20.1	S20 34.9	17 33.7	14.3	N11 23.8	8.1	54.3
07	288 19.9	35.4	32 07.0	14.4	11 15.7	8.3	54.4
08	303 19.7	35.9	46 40.4	14.3	11 07.4	8.3	54.4
S 09	318 19.6	.. 36.4	61 13.7	14.4	10 59.1	8.3	54.4
U 10	333 19.4	36.9	75 47.1	14.4	10 50.8	8.4	54.4
N 11	348 19.2	37.4	90 20.5	14.4	10 42.4	8.5	54.4
D 12	3 19.0	S20 37.9	104 53.9	14.4	N10 33.9	8.5	54.4
A 13	18 18.8	38.4	119 27.3	14.4	10 25.4	8.5	54.4
Y 14	33 18.6	38.9	134 00.7	14.5	10 16.9	8.6	54.5
15	48 18.5	.. 39.4	148 34.2	14.4	10 08.3	8.6	54.5
16	63 18.3	39.9	163 07.6	14.5	9 59.7	8.7	54.5
17	78 18.1	40.4	177 41.1	14.5	9 51.0	8.7	54.5
18	93 17.9	S20 40.8	192 14.6	14.5	N 9 42.3	8.8	54.5
19	108 17.7	41.3	206 48.1	14.4	9 33.5	8.8	54.5
20	123 17.5	41.8	221 21.5	14.5	9 24.7	8.9	54.5
21	138 17.3	.. 42.3	235 55.0	14.6	9 15.8	8.9	54.6
22	153 17.2	42.8	250 28.6	14.5	9 06.9	8.9	54.6
23	168 17.0	43.3	265 02.1	14.5	8 58.0	9.0	54.6
25 00	183 16.8	S20 43.8	279 35.6	14.5	N 8 49.0	9.0	54.6
01	198 16.6	44.3	294 09.1	14.6	8 40.0	9.1	54.6
02	213 16.4	44.8	308 42.6	14.6	8 30.9	9.1	54.6
03	228 16.2	.. 45.3	323 16.2	14.5	8 21.8	9.2	54.7
04	243 16.0	45.8	337 49.7	14.6	8 12.6	9.2	54.7
05	258 15.8	46.2	352 23.3	14.5	8 03.4	9.2	54.7
06	273 15.7	S20 46.7	6 56.8	14.6	N 7 54.2	9.3	54.7
07	288 15.5	47.2	21 30.4	14.5	7 44.9	9.3	54.7
08	303 15.3	47.7	36 03.9	14.6	7 35.6	9.4	54.8
M 09	318 15.1	.. 48.2	50 37.5	14.5	7 26.2	9.4	54.8
O 10	333 14.9	48.7	65 11.0	14.6	7 16.8	9.4	54.8
N 11	348 14.7	49.2	79 44.6	14.5	7 07.4	9.5	54.8
D 12	3 14.5	S20 49.6	94 18.1	14.5	N 6 57.9	9.5	54.8
A 13	18 14.3	50.1	108 51.6	14.6	6 48.4	9.5	54.9
Y 14	33 14.1	50.6	123 25.2	14.6	6 38.9	9.6	54.9
15	48 13.9	.. 51.1	137 58.7	14.6	6 29.3	9.6	54.9
16	63 13.7	51.6	152 32.3	14.5	6 19.7	9.6	54.9
17	78 13.5	52.0	167 05.8	14.5	6 10.1	9.7	55.0
18	93 13.3	S20 52.5	181 39.3	14.5	N 6 00.4	9.7	55.0
19	108 13.2	53.0	196 12.8	14.5	5 50.7	9.8	55.0
20	123 13.0	53.5	210 46.3	14.5	5 40.9	9.7	55.0
21	138 12.8	.. 53.9	225 19.8	14.5	5 31.2	9.8	55.0
22	153 12.6	54.4	239 53.3	14.5	5 21.4	9.9	55.1
23	168 12.4	54.9	254 26.8	14.5	5 11.5	9.9	55.1
26 00	183 12.2	S20 55.4	269 00.3	14.4	N 5 01.6	9.9	55.1
01	198 12.0	55.8	283 33.7	14.5	4 51.7	9.9	55.1
02	213 11.8	56.3	298 07.2	14.4	4 41.8	9.9	55.2
03	228 11.6	.. 56.8	312 40.6	14.4	4 31.9	10.0	55.2
04	243 11.4	57.3	327 14.0	14.4	4 21.9	10.0	55.2
05	258 11.2	57.7	341 47.4	14.4	4 11.9	10.1	55.2
06	273 11.0	S20 58.2	356 20.8	14.4	N 4 01.8	10.1	55.3
07	288 10.8	58.7	10 54.2	14.3	3 51.7	10.1	55.3
08	303 10.6	59.1	25 27.5	14.4	3 41.6	10.1	55.3
T 09	318 10.4	20 59.6	40 00.9	14.3	3 31.5	10.1	55.4
U 10	333 10.2	21 00.1	54 34.2	14.3	3 21.4	10.2	55.4
E 11	348 10.0	00.5	69 07.5	14.3	3 11.2	10.2	55.4
S 12	3 09.8	S21 01.0	83 40.8	14.2	N 3 01.0	10.2	55.4
D 13	18 09.6	01.5	98 14.0	14.3	2 50.8	10.3	55.5
A 14	33 09.4	01.9	112 47.3	14.2	2 40.5	10.3	55.5
Y 15	48 09.2	.. 02.4	127 20.5	14.2	2 30.3	10.3	55.5
16	63 09.0	02.9	141 53.7	14.2	2 20.0	10.3	55.5
17	78 08.8	03.3	156 26.9	14.1	2 09.7	10.3	55.6
18	93 08.6	S21 03.8	171 00.0	14.1	N 1 59.4	10.4	55.6
19	108 08.4	04.3	185 33.1	14.1	1 49.0	10.4	55.6
20	123 08.2	04.7	200 06.2	14.1	1 38.6	10.3	55.7
21	138 08.0	.. 05.2	214 39.3	14.0	1 28.3	10.4	55.7
22	153 07.8	05.6	229 12.3	14.0	1 17.9	10.5	55.7
23	168 07.6	06.1	243 45.3	14.0	N 1 07.4	10.4	55.8
	SD 16.2	d 0.5	SD 14.8		14.9		15.1

Lat.	Twilight Naut.	Twilight Civil	Sunrise	Moonrise 24	Moonrise 25	Moonrise 26	Moonrise 27
o	h m	h m	h m	h m	h m	h m	h m
N 72	07 34	09 22	■	21 18	22 59	24 39	00 39
N 70	07 19	08 50	11 40	21 33	23 06	24 40	00 40
68	07 08	08 27	10 03	21 45	23 12	24 41	00 40
66	06 58	08 08	09 25	21 54	23 17	24 42	00 42
64	06 50	07 53	08 59	22 02	23 21	24 42	00 42
62	06 43	07 41	08 39	22 09	23 25	24 43	00 43
60	06 36	07 30	08 22	22 15	23 28	24 43	00 43
N 58	06 30	07 20	08 08	22 20	23 31	24 44	00 44
56	06 25	07 12	07 56	22 25	23 34	24 44	00 44
54	06 20	07 05	07 46	22 29	23 36	24 44	00 44
52	06 16	06 58	07 37	22 33	23 38	24 45	00 45
50	06 11	06 52	07 28	22 36	23 40	24 45	00 45
45	06 02	06 38	07 11	22 43	23 44	24 45	00 45
N 40	05 53	06 27	06 56	22 50	23 47	24 46	00 46
35	05 46	06 17	06 44	22 55	23 50	24 46	00 46
30	05 38	06 08	06 33	22 59	23 53	24 47	00 47
20	05 24	05 51	06 15	23 07	23 57	24 47	00 47
N 10	05 10	05 36	05 59	23 14	24 01	00 01	00 48
0	04 56	05 21	05 43	23 21	24 05	00 05	00 49
S 10	04 39	05 05	05 28	23 27	24 08	00 08	00 49
20	04 19	04 47	05 11	23 34	24 12	00 12	00 50
30	03 53	04 25	04 52	23 42	24 16	00 16	00 51
35	03 37	04 12	04 41	23 47	24 19	00 19	00 51
40	03 17	03 56	04 28	23 52	24 22	00 22	00 52
45	02 51	03 37	04 12	23 58	24 25	00 25	00 52
S 50	02 15	03 12	03 53	24 05	00 05	00 29	00 53
52	01 56	03 00	03 44	24 08	00 08	00 31	00 53
54	01 31	02 45	03 34	24 12	00 12	00 33	00 54
56	00 53	02 28	03 22	24 16	00 16	00 35	00 54
58	////	02 08	03 09	00 01	00 20	00 38	00 54
S 60	////	01 41	02 53	00 08	00 25	00 40	00 55

Lat.	Sunset	Twilight Civil	Twilight Naut.	Moonset 24	Moonset 25	Moonset 26	Moonset 27
o	h m	h m	h m	h m	h m	h m	h m
N 72	■	14 11	15 59	13 19	13 09	13 01	12 53
N 70	11 53	14 43	16 14	13 02	13 00	12 57	12 54
68	13 30	15 07	16 25	12 49	12 52	12 54	12 56
66	14 08	15 25	16 35	12 39	12 46	12 52	12 57
64	14 34	15 40	16 43	12 30	12 40	12 49	12 58
62	14 55	15 53	16 51	12 22	12 35	12 48	12 59
60	15 11	16 04	16 57	12 15	12 31	12 46	13 00
N 58	15 25	16 13	17 03	12 09	12 27	12 44	13 01
56	15 37	16 21	17 09	12 04	12 24	12 43	13 02
54	15 48	16 29	17 13	11 59	12 21	12 42	13 02
52	15 57	16 36	17 18	11 55	12 18	12 41	13 03
50	16 05	16 42	17 23	11 51	12 16	12 41	13 03
45	16 23	16 56	17 32	11 43	12 10	12 37	13 05
N 40	16 37	17 07	17 40	11 35	12 06	12 36	13 05
35	16 50	17 17	17 48	11 29	12 02	12 34	13 06
30	17 00	17 26	17 56	11 24	11 58	12 33	13 07
20	17 19	17 43	18 10	11 14	11 52	12 30	13 08
N 10	17 35	17 58	18 24	11 06	11 47	12 28	13 09
0	17 51	18 13	18 39	10 58	11 42	12 26	13 10
S 10	18 06	18 29	18 55	10 50	11 37	12 23	13 11
20	18 23	18 47	19 15	10 42	11 31	12 21	13 12
30	18 42	19 09	19 41	10 32	11 25	12 18	13 13
35	18 54	19 22	19 58	10 27	11 21	12 17	13 14
40	19 07	19 38	20 18	10 20	11 17	12 15	13 15
45	19 22	19 58	20 44	10 13	11 12	12 13	13 15
S 50	19 42	20 23	21 20	10 04	11 06	12 11	13 17
52	19 51	20 36	21 40	09 59	11 04	12 10	13 17
54	20 01	20 50	22 06	09 55	11 01	12 08	13 18
56	20 13	21 07	22 46	09 50	10 57	12 07	13 18
58	20 26	21 28	////	09 44	10 54	12 05	13 19
S 60	20 42	21 56	////	09 37	10 50	12 04	13 20

	SUN			MOON			
Day	Eqn. of Time 00h	Eqn. of Time 12h	Mer. Pass.	Mer. Pass. Upper	Mer. Pass. Lower	Age	Phase
d	m s	m s	h m	h m	h m	d	%
24	13 25	13 16	11 47	04 48	17 10	21	63
25	13 08	12 58	11 47	05 31	17 53	22	53
26	12 49	12 40	11 47	06 15	18 37	23	43

UT	ARIES	VENUS −4.8		MARS +1.3		JUPITER −2.6		SATURN +0.6		STARS		
	GHA	GHA	Dec	GHA	Dec	GHA	Dec	GHA	Dec	Name	SHA	Dec
d h	° ′	° ′	° ′	° ′	° ′	° ′	° ′	° ′	° ′		° ′	° ′
27 00	66 04.4	135 19.8	S25 21.0	250 36.7	N 3 55.8	314 34.4	N22 00.3	201 14.5	S14 47.1	Acamar	315 17.7	S40 15.1
01	81 06.9	150 20.3	20.6	265 37.9	55.3	329 37.1	00.3	216 16.7	47.1	Achernar	335 26.2	S57 10.2
02	96 09.3	165 20.8	20.2	280 39.1	54.7	344 39.7	00.3	231 18.9	47.2	Acrux	173 09.2	S63 10.3
03	111 11.8	180 21.3	.. 19.7	295 40.3	.. 54.2	359 42.4	.. 00.4	246 21.0	.. 47.3	Adhara	255 12.0	S28 59.5
04	126 14.2	195 21.9	19.3	310 41.5	53.7	14 45.0	00.4	261 23.2	47.4	Aldebaran	290 48.7	N16 32.1
05	141 16.7	210 22.4	18.9	325 42.8	53.2	29 47.6	00.4	276 25.4	47.5			
06	156 19.2	225 22.9	S25 18.5	340 44.0	N 3 52.7	44 50.3	N22 00.5	291 27.6	S14 47.5	Alioth	166 20.9	N55 52.8
W 07	171 21.6	240 23.4	18.1	355 45.2	52.2	59 52.9	00.5	306 29.7	47.6	Alkaid	152 59.1	N49 14.5
E 08	186 24.1	255 24.0	17.7	10 46.4	51.7	74 55.5	00.5	321 31.9	47.7	Al Na'ir	27 43.5	S46 53.7
D 09	201 26.6	270 24.5	.. 17.2	25 47.6	.. 51.2	89 58.2	.. 00.6	336 34.1	.. 47.8	Alnilam	275 45.7	S 1 11.7
N 10	216 29.0	285 25.1	16.8	40 48.8	50.7	105 00.8	00.6	351 36.3	47.9	Alphard	217 55.7	S 8 43.2
E 11	231 31.5	300 25.6	16.4	55 50.1	50.1	120 03.5	00.6	6 38.4	47.9			
S 12	246 34.0	315 26.1	S25 16.0	70 51.3	N 3 49.6	135 06.1	N22 00.6	21 40.6	S14 48.0	Alphecca	126 11.1	N26 40.2
D 13	261 36.4	330 26.7	15.6	85 52.5	49.1	150 08.7	00.7	36 42.8	48.1	Alpheratz	357 43.0	N29 10.3
A 14	276 38.9	345 27.2	15.1	100 53.7	48.6	165 11.4	00.7	51 45.0	48.2	Altair	62 08.2	N 8 54.6
Y 15	291 41.3	0 27.8	.. 14.7	115 54.9	.. 48.1	180 14.0	.. 00.7	66 47.2	.. 48.3	Ankaa	353 15.2	S42 13.9
16	306 43.8	15 28.3	14.3	130 56.2	47.6	195 16.7	00.8	81 49.3	48.3	Antares	112 26.3	S26 27.6
17	321 46.3	30 28.9	13.9	145 57.4	47.1	210 19.3	00.8	96 51.5	48.4			
18	336 48.7	45 29.5	S25 13.5	160 58.6	N 3 46.6	225 21.9	N22 00.8	111 53.7	S14 48.5	Arcturus	145 55.8	N19 06.6
19	351 51.2	60 30.0	13.0	175 59.8	46.1	240 24.6	00.8	126 55.9	48.6	Atria	107 28.3	S69 03.0
20	6 53.7	75 30.6	12.6	191 01.0	45.6	255 27.2	00.9	141 58.0	48.7	Avior	234 17.5	S59 33.1
21	21 56.1	90 31.2	.. 12.2	206 02.3	.. 45.1	270 29.9	.. 00.9	157 00.2	.. 48.7	Bellatrix	278 31.3	N 6 21.6
22	36 58.6	105 31.7	11.8	221 03.5	44.5	285 32.5	00.9	172 02.4	48.8	Betelgeuse	271 00.7	N 7 24.4
23	52 01.1	120 32.3	11.3	236 04.7	44.0	300 35.2	01.0	187 04.6	48.9			
28 00	67 03.5	135 32.9	S25 10.9	251 05.9	N 3 43.5	315 37.8	N22 01.0	202 06.7	S14 49.0	Canopus	263 55.5	S52 42.2
01	82 06.0	150 33.4	10.5	266 07.2	43.0	330 40.4	01.0	217 08.9	49.1	Capella	280 33.5	N46 00.5
02	97 08.5	165 34.0	10.1	281 08.4	42.5	345 43.1	01.1	232 11.1	49.1	Deneb	49 31.5	N45 20.2
03	112 10.9	180 34.6	.. 09.6	296 09.6	.. 42.0	0 45.7	.. 01.1	247 13.3	.. 49.2	Denebola	182 33.5	N14 29.6
04	127 13.4	195 35.2	09.2	311 10.8	41.5	15 48.4	01.1	262 15.5	49.3	Diphda	348 55.4	S17 54.6
05	142 15.8	210 35.8	08.8	326 12.0	41.0	30 51.0	01.2	277 17.6	49.4			
06	157 18.3	225 36.3	S25 08.3	341 13.3	N 3 40.5	45 53.7	N22 01.2	292 19.8	S14 49.5	Dubhe	193 51.5	N61 40.2
T 07	172 20.8	240 36.9	07.9	356 14.5	40.0	60 56.3	01.2	307 22.0	49.5	Elnath	278 11.9	N28 37.0
H 08	187 23.2	255 37.5	07.5	11 15.7	39.5	75 59.0	01.2	322 24.2	49.6	Eltanin	90 46.5	N51 29.5
U 09	202 25.7	270 38.1	.. 07.0	26 16.9	.. 38.9	91 01.6	.. 01.3	337 26.3	.. 49.7	Enif	33 46.9	N 9 56.6
R 10	217 28.2	285 38.7	06.6	41 18.2	38.4	106 04.3	01.3	352 28.5	49.8	Fomalhaut	15 23.6	S29 32.9
R 11	232 30.6	300 39.3	06.2	56 19.4	37.9	121 06.9	01.3	7 30.7	49.9			
S 12	247 33.1	315 39.9	S25 05.7	71 20.6	N 3 37.4	136 09.5	N22 01.4	22 32.9	S14 49.9	Gacrux	172 00.8	S57 11.2
D 13	262 35.6	330 40.5	05.3	86 21.8	36.9	151 12.2	01.4	37 35.0	50.0	Gienah	175 52.1	S17 37.1
A 14	277 38.0	345 41.1	04.9	101 23.1	36.4	166 14.8	01.4	52 37.2	50.1	Hadar	148 47.9	S60 26.1
Y 15	292 40.5	0 41.7	.. 04.4	116 24.3	.. 35.9	181 17.5	.. 01.5	67 39.4	.. 50.2	Hamal	328 00.1	N23 31.8
16	307 42.9	15 42.3	04.0	131 25.5	35.4	196 20.1	01.5	82 41.6	50.3	Kaus Aust.	83 43.8	S34 22.5
17	322 45.4	30 42.9	03.6	146 26.7	34.9	211 22.8	01.5	97 43.8	50.3			
18	337 47.9	45 43.6	S25 03.1	161 28.0	N 3 34.4	226 25.4	N22 01.6	112 45.9	S14 50.4	Kochab	137 21.3	N74 05.8
19	352 50.3	60 44.2	02.7	176 29.2	33.9	241 28.1	01.6	127 48.1	50.5	Markab	13 48.0	N15 17.0
20	7 52.8	75 44.8	02.3	191 30.4	33.4	256 30.7	01.6	142 50.3	50.6	Menkar	314 14.4	N 4 08.6
21	22 55.3	90 45.4	.. 01.8	206 31.6	.. 32.9	271 33.4	.. 01.6	157 52.5	.. 50.7	Menkent	148 07.5	S36 26.1
22	37 57.7	105 46.0	01.4	221 32.9	32.3	286 36.0	01.7	172 54.6	50.7	Miaplacidus	221 39.2	S69 46.3
23	53 00.2	120 46.7	00.9	236 34.1	31.8	301 38.7	01.7	187 56.8	50.8			
29 00	68 02.7	135 47.3	S25 00.5	251 35.3	N 3 31.3	316 41.3	N22 01.7	202 59.0	S14 50.9	Mirfak	308 39.4	N49 54.6
01	83 05.1	150 47.9	25 00.1	266 36.5	30.8	331 44.0	01.8	218 01.2	51.0	Nunki	75 58.3	S26 16.6
02	98 07.6	165 48.6	24 59.6	281 37.8	30.3	346 46.6	01.8	233 03.4	51.0	Peacock	53 19.1	S56 41.4
03	113 10.1	180 49.2	.. 59.2	296 39.0	.. 29.8	1 49.3	.. 01.8	248 05.5	.. 51.1	Pollux	243 27.1	N27 59.3
04	128 12.5	195 49.8	58.7	311 40.2	29.3	16 52.0	01.9	263 07.7	51.2	Procyon	244 59.2	N 5 11.2
05	143 15.0	210 50.5	58.3	326 41.5	28.8	31 54.6	01.9	278 09.9	51.3			
06	158 17.4	225 51.1	S24 57.8	341 42.7	N 3 28.3	46 57.3	N22 01.9	293 12.1	S14 51.4	Rasalhague	96 06.5	N12 33.2
07	173 19.9	240 51.8	57.4	356 43.9	27.8	61 59.9	02.0	308 14.2	51.4	Regulus	207 43.2	N11 53.8
08	188 22.4	255 52.4	57.0	11 45.1	27.3	77 02.6	02.0	323 16.4	51.5	Rigel	281 11.4	S 8 11.2
F 09	203 24.8	270 53.1	.. 56.5	26 46.4	.. 26.8	92 05.2	.. 02.0	338 18.6	.. 51.6	Rigil Kent.	139 51.8	S60 53.3
R 10	218 27.3	285 53.7	56.1	41 47.6	26.3	107 07.9	02.1	353 20.8	51.7	Sabik	102 12.5	S15 44.3
I 11	233 29.8	300 54.4	55.6	56 48.8	25.8	122 10.5	02.1	8 23.0	51.8			
D 12	248 32.2	315 55.0	S24 55.2	71 50.1	N 3 25.2	137 13.2	N22 02.1	23 25.1	S14 51.8	Schedar	349 39.8	N56 37.1
A 13	263 34.7	330 55.7	54.7	86 51.3	24.7	152 15.8	02.2	38 27.3	51.9	Shaula	96 21.9	S37 06.6
Y 14	278 37.2	345 56.4	54.3	101 52.5	24.2	167 18.5	02.2	53 29.5	52.0	Sirius	258 33.1	S16 44.2
15	293 39.6	0 57.0	.. 53.8	116 53.7	.. 23.7	182 21.2	.. 02.2	68 31.7	.. 52.1	Spica	158 31.2	S11 13.9
16	308 42.1	15 57.7	53.4	131 55.0	23.2	197 23.8	02.2	83 33.8	52.2	Suhail	222 52.0	S43 29.2
17	323 44.6	30 58.4	52.9	146 56.2	22.7	212 26.5	02.3	98 36.0	52.2			
18	338 47.0	45 59.0	S24 52.5	161 57.4	N 3 22.2	227 29.1	N22 02.3	113 38.2	S14 52.3	Vega	80 39.1	N38 48.1
19	353 49.5	60 59.7	52.0	176 58.7	21.7	242 31.8	02.3	128 40.4	52.4	Zuben'ubi	137 05.4	S16 05.8
20	8 51.9	76 00.4	51.5	191 59.9	21.2	257 34.4	02.4	143 42.6	52.5		SHA	Mer.Pass.
21	23 54.4	91 01.1	.. 51.1	207 01.1	.. 20.7	272 37.1	.. 02.4	158 44.7	.. 52.5	Venus	68 29.3	14 57
22	38 56.9	106 01.7	50.7	222 02.4	20.2	287 39.8	02.4	173 46.9	52.6	Mars	184 02.4	7 15
23	53 59.3	121 02.4	50.2	237 03.6	19.7	302 42.4	02.5	188 49.1	52.7	Jupiter	248 34.3	2 57
Mer.Pass. 19 28.6		v 0.6 d 0.4		v 1.2 d 0.5		v 2.6 d 0.0		v 2.2 d 0.1		Saturn	135 03.2	10 30

SUN and MOON

UT	SUN GHA	SUN Dec	MOON GHA	v	MOON Dec	d	HP
d h	° ′	° ′	° ′	′	° ′	′	′
27 00	183 07.4	S21 06.6	258 18.3	13.9	N 0 57.0	10.5	55.8
01	198 07.2	07.0	272 51.2	14.0	0 46.5	10.4	55.8
02	213 07.0	07.5	287 24.2	13.8	0 36.1	10.5	55.8
03	228 06.8	.. 07.9	301 57.0	13.9	0 25.6	10.5	55.9
04	243 06.6	08.4	316 29.9	13.8	0 15.1	10.5	55.9
05	258 06.4	08.8	331 02.7	13.8	N 0 04.6	10.6	55.9
W 06	273 06.2	S21 09.3	345 35.5	13.7	S 0 06.0	10.5	56.0
E 07	288 05.9	09.7	0 08.2	13.7	0 16.5	10.5	56.0
D 08	303 05.7	10.2	14 40.9	13.7	0 27.0	10.6	56.0
N 09	318 05.5	.. 10.6	29 13.6	13.6	0 37.6	10.6	56.1
E 10	333 05.3	11.1	43 46.2	13.6	0 48.2	10.6	56.1
S 11	348 05.1	11.5	58 18.8	13.6	0 58.8	10.5	56.1
D 12	3 04.9	S21 12.0	72 51.4	13.5	S 1 09.3	10.6	56.2
A 13	18 04.7	12.4	87 23.9	13.5	1 19.9	10.7	56.2
Y 14	33 04.5	12.9	101 56.4	13.4	1 30.6	10.6	56.2
15	48 04.3	.. 13.3	116 28.8	13.4	1 41.2	10.6	56.3
16	63 04.1	13.8	131 01.2	13.3	1 51.8	10.6	56.3
17	78 03.9	14.2	145 33.5	13.3	2 02.4	10.6	56.3
18	93 03.7	S21 14.7	160 05.8	13.2	S 2 13.0	10.7	56.4
19	108 03.5	15.1	174 38.0	13.2	2 23.7	10.6	56.4
20	123 03.2	15.6	189 10.2	13.2	2 34.3	10.6	56.4
21	138 03.0	.. 16.0	203 42.4	13.1	2 44.9	10.7	56.5
22	153 02.8	16.4	218 14.5	13.1	2 55.6	10.6	56.5
23	168 02.6	16.9	232 46.6	13.0	3 06.2	10.6	56.6
28 00	183 02.4	S21 17.3	247 18.6	12.9	S 3 16.8	10.7	56.6
01	198 02.2	17.8	261 50.5	12.9	3 27.5	10.6	56.6
02	213 02.0	18.2	276 22.4	12.9	3 38.1	10.6	56.7
03	228 01.8	.. 18.7	290 54.3	12.7	3 48.7	10.7	56.7
04	243 01.5	19.1	305 26.0	12.8	3 59.4	10.6	56.7
05	258 01.3	19.5	319 57.8	12.7	4 10.0	10.6	56.8
T 06	273 01.1	S21 20.0	334 29.5	12.6	S 4 20.6	10.6	56.8
H 07	288 00.9	20.4	349 01.1	12.6	4 31.2	10.6	56.8
U 08	303 00.7	20.8	3 32.7	12.5	4 41.8	10.6	56.9
R 09	318 00.5	.. 21.3	18 04.2	12.4	4 52.4	10.6	56.9
S 10	333 00.3	21.7	32 35.6	12.4	5 03.0	10.6	57.0
D 11	348 00.1	22.1	47 07.0	12.3	5 13.6	10.5	57.0
A 12	2 59.8	S21 22.6	61 38.3	12.3	S 5 24.1	10.6	57.0
Y 13	17 59.6	23.0	76 09.6	12.2	5 34.7	10.5	57.1
14	32 59.4	23.4	90 40.8	12.2	5 45.2	10.6	57.1
15	47 59.2	.. 23.9	105 12.0	12.0	5 55.8	10.5	57.1
16	62 59.0	24.3	119 43.0	12.1	6 06.3	10.5	57.2
17	77 58.8	24.7	134 14.1	11.9	6 16.8	10.4	57.2
18	92 58.5	S21 25.2	148 45.0	11.9	S 6 27.2	10.5	57.3
19	107 58.3	25.6	163 15.9	11.8	6 37.7	10.5	57.3
20	122 58.1	26.0	177 46.7	11.8	6 48.2	10.4	57.3
21	137 57.9	.. 26.4	192 17.5	11.6	6 58.6	10.4	57.4
22	152 57.7	26.9	206 48.1	11.7	7 09.0	10.4	57.4
23	167 57.5	27.3	221 18.8	11.5	7 19.4	10.3	57.4
29 00	182 57.2	S21 27.7	235 49.3	11.5	S 7 29.7	10.4	57.5
01	197 57.0	28.1	250 19.8	11.4	7 40.1	10.3	57.5
02	212 56.8	28.6	264 50.2	11.3	7 50.4	10.3	57.6
03	227 56.6	.. 29.0	279 20.5	11.3	8 00.7	10.2	57.6
04	242 56.4	29.4	293 50.8	11.1	8 10.9	10.3	57.6
05	257 56.1	29.8	308 20.9	11.1	8 21.2	10.2	57.7
F 06	272 55.9	S21 30.2	322 51.0	11.1	S 8 31.4	10.1	57.7
R 07	287 55.7	30.7	337 21.1	10.9	8 41.5	10.2	57.8
I 08	302 55.5	31.1	351 51.0	10.9	8 51.7	10.1	57.8
D 09	317 55.2	.. 31.5	6 20.9	10.8	9 01.8	10.1	57.8
A 10	332 55.0	31.9	20 50.7	10.7	9 11.9	10.0	57.9
Y 11	347 54.8	32.3	35 20.4	10.7	9 21.9	10.0	57.9
12	2 54.6	S21 32.8	49 50.1	10.6	S 9 31.9	10.0	58.0
13	17 54.4	33.2	64 19.7	10.4	9 41.9	9.9	58.0
14	32 54.1	33.6	78 49.1	10.5	9 51.8	9.9	58.0
15	47 53.9	.. 34.0	93 18.6	10.3	10 01.7	9.9	58.1
16	62 53.7	34.4	107 47.9	10.2	10 11.6	9.8	58.1
17	77 53.5	34.8	122 17.1	10.2	10 21.4	9.7	58.1
18	92 53.2	S21 35.2	136 46.3	10.1	S10 31.1	9.8	58.2
19	107 53.0	35.6	151 15.4	10.0	10 40.9	9.6	58.2
20	122 52.8	36.1	165 44.4	9.9	10 50.5	9.7	58.3
21	137 52.6	.. 36.5	180 13.3	9.8	11 00.2	9.6	58.3
22	152 52.3	36.9	194 42.1	9.8	11 09.8	9.5	58.3
23	167 52.1	37.3	209 10.9	9.6	S11 19.3	9.5	58.4
	SD 16.2	d 0.4	SD 15.3		15.5		15.8

Twilight, Sunrise and Moonrise

Lat.	Naut.	Civil	Sunrise	Moonrise 27	28	29	30
°	h m	h m	h m	h m	h m	h m	h m
N 72	07 43	09 37	■■	00 39	02 23	04 13	06 12
N 70	07 28	09 01	■■	00 40	02 17	03 59	05 48
68	07 15	08 36	10 20	00 41	02 13	03 49	05 30
66	07 05	08 16	09 37	00 42	02 09	03 40	05 15
64	06 56	08 00	09 08	00 42	02 06	03 33	05 03
62	06 48	07 47	08 46	00 43	02 03	03 27	04 53
60	06 41	07 36	08 29	00 43	02 01	03 21	04 45
N 58	06 35	07 26	08 14	00 44	01 59	03 17	04 37
56	06 29	07 17	08 02	00 44	01 57	03 12	04 31
54	06 24	07 09	07 51	00 44	01 55	03 09	04 25
52	06 20	07 02	07 41	00 45	01 54	03 05	04 19
50	06 15	06 56	07 33	00 45	01 52	03 02	04 15
45	06 05	06 42	07 14	00 45	01 49	02 56	04 04
N 40	05 56	06 30	07 00	00 46	01 47	02 50	03 56
35	05 48	06 19	06 47	00 46	01 45	02 45	03 49
30	05 41	06 10	06 36	00 47	01 43	02 41	03 42
20	05 26	05 53	06 17	00 47	01 40	02 34	03 31
N 10	05 12	05 38	06 00	00 48	01 37	02 28	03 22
0	04 56	05 22	05 44	00 49	01 34	02 22	03 13
S 10	04 39	05 06	05 28	00 49	01 32	02 16	03 04
20	04 19	04 47	05 11	00 50	01 29	02 10	02 54
30	03 52	04 25	04 52	00 51	01 26	02 03	02 44
35	03 36	04 11	04 40	00 51	01 24	01 59	02 38
40	03 15	03 55	04 26	00 52	01 22	01 55	02 31
45	02 48	03 35	04 10	00 52	01 20	01 50	02 23
S 50	02 11	03 09	03 51	00 53	01 17	01 43	02 13
52	01 50	02 56	03 41	00 53	01 16	01 41	02 09
54	01 22	02 41	03 31	00 54	01 15	01 37	02 04
56	00 37	02 23	03 19	00 54	01 13	01 34	01 58
58	////	02 01	03 05	00 54	01 11	01 30	01 53
S 60	////	01 31	02 48	00 55	01 10	01 26	01 46

Sunset, Twilight and Moonset

Lat.	Sunset	Civil	Naut.	Moonset 27	28	29	30
°	h m	h m	h m	h m	h m	h m	h m
N 72	■■	13 59	15 52	12 53	12 44	12 34	12 21
N 70	■■	14 34	16 08	12 54	12 52	12 49	12 46
68	13 16	15 00	16 20	12 56	12 58	13 01	13 06
66	13 59	15 19	16 31	12 57	13 03	13 11	13 22
64	14 27	15 35	16 40	12 58	13 08	13 19	13 34
62	14 49	15 49	16 47	12 59	13 12	13 27	13 45
60	15 07	16 00	16 54	13 00	13 16	13 33	13 55
N 58	15 21	16 10	17 00	13 01	13 19	13 39	14 03
56	15 34	16 19	17 06	13 02	13 21	13 44	14 10
54	15 45	16 26	17 11	13 02	13 24	13 48	14 17
52	15 54	16 34	17 16	13 03	13 26	13 52	14 23
50	16 03	16 40	17 21	13 03	13 28	13 56	14 28
45	16 21	16 54	17 31	13 05	13 33	14 04	14 39
N 40	16 36	17 06	17 39	13 05	13 37	14 11	14 49
35	16 49	17 16	17 48	13 06	13 40	14 16	14 57
30	17 00	17 26	17 55	13 07	13 43	14 22	15 04
20	17 19	17 43	18 10	13 08	13 48	14 31	15 17
N 10	17 36	17 58	18 24	13 09	13 52	14 38	15 28
0	17 52	18 14	18 40	13 10	13 57	14 46	15 38
S 10	18 08	18 30	18 57	13 11	14 01	14 53	15 48
20	18 25	18 49	19 18	13 12	14 05	15 01	16 00
30	18 45	19 12	19 44	13 13	14 10	15 10	16 12
35	18 56	19 25	20 01	13 14	14 13	15 15	16 20
40	19 10	19 42	20 22	13 15	14 17	15 21	16 28
45	19 26	20 02	20 49	13 16	14 21	15 28	16 38
S 50	19 46	20 28	21 27	13 17	14 25	15 36	16 49
52	19 56	20 41	21 48	13 17	14 27	15 40	16 55
54	20 06	20 56	22 16	13 18	14 30	15 44	17 01
56	20 18	21 14	23 05	13 18	14 32	15 49	17 08
58	20 33	21 37	////	13 19	14 35	15 54	17 16
S 60	20 50	22 07	////	13 20	14 38	16 00	17 24

SUN and MOON

Day	Eqn. of Time 00h	12h	Mer. Pass.	Mer. Pass. Upper	Lower	Age	Phase
d	m s	m s	h m	h m	h m	d	%
27	12 30	12 20	11 48	06 59	19 22	24	34
28	12 10	12 00	11 48	07 45	20 09	25	24
29	11 49	11 39	11 48	08 34	20 59	26	16

UT	ARIES GHA	VENUS −4.9 GHA	Dec	MARS +1.2 GHA	Dec	JUPITER −2.6 GHA	Dec	SATURN +0.6 GHA	Dec	STARS Name	SHA	Dec
30 00	69 01.8	136 03.1	S24 49.8	252 04.8	N 3 19.2	317 45.1	N22 02.5	203 51.3	S14 52.8	Acamar	315 17.7	S40 15.1
01	84 04.3	151 03.8	49.3	267 06.1	18.7	332 47.7	02.5	218 53.4	52.9	Achernar	335 26.2	S57 10.2
02	99 06.7	166 04.5	48.9	282 07.3	18.2	347 50.4	02.6	233 55.6	52.9	Acrux	173 09.1	S63 10.3
03	114 09.2	181 05.2	.. 48.4	297 08.5	.. 17.7	2 53.1	.. 02.6	248 57.8	.. 53.0	Adhara	255 12.0	S28 59.5
04	129 11.7	196 05.9	48.0	312 09.7	17.2	17 55.7	02.6	264 00.0	53.1	Aldebaran	290 48.7	N16 32.1
05	144 14.1	211 06.6	47.5	327 11.0	16.7	32 58.4	02.7	279 02.2	53.2			
06	159 16.6	226 07.3	S24 47.0	342 12.2	N 3 16.1	48 01.0	N22 02.7	294 04.3	S14 53.3	Alioth	166 20.8	N55 52.8
07	174 19.0	241 08.0	46.6	357 13.4	15.6	63 03.7	02.7	309 06.5	53.3	Alkaid	152 59.1	N49 14.5
S 08	189 21.5	256 08.7	46.1	12 14.7	15.1	78 06.4	02.8	324 08.7	53.4	Al Na'ir	27 43.5	S46 53.7
A 09	204 24.0	271 09.4	.. 45.7	27 15.9	.. 14.6	93 09.0	.. 02.8	339 10.9	.. 53.5	Alnilam	275 45.7	S 1 11.7
T 10	219 26.4	286 10.1	45.2	42 17.1	14.1	108 11.7	02.8	354 13.1	53.6	Alphard	217 55.7	S 8 43.2
U 11	234 28.9	301 10.8	44.8	57 18.4	13.6	123 14.4	02.9	9 15.2	53.6			
R 12	249 31.4	316 11.6	S24 44.3	72 19.6	N 3 13.1	138 17.0	N22 02.9	24 17.4	S14 53.7	Alphecca	126 11.1	N26 40.2
D 13	264 33.8	331 12.3	43.8	87 20.9	12.6	153 19.7	02.9	39 19.6	53.8	Alpheratz	357 43.0	N29 10.3
A 14	279 36.3	346 13.0	43.4	102 22.1	12.1	168 22.4	03.0	54 21.8	53.9	Altair	62 08.2	N 8 54.6
Y 15	294 38.8	1 13.7	.. 42.9	117 23.3	.. 11.6	183 25.0	.. 03.0	69 24.0	.. 54.0	Ankaa	353 15.2	S42 14.0
16	309 41.2	16 14.5	42.5	132 24.6	11.1	198 27.7	03.0	84 26.1	54.0	Antares	112 26.2	S26 27.6
17	324 43.7	31 15.2	42.0	147 25.8	10.6	213 30.3	03.1	99 28.3	54.1			
18	339 46.2	46 15.9	S24 41.5	162 27.0	N 3 10.1	228 33.0	N22 03.1	114 30.5	S14 54.2	Arcturus	145 55.8	N19 06.6
19	354 48.6	61 16.7	41.1	177 28.3	09.6	243 35.7	03.1	129 32.7	54.3	Atria	107 28.3	S69 03.0
20	9 51.1	76 17.4	40.6	192 29.5	09.1	258 38.3	03.2	144 34.8	54.3	Avior	234 17.4	S59 33.2
21	24 53.5	91 18.1	.. 40.1	207 30.7	.. 08.6	273 41.0	.. 03.2	159 37.0	.. 54.4	Bellatrix	278 31.3	N 6 21.6
22	39 56.0	106 18.9	39.7	222 32.0	08.1	288 43.7	03.2	174 39.2	54.5	Betelgeuse	271 00.6	N 7 24.4
23	54 58.5	121 19.6	39.2	237 33.2	07.6	303 46.3	03.3	189 41.4	54.6			
1 00	70 00.9	136 20.4	S24 38.7	252 34.4	N 3 07.1	318 49.0	N22 03.3	204 43.6	S14 54.7	Canopus	263 55.5	S52 42.2
01	85 03.4	151 21.1	38.3	267 35.7	06.6	333 51.7	03.3	219 45.7	54.7	Capella	280 33.5	N46 00.5
02	100 05.9	166 21.9	37.8	282 36.9	06.1	348 54.4	03.4	234 47.9	54.8	Deneb	49 31.5	N45 20.2
03	115 08.3	181 22.6	.. 37.3	297 38.2	.. 05.6	3 57.0	.. 03.4	249 50.1	.. 54.9	Denebola	182 33.5	N14 29.6
04	130 10.8	196 23.4	36.9	312 39.4	05.1	18 59.7	03.4	264 52.3	55.0	Diphda	348 55.4	S17 54.6
05	145 13.3	211 24.2	36.4	327 40.6	04.6	34 02.4	03.5	279 54.5	55.1			
06	160 15.7	226 24.9	S24 36.0	342 41.9	N 3 04.0	49 05.0	N22 03.5	294 56.6	S14 55.1	Dubhe	193 51.5	N61 40.2
07	175 18.2	241 25.7	35.5	357 43.1	03.5	64 07.7	03.5	309 58.8	55.2	Elnath	278 11.8	N28 37.0
S 08	190 20.7	256 26.5	35.0	12 44.3	03.0	79 10.4	03.6	325 01.0	55.3	Eltanin	90 46.5	N51 29.5
U 09	205 23.1	271 27.2	.. 34.5	27 45.6	.. 02.5	94 13.0	.. 03.6	340 03.2	.. 55.4	Enif	33 46.9	N 9 56.6
N 10	220 25.6	286 28.0	34.1	42 46.8	02.0	109 15.7	03.6	355 05.4	55.4	Fomalhaut	15 23.7	S29 32.9
N 11	235 28.0	301 28.8	33.6	57 48.1	01.5	124 18.4	03.7	10 07.5	55.5			
D 12	250 30.5	316 29.6	S24 33.1	72 49.3	N 3 01.0	139 21.1	N22 03.7	25 09.7	S14 55.6	Gacrux	172 00.7	S57 11.2
A 13	265 33.0	331 30.3	32.6	87 50.5	00.5	154 23.7	03.7	40 11.9	55.7	Gienah	175 52.1	S17 37.1
Y 14	280 35.4	346 31.1	32.2	102 51.8	3 00.0	169 26.4	03.8	55 14.1	55.8	Hadar	148 47.9	S60 26.1
15	295 37.9	1 31.9	.. 31.7	117 53.0	2 59.5	184 29.1	.. 03.8	70 16.3	.. 55.8	Hamal	328 00.1	N23 31.8
16	310 40.4	16 32.7	31.2	132 54.3	59.0	199 31.7	03.8	85 18.4	55.9	Kaus Aust.	83 43.8	S34 22.5
17	325 42.8	31 33.5	30.8	147 55.5	58.5	214 34.4	03.9	100 20.6	56.0			
18	340 45.3	46 34.3	S24 30.3	162 56.7	N 2 58.0	229 37.1	N22 03.9	115 22.8	S14 56.1	Kochab	137 21.3	N74 05.8
19	355 47.8	61 35.1	29.8	177 58.0	57.5	244 39.8	03.9	130 25.0	56.1	Markab	13 38.0	N15 17.0
20	10 50.2	76 35.9	29.3	192 59.2	57.0	259 42.4	04.0	145 27.2	56.2	Menkar	314 14.4	N 4 08.6
21	25 52.7	91 36.7	.. 28.9	208 00.5	.. 56.5	274 45.1	.. 04.0	160 29.3	.. 56.3	Menkent	148 07.5	S36 26.1
22	40 55.2	106 37.5	28.4	223 01.7	56.0	289 47.8	04.0	175 31.5	56.4	Miaplacidus	221 39.1	S69 46.3
23	55 57.6	121 38.3	27.9	238 02.9	55.5	304 50.5	04.1	190 33.7	56.5			
2 00	71 00.1	136 39.1	S24 27.4	253 04.2	N 2 55.0	319 53.1	N22 04.1	205 35.9	S14 56.5	Mirfak	308 39.4	N49 54.6
01	86 02.5	151 39.9	27.0	268 05.4	54.5	334 55.8	04.1	220 38.1	56.6	Nunki	75 58.3	S26 16.6
02	101 05.0	166 40.8	26.5	283 06.7	54.0	349 58.5	04.2	235 40.3	56.7	Peacock	53 19.2	S56 41.4
03	116 07.5	181 41.6	.. 26.0	298 07.9	.. 53.5	5 01.2	.. 04.2	250 42.4	.. 56.8	Pollux	243 27.1	N27 59.3
04	131 09.9	196 42.4	25.5	313 09.2	53.0	20 03.8	04.2	265 44.6	56.8	Procyon	244 59.2	N 5 11.2
05	146 12.4	211 43.2	25.0	328 10.4	52.5	35 06.5	04.3	280 46.8	56.9			
06	161 14.9	226 44.1	S24 24.6	343 11.6	N 2 52.0	50 09.2	N22 04.3	295 49.0	S14 57.0	Rasalhague	96 06.5	N12 33.2
07	176 17.3	241 44.9	24.1	358 12.9	51.5	65 11.9	04.3	310 51.2	57.1	Regulus	207 43.1	N11 53.8
08	191 19.8	256 45.7	23.6	13 14.1	51.0	80 14.6	04.4	325 53.3	57.1	Rigel	281 11.4	S 8 11.3
M 09	206 22.3	271 46.6	.. 23.1	28 15.4	.. 50.5	95 17.2	.. 04.4	340 55.5	.. 57.2	Rigil Kent.	139 51.8	S60 53.3
O 10	221 24.7	286 47.4	22.6	43 16.6	50.0	110 19.9	04.5	355 57.7	57.3	Sabik	102 12.5	S15 44.3
N 11	236 27.2	301 48.2	22.2	58 17.9	49.5	125 22.6	04.5	10 59.9	57.4			
D 12	251 29.6	316 49.1	S24 21.7	73 19.1	N 2 49.0	140 25.3	N22 04.5	26 02.1	S14 57.5	Schedar	349 39.8	N56 37.1
A 13	266 32.1	331 49.9	21.2	88 20.4	48.5	155 27.9	04.6	41 04.2	57.5	Shaula	96 21.9	S37 06.6
Y 14	281 34.6	346 50.8	20.7	103 21.6	48.0	170 30.6	04.6	56 06.4	57.6	Sirius	258 33.1	S16 44.2
15	296 37.0	1 51.6	.. 20.2	118 22.8	.. 47.5	185 33.3	.. 04.6	71 08.6	.. 57.7	Spica	158 31.1	S11 13.9
16	311 39.5	16 52.5	19.7	133 24.1	47.0	200 36.0	04.7	86 10.8	57.8	Suhail	222 52.0	S43 29.2
17	326 42.0	31 53.3	19.3	148 25.3	46.5	215 38.7	04.7	101 13.0	57.8			
18	341 44.4	46 54.2	S24 18.8	163 26.6	N 2 46.0	230 41.4	N22 04.7	116 15.1	S14 57.9	Vega	80 39.1	N38 48.1
19	356 46.9	61 55.1	18.3	178 27.8	45.5	245 44.0	04.8	131 17.3	58.0	Zuben'ubi	137 05.4	S16 05.8
20	11 49.4	76 55.9	17.8	193 29.1	45.0	260 46.7	04.8	146 19.5	58.1		SHA	Mer.Pass.
21	26 51.8	91 56.8	.. 17.3	208 30.3	.. 44.5	275 49.4	.. 04.8	161 21.7	.. 58.1		° ′	h m
22	41 54.3	106 57.7	16.8	223 31.6	44.0	290 52.1	04.9	176 23.9	58.2	Venus	66 19.4	14 54
23	56 56.8	121 58.5	16.3	238 32.8	43.5	305 54.8	04.9	191 26.1	58.3	Mars	182 33.5	7 09
										Jupiter	248 48.1	2 44
Mer. Pass.	19 16.8	v 0.8	d 0.5	v 1.2	d 0.5	v 2.7	d 0.0	v 2.2	d 0.1	Saturn	134 42.6	10 20

UT	SUN GHA	SUN Dec	MOON GHA	v	MOON Dec	d	HP
d h	° ′	° ′	° ′	′	° ′	′	′
30 00	182 51.9	S21 37.7	223 39.5	9.6	S11 28.8	9.4	58.4
01	197 51.7	38.1	238 08.1	9.5	11 38.2	9.4	58.5
02	212 51.4	38.5	252 36.6	9.4	11 47.6	9.3	58.5
03	227 51.2 ..	38.9	267 05.0	9.4	11 56.9	9.3	58.5
04	242 51.0	39.3	281 33.4	9.2	12 06.2	9.2	58.6
05	257 50.8	39.7	296 01.6	9.1	12 15.4	9.2	58.6
06	272 50.5	S21 40.1	310 29.7	9.1	S12 24.6	9.1	58.6
S 07	287 50.3	40.5	324 57.8	9.0	12 33.7	9.0	58.7
A 08	302 50.1	40.9	339 25.8	8.9	12 42.7	9.0	58.7
T 09	317 49.8 ..	41.3	353 53.7	8.8	12 51.7	8.9	58.8
U 10	332 49.6	41.7	8 21.5	8.7	13 00.6	8.8	58.8
R 11	347 49.4	42.1	22 49.2	8.6	13 09.4	8.8	58.8
D 12	2 49.2	S21 42.5	37 16.8	8.5	S13 18.2	8.7	58.9
A 13	17 48.9	42.9	51 44.3	8.5	13 26.9	8.7	58.9
Y 14	32 48.7	43.3	66 11.8	8.3	13 35.6	8.5	58.9
15	47 48.5 ..	43.7	80 39.1	8.3	13 44.1	8.5	59.0
16	62 48.2	44.1	95 06.4	8.2	13 52.6	8.5	59.0
17	77 48.0	44.5	109 33.6	8.1	14 01.1	8.3	59.1
18	92 47.8	S21 44.9	124 00.7	8.0	S14 09.4	8.3	59.1
19	107 47.5	45.3	138 27.7	7.9	14 17.7	8.2	59.1
20	122 47.3	45.7	152 54.6	7.8	14 25.9	8.1	59.2
21	137 47.1 ..	46.1	167 21.4	7.7	14 34.0	8.1	59.2
22	152 46.8	46.5	181 48.1	7.7	14 42.1	7.9	59.2
23	167 46.6	46.9	196 14.8	7.6	14 50.0	7.9	59.3
1 00	182 46.4	S21 47.3	210 41.4	7.4	S14 57.9	7.8	59.3
01	197 46.1	47.6	225 07.8	7.4	15 05.7	7.7	59.3
02	212 45.9	48.0	239 34.2	7.3	15 13.4	7.6	59.4
03	227 45.7 ..	48.4	254 00.5	7.2	15 21.0	7.6	59.4
04	242 45.4	48.8	268 26.7	7.1	15 28.6	7.4	59.4
05	257 45.2	49.2	282 52.8	7.1	15 36.0	7.4	59.5
06	272 45.0	S21 49.6	297 18.9	6.9	S15 43.4	7.2	59.5
S 07	287 44.7	50.0	311 44.8	6.9	15 50.6	7.2	59.5
U 08	302 44.5	50.4	326 10.7	6.7	15 57.8	7.1	59.6
N 09	317 44.3 ..	50.7	340 36.4	6.7	16 04.9	7.0	59.6
10	332 44.0	51.1	355 02.1	6.6	16 11.9	6.8	59.6
N 11	347 43.8	51.5	9 27.7	6.6	16 18.7	6.8	59.7
D 12	2 43.6	S21 51.9	23 53.3	6.4	S16 25.5	6.7	59.7
A 13	17 43.3	52.3	38 18.7	6.3	16 32.2	6.6	59.7
Y 14	32 43.1	52.6	52 44.0	6.3	16 38.8	6.5	59.8
15	47 42.9 ..	53.0	67 09.3	6.2	16 45.3	6.4	59.8
16	62 42.6	53.4	81 34.5	6.1	16 51.7	6.2	59.8
17	77 42.4	53.8	95 59.6	6.0	16 57.9	6.2	59.9
18	92 42.1	S21 54.2	110 24.6	6.0	S17 04.1	6.0	59.9
19	107 41.9	54.5	124 49.6	5.9	17 10.1	6.0	59.9
20	122 41.7	54.9	139 14.5	5.7	17 16.1	5.8	59.9
21	137 41.4 ..	55.3	153 39.2	5.8	17 21.9	5.7	60.0
22	152 41.2	55.7	168 04.0	5.6	17 27.6	5.7	60.0
23	167 40.9	56.0	182 28.6	5.6	17 33.3	5.4	60.0
2 00	182 40.7	S21 56.4	196 53.2	5.4	S17 38.7	5.4	60.1
01	197 40.5	56.8	211 17.6	5.5	17 44.1	5.3	60.1
02	212 40.2	57.1	225 42.1	5.3	17 49.4	5.1	60.1
03	227 40.0 ..	57.5	240 06.4	5.3	17 54.5	5.1	60.1
04	242 39.7	57.9	254 30.7	5.2	17 59.6	4.9	60.2
05	257 39.5	58.3	268 54.9	5.1	18 04.5	4.8	60.2
06	272 39.3	S21 58.6	283 19.0	5.1	S18 09.3	4.6	60.2
07	287 39.0	59.0	297 43.1	5.0	18 13.9	4.6	60.2
08	302 38.8	59.4	312 07.1	4.9	18 18.5	4.4	60.3
M 09	317 38.5	21 59.7	326 31.0	4.9	18 22.9	4.3	60.3
O 10	332 38.3	22 00.1	340 54.9	4.8	18 27.2	4.1	60.3
N 11	347 38.0	00.5	355 18.7	4.7	18 31.3	4.1	60.3
D 12	2 37.8	S22 00.8	9 42.4	4.7	S18 35.4	3.9	60.4
A 13	17 37.6	01.2	24 06.1	4.6	18 39.3	3.7	60.4
Y 14	32 37.3	01.5	38 29.7	4.6	18 43.0	3.7	60.4
15	47 37.1 ..	01.9	52 53.3	4.5	18 46.7	3.5	60.4
16	62 36.8	02.3	67 16.8	4.5	18 50.2	3.4	60.4
17	77 36.6	02.6	81 40.3	4.4	18 53.6	3.2	60.5
18	92 36.3	S22 03.0	96 03.7	4.3	S18 56.8	3.1	60.5
19	107 36.1	03.3	110 27.0	4.4	18 59.9	3.0	60.5
20	122 35.9	03.7	124 50.4	4.2	19 02.9	2.9	60.5
21	137 35.6 ..	04.1	139 13.6	4.2	19 05.8	2.7	60.5
22	152 35.4	04.4	153 36.8	4.2	19 08.5	2.5	60.6
23	167 35.1	04.8	168 00.0	4.1	S19 11.0	2.5	60.6
	SD 16.2	d 0.4	SD 16.0		16.3		16.4

Twilight / Sunrise / Moonrise

Lat.	Naut.	Civil	Sunrise	Moonrise 30	1	2	3
°	h m	h m	h m	h m	h m	h m	h m
N 72	07 51	09 51	■	06 12	08 29	■	■
N 70	07 35	09 11	■	05 48	07 44	09 46	11 37
68	07 22	08 44	10 37	05 30	07 15	08 58	10 25
66	07 11	08 23	09 47	05 15	06 53	08 28	09 48
64	07 01	08 07	09 16	05 03	06 36	08 05	09 22
62	06 53	07 53	08 53	04 53	06 21	07 47	09 02
60	06 46	07 41	08 35	04 45	06 10	07 32	08 45
N 58	06 39	07 31	08 20	04 37	05 59	07 19	08 31
56	06 34	07 21	08 07	04 31	05 50	07 08	08 19
54	06 29	07 13	07 56	04 25	05 42	06 58	08 08
52	06 23	07 06	07 46	04 19	05 35	06 50	07 59
50	06 19	06 59	07 37	04 15	05 29	06 42	07 51
45	06 08	06 45	07 18	04 04	05 15	06 26	07 33
N 40	05 59	06 33	07 03	03 56	05 04	06 12	07 18
35	05 51	06 22	06 50	03 49	04 54	06 01	07 06
30	05 43	06 12	06 38	03 42	04 46	05 51	06 55
20	05 28	05 55	06 19	03 31	04 31	05 34	06 37
N 10	05 13	05 39	06 02	03 22	04 19	05 19	06 21
0	04 57	05 23	05 45	03 13	04 07	05 05	06 06
S 10	04 40	05 06	05 29	03 04	03 56	04 52	05 51
20	04 19	04 47	05 12	02 54	03 43	04 37	05 36
30	03 52	04 24	04 51	02 44	03 29	04 20	05 17
35	03 34	04 10	04 39	02 38	03 21	04 11	05 07
40	03 13	03 53	04 25	02 31	03 12	04 00	04 55
45	02 46	03 33	04 09	02 23	03 01	03 47	04 41
S 50	02 07	03 06	03 49	02 13	02 48	03 31	04 23
52	01 44	02 53	03 39	02 09	02 42	03 24	04 15
54	01 14	02 37	03 28	02 04	02 36	03 16	04 06
56	00 16	02 19	03 15	01 58	02 28	03 07	03 56
58	////	01 55	03 01	01 53	02 20	02 56	03 44
S 60	////	01 22	02 43	01 46	02 11	02 45	03 31

Sunset / Twilight / Moonset

Lat.	Sunset	Civil	Naut.	Moonset 30	1	2	3
°	h m	h m	h m	h m	h m	h m	h m
N 72	■	13 47	15 46	12 21	11 59	■	■
N 70	■	14 26	16 02	12 46	12 45	12 46	13 04
68	13 01	14 54	16 16	13 06	13 15	13 34	14 16
66	13 50	15 14	16 27	13 22	13 38	14 05	14 53
64	14 21	15 31	16 36	13 34	13 56	14 29	15 19
62	14 44	15 45	16 44	13 45	14 11	14 47	15 40
60	15 03	15 57	16 52	13 55	14 23	15 02	15 56
N 58	15 18	16 07	16 58	14 03	14 34	15 16	16 10
56	15 31	16 16	17 04	14 10	14 44	15 27	16 22
54	15 42	16 24	17 10	14 17	14 52	15 37	16 33
52	15 52	16 32	17 15	14 23	15 00	15 46	16 42
50	16 01	16 38	17 19	14 28	15 06	15 54	16 51
45	16 20	16 53	17 30	14 39	15 21	16 10	17 09
N 40	16 35	17 05	17 39	14 49	15 33	16 24	17 23
35	16 48	17 16	17 47	14 57	15 43	16 36	17 36
30	17 00	17 26	17 55	15 04	15 52	16 46	17 46
20	17 19	17 43	18 10	15 17	16 08	17 04	18 05
N 10	17 37	17 59	18 25	15 28	16 22	17 20	18 21
0	17 53	18 15	18 41	15 38	16 34	17 34	18 36
S 10	18 09	18 32	18 59	15 48	16 47	17 48	18 51
20	18 27	18 51	19 20	16 00	17 01	18 04	19 07
30	18 47	19 14	19 47	16 12	17 17	18 22	19 25
35	18 59	19 28	20 04	16 20	17 26	18 32	19 36
40	19 13	19 45	20 25	16 28	17 36	18 44	19 48
45	19 30	20 06	20 53	16 38	17 48	18 58	20 02
S 50	19 50	20 33	21 33	16 49	18 03	19 15	20 20
52	20 00	20 46	21 55	16 55	18 10	19 23	20 28
54	20 11	21 02	22 26	17 01	18 18	19 31	20 37
56	20 24	21 21	23 35	17 08	18 27	19 41	20 47
58	20 39	21 45	////	17 16	18 37	19 53	20 59
S 60	20 56	22 19	////	17 24	18 48	20 06	21 13

SUN / MOON

Day	Eqn. of Time 00h	12h	Mer. Pass.	Mer. Pass. Upper	Lower	Age	Phase
d	m s	m s	h m	h m	h m	d	%
30	11 28	11 17	11 49	09 25	21 53	27	9
1	11 06	10 55	11 49	10 21	22 50	28	3
2	10 43	10 32	11 49	11 20	23 50	29	0 ●

UT	ARIES GHA	VENUS −4.9 GHA	Dec	MARS +1.2 GHA	Dec	JUPITER −2.6 GHA	Dec	SATURN +0.6 GHA	Dec	STARS Name	SHA	Dec
3 00	71 59.2	136 59.4	S24 15.9	253 34.1	N 2 43.0	320 57.4	N22 04.9	206 28.2	S14 58.4	Acamar	315 17.7	S40 15.1
01	87 01.7	152 00.3	15.4	268 35.3	42.5	336 00.1	05.0	221 30.4	58.5	Achernar	335 26.2	S57 10.2
02	102 04.1	167 01.2	14.9	283 36.6	42.0	351 02.8	05.0	236 32.6	58.5	Acrux	173 09.1	S63 10.3
03	117 06.6	182 02.1 ..	14.4	298 37.8 ..	41.5	6 05.5 ..	05.0	251 34.8 ..	58.6	Adhara	255 11.9	S28 59.5
04	132 09.1	197 03.0	13.9	313 39.0	41.0	21 08.2	05.1	266 37.0	58.7	Aldebaran	290 48.6	N16 32.1
05	147 11.5	212 03.9	13.4	328 40.3	40.5	36 10.9	05.1	281 39.1	58.8			
06	162 14.0	227 04.7	S24 12.9	343 41.5	N 2 40.0	51 13.6	N22 05.2	296 41.3	S14 58.8	Alioth	166 20.8	N55 52.8
07	177 16.5	242 05.6	12.4	358 42.8	39.5	66 16.2	05.2	311 43.5	58.9	Alkaid	152 59.1	N49 14.5
08	192 18.9	257 06.5	11.9	13 44.0	39.0	81 18.9	05.2	326 45.7	59.0	Al Na'ir	27 43.5	S46 53.7
T 09	207 21.4	272 07.4 ..	11.4	28 45.3 ..	38.5	96 21.6 ..	05.3	341 47.9 ..	59.1	Alnilam	275 45.7	S 1 11.7
U 10	222 23.9	287 08.3	11.0	43 46.5	38.0	111 24.3	05.3	356 50.1	59.1	Alphard	217 55.6	S 8 43.2
E 11	237 26.3	302 09.3	10.5	58 47.8	37.5	126 27.0	05.3	11 52.2	59.2			
S 12	252 28.8	317 10.2	S24 10.0	73 49.0	N 2 37.0	141 29.7	N22 05.4	26 54.4	S14 59.3	Alphecca	126 11.1	N26 40.2
D 13	267 31.3	332 11.1	09.5	88 50.3	36.5	156 32.4	05.4	41 56.6	59.4	Alpheratz	357 43.0	N29 10.3
A 14	282 33.7	347 12.0	09.0	103 51.5	36.0	171 35.0	05.4	56 58.8	59.5	Altair	62 08.2	N 8 54.6
Y 15	297 36.2	2 12.9 ..	08.5	118 52.8 ..	35.5	186 37.7 ..	05.5	72 01.0 ..	59.5	Ankaa	353 15.3	S42 14.0
16	312 38.6	17 13.8	08.0	133 54.0	35.0	201 40.4	05.5	87 03.2	59.6	Antares	112 26.2	S26 27.6
17	327 41.1	32 14.8	07.5	148 55.3	34.5	216 43.1	05.5	102 05.3	59.7			
18	342 43.6	47 15.7	S24 07.0	163 56.5	N 2 34.0	231 45.8	N22 05.6	117 07.5	S14 59.8	Arcturus	145 55.7	N19 06.6
19	357 46.0	62 16.6	06.5	178 57.8	33.5	246 48.5	05.6	132 09.7	59.8	Atria	107 28.3	S69 02.9
20	12 48.5	77 17.6	06.0	193 59.0	33.0	261 51.2	05.7	147 11.9	14 59.9	Avior	234 17.4	S59 33.2
21	27 51.0	92 18.5 ..	05.5	209 00.3 ..	32.5	276 53.9 ..	05.7	162 14.1	15 00.0	Bellatrix	278 31.3	N 6 21.6
22	42 53.4	107 19.4	05.0	224 01.5	32.0	291 56.6	05.7	177 16.2	00.1	Betelgeuse	271 00.6	N 7 24.4
23	57 55.9	122 20.4	04.5	239 02.8	31.5	306 59.2	05.8	192 18.4	00.1			
4 00	72 58.4	137 21.3	S24 04.0	254 04.0	N 2 31.0	322 01.9	N22 05.8	207 20.6	S15 00.2	Canopus	263 55.5	S52 42.2
01	88 00.8	152 22.3	03.5	269 05.3	30.5	337 04.6	05.8	222 22.8	00.3	Capella	280 33.5	N46 00.5
02	103 03.3	167 23.2	03.0	284 06.6	30.0	352 07.3	05.9	237 25.0	00.4	Deneb	49 31.5	N45 20.2
03	118 05.8	182 24.2 ..	02.5	299 07.8 ..	29.5	7 10.0 ..	05.9	252 27.2 ..	00.4	Denebola	182 33.4	N14 29.5
04	133 08.2	197 25.1	02.0	314 09.1	29.0	22 12.7	05.9	267 29.3	00.5	Diphda	348 55.4	S17 54.6
05	148 10.7	212 26.1	01.5	329 10.3	28.5	37 15.4	06.0	282 31.5	00.6			
06	163 13.1	227 27.0	S24 01.0	344 11.6	N 2 28.0	52 18.1	N22 06.0	297 33.7	S15 00.7	Dubhe	193 51.5	N61 40.2
W 07	178 15.6	242 28.0	00.5	359 12.8	27.5	67 20.8	06.1	312 35.9	00.7	Elnath	278 11.8	N28 37.0
E 08	193 18.1	257 29.0	24 00.0	14 14.1	27.1	82 23.5	06.1	327 38.1	00.8	Eltanin	90 46.5	N51 29.5
D 09	208 20.5	272 30.0	23 59.5	29 15.3 ..	26.6	97 26.2 ..	06.1	342 40.3 ..	00.9	Enif	33 46.9	N 9 56.6
N 10	223 23.0	287 30.9	59.0	44 16.6	26.1	112 28.9	06.2	357 42.4	01.0	Fomalhaut	15 23.7	S29 32.9
E 11	238 25.5	302 31.9	58.5	59 17.8	25.6	127 31.6	06.2	12 44.6	01.1			
S 12	253 27.9	317 32.9	S23 58.0	74 19.1	N 2 25.1	142 34.2	N22 06.2	27 46.8	S15 01.1	Gacrux	172 00.7	S57 11.2
D 13	268 30.4	332 33.9	57.5	89 20.3	24.6	157 36.9	06.3	42 49.0	01.2	Gienah	175 52.1	S17 37.1
A 14	283 32.9	347 34.8	57.0	104 21.6	24.1	172 39.6	06.3	57 51.2	01.3	Hadar	148 47.8	S60 26.1
Y 15	298 35.3	2 35.8 ..	56.5	119 22.9 ..	23.6	187 42.3 ..	06.3	72 53.4 ..	01.4	Hamal	328 00.1	N23 31.8
16	313 37.8	17 36.8	56.0	134 24.1	23.1	202 45.0	06.4	87 55.5	01.4	Kaus Aust.	83 43.8	S34 22.5
17	328 40.3	32 37.8	55.5	149 25.4	22.6	217 47.7	06.4	102 57.7	01.5			
18	343 42.7	47 38.8	S23 55.0	164 26.6	N 2 22.1	232 50.4	N22 06.5	117 59.9	S15 01.6	Kochab	137 21.2	N74 05.8
19	358 45.2	62 39.8	54.5	179 27.9	21.6	247 53.1	06.5	133 02.1	01.7	Markab	13 38.0	N15 17.0
20	13 47.6	77 40.8	54.0	194 29.1	21.1	262 55.8	06.6	148 04.3	01.7	Menkar	314 14.4	N 4 08.6
21	28 50.1	92 41.8 ..	53.5	209 30.4 ..	20.6	277 58.5 ..	06.6	163 06.5 ..	01.8	Menkent	148 07.5	S36 26.1
22	43 52.6	107 42.8	53.0	224 31.7	20.1	293 01.2	06.6	178 08.6	01.9	Miaplacidus	221 39.0	S69 46.3
23	58 55.0	122 43.8	52.5	239 32.9	19.6	308 03.9	06.6	193 10.8	02.0			
5 00	73 57.5	137 44.9	S23 52.0	254 34.2	N 2 19.1	323 06.6	N22 06.7	208 13.0	S15 02.0	Mirfak	308 39.3	N49 54.6
01	89 00.0	152 45.9	51.5	269 35.4	18.6	338 09.3	06.7	223 15.2	02.1	Nunki	75 58.3	S26 16.6
02	104 02.4	167 46.9	51.0	284 36.7	18.1	353 12.0	06.8	238 17.4	02.2	Peacock	53 19.2	S56 41.4
03	119 04.9	182 47.9 ..	50.5	299 37.9 ..	17.6	8 14.7 ..	06.8	253 19.6 ..	02.3	Pollux	243 27.1	N27 59.3
04	134 07.4	197 49.0	50.0	314 39.2	17.1	23 17.4	06.8	268 21.8	02.3	Procyon	244 59.1	N 5 11.2
05	149 09.8	212 50.0	49.5	329 40.5	16.6	38 20.1	06.9	283 23.9	02.4			
06	164 12.3	227 51.0	S23 48.9	344 41.7	N 2 16.1	53 22.8	N22 06.9	298 26.1	S15 02.5	Rasalhague	96 06.5	N12 33.2
07	179 14.8	242 52.1	48.4	359 43.0	15.7	68 25.5	06.9	313 28.3	02.6	Regulus	207 43.1	N11 53.8
T 08	194 17.2	257 53.1	47.9	14 44.2	15.2	83 28.2	07.0	328 30.5	02.6	Rigel	281 11.4	S 8 11.3
H 09	209 19.7	272 54.1 ..	47.4	29 45.5 ..	14.7	98 30.9 ..	07.0	343 32.7 ..	02.7	Rigil Kent.	139 51.8	S60 53.3
U 10	224 22.1	287 55.2	46.9	44 46.8	14.2	113 33.6	07.1	358 34.9	02.8	Sabik	102 12.5	S15 44.3
R 11	239 24.6	302 56.2	46.4	59 48.0	13.7	128 36.3	07.1	13 37.0	02.9			
S 12	254 27.1	317 57.3	S23 45.9	74 49.3	N 2 13.2	143 39.0	N22 07.1	28 39.2	S15 02.9	Schedar	349 39.8	N56 37.1
D 13	269 29.5	332 58.3	45.4	89 50.5	12.7	158 41.7	07.2	43 41.4	03.0	Shaula	96 21.9	S37 06.6
A 14	284 32.0	347 59.4	44.9	104 51.8	12.2	173 44.4	07.2	58 43.6	03.1	Sirius	258 33.1	S16 44.2
Y 15	299 34.5	3 00.5 ..	44.4	119 53.1 ..	11.7	188 47.1 ..	07.2	73 45.8 ..	03.2	Spica	158 31.1	S11 13.9
16	314 36.9	18 01.5	43.8	134 54.3	11.2	203 49.8	07.3	88 48.0	03.2	Suhail	222 52.0	S43 29.3
17	329 39.4	33 02.6	43.3	149 55.6	10.7	218 52.5	07.3	103 50.2	03.3			
18	344 41.9	48 03.6	S23 42.8	164 56.8	N 2 10.2	233 55.2	N22 07.4	118 52.3	S15 03.4	Vega	80 39.1	N38 48.1
19	359 44.3	63 04.7	42.3	179 58.1	09.7	248 57.9	07.4	133 54.5	03.5	Zuben'ubi	137 05.4	S16 05.8
20	14 46.8	78 05.8	41.8	194 59.4	09.2	264 00.6	07.4	148 56.7	03.5		SHA	Mer. Pass.
21	29 49.3	93 06.9 ..	41.3	210 00.6 ..	08.7	279 03.3 ..	07.5	163 58.9 ..	03.6		° ′	h m
22	44 51.7	108 08.0	40.8	225 01.9	08.2	294 06.0	07.5	179 01.1	03.7	Venus	64 23.0	14 50
23	59 54.2	123 09.0	40.3	240 03.2	07.8	309 08.7	07.5	194 03.3	03.8	Mars	181 05.7	7 03
	h m									Jupiter	249 03.6	2 31
Mer. Pass. 19 05.0	v 1.0 d 0.5			v 1.3 d 0.5		v 2.7 d 0.0		v 2.2 d 0.1		Saturn	134 22.3	10 09

UT	SUN GHA	SUN Dec	MOON GHA	v	MOON Dec	d	HP
d h	o ′	o ′	o ′	′	o ′	′	′
3 00	182 34.9	S22 05.1	182 23.1	4.1	S19 13.5	2.3	60.6
01	197 34.6	05.5	196 46.2	4.0	19 15.8	2.1	60.6
02	212 34.4	05.8	211 09.2	4.1	19 17.9	2.0	60.6
03	227 34.1	.. 06.2	225 32.3	3.9	19 19.9	1.9	60.7
04	242 33.9	06.5	239 55.2	4.0	19 21.8	1.7	60.7
05	257 33.6	06.9	254 18.2	3.9	19 23.5	1.6	60.7
06	272 33.4	S22 07.2	268 41.1	3.8	S19 25.1	1.5	60.7
07	287 33.1	07.6	283 03.9	3.9	19 26.6	1.3	60.7
T 08	302 32.9	07.9	297 26.8	3.8	19 27.9	1.2	60.7
U 09	317 32.6	.. 08.3	311 49.6	3.8	19 29.1	1.0	60.7
E 10	332 32.4	08.6	326 12.4	3.8	19 30.1	0.9	60.7
S 11	347 32.1	09.0	340 35.2	3.7	19 31.0	0.7	60.8
D 12	2 31.9	S22 09.3	354 57.9	3.7	S19 31.7	0.6	60.8
A 13	17 31.6	09.7	9 20.6	3.7	19 32.3	0.4	60.8
Y 14	32 31.4	10.0	23 43.3	3.7	19 32.7	0.3	60.8
15	47 31.1	.. 10.4	38 06.0	3.7	19 33.0	0.2	60.8
16	62 30.9	10.7	52 28.7	3.7	19 33.2	0.0	60.8
17	77 30.6	11.1	66 51.4	3.6	19 33.2	0.1	60.8
18	92 30.4	S22 11.4	81 14.0	3.7	S19 33.1	0.3	60.8
19	107 30.1	11.7	95 36.7	3.6	19 32.8	0.4	60.8
20	122 29.9	12.1	109 59.3	3.7	19 32.4	0.6	60.9
21	137 29.6	.. 12.4	124 22.0	3.6	19 31.8	0.7	60.9
22	152 29.4	12.8	138 44.6	3.7	19 31.1	0.9	60.9
23	167 29.1	13.1	153 07.3	3.6	19 30.2	1.0	60.9
4 00	182 28.9	S22 13.4	167 29.9	3.6	S19 29.2	1.1	60.9
01	197 28.6	13.8	181 52.5	3.7	19 28.1	1.3	60.9
02	212 28.4	14.1	196 15.2	3.6	19 26.8	1.4	60.9
03	227 28.1	.. 14.4	210 37.8	3.7	19 25.4	1.6	60.9
04	242 27.9	14.8	225 00.5	3.7	19 23.8	1.8	60.9
05	257 27.6	15.1	239 23.2	3.7	19 22.0	1.8	60.9
06	272 27.4	S22 15.4	253 45.9	3.7	S19 20.2	2.0	60.9
W 07	287 27.1	15.8	268 08.6	3.7	19 18.2	2.2	60.9
E 08	302 26.9	16.1	282 31.3	3.7	19 16.0	2.3	60.9
D 09	317 26.3	.. 16.4	296 54.0	3.8	19 13.7	2.4	60.9
N 10	332 26.3	16.8	311 16.8	3.8	19 11.3	2.6	60.9
E 11	347 26.1	17.1	325 39.6	3.8	19 08.7	2.7	60.9
S 12	2 25.8	S22 17.4	340 02.4	3.8	S19 06.0	2.9	60.9
D 13	17 25.6	17.7	354 25.2	3.8	19 03.1	3.0	60.9
A 14	32 25.3	18.1	8 48.0	3.9	19 00.1	3.2	60.9
Y 15	47 25.1	.. 18.4	23 10.9	3.9	18 56.9	3.2	60.9
16	62 24.8	18.7	37 33.8	4.0	18 53.7	3.5	60.9
17	77 24.6	19.0	51 56.8	4.0	18 50.2	3.5	60.9
18	92 24.3	S22 19.4	66 19.8	4.0	S18 46.7	3.7	60.9
19	107 24.0	19.7	80 42.8	4.0	18 43.0	3.9	60.9
20	122 23.8	20.0	95 05.8	4.1	18 39.1	3.9	60.9
21	137 23.5	.. 20.3	109 28.9	4.2	18 35.2	4.1	60.9
22	152 23.3	20.7	123 52.1	4.1	18 31.1	4.3	60.9
23	167 23.0	21.0	138 15.2	4.3	18 26.8	4.4	60.9
5 00	182 22.8	S22 21.3	152 38.5	4.2	S18 22.4	4.5	60.9
01	197 22.5	21.6	167 01.7	4.3	18 17.9	4.6	60.8
02	212 22.2	21.9	181 25.0	4.4	18 13.3	4.8	60.8
03	227 22.0	.. 22.3	195 48.4	4.4	18 08.5	4.9	60.8
04	242 21.7	22.6	210 11.8	4.5	18 03.6	5.0	60.8
05	257 21.5	22.9	224 35.3	4.5	17 58.6	5.1	60.8
06	272 21.2	S22 23.2	238 58.8	4.5	S17 53.5	5.3	60.8
T 07	287 20.9	23.5	253 22.3	4.6	17 48.2	5.4	60.8
H 08	302 20.7	23.8	267 45.9	4.7	17 42.8	5.6	60.8
U 09	317 20.4	.. 24.1	282 09.6	4.7	17 37.2	5.6	60.8
R 10	332 20.2	24.5	296 33.3	4.8	17 31.6	5.7	60.8
S 11	347 19.9	24.8	310 57.1	4.9	17 25.8	5.9	60.7
D 12	2 19.6	S22 25.1	325 21.0	4.9	S17 19.9	6.0	60.7
A 13	17 19.4	25.4	339 44.9	4.9	17 13.9	6.1	60.7
Y 14	32 19.1	25.7	354 08.8	5.1	17 07.8	6.3	60.7
15	47 18.9	.. 26.0	8 32.9	5.1	17 01.5	6.4	60.7
16	62 18.6	26.3	22 57.0	5.1	16 55.1	6.5	60.7
17	77 18.3	26.6	37 21.1	5.2	16 48.6	6.6	60.7
18	92 18.1	S22 26.9	51 45.3	5.3	S16 42.0	6.7	60.7
19	107 17.8	27.2	66 09.6	5.4	16 35.3	6.8	60.6
20	122 17.5	27.5	80 34.0	5.4	16 28.5	6.9	60.6
21	137 17.3	.. 27.8	94 58.4	5.5	16 21.6	7.1	60.6
22	152 17.0	28.1	109 22.9	5.6	16 14.5	7.1	60.6
23	167 16.8	28.4	123 47.5	5.6	S16 07.4	7.3	60.6
	SD 16.3	d 0.3	SD 16.6		16.6		16.5

Lat.	Twilight Naut.	Twilight Civil	Sunrise	Moonrise 3	4	5	6
°	h m	h m	h m	h m	h m	h m	h m
N 72	07 59	10 04	■	■	■	13 19	12 47
N 70	07 42	09 21	■	11 37	12 15	12 19	12 18
68	07 28	08 52	10 56	10 25	11 19	11 44	11 56
66	07 16	08 30	09 58	09 48	10 45	11 18	11 38
64	07 07	08 13	09 24	09 22	10 20	10 59	11 24
62	06 58	07 58	09 00	09 02	10 00	10 42	11 12
60	06 50	07 46	08 41	08 45	09 44	10 29	11 01
N 58	06 44	07 35	08 25	08 31	09 31	10 17	10 52
56	06 38	07 26	08 12	08 19	09 19	10 07	10 44
54	06 32	07 17	08 00	08 08	09 09	09 58	10 37
52	06 27	07 10	07 50	07 59	09 00	09 50	10 31
50	06 22	07 03	07 41	07 51	08 52	09 43	10 25
45	06 11	06 48	07 21	07 33	08 34	09 27	10 13
N 40	06 02	06 35	07 06	07 18	08 20	09 15	10 02
35	05 53	06 24	06 52	07 06	08 08	09 04	09 53
30	05 45	06 14	06 41	06 55	07 57	08 54	09 46
20	05 29	05 57	06 21	06 37	07 39	08 38	09 32
N 10	05 14	05 40	06 03	06 21	07 23	08 24	09 20
0	04 58	05 24	05 47	06 06	07 09	08 10	09 09
S 10	04 40	05 07	05 30	05 51	06 54	07 57	08 58
20	04 19	04 48	05 12	05 36	06 38	07 42	08 46
30	03 51	04 24	04 51	05 17	06 20	07 26	08 33
35	03 34	04 10	04 39	05 07	06 09	07 16	08 25
40	03 12	03 53	04 25	04 55	05 57	07 05	08 16
45	02 44	03 31	04 08	04 41	05 43	06 52	08 05
S 50	02 03	03 04	03 47	04 23	05 26	06 37	07 52
52	01 40	02 50	03 37	04 15	05 18	06 29	07 46
54	01 07	02 34	03 26	04 06	05 09	06 21	07 40
56	////	02 14	03 13	03 56	04 58	06 12	07 32
58	////	01 50	02 57	03 44	04 47	06 01	07 24
S 60	////	01 14	02 39	03 31	04 33	05 49	07 14

Lat.	Sunset	Twilight Civil	Twilight Naut.	Moonset 3	4	5	6
°	h m	h m	h m	h m	h m	h m	h m
N 72	■	13 35	15 41	■	■	15 42	18 15
N 70	■	14 19	15 58	13 04	14 36	16 41	18 44
68	12 44	14 48	16 12	14 16	15 33	17 15	19 05
66	13 43	15 10	16 24	14 53	16 06	17 40	19 21
64	14 16	15 28	16 34	15 19	16 31	17 59	19 35
62	14 40	15 42	16 42	15 40	16 50	18 15	19 46
60	14 59	15 54	16 50	15 56	17 06	18 28	19 55
N 58	15 15	16 05	16 57	16 10	17 19	18 39	20 04
56	15 28	16 14	17 03	16 22	17 31	18 48	20 11
54	15 40	16 23	17 08	16 33	17 41	18 57	20 17
52	15 50	16 30	17 13	16 42	17 50	19 05	20 23
50	16 00	16 37	17 18	16 51	17 58	19 12	20 29
45	16 19	16 52	17 29	17 09	18 15	19 26	20 40
N 40	16 35	17 05	17 39	17 23	18 29	19 38	20 49
35	16 48	17 16	17 47	17 36	18 40	19 49	20 57
30	17 00	17 26	17 56	17 46	18 51	19 57	21 04
20	17 20	17 44	18 11	18 05	19 08	20 13	21 16
N 10	17 37	18 00	18 26	18 21	19 24	20 26	21 27
0	17 54	18 16	18 42	18 36	19 38	20 39	21 36
S 10	18 11	18 34	19 00	18 51	19 52	20 51	21 46
20	18 29	18 53	19 22	19 07	20 07	21 04	21 56
30	18 50	19 17	19 50	19 25	20 25	21 19	22 08
35	19 02	19 31	20 07	19 36	20 35	21 28	22 14
40	19 16	19 48	20 29	19 48	20 46	21 37	22 22
45	19 33	20 10	20 58	20 02	21 00	21 49	22 31
S 50	19 54	20 37	21 39	20 20	21 16	22 03	22 41
52	20 04	20 51	22 03	20 28	21 24	22 09	22 46
54	20 16	21 08	22 36	20 37	21 32	22 16	22 51
56	20 29	21 27	////	20 47	21 42	22 24	22 57
58	20 44	21 53	////	20 59	21 51	22 33	23 04
S 60	21 02	22 29	////	21 13	22 05	22 43	23 11

	SUN Eqn. of Time 00h	12h	Mer. Pass.	MOON Mer. Pass. Upper	Lower	Age	Phase
Day	m s	m s	h m	h m	h m	d	%
3	10 20	10 08	11 50	12 21	24 52	00	0
4	09 56	09 44	11 50	13 23	00 52	01	3
5	09 32	09 19	11 51	14 24	01 54	02	9

UT	ARIES GHA	VENUS −4.9 GHA	Dec	MARS +1.2 GHA	Dec	JUPITER −2.6 GHA	Dec	SATURN +0.6 GHA	Dec	STARS Name	SHA	Dec
d h	° ′	° ′	° ′	° ′	° ′	° ′	° ′	° ′	° ′		° ′	° ′
6 00	74 56.6	138 10.1	S23 39.7	255 04.4	N 2 07.3	324 11.4	N22 07.6	209 05.5	S15 03.8	Acamar	315 17.7	S40 15.1
01	89 59.1	153 11.2	39.2	270 05.7	06.8	339 14.2	07.6	224 07.6	03.9	Achernar	335 26.2	S57 10.2
02	105 01.6	168 12.3	38.7	285 06.9	06.3	354 16.9	07.7	239 09.8	04.0	Acrux	173 09.0	S63 10.3
03	120 04.0	183 13.4	.. 38.2	300 08.2	.. 05.8	9 19.6	.. 07.7	254 12.0	.. 04.1	Adhara	255 11.9	S28 59.5
04	135 06.5	198 14.5	37.7	315 09.5	05.3	24 22.3	07.7	269 14.2	04.1	Aldebaran	290 48.6	N16 32.1
05	150 09.0	213 15.6	37.2	330 10.7	04.8	39 25.0	07.8	284 16.4	04.2			
06	165 11.4	228 16.7	S23 36.6	345 12.0	N 2 04.3	54 27.7	N22 07.8	299 18.6	S15 04.3	Alioth	166 20.8	N55 52.8
07	180 13.9	243 17.8	36.1	0 13.3	03.8	69 30.4	07.8	314 20.8	04.4	Alkaid	152 59.0	N49 14.5
08	195 16.4	258 18.9	35.6	15 14.5	03.3	84 33.1	07.9	329 22.9	04.4	Al Na'ir	27 43.5	S46 53.7
F 09	210 18.8	273 20.1	.. 35.1	30 15.8	.. 02.8	99 35.8	.. 07.9	344 25.1	.. 04.5	Alnilam	275 45.7	S 1 11.7
R 10	225 21.3	288 21.2	34.6	45 17.1	02.3	114 38.5	08.0	359 27.3	04.6	Alphard	217 55.6	S 8 43.2
I 11	240 23.7	303 22.3	34.1	60 18.3	01.8	129 41.2	08.0	14 29.5	04.7			
D 12	255 26.2	318 23.4	S23 33.5	75 19.6	N 2 01.4	144 43.9	N22 08.0	29 31.7	S15 04.7	Alphecca	126 11.1	N26 40.1
A 13	270 28.7	333 24.6	33.0	90 20.9	00.9	159 46.6	08.1	44 33.9	04.8	Alpheratz	357 43.0	N29 10.3
Y 14	285 31.1	348 25.7	32.5	105 22.1	2 00.4	174 49.4	08.1	59 36.1	04.9	Altair	62 08.2	N 8 54.6
15	300 33.6	3 26.8	.. 32.0	120 23.4	1 59.9	189 52.1	.. 08.1	74 38.2	.. 05.0	Ankaa	353 15.3	S42 14.0
16	315 36.1	18 28.0	31.5	135 24.7	59.4	204 54.8	08.2	89 40.4	05.0	Antares	112 26.2	S26 27.6
17	330 38.5	33 29.1	30.9	150 25.9	58.9	219 57.5	08.2	104 42.6	05.1			
18	345 41.0	48 30.2	S23 30.4	165 27.2	N 1 58.4	235 00.2	N22 08.3	119 44.8	S15 05.2	Arcturus	145 55.7	N19 06.6
19	0 43.5	63 31.4	29.9	180 28.5	57.9	250 02.9	08.3	134 47.0	05.3	Atria	107 28.3	S69 02.9
20	15 45.9	78 32.5	29.4	195 29.7	57.4	265 05.6	08.3	149 49.2	05.3	Avior	234 17.4	S59 33.2
21	30 48.4	93 33.7	.. 28.9	210 31.0	.. 56.9	280 08.3	.. 08.4	164 51.4	.. 05.4	Bellatrix	278 31.3	N 6 21.6
22	45 50.9	108 34.8	28.3	225 32.3	56.4	295 11.0	08.4	179 53.5	05.5	Betelgeuse	271 00.6	N 7 24.4
23	60 53.3	123 36.0	27.8	240 33.5	56.0	310 13.8	08.5	194 55.7	05.6			
7 00	75 55.8	138 37.2	S23 27.3	255 34.8	N 1 55.5	325 16.5	N22 08.5	209 57.9	S15 05.6	Canopus	263 55.5	S52 42.3
01	90 58.2	153 38.3	26.8	270 36.1	55.0	340 19.2	08.5	225 00.1	05.7	Capella	280 33.5	N46 00.5
02	106 00.7	168 39.5	26.3	285 37.3	54.5	355 21.9	08.6	240 02.3	05.8	Deneb	49 31.5	N45 20.2
03	121 03.2	183 40.7	.. 25.7	300 38.6	.. 54.0	10 24.6	.. 08.6	255 04.5	.. 05.9	Denebola	182 33.4	N14 29.5
04	136 05.6	198 41.9	25.2	315 39.9	53.5	25 27.3	08.7	270 06.7	05.9	Diphda	348 55.4	S17 54.6
05	151 08.1	213 43.0	24.7	330 41.1	53.0	40 30.0	08.7	285 08.9	06.0			
06	166 10.6	228 44.2	S23 24.2	345 42.4	N 1 52.5	55 32.7	N22 08.7	300 11.0	S15 06.1	Dubhe	193 51.4	N61 40.2
07	181 13.0	243 45.4	23.6	0 43.7	52.0	70 35.5	08.8	315 13.2	06.2	Elnath	278 11.8	N28 37.0
S 08	196 15.5	258 46.6	23.1	15 44.9	51.5	85 38.2	08.8	330 15.4	06.2	Eltanin	90 46.5	N51 29.5
A 09	211 18.0	273 47.8	.. 22.6	30 46.2	.. 51.1	100 40.9	.. 08.8	345 17.6	.. 06.3	Enif	33 46.9	N 9 56.6
T 10	226 20.4	288 49.0	22.1	45 47.5	50.6	115 43.6	08.9	0 19.8	06.4	Fomalhaut	15 23.7	S29 32.9
U 11	241 22.9	303 50.2	21.5	60 48.8	50.1	130 46.3	08.9	15 22.0	06.4			
R 12	256 25.4	318 51.4	S23 21.0	75 50.0	N 1 49.6	145 49.0	N22 09.0	30 24.2	S15 06.5	Gacrux	172 00.7	S57 11.2
D 13	271 27.8	333 52.6	20.5	90 51.3	49.1	160 51.8	09.0	45 26.4	06.6	Gienah	175 52.0	S17 37.1
A 14	286 30.3	348 53.8	20.0	105 52.6	48.6	175 54.5	09.0	60 28.5	06.7	Hadar	148 47.8	S60 26.1
Y 15	301 32.7	3 55.0	.. 19.4	120 53.8	.. 48.1	190 57.2	.. 09.1	75 30.7	.. 06.7	Hamal	328 00.1	N23 31.8
16	316 35.2	18 56.2	18.9	135 55.1	47.6	205 59.9	09.1	90 32.9	06.8	Kaus Aust.	83 43.8	S34 22.5
17	331 37.7	33 57.4	18.4	150 56.4	47.1	221 02.6	09.2	105 35.1	06.9			
18	346 40.1	48 58.7	S23 17.9	165 57.7	N 1 46.6	236 05.3	N22 09.2	120 37.3	S15 07.0	Kochab	137 21.2	N74 05.8
19	1 42.6	63 59.9	17.3	180 58.9	46.2	251 08.1	09.2	135 39.5	07.0	Markab	13 38.0	N15 17.0
20	16 45.1	79 01.1	16.8	196 00.2	45.7	266 10.8	09.3	150 41.7	07.1	Menkar	314 14.4	N 4 08.6
21	31 47.5	94 02.3	.. 16.3	211 01.5	.. 45.2	281 13.5	.. 09.3	165 43.9	.. 07.2	Menkent	148 07.4	S36 26.1
22	46 50.0	109 03.6	15.8	226 02.8	44.7	296 16.2	09.4	180 46.0	07.3	Miaplacidus	221 39.0	S69 46.3
23	61 52.5	124 04.8	15.2	241 04.0	44.2	311 18.9	09.4	195 48.2	07.3			
8 00	76 54.9	139 06.1	S23 14.7	256 05.3	N 1 43.7	326 21.7	N22 09.4	210 50.4	S15 07.4	Mirfak	308 39.3	N49 54.7
01	91 57.4	154 07.3	14.2	271 06.6	43.2	341 24.4	09.5	225 52.6	07.5	Nunki	75 58.3	S26 16.6
02	106 59.9	169 08.5	13.6	286 07.8	42.7	356 27.1	09.5	240 54.8	07.6	Peacock	53 19.2	S56 41.4
03	122 02.3	184 09.8	.. 13.1	301 09.1	.. 42.3	11 29.8	.. 09.6	255 57.0	.. 07.6	Pollux	243 27.0	N27 59.3
04	137 04.8	199 11.0	12.6	316 10.4	41.8	26 32.5	09.6	270 59.2	07.7	Procyon	244 59.1	N 5 11.2
05	152 07.2	214 12.3	12.1	331 11.7	41.3	41 35.3	09.6	286 01.4	07.8			
06	167 09.7	229 13.6	S23 11.5	346 12.9	N 1 40.8	56 38.0	N22 09.7	301 03.5	S15 07.8	Rasalhague	96 06.5	N12 33.2
07	182 12.2	244 14.8	11.0	1 14.2	40.3	71 40.7	09.7	316 05.7	07.9	Regulus	207 43.1	N11 53.8
08	197 14.6	259 16.1	10.5	16 15.5	39.8	86 43.4	09.8	331 07.9	08.0	Rigel	281 11.4	S 8 11.3
S 09	212 17.1	274 17.4	.. 09.9	31 16.8	.. 39.3	101 46.1	.. 09.8	346 10.1	.. 08.1	Rigil Kent.	139 51.7	S60 53.3
U 10	227 19.6	289 18.6	09.4	46 18.1	38.8	116 48.9	09.8	1 12.3	08.1	Sabik	102 12.5	S15 44.3
N 11	242 22.0	304 19.9	08.9	61 19.3	38.4	131 51.6	09.9	16 14.5	08.2			
D 12	257 24.5	319 21.2	S23 08.3	76 20.6	N 1 37.9	146 54.3	N22 09.9	31 16.7	S15 08.3	Schedar	349 39.8	N56 37.1
A 13	272 27.0	334 22.5	07.8	91 21.9	37.4	161 57.0	09.9	46 18.9	08.4	Shaula	96 21.9	S37 06.6
Y 14	287 29.4	349 23.8	07.3	106 23.2	36.9	176 59.8	10.0	61 21.1	08.4	Sirius	258 33.1	S16 44.2
15	302 31.9	4 25.1	.. 06.8	121 24.4	.. 36.4	192 02.5	.. 10.0	76 23.2	.. 08.5	Spica	158 31.1	S11 13.9
16	317 34.3	19 26.4	06.2	136 25.7	35.9	207 05.2	10.1	91 25.4	08.6	Suhail	222 51.9	S43 29.3
17	332 36.8	34 27.7	05.7	151 27.0	35.4	222 07.9	10.1	106 27.6	08.7			
18	347 39.3	49 29.0	S23 05.2	166 28.3	N 1 35.0	237 10.6	N22 10.1	121 29.8	S15 08.7	Vega	80 39.1	N38 48.1
19	2 41.7	64 30.3	04.6	181 29.6	34.5	252 13.4	10.2	136 32.0	08.8	Zuben'ubi	137 05.3	S16 05.8
20	17 44.2	79 31.6	04.1	196 30.8	34.0	267 16.1	10.2	151 34.2	08.9		SHA	Mer. Pass.
21	32 46.7	94 32.9	.. 03.6	211 32.1	.. 33.5	282 18.8	.. 10.3	166 36.4	.. 08.9		° ′	h m
22	47 49.1	109 34.2	03.0	226 33.4	33.0	297 21.5	10.3	181 38.6	09.0	Venus	62 41.4	14 44
23	62 51.6	124 35.5	02.5	241 34.7	32.5	312 24.3	10.3	196 40.8	09.1	Mars	179 39.0	6 57
	h m									Jupiter	249 20.7	2 18
Mer. Pass. 18 53.2	v 1.2 d 0.5			v 1.3 d 0.5		v 2.7 d 0.0		v 2.2 d 0.1		Saturn	134 02.1	9 59

UT	SUN GHA	SUN Dec	MOON GHA	v	MOON Dec	d	HP
d h	° ′	° ′	° ′	′	° ′	′	′
6 00	182 16.5	S22 28.7	138 12.1	5.7	S16 00.1	7.3	60.6
01	197 16.2	29.0	152 36.8	5.7	15 52.8	7.5	60.5
02	212 16.0	29.3	167 01.5	5.9	15 45.3	7.6	60.5
03	227 15.7	.. 29.6	181 26.4	5.9	15 37.7	7.7	60.5
04	242 15.4	29.9	195 51.3	6.0	15 30.0	7.7	60.5
05	257 15.2	30.2	210 16.3	6.0	15 22.3	7.9	60.5
06	272 14.9	S22 30.5	224 41.3	6.2	S15 14.4	8.0	60.4
07	287 14.6	30.8	239 06.5	6.2	15 06.4	8.0	60.4
F 08	302 14.4	31.1	253 31.7	6.3	14 58.4	8.2	60.4
R 09	317 14.1	.. 31.4	267 57.0	6.3	14 50.2	8.2	60.4
I 10	332 13.8	31.7	282 22.3	6.4	14 42.0	8.4	60.4
11	347 13.6	32.0	296 47.7	6.6	14 33.6	8.4	60.3
D 12	2 13.3	S22 32.3	311 13.3	6.5	S14 25.2	8.5	60.3
A 13	17 13.0	32.6	325 38.8	6.7	14 16.7	8.6	60.3
Y 14	32 12.8	32.9	340 04.5	6.7	14 08.1	8.7	60.3
15	47 12.5	.. 33.2	354 30.2	6.8	13 59.4	8.8	60.3
16	62 12.2	33.5	8 56.0	6.9	13 50.6	8.9	60.2
17	77 12.0	33.7	23 21.9	7.0	13 41.7	8.9	60.2
18	92 11.7	S22 34.0	37 47.9	7.0	S13 32.8	9.0	60.2
19	107 11.4	34.3	52 13.9	7.1	13 23.8	9.1	60.2
20	122 11.2	34.6	66 40.0	7.2	13 14.7	9.2	60.1
21	137 10.9	.. 34.9	81 06.2	7.3	13 05.5	9.3	60.1
22	152 10.6	35.2	95 32.5	7.4	12 56.2	9.3	60.1
23	167 10.4	35.5	109 58.9	7.4	12 46.9	9.4	60.1
7 00	182 10.1	S22 35.7	124 25.3	7.5	S12 37.5	9.5	60.0
01	197 09.8	36.0	138 51.8	7.6	12 28.0	9.5	60.0
02	212 09.6	36.3	153 18.4	7.6	12 18.5	9.6	60.0
03	227 09.3	.. 36.6	167 45.0	7.7	12 08.9	9.7	60.0
04	242 09.0	36.9	182 11.7	7.9	11 59.2	9.8	59.9
05	257 08.8	37.1	196 38.6	7.8	11 49.4	9.8	59.9
06	272 08.5	S22 37.4	211 05.4	8.0	S11 39.6	9.9	59.9
S 07	287 08.2	37.7	225 32.4	8.0	11 29.7	9.9	59.9
A 08	302 07.9	38.0	239 59.4	8.1	11 19.8	10.0	59.8
T 09	317 07.7	.. 38.2	254 26.5	8.2	11 09.8	10.1	59.8
U 10	332 07.4	38.5	268 53.7	8.3	10 59.7	10.1	59.8
R 11	347 07.1	38.8	283 21.0	8.3	10 49.6	10.2	59.8
D 12	2 06.9	S22 39.1	297 48.3	8.4	S10 39.4	10.2	59.7
A 13	17 06.6	39.3	312 15.7	8.5	10 29.2	10.3	59.7
Y 14	32 06.3	39.6	326 43.2	8.5	10 18.9	10.3	59.7
15	47 06.0	.. 39.9	341 10.7	8.7	10 08.6	10.4	59.6
16	62 05.8	40.2	355 38.4	8.7	9 58.2	10.4	59.6
17	77 05.5	40.4	10 06.1	8.7	9 47.8	10.5	59.6
18	92 05.2	S22 40.7	24 33.8	8.9	S 9 37.3	10.5	59.6
19	107 05.0	41.0	39 01.7	8.9	9 26.8	10.6	59.5
20	122 04.7	41.2	53 29.6	9.0	9 16.2	10.6	59.5
21	137 04.4	.. 41.5	67 57.6	9.0	9 05.6	10.7	59.5
22	152 04.1	41.8	82 25.6	9.1	8 54.9	10.7	59.4
23	167 03.9	42.0	96 53.7	9.2	8 44.2	10.7	59.4
8 00	182 03.6	S22 42.3	111 21.9	9.3	S 8 33.5	10.8	59.4
01	197 03.3	42.6	125 50.2	9.3	8 22.7	10.8	59.4
02	212 03.0	42.8	140 18.5	9.4	8 11.9	10.9	59.3
03	227 02.8	.. 43.1	154 46.9	9.4	8 01.0	10.9	59.3
04	242 02.5	43.3	169 15.3	9.5	7 50.1	10.9	59.2
05	257 02.2	43.6	183 43.8	9.6	7 39.2	10.9	59.2
06	272 01.9	S22 43.9	198 12.4	9.7	S 7 28.3	11.0	59.2
07	287 01.7	44.1	212 41.1	9.7	7 17.3	11.0	59.2
S 08	302 01.4	44.4	227 09.8	9.8	7 06.3	11.1	59.1
U 09	317 01.1	.. 44.6	241 38.6	9.8	6 55.2	11.1	59.1
N 10	332 00.8	44.9	256 07.4	9.9	6 44.1	11.1	59.1
11	347 00.6	45.1	270 36.3	10.0	6 33.0	11.1	59.1
D 12	2 00.3	S22 45.4	285 05.3	10.0	S 6 21.9	11.1	59.0
A 13	17 00.0	45.7	299 34.3	10.1	6 10.8	11.2	59.0
Y 14	31 59.7	45.9	314 03.4	10.1	5 59.6	11.2	59.0
15	46 59.5	.. 46.2	328 32.5	10.2	5 48.4	11.2	58.9
16	61 59.2	46.4	343 01.7	10.3	5 37.2	11.2	58.9
17	76 58.9	46.7	357 31.0	10.3	5 26.0	11.3	58.9
18	91 58.6	S22 46.9	12 00.3	10.3	S 5 14.7	11.3	58.8
19	106 58.3	47.2	26 29.6	10.4	5 03.4	11.2	58.8
20	121 58.1	47.4	40 59.0	10.5	4 52.2	11.3	58.8
21	136 57.8	.. 47.7	55 28.5	10.6	4 40.9	11.3	58.8
22	151 57.5	47.9	69 58.1	10.5	4 29.6	11.4	58.7
23	166 57.2	48.2	84 27.6	10.7	S 4 18.2	11.3	58.7
	SD 16.3	d 0.3	SD 16.4		16.3		16.1

Twilight, Sunrise, Moonrise

Lat.	Naut.	Civil	Sunrise	Moonrise 6	7	8	9
°	h m	h m	h m	h m	h m	h m	h m
N 72	08 06	10 18	■	12 47	12 33	12 22	12 13
N 70	07 48	09 30	■	12 18	12 15	12 13	12 10
68	07 33	08 59	11 20	11 56	12 02	12 05	12 08
66	07 21	08 36	10 07	11 38	11 50	11 59	12 06
64	07 11	08 18	09 32	11 24	11 41	11 54	12 05
62	07 02	08 03	09 06	11 12	11 33	11 49	12 03
60	06 54	07 50	08 46	11 01	11 26	11 45	12 02
N 58	06 47	07 39	08 30	10 52	11 19	11 42	12 01
56	06 41	07 30	08 16	10 44	11 14	11 38	12 00
54	06 35	07 21	08 04	10 37	11 09	11 36	11 59
52	06 30	07 13	07 54	10 31	11 04	11 33	11 59
50	06 25	07 06	07 44	10 25	11 00	11 31	11 58
45	06 14	06 51	07 24	10 13	10 51	11 25	11 56
N 40	06 04	06 38	07 08	10 02	10 44	11 21	11 55
35	05 55	06 27	06 55	09 53	10 38	11 17	11 54
30	05 47	06 17	06 43	09 46	10 32	11 14	11 53
20	05 31	05 59	06 22	09 32	10 22	11 08	11 51
N 10	05 16	05 42	06 05	09 20	10 13	11 03	11 50
0	04 59	05 25	05 48	09 09	10 05	10 58	11 48
S 10	04 41	05 08	05 31	08 58	09 57	10 53	11 47
20	04 19	04 48	05 13	08 46	09 48	10 48	11 46
30	03 51	04 24	04 51	08 33	09 38	10 42	11 44
35	03 33	04 10	04 39	08 25	09 33	10 39	11 43
40	03 11	03 52	04 25	08 16	09 26	10 35	11 42
45	02 42	03 31	04 07	08 05	09 19	10 31	11 41
S 50	02 00	03 02	03 46	07 52	09 09	10 25	11 39
52	01 35	02 48	03 36	07 46	09 05	10 23	11 39
54	01 00	02 31	03 24	07 40	09 00	10 20	11 38
56	////	02 11	03 11	07 32	08 55	10 17	11 37
58	////	01 45	02 55	07 24	08 49	10 14	11 36
S 60	////	01 06	02 36	07 14	08 43	10 10	11 35

Sunset, Twilight, Moonset

Lat.	Sunset	Civil	Naut.	Moonset 6	7	8	9
°	h m	h m	h m	h m	h m	h m	h m
N 72	■	13 25	15 36	18 15	20 25	22 24	24 17
N 70	■	14 13	15 55	18 44	20 40	22 31	24 16
68	12 23	14 44	16 09	19 05	20 52	22 36	24 16
66	13 36	15 07	16 21	19 21	21 02	22 41	24 15
64	14 11	15 25	16 32	19 35	21 11	22 44	24 15
62	14 37	15 40	16 40	19 46	21 18	22 48	24 15
60	14 57	15 52	16 48	19 55	21 24	22 50	24 15
N 58	15 13	16 03	16 55	20 04	21 29	22 53	24 14
56	15 27	16 13	17 02	20 11	21 34	22 55	24 14
54	15 39	16 22	17 07	20 17	21 38	22 57	24 14
52	15 49	16 30	17 13	20 23	21 42	22 59	24 14
50	15 59	16 37	17 18	20 29	21 45	23 01	24 14
45	16 18	16 52	17 29	20 40	21 53	23 04	24 13
N 40	16 35	17 05	17 39	20 49	21 59	23 07	24 13
35	16 48	17 16	17 48	20 57	22 04	23 10	24 13
30	17 00	17 26	17 56	21 04	22 09	23 12	24 12
20	17 21	17 44	18 12	21 16	22 17	23 16	24 12
N 10	17 38	18 01	18 27	21 27	22 24	23 19	24 12
0	17 55	18 18	18 44	21 36	22 31	23 22	24 12
S 10	18 12	18 35	19 02	21 46	22 37	23 25	24 11
20	18 31	18 55	19 24	21 56	22 44	23 29	24 11
30	18 52	19 19	19 52	22 08	22 52	23 32	24 11
35	19 04	19 34	20 10	22 14	22 56	23 34	24 10
40	19 19	19 51	20 32	22 22	23 01	23 37	24 10
45	19 36	20 13	21 02	22 31	23 07	23 39	24 10
S 50	19 58	20 41	21 44	22 41	23 14	23 43	24 09
52	20 08	20 55	22 09	22 46	23 17	23 44	24 09
54	20 20	21 13	22 46	22 51	23 21	23 46	24 09
56	20 33	21 33	////	22 57	23 24	23 47	24 08
58	20 48	22 00	////	23 04	23 29	23 49	24 08
S 60	21 08	22 40	////	23 11	23 33	23 52	24 08

SUN / MOON

Day	Eqn. of Time 00h	Eqn. of Time 12h	Mer. Pass.	Mer. Pass. Upper	Mer. Pass. Lower	Age	Phase
d	m s	m s	h m	h m	h m	d	%
6	09 06	08 54	11 51	15 23	02 54	03	17
7	08 41	08 28	11 52	16 18	03 51	04	27
8	08 15	08 02	11 52	17 10	04 45	05	38

UT	ARIES	VENUS −4.9		MARS +1.1		JUPITER −2.6		SATURN +0.6		STARS		
	GHA	GHA	Dec	GHA	Dec	GHA	Dec	GHA	Dec	Name	SHA	Dec
d h	° ′	° ′	° ′	° ′	° ′	° ′	° ′	° ′	° ′		° ′	° ′
9 00	77 54.1	139 36.8	S23 02.0	256 35.9	N 1 32.0	327 27.0	N22 10.4	211 43.0	S15 09.2	Acamar	315 17.8	S40 15.1
01	92 56.5	154 38.2	01.4	271 37.2	31.6	342 29.7	10.4	226 45.1	09.2	Achernar	335 26.2	S57 10.2
02	107 59.0	169 39.5	00.9	286 38.5	31.1	357 32.5	10.5	241 47.3	09.3	Acrux	173 09.0	S63 10.3
03	123 01.5	184 40.8	23 00.4	301 39.8	30.6	12 35.2	10.5	256 49.5	09.4	Adhara	255 11.9	S28 59.6
04	138 03.9	199 42.2	22 59.8	316 41.1	30.1	27 37.9	10.5	271 51.7	09.5	Aldebaran	290 48.6	N16 32.1
05	153 06.4	214 43.5	59.3	331 42.3	29.6	42 40.6	10.6	286 53.9	09.5			
06	168 08.8	229 44.8	S22 58.8	346 43.6	N 1 29.1	57 43.4	N22 10.6	301 56.1	S15 09.6	Alioth	166 20.7	N55 52.8
07	183 11.3	244 46.2	58.2	1 44.9	28.6	72 46.1	10.7	316 58.3	09.7	Alkaid	152 59.0	N49 14.5
08	198 13.8	259 47.5	57.7	16 46.2	28.2	87 48.8	10.7	332 00.5	09.7	Al Na'ir	27 43.5	S46 53.7
M 09	213 16.2	274 48.9	. . 57.1	31 47.5	. . 27.7	102 51.5	. . 10.8	347 02.7	. . 09.8	Alnilam	275 45.7	S 1 11.7
O 10	228 18.7	289 50.2	56.6	46 48.7	27.2	117 54.3	10.8	2 04.9	09.9	Alphard	217 55.6	S 8 43.2
N 11	243 21.2	304 51.6	56.1	61 50.0	26.7	132 57.0	10.8	17 07.0	09.9			
D 12	258 23.6	319 53.0	S22 55.5	76 51.3	N 1 26.2	147 59.7	N22 10.9	32 09.2	S15 10.0	Alphecca	126 11.1	N26 40.1
A 13	273 26.1	334 54.3	55.0	91 52.6	25.7	163 02.5	10.9	47 11.4	10.1	Alpheratz	357 43.0	N29 10.3
Y 14	288 28.6	349 55.7	54.5	106 53.9	25.2	178 05.2	11.0	62 13.6	10.2	Altair	62 08.2	N 8 54.6
15	303 31.0	4 57.1	. . 53.9	121 55.2	. . 24.8	193 07.9	. . 11.0	77 15.8	. . 10.3	Ankaa	353 15.3	S42 14.0
16	318 33.5	19 58.5	53.4	136 56.4	24.3	208 10.7	11.0	92 18.0	10.3	Antares	112 26.2	S26 27.6
17	333 36.0	34 59.8	52.9	151 57.7	23.8	223 13.4	11.1	107 20.2	10.4			
18	348 38.4	50 01.2	S22 52.3	166 59.0	N 1 23.3	238 16.1	N22 11.1	122 22.4	S15 10.5	Arcturus	145 55.7	N19 06.6
19	3 40.9	65 02.6	51.8	182 00.3	22.8	253 18.8	11.2	137 24.6	10.5	Atria	107 28.3	S69 02.9
20	18 43.3	80 04.0	51.2	197 01.6	22.3	268 21.6	11.2	152 26.8	10.6	Avior	234 17.3	S59 33.2
21	33 45.8	95 05.4	. . 50.7	212 02.9	. . 21.9	283 24.3	. . 11.2	167 28.9	. . 10.7	Bellatrix	278 31.3	N 6 21.6
22	48 48.3	110 06.8	50.2	227 04.1	21.4	298 27.0	11.3	182 31.1	10.8	Betelgeuse	271 00.6	N 7 24.4
23	63 50.7	125 08.2	49.6	242 05.4	20.9	313 29.8	11.3	197 33.3	10.8			
10 00	78 53.2	140 09.6	S22 49.1	257 06.7	N 1 20.4	328 32.5	N22 11.4	212 35.5	S15 10.9	Canopus	263 55.4	S52 42.3
01	93 55.7	155 11.0	48.6	272 08.0	19.9	343 35.2	11.4	227 37.7	11.0	Capella	280 33.4	N46 00.5
02	108 58.1	170 12.4	48.0	287 09.3	19.4	358 38.0	11.4	242 39.9	11.0	Deneb	49 31.5	N45 20.2
03	124 00.6	185 13.8	. . 47.5	302 10.6	. . 19.0	13 40.7	. . 11.5	257 42.1	. . 11.1	Denebola	182 33.4	N14 29.5
04	139 03.1	200 15.3	46.9	317 11.9	18.5	28 43.4	11.5	272 44.3	11.2	Diphda	348 55.4	S17 54.7
05	154 05.5	215 16.7	46.4	332 13.1	18.0	43 46.2	11.6	287 46.5	11.3			
06	169 08.0	230 18.1	S22 45.9	347 14.4	N 1 17.5	58 48.9	N22 11.6	302 48.7	S15 11.3	Dubhe	193 51.4	N61 40.1
07	184 10.4	245 19.5	45.3	2 15.7	17.0	73 51.6	11.6	317 50.9	11.4	Elnath	278 11.8	N28 37.0
08	199 12.9	260 21.0	44.8	17 17.0	16.6	88 54.4	11.7	332 53.0	11.5	Eltanin	90 46.5	N51 29.5
T 09	214 15.4	275 22.4	. . 44.2	32 18.3	. . 16.1	103 57.1	. . 11.7	347 55.2	. . 11.5	Enif	33 46.9	N 9 56.6
U 10	229 17.8	290 23.8	43.7	47 19.6	15.6	118 59.8	11.8	2 57.4	11.6	Fomalhaut	15 23.7	S29 32.9
E 11	244 20.3	305 25.3	43.2	62 20.9	15.1	134 02.6	11.8	17 59.6	11.7			
S 12	259 22.8	320 26.7	S22 42.6	77 22.1	N 1 14.6	149 05.3	N22 11.9	33 01.8	S15 11.8	Gacrux	172 00.6	S57 11.2
D 13	274 25.2	335 28.2	42.1	92 23.4	14.1	164 08.1	11.9	48 04.0	11.8	Gienah	175 52.0	S17 37.1
A 14	289 27.7	350 29.6	41.5	107 24.7	13.7	179 10.8	11.9	63 06.2	11.9	Hadar	148 47.8	S60 26.1
Y 15	304 30.2	5 31.1	. . 41.0	122 26.0	. . 13.2	194 13.5	. . 12.0	78 08.4	. . 12.0	Hamal	328 00.1	N23 31.8
16	319 32.6	20 32.6	40.5	137 27.3	12.7	209 16.3	12.0	93 10.6	12.1	Kaus Aust.	83 43.8	S34 22.5
17	334 35.1	35 34.0	39.9	152 28.6	12.2	224 19.0	12.1	108 12.8	12.1			
18	349 37.6	50 35.5	S22 39.4	167 29.9	N 1 11.7	239 21.7	N22 12.1	123 15.0	S15 12.2	Kochab	137 21.2	N74 05.8
19	4 40.0	65 37.0	38.8	182 31.2	11.3	254 24.5	12.1	138 17.2	12.3	Markab	13 51.5	N15 17.0
20	19 42.5	80 38.4	38.3	197 32.5	10.8	269 27.2	12.2	153 19.4	12.3	Menkar	314 14.4	N 4 08.6
21	34 44.9	95 39.9	. . 37.7	212 33.7	. . 10.3	284 30.0	. . 12.2	168 21.5	. . 12.4	Menkent	148 07.4	S36 26.1
22	49 47.4	110 41.4	37.2	227 35.0	09.8	299 32.7	12.3	183 23.7	12.5	Miaplacidus	221 39.0	S69 46.3
23	64 49.9	125 42.9	36.7	242 36.3	09.3	314 35.4	12.3	198 25.9	12.6			
11 00	79 52.3	140 44.4	S22 36.1	257 37.6	N 1 08.9	329 38.2	N22 12.3	213 28.1	S15 12.6	Mirfak	308 39.3	N49 54.7
01	94 54.8	155 45.9	35.6	272 38.9	08.4	344 40.9	12.4	228 30.3	12.7	Nunki	75 58.3	S26 16.6
02	109 57.3	170 47.4	35.0	287 40.2	07.9	359 43.7	12.4	243 32.5	12.8	Peacock	53 19.2	S56 41.4
03	124 59.7	185 48.9	. . 34.5	302 41.5	. . 07.4	14 46.4	. . 12.5	258 34.7	. . 12.8	Pollux	243 27.0	N27 59.3
04	140 02.2	200 50.4	33.9	317 42.8	06.9	29 49.1	12.5	273 36.9	12.9	Procyon	244 59.1	N 5 11.2
05	155 04.7	215 51.9	33.4	332 44.1	06.5	44 51.9	12.6	288 39.1	13.0			
06	170 07.1	230 53.4	S22 32.9	347 45.4	N 1 06.0	59 54.6	N22 12.6	303 41.3	S15 13.1	Rasalhague	96 06.5	N12 33.2
W 07	185 09.6	245 54.9	32.3	2 46.7	05.5	74 57.4	12.6	318 43.5	13.1	Regulus	207 43.1	N11 53.8
E 08	200 12.0	260 56.4	31.8	17 47.9	05.0	90 00.1	12.7	333 45.7	13.2	Rigel	281 11.4	S 8 11.3
D 09	215 14.5	275 58.0	. . 31.2	32 49.2	. . 04.5	105 02.8	. . 12.7	348 47.9	. . 13.3	Rigil Kent.	139 51.7	S60 53.2
N 10	230 17.0	290 59.5	30.7	47 50.5	04.1	120 05.6	12.8	3 50.1	13.3	Sabik	102 12.5	S15 44.3
E 11	245 19.4	306 01.0	30.1	62 51.8	03.6	135 08.3	12.8	18 52.2	13.4			
S 12	260 21.9	321 02.6	S22 29.6	77 53.1	N 1 03.1	150 11.1	N22 12.8	33 54.4	S15 13.5	Schedar	349 39.8	N56 37.1
D 13	275 24.4	336 04.1	29.1	92 54.4	02.6	165 13.8	12.9	48 56.6	13.5	Shaula	96 21.9	S37 06.6
A 14	290 26.8	351 05.6	28.5	107 55.7	02.1	180 16.5	12.9	63 58.8	13.6	Sirius	258 33.5	S16 44.3
Y 15	305 29.3	6 07.2	. . 28.0	122 57.0	. . 01.7	195 19.3	. . 13.0	79 01.0	. . 13.7	Spica	158 31.1	S11 13.9
16	320 31.8	21 08.7	27.4	137 58.3	01.2	210 22.0	13.0	94 03.2	13.8	Suhail	222 51.9	S43 29.3
17	335 34.2	36 10.3	26.9	152 59.6	00.7	225 24.8	13.1	109 05.4	13.8			
18	350 36.7	51 11.8	S22 26.3	168 00.9	N 1 00.2	240 27.5	N22 13.1	124 07.6	S15 13.9	Vega	80 39.1	N38 48.1
19	5 39.2	66 13.4	25.8	183 02.2	0 59.7	255 30.3	13.1	139 09.8	14.0	Zuben'ubi	137 05.3	S16 05.8
20	20 41.6	81 15.0	25.2	198 03.5	59.3	270 33.0	13.2	154 12.0	14.0		SHA	Mer. Pass.
21	35 44.1	96 16.5	24.7	213 04.8	58.8	285 35.8	13.2	169 14.2	14.1		° ′	h m
22	50 46.5	111 18.1	24.1	228 06.1	58.3	300 38.5	13.3	184 16.4	14.2	Venus	61 16.4	14 38
23	65 49.0	126 19.7	23.6	243 07.4	57.8	315 41.2	13.3	199 18.6	14.3	Mars	178 13.5	6 51
	h m									Jupiter	249 39.3	2 05
Mer. Pass. 18 41.4		v 1.4	d 0.5	v 1.3	d 0.5	v 2.7	d 0.0	v 2.2	d 0.1	Saturn	133 42.3	9 48

SUN and MOON — GHA / Dec

UT (d h)	SUN GHA	SUN Dec	MOON GHA	v	MOON Dec	d	HP
9 00	181 57.0	S22 48.4	98 57.3	10.6	S 4 06.9	11.3	58.7
01	196 56.7	48.6	113 26.9	10.8	3 55.6	11.4	58.6
02	211 56.4	48.9	127 56.7	10.8	3 44.2	11.4	58.6
03	226 56.1 ..	49.1	142 26.5	10.8	3 32.8	11.3	58.6
04	241 55.8	49.4	156 56.3	10.9	3 21.5	11.4	58.5
05	256 55.6	49.6	171 26.2	10.9	3 10.1	11.4	58.5
06	271 55.3	S22 49.9	185 56.1	11.0	S 2 58.7	11.4	58.5
07	286 55.0	50.1	200 26.1	11.0	2 47.3	11.3	58.4
M 08	301 54.7	50.3	214 56.1	11.1	2 36.0	11.4	58.4
O 09	316 54.4 ..	50.6	229 26.2	11.1	2 24.6	11.4	58.4
N 10	331 54.2	50.8	243 56.3	11.1	2 13.2	11.4	58.3
D 11	346 53.9	51.1	258 26.4	11.2	2 01.8	11.4	58.3
A 12	1 53.6	S22 51.3	272 56.6	11.2	S 1 50.4	11.4	58.3
Y 13	16 53.3	51.5	287 26.8	11.3	1 39.0	11.4	58.3
14	31 53.0	51.8	301 57.1	11.3	1 27.6	11.3	58.2
15	46 52.8 ..	52.0	316 27.4	11.4	1 16.3	11.4	58.2
16	61 52.5	52.2	330 57.8	11.4	1 04.9	11.4	58.2
17	76 52.2	52.5	345 28.2	11.4	0 53.5	11.3	58.1
18	91 51.9	S22 52.7	359 58.6	11.5	S 0 42.2	11.4	58.1
19	106 51.6	52.9	14 29.1	11.5	0 30.8	11.3	58.1
20	121 51.4	53.2	28 59.6	11.5	0 19.5	11.3	58.0
21	136 51.1 ..	53.4	43 30.1	11.6	S 0 08.2	11.3	58.0
22	151 50.8	53.6	58 00.7	11.6	N 0 03.1	11.4	58.0
23	166 50.5	53.8	72 31.3	11.6	0 14.5	11.2	57.9
10 00	181 50.2	S22 54.1	87 01.9	11.7	N 0 25.7	11.3	57.9
01	196 49.9	54.3	101 32.6	11.7	0 37.0	11.3	57.9
02	211 49.7	54.5	116 03.3	11.7	0 48.3	11.2	57.9
03	226 49.4 ..	54.7	130 34.0	11.7	0 59.5	11.3	57.8
04	241 49.1	55.0	145 04.7	11.8	1 10.8	11.2	57.8
05	256 48.8	55.2	159 35.5	11.8	1 22.0	11.2	57.8
06	271 48.5	S22 55.4	174 06.3	11.9	N 1 33.2	11.1	57.7
07	286 48.2	55.6	188 37.2	11.8	1 44.3	11.2	57.7
T 08	301 48.0	55.9	203 08.0	11.9	1 55.5	11.1	57.7
U 09	316 47.7 ..	56.1	217 38.9	11.9	2 06.6	11.1	57.6
E 10	331 47.4	56.3	232 09.8	12.0	2 17.7	11.1	57.6
S 11	346 47.1	56.5	246 40.8	11.9	2 28.8	11.1	57.6
D 12	1 46.8	S22 56.7	261 11.7	12.0	N 2 39.9	11.0	57.6
A 13	16 46.5	56.9	275 42.7	12.0	2 50.9	11.1	57.5
Y 14	31 46.3	57.2	290 13.7	12.0	3 02.0	10.9	57.5
15	46 46.0 ..	57.4	304 44.7	12.1	3 12.9	11.0	57.5
16	61 45.7	57.6	319 15.8	12.0	3 23.9	10.9	57.4
17	76 45.4	57.8	333 46.8	12.1	3 34.8	11.0	57.4
18	91 45.1	S22 58.0	348 17.9	12.1	N 3 45.8	10.8	57.4
19	106 44.8	58.2	2 49.0	12.1	3 56.6	10.9	57.4
20	121 44.5	58.4	17 20.1	12.2	4 07.5	10.8	57.3
21	136 44.3 ..	58.6	31 51.3	12.1	4 18.3	10.8	57.3
22	151 44.0	58.9	46 22.4	12.2	4 29.1	10.7	57.3
23	166 43.7	59.1	60 53.6	12.1	4 39.8	10.8	57.2
11 00	181 43.4	S22 59.3	75 24.7	12.2	N 4 50.6	10.6	57.2
01	196 43.1	59.5	89 55.9	12.2	5 01.2	10.7	57.2
02	211 42.8	59.7	104 27.1	12.3	5 11.9	10.6	57.1
03	226 42.5	22 59.9	118 58.4	12.2	5 22.5	10.6	57.1
04	241 42.3	23 00.1	133 29.6	12.2	5 33.1	10.5	57.1
05	256 42.0	00.3	148 00.8	12.3	5 43.6	10.5	57.1
06	271 41.7	S23 00.5	162 32.1	12.2	N 5 54.1	10.5	57.0
07	286 41.4	00.7	177 03.3	12.3	6 04.6	10.4	57.0
W 08	301 41.1	00.9	191 34.6	12.2	6 15.0	10.4	57.0
E 09	316 40.8 ..	01.1	206 05.8	12.3	6 25.4	10.4	57.0
D 10	331 40.5	01.3	220 37.1	12.3	6 35.8	10.3	56.9
N 11	346 40.2	01.5	235 08.4	12.3	6 46.1	10.2	56.9
E 12	1 39.9	S23 01.7	249 39.7	12.3	N 6 56.3	10.2	56.9
S 13	16 39.7	01.9	264 11.0	12.3	7 06.5	10.2	56.9
D 14	31 39.4	02.1	278 42.3	12.3	7 16.7	10.1	56.8
A 15	46 39.1 ..	02.3	293 13.6	12.3	7 26.8	10.1	56.8
Y 16	61 38.8	02.5	307 44.9	12.3	7 36.9	10.1	56.8
17	76 38.5	02.7	322 16.2	12.3	7 47.0	10.0	56.7
18	91 38.2	S23 02.9	336 47.5	12.3	N 7 57.0	9.9	56.7
19	106 37.9	03.1	351 18.8	12.3	8 06.9	9.9	56.7
20	121 37.6	03.3	5 50.1	12.4	8 16.8	9.9	56.7
21	136 37.3 ..	03.5	20 21.5	12.3	8 26.7	9.8	56.6
22	151 37.1	03.6	34 52.8	12.3	8 36.5	9.7	56.6
23	166 36.8	03.8	49 24.1	12.3	N 8 46.2	9.7	56.6
	SD 16.3	d 0.2	SD 15.9		15.7		15.5

Twilight / Sunrise / Moonrise

Lat.	Twilight Naut.	Civil	Sunrise	Moonrise 9	10	11	12
N 72	08 12	10 30	■	12 13	12 04	11 55	11 45
N 70	07 53	09 38	■	12 10	12 07	12 05	12 02
68	07 38	09 05	■	12 08	12 10	12 13	12 16
66	07 26	08 41	10 16	12 06	12 13	12 19	12 27
64	07 15	08 23	09 38	12 05	12 15	12 25	12 37
62	07 06	08 07	09 11	12 03	12 16	12 30	12 45
60	06 58	07 54	08 51	12 02	12 18	12 34	12 52
N 58	06 51	07 43	08 34	12 01	12 19	12 38	12 58
56	06 44	07 33	08 20	12 00	12 21	12 41	13 03
54	06 38	07 24	08 08	11 59	12 22	12 44	13 08
52	06 33	07 16	07 57	11 59	12 23	12 47	13 13
50	06 28	07 09	07 47	11 58	12 24	12 50	13 17
45	06 17	06 54	07 27	11 56	12 26	12 55	13 26
N 40	06 07	06 40	07 11	11 55	12 28	13 00	13 33
35	05 57	06 29	06 57	11 54	12 29	13 04	13 40
30	05 49	06 19	06 45	11 53	12 30	13 08	13 45
20	05 33	06 00	06 24	11 51	12 33	13 14	13 55
N 10	05 17	05 43	06 06	11 50	12 35	13 19	14 04
0	05 01	05 27	05 49	11 48	12 37	13 25	14 12
S 10	04 42	05 09	05 32	11 47	12 39	13 30	14 20
20	04 20	04 49	05 13	11 46	12 41	13 35	14 29
30	03 51	04 25	04 52	11 44	12 44	13 42	14 39
35	03 33	04 10	04 39	11 43	12 45	13 46	14 45
40	03 11	03 52	04 25	11 42	12 47	13 50	14 52
45	02 41	03 30	04 07	11 41	12 49	13 55	15 00
S 50	01 58	03 01	03 45	11 39	12 51	14 01	15 09
52	01 32	02 47	03 35	11 39	12 52	14 04	15 13
54	00 53	02 30	03 23	11 38	12 53	14 07	15 18
56	////	02 09	03 09	11 37	12 55	14 10	15 24
58	////	01 41	02 53	11 36	12 56	14 14	15 30
S 60	////	00 59	02 34	11 35	12 58	14 18	15 36

Sunset / Twilight / Moonset

Lat.	Sunset	Twilight Civil	Naut.	Moonset 9	10	11	12
N 72	■	13 15	15 33	24 17	00 17	02 06	03 55
N 70	■	14 08	15 52	24 16	00 16	01 58	03 39
68	■	14 40	16 07	24 16	00 16	01 52	03 27
66	13 30	15 04	16 20	24 15	00 15	01 47	03 17
64	14 08	15 23	16 30	24 15	00 15	01 43	03 09
62	14 34	15 38	16 39	24 15	00 15	01 39	03 02
60	14 55	15 51	16 47	24 15	00 15	01 36	02 56
N 58	15 11	16 02	16 55	24 14	00 14	01 33	02 50
56	15 26	16 12	17 01	24 14	00 14	01 31	02 45
54	15 38	16 21	17 07	24 14	00 14	01 29	02 41
52	15 49	16 29	17 13	24 14	00 14	01 27	02 37
50	15 58	16 36	17 18	24 13	00 13	01 25	02 34
45	16 18	16 52	17 29	24 13	00 13	01 21	02 26
N 40	16 35	17 05	17 39	24 13	00 13	01 17	02 20
35	16 49	17 17	17 48	24 13	00 13	01 14	02 14
30	17 01	17 27	17 57	24 13	00 13	01 12	02 10
20	17 21	17 45	18 13	24 12	00 12	01 07	02 01
N 10	17 40	18 02	18 29	24 12	00 12	01 03	01 54
0	17 57	18 19	18 45	24 12	00 12	01 00	01 47
S 10	18 14	18 37	19 04	24 11	00 11	00 56	01 40
20	18 32	18 57	19 26	24 11	00 11	00 52	01 33
30	18 54	19 21	19 54	24 11	00 11	00 48	01 25
35	19 07	19 36	20 13	24 10	00 10	00 45	01 20
40	19 22	19 54	20 35	24 10	00 10	00 42	01 15
45	19 39	20 16	21 05	24 10	00 10	00 39	01 09
S 50	20 01	20 45	21 49	24 09	00 09	00 35	01 01
52	20 12	21 00	22 15	24 09	00 09	00 33	00 58
54	20 24	21 17	22 55	24 09	00 09	00 31	00 54
56	20 37	21 38	////	24 08	00 08	00 29	00 50
58	20 53	22 06	////	24 08	00 08	00 27	00 46
S 60	21 13	22 49	////	24 08	00 08	00 24	00 41

SUN / MOON

Day	Eqn. of Time 00h	12h	Mer. Pass.	Mer. Pass. Upper	Lower	Age	Phase %
9	07 48	07 35	11 52	18 00	05 35	06	49
10	07 21	07 08	11 53	18 48	06 24	07	59
11	06 54	06 40	11 53	19 36	07 12	08	70

UT	ARIES GHA	VENUS −4.9 GHA	Dec	MARS +1.1 GHA	Dec	JUPITER −2.6 GHA	Dec	SATURN +0.6 GHA	Dec	Name	SHA	Dec
12 00	80 51.5	141 21.3	S22 23.1	258 08.7	N 0 57.4	330 44.0	N22 13.3	214 20.8	S15 14.3	Acamar	315 17.8	S40 15.1
01	95 53.9	156 22.8	22.5	273 09.9	56.9	345 46.7	13.4	229 23.0	14.4	Achernar	335 26.3	S57 10.2
02	110 56.4	171 24.4	22.0	288 11.2	56.4	0 49.5	13.4	244 25.2	14.5	Acrux	173 09.0	S63 10.3
03	125 58.9	186 26.0	.. 21.4	303 12.5	.. 55.9	15 52.2	.. 13.5	259 27.3	.. 14.5	Adhara	255 11.9	S28 59.6
04	141 01.3	201 27.6	20.9	318 13.8	55.4	30 55.0	13.5	274 29.5	14.6	Aldebaran	290 48.6	N16 32.1
05	156 03.8	216 29.2	20.3	333 15.1	55.0	45 57.7	13.6	289 31.7	14.7			
06	171 06.3	231 30.8	S22 19.8	348 16.4	N 0 54.5	61 00.5	N22 13.6	304 33.9	S15 14.8	Alioth	166 20.7	N55 52.8
07	186 08.7	246 32.4	19.2	3 17.7	54.0	76 03.2	13.6	319 36.1	14.8	Alkaid	152 59.0	N49 14.4
T 08	201 11.2	261 34.0	18.7	18 19.0	53.5	91 06.0	13.7	334 38.3	14.9	Al Na'ir	27 43.5	S46 53.7
H 09	216 13.7	276 35.6	.. 18.1	33 20.3	.. 53.1	106 08.7	.. 13.7	349 40.5	.. 15.0	Alnilam	275 45.7	S 1 11.7
U 10	231 16.1	291 37.3	17.6	48 21.6	52.6	121 11.5	13.8	4 42.7	15.0	Alphard	217 55.6	S 8 43.2
R 11	246 18.6	306 38.9	17.0	63 22.9	52.1	136 14.2	13.8	19 44.9	15.1			
S 12	261 21.0	321 40.5	S22 16.5	78 24.2	N 0 51.6	151 16.9	N22 13.9	34 47.1	S15 15.2	Alphecca	126 11.1	N26 40.1
D 13	276 23.5	336 42.1	16.0	93 25.5	51.2	166 19.7	13.9	49 49.3	15.2	Alpheratz	357 43.0	N29 10.3
A 14	291 26.0	351 43.8	15.4	108 26.8	50.7	181 22.4	14.0	64 51.5	15.3	Altair	62 08.2	N 8 54.6
Y 15	306 28.4	6 45.4	.. 14.9	123 28.1	.. 50.2	196 25.2	.. 14.0	79 53.7	.. 15.4	Ankaa	353 15.3	S42 14.0
16	321 30.9	21 47.0	14.3	138 29.4	49.7	211 27.9	14.0	94 55.9	15.5	Antares	112 26.2	S26 27.6
17	336 33.4	36 48.7	13.8	153 30.7	49.3	226 30.7	14.1	109 58.1	15.5			
18	351 35.8	51 50.3	S22 13.2	168 32.0	N 0 48.8	241 33.4	N22 14.1	125 00.3	S15 15.6	Arcturus	145 55.7	N19 06.6
19	6 38.3	66 52.0	12.7	183 33.3	48.3	256 36.2	14.2	140 02.5	15.7	Atria	107 28.2	S69 02.9
20	21 40.8	81 53.6	12.1	198 34.6	47.8	271 38.9	14.2	155 04.7	15.7	Avior	234 17.3	S59 33.2
21	36 43.2	96 55.3	.. 11.6	213 35.9	.. 47.4	286 41.7	.. 14.2	170 06.9	.. 15.8	Bellatrix	278 31.3	N 6 21.6
22	51 45.7	111 57.0	11.0	228 37.2	46.9	301 44.4	14.3	185 09.1	15.9	Betelgeuse	271 00.6	N 7 24.4
23	66 48.1	126 58.6	10.5	243 38.5	46.4	316 47.2	14.3	200 11.2	15.9			
13 00	81 50.6	142 00.3	S22 09.9	258 39.8	N 0 45.9	331 49.9	N22 14.4	215 13.4	S15 16.0	Canopus	263 55.4	S52 42.3
01	96 53.1	157 02.0	09.4	273 41.1	45.5	346 52.7	14.4	230 15.6	16.1	Capella	280 33.4	N46 00.6
02	111 55.5	172 03.7	08.8	288 42.4	45.0	1 55.4	14.4	245 17.8	16.2	Deneb	49 31.5	N45 20.2
03	126 58.0	187 05.3	.. 08.3	303 43.7	.. 44.5	16 58.2	.. 14.5	260 20.0	.. 16.2	Denebola	182 33.4	N14 29.5
04	142 00.5	202 07.0	07.7	318 45.0	44.0	32 01.0	14.5	275 22.2	16.3	Diphda	348 55.5	S17 54.7
05	157 02.9	217 08.7	07.2	333 46.3	43.6	47 03.7	14.6	290 24.4	16.4			
06	172 05.4	232 10.4	S22 06.6	348 47.6	N 0 43.1	62 06.5	N22 14.6	305 26.6	S15 16.4	Dubhe	193 51.3	N61 40.1
07	187 07.9	247 12.1	06.1	3 48.9	42.6	77 09.2	14.7	320 28.8	16.5	Elnath	278 11.8	N28 37.0
F 08	202 10.3	262 13.8	05.5	18 50.2	42.1	92 12.0	14.7	335 31.0	16.6	Eltanin	90 46.5	N51 29.4
R 09	217 12.8	277 15.5	.. 05.0	33 51.6	.. 41.7	107 14.7	.. 14.7	350 33.2	.. 16.6	Enif	33 46.9	N 9 56.6
I 10	232 15.3	292 17.2	04.5	48 52.9	41.2	122 17.5	14.8	5 35.4	16.7	Fomalhaut	15 23.7	S29 32.9
D 11	247 17.7	307 18.9	03.9	63 54.2	40.7	137 20.2	14.8	20 37.6	16.8			
A 12	262 20.2	322 20.7	S22 03.4	78 55.5	N 0 40.2	152 23.0	N22 14.9	35 39.8	S15 16.9	Gacrux	172 00.6	S57 11.2
Y 13	277 22.6	337 22.4	02.8	93 56.8	39.8	167 25.7	14.9	50 42.0	16.9	Gienah	175 52.0	S17 37.1
14	292 25.1	352 24.1	02.3	108 58.1	39.3	182 28.5	15.0	65 44.2	17.0	Hadar	148 47.7	S60 26.1
15	307 27.6	7 25.8	.. 01.7	123 59.4	.. 38.8	197 31.2	.. 15.0	80 46.4	.. 17.1	Hamal	328 00.1	N23 31.8
16	322 30.0	22 27.6	01.2	139 00.7	38.3	212 34.0	15.0	95 48.6	17.1	Kaus Aust.	83 43.8	S34 22.5
17	337 32.5	37 29.3	00.6	154 02.0	37.9	227 36.8	15.1	110 50.8	17.2			
18	352 35.0	52 31.0	S22 00.1	169 03.3	N 0 37.4	242 39.5	N22 15.2	125 53.0	S15 17.3	Kochab	137 21.1	N74 05.7
19	7 37.4	67 32.8	21 59.5	184 04.6	36.9	257 42.3	15.2	140 55.2	17.3	Markab	13 38.0	N15 17.0
20	22 39.9	82 34.5	59.0	199 05.9	36.5	272 45.0	15.2	155 57.4	17.4	Menkar	314 14.4	N 4 08.6
21	37 42.4	97 36.3	.. 58.4	214 07.2	.. 36.0	287 47.8	.. 15.3	170 59.6	.. 17.5	Menkent	148 07.4	S36 26.1
22	52 44.8	112 38.0	57.9	229 08.5	35.5	302 50.5	15.3	186 01.8	17.5	Miaplacidus	221 38.9	S69 46.3
23	67 47.3	127 39.8	57.3	244 09.8	35.0	317 53.3	15.3	201 04.0	17.6			
14 00	82 49.8	142 41.6	S21 56.8	259 11.1	N 0 34.6	332 56.0	N22 15.4	216 06.2	S15 17.7	Mirfak	308 39.4	N49 54.7
01	97 52.2	157 43.3	56.2	274 12.4	34.1	347 58.8	15.4	231 08.4	17.8	Nunki	75 58.3	S26 16.6
02	112 54.7	172 45.1	55.7	289 13.8	33.6	3 01.6	15.5	246 10.6	17.8	Peacock	53 19.2	S56 41.4
03	127 57.1	187 46.9	.. 55.1	304 15.1	.. 33.2	18 04.3	.. 15.5	261 12.8	.. 17.9	Pollux	243 27.0	N27 59.3
04	142 59.6	202 48.7	54.6	319 16.4	32.7	33 07.1	15.6	276 15.0	18.0	Procyon	244 59.1	N 5 11.1
05	158 02.1	217 50.4	54.0	334 17.7	32.2	48 09.8	15.6	291 17.2	18.0			
06	173 04.5	232 52.2	S21 53.5	349 19.0	N 0 31.7	63 12.6	N22 15.7	306 19.3	S15 18.1	Rasalhague	96 06.5	N12 33.2
07	188 07.0	247 54.0	52.9	4 20.3	31.3	78 15.4	15.7	321 21.5	18.2	Regulus	207 43.0	N11 53.7
S 08	203 09.5	262 55.8	52.4	19 21.6	30.8	93 18.1	15.7	336 23.7	18.2	Rigel	281 11.4	S 8 11.3
A 09	218 11.9	277 57.6	.. 51.8	34 22.9	.. 30.3	108 20.9	.. 15.8	351 25.9	.. 18.3	Rigil Kent.	139 51.7	S60 53.2
T 10	233 14.4	292 59.4	51.3	49 24.2	29.9	123 23.6	15.8	6 28.1	18.4	Sabik	102 12.5	S15 44.3
U 11	248 16.9	308 01.2	50.7	64 25.5	29.4	138 26.4	15.9	21 30.3	18.4			
R 12	263 19.3	323 03.0	S21 50.2	79 26.8	N 0 28.9	153 29.2	N22 15.9	36 32.5	S15 18.5	Schedar	349 39.8	N56 37.1
D 13	278 21.8	338 04.9	49.6	94 28.2	28.4	168 31.9	16.0	51 34.7	18.6	Shaula	96 21.9	S37 06.3
A 14	293 24.3	353 06.7	49.1	109 29.5	28.0	183 34.7	16.0	66 36.9	18.7	Sirius	258 33.1	S16 44.3
Y 15	308 26.7	8 08.5	.. 48.5	124 30.8	.. 27.5	198 37.4	.. 16.0	81 39.1	.. 18.7	Spica	158 31.1	S11 14.0
16	323 29.2	23 10.3	48.0	139 32.1	27.0	213 40.2	16.1	96 41.3	18.8	Suhail	222 51.9	S43 29.3
17	338 31.6	38 12.2	47.4	154 33.4	26.6	228 43.0	16.1	111 43.5	18.9			
18	353 34.1	53 14.0	S21 46.9	169 34.7	N 0 26.1	243 45.7	N22 16.2	126 45.7	S15 18.9	Vega	80 39.1	N38 48.1
19	8 36.6	68 15.8	46.3	184 36.0	25.6	258 48.5	16.2	141 47.9	19.0	Zuben'ubi	137 05.3	S16 05.8
20	23 39.0	83 17.7	45.8	199 37.3	25.2	273 51.2	16.3	156 50.1	19.1		SHA	Mer.Pass.
21	38 41.5	98 19.5	.. 45.2	214 38.7	.. 24.7	288 54.0	.. 16.3	171 52.3	.. 19.1	Venus	60 09.7	14 30
22	53 44.0	113 21.4	44.7	229 40.0	24.2	303 56.8	16.3	186 54.5	19.2	Mars	176 49.2	6 45
23	68 46.4	128 23.2	44.1	244 41.3	23.7	318 59.5	16.4	201 56.7	19.3	Jupiter	249 59.3	1 52
Mer.Pass. 18 29.6		v 1.7 d 0.5		v 1.3 d 0.5		v 2.8 d 0.0		v 2.2 d 0.1		Saturn	133 22.8	9 38

UT	SUN GHA	SUN Dec	MOON GHA	v	Dec	d	HP
d h	° ′	° ′	° ′	′	° ′	′	′
12 00	181 36.5	S23 04.0	63 55.4	12.3	N 8 55.9	9.7	56.6
01	196 36.2	04.2	78 26.7	12.3	9 05.6	9.6	56.5
02	211 35.9	04.4	92 58.0	12.3	9 15.2	9.5	56.5
03	226 35.6 ..	04.6	107 29.3	12.3	9 24.7	9.5	56.5
04	241 35.3	04.8	122 00.6	12.3	9 34.2	9.4	56.5
05	256 35.0	05.0	136 31.9	12.3	9 43.6	9.4	56.4
06	271 34.7	S23 05.1	151 03.2	12.3	N 9 53.0	9.4	56.4
T 07	286 34.4	05.3	165 34.5	12.3	10 02.4	9.2	56.4
H 08	301 34.2	05.5	180 05.8	12.3	10 11.6	9.2	56.4
U 09	316 33.9 ..	05.7	194 37.1	12.3	10 20.8	9.2	56.3
R 10	331 33.6	05.9	209 08.4	12.2	10 30.0	9.1	56.3
S 11	346 33.3	06.1	223 39.6	12.3	10 39.1	9.0	56.3
D 12	1 33.0	S23 06.2	238 10.9	12.3	N10 48.1	9.0	56.3
A 13	16 32.7	06.4	252 42.2	12.2	10 57.1	9.0	56.2
Y 14	31 32.4	06.6	267 13.4	12.3	11 06.1	8.8	56.2
15	46 32.1 ..	06.8	281 44.7	12.2	11 14.9	8.8	56.2
16	61 31.8	06.9	296 15.9	12.2	11 23.7	8.8	56.2
17	76 31.5	07.1	310 47.1	12.2	11 32.5	8.6	56.1
18	91 31.2	S23 07.3	325 18.3	12.2	N11 41.1	8.7	56.1
19	106 30.9	07.5	339 49.5	12.2	11 49.8	8.5	56.1
20	121 30.6	07.6	354 20.7	12.2	11 58.3	8.5	56.1
21	136 30.4 ..	07.8	8 51.9	12.2	12 06.8	8.4	56.0
22	151 30.1	08.0	23 23.1	12.2	12 15.2	8.4	56.0
23	166 29.8	08.2	37 54.3	12.1	12 23.6	8.3	56.0
13 00	181 29.5	S23 08.3	52 25.4	12.2	N12 31.9	8.2	56.0
01	196 29.2	08.5	66 56.6	12.1	12 40.1	8.2	56.0
02	211 28.9	08.7	81 27.7	12.2	12 48.3	8.1	55.9
03	226 28.6 ..	08.8	95 58.9	12.1	12 56.4	8.0	55.9
04	241 28.3	09.0	110 30.0	12.1	13 04.4	8.0	55.9
05	256 28.0	09.2	125 01.1	12.1	13 12.4	7.8	55.9
06	271 27.7	S23 09.3	139 32.2	12.0	N13 20.2	7.9	55.8
07	286 27.4	09.5	154 03.2	12.1	13 28.1	7.7	55.8
F 08	301 27.1	09.7	168 34.3	12.1	13 35.8	7.7	55.8
R 09	316 26.8 ..	09.8	183 05.4	12.0	13 43.5	7.6	55.8
I 10	331 26.5	10.0	197 36.4	12.0	13 51.1	7.5	55.8
D 11	346 26.2	10.1	212 07.4	12.0	13 58.6	7.5	55.7
A 12	1 25.9	S23 10.3	226 38.4	12.0	N14 06.1	7.4	55.7
Y 13	16 25.6	10.5	241 09.4	12.0	14 13.5	7.3	55.7
14	31 25.3	10.6	255 40.4	12.0	14 20.8	7.3	55.7
15	46 25.1 ..	10.8	270 11.4	12.0	14 28.1	7.1	55.6
16	61 24.8	10.9	284 42.4	11.9	14 35.2	7.1	55.6
17	76 24.5	11.1	299 13.3	11.9	14 42.3	7.1	55.6
18	91 24.2	S23 11.2	313 44.2	12.0	N14 49.4	6.9	55.6
19	106 23.9	11.4	328 15.2	11.9	14 56.3	6.9	55.5
20	121 23.6	11.6	342 46.1	11.9	15 03.2	6.8	55.5
21	136 23.3 ..	11.7	357 17.0	11.8	15 10.0	6.7	55.5
22	151 23.0	11.9	11 47.8	11.9	15 16.7	6.6	55.5
23	166 22.7	12.0	26 18.7	11.9	15 23.3	6.6	55.5
14 00	181 22.4	S23 12.2	40 49.6	11.8	N15 29.9	6.5	55.5
01	196 22.1	12.3	55 20.4	11.8	15 36.4	6.4	55.5
02	211 21.8	12.5	69 51.2	11.8	15 42.8	6.3	55.4
03	226 21.5 ..	12.6	84 22.0	11.8	15 49.1	6.2	55.4
04	241 21.2	12.8	98 52.8	11.8	15 55.3	6.2	55.4
05	256 20.9	12.9	113 23.6	11.8	16 01.5	6.1	55.4
06	271 20.6	S23 13.1	127 54.4	11.7	N16 07.6	6.0	55.3
S 07	286 20.3	13.2	142 25.1	11.8	16 13.6	5.9	55.3
A 08	301 20.0	13.3	156 55.9	11.7	16 19.5	5.8	55.3
T 09	316 19.7 ..	13.5	171 26.6	11.7	16 25.3	5.8	55.3
U 10	331 19.4	13.6	185 57.3	11.7	16 31.1	5.6	55.3
R 11	346 19.1	13.8	200 28.0	11.7	16 36.7	5.6	55.3
D 12	1 18.8	S23 13.9	214 58.7	11.7	N16 42.3	5.5	55.2
A 13	16 18.5	14.0	229 29.4	11.7	16 47.8	5.4	55.2
Y 14	31 18.2	14.2	244 00.1	11.6	16 53.2	5.4	55.2
15	46 17.9 ..	14.3	258 30.7	11.7	16 58.6	5.2	55.2
16	61 17.6	14.5	273 01.4	11.6	17 03.8	5.2	55.2
17	76 17.3	14.6	287 32.0	11.6	17 09.0	5.1	55.2
18	91 17.0	S23 14.7	302 02.6	11.6	N17 14.1	5.0	55.1
19	106 16.7	14.9	316 33.2	11.6	17 19.1	4.9	55.1
20	121 16.4	15.0	331 03.8	11.6	17 24.0	4.8	55.1
21	136 16.1 ..	15.1	345 34.4	11.6	17 28.8	4.7	55.1
22	151 15.8	15.3	0 05.0	11.5	17 33.5	4.7	55.1
23	166 15.5	15.4	14 35.5	11.6	N17 38.2	4.5	55.1
	SD 16.3	d 0.2	SD 15.3		15.2		15.1

Lat.	Twilight Naut.	Twilight Civil	Sunrise	Moonrise 12	13	14	15
°	h m	h m	h m	h m	h m	h m	h m
N 72	08 17	10 41	■	11 45	11 33	11 15	□
N 70	07 58	09 44	■	12 02	12 01	12 00	12 03
68	07 42	09 10	■	12 16	12 21	12 30	12 46
66	07 30	08 46	10 23	12 27	12 38	12 53	13 15
64	07 19	08 27	09 43	12 37	12 51	13 11	13 37
62	07 09	08 11	09 16	12 45	13 03	13 25	13 55
60	07 01	07 58	08 55	12 52	13 12	13 38	14 10
N 58	06 54	07 46	08 38	12 58	13 21	13 48	14 22
56	06 47	07 36	08 23	13 03	13 28	13 58	14 33
54	06 41	07 27	08 11	13 08	13 35	14 06	14 43
52	06 36	07 19	08 00	13 13	13 41	14 14	14 51
50	06 30	07 12	07 50	13 17	13 47	14 20	14 59
45	06 19	06 56	07 30	13 26	13 59	14 35	15 15
N 40	06 09	06 43	07 13	13 33	14 09	14 47	15 29
35	06 00	06 31	06 59	13 40	14 17	14 57	15 40
30	05 51	06 21	06 47	13 45	14 25	15 06	15 50
20	05 35	06 02	06 26	13 55	14 38	15 22	16 07
N 10	05 19	05 45	06 08	14 04	14 49	15 35	16 23
0	05 01	05 28	05 51	14 12	15 00	15 48	16 37
S 10	04 43	05 10	05 33	14 20	15 10	16 01	16 51
20	04 21	04 50	05 14	14 29	15 22	16 15	17 06
30	03 52	04 25	04 53	14 39	15 35	16 30	17 24
35	03 34	04 10	04 40	14 45	15 43	16 40	17 34
40	03 11	03 52	04 25	14 52	15 52	16 50	17 46
45	02 41	03 30	04 07	15 00	16 02	17 02	17 59
S 50	01 56	03 01	03 45	15 09	16 15	17 18	18 16
52	01 30	02 46	03 34	15 13	16 21	17 25	18 24
54	00 48	02 28	03 22	15 18	16 27	17 33	18 33
56	////	02 07	03 08	15 24	16 34	17 41	18 43
58	////	01 38	02 52	15 30	16 43	17 51	18 54
S 60	////	00 53	02 32	15 36	16 52	18 03	19 08

Lat.	Sunset	Twilight Civil	Twilight Naut.	Moonset 12	13	14	15
°	h m	h m	h m	h m	h m	h m	h m
N 72	■	13 07	15 31	03 55	05 46	07 45	□
N 70	■	14 04	15 50	03 39	05 20	07 01	08 39
68	■	14 38	16 06	03 27	05 01	06 31	07 56
66	13 25	15 02	16 19	03 17	04 45	06 09	07 28
64	14 05	15 21	16 29	03 09	04 32	05 52	07 06
62	14 32	15 37	16 39	03 02	04 22	05 38	06 49
60	14 53	15 51	16 47	02 56	04 13	05 26	06 34
N 58	15 11	16 03	16 55	02 50	04 05	05 16	06 22
56	15 25	16 12	17 01	02 45	03 58	05 07	06 11
54	15 37	16 21	17 07	02 41	03 51	04 59	06 02
52	15 48	16 29	17 13	02 37	03 46	04 52	05 54
50	15 58	16 36	17 18	02 34	03 41	04 45	05 46
45	16 19	16 52	17 29	02 26	03 30	04 31	05 30
N 40	16 35	17 06	17 40	02 20	03 21	04 20	05 17
35	16 49	17 17	17 49	02 14	03 13	04 10	05 06
30	17 01	17 28	17 58	02 10	03 06	04 02	04 56
20	17 22	17 46	18 14	02 01	02 55	03 47	04 40
N 10	17 41	18 04	18 30	01 54	02 44	03 35	04 25
0	17 58	18 21	18 47	01 47	02 35	03 23	04 11
S 10	18 15	18 38	19 05	01 40	02 25	03 11	03 58
20	18 34	18 59	19 28	01 33	02 15	02 58	03 43
30	18 56	19 23	19 57	01 25	02 04	02 44	03 27
35	19 09	19 39	20 15	01 20	01 57	02 36	03 17
40	19 24	19 57	20 38	01 15	01 49	02 26	03 06
45	19 42	20 19	21 08	01 09	01 41	02 15	02 53
S 50	20 04	20 48	21 53	01 01	01 30	02 02	02 37
52	20 15	21 03	22 20	00 58	01 25	01 55	02 30
54	20 27	21 21	23 03	00 54	01 20	01 48	02 22
56	20 41	21 42	////	00 50	01 14	01 41	02 13
58	20 57	22 11	////	00 46	01 07	01 32	02 02
S 60	21 17	22 58	////	00 41	01 00	01 22	01 51

Day	SUN Eqn. of Time 00h	12h	Mer. Pass.	MOON Mer. Pass. Upper	Lower	Age	Phase
d	m s	m s	h m	h m	h m	d	%
12	06 26	06 13	11 54	20 23	08 00	09	79
13	05 58	05 44	11 54	21 11	08 47	10	86
14	05 30	05 16	11 55	22 00	09 35	11	92

2013 DECEMBER 15, 16, 17 (SUN., MON., TUES.)

UT	ARIES GHA	VENUS −4.9 GHA	Dec	MARS +1.1 GHA	Dec	JUPITER −2.7 GHA	Dec	SATURN +0.6 GHA	Dec	STARS Name	SHA	Dec
15 00	83 48.9	143 25.1	S21 43.6	259 42.6	N 0 23.3	334 02.3	N22 16.4	216 58.9	S15 19.3	Acamar	315 17.8	S40 15.1
01	98 51.4	158 27.0	43.0	274 43.9	22.8	349 05.1	16.5	232 01.1	19.4	Achernar	335 26.3	S57 10.2
02	113 53.8	173 28.8	42.5	289 45.2	22.3	4 07.8	16.5	247 03.3	19.5	Acrux	173 08.9	S63 10.3
03	128 56.3	188 30.7 ..	41.9	304 46.5 ..	21.9	19 10.6 ..	16.6	262 05.5 ..	19.5	Adhara	255 11.9	S28 59.6
04	143 58.7	203 32.6	41.4	319 47.8	21.4	34 13.3	16.6	277 07.7	19.6	Aldebaran	290 48.6	N16 32.1
05	159 01.2	218 34.5	40.8	334 49.2	20.9	49 16.1	16.7	292 09.9	19.7			
06	174 03.7	233 36.3	S21 40.3	349 50.5	N 0 20.5	64 18.9	N22 16.7	307 12.1	S15 19.7	Alioth	166 20.7	N55 52.8
07	189 06.1	248 38.2	39.7	4 51.8	20.0	79 21.6	16.7	322 14.3	19.8	Alkaid	152 59.0	N49 14.4
08	204 08.6	263 40.1	39.2	19 53.1	19.5	94 24.4	16.8	337 16.5	19.9	Al Na'ir	27 43.6	S46 53.7
S 09	219 11.1	278 42.0 ..	38.6	34 54.4 ..	19.1	109 27.2 ..	16.8	352 18.7 ..	20.0	Alnilam	275 45.7	S 1 11.8
U 10	234 13.5	293 43.9	38.1	49 55.7	18.6	124 29.9	16.9	7 20.9	20.0	Alphard	217 55.5	S 8 43.3
N 11	249 16.0	308 45.8	37.5	64 57.1	18.1	139 32.7	16.9	22 23.1	20.1			
D 12	264 18.5	323 47.7	S21 37.0	79 58.4	N 0 17.7	154 35.5	N22 17.0	37 25.3	S15 20.2	Alphecca	126 11.1	N26 40.1
A 13	279 20.9	338 49.7	36.4	94 59.7	17.2	169 38.2	17.0	52 27.5	20.2	Alpheratz	357 43.0	N29 10.3
Y 14	294 23.4	353 51.6	35.9	110 01.0	16.7	184 41.0	17.0	67 29.7	20.3	Altair	62 08.2	N 8 54.6
15	309 25.9	8 53.5 ..	35.3	125 02.3 ..	16.3	199 43.8 ..	17.1	82 31.9 ..	20.4	Ankaa	353 15.3	S42 14.0
16	324 28.3	23 55.4	34.8	140 03.6	15.8	214 46.5	17.1	97 34.1	20.4	Antares	112 26.2	S26 27.6
17	339 30.8	38 57.4	34.2	155 05.0	15.3	229 49.3	17.2	112 36.3	20.5			
18	354 33.2	53 59.3	S21 33.7	170 06.3	N 0 14.8	244 52.1	N22 17.2	127 38.5	S15 20.6	Arcturus	145 55.7	N19 06.6
19	9 35.7	69 01.2	33.1	185 07.6	14.4	259 54.8	17.3	142 40.7	20.6	Atria	107 28.2	S69 02.9
20	24 38.2	84 03.2	32.6	200 08.9	13.9	274 57.6	17.3	157 42.9	20.7	Avior	234 17.3	S59 33.2
21	39 40.6	99 05.1 ..	32.0	215 10.2 ..	13.4	290 00.4 ..	17.4	172 45.1 ..	20.8	Bellatrix	278 31.3	N 6 21.6
22	54 43.1	114 07.1	31.5	230 11.5	13.0	305 03.1	17.4	187 47.3	20.8	Betelgeuse	271 00.6	N 7 24.4
23	69 45.6	129 09.0	30.9	245 12.9	12.5	320 05.9	17.4	202 49.5	20.9			
16 00	84 48.0	144 11.0	S21 30.4	260 14.2	N 0 12.1	335 08.7	N22 17.5	217 51.7	S15 21.0	Canopus	263 55.4	S52 42.3
01	99 50.5	159 12.9	29.8	275 15.5	11.6	350 11.4	17.5	232 53.9	21.0	Capella	280 33.4	N46 00.6
02	114 53.0	174 14.9	29.3	290 16.8	11.1	5 14.2	17.6	247 56.1	21.1	Deneb	49 31.5	N45 20.2
03	129 55.4	189 16.9 ..	28.7	305 18.1 ..	10.7	20 17.0 ..	17.6	262 58.3 ..	21.2	Denebola	182 33.3	N14 29.5
04	144 57.9	204 18.9	28.2	320 19.5	10.2	35 19.7	17.7	278 00.5	21.2	Diphda	348 55.5	S17 54.7
05	160 00.4	219 20.8	27.6	335 20.8	09.7	50 22.5	17.7	293 02.7	21.3			
06	175 02.8	234 22.8	S21 27.1	350 22.1	N 0 09.3	65 25.3	N22 17.8	308 04.9	S15 21.4	Dubhe	193 51.3	N61 40.1
07	190 05.3	249 24.8	26.5	5 23.4	08.8	80 28.0	17.8	323 07.1	21.4	Elnath	278 11.8	N28 37.0
08	205 07.7	264 26.8	26.0	20 24.7	08.3	95 30.8	17.8	338 09.3	21.5	Eltanin	90 46.5	N51 29.4
M 09	220 10.2	279 28.8 ..	25.4	35 26.1 ..	07.9	110 33.6 ..	17.9	353 11.5 ..	21.6	Enif	33 46.9	N 9 56.6
O 10	235 12.7	294 30.8	24.9	50 27.4	07.4	125 36.4	17.9	8 13.7	21.6	Fomalhaut	15 23.7	S29 32.9
N 11	250 15.1	309 32.8	24.3	65 28.7	06.9	140 39.1	18.0	23 15.9	21.7			
D 12	265 17.6	324 34.8	S21 23.8	80 30.0	N 0 06.5	155 41.9	N22 18.0	38 18.1	S15 21.8	Gacrux	172 00.5	S57 11.2
A 13	280 20.1	339 36.8	23.2	95 31.3	06.0	170 44.7	18.1	53 20.3	21.9	Gienah	175 52.0	S17 37.1
Y 14	295 22.5	354 38.8	22.7	110 32.7	05.5	185 47.4	18.1	68 22.5	21.9	Hadar	148 47.7	S60 26.1
15	310 25.0	9 40.9 ..	22.1	125 34.0 ..	05.1	200 50.2 ..	18.1	83 24.7 ..	22.0	Hamal	328 00.1	N23 31.8
16	325 27.5	24 42.9	21.6	140 35.3	04.6	215 53.0	18.2	98 26.9	22.1	Kaus Aust.	83 43.8	S34 22.5
17	340 29.9	39 44.9	21.0	155 36.6	04.1	230 55.8	18.2	113 29.2	22.1			
18	355 32.4	54 47.0	S21 20.5	170 37.9	N 0 03.7	245 58.5	N22 18.3	128 31.4	S15 22.2	Kochab	137 21.1	N74 05.7
19	10 34.9	69 49.0	19.9	185 39.3	03.2	261 01.3	18.3	143 33.6	22.3	Markab	13 38.0	N15 17.0
20	25 37.3	84 51.0	19.4	200 40.6	02.8	276 04.1	18.4	158 35.8	22.3	Menkar	314 14.4	N 4 08.6
21	40 39.8	99 53.1 ..	18.8	215 41.9 ..	02.3	291 06.8 ..	18.4	173 38.0 ..	22.4	Menkent	148 07.4	S36 26.1
22	55 42.2	114 55.1	18.3	230 43.3	01.8	306 09.6	18.5	188 40.2	22.5	Miaplacidus	221 38.9	S69 46.4
23	70 44.7	129 57.2	17.7	245 44.6	01.4	321 12.4	18.5	203 42.4	22.5			
17 00	85 47.2	144 59.2	S21 17.2	260 45.9	N 0 00.9	336 15.2	N22 18.5	218 44.6	S15 22.6	Mirfak	308 39.3	N49 54.7
01	100 49.6	160 01.3	16.6	275 47.2	N 00.4	351 17.9	18.6	233 46.8	22.7	Nunki	75 58.3	S26 16.6
02	115 52.1	175 03.4	16.1	290 48.6	00.0	6 20.7	18.6	248 49.0	.22.7	Peacock	53 19.2	S56 41.4
03	130 54.6	190 05.5 ..	15.5	305 49.9	S 00.5	21 23.5 ..	18.7	263 51.2 ..	22.8	Pollux	243 27.0	N27 59.3
04	145 57.0	205 07.5	15.0	320 51.2	01.0	36 26.3	18.7	278 53.4	22.9	Procyon	244 59.1	N 5 11.1
05	160 59.5	220 09.6	14.4	335 52.5	01.4	51 29.0	18.8	293 55.6	22.9			
06	176 02.0	235 11.7	S21 13.9	350 53.9	S 0 01.9	66 31.8	N22 18.8	308 57.8	S15 23.0	Rasalhague	96 06.5	N12 33.2
07	191 04.4	250 13.8	13.3	5 55.2	02.3	81 34.6	18.9	324 00.0	23.1	Regulus	207 43.0	N11 53.7
08	206 06.9	265 15.9	12.8	20 56.5	02.8	96 37.4	18.9	339 02.2	23.1	Rigel	281 11.4	S 8 11.3
T 09	221 09.4	280 18.0 ..	12.2	35 57.8 ..	03.3	111 40.1 ..	19.0	354 04.4 ..	23.2	Rigil Kent.	139 51.6	S60 53.2
U 10	236 11.8	295 20.1	11.7	50 59.2	03.7	126 42.9	19.0	9 06.6	23.3	Sabik	102 12.5	S15 44.3
E 11	251 14.3	310 22.2	11.2	66 00.5	04.2	141 45.7	19.0	24 08.8	23.3			
S 12	266 16.7	325 24.3	S21 10.6	81 01.8	S 0 04.6	156 48.5	N22 19.1	39 11.0	S15 23.4	Schedar	349 39.9	N56 37.1
D 13	281 19.2	340 26.4	10.1	96 03.2	05.1	171 51.2	19.1	54 13.2	23.5	Shaula	96 21.9	S37 06.6
A 14	296 21.7	355 28.5	09.5	111 04.5	05.6	186 54.0	19.2	69 15.4	23.5	Sirius	258 33.1	S16 44.3
Y 15	311 24.1	10 30.7 ..	09.0	126 05.8 ..	06.0	201 56.8 ..	19.2	84 17.6 ..	23.6	Spica	158 31.0	S11 14.0
16	326 26.6	25 32.8	08.4	141 07.1	06.5	216 59.6	19.3	99 19.8	23.7	Suhail	222 51.8	S43 29.3
17	341 29.1	40 34.9	07.9	156 08.5	07.0	232 02.3	19.3	114 22.0	23.7			
18	356 31.5	55 37.1	S21 07.3	171 09.8	S 0 07.4	247 05.1	N22 19.4	129 24.2	S15 23.8	Vega	80 39.1	N38 48.0
19	11 34.0	70 39.2	06.8	186 11.2	07.9	262 07.9	19.4	144 26.4	23.9	Zuben'ubi	137 05.3	S16 05.8
20	26 36.5	85 41.3	06.2	201 12.5	08.3	277 10.7	19.4	159 28.6	23.9		SHA	Mer. Pass.
21	41 38.9	100 43.5 ..	05.7	216 13.8 ..	08.8	292 13.5 ..	19.5	174 30.8 ..	24.0		° ′	h m
22	56 41.4	115 45.6	05.1	231 15.1	09.3	307 16.2	19.5	189 33.0	24.1	Venus	59 22.9	14 21
23	71 43.8	130 47.8	04.6	246 16.5	09.7	322 19.0	19.6	204 35.3	24.1	Mars	175 26.1	6 38
	h m									Jupiter	250 20.6	1 39
Mer. Pass. 18 17.8	v 2.0 d 0.5		v 1.3 d 0.5		v 2.8 d 0.0		v 2.2 d 0.1			Saturn	133 03.7	9 27

UT	SUN GHA	SUN Dec	MOON GHA	v	MOON Dec	d	HP
15 00	181 15.2	S23 15.5	29 06.1	11.5	N17 42.7	4.5	55.0
01	196 14.9	15.7	43 36.6	11.6	17 47.2	4.4	55.0
02	211 14.6	15.8	58 07.2	11.5	17 51.6	4.3	55.0
03	226 14.3	.. 15.9	72 37.7	11.5	17 55.9	4.2	55.0
04	241 14.0	16.1	87 08.2	11.5	18 00.1	4.1	55.0
05	256 13.7	16.2	101 38.7	11.5	18 04.2	4.0	55.0
S 06	271 13.4	S23 16.3	116 09.2	11.5	N18 08.2	3.9	54.9
U 07	286 13.1	16.4	130 39.7	11.5	18 12.1	3.9	54.9
N 08	301 12.8	16.6	145 10.2	11.5	18 16.0	3.8	54.9
D 09	316 12.5	.. 16.7	159 40.7	11.4	18 19.8	3.6	54.9
A 10	331 12.2	16.8	174 11.1	11.5	18 23.4	3.6	54.9
Y 11	346 11.9	16.9	188 41.6	11.4	18 27.0	3.5	54.9
12	1 11.6	S23 17.1	203 12.0	11.5	N18 30.5	3.4	54.8
13	16 11.3	17.2	217 42.5	11.4	18 33.9	3.3	54.8
14	31 11.0	17.3	232 12.9	11.5	18 37.2	3.2	54.8
15	46 10.7	.. 17.4	246 43.4	11.4	18 40.4	3.1	54.8
16	61 10.4	17.5	261 13.8	11.4	18 43.5	3.0	54.8
17	76 10.1	17.7	275 44.2	11.5	18 46.5	3.0	54.8
18	91 09.8	S23 17.8	290 14.7	11.4	N18 49.5	2.8	54.8
19	106 09.5	17.9	304 45.1	11.4	18 52.3	2.8	54.7
20	121 09.2	18.0	319 15.5	11.4	18 55.1	2.6	54.7
21	136 08.9	.. 18.1	333 45.9	11.5	18 57.7	2.6	54.7
22	151 08.6	18.2	348 16.4	11.4	19 00.3	2.4	54.7
23	166 08.3	18.3	2 46.8	11.4	19 02.7	2.4	54.7
16 00	181 08.0	S23 18.5	17 17.2	11.4	N19 05.1	2.3	54.7
01	196 07.7	18.6	31 47.6	11.4	19 07.4	2.2	54.7
02	211 07.4	18.7	46 18.0	11.4	19 09.6	2.1	54.7
03	226 07.1	.. 18.8	60 48.4	11.5	19 11.7	2.0	54.6
04	241 06.8	18.9	75 18.9	11.4	19 13.7	1.9	54.6
05	256 06.5	19.0	89 49.3	11.4	19 15.6	1.8	54.6
06	271 06.2	S23 19.1	104 19.7	11.4	N19 17.4	1.8	54.6
07	286 05.9	19.2	118 50.1	11.4	19 19.2	1.6	54.6
M 08	301 05.6	19.3	133 20.5	11.5	19 20.8	1.5	54.6
O 09	316 05.3	.. 19.4	147 51.0	11.4	19 22.3	1.5	54.6
N 10	331 05.0	19.5	162 21.4	11.4	19 23.8	1.3	54.5
N 11	346 04.7	19.6	176 51.8	11.5	19 25.1	1.3	54.5
D 12	1 04.4	S23 19.7	191 22.3	11.4	N19 26.4	1.2	54.5
A 13	16 04.1	19.8	205 52.7	11.5	19 27.6	1.0	54.5
Y 14	31 03.8	19.9	220 23.2	11.4	19 28.6	1.0	54.5
15	46 03.5	.. 20.0	234 53.6	11.5	19 29.6	0.9	54.5
16	61 03.2	20.1	249 24.1	11.5	19 30.5	0.8	54.5
17	76 02.9	20.2	263 54.6	11.5	19 31.3	0.7	54.5
18	91 02.6	S23 20.3	278 25.1	11.5	N19 32.0	0.6	54.5
19	106 02.3	20.4	292 55.6	11.5	19 32.6	0.5	54.4
20	121 02.0	20.5	307 26.1	11.5	19 33.1	0.4	54.4
21	136 01.7	.. 20.6	321 56.6	11.5	19 33.5	0.3	54.4
22	151 01.4	20.7	336 27.1	11.5	19 33.8	0.2	54.4
23	166 01.0	20.8	350 57.6	11.5	19 34.0	0.1	54.4
17 00	181 00.7	S23 20.9	5 28.1	11.6	N19 34.2	0.0	54.4
01	196 00.4	21.0	19 58.7	11.6	19 34.2	0.0	54.4
02	211 00.1	21.1	34 29.3	11.5	19 34.2	0.2	54.4
03	225 59.8	.. 21.2	48 59.8	11.6	19 34.0	0.2	54.3
04	240 59.5	21.3	63 30.4	11.6	19 33.8	0.3	54.3
05	255 59.2	21.3	78 01.0	11.7	19 33.5	0.5	54.3
06	270 58.9	S23 21.4	92 31.7	11.6	N19 33.0	0.5	54.3
07	285 58.6	21.5	107 02.3	11.6	19 32.5	0.6	54.3
T 08	300 58.3	21.6	121 32.9	11.7	19 31.9	0.7	54.3
U 09	315 58.0	.. 21.7	136 03.6	11.7	19 31.2	0.8	54.3
E 10	330 57.7	21.8	150 34.3	11.7	19 30.4	0.9	54.3
S 11	345 57.4	21.9	165 05.0	11.7	19 29.5	0.9	54.3
D 12	0 57.1	S23 21.9	179 35.7	11.7	N19 28.6	1.1	54.3
A 13	15 56.8	22.0	194 06.4	11.8	19 27.5	1.2	54.3
Y 14	30 56.5	22.1	208 37.2	11.7	19 26.3	1.2	54.2
15	45 56.2	.. 22.2	223 07.9	11.8	19 25.1	1.4	54.2
16	60 55.9	22.3	237 38.7	11.8	19 23.7	1.4	54.2
17	75 55.6	22.3	252 09.5	11.9	19 22.3	1.5	54.2
18	90 55.3	S23 22.4	266 40.4	11.8	N19 20.8	1.6	54.2
19	105 55.0	22.5	281 11.2	11.9	19 19.2	1.7	54.2
20	120 54.6	22.6	295 42.1	11.9	19 17.5	1.8	54.2
21	135 54.3	.. 22.7	310 13.0	11.9	19 15.7	1.9	54.2
22	150 54.0	22.7	324 43.9	11.9	19 13.8	2.0	54.2
23	165 53.7	22.8	339 14.8	12.0	N19 11.8	2.0	54.2
SD	16.3	d 0.1	SD 14.9	14.9	14.8		

Twilight / Sunrise / Moonrise

Lat.	Naut.	Civil	Sunrise	Moonrise 15	16	17	18
N 72	08 21	10 50	■	□	□	□	□
N 70	08 02	09 49	■	12 03	12 16	13 04	14 28
68	07 46	09 15	■	12 46	13 15	14 04	15 13
66	07 33	08 50	10 29	13 15	13 49	14 39	15 43
64	07 22	08 30	09 48	13 37	14 14	15 04	16 05
62	07 12	08 14	09 20	13 55	14 34	15 23	16 23
60	07 04	08 01	08 58	14 10	14 50	15 39	16 37
N 58	06 57	07 49	08 41	14 22	15 03	15 53	16 50
56	06 50	07 39	08 26	14 33	15 15	16 05	17 01
54	06 44	07 30	08 14	14 43	15 25	16 15	17 10
52	06 38	07 22	08 03	14 51	15 34	16 24	17 18
50	06 33	07 14	07 53	14 59	15 43	16 32	17 26
45	06 21	06 58	07 32	15 15	16 00	16 49	17 42
N 40	06 11	06 45	07 15	15 29	16 14	17 03	17 55
35	06 01	06 33	07 01	15 40	16 26	17 15	18 07
30	05 53	06 23	06 49	15 50	16 37	17 26	18 16
20	05 36	06 04	06 28	16 07	16 55	17 44	18 33
N 10	05 20	05 46	06 09	16 23	17 11	17 59	18 48
0	05 03	05 29	05 52	16 37	17 26	18 14	19 02
S 10	04 44	05 11	05 34	16 51	17 40	18 29	19 16
20	04 22	04 51	05 16	17 06	17 56	18 44	19 30
30	03 53	04 26	04 54	17 24	18 15	19 02	19 47
35	03 34	04 11	04 41	17 34	18 25	19 13	19 57
40	03 11	03 53	04 26	17 46	18 37	19 25	20 08
45	02 41	03 30	04 08	17 59	18 52	19 39	20 21
S 50	01 56	03 01	03 45	18 16	19 09	19 56	20 37
52	01 28	02 46	03 34	18 24	19 18	20 04	20 44
54	00 43	02 28	03 22	18 33	19 27	20 14	20 53
56	////	02 06	03 08	18 43	19 37	20 24	21 02
58	////	01 37	02 51	18 54	19 49	20 35	21 13
S 60	////	00 48	02 31	19 08	20 03	20 49	21 25

Sunset / Twilight / Moonset

Lat.	Sunset	Civil	Naut.	Moonset 15	16	17	18
N 72	■	13 02	15 30	□	□	□	□
N 70	■	14 02	15 50	08 39	10 08	11 01	11 17
68	■	14 37	16 05	07 56	09 09	10 11	10 31
66	13 22	15 02	16 18	07 28	08 35	09 26	10 01
64	14 04	15 21	16 29	07 06	08 10	09 01	09 39
62	14 32	15 37	16 39	06 49	07 50	08 41	09 21
60	14 53	15 51	16 47	06 34	07 34	08 25	09 06
N 58	15 10	16 02	16 55	06 22	07 21	08 12	08 53
56	15 25	16 12	17 02	06 11	07 09	08 00	08 42
54	15 38	16 21	17 08	06 02	06 59	07 50	08 33
52	15 49	16 30	17 13	05 54	06 50	07 40	08 24
50	15 59	16 37	17 19	05 46	06 42	07 32	08 16
45	16 19	16 53	17 30	05 30	06 25	07 15	08 00
N 40	16 36	17 07	17 41	05 17	06 11	07 01	07 46
35	16 50	17 18	17 50	05 06	05 59	06 49	07 34
30	17 02	17 29	17 59	04 56	05 48	06 38	07 24
20	17 24	17 48	18 15	04 40	05 31	06 20	07 07
N 10	17 42	18 05	18 31	04 25	05 15	06 04	06 52
0	17 59	18 22	18 48	04 11	05 00	05 49	06 37
S 10	18 17	18 40	19 07	03 58	04 46	05 34	06 23
20	18 36	19 00	19 30	03 43	04 30	05 18	06 08
30	18 58	19 25	19 59	03 27	04 12	05 00	05 50
35	19 11	19 41	20 17	03 17	04 02	04 49	05 40
40	19 26	19 59	20 40	03 06	03 50	04 37	05 28
45	19 44	20 21	21 11	02 53	03 36	04 23	05 14
S 50	20 06	20 51	21 56	02 37	03 19	04 05	04 57
52	20 17	21 06	22 24	02 30	03 10	03 57	04 49
54	20 29	21 24	23 09	02 22	03 02	03 48	04 40
56	20 44	21 46	////	02 13	02 51	03 37	04 30
58	21 00	22 16	////	02 02	02 40	03 25	04 19
S 60	21 21	23 05	////	01 51	02 27	03 11	04 05

SUN / MOON

Day	Eqn. of Time 00h	12h	Mer. Pass.	Mer. Pass. Upper	Lower	Age	Phase
	m s	m s	h m	h m	h m	d	%
15	05 02	04 47	11 55	22 49	10 24	12	97
16	04 33	04 18	11 56	23 37	11 13	13	99
17	04 04	03 49	11 56	24 26	12 02	14	100

UT	ARIES GHA	VENUS −4.8 GHA	Dec	MARS +1.0 GHA	Dec	JUPITER −2.7 GHA	Dec	SATURN +0.6 GHA	Dec	Star Name	SHA	Dec
18 00	86 46.3	145 50.0	S21 04.0	261 17.8	S 0 10.2	337 21.8	N22 19.6	219 37.5	S15 24.2	Acamar	315 17.8	S40 15.2
01	101 48.8	160 52.1	03.5	276 19.1	10.6	352 24.6	19.7	234 39.7	24.3	Achernar	335 26.3	S57 10.2
02	116 51.2	175 54.3	02.9	291 20.5	11.1	7 27.3	19.7	249 41.9	24.3	Acrux	173 08.9	S63 10.3
03	131 53.7	190 56.5	.. 02.4	306 21.8	.. 11.6	22 30.1	.. 19.8	264 44.1	.. 24.4	Adhara	255 11.9	S28 59.6
04	146 56.2	205 58.7	01.8	321 23.1	12.0	37 32.9	19.8	279 46.3	24.5	Aldebaran	290 48.6	N16 32.1
05	161 58.6	221 00.8	01.3	336 24.4	12.5	52 35.7	19.8	294 48.5	24.5			
W 06	177 01.1	236 03.0	S21 00.8	351 25.8	S 0 12.9	67 38.5	N22 19.9	309 50.7	S15 24.6	Alioth	166 20.6	N55 52.7
E 07	192 03.6	251 05.2	21 00.2	6 27.1	13.4	82 41.2	19.9	324 52.9	24.6	Alkaid	152 58.9	N49 14.4
D 08	207 06.0	266 07.4	20 59.7	21 28.4	13.8	97 44.0	20.0	339 55.1	24.7	Al Na'ir	27 43.6	S46 53.7
N 09	222 08.5	281 09.6	.. 59.1	36 29.8	.. 14.3	112 46.8	.. 20.0	354 57.3	.. 24.8	Alnilam	275 45.7	S 1 11.8
E 10	237 11.0	296 11.8	58.6	51 31.1	14.8	127 49.6	20.1	9 59.5	24.8	Alphard	217 55.5	S 8 43.3
S 11	252 13.4	311 14.0	58.0	66 32.4	15.2	142 52.4	20.1	25 01.7	24.9			
D 12	267 15.9	326 16.3	S20 57.5	81 33.8	S 0 15.7	157 55.1	N22 20.2	40 03.9	S15 25.0	Alphecca	126 11.0	N26 40.1
A 13	282 18.3	341 18.5	56.9	96 35.1	16.1	172 57.9	20.2	55 06.1	25.0	Alpheratz	357 43.1	N29 10.3
Y 14	297 20.8	356 20.7	56.4	111 36.5	16.6	188 00.7	20.3	70 08.3	25.1	Altair	62 08.2	N 8 54.5
15	312 23.3	11 22.9	.. 55.8	126 37.8	.. 17.1	203 03.5	.. 20.3	85 10.5	.. 25.2	Ankaa	353 15.3	S42 14.0
16	327 25.7	26 25.2	55.3	141 39.1	17.5	218 06.3	20.4	100 12.7	25.2	Antares	112 26.2	S26 27.6
17	342 28.2	41 27.4	54.7	156 40.5	18.0	233 09.1	20.4	115 14.9	25.3			
18	357 30.7	56 29.6	S20 54.2	171 41.8	S 0 18.4	248 11.8	N22 20.4	130 17.2	S15 25.4	Arcturus	145 55.6	N19 06.5
19	12 33.1	71 31.9	53.7	186 43.1	18.9	263 14.6	20.5	145 19.4	25.4	Atria	107 28.2	S69 02.9
20	27 35.6	86 34.1	53.1	201 44.5	19.3	278 17.4	20.5	160 21.6	25.5	Avior	234 17.3	S59 33.2
21	42 38.1	101 36.4	.. 52.6	216 45.8	.. 19.8	293 20.2	.. 20.6	175 23.8	.. 25.6	Bellatrix	278 31.3	N 6 21.6
22	57 40.5	116 38.6	52.0	231 47.1	20.3	308 23.0	20.6	190 26.0	25.6	Betelgeuse	271 00.6	N 7 24.4
23	72 43.0	131 40.9	51.5	246 48.5	20.7	323 25.7	20.7	205 28.2	25.7			
19 00	87 45.5	146 43.2	S20 50.9	261 49.8	S 0 21.2	338 28.5	N22 20.7	220 30.4	S15 25.8	Canopus	263 55.4	S52 42.3
01	102 47.9	161 45.4	50.4	276 51.1	21.6	353 31.3	20.7	235 32.6	25.8	Capella	280 33.4	N46 00.6
02	117 50.4	176 47.7	49.8	291 52.5	22.1	8 34.1	20.8	250 34.8	25.9	Deneb	49 31.5	N45 20.2
03	132 52.8	191 50.0	.. 49.3	306 53.8	.. 22.5	23 36.9	.. 20.8	265 37.0	.. 26.0	Denebola	182 33.3	N14 29.5
04	147 55.3	206 52.3	48.8	321 55.2	23.0	38 39.7	20.9	280 39.2	26.0	Diphda	348 55.5	S17 54.7
05	162 57.8	221 54.6	48.2	336 56.5	23.5	53 42.4	20.9	295 41.4	26.1			
T 06	178 00.2	236 56.9	S20 47.7	351 57.8	S 0 23.9	68 45.2	N22 21.0	310 43.6	S15 26.2	Dubhe	193 51.2	N61 40.1
H 07	193 02.7	251 59.2	47.1	6 59.2	24.4	83 48.0	21.0	325 45.8	26.2	Elnath	278 11.8	N28 37.0
U 08	208 05.2	267 01.5	46.6	22 00.5	24.8	98 50.8	21.1	340 48.0	26.3	Eltanin	90 46.5	N51 29.4
R 09	223 07.6	282 03.8	.. 46.0	37 01.9	.. 25.3	113 53.6	.. 21.1	355 50.2	.. 26.4	Enif	33 46.9	N 9 56.6
S 10	238 10.1	297 06.1	45.5	52 03.2	25.7	128 56.4	21.2	10 52.5	26.4	Fomalhaut	15 23.7	S29 32.9
D 11	253 12.6	312 08.4	44.9	67 04.5	26.2	143 59.2	21.2	25 54.7	26.5			
A 12	268 15.0	327 10.7	S20 44.4	82 05.9	S 0 26.6	159 01.9	N22 21.2	40 56.9	S15 26.5	Gacrux	172 00.5	S57 11.2
Y 13	283 17.5	342 13.1	43.9	97 07.2	27.1	174 04.7	21.3	55 59.1	26.6	Gienah	175 51.9	S17 37.1
14	298 20.0	357 15.4	43.3	112 08.6	27.6	189 07.5	21.3	71 01.3	26.7	Hadar	148 47.7	S60 26.1
15	313 22.4	12 17.7	.. 42.8	127 09.9	.. 28.0	204 10.3	.. 21.4	86 03.5	.. 26.7	Hamal	328 00.1	N23 31.8
16	328 24.9	27 20.1	42.2	142 11.2	28.5	219 13.1	21.4	101 05.7	26.8	Kaus Aust.	83 43.7	S34 22.5
17	343 27.3	42 22.4	41.7	157 12.6	28.9	234 15.9	21.5	116 07.9	26.9			
18	358 29.8	57 24.7	S20 41.1	172 13.9	S 0 29.4	249 18.7	N22 21.6	131 10.1	S15 26.9	Kochab	137 21.1	N74 05.7
19	13 32.3	72 27.1	40.6	187 15.3	29.8	264 21.4	21.6	146 12.3	27.0	Markab	13 38.0	N15 17.0
20	28 34.7	87 29.5	40.1	202 16.6	30.3	279 24.2	21.6	161 14.5	27.1	Menkar	314 14.4	N 4 08.6
21	43 37.2	102 31.8	.. 39.5	217 18.0	.. 30.7	294 27.0	.. 21.7	176 16.7	.. 27.1	Menkent	148 07.3	S36 26.1
22	58 39.7	117 34.2	39.0	232 19.3	31.2	309 29.8	21.7	191 19.0	27.2	Miaplacidus	221 38.8	S69 46.4
23	73 42.1	132 36.5	38.4	247 20.6	31.6	324 32.6	21.7	206 21.2	27.3			
20 00	88 44.6	147 38.9	S20 37.9	262 22.0	S 0 32.1	339 35.4	N22 21.8	221 23.4	S15 27.3	Mirfak	308 39.3	N49 54.7
01	103 47.1	162 41.3	37.4	277 23.3	32.5	354 38.2	21.8	236 25.6	27.4	Nunki	75 58.2	S26 16.6
02	118 49.5	177 43.7	36.8	292 24.7	33.0	9 41.0	21.9	251 27.8	27.5	Peacock	53 19.2	S56 41.4
03	133 52.0	192 46.1	.. 36.3	307 26.0	.. 33.5	24 43.7	.. 21.9	266 30.0	.. 27.5	Pollux	243 27.0	N27 59.3
04	148 54.4	207 48.5	35.7	322 27.4	33.9	39 46.5	22.0	281 32.2	27.6	Procyon	244 59.1	N 5 11.1
05	163 56.9	222 50.9	35.2	337 28.7	34.4	54 49.3	22.0	296 34.4	27.6			
F 06	178 59.4	237 53.3	S20 34.7	352 30.1	S 0 34.8	69 52.1	N22 22.1	311 36.6	S15 27.7	Rasalhague	96 06.5	N12 33.2
R 07	194 01.8	252 55.7	34.1	7 31.4	35.3	84 54.9	22.1	326 38.8	27.8	Regulus	207 43.0	N11 53.7
I 08	209 04.3	267 58.1	33.6	22 32.7	35.7	99 57.7	22.2	341 41.0	27.8	Rigel	281 11.4	S 8 11.3
D 09	224 06.8	283 00.5	.. 33.0	37 34.1	.. 36.2	115 00.5	.. 22.2	356 43.2	.. 27.9	Rigil Kent.	139 51.6	S60 53.2
A 10	239 09.2	298 02.9	32.5	52 35.4	36.6	130 03.3	22.2	11 45.5	28.0	Sabik	102 12.5	S15 44.3
Y 11	254 11.7	313 05.3	32.0	67 36.8	37.1	145 06.1	22.3	26 47.7	28.0			
12	269 14.2	328 07.8	S20 31.4	82 38.1	S 0 37.5	160 08.9	N22 22.3	41 49.9	S15 28.1	Schedar	349 39.9	N56 37.1
13	284 16.6	343 10.2	30.9	97 39.5	38.0	175 11.6	22.4	56 52.1	28.2	Shaula	96 21.8	S37 06.6
14	299 19.1	358 12.6	30.3	112 40.8	38.4	190 14.4	22.4	71 54.3	28.2	Sirius	258 33.0	S16 44.3
15	314 21.6	13 15.1	.. 29.8	127 42.2	.. 38.9	205 17.2	.. 22.5	86 56.5	.. 28.3	Spica	158 31.0	S11 14.0
16	329 24.0	28 17.5	29.3	142 43.5	39.3	220 20.0	22.5	101 58.7	28.4	Suhail	222 51.8	S43 29.3
17	344 26.5	43 20.0	28.7	157 44.9	39.8	235 22.8	22.6	117 00.9	28.4			
18	359 28.9	58 22.4	S20 28.2	172 46.2	S 0 40.2	250 25.6	N22 22.6	132 03.1	S15 28.5	Vega	80 39.1	N38 48.0
19	14 31.4	73 24.9	27.6	187 47.6	40.7	265 28.4	22.7	147 05.3	28.5	Zuben'ubi	137 05.3	S16 05.8
20	29 33.9	88 27.3	27.1	202 48.9	41.1	280 31.2	22.7	162 07.6	28.6		SHA	Mer. Pass.
21	44 36.3	103 29.8	.. 26.6	217 50.3	.. 41.6	295 34.0	.. 22.8	177 09.8	.. 28.7	Venus	58 57.7	14 11
22	59 38.8	118 32.3	26.0	232 51.6	42.0	310 36.8	22.8	192 12.0	28.7	Mars	174 04.4	6 32
23	74 41.3	133 34.8	25.5	247 53.0	42.5	325 39.6	22.8	207 14.2	28.8	Jupiter	250 43.1	1 26
Mer. Pass. 18 06.0		v 2.3	d 0.5	v 1.3	d 0.5	v 2.8	d 0.0	v 2.2	d 0.1	Saturn	132 44.9	9 17

UT	SUN GHA	SUN Dec	MOON GHA	v	Dec	d	HP
d h	° ′	° ′	° ′	′	° ′	′	′
18 00	180 53.4	S23 22.9	353 45.8	11.9	N19 09.8	2.2	54.2
01	195 53.1	23.0	8 16.7	12.0	19 07.6	2.2	54.2
02	210 52.8	23.0	22 47.7	12.1	19 05.4	2.3	54.1
03	225 52.5	.. 23.1	37 18.8	12.0	19 03.1	2.4	54.1
04	240 52.2	23.2	51 49.8	12.1	19 00.7	2.5	54.1
05	255 51.9	23.2	66 20.9	12.1	18 58.2	2.6	54.1
06	270 51.6	S23 23.3	80 52.0	12.1	N18 55.6	2.7	54.1
W 07	285 51.3	23.4	95 23.1	12.1	18 52.9	2.7	54.1
E 08	300 51.0	23.4	109 54.2	12.2	18 50.2	2.9	54.1
D 09	315 50.7	.. 23.5	124 25.4	12.2	18 47.3	2.9	54.1
N 10	330 50.4	23.6	138 56.6	12.2	18 44.4	3.0	54.1
E 11	345 50.1	23.6	153 27.8	12.3	18 41.4	3.1	54.1
S 12	0 49.7	S23 23.7	167 59.1	12.3	N18 38.3	3.2	54.1
D 13	15 49.4	23.8	182 30.4	12.3	18 35.1	3.3	54.1
A 14	30 49.1	23.8	197 01.7	12.3	18 31.8	3.3	54.1
Y 15	45 48.8	.. 23.9	211 33.0	12.4	18 28.5	3.4	54.1
16	60 48.5	23.9	226 04.4	12.4	18 25.1	3.6	54.1
17	75 48.2	24.0	240 35.8	12.4	18 21.5	3.6	54.1
18	90 47.9	S23 24.1	255 07.2	12.5	N18 17.9	3.6	54.0
19	105 47.6	24.1	269 38.7	12.4	18 14.3	3.8	54.0
20	120 47.3	24.2	284 10.1	12.5	18 10.5	3.9	54.0
21	135 47.0	.. 24.2	298 41.6	12.6	18 06.6	3.9	54.0
22	150 46.7	24.3	313 13.2	12.6	18 02.7	4.0	54.0
23	165 46.4	24.3	327 44.8	12.6	17 58.7	4.1	54.0
19 00	180 46.1	S23 24.4	342 16.4	12.6	N17 54.6	4.1	54.0
01	195 45.8	24.4	356 48.0	12.6	17 50.5	4.3	54.0
02	210 45.4	24.5	11 19.6	12.7	17 46.2	4.3	54.0
03	225 45.1	.. 24.5	25 51.3	12.8	17 41.9	4.4	54.0
04	240 44.8	24.6	40 23.1	12.7	17 37.5	4.5	54.0
05	255 44.5	24.6	54 54.8	12.8	17 33.0	4.6	54.0
06	270 44.2	S23 24.7	69 26.6	12.8	N17 28.4	4.6	54.0
T 07	285 43.9	24.7	83 58.4	12.8	17 23.8	4.7	54.0
H 08	300 43.6	24.8	98 30.2	12.9	17 19.1	4.8	54.0
U 09	315 43.3	.. 24.8	113 02.1	12.9	17 14.3	4.9	54.0
R 10	330 43.0	24.9	127 34.0	13.0	17 09.4	4.9	54.0
S 11	345 42.7	24.9	142 06.0	12.9	17 04.5	5.0	54.0
D 12	0 42.4	S23 25.0	156 37.9	13.0	N16 59.5	5.1	54.0
A 13	15 42.1	25.0	171 09.9	13.1	16 54.4	5.2	54.0
Y 14	30 41.8	25.1	185 42.0	13.0	16 49.2	5.2	54.0
15	45 41.4	.. 25.1	200 14.0	13.1	16 44.0	5.3	54.0
16	60 41.1	25.1	214 46.1	13.2	16 38.7	5.4	54.0
17	75 40.8	25.2	229 18.3	13.1	16 33.3	5.5	54.0
18	90 40.5	S23 25.2	243 50.4	13.2	N16 27.8	5.5	54.0
19	105 40.2	25.3	258 22.6	13.3	16 22.3	5.6	54.0
20	120 39.9	25.3	272 54.9	13.2	16 16.7	5.7	54.0
21	135 39.6	.. 25.3	287 27.1	13.3	16 11.0	5.7	54.0
22	150 39.3	25.4	301 59.4	13.3	16 05.3	5.8	54.0
23	165 39.0	25.4	316 31.7	13.4	15 59.5	5.9	54.0
20 00	180 38.7	S23 25.4	331 04.1	13.4	N15 53.6	5.9	54.0
01	195 38.4	25.5	345 36.5	13.4	15 47.7	6.0	54.0
02	210 38.0	25.5	0 08.9	13.4	15 41.7	6.1	54.0
03	225 37.7	.. 25.5	14 41.3	13.5	15 35.6	6.2	54.0
04	240 37.4	25.6	29 13.8	13.5	15 29.4	6.2	54.0
05	255 37.1	25.6	43 46.3	13.6	15 23.2	6.3	54.0
06	270 36.8	S23 25.6	58 18.9	13.5	N15 16.9	6.3	54.0
07	285 36.5	25.6	72 51.4	13.6	15 10.6	6.4	54.0
08	300 36.2	25.7	87 24.0	13.7	15 04.2	6.5	54.0
F 09	315 35.9	.. 25.7	101 56.7	13.6	14 57.7	6.5	54.0
R 10	330 35.6	25.7	116 29.3	13.7	14 51.2	6.7	54.0
I 11	345 35.3	25.8	131 02.0	13.8	14 44.5	6.6	54.0
D 12	0 35.0	S23 25.8	145 34.8	13.7	N14 37.9	6.8	54.0
A 13	15 34.6	25.8	160 07.5	13.8	14 31.1	6.7	54.0
Y 14	30 34.3	25.8	174 40.3	13.8	14 24.4	6.9	54.0
15	45 34.0	.. 25.8	189 13.1	13.9	14 17.5	6.9	54.0
16	60 33.7	25.9	203 46.0	13.8	14 10.6	7.0	54.0
17	75 33.4	25.9	218 18.8	14.0	14 03.6	7.0	54.0
18	90 33.1	S23 25.9	232 51.8	13.9	N13 56.6	7.1	54.0
19	105 32.8	25.9	247 24.7	13.9	13 49.5	7.2	54.0
20	120 32.5	26.0	261 57.6	14.0	13 42.3	7.2	54.0
21	135 32.2	.. 26.0	276 30.6	14.1	13 35.1	7.2	54.0
22	150 31.9	26.0	291 03.7	14.0	13 27.9	7.4	54.0
23	165 31.6	26.0	305 36.7	14.1	N13 20.5	7.4	54.0
	SD 16.3	d 0.0	SD 14.7		14.7		14.7

Lat.	Twilight Naut.	Twilight Civil	Sunrise	Moonrise 18	19	20	21
°	h m	h m	h m	h m	h m	h m	h m
N 72	08 24	10 56	▬	▭	15 12	17 07	18 52
N 70	08 04	09 53	▬	14 28	16 02	17 37	19 10
68	07 48	09 18	▬	15 13	16 33	17 58	19 24
66	07 35	08 52	10 33	15 43	16 56	18 15	19 35
64	07 24	08 33	09 51	16 05	17 14	18 29	19 45
62	07 15	08 17	09 22	16 23	17 29	18 40	19 53
60	07 06	08 03	09 01	16 37	17 42	18 50	20 00
N 58	06 59	07 51	08 43	16 50	17 52	18 58	20 06
56	06 52	07 41	08 29	17 01	18 01	19 06	20 12
54	06 46	07 32	08 16	17 10	18 10	19 12	20 17
52	06 40	07 24	08 05	17 18	18 17	19 18	20 21
50	06 35	07 16	07 55	17 26	18 24	19 24	20 25
45	06 23	07 00	07 34	17 42	18 38	19 35	20 34
N 40	06 13	06 47	07 17	17 55	18 50	19 45	20 41
35	06 03	06 35	07 03	18 07	18 59	19 53	20 47
30	05 54	06 24	06 51	18 16	19 08	20 00	20 52
20	05 38	06 05	06 29	18 33	19 23	20 13	21 02
N 10	05 22	05 48	06 11	18 48	19 36	20 23	21 10
0	05 05	05 31	05 53	19 02	19 48	20 34	21 18
S 10	04 46	05 13	05 36	19 16	20 01	20 44	21 25
20	04 23	04 52	05 17	19 30	20 14	20 54	21 33
30	03 54	04 27	04 55	19 47	20 28	21 07	21 43
35	03 35	04 12	04 42	19 57	20 37	21 14	21 48
40	03 12	03 54	04 27	20 08	20 47	21 22	21 54
45	02 41	03 31	04 09	20 21	20 58	21 31	22 01
S 50	01 56	03 01	03 46	20 37	21 12	21 42	22 09
52	01 28	02 46	03 35	20 44	21 18	21 48	22 13
54	00 41	02 28	03 23	20 53	21 26	21 53	22 17
56	////	02 06	03 09	21 02	21 34	22 00	22 22
58	////	01 36	02 52	21 13	21 42	22 07	22 27
S 60	////	00 46	02 31	21 25	21 53	22 15	22 33

Lat.	Sunset	Twilight Civil	Twilight Naut.	Moonset 18	19	20	21
°	h m	h m	h m	h m	h m	h m	h m
N 72	▬	12 59	15 30	▭	12 10	11 50	11 37
N 70	▬	14 01	15 50	11 17	11 20	11 20	11 18
68	▬	14 37	16 06	10 31	10 48	10 57	11 02
66	13 21	15 02	16 19	10 01	10 24	10 39	10 50
64	14 04	15 22	16 30	09 39	10 06	10 25	10 39
62	14 32	15 38	16 40	09 21	09 51	10 13	10 30
60	14 54	15 51	16 48	09 06	09 38	10 03	10 23
N 58	15 11	16 03	16 56	08 53	09 27	09 54	10 16
56	15 26	16 13	17 02	08 42	09 17	09 46	10 10
54	15 38	16 22	17 09	08 33	09 08	09 39	10 04
52	15 50	16 31	17 14	08 24	09 01	09 32	09 59
50	15 59	16 38	17 20	08 16	08 54	09 26	09 55
45	16 20	16 54	17 31	08 00	08 39	09 14	09 45
N 40	16 37	17 08	17 42	07 46	08 27	09 04	09 37
35	16 51	17 19	17 51	07 34	08 16	08 55	09 30
30	17 04	17 30	18 00	07 24	08 07	08 47	09 24
20	17 25	17 49	18 16	07 07	07 51	08 33	09 13
N 10	17 43	18 06	18 33	06 52	07 38	08 22	09 04
0	18 01	18 23	18 50	06 37	07 25	08 10	08 55
S 10	18 19	18 42	19 09	06 23	07 11	07 59	08 46
20	18 38	19 02	19 31	06 08	06 57	07 47	08 36
30	19 00	19 27	20 00	05 50	06 41	07 33	08 25
35	19 13	19 42	20 19	05 40	06 32	07 25	08 19
40	19 28	20 01	20 42	05 28	06 21	07 16	08 12
45	19 46	20 23	21 13	05 14	06 09	07 05	08 03
S 50	20 08	20 53	21 59	04 57	05 53	06 52	07 53
52	20 19	21 08	22 27	04 49	05 46	06 46	07 48
54	20 32	21 26	23 14	04 40	05 38	06 39	07 43
56	20 46	21 48	////	04 30	05 29	06 32	07 37
58	21 03	22 18	////	04 19	05 19	06 25	07 31
S 60	21 23	23 09	////	04 05	05 07	06 14	07 23

	SUN			MOON			
Day	Eqn. of Time 00ʰ	12ʰ	Mer. Pass.	Mer. Pass. Upper	Lower	Age	Phase
d	m s	m s	h m	h m	h m	d	%
18	03 34	03 20	11 57	00 26	12 50	15	99
19	03 05	02 50	11 57	01 13	13 36	16	96
20	02 35	02 20	11 58	01 59	14 22	17	91

2013 DECEMBER 21, 22, 23 (SAT., SUN., MON.)

UT	ARIES	VENUS −4.8		MARS +1.0		JUPITER −2.7		SATURN +0.6		STARS		
	GHA	GHA	Dec	GHA	Dec	GHA	Dec	GHA	Dec	Name	SHA	Dec
d h	° ′	° ′	° ′	° ′	° ′	° ′	° ′	° ′	° ′		° ′	° ′
21 00	89 43.7	148 37.2	S20 24.9	262 54.3	S 0 42.9	340 42.3	N22 22.9	222 16.4	S15 28.9	Acamar	315 17.8	S40 15.2
01	104 46.2	163 39.7	24.4	277 55.7	43.4	355 45.1	22.9	237 18.6	28.9	Achernar	335 26.3	S57 10.2
02	119 48.7	178 42.2	23.9	292 57.0	43.8	10 47.9	23.0	252 20.8	29.0	Acrux	173 08.8	S63 10.3
03	134 51.1	193 44.7 ..	23.3	307 58.4 ..	44.3	25 50.7 ..	23.0	267 23.0 ..	29.1	Adhara	255 11.8	S28 59.6
04	149 53.6	208 47.2	22.8	322 59.7	44.7	40 53.5	23.1	282 25.2	29.1	Aldebaran	290 48.6	N16 32.1
05	164 56.1	223 49.7	22.3	338 01.1	45.2	55 56.3	23.1	297 27.4	29.2			
06	179 58.5	238 52.2	S20 21.7	353 02.4	S 0 45.6	70 59.1	N22 23.2	312 29.7	S15 29.3	Alioth	166 20.6	N55 52.7
07	195 01.0	253 54.7	21.2	8 03.8	46.1	86 01.9	23.2	327 31.9	29.3	Alkaid	152 58.9	N49 14.4
S 08	210 03.4	268 57.3	20.7	23 05.1	46.5	101 04.7	23.3	342 34.1	29.4	Al Na'ir	27 43.6	S46 53.7
A 09	225 05.9	283 59.8 ..	20.1	38 06.5 ..	47.0	116 07.5 ..	23.3	357 36.3 ..	29.4	Alnilam	275 45.7	S 1 11.8
T 10	240 08.4	299 02.3	19.6	53 07.8	47.4	131 10.3	23.3	12 38.5	29.5	Alphard	217 55.5	S 8 43.3
U 11	255 10.8	314 04.8	19.0	68 09.2	47.9	146 13.1	23.4	27 40.8	29.5			
R 12	270 13.3	329 07.4	S20 18.5	83 10.5	S 0 48.3	161 15.9	N22 23.4	42 42.9	S15 29.6	Alphecca	126 11.0	N26 40.1
D 13	285 15.8	344 09.9	18.0	98 11.9	48.8	176 18.7	23.5	57 45.1	29.7	Alpheratz	357 43.1	N29 10.3
A 14	300 18.2	359 12.5	17.4	113 13.2	49.2	191 21.5	23.5	72 47.3	29.8	Altair	62 08.2	N 8 54.5
Y 15	315 20.7	14 15.0 ..	16.9	128 14.6 ..	49.7	206 24.3 ..	23.6	87 49.6 ..	29.8	Ankaa	353 15.3	S42 14.0
16	330 23.2	29 17.6	16.4	143 15.9	50.1	221 27.0	23.6	102 51.8	29.9	Antares	112 26.1	S26 27.6
17	345 25.6	44 20.1	15.8	158 17.3	50.6	236 29.8	23.7	117 54.0	29.9			
18	0 28.1	59 22.7	S20 15.3	173 18.7	S 0 51.0	251 32.6	N22 23.7	132 56.2	S15 30.0	Arcturus	145 55.6	N19 06.5
19	15 30.6	74 25.3	14.8	188 20.0	51.5	266 35.4	23.8	147 58.4	30.1	Atria	107 28.2	S69 02.9
20	30 33.0	89 27.8	14.2	203 21.4	51.9	281 38.2	23.8	163 00.6	30.1	Avior	234 17.2	S59 33.3
21	45 35.5	104 30.4 ..	13.7	218 22.7 ..	52.3	296 41.0 ..	23.9	178 02.8 ..	30.2	Bellatrix	278 31.3	N 6 21.6
22	60 37.9	119 33.0	13.2	233 24.1	52.8	311 43.8	23.9	193 05.0	30.3	Betelgeuse	271 00.6	N 7 24.4
23	75 40.4	134 35.6	12.6	248 25.4	53.2	326 46.6	23.9	208 07.3	30.3			
22 00	90 42.9	149 38.2	S20 12.1	263 26.8	S 0 53.7	341 49.4	N22 24.0	223 09.5	S15 30.4	Canopus	263 55.4	S52 42.3
01	105 45.3	164 40.8	11.6	278 28.1	54.1	356 52.2	24.0	238 11.7	30.5	Capella	280 33.4	N46 00.6
02	120 47.8	179 43.4	11.0	293 29.5	54.6	11 55.0	24.1	253 13.9	30.5	Deneb	49 31.6	N45 20.1
03	135 50.3	194 46.0 ..	10.5	308 30.9 ..	55.0	26 57.8 ..	24.1	268 16.1 ..	30.6	Denebola	182 33.3	N14 29.5
04	150 52.7	209 48.6	10.0	323 32.2	55.5	42 00.6	24.2	283 18.3	30.6	Diphda	348 55.5	S17 54.2
05	165 55.2	224 51.2	09.4	338 33.6	55.9	57 03.4	24.2	298 20.5	30.7			
06	180 57.7	239 53.8	S20 08.9	353 34.9	S 0 56.4	72 06.2	N22 24.3	313 22.7	S15 30.8	Dubhe	193 51.2	N61 40.1
07	196 00.1	254 56.4	08.4	8 36.3	56.8	87 09.0	24.3	328 25.0	30.8	Elnath	278 11.8	N28 37.0
08	211 02.6	269 59.1	07.9	23 37.6	57.3	102 11.8	24.4	343 27.2	30.9	Eltanin	90 46.5	N51 29.4
S 09	226 05.0	285 01.7 ..	07.3	38 39.0 ..	57.7	117 14.6 ..	24.4	358 29.4 ..	31.0	Enif	33 46.9	N 9 56.6
U 10	241 07.5	300 04.3	06.8	53 40.4	58.1	132 17.4	24.5	13 31.6	31.0	Fomalhaut	15 23.7	S29 32.9
N 11	256 10.0	315 07.0	06.3	68 41.7	58.6	147 20.2	24.5	28 33.8	31.1			
D 12	271 12.4	330 09.6	S20 05.7	83 43.1	S 0 59.0	162 23.0	N22 24.5	43 36.0	S15 31.1	Gacrux	172 00.5	S57 11.2
A 13	286 14.9	345 12.3	05.2	98 44.4	59.5	177 25.8	24.6	58 38.2	31.2	Gienah	175 51.9	S17 37.1
Y 14	301 17.4	0 14.9	04.7	113 45.8	0 59.9	192 28.6	24.6	73 40.5	31.2	Hadar	148 47.6	S60 26.1
15	316 19.8	15 17.6 ..	04.1	128 47.2	1 00.4	207 31.4 ..	24.7	88 42.7 ..	31.3	Hamal	328 00.1	N23 31.8
16	331 22.3	30 20.3	03.6	143 48.5	00.8	222 34.2	24.7	103 44.9	31.4	Kaus Aust.	83 43.7	S34 22.5
17	346 24.8	45 22.9	03.1	158 49.9	01.3	237 37.0	24.8	118 47.1	31.5			
18	1 27.2	60 25.6	S20 02.6	173 51.3	S 1 01.7	252 39.8	N22 24.8	133 49.3	S15 31.5	Kochab	137 21.0	N74 05.7
19	16 29.7	75 28.3	02.0	188 52.6	02.1	267 42.6	24.9	148 51.5	31.6	Markab	13 38.0	N15 17.0
20	31 32.2	90 31.0	01.5	203 54.0	02.6	282 45.4	24.9	163 53.7	31.6	Menkar	314 14.4	N 4 08.6
21	46 34.6	105 33.6 ..	01.0	218 55.3 ..	03.0	297 48.2 ..	25.0	178 55.9 ..	31.7	Menkent	148 07.3	S36 26.1
22	61 37.1	120 36.3	20 00.4	233 56.7	03.5	312 51.0	25.0	193 58.1	31.8	Miaplacidus	221 38.8	S69 46.4
23	76 39.5	135 39.0	19 59.9	248 58.1	03.9	327 53.8	25.1	209 00.4	31.8			
23 00	91 42.0	150 41.7	S19 59.4	263 59.4	S 1 04.4	342 56.6	N22 25.1	224 02.6	S15 31.9	Mirfak	308 39.4	N49 54.7
01	106 44.5	165 44.4	58.9	279 00.8	04.8	357 59.4	25.1	239 04.8	32.0	Nunki	75 58.2	S26 16.6
02	121 46.9	180 47.1	58.3	294 02.2	05.2	13 02.2	25.2	254 07.0	32.0	Peacock	53 19.2	S56 41.4
03	136 49.4	195 49.9 ..	57.8	309 03.5 ..	05.7	28 05.0 ..	25.2	269 09.2 ..	32.1	Pollux	243 27.0	N27 59.3
04	151 51.9	210 52.6	57.3	324 04.9	06.1	43 07.8	25.3	284 11.5	32.1	Procyon	244 59.0	N 5 11.1
05	166 54.3	225 55.3	56.8	339 06.2	06.6	58 10.6	25.3	299 13.7	32.2			
06	181 56.8	240 58.0	S19 56.2	354 07.6	S 1 07.0	73 13.4	N22 25.4	314 15.9	S15 32.3	Rasalhague	96 06.5	N12 33.2
07	196 59.3	256 00.8	55.7	9 09.0	07.5	88 16.2	25.4	329 18.1	32.3	Regulus	207 43.0	N11 53.7
08	212 01.7	271 03.5	55.2	24 10.3	07.9	103 19.0	25.5	344 20.3	32.4	Rigel	281 11.4	S 8 11.3
M 09	227 04.2	286 06.2 ..	54.7	39 11.7 ..	08.3	118 21.8 ..	25.5	359 22.5 ..	32.4	Rigil Kent.	139 51.6	S60 53.2
O 10	242 06.7	301 09.0	54.1	54 13.1	08.8	133 24.6	25.6	14 24.7	32.5	Sabik	102 12.5	S15 44.3
N 11	257 09.1	316 11.7	53.6	69 14.4	09.2	148 27.4	25.6	29 26.9	32.6			
D 12	272 11.6	331 14.5	S19 53.1	84 15.8	S 1 09.7	163 30.2	N22 25.7	44 29.2	S15 32.6	Schedar	349 39.9	N56 37.2
A 13	287 14.0	346 17.3	52.6	99 17.2	10.1	178 33.0	25.7	59 31.4	32.7	Shaula	96 21.8	S37 06.6
Y 14	302 16.5	1 20.0	52.0	114 18.5	10.5	193 35.8	25.8	74 33.6	32.8	Sirius	258 33.0	S16 44.3
15	317 19.0	16 22.8 ..	51.5	129 19.9 ..	11.0	208 38.6 ..	25.8	89 35.8 ..	32.8	Spica	158 31.0	S11 14.0
16	332 21.4	31 25.6	51.0	144 21.3	11.4	223 41.4	25.8	104 38.0	32.9	Suhail	222 51.8	S43 29.3
17	347 23.9	46 28.3	50.5	159 22.6	11.9	238 44.2	25.9	119 40.3	32.9			
18	2 26.4	61 31.1	S19 49.9	174 24.0	S 1 12.3	253 47.0	N22 25.9	134 42.5	S15 33.0	Vega	80 39.1	N38 48.0
19	17 28.8	76 33.9	49.4	189 25.4	12.7	268 49.8	26.0	149 44.7	33.1	Zuben'ubi	137 05.2	S16 05.8
20	32 31.3	91 36.7	48.9	204 26.7	13.2	283 52.6	26.0	164 46.9	33.1		SHA	Mer.Pass.
21	47 33.8	106 39.5 ..	48.4	219 28.1 ..	13.6	298 55.4 ..	26.1	179 49.1 ..	33.2		° ′	h m
22	62 36.2	121 42.3	47.9	234 29.5	14.1	313 58.2	26.1	194 51.3	33.2	Venus	58 55.3	13 59
23	77 38.7	136 45.1	47.3	249 30.9	14.5	329 01.0	26.2	209 53.6	33.3	Mars	172 43.9	6 26
	h m									Jupiter	251 06.5	1 12
Mer.Pass. 17 54.2	v 2.6 d 0.5		v 1.4 d 0.4		v 2.8 d 0.0		v 2.2 d 0.1		Saturn	132 26.6	9 06

SUN / MOON

UT	SUN GHA	SUN Dec	MOON GHA	v	MOON Dec	d	HP
d h	° ′	° ′	° ′	′	° ′	′	′
21 00	180 31.2	S23 26.0	320 09.8	14.1	N13 13.1	7.4	54.0
01	195 30.9	26.0	334 42.9	14.1	13 05.7	7.5	54.0
02	210 30.6	26.0	349 16.0	14.2	12 58.2	7.5	54.0
03	225 30.3 ..	26.0	3 49.2	14.1	12 50.7	7.6	54.0
04	240 30.0	26.1	18 22.3	14.2	12 43.1	7.7	54.1
05	255 29.7	26.1	32 55.5	14.3	12 35.4	7.7	54.1
06	270 29.4	S23 26.1	47 28.8	14.2	N12 27.7	7.8	54.1
07	285 29.1	26.1	62 02.0	14.3	12 19.9	7.8	54.1
S 08	300 28.8	26.1	76 35.3	14.3	12 12.1	7.9	54.1
A 09	315 28.5 ..	26.1	91 08.6	14.3	12 04.2	7.9	54.1
T 10	330 28.1	26.1	105 41.9	14.4	11 56.3	8.0	54.1
U 11	345 27.8	26.1	120 15.3	14.4	11 48.3	8.0	54.1
R 12	0 27.5	S23 26.1	134 48.7	14.4	N11 40.3	8.1	54.1
D 13	15 27.2	26.1	149 22.1	14.4	11 32.2	8.1	54.1
A 14	30 26.9	26.1	163 55.5	14.4	11 24.1	8.2	54.1
Y 15	45 26.6 ..	26.1	178 28.9	14.5	11 15.9	8.2	54.1
16	60 26.3	26.1	193 02.4	14.5	11 07.7	8.2	54.1
17	75 26.0	26.1	207 35.9	14.5	10 59.5	8.4	54.1
18	90 25.7	S23 26.1	222 09.4	14.5	N10 51.1	8.3	54.2
19	105 25.4	26.1	236 42.9	14.6	10 42.8	8.4	54.2
20	120 25.0	26.1	251 16.5	14.5	10 34.4	8.5	54.2
21	135 24.7 ..	26.1	265 50.0	14.6	10 25.9	8.5	54.2
22	150 24.4	26.1	280 23.6	14.6	10 17.4	8.5	54.2
23	165 24.1	26.1	294 57.2	14.6	10 08.9	8.6	54.2
22 00	180 23.8	S23 26.1	309 30.8	14.7	N10 00.3	8.7	54.2
01	195 23.5	26.1	324 04.5	14.6	9 51.7	8.7	54.2
02	210 23.2	26.1	338 38.1	14.7	9 43.0	8.7	54.2
03	225 22.9 ..	26.1	353 11.8	14.7	9 34.3	8.8	54.2
04	240 22.6	26.1	7 45.5	14.7	9 25.5	8.8	54.3
05	255 22.3	26.1	22 19.2	14.7	9 16.7	8.8	54.3
06	270 21.9	S23 26.1	36 52.9	14.7	N 9 07.9	8.9	54.3
07	285 21.6	26.0	51 26.6	14.7	8 59.0	8.9	54.3
08	300 21.3	26.0	66 00.3	14.8	8 50.1	9.0	54.3
S 09	315 21.0 ..	26.0	80 34.1	14.8	8 41.1	9.0	54.3
U 10	330 20.7	26.0	95 07.9	14.7	8 32.1	9.0	54.3
N 11	345 20.4	26.0	109 41.6	14.8	8 23.1	9.1	54.3
D 12	0 20.1	S23 26.0	124 15.4	14.8	N 8 14.0	9.1	54.4
A 13	15 19.8	26.0	138 49.2	14.8	8 04.9	9.2	54.4
Y 14	30 19.5	25.9	153 23.0	14.8	7 55.7	9.2	54.4
15	45 19.2 ..	25.9	167 56.8	14.9	7 46.5	9.2	54.4
16	60 18.8	25.9	182 30.7	14.8	7 37.3	9.3	54.4
17	75 18.5	25.9	197 04.5	14.8	7 28.0	9.2	54.4
18	90 18.2	S23 25.9	211 38.3	14.9	N 7 18.8	9.4	54.4
19	105 17.9	25.9	226 12.2	14.8	7 09.4	9.4	54.4
20	120 17.6	25.8	240 46.0	14.9	7 00.1	9.4	54.5
21	135 17.3 ..	25.8	255 19.9	14.9	6 50.7	9.5	54.5
22	150 17.0	25.8	269 53.8	14.8	6 41.2	9.4	54.5
23	165 16.7	25.8	284 27.6	14.9	6 31.8	9.5	54.5
23 00	180 16.4	S23 25.7	299 01.5	14.9	N 6 22.3	9.5	54.5
01	195 16.0	25.7	313 35.4	14.8	6 12.8	9.6	54.5
02	210 15.7	25.7	328 09.2	14.9	6 03.2	9.6	54.6
03	225 15.4 ..	25.7	342 43.1	14.9	5 53.6	9.6	54.6
04	240 15.1	25.6	357 17.0	14.9	5 44.0	9.6	54.6
05	255 14.8	25.6	11 50.9	14.8	5 34.4	9.7	54.6
06	270 14.5	S23 25.6	26 24.7	14.9	N 5 24.7	9.7	54.6
07	285 14.2	25.5	40 58.6	14.9	5 15.0	9.7	54.7
08	300 13.9	25.5	55 32.5	14.9	5 05.3	9.7	54.7
M 09	315 13.6 ..	25.5	70 06.4	14.8	4 55.6	9.8	54.7
O 10	330 13.3	25.4	84 40.2	14.9	4 45.8	9.8	54.7
N 11	345 12.9	25.4	99 14.1	14.8	4 36.0	9.8	54.7
D 12	0 12.6	S23 25.4	113 47.9	14.9	N 4 26.2	9.9	54.7
A 13	15 12.3	25.3	128 21.8	14.8	4 16.3	9.9	54.8
Y 14	30 12.0	25.3	142 55.6	14.9	4 06.4	9.9	54.8
15	45 11.7 ..	25.3	157 29.5	14.8	3 56.5	9.9	54.8
16	60 11.4	25.2	172 03.3	14.8	3 46.6	9.9	54.8
17	75 11.1	25.2	186 37.1	14.8	3 36.7	10.0	54.8
18	90 10.8	S23 25.2	201 10.9	14.8	N 3 26.7	10.0	54.9
19	105 10.5	25.1	215 44.7	14.8	3 16.7	10.0	54.9
20	120 10.1	25.1	230 18.5	14.8	3 06.7	10.0	54.9
21	135 09.8 ..	25.0	244 52.3	14.8	2 56.7	10.1	54.9
22	150 09.5	25.0	259 26.1	14.7	2 46.6	10.1	55.0
23	165 09.2	24.9	273 59.8	14.7	N 2 36.6	10.1	55.0
	SD 16.3	d 0.0	SD 14.7		14.8		14.9

Moonrise

Lat.	Twilight Naut.	Twilight Civil	Sunrise	21	22	23	24
°	h m	h m	h m	h m	h m	h m	h m
N 72	08 26	10 58	■	18 52	20 31	22 10	23 49
N 70	08 06	09 55	■	19 10	20 42	22 14	23 47
68	07 50	09 20	■	19 24	20 50	22 17	23 45
66	07 37	08 54	10 35	19 35	20 57	22 19	23 43
64	07 26	08 34	09 53	19 45	21 03	22 21	23 42
62	07 16	08 18	09 24	19 53	21 08	22 23	23 41
60	07 08	08 05	09 02	20 00	21 12	22 25	23 40
N 58	07 00	07 53	08 45	20 06	21 16	22 26	23 39
56	06 53	07 43	08 30	20 12	21 19	22 28	23 38
54	06 47	07 34	08 17	20 17	21 22	22 29	23 37
52	06 42	07 25	08 06	20 21	21 25	22 30	23 36
50	06 36	07 18	07 56	20 25	21 28	22 31	23 36
45	06 24	07 02	07 36	20 34	21 33	22 33	23 34
N 40	06 14	06 48	07 19	20 41	21 37	22 35	23 33
35	06 05	06 36	07 05	20 47	21 41	22 36	23 32
30	05 56	06 26	06 52	20 52	21 45	22 38	23 32
20	05 39	06 07	06 31	21 02	21 51	22 40	23 30
N 10	05 23	05 50	06 12	21 10	21 56	22 42	23 29
0	05 06	05 32	05 55	21 18	22 01	22 44	23 28
S 10	04 47	05 14	05 37	21 25	22 06	22 46	23 27
20	04 24	04 54	05 18	21 33	22 11	22 48	23 25
30	03 55	04 29	04 56	21 43	22 17	22 50	23 24
35	03 37	04 13	04 43	21 48	22 20	22 52	23 23
40	03 13	03 55	04 28	21 54	22 24	22 53	23 22
45	02 43	03 33	04 10	22 01	22 28	22 55	23 21
S 50	01 57	03 03	03 47	22 09	22 34	22 57	23 20
52	01 29	02 48	03 37	22 13	22 36	22 58	23 20
54	00 42	02 30	03 24	22 17	22 39	22 59	23 19
56	////	02 07	03 10	22 22	22 42	23 00	23 19
58	////	01 37	02 53	22 27	22 45	23 02	23 18
S 60	////	00 46	02 33	22 33	22 49	23 03	23 17

Moonset

Lat.	Sunset	Twilight Civil	Twilight Naut.	21	22	23	24
°	h m	h m	h m	h m	h m	h m	h m
N 72	■	12 59	15 31	11 37	11 28	11 19	11 11
N 70	■	14 02	15 51	11 18	11 16	11 13	11 10
68	■	14 38	16 07	11 02	11 06	11 08	11 10
66	13 22	15 03	16 20	10 50	10 58	11 04	11 09
64	14 05	15 23	16 31	10 39	10 51	11 00	11 09
62	14 33	15 39	16 41	10 30	10 45	10 57	11 09
60	14 55	15 53	16 50	10 23	10 39	10 54	11 08
N 58	15 12	16 04	16 57	10 16	10 35	10 52	11 08
56	15 27	16 15	17 04	10 10	10 31	10 50	11 08
54	15 40	16 24	17 10	10 04	10 27	10 48	11 08
52	15 51	16 32	17 16	09 59	10 24	10 46	11 07
50	16 01	16 39	17 21	09 55	10 20	10 44	11 07
45	16 22	16 56	17 33	09 45	10 14	10 41	11 07
N 40	16 39	17 09	17 43	09 37	10 08	10 38	11 07
35	16 53	17 21	17 53	09 30	10 03	10 35	11 06
30	17 05	17 32	18 01	09 24	09 59	10 33	11 06
20	17 26	17 50	18 18	09 13	09 51	10 29	11 06
N 10	17 45	18 08	18 34	09 04	09 45	10 25	11 05
0	18 02	18 25	18 51	08 55	09 38	10 22	11 05
S 10	18 20	18 43	19 10	08 46	09 32	10 18	11 04
20	18 39	19 04	19 33	08 36	09 25	10 14	11 04
30	19 01	19 29	20 02	08 25	09 18	10 10	11 03
35	19 14	19 44	20 21	08 19	09 13	10 08	11 03
40	19 29	20 02	20 44	08 12	09 08	10 05	11 03
45	19 47	20 25	21 15	08 03	09 02	10 02	11 02
S 50	20 10	20 55	22 00	07 53	08 55	09 58	11 02
52	20 21	21 10	22 28	07 48	08 52	09 56	11 02
54	20 33	21 28	23 15	07 43	08 48	09 54	11 01
56	20 47	21 50	////	07 37	08 44	09 52	11 01
58	21 04	22 20	////	07 31	08 39	09 49	11 01
S 60	21 25	23 11	////	07 23	08 34	09 47	11 00

Day	SUN Eqn. of Time 00h	SUN Eqn. of Time 12h	SUN Mer. Pass.	MOON Mer. Pass. Upper	MOON Mer. Pass. Lower	Age	Phase
d	m s	m s	h m	h m	h m	d	%
21	02 06	01 51	11 58		15 06	18	85
22	01 36	01 21	11 59	03 28	15 50	19	78
23	01 06	00 51	11 59	04 11	16 33	20	70

UT	ARIES	VENUS −4.7		MARS +0.9		JUPITER −2.7		SATURN +0.6		STARS		
	GHA	GHA	Dec	GHA	Dec	GHA	Dec	GHA	Dec	Name	SHA	Dec
d h	° ′	° ′	° ′	° ′	° ′	° ′	° ′	° ′	° ′		° ′	° ′
24 00	92 41.1	151 47.9	S19 46.8	264 32.2	S 1 14.9	344 03.8	N22 26.2	224 55.8	S15 33.4	Acamar	315 17.8	S40 15.2
01	107 43.6	166 50.7	46.3	279 33.6	15.4	359 06.6	26.3	239 58.0	33.4	Achernar	335 26.4	S57 10.2
02	122 46.1	181 53.6	45.8	294 35.0	15.8	14 09.4	26.3	255 00.2	33.5	Acrux	173 08.8	S63 10.3
03	137 48.5	196 56.4	. . 45.2	309 36.3	. . 16.3	29 12.2	. . 26.3	270 02.4	. . 33.6	Adhara	255 11.8	S28 59.6
04	152 51.0	211 59.2	44.7	324 37.7	16.7	44 15.0	26.4	285 04.6	33.6	Aldebaran	290 48.6	N16 32.1
05	167 53.5	227 02.1	44.2	339 39.1	17.1	59 17.9	26.4	300 06.9	33.7			
06	182 55.9	242 04.9	S19 43.7	354 40.4	S 1 17.6	74 20.7	N22 26.5	315 09.1	S15 33.7	Alioth	166 20.6	N55 52.7
07	197 58.4	257 07.7	43.2	9 41.8	18.0	89 23.5	26.5	330 11.3	33.8	Alkaid	152 58.9	N49 14.4
T 08	213 00.9	272 10.6	42.6	24 43.2	18.5	104 26.3	26.6	345 13.5	33.9	Al Na'ir	27 43.6	S46 53.7
U 09	228 03.3	287 13.4	. . 42.1	39 44.6	. . 18.9	119 29.1	. . 26.6	0 15.7	. . 33.9	Alnilam	275 45.7	S 1 11.8
E 10	243 05.8	302 16.3	41.6	54 45.9	19.3	134 31.9	26.7	15 17.9	34.0	Alphard	217 55.5	S 8 43.3
S 11	258 08.3	317 19.2	41.1	69 47.3	19.8	149 34.7	26.7	30 20.2	34.0			
D 12	273 10.7	332 22.0	S19 40.6	84 48.7	S 1 20.2	164 37.5	N22 26.8	45 22.4	S15 34.1	Alphecca	126 11.0	N26 40.1
A 13	288 13.2	347 24.9	40.1	99 50.1	20.6	179 40.3	26.8	60 24.6	34.2	Alpheratz	357 43.1	N29 10.3
Y 14	303 15.6	2 27.8	39.5	114 51.4	21.1	194 43.1	26.9	75 26.8	34.2	Altair	62 08.2	N 8 54.5
15	318 18.1	17 30.6	. . 39.0	129 52.8	. . 21.5	209 45.9	. . 26.9	90 29.0	. . 34.3	Ankaa	353 15.4	S42 14.0
16	333 20.6	32 33.5	38.5	144 54.2	21.9	224 48.7	27.0	105 31.2	34.3	Antares	112 26.1	S26 27.6
17	348 23.0	47 36.4	38.0	159 55.6	22.4	239 51.5	27.0	120 33.5	34.4			
18	3 25.5	62 39.3	S19 37.5	174 56.9	S 1 22.8	254 54.3	N22 27.0	135 35.7	S15 34.5	Arcturus	145 55.6	N19 06.5
19	18 28.0	77 42.2	37.0	189 58.3	23.3	269 57.1	27.1	150 37.9	34.5	Atria	107 28.1	S69 02.9
20	33 30.4	92 45.1	36.4	204 59.7	23.7	284 59.9	27.1	165 40.1	34.6	Avior	234 17.2	S59 33.3
21	48 32.9	107 48.0	. . 35.9	220 01.1	. . 24.1	300 02.7	. . 27.2	180 42.3	. . 34.7	Bellatrix	278 31.3	N 6 21.6
22	63 35.4	122 50.9	35.4	235 02.4	24.6	315 05.6	27.2	195 44.6	34.7	Betelgeuse	271 00.6	N 7 24.4
23	78 37.8	137 53.8	34.9	250 03.8	25.0	330 08.4	27.3	210 46.8	34.8			
25 00	93 40.3	152 56.8	S19 34.4	265 05.2	S 1 25.4	345 11.2	N22 27.3	225 49.0	S15 34.8	Canopus	263 55.4	S52 42.4
01	108 42.8	167 59.7	33.9	280 06.6	25.9	0 14.0	27.4	240 51.2	34.9	Capella	280 33.4	N46 00.6
02	123 45.2	183 02.6	33.4	295 07.9	26.3	15 16.8	27.4	255 53.4	35.0	Deneb	49 31.6	N45 20.1
03	138 47.7	198 05.6	. . 32.8	310 09.3	. . 26.7	30 19.6	. . 27.5	270 55.7	. . 35.0	Denebola	182 33.3	N14 29.5
04	153 50.1	213 08.5	32.3	325 10.7	27.2	45 22.4	27.5	285 57.9	35.1	Diphda	348 55.5	S17 54.7
05	168 52.6	228 11.4	31.8	340 12.1	27.6	60 25.2	27.6	301 00.1	35.1			
06	183 55.1	243 14.4	S19 31.3	355 13.5	S 1 28.0	75 28.0	N22 27.6	316 02.3	S15 35.2	Dubhe	193 51.1	N61 40.1
W 07	198 57.5	258 17.3	30.8	10 14.8	28.5	90 30.8	27.6	331 04.5	35.3	Elnath	278 11.8	N28 37.0
E 08	214 00.0	273 20.3	30.3	25 16.2	28.9	105 33.6	27.7	346 06.7	35.3	Eltanin	90 46.5	N51 29.4
D 09	229 02.5	288 23.3	. . 29.8	40 17.6	. . 29.4	120 36.4	. . 27.7	1 09.0	. . 35.4	Enif	33 47.0	N 9 56.5
N 10	244 04.9	303 26.2	29.3	55 19.0	29.8	135 39.2	27.8	16 11.2	35.4	Fomalhaut	15 23.7	S29 32.9
E 11	259 07.4	318 29.2	28.7	70 20.4	30.2	150 42.1	27.8	31 13.4	35.5			
S 12	274 09.9	333 32.2	S19 28.2	85 21.7	S 1 30.7	165 44.9	N22 27.9	46 15.6	S15 35.6	Gacrux	172 00.4	S57 11.2
D 13	289 12.3	348 35.2	27.7	100 23.1	31.1	180 47.7	27.9	61 17.8	35.6	Gienah	175 51.9	S17 37.1
A 14	304 14.8	3 38.1	27.2	115 24.5	31.5	195 50.5	28.0	76 20.1	35.7	Hadar	148 47.6	S60 26.1
Y 15	319 17.2	18 41.1	. . 26.7	130 25.9	. . 32.0	210 53.3	. . 28.0	91 22.3	. . 35.7	Hamal	328 00.1	N23 31.8
16	334 19.7	33 44.1	26.2	145 27.3	32.4	225 56.1	28.1	106 24.5	35.8	Kaus Aust.	83 43.7	S34 22.5
17	349 22.2	48 47.1	25.7	160 28.6	32.8	240 58.9	28.1	121 26.7	35.9			
18	4 24.6	63 50.1	S19 25.2	175 30.0	S 1 33.3	256 01.7	N22 28.2	136 28.9	S15 35.9	Kochab	137 21.0	N74 05.7
19	19 27.1	78 53.1	24.7	190 31.4	33.7	271 04.5	28.2	151 31.2	36.0	Markab	13 38.0	N15 17.0
20	34 29.6	93 56.1	24.2	205 32.8	34.1	286 07.3	28.3	166 33.4	36.0	Menkar	314 14.4	N 4 08.6
21	49 32.0	108 59.2	. . 23.6	220 34.2	. . 34.5	301 10.2	. . 28.3	181 35.6	. . 36.1	Menkent	148 07.3	S36 26.1
22	64 34.5	124 02.2	23.1	235 35.6	35.0	316 13.0	28.3	196 37.8	36.2	Miaplacidus	221 38.8	S69 46.4
23	79 37.0	139 05.2	22.6	250 36.9	35.4	331 15.8	28.4	211 40.1	36.2			
26 00	94 39.4	154 08.2	S19 22.1	265 38.3	S 1 35.8	346 18.6	N22 28.4	226 42.3	S15 36.3	Mirfak	308 39.4	N49 54.7
01	109 41.9	169 11.3	21.6	280 39.7	36.3	1 21.4	28.5	241 44.5	36.3	Nunki	75 58.2	S26 16.6
02	124 44.4	184 14.3	21.1	295 41.1	36.7	16 24.2	28.5	256 46.7	36.4	Peacock	53 19.2	S56 41.4
03	139 46.8	199 17.4	. . 20.6	310 42.5	. . 37.1	31 27.0	. . 28.6	271 48.9	. . 36.5	Pollux	243 26.9	N27 59.3
04	154 49.3	214 20.4	20.1	325 43.9	37.6	46 29.8	28.6	286 51.2	36.5	Procyon	244 59.0	N 5 11.1
05	169 51.7	229 23.5	19.6	340 45.2	38.0	61 32.6	28.7	301 53.4	36.6			
06	184 54.2	244 26.5	S19 19.1	355 46.6	S 1 38.4	76 35.5	N22 28.7	316 55.6	S15 36.6	Rasalhague	96 06.5	N12 33.2
07	199 56.7	259 29.6	18.6	10 48.0	38.9	91 38.3	28.8	331 57.8	36.7	Regulus	207 43.0	N11 53.7
T 08	214 59.1	274 32.6	18.1	25 49.4	39.3	106 41.1	28.8	347 00.0	36.8	Rigel	281 11.4	S 8 11.3
H 09	230 01.6	289 35.7	. . 17.6	40 50.8	. . 39.7	121 43.9	. . 28.9	2 02.3	. . 36.8	Rigil Kent.	139 51.5	S60 53.2
U 10	245 04.1	304 38.8	17.1	55 52.2	40.2	136 46.7	28.9	17 04.5	36.9	Sabik	102 12.5	S15 44.3
R 11	260 06.5	319 41.9	16.6	70 53.6	40.6	151 49.5	29.0	32 06.7	36.9			
S 12	275 09.0	334 45.0	S19 16.1	85 54.9	S 1 41.0	166 52.3	N22 29.0	47 08.9	S15 37.0	Schedar	349 39.9	N56 37.2
D 13	290 11.5	349 48.0	15.6	100 56.3	41.4	181 55.1	29.0	62 11.2	37.0	Shaula	96 21.8	S37 06.6
A 14	305 13.9	4 51.1	15.1	115 57.7	41.9	196 57.9	29.1	77 13.4	37.1	Sirius	258 33.0	S16 44.3
Y 15	320 16.4	19 54.2	. . 14.6	130 59.1	. . 42.3	212 00.8	. . 29.1	92 15.6	. . 37.2	Spica	158 31.0	S11 14.0
16	335 18.9	34 57.3	14.1	146 00.5	42.7	227 03.6	29.2	107 17.8	37.2	Suhail	222 51.8	S43 29.4
17	350 21.3	50 00.5	13.6	161 01.9	43.2	242 06.4	29.2	122 20.0	37.3			
18	5 23.8	65 03.6	S19 13.1	176 03.3	S 1 43.6	257 09.2	N22 29.3	137 22.3	S15 37.3	Vega	80 39.1	N38 48.0
19	20 26.2	80 06.7	12.6	191 04.7	44.0	272 12.0	29.3	152 24.5	37.4	Zuben'ubi	137 05.2	S16 05.8
20	35 28.7	95 09.8	12.1	206 06.1	44.4	287 14.8	29.4	167 26.7	37.5		SHA	Mer. Pass.
21	50 31.2	110 12.9	. . 11.6	221 07.4	. . 44.9	302 17.6	. . 29.4	182 28.9	. . 37.5		° ′	h m
22	65 33.6	125 16.1	11.1	236 08.8	45.3	317 20.5	29.5	197 31.2	37.6	Venus	59 16.5	13 46
23	80 36.1	140 19.2	10.6	251 10.2	45.7	332 23.3	29.5	212 33.4	37.6	Mars	171 24.9	6 19
	h m									Jupiter	251 30.9	0 59
Mer. Pass. 17 42.4		v 3.0	d 0.5	v 1.4	d 0.4	v 2.8	d 0.0	v 2.2	d 0.1	Saturn	132 08.7	8 55

UT	SUN GHA	SUN Dec	MOON GHA	v	MOON Dec	d	HP
d h	° '	° '	° '	'	° '	'	'
24 00	180 08.9	S23 24.9	288 33.5	14.8	N 2 26.5	10.1	55.0
01	195 08.6	24.9	303 07.3	14.7	2 16.4	10.2	55.0
02	210 08.3	24.8	317 41.0	14.7	2 06.2	10.1	55.0
03	225 08.0 ..	24.8	332 14.7	14.6	1 56.1	10.1	55.1
04	240 07.7	24.7	346 48.3	14.7	1 46.0	10.2	55.1
05	255 07.4	24.7	1 22.0	14.6	1 35.8	10.2	55.1
06	270 07.0	S23 24.6	15 55.6	14.6	N 1 25.6	10.2	55.1
07	285 06.7	24.6	30 29.2	14.6	1 15.4	10.2	55.2
08	300 06.4	24.5	45 02.8	14.6	1 05.2	10.2	55.2
T 09	315 06.1 ..	24.5	59 36.4	14.5	0 55.0	10.3	55.2
U 10	330 05.8	24.4	74 09.9	14.6	0 44.7	10.2	55.2
E 11	345 05.5	24.4	88 43.5	14.5	0 34.5	10.3	55.3
S 12	0 05.2	S23 24.3	103 17.0	14.4	N 0 24.2	10.3	55.3
D 13	15 04.9	24.2	117 50.4	14.5	0 13.9	10.2	55.3
A 14	30 04.6	24.2	132 23.9	14.4	N 0 03.7	10.3	55.3
Y 15	45 04.3 ..	24.1	146 57.3	14.4	S 0 06.6	10.3	55.4
16	60 03.9	24.1	161 30.7	14.4	0 16.9	10.4	55.4
17	75 03.6	24.0	176 04.1	14.3	0 27.3	10.3	55.4
18	90 03.3	S23 24.0	190 37.4	14.3	S 0 37.6	10.3	55.5
19	105 03.0	23.9	205 10.7	14.3	0 47.9	10.3	55.5
20	120 02.7	23.8	219 44.0	14.2	0 58.2	10.4	55.5
21	135 02.4 ..	23.8	234 17.2	14.2	1 08.6	10.3	55.5
22	150 02.1	23.7	248 50.4	14.2	1 18.9	10.4	55.6
23	165 01.8	23.6	263 23.6	14.2	1 29.3	10.3	55.6
25 00	180 01.5	S23 23.6	277 56.8	14.1	S 1 39.6	10.4	55.6
01	195 01.2	23.5	292 29.9	14.1	1 50.0	10.3	55.7
02	210 00.8	23.5	307 03.0	14.0	2 00.3	10.4	55.7
03	225 00.5 ..	23.4	321 36.0	14.0	2 10.7	10.3	55.7
04	240 00.2	23.3	336 09.0	13.9	2 21.0	10.4	55.7
05	254 59.9	23.3	350 41.9	14.0	2 31.4	10.4	55.8
06	269 59.6	S23 23.2	5 14.9	13.8	S 2 41.8	10.3	55.8
W 07	284 59.3	23.1	19 47.7	13.9	2 52.1	10.4	55.8
E 08	299 59.0	23.0	34 20.6	13.8	3 02.5	10.3	55.9
D 09	314 58.7 ..	23.0	48 53.4	13.7	3 12.8	10.4	55.9
N 10	329 58.4	22.9	63 26.1	13.7	3 23.2	10.4	55.9
E 11	344 58.1	22.8	77 58.8	13.7	3 33.6	10.3	56.0
S 12	359 57.7	S23 22.8	92 31.5	13.6	S 3 43.9	10.3	56.0
D 13	14 57.4	22.7	107 04.1	13.6	3 54.2	10.4	56.0
A 14	29 57.1	22.6	121 36.7	13.5	4 04.6	10.3	56.1
Y 15	44 56.8 ..	22.5	136 09.2	13.5	4 14.9	10.3	56.1
16	59 56.5	22.4	150 41.7	13.4	4 25.2	10.3	56.1
17	74 56.2	22.4	165 14.1	13.4	4 35.5	10.4	56.2
18	89 55.9	S23 22.3	179 46.5	13.3	S 4 45.9	10.2	56.2
19	104 55.6	22.2	194 18.8	13.3	4 56.1	10.3	56.2
20	119 55.3	22.1	208 51.1	13.2	5 06.4	10.3	56.3
21	134 55.0 ..	22.1	223 23.3	13.2	5 16.7	10.3	56.3
22	149 54.7	22.0	237 55.5	13.1	5 27.0	10.2	56.3
23	164 54.3	21.9	252 27.6	13.1	5 37.2	10.3	56.4
26 00	179 54.0	S23 21.8	266 59.7	13.0	S 5 47.5	10.2	56.4
01	194 53.7	21.7	281 31.7	12.9	5 57.7	10.2	56.4
02	209 53.4	21.6	296 03.6	12.9	6 07.9	10.2	56.5
03	224 53.1 ..	21.5	310 35.5	12.8	6 18.1	10.2	56.5
04	239 52.8	21.5	325 07.3	12.8	6 28.3	10.1	56.5
05	254 52.5	21.4	339 39.1	12.7	6 38.4	10.2	56.6
06	269 52.2	S23 21.3	354 10.8	12.6	S 6 48.6	10.1	56.6
07	284 51.9	21.2	8 42.4	12.6	6 58.7	10.1	56.6
T 08	299 51.6	21.1	23 14.0	12.5	7 08.8	10.1	56.7
H 09	314 51.3 ..	21.0	37 45.5	12.5	7 18.9	10.0	56.7
U 10	329 50.9	20.9	52 17.0	12.4	7 28.9	10.0	56.7
R 11	344 50.6	20.8	66 48.4	12.3	7 38.9	10.1	56.8
S 12	359 50.3	S23 20.7	81 19.7	12.3	S 7 49.0	9.9	56.8
D 13	14 50.0	20.6	95 51.0	12.1	7 58.9	10.0	56.9
A 14	29 49.7	20.5	110 22.1	12.2	8 08.9	9.9	56.9
Y 15	44 49.4 ..	20.4	124 53.3	12.0	8 18.8	9.9	56.9
16	59 49.1	20.4	139 24.3	12.0	8 28.7	9.9	57.0
17	74 48.8	20.3	153 55.3	11.9	8 38.6	9.9	57.0
18	89 48.5	S23 20.2	168 26.2	11.9	S 8 48.5	9.8	57.0
19	104 48.2	20.1	182 57.1	11.7	8 58.3	9.8	57.1
20	119 47.9	20.0	197 27.8	11.7	9 08.1	9.7	57.1
21	134 47.6 ..	19.9	211 58.5	11.6	9 17.8	9.8	57.2
22	149 47.2	19.8	226 29.1	11.6	9 27.6	9.6	57.2
23	164 46.9	19.7	240 59.7	11.5	S 9 37.2	9.7	57.2
SD	16.3	d 0.1	SD 15.1		15.3		15.5

Lat.	Twilight Naut.	Twilight Civil	Sunrise	Moonrise 24	Moonrise 25	Moonrise 26	Moonrise 27
°	h m	h m	h m	h m	h m	h m	h m
N 72	08 27	10 57	■	23 49	25 33	01 33	03 23
N 70	08 07	09 55	■	23 47	25 24	01 24	03 05
68	07 51	09 20	■	23 45	25 16	01 16	02 51
66	07 38	08 55	10 35	23 43	25 10	01 10	02 40
64	07 27	08 35	09 53	23 42	25 05	01 05	02 31
62	07 17	08 19	09 25	23 41	25 00	01 00	02 23
60	07 09	08 06	09 03	23 40	24 56	00 56	02 16
N 58	07 01	07 54	08 46	23 39	24 53	00 53	02 10
56	06 55	07 44	08 31	23 38	24 50	00 50	02 04
54	06 48	07 35	08 19	23 37	24 47	00 47	02 00
52	06 43	07 27	08 07	23 36	24 45	00 45	01 55
50	06 38	07 19	07 58	23 36	24 42	00 42	01 51
45	06 26	07 03	07 37	23 34	24 38	00 38	01 43
N 40	06 15	06 50	07 20	23 33	24 34	00 34	01 36
35	06 06	06 38	07 06	23 32	24 30	00 30	01 30
30	05 57	06 27	06 54	23 32	24 27	00 27	01 25
20	05 41	06 08	06 32	23 30	24 22	00 22	01 16
N 10	05 25	05 51	06 14	23 29	24 17	00 17	01 08
0	05 08	05 34	05 56	23 28	24 13	00 13	01 00
S 10	04 49	05 16	05 39	23 27	24 09	00 09	00 53
20	04 26	04 55	05 20	23 25	24 04	00 04	00 45
30	03 57	04 30	04 58	23 24	23 59	24 37	00 37
35	03 38	04 15	04 45	23 23	23 56	24 32	00 32
40	03 15	03 57	04 30	23 22	23 53	24 26	00 26
45	02 45	03 34	04 12	23 21	23 49	24 19	00 19
S 50	01 59	03 05	03 49	23 20	23 45	24 12	00 12
52	01 31	02 50	03 38	23 20	23 43	24 08	00 08
54	00 45	02 32	03 26	23 19	23 40	24 04	00 04
56	////	02 09	03 12	23 19	23 38	24 00	00 00
58	////	01 39	02 55	23 18	23 35	23 55	24 19
S 60	////	00 49	02 35	23 17	23 32	23 49	24 11

Lat.	Sunset	Twilight Civil	Twilight Naut.	Moonset 24	Moonset 25	Moonset 26	Moonset 27
°	h m	h m	h m	h m	h m	h m	h m
N 72	■	13 04	15 34	11 11	11 02	10 53	10 43
N 70	■	14 05	15 53	11 10	11 07	11 05	11 02
68	■	14 40	16 09	11 10	11 11	11 13	11 17
66	13 25	15 05	16 22	11 09	11 15	11 21	11 30
64	14 07	15 25	16 34	11 09	11 18	11 28	11 40
62	14 35	15 41	16 43	11 09	11 20	11 33	11 49
60	14 57	15 55	16 51	11 08	11 23	11 38	11 57
N 58	15 14	16 06	16 59	11 08	11 25	11 43	12 04
56	15 29	16 17	17 06	11 08	11 26	11 47	12 10
54	15 42	16 26	17 12	11 08	11 28	11 50	12 15
52	15 53	16 34	17 18	11 07	11 30	11 53	12 20
50	16 03	16 41	17 25	11 07	11 31	11 56	12 25
45	16 23	16 57	17 35	11 07	11 34	12 02	12 34
N 40	16 40	17 11	17 45	11 07	11 36	12 08	12 42
35	16 54	17 23	17 54	11 06	11 38	12 13	12 49
30	17 07	17 33	18 03	11 06	11 40	12 16	12 56
20	17 28	17 52	18 19	11 06	11 44	12 23	13 06
N 10	17 46	18 09	18 36	11 05	11 46	12 30	13 16
0	18 04	18 26	18 53	11 05	11 49	12 35	13 24
S 10	18 21	18 45	19 12	11 04	11 52	12 41	13 33
20	18 40	19 05	19 34	11 04	11 55	12 47	13 43
30	19 02	19 30	20 03	11 03	11 58	12 54	13 53
35	19 15	19 45	20 22	11 03	12 00	12 58	14 00
40	19 30	20 03	20 45	11 03	12 02	13 03	14 07
45	19 48	20 26	21 16	11 02	12 04	13 09	14 15
S 50	20 11	20 55	22 01	11 02	12 07	13 15	14 25
52	20 22	21 11	22 29	11 02	12 09	13 18	14 30
54	20 34	21 28	23 14	11 01	12 10	13 21	14 35
56	20 48	21 51	////	11 01	12 12	13 25	14 40
58	21 05	22 20	////	11 01	12 14	13 29	14 47
S 60	21 25	23 10	////	11 00	12 16	13 34	14 54

Day	SUN Eqn. of Time 00h	SUN Eqn. of Time 12h	SUN Mer. Pass.	MOON Mer. Pass. Upper	MOON Mer. Pass. Lower	MOON Age	MOON Phase
	m s	m s	h m	h m	h m	d	%
24	00 36	00 21	12 00	04 54	17 16	21	61
25	00 06	00 08	12 00	05 38	18 01	22	51
26	00 23	00 38	12 01	06 24	18 48	23	41

UT	ARIES	VENUS −4.6		MARS +0.9		JUPITER −2.7		SATURN +0.6		STARS		
	GHA	GHA	Dec	GHA	Dec	GHA	Dec	GHA	Dec	Name	SHA	Dec
d h	° ′	° ′	° ′	° ′	° ′	° ′	° ′	° ′	° ′		° ′	° ′
27 00	95 38.6	155 22.3	S19 10.1	266 11.6	S 1 46.2	347 26.1	N22 29.6	227 35.6	S15 37.7	Acamar	315 17.8	S40 15.2
01	110 41.0	170 25.5	09.6	281 13.0	46.6	2 28.9	29.6	242 37.8	37.8	Achernar	335 26.4	S57 10.2
02	125 43.5	185 28.6	09.1	296 14.4	47.0	17 31.7	29.6	257 40.1	37.8	Acrux	173 08.7	S63 10.3
03	140 46.0	200 31.8	08.6	311 15.8	47.4	32 34.5	29.7	272 42.3	37.9	Adhara	255 11.8	S28 59.7
04	155 48.4	215 34.9	08.1	326 17.2	47.9	47 37.3	29.7	287 44.5	37.9	Aldebaran	290 48.6	N16 32.1
05	170 50.9	230 38.1	07.6	341 18.6	48.3	62 40.1	29.8	302 46.7	38.0			
06	185 53.3	245 41.3	S19 07.1	356 20.0	S 1 48.7	77 43.0	N22 29.8	317 49.0	S15 38.0	Alioth	166 20.5	N55 52.7
07	200 55.8	260 44.4	06.6	11 21.4	49.1	92 45.8	29.9	332 51.2	38.1	Alkaid	152 58.8	N49 14.4
08	215 58.3	275 47.6	06.1	26 22.8	49.6	107 48.6	29.9	347 53.4	38.2	Al Na'ir	27 43.6	S46 53.7
F 09	231 00.7	290 50.8	05.6	41 24.2	50.0	122 51.4	30.0	2 55.6	38.2	Alnilam	275 45.6	S 1 11.8
R 10	246 03.2	305 54.0	05.1	56 25.6	50.4	137 54.2	30.0	17 57.8	38.3	Alphard	217 55.5	S 8 43.3
I 11	261 05.7	320 57.1	04.6	71 26.9	50.8	152 57.0	30.1	33 00.1	38.3			
D 12	276 08.1	336 00.3	S19 04.1	86 28.3	S 1 51.3	167 59.9	N22 30.1	48 02.3	S15 38.4	Alphecca	126 11.0	N26 40.0
A 13	291 10.6	351 03.5	03.6	101 29.7	51.7	183 02.7	30.2	63 04.5	38.5	Alpheratz	357 43.1	N29 10.3
Y 14	306 13.1	6 06.7	03.1	116 31.1	52.1	198 05.5	30.2	78 06.7	38.5	Altair	62 08.2	N 8 54.5
15	321 15.5	21 09.9	02.6	131 32.5	52.6	213 08.3	30.3	93 09.0	38.6	Ankaa	353 15.4	S42 14.0
16	336 18.0	36 13.1	02.1	146 33.9	53.0	228 11.1	30.3	108 11.2	38.6	Antares	112 26.1	S26 27.6
17	351 20.5	51 16.4	01.6	161 35.3	53.4	243 13.9	30.3	123 13.4	38.7			
18	6 22.9	66 19.6	S19 01.1	176 36.7	S 1 53.8	258 16.7	N22 30.4	138 15.6	S15 38.7	Arcturus	145 55.6	N19 06.5
19	21 25.4	81 22.8	00.6	191 38.1	54.2	273 19.6	30.4	153 17.9	38.8	Atria	107 28.1	S69 02.9
20	36 27.8	96 26.0	19 00.2	206 39.5	54.7	288 22.4	30.5	168 20.1	38.9	Avior	234 17.2	S59 33.3
21	51 30.3	111 29.3	18 59.7	221 40.9	55.1	303 25.2	30.5	183 22.3	38.9	Bellatrix	278 31.3	N 6 21.5
22	66 32.8	126 32.5	59.2	236 42.3	55.5	318 28.0	30.6	198 24.5	39.0	Betelgeuse	271 00.5	N 7 24.4
23	81 35.2	141 35.7	58.7	251 43.7	55.9	333 30.8	30.6	213 26.8	39.0			
28 00	96 37.7	156 39.0	S18 58.2	266 45.1	S 1 56.4	348 33.6	N22 30.7	228 29.0	S15 39.1	Canopus	263 55.4	S52 42.4
01	111 40.2	171 42.2	57.7	281 46.5	56.8	3 36.5	30.7	243 31.2	39.2	Capella	280 33.4	N46 00.6
02	126 42.6	186 45.5	57.2	296 47.9	57.2	18 39.3	30.8	258 33.5	39.2	Deneb	49 31.6	N45 20.1
03	141 45.1	201 48.7	56.7	311 49.3	57.6	33 42.1	30.8	273 35.7	39.3	Denebola	182 33.2	N14 29.5
04	156 47.6	216 52.0	56.2	326 50.7	58.1	48 44.9	30.9	288 37.9	39.3	Diphda	348 55.5	S17 54.7
05	171 50.0	231 55.3	55.7	341 52.1	58.5	63 47.7	30.9	303 40.1	39.4			
06	186 52.5	246 58.5	S18 55.3	356 53.5	S 1 58.9	78 50.5	N22 30.9	318 42.4	S15 39.4	Dubhe	193 51.1	N61 40.1
07	201 55.0	262 01.8	54.8	11 54.9	59.3	93 53.4	31.0	333 44.6	39.5	Elnath	278 11.8	N28 37.0
S 08	216 57.4	277 05.1	54.3	26 56.3	1 59.8	108 56.2	31.0	348 46.8	39.6	Eltanin	90 46.5	N51 29.4
A 09	231 59.9	292 08.4	53.8	41 57.7	2 00.2	123 59.0	31.1	3 49.0	39.6	Enif	33 47.0	N 9 56.5
T 10	247 02.3	307 11.7	53.3	56 59.1	00.6	139 01.8	31.1	18 51.3	39.7	Fomalhaut	15 23.7	S29 32.9
U 11	262 04.8	322 15.0	52.8	72 00.5	01.0	154 04.6	31.2	33 53.5	39.7			
R 12	277 07.3	337 18.3	S18 52.3	87 01.9	S 2 01.4	169 07.4	N22 31.2	48 55.7	S15 39.8	Gacrux	172 00.4	S57 11.2
D 13	292 09.7	352 21.6	51.9	102 03.3	01.9	184 10.3	31.3	63 57.9	39.8	Gienah	175 51.9	S17 37.1
A 14	307 12.2	7 24.9	51.4	117 04.7	02.3	199 13.1	31.3	79 00.2	39.9	Hadar	148 47.5	S60 26.1
Y 15	322 14.7	22 28.2	50.9	132 06.1	02.7	214 15.9	31.4	94 02.4	40.0	Hamal	328 00.1	N23 31.8
16	337 17.1	37 31.5	50.4	147 07.5	03.1	229 18.7	31.4	109 04.6	40.0	Kaus Aust.	83 43.7	S34 22.5
17	352 19.6	52 34.8	49.9	162 08.9	03.5	244 21.5	31.5	124 06.9	40.1			
18	7 22.1	67 38.1	S18 49.4	177 10.3	S 2 04.0	259 24.3	N22 31.5	139 09.1	S15 40.1	Kochab	137 20.9	N74 05.7
19	22 24.5	82 41.5	49.0	192 11.7	04.4	274 27.2	31.6	154 11.3	40.2	Markab	13 38.1	N15 17.0
20	37 27.0	97 44.8	48.5	207 13.1	04.8	289 30.0	31.6	169 13.5	40.2	Menkar	314 14.4	N 4 08.6
21	52 29.4	112 48.1	48.0	222 14.5	05.2	304 32.8	31.6	184 15.8	40.3	Menkent	148 07.3	S36 26.1
22	67 31.9	127 51.5	47.5	237 16.0	05.6	319 35.6	31.7	199 18.0	40.4	Miaplacidus	221 38.7	S69 46.4
23	82 34.4	142 54.8	47.0	252 17.4	06.1	334 38.4	31.7	214 20.2	40.4			
29 00	97 36.8	157 58.2	S18 46.5	267 18.8	S 2 06.5	349 41.3	N22 31.8	229 22.4	S15 40.5	Mirfak	308 39.4	N49 54.7
01	112 39.3	173 01.5	46.1	282 20.2	06.9	4 44.1	31.8	244 24.7	40.5	Nunki	75 58.2	S26 16.6
02	127 41.8	188 04.9	45.6	297 21.6	07.3	19 46.9	31.9	259 26.9	40.6	Peacock	53 19.2	S56 41.3
03	142 44.2	203 08.2	45.1	312 23.0	07.7	34 49.7	31.9	274 29.1	40.6	Pollux	243 26.9	N27 59.3
04	157 46.7	218 11.6	44.6	327 24.4	08.2	49 52.5	32.0	289 31.4	40.7	Procyon	244 59.0	N 5 11.1
05	172 49.2	233 15.0	44.2	342 25.8	08.6	64 55.4	32.0	304 33.6	40.8			
06	187 51.6	248 18.3	S18 43.7	357 27.2	S 2 09.0	79 58.2	N22 32.1	319 35.8	S15 40.8	Rasalhague	96 06.4	N12 33.1
07	202 54.1	263 21.7	43.2	12 28.6	09.4	95 01.0	32.1	334 38.0	40.9	Regulus	207 42.9	N11 53.7
08	217 56.6	278 25.1	42.7	27 30.0	09.8	110 03.8	32.2	349 40.3	40.9	Rigel	281 11.4	S 8 11.3
S 09	232 59.0	293 28.5	42.2	42 31.4	10.3	125 06.6	32.2	4 42.5	41.0	Rigil Kent.	139 51.5	S60 53.2
U 10	248 01.5	308 31.9	41.8	57 32.8	10.7	140 09.5	32.2	19 44.7	41.0	Sabik	102 12.4	S15 44.3
N 11	263 03.9	323 35.3	41.3	72 34.3	11.1	155 12.3	32.3	34 47.0	41.1			
D 12	278 06.4	338 38.7	S18 40.8	87 35.7	S 2 11.5	170 15.1	N22 32.3	49 49.2	S15 41.2	Schedar	349 39.9	N56 37.2
A 13	293 08.9	353 42.1	40.3	102 37.1	11.9	185 17.9	32.4	64 51.4	41.2	Shaula	96 21.8	S37 06.6
Y 14	308 11.3	8 45.5	39.9	117 38.5	12.3	200 20.7	32.4	79 53.7	41.3	Sirius	258 33.0	S16 44.3
15	323 13.8	23 48.9	39.4	132 39.9	12.8	215 23.5	32.5	94 55.9	41.3	Spica	158 30.9	S11 14.0
16	338 16.3	38 52.3	38.9	147 41.3	13.2	230 26.4	32.5	109 58.1	41.4	Suhail	222 51.8	S43 29.4
17	353 18.7	53 55.7	38.4	162 42.7	13.6	245 29.2	32.6	125 00.3	41.4			
18	8 21.2	68 59.2	S18 38.0	177 44.1	S 2 14.0	260 32.0	N22 32.6	140 02.6	S15 41.5	Vega	80 39.1	N38 48.0
19	23 23.7	84 02.6	37.5	192 45.5	14.4	275 34.8	32.7	155 04.8	41.5	Zuben'ubi	137 05.2	S16 05.8
20	38 26.1	99 06.0	37.0	207 47.0	14.8	290 37.7	32.7	170 07.0	41.6		SHA	Mer. Pass.
21	53 28.6	114 09.5	36.5	222 48.4	15.3	305 40.5	32.8	185 09.3	41.7		° ′	h m
22	68 31.1	129 12.9	36.1	237 49.8	15.7	320 43.3	32.8	200 11.5	41.7	Venus	60 01.3	13 30
23	83 33.5	144 16.3	35.6	252 51.2	16.1	335 46.1	32.9	215 13.7	41.8	Mars	170 07.4	6 12
	h m									Jupiter	251 55.9	0 46
Mer. Pass. 17 30.6		v 3.3	d 0.5	v 1.4	d 0.4	v 2.8	d 0.0	v 2.2	d 0.1	Saturn	131 51.3	8 45

UT	SUN		MOON					Lat.	Twilight		Sunrise	Moonrise			
									Naut.	Civil		27	28	29	30
	GHA	Dec	GHA	v	Dec	d	HP		h m	h m	h m	h m	h m	h m	h m
d h	° '	° '	° '	'	° '	'	'	N 72	08 26	10 52	▬	03 23	05 25	07 57	▬
27 00	179 46.6	S23 19.5	255 30.2	11.3	S 9 46.9	9.6	57.3	N 70	08 07	09 54	▬	03 05	04 54	06 50	08 50
01	194 46.3	19.4	270 00.5	11.4	9 56.5	9.6	57.3	68	07 51	09 19	▬	02 51	04 32	06 14	07 52
02	209 46.0	19.3	284 30.9	11.2	10 06.1	9.5	57.4	66	07 38	08 55	10 33	02 40	04 14	05 49	07 18
03	224 45.7	.. 19.2	299 01.1	11.2	10 15.6	9.5	57.4	64	07 27	08 35	09 52	02 31	04 00	05 29	06 53
04	239 45.4	19.1	313 31.3	11.0	10 25.1	9.5	57.4	62	07 18	08 19	09 25	02 23	03 48	05 13	06 34
05	254 45.1	19.0	328 01.3	11.1	10 34.6	9.4	57.5	60	07 09	08 06	09 03	02 16	03 38	05 00	06 18
06	269 44.8	S23 18.9	342 31.4	10.9	S10 44.0	9.4	57.5	N 58	07 02	07 55	08 46	02 10	03 29	04 48	06 04
07	284 44.5	18.8	357 01.3	10.8	10 53.4	9.3	57.6	56	06 55	07 44	08 32	02 04	03 21	04 38	05 53
08	299 44.2	18.7	11 31.1	10.8	11 02.7	9.3	57.6	54	06 49	07 35	08 19	02 00	03 14	04 30	05 43
F 09	314 43.9	.. 18.6	26 00.9	10.7	11 12.0	9.2	57.6	52	06 44	07 27	08 08	01 55	03 08	04 22	05 34
R 10	329 43.6	18.5	40 30.6	10.5	11 21.2	9.2	57.7	50	06 38	07 20	07 58	01 51	03 03	04 15	05 25
I 11	344 43.2	18.4	55 00.1	10.6	11 30.4	9.2	57.7	45	06 27	07 04	07 38	01 43	02 51	04 00	05 08
D 12	359 42.9	S23 18.2	69 29.7	10.4	S11 39.6	9.1	57.8	N 40	06 16	06 51	07 21	01 36	02 41	03 48	04 54
A 13	14 42.6	18.1	83 59.1	10.3	11 48.7	9.0	57.8	35	06 07	06 39	07 07	01 30	02 32	03 37	04 42
Y 14	29 42.3	18.0	98 28.4	10.3	11 57.7	9.0	57.8	30	05 59	06 28	06 55	01 25	02 25	03 28	04 32
15	44 42.0	.. 17.9	112 57.7	10.2	12 06.7	9.0	57.9	20	05 42	06 10	06 34	01 16	02 13	03 12	04 14
16	59 41.7	17.8	127 26.9	10.0	12 15.7	8.9	57.9	N 10	05 26	05 52	06 15	01 08	02 02	02 59	03 59
17	74 41.4	17.7	141 55.9	10.0	12 24.6	8.8	58.0	0	05 09	05 35	05 58	01 00	01 51	02 46	03 45
18	89 41.1	S23 17.6	156 24.9	9.9	S12 33.4	8.8	58.0	S 10	04 50	05 17	05 40	00 53	01 41	02 33	03 30
19	104 40.8	17.4	170 53.8	9.9	12 42.2	8.7	58.0	20	04 28	04 57	05 22	00 45	01 30	02 20	03 15
20	119 40.5	17.3	185 22.7	9.7	12 50.9	8.7	58.1	30	03 59	04 32	05 00	00 37	01 18	02 05	02 58
21	134 40.2	.. 17.2	199 51.4	9.6	12 59.6	8.6	58.1	35	03 40	04 17	04 47	00 32	01 11	01 56	02 48
22	149 39.9	17.1	214 20.0	9.6	13 08.2	8.5	58.2	40	03 17	03 59	04 32	00 26	01 03	01 46	02 36
23	164 39.6	17.0	228 48.6	9.5	13 16.7	8.5	58.2	45	02 47	03 37	04 14	00 19	00 54	01 34	02 22
28 00	179 39.3	S23 16.8	243 17.1	9.3	S13 25.2	8.4	58.2	S 50	02 02	03 07	03 51	00 12	00 43	01 20	02 06
01	194 38.9	16.7	257 45.4	9.3	13 33.6	8.4	58.3	52	01 35	02 52	03 41	00 08	00 38	01 13	01 58
02	209 38.6	16.6	272 13.7	9.2	13 42.0	8.2	58.3	54	00 50	02 34	03 28	00 04	00 32	01 06	01 50
03	224 38.3	.. 16.5	286 41.9	9.1	13 50.2	8.3	58.4	56	////	02 12	03 14	00 00	00 26	00 58	01 40
04	239 38.0	16.3	301 10.0	9.0	13 58.5	8.1	58.4	58	////	01 43	02 58	24 19	00 19	00 49	01 29
05	254 37.7	16.2	315 38.0	8.9	14 06.6	8.1	58.5	S 60	////	00 55	02 38	24 11	00 11	00 38	01 17

06	269 37.4	S23 16.1	330 05.9	8.9	S14 14.7	8.0	58.5	Lat.	Sunset	Twilight		Moonset			
07	284 37.1	15.9	344 33.8	8.7	14 22.7	7.9	58.5			Civil	Naut.	27	28	29	30
S 08	299 36.8	15.8	359 01.5	8.7	14 30.6	7.9	58.6								
A 09	314 36.5	.. 15.7	13 29.2	8.5	14 38.5	7.8	58.6	°	h m	h m	h m	h m	h m	h m	h m
T 10	329 36.2	15.6	27 56.7	8.5	14 46.3	7.7	58.7	N 72	▬	13 11	15 37	10 43	10 27	09 52	▬
U 11	344 35.9	15.4	42 24.2	8.3	14 54.0	7.6	58.7	N 70	▬	14 10	15 57	11 02	11 00	10 59	11 04
R 12	359 35.6	S23 15.3	56 51.5	8.3	S15 01.6	7.6	58.7	68	▬	14 44	16 12	11 17	11 24	11 36	12 02
D 13	14 35.3	15.2	71 18.8	8.2	15 09.2	7.5	58.8	66	13 30	15 09	16 25	11 30	11 42	12 02	12 36
A 14	29 35.0	15.0	85 46.0	8.0	15 16.7	7.4	58.8	64	14 11	15 28	16 36	11 40	11 57	12 22	13 01
Y 15	44 34.7	.. 14.9	100 13.0	8.0	15 24.1	7.3	58.9	62	14 39	15 44	16 46	11 49	12 10	12 39	13 21
16	59 34.4	14.8	114 40.0	7.9	15 31.4	7.2	58.9	60	15 00	15 57	16 54	11 57	12 21	12 53	13 37
17	74 34.1	14.6	129 06.9	7.8	15 38.6	7.2	58.9	N 58	15 17	16 09	17 01	12 04	12 30	13 05	13 51
18	89 33.7	S23 14.5	143 33.7	7.7	S15 45.8	7.0	59.0	56	15 32	16 19	17 08	12 10	12 38	13 15	14 03
19	104 33.4	14.3	158 00.4	7.7	15 52.8	7.0	59.0	54	15 44	16 28	17 14	12 15	12 46	13 24	14 13
20	119 33.1	14.2	172 27.1	7.5	15 59.8	6.9	59.1	52	15 55	16 36	17 20	12 20	12 52	13 32	14 22
21	134 32.8	.. 14.1	186 53.6	7.4	16 06.7	6.8	59.1	50	16 05	16 43	17 25	12 25	12 58	13 39	14 30
22	149 32.5	13.9	201 20.0	7.4	16 13.5	6.7	59.1	45	16 26	16 59	17 37	12 34	13 11	13 55	14 48
23	164 32.2	13.8	215 46.4	7.2	16 20.2	6.6	59.2								
29 00	179 31.9	S23 13.6	230 12.6	7.1	S16 26.8	6.5	59.2	N 40	16 42	17 13	17 47	12 42	13 22	14 08	15 02
01	194 31.6	13.5	244 38.7	7.1	16 33.3	6.4	59.3	35	16 56	17 24	17 56	12 49	13 31	14 19	15 14
02	209 31.3	13.4	259 04.8	7.0	16 39.7	6.3	59.3	30	17 09	17 35	18 05	12 56	13 39	14 29	15 25
03	224 31.0	.. 13.2	273 30.8	6.9	16 46.0	6.2	59.3	20	17 30	17 54	18 21	13 06	13 53	14 45	15 43
04	239 30.7	13.1	287 56.7	6.7	16 52.2	6.2	59.4	N 10	17 48	18 11	18 37	13 16	14 05	15 00	15 59
05	254 30.4	12.9	302 22.4	6.7	16 58.4	6.0	59.4	0	18 05	18 28	18 54	13 24	14 17	15 13	16 14
06	269 30.1	S23 12.8	316 48.1	6.6	S17 04.4	5.9	59.5	S 10	18 23	18 46	19 13	13 33	14 28	15 27	16 28
07	284 29.8	12.6	331 13.7	6.6	17 10.3	5.8	59.5	20	18 42	19 06	19 35	13 43	14 41	15 42	16 44
08	299 29.5	12.5	345 39.3	6.4	17 16.1	5.7	59.5	30	19 04	19 31	20 04	13 55	14 55	15 58	17 02
S 09	314 29.2	.. 12.3	0 04.7	6.3	17 21.8	5.6	59.6	35	19 16	19 46	20 23	14 00	15 03	16 08	17 13
U 10	329 28.9	12.2	14 30.0	6.3	17 27.4	5.5	59.6	40	19 31	20 04	20 46	14 07	15 12	16 19	17 25
N 11	344 28.6	12.0	28 55.3	6.1	17 32.9	5.4	59.7	45	19 49	20 26	21 16	14 15	15 23	16 32	17 39
D 12	359 28.3	S23 11.9	43 20.4	6.1	S17 38.3	5.3	59.7	S 50	20 12	20 56	22 01	14 25	15 37	16 48	17 57
A 13	14 28.0	11.7	57 45.5	6.0	17 43.6	5.2	59.7	52	20 22	21 11	22 28	14 30	15 43	16 56	18 05
Y 14	29 27.7	11.6	72 10.5	5.9	17 48.8	5.0	59.8	54	20 34	21 28	23 11	14 35	15 50	17 04	18 14
15	44 27.4	.. 11.4	86 35.4	5.8	17 53.8	5.0	59.8	56	20 48	21 50	////	14 40	15 57	17 13	18 24
16	59 27.1	11.3	101 00.2	5.8	17 58.8	4.8	59.8	58	21 05	22 19	////	14 47	16 06	17 24	18 36
17	74 26.7	11.1	115 25.0	5.6	18 03.6	4.7	59.9	S 60	21 25	23 06	////	14 54	16 16	17 36	18 49
18	89 26.4	S23 10.9	129 49.6	5.6	S18 08.3	4.6	59.9								
19	104 26.1	10.8	144 14.2	5.5	18 12.9	4.5	59.9			SUN		MOON			
20	119 25.8	10.6	158 38.7	5.3	18 17.4	4.4	60.0	Day	Eqn. of Time		Mer.	Mer. Pass.		Age	Phase
21	134 25.5	.. 10.5	173 03.1	5.3	18 21.8	4.2	60.0		00h	12h	Pass.	Upper	Lower		
22	149 25.2	10.3	187 27.4	5.3	18 26.0	4.1	60.1	d	m s	m s	h m	h m	h m	d %	
23	164 24.9	10.1	201 51.7	5.2	S18 30.1	4.0	60.1	27	00 53	01 08	12 01	02 11	19 38	24 31	
								28	01 22	01 37	12 02	08 04	20 31	25 21	
	SD 16.3	d 0.1	SD 15.7		16.0		16.3	29	01 52	02 06	12 02	09 00	21 29	26 13	

UT	ARIES GHA	VENUS −4.4 GHA	Dec	MARS +0.9 GHA	Dec	JUPITER −2.7 GHA	Dec	SATURN +0.6 GHA	Dec	STARS Name	SHA	Dec
30 00	98 36.0	159 19.8	S18 35.1	267 52.6	S 2 16.5	350 48.9	N22 32.9	230 16.0	S15 41.8	Acamar	315 17.8	S40 15.2
01	113 38.4	174 23.2	34.7	282 54.0	16.9	5 51.8	32.9	245 18.2	41.9	Achernar	335 26.4	S57 10.2
02	128 40.9	189 26.7	34.2	297 55.4	17.3	20 54.6	33.0	260 20.4	41.9	Acrux	173 08.7	S63 10.4
03	143 43.4	204 30.2	.. 33.7	312 56.9	.. 17.8	35 57.4	.. 33.0	275 22.6	.. 42.0	Adhara	255 11.8	S28 59.7
04	158 45.8	219 33.6	33.3	327 58.3	18.2	51 00.2	33.1	290 24.9	42.1	Aldebaran	290 48.6	N16 32.1
05	173 48.3	234 37.1	32.8	342 59.7	18.6	66 03.0	33.1	305 27.1	42.1			
06	188 50.8	249 40.6	S18 32.3	358 01.1	S 2 19.0	81 05.9	N22 33.2	320 29.3	S15 42.2	Alioth	166 20.5	N55 52.7
07	203 53.2	264 44.0	31.9	13 02.5	19.4	96 08.7	33.2	335 31.6	42.2	Alkaid	152 58.8	N49 14.4
M 08	218 55.7	279 47.5	31.4	28 03.9	19.8	111 11.5	33.3	350 33.8	42.3	Al Na'ir	27 43.6	S46 53.7
O 09	233 58.2	294 51.0	.. 30.9	43 05.4	.. 20.2	126 14.3	.. 33.3	5 36.0	.. 42.3	Alnilam	275 45.6	S 1 11.8
N 10	249 00.6	309 54.5	30.5	58 06.8	20.7	141 17.1	33.4	20 38.3	42.4	Alphard	217 55.4	S 8 43.3
D 11	264 03.1	324 58.0	30.0	73 08.2	21.1	156 20.0	33.4	35 40.5	42.4			
A 12	279 05.6	340 01.5	S18 29.5	88 09.6	S 2 21.5	171 22.8	N22 33.5	50 42.7	S15 42.5	Alphecca	126 11.0	N26 40.0
Y 13	294 08.0	355 05.0	29.1	103 11.0	21.9	186 25.6	33.5	65 45.0	42.6	Alpheratz	357 43.1	N29 10.3
14	309 10.5	10 08.5	28.6	118 12.4	22.3	201 28.4	33.5	80 47.2	42.6	Altair	62 08.2	N 8 54.5
15	324 12.9	25 12.0	.. 28.1	133 13.9	.. 22.7	216 31.3	.. 33.6	95 49.4	.. 42.7	Ankaa	353 15.4	S42 14.0
16	339 15.4	40 15.5	27.7	148 15.3	23.1	231 34.1	33.6	110 51.7	42.7	Antares	112 26.1	S26 27.6
17	354 17.9	55 19.0	27.2	163 16.7	23.5	246 36.9	33.7	125 53.9	42.8			
18	9 20.3	70 22.6	S18 26.7	178 18.1	S 2 24.0	261 39.7	N22 33.7	140 56.1	S15 42.8	Arcturus	145 55.5	N19 06.5
19	24 22.8	85 26.1	26.3	193 19.5	24.4	276 42.5	33.8	155 58.4	42.9	Atria	107 28.1	S69 02.8
20	39 25.3	100 29.6	25.8	208 21.0	24.8	291 45.4	33.8	171 00.6	42.9	Avior	234 17.2	S59 33.3
21	54 27.7	115 33.2	.. 25.4	223 22.4	.. 25.2	306 48.2	.. 33.9	186 02.8	.. 43.0	Bellatrix	278 31.3	N 6 21.5
22	69 30.2	130 36.7	24.9	238 23.8	25.6	321 51.0	33.9	201 05.1	43.1	Betelgeuse	271 00.5	N 7 24.4
23	84 32.7	145 40.2	24.4	253 25.2	26.0	336 53.8	34.0	216 07.3	43.1			
31 00	99 35.1	160 43.8	S18 24.0	268 26.6	S 2 26.4	351 56.7	N22 34.0	231 09.5	S15 43.2	Canopus	263 55.4	S52 42.4
01	114 37.6	175 47.3	23.5	283 28.1	26.8	6 59.5	34.1	246 11.8	43.2	Capella	280 33.4	N46 00.6
02	129 40.1	190 50.9	23.1	298 29.5	27.2	22 02.3	34.1	261 14.0	43.3	Deneb	49 31.6	N45 20.1
03	144 42.5	205 54.4	.. 22.6	313 30.9	.. 27.7	37 05.1	.. 34.1	276 16.2	.. 43.3	Denebola	182 33.2	N14 29.4
04	159 45.0	220 58.0	22.1	328 32.3	28.1	52 07.9	34.2	291 18.5	43.4	Diphda	348 55.5	S17 54.7
05	174 47.4	236 01.6	21.7	343 33.8	28.5	67 10.8	34.2	306 20.7	43.4			
06	189 49.9	251 05.1	S18 21.2	358 35.2	S 2 28.9	82 13.6	N22 34.3	321 22.9	S15 43.5	Dubhe	193 51.1	N61 40.1
07	204 52.4	266 08.7	20.8	13 36.6	29.3	97 16.4	34.3	336 25.2	43.6	Elnath	278 11.7	N28 37.0
T 08	219 54.8	281 12.3	20.3	28 38.0	29.7	112 19.2	34.4	351 27.4	43.6	Eltanin	90 46.5	N51 29.3
U 09	234 57.3	296 15.9	.. 19.9	43 39.5	.. 30.1	127 22.1	.. 34.4	6 29.6	.. 43.7	Enif	33 47.0	N 9 56.5
E 10	249 59.8	311 19.5	19.4	58 40.9	30.5	142 24.9	34.5	21 31.9	43.7	Fomalhaut	15 23.8	S29 32.9
S 11	265 02.2	326 23.0	18.9	73 42.3	30.9	157 27.7	34.5	36 34.1	43.8			
D 12	280 04.7	341 26.6	S18 18.5	88 43.7	S 2 31.3	172 30.5	N22 34.6	51 36.3	S15 43.8	Gacrux	172 00.3	S57 11.3
A 13	295 07.2	356 30.2	18.0	103 45.2	31.8	187 33.4	34.6	66 38.6	43.9	Gienah	175 51.8	S17 37.2
Y 14	310 09.6	11 33.8	17.6	118 46.6	32.2	202 36.2	34.7	81 40.8	43.9	Hadar	148 47.5	S60 26.1
15	325 12.1	26 37.4	.. 17.1	133 48.0	.. 32.6	217 39.0	.. 34.7	96 43.0	.. 44.0	Hamal	328 00.1	N23 31.8
16	340 14.6	41 41.0	16.7	148 49.4	33.0	232 41.8	34.7	111 45.3	44.0	Kaus Aust.	83 43.7	S34 22.5
17	355 17.0	56 44.7	16.2	163 50.9	33.4	247 44.7	34.8	126 47.5	44.1			
18	10 19.5	71 48.3	S18 15.8	178 52.3	S 2 33.8	262 47.5	N22 34.8	141 49.7	S15 44.2	Kochab	137 20.9	N74 05.7
19	25 21.9	86 51.9	15.3	193 53.7	34.2	277 50.3	34.9	156 52.0	44.2	Markab	13 38.1	N15 17.0
20	40 24.4	101 55.5	14.9	208 55.2	34.6	292 53.1	34.9	171 54.2	44.3	Menkar	314 14.4	N 4 08.6
21	55 26.9	116 59.1	.. 14.4	223 56.6	.. 35.0	307 55.9	.. 35.0	186 56.4	.. 44.3	Menkent	148 07.2	S36 26.1
22	70 29.3	132 02.8	14.0	238 58.0	35.4	322 58.8	35.0	201 58.7	44.4	Miaplacidus	221 38.7	S69 46.4
23	85 31.8	147 06.4	13.5	253 59.5	35.8	338 01.6	35.1	217 00.9	44.4			
1 00	100 34.3	162 10.0	S18 13.1	269 00.9	S 2 36.2	353 04.4	N22 35.1	232 03.1	S15 44.5	Mirfak	308 39.4	N49 54.7
01	115 36.7	177 13.7	12.6	284 02.3	36.6	8 07.2	35.2	247 05.4	44.5	Nunki	75 58.2	S26 16.6
02	130 39.2	192 17.3	12.2	299 03.7	37.1	23 10.1	35.2	262 07.6	44.6	Peacock	53 19.2	S56 41.3
03	145 41.7	207 21.0	.. 11.7	314 05.2	.. 37.5	38 12.9	.. 35.3	277 09.9	.. 44.6	Pollux	243 26.9	N27 59.3
04	160 44.1	222 24.6	11.3	329 06.6	37.9	53 15.7	35.3	292 12.1	44.7	Procyon	244 59.0	N 5 11.1
05	175 46.6	237 28.3	10.8	344 08.0	38.3	68 18.5	35.3	307 14.3	44.8			
06	190 49.0	252 31.9	S18 10.4	359 09.5	S 2 38.7	83 21.4	N22 35.4	322 16.6	S15 44.8	Rasalhague	96 06.4	N12 33.1
W 07	205 51.5	267 35.6	10.0	14 10.9	39.1	98 24.2	35.4	337 18.8	44.9	Regulus	207 42.9	N11 53.7
E 08	220 54.0	282 39.3	09.5	29 12.3	39.5	113 27.0	35.5	352 21.0	44.9	Rigel	281 11.4	S 8 11.3
D 09	235 56.4	297 42.9	.. 09.1	44 13.8	.. 39.9	128 29.8	.. 35.5	7 23.3	.. 45.0	Rigil Kent.	139 51.4	S60 53.2
N 10	250 58.9	312 46.6	08.6	59 15.2	40.3	143 32.7	35.6	22 25.5	45.0	Sabik	102 12.4	S15 44.3
E 11	266 01.4	327 50.3	08.2	74 16.6	40.7	158 35.5	35.6	37 27.7	45.1			
S 12	281 03.8	342 54.0	S18 07.7	89 18.1	S 2 41.1	173 38.3	N22 35.7	52 30.0	S15 45.1	Schedar	349 40.0	N56 37.2
D 13	296 06.3	357 57.7	07.3	104 19.5	41.5	188 41.1	35.7	67 32.2	45.2	Shaula	96 21.8	S37 06.6
A 14	311 08.8	13 01.4	06.9	119 20.9	41.9	203 44.0	35.8	82 34.5	45.2	Sirius	258 33.0	S16 44.3
Y 15	326 11.2	28 05.0	.. 06.4	134 22.4	.. 42.3	218 46.8	.. 35.8	97 36.7	.. 45.3	Spica	158 30.9	S11 14.0
16	341 13.7	43 08.7	06.0	149 23.8	42.7	233 49.6	35.9	112 38.9	45.3	Suhail	222 51.7	S43 29.4
17	356 16.2	58 12.4	05.5	164 25.3	43.1	248 52.4	35.9	127 41.2	45.4			
18	11 18.6	73 16.1	S18 05.1	179 26.7	S 2 43.5	263 55.3	N22 35.9	142 43.4	S15 45.5	Vega	80 39.1	N38 48.0
19	26 21.1	88 19.8	04.7	194 28.1	43.9	278 58.1	36.0	157 45.6	45.5	Zuben'ubi	137 05.2	S16 05.9
20	41 23.5	103 23.6	04.2	209 29.6	44.3	294 00.9	36.0	172 47.9	45.6		SHA	Mer.Pass.
21	56 26.0	118 27.3	.. 03.8	224 31.0	.. 44.7	309 03.7	.. 36.1	187 50.1	.. 45.6		° ′	h m
22	71 28.5	133 31.0	03.3	239 32.4	45.1	324 06.6	36.1	202 52.4	45.7	Venus	61 08.7	13 14
23	86 30.9	148 34.7	02.9	254 33.9	45.5	339 09.4	36.2	217 54.6	45.7	Mars	168 51.5	6 06
Mer.Pass.	17 18.8	v 3.6	d 0.5	v 1.4	d 0.4	v 2.8	d 0.0	v 2.2	d 0.1	Jupiter	252 21.5	0 32
										Saturn	131 34.4	8 34

UT	SUN GHA	SUN Dec	MOON GHA	v	MOON Dec	d	HP
d h	° ′	° ′	° ′	′	° ′	′	′
30 00	179 24.6	S23 10.0	216 15.9	5.1	S18 34.1	3.9	60.1
01	194 24.3	09.8	230 40.0	5.0	18 38.0	3.7	60.2
02	209 24.0	09.7	245 04.0	4.9	18 41.7	3.6	60.2
03	224 23.7	.. 09.5	259 27.9	4.9	18 45.3	3.5	60.2
04	239 23.4	09.3	273 51.8	4.8	18 48.8	3.4	60.3
05	254 23.1	09.2	288 15.6	4.7	18 52.2	3.2	60.3
06	269 22.8	S23 09.0	302 39.3	4.7	S18 55.4	3.1	60.3
07	284 22.5	08.8	317 03.0	4.6	18 58.5	3.0	60.4
08	299 22.2	08.7	331 26.6	4.6	19 01.5	2.9	60.4
M 09	314 21.9	.. 08.5	345 50.2	4.4	19 04.4	2.7	60.4
O 10	329 21.6	08.3	0 13.6	4.4	19 07.1	2.5	60.5
N 11	344 21.3	08.2	14 37.0	4.4	19 09.6	2.5	60.5
D 12	359 21.0	S23 08.0	29 00.4	4.3	S19 12.1	2.3	60.5
A 13	14 20.7	07.8	43 23.7	4.2	19 14.4	2.2	60.5
Y 14	29 20.4	07.6	57 46.9	4.1	19 16.6	2.0	60.6
15	44 20.1	.. 07.5	72 10.0	4.2	19 18.6	1.9	60.6
16	59 19.8	07.3	86 33.2	4.0	19 20.5	1.7	60.6
17	74 19.5	07.1	100 56.2	4.0	19 22.2	1.6	60.7
18	89 19.2	S23 06.9	115 19.2	4.0	S19 23.8	1.5	60.7
19	104 18.9	06.8	129 42.2	3.9	19 25.3	1.4	60.7
20	119 18.6	06.6	144 05.1	3.8	19 26.7	1.1	60.7
21	134 18.3	.. 06.4	158 27.9	3.9	19 27.8	1.1	60.8
22	149 18.0	06.2	172 50.8	3.7	19 28.9	0.9	60.8
23	164 17.7	06.0	187 13.5	3.7	19 29.8	0.8	60.8
31 00	179 17.4	S23 05.9	201 36.2	3.7	S19 30.6	0.6	60.8
01	194 17.1	05.7	215 58.9	3.7	19 31.2	0.5	60.9
02	209 16.8	05.5	230 21.6	3.6	19 31.7	0.3	60.9
03	224 16.5	.. 05.3	244 44.2	3.6	19 32.0	0.2	60.9
04	239 16.2	05.1	259 06.8	3.5	19 32.2	0.0	60.9
05	254 15.9	05.0	273 29.3	3.5	19 32.2	0.1	61.0
06	269 15.6	S23 04.8	287 51.8	3.5	S19 32.1	0.2	61.0
07	284 15.3	04.6	302 14.3	3.4	19 31.9	0.4	61.0
T 08	299 15.0	04.4	316 36.7	3.5	19 31.5	0.6	61.0
U 09	314 14.7	.. 04.2	330 59.2	3.4	19 30.9	0.7	61.1
E 10	329 14.4	04.0	345 21.6	3.4	19 30.2	0.8	61.1
S 11	344 14.1	03.8	359 44.0	3.3	19 29.4	1.0	61.1
D 12	359 13.8	S23 03.6	14 06.3	3.4	S19 28.4	1.1	61.1
A 13	14 13.5	03.4	28 28.7	3.3	19 27.3	1.3	61.1
Y 14	29 13.2	03.3	42 51.0	3.3	19 26.0	1.4	61.2
15	44 12.9	.. 03.1	57 13.3	3.4	19 24.6	1.6	61.2
16	59 12.6	02.9	71 35.6	3.3	19 23.0	1.7	61.2
17	74 12.3	02.7	85 57.9	3.3	19 21.3	1.9	61.2
18	89 12.0	S23 02.5	100 20.2	3.3	S19 19.4	2.0	61.2
19	104 11.7	02.3	114 42.5	3.3	19 17.4	2.2	61.2
20	119 11.4	02.1	129 04.8	3.2	19 15.2	2.3	61.3
21	134 11.1	.. 01.9	143 27.0	3.3	19 12.9	2.4	61.3
22	149 10.8	01.7	157 49.3	3.3	19 10.5	2.6	61.3
23	164 10.5	01.5	172 11.6	3.3	19 07.9	2.8	61.3
1 00	179 10.2	S23 01.3	186 33.9	3.3	S19 05.1	2.9	61.3
01	194 09.9	01.1	200 56.2	3.2	19 02.2	3.0	61.3
02	209 09.6	00.9	215 18.4	3.3	18 59.2	3.2	61.3
03	224 09.3	.. 00.7	229 40.7	3.4	18 56.0	3.3	61.3
04	239 09.0	00.5	244 03.1	3.3	18 52.7	3.5	61.3
05	254 08.8	00.3	258 25.4	3.3	18 49.2	3.6	61.4
06	269 08.5	S23 00.1	272 47.7	3.4	S18 45.6	3.8	61.4
W 07	284 08.2	22 59.9	287 10.1	3.4	18 41.8	3.9	61.4
E 08	299 07.9	59.7	301 32.5	3.4	18 37.9	4.0	61.4
D 09	314 07.6	.. 59.5	315 54.9	3.4	18 33.9	4.2	61.4
N 10	329 07.3	59.2	330 17.3	3.4	18 29.7	4.4	61.4
E 11	344 07.0	59.0	344 39.7	3.5	18 25.3	4.4	61.4
S 12	359 06.7	S22 58.8	359 02.2	3.5	S18 20.9	4.6	61.4
D 13	14 06.4	58.6	13 24.7	3.6	18 16.3	4.8	61.4
A 14	29 06.1	58.4	27 47.3	3.5	18 11.5	4.9	61.4
Y 15	44 05.8	.. 58.2	42 09.8	3.6	18 06.6	5.2	61.4
16	59 05.5	58.0	56 32.4	3.6	18 01.6	5.2	61.4
17	74 05.2	57.8	70 55.0	3.7	17 56.4	5.2	61.4
18	89 04.9	S22 57.6	85 17.7	3.7	S17 51.2	5.5	61.4
19	104 04.6	57.3	99 40.4	3.8	17 45.7	5.5	61.4
20	119 04.3	57.1	114 03.2	3.7	17 40.2	5.7	61.4
21	134 04.0	.. 56.9	128 25.9	3.9	17 34.5	5.8	61.4
22	149 03.7	56.7	142 48.8	3.8	17 28.7	6.0	61.4
23	164 03.4	56.5	157 11.6	4.0	S17 22.7	6.1	61.4
	SD 16.3	d 0.2	SD 16.5		16.7		16.7

Lat.	Twilight Naut.	Twilight Civil	Sunrise	Moonrise 30	31	1	2
°	h m	h m	h m	h m	h m	h m	h m
N 72	08 25	10 45	■	■	■	■	11 14
N 70	08 06	09 51	■	08 50	10 16	10 32	10 33
68	07 50	09 18	■	07 52	09 06	09 46	10 04
66	07 38	08 54	10 29	07 18	08 29	09 15	09 43
64	07 27	08 35	09 50	06 53	08 03	08 53	09 25
62	07 18	08 19	09 23	06 34	07 42	08 34	09 11
60	07 09	08 06	09 03	06 18	07 26	08 19	08 59
N 58	07 02	07 54	08 46	06 04	07 12	08 06	08 48
56	06 56	07 44	08 31	05 53	07 00	07 55	08 39
54	06 50	07 36	08 19	05 43	06 49	07 45	08 31
52	06 44	07 28	08 08	05 34	06 40	07 37	08 24
50	06 39	07 20	07 59	05 25	06 31	07 29	08 17
45	06 27	07 05	07 38	05 08	06 13	07 12	08 03
N 40	06 17	06 51	07 22	04 54	05 59	06 58	07 51
35	06 08	06 40	07 08	04 42	05 46	06 47	07 41
30	06 00	06 29	06 56	04 32	05 36	06 36	07 32
20	05 43	06 11	06 35	04 14	05 17	06 19	07 17
N 10	05 27	05 54	06 17	03 59	05 01	06 03	07 04
0	05 11	05 39	06 00	03 45	04 46	05 49	06 51
S 10	04 52	05 19	05 42	03 30	04 31	05 35	06 39
20	04 30	04 59	05 23	03 15	04 15	05 19	06 25
30	04 01	04 34	05 02	02 58	03 57	05 02	06 10
35	03 43	04 19	04 49	02 48	03 46	04 52	06 01
40	03 20	04 01	04 34	02 36	03 34	04 40	05 51
45	02 50	03 39	04 16	02 22	03 20	04 26	05 39
S 50	02 06	03 10	03 54	02 06	03 02	04 09	05 25
52	01 39	02 55	03 44	01 58	02 54	04 01	05 18
54	00 58	02 38	03 31	01 50	02 45	03 53	05 10
56	////	02 16	03 18	01 40	02 35	03 43	05 02
58	////	01 48	03 01	01 29	02 23	03 31	04 52
S 60	////	01 03	02 41	01 17	02 09	03 18	04 41

Lat.	Sunset	Twilight Civil	Twilight Naut.	Moonset 30	31	1	2
°	h m	h m	h m	h m	h m	h m	h m
N 72	■	13 21	15 42	■	■	■	15 12
N 70	■	14 16	16 01	11 04	11 48	13 44	15 52
68	■	14 49	16 16	12 02	12 58	14 30	16 20
66	13 37	15 13	16 29	12 36	13 35	14 59	16 41
64	14 16	15 32	16 41	13 01	14 01	15 22	16 57
62	14 43	15 47	16 49	13 21	14 21	15 40	17 11
60	15 04	16 01	16 57	13 37	14 38	15 54	17 22
N 58	15 21	16 12	17 04	13 51	14 52	16 07	17 32
56	15 35	16 22	17 11	14 03	15 04	16 18	17 41
54	15 47	16 31	17 17	14 13	15 14	16 27	17 48
52	15 58	16 39	17 22	14 22	15 24	16 36	17 55
50	16 08	16 46	17 27	14 30	15 32	16 43	18 01
45	16 28	17 02	17 39	14 48	15 50	17 00	18 15
N 40	16 45	17 16	17 49	15 02	16 04	17 13	18 25
35	16 59	17 27	17 50	15 14	16 16	17 24	18 35
30	17 11	17 37	18 07	15 25	16 27	17 34	18 43
20	17 31	17 55	18 23	15 43	16 45	17 51	18 57
N 10	17 50	18 12	18 39	15 59	17 01	18 05	19 09
0	18 07	18 29	18 55	16 14	17 16	18 19	19 20
S 10	18 24	18 47	19 14	16 28	17 31	18 32	19 31
20	18 43	19 07	19 36	16 44	17 47	18 47	19 43
30	19 04	19 32	20 05	17 02	18 05	19 03	19 57
35	19 17	19 47	20 23	17 13	18 15	19 13	20 04
40	19 32	20 05	20 46	17 25	18 27	19 23	20 13
45	19 50	20 27	21 16	17 39	18 41	19 36	20 23
S 50	20 12	20 56	22 00	17 57	18 58	19 51	20 36
52	20 22	21 10	22 26	18 05	19 07	19 59	20 41
54	20 34	21 28	23 06	18 14	19 15	20 07	20 48
56	20 48	21 49	////	18 24	19 26	20 15	20 55
58	21 04	22 17	////	18 36	19 37	20 25	21 03
S 60	21 24	23 01	////	18 49	19 50	20 37	21 11

Day	SUN Eqn. of Time 00h	12h	SUN Mer. Pass.	MOON Mer. Pass. Upper	Lower	Age	Phase
d	m s	m s	h m	h m	h m	d	%
30	02 21	02 35	12 03	09 59	22 30	27	6
31	02 50	03 04	12 03	11 01	23 33	28	2
1	03 18	03 33	12 04	12 04	24 35	00	0

EXPLANATION

PRINCIPLE AND ARRANGEMENT

1. *Object.* The object of this Almanac is to provide, in a convenient form, the data required for the practice of astronomical navigation at sea.

2. *Principle.* The main contents of the Almanac consist of data from which the *Greenwich Hour Angle* (GHA) and the *Declination* (Dec) of all the bodies used for navigation can be obtained for any instant of *Universal Time* (UT, specifically UT1, or previously Greenwich Mean Time (GMT)).

The *Local Hour Angle* (LHA) can then be obtained by means of the formula:

$$\text{LHA} = \text{GHA} \; {- \text{ west} \atop + \text{ east}} \; \text{longitude}$$

The remaining data consist of: times of rising and setting of the Sun and Moon, and times of twilight; miscellaneous calendarial and planning data and auxiliary tables, including a list of Standard Times; corrections to be applied to observed altitude.

For the Sun, Moon, and planets the GHA and Dec are tabulated directly for each hour of UT throughout the year. For the stars the *Sidereal Hour Angle* (SHA) is given, and the GHA is obtained from:

$$\text{GHA Star} = \text{GHA Aries} + \text{SHA Star}$$

The SHA and Dec of the stars change slowly and may be regarded as constant over periods of several days. GHA Aries, or the Greenwich Hour Angle of the first point of Aries (the Vernal Equinox), is tabulated for each hour. Permanent tables give the appropriate increments and corrections to the tabulated hourly values of GHA and Dec for the minutes and seconds of UT.

The six-volume series of *Sight Reduction Tables for Marine Navigation* (published in U.S.A. as Pub. No. 229 and in U.K. as N.P. 401) has been designed for the solution of the navigational triangle and is intended for use with *The Nautical Almanac*.

Two alternative procedures for sight reduction are described on pages 277–318. The first requires the use of programmable calculators or computers, while the second uses a set of concise tables that is given on pages 286–317.

The tabular accuracy is $0\!\!\stackrel{\prime}{.}1$ throughout. The time argument on the daily pages of this Almanac is UT1 denoted throughout by UT. This scale may differ from the broadcast time signals (UTC) by an amount which, if ignored, will introduce an error of up to $0\!\!\stackrel{\prime}{.}2$ in longitude determined from astronomical observations. The difference arises because the time argument depends on the variable rate of rotation of the Earth while the broadcast time signals are based on an atomic time-scale. Step adjustments of exactly one second are made to the time signals as required (normally at 24^h on December 31 and June 30) so that the difference between the time signals and UT, as used in this Almanac, may not exceed $0\!\!\stackrel{s}{.}9$. Those who require to reduce observations to a precision of better than 1^s must therefore obtain the correction (DUT1) to the time signals from coding in the signal, or from other sources; the required time is given by UT1=UTC+DUT1 to a precision of $0\!\!\stackrel{s}{.}1$. Alternatively, the longitude, when determined from astronomical observations, may be corrected by the corresponding amount shown in the following table:

Correction to time signals	Correction to longitude
$-0\!\!\stackrel{s}{.}9$ to $-0\!\!\stackrel{s}{.}7$	$0\!\!\stackrel{\prime}{.}2$ to east
$-0\!\!\stackrel{s}{.}6$ to $-0\!\!\stackrel{s}{.}3$	$0\!\!\stackrel{\prime}{.}1$ to east
$-0\!\!\stackrel{s}{.}2$ to $+0\!\!\stackrel{s}{.}2$	no correction
$+0\!\!\stackrel{s}{.}3$ to $+0\!\!\stackrel{s}{.}6$	$0\!\!\stackrel{\prime}{.}1$ to west
$+0\!\!\stackrel{s}{.}7$ to $+0\!\!\stackrel{s}{.}9$	$0\!\!\stackrel{\prime}{.}2$ to west

3. *Lay-out.* The ephemeral data for three days are presented on an opening of two pages: the left-hand page contains the data for the planets and stars; the right-hand page contains the data for the Sun and Moon, together with times of twilight, sunrise, sunset, moonrise and moonset.

The remaining contents are arranged as follows: for ease of reference the altitude-correction tables are given on pages A2, A3, A4, xxxiv and xxxv; calendar, Moon's phases, eclipses, and planet notes (i.e. data of general interest) precede the main tabulations. The Explanation is followed by information on standard times, star charts and list of star positions, sight reduction procedures and concise sight reduction tables, tables of increments and corrections and other auxiliary tables that are frequently used.

MAIN DATA

4. *Daily pages.* The daily pages give the GHA of Aries, the GHA and Dec of the Sun, Moon, and the four navigational planets, for each hour of UT. For the Moon, values of v and d are also tabulated for each hour to facilitate the correction of GHA and Dec to intermediate times; v and d for the Sun and planets change so slowly that they are given, at the foot of the appropriate columns, once only on the page; v is zero for Aries and negligible for the Sun, and is omitted. The SHA and Dec of the 57 selected stars, arranged in alphabetical order of proper name, are also given.

5. *Stars.* The SHA and Dec of 173 stars, including the 57 selected stars, are tabulated for each month on pages 268–273; no interpolation is required and the data can be used in precisely the same way as those for the selected stars on the daily pages. The stars are arranged in order of SHA.

The list of 173 includes all stars down to magnitude 3·0, together with a few fainter ones to fill the larger gaps. The 57 selected stars have been chosen from amongst these on account of brightness and distribution in the sky; they will suffice for the majority of observations.

The 57 selected stars are known by their proper names, but they are also numbered in descending order of SHA. In the list of 173 stars, the constellation names are always given on the left-hand page; on the facing page proper names are given where well-known names exist. Numbers for the selected stars are given in both columns.

An index to the selected stars, containing lists in both alphabetical and numerical order, is given on page xxxiii and is also reprinted on the bookmark.

6. *Increments and corrections.* The tables printed on tinted paper (pages ii–xxxi) at the back of the Almanac provide the increments and corrections for minutes and seconds to be applied to the hourly values of GHA and Dec. They consist of sixty tables, one for each minute, separated into two parts: increments to GHA for Sun and planets, Aries, and Moon for every minute and second; and, for each minute, corrections to be applied to GHA and Dec corresponding to the values of v and d given on the daily pages.

The increments are based on the following adopted hourly rates of increase of the GHA: Sun and planets, 15° precisely; Aries, 15° 02ʹ46; Moon, 14° 19ʹ0. The values of v on the daily pages are the excesses of the actual hourly motions over the adopted values; they are generally positive, except for Venus. The tabulated hourly values of the Sun's GHA have been adjusted to reduce to a minimum the error caused by treating v as negligible. The values of d on the daily pages are the hourly differences of the Dec. For the Moon, the true values of v and d are given for each hour; otherwise mean values are given for the three days on the page.

7. *Method of entry.* The UT of an observation is expressed as a day and hour, followed by a number of minutes and seconds. The tabular values of GHA and Dec, and, where necessary, the corresponding values of v and d, are taken directly from the daily pages for the day and hour of UT; this hour is always *before* the time of observation. SHA and Dec of the selected stars are also taken from the daily pages.

The table of Increments and Corrections for the minute of UT is then selected. For the GHA, the increment for minutes and seconds is taken from the appropriate column opposite the seconds of UT; the v-correction is taken from the second part of the same table opposite the value of v as given on the daily pages. Both increment and v-correction are to be added to the GHA, except for Venus when v is prefixed by a minus sign and the v-correction is to be subtracted. For the Dec there is no increment, but a d-correction is applied in the same way as the v-correction; d is given without sign on the daily pages and the sign of the correction is to be supplied by inspection of the Dec column. In many cases the correction may be applied mentally.

8. *Examples.* (a) Sun and Moon. Required the GHA and Dec of the Sun and Moon on 2013 November 13 at 15^h 47^m 13^s UT.

		SUN			MOON			
		GHA	Dec	d	GHA	v	Dec	d
		° ′	° ′	′	° ′	′	° ′	′
Daily page, November 13^d 15^h		48 55·0	S 18 06·5	0·7	275 19·7	12·0	N 4 18·4	10·8
Increments for	47^m 13^s	11 48·3			11 16·0			
v or d corrections for	47^m		+0·6		+9·5		+8·6	
Sum for November 13^d 15^h 47^m 13^s		60 43·3	S 18 07·1		286 45·2		N 4 27·0	

(b) Planets. Required the LHA and Dec of (i) Venus on 2013 November 13 at 13^h 58^m 16^s UT in longitude E $70°$ $19'$; (ii) Mars on 2013 November 13 at 8^h 44^m 06^s UT in longitude W $53°$ $11'$.

		VENUS				MARS			
		GHA	v	Dec	d		GHA	v	Dec	d
		° ′	′	° ′	′		° ′	′	° ′	′
Daily page, Nov. 13^d	(13^h)	329 12·5	−0·1	S 26 56·2	0·2	(8^h)	4 07·8	1·2	N 6 46·0	0·5
Increments (planets)	(58^m 16^s)	14 34·0				(44^m 06^s)	11 01·5			
v or d corrections	(58^m)	−0·1		−0·2		(44^m)	+0·9		−0·4	
Sum = GHA and Dec.		343 46·4		S 26 56·0			15 10·2		N 6 45·6	
Longitude	(east)	+ 70 19·0				(west)	− 53 11·0			
Multiples of 360°		−360					+360			
LHA planet		54 05·4					321 59·2			

(c) Stars. Required the GHA and Dec of (i) *Sirius* on 2013 November 13 at 8^h 44^m 06^s UT; (ii) *Vega* on 2013 November 13 at 21^h 45^m 38^s UT.

		Sirius			Vega	
		GHA	Dec		GHA	Dec
		° ′	° ′		° ′	° ′
Daily page (SHA and Dec)		258 33·2	S 16 44·1		80 39·1	N 38 48·2
Daily page (GHA Aries)	(8^h)	172 36·2		(21^h)	8 08·2	
Increments (Aries)	(44^m 06^s)	11 03·3		(45^m 38^s)	11 26·4	
Sum = GHA star		442 12·7			100 13·7	
Multiples of 360°		−360				
GHA star		82 12·7			100 13·7	

9. *Polaris (Pole Star) tables.* The tables on pages 274–276 provide means by which the latitude can be deduced from an observed altitude of *Polaris*, and they also give its azimuth; their use is explained and illustrated on those pages. They are based on the following formula:

$$\text{Latitude} - H_0 = -p \cos h + \tfrac{1}{2} p \sin p \sin^2 h \tan (\text{latitude})$$

where

H_0 = Apparent altitude (corrected for refraction)

p = polar distance of *Polaris* = $90°$ − Dec

h = local hour angle of *Polaris* = LHA Aries + SHA

a_0, which is a function of LHA Aries only, is the value of both terms of the above formula calculated for mean values of the SHA ($317°$ $43'$) and Dec (N $89°$ $19\!\cdot\!3$) of *Polaris*, for a mean latitude of $50°$, and adjusted by the addition of a constant ($58\!\cdot\!8$).

a_1, which is a function of LHA Aries and latitude, is the excess of the value of the second term over its mean value for latitude 50°, increased by a constant (0.6) to make it always positive. a_2, which is a function of LHA Aries and date, is the correction to the first term for the variation of *Polaris* from its adopted mean position; it is increased by a constant (0.6) to make it positive. The sum of the added constants is 1°, so that:

Latitude = Apparent altitude (corrected for refraction) − 1° + a_0 + a_1 + a_2

RISING AND SETTING PHENOMENA

10. *General.* On the right-hand daily pages are given the times of sunrise and sunset, of the beginning and end of civil and nautical twilights, and of moonrise and moonset for a range of latitudes from N 72° to S 60°. These times, which are given to the nearest minute, are strictly the UT of the phenomena on the Greenwich meridian; they are given for every day for moonrise and moonset, but only for the middle day of the three on each page for the solar phenomena.

They are approximately the Local Mean Times (LMT) of the corresponding phenomena on other meridians; they can be formally interpolated if desired. The UT of a phenomenon is obtained from the LMT by:

$$UT = LMT \, {}^{+ \text{ west}}_{- \text{ east}} \text{ longitude}$$

in which the longitude must first be converted to time by the table on page i or otherwise.

Interpolation for latitude can be done mentally or with the aid of Table I on page xxxii.

The following symbols are used to indicate the conditions under which, in high latitudes, some of the phenomena do not occur:

▭ Sun or Moon remains continuously above the horizon;

■ Sun or Moon remains continuously below the horizon;

//// twilight lasts all night.

Basis of the tabulations. At sunrise and sunset 16′ is allowed for semi-diameter and 34′ for horizontal refraction, so that at the times given the Sun's upper limb is on the visible horizon; all times refer to phenomena as seen from sea level with a clear horizon.

At the times given for the beginning and end of twilight, the Sun's zenith distance is 96° for civil, and 102° for nautical twilight. The degree of illumination at the times given for civil twilight (in good conditions and in the absence of other illumination) is such that the brightest stars are visible and the horizon is clearly defined. At the times given for nautical twilight the horizon is in general not visible, and it is too dark for observation with a marine sextant

Times corresponding to other depressions of the Sun may be obtained by interpolation or, for depressions of more than 12°, less reliably, by extrapolation; times so obtained will be subject to considerable uncertainty near extreme conditions.

At moonrise and moonset allowance is made for semi-diameter, parallax, and refraction (34′), so that at the times given the Moon's upper limb is on the visible horizon as seen from sea level.

11. *Sunrise, sunset, twilight.* The tabulated times may be regarded, without serious error, as the LMT of the phenomena on any of the three days on the page and in any longitude. Precise times may normally be obtained by interpolating the tabular values for latitude and to the correct day and longitude, the latter being expressed as a fraction of a day by dividing it by 360°, positive for west and negative for east longitudes. In the extreme conditions near ▭, ■ or //// interpolation may not be possible in one direction, but accurate times are of little value in these circumstances.

Examples. Required the UT of (a) the beginning of morning twilights and sunrise on 2013 January 13 for latitude S 48° 55′, longitude E 75° 18′; (b) sunset and the end of evening twilights on 2013 January 15 for latitude N 67° 10′, longitude W 168° 05′.

	(a)	Twilight Nautical	Civil	Sunrise	(b)	Sunset	Twilight Civil	Nautical
		d h m	d h m	d h m		d h m	d h m	d h m
From p. 19								
LMT for Lat	S 45°	13 03 10	13 03 56	13 04 32	N 66°	15 14 24	15 15 43	15 16 54
Corr. to	S 48° 55′	−30	−20	−16	N 67° 10′	−22	−12	−6
(p. xxxii, Table I)								
Long (p. i)	E 75° 18′	−5 01	−5 01	−5 01	W 168° 05′	+11 12	+11 12	+11 12
UT		12 21 39	12 22 35	12 23 15		16 01 14	16 02 43	16 04 00

The LMT are strictly for January 14 (middle date on page) and 0° longitude; for more precise times it is necessary to interpolate, but rounding errors may accumulate to about 2^m.

(a) to January $13^d − 75°/360°$ = Jan. 12^d8, i.e. $\frac{1}{3}(1\cdot2) = 0\cdot4$ backwards towards the data for the same latitude interpolated similarly from page 17; the corrections are $−2^m$ to nautical twilight, $−2^m$ to civil twilight and $−2^m$ to sunrise.

(b) to January $15^d + 168°/360°$ = Jan. 15^d5, i.e. $\frac{1}{3}(1\cdot5) = 0\cdot5$ forwards towards the data for the same latitude interpolated similarly from page 21; the corrections are $+7^m$ to sunset, $+4^m$ to civil twilight, and $+4^m$ to nautical twilight.

12. *Moonrise, moonset.* Precise times of moonrise and moonset are rarely needed; a glance at the tables will generally give sufficient indication of whether the Moon is available for observation and of the hours of rising and setting. If needed, precise times may be obtained as follows. Interpolate for latitude, using Table I on page xxxii, on the day wanted and also on the preceding day in east longitudes or the following day in west longitudes; take the difference between these times and interpolate for longitude by applying to the time for the day wanted the correction from Table II on page xxxii, so that the resulting time is between the two times used. In extreme conditions near $\square$ or ■ interpolation for latitude or longitude may be possible only in one direction; accurate times are of little value in these circumstances.

To facilitate this interpolation the times of moonrise and moonset are given for four days on each page; where no phenomenon occurs during a particular day (as happens once a month) the time of the phenomenon on the following day, increased by 24^h, is given; extra care must be taken when interpolating between two values, when one of those values exceeds 24^h. In practice it suffices to use the daily difference between the times for the nearest tabular latitude, and generally, to enter Table II with the nearest tabular arguments as in the examples below.

Examples. Required the UT of moonrise and moonset in latitude S 47° 10′, longitudes E 124° 00′ and W 78° 31′ on 2013 January 17.

	Longitude E 124° 00′ Moonrise	Moonset	Longitude W 78° 31′ Moonrise	Moonset
	d h m	d h m	d h m	d h m
LMT for Lat. S 45°	17 11 14	17 22 26	17 11 14	17 22 26
Lat correction (p. xxxii, Table I)	+02	−02	+02	−02
Long correction (p. xxxii, Table II)	−23	−10	+16	+07
Correct LMT	17 10 53	17 22 14	17 11 32	17 22 31
Longitude (p. i)	−8 16	−8 16	+5 14	+5 14
UT	17 02 37	17 13 58	17 16 46	18 03 45

ALTITUDE CORRECTION TABLES

13. *General.* In general two corrections are given for application to altitudes observed with a marine sextant; additional corrections are required for Venus and Mars and also for very low altitudes.

Tables of the correction for dip of the horizon, due to height of eye above sea level, are given on pages A2 and xxxiv. Strictly this correction should be applied first and subtracted from the sextant altitude to give apparent altitude, which is the correct argument for the other tables.

Separate tables are given of the second correction for the Sun, for stars and planets (on pages A2 and A3), and for the Moon (on pages xxxiv and xxxv). For the Sun, values are given for both lower and upper limbs, for two periods of the year. The star tables are used for the planets, but additional corrections for parallax (page A2) are required for Venus and Mars. The Moon tables are in two parts: the main correction is a function of apparent altitude only and is tabulated for the lower limb (30′ must be subtracted to obtain the correction for the upper limb); the other, which is given for both lower and upper limbs, depends also on the horizontal parallax, which has to be taken from the daily pages.

An additional correction, given on page A4, is required for the change in the refraction, due to variations of pressure and temperature from the adopted standard conditions; it may generally be ignored for altitudes greater than 10°, except possibly in extreme conditions. The correction tables for the Sun, stars, and planets are in two parts; only those for altitudes greater than 10° are reprinted on the bookmark.

14. *Critical tables.*   Some of the altitude correction tables are arranged as critical tables. In these an interval of apparent altitude (or height of eye) corresponds to a single value of the correction; no interpolation is required. At a "critical" entry the upper of the two possible values of the correction is to be taken. For example, in the table of dip, a correction of −4′.1 corresponds to all values of the height of eye from 5·3 to 5·5 metres (17·5 to 18·3 feet) inclusive.

15. *Examples.*   The following examples illustrate the use of the altitude correction tables; the sextant altitudes given are assumed to be taken on 2013 August 12 with a marine sextant at height 5·4 metres (18 feet), temperature −3°C and pressure 982 mb, the Moon sights being taken at about 10^h UT.

	SUN lower limb	SUN upper limb	MOON lower limb	MOON upper limb	VENUS	*Polaris*
	° ′	° ′	° ′	° ′	° ′	° ′
Sextant altitude	21 19·7	3 20·2	33 27·6	26 06·7	4 32·6	49 36·5
Dip, height 5·4 metres (18 feet)	−4·1	−4·1	−4·1	−4·1	−4·1	−4·1
Main correction	+13·6	−29·3	+57·4	+60·5	−10·8	−0·8
−30′ for upper limb (Moon)	—	—	—	−30·0	—	—
L, U correction for Moon	—	—	+4·6	+3·4	—	—
Additional correction for Venus	—	—	—	—	+0·1	—
Additional refraction correction	−0·1	−0·6	−0·1	−0·1	−0·5	0·0
Corrected sextant altitude	21 29·1	2 46·2	34 25·4	26 36·4	4 17·3	49 31·6

The main corrections have been taken out with apparent altitude (sextant altitude corrected for index error and dip) as argument, interpolating where possible. These refinements are rarely necessary.

16. *Composition of the Corrections.*   The table for the dip of the sea horizon is based on the formula:

Correction for dip $= -1′.76\sqrt{\text{(height of eye in metres)}} = -0′.97\sqrt{\text{(height of eye in feet)}}$

The correction table for the Sun includes the effects of semi-diameter, parallax and mean refraction.

The correction tables for the stars and planets allow for the effect of mean refraction.

The phase correction for Venus has been incorporated in the tabulations for GHA and Dec, and no correction for phase is required. The additional corrections for Venus and Mars allow for parallax. Alternatively, the correction for parallax may be calculated from $p\cos H$, where p is the parallax and H is the altitude. In 2013 the values for p are:

	Jan. 1	Sept. 21	Nov. 11	Dec. 5	Dec. 20	Dec. 31
Venus	0′.1	0′.2	0′.3	0′.4	0′.5	

	Jan. 1	Dec. 31
Mars	0′.1	

The correction table for the Moon includes the effect of semi-diameter, parallax, augmentation and mean refraction.

Mean refraction is calculated for a temperature of 10°C (50°F), a pressure of 1010 mb (29·83 inches), humidity of 80% and wavelength 0·50169 μm.

17. *Bubble sextant observations.* When observing with a bubble sextant no correction is necessary for dip, semi-diameter, or augmentation. The altitude corrections for the stars and planets on page A2 and on the bookmark should be used for the Sun as well as for the stars and planets; for the Moon it is easiest to take the mean of the corrections for lower and upper limbs and subtract 15′ from the altitude; the correction for dip must not be applied.

AUXILIARY AND PLANNING DATA

18. *Sun and Moon.* On the daily pages are given: hourly values of the horizontal parallax of the Moon; the semi-diameters and the times of meridian passage of both Sun and Moon over the Greenwich meridian; the equation of time; the age of the Moon, the percent (%) illuminated and a symbol indicating the phase. The times of the phases of the Moon are given in UT on page 4. For the Moon, the semi-diameters for each of the three days are given at the foot of the column; for the Sun a single value is sufficient. Table II on page xxxii may be used for interpolating the time of the Moon's meridian passage for longitude. The equation of time is given daily at 00^h and 12^h UT. The sign is *positive* for unshaded values and *negative* for shaded values. To obtain apparent time add the equation of time to mean time when the sign is *positive*. Subtract the equation of time from mean time when the sign is *negative*. At 12^h UT, when the sign is *positive*, meridian passage of the Sun occurs *before* 12^h UT, otherwise it occurs *after* 12^h UT.

19. *Planets.* The magnitudes of the planets are given immediately following their names in the headings on the daily pages; also given, for the middle day of the three on the page, are their SHA at 00^h UT and their times of meridian passage.

The planet notes and diagram on pages 8 and 9 provide descriptive information as to the suitability of the planets for observation during the year, and of their positions and movements.

20. *Stars.* The time of meridian passage of the first point of Aries over the Greenwich meridian is given on the daily pages, for the middle day of the three on the page, to 0^m1. The interval between successive meridian passages is $23^h 56^m1$ (24^h less 3^m9) so that times for intermediate days and other meridians can readily be derived. If a precise time is required it may be obtained by finding the UT at which LHA Aries is zero.

The meridian passage of a star occurs when its LHA is zero, that is when LHA Aries + SHA = 360°. An approximate time can be obtained from the planet diagram on page 9.

The star charts on pages 266 and 267 are intended to assist identification. They show the relative positions of the stars in the sky as seen from the Earth and include all 173 stars used in the Almanac, together with a few others to complete the main constellation configurations. The local meridian at any time may be located on the chart by means of its SHA which is 360° − LHA Aries, or west longitude − GHA Aries.

21. *Star globe.* To set a star globe on which is printed a scale of LHA Aries, first set the globe for latitude and then rotate about the polar axis until the scale under the edge of the meridian circle reads LHA Aries.

To mark the positions of the Sun, Moon, and planets on the star globe, take the difference GHA Aries − GHA body and use this along the LHA Aries scale, in conjunction with the declination, to plot the position. GHA Aries − GHA body is most conveniently found by taking the difference when the GHA of the body is small (less than 15°), which happens once a day.

22. *Calendar.* On page 4 are given lists of ecclesiastical festivals, and of the principal anniversaries and holidays in the United Kingdom and the United States of America. The calendar on page 5 includes the day of the year as well as the day of the week.

Brief particulars are given, at the foot of page 5, of the solar and lunar eclipses occurring during the year; the times given are in UT. The principal features of the more important solar eclipses are shown on the maps on pages 6 and 7.

23. *Standard times.* The lists on pages 262–265 give the standard times used in most countries. In general no attempt is made to give details of the beginning and end of summer time, since they are liable to frequent changes at short notice. For the latest information consult Admiralty List of Radio Signals Volume 2 (NP 282) corrected by Section VI of the weekly edition of Admiralty Notices to Mariners.

The Date or Calendar Line is an arbitrary line, on either side of which the date differs by one day; when crossing this line on a westerly course, the date must be advanced one day; when crossing it on an easterly course, the date must be put back one day. The line is a modification of the line of the 180th meridian, and is drawn so as to include, as far as possible, islands of any one group, etc., on the same side of the line. It may be traced by starting at the South Pole and joining up to the following positions:

Lat	S 51·0	S 45·0	S 15·0	S 5·0	N 48·0	N 53·0	N 65·5
Long	180·0	W 172·5	W 172·5	180·0	180·0	E 170·0	W 169·0

thence through the middle of the Diomede Islands to Lat N 68°0, Long W 169°0, passing east of Ostrov Vrangelya (Wrangel Island) to Lat N 75°0, Long 180°0, and thence to the North Pole.

ACCURACY

24. *Main data.* The quantities tabulated in this Almanac are generally correct to the nearest 0′.1; the exception is the Sun's GHA which is deliberately adjusted by up to 0′.15 to reduce the error due to ignoring the v-correction. The GHA and Dec at intermediate times cannot be obtained to this precision, since at least two quantities must be added; moreover, the v- and d-corrections are based on mean values of v and d and are taken from tables for the whole minute only. The largest error that can occur in the GHA or Dec of any body other than the Sun or Moon is less than 0′.2; it may reach 0′.25 for the GHA of the Sun and 0′.3 for that of the Moon.

In practice it may be expected that only one third of the values of GHA and Dec taken out will have errors larger than 0′.05 and less than one tenth will have errors larger than 0′.1.

25. *Altitude corrections.* The errors in the altitude corrections are nominally of the same order as those in GHA and Dec, as they result from the addition of several quantities each correctly rounded off to 0′.1. But the actual values of the dip and of the refraction at low altitudes may, in extreme atmospheric conditions, differ considerably from the mean values used in the tables.

USE OF THIS ALMANAC IN 2014

This Almanac may be used for the Sun and stars in 2014 in the following manner.

For the Sun, take out the GHA and Dec for the same date but for a time $5^h 48^m 00^s$ *earlier* than the UT of observation; add 87° 00′ to the GHA so obtained. The error, mainly due to planetary perturbations of the Earth, is unlikely to exceed 0′.4.

For the stars, calculate the GHA and Dec for the same date and the same time, but *subtract* 15′.1 from the GHA so found. The error, due to incomplete correction for precession and nutation, is unlikely to exceed 0′.4. If preferred, the same result can be obtained by using a time $5^h 48^m 00^s$ earlier than the UT of observation (as for the Sun) and adding 86° 59′.2 to the GHA (or adding 87° as for the Sun and subtracting 0′.8, for precession, from the SHA of the star).

The Almanac cannot be so used for the Moon or planets.

LIST I — PLACES FAST ON UTC (mainly those EAST OF GREENWICH)

The times given ⎱ *added* to UTC to give Standard Time
below should be ⎰ *subtracted* from Standard Time to give UTC.

	h	m		h	m
Admiralty Islands	10		Denmark*†	01	
Afghanistan	04	30	Djibouti	03	
Albania*	01				
Algeria	01		Egypt, Arab Republic of	02	
Amirante Islands	04		Equatorial Guinea, Republic of	01	
Andaman Islands	05	30	Eritrea	03	
Angola	01		Estonia*†	02	
Armenia*	04		Ethiopia	03	
Australia			Fiji*	12	
Australian Capital Territory*	10		Finland*†	02	
New South Wales*[1]	10		France*†	01	
Northern Territory	09	30	Gabon	01	
Queensland	10		Georgia	04	
South Australia*	09	30	Germany*†	01	
Tasmania*	10		Gibraltar*	01	
Victoria*	10		Greece*†	02	
Western Australia	08		Guam	10	
Whitsunday Islands	10				
Austria*†	01		Hong Kong	08	
Azerbaijan*	04		Hungary*†	01	
Bahrain	03		India	05	30
Balearic Islands*†	01		Indonesia, Republic of		
Bangladesh	06		Bangka, Billiton, Java, West and		
Belarus	03		Central Kalimantan, Madura, Sumatra	07	
Belgium*†	01		Bali, Flores, South and East		
Benin	01		Kalimantan, Lombok, Sulawesi,		
Bosnia and Herzegovina*	01		Sumba, Sumbawa, West Timor	08	
Botswana, Republic of	02		Aru, Irian Jaya, Kai, Moluccas		
Brunei	08		Tanimbar	09	
Bulgaria*†	02		Iran*	03	30
Burma (Myanmar)	06	30	Iraq	03	
Burundi	02		Israel*	02	
			Italy*†	01	
Cambodia	07		Jan Mayen Island*	01	
Cameroon Republic	01		Japan	09	
Caroline Islands[2]	10		Jordan*	02	
Central African Republic	01				
Chad	01		Kazakhstan		
Chagos Archipelago & Diego Garcia	06		Western: Aktau, Uralsk, Atyrau	05	
Chatham Islands*	12	45	Eastern & Central: Kzyl-Orda, Astana	06	
China, People's Republic of	08		Kenya	03	
Christmas Island, Indian Ocean	07		Kerguelen Islands	05	
Cocos (Keeling) Islands	06	30	Kiribati Republic		
Comoro Islands (Comoros)	03		Gilbert Islands	12	
Congo, Democratic Republic			Phoenix Islands[3]	13	
West: Kinshasa, Equateur	01		Line Islands[3]	14	
East: Orientale, Kasai, Kivu, Shaba	02		Korea, North	09	
Congo Republic	01		Korea, South	09	
Corsica*†	01		Kuwait	03	
Crete*†	02		Kyrgyzstan	06	
Croatia*	01				
Cyprus†: Ercan*, Larnaca*	02		Laccadive Islands	05	30
Czech Republic*†	01		Laos	07	
			Latvia*†	02	

---

* Daylight-saving time may be kept in these places.   † For Summer time dates see List II footnotes.
[1] Except Broken Hill Area* which keeps 09h 30m.
[2] Except Pohnpei, Pingelap and Kosrae which keep 11h and Palau which keeps 09h.
[3] The Line and Phoenix Is. not part of the Kiribati Republic keep 10h and 11h, respectively, slow on UTC.

LIST I — (continued)

	h	m
Lebanon*	02	
Lesotho	02	
Libya	02	
Liechtenstein*	01	
Lithuania*†	02	
Lord Howe Island*	10	30
Luxembourg*†	01	
Macau	08	
Macedonia*, former Yugoslav Republic	01	
Macias Nguema (Fernando Póo) ...	01	
Madagascar, Democratic Republic of	03	
Malawi	02	
Malaysia, Malaya, Sabah, Sarawak ...	08	
Maldives, Republic of The	05	
Malta*†	01	
Mariana Islands	10	
Marshall Islands	12	
Mauritius	04	
Moldova*	02	
Monaco*	01	
Mongolia	08	
Montenegro*	01	
Mozambique	02	
Namibia*	01	
Nauru	12	
Nepal	05	45
Netherlands, The*†	01	
New Caledonia	11	
New Zealand*	12	
Nicobar Islands	05	30
Niger	01	
Nigeria, Republic of	01	
Norfolk Island	11	30
Norway*	01	
Novaya Zemlya	04	
Okinawa	09	
Oman	04	
Pagalu (Annobon Islands)	01	
Pakistan	05	
Palau Islands	09	
Papua New Guinea	10	
Pescadores Islands	08	
Philippine Republic	08	
Poland*†	01	
Qatar	03	
Reunion	04	
Romania*†	02	
Russia [1]		
Kaliningrad	03	
Moscow, St. Petersburg, Volgograd		
Arkhangelsk, Astrakhan, Samara	04	
Ekaterinburg, Ufa, Perm, Novyy Port	06	
Omsk, Novosibirsk, Tomsk	07	
Norilsk, Krasnoyarsk, Dikson	08	

	h	m
Irkutsk, Bratsk, Ulan-Ude	09	
Tiksi, Yakutsk, Chita	10	
Vladivostok, Khabarovsk, Okhotsk		
Sakhalin Island	11	
Petropavlovsk-K., Magadan, Anadyr		
Kuril Islands	12	
Rwanda	02	
Ryukyu Islands	09	
Samoa*	13	
Santa Cruz Islands	11	
Sardinia*†	01	
Saudi Arabia	03	
Schouten Islands	09	
Serbia*	01	
Seychelles	04	
Sicily*†	01	
Singapore	08	
Slovakia*†	01	
Slovenia*†	01	
Socotra	03	
Solomon Islands	11	
Somalia Republic	03	
South Africa, Republic of	02	
Spain*†	01	
Spanish Possessions in North Africa*	01	
Spitsbergen (Svalbard)*	01	
Sri Lanka	05	30
Sudan, Republic of	03	
Swaziland	02	
Sweden*†	01	
Switzerland*	01	
Syria (Syrian Arab Republic)*	02	
Taiwan	08	
Tajikistan	05	
Tanzania	03	
Thailand	07	
Timor-Leste	09	
Tonga	13	
Tunisia	01	
Turkey*	02	
Turkmenistan	05	
Tuvalu	12	
Uganda	03	
Ukraine*	02	
United Arab Emirates	04	
Uzbekistan	05	
Vanuatu, Republic of	11	
Vietnam, Socialist Republic of	07	
Yemen	03	
Zambia, Republic of	02	
Zimbabwe	02	

* Daylight-saving time may be kept in these places.   † For Summer time dates see List II footnotes.
[1] The boundaries between the zones are irregular; listed are chief towns in each zone.

LIST II — PLACES NORMALLY KEEPING UTC

Ascension Island	Ghana	Irish Republic*†	Morocco*	Sierra Leone
Burkina-Faso	Great Britain†	Ivory Coast	Portugal*†	Togo Republic
Canary Islands*†	Guinea-Bissau	Liberia	Principe	Tristan da Cunha
Channel Islands†	Guinea Republic	Madeira*†	St. Helena	
Faeroes*, The	Iceland	Mali	São Tomé	
Gambia, The	Ireland, Northern†	Mauritania	Senegal	

* Daylight-saving time may be kept in these places.

† Summer time (daylight-saving time), one hour in advance of UTC, will be kept from 2013 March 31$^\text{d}$ 01$^\text{h}$ to October 27$^\text{d}$ 01$^\text{h}$ UTC (Ninth Summer Time Directive of the European Union). Ratification by member countries has not been verified.

LIST III — PLACES SLOW ON UTC (WEST OF GREENWICH)

The times given ⎱ *subtracted* from UTC to give Standard Time
below should be ⎰ *added* to Standard Time to give UTC.

	h	m		h	m
American Samoa	11		Canada (*continued*)		
Argentina	03		Prince Edward Island*	04	
Austral (Tubuai) Islands[1]	10		Quebec, east of long. W. 63°	04	
Azores*†	01		west of long. W. 63°* ...	05	
			Saskatchewan	06	
Bahamas*	05		Yukon*	08	
Barbados	04		Cape Verde Islands	01	
Belize	06		Cayman Islands	05	
Bermuda*	04		Chile*	04	
Bolivia	04		Colombia	05	
Brazil			Cook Islands	10	
Fernando de Noronha I., Trindade I.,			Costa Rica	06	
Oceanic Is.	02		Cuba*	05	
N and NE coastal states, Bahia,			Curaçao Island	04	
Tocantins, Goiás*, Brasilia*,					
Minas Gerais*, Espirito Santo*,					
S and E coastal states*	03		Dominican Republic	04	
Mato Grosso do Sul*, Mato Grosso*,					
Rondônia, Amazonas, Roraima, Acre	04		Easter Island (I. de Pascua)*	06	
British Antarctic Territory[2,3]	03		Ecuador	05	
			El Salvador	06	
Canada[3]‡					
Alberta*	07		Falkland Islands*	04	
British Columbia*	08		Fernando de Noronha Island	02	
Labrador*	04		French Guiana	03	
Manitoba*	06				
New Brunswick*	04		Galápagos Islands	06	
Newfoundland*	03	30	Greenland		
Nunavut*			Danmarkshavn, Mesters Vig	00	
east of long. W. 85°	05		General*	03	
long. W. 85° to W. 102°	06		Scoresby Sound*	01	
west of long. W. 102°	07		Thule*, Pituffik*	04	
Northwest Territories*	07		Grenada	04	
Nova Scotia*	04		Guadeloupe	04	
Ontario, east of long. W. 90°*	05		Guatemala	06	
Ontario, west of long. W. 90°* ...	06		Guyana, Republic of	04	

* Daylight-saving time may be kept in these places.   ‡ Dates for DST are given at the end of List III.

[1] This is the legal standard time, but local mean time is generally used.

[2] Stations may use UTC.

[3] Some areas may keep another time zone.

LIST III — (continued)

	h m		h m
Haiti	05	United States of America ‡(continued)	
Honduras	06	Idaho, southern part	07
		northern part	08
Jamaica	05	Illinois	06
Johnston Island	10	Indiana[2]	05
Juan Fernandez Islands*	04	Iowa	06
		Kansas[2]	06
Leeward Islands	04	Kentucky, eastern part	05
		western part	06
Marquesas Islands	09 30	Louisiana	06
Martinique	04	Maine	05
Mexico		Maryland	05
General*	06	Massachusetts	05
Sonora, Sinaloa*, Nayarit*,		Michigan[2]	05
Chihuahua*, Southern District		Minnesota	06
of Lower California*	07	Mississippi	06
Northern District of Lower California*	08	Missouri	06
Midway Islands	11	Montana	07
		Nebraska, eastern part	06
Nicaragua	06	western part	07
Niue	11	Nevada	08
		New Hampshire	05
Panama, Republic of	05	New Jersey	05
Paraguay*	04	New Mexico	07
Peru	05	New York	05
Pitcairn Island	08	North Carolina	05
Puerto Rico	04	North Dakota, eastern part	06
		western part	07
St. Pierre and Miquelon*	03	Ohio	05
Society Islands	10	Oklahoma	06
South Georgia	02	Oregon[2]	08
Suriname	03	Pennsylvania	05
		Rhode Island	05
Trindade Island, South Atlantic ...	02	South Carolina	05
Trinidad and Tobago	04	South Dakota, eastern part	06
Tuamotu Archipelago	10	western part	07
Tubuai (Austral) Islands	10	Tennessee, eastern part	05
Turks and Caicos Islands*	05	western part	06
		Texas[2]	06
United States of America ‡		Utah	07
Alabama	06	Vermont	05
Alaska	09	Virginia	05
Aleutian Islands, east of W. 169° 30'	09	Washington D.C.	05
Aleutian Islands, west of W. 169° 30'	10	Washington	08
Arizona[1]	07	West Virginia	05
Arkansas	06	Wisconsin	06
California	08	Wyoming	07
Colorado	07	Uruguay*	03
Connecticut	05		
Delaware	05	Venezuela	04 30
District of Columbia	05	Virgin Islands	04
Florida[2]	05		
Georgia	05	Windward Islands	04
Hawaii[1]	10		

* Daylight-saving time may be kept in these places.

‡ Daylight-saving (Summer) time, one hour fast on the time given, is kept during 2013 from March 10 (second Sunday) to November 3 (first Sunday), changing at 02ʰ 00ᵐ local clock time.

[1] Exempt from keeping daylight-saving time, except for a portion of Arizona.

[2] A small portion of the state is in another time zone.

NORTHERN STARS

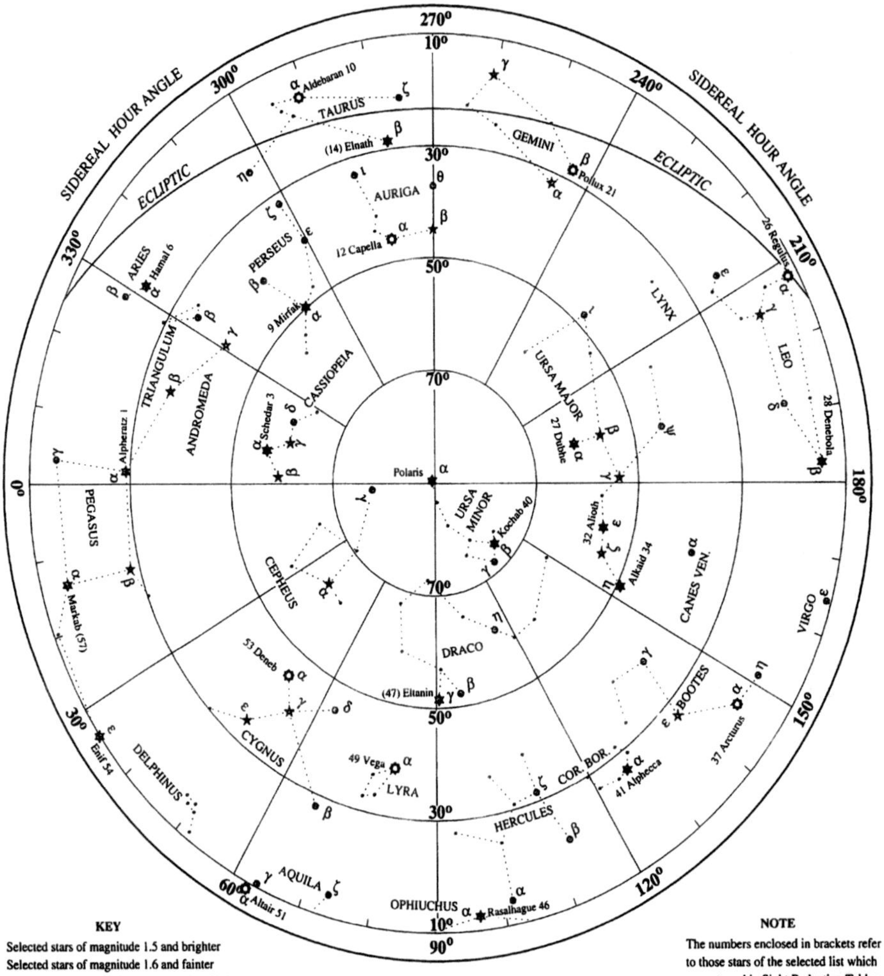

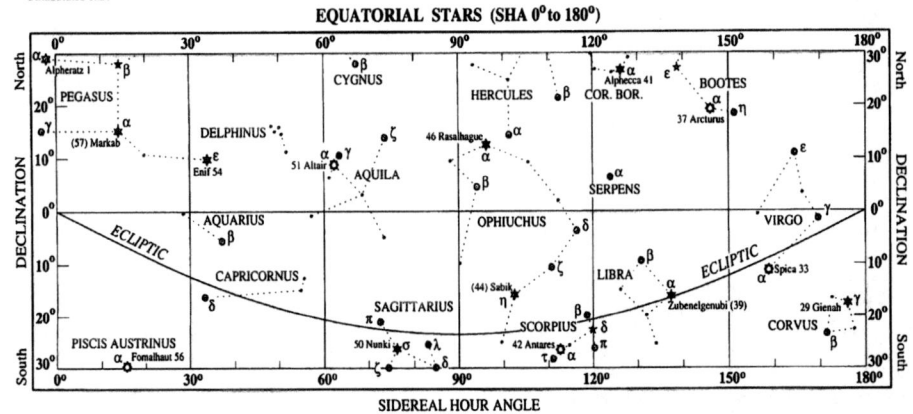

KEY

✪ Selected stars of magnitude 1.5 and brighter
✸ Selected stars of magnitude 1.6 and fainter
★ Other tabulated stars of magnitude 2.5 and brighter
● Other tabulated stars of magnitude 2.6 and fainter
· Untabulated stars

NOTE

The numbers enclosed in brackets refer to those stars of the selected list which are not used in Sight Reduction Tables H.O. 249, A.P. 3270, N.P. 303.

EQUATORIAL STARS (SHA 0° to 180°)

SOUTHERN STARS

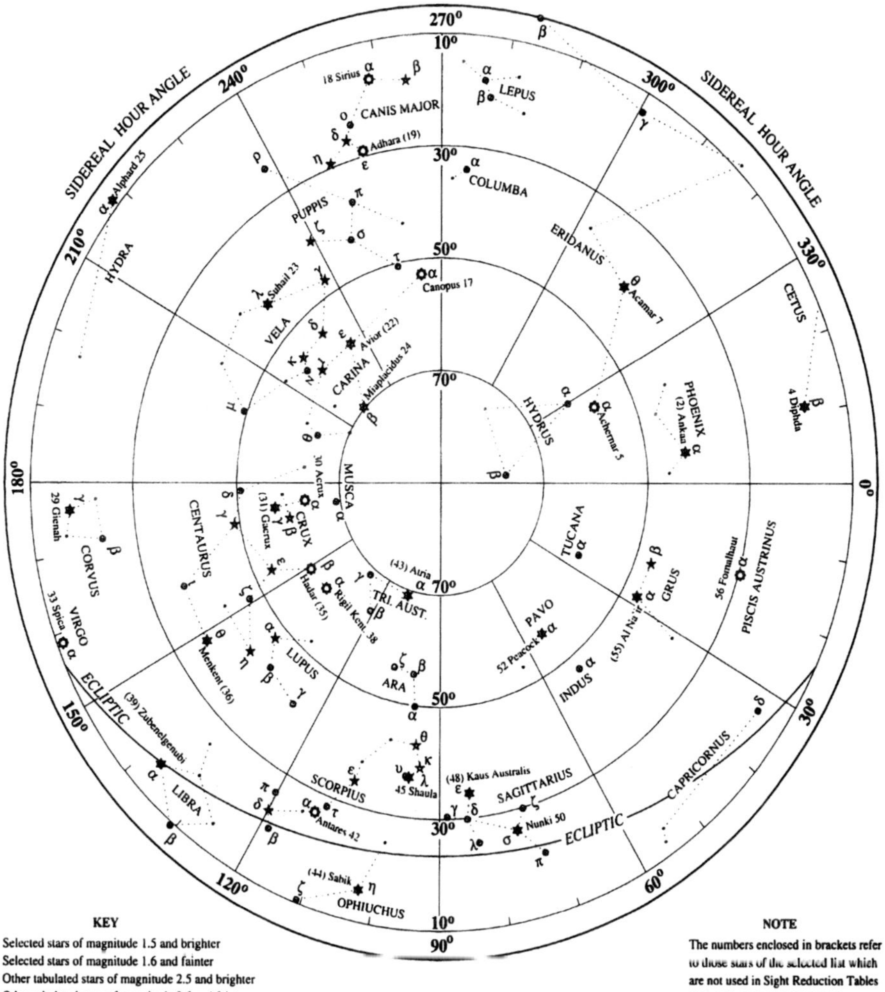

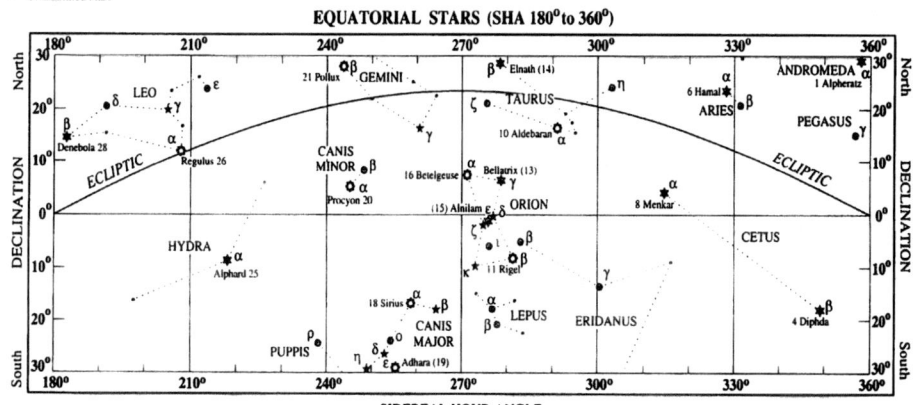

KEY

- ✪ Selected stars of magnitude 1.5 and brighter
- ✸ Selected stars of magnitude 1.6 and fainter
- ★ Other tabulated stars of magnitude 2.5 and brighter
- ● Other tabulated stars of magnitude 2.6 and fainter
- · Untabulated stars

NOTE

The numbers enclosed in brackets refer to those stars of the selected list which are not used in Sight Reduction Tables H.O. 249, A.P. 3270, N.P. 303.

EQUATORIAL STARS (SHA 180° to 360°)

SIDEREAL HOUR ANGLE

Mag.	Name and Number		SHA							Declination						
			°	JAN.	FEB.	MAR.	APR.	MAY	JUNE		°	JAN.	FEB.	MAR.	APR.	MAY	JUNE
3·2	γ Cephei		5	01·7	02·2	02·4	02·1	01·5	00·6	N 77	42·7	42·6	42·4	42·3	42·2	42·2
2·5	α Pegasi	57	13	38·8	38·8	38·8	38·7	38·5	38·3	N 15	16·7	16·6	16·6	16·5	16·6	16·7
2·4	β Pegasi		13	53·8	53·9	53·9	53·7	53·5	53·3	N 28	09·4	09·3	09·2	09·2	09·2	09·3
1·2	α Piscis Aust.	56	15	24·5	24·6	24·5	24·4	24·2	23·9	S 29	33·2	33·2	33·1	33·0	32·9	32·8
2·1	β Gruis		19	08·6	08·6	08·5	08·4	08·1	07·8	S 46	49·1	49·0	48·8	48·7	48·6	48·5
2·9	α Tucanæ		25	09·6	09·6	09·5	09·3	08·9	08·5	S 60	11·7	11·6	11·5	11·3	11·2	11·1
1·7	α Gruis	55	27	44·5	44·5	44·4	44·2	43·9	43·6	S 46	53·9	53·8	53·7	53·5	53·4	53·4
2·9	δ Capricorni		33	03·7	03·7	03·6	03·4	03·2	02·9	S 16	04·0	04·0	04·0	03·9	03·8	03·7
2·4	ε Pegasi	54	33	47·7	47·6	47·6	47·4	47·2	46·9	N 9	56·2	56·2	56·1	56·1	56·2	56·3
2·9	β Aquarii		36	56·4	56·4	56·3	56·1	55·9	55·7	S 5	30·7	30·8	30·7	30·7	30·6	30·5
2·4	α Cephei		40	17·1	17·1	16·9	16·6	16·2	15·8	N 62	38·7	38·6	38·4	38·3	38·4	38·5
2·5	ε Cygni		48	19·1	19·0	18·9	18·7	18·4	18·2	N 34	01·3	01·2	01·1	01·1	01·1	01·3
1·3	α Cygni	53	49	32·1	32·0	31·9	31·6	31·4	31·1	N 45	19·8	19·7	19·6	19·5	19·6	19·7
3·1	α Indi		50	23·0	23·0	22·8	22·5	22·2	21·9	S 47	14·7	14·6	14·5	14·4	14·3	14·3
1·9	α Pavonis	52	53	20·3	20·1	19·9	19·6	19·2	18·8	S 56	41·5	41·4	41·3	41·2	41·1	41·1
2·2	γ Cygni		54	19·8	19·7	19·6	19·3	19·0	18·8	N 40	18·1	17·9	17·8	17·8	17·9	18·0
0·8	α Aquilæ	51	62	08·8	08·7	08·6	08·4	08·1	07·9	N 8	54·3	54·2	54·2	54·2	54·3	54·4
2·7	γ Aquilæ		63	16·9	16·8	16·7	16·5	16·2	16·0	N 10	38·8	38·7	38·7	38·7	38·8	38·9
2·9	δ Cygni		63	39·6	39·5	39·3	39·0	38·7	38·5	N 45	09·9	09·7	09·6	09·6	09·7	09·9
3·1	β Cygni		67	11·5	11·4	11·2	11·0	10·7	10·5	N 27	59·3	59·2	59·2	59·2	59·2	59·4
2·9	π Sagittarii		72	22·0	21·9	21·7	21·5	21·2	21·0	S 20	60·0	60·0	60·0	60·0	59·9	59·9
3·0	ζ Aquilæ		73	30·0	29·9	29·7	29·5	29·2	29·1	N 13	53·1	53·0	52·9	53·0	53·0	53·1
2·6	ζ Sagittarii		74	08·5	08·3	08·1	07·9	07·6	07·4	S 29	51·5	51·5	51·5	51·4	51·4	51·4
2·0	σ Sagittarii	50	75	59·0	58·8	58·6	58·4	58·2	58·0	S 26	16·7	16·7	16·6	16·6	16·6	16·6
0·0	α Lyræ	49	80	39·6	39·4	39·2	38·9	38·7	38·5	N 38	47·8	47·7	47·6	47·6	47·7	47·9
2·8	λ Sagittarii		82	48·5	48·3	48·1	47·8	47·6	47·4	S 25	24·7	24·7	24·7	24·7	24·7	24·6
1·9	ε Sagittarii	48	83	44·5	44·3	44·1	43·8	43·6	43·4	S 34	22·5	22·5	22·5	22·5	22·5	22·5
2·7	δ Sagittarii		84	32·7	32·5	32·2	32·0	31·7	31·6	S 29	49·2	49·2	49·1	49·1	49·1	49·1
3·0	γ Sagittarii		88	20·4	20·2	20·0	19·7	19·5	19·3	S 30	25·3	25·2	25·2	25·2	25·2	25·2
2·2	γ Draconis	47	90	46·8	46·5	46·3	46·0	45·7	45·6	N 51	29·2	29·1	29·0	29·1	29·2	29·3
2·8	β Ophiuchi		93	58·3	58·1	57·9	57·7	57·5	57·4	N 4	33·8	33·7	33·7	33·7	33·8	33·9
2·4	κ Scorpii		94	09·2	09·0	08·7	08·4	08·2	08·1	S 39	02·0	02·0	02·0	02·0	02·0	02·0
1·9	θ Scorpii		95	26·2	26·0	25·7	25·4	25·1	25·0	S 43	00·1	00·1	00·1	00·1	00·2	00·2
2·1	α Ophiuchi	46	96	07·0	06·8	06·6	06·4	06·2	06·1	N 12	33·1	33·0	33·0	33·0	33·1	33·2
1·6	λ Scorpii	45	96	22·6	22·4	22·1	21·9	21·6	21·5	S 37	06·6	06·6	06·6	06·6	06·6	06·6
3·0	α Aræ		96	47·3	47·0	46·7	46·4	46·1	45·9	S 49	52·9	52·9	52·9	52·9	53·0	53·0
2·7	υ Scorpii		97	05·3	05·0	04·8	04·5	04·3	04·1	S 37	18·2	18·1	18·1	18·2	18·2	18·2
2·8	β Draconis		97	19·5	19·2	18·9	18·6	18·4	18·3	N 52	17·4	17·3	17·3	17·3	17·4	17·6
2·8	β Aræ		98	24·3	24·0	23·6	23·3	23·0	22·8	S 55	32·2	32·2	32·2	32·2	32·3	32·3
Var.‡	α Herculis		101	11·4	11·3	11·0	10·8	10·7	10·6	N 14	22·5	22·5	22·4	22·5	22·5	22·6
2·4	η Ophiuchi	44	102	13·1	12·9	12·7	12·5	12·3	12·2	S 15	44·3	44·4	44·4	44·4	44·4	44·4
3·1	ζ Aræ		105	04·5	04·2	03·8	03·4	03·2	03·0	S 56	00·3	00·3	00·3	00·4	00·5	00·6
2·3	ε Scorpii		107	14·8	14·6	14·3	14·1	13·9	13·8	S 34	18·8	18·8	18·8	18·9	18·9	19·0
1·9	α Triang. Aust.	43	107	29·3	28·8	28·2	27·7	27·3	27·1	S 69	02·7	02·7	02·7	02·8	02·9	03·0
2·8	ζ Herculis		109	33·5	33·2	33·0	32·8	32·7	32·6	N 31	34·7	34·6	34·5	34·6	34·7	34·8
2·6	ζ Ophiuchi		110	31·8	31·6	31·4	31·2	31·0	30·9	S 10	35·5	35·6	35·6	35·6	35·6	35·6
2·8	τ Scorpii		110	49·5	49·3	49·0	48·8	48·6	48·6	S 28	14·4	14·4	14·5	14·5	14·5	14·5
2·8	β Herculis		112	18·4	18·1	17·9	17·7	17·6	17·5	N 21	27·6	27·5	27·5	27·6	27·6	27·8
1·0	α Scorpii	42	112	26·8	26·6	26·4	26·1	26·0	25·9	S 26	27·5	27·5	27·6	27·6	27·6	27·6
2·7	η Draconis		113	57·9	57·6	57·2	56·9	56·7	56·7	N 61	28·9	28·8	28·8	28·9	29·0	29·2
2·7	δ Ophiuchi		116	14·5	14·3	14·1	13·9	13·8	13·7	S 3	43·6	43·7	43·7	43·7	43·7	43·6
2·6	β Scorpii		118	27·0	26·7	26·5	26·3	26·2	26·1	S 19	50·3	50·4	50·4	50·5	50·5	50·6
2·3	δ Scorpii		119	43·3	43·1	42·9	42·8	42·5	42·5	S 22	39·4	39·4	39·5	39·5	39·5	39·6
2·9	π Scorpii		120	05·3	05·0	04·8	04·6	04·5	04·4	S 26	08·9	09·0	09·0	09·1	09·1	09·1
2·8	β Trianguli Aust.		120	55·4	54·9	54·5	54·1	53·9	53·8	S 63	27·9	27·9	28·0	28·1	28·2	28·3
2·6	α Serpentis		123	46·3	46·1	45·9	45·7	45·6	45·6	N 6	23·1	23·0	22·9	23·0	23·0	23·1
2·8	γ Lupi		125	59·7	59·4	59·1	58·9	58·7	58·7	S 41	12·4	12·4	12·5	12·6	12·7	12·7
2·2	α Coronæ Bor.	41	126	11·4	11·2	11·0	10·8	10·7	10·7	N 26	40·1	40·0	40·0	40·1	40·2	40·3

‡ 2·9 — 3·6

Mag.	Name and Number		SHA						Declination						
			JULY	AUG.	SEPT.	OCT.	NOV.	DEC.		JULY	AUG.	SEPT.	OCT.	NOV.	DEC.
		°	′	′	′	′	′	′	°	′	′	′	′	′	′
3·2	γ Cephei	4	59·9	59·3	59·1	59·2	59·6	60·2	N 77	42·3	42·4	42·6	42·8	43·0	43·0
2·5	Markab 57	13	38·0	37·9	37·8	37·8	37·9	38·0	N 15	16·8	16·9	17·0	17·0	17·1	17·0
2·4	Scheat	13	53·1	52·9	52·8	52·8	52·9	53·1	N 28	09·4	09·6	09·7	09·8	09·8	09·8
1·2	Fomalhaut 56	15	23·7	23·5	23·4	23·5	23·6	23·7	S 29	32·7	32·7	32·8	32·8	32·9	32·9
2·1	β Gruis	19	07·5	07·3	07·3	07·3	07·5	07·7	S 46	48·5	48·5	48·6	48·7	48·8	48·8
2·9	α Tucanæ	25	08·2	07·9	07·9	08·0	08·3	08·6	S 60	11·1	11·2	11·3	11·5	11·5	11·5
1·7	Al Na'ir 55	27	43·3	43·1	43·1	43·2	43·4	43·5	S 46	53·4	53·4	53·5	53·6	53·7	53·7
2·9	δ Capricorni	33	02·7	02·6	02·6	02·7	02·8	02·9	S 16	03·7	03·7	03·7	03·7	03·7	03·7
2·4	Enif 54	33	46·8	46·7	46·6	46·7	46·8	46·9	N 9	56·4	56·5	56·6	56·6	56·6	56·6
2·9	β Aquarii	36	55·5	55·4	55·4	55·4	55·6	55·7	S 5	30·5	30·4	30·4	30·4	30·4	30·4
2·4	Alderamin	40	15·6	15·5	15·6	15·9	16·2	16·5	N 62	38·6	38·8	39·0	39·1	39·1	39·1
2·5	ε Cygni	48	18·0	18·0	18·0	18·1	18·3	18·5	N 34	01·4	01·6	01·7	01·8	01·8	01·7
1·3	Deneb 53	49	30·9	30·9	31·0	31·2	31·4	31·5	N 45	19·9	20·0	20·2	20·2	20·2	20·2
3·1	α Indi	50	21·6	21·6	21·6	21·8	22·0	22·1	S 47	14·3	14·4	14·5	14·6	14·6	14·5
1·9	Peacock 52	53	18·6	18·5	18·6	18·8	19·1	19·2	S 56	41·2	41·3	41·4	41·4	41·5	41·4
2·2	γ Cygni	54	18·7	18·6	18·7	18·9	19·1	19·2	N 40	18·2	18·3	18·5	18·5	18·5	18·4
0·8	Altair 51	62	07·8	07·8	07·9	08·0	08·1	08·2	N 8	54·5	54·6	54·6	54·6	54·6	54·6
2·7	γ Aquilæ	63	15·9	15·9	16·0	16·1	16·2	16·3	N 10	39·0	39·1	39·2	39·2	39·1	39·1
2·9	δ Cygni	63	38·4	38·4	38·6	38·8	39·0	39·1	N 45	10·0	10·2	10·3	10·3	10·3	10·2
3·1	Albireo	67	10·4	10·4	10·5	10·7	10·9	10·9	N 27	59·5	59·6	59·7	59·8	59·7	59·6
2·9	π Sagittarii	72	20·9	20·9	21·0	21·1	21·3	21·3	S 20	59·9	59·9	59·9	59·9	59·9	59·9
3·0	ζ Aquilæ	73	29·0	29·0	29·1	29·2	29·4	29·4	N 13	53·3	53·4	53·4	53·4	53·4	53·3
2·6	ζ Sagittarii	74	07·3	07·3	07·4	07·6	07·7	07·7	S 29	51·4	51·4	51·5	51·5	51·5	51·4
2·0	Nunki 50	75	57·9	57·9	58·0	58·1	58·2	58·3	S 26	16·6	16·6	16·6	16·6	16·6	16·6
0·0	Vega 49	80	38·5	38·5	38·7	38·9	39·1	39·1	N 38	48·0	48·2	48·2	48·2	48·2	48·1
2·8	λ Sagittarii	82	47·3	47·4	47·5	47·6	47·7	47·7	S 25	24·6	24·7	24·7	24·7	24·7	24·6
1·9	Kaus Australis 48	83	43·3	43·3	43·5	43·6	43·8	43·8	S 34	22·5	22·5	22·6	22·6	22·5	22·5
2·7	δ Sagittarii	84	31·5	31·5	31·6	31·8	31·9	31·9	S 29	49·1	49·2	49·2	49·2	49·2	49·1
3·0	γ Sagittarii	88	19·2	19·3	19·4	19·5	19·7	19·6	S 30	25·3	25·3	25·3	25·3	25·3	25·2
2·2	Eltanin 47	90	45·6	45·8	46·0	46·2	46·5	46·5	N 51	29·5	29·6	29·7	29·7	29·6	29·4
2·8	β Ophiuchi	93	57·4	57·4	57·6	57·7	57·8	57·8	N 4	33·9	34·0	34·0	34·0	34·0	33·9
2·4	κ Scorpii	94	08·0	08·0	08·2	08·3	08·5	08·5	S 39	02·1	02·1	02·1	02·1	02·1	02·0
1·9	θ Scorpii	95	24·9	25·0	25·2	25·3	25·4	25·4	S 43	00·3	00·3	00·3	00·3	00·3	00·2
2·1	Rasalhague 46	96	06·1	06·1	06·3	06·4	06·5	06·5	N 12	33·3	33·3	33·4	33·3	33·3	33·2
1·6	Shaula 45	96	21·4	21·5	21·6	21·8	21·9	21·9	S 37	06·7	06·7	06·7	06·7	06·7	06·6
3·0	α Aræ	96	45·9	46·0	46·2	46·4	46·5	46·5	S 49	53·1	53·2	53·2	53·2	53·1	53·0
2·7	υ Scorpii	97	04·1	04·2	04·3	04·5	04·6	04·5	S 37	18·3	18·3	18·3	18·3	18·2	18·2
2·8	β Draconis	97	18·4	18·5	18·8	19·1	19·2	19·3	N 52	17·8	17·9	17·9	17·9	17·8	17·6
2·8	β Aræ	98	22·7	22·9	23·1	23·3	23·5	23·4	S 55	32·5	32·5	32·6	32·5	32·4	32·3
Var.‡	α Herculis	101	10·6	10·6	10·8	10·9	11·0	11·0	N 14	22·7	22·8	22·8	22·8	22·7	22·6
2·4	Sabik 44	102	12·2	12·2	12·3	12·5	12·5	12·5	S 15	44·3	44·3	44·3	44·3	44·3	44·3
3·1	ζ Aræ	105	03·0	03·1	03·4	03·6	03·7	03·6	S 56	00·6	00·7	00·7	00·7	00·6	00·5
2·3	ε Scorpii	107	13·8	13·9	14·0	14·2	14·2	14·2	S 34	19·0	19·0	19·0	19·0	18·9	18·9
1·9	Atria 43	107	27·1	27·4	27·8	28·2	28·3	28·2	S 69	03·1	03·2	03·2	03·2	03·0	02·9
2·8	ζ Herculis	109	32·6	32·8	32·9	33·1	33·2	33·1	N 31	35·0	35·0	35·1	35·0	34·9	34·8
2·6	ζ Ophiuchi	110	30·9	31·0	31·2	31·3	31·3	31·2	S 10	35·5	35·5	35·5	35·5	35·5	35·5
2·8	τ Scorpii	110	48·6	48·6	48·8	48·9	49·0	48·9	S 28	14·6	14·6	14·6	14·5	14·5	14·5
2·8	β Herculis	112	17·6	17·7	17·8	17·9	18·0	17·9	N 21	27·9	27·9	27·9	27·9	27·8	27·7
1·0	Antares 42	112	25·9	26·0	26·1	26·2	26·3	26·2	S 26	27·6	27·6	27·6	27·6	27·6	27·6
2·7	η Draconis	113	56·9	57·2	57·5	57·8	58·0	58·0	N 61	29·3	29·4	29·4	29·3	29·2	29·0
2·7	δ Ophiuchi	116	13·7	13·8	13·9	14·0	14·1	14·0	S 3	43·6	43·6	43·5	43·5	43·6	43·6
2·6	β Scorpii	118	26·1	26·2	26·4	26·5	26·5	26·4	S 19	50·5	50·5	50·4	50·4	50·4	50·4
2·3	Dschubba	119	42·5	42·6	42·7	42·8	42·8	42·7	S 22	39·6	39·5	39·5	39·5	39·5	39·5
2·9	π Scorpii	120	04·4	04·5	04·6	04·8	04·8	04·7	S 26	09·1	09·1	09·1	09·1	09·0	09·0
2·8	β Trianguli Aust.	120	53·9	54·1	54·4	54·7	54·7	54·5	S 63	28·4	28·5	28·4	28·4	28·2	28·1
2·6	α Serpentis	123	45·6	45·7	45·8	45·9	45·9	45·8	N 6	23·2	23·2	23·2	23·2	23·1	23·0
2·8	γ Lupi	125	58·8	58·9	59·0	59·2	59·2	59·0	S 41	12·8	12·8	12·7	12·7	12·6	12·6
2·2	Alphecca 41	126	10·8	10·9	11·0	11·1	11·2	11·1	N 26	40·4	40·5	40·4	40·4	40·3	40·1

‡ 2·9 — 3·6

Mag.	Name and Number		SHA						Declination					
			JAN.	FEB.	MAR.	APR.	MAY	JUNE	JAN.	FEB.	MAR.	APR.	MAY	JUNE
			° ′	′	′	′	′	′	° ′	′	′	′	′	′
3·1	γ Ursæ Minoris		129 49·9	49·4	48·9	48·5	48·4	48·6	N 71 47·0	46·9	46·9	47·1	47·2	47·4
2·9	γ Trianguli Aust.		129 57·7	57·1	56·6	56·2	55·9	55·9	S 68 43·3	43·3	43·4	43·5	43·7	43·8
2·6	β Libræ		130 34·2	34·0	33·8	33·6	33·6	33·5	S 9 25·8	25·9	25·9	26·0	25·9	25·9
2·7	β Lupi		135 08·9	08·6	08·4	08·2	08·1	08·0	S 43 11·0	11·0	11·1	11·2	11·3	11·4
2·8	α Libræ	39	137 05·8	05·6	05·4	05·2	05·1	05·1	S 16 05·7	05·8	05·8	05·9	05·9	05·9
2·1	β Ursæ Minoris	40	137 20·5	19·8	19·3	19·0	18·9	19·2	N 74 05·8	05·8	05·8	06·0	06·1	06·3
2·4	ε Bootis		138 36·6	36·4	36·2	36·0	36·0	36·0	N 27 01·0	01·0	01·0	01·0	01·1	01·2
2·3	α Lupi		139 17·7	17·4	17·1	16·9	16·8	16·8	S 47 26·4	26·5	26·6	26·7	26·8	26·9
−0·3	α Centauri	38	139 52·2	51·8	51·4	51·2	51·1	51·2	S 60 53·0	53·1	53·2	53·3	53·5	53·6
2·3	η Centauri		140 54·7	54·4	54·1	53·9	53·9	53·9	S 42 12·7	12·8	12·9	13·0	13·1	13·1
3·0	γ Bootis		141 51·0	50·7	50·5	50·3	50·3	50·3	N 38 14·8	14·8	14·8	14·9	15·0	15·1
0·0	α Bootis	37	145 56·0	55·8	55·6	55·5	55·5	55·5	N 19 06·7	06·6	06·6	06·7	06·8	06·8
2·1	θ Centauri	36	148 07·9	07·6	07·4	07·3	07·2	07·3	S 36 25·9	26·0	26·1	26·2	26·3	26·3
0·6	β Centauri	35	148 48·3	47·9	47·6	47·4	47·3	47·4	S 60 25·9	26·0	26·1	26·2	26·4	26·5
2·6	ζ Centauri		150 54·3	54·0	53·7	53·6	53·5	53·6	S 47 21·0	21·0	21·2	21·3	21·4	21·5
2·7	η Bootis		151 10·3	10·0	09·9	09·8	09·7	09·8	N 18 19·8	19·7	19·7	19·7	19·8	19·9
1·9	η Ursæ Majoris	34	152 59·2	58·9	58·6	58·5	58·5	58·7	N 49 14·6	14·5	14·6	14·7	14·9	15·0
2·3	ε Centauri		154 48·8	48·4	48·2	48·1	48·0	48·1	S 53 31·7	31·8	32·0	32·1	32·2	32·3
1·0	α Virginis	33	158 31·5	31·3	31·1	31·1	31·0	31·1	S 11 13·8	13·9	13·9	14·0	14·0	14·0
2·3	ζ Ursæ Majoris		158 53·2	52·9	52·6	52·6	52·6	52·8	N 54 51·1	51·1	51·2	51·3	51·4	51·5
2·8	ι Centauri		159 39·6	39·4	39·2	39·1	39·1	39·2	S 36 46·7	46·9	47·0	47·1	47·2	47·2
2·8	ε Virginis		164 17·4	17·1	17·0	17·0	17·0	17·0	N 10 53·2	53·1	53·1	53·1	53·2	53·2
2·9	α Canum Venat.		165 50·3	50·0	49·9	49·8	49·8	49·9	N 38 14·6	14·5	14·6	14·7	14·8	14·9
1·8	ε Ursæ Majoris	32	166 20·9	20·5	20·3	20·3	20·4	20·5	N 55 53·0	53·0	53·1	53·2	53·3	53·4
1·3	β Crucis		167 52·1	51·7	51·5	51·4	51·5	51·6	S 59 45·4	45·5	45·7	45·9	46·0	46·1
2·9	γ Virginis		169 24·9	24·7	24·6	24·5	24·5	24·6	S 1 31·4	31·5	31·5	31·5	31·5	31·5
2·2	γ Centauri		169 25·9	25·6	25·4	25·4	25·4	25·5	S 49 01·7	01·9	02·0	02·2	02·3	02·3
2·7	α Muscæ		170 29·6	29·2	28·9	28·8	28·9	29·2	S 69 12·2	12·4	12·5	12·7	12·9	12·9
2·7	β Corvi		171 13·5	13·3	13·2	13·1	13·1	13·2	S 23 28·1	28·2	28·3	28·4	28·5	28·5
1·6	γ Crucis	31	172 01·0	00·7	00·5	00·4	00·5	00·7	S 57 11·0	11·1	11·3	11·5	11·6	11·6
1·3	α Crucis	30	173 09·3	08·9	08·7	08·7	08·8	09·0	S 63 10·1	10·2	10·4	10·6	10·7	10·8
2·6	γ Corvi	29	175 52·4	52·2	52·1	52·1	52·1	52·2	S 17 36·9	37·0	37·1	37·2	37·2	37·2
2·6	δ Centauri		177 43·9	43·6	43·5	43·5	43·5	43·7	S 50 47·6	47·7	47·9	48·0	48·1	48·2
2·4	γ Ursæ Majoris		181 22·0	21·7	21·6	21·6	21·7	21·9	N 53 36·9	37·0	37·1	37·2	37·3	37·4
2·1	β Leonis	28	182 33·8	33·6	33·5	33·5	33·6	33·7	N 14 29·7	29·7	29·7	29·7	29·7	29·8
2·6	δ Leonis		191 17·6	17·4	17·4	17·4	17·5	17·6	N 20 26·9	26·8	26·8	26·9	27·0	27·0
3·0	ψ Ursæ Majoris		192 23·7	23·5	23·4	23·5	23·6	23·7	N 44 25·3	25·3	25·4	25·5	25·6	25·6
1·8	α Ursæ Majoris	27	193 51·6	51·4	51·3	51·4	51·6	51·9	N 61 40·4	40·5	40·6	40·8	40·9	40·9
2·4	β Ursæ Majoris		194 20·2	19·9	19·9	20·0	20·2	20·4	N 56 18·4	18·4	18·5	18·7	18·8	18·8
2·7	μ Velorum		198 09·4	09·2	09·1	09·2	09·4	09·6	S 49 29·3	29·5	29·7	29·8	29·9	29·9
2·8	θ Carinæ		199 07·7	07·5	07·5	07·7	07·9	08·2	S 64 27·7	27·9	28·1	28·2	28·3	28·3
2·3	γ Leonis		204 49·2	49·0	49·0	49·1	49·2	49·3	N 19 46·2	46·2	46·2	46·3	46·3	46·4
1·4	α Leonis	26	207 43·5	43·4	43·4	43·5	43·6	43·7	N 11 53·9	53·9	53·9	53·9	54·0	54·0
3·0	ε Leonis		213 20·6	20·5	20·5	20·6	20·7	20·8	N 23 42·6	42·6	42·6	42·6	42·7	42·7
3·1	N Velorum		217 04·9	04·8	04·9	05·1	05·4	05·6	S 57 05·6	05·7	05·9	06·0	06·1	06·0
2·0	α Hydræ	25	217 56·0	56·0	56·0	56·1	56·2	56·3	S 8 43·1	43·2	43·3	43·3	43·3	43·2
2·5	κ Velorum		219 21·5	21·5	21·5	21·7	21·9	22·1	S 55 04·0	04·2	04·4	04·5	04·5	04·4
2·2	ι Carinæ		220 37·6	37·5	37·6	37·8	38·1	38·4	S 59 19·9	20·0	20·2	20·3	20·3	20·3
1·7	β Carinæ	24	221 38·8	38·7	38·9	39·3	39·7	40·2	S 69 46·3	46·5	46·6	46·8	46·8	46·8
2·2	λ Velorum	23	222 52·2	52·1	52·2	52·4	52·5	52·7	S 43 29·2	29·4	29·5	29·6	29·6	29·6
3·1	ι Ursæ Majoris		224 57·9	57·8	57·8	58·0	58·2	58·3	N 47 59·1	59·2	59·3	59·3	59·4	59·3
2·0	δ Velorum		228 43·3	43·2	43·4	43·6	43·9	44·1	S 54 45·5	45·7	45·8	45·9	45·9	45·9
1·9	ε Carinæ	22	234 17·4	17·5	17·6	17·9	18·2	18·5	S 59 33·2	33·4	33·5	33·6	33·6	33·5
1·8	γ Velorum		237 30·3	30·3	30·4	30·6	30·9	31·0	S 47 22·7	22·8	23·0	23·0	23·0	22·9
2·8	ρ Puppis		237 57·9	57·9	58·0	58·1	58·3	58·3	S 24 20·7	20·8	20·9	21·0	20·9	20·9
2·3	ζ Puppis		238 58·7	58·7	58·8	59·0	59·2	59·3	S 40 02·6	02·7	02·8	02·9	02·9	02·8
1·1	β Geminorum	21	243 27·7	27·7	27·7	27·9	28·0	28·1	N 27 59·4	59·5	59·5	59·5	59·5	59·5
0·4	α Canis Minoris	20	244 59·7	59·7	59·7	59·9	60·0	60·0	N 5 11·2	11·2	11·2	11·2	11·2	11·2

Mag.	Name and Number		SHA							Declination						
		°	JULY	AUG.	SEPT.	OCT.	NOV.	DEC.		°	JULY	AUG.	SEPT.	OCT.	NOV.	DEC.
3·1	γ Ursæ Minoris	129	49·0	49·5	50·0	50·0	50·6	50·4	N 71		47·5	47·5	47·4	47·3	47·1	46·9
2·9	γ Trianguli Aust.	129	56·1	56·5	56·8	57·1	57·1	56·8	S 68		43·9	43·9	43·9	43·8	43·6	43·5
2·6	β Libræ	130	33·6	33·7	33·8	33·9	33·9	33·7	S 9		25·9	25·9	25·8	25·8	25·9	25·9
2·7	β Lupi	135	08·1	08·3	08·4	08·5	08·5	08·3	S 43		11·4	11·4	11·3	11·3	11·2	11·1
2·8	Zubenelgenubi 39	137	05·2	05·3	05·4	05·5	05·4	05·3	S 16		05·9	05·8	05·8	05·8	05·8	05·8
2·1	Kochab 40	137	19·7	20·3	20·8	21·2	21·3	21·1	N 74		06·3	06·3	06·3	06·1	05·9	05·7
2·4	ε Bootis	138	36·1	36·2	36·4	36·4	36·4	36·3	N 27		01·3	01·3	01·3	01·2	01·1	01·0
2·3	α Lupi	139	16·9	17·1	17·3	17·4	17·3	17·1	S 47		26·9	26·9	26·8	26·8	26·7	26·6
−0·3	Rigil Kent. 38	139	51·3	51·6	51·9	52·0	51·9	51·7	S 60		53·6	53·6	53·6	53·4	53·3	53·2
2·3	η Centauri	140	54·0	54·1	54·3	54·3	54·3	54·1	S 42		13·2	13·1	13·1	13·0	12·9	12·9
3·0	γ Bootis	141	50·5	50·6	50·8	50·9	50·8	50·7	N 38		15·2	15·2	15·2	15·1	14·9	14·8
0·0	Arcturus 37	145	55·6	55·7	55·8	55·9	55·8	55·7	N 19		06·9	06·9	06·9	06·8	06·7	06·6
2·1	Menkent 36	148	07·4	07·5	07·6	07·7	07·6	07·4	S 36		26·3	26·3	26·2	26·2	26·1	26·1
0·6	Hadar 35	148	47·6	47·8	48·0	48·1	48·0	47·7	S 60		26·5	26·5	26·4	26·3	26·2	26·1
2·6	ζ Centauri	150	53·7	53·9	54·0	54·1	54·0	53·7	S 47		21·5	21·5	21·4	21·3	21·2	21·2
2·7	η Bootis	151	09·9	10·0	10·1	10·1	10·0	09·9	N 18		20·0	20·0	19·9	19·9	19·8	19·6
1·9	Alkaid 34	152	58·8	59·0	59·2	59·2	59·2	59·0	N 49		15·0	15·0	14·9	14·8	14·6	14·4
2·3	ε Centauri	154	48·3	48·5	48·6	48·7	48·5	48·2	S 53		32·3	32·3	32·2	32·1	32·0	32·0
1·0	Spica 33	158	31·2	31·3	31·3	31·3	31·2	31·0	S 11		13·9	13·9	13·9	13·9	13·9	14·0
2·3	Mizar	158	53·0	53·2	53·4	53·4	53·3	53·1	N 54		51·6	51·5	51·4	51·3	51·1	50·9
2·8	ι Centauri	159	39·3	39·4	39·5	39·5	39·4	39·1	S 36		47·2	47·1	47·1	47·0	46·9	46·9
2·8	ε Virginis	164	17·1	17·2	17·3	17·2	17·1	16·9	N 10		53·3	53·3	53·3	53·2	53·1	53·0
2·9	Cor Caroli	165	50·1	50·2	50·3	50·3	50·2	49·9	N 38		14·9	14·9	14·8	14·7	14·5	14·4
1·8	Alioth 32	166	20·8	21·0	21·1	21·1	21·0	20·7	N 55		53·4	53·4	53·3	53·1	52·9	52·8
1·3	Mimosa	167	51·9	52·1	52·2	52·2	52·0	51·6	S 59		46·1	46·0	45·9	45·8	45·7	45·6
2·9	γ Virginis	169	24·7	24·8	24·8	24·8	24·6	24·4	S 1		31·4	31·4	31·4	31·4	31·5	31·6
2·2	Muhlifain	169	25·7	25·9	25·9	25·9	25·7	25·4	S 49		02·3	02·2	02·1	02·0	02·0	02·0
2·7	α Muscæ	170	29·6	29·9	30·1	30·1	29·8	29·3	S 69		12·9	12·9	12·7	12·6	12·5	12·5
2·7	β Corvi	171	13·3	13·4	13·5	13·4	13·3	13·0	S 23		28·4	28·4	28·3	28·3	28·3	28·3
1·6	Gacrux 31	172	00·9	01·1	01·2	01·1	00·9	00·6	S 57		11·6	11·6	11·4	11·3	11·2	11·2
1·3	Acrux 30	173	09·3	09·5	09·7	09·6	09·3	08·9	S 63		10·8	10·7	10·6	10·4	10·3	10·3
2·6	Gienah 29	175	52·3	52·4	52·4	52·4	52·2	52·0	S 17		37·1	37·1	37·0	37·0	37·0	37·1
2·6	δ Centauri	177	43·9	44·0	44·1	44·0	43·8	43·5	S 50		48·2	48·1	47·9	47·8	47·8	47·8
2·4	Phecda	181	22·1	22·3	22·3	22·2	22·0	21·7	N 53		37·4	37·3	37·1	37·0	36·8	36·7
2·1	Denebola 28	182	33·7	33·8	33·8	33·7	33·6	33·4	N 14		29·8	29·8	29·8	29·7	29·6	29·5
2·6	δ Leonis	191	17·6	17·7	17·7	17·6	17·4	17·1	N 20		27·0	27·0	26·9	26·8	26·7	26·6
3·0	ψ Ursæ Majoris	192	23·9	23·9	23·9	23·8	23·6	23·3	N 44		25·6	25·5	25·4	25·3	25·1	25·0
1·8	Dubhe 27	193	52·1	52·2	52·2	52·0	51·7	51·3	N 61		40·8	40·7	40·5	40·4	40·2	40·1
2·4	Merak	194	20·5	20·6	20·6	20·5	20·2	19·8	N 56		18·7	18·6	18·5	18·3	18·2	18·1
2·7	μ Velorum	198	09·7	09·8	09·8	09·6	09·4	09·0	S 49		29·8	29·7	29·6	29·5	29·4	29·5
2·8	θ Carinæ	199	08·5	08·7	08·6	08·4	08·0	07·6	S 64		28·3	28·1	28·0	27·9	27·8	27·9
2·3	Algeiba	204	49·3	49·3	49·3	49·1	48·9	48·7	N 19		46·4	46·3	46·3	46·2	46·1	46·0
1·4	Regulus 26	207	43·7	43·7	43·6	43·5	43·3	43·0	N 11		54·0	54·0	54·0	53·9	53·8	53·7
3·0	ε Leonis	213	20·9	20·8	20·7	20·6	20·4	20·1	N 23		42·7	42·6	42·6	42·5	42·4	42·3
3·1	N Velorum	217	05·8	05·8	05·7	05·4	05·1	04·7	S 57		05·9	05·8	05·6	05·5	05·6	05·7
2·0	Alphard 25	217	56·3	56·3	56·2	56·0	55·8	55·6	S 8		43·2	43·1	43·1	43·1	43·2	43·3
2·5	κ Velorum	219	22·3	22·3	22·2	21·9	21·6	21·2	S 55		04·4	04·2	04·1	04·0	04·0	04·1
2·2	ι Carinæ	220	38·5	38·6	38·4	38·2	37·8	37·4	S 59		20·2	20·0	19·9	19·8	19·8	19·9
1·7	Miaplacidus 24	221	40·4	40·5	40·3	39·9	39·4	38·9	S 69		46·6	46·5	46·3	46·3	46·3	46·4
2·2	Suhail 23	222	52·8	52·8	52·6	52·4	52·1	51·9	S 43		29·5	29·3	29·2	29·2	29·2	29·3
3·1	ι Ursæ Majoris	224	58·4	58·3	58·1	57·9	57·5	57·2	N 47		59·3	59·2	59·0	58·9	58·9	58·8
2·0	δ Velorum	228	44·2	44·1	44·0	43·7	43·4	43·0	S 54		45·7	45·6	45·5	45·4	45·4	45·6
1·9	Avior 22	234	18·6	18·5	18·3	18·0	17·6	17·3	S 59		33·4	33·2	33·1	33·0	33·1	33·2
1·8	γ Velorum	237	31·0	31·0	30·8	30·5	30·2	30·0	S 47		22·8	22·6	22·5	22·5	22·5	22·7
2·8	ρ Puppis	237	58·4	58·3	58·1	57·9	57·7	57·5	S 24		20·8	20·7	20·6	20·6	20·6	20·8
2·3	ζ Puppis	238	59·3	59·3	59·1	58·9	58·6	58·4	S 40		02·7	02·5	02·4	02·4	02·4	02·6
1·1	Pollux 21	243	28·0	27·9	27·7	27·5	27·2	27·0	N 27		59·5	59·4	59·4	59·3	59·3	59·3
0·4	Procyon 20	244	60·0	59·9	59·7	59·5	59·3	59·1	N 5		11·3	11·3	11·3	11·3	11·2	11·1

Mag.	Name and Number		SHA							Declination					
			JAN.	FEB.	MAR.	APR.	MAY	JUNE		JAN.	FEB.	MAR.	APR.	MAY	JUNE
		°	′	′	′	′	′	′	°	′	′	′	′	′	′
1·6	α Geminorum	246	07·9	07·9	08·0	08·2	08·3	08·3	N 31	51·3	51·4	51·4	51·4	51·4	51·4
3·3	σ Puppis	247	34·7	34·7	34·9	35·1	35·3	35·4	S 43	19·9	20·0	20·1	20·2	20·1	20·0
2·9	β Canis Minoris	248	01·6	01·6	01·6	01·8	01·9	01·9	N 8	15·5	15·5	15·5	15·5	15·5	15·5
2·4	η Canis Majoris	248	50·2	50·3	50·4	50·6	50·7	50·8	S 29	19·9	20·1	20·1	20·2	20·1	20·0
2·7	π Puppis	250	35·3	35·4	35·5	35·7	35·9	36·0	S 37	07·5	07·6	07·7	07·7	07·7	07·6
1·8	δ Canis Majoris	252	45·6	45·6	45·8	45·9	46·0	46·1	S 26	25·1	25·2	25·3	25·3	25·2	25·1
3·0	o Canis Majoris	254	05·9	05·9	06·0	06·2	06·3	06·4	S 23	51·4	51·5	51·6	51·6	51·5	51·4
1·5	ε Canis Majoris	19	255	12·3	12·4	12·5	12·7	12·8	12·9	S 28	59·6	59·7	59·8	59·8	59·8	59·7
2·9	τ Puppis	257	25·4	25·5	25·8	26·0	26·2	26·3	S 50	38·0	38·2	38·3	38·3	38·2	38·1
−1·5	α Canis Majoris	18	258	33·6	33·6	33·8	33·9	34·0	34·0	S 16	44·3	44·4	44·4	44·4	44·4	44·3
1·9	γ Geminorum	260	22·4	22·5	22·6	22·7	22·8	22·8	N 16	23·1	23·1	23·1	23·1	23·1	23·1
−0·7	α Carinæ	17	263	55·7	55·9	56·1	56·4	56·6	56·7	S 52	42·4	42·6	42·6	42·6	42·5	42·4
2·0	β Canis Majoris	264	10·3	10·4	10·5	10·7	10·8	10·8	S 17	58·0	58·1	58·1	58·1	58·1	58·0
2·6	θ Aurigæ	269	50·1	50·2	50·4	50·5	50·6	50·6	N 37	12·7	12·7	12·7	12·7	12·7	12·6
1·9	β Aurigæ	269	51·9	52·0	52·2	52·4	52·5	52·5	N 44	56·8	56·9	56·9	56·9	56·8	56·7
Var.‡	α Orionis	16	271	01·3	01·3	01·4	01·6	01·7	01·6	N 7	24·4	24·3	24·3	24·3	24·3	24·4
2·1	κ Orionis	272	53·8	53·9	54·0	54·2	54·3	54·2	S 9	40·1	40·2	40·2	40·2	40·2	40·1
1·9	ζ Orionis	274	38·2	38·3	38·4	38·5	38·6	38·6	S 1	56·3	56·4	56·4	56·4	56·4	56·3
2·6	α Columbæ	274	57·7	57·8	57·9	58·1	58·2	58·2	S 34	04·3	04·4	04·4	04·4	04·3	04·2
3·0	ζ Tauri	275	23·0	23·1	23·2	23·4	23·4	23·4	N 21	08·9	08·9	08·9	08·9	08·9	08·9
1·7	ε Orionis	15	275	46·3	46·4	46·5	46·7	46·7	46·7	S 1	11·8	11·9	11·9	11·9	11·8	11·8
2·8	ι Orionis	275	58·4	58·5	58·6	58·7	58·8	58·8	S 5	54·3	54·4	54·4	54·4	54·3	54·2
2·6	α Leporis	276	39·9	40·0	40·1	40·3	40·4	40·3	S 17	49·0	49·1	49·1	49·1	49·0	48·9
2·2	δ Orionis	276	49·4	49·4	49·6	49·7	49·8	49·7	S 0	17·6	17·6	17·6	17·6	17·6	17·5
2·8	β Leporis	277	47·4	47·5	47·7	47·8	47·9	47·9	S 20	45·2	45·3	45·3	45·3	45·2	45·1
1·7	β Tauri	14	278	12·6	12·7	12·8	13·0	13·0	13·0	N 28	37·0	37·0	37·0	37·0	37·0	36·9
1·6	γ Orionis	13	278	32·0	32·1	32·2	32·3	32·4	32·3	N 6	21·5	21·5	21·5	21·5	21·5	21·5
0·1	α Aurigæ	12	280	34·4	34·5	34·7	34·9	35·0	34·9	N 46	00·6	00·7	00·7	00·6	00·6	00·5
0·1	β Orionis	11	281	12·0	12·1	12·2	12·4	12·4	12·4	S 8	11·4	11·5	11·5	11·5	11·4	11·3
2·8	β Eridani	282	52·1	52·2	52·3	52·5	52·5	52·5	S 5	04·4	04·4	04·4	04·4	04·4	04·3
2·7	ι Aurigæ	285	31·7	31·8	31·9	32·1	32·1	32·1	N 33	11·1	11·2	11·1	11·1	11·1	11·0
0·9	α Tauri	10	290	49·4	49·5	49·6	49·8	49·8	49·7	N 16	32·0	32·0	32·0	32·0	32·0	32·0
2·9	ε Persei	300	18·4	18·5	18·7	18·8	18·8	18·7	N 40	02·9	02·9	02·9	02·8	02·8	02·7
3·0	γ Eridani	300	20·0	20·1	20·3	20·4	20·4	20·3	S 13	28·5	28·5	28·5	28·5	28·4	28·3
2·9	ζ Persei	301	15·1	15·2	15·4	15·5	15·5	15·4	N 31	55·3	55·3	55·3	55·3	55·2	55·2
2·9	η Tauri	302	55·6	55·7	55·8	55·9	55·9	55·8	N 24	08·7	08·7	08·7	08·6	08·6	08·6
1·8	α Persei	9	308	40·4	40·6	40·8	40·9	40·9	40·7	N 49	54·6	54·6	54·5	54·4	54·4	54·3
Var.§	β Persei	312	44·1	44·3	44·4	44·5	44·5	44·3	N 41	00·5	00·4	00·4	00·3	00·3	00·2
2·5	α Ceti	8	314	15·2	15·3	15·4	15·5	15·4	15·3	N 4	08·4	08·3	08·3	08·3	08·4	08·4
3·2	θ Eridani	7	315	18·4	18·6	18·7	18·8	18·8	18·7	S 40	15·4	15·4	15·4	15·3	15·1	15·0
2·0	α Ursæ Minoris	317	45·3	57·9	68·9	75·1	73·6	65·5	N 89	19·5	19·5	19·5	19·3	19·2	19·0
3·0	β Trianguli	327	24·7	24·9	25·0	25·0	24·9	24·7	N 35	03·1	03·0	03·0	02·9	02·9	02·9
2·0	α Arietis	6	328	01·0	01·1	01·2	01·2	01·1	01·0	N 23	31·5	31·5	31·4	31·4	31·4	31·4
2·3	γ Andromedæ	328	49·0	49·2	49·3	49·3	49·2	49·0	N 42	23·7	23·7	23·6	23·5	23·5	23·4
2·9	α Hydri	330	12·2	12·5	12·8	12·9	12·8	12·6	S 61	30·7	30·7	30·6	30·4	30·2	30·0
2·6	β Arietis	331	09·2	09·3	09·4	09·4	09·4	09·2	N 20	52·4	52·3	52·3	52·3	52·3	52·3
0·5	α Eridani	5	335	27·0	27·2	27·4	27·5	27·4	27·1	S 57	10·5	10·5	10·4	10·2	10·0	09·9
2·7	δ Cassiopeiæ	338	19·4	19·6	19·8	19·8	19·6	19·3	N 60	18·5	18·4	18·3	18·2	18·1	18·0
2·1	β Andromedæ	342	22·7	22·9	22·9	22·9	22·8	22·5	N 35	41·6	41·5	41·4	41·4	41·3	41·3
Var.‖	γ Cassiopeiæ	345	37·1	37·3	37·5	37·4	37·2	36·8	N 60	47·6	47·5	47·4	47·2	47·1	47·1
2·0	β Ceti	4	348	56·2	56·3	56·4	56·3	56·2	56·0	S 17	55·0	55·0	54·9	54·9	54·8	54·6
2·2	α Cassiopeiæ	3	349	40·9	41·1	41·2	41·2	40·9	40·6	N 56	36·8	36·8	36·6	36·5	36·4	36·4
2·4	α Phœnicis	2	353	16·1	16·2	16·3	16·2	16·1	15·8	S 42	14·3	14·2	14·1	14·0	13·8	13·7
2·8	β Hydri	353	24·4	24·9	25·2	25·1	24·8	24·1	S 77	11·1	11·0	10·8	10·6	10·5	10·3
2·8	γ Pegasi	356	31·2	31·3	31·3	31·3	31·1	30·9	N 15	15·5	15·5	15·4	15·4	15·4	15·5
2·3	β Cassiopeiæ	357	31·6	31·8	31·9	31·8	31·5	31·1	N 59	13·6	13·5	13·4	13·3	13·2	13·2
2·1	α Andromedæ	1	357	43·9	44·0	44·0	43·9	43·8	43·5	N 29	09·9	09·9	09·8	09·7	09·7	09·8

‡ 0·1 — 1·2   § 2·1 — 3·4   ‖ Irregular variable; 2011 mag. 2·2

Mag.	Name and Number		SHA °	JULY	AUG.	SEPT.	OCT.	NOV.	DEC.	Declination	JULY	AUG.	SEPT.	OCT.	NOV.	DEC.
1·6	*Castor*		246	08·3	08·2	07·9	07·7	07·4	07·2	N 31	51·4	51·3	51·3	51·2	51·2	51·2
3·3	σ *Puppis*		247	35·4	35·3	35·1	34·8	34·6	34·3	S 43	19·9	19·7	19·6	19·6	19·7	19·8
2·9	β *Canis Minoris*		248	01·9	01·8	01·6	01·4	01·1	00·9	N 8	15·6	15·6	15·6	15·6	15·5	15·5
2·4	η *Canis Majoris*		248	50·7	50·6	50·4	50·2	50·0	49·8	S 29	19·9	19·8	19·7	19·7	19·8	19·9
2·7	π *Puppis*		250	35·9	35·8	35·6	35·4	35·1	34·9	S 37	07·4	07·3	07·2	07·2	07·3	07·4
1·8	*Wezen*		252	46·1	45·9	45·8	45·5	45·3	45·1	S 26	25·0	24·9	24·8	24·8	24·9	25·0
3·0	o *Canis Majoris*		254	06·3	06·2	06·0	05·8	05·6	05·4	S 23	51·3	51·2	51·1	51·1	51·2	51·3
1·5	*Adhara*	19	255	12·8	12·7	12·5	12·3	12·1	11·9	S 28	59·5	59·4	59·4	59·4	59·4	59·6
2·9	τ *Puppis*		257	26·3	26·2	25·9	25·6	25·3	25·1	S 50	37·9	37·8	37·7	37·7	37·8	38·0
−1·5	*Sirius*	18	258	34·0	33·9	33·7	33·4	33·2	33·1	S 16	44·2	44·1	44·1	44·1	44·2	44·3
1·9	*Alhena*		260	22·7	22·6	22·4	22·1	21·9	21·7	N 16	23·1	23·1	23·1	23·1	23·1	23·0
−0·7	*Canopus*	17	263	56·6	56·5	56·2	55·9	55·6	55·4	S 52	42·2	42·1	42·0	42·0	42·1	42·3
2·0	*Mirzam*		264	10·7	10·6	10·4	10·1	09·9	09·8	S 17	57·9	57·8	57·7	57·7	57·8	57·9
2·6	θ *Aurigæ*		269	50·5	50·2	50·0	49·7	49·5	49·3	N 37	12·6	12·6	12·5	12·5	12·6	12·6
1·9	*Menkalinan*		269	52·3	52·1	51·8	51·5	51·2	51·0	N 44	56·7	56·6	56·6	56·6	56·6	56·7
Var.‡	*Betelgeuse*	16	271	01·5	01·4	01·1	00·9	00·7	00·6	N 7	24·4	24·5	24·5	24·5	24·4	24·4
2·1	κ *Orionis*		272	54·1	54·0	53·8	53·5	53·4	53·2	S 9	40·0	39·9	39·9	39·9	39·9	40·0
1·9	*Alnitak*		274	38·5	38·3	38·1	37·9	37·7	37·6	S 1	56·2	56·2	56·1	56·1	56·2	56·3
2·6	*Phact*		274	58·1	57·9	57·7	57·5	57·3	57·2	S 34	04·0	03·9	03·9	03·9	04·0	04·2
3·0	ζ *Tauri*		275	23·3	23·1	22·8	22·6	22·4	22·3	N 21	08·9	08·9	08·9	08·9	08·9	08·9
1·7	*Alnilam*	15	275	46·6	46·4	46·2	46·0	45·8	45·7	S 1	11·7	11·6	11·6	11·6	11·7	11·8
2·8	ι *Orionis*		275	58·7	58·5	58·3	58·1	57·9	57·8	S 5	54·2	54·1	54·0	54·1	54·1	54·2
2·6	α *Leporis*		276	40·2	40·0	39·8	39·6	39·4	39·3	S 17	48·8	48·7	48·7	48·7	48·8	48·9
2·2	δ *Orionis*		276	49·6	49·4	49·2	49·0	48·8	48·7	S 0	17·5	17·4	17·4	17·4	17·4	17·5
2·8	β *Leporis*		277	47·8	47·6	47·4	47·1	47·0	46·9	S 20	45·0	44·9	44·8	44·8	44·9	45·1
1·7	*Elnath*	14	278	12·9	12·6	12·4	12·1	11·9	11·8	N 28	36·9	36·9	36·9	37·0	37·0	37·0
1·6	*Bellatrix*	13	278	32·2	32·0	31·8	31·6	31·4	31·3	N 6	21·6	21·6	21·7	21·7	21·6	21·6
0·1	*Capella*	12	280	34·7	34·5	34·1	33·8	33·6	33·4	N 46	00·4	00·4	00·4	00·4	00·5	00·6
0·1	*Rigel*	11	281	12·3	12·1	11·9	11·7	11·5	11·4	S 8	11·2	11·2	11·1	11·1	11·2	11·3
2·8	β *Eridani*		282	52·4	52·2	51·9	51·7	51·6	51·5	S 5	04·2	04·1	04·1	04·1	04·2	04·3
2·7	ι *Aurigæ*		285	31·9	31·7	31·4	31·1	30·9	30·8	N 33	11·0	11·0	11·1	11·1	11·1	11·1
0·9	*Aldebaran*	10	290	49·5	49·3	49·1	48·9	48·7	48·6	N 16	32·0	32·1	32·1	32·1	32·1	32·1
2·9	ε *Persei*		300	18·5	18·2	17·9	17·7	17·5	17·4	N 40	02·7	02·7	02·8	02·9	02·9	03·0
3·0	γ *Eridani*		300	20·1	19·9	19·7	19·5	19·4	19·3	S 13	28·2	28·1	28·1	28·1	28·2	28·3
2·9	ζ *Persei*		301	15·2	14·9	14·6	14·4	14·3	14·2	N 31	55·2	55·3	55·3	55·4	55·4	55·4
2·9	*Alcyone*		302	55·6	55·3	55·1	54·9	54·8	54·7	N 24	08·6	08·7	08·8	08·8	08·8	08·8
1·8	*Mirfak*	9	308	40·5	40·1	39·8	39·6	39·4	39·4	N 49	54·3	54·3	54·4	54·5	54·6	54·7
Var.§	*Algol*		312	44·1	43·8	43·5	43·3	43·2	43·1	N 41	00·2	00·3	00·4	00·4	00·5	00·6
2·5	*Menkar*	8	314	15·1	14·9	14·7	14·5	14·4	14·4	N 4	08·5	08·6	08·7	08·7	08·6	08·6
3·2	*Acamar*	7	315	18·5	18·2	18·0	17·8	17·7	17·8	S 40	14·8	14·8	14·8	14·9	15·0	15·1
2·0	*Polaris*		317	52·6	37·7	24·3	14·9	10·8	14·6	N 89	19·0	19·0	19·1	19·3	19·4	19·6
3·0	β *Trianguli*		327	24·5	24·2	24·0	23·8	23·8	23·8	N 35	02·9	03·0	03·1	03·2	03·3	03·3
2·0	*Hamal*	6	328	00·7	00·5	00·3	00·1	00·1	00·1	N 23	31·5	31·6	31·7	31·7	31·8	31·8
2·3	*Almak*		328	48·7	48·4	48·2	48·0	48·0	48·0	N 42	23·5	23·6	23·7	23·8	23·9	23·9
2·9	α *Hydri*		330	12·2	11·8	11·5	11·4	11·4	11·6	S 61	29·9	29·9	30·0	30·1	30·3	30·4
2·6	*Sheratan*		331	08·9	08·7	08·5	08·4	08·4	08·4	N 20	52·4	52·5	52·5	52·6	52·6	52·6
0·5	*Achernar*	5	335	26·8	26·5	26·2	26·1	26·1	26·3	S 57	09·8	09·7	09·8	09·9	10·1	10·2
2·7	*Ruchbah*		338	18·9	18·5	18·2	18·0	18·0	18·2	N 60	18·1	18·2	18·3	18·5	18·6	18·7
2·1	*Mirach*		342	22·3	22·0	21·8	21·7	21·7	21·8	N 35	41·4	41·5	41·6	41·8	41·8	41·9
Var.‖	γ *Cassiopeiæ*		345	36·4	36·1	35·8	35·7	35·8	35·9	N 60	47·2	47·3	47·5	47·6	47·8	47·8
2·0	*Diphda*	4	348	55·8	55·5	55·4	55·3	55·4	55·5	S 17	54·5	54·5	54·5	54·5	54·6	54·7
2·2	*Schedar*	3	349	40·2	39·9	39·7	39·6	39·7	39·8	N 56	36·5	36·6	36·8	36·9	37·1	37·1
2·4	*Ankaa*	2	353	15·5	15·3	15·1	15·1	15·2	15·3	S 42	13·6	13·6	13·7	13·8	13·9	14·0
2·8	β *Hydri*		353	23·3	22·6	22·2	22·1	22·5	23·2	S 77	10·3	10·3	10·5	10·6	10·8	10·9
2·8	*Algenib*		356	30·7	30·4	30·3	30·3	30·3	30·4	N 15	15·6	15·7	15·8	15·8	15·8	15·8
2·3	*Caph*		357	30·8	30·5	30·3	30·3	30·4	30·6	N 59	13·3	13·4	13·6	13·8	13·9	14·0
2·1	*Alpheratz*	1	357	43·3	43·1	42·9	42·9	43·0	43·0	N 29	09·9	10·0	10·1	10·2	10·3	10·3

‡ 0·1 — 1·2　　§ 2·1 — 3·4　　‖ Irregular variable; 2011 mag. 2·2

POLARIS (POLE STAR) TABLES, 2013
FOR DETERMINING LATITUDE FROM SEXTANT ALTITUDE AND FOR AZIMUTH

LHA ARIES	0° – 9°	10° – 19°	20° – 29°	30° – 39°	40° – 49°	50° – 59°	60° – 69°	70° – 79°	80° – 89°	90° – 99°	100° – 109°	110° – 119°
	a_0	a_0	a_0	a_0	a_0	a_0	a_0	a_0	a_0	a_0	a_0	a_0
0	0 28·8	0 24·5	0 21·2	0 19·0	0 18·1	0 18·5	0 20·1	0 22·8	0 26·7	0 31·6	0 37·3	0 43·6
1	28·3	24·1	20·9	18·9	18·1	18·6	20·3	23·2	27·2	32·1	37·9	44·3
2	27·9	23·7	20·7	18·8	18·1	18·7	20·5	23·5	27·6	32·7	38·5	44·9
3	27·4	23·4	20·4	18·6	18·1	18·8	20·8	23·9	28·1	33·2	39·1	45·6
4	27·0	23·0	20·2	18·5	18·1	19·0	21·0	24·3	28·5	33·8	39·7	46·3
5	0 26·5	0 22·7	0 20·0	0 18·4	0 18·1	0 19·1	0 21·3	0 24·6	0 29·0	0 34·3	0 40·4	0 47·0
6	26·1	22·4	19·8	18·3	18·2	19·3	21·6	25·0	29·5	34·9	41·0	47·7
7	25·7	22·1	19·6	18·3	18·2	19·5	21·9	25·4	30·0	35·5	41·7	48·3
8	25·3	21·7	19·4	18·2	18·3	19·6	22·2	25·9	30·5	36·1	42·3	49·0
9	24·9	21·5	19·2	18·2	18·4	19·8	22·5	26·3	31·0	36·7	43·0	49·7
10	0 24·5	0 21·2	0 19·0	0 18·1	0 18·5	0 20·1	0 22·8	0 26·7	0 31·6	0 37·3	0 43·6	0 50·4

Lat.	a_1	a_1	a_1	a_1	a_1	a_1	a_1	a_1	a_1	a_1	a_1	a_1
0	0·5	0·5	0·6	0·6	0·6	0·6	0·6	0·5	0·5	0·4	0·4	0·3
10	·5	·5	·6	·6	·6	·6	·6	·5	·5	·4	·4	·4
20	·5	·6	·6	·6	·6	·6	·6	·5	·5	·5	·4	·4
30	·5	·6	·6	·6	·6	·6	·6	·6	·5	·5	·5	·5
40	0·6	0·6	0·6	0·6	0·6	0·6	0·6	0·6	0·6	0·5	0·5	0·5
45	·6	·6	·6	·6	·6	·6	·6	·6	·6	·6	·6	·6
50	·6	·6	·6	·6	·6	·6	·6	·6	·6	·6	·6	·6
55	·6	·6	·6	·6	·6	·6	·6	·6	·6	·6	·6	·7
60	·6	·6	·6	·6	·6	·6	·6	·6	·7	·7	·7	·7
62	0·7	0·6	0·6	0·6	0·6	0·6	0·6	0·6	0·7	0·7	0·7	0·8
64	·7	·6	·6	·6	·6	·6	·6	·7	·7	·7	·8	·8
66	·7	·7	·6	·6	·6	·6	·6	·7	·7	·8	·8	·8
68	0·7	0·7	0·6	0·6	0·6	0·6	0·6	0·7	0·7	0·8	0·8	0·9

Month	a_2	a_2	a_2	a_2	a_2	a_2	a_2	a_2	a_2	a_2	a_2	a_2
Jan.	0·7	0·8	0·8	0·8	0·8	0·8	0·8	0·8	0·8	0·7	0·7	0·7
Feb.	·7	·7	·8	·8	·8	·9	·9	·9	·9	·9	·9	·8
Mar.	·5	·6	·7	·7	·8	·8	·9	·9	·9	·9	·9	0·9
Apr.	0·4	0·4	0·5	0·6	0·6	0·7	0·8	0·8	0·9	0·9	0·9	1·0
May	·3	·3	·4	·4	·5	·6	·6	·7	·7	·8	·9	0·9
June	·2	·3	·3	·3	·4	·4	·5	·5	·6	·7	·7	·8
July	0·3	0·3	0·3	0·3	0·3	0·3	0·4	0·4	0·5	0·5	0·6	0·6
Aug.	·4	·4	·3	·3	·3	·3	·3	·3	·3	·4	·4	·5
Sept.	·6	·5	·5	·4	·4	·4	·3	·3	·3	·3	·3	·3
Oct.	0·8	0·7	0·7	0·6	0·5	0·5	0·4	0·4	0·3	0·3	0·3	0·3
Nov.	0·9	0·9	0·8	·8	·7	·6	·6	·5	·4	·4	·3	·3
Dec.	1·0	1·0	1·0	0·9	0·9	0·8	0·7	0·7	0·6	0·5	0·4	0·4

Lat.	AZIMUTH											
°	°	°	°	°	°	°	°	°	°	°	°	°
0	0·4	0·3	0·2	0·1	0·0	359·9	359·7	359·6	359·5	359·5	359·4	359·4
20	0·4	0·3	0·2	0·1	0·0	359·8	359·7	359·6	359·5	359·4	359·4	359·3
40	0·5	0·4	0·3	0·1	0·0	359·8	359·7	359·5	359·4	359·3	359·2	359·2
50	0·6	0·5	0·3	0·1	359·9	359·8	359·6	359·4	359·3	359·2	359·1	359·0
55	0·7	0·6	0·4	0·2	359·9	359·7	359·5	359·4	359·2	359·0	358·9	358·9
60	0·8	0·6	0·4	0·2	359·9	359·7	359·5	359·3	359·1	358·9	358·8	358·7
65	1·0	0·8	0·5	0·2	359·9	359·6	359·4	359·1	358·9	358·7	358·6	358·5

Latitude = Apparent altitude (corrected for refraction) $-1° + a_0 + a_1 + a_2$

The table is entered with LHA Aries to determine the column to be used; each column refers to a range of 10°. a_0 is taken, with mental interpolation, from the upper table with the units of LHA Aries in degrees as argument; a_1, a_2 are taken, without interpolation, from the second and third tables with arguments latitude and month respectively. a_0, a_1, a_2, are always positive. The final table gives the azimuth of *Polaris*.

FOR DETERMINING LATITUDE FROM SEXTANT ALTITUDE AND FOR AZIMUTH

LHA ARIES	120° – 129°	130° – 139°	140° – 149°	150° – 159°	160° – 169°	170° – 179°	180° – 189°	190° – 199°	200° – 209°	210° – 219°	220° – 229°	230° – 239°
	a_0	a_0	a_0	a_0	a_0	a_0	a_0	a_0	a_0	a_0	a_0	a_0
0	0 50·4	0 57·5	1 04·5	1 11·4	1 18·0	1 23·9	1 29·0	1 33·3	1 36·5	1 38·6	1 39·5	1 39·1
1	51·1	58·2	05·2	12·1	18·6	24·4	29·5	33·7	36·8	38·7	39·5	39·0
2	51·8	58·9	05·9	12·8	19·2	25·0	30·0	34·0	37·0	38·9	39·5	38·9
3	52·5	0 59·6	06·6	13·4	19·8	25·5	30·4	34·4	37·2	39·0	39·5	38·8
4	53·2	1 00·3	07·3	14·1	20·4	26·0	30·9	34·7	37·5	39·1	39·5	38·7
5	0 53·9	1 01·0	1 08·0	1 14·8	1 21·0	1 26·6	1 31·3	1 35·0	1 37·7	1 39·2	1 39·5	1 38·5
6	54·6	01·7	08·7	15·4	21·6	27·1	31·7	35·3	37·9	39·3	39·4	38·4
7	55·3	02·4	09·4	16·1	22·2	27·6	32·1	35·7	38·1	39·3	39·4	38·2
8	56·0	03·1	10·1	16·7	22·7	28·1	32·5	35·9	38·3	39·4	39·3	38·0
9	56·8	03·8	10·8	17·3	23·3	28·6	32·9	36·2	38·4	39·4	39·2	37·8
10	0 57·5	1 04·5	1 11·4	1 18·0	1 23·9	1 29·0	1 33·3	1 36·5	1 38·6	1 39·5	1 39·1	1 37·6
Lat.	a_1	a_1	a_1	a_1	a_1	a_1	a_1	a_1	a_1	a_1	a_1	a_1
0	0·3	0·3	0·3	0·4	0·4	0·4	0·5	0·5	0·6	0·6	0·6	0·6
10	·4	·4	·4	·4	·4	·5	·5	·5	·6	·6	·6	·6
20	·4	·4	·4	·4	·5	·5	·5	·6	·6	·6	·6	·6
30	·5	·5	·5	·5	·5	·5	·5	·6	·6	·6	·6	·6
40	0·5	0·5	0·5	0·5	0·5	0·6	0·6	0·6	0·6	0·6	0·6	0·6
45	·6	·6	·6	·6	·6	·6	·6	·6	·6	·6	·6	·6
50	·6	·6	·6	·6	·6	·6	·6	·6	·6	·6	·6	·6
55	·7	·7	·7	·6	·6	·6	·6	·6	·6	·6	·6	·6
60	·7	·7	·7	·7	·7	·7	·6	·6	·6	·6	·6	·6
62	0·8	0·8	0·8	0·7	0·7	0·7	0·7	0·6	0·6	0·6	0·6	0·6
64	·8	·8	·8	·8	·7	·7	·7	·6	·6	·6	·6	·6
66	·8	·9	·8	·8	·8	·7	·7	·7	·6	·6	·6	·6
68	0·9	0·9	0·9	0·9	0·8	0·8	0·7	0·7	0·6	0·6	0·6	0·6
Month	a_2	a_2	a_2	a_2	a_2	a_2	a_2	a_2	a_2	a_2	a_2	a_2
Jan.	0·7	0·6	0·6	0·5	0·5	0·5	0·5	0·4	0·4	0·4	0·4	0·4
Feb.	·8	·8	·7	·7	·6	·6	·5	·5	·4	·4	·4	·3
Mar.	0·9	0·9	0·9	·8	·8	·7	·7	·6	·5	·5	·4	·4
Apr.	1·0	1·0	1·0	0·9	0·9	0·9	0·8	0·8	0·7	0·6	0·6	0·5
May	0·9	1·0	1·0	1·0	1·0	1·0	0·9	·9	·8	·8	·7	·6
June	·8	0·9	0·9	0·9	1·0	1·0	1·0	·9	·9	·9	·8	·8
July	0·7	0·7	0·8	0·8	0·9	0·9	0·9	0·9	0·9	0·9	0·9	0·9
Aug.	·5	·6	·6	·7	·7	·7	·8	·8	·9	·9	·9	·9
Sept.	·4	·4	·4	·5	·5	·6	·6	·7	·7	·8	·8	·8
Oct.	0·3	0·3	0·3	0·3	0·3	0·4	0·4	0·5	0·5	0·6	0·7	0·7
Nov.	·2	·2	·2	·2	·2	·2	·3	·3	·4	·4	·5	·6
Dec.	0·3	0·2	0·2	0·2	0·2	0·2	0·2	0·2	0·2	0·3	·0·3	0·4
Lat.	AZIMUTH											
0	359·3	359·3	359·3	359·4	359·4	359·5	359·6	359·7	359·8	359·9	0·0	0·1
20	359·3	359·3	359·3	359·3	359·4	359·5	359·6	359·6	359·8	359·9	0·0	0·2
40	359·1	359·1	359·1	359·2	359·3	359·4	359·5	359·6	359·7	359·9	0·0	0·2
50	359·0	358·9	359·0	359·0	359·1	359·2	359·4	359·5	359·7	359·9	0·0	0·2
55	358·8	358·8	358·9	358·9	359·0	359·1	359·3	359·5	359·7	359·9	0·1	0·3
60	358·7	358·6	358·7	358·8	358·9	359·0	359·2	359·4	359·6	359·8	0·1	0·3
65	358·4	358·4	358·4	358·5	358·7	358·8	359·0	359·3	359·5	359·8	0·1	0·3

ILLUSTRATION

On 2013 April 21 at 23^h 18^m 56^s UT in longitude W 37° 14′ the apparent altitude (corrected for refraction), H_0, of Polaris was 49° 21′6

From the daily pages:	°	′
GHA Aries (23^h)	195	10·6
Increment (18^m 56^s)	4	44·8
Longitude (west)	−37	14
LHA Aries	162	41

	°	′
H_0	49	31·6
a_0 (argument 162° 41′)	1	19·6
a_1 (Lat 50° approx.)		0·6
a_2 (April)		0·9
Sum − 1° = Lat =	49	52·7

POLARIS (POLE STAR) TABLES, 2013
FOR DETERMINING LATITUDE FROM SEXTANT ALTITUDE AND FOR AZIMUTH

LHA ARIES	240°–249°	250°–259°	260°–269°	270°–279°	280°–289°	290°–299°	300°–309°	310°–319°	320°–329°	330°–339°	340°–349°	350°–359°
	a_0	a_0	a_0	a_0	a_0	a_0	a_0	a_0	a_0	a_0	a_0	a_0
0	I 37·6	I 34·9	I 31·1	I 26·3	I 20·7	I 14·5	I 07·7	I 00·7	0 53·6	0 46·7	0 40·1	0 34·1
1	37·4	34·6	30·7	25·8	20·1	13·8	07·0	I 00·0	52·9	46·0	39·5	33·5
2	37·1	34·2	30·2	25·3	19·5	13·2	06·3	0 59·3	52·2	45·3	38·8	33·0
3	36·9	33·9	29·8	24·7	18·9	12·5	05·6	58·6	51·5	44·7	38·2	32·4
4	36·7	33·5	29·3	24·2	18·3	11·8	04·9	57·9	50·8	44·0	37·6	31·9
5	I 36·4	I 33·1	I 28·8	I 23·6	I 17·7	I 11·2	I 04·2	0 57·2	0 50·1	0 43·3	0 37·0	0 31·3
6	36·1	32·7	28·4	23·1	17·1	10·5	03·5	56·4	49·4	42·7	36·4	30·8
7	35·8	32·3	27·9	22·5	16·4	09·8	02·8	55·7	48·7	42·0	35·8	30·3
8	35·5	31·9	27·4	21·9	15·8	09·1	02·1	55·0	48·0	41·4	35·2	29·8
9	35·2	31·5	26·9	21·3	15·1	08·4	01·4	54·3	47·4	40·7	34·7	29·3
10	I 34·9	I 31·1	I 26·3	I 20·7	I 14·5	I 07·7	I 00·7	0 53·6	0 46·7	0 40·1	0 34·1	0 28·8

Lat.	a_1	a_1	a_1	a_1	a_1	a_1	a_1	a_1	a_1	a_1	a_1	a_1
0	0·6	0·5	0·5	0·4	0·4	0·3	0·3	0·3	0·3	0·4	0·4	0·4
10	·6	·5	·5	·4	·4	·4	·4	·4	·4	·4	·4	·5
20	·6	·5	·5	·5	·4	·4	·4	·4	·4	·4	·5	·5
30	·6	·6	·5	·5	·5	·5	·5	·5	·5	·5	·5	·5
40	0·6	0·6	0·6	0·5	0·5	0·5	0·5	0·5	0·5	0·5	0·5	0·6
45	·6	·6	·6	·6	·6	·6	·6	·6	·6	·6	·6	·6
50	·6	·6	·6	·6	·6	·6	·6	·6	·6	·6	·6	·6
55	·6	·6	·6	·6	·6	·7	·7	·7	·7	·6	·6	·6
60	·6	·6	·7	·7	·7	·7	·7	·7	·7	·7	·7	·7
62	0·6	0·6	0·7	0·7	0·7	0·8	0·8	0·8	0·8	0·7	0·7	0·7
64	·6	·7	·7	·7	·8	·8	·8	·8	·8	·8	·7	·7
66	·6	·7	·7	·8	·8	·8	·8	·9	·8	·8	·8	·7
68	0·6	0·7	0·7	0·8	0·8	0·9	0·9	0·9	0·9	0·9	0·8	0·8

Month	a_2	a_2	a_2	a_2	a_2	a_2	a_2	a_2	a_2	a_2	a_2	a_2
Jan.	0·4	0·4	0·4	0·5	0·5	0·5	0·5	0·6	0·6	0·7	0·7	0·7
Feb.	·3	·3	·3	·3	·3	·4	·4	·4	·5	·5	·6	·6
Mar.	·3	·3	·3	·3	·3	·3	·3	·3	·3	·4	·4	·5
Apr.	0·4	0·4	0·3	0·3	0·3	0·2	0·2	0·2	0·2	0·3	0·3	0·3
May	·6	·5	·5	·4	·3	·3	·3	·2	·2	·2	·2	·2
June	·7	·7	·6	·5	·5	·4	·4	·3	·3	·3	·2	·2
July	0·8	0·8	0·7	0·7	0·6	0·6	0·5	0·5	0·4	0·4	0·3	0·3
Aug.	·9	·9	·9	·8	·8	·7	·7	·6	·6	·5	·5	·5
Sept.	·9	·9	·9	·9	·9	·9	·8	·8	·8	·7	·7	·6
Oct.	0·8	0·8	0·9	0·9	0·9	0·9	0·9	0·9	0·9	0·9	0·9	0·8
Nov.	·6	·7	·8	·8	·9	·9	1·0	1·0	1·0	1·0	1·0	1·0
Dec.	0·5	0·5	0·6	0·7	0·8	0·9	0·9	1·0	1·0	1·0	1·0	1·0

Lat.	AZIMUTH											
0	0·3	0·4	0·5	0·5	0·6	0·6	0·7	0·7	0·7	0·6	0·6	0·5
20	0·3	0·4	0·5	0·6	0·6	0·7	0·7	0·7	0·7	0·7	0·6	0·5
40	0·3	0·5	0·6	0·7	0·8	0·8	0·9	0·9	0·9	0·8	0·7	0·7
50	0·4	0·6	0·7	0·8	0·9	1·0	1·0	1·1	1·0	1·0	0·9	0·8
55	0·4	0·6	0·8	0·9	1·0	1·1	1·2	1·2	1·2	1·1	1·0	0·9
60	0·5	0·7	0·9	1·1	1·2	1·3	1·3	1·4	1·3	1·3	1·2	1·0
65	0·6	0·8	1·1	1·3	1·4	1·5	1·6	1·6	1·6	1·5	1·4	1·2

Latitude = Apparent altitude (corrected for refraction) $-1° + a_0 + a_1 + a_2$

The table is entered with LHA Aries to determine the column to be used; each column refers to a range of 10°. a_0 is taken, with mental interpolation, from the upper table with the units of LHA Aries in degrees as argument; a_1, a_2 are taken, without interpolation, from the second and third tables with arguments latitude and month respectively. a_0, a_1, a_2, are always positive. The final table gives the azimuth of *Polaris*.

SIGHT REDUCTION PROCEDURES

METHODS AND FORMULAE FOR DIRECT COMPUTATION

1. *Introduction.* In this section formulae and methods are provided for *calculating* position at sea from observed altitudes taken with a marine sextant using a computer or programmable calculator.

The method uses analogous concepts and similar terminology as that used in *manual* methods of astro-navigation, where position is found by plotting position lines from their intercept and azimuth on a marine chart.

The algorithms are presented in standard algebra suitable for translating into the programming language of the user's computer. The basic ephemeris data may be taken directly from the main tabular pages of a current version of *The Nautical Almanac*. Formulae are given for calculating altitude and azimuth from the *GHA* and *Dec* of a body, and the estimated position of the observer. Formulae are also given for reducing sextant observations to observed altitudes by applying the corrections for dip, refraction, parallax and semi-diameter.

The intercept and azimuth obtained from each observation determine a position line, and the observer should lie on or close to each position line. The method of least squares is used to calculate the fix by finding the position where the sum of the squares of the distances from the position lines is a minimum. The use of least squares has other advantages. For example it is possible to improve the estimated position at the time of fix by repeating the calculation. It is also possible to include more observations in the solution and to reject doubtful ones.

2. *Notation.*

GHA = Greenwich hour angle. The range of *GHA* is from 0° to 360° starting at 0° on the Greenwich meridian increasing to the west, back to 360° on the Greenwich meridian.

SHA = sidereal hour angle. The range is 0° to 360°.

Dec = declination. The sign convention for declination is north is positive, south is negative. The range is from −90° at the south celestial pole to +90° at the north celestial pole.

$Long$ = longitude. The sign convention is east is positive, west is negative. The range is −180° to +180°.

Lat − latitude. The sign convention is north is positive, south is negative. The range is from −90° to +90°.

LHA = $GHA + Long$ = local hour angle. The *LHA* increases to the west from 0° on the local meridian to 360°.

H_C = calculated altitude. Above the horizon is positive, below the horizon is negative. The range is from −90° in the nadir to +90° in the zenith.

H_S = sextant altitude.

H = apparent altitude = sextant altitude corrected for instrumental error and dip.

H_O = observed altitude = apparent altitude corrected for refraction and, in appropriate cases, corrected for parallax and semi-diameter.

Z = Z_n = true azimuth. Z is measured from true north through east, south, west and back to north. The range is from 0° to 360°.

I = sextant index error.

D = dip of horizon.

R = atmospheric refraction.

HP = horizontal parallax of the Sun, Moon, Venus or Mars.
PA = parallax in altitude of the Sun, Moon, Venus or Mars.
SD = semi-diameter of the Sun or Moon.
p = intercept = $H_O - H_C$. Towards is positive, away is negative.
T = course or track, measured as for azimuth from the north.
V = speed in knots.

3. *Entering Basic Data.*   When quantities such as *GHA* are entered, which in *The Nautical Almanac* are given in degrees and minutes, convert them to degrees and decimals of a degree by dividing the minutes by 60 and adding to the degrees; for example, if $GHA = 123°\ 45\!'6$, enter the two numbers 123 and 45·6 into the memory and set $GHA = 123 + 45·6/60 = 123°7600$. Although four decimal places of a degree are shown in the examples, it is assumed that full precision is maintained in the calculations.

When using a computer or programmable calculator, write a subroutine to convert degrees and minutes to degrees and decimals. Scientific calculators usually have a special key for this purpose. For quantities like *Dec* which require a minus sign for southern declination, change the sign from plus to minus after the value has been converted to degrees and decimals, *e.g. Dec* = $S\,0°\ 12\!'3 = S\,0°2050 = -0°2050$. Other quantities which require conversion are semi-diameter, horizontal parallax, longitude and latitude.

4. *Interpolation of GHA and Dec*   The *GHA* and *Dec* of the Sun, Moon and planets are interpolated to the time of observation by direct calculation as follows: If the universal time is $a^h\ b^m\ c^s$, form the interpolation factor $x = b/60 + c/3600$. Enter the tabular value GHA_0 for the preceding hour (a) and the tabular value GHA_1 for the following hour $(a+1)$ then the interpolated value *GHA* is given by

$$GHA = GHA_0 + x(GHA_1 - GHA_0)$$

If the *GHA* passes through 360° between tabular values add 360° to GHA_1 before interpolation. If the interpolated value exceeds 360°, subtract 360° from *GHA*.

Similarly for declination, enter the tabular value Dec_0 for the preceding hour (a) and the tabular value Dec_1 for the following hour $(a+1)$, then the interpolated value *Dec* is given by

$$Dec = Dec_0 + x(Dec_1 - Dec_0)$$

5. *Example.*   (a) Find the *GHA* and *Dec* of the Sun on 2013 November 13 at $20^h\ 47^m\ 13^s$ UT.

The interpolation factor $x = 47/60 + 13/3600 = 0^h7869$

page 221 $20^h\ GHA_0 = 123°\ 54\!'6 = 123°9100$

$21^h\ GHA_1 = 138°\ 54\!'5 = 138°9083$

$20^h7869\ GHA = 123·9100 + 0·7869(138·9083 - 123·9100) = 135°7129$

$20^h\ Dec_0 = S\,18°\ 09\!'8 = -18°1633$

$21^h\ Dec_1 = S\,18°\ 10\!'4 = -18°1733$

$20^h7869\ Dec = -18·1633 + 0·7869(-18·1733 + 18·1633) = -18°1712$

GHA Aries is interpolated in the same way as *GHA* of a body. For a star the *SHA* and *Dec* are taken from the tabular page and do not require interpolation, then

$$GHA = GHA\ \text{Aries} + SHA$$

where *GHA* Aries is interpolated to the time of observation.

(b) Find the *GHA* and *Dec* of *Vega* on 2013 November 13 at $20^h\ 47^m\ 13^s$ UT.

The interpolation factor $x = 0^h\!7869$ as in the previous example

page 220 $20^h\ GHA\ Aries_0 = 353°\ 05\!.7 = 353°\!0950$

$21^h\ GHA\ Aries_1 = 8°\ 08\!.2 = 368°\!1367$ (360° added)

$20^h\!7869\ GHA\ Aries = 353·0950 + 0·7869(368·1367 - 353·0950) = 364°\!9320$

$SHA = 80°\ 39\!.1 = 80°\!6517$

$GHA = GHA\ Aries + SHA = 85°\!5836$ (multiple of 360° removed)

$Dec = N\,38°\ 48\!.2 = +38°\!8033$

6. *The calculated altitude and azimuth.* The calculated altitude H_C and true azimuth Z are determined from the *GHA* and *Dec* interpolated to the time of observation and from the *Long* and *Lat* estimated at the time of observation as follows:

Step 1.   Calculate the local hour angle

$$LHA = GHA + Long$$

Add or subtract multiples of 360° to set *LHA* in the range 0° to 360°.

Step 2.   Calculate S, C and the altitude H_C from

$$S = \sin Dec$$
$$C = \cos Dec\ \cos LHA$$
$$H_C = \sin^{-1}(S\ \sin Lat + C\ \cos Lat)$$

where $\sin^{-1}$ is the inverse function of sine.

Step 3.   Calculate X and A from

$$X = (S\ \cos Lat - C\ \sin Lat)/\cos H_C$$
$$\text{If}\ \ X > +1\ \ \text{set}\ \ X = +1$$
$$\text{If}\ \ X < -1\ \ \text{set}\ \ X = -1$$
$$A = \cos^{-1} X$$

where $\cos^{-1}$ is the inverse function of cosine.

Step 4.   Determine the azimuth Z

$$\text{If}\ LHA > 180°\ \ \text{then}\ \ Z = A$$
$$\text{Otherwise}\ \ Z = 360° - A$$

7. *Example.*   Find the calculated altitude H_C and azimuth Z when

$$GHA = 53°\quad Dec = S\,15°\quad Lat = N\,32°\quad Long = W\,16°$$

For the calculation

$$GHA = 53°\!0000\quad Dec = -15°\!0000\quad Lat = +32°\!0000\quad Long = -16°\!0000$$

Step 1. $LHA = 53·0000 - 16·0000 = 37·0000$

Step 2. $S = -0·2588$

$C = +0·9659 \times 0·7986 = 0·7714$

$\sin H_C = -0·2588 \times 0·5299 + 0·7714 \times 0·8480 = 0·5171$

$H_C = 31°\!1346$

Step 3. $$X = (-0{\cdot}2588 \times 0{\cdot}8480 - 0{\cdot}7714 \times 0{\cdot}5299)/0{\cdot}8560 = -0{\cdot}7340$$
$$A = 137{\cdot}^\circ 2239$$

Step 4.   Since $LHA \leq 180°$ then $Z = 360° - A = 222{\cdot}^\circ 7761$

8. *Reduction from sextant altitude to observed altitude.*   The sextant altitude H_S is corrected for both dip and index error to produce the apparent altitude. The observed altitude H_O is calculated by applying a correction for refraction. For the Sun, Moon, Venus and Mars a correction for parallax is also applied to H, and for the Sun and Moon a further correction for semi-diameter is required. The corrections are calculated as follows:

Step 1.   Calculate dip

$$D = 0{\cdot}^\circ 0293\sqrt{h}$$

where h is the height of eye above the horizon in metres.

Step 2.   Calculate apparent altitude

$$H = H_S + I - D$$

where I is the sextant index error.

Step 3.   Calculate refraction (R) at a standard temperature of $10°$ Celsius (C) and pressure of 1010 millibars (mb)

$$R_0 = 0{\cdot}^\circ 0167/\tan(H + 7{\cdot}32/(H + 4{\cdot}32))$$

If the temperature $T°$ C and pressure P mb are known calculate the refraction from

$$R = fR_0 \qquad \text{where} \qquad f = 0{\cdot}28P/(T + 273)$$

otherwise set $R = R_0$

Step 4.   Calculate the parallax in altitude (PA) from the horizontal parallax (HP) and the apparent altitude (H) for the Sun, Moon, Venus and Mars as follows:

$$PA = HP\cos H$$

For the Sun $HP = 0{\cdot}^\circ 0024$. This correction is very small and could be ignored.

For the Moon HP is taken for the nearest hour from the main tabular page and converted to degrees.

For Venus and Mars the HP is taken from the critical table at the bottom of page 259 and converted to degrees.

For the navigational stars and the remaining planets, Jupiter and Saturn set $PA = 0$.

If an error of $0'{\cdot}2$ is significant the expression for the parallax in altitude for the Moon should include a small correction OB for the oblateness of the Earth as follows:

$$PA = HP\cos H + OB$$
$$\text{where} \quad OB = -0{\cdot}^\circ 0032\sin^2 Lat\,\cos H + 0{\cdot}^\circ 0032\sin(2Lat)\cos Z \sin H$$

At mid-latitudes and for altitudes of the Moon below $60°$ a simple approximation to OB is

$$OB = -0{\cdot}^\circ 0017\cos H$$

Step 5. Calculate the semi-diameter for the Sun and Moon as follows:

Sun: *SD* is taken from the main tabular page and converted to degrees.

Moon: $SD = 0°2724 HP$ where *HP* is taken for the nearest hour from the main tabular page and converted to degrees.

Step 6. Calculate the observed altitude

$$H_O = H - R + PA \pm SD$$

where the plus sign is used if the lower limb of the Sun or Moon was observed and the minus sign if the upper limb was observed.

9. *Example.* The following example illustrates how to use a calculator to reduce the sextant altitude (H_S) to observed altitude (H_O); the sextant altitudes given are assumed to be taken on 2013 August 12 with a marine sextant, zero index error, at height 5·4 m, temperature $-3°$ C and pressure 982 mb, the Moon sights are assumed to be taken at 10^h UT.

Body limb	Sun lower	Sun upper	Moon lower	Moon upper	Venus –	*Polaris* –
Sextant altitude: H_S	21·3283	3·3367	33·4600	26·1117	4·5433	49·6083
Step 1. Dip: $D = 0·0293\sqrt{h}$	0·0681	0·0681	0·0681	0·0681	0·0681	0·0681
Step 2. Apparent altitude: $H = H_S + I - D$	21·2602	3·2686	33·3919	26·0436	4·4752	49·5402
Step 3. Refraction: R_0	0·0423	0·2256	0·0251	0·0338	0·1798	0·0142
f	1·0184	1·0184	1·0184	1·0184	1·0184	1·0184
$R = fR_0$	0·0431	0·2298	0·0256	0·0344	0·1831	0·0144
Step 4. Parallax:			(57ʹ3)	(57ʹ3)	(0ʹ1)	
HP	0·0024	0·0024	0·9550	0·9550	0·0017	–
Parallax in altitude: $PA = HP \cos H$	0·0022	0·0024	0·7974	0·8580	0·0017	–
Step 5. Semi-diameter: Sun : $SD = 15·8/60$	0·2633	0·2633	–	–	–	–
Moon : $SD = 0·2724 HP$	–	–	0·2601	0·2601	–	–
Step 6. Observed altitude: $H_O = H - R + PA \pm SD$	21·4827	2·7779	34·4238	26·6071	4·2938	49·5258

Note that for the Moon the correction for the oblateness of the Earth of about $-0°0017 \cos H$, which equals $-0°0014$ for the lower limb and $-0°0015$ for the upper limb, has been ignored in the above calculation.

10. *Position from intercept and azimuth using a chart.* An estimate is made of the position at the adopted time of fix. The position at the time of observation is then calculated by dead reckoning from the time of fix. For example if the course (track) *T* and the speed *V* (in knots) of the observer are constant then *Long* and *Lat* at the time of observation are calculated from

$$Long = L_F + t(V/60)\sin T / \cos B_F$$
$$Lat = B_F + t(V/60)\cos T$$

where L_F and B_F are the estimated longitude and latitude at the time of fix and t is the time interval in hours from the time of fix to the time of observation, t is positive if the time of observation is after the time of fix and negative if it was before.

The position line of an observation is plotted on a chart using the intercept

$$p = H_O - H_C$$

and azimuth Z with origin at the calculated position $(Long, Lat)$ at the time of observation, where H_C and Z are calculated using the method in section 6, page 279. Starting from this calculated position a line is drawn on the chart along the direction of the azimuth to the body. Convert p to nautical miles by multiplying by 60. The position line is drawn at right angles to the azimuth line, distance p from $(Long, Lat)$ towards the body if p is positive and distance p away from the body if p is negative. Provided there are no gross errors the navigator should be somewhere on or near the position line at the time of observation. Two or more position lines are required to determine a fix.

11. *Position from intercept and azimuth by calculation.* The position of the fix may be calculated from two or more sextant observations as follows.

If p_1, Z_1, are the intercept and azimuth of the first observation, p_2, Z_2, of the second observation and so on, form the summations

$$A = \cos^2 Z_1 + \cos^2 Z_2 + \cdots$$
$$B = \cos Z_1 \sin Z_1 + \cos Z_2 \sin Z_2 + \cdots$$
$$C = \sin^2 Z_1 + \sin^2 Z_2 + \cdots$$
$$D = p_1 \cos Z_1 + p_2 \cos Z_2 + \cdots$$
$$E = p_1 \sin Z_1 + p_2 \sin Z_2 + \cdots$$

where the number of terms in each summation is equal to the number of observations.

With $G = AC - B^2$, an improved estimate of the position at the time of fix (L_I, B_I) is given by

$$L_I = L_F + (AE - BD)/(G\cos B_F), \qquad B_I = B_F + (CD - BE)/G$$

Calculate the distance d between the initial estimated position (L_F, B_F) at the time of fix and the improved estimated position (L_I, B_I) in nautical miles from

$$d = 60\sqrt{((L_I - L_F)^2 \cos^2 B_F + (B_I - B_F)^2)}$$

If d exceeds about 20 nautical miles set $L_F = L_I$, $B_F = B_I$ and repeat the calculation until d, the distance between the position at the previous estimate and the improved estimate, is less than about 20 nautical miles.

12. *Example of direct computation.* Using the method described above, calculate the position of a ship on 2013 July 4 at $21^h\ 00^m\ 00^s$ UT from the marine sextant observations of the three stars *Antares* (No. 42) at $20^h\ 45^m\ 47^s$ UT, *Kochab* (No. 40) at $20^h\ 58^m\ 37^s$ UT and *Regulus* (No. 26) at $21^h\ 05^m\ 34^s$ UT, where the observed altitudes of the three stars corrected for the effects of refraction, dip and instrumental error, are $26°0803$, $47°4886$ and $21°3601$ respectively. The ship was travelling at a constant speed of 20 knots on a course of 325° during the period of observation, and the position of the ship at the time of fix $21^h\ 00^m\ 00^s$ UT is only known to the nearest whole degree W 15°, N 32°.

Intermediate values for the first iteration are shown in the table. *GHA* Aries was interpolated from the nearest tabular values on page 132. For the first iteration set $L_F = -15°0000$, $B_F = +32°0000$ at the time of fix at 21^h 00^m 00^s UT.

First Iteration

Body No.	Antares 42	Kochab 40	Regulus 26
time of observation	20^h 45^m 47^s	20^h 58^m 37^s	21^h 05^m 34^s
H_O	26·0803	47·4886	21·3601
interpolation factor	0·7631	0·9769	0·0928
GHA Aries	234·4676	237·6849	239·4272
SHA (page 132)	112·4317	137·3250	207·7283
GHA	346·8993	15·0099	87·1555
Dec (page 132)	−26·4600	+74·1050	+11·9000
t	−0·2369	−0·0231	+0·0928
Long	−14·9466	−14·9948	−15·0209
Lat	+31·9353	+31·9937	+32·0253
Z	152·1311	359·9938	270·9618
H_C	25·7745	47·8887	21·3370
p	+0·3058	−0·4001	+0·0231

$$A = 1·7818 \quad B = -0·4301 \quad C = 1·2182 \quad D = -0·6700 \quad E = 0·1199 \quad G = 1·9856$$
$$(A E - B D)/(G \cos B_F) = -0·0443, \quad (C D - B E)/G = -0·3851$$

An improved estimate of the position at the time of fix is

$$L_I = L_F - 0·0443 = -15·0443 \quad \text{and} \quad B_I = B_F - 0·3851 = +31·6149$$

Since the distance between the previous estimated position and the improved estimate $d = 23·2$ nautical miles set $L_F = -15·0443$, and $B_F = +31·6149$ and repeat the calculation. The table shows the intermediate values of the calculation for the second iteration. In each iteration the quantities H_O, *GHA*, *Dec* and *t* do not change.

Second Iteration

Body No.	Antares 42	Kochab 40	Regulus 26
Long	−14·9911	−15·0391	−15·0651
Lat	+31·5502	+31·6086	+31·6402
Z	152·0037	0·0119	271·0892
H_C	26·0971	47·5036	21·3677
p	−0·0167	−0·0150	−0·0076

$$A = 1·7800 \quad B = -0·4333 \quad C = 1·2200 \quad D = -0·0004 \quad E = -0·0003 \quad G = 1·9839$$
$$(A E - B D)/(G \cos B_F) = -0·0004, \quad (C D - B E)/G = -0·0003$$

An improved estimate of the position at the time of fix is

$$L_I = L_F - 0·0004 = -15·0447 \quad \text{and} \quad B_I = B_F - 0·0003 = +31·6146$$

The distance between the previous estimated position and the improved estimated position $d = 0·03$ nautical miles is so small that a third iteration would produce a negligible improvement to the estimate of the position.

USE OF CONCISE SIGHT REDUCTION TABLES

1. *Introduction.* The concise sight reduction tables given on pages 286 to 317 are intended for use when neither more extensive tables nor electronic computing aids are available. These "NAO sight reduction tables" provide for the reduction of the local hour angle and declination of a celestial object to azimuth and altitude, referred to an assumed position on the Earth, for use in the intercept method of celestial navigation which is now standard practice.

2. *Form of tables.* Entries in the reduction table are at a fixed interval of one degree for all latitudes and hour angles. A compact arrangement results from division of the navigational triangle into two right spherical triangles, so that the table has to be entered twice. Assumed latitude and local hour angle are the arguments for the first entry. The reduction table responds with the intermediate arguments A, B, and Z_1, where A is used as one of the arguments for the second entry to the table, B has to be incremented by the declination to produce the quantity F, and Z_1 is a component of the azimuth angle. The reduction table is then reentered with A and F and yields H, P, and Z_2 where H is the altitude, P is the complement of the parallactic angle, and Z_2 is the second component of the azimuth angle. It is usually necessary to adjust the tabular altitude for the fractional parts of the intermediate entering arguments to derive computed altitude, and an auxiliary table is provided for the purpose. Rules governing signs of the quantities which must be added or subtracted are given in the instructions and summarized on each tabular page. Azimuth angle is the sum of two components and is converted to true azimuth by familiar rules, repeated at the bottom of the tabular pages.

Tabular altitude and intermediate quantities are given to the nearest minute of arc, although errors of $2'$ in computed altitude may accrue during adjustment for the minutes parts of entering arguments. Components of azimuth angle are stated to $0°.1$; for derived true azimuth, only whole degrees are warranted. Since objects near the zenith are difficult to observe with a marine sextant, they should be avoided; altitudes greater than about 80° are not suited to reduction by this method.

In many circumstances the accuracy provided by these tables is sufficient. However, to maintain the full accuracy $(0'.1)$ of the ephemeral data in the almanac throughout their reduction to altitude and azimuth, more extensive tables or a calculator should be used.

3. *Use of Tables.*

Step 1. Determine the Greenwich hour angle (GHA) and Declination (Dec) of the body from the almanac. Select an assumed latitude (Lat) of integral degrees nearest to the estimated latitude. Choose an assumed longitude nearest to the estimated longitude such that the local hour angle

$$LHA = GHA \begin{array}{c} - \text{ west} \\ + \text{ east} \end{array} \text{longitude}$$

has integral degrees.

Step 2. Enter the reduction table with Lat and LHA as arguments. Record the quantities A, B and Z_1. Apply the rules for the sign of B and Z_1: B is minus if $90° < LHA < 270°$: Z_1 has the same sign as B. Set $A° =$ nearest whole degree of A and $A' =$ minutes part of A. This step may be repeated for all reductions before leaving the latitude opening of the table.

Step 3. Record the declination Dec. Apply the rules for the sign of Dec: Dec is minus if the name of Dec (*i.e.* N or S) is contrary to latitude. Add B and Dec algebraically to produce F. If F is negative, the object is below the horizon (in sight reduction, this can occur when the objects are close to the horizon). Regard F as positive until step 7. Set $F° =$ nearest whole degree of F and $F' =$ minutes part of F.

Step 4. Enter the reduction table a second time with $A°$ and $F°$ as arguments and record H, P, and Z_2. Set $P° =$ nearest whole degree of P and $Z_2° =$ nearest whole degree of Z_2.

Step 5. Enter the auxiliary table with F' and $P°$ as arguments to obtain $corr_1$ to H for F'. Apply the rule for the sign of $corr_1$: $corr_1$ is minus if $F < 90°$ and $F' > 29'$ or if $F > 90°$ and $F' < 30'$, otherwise $corr_1$ is plus.

Step 6. Enter the auxiliary table with A' and $Z_2°$ as arguments to obtain $corr_2$ to H for A'. Apply the rule for the sign of $corr_2$: $corr_2$ is minus if $A' < 30'$, otherwise $corr_2$ is plus.

Step 7. Calculate the computed altitude H_C as the sum of H, $corr_1$ and $corr_2$. Apply the rule for the sign of H_C: H_C is minus if F is negative.

Step 8. Apply the rule for the sign of Z_2: Z_2 is minus if $F > 90°$. If F is negative, replace Z_2 by $180° - Z_2$. Set the azimuth angle Z equal to the algebraic sum of Z_1 and Z_2 and ignore the resulting sign. Obtain the true azimuth Z_n from the rules

$$\text{For N latitude, if } LHA > 180° \quad Z_n = Z$$
$$\text{if } LHA < 180° \quad Z_n = 360° - Z$$

$$\text{For S latitude, if } LHA > 180° \quad Z_n = 180° - Z$$
$$\text{if } LHA < 180° \quad Z_n = 180° + Z$$

Observed altitude H_O is compared with H_C to obtain the altitude difference, which, with Z_n, is used to plot the position line.

4. *Example.* (a) Required the altitude and azimuth of *Schedar* on 2013 February 4 at UT 06^h 30^m from the estimated position 5° east, 53° north.

1. Assumed latitude $Lat =$ 53° N
   From the almanac $GHA =$ 221° 46'
   Assumed longitude   5° 14' E
   Local hour angle $LHA =$ 227

2. Reduction table, 1st entry
   $(Lat, LHA) = (53, 227)$ $A =$ 26 07 $A° = 26, A' = 7$
                               $B = -27$ 12 $Z_1 = -49.4,$ $90° < LHA < 270°$
3. From the almanac $Dec = +56$ 37   *Lat* and *Dec* same
   Sum $= B + Dec$ $F = +29$ 25 $F° = 29, F' = 25$

4. Reduction table, 2nd entry
   $(A°, F°) = (26, 29)$ $H =$ 25 50 $P° = 61$
                                               $Z_2 = 76.3, Z_2° = 76$

5. Auxiliary table, 1st entry
   $(F', P°) = (25, 61)$ $corr_1 =$ +22 $F < 90°, F' < 29'$
   Sum   26 12
6. Auxiliary table, 2nd entry
   $(A', Z_2°) = (7, 76)$ $corr_2 =$ −2 $A' < 30'$
7. Sum $=$ computed altitude $H_C = +26°$ 10' $F > 0°$

8. Azimuth, first component $Z_1 = -49.4$ same sign as B
           second component $Z_2 = +76.3$ $F < 90°, F > 0°$
   Sum $=$ azimuth angle $Z =$ 26.9

   True azimuth $Z_n =$ 027°   N *Lat*, $LHA > 180°$

continued on page 318

SIGHT REDUCTION TABLE

B: (−) for 90° < LHA < 270°
Dec:(−) for Lat. contrary name

Z₁: same sign as B
Z₂: (−) for F > 90°

LHA/F	Lat./A	0° A/H	0° B/P	0° Z₁/Z₂	1° A/H	1° B/P	1° Z₁/Z₂	2° A/H	2° B/P	2° Z₁/Z₂	3° A/H	3° B/P	3° Z₁/Z₂	4° A/H	4° B/P	4° Z₁/Z₂	5° A/H	5° B/P	5° Z₁/Z₂	Lat./A	LHA
0	180	0 00	90 00	90·0	0 00	89 00	90·0	0 00	88 00	90·0	0 00	87 00	90·0	0 00	86 00	90·0	0 00	85 00	90·0	180	360
1	179	1 00	90 00	90·0	1 00	89 00	90·0	1 00	88 00	90·0	1 00	87 00	90·0	1 00	86 00	89·9	1 00	85 00	89·9	181	359
2	178	2 00	90 00	90·0	2 00	89 00	90·0	2 00	88 00	89·9	2 00	87 00	89·9	2 00	86 00	89·9	2 00	85 00	89·8	182	358
3	177	3 00	90 00	90·0	3 00	89 00	89·9	3 00	88 00	89·9	3 00	87 00	89·8	3 00	86 00	89·8	3 00	85 00	89·7	183	357
4	176	4 00	90 00	90·0	4 00	89 00	89·9	4 00	88 00	89·9	4 00	87 00	89·8	4 00	85 59	89·8	3 59	84 59	89·7	184	356
5	175	5 00	90 00	90·0	5 00	89 00	89·8	5 00	88 00	89·8	5 00	86 59	89·7	4 59	85 59	89·7	4 59	84 59	89·6	185	355
6	174	6 00	90 00	90·0	6 00	89 00	89·8	6 00	87 59	89·8	6 00	86 59	89·7	5 59	85 59	89·6	5 59	84 58	89·5	186	354
7	173	7 00	90 00	90·0	7 00	89 00	89·8	7 00	87 59	89·8	6 59	86 59	89·6	6 59	85 58	89·5	6 58	84 58	89·4	187	353
8	172	8 00	90 00	90·0	8 00	88 59	89·8	8 00	87 59	89·7	7 59	86 58	89·6	7 59	85 58	89·5	7 58	84 57	89·3	188	352
9	171	9 00	90 00	90·0	9 00	88 59	89·8	9 00	87 59	89·6	8 59	86 58	89·5	8 59	85 57	89·4	8 58	84 56	89·2	189	351
10	170	10 00	90 00	90·0	10 00	88 59	89·8	10 00	87 58	89·6	9 59	86 57	89·5	9 59	85 56	89·3	9 57	84 55	89·1	190	350
11	169	11 00	90 00	90·0	11 00	88 59	89·8	11 00	87 58	89·6	10 59	86 57	89·4	10 58	85 56	89·2	10 57	84 54	89·0	191	349
12	168	12 00	90 00	90·0	12 00	88 59	89·8	12 00	87 57	89·6	11 59	86 56	89·4	11 58	85 55	89·2	11 57	84 53	88·9	192	348
13	167	13 00	90 00	90·0	13 00	88 58	89·8	13 00	87 57	89·5	12 59	86 55	89·3	12 58	85 54	89·1	12 57	84 52	88·8	193	347
14	166	14 00	90 00	90·0	14 00	88 58	89·8	14 00	87 56	89·5	13 59	86 54	89·2	13 58	85 53	89·0	13 57	84 51	88·8	194	346
15	165	15 00	90 00	90·0	15 00	88 58	89·7	14 59	87 56	89·5	14 59	86 54	89·1	14 58	85 52	89·0	14 56	84 49	88·7	195	345
16	164	16 00	90 00	90·0	16 00	88 57	89·7	15 59	87 55	89·4	15 59	86 53	89·1	15 58	85 50	88·9	15 56	84 48	88·6	196	344
17	163	17 00	90 00	90·0	17 00	88 57	89·7	16 59	87 55	89·4	16 59	86 52	89·0	16 57	85 49	88·8	16 56	84 46	88·5	197	343
18	162	18 00	90 00	90·0	18 00	88 57	89·7	17 59	87 54	89·4	17 58	86 51	89·0	17 57	85 48	88·7	17 56	84 45	88·4	198	342
19	161	19 00	90 00	90·0	19 00	88 56	89·7	18 59	87 53	89·3	18 58	86 50	89·0	18 57	85 45	88·7	18 55	84 43	88·3	199	341
20	160	20 00	90 00	90·0	20 00	88 56	89·6	19 59	87 52	89·3	19 58	86 48	88·9	19 57	85 43	88·6	19 55	84 41	88·2	200	340
21	159	21 00	90 00	90·0	21 00	88 56	89·6	20 59	87 51	89·2	20 58	86 47	88·8	20 57	85 41	88·5	20 55	84 39	88·1	201	339
22	158	22 00	90 00	90·0	22 00	88 55	89·6	21 59	87 51	89·2	21 58	86 46	88·8	21 57	85 39	88·4	21 54	84 37	88·1	202	338
23	157	23 00	90 00	90·0	23 00	88 55	89·6	22 59	87 50	89·2	22 58	86 44	88·7	22 56	85 37	88·3	22 54	84 34	87·9	203	337
24	156	24 00	90 00	90·0	24 00	88 54	89·6	23 59	87 49	89·1	23 58	86 43	88·7	23 56	85 35	88·2	23 54	84 32	87·8	204	336
25	155	25 00	90 00	90·0	25 00	88 54	89·5	24 59	87 48	89·1	24 58	86 41	88·6	24 56	85 33	88·1	24 54	84 29	87·6	205	335
26	154	26 00	90 00	90·0	26 00	88 53	89·5	25 59	87 47	89·0	25 58	86 40	88·5	25 56	85 31	88·1	25 53	84 26	87·5	206	334
27	153	27 00	90 00	90·0	27 00	88 53	89·5	26 59	87 46	89·0	26 57	86 38	88·4	26 56	85 28	88·0	26 53	84 24	87·4	207	333
28	152	28 00	90 00	90·0	28 00	88 52	89·5	27 59	87 45	88·9	27 57	86 36	88·4	27 56	85 26	87·9	27 53	84 20	87·3	208	332
29	151	29 00	90 00	90·0	29 00	88 51	89·4	28 59	87 43	88·9	28 57	86 34	88·3	28 55	85 23	87·8	28 53	84 17	87·2	209	331
30	150	30 00	90 00	90·0	30 00	88 51	89·4	29 59	87 41	88·8	29 57	86 32	88·2	29 55	85 20	87·7	29 52	84 14	87·1	210	330
31	149	31 00	90 00	90·0	31 00	88 50	89·4	30 59	87 40	88·8	30 57	86 30	88·2	30 55	85 17	87·6	30 52	84 10	87·0	211	329
32	148	32 00	90 00	90·0	32 00	88 49	89·4	31 59	87 39	88·8	31 57	86 28	88·1	31 55	85 14	87·5	31 52	84 07	86·9	212	328
33	147	33 00	90 00	90·0	33 00	88 48	89·3	32 59	87 37	88·7	32 57	86 25	88·1	32 54	85 11	87·4	32 51	84 03	86·8	213	327
34	146	34 00	90 00	90·0	34 00	88 48	89·3	33 59	87 35	88·7	33 57	86 23	88·0	33 54	85 07	87·3	33 51	83 59	86·6	214	326
35	145	35 00	90 00	90·0	35 00	88 47	89·3	34 59	87 34	88·6	34 57	86 20	87·9	34 54	85 04	87·2	34 51	83 55	86·5	215	325
36	144	36 00	90 00	90·0	36 00	88 46	89·3	35 58	87 32	88·5	35 57	86 18	87·8	35 54	85 00	87·1	35 50	83 50	86·4	216	324
37	143	37 00	90 00	90·0	37 00	88 45	89·2	36 58	87 30	88·5	36 56	86 15	87·7	36 54	84 56	87·0	36 50	83 45	86·2	217	323
38	142	38 00	90 00	90·0	38 00	88 44	89·2	37 58	87 28	88·4	37 56	86 12	87·7	37 53	84 52	86·9	37 49	83 39	86·1	218	322
39	141	39 00	90 00	90·0	39 00	88 43	89·2	38 58	87 26	88·4	38 56	86 09	87·6	38 53	84 47	86·8	38 49	83 35	86·0	219	321
40	140	40 00	90 00	90·0	40 00	88 42	89·1	39 58	87 23	88·3	39 56	86 05	87·5	39 53	84 42	86·7	39 49	83 29	85·8	220	320
41	139	41 00	90 00	90·0	41 00	88 41	89·1	40 58	87 21	88·3	40 56	86 02	87·4	40 52	84 37	86·5	40 49	83 23	85·7	221	319
42	138	42 00	90 00	90·0	42 00	88 39	89·1	41 58	87 19	88·2	41 56	85 58	87·3	41 52	84 32	86·4	41 48	83 17	85·5	222	318
43	137	43 00	90 00	90·0	43 00	88 38	89·1	42 58	87 16	88·2	42 56	85 54	87·2	42 52	84 27	86·3	42 48	83 11	85·4	223	317
44	136	44 00	90 00	90·0	43 59	88 37	89·0	43 58	87 13	88·1	43 55	85 50	87·2	43 52	84 21	86·1	43 47	83 04	85·2	224	316
45	135	45 00	90 00	90·0	44 59	88 35	89·0	44 58	87 10	88·0	44 55	85 46	87·0	44 52	84 21	86·0	44 47	82 57	85·0	225	315

Lat./A	LHA/F	0° A/H	0° B/P	0° Z₁/Z₂	1° A/H	1° B/P	1° Z₁/Z₂	2° A/H	2° B/P	2° Z₁/Z₂	3° A/H	3° B/P	3° Z₁/Z₂	4° A/H	4° B/P	4° Z₁/Z₂	5° A/H	5° B/P	5° Z₁/Z₂	Lat./A	LHA
45	135	45 00	90 00	90·0	44 59	88 35	89·0	44 58	87 10	88·0	44 55	85 46	87·0	44 52	84 21	86·0	44 47	82 57	85·0	225	315
46	134	46 00	90 00	90·0	45 59	88 34	89·0	45 58	87 07	87·9	45 55	85 41	86·9	45 51	84 15	85·9	45 46	82 49	84·8	226	314
47	133	47 00	90 00	90·0	46 59	88 32	89·0	46 58	87 04	87·9	46 55	85 36	86·8	46 51	84 09	85·8	46 46	82 41	84·7	227	313
48	132	48 00	90 00	90·0	47 59	88 30	88·9	47 58	87 01	87·8	47 55	85 31	86·7	47 51	84 02	85·6	47 46	82 33	84·5	228	312
49	131	49 00	90 00	90·0	48 59	88 29	88·8	48 58	86 57	87·7	48 55	85 26	86·6	48 50	83 55	85·4	48 45	82 24	84·3	229	311
50	130	50 00	90 00	90·0	49 59	88 27	88·8	49 58	86 53	87·6	49 54	85 20	86·4	49 50	83 47	85·2	49 44	82 15	84·1	230	310
51	129	51 00	90 00	90·0	50 59	88 25	88·8	50 57	86 49	87·5	50 54	85 14	86·3	50 50	83 40	85·1	50 44	82 05	83·9	231	309
52	128	52 00	90 00	90·0	51 59	88 23	88·7	51 57	86 45	87·4	51 54	85 08	86·2	51 49	83 31	84·9	51 43	81 55	83·6	232	308
53	127	53 00	90 00	90·0	52 59	88 20	88·7	52 57	86 41	87·3	52 54	85 01	86·0	52 49	83 22	84·7	52 43	81 44	83·4	233	307
54	126	54 00	90 00	90·0	53 59	88 18	88·6	53 57	86 36	87·2	53 54	84 54	85·9	53 49	83 13	84·5	53 42	81 32	83·2	234	306
55	125	55 00	90 00	90·0	54 59	88 15	88·6	54 57	86 31	87·1	54 53	84 47	85·7	54 48	83 03	84·3	54 41	81 20	82·9	235	305
56	124	56 00	90 00	90·0	55 59	88 13	88·5	55 57	86 26	87·0	55 53	84 39	85·6	55 48	82 52	84·1	55 41	81 06	82·6	236	304
57	123	57 00	90 00	90·0	56 59	88 10	88·5	56 57	86 20	86·9	56 53	84 30	85·4	56 47	82 41	83·9	56 40	80 52	82·4	237	303
58	122	58 00	90 00	90·0	57 59	88 07	88·4	57 57	86 14	86·8	57 52	84 21	85·2	57 47	82 29	83·6	57 39	80 38	82·1	238	302
59	121	59 00	90 00	90·0	58 59	88 04	88·3	58 57	86 07	86·7	58 52	84 11	85·0	58 46	82 16	83·4	58 38	80 23	81·7	239	301
60	120	60 00	90 00	90·0	59 59	88 00	88·3	59 56	86 00	86·5	59 52	84 01	84·8	59 46	82 02	83·1	59 37	80 04	81·4	240	300
61	119	61 00	90 00	90·0	60 59	87 56	88·2	60 56	85 53	86·4	60 52	83 50	84·6	60 45	81 48	82·8	60 37	79 46	81·1	241	299
62	118	62 00	90 00	90·0	61 59	87 52	88·1	61 56	85 45	86·2	61 51	83 38	84·4	61 44	81 32	82·5	61 36	79 27	80·7	242	298
63	117	63 00	90 00	90·0	62 59	87 48	88·0	62 56	85 36	86·1	62 51	83 25	84·1	62 44	81 15	82·2	62 35	79 06	80·3	243	297
64	116	64 00	90 00	90·0	63 59	87 43	88·0	63 56	85 27	85·9	63 50	83 11	83·9	63 43	80 56	81·9	63 33	78 43	79·9	244	296
65	115	65 00	90 00	90·0	64 59	87 38	87·9	64 56	85 17	85·7	64 50	82 56	83·6	64 42	80 36	81·5	64 32	78 19	79·4	245	295
66	114	66 00	90 00	90·0	65 58	87 33	87·8	65 55	85 06	85·5	65 49	82 39	83·3	65 41	80 15	81·1	65 31	77 52	78·9	246	294
67	113	67 00	90 00	90·0	66 58	87 27	87·6	66 55	84 54	85·3	66 48	82 22	83·0	66 40	79 52	80·7	66 29	77 23	78·4	247	293
68	112	68 00	90 00	90·0	67 58	87 20	87·5	67 55	84 40	85·1	67 48	82 02	82·6	67 39	79 26	80·2	67 28	76 51	77·8	248	292
69	111	69 00	90 00	90·0	68 59	87 13	87·4	68 55	84 26	84·8	68 48	81 41	82·2	68 38	78 58	79·7	68 26	76 17	77·2	249	291
70	110	70 00	90 00	90·0	69 58	87 05	87·3	69 54	84 10	84·5	69 47	81 17	81·8	69 37	78 27	79·2	69 25	75 39	76·5	250	290
71	109	71 00	90 00	90·0	70 58	86 56	87·1	70 54	83 53	84·2	70 46	80 51	81·4	70 36	77 53	78·5	70 23	74 58	75·8	251	289
72	108	72 00	90 00	90·0	71 57	86 46	86·9	71 53	83 33	83·9	71 46	80 22	80·8	71 35	77 16	77·9	71 20	74 12	75·0	252	288
73	107	73 00	90 00	90·0	72 57	86 35	86·7	72 53	83 11	83·5	72 45	79 50	80·3	72 33	76 33	77·1	72 17	73 23	74·1	253	287
74	106	74 00	90 00	90·0	73 57	86 23	86·5	73 53	82 47	83·1	73 44	79 14	79·7	73 31	75 46	76·3	73 15	72 23	73·1	254	286
75	105	75 00	90 00	90·0	74 58	86 09	86·3	74 52	82 19	82·6	74 43	78 33	78·9	74 29	74 53	75·4	74 12	71 19	72·0	255	285
76	104	76 00	90 00	90·0	75 56	85 52	86·0	75 51	81 48	82·0	75 41	77 47	78·1	75 27	73 55	74·4	75 07	70 07	70·7	256	284
77	103	77 00	90 00	90·0	76 56	85 34	85·7	76 50	81 11	81·4	76 40	76 53	77·2	76 25	72 44	73·2	76 05	68 45	69·3	257	283
78	102	78 00	90 00	90·0	77 55	85 12	85·3	77 49	80 28	80·7	77 38	75 51	76·2	77 22	71 20	71·8	77 02	67 11	67·7	258	282
79	101	79 00	90 00	90·0	78 57	84 46	84·9	78 48	79 38	79·8	78 36	74 38	74·9	78 18	69 52	70·3	77 56	65 22	65·8	259	281
80	100	80 00	90 00	90·0	79 57	84 16	84·3	79 48	78 38	78·8	79 34	73 12	73·5	79 14	68 04	68·4	78 50	63 16	63·7	260	280
81	99	81 00	90 00	90·0	80 57	83 38	83·7	80 47	77 25	77·6	80 31	71 29	71·7	80 09	65 55	66·2	79 43	60 47	61·2	261	279
82	98	82 00	90 00	90·0	81 56	82 51	82·9	81 45	75 55	76·1	81 28	69 22	69·6	81 04	63 19	63·6	80 34	57 51	58·2	262	278
83	97	83 00	90 00	90·0	82 56	81 51	81·9	82 43	74 01	74·1	82 23	66 44	66·9	81 57	60 09	60·4	81 24	54 20	54·6	263	277
84	96	84 00	90 00	90·0	83 54	80 31	80·6	83 41	71 32	71·6	83 10	63 24	63·5	82 48	56 13	56·4	82 12	50 04	50·3	264	276
85	95	85 00	90 00	90·0	84 54	78 40	78·7	84 37	68 10	68·3	84 00	58 59	59·1	83 36	51 16	51·4	82 56	44 53	45·1	265	275
86	94	86 00	90 00	90·0	85 53	75 57	76·0	85 32	63 24	63·5	84 55	53 05	53·2	84 21	44 56	45·1	83 36	38 34	38·7	266	274
87	93	87 00	90 00	90·0	86 50	71 33	71·6	86 24	56 17	56·3	85 45	45 58	45·0	85 00	36 49	36·9	84 10	30 53	31·0	267	273
88	92	88 00	90 00	90·0	87 46	63 26	63·4	87 10	44 59	45·0	86 24	33 40	33·7	85 32	26 31	26·6	84 37	21 45	21·8	268	272
89	91	89 00	90 00	90·0	88 35	45 00	45·0	87 46	26 33	26·6	86 50	18 25	18·4	85 53	14 01	14·0	84 54	11 17	11·3	269	271
90	90	90 00	0 00		89 00	0 00	0·0	88 00	0 00	0·0	87 00	0 00	0·0	86 00	0 00	0·0	85 00	0 00	0·0	270	270

N. Lat.: for LHA > 180° ... Zₙ = Z
for LHA < 180° ... Zₙ = 360° − Z

S. Lat.: for LHA > 180° ... Zₙ = 180° − Z
for LHA < 180° ... Zₙ = 180° + Z

SIGHT REDUCTION TABLE

B: (−) for 90° < LHA < 270°
Dec:(−) for Lat. contrary name

Z_1: same sign as B
Z_2:(−) for F > 90°

Lat./A LHA/F	6° A/H	6° B/P	6° Z_1/Z_2	7° A/H	7° B/P	7° Z_1/Z_2	8° A/H	8° B/P	8° Z_1/Z_2	9° A/H	9° B/P	9° Z_1/Z_2	10° A/H	10° B/P	10° Z_1/Z_2	11° A/H	11° B/P	11° Z_1/Z_2	Lat./A LHA
0	0 00	84 00	90·0	0 00	83 00	90·0	0 00	82 00	90·0	0 00	81 00	90·0	0 00	80 00	90·0	0 00	79 00	90·0	180
1	1 00	84 00	89·9	1 00	83 00	89·9	0 59	82 00	89·9	0 59	81 00	89·8	0 59	80 00	89·8	0 59	79 00	89·8	181
2	1 59	84 00	89·8	1 59	82 59	89·8	1 59	81 59	89·7	1 58	80 59	89·7	1 58	79 59	89·6	1 58	78 59	89·6	182
3	2 59	83 59	89·7	2 59	82 59	89·6	2 58	81 59	89·6	2 58	80 59	89·5	2 57	79 59	89·5	2 57	78 59	89·4	183
4	3 59	83 59	89·6	3 58	82 58	89·5	3 58	81 59	89·4	3 57	80 58	89·4	3 57	79 58	89·3	3 56	78 58	89·2	184
5	4 58	83 59	89·5	4 58	82 58	89·4	4 57	81 58	89·3	4 56	80 58	89·2	4 55	79 58	89·1	4 54	78 58	89·0	185
6	5 58	83 58	89·4	5 57	82 58	89·3	5 56	81 57	89·2	5 56	80 57	89·1	5 56	79 56	89·0	5 53	78 56	88·9	186
7	6 58	83 57	89·3	6 57	82 57	89·1	6 56	81 55	89·0	6 55	80 55	88·9	6 54	79 55	88·8	6 52	78 55	88·7	187
8	7 57	83 56	89·2	7 56	82 56	89·0	7 55	81 54	88·9	7 54	80 53	88·7	7 53	79 54	88·6	7 51	78 54	88·5	188
9	8 57	83 56	89·1	8 56	82 54	88·9	8 55	81 52	88·7	8 53	80 52	88·6	8 52	79 52	88·4	8 50	78 52	88·3	189
10	9 57	83 55	88·9	9 55	82 52	88·8	9 54	81 51	88·6	9 53	80 50	88·4	9 51	79 50	88·2	9 49	78 50	88·1	190
11	10 56	83 53	88·8	10 55	82 51	88·6	10 53	81 50	88·5	10 52	80 48	88·3	10 50	79 48	88·1	10 48	78 48	87·9	191
12	11 56	83 52	88·7	11 55	82 49	88·5	11 53	81 49	88·3	11 51	80 46	88·1	11 49	79 46	87·9	11 47	78 46	87·7	192
13	12 56	83 51	88·6	12 54	82 47	88·3	12 52	81 48	88·2	12 50	80 44	87·9	12 48	79 44	87·7	12 46	78 43	87·5	193
14	13 55	83 49	88·5	13 54	82 45	88·1	13 52	81 46	88·0	13 49	80 42	87·8	13 47	79 41	87·5	13 44	78 40	87·3	194
15	14 55	83 47	88·4	14 53	82 43	88·0	14 51	81 44	87·9	14 48	80 40	87·7	14 46	79 39	87·3	14 43	78 37	87·1	195
16	15 55	83 46	88·3	15 53	82 41	87·9	15 50	81 41	87·7	15 48	80 38	87·4	15 45	79 36	87·1	15 42	78 34	86·9	196
17	16 54	83 44	88·2	16 52	82 41	87·7	16 50	81 38	87·6	16 47	80 36	87·3	16 44	79 34	87·0	16 41	78 31	86·7	197
18	17 54	83 42	88·1	17 52	82 39	87·7	17 49	81 36	87·4	17 46	80 33	87·1	17 43	79 30	86·8	17 39	78 27	86·5	198
19	18 54	83 40	87·9	18 51	82 36	87·6	18 48	81 33	87·3	18 45	80 29	86·9	18 42	79 26	86·6	18 38	78 23	86·2	199
20	19 53	83 37	87·8	19 51	82 33	87·5	19 47	81 30	87·1	19 44	80 25	86·7	19 41	79 22	86·4	19 37	78 19	86·0	200
21	20 52	83 35	87·7	20 50	82 30	87·3	20 47	81 26	86·9	20 44	80 22	86·6	20 40	79 18	86·2	20 36	78 14	85·8	201
22	21 52	83 32	87·6	21 50	82 27	87·2	21 46	81 23	86·8	21 43	80 18	86·4	21 39	79 14	86·0	21 35	78 10	85·6	202
23	22 52	83 29	87·5	22 49	82 24	87·0	22 45	81 19	86·6	22 42	80 14	86·2	22 38	79 10	85·8	22 33	78 05	85·4	203
24	23 52	83 26	87·3	23 49	82 21	86·9	23 45	81 15	86·5	23 41	80 10	86·0	23 37	79 05	85·6	23 32	77 59	85·1	204
25	24 51	83 23	87·2	24 48	82 17	86·7	24 44	81 11	86·3	24 40	80 05	85·8	24 36	79 00	85·4	24 31	77 54	84·9	205
26	25 51	83 20	87·1	25 48	82 13	86·6	25 44	81 07	86·1	25 39	80 00	85·6	25 35	78 54	85·2	25 30	77 48	84·7	206
27	26 50	83 16	87·0	26 47	82 09	86·4	26 43	81 02	85·9	26 38	79 55	85·4	26 33	78 49	84·9	26 28	77 42	84·4	207
28	27 50	83 13	86·8	27 46	82 05	86·3	27 42	80 57	85·8	27 38	79 50	85·2	27 32	78 43	84·7	27 27	77 35	84·2	208
29	28 49	83 09	86·7	28 46	82 01	86·1	28 41	80 52	85·6	28 37	79 44	85·0	28 31	78 36	84·5	28 25	77 28	84·0	209
30	29 49	83 05	86·5	29 45	81 56	86·0	29 41	80 47	85·4	29 36	79 38	84·8	29 30	78 29	84·3	29 24	77 21	83·7	210
31	30 49	83 01	86·4	30 45	81 51	85·8	30 40	80 41	85·2	30 35	79 32	84·6	30 29	78 23	84·0	30 22	77 13	83·5	211
32	31 48	82 56	86·3	31 44	81 46	85·6	31 39	80 35	85·0	31 34	79 25	84·4	31 27	78 15	83·8	31 21	77 05	83·2	212
33	32 48	82 51	86·1	32 43	81 40	85·5	32 38	80 29	84·8	32 33	79 18	84·2	32 26	78 08	83·6	32 19	76 57	82·9	213
34	33 47	82 46	86·0	33 43	81 35	85·3	33 37	80 23	84·6	33 31	79 11	84·0	33 25	78 00	83·3	33 18	76 48	82·7	214
35	34 47	82 41	85·8	34 42	81 29	85·1	34 37	80 16	84·4	34 30	79 03	83·7	34 24	77 51	83·1	34 16	76 39	82·4	215
36	35 46	82 36	85·7	35 41	81 22	84·9	35 36	80 09	84·2	35 29	78 55	83·5	35 22	77 42	82·8	35 14	76 29	82·1	216
37	36 46	82 30	85·5	36 41	81 16	84·8	36 35	80 01	84·0	36 28	78 47	83·3	36 21	77 33	82·5	36 13	76 19	81·8	217
38	37 45	82 24	85·3	37 40	81 09	84·6	37 34	79 53	83·8	37 27	78 38	83·0	37 19	77 24	82·3	37 11	76 09	81·5	218
39	38 45	82 18	85·2	38 39	81 01	84·4	38 33	79 45	83·6	38 26	78 29	82·8	38 18	77 13	82·0	38 09	75 57	81·2	219
40	39 44	82 11	85·0	39 39	80 54	84·2	39 32	79 36	83·3	39 24	78 19	82·5	39 16	77 03	81·7	39 08	75 46	80·9	220
41	40 44	82 04	84·8	40 38	80 46	84·0	40 31	79 27	83·1	40 23	78 09	82·3	40 15	76 51	81·4	40 05	75 33	80·6	221
42	41 43	81 57	84·6	41 37	80 37	83·7	41 30	79 17	82·9	41 22	77 58	82·0	41 13	76 39	81·1	41 04	75 21	80·3	222
43	42 42	81 49	84·4	42 36	80 28	83·5	42 29	79 07	82·6	42 21	77 47	81·7	42 12	76 27	80·8	42 02	75 07	79·9	223
44	43 42	81 41	84·2	43 35	80 19	83·3	43 28	78 57	82·3	43 19	77 35	81·4	43 10	76 14	80·5	43 00	74 53	79·6	224
45	44 41	81 33	84·0	44 34	80 09	83·1	44 27	78 46	82·1	44 18	77 22	81·1	44 08	76 00	80·1	43 57	74 38	79·2	225

Lat./A		6°			7°			8°			9°			10°			11°			Lat./A	
LHA/F		A/H	B/P	Z1/Z2	A/H	B/P	Z1/Z2	A/H	B/P	Z1/Z2	A/H	B/P	Z1/Z2	A/H	B/P	Z1/Z2	A/H	B/P	Z1/Z2	LHA	
45	135	44 41	81 33	84.0	44 34	80 09	83.1	44 27	78 46	82.1	44 18	77 22	81.1	44 08	76 00	80.1	43 57	74 38	79.2	225	315
46	134	45 41	81 24	83.8	45 34	79 59	82.8	45 26	78 34	81.8	45 16	77 09	80.8	45 06	75 45	79.8	44 55	74 22	78.8	226	314
47	133	46 40	81 14	83.6	46 33	79 48	82.6	46 24	78 21	81.5	46 15	76 56	80.5	46 04	75 30	79.5	45 53	74 05	78.4	227	313
48	132	47 39	81 04	83.3	47 32	79 36	82.3	47 23	78 08	81.2	47 13	76 41	80.1	47 03	75 14	79.1	46 51	73 48	78.0	228	312
49	131	48 38	80 54	83.1	48 31	79 24	82.0	48 22	77 55	80.9	48 12	76 26	79.8	48 01	74 57	78.7	47 48	73 30	77.6	229	311
50	130	49 38	80 43	82.9	49 30	79 11	81.7	49 20	77 40	80.6	49 10	76 09	79.4	48 58	74 40	78.3	48 46	73 10	77.2	230	310
51	129	50 37	80 31	82.6	50 29	78 58	81.4	50 19	77 25	80.2	50 08	75 52	79.1	49 56	74 21	77.9	49 43	72 50	76.7	231	309
52	128	51 36	80 19	82.4	51 27	78 43	81.1	51 18	77 09	79.9	51 06	75 34	78.7	50 54	74 01	77.5	50 40	72 29	76.3	232	308
53	127	52 35	80 06	82.1	52 26	78 28	80.8	52 16	76 51	79.5	52 04	75 15	78.3	51 52	73 40	77.0	51 37	72 06	75.8	233	307
54	126	53 34	79 52	81.8	53 25	78 12	80.5	53 14	76 33	79.2	53 02	74 55	77.8	52 49	73 18	76.6	52 34	71 42	75.3	234	306
55	125	54 33	79 37	81.5	54 24	77 55	80.1	54 13	76 14	78.8	54 00	74 34	77.4	53 47	72 55	76.1	53 31	71 17	74.8	235	305
56	124	55 32	79 21	81.2	55 22	77 37	79.8	55 11	75 54	78.3	54 58	74 11	76.9	54 44	72 30	75.6	54 28	70 50	74.2	236	304
57	123	56 31	79 05	80.9	56 21	77 18	79.4	56 09	75 32	77.9	55 56	73 47	76.5	55 41	72 04	75.0	55 25	70 22	73.6	237	303
58	122	57 30	78 47	80.5	57 19	76 57	79.0	57 07	75 09	77.4	56 53	73 22	75.9	56 38	71 36	74.5	56 21	69 51	73.0	238	302
59	121	58 29	78 28	80.1	58 18	76 35	78.5	58 05	74 44	76.9	57 51	72 54	75.4	57 35	71 06	73.9	57 17	69 19	72.4	239	301
60	120	59 28	78 08	79.7	59 16	76 12	78.1	59 03	74 18	76.4	58 48	72 24	74.8	58 32	70 34	73.3	58 13	68 45	71.7	240	300
61	119	60 26	77 46	79.3	60 14	75 47	77.6	60 01	73 50	75.9	59 45	71 54	74.2	59 28	70 01	72.6	59 09	68 09	71.0	241	299
62	118	61 25	77 23	78.9	61 12	75 21	77.1	60 58	73 20	75.3	60 42	71 21	73.6	60 24	69 25	71.9	60 05	67 31	70.3	242	298
63	117	62 23	76 58	78.4	62 10	74 52	76.5	61 56	72 48	74.7	61 38	70 46	72.9	61 20	68 46	71.2	61 00	66 49	69.5	243	297
64	116	63 22	76 31	77.9	63 08	74 21	76.0	62 53	72 13	74.1	62 35	70 08	72.2	62 16	68 05	70.4	61 55	66 05	68.6	244	296
65	115	64 20	76 02	77.4	64 06	73 48	75.4	63 50	71 36	73.4	63 32	69 27	71.5	63 12	67 21	69.6	62 50	65 18	67.7	245	295
66	114	65 18	75 31	76.8	65 03	73 12	74.7	64 47	70 56	72.6	64 28	68 43	70.6	64 07	66 34	68.7	63 44	64 27	66.8	246	294
67	113	66 16	74 57	76.2	66 01	72 33	74.0	65 43	70 13	71.8	65 23	67 55	69.8	65 02	65 43	67.8	64 38	63 33	65.8	247	293
68	112	67 14	74 20	75.5	66 58	71 51	73.2	66 40	69 26	71.0	66 18	67 05	68.8	65 56	64 48	66.7	65 32	62 35	64.7	248	292
69	111	68 12	73 39	74.8	67 55	71 05	72.4	67 36	68 35	70.1	67 14	66 09	67.8	66 50	63 48	65.7	66 25	61 31	63.6	249	291
70	110	69 09	72 55	74.0	68 51	70 15	71.5	68 31	67 40	69.1	68 08	65 09	66.7	67 44	62 44	64.5	67 17	60 23	62.3	250	290
71	109	70 07	72 06	73.1	69 48	69 20	70.5	69 26	66 39	68.0	69 03	64 03	65.6	68 37	61 34	63.2	68 09	59 10	61.0	251	289
72	108	71 03	71 13	72.2	70 44	68 20	69.4	70 21	65 33	66.8	69 57	62 52	64.3	69 29	60 17	61.9	69 00	57 51	59.6	252	288
73	107	72 00	70 14	71.1	71 39	67 14	68.3	71 16	64 20	65.5	70 50	61 33	62.9	70 21	58 54	60.4	69 50	56 23	58.0	253	287
74	106	72 56	69 08	70.0	72 34	65 59	67.0	72 09	62 59	64.1	71 42	60 07	61.4	71 12	57 24	58.8	70 40	54 48	56.4	254	286
75	105	73 52	67 54	68.7	73 29	64 37	65.5	73 03	61 30	62.6	72 34	58 32	59.7	72 02	55 44	57.1	71 28	53 06	54.5	255	285
76	104	74 48	66 31	67.3	74 23	63 05	64.0	73 55	59 51	60.8	73 24	56 47	57.9	72 51	53 55	55.1	72 16	51 13	52.6	256	284
77	103	75 42	64 57	65.7	75 16	61 22	62.2	74 46	58 01	58.9	74 14	54 51	55.9	73 39	51 55	53.1	73 03	49 10	50.4	257	283
78	102	76 36	63 11	63.8	76 08	59 26	60.2	75 37	55 57	56.8	75 02	52 42	53.6	74 26	49 42	50.8	73 47	46 56	48.1	258	282
79	101	77 29	61 09	61.7	76 59	57 16	57.9	76 26	53 38	54.4	75 49	50 20	51.2	75 11	47 16	48.2	74 30	44 28	45.5	259	281
80	100	78 21	58 49	59.3	77 49	54 44	55.3	77 13	51 01	51.7	76 35	47 38	48.4	75 54	44 35	45.4	75 11	41 47	42.7	260	280
81	99	79 12	56 06	56.6	78 37	51 52	52.4	77 59	48 04	48.7	77 18	44 39	45.4	76 35	41 35	42.4	75 49	38 50	39.7	261	279
82	98	80 01	52 56	53.4	79 23	48 35	49.1	78 42	44 43	45.3	77 59	41 18	41.9	77 13	38 17	39.0	76 26	35 36	36.4	262	278
83	97	80 47	49 13	49.6	80 07	44 47	45.2	79 23	40 55	41.4	78 37	37 33	38.1	77 49	34 39	35.3	77 00	32 05	32.8	263	277
84	96	81 31	44 51	45.2	80 47	40 24	40.8	80 01	36 38	37.1	79 12	33 25	33.9	78 21	30 40	31.2	77 29	28 16	28.8	264	276
85	95	82 12	39 40	39.9	81 24	35 22	35.7	80 35	31 48	32.2	79 44	29 02	29.2	78 48	26 35	26.7	77 56	24 09	24.6	265	275
86	94	82 48	33 34	33.8	81 57	29 36	29.8	81 04	26 24	26.7	80 11	23 46	24.1	79 12	21 35	21.9	78 18	19 44	20.1	266	274
87	93	83 18	26 28	26.6	82 23	23 05	23.3	81 28	20 25	20.6	80 31	18 17	18.5	79 34	16 32	16.8	78 36	15 04	15.4	267	273
88	92	83 41	18 22	18.5	82 43	15 46	16.0	81 45	13 51	14.1	80 47	12 26	12.6	79 48	11 12	11.4	78 49	10 11	10.4	268	272
89	91	83 55	9 26	9.5	82 56	8 05	8.2	81 56	7 05	7.1	80 57	6 17	6.3	79 57	5 00	5.7	78 57	5 08	5.2	269	271
90	90	84 00	0 00	0.0	83 00	0 00	0.0	82 00	0 00	0.0	81 00	0 00	0.0	80 00	0 00	0.0	79 00	0 00	0.0	270	270

N. Lat: for LHA > 180° ... $Z_n = Z$
for LHA < 180° ... $Z_n = 360° - Z$

S. Lat.: for LHA > 180° ... $Z_n = 180° - Z$
for LHA < 180° ... $Z_n = 180° + Z$

SIGHT REDUCTION TABLE

B: (−) for 90° < LHA < 270°
Dec:(−) for Lat. contrary name

Z₁: same sign as B
Z₂:(−) for F > 90°

Z₁: for 90° < LHA < 270°
Dec:(−) for Lat. contrary name

Lat./A (LHA/F)	12° A/H	12° B/P	12° Z₁/Z₂	13° A/H	13° B/P	13° Z₁/Z₂	14° A/H	14° B/P	14° Z₁/Z₂	15° A/H	15° B/P	15° Z₁/Z₂	16° A/H	16° B/P	16° Z₁/Z₂	17° A/H	17° B/P	17° Z₁/Z₂	Lat./A (LHA)
0 / 180	0 00	78 00	90.0	0 00	77 00	90.0	0 00	76 00	90.0	0 00	75 00	90.0	0 00	74 00	90.0	0 00	73 00	90.0	180 / 360
1 / 179	0 59	78 00	89.8	0 58	77 00	89.8	0 58	76 00	89.8	0 58	75 00	89.7	0 58	74 00	89.7	0 57	73 00	89.7	181 / 359
2 / 178	1 57	78 00	89.6	1 57	77 00	89.6	1 56	76 00	89.5	1 56	75 00	89.5	1 55	74 00	89.4	1 55	72 59	89.4	182 / 358
3 / 177	2 56	77 59	89.4	2 55	76 59	89.4	2 55	75 59	89.3	2 54	74 59	89.2	2 53	73 59	89.2	2 52	72 58	89.1	183 / 357
4 / 176	3 55	77 58	89.1	3 54	76 58	89.1	3 53	75 58	89.0	3 52	74 58	89.0	3 51	73 58	88.9	3 49	72 57	88.8	184 / 356
5 / 175	4 53	77 57	89.0	4 52	76 57	88.9	4 51	75 57	88.8	4 50	74 57	88.7	4 48	73 57	88.6	4 47	72 56	88.5	185 / 355
6 / 174	5 52	77 56	88.7	5 51	76 56	88.6	5 49	75 56	88.5	5 48	74 55	88.4	5 46	73 55	88.3	5 44	72 55	88.2	186 / 354
7 / 173	6 51	77 55	88.5	6 49	76 54	88.4	6 47	75 54	88.3	6 46	74 54	88.2	6 44	73 53	88.1	6 42	72 53	87.9	187 / 353
8 / 172	7 49	77 53	88.3	7 48	76 53	88.2	7 46	75 52	88.1	7 44	74 52	87.9	7 41	73 51	87.8	7 39	72 51	87.6	188 / 352
9 / 171	8 48	77 51	88.1	8 46	76 51	88.0	8 44	75 50	87.8	8 41	74 49	87.7	8 39	73 48	87.5	8 36	72 48	87.3	189 / 351
10 / 170	9 47	77 49	87.9	9 44	76 48	87.8	9 42	75 48	87.6	9 39	74 47	87.4	9 37	73 46	87.2	9 34	72 45	87.0	190 / 350
11 / 169	10 45	77 47	87.7	10 43	76 46	87.5	10 40	75 45	87.3	10 37	74 44	87.1	10 34	73 43	86.9	10 31	72 42	86.7	191 / 349
12 / 168	11 44	77 44	87.5	11 41	76 43	87.3	11 38	75 42	87.0	11 35	74 41	86.9	11 32	73 40	86.6	11 28	72 39	86.4	192 / 348
13 / 167	12 43	77 42	87.3	12 40	76 40	87.0	12 36	75 39	86.8	12 33	74 37	86.6	12 29	73 36	86.4	12 25	72 35	86.1	193 / 347
14 / 166	13 41	77 39	87.0	13 38	76 37	86.8	13 35	75 35	86.5	13 31	74 34	86.3	13 27	73 32	86.1	13 23	72 31	85.8	194 / 346
15 / 165	14 40	77 35	86.8	14 36	76 33	86.6	14 33	75 32	86.3	14 28	74 30	86.0	14 24	73 28	85.8	14 20	72 26	85.5	195 / 345
16 / 164	15 38	77 32	86.6	15 35	76 30	86.3	15 31	75 28	86.0	15 26	74 25	85.8	15 22	73 23	85.5	15 17	72 21	85.2	196 / 344
17 / 163	16 37	77 28	86.4	16 33	76 26	86.1	16 29	75 23	85.8	16 24	74 21	85.5	16 19	73 19	85.2	16 14	72 16	84.9	197 / 343
18 / 162	17 36	77 24	86.1	17 31	76 21	85.8	17 27	75 19	85.5	17 22	74 16	85.2	17 17	73 13	84.9	17 11	72 11	84.6	198 / 342
19 / 161	18 35	77 20	85.9	18 30	76 17	85.6	18 25	75 14	85.2	18 20	74 11	84.9	18 14	73 08	84.6	18 08	72 05	84.3	199 / 341
20 / 160	19 33	77 15	85.7	19 28	76 12	85.3	19 23	75 08	85.0	19 17	74 05	84.6	19 12	73 02	84.3	19 05	71 59	83.9	200 / 340
21 / 159	20 31	77 10	85.4	20 26	76 07	85.1	20 21	75 02	84.7	20 15	73 59	84.3	20 09	72 56	84.0	20 03	71 52	83.6	201 / 339
22 / 158	21 30	77 05	85.2	21 24	76 01	84.8	21 19	74 57	84.4	21 13	73 53	84.0	21 06	72 49	83.6	21 00	71 45	83.3	202 / 338
23 / 157	22 28	77 00	85.0	22 23	75 55	84.5	22 17	74 51	84.1	22 10	73 46	83.7	22 04	72 42	83.3	21 56	71 38	82.9	203 / 337
24 / 156	23 27	76 54	84.7	23 21	75 49	84.3	23 15	74 44	83.9	23 08	73 39	83.4	23 01	72 34	83.0	22 53	71 30	82.6	204 / 336
25 / 155	24 25	76 48	84.5	24 19	75 43	84.0	24 13	74 37	83.6	24 06	73 32	83.1	23 58	72 27	82.7	23 50	71 22	82.2	205 / 335
26 / 154	25 23	76 42	84.2	25 17	75 36	83.7	25 10	74 30	83.3	25 04	73 24	82.8	24 55	72 18	82.3	24 47	71 13	81.9	206 / 334
27 / 153	26 21	76 35	84.0	26 15	75 28	83.5	26 08	74 22	83.0	26 01	73 16	82.5	25 52	72 10	82.0	25 44	71 04	81.5	207 / 333
28 / 152	27 20	76 28	83.7	27 13	75 21	83.2	27 06	74 14	82.7	26 58	73 07	82.2	26 50	72 00	81.7	26 41	70 54	81.2	208 / 332
29 / 151	28 18	76 20	83.4	28 11	75 13	82.9	28 04	74 05	82.4	27 55	72 58	81.8	27 47	71 51	81.3	27 37	70 44	80.8	209 / 331
30 / 150	29 17	76 13	83.2	29 09	75 04	82.6	29 01	73 56	82.0	28 53	72 48	81.5	28 44	71 41	81.0	28 34	70 33	80.4	210 / 330
31 / 149	30 15	76 04	82.9	30 07	74 56	82.3	29 59	73 47	81.7	29 50	72 38	81.2	29 41	71 30	80.6	29 30	70 22	80.0	211 / 329
32 / 148	31 13	75 56	82.6	31 05	74 47	82.0	30 57	73 37	81.4	30 47	72 28	80.8	30 37	71 19	80.2	30 27	70 11	79.6	212 / 328
33 / 147	32 11	75 47	82.3	32 03	74 37	81.7	31 54	73 27	81.1	31 44	72 17	80.5	31 34	71 07	79.9	31 23	69 58	79.2	213 / 327
34 / 146	33 10	75 37	82.0	33 01	74 26	81.4	32 52	73 16	80.7	32 41	72 05	80.1	32 31	70 55	79.5	32 20	69 45	78.8	214 / 326
35 / 145	34 08	75 27	81.7	33 59	74 16	81.0	33 49	73 04	80.4	33 38	71 53	79.7	33 28	70 42	79.1	33 16	69 32	78.4	215 / 325
36 / 144	35 06	75 17	81.4	34 56	74 04	80.7	34 46	72 52	80.0	34 36	71 40	79.4	34 24	70 29	78.7	34 12	69 18	78.0	216 / 324
37 / 143	36 04	75 06	81.1	35 54	73 53	80.4	35 44	72 40	79.7	35 33	71 27	79.0	35 21	70 15	78.3	35 08	69 03	77.6	217 / 323
38 / 142	37 03	74 54	80.8	36 52	73 40	80.0	36 41	72 27	79.3	36 29	71 13	78.6	36 17	70 00	77.8	36 04	68 48	77.1	218 / 322
39 / 141	38 00	74 42	80.4	37 49	73 27	79.7	37 38	72 13	78.9	37 26	70 59	78.2	37 13	69 45	77.4	37 00	68 32	76.7	219 / 321
40 / 140	38 58	74 30	80.1	38 47	73 14	79.3	38 35	71 58	78.5	38 22	70 43	77.8	38 10	69 29	77.0	37 56	68 15	76.2	220 / 320
41 / 139	39 55	74 16	79.8	39 44	72 59	78.9	39 32	71 43	78.1	39 19	70 27	77.3	39 06	69 12	76.5	38 51	67 57	75.7	221 / 319
42 / 138	40 53	74 02	79.4	40 41	72 45	78.5	40 29	71 27	77.7	40 16	70 10	76.9	40 02	68 54	76.1	39 47	67 38	75.3	222 / 318
43 / 137	41 51	73 48	79.0	41 39	72 29	78.2	41 26	71 11	77.3	41 12	69 53	76.4	40 58	68 35	75.6	40 42	67 19	74.7	223 / 317
44 / 136	42 48	73 32	78.6	42 36	72 12	77.7	42 23	70 53	76.9	42 09	69 34	76.0	41 54	68 16	75.1	41 38	66 59	74.2	224 / 316
45 / 135	43 46	73 16	78.3	43 33	71 55	77.3	43 19	70 35	76.4	43 05	69 15	75.5	42 49	67 56	74.6	42 33	66 37	73.7	225 / 315

Lat.	LHA/F	12° A/H	12° B/P	12° Z₁/Z₂	13° A/H	13° B/P	13° Z₁/Z₂	14° A/H	14° B/P	14° Z₁/Z₂	15° A/H	15° B/P	15° Z₁/Z₂	16° A/H	16° B/P	16° Z₁/Z₂	17° A/H	17° B/P	17° Z₁/Z₂	LHA	A
45	135	43 46	73 16	78·3	43 33	71 55	77·3	43 19	70 35	76·4	43 05	69 15	75·5	42 49	67 56	74·6	42 33	66 37	73·7	225	315
46	134	44 43	72 59	77·8	44 30	71 37	76·9	44 16	70 15	75·9	44 01	68 54	75·0	43 45	67 34	74·1	43 28	66 15	73·2	226	314
47	133	45 40	72 41	77·4	45 27	71 18	76·4	45 13	69 55	75·5	44 57	68 33	74·5	44 40	67 12	73·5	44 23	65 51	72·6	227	313
48	132	46 38	72 23	77·0	46 24	70 58	76·0	46 09	69 34	75·0	45 53	68 11	74·0	45 35	66 48	73·0	45 17	65 27	72·0	228	312
49	131	47 35	72 03	76·5	47 20	70 37	75·5	47 05	69 11	74·4	46 48	67 47	73·4	46 30	66 23	72·4	46 12	65 01	71·4	229	311
50	130	48 32	71 42	76·1	48 17	70 15	75·0	48 01	68 48	73·9	47 44	67 22	72·9	47 25	65 58	71·8	47 06	64 34	70·8	230	310
51	129	49 29	71 20	75·6	49 13	69 51	74·5	48 57	68 23	73·4	48 39	66 56	72·3	48 20	65 30	71·2	48 00	64 05	70·1	231	309
52	128	50 25	70 57	75·1	50 09	69 27	73·9	49 52	67 57	72·8	49 34	66 29	71·7	49 15	65 02	70·6	48 54	63 35	69·5	232	308
53	127	51 22	70 33	74·6	51 06	69 01	73·4	50 48	67 30	72·2	50 29	66 00	71·0	50 09	64 31	69·9	49 48	63 04	68·8	233	307
54	126	52 19	70 07	74·0	52 02	68 33	72·8	51 43	67 01	71·6	51 24	65 30	70·4	51 03	64 00	69·3	50 41	62 31	68·1	234	306
55	125	53 15	69 40	73·5	52 57	68 04	72·2	52 38	66 30	70·9	52 18	64 58	69·7	51 57	63 26	68·5	51 34	61 56	67·3	235	305
56	124	54 11	69 11	72·9	53 53	67 34	71·6	53 33	65 58	70·3	53 12	64 24	69·0	52 50	62 51	67·8	52 27	61 20	66·6	236	304
57	123	55 07	68 41	72·2	54 48	67 02	70·9	54 28	65 24	69·6	54 06	63 48	68·3	53 43	62 14	67·0	53 19	60 42	65·8	237	303
58	122	56 03	68 09	71·6	55 43	66 28	70·2	55 22	64 48	68·8	55 00	63 11	67·5	54 36	61 35	66·2	54 12	60 01	64·9	238	302
59	121	56 59	67 34	70·9	56 38	65 51	69·5	56 16	64 10	68·1	55 53	62 31	66·7	55 29	60 54	65·4	55 03	59 18	64·1	239	301
60	120	57 54	66 58	70·2	57 33	65 13	68·7	57 10	63 30	67·3	56 46	61 49	65·9	56 21	60 10	64·5	55 55	58 33	63·1	240	300
61	119	58 49	66 20	69·4	58 27	64 32	67·9	58 04	62 47	66·4	57 39	61 04	65·0	57 13	59 24	63·6	56 46	57 46	62·2	241	299
62	118	59 44	65 38	68·6	59 21	63 49	67·1	58 57	62 02	65·5	58 31	60 17	64·0	58 05	58 35	62·6	57 36	56 56	61·2	242	298
63	117	60 38	64 55	67·8	60 15	63 03	66·2	59 50	61 13	64·6	59 23	59 27	63·1	58 55	57 43	61·6	58 26	56 03	60·2	243	297
64	116	61 32	64 08	66·9	61 08	62 14	65·2	60 42	60 22	63·6	60 15	58 34	62·0	59 46	56 49	60·5	59 16	55 06	59·1	244	296
65	115	62 26	63 18	66·0	62 01	61 21	64·2	61 34	59 28	62·6	61 06	57 37	61·0	60 36	55 49	59·4	60 05	54 04	57·9	245	295
66	114	63 19	62 25	65·0	62 53	60 25	63·2	62 26	58 30	61·5	61 56	56 37	59·8	61 25	54 49	58·2	60 53	53 04	56·7	246	294
67	113	64 13	61 27	63·9	63 45	59 25	62·1	63 16	57 27	60·3	62 46	55 34	58·6	62 14	53 44	57·0	61 41	51 57	55·4	247	293
68	112	65 05	60 26	62·8	64 37	58 21	60·9	64 07	56 21	59·1	63 35	54 25	57·4	63 02	52 34	55·7	62 27	50 47	54·1	248	292
69	111	65 57	59 20	61·6	65 27	57 13	59·6	64 56	55 10	57·8	64 23	53 13	56·0	63 49	51 20	54·3	63 14	49 32	52·7	249	291
70	110	66 48	58 08	60·4	66 18	55 55	58·3	65 45	53 53	56·0	65 11	51 55	54·9	64 36	50 01	52·9	63 59	48 12	51·2	250	290
71	109	67 39	56 52	59·0	67 07	54 40	56·8	66 33	52 33	54·9	65 58	50 33	53·1	65 21	48 38	51·3	64 43	46 48	49·7	251	289
72	108	68 28	55 29	57·4	67 55	53 10	55·3	67 20	51 06	53·3	66 44	49 04	51·5	66 06	47 08	49·7	65 26	45 18	48·0	252	288
73	107	69 18	54 01	55·8	68 43	51 42	53·7	68 07	49 33	51·6	67 29	47 30	49·8	66 49	45 32	48·0	66 08	43 43	46·3	253	287
74	106	70 06	52 26	54·1	69 30	50 03	51·9	68 52	47 52	49·8	68 12	45 49	47·9	67 31	43 52	46·1	66 49	42 02	44·4	254	286
75	105	70 53	50 36	52·2	70 15	48 16	50·0	69 36	46 04	47·9	68 55	44 05	46·0	68 12	42 04	44·2	67 29	40 15	42·5	255	285
76	104	71 38	48 42	50·1	70 59	46 20	47·9	70 18	44 04	45·9	69 36	42 04	43·9	68 52	40 04	42·1	68 07	38 21	40·5	256	284
77	103	72 23	46 37	48·0	71 42	44 15	45·7	70 59	42 03	43·7	70 15	40 01	41·7	69 30	38 07	39·9	68 43	36 21	38·3	257	283
78	102	73 06	44 32	45·6	72 23	42 00	43·4	71 38	39 48	41·3	70 53	37 52	39·4	70 06	35 57	37·6	69 18	34 13	36·0	258	282
79	101	73 47	41 55	43·1	73 02	39 34	40·8	72 16	37 26	38·8	71 28	35 32	36·9	70 40	33 38	35·2	69 50	31 58	33·6	259	281
80	100	74 26	39 15	40·3	73 39	36 57	38·1	72 51	34 51	36·1	72 02	32 57	34·3	71 12	31 12	32·6	70 21	29 36	31·1	260	280
81	99	75 13	36 21	37·3	74 14	34 07	35·1	73 24	32 06	33·2	72 34	30 17	31·5	71 42	28 37	29·9	70 50	27 06	28·4	261	279
82	98	75 45	33 13	34·1	74 46	31 05	32·0	73 55	29 12	30·2	73 03	27 27	28·5	72 09	25 53	27·0	71 16	24 29	25·7	262	278
83	97	76 14	29 50	30·6	75 16	27 50	28·6	74 23	26 08	26·9	73 29	24 27	25·4	72 34	23 02	24·0	71 39	21 44	22·8	263	277
84	96	76 40	26 11	26·8	75 42	24 24	25·0	74 48	22 49	23·5	73 52	21 13	22·1	72 56	20 02	20·9	72 00	18 53	19·8	264	276
85	95	77 02	22 10	22·8	76 05	20 41	21·3	75 09	19 21	19·9	74 12	18 01	18·7	73 15	16 54	17·6	72 18	15 51	16·7	265	275
86	94	77 22	18 10	18·6	76 25	16 49	17·3	75 27	15 42	16·1	74 29	14 36	15·1	73 31	13 40	14·2	72 33	12 51	13·5	266	274
87	93	77 38	13 50	14·1	76 40	12 46	13·1	75 41	11 54	12·2	74 43	11 03	11·4	73 44	10 21	10·8	72 45	9 43	10·2	267	273
88	92	77 50	9 19	9·5	76 51	8 36	8·8	75 52	8 00	8·2	74 53	7 25	7·7	73 53	6 56	7·2	72 53	6 31	6·8	268	272
89	91	77 58	4 42	4·8	76 58	4 19	4·4	75 58	4 00	4·1	74 58	3 44	3·9	73 58	3 29	3·6	72 58	3 16	3·4	269	271
90	90	78 00	0 00	0·0	77 00	0 00	0·0	76 00	0 00	0·0	75 00	0 00	0·0	74 00	0 00	0·0	73 00	0 00	0·0	270	270

N. Lat.: for LHA > 180° ..... Zₙ = Z
for LHA < 180° ..... Zₙ = 360° − Z

S. Lat.: for LHA > 180° ..... Zₙ = 180° − Z
for LHA < 180° ..... Zₙ = 180° + Z

SIGHT REDUCTION TABLE

B: (−) for 90° < LHA < 270°
Dec: (−) for Lat. contrary name

Z₁: same sign as B
Z₂: (−) for F > 90°

Lat./A LHA/F	A	18° A/H	18° B/P	18° Z₁/Z₂	19° A/H	19° B/P	19° Z₁/Z₂	20° A/H	20° B/P	20° Z₁/Z₂	21° A/H	21° B/P	21° Z₁/Z₂	22° A/H	22° B/P	22° Z₁/Z₂	23° A/H	23° B/P	23° Z₁/Z₂	LHA	LHA
0	180	0 00	72 00	90·0	0 00	71 00	90·0	0 00	70 00	90·0	0 00	69 00	90·0	0 00	68 00	90·0	0 00	67 00	90·0	180	360
1	179	0 57	72 00	89·7	0 57	71 00	89·7	0 56	70 00	89·7	0 56	69 00	89·6	0 56	68 00	89·6	0 55	67 00	89·6	181	359
2	178	1 54	71 59	89·4	1 53	70 59	89·3	1 53	69 59	89·3	1 52	68 59	89·3	1 51	67 59	89·3	1 50	66 59	89·2	182	358
3	177	2 51	71 58	89·1	2 50	70 59	89·0	2 49	69 59	89·0	2 48	68 58	88·9	2 47	67 58	88·9	2 46	66 58	88·8	183	357
4	176	3 48	71 58	88·8	3 47	70 57	88·7	3 46	69 57	88·6	3 44	68 57	88·6	3 42	67 57	88·5	3 41	66 57	88·4	184	356
5	175	4 45	71 56	88·5	4 44	70 56	88·4	4 42	69 56	88·3	4 40	68 56	88·2	4 38	67 55	88·1	4 36	66 55	88·0	185	355
6	174	5 42	71 54	88·1	5 40	70 54	88·0	5 38	69 54	87·9	5 36	68 54	87·8	5 34	67 53	87·8	5 31	66 53	87·6	186	354
7	173	6 39	71 52	87·8	6 37	70 52	87·6	6 35	69 51	87·6	6 32	68 51	87·5	6 29	67 51	87·4	6 26	66 51	87·3	187	353
8	172	7 36	71 50	87·5	7 34	70 50	87·4	7 31	69 49	87·2	7 28	68 49	87·1	7 25	67 48	87·0	7 22	66 48	86·9	188	352
9	171	8 33	71 47	87·2	8 30	70 47	87·0	8 27	69 46	86·9	8 24	68 46	86·8	8 20	67 45	86·6	8 17	66 45	86·5	189	351
10	170	9 30	71 44	86·9	9 27	70 44	86·7	9 23	69 43	86·5	9 20	68 42	86·4	9 16	67 42	86·2	9 12	66 42	86·1	190	350
11	169	10 27	71 41	86·6	10 24	70 40	86·4	10 20	69 39	86·2	10 16	68 39	86·0	10 11	67 38	85·8	10 07	66 37	85·7	191	349
12	168	11 24	71 37	86·2	11 20	70 36	86·0	11 16	69 35	85·8	11 12	68 34	85·6	11 07	67 33	85·4	11 02	66 32	85·3	192	348
13	167	12 21	71 33	85·9	12 17	70 32	85·7	12 12	69 31	85·5	12 07	68 30	85·1	12 02	67 29	85·1	11 57	66 28	84·8	193	347
14	166	13 18	71 29	85·6	13 13	70 28	85·4	13 08	69 26	85·1	13 03	68 25	84·9	12 58	67 24	84·7	12 52	66 22	84·4	194	346
15	165	14 15	71 24	85·3	14 10	70 23	85·0	14 05	69 21	84·8	13 59	68 20	84·5	13 53	67 18	84·3	13 47	66 17	84·0	195	345
16	164	15 12	71 19	84·9	15 06	70 18	84·7	15 01	69 16	84·4	14 55	68 14	84·1	14 48	67 12	83·9	14 42	66 10	83·6	196	344
17	163	16 09	71 14	84·6	16 03	70 12	84·3	15 57	69 10	84·0	15 50	68 08	83·7	15 44	67 06	83·5	15 37	66 04	83·2	197	343
18	162	17 05	71 08	84·3	16 59	70 06	84·0	16 53	69 03	83·7	16 46	68 01	83·4	16 39	66 59	83·1	16 32	65 57	82·8	198	342
19	161	18 02	71 02	83·9	17 56	70 00	83·6	17 49	68 57	83·3	17 42	67 54	83·0	17 34	66 52	82·7	17 26	65 49	82·3	199	341
20	160	18 59	70 56	83·6	18 52	69 53	83·2	18 45	68 50	82·9	18 37	67 47	82·6	18 29	66 44	82·2	18 21	65 41	81·9	200	340
21	159	19 56	70 49	83·2	19 48	69 45	82·9	19 41	68 42	82·5	19 33	67 39	82·2	19 24	66 36	81·8	19 16	65 33	81·5	201	339
22	158	20 52	70 41	82·9	20 45	69 38	82·5	20 37	68 34	82·1	20 28	67 31	81·8	20 19	66 27	81·4	20 10	65 24	81·0	202	338
23	157	21 49	70 33	82·5	21 41	69 29	82·1	21 32	68 26	81·7	21 24	67 22	81·4	21 14	66 18	81·0	21 05	65 15	80·6	203	337
24	156	22 45	70 25	82·2	22 37	69 21	81·8	22 28	68 17	81·3	22 19	67 12	81·0	22 09	66 09	80·5	21 59	65 05	80·1	204	336
25	155	23 42	70 17	81·8	23 33	69 12	81·4	23 24	68 07	80·9	23 14	67 03	80·5	23 04	65 58	80·1	22 54	64 54	79·7	205	335
26	154	24 38	70 07	81·4	24 29	69 02	81·0	24 20	67 57	80·5	24 09	66 53	80·1	23 59	65 48	79·6	23 48	64 43	79·2	206	334
27	153	25 35	69 58	81·1	25 25	68 52	80·6	25 15	67 47	80·1	25 05	66 42	79·6	24 54	65 36	79·2	24 42	64 32	78·7	207	333
28	152	26 31	69 48	80·7	26 21	68 41	80·2	26 11	67 36	79·7	26 00	66 30	79·2	25 48	65 24	78·7	25 36	64 19	78·3	208	332
29	151	27 27	69 37	80·3	27 17	68 30	79·8	27 06	67 24	79·2	26 55	66 18	78·7	26 43	65 12	78·3	26 30	64 07	77·8	209	331
30	150	28 24	69 26	79·9	28 13	68 19	79·4	28 01	67 12	78·8	27 50	66 06	78·3	27 37	64 59	77·8	27 24	63 53	77·3	210	330
31	149	29 20	69 14	79·5	29 09	68 07	78·9	28 57	67 00	78·4	28 44	65 53	77·8	28 31	64 46	77·3	28 18	63 39	76·8	211	329
32	148	30 16	69 02	79·1	30 04	67 54	78·5	29 52	66 46	77·9	29 39	65 39	77·3	29 26	64 32	76·8	29 12	63 25	76·3	212	328
33	147	31 12	68 49	78·7	31 00	67 41	78·1	30 47	66 32	77·5	30 34	65 24	76·8	30 20	64 17	76·3	30 05	63 09	75·8	213	327
34	146	32 08	68 36	78·2	31 55	67 27	77·6	31 42	66 18	77·0	31 28	65 09	76·3	31 14	64 01	75·8	30 59	62 53	75·2	214	326
35	145	33 04	68 22	77·8	32 51	67 12	77·2	32 37	66 03	76·5	32 22	64 54	75·9	32 08	63 45	75·3	31 52	62 36	74·7	215	325
36	144	33 59	68 07	77·3	33 46	66 57	76·7	33 32	65 47	76·0	33 17	64 37	75·4	33 01	63 28	74·8	32 45	62 19	74·2	216	324
37	143	34 55	67 52	76·9	34 41	66 41	76·2	34 26	65 30	75·5	34 11	64 20	74·9	33 55	63 10	74·2	33 38	62 01	73·6	217	323
38	142	35 50	67 36	76·4	35 36	66 24	75·7	35 21	65 12	75·0	35 05	64 02	74·4	34 48	62 51	73·7	34 31	61 42	73·0	218	322
39	141	36 46	67 19	76·0	36 31	66 06	75·2	36 15	64 54	74·5	35 59	63 43	73·8	35 42	62 32	73·1	35 24	61 21	72·4	219	321
40	140	37 41	67 01	75·5	37 26	65 48	74·7	37 09	64 35	74·0	36 52	63 23	73·3	36 35	62 11	72·6	36 17	61 00	71·8	220	320
41	139	38 36	66 42	75·0	38 20	65 29	74·2	38 04	64 15	73·4	37 46	63 02	72·7	37 28	61 50	72·0	37 09	60 39	71·2	221	319
42	138	39 31	66 23	74·5	39 15	65 08	73·7	38 58	63 54	72·9	38 40	62 41	72·1	38 21	61 28	71·4	38 01	60 16	70·6	222	318
43	137	40 26	66 03	73·9	40 09	64 47	73·1	39 51	63 33	72·3	39 33	62 18	71·5	39 13	61 05	70·7	38 53	59 52	70·0	223	317
44	136	41 21	65 42	73·4	41 03	64 25	72·5	40 45	63 10	71·7	40 26	61 55	70·9	40 06	60 41	70·1	39 45	59 27	69·3	224	316
45	135	42 16	65 19	72·8	41 57	64 02	72·0	41 38	62 46	71·1	41 19	61 30	70·3	40 58	60 15	69·5	40 37	59 01	68·7	225	315

Lat. contrary name

Lat./A	LHA/F	18° A/H	18° B/P	18° Z₁/Z₂	19° A/H	19° B/P	19° Z₁/Z₂	20° A/H	20° B/P	20° Z₁/Z₂	21° A/H	21° B/P	21° Z₁/Z₂	22° A/H	22° B/P	22° Z₁/Z₂	23° A/H	23° B/P	23° Z₁/Z₂	LHA	LHA/A
45	135	42 16	65 19	72.8	41 57	64 02	72.0	41 38	62 46	71.1	41 19	61 30	70.3	40 58	60 15	69.5	40 37	59 01	68.7	225	315
46	134	43 10	64 56	72.3	42 51	63 38	71.4	42 32	62 21	70.5	42 12	61 05	69.6	41 50	59 49	68.8	41 28	58 34	68.0	226	314
47	133	44 04	64 32	71.7	43 45	63 13	70.8	43 25	61 55	69.9	43 04	60 38	69.0	42 42	59 21	68.1	42 19	58 06	67.3	227	313
48	132	44 58	64 06	71.1	44 38	62 46	70.1	44 18	61 27	69.2	43 56	60 10	68.3	43 33	58 53	67.4	43 10	57 37	66.5	228	312
49	131	45 52	63 39	70.4	45 32	62 18	69.5	45 10	60 59	68.5	44 48	59 40	67.6	44 24	58 23	66.7	44 00	57 06	65.8	229	311
50	130	46 46	63 11	69.8	46 25	61 49	68.8	46 03	60 29	67.8	45 39	59 09	66.9	45 15	57 51	65.9	44 50	56 34	65.0	230	310
51	129	47 39	62 42	69.1	47 17	61 19	68.1	46 55	59 57	67.1	46 31	58 37	66.1	46 06	57 18	65.2	45 40	56 00	64.2	231	309
52	128	48 33	62 11	68.4	48 10	60 47	67.4	47 46	59 25	66.4	47 22	58 03	65.4	46 56	56 44	64.4	46 30	55 25	63.4	232	308
53	127	49 25	61 38	67.7	49 02	60 13	66.6	48 38	58 50	65.6	48 13	57 28	64.6	47 46	56 07	63.6	47 19	54 48	62.6	233	307
54	126	50 18	61 04	67.0	49 54	59 38	65.9	49 29	58 14	64.9	49 03	56 51	63.7	48 36	55 30	62.7	48 08	54 10	61.7	234	306
55	125	51 10	60 28	66.2	50 46	59 01	65.1	50 20	57 36	64.0	49 53	56 12	62.9	49 25	54 50	61.9	48 56	53 30	60.8	235	305
56	124	52 03	59 50	65.4	51 37	58 23	64.2	51 10	56 56	63.1	50 43	55 32	62.0	50 14	54 09	61.0	49 44	52 48	59.9	236	304
57	123	52 54	59 11	64.6	52 28	57 42	63.4	52 00	56 15	62.2	51 32	54 49	61.1	51 02	53 26	60.0	50 32	52 04	59.0	237	303
58	122	53 46	58 29	63.7	53 18	56 59	62.5	52 49	55 31	61.3	52 21	54 05	60.2	51 50	52 41	59.1	51 19	51 18	58.0	238	302
59	121	54 37	57 45	62.8	54 08	56 14	61.5	53 39	54 45	60.4	53 09	53 18	59.2	52 38	51 53	58.1	52 06	50 30	57.0	239	301
60	120	55 27	57 00	61.8	54 57	55 27	60.6	54 28	53 57	59.4	53 57	52 28	58.2	53 25	51 04	57.0	52 52	49 40	55.9	240	300
61	119	56 17	56 10	60.9	55 47	54 37	59.6	55 16	53 06	58.3	54 44	51 38	57.1	54 11	50 12	55.9	53 37	48 48	54.8	241	299
62	118	57 07	55 19	59.8	56 36	53 45	58.5	56 04	52 13	57.2	55 31	50 44	56.0	54 57	49 17	54.8	54 22	47 53	53.7	242	298
63	117	57 56	54 25	58.8	57 24	52 49	57.4	56 51	51 17	56.1	56 17	49 47	54.9	55 42	48 20	53.7	55 06	46 55	52.5	243	297
64	116	58 44	53 27	57.6	58 12	51 51	56.3	57 38	50 18	55.0	57 03	48 48	53.7	56 27	47 20	52.5	55 49	45 55	51.3	244	296
65	115	59 32	52 27	56.5	58 58	50 50	55.1	58 24	49 16	53.7	57 47	47 48	52.5	57 10	46 17	51.2	56 32	44 52	50.0	245	295
66	114	60 19	51 23	55.3	59 45	49 46	53.8	59 09	48 11	52.5	58 31	46 39	51.2	57 53	45 11	49.9	57 14	43 45	48.7	246	294
67	113	61 06	50 15	53.9	60 30	48 37	52.5	59 54	47 02	51.1	59 15	45 30	49.8	58 36	44 02	48.6	57 55	42 38	47.4	247	293
68	112	61 52	49 04	52.6	61 15	47 25	51.1	60 38	45 50	49.8	59 57	44 18	48.4	59 17	42 50	47.2	58 36	41 26	46.0	248	292
69	111	62 37	47 48	51.2	61 58	46 09	49.7	61 19	44 33	48.3	60 39	43 02	47.0	59 57	41 34	45.7	59 15	40 10	44.5	249	291
70	110	63 21	46 28	49.7	62 41	44 48	48.2	62 01	43 13	46.8	61 19	41 42	45.4	60 36	40 15	44.2	59 53	38 52	43.0	250	290
71	109	64 04	45 03	48.1	63 23	43 24	46.6	62 41	41 49	45.2	61 59	40 18	43.9	61 15	38 52	42.6	60 30	37 29	41.4	251	289
72	108	64 45	43 34	46.4	64 04	41 54	44.9	63 21	40 20	43.5	62 37	38 50	42.2	61 52	37 25	40.9	61 06	36 03	39.7	252	288
73	107	65 26	41 59	44.7	64 43	40 20	43.2	63 59	38 46	41.8	63 14	37 18	40.5	62 27	35 53	39.2	61 41	34 34	38.0	253	287
74	106	66 06	40 19	42.9	65 21	38 41	41.4	64 36	37 08	40.0	63 49	35 41	38.7	63 02	34 18	37.4	62 14	33 00	36.3	254	286
75	105	66 44	38 32	40.9	65 58	36 56	39.5	65 11	35 25	38.1	64 23	33 59	36.8	63 35	32 39	35.6	62 46	31 22	34.4	255	285
76	104	67 20	36 40	38.9	66 33	35 05	37.4	65 45	33 37	36.1	64 56	32 13	34.8	64 07	30 55	33.6	63 16	29 41	32.5	256	284
77	103	67 55	34 42	36.8	67 06	33 07	35.3	66 18	31 43	34.0	65 27	30 22	32.8	64 37	29 06	31.6	63 45	27 55	30.6	257	283
78	102	68 29	32 37	34.5	67 39	31 07	33.1	66 48	29 44	31.9	65 57	28 26	30.7	65 05	27 14	29.6	64 13	26 06	28.5	258	282
79	101	69 00	30 25	32.2	68 09	29 01	30.8	67 17	27 40	29.6	66 25	26 26	28.5	65 32	25 17	27.4	64 38	24 12	26.4	259	281
80	100	69 29	28 07	29.7	68 37	26 46	28.4	67 44	25 30	27.3	66 55	24 20	26.2	65 56	23 15	25.2	65 02	22 15	24.3	260	280
81	99	69 57	25 43	27.1	69 03	24 26	25.9	68 09	23 15	24.8	67 14	22 10	23.8	66 19	21 10	22.9	65 23	20 14	22.1	261	279
82	98	70 21	23 11	24.5	69 27	22 00	23.3	68 31	20 56	22.3	67 36	19 56	21.4	66 40	19 00	20.6	65 43	18 09	19.8	262	278
83	97	70 44	20 34	21.7	69 48	19 29	20.7	68 52	18 31	19.7	67 55	17 37	18.9	66 58	16 47	18.1	66 01	16 01	17.4	263	277
84	96	71 03	17 50	18.8	70 07	16 53	17.9	69 09	16 01	17.1	68 12	15 14	16.3	67 14	14 30	15.7	66 16	13 50	15.1	264	276
85	95	71 20	15 01	15.8	70 23	14 11	15.0	69 25	13 28	14.3	68 26	12 48	13.7	67 28	12 10	13.1	66 29	11 36	12.6	265	275
86	94	71 35	12 07	12.8	70 36	11 27	12.1	69 37	10 51	11.6	68 38	10 18	11.0	67 39	9 48	10.6	66 40	9 20	10.1	266	274
87	93	71 46	9 09	9.6	70 46	8 39	9.1	69 47	8 11	8.7	68 48	7 46	8.3	67 48	7 23	8.0	66 49	7 02	7.6	267	273
88	92	71 54	6 08	6.4	70 54	5 47	6.1	69 54	5 29	5.8	68 55	5 12	5.6	67 55	4 56	5.3	66 55	4 42	5.1	268	272
89	91	71 58	3 04	3.2	70 58	2 54	3.1	69 59	2 45	2.9	68 59	2 36	2.8	67 59	2 28	2.7	66 59	2 21	2.6	269	271
90	90	72 00	0 00	0.0	71 00	0 00	0.0	70 00	0 00	0.0	69 00	0 00	0.0	68 00	0 00	0.0	67 00	0 00	0.0	270	270

N. Lat.: for LHA > 180° ... $Z_n = Z$
for LHA < 180° ... $Z_n = 360° - Z$

S. Lat.: for LHA > 180° ... $Z_n = 180° - Z$
for LHA < 180° ... $Z_n = 180° + Z$

SIGHT REDUCTION TABLE

B: (−) for 90° < LHA < 270°
Dec:(−) for Lat. contrary name

Z_1: same sign as B
Z_2: (−) for F > 90°

LHA/F	24° A/H	B/P	Z_1/Z_2	25° A/H	B/P	Z_1/Z_2	26° A/H	B/P	Z_1/Z_2	27° A/H	B/P	Z_1/Z_2	28° A/H	B/P	Z_1/Z_2	29° A/H	B/P	Z_1/Z_2	Lat./A	LHA
180	0 00	66 00	90·0	0 00	65 00	90·0	0 00	64 00	90·0	0 00	63 00	90·0	0 00	62 00	90·0	0 00	61 00	90·0	180	360
179	0 55	66 00	89·6	0 54	65 00	89·6	0 54	64 00	89·6	0 53	63 00	89·5	0 53	62 00	89·5	0 52	61 00	89·5	181	359
178	1 50	65 59	89·2	1 49	64 59	89·2	1 48	63 59	89·1	1 47	62 59	89·1	1 46	61 59	89·1	1 45	60 59	89·0	182	358
177	2 44	65 58	88·8	2 43	64 58	88·7	2 42	63 58	88·7	2 40	62 58	88·6	2 39	61 58	88·6	2 37	60 58	88·5	183	357
176	3 39	65 57	88·4	3 37	64 57	88·3	3 36	63 57	88·2	3 34	62 57	88·2	3 32	61 57	88·1	3 30	60 57	88·1	184	356
175	4 34	65 55	88·0	4 32	64 55	87·9	4 30	63 55	87·8	4 27	62 55	87·7	4 25	61 55	87·6	4 22	60 55	87·6	185	355
174	5 29	65 53	87·6	5 26	64 53	87·5	5 24	63 53	87·4	5 21	62 53	87·3	5 18	61 53	87·2	5 15	60 53	87·1	186	354
173	6 24	65 50	87·1	6 20	64 50	87·0	6 17	63 50	86·9	6 14	62 50	86·8	6 11	61 50	86·7	6 07	60 50	86·6	187	353
172	7 18	65 47	86·7	7 15	64 47	86·6	7 11	63 47	86·4	7 07	62 46	86·3	7 04	61 46	86·2	6 59	60 46	86·1	188	352
171	8 13	65 44	86·3	8 09	64 44	86·2	8 05	63 43	86·0	8 01	62 43	85·9	7 56	61 43	85·7	7 52	60 42	85·6	189	351
170	9 08	65 40	85·9	9 03	64 40	85·7	8 59	63 39	85·5	8 54	62 39	85·4	8 49	61 39	85·3	8 44	60 38	85·1	190	350
169	10 02	65 36	85·5	9 57	64 35	85·3	9 53	63 35	85·1	9 47	62 34	85·0	9 42	61 34	84·8	9 36	60 33	84·6	191	349
168	10 57	65 32	85·1	10 52	64 31	84·9	10 46	63 30	84·7	10 41	62 29	84·5	10 35	61 29	84·3	10 29	60 28	84·1	192	348
167	11 52	65 27	84·6	11 46	64 26	84·4	11 40	63 25	84·2	11 34	62 24	84·0	11 27	61 24	83·8	11 21	60 22	83·6	193	347
166	12 46	65 21	84·2	12 40	64 20	84·0	12 34	63 19	83·8	12 27	62 18	83·5	12 20	61 18	83·3	12 13	60 16	83·1	194	346
165	13 41	65 15	83·8	13 34	64 14	83·5	13 27	63 13	83·3	13 20	62 11	83·1	13 13	61 10	82·8	13 05	60 09	82·6	195	345
164	14 35	65 09	83·3	14 28	64 07	83·1	14 21	63 06	82·8	14 13	62 04	82·6	14 05	61 03	82·3	13 57	60 02	82·1	196	344
163	15 29	65 02	82·9	15 22	64 00	82·6	15 14	62 59	82·4	15 06	61 57	82·1	14 58	60 56	81·8	14 49	59 54	81·6	197	343
162	16 24	64 55	82·5	16 16	63 53	82·2	16 08	62 51	81·9	15 59	61 49	81·6	15 50	60 47	81·3	15 41	59 46	81·0	198	342
161	17 18	64 47	82·0	17 10	63 45	81·7	17 01	62 43	81·4	16 52	61 41	81·1	16 42	60 39	80·8	16 33	59 37	80·5	199	341
160	18 12	64 39	81·6	18 03	63 36	81·3	17 54	62 34	80·9	17 45	61 32	80·6	17 35	60 30	80·3	17 24	59 28	80·0	200	340
159	19 07	64 30	81·1	18 57	63 28	80·8	18 47	62 25	80·4	18 37	61 23	80·1	18 27	60 20	79·8	18 16	59 18	79·5	201	339
158	20 01	64 21	80·7	19 51	63 18	80·3	19 41	62 15	79·9	19 30	61 13	79·6	19 19	60 10	79·3	19 08	59 08	78·9	202	338
157	20 55	64 11	80·2	20 44	63 08	79·8	20 34	62 05	79·5	20 22	61 02	79·1	20 11	59 59	78·7	19 59	58 57	78·4	203	337
156	21 49	64 01	79·7	21 38	62 58	79·3	21 27	61 54	79·0	21 15	60 51	78·6	21 03	59 48	78·2	20 50	58 45	77·8	204	336
155	22 43	63 50	79·3	22 31	62 46	78·8	22 19	61 43	78·4	22 07	60 39	78·0	21 55	59 36	77·7	21 42	58 33	77·3	205	335
154	23 36	63 39	78·8	23 25	62 35	78·3	23 12	61 31	77·9	22 59	60 27	77·5	22 46	59 24	77·1	22 33	58 20	76·7	206	334
153	24 30	63 27	78·3	24 18	62 22	77·8	24 05	61 18	77·4	23 52	60 14	77·0	23 38	59 10	76·5	23 24	58 07	76·1	207	333
152	25 24	63 14	77·8	25 11	62 10	77·3	24 58	61 05	76·9	24 44	60 01	76·4	24 30	58 57	76·0	24 15	57 53	75·5	208	332
151	26 17	63 01	77·3	26 04	61 56	76·8	25 50	60 51	76·3	25 36	59 47	75·9	25 21	58 42	75·4	25 05	57 38	75·0	209	331
150	27 11	62 48	76·8	26 57	61 42	76·3	26 42	60 37	75·8	26 27	59 32	75·3	26 12	58 27	74·8	25 56	57 23	74·4	210	330
149	28 04	62 33	76·3	27 50	61 27	75·8	27 35	60 22	75·2	27 19	59 16	74·7	27 03	58 11	74·2	26 46	57 07	73·8	211	329
148	28 57	62 18	75·7	28 42	61 12	75·2	28 27	60 06	74·7	28 10	59 00	74·2	27 54	57 55	73·7	27 37	56 50	73·1	212	328
147	29 50	62 02	75·2	29 35	60 56	74·7	29 19	59 49	74·1	29 02	58 43	73·6	28 45	57 38	73·0	28 27	56 32	72·4	213	327
146	30 43	61 46	74·7	30 27	60 39	74·1	30 10	59 32	73·5	29 53	58 26	73·0	29 35	57 20	72·4	29 17	56 14	71·9	214	326
145	31 36	61 28	74·1	31 19	60 21	73·5	31 02	59 14	72·9	30 44	58 07	72·4	30 26	57 01	71·8	30 07	55 55	71·2	215	325
144	32 29	61 10	73·5	32 11	60 02	72·9	31 53	58 55	72·3	31 35	57 48	71·7	31 16	56 41	71·2	30 56	55 35	70·6	216	324
143	33 21	60 51	73·0	33 03	59 42	72·3	32 45	58 35	71·7	32 26	57 28	71·1	32 06	56 21	70·5	31 46	55 14	69·9	217	323
142	34 13	60 32	72·4	33 55	59 23	71·7	33 36	58 15	71·1	33 16	57 07	70·5	32 56	55 59	69·9	32 35	54 53	69·3	218	322
141	35 06	60 11	71·8	34 47	59 02	71·1	34 27	57 54	70·5	34 06	56 45	69·8	33 45	55 37	69·2	33 25	54 30	68·6	219	321
140	35 58	59 50	71·2	35 38	58 40	70·5	35 17	57 31	69·8	34 56	56 22	69·1	34 35	55 14	68·5	34 12	54 07	67·9	220	320
139	36 49	59 28	70·5	36 29	58 17	69·8	36 08	57 08	69·2	35 46	55 59	68·5	35 24	54 50	67·8	35 01	53 42	67·1	221	319
138	37 41	59 04	69·9	37 20	57 54	69·2	36 58	56 43	68·5	36 36	55 34	67·8	36 13	54 25	67·1	35 49	53 17	66·4	222	318
137	38 32	58 40	69·2	38 11	57 29	68·5	37 48	56 18	67·8	37 25	55 08	67·1	37 02	53 59	66·4	36 37	52 50	65·7	223	317
136	39 23	58 15	68·6	39 01	57 03	67·8	38 38	55 52	67·1	38 14	54 41	66·3	37 50	53 32	65·6	37 25	52 23	64·9	224	316
135	40 14	57 48	67·9	39 51	56 36	67·1	39 28	55 24	66·3	39 03	54 13	65·6	38 38	53 04	64·9	38 12	51 54	64·1	225	315

| Lat. / A | 24° | | | 25° | | | 26° | | | 27° | | | 28° | | | 29° | | | Lat. / A |
LHA/F	A/H	B/P	Z_1/Z_2	A/H	B/P	Z_1/Z_2	A/H	B/P	Z_1/Z_2	A/H	B/P	Z_1/Z_2	A/H	B/P	Z_1/Z_2	A/H	B/P	Z_1/Z_2	LHA
45 / 135	40 14	57 48	67·9	39 51	56 36	67·1	39 28	55 24	66·3	39 03	54 13	65·6	38 38	53 04	64·8	38 12	51 54	64·1	225 / 315
46 / 134	41 05	57 21	67·2	40 41	56 08	66·4	40 17	54 56	65·6	39 52	53 44	64·8	39 26	52 34	64·1	38 59	51 25	63·3	226 / 314
47 / 133	41 55	56 52	66·4	41 31	55 38	65·6	41 06	54 26	64·8	40 40	53 14	64·0	40 13	52 04	63·3	39 46	50 54	62·5	227 / 313
48 / 132	42 45	56 22	65·7	42 20	55 08	64·9	41 54	53 55	64·0	41 28	52 43	63·2	41 00	51 32	62·5	40 32	50 22	61·7	228 / 312
49 / 131	43 35	55 50	64·9	43 09	54 36	64·1	42 43	53 22	63·2	42 15	52 10	62·4	41 47	50 59	61·6	41 18	49 48	60·9	229 / 311
50 / 130	44 25	55 17	64·1	43 58	54 02	63·3	43 31	52 49	62·4	43 03	51 36	61·6	42 34	50 24	60·8	42 04	49 14	60·0	230 / 310
51 / 129	45 14	54 43	63·3	44 47	53 28	62·4	44 18	52 13	61·6	43 49	51 00	60·7	43 20	49 48	59·9	42 49	48 38	59·1	231 / 309
52 / 128	46 03	54 08	62·5	45 35	52 52	61·6	45 06	51 37	60·7	44 36	50 23	59·8	44 05	49 11	59·0	43 34	48 00	58·2	232 / 308
53 / 127	46 51	53 32	61·6	46 22	52 14	60·7	45 52	50 59	59·8	45 21	49 45	58·9	44 49	48 32	58·1	44 18	47 21	57·2	233 / 307
54 / 126	47 39	52 55	60·8	47 09	51 34	59·9	46 39	50 19	58·9	46 07	49 05	58·0	45 35	47 52	57·1	45 02	46 41	56·3	234 / 306
55 / 125	48 27	52 11	59·9	47 56	50 53	58·9	47 25	49 37	58·0	46 54	48 23	57·1	46 19	47 10	56·2	45 46	45 59	55·3	235 / 305
56 / 124	49 14	51 28	58·9	48 43	50 11	57·9	48 10	48 54	57·0	47 37	47 40	56·1	47 03	46 27	55·2	46 29	45 15	54·3	236 / 304
57 / 123	50 01	50 44	57·9	49 28	49 26	56·9	48 55	48 09	56·0	48 21	46 54	55·0	47 46	45 41	54·1	47 11	44 30	53·3	237 / 303
58 / 122	50 47	49 58	56·9	50 14	48 39	55·9	49 40	47 22	54·9	49 05	46 07	54·0	48 29	44 54	53·1	47 53	43 43	52·2	238 / 302
59 / 121	51 33	49 09	55·9	50 58	47 51	54·9	50 23	46 34	53·9	49 48	45 18	52·9	49 11	44 05	52·0	48 34	42 54	51·1	239 / 301
60 / 120	52 18	48 19	54·8	51 43	47 00	53·8	51 07	45 43	52·8	50 30	44 28	51·8	49 53	43 14	50·9	49 14	42 03	50·0	240 / 300
61 / 119	53 02	47 26	53·7	52 26	46 07	52·7	51 49	44 50	51·8	51 12	43 35	50·7	50 34	42 22	49·7	49 54	41 10	48·8	241 / 299
62 / 118	53 46	46 31	52·6	53 09	45 12	51·5	52 31	43 54	50·5	51 53	42 39	49·5	51 13	41 27	48·6	50 33	40 16	47·6	242 / 298
63 / 117	54 29	45 33	51·4	53 51	44 14	50·3	53 13	42 57	49·3	52 33	41 42	48·3	51 52	40 30	47·3	51 12	39 19	46·4	243 / 297
64 / 116	55 12	44 33	50·1	54 33	43 14	49·1	53 53	41 57	48·1	53 12	40 42	47·1	52 32	39 30	46·1	51 51	38 20	45·2	244 / 296
65 / 115	55 53	43 30	48·9	55 13	42 11	47·8	54 33	40 55	46·8	53 51	39 40	45·8	53 08	38 29	44·8	52 26	37 19	43·9	245 / 295
66 / 114	56 34	42 25	47·6	55 53	41 06	46·5	55 12	39 50	45·4	54 29	38 36	44·4	53 45	37 25	43·5	53 02	36 16	42·6	246 / 294
67 / 113	57 14	41 16	46·2	56 32	39 58	45·1	55 50	38 42	44·1	55 06	37 29	43·1	54 21	36 19	42·1	53 37	35 11	41·2	247 / 293
68 / 112	57 53	40 05	44·8	57 10	38 47	43·7	56 27	37 32	42·7	55 42	36 19	41·7	54 56	35 10	40·7	54 11	34 03	39·8	248 / 292
69 / 111	58 32	38 50	43·3	57 47	37 33	42·2	57 03	36 18	41·2	56 17	35 07	40·2	55 30	33 59	39·3	54 44	32 53	38·4	249 / 291
70 / 110	59 09	37 32	41·8	58 24	36 16	40·7	57 38	35 02	39·7	56 51	33 52	38·7	56 03	32 45	37·8	55 16	31 41	37·0	250 / 290
71 / 109	59 45	36 11	40·2	58 58	34 55	39·2	58 12	33 43	38·1	57 24	32 34	37·2	56 35	31 29	36·3	55 47	30 26	35·4	251 / 289
72 / 108	60 19	34 46	38·6	59 32	33 31	37·6	58 45	32 21	36·5	57 56	31 14	35·6	57 06	30 10	34·7	56 17	29 08	33·8	252 / 288
73 / 107	60 53	33 18	36·9	60 05	32 05	35·9	59 16	30 56	34·9	58 26	29 51	33·9	57 36	28 48	33·1	56 46	27 49	32·2	253 / 287
74 / 106	61 25	31 46	35·2	60 36	30 35	34·2	59 46	29 28	33·2	58 55	28 25	32·3	58 04	27 24	31·4	57 13	26 26	30·6	254 / 286
75 / 105	61 56	30 10	33·4	61 06	29 02	32·4	60 15	27 57	31·4	59 23	26 56	30·5	58 31	25 57	29·7	57 39	25 02	28·9	255 / 285
76 / 104	62 26	28 31	31·5	61 34	27 25	30·5	60 42	26 23	29·6	59 50	25 24	28·8	58 57	24 28	28·0	58 04	23 35	27·2	256 / 284
77 / 103	62 53	26 48	29·6	62 01	25 45	28·6	61 08	24 46	27·8	60 15	23 49	27·0	59 21	22 56	26·2	58 27	22 05	25·5	257 / 283
78 / 102	63 20	25 02	27·6	62 26	24 02	26·7	61 32	23 05	25·9	60 38	22 12	25·1	59 43	21 22	24·4	58 49	20 34	23·7	258 / 282
79 / 101	63 44	23 12	25·5	62 50	22 15	24·7	61 55	21 22	23·9	61 00	20 32	23·2	60 04	19 44	22·5	59 09	19 00	21·8	259 / 281
80 / 100	64 07	21 18	23·4	63 12	20 25	22·6	62 16	19 36	21·9	61 20	18 49	21·2	60 24	18 05	20·6	59 28	17 24	20·0	260 / 280
81 / 99	64 28	19 22	21·3	63 32	18 33	20·5	62 35	17 47	19·9	61 39	17 04	19·2	60 42	16 24	18·6	59 45	15 46	18·1	261 / 279
82 / 98	64 47	17 22	19·1	63 50	16 37	18·4	62 53	15 56	17·8	61 56	15 17	17·2	60 58	14 40	16·7	60 01	14 06	16·2	262 / 278
83 / 97	65 03	15 18	16·8	64 06	14 39	16·2	63 08	14 02	15·6	62 10	13 27	15·1	61 12	12 55	14·7	60 14	12 24	14·2	263 / 277
84 / 96	65 18	13 13	14·5	64 20	12 38	14·0	63 22	12 06	13·5	62 23	11 36	13·0	61 25	11 07	12·6	60 26	10 41	12·2	264 / 276
85 / 95	65 31	11 05	12·1	64 32	10 35	11·7	63 33	10 08	11·3	62 35	9 42	10·9	61 36	9 19	10·6	60 37	8 56	10·2	265 / 275
86 / 94	65 41	8 54	9·7	64 42	8 30	9·4	63 43	8 08	9·1	62 44	7 48	8·8	61 44	7 28	8·5	60 45	7 10	8·2	266 / 274
87 / 93	65 49	6 42	7·3	64 50	6 24	7·1	63 50	6 07	6·8	62 51	5 52	6·6	61 51	5 37	6·4	60 52	5 24	6·2	267 / 273
88 / 92	65 55	4 29	4·9	64 56	4 17	4·7	63 56	4 06	4·6	62 56	3 55	4·4	61 56	3 45	4·3	60 56	3 36	4·1	268 / 272
89 / 91	65 59	2 15	2·5	64 59	2 09	2·4	63 59	2 03	2·3	62 59	1 58	2·2	61 59	1 53	2·1	60 59	1 48	2·1	269 / 271
90 / 90	66 00	0 00	0·0	65 00	0 00	0·0	64 00	0 00	0·0	63 00	0 00	0·0	62 00	0 00	0·0	61 00	0 00	0·0	270 / 270

N. Lat.: for LHA > 180° ... $Z_n = Z$
for LHA < 180° ... $Z_n = 360° - Z$

S. Lat.: for LHA > 180° ... $Z_n = 180° - Z$
for LHA < 180° ... $Z_n = 180° + Z$

SIGHT REDUCTION TABLE

B: (–) for 90° < LHA < 270°
Dec:(–) for Lat. contrary name

Z₁: same sign as B
Z₂: (–) for F > 90°

Lat./A	LHA/F	30° A/H	30° B/P	30° Z₁/Z₂	31° A/H	31° B/P	31° Z₁/Z₂	32° A/H	32° B/P	32° Z₁/Z₂	33° A/H	33° B/P	33° Z₁/Z₂	34° A/H	34° B/P	34° Z₁/Z₂	35° A/H	35° B/P	35° Z₁/Z₂	LHA	Lat./A
180	0	0 00	60 00	90·0	0 00	59 00	90·0	0 00	58 00	90·0	0 00	57 00	90·0	0 00	56 00	90·0	0 00	55 00	90·0	180	360
179	1	0 52	59 59	89·5	0 51	59 00	89·5	0 51	58 00	89·5	0 50	57 00	89·5	0 50	56 00	89·4	0 49	55 00	89·4	181	359
178	2	1 44	59 59	89·0	1 43	58 59	89·0	1 42	57 59	88·9	1 41	56 59	88·9	1 39	55 59	88·9	1 38	54 59	88·9	182	358
177	3	2 36	59 58	88·5	2 34	58 58	88·5	2 33	57 58	88·4	2 31	56 58	88·4	2 29	55 58	88·3	2 27	54 58	88·3	183	357
176	4	3 28	59 56	88·0	3 26	58 56	88·0	3 23	57 57	87·9	3 21	56 56	87·8	3 19	55 56	87·8	3 17	54 56	87·7	184	356
175	5	4 20	59 54	87·5	4 17	58 54	87·4	4 14	57 54	87·3	4 12	56 54	87·3	4 09	55 54	87·2	4 06	54 54	87·1	185	355
174	6	5 12	59 52	87·0	5 08	58 52	86·9	5 05	57 52	86·8	5 02	56 51	86·7	4 58	55 51	86·6	4 55	54 51	86·6	186	354
173	7	6 04	59 49	86·5	6 00	58 49	86·4	5 56	57 48	86·3	5 52	56 48	86·2	5 48	55 48	86·1	5 44	54 48	86·0	187	353
172	8	6 55	59 45	86·0	6 51	58 45	85·9	6 47	57 45	85·7	6 42	56 45	85·6	6 38	55 44	85·5	6 33	54 44	85·4	188	352
171	9	7 47	59 42	85·5	7 42	58 41	85·3	7 37	57 41	85·2	7 32	56 40	85·1	7 27	55 40	84·9	7 22	54 40	84·8	189	351
170	10	8 39	59 37	85·0	8 34	58 37	84·8	8 28	57 36	84·7	8 22	56 36	84·5	8 17	55 36	84·4	8 11	54 35	84·2	190	350
169	11	9 31	59 32	84·4	9 25	58 32	84·3	9 19	57 31	84·1	9 13	56 31	84·0	9 06	55 30	83·8	9 00	54 30	83·6	191	349
168	12	10 22	59 27	83·9	10 16	58 26	83·8	10 09	57 26	83·6	10 03	56 25	83·4	9 56	55 25	83·2	9 48	54 24	83·0	192	348
167	13	11 14	59 21	83·4	11 07	58 20	83·2	11 00	57 20	83·0	10 52	56 19	82·8	10 45	55 18	82·6	10 37	54 18	82·5	193	347
166	14	12 06	59 15	82·9	11 58	58 14	82·7	11 50	57 13	82·5	11 42	56 12	82·3	11 34	55 12	82·1	11 26	54 11	81·9	194	346
165	15	12 57	59 08	82·4	12 49	58 07	82·1	12 41	57 07	81·9	12 32	56 05	81·7	12 23	55 04	81·5	12 14	54 03	81·3	195	345
164	16	13 49	59 01	81·8	13 40	57 59	81·6	13 31	56 58	81·4	13 22	55 57	81·1	13 13	54 57	80·9	13 03	53 56	80·7	196	344
163	17	14 40	58 53	81·3	14 31	57 51	81·1	14 21	56 50	80·8	14 12	55 49	80·5	14 02	54 48	80·3	13 51	53 47	80·1	197	343
162	18	15 31	58 44	80·8	15 22	57 43	80·5	15 12	56 42	80·2	15 01	55 40	80·0	14 51	54 39	79·7	14 40	53 38	79·4	198	342
161	19	16 23	58 35	80·2	16 12	57 34	79·9	16 02	56 33	79·7	15 50	55 31	79·4	15 40	54 30	79·1	15 28	53 29	78·8	199	341
160	20	17 14	58 26	79·7	17 03	57 24	79·4	16 52	56 23	79·1	16 40	55 21	78·8	16 28	54 20	78·5	16 16	53 19	78·2	200	340
159	21	18 05	58 16	79·1	17 53	57 14	78·8	17 42	56 12	78·5	17 29	55 11	78·2	17 17	54 09	77·9	17 04	53 08	77·6	201	339
158	22	18 56	58 05	78·6	18 44	57 03	78·2	18 31	56 01	77·9	18 19	55 00	77·6	18 06	53 58	77·3	17 52	52 56	77·0	202	338
157	23	19 47	57 54	78·0	19 34	56 52	77·7	19 21	55 50	77·3	19 08	54 48	77·0	18 54	53 46	76·6	18 40	52 44	76·3	203	337
156	24	20 37	57 42	77·4	20 24	56 40	77·1	20 11	55 38	76·7	19 57	54 36	76·4	19 42	53 34	76·0	19 28	52 32	75·7	204	336
155	25	21 28	57 30	76·9	21 14	56 27	76·5	21 00	55 25	76·1	20 46	54 23	75·7	20 31	53 21	75·4	20 15	52 19	75·0	205	335
154	26	22 19	57 17	76·3	22 04	56 14	75·9	21 49	55 12	75·5	21 34	54 09	75·1	21 19	53 07	74·7	21 02	52 05	74·4	206	334
153	27	23 09	57 03	75·7	22 54	56 00	75·3	22 38	54 59	74·9	22 23	53 56	74·5	22 07	52 53	74·1	21 50	51 50	73·7	207	333
152	28	23 59	56 49	75·1	23 44	55 46	74·7	23 27	54 43	74·3	23 11	53 40	73·8	22 54	52 37	73·4	22 37	51 35	73·1	208	332
151	29	24 50	56 34	74·5	24 33	55 31	74·1	24 16	54 27	73·6	23 59	53 24	73·2	23 42	52 22	72·8	23 24	51 19	72·4	209	331
150	30	25 40	56 19	73·9	25 23	55 15	73·4	25 05	54 11	73·0	24 48	53 08	72·5	24 29	52 05	72·1	24 11	51 03	71·7	210	330
149	31	26 29	56 02	73·3	26 12	54 58	72·8	25 54	53 54	72·3	25 36	52 51	71·9	25 17	51 48	71·4	24 57	50 45	71·0	211	329
148	32	27 19	55 45	72·6	27 01	54 41	72·2	26 42	53 37	71·7	26 24	52 33	71·2	26 04	51 30	70·7	25 43	50 27	70·3	212	328
147	33	28 09	55 27	72·0	27 50	54 23	71·5	27 31	53 19	71·0	27 11	52 15	70·5	26 50	51 12	70·0	26 30	50 08	69·6	213	327
146	34	28 58	55 09	71·4	28 38	54 04	70·8	28 19	53 00	70·3	27 58	51 56	69·8	27 37	50 52	69·3	27 16	49 49	68·8	214	326
145	35	29 47	54 49	70·7	29 27	53 44	70·2	29 06	52 42	69·6	28 45	51 36	69·1	28 24	50 32	68·6	28 01	49 29	68·1	215	325
144	36	30 36	54 29	70·0	30 15	53 24	69·5	29 54	52 19	68·9	29 32	51 15	68·4	29 10	50 11	67·9	28 47	49 07	67·4	216	324
143	37	31 25	54 08	69·4	31 03	53 03	68·8	30 41	51 58	68·2	30 19	50 53	67·7	29 56	49 49	67·2	29 32	48 45	66·6	217	323
142	38	32 13	53 46	68·8	31 51	52 40	68·1	31 28	51 35	67·5	31 06	50 30	66·9	30 41	49 26	66·4	30 17	48 23	65·9	218	322
141	39	33 02	53 23	68·0	32 39	52 17	67·4	32 15	51 12	66·8	31 51	50 07	66·2	31 27	49 03	65·6	31 02	47 59	65·1	219	321
140	40	33 50	53 00	67·2	33 26	51 53	66·6	33 02	50 48	66·0	32 37	49 43	65·4	32 12	48 38	64·9	31 46	47 34	64·3	220	320
139	41	34 37	52 35	66·5	34 13	51 29	65·9	33 48	50 23	65·3	33 23	49 18	64·7	32 57	48 13	64·1	32 30	47 09	63·5	221	319
138	42	35 25	52 09	65·8	35 00	51 03	65·1	34 34	49 56	64·5	34 08	48 51	63·9	33 42	47 46	63·3	33 14	46 42	62·7	222	318
137	43	36 12	51 43	65·0	35 46	50 36	64·3	35 20	49 29	63·7	34 53	48 24	63·1	34 26	47 19	62·5	33 58	46 15	61·9	223	317
136	44	36 59	51 15	64·2	36 33	50 08	63·6	36 06	49 01	62·9	35 38	47 56	62·3	35 10	46 51	61·6	34 41	45 46	61·0	224	316
135	45	37 46	50 46	63·4	37 19	49 39	62·7	36 51	48 32	62·1	36 22	47 26	61·4	35 53	46 21	60·8	35 24	45 17	60·2	225	315

Lat. / F	30°			31°			32°			33°			34°			35°			Lat. / A
LHA/F	A/H	B/P	Z₁/Z₂	A/H	B/P	Z₁/Z₂	A/H	B/P	Z₁/Z₂	A/H	B/P	Z₁/Z₂	A/H	B/P	Z₁/Z₂	A/H	B/P	Z₁/Z₂	LHA
45 / 135	37 46	50 46	63·4	37 19	49 39	62·7	36 51	48 32	62·1	36 22	47 26	61·4	35 53	46 21	60·8	35 24	45 17	60·2	225 / 315
46 / 134	38 32	50 16	62·6	38 04	49 08	61·9	37 36	48 02	61·2	37 06	46 56	60·6	36 37	45 51	59·9	36 06	44 46	59·3	226 / 314
47 / 133	39 18	49 45	61·8	38 49	48 37	61·1	38 20	47 30	60·4	37 50	46 24	59·7	37 19	45 19	59·1	36 48	44 15	58·4	227 / 313
48 / 132	40 04	49 13	61·0	39 34	48 05	60·2	39 04	46 58	59·5	38 33	45 51	58·8	38 02	44 46	58·2	37 30	43 42	57·5	228 / 312
49 / 131	40 49	48 39	60·1	40 19	47 31	59·4	39 48	46 24	58·6	39 16	45 18	57·9	38 44	44 12	57·2	38 11	43 08	56·6	229 / 311
50 / 130	41 34	48 04	59·2	41 03	46 56	58·5	40 31	45 49	57·7	39 59	44 42	57·0	39 26	43 37	56·3	38 52	42 33	55·6	230 / 310
51 / 129	42 18	47 28	58·3	41 46	46 20	57·5	41 14	45 12	56·8	40 41	44 06	56·1	40 07	43 01	55·4	39 32	41 57	54·7	231 / 309
52 / 128	43 02	46 50	57·4	42 29	45 42	56·6	41 56	44 34	55·9	41 22	43 28	55·1	40 47	42 23	54·4	40 12	41 19	53·7	232 / 308
53 / 127	43 46	46 11	56·4	43 12	45 03	55·6	42 38	43 55	54·9	42 03	42 49	54·1	41 28	41 44	53·4	40 52	40 41	52·7	233 / 307
54 / 126	44 29	45 31	55·5	43 54	44 22	54·7	43 19	43 15	53·9	42 44	42 09	53·1	42 07	41 04	52·4	41 30	40 01	51·7	234 / 306
55 / 125	45 11	44 49	54·5	44 36	43 40	53·7	44 00	42 33	52·9	43 24	41 27	52·1	42 46	40 23	51·4	42 09	39 19	50·7	235 / 305
56 / 124	45 53	44 05	53·5	45 17	42 57	52·6	44 40	41 50	51·8	44 03	40 44	51·1	43 25	39 40	50·3	42 46	38 37	49·6	236 / 304
57 / 123	46 35	43 20	52·4	45 58	42 11	51·6	45 20	41 05	50·8	44 42	39 59	50·0	44 03	38 55	49·3	43 24	37 53	48·5	237 / 303
58 / 122	47 16	42 33	51·3	46 38	41 25	50·5	45 59	40 18	49·7	45 20	39 13	48·9	44 40	38 09	48·2	44 00	37 07	47·5	238 / 302
59 / 121	47 56	41 44	50·2	47 17	40 36	49·4	46 38	39 30	48·6	45 58	38 25	47·8	45 17	37 22	47·1	44 36	36 20	46·3	239 / 301
60 / 120	48 35	40 54	49·1	47 56	39 46	48·3	47 16	38 40	47·5	46 35	37 35	46·7	45 53	36 33	45·9	45 11	35 32	45·2	240 / 300
61 / 119	49 14	40 01	47·9	48 34	38 54	47·1	47 53	37 48	46·3	47 11	36 45	45·5	46 29	35 42	44·7	45 46	34 42	44·0	241 / 299
62 / 118	49 53	39 07	46·8	49 11	38 00	45·9	48 29	36 55	45·1	47 46	35 52	44·3	47 03	34 50	43·6	46 19	33 50	42·8	242 / 298
63 / 117	50 30	38 11	45·5	49 48	37 04	44·7	49 05	36 00	43·9	48 21	34 57	43·1	47 37	33 57	42·3	46 53	32 57	41·6	243 / 297
64 / 116	51 07	37 13	44·3	50 23	36 07	43·4	49 40	35 03	42·6	48 55	34 01	41·8	48 10	33 04	41·1	47 25	32 02	40·4	244 / 296
65 / 115	51 43	36 12	43·0	50 58	35 08	42·2	50 14	34 04	41·3	49 28	33 03	40·6	48 43	32 08	39·8	47 56	31 07	39·1	245 / 295
66 / 114	52 18	35 10	41·7	51 33	34 06	40·8	50 48	33 01	40·0	50 01	32 02	39·3	49 14	31 05	38·5	48 27	30 10	37·8	246 / 294
67 / 113	52 52	34 05	40·3	52 06	33 02	39·5	51 20	31 57	38·7	50 32	31 00	37·9	49 44	30 05	37·2	48 56	29 10	36·5	247 / 293
68 / 112	53 25	32 59	38·9	52 38	31 56	38·1	51 52	30 50	37·3	51 02	29 57	36·6	50 14	29 03	35·8	49 25	28 09	35·2	248 / 292
69 / 111	53 57	31 50	37·5	53 09	30 49	36·7	52 23	29 53	35·9	51 31	28 57	35·2	50 43	28 01	34·5	49 53	27 06	33·8	249 / 291
70 / 110	54 28	30 39	36·1	53 39	29 39	35·2	52 49	28 45	34·5	52 00	27 50	33·8	51 10	26 56	33·1	50 20	26 02	32·4	250 / 290
71 / 109	54 58	29 25	34·6	54 08	28 27	33·8	53 17	27 34	33·0	52 27	26 41	32·3	51 37	25 49	31·6	50 46	24 56	31·0	251 / 289
72 / 108	55 27	28 09	33·0	54 37	27 13	32·2	53 45	26 22	31·5	52 54	25 31	30·8	52 03	24 40	30·2	51 11	23 49	29·5	252 / 288
73 / 107	55 55	26 51	31·4	55 03	25 57	30·7	54 10	25 08	30·0	53 18	24 18	29·3	52 27	23 29	28·7	51 34	22 40	28·1	253 / 287
74 / 106	56 21	25 31	29·8	55 29	24 38	29·1	54 36	23 51	28·4	53 43	23 03	27·8	52 50	22 16	27·1	51 57	21 29	26·6	254 / 286
75 / 105	56 46	24 09	28·2	55 53	23 18	27·5	55 00	22 33	26·8	54 06	21 48	26·2	53 12	21 03	25·6	52 18	20 18	25·0	255 / 285
76 / 104	57 10	22 44	26·5	56 16	21 56	25·8	55 22	21 13	25·2	54 27	20 30	24·6	53 33	19 47	24·0	52 38	19 04	23·5	256 / 284
77 / 103	57 33	21 17	24·8	56 37	20 31	24·1	55 42	19 50	23·5	54 47	19 10	23·0	53 53	18 29	22·4	52 57	17 49	21·9	257 / 283
78 / 102	57 54	19 48	23·0	56 57	19 05	22·4	56 02	18 27	21·9	55 06	17 49	21·3	54 11	17 10	20·8	53 15	16 32	20·3	258 / 282
79 / 101	58 14	18 17	21·2	57 17	17 35	20·7	56 21	17 00	20·1	55 24	16 25	19·6	54 28	15 50	19·2	53 31	15 15	18·7	259 / 281
80 / 100	58 32	16 44	19·4	57 35	16 03	18·9	56 38	15 31	18·4	55 41	14 59	17·9	54 44	14 28	17·5	53 47	13 56	17·1	260 / 280
81 / 99	58 48	15 10	17·6	57 51	14 36	17·1	56 53	14 03	16·6	55 56	13 33	16·2	54 58	13 03	15·8	54 00	12 36	15·4	261 / 279
82 / 98	59 03	13 33	15·7	58 05	13 02	15·3	57 07	12 33	14·9	56 09	12 06	14·5	55 11	11 40	14·1	54 13	11 14	13·8	262 / 278
83 / 97	59 16	11 55	13·8	58 18	11 28	13·4	57 19	11 02	13·0	56 21	10 38	12·7	55 22	10 14	12·4	54 24	9 52	12·1	263 / 277
84 / 96	59 28	10 16	11·9	58 29	9 52	11·5	57 30	9 30	11·2	56 31	9 09	10·9	55 32	8 49	10·6	54 33	8 29	10·4	264 / 276
85 / 95	59 38	8 35	9·9	58 39	8 15	9·6	57 39	7 56	9·4	56 40	7 39	9·1	55 41	7 22	8·9	54 41	7 06	8·7	265 / 275
86 / 94	59 46	6 53	8·0	58 46	6 37	7·7	57 47	6 22	7·5	56 47	6 08	7·3	55 48	5 54	7·1	54 48	5 41	7·0	266 / 274
87 / 93	59 52	5 11	6·0	58 52	4 59	5·8	57 52	4 47	5·6	56 53	4 36	5·5	55 53	4 26	5·4	54 53	4 16	5·2	267 / 273
88 / 92	59 56	3 28	4·0	58 57	3 19	3·9	57 57	3 12	3·8	56 57	3 05	3·7	55 57	2 58	3·6	54 57	2 51	3·5	268 / 272
89 / 91	59 59	1 44	2·0	58 59	1 40	1·9	57 59	1 36	1·9	56 59	1 32	1·8	55 59	1 29	1·8	54 59	1 26	1·7	269 / 271
90 / 90	60 00	0 00	0·0	59 00	0 00	0·0	58 00	0 00	0·0	57 00	0 00	0·0	56 00	0 00	0·0	55 00	0 00	0·0	270 / 270

N. Lat.: for LHA > 180° .... Zₙ = Z; for LHA < 180° .... Zₙ = 360° − Z

S. Lat.: for LHA > 180° .... Zₙ = 180° − Z; for LHA < 180° .... Zₙ = 180° + Z

SIGHT REDUCTION TABLE

B: (−) for 90° < LHA < 270°
Dec: (−) for Lat. contrary name

Z₁: same sign as B
Z₂: (−) for F > 90°

Lat./A	LHA/F	36° A/H	36° B/P	36° Z₁/Z₂	37° A/H	37° B/P	37° Z₁/Z₂	38° A/H	38° B/P	38° Z₁/Z₂	39° A/H	39° B/P	39° Z₁/Z₂	40° A/H	40° B/P	40° Z₁/Z₂	41° A/H	41° B/P	41° Z₁/Z₂	Lat./A	LHA
0	180	0 00	54 00	90·0	0 00	53 00	90·0	0 00	52 00	90·0	0 00	51 00	90·0	0 00	50 00	90·0	0 00	49 00	90·0	180	360
1	179	0 49	54 00	89·4	0 48	53 00	89·4	0 47	52 00	89·4	0 47	51 00	89·4	0 46	50 00	89·4	0 45	49 00	89·3	181	359
2	178	1 37	53 59	88·8	1 36	52 59	88·8	1 35	51 59	88·8	1 33	50 59	88·7	1 32	49 59	88·7	1 31	48 59	88·7	182	358
3	177	2 26	53 58	88·2	2 24	52 58	88·2	2 22	51 58	88·1	2 20	50 58	88·1	2 18	49 58	88·1	2 16	48 58	88·0	183	357
4	176	3 14	53 56	87·6	3 12	52 56	87·6	3 09	51 56	87·5	3 06	50 56	87·5	3 04	49 56	87·4	3 01	48 56	87·4	184	356
5	175	4 03	53 54	87·1	3 59	52 54	87·0	3 56	51 54	86·9	3 53	50 54	86·8	3 50	49 54	86·8	3 46	48 54	86·7	185	355
6	174	4 51	53 51	86·5	4 47	52 51	86·4	4 43	51 51	86·3	4 40	50 51	86·2	4 36	49 51	86·1	4 31	48 51	86·1	186	354
7	173	5 39	53 48	85·9	5 35	52 48	85·8	5 31	51 48	85·6	5 26	50 47	85·6	5 21	49 47	85·5	5 17	48 47	85·4	187	353
8	172	6 28	53 44	85·3	6 23	52 44	85·2	6 18	51 44	85·1	6 13	50 44	84·9	6 07	49 43	84·9	6 02	48 43	84·7	188	352
9	171	7 16	53 40	84·7	7 11	52 39	84·6	7 05	51 39	84·4	6 59	50 39	84·3	6 53	49 39	84·2	6 47	48 39	84·1	189	351
10	170	8 05	53 35	84·1	7 58	52 35	83·9	7 52	51 34	83·8	7 45	50 34	83·7	7 39	49 34	83·5	7 32	48 34	83·4	190	350
11	169	8 53	53 30	83·5	8 46	52 29	83·3	8 39	51 29	83·2	8 32	50 29	83·0	8 24	49 29	82·9	8 17	48 28	82·7	191	349
12	168	9 41	53 24	82·9	9 33	52 23	82·7	9 26	51 23	82·5	9 18	50 23	82·4	9 10	49 23	82·2	9 02	48 22	82·1	192	348
13	167	10 29	53 17	82·3	10 21	52 17	82·1	10 13	51 17	81·9	10 04	50 16	81·7	9 55	49 16	81·6	9 46	48 16	81·4	193	347
14	166	11 17	53 10	81·7	11 08	52 10	81·5	10 59	51 10	81·3	10 50	50 09	81·1	10 41	49 09	80·9	10 31	48 09	80·7	194	346
15	165	12 05	53 03	81·0	11 56	52 02	80·8	11 46	51 02	80·6	11 36	50 02	80·4	11 26	49 01	80·2	11 16	48 01	80·0	195	345
16	164	12 53	52 55	80·4	12 43	51 54	80·2	12 33	50 54	80·0	12 21	49 53	79·8	12 11	48 53	79·6	12 00	47 53	79·3	196	344
17	163	13 41	52 46	79·8	13 30	51 46	79·6	13 19	50 46	79·3	13 08	49 45	79·1	12 57	48 44	78·9	12 45	47 44	78·7	197	343
18	162	14 29	52 37	79·2	14 17	51 37	78·9	14 06	50 36	78·7	13 54	49 35	78·4	13 42	48 35	78·2	13 29	47 34	78·0	198	342
19	161	15 16	52 28	78·6	15 04	51 27	78·3	14 52	50 26	78·0	14 39	49 25	77·8	14 27	48 25	77·5	14 13	47 24	77·3	199	341
20	160	16 04	52 17	77·9	15 51	51 16	77·6	15 38	50 16	77·4	15 25	49 15	77·1	15 11	48 14	76·8	14 58	47 14	76·6	200	340
21	159	16 51	52 07	77·3	16 38	51 05	77·0	16 24	50 05	76·7	16 10	49 04	76·4	15 56	48 03	76·1	15 42	47 03	75·9	201	339
22	158	17 38	51 55	76·6	17 24	50 54	76·3	17 10	49 53	76·0	16 56	48 52	75·7	16 41	47 51	75·4	16 25	46 51	75·2	202	338
23	157	18 26	51 43	76·0	18 11	50 42	75·7	17 56	49 41	75·4	17 41	48 40	75·0	17 25	47 39	74·7	17 09	46 38	74·4	203	337
24	156	19 13	51 30	75·3	18 57	50 29	75·0	18 42	49 28	74·7	18 26	48 27	74·3	18 09	47 26	74·0	17 53	46 25	73·7	204	336
25	155	20 00	51 17	74·7	19 44	50 15	74·3	19 27	49 14	74·0	19 11	48 13	73·6	18 53	47 12	73·3	18 36	46 12	73·0	205	335
26	154	20 46	51 03	74·0	20 30	50 01	73·6	20 13	49 00	73·3	19 55	47 58	72·9	19 37	46 58	72·6	19 19	45 57	72·3	206	334
27	153	21 33	50 48	73·3	21 15	49 47	73·0	20 58	48 45	72·6	20 40	47 44	72·2	20 21	46 43	71·9	20 02	45 42	71·5	207	333
28	152	22 19	50 33	72·6	22 01	49 31	72·3	21 43	48 30	71·9	21 24	47 28	71·5	21 05	46 28	71·1	20 45	45 27	70·8	208	332
29	151	23 06	50 17	72·0	22 47	49 15	71·6	22 28	48 14	71·2	22 08	47 12	70·8	21 48	46 11	70·4	21 28	45 11	70·0	209	331
30	150	23 52	50 00	71·3	23 32	48 58	70·8	23 12	47 57	70·4	22 52	46 55	70·0	22 31	45 54	69·6	22 10	44 54	69·3	210	330
31	149	24 37	49 43	70·5	24 17	48 41	70·1	23 57	47 39	69·7	23 36	46 37	69·3	23 14	45 37	68·9	22 52	44 36	68·5	211	329
32	148	25 23	49 25	69·8	25 02	48 23	69·4	24 41	47 21	69·0	24 19	46 19	68·5	23 57	45 18	68·1	23 34	44 17	67·7	212	328
33	147	26 09	49 06	69·1	25 47	48 04	68·7	25 25	47 02	68·2	25 02	46 00	67·8	24 40	44 59	67·3	24 16	43 58	66·9	213	327
34	146	26 54	48 48	68·4	26 32	47 44	67·9	26 09	46 42	67·4	25 45	45 40	67·0	25 22	44 39	66·6	24 58	43 39	66·1	214	326
35	145	27 39	48 26	67·6	27 16	47 23	67·1	26 52	46 21	66·7	26 28	45 20	66·2	26 04	44 19	65·8	25 39	43 18	65·3	215	325
36	144	28 24	48 04	66·9	28 00	47 02	66·4	27 36	46 00	65·9	27 11	44 58	65·4	26 46	43 57	65·0	26 20	42 57	64·5	216	324
37	143	29 08	47 42	66·1	28 44	46 40	65·6	28 19	45 38	65·1	27 53	44 36	64·6	27 27	43 35	64·2	27 01	42 34	63·7	217	323
38	142	29 52	47 19	65·3	29 27	46 17	64·8	29 01	45 15	64·3	28 35	44 13	63·8	28 08	43 12	63·3	27 41	42 12	62·9	218	322
39	141	30 36	46 56	64·5	30 10	45 53	64·0	29 44	44 51	63·5	29 17	43 49	63·0	28 50	42 48	62·5	28 21	41 48	62·0	219	321
40	140	31 20	46 31	63·7	30 53	45 28	63·2	30 26	44 26	62·7	29 58	43 25	62·2	29 30	42 24	61·7	29 01	41 23	61·2	220	320
41	139	32 03	46 05	62·9	31 36	45 03	62·4	31 08	44 01	61·8	30 39	42 59	61·3	30 10	41 58	60·8	29 41	40 58	60·3	221	319
42	138	32 46	45 39	62·1	32 18	44 36	61·5	31 49	43 34	61·0	31 20	42 33	60·5	30 50	41 32	59·9	30 20	40 32	59·4	222	318
43	137	33 29	45 11	61·3	33 00	44 09	60·7	32 30	43 07	60·1	32 00	42 05	59·6	31 30	41 05	59·1	30 59	40 05	58·5	223	317
44	136	34 12	44 43	60·4	33 42	43 40	59·8	33 11	42 38	59·3	32 40	41 37	58·7	32 09	40 36	58·2	31 37	39 36	57·6	224	316
45	135	34 54	44 13	59·6	34 23	43 11	59·0	33 52	42 09	58·4	33 20	41 08	57·8	32 48	40 07	57·3	32 15	39 08	56·7	225	315

Lat./A	LHA/F	36° A/H	36° B/P	36° Z1/Z2	37° A/H	37° B/P	37° Z1/Z2	38° A/H	38° B/P	38° Z1/Z2	39° A/H	39° B/P	39° Z1/Z2	40° A/H	40° B/P	40° Z1/Z2	41° A/H	41° B/P	41° Z1/Z2	LHA	Lat./A
45	135	34 54	44 13	59.6	34 23	43 11	59.0	33 52	42 09	58.4	33 20	41 08	57.8	32 48	40 07	57.3	32 15	39 08	56.7	225	315
46	134	35 35	43 43	58.7	35 05	42 40	58.1	34 32	41 38	57.5	33 59	40 37	56.9	33 26	39 37	56.4	32 53	38 38	55.8	226	314
47	133	36 17	43 11	57.8	35 44	42 09	57.2	35 12	41 07	56.6	34 38	40 06	56.0	34 04	39 06	55.4	33 30	38 07	54.9	227	313
48	132	36 57	42 39	56.9	36 24	41 36	56.2	35 51	40 35	55.6	35 17	39 34	55.0	34 42	38 34	54.5	34 07	37 35	53.9	228	312
49	131	37 38	42 05	55.9	37 04	41 04	55.3	36 30	40 01	54.7	35 55	39 01	54.1	35 19	38 01	53.5	34 43	37 03	53.0	229	311
50	130	38 18	41 30	55.0	37 43	40 28	54.4	37 08	39 27	53.7	36 32	38 27	53.1	35 56	37 27	52.5	35 19	36 29	52.0	230	310
51	129	38 57	40 54	54.0	38 22	39 52	53.4	37 46	38 51	52.8	37 09	37 51	52.1	36 32	36 52	51.6	35 55	35 54	51.0	231	309
52	128	39 36	40 17	53.0	39 00	39 15	52.4	38 23	38 14	51.8	37 46	37 15	51.1	37 08	36 16	50.6	36 30	35 18	50.0	232	308
53	127	40 15	39 38	52.0	39 38	38 37	51.4	39 00	37 36	50.8	38 22	36 37	50.1	37 43	35 39	49.5	37 04	34 42	49.0	233	307
54	126	40 53	38 58	51.0	40 15	37 57	50.4	39 36	36 57	49.7	38 57	35 58	49.1	38 18	35 01	48.5	37 38	34 04	47.9	234	306
55	125	41 30	38 17	50.0	40 52	37 17	49.3	40 12	36 17	48.7	39 32	35 18	48.1	38 52	34 21	47.4	38 11	33 25	46.9	235	305
56	124	42 07	37 35	48.9	41 28	36 35	48.3	40 47	35 36	47.6	40 07	34 38	47.0	39 26	33 41	46.4	38 44	32 45	45.8	236	304
57	123	42 44	36 51	47.9	42 03	35 51	47.2	41 22	34 53	46.5	40 41	33 55	45.9	39 59	32 59	45.3	39 16	32 04	44.7	237	303
58	122	43 19	36 06	46.8	42 38	35 07	46.1	41 56	34 09	45.4	41 14	33 12	44.8	40 31	32 16	44.2	39 48	31 22	43.6	238	302
59	121	43 54	35 20	45.6	43 12	34 21	45.0	42 29	33 24	44.3	41 46	32 27	43.7	41 03	31 32	43.1	40 19	30 39	42.5	239	301
60	120	44 29	34 32	44.5	43 46	33 34	43.8	43 02	32 37	43.2	42 18	31 42	42.5	41 34	30 47	41.9	40 49	29 54	41.3	240	300
61	119	45 02	33 43	43.3	44 18	32 45	42.6	43 34	31 49	42.0	42 49	30 53	41.4	42 04	30 01	40.8	41 18	29 09	40.2	241	299
62	118	45 35	32 52	42.1	44 51	31 55	41.5	44 05	31 00	40.8	43 20	30 06	40.2	42 34	29 14	39.6	41 47	28 22	39.0	242	298
63	117	46 07	32 00	40.9	45 22	31 04	40.3	44 36	30 10	39.6	43 49	29 17	39.0	43 03	28 25	38.4	42 15	27 35	37.8	243	297
64	116	46 39	31 06	39.7	45 52	30 11	39.0	45 06	29 18	38.4	44 18	28 26	37.8	43 31	27 35	37.2	42 43	26 46	36.6	244	296
65	115	47 09	30 11	38.4	46 21	29 17	37.8	45 35	28 25	37.1	44 47	27 34	36.5	43 58	26 44	36.0	43 09	25 56	35.4	245	295
66	114	47 39	29 14	37.1	46 50	28 21	36.5	46 03	27 30	35.9	45 14	26 40	35.3	44 24	25 52	34.7	43 35	25 04	34.2	246	294
67	113	48 08	28 16	35.8	47 19	27 24	35.2	46 30	26 34	34.6	45 40	25 45	34.0	44 50	24 58	33.4	44 00	24 12	32.9	247	293
68	112	48 36	27 17	34.5	47 47	26 26	33.9	46 56	25 37	33.3	46 06	24 50	32.7	45 15	24 03	32.2	44 24	23 19	31.6	248	292
69	111	49 03	26 15	33.1	48 13	25 26	32.5	47 22	24 38	31.9	46 31	23 52	31.4	45 39	23 08	30.8	44 48	22 24	30.3	249	291
70	110	49 29	25 13	31.8	48 38	24 25	31.2	47 46	23 39	30.6	46 55	22 53	30.0	46 03	22 12	29.5	45 10	21 28	29.0	250	290
71	109	49 54	24 08	30.4	49 02	23 22	29.8	48 10	22 37	29.2	47 17	21 54	28.7	46 25	21 12	28.2	45 32	20 32	27.7	251	289
72	108	50 18	23 02	28.9	49 25	22 18	28.4	48 33	21 35	27.8	47 39	20 53	27.3	46 48	20 13	26.8	45 54	19 34	26.3	252	288
73	107	50 41	21 55	27.5	49 48	21 12	26.9	48 54	20 31	26.4	48 00	19 51	25.9	47 06	19 13	25.4	46 12	18 35	25.0	253	287
74	106	51 03	20 47	26.0	50 09	20 06	25.4	49 15	19 26	25.0	48 20	18 48	24.5	47 25	18 11	24.0	46 30	17 36	23.6	254	286
75	105	51 24	19 36	24.5	50 29	18 57	24.0	49 34	18 20	23.5	48 39	17 43	23.1	47 44	17 09	22.6	46 48	16 35	22.2	255	285
76	104	51 43	18 25	23.0	50 48	17 48	22.5	49 52	17 12	22.0	48 57	16 38	21.6	48 01	16 05	21.2	47 05	15 33	20.8	256	284
77	103	52 02	17 12	21.4	51 06	16 37	21.0	50 09	16 04	20.6	49 13	15 31	20.1	48 17	15 00	19.8	47 20	14 31	19.4	257	283
78	102	52 19	15 58	19.9	51 22	15 25	19.5	50 25	14 54	19.0	49 29	14 24	18.7	48 32	13 55	18.3	47 38	13 27	18.0	258	282
79	101	52 35	14 43	18.3	51 37	14 13	17.9	50 40	13 43	17.5	49 43	13 16	17.2	48 46	12 49	16.8	47 48	12 23	16.5	259	281
80	100	52 49	13 27	16.7	51 52	12 59	16.3	50 54	12 32	16.0	49 56	12 06	15.7	48 58	11 42	15.3	48 01	11 18	15.0	260	280
81	99	53 02	12 09	15.1	52 04	11 44	14.7	51 06	11 19	14.4	50 08	10 56	14.1	49 10	10 34	13.8	48 12	10 12	13.6	261	279
82	98	53 14	10 51	13.4	52 16	10 28	13.1	51 18	10 06	12.9	50 19	9 45	12.6	49 20	9 25	12.3	48 22	9 06	12.1	262	278
83	97	53 25	9 31	11.8	52 26	9 11	11.5	51 29	8 52	11.3	50 29	8 34	11.0	49 30	8 16	10.8	48 31	7 59	10.6	263	277
84	96	53 34	8 11	10.1	52 35	7 54	9.9	51 36	7 37	9.7	50 37	7 21	9.5	49 38	7 06	9.3	48 38	6 51	9.1	264	276
85	95	53 42	6 50	8.5	52 43	6 36	8.3	51 43	6 22	8.1	50 44	6 09	7.9	49 44	5 56	7.8	48 45	5 44	7.6	265	275
86	94	53 49	5 29	6.8	52 49	5 17	6.6	51 49	5 06	6.5	50 50	4 55	6.3	49 50	4 45	6.2	48 50	4 35	6.1	266	274
87	93	53 54	4 07	5.1	52 54	3 58	5.0	51 54	3 50	4.9	50 54	3 42	4.8	49 54	3 34	4.7	48 55	3 27	4.6	267	273
88	92	53 57	2 45	3.4	52 57	2 39	3.3	51 57	2 33	3.2	50 57	2 28	3.2	49 58	2 23	3.1	48 58	2 18	3.0	268	272
89	91	53 59	1 23	1.7	52 59	1 20	1.7	51 59	1 17	1.6	50 59	1 14	1.6	49 59	1 11	1.6	48 59	1 09	1.5	269	271
90	90	54 00	0 00	0.0	53 00	0 00	0.0	52 00	0 00	0.0	51 00	0 00	0.0	50 00	0 00	0.0	49 00	0 00	0.0	270	270

N. Lat.: for LHA > 180° .... $Z_n = Z$
for LHA < 180° .... $Z_n = 360° - Z$

S. Lat.: for LHA > 180° .... $Z_n = 180° - Z$
for LHA < 180° .... $Z_n = 180° + Z$

SIGHT REDUCTION TABLE

B: (−) for 90° < LHA < 270°
Dec:(−) for Lat. contrary name

Z₁: same sign as B
Z₂:(−) for F > 90°

Lat./A LHA/F	42° A/H	42° B/P	42° Z₁/Z₂	43° A/H	43° B/P	43° Z₁/Z₂	44° A/H	44° B/P	44° Z₁/Z₂	45° A/H	45° B/P	45° Z₁/Z₂	46° A/H	46° B/P	46° Z₁/Z₂	47° A/H	47° B/P	47° Z₁/Z₂	Lat./A LHA
0 180	0 00	48 00	90·0	0 00	47 00	90·0	0 00	46 00	90·0	0 00	45 00	90·0	0 00	44 00	90·0	0 00	43 00	90·0	180 360
1 179	0 45	48 00	89·3	0 44	47 00	89·3	0 43	46 00	89·3	0 42	45 00	89·3	0 42	44 00	89·3	0 41	43 00	89·3	181 359
2 178	1 29	47 59	88·7	1 28	46 59	88·6	1 26	45 59	88·6	1 25	44 59	88·6	1 23	43 59	88·6	1 22	42 59	88·5	182 358
3 177	2 14	47 58	88·0	2 12	46 58	88·0	2 09	45 58	87·9	2 07	44 58	87·9	2 05	43 58	87·9	2 03	42 58	87·8	183 357
4 176	2 58	47 56	87·3	2 55	46 56	87·3	2 53	45 56	87·2	2 50	44 56	87·2	2 47	43 56	87·1	2 44	42 56	87·1	184 356
5 175	3 43	47 53	86·6	3 39	46 53	86·6	3 36	45 53	86·5	3 32	44 53	86·5	3 28	43 53	86·4	3 24	42 53	86·3	185 355
6 174	4 27	47 51	86·0	4 23	46 51	85·9	4 19	45 51	85·8	4 14	44 51	85·7	4 10	43 51	85·7	4 05	42 51	85·6	186 354
7 173	5 12	47 47	85·3	5 07	46 47	85·2	5 02	45 47	85·1	4 57	44 47	85·0	4 51	43 47	85·0	4 46	42 47	84·9	187 353
8 172	5 56	47 43	84·6	5 51	46 43	84·5	5 45	45 43	84·4	5 39	44 43	84·3	5 33	43 43	84·2	5 27	42 43	84·1	188 352
9 171	6 41	47 39	84·0	6 34	46 39	83·8	6 28	45 39	83·7	6 21	44 39	83·6	6 14	43 39	83·5	6 07	42 39	83·4	189 351
10 170	7 25	47 34	83·3	7 18	46 34	83·1	7 11	45 34	83·0	7 03	44 34	82·9	6 56	43 34	82·8	6 48	42 34	82·7	190 350
11 169	8 09	47 28	82·6	8 01	46 28	82·4	7 53	45 28	82·3	7 45	44 28	82·2	7 37	43 28	82·0	7 29	42 28	81·9	191 349
12 168	8 53	47 22	81·9	8 45	46 22	81·8	8 36	45 22	81·6	8 27	44 22	81·5	8 18	43 22	81·3	8 09	42 22	81·2	192 348
13 167	9 37	47 16	81·2	9 28	46 15	81·1	9 19	45 15	80·9	9 09	44 15	80·7	8 59	43 15	80·6	8 49	42 15	80·4	193 347
14 166	10 21	47 08	80·5	10 11	46 08	80·3	10 01	45 08	80·2	9 51	44 08	80·0	9 40	43 08	79·8	9 30	42 08	79·7	194 346
15 165	11 05	47 01	79·8	10 55	46 00	79·6	10 44	45 00	79·5	10 33	44 00	79·3	10 21	43 00	79·1	10 10	42 01	78·9	195 345
16 164	11 49	46 52	79·1	11 38	45 52	78·9	11 26	44 52	78·7	11 14	43 52	78·5	11 02	42 52	78·3	10 50	41 52	78·2	196 344
17 163	12 33	46 43	78·4	12 21	45 43	78·2	12 08	44 43	78·0	11 56	43 43	77·8	11 43	42 43	77·6	11 30	41 44	77·4	197 343
18 162	13 17	46 34	77·7	13 04	45 34	77·5	12 51	44 34	77·3	12 37	43 34	77·1	12 24	42 34	76·8	12 10	41 34	76·6	198 342
19 161	14 00	46 24	77·0	13 46	45 24	76·8	13 33	44 24	76·5	13 19	43 24	76·3	13 04	42 24	76·1	12 50	41 24	75·9	199 341
20 160	14 43	46 13	76·3	14 29	45 13	76·1	14 15	44 13	75·8	14 00	43 13	75·6	13 45	42 13	75·3	13 29	41 14	75·1	200 340
21 159	15 27	46 02	75·6	15 12	45 02	75·3	14 56	44 02	75·1	14 41	43 02	74·8	14 25	42 02	74·6	14 09	41 03	74·3	201 339
22 158	16 10	45 50	74·9	15 54	44 50	74·6	15 38	43 50	74·3	15 22	42 50	74·1	15 05	41 50	73·8	14 48	40 51	73·5	202 338
23 157	16 53	45 38	74·1	16 36	44 38	73·9	16 19	43 38	73·6	16 02	42 38	73·3	15 45	41 38	73·0	15 27	40 39	72·8	203 337
24 156	17 36	45 25	73·4	17 18	44 25	73·1	17 01	43 25	72·8	16 43	42 25	72·5	16 25	41 25	72·2	16 06	40 26	72·0	204 336
25 155	18 18	45 11	72·7	18 00	44 11	72·4	17 42	43 11	72·1	17 23	42 11	71·8	17 04	41 12	71·5	16 45	40 12	71·2	205 335
26 154	19 01	44 57	71·9	18 42	43 57	71·6	18 23	42 57	71·3	18 03	41 57	71·0	17 44	40 57	70·7	17 24	39 58	70·4	206 334
27 153	19 43	44 42	71·2	19 24	43 42	70·8	19 04	42 42	70·5	18 43	41 42	70·2	18 23	40 43	69·9	18 02	39 43	69·6	207 333
28 152	20 25	44 26	70·4	20 05	43 26	70·1	19 44	42 26	69·7	19 23	41 27	69·4	19 02	40 27	69·1	18 40	39 27	68·8	208 332
29 151	21 07	44 10	69·6	20 46	43 10	69·3	20 25	42 10	68·9	20 03	41 11	68·6	19 41	40 11	68·3	19 18	39 12	67·9	209 331
30 150	21 49	43 53	68·9	21 27	42 53	68·5	21 05	41 53	68·1	20 42	40 54	67·8	20 19	39 54	67·4	19 56	38 55	67·1	210 330
31 149	22 31	43 35	68·1	22 08	42 35	67·7	21 45	41 36	67·3	21 21	40 36	67·0	20 58	39 37	66·6	20 34	38 38	66·3	211 329
32 148	23 11	43 17	67·3	22 48	42 17	66·9	22 24	41 17	66·5	22 00	40 18	66·2	21 36	39 19	65·8	21 11	38 20	65·4	212 328
33 147	23 52	42 58	66·5	23 28	41 58	66·1	23 04	40 58	65·7	22 39	39 59	65·3	22 14	39 00	65·0	21 48	38 02	64·6	213 327
34 146	24 33	42 38	65·7	24 08	41 38	65·3	23 43	40 39	64·9	23 17	39 40	64·5	22 51	38 41	64·1	22 25	37 42	63·7	214 326
35 145	25 14	42 18	64·9	24 48	41 18	64·5	24 22	40 18	64·1	23 56	39 19	63·7	23 29	38 21	63·3	23 02	37 23	62·9	215 325
36 144	25 54	41 56	64·1	25 28	40 57	63·6	25 01	39 57	63·2	24 34	38 58	62·8	24 06	38 00	62·4	23 38	37 02	62·0	216 324
37 143	26 34	41 34	63·2	26 07	40 35	62·8	25 39	39 35	62·4	25 11	38 37	61·9	24 43	37 38	61·5	24 14	36 41	61·1	217 323
38 142	27 14	41 11	62·4	26 46	40 12	62·0	26 17	39 13	61·5	25 48	38 14	61·1	25 19	37 16	60·7	24 50	36 19	60·3	218 322
39 141	27 53	40 48	61·5	27 24	39 48	61·1	26 55	38 50	60·6	26 25	37 51	60·2	25 55	36 53	59·8	25 26	35 56	59·4	219 321
40 140	28 32	40 23	60·7	28 02	39 24	60·2	27 32	38 25	59·8	27 02	37 27	59·3	26 31	36 30	58·9	26 00	35 33	58·5	220 320
41 139	29 11	39 58	59·8	28 40	38 59	59·3	28 10	38 01	58·9	27 38	37 03	58·4	27 07	36 05	58·0	26 35	35 08	57·6	221 319
42 138	29 49	39 32	58·9	29 18	38 33	58·4	28 46	37 35	58·0	28 14	36 37	57·5	27 42	35 40	57·1	27 09	34 43	56·6	222 318
43 137	30 27	39 05	58·0	29 55	38 06	57·5	29 23	37 08	57·1	28 50	36 11	56·6	28 17	35 14	56·1	27 43	34 18	55·7	223 317
44 136	31 05	38 37	57·1	30 32	37 39	56·6	29 59	36 41	56·2	29 25	35 44	55·7	28 51	34 47	55·2	28 17	33 51	54·8	224 316
45 135	31 42	38 09	56·2	31 08	37 10	55·7	30 34	36 13	55·2	30 00	35 16	54·7	29 25	34 20	54·3	28 50	33 24	53·8	225 315

Lat./A	LHA/F	42° A/H	42° B/P	42° Z_1/Z_2	43° A/H	43° B/P	43° Z_1/Z_2	44° A/H	44° B/P	44° Z_1/Z_2	45° A/H	45° B/P	45° Z_1/Z_2	46° A/H	46° B/P	46° Z_1/Z_2	47° A/H	47° B/P	47° Z_1/Z_2	Lat./A	LHA
135	45	31 42	38 09	56·2	31 08	37 10	55·7	30 34	36 13	55·2	30 00	35 16	54·7	29 25	34 20	54·3	28 50	33 24	53·8	225	315
134	46	32 19	37 39	55·3	31 45	36 41	54·8	31 11	35 44	54·3	30 34	34 47	53·8	29 59	33 51	53·3	29 23	32 56	52·9	226	314
133	47	32 55	37 08	54·3	32 20	36 11	53·8	31 45	35 14	53·3	31 08	34 18	52·8	30 32	33 22	52·4	29 55	32 27	51·9	227	313
132	48	33 31	36 37	53·4	32 55	35 40	52·9	32 19	34 43	52·3	31 42	33 47	51·9	31 05	32 52	51·4	30 27	31 58	50·9	228	312
131	49	34 07	36 05	52·4	33 30	35 08	51·9	32 53	34 11	51·4	32 15	33 16	50·9	31 37	32 22	50·4	30 59	31 27	49·9	229	311
130	50	34 42	35 31	51·4	34 04	34 35	50·9	33 26	33 39	50·4	32 48	32 44	49·9	32 09	31 50	49·4	31 30	30 56	48·9	230	310
129	51	35 17	34 57	50·4	34 38	34 01	49·9	33 59	33 05	49·4	33 20	32 11	48·9	32 40	31 17	48·4	32 00	30 24	47·9	231	309
128	52	35 51	34 22	49·4	35 12	33 26	48·9	34 30	32 31	48·4	33 52	31 37	47·9	33 11	30 44	47·4	32 30	29 52	46·9	232	308
127	53	36 24	33 45	48·4	35 44	32 50	47·9	35 04	31 56	47·3	34 23	31 02	46·8	33 42	30 10	46·3	33 00	29 18	45·9	233	307
126	54	36 57	33 08	47·4	36 17	32 13	46·8	35 35	31 20	46·3	34 54	30 27	45·8	34 12	29 35	45·3	33 29	28 44	44·8	234	306
125	55	37 30	32 30	46·3	36 48	31 36	45·8	36 07	30 43	45·2	35 24	29 50	44·7	34 41	28 59	44·2	33 58	28 08	43·8	235	305
124	56	38 02	31 51	45·2	37 19	30 57	44·7	36 37	30 04	44·2	35 53	29 13	43·6	35 10	28 22	43·2	34 26	27 32	42·7	236	304
123	57	38 33	31 10	44·1	37 50	30 17	43·6	37 06	29 25	43·1	36 22	28 34	42·6	35 38	27 45	42·1	34 53	26 56	41·6	237	303
122	58	39 04	30 29	43·0	38 20	29 36	42·5	37 36	28 45	42·0	36 51	27 55	41·5	36 06	27 06	41·0	35 20	26 18	40·5	238	302
121	59	39 34	29 46	41·9	38 49	28 55	41·4	38 04	28 04	40·9	37 19	27 15	40·4	36 33	26 27	39·9	35 46	25 39	39·4	239	301
120	60	40 04	29 03	40·8	39 18	28 13	40·2	38 31	27 22	39·7	37 46	26 34	39·2	36 59	25 46	38·8	36 12	25 00	38·3	240	300
119	61	40 32	28 18	39·6	39 46	27 28	39·1	38 59	26 39	38·6	38 12	25 52	38·1	37 25	25 05	37·6	36 37	24 20	37·2	241	299
118	62	41 00	27 32	38·5	40 13	26 43	37·9	39 26	25 56	37·4	38 38	25 09	36·9	37 50	24 23	36·5	37 02	23 39	36·0	242	298
117	63	41 28	26 45	37·3	40 40	25 58	36·8	39 52	25 11	36·3	39 03	24 25	35·8	38 14	23 40	35·3	37 25	22 57	34·9	243	297
116	64	41 54	25 58	36·1	41 06	25 11	35·6	40 17	24 25	35·1	39 28	23 40	34·6	38 38	22 57	34·1	37 48	22 14	33·7	244	296
115	65	42 20	25 09	34·9	41 31	24 23	34·4	40 41	23 38	33·9	39 51	22 54	33·4	39 01	22 12	33·0	38 11	21 31	32·5	245	295
114	66	42 45	24 19	33·6	41 55	23 34	33·1	41 05	22 50	32·7	40 14	22 08	32·2	39 23	21 27	31·8	38 33	20 46	31·3	246	294
113	67	43 10	23 28	32·4	42 19	22 44	31·9	41 28	22 02	31·4	40 37	21 21	31·0	39 45	20 40	30·5	38 53	20 01	30·1	247	293
112	68	43 33	22 35	31·1	42 42	21 53	30·6	41 50	21 12	30·2	40 58	20 32	29·7	40 06	19 53	29·3	39 13	19 15	28·9	248	292
111	69	43 56	21 42	29·8	43 04	21 01	29·4	42 12	20 22	28·9	41 18	19 43	28·5	40 26	19 05	28·1	39 33	18 29	27·7	249	291
110	70	44 18	20 48	28·5	43 25	20 08	28·1	42 32	19 30	27·7	41 38	18 53	27·2	40 45	18 17	26·8	39 50	17 41	26·5	250	290
109	71	44 38	19 53	27·2	43 45	19 15	26·8	42 51	18 38	26·4	41 57	18 02	26·0	41 03	17 27	25·6	40 09	16 53	25·2	251	289
108	72	44 58	18 57	25·9	44 04	18 20	25·5	43 10	17 45	25·1	42 16	17 10	24·7	41 21	16 37	24·3	40 26	16 05	24·0	252	288
107	73	45 17	17 59	24·6	44 23	17 24	24·1	43 28	16 51	23·8	42 33	16 18	23·4	41 38	15 46	23·0	40 42	15 15	22·7	253	287
106	74	45 35	17 01	23·2	44 40	16 28	22·8	43 45	15 56	22·4	42 49	15 25	22·1	41 54	14 54	21·7	40 58	14 25	21·4	254	286
105	75	45 53	16 02	21·8	44 57	15 31	21·4	44 01	15 00	21·1	43 05	14 31	20·8	42 09	14 02	20·4	41 12	13 34	20·1	255	285
104	76	46 09	15 02	20·4	45 12	14 33	20·1	44 16	14 04	19·7	43 19	13 36	19·4	42 23	13 09	19·1	41 26	12 43	18·8	256	284
103	77	46 24	14 02	19·0	45 27	13 34	18·7	44 30	13 07	18·4	43 32	12 41	18·1	42 36	12 15	17·8	41 39	11 51	17·5	257	283
102	78	46 38	13 00	17·6	45 40	12 34	17·3	44 43	12 09	17·0	43 46	11 45	16·7	42 48	11 21	16·5	41 51	10 58	16·2	258	282
101	79	46 51	11 58	16·2	45 53	11 34	15·9	44 55	11 11	15·6	43 57	10 48	15·4	43 00	10 26	15·1	42 02	10 05	14·9	259	281
100	80	47 03	10 55	14·8	46 04	10 33	14·5	45 06	10 12	14·2	44 08	9 51	14·0	43 12	9 30	13·8	42 12	9 12	13·6	260	280
99	81	47 13	9 51	13·3	46 15	9 31	13·1	45 16	9 12	12·8	44 18	8 53	12·6	43 19	8 35	12·4	42 21	8 18	12·2	261	279
98	82	47 23	8 47	11·9	46 24	8 29	11·6	45 26	8 12	11·4	44 27	7 55	11·2	43 28	7 39	11·1	42 29	7 24	10·9	262	278
97	83	47 32	7 42	10·4	46 33	7 27	10·2	45 34	7 11	10·0	44 34	6 57	9·9	43 35	6 43	9·7	42 36	6 29	9·5	263	277
96	84	47 39	6 37	8·9	46 40	6 24	8·8	45 41	6 09	8·6	44 41	5 58	8·5	43 42	5 46	8·3	42 42	5 34	8·2	264	276
95	85	47 46	5 32	7·4	46 46	5 21	7·3	45 46	5 08	7·1	44 47	4 59	7·1	43 48	4 49	6·9	42 48	4 39	6·8	265	275
94	86	47 51	4 26	6·0	46 51	4 17	5·9	45 51	4 06	5·7	44 52	3 59	5·6	43 52	3 51	5·6	42 52	3 43	5·5	266	274
93	87	47 55	3 20	4·5	46 55	3 13	4·4	45 55	3 06	4·3	44 55	3 00	4·2	43 55	2 54	4·2	42 56	2 48	4·1	267	273
92	88	47 58	2 13	3·0	46 58	2 09	3·0	45 58	2 04	2·9	44 58	2 00	2·8	43 58	1 56	2·8	42 58	1 52	2·7	268	272
91	89	47 59	1 07	1·5	46 59	1 04	1·5	45 59	1 02	1·4	44 59	1 00	1·4	43 59	0 58	1·4	43 00	0 56	1·4	269	271
90	90	48 00	0 00	0·0	47 00	0 00	0·0	46 00	0 00	0·0	45 00	0 00	0·0	44 00	0 00	0·0	43 00	0 00	0·0	270	270

N. Lat.: for LHA > 180° .... $Z_n = Z$
for LHA < 180° .... $Z_n = 360° − Z$

S. Lat.: for LHA > 180° .... $Z_n = 180° − Z$
for LHA < 180° .... $Z_n = 180° + Z$

B: (–) for 90° < LHA < 270°
Dec:(–) for Lat. contrary name

Z₁: same sign as B
Z₂: (–) for F > 90°

SIGHT REDUCTION TABLE

LHA/F	F	48° A/H	48° B/P	48° Z_1/Z_2	49° A/H	49° B/P	49° Z_1/Z_2	50° A/H	50° B/P	50° Z_1/Z_2	51° A/H	51° B/P	51° Z_1/Z_2	52° A/H	52° B/P	52° Z_1/Z_2	53° A/H	53° B/P	53° Z_1/Z_2	LHA
0	180	0 00	42 00	90·0	0 00	41 00	90·0	0 00	40 00	90·0	0 00	39 00	90·0	0 00	38 00	90·0	0 00	37 00	90·0	180
1	179	0 40	42 00	89·3	0 39	41 00	89·3	0 39	40 00	89·2	0 38	39 00	89·2	0 37	38 00	89·2	0 36	37 00	89·2	181
2	178	1 20	41 59	88·5	1 19	40 59	88·5	1 17	39 59	88·5	1 16	38 59	88·4	1 14	37 59	88·4	1 12	36 59	88·4	182
3	177	2 00	41 58	87·8	1 58	40 58	87·8	1 56	39 58	87·7	1 53	38 58	87·7	1 51	37 58	87·6	1 48	36 58	87·6	183
4	176	2 41	41 56	87·0	2 37	40 56	87·0	2 34	39 56	87·0	2 31	38 56	86·9	2 28	37 56	86·8	2 24	36 56	86·8	184
5	175	3 21	41 53	86·3	3 17	40 54	86·3	3 13	39 54	86·2	3 09	38 54	86·1	3 05	37 54	86·1	3 00	36 54	86·0	185
6	174	4 01	41 51	85·5	3 56	40 51	85·5	3 51	39 51	85·4	3 46	38 51	85·3	3 41	37 51	85·3	3 36	36 51	85·2	186
7	173	4 41	41 47	84·8	4 35	40 47	84·7	4 30	39 47	84·6	4 24	38 47	84·5	4 18	37 48	84·5	4 12	36 48	84·4	187
8	172	5 21	41 43	84·0	5 14	40 43	84·0	5 08	39 43	83·9	5 01	38 44	83·8	4 55	37 44	83·7	4 48	36 44	83·7	188
9	171	6 01	41 39	83·3	5 53	40 39	83·2	5 46	39 39	83·2	5 39	38 39	83·0	5 32	37 39	82·9	5 24	36 40	82·9	189
10	170	6 40	41 34	82·5	6 32	40 34	82·5	6 25	39 34	82·4	6 16	38 34	82·2	6 09	37 35	82·1	6 00	36 35	82·0	190
11	169	7 20	41 28	81·8	7 11	40 28	81·8	7 03	39 29	81·7	6 54	38 29	81·4	6 45	37 29	81·3	6 36	36 29	81·2	191
12	168	8 00	41 22	81·0	7 50	40 22	81·0	7 41	39 23	80·9	7 31	38 23	80·6	7 21	37 23	80·5	7 11	36 24	80·4	192
13	167	8 39	41 16	80·3	8 29	40 16	80·3	8 19	39 16	80·1	8 08	38 16	79·8	7 58	37 17	79·7	7 47	36 16	79·6	193
14	166	9 19	41 09	79·5	9 08	40 09	79·5	8 57	39 09	79·3	8 45	38 09	79·0	8 34	37 10	78·9	8 22	36 10	78·7	194
15	165	9 58	41 01	78·7	9 47	40 01	78·7	9 35	39 02	78·6	9 22	38 02	78·2	9 10	37 02	78·1	8 58	36 03	77·9	195
16	164	10 38	40 53	78·0	10 25	39 53	78·0	10 12	38 53	77·8	9 59	37 54	77·4	9 46	36 54	77·3	9 33	35 55	77·1	196
17	163	11 17	40 44	77·2	11 04	39 44	77·2	10 50	38 45	77·0	10 36	37 45	76·6	10 22	36 46	76·5	10 08	35 47	76·3	197
18	162	11 56	40 34	76·4	11 42	39 35	76·4	11 27	38 35	76·2	11 13	37 36	75·8	10 58	36 37	75·6	10 43	35 38	75·5	198
19	161	12 35	40 25	75·6	12 20	39 25	75·6	12 05	38 26	75·4	11 49	37 26	75·0	11 34	36 27	74·8	11 18	35 28	74·6	199
20	160	13 14	40 14	74·9	12 58	39 15	74·9	12 42	38 15	74·6	12 26	37 16	74·2	12 09	36 17	74·0	11 53	35 18	73·8	200
21	159	13 52	40 03	74·1	13 36	39 04	74·1	13 19	38 04	73·8	13 02	37 05	73·4	12 45	36 06	73·2	12 27	35 08	73·0	201
22	158	14 31	39 51	73·3	14 14	38 52	73·3	13 56	37 53	73·0	13 38	36 54	72·6	13 20	35 55	72·3	13 02	34 56	72·1	202
23	157	15 09	39 39	72·5	14 51	38 40	72·5	14 33	37 41	72·2	14 14	36 42	71·7	13 55	35 43	71·5	13 36	34 45	71·3	203
24	156	15 48	39 26	71·7	15 29	38 27	71·7	15 09	37 28	71·4	14 50	36 30	70·9	14 30	35 31	70·7	14 10	34 33	70·4	204
25	155	16 26	39 13	70·9	16 06	38 14	70·8	15 46	37 15	70·6	15 25	36 17	70·1	15 05	35 18	69·8	14 44	34 20	69·6	205
26	154	17 03	38 59	70·1	16 43	38 00	70·1	16 22	37 01	69·8	16 01	36 03	69·2	15 39	35 05	69·0	15 18	34 07	68·7	206
27	153	17 41	38 44	69·3	17 20	37 46	69·3	16 58	36 47	69·0	16 36	35 49	68·4	16 14	34 51	68·1	15 51	33 53	67·9	207
28	152	18 19	38 29	68·4	17 56	37 30	68·4	17 34	36 32	68·1	17 11	35 34	67·5	16 48	34 36	67·3	16 25	33 38	67·0	208
29	151	18 56	38 13	67·6	18 33	37 15	67·6	18 09	36 16	67·3	17 46	35 18	66·7	17 22	34 21	66·4	16 58	33 23	66·1	209
30	150	19 33	37 57	66·8	19 09	36 58	66·8	18 45	36 00	66·5	18 20	35 03	65·8	17 56	34 05	65·5	17 31	33 08	65·2	210
31	149	20 10	37 40	65·9	19 45	36 41	65·9	19 20	35 44	65·6	18 55	34 46	65·0	18 29	33 49	64·7	18 03	32 52	64·3	211
32	148	20 46	37 22	65·1	20 21	36 24	65·1	19 55	35 26	64·8	19 29	34 29	64·1	19 02	33 32	63·8	18 36	32 35	63·5	212
33	147	21 22	37 03	64·2	20 56	36 06	64·2	20 30	35 08	63·9	20 03	34 11	63·2	19 35	33 14	62·9	19 08	32 18	62·6	213
34	146	21 58	36 44	63·4	21 31	35 47	63·4	21 04	34 49	63·0	20 36	33 53	62·3	20 08	32 56	62·0	19 40	32 00	61·7	214
35	145	22 34	36 25	62·5	22 06	35 27	62·5	21 38	34 30	62·1	21 10	33 33	61·4	20 41	32 37	61·1	20 12	31 41	60·8	215
36	144	23 10	36 04	61·6	22 41	35 07	61·6	22 12	34 10	61·3	21 43	33 14	60·5	21 13	32 18	60·2	20 43	31 22	59·9	216
37	143	23 45	35 43	60·8	23 15	34 46	60·8	22 45	33 50	60·4	22 15	32 53	59·6	21 45	31 57	59·3	21 15	31 02	59·0	217
38	142	24 20	35 21	59·9	23 49	34 25	59·9	23 19	33 28	59·5	22 48	32 33	58·7	22 16	31 37	58·4	21 45	30 42	58·0	218
39	141	24 54	34 59	59·0	24 23	34 03	59·0	23 52	33 07	58·6	23 20	32 11	57·8	22 48	31 16	57·5	22 15	30 21	57·1	219
40	140	25 28	34 36	58·1	24 57	33 40	58·1	24 24	32 44	57·7	23 52	31 49	56·9	23 19	30 54	56·5	22 45	30 00	56·2	220
41	139	26 02	34 12	57·1	25 30	33 16	57·1	24 57	32 21	56·7	24 23	31 26	56·0	23 49	30 32	55·6	23 15	29 38	55·2	221
42	138	26 36	33 47	56·2	26 02	32 52	56·2	25 28	31 57	55·8	24 54	31 02	55·0	24 20	30 08	54·6	23 45	29 15	54·3	222
43	137	27 09	33 22	55·3	26 35	32 27	55·3	26 00	31 32	54·9	25 25	30 38	54·1	24 50	29 45	53·7	24 14	28 52	53·3	223
44	136	27 42	32 56	54·3	27 07	32 01	54·3	26 31	31 07	53·9	25 55	30 13	53·1	25 19	29 20	52·7	24 43	28 28	52·4	224
45	135	28 14	32 29	53·4	27 38	31 35	53·4	27 02	30 41	53·0	26 25	29 48	52·1	25 48	28 55	51·8	25 11	28 03	51·4	225

Lat. / A		48°			49°			50°			51°			52°			53°			Lat. / A	
LHA/F		A/H	B/P	Z₁/Z₂	A/H	B/P	Z₁/Z₂	A/H	B/P	Z₁/Z₂	A/H	B/P	Z₁/Z₂	A/H	B/P	Z₁/Z₂	A/H	B/P	Z₁/Z₂	LHA	
°	°	° ′	° ′		° ′	° ′		° ′	° ′		° ′	° ′		° ′	° ′		° ′	° ′		°	°
45	135	28 14	32 29	53.4	27 38	31 35	53.0	27 02	30 41	52.5	26 25	29 48	52.1	25 48	28 55	51.8	25 11	28 03	51.4	225	315
46	134	28 46	32 01	52.4	28 10	31 08	52.0	27 32	30 14	51.6	26 55	29 22	51.2	26 17	28 29	50.8	25 39	27 38	50.4	226	314
47	133	29 18	31 33	51.4	28 40	30 40	51.0	28 02	29 47	50.6	27 25	28 55	50.2	26 46	28 03	49.8	26 07	27 12	49.4	227	313
48	132	29 49	31 04	50.5	29 11	30 11	50.0	28 32	29 19	49.6	27 53	28 27	49.2	27 14	27 36	48.8	26 34	26 46	48.4	228	312
49	131	30 20	30 34	49.5	29 41	29 42	49.0	29 01	28 50	48.6	28 21	27 59	48.2	27 41	27 08	47.8	27 01	26 18	47.4	229	311
50	130	30 50	30 04	48.5	30 10	29 12	48.0	29 30	28 20	47.6	28 49	27 30	47.2	28 08	26 40	46.8	27 27	25 51	46.4	230	310
51	129	31 20	29 32	47.5	30 39	28 41	47.0	29 58	27 50	46.6	29 17	27 00	46.2	28 35	26 11	45.8	27 53	25 22	45.4	231	309
52	128	31 49	29 00	46.4	31 08	28 09	46.0	30 26	27 19	45.6	29 44	26 30	45.2	29 01	25 41	44.8	28 19	24 53	44.4	232	308
53	127	32 18	28 27	45.4	31 36	27 37	45.0	30 53	26 48	44.5	30 10	25 59	44.1	29 27	25 11	43.7	28 44	24 24	43.3	233	307
54	126	32 46	27 53	44.4	32 03	27 04	43.9	31 19	26 15	43.5	30 36	25 27	43.1	29 52	24 40	42.7	29 08	23 53	42.3	234	306
55	125	33 14	27 19	43.3	32 30	26 30	42.9	31 46	25 42	42.4	31 02	24 55	42.0	30 17	24 09	41.6	29 32	23 23	41.2	235	305
56	124	33 42	26 44	42.2	32 57	25 55	41.8	32 12	25 08	41.4	31 27	24 22	41.0	30 41	23 36	40.6	29 56	22 51	40.2	236	304
57	123	34 08	26 07	41.1	33 23	25 20	40.7	32 37	24 34	40.3	31 51	23 48	39.9	31 05	23 03	39.5	30 19	22 19	39.1	237	303
58	122	34 34	25 30	40.0	33 48	24 44	39.6	33 01	23 58	39.2	32 15	23 14	38.8	31 28	22 29	38.4	30 41	21 46	38.0	238	302
59	121	35 00	24 53	39.0	34 13	24 07	38.5	33 26	23 22	38.1	32 39	22 38	37.7	31 51	21 55	37.3	31 03	21 13	37.0	239	301
60	120	35 25	24 14	37.8	34 37	23 30	37.4	33 50	22 46	37.0	33 02	22 03	36.6	32 13	21 20	36.2	31 25	20 39	35.9	240	300
61	119	35 49	23 35	36.7	35 01	22 51	36.3	34 12	22 08	35.9	33 24	21 26	35.5	32 35	20 45	35.1	31 46	20 04	34.8	241	299
62	118	36 13	22 55	35.6	35 24	22 12	35.2	34 35	21 30	34.8	33 45	20 49	34.4	32 56	20 09	34.0	32 06	19 29	33.7	242	298
63	117	36 36	22 14	34.4	35 46	21 32	34.0	34 56	20 51	33.6	34 06	20 11	33.3	33 16	19 32	32.9	32 26	18 53	32.5	243	297
64	116	36 58	21 32	33.3	36 08	20 51	32.9	35 17	20 11	32.5	34 27	19 33	32.1	33 35	18 54	31.8	32 45	18 17	31.4	244	296
65	115	37 20	20 50	32.1	36 29	20 10	31.7	35 38	19 32	31.3	34 47	18 54	31.0	33 55	18 16	30.6	33 03	17 40	30.3	245	295
66	114	37 41	20 07	30.9	36 49	19 28	30.5	35 58	18 52	30.2	35 06	18 14	29.8	34 13	17 38	29.5	33 21	17 02	29.1	246	294
67	113	38 01	19 23	29.7	37 09	18 46	29.4	36 17	18 09	29.0	35 24	17 33	28.6	34 31	16 59	28.3	33 38	16 24	28.0	247	293
68	112	38 21	18 38	28.5	37 28	18 02	28.2	36 35	17 27	27.8	35 42	16 53	27.5	34 48	16 19	27.1	33 55	15 46	26.8	248	292
69	111	38 40	17 53	27.3	37 46	17 18	27.0	36 53	16 43	26.6	35 59	16 11	26.3	35 05	15 38	26.0	34 11	15 07	25.7	249	291
70	110	38 58	17 07	26.1	38 04	16 33	25.7	37 09	16 01	25.4	36 15	15 29	25.1	35 21	14 58	24.8	34 26	14 27	24.5	250	290
71	109	39 15	16 20	24.9	38 20	15 48	24.5	37 26	15 17	24.2	36 31	14 46	23.9	35 36	14 16	23.6	34 41	13 47	23.3	251	289
72	108	39 31	15 33	23.6	38 36	15 02	23.3	37 41	14 32	23.0	36 46	14 03	22.7	35 50	13 34	22.4	34 55	13 06	22.1	252	288
73	107	39 47	14 45	22.4	38 51	14 16	22.1	37 56	13 47	21.8	37 00	13 19	21.5	36 04	12 52	21.2	35 08	12 25	20.9	253	287
74	106	40 02	13 56	21.1	39 06	13 28	20.8	38 10	13 01	20.5	37 13	12 35	20.3	36 17	12 09	20.0	35 21	11 44	19.8	254	286
75	105	40 16	13 07	19.8	39 19	12 41	19.5	38 23	12 15	19.3	37 26	11 50	19.0	36 29	11 26	18.8	35 33	11 02	18.3	255	285
76	104	40 29	12 17	18.5	39 32	11 53	18.3	38 35	11 28	18.0	37 38	11 05	17.8	36 41	10 42	17.6	35 44	10 20	17.3	256	284
77	103	40 41	11 27	17.3	39 44	11 04	17.0	38 47	10 41	16.8	37 49	10 19	16.5	36 52	9 58	16.3	35 54	9 37	16.1	257	283
78	102	40 53	10 36	16.0	39 55	10 15	15.7	38 57	9 54	15.5	38 00	9 33	15.3	37 02	9 14	15.1	36 04	8 54	14.9	258	282
79	101	41 04	9 45	14.7	40 05	9 25	14.4	39 07	9 06	14.2	38 09	8 47	14.0	37 11	8 29	13.9	36 13	8 11	13.7	259	281
80	100	41 13	8 53	13.3	40 15	8 53	13.2	39 16	8 17	13.0	38 18	8 00	12.8	37 19	7 44	12.6	36 21	7 27	12.5	260	280
81	99	41 22	8 01	12.0	40 23	7 45	11.9	39 25	7 29	11.7	38 26	7 13	11.5	37 27	6 58	11.4	36 28	6 43	11.2	261	279
82	98	41 30	7 09	10.7	40 31	6 54	10.5	39 32	6 40	10.4	38 33	6 26	10.3	37 34	6 12	10.1	36 35	5 59	10.0	262	278
83	97	41 37	6 16	9.4	40 38	6 03	9.2	39 39	5 50	9.1	38 40	5 38	9.0	37 40	5 26	8.9	36 41	5 15	8.7	263	277
84	96	41 43	5 23	8.1	40 44	5 12	7.9	39 44	5 01	7.8	38 45	4 50	7.7	37 45	4 40	7.6	36 46	4 30	7.5	264	276
85	95	41 48	4 29	6.7	40 49	4 20	6.6	39 49	4 11	6.5	38 49	4 02	6.4	37 50	3 54	6.3	36 50	3 45	6.3	265	275
86	94	41 52	3 36	5.4	40 53	3 28	5.3	39 53	3 21	5.2	38 53	3 14	5.1	37 53	3 07	5.1	36 54	3 01	5.0	266	274
87	93	41 56	2 42	4.0	40 56	2 36	4.0	39 56	2 31	3.9	38 56	2 26	3.9	37 56	2 20	3.8	36 56	2 16	3.8	267	273
88	92	41 58	1 48	2.7	40 58	1 44	2.6	39 58	1 41	2.6	38 58	1 37	2.6	37 58	1 34	2.5	36 58	1 30	2.5	268	272
89	91	42 00	0 54	1.3	41 00	0 52	1.3	40 00	0 50	1.3	39 00	0 49	1.3	38 00	0 47	1.3	37 00	0 00	1.3	269	271
90	90	42 00	0 00	0.0	41 00	0 00	0.0	40 00	0 00	0.0	39 00	0 00	0.0	38 00	0 00	0.0	37 00	0 00	0.0	270	270

N. Lat.: for LHA > 180° ... $Z_n = Z$
for LHA < 180° ... $Z_n = 360° - Z$

S. Lat.: for LHA > 180° ... $Z_n = 180° - Z$
for LHA < 180° ... $Z_n = 180° + Z$

B: (−) for 90° < LHA < 270°
Dec: (−) for Lat. contrary name

Z₁: same sign as B
Z₂: (−) for F > 90°

SIGHT REDUCTION TABLE

LHA/F	54° A/H	54° B/P	54° Z₁/Z₂	55° A/H	55° B/P	55° Z₁/Z₂	56° A/H	56° B/P	56° Z₁/Z₂	57° A/H	57° B/P	57° Z₁/Z₂	58° A/H	58° B/P	58° Z₁/Z₂	59° A/H	59° B/P	59° Z₁/Z₂	LHA	LHA
180	0 00	36 00	90.0	0 00	35 00	90.0	0 00	34 00	90.0	0 00	33 00	90.0	0 00	32 00	90.0	0 00	31 00	90.0	360	180
179	0 35	36 00	89.2	0 34	35 00	89.2	0 34	34 00	89.2	0 33	33 00	89.2	0 32	32 00	89.2	0 31	31 00	89.1	359	181
178	1 11	35 59	88.4	1 09	34 59	88.4	1 07	33 59	88.3	1 05	32 59	88.3	1 04	31 59	88.3	1 02	30 59	88.3	358	182
177	1 46	35 58	87.6	1 43	34 58	87.5	1 41	33 58	87.5	1 38	32 58	87.5	1 35	31 58	87.5	1 33	30 58	87.4	357	183
176	2 21	35 56	86.8	2 18	34 56	86.7	2 14	33 56	86.7	2 11	32 56	86.7	2 07	31 56	86.6	2 04	30 56	86.6	356	184
175	2 56	35 54	86.0	2 52	34 54	85.9	2 48	33 54	85.9	2 43	32 54	85.9	2 39	31 54	85.8	2 34	30 54	85.7	355	185
174	3 31	35 51	85.1	3 26	34 51	85.1	3 21	33 51	85.0	3 16	32 51	85.0	3 11	31 52	84.9	3 05	30 52	84.9	354	186
173	4 06	35 48	84.3	4 00	34 48	84.3	3 54	33 48	84.2	3 48	32 48	84.2	3 42	31 48	84.1	3 36	30 49	84.0	353	187
172	4 42	35 44	83.5	4 35	34 44	83.4	4 28	33 44	83.4	4 21	32 44	83.3	4 14	31 45	83.3	4 07	30 45	83.2	352	188
171	5 17	35 40	82.7	5 09	34 40	82.6	5 01	33 40	82.5	4 53	32 40	82.5	4 45	31 41	82.4	4 37	30 41	82.3	351	189
170	5 51	35 35	81.9	5 43	34 35	81.8	5 34	33 35	81.7	5 26	32 36	81.6	5 17	31 37	81.5	5 08	30 37	81.4	350	190
169	6 26	35 30	81.1	6 17	34 30	81.0	6 08	33 31	80.8	5 58	32 31	80.7	5 48	31 31	80.6	5 38	30 32	80.5	349	191
168	7 01	35 24	80.2	6 51	34 24	80.1	6 41	33 25	80.0	6 30	32 25	79.9	6 20	31 26	79.8	6 09	30 27	79.7	348	192
167	7 36	35 18	79.4	7 25	34 18	79.3	7 14	33 19	79.2	7 02	32 19	79.0	6 51	31 20	78.9	6 39	30 20	78.8	347	193
166	8 11	35 11	78.6	7 59	34 12	78.5	7 46	33 12	78.3	7 34	32 13	78.2	7 22	31 14	78.1	7 09	30 15	77.9	346	194
165	8 45	35 04	77.8	8 32	34 04	77.6	8 19	33 05	77.5	8 06	32 06	77.3	7 53	31 07	77.2	7 40	30 08	77.1	345	195
164	9 19	34 57	76.9	9 06	33 57	76.8	8 52	32 58	76.6	8 38	31 58	76.5	8 24	31 00	76.3	8 10	30 01	76.2	344	196
163	9 54	34 47	76.1	9 39	33 48	75.9	9 25	32 49	75.8	9 10	31 50	75.6	8 55	30 52	75.5	8 40	29 53	75.3	343	197
162	10 28	34 39	75.3	10 13	33 40	75.1	9 57	32 41	74.9	9 41	31 42	74.8	9 25	30 43	74.6	9 09	29 45	74.4	342	198
161	11 02	34 30	74.4	10 46	33 30	74.2	10 29	32 32	74.1	10 13	31 33	73.9	9 56	30 35	73.7	9 39	29 36	73.6	341	199
160	11 36	34 19	73.6	11 19	33 21	73.4	11 02	32 22	73.2	10 44	31 24	73.0	10 27	30 25	72.8	10 09	29 27	72.7	340	200
159	12 10	34 09	72.7	11 52	33 10	72.5	11 34	32 12	72.3	11 15	31 14	72.2	10 57	30 16	72.0	10 38	29 17	71.8	339	201
158	12 43	33 58	71.9	12 24	33 00	71.7	12 06	32 01	71.5	11 46	31 03	71.3	11 27	30 05	71.1	11 07	29 07	70.9	338	202
157	13 17	33 46	71.0	12 57	32 48	70.8	12 37	31 50	70.6	12 17	30 52	70.4	11 57	29 54	70.2	11 37	28 57	70.0	337	203
156	13 50	33 34	70.2	13 29	32 36	70.0	13 09	31 38	69.7	12 48	30 41	69.5	12 27	29 43	69.3	12 06	28 46	69.1	336	204
155	14 23	33 22	69.3	14 01	32 24	69.1	13 40	31 26	68.9	13 18	30 29	68.6	12 56	29 31	68.4	12 34	28 34	68.2	335	205
154	14 56	33 09	68.5	14 34	32 11	68.2	14 11	31 14	68.0	13 49	30 16	67.8	13 26	29 19	67.5	13 03	28 22	67.3	334	206
153	15 29	32 55	67.6	15 05	31 58	67.3	14 42	31 00	67.1	14 19	30 03	66.9	13 55	29 06	66.6	13 31	28 10	66.4	333	207
152	16 01	32 41	66.7	15 37	31 44	66.5	15 13	30 47	66.2	14 49	29 50	66.0	14 24	28 53	65.7	14 00	27 57	65.5	332	208
151	16 33	32 26	65.8	16 09	31 29	65.6	15 44	30 32	65.3	15 19	29 36	65.1	14 53	28 39	64.8	14 28	27 43	64.6	331	209
150	17 05	32 11	65.0	16 40	31 14	64.7	16 14	30 17	64.4	15 48	29 21	64.2	15 22	28 25	63.9	14 55	27 29	63.7	330	210
149	17 37	31 55	64.1	17 11	30 58	63.8	16 44	30 02	63.5	16 17	29 06	63.3	15 50	28 10	63.0	15 23	27 15	62.7	329	211
148	18 09	31 38	63.2	17 42	30 42	62.9	17 14	29 46	62.6	16 47	28 51	62.3	16 19	27 55	62.1	15 50	27 00	61.8	328	212
147	18 40	31 21	62.3	18 12	30 25	62.0	17 44	29 30	61.7	17 15	28 34	61.4	16 47	27 39	61.2	16 17	26 45	60.9	327	213
146	19 11	31 04	61.4	18 42	30 08	61.1	18 13	29 13	60.8	17 44	28 18	60.5	17 14	27 23	60.2	16 44	26 29	60.0	326	214
145	19 42	30 46	60.5	19 12	29 50	60.2	18 42	28 55	59.9	18 12	28 01	59.6	17 42	27 06	59.3	17 11	26 12	59.0	325	215
144	20 13	30 27	59.6	19 42	29 32	59.2	19 11	28 37	58.9	18 40	27 43	58.6	18 09	26 49	58.4	17 37	25 55	58.1	324	216
143	20 43	30 07	58.6	20 12	29 13	58.3	19 40	28 19	58.0	19 08	27 25	57.7	18 36	26 31	57.4	18 03	25 38	57.1	323	217
142	21 13	29 48	57.7	20 41	28 53	57.4	20 08	27 59	57.1	19 35	27 06	56.7	19 02	26 13	56.5	18 29	25 20	56.2	322	218
141	21 43	29 27	56.8	21 10	28 33	56.4	20 36	27 40	56.1	20 03	26 47	55.8	19 29	25 55	55.5	18 55	25 02	55.2	321	219
140	22 12	29 06	55.8	21 38	28 13	55.5	21 04	27 20	55.2	20 30	26 27	54.9	19 55	25 35	54.6	19 20	24 43	54.3	320	220
139	22 41	28 44	54.9	22 06	27 51	54.5	21 31	26 59	54.2	20 56	26 07	53.9	20 21	25 15	53.6	19 45	24 24	53.3	319	221
138	23 10	28 22	53.9	22 34	27 29	53.6	21 58	26 37	53.3	21 23	25 46	52.9	20 46	24 55	52.6	20 10	24 04	52.3	318	222
137	23 38	27 59	53.0	23 02	27 07	52.6	22 25	26 15	52.3	21 48	25 24	52.0	21 11	24 34	51.7	20 34	23 43	51.4	317	223
136	24 06	27 36	52.0	23 29	26 44	51.7	22 51	25 53	51.3	22 14	25 02	51.0	21 36	24 12	50.7	20 58	23 23	50.4	316	224
135	24 34	27 11	51.0	23 56	26 20	50.7	23 17	25 30	50.3	22 39	24 40	50.0	22 00	23 50	49.7	21 21	23 01	49.4	315	225

Top header (right-reading): Lat. / A — 59°, 58°, 57°, 56°, 55°, 54° — Lat. / A (LHA)
Bottom header (left-reading): Lat. / A (LHA/F) — 54°, 55°, 56°, 57°, 58°, 59° — Lat. / A

Each latitude column is given as A/H, B/P, Z_1/Z_2.

A	LHA/F	54° A/H	54° B/P	54° Z_1/Z_2	55° A/H	55° B/P	55° Z_1/Z_2	56° A/H	56° B/P	56° Z_1/Z_2	57° A/H	57° B/P	57° Z_1/Z_2	58° A/H	58° B/P	58° Z_1/Z_2	59° A/H	59° B/P	59° Z_1/Z_2	LHA	A
135	45	24 34	27 11	51·0	23 56	26 20	50·7	23 17	25 30	50·3	22 39	24 40	50·0	22 00	23 50	49·7	21 21	23 01	49·4	225	315
134	46	25 01	26 47	50·0	24 22	25 56	49·7	23 43	25 06	49·4	23 04	24 17	49·0	22 24	23 28	48·7	21 45	22 39	48·4	226	314
133	47	25 28	26 22	49·1	24 48	25 32	48·7	24 08	24 42	48·4	23 28	23 53	48·0	22 48	23 05	47·7	22 08	22 17	47·4	227	313
132	48	25 55	25 56	48·1	25 14	25 06	47·7	24 33	24 17	47·4	23 53	23 29	47·0	23 11	22 41	46·7	22 30	21 54	46·4	228	312
131	49	26 21	25 29	47·1	25 39	24 40	46·7	24 58	23 52	46·4	24 16	23 05	46·0	23 34	22 17	45·7	22 52	21 31	45·4	229	311
130	50	26 46	25 02	46·0	26 04	24 14	45·7	25 22	23 26	45·3	24 40	22 39	45·0	23 57	21 53	44·7	23 14	21 07	44·4	230	310
129	51	27 11	24 34	45·0	26 28	23 47	44·7	25 45	23 00	44·3	25 02	22 14	44·0	24 19	21 28	43·7	23 36	20 43	43·4	231	309
128	52	27 36	24 06	44·0	26 52	23 19	43·6	26 09	22 33	43·3	25 25	21 48	43·0	24 41	21 03	42·7	23 57	20 18	42·3	232	308
127	53	28 00	23 37	43·0	27 16	22 51	42·6	26 32	22 06	42·3	25 47	21 21	41·9	25 02	20 37	41·6	24 17	19 53	41·3	233	307
126	54	28 24	23 07	41·9	27 39	22 22	41·6	26 55	21 38	41·2	26 09	20 54	40·9	25 23	20 10	40·6	24 37	19 27	40·3	234	306
125	55	28 47	22 37	40·9	28 01	21 53	40·5	27 16	21 09	40·2	26 30	20 26	39·9	25 44	19 43	39·5	24 57	19 01	39·2	235	305
124	56	29 10	22 07	39·8	28 24	21 23	39·5	27 37	20 40	39·1	26 50	19 57	38·8	26 04	19 16	38·5	25 17	18 34	38·2	236	304
123	57	29 32	21 35	38·7	28 45	20 52	38·4	27 58	20 10	38·1	27 11	19 29	37·8	26 23	18 48	37·4	25 35	18 07	37·4	237	303
122	58	29 54	21 03	37·7	29 06	20 21	37·3	28 18	19 40	37·0	27 31	18 59	36·7	26 42	18 19	36·4	25 54	17 40	36·1	238	302
121	59	30 15	20 31	36·6	29 27	19 50	36·3	28 38	19 09	35·9	27 50	18 30	35·6	27 01	17 50	35·3	26 12	17 12	35·0	239	301
120	60	30 36	19 58	35·5	29 47	19 18	35·2	28 58	18 38	34·9	28 09	17 59	34·5	27 19	17 21	34·2	26 29	16 43	34·0	240	300
119	61	30 56	19 25	34·4	30 07	18 45	34·1	29 17	18 06	33·8	28 27	17 29	33·5	27 37	16 51	33·2	26 46	16 14	32·9	241	299
118	62	31 16	18 50	33·3	30 26	18 12	33·0	29 35	17 34	32·7	28 45	16 57	32·4	27 54	16 21	32·1	27 03	15 45	31·8	242	298
117	63	31 35	18 15	32·2	30 44	17 38	31·9	29 53	17 02	31·6	29 02	16 26	31·3	28 10	15 50	31·0	27 19	15 15	30·7	243	297
116	64	31 53	17 40	31·1	31 02	17 04	30·8	30 10	16 28	30·5	29 19	15 53	30·2	28 27	15 19	29·9	27 35	14 45	29·6	244	296
115	65	32 11	17 04	30·0	31 19	16 29	29·7	30 27	15 55	29·3	29 35	15 20	29·1	28 42	14 48	28·8	27 50	14 15	28·5	245	295
114	66	32 29	16 28	28·8	31 36	15 54	28·5	30 43	15 20	28·2	29 50	14 48	28·0	28 57	14 16	27·7	28 04	13 44	27·4	246	294
113	67	32 45	15 51	27·7	31 52	15 18	27·3	30 59	14 46	27·1	30 05	14 14	26·8	29 12	13 43	26·6	28 18	13 13	26·3	247	293
112	68	33 01	15 14	26·5	32 08	14 42	26·1	31 14	14 11	26·0	30 20	13 40	25·7	29 26	13 10	25·5	28 31	12 41	25·2	248	292
111	69	33 17	14 36	25·4	32 23	14 05	25·1	31 28	13 35	24·8	30 34	13 06	24·6	29 39	12 37	24·4	28 44	12 09	24·1	249	291
110	70	33 32	13 57	24·2	32 37	13 28	24·0	31 42	12 59	23·7	30 47	12 31	23·5	29 52	12 04	23·2	28 57	11 37	23·0	250	290
109	71	33 46	13 18	23·1	32 51	12 51	22·8	31 56	12 23	22·6	31 00	11 56	22·3	30 04	11 30	22·1	29 09	11 04	21·9	251	289
108	72	33 59	12 39	21·9	33 04	12 13	21·6	32 08	11 46	21·4	31 12	11 21	21·2	30 16	10 56	21·0	29 20	10 31	20·8	252	288
107	73	34 12	12 00	20·7	33 16	11 34	20·5	32 20	11 09	20·3	31 23	10 45	20·0	30 27	10 21	19·8	29 30	9 58	19·6	253	287
106	74	34 24	11 19	19·5	33 28	10 55	19·3	32 31	10 32	19·1	31 34	10 09	18·9	30 37	9 46	18·5	29 41	9 24	18·5	254	286
105	75	34 36	10 39	18·3	33 39	10 16	18·1	32 42	9 54	17·9	31 44	9 32	17·7	30 47	9 11	17·5	29 50	8 50	17·4	255	285
104	76	34 46	9 58	17·1	33 49	9 37	16·9	32 52	9 16	16·7	31 54	8 56	16·6	30 57	8 36	16·4	29 59	8 16	16·2	256	284
103	77	34 56	9 17	15·9	33 59	8 57	15·7	33 01	8 38	15·6	32 03	8 19	15·4	31 05	8 00	15·2	30 07	7 42	15·1	257	283
102	78	35 06	8 35	14·7	34 08	8 17	14·5	33 10	7 59	14·4	32 11	7 41	14·2	31 13	7 24	14·1	30 15	7 07	13·9	258	282
101	79	35 15	7 54	13·5	34 16	7 37	13·3	33 18	7 20	13·2	32 19	7 04	13·0	31 21	6 48	12·9	30 22	6 32	12·8	259	281
100	80	35 22	7 11	12·3	34 24	6 56	12·1	33 25	6 41	12·0	32 26	6 26	11·9	31 27	6 12	11·7	30 29	5 57	11·6	260	280
99	81	35 29	6 29	11·1	34 30	6 15	10·9	33 32	6 01	10·8	32 33	5 48	10·7	31 34	5 35	10·6	30 35	5 22	10·5	261	279
98	82	35 36	5 46	9·9	34 37	5 34	9·7	33 37	5 22	9·6	32 38	5 10	9·5	31 39	4 58	9·4	30 40	4 47	9·3	262	278
97	83	35 41	5 04	8·6	34 42	4 53	8·5	33 43	4 42	8·4	32 43	4 32	8·3	31 43	4 21	8·2	30 45	4 11	8·2	263	277
96	84	35 46	4 21	7·4	34 47	4 11	7·3	33 47	4 02	7·2	32 48	3 53	7·1	31 48	3 44	7·1	30 49	3 36	7·0	264	276
95	85	35 50	3 37	6·2	34 51	3 30	6·1	33 51	3 22	6·0	32 52	3 14	6·0	31 52	3 07	5·9	30 53	3 00	5·8	265	275
94	86	35 54	2 54	4·9	34 54	2 48	4·9	33 54	2 42	4·8	32 55	2 36	4·8	31 55	2 30	4·7	30 55	2 24	4·7	266	274
93	87	35 57	2 11	3·7	34 57	2 06	3·7	33 57	2 01	3·6	32 57	1 57	3·6	31 57	1 52	3·5	30 57	1 48	3·5	267	273
92	88	35 59	1 27	2·5	34 59	1 24	2·4	33 59	1 21	2·4	32 59	1 18	2·4	31 59	1 15	2·4	30 59	1 12	2·3	268	272
91	89	36 00	0 44	1·2	35 00	0 42	1·2	34 00	0 40	1·2	33 00	0 39	1·2	32 00	0 37	1·2	31 00	0 36	1·2	269	271
90	90	36 00	0 00	0·0	35 00	0 00	0·0	34 00	0 00	0·0	33 00	0 00	0·0	32 00	0 00	0·0	31 00	0 00	0·0	270	270

N. Lat.: for LHA > 180° ... $Z_n = Z$
　　　　for LHA < 180° ... $Z_n = 360° − Z$

S. Lat.: for LHA > 180° ... $Z_n = 180° − Z$
　　　　for LHA < 180° ... $Z_n = 180° + Z$

B: (−) for 90° < LHA < 270°
Dec:(−) for Lat. contrary name

Z1: same sign as B
Z2:(−) for F > 90°

SIGHT REDUCTION TABLE

LHA/F	Lat./A	60° A/H	60° B/P	60° Z1/Z2	61° A/H	61° B/P	61° Z1/Z2	62° A/H	62° B/P	62° Z1/Z2	63° A/H	63° B/P	63° Z1/Z2	64° A/H	64° B/P	64° Z1/Z2	65° A/H	65° B/P	65° Z1/Z2	Lat./A	LHA
0	180	0 00	30 00	90·0	0 00	29 00	90·0	0 00	28 00	90·0	0 00	27 00	90·0	0 00	26 00	90·0	0 00	25 00	90·0	180	360
1	179	0 30	30 00	89·1	0 30	29 00	89·1	0 28	28 00	89·1	0 27	27 00	89·1	0 26	26 00	89·1	0 25	25 00	89·1	181	359
2	178	1 00	29 59	88·3	0 58	28 59	88·3	0 56	27 59	88·2	0 54	26 59	88·2	0 53	25 59	88·2	0 51	24 59	88·2	182	358
3	177	1 30	29 58	87·4	1 27	28 58	87·4	1 24	27 58	87·4	1 22	26 58	87·3	1 19	25 58	87·3	1 16	24 58	87·3	183	357
4	176	2 00	29 56	86·5	1 56	28 56	86·5	1 53	27 57	86·5	1 49	26 57	86·4	1 45	25 57	86·4	1 41	24 57	86·4	184	356
5	175	2 30	29 54	85·7	2 25	28 54	85·6	2 21	27 55	85·6	2 16	26 55	85·5	2 11	25 55	85·5	2 07	24 55	85·5	185	355
6	174	3 00	29 52	84·8	2 54	28 52	84·7	2 49	27 52	84·7	2 43	26 52	84·6	2 38	25 53	84·6	2 32	24 53	84·6	186	354
7	173	3 30	29 49	83·9	3 23	28 49	83·9	3 17	27 49	83·8	3 10	26 50	83·8	3 04	25 50	83·7	2 57	24 50	83·7	187	353
8	172	3 59	29 45	83·1	3 52	28 46	83·0	3 45	27 46	83·0	3 37	26 46	82·9	3 30	25 47	82·8	3 22	24 47	82·7	188	352
9	171	4 29	29 42	82·2	4 21	28 42	82·1	4 13	27 42	82·0	4 04	26 43	82·0	3 56	25 43	81·9	3 47	24 44	81·8	189	351
10	170	4 59	29 37	81·3	4 50	28 38	81·2	4 41	27 38	81·2	4 31	26 39	81·1	4 22	25 39	81·0	4 13	24 40	80·9	190	350
11	169	5 28	29 33	80·4	5 18	28 33	80·4	5 08	27 34	80·3	4 58	26 34	80·2	4 48	25 35	80·1	4 38	24 36	80·0	191	349
12	168	5 58	29 27	79·6	5 47	28 28	79·5	5 36	27 29	79·4	5 25	26 29	79·3	5 14	25 30	79·2	5 02	24 31	79·1	192	348
13	167	6 27	29 22	78·7	6 16	28 22	78·6	6 04	27 23	78·5	5 52	26 24	78·4	5 40	25 25	78·3	5 27	24 26	78·2	193	347
14	166	6 57	29 15	77·8	6 44	28 16	77·8	6 31	27 17	77·6	6 19	26 18	77·5	6 05	25 20	77·4	5 52	24 21	77·2	194	346
15	165	7 26	29 09	76·9	7 13	28 10	76·9	6 59	27 11	76·7	6 45	26 12	76·6	6 31	25 14	76·5	6 17	24 15	76·4	195	345
16	164	7 55	29 02	76·1	7 41	28 03	76·0	7 26	27 04	75·8	7 11	26 06	75·7	6 56	25 07	75·5	6 41	24 09	75·4	196	344
17	163	8 24	28 54	75·2	8 09	27 56	75·0	7 53	26 57	74·9	7 38	25 59	74·8	7 22	25 00	74·6	7 06	24 02	74·5	197	343
18	162	8 53	28 46	74·3	8 37	27 48	74·1	8 20	26 50	74·0	8 04	25 51	73·9	7 47	24 53	73·7	7 30	23 55	73·6	198	342
19	161	9 22	28 38	73·4	9 05	27 40	73·2	8 48	26 41	73·1	8 30	25 43	72·9	8 12	24 45	72·8	7 55	23 47	72·7	199	341
20	160	9 51	28 29	72·5	9 33	27 31	72·3	9 14	26 33	72·2	8 56	25 35	72·0	8 37	24 37	71·9	8 19	23 40	71·7	200	340
21	159	10 19	28 20	71·6	10 00	27 22	71·4	9 41	26 24	71·3	9 22	25 26	71·1	9 02	24 29	71·0	8 43	23 32	70·8	201	339
22	158	10 48	28 10	70·7	10 28	27 12	70·5	10 08	26 15	70·4	9 48	25 17	70·2	9 27	24 20	70·0	9 07	23 23	69·9	202	338
23	157	11 16	27 59	69·8	10 55	27 02	69·6	10 34	26 05	69·5	10 13	25 08	69·3	9 52	24 11	69·1	9 30	23 14	69·0	203	337
24	156	11 44	27 49	68·9	11 22	26 51	68·7	11 00	25 54	68·5	10 38	24 58	68·4	10 16	24 01	68·2	9 54	23 04	68·0	204	336
25	155	12 12	27 37	68·0	11 49	26 40	67·8	11 27	25 44	67·6	11 04	24 47	67·4	10 41	23 51	67·3	10 17	22 55	67·1	205	335
26	154	12 40	27 26	67·1	12 16	26 29	66·9	11 53	25 33	66·7	11 29	24 36	66·5	11 05	23 40	66·3	10 41	22 44	66·2	206	334
27	153	13 07	27 13	66·2	12 43	26 17	66·0	12 18	25 21	65·8	11 54	24 25	65·6	11 29	23 29	65·4	11 04	22 34	65·2	207	333
28	152	13 35	27 01	65·3	13 09	26 05	65·1	12 44	25 09	64·9	12 18	24 13	64·7	11 53	23 18	64·5	11 27	22 23	64·3	208	332
29	151	14 02	26 48	64·4	13 36	25 52	64·1	13 09	24 56	63·9	12 43	24 01	63·7	12 16	23 06	63·5	11 49	22 11	63·3	209	331
30	150	14 29	26 34	63·4	14 02	25 39	63·2	13 35	24 43	63·0	13 07	23 49	62·8	12 40	22 54	62·6	12 12	21 59	62·4	210	330
31	149	14 55	26 20	62·5	14 28	25 25	62·3	14 00	24 30	62·1	13 31	23 36	61·8	13 03	22 42	61·6	12 34	21 47	61·4	211	329
32	148	15 22	26 05	61·6	14 53	25 11	61·3	14 24	24 16	61·1	13 55	23 22	60·9	13 26	22 28	60·7	12 56	21 35	60·5	212	328
33	147	15 48	25 50	60·6	15 19	24 56	60·4	14 49	24 02	60·2	14 19	23 08	59·9	13 49	22 15	59·7	13 18	21 22	59·5	213	327
34	146	16 14	25 35	59·7	15 44	24 41	59·5	15 13	23 47	59·2	14 42	22 54	59·0	14 11	22 01	58·8	13 40	21 08	58·6	214	326
35	145	16 40	25 19	58·8	16 09	24 25	58·5	15 37	23 32	58·3	15 06	22 39	58·0	14 34	21 47	57·8	14 02	20 54	57·6	215	325
36	144	17 05	25 02	57·8	16 33	24 09	57·6	16 01	23 17	57·3	15 29	22 24	57·1	14 56	21 32	56·9	14 23	20 40	56·6	216	324
37	143	17 31	24 45	56·9	16 58	23 53	56·6	16 24	23 00	56·4	15 51	22 09	56·1	15 18	21 17	55·9	14 44	20 25	55·7	217	323
38	142	17 56	24 28	55·9	17 22	23 36	55·7	16 48	22 44	55·4	16 14	21 53	55·2	15 39	21 01	54·9	15 05	20 11	54·7	218	322
39	141	18 20	24 10	55·0	17 46	23 18	54·7	17 11	22 27	54·4	16 36	21 37	54·2	16 01	20 46	54·0	15 25	19 55	53·7	219	321
40	140	18 45	23 52	54·0	18 09	23 00	53·7	17 34	22 10	53·5	16 58	21 19	53·2	16 22	20 29	53·0	15 46	19 39	52·7	220	320
41	139	19 09	23 33	53·0	18 33	22 42	52·8	17 56	21 52	52·5	17 20	21 02	52·2	16 43	20 13	52·0	16 06	19 23	51·8	221	319
42	138	19 33	23 13	52·1	18 56	22 23	51·8	18 19	21 34	51·5	17 41	20 44	51·3	17 03	19 55	51·0	16 26	19 07	50·8	222	318
43	137	19 56	22 53	51·1	19 18	22 03	50·8	18 40	21 15	50·5	18 02	20 26	50·3	17 24	19 38	50·0	16 45	18 50	49·8	223	317
44	136	20 19	22 33	50·1	19 41	21 44	49·8	19 02	20 56	49·5	18 23	20 08	49·3	17 44	19 20	49·0	17 04	18 33	48·8	224	316
45	135	20 42	22 12	49·1	20 03	21 24	48·8	19 23	20 36	48·6	18 43	19 49	48·3	18 03	19 02	48·1	17 23	18 15	47·8	225	315

Lat./A LHA	F	60° A/H	60° B/P	60° Z₁/Z₂	61° A/H	61° B/P	61° Z₁/Z₂	62° A/H	62° B/P	62° Z₁/Z₂	63° A/H	63° B/P	63° Z₁/Z₂	64° A/H	64° B/P	64° Z₁/Z₂	65° A/H	65° B/P	65° Z₁/Z₂	Lat./A LHA	
45	135	20 42	22 12	49.1	20 03	21 24	48.8	19 23	20 36	48.6	18 43	19 49	48.3	18 03	19 02	48.1	17 23	18 15	47.8	225	315
46	134	21 05	21 51	48.1	20 25	21 04	47.8	19 44	20 16	47.6	19 04	19 29	47.3	18 23	18 43	47.1	17 42	17 57	46.8	226	314
47	133	21 27	21 30	47.1	20 46	20 43	46.8	20 05	19 56	46.6	19 24	19 10	46.3	18 42	18 24	46.1	18 00	17 39	45.8	227	313
48	132	21 49	21 07	46.1	21 07	20 21	45.8	20 25	19 35	45.6	19 43	18 50	45.3	19 01	18 04	45.1	18 18	17 20	44.8	228	312
49	131	22 10	20 45	45.1	21 28	19 59	44.8	20 45	19 14	44.6	20 02	18 29	44.3	19 19	17 45	44.1	18 36	17 01	43.8	229	311
50	130	22 31	20 22	44.1	21 48	19 37	43.8	21 05	18 52	43.5	20 21	18 08	43.3	19 37	17 24	43.0	18 53	16 41	42.8	230	310
51	129	22 52	19 58	43.1	22 08	19 14	42.8	21 24	18 30	42.5	20 40	17 47	42.3	19 55	17 04	42.0	19 10	16 21	41.8	231	309
52	128	23 12	19 34	42.1	22 28	18 51	41.8	21 43	18 08	41.5	20 58	17 25	41.2	20 13	16 43	41.0	19 27	16 01	40.8	232	308
53	127	23 32	19 10	41.0	22 47	18 27	40.7	22 01	17 45	40.5	21 15	17 03	40.2	20 30	16 21	40.0	19 44	15 41	39.7	233	307
54	126	23 52	18 45	40.0	23 06	18 03	39.7	22 19	17 21	39.4	21 33	16 40	39.2	20 46	16 00	39.0	20 00	15 20	38.7	234	306
55	125	24 11	18 19	39.0	23 24	17 38	38.7	22 37	16 58	38.4	21 50	16 17	38.2	21 03	15 38	37.9	20 15	14 58	37.7	235	305
56	124	24 29	17 54	37.9	23 42	17 13	37.6	22 54	16 34	37.4	22 07	15 54	37.1	21 19	15 15	36.9	20 31	14 37	36.7	236	304
57	123	24 48	17 27	36.9	23 59	16 48	36.6	23 11	16 09	36.3	22 23	15 31	36.1	21 34	14 53	35.8	20 46	14 15	35.6	237	303
58	122	25 05	17 01	35.8	24 16	16 22	35.5	23 28	15 44	35.3	22 39	15 07	35.0	21 49	14 29	34.8	21 00	13 53	34.6	238	302
59	121	25 23	16 34	34.8	24 33	15 56	34.4	23 44	15 19	34.2	22 54	14 42	34.0	22 04	14 06	33.8	21 14	13 30	33.5	239	301
60	120	25 40	16 06	33.7	24 50	15 30	33.4	23 59	14 53	33.2	23 09	14 18	32.9	22 19	13 42	32.7	21 28	13 07	32.5	240	300
61	119	25 56	15 38	32.6	25 05	15 03	32.4	24 15	14 27	32.1	23 24	13 53	31.9	22 33	13 18	31.7	21 42	12 44	31.5	241	299
62	118	26 12	15 10	31.5	25 21	14 35	31.3	24 29	14 01	31.1	23 38	13 27	30.8	22 46	12 54	30.6	21 55	12 21	30.4	242	298
63	117	26 27	14 41	30.5	25 36	14 08	30.2	24 44	13 34	30.0	23 52	13 01	29.7	22 59	12 29	29.5	22 07	11 57	29.3	243	297
64	116	26 42	14 12	29.4	25 50	13 39	29.1	24 58	13 07	28.8	24 05	12 35	28.7	23 12	12 04	28.5	22 19	11 33	28.3	244	296
65	115	26 57	13 43	28.3	26 04	13 11	28.1	25 11	12 40	27.8	24 18	12 09	27.6	23 25	11 39	27.4	22 31	11 09	27.2	245	295
66	114	27 10	13 13	27.2	26 18	12 42	27.0	25 24	12 12	26.8	24 30	11 43	26.6	23 36	11 13	26.4	22 43	10 44	26.2	246	294
67	113	27 24	12 43	26.1	26 30	12 13	25.9	25 36	11 44	25.7	24 42	11 16	25.5	23 48	10 47	25.3	22 54	10 20	25.1	247	293
68	112	27 37	12 12	25.0	26 43	11 44	24.8	25 48	11 16	24.6	24 54	10 48	24.4	23 59	10 21	24.2	23 04	9 55	24.0	248	292
69	111	27 50	11 41	23.9	26 55	11 14	23.7	26 00	10 47	23.5	25 05	10 21	23.3	24 09	9 55	23.1	23 14	9 29	23.0	249	291
70	110	28 01	11 10	22.8	27 06	10 44	22.6	26 11	10 18	22.4	25 15	9 53	22.2	24 19	9 28	22.0	23 23	9 04	21.9	250	290
71	109	28 13	10 39	21.7	27 17	10 14	21.5	26 21	9 49	21.3	25 25	9 25	21.1	24 28	9 01	21.0	23 33	8 38	20.7	251	289
72	108	28 24	10 07	20.6	27 27	9 43	20.4	26 31	9 20	20.2	25 35	8 57	20.0	24 38	8 34	19.9	23 42	8 12	19.6	252	288
73	107	28 34	9 35	19.4	27 37	9 12	19.3	26 41	8 50	19.1	25 44	8 28	18.9	24 47	8 07	18.8	23 50	7 46	18.6	253	287
74	106	28 44	9 03	18.3	27 47	8 41	18.2	26 50	8 20	18.0	25 52	8 00	17.8	24 55	7 39	17.7	23 58	7 19	17.6	254	286
75	105	28 53	8 30	17.2	27 55	8 10	17.0	26 58	7 50	16.9	26 01	7 31	16.7	25 03	7 12	16.5	24 06	6 53	16.5	255	285
76	104	29 01	7 57	16.1	28 04	7 38	15.9	27 06	7 20	15.8	26 08	7 02	15.6	25 10	6 44	15.5	24 13	6 26	15.4	256	284
77	103	29 09	7 24	14.9	28 11	7 06	14.8	27 13	6 49	14.7	26 15	6 32	14.5	25 17	6 16	14.4	24 19	5 59	14.3	257	283
78	102	29 17	6 51	13.8	28 18	6 34	13.7	27 20	6 19	13.5	26 22	6 03	13.4	25 23	5 47	13.3	24 26	5 32	13.2	258	282
79	101	29 24	6 17	12.7	28 25	6 02	12.5	27 27	5 48	12.4	26 28	5 33	12.3	25 29	5 19	12.2	24 31	5 05	12.1	259	281
80	100	29 30	5 44	11.5	28 31	5 30	11.4	27 33	5 17	11.3	26 33	5 03	11.2	25 35	4 50	11.1	24 36	4 38	11.0	260	280
81	99	29 36	5 10	10.4	28 37	4 57	10.3	27 38	4 45	10.2	26 38	4 33	10.1	25 39	4 22	10.0	24 40	4 10	9.9	261	279
82	98	29 41	4 36	9.2	28 41	4 25	9.1	27 42	4 14	9.0	26 43	4 03	9.0	25 44	3 53	8.9	24 44	3 43	8.8	262	278
83	97	29 45	4 01	8.1	28 46	3 52	8.0	27 46	3 42	7.9	26 47	3 33	7.8	25 48	3 24	7.8	24 48	3 15	7.7	263	277
84	96	29 49	3 27	6.9	28 50	3 19	6.9	27 50	3 11	6.8	26 50	3 02	6.7	25 51	2 55	6.7	24 51	2 47	6.6	264	276
85	95	29 52	2 53	5.8	28 53	2 46	5.7	27 53	2 39	5.7	26 53	2 32	5.6	25 54	2 26	5.6	24 54	2 20	5.5	265	275
86	94	29 55	2 18	4.6	28 55	2 13	4.6	27 55	2 07	4.5	26 56	2 02	4.5	25 56	1 57	4.4	24 56	1 52	4.4	266	274
87	93	29 57	1 44	3.5	28 57	1 40	3.4	27 57	1 36	3.4	26 58	1 32	3.4	25 58	1 28	3.3	24 58	1 24	3.3	267	273
88	92	29 59	1 09	2.3	28 59	1 06	2.3	27 59	1 04	2.3	26 59	1 01	2.2	25 59	0 59	2.2	24 59	0 56	2.2	268	272
89	91	30 00	0 35	1.2	29 00	0 33	1.1	28 00	0 32	1.1	27 00	0 31	1.1	26 00	0 29	1.1	25 00	0 28	1.1	269	271
90	90	30 00	0 00	0.0	29 00	0 00	0.0	28 00	0 00	0.0	27 00	0 00	0.0	26 00	0 00	0.0	25 00	0 00	0.0	270	270

N. Lat.: for LHA > 180° ... Zₙ = Z
for LHA < 180° ... Zₙ = 360° − Z

S. Lat.: for LHA > 180° ... Zₙ = 180° − Z
for LHA < 180° ... Zₙ = 180° + Z

SIGHT REDUCTION TABLE

B: (−) for 90° < LHA < 270°
Dec:(−) for Lat. contrary name

Z₁ : same sign as B
Z₂:(−) for F > 90°

Lat./A	LHA/F	66° A/H	B/P	Z₁/Z₂	67° A/H	B/P	Z₁/Z₂	68° A/H	B/P	Z₁/Z₂	69° A/H	B/P	Z₁/Z₂	70° A/H	B/P	Z₁/Z₂	71° A/H	B/P	Z₁/Z₂	Lat./A	LHA
0	180	0 00	24 00	90·0	0 00	23 00	90·0	0 00	22 00	90·0	0 00	21 00	90·0	0 00	20 00	90·0	0 00	19 00	90·0	0	180
1	179	0 24	24 00	89·1	0 23	23 00	89·1	0 22	22 00	89·1	0 22	21 00	89·1	0 21	20 00	89·1	0 20	19 00	89·1	1	181
2	178	0 49	23 59	88·2	0 47	22 59	88·1	0 45	21 59	88·2	0 43	20 59	88·1	0 41	19 59	88·1	0 39	18 59	88·1	2	182
3	177	1 13	23 58	87·3	1 10	22 58	87·2	1 07	21 58	87·2	1 04	20 58	87·2	1 02	19 58	87·2	0 59	18 58	87·2	3	183
4	176	1 38	23 57	86·3	1 34	22 57	86·3	1 30	21 57	86·3	1 26	20 57	86·3	1 22	19 57	86·3	1 18	18 57	86·2	4	184
5	175	2 02	23 55	85·4	1 57	22 55	85·4	1 52	21 55	85·4	1 47	20 56	85·3	1 42	19 56	85·3	1 38	18 56	85·3	5	185
6	174	2 26	23 53	84·5	2 20	22 53	84·5	2 15	21 53	84·4	2 09	20 54	84·4	2 03	19 54	84·4	1 57	18 54	84·3	6	186
7	173	2 50	23 50	83·6	2 44	22 51	83·6	2 37	21 51	83·5	2 30	20 51	83·5	2 23	19 52	83·4	2 16	18 52	83·4	7	187
8	172	3 15	23 47	82·7	3 07	22 48	82·6	3 00	21 48	82·6	2 52	20 49	82·5	2 44	19 49	82·5	2 36	18 50	82·4	8	188
9	171	3 39	23 44	81·8	3 30	22 45	81·7	3 22	21 45	81·6	3 13	20 46	81·6	3 04	19 46	81·6	2 55	18 47	81·5	9	189
10	170	4 03	23 41	80·8	3 53	22 41	80·8	3 44	21 42	80·7	3 34	20 42	80·7	3 24	19 43	80·7	3 14	18 44	80·5	10	190
11	169	4 27	23 36	79·9	4 17	22 37	79·9	4 06	21 38	79·8	3 55	20 39	79·7	3 45	19 40	79·7	3 34	18 41	79·6	11	191
12	168	4 51	23 32	79·0	4 40	22 33	78·9	4 28	21 34	78·9	4 16	20 35	78·8	4 05	19 36	78·7	3 53	18 37	78·6	12	192
13	167	5 15	23 27	78·1	5 03	22 28	78·0	4 50	21 29	78·0	4 37	20 30	77·9	4 25	19 32	77·8	4 12	18 33	77·7	13	193
14	166	5 39	23 22	77·2	5 25	22 23	77·1	5 12	21 24	77·0	4 58	20 26	77·0	4 45	19 27	76·8	4 31	18 28	76·7	14	194
15	165	6 03	23 16	76·2	5 48	22 18	76·1	5 34	21 19	76·1	5 19	20 21	76·0	5 05	19 22	75·9	4 50	18 24	75·8	15	195
16	164	6 26	23 10	75·3	6 11	22 12	75·2	5 56	21 13	75·1	5 40	20 15	75·1	5 25	19 17	74·9	5 09	18 19	74·8	16	196
17	163	6 50	23 04	74·4	6 34	22 06	74·3	6 17	21 08	74·2	6 01	20 09	74·1	5 44	19 11	74·0	5 28	18 14	73·9	17	197
18	162	7 13	22 57	73·5	6 56	21 59	73·3	6 39	21 01	73·2	6 21	20 03	73·1	6 04	19 06	73·0	5 46	18 08	72·9	18	198
19	161	7 37	22 50	72·5	7 19	21 51	72·4	7 00	20 54	72·3	6 42	19 57	72·2	6 23	18 59	72·1	6 05	18 02	72·0	19	199
20	160	8 00	22 42	71·6	7 41	21 45	71·5	7 22	20 47	71·4	7 02	19 50	71·2	6 43	18 53	71·1	6 24	17 56	71·0	20	200
21	159	8 23	22 34	70·7	8 03	21 37	70·5	7 43	20 40	70·4	7 23	19 43	70·3	7 02	18 46	70·2	6 42	17 49	70·1	21	201
22	158	8 46	22 26	69·7	8 25	21 29	69·6	8 04	20 32	69·5	7 43	19 35	69·3	7 22	18 39	69·2	7 00	17 42	69·1	22	202
23	157	9 09	22 17	68·8	8 47	21 21	68·7	8 25	20 24	68·5	8 03	19 28	68·4	7 41	18 31	68·3	7 19	17 35	68·1	23	203
24	156	9 31	22 08	67·9	9 09	21 12	67·7	8 46	20 16	67·6	8 23	19 19	67·4	8 00	18 24	67·3	7 37	17 28	67·2	24	204
25	155	9 54	21 58	66·9	9 30	21 03	66·8	9 07	20 07	66·6	8 43	19 11	66·5	8 19	18 15	66·4	7 55	17 20	66·2	25	205
26	154	10 16	21 49	66·0	9 52	20 53	65·8	9 27	19 57	65·7	9 02	19 02	65·5	8 37	18 07	65·4	8 12	17 12	65·3	26	206
27	153	10 38	21 38	65·0	10 14	20 43	64·9	9 48	19 48	64·7	9 22	18 53	64·6	8 56	17 58	64·4	8 30	17 03	64·3	27	207
28	152	11 00	21 28	64·1	10 34	20 33	63·9	10 08	19 38	63·8	9 41	18 43	63·6	9 14	17 49	63·5	8 48	16 55	63·3	28	208
29	151	11 22	21 17	63·1	10 55	20 22	63·0	10 28	19 28	62·8	10 00	18 34	62·6	9 33	17 39	62·5	9 05	16 46	62·3	29	209
30	150	11 44	21 05	62·2	11 16	20 11	62·0	10 48	19 17	61·8	10 19	18 23	61·7	9 51	17 30	61·5	9 22	16 36	61·4	30	210
31	149	12 06	20 53	61·2	11 37	20 00	61·1	11 07	19 06	60·9	10 38	18 13	60·7	10 09	17 20	60·5	9 39	16 27	60·4	31	211
32	148	12 27	20 41	60·3	11 57	19 48	60·1	11 27	18 55	59·9	10 57	18 02	59·7	10 27	17 09	59·6	9 56	16 17	59·4	32	212
33	147	12 48	20 29	59·3	12 17	19 36	59·1	11 46	18 43	58·9	11 15	17 51	58·8	10 44	16 58	58·6	10 13	16 06	58·4	33	213
34	146	13 09	20 16	58·4	12 37	19 23	58·2	12 06	18 31	58·0	11 34	17 39	57·8	11 02	16 47	57·6	10 29	15 56	57·5	34	214
35	145	13 29	20 02	57·4	12 57	19 10	57·2	12 24	18 19	57·0	11 52	17 27	56·8	11 19	16 36	56·7	10 46	15 45	56·5	35	215
36	144	13 50	19 49	56·4	13 17	18 57	56·2	12 43	18 06	56·0	12 10	17 15	55·9	11 36	16 24	55·7	11 02	15 34	55·5	36	216
37	143	14 10	19 34	55·5	13 36	18 44	55·3	13 02	17 53	55·1	12 27	17 03	54·9	11 53	16 12	54·7	11 18	15 23	54·5	37	217
38	142	14 30	19 20	54·5	13 55	18 30	54·3	13 20	17 40	54·1	12 45	16 50	53·9	12 09	16 00	53·7	11 34	15 11	53·5	38	218
39	141	14 50	19 05	53·5	14 14	18 15	53·3	13 38	17 26	53·1	13 02	16 37	52·9	12 26	15 48	52·7	11 49	14 59	52·6	39	219
40	140	15 09	18 50	52·5	14 33	18 01	52·3	13 56	17 12	52·1	13 19	16 23	51·9	12 42	15 35	51·7	12 05	14 47	51·6	40	220
41	139	15 29	18 34	51·5	14 51	17 46	51·3	14 14	16 57	51·1	13 36	16 09	50·9	12 58	15 22	50·8	12 20	14 34	50·6	41	221
42	138	15 48	18 18	50·6	15 09	17 30	50·3	14 31	16 43	50·1	13 52	15 55	49·9	13 14	15 08	49·8	12 35	14 21	49·6	42	222
43	137	16 06	18 02	49·6	15 27	17 15	49·4	14 48	16 28	49·2	14 09	15 41	49·0	13 29	14 54	48·8	12 50	14 08	48·6	43	223
44	136	16 25	17 46	48·6	15 45	16 59	48·4	15 05	16 12	48·2	14 25	15 26	48·0	13 45	14 40	47·8	13 04	13 55	47·6	44	224
45	135	16 43	17 29	47·6	16 02	16 42	47·4	15 22	15 57	47·2	14 41	15 11	47·0	14 00	14 26	46·8	13 19	13 41	46·6	45	225

Lat./A	66°			67°			68°			69°			70°			71°			Lat./A
LHA/F	A/H	B/P	Z_1/Z_2	A/H	B/P	Z_1/Z_2	A/H	B/P	Z_1/Z_2	A/H	B/P	Z_1/Z_2	A/H	B/P	Z_1/Z_2	A/H	B/P	Z_1/Z_2	LHA
45 135	16 43	17 29	47·6	16 02	16 42	47·4	15 22	15 57	47·2	14 41	15 11	47·0	14 00	14 26	46·8	13 19	13 41	46·6	225 315
46 134	17 01	17 11	46·6	16 19	16 26	46·4	15 38	15 41	46·2	14 56	14 56	46·0	14 15	14 11	45·8	13 33	13 27	45·6	226 314
47 133	17 18	16 53	45·6	16 36	16 09	45·4	15 54	15 24	45·2	15 12	14 40	45·0	14 29	13 56	44·8	13 46	13 13	44·6	227 313
48 132	17 36	16 35	44·6	16 53	15 51	44·4	16 10	15 08	44·2	15 27	14 24	44·0	14 43	13 41	43·8	14 00	12 58	43·6	228 312
49 131	17 53	16 17	43·6	17 09	15 34	43·4	16 25	14 51	43·2	15 42	14 08	43·0	14 58	13 26	42·8	14 13	12 44	42·6	229 311
50 130	18 09	15 58	42·6	17 25	15 16	42·4	16 41	14 33	42·1	15 56	13 52	41·9	15 11	13 10	41·8	14 27	12 29	41·6	230 310
51 129	18 26	15 39	41·6	17 41	14 57	41·3	16 56	14 16	41·1	16 10	13 35	40·9	15 25	12 54	40·8	14 39	12 14	40·6	231 309
52 128	18 42	15 20	40·5	17 56	14 39	40·3	17 10	13 58	40·1	16 24	13 18	39·9	15 38	12 38	39·8	14 52	11 58	39·6	232 308
53 127	18 57	15 00	39·5	18 11	14 20	39·3	17 24	13 40	39·1	16 38	13 00	38·9	15 51	12 21	38·7	15 04	11 42	38·6	233 307
54 126	19 13	14 40	38·5	18 26	14 01	38·3	17 39	13 22	38·1	16 51	12 43	37·9	16 04	12 05	37·7	15 16	11 26	37·5	234 306
55 125	19 28	14 20	37·5	18 40	13 41	37·3	17 52	13 03	37·1	17 04	12 25	36·9	16 16	11 48	36·7	15 28	11 10	36·5	235 305
56 124	19 42	13 59	36·4	18 54	13 21	36·2	18 06	12 44	36·0	17 17	12 07	35·8	16 28	11 30	35·7	15 40	10 54	35·5	236 304
57 123	19 57	13 38	35·4	19 08	13 01	35·2	18 19	12 24	35·0	17 29	11 49	34·8	16 40	11 13	34·6	15 51	10 37	34·5	237 303
58 122	20 11	13 17	34·4	19 21	12 41	34·2	18 31	12 05	34·0	17 42	11 30	33·8	16 52	10 55	33·6	16 02	10 20	33·5	238 302
59 121	20 24	12 55	33·3	19 34	12 20	33·1	18 44	11 45	32·9	17 54	11 11	32·8	17 03	10 37	32·6	16 12	10 03	32·4	239 301
60 120	20 37	12 33	32·3	19 47	11 59	32·1	18 56	11 25	31·9	18 05	10 52	31·8	17 14	10 19	31·6	16 23	9 46	31·4	240 300
61 119	20 50	12 11	31·2	19 59	11 38	31·1	19 08	11 05	30·9	18 16	10 33	30·7	17 24	10 00	30·5	16 33	9 29	30·4	241 299
62 118	21 03	11 48	30·2	20 11	11 16	30·0	19 19	10 44	29·8	18 27	10 13	29·7	17 35	9 42	29·5	16 42	9 11	29·4	242 298
63 117	21 15	11 26	29·2	20 22	10 54	29·0	19 30	10 24	28·8	18 37	9 53	28·6	17 45	9 23	28·5	16 52	8 53	28·3	243 297
64 116	21 27	11 03	28·1	20 34	10 32	27·9	19 41	10 03	27·7	18 47	9 33	27·6	17 54	9 04	27·4	17 01	8 35	27·3	244 296
65 115	21 38	10 39	27·0	20 44	10 10	26·9	19 51	9 41	26·7	18 57	9 13	26·5	18 03	8 45	26·4	17 10	8 17	26·3	245 295
66 114	21 49	10 16	26·0	20 55	9 48	25·8	20 01	9 20	25·7	19 06	8 52	25·5	18 12	8 25	25·4	17 18	7 58	25·2	246 294
67 113	21 59	9 52	24·9	21 05	9 25	24·8	20 10	8 58	24·6	19 15	8 32	24·5	18 21	8 06	24·3	17 26	7 40	24·2	247 293
68 112	22 09	9 28	23·9	21 14	9 02	23·7	20 19	8 36	23·5	19 24	8 11	23·4	18 29	7 46	23·3	17 34	7 21	23·1	248 292
69 111	22 19	9 04	22·8	21 24	8 39	22·6	20 28	8 14	22·5	19 32	7 50	22·4	18 37	7 26	22·2	17 42	7 02	22·1	249 291
70 110	22 28	8 39	21·7	21 32	8 16	21·6	20 37	7 52	21·4	19 41	7 29	21·3	18 45	7 06	21·2	17 49	6 43	21·1	250 290
71 109	22 37	8 15	20·7	21 41	7 52	20·5	20 45	7 30	20·4	19 48	7 07	20·2	18 52	6 45	20·1	17 56	6 23	20·0	251 289
72 108	22 45	7 50	19·6	21 49	7 28	19·4	20 52	7 07	19·3	19 55	6 46	19·2	18 59	6 25	19·1	18 02	6 04	19·0	252 288
73 107	22 53	7 25	18·5	21 56	7 04	18·4	20 59	6 44	18·2	20 02	6 24	18·1	19 05	6 04	18·0	18 08	5 45	17·9	253 287
74 106	23 01	7 00	17·4	22 04	6 40	17·3	21 06	6 21	17·2	20 09	6 02	17·1	19 12	5 44	17·0	18 14	5 25	16·9	254 286
75 105	23 08	6 34	16·3	22 10	6 16	16·2	21 13	5 58	16·1	20 15	5 40	16·0	19 17	5 23	15·9	18 20	5 06	15·8	255 285
76 104	23 15	6 09	15·2	22 17	5 52	15·1	21 19	5 35	15·1	20 21	5 18	15·0	19 23	5 02	14·9	18 25	4 46	14·8	256 284
77 103	23 21	5 43	14·2	22 23	5 27	14·1	21 24	5 12	14·0	20 26	4 56	13·9	19 28	4 41	13·8	18 30	4 26	13·7	257 283
78 102	23 27	5 17	13·1	22 28	5 03	13·0	21 30	4 48	12·9	20 31	4 34	12·8	19 33	4 20	12·7	18 34	4 06	12·7	258 282
79 101	23 32	4 51	12·0	22 33	4 38	11·9	21 35	4 24	11·8	20 36	4 11	11·8	19 37	3 58	11·7	18 38	3 46	11·6	259 281
80 100	23 37	4 25	10·9	22 38	4 13	10·8	21 39	4 01	10·8	20 40	3 49	10·7	19 41	3 37	10·6	18 42	3 25	10·6	260 280
81 99	23 41	3 59	9·8	22 42	3 48	9·8	21 43	3 37	9·7	20 44	3 26	9·6	19 45	3 16	9·6	18 45	3 05	9·5	261 279
82 98	23 45	3 33	8·7	22 46	3 23	8·7	21 46	3 13	8·6	20 47	3 03	8·6	19 48	2 54	8·5	18 48	2 45	8·5	262 278
83 97	23 49	3 06	7·7	22 49	2 58	7·6	21 50	2 49	7·5	20 50	2 41	7·5	19 51	2 32	7·4	18 51	2 24	7·4	263 277
84 96	23 52	2 40	6·6	22 52	2 32	6·5	21 52	2 25	6·5	20 53	2 18	6·4	19 53	2 11	6·4	18 54	2 04	6·3	264 276
85 95	23 54	2 13	5·5	22 54	2 07	5·5	21 55	2 01	5·4	20 55	1 55	5·4	19 55	1 49	5·3	18 55	1 43	5·3	265 275
86 94	23 56	1 47	4·4	22 56	1 42	4·3	21 57	1 37	4·3	20 57	1 32	4·3	19 57	1 27	4·3	18 57	1 23	4·2	266 274
87 93	23 58	1 20	3·3	22 58	1 16	3·3	21 58	1 13	3·2	20 58	1 09	3·2	19 58	1 05	3·2	18 58	1 02	3·2	267 273
88 92	23 59	0 53	2·2	22 59	0 51	2·2	21 59	0 48	2·2	20 59	0 46	2·1	19 59	0 44	2·1	18 59	0 41	2·1	268 272
89 91	24 00	0 27	1·1	23 00	0 25	1·1	22 00	0 24	1·1	21 00	0 23	1·1	20 00	0 22	1·1	19 00	0 21	1·1	269 271
90 90	24 00	0 00	0·0	23 00	0 00	0·0	22 00	0 00	0·0	21 00	0 00	0·0	20 00	0 00	0·0	19 00	0 00	0·0	270 270

N. Lat.: for LHA > 180° ... $Z_n = Z$
for LHA < 180° ... $Z_n = 360° − Z$

S. Lat.: for LHA > 180° ... $Z_n = 180° − Z$
for LHA < 180° ... $Z_n = 180° + Z$

SIGHT REDUCTION TABLE

B: (−) for 90° < LHA < 270°
Dec:(−) for Lat. contrary name

Z₁: same sign as B
Z₂:(−) for F > 90°

Lat./F	72° A/H	72° B/P	72° Z_1/Z_2	73° A/H	73° B/P	73° Z_1/Z_2	74° A/H	74° B/P	74° Z_1/Z_2	75° A/H	75° B/P	75° Z_1/Z_2	76° A/H	76° B/P	76° Z_1/Z_2	77° A/H	77° B/P	77° Z_1/Z_2	Lat./A	LHA
0	0 00	18 00	90·0	0 00	17 00	90·0	0 00	16 00	90·0	0 00	15 00	90·0	0 00	14 00	90·0	0 00	13 00	90·0	180	360
1	0 19	18 00	89·0	0 18	17 00	89·0	0 17	16 00	89·0	0 16	15 00	89·0	0 15	14 00	89·0	0 13	13 00	89·0	181	359
2	0 37	17 59	88·1	0 35	16 59	88·1	0 33	15 59	88·1	0 31	14 59	88·1	0 29	14 00	88·1	0 27	13 00	88·1	182	358
3	0 56	17 59	87·1	0 53	16 59	87·1	0 50	15 59	87·1	0 47	14 59	87·1	0 44	13 59	87·1	0 40	12 58	87·1	183	357
4	1 14	17 58	86·2	1 10	16 58	86·2	1 06	15 58	86·2	1 02	14 58	86·1	0 58	13 58	86·1	0 54	12 57	86·1	184	356
5	1 33	17 56	85·2	1 28	16 56	85·2	1 23	15 57	85·2	1 18	14 57	85·1	1 12	13 57	85·1	1 07	12 57	85·1	185	355
6	1 51	17 54	84·3	1 45	16 55	84·3	1 39	15 55	84·2	1 33	14 55	84·2	1 27	13 54	84·2	1 21	12 56	84·2	186	354
7	2 09	17 52	83·3	2 03	16 53	83·3	1 56	15 53	83·3	1 48	14 54	83·2	1 41	13 54	83·2	1 34	12 54	83·2	187	353
8	2 28	17 50	82·4	2 20	16 51	82·3	2 12	15 51	82·3	2 04	14 52	82·3	1 56	13 51	82·2	1 48	12 53	82·2	188	352
9	2 46	17 48	81·4	2 37	16 48	81·4	2 28	15 49	81·3	2 19	14 49	81·3	2 10	13 50	81·3	2 01	12 51	81·2	189	351
10	3 05	17 45	80·5	2 55	16 45	80·4	2 45	15 46	80·4	2 35	14 47	80·3	2 24	13 48	80·3	2 14	12 49	80·3	190	350
11	3 23	17 41	79·5	3 12	16 42	79·5	3 01	15 43	79·4	2 50	14 44	79·4	2 39	13 45	79·3	2 28	12 46	79·3	191	349
12	3 41	17 38	78·6	3 29	16 39	78·5	3 17	15 40	78·5	3 05	14 41	78·4	2 53	13 42	78·3	2 41	12 44	78·3	192	348
13	3 59	17 34	77·6	3 46	16 35	77·5	3 33	15 37	77·5	3 20	14 38	77·4	3 07	13 39	77·3	2 54	12 41	77·3	193	347
14	4 17	17 30	76·7	4 03	16 31	76·6	3 49	15 33	76·6	3 35	14 34	76·5	3 21	13 36	76·4	3 07	12 38	76·3	194	346
15	4 35	17 25	75·7	4 20	16 27	75·6	4 05	15 29	75·6	3 50	14 31	75·5	3 35	13 32	75·4	3 20	12 34	75·4	195	345
16	4 53	17 21	74·7	4 37	16 23	74·7	4 21	15 25	74·6	4 05	14 27	74·6	3 49	13 29	74·5	3 33	12 31	74·4	196	344
17	5 11	17 16	73·8	4 54	16 18	73·7	4 37	15 20	73·6	4 20	14 22	73·5	4 03	13 25	73·5	3 46	12 27	73·4	197	343
18	5 29	17 10	72·8	5 11	16 13	72·7	4 53	15 15	72·7	4 35	14 18	72·6	4 17	13 20	72·5	3 59	12 23	72·4	198	342
19	5 46	17 05	71·9	5 28	16 07	71·8	5 09	15 10	71·7	4 50	14 13	71·6	4 31	13 16	71·5	4 12	12 19	71·5	199	341
20	6 04	16 59	70·9	5 44	16 02	70·8	5 25	15 05	70·7	5 05	14 08	70·6	4 45	13 11	70·5	4 25	12 14	70·5	200	340
21	6 21	16 52	69·9	6 01	15 56	69·8	5 40	14 59	69·7	5 19	14 03	69·7	4 58	13 06	69·6	4 37	12 10	69·5	201	339
22	6 39	16 46	69·0	6 17	15 50	68·9	5 56	14 53	68·8	5 34	13 57	68·7	5 12	13 01	68·6	4 50	12 05	68·5	202	338
23	6 56	16 39	68·0	6 34	15 43	67·9	6 11	14 47	67·8	5 48	13 51	67·7	5 25	12 56	67·6	5 03	12 00	67·5	203	337
24	7 13	16 32	67·1	6 50	15 36	66·9	6 26	14 41	66·8	6 03	13 45	66·7	5 39	12 50	66·6	5 15	11 55	66·5	204	336
25	7 30	16 25	66·1	7 06	15 29	66·0	6 41	14 34	65·9	6 17	13 39	65·7	5 52	12 44	65·7	5 27	11 49	65·6	205	335
26	7 47	16 17	65·1	7 22	15 22	65·0	6 56	14 27	64·9	6 31	13 32	64·8	6 05	12 38	64·7	5 40	11 43	64·6	206	334
27	8 04	16 09	64·1	7 38	15 14	64·0	7 11	14 20	63·9	6 45	13 26	63·8	6 18	12 32	63·7	5 52	11 37	63·6	207	333
28	8 20	16 00	63·2	7 53	15 06	63·0	7 26	14 12	62·9	6 59	13 19	62·8	6 31	12 25	62·7	6 04	11 31	62·6	208	332
29	8 37	15 52	62·2	8 09	14 58	62·1	7 41	14 05	61·9	7 13	13 11	61·8	6 44	12 18	61·7	6 16	11 25	61·6	209	331
30	8 53	15 43	61·2	8 24	14 50	61·1	7 55	13 57	61·0	7 26	13 04	60·9	6 57	12 11	60·7	6 27	11 18	60·6	210	330
31	9 09	15 34	60·3	8 40	14 41	60·1	8 10	13 49	60·0	7 40	12 56	59·9	7 09	12 04	59·8	6 39	11 12	59·7	211	329
32	9 25	15 24	59·3	8 55	14 32	59·1	8 24	13 40	59·0	7 53	12 48	58·9	7 22	11 56	58·8	6 51	11 05	58·7	212	328
33	9 41	15 15	58·3	9 10	14 23	58·2	8 38	13 31	58·0	8 06	12 40	57·9	7 34	11 49	57·8	7 02	10 57	57·7	213	327
34	9 57	15 05	57·3	9 25	14 13	57·2	8 52	13 22	57·0	8 19	12 31	56·9	7 46	11 41	56·8	7 14	10 50	56·7	214	326
35	10 13	14 54	56·3	9 39	14 04	56·3	9 06	13 13	56·1	8 32	12 23	55·9	7 59	11 33	55·8	7 25	10 43	55·7	215	325
36	10 28	14 44	55·4	9 54	13 54	55·2	9 19	13 04	55·1	8 45	12 14	54·9	8 11	11 24	54·8	7 36	10 35	54·7	216	324
37	10 43	14 33	54·4	10 08	13 43	54·2	9 32	12 54	54·1	8 58	12 05	53·9	8 22	11 15	53·8	7 47	10 27	53·7	217	323
38	10 58	14 22	53·4	10 22	13 33	53·2	9 46	12 44	53·1	9 10	11 55	53·0	8 34	11 07	52·8	7 58	10 19	52·7	218	322
39	11 13	14 10	52·4	10 36	13 22	52·2	9 59	12 34	52·1	9 22	11 46	52·0	8 45	10 58	51·8	8 09	10 10	51·7	219	321
40	11 27	13 59	51·4	10 50	13 11	51·3	10 12	12 23	51·1	9 35	11 36	51·0	8 57	10 49	50·8	8 19	10 02	50·7	220	320
41	11 42	13 47	50·4	11 04	13 00	50·3	10 25	12 13	50·0	9 47	11 26	50·0	9 08	10 39	49·9	8 29	9 53	49·7	221	319
42	11 56	13 34	49·4	11 17	12 48	49·3	10 38	12 02	49·3	9 58	11 16	49·1	9 19	10 30	48·9	8 39	9 44	48·7	222	318
43	12 11	13 22	48·3	11 30	12 36	48·3	10 50	11 51	48·3	10 10	11 05	48·0	9 30	10 20	47·9	8 49	9 34	47·7	223	317
44	12 24	13 09	47·4	11 43	12 24	47·3	11 02	11 39	47·3	10 21	10 55	47·1	9 40	10 10	46·9	8 59	9 26	46·7	224	316
45	12 37	12 56	46·4	11 56	12 12	46·3	11 14	11 28	46·1	10 33	10 44	46·0	9 51	10 00	45·9	9 09	9 16	45·7	225	315

Lat. / A LHA/F	72° A/H	72° B/P	72° Z₁/Z₂	73° A/H	73° B/P	73° Z₁/Z₂	74° A/H	74° B/P	74° Z₁/Z₂	75° A/H	75° B/P	75° Z₁/Z₂	76° A/H	76° B/P	76° Z₁/Z₂	77° A/H	77° B/P	77° Z₁/Z₂	Lat. / A LHA
45 / 135	12 37	12 56	46.4	11 56	12 12	46.3	11 14	11 28	46.1	10 33	10 44	46.0	9 51	10 00	45.9	9 09	9 16	45.7	225 / 315
46 / 134	12 51	12 43	45.4	12 08	11 59	45.3	11 26	11 16	45.1	10 44	10 33	45.0	10 01	9 50	44.9	9 19	9 07	44.7	226 / 314
47 / 133	13 04	12 30	44.4	12 21	11 47	44.3	11 38	11 04	44.1	10 55	10 21	44.0	10 11	9 39	43.9	9 28	8 57	43.7	227 / 313
48 / 132	13 17	12 16	43.4	12 33	11 34	43.3	11 49	10 52	43.1	11 05	10 10	43.0	10 21	9 28	42.9	9 37	8 47	42.7	228 / 312
49 / 131	13 29	12 02	42.4	12 45	11 21	42.3	12 00	10 39	42.1	11 16	9 58	42.0	10 31	9 17	41.9	9 46	8 37	41.7	229 / 311
50 / 130	13 42	11 48	41.4	12 57	11 07	41.3	12 11	10 27	41.1	11 26	9 46	41.0	10 41	9 06	40.9	9 55	8 26	40.7	230 / 310
51 / 129	13 54	11 33	40.4	13 08	10 53	40.3	12 22	10 14	40.1	11 36	9 34	40.0	10 50	8 55	39.8	10 04	8 16	39.7	231 / 309
52 / 128	14 06	11 19	39.4	13 19	10 40	39.2	12 33	10 01	39.1	11 46	9 22	39.0	10 59	8 44	38.8	10 13	8 05	38.7	232 / 308
53 / 127	14 17	11 04	38.4	13 30	10 26	38.2	12 43	9 47	38.1	11 56	9 10	38.0	11 08	8 32	37.8	10 21	7 55	37.7	233 / 307
54 / 126	14 29	10 49	37.4	13 41	10 11	37.2	12 53	9 34	37.1	12 05	8 57	36.9	11 17	8 20	36.8	10 29	7 44	36.7	234 / 306
55 / 125	14 40	10 33	36.4	13 51	9 57	36.2	13 03	9 20	36.1	12 14	8 44	35.9	11 26	8 08	35.8	10 37	7 33	35.7	235 / 305
56 / 124	14 51	10 18	35.3	14 02	9 42	35.2	13 13	9 07	35.1	12 23	8 31	34.9	11 34	7 56	34.8	10 45	7 21	34.7	236 / 304
57 / 123	15 01	10 02	34.3	14 12	9 27	34.2	13 22	8 53	34.0	12 32	8 18	33.9	11 42	7 44	33.8	10 52	7 10	33.7	237 / 303
58 / 122	15 12	9 46	33.3	14 21	9 12	33.2	13 31	8 38	33.0	12 41	8 05	32.9	11 50	7 32	32.8	11 00	6 58	32.7	238 / 302
59 / 121	15 22	9 30	32.3	14 31	8 57	32.1	13 40	8 24	32.0	12 49	7 51	31.9	11 58	7 19	31.8	11 07	6 47	31.7	239 / 301
60 / 120	15 31	9 14	31.3	14 40	8 41	31.1	13 49	8 10	31.0	12 57	7 38	30.9	12 06	7 06	30.8	11 14	6 35	30.6	240 / 300
61 / 119	15 41	8 57	30.2	14 49	8 26	30.1	13 57	7 55	30.0	13 05	7 24	29.8	12 13	6 54	29.7	11 21	6 23	29.6	241 / 299
62 / 118	15 50	8 40	29.2	14 58	8 10	29.1	14 05	7 40	28.9	13 13	7 10	28.8	12 20	6 41	28.7	11 27	6 11	28.6	242 / 298
63 / 117	15 59	8 23	28.2	15 06	7 54	28.0	14 13	7 25	27.9	13 20	6 56	27.8	12 27	6 27	27.7	11 34	5 59	27.6	243 / 297
64 / 116	16 08	8 06	27.2	15 14	7 38	27.0	14 21	7 10	26.9	13 27	6 42	26.8	12 34	6 14	26.7	11 40	5 47	26.6	244 / 296
65 / 115	16 16	7 49	26.1	15 22	7 22	26.0	14 28	6 55	25.9	13 34	6 28	25.8	12 40	6 01	25.7	11 46	5 34	25.6	245 / 295
66 / 114	16 24	7 32	25.1	15 29	7 05	25.0	14 35	6 39	24.9	13 41	6 13	24.7	12 46	5 47	24.6	11 52	5 22	24.6	246 / 294
67 / 113	16 32	7 14	24.1	15 37	6 49	23.9	14 42	6 24	23.8	13 47	5 59	23.7	12 52	5 34	23.6	11 57	5 09	23.5	247 / 293
68 / 112	16 39	6 56	23.0	15 44	6 32	22.9	14 48	6 08	22.8	13 53	5 44	22.7	12 58	5 20	22.6	12 02	4 57	22.5	248 / 292
69 / 111	16 46	6 38	22.0	15 50	6 15	21.9	14 55	5 52	21.8	13 59	5 29	21.7	13 03	5 06	21.6	12 07	4 44	21.5	249 / 291
70 / 110	16 53	6 20	20.9	15 57	5 58	20.8	15 01	5 36	20.7	14 05	5 14	20.6	13 08	4 52	20.6	12 12	4 31	20.5	250 / 290
71 / 109	16 59	6 02	19.9	16 03	5 41	19.8	15 06	5 20	19.7	14 10	4 59	19.6	13 13	4 38	19.5	12 17	4 18	19.5	251 / 289
72 / 108	17 05	5 44	18.9	16 09	5 24	18.8	15 12	5 04	18.7	14 15	4 44	18.6	13 18	4 24	18.5	12 21	4 05	18.4	252 / 288
73 / 107	17 11	5 26	17.8	16 14	5 06	17.7	15 17	4 48	17.6	14 20	4 29	17.6	13 23	4 10	17.5	12 25	3 52	17.4	253 / 287
74 / 106	17 17	5 07	16.8	16 19	4 49	16.7	15 22	4 31	16.6	14 24	4 13	16.5	13 27	3 56	16.5	12 29	3 38	16.4	254 / 286
75 / 105	17 22	4 48	15.7	16 24	4 31	15.7	15 26	4 15	15.6	14 29	3 58	15.5	13 31	3 42	15.4	12 33	3 25	15.4	255 / 285
76 / 104	17 27	4 30	14.7	16 29	4 14	14.6	15 31	3 58	14.6	14 33	3 43	14.5	13 35	3 27	14.4	12 36	3 12	14.4	256 / 284
77 / 103	17 31	4 11	13.6	16 33	3 56	13.6	15 35	3 41	13.6	14 36	3 27	13.4	13 38	3 13	13.4	12 40	2 58	13.3	257 / 283
78 / 102	17 36	3 52	12.6	16 37	3 38	12.5	15 38	3 25	12.5	14 40	3 11	12.4	13 41	2 58	12.4	12 43	2 45	12.3	258 / 282
79 / 101	17 39	3 33	11.6	16 41	3 20	11.5	15 42	3 08	11.5	14 43	2 56	11.4	13 44	2 43	11.3	12 45	2 31	11.3	259 / 281
80 / 100	17 43	3 14	10.5	16 44	3 02	10.4	15 45	2 51	10.4	14 46	2 40	10.3	13 47	2 29	10.3	12 48	2 18	10.3	260 / 280
81 / 99	17 46	2 55	9.5	16 47	2 44	9.4	15 48	2 34	9.4	14 49	2 24	9.3	13 49	2 14	9.3	12 50	2 04	9.2	261 / 279
82 / 98	17 49	2 35	8.4	16 50	2 26	8.4	15 50	2 17	8.3	14 51	2 08	8.3	13 52	1 59	8.2	12 52	1 50	8.2	262 / 278
83 / 97	17 52	2 16	7.4	16 52	2 08	7.3	15 52	2 00	7.3	14 53	1 52	7.2	13 54	1 44	7.2	12 54	1 37	7.2	263 / 277
84 / 96	17 54	1 57	6.3	16 54	1 50	6.3	15 55	1 43	6.3	14 55	1 36	6.2	13 55	1 30	6.2	12 56	1 23	6.2	264 / 276
85 / 95	17 56	1 37	5.3	16 56	1 32	5.2	15 56	1 26	5.2	14 56	1 20	5.2	13 57	1 15	5.2	12 57	1 09	5.1	265 / 275
86 / 94	17 57	1 18	4.2	16 57	1 13	4.2	15 58	1 09	4.2	14 58	1 04	4.1	13 58	1 00	4.1	12 58	0 55	4.1	266 / 274
87 / 93	17 58	0 58	3.2	16 59	0 55	3.1	15 59	0 52	3.1	14 59	0 48	3.1	13 59	0 45	3.1	12 59	0 42	3.1	267 / 273
88 / 92	17 59	0 39	2.1	16 59	0 37	2.1	15 59	0 34	2.1	14 59	0 32	2.1	13 59	0 30	2.1	13 00	0 28	2.1	268 / 272
89 / 91	18 00	0 19	1.1	17 00	0 18	1.0	16 00	0 17	1.0	15 00	0 16	1.0	14 00	0 15	1.0	13 00	0 14	1.0	269 / 271
90 / 90	18 00	0 00	0.0	17 00	0 00	0.0	16 00	0 00	0.0	15 00	0 00	0.0	14 00	0 00	0.0	13 00	0 00	0.0	270 / 270

N. Lat.: for LHA > 180° .... Zₙ = Z
for LHA < 180° .... Zₙ = 360° − Z

S. Lat.: for LHA > 180° .... Zₙ = 180° − Z
for LHA < 180° .... Zₙ = 180° + Z

LATITUDE / A: 78° – 83°

SIGHT REDUCTION TABLE

B: (−) for 90° < LHA < 270°
Dec:(−) for Lat. contrary name

Z₁: same sign as B
Z₂: (−) for F > 90°

Lat./A LHA/F	180…135	78° A/H	78° B/P	78° Z₁/Z₂	79° A/H	79° B/P	79° Z₁/Z₂	80° A/H	80° B/P	80° Z₁/Z₂	81° A/H	81° B/P	81° Z₁/Z₂	82° A/H	82° B/P	82° Z₁/Z₂	83° A/H	83° B/P	83° Z₁/Z₂	Lat./A	LHA
0	180	0 00	12 00	90·0	0 00	11 00	90·0	0 00	10 00	90·0	0 00	9 00	90·0	0 00	8 00	90·0	0 00	7 00	90·0	180	360
1	179	0 12	12 00	89·0	0 11	11 00	89·0	0 10	10 00	89·0	0 09	9 00	89·0	0 08	8 00	89·0	0 07	7 00	89·0	181	359
2	178	0 25	12 00	88·0	0 23	11 00	88·0	0 21	10 00	88·0	0 19	8 59	88·0	0 17	7 59	88·0	0 15	7 00	88·0	182	358
3	177	0 37	11 59	87·1	0 34	10 59	87·1	0 31	9 59	87·1	0 28	8 59	87·1	0 25	7 59	87·0	0 22	6 59	87·0	183	357
4	176	0 50	11 58	86·1	0 46	10 58	86·1	0 42	9 59	86·1	0 38	8 59	86·1	0 33	7 58	86·0	0 29	6 59	86·0	184	356
5	175	1 02	11 58	85·1	0 57	10 58	85·1	0 52	9 58	85·1	0 47	8 58	85·1	0 42	7 58	85·0	0 37	6 58	85·0	185	355
6	174	1 15	11 56	84·1	1 09	10 56	84·1	1 02	9 57	84·1	0 56	8 57	84·1	0 50	7 57	84·1	0 44	6 58	84·0	186	354
7	173	1 27	11 55	83·2	1 20	10 55	83·1	1 13	9 56	83·1	1 06	8 56	83·1	0 58	7 56	83·1	0 51	6 57	83·1	187	353
8	172	1 39	11 53	82·2	1 31	10 54	82·2	1 23	9 54	82·1	1 15	8 55	82·1	1 07	7 55	82·1	0 58	6 56	82·1	188	352
9	171	1 52	11 51	81·2	1 43	10 52	81·2	1 33	9 53	81·2	1 24	8 53	81·1	1 15	7 54	81·1	1 06	6 55	81·1	189	351
10	170	2 04	11 49	80·2	1 54	10 50	80·2	1 44	9 51	80·2	1 33	8 52	80·1	1 23	7 52	80·1	1 13	6 54	80·1	190	350
11	169	2 16	11 47	79·2	2 05	10 48	79·2	1 54	9 49	79·2	1 43	8 50	79·2	1 31	7 51	79·1	1 20	6 52	79·1	191	349
12	168	2 29	11 45	78·3	2 16	10 46	78·2	2 04	9 47	78·2	1 52	8 48	78·1	1 39	7 50	78·1	1 27	6 51	78·1	192	348
13	167	2 41	11 42	77·3	2 28	10 43	77·2	2 14	9 45	77·2	2 01	8 46	77·2	1 48	7 48	77·1	1 34	6 49	77·1	193	347
14	166	2 53	11 39	76·3	2 39	10 41	76·2	2 24	9 43	76·2	2 10	8 44	76·2	1 56	7 46	76·1	1 41	6 48	76·1	194	346
15	165	3 05	11 36	75·3	2 50	10 38	75·3	2 35	9 40	75·2	2 19	8 42	75·2	2 04	7 44	75·2	1 48	6 46	75·1	195	345
16	164	3 17	11 33	74·4	3 01	10 35	74·3	2 45	9 38	74·3	2 28	8 39	74·2	2 12	7 42	74·1	1 56	6 44	74·1	196	344
17	163	3 29	11 29	73·4	3 12	10 32	73·3	2 55	9 34	73·3	2 37	8 37	73·2	2 20	7 39	73·2	2 03	6 42	73·1	197	343
18	162	3 41	11 26	72·4	3 23	10 28	72·3	3 05	9 31	72·3	2 46	8 34	72·2	2 28	7 37	72·2	2 09	6 40	72·1	198	342
19	161	3 53	11 22	71·4	3 34	10 24	71·3	3 14	9 28	71·3	2 55	8 31	71·2	2 36	7 34	71·2	2 16	6 37	71·1	199	341
20	160	4 05	11 18	70·4	3 45	10 21	70·3	3 24	9 24	70·3	3 04	8 28	70·2	2 44	7 31	70·1	2 23	6 35	70·1	200	340
21	159	4 16	11 13	69·4	3 55	10 17	69·4	3 34	9 21	69·4	3 13	8 24	69·2	2 52	7 28	69·2	2 30	6 32	69·1	201	339
22	158	4 28	11 09	68·4	4 06	10 13	68·4	3 44	9 17	68·4	3 22	8 21	68·2	2 59	7 25	68·2	2 37	6 30	68·1	202	338
23	157	4 40	11 04	67·5	4 17	10 09	67·4	3 53	9 13	67·3	3 30	8 18	67·3	3 07	7 22	67·2	2 44	6 27	67·2	203	337
24	156	4 51	10 59	66·5	4 27	10 04	66·4	4 03	9 09	66·4	3 39	8 14	66·3	3 15	7 19	66·2	2 50	6 24	66·2	204	336
25	155	5 02	10 54	65·5	4 38	9 59	65·4	4 13	9 05	65·3	3 47	8 10	65·3	3 22	7 16	65·2	2 57	6 21	65·2	205	335
26	154	5 14	10 49	64·5	4 48	9 55	64·4	4 22	9 00	64·3	3 56	8 06	64·3	3 30	7 12	64·2	3 04	6 18	64·2	206	334
27	153	5 25	10 43	63·5	4 58	9 50	63·4	4 31	8 56	63·4	4 04	8 02	63·3	3 37	7 08	63·2	3 10	6 15	63·2	207	333
28	152	5 36	10 38	62·5	5 08	9 44	62·4	4 41	8 51	62·4	4 13	7 58	62·3	3 45	7 04	62·2	3 17	6 11	62·2	208	332
29	151	5 47	10 32	61·5	5 18	9 39	61·4	4 50	8 46	61·4	4 21	7 53	61·3	3 52	7 00	61·3	3 23	6 08	61·2	209	331
30	150	5 58	10 26	60·5	5 28	9 33	60·5	4 59	8 41	60·4	4 29	7 49	60·3	3 59	6 56	60·2	3 30	6 04	60·2	210	330
31	149	6 09	10 20	59·6	5 38	9 28	59·5	5 08	8 36	59·4	4 37	7 44	59·3	4 07	6 52	59·2	3 36	6 00	59·2	211	329
32	148	6 20	10 13	58·6	5 48	9 22	58·5	5 17	8 30	58·4	4 45	7 39	58·3	4 14	6 48	58·3	3 42	5 57	58·2	212	328
33	147	6 30	10 06	57·6	5 58	9 16	57·5	5 26	8 25	57·5	4 53	7 34	57·3	4 21	6 43	57·2	3 48	5 53	57·2	213	327
34	146	6 41	10 00	56·6	6 08	9 09	56·6	5 34	8 19	56·4	5 01	7 29	56·3	4 28	6 39	56·2	3 54	5 49	56·2	214	326
35	145	6 51	9 53	55·6	6 17	9 03	55·5	5 43	8 13	55·4	5 09	7 24	55·3	4 35	6 34	55·3	4 00	5 45	55·2	215	325
36	144	7 01	9 46	54·6	6 26	8 56	54·6	5 51	8 07	54·4	5 17	7 18	54·3	4 42	6 29	54·3	4 06	5 40	54·2	216	324
37	143	7 11	9 38	53·6	6 36	8 49	53·5	6 00	8 01	53·4	5 24	7 13	53·3	4 48	6 24	53·3	4 12	5 36	53·2	217	323
38	142	7 21	9 31	52·6	6 45	8 43	52·6	6 08	7 55	52·4	5 32	7 07	52·3	4 55	6 19	52·3	4 18	5 32	52·2	218	322
39	141	7 31	9 23	51·6	6 54	8 35	51·6	6 16	7 48	51·4	5 39	7 01	51·3	5 01	6 14	51·3	4 24	5 27	51·2	219	321
40	140	7 41	9 15	50·6	7 03	8 28	50·5	6 25	7 42	50·4	5 46	6 55	50·3	5 08	6 09	50·3	4 30	5 22	50·2	220	320
41	139	7 50	9 07	49·6	7 11	8 21	49·5	6 32	7 35	49·4	5 53	6 49	49·4	5 14	6 03	49·3	4 35	5 18	49·2	221	319
42	138	8 00	8 59	48·6	7 20	8 13	48·5	6 40	7 28	48·5	6 01	6 43	48·4	5 21	5 58	48·3	4 41	5 13	48·2	222	318
43	137	8 09	8 50	47·6	7 29	8 05	47·5	6 48	7 21	47·4	6 07	6 36	47·3	5 27	5 52	47·3	4 46	5 08	47·2	223	317
44	136	8 18	8 42	46·6	7 37	7 58	46·5	6 56	7 14	46·4	6 14	6 30	46·4	5 33	5 46	46·3	4 52	5 03	46·2	224	316
45	135	8 27	8 33	45·6	7 45	7 50	45·5	7 03	7 06	45·4	6 21	6 23	45·4	5 39	5 41	45·3	4 58	4 58	45·2	225	315

Lat./A LHA/F	78° A/H	78° B/P	78° Z1/Z2	79° A/H	79° B/P	79° Z1/Z2	80° A/H	80° B/P	80° Z1/Z2	81° A/H	81° B/P	81° Z1/Z2	82° A/H	82° B/P	82° Z1/Z2	83° A/H	83° B/P	83° Z1/Z2	Lat./A LHA
45 135	8 27	8 33	45·6	7 45	7 50	45·5	7 03	7 06	45·4	6 21	6 23	45·4	5 39	5 41	45·3	4 57	4 58	45·2	225 315
46 134	8 36	8 24	44·6	7 53	7 41	44·5	7 11	6 59	44·4	6 28	6 17	44·4	5 45	5 35	44·3	5 02	4 53	44·2	226 314
47 133	8 45	8 15	43·6	8 01	7 33	43·5	7 18	6 51	43·4	6 34	6 10	43·4	5 51	5 28	43·3	5 07	4 47	43·2	227 313
48 132	8 53	8 06	42·6	8 09	7 25	42·5	7 25	6 44	42·4	6 41	6 03	42·4	5 56	5 22	42·3	5 12	4 42	42·2	228 312
49 131	9 02	7 56	41·6	8 17	7 16	41·5	7 32	6 36	41·4	6 47	5 56	41·4	6 02	5 16	41·3	5 17	4 36	41·2	229 311
50 130	9 10	7 47	40·6	8 24	7 07	40·5	7 39	6 28	40·4	6 53	5 49	40·4	6 07	5 10	40·3	5 21	4 31	40·2	230 310
51 129	9 18	7 37	39·6	8 32	6 58	39·5	7 45	6 20	39·4	6 59	5 42	39·3	6 13	5 03	39·3	5 26	4 25	39·2	231 309
52 128	9 26	7 27	38·6	8 39	6 49	38·5	7 52	6 12	38·4	7 05	5 34	38·3	6 18	4 57	38·3	5 31	4 19	38·2	232 308
53 127	9 33	7 17	37·6	8 46	6 40	37·5	7 58	6 03	37·4	7 11	5 27	37·3	6 23	4 50	37·3	5 35	4 14	37·2	233 307
54 126	9 41	7 07	36·6	8 53	6 31	36·5	8 05	5 55	36·4	7 16	5 19	36·3	6 28	4 43	36·3	5 39	4 08	36·2	234 306
55 125	9 48	6 57	35·6	9 00	6 22	35·5	8 11	5 47	35·4	7 22	5 11	35·3	6 33	4 37	35·3	5 44	4 02	35·2	235 305
56 124	9 56	6 47	34·6	9 06	6 12	34·5	8 17	5 38	34·4	7 27	5 04	34·3	6 38	4 30	34·3	5 48	3 56	34·2	236 304
57 123	10 03	6 36	33·6	9 13	6 03	33·5	8 22	5 29	33·4	7 32	4 56	33·3	6 42	4 23	33·3	5 52	3 50	33·2	237 303
58 122	10 09	6 26	32·6	9 19	5 53	32·5	8 28	5 20	32·4	7 37	4 48	32·3	6 47	4 16	32·3	5 56	3 43	32·2	238 302
59 121	10 16	6 15	31·6	9 25	5 43	31·5	8 34	5 11	31·4	7 42	4 40	31·3	6 51	4 08	31·2	6 00	3 37	31·2	239 301
60 120	10 22	6 04	30·6	9 31	5 33	30·5	8 39	5 02	30·4	7 47	4 32	30·3	6 55	4 01	30·2	6 04	3 31	30·2	240 300
61 119	10 29	5 53	29·5	9 36	5 23	29·4	8 44	4 53	29·4	7 52	4 23	29·3	6 59	3 54	29·2	6 07	3 24	29·2	241 299
62 118	10 35	5 42	28·5	9 42	5 13	28·4	8 49	4 44	28·4	7 56	4 15	28·3	7 04	3 46	28·2	6 11	3 18	28·2	242 298
63 117	10 41	5 31	27·5	9 47	5 03	27·4	8 54	4 35	27·4	8 01	4 07	27·3	7 07	3 39	27·2	6 14	3 11	27·2	243 297
64 116	10 46	5 19	26·5	9 52	4 52	26·4	8 59	4 26	26·3	8 05	3 58	26·3	7 11	3 32	26·2	6 17	3 05	26·2	244 296
65 115	10 52	5 08	25·5	9 57	4 41	25·4	9 03	4 16	25·3	8 09	3 49	25·3	7 15	3 24	25·2	6 20	2 58	25·2	245 295
66 114	10 57	4 56	24·5	10 02	4 31	24·4	9 08	4 06	24·3	8 13	3 41	24·3	7 18	3 16	24·2	6 24	2 52	24·2	246 294
67 113	11 02	4 45	23·5	10 07	4 21	23·4	9 12	3 57	23·3	8 17	3 32	23·3	7 22	3 09	23·2	6 26	2 45	23·2	247 293
68 112	11 07	4 33	22·4	10 11	4 10	22·4	9 16	3 47	22·3	8 20	3 24	22·2	7 25	3 01	22·2	6 29	2 38	22·1	248 292
69 111	11 12	4 21	21·4	10 16	3 59	21·4	9 20	3 37	21·3	8 24	3 15	21·2	7 28	2 53	21·2	6 32	2 31	21·1	249 291
70 110	11 16	4 09	20·4	10 20	3 48	20·3	9 23	3 27	20·3	8 27	3 06	20·2	7 31	2 45	20·2	6 35	2 24	20·1	250 290
71 109	11 20	3 58	19·4	10 24	3 37	19·3	9 27	3 17	19·3	8 30	2 57	19·2	7 34	2 37	19·2	6 37	2 17	19·1	251 289
72 108	11 24	3 45	18·4	10 27	3 26	18·3	9 30	3 07	18·3	8 33	2 48	18·2	7 36	2 29	18·2	6 39	2 10	18·1	252 288
73 107	11 28	3 33	17·4	10 31	3 15	17·3	9 34	2 57	17·3	8 36	2 39	17·2	7 39	2 21	17·2	6 42	2 03	17·1	253 287
74 106	11 32	3 21	16·3	10 34	3 04	16·3	9 37	2 47	16·2	8 39	2 30	16·2	7 41	2 13	16·1	6 44	1 56	16·1	254 286
75 105	11 35	3 09	15·3	10 37	2 53	15·3	9 39	2 37	15·3	8 41	2 21	15·2	7 44	2 05	15·1	6 46	1 49	15·1	255 285
76 104	11 38	2 57	14·3	10 40	2 42	14·3	9 42	2 27	14·3	8 44	2 12	14·2	7 46	1 57	14·1	6 47	1 42	14·1	256 284
77 103	11 41	2 44	13·3	10 43	2 30	13·3	9 44	2 16	13·2	8 46	2 02	13·2	7 48	1 49	13·1	6 49	1 35	13·1	257 283
78 102	11 44	2 32	12·3	10 45	2 19	12·2	9 47	2 06	12·2	8 48	1 53	12·1	7 49	1 40	12·1	6 51	1 28	12·1	258 282
79 101	11 47	2 19	11·2	10 48	2 07	11·2	9 49	1 56	11·2	8 50	1 44	11·1	7 51	1 32	11·1	6 52	1 21	11·1	259 281
80 100	11 49	2 07	10·2	10 50	1 56	10·2	9 51	1 45	10·2	8 52	1 35	10·1	7 53	1 24	10·1	6 54	1 13	10·1	260 280
81 99	11 51	1 54	9·2	10 52	1 45	9·2	9 53	1 35	9·1	8 53	1 25	9·1	7 54	1 16	9·1	6 55	1 06	9·1	261 279
82 98	11 53	1 42	8·2	10 53	1 33	8·1	9 54	1 24	8·1	8 55	1 16	8·1	7 55	1 07	8·1	6 56	0 59	8·1	262 278
83 97	11 55	1 29	7·2	10 55	1 21	7·1	9 55	1 14	7·1	8 56	1 06	7·1	7 56	0 59	7·1	6 57	0 51	7·0	263 277
84 96	11 56	1 16	6·1	10 56	1 10	6·1	9 57	1 03	6·1	8 57	0 57	6·1	7 57	0 50	6·1	6 58	0 44	6·0	264 276
85 95	11 57	1 04	5·1	10 57	0 58	5·1	9 58	0 53	5·1	8 58	0 47	5·1	7 58	0 42	5·0	6 59	0 37	5·0	265 275
86 94	11 58	0 51	4·1	10 58	0 47	4·1	9 59	0 42	4·1	8 59	0 38	4·0	7 59	0 34	4·0	6 59	0 29	4·0	266 274
87 93	11 59	0 38	3·1	10 59	0 35	3·1	9 59	0 32	3·0	8 59	0 28	3·0	7 59	0 25	3·0	6 59	0 22	3·0	267 273
88 92	12 00	0 26	2·0	11 00	0 23	2·0	10 00	0 21	2·0	9 00	0 19	2·0	8 00	0 17	2·0	7 00	0 15	2·0	268 272
89 91	12 00	0 13	1·0	11 00	0 12	1·0	10 00	0 11	1·0	9 00	0 10	1·0	8 00	0 08	1·0	7 00	0 07	1·0	269 271
90 90	12 00	0 00	0·0	11 00	0 00	0·0	10 00	0 00	0·0	9 00	0 00	0·0	8 00	0 00	0·0	7 00	0 00	0·0	270 270

N. Lat: for LHA > 180° .... Zn = Z
for LHA < 180° .... Zn = 360° − Z

S. Lat: for LHA > 180° .... Zn = 180° − Z
for LHA < 180° .... Zn = 180° + Z

B: (−) for 90° < LHA < 270°
Dec:(−) for Lat. contrary name

Z_1: same sign as B
Z_2: (−) for F > 90°

SIGHT REDUCTION TABLE

LHA	F	84° A/H	84° B/P	84° Z_1/Z_2	85° A/H	85° B/P	85° Z_1/Z_2	86° A/H	86° B/P	86° Z_1/Z_2	87° A/H	87° B/P	87° Z_1/Z_2	88° A/H	88° B/P	88° Z_1/Z_2	89° A/H	89° B/P	89° Z_1/Z_2	LHA	LHA
0	180	0 00	6 00	90.0	0 00	5 00	90.0	0 00	4 00	90.0	0 00	3 00	90.0	0 00	2 00	90.0	0 00	1 00	90.0	180	360
1	179	0 06	6 00	89.0	0 05	5 00	89.0	0 04	4 00	89.0	0 03	3 00	89.0	0 02	2 00	89.0	0 01	1 00	89.0	181	359
2	178	0 13	6 00	88.0	0 10	5 00	88.0	0 08	4 00	88.0	0 06	3 00	88.0	0 04	2 00	88.0	0 02	1 00	88.0	182	358
3	177	0 19	5 59	87.0	0 16	5 00	87.0	0 13	4 00	87.0	0 09	3 00	87.0	0 06	2 00	87.0	0 03	1 00	87.0	183	357
4	176	0 25	5 59	86.0	0 21	4 59	86.0	0 17	3 59	86.0	0 13	3 00	86.0	0 08	2 00	86.0	0 04	1 00	86.0	184	356
5	175	0 31	5 59	85.0	0 26	4 59	85.0	0 21	3 59	85.0	0 16	2 59	85.0	0 10	2 00	85.0	0 05	1 00	85.0	185	355
6	174	0 38	5 58	84.0	0 31	4 58	84.0	0 25	3 58	84.0	0 19	2 59	84.0	0 13	1 59	84.0	0 06	1 00	84.0	186	354
7	173	0 44	5 57	83.0	0 37	4 58	83.0	0 29	3 58	83.0	0 22	2 59	83.0	0 15	1 59	83.0	0 07	1 00	83.0	187	353
8	172	0 50	5 57	82.0	0 42	4 57	82.0	0 33	3 57	82.0	0 25	2 58	82.0	0 17	1 59	82.0	0 08	0 59	82.0	188	352
9	171	0 56	5 56	81.0	0 47	4 56	81.0	0 38	3 56	81.0	0 28	2 58	81.0	0 19	1 59	81.0	0 09	0 59	81.0	189	351
10	170	1 02	5 55	80.1	0 52	4 55	80.0	0 42	3 55	80.0	0 31	2 57	80.0	0 21	1 58	80.0	0 10	0 59	80.0	190	350
11	169	1 09	5 53	79.1	0 57	4 55	79.1	0 46	3 53	79.0	0 34	2 57	79.0	0 23	1 58	79.0	0 11	0 59	79.0	191	349
12	168	1 15	5 52	78.1	1 02	4 53	78.1	0 50	3 52	78.0	0 37	2 56	78.0	0 25	1 57	78.0	0 12	0 59	78.0	192	348
13	167	1 21	5 51	77.1	1 07	4 52	77.1	0 54	3 51	77.0	0 40	2 55	77.0	0 27	1 57	77.0	0 13	0 59	77.0	193	347
14	166	1 27	5 49	76.1	1 12	4 51	76.1	0 58	3 50	76.0	0 44	2 55	76.0	0 29	1 56	76.0	0 15	0 58	76.0	194	346
15	165	1 33	5 48	75.1	1 18	4 50	75.1	1 02	3 48	75.0	0 47	2 54	75.0	0 31	1 56	75.0	0 16	0 58	75.0	195	345
16	164	1 39	5 46	74.1	1 23	4 48	74.1	1 06	3 47	74.0	0 50	2 53	74.0	0 33	1 55	74.0	0 17	0 58	74.0	196	344
17	163	1 45	5 44	73.1	1 28	4 47	73.1	1 10	3 45	73.0	0 53	2 52	73.0	0 35	1 55	73.0	0 18	0 58	73.0	197	343
18	162	1 51	5 42	72.1	1 33	4 45	72.1	1 14	3 44	72.0	0 56	2 51	72.0	0 37	1 54	72.0	0 19	0 57	72.0	198	342
19	161	1 57	5 41	71.1	1 38	4 44	71.1	1 18	3 42	71.0	0 59	2 50	71.0	0 39	1 53	71.0	0 20	0 57	71.0	199	341
20	160	2 03	5 38	70.1	1 42	4 42	70.1	1 22	3 40	70.0	1 02	2 49	70.0	0 41	1 53	70.0	0 21	0 57	70.0	200	340
21	159	2 09	5 36	69.1	1 47	4 40	69.1	1 26	3 39	69.0	1 04	2 48	69.0	0 43	1 52	69.0	0 22	0 56	69.0	201	339
22	158	2 15	5 34	68.1	1 52	4 38	68.1	1 30	3 37	68.0	1 07	2 47	68.0	0 45	1 51	68.0	0 22	0 56	68.0	202	338
23	157	2 20	5 32	67.1	1 57	4 36	67.1	1 34	3 35	67.0	1 10	2 46	67.0	0 47	1 50	67.0	0 23	0 56	67.0	203	337
24	156	2 26	5 29	66.1	2 02	4 34	66.1	1 38	3 34	66.1	1 13	2 44	66.0	0 49	1 50	66.0	0 24	0 55	66.0	204	336
25	155	2 32	5 26	65.1	2 07	4 32	65.1	1 41	3 32	65.1	1 16	2 43	65.0	0 51	1 49	65.0	0 25	0 55	65.0	205	335
26	154	2 38	5 24	64.1	2 11	4 30	64.1	1 45	3 30	64.1	1 19	2 42	64.0	0 53	1 48	64.0	0 26	0 54	64.0	206	334
27	153	2 43	5 21	63.1	2 16	4 27	63.1	1 49	3 28	63.1	1 22	2 40	63.0	0 54	1 47	63.0	0 27	0 54	63.0	207	333
28	152	2 49	5 18	62.1	2 21	4 25	62.1	1 53	3 27	62.1	1 24	2 39	62.0	0 56	1 46	62.0	0 28	0 53	62.0	208	332
29	151	2 54	5 15	61.1	2 25	4 23	61.1	1 56	3 25	61.1	1 27	2 37	61.0	0 58	1 45	61.0	0 29	0 53	61.0	209	331
30	150	3 00	5 12	60.1	2 30	4 20	60.1	2 00	3 23	60.1	1 30	2 36	60.0	1 00	1 44	60.0	0 30	0 52	60.0	210	330
31	149	3 05	5 09	59.1	2 34	4 17	59.1	2 04	3 21	59.1	1 33	2 34	59.0	1 02	1 43	59.0	0 31	0 52	59.0	211	329
32	148	3 11	5 06	58.1	2 39	4 15	58.1	2 07	3 19	58.1	1 35	2 33	58.0	1 04	1 42	58.0	0 32	0 51	58.0	212	328
33	147	3 16	5 02	57.1	2 43	4 12	57.1	2 11	3 17	57.1	1 38	2 31	57.0	1 05	1 41	57.0	0 33	0 50	57.0	213	327
34	146	3 21	4 59	56.1	2 48	4 09	56.1	2 14	3 15	56.1	1 41	2 29	56.0	1 07	1 39	56.0	0 34	0 50	56.0	214	326
35	145	3 26	4 55	55.1	2 52	4 06	55.1	2 18	3 13	55.1	1 43	2 27	55.0	1 09	1 38	55.0	0 34	0 49	55.0	215	325
36	144	3 31	4 52	54.1	2 56	4 03	54.1	2 21	3 11	54.1	1 46	2 26	54.0	1 11	1 37	54.0	0 35	0 49	54.0	216	324
37	143	3 36	4 48	53.2	3 00	4 00	53.1	2 24	3 09	53.1	1 49	2 24	53.0	1 12	1 36	53.0	0 36	0 48	53.0	217	323
38	142	3 41	4 44	52.2	3 05	3 57	52.1	2 28	3 07	52.1	1 51	2 22	52.0	1 14	1 34	52.0	0 37	0 47	52.0	218	322
39	141	3 46	4 40	51.2	3 09	3 53	51.1	2 31	3 05	51.1	1 53	2 20	51.0	1 16	1 33	51.0	0 38	0 47	51.0	219	321
40	140	3 51	4 36	50.2	3 13	3 50	50.1	2 34	3 03	50.1	1 56	2 18	50.0	1 17	1 32	50.0	0 39	0 46	50.0	220	320
41	139	3 56	4 32	49.2	3 17	3 47	49.1	2 37	3 01	49.1	1 58	2 16	49.0	1 19	1 31	49.0	0 39	0 45	49.0	221	319
42	138	4 01	4 28	48.2	3 21	3 43	48.1	2 41	2 58	48.1	2 00	2 14	48.0	1 20	1 29	48.0	0 40	0 45	48.0	222	318
43	137	4 05	4 24	47.2	3 24	3 40	47.1	2 44	2 56	47.1	2 03	2 12	47.0	1 22	1 28	47.0	0 41	0 44	47.0	223	317
44	136	4 10	4 19	46.2	3 28	3 36	46.1	2 47	2 53	46.1	2 05	2 10	46.0	1 23	1 26	46.0	0 42	0 43	46.0	224	316
45	135	4 14	4 15	45.2	3 32	3 32	45.1	2 50	2 50	45.1	2 07	2 07	45.0	1 25	1 25	45.0	0 42	0 42	45.0	225	315

Lat. / A	LHA/F	84° A/H	84° B/P	84° Z₁/Z₂	85° A/H	85° B/P	85° Z₁/Z₂	86° A/H	86° B/P	86° Z₁/Z₂	87° A/H	87° B/P	87° Z₁/Z₂	88° A/H	88° B/P	88° Z₁/Z₂	89° A/H	89° B/P	89° Z₁/Z₂	Lat. / A LHA	
45	135	4 14	4 15	45·2	3 32	3 32	45·1	2 50	2 50	45·1	2 07	2 07	45·0	1 25	1 25	45·0	0 42	0 42	45·0	225	315
46	134	4 19	4 11	44·2	3 36	3 29	44·1	2 53	2 47	44·1	2 09	2 05	44·0	1 26	1 23	44·0	0 43	0 42	44·0	226	314
47	133	4 23	4 06	43·2	3 39	3 25	43·1	2 55	2 44	43·1	2 12	2 03	43·0	1 28	1 22	43·0	0 44	0 41	43·0	227	313
48	132	4 27	4 01	42·2	3 43	3 21	42·1	2 58	2 41	42·1	2 14	2 01	42·0	1 29	1 20	42·0	0 45	0 40	42·0	228	312
49	131	4 31	3 57	41·2	3 46	3 17	41·1	3 01	2 38	41·1	2 16	1 58	41·0	1 31	1 19	41·0	0 45	0 39	41·0	229	311
50	130	4 36	3 52	40·2	3 50	3 13	40·1	3 04	2 34	40·1	2 18	1 56	40·0	1 32	1 17	40·0	0 46	0 39	40·0	230	310
51	129	4 40	3 47	39·2	3 53	3 09	39·1	3 06	2 31	39·1	2 20	1 53	39·0	1 33	1 16	39·0	0 47	0 38	39·0	231	309
52	128	4 43	3 42	38·2	3 56	3 05	38·1	3 09	2 28	38·1	2 22	1 51	38·0	1 35	1 14	38·0	0 47	0 37	38·0	232	308
53	127	4 47	3 37	37·2	3 59	3 01	37·1	3 12	2 25	37·1	2 24	1 48	37·0	1 36	1 12	37·0	0 48	0 36	37·0	233	307
54	126	4 51	3 32	36·1	4 03	2 57	36·1	3 14	2 21	36·1	2 26	1 46	36·0	1 37	1 11	36·0	0 49	0 35	36·0	234	306
55	125	4 55	3 27	35·1	4 06	2 52	35·1	3 17	2 18	35·1	2 27	1 43	35·0	1 38	1 09	35·0	0 49	0 34	35·0	235	305
56	124	4 58	3 22	34·1	4 09	2 48	34·1	3 19	2 14	34·1	2 29	1 41	34·0	1 39	1 07	34·0	0 50	0 34	34·0	236	304
57	123	5 02	3 17	33·1	4 12	2 44	33·1	3 21	2 11	33·1	2 31	1 38	33·0	1 41	1 05	33·0	0 50	0 33	33·0	237	303
58	122	5 05	3 11	32·1	4 14	2 39	32·1	3 23	2 07	32·1	2 33	1 35	32·0	1 42	1 04	32·0	0 51	0 32	32·0	238	302
59	121	5 08	3 06	31·1	4 17	2 35	31·1	3 26	2 04	31·1	2 34	1 33	31·0	1 43	1 02	31·0	0 51	0 31	31·0	239	301
60	120	5 12	3 00	30·1	4 20	2 30	30·1	3 28	2 00	30·1	2 36	1 30	30·0	1 44	1 00	30·0	0 52	0 30	30·0	240	300
61	119	5 15	2 55	29·1	4 22	2 26	29·1	3 30	1 56	29·1	2 37	1 27	29·0	1 45	0 58	29·0	0 52	0 29	29·0	241	299
62	118	5 18	2 49	28·1	4 25	2 21	28·1	3 32	1 53	28·1	2 39	1 25	28·0	1 46	0 56	28·0	0 53	0 28	28·0	242	298
63	117	5 21	2 44	27·1	4 27	2 16	27·1	3 34	1 49	27·1	2 40	1 22	27·0	1 47	0 54	27·0	0 53	0 27	27·0	243	297
64	116	5 23	2 38	26·1	4 30	2 12	26·1	3 36	1 45	26·1	2 42	1 19	26·0	1 48	0 53	26·0	0 54	0 26	26·0	244	296
65	115	5 26	2 33	25·1	4 32	2 07	25·1	3 37	1 42	25·1	2 43	1 16	25·0	1 49	0 51	25·0	0 54	0 25	25·0	245	295
66	114	5 29	2 27	24·1	4 34	2 02	24·1	3 39	1 38	24·1	2 44	1 13	24·0	1 50	0 49	24·0	0 55	0 24	24·0	246	294
67	113	5 31	2 21	23·1	4 36	1 57	23·1	3 41	1 34	23·1	2 46	1 10	23·0	1 51	0 47	23·0	0 55	0 23	23·0	247	293
68	112	5 34	2 15	22·1	4 38	1 53	22·1	3 42	1 30	22·1	2 47	1 07	22·0	1 51	0 45	22·0	0 56	0 22	22·0	248	292
69	111	5 36	2 09	21·1	4 40	1 48	21·1	3 44	1 26	21·0	2 48	1 05	21·0	1 52	0 43	21·0	0 56	0 22	21·0	249	291
70	110	5 38	2 04	20·1	4 42	1 43	20·1	3 46	1 22	20·0	2 49	1 02	20·0	1 53	0 41	20·0	0 56	0 21	20·0	250	290
71	109	5 40	1 58	19·1	4 44	1 38	19·1	3 47	1 18	19·0	2 50	0 59	19·0	1 53	0 39	19·0	0 57	0 20	19·0	251	289
72	108	5 42	1 52	18·1	4 45	1 33	18·1	3 48	1 14	18·0	2 51	0 56	18·0	1 54	0 37	18·0	0 57	0 19	18·0	252	288
73	107	5 44	1 46	17·1	4 47	1 28	17·1	3 49	1 10	17·0	2 52	0 53	17·0	1 55	0 35	17·0	0 57	0 18	17·0	253	287
74	106	5 46	1 40	16·1	4 48	1 23	16·1	3 51	1 06	16·0	2 53	0 50	16·0	1 55	0 33	16·0	0 58	0 17	16·0	254	286
75	105	5 48	1 33	15·1	4 50	1 18	15·1	3 52	1 02	15·0	2 54	0 47	15·0	1 56	0 31	15·0	0 58	0 16	15·0	255	285
76	104	5 49	1 27	14·1	4 51	1 13	14·1	3 53	0 58	14·0	2 55	0 44	14·0	1 56	0 29	14·0	0 58	0 15	14·0	256	284
77	103	5 51	1 21	13·1	4 52	1 08	13·0	3 54	0 54	13·0	2 56	0 41	13·0	1 57	0 27	13·0	0 58	0 14	13·0	257	283
78	102	5 52	1 15	12·1	4 53	1 03	12·0	3 55	0 50	12·0	2 56	0 37	12·0	1 57	0 25	12·0	0 59	0 13	12·0	258	282
79	101	5 53	1 09	11·1	4 54	0 57	11·0	3 56	0 46	11·0	2 57	0 34	11·0	1 58	0 23	11·0	0 59	0 12	11·0	259	281
80	100	5 55	1 03	10·1	4 55	0 52	10·0	3 56	0 42	10·0	2 58	0 31	10·0	1 58	0 21	10·0	0 59	0 11	10·0	260	280
81	99	5 56	0 57	9·0	4 56	0 47	9·0	3 57	0 38	9·0	2 58	0 28	9·0	1 59	0 19	9·0	0 59	0 09	9·0	261	279
82	98	5 57	0 50	8·0	4 57	0 42	8·0	3 58	0 33	8·0	2 59	0 25	8·0	1 59	0 17	8·0	0 59	0 08	8·0	262	278
83	97	5 58	0 44	7·0	4 58	0 37	7·0	3 59	0 29	7·0	2 59	0 22	7·0	1 59	0 15	7·0	1 00	0 07	7·0	263	277
84	96	5 59	0 38	6·0	4 58	0 31	6·0	3 59	0 25	6·0	2 59	0 19	6·0	1 59	0 13	6·0	1 00	0 06	6·0	264	276
85	95	5 59	0 31	5·0	4 59	0 26	5·0	3 59	0 21	5·0	3 00	0 16	5·0	1 59	0 10	5·0	1 00	0 05	5·0	265	275
86	94	6 00	0 25	4·0	4 59	0 21	4·0	4 00	0 17	4·0	3 00	0 13	4·0	2 00	0 08	4·0	1 00	0 04	4·0	266	274
87	93	6 00	0 19	3·0	5 00	0 16	3·0	4 00	0 13	3·0	3 00	0 09	3·0	2 00	0 06	3·0	1 00	0 03	3·0	267	273
88	92	6 00	0 13	2·0	5 00	0 10	2·0	4 00	0 08	2·0	3 00	0 06	2·0	2 00	0 04	2·0	1 00	0 02	2·0	268	272
89	91	6 00	0 06	1·0	5 00	0 05	1·0	4 00	0 04	1·0	3 00	0 03	1·0	2 00	0 02	1·0	1 00	0 01	1·0	269	271
90	90	6 00	0 00	0·0	5 00	0 00	0·0	4 00	0 00	0·0	3 00	0 00	0·0	2 00	0 00	0·0	1 00	0 00	0·0	270	270

N. Lat.: for LHA > 180° .... Zₙ = Z
for LHA < 180° .... Zₙ = 360° − Z

S. Lat.: for LHA > 180° .... Zₙ = 180° − Z
for LHA < 180° .... Zₙ = 180° + Z

AUXILIARY TABLE

Sign for corr$_2$ for A'. → $-/+$ (A')

Sign of corr$_1$ for F'. Reverse sign if F' > 90°.

Sign → $+/-$ (F'/−)

P°	30	29/31	28/32	27/33	26/34	25/35	24/36	23/37	22/38	21/39	20/40	19/41	18/42	17/43	16/44	15/45	14/46	13/47	12/48	11/49	10/50	9/51	8/52	7/53	6/54	5/55	4/56	3/57	2/58	1/59	Z°$_2$
1	~	~	~	~	~	~	~	~	~	~	~	~	~	~	~	~	~	~	~	~	~	~	~	~	~	~	~	~	~	~	89
2	1	1	0	0	0	0	0	0	0	0	0	0	0	0	0	0	0	0	0	0	0	0	0	0	0	0	0	0	0	0	88
3	1	1	1	1	1	1	1	1	1	1	1	1	1	1	1	1	0	0	0	0	0	0	0	0	0	0	0	0	0	0	87
4	2	2	1	1	1	1	1	1	1	1	1	1	1	1	1	1	1	1	1	1	1	0	0	0	0	0	0	0	0	0	86
5	3	3	2	2	2	2	2	2	2	1	2	2	1	1	1	1	1	1	1	1	1	1	1	0	0	0	0	0	0	0	85
6	3	3	2	2	2	2	2	2	2	2	2	2	2	2	2	2	1	1	1	1	1	1	1	1	1	0	0	0	0	0	84
7	4	4	3	3	3	3	3	3	3	2	2	2	2	2	2	2	2	2	1	1	1	1	1	1	1	1	0	0	0	0	83
8	4	4	3	3	3	3	3	3	3	3	3	3	2	2	2	2	2	2	2	2	2	1	1	1	1	1	1	0	0	0	82
9	5	5	4	4	4	3	3	4	4	3	3	3	3	3	3	2	2	2	2	2	2	2	1	1	1	1	1	0	0	0	81
10	5	5	4	4	4	4	4	4	4	4	3	3	3	3	3	3	2	2	2	2	2	2	2	1	1	1	1	1	0	0	80
11	6	6	5	5	5	4	4	4	4	4	4	4	3	3	3	3	3	2	2	2	2	2	2	1	1	1	1	1	0	0	79
12	6	6	5	5	5	5	5	5	5	4	4	4	4	3	3	3	3	3	2	2	2	2	2	2	1	1	1	1	1	0	78
13	7	7	6	6	5	5	5	5	5	5	4	4	4	4	4	3	3	3	3	3	3	2	2	2	2	1	1	1	1	0	77
14	7	7	6	6	6	6	6	6	5	5	5	5	4	4	4	4	3	3	3	3	3	2	2	2	2	1	1	1	1	0	76
15	8	8	7	7	6	6	6	6	6	5	5	5	5	4	4	4	4	3	3	3	3	3	2	2	2	2	1	1	1	0	75
16	8	8	7	7	7	6	7	6	6	6	5	5	5	4	4	4	4	4	3	3	3	3	3	2	2	2	1	1	1	0	74
17	9	8	8	7	7	7	7	7	7	6	6	6	5	5	5	4	4	4	4	3	3	3	3	2	2	2	2	1	1	0	73
18	9	9	8	8	8	7	7	7	7	6	6	6	5	5	5	5	4	4	4	4	4	3	3	3	2	2	2	1	1	0	72
19	10	9	9	8	8	8	8	8	8	7	6	6	6	5	5	5	5	4	4	4	4	3	3	3	2	2	2	1	1	0	71
20	10	10	9	9	9	8	8	8	8	7	7	6	6	6	5	5	5	5	4	4	4	4	3	3	2	2	2	1	1	0	70
21	11	10	10	9	9	9	9	8	8	7	7	7	6	6	6	5	5	5	5	4	4	4	3	3	3	2	2	1	1	1	69
22	11	11	10	10	10	9	9	9	9	8	7	7	7	6	6	6	5	5	5	5	4	4	4	3	3	2	2	1	1	1	68
23	12	11	11	10	10	9	9	9	9	8	8	7	7	6	6	6	5	5	5	5	5	4	4	3	3	2	2	1	1	1	67
24	12	12	11	11	10	10	10	9	9	8	8	8	7	7	7	6	6	6	5	5	5	4	4	3	3	3	2	2	1	1	66
25	13	12	12	11	11	10	10	10	10	9	8	8	8	7	7	6	6	6	6	5	5	5	4	3	3	3	2	2	1	1	65
26	13	13	12	11	11	11	11	10	10	9	9	8	8	7	7	7	6	6	6	5	5	5	4	4	3	3	2	2	1	1	64
27	14	13	13	12	12	11	11	11	11	9	9	9	8	8	8	7	6	7	6	6	5	5	5	4	3	3	2	2	1	1	63
28	14	14	13	12	12	11	11	11	11	10	9	9	8	8	8	7	7	7	6	6	6	5	5	4	4	3	2	2	1	1	62
29	15	14	14	13	13	12	12	11	11	10	10	9	9	8	8	7	7	7	7	6	6	5	5	4	4	3	2	2	1	1	61
30	15	14	14	13	13	12	12	12	12	10	10	9	9	8	8	8	7	7	7	6	6	5	5	4	4	3	2	2	1	1	60
31	15	15	14	13	13	13	12	12	12	11	10	10	9	8	8	8	7	7	7	6	6	5	5	4	4	3	2	2	1	1	59
32	16	15	15	14	14	13	13	12	12	11	11	10	10	9	9	8	8	8	7	7	6	5	5	4	4	3	2	2	1	1	58
33	16	16	15	14	14	13	13	13	13	11	11	11	10	9	9	8	8	8	7	7	6	5	5	4	4	3	2	2	1	1	57
34	17	16	16	15	15	14	14	13	13	12	11	11	10	9	9	9	8	8	7	7	6	5	5	4	4	3	2	2	1	1	56
35	17	17	16	15	15	14	14	13	14	12	12	11	10	10	9	9	8	8	8	7	6	5	5	4	4	3	3	2	1	1	55
36	18	17	16	15	15	15	14	14	14	12	12	11	11	10	10	9	8	8	8	7	6	5	5	4	4	3	3	2	1	1	54
37	18	17	17	16	16	15	15	14	14	13	12	12	11	10	10	9	9	8	8	7	6	5	5	4	4	3	3	2	1	1	53
38	18	18	17	16	16	15	15	14	14	13	12	12	11	10	10	9	9	8	8	7	6	6	5	4	4	3	3	2	1	1	52
39	19	18	18	17	16	16	15	15	14	13	13	12	11	11	10	9	9	8	8	7	6	6	5	4	4	3	3	2	1	1	51
40	19	19	18	17	17	16	15	15	14	13	13	12	12	11	10	10	9	8	8	7	6	6	5	4	4	3	3	2	1	1	50

Sign for corr$_1$ for F'. Reverse sign if F' > 90°.

For Z₂ < 10°, use 10°

For P > 80°, use 80°

$\mp A'$ (top) / $+\ -$; Z_2°

P°	30	29	28	27	26	25	24	23	22	21	20	19	18	17	16	15	14	13	12	11	10	9	8	7	6	5	4	3	2	1	Z₂
	30	31	32	33	34	35	36	37	38	39	40	41	42	43	44	45	46	47	48	49	50	51	52	53	54	55	56	57	58	59	
41	‸	‸	‸	‸	‸	‸	‸	‸	‸	‸	‸	‸	‸	‸	‸	‸	‸	‸	‸	‸	‸	‸	‸	‸	‸	‸	‸	‸	‸	‸	49
42	20	19	18	18	17	16	16	15	14	14	13	12	12	11	10	10	9	9	8	7	7	6	5	5	4	3	3	2	1	1	48
43	20	19	18	18	17	16	16	15	14	14	13	12	12	11	10	10	9	9	8	7	7	6	5	5	4	3	3	2	1	1	47
44	20	20	19	18	17	16	16	15	14	14	13	12	12	11	10	10	9	9	8	7	7	6	5	5	4	3	3	2	1	1	46
45	21	20	19	19	18	17	17	16	15	15	14	13	12	11	10	10	9	9	8	7	7	6	5	5	4	3	3	2	1	1	45
46	21	20	19	19	18	17	17	16	15	15	14	13	13	12	11	11	10	9	8	7	7	6	5	5	4	3	3	2	1	1	44
47	21	20	19	19	18	17	17	16	15	15	14	13	13	12	11	11	10	10	9	8	7	6	5	5	4	3	3	2	1	1	43
48	22	21	20	20	19	18	17	16	15	15	14	13	13	12	11	11	10	10	9	8	8	7	6	5	4	3	3	2	1	1	42
49	22	21	20	20	19	18	18	17	16	15	14	13	13	12	11	11	10	10	9	8	8	7	6	5	4	3	3	2	1	1	41
50	22	21	20	20	19	18	18	17	16	16	15	14	13	12	11	11	10	10	9	8	8	7	6	5	4	3	3	2	1	1	40
51	23	22	21	20	19	18	18	17	16	16	15	14	14	13	12	11	10	10	9	8	8	7	6	6	5	4	3	2	2	2	39
52	23	22	21	21	20	19	18	17	16	16	15	14	14	13	12	11	10	10	9	8	8	7	6	6	5	4	3	2	2	2	38
53	23	22	21	21	20	19	18	17	16	16	15	14	14	13	12	11	10	10	9	8	8	7	6	6	5	4	3	2	2	2	37
54	23	22	21	21	20	19	19	18	17	16	15	14	14	13	12	12	11	10	9	8	8	7	6	6	5	4	3	2	2	2	36
55	23	22	21	21	20	19	19	18	17	16	15	14	14	13	12	12	11	10	9	8	8	7	6	6	5	4	3	2	2	2	35
56	24	23	22	22	21	20	19	18	17	17	16	15	14	13	12	12	11	11	10	9	8	7	6	6	5	4	3	2	2	2	34
57	24	23	22	22	21	20	19	18	17	17	16	15	15	14	13	12	11	11	10	9	8	7	6	6	5	4	3	2	2	2	33
58	24	23	22	22	21	20	20	19	18	17	16	15	15	14	13	12	11	11	10	9	8	7	6	6	5	4	3	2	2	2	32
59	24	23	22	22	21	20	20	19	18	17	16	15	15	14	13	12	11	11	10	9	8	7	6	6	5	4	3	2	2	2	31
60	25	24	23	22	21	20	20	19	18	17	16	15	15	14	13	12	11	11	10	9	8	7	6	6	5	4	3	2	2	2	30
61	25	24	23	23	22	21	20	19	18	18	17	16	15	14	13	13	12	11	10	9	9	8	7	6	5	4	4	3	2	2	29
62	25	24	23	23	22	21	20	19	18	18	17	16	15	14	13	13	12	11	10	9	9	8	7	6	5	4	4	3	2	2	28
63	26	25	24	23	22	21	21	20	19	18	17	16	15	14	13	13	12	11	10	9	9	8	7	6	5	4	4	3	2	2	27
64	26	25	24	23	22	21	21	20	19	18	17	16	16	15	14	13	12	11	10	9	9	8	7	6	5	4	4	3	2	2	26
65	26	25	24	24	23	22	21	20	19	18	17	16	16	15	14	13	12	12	11	10	9	8	7	6	5	4	4	3	2	2	25
66	27	26	25	24	23	22	21	20	19	19	18	17	16	15	14	13	12	12	11	10	9	8	7	6	5	4	4	3	2	2	24
67	27	26	25	24	23	22	21	20	19	19	18	17	16	15	14	13	12	12	11	10	9	8	7	6	5	4	4	3	2	2	23
68	27	26	25	24	23	22	22	21	20	19	18	17	16	15	14	13	12	12	11	10	9	8	7	6	5	4	4	3	2	2	22
69	27	26	25	24	23	22	22	21	20	19	18	17	16	15	14	14	13	12	11	10	9	8	7	6	5	4	4	3	2	2	21
70	27	26	25	25	24	23	22	21	20	19	18	17	16	15	14	14	13	12	11	10	9	8	7	6	5	4	4	3	2	2	20
71	28	27	26	25	24	23	22	21	20	19	18	17	17	16	15	14	13	12	11	10	9	8	7	7	6	5	4	3	3	3	19
72	28	27	26	25	24	23	22	21	20	19	18	17	17	16	15	14	13	12	11	10	9	8	7	7	6	5	4	3	3	3	18
73	28	27	26	25	24	23	22	21	20	19	18	17	17	16	15	14	13	12	11	10	9	8	7	7	6	5	4	3	3	3	17
74	28	27	26	25	24	23	23	22	21	20	19	18	17	16	15	14	13	12	11	10	9	8	7	7	6	5	4	3	3	3	16
75	29	28	27	26	25	24	23	22	21	20	19	18	17	16	15	14	13	12	11	10	9	8	7	7	6	5	4	3	3	3	15
76	29	28	27	26	25	24	23	22	21	20	19	18	18	17	16	15	14	13	12	11	10	9	8	7	6	5	4	3	3	3	14
77	29	28	27	26	25	24	23	22	21	20	19	18	18	17	16	15	14	13	12	11	10	9	8	7	6	5	4	3	3	3	13
78	29	28	27	27	26	25	24	23	22	21	20	19	18	17	16	15	14	13	12	11	10	9	8	7	6	5	4	3	3	3	12
79	30	29	28	27	26	25	24	23	22	21	20	19	18	17	16	15	14	13	12	11	10	9	8	7	6	5	4	3	3	3	11
80	30	29	28	27	26	25	24	23	22	21	20	19	18	17	16	15	14	13	12	11	10	9	8	7	6	5	4	3	3	3	10

For Z₂ < 10°, use 10°

For P > 80°, use 80°

USE OF CONCISE SIGHT REDUCTION TABLES (continued)

4. *Example.* (b) Required the altitude and azimuth of *Vega* on 2013 July 29 at UT 04^h 50^m from the estimated position 152° west, 15° south.

1. Assumed latitude	$Lat =$	15° S
From the almanac	$GHA =$	100° 09'
Assumed longitude		152° 09' W
Local hour angle	$LHA =$	308

2. Reduction table, 1st entry
$(Lat, LHA) = (15, 308)$ $A =$ 49   34 $A° = 50, A' = 34$

                        $B = +66$ 29 $Z_1 = +71.7,$ $LHA > 270°$

3. From the almanac $Dec = -38$ 48 Lat and Dec contrary

    $Sum = B + Dec$ $F = +27$ 41 $F° = 28, F' = 41$

4. Reduction table, 2nd entry
$(A°, F°) = (50, 28)$ $H =$ 17   34 $P° = 37$

                                           $Z_2 = 67.8, Z_2° = 68$

5. Auxiliary table, 1st entry
$(F', P°) = (41, 37)$ $corr_1 =$ -11 $F < 90°, F' > 29'$

    Sum   17   23

6. Auxiliary table, 2nd entry
$(A', Z_2°) = (34, 68)$ $corr_2 =$ $+10$ $A' > 30'$

7. Sum = computed altitude $H_C = +17°$ 33' $F > 0°$

8. Azimuth, first component $Z_1 = +71.7$ same sign as B

         second component $Z_2 = +67.8$ $F < 90°, F > 0°$

    Sum = azimuth angle $Z = 139.5$

    True azimuth $Z_n = 040°$ S *Lat*, $LHA > 180°$

5. *Form for use with the Concise Sight Reduction Tables.* The form on the following page lays out the procedure explained on pages 284-285. Each step is shown, with notes and rules to ensure accuracy, rather than speed, throughout the calculation. The form is mainly intended for the calculation of star positions. It therefore includes the formation of the Greenwich hour of Aries (*GHA* Aries), and thus the Greenwich hour angle of the star (*GHA*) from its tabular sidereal hour angle (*SHA*). These calculations, included in step 1 of the form, can easily be replaced by the interpolation of *GHA* and *Dec* for the Sun, Moon or planets.

The form may be freely copied, however, acknowledgement of the source is requested.

Date & UT of observation		Body	Estimated Latitude & Longitude
	h m s		° ′ · ° ′

Step	Calculate Altitude & Azimuth	Summary of Rules & Notes
Assumed latitude	$Lat =$ °	Nearest estimated latitude, integral number of degrees.
Assumed longitude	$Long =$ ° ′	Choose $Long$ so that LHA has integral number of degrees.
1. From the almanac:	$Dec =$ ° ′	Record the Dec for use in Step 3.
GHA Aries h	$=$ ° !	Needed if using SHA. Tabular value.
Increment m s	$=$ ° !	for minutes and seconds of time.
SHA	$SHA =$ ° !	
$GHA = GHA\ Aries + SHA$	$GHA =$ ° ′	Remove multiples of 360°.
Assumed longitude	$Long =$ ° ′	West longitudes are negative.
$LHA = GHA + Long$	$LHA =$ °	Remove multiples of 360°.
2. Reduction table, 1st entry		
$(Lat, LHA) = ($ °, ° $)$	$A =$ ° ′ $A° =$ °	nearest whole degree of A.
record A, B and Z_1.	$A' =$ ′	minutes part of A.
	$B =$ ° ′	B is minus if $90° < LHA < 270°$.
	$Z_1 =$ °	Z_1 has the same sign as B.
3. From step 1	$Dec =$ ° ′	Dec is minus if contrary to Lat.
$F = B + Dec$	$F =$ ° ′	Regard F as positive until step 7.
	$F° =$ °	nearest whole degree of F.
	$F' =$ ′	minutes part of F.
4. Reduction table, 2nd entry		
$(A°, F°) = ($ °, ° $)$	$H =$ ° ′ $P° =$ °	nearest whole degree of P.
record H, P and Z_2.	$Z_2 =$ °	
5. Auxiliary table, 1st entry		
$(F', P°) = ($ ′, ° $)$	$corr_1 =$ ′	$corr_1$ is minus if $F < 90°$ & $F' > 29'$,
record $corr_1$		or if $F > 90°$ & $F' < 30'$.
6. Auxiliary table, 2nd entry		$Z_2°$ nearest whole degree of Z_2.
$(A', Z_2°) = ($ ′, ° $)$	$corr_2 =$ ′	$corr_2$ is minus if $A' < 30'$.
record $corr_2$		
7. Calculated altitude =	$H_C =$ ° ′	H_C is minus if F is negative, and
$H_C = H + corr_1 + corr_2$		object is below the horizon.
8. Azimuth, 1st component	$Z_1 =$ °	Z_1 has the same sign as B.
2nd component	$Z_2 =$ °	Z_2 is minus if $F > 90°$.
		If F is negative, $Z_2 = 180° - Z_2$
$Z = Z_1 + Z_2$	$Z =$ °	Ignore the sign of Z.
		N Lat: If $LHA > 180°$, $Z_n = Z$, or
		if $LHA < 180°$, $Z_n = 360° - Z$,
		S Lat: If $LHA > 180°$, $Z_n = 180° - Z$, or
True azimuth	$Z_n =$ °	if $LHA < 180°$, $Z_n = 180° + Z$.
		©HMNAO

For use with *The Nautical Almanac's* Concise Sight Reduction Tables pages 284-318

CONVERSION OF ARC TO TIME

0°–59°		60°–119°		120°–179°		180°–239°		240°–299°		300°–359°		0′.00	0′.25	0′.50	0′.75
°	h m	°	h m	°	h m	°	h m	°	h m	°	h m	′ m s	m s	m s	m s
0	0 00	60	4 00	120	8 00	180	12 00	240	16 00	300	20 00	0 — 0 00	0 01	0 02	0 03
1	0 04	61	4 04	121	8 04	181	12 04	241	16 04	301	20 04	1 — 0 04	0 05	0 06	0 07
2	0 08	62	4 08	122	8 08	182	12 08	242	16 08	302	20 08	2 — 0 08	0 09	0 10	0 11
3	0 12	63	4 12	123	8 12	183	12 12	243	16 12	303	20 12	3 — 0 12	0 13	0 14	0 15
4	0 16	64	4 16	124	8 16	184	12 16	244	16 16	304	20 16	4 — 0 16	0 17	0 18	0 19
5	0 20	65	4 20	125	8 20	185	12 20	245	16 20	305	20 20	5 — 0 20	0 21	0 22	0 23
6	0 24	66	4 24	126	8 24	186	12 24	246	16 24	306	20 24	6 — 0 24	0 25	0 26	0 27
7	0 28	67	4 28	127	8 28	187	12 28	247	16 28	307	20 28	7 — 0 28	0 29	0 30	0 31
8	0 32	68	4 32	128	8 32	188	12 32	248	16 32	308	20 32	8 — 0 32	0 33	0 34	0 35
9	0 36	69	4 36	129	8 36	189	12 36	249	16 36	309	20 36	9 — 0 36	0 37	0 38	0 39
10	0 40	70	4 40	130	8 40	190	12 40	250	16 40	310	20 40	10 — 0 40	0 41	0 42	0 43
11	0 44	71	4 44	131	8 44	191	12 44	251	16 44	311	20 44	11 — 0 44	0 45	0 46	0 47
12	0 48	72	4 48	132	8 48	192	12 48	252	16 48	312	20 48	12 — 0 48	0 49	0 50	0 51
13	0 52	73	4 52	133	8 52	193	12 52	253	16 52	313	20 52	13 — 0 52	0 53	0 54	0 55
14	0 56	74	4 56	134	8 56	194	12 56	254	16 56	314	20 56	14 — 0 56	0 57	0 58	0 59
15	1 00	75	5 00	135	9 00	195	13 00	255	17 00	315	21 00	15 — 1 00	1 01	1 02	1 03
16	1 04	76	5 04	136	9 04	196	13 04	256	17 04	316	21 04	16 — 1 04	1 05	1 06	1 07
17	1 08	77	5 08	137	9 08	197	13 08	257	17 08	317	21 08	17 — 1 08	1 09	1 10	1 11
18	1 12	78	5 12	138	9 12	198	13 12	258	17 12	318	21 12	18 — 1 12	1 13	1 14	1 15
19	1 16	79	5 16	139	9 16	199	13 16	259	17 16	319	21 16	19 — 1 16	1 17	1 18	1 19
20	1 20	80	5 20	140	9 20	200	13 20	260	17 20	320	21 20	20 — 1 20	1 21	1 22	1 23
21	1 24	81	5 24	141	9 24	201	13 24	261	17 24	321	21 24	21 — 1 24	1 25	1 26	1 27
22	1 28	82	5 28	142	9 28	202	13 28	262	17 28	322	21 28	22 — 1 28	1 29	1 30	1 31
23	1 32	83	5 32	143	9 32	203	13 32	263	17 32	323	21 32	23 — 1 32	1 33	1 34	1 35
24	1 36	84	5 36	144	9 36	204	13 36	264	17 36	324	21 36	24 — 1 36	1 37	1 38	1 39
25	1 40	85	5 40	145	9 40	205	13 40	265	17 40	325	21 40	25 — 1 40	1 41	1 42	1 43
26	1 44	86	5 44	146	9 44	206	13 44	266	17 44	326	21 44	26 — 1 44	1 45	1 46	1 47
27	1 48	87	5 48	147	9 48	207	13 48	267	17 48	327	21 48	27 — 1 48	1 49	1 50	1 51
28	1 52	88	5 52	148	9 52	208	13 52	268	17 52	328	21 52	28 — 1 52	1 53	1 54	1 55
29	1 56	89	5 56	149	9 56	209	13 56	269	17 56	329	21 56	29 — 1 56	1 57	1 58	1 59
30	2 00	90	6 00	150	10 00	210	14 00	270	18 00	330	22 00	30 — 2 00	2 01	2 02	2 03
31	2 04	91	6 04	151	10 04	211	14 04	271	18 04	331	22 04	31 — 2 04	2 05	2 06	2 07
32	2 08	92	6 08	152	10 08	212	14 08	272	18 08	332	22 08	32 — 2 08	2 09	2 10	2 11
33	2 12	93	6 12	153	10 12	213	14 12	273	18 12	333	22 12	33 — 2 12	2 13	2 14	2 15
34	2 16	94	6 16	154	10 16	214	14 16	274	18 16	334	22 16	34 — 2 16	2 17	2 18	2 19
35	2 20	95	6 20	155	10 20	215	14 20	275	18 20	335	22 20	35 — 2 20	2 21	2 22	2 23
36	2 24	96	6 24	156	10 24	216	14 24	276	18 24	336	22 24	36 — 2 24	2 25	2 26	2 27
37	2 28	97	6 28	157	10 28	217	14 28	277	18 28	337	22 28	37 — 2 28	2 29	2 30	2 31
38	2 32	98	6 32	158	10 32	218	14 32	278	18 32	338	22 32	38 — 2 32	2 33	2 34	2 35
39	2 36	99	6 36	159	10 36	219	14 36	279	18 36	339	22 36	39 — 2 36	2 37	2 38	2 39
40	2 40	100	6 40	160	10 40	220	14 40	280	18 40	340	22 40	40 — 2 40	2 41	2 42	2 43
41	2 44	101	6 44	161	10 44	221	14 44	281	18 44	341	22 44	41 — 2 44	2 45	2 46	2 47
42	2 48	102	6 48	162	10 48	222	14 48	282	18 48	342	22 48	42 — 2 48	2 49	2 50	2 51
43	2 52	103	6 52	163	10 52	223	14 52	283	18 52	343	22 52	43 — 2 52	2 53	2 54	2 55
44	2 56	104	6 56	164	10 56	224	14 56	284	18 56	344	22 56	44 — 2 56	2 57	2 58	2 59
45	3 00	105	7 00	165	11 00	225	15 00	285	19 00	345	23 00	45 — 3 00	3 01	3 02	3 03
46	3 04	106	7 04	166	11 04	226	15 04	286	19 04	346	23 04	46 — 3 04	3 05	3 06	3 07
47	3 08	107	7 08	167	11 08	227	15 08	287	19 08	347	23 08	47 — 3 08	3 09	3 10	3 11
48	3 12	108	7 12	168	11 12	228	15 12	288	19 12	348	23 12	48 — 3 12	3 13	3 14	3 15
49	3 16	109	7 16	169	11 16	229	15 16	289	19 16	349	23 16	49 — 3 16	3 17	3 18	3 19
50	3 20	110	7 20	170	11 20	230	15 20	290	19 20	350	23 20	50 — 3 20	3 21	3 22	3 23
51	3 24	111	7 24	171	11 24	231	15 24	291	19 24	351	23 24	51 — 3 24	3 25	3 26	3 27
52	3 28	112	7 28	172	11 28	232	15 28	292	19 28	352	23 28	52 — 3 28	3 29	3 30	3 31
53	3 32	113	7 32	173	11 32	233	15 32	293	19 32	353	23 32	53 — 3 32	3 33	3 34	3 35
54	3 36	114	7 36	174	11 36	234	15 36	294	19 36	354	23 36	54 — 3 36	3 37	3 38	3 39
55	3 40	115	7 40	175	11 40	235	15 40	295	19 40	355	23 40	55 — 3 40	3 41	3 42	3 43
56	3 44	116	7 44	176	11 44	236	15 44	296	19 44	356	23 44	56 — 3 44	3 45	3 46	3 47
57	3 48	117	7 48	177	11 48	237	15 48	297	19 48	357	23 48	57 — 3 48	3 49	3 50	3 51
58	3 52	118	7 52	178	11 52	238	15 52	298	19 52	358	23 52	58 — 3 52	3 53	3 54	3 55
59	3 56	119	7 56	179	11 56	239	15 56	299	19 56	359	23 56	59 — 3 56	3 57	3 58	3 59

The above table is for converting expressions in arc to their equivalent in time; its main use in this Almanac is for the conversion of longitude for application to LMT (*added* if *west*, *subtracted* if *east*) to give UT or vice versa, particularly in the case of sunrise, sunset, etc.

INCREMENTS AND CORRECTIONS

m 0	SUN PLANETS	ARIES	MOON	v or Corrⁿ d	v or Corrⁿ d	v or Corrⁿ d
s	° ′	° ′	° ′	′ ′	′ ′	′ ′
00	0 00.0	0 00.0	0 00.0	0.0 0.0	6.0 0.1	12.0 0.1
01	0 00.3	0 00.3	0 00.2	0.1 0.0	6.1 0.1	12.1 0.1
02	0 00.5	0 00.5	0 00.5	0.2 0.0	6.2 0.1	12.2 0.1
03	0 00.8	0 00.8	0 00.7	0.3 0.0	6.3 0.1	12.3 0.1
04	0 01.0	0 01.0	0 01.0	0.4 0.0	6.4 0.1	12.4 0.1
05	0 01.3	0 01.3	0 01.2	0.5 0.0	6.5 0.1	12.5 0.1
06	0 01.5	0 01.5	0 01.4	0.6 0.0	6.6 0.1	12.6 0.1
07	0 01.8	0 01.8	0 01.7	0.7 0.0	6.7 0.1	12.7 0.1
08	0 02.0	0 02.0	0 01.9	0.8 0.0	6.8 0.1	12.8 0.1
09	0 02.3	0 02.3	0 02.1	0.9 0.0	6.9 0.1	12.9 0.1
10	0 02.5	0 02.5	0 02.4	1.0 0.0	7.0 0.1	13.0 0.1
11	0 02.8	0 02.8	0 02.6	1.1 0.0	7.1 0.1	13.1 0.1
12	0 03.0	0 03.0	0 02.9	1.2 0.0	7.2 0.1	13.2 0.1
13	0 03.3	0 03.3	0 03.1	1.3 0.0	7.3 0.1	13.3 0.1
14	0 03.5	0 03.5	0 03.3	1.4 0.0	7.4 0.1	13.4 0.1
15	0 03.8	0 03.8	0 03.6	1.5 0.0	7.5 0.1	13.5 0.1
16	0 04.0	0 04.0	0 03.8	1.6 0.0	7.6 0.1	13.6 0.1
17	0 04.3	0 04.3	0 04.1	1.7 0.0	7.7 0.1	13.7 0.1
18	0 04.5	0 04.5	0 04.3	1.8 0.0	7.8 0.1	13.8 0.1
19	0 04.8	0 04.8	0 04.5	1.9 0.0	7.9 0.1	13.9 0.1
20	0 05.0	0 05.0	0 04.8	2.0 0.0	8.0 0.1	14.0 0.1
21	0 05.3	0 05.3	0 05.0	2.1 0.0	8.1 0.1	14.1 0.1
22	0 05.5	0 05.5	0 05.2	2.2 0.0	8.2 0.1	14.2 0.1
23	0 05.8	0 05.8	0 05.5	2.3 0.0	8.3 0.1	14.3 0.1
24	0 06.0	0 06.0	0 05.7	2.4 0.0	8.4 0.1	14.4 0.1
25	0 06.3	0 06.3	0 06.0	2.5 0.0	8.5 0.1	14.5 0.1
26	0 06.5	0 06.5	0 06.2	2.6 0.0	8.6 0.1	14.6 0.1
27	0 06.8	0 06.8	0 06.4	2.7 0.0	8.7 0.1	14.7 0.1
28	0 07.0	0 07.0	0 06.7	2.8 0.0	8.8 0.1	14.8 0.1
29	0 07.3	0 07.3	0 06.9	2.9 0.0	8.9 0.1	14.9 0.1
30	0 07.5	0 07.5	0 07.2	3.0 0.0	9.0 0.1	15.0 0.1
31	0 07.8	0 07.8	0 07.4	3.1 0.0	9.1 0.1	15.1 0.1
32	0 08.0	0 08.0	0 07.6	3.2 0.0	9.2 0.1	15.2 0.1
33	0 08.3	0 08.3	0 07.9	3.3 0.0	9.3 0.1	15.3 0.1
34	0 08.5	0 08.5	0 08.1	3.4 0.0	9.4 0.1	15.4 0.1
35	0 08.8	0 08.8	0 08.4	3.5 0.0	9.5 0.1	15.5 0.1
36	0 09.0	0 09.0	0 08.6	3.6 0.0	9.6 0.1	15.6 0.1
37	0 09.3	0 09.3	0 08.8	3.7 0.0	9.7 0.1	15.7 0.1
38	0 09.5	0 09.5	0 09.1	3.8 0.0	9.8 0.1	15.8 0.1
39	0 09.8	0 09.8	0 09.3	3.9 0.0	9.9 0.1	15.9 0.1
40	0 10.0	0 10.0	0 09.5	4.0 0.0	10.0 0.1	16.0 0.1
41	0 10.3	0 10.3	0 09.8	4.1 0.0	10.1 0.1	16.1 0.1
42	0 10.5	0 10.5	0 10.0	4.2 0.0	10.2 0.1	16.2 0.1
43	0 10.8	0 10.8	0 10.3	4.3 0.0	10.3 0.1	16.3 0.1
44	0 11.0	0 11.0	0 10.5	4.4 0.0	10.4 0.1	16.4 0.1
45	0 11.3	0 11.3	0 10.7	4.5 0.0	10.5 0.1	16.5 0.1
46	0 11.5	0 11.5	0 11.0	4.6 0.0	10.6 0.1	16.6 0.1
47	0 11.8	0 11.8	0 11.2	4.7 0.0	10.7 0.1	16.7 0.1
48	0 12.0	0 12.0	0 11.5	4.8 0.0	10.8 0.1	16.8 0.1
49	0 12.3	0 12.3	0 11.7	4.9 0.0	10.9 0.1	16.9 0.1
50	0 12.5	0 12.5	0 11.9	5.0 0.0	11.0 0.1	17.0 0.1
51	0 12.8	0 12.8	0 12.2	5.1 0.0	11.1 0.1	17.1 0.1
52	0 13.0	0 13.0	0 12.4	5.2 0.0	11.2 0.1	17.2 0.1
53	0 13.3	0 13.3	0 12.6	5.3 0.0	11.3 0.1	17.3 0.1
54	0 13.5	0 13.5	0 12.9	5.4 0.0	11.4 0.1	17.4 0.1
55	0 13.8	0 13.8	0 13.1	5.5 0.0	11.5 0.1	17.5 0.1
56	0 14.0	0 14.0	0 13.4	5.6 0.0	11.6 0.1	17.6 0.1
57	0 14.3	0 14.3	0 13.6	5.7 0.0	11.7 0.1	17.7 0.1
58	0 14.5	0 14.5	0 13.8	5.8 0.0	11.8 0.1	17.8 0.1
59	0 14.8	0 14.8	0 14.1	5.9 0.0	11.9 0.1	17.9 0.1
60	0 15.0	0 15.0	0 14.3	6.0 0.1	12.0 0.1	18.0 0.2

m 1	SUN PLANETS	ARIES	MOON	v or Corrⁿ d	v or Corrⁿ d	v or Corrⁿ d
s	° ′	° ′	° ′	′ ′	′ ′	′ ′
00	0 15.0	0 15.0	0 14.3	0.0 0.0	6.0 0.2	12.0 0.3
01	0 15.3	0 15.3	0 14.6	0.1 0.0	6.1 0.2	12.1 0.3
02	0 15.5	0 15.5	0 14.8	0.2 0.0	6.2 0.2	12.2 0.3
03	0 15.8	0 15.8	0 15.0	0.3 0.0	6.3 0.2	12.3 0.3
04	0 16.0	0 16.0	0 15.3	0.4 0.0	6.4 0.2	12.4 0.3
05	0 16.3	0 16.3	0 15.5	0.5 0.0	6.5 0.2	12.5 0.3
06	0 16.5	0 16.5	0 15.7	0.6 0.0	6.6 0.2	12.6 0.3
07	0 16.8	0 16.8	0 16.0	0.7 0.0	6.7 0.2	12.7 0.3
08	0 17.0	0 17.0	0 16.2	0.8 0.0	6.8 0.2	12.8 0.3
09	0 17.3	0 17.3	0 16.5	0.9 0.0	6.9 0.2	12.9 0.3
10	0 17.5	0 17.5	0 16.7	1.0 0.0	7.0 0.2	13.0 0.3
11	0 17.8	0 17.8	0 16.9	1.1 0.0	7.1 0.2	13.1 0.3
12	0 18.0	0 18.0	0 17.2	1.2 0.0	7.2 0.2	13.2 0.3
13	0 18.3	0 18.3	0 17.4	1.3 0.0	7.3 0.2	13.3 0.3
14	0 18.5	0 18.6	0 17.7	1.4 0.0	7.4 0.2	13.4 0.3
15	0 18.8	0 18.8	0 17.9	1.5 0.0	7.5 0.2	13.5 0.3
16	0 19.0	0 19.1	0 18.1	1.6 0.0	7.6 0.2	13.6 0.3
17	0 19.3	0 19.3	0 18.4	1.7 0.0	7.7 0.2	13.7 0.3
18	0 19.5	0 19.6	0 18.6	1.8 0.0	7.8 0.2	13.8 0.3
19	0 19.8	0 19.8	0 18.9	1.9 0.0	7.9 0.2	13.9 0.3
20	0 20.0	0 20.1	0 19.1	2.0 0.1	8.0 0.2	14.0 0.4
21	0 20.3	0 20.3	0 19.3	2.1 0.1	8.1 0.2	14.1 0.4
22	0 20.5	0 20.6	0 19.6	2.2 0.1	8.2 0.2	14.2 0.4
23	0 20.8	0 20.8	0 19.8	2.3 0.1	8.3 0.2	14.3 0.4
24	0 21.0	0 21.1	0 20.0	2.4 0.1	8.4 0.2	14.4 0.4
25	0 21.3	0 21.3	0 20.3	2.5 0.1	8.5 0.2	14.5 0.4
26	0 21.5	0 21.6	0 20.5	2.6 0.1	8.6 0.2	14.6 0.4
27	0 21.8	0 21.8	0 20.8	2.7 0.1	8.7 0.2	14.7 0.4
28	0 22.0	0 22.1	0 21.0	2.8 0.1	8.8 0.2	14.8 0.4
29	0 22.3	0 22.3	0 21.2	2.9 0.1	8.9 0.2	14.9 0.4
30	0 22.5	0 22.6	0 21.5	3.0 0.1	9.0 0.2	15.0 0.4
31	0 22.8	0 22.8	0 21.7	3.1 0.1	9.1 0.2	15.1 0.4
32	0 23.0	0 23.1	0 22.0	3.2 0.1	9.2 0.2	15.2 0.4
33	0 23.3	0 23.3	0 22.2	3.3 0.1	9.3 0.2	15.3 0.4
34	0 23.5	0 23.6	0 22.4	3.4 0.1	9.4 0.2	15.4 0.4
35	0 23.8	0 23.8	0 22.7	3.5 0.1	9.5 0.2	15.5 0.4
36	0 24.0	0 24.1	0 22.9	3.6 0.1	9.6 0.2	15.6 0.4
37	0 24.3	0 24.3	0 23.1	3.7 0.1	9.7 0.2	15.7 0.4
38	0 24.5	0 24.6	0 23.4	3.8 0.1	9.8 0.2	15.8 0.4
39	0 24.8	0 24.8	0 23.6	3.9 0.1	9.9 0.2	15.9 0.4
40	0 25.0	0 25.1	0 23.9	4.0 0.1	10.0 0.3	16.0 0.4
41	0 25.3	0 25.3	0 24.1	4.1 0.1	10.1 0.3	16.1 0.4
42	0 25.5	0 25.6	0 24.3	4.2 0.1	10.2 0.3	16.2 0.4
43	0 25.8	0 25.8	0 24.6	4.3 0.1	10.3 0.3	16.3 0.4
44	0 26.0	0 26.1	0 24.8	4.4 0.1	10.4 0.3	16.4 0.4
45	0 26.3	0 26.3	0 25.1	4.5 0.1	10.5 0.3	16.5 0.4
46	0 26.5	0 26.6	0 25.3	4.6 0.1	10.6 0.3	16.6 0.4
47	0 26.8	0 26.8	0 25.5	4.7 0.1	10.7 0.3	16.7 0.4
48	0 27.0	0 27.1	0 25.8	4.8 0.1	10.8 0.3	16.8 0.4
49	0 27.3	0 27.3	0 26.0	4.9 0.1	10.9 0.3	16.9 0.4
50	0 27.5	0 27.6	0 26.2	5.0 0.1	11.0 0.3	17.0 0.4
51	0 27.8	0 27.8	0 26.5	5.1 0.1	11.1 0.3	17.1 0.4
52	0 28.0	0 28.1	0 26.7	5.2 0.1	11.2 0.3	17.2 0.4
53	0 28.3	0 28.3	0 27.0	5.3 0.1	11.3 0.3	17.3 0.4
54	0 28.5	0 28.6	0 27.2	5.4 0.1	11.4 0.3	17.4 0.4
55	0 28.8	0 28.8	0 27.4	5.5 0.1	11.5 0.3	17.5 0.4
56	0 29.0	0 29.1	0 27.7	5.6 0.1	11.6 0.3	17.6 0.4
57	0 29.3	0 29.3	0 27.9	5.7 0.1	11.7 0.3	17.7 0.4
58	0 29.5	0 29.6	0 28.2	5.8 0.1	11.8 0.3	17.8 0.4
59	0 29.8	0 29.8	0 28.4	5.9 0.1	11.9 0.3	17.9 0.4
60	0 30.0	0 30.1	0 28.6	6.0 0.2	12.0 0.3	18.0 0.5

m 2	SUN PLANETS	ARIES	MOON	v or Corrⁿ d		v or Corrⁿ d		v or Corrⁿ d	
s	° ′	° ′	° ′	′	′	′	′	′	′
00	0 30·0	0 30·1	0 28·6	0·0	0·0	6·0	0·3	12·0	0·5
01	0 30·3	0 30·3	0 28·9	0·1	0·0	6·1	0·3	12·1	0·5
02	0 30·5	0 30·6	0 29·1	0·2	0·0	6·2	0·3	12·2	0·5
03	0 30·8	0 30·8	0 29·3	0·3	0·0	6·3	0·3	12·3	0·5
04	0 31·0	0 31·1	0 29·6	0·4	0·0	6·4	0·3	12·4	0·5
05	0 31·3	0 31·3	0 29·8	0·5	0·0	6·5	0·3	12·5	0·5
06	0 31·5	0 31·6	0 30·1	0·6	0·0	6·6	0·3	12·6	0·5
07	0 31·8	0 31·8	0 30·3	0·7	0·0	6·7	0·3	12·7	0·5
08	0 32·0	0 32·1	0 30·5	0·8	0·0	6·8	0·3	12·8	0·5
09	0 32·3	0 32·3	0 30·8	0·9	0·0	6·9	0·3	12·9	0·5
10	0 32·5	0 32·6	0 31·0	1·0	0·0	7·0	0·3	13·0	0·5
11	0 32·8	0 32·8	0 31·3	1·1	0·0	7·1	0·3	13·1	0·5
12	0 33·0	0 33·1	0 31·5	1·2	0·1	7·2	0·3	13·2	0·6
13	0 33·3	0 33·3	0 31·7	1·3	0·1	7·3	0·3	13·3	0·6
14	0 33·5	0 33·6	0 32·0	1·4	0·1	7·4	0·3	13·4	0·6
15	0 33·8	0 33·8	0 32·2	1·5	0·1	7·5	0·3	13·5	0·6
16	0 34·0	0 34·1	0 32·5	1·6	0·1	7·6	0·3	13·6	0·6
17	0 34·3	0 34·3	0 32·7	1·7	0·1	7·7	0·3	13·7	0·6
18	0 34·5	0 34·6	0 32·9	1·8	0·1	7·8	0·3	13·8	0·6
19	0 34·8	0 34·8	0 33·2	1·9	0·1	7·9	0·3	13·9	0·6
20	0 35·0	0 35·1	0 33·4	2·0	0·1	8·0	0·3	14·0	0·6
21	0 35·3	0 35·3	0 33·6	2·1	0·1	8·1	0·3	14·1	0·6
22	0 35·5	0 35·6	0 33·9	2·2	0·1	8·2	0·3	14·2	0·6
23	0 35·8	0 35·8	0 34·1	2·3	0·1	8·3	0·3	14·3	0·6
24	0 36·0	0 36·1	0 34·4	2·4	0·1	8·4	0·4	14·4	0·6
25	0 36·3	0 36·3	0 34·6	2·5	0·1	8·5	0·4	14·5	0·6
26	0 36·5	0 36·6	0 34·8	2·6	0·1	8·6	0·4	14·6	0·6
27	0 36·8	0 36·9	0 35·1	2·7	0·1	8·7	0·4	14·7	0·6
28	0 37·0	0 37·1	0 35·3	2·8	0·1	8·8	0·4	14·8	0·6
29	0 37·3	0 37·4	0 35·6	2·9	0·1	8·9	0·4	14·9	0·6
30	0 37·5	0 37·6	0 35·8	3·0	0·1	9·0	0·4	15·0	0·6
31	0 37·8	0 37·9	0 36·0	3·1	0·1	9·1	0·4	15·1	0·6
32	0 38·0	0 38·1	0 36·3	3·2	0·1	9·2	0·4	15·2	0·6
33	0 38·3	0 38·4	0 36·5	3·3	0·1	9·3	0·4	15·3	0·6
34	0 38·5	0 38·6	0 36·7	3·4	0·1	9·4	0·4	15·4	0·6
35	0 38·8	0 38·9	0 37·0	3·5	0·1	9·5	0·4	15·5	0·6
36	0 39·0	0 39·1	0 37·2	3·6	0·2	9·6	0·4	15·6	0·7
37	0 39·3	0 39·4	0 37·5	3·7	0·2	9·7	0·4	15·7	0·7
38	0 39·5	0 39·6	0 37·7	3·8	0·2	9·8	0·4	15·8	0·7
39	0 39·8	0 39·9	0 37·9	3·9	0·2	9·9	0·4	15·9	0·7
40	0 40·0	0 40·1	0 38·2	4·0	0·2	10·0	0·4	16·0	0·7
41	0 40·3	0 40·4	0 38·4	4·1	0·2	10·1	0·4	16·1	0·7
42	0 40·5	0 40·6	0 38·7	4·2	0·2	10·2	0·4	16·2	0·7
43	0 40·8	0 40·9	0 38·9	4·3	0·2	10·3	0·4	16·3	0·7
44	0 41·0	0 41·1	0 39·1	4·4	0·2	10·4	0·4	16·4	0·7
45	0 41·3	0 41·4	0 39·4	4·5	0·2	10·5	0·4	16·5	0·7
46	0 41·5	0 41·6	0 39·6	4·6	0·2	10·6	0·4	16·6	0·7
47	0 41·8	0 41·9	0 39·8	4·7	0·2	10·7	0·4	16·7	0·7
48	0 42·0	0 42·1	0 40·1	4·8	0·2	10·8	0·5	16·8	0·7
49	0 42·3	0 42·4	0 40·3	4·9	0·2	10·9	0·5	16·9	0·7
50	0 42·5	0 42·6	0 40·6	5·0	0·2	11·0	0·5	17·0	0·7
51	0 42·8	0 42·9	0 40·8	5·1	0·2	11·1	0·5	17·1	0·7
52	0 43·0	0 43·1	0 41·0	5·2	0·2	11·2	0·5	17·2	0·7
53	0 43·3	0 43·4	0 41·3	5·3	0·2	11·3	0·5	17·3	0·7
54	0 43·5	0 43·6	0 41·5	5·4	0·2	11·4	0·5	17·4	0·7
55	0 43·8	0 43·9	0 41·8	5·5	0·2	11·5	0·5	17·5	0·7
56	0 44·0	0 44·1	0 42·0	5·6	0·2	11·6	0·5	17·6	0·7
57	0 44·3	0 44·4	0 42·2	5·7	0·2	11·7	0·5	17·7	0·7
58	0 44·5	0 44·6	0 42·5	5·8	0·2	11·8	0·5	17·8	0·7
59	0 44·8	0 44·9	0 42·7	5·9	0·2	11·9	0·5	17·9	0·7
60	0 45·0	0 45·1	0 43·0	6·0	0·3	12·0	0·5	18·0	0·8

m 3	SUN PLANETS	ARIES	MOON	v or Corrⁿ d		v or Corrⁿ d		v or Corrⁿ d	
s	° ′	° ′	° ′	′	′	′	′	′	′
00	0 45·0	0 45·1	0 43·0	0·0	0·0	6·0	0·4	12·0	0·7
01	0 45·3	0 45·4	0 43·2	0·1	0·0	6·1	0·4	12·1	0·7
02	0 45·5	0 45·6	0 43·4	0·2	0·0	6·2	0·4	12·2	0·7
03	0 45·8	0 45·9	0 43·7	0·3	0·0	6·3	0·4	12·3	0·7
04	0 46·0	0 46·1	0 43·9	0·4	0·0	6·4	0·4	12·4	0·7
05	0 46·3	0 46·4	0 44·1	0·5	0·0	6·5	0·4	12·5	0·7
06	0 46·5	0 46·6	0 44·4	0·6	0·0	6·6	0·4	12·6	0·7
07	0 46·8	0 46·9	0 44·6	0·7	0·0	6·7	0·4	12·7	0·7
08	0 47·0	0 47·1	0 44·9	0·8	0·0	6·8	0·4	12·8	0·7
09	0 47·3	0 47·4	0 45·1	0·9	0·1	6·9	0·4	12·9	0·8
10	0 47·5	0 47·6	0 45·3	1·0	0·1	7·0	0·4	13·0	0·8
11	0 47·8	0 47·9	0 45·6	1·1	0·1	7·1	0·4	13·1	0·8
12	0 48·0	0 48·1	0 45·8	1·2	0·1	7·2	0·4	13·2	0·8
13	0 48·3	0 48·4	0 46·1	1·3	0·1	7·3	0·4	13·3	0·8
14	0 48·5	0 48·6	0 46·3	1·4	0·1	7·4	0·4	13·4	0·8
15	0 48·8	0 48·9	0 46·5	1·5	0·1	7·5	0·4	13·5	0·8
16	0 49·0	0 49·1	0 46·8	1·6	0·1	7·6	0·4	13·6	0·8
17	0 49·3	0 49·4	0 47·0	1·7	0·1	7·7	0·4	13·7	0·8
18	0 49·5	0 49·6	0 47·2	1·8	0·1	7·8	0·5	13·8	0·8
19	0 49·8	0 49·9	0 47·5	1·9	0·1	7·9	0·5	13·9	0·8
20	0 50·0	0 50·1	0 47·7	2·0	0·1	8·0	0·5	14·0	0·8
21	0 50·3	0 50·4	0 48·0	2·1	0·1	8·1	0·5	14·1	0·8
22	0 50·5	0 50·6	0 48·2	2·2	0·1	8·2	0·5	14·2	0·8
23	0 50·8	0 50·9	0 48·4	2·3	0·1	8·3	0·5	14·3	0·8
24	0 51·0	0 51·1	0 48·7	2·4	0·1	8·4	0·5	14·4	0·8
25	0 51·3	0 51·4	0 48·9	2·5	0·1	8·5	0·5	14·5	0·8
26	0 51·5	0 51·6	0 49·2	2·6	0·2	8·6	0·5	14·6	0·9
27	0 51·8	0 51·9	0 49·6	2·7	0·2	8·7	0·5	14·7	0·9
28	0 52·0	0 52·1	0 49·6	2·8	0·2	8·8	0·5	14·8	0·9
29	0 52·3	0 52·4	0 49·9	2·9	0·2	8·9	0·5	14·9	0·9
30	0 52·5	0 52·6	0 50·1	3·0	0·2	9·0	0·5	15·0	0·9
31	0 52·8	0 52·9	0 50·3	3·1	0·2	9·1	0·5	15·1	0·9
32	0 53·0	0 53·1	0 50·6	3·2	0·2	9·2	0·5	15·2	0·9
33	0 53·3	0 53·4	0 50·8	3·3	0·2	9·3	0·5	15·3	0·9
34	0 53·5	0 53·6	0 51·1	3·4	0·2	9·4	0·5	15·4	0·9
35	0 53·8	0 53·9	0 51·3	3·5	0·2	9·5	0·6	15·5	0·9
36	0 54·0	0 54·1	0 51·5	3·6	0·2	9·6	0·6	15·6	0·9
37	0 54·3	0 54·4	0 51·8	3·7	0·2	9·7	0·6	15·7	0·9
38	0 54·5	0 54·6	0 52·0	3·8	0·2	9·8	0·6	15·8	0·9
39	0 54·8	0 54·9	0 52·3	3·9	0·2	9·9	0·6	15·9	0·9
40	0 55·0	0 55·2	0 52·5	4·0	0·2	10·0	0·6	16·0	0·9
41	0 55·3	0 55·4	0 52·7	4·1	0·2	10·1	0·6	16·1	0·9
42	0 55·5	0 55·7	0 53·0	4·2	0·2	10·2	0·6	16·2	0·9
43	0 55·8	0 55·9	0 53·2	4·3	0·3	10·3	0·6	16·3	1·0
44	0 56·0	0 56·2	0 53·4	4·4	0·3	10·4	0·6	16·4	1·0
45	0 56·3	0 56·4	0 53·7	4·5	0·3	10·5	0·6	16·5	1·0
46	0 56·5	0 56·7	0 53·9	4·6	0·3	10·6	0·6	16·6	1·0
47	0 56·8	0 56·9	0 54·2	4·7	0·3	10·7	0·6	16·7	1·0
48	0 57·0	0 57·2	0 54·4	4·8	0·3	10·8	0·6	16·8	1·0
49	0 57·3	0 57·4	0 54·6	4·9	0·3	10·9	0·6	16·9	1·0
50	0 57·5	0 57·7	0 54·9	5·0	0·3	11·0	0·6	17·0	1·0
51	0 57·8	0 57·9	0 55·1	5·1	0·3	11·1	0·6	17·1	1·0
52	0 58·0	0 58·2	0 55·4	5·2	0·3	11·2	0·7	17·2	1·0
53	0 58·3	0 58·4	0 55·6	5·3	0·3	11·3	0·7	17·3	1·0
54	0 58·5	0 58·7	0 55·8	5·4	0·3	11·4	0·7	17·4	1·0
55	0 58·8	0 58·9	0 56·1	5·5	0·3	11·5	0·7	17·5	1·0
56	0 59·0	0 59·2	0 56·3	5·6	0·3	11·6	0·7	17·6	1·0
57	0 59·3	0 59·4	0 56·5	5·7	0·3	11·7	0·7	17·7	1·0
58	0 59·5	0 59·7	0 56·8	5·8	0·3	11·8	0·7	17·8	1·0
59	0 59·8	0 59·9	0 57·0	5·9	0·3	11·9	0·7	17·9	1·0
60	1 00·0	1 00·2	0 57·3	6·0	0·4	12·0	0·7	18·0	1·1

4 ᵐ s	SUN PLANETS ° '	ARIES ° '	MOON ° '	v or d '	Corrⁿ '	v or d '	Corrⁿ '	v or d '	Corrⁿ '
00	1 00·0	1 00·2	0 57·3	0·0	0·0	6·0	0·5	12·0	0·9
01	1 00·3	1 00·4	0 57·5	0·1	0·0	6·1	0·5	12·1	0·9
02	1 00·5	1 00·7	0 57·7	0·2	0·0	6·2	0·5	12·2	0·9
03	1 00·8	1 00·9	0 58·0	0·3	0·0	6·3	0·5	12·3	0·9
04	1 01·0	1 01·2	0 58·2	0·4	0·0	6·4	0·5	12·4	0·9
05	1 01·3	1 01·4	0 58·5	0·5	0·0	6·5	0·5	12·5	0·9
06	1 01·5	1 01·7	0 58·7	0·6	0·0	6·6	0·5	12·6	0·9
07	1 01·8	1 01·9	0 58·9	0·7	0·1	6·7	0·5	12·7	1·0
08	1 02·0	1 02·2	0 59·2	0·8	0·1	6·8	0·5	12·8	1·0
09	1 02·3	1 02·4	0 59·4	0·9	0·1	6·9	0·5	12·9	1·0
10	1 02·5	1 02·7	0 59·7	1·0	0·1	7·0	0·5	13·0	1·0
11	1 02·8	1 02·9	0 59·9	1·1	0·1	7·1	0·5	13·1	1·0
12	1 03·0	1 03·2	1 00·1	1·2	0·1	7·2	0·5	13·2	1·0
13	1 03·3	1 03·4	1 00·4	1·3	0·1	7·3	0·5	13·3	1·0
14	1 03·5	1 03·7	1 00·6	1·4	0·1	7·4	0·5	13·4	1·0
15	1 03·8	1 03·9	1 00·8	1·5	0·1	7·5	0·6	13·5	1·0
16	1 04·0	1 04·2	1 01·1	1·6	0·1	7·6	0·6	13·6	1·0
17	1 04·3	1 04·4	1 01·3	1·7	0·1	7·7	0·6	13·7	1·0
18	1 04·5	1 04·7	1 01·6	1·8	0·1	7·8	0·6	13·8	1·0
19	1 04·8	1 04·9	1 01·8	1·9	0·1	7·9	0·6	13·9	1·0
20	1 05·0	1 05·2	1 02·0	2·0	0·2	8·0	0·6	14·0	1·1
21	1 05·3	1 05·4	1 02·3	2·1	0·2	8·1	0·6	14·1	1·1
22	1 05·5	1 05·7	1 02·5	2·2	0·2	8·2	0·6	14·2	1·1
23	1 05·8	1 05·9	1 02·8	2·3	0·2	8·3	0·6	14·3	1·1
24	1 06·0	1 06·2	1 03·0	2·4	0·2	8·4	0·6	14·4	1·1
25	1 06·3	1 06·4	1 03·2	2·5	0·2	8·5	0·6	14·5	1·1
26	1 06·5	1 06·7	1 03·5	2·6	0·2	8·6	0·6	14·6	1·1
27	1 06·8	1 06·9	1 03·7	2·7	0·2	8·7	0·6	14·7	1·1
28	1 07·0	1 07·2	1 03·9	2·8	0·2	8·8	0·7	14·8	1·1
29	1 07·3	1 07·4	1 04·2	2·9	0·2	8·9	0·7	14·9	1·1
30	1 07·5	1 07·7	1 04·4	3·0	0·2	9·0	0·7	15·0	1·1
31	1 07·8	1 07·9	1 04·7	3·1	0·2	9·1	0·7	15·1	1·1
32	1 08·0	1 08·2	1 04·9	3·2	0·2	9·2	0·7	15·2	1·1
33	1 08·3	1 08·4	1 05·1	3·3	0·2	9·3	0·7	15·3	1·1
34	1 08·5	1 08·7	1 05·4	3·4	0·3	9·4	0·7	15·4	1·2
35	1 08·8	1 08·9	1 05·6	3·5	0·3	9·5	0·7	15·5	1·2
36	1 09·0	1 09·2	1 05·9	3·6	0·3	9·6	0·7	15·6	1·2
37	1 09·3	1 09·4	1 06·1	3·7	0·3	9·7	0·7	15·7	1·2
38	1 09·5	1 09·7	1 06·3	3·8	0·3	9·8	0·7	15·8	1·2
39	1 09·8	1 09·9	1 06·6	3·9	0·3	9·9	0·7	15·9	1·2
40	1 10·0	1 10·2	1 06·8	4·0	0·3	10·0	0·8	16·0	1·2
41	1 10·3	1 10·4	1 07·0	4·1	0·3	10·1	0·8	16·1	1·2
42	1 10·5	1 10·7	1 07·3	4·2	0·3	10·2	0·8	16·2	1·2
43	1 10·8	1 10·9	1 07·5	4·3	0·3	10·3	0·8	16·3	1·2
44	1 11·0	1 11·2	1 07·8	4·4	0·3	10·4	0·8	16·4	1·2
45	1 11·3	1 11·4	1 08·0	4·5	0·3	10·5	0·8	16·5	1·2
46	1 11·5	1 11·7	1 08·2	4·6	0·3	10·6	0·8	16·6	1·2
47	1 11·8	1 11·9	1 08·5	4·7	0·4	10·7	0·8	16·7	1·3
48	1 12·0	1 12·2	1 08·7	4·8	0·4	10·8	0·8	16·8	1·3
49	1 12·3	1 12·4	1 09·0	4·9	0·4	10·9	0·8	16·9	1·3
50	1 12·5	1 12·7	1 09·2	5·0	0·4	11·0	0·8	17·0	1·3
51	1 12·8	1 12·9	1 09·4	5·1	0·4	11·1	0·8	17·1	1·3
52	1 13·0	1 13·2	1 09·7	5·2	0·4	11·2	0·8	17·2	1·3
53	1 13·3	1 13·5	1 09·9	5·3	0·4	11·3	0·8	17·3	1·3
54	1 13·5	1 13·7	1 10·2	5·4	0·4	11·4	0·9	17·4	1·3
55	1 13·8	1 14·0	1 10·4	5·5	0·4	11·5	0·9	17·5	1·3
56	1 14·0	1 14·2	1 10·6	5·6	0·4	11·6	0·9	17·6	1·3
57	1 14·3	1 14·5	1 10·9	5·7	0·4	11·7	0·9	17·7	1·3
58	1 14·5	1 14·7	1 11·1	5·8	0·4	11·8	0·9	17·8	1·3
59	1 14·8	1 15·0	1 11·3	5·9	0·4	11·9	0·9	17·9	1·3
60	1 15·0	1 15·2	1 11·6	6·0	0·5	12·0	0·9	18·0	1·4

5 ᵐ s	SUN PLANETS ° '	ARIES ° '	MOON ° '	v or d '	Corrⁿ '	v or d '	Corrⁿ '	v or d '	Corrⁿ '
00	1 15·0	1 15·2	1 11·6	0·0	0·0	6·0	0·6	12·0	1·1
01	1 15·3	1 15·5	1 11·8	0·1	0·0	6·1	0·6	12·1	1·1
02	1 15·5	1 15·7	1 12·1	0·2	0·0	6·2	0·6	12·2	1·1
03	1 15·8	1 16·0	1 12·3	0·3	0·0	6·3	0·6	12·3	1·1
04	1 16·0	1 16·2	1 12·5	0·4	0·0	6·4	0·6	12·4	1·1
05	1 16·3	1 16·5	1 12·8	0·5	0·0	6·5	0·6	12·5	1·1
06	1 16·5	1 16·7	1 13·0	0·6	0·1	6·6	0·6	12·6	1·2
07	1 16·8	1 17·0	1 13·3	0·7	0·1	6·7	0·6	12·7	1·2
08	1 17·0	1 17·2	1 13·5	0·8	0·1	6·8	0·6	12·8	1·2
09	1 17·3	1 17·5	1 13·7	0·9	0·1	6·9	0·6	12·9	1·2
10	1 17·5	1 17·7	1 14·0	1·0	0·1	7·0	0·6	13·0	1·2
11	1 17·8	1 18·0	1 14·2	1·1	0·1	7·1	0·7	13·1	1·2
12	1 18·0	1 18·2	1 14·4	1·2	0·1	7·2	0·7	13·2	1·2
13	1 18·3	1 18·5	1 14·7	1·3	0·1	7·3	0·7	13·3	1·2
14	1 18·5	1 18·7	1 14·9	1·4	0·1	7·4	0·7	13·4	1·2
15	1 18·8	1 19·0	1 15·2	1·5	0·1	7·5	0·7	13·5	1·2
16	1 19·0	1 19·2	1 15·4	1·6	0·1	7·6	0·7	13·6	1·2
17	1 19·3	1 19·5	1 15·6	1·7	0·2	7·7	0·7	13·7	1·3
18	1 19·5	1 19·7	1 15·9	1·8	0·2	7·8	0·7	13·8	1·3
19	1 19·8	1 20·0	1 16·1	1·9	0·2	7·9	0·7	13·9	1·3
20	1 20·0	1 20·2	1 16·4	2·0	0·2	8·0	0·7	14·0	1·3
21	1 20·3	1 20·5	1 16·6	2·1	0·2	8·1	0·7	14·1	1·3
22	1 20·5	1 20·7	1 16·8	2·2	0·2	8·2	0·8	14·2	1·3
23	1 20·8	1 21·0	1 17·1	2·3	0·2	8·3	0·8	14·3	1·3
24	1 21·0	1 21·2	1 17·3	2·4	0·2	8·4	0·8	14·4	1·3
25	1 21·3	1 21·5	1 17·5	2·5	0·2	8·5	0·8	14·5	1·3
26	1 21·5	1 21·7	1 17·8	2·6	0·2	8·6	0·8	14·6	1·3
27	1 21·8	1 22·0	1 18·0	2·7	0·2	8·7	0·8	14·7	1·3
28	1 22·0	1 22·2	1 18·3	2·8	0·3	8·8	0·8	14·8	1·4
29	1 22·3	1 22·5	1 18·5	2·9	0·3	8·9	0·8	14·9	1·4
30	1 22·5	1 22·7	1 18·7	3·0	0·3	9·0	0·8	15·0	1·4
31	1 22·8	1 23·0	1 19·0	3·1	0·3	9·1	0·8	15·1	1·4
32	1 23·0	1 23·2	1 19·2	3·2	0·3	9·2	0·8	15·2	1·4
33	1 23·3	1 23·5	1 19·5	3·3	0·3	9·3	0·9	15·3	1·4
34	1 23·5	1 23·7	1 19·7	3·4	0·3	9·4	0·9	15·4	1·4
35	1 23·8	1 24·0	1 19·9	3·5	0·3	9·5	0·9	15·5	1·4
36	1 24·0	1 24·2	1 20·2	3·6	0·3	9·6	0·9	15·6	1·4
37	1 24·3	1 24·5	1 20·4	3·7	0·3	9·7	0·9	15·7	1·4
38	1 24·5	1 24·7	1 20·7	3·8	0·3	9·8	0·9	15·8	1·4
39	1 24·8	1 25·0	1 20·9	3·9	0·4	9·9	0·9	15·9	1·5
40	1 25·0	1 25·2	1 21·1	4·0	0·4	10·0	0·9	16·0	1·5
41	1 25·3	1 25·5	1 21·4	4·1	0·4	10·1	0·9	16·1	1·5
42	1 25·5	1 25·7	1 21·6	4·2	0·4	10·2	0·9	16·2	1·5
43	1 25·8	1 26·0	1 21·8	4·3	0·4	10·3	0·9	16·3	1·5
44	1 26·0	1 26·2	1 22·1	4·4	0·4	10·4	1·0	16·4	1·5
45	1 26·3	1 26·5	1 22·3	4·5	0·4	10·5	1·0	16·5	1·5
46	1 26·5	1 26·7	1 22·6	4·6	0·4	10·6	1·0	16·6	1·5
47	1 26·8	1 27·0	1 22·8	4·7	0·4	10·7	1·0	16·7	1·5
48	1 27·0	1 27·2	1 23·0	4·8	0·4	10·8	1·0	16·8	1·5
49	1 27·3	1 27·5	1 23·3	4·9	0·4	10·9	1·0	16·9	1·5
50	1 27·5	1 27·7	1 23·5	5·0	0·5	11·0	1·0	17·0	1·6
51	1 27·8	1 28·0	1 23·8	5·1	0·5	11·1	1·0	17·1	1·6
52	1 28·0	1 28·2	1 24·0	5·2	0·5	11·2	1·0	17·2	1·6
53	1 28·3	1 28·5	1 24·2	5·3	0·5	11·3	1·0	17·3	1·6
54	1 28·5	1 28·7	1 24·5	5·4	0·5	11·4	1·0	17·4	1·6
55	1 28·8	1 29·0	1 24·7	5·5	0·5	11·5	1·1	17·5	1·6
56	1 29·0	1 29·2	1 24·9	5·6	0·5	11·6	1·1	17·6	1·6
57	1 29·3	1 29·5	1 25·2	5·7	0·5	11·7	1·1	17·7	1·6
58	1 29·5	1 29·7	1 25·4	5·8	0·5	11·8	1·1	17·8	1·6
59	1 29·8	1 30·0	1 25·7	5·9	0·5	11·9	1·1	17·9	1·6
60	1 30·0	1 30·2	1 25·9	6·0	0·6	12·0	1·1	18·0	1·7

m 6	SUN PLANETS	ARIES	MOON	v or Corrⁿ d		v or Corrⁿ d		v or Corrⁿ d		m 7	SUN PLANETS	ARIES	MOON	v or Corrⁿ d		v or Corrⁿ d		v or Corrⁿ d	
s	° ′	° ′	° ′	′	′	′	′	′	′	s	° ′	° ′	° ′	′	′	′	′	′	′
00	1 30·0	1 30·2	1 25·9	0·0	0·0	6·0	0·7	12·0	1·3	00	1 45·0	1 45·3	1 40·2	0·0	0·0	6·0	0·8	12·0	1·5
01	1 30·3	1 30·5	1 26·1	0·1	0·0	6·1	0·7	12·1	1·3	01	1 45·3	1 45·5	1 40·5	0·1	0·0	6·1	0·8	12·1	1·5
02	1 30·5	1 30·7	1 26·4	0·2	0·0	6·2	0·7	12·2	1·3	02	1 45·5	1 45·8	1 40·7	0·2	0·0	6·2	0·8	12·2	1·5
03	1 30·8	1 31·0	1 26·6	0·3	0·0	6·3	0·7	12·3	1·3	03	1 45·8	1 46·0	1 40·9	0·3	0·0	6·3	0·8	12·3	1·5
04	1 31·0	1 31·2	1 26·9	0·4	0·0	6·4	0·7	12·4	1·3	04	1 46·0	1 46·3	1 41·2	0·4	0·1	6·4	0·8	12·4	1·6
05	1 31·3	1 31·5	1 27·1	0·5	0·1	6·5	0·7	12·5	1·4	05	1 46·3	1 46·5	1 41·4	0·5	0·1	6·5	0·8	12·5	1·6
06	1 31·5	1 31·8	1 27·3	0·6	0·1	6·6	0·7	12·6	1·4	06	1 46·5	1 46·8	1 41·6	0·6	0·1	6·6	0·8	12·6	1·6
07	1 31·8	1 32·0	1 27·6	0·7	0·1	6·7	0·7	12·7	1·4	07	1 46·8	1 47·0	1 41·9	0·7	0·1	6·7	0·8	12·7	1·6
08	1 32·0	1 32·3	1 27·8	0·8	0·1	6·8	0·7	12·8	1·4	08	1 47·0	1 47·3	1 42·1	0·8	0·1	6·8	0·9	12·8	1·6
09	1 32·3	1 32·5	1 28·0	0·9	0·1	6·9	0·7	12·9	1·4	09	1 47·3	1 47·5	1 42·4	0·9	0·1	6·9	0·9	12·9	1·6
10	1 32·5	1 32·8	1 28·3	1·0	0·1	7·0	0·8	13·0	1·4	10	1 47·5	1 47·8	1 42·6	1·0	0·1	7·0	0·9	13·0	1·6
11	1 32·8	1 33·0	1 28·5	1·1	0·1	7·1	0·8	13·1	1·4	11	1 47·8	1 48·0	1 42·8	1·1	0·1	7·1	0·9	13·1	1·6
12	1 33·0	1 33·3	1 28·8	1·2	0·1	7·2	0·8	13·2	1·4	12	1 48·0	1 48·3	1 43·1	1·2	0·2	7·2	0·9	13·2	1·7
13	1 33·3	1 33·5	1 29·0	1·3	0·1	7·3	0·8	13·3	1·4	13	1 48·3	1 48·5	1 43·3	1·3	0·2	7·3	0·9	13·3	1·7
14	1 33·5	1 33·8	1 29·2	1·4	0·2	7·4	0·8	13·4	1·5	14	1 48·5	1 48·8	1 43·6	1·4	0·2	7·4	0·9	13·4	1·7
15	1 33·8	1 34·0	1 29·5	1·5	0·2	7·5	0·8	13·5	1·5	15	1 48·8	1 49·0	1 43·8	1·5	0·2	7·5	0·9	13·5	1·7
16	1 34·0	1 34·3	1 29·7	1·6	0·2	7·6	0·8	13·6	1·5	16	1 49·0	1 49·3	1 44·0	1·6	0·2	7·6	1·0	13·6	1·7
17	1 34·3	1 34·5	1 30·0	1·7	0·2	7·7	0·8	13·7	1·5	17	1 49·3	1 49·5	1 44·3	1·7	0·2	7·7	1·0	13·7	1·7
18	1 34·5	1 34·8	1 30·2	1·8	0·2	7·8	0·8	13·8	1·5	18	1 49·5	1 49·8	1 44·5	1·8	0·2	7·8	1·0	13·8	1·7
19	1 34·8	1 35·0	1 30·4	1·9	0·2	7·9	0·9	13·9	1·5	19	1 49·8	1 50·1	1 44·8	1·9	0·2	7·9	1·0	13·9	1·7
20	1 35·0	1 35·3	1 30·7	2·0	0·2	8·0	0·9	14·0	1·5	20	1 50·0	1 50·3	1 45·0	2·0	0·3	8·0	1·0	14·0	1·8
21	1 35·3	1 35·5	1 30·9	2·1	0·2	8·1	0·9	14·1	1·5	21	1 50·3	1 50·6	1 45·2	2·1	0·3	8·1	1·0	14·1	1·8
22	1 35·5	1 35·8	1 31·1	2·2	0·2	8·2	0·9	14·2	1·5	22	1 50·5	1 50·8	1 45·5	2·2	0·3	8·2	1·0	14·2	1·8
23	1 35·8	1 36·0	1 31·4	2·3	0·2	8·3	0·9	14·3	1·5	23	1 50·8	1 51·1	1 45·7	2·3	0·3	8·3	1·0	14·3	1·8
24	1 36·0	1 36·3	1 31·6	2·4	0·3	8·4	0·9	14·4	1·6	24	1 51·0	1 51·3	1 45·9	2·4	0·3	8·4	1·1	14·4	1·8
25	1 36·3	1 36·5	1 31·9	2·5	0·3	8·5	0·9	14·5	1·6	25	1 51·3	1 51·6	1 46·2	2·5	0·3	8·5	1·1	14·5	1·8
26	1 36·5	1 36·8	1 32·1	2·6	0·3	8·6	0·9	14·6	1·6	26	1 51·5	1 51·8	1 46·4	2·6	0·3	8·6	1·1	14·6	1·8
27	1 36·8	1 37·0	1 32·3	2·7	0·3	8·7	0·9	14·7	1·6	27	1 51·8	1 52·1	1 46·7	2·7	0·3	8·7	1·1	14·7	1·8
28	1 37·0	1 37·3	1 32·6	2·8	0·3	8·8	1·0	14·8	1·6	28	1 52·0	1 52·3	1 46·9	2·8	0·4	8·8	1·1	14·8	1·9
29	1 37·3	1 37·5	1 32·8	2·9	0·3	8·9	1·0	14·9	1·6	29	1 52·3	1 52·6	1 47·1	2·9	0·4	8·9	1·1	14·9	1·9
30	1 37·5	1 37·8	1 33·1	3·0	0·3	9·0	1·0	15·0	1·6	30	1 52·5	1 52·8	1 47·4	3·0	0·4	9·0	1·1	15·0	1·9
31	1 37·8	1 38·0	1 33·3	3·1	0·3	9·1	1·0	15·1	1·6	31	1 52·8	1 53·1	1 47·6	3·1	0·4	9·1	1·1	15·1	1·9
32	1 38·0	1 38·3	1 33·5	3·2	0·3	9·2	1·0	15·2	1·6	32	1 53·0	1 53·3	1 47·9	3·2	0·4	9·2	1·2	15·2	1·9
33	1 38·3	1 38·5	1 33·8	3·3	0·4	9·3	1·0	15·3	1·7	33	1 53·3	1 53·6	1 48·1	3·3	0·4	9·3	1·2	15·3	1·9
34	1 38·5	1 38·8	1 34·0	3·4	0·4	9·4	1·0	15·4	1·7	34	1 53·5	1 53·8	1 48·3	3·4	0·4	9·4	1·2	15·4	1·9
35	1 38·8	1 39·0	1 34·3	3·5	0·4	9·5	1·0	15·5	1·7	35	1 53·8	1 54·1	1 48·6	3·5	0·4	9·5	1·2	15·5	1·9
36	1 39·0	1 39·3	1 34·5	3·6	0·4	9·6	1·0	15·6	1·7	36	1 54·0	1 54·3	1 48·8	3·6	0·5	9·6	1·2	15·6	2·0
37	1 39·3	1 39·5	1 34·7	3·7	0·4	9·7	1·1	15·7	1·7	37	1 54·3	1 54·6	1 49·0	3·7	0·5	9·7	1·2	15·7	2·0
38	1 39·5	1 39·8	1 35·0	3·8	0·4	9·8	1·1	15·8	1·7	38	1 54·5	1 54·8	1 49·3	3·8	0·5	9·8	1·2	15·8	2·0
39	1 39·8	1 40·0	1 35·2	3·9	0·4	9·9	1·1	15·9	1·7	39	1 54·8	1 55·1	1 49·5	3·9	0·5	9·9	1·2	15·9	2·0
40	1 40·0	1 40·3	1 35·4	4·0	0·4	10·0	1·1	16·0	1·7	40	1 55·0	1 55·3	1 49·8	4·0	0·5	10·0	1·3	16·0	2·0
41	1 40·3	1 40·5	1 35·7	4·1	0·4	10·1	1·1	16·1	1·7	41	1 55·3	1 55·6	1 50·0	4·1	0·5	10·1	1·3	16·1	2·0
42	1 40·5	1 40·8	1 35·9	4·2	0·5	10·2	1·1	16·2	1·8	42	1 55·5	1 55·8	1 50·2	4·2	0·5	10·2	1·3	16·2	2·0
43	1 40·8	1 41·0	1 36·2	4·3	0·5	10·3	1·1	16·3	1·8	43	1 55·8	1 56·1	1 50·5	4·3	0·5	10·3	1·3	16·3	2·0
44	1 41·0	1 41·3	1 36·4	4·4	0·5	10·4	1·1	16·4	1·8	44	1 56·0	1 56·3	1 50·7	4·4	0·6	10·4	1·3	16·4	2·1
45	1 41·3	1 41·5	1 36·6	4·5	0·5	10·5	1·1	16·5	1·8	45	1 56·3	1 56·6	1 51·0	4·5	0·6	10·5	1·3	16·5	2·1
46	1 41·5	1 41·8	1 36·9	4·6	0·5	10·6	1·1	16·6	1·8	46	1 56·5	1 56·8	1 51·2	4·6	0·6	10·6	1·3	16·6	2·1
47	1 41·8	1 42·0	1 37·1	4·7	0·5	10·7	1·2	16·7	1·8	47	1 56·8	1 57·1	1 51·4	4·7	0·6	10·7	1·3	16·7	2·1
48	1 42·0	1 42·3	1 37·4	4·8	0·5	10·8	1·2	16·8	1·8	48	1 57·0	1 57·3	1 51·7	4·8	0·6	10·8	1·4	16·8	2·1
49	1 42·3	1 42·5	1 37·6	4·9	0·5	10·9	1·2	16·9	1·8	49	1 57·3	1 57·6	1 51·9	4·9	0·6	10·9	1·4	16·9	2·1
50	1 42·5	1 42·8	1 37·8	5·0	0·5	11·0	1·2	17·0	1·8	50	1 57·5	1 57·8	1 52·1	5·0	0·6	11·0	1·4	17·0	2·1
51	1 42·8	1 43·0	1 38·1	5·1	0·6	11·1	1·2	17·1	1·9	51	1 57·8	1 58·1	1 52·4	5·1	0·6	11·1	1·4	17·1	2·1
52	1 43·0	1 43·3	1 38·3	5·2	0·6	11·2	1·2	17·2	1·9	52	1 58·0	1 58·3	1 52·6	5·2	0·7	11·2	1·4	17·2	2·2
53	1 43·3	1 43·5	1 38·5	5·3	0·6	11·3	1·2	17·3	1·9	53	1 58·3	1 58·6	1 52·9	5·3	0·7	11·3	1·4	17·3	2·2
54	1 43·5	1 43·8	1 38·8	5·4	0·6	11·4	1·2	17·4	1·9	54	1 58·5	1 58·8	1 53·1	5·4	0·7	11·4	1·4	17·4	2·2
55	1 43·8	1 44·0	1 39·0	5·5	0·6	11·5	1·2	17·5	1·9	55	1 58·8	1 59·1	1 53·3	5·5	0·7	11·5	1·4	17·5	2·2
56	1 44·0	1 44·3	1 39·3	5·6	0·6	11·6	1·3	17·6	1·9	56	1 59·0	1 59·3	1 53·6	5·6	0·7	11·6	1·5	17·6	2·2
57	1 44·3	1 44·5	1 39·5	5·7	0·6	11·7	1·3	17·7	1·9	57	1 59·3	1 59·6	1 53·8	5·7	0·7	11·7	1·5	17·7	2·2
58	1 44·5	1 44·8	1 39·7	5·8	0·6	11·8	1·3	17·8	1·9	58	1 59·5	1 59·8	1 54·1	5·8	0·7	11·8	1·5	17·8	2·2
59	1 44·8	1 45·0	1 40·0	5·9	0·6	11·9	1·3	17·9	1·9	59	1 59·8	2 00·1	1 54·3	5·9	0·7	11·9	1·5	17·9	2·2
60	1 45·0	1 45·3	1 40·2	6·0	0·7	12·0	1·3	18·0	2·0	60	2 00·0	2 00·3	1 54·5	6·0	0·8	12·0	1·5	18·0	2·3

8 s	SUN PLANETS ° '	ARIES ° '	MOON ° '	v or d '	Corrⁿ '	v or d '	Corrⁿ '	v or d '	Corrⁿ '
00	2 00·0	2 00·3	1 54·5	0·0	0·0	6·0	0·9	12·0	1·7
01	2 00·3	2 00·6	1 54·8	0·1	0·0	6·1	0·9	12·1	1·7
02	2 00·5	2 00·8	1 55·0	0·2	0·0	6·2	0·9	12·2	1·7
03	2 00·8	2 01·1	1 55·2	0·3	0·0	6·3	0·9	12·3	1·7
04	2 01·0	2 01·3	1 55·5	0·4	0·1	6·4	0·9	12·4	1·8
05	2 01·3	2 01·6	1 55·7	0·5	0·1	6·5	0·9	12·5	1·8
06	2 01·5	2 01·8	1 56·0	0·6	0·1	6·6	0·9	12·6	1·8
07	2 01·8	2 02·1	1 56·2	0·7	0·1	6·7	0·9	12·7	1·8
08	2 02·0	2 02·3	1 56·4	0·8	0·1	6·8	1·0	12·8	1·8
09	2 02·3	2 02·6	1 56·7	0·9	0·1	6·9	1·0	12·9	1·8
10	2 02·5	2 02·8	1 56·9	1·0	0·1	7·0	1·0	13·0	1·8
11	2 02·8	2 03·1	1 57·2	1·1	0·2	7·1	1·0	13·1	1·9
12	2 03·0	2 03·3	1 57·4	1·2	0·2	7·2	1·0	13·2	1·9
13	2 03·3	2 03·6	1 57·6	1·3	0·2	7·3	1·0	13·3	1·9
14	2 03·5	2 03·8	1 57·9	1·4	0·2	7·4	1·0	13·4	1·9
15	2 03·8	2 04·1	1 58·1	1·5	0·2	7·5	1·1	13·5	1·9
16	2 04·0	2 04·3	1 58·4	1·6	0·2	7·6	1·1	13·6	1·9
17	2 04·3	2 04·6	1 58·6	1·7	0·2	7·7	1·1	13·7	1·9
18	2 04·5	2 04·8	1 58·8	1·8	0·3	7·8	1·1	13·8	2·0
19	2 04·8	2 05·1	1 59·1	1·9	0·3	7·9	1·1	13·9	2·0
20	2 05·0	2 05·3	1 59·3	2·0	0·3	8·0	1·1	14·0	2·0
21	2 05·3	2 05·6	1 59·5	2·1	0·3	8·1	1·1	14·1	2·0
22	2 05·5	2 05·8	1 59·8	2·2	0·3	8·2	1·2	14·2	2·0
23	2 05·8	2 06·1	2 00·0	2·3	0·3	8·3	1·2	14·3	2·0
24	2 06·0	2 06·3	2 00·3	2·4	0·3	8·4	1·2	14·4	2·0
25	2 06·3	2 06·6	2 00·5	2·5	0·4	8·5	1·2	14·5	2·1
26	2 06·5	2 06·8	2 00·7	2·6	0·4	8·6	1·2	14·6	2·1
27	2 06·8	2 07·1	2 01·0	2·7	0·4	8·7	1·2	14·7	2·1
28	2 07·0	2 07·3	2 01·2	2·8	0·4	8·8	1·2	14·8	2·1
29	2 07·3	2 07·6	2 01·5	2·9	0·4	8·9	1·3	14·9	2·1
30	2 07·5	2 07·8	2 01·7	3·0	0·4	9·0	1·3	15·0	2·1
31	2 07·8	2 08·1	2 01·9	3·1	0·4	9·1	1·3	15·1	2·1
32	2 08·0	2 08·4	2 02·2	3·2	0·5	9·2	1·3	15·2	2·2
33	2 08·3	2 08·6	2 02·4	3·3	0·5	9·3	1·3	15·3	2·2
34	2 08·5	2 08·9	2 02·6	3·4	0·5	9·4	1·3	15·4	2·2
35	2 08·8	2 09·1	2 02·9	3·5	0·5	9·5	1·3	15·5	2·2
36	2 09·0	2 09·4	2 03·1	3·6	0·5	9·6	1·4	15·6	2·2
37	2 09·3	2 09·6	2 03·4	3·7	0·5	9·7	1·4	15·7	2·2
38	2 09·5	2 09·9	2 03·6	3·8	0·5	9·8	1·4	15·8	2·2
39	2 09·8	2 10·1	2 03·8	3·9	0·6	9·9	1·4	15·9	2·3
40	2 10·0	2 10·4	2 04·1	4·0	0·6	10·0	1·4	16·0	2·3
41	2 10·3	2 10·6	2 04·3	4·1	0·6	10·1	1·4	16·1	2·3
42	2 10·5	2 10·9	2 04·6	4·2	0·6	10·2	1·4	16·2	2·3
43	2 10·8	2 11·1	2 04·8	4·3	0·6	10·3	1·5	16·3	2·3
44	2 11·0	2 11·4	2 05·0	4·4	0·6	10·4	1·5	16·4	2·3
45	2 11·3	2 11·6	2 05·3	4·5	0·6	10·5	1·5	16·5	2·3
46	2 11·5	2 11·9	2 05·5	4·6	0·7	10·6	1·5	16·6	2·4
47	2 11·8	2 12·1	2 05·7	4·7	0·7	10·7	1·5	16·7	2·4
48	2 12·0	2 12·4	2 06·0	4·8	0·7	10·8	1·5	16·8	2·4
49	2 12·3	2 12·6	2 06·2	4·9	0·7	10·9	1·5	16·9	2·4
50	2 12·5	2 12·9	2 06·5	5·0	0·7	11·0	1·6	17·0	2·4
51	2 12·8	2 13·1	2 06·7	5·1	0·7	11·1	1·6	17·1	2·4
52	2 13·0	2 13·4	2 06·9	5·2	0·7	11·2	1·6	17·2	2·4
53	2 13·3	2 13·6	2 07·2	5·3	0·8	11·3	1·6	17·3	2·5
54	2 13·5	2 13·9	2 07·4	5·4	0·8	11·4	1·6	17·4	2·5
55	2 13·8	2 14·1	2 07·7	5·5	0·8	11·5	1·6	17·5	2·5
56	2 14·0	2 14·4	2 07·9	5·6	0·8	11·6	1·6	17·6	2·5
57	2 14·3	2 14·6	2 08·1	5·7	0·8	11·7	1·7	17·7	2·5
58	2 14·5	2 14·9	2 08·4	5·8	0·8	11·8	1·7	17·8	2·5
59	2 14·8	2 15·1	2 08·6	5·9	0·8	11·9	1·7	17·9	2·5
60	2 15·0	2 15·4	2 08·9	6·0	0·9	12·0	1·7	18·0	2·6

9 s	SUN PLANETS ° '	ARIES ° '	MOON ° '	v or d '	Corrⁿ '	v or d '	Corrⁿ '	v or d '	Corrⁿ '
00	2 15·0	2 15·4	2 08·9	0·0	0·0	6·0	1·0	12·0	1·9
01	2 15·3	2 15·6	2 09·1	0·1	0·0	6·1	1·0	12·1	1·9
02	2 15·5	2 15·9	2 09·3	0·2	0·0	6·2	1·0	12·2	1·9
03	2 15·8	2 16·1	2 09·6	0·3	0·0	6·3	1·0	12·3	1·9
04	2 16·0	2 16·4	2 09·8	0·4	0·1	6·4	1·0	12·4	2·0
05	2 16·3	2 16·6	2 10·0	0·5	0·1	6·5	1·0	12·5	2·0
06	2 16·5	2 16·9	2 10·3	0·6	0·1	6·6	1·0	12·6	2·0
07	2 16·8	2 17·1	2 10·5	0·7	0·1	6·7	1·1	12·7	2·0
08	2 17·0	2 17·4	2 10·8	0·8	0·1	6·8	1·1	12·8	2·0
09	2 17·3	2 17·6	2 11·0	0·9	0·1	6·9	1·1	12·9	2·0
10	2 17·5	2 17·9	2 11·2	1·0	0·2	7·0	1·1	13·0	2·1
11	2 17·8	2 18·1	2 11·5	1·1	0·2	7·1	1·1	13·1	2·1
12	2 18·0	2 18·4	2 11·7	1·2	0·2	7·2	1·1	13·2	2·1
13	2 18·3	2 18·6	2 12·0	1·3	0·2	7·3	1·2	13·3	2·1
14	2 18·5	2 18·9	2 12·2	1·4	0·2	7·4	1·2	13·4	2·1
15	2 18·8	2 19·1	2 12·4	1·5	0·2	7·5	1·2	13·5	2·1
16	2 19·0	2 19·4	2 12·7	1·6	0·3	7·6	1·2	13·6	2·2
17	2 19·3	2 19·6	2 12·9	1·7	0·3	7·7	1·2	13·7	2·2
18	2 19·5	2 19·9	2 13·1	1·8	0·3	7·8	1·2	13·8	2·2
19	2 19·8	2 20·1	2 13·4	1·9	0·3	7·9	1·3	13·9	2·2
20	2 20·0	2 20·4	2 13·6	2·0	0·3	8·0	1·3	14·0	2·2
21	2 20·3	2 20·6	2 13·9	2·1	0·3	8·1	1·3	14·1	2·2
22	2 20·5	2 20·9	2 14·1	2·2	0·3	8·2	1·3	14·2	2·2
23	2 20·8	2 21·1	2 14·3	2·3	0·4	8·3	1·3	14·3	2·3
24	2 21·0	2 21·4	2 14·6	2·4	0·4	8·4	1·3	14·4	2·3
25	2 21·3	2 21·6	2 14·8	2·5	0·4	8·5	1·3	14·5	2·3
26	2 21·5	2 21·9	2 15·1	2·6	0·4	8·6	1·4	14·6	2·3
27	2 21·8	2 22·1	2 15·3	2·7	0·4	8·7	1·4	14·7	2·3
28	2 22·0	2 22·4	2 15·5	2·8	0·4	8·8	1·4	14·8	2·3
29	2 22·3	2 22·6	2 15·8	2·9	0·5	8·9	1·4	14·9	2·4
30	2 22·5	2 22·9	2 16·0	3·0	0·5	9·0	1·4	15·0	2·4
31	2 22·8	2 23·1	2 16·2	3·1	0·5	9·1	1·4	15·1	2·4
32	2 23·0	2 23·4	2 16·5	3·2	0·5	9·2	1·5	15·2	2·4
33	2 23·3	2 23·6	2 16·7	3·3	0·5	9·3	1·5	15·3	2·4
34	2 23·5	2 23·9	2 17·0	3·4	0·5	9·4	1·5	15·4	2·4
35	2 23·8	2 24·1	2 17·2	3·5	0·6	9·5	1·5	15·5	2·5
36	2 24·0	2 24·4	2 17·4	3·6	0·6	9·6	1·5	15·6	2·5
37	2 24·3	2 24·6	2 17·7	3·7	0·6	9·7	1·5	15·7	2·5
38	2 24·5	2 24·9	2 17·9	3·8	0·6	9·8	1·6	15·8	2·5
39	2 24·8	2 25·1	2 18·2	3·9	0·6	9·9	1·6	15·9	2·5
40	2 25·0	2 25·4	2 18·4	4·0	0·6	10·0	1·6	16·0	2·5
41	2 25·3	2 25·6	2 18·6	4·1	0·6	10·1	1·6	16·1	2·6
42	2 25·5	2 25·9	2 18·9	4·2	0·7	10·2	1·6	16·2	2·6
43	2 25·8	2 26·1	2 19·1	4·3	0·7	10·3	1·6	16·3	2·6
44	2 26·0	2 26·4	2 19·3	4·4	0·7	10·4	1·6	16·4	2·6
45	2 26·3	2 26·7	2 19·6	4·5	0·7	10·5	1·7	16·5	2·6
46	2 26·5	2 26·9	2 19·8	4·6	0·7	10·6	1·7	16·6	2·6
47	2 26·8	2 27·2	2 20·1	4·7	0·7	10·7	1·7	16·7	2·6
48	2 27·0	2 27·4	2 20·3	4·8	0·8	10·8	1·7	16·8	2·7
49	2 27·3	2 27·7	2 20·5	4·9	0·8	10·9	1·7	16·9	2·7
50	2 27·5	2 27·9	2 20·8	5·0	0·8	11·0	1·7	17·0	2·7
51	2 27·8	2 28·2	2 21·0	5·1	0·8	11·1	1·8	17·1	2·7
52	2 28·0	2 28·4	2 21·3	5·2	0·8	11·2	1·8	17·2	2·7
53	2 28·3	2 28·7	2 21·5	5·3	0·8	11·3	1·8	17·3	2·7
54	2 28·5	2 28·9	2 21·7	5·4	0·9	11·4	1·8	17·4	2·8
55	2 28·8	2 29·2	2 22·0	5·5	0·9	11·5	1·8	17·5	2·8
56	2 29·0	2 29·4	2 22·2	5·6	0·9	11·6	1·8	17·6	2·8
57	2 29·3	2 29·7	2 22·5	5·7	0·9	11·7	1·9	17·7	2·8
58	2 29·5	2 29·9	2 22·7	5·8	0·9	11·8	1·9	17·8	2·8
59	2 29·8	2 30·2	2 22·9	5·9	0·9	11·9	1·9	17·9	2·8
60	2 30·0	2 30·4	2 23·2	6·0	1·0	12·0	1·9	18·0	2·9

10ᵐ

m 10	SUN PLANETS	ARIES	MOON	v or Corrⁿ d	v or Corrⁿ d	v or Corrⁿ d
s	° ′	° ′	° ′	′ ′	′ ′	′ ′
00	2 30·0	2 30·4	2 23·2	0·0 0·0	6·0 1·1	12·0 2·1
01	2 30·3	2 30·7	2 23·4	0·1 0·0	6·1 1·1	12·1 2·1
02	2 30·5	2 30·9	2 23·6	0·2 0·0	6·2 1·1	12·2 2·1
03	2 30·8	2 31·2	2 23·9	0·3 0·1	6·3 1·1	12·3 2·2
04	2 31·0	2 31·4	2 24·1	0·4 0·1	6·4 1·1	12·4 2·2
05	2 31·3	2 31·7	2 24·4	0·5 0·1	6·5 1·1	12·5 2·2
06	2 31·5	2 31·9	2 24·6	0·6 0·1	6·6 1·2	12·6 2·2
07	2 31·8	2 32·2	2 24·8	0·7 0·1	6·7 1·2	12·7 2·2
08	2 32·0	2 32·4	2 25·1	0·8 0·1	6·8 1·2	12·8 2·2
09	2 32·3	2 32·7	2 25·3	0·9 0·2	6·9 1·2	12·9 2·3
10	2 32·5	2 32·9	2 25·6	1·0 0·2	7·0 1·2	13·0 2·3
11	2 32·8	2 33·2	2 25·8	1·1 0·2	7·1 1·2	13·1 2·3
12	2 33·0	2 33·4	2 26·0	1·2 0·2	7·2 1·3	13·2 2·3
13	2 33·3	2 33·7	2 26·3	1·3 0·2	7·3 1·3	13·3 2·3
14	2 33·5	2 33·9	2 26·5	1·4 0·2	7·4 1·3	13·4 2·3
15	2 33·8	2 34·2	2 26·7	1·5 0·3	7·5 1·3	13·5 2·4
16	2 34·0	2 34·4	2 27·0	1·6 0·3	7·6 1·3	13·6 2·4
17	2 34·3	2 34·7	2 27·2	1·7 0·3	7·7 1·3	13·7 2·4
18	2 34·5	2 34·9	2 27·5	1·8 0·3	7·8 1·4	13·8 2·4
19	2 34·8	2 35·2	2 27·7	1·9 0·3	7·9 1·4	13·9 2·4
20	2 35·0	2 35·4	2 27·9	2·0 0·4	8·0 1·4	14·0 2·5
21	2 35·3	2 35·7	2 28·2	2·1 0·4	8·1 1·4	14·1 2·5
22	2 35·5	2 35·9	2 28·4	2·2 0·4	8·2 1·4	14·2 2·5
23	2 35·8	2 36·2	2 28·7	2·3 0·4	8·3 1·5	14·3 2·5
24	2 36·0	2 36·4	2 28·9	2·4 0·4	8·4 1·5	14·4 2·5
25	2 36·3	2 36·7	2 29·1	2·5 0·4	8·5 1·5	14·5 2·5
26	2 36·5	2 36·9	2 29·4	2·6 0·5	8·6 1·5	14·6 2·6
27	2 36·8	2 37·2	2 29·6	2·7 0·5	8·7 1·5	14·7 2·6
28	2 37·0	2 37·4	2 29·8	2·8 0·5	8·8 1·5	14·8 2·6
29	2 37·3	2 37·7	2 30·1	2·9 0·5	8·9 1·6	14·9 2·6
30	2 37·5	2 37·9	2 30·3	3·0 0·5	9·0 1·6	15·0 2·6
31	2 37·8	2 38·2	2 30·6	3·1 0·5	9·1 1·6	15·1 2·6
32	2 38·0	2 38·4	2 30·8	3·2 0·6	9·2 1·6	15·2 2·7
33	2 38·3	2 38·7	2 31·0	3·3 0·6	9·3 1·6	15·3 2·7
34	2 38·5	2 38·9	2 31·3	3·4 0·6	9·4 1·6	15·4 2·7
35	2 38·8	2 39·2	2 31·5	3·5 0·6	9·5 1·7	15·5 2·7
36	2 39·0	2 39·4	2 31·8	3·6 0·6	9·6 1·7	15·6 2·7
37	2 39·3	2 39·7	2 32·0	3·7 0·6	9·7 1·7	15·7 2·7
38	2 39·5	2 39·9	2 32·2	3·8 0·7	9·8 1·7	15·8 2·8
39	2 39·8	2 40·2	2 32·5	3·9 0·7	9·9 1·7	15·9 2·8
40	2 40·0	2 40·4	2 32·7	4·0 0·7	10·0 1·8	16·0 2·8
41	2 40·3	2 40·7	2 32·9	4·1 0·7	10·1 1·8	16·1 2·8
42	2 40·5	2 40·9	2 33·2	4·2 0·7	10·2 1·8	16·2 2·8
43	2 40·8	2 41·2	2 33·4	4·3 0·8	10·3 1·8	16·3 2·9
44	2 41·0	2 41·4	2 33·7	4·4 0·8	10·4 1·8	16·4 2·9
45	2 41·3	2 41·7	2 33·9	4·5 0·8	10·5 1·8	16·5 2·9
46	2 41·5	2 41·9	2 34·1	4·6 0·8	10·6 1·9	16·6 2·9
47	2 41·8	2 42·2	2 34·4	4·7 0·8	10·7 1·9	16·7 2·9
48	2 42·0	2 42·4	2 34·6	4·8 0·8	10·8 1·9	16·8 2·9
49	2 42·3	2 42·7	2 34·9	4·9 0·9	10·9 1·9	16·9 3·0
50	2 42·5	2 42·9	2 35·1	5·0 0·9	11·0 1·9	17·0 3·0
51	2 42·8	2 43·2	2 35·3	5·1 0·9	11·1 1·9	17·1 3·0
52	2 43·0	2 43·4	2 35·6	5·2 0·9	11·2 2·0	17·2 3·0
53	2 43·3	2 43·7	2 35·8	5·3 0·9	11·3 2·0	17·3 3·0
54	2 43·5	2 43·9	2 36·1	5·4 0·9	11·4 2·0	17·4 3·0
55	2 43·8	2 44·2	2 36·3	5·5 1·0	11·5 2·0	17·5 3·1
56	2 44·0	2 44·4	2 36·5	5·6 1·0	11·6 2·0	17·6 3·1
57	2 44·3	2 44·7	2 36·8	5·7 1·0	11·7 2·0	17·7 3·1
58	2 44·5	2 45·0	2 37·0	5·8 1·0	11·8 2·1	17·8 3·1
59	2 44·8	2 45·2	2 37·2	5·9 1·0	11·9 2·1	17·9 3·1
60	2 45·0	2 45·5	2 37·5	6·0 1·1	12·0 2·1	18·0 3·2

11ᵐ

m 11	SUN PLANETS	ARIES	MOON	v or Corrⁿ d	v or Corrⁿ d	v or Corrⁿ d
s	° ′	° ′	° ′	′ ′	′ ′	′ ′
00	2 45·0	2 45·5	2 37·5	0·0 0·0	6·0 1·2	12·0 2·3
01	2 45·3	2 45·7	2 37·7	0·1 0·0	6·1 1·2	12·1 2·3
02	2 45·5	2 46·0	2 38·0	0·2 0·0	6·2 1·2	12·2 2·3
03	2 45·8	2 46·2	2 38·2	0·3 0·1	6·3 1·2	12·3 2·4
04	2 46·0	2 46·5	2 38·4	0·4 0·1	6·4 1·2	12·4 2·4
05	2 46·3	2 46·7	2 38·7	0·5 0·1	6·5 1·2	12·5 2·4
06	2 46·5	2 47·0	2 38·9	0·6 0·1	6·6 1·3	12·6 2·4
07	2 46·8	2 47·2	2 39·2	0·7 0·1	6·7 1·3	12·7 2·4
08	2 47·0	2 47·5	2 39·4	0·8 0·2	6·8 1·3	12·8 2·5
09	2 47·3	2 47·7	2 39·6	0·9 0·2	6·9 1·3	12·9 2·5
10	2 47·5	2 48·0	2 39·9	1·0 0·2	7·0 1·3	13·0 2·5
11	2 47·8	2 48·2	2 40·1	1·1 0·2	7·1 1·4	13·1 2·5
12	2 48·0	2 48·5	2 40·3	1·2 0·2	7·2 1·4	13·2 2·5
13	2 48·3	2 48·7	2 40·6	1·3 0·2	7·3 1·4	13·3 2·5
14	2 48·5	2 49·0	2 40·8	1·4 0·3	7·4 1·4	13·4 2·6
15	2 48·8	2 49·2	2 41·1	1·5 0·3	7·5 1·4	13·5 2·6
16	2 49·0	2 49·5	2 41·3	1·6 0·3	7·6 1·5	13·6 2·6
17	2 49·3	2 49·7	2 41·5	1·7 0·3	7·7 1·5	13·7 2·6
18	2 49·5	2 50·0	2 41·8	1·8 0·3	7·8 1·5	13·8 2·6
19	2 49·8	2 50·2	2 42·0	1·9 0·4	7·9 1·5	13·9 2·7
20	2 50·0	2 50·5	2 42·3	2·0 0·4	8·0 1·5	14·0 2·7
21	2 50·3	2 50·7	2 42·5	2·1 0·4	8·1 1·6	14·1 2·7
22	2 50·5	2 51·0	2 42·7	2·2 0·4	8·2 1·6	14·2 2·7
23	2 50·8	2 51·2	2 43·0	2·3 0·4	8·3 1·6	14·3 2·7
24	2 51·0	2 51·5	2 43·2	2·4 0·5	8·4 1·6	14·4 2·8
25	2 51·3	2 51·7	2 43·4	2·5 0·5	8·5 1·6	14·5 2·8
26	2 51·5	2 52·0	2 43·7	2·6 0·5	8·6 1·6	14·6 2·8
27	2 51·8	2 52·2	2 43·9	2·7 0·5	8·7 1·7	14·7 2·8
28	2 52·0	2 52·5	2 44·2	2·8 0·5	8·8 1·7	14·8 2·8
29	2 52·3	2 52·7	2 44·4	2·9 0·6	8·9 1·7	14·9 2·9
30	2 52·5	2 53·0	2 44·6	3·0 0·6	9·0 1·7	15·0 2·9
31	2 52·8	2 53·2	2 44·9	3·1 0·6	9·1 1·7	15·1 2·9
32	2 53·0	2 53·5	2 45·1	3·2 0·6	9·2 1·8	15·2 2·9
33	2 53·3	2 53·7	2 45·4	3·3 0·6	9·3 1·8	15·3 2·9
34	2 53·5	2 54·0	2 45·6	3·4 0·7	9·4 1·8	15·4 3·0
35	2 53·8	2 54·2	2 45·8	3·5 0·7	9·5 1·8	15·5 3·0
36	2 54·0	2 54·5	2 46·1	3·6 0·7	9·6 1·8	15·6 3·0
37	2 54·3	2 54·7	2 46·3	3·7 0·7	9·7 1·9	15·7 3·0
38	2 54·5	2 55·0	2 46·6	3·8 0·7	9·8 1·9	15·8 3·0
39	2 54·8	2 55·2	2 46·8	3·9 0·7	9·9 1·9	15·9 3·0
40	2 55·0	2 55·5	2 47·0	4·0 0·8	10·0 1·9	16·0 3·1
41	2 55·3	2 55·7	2 47·3	4·1 0·8	10·1 1·9	16·1 3·1
42	2 55·5	2 56·0	2 47·5	4·2 0·8	10·2 2·0	16·2 3·1
43	2 55·8	2 56·2	2 47·7	4·3 0·8	10·3 2·0	16·3 3·1
44	2 56·0	2 56·5	2 48·0	4·4 0·8	10·4 2·0	16·4 3·1
45	2 56·3	2 56·7	2 48·2	4·5 0·9	10·5 2·0	16·5 3·2
46	2 56·5	2 57·0	2 48·5	4·6 0·9	10·6 2·0	16·6 3·2
47	2 56·8	2 57·2	2 48·7	4·7 0·9	10·7 2·1	16·7 3·2
48	2 57·0	2 57·5	2 48·9	4·8 0·9	10·8 2·1	16·8 3·2
49	2 57·3	2 57·7	2 49·2	4·9 0·9	10·9 2·1	16·9 3·2
50	2 57·5	2 58·0	2 49·4	5·0 1·0	11·0 2·1	17·0 3·3
51	2 57·8	2 58·2	2 49·7	5·1 1·0	11·1 2·1	17·1 3·3
52	2 58·0	2 58·5	2 49·9	5·2 1·0	11·2 2·1	17·2 3·3
53	2 58·3	2 58·7	2 50·1	5·3 1·0	11·3 2·2	17·3 3·3
54	2 58·5	2 59·0	2 50·4	5·4 1·0	11·4 2·2	17·4 3·3
55	2 58·8	2 59·2	2 50·6	5·5 1·1	11·5 2·2	17·5 3·4
56	2 59·0	2 59·5	2 50·8	5·6 1·1	11·6 2·2	17·6 3·4
57	2 59·3	2 59·7	2 51·1	5·7 1·1	11·7 2·2	17·7 3·4
58	2 59·5	3 00·0	2 51·3	5·8 1·1	11·8 2·3	17·8 3·4
59	2 59·8	3 00·2	2 51·6	5·9 1·1	11·9 2·3	17·9 3·4
60	3 00·0	3 00·5	2 51·8	6·0 1·2	12·0 2·3	18·0 3·5

12	SUN PLANETS	ARIES	MOON	v or d / Corrⁿ	v or d / Corrⁿ	v or d / Corrⁿ
s	° ′	° ′	° ′	′ ′	′ ′	′ ′
00	3 00·0	3 00·5	2 51·8	0·0 0·0	6·0 1·3	12·0 2·5
01	3 00·3	3 00·7	2 52·0	0·1 0·0	6·1 1·3	12·1 2·5
02	3 00·5	3 01·0	2 52·3	0·2 0·0	6·2 1·3	12·2 2·5
03	3 00·8	3 01·2	2 52·5	0·3 0·1	6·3 1·3	12·3 2·6
04	3 01·0	3 01·5	2 52·8	0·4 0·1	6·4 1·3	12·4 2·6
05	3 01·3	3 01·7	2 53·0	0·5 0·1	6·5 1·4	12·5 2·6
06	3 01·5	3 02·0	2 53·2	0·6 0·1	6·6 1·4	12·6 2·6
07	3 01·8	3 02·2	2 53·5	0·7 0·1	6·7 1·4	12·7 2·6
08	3 02·0	3 02·5	2 53·7	0·8 0·2	6·8 1·4	12·8 2·7
09	3 02·3	3 02·7	2 53·9	0·9 0·2	6·9 1·4	12·9 2·7
10	3 02·5	3 03·0	2 54·2	1·0 0·2	7·0 1·5	13·0 2·7
11	3 02·8	3 03·3	2 54·4	1·1 0·2	7·1 1·5	13·1 2·7
12	3 03·0	3 03·5	2 54·7	1·2 0·3	7·2 1·5	13·2 2·8
13	3 03·3	3 03·8	2 54·9	1·3 0·3	7·3 1·5	13·3 2·8
14	3 03·5	3 04·0	2 55·1	1·4 0·3	7·4 1·5	13·4 2·8
15	3 03·8	3 04·3	2 55·4	1·5 0·3	7·5 1·6	13·5 2·8
16	3 04·0	3 04·5	2 55·6	1·6 0·3	7·6 1·6	13·6 2·8
17	3 04·3	3 04·8	2 55·9	1·7 0·4	7·7 1·6	13·7 2·9
18	3 04·5	3 05·0	2 56·1	1·8 0·4	7·8 1·6	13·8 2·9
19	3 04·8	3 05·3	2 56·3	1·9 0·4	7·9 1·6	13·9 2·9
20	3 05·0	3 05·5	2 56·6	2·0 0·4	8·0 1·7	14·0 2·9
21	3 05·3	3 05·8	2 56·8	2·1 0·4	8·1 1·7	14·1 2·9
22	3 05·5	3 06·0	2 57·0	2·2 0·5	8·2 1·7	14·2 3·0
23	3 05·8	3 06·3	2 57·3	2·3 0·5	8·3 1·7	14·3 3·0
24	3 06·0	3 06·5	2 57·5	2·4 0·5	8·4 1·8	14·4 3·0
25	3 06·3	3 06·8	2 57·8	2·5 0·5	8·5 1·8	14·5 3·0
26	3 06·5	3 07·0	2 58·0	2·6 0·5	8·6 1·8	14·6 3·0
27	3 06·8	3 07·3	2 58·2	2·7 0·6	8·7 1·8	14·7 3·1
28	3 07·0	3 07·5	2 58·5	2·8 0·6	8·8 1·8	14·8 3·1
29	3 07·3	3 07·8	2 58·7	2·9 0·6	8·9 1·9	14·9 3·1
30	3 07·5	3 08·0	2 59·0	3·0 0·6	9·0 1·9	15·0 3·1
31	3 07·8	3 08·3	2 59·2	3·1 0·6	9·1 1·9	15·1 3·1
32	3 08·0	3 08·5	2 59·4	3·2 0·7	9·2 1·9	15·2 3·2
33	3 08·3	3 08·8	2 59·7	3·3 0·7	9·3 1·9	15·3 3·2
34	3 08·5	3 09·0	2 59·9	3·4 0·7	9·4 2·0	15·4 3·2
35	3 08·8	3 09·3	3 00·2	3·5 0·7	9·5 2·0	15·5 3·2
36	3 09·0	3 09·5	3 00·4	3·6 0·8	9·6 2·0	15·6 3·3
37	3 09·3	3 09·8	3 00·6	3·7 0·8	9·7 2·0	15·7 3·3
38	3 09·5	3 10·0	3 00·9	3·8 0·8	9·8 2·0	15·8 3·3
39	3 09·8	3 10·3	3 01·1	3·9 0·8	9·9 2·1	15·9 3·3
40	3 10·0	3 10·5	3 01·3	4·0 0·8	10·0 2·1	16·0 3·3
41	3 10·3	3 10·8	3 01·6	4·1 0·9	10·1 2·1	16·1 3·4
42	3 10·5	3 11·0	3 01·8	4·2 0·9	10·2 2·1	16·2 3·4
43	3 10·8	3 11·3	3 02·1	4·3 0·9	10·3 2·1	16·3 3·4
44	3 11·0	3 11·5	3 02·3	4·4 0·9	10·4 2·2	16·4 3·4
45	3 11·3	3 11·8	3 02·5	4·5 0·9	10·5 2·2	16·5 3·4
46	3 11·5	3 12·0	3 02·8	4·6 1·0	10·6 2·2	16·6 3·5
47	3 11·8	3 12·3	3 03·0	4·7 1·0	10·7 2·2	16·7 3·5
48	3 12·0	3 12·5	3 03·3	4·8 1·0	10·8 2·3	16·8 3·5
49	3 12·3	3 12·8	3 03·5	4·9 1·0	10·9 2·3	16·9 3·5
50	3 12·5	3 13·0	3 03·7	5·0 1·0	11·0 2·3	17·0 3·5
51	3 12·8	3 13·3	3 04·0	5·1 1·1	11·1 2·3	17·1 3·6
52	3 13·0	3 13·5	3 04·2	5·2 1·1	11·2 2·3	17·2 3·6
53	3 13·3	3 13·8	3 04·4	5·3 1·1	11·3 2·4	17·3 3·6
54	3 13·5	3 14·0	3 04·7	5·4 1·1	11·4 2·4	17·4 3·6
55	3 13·8	3 14·3	3 04·9	5·5 1·1	11·5 2·4	17·5 3·6
56	3 14·0	3 14·5	3 05·2	5·6 1·2	11·6 2·4	17·6 3·7
57	3 14·3	3 14·8	3 05·4	5·7 1·2	11·7 2·4	17·7 3·7
58	3 14·5	3 15·0	3 05·6	5·8 1·2	11·8 2·5	17·8 3·7
59	3 14·8	3 15·3	3 05·9	5·9 1·2	11·9 2·5	17·9 3·7
60	3 15·0	3 15·5	3 06·1	6·0 1·3	12·0 2·5	18·0 3·8

13	SUN PLANETS	ARIES	MOON	v or d / Corrⁿ	v or d / Corrⁿ	v or d / Corrⁿ
s	° ′	° ′	° ′	′ ′	′ ′	′ ′
00	3 15·0	3 15·5	3 06·1	0·0 0·0	6·0 1·4	12·0 2·7
01	3 15·3	3 15·8	3 06·4	0·1 0·0	6·1 1·4	12·1 2·7
02	3 15·5	3 16·0	3 06·6	0·2 0·0	6·2 1·4	12·2 2·8
03	3 15·8	3 16·3	3 06·8	0·3 0·1	6·3 1·4	12·3 2·8
04	3 16·0	3 16·5	3 07·1	0·4 0·1	6·4 1·4	12·4 2·8
05	3 16·3	3 16·8	3 07·3	0·5 0·1	6·5 1·5	12·5 2·8
06	3 16·5	3 17·0	3 07·5	0·6 0·1	6·6 1·5	12·6 2·8
07	3 16·8	3 17·3	3 07·8	0·7 0·2	6·7 1·5	12·7 2·9
08	3 17·0	3 17·5	3 08·0	0·8 0·2	6·8 1·5	12·8 2·9
09	3 17·3	3 17·8	3 08·3	0·9 0·2	6·9 1·6	12·9 2·9
10	3 17·5	3 18·0	3 08·5	1·0 0·2	7·0 1·6	13·0 2·9
11	3 17·8	3 18·3	3 08·7	1·1 0·2	7·1 1·6	13·1 2·9
12	3 18·0	3 18·5	3 09·0	1·2 0·3	7·2 1·6	13·2 3·0
13	3 18·3	3 18·8	3 09·2	1·3 0·3	7·3 1·6	13·3 3·0
14	3 18·5	3 19·0	3 09·5	1·4 0·3	7·4 1·7	13·4 3·0
15	3 18·8	3 19·3	3 09·7	1·5 0·3	7·5 1·7	13·5 3·0
16	3 19·0	3 19·5	3 09·9	1·6 0·4	7·6 1·7	13·6 3·1
17	3 19·3	3 19·8	3 10·2	1·7 0·4	7·7 1·7	13·7 3·1
18	3 19·5	3 20·0	3 10·4	1·8 0·4	7·8 1·8	13·8 3·1
19	3 19·8	3 20·3	3 10·7	1·9 0·4	7·9 1·8	13·9 3·1
20	3 20·0	3 20·5	3 10·9	2·0 0·5	8·0 1·8	14·0 3·2
21	3 20·3	3 20·8	3 11·1	2·1 0·5	8·1 1·8	14·1 3·2
22	3 20·5	3 21·0	3 11·4	2·2 0·5	8·2 1·8	14·2 3·2
23	3 20·8	3 21·3	3 11·6	2·3 0·5	8·3 1·9	14·3 3·2
24	3 21·0	3 21·6	3 11·8	2·4 0·5	8·4 1·9	14·4 3·2
25	3 21·3	3 21·8	3 12·1	2·5 0·6	8·5 1·9	14·5 3·3
26	3 21·5	3 22·1	3 12·3	2·6 0·6	8·6 1·9	14·6 3·3
27	3 21·8	3 22·3	3 12·6	2·7 0·6	8·7 2·0	14·7 3·3
28	3 22·0	3 22·6	3 12·8	2·8 0·6	8·8 2·0	14·8 3·3
29	3 22·3	3 22·8	3 13·0	2·9 0·7	8·9 2·0	14·9 3·4
30	3 22·5	3 23·1	3 13·3	3·0 0·7	9·0 2·0	15·0 3·4
31	3 22·8	3 23·3	3 13·5	3·1 0·7	9·1 2·0	15·1 3·4
32	3 23·0	3 23·6	3 13·8	3·2 0·7	9·2 2·1	15·2 3·4
33	3 23·3	3 23·8	3 14·0	3·3 0·7	9·3 2·1	15·3 3·4
34	3 23·5	3 24·1	3 14·2	3·4 0·8	9·4 2·1	15·4 3·5
35	3 23·8	3 24·3	3 14·5	3·5 0·8	9·5 2·1	15·5 3·5
36	3 24·0	3 24·6	3 14·7	3·6 0·8	9·6 2·2	15·6 3·5
37	3 24·3	3 24·8	3 14·9	3·7 0·8	9·7 2·2	15·7 3·5
38	3 24·5	3 25·1	3 15·2	3·8 0·9	9·8 2·2	15·8 3·6
39	3 24·8	3 25·3	3 15·4	3·9 0·9	9·9 2·2	15·9 3·6
40	3 25·0	3 25·6	3 15·7	4·0 0·9	10·0 2·3	16·0 3·6
41	3 25·3	3 25·8	3 15·9	4·1 0·9	10·1 2·3	16·1 3·6
42	3 25·5	3 26·1	3 16·1	4·2 0·9	10·2 2·3	16·2 3·6
43	3 25·8	3 26·3	3 16·4	4·3 1·0	10·3 2·3	16·3 3·7
44	3 26·0	3 26·6	3 16·6	4·4 1·0	10·4 2·3	16·4 3·7
45	3 26·3	3 26·8	3 16·9	4·5 1·0	10·5 2·4	16·5 3·7
46	3 26·5	3 27·1	3 17·1	4·6 1·0	10·6 2·4	16·6 3·7
47	3 26·8	3 27·3	3 17·3	4·7 1·1	10·7 2·4	16·7 3·8
48	3 27·0	3 27·6	3 17·6	4·8 1·1	10·8 2·4	16·8 3·8
49	3 27·3	3 27·8	3 17·8	4·9 1·1	10·9 2·5	16·9 3·8
50	3 27·5	3 28·1	3 18·0	5·0 1·1	11·0 2·5	17·0 3·8
51	3 27·8	3 28·3	3 18·3	5·1 1·1	11·1 2·5	17·1 3·8
52	3 28·0	3 28·6	3 18·5	5·2 1·2	11·2 2·5	17·2 3·9
53	3 28·3	3 28·8	3 18·8	5·3 1·2	11·3 2·5	17·3 3·9
54	3 28·5	3 29·1	3 19·0	5·4 1·2	11·4 2·6	17·4 3·9
55	3 28·8	3 29·3	3 19·2	5·5 1·2	11·5 2·6	17·5 3·9
56	3 29·0	3 29·6	3 19·5	5·6 1·3	11·6 2·6	17·6 4·0
57	3 29·3	3 29·8	3 19·7	5·7 1·3	11·7 2·6	17·7 4·0
58	3 29·5	3 30·1	3 20·0	5·8 1·3	11·8 2·7	17·8 4·0
59	3 29·8	3 30·3	3 20·2	5·9 1·3	11·9 2·7	17·9 4·0
60	3 30·0	3 30·6	3 20·4	6·0 1·4	12·0 2·7	18·0 4·1

14 m	SUN PLANETS	ARIES	MOON	v or Corrⁿ d		v or Corrⁿ d		v or Corrⁿ d	
s	° ′	° ′	° ′	′	′	′	′	′	′
00	3 30·0	3 30·6	3 20·4	0·0	0·0	6·0	1·5	12·0	2·9
01	3 30·3	3 30·8	3 20·7	0·1	0·0	6·1	1·5	12·1	2·9
02	3 30·5	3 31·1	3 20·9	0·2	0·0	6·2	1·5	12·2	2·9
03	3 30·8	3 31·3	3 21·1	0·3	0·1	6·3	1·5	12·3	3·0
04	3 31·0	3 31·6	3 21·4	0·4	0·1	6·4	1·5	12·4	3·0
05	3 31·3	3 31·8	3 21·6	0·5	0·1	6·5	1·6	12·5	3·0
06	3 31·5	3 32·1	3 21·9	0·6	0·1	6·6	1·6	12·6	3·0
07	3 31·8	3 32·3	3 22·1	0·7	0·2	6·7	1·6	12·7	3·1
08	3 32·0	3 32·6	3 22·3	0·8	0·2	6·8	1·6	12·8	3·1
09	3 32·3	3 32·8	3 22·6	0·9	0·2	6·9	1·7	12·9	3·1
10	3 32·5	3 33·1	3 22·8	1·0	0·2	7·0	1·7	13·0	3·1
11	3 32·8	3 33·3	3 23·1	1·1	0·3	7·1	1·7	13·1	3·2
12	3 33·0	3 33·6	3 23·3	1·2	0·3	7·2	1·7	13·2	3·2
13	3 33·3	3 33·8	3 23·5	1·3	0·3	7·3	1·8	13·3	3·2
14	3 33·5	3 34·1	3 23·8	1·4	0·3	7·4	1·8	13·4	3·2
15	3 33·8	3 34·3	3 24·0	1·5	0·4	7·5	1·8	13·5	3·3
16	3 34·0	3 34·6	3 24·3	1·6	0·4	7·6	1·8	13·6	3·3
17	3 34·3	3 34·8	3 24·5	1·7	0·4	7·7	1·9	13·7	3·3
18	3 34·5	3 35·1	3 24·7	1·8	0·4	7·8	1·9	13·8	3·3
19	3 34·8	3 35·3	3 25·0	1·9	0·5	7·9	1·9	13·9	3·4
20	3 35·0	3 35·6	3 25·2	2·0	0·5	8·0	1·9	14·0	3·4
21	3 35·3	3 35·8	3 25·4	2·1	0·5	8·1	2·0	14·1	3·4
22	3 35·5	3 36·1	3 25·7	2·2	0·5	8·2	2·0	14·2	3·4
23	3 35·8	3 36·3	3 25·9	2·3	0·6	8·3	2·0	14·3	3·5
24	3 36·0	3 36·6	3 26·2	2·4	0·6	8·4	2·0	14·4	3·5
25	3 36·3	3 36·8	3 26·4	2·5	0·6	8·5	2·1	14·5	3·5
26	3 36·5	3 37·1	3 26·6	2·6	0·6	8·6	2·1	14·6	3·5
27	3 36·8	3 37·3	3 26·9	2·7	0·7	8·7	2·1	14·7	3·6
28	3 37·0	3 37·6	3 27·1	2·8	0·7	8·8	2·1	14·8	3·6
29	3 37·3	3 37·8	3 27·4	2·9	0·7	8·9	2·2	14·9	3·6
30	3 37·5	3 38·1	3 27·6	3·0	0·7	9·0	2·2	15·0	3·6
31	3 37·8	3 38·3	3 27·8	3·1	0·7	9·1	2·2	15·1	3·6
32	3 38·0	3 38·6	3 28·1	3·2	0·8	9·2	2·2	15·2	3·7
33	3 38·3	3 38·8	3 28·3	3·3	0·8	9·3	2·2	15·3	3·7
34	3 38·5	3 39·1	3 28·5	3·4	0·8	9·4	2·3	15·4	3·7
35	3 38·8	3 39·3	3 28·8	3·5	0·8	9·5	2·3	15·5	3·7
36	3 39·0	3 39·6	3 29·0	3·6	0·9	9·6	2·3	15·6	3·8
37	3 39·3	3 39·9	3 29·3	3·7	0·9	9·7	2·3	15·7	3·8
38	3 39·5	3 40·1	3 29·5	3·8	0·9	9·8	2·4	15·8	3·8
39	3 39·8	3 40·4	3 29·7	3·9	0·9	9·9	2·4	15·9	3·8
40	3 40·0	3 40·6	3 30·0	4·0	1·0	10·0	2·4	16·0	3·9
41	3 40·3	3 40·9	3 30·2	4·1	1·0	10·1	2·4	16·1	3·9
42	3 40·5	3 41·1	3 30·5	4·2	1·0	10·2	2·5	16·2	3·9
43	3 40·8	3 41·4	3 30·7	4·3	1·0	10·3	2·5	16·3	3·9
44	3 41·0	3 41·6	3 30·9	4·4	1·1	10·4	2·5	16·4	4·0
45	3 41·3	3 41·9	3 31·2	4·5	1·1	10·5	2·5	16·5	4·0
46	3 41·5	3 42·1	3 31·4	4·6	1·1	10·6	2·6	16·6	4·0
47	3 41·8	3 42·4	3 31·6	4·7	1·1	10·7	2·6	16·7	4·0
48	3 42·0	3 42·6	3 31·9	4·8	1·2	10·8	2·6	16·8	4·1
49	3 42·3	3 42·9	3 32·1	4·9	1·2	10·9	2·6	16·9	4·1
50	3 42·5	3 43·1	3 32·4	5·0	1·2	11·0	2·7	17·0	4·1
51	3 42·8	3 43·4	3 32·6	5·1	1·2	11·1	2·7	17·1	4·1
52	3 43·0	3 43·6	3 32·8	5·2	1·3	11·2	2·7	17·2	4·2
53	3 43·3	3 43·9	3 33·1	5·3	1·3	11·3	2·7	17·3	4·2
54	3 43·5	3 44·1	3 33·3	5·4	1·3	11·4	2·8	17·4	4·2
55	3 43·8	3 44·4	3 33·6	5·5	1·3	11·5	2·8	17·5	4·2
56	3 44·0	3 44·6	3 33·8	5·6	1·4	11·6	2·8	17·6	4·3
57	3 44·3	3 44·9	3 34·0	5·7	1·4	11·7	2·8	17·7	4·3
58	3 44·5	3 45·1	3 34·3	5·8	1·4	11·8	2·9	17·8	4·3
59	3 44·8	3 45·4	3 34·5	5·9	1·4	11·9	2·9	17·9	4·3
60	3 45·0	3 45·6	3 34·8	6·0	1·5	12·0	2·9	18·0	4·4

15 m	SUN PLANETS	ARIES	MOON	v or Corrⁿ d		v or Corrⁿ d		v or Corrⁿ d	
s	° ′	° ′	° ′	′	′	′	′	′	′
00	3 45·0	3 45·6	3 34·8	0·0	0·0	6·0	1·6	12·0	3·1
01	3 45·3	3 45·9	3 35·0	0·1	0·0	6·1	1·6	12·1	3·1
02	3 45·5	3 46·1	3 35·2	0·2	0·1	6·2	1·6	12·2	3·2
03	3 45·8	3 46·4	3 35·5	0·3	0·1	6·3	1·6	12·3	3·2
04	3 46·0	3 46·6	3 35·7	0·4	0·1	6·4	1·7	12·4	3·2
05	3 46·3	3 46·9	3 35·9	0·5	0·1	6·5	1·7	12·5	3·2
06	3 46·5	3 47·1	3 36·2	0·6	0·2	6·6	1·7	12·6	3·3
07	3 46·8	3 47·4	3 36·4	0·7	0·2	6·7	1·7	12·7	3·3
08	3 47·0	3 47·6	3 36·7	0·8	0·2	6·8	1·8	12·8	3·3
09	3 47·3	3 47·9	3 36·9	0·9	0·2	6·9	1·8	12·9	3·3
10	3 47·5	3 48·1	3 37·1	1·0	0·3	7·0	1·8	13·0	3·4
11	3 47·8	3 48·4	3 37·4	1·1	0·3	7·1	1·8	13·1	3·4
12	3 48·0	3 48·6	3 37·6	1·2	0·3	7·2	1·9	13·2	3·4
13	3 48·3	3 48·9	3 37·9	1·3	0·3	7·3	1·9	13·3	3·4
14	3 48·5	3 49·1	3 38·1	1·4	0·4	7·4	1·9	13·4	3·5
15	3 48·8	3 49·4	3 38·3	1·5	0·4	7·5	1·9	13·5	3·5
16	3 49·0	3 49·6	3 38·6	1·6	0·4	7·6	2·0	13·6	3·5
17	3 49·3	3 49·9	3 38·8	1·7	0·4	7·7	2·0	13·7	3·5
18	3 49·5	3 50·1	3 39·0	1·8	0·5	7·8	2·0	13·8	3·6
19	3 49·8	3 50·4	3 39·3	1·9	0·5	7·9	2·0	13·9	3·6
20	3 50·0	3 50·6	3 39·5	2·0	0·5	8·0	2·1	14·0	3·6
21	3 50·3	3 50·9	3 39·8	2·1	0·5	8·1	2·1	14·1	3·6
22	3 50·5	3 51·1	3 40·0	2·2	0·6	8·2	2·1	14·2	3·7
23	3 50·8	3 51·4	3 40·2	2·3	0·6	8·3	2·1	14·3	3·7
24	3 51·0	3 51·6	3 40·5	2·4	0·6	8·4	2·2	14·4	3·7
25	3 51·3	3 51·9	3 40·7	2·5	0·6	8·5	2·2	14·5	3·7
26	3 51·5	3 52·1	3 41·0	2·6	0·7	8·6	2·2	14·6	3·8
27	3 51·8	3 52·4	3 41·2	2·7	0·7	8·7	2·2	14·7	3·8
28	3 52·0	3 52·6	3 41·4	2·8	0·7	8·8	2·3	14·8	3·8
29	3 52·3	3 52·9	3 41·7	2·9	0·7	8·9	2·3	14·9	3·8
30	3 52·5	3 53·1	3 41·9	3·0	0·8	9·0	2·3	15·0	3·9
31	3 52·8	3 53·4	3 42·1	3·1	0·8	9·1	2·4	15·1	3·9
32	3 53·0	3 53·6	3 42·4	3·2	0·8	9·2	2·4	15·2	3·9
33	3 53·3	3 53·9	3 42·6	3·3	0·9	9·3	2·4	15·3	4·0
34	3 53·5	3 54·1	3 42·9	3·4	0·9	9·4	2·4	15·4	4·0
35	3 53·8	3 54·4	3 43·1	3·5	0·9	9·5	2·5	15·5	4·0
36	3 54·0	3 54·6	3 43·3	3·6	0·9	9·6	2·5	15·6	4·0
37	3 54·3	3 54·9	3 43·6	3·7	1·0	9·7	2·5	15·7	4·1
38	3 54·5	3 55·1	3 43·8	3·8	1·0	9·8	2·5	15·8	4·1
39	3 54·8	3 55·4	3 44·1	3·9	1·0	9·9	2·6	15·9	4·1
40	3 55·0	3 55·6	3 44·3	4·0	1·0	10·0	2·6	16·0	4·1
41	3 55·3	3 55·9	3 44·5	4·1	1·1	10·1	2·6	16·1	4·2
42	3 55·5	3 56·1	3 44·8	4·2	1·1	10·2	2·6	16·2	4·2
43	3 55·8	3 56·4	3 45·0	4·3	1·1	10·3	2·7	16·3	4·2
44	3 56·0	3 56·6	3 45·2	4·4	1·1	10·4	2·7	16·4	4·2
45	3 56·3	3 56·9	3 45·5	4·5	1·2	10·5	2·7	16·5	4·3
46	3 56·5	3 57·1	3 45·7	4·6	1·2	10·6	2·7	16·6	4·3
47	3 56·8	3 57·4	3 46·0	4·7	1·2	10·7	2·8	16·7	4·3
48	3 57·0	3 57·6	3 46·2	4·8	1·2	10·8	2·8	16·8	4·3
49	3 57·3	3 57·9	3 46·4	4·9	1·3	10·9	2·8	16·9	4·4
50	3 57·5	3 58·2	3 46·7	5·0	1·3	11·0	2·8	17·0	4·4
51	3 57·8	3 58·4	3 46·9	5·1	1·3	11·1	2·9	17·1	4·4
52	3 58·0	3 58·7	3 47·2	5·2	1·3	11·2	2·9	17·2	4·4
53	3 58·3	3 58·9	3 47·4	5·3	1·4	11·3	2·9	17·3	4·5
54	3 58·5	3 59·2	3 47·6	5·4	1·4	11·4	2·9	17·4	4·5
55	3 58·8	3 59·4	3 47·9	5·5	1·4	11·5	3·0	17·5	4·5
56	3 59·0	3 59·7	3 48·1	5·6	1·4	11·6	3·0	17·6	4·5
57	3 59·3	3 59·9	3 48·4	5·7	1·5	11·7	3·0	17·7	4·6
58	3 59·5	4 00·2	3 48·6	5·8	1·5	11·8	3·0	17·8	4·6
59	3 59·8	4 00·4	3 48·8	5·9	1·5	11·9	3·1	17·9	4·6
60	4 00·0	4 00·7	3 49·1	6·0	1·6	12·0	3·1	18·0	4·7

16ᵐ

16 m/s	SUN PLANETS	ARIES	MOON	v or d	Corrⁿ	v or d	Corrⁿ	v or d	Corrⁿ
s	° ′	° ′	° ′	′	′	′	′	′	′
00	4 00·0	4 00·7	3 49·1	0·0	0·0	6·0	1·7	12·0	3·3
01	4 00·3	4 00·9	3 49·3	0·1	0·0	6·1	1·7	12·1	3·3
02	4 00·5	4 01·2	3 49·5	0·2	0·1	6·2	1·7	12·2	3·4
03	4 00·8	4 01·4	3 49·8	0·3	0·1	6·3	1·7	12·3	3·4
04	4 01·0	4 01·7	3 50·0	0·4	0·1	6·4	1·8	12·4	3·4
05	4 01·3	4 01·9	3 50·3	0·5	0·1	6·5	1·8	12·5	3·4
06	4 01·5	4 02·2	3 50·5	0·6	0·2	6·6	1·8	12·6	3·5
07	4 01·8	4 02·4	3 50·7	0·7	0·2	6·7	1·8	12·7	3·5
08	4 02·0	4 02·7	3 51·0	0·8	0·2	6·8	1·9	12·8	3·5
09	4 02·3	4 02·9	3 51·2	0·9	0·2	6·9	1·9	12·9	3·5
10	4 02·5	4 03·2	3 51·5	1·0	0·3	7·0	1·9	13·0	3·6
11	4 02·8	4 03·4	3 51·7	1·1	0·3	7·1	2·0	13·1	3·6
12	4 03·0	4 03·7	3 51·9	1·2	0·3	7·2	2·0	13·2	3·6
13	4 03·3	4 03·9	3 52·2	1·3	0·4	7·3	2·0	13·3	3·7
14	4 03·5	4 04·2	3 52·4	1·4	0·4	7·4	2·0	13·4	3·7
15	4 03·8	4 04·4	3 52·6	1·5	0·4	7·5	2·1	13·5	3·7
16	4 04·0	4 04·7	3 52·9	1·6	0·4	7·6	2·1	13·6	3·7
17	4 04·3	4 04·9	3 53·1	1·7	0·5	7·7	2·1	13·7	3·8
18	4 04·5	4 05·2	3 53·4	1·8	0·5	7·8	2·1	13·8	3·8
19	4 04·8	4 05·4	3 53·6	1·9	0·5	7·9	2·2	13·9	3·8
20	4 05·0	4 05·7	3 53·8	2·0	0·6	8·0	2·2	14·0	3·9
21	4 05·3	4 05·9	3 54·1	2·1	0·6	8·1	2·2	14·1	3·9
22	4 05·5	4 06·2	3 54·3	2·2	0·6	8·2	2·3	14·2	3·9
23	4 05·8	4 06·4	3 54·6	2·3	0·6	8·3	2·3	14·3	3·9
24	4 06·0	4 06·7	3 54·8	2·4	0·7	8·4	2·3	14·4	4·0
25	4 06·3	4 06·9	3 55·0	2·5	0·7	8·5	2·3	14·5	4·0
26	4 06·5	4 07·2	3 55·3	2·6	0·7	8·6	2·4	14·6	4·0
27	4 06·8	4 07·4	3 55·5	2·7	0·7	8·7	2·4	14·7	4·0
28	4 07·0	4 07·7	3 55·7	2·8	0·8	8·8	2·4	14·8	4·1
29	4 07·3	4 07·9	3 56·0	2·9	0·8	8·9	2·4	14·9	4·1
30	4 07·5	4 08·2	3 56·2	3·0	0·8	9·0	2·5	15·0	4·1
31	4 07·8	4 08·4	3 56·5	3·1	0·9	9·1	2·5	15·1	4·2
32	4 08·0	4 08·7	3 56·7	3·2	0·9	9·2	2·5	15·2	4·2
33	4 08·3	4 08·9	3 56·9	3·3	0·9	9·3	2·6	15·3	4·2
34	4 08·5	4 09·2	3 57·2	3·4	0·9	9·4	2·6	15·4	4·2
35	4 08·8	4 09·4	3 57·4	3·5	1·0	9·5	2·6	15·5	4·3
36	4 09·0	4 09·7	3 57·7	3·6	1·0	9·6	2·6	15·6	4·3
37	4 09·3	4 09·9	3 57·9	3·7	1·0	9·7	2·7	15·7	4·3
38	4 09·5	4 10·2	3 58·1	3·8	1·0	9·8	2·7	15·8	4·3
39	4 09·8	4 10·4	3 58·4	3·9	1·1	9·9	2·7	15·9	4·4
40	4 10·0	4 10·7	3 58·6	4·0	1·1	10·0	2·8	16·0	4·4
41	4 10·3	4 10·9	3 58·8	4·1	1·1	10·1	2·8	16·1	4·4
42	4 10·5	4 11·2	3 59·1	4·2	1·2	10·2	2·8	16·2	4·5
43	4 10·8	4 11·4	3 59·3	4·3	1·2	10·3	2·8	16·3	4·5
44	4 11·0	4 11·7	3 59·6	4·4	1·2	10·4	2·9	16·4	4·5
45	4 11·3	4 11·9	3 59·8	4·5	1·2	10·5	2·9	16·5	4·5
46	4 11·5	4 12·2	4 00·0	4·6	1·3	10·6	2·9	16·6	4·6
47	4 11·8	4 12·4	4 00·3	4·7	1·3	10·7	2·9	16·7	4·6
48	4 12·0	4 12·7	4 00·5	4·8	1·3	10·8	3·0	16·8	4·6
49	4 12·3	4 12·9	4 00·8	4·9	1·3	10·9	3·0	16·9	4·6
50	4 12·5	4 13·2	4 01·0	5·0	1·4	11·0	3·0	17·0	4·7
51	4 12·8	4 13·4	4 01·2	5·1	1·4	11·1	3·1	17·1	4·7
52	4 13·0	4 13·7	4 01·5	5·2	1·4	11·2	3·1	17·2	4·7
53	4 13·3	4 13·9	4 01·7	5·3	1·5	11·3	3·1	17·3	4·8
54	4 13·5	4 14·2	4 02·0	5·4	1·5	11·4	3·1	17·4	4·8
55	4 13·8	4 14·4	4 02·2	5·5	1·5	11·5	3·2	17·5	4·8
56	4 14·0	4 14·7	4 02·4	5·6	1·5	11·6	3·2	17·6	4·8
57	4 14·3	4 14·9	4 02·7	5·7	1·6	11·7	3·2	17·7	4·9
58	4 14·5	4 15·2	4 02·9	5·8	1·6	11·8	3·2	17·8	4·9
59	4 14·8	4 15·4	4 03·1	5·9	1·6	11·9	3·3	17·9	4·9
60	4 15·0	4 15·7	4 03·4	6·0	1·7	12·0	3·3	18·0	5·0

17ᵐ

17 m/s	SUN PLANETS	ARIES	MOON	v or d	Corrⁿ	v or d	Corrⁿ	v or d	Corrⁿ
s	° ′	° ′	° ′	′	′	′	′	′	′
00	4 15·0	4 15·7	4 03·4	0·0	0·0	6·0	1·8	12·0	3·5
01	4 15·3	4 15·9	4 03·6	0·1	0·0	6·1	1·8	12·1	3·5
02	4 15·5	4 16·2	4 03·9	0·2	0·1	6·2	1·8	12·2	3·6
03	4 15·8	4 16·5	4 04·1	0·3	0·1	6·3	1·8	12·3	3·6
04	4 16·0	4 16·7	4 04·3	0·4	0·1	6·4	1·9	12·4	3·6
05	4 16·3	4 17·0	4 04·6	0·5	0·1	6·5	1·9	12·5	3·6
06	4 16·5	4 17·2	4 04·8	0·6	0·2	6·6	1·9	12·6	3·7
07	4 16·8	4 17·5	4 05·1	0·7	0·2	6·7	2·0	12·7	3·7
08	4 17·0	4 17·7	4 05·3	0·8	0·2	6·8	2·0	12·8	3·7
09	4 17·3	4 18·0	4 05·5	0·9	0·3	6·9	2·0	12·9	3·8
10	4 17·5	4 18·2	4 05·8	1·0	0·3	7·0	2·0	13·0	3·8
11	4 17·8	4 18·5	4 06·0	1·1	0·3	7·1	2·1	13·1	3·8
12	4 18·0	4 18·7	4 06·2	1·2	0·4	7·2	2·1	13·2	3·9
13	4 18·3	4 19·0	4 06·5	1·3	0·4	7·3	2·1	13·3	3·9
14	4 18·5	4 19·2	4 06·7	1·4	0·4	7·4	2·2	13·4	3·9
15	4 18·8	4 19·5	4 07·0	1·5	0·4	7·5	2·2	13·5	3·9
16	4 19·0	4 19·7	4 07·2	1·6	0·5	7·6	2·2	13·6	4·0
17	4 19·3	4 20·0	4 07·4	1·7	0·5	7·7	2·2	13·7	4·0
18	4 19·5	4 20·2	4 07·7	1·8	0·5	7·8	2·3	13·8	4·0
19	4 19·8	4 20·5	4 07·9	1·9	0·6	7·9	2·3	13·9	4·1
20	4 20·0	4 20·7	4 08·2	2·0	0·6	8·0	2·3	14·0	4·1
21	4 20·3	4 21·0	4 08·4	2·1	0·6	8·1	2·4	14·1	4·1
22	4 20·5	4 21·2	4 08·6	2·2	0·6	8·2	2·4	14·2	4·1
23	4 20·8	4 21·5	4 08·9	2·3	0·7	8·3	2·4	14·3	4·2
24	4 21·0	4 21·7	4 09·1	2·4	0·7	8·4	2·5	14·4	4·2
25	4 21·3	4 22·0	4 09·3	2·5	0·7	8·5	2·5	14·5	4·2
26	4 21·5	4 22·2	4 09·6	2·6	0·8	8·6	2·5	14·6	4·3
27	4 21·8	4 22·5	4 09·8	2·7	0·8	8·7	2·5	14·7	4·3
28	4 22·0	4 22·7	4 10·1	2·8	0·8	8·8	2·6	14·8	4·3
29	4 22·3	4 23·0	4 10·3	2·9	0·8	8·9	2·6	14·9	4·3
30	4 22·5	4 23·2	4 10·5	3·0	0·9	9·0	2·6	15·0	4·4
31	4 22·8	4 23·5	4 10·8	3·1	0·9	9·1	2·7	15·1	4·4
32	4 23·0	4 23·7	4 11·0	3·2	0·9	9·2	2·7	15·2	4·4
33	4 23·3	4 24·0	4 11·3	3·3	1·0	9·3	2·7	15·3	4·5
34	4 23·5	4 24·2	4 11·5	3·4	1·0	9·4	2·7	15·4	4·5
35	4 23·8	4 24·5	4 11·7	3·5	1·0	9·5	2·8	15·5	4·5
36	4 24·0	4 24·7	4 12·0	3·6	1·1	9·6	2·8	15·6	4·6
37	4 24·3	4 25·0	4 12·2	3·7	1·1	9·7	2·8	15·7	4·6
38	4 24·5	4 25·2	4 12·5	3·8	1·1	9·8	2·9	15·8	4·6
39	4 24·8	4 25·5	4 12·7	3·9	1·1	9·9	2·9	15·9	4·6
40	4 25·0	4 25·7	4 12·9	4·0	1·2	10·0	2·9	16·0	4·7
41	4 25·3	4 26·0	4 13·2	4·1	1·2	10·1	2·9	16·1	4·7
42	4 25·5	4 26·2	4 13·4	4·2	1·2	10·2	3·0	16·2	4·7
43	4 25·8	4 26·5	4 13·6	4·3	1·3	10·3	3·0	16·3	4·8
44	4 26·0	4 26·7	4 13·9	4·4	1·3	10·4	3·0	16·4	4·8
45	4 26·3	4 27·0	4 14·1	4·5	1·3	10·5	3·1	16·5	4·8
46	4 26·5	4 27·2	4 14·4	4·6	1·3	10·6	3·1	16·6	4·8
47	4 26·8	4 27·5	4 14·6	4·7	1·4	10·7	3·1	16·7	4·9
48	4 27·0	4 27·7	4 14·8	4·8	1·4	10·8	3·2	16·8	4·9
49	4 27·3	4 28·0	4 15·1	4·9	1·4	10·9	3·2	16·9	4·9
50	4 27·5	4 28·2	4 15·3	5·0	1·5	11·0	3·2	17·0	5·0
51	4 27·8	4 28·5	4 15·6	5·1	1·5	11·1	3·2	17·1	5·0
52	4 28·0	4 28·7	4 15·8	5·2	1·5	11·2	3·3	17·2	5·0
53	4 28·3	4 29·0	4 16·0	5·3	1·5	11·3	3·3	17·3	5·0
54	4 28·5	4 29·2	4 16·3	5·4	1·6	11·4	3·3	17·4	5·1
55	4 28·8	4 29·5	4 16·5	5·5	1·6	11·5	3·4	17·5	5·1
56	4 29·0	4 29·7	4 16·7	5·6	1·6	11·6	3·4	17·6	5·1
57	4 29·3	4 30·0	4 17·0	5·7	1·7	11·7	3·4	17·7	5·2
58	4 29·5	4 30·2	4 17·2	5·8	1·7	11·8	3·4	17·8	5·2
59	4 29·8	4 30·5	4 17·5	5·9	1·7	11·9	3·5	17·9	5·2
60	4 30·0	4 30·7	4 17·7	6·0	1·8	12·0	3·5	18·0	5·3

18ᵐ

18 s	SUN PLANETS	ARIES	MOON	v or d	Corrⁿ	v or d	Corrⁿ	v or d	Corrⁿ
	° ′	° ′	° ′	′	′	′	′	′	′
00	4 30.0	4 30.7	4 17.7	0.0	0.0	6.0	1.9	12.0	3.7
01	4 30.3	4 31.0	4 17.9	0.1	0.0	6.1	1.9	12.1	3.7
02	4 30.5	4 31.2	4 18.2	0.2	0.1	6.2	1.9	12.2	3.8
03	4 30.8	4 31.5	4 18.4	0.3	0.1	6.3	1.9	12.3	3.8
04	4 31.0	4 31.7	4 18.7	0.4	0.1	6.4	2.0	12.4	3.8
05	4 31.3	4 32.0	4 18.9	0.5	0.2	6.5	2.0	12.5	3.9
06	4 31.5	4 32.2	4 19.1	0.6	0.2	6.6	2.0	12.6	3.9
07	4 31.8	4 32.5	4 19.4	0.7	0.2	6.7	2.1	12.7	3.9
08	4 32.0	4 32.7	4 19.6	0.8	0.2	6.8	2.1	12.8	3.9
09	4 32.3	4 33.0	4 19.8	0.9	0.3	6.9	2.1	12.9	4.0
10	4 32.5	4 33.2	4 20.1	1.0	0.3	7.0	2.2	13.0	4.0
11	4 32.8	4 33.5	4 20.3	1.1	0.3	7.1	2.2	13.1	4.0
12	4 33.0	4 33.7	4 20.6	1.2	0.4	7.2	2.2	13.2	4.1
13	4 33.3	4 34.0	4 20.8	1.3	0.4	7.3	2.3	13.3	4.1
14	4 33.5	4 34.2	4 21.0	1.4	0.4	7.4	2.3	13.4	4.1
15	4 33.8	4 34.5	4 21.3	1.5	0.5	7.5	2.3	13.5	4.2
16	4 34.0	4 34.8	4 21.5	1.6	0.5	7.6	2.3	13.6	4.2
17	4 34.3	4 35.0	4 21.8	1.7	0.5	7.7	2.4	13.7	4.2
18	4 34.5	4 35.3	4 22.0	1.8	0.6	7.8	2.4	13.8	4.3
19	4 34.8	4 35.5	4 22.2	1.9	0.6	7.9	2.4	13.9	4.3
20	4 35.0	4 35.8	4 22.5	2.0	0.6	8.0	2.5	14.0	4.3
21	4 35.3	4 36.0	4 22.7	2.1	0.6	8.1	2.5	14.1	4.3
22	4 35.5	4 36.3	4 22.9	2.2	0.7	8.2	2.5	14.2	4.4
23	4 35.8	4 36.5	4 23.2	2.3	0.7	8.3	2.6	14.3	4.4
24	4 36.0	4 36.8	4 23.4	2.4	0.7	8.4	2.6	14.4	4.4
25	4 36.3	4 37.0	4 23.7	2.5	0.8	8.5	2.6	14.5	4.5
26	4 36.5	4 37.3	4 23.9	2.6	0.8	8.6	2.7	14.6	4.5
27	4 36.8	4 37.5	4 24.1	2.7	0.8	8.7	2.7	14.7	4.5
28	4 37.0	4 37.8	4 24.4	2.8	0.9	8.8	2.7	14.8	4.6
29	4 37.3	4 38.0	4 24.6	2.9	0.9	8.9	2.7	14.9	4.6
30	4 37.5	4 38.3	4 24.9	3.0	0.9	9.0	2.8	15.0	4.6
31	4 37.8	4 38.5	4 25.1	3.1	1.0	9.1	2.8	15.1	4.7
32	4 38.0	4 38.8	4 25.3	3.2	1.0	9.2	2.8	15.2	4.7
33	4 38.3	4 39.0	4 25.6	3.3	1.0	9.3	2.9	15.3	4.7
34	4 38.5	4 39.3	4 25.8	3.4	1.0	9.4	2.9	15.4	4.7
35	4 38.8	4 39.5	4 26.1	3.5	1.1	9.5	2.9	15.5	4.8
36	4 39.0	4 39.8	4 26.3	3.6	1.1	9.6	3.0	15.6	4.8
37	4 39.3	4 40.0	4 26.5	3.7	1.1	9.7	3.0	15.7	4.8
38	4 39.5	4 40.3	4 26.8	3.8	1.2	9.8	3.0	15.8	4.9
39	4 39.8	4 40.5	4 27.0	3.9	1.2	9.9	3.1	15.9	4.9
40	4 40.0	4 40.8	4 27.2	4.0	1.2	10.0	3.1	16.0	4.9
41	4 40.3	4 41.0	4 27.5	4.1	1.3	10.1	3.1	16.1	5.0
42	4 40.5	4 41.3	4 27.7	4.2	1.3	10.2	3.1	16.2	5.0
43	4 40.8	4 41.5	4 28.0	4.3	1.3	10.3	3.2	16.3	5.0
44	4 41.0	4 41.8	4 28.2	4.4	1.4	10.4	3.2	16.4	5.1
45	4 41.3	4 42.0	4 28.4	4.5	1.4	10.5	3.2	16.5	5.1
46	4 41.5	4 42.3	4 28.7	4.6	1.4	10.6	3.3	16.6	5.1
47	4 41.8	4 42.5	4 28.9	4.7	1.4	10.7	3.3	16.7	5.1
48	4 42.0	4 42.8	4 29.2	4.8	1.5	10.8	3.3	16.8	5.2
49	4 42.3	4 43.0	4 29.4	4.9	1.5	10.9	3.4	16.9	5.2
50	4 42.5	4 43.3	4 29.6	5.0	1.5	11.0	3.4	17.0	5.2
51	4 42.8	4 43.5	4 29.9	5.1	1.6	11.1	3.4	17.1	5.3
52	4 43.0	4 43.8	4 30.1	5.2	1.6	11.2	3.5	17.2	5.3
53	4 43.3	4 44.0	4 30.3	5.3	1.6	11.3	3.5	17.3	5.3
54	4 43.5	4 44.3	4 30.6	5.4	1.7	11.4	3.5	17.4	5.4
55	4 43.8	4 44.5	4 30.8	5.5	1.7	11.5	3.5	17.5	5.4
56	4 44.0	4 44.8	4 31.1	5.6	1.7	11.6	3.6	17.6	5.4
57	4 44.3	4 45.0	4 31.3	5.7	1.8	11.7	3.6	17.7	5.5
58	4 44.5	4 45.3	4 31.5	5.8	1.8	11.8	3.6	17.8	5.5
59	4 44.8	4 45.5	4 31.8	5.9	1.8	11.9	3.7	17.9	5.5
60	4 45.0	4 45.8	4 32.0	6.0	1.9	12.0	3.7	18.0	5.6

19ᵐ

19 s	SUN PLANETS	ARIES	MOON	v or d	Corrⁿ	v or d	Corrⁿ	v or d	Corrⁿ
	° ′	° ′	° ′	′	′	′	′	′	′
00	4 45.0	4 45.8	4 32.0	0.0	0.0	6.0	2.0	12.0	3.9
01	4 45.3	4 46.0	4 32.3	0.1	0.0	6.1	2.0	12.1	3.9
02	4 45.5	4 46.3	4 32.5	0.2	0.1	6.2	2.0	12.2	4.0
03	4 45.8	4 46.5	4 32.7	0.3	0.1	6.3	2.0	12.3	4.0
04	4 46.0	4 46.8	4 33.0	0.4	0.1	6.4	2.1	12.4	4.0
05	4 46.3	4 47.0	4 33.2	0.5	0.2	6.5	2.1	12.5	4.1
06	4 46.5	4 47.3	4 33.4	0.6	0.2	6.6	2.1	12.6	4.1
07	4 46.8	4 47.5	4 33.7	0.7	0.2	6.7	2.2	12.7	4.1
08	4 47.0	4 47.8	4 33.9	0.8	0.3	6.8	2.2	12.8	4.2
09	4 47.3	4 48.0	4 34.2	0.9	0.3	6.9	2.2	12.9	4.2
10	4 47.5	4 48.3	4 34.4	1.0	0.3	7.0	2.3	13.0	4.2
11	4 47.8	4 48.5	4 34.6	1.1	0.4	7.1	2.3	13.1	4.3
12	4 48.0	4 48.8	4 34.9	1.2	0.4	7.2	2.3	13.2	4.3
13	4 48.3	4 49.0	4 35.1	1.3	0.4	7.3	2.4	13.3	4.3
14	4 48.5	4 49.3	4 35.4	1.4	0.5	7.4	2.4	13.4	4.4
15	4 48.8	4 49.5	4 35.6	1.5	0.5	7.5	2.4	13.5	4.4
16	4 49.0	4 49.8	4 35.8	1.6	0.5	7.6	2.5	13.6	4.4
17	4 49.3	4 50.0	4 36.1	1.7	0.6	7.7	2.5	13.7	4.5
18	4 49.5	4 50.3	4 36.3	1.8	0.6	7.8	2.5	13.8	4.5
19	4 49.8	4 50.5	4 36.6	1.9	0.6	7.9	2.6	13.9	4.5
20	4 50.0	4 50.8	4 36.8	2.0	0.7	8.0	2.6	14.0	4.6
21	4 50.3	4 51.0	4 37.0	2.1	0.7	8.1	2.6	14.1	4.6
22	4 50.5	4 51.3	4 37.3	2.2	0.7	8.2	2.7	14.2	4.6
23	4 50.8	4 51.5	4 37.5	2.3	0.7	8.3	2.7	14.3	4.6
24	4 51.0	4 51.8	4 37.7	2.4	0.8	8.4	2.7	14.4	4.7
25	4 51.3	4 52.0	4 38.0	2.5	0.8	8.5	2.8	14.5	4.7
26	4 51.5	4 52.3	4 38.2	2.6	0.8	8.6	2.8	14.6	4.7
27	4 51.8	4 52.5	4 38.5	2.7	0.9	8.7	2.8	14.7	4.8
28	4 52.0	4 52.8	4 38.7	2.8	0.9	8.8	2.9	14.8	4.8
29	4 52.3	4 53.1	4 38.9	2.9	0.9	8.9	2.9	14.9	4.8
30	4 52.5	4 53.3	4 39.2	3.0	1.0	9.0	2.9	15.0	4.9
31	4 52.8	4 53.6	4 39.4	3.1	1.0	9.1	3.0	15.1	4.9
32	4 53.0	4 53.8	4 39.7	3.2	1.0	9.2	3.0	15.2	4.9
33	4 53.3	4 54.1	4 39.9	3.3	1.1	9.3	3.0	15.3	5.0
34	4 53.5	4 54.3	4 40.1	3.4	1.1	9.4	3.1	15.4	5.0
35	4 53.8	4 54.6	4 40.4	3.5	1.1	9.5	3.1	15.5	5.0
36	4 54.0	4 54.8	4 40.6	3.6	1.1	9.6	3.1	15.6	5.1
37	4 54.3	4 55.1	4 40.8	3.7	1.2	9.7	3.2	15.7	5.1
38	4 54.5	4 55.3	4 41.1	3.8	1.2	9.8	3.2	15.8	5.1
39	4 54.8	4 55.6	4 41.3	3.9	1.3	9.9	3.2	15.9	5.2
40	4 55.0	4 55.8	4 41.6	4.0	1.3	10.0	3.3	16.0	5.2
41	4 55.3	4 56.1	4 41.8	4.1	1.3	10.1	3.3	16.1	5.2
42	4 55.5	4 56.3	4 42.0	4.2	1.4	10.2	3.3	16.2	5.3
43	4 55.8	4 56.6	4 42.3	4.3	1.4	10.3	3.3	16.3	5.3
44	4 56.0	4 56.8	4 42.5	4.4	1.4	10.4	3.4	16.4	5.3
45	4 56.3	4 57.1	4 42.8	4.5	1.5	10.5	3.4	16.5	5.4
46	4 56.5	4 57.3	4 43.0	4.6	1.5	10.6	3.4	16.6	5.4
47	4 56.8	4 57.6	4 43.2	4.7	1.5	10.7	3.5	16.7	5.4
48	4 57.0	4 57.8	4 43.5	4.8	1.6	10.8	3.5	16.8	5.5
49	4 57.3	4 58.1	4 43.7	4.9	1.6	10.9	3.5	16.9	5.5
50	4 57.5	4 58.3	4 43.9	5.0	1.6	11.0	3.6	17.0	5.5
51	4 57.8	4 58.6	4 44.2	5.1	1.7	11.1	3.6	17.1	5.6
52	4 58.0	4 58.8	4 44.4	5.2	1.7	11.2	3.6	17.2	5.6
53	4 58.3	4 59.1	4 44.7	5.3	1.7	11.3	3.7	17.3	5.6
54	4 58.5	4 59.3	4 44.9	5.4	1.8	11.4	3.7	17.4	5.7
55	4 58.8	4 59.6	4 45.1	5.5	1.8	11.5	3.7	17.5	5.7
56	4 59.0	4 59.8	4 45.4	5.6	1.8	11.6	3.8	17.6	5.7
57	4 59.3	5 00.1	4 45.6	5.7	1.9	11.7	3.8	17.7	5.8
58	4 59.5	5 00.3	4 45.9	5.8	1.9	11.8	3.8	17.8	5.8
59	4 59.8	5 00.6	4 46.1	5.9	1.9	11.9	3.9	17.9	5.8
60	5 00.0	5 00.8	4 46.3	6.0	2.0	12.0	3.9	18.0	5.9

20ᵐ

m 20 s	SUN PLANETS	ARIES	MOON	v or d	Corrⁿ	v or d	Corrⁿ	v or d	Corrⁿ
00	5 00·0	5 00·8	4 46·3	0·0	0·0	6·0	2·1	12·0	4·1
01	5 00·3	5 01·1	4 46·6	0·1	0·0	6·1	2·1	12·1	4·1
02	5 00·5	5 01·3	4 46·8	0·2	0·1	6·2	2·1	12·2	4·2
03	5 00·8	5 01·6	4 47·0	0·3	0·1	6·3	2·2	12·3	4·2
04	5 01·0	5 01·8	4 47·3	0·4	0·1	6·4	2·2	12·4	4·2
05	5 01·3	5 02·1	4 47·5	0·5	0·2	6·5	2·2	12·5	4·3
06	5 01·5	5 02·3	4 47·8	0·6	0·2	6·6	2·3	12·6	4·3
07	5 01·8	5 02·6	4 48·0	0·7	0·2	6·7	2·3	12·7	4·3
08	5 02·0	5 02·8	4 48·2	0·8	0·3	6·8	2·3	12·8	4·4
09	5 02·3	5 03·1	4 48·5	0·9	0·3	6·9	2·4	12·9	4·4
10	5 02·5	5 03·3	4 48·7	1·0	0·3	7·0	2·4	13·0	4·4
11	5 02·8	5 03·6	4 49·0	1·1	0·4	7·1	2·4	13·1	4·5
12	5 03·0	5 03·8	4 49·2	1·2	0·4	7·2	2·5	13·2	4·5
13	5 03·3	5 04·1	4 49·4	1·3	0·4	7·3	2·5	13·3	4·5
14	5 03·5	5 04·3	4 49·7	1·4	0·5	7·4	2·5	13·4	4·6
15	5 03·8	5 04·6	4 49·9	1·5	0·5	7·5	2·6	13·5	4·6
16	5 04·0	5 04·8	4 50·2	1·6	0·5	7·6	2·6	13·6	4·6
17	5 04·3	5 05·1	4 50·4	1·7	0·6	7·7	2·6	13·7	4·7
18	5 04·5	5 05·3	4 50·6	1·8	0·6	7·8	2·7	13·8	4·7
19	5 04·8	5 05·6	4 50·9	1·9	0·6	7·9	2·7	13·9	4·7
20	5 05·0	5 05·8	4 51·1	2·0	0·7	8·0	2·7	14·0	4·8
21	5 05·3	5 06·1	4 51·3	2·1	0·7	8·1	2·8	14·1	4·8
22	5 05·5	5 06·3	4 51·6	2·2	0·8	8·2	2·8	14·2	4·9
23	5 05·8	5 06·6	4 51·8	2·3	0·8	8·3	2·8	14·3	4·9
24	5 06·0	5 06·8	4 52·1	2·4	0·8	8·4	2·9	14·4	4·9
25	5 06·3	5 07·1	4 52·3	2·5	0·9	8·5	2·9	14·5	5·0
26	5 06·5	5 07·3	4 52·5	2·6	0·9	8·6	2·9	14·6	5·0
27	5 06·8	5 07·6	4 52·8	2·7	0·9	8·7	3·0	14·7	5·0
28	5 07·0	5 07·8	4 53·0	2·8	1·0	8·8	3·0	14·8	5·1
29	5 07·3	5 08·1	4 53·3	2·9	1·0	8·9	3·0	14·9	5·1
30	5 07·5	5 08·3	4 53·5	3·0	1·0	9·0	3·1	15·0	5·1
31	5 07·8	5 08·6	4 53·7	3·1	1·1	9·1	3·1	15·1	5·2
32	5 08·0	5 08·8	4 54·0	3·2	1·1	9·2	3·1	15·2	5·2
33	5 08·3	5 09·1	4 54·2	3·3	1·1	9·3	3·2	15·3	5·2
34	5 08·5	5 09·3	4 54·4	3·4	1·2	9·4	3·2	15·4	5·3
35	5 08·8	5 09·6	4 54·7	3·5	1·2	9·5	3·2	15·5	5·3
36	5 09·0	5 09·8	4 54·9	3·6	1·2	9·6	3·3	15·6	5·3
37	5 09·3	5 10·1	4 55·2	3·7	1·3	9·7	3·3	15·7	5·4
38	5 09·5	5 10·3	4 55·4	3·8	1·3	9·8	3·3	15·8	5·4
39	5 09·8	5 10·6	4 55·6	3·9	1·3	9·9	3·4	15·9	5·4
40	5 10·0	5 10·8	4 55·9	4·0	1·4	10·0	3·4	16·0	5·5
41	5 10·3	5 11·1	4 56·1	4·1	1·4	10·1	3·5	16·1	5·5
42	5 10·5	5 11·4	4 56·4	4·2	1·4	10·2	3·5	16·2	5·5
43	5 10·8	5 11·6	4 56·6	4·3	1·5	10·3	3·5	16·3	5·6
44	5 11·0	5 11·9	4 56·8	4·4	1·5	10·4	3·6	16·4	5·6
45	5 11·3	5 12·1	4 57·1	4·5	1·5	10·5	3·6	16·5	5·6
46	5 11·5	5 12·4	4 57·3	4·6	1·6	10·6	3·6	16·6	5·7
47	5 11·8	5 12·6	4 57·5	4·7	1·6	10·7	3·7	16·7	5·7
48	5 12·0	5 12·9	4 57·8	4·8	1·6	10·8	3·7	16·8	5·7
49	5 12·3	5 13·1	4 58·0	4·9	1·7	10·9	3·7	16·9	5·8
50	5 12·5	5 13·4	4 58·3	5·0	1·7	11·0	3·8	17·0	5·8
51	5 12·8	5 13·6	4 58·5	5·1	1·7	11·1	3·8	17·1	5·8
52	5 13·0	5 13·9	4 58·7	5·2	1·8	11·2	3·8	17·2	5·9
53	5 13·3	5 14·1	4 59·0	5·3	1·8	11·3	3·9	17·3	5·9
54	5 13·5	5 14·4	4 59·2	5·4	1·8	11·4	3·9	17·4	5·9
55	5 13·8	5 14·6	4 59·5	5·5	1·9	11·5	3·9	17·5	6·0
56	5 14·0	5 14·9	4 59·7	5·6	1·9	11·6	4·0	17·6	6·0
57	5 14·3	5 15·1	4 59·9	5·7	1·9	11·7	4·0	17·7	6·0
58	5 14·5	5 15·4	5 00·2	5·8	2·0	11·8	4·0	17·8	6·1
59	5 14·8	5 15·6	5 00·4	5·9	2·0	11·9	4·1	17·9	6·1
60	5 15·0	5 15·9	5 00·7	6·0	2·1	12·0	4·1	18·0	6·2

21ᵐ

m 21 s	SUN PLANETS	ARIES	MOON	v or d	Corrⁿ	v or d	Corrⁿ	v or d	Corrⁿ
00	5 15·0	5 15·9	5 00·7	0·0	0·0	6·0	2·2	12·0	4·3
01	5 15·3	5 16·1	5 00·9	0·1	0·0	6·1	2·2	12·1	4·3
02	5 15·5	5 16·4	5 01·1	0·2	0·1	6·2	2·2	12·2	4·4
03	5 15·8	5 16·6	5 01·4	0·3	0·1	6·3	2·3	12·3	4·4
04	5 16·0	5 16·9	5 01·6	0·4	0·1	6·4	2·3	12·4	4·4
05	5 16·3	5 17·1	5 01·8	0·5	0·2	6·5	2·3	12·5	4·5
06	5 16·5	5 17·4	5 02·1	0·6	0·2	6·6	2·4	12·6	4·5
07	5 16·8	5 17·6	5 02·3	0·7	0·3	6·7	2·4	12·7	4·6
08	5 17·0	5 17·9	5 02·6	0·8	0·3	6·8	2·4	12·8	4·6
09	5 17·3	5 18·1	5 02·8	0·9	0·3	6·9	2·5	12·9	4·6
10	5 17·5	5 18·4	5 03·0	1·0	0·4	7·0	2·5	13·0	4·7
11	5 17·8	5 18·6	5 03·3	1·1	0·4	7·1	2·5	13·1	4·7
12	5 18·0	5 18·9	5 03·5	1·2	0·4	7·2	2·6	13·2	4·7
13	5 18·3	5 19·1	5 03·8	1·3	0·5	7·3	2·6	13·3	4·8
14	5 18·5	5 19·4	5 04·0	1·4	0·5	7·4	2·7	13·4	4·8
15	5 18·8	5 19·6	5 04·2	1·5	0·5	7·5	2·7	13·5	4·8
16	5 19·0	5 19·9	5 04·5	1·6	0·6	7·6	2·7	13·6	4·9
17	5 19·3	5 20·1	5 04·7	1·7	0·6	7·7	2·8	13·7	4·9
18	5 19·5	5 20·4	5 04·9	1·8	0·6	7·8	2·8	13·8	4·9
19	5 19·8	5 20·6	5 05·2	1·9	0·7	7·9	2·8	13·9	5·0
20	5 20·0	5 20·9	5 05·4	2·0	0·7	8·0	2·9	14·0	5·0
21	5 20·3	5 21·1	5 05·7	2·1	0·8	8·1	2·9	14·1	5·1
22	5 20·5	5 21·4	5 05·9	2·2	0·8	8·2	2·9	14·2	5·1
23	5 20·8	5 21·6	5 06·1	2·3	0·8	8·3	3·0	14·3	5·1
24	5 21·0	5 21·9	5 06·4	2·4	0·9	8·4	3·0	14·4	5·2
25	5 21·3	5 22·1	5 06·6	2·5	0·9	8·5	3·0	14·5	5·2
26	5 21·5	5 22·4	5 06·9	2·6	0·9	8·6	3·1	14·6	5·2
27	5 21·8	5 22·6	5 07·1	2·7	1·0	8·7	3·1	14·7	5·3
28	5 22·0	5 22·9	5 07·3	2·8	1·0	8·8	3·2	14·8	5·3
29	5 22·3	5 23·1	5 07·6	2·9	1·0	8·9	3·2	14·9	5·3
30	5 22·5	5 23·4	5 07·8	3·0	1·1	9·0	3·2	15·0	5·4
31	5 22·8	5 23·6	5 08·0	3·1	1·1	9·1	3·3	15·1	5·4
32	5 23·0	5 23·9	5 08·3	3·2	1·1	9·2	3·3	15·2	5·4
33	5 23·3	5 24·1	5 08·5	3·3	1·2	9·3	3·3	15·3	5·5
34	5 23·5	5 24·4	5 08·8	3·4	1·2	9·4	3·4	15·4	5·5
35	5 23·8	5 24·6	5 09·0	3·5	1·3	9·5	3·4	15·5	5·6
36	5 24·0	5 24·9	5 09·2	3·6	1·3	9·6	3·4	15·6	5·6
37	5 24·3	5 25·1	5 09·5	3·7	1·3	9·7	3·5	15·7	5·6
38	5 24·5	5 25·4	5 09·7	3·8	1·4	9·8	3·5	15·8	5·7
39	5 24·8	5 25·6	5 10·0	3·9	1·4	9·9	3·5	15·9	5·7
40	5 25·0	5 25·9	5 10·2	4·0	1·4	10·0	3·6	16·0	5·7
41	5 25·3	5 26·1	5 10·4	4·1	1·5	10·1	3·6	16·1	5·8
42	5 25·5	5 26·4	5 10·7	4·2	1·5	10·2	3·7	16·2	5·8
43	5 25·8	5 26·6	5 10·9	4·3	1·5	10·3	3·7	16·3	5·8
44	5 26·0	5 26·9	5 11·1	4·4	1·6	10·4	3·7	16·4	5·9
45	5 26·3	5 27·1	5 11·4	4·5	1·6	10·5	3·8	16·5	5·9
46	5 26·5	5 27·4	5 11·6	4·6	1·6	10·6	3·8	16·6	5·9
47	5 26·8	5 27·6	5 11·9	4·7	1·7	10·7	3·8	16·7	6·0
48	5 27·0	5 27·9	5 12·1	4·8	1·7	10·8	3·9	16·8	6·0
49	5 27·3	5 28·1	5 12·3	4·9	1·8	10·9	3·9	16·9	6·1
50	5 27·5	5 28·4	5 12·6	5·0	1·8	11·0	3·9	17·0	6·1
51	5 27·8	5 28·6	5 12·8	5·1	1·8	11·1	4·0	17·1	6·1
52	5 28·0	5 28·9	5 13·1	5·2	1·9	11·2	4·0	17·2	6·2
53	5 28·3	5 29·1	5 13·3	5·3	1·9	11·3	4·0	17·3	6·2
54	5 28·5	5 29·4	5 13·5	5·4	1·9	11·4	4·1	17·4	6·2
55	5 28·8	5 29·7	5 13·8	5·5	2·0	11·5	4·1	17·5	6·3
56	5 29·0	5 29·9	5 14·0	5·6	2·0	11·6	4·2	17·6	6·3
57	5 29·3	5 30·2	5 14·3	5·7	2·0	11·7	4·2	17·7	6·3
58	5 29·5	5 30·4	5 14·5	5·8	2·1	11·8	4·2	17·8	6·4
59	5 29·8	5 30·7	5 14·7	5·9	2·1	11·9	4·3	17·9	6·4
60	5 30·0	5 30·9	5 15·0	6·0	2·2	12·0	4·3	18·0	6·5

22^m

22	SUN PLANETS	ARIES	MOON	v or d	Corrn	v or d	Corrn	v or d	Corrn
s	° ′	° ′	° ′	′	′	′	′	′	′
00	5 30·0	5 30·9	5 15·0	0·0	0·0	6·0	2·3	12·0	4·5
01	5 30·3	5 31·2	5 15·2	0·1	0·0	6·1	2·3	12·1	4·5
02	5 30·5	5 31·4	5 15·4	0·2	0·1	6·2	2·3	12·2	4·6
03	5 30·8	5 31·7	5 15·7	0·3	0·1	6·3	2·4	12·3	4·6
04	5 31·0	5 31·9	5 15·9	0·4	0·2	6·4	2·4	12·4	4·7
05	5 31·3	5 32·2	5 16·2	0·5	0·2	6·5	2·4	12·5	4·7
06	5 31·5	5 32·4	5 16·4	0·6	0·2	6·6	2·5	12·6	4·7
07	5 31·8	5 32·7	5 16·6	0·7	0·3	6·7	2·5	12·7	4·8
08	5 32·0	5 32·9	5 16·9	0·8	0·3	6·8	2·6	12·8	4·8
09	5 32·3	5 33·2	5 17·1	0·9	0·3	6·9	2·6	12·9	4·8
10	5 32·5	5 33·4	5 17·4	1·0	0·4	7·0	2·6	13·0	4·9
11	5 32·8	5 33·7	5 17·6	1·1	0·4	7·1	2·7	13·1	4·9
12	5 33·0	5 33·9	5 17·8	1·2	0·5	7·2	2·7	13·2	5·0
13	5 33·3	5 34·2	5 18·1	1·3	0·5	7·3	2·7	13·3	5·0
14	5 33·5	5 34·4	5 18·3	1·4	0·5	7·4	2·8	13·4	5·0
15	5 33·8	5 34·7	5 18·5	1·5	0·6	7·5	2·8	13·5	5·1
16	5 34·0	5 34·9	5 18·8	1·6	0·6	7·6	2·9	13·6	5·1
17	5 34·3	5 35·2	5 19·0	1·7	0·6	7·7	2·9	13·7	5·1
18	5 34·5	5 35·4	5 19·3	1·8	0·7	7·8	2·9	13·8	5·2
19	5 34·8	5 35·7	5 19·5	1·9	0·7	7·9	3·0	13·9	5·2
20	5 35·0	5 35·9	5 19·7	2·0	0·8	8·0	3·0	14·0	5·3
21	5 35·3	5 36·2	5 20·0	2·1	0·8	8·1	3·0	14·1	5·3
22	5 35·5	5 36·4	5 20·2	2·2	0·8	8·2	3·1	14·2	5·3
23	5 35·8	5 36·7	5 20·5	2·3	0·9	8·3	3·1	14·3	5·4
24	5 36·0	5 36·9	5 20·7	2·4	0·9	8·4	3·2	14·4	5·4
25	5 36·3	5 37·2	5 20·9	2·5	0·9	8·5	3·2	14·5	5·4
26	5 36·5	5 37·4	5 21·2	2·6	1·0	8·6	3·2	14·6	5·5
27	5 36·8	5 37·7	5 21·4	2·7	1·0	8·7	3·3	14·7	5·5
28	5 37·0	5 37·9	5 21·6	2·8	1·0	8·8	3·3	14·8	5·6
29	5 37·3	5 38·2	5 21·9	2·9	1·1	8·9	3·3	14·9	5·6
30	5 37·5	5 38·4	5 22·1	3·0	1·1	9·0	3·4	15·0	5·6
31	5 37·8	5 38·7	5 22·4	3·1	1·2	9·1	3·4	15·1	5·7
32	5 38·0	5 38·9	5 22·6	3·2	1·2	9·2	3·5	15·2	5·7
33	5 38·3	5 39·2	5 22·8	3·3	1·2	9·3	3·5	15·3	5·7
34	5 38·5	5 39·4	5 23·1	3·4	1·3	9·4	3·5	15·4	5·8
35	5 38·8	5 39·7	5 23·3	3·5	1·3	9·5	3·6	15·5	5·8
36	5 39·0	5 39·9	5 23·6	3·6	1·4	9·6	3·6	15·6	5·9
37	5 39·3	5 40·2	5 23·8	3·7	1·4	9·7	3·6	15·7	5·9
38	5 39·5	5 40·4	5 24·0	3·8	1·4	9·8	3·7	15·8	5·9
39	5 39·8	5 40·7	5 24·3	3·9	1·5	9·9	3·7	15·9	6·0
40	5 40·0	5 40·9	5 24·5	4·0	1·5	10·0	3·8	16·0	6·0
41	5 40·3	5 41·2	5 24·7	4·1	1·5	10·1	3·8	16·1	6·0
42	5 40·5	5 41·4	5 25·0	4·2	1·6	10·2	3·8	16·2	6·1
43	5 40·8	5 41·7	5 25·2	4·3	1·6	10·3	3·9	16·3	6·1
44	5 41·0	5 41·9	5 25·5	4·4	1·7	10·4	3·9	16·4	6·1
45	5 41·3	5 42·2	5 25·7	4·5	1·7	10·5	3·9	16·5	6·2
46	5 41·5	5 42·4	5 25·9	4·6	1·7	10·6	4·0	16·6	6·2
47	5 41·8	5 42·7	5 26·2	4·7	1·8	10·7	4·0	16·7	6·3
48	5 42·0	5 42·9	5 26·4	4·8	1·8	10·8	4·1	16·8	6·3
49	5 42·3	5 43·2	5 26·7	4·9	1·8	10·9	4·1	16·9	6·3
50	5 42·5	5 43·4	5 26·9	5·0	1·9	11·0	4·1	17·0	6·4
51	5 42·8	5 43·7	5 27·1	5·1	1·9	11·1	4·2	17·1	6·4
52	5 43·0	5 43·9	5 27·4	5·2	2·0	11·2	4·2	17·2	6·5
53	5 43·3	5 44·2	5 27·6	5·3	2·0	11·3	4·2	17·3	6·5
54	5 43·5	5 44·4	5 27·9	5·4	2·0	11·4	4·3	17·4	6·5
55	5 43·8	5 44·7	5 28·1	5·5	2·1	11·5	4·3	17·5	6·6
56	5 44·0	5 44·9	5 28·3	5·6	2·1	11·6	4·4	17·6	6·6
57	5 44·3	5 45·2	5 28·6	5·7	2·1	11·7	4·4	17·7	6·6
58	5 44·5	5 45·4	5 28·8	5·8	2·2	11·8	4·4	17·8	6·7
59	5 44·8	5 45·7	5 29·0	5·9	2·2	11·9	4·5	17·9	6·7
60	5 45·0	5 45·9	5 29·3	6·0	2·3	12·0	4·5	18·0	6·8

23^m

23	SUN PLANETS	ARIES	MOON	v or d	Corrn	v or d	Corrn	v or d	Corrn
s	° ′	° ′	° ′	′	′	′	′	′	′
00	5 45·0	5 45·9	5 29·3	0·0	0·0	6·0	2·4	12·0	4·7
01	5 45·3	5 46·2	5 29·5	0·1	0·0	6·1	2·4	12·1	4·7
02	5 45·5	5 46·4	5 29·8	0·2	0·1	6·2	2·4	12·2	4·8
03	5 45·8	5 46·7	5 30·0	0·3	0·1	6·3	2·5	12·3	4·8
04	5 46·0	5 46·9	5 30·2	0·4	0·2	6·4	2·5	12·4	4·9
05	5 46·3	5 47·2	5 30·5	0·5	0·2	6·5	2·5	12·5	4·9
06	5 46·5	5 47·4	5 30·7	0·6	0·2	6·6	2·6	12·6	4·9
07	5 46·8	5 47·7	5 31·0	0·7	0·3	6·7	2·6	12·7	5·0
08	5 47·0	5 48·0	5 31·2	0·8	0·3	6·8	2·7	12·8	5·0
09	5 47·3	5 48·2	5 31·4	0·9	0·4	6·9	2·7	12·9	5·1
10	5 47·5	5 48·5	5 31·7	1·0	0·4	7·0	2·7	13·0	5·1
11	5 47·8	5 48·7	5 31·9	1·1	0·4	7·1	2·8	13·1	5·1
12	5 48·0	5 49·0	5 32·1	1·2	0·5	7·2	2·8	13·2	5·2
13	5 48·3	5 49·2	5 32·4	1·3	0·5	7·3	2·9	13·3	5·2
14	5 48·5	5 49·5	5 32·6	1·4	0·5	7·4	2·9	13·4	5·2
15	5 48·8	5 49·7	5 32·9	1·5	0·6	7·5	2·9	13·5	5·3
16	5 49·0	5 50·0	5 33·1	1·6	0·6	7·6	3·0	13·6	5·3
17	5 49·3	5 50·2	5 33·3	1·7	0·7	7·7	3·0	13·7	5·4
18	5 49·5	5 50·5	5 33·6	1·8	0·7	7·8	3·1	13·8	5·4
19	5 49·8	5 50·7	5 33·8	1·9	0·7	7·9	3·1	13·9	5·4
20	5 50·0	5 51·0	5 34·1	2·0	0·8	8·0	3·1	14·0	5·5
21	5 50·3	5 51·2	5 34·3	2·1	0·8	8·1	3·2	14·1	5·5
22	5 50·5	5 51·5	5 34·5	2·2	0·9	8·2	3·2	14·2	5·6
23	5 50·8	5 51·7	5 34·8	2·3	0·9	8·3	3·3	14·3	5·6
24	5 51·0	5 52·0	5 35·0	2·4	0·9	8·4	3·3	14·4	5·6
25	5 51·3	5 52·2	5 35·2	2·5	1·0	8·5	3·3	14·5	5·7
26	5 51·5	5 52·5	5 35·5	2·6	1·0	8·6	3·4	14·6	5·7
27	5 51·8	5 52·7	5 35·7	2·7	1·1	8·7	3·4	14·7	5·8
28	5 52·0	5 53·0	5 36·0	2·8	1·1	8·8	3·4	14·8	5·8
29	5 52·3	5 53·2	5 36·2	2·9	1·1	8·9	3·5	14·9	5·8
30	5 52·5	5 53·5	5 36·4	3·0	1·2	9·0	3·5	15·0	5·9
31	5 52·8	5 53·7	5 36·7	3·1	1·2	9·1	3·6	15·1	5·9
32	5 53·0	5 54·0	5 36·9	3·2	1·3	9·2	3·6	15·2	6·0
33	5 53·3	5 54·2	5 37·2	3·3	1·3	9·3	3·6	15·3	6·0
34	5 53·5	5 54·5	5 37·4	3·4	1·3	9·4	3·7	15·4	6·0
35	5 53·8	5 54·7	5 37·6	3·5	1·4	9·5	3·7	15·5	6·1
36	5 54·0	5 55·0	5 37·9	3·6	1·4	9·6	3·8	15·6	6·1
37	5 54·3	5 55·2	5 38·1	3·7	1·4	9·7	3·8	15·7	6·1
38	5 54·5	5 55·5	5 38·4	3·8	1·5	9·8	3·8	15·8	6·2
39	5 54·8	5 55·7	5 38·6	3·9	1·5	9·9	3·9	15·9	6·2
40	5 55·0	5 56·0	5 38·8	4·0	1·6	10·0	3·9	16·0	6·3
41	5 55·3	5 56·2	5 39·1	4·1	1·6	10·1	4·0	16·1	6·3
42	5 55·5	5 56·5	5 39·3	4·2	1·6	10·2	4·0	16·2	6·3
43	5 55·8	5 56·7	5 39·5	4·3	1·7	10·3	4·0	16·3	6·4
44	5 56·0	5 57·0	5 39·8	4·4	1·7	10·4	4·1	16·4	6·4
45	5 56·3	5 57·2	5 40·0	4·5	1·8	10·5	4·1	16·5	6·5
46	5 56·5	5 57·5	5 40·3	4·6	1·8	10·6	4·2	16·6	6·5
47	5 56·8	5 57·7	5 40·5	4·7	1·8	10·7	4·2	16·7	6·5
48	5 57·0	5 58·0	5 40·7	4·8	1·9	10·8	4·2	16·8	6·6
49	5 57·3	5 58·2	5 41·0	4·9	1·9	10·9	4·3	16·9	6·6
50	5 57·5	5 58·5	5 41·2	5·0	2·0	11·0	4·3	17·0	6·7
51	5 57·8	5 58·7	5 41·5	5·1	2·0	11·1	4·3	17·1	6·7
52	5 58·0	5 59·0	5 41·7	5·2	2·0	11·2	4·4	17·2	6·7
53	5 58·3	5 59·2	5 41·9	5·3	2·1	11·3	4·4	17·3	6·8
54	5 58·5	5 59·5	5 42·2	5·4	2·1	11·4	4·5	17·4	6·8
55	5 58·8	5 59·7	5 42·4	5·5	2·2	11·5	4·5	17·5	6·9
56	5 59·0	6 00·0	5 42·6	5·6	2·2	11·6	4·5	17·6	6·9
57	5 59·3	6 00·2	5 42·9	5·7	2·2	11·7	4·6	17·7	6·9
58	5 59·5	6 00·5	5 43·1	5·8	2·3	11·8	4·6	17·8	7·0
59	5 59·8	6 00·7	5 43·4	5·9	2·3	11·9	4·7	17·9	7·0
60	6 00·0	6 01·0	5 43·6	6·0	2·4	12·0	4·7	18·0	7·1

24ᵐ	SUN PLANETS	ARIES	MOON	v or d	Corrⁿ	v or d	Corrⁿ	v or d	Corrⁿ
s	° ′	° ′	° ′	′	′	′	′	′	′
00	6 00·0	6 01·0	5 43·6	0·0	0·0	6·0	2·5	12·0	4·9
01	6 00·3	6 01·2	5 43·8	0·1	0·0	6·1	2·5	12·1	4·9
02	6 00·5	6 01·5	5 44·1	0·2	0·1	6·2	2·5	12·2	5·0
03	6 00·8	6 01·7	5 44·3	0·3	0·1	6·3	2·6	12·3	5·0
04	6 01·0	6 02·0	5 44·6	0·4	0·2	6·4	2·6	12·4	5·1
05	6 01·3	6 02·2	5 44·8	0·5	0·2	6·5	2·7	12·5	5·1
06	6 01·5	6 02·5	5 45·0	0·6	0·2	6·6	2·7	12·6	5·1
07	6 01·8	6 02·7	5 45·3	0·7	0·3	6·7	2·7	12·7	5·2
08	6 02·0	6 03·0	5 45·5	0·8	0·3	6·8	2·8	12·8	5·2
09	6 02·3	6 03·2	5 45·7	0·9	0·4	6·9	2·8	12·9	5·3
10	6 02·5	6 03·5	5 46·0	1·0	0·4	7·0	2·9	13·0	5·3
11	6 02·8	6 03·7	5 46·2	1·1	0·4	7·1	2·9	13·1	5·3
12	6 03·0	6 04·0	5 46·5	1·2	0·5	7·2	2·9	13·2	5·4
13	6 03·3	6 04·2	5 46·7	1·3	0·5	7·3	3·0	13·3	5·4
14	6 03·5	6 04·5	5 46·9	1·4	0·6	7·4	3·0	13·4	5·5
15	6 03·8	6 04·7	5 47·2	1·5	0·6	7·5	3·1	13·5	5·5
16	6 04·0	6 05·0	5 47·4	1·6	0·7	7·6	3·1	13·6	5·6
17	6 04·3	6 05·2	5 47·7	1·7	0·7	7·7	3·1	13·7	5·6
18	6 04·5	6 05·5	5 47·9	1·8	0·7	7·8	3·2	13·8	5·6
19	6 04·8	6 05·7	5 48·1	1·9	0·8	7·9	3·2	13·9	5·7
20	6 05·0	6 06·0	5 48·4	2·0	0·8	8·0	3·3	14·0	5·7
21	6 05·3	6 06·3	5 48·6	2·1	0·9	8·1	3·3	14·1	5·8
22	6 05·5	6 06·5	5 48·8	2·2	0·9	8·2	3·3	14·2	5·8
23	6 05·8	6 06·8	5 49·1	2·3	0·9	8·3	3·4	14·3	5·8
24	6 06·0	6 07·0	5 49·3	2·4	1·0	8·4	3·4	14·4	5·9
25	6 06·3	6 07·3	5 49·6	2·5	1·0	8·5	3·5	14·5	5·9
26	6 06·5	6 07·5	5 49·8	2·6	1·1	8·6	3·5	14·6	6·0
27	6 06·8	6 07·8	5 50·0	2·7	1·1	8·7	3·6	14·7	6·0
28	6 07·0	6 08·0	5 50·3	2·8	1·1	8·8	3·6	14·8	6·0
29	6 07·3	6 08·3	5 50·5	2·9	1·2	8·9	3·6	14·9	6·1
30	6 07·5	6 08·5	5 50·8	3·0	1·2	9·0	3·7	15·0	6·1
31	6 07·8	6 08·8	5 51·0	3·1	1·3	9·1	3·7	15·1	6·2
32	6 08·0	6 09·0	5 51·2	3·2	1·3	9·2	3·8	15·2	6·2
33	6 08·3	6 09·3	5 51·5	3·3	1·3	9·3	3·8	15·3	6·2
34	6 08·5	6 09·5	5 51·7	3·4	1·4	9·4	3·8	15·4	6·3
35	6 08·8	6 09·8	5 52·0	3·5	1·4	9·5	3·9	15·5	6·3
36	6 09·0	6 10·0	5 52·2	3·6	1·5	9·6	3·9	15·6	6·4
37	6 09·3	6 10·3	5 52·4	3·7	1·5	9·7	4·0	15·7	6·4
38	6 09·5	6 10·5	5 52·7	3·8	1·6	9·8	4·0	15·8	6·5
39	6 09·8	6 10·8	5 52·9	3·9	1·6	9·9	4·0	15·9	6·5
40	6 10·0	6 11·0	5 53·1	4·0	1·6	10·0	4·1	16·0	6·5
41	6 10·3	6 11·3	5 53·4	4·1	1·7	10·1	4·1	16·1	6·6
42	6 10·5	6 11·5	5 53·6	4·2	1·7	10·2	4·2	16·2	6·6
43	6 10·8	6 11·8	5 53·9	4·3	1·8	10·3	4·2	16·3	6·7
44	6 11·0	6 12·0	5 54·1	4·4	1·8	10·4	4·2	16·4	6·7
45	6 11·3	6 12·3	5 54·3	4·5	1·8	10·5	4·3	16·5	6·7
46	6 11·5	6 12·5	5 54·6	4·6	1·9	10·6	4·3	16·6	6·8
47	6 11·8	6 12·8	5 54·8	4·7	1·9	10·7	4·4	16·7	6·8
48	6 12·0	6 13·0	5 55·1	4·8	2·0	10·8	4·4	16·8	6·9
49	6 12·3	6 13·3	5 55·3	4·9	2·0	10·9	4·5	16·9	6·9
50	6 12·5	6 13·5	5 55·5	5·0	2·0	11·0	4·5	17·0	6·9
51	6 12·8	6 13·8	5 55·8	5·1	2·1	11·1	4·5	17·1	7·0
52	6 13·0	6 14·0	5 56·0	5·2	2·1	11·2	4·6	17·2	7·0
53	6 13·3	6 14·3	5 56·2	5·3	2·2	11·3	4·6	17·3	7·1
54	6 13·5	6 14·5	5 56·5	5·4	2·2	11·4	4·7	17·4	7·1
55	6 13·8	6 14·8	5 56·7	5·5	2·2	11·5	4·7	17·5	7·1
56	6 14·0	6 15·0	5 57·0	5·6	2·3	11·6	4·7	17·6	7·2
57	6 14·3	6 15·3	5 57·2	5·7	2·3	11·7	4·8	17·7	7·2
58	6 14·5	6 15·5	5 57·4	5·8	2·4	11·8	4·8	17·8	7·3
59	6 14·8	6 15·8	5 57·7	5·9	2·4	11·9	4·9	17·9	7·3
60	6 15·0	6 16·0	5 57·9	6·0	2·5	12·0	4·9	18·0	7·4

25ᵐ	SUN PLANETS	ARIES	MOON	v or d	Corrⁿ	v or d	Corrⁿ	v or d	Corrⁿ
s	° ′	° ′	° ′	′	′	′	′	′	′
00	6 15·0	6 16·0	5 57·9	0·0	0·0	6·0	2·6	12·0	5·1
01	6 15·3	6 16·3	5 58·2	0·1	0·0	6·1	2·6	12·1	5·1
02	6 15·5	6 16·5	5 58·4	0·2	0·1	6·2	2·6	12·2	5·2
03	6 15·8	6 16·8	5 58·6	0·3	0·1	6·3	2·7	12·3	5·2
04	6 16·0	6 17·0	5 58·9	0·4	0·2	6·4	2·7	12·4	5·3
05	6 16·3	6 17·3	5 59·1	0·5	0·2	6·5	2·8	12·5	5·3
06	6 16·5	6 17·5	5 59·3	0·6	0·3	6·6	2·8	12·6	5·4
07	6 16·8	6 17·8	5 59·6	0·7	0·3	6·7	2·8	12·7	5·4
08	6 17·0	6 18·0	5 59·8	0·8	0·3	6·8	2·9	12·8	5·4
09	6 17·3	6 18·3	6 00·1	0·9	0·4	6·9	2·9	12·9	5·5
10	6 17·5	6 18·5	6 00·3	1·0	0·4	7·0	3·0	13·0	5·5
11	6 17·8	6 18·8	6 00·5	1·1	0·5	7·1	3·0	13·1	5·6
12	6 18·0	6 19·0	6 00·8	1·2	0·5	7·2	3·1	13·2	5·6
13	6 18·3	6 19·3	6 01·0	1·3	0·6	7·3	3·1	13·3	5·7
14	6 18·5	6 19·5	6 01·3	1·4	0·6	7·4	3·1	13·4	5·7
15	6 18·8	6 19·8	6 01·5	1·5	0·6	7·5	3·2	13·5	5·7
16	6 19·0	6 20·0	6 01·7	1·6	0·7	7·6	3·2	13·6	5·8
17	6 19·3	6 20·3	6 02·0	1·7	0·7	7·7	3·3	13·7	5·8
18	6 19·5	6 20·5	6 02·2	1·8	0·8	7·8	3·3	13·8	5·9
19	6 19·8	6 20·8	6 02·5	1·9	0·8	7·9	3·4	13·9	5·9
20	6 20·0	6 21·0	6 02·7	2·0	0·9	8·0	3·4	14·0	6·0
21	6 20·3	6 21·3	6 02·9	2·1	0·9	8·1	3·4	14·1	6·0
22	6 20·5	6 21·5	6 03·2	2·2	0·9	8·2	3·5	14·2	6·0
23	6 20·8	6 21·8	6 03·4	2·3	1·0	8·3	3·5	14·3	6·1
24	6 21·0	6 22·0	6 03·6	2·4	1·0	8·4	3·6	14·4	6·1
25	6 21·3	6 22·3	6 03·9	2·5	1·1	8·5	3·6	14·5	6·2
26	6 21·5	6 22·5	6 04·1	2·6	1·1	8·6	3·7	14·6	6·2
27	6 21·8	6 22·8	6 04·4	2·7	1·1	8·7	3·7	14·7	6·2
28	6 22·0	6 23·0	6 04·6	2·8	1·2	8·8	3·7	14·8	6·3
29	6 22·3	6 23·3	6 04·8	2·9	1·2	8·9	3·8	14·9	6·3
30	6 22·5	6 23·5	6 05·1	3·0	1·3	9·0	3·8	15·0	6·4
31	6 22·8	6 23·8	6 05·3	3·1	1·3	9·1	3·9	15·1	6·4
32	6 23·0	6 24·0	6 05·6	3·2	1·4	9·2	3·9	15·2	6·5
33	6 23·3	6 24·3	6 05·8	3·3	1·4	9·3	4·0	15·3	6·5
34	6 23·5	6 24·5	6 06·0	3·4	1·4	9·4	4·0	15·4	6·5
35	6 23·8	6 24·8	6 06·3	3·5	1·5	9·5	4·0	15·5	6·6
36	6 24·0	6 25·1	6 06·5	3·6	1·5	9·6	4·1	15·6	6·6
37	6 24·3	6 25·3	6 06·7	3·7	1·6	9·7	4·1	15·7	6·7
38	6 24·5	6 25·6	6 07·0	3·8	1·6	9·8	4·2	15·8	6·7
39	6 24·8	6 25·8	6 07·2	3·9	1·7	9·9	4·2	15·9	6·8
40	6 25·0	6 26·1	6 07·5	4·0	1·7	10·0	4·3	16·0	6·8
41	6 25·3	6 26·3	6 07·7	4·1	1·7	10·1	4·3	16·1	6·8
42	6 25·5	6 26·6	6 07·9	4·2	1·8	10·2	4·3	16·2	6·9
43	6 25·8	6 26·8	6 08·2	4·3	1·8	10·3	4·4	16·3	6·9
44	6 26·0	6 27·1	6 08·4	4·4	1·9	10·4	4·4	16·4	7·0
45	6 26·3	6 27·3	6 08·7	4·5	1·9	10·5	4·5	16·5	7·0
46	6 26·5	6 27·6	6 08·9	4·6	2·0	10·6	4·5	16·6	7·1
47	6 26·8	6 27·8	6 09·1	4·7	2·0	10·7	4·5	16·7	7·1
48	6 27·0	6 28·1	6 09·4	4·8	2·0	10·8	4·6	16·8	7·1
49	6 27·3	6 28·3	6 09·6	4·9	2·1	10·9	4·6	16·9	7·2
50	6 27·5	6 28·6	6 09·8	5·0	2·1	11·0	4·7	17·0	7·2
51	6 27·8	6 28·8	6 10·1	5·1	2·2	11·1	4·7	17·1	7·3
52	6 28·0	6 29·1	6 10·3	5·2	2·2	11·2	4·8	17·2	7·3
53	6 28·3	6 29·3	6 10·6	5·3	2·3	11·3	4·8	17·3	7·4
54	6 28·5	6 29·6	6 10·8	5·4	2·3	11·4	4·8	17·4	7·4
55	6 28·8	6 29·8	6 11·0	5·5	2·3	11·5	4·9	17·5	7·4
56	6 29·0	6 30·1	6 11·3	5·6	2·4	11·6	4·9	17·6	7·5
57	6 29·3	6 30·3	6 11·5	5·7	2·4	11·7	5·0	17·7	7·5
58	6 29·5	6 30·6	6 11·8	5·8	2·5	11·8	5·0	17·8	7·6
59	6 29·8	6 30·8	6 12·0	5·9	2·5	11·9	5·1	17·9	7·6
60	6 30·0	6 31·1	6 12·2	6·0	2·6	12·0	5·1	18·0	7·7

26 s	SUN PLANETS	ARIES	MOON	v or Corrⁿ d		v or Corrⁿ d		v or Corrⁿ d	
	° ′	° ′	° ′	′	′	′	′	′	′
00	6 30.0	6 31.1	6 12.2	0.0	0.0	6.0	2.7	12.0	5.3
01	6 30.3	6 31.3	6 12.5	0.1	0.0	6.1	2.7	12.1	5.3
02	6 30.5	6 31.6	6 12.7	0.2	0.1	6.2	2.7	12.2	5.4
03	6 30.8	6 31.8	6 12.9	0.3	0.1	6.3	2.8	12.3	5.4
04	6 31.0	6 32.1	6 13.2	0.4	0.2	6.4	2.8	12.4	5.5
05	6 31.3	6 32.3	6 13.4	0.5	0.2	6.5	2.9	12.5	5.5
06	6 31.5	6 32.6	6 13.7	0.6	0.3	6.6	2.9	12.6	5.6
07	6 31.8	6 32.8	6 13.9	0.7	0.3	6.7	3.0	12.7	5.6
08	6 32.0	6 33.1	6 14.1	0.8	0.4	6.8	3.0	12.8	5.7
09	6 32.3	6 33.3	6 14.4	0.9	0.4	6.9	3.0	12.9	5.7
10	6 32.5	6 33.6	6 14.6	1.0	0.4	7.0	3.1	13.0	5.7
11	6 32.8	6 33.8	6 14.9	1.1	0.5	7.1	3.1	13.1	5.8
12	6 33.0	6 34.1	6 15.1	1.2	0.5	7.2	3.2	13.2	5.8
13	6 33.3	6 34.3	6 15.3	1.3	0.6	7.3	3.2	13.3	5.9
14	6 33.5	6 34.6	6 15.6	1.4	0.6	7.4	3.3	13.4	5.9
15	6 33.8	6 34.8	6 15.8	1.5	0.7	7.5	3.3	13.5	6.0
16	6 34.0	6 35.1	6 16.1	1.6	0.7	7.6	3.4	13.6	6.0
17	6 34.3	6 35.3	6 16.3	1.7	0.8	7.7	3.4	13.7	6.1
18	6 34.5	6 35.6	6 16.5	1.8	0.8	7.8	3.4	13.8	6.1
19	6 34.8	6 35.8	6 16.8	1.9	0.8	7.9	3.5	13.9	6.1
20	6 35.0	6 36.1	6 17.0	2.0	0.9	8.0	3.5	14.0	6.2
21	6 35.3	6 36.3	6 17.2	2.1	0.9	8.1	3.6	14.1	6.2
22	6 35.5	6 36.6	6 17.5	2.2	1.0	8.2	3.6	14.2	6.3
23	6 35.8	6 36.8	6 17.7	2.3	1.0	8.3	3.6	14.3	6.3
24	6 36.0	6 37.1	6 18.0	2.4	1.1	8.4	3.7	14.4	6.4
25	6 36.3	6 37.3	6 18.2	2.5	1.1	8.5	3.8	14.5	6.4
26	6 36.5	6 37.6	6 18.4	2.6	1.1	8.6	3.8	14.6	6.4
27	6 36.8	6 37.8	6 18.7	2.7	1.2	8.7	3.8	14.7	6.5
28	6 37.0	6 38.1	6 18.9	2.8	1.2	8.8	3.9	14.8	6.5
29	6 37.3	6 38.3	6 19.2	2.9	1.3	8.9	3.9	14.9	6.6
30	6 37.5	6 38.6	6 19.4	3.0	1.3	9.0	4.0	15.0	6.6
31	6 37.8	6 38.8	6 19.6	3.1	1.4	9.1	4.0	15.1	6.7
32	6 38.0	6 39.1	6 19.9	3.2	1.4	9.2	4.1	15.2	6.7
33	6 38.3	6 39.3	6 20.1	3.3	1.5	9.3	4.1	15.3	6.8
34	6 38.5	6 39.6	6 20.3	3.4	1.5	9.4	4.2	15.4	6.8
35	6 38.8	6 39.8	6 20.6	3.5	1.5	9.5	4.2	15.5	6.8
36	6 39.0	6 40.1	6 20.8	3.6	1.6	9.6	4.2	15.6	6.9
37	6 39.3	6 40.3	6 21.1	3.7	1.6	9.7	4.3	15.7	6.9
38	6 39.5	6 40.6	6 21.3	3.8	1.7	9.8	4.3	15.8	7.0
39	6 39.8	6 40.8	6 21.5	3.9	1.7	9.9	4.4	15.9	7.0
40	6 40.0	6 41.1	6 21.8	4.0	1.8	10.0	4.4	16.0	7.1
41	6 40.3	6 41.3	6 22.0	4.1	1.8	10.1	4.5	16.1	7.1
42	6 40.5	6 41.6	6 22.3	4.2	1.9	10.2	4.5	16.2	7.2
43	6 40.8	6 41.8	6 22.5	4.3	1.9	10.3	4.5	16.3	7.2
44	6 41.0	6 42.1	6 22.7	4.4	1.9	10.4	4.6	16.4	7.2
45	6 41.3	6 42.3	6 23.0	4.5	2.0	10.5	4.6	16.5	7.3
46	6 41.5	6 42.6	6 23.2	4.6	2.0	10.6	4.7	16.6	7.3
47	6 41.8	6 42.8	6 23.4	4.7	2.1	10.7	4.7	16.7	7.4
48	6 42.0	6 43.1	6 23.7	4.8	2.1	10.8	4.8	16.8	7.4
49	6 42.3	6 43.4	6 23.9	4.9	2.2	10.9	4.8	16.9	7.5
50	6 42.5	6 43.6	6 24.2	5.0	2.2	11.0	4.9	17.0	7.5
51	6 42.8	6 43.9	6 24.4	5.1	2.3	11.1	4.9	17.1	7.6
52	6 43.0	6 44.1	6 24.6	5.2	2.3	11.2	4.9	17.2	7.6
53	6 43.3	6 44.4	6 24.9	5.3	2.3	11.3	5.0	17.3	7.6
54	6 43.5	6 44.6	6 25.1	5.4	2.4	11.4	5.0	17.4	7.7
55	6 43.8	6 44.9	6 25.4	5.5	2.4	11.5	5.1	17.5	7.7
56	6 44.0	6 45.1	6 25.6	5.6	2.5	11.6	5.1	17.6	7.8
57	6 44.3	6 45.4	6 25.8	5.7	2.5	11.7	5.2	17.7	7.8
58	6 44.5	6 45.6	6 26.1	5.8	2.6	11.8	5.2	17.8	7.9
59	6 44.8	6 45.9	6 26.3	5.9	2.6	11.9	5.3	17.9	7.9
60	6 45.0	6 46.1	6 26.6	6.0	2.7	12.0	5.3	18.0	8.0

27 s	SUN PLANETS	ARIES	MOON	v or Corrⁿ d		v or Corrⁿ d		v or Corrⁿ d	
	° ′	° ′	° ′	′	′	′	′	′	′
00	6 45.0	6 46.1	6 26.6	0.0	0.0	6.0	2.8	12.0	5.5
01	6 45.3	6 46.4	6 26.8	0.1	0.0	6.1	2.8	12.1	5.5
02	6 45.5	6 46.6	6 27.0	0.2	0.1	6.2	2.8	12.2	5.6
03	6 45.8	6 46.9	6 27.3	0.3	0.1	6.3	2.9	12.3	5.6
04	6 46.0	6 47.1	6 27.5	0.4	0.2	6.4	2.9	12.4	5.7
05	6 46.3	6 47.4	6 27.7	0.5	0.2	6.5	3.0	12.5	5.7
06	6 46.5	6 47.6	6 28.0	0.6	0.3	6.6	3.0	12.6	5.8
07	6 46.8	6 47.9	6 28.2	0.7	0.3	6.7	3.1	12.7	5.8
08	6 47.0	6 48.1	6 28.5	0.8	0.4	6.8	3.1	12.8	5.9
09	6 47.3	6 48.4	6 28.7	0.9	0.4	6.9	3.2	12.9	5.9
10	6 47.5	6 48.6	6 28.9	1.0	0.5	7.0	3.2	13.0	6.0
11	6 47.8	6 48.9	6 29.2	1.1	0.5	7.1	3.3	13.1	6.0
12	6 48.0	6 49.1	6 29.4	1.2	0.6	7.2	3.3	13.2	6.1
13	6 48.3	6 49.4	6 29.7	1.3	0.6	7.3	3.3	13.3	6.1
14	6 48.5	6 49.6	6 29.9	1.4	0.6	7.4	3.4	13.4	6.1
15	6 48.8	6 49.9	6 30.1	1.5	0.7	7.5	3.4	13.5	6.2
16	6 49.0	6 50.1	6 30.4	1.6	0.7	7.6	3.5	13.6	6.2
17	6 49.3	6 50.4	6 30.6	1.7	0.8	7.7	3.5	13.7	6.3
18	6 49.5	6 50.6	6 30.8	1.8	0.8	7.8	3.6	13.8	6.3
19	6 49.8	6 50.9	6 31.1	1.9	0.9	7.9	3.6	13.9	6.4
20	6 50.0	6 51.1	6 31.3	2.0	0.9	8.0	3.7	14.0	6.4
21	6 50.3	6 51.4	6 31.6	2.1	1.0	8.1	3.7	14.1	6.5
22	6 50.5	6 51.6	6 31.8	2.2	1.0	8.2	3.8	14.2	6.5
23	6 50.8	6 51.9	6 32.0	2.3	1.1	8.3	3.8	14.3	6.6
24	6 51.0	6 52.1	6 32.3	2.4	1.1	8.4	3.9	14.4	6.6
25	6 51.3	6 52.4	6 32.5	2.5	1.1	8.5	3.9	14.5	6.6
26	6 51.5	6 52.6	6 32.8	2.6	1.2	8.6	3.9	14.6	6.7
27	6 51.8	6 52.9	6 33.0	2.7	1.2	8.7	4.0	14.7	6.7
28	6 52.0	6 53.1	6 33.2	2.8	1.3	8.8	4.0	14.8	6.8
29	6 52.3	6 53.4	6 33.5	2.9	1.3	8.9	4.1	14.9	6.8
30	6 52.5	6 53.6	6 33.7	3.0	1.4	9.0	4.1	15.0	6.9
31	6 52.8	6 53.9	6 33.9	3.1	1.4	9.1	4.2	15.1	6.9
32	6 53.0	6 54.1	6 34.2	3.2	1.5	9.2	4.2	15.2	7.0
33	6 53.3	6 54.4	6 34.4	3.3	1.5	9.3	4.3	15.3	7.0
34	6 53.5	6 54.6	6 34.7	3.4	1.6	9.4	4.3	15.4	7.1
35	6 53.8	6 54.9	6 34.9	3.5	1.6	9.5	4.4	15.5	7.1
36	6 54.0	6 55.1	6 35.1	3.6	1.7	9.6	4.4	15.6	7.2
37	6 54.3	6 55.4	6 35.4	3.7	1.7	9.7	4.4	15.7	7.2
38	6 54.5	6 55.6	6 35.6	3.8	1.7	9.8	4.5	15.8	7.2
39	6 54.8	6 55.9	6 35.9	3.9	1.8	9.9	4.5	15.9	7.3
40	6 55.0	6 56.1	6 36.1	4.0	1.8	10.0	4.6	16.0	7.3
41	6 55.3	6 56.4	6 36.3	4.1	1.9	10.1	4.6	16.1	7.4
42	6 55.5	6 56.6	6 36.6	4.2	1.9	10.2	4.7	16.2	7.4
43	6 55.8	6 56.9	6 36.8	4.3	2.0	10.3	4.7	16.3	7.5
44	6 56.0	6 57.1	6 37.0	4.4	2.0	10.4	4.8	16.4	7.5
45	6 56.3	6 57.4	6 37.3	4.5	2.1	10.5	4.8	16.5	7.6
46	6 56.5	6 57.6	6 37.5	4.6	2.1	10.6	4.9	16.6	7.6
47	6 56.8	6 57.9	6 37.8	4.7	2.2	10.7	4.9	16.7	7.7
48	6 57.0	6 58.1	6 38.0	4.8	2.2	10.8	5.0	16.8	7.7
49	6 57.3	6 58.4	6 38.2	4.9	2.2	10.9	5.0	16.9	7.7
50	6 57.5	6 58.6	6 38.5	5.0	2.3	11.0	5.0	17.0	7.8
51	6 57.8	6 58.9	6 38.7	5.1	2.3	11.1	5.1	17.1	7.8
52	6 58.0	6 59.1	6 39.0	5.2	2.4	11.2	5.1	17.2	7.9
53	6 58.3	6 59.4	6 39.2	5.3	2.4	11.3	5.2	17.3	7.9
54	6 58.5	6 59.6	6 39.4	5.4	2.5	11.4	5.2	17.4	8.0
55	6 58.8	6 59.9	6 39.7	5.5	2.5	11.5	5.3	17.5	8.0
56	6 59.0	7 00.1	6 39.9	5.6	2.6	11.6	5.3	17.6	8.1
57	6 59.3	7 00.4	6 40.2	5.7	2.6	11.7	5.4	17.7	8.1
58	6 59.5	7 00.6	6 40.4	5.8	2.7	11.8	5.4	17.8	8.2
59	6 59.8	7 00.9	6 40.6	5.9	2.7	11.9	5.5	17.9	8.2
60	7 00.0	7 01.1	6 40.9	6.0	2.8	12.0	5.5	18.0	8.3

28ᵐ

28 m	SUN PLANETS	ARIES	MOON	v or d	Corrⁿ	v or d	Corrⁿ	v or d	Corrⁿ
s	° ′	° ′	° ′	′	′	′	′	′	′
00	7 00·0	7 01·1	6 40·9	0·0	0·0	6·0	2·9	12·0	5·7
01	7 00·3	7 01·4	6 41·1	0·1	0·0	6·1	2·9	12·1	5·7
02	7 00·5	7 01·7	6 41·3	0·2	0·1	6·2	2·9	12·2	5·8
03	7 00·8	7 01·9	6 41·6	0·3	0·1	6·3	3·0	12·3	5·8
04	7 01·0	7 02·2	6 41·8	0·4	0·2	6·4	3·0	12·4	5·9
05	7 01·3	7 02·4	6 42·1	0·5	0·2	6·5	3·1	12·5	5·9
06	7 01·5	7 02·7	6 42·3	0·6	0·3	6·6	3·1	12·6	6·0
07	7 01·8	7 02·9	6 42·5	0·7	0·3	6·7	3·2	12·7	6·0
08	7 02·0	7 03·2	6 42·8	0·8	0·4	6·8	3·2	12·8	6·1
09	7 02·3	7 03·4	6 43·0	0·9	0·4	6·9	3·3	12·9	6·1
10	7 02·5	7 03·7	6 43·3	1·0	0·5	7·0	3·3	13·0	6·2
11	7 02·8	7 03·9	6 43·5	1·1	0·5	7·1	3·4	13·1	6·2
12	7 03·0	7 04·2	6 43·7	1·2	0·6	7·2	3·4	13·2	6·3
13	7 03·3	7 04·4	6 44·0	1·3	0·6	7·3	3·5	13·3	6·3
14	7 03·5	7 04·7	6 44·2	1·4	0·7	7·4	3·5	13·4	6·4
15	7 03·8	7 04·9	6 44·4	1·5	0·7	7·5	3·6	13·5	6·4
16	7 04·0	7 05·2	6 44·7	1·6	0·8	7·6	3·6	13·6	6·5
17	7 04·3	7 05·4	6 44·9	1·7	0·8	7·7	3·7	13·7	6·5
18	7 04·5	7 05·7	6 45·2	1·8	0·9	7·8	3·7	13·8	6·6
19	7 04·8	7 05·9	6 45·4	1·9	0·9	7·9	3·8	13·9	6·6
20	7 05·0	7 06·2	6 45·6	2·0	1·0	8·0	3·8	14·0	6·7
21	7 05·3	7 06·4	6 45·9	2·1	1·0	8·1	3·8	14·1	6·7
22	7 05·5	7 06·7	6 46·1	2·2	1·0	8·2	3·9	14·2	6·7
23	7 05·8	7 06·9	6 46·4	2·3	1·1	8·3	3·9	14·3	6·8
24	7 06·0	7 07·2	6 46·6	2·4	1·1	8·4	4·0	14·4	6·8
25	7 06·3	7 07·4	6 46·8	2·5	1·2	8·5	4·0	14·5	6·9
26	7 06·5	7 07·7	6 47·1	2·6	1·2	8·6	4·1	14·6	6·9
27	7 06·8	7 07·9	6 47·3	2·7	1·3	8·7	4·1	14·7	7·0
28	7 07·0	7 08·2	6 47·5	2·8	1·3	8·8	4·2	14·8	7·0
29	7 07·3	7 08·4	6 47·8	2·9	1·4	8·9	4·2	14·9	7·1
30	7 07·5	7 08·7	6 48·0	3·0	1·4	9·0	4·3	15·0	7·1
31	7 07·8	7 08·9	6 48·3	3·1	1·5	9·1	4·3	15·1	7·2
32	7 08·0	7 09·2	6 48·5	3·2	1·5	9·2	4·4	15·2	7·2
33	7 08·3	7 09·4	6 48·7	3·3	1·6	9·3	4·4	15·3	7·3
34	7 08·5	7 09·7	6 49·0	3·4	1·6	9·4	4·5	15·4	7·3
35	7 08·8	7 09·9	6 49·2	3·5	1·7	9·5	4·5	15·5	7·4
36	7 09·0	7 10·2	6 49·5	3·6	1·8	9·6	4·6	15·6	7·4
37	7 09·3	7 10·4	6 49·7	3·7	1·8	9·7	4·6	15·7	7·5
38	7 09·5	7 10·7	6 49·9	3·8	1·8	9·8	4·7	15·8	7·5
39	7 09·8	7 10·9	6 50·2	3·9	1·9	9·9	4·7	15·9	7·6
40	7 10·0	7 11·2	6 50·4	4·0	1·9	10·0	4·8	16·0	7·6
41	7 10·3	7 11·4	6 50·6	4·1	1·9	10·1	4·8	16·1	7·6
42	7 10·5	7 11·7	6 50·9	4·2	2·0	10·2	4·8	16·2	7·7
43	7 10·8	7 11·9	6 51·1	4·3	2·0	10·3	4·9	16·3	7·7
44	7 11·0	7 12·2	6 51·4	4·4	2·1	10·4	4·9	16·4	7·8
45	7 11·3	7 12·4	6 51·6	4·5	2·1	10·5	5·0	16·5	7·8
46	7 11·5	7 12·7	6 51·8	4·6	2·2	10·6	5·0	16·6	7·9
47	7 11·8	7 12·9	6 52·1	4·7	2·2	10·7	5·1	16·7	7·9
48	7 12·0	7 13·2	6 52·3	4·8	2·3	10·8	5·1	16·8	8·0
49	7 12·3	7 13·4	6 52·6	4·9	2·3	10·9	5·2	16·9	8·0
50	7 12·5	7 13·7	6 52·8	5·0	2·4	11·0	5·2	17·0	8·1
51	7 12·8	7 13·9	6 53·0	5·1	2·4	11·1	5·3	17·1	8·1
52	7 13·0	7 14·2	6 53·3	5·2	2·5	11·2	5·3	17·2	8·2
53	7 13·3	7 14·4	6 53·5	5·3	2·5	11·3	5·4	17·3	8·2
54	7 13·5	7 14·7	6 53·8	5·4	2·6	11·4	5·4	17·4	8·3
55	7 13·8	7 14·9	6 54·0	5·5	2·6	11·5	5·5	17·5	8·3
56	7 14·0	7 15·2	6 54·2	5·6	2·7	11·6	5·5	17·6	8·4
57	7 14·3	7 15·4	6 54·5	5·7	2·7	11·7	5·6	17·7	8·4
58	7 14·5	7 15·7	6 54·7	5·8	2·8	11·8	5·6	17·8	8·5
59	7 14·8	7 15·9	6 54·9	5·9	2·8	11·9	5·7	17·9	8·5
60	7 15·0	7 16·2	6 55·2	6·0	2·9	12·0	5·7	18·0	8·6

29ᵐ

29 m	SUN PLANETS	ARIES	MOON	v or d	Corrⁿ	v or d	Corrⁿ	v or d	Corrⁿ
s	° ′	° ′	° ′	′	′	′	′	′	′
00	7 15·0	7 16·2	6 55·2	0·0	0·0	6·0	3·0	12·0	5·9
01	7 15·3	7 16·4	6 55·4	0·1	0·0	6·1	3·0	12·1	5·9
02	7 15·5	7 16·7	6 55·7	0·2	0·1	6·2	3·0	12·2	6·0
03	7 15·8	7 16·9	6 55·9	0·3	0·1	6·3	3·1	12·3	6·0
04	7 16·0	7 17·2	6 56·1	0·4	0·2	6·4	3·1	12·4	6·1
05	7 16·3	7 17·4	6 56·4	0·5	0·2	6·5	3·2	12·5	6·1
06	7 16·5	7 17·7	6 56·6	0·6	0·3	6·6	3·2	12·6	6·2
07	7 16·8	7 17·9	6 56·9	0·7	0·3	6·7	3·3	12·7	6·2
08	7 17·0	7 18·2	6 57·1	0·8	0·4	6·8	3·3	12·8	6·3
09	7 17·3	7 18·4	6 57·3	0·9	0·4	6·9	3·4	12·9	6·3
10	7 17·5	7 18·7	6 57·6	1·0	0·5	7·0	3·4	13·0	6·4
11	7 17·8	7 18·9	6 57·8	1·1	0·5	7·1	3·5	13·1	6·4
12	7 18·0	7 19·2	6 58·0	1·2	0·6	7·2	3·5	13·2	6·5
13	7 18·3	7 19·4	6 58·3	1·3	0·6	7·3	3·6	13·3	6·5
14	7 18·5	7 19·7	6 58·5	1·4	0·7	7·4	3·6	13·4	6·6
15	7 18·8	7 20·0	6 58·8	1·5	0·7	7·5	3·7	13·5	6·6
16	7 19·0	7 20·2	6 59·0	1·6	0·8	7·6	3·7	13·6	6·7
17	7 19·3	7 20·5	6 59·2	1·7	0·8	7·7	3·8	13·7	6·7
18	7 19·5	7 20·7	6 59·5	1·8	0·9	7·8	3·8	13·8	6·8
19	7 19·8	7 21·0	6 59·7	1·9	0·9	7·9	3·9	13·9	6·8
20	7 20·0	7 21·2	7 00·0	2·0	1·0	8·0	3·9	14·0	6·9
21	7 20·3	7 21·5	7 00·2	2·1	1·0	8·1	4·0	14·1	6·9
22	7 20·5	7 21·7	7 00·4	2·2	1·1	8·2	4·0	14·2	7·0
23	7 20·8	7 22·0	7 00·7	2·3	1·1	8·3	4·1	14·3	7·0
24	7 21·0	7 22·2	7 00·9	2·4	1·2	8·4	4·1	14·4	7·1
25	7 21·3	7 22·5	7 01·1	2·5	1·2	8·5	4·2	14·5	7·1
26	7 21·5	7 22·7	7 01·4	2·6	1·3	8·6	4·2	14·6	7·2
27	7 21·8	7 23·0	7 01·6	2·7	1·3	8·7	4·3	14·7	7·2
28	7 22·0	7 23·2	7 01·9	2·8	1·4	8·8	4·3	14·8	7·3
29	7 22·3	7 23·5	7 02·1	2·9	1·4	8·9	4·4	14·9	7·3
30	7 22·5	7 23·7	7 02·3	3·0	1·5	9·0	4·4	15·0	7·4
31	7 22·8	7 24·0	7 02·6	3·1	1·5	9·1	4·5	15·1	7·4
32	7 23·0	7 24·2	7 02·8	3·2	1·6	9·2	4·5	15·2	7·5
33	7 23·3	7 24·5	7 03·1	3·3	1·6	9·3	4·6	15·3	7·5
34	7 23·5	7 24·7	7 03·3	3·4	1·7	9·4	4·6	15·4	7·6
35	7 23·8	7 25·0	7 03·5	3·5	1·7	9·5	4·7	15·5	7·6
36	7 24·0	7 25·2	7 03·8	3·6	1·8	9·6	4·7	15·6	7·7
37	7 24·3	7 25·5	7 04·0	3·7	1·8	9·7	4·8	15·7	7·7
38	7 24·5	7 25·7	7 04·3	3·8	1·9	9·8	4·8	15·8	7·8
39	7 24·8	7 26·0	7 04·5	3·9	1·9	9·9	4·9	15·9	7·8
40	7 25·0	7 26·2	7 04·7	4·0	2·0	10·0	4·9	16·0	7·9
41	7 25·3	7 26·5	7 05·0	4·1	2·0	10·1	5·0	16·1	7·9
42	7 25·5	7 26·7	7 05·2	4·2	2·1	10·2	5·0	16·2	8·0
43	7 25·8	7 27·0	7 05·4	4·3	2·1	10·3	5·1	16·3	8·0
44	7 26·0	7 27·2	7 05·7	4·4	2·2	10·4	5·1	16·4	8·1
45	7 26·3	7 27·5	7 05·9	4·5	2·2	10·5	5·2	16·5	8·1
46	7 26·5	7 27·7	7 06·2	4·6	2·3	10·6	5·2	16·6	8·2
47	7 26·8	7 28·0	7 06·4	4·7	2·3	10·7	5·3	16·7	8·2
48	7 27·0	7 28·2	7 06·6	4·8	2·4	10·8	5·3	16·8	8·3
49	7 27·3	7 28·5	7 06·9	4·9	2·4	10·9	5·4	16·9	8·3
50	7 27·5	7 28·7	7 07·1	5·0	2·5	11·0	5·4	17·0	8·4
51	7 27·8	7 29·0	7 07·4	5·1	2·5	11·1	5·5	17·1	8·4
52	7 28·0	7 29·2	7 07·6	5·2	2·6	11·2	5·5	17·2	8·5
53	7 28·3	7 29·5	7 07·8	5·3	2·6	11·3	5·6	17·3	8·5
54	7 28·5	7 29·7	7 08·1	5·4	2·7	11·4	5·6	17·4	8·6
55	7 28·8	7 30·0	7 08·3	5·5	2·7	11·5	5·7	17·5	8·6
56	7 29·0	7 30·2	7 08·5	5·6	2·8	11·6	5·7	17·6	8·7
57	7 29·3	7 30·5	7 08·8	5·7	2·8	11·7	5·8	17·7	8·7
58	7 29·5	7 30·7	7 09·0	5·8	2·9	11·8	5·8	17·8	8·8
59	7 29·8	7 31·0	7 09·3	5·9	2·9	11·9	5·9	17·9	8·8
60	7 30·0	7 31·2	7 09·5	6·0	3·0	12·0	5·9	18·0	8·9

30	SUN PLANETS	ARIES	MOON	v or d Corrⁿ		v or d Corrⁿ		v or d Corrⁿ		31	SUN PLANETS	ARIES	MOON	v or d Corrⁿ		v or d Corrⁿ		v or d Corrⁿ	
s	° ′	° ′	° ′	′	′	′	′	′	′	s	° ′	° ′	° ′	′	′	′	′	′	′
00	7 30·0	7 31·2	7 09·5	0·0	0·0	6·0	3·1	12·0	6·1	00	7 45·0	7 46·3	7 23·8	0·0	0·0	6·0	3·2	12·0	6·3
01	7 30·3	7 31·5	7 09·7	0·1	0·1	6·1	3·1	12·1	6·2	01	7 45·3	7 46·5	7 24·1	0·1	0·1	6·1	3·2	12·1	6·4
02	7 30·5	7 31·7	7 10·0	0·2	0·1	6·2	3·2	12·2	6·2	02	7 45·5	7 46·8	7 24·3	0·2	0·1	6·2	3·3	12·2	6·4
03	7 30·8	7 32·0	7 10·2	0·3	0·2	6·3	3·2	12·3	6·3	03	7 45·8	7 47·0	7 24·5	0·3	0·2	6·3	3·3	12·3	6·5
04	7 31·0	7 32·2	7 10·5	0·4	0·2	6·4	3·3	12·4	6·3	04	7 46·0	7 47·3	7 24·8	0·4	0·2	6·4	3·4	12·4	6·5
05	7 31·3	7 32·5	7 10·7	0·5	0·3	6·5	3·3	12·5	6·4	05	7 46·3	7 47·5	7 25·0	0·5	0·3	6·5	3·4	12·5	6·6
06	7 31·5	7 32·7	7 10·9	0·6	0·3	6·6	3·4	12·6	6·4	06	7 46·5	7 47·8	7 25·2	0·6	0·3	6·6	3·5	12·6	6·6
07	7 31·8	7 33·0	7 11·2	0·7	0·4	6·7	3·4	12·7	6·5	07	7 46·8	7 48·0	7 25·5	0·7	0·4	6·7	3·5	12·7	6·7
08	7 32·0	7 33·2	7 11·4	0·8	0·4	6·8	3·5	12·8	6·5	08	7 47·0	7 48·3	7 25·7	0·8	0·4	6·8	3·6	12·8	6·7
09	7 32·3	7 33·5	7 11·6	0·9	0·5	6·9	3·5	12·9	6·6	09	7 47·3	7 48·5	7 26·0	0·9	0·5	6·9	3·6	12·9	6·8
10	7 32·5	7 33·7	7 11·9	1·0	0·5	7·0	3·6	13·0	6·6	10	7 47·5	7 48·8	7 26·2	1·0	0·5	7·0	3·7	13·0	6·8
11	7 32·8	7 34·0	7 12·1	1·1	0·6	7·1	3·6	13·1	6·7	11	7 47·8	7 49·0	7 26·4	1·1	0·6	7·1	3·7	13·1	6·9
12	7 33·0	7 34·2	7 12·4	1·2	0·6	7·2	3·7	13·2	6·7	12	7 48·0	7 49·3	7 26·7	1·2	0·6	7·2	3·8	13·2	6·9
13	7 33·3	7 34·5	7 12·6	1·3	0·7	7·3	3·7	13·3	6·8	13	7 48·3	7 49·5	7 26·9	1·3	0·7	7·3	3·8	13·3	7·0
14	7 33·5	7 34·7	7 12·8	1·4	0·7	7·4	3·8	13·4	6·8	14	7 48·5	7 49·8	7 27·2	1·4	0·7	7·4	3·9	13·4	7·0
15	7 33·8	7 35·0	7 13·1	1·5	0·8	7·5	3·8	13·5	6·9	15	7 48·8	7 50·0	7 27·4	1·5	0·8	7·5	3·9	13·5	7·1
16	7 34·0	7 35·2	7 13·3	1·6	0·8	7·6	3·9	13·6	6·9	16	7 49·0	7 50·3	7 27·6	1·6	0·8	7·6	4·0	13·6	7·1
17	7 34·3	7 35·5	7 13·6	1·7	0·9	7·7	3·9	13·7	7·0	17	7 49·3	7 50·5	7 27·9	1·7	0·9	7·7	4·0	13·7	7·2
18	7 34·5	7 35·7	7 13·8	1·8	0·9	7·8	4·0	13·8	7·0	18	7 49·5	7 50·8	7 28·1	1·8	0·9	7·8	4·1	13·8	7·2
19	7 34·8	7 36·0	7 14·0	1·9	1·0	7·9	4·0	13·9	7·1	19	7 49·8	7 51·0	7 28·4	1·9	1·0	7·9	4·1	13·9	7·3
20	7 35·0	7 36·2	7 14·3	2·0	1·0	8·0	4·1	14·0	7·1	20	7 50·0	7 51·3	7 28·6	2·0	1·1	8·0	4·2	14·0	7·4
21	7 35·3	7 36·5	7 14·5	2·1	1·1	8·1	4·1	14·1	7·2	21	7 50·3	7 51·5	7 28·8	2·1	1·1	8·1	4·3	14·1	7·4
22	7 35·5	7 36·7	7 14·7	2·2	1·1	8·2	4·2	14·2	7·2	22	7 50·5	7 51·8	7 29·1	2·2	1·2	8·2	4·3	14·2	7·5
23	7 35·8	7 37·0	7 15·0	2·3	1·2	8·3	4·2	14·3	7·3	23	7 50·8	7 52·0	7 29·3	2·3	1·2	8·3	4·4	14·3	7·5
24	7 36·0	7 37·2	7 15·2	2·4	1·2	8·4	4·3	14·4	7·3	24	7 51·0	7 52·3	7 29·5	2·4	1·3	8·4	4·4	14·4	7·6
25	7 36·3	7 37·5	7 15·5	2·5	1·3	8·5	4·3	14·5	7·4	25	7 51·3	7 52·5	7 29·8	2·5	1·3	8·5	4·5	14·5	7·6
26	7 36·5	7 37·7	7 15·7	2·6	1·3	8·6	4·4	14·6	7·4	26	7 51·5	7 52·8	7 30·0	2·6	1·4	8·6	4·5	14·6	7·7
27	7 36·8	7 38·0	7 15·9	2·7	1·4	8·7	4·4	14·7	7·5	27	7 51·8	7 53·0	7 30·3	2·7	1·4	8·7	4·6	14·7	7·7
28	7 37·0	7 38·3	7 16·2	2·8	1·4	8·8	4·5	14·8	7·5	28	7 52·0	7 53·3	7 30·5	2·8	1·5	8·8	4·6	14·8	7·8
29	7 37·3	7 38·5	7 16·4	2·9	1·5	8·9	4·5	14·9	7·6	29	7 52·3	7 53·5	7 30·7	2·9	1·5	8·9	4·7	14·9	7·8
30	7 37·5	7 38·8	7 16·7	3·0	1·5	9·0	4·6	15·0	7·6	30	7 52·5	7 53·8	7 31·0	3·0	1·6	9·0	4·7	15·0	7·9
31	7 37·8	7 39·0	7 16·9	3·1	1·6	9·1	4·6	15·1	7·7	31	7 52·8	7 54·0	7 31·2	3·1	1·6	9·1	4·8	15·1	7·9
32	7 38·0	7 39·3	7 17·1	3·2	1·6	9·2	4·7	15·2	7·7	32	7 53·0	7 54·3	7 31·5	3·2	1·7	9·2	4·8	15·2	8·0
33	7 38·3	7 39·5	7 17·4	3·3	1·7	9·3	4·7	15·3	7·8	33	7 53·3	7 54·5	7 31·7	3·3	1·7	9·3	4·9	15·3	8·0
34	7 38·5	7 39·8	7 17·6	3·4	1·7	9·4	4·8	15·4	7·8	34	7 53·5	7 54·8	7 31·9	3·4	1·8	9·4	4·9	15·4	8·1
35	7 38·8	7 40·0	7 17·9	3·5	1·8	9·5	4·8	15·5	7·9	35	7 53·8	7 55·0	7 32·2	3·5	1·8	9·5	5·0	15·5	8·1
36	7 39·0	7 40·3	7 18·1	3·6	1·8	9·6	4·9	15·6	7·9	36	7 54·0	7 55·3	7 32·4	3·6	1·9	9·6	5·0	15·6	8·2
37	7 39·3	7 40·5	7 18·3	3·7	1·9	9·7	4·9	15·7	8·0	37	7 54·3	7 55·5	7 32·6	3·7	1·9	9·7	5·1	15·7	8·2
38	7 39·5	7 40·8	7 18·6	3·8	1·9	9·8	5·0	15·8	8·0	38	7 54·5	7 55·8	7 32·9	3·8	2·0	9·8	5·1	15·8	8·3
39	7 39·8	7 41·0	7 18·8	3·9	2·0	9·9	5·0	15·9	8·1	39	7 54·8	7 56·0	7 33·1	3·9	2·0	9·9	5·2	15·9	8·3
40	7 40·0	7 41·3	7 19·0	4·0	2·0	10·0	5·1	16·0	8·1	40	7 55·0	7 56·3	7 33·4	4·0	2·1	10·0	5·3	16·0	8·4
41	7 40·3	7 41·5	7 19·3	4·1	2·1	10·1	5·1	16·1	8·2	41	7 55·3	7 56·5	7 33·6	4·1	2·2	10·1	5·3	16·1	8·5
42	7 40·5	7 41·8	7 19·5	4·2	2·1	10·2	5·2	16·2	8·2	42	7 55·5	7 56·8	7 33·8	4·2	2·2	10·2	5·4	16·2	8·5
43	7 40·8	7 42·0	7 19·8	4·3	2·2	10·3	5·2	16·3	8·3	43	7 55·8	7 57·1	7 34·1	4·3	2·3	10·3	5·4	16·3	8·6
44	7 41·0	7 42·3	7 20·0	4·4	2·2	10·4	5·3	16·4	8·3	44	7 56·0	7 57·3	7 34·3	4·4	2·3	10·4	5·5	16·4	8·6
45	7 41·3	7 42·5	7 20·2	4·5	2·3	10·5	5·3	16·5	8·4	45	7 56·3	7 57·6	7 34·6	4·5	2·4	10·5	5·5	16·5	8·7
46	7 41·5	7 42·8	7 20·5	4·6	2·3	10·6	5·4	16·6	8·4	46	7 56·5	7 57·8	7 34·8	4·6	2·4	10·6	5·6	16·6	8·7
47	7 41·8	7 43·0	7 20·7	4·7	2·4	10·7	5·4	16·7	8·5	47	7 56·8	7 58·1	7 35·0	4·7	2·5	10·7	5·6	16·7	8·8
48	7 42·0	7 43·3	7 21·0	4·8	2·4	10·8	5·5	16·8	8·5	48	7 57·0	7 58·3	7 35·3	4·8	2·5	10·8	5·7	16·8	8·8
49	7 42·3	7 43·5	7 21·2	4·9	2·5	10·9	5·5	16·9	8·6	49	7 57·3	7 58·6	7 35·5	4·9	2·6	10·9	5·7	16·9	8·9
50	7 42·5	7 43·8	7 21·4	5·0	2·5	11·0	5·6	17·0	8·6	50	7 57·5	7 58·8	7 35·7	5·0	2·6	11·0	5·8	17·0	8·9
51	7 42·8	7 44·0	7 21·7	5·1	2·6	11·1	5·6	17·1	8·7	51	7 57·8	7 59·1	7 36·0	5·1	2·7	11·1	5·8	17·1	9·0
52	7 43·0	7 44·3	7 21·9	5·2	2·6	11·2	5·7	17·2	8·7	52	7 58·0	7 59·3	7 36·2	5·2	2·7	11·2	5·9	17·2	9·0
53	7 43·3	7 44·5	7 22·1	5·3	2·7	11·3	5·7	17·3	8·8	53	7 58·3	7 59·6	7 36·5	5·3	2·8	11·3	5·9	17·3	9·1
54	7 43·5	7 44·8	7 22·4	5·4	2·7	11·4	5·8	17·4	8·8	54	7 58·5	7 59·8	7 36·7	5·4	2·8	11·4	6·0	17·4	9·1
55	7 43·8	7 45·0	7 22·6	5·5	2·8	11·5	5·8	17·5	8·9	55	7 58·8	8 00·1	7 36·9	5·5	2·9	11·5	6·0	17·5	9·2
56	7 44·0	7 45·3	7 22·9	5·6	2·8	11·6	5·9	17·6	8·9	56	7 59·0	8 00·3	7 37·2	5·6	2·9	11·6	6·1	17·6	9·2
57	7 44·3	7 45·5	7 23·1	5·7	2·9	11·7	5·9	17·7	9·0	57	7 59·3	8 00·6	7 37·4	5·7	3·0	11·7	6·1	17·7	9·3
58	7 44·5	7 45·8	7 23·3	5·8	2·9	11·8	6·0	17·8	9·0	58	7 59·5	8 00·8	7 37·7	5·8	3·0	11·8	6·2	17·8	9·3
59	7 44·8	7 46·0	7 23·6	5·9	3·0	11·9	6·0	17·9	9·1	59	7 59·8	8 01·1	7 37·9	5·9	3·1	11·9	6·2	17·9	9·4
60	7 45·0	7 46·3	7 23·8	6·0	3·1	12·0	6·1	18·0	9·2	60	8 00·0	8 01·3	7 38·1	6·0	3·2	12·0	6·3	18·0	9·5

32 m	SUN PLANETS	ARIES	MOON	v or d	Corrⁿ	v or d	Corrⁿ	v or d	Corrⁿ
s	° ′	° ′	° ′	′	′	′	′	′	′
00	8 00·0	8 01·3	7 38·1	0·0	0·0	6·0	3·3	12·0	6·5
01	8 00·3	8 01·6	7 38·4	0·1	0·1	6·1	3·3	12·1	6·6
02	8 00·5	8 01·8	7 38·6	0·2	0·1	6·2	3·4	12·2	6·6
03	8 00·8	8 02·1	7 38·8	0·3	0·2	6·3	3·4	12·3	6·7
04	8 01·0	8 02·3	7 39·1	0·4	0·2	6·4	3·5	12·4	6·7
05	8 01·3	8 02·6	7 39·3	0·5	0·3	6·5	3·5	12·5	6·8
06	8 01·5	8 02·8	7 39·6	0·6	0·3	6·6	3·6	12·6	6·8
07	8 01·8	8 03·1	7 39·8	0·7	0·4	6·7	3·6	12·7	6·9
08	8 02·0	8 03·3	7 40·0	0·8	0·4	6·8	3·7	12·8	6·9
09	8 02·3	8 03·6	7 40·3	0·9	0·5	6·9	3·7	12·9	7·0
10	8 02·5	8 03·8	7 40·5	1·0	0·5	7·0	3·8	13·0	7·0
11	8 02·8	8 04·1	7 40·8	1·1	0·6	7·1	3·8	13·1	7·1
12	8 03·0	8 04·3	7 41·0	1·2	0·7	7·2	3·9	13·2	7·2
13	8 03·3	8 04·6	7 41·2	1·3	0·7	7·3	4·0	13·3	7·2
14	8 03·5	8 04·8	7 41·5	1·4	0·8	7·4	4·0	13·4	7·3
15	8 03·8	8 05·1	7 41·7	1·5	0·8	7·5	4·1	13·5	7·3
16	8 04·0	8 05·3	7 42·0	1·6	0·9	7·6	4·1	13·6	7·4
17	8 04·3	8 05·6	7 42·2	1·7	0·9	7·7	4·2	13·7	7·4
18	8 04·5	8 05·8	7 42·4	1·8	1·0	7·8	4·2	13·8	7·5
19	8 04·8	8 06·1	7 42·7	1·9	1·0	7·9	4·3	13·9	7·5
20	8 05·0	8 06·3	7 42·9	2·0	1·1	8·0	4·3	14·0	7·6
21	8 05·3	8 06·6	7 43·1	2·1	1·1	8·1	4·4	14·1	7·6
22	8 05·5	8 06·8	7 43·4	2·2	1·2	8·2	4·4	14·2	7·7
23	8 05·8	8 07·1	7 43·6	2·3	1·2	8·3	4·5	14·3	7·7
24	8 06·0	8 07·3	7 43·9	2·4	1·3	8·4	4·6	14·4	7·8
25	8 06·3	8 07·6	7 44·1	2·5	1·4	8·5	4·6	14·5	7·9
26	8 06·5	8 07·8	7 44·3	2·6	1·4	8·6	4·7	14·6	7·9
27	8 06·8	8 08·1	7 44·6	2·7	1·5	8·7	4·7	14·7	8·0
28	8 07·0	8 08·3	7 44·8	2·8	1·5	8·8	4·8	14·8	8·0
29	8 07·3	8 08·6	7 45·1	2·9	1·6	8·9	4·8	14·9	8·1
30	8 07·5	8 08·8	7 45·3	3·0	1·6	9·0	4·9	15·0	8·1
31	8 07·8	8 09·1	7 45·5	3·1	1·7	9·1	4·9	15·1	8·2
32	8 08·0	8 09·3	7 45·8	3·2	1·7	9·2	5·0	15·2	8·2
33	8 08·3	8 09·6	7 46·0	3·3	1·8	9·3	5·0	15·3	8·3
34	8 08·5	8 09·8	7 46·2	3·4	1·8	9·4	5·1	15·4	8·3
35	8 08·8	8 10·1	7 46·5	3·5	1·9	9·5	5·1	15·5	8·4
36	8 09·0	8 10·3	7 46·7	3·6	2·0	9·6	5·2	15·6	8·5
37	8 09·3	8 10·6	7 47·0	3·7	2·0	9·7	5·3	15·7	8·5
38	8 09·5	8 10·8	7 47·2	3·8	2·1	9·8	5·3	15·8	8·6
39	8 09·8	8 11·1	7 47·4	3·9	2·1	9·9	5·4	15·9	8·6
40	8 10·0	8 11·3	7 47·7	4·0	2·2	10·0	5·4	16·0	8·7
41	8 10·3	8 11·6	7 47·9	4·1	2·2	10·1	5·5	16·1	8·7
42	8 10·5	8 11·8	7 48·2	4·2	2·3	10·2	5·5	16·2	8·8
43	8 10·8	8 12·1	7 48·4	4·3	2·3	10·3	5·6	16·3	8·8
44	8 11·0	8 12·3	7 48·6	4·4	2·4	10·4	5·6	16·4	8·9
45	8 11·3	8 12·6	7 48·9	4·5	2·4	10·5	5·7	16·5	8·9
46	8 11·5	8 12·8	7 49·1	4·6	2·5	10·6	5·7	16·6	9·0
47	8 11·8	8 13·1	7 49·3	4·7	2·5	10·7	5·8	16·7	9·0
48	8 12·0	8 13·3	7 49·6	4·8	2·6	10·8	5·9	16·8	9·1
49	8 12·3	8 13·6	7 49·8	4·9	2·7	10·9	5·9	16·9	9·2
50	8 12·5	8 13·8	7 50·1	5·0	2·7	11·0	6·0	17·0	9·2
51	8 12·8	8 14·1	7 50·3	5·1	2·8	11·1	6·0	17·1	9·3
52	8 13·0	8 14·3	7 50·5	5·2	2·8	11·2	6·1	17·2	9·3
53	8 13·3	8 14·6	7 50·8	5·3	2·9	11·3	6·1	17·3	9·4
54	8 13·5	8 14·9	7 51·0	5·4	2·9	11·4	6·2	17·4	9·4
55	8 13·8	8 15·1	7 51·3	5·5	3·0	11·5	6·2	17·5	9·5
56	8 14·0	8 15·4	7 51·5	5·6	3·0	11·6	6·3	17·6	9·5
57	8 14·3	8 15·6	7 51·7	5·7	3·1	11·7	6·3	17·7	9·6
58	8 14·5	8 15·9	7 52·0	5·8	3·1	11·8	6·4	17·8	9·6
59	8 14·8	8 16·1	7 52·2	5·9	3·2	11·9	6·4	17·9	9·7
60	8 15·0	8 16·4	7 52·5	6·0	3·3	12·0	6·5	18·0	9·8

33 m	SUN PLANETS	ARIES	MOON	v or d	Corrⁿ	v or d	Corrⁿ	v or d	Corrⁿ
s	° ′	° ′	° ′	′	′	′	′	′	′
00	8 15·0	8 16·4	7 52·5	0·0	0·0	6·0	3·4	12·0	6·7
01	8 15·3	8 16·6	7 52·7	0·1	0·1	6·1	3·4	12·1	6·8
02	8 15·5	8 16·9	7 52·9	0·2	0·1	6·2	3·5	12·2	6·8
03	8 15·8	8 17·1	7 53·2	0·3	0·2	6·3	3·5	12·3	6·9
04	8 16·0	8 17·4	7 53·4	0·4	0·2	6·4	3·6	12·4	6·9
05	8 16·3	8 17·6	7 53·6	0·5	0·3	6·5	3·6	12·5	7·0
06	8 16·5	8 17·9	7 53·9	0·6	0·3	6·6	3·7	12·6	7·0
07	8 16·8	8 18·1	7 54·1	0·7	0·4	6·7	3·7	12·7	7·1
08	8 17·0	8 18·4	7 54·4	0·8	0·4	6·8	3·8	12·8	7·1
09	8 17·3	8 18·6	7 54·6	0·9	0·5	6·9	3·9	12·9	7·2
10	8 17·5	8 18·9	7 54·8	1·0	0·6	7·0	3·9	13·0	7·3
11	8 17·8	8 19·1	7 55·1	1·1	0·6	7·1	4·0	13·1	7·3
12	8 18·0	8 19·4	7 55·3	1·2	0·7	7·2	4·0	13·2	7·4
13	8 18·3	8 19·6	7 55·6	1·3	0·7	7·3	4·1	13·3	7·4
14	8 18·5	8 19·9	7 55·8	1·4	0·8	7·4	4·1	13·4	7·5
15	8 18·8	8 20·1	7 56·0	1·5	0·8	7·5	4·2	13·5	7·5
16	8 19·0	8 20·4	7 56·3	1·6	0·9	7·6	4·2	13·6	7·6
17	8 19·3	8 20·6	7 56·5	1·7	0·9	7·7	4·3	13·7	7·6
18	8 19·5	8 20·9	7 56·7	1·8	1·0	7·8	4·4	13·8	7·7
19	8 19·8	8 21·1	7 57·0	1·9	1·1	7·9	4·4	13·9	7·8
20	8 20·0	8 21·4	7 57·2	2·0	1·1	8·0	4·5	14·0	7·8
21	8 20·3	8 21·6	7 57·5	2·1	1·2	8·1	4·5	14·1	7·9
22	8 20·5	8 21·9	7 57·7	2·2	1·2	8·2	4·6	14·2	7·9
23	8 20·8	8 22·1	7 57·9	2·3	1·3	8·3	4·6	14·3	8·0
24	8 21·0	8 22·4	7 58·2	2·4	1·3	8·4	4·7	14·4	8·0
25	8 21·3	8 22·6	7 58·4	2·5	1·4	8·5	4·7	14·5	8·1
26	8 21·5	8 22·9	7 58·7	2·6	1·5	8·6	4·8	14·6	8·2
27	8 21·8	8 23·1	7 58·9	2·7	1·5	8·7	4·9	14·7	8·2
28	8 22·0	8 23·4	7 59·1	2·8	1·6	8·8	4·9	14·8	8·3
29	8 22·3	8 23·6	7 59·4	2·9	1·6	8·9	5·0	14·9	8·3
30	8 22·5	8 23·9	7 59·6	3·0	1·7	9·0	5·0	15·0	8·4
31	8 22·8	8 24·1	7 59·8	3·1	1·7	9·1	5·1	15·1	8·4
32	8 23·0	8 24·4	8 00·1	3·2	1·8	9·2	5·1	15·2	8·5
33	8 23·3	8 24·6	8 00·3	3·3	1·8	9·3	5·2	15·3	8·5
34	8 23·5	8 24·9	8 00·6	3·4	1·9	9·4	5·2	15·4	8·6
35	8 23·8	8 25·1	8 00·8	3·5	2·0	9·5	5·3	15·5	8·7
36	8 24·0	8 25·4	8 01·0	3·6	2·0	9·6	5·4	15·6	8·7
37	8 24·3	8 25·6	8 01·3	3·7	2·1	9·7	5·4	15·7	8·8
38	8 24·5	8 25·9	8 01·5	3·8	2·1	9·8	5·5	15·8	8·8
39	8 24·8	8 26·1	8 01·8	3·9	2·2	9·9	5·5	15·9	8·9
40	8 25·0	8 26·4	8 02·0	4·0	2·2	10·0	5·6	16·0	8·9
41	8 25·3	8 26·6	8 02·2	4·1	2·3	10·1	5·6	16·1	9·0
42	8 25·5	8 26·9	8 02·5	4·2	2·3	10·2	5·7	16·2	9·0
43	8 25·8	8 27·1	8 02·7	4·3	2·4	10·3	5·8	16·3	9·1
44	8 26·0	8 27·4	8 02·9	4·4	2·5	10·4	5·8	16·4	9·2
45	8 26·3	8 27·6	8 03·2	4·5	2·5	10·5	5·9	16·5	9·2
46	8 26·5	8 27·9	8 03·4	4·6	2·6	10·6	5·9	16·6	9·3
47	8 26·8	8 28·1	8 03·7	4·7	2·6	10·7	6·0	16·7	9·3
48	8 27·0	8 28·4	8 03·9	4·8	2·7	10·8	6·0	16·8	9·4
49	8 27·3	8 28·6	8 04·1	4·9	2·7	10·9	6·1	16·9	9·4
50	8 27·5	8 28·9	8 04·4	5·0	2·8	11·0	6·1	17·0	9·5
51	8 27·8	8 29·1	8 04·6	5·1	2·8	11·1	6·2	17·1	9·5
52	8 28·0	8 29·4	8 04·9	5·2	2·9	11·2	6·3	17·2	9·6
53	8 28·3	8 29·6	8 05·1	5·3	3·0	11·3	6·3	17·3	9·7
54	8 28·5	8 29·9	8 05·3	5·4	3·0	11·4	6·4	17·4	9·7
55	8 28·8	8 30·1	8 05·6	5·5	3·1	11·5	6·4	17·5	9·8
56	8 29·0	8 30·4	8 05·8	5·6	3·1	11·6	6·5	17·6	9·8
57	8 29·3	8 30·6	8 06·1	5·7	3·2	11·7	6·5	17·7	9·9
58	8 29·5	8 30·9	8 06·3	5·8	3·2	11·8	6·6	17·8	9·9
59	8 29·8	8 31·1	8 06·5	5·9	3·3	11·9	6·6	17·9	10·0
60	8 30·0	8 31·4	8 06·8	6·0	3·4	12·0	6·7	18·0	10·1

34^m

m 34 s	SUN PLANETS	ARIES	MOON	v or d	Corrⁿ	v or d	Corrⁿ	v or d	Corrⁿ
00	8 30.0	8 31.4	8 06.8	0.0	0.0	6.0	3.5	12.0	6.9
01	8 30.3	8 31.6	8 07.0	0.1	0.1	6.1	3.5	12.1	7.0
02	8 30.5	8 31.9	8 07.2	0.2	0.1	6.2	3.6	12.2	7.0
03	8 30.8	8 32.1	8 07.5	0.3	0.2	6.3	3.6	12.3	7.1
04	8 31.0	8 32.4	8 07.7	0.4	0.2	6.4	3.7	12.4	7.1
05	8 31.3	8 32.6	8 08.0	0.5	0.3	6.5	3.7	12.5	7.2
06	8 31.5	8 32.9	8 08.2	0.6	0.3	6.6	3.8	12.6	7.2
07	8 31.8	8 33.2	8 08.4	0.7	0.4	6.7	3.9	12.7	7.3
08	8 32.0	8 33.4	8 08.7	0.8	0.5	6.8	3.9	12.8	7.4
09	8 32.3	8 33.7	8 08.9	0.9	0.5	6.9	4.0	12.9	7.4
10	8 32.5	8 33.9	8 09.2	1.0	0.6	7.0	4.0	13.0	7.5
11	8 32.8	8 34.2	8 09.4	1.1	0.6	7.1	4.1	13.1	7.5
12	8 33.0	8 34.4	8 09.6	1.2	0.7	7.2	4.1	13.2	7.6
13	8 33.3	8 34.7	8 09.9	1.3	0.7	7.3	4.2	13.3	7.6
14	8 33.5	8 34.9	8 10.1	1.4	0.8	7.4	4.3	13.4	7.7
15	8 33.8	8 35.2	8 10.3	1.5	0.9	7.5	4.3	13.5	7.8
16	8 34.0	8 35.4	8 10.6	1.6	0.9	7.6	4.4	13.6	7.8
17	8 34.3	8 35.7	8 10.8	1.7	1.0	7.7	4.4	13.7	7.9
18	8 34.5	8 35.9	8 11.1	1.8	1.0	7.8	4.5	13.8	7.9
19	8 34.8	8 36.2	8 11.3	1.9	1.1	7.9	4.5	13.9	8.0
20	8 35.0	8 36.4	8 11.5	2.0	1.2	8.0	4.6	14.0	8.1
21	8 35.3	8 36.7	8 11.8	2.1	1.2	8.1	4.7	14.1	8.1
22	8 35.5	8 36.9	8 12.0	2.2	1.3	8.2	4.7	14.2	8.2
23	8 35.8	8 37.2	8 12.3	2.3	1.3	8.3	4.8	14.3	8.2
24	8 36.0	8 37.4	8 12.5	2.4	1.4	8.4	4.8	14.4	8.3
25	8 36.3	8 37.7	8 12.7	2.5	1.4	8.5	4.9	14.5	8.3
26	8 36.5	8 37.9	8 13.0	2.6	1.5	8.6	4.9	14.6	8.4
27	8 36.8	8 38.2	8 13.2	2.7	1.6	8.7	5.0	14.7	8.5
28	8 37.0	8 38.4	8 13.4	2.8	1.6	8.8	5.1	14.8	8.5
29	8 37.3	8 38.7	8 13.7	2.9	1.7	8.9	5.1	14.9	8.6
30	8 37.5	8 38.9	8 13.9	3.0	1.7	9.0	5.2	15.0	8.6
31	8 37.8	8 39.2	8 14.2	3.1	1.8	9.1	5.2	15.1	8.7
32	8 38.0	8 39.4	8 14.4	3.2	1.8	9.2	5.3	15.2	8.7
33	8 38.3	8 39.7	8 14.6	3.3	1.9	9.3	5.3	15.3	8.8
34	8 38.5	8 39.9	8 14.9	3.4	2.0	9.4	5.4	15.4	8.9
35	8 38.8	8 40.2	8 15.1	3.5	2.0	9.5	5.5	15.5	8.9
36	8 39.0	8 40.4	8 15.4	3.6	2.1	9.6	5.5	15.6	9.0
37	8 39.3	8 40.7	8 15.6	3.7	2.1	9.7	5.6	15.7	9.0
38	8 39.5	8 40.9	8 15.8	3.8	2.2	9.8	5.6	15.8	9.1
39	8 39.8	8 41.2	8 16.1	3.9	2.2	9.9	5.7	15.9	9.1
40	8 40.0	8 41.4	8 16.3	4.0	2.3	10.0	5.8	16.0	9.2
41	8 40.3	8 41.7	8 16.5	4.1	2.4	10.1	5.8	16.1	9.3
42	8 40.5	8 41.9	8 16.8	4.2	2.4	10.2	5.9	16.2	9.3
43	8 40.8	8 42.2	8 17.0	4.3	2.5	10.3	5.9	16.3	9.4
44	8 41.0	8 42.4	8 17.3	4.4	2.5	10.4	6.0	16.4	9.4
45	8 41.3	8 42.7	8 17.5	4.5	2.6	10.5	6.0	16.5	9.5
46	8 41.5	8 42.9	8 17.7	4.6	2.6	10.6	6.1	16.6	9.5
47	8 41.8	8 43.2	8 18.0	4.7	2.7	10.7	6.2	16.7	9.6
48	8 42.0	8 43.4	8 18.2	4.8	2.8	10.8	6.2	16.8	9.7
49	8 42.3	8 43.7	8 18.5	4.9	2.8	10.9	6.3	16.9	9.7
50	8 42.5	8 43.9	8 18.7	5.0	2.9	11.0	6.3	17.0	9.8
51	8 42.8	8 44.2	8 18.9	5.1	2.9	11.1	6.4	17.1	9.8
52	8 43.0	8 44.4	8 19.2	5.2	3.0	11.2	6.4	17.2	9.9
53	8 43.3	8 44.7	8 19.4	5.3	3.0	11.3	6.5	17.3	9.9
54	8 43.5	8 44.9	8 19.7	5.4	3.1	11.4	6.6	17.4	10.0
55	8 43.8	8 45.2	8 19.9	5.5	3.2	11.5	6.6	17.5	10.1
56	8 44.0	8 45.4	8 20.1	5.6	3.2	11.6	6.7	17.6	10.1
57	8 44.3	8 45.7	8 20.4	5.7	3.3	11.7	6.7	17.7	10.2
58	8 44.5	8 45.9	8 20.6	5.8	3.3	11.8	6.8	17.8	10.2
59	8 44.8	8 46.2	8 20.8	5.9	3.4	11.9	6.8	17.9	10.3
60	8 45.0	8 46.4	8 21.1	6.0	3.5	12.0	6.9	18.0	10.4

35^m

m 35 s	SUN PLANETS	ARIES	MOON	v or d	Corrⁿ	v or d	Corrⁿ	v or d	Corrⁿ
00	8 45.0	8 46.4	8 21.1	0.0	0.0	6.0	3.6	12.0	7.1
01	8 45.3	8 46.7	8 21.3	0.1	0.1	6.1	3.6	12.1	7.2
02	8 45.5	8 46.9	8 21.6	0.2	0.1	6.2	3.7	12.2	7.2
03	8 45.8	8 47.2	8 21.8	0.3	0.2	6.3	3.7	12.3	7.3
04	8 46.0	8 47.4	8 22.0	0.4	0.2	6.4	3.8	12.4	7.3
05	8 46.3	8 47.7	8 22.3	0.5	0.3	6.5	3.8	12.5	7.4
06	8 46.5	8 47.9	8 22.5	0.6	0.4	6.6	3.9	12.6	7.5
07	8 46.8	8 48.2	8 22.8	0.7	0.4	6.7	4.0	12.7	7.5
08	8 47.0	8 48.4	8 23.0	0.8	0.5	6.8	4.0	12.8	7.6
09	8 47.3	8 48.7	8 23.2	0.9	0.5	6.9	4.1	12.9	7.6
10	8 47.5	8 48.9	8 23.5	1.0	0.6	7.0	4.1	13.0	7.7
11	8 47.8	8 49.2	8 23.7	1.1	0.7	7.1	4.2	13.1	7.8
12	8 48.0	8 49.4	8 23.9	1.2	0.7	7.2	4.3	13.2	7.8
13	8 48.3	8 49.7	8 24.2	1.3	0.8	7.3	4.3	13.3	7.9
14	8 48.5	8 49.9	8 24.4	1.4	0.8	7.4	4.4	13.4	7.9
15	8 48.8	8 50.2	8 24.7	1.5	0.9	7.5	4.4	13.5	8.0
16	8 49.0	8 50.4	8 24.9	1.6	0.9	7.6	4.5	13.6	8.0
17	8 49.3	8 50.7	8 25.1	1.7	1.0	7.7	4.6	13.7	8.1
18	8 49.5	8 50.9	8 25.4	1.8	1.1	7.8	4.6	13.8	8.2
19	8 49.8	8 51.2	8 25.6	1.9	1.1	7.9	4.7	13.9	8.2
20	8 50.0	8 51.5	8 25.9	2.0	1.2	8.0	4.7	14.0	8.3
21	8 50.3	8 51.7	8 26.1	2.1	1.2	8.1	4.8	14.1	8.3
22	8 50.5	8 52.0	8 26.3	2.2	1.3	8.2	4.9	14.2	8.4
23	8 50.8	8 52.2	8 26.6	2.3	1.4	8.3	4.9	14.3	8.5
24	8 51.0	8 52.5	8 26.8	2.4	1.4	8.4	5.0	14.4	8.5
25	8 51.3	8 52.7	8 27.0	2.5	1.5	8.5	5.0	14.5	8.6
26	8 51.5	8 53.0	8 27.3	2.6	1.5	8.6	5.1	14.6	8.6
27	8 51.8	8 53.2	8 27.5	2.7	1.6	8.7	5.1	14.7	8.7
28	8 52.0	8 53.5	8 27.8	2.8	1.7	8.8	5.2	14.8	8.8
29	8 52.3	8 53.7	8 28.0	2.9	1.7	8.9	5.3	14.9	8.8
30	8 52.5	8 54.0	8 28.2	3.0	1.8	9.0	5.3	15.0	8.9
31	8 52.8	8 54.2	8 28.5	3.1	1.8	9.1	5.4	15.1	8.9
32	8 53.0	8 54.5	8 28.7	3.2	1.9	9.2	5.4	15.2	9.0
33	8 53.3	8 54.7	8 29.0	3.3	2.0	9.3	5.5	15.3	9.1
34	8 53.5	8 55.0	8 29.2	3.4	2.0	9.4	5.6	15.4	9.1
35	8 53.8	8 55.2	8 29.4	3.5	2.1	9.5	5.6	15.5	9.2
36	8 54.0	8 55.5	8 29.7	3.6	2.1	9.6	5.7	15.6	9.2
37	8 54.3	8 55.7	8 29.9	3.7	2.2	9.7	5.7	15.7	9.3
38	8 54.5	8 56.0	8 30.2	3.8	2.2	9.8	5.8	15.8	9.3
39	8 54.8	8 56.2	8 30.4	3.9	2.3	9.9	5.9	15.9	9.4
40	8 55.0	8 56.5	8 30.6	4.0	2.4	10.0	5.9	16.0	9.5
41	8 55.3	8 56.7	8 30.9	4.1	2.4	10.1	6.0	16.1	9.5
42	8 55.5	8 57.0	8 31.1	4.2	2.5	10.2	6.0	16.2	9.6
43	8 55.8	8 57.2	8 31.3	4.3	2.5	10.3	6.1	16.3	9.6
44	8 56.0	8 57.5	8 31.6	4.4	2.6	10.4	6.2	16.4	9.7
45	8 56.3	8 57.7	8 31.8	4.5	2.7	10.5	6.2	16.5	9.8
46	8 56.5	8 58.0	8 32.1	4.6	2.7	10.6	6.3	16.6	9.8
47	8 56.8	8 58.2	8 32.3	4.7	2.8	10.7	6.3	16.7	9.9
48	8 57.0	8 58.5	8 32.5	4.8	2.8	10.8	6.4	16.8	9.9
49	8 57.3	8 58.7	8 32.8	4.9	2.9	10.9	6.4	16.9	10.0
50	8 57.5	8 59.0	8 33.0	5.0	3.0	11.0	6.5	17.0	10.1
51	8 57.8	8 59.2	8 33.3	5.1	3.0	11.1	6.6	17.1	10.1
52	8 58.0	8 59.5	8 33.5	5.2	3.1	11.2	6.6	17.2	10.2
53	8 58.3	8 59.7	8 33.7	5.3	3.1	11.3	6.7	17.3	10.2
54	8 58.5	9 00.0	8 34.0	5.4	3.2	11.4	6.7	17.4	10.3
55	8 58.8	9 00.2	8 34.2	5.5	3.3	11.5	6.8	17.5	10.4
56	8 59.0	9 00.5	8 34.4	5.6	3.3	11.6	6.9	17.6	10.4
57	8 59.3	9 00.7	8 34.7	5.7	3.4	11.7	6.9	17.7	10.5
58	8 59.5	9 01.0	8 34.9	5.8	3.4	11.8	7.0	17.8	10.5
59	8 59.8	9 01.2	8 35.2	5.9	3.5	11.9	7.0	17.9	10.6
60	9 00.0	9 01.5	8 35.4	6.0	3.6	12.0	7.1	18.0	10.7

36	SUN PLANETS	ARIES	MOON	v or d Corrⁿ		v or d Corrⁿ		v or d Corrⁿ	
s	° ′	° ′	° ′	′	′	′	′	′	′
00	9 00·0	9 01·5	8 35·4	0·0	0·0	6·0	3·7	12·0	7·3
01	9 00·3	9 01·7	8 35·6	0·1	0·1	6·1	3·7	12·1	7·4
02	9 00·5	9 02·0	8 35·9	0·2	0·1	6·2	3·8	12·2	7·4
03	9 00·8	9 02·2	8 36·1	0·3	0·2	6·3	3·8	12·3	7·5
04	9 01·0	9 02·5	8 36·4	0·4	0·2	6·4	3·9	12·4	7·5
05	9 01·3	9 02·7	8 36·6	0·5	0·3	6·5	4·0	12·5	7·6
06	9 01·5	9 03·0	8 36·8	0·6	0·4	6·6	4·0	12·6	7·7
07	9 01·8	9 03·2	8 37·1	0·7	0·4	6·7	4·1	12·7	7·7
08	9 02·0	9 03·5	8 37·3	0·8	0·5	6·8	4·1	12·8	7·8
09	9 02·3	9 03·7	8 37·5	0·9	0·5	6·9	4·2	12·9	7·8
10	9 02·5	9 04·0	8 37·8	1·0	0·6	7·0	4·3	13·0	7·9
11	9 02·8	9 04·2	8 38·0	1·1	0·7	7·1	4·3	13·1	8·0
12	9 03·0	9 04·5	8 38·3	1·2	0·7	7·2	4·4	13·2	8·0
13	9 03·3	9 04·7	8 38·5	1·3	0·8	7·3	4·4	13·3	8·1
14	9 03·5	9 05·0	8 38·7	1·4	0·9	7·4	4·5	13·4	8·2
15	9 03·8	9 05·2	8 39·0	1·5	0·9	7·5	4·6	13·5	8·2
16	9 04·0	9 05·5	8 39·2	1·6	1·0	7·6	4·6	13·6	8·3
17	9 04·3	9 05·7	8 39·5	1·7	1·0	7·7	4·7	13·7	8·3
18	9 04·5	9 06·0	8 39·7	1·8	1·1	7·8	4·7	13·8	8·4
19	9 04·8	9 06·2	8 39·9	1·9	1·2	7·9	4·8	13·9	8·5
20	9 05·0	9 06·5	8 40·2	2·0	1·2	8·0	4·9	14·0	8·5
21	9 05·3	9 06·7	8 40·4	2·1	1·3	8·1	4·9	14·1	8·6
22	9 05·5	9 07·0	8 40·6	2·2	1·3	8·2	5·0	14·2	8·6
23	9 05·8	9 07·2	8 40·9	2·3	1·4	8·3	5·0	14·3	8·7
24	9 06·0	9 07·5	8 41·1	2·4	1·5	8·4	5·1	14·4	8·8
25	9 06·3	9 07·7	8 41·4	2·5	1·5	8·5	5·2	14·5	8·8
26	9 06·5	9 08·0	8 41·6	2·6	1·6	8·6	5·2	14·6	8·9
27	9 06·8	9 08·2	8 41·8	2·7	1·6	8·7	5·3	14·7	9·2
28	9 07·0	9 08·5	8 42·1	2·8	1·7	8·8	5·4	14·8	9·0
29	9 07·3	9 08·7	8 42·3	2·9	1·8	8·9	5·4	14·9	9·1
30	9 07·5	9 09·0	8 42·6	3·0	1·8	9·0	5·5	15·0	9·1
31	9 07·8	9 09·2	8 42·8	3·1	1·9	9·1	5·5	15·1	9·2
32	9 08·0	9 09·5	8 43·0	3·2	1·9	9·2	5·6	15·2	9·2
33	9 08·3	9 09·8	8 43·3	3·3	2·0	9·3	5·7	15·3	9·3
34	9 08·5	9 10·0	8 43·5	3·4	2·1	9·4	5·7	15·4	9·4
35	9 08·8	9 10·3	8 43·8	3·5	2·1	9·5	5·8	15·5	9·4
36	9 09·0	9 10·5	8 44·0	3·6	2·2	9·6	5·8	15·6	9·5
37	9 09·3	9 10·8	8 44·2	3·7	2·3	9·7	5·9	15·7	9·6
38	9 09·5	9 11·0	8 44·5	3·8	2·3	9·8	6·0	15·8	9·6
39	9 09·8	9 11·3	8 44·7	3·9	2·4	9·9	6·0	15·9	9·7
40	9 10·0	9 11·5	8 44·9	4·0	2·4	10·0	6·1	16·0	9·7
41	9 10·3	9 11·8	8 45·2	4·1	2·5	10·1	6·1	16·1	9·8
42	9 10·5	9 12·0	8 45·4	4·2	2·6	10·2	6·2	16·2	9·9
43	9 10·8	9 12·3	8 45·7	4·3	2·6	10·3	6·3	16·3	9·9
44	9 11·0	9 12·5	8 45·9	4·4	2·7	10·4	6·3	16·4	10·0
45	9 11·3	9 12·8	8 46·1	4·5	2·7	10·5	6·4	16·5	10·0
46	9 11·5	9 13·0	8 46·4	4·6	2·8	10·6	6·4	16·6	10·1
47	9 11·8	9 13·3	8 46·6	4·7	2·9	10·7	6·5	16·7	10·2
48	9 12·0	9 13·5	8 46·9	4·8	3·0	10·8	6·6	16·8	10·2
49	9 12·3	9 13·8	8 47·1	4·9	3·0	10·9	6·6	16·9	10·3
50	9 12·5	9 14·0	8 47·3	5·0	3·0	11·0	6·7	17·0	10·3
51	9 12·8	9 14·3	8 47·6	5·1	3·1	11·1	6·8	17·1	10·4
52	9 13·0	9 14·5	8 47·8	5·2	3·2	11·2	6·8	17·2	10·5
53	9 13·3	9 14·8	8 48·0	5·3	3·2	11·3	6·9	17·3	10·5
54	9 13·5	9 15·0	8 48·3	5·4	3·3	11·4	6·9	17·4	10·6
55	9 13·8	9 15·3	8 48·5	5·5	3·3	11·5	7·0	17·5	10·6
56	9 14·0	9 15·5	8 48·8	5·6	3·4	11·6	7·1	17·6	10·7
57	9 14·3	9 15·8	8 49·0	5·7	3·5	11·7	7·1	17·7	10·8
58	9 14·5	9 16·0	8 49·2	5·8	3·5	11·8	7·2	17·8	10·8
59	9 14·8	9 16·3	8 49·5	5·9	3·6	11·9	7·2	17·9	10·9
60	9 15·0	9 16·5	8 49·7	6·0	3·7	12·0	7·3	18·0	11·0

37	SUN PLANETS	ARIES	MOON	v or d Corrⁿ		v or d Corrⁿ		v or d Corrⁿ	
s	° ′	° ′	° ′	′	′	′	′	′	′
00	9 15·0	9 16·5	8 49·7	0·0	0·0	6·0	3·8	12·0	7·5
01	9 15·3	9 16·8	8 50·0	0·1	0·1	6·1	3·8	12·1	7·6
02	9 15·5	9 17·0	8 50·2	0·2	0·1	6·2	3·9	12·2	7·7
03	9 15·8	9 17·3	8 50·4	0·3	0·2	6·3	3·9	12·3	7·7
04	9 16·0	9 17·5	8 50·7	0·4	0·3	6·4	4·0	12·4	7·8
05	9 16·3	9 17·8	8 50·9	0·5	0·3	6·5	4·1	12·5	7·8
06	9 16·5	9 18·0	8 51·1	0·6	0·4	6·6	4·1	12·6	7·9
07	9 16·8	9 18·3	8 51·4	0·7	0·4	6·7	4·2	12·7	7·9
08	9 17·0	9 18·5	8 51·6	0·8	0·5	6·8	4·3	12·8	8·0
09	9 17·3	9 18·8	8 51·9	0·9	0·6	6·9	4·3	12·9	8·1
10	9 17·5	9 19·0	8 52·1	1·0	0·6	7·0	4·4	13·0	8·1
11	9 17·8	9 19·3	8 52·3	1·1	0·7	7·1	4·4	13·1	8·2
12	9 18·0	9 19·5	8 52·6	1·2	0·8	7·2	4·5	13·2	8·3
13	9 18·3	9 19·8	8 52·8	1·3	0·8	7·3	4·6	13·3	8·3
14	9 18·5	9 20·0	8 53·1	1·4	0·9	7·4	4·6	13·4	8·4
15	9 18·8	9 20·3	8 53·3	1·5	0·9	7·5	4·7	13·5	8·4
16	9 19·0	9 20·5	8 53·5	1·6	1·0	7·6	4·8	13·6	8·5
17	9 19·3	9 20·8	8 53·8	1·7	1·1	7·7	4·8	13·7	8·6
18	9 19·5	9 21·0	8 54·0	1·8	1·1	7·8	4·9	13·8	8·6
19	9 19·8	9 21·3	8 54·3	1·9	1·2	7·9	4·9	13·9	8·7
20	9 20·0	9 21·5	8 54·5	2·0	1·3	8·0	5·0	14·0	8·8
21	9 20·3	9 21·8	8 54·7	2·1	1·3	8·1	5·1	14·1	8·8
22	9 20·5	9 22·0	8 55·0	2·2	1·4	8·2	5·1	14·2	8·9
23	9 20·8	9 22·3	8 55·2	2·3	1·4	8·3	5·2	14·3	8·9
24	9 21·0	9 22·5	8 55·4	2·4	1·5	8·4	5·3	14·4	9·0
25	9 21·3	9 22·8	8 55·7	2·5	1·6	8·5	5·3	14·5	9·1
26	9 21·5	9 23·0	8 55·9	2·6	1·6	8·6	5·4	14·6	9·1
27	9 21·8	9 23·3	8 56·2	2·7	1·7	8·7	5·4	14·7	9·2
28	9 22·0	9 23·5	8 56·4	2·8	1·8	8·8	5·5	14·8	9·3
29	9 22·3	9 23·8	8 56·6	2·9	1·8	8·9	5·6	14·9	9·3
30	9 22·5	9 24·0	8 56·9	3·0	1·9	9·0	5·6	15·0	9·4
31	9 22·8	9 24·3	8 57·1	3·1	1·9	9·1	5·7	15·1	9·4
32	9 23·0	9 24·5	8 57·4	3·2	2·0	9·2	5·8	15·2	9·5
33	9 23·3	9 24·8	8 57·6	3·3	2·1	9·3	5·8	15·3	9·6
34	9 23·5	9 25·0	8 57·8	3·4	2·1	9·4	5·9	15·4	9·6
35	9 23·8	9 25·3	8 58·1	3·5	2·2	9·5	5·9	15·5	9·7
36	9 24·0	9 25·5	8 58·3	3·6	2·3	9·6	6·0	15·6	9·8
37	9 24·3	9 25·8	8 58·5	3·7	2·3	9·7	6·1	15·7	9·8
38	9 24·5	9 26·0	8 58·8	3·8	2·4	9·8	6·1	15·8	9·9
39	9 24·8	9 26·3	8 59·0	3·9	2·4	9·9	6·2	15·9	9·9
40	9 25·0	9 26·5	8 59·3	4·0	2·5	10·0	6·3	16·0	10·0
41	9 25·3	9 26·8	8 59·5	4·1	2·6	10·1	6·3	16·1	10·1
42	9 25·5	9 27·0	8 59·7	4·2	2·6	10·2	6·4	16·2	10·1
43	9 25·8	9 27·3	9 00·0	4·3	2·7	10·3	6·4	16·3	10·2
44	9 26·0	9 27·5	9 00·2	4·4	2·8	10·4	6·5	16·4	10·3
45	9 26·3	9 27·8	9 00·5	4·5	2·8	10·5	6·6	16·5	10·3
46	9 26·5	9 28·1	9 00·7	4·6	2·9	10·6	6·6	16·6	10·4
47	9 26·8	9 28·3	9 00·9	4·7	2·9	10·7	6·7	16·7	10·4
48	9 27·0	9 28·6	9 01·2	4·8	3·0	10·8	6·8	16·8	10·5
49	9 27·3	9 28·8	9 01·4	4·9	3·1	10·9	6·8	16·9	10·6
50	9 27·5	9 29·1	9 01·6	5·0	3·1	11·0	6·9	17·0	10·6
51	9 27·8	9 29·3	9 01·9	5·1	3·2	11·1	6·9	17·1	10·7
52	9 28·0	9 29·6	9 02·1	5·2	3·3	11·2	7·0	17·2	10·8
53	9 28·3	9 29·8	9 02·4	5·3	3·3	11·3	7·1	17·3	10·8
54	9 28·5	9 30·1	9 02·6	5·4	3·4	11·4	7·1	17·4	10·9
55	9 28·8	9 30·3	9 02·8	5·5	3·4	11·5	7·2	17·5	10·9
56	9 29·0	9 30·6	9 03·1	5·6	3·5	11·6	7·3	17·6	11·0
57	9 29·3	9 30·8	9 03·3	5·7	3·5	11·7	7·3	17·7	11·1
58	9 29·5	9 31·1	9 03·6	5·8	3·6	11·8	7·4	17·8	11·1
59	9 29·8	9 31·3	9 03·8	5·9	3·7	11·9	7·4	17·9	11·2
60	9 30·0	9 31·6	9 04·0	6·0	3·8	12·0	7·5	18·0	11·3

38ᵐ

38	SUN PLANETS	ARIES	MOON	v or Corrⁿ d		v or Corrⁿ d		v or Corrⁿ d	
s	° ′	° ′	° ′	′	′	′	′	′	′
00	9 30·0	9 31·6	9 04·0	0·0	0·0	6·0	3·9	12·0	7·7
01	9 30·3	9 31·8	9 04·3	0·1	0·1	6·1	3·9	12·1	7·8
02	9 30·5	9 32·1	9 04·5	0·2	0·1	6·2	4·0	12·2	7·8
03	9 30·8	9 32·3	9 04·7	0·3	0·2	6·3	4·0	12·3	7·9
04	9 31·0	9 32·6	9 05·0	0·4	0·3	6·4	4·1	12·4	8·0
05	9 31·3	9 32·8	9 05·2	0·5	0·3	6·5	4·2	12·5	8·0
06	9 31·5	9 33·1	9 05·5	0·6	0·4	6·6	4·2	12·6	8·1
07	9 31·8	9 33·3	9 05·7	0·7	0·4	6·7	4·3	12·7	8·1
08	9 32·0	9 33·6	9 05·9	0·8	0·5	6·8	4·4	12·8	8·2
09	9 32·3	9 33·8	9 06·2	0·9	0·6	6·9	4·4	12·9	8·3
10	9 32·5	9 34·1	9 06·4	1·0	0·6	7·0	4·5	13·0	8·3
11	9 32·8	9 34·3	9 06·7	1·1	0·7	7·1	4·6	13·1	8·4
12	9 33·0	9 34·6	9 06·9	1·2	0·8	7·2	4·6	13·2	8·5
13	9 33·3	9 34·8	9 07·1	1·3	0·8	7·3	4·7	13·3	8·5
14	9 33·5	9 35·1	9 07·4	1·4	0·9	7·4	4·7	13·4	8·6
15	9 33·8	9 35·3	9 07·6	1·5	1·0	7·5	4·8	13·5	8·7
16	9 34·0	9 35·6	9 07·9	1·6	1·0	7·6	4·9	13·6	8·7
17	9 34·3	9 35·8	9 08·1	1·7	1·1	7·7	4·9	13·7	8·8
18	9 34·5	9 36·1	9 08·3	1·8	1·2	7·8	5·0	13·8	8·9
19	9 34·8	9 36·3	9 08·6	1·9	1·2	7·9	5·1	13·9	8·9
20	9 35·0	9 36·6	9 08·8	2·0	1·3	8·0	5·1	14·0	9·0
21	9 35·3	9 36·8	9 09·0	2·1	1·3	8·1	5·2	14·1	9·0
22	9 35·5	9 37·1	9 09·3	2·2	1·4	8·2	5·3	14·2	9·1
23	9 35·8	9 37·3	9 09·5	2·3	1·5	8·3	5·3	14·3	9·2
24	9 36·0	9 37·6	9 09·8	2·4	1·5	8·4	5·4	14·4	9·2
25	9 36·3	9 37·8	9 10·0	2·5	1·6	8·5	5·5	14·5	9·3
26	9 36·5	9 38·1	9 10·2	2·6	1·7	8·6	5·5	14·6	9·4
27	9 36·8	9 38·3	9 10·5	2·7	1·7	8·7	5·6	14·7	9·4
28	9 37·0	9 38·6	9 10·7	2·8	1·8	8·8	5·6	14·8	9·5
29	9 37·3	9 38·8	9 11·0	2·9	1·9	8·9	5·7	14·9	9·6
30	9 37·5	9 39·1	9 11·2	3·0	1·9	9·0	5·8	15·0	9·6
31	9 37·8	9 39·3	9 11·4	3·1	2·0	9·1	5·8	15·1	9·7
32	9 38·0	9 39·6	9 11·7	3·2	2·1	9·2	5·9	15·2	9·8
33	9 38·3	9 39·8	9 11·9	3·3	2·1	9·3	6·0	15·3	9·8
34	9 38·5	9 40·1	9 12·1	3·4	2·2	9·4	6·0	15·4	9·9
35	9 38·8	9 40·3	9 12·4	3·5	2·2	9·5	6·1	15·5	9·9
36	9 39·0	9 40·6	9 12·6	3·6	2·3	9·6	6·2	15·6	10·0
37	9 39·3	9 40·8	9 12·9	3·7	2·4	9·7	6·2	15·7	10·1
38	9 39·5	9 41·1	9 13·1	3·8	2·4	9·8	6·3	15·8	10·1
39	9 39·8	9 41·3	9 13·3	3·9	2·5	9·9	6·4	15·9	10·2
40	9 40·0	9 41·6	9 13·6	4·0	2·6	10·0	6·4	16·0	10·3
41	9 40·3	9 41·8	9 13·8	4·1	2·6	10·1	6·5	16·1	10·3
42	9 40·5	9 42·1	9 14·1	4·2	2·7	10·2	6·5	16·2	10·4
43	9 40·8	9 42·3	9 14·3	4·3	2·8	10·3	6·6	16·3	10·5
44	9 41·0	9 42·6	9 14·5	4·4	2·8	10·4	6·7	16·4	10·5
45	9 41·3	9 42·8	9 14·8	4·5	2·9	10·5	6·7	16·5	10·6
46	9 41·5	9 43·1	9 15·0	4·6	3·0	10·6	6·8	16·6	10·7
47	9 41·8	9 43·3	9 15·2	4·7	3·0	10·7	6·9	16·7	11·0
48	9 42·0	9 43·6	9 15·5	4·8	3·1	10·8	6·9	16·8	10·8
49	9 42·3	9 43·8	9 15·7	4·9	3·1	10·9	7·0	16·9	10·8
50	9 42·5	9 44·1	9 16·0	5·0	3·2	11·0	7·1	17·0	10·9
51	9 42·8	9 44·3	9 16·2	5·1	3·3	11·1	7·1	17·1	11·0
52	9 43·0	9 44·6	9 16·4	5·2	3·3	11·2	7·2	17·2	11·0
53	9 43·3	9 44·8	9 16·7	5·3	3·4	11·3	7·3	17·3	11·1
54	9 43·5	9 45·1	9 16·9	5·4	3·5	11·4	7·3	17·4	11·2
55	9 43·8	9 45·3	9 17·2	5·5	3·5	11·5	7·4	17·5	11·2
56	9 44·0	9 45·6	9 17·4	5·6	3·6	11·6	7·4	17·6	11·3
57	9 44·3	9 45·8	9 17·6	5·7	3·7	11·7	7·5	17·7	11·4
58	9 44·5	9 46·1	9 17·9	5·8	3·7	11·8	7·6	17·8	11·4
59	9 44·8	9 46·4	9 18·1	5·9	3·8	11·9	7·6	17·9	11·5
60	9 45·0	9 46·6	9 18·4	6·0	3·9	12·0	7·7	18·0	11·6

39ᵐ

39	SUN PLANETS	ARIES	MOON	v or Corrⁿ d		v or Corrⁿ d		v or Corrⁿ d	
s	° ′	° ′	° ′	′	′	′	′	′	′
00	9 45·0	9 46·6	9 18·4	0·0	0·0	6·0	4·0	12·0	7·9
01	9 45·3	9 46·9	9 18·6	0·1	0·1	6·1	4·0	12·1	8·0
02	9 45·5	9 47·1	9 18·8	0·2	0·1	6·2	4·1	12·2	8·0
03	9 45·8	9 47·4	9 19·1	0·3	0·2	6·3	4·1	12·3	8·1
04	9 46·0	9 47·6	9 19·3	0·4	0·3	6·4	4·2	12·4	8·2
05	9 46·3	9 47·9	9 19·5	0·5	0·3	6·5	4·3	12·5	8·2
06	9 46·5	9 48·1	9 19·8	0·6	0·4	6·6	4·3	12·6	8·3
07	9 46·8	9 48·4	9 20·0	0·7	0·5	6·7	4·4	12·7	8·4
08	9 47·0	9 48·6	9 20·3	0·8	0·5	6·8	4·5	12·8	8·4
09	9 47·3	9 48·9	9 20·5	0·9	0·6	6·9	4·5	12·9	8·5
10	9 47·5	9 49·1	9 20·7	1·0	0·7	7·0	4·6	13·0	8·6
11	9 47·8	9 49·4	9 21·0	1·1	0·7	7·1	4·7	13·1	8·6
12	9 48·0	9 49·6	9 21·2	1·2	0·8	7·2	4·7	13·2	8·7
13	9 48·3	9 49·9	9 21·5	1·3	0·9	7·3	4·8	13·3	8·8
14	9 48·5	9 50·1	9 21·7	1·4	0·9	7·4	4·9	13·4	8·8
15	9 48·8	9 50·4	9 21·9	1·5	1·0	7·5	4·9	13·5	8·9
16	9 49·0	9 50·6	9 22·2	1·6	1·1	7·6	5·0	13·6	9·0
17	9 49·3	9 50·9	9 22·4	1·7	1·1	7·7	5·1	13·7	9·0
18	9 49·5	9 51·1	9 22·6	1·8	1·2	7·8	5·1	13·8	9·1
19	9 49·8	9 51·4	9 22·9	1·9	1·3	7·9	5·2	13·9	9·2
20	9 50·0	9 51·6	9 23·1	2·0	1·3	8·0	5·3	14·0	9·2
21	9 50·3	9 51·9	9 23·4	2·1	1·4	8·1	5·3	14·1	9·3
22	9 50·5	9 52·1	9 23·6	2·2	1·4	8·2	5·4	14·2	9·3
23	9 50·8	9 52·4	9 23·8	2·3	1·5	8·3	5·5	14·3	9·4
24	9 51·0	9 52·6	9 24·1	2·4	1·6	8·4	5·5	14·4	9·5
25	9 51·3	9 52·9	9 24·3	2·5	1·6	8·5	5·6	14·5	9·5
26	9 51·5	9 53·1	9 24·6	2·6	1·7	8·6	5·7	14·6	9·6
27	9 51·8	9 53·4	9 24·8	2·7	1·8	8·7	5·7	14·7	9·7
28	9 52·0	9 53·6	9 25·0	2·8	1·8	8·8	5·8	14·8	9·7
29	9 52·3	9 53·9	9 25·3	2·9	1·9	8·9	5·9	14·9	9·8
30	9 52·5	9 54·1	9 25·5	3·0	2·0	9·0	5·9	15·0	9·9
31	9 52·8	9 54·4	9 25·7	3·1	2·0	9·1	6·0	15·1	9·9
32	9 53·0	9 54·6	9 26·0	3·2	2·1	9·2	6·1	15·2	10·0
33	9 53·3	9 54·9	9 26·2	3·3	2·2	9·3	6·1	15·3	10·1
34	9 53·5	9 55·1	9 26·5	3·4	2·2	9·4	6·2	15·4	10·1
35	9 53·8	9 55·4	9 26·7	3·5	2·3	9·5	6·3	15·5	10·2
36	9 54·0	9 55·6	9 26·9	3·6	2·4	9·6	6·3	15·6	10·3
37	9 54·3	9 55·9	9 27·2	3·7	2·4	9·7	6·4	15·7	10·3
38	9 54·5	9 56·1	9 27·4	3·8	2·5	9·8	6·5	15·8	10·4
39	9 54·8	9 56·4	9 27·7	3·9	2·6	9·9	6·5	15·9	10·5
40	9 55·0	9 56·6	9 27·9	4·0	2·6	10·0	6·6	16·0	10·5
41	9 55·3	9 56·9	9 28·1	4·1	2·7	10·1	6·6	16·1	10·6
42	9 55·5	9 57·1	9 28·4	4·2	2·8	10·2	6·7	16·2	10·7
43	9 55·8	9 57·4	9 28·6	4·3	2·8	10·3	6·8	16·3	10·7
44	9 56·0	9 57·6	9 28·8	4·4	2·9	10·4	6·8	16·4	10·8
45	9 56·3	9 57·9	9 29·1	4·5	3·0	10·5	6·9	16·5	10·9
46	9 56·5	9 58·1	9 29·3	4·6	3·0	10·6	7·0	16·6	10·9
47	9 56·8	9 58·4	9 29·6	4·7	3·1	10·7	7·0	16·7	11·0
48	9 57·0	9 58·6	9 29·8	4·8	3·2	10·8	7·1	16·8	11·1
49	9 57·3	9 58·9	9 30·0	4·9	3·2	10·9	7·2	16·9	11·1
50	9 57·5	9 59·1	9 30·3	5·0	3·3	11·0	7·2	17·0	11·2
51	9 57·8	9 59·4	9 30·5	5·1	3·4	11·1	7·3	17·1	11·3
52	9 58·0	9 59·6	9 30·8	5·2	3·4	11·2	7·4	17·2	11·3
53	9 58·3	9 59·9	9 31·0	5·3	3·5	11·3	7·4	17·3	11·4
54	9 58·5	10 00·1	9 31·2	5·4	3·6	11·4	7·5	17·4	11·5
55	9 58·8	10 00·4	9 31·5	5·5	3·6	11·5	7·6	17·5	11·5
56	9 59·0	10 00·6	9 31·7	5·6	3·7	11·6	7·6	17·6	11·6
57	9 59·3	10 00·9	9 32·0	5·7	3·8	11·7	7·7	17·7	11·7
58	9 59·5	10 01·1	9 32·2	5·8	3·8	11·8	7·8	17·8	11·7
59	9 59·8	10 01·4	9 32·4	5·9	3·9	11·9	7·8	17·9	11·8
60	10 00·0	10 01·6	9 32·7	6·0	4·0	12·0	7·9	18·0	11·9

m 40	SUN PLANETS	ARIES	MOON	v or d	Corrⁿ	v or d	Corrⁿ	v or d	Corrⁿ	m 41	SUN PLANETS	ARIES	MOON	v or d	Corrⁿ	v or d	Corrⁿ	v or d	Corrⁿ
s	° ′	° ′	° ′	′	′	′	′	′	′	s	° ′	° ′	° ′	′	′	′	′	′	′
00	10 00·0	10 01·6	9 32·7	0·0	0·0	6·0	4·1	12·0	8·1	00	10 15·0	10 16·7	9 47·0	0·0	0·0	6·0	4·2	12·0	8·3
01	10 00·3	10 01·9	9 32·9	0·1	0·1	6·1	4·1	12·1	8·2	01	10 15·3	10 16·9	9 47·2	0·1	0·1	6·1	4·2	12·1	8·4
02	10 00·5	10 02·1	9 33·1	0·2	0·1	6·2	4·2	12·2	8·2	02	10 15·5	10 17·2	9 47·5	0·2	0·1	6·2	4·3	12·2	8·4
03	10 00·8	10 02·4	9 33·4	0·3	0·2	6·3	4·3	12·3	8·3	03	10 15·8	10 17·4	9 47·7	0·3	0·2	6·3	4·4	12·3	8·5
04	10 01·0	10 02·6	9 33·6	0·4	0·3	6·4	4·3	12·4	8·4	04	10 16·0	10 17·7	9 47·9	0·4	0·3	6·4	4·4	12·4	8·6
05	10 01·3	10 02·9	9 33·9	0·5	0·3	6·5	4·4	12·5	8·4	05	10 16·3	10 17·9	9 48·2	0·5	0·3	6·5	4·5	12·5	8·6
06	10 01·5	10 03·1	9 34·1	0·6	0·4	6·6	4·5	12·6	8·5	06	10 16·5	10 18·2	9 48·4	0·6	0·4	6·6	4·6	12·6	8·7
07	10 01·8	10 03·4	9 34·3	0·7	0·5	6·7	4·5	12·7	8·6	07	10 16·8	10 18·4	9 48·7	0·7	0·5	6·7	4·6	12·7	8·8
08	10 02·0	10 03·6	9 34·6	0·8	0·5	6·8	4·6	12·8	8·6	08	10 17·0	10 18·7	9 48·9	0·8	0·6	6·8	4·7	12·8	8·9
09	10 02·3	10 03·9	9 34·8	0·9	0·6	6·9	4·7	12·9	8·7	09	10 17·3	10 18·9	9 49·1	0·9	0·6	6·9	4·8	12·9	8·9
10	10 02·5	10 04·1	9 35·1	1·0	0·7	7·0	4·7	13·0	8·8	10	10 17·5	10 19·2	9 49·4	1·0	0·7	7·0	4·8	13·0	9·0
11	10 02·8	10 04·4	9 35·3	1·1	0·7	7·1	4·8	13·1	8·8	11	10 17·8	10 19·4	9 49·6	1·1	0·8	7·1	4·9	13·1	9·1
12	10 03·0	10 04·7	9 35·5	1·2	0·8	7·2	4·9	13·2	8·9	12	10 18·0	10 19·7	9 49·8	1·2	0·8	7·2	5·0	13·2	9·1
13	10 03·3	10 04·9	9 35·8	1·3	0·9	7·3	4·9	13·3	9·0	13	10 18·3	10 19·9	9 50·1	1·3	0·9	7·3	5·0	13·3	9·2
14	10 03·5	10 05·2	9 36·0	1·4	0·9	7·4	5·0	13·4	9·0	14	10 18·5	10 20·2	9 50·3	1·4	1·0	7·4	5·1	13·4	9·3
15	10 03·8	10 05·4	9 36·2	1·5	1·0	7·5	5·1	13·5	9·1	15	10 18·8	10 20·4	9 50·6	1·5	1·0	7·5	5·2	13·5	9·3
16	10 04·0	10 05·7	9 36·5	1·6	1·1	7·6	5·1	13·6	9·2	16	10 19·0	10 20·7	9 50·8	1·6	1·1	7·6	5·3	13·6	9·4
17	10 04·3	10 05·9	9 36·7	1·7	1·1	7·7	5·2	13·7	9·2	17	10 19·3	10 20·9	9 51·0	1·7	1·2	7·7	5·3	13·7	9·5
18	10 04·5	10 06·2	9 37·0	1·8	1·2	7·8	5·3	13·8	9·3	18	10 19·5	10 21·2	9 51·3	1·8	1·2	7·8	5·4	13·8	9·5
19	10 04·8	10 06·4	9 37·2	1·9	1·3	7·9	5·3	13·9	9·4	19	10 19·8	10 21·4	9 51·5	1·9	1·3	7·9	5·5	13·9	9·6
20	10 05·0	10 06·7	9 37·4	2·0	1·4	8·0	5·4	14·0	9·5	20	10 20·0	10 21·7	9 51·8	2·0	1·4	8·0	5·5	14·0	9·7
21	10 05·3	10 06·9	9 37·7	2·1	1·4	8·1	5·5	14·1	9·5	21	10 20·3	10 21·9	9 52·0	2·1	1·5	8·1	5·6	14·1	9·8
22	10 05·5	10 07·2	9 37·9	2·2	1·5	8·2	5·5	14·2	9·6	22	10 20·5	10 22·2	9 52·2	2·2	1·5	8·2	5·7	14·2	9·8
23	10 05·8	10 07·4	9 38·2	2·3	1·6	8·3	5·6	14·3	9·7	23	10 20·8	10 22·4	9 52·5	2·3	1·6	8·3	5·7	14·3	9·9
24	10 06·0	10 07·7	9 38·4	2·4	1·6	8·4	5·7	14·4	9·7	24	10 21·0	10 22·7	9 52·7	2·4	1·7	8·4	5·8	14·4	10·0
25	10 06·3	10 07·9	9 38·6	2·5	1·7	8·5	5·7	14·5	9·8	25	10 21·3	10 23·0	9 52·9	2·5	1·7	8·5	5·9	14·5	10·0
26	10 06·5	10 08·2	9 38·9	2·6	1·8	8·6	5·8	14·6	9·9	26	10 21·5	10 23·2	9 53·2	2·6	1·8	8·6	5·9	14·6	10·1
27	10 06·8	10 08·4	9 39·1	2·7	1·8	8·7	5·9	14·7	9·9	27	10 21·8	10 23·5	9 53·4	2·7	1·9	8·7	6·0	14·7	10·2
28	10 07·0	10 08·7	9 39·3	2·8	1·9	8·8	5·9	14·8	10·0	28	10 22·0	10 23·7	9 53·7	2·8	1·9	8·8	6·1	14·8	10·2
29	10 07·3	10 08·9	9 39·6	2·9	2·0	8·9	6·0	14·9	10·1	29	10 22·3	10 24·0	9 53·9	2·9	2·0	8·9	6·2	14·9	10·3
30	10 07·5	10 09·2	9 39·8	3·0	2·0	9·0	6·1	15·0	10·1	30	10 22·5	10 24·2	9 54·1	3·0	2·1	9·0	6·2	15·0	10·4
31	10 07·8	10 09·4	9 40·1	3·1	2·1	9·1	6·1	15·1	10·2	31	10 22·8	10 24·5	9 54·4	3·1	2·1	9·1	6·3	15·1	10·4
32	10 08·0	10 09·7	9 40·3	3·2	2·2	9·2	6·2	15·2	10·3	32	10 23·0	10 24·7	9 54·6	3·2	2·2	9·2	6·4	15·2	10·5
33	10 08·3	10 09·9	9 40·5	3·3	2·2	9·3	6·3	15·3	10·3	33	10 23·3	10 25·0	9 54·9	3·3	2·3	9·3	6·4	15·3	10·6
34	10 08·5	10 10·2	9 40·8	3·4	2·3	9·4	6·3	15·4	10·4	34	10 23·5	10 25·2	9 55·1	3·4	2·4	9·4	6·5	15·4	10·7
35	10 08·8	10 10·4	9 41·0	3·5	2·4	9·5	6·4	15·5	10·5	35	10 23·8	10 25·5	9 55·3	3·5	2·4	9·5	6·6	15·5	10·7
36	10 09·0	10 10·7	9 41·3	3·6	2·4	9·6	6·5	15·6	10·5	36	10 24·0	10 25·7	9 55·6	3·6	2·5	9·6	6·6	15·6	10·8
37	10 09·3	10 10·9	9 41·5	3·7	2·5	9·7	6·5	15·7	10·6	37	10 24·3	10 26·0	9 55·8	3·7	2·6	9·7	6·7	15·7	10·9
38	10 09·5	10 11·2	9 41·7	3·8	2·6	9·8	6·6	15·8	10·7	38	10 24·5	10 26·2	9 56·1	3·8	2·6	9·8	6·8	15·8	10·9
39	10 09·8	10 11·4	9 42·0	3·9	2·6	9·9	6·7	15·9	10·7	39	10 24·8	10 26·5	9 56·3	3·9	2·7	9·9	6·8	15·9	11·0
40	10 10·0	10 11·7	9 42·2	4·0	2·7	10·0	6·8	16·0	10·8	40	10 25·0	10 26·7	9 56·5	4·0	2·8	10·0	6·9	16·0	11·1
41	10 10·3	10 11·9	9 42·4	4·1	2·8	10·1	6·8	16·1	10·9	41	10 25·3	10 27·0	9 56·8	4·1	2·8	10·1	7·0	16·1	11·1
42	10 10·5	10 12·2	9 42·7	4·2	2·8	10·2	6·9	16·2	10·9	42	10 25·5	10 27·2	9 57·0	4·2	2·9	10·2	7·1	16·2	11·2
43	10 10·8	10 12·4	9 42·9	4·3	2·9	10·3	7·0	16·3	11·0	43	10 25·8	10 27·5	9 57·2	4·3	3·0	10·3	7·1	16·3	11·3
44	10 11·0	10 12·7	9 43·2	4·4	3·0	10·4	7·0	16·4	11·1	44	10 26·0	10 27·7	9 57·5	4·4	3·0	10·4	7·2	16·4	11·3
45	10 11·3	10 12·9	9 43·4	4·5	3·0	10·5	7·1	16·5	11·1	45	10 26·3	10 28·0	9 57·7	4·5	3·1	10·5	7·3	16·5	11·4
46	10 11·5	10 13·2	9 43·6	4·6	3·1	10·6	7·2	16·6	11·2	46	10 26·5	10 28·2	9 58·0	4·6	3·2	10·6	7·3	16·6	11·5
47	10 11·8	10 13·4	9 43·9	4·7	3·2	10·7	7·2	16·7	11·3	47	10 26·8	10 28·5	9 58·2	4·7	3·3	10·7	7·4	16·7	11·6
48	10 12·0	10 13·7	9 44·1	4·8	3·2	10·8	7·3	16·8	11·3	48	10 27·0	10 28·7	9 58·4	4·8	3·3	10·8	7·5	16·8	11·6
49	10 12·3	10 13·9	9 44·4	4·9	3·3	10·9	7·4	16·9	11·4	49	10 27·3	10 29·0	9 58·7	4·9	3·4	10·9	7·5	16·9	11·7
50	10 12·5	10 14·2	9 44·6	5·0	3·4	11·0	7·4	17·0	11·5	50	10 27·5	10 29·2	9 58·9	5·0	3·5	11·0	7·6	17·0	11·8
51	10 12·8	10 14·4	9 44·8	5·1	3·4	11·1	7·5	17·1	11·5	51	10 27·8	10 29·5	9 59·2	5·1	3·5	11·1	7·7	17·1	11·8
52	10 13·0	10 14·7	9 45·1	5·2	3·5	11·2	7·6	17·2	11·6	52	10 28·0	10 29·7	9 59·4	5·2	3·6	11·2	7·7	17·2	11·9
53	10 13·3	10 14·9	9 45·3	5·3	3·6	11·3	7·6	17·3	11·7	53	10 28·3	10 30·0	9 59·6	5·3	3·7	11·3	7·8	17·3	12·0
54	10 13·5	10 15·2	9 45·6	5·4	3·6	11·4	7·7	17·4	11·7	54	10 28·5	10 30·2	9 59·9	5·4	3·7	11·4	7·9	17·4	12·0
55	10 13·8	10 15·4	9 45·8	5·5	3·7	11·5	7·8	17·5	11·8	55	10 28·8	10 30·5	10 00·1	5·5	3·8	11·5	8·0	17·5	12·1
56	10 14·0	10 15·7	9 46·0	5·6	3·8	11·6	7·8	17·6	11·9	56	10 29·0	10 30·7	10 00·3	5·6	3·9	11·6	8·0	17·6	12·2
57	10 14·3	10 15·9	9 46·3	5·7	3·8	11·7	7·9	17·7	11·9	57	10 29·3	10 31·0	10 00·6	5·7	3·9	11·7	8·1	17·7	12·2
58	10 14·5	10 16·2	9 46·5	5·8	3·9	11·8	8·0	17·8	12·0	58	10 29·5	10 31·2	10 00·8	5·8	4·0	11·8	8·2	17·8	12·3
59	10 14·8	10 16·4	9 46·7	5·9	4·0	11·9	8·0	17·9	12·1	59	10 29·8	10 31·5	10 01·1	5·9	4·1	11·9	8·2	17·9	12·4
60	10 15·0	10 16·7	9 47·0	6·0	4·1	12·0	8·1	18·0	12·2	60	10 30·0	10 31·7	10 01·3	6·0	4·2	12·0	8·3	18·0	12·5

42^m

42 s	SUN PLANETS	ARIES	MOON	v or d	Corr^n	v or d	Corr^n	v or d	Corr^n
00	10 30.0	10 31.7	10 01.3	0.0	0.0	6.0	4.3	12.0	8.5
01	10 30.3	10 32.0	10 01.5	0.1	0.1	6.1	4.3	12.1	8.6
02	10 30.5	10 32.2	10 01.8	0.2	0.1	6.2	4.4	12.2	8.6
03	10 30.8	10 32.5	10 02.0	0.3	0.2	6.3	4.5	12.3	8.7
04	10 31.0	10 32.7	10 02.3	0.4	0.3	6.4	4.5	12.4	8.8
05	10 31.3	10 33.0	10 02.5	0.5	0.4	6.5	4.6	12.5	8.9
06	10 31.5	10 33.2	10 02.7	0.6	0.4	6.6	4.7	12.6	8.9
07	10 31.8	10 33.5	10 03.0	0.7	0.5	6.7	4.7	12.7	9.0
08	10 32.0	10 33.7	10 03.2	0.8	0.6	6.8	4.8	12.8	9.1
09	10 32.3	10 34.0	10 03.4	0.9	0.6	6.9	4.9	12.9	9.1
10	10 32.5	10 34.2	10 03.7	1.0	0.7	7.0	5.0	13.0	9.2
11	10 32.8	10 34.5	10 03.9	1.1	0.8	7.1	5.0	13.1	9.3
12	10 33.0	10 34.7	10 04.2	1.2	0.9	7.2	5.1	13.2	9.4
13	10 33.3	10 35.0	10 04.4	1.3	0.9	7.3	5.2	13.3	9.4
14	10 33.5	10 35.2	10 04.6	1.4	1.0	7.4	5.2	13.4	9.5
15	10 33.8	10 35.5	10 04.9	1.5	1.1	7.5	5.3	13.5	9.6
16	10 34.0	10 35.7	10 05.1	1.6	1.1	7.6	5.4	13.6	9.6
17	10 34.3	10 36.0	10 05.4	1.7	1.2	7.7	5.5	13.7	9.7
18	10 34.5	10 36.2	10 05.6	1.8	1.3	7.8	5.5	13.8	9.8
19	10 34.8	10 36.5	10 05.8	1.9	1.3	7.9	5.6	13.9	9.8
20	10 35.0	10 36.7	10 06.1	2.0	1.4	8.0	5.7	14.0	9.9
21	10 35.3	10 37.0	10 06.3	2.1	1.5	8.1	5.7	14.1	10.0
22	10 35.5	10 37.2	10 06.5	2.2	1.6	8.2	5.8	14.2	10.1
23	10 35.8	10 37.5	10 06.8	2.3	1.6	8.3	5.9	14.3	10.1
24	10 36.0	10 37.7	10 07.0	2.4	1.7	8.4	6.0	14.4	10.2
25	10 36.3	10 38.0	10 07.3	2.5	1.8	8.5	6.0	14.5	10.3
26	10 36.5	10 38.2	10 07.5	2.6	1.8	8.6	6.1	14.6	10.3
27	10 36.8	10 38.5	10 07.7	2.7	1.9	8.7	6.2	14.7	10.4
28	10 37.0	10 38.7	10 08.0	2.8	2.0	8.8	6.2	14.8	10.5
29	10 37.3	10 39.0	10 08.2	2.9	2.1	8.9	6.3	14.9	10.6
30	10 37.5	10 39.2	10 08.5	3.0	2.1	9.0	6.4	15.0	10.6
31	10 37.8	10 39.5	10 08.7	3.1	2.2	9.1	6.4	15.1	10.7
32	10 38.0	10 39.7	10 08.9	3.2	2.3	9.2	6.5	15.2	10.8
33	10 38.3	10 40.0	10 09.2	3.3	2.3	9.3	6.6	15.3	10.8
34	10 38.5	10 40.2	10 09.4	3.4	2.4	9.4	6.7	15.4	10.9
35	10 38.8	10 40.5	10 09.7	3.5	2.5	9.5	6.7	15.5	11.0
36	10 39.0	10 40.7	10 09.9	3.6	2.6	9.6	6.8	15.6	11.1
37	10 39.3	10 41.0	10 10.1	3.7	2.6	9.7	6.9	15.7	11.1
38	10 39.5	10 41.3	10 10.4	3.8	2.7	9.8	6.9	15.8	11.2
39	10 39.8	10 41.5	10 10.6	3.9	2.8	9.9	7.0	15.9	11.3
40	10 40.0	10 41.8	10 10.8	4.0	2.8	10.0	7.1	16.0	11.3
41	10 40.3	10 42.0	10 11.1	4.1	2.9	10.1	7.2	16.1	11.4
42	10 40.5	10 42.3	10 11.3	4.2	3.0	10.2	7.2	16.2	11.5
43	10 40.8	10 42.5	10 11.6	4.3	3.0	10.3	7.3	16.3	11.5
44	10 41.0	10 42.8	10 11.8	4.4	3.1	10.4	7.4	16.4	11.6
45	10 41.3	10 43.0	10 12.0	4.5	3.2	10.5	7.4	16.5	11.7
46	10 41.5	10 43.3	10 12.3	4.6	3.3	10.6	7.5	16.6	11.8
47	10 41.8	10 43.5	10 12.5	4.7	3.3	10.7	7.6	16.7	11.8
48	10 42.0	10 43.8	10 12.8	4.8	3.4	10.8	7.7	16.8	11.9
49	10 42.3	10 44.0	10 13.0	4.9	3.5	10.9	7.7	16.9	12.0
50	10 42.5	10 44.3	10 13.2	5.0	3.5	11.0	7.8	17.0	12.0
51	10 42.8	10 44.5	10 13.5	5.1	3.6	11.1	7.9	17.1	12.1
52	10 43.0	10 44.8	10 13.7	5.2	3.7	11.2	7.9	17.2	12.2
53	10 43.3	10 45.0	10 13.9	5.3	3.8	11.3	8.0	17.3	12.3
54	10 43.5	10 45.3	10 14.2	5.4	3.8	11.4	8.1	17.4	12.3
55	10 43.8	10 45.5	10 14.4	5.5	3.9	11.5	8.1	17.5	12.4
56	10 44.0	10 45.8	10 14.7	5.6	4.0	11.6	8.2	17.6	12.5
57	10 44.3	10 46.0	10 14.9	5.7	4.0	11.7	8.3	17.7	12.5
58	10 44.5	10 46.3	10 15.1	5.8	4.1	11.8	8.4	17.8	12.6
59	10 44.8	10 46.5	10 15.4	5.9	4.2	11.9	8.4	17.9	12.7
60	10 45.0	10 46.8	10 15.6	6.0	4.3	12.0	8.5	18.0	12.8

43^m

43 s	SUN PLANETS	ARIES	MOON	v or d	Corr^n	v or d	Corr^n	v or d	Corr^n
00	10 45.0	10 46.8	10 15.6	0.0	0.0	6.0	4.4	12.0	8.7
01	10 45.3	10 47.0	10 15.9	0.1	0.1	6.1	4.4	12.1	8.8
02	10 45.5	10 47.3	10 16.1	0.2	0.1	6.2	4.5	12.2	8.8
03	10 45.8	10 47.5	10 16.3	0.3	0.2	6.3	4.6	12.3	8.9
04	10 46.0	10 47.8	10 16.6	0.4	0.3	6.4	4.6	12.4	9.0
05	10 46.3	10 48.0	10 16.8	0.5	0.4	6.5	4.7	12.5	9.1
06	10 46.5	10 48.3	10 17.0	0.6	0.4	6.6	4.8	12.6	9.1
07	10 46.8	10 48.5	10 17.3	0.7	0.5	6.7	4.9	12.7	9.2
08	10 47.0	10 48.8	10 17.5	0.8	0.6	6.8	4.9	12.8	9.3
09	10 47.3	10 49.0	10 17.8	0.9	0.7	6.9	5.0	12.9	9.4
10	10 47.5	10 49.3	10 18.0	1.0	0.7	7.0	5.1	13.0	9.4
11	10 47.8	10 49.5	10 18.2	1.1	0.8	7.1	5.1	13.1	9.5
12	10 48.0	10 49.8	10 18.5	1.2	0.9	7.2	5.2	13.2	9.6
13	10 48.3	10 50.0	10 18.7	1.3	0.9	7.3	5.3	13.3	9.6
14	10 48.5	10 50.3	10 19.0	1.4	1.0	7.4	5.4	13.4	9.7
15	10 48.8	10 50.5	10 19.2	1.5	1.1	7.5	5.4	13.5	9.8
16	10 49.0	10 50.8	10 19.4	1.6	1.2	7.6	5.5	13.6	9.9
17	10 49.3	10 51.0	10 19.7	1.7	1.2	7.7	5.6	13.7	9.9
18	10 49.5	10 51.3	10 19.9	1.8	1.3	7.8	5.7	13.8	10.0
19	10 49.8	10 51.5	10 20.2	1.9	1.4	7.9	5.7	13.9	10.1
20	10 50.0	10 51.8	10 20.4	2.0	1.5	8.0	5.8	14.0	10.2
21	10 50.3	10 52.0	10 20.6	2.1	1.5	8.1	5.9	14.1	10.2
22	10 50.5	10 52.3	10 20.9	2.2	1.6	8.2	5.9	14.2	10.3
23	10 50.8	10 52.5	10 21.1	2.3	1.7	8.3	6.0	14.3	10.4
24	10 51.0	10 52.8	10 21.3	2.4	1.7	8.4	6.1	14.4	10.4
25	10 51.3	10 53.0	10 21.6	2.5	1.8	8.5	6.2	14.5	10.5
26	10 51.5	10 53.3	10 21.8	2.6	1.9	8.6	6.2	14.6	10.6
27	10 51.8	10 53.5	10 22.1	2.7	2.0	8.7	6.3	14.7	10.7
28	10 52.0	10 53.8	10 22.3	2.8	2.0	8.8	6.4	14.8	10.7
29	10 52.3	10 54.0	10 22.5	2.9	2.1	8.9	6.5	14.9	10.8
30	10 52.5	10 54.3	10 22.8	3.0	2.2	9.0	6.5	15.0	10.9
31	10 52.8	10 54.5	10 23.0	3.1	2.2	9.1	6.6	15.1	10.9
32	10 53.0	10 54.8	10 23.3	3.2	2.3	9.2	6.7	15.2	11.0
33	10 53.3	10 55.0	10 23.5	3.3	2.4	9.3	6.7	15.3	11.1
34	10 53.5	10 55.3	10 23.7	3.4	2.5	9.4	6.8	15.4	11.2
35	10 53.8	10 55.5	10 24.0	3.5	2.5	9.5	6.9	15.5	11.2
36	10 54.0	10 55.8	10 24.2	3.6	2.6	9.6	7.0	15.6	11.3
37	10 54.3	10 56.0	10 24.4	3.7	2.7	9.7	7.0	15.7	11.4
38	10 54.5	10 56.3	10 24.7	3.8	2.8	9.8	7.1	15.8	11.5
39	10 54.8	10 56.5	10 24.9	3.9	2.8	9.9	7.2	15.9	11.5
40	10 55.0	10 56.8	10 25.2	4.0	2.9	10.0	7.3	16.0	11.6
41	10 55.3	10 57.0	10 25.4	4.1	3.0	10.1	7.3	16.1	11.7
42	10 55.5	10 57.3	10 25.6	4.2	3.0	10.2	7.4	16.2	11.7
43	10 55.8	10 57.5	10 25.9	4.3	3.1	10.3	7.5	16.3	11.8
44	10 56.0	10 57.8	10 26.1	4.4	3.2	10.4	7.5	16.4	11.9
45	10 56.3	10 58.0	10 26.4	4.5	3.3	10.5	7.6	16.5	12.0
46	10 56.5	10 58.3	10 26.6	4.6	3.3	10.6	7.7	16.6	12.0
47	10 56.8	10 58.5	10 26.8	4.7	3.4	10.7	7.8	16.7	12.1
48	10 57.0	10 58.8	10 27.1	4.8	3.5	10.8	7.8	16.8	12.2
49	10 57.3	10 59.0	10 27.3	4.9	3.6	10.9	7.9	16.9	12.3
50	10 57.5	10 59.3	10 27.5	5.0	3.6	11.0	8.0	17.0	12.3
51	10 57.8	10 59.6	10 27.8	5.1	3.7	11.1	8.0	17.1	12.4
52	10 58.0	10 59.9	10 28.0	5.2	3.8	11.2	8.1	17.2	12.5
53	10 58.3	11 00.1	10 28.3	5.3	3.8	11.3	8.2	17.3	12.5
54	10 58.5	11 00.3	10 28.5	5.4	3.9	11.4	8.3	17.4	12.6
55	10 58.8	11 00.6	10 28.7	5.5	4.0	11.5	8.3	17.5	12.7
56	10 59.0	11 00.8	10 29.0	5.6	4.1	11.6	8.4	17.6	12.8
57	10 59.3	11 01.1	10 29.2	5.7	4.1	11.7	8.5	17.7	12.8
58	10 59.5	11 01.3	10 29.5	5.8	4.2	11.8	8.6	17.8	12.9
59	10 59.8	11 01.6	10 29.7	5.9	4.3	11.9	8.6	17.9	13.0
60	11 00.0	11 01.8	10 29.9	6.0	4.4	12.0	8.7	18.0	13.1

44ᵐ

44	SUN PLANETS	ARIES	MOON	v or d	Corrⁿ	v or d	Corrⁿ	v or d	Corrⁿ
s	° ′	° ′	° ′	′	′	′	′	′	′
00	11 00.0	11 01.8	10 29.9	0.0	0.0	6.0	4.5	12.0	8.9
01	11 00.3	11 02.1	10 30.2	0.1	0.1	6.1	4.5	12.1	9.0
02	11 00.5	11 02.3	10 30.4	0.2	0.1	6.2	4.6	12.2	9.0
03	11 00.8	11 02.6	10 30.6	0.3	0.2	6.3	4.7	12.3	9.1
04	11 01.0	11 02.8	10 30.9	0.4	0.3	6.4	4.7	12.4	9.2
05	11 01.3	11 03.1	10 31.1	0.5	0.4	6.5	4.8	12.5	9.3
06	11 01.5	11 03.3	10 31.4	0.6	0.4	6.6	4.9	12.6	9.3
07	11 01.8	11 03.6	10 31.6	0.7	0.5	6.7	5.0	12.7	9.4
08	11 02.0	11 03.8	10 31.8	0.8	0.6	6.8	5.0	12.8	9.5
09	11 02.3	11 04.1	10 32.1	0.9	0.7	6.9	5.1	12.9	9.6
10	11 02.5	11 04.3	10 32.3	1.0	0.7	7.0	5.2	13.0	9.6
11	11 02.8	11 04.6	10 32.6	1.1	0.8	7.1	5.3	13.1	9.7
12	11 03.0	11 04.8	10 32.8	1.2	0.9	7.2	5.3	13.2	9.8
13	11 03.3	11 05.1	10 33.0	1.3	1.0	7.3	5.4	13.3	9.9
14	11 03.5	11 05.3	10 33.3	1.4	1.0	7.4	5.5	13.4	9.9
15	11 03.8	11 05.6	10 33.5	1.5	1.1	7.5	5.6	13.5	10.0
16	11 04.0	11 05.8	10 33.8	1.6	1.2	7.6	5.6	13.6	10.1
17	11 04.3	11 06.1	10 34.0	1.7	1.3	7.7	5.7	13.7	10.2
18	11 04.5	11 06.3	10 34.2	1.8	1.3	7.8	5.8	13.8	10.2
19	11 04.8	11 06.6	10 34.5	1.9	1.4	7.9	5.9	13.9	10.3
20	11 05.0	11 06.8	10 34.7	2.0	1.5	8.0	5.9	14.0	10.4
21	11 05.3	11 07.1	10 34.9	2.1	1.6	8.1	6.0	14.1	10.5
22	11 05.5	11 07.3	10 35.2	2.2	1.6	8.2	6.1	14.2	10.5
23	11 05.8	11 07.6	10 35.4	2.3	1.7	8.3	6.2	14.3	10.6
24	11 06.0	11 07.8	10 35.7	2.4	1.8	8.4	6.2	14.4	10.7
25	11 06.3	11 08.1	10 35.9	2.5	1.9	8.5	6.3	14.5	10.8
26	11 06.5	11 08.3	10 36.1	2.6	1.9	8.6	6.4	14.6	10.8
27	11 06.8	11 08.6	10 36.4	2.7	2.0	8.7	6.5	14.7	10.9
28	11 07.0	11 08.8	10 36.6	2.8	2.1	8.8	6.5	14.8	11.0
29	11 07.3	11 09.1	10 36.9	2.9	2.2	8.9	6.6	14.9	11.1
30	11 07.5	11 09.3	10 37.1	3.0	2.2	9.0	6.7	15.0	11.1
31	11 07.8	11 09.6	10 37.3	3.1	2.3	9.1	6.7	15.1	11.2
32	11 08.0	11 09.8	10 37.6	3.2	2.4	9.2	6.8	15.2	11.3
33	11 08.3	11 10.1	10 37.8	3.3	2.4	9.3	6.9	15.3	11.3
34	11 08.5	11 10.3	10 38.0	3.4	2.5	9.4	7.0	15.4	11.4
35	11 08.8	11 10.6	10 38.3	3.5	2.6	9.5	7.0	15.5	11.5
36	11 09.0	11 10.8	10 38.5	3.6	2.7	9.6	7.1	15.6	11.6
37	11 09.3	11 11.1	10 38.8	3.7	2.7	9.7	7.2	15.7	11.6
38	11 09.5	11 11.3	10 39.0	3.8	2.8	9.8	7.3	15.8	11.7
39	11 09.8	11 11.6	10 39.2	3.9	2.9	9.9	7.3	15.9	11.8
40	11 10.0	11 11.8	10 39.5	4.0	3.0	10.0	7.4	16.0	11.9
41	11 10.3	11 12.1	10 39.7	4.1	3.0	10.1	7.5	16.1	11.9
42	11 10.5	11 12.3	10 40.0	4.2	3.1	10.2	7.6	16.2	12.0
43	11 10.8	11 12.6	10 40.2	4.3	3.2	10.3	7.6	16.3	12.1
44	11 11.0	11 12.8	10 40.4	4.4	3.3	10.4	7.7	16.4	12.2
45	11 11.3	11 13.1	10 40.7	4.5	3.3	10.5	7.8	16.5	12.2
46	11 11.5	11 13.3	10 40.9	4.6	3.4	10.6	7.9	16.6	12.3
47	11 11.8	11 13.6	10 41.1	4.7	3.5	10.7	7.9	16.7	12.4
48	11 12.0	11 13.8	10 41.4	4.8	3.6	10.8	8.0	16.8	12.5
49	11 12.3	11 14.1	10 41.6	4.9	3.6	10.9	8.1	16.9	12.5
50	11 12.5	11 14.3	10 41.9	5.0	3.7	11.0	8.2	17.0	12.6
51	11 12.8	11 14.6	10 42.1	5.1	3.8	11.1	8.2	17.1	12.7
52	11 13.0	11 14.8	10 42.3	5.2	3.9	11.2	8.3	17.2	12.8
53	11 13.3	11 15.1	10 42.6	5.3	3.9	11.3	8.4	17.3	12.8
54	11 13.5	11 15.3	10 42.8	5.4	4.0	11.4	8.5	17.4	12.9
55	11 13.8	11 15.6	10 43.1	5.5	4.1	11.5	8.5	17.5	13.0
56	11 14.0	11 15.8	10 43.3	5.6	4.2	11.6	8.6	17.6	13.1
57	11 14.3	11 16.1	10 43.5	5.7	4.2	11.7	8.7	17.7	13.1
58	11 14.5	11 16.3	10 43.8	5.8	4.3	11.8	8.8	17.8	13.2
59	11 14.8	11 16.6	10 44.0	5.9	4.4	11.9	8.8	17.9	13.3
60	11 15.0	11 16.8	10 44.3	6.0	4.5	12.0	8.9	18.0	13.4

45ᵐ

45	SUN PLANETS	ARIES	MOON	v or d	Corrⁿ	v or d	Corrⁿ	v or d	Corrⁿ
s	° ′	° ′	° ′	′	′	′	′	′	′
00	11 15.0	11 16.8	10 44.3	0.0	0.0	6.0	4.6	12.0	9.1
01	11 15.3	11 17.1	10 44.5	0.1	0.1	6.1	4.6	12.1	9.2
02	11 15.5	11 17.3	10 44.7	0.2	0.2	6.2	4.7	12.2	9.3
03	11 15.8	11 17.6	10 45.0	0.3	0.2	6.3	4.8	12.3	9.3
04	11 16.0	11 17.9	10 45.2	0.4	0.3	6.4	4.9	12.4	9.4
05	11 16.3	11 18.1	10 45.4	0.5	0.4	6.5	4.9	12.5	9.5
06	11 16.5	11 18.4	10 45.7	0.6	0.5	6.6	5.0	12.6	9.6
07	11 16.8	11 18.6	10 45.9	0.7	0.5	6.7	5.1	12.7	9.6
08	11 17.0	11 18.9	10 46.2	0.8	0.6	6.8	5.2	12.8	9.7
09	11 17.3	11 19.1	10 46.4	0.9	0.7	6.9	5.2	12.9	9.8
10	11 17.5	11 19.4	10 46.6	1.0	0.8	7.0	5.3	13.0	9.9
11	11 17.8	11 19.6	10 46.9	1.1	0.8	7.1	5.4	13.1	9.9
12	11 18.0	11 19.9	10 47.1	1.2	0.9	7.2	5.5	13.2	10.0
13	11 18.3	11 20.1	10 47.4	1.3	1.0	7.3	5.5	13.3	10.1
14	11 18.5	11 20.4	10 47.6	1.4	1.1	7.4	5.6	13.4	10.2
15	11 18.8	11 20.6	10 47.8	1.5	1.1	7.5	5.7	13.5	10.2
16	11 19.0	11 20.9	10 48.1	1.6	1.2	7.6	5.8	13.6	10.3
17	11 19.3	11 21.1	10 48.3	1.7	1.3	7.7	5.8	13.7	10.4
18	11 19.5	11 21.4	10 48.5	1.8	1.4	7.8	5.9	13.8	10.5
19	11 19.8	11 21.6	10 48.8	1.9	1.4	7.9	6.0	13.9	10.5
20	11 20.0	11 21.9	10 49.0	2.0	1.5	8.0	6.1	14.0	10.6
21	11 20.3	11 22.1	10 49.3	2.1	1.6	8.1	6.1	14.1	10.7
22	11 20.5	11 22.4	10 49.5	2.2	1.7	8.2	6.2	14.2	10.8
23	11 20.8	11 22.6	10 49.7	2.3	1.7	8.3	6.3	14.3	10.8
24	11 21.0	11 22.9	10 50.0	2.4	1.8	8.4	6.4	14.4	10.9
25	11 21.3	11 23.1	10 50.2	2.5	1.9	8.5	6.4	14.5	11.0
26	11 21.5	11 23.4	10 50.5	2.6	2.0	8.6	6.5	14.6	11.1
27	11 21.8	11 23.6	10 50.7	2.7	2.0	8.7	6.6	14.7	11.1
28	11 22.0	11 23.9	10 50.9	2.8	2.1	8.8	6.7	14.8	11.2
29	11 22.3	11 24.1	10 51.2	2.9	2.2	8.9	6.7	14.9	11.3
30	11 22.5	11 24.4	10 51.4	3.0	2.3	9.0	6.8	15.0	11.4
31	11 22.8	11 24.6	10 51.6	3.1	2.4	9.1	6.9	15.1	11.5
32	11 23.0	11 24.9	10 51.9	3.2	2.4	9.2	7.0	15.2	11.5
33	11 23.3	11 25.1	10 52.1	3.3	2.5	9.3	7.1	15.3	11.6
34	11 23.5	11 25.4	10 52.4	3.4	2.6	9.4	7.1	15.4	11.7
35	11 23.8	11 25.6	10 52.6	3.5	2.7	9.5	7.2	15.5	11.8
36	11 24.0	11 25.9	10 52.8	3.6	2.7	9.6	7.3	15.6	11.8
37	11 24.3	11 26.1	10 53.1	3.7	2.8	9.7	7.4	15.7	11.9
38	11 24.5	11 26.4	10 53.3	3.8	2.9	9.8	7.4	15.8	12.0
39	11 24.8	11 26.6	10 53.6	3.9	3.0	9.9	7.5	15.9	12.1
40	11 25.0	11 26.9	10 53.8	4.0	3.0	10.0	7.6	16.0	12.1
41	11 25.3	11 27.1	10 54.0	4.1	3.1	10.1	7.7	16.1	12.2
42	11 25.5	11 27.4	10 54.3	4.2	3.2	10.2	7.7	16.2	12.3
43	11 25.8	11 27.6	10 54.5	4.3	3.3	10.3	7.8	16.3	12.4
44	11 26.0	11 27.9	10 54.7	4.4	3.3	10.4	7.9	16.4	12.4
45	11 26.3	11 28.1	10 55.0	4.5	3.4	10.5	8.0	16.5	12.5
46	11 26.5	11 28.4	10 55.2	4.6	3.5	10.6	8.0	16.6	12.6
47	11 26.8	11 28.6	10 55.5	4.7	3.6	10.7	8.1	16.7	12.7
48	11 27.0	11 28.9	10 55.7	4.8	3.6	10.8	8.2	16.8	12.7
49	11 27.3	11 29.1	10 55.9	4.9	3.7	10.9	8.3	16.9	12.8
50	11 27.5	11 29.4	10 56.2	5.0	3.8	11.0	8.3	17.0	12.9
51	11 27.8	11 29.6	10 56.4	5.1	3.9	11.1	8.4	17.1	13.0
52	11 28.0	11 29.9	10 56.7	5.2	3.9	11.2	8.5	17.2	13.0
53	11 28.3	11 30.1	10 56.9	5.3	4.0	11.3	8.6	17.3	13.1
54	11 28.5	11 30.4	10 57.1	5.4	4.1	11.4	8.6	17.4	13.2
55	11 28.8	11 30.6	10 57.4	5.5	4.2	11.5	8.7	17.5	13.3
56	11 29.0	11 30.9	10 57.6	5.6	4.2	11.6	8.8	17.6	13.3
57	11 29.3	11 31.1	10 57.9	5.7	4.3	11.7	8.9	17.7	13.4
58	11 29.5	11 31.4	10 58.1	5.8	4.4	11.8	8.9	17.8	13.5
59	11 29.8	11 31.6	10 58.3	5.9	4.5	11.9	9.0	17.9	13.6
60	11 30.0	11 31.9	10 58.6	6.0	4.6	12.0	9.1	18.0	13.7

46 m s	SUN PLANETS	ARIES	MOON	v or d	Corrⁿ	v or d	Corrⁿ	v or d	Corrⁿ
00	11 30.0	11 31.9	10 58.6	0.0	0.0	6.0	4.7	12.0	9.3
01	11 30.3	11 32.1	10 58.8	0.1	0.1	6.1	4.7	12.1	9.4
02	11 30.5	11 32.4	10 59.0	0.2	0.2	6.2	4.8	12.2	9.5
03	11 30.8	11 32.6	10 59.3	0.3	0.2	6.3	4.9	12.3	9.5
04	11 31.0	11 32.9	10 59.5	0.4	0.3	6.4	5.0	12.4	9.6
05	11 31.3	11 33.1	10 59.8	0.5	0.4	6.5	5.0	12.5	9.7
06	11 31.5	11 33.4	11 00.0	0.6	0.5	6.6	5.1	12.6	9.8
07	11 31.8	11 33.6	11 00.2	0.7	0.5	6.7	5.2	12.7	9.8
08	11 32.0	11 33.9	11 00.5	0.8	0.6	6.8	5.3	12.8	9.9
09	11 32.3	11 34.1	11 00.7	0.9	0.7	6.9	5.3	12.9	10.0
10	11 32.5	11 34.4	11 01.0	1.0	0.8	7.0	5.4	13.0	10.1
11	11 32.8	11 34.6	11 01.2	1.1	0.9	7.1	5.5	13.1	10.2
12	11 33.0	11 34.9	11 01.4	1.2	0.9	7.2	5.6	13.2	10.2
13	11 33.3	11 35.1	11 01.7	1.3	1.0	7.3	5.7	13.3	10.3
14	11 33.5	11 35.4	11 01.9	1.4	1.1	7.4	5.7	13.4	10.4
15	11 33.8	11 35.6	11 02.1	1.5	1.2	7.5	5.8	13.5	10.5
16	11 34.0	11 35.9	11 02.4	1.6	1.2	7.6	5.9	13.6	10.5
17	11 34.3	11 36.2	11 02.6	1.7	1.3	7.7	6.0	13.7	10.6
18	11 34.5	11 36.4	11 02.9	1.8	1.4	7.8	6.0	13.8	10.7
19	11 34.8	11 36.7	11 03.1	1.9	1.5	7.9	6.1	13.9	10.8
20	11 35.0	11 36.9	11 03.3	2.0	1.6	8.0	6.2	14.0	10.9
21	11 35.3	11 37.2	11 03.6	2.1	1.6	8.1	6.3	14.1	10.9
22	11 35.5	11 37.4	11 03.8	2.2	1.7	8.2	6.4	14.2	11.0
23	11 35.8	11 37.7	11 04.1	2.3	1.8	8.3	6.4	14.3	11.1
24	11 36.0	11 37.9	11 04.3	2.4	1.9	8.4	6.5	14.4	11.2
25	11 36.3	11 38.2	11 04.5	2.5	1.9	8.5	6.6	14.5	11.2
26	11 36.5	11 38.4	11 04.8	2.6	2.0	8.6	6.7	14.6	11.3
27	11 36.8	11 38.7	11 05.0	2.7	2.1	8.7	6.7	14.7	11.4
28	11 37.0	11 38.9	11 05.2	2.8	2.2	8.8	6.8	14.8	11.5
29	11 37.3	11 39.2	11 05.5	2.9	2.2	8.9	6.9	14.9	11.5
30	11 37.5	11 39.4	11 05.7	3.0	2.3	9.0	7.0	15.0	11.6
31	11 37.8	11 39.7	11 06.0	3.1	2.4	9.1	7.1	15.1	11.7
32	11 38.0	11 39.9	11 06.2	3.2	2.5	9.2	7.1	15.2	11.8
33	11 38.3	11 40.2	11 06.4	3.3	2.6	9.3	7.2	15.3	11.9
34	11 38.5	11 40.4	11 06.7	3.4	2.6	9.4	7.3	15.4	11.9
35	11 38.8	11 40.7	11 06.9	3.5	2.7	9.5	7.4	15.5	12.0
36	11 39.0	11 40.9	11 07.2	3.6	2.8	9.6	7.4	15.6	12.1
37	11 39.3	11 41.2	11 07.4	3.7	2.9	9.7	7.5	15.7	12.2
38	11 39.5	11 41.4	11 07.6	3.8	2.9	9.8	7.6	15.8	12.2
39	11 39.8	11 41.7	11 07.9	3.9	3.0	9.9	7.7	15.9	12.3
40	11 40.0	11 41.9	11 08.1	4.0	3.1	10.0	7.8	16.0	12.4
41	11 40.3	11 42.2	11 08.3	4.1	3.2	10.1	7.8	16.1	12.5
42	11 40.5	11 42.4	11 08.6	4.2	3.3	10.2	7.9	16.2	12.6
43	11 40.8	11 42.7	11 08.8	4.3	3.3	10.3	8.0	16.3	12.6
44	11 41.0	11 42.9	11 09.1	4.4	3.4	10.4	8.1	16.4	12.7
45	11 41.3	11 43.2	11 09.3	4.5	3.5	10.5	8.1	16.5	12.8
46	11 41.5	11 43.4	11 09.5	4.6	3.6	10.6	8.2	16.6	12.9
47	11 41.8	11 43.7	11 09.8	4.7	3.6	10.7	8.3	16.7	12.9
48	11 42.0	11 43.9	11 10.0	4.8	3.7	10.8	8.4	16.8	13.0
49	11 42.3	11 44.2	11 10.3	4.9	3.8	10.9	8.4	16.9	13.1
50	11 42.5	11 44.4	11 10.5	5.0	3.9	11.0	8.5	17.0	13.2
51	11 42.8	11 44.7	11 10.7	5.1	4.0	11.1	8.6	17.1	13.3
52	11 43.0	11 44.9	11 11.0	5.2	4.0	11.2	8.7	17.2	13.3
53	11 43.3	11 45.2	11 11.2	5.3	4.1	11.3	8.8	17.3	13.4
54	11 43.5	11 45.4	11 11.5	5.4	4.2	11.4	8.8	17.4	13.5
55	11 43.8	11 45.7	11 11.7	5.5	4.3	11.5	8.9	17.5	13.6
56	11 44.0	11 45.9	11 11.9	5.6	4.3	11.6	9.0	17.6	13.6
57	11 44.3	11 46.2	11 12.2	5.7	4.4	11.7	9.1	17.7	13.7
58	11 44.5	11 46.4	11 12.4	5.8	4.5	11.8	9.1	17.8	13.8
59	11 44.8	11 46.7	11 12.6	5.9	4.6	11.9	9.2	17.9	13.9
60	11 45.0	11 46.9	11 12.9	6.0	4.7	12.0	9.3	18.0	14.0

47 m s	SUN PLANETS	ARIES	MOON	v or d	Corrⁿ	v or d	Corrⁿ	v or d	Corrⁿ
00	11 45.0	11 46.9	11 12.9	0.0	0.0	6.0	4.8	12.0	9.5
01	11 45.3	11 47.2	11 13.1	0.1	0.1	6.1	4.8	12.1	9.6
02	11 45.5	11 47.4	11 13.4	0.2	0.2	6.2	4.9	12.2	9.7
03	11 45.8	11 47.7	11 13.6	0.3	0.2	6.3	5.0	12.3	9.7
04	11 46.0	11 47.9	11 13.8	0.4	0.3	6.4	5.1	12.4	9.8
05	11 46.3	11 48.2	11 14.1	0.5	0.4	6.5	5.1	12.5	9.9
06	11 46.5	11 48.4	11 14.3	0.6	0.5	6.6	5.2	12.6	10.0
07	11 46.8	11 48.7	11 14.6	0.7	0.6	6.7	5.3	12.7	10.1
08	11 47.0	11 48.9	11 14.8	0.8	0.6	6.8	5.4	12.8	10.1
09	11 47.3	11 49.2	11 15.0	0.9	0.7	6.9	5.5	12.9	10.2
10	11 47.5	11 49.4	11 15.3	1.0	0.8	7.0	5.5	13.0	10.3
11	11 47.8	11 49.7	11 15.5	1.1	0.9	7.1	5.6	13.1	10.4
12	11 48.0	11 49.9	11 15.7	1.2	1.0	7.2	5.7	13.2	10.5
13	11 48.3	11 50.2	11 16.0	1.3	1.0	7.3	5.8	13.3	10.5
14	11 48.5	11 50.4	11 16.2	1.4	1.1	7.4	5.9	13.4	10.6
15	11 48.8	11 50.7	11 16.5	1.5	1.2	7.5	5.9	13.5	10.7
16	11 49.0	11 50.9	11 16.7	1.6	1.3	7.6	6.0	13.6	10.8
17	11 49.3	11 51.2	11 16.9	1.7	1.3	7.7	6.1	13.7	10.8
18	11 49.5	11 51.4	11 17.2	1.8	1.4	7.8	6.2	13.8	10.9
19	11 49.8	11 51.7	11 17.4	1.9	1.5	7.9	6.3	13.9	11.0
20	11 50.0	11 51.9	11 17.7	2.0	1.6	8.0	6.3	14.0	11.1
21	11 50.3	11 52.2	11 17.9	2.1	1.7	8.1	6.4	14.1	11.2
22	11 50.5	11 52.4	11 18.1	2.2	1.7	8.2	6.5	14.2	11.2
23	11 50.8	11 52.7	11 18.4	2.3	1.8	8.3	6.6	14.3	11.3
24	11 51.0	11 52.9	11 18.6	2.4	1.9	8.4	6.7	14.4	11.4
25	11 51.3	11 53.2	11 18.8	2.5	2.0	8.5	6.7	14.5	11.5
26	11 51.5	11 53.4	11 19.1	2.6	2.1	8.6	6.8	14.6	11.6
27	11 51.8	11 53.7	11 19.3	2.7	2.1	8.7	6.9	14.7	11.6
28	11 52.0	11 53.9	11 19.6	2.8	2.2	8.8	7.0	14.8	11.7
29	11 52.3	11 54.2	11 19.8	2.9	2.3	8.9	7.0	14.9	11.8
30	11 52.5	11 54.5	11 20.0	3.0	2.4	9.0	7.1	15.0	11.9
31	11 52.8	11 54.7	11 20.3	3.1	2.5	9.1	7.2	15.1	12.0
32	11 53.0	11 55.0	11 20.5	3.2	2.5	9.2	7.3	15.2	12.0
33	11 53.3	11 55.2	11 20.8	3.3	2.6	9.3	7.4	15.3	12.1
34	11 53.5	11 55.5	11 21.0	3.4	2.7	9.4	7.4	15.4	12.2
35	11 53.8	11 55.7	11 21.2	3.5	2.8	9.5	7.5	15.5	12.3
36	11 54.0	11 56.0	11 21.5	3.6	2.9	9.6	7.6	15.6	12.4
37	11 54.3	11 56.2	11 21.7	3.7	2.9	9.7	7.7	15.7	12.4
38	11 54.5	11 56.5	11 22.0	3.8	3.0	9.8	7.8	15.8	12.5
39	11 54.8	11 56.7	11 22.2	3.9	3.1	9.9	7.8	15.9	12.6
40	11 55.0	11 57.0	11 22.4	4.0	3.2	10.0	7.9	16.0	12.7
41	11 55.3	11 57.2	11 22.7	4.1	3.2	10.1	8.0	16.1	12.7
42	11 55.5	11 57.5	11 22.9	4.2	3.3	10.2	8.1	16.2	12.8
43	11 55.8	11 57.7	11 23.1	4.3	3.4	10.3	8.2	16.3	12.9
44	11 56.0	11 58.0	11 23.4	4.4	3.5	10.4	8.2	16.4	13.0
45	11 56.3	11 58.2	11 23.6	4.5	3.6	10.5	8.3	16.5	13.1
46	11 56.5	11 58.5	11 23.9	4.6	3.6	10.6	8.4	16.6	13.1
47	11 56.8	11 58.7	11 24.1	4.7	3.7	10.7	8.5	16.7	13.2
48	11 57.0	11 59.0	11 24.3	4.8	3.8	10.8	8.6	16.8	13.3
49	11 57.3	11 59.2	11 24.6	4.9	3.9	10.9	8.6	16.9	13.4
50	11 57.5	11 59.5	11 24.8	5.0	4.0	11.0	8.7	17.0	13.5
51	11 57.8	11 59.7	11 25.1	5.1	4.0	11.1	8.8	17.1	13.5
52	11 58.0	12 00.0	11 25.3	5.2	4.1	11.2	8.9	17.2	13.6
53	11 58.3	12 00.2	11 25.5	5.3	4.2	11.3	8.9	17.3	13.7
54	11 58.5	12 00.5	11 25.8	5.4	4.3	11.4	9.0	17.4	13.8
55	11 58.8	12 00.7	11 26.0	5.5	4.4	11.5	9.1	17.5	13.9
56	11 59.0	12 01.0	11 26.2	5.6	4.4	11.6	9.2	17.6	13.9
57	11 59.3	12 01.2	11 26.5	5.7	4.5	11.7	9.3	17.7	14.0
58	11 59.5	12 01.5	11 26.7	5.8	4.6	11.8	9.3	17.8	14.1
59	11 59.8	12 01.7	11 27.0	5.9	4.7	11.9	9.4	17.9	14.2
60	12 00.0	12 02.0	11 27.2	6.0	4.8	12.0	9.5	18.0	14.3

48ᵐ

48	SUN PLANETS	ARIES	MOON	v or d	Corrⁿ	v or d	Corrⁿ	v or d	Corrⁿ
s	° ′	° ′	° ′	′	′	′	′	′	′
00	12 00·0	12 02·0	11 27·2	0·0	0·0	6·0	4·9	12·0	9·7
01	12 00·3	12 02·2	11 27·4	0·1	0·1	6·1	4·9	12·1	9·8
02	12 00·5	12 02·5	11 27·7	0·2	0·2	6·2	5·0	12·2	9·9
03	12 00·8	12 02·7	11 27·9	0·3	0·2	6·3	5·1	12·3	9·9
04	12 01·0	12 03·0	11 28·2	0·4	0·3	6·4	5·2	12·4	10·0
05	12 01·3	12 03·2	11 28·4	0·5	0·4	6·5	5·3	12·5	10·1
06	12 01·5	12 03·5	11 28·6	0·6	0·5	6·6	5·3	12·6	10·2
07	12 01·8	12 03·7	11 28·9	0·7	0·6	6·7	5·4	12·7	10·3
08	12 02·0	12 04·0	11 29·1	0·8	0·6	6·8	5·5	12·8	10·3
09	12 02·3	12 04·2	11 29·3	0·9	0·7	6·9	5·6	12·9	10·4
10	12 02·5	12 04·5	11 29·6	1·0	0·8	7·0	5·7	13·0	10·5
11	12 02·8	12 04·7	11 29·8	1·1	0·9	7·1	5·7	13·1	10·6
12	12 03·0	12 05·0	11 30·1	1·2	1·0	7·2	5·8	13·2	10·7
13	12 03·3	12 05·2	11 30·3	1·3	1·1	7·3	5·9	13·3	10·8
14	12 03·5	12 05·5	11 30·5	1·4	1·1	7·4	6·0	13·4	10·8
15	12 03·8	12 05·7	11 30·8	1·5	1·2	7·5	6·1	13·5	10·9
16	12 04·0	12 06·0	11 31·0	1·6	1·3	7·6	6·1	13·6	11·0
17	12 04·3	12 06·2	11 31·3	1·7	1·4	7·7	6·2	13·7	11·1
18	12 04·5	12 06·5	11 31·5	1·8	1·5	7·8	6·3	13·8	11·2
19	12 04·8	12 06·7	11 31·7	1·9	1·5	7·9	6·4	13·9	11·2
20	12 05·0	12 07·0	11 32·0	2·0	1·6	8·0	6·5	14·0	11·3
21	12 05·3	12 07·2	11 32·2	2·1	1·7	8·1	6·5	14·1	11·4
22	12 05·5	12 07·5	11 32·4	2·2	1·8	8·2	6·6	14·2	11·5
23	12 05·8	12 07·7	11 32·7	2·3	1·9	8·3	6·7	14·3	11·6
24	12 06·0	12 08·0	11 32·9	2·4	1·9	8·4	6·8	14·4	11·6
25	12 06·3	12 08·2	11 33·2	2·5	2·0	8·5	6·9	14·5	11·7
26	12 06·5	12 08·5	11 33·4	2·6	2·1	8·6	7·0	14·6	11·8
27	12 06·8	12 08·7	11 33·6	2·7	2·2	8·7	7·0	14·7	11·9
28	12 07·0	12 09·0	11 33·9	2·8	2·3	8·8	7·1	14·8	12·0
29	12 07·3	12 09·2	11 34·1	2·9	2·3	8·9	7·2	14·9	12·0
30	12 07·5	12 09·5	11 34·4	3·0	2·4	9·0	7·3	15·0	12·1
31	12 07·8	12 09·7	11 34·6	3·1	2·5	9·1	7·4	15·1	12·2
32	12 08·0	12 10·0	11 34·8	3·2	2·6	9·2	7·4	15·2	12·3
33	12 08·3	12 10·2	11 35·1	3·3	2·7	9·3	7·5	15·3	12·4
34	12 08·5	12 10·5	11 35·3	3·4	2·7	9·4	7·6	15·4	12·4
35	12 08·8	12 10·7	11 35·6	3·5	2·8	9·5	7·7	15·5	12·5
36	12 09·0	12 11·0	11 35·8	3·6	2·9	9·6	7·8	15·6	12·6
37	12 09·3	12 11·2	11 36·0	3·7	3·0	9·7	7·8	15·7	12·7
38	12 09·5	12 11·5	11 36·3	3·8	3·1	9·8	7·9	15·8	12·8
39	12 09·8	12 11·7	11 36·5	3·9	3·2	9·9	8·0	15·9	12·9
40	12 10·0	12 12·0	11 36·7	4·0	3·2	10·0	8·1	16·0	12·9
41	12 10·3	12 12·2	11 37·0	4·1	3·3	10·1	8·2	16·1	13·0
42	12 10·5	12 12·5	11 37·2	4·2	3·4	10·2	8·2	16·2	13·1
43	12 10·8	12 12·8	11 37·5	4·3	3·5	10·3	8·3	16·3	13·2
44	12 11·0	12 13·0	11 37·7	4·4	3·6	10·4	8·4	16·4	13·3
45	12 11·3	12 13·3	11 37·9	4·5	3·6	10·5	8·5	16·5	13·3
46	12 11·5	12 13·5	11 38·2	4·6	3·7	10·6	8·6	16·6	13·4
47	12 11·8	12 13·8	11 38·4	4·7	3·8	10·7	8·6	16·7	13·5
48	12 12·0	12 14·0	11 38·7	4·8	3·9	10·8	8·7	16·8	13·6
49	12 12·3	12 14·3	11 38·9	4·9	4·0	10·9	8·8	16·9	13·7
50	12 12·5	12 14·5	11 39·1	5·0	4·0	11·0	8·9	17·0	13·7
51	12 12·8	12 14·8	11 39·4	5·1	4·1	11·1	9·0	17·1	13·8
52	12 13·0	12 15·0	11 39·6	5·2	4·2	11·2	9·1	17·2	13·9
53	12 13·3	12 15·3	11 39·8	5·3	4·3	11·3	9·1	17·3	14·0
54	12 13·5	12 15·5	11 40·1	5·4	4·4	11·4	9·2	17·4	14·1
55	12 13·8	12 15·8	11 40·3	5·5	4·4	11·5	9·3	17·5	14·1
56	12 14·0	12 16·0	11 40·6	5·6	4·5	11·6	9·4	17·6	14·2
57	12 14·3	12 16·3	11 40·8	5·7	4·6	11·7	9·5	17·7	14·3
58	12 14·5	12 16·5	11 41·0	5·8	4·7	11·8	9·5	17·8	14·4
59	12 14·8	12 16·8	11 41·3	5·9	4·8	11·9	9·6	17·9	14·5
60	12 15·0	12 17·0	11 41·5	6·0	4·9	12·0	9·7	18·0	14·6

49ᵐ

49	SUN PLANETS	ARIES	MOON	v or d	Corrⁿ	v or d	Corrⁿ	v or d	Corrⁿ
s	° ′	° ′	° ′	′	′	′	′	′	′
00	12 15·0	12 17·0	11 41·5	0·0	0·0	6·0	5·0	12·0	9·9
01	12 15·3	12 17·3	11 41·8	0·1	0·1	6·1	5·0	12·1	10·0
02	12 15·5	12 17·5	11 42·0	0·2	0·2	6·2	5·1	12·2	10·1
03	12 15·8	12 17·8	11 42·2	0·3	0·2	6·3	5·2	12·3	10·1
04	12 16·0	12 18·0	11 42·5	0·4	0·3	6·4	5·3	12·4	10·2
05	12 16·3	12 18·3	11 42·7	0·5	0·4	6·5	5·4	12·5	10·3
06	12 16·5	12 18·5	11 42·9	0·6	0·5	6·6	5·4	12·6	10·4
07	12 16·8	12 18·8	11 43·2	0·7	0·6	6·7	5·5	12·7	10·5
08	12 17·0	12 19·0	11 43·4	0·8	0·7	6·8	5·6	12·8	10·6
09	12 17·3	12 19·3	11 43·7	0·9	0·7	6·9	5·7	12·9	10·6
10	12 17·5	12 19·5	11 43·9	1·0	0·8	7·0	5·8	13·0	10·7
11	12 17·8	12 19·8	11 44·1	1·1	0·9	7·1	5·9	13·1	10·8
12	12 18·0	12 20·0	11 44·4	1·2	1·0	7·2	5·9	13·2	10·9
13	12 18·3	12 20·3	11 44·6	1·3	1·1	7·3	6·0	13·3	11·0
14	12 18·5	12 20·5	11 44·9	1·4	1·2	7·4	6·1	13·4	11·1
15	12 18·8	12 20·8	11 45·1	1·5	1·2	7·5	6·2	13·5	11·1
16	12 19·0	12 21·0	11 45·3	1·6	1·3	7·6	6·3	13·6	11·2
17	12 19·3	12 21·3	11 45·6	1·7	1·4	7·7	6·4	13·7	11·3
18	12 19·5	12 21·5	11 45·8	1·8	1·5	7·8	6·4	13·8	11·4
19	12 19·8	12 21·8	11 46·1	1·9	1·6	7·9	6·5	13·9	11·5
20	12 20·0	12 22·0	11 46·3	2·0	1·7	8·0	6·6	14·0	11·6
21	12 20·3	12 22·3	11 46·5	2·1	1·7	8·1	6·7	14·1	11·6
22	12 20·5	12 22·5	11 46·8	2·2	1·8	8·2	6·8	14·2	11·7
23	12 20·8	12 22·8	11 47·0	2·3	1·9	8·3	6·8	14·3	11·8
24	12 21·0	12 23·0	11 47·2	2·4	2·0	8·4	6·9	14·4	11·9
25	12 21·3	12 23·3	11 47·5	2·5	2·1	8·5	7·0	14·5	12·0
26	12 21·5	12 23·5	11 47·7	2·6	2·1	8·6	7·1	14·6	12·0
27	12 21·8	12 23·8	11 48·0	2·7	2·2	8·7	7·2	14·7	12·1
28	12 22·0	12 24·0	11 48·2	2·8	2·3	8·8	7·3	14·8	12·2
29	12 22·3	12 24·3	11 48·4	2·9	2·4	8·9	7·3	14·9	12·3
30	12 22·5	12 24·5	11 48·7	3·0	2·5	9·0	7·4	15·0	12·4
31	12 22·8	12 24·8	11 48·9	3·1	2·6	9·1	7·5	15·1	12·5
32	12 23·0	12 25·0	11 49·2	3·2	2·6	9·2	7·6	15·2	12·5
33	12 23·3	12 25·3	11 49·4	3·3	2·7	9·3	7·7	15·3	12·6
34	12 23·5	12 25·5	11 49·6	3·4	2·8	9·4	7·8	15·4	12·7
35	12 23·8	12 25·8	11 49·9	3·5	2·9	9·5	7·8	15·5	12·8
36	12 24·0	12 26·0	11 50·1	3·6	3·0	9·6	7·9	15·6	12·9
37	12 24·3	12 26·3	11 50·3	3·7	3·1	9·7	8·0	15·7	13·0
38	12 24·5	12 26·5	11 50·6	3·8	3·1	9·8	8·1	15·8	13·0
39	12 24·8	12 26·8	11 50·8	3·9	3·2	9·9	8·2	15·9	13·1
40	12 25·0	12 27·0	11 51·1	4·0	3·3	10·0	8·3	16·0	13·2
41	12 25·3	12 27·3	11 51·3	4·1	3·4	10·1	8·3	16·1	13·3
42	12 25·5	12 27·5	11 51·5	4·2	3·5	10·2	8·4	16·2	13·4
43	12 25·8	12 27·8	11 51·8	4·3	3·5	10·3	8·5	16·3	13·4
44	12 26·0	12 28·0	11 52·0	4·4	3·6	10·4	8·6	16·4	13·5
45	12 26·3	12 28·3	11 52·3	4·5	3·7	10·5	8·7	16·5	13·6
46	12 26·5	12 28·5	11 52·5	4·6	3·8	10·6	8·7	16·6	13·7
47	12 26·8	12 28·8	11 52·7	4·7	3·9	10·7	8·8	16·7	13·8
48	12 27·0	12 29·0	11 53·0	4·8	4·0	10·8	8·9	16·8	13·9
49	12 27·3	12 29·3	11 53·2	4·9	4·0	10·9	9·0	16·9	13·9
50	12 27·5	12 29·5	11 53·4	5·0	4·1	11·0	9·1	17·0	14·0
51	12 27·8	12 29·8	11 53·7	5·1	4·2	11·1	9·2	17·1	14·1
52	12 28·0	12 30·0	11 53·9	5·2	4·3	11·2	9·2	17·2	14·2
53	12 28·3	12 30·3	11 54·2	5·3	4·4	11·3	9·3	17·3	14·3
54	12 28·5	12 30·5	11 54·4	5·4	4·5	11·4	9·4	17·4	14·4
55	12 28·8	12 30·8	11 54·6	5·5	4·5	11·5	9·5	17·5	14·4
56	12 29·0	12 31·1	11 54·9	5·6	4·6	11·6	9·6	17·6	14·5
57	12 29·3	12 31·3	11 55·1	5·7	4·7	11·7	9·7	17·7	14·6
58	12 29·5	12 31·6	11 55·4	5·8	4·8	11·8	9·7	17·8	14·7
59	12 29·8	12 31·8	11 55·6	5·9	4·9	11·9	9·8	17·9	14·8
60	12 30·0	12 32·1	11 55·8	6·0	5·0	12·0	9·9	18·0	14·9

m 50	SUN PLANETS	ARIES	MOON	v or Corrⁿ d		v or Corrⁿ d		v or Corrⁿ d		m 51	SUN PLANETS	ARIES	MOON	v or Corrⁿ d		v or Corrⁿ d		v or Corrⁿ d	
s	° ′	° ′	° ′	′	′	′	′	′	′	s	° ′	° ′	° ′	′	′	′	′	′	′
00	12 30·0	12 32·1	11 55·8	0·0	0·0	6·0	5·1	12·0	10·1	00	12 45·0	12 47·1	12 10·2	0·0	0·0	6·0	5·2	12·0	10·3
01	12 30·3	12 32·3	11 56·1	0·1	0·1	6·1	5·1	12·1	10·2	01	12 45·3	12 47·3	12 10·4	0·1	0·1	6·1	5·2	12·1	10·4
02	12 30·5	12 32·6	11 56·3	0·2	0·2	6·2	5·2	12·2	10·3	02	12 45·5	12 47·6	12 10·6	0·2	0·2	6·2	5·3	12·2	10·5
03	12 30·8	12 32·8	11 56·5	0·3	0·3	6·3	5·3	12·3	10·4	03	12 45·8	12 47·8	12 10·9	0·3	0·3	6·3	5·4	12·3	10·6
04	12 31·0	12 33·1	11 56·8	0·4	0·3	6·4	5·4	12·4	10·4	04	12 46·0	12 48·1	12 11·1	0·4	0·3	6·4	5·5	12·4	10·6
05	12 31·3	12 33·3	11 57·0	0·5	0·4	6·5	5·5	12·5	10·5	05	12 46·3	12 48·3	12 11·3	0·5	0·4	6·5	5·6	12·5	10·7
06	12 31·5	12 33·6	11 57·3	0·6	0·5	6·6	5·6	12·6	10·6	06	12 46·5	12 48·6	12 11·6	0·6	0·5	6·6	5·7	12·6	10·8
07	12 31·8	12 33·8	11 57·5	0·7	0·6	6·7	5·6	12·7	10·7	07	12 46·8	12 48·8	12 11·8	0·7	0·6	6·7	5·8	12·7	10·9
08	12 32·0	12 34·1	11 57·7	0·8	0·7	6·8	5·7	12·8	10·8	08	12 47·0	12 49·1	12 12·1	0·8	0·7	6·8	5·8	12·8	11·0
09	12 32·3	12 34·3	11 58·0	0·9	0·8	6·9	5·8	12·9	10·9	09	12 47·3	12 49·4	12 12·3	0·9	0·8	6·9	5·9	12·9	11·1
10	12 32·5	12 34·6	11 58·2	1·0	0·8	7·0	5·9	13·0	10·9	10	12 47·5	12 49·6	12 12·5	1·0	0·9	7·0	6·0	13·0	11·2
11	12 32·8	12 34·8	11 58·5	1·1	0·9	7·1	6·0	13·1	11·0	11	12 47·8	12 49·9	12 12·8	1·1	0·9	7·1	6·1	13·1	11·2
12	12 33·0	12 35·1	11 58·7	1·2	1·0	7·2	6·1	13·2	11·1	12	12 48·0	12 50·1	12 13·0	1·2	1·0	7·2	6·2	13·2	11·3
13	12 33·3	12 35·3	11 58·9	1·3	1·1	7·3	6·1	13·3	11·2	13	12 48·3	12 50·4	12 13·3	1·3	1·1	7·3	6·3	13·3	11·4
14	12 33·5	12 35·6	11 59·2	1·4	1·2	7·4	6·2	13·4	11·3	14	12 48·5	12 50·6	12 13·5	1·4	1·2	7·4	6·4	13·4	11·5
15	12 33·8	12 35·8	11 59·4	1·5	1·3	7·5	6·3	13·5	11·4	15	12 48·8	12 50·9	12 13·7	1·5	1·3	7·5	6·4	13·5	11·6
16	12 34·0	12 36·1	11 59·7	1·6	1·3	7·6	6·4	13·6	11·4	16	12 49·0	12 51·1	12 14·0	1·6	1·4	7·6	6·5	13·6	11·7
17	12 34·3	12 36·3	11 59·9	1·7	1·4	7·7	6·5	13·7	11·5	17	12 49·3	12 51·4	12 14·2	1·7	1·5	7·7	6·6	13·7	11·8
18	12 34·5	12 36·6	12 00·1	1·8	1·5	7·8	6·6	13·8	11·6	18	12 49·5	12 51·6	12 14·4	1·8	1·5	7·8	6·7	13·8	11·8
19	12 34·8	12 36·8	12 00·4	1·9	1·6	7·9	6·6	13·9	11·7	19	12 49·8	12 51·9	12 14·7	1·9	1·6	7·9	6·8	13·9	11·9
20	12 35·0	12 37·1	12 00·6	2·0	1·7	8·0	6·7	14·0	11·8	20	12 50·0	12 52·1	12 14·9	2·0	1·7	8·0	6·9	14·0	12·0
21	12 35·3	12 37·3	12 00·8	2·1	1·8	8·1	6·8	14·1	11·9	21	12 50·3	12 52·4	12 15·2	2·1	1·8	8·1	7·0	14·1	12·1
22	12 35·5	12 37·6	12 01·1	2·2	1·9	8·2	6·9	14·2	12·0	22	12 50·5	12 52·6	12 15·4	2·2	1·9	8·2	7·0	14·2	12·2
23	12 35·8	12 37·8	12 01·3	2·3	1·9	8·3	7·0	14·3	12·0	23	12 50·8	12 52·9	12 15·6	2·3	2·0	8·3	7·1	14·3	12·3
24	12 36·0	12 38·1	12 01·6	2·4	2·0	8·4	7·1	14·4	12·1	24	12 51·0	12 53·1	12 15·9	2·4	2·1	8·4	7·2	14·4	12·4
25	12 36·3	12 38·3	12 01·8	2·5	2·1	8·5	7·2	14·5	12·2	25	12 51·3	12 53·4	12 16·1	2·5	2·1	8·5	7·3	14·5	12·4
26	12 36·5	12 38·6	12 02·0	2·6	2·2	8·6	7·2	14·6	12·3	26	12 51·5	12 53·6	12 16·4	2·6	2·2	8·6	7·4	14·6	12·5
27	12 36·8	12 38·8	12 02·3	2·7	2·3	8·7	7·3	14·7	12·4	27	12 51·8	12 53·9	12 16·6	2·7	2·3	8·7	7·5	14·7	12·6
28	12 37·0	12 39·1	12 02·5	2·8	2·4	8·8	7·4	14·8	12·5	28	12 52·0	12 54·1	12 16·8	2·8	2·4	8·8	7·6	14·8	12·7
29	12 37·3	12 39·3	12 02·8	2·9	2·4	8·9	7·5	14·9	12·5	29	12 52·3	12 54·4	12 17·1	2·9	2·5	8·9	7·6	14·9	12·8
30	12 37·5	12 39·6	12 03·0	3·0	2·5	9·0	7·6	15·0	12·6	30	12 52·5	12 54·6	12 17·3	3·0	2·6	9·0	7·7	15·0	12·9
31	12 37·8	12 39·8	12 03·2	3·1	2·6	9·1	7·7	15·1	12·7	31	12 52·8	12 54·9	12 17·5	3·1	2·7	9·1	7·8	15·1	13·0
32	12 38·0	12 40·1	12 03·5	3·2	2·7	9·2	7·7	15·2	12·8	32	12 53·0	12 55·1	12 17·8	3·2	2·7	9·2	7·9	15·2	13·0
33	12 38·3	12 40·3	12 03·7	3·3	2·8	9·3	7·8	15·3	12·9	33	12 53·3	12 55·4	12 18·0	3·3	2·8	9·3	8·0	15·3	13·1
34	12 38·5	12 40·6	12 03·9	3·4	2·9	9·4	7·9	15·4	13·0	34	12 53·5	12 55·6	12 18·3	3·4	2·9	9·4	8·1	15·4	13·2
35	12 38·8	12 40·8	12 04·2	3·5	2·9	9·5	8·0	15·5	13·0	35	12 53·8	12 55·9	12 18·5	3·5	3·0	9·5	8·2	15·5	13·3
36	12 39·0	12 41·1	12 04·4	3·6	3·0	9·6	8·1	15·6	13·1	36	12 54·0	12 56·1	12 18·7	3·6	3·1	9·6	8·2	15·6	13·4
37	12 39·3	12 41·3	12 04·7	3·7	3·1	9·7	8·2	15·7	13·2	37	12 54·3	12 56·4	12 19·0	3·7	3·2	9·7	8·3	15·7	13·5
38	12 39·5	12 41·6	12 04·9	3·8	3·2	9·8	8·2	15·8	13·3	38	12 54·5	12 56·6	12 19·2	3·8	3·3	9·8	8·4	15·8	13·6
39	12 39·8	12 41·8	12 05·1	3·9	3·3	9·9	8·3	15·9	13·4	39	12 54·8	12 56·9	12 19·5	3·9	3·3	9·9	8·5	15·9	13·6
40	12 40·0	12 42·1	12 05·4	4·0	3·4	10·0	8·4	16·0	13·5	40	12 55·0	12 57·1	12 19·7	4·0	3·4	10·0	8·6	16·0	13·7
41	12 40·3	12 42·3	12 05·6	4·1	3·5	10·1	8·5	16·1	13·6	41	12 55·3	12 57·4	12 19·9	4·1	3·5	10·1	8·7	16·1	13·8
42	12 40·5	12 42·6	12 05·9	4·2	3·5	10·2	8·6	16·2	13·6	42	12 55·5	12 57·6	12 20·2	4·2	3·6	10·2	8·8	16·2	13·9
43	12 40·8	12 42·8	12 06·1	4·3	3·6	10·3	8·7	16·3	13·7	43	12 55·8	12 57·9	12 20·4	4·3	3·7	10·3	8·8	16·3	14·0
44	12 41·0	12 43·1	12 06·3	4·4	3·7	10·4	8·8	16·4	13·8	44	12 56·0	12 58·1	12 20·6	4·4	3·8	10·4	8·9	16·4	14·1
45	12 41·3	12 43·3	12 06·6	4·5	3·8	10·5	8·8	16·5	13·9	45	12 56·3	12 58·4	12 20·9	4·5	3·9	10·5	9·0	16·5	14·2
46	12 41·5	12 43·6	12 06·8	4·6	3·9	10·6	8·9	16·6	14·0	46	12 56·5	12 58·6	12 21·1	4·6	3·9	10·6	9·1	16·6	14·2
47	12 41·8	12 43·8	12 07·0	4·7	4·0	10·7	9·0	16·7	14·1	47	12 56·8	12 58·9	12 21·4	4·7	4·0	10·7	9·2	16·7	14·3
48	12 42·0	12 44·1	12 07·3	4·8	4·0	10·8	9·1	16·8	14·1	48	12 57·0	12 59·1	12 21·6	4·8	4·1	10·8	9·3	16·8	14·4
49	12 42·3	12 44·3	12 07·5	4·9	4·1	10·9	9·2	16·9	14·2	49	12 57·3	12 59·4	12 21·8	4·9	4·2	10·9	9·4	16·9	14·5
50	12 42·5	12 44·6	12 07·8	5·0	4·2	11·0	9·3	17·0	14·3	50	12 57·5	12 59·6	12 22·1	5·0	4·3	11·0	9·4	17·0	14·6
51	12 42·8	12 44·8	12 08·0	5·1	4·3	11·1	9·3	17·1	14·4	51	12 57·8	12 59·9	12 22·3	5·1	4·4	11·1	9·5	17·1	14·7
52	12 43·0	12 45·1	12 08·2	5·2	4·4	11·2	9·4	17·2	14·5	52	12 58·0	13 00·1	12 22·6	5·2	4·5	11·2	9·6	17·2	14·8
53	12 43·3	12 45·3	12 08·5	5·3	4·5	11·3	9·5	17·3	14·6	53	12 58·3	13 00·4	12 22·8	5·3	4·5	11·3	9·7	17·3	14·8
54	12 43·5	12 45·6	12 08·7	5·4	4·5	11·4	9·6	17·4	14·6	54	12 58·5	13 00·6	12 23·0	5·4	4·6	11·4	9·8	17·4	14·9
55	12 43·8	12 45·8	12 09·0	5·5	4·6	11·5	9·7	17·5	14·7	55	12 58·8	13 00·9	12 23·3	5·5	4·7	11·5	9·9	17·5	15·0
56	12 44·0	12 46·1	12 09·2	5·6	4·7	11·6	9·8	17·6	14·8	56	12 59·0	13 01·1	12 23·5	5·6	4·8	11·6	10·0	17·6	15·1
57	12 44·3	12 46·3	12 09·4	5·7	4·8	11·7	9·8	17·7	14·9	57	12 59·3	13 01·4	12 23·8	5·7	4·9	11·7	10·0	17·7	15·2
58	12 44·5	12 46·6	12 09·7	5·8	4·9	11·8	9·9	17·8	15·0	58	12 59·5	13 01·6	12 24·0	5·8	5·0	11·8	10·1	17·8	15·3
59	12 44·8	12 46·8	12 09·9	5·9	5·0	11·9	10·0	17·9	15·1	59	12 59·8	13 01·9	12 24·2	5·9	5·1	11·9	10·2	17·9	15·4
60	12 45·0	12 47·1	12 10·2	6·0	5·1	12·0	10·1	18·0	15·2	60	13 00·0	13 02·1	12 24·5	6·0	5·2	12·0	10·3	18·0	15·5

52	SUN PLANETS	ARIES	MOON	v or d	Corrⁿ	v or d	Corrⁿ	v or d	Corrⁿ
s	° ′	° ′	° ′	′	′	′	′	′	′
00	13 00·0	13 02·1	12 24·5	0·0	0·0	6·0	5·3	12·0	10·5
01	13 00·3	13 02·4	12 24·7	0·1	0·1	6·1	5·3	12·1	10·6
02	13 00·5	13 02·6	12 24·9	0·2	0·2	6·2	5·4	12·2	10·7
03	13 00·8	13 02·9	12 25·2	0·3	0·3	6·3	5·5	12·3	10·8
04	13 01·0	13 03·1	12 25·4	0·4	0·4	6·4	5·6	12·4	10·9
05	13 01·3	13 03·4	12 25·7	0·5	0·4	6·5	5·7	12·5	10·9
06	13 01·5	13 03·6	12 25·9	0·6	0·5	6·6	5·8	12·6	11·0
07	13 01·8	13 03·9	12 26·1	0·7	0·6	6·7	5·9	12·7	11·1
08	13 02·0	13 04·1	12 26·4	0·8	0·7	6·8	6·0	12·8	11·2
09	13 02·3	13 04·4	12 26·6	0·9	0·8	6·9	6·0	12·9	11·3
10	13 02·5	13 04·6	12 26·9	1·0	0·9	7·0	6·1	13·0	11·4
11	13 02·8	13 04·9	12 27·1	1·1	1·0	7·1	6·2	13·1	11·5
12	13 03·0	13 05·1	12 27·3	1·2	1·1	7·2	6·3	13·2	11·6
13	13 03·3	13 05·4	12 27·6	1·3	1·1	7·3	6·4	13·3	11·6
14	13 03·5	13 05·6	12 27·8	1·4	1·2	7·4	6·5	13·4	11·7
15	13 03·8	13 05·9	12 28·0	1·5	1·3	7·5	6·6	13·5	11·8
16	13 04·0	13 06·1	12 28·3	1·6	1·4	7·6	6·7	13·6	11·9
17	13 04·3	13 06·4	12 28·5	1·7	1·5	7·7	6·7	13·7	12·0
18	13 04·5	13 06·6	12 28·8	1·8	1·6	7·8	6·8	13·8	12·1
19	13 04·8	13 06·9	12 29·0	1·9	1·7	7·9	6·9	13·9	12·2
20	13 05·0	13 07·1	12 29·2	2·0	1·8	8·0	7·0	14·0	12·3
21	13 05·3	13 07·4	12 29·5	2·1	1·8	8·1	7·1	14·1	12·3
22	13 05·5	13 07·7	12 29·7	2·2	1·9	8·2	7·2	14·2	12·4
23	13 05·8	13 07·9	12 30·0	2·3	2·0	8·3	7·3	14·3	12·5
24	13 06·0	13 08·2	12 30·2	2·4	2·1	8·4	7·4	14·4	12·6
25	13 06·3	13 08·4	12 30·4	2·5	2·2	8·5	7·4	14·5	12·7
26	13 06·5	13 08·7	12 30·7	2·6	2·3	8·6	7·5	14·6	12·8
27	13 06·8	13 08·9	12 30·9	2·7	2·4	8·7	7·6	14·7	12·9
28	13 07·0	13 09·2	12 31·1	2·8	2·5	8·8	7·7	14·8	13·0
29	13 07·3	13 09·4	12 31·4	2·9	2·5	8·9	7·8	14·9	13·0
30	13 07·5	13 09·7	12 31·6	3·0	2·6	9·0	7·9	15·0	13·1
31	13 07·8	13 09·9	12 31·9	3·1	2·7	9·1	8·0	15·1	13·2
32	13 08·0	13 10·2	12 32·1	3·2	2·8	9·2	8·0	15·2	13·3
33	13 08·3	13 10·4	12 32·3	3·3	2·9	9·3	8·1	15·3	13·4
34	13 08·5	13 10·7	12 32·6	3·4	3·0	9·4	8·2	15·4	13·5
35	13 08·8	13 10·9	12 32·8	3·5	3·1	9·5	8·3	15·5	13·6
36	13 09·0	13 11·2	12 33·1	3·6	3·2	9·6	8·4	15·6	13·7
37	13 09·3	13 11·4	12 33·3	3·7	3·2	9·7	8·5	15·7	13·7
38	13 09·5	13 11·7	12 33·5	3·8	3·3	9·8	8·6	15·8	13·8
39	13 09·8	13 11·9	12 33·8	3·9	3·4	9·9	8·7	15·9	13·9
40	13 10·0	13 12·2	12 34·0	4·0	3·5	10·0	8·8	16·0	14·0
41	13 10·3	13 12·4	12 34·2	4·1	3·6	10·1	8·8	16·1	14·1
42	13 10·5	13 12·7	12 34·5	4·2	3·7	10·2	8·9	16·2	14·2
43	13 10·8	13 12·9	12 34·7	4·3	3·8	10·3	9·0	16·3	14·3
44	13 11·0	13 13·2	12 35·0	4·4	3·9	10·4	9·1	16·4	14·3
45	13 11·3	13 13·4	12 35·2	4·5	3·9	10·5	9·2	16·5	14·4
46	13 11·5	13 13·7	12 35·4	4·6	4·0	10·6	9·3	16·6	14·5
47	13 11·8	13 13·9	12 35·7	4·7	4·1	10·7	9·4	16·7	14·6
48	13 12·0	13 14·2	12 35·9	4·8	4·2	10·8	9·5	16·8	14·7
49	13 12·3	13 14·4	12 36·2	4·9	4·3	10·9	9·5	16·9	14·8
50	13 12·5	13 14·7	12 36·4	5·0	4·4	11·0	9·6	17·0	14·9
51	13 12·8	13 14·9	12 36·6	5·1	4·5	11·1	9·7	17·1	15·0
52	13 13·0	13 15·2	12 36·9	5·2	4·6	11·2	9·8	17·2	15·1
53	13 13·3	13 15·4	12 37·1	5·3	4·6	11·3	9·9	17·3	15·1
54	13 13·5	13 15·7	12 37·4	5·4	4·7	11·4	10·0	17·4	15·2
55	13 13·8	13 15·9	12 37·6	5·5	4·8	11·5	10·1	17·5	15·3
56	13 14·0	13 16·2	12 37·8	5·6	4·9	11·6	10·2	17·6	15·4
57	13 14·3	13 16·4	12 38·1	5·7	5·0	11·7	10·2	17·7	15·5
58	13 14·5	13 16·7	12 38·3	5·8	5·1	11·8	10·3	17·8	15·6
59	13 14·8	13 16·9	12 38·5	5·9	5·2	11·9	10·4	17·9	15·7
60	13 15·0	13 17·2	12 38·8	6·0	5·3	12·0	10·5	18·0	15·8

53	SUN PLANETS	ARIES	MOON	v or d	Corrⁿ	v or d	Corrⁿ	v or d	Corrⁿ
s	° ′	° ′	° ′	′	′	′	′	′	′
00	13 15·0	13 17·2	12 38·8	0·0	0·0	6·0	5·4	12·0	10·7
01	13 15·3	13 17·4	12 39·0	0·1	0·1	6·1	5·4	12·1	10·8
02	13 15·5	13 17·7	12 39·3	0·2	0·2	6·2	5·5	12·2	10·9
03	13 15·8	13 17·9	12 39·5	0·3	0·3	6·3	5·6	12·3	11·0
04	13 16·0	13 18·2	12 39·7	0·4	0·4	6·4	5·7	12·4	11·1
05	13 16·3	13 18·4	12 40·0	0·5	0·4	6·5	5·8	12·5	11·1
06	13 16·5	13 18·7	12 40·2	0·6	0·5	6·6	5·9	12·6	11·2
07	13 16·8	13 18·9	12 40·5	0·7	0·6	6·7	6·0	12·7	11·3
08	13 17·0	13 19·2	12 40·7	0·8	0·7	6·8	6·1	12·8	11·4
09	13 17·3	13 19·4	12 40·9	0·9	0·8	6·9	6·2	12·9	11·5
10	13 17·5	13 19·7	12 41·2	1·0	0·9	7·0	6·2	13·0	11·6
11	13 17·8	13 19·9	12 41·4	1·1	1·0	7·1	6·3	13·1	11·7
12	13 18·0	13 20·2	12 41·6	1·2	1·1	7·2	6·4	13·2	11·8
13	13 18·3	13 20·4	12 41·9	1·3	1·2	7·3	6·5	13·3	11·9
14	13 18·5	13 20·7	12 42·1	1·4	1·2	7·4	6·6	13·4	11·9
15	13 18·8	13 20·9	12 42·4	1·5	1·3	7·5	6·7	13·5	12·0
16	13 19·0	13 21·2	12 42·6	1·6	1·4	7·6	6·8	13·6	12·1
17	13 19·3	13 21·4	12 42·8	1·7	1·5	7·7	6·9	13·7	12·2
18	13 19·5	13 21·7	12 43·1	1·8	1·6	7·8	7·0	13·8	12·3
19	13 19·8	13 21·9	12 43·3	1·9	1·7	7·9	7·0	13·9	12·4
20	13 20·0	13 22·2	12 43·6	2·0	1·8	8·0	7·1	14·0	12·5
21	13 20·3	13 22·4	12 43·8	2·1	1·9	8·1	7·2	14·1	12·6
22	13 20·5	13 22·7	12 44·0	2·2	2·0	8·2	7·3	14·2	12·7
23	13 20·8	13 22·9	12 44·3	2·3	2·1	8·3	7·4	14·3	12·8
24	13 21·0	13 23·2	12 44·5	2·4	2·1	8·4	7·5	14·4	12·8
25	13 21·3	13 23·4	12 44·7	2·5	2·2	8·5	7·6	14·5	12·9
26	13 21·5	13 23·7	12 45·0	2·6	2·3	8·6	7·7	14·6	13·0
27	13 21·8	13 23·9	12 45·2	2·7	2·4	8·7	7·8	14·7	13·1
28	13 22·0	13 24·2	12 45·5	2·8	2·5	8·8	7·8	14·8	13·2
29	13 22·3	13 24·4	12 45·7	2·9	2·6	8·9	7·9	14·9	13·3
30	13 22·5	13 24·7	12 45·9	3·0	2·7	9·0	8·0	15·0	13·4
31	13 22·8	13 24·9	12 46·2	3·1	2·8	9·1	8·1	15·1	13·5
32	13 23·0	13 25·2	12 46·4	3·2	2·9	9·2	8·2	15·2	13·6
33	13 23·3	13 25·4	12 46·7	3·3	2·9	9·3	8·3	15·3	13·6
34	13 23·5	13 25·7	12 46·9	3·4	3·0	9·4	8·4	15·4	13·7
35	13 23·8	13 26·0	12 47·1	3·5	3·1	9·5	8·5	15·5	13·8
36	13 24·0	13 26·2	12 47·4	3·6	3·2	9·6	8·6	15·6	13·9
37	13 24·3	13 26·5	12 47·6	3·7	3·3	9·7	8·6	15·7	14·0
38	13 24·5	13 26·7	12 47·9	3·8	3·4	9·8	8·7	15·8	14·1
39	13 24·8	13 27·0	12 48·1	3·9	3·5	9·9	8·8	15·9	14·2
40	13 25·0	13 27·2	12 48·3	4·0	3·6	10·0	8·9	16·0	14·3
41	13 25·3	13 27·5	12 48·6	4·1	3·7	10·1	9·0	16·1	14·4
42	13 25·5	13 27·7	12 48·8	4·2	3·7	10·2	9·1	16·2	14·4
43	13 25·8	13 28·0	12 49·0	4·3	3·8	10·3	9·2	16·3	14·5
44	13 26·0	13 28·2	12 49·3	4·4	3·9	10·4	9·3	16·4	14·6
45	13 26·3	13 28·5	12 49·5	4·5	4·0	10·5	9·4	16·5	14·7
46	13 26·5	13 28·7	12 49·8	4·6	4·1	10·6	9·5	16·6	14·8
47	13 26·8	13 29·0	12 50·0	4·7	4·2	10·7	9·5	16·7	14·9
48	13 27·0	13 29·2	12 50·2	4·8	4·3	10·8	9·6	16·8	15·0
49	13 27·3	13 29·5	12 50·5	4·9	4·4	10·9	9·7	16·9	15·1
50	13 27·5	13 29·7	12 50·7	5·0	4·5	11·0	9·8	17·0	15·2
51	13 27·8	13 30·0	12 51·0	5·1	4·5	11·1	9·9	17·1	15·2
52	13 28·0	13 30·2	12 51·2	5·2	4·6	11·2	10·0	17·2	15·3
53	13 28·3	13 30·5	12 51·4	5·3	4·7	11·3	10·1	17·3	15·4
54	13 28·5	13 30·7	12 51·7	5·4	4·8	11·4	10·2	17·4	15·5
55	13 28·8	13 31·0	12 51·9	5·5	4·9	11·5	10·3	17·5	15·6
56	13 29·0	13 31·2	12 52·1	5·6	5·0	11·6	10·3	17·6	15·7
57	13 29·3	13 31·5	12 52·4	5·7	5·1	11·7	10·4	17·7	15·8
58	13 29·5	13 31·7	12 52·6	5·8	5·2	11·8	10·5	17·8	15·9
59	13 29·8	13 32·0	12 52·9	5·9	5·3	11·9	10·6	17·9	16·0
60	13 30·0	13 32·2	12 53·1	6·0	5·4	12·0	10·7	18·0	16·1

54ᵐ

54 s	SUN PLANETS	ARIES	MOON	v or d Corrⁿ	v or d Corrⁿ	v or d Corrⁿ
00	13 30.0	13 32.2	12 53.1	0.0 0.0	6.0 5.5	12.0 10.9
01	13 30.3	13 32.5	12 53.3	0.1 0.1	6.1 5.5	12.1 11.0
02	13 30.5	13 32.7	12 53.6	0.2 0.2	6.2 5.6	12.2 11.1
03	13 30.8	13 33.0	12 53.8	0.3 0.3	6.3 5.7	12.3 11.2
04	13 31.0	13 33.2	12 54.1	0.4 0.4	6.4 5.8	12.4 11.3
05	13 31.3	13 33.5	12 54.3	0.5 0.5	6.5 5.9	12.5 11.4
06	13 31.5	13 33.7	12 54.5	0.6 0.5	6.6 6.0	12.6 11.4
07	13 31.8	13 34.0	12 54.8	0.7 0.6	6.7 6.1	12.7 11.5
08	13 32.0	13 34.2	12 55.0	0.8 0.7	6.8 6.2	12.8 11.6
09	13 32.3	13 34.5	12 55.2	0.9 0.8	6.9 6.3	12.9 11.7
10	13 32.5	13 34.7	12 55.5	1.0 0.9	7.0 6.4	13.0 11.8
11	13 32.8	13 35.0	12 55.7	1.1 1.0	7.1 6.4	13.1 11.9
12	13 33.0	13 35.2	12 56.0	1.2 1.1	7.2 6.5	13.2 12.0
13	13 33.3	13 35.5	12 56.2	1.3 1.2	7.3 6.6	13.3 12.1
14	13 33.5	13 35.7	12 56.4	1.4 1.3	7.4 6.7	13.4 12.2
15	13 33.8	13 36.0	12 56.7	1.5 1.4	7.5 6.8	13.5 12.3
16	13 34.0	13 36.2	12 56.9	1.6 1.5	7.6 6.9	13.6 12.4
17	13 34.3	13 36.5	12 57.2	1.7 1.5	7.7 7.0	13.7 12.4
18	13 34.5	13 36.7	12 57.4	1.8 1.6	7.8 7.1	13.8 12.5
19	13 34.8	13 37.0	12 57.6	1.9 1.7	7.9 7.2	13.9 12.6
20	13 35.0	13 37.2	12 57.9	2.0 1.8	8.0 7.3	14.0 12.7
21	13 35.3	13 37.5	12 58.1	2.1 1.9	8.1 7.4	14.1 12.8
22	13 35.5	13 37.7	12 58.3	2.2 2.0	8.2 7.4	14.2 12.9
23	13 35.8	13 38.0	12 58.6	2.3 2.1	8.3 7.5	14.3 13.0
24	13 36.0	13 38.2	12 58.8	2.4 2.2	8.4 7.6	14.4 13.1
25	13 36.3	13 38.5	12 59.1	2.5 2.3	8.5 7.7	14.5 13.2
26	13 36.5	13 38.7	12 59.3	2.6 2.4	8.6 7.8	14.6 13.3
27	13 36.8	13 39.0	12 59.5	2.7 2.5	8.7 7.9	14.7 13.4
28	13 37.0	13 39.2	12 59.8	2.8 2.5	8.8 8.0	14.8 13.4
29	13 37.3	13 39.5	13 00.0	2.9 2.6	8.9 8.1	14.9 13.5
30	13 37.5	13 39.7	13 00.3	3.0 2.7	9.0 8.2	15.0 13.6
31	13 37.8	13 40.0	13 00.5	3.1 2.8	9.1 8.3	15.1 13.7
32	13 38.0	13 40.2	13 00.7	3.2 2.9	9.2 8.4	15.2 13.8
33	13 38.3	13 40.5	13 01.0	3.3 3.0	9.3 8.4	15.3 13.9
34	13 38.5	13 40.7	13 01.2	3.4 3.1	9.4 8.5	15.4 14.0
35	13 38.8	13 41.0	13 01.5	3.5 3.2	9.5 8.6	15.5 14.1
36	13 39.0	13 41.2	13 01.7	3.6 3.3	9.6 8.7	15.6 14.2
37	13 39.3	13 41.5	13 01.9	3.7 3.4	9.7 8.8	15.7 14.3
38	13 39.5	13 41.7	13 02.2	3.8 3.5	9.8 8.9	15.8 14.4
39	13 39.8	13 42.0	13 02.4	3.9 3.5	9.9 9.0	15.9 14.4
40	13 40.0	13 42.2	13 02.6	4.0 3.6	10.0 9.1	16.0 14.5
41	13 40.3	13 42.5	13 02.9	4.1 3.7	10.1 9.2	16.1 14.6
42	13 40.5	13 42.7	13 03.1	4.2 3.8	10.2 9.3	16.2 14.7
43	13 40.8	13 43.0	13 03.4	4.3 3.9	10.3 9.4	16.3 14.8
44	13 41.0	13 43.2	13 03.6	4.4 4.0	10.4 9.4	16.4 14.9
45	13 41.3	13 43.5	13 03.8	4.5 4.1	10.5 9.5	16.5 15.0
46	13 41.5	13 43.7	13 04.1	4.6 4.2	10.6 9.6	16.6 15.1
47	13 41.8	13 44.0	13 04.3	4.7 4.3	10.7 9.7	16.7 15.2
48	13 42.0	13 44.3	13 04.6	4.8 4.4	10.8 9.8	16.8 15.3
49	13 42.3	13 44.5	13 04.8	4.9 4.5	10.9 9.9	16.9 15.4
50	13 42.5	13 44.8	13 05.0	5.0 4.5	11.0 10.0	17.0 15.4
51	13 42.8	13 45.0	13 05.3	5.1 4.6	11.1 10.1	17.1 15.5
52	13 43.0	13 45.3	13 05.5	5.2 4.7	11.2 10.2	17.2 15.6
53	13 43.3	13 45.5	13 05.7	5.3 4.8	11.3 10.3	17.3 15.7
54	13 43.5	13 45.8	13 06.0	5.4 4.9	11.4 10.4	17.4 15.8
55	13 43.8	13 46.0	13 06.2	5.5 5.0	11.5 10.4	17.5 15.9
56	13 44.0	13 46.3	13 06.5	5.6 5.1	11.6 10.5	17.6 16.0
57	13 44.3	13 46.5	13 06.7	5.7 5.2	11.7 10.6	17.7 16.1
58	13 44.5	13 46.8	13 06.9	5.8 5.3	11.8 10.7	17.8 16.2
59	13 44.8	13 47.0	13 07.2	5.9 5.4	11.9 10.8	17.9 16.3
60	13 45.0	13 47.3	13 07.4	6.0 5.5	12.0 10.9	18.0 16.4

55ᵐ

55 s	SUN PLANETS	ARIES	MOON	v or d Corrⁿ	v or d Corrⁿ	v or d Corrⁿ
00	13 45.0	13 47.3	13 07.4	0.0 0.0	6.0 5.6	12.0 11.1
01	13 45.3	13 47.5	13 07.7	0.1 0.1	6.1 5.6	12.1 11.2
02	13 45.5	13 47.8	13 07.9	0.2 0.2	6.2 5.7	12.2 11.3
03	13 45.8	13 48.0	13 08.1	0.3 0.3	6.3 5.8	12.3 11.4
04	13 46.0	13 48.3	13 08.4	0.4 0.4	6.4 5.9	12.4 11.5
05	13 46.3	13 48.5	13 08.6	0.5 0.5	6.5 6.0	12.5 11.6
06	13 46.5	13 48.8	13 08.8	0.6 0.6	6.6 6.1	12.6 11.7
07	13 46.8	13 49.0	13 09.1	0.7 0.6	6.7 6.2	12.7 11.7
08	13 47.0	13 49.3	13 09.3	0.8 0.7	6.8 6.3	12.8 11.8
09	13 47.3	13 49.5	13 09.5	0.9 0.8	6.9 6.4	12.9 11.9
10	13 47.5	13 49.8	13 09.8	1.0 0.9	7.0 6.5	13.0 12.0
11	13 47.8	13 50.0	13 10.0	1.1 1.0	7.1 6.6	13.1 12.1
12	13 48.0	13 50.3	13 10.3	1.2 1.1	7.2 6.7	13.2 12.2
13	13 48.3	13 50.5	13 10.5	1.3 1.2	7.3 6.8	13.3 12.3
14	13 48.5	13 50.8	13 10.8	1.4 1.3	7.4 6.8	13.4 12.4
15	13 48.8	13 51.0	13 11.0	1.5 1.4	7.5 6.9	13.5 12.5
16	13 49.0	13 51.3	13 11.2	1.6 1.5	7.6 7.0	13.6 12.6
17	13 49.3	13 51.5	13 11.5	1.7 1.6	7.7 7.1	13.7 12.7
18	13 49.5	13 51.8	13 11.7	1.8 1.7	7.8 7.2	13.8 12.8
19	13 49.8	13 52.0	13 12.0	1.9 1.8	7.9 7.3	13.9 12.9
20	13 50.0	13 52.3	13 12.2	2.0 1.9	8.0 7.4	14.0 13.0
21	13 50.3	13 52.5	13 12.4	2.1 1.9	8.1 7.5	14.1 13.0
22	13 50.5	13 52.8	13 12.7	2.2 2.0	8.2 7.6	14.2 13.1
23	13 50.8	13 53.0	13 12.9	2.3 2.1	8.3 7.7	14.3 13.2
24	13 51.0	13 53.3	13 13.1	2.4 2.2	8.4 7.8	14.4 13.3
25	13 51.3	13 53.5	13 13.4	2.5 2.3	8.5 7.9	14.5 13.4
26	13 51.5	13 53.8	13 13.6	2.6 2.4	8.6 8.0	14.6 13.5
27	13 51.8	13 54.0	13 13.9	2.7 2.5	8.7 8.0	14.7 13.6
28	13 52.0	13 54.3	13 14.1	2.8 2.6	8.8 8.1	14.8 13.7
29	13 52.3	13 54.5	13 14.3	2.9 2.7	8.9 8.2	14.9 13.8
30	13 52.5	13 54.8	13 14.6	3.0 2.8	9.0 8.3	15.0 13.9
31	13 52.8	13 55.0	13 14.8	3.1 2.9	9.1 8.4	15.1 14.0
32	13 53.0	13 55.3	13 15.1	3.2 3.0	9.2 8.5	15.2 14.1
33	13 53.3	13 55.5	13 15.3	3.3 3.1	9.3 8.6	15.3 14.2
34	13 53.5	13 55.8	13 15.5	3.4 3.1	9.4 8.7	15.4 14.2
35	13 53.8	13 56.0	13 15.8	3.5 3.2	9.5 8.8	15.5 14.3
36	13 54.0	13 56.3	13 16.0	3.6 3.3	9.6 8.9	15.6 14.4
37	13 54.3	13 56.5	13 16.2	3.7 3.4	9.7 9.0	15.7 14.5
38	13 54.5	13 56.8	13 16.5	3.8 3.5	9.8 9.1	15.8 14.6
39	13 54.8	13 57.0	13 16.7	3.9 3.6	9.9 9.2	15.9 14.7
40	13 55.0	13 57.3	13 17.0	4.0 3.7	10.0 9.3	16.0 14.8
41	13 55.3	13 57.5	13 17.2	4.1 3.8	10.1 9.3	16.1 14.9
42	13 55.5	13 57.8	13 17.4	4.2 3.9	10.2 9.4	16.2 15.0
43	13 55.8	13 58.0	13 17.7	4.3 4.0	10.3 9.5	16.3 15.1
44	13 56.0	13 58.3	13 17.9	4.4 4.1	10.4 9.6	16.4 15.2
45	13 56.3	13 58.5	13 18.2	4.5 4.2	10.5 9.7	16.5 15.3
46	13 56.5	13 58.8	13 18.4	4.6 4.3	10.6 9.8	16.6 15.4
47	13 56.8	13 59.0	13 18.6	4.7 4.3	10.7 9.9	16.7 15.4
48	13 57.0	13 59.3	13 18.9	4.8 4.4	10.8 10.0	16.8 15.5
49	13 57.3	13 59.5	13 19.1	4.9 4.5	10.9 10.1	16.9 15.6
50	13 57.5	13 59.8	13 19.3	5.0 4.6	11.0 10.2	17.0 15.7
51	13 57.8	14 00.0	13 19.6	5.1 4.7	11.1 10.3	17.1 15.8
52	13 58.0	14 00.3	13 19.8	5.2 4.8	11.2 10.4	17.2 15.9
53	13 58.3	14 00.5	13 20.1	5.3 4.9	11.3 10.5	17.3 16.0
54	13 58.5	14 00.8	13 20.3	5.4 5.0	11.4 10.5	17.4 16.1
55	13 58.8	14 01.0	13 20.5	5.5 5.1	11.5 10.6	17.5 16.2
56	13 59.0	14 01.3	13 20.8	5.6 5.2	11.6 10.7	17.6 16.3
57	13 59.3	14 01.5	13 21.0	5.7 5.3	11.7 10.8	17.7 16.4
58	13 59.5	14 01.8	13 21.3	5.8 5.4	11.8 10.9	17.8 16.5
59	13 59.8	14 02.0	13 21.5	5.9 5.5	11.9 11.0	17.9 16.6
60	14 00.0	14 02.3	13 21.7	6.0 5.6	12.0 11.1	18.0 16.7

56ᵐ

56	SUN PLANETS	ARIES	MOON	v or Corrⁿ d		v or Corrⁿ d		v or Corrⁿ d	
s	° ′	° ′	° ′	′	′	′	′	′	′
00	14 00.0	14 02.3	13 21.7	0.0	0.0	6.0	5.7	12.0	11.3
01	14 00.3	14 02.6	13 22.0	0.1	0.1	6.1	5.7	12.1	11.4
02	14 00.5	14 02.8	13 22.2	0.2	0.2	6.2	5.8	12.2	11.5
03	14 00.8	14 03.1	13 22.4	0.3	0.3	6.3	5.9	12.3	11.6
04	14 01.0	14 03.3	13 22.7	0.4	0.4	6.4	6.0	12.4	11.7
05	14 01.3	14 03.6	13 22.9	0.5	0.5	6.5	6.1	12.5	11.8
06	14 01.5	14 03.8	13 23.2	0.6	0.6	6.6	6.2	12.6	11.9
07	14 01.8	14 04.1	13 23.4	0.7	0.7	6.7	6.3	12.7	12.0
08	14 02.0	14 04.3	13 23.6	0.8	0.8	6.8	6.4	12.8	12.1
09	14 02.3	14 04.6	13 23.9	0.9	0.8	6.9	6.5	12.9	12.1
10	14 02.5	14 04.8	13 24.1	1.0	0.9	7.0	6.6	13.0	12.2
11	14 02.8	14 05.1	13 24.4	1.1	1.0	7.1	6.7	13.1	12.3
12	14 03.0	14 05.3	13 24.6	1.2	1.1	7.2	6.8	13.2	12.4
13	14 03.3	14 05.6	13 24.8	1.3	1.2	7.3	6.9	13.3	12.5
14	14 03.5	14 05.8	13 25.1	1.4	1.3	7.4	7.0	13.4	12.6
15	14 03.8	14 06.1	13 25.3	1.5	1.4	7.5	7.1	13.5	12.7
16	14 04.0	14 06.3	13 25.6	1.6	1.5	7.6	7.2	13.6	12.8
17	14 04.3	14 06.6	13 25.8	1.7	1.6	7.7	7.3	13.7	12.9
18	14 04.5	14 06.8	13 26.0	1.8	1.7	7.8	7.3	13.8	13.0
19	14 04.8	14 07.1	13 26.3	1.9	1.8	7.9	7.4	13.9	13.1
20	14 05.0	14 07.3	13 26.5	2.0	1.9	8.0	7.5	14.0	13.2
21	14 05.3	14 07.6	13 26.7	2.1	2.0	8.1	7.6	14.1	13.3
22	14 05.5	14 07.8	13 27.0	2.2	2.1	8.2	7.7	14.2	13.4
23	14 05.8	14 08.1	13 27.2	2.3	2.2	8.3	7.8	14.3	13.5
24	14 06.0	14 08.3	13 27.5	2.4	2.3	8.4	7.9	14.4	13.6
25	14 06.3	14 08.6	13 27.7	2.5	2.4	8.5	8.0	14.5	13.7
26	14 06.5	14 08.8	13 27.9	2.6	2.4	8.6	8.1	14.6	13.7
27	14 06.8	14 09.1	13 28.2	2.7	2.5	8.7	8.2	14.7	13.8
28	14 07.0	14 09.3	13 28.4	2.8	2.6	8.8	8.3	14.8	13.9
29	14 07.3	14 09.6	13 28.7	2.9	2.7	8.9	8.4	14.9	14.0
30	14 07.5	14 09.8	13 28.9	3.0	2.8	9.0	8.5	15.0	14.1
31	14 07.8	14 10.1	13 29.1	3.1	2.9	9.1	8.6	15.1	14.2
32	14 08.0	14 10.3	13 29.4	3.2	3.0	9.2	8.7	15.2	14.3
33	14 08.3	14 10.6	13 29.6	3.3	3.1	9.3	8.8	15.3	14.4
34	14 08.5	14 10.8	13 29.8	3.4	3.2	9.4	8.9	15.4	14.5
35	14 08.8	14 11.1	13 30.1	3.5	3.3	9.5	8.9	15.5	14.6
36	14 09.0	14 11.3	13 30.3	3.6	3.4	9.6	9.0	15.6	14.7
37	14 09.3	14 11.6	13 30.6	3.7	3.5	9.7	9.1	15.7	14.8
38	14 09.5	14 11.8	13 30.8	3.8	3.6	9.8	9.2	15.8	14.9
39	14 09.8	14 12.1	13 31.0	3.9	3.7	9.9	9.3	15.9	15.0
40	14 10.0	14 12.3	13 31.3	4.0	3.8	10.0	9.4	16.0	15.1
41	14 10.3	14 12.6	13 31.5	4.1	3.9	10.1	9.5	16.1	15.2
42	14 10.5	14 12.8	13 31.8	4.2	4.0	10.2	9.6	16.2	15.3
43	14 10.8	14 13.1	13 32.0	4.3	4.0	10.3	9.7	16.3	15.3
44	14 11.0	14 13.3	13 32.2	4.4	4.1	10.4	9.8	16.4	15.4
45	14 11.3	14 13.6	13 32.5	4.5	4.2	10.5	9.9	16.5	15.5
46	14 11.5	14 13.8	13 32.7	4.6	4.3	10.6	10.0	16.6	15.6
47	14 11.8	14 14.1	13 32.9	4.7	4.4	10.7	10.1	16.7	15.7
48	14 12.0	14 14.3	13 33.2	4.8	4.5	10.8	10.2	16.8	15.8
49	14 12.3	14 14.6	13 33.4	4.9	4.6	10.9	10.3	16.9	15.9
50	14 12.5	14 14.8	13 33.7	5.0	4.7	11.0	10.4	17.0	16.0
51	14 12.8	14 15.1	13 33.9	5.1	4.8	11.1	10.5	17.1	16.1
52	14 13.0	14 15.3	13 34.1	5.2	4.9	11.2	10.5	17.2	16.2
53	14 13.3	14 15.6	13 34.4	5.3	5.0	11.3	10.6	17.3	16.3
54	14 13.5	14 15.8	13 34.6	5.4	5.1	11.4	10.7	17.4	16.4
55	14 13.8	14 16.1	13 34.9	5.5	5.2	11.5	10.8	17.5	16.5
56	14 14.0	14 16.3	13 35.1	5.6	5.3	11.6	10.9	17.6	16.6
57	14 14.3	14 16.6	13 35.3	5.7	5.4	11.7	11.0	17.7	16.7
58	14 14.5	14 16.8	13 35.6	5.8	5.5	11.8	11.1	17.8	16.8
59	14 14.8	14 17.1	13 35.8	5.9	5.6	11.9	11.2	17.9	16.9
60	14 15.0	14 17.3	13 36.1	6.0	5.7	12.0	11.3	18.0	17.0

57ᵐ

57	SUN PLANETS	ARIES	MOON	v or Corrⁿ d		v or Corrⁿ d		v or Corrⁿ d	
s	° ′	° ′	° ′	′	′	′	′	′	′
00	14 15.0	14 17.3	13 36.1	0.0	0.0	6.0	5.8	12.0	11.5
01	14 15.3	14 17.6	13 36.3	0.1	0.1	6.1	5.8	12.1	11.6
02	14 15.5	14 17.8	13 36.5	0.2	0.2	6.2	5.9	12.2	11.7
03	14 15.8	14 18.1	13 36.8	0.3	0.3	6.3	6.0	12.3	11.8
04	14 16.0	14 18.3	13 37.0	0.4	0.4	6.4	6.1	12.4	11.9
05	14 16.3	14 18.6	13 37.2	0.5	0.5	6.5	6.2	12.5	12.0
06	14 16.5	14 18.8	13 37.5	0.6	0.6	6.6	6.3	12.6	12.1
07	14 16.8	14 19.1	13 37.7	0.7	0.7	6.7	6.4	12.7	12.2
08	14 17.0	14 19.3	13 38.0	0.8	0.8	6.8	6.5	12.8	12.3
09	14 17.3	14 19.6	13 38.2	0.9	0.9	6.9	6.6	12.9	12.4
10	14 17.5	14 19.8	13 38.4	1.0	1.0	7.0	6.7	13.0	12.5
11	14 17.8	14 20.1	13 38.7	1.1	1.1	7.1	6.8	13.1	12.6
12	14 18.0	14 20.3	13 38.9	1.2	1.2	7.2	6.9	13.2	12.7
13	14 18.3	14 20.6	13 39.2	1.3	1.2	7.3	7.0	13.3	12.7
14	14 18.5	14 20.9	13 39.4	1.4	1.3	7.4	7.1	13.4	12.8
15	14 18.8	14 21.1	13 39.6	1.5	1.4	7.5	7.2	13.5	12.9
16	14 19.0	14 21.4	13 39.9	1.6	1.5	7.6	7.3	13.6	13.0
17	14 19.3	14 21.6	13 40.1	1.7	1.6	7.7	7.4	13.7	13.1
18	14 19.5	14 21.9	13 40.3	1.8	1.7	7.8	7.5	13.8	13.2
19	14 19.8	14 22.1	13 40.6	1.9	1.8	7.9	7.6	13.9	13.3
20	14 20.0	14 22.4	13 40.8	2.0	1.9	8.0	7.7	14.0	13.4
21	14 20.3	14 22.6	13 41.1	2.1	2.0	8.1	7.8	14.1	13.5
22	14 20.5	14 22.9	13 41.3	2.2	2.1	8.2	7.9	14.2	13.6
23	14 20.8	14 23.1	13 41.5	2.3	2.2	8.3	8.0	14.3	13.7
24	14 21.0	14 23.4	13 41.8	2.4	2.3	8.4	8.1	14.4	13.8
25	14 21.3	14 23.6	13 42.0	2.5	2.4	8.5	8.1	14.5	13.9
26	14 21.5	14 23.9	13 42.3	2.6	2.5	8.6	8.2	14.6	14.0
27	14 21.8	14 24.1	13 42.5	2.7	2.6	8.7	8.3	14.7	14.1
28	14 22.0	14 24.4	13 42.7	2.8	2.7	8.8	8.4	14.8	14.2
29	14 22.3	14 24.6	13 43.0	2.9	2.8	8.9	8.5	14.9	14.3
30	14 22.5	14 24.9	13 43.2	3.0	2.9	9.0	8.6	15.0	14.4
31	14 22.8	14 25.1	13 43.4	3.1	3.0	9.1	8.7	15.1	14.5
32	14 23.0	14 25.4	13 43.7	3.2	3.1	9.2	8.8	15.2	14.6
33	14 23.3	14 25.6	13 43.9	3.3	3.2	9.3	8.9	15.3	14.7
34	14 23.5	14 25.9	13 44.2	3.4	3.3	9.4	9.0	15.4	14.8
35	14 23.8	14 26.1	13 44.4	3.5	3.4	9.5	9.1	15.5	14.9
36	14 24.0	14 26.4	13 44.6	3.6	3.5	9.6	9.2	15.6	15.0
37	14 24.3	14 26.6	13 44.9	3.7	3.5	9.7	9.3	15.7	15.0
38	14 24.5	14 26.9	13 45.1	3.8	3.6	9.8	9.4	15.8	15.1
39	14 24.8	14 27.1	13 45.4	3.9	3.7	9.9	9.5	15.9	15.2
40	14 25.0	14 27.4	13 45.6	4.0	3.8	10.0	9.6	16.0	15.3
41	14 25.3	14 27.6	13 45.8	4.1	3.9	10.1	9.7	16.1	15.4
42	14 25.5	14 27.9	13 46.1	4.2	4.0	10.2	9.8	16.2	15.5
43	14 25.8	14 28.1	13 46.3	4.3	4.1	10.3	9.9	16.3	15.6
44	14 26.0	14 28.4	13 46.5	4.4	4.2	10.4	10.0	16.4	15.7
45	14 26.3	14 28.6	13 46.8	4.5	4.3	10.5	10.1	16.5	15.8
46	14 26.5	14 28.9	13 47.0	4.6	4.4	10.6	10.2	16.6	15.9
47	14 26.8	14 29.1	13 47.3	4.7	4.5	10.7	10.3	16.7	16.0
48	14 27.0	14 29.4	13 47.5	4.8	4.6	10.8	10.4	16.8	16.1
49	14 27.3	14 29.6	13 47.7	4.9	4.7	10.9	10.4	16.9	16.2
50	14 27.5	14 29.9	13 48.0	5.0	4.8	11.0	10.5	17.0	16.3
51	14 27.8	14 30.1	13 48.2	5.1	4.9	11.1	10.6	17.1	16.4
52	14 28.0	14 30.4	13 48.5	5.2	5.0	11.2	10.7	17.2	16.5
53	14 28.3	14 30.6	13 48.7	5.3	5.1	11.3	10.8	17.3	16.6
54	14 28.5	14 30.9	13 48.9	5.4	5.2	11.4	10.9	17.4	16.7
55	14 28.8	14 31.1	13 49.2	5.5	5.3	11.5	11.0	17.5	16.8
56	14 29.0	14 31.4	13 49.4	5.6	5.4	11.6	11.1	17.6	16.9
57	14 29.3	14 31.6	13 49.7	5.7	5.5	11.7	11.2	17.7	17.0
58	14 29.5	14 31.9	13 49.9	5.8	5.6	11.8	11.3	17.8	17.1
59	14 29.8	14 32.1	13 50.1	5.9	5.7	11.9	11.4	17.9	17.2
60	14 30.0	14 32.4	13 50.4	6.0	5.8	12.0	11.5	18.0	17.3

58m

58	SUN PLANETS	ARIES	MOON	v or Corrn d		v or Corrn d		v or Corrn d	
s	° ′	° ′	° ′	′	′	′	′	′	′
00	14 30.0	14 32.4	13 50.4	0.0	0.0	6.0	5.9	12.0	11.7
01	14 30.3	14 32.6	13 50.6	0.1	0.1	6.1	5.9	12.1	11.8
02	14 30.5	14 32.9	13 50.8	0.2	0.2	6.2	6.0	12.2	11.9
03	14 30.8	14 33.1	13 51.1	0.3	0.3	6.3	6.1	12.3	12.0
04	14 31.0	14 33.4	13 51.3	0.4	0.4	6.4	6.2	12.4	12.1
05	14 31.3	14 33.6	13 51.6	0.5	0.5	6.5	6.3	12.5	12.2
06	14 31.5	14 33.9	13 51.8	0.6	0.6	6.6	6.4	12.6	12.3
07	14 31.8	14 34.1	13 52.0	0.7	0.7	6.7	6.5	12.7	12.4
08	14 32.0	14 34.4	13 52.3	0.8	0.8	6.8	6.6	12.8	12.5
09	14 32.3	14 34.6	13 52.5	0.9	0.9	6.9	6.7	12.9	12.6
10	14 32.5	14 34.9	13 52.8	1.0	1.0	7.0	6.8	13.0	12.7
11	14 32.8	14 35.1	13 53.0	1.1	1.1	7.1	6.9	13.1	12.8
12	14 33.0	14 35.4	13 53.2	1.2	1.2	7.2	7.0	13.2	12.9
13	14 33.3	14 35.6	13 53.5	1.3	1.3	7.3	7.1	13.3	13.0
14	14 33.5	14 35.9	13 53.7	1.4	1.4	7.4	7.2	13.4	13.1
15	14 33.8	14 36.1	13 53.9	1.5	1.5	7.5	7.3	13.5	13.2
16	14 34.0	14 36.4	13 54.2	1.6	1.6	7.6	7.4	13.6	13.3
17	14 34.3	14 36.6	13 54.4	1.7	1.7	7.7	7.5	13.7	13.4
18	14 34.5	14 36.9	13 54.7	1.8	1.8	7.8	7.6	13.8	13.5
19	14 34.8	14 37.1	13 54.9	1.9	1.9	7.9	7.7	13.9	13.6
20	14 35.0	14 37.4	13 55.1	2.0	2.0	8.0	7.8	14.0	13.7
21	14 35.3	14 37.6	13 55.4	2.1	2.0	8.1	7.9	14.1	13.7
22	14 35.5	14 37.9	13 55.6	2.2	2.1	8.2	8.0	14.2	13.8
23	14 35.8	14 38.1	13 55.9	2.3	2.2	8.3	8.1	14.3	13.9
24	14 36.0	14 38.4	13 56.1	2.4	2.3	8.4	8.2	14.4	14.0
25	14 36.3	14 38.6	13 56.3	2.5	2.4	8.5	8.3	14.5	14.1
26	14 36.5	14 38.9	13 56.6	2.6	2.5	8.6	8.4	14.6	14.2
27	14 36.8	14 39.2	13 56.8	2.7	2.6	8.7	8.5	14.7	14.3
28	14 37.0	14 39.4	13 57.0	2.8	2.7	8.8	8.6	14.8	14.4
29	14 37.3	14 39.7	13 57.3	2.9	2.8	8.9	8.7	14.9	14.5
30	14 37.5	14 39.9	13 57.5	3.0	2.9	9.0	8.8	15.0	14.6
31	14 37.8	14 40.2	13 57.8	3.1	3.0	9.1	8.9	15.1	14.7
32	14 38.0	14 40.4	13 58.0	3.2	3.1	9.2	9.0	15.2	14.8
33	14 38.3	14 40.7	13 58.2	3.3	3.2	9.3	9.1	15.3	14.9
34	14 38.5	14 40.9	13 58.5	3.4	3.3	9.4	9.2	15.4	15.0
35	14 38.8	14 41.2	13 58.7	3.5	3.4	9.5	9.3	15.5	15.1
36	14 39.0	14 41.4	13 59.0	3.6	3.5	9.6	9.4	15.6	15.2
37	14 39.3	14 41.7	13 59.2	3.7	3.6	9.7	9.5	15.7	15.3
38	14 39.5	14 41.9	13 59.4	3.8	3.7	9.8	9.6	15.8	15.4
39	14 39.8	14 42.2	13 59.7	3.9	3.8	9.9	9.7	15.9	15.5
40	14 40.0	14 42.4	13 59.9	4.0	3.9	10.0	9.8	16.0	15.6
41	14 40.3	14 42.7	14 00.1	4.1	4.0	10.1	9.9	16.1	15.7
42	14 40.5	14 42.9	14 00.4	4.2	4.1	10.2	9.9	16.2	15.8
43	14 40.8	14 43.2	14 00.6	4.3	4.2	10.3	10.0	16.3	15.9
44	14 41.0	14 43.4	14 00.9	4.4	4.3	10.4	10.1	16.4	16.0
45	14 41.3	14 43.7	14 01.1	4.5	4.4	10.5	10.2	16.5	16.1
46	14 41.5	14 43.9	14 01.3	4.6	4.5	10.6	10.3	16.6	16.2
47	14 41.8	14 44.2	14 01.6	4.7	4.6	10.7	10.4	16.7	16.3
48	14 42.0	14 44.4	14 01.8	4.8	4.7	10.8	10.5	16.8	16.4
49	14 42.3	14 44.7	14 02.1	4.9	4.8	10.9	10.6	16.9	16.5
50	14 42.5	14 44.9	14 02.3	5.0	4.9	11.0	10.7	17.0	16.6
51	14 42.8	14 45.2	14 02.5	5.1	5.0	11.1	10.8	17.1	16.7
52	14 43.0	14 45.4	14 02.8	5.2	5.1	11.2	10.9	17.2	16.8
53	14 43.3	14 45.7	14 03.0	5.3	5.2	11.3	11.0	17.3	16.9
54	14 43.5	14 45.9	14 03.3	5.4	5.3	11.4	11.1	17.4	17.0
55	14 43.8	14 46.2	14 03.5	5.5	5.4	11.5	11.2	17.5	17.1
56	14 44.0	14 46.4	14 03.7	5.6	5.5	11.6	11.3	17.6	17.2
57	14 44.3	14 46.7	14 04.0	5.7	5.6	11.7	11.4	17.7	17.3
58	14 44.5	14 46.9	14 04.2	5.8	5.7	11.8	11.5	17.8	17.4
59	14 44.8	14 47.2	14 04.4	5.9	5.8	11.9	11.6	17.9	17.5
60	14 45.0	14 47.4	14 04.7	6.0	5.9	12.0	11.7	18.0	17.6

59m

59	SUN PLANETS	ARIES	MOON	v or Corrn d		v or Corrn d		v or Corrn d	
s	° ′	° ′	° ′	′	′	′	′	′	′
00	14 45.0	14 47.4	14 04.7	0.0	0.0	6.0	6.0	12.0	11.9
01	14 45.3	14 47.7	14 04.9	0.1	0.1	6.1	6.0	12.1	12.0
02	14 45.5	14 47.9	14 05.2	0.2	0.2	6.2	6.1	12.2	12.1
03	14 45.8	14 48.2	14 05.4	0.3	0.3	6.3	6.2	12.3	12.2
04	14 46.0	14 48.4	14 05.6	0.4	0.4	6.4	6.3	12.4	12.3
05	14 46.3	14 48.7	14 05.9	0.5	0.5	6.5	6.4	12.5	12.4
06	14 46.5	14 48.9	14 06.1	0.6	0.6	6.6	6.5	12.6	12.5
07	14 46.8	14 49.2	14 06.4	0.7	0.7	6.7	6.6	12.7	12.6
08	14 47.0	14 49.4	14 06.6	0.8	0.8	6.8	6.7	12.8	12.7
09	14 47.3	14 49.7	14 06.8	0.9	0.9	6.9	6.8	12.9	12.8
10	14 47.5	14 49.9	14 07.1	1.0	1.0	7.0	6.9	13.0	12.9
11	14 47.8	14 50.2	14 07.3	1.1	1.1	7.1	7.0	13.1	13.0
12	14 48.0	14 50.4	14 07.5	1.2	1.2	7.2	7.1	13.2	13.1
13	14 48.3	14 50.7	14 07.8	1.3	1.3	7.3	7.2	13.3	13.2
14	14 48.5	14 50.9	14 08.0	1.4	1.4	7.4	7.3	13.4	13.3
15	14 48.8	14 51.2	14 08.3	1.5	1.5	7.5	7.4	13.5	13.4
16	14 49.0	14 51.4	14 08.5	1.6	1.6	7.6	7.5	13.6	13.5
17	14 49.3	14 51.7	14 08.7	1.7	1.7	7.7	7.6	13.7	13.6
18	14 49.5	14 51.9	14 09.0	1.8	1.8	7.8	7.7	13.8	13.7
19	14 49.8	14 52.2	14 09.2	1.9	1.9	7.9	7.8	13.9	13.8
20	14 50.0	14 52.4	14 09.5	2.0	2.0	8.0	7.9	14.0	13.9
21	14 50.3	14 52.7	14 09.7	2.1	2.1	8.1	8.0	14.1	14.0
22	14 50.5	14 52.9	14 09.9	2.2	2.2	8.2	8.1	14.2	14.1
23	14 50.8	14 53.2	14 10.2	2.3	2.3	8.3	8.2	14.3	14.2
24	14 51.0	14 53.4	14 10.4	2.4	2.4	8.4	8.3	14.4	14.3
25	14 51.3	14 53.7	14 10.6	2.5	2.5	8.5	8.4	14.5	14.4
26	14 51.5	14 53.9	14 10.9	2.6	2.6	8.6	8.5	14.6	14.5
27	14 51.8	14 54.2	14 11.1	2.7	2.7	8.7	8.6	14.7	14.6
28	14 52.0	14 54.4	14 11.4	2.8	2.8	8.8	8.7	14.8	14.7
29	14 52.3	14 54.7	14 11.6	2.9	2.9	8.9	8.8	14.9	14.8
30	14 52.5	14 54.9	14 11.8	3.0	3.0	9.0	8.9	15.0	14.9
31	14 52.8	14 55.2	14 12.1	3.1	3.1	9.1	9.0	15.1	15.0
32	14 53.0	14 55.4	14 12.3	3.2	3.2	9.2	9.1	15.2	15.1
33	14 53.3	14 55.7	14 12.6	3.3	3.3	9.3	9.2	15.3	15.2
34	14 53.5	14 55.9	14 12.8	3.4	3.4	9.4	9.3	15.4	15.3
35	14 53.8	14 56.2	14 13.0	3.5	3.5	9.5	9.4	15.5	15.4
36	14 54.0	14 56.4	14 13.3	3.6	3.6	9.6	9.5	15.6	15.5
37	14 54.3	14 56.7	14 13.5	3.7	3.7	9.7	9.6	15.7	15.6
38	14 54.5	14 56.9	14 13.8	3.8	3.8	9.8	9.7	15.8	15.7
39	14 54.8	14 57.2	14 14.0	3.9	3.9	9.9	9.8	15.9	15.8
40	14 55.0	14 57.5	14 14.2	4.0	4.0	10.0	9.9	16.0	15.9
41	14 55.3	14 57.7	14 14.5	4.1	4.1	10.1	10.0	16.1	16.0
42	14 55.5	14 58.0	14 14.7	4.2	4.2	10.2	10.1	16.2	16.1
43	14 55.8	14 58.2	14 14.9	4.3	4.3	10.3	10.2	16.3	16.2
44	14 56.0	14 58.5	14 15.2	4.4	4.4	10.4	10.3	16.4	16.3
45	14 56.3	14 58.7	14 15.4	4.5	4.5	10.5	10.4	16.5	16.4
46	14 56.5	14 59.0	14 15.7	4.6	4.6	10.6	10.5	16.6	16.5
47	14 56.8	14 59.2	14 15.9	4.7	4.7	10.7	10.6	16.7	16.6
48	14 57.0	14 59.5	14 16.1	4.8	4.8	10.8	10.7	16.8	16.7
49	14 57.3	14 59.7	14 16.4	4.9	4.9	10.9	10.8	16.9	16.8
50	14 57.5	15 00.0	14 16.6	5.0	5.0	11.0	10.9	17.0	16.9
51	14 57.8	15 00.2	14 16.9	5.1	5.1	11.1	11.0	17.1	17.0
52	14 58.0	15 00.5	14 17.1	5.2	5.2	11.2	11.1	17.2	17.1
53	14 58.3	15 00.7	14 17.3	5.3	5.3	11.3	11.2	17.3	17.2
54	14 58.5	15 01.0	14 17.6	5.4	5.4	11.4	11.3	17.4	17.3
55	14 58.8	15 01.2	14 17.8	5.5	5.5	11.5	11.4	17.5	17.4
56	14 59.0	15 01.5	14 18.0	5.6	5.6	11.6	11.5	17.6	17.5
57	14 59.3	15 01.7	14 18.3	5.7	5.7	11.7	11.6	17.7	17.6
58	14 59.5	15 02.0	14 18.5	5.8	5.8	11.8	11.7	17.8	17.7
59	14 59.8	15 02.2	14 18.8	5.9	5.9	11.9	11.8	17.9	17.8
60	15 00.0	15 02.5	14 19.0	6.0	6.0	12.0	11.9	18.0	17.9

TABLES FOR INTERPOLATING SUNRISE, MOONRISE, ETC.

TABLE I—FOR LATITUDE

10°	5°	2°	5ᵐ	10ᵐ	15ᵐ	20ᵐ	25ᵐ	30ᵐ	35ᵐ	40ᵐ	45ᵐ	50ᵐ	55ᵐ	60ᵐ	1ʰ05ᵐ	1ʰ10ᵐ	1ʰ15ᵐ	1ʰ20ᵐ
0 30	0 15	0 06	0	0	1	1	1	1	1	2	2	2	2	2	0 02	0 02	0 02	0 02
1 00	0 30	0 12	0	1	1	2	2	3	3	3	4	4	4	5	05	05	05	05
1 30	0 45	0 18	1	1	2	3	3	4	4	5	5	6	7	7	07	07	07	07
2 00	1 00	0 24	1	2	3	4	5	5	6	7	7	8	9	10	10	10	10	10
2 30	1 15	0 30	1	2	4	5	6	7	8	9	9	10	11	12	12	13	13	13
3 00	1 30	0 36	1	3	4	6	7	8	9	10	11	12	13	14	0 15	0 15	0 16	0 16
3 30	1 45	0 42	2	3	5	7	8	10	11	12	13	14	16	17	18	18	19	19
4 00	2 00	0 48	2	4	6	8	9	11	13	14	15	16	18	19	20	21	22	22
4 30	2 15	0 54	2	4	7	9	11	13	15	16	18	19	21	22	23	24	25	26
5 00	2 30	1 00	2	5	7	10	12	14	16	18	20	22	23	25	26	27	28	29
5 30	2 45	1 06	3	5	8	11	13	16	18	20	22	24	26	28	0 29	0 30	0 31	0 32
6 00	3 00	1 12	3	6	9	12	14	17	20	22	24	26	29	31	32	33	34	36
6 30	3 15	1 18	3	6	10	13	16	19	22	24	26	29	31	34	36	37	38	40
7 00	3 30	1 24	3	7	10	14	17	20	23	26	29	31	34	37	39	41	42	44
7 30	3 45	1 30	4	7	11	15	18	22	25	28	31	34	37	40	43	44	46	48
8 00	4 00	1 36	4	8	12	16	20	23	27	30	34	37	41	44	0 47	0 48	0 51	0 53
8 30	4 15	1 42	4	8	13	17	21	25	29	33	36	40	44	48	0 51	0 53	0 56	0 58
9 00	4 30	1 48	4	9	13	18	22	27	31	35	39	43	47	52	0 55	0 58	1 01	1 04
9 30	4 45	1 54	5	9	14	19	24	28	33	38	42	47	51	56	1 00	1 04	1 08	1 12
10 00	5 00	2 00	5	10	15	20	25	30	35	40	45	50	55	60	1 05	1 10	1 15	1 20

(Tabular Interval columns: 10°, 5°, 2°. Top argument: Difference between the times for consecutive latitudes.)

Table I is for interpolating the LMT of sunrise, twilight, moonrise, etc., for latitude. It is to be entered, in the appropriate column on the left, with the difference between true latitude and the nearest tabular latitude which is *less* than the true latitude; and with the argument at the top which is the nearest value of the difference between the times for the tabular latitude and the next higher one; the correction so obtained is applied to the time for the tabular latitude; the sign of the correction can be seen by inspection. It is to be noted that the interpolation is not linear, so that when using this table it is essential to take out the tabular phenomenon for the latitude *less* than the true latitude.

TABLE II—FOR LONGITUDE

Difference between the times for given date and preceding date (for east longitude) or for given date and following date (for west longitude)

Long. East or West	10ᵐ	20ᵐ	30ᵐ	40ᵐ	50ᵐ	60ᵐ	1ʰ+ 10ᵐ	20ᵐ	30ᵐ	1ʰ+ 40ᵐ	50ᵐ	60ᵐ	2ʰ10ᵐ	2ʰ20ᵐ	2ʰ30ᵐ	2ʰ40ᵐ	2ʰ50ᵐ	3ʰ00ᵐ
0	0	0	0	0	0	0	0	0	0	0	0	0	0 00	0 00	0 00	0 00	0 00	0 00
10	0	1	1	1	1	2	2	2	2	3	3	3	04	04	04	04	05	05
20	1	1	2	2	3	3	4	4	5	6	6	7	07	08	08	09	09	10
30	1	2	2	3	4	5	6	7	7	8	9	10	11	12	12	13	14	15
40	1	2	3	4	6	7	8	9	10	11	12	13	14	16	17	18	19	20
50	1	3	4	6	7	8	10	11	12	14	15	17	0 18	0 19	0 21	0 22	0 24	0 25
60	2	3	5	7	8	10	12	13	15	17	18	20	22	23	25	27	28	30
70	2	4	6	8	10	12	14	16	17	19	21	23	25	27	29	31	33	35
80	2	4	7	9	11	13	16	18	20	22	24	27	29	31	33	36	38	40
90	2	5	7	10	12	15	17	20	22	25	27	30	32	35	37	40	42	45
100	3	6	8	11	14	17	19	22	25	28	31	33	0 36	0 39	0 42	0 44	0 47	0 50
110	3	6	9	12	15	18	21	24	27	31	34	37	40	43	46	49	0 52	0 55
120	3	7	10	13	17	20	23	27	30	33	37	40	43	47	50	53	0 57	1 00
130	4	7	11	14	18	22	25	29	32	36	40	43	47	51	54	0 58	1 01	1 05
140	4	8	12	16	19	23	27	31	35	39	43	47	51	54	0 58	1 02	1 06	1 10
150	4	8	13	17	21	25	29	33	38	42	46	50	0 54	0 58	1 03	1 07	1 11	1 15
160	4	9	13	18	22	27	31	36	40	44	49	53	0 58	1 02	1 07	1 11	1 16	1 20
170	5	9	14	19	24	28	33	38	42	47	52	57	1 01	1 06	1 11	1 16	1 20	1 25
180	5	10	15	20	25	30	35	40	45	50	55	60	1 05	1 10	1 15	1 20	1 25	1 30

Table II is for interpolating the LMT of moonrise, moonset and the Moon's meridian passage for longitude. It is entered with longitude and with the difference between the times for the given date and for the preceding date (in east longitudes) or following date (in west longitudes). The correction is normally *added* for west longitudes and *subtracted* for east longitudes, but if, as occasionally happens, the times become earlier each day instead of later, the signs of the corrections must be reversed.

INDEX TO SELECTED STARS, 2013

Name	No	Mag	SHA	Dec		No	Name	Mag	SHA	Dec
			°	°					°	°
Acamar	7	3·2	315	S 40		1	Alpheratz	2·1	358	N 29
Achernar	5	0·5	335	S 57		2	Ankaa	2·4	353	S 42
Acrux	30	1·3	173	S 63		3	Schedar	2·2	350	N 57
Adhara	19	1·5	255	S 29		4	Diphda	2·0	349	S 18
Aldebaran	10	0·9	291	N 17		5	Achernar	0·5	335	S 57
Alioth	32	1·8	166	N 56		6	Hamal	2·0	328	N 24
Alkaid	34	1·9	153	N 49		7	Acamar	3·2	315	S 40
Al Na'ir	55	1·7	28	S 47		8	Menkar	2·5	314	N 4
Alnilam	15	1·7	276	S 1		9	Mirfak	1·8	309	N 50
Alphard	25	2·0	218	S 9		10	Aldebaran	0·9	291	N 17
Alphecca	41	2·2	126	N 27		11	Rigel	0·1	281	S 8
Alpheratz	1	2·1	358	N 29		12	Capella	0·1	281	N 46
Altair	51	0·8	62	N 9		13	Bellatrix	1·6	279	N 6
Ankaa	2	2·4	353	S 42		14	Elnath	1·7	278	N 29
Antares	42	1·0	112	S 26		15	Alnilam	1·7	276	S 1
Arcturus	37	0·0	146	N 19		16	Betelgeuse	Var.*	271	N 7
Atria	43	1·9	107	S 69		17	Canopus	−0·7	264	S 53
Avior	22	1·9	234	S 60		18	Sirius	−1·5	259	S 17
Bellatrix	13	1·6	279	N 6		19	Adhara	1·5	255	S 29
Betelgeuse	16	Var.*	271	N 7		20	Procyon	0·4	245	N 5
Canopus	17	−0·7	264	S 53		21	Pollux	1·1	243	N 28
Capella	12	0·1	281	N 46		22	Avior	1·9	234	S 60
Deneb	53	1·3	50	N 45		23	Suhail	2·2	223	S 43
Denebola	28	2·1	183	N 14		24	Miaplacidus	1·7	222	S 70
Diphda	4	2·0	349	S 18		25	Alphard	2·0	218	S 9
Dubhe	27	1·8	194	N 62		26	Regulus	1·4	208	N 12
Elnath	14	1·7	278	N 29		27	Dubhe	1·8	194	N 62
Eltanin	47	2·2	91	N 51		28	Denebola	2·1	183	N 14
Enif	54	2·4	34	N 10		29	Gienah	2·6	176	S 18
Fomalhaut	56	1·2	15	S 30		30	Acrux	1·3	173	S 63
Gacrux	31	1·6	172	S 57		31	Gacrux	1·6	172	S 57
Gienah	29	2·6	176	S 18		32	Alioth	1·8	166	N 56
Hadar	35	0·6	149	S 60		33	Spica	1·0	159	S 11
Hamal	6	2·0	328	N 24		34	Alkaid	1·9	153	N 49
Kaus Australis	48	1·9	84	S 34		35	Hadar	0·6	149	S 60
Kochab	40	2·1	137	N 74		36	Menkent	2·1	148	S 36
Markab	57	2·5	14	N 15		37	Arcturus	0·0	146	N 19
Menkar	8	2·5	314	N 4		38	Rigil Kentaurus	−0·3	140	S 61
Menkent	36	2·1	148	S 36		39	Zubenelgenubi	2·8	137	S 16
Miaplacidus	24	1·7	222	S 70		40	Kochab	2·1	137	N 74
Mirfak	9	1·8	309	N 50		41	Alphecca	2·2	126	N 27
Nunki	50	2·0	76	S 26		42	Antares	1·0	112	S 26
Peacock	52	1·9	53	S 57		43	Atria	1·9	107	S 69
Pollux	21	1·1	243	N 28		44	Sabik	2·4	102	S 16
Procyon	20	0·4	245	N 5		45	Shaula	1·6	96	S 37
Rasalhague	46	2·1	96	N 13		46	Rasalhague	2·1	96	N 13
Regulus	26	1·4	208	N 12		47	Eltanin	2·2	91	N 51
Rigel	11	0·1	281	S 8		48	Kaus Australis	1·9	84	S 34
Rigil Kentaurus	38	−0·3	140	S 61		49	Vega	0·0	81	N 39
Sabik	44	2·4	102	S 16		50	Nunki	2·0	76	S 26
Schedar	3	2·2	350	N 57		51	Altair	0·8	62	N 9
Shaula	45	1·6	96	S 37		52	Peacock	1·9	53	S 57
Sirius	18	−1·5	259	S 17		53	Deneb	1·3	50	N 45
Spica	33	1·0	159	S 11		54	Enif	2·4	34	N 10
Suhail	23	2·2	223	S 43		55	Al Na'ir	1·7	28	S 47
Vega	49	0·0	81	N 39		56	Fomalhaut	1·2	15	S 30
Zubenelgenubi	39	2·8	137	S 16		57	Markab	2·5	14	N 15

*0·1 — 1·2

ALTITUDE CORRECTION TABLES 0°–35°— MOON

App. Alt.	0°–4° Corrⁿ	5°–9° Corrⁿ	10°–14° Corrⁿ	15°–19° Corrⁿ	20°–24° Corrⁿ	25°–29° Corrⁿ	30°–34° Corrⁿ	App. Alt.
00	0° 34·5	5° 58·2	10° 62·1	15° 62·8	20° 62·2	25° 60·8	30° 58·9	00
10	36·5	58·5	62·2	62·8	62·2	60·8	58·8	10
20	38·3	58·7	62·2	62·8	62·1	60·7	58·8	20
30	40·0	58·9	62·3	62·8	62·1	60·7	58·7	30
40	41·5	59·1	62·3	62·8	62·0	60·6	58·6	40
50	42·9	59·3	62·4	62·7	62·0	60·6	58·5	50
00	1° 44·2	6° 59·5	11° 62·4	16° 62·7	21° 62·0	26° 60·5	31° 58·5	00
10	45·4	59·7	62·4	62·7	61·9	60·4	58·4	10
20	46·5	59·9	62·5	62·7	61·9	60·4	58·3	20
30	47·5	60·0	62·5	62·7	61·9	60·3	58·2	30
40	48·4	60·2	62·5	62·7	61·8	60·3	58·2	40
50	49·3	60·3	62·6	62·7	61·8	60·2	58·1	50
00	2° 50·1	7° 60·5	12° 62·6	17° 62·7	22° 61·7	27° 60·1	32° 58·0	00
10	50·8	60·6	62·6	62·6	61·7	60·1	57·9	10
20	51·5	60·7	62·6	62·6	61·6	60·0	57·8	20
30	52·2	60·9	62·7	62·6	61·6	59·9	57·8	30
40	52·8	61·0	62·7	62·6	61·6	59·9	57·7	40
50	53·4	61·1	62·7	62·6	61·5	59·8	57·6	50
00	3° 53·9	8° 61·2	13° 62·7	18° 62·5	23° 61·5	28° 59·7	33° 57·5	00
10	54·4	61·3	62·7	62·5	61·4	59·7	57·4	10
20	54·9	61·4	62·7	62·5	61·4	59·6	57·4	20
30	55·3	61·5	62·8	62·5	61·3	59·5	57·3	30
40	55·7	61·6	62·8	62·4	61·3	59·5	57·2	40
50	56·1	61·6	62·8	62·4	61·2	59·4	57·1	50
00	4° 56·4	9° 61·7	14° 62·8	19° 62·4	24° 61·2	29° 59·3	34° 57·0	00
10	56·8	61·8	62·8	62·4	61·1	59·3	56·9	10
20	57·1	61·9	62·8	62·3	61·1	59·2	56·9	20
30	57·4	61·9	62·8	62·3	61·0	59·1	56·8	30
40	57·7	62·0	62·8	62·3	61·0	59·1	56·7	40
50	58·0	62·1	62·8	62·2	60·9	59·0	56·6	50

HP	L	U	L	U	L	U	L	U	L	U	L	U	L	U	HP
54·0	0·3	0·9	0·3	0·9	0·4	1·0	0·5	1·1	0·6	1·2	0·7	1·3	0·9	1·5	54·0
54·3	0·7	1·1	0·7	1·2	0·8	1·2	0·8	1·3	0·9	1·4	1·1	1·5	1·2	1·7	54·3
54·6	1·1	1·4	1·1	1·4	1·1	1·4	1·2	1·5	1·3	1·6	1·4	1·7	1·5	1·8	54·6
54·9	1·4	1·6	1·5	1·6	1·5	1·6	1·6	1·7	1·6	1·8	1·8	1·9	1·9	2·0	54·9
55·2	1·8	1·8	1·8	1·8	1·9	1·8	1·9	1·9	2·0	2·0	2·1	2·1	2·2	2·2	55·2
55·5	2·2	2·0	2·2	2·0	2·3	2·1	2·3	2·1	2·4	2·2	2·4	2·3	2·5	2·4	55·5
55·8	2·6	2·2	2·6	2·2	2·6	2·3	2·7	2·3	2·7	2·4	2·8	2·4	2·9	2·5	55·8
56·1	3·0	2·4	3·0	2·5	3·0	2·5	3·1	2·6	3·1	2·6	3·2	2·7	3·2	2·7	56·1
56·4	3·3	2·7	3·4	2·7	3·4	2·7	3·4	2·7	3·5	2·8	3·5	2·8	3·5	2·9	56·4
56·7	3·7	2·9	3·7	2·9	3·8	2·9	3·8	2·9	3·8	3·0	3·8	3·0	3·9	3·0	56·7
57·0	4·1	3·1	4·1	3·1	4·1	3·1	4·1	3·1	4·2	3·2	4·2	3·2	4·2	3·2	57·0
57·3	4·5	3·3	4·5	3·3	4·5	3·3	4·5	3·3	4·5	3·3	4·5	3·4	4·6	3·4	57·3
57·6	4·9	3·5	4·9	3·5	4·9	3·5	4·9	3·5	4·9	3·5	4·9	3·5	4·9	3·6	57·6
57·9	5·3	3·8	5·3	3·8	5·2	3·8	5·2	3·7	5·2	3·7	5·2	3·7	5·2	3·7	57·9
58·2	5·6	4·0	5·6	4·0	5·6	4·0	5·6	4·0	5·6	3·9	5·6	3·9	5·6	3·9	58·2
58·5	6·0	4·2	6·0	4·2	6·0	4·2	6·0	4·2	6·0	4·1	5·9	4·1	5·9	4·1	58·5
58·8	6·4	4·4	6·4	4·4	6·4	4·4	6·3	4·3	6·3	4·3	6·3	4·3	6·2	4·2	58·8
59·1	6·8	4·6	6·8	4·6	6·8	4·6	6·7	4·6	6·7	4·5	6·6	4·5	6·6	4·4	59·1
59·4	7·2	4·8	7·1	4·8	7·1	4·8	7·1	4·8	7·0	4·7	7·0	4·7	6·9	4·6	59·4
59·7	7·5	5·1	7·5	5·0	7·5	5·0	7·5	5·0	7·4	4·9	7·3	4·8	7·2	4·8	59·7
60·0	7·9	5·3	7·9	5·3	7·9	5·2	7·8	5·2	7·8	5·1	7·7	5·0	7·6	4·9	60·0
60·3	8·3	5·5	8·3	5·5	8·2	5·4	8·2	5·4	8·1	5·3	8·0	5·2	7·9	5·1	60·3
60·6	8·7	5·7	8·7	5·7	8·6	5·7	8·6	5·6	8·5	5·5	8·4	5·4	8·2	5·3	60·6
60·9	9·1	5·9	9·0	5·9	9·0	5·9	8·9	5·8	8·8	5·7	8·7	5·6	8·6	5·4	60·9
61·2	9·5	6·2	9·4	6·1	9·4	6·1	9·3	6·0	9·2	5·9	9·1	5·8	8·9	5·6	61·2
61·5	9·8	6·4	9·8	6·3	9·7	6·3	9·7	6·2	9·5	6·1	9·4	5·9	9·2	5·8	61·5

DIP

Ht. of Eye (m)	Corrⁿ	Ht. of Eye (ft)	Ht. of Eye (m)	Corrⁿ	Ht. of Eye (ft)
2·4	−2·8	8·0	9·5	−5·5	31·5
2·6	−2·9	8·6	9·9	−5·6	32·7
2·8	−3·0	9·2	10·3	−5·7	33·9
3·0	−3·1	9·8	10·6	−5·8	35·1
3·2	−3·2	10·5	11·0	−5·9	36·3
3·4	−3·3	11·2	11·4	−6·0	37·6
3·6	−3·4	11·9	11·8	−6·1	38·9
3·8	−3·5	12·6	12·2	−6·2	40·1
4·0	−3·6	13·3	12·6	−6·3	41·5
4·3	−3·7	14·1	13·0	−6·4	42·8
4·5	−3·8	14·9	13·4	−6·5	44·2
4·7	−3·9	15·7	13·8	−6·6	45·5
5·0	−4·0	16·5	14·2	−6·7	46·9
5·2	−4·1	17·4	14·7	−6·8	48·4
5·5	−4·2	18·3	15·1	−6·9	49·8
5·8	−4·3	19·1	15·5	−7·0	51·3
6·1	−4·4	20·1	16·0	−7·1	52·8
6·3	−4·5	21·0	16·5	−7·2	54·3
6·6	−4·6	22·0	16·9	−7·3	55·8
6·9	−4·7	22·9	17·4	−7·4	57·4
7·2	−4·8	23·9	17·9	−7·5	58·9
7·5	−4·9	24·9	18·4	−7·6	60·5
7·9	−5·0	26·0	18·8	−7·7	62·1
8·2	−5·1	27·1	19·3	−7·8	63·8
8·5	−5·2	28·1	19·8	−7·9	65·4
8·8	−5·3	29·2	20·4	−8·0	67·1
9·2	−5·4	30·4	20·9	−8·1	68·8
9·5		31·5	21·4		70·5

MOON CORRECTION TABLE

The correction is in two parts; the first correction is taken from the upper part of the table with argument apparent altitude, and the second from the lower part, with argument HP, in the same column as that from which the first correction was taken. Separate corrections are given in the lower part for lower (L) and upper (U) limbs. All corrections are to be **added** to apparent altitude, *but 30′ is to be subtracted from the altitude of the upper limb.*

For corrections for pressure and temperature see page A4.

For bubble sextant observations ignore dip, take the mean of upper and lower limb corrections and subtract 15′ from the altitude.

App. Alt. = Apparent altitude = Sextant altitude corrected for index error and dip.

ALTITUDE CORRECTION TABLES 35°–90°— MOON

App. Alt.	35°–39° Corrn	40°–44° Corrn	45°–49° Corrn	50°–54° Corrn	55°–59° Corrn	60°–64° Corrn	65°–69° Corrn	70°–74° Corrn	75°–79° Corrn	80°–84° Corrn	85°–89° Corrn	App. Alt.
00	35° 56.5	40° 53.7	45° 50.5	50° 46.9	55° 43.1	60° 38.9	65° 34.6	70° 30.0	75° 25.3	80° 20.5	85° 15.6	00
10	56.4	53.6	50.4	46.8	42.9	38.8	34.4	29.9	25.2	20.4	15.5	10
20	56.3	53.5	50.2	46.7	42.8	38.7	34.3	29.7	25.0	20.2	15.3	20
30	56.2	53.4	50.1	46.5	42.7	38.5	34.1	29.6	24.9	20.0	15.1	30
40	56.2	53.3	50.0	46.4	42.5	38.4	34.0	29.4	24.7	19.9	15.0	40
50	56.1	53.2	49.9	46.3	42.4	38.2	33.8	29.3	24.5	19.7	14.8	50
00	36° 56.0	41° 53.1	46° 49.8	51° 46.2	56° 42.3	61° 38.1	66° 33.7	71° 29.1	76° 24.4	81° 19.6	86° 14.6	00
10	55.9	53.0	49.7	46.0	42.1	37.9	33.5	29.0	24.2	19.4	14.5	10
20	55.8	52.9	49.5	45.9	42.0	37.8	33.4	28.8	24.1	19.2	14.3	20
30	55.7	52.8	49.4	45.8	41.9	37.7	33.2	28.7	23.9	19.1	14.2	30
40	55.6	52.6	49.3	45.7	41.7	37.5	33.1	28.5	23.8	18.9	14.0	40
50	55.5	52.5	49.2	45.5	41.6	37.4	32.9	28.3	23.6	18.7	13.8	50
00	37° 55.4	42° 52.4	47° 49.1	52° 45.4	57° 41.4	62° 37.2	67° 32.8	72° 28.2	77° 23.4	82° 18.6	87° 13.7	00
10	55.3	52.3	49.0	45.3	41.3	37.1	32.6	28.0	23.3	18.4	13.5	10
20	55.2	52.2	48.8	45.2	41.2	36.9	32.5	27.9	23.1	18.2	13.3	20
30	55.1	52.1	48.7	45.0	41.0	36.8	32.3	27.7	22.9	18.1	13.2	30
40	55.0	52.0	48.6	44.9	40.9	36.6	32.2	27.6	22.8	17.9	13.0	40
50	55.0	51.9	48.5	44.8	40.8	36.5	32.0	27.4	22.6	17.8	12.8	50
00	38° 54.9	43° 51.8	48° 48.4	53° 44.6	58° 40.6	63° 36.4	68° 31.9	73° 27.2	78° 22.5	83° 17.6	88° 12.7	00
10	54.8	51.7	48.3	44.5	40.5	36.2	31.7	27.1	22.3	17.4	12.5	10
20	54.7	51.6	48.1	44.4	40.3	36.1	31.6	26.9	22.1	17.3	12.3	20
30	54.6	51.5	48.0	44.2	40.2	35.9	31.4	26.8	22.0	17.1	12.2	30
40	54.5	51.4	47.9	44.1	40.1	35.8	31.3	26.6	21.8	16.9	12.0	40
50	54.4	51.2	47.8	44.0	39.9	35.6	31.1	26.5	21.7	16.8	11.8	50
00	39° 54.3	44° 51.1	49° 47.7	54° 43.9	59° 39.8	64° 35.5	69° 31.0	74° 26.3	79° 21.5	84° 16.6	89° 11.7	00
10	54.2	51.0	47.5	43.7	39.6	35.3	30.8	26.1	21.3	16.4	11.5	10
20	54.1	50.9	47.4	43.6	39.5	35.2	30.7	26.0	21.2	16.3	11.4	20
30	54.0	50.8	47.3	43.5	39.4	35.0	30.5	25.8	21.0	16.1	11.2	30
40	53.9	50.7	47.2	43.3	39.2	34.9	30.4	25.7	20.9	16.0	11.0	40
50	53.8	50.6	47.0	43.2	39.1	34.7	30.2	25.5	20.7	15.8	10.9	50

HP	L	U	L	U	L	U	L	U	L	U	L	U	L	U	L	U	L	U	L	U	L	U	HP
54.0	1.1	1.7	1.3	1.9	1.5	2.1	1.7	2.4	2.0	2.6	2.3	2.9	2.6	3.2	2.9	3.5	3.2	3.8	3.5	4.1	3.8	4.5	54.0
54.3	1.4	1.8	1.6	2.0	1.8	2.2	2.0	2.5	2.2	2.7	2.5	3.0	2.8	3.2	3.1	3.5	3.3	3.8	3.6	4.1	3.9	4.4	54.3
54.6	1.7	2.0	1.9	2.2	2.1	2.4	2.3	2.6	2.5	2.8	2.7	3.0	3.0	3.3	3.2	3.5	3.5	3.8	3.8	4.0	4.0	4.3	54.6
54.9	2.0	2.2	2.2	2.3	2.3	2.5	2.5	2.7	2.7	2.9	2.9	3.1	3.2	3.3	3.4	3.5	3.6	3.8	3.9	4.0	4.1	4.3	54.9
55.2	2.3	2.3	2.5	2.4	2.6	2.6	2.8	2.8	3.0	2.9	3.2	3.1	3.4	3.3	3.6	3.5	3.8	3.7	4.0	4.0	4.2	4.2	55.2
55.5	2.7	2.5	2.8	2.6	2.9	2.7	3.1	2.9	3.2	3.0	3.4	3.2	3.6	3.4	3.7	3.5	3.9	3.7	4.1	3.9	4.3	4.1	55.5
55.8	3.0	2.6	3.1	2.7	3.2	2.8	3.3	3.0	3.5	3.1	3.6	3.3	3.8	3.4	3.9	3.6	4.1	3.7	4.2	3.9	4.4	4.0	55.8
56.1	3.3	2.8	3.4	2.9	3.5	3.0	3.6	3.1	3.7	3.2	3.8	3.3	4.0	3.4	4.1	3.6	4.2	3.7	4.4	3.8	4.5	4.0	56.1
56.4	3.6	2.9	3.7	3.0	3.8	3.1	3.9	3.2	3.9	3.3	4.0	3.4	4.1	3.5	4.3	3.6	4.4	3.7	4.5	3.8	4.6	3.9	56.4
56.7	3.9	3.1	4.0	3.1	4.1	3.2	4.1	3.3	4.2	3.3	4.3	3.4	4.3	3.5	4.4	3.6	4.5	3.7	4.6	3.8	4.7	3.8	56.7
57.0	4.3	3.2	4.3	3.3	4.3	3.3	4.4	3.4	4.4	3.4	4.5	3.5	4.5	3.5	4.6	3.6	4.7	3.6	4.7	3.7	4.8	3.8	57.0
57.3	4.6	3.4	4.6	3.4	4.6	3.5	4.7	3.5	4.7	3.5	4.7	3.5	4.8	3.6	4.8	3.6	4.7	3.6	4.8	3.7	4.9	3.7	57.3
57.6	4.9	3.6	4.9	3.6	4.9	3.6	4.9	3.6	4.9	3.6	4.9	3.6	4.9	3.6	5.0	3.6	5.0	3.6	5.0	3.6	5.0	3.6	57.6
57.9	5.2	3.7	5.2	3.7	5.2	3.7	5.2	3.7	5.2	3.7	5.1	3.6	5.1	3.6	5.1	3.6	5.1	3.6	5.1	3.6	5.1	3.6	57.9
58.2	5.5	3.9	5.5	3.8	5.5	3.8	5.4	3.8	5.4	3.8	5.4	3.7	5.4	3.7	5.3	3.7	5.3	3.6	5.2	3.6	5.2	3.5	58.2
58.5	5.9	4.0	5.8	4.0	5.8	3.9	5.7	3.9	5.6	3.8	5.6	3.8	5.5	3.7	5.5	3.6	5.4	3.6	5.3	3.5	5.3	3.4	58.5
58.8	6.2	4.2	6.1	4.1	6.0	4.1	6.0	4.0	5.9	3.9	5.8	3.8	5.7	3.7	5.6	3.6	5.5	3.5	5.4	3.5	5.3	3.4	58.8
59.1	6.5	4.3	6.4	4.3	6.3	4.2	6.2	4.1	6.1	4.0	6.0	3.9	5.9	3.8	5.8	3.6	5.7	3.5	5.6	3.4	5.4	3.3	59.1
59.4	6.8	4.5	6.7	4.4	6.6	4.3	6.5	4.2	6.4	4.1	6.3	4.0	6.1	3.8	6.0	3.7	5.8	3.5	5.7	3.4	5.5	3.2	59.4
59.7	7.1	4.7	7.0	4.5	6.9	4.4	6.8	4.3	6.6	4.1	6.5	4.0	6.3	3.8	6.1	3.7	6.0	3.5	5.8	3.3	5.6	3.2	59.7
60.0	7.5	4.8	7.3	4.7	7.2	4.5	7.0	4.4	6.9	4.2	6.7	4.0	6.5	3.9	6.3	3.7	6.1	3.5	5.9	3.3	5.7	3.1	60.0
60.3	7.8	5.0	7.6	4.8	7.5	4.7	7.3	4.5	7.1	4.3	6.9	4.1	6.7	3.9	6.5	3.7	6.3	3.5	6.0	3.2	5.8	3.0	60.3
60.6	8.1	5.1	7.9	5.0	7.7	4.8	7.6	4.6	7.3	4.4	7.1	4.2	6.9	3.9	6.7	3.7	6.4	3.4	6.2	3.2	5.9	2.9	60.6
60.9	8.4	5.3	8.2	5.1	8.0	4.9	7.8	4.7	7.6	4.5	7.3	4.2	7.1	4.0	6.8	3.7	6.6	3.4	6.3	3.2	6.0	2.9	60.9
61.2	8.7	5.4	8.5	5.2	8.3	5.0	8.1	4.8	7.8	4.5	7.6	4.3	7.3	4.0	7.0	3.7	6.7	3.4	6.4	3.1	6.1	2.8	61.2
61.5	9.1	5.6	8.8	5.4	8.6	5.1	8.3	4.9	8.1	4.6	7.8	4.3	7.5	4.0	7.2	3.7	6.9	3.4	6.5	3.1	6.2	2.7	61.5

CPSIA information can be obtained at www.ICGtesting.com
Printed in the USA
LVOW112138030213

318442LV00004B/143/P